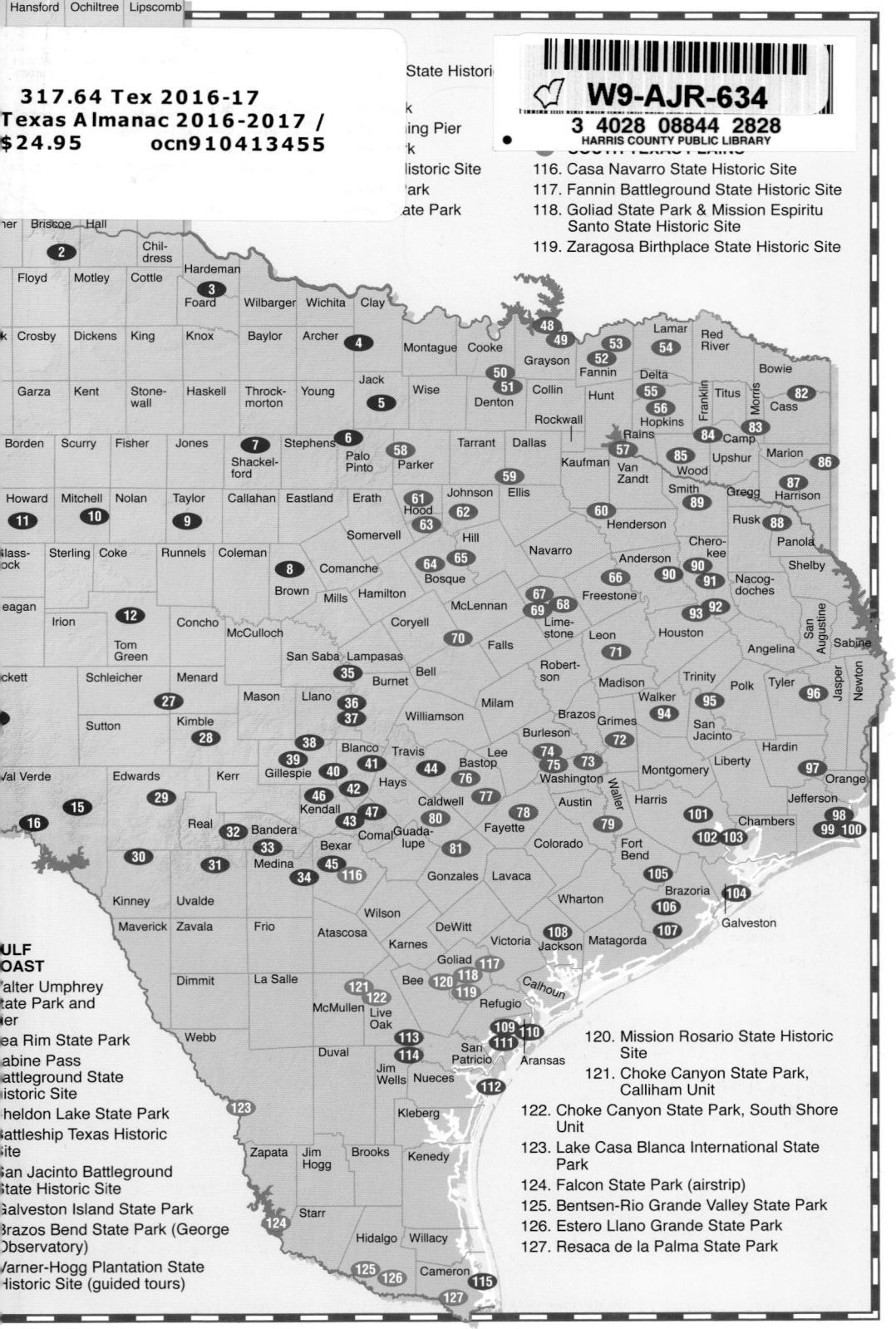

SOUTH TEXAS PLAINS

116. Casa Navarro State Historic Site
117. Fannin Battleground State Historic Site
118. Goliad State Park & Mission Espiritu Santo State Historic Site
119. Zaragosa Birthplace State Historic Site

120. Mission Rosario State Historic Site
121. Choke Canyon State Park, Calliham Unit
122. Choke Canyon State Park, South Shore Unit
123. Lake Casa Blanca International State Park
124. Falcon State Park (airstrip)
125. Bentsen-Rio Grande Valley State Park
126. Estero Llano Grande State Park
127. Resaca de la Palma State Park

GULF COAST

Walter Umphrey State Park and Pier
Sea Rim State Park
Sabine Pass Battleground State Historic Site
Sheldon Lake State Park
Battleship Texas Historic Site
San Jacinto Battleground State Historic Site
Galveston Island State Park
Brazos Bend State Park (George Observatory)
Varner-Hogg Plantation State Historic Site (guided tours)

# TEXAS ALMANAC

2016
2017

Published by

TEXAS STATE HISTORICAL ASSOCIATION

Austin, Texas

# TEXAS ALMANAC
## 2016 ★ 2017

EDITOR
### Elizabeth Cruce Alvarez

ASSOCIATE EDITOR
### Robert Plocheck

COVER ARTWORK
### *Texas Bounty*
### by Lamberto Alvarez

**ISBN (hardcover)** 978-1-62511-032-9
**ISBN (flexbound)** 978-1-62511-033-6
**ISBN (ebook)** 978-1-62511-034-3
**Library of Congress ISSN:** 2378-2188 (Print)
**Library of Congress ISSN:** 2378-2234 (Digital)

## TEXAS STATE HISTORICAL ASSOCIATION

**The University of Texas at Austin**
3001 Lake Austin Blvd., Suite 3.116, Austin, TX 78703; (512) 471-2600
**www.tshaonline.org**

Printed in Dallas, Texas, by Quad Williamson.
Bound in San Antonio, Texas, by Universal Bookbindery.

For permission requests, contact Elizabeth.Alvarez@TSHAonline.org.

Distributed by Texas A&M University Press and the Texas Book Consortium
4354 TAMU, College Station, Texas, 77843-4354

Order hardcover or flexbound editions at **(800) 826-8911** or log on to:
www.tamupress.com

**www.TexasAlmanac.com**

## THE SOURCE FOR ALL THINGS TEXAN SINCE 1857

# PREFACE

This edition of the Texas Almanac — the 68th in its 159-year history — is a celebration of many aspects of Texas life. Our feature articles celebrate the glorious food of The Lone Star State, a rich blend of many cultures over hundreds of years, and the vineyards and wineries that produce unique wines that have become a booming business for our state.

We also celebrate the 70th anniversary of the state's one and only Triple Crown Champion. The story of Assault, a Thoroughbred colt from the historic King Ranch who had a life-threatening injury as a yearling, is an incredible tale of the will to live and to win. My thanks to all of the authors who have enriched this edition with their wonderful articles and unique perspectives.

Art and photography also are celebrated in this Texas Almanac. The cover, which illustrates Texas' one-of-a-kind heritage of food and wine *(see About the Cover, below),* and the hundreds of photographs that capture special moments across Texas make this edition the most colorful and picturesque of all. In this era of video and digital images, we continue to celebrate still photography. There is something special, almost magical, about a photograph. The black and white image, which opens the History section on page 27 and illustrates the "Lone Star Cuisine" article by Dotty Griffith, is amazing to behold. Taken by *San Antonio Light* photographer Jack Specht on a January evening in 1933, this photograph captures a group of people at a chili stand in Haymarket Plaza. All of the faces, with their diverse expressions — some haunting, some happy — is worth a close look. It is a moment during Depression-era San Antonio that would have been lost to time except for one roving photographer.

This edition is filled with photos that are fun, historic, and show the many faces and moods of Texas. My heartfelt thanks to all of the photographers and organizations that contributed to this edition: Dr. Ron Billings of the Texas A&M Forest Service, who always contributes so many, the photographers at the Texas Parks and Wildlife Department, the U.S. Fish and Wildlife Service, the USDA/Natural Resources Conservation Service, our own associate editor Robert Plocheck, Traces of Texas.com, and all of the news agencies, libraries, chambers of commerce, and the many individuals who responded to our "Call for Photos" and submitted wonderful images from around the state. As you look through this volume, please take time to notice the photo credit for each photograph. I also want to credit www.goodtextures.com, which supplied the "Damaged Plaster" texture that is the warm and rugged backdrop for all of the section openers.

**Photo by Veronica Elinor Alvarez.**

**Elizabeth Cruce Alvarez**
**Editor, 2015**

Thank you to all of the loyal readers of the Texas Almanac and to those new readers who are seeing this historic book for the first time. We appreciate you, and we hope you enjoy the *Texas Almanac 2016–2017.*

## About the Cover

Finding the perfect image for this edition with its dual theme of food and wine was a challenge. Artist Lamberto Alvarez is known as a problem solver. His years of working as an illustrator for many major newspapers and as illustration director at *The Dallas Morning News* equipped him with the talent for finding visual solutions. As we discussed the theme, he was inspired by a photograph of a vineyard worker taken at Fall Creek Vineyards near Tow in Llano County by Melinda Esco, author of our "Texas Wine Country" article *(see page 38).*

That was all Lamberto needed to work out a concept and begin painting. The finished piece, *Texas Bounty,* is a beautifully layered and complex painting that shows a colorful dawn breaking over a Texas vineyard. The viewer sits behind a set table, with the expectancy of a sumptuous meal to come and looking out at the lush scenery and a hacienda in the distance.

"Although I work in diverse media, even concrete and assemblage," Lamberto said, "this painting for the Texas Almanac has inspired me to create more, even larger-scale canvas paintings that capture the magnificent vineyards of Texas." Creating the cover painting was truly a labor of love for this artist. ☆

**Photo by Veronica Elinor Alvarez.**

**Lamberto™ works on the cover painting.**

# TSHA Returns to Its First Home at UT Austin

After seven successful years in Denton, the Texas State Historical Association (TSHA) returned to its original home of Austin in the spring of 2015.

Like the amazing Texas cuisine chronicled in this edition of the Texas Almanac, the unique city of Austin encapsulates the diverse flavors of The Lone Star State. With the barbecue capital of Texas just down the road and home-grown vineyards to the west, Austin has a rich flavor all its own.

*Brian A. Bolinger*

Established on The University of Texas campus in Austin on March 2, 1897, TSHA engages its members and the public at large through publications and outreach events.

In addition to the Handbook of Texas Online and the Texas Almanac, TSHA members receive the *Southwestern Historical Quarterly,* access to TSHA's digital resource center, and exclusive invitations and discounts to Texas history programs and events.

I invite you to visit us in Austin or online at www.tshaonline.org to explore Texas history and see what we are cooking up next.

It's good to be back home in our state's capital city, and there is no better place to call home than Texas!

**Brian A. Bolinger**
**Chief Executive Officer**
**Texas State Historical Association**

## TSHA Board of Directors

### OFFICERS

| | | | | |
|---|---|---|---|---|
| **Lynn Denton** Austin | President | **John L. Nau III** Houston | Past President (2014) |
| **Stephen C. Cook** Houston | First Vice President | **Gregg Cantrell** Fort Worth | Past President (2013) |
| **Paula Mitchell Marks** Austin | Second Vice President | **John Miller Morris Jr.** Austin | Secretary (2013–2016) |

### BOARD MEMBERS

| | | | |
|---|---|---|---|
| **Carlos K. Blanton** College Station | (2013–2016) | **Thomas R. Phillips** Austin | (2014–2017) |
| **Jessica Brannon-Wranosky** McKinney | (2015–2018) | **Rebecca Sharpless** Fort Worth | (2013–2016) |
| **James H. Clement Jr.** Dallas | (2015–2018) | **Jean A. Stuntz** Canyon | (2013–2016) |
| **W. Marvin Dulaney** Arlington | (2013–2016) | **Homero S. Vera** Premont and Sarita | (2015–2018) |
| **Jeffrey Dunn** Dallas | (2013–2016) | **Emilio Zamora** Austin | (2015–2018) |
| **David A. Gravelle** Dallas | (2014–2017) | **J.P. Bryan** Houston | Honorary Life Member |
| **Kay Bailey Hutchison** Dallas | (2015–2018) | **Walter L. Buenger** College Station | Honorary Life Member |
| **Mary Margaret McAllen** San Antonio | (2013–2016) | **John W. Crain** Dallas | Honorary Life Member |
| **Richard B. McCaslin** Denton | (2014–2017) | **Brian A. Bolinger** Austin | Chief Executive Officer (ex officio) |
| **Nancy Painter Paup** Fort Worth | (2014–2017) | **Randolph (Mike) Campbell** Denton | Chief Historian (ex officio) |

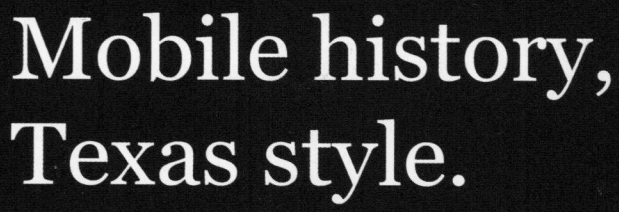
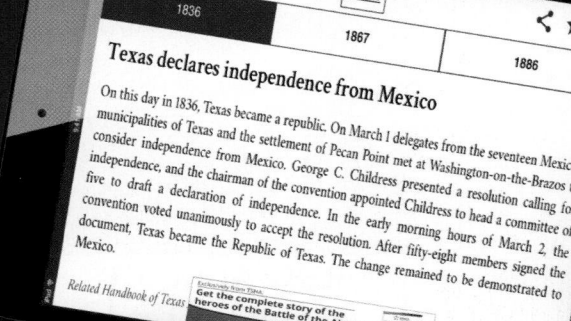
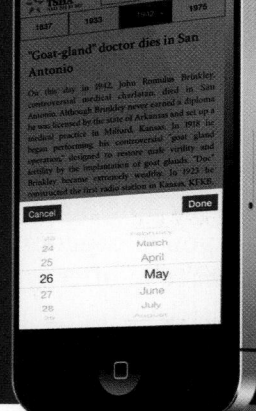

**GREG ABBOTT**
**Governor of Texas**

The Lone Star State is a fascinating place, full of beautiful natural landscapes, a diverse culture and legendary history. Home to more than 50 Fortune 500 companies and named Best State for Business 11 years in a row, Texas also boasts one of the strongest economies in the world.

Whether you are exploring our unique communities and attractions, learning about our storied past or seeking to unleash the potential for innovation and economic success, I invite you to experience everything that Texas and its people have to offer.

Greg Abbott
Governor

Fellow Texans,

I hope you enjoy the *Texas Almanac 2016-2017*. This book offers an extensive tutorial in the geography, economy, history, and people of our beautiful state. It is an excellent resource for anyone who wants to know more about our rich history and our dynamic population.

From the iconic courthouses that anchor our rural counties to the internationally recognized skylines in our largest cities, Texas is unlike any other place in the world. Throughout our

**JOE STRAUS**
**Texas House Speaker**

history, Texas has valued and encouraged exploration, discovery, and innovation. While the mechanics of our economy have changed significantly throughout our history, the determination and drive that make Texans successful have remained constant.

Today, our state is changing. Our population is growing rapidly and becoming increasingly diverse. New opportunities arise each day here, and our economy matters more and more to the rest of the world. As Texans, we embrace these changes because we know that the values that have made this such an exceptional place will continue to endure, and that Texas will remain a land of opportunity for all of its people.

After spending just a few minutes with this Almanac, you are likely to have a better understanding of the kind of state Texans have built over the last couple of centuries — and what can be built in the centuries to come. I want to thank the Texas State Historical Association for producing this thorough and engaging guide to the wonders of this state.

**Joe Straus**
Speaker
Texas House of Representatives

# TABLE OF CONTENTS

# INDEX OF TABLES

# CRIME

# CULTURE & THE ARTS

# HEALTH & SCIENCE

# EDUCATION

# BUSINESS

# TRANSPORTATION

# AGRICULTURE

*Experience life on the 19th-century farm of Anson Jones, the last president of the Republic of Texas. Barrington Living History Farm is part of the Washington-on-the-Brazos State Historic Site. Texas Parks & Wildlife Photo.*

# INDEX OF MAPS

# TEXAS
## *The Lone Star State*

*On this and the following page is a demographic and geographic profile of the second-largest, second-most-populous state in the United States. Look in the Index to find more-detailed information about each subject.*

## GOVERNMENT

**Capital:** Austin
**Government:** Bicameral Legislature
**28th State to enter the Union:** Dec. 29, 1845
**Present Constitution adopted:** 1876
**State motto:** Friendship (1930)
**State symbols:**
    **Flower:** . . . .Bluebonnet . . . . . . . (1901)
    **Bird:** . . . . . .Mockingbird. . . . . . (1927)
    **Tree:** . . . . . .Pecan . . . . . . . . . . (1919)
    **Song:** . . . . ."Texas, Our Texas" . . . (1929)
**Origin of name:** Texas, or Tejas, was the Spanish pronunciation of a Caddo Indian word meaning "friends" or "allies."
**Nickname:** Texas is called **The Lone Star State** because of the design of the state flag: a broad vertical blue stripe at left centered by a single white star, and at right, horizontal bars of white (top) and red.

## PEOPLE

**Population, 2014\***. . . . . . . . . . . . . . 26,956,958
**Population, 2010** U.S. Census. . . . . . 25,145,561
**Population increase, 2010–2014**. . . . . . . 7.2%
**Population, 2000** U.S. Census. . . . . . 20,851,820
**Population increase, 2000–2010**. . . . . . 20.6%
**Ethnicity, 2013** *(for explanation, see page 238)*:

|          | Number      | Percent |
|----------|-------------|---------|
| Anglo    | 11,637,204  | 44.0%   |
| Hispanic | 10,156,106  | 38.4%   |
| Black    | 3,279,576   | 12.4%   |
| Asian    | 1,137,272   | 4.3%    |
| Other    | 766,998     | 2.9%    |

Population density (2010) . . . . . . . 96.3 per sq. mi.
Voting-age population (2012) . . . . . . 18,279,737

\* *Jan. 1, 2014, Texas State Data Center estimate.*
*(U.S. Census Bureau, State Data Center, Texas Secretary of State.)*

### On an Average Day in Texas in 2013:

There were 1,061 resident live births.
There were 489 resident deaths.
There were 572 more births than deaths.
There were 491 marriages.
There were 209 divorces.

*(2013 Texas Vital Statistics, Dept. of State Health Services)*

## TEN LARGEST CITIES

Houston (Harris Co.) . . . . . . . . . . . . . .2,201,974
San Antonio (Bexar Co.) . . . . . . . . . . . .1,419,762
Dallas (Dallas Co.) . . . . . . . . . . . . . . . .1,255,343
Austin (Travis Co.) . . . . . . . . . . . . . . . . .877,210
Fort Worth (Tarrant Co.) . . . . . . . . . . . .798,382
El Paso (El Paso Co.) . . . . . . . . . . . . . . .669,882
Arlington (Tarrant Co.). . . . . . . . . . . . . .380,698
Corpus Christi (Nueces Co.) . . . . . . . . . .317,004
Plano (Collin Co.) . . . . . . . . . . . . . . . . .278,495
Laredo (Webb Co.) . . . . . . . . . . . . . . . .254,190

*(Texas State Data Center estimates as of Jan. 1, 2014.)*

**Number of counties.** . . . . . . . . . . . . **254**
Largest by pop . . . . . 4,441,370 . . . . . Harris Co.
Smallest by pop. . . . . . . . . .86 . . . . . Loving Co.

Number of incorporated cities . . . . . . . . . . 1,215
Number of cities of 100,000 pop. or more. . . . . 35
Number of cities of 50,000 pop. or more . . . . . 64
Number of cities of 10,000 pop. or more . . . . .221

## BUSINESS

Gross State Product (2014). . . . . . . $1.447 trillion
Per Capita Personal Income (2013). . . . . . $43,862
Civilian Labor Force (July 2015) . . . . . . 13,081,500

*(GSP: Texas Comptroller of Public Accounts and U.S. Bureau of Economic Analysis; per capita income: U.S. Bureau of Economic Analysis; civilian labor force: Texas Workforce Commission.)*

## NATURAL ENVIRONMENT

**AREA** (total) . . . . . . . . . 268,596 sq. miles
(171,901,440 acres)

**LAND AREA**. . . . . . . . . 261,232 sq. miles
(167,188,480 acres)

**WATER AREA** . . . . . . . . . 7,365 sq. miles
(4,713,600 acres)

**GEOGRAPHIC CENTER:**
About 15 miles northeast of Brady in northern McCulloch County.

**HIGHEST POINT:** Guadalupe Peak (8,749 ft.) in Culberson County in far West Texas.

**LOWEST POINT:** Gulf of Mexico (sea level).

**NORMAL AVERAGE ANNUAL PRECIPITATION RANGE:**
From 60.57 inches at Jasper County in far East Texas to 9.43 inches at El Paso, in far West Texas.

**RECORD HIGHEST TEMPERATURE:**

| | | |
|---|---|---|
| Seymour, Baylor Co., | Aug. 12, 1936 | 120°F |
| Monahans, Ward Co., | June 28, 1994 | 120°F |

**RECORD LOWEST TEMPERATURE:**

| | | |
|---|---|---|
| Tulia, Swisher Co., | Feb. 12, 1899 | −23°F |
| Seminole, Gaines Co., | Feb. 8, 1933 | −23°F |

## PRINCIPAL PRODUCTS

**MANUFACTURES:** Chemicals and allied products, petroleum and coal products, food and kindred products, transportation equipment.

**FARM PRODUCTS:** Cattle, cotton, vegetables, fruits, nursery and greenhouse, dairy products.

**MINERALS:** Petroleum, natural gas, and natural gas liquids.

**FINANCE** (as of 12/31/2014):

| | |
|---|---|
| Number of banks . . . . . . . . . . . . . . . . . . . . . | .470 |
| Total deposits . . . . . . . . . . . . | $305,584,530,000 |
| Number of savings & loan associations . . . . . . | 8 |
| Total assets . . . . . . . . . . . . . . | $62,899,043,000 |
| Number of savings banks . . . . . . . . . . . . . | 29 |
| Total assets. . . . . . . . . . . . . . . | $8,257,801,000 |

*(Banks: Federal Reserve Bank of Dallas; savings and loans and savings banks: Texas Savings and Loan Department.)*

**AGRICULTURE:**

| | |
|---|---|
| Total cash receipts, 2013 . . . . . . . . | $21.6 billion |
| Number of farms, 2010. . . . . . . . . . . | 247,500 |
| Land in farms (acres, 2010) . . . . . . . | 130.4 million |
| Cropland (acres, 2007) . . . . . . . . . | 33,667,177 |
| Harvested land (acres, 2007) . . . . . . | 19,174,301 |
| Irrigated land (acres, 2007) . . . . . . . . | 5,010,416 |

*(The Statistical Abstract of the United States 2010; 2007 Census of Agriculture.)*

The Stevie Ray Vaughan statue stands on the bank of Lady Bird Lake with the Austin skyline as its backdrop. Stevie Ray Vaughan & Double Trouble were inducted into the Rock & Roll Hall of Fame in 2015. Photo courtesy of Traces of Texas.com.

# TEXAS' Rank
## Among the United States

Texas' rank among the United States in selected categories are given below. Others categories are covered in other sections, such as Agriculture, Business, Transportation, Health & Science.

Source (unless otherwise noted): The 2013 Statistical Abstract, U.S. Census Bureau;
www.census.gov/compendia/statab

## Ten Most Populous States, 2012

| Rank | State | Population 2012 | %Change 2010–2012 |
|------|-------|------------|----------|
| 1. | California | 38,041,430 | 2.1 |
| **2.** | **Texas** | **26,059,203** | **3.6** |
| 3. | New York | 19,570,261 | 1.0 |
| 4. | Florida | 19,317,568 | 2.7 |
| 5. | Illinois | 12,875,255 | 0.3 |
| 6. | Pennsylvania | 12,763,536 | 0.5 |
| 7. | Ohio | 11,544,225 | 0.1 |
| 8. | Georgia | 9,919,945 | 2.4 |
| 9. | Michigan | 9,883,360 | 0.0 |
| 10. | North Carolina | 9,752,073 | 2.3 |

*(United States,        308,747,508        1.7)*

## Ten Fastest Growing States, 2012

| Rank | State | Population Change 2010–2012 |
|------|-------|--------------|
| 1. | North Dakota | 4.0% |
| **2.** | **Texas** | **3.6%** |
| 3. | Utah | 3.3% |
| 4. | Colorado | 3.1% |
| 5. | Alaska | 3.0% |
| 6. | Florida | 2.7% |
| 7. | Washington | 2.6% |
| 8. | Arizona | 2.5% |
| 9. | Georgia | 2.4% |
| 10. | South Dakota | 2.4% |

## Unauthorized Immigrants, 2009

| Rank | State | Estimated |
|------|-------|-----------|
| 1. | California | 2,600,000 |
| **2.** | **Texas** | **1,680,000** |
| 3. | Florida | 720,000 |
| 4. | New York | 550,000 |
| 5. | Illinois | 540,000 |
| 6. | Georgia | 480,000 |
| 7. | Arizona | 460,000 |
| 8. | North Carolina | 370,000 |
| 9. | New Jersey | 360,000 |
| 10. | Nevada | 260,000 |
| | Other states | 2,730,000 |

*(United States ............................ 10,750,000)*

## States with Most Live Births, 2009

| Rank | State | Births |
|------|-------|--------|
| 1. | California | 527,011 |
| **2.** | **Texas** | **402,011** |
| 3. | New York | 248,110 |
| 4. | Florida | 221,391 |
| 5. | Illinois | 171,255 |
| 6. | Pennsylvania | 146,432 |
| 7. | Ohio | 144,772 |

*(United States        4,131,019)*

## ... Highest Birth Rates, 2009

| Rank | State | Births per 1,000 Pop. |
|------|-------|-----------|
| 1. | Utah | 19.4 |
| **2.** | **Texas** | **16.2** |
| 2. | Alaska | 16.2 |
| 3. | Idaho | 15.4 |
| 4. | Nebraska | 15.0 |
| 5. | Oklahoma | 14.8 |
| 6. | Kansas and South Dakota | 14.7 |

*(United States            13.5)*

## States with Most Farms, 2009

| Rank | State | No. of Farms |
|------|-------|-----------|
| **1.** | **Texas** | **247,500** |
| 2. | Missouri | 108,000 |
| 3. | Iowa | 93,000 |
| 4. | Oklahoma | 87,000 |
| 5. | Kentucky | 86,000 |
| 6. | California | 82,000 |
| 7. | Minnesota | 81,000 |
| 8. | Tennessee | 79,000 |

*(United States            2,200,000)*

## ... Most Land in Farms, 2009

| Rank | State | Farm Acreage |
|------|-------|-----------|
| **1.** | **Texas** | **130,400,000** |
| 2. | Montana | 60,800,000 |
| 3. | Kansas | 46,200,000 |
| 4. | Nebraska | 45,600,000 |
| 5. | South Dakota | 43,700,000 |
| 6. | New Mexico | 43,000,000 |
| 7. | North Dakota | 39,600,000 |

*(United States            919,800,000)*

# FLAGS OF TEXAS

**United States**
1845-Present

**Spain**
1519-1821

**France**
1685-1690

**Republic**
Republic: 1836-1845; State: 1845-Present

**Mexico**
1821-1836

**Confederate States of America**
1861-1865

Texas often is called the **Lone Star State** because of its state flag with a single star. The state flag was also the **flag of the Republic of Texas.**

The following information about historic Texas flags, the current flag, and other Texas symbols may be supplemented by information from the **Texas State Library & Archives** in Austin. (On the web: **www.texasalmanac.com/topics/flags-symbols** and **www.tsl.state.tx.us/ref/abouttx/index.html#flags**)

## Six Flags of Texas

Six different flags have flown over Texas during eight changes of sovereignty. The accepted sequence of these flags follows:

**Spanish – 1519–1821**

**French – 1685–1690**

**Mexican – 1821–1836**

**Republic of Texas – 1836–1845**

**Confederate States of America – 1861–1865**

**United States – 1845 to the present.**

## Evolution of the Lone Star Flag

The Convention at Washington-on-the-Brazos in March 1836 allegedly adopted a flag for the Republic that was designed by **Lorenzo de Zavala.** The design of de Zavala's flag is unknown, but the convention journals state that a "Rainbow and star of five points above the western horizon; and a star of six points sinking below" was added to de Zavala's flag.

There was a suggestion the letters "T E X A S" be placed around the star in the flag, but there is no evidence that the Convention ever approved a final flag design. Probably because of the hasty dispersion of the Convention and loss of part of the Convention notes, nothing further was done with the Convention's proposals for a national flag.

A so-called **"Zavala flag"** is sometimes flown in Texas today that consists of a blue field with a white five-pointed star in the center and the letters "T E X A S" between the star points, but there is no historical evidence to support this flag's design.

The **first official flag of the Republic,** known as

the **National Standard of Texas** or **David G. Burnet's flag,** was adopted by the Texas Congress and approved by President Sam Houston on Dec. 10, 1836. The design "shall be an azure ground with a large golden star central."

## The Lone Star Flag

On Jan. 25, 1839, President Mirabeau B. Lamar approved the adoption by Congress of a new national flag. This flag consisted of "a blue perpendicular stripe of the width of one third of the whole length of the flag, with a white star of five points in the centre thereof, and two horizontal stripes of equal breadth, the upper stripe white, the lower red, of the length of two thirds of the length of the whole flag." This is the **Lone Star Flag,** which later became the state flag. Although Senator William H. Wharton proposed the adoption of the Lone Star Flag in 1838, no one knows who actually designed the flag. The legislature in 1879 inadvertently repealed the law establishing the state flag, but the legislature adopted a new law in 1933 that legally re-established the flag's design.

The red, white, and blue of the state flag stand, respectively, for bravery, purity, and loyalty. The proper **finial** for use with the state flag is either **a star or a spearhead.** Texas is one of only two states that has a flag that formerly served as the flag of an independent nation. The other is Hawaii.

## Rules for Display of the State Flag

The Texas Flag Code was first adopted in 1933 and completely revised in 1993. Laws governing display of the state flag are found in sections 3100.051 through 3100.072 of the Texas Government Code. (On the web: **www.tsl.state.tx.us/ref/abouttx/flagcode. html**). A summary of those rules follows:

★ The Texas flag should be displayed on state and national holidays and on special occasions of historical significance, and it should be displayed at every school on regular school days. **When flown out-of-doors,** the Texas flag should not be flown earlier than sunrise nor later than sunset unless properly illuminated. It should not be left out in inclement weather unless a weather-proof flag is used. It should be flown with the white stripe uppermost **except in case of distress.**

★ No flag other than the **United States flag** should be placed above or, if on the same level, to the state flag's right (observer's left). The state flag should be underneath the national flag when the two are flown from the same halyard. **When flown from adjacent flagpoles,** the national flag and the state flag should be of approximately the same size and on flagpoles of equal height; the national flag should be on the flag's own right (observer's left).

★ **If the state flag is displayed with the flag of another U.S. state, a nation other than the U.S., or an international organization,** the state flag should be, from an observer's perspective, to the left of the other flag on a separate flagpole or flagstaff, and the state flag should be underneath the other flag on the same flagpole or flagstaff or on a taller flagpole or flagstaff. If the state flag and the U.S. flag are displayed from crossed flagstaffs, the state flag should be, from an observer's perspective, to the right of the U.S. flag and the state flag's flagstaff should be behind the U.S.

flag's flagstaff.

★ **When the flag is displayed horizontally,** the white stripe should be above the red stripe and, from an observer's perspective, to the right of the blue stripe. **When the flag is displayed vertically,** the blue stripe should be uppermost and the white stripe should be to the state flag's right (observer's left).

★ If the state and national flags are both **carried in a procession,** the national flag should be on the marching right and state flag should be on the national flag's left (observer's right).

★ **On Memorial Day,** the state flag should be displayed at half-staff until noon and at that time raised to the peak of the flagpole. **On Peace Officers Memorial Day** (May 15), the state flag should be displayed at half-staff all day, unless that day is also Armed Forces Day.

★ The state flag should not touch anything beneath it or be dipped to any person or things except the U.S. flag. Advertising should not be fastened to a flagpole, flagstaff, or halyard on which the state flag is displayed.

★ If a state flag is no longer used or useful as an emblem for display, it should be destroyed, preferably by burning. A **flag retirement ceremony** is set out in the Texas Government Code at the Texas State Library & Archives website mentioned earlier.

## Pledge to the Texas Flag

*Honor the Texas flag; I pledge allegiance to thee, Texas, one state under God, one and indivisible.*

A pledge to the Texas flag was adopted in 1933 by the 43rd Legislature. It contained a phrase, "Flag of 1836," which inadvertently referred to the **David G. Burnet flag** instead of the Lone Star Flag adopted in 1839. In 2007, the 80th Legislature changed the pledge to its current form:

A person reciting the pledge to the state flag should face the flag, place the right hand over the heart, and remove any easily removable hat.

The pledge to the Texas flag may be recited at all public and private meetings at which the Pledge of Allegiance to the national flag is recited and at state historical events and celebrations.

The pledge to the Texas flag should be recited after the pledge of allegiance to the United States flag, if both are recited.

# TEXAS STATE SYMBOLS

## State Song

The state song of Texas is **"Texas, Our Texas."** The music was written by the late William J. Marsh (who died Feb. 1, 1971, in Fort Worth at age 90), and the words by Marsh and Gladys Yoakum Wright, also of Fort Worth. It was the winner of a state song contest sponsored by the 41st Legislature and was **adopted in 1929.** The wording has been changed once: Shortly after Alaska became a state in January 1959, the word "Largest" in the third line was changed by Mr. Marsh to "Boldest." The text follows:

# TEXAS, OUR TEXAS

Texas, our Texas! All hail the mighty State!
Texas, our Texas! So wonderful, so great!
Boldest and grandest, Withstanding ev'ry test;
O Empire wide and glorious, You stand supremely blest.

### CHORUS

God bless you Texas!
And keep you brave and strong,
That you may grow in power and worth,
Thro'out the ages long.

### REFRAIN

Texas, O Texas! Your freeborn single star,
Sends out its radiance to nations near and far.
Emblem of freedom! It sets our hearts aglow,
With thoughts of San Jacinto and glorious Alamo.

Texas, dear Texas! From tyrant grip now free,
Shines forth in splendor your star of destiny!
Mother of heroes! We come your children true,
Proclaiming our allegiance, our faith, our love for you.

## State Motto

The state motto is **"Friendship."** The word Texas, or Tejas, was the Spanish pronunciation of a Caddo Indian word meaning "friends" or "allies." It was designated by the 41st Legislature in 1930.

## State Citizenship Designation

The people of Texas usually call themselves Texans. However, **Texian** was generally used in the early period of the state's history.

## State Seal

The design of the **obverse (front)** of the State Seal consists of "a star of five points encircled by olive and live oak branches, and the words, 'The State of Texas.' " (State Constitution, Art. IV, Sec. 19.) This design is a slight modification of the Great Seal of the Republic of Texas, adopted by the Congress of the Republic, Dec. 10, 1836, and readopted with modifications in 1839.

**Front of Seal**

An official design for the **reverse (back)** of the seal was adopted by the 57th Legislature in 1961, but there were discrepancies between the written description and the artistic rendering that was adopted at the same time. To resolve the problems, the 72nd Legislature in 1991 adopted an official design.

The 73rd Legislature in 1993 finally adopted the reverse by law. The current description is in the Texas Government Code, section 3101.001:

**Back of Seal**

"(b) The reverse side of the state seal contains a shield displaying a depiction of:

(1) the Alamo; (2) the cannon of the Battle of Gonzales; and (3) Vince's Bridge.

(c) The shield on the reverse side of the state seal is encircled by:

(1) live oak and olive branches; and (2) the

unfurled flags of: (A) the Kingdom of France; (B) the Kingdom of Spain; (C) the United Mexican States; (D) the Republic of Texas; (E) the Confederate States of America; and (F) the United States of America.

(d) Above the shield is emblazoned the motto, "REMEMBER THE ALAMO," and beneath the shield are the words, "TEXAS ONE AND INDIVISIBLE."

(e) A white five-pointed star hangs over the shield, centered between the flags."

## Texas State Symbols

**State Bird** — The **mockingbird** (*Mimus polyglottos*) is the state bird of Texas, adopted by the 40th Legislature of 1927 at the request of the Texas Federation of Women's Clubs.

**State Flower** — The state flower of Texas is the **bluebonnet,** also called **buffalo clover, wolf flower,** and *el conejo* (the rabbit). The bluebonnet was adopted as the state flower, at the request of the Society of Colonial Dames in Texas, by the 27th Legislature in 1901. The original resolution made *Lupinus subcarnosus* the state flower, but a resolution by the 62nd Legislature in 1971 provided legal status as the state flower of Texas for "*Lupinus Texensis* and any other variety of bluebonnet."

**State Tree** — The **pecan tree** (*Carya illinoinensis*) is the state tree of Texas. The sentiment that led to its official adoption probably grew out of the request of Gov. James Stephen Hogg that a pecan tree be planted at his grave. The 36th Legislature in 1919 adopted the pecan tree.

## Other Symbols

*(In 2001, the Texas Legislature placed restrictions on the adoption of future symbols by requiring that a joint resolution to designate a symbol must specify the item's historical or cultural significance to the state.)*

**State Air Force** — **The Commemorative Air Force** (formerly known as the Confederate Air Force), based in Midland at Midland International Airport, was proclaimed the state air force of Texas by the 71st Legislature in 1989.

**State Amphibian** — The **Texas toad** was named the state amphibian by the 81st Legislature in 2009.

**State Aquarium** — The **Texas State Aquarium** in Corpus Christi was designated the state aquarium of Texas by the 69th Legislature in 1985.

**State Bison Herd** — The **bison herd** at Caprock Canyons State Park was named the official Texas State

The American Quarter Horse was named the state horse in 2009. Photo courtesy of the Greater Houston Quarter Horse Association.

Bison Herd by the 82nd Legislature in 2011.

**State Bluebonnet City** — The city of **Ennis** in Ellis County was designated the state bluebonnet city by the 75th Legislature in 1997.

**State Bluebonnet Festival** — The **Chappell Hill Bluebonnet Festival,** held in April, was named state bluebonnet festival by the 75th Legislature in 1997.

**State Bluebonnet Trail** — The city of **Ennis** was proclaimed the official state bluebonnet trail by the 75th Legislature in 1997.

**State Bread** — *Pan de campo,* translated "camp bread" and often called cowboy bread, was named the state bread by the 79th Legislature in 2005. It is a simple baking-powder bread that was a staple of early Texans and often baked in a Dutch oven.

**State Cobbler** — **Peach cobbler** was named the state cobbler of Texas by the 83rd Legislature in 2013.

**State Cooking Implement** — The **cast iron Dutch oven** was named the cooking implement of Texas by the 79th Legislature in 2005.

**State Crustacean** — **Texas Gulf Shrimp** was designated the state crustacean by the 84th Legislature in 2015.

**State Dinosaur** — *Paluxysaurus jonesi* was proclaimed the state dinosaur by the 81st Legislature in 2009. It replaced *Brachiosaur Sauropod, Pleurocoelus,* which was named by the 75th Legislature in 1997.

**State Dish** — **Chili** was proclaimed the Texas state dish by the 65th Legislature in 1977.

**State Dog Breed** — The **Blue Lacy** was designated the state dog breed by the 79th Legislature in 2005. The Blue

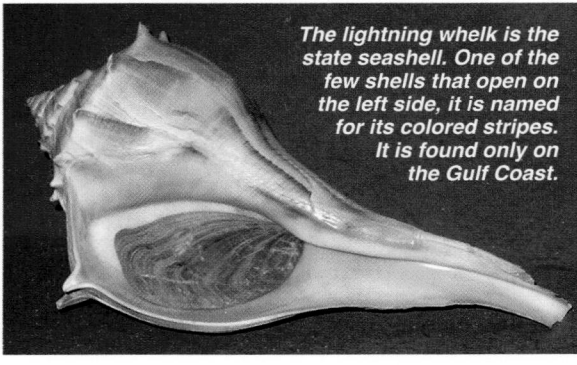

The lightning whelk is the state seashell. One of the few shells that open on the left side, it is named for its colored stripes. It is found only on the Gulf Coast.

*The State Longhorn Herd resides at Fort Griffin State Historic Site northeast of Albany in Shackelford County. Photo courtesy of Fort Griffin State Historic Site.*

Lacy is a herding and hunting breed descended from greyhound, scent-hound, and coyote stock and developed by the Lacy brothers, who left Kentucky and settled near Marble Falls in 1858.

**State Domino Game** — **42** was named the state domino game by the 82nd Legislature in 2011.

**State Epic Poem** — **"The Legend of Old Stone Ranch,"** written by John Worth Cloud, was named the epic poem of Texas by the 61st Legislature in 1969. The work is a 400-page history of the Albany–Fort Griffin area written in verse form.

**State Fiber and Fabric** — **Cotton** was designated the state fiber and fabric of Texas by the 75th Legislature in 1997.

**State Fish** — The **Guadalupe bass,** a member of the genus *Micropterus* within the sunfish family, was named the state fish of Texas by the 71st Legislature in 1989. It is one of a group of fish collectively known as black bass.

**State Flower Song** — **"Bluebonnets,"** written by Julia D. Booth and Lora C. Crockett, was named the state flower song by the 43rd Legislature in 1933.

**State Folk Dance** — The **square dance** was designated the state folk dance by the 72nd Legislature in 1991.

**State Footwear** — the **cowboy boot** was named the state footwear by the 80th Legislature in 2007.

**State Fruit** — **Texas red grapefruit** was designated the state fruit by the 73rd Legislature in 1993.

**State Gem** — **Texas blue topaz,** the state gem of Texas, is found in the Llano uplift area in Central Texas, especially west to northwest of Mason. It was

designated by the 61st Legislature in 1969.

**State Gemstone Cut** — The **Lone Star Cut** was named the state gemstone cut by the 65th Legislature in 1977.

**State Grass** — **Sideoats grama** (*Bouteloua curtipendula*), a native grass found on many different Texas soils, was designated the state grass of Texas by the 62nd Legislature in 1971.

**State Hashtag** — **#Texas** was designated the state hashtag by the 84th Legislature in 2015.

**State Tourism Hashtag** — **#TexasToDo** was designated the hashtag of Texas tourism by the 84th Legislature in 2015.

**State Legislative Hashtag** — **#txlege** was proclaimed the hashtag of the Texas Legislature by the 84th Legislature in 2015.

**State Hat** — The **cowboy hat** was named the state hat of Texas by the 84th Legislature in 2015.

**State Health Nut** — The **pecan** was designated the state health nut by the 77th Legislature in 2001.

**State Horse** — The **American Quarter Horse** was named state horse by the 81st Legislature in 2009.

**State Insect** — The **Monarch butterfly** (*Danaus plexippus*) was designated the state insect by the 74th Legislature in 1995.

**State Longhorn Herd** — The **longhorn herd** at Fort Griffin State Historic Site was named the state longhorn herd by the 61st Legislature in 1969.

**State Mammals** — The state mammals were all designated by the 74th Legislature in 1995:

• **Flying** — **Mexican free-tailed bat** (*Tadarida*

*brasiliensis);*
- **Large** — **Longhorn** *(Bos Texanus);*
- **Small** — **Armadillo** *(Dasypus novemcinctus).*

**State Maritime Museum** — The **Texas Maritime Museum** in Rockport was named the state maritime museum by the 70th Legislature in 1987.

**State Music** — **Western swing** was named the state's official music by the 82nd Legislature in 2011.

**State Musical Instrument** — The **guitar** was designated the state musical instrument by the 75th Legislature in 1997.

**State Native Pepper** — The **chiltepin** *(Capsicum annuum var. glabriusculum)* was named the native pepper of Texas by the 75th Legislature in 1997.

**State Native Shrub** — **Texas purple sage** *(Leucophyllum frutescens)* was designated the state native shrub by the 79th Legislature in 2005.

**State Nickname** — **"The Lone Star State"** was designated the state nickname of Texas by the 84th Legislature in 2015.

**State Pastries** — Both the **sopaipilla** and **strudel** were named the state pastries of Texas by the 78th Legislature in 2003.

**State Pepper** — The **jalapeño pepper** *(Capsicum annuum)* was designated the state pepper by the 74th Legislature in 1995.

**State Pie** — **Pecan pie** was named the state pie by the 83rd Legislature in 2013.

**State Plant** — The **prickly pear cactus** (Genus *Opuntia)* was named the state plant by the 74th Legislature in 1995.

**State Plays** — There are four official state plays that were designated by the 66th Legislature in 1979:
1. *The Lone Star*      2. *Texas*
3. *Beyond the Sundown*      4. *Fandangle*

**State Pollinator** — The **Western Honey Bee** *(Apis mellifera)* was designated the official pollinator of Texas by the 84th Legislature in 2015.

**State Precious Metal** — **Silver** was named the official precious metal by the 80th Legislature in 2007.

**State Railroad** — The **Texas State Railroad** was designated the state railroad by the 78th Legislature in 2003. It is a steam-powered tourist excursion train that runs between the towns of Rusk and Palestine.

**State Reptile** — The **Texas horned lizard** *(Phrynosoma cornutum)* was named the state reptile by the 73rd Legislature in 1993.

**State Rodeo Drill Team** — **Ghostriders** were named the official rodeo drill team of Texas by the 80th Legislature in 2007.

**State Saltwater Fish** — Red Drum *(Sciaenops ocellatus)* was named the state's saltwater fish by the 82nd Legislature in 2011.

**State Sea Turtle** — **Kemp's Ridley Sea Turtle** was named the state sea turtle of Texas by the 83rd Legislature in 2013.

**State Seashell** — The **lightning whelk** *(Busycon perversum pulleyi)* was named the state seashell by the 70th Legislature in 1987. One of the few shells that open on the left side, the lightning whelk is named for its colored stripes and is found only on the Gulf Coast.

**State Ship** — The battleship **USS Texas** was designated the state ship by the 74th Legislature in 1995. The USS Texas was launched on May 18, 1912, from Newport News, Virginia, and commissioned on March

*The Nymphaea "Texas Dawn" was named the state waterlily by the 82nd Legislature in 2011. Texas Parks and Wildlife photo.*

12, 1914. In 1919, it became the first U.S. battleship to launch an aircraft, and in 1939, it received the first commercial radar in the U.S. Navy. In 1940, the Texas was designated flagship of the U.S. Atlantic Fleet and was the last of the battleships to participate in both World Wars I and II. It was decommissioned on April 21, 1948, and is a National Historic Landmark and a National Mechanical Engineering Landmark. It is docked along the Houston Ship Channel.

**State Shrub** — The **crape myrtle** *(Lagerstroemia indica)* was designated the official state shrub by the 75th Legislature in 1997.

**State Snack** — **Tortilla chips and salsa** was named the state snack by the 78th Legislature in 2003.

**State Sport** — **Rodeo** was named the state sport of Texas by the 75th Legislature in 1997.

**State Squash** — **Pumpkin** was designated the state squash of Texas by the 83rd Legislature in 2013.

**State Stone** — **Petrified palmwood,** found in Texas principally near the Gulf Coast, was designated the state stone by the 61st Legislature in 1969.

**State Tall Ship** — The **Elissa** was named the state tall ship by the 79th Legislature in 2005. The 1877 ship makes its home at the Texas Seaport Museum at the port of Galveston.

**State Tartan** — The **Texas Bluebonnet Tartan** was named the official state tartan by the 71st Texas Legislature in 1989.

**State 10K** — The **Texas Roundup 10K** was named the official state 10K by the 79th Legislature in 2005 to encourage Texans to exercise and incorporate physical activity into their daily lives.

**State Tie** — The **bolo tie** was designated the state tie by the 80th Legislature in 2007.

**State Vegetable** — The **Texas sweet onion** was designated the state vegetable by the 75th Legislature in 1997.

**State Vehicle** — The **chuck wagon** was named the state vehicle by the 79th Legislature in 2005. Texas rancher Charles Goodnight is credited with inventing the chuck wagon to carry food and supplies for the cowboys on trail drives.

**State Waterlily** — The **Nymphaea "Texas Dawn"** was named the state waterlily by the 82nd Legislature in 2011. ☆

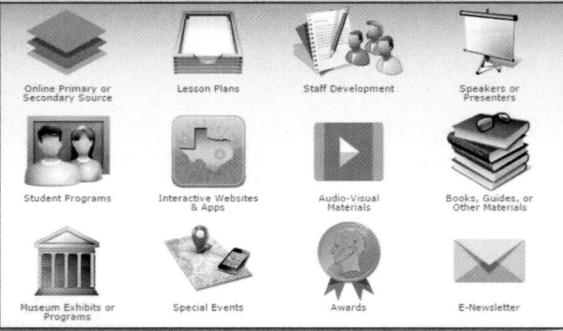

# History

*A chili stand in San Antonio's Haymarket Plaza in 1933 shows food vendors, known as "chili queens," with customers seated and spectators. San Antonio Light Collection, Institute of Texan Cultures, UT San Antonio.*

## Lone Star Cuisine
## Texas Wine Country
## A Brief Sketch of Texas History

*A couple tend to their chili stand in Haymarket Plaza in San Antonio, circa 1902–1904. Photo courtesy of the UT San Antonio collection; Virginia Essington, lender.*

# Many Cultures Converge to Create One-of-a-Kind Lone Star Cuisine

### By Dotty Griffith

What do Texas' three iconic food groups — Tex-Mex, barbecue, and chicken fried steak — have to do with six flags and five states?

Melding the six flags that have flown over Texas with five sub-states or regions cooks up a distinctive Texas cuisine; a veritable state stew, gumbo, or chili — take your pick — that reflects a land and its people. Because Texas is so big and encompasses so many different climates, terra, flora, and fauna, there are regional variations on even the most basic of Texas dishes. Similarly, the influences of indigenous people, settlers, and immigrants greatly shaped the foods we think of as Texan.

Within broad similarities, regional differences abound. That's one reason stacked enchiladas are very much a part of West Texas, that is, Marfa north to El Paso, while rolled enchiladas define enchiladas south of the Big Bend to the tip of Texas, as well as most of the rest of the state and the Tex-Mex universe.

Barbecue in East Texas reflects more Southern and African-American traditions, while barbecue in the Texas Hill Country draws heavily on the smoked sausage–making customs brought by a wave of German settlers, beginning in the early 1800s. East Texas 'cue is often served dripping with a sweeter-profile sauce than that found in the Hill Country, where smoke is a dominant seasoning and sauce (on the side) isn't nearly as sweet. Then there's chicken fried steak with white gravy, a staple of Texas cafes from the Panhandle to Brownsville, and El Paso to Texarkana. The basic idea is the same — a pounded piece of lean, tough beef, battered and fried — but with regional differences within that basic technique.

Not surprisingly, Tex-Mex ranks high on the palates, and in the hearts, of Texans. Moreover, Tex-Mex, recognized all over the United States and in many parts of the globe, is Texas' culinary gift to the world. Beloved in Paris, France, and Paris, Texas, Tex-Mex has spread far beyond the borders of the state.

Still, no place loves Tex-Mex as much as

Texas. Yelp, the website of people's choices and snarky, sometimes mean, and just plain stupid comments, calculated that Tex-Mex is the most popular cuisine in Texas, in terms of the number of restaurants. Cajun ranks second; and barbecue third, as reported in the *Huffington Post*.

To compile that information, Yelp calculated the most common cuisines in Texas based on the restaurant listings on the site. The rankings reflect the percentage of total restaurants in the state represented by each cuisine. Yelp's review service uses information pulled by third-party data providers from public records and other sources in order to create its online restaurant listings. (Are there really *that* many Popeye's and Pappadeaux restaurants in Texas?)

The same Yelp report noted that Tex-Mex is 174 percent more popular in Texas than the national average; Cajun, 171 percent; barbecue, 80 percent. Where's the other Texas food icon, chicken fried steak? It didn't make the list, but it's still a major Texas food group in my opinion, although considered by many to be a dying art form. Sadly, most chicken fried steaks served up today go from freezer to deep fryer instead of being hand-pounded to tenderize a piece of round steak, then breaded or battered to order. Be that as it may, chicken fried steak — even as a handmade rarity — is recognized as a distinctly Texas food *thang*.

To truly understand the state and its food, let's take a look at some of the influences:

★ **THE 6 FLAGS:** Spain, France, Mexico, Republic of Texas (Lone Star flag), Confederacy, and United States of America. *See* Flags box on page 35.

★ **THE 5 CULINARY SUB-STATES:** Let's begin at the beginning, with the often-talked-about provision that many people mistakenly believe is in the Texas Constitution that allows for the division of Texas into five states. Actually the 5-for-1 proposition is embodied in the March 1, 1845, Congressional Joint Resolution for Annexing Texas to the United States. The resolution allows for new states "of convenient size," not to exceed four, to be carved out of the whole. That clause is interpreted to mean one state, called "Texas," plus four within the distinctive boundary profile recognized worldwide as Texas. ***See page 466.***

To help us understand the regions of Texas cuisine, let's divide our great state into five mini-culinary states and match the flags.

1. **Tex-Mex Land — Spain and Mexico**
2. **Coastal Bend — France**
3. **New Texas — Republic of Texas**
4. **The Old South East — Confederacy**
5. **Cowboy Country — United States and Lone Star flags**

Now, let's take a closer look at each of the five culinary states of Texas.

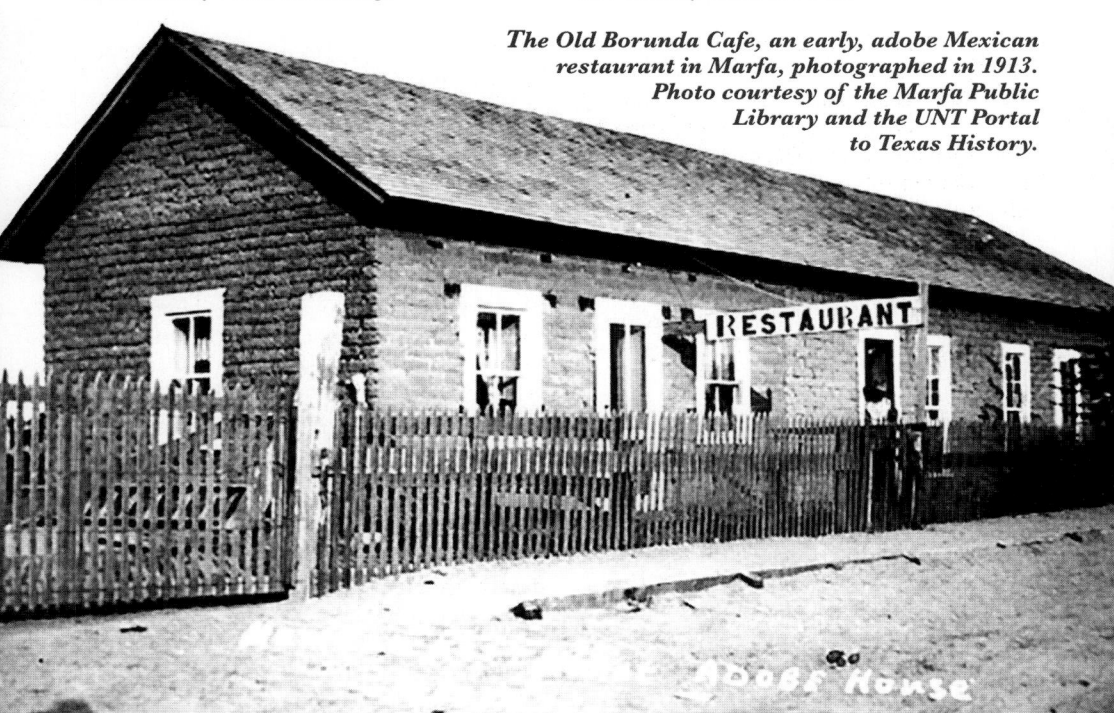

*The Old Borunda Cafe, an early, adobe Mexican restaurant in Marfa, photographed in 1913. Photo courtesy of the Marfa Public Library and the UNT Portal to Texas History.*

# Tex-Mex Land

We'll start at the beginning, in the cradle of Texas cuisine: South Texas and San Antonio. The official state dish, chili con carne, is a meat stew flavored by dried, ground chile peppers. This totally Texas dish reflects Tejano cooking — Native American, Spanish, and Mexican. The chili queens of the Spanish mission town of San Antonio made it famous. For more than 100 years, women would arrive at twilight in the plazas of San Antonio, where they cooked chili over open fires and served it outdoors at makeshift tables. Texians, the term that distinguished Anglo-American Texans from Tejanos (Mexican Texans), ate it up, as did Tejanos.

What we're calling Tex-Mex Land, the vast region from Brownsville to San Antonio to El Paso, bordered on the west by the Rio Grande and Mexico, is the Garden of Eden for Tex-Mex: nachos, flautas, tamales, tacos, enchiladas, refried beans, Mexican red rice with tomatoes, and, of course, fajitas. Chili con carne and fajitas are the truest Tex-Mex dishes, more Texas than Mexican.

Fajitas, commercialized and popularized by Ninfa Laurenzo (1924–2001) at her Ninfa's restaurant in Houston, can be traced back to the vast ranches of South Texas. Mama Ninfa, as she came to be known, grew up in South Texas where *vaqueros* (Tejano ranch hands) made something out of nothing. In this case, grilling what was once a throwaway cut of beef, the skirt steak, into delicious mesquite-flavored strips of beef. Fajitas were a very local food tradition until Ninfa Laurenzo started serving them in her restaurant. Originally beef, now fajitas can be served as grilled chicken, seafood, or vegetables. Like many other Tex-Mex favorites, fajitas are finger food, with the strips rolled into flour or corn tortillas and eaten out of hand.

*Ninfa Laurenzo at her original Ninfa's on Navigation in Houston. Photo courtesy of the Laurenzo family.*

And speaking of tortillas, flour tortillas are another Tex-Mex melting-pot creation. American and European settlers brought wheat flour with them, and soon the classic Mexican corn tortilla made of corn flour, i.e. masa, was adapted to a flat bread made of wheat flour.

Although Tex-Mex can be traced to San Antonio and South Texas, two major old-school Tex-Mex chains, El Fenix and El Chico, were developed in the Dallas area. The very fact that salsa beat out ketchup as America's favorite condiment starting in 1992 pretty much tells the story of the ascendancy of Tex-Mex.

## Coastal Bend

Cajun and Creole cuisines from Louisiana and New Orleans manifest considerable influence from Beaumont and Houston and all along the Gulf Coast. Certainly there are some Mexican seafood influences as well, but the many Cajun- and Creole-inspired  dishes and traditions dominate along the Texas Gulf Coast.

Here, let's distinguish between Cajun and Creole. In a nutshell, Creole cuisine is the classic cuisine prepared in New Orleans, reflecting French, Spanish, Caribbean, and African traditions. Cajun is the rest of the state, reflecting traditions and ingredients available to *Les Acadians*, who immigrated from French Canada to Louisiana's coasts, bayous, and prairies.

The post-Katrina diaspora gave a major boost to Cajun food in Texas, as refugees of the 2005 category-5 hurricane found new homes all over the state, particularly in Southeast Texas. Seafood gumbo, shrimp, crab, and crawfish boils; po'boy sandwiches; and boudin (rice and meat-stuffed sausage) are staples all along the Texas Gulf Coast.

But prior to Katrina, Cajun and Creole influence on Texas dates to the migration of Louisiana ranchers and their ranch hands in the early 1800s. They liked Texas' coastal prairies and salt grass flats for running cattle. The 1901 discovery of oil at Spindletop Hill near Beaumont started attracting Louisiana oilfield workers to the area, including Houston, where much of the industry is headquartered. Naturally, they brought their culinary traditions — wild game, water fowl, and seafood — with them. Various oil booms throughout the 1970s continued to draw workers in the petroleum industry.

In 1976, Louisiana restaurateurs Floyd and Billy Landry opened their first Cajun restaurant in Texas. Immensely successful, they sold what became their chain of restaurants to Galveston native and food industry magnate Tilman Fertitta, who today operates Landry's Restaurants, Inc., as well as other hospitality

*Cajun food is featured at Landry's, above; photo courtesy of Landry's website. Below, a Cajun gumbo is prepared at the Texas Folklife Festival in 1976. Photo courtesy of the Institute of Texan Cultures, UT San Antonio.*

entities. After disastrous Hurricane Katrina flooded parts of New Orleans in 2005, restaurateurs, chefs, and other food service workers evacuated to Texas towns and cities. Many stayed to rebuild their lives and livelihoods.

Today, Texans — particularly those in Southeast Texas — love crawfish, shrimp, and crab boils. Texas backyard cooks, like many others in the South and now the rest of the country, use their big seafood boiling pots and propane cookers for another Cajun specialty: fried turkey. Seafood shacks from Galveston Island to South Padre serve gumbo and "blackened" fish fillets, associated with famed Louisiana chef Paul Prudhomme. Blackening refers to the technique of coating fish with a blend of spices, then sautéing in a hot cast iron skillet. The spicy crust turns a brownish black. The increasing popularity of Cajun cuisine throughout the state, particularly along the upper Gulf Coast, reflects the influence of our Louisiana neighbors.

## New Texas

Today, the center of Texas, dominated by Austin and the Texas Hill Country, is the land of breakfast tacos and food trucks. Still, the roots of a couple of Texas iconic foods — barbecue and chicken fried steak — run deep in these parts. The Texas barbecue belt runs through towns like Taylor, Luling, Lockhart, and Elgin. This is where the German smokehouse, butcher shop, barbecue tradition rules.

Waves of German, as well as Czech and Polish, immigrants came to Texas in the 30 years before the Civil War and a couple of decades following. They, of course, brought their food traditions and adapted to the land and what it provided. Wurst meet brisket. Butcher shops and smokehouses soon morphed into barbecue emporiums. As usual, barbecue was the technique used to make the tougher cuts, like brisket, tender and palatable.

Pecan wood and oak often get the nod here when it's time to build or flavor a fire with aromatics. This is the land of dry spice rubs, while mops and basting marinades often carry the seasoning load in East Texas.

Chicken fried steak is eaten and loved all over Texas. It's thought by some that the roots of this Lone Star favorite go deep in the areas of Texas influenced by the German foodways of immigrants. It's also a dish that translated well to the Southern penchant for frying, and, of course, all Texans love beef cooked just about any and every way.

No one has made a closer study of chicken fried steak than author Robb Walsh. His *Texas Eats: The New Lone Star Heritage Cookbook* identifies three kinds of chicken fried steak

with slightly different origins. Similar to Southern fried chicken, the East Texas version is dipped in egg and then flour. There are versions in Central Texas made with bread crumbs rather than flour, much like wiener schnitzel. Cowboy style pan-fried steak in West Texas is dredged in flour and then fried, without egg batter.

Fact is, frying battered or floured meat isn't exactly a new or unique technique. But when it is called "chicken fried steak" and served with white gravy, it is Texas food. The same basic dish, served in Missouri, might be called country fried steak. Finding a fresh, hand-battered chicken fried steak at a Texas restaurant or café today can be a rare treat indeed.

## The Old South East

Culturally and economically, East Texas had a lot in common with the antebellum South. Although Texas entered the Union as a slave state, most of the plantations that operated on slave labor were in the eastern part of the state. Many of the settlers who came to Texas were from the upper South, most notably Tennessee, including Alamo hero Davy Crockett. More Alamo defenders were from Tennessee than any other state or country, including Texas. Kentucky is another state where "gone to Texas" became a frequent answer to the question of "Where  is ol' so-and so?" Of course, the lower Southern states also contributed their fair share of adventurers, entrepreneurs, schemers, dreamers, outlaws, and scofflaws. William Barret Travis is one such. The 26-year-old commander of the Alamo deserted South Carolina — and his pregnant wife and son — for Texas, arriving in 1831 where he began his new, although brief, life as a Texan.

There were basically two types of Southerners who found their way to Texas. Many from the mountainous Southern states — Arkansas, Kentucky, Tennessee — were hard scrabblers, call them hillbillies if you insist. Though not everyone from the lower Southern states — Georgia, Alabama, Mississippi, Louisiana — were aligned with wealthy plantation owners and slave holders, many were. Guess who did the cooking in those households? The influence of African-American cooks, many of whom were former slaves, on the South and on Texas can't be overstated. Their foodways impacted Texas before and well after the Civil War.

*An underground pit is used to barbecue meat at Camp George near Richmond in Fort Bend County in 1920. Photo from the George Ranch Museum Collection.*

Especially when it comes to barbecue, particularly in East Texas, black barbecue masters reigned at roadside stands, church picnics, and fundraisers. Barbecue in East Texas is often a saucy mess, whether you're eating brisket, sausage, ribs, or chicken. Though wood fuel and sauces may differ from one part of the state to the other, beef brisket is the defining meat of Texas barbecue — the piece de résistance from east to west, north to south. But in the eastern part of the state, where it abuts the Deep South, pork shoulder and whole hogs steal the show. Seems everybody everywhere loves pork ribs.

Frying is truly an art form in the South, as well as in East Texas, where "fry that sucker" is recognized as a recipe. Fried chicken and cornmeal-battered fried fish, particularly catfish, are two of the typically Southern dishes wholeheartedly adopted all over East Texas, both in homes and in restaurants, even today in the era of quinoa and kale.

Boarding house fare or country cooking — a plate with (often fried) meat and gravy, starch (potatoes or rice) and (usually overcooked) vegetables, such as green beans and corn — is typical of this part of the state, as well. Also known as meat-and-three (sides), this tradition finds expression all over Texas but nowhere more than in The Old South East.

White gravy often graces plates of fried chicken and chicken fried steak. It's a must with mashed potatoes and biscuits. Though made from golden brown pan drippings like most gravies, white or cream gravy is distinguished by the use of milk or cream as the

main liquid, not broth or water. Hence, the milky color that differentiates it from pan or brown gravy.

## Cowboy Country

The era of big cattle drives came after the Civil War. Texas was back in the Union and selling beef was a major rebuilding effort all over the state. This vast plains area was ripe for settlement. There's lots of space on these open plains for driving or raising cattle. Stands to reason that cowboy chuck wagon fare and steaks rule menus around here.

Famed rancher and cattleman Charles Goodnight invented the portable cowboy kitchen known as the chuckwagon in 1866 as a way to provision the cowboys who would drive 2,000 longhorns from the Panhandle to Denver. Chuckwagon  menus often included black-eyed peas, pinto beans, corn, and cabbage, all very portable and non-perishable. Not surprisingly beef, as well as bison, steaks and stews were common fare. Chiles, garlic, and onion were the main flavoring agents. Fish or frog legs from rivers and lakes provided welcome variety on occasion. Staples like sourdough bread, biscuits, or corn bread and boiled cowboy coffee were always available.

Cowboy chef and restaurateur Tom Perini embodies this era of Texas food in his restaurant and catering operation. Perini Ranch

*Tom and Lisa Perini at their Perini Ranch Steakhouse in Buffalo Gap. Photo courtesy of the Perini Ranch website.*

Steakhouse in Buffalo Gap, just south of Abilene, is known for its range of Texas dishes, particularly his signature steaks. In addition to beef served in his restaurant, Perini ships thousands of pounds of his famous smoked beef tenderloin all over the world. Perini's menu reflects the coming together of all types of Texas cuisines in this region and, today, over much of Texas. Perini serves killer fried chicken, barbecue, chicken fried steak, and grilled steaks. His sides reflect a panoply of homestyle Texas vegetables, stewed green beans and mashed potatoes, and desserts like peach cobbler.

This part of Texas is ground zero for the Saturday night steak special at small town steakhouses, where all-you-can-eat sirloin is the favored fare, especially during fall hunting season when small towns are flooded with dove, deer, quail, and turkey hunters. The Big Texan Steak Ranch in Amarillo is another well-known Texas venue, where big appetites eat free if they can finish off 72-ounces of beef in an hour.

Nothing is more identified with Texas than a big ol' steak dinner. Even in an era when chefs serve very complex and sophisticated dishes, a prime steak remains a top-tier dining experience. Big cities like Houston and Dallas are home to luxe steakhouses, charging as much as $100 for some magnificent cuts. Smaller towns are the places where family-owned steakhouses may be the only restaurant in town. Yep, they'll have chicken fried steak, barbecue, and

Mexican food on the menu, too.

Texas cuisine is a fascinating blend of old and new. Regional differences abound. Still the big three of Lone Star cuisine — Tex-Mex, barbecue, and chicken fried steak — symbolize the state's foodways to Texans and wannabe Texans.

### SOURCES

Harry Bradford. "Here Is the Most Disproportionately Popular Cuisine in Each State," Huffington Post. Jan. 14, 2015.

Rob Walsh. *Texas Eats: The New Lone Star Heritage Cookbook*. Berkeley: Ten Speed Press, 2012.

*Dotty Griffith spent most of her 34-year career with* The Dallas Morning News *as food editor and restaurant critic. She is the author of nine cookbooks, most about Texas-style cuisine. She hosted a radio show about Texas cuisine, "In the Kitchen with Dotty," on KRLD radio in Dallas and has written about Texas cuisine for John Mariani's* Virtual Gourmet, The New York Times, Gourmet Magazine, Modern Luxury Magazine Dallas, *and* Houston Magazine.

# Six Flags and Five Culinary States
## *More than roller coasters and Wild West shootouts*

*Six Flags isn't just the brand of an amusement park empire, although the parks are tangible memes that keep this Texas history alive: six national flags have flown over Texas.*

### Spain 1519–1821  Mexico 1821–1836

Spain was the first European power to claim Texas beginning with the explorations of colonial marauder Hernán Cortéz in 1519. Spanish influence continued for 300 years, with a significant legacy. Spanish remained the language of

the Mexican nation that freed itself from Spain in 1821, including parts of Texas today. Many towns in Texas bear Spanish names, prominently San Antonio, the hub of Spanish missions. On the culinary side, the chili queens of San Antonio symbolize roots of the cuisine we know as Tex-Mex.

### France 1685–1690

France's tenure in Texas was brief, a short-lived attempt to expand its base from French Louisiana. The flag bearing the fleur de lys

was planted in East Texas near the Gulf Coast. The French in Texas didn't last long and their impact was not particularly significant. Most of the French influence in Texas cuisine, like the fleeting French presence in Texas, comes from Louisiana in the form of Cajun and Creole dishes, particularly since the post-Katrina migrations. Think gumbo and crawfish boils.

### The Republic of Texas 1836–1845

The war for independence from Mexico established Texas as a republic. Though Texas wasn't an

independent nation all that long before joining the United States, that status has forever marked the Lone Star State as a bastion of bravado. This is just one of the unique features defining our state. Texas as a fledgling nation blended European cultures into a new identity, much the same way schnitzel may have become chicken fried steak.

### The Confederacy 1861–1865

Sixteen years after joining the Union, Texas went along with Southern states in a bloody and

ill-fated attempt to secede. The eastern parts of the state were closely aligned with the South culturally and economically. This sentiment prevailed in the debate over joining the doomed rebel cause. The culinary legacy of the South had a great influence on Texas cuisine, especially in East Texas where saucy barbecue and fried chicken are as much a part of the fabric of life as sweet tea.

### United State of America 1845–1861; 1865–present

Beef in the shape of longhorns helped define Texas in the years immediately following the Civil War. This was the era of cattle drives and sprawling ranches, driving the lore that symbolizes Texas to much of the world. Add oil wells to the image of much

land and many cattle and you have the bigger-than-life mystique of 16-ounce T-bone steaks. Yes, there's more to Texas cuisine, but for many Texans a big steak remains tops when it comes to big deal meals.

# Good Eats from the Five Culinary States of Texas

*These recipes are from Dotty Griffith's* **The Texas Holiday Cookbook, Second Edition,** *Taylor Trade Publishing. It is her ninth cookbook, and recipes are tied to major Texas holidays from Thanksgiving to New Year's. Each was selected to reflect traditions of one of the six flags of Texas: https://rowman.com/ISBN/9781589798649/The-Texas-Holiday-Cookbook-Second-Edition. Photos are by Dallas-based photographer Rick Turner: http://www.rickturnerphotography.com.*

## Tex-Mex Land — Spain & Mexico

Chili con carne is the official state dish. A meat stew flavored by dried, ground chile peppers, this dish reflects Tejano cooking — Native American, Spanish, and Mexican. The chili queens of the Spanish mission town of San Antonio made it famous.

### CHILI CON CARNE

3 pounds coarsely ground beef or venison, or a mixture
4 cloves garlic, crushed
7 tablespoons chili powder
1 tablespoon ground cumin
1 (8-ounce) can tomato sauce or enchilada sauce
2 cups water, or as needed
3 tablespoons masa harina or instant dissolving flour
1 teaspoon salt, or to taste
1 teaspoon cayenne pepper, or to taste, optional
1 tablespoon paprika, optional

Place one-third of meat in a large saucepan or Dutch oven over medium-high heat. Cook until juices evaporate and meat begins to turn brown. Remove from pot and reserve. Repeat until all meat is cooked. Return meat to pot.

Lower heat and add garlic. Cook and stir until garlic softens and the fragrance is compelling. Stir

in 6 tablespoons chili powder and cumin, mixing well to coat meat evenly. Add tomato or enchilada sauce and enough water to just barely cover the meat.

Raise heat and bring liquid to a boil. Lower heat and simmer, covered, about 1 hour or until meat is tender.

While stirring, sprinkle masa harina or flour over chili, 1 tablespoon at a time. Allow chili to cook and thicken between additions. Adjust thickness with additional masa or flour, as desired. Some Texans like soupy chili, others like theirs thick, like stew.

Cook, uncovered, for 20 minutes longer, or until liquid is slightly reduced and thickened. Add salt and cayenne pepper to taste.

Stir in paprika for a brighter red color. About 5 minutes before serving, stir in 1 tablespoon chili powder for a fresher chili flavor.

Makes 8 servings.

## Coastal Bend — France

No dish says Cajun and Creole like gumbo. Rice may be the bed or crown for this traditional seafood and okra stew. Use shrimp and oysters from the Texas Gulf Coast.

### GULF GUMBO

3 tablespoons vegetable oil
⅓ cup flour
1 cup chopped onion
½ cup green bell pepper, chopped
½ cup celery, chopped
2 cloves garlic, chopped
1 (28-ounce) can tomatoes, chopped (juice reserved)
6 cups chicken stock
½ cup bottled clam juice
1 (8-ounce) package frozen sliced okra
½ teaspoon leaf oregano
1 bay leaf
1 teaspoon black pepper
½ teaspoon cayenne pepper, or to taste
1 teaspoon salt, or to taste
1 pound Texas seafood: peeled shrimp, crab, or whitefish (such as snapper or catfish), cut into 1-inch cubes (or a combination of seafood)
12 fresh Texas oysters, liquid reserved, optional
1 tablespoon filé powder
6 cups cooked rice

Heat vegetable oil in a large pot or Dutch oven over low heat. Stir in flour and cook, stirring constantly, until flour is dark brown, about 30 minutes. Add onion, green pepper, celery and garlic. Cook until vegetables soften and onion begins to brown.

Stir tomatoes and their juice, stock, and clam juice into vegetables.

Add okra, oregano, bay leaf, black pepper, cayenne, and salt. Bring liquid to a boil; reduce heat and simmer, uncovered, about 30 minutes until vegetables are tender.

Add seafood, except oysters, and cook just until seafood texture firms, about 5 minutes. Fish will turn white; shrimp will turn pink. If using, add oysters and their liquid during the last minute or so of cooking. Adjust seasoning to taste.

Just before serving, add filé (ground sassafras) to thicken gumbo to desired consistency. Do not allow liquid to boil again or filé will appear stringy; and oysters will overcook. Cook oysters just until the edges curl.

Ladle cooked gumbo into rice in shallow bowls. Or top gumbo with a scoop of rice.

Makes 12 servings.

## New Texas — Republic of Texas

Brisket has a deserved reputation as a tough cut of meat. Long, slow cooking over indirect heat and smoke is the key to tenderness. The technique in this recipe provides great smoke flavor without a giant outdoor smoker. It produces foolproof, tender, flavorful brisket.

### SMOKY BRISKET

1 (8 to 10 lb.) whole beef brisket, with fat layer
2 tablespoons garlic salt
2 tablespoons lemon pepper
2 tablespoons paprika
1 tablespoon chili powder
1 tablespoon sugar

Remove brisket from refrigerator about 1 hour before grilling. Combine garlic, salt, lemon pepper, paprika, chili powder, and sugar. Sprinkle over entire surface of meat, concentrating on fat layer. Rub or press seasoning into meat.

Cover and let meat come to room temperature. Light a fire in a charcoal grill big enough to hold the brisket. Allow coals to burn down to gray ash. Place brisket on grill, fat side up.

Grill until fat is charred, turning occasionally, when necessary, to stop fat from dripping into fire. Squirt flare-ups with water to douse the flames. It will take about 45 minutes to grill the brisket. Remove brisket from grill.

Preheat oven to 300 degrees F. Place brisket on a double thickness of foil in a shallow roasting pan. Wrap brisket tightly and bake for 5 to 8 hours, or until meat is very tender. Remove brisket from oven and peel back foil.

Raise oven temperature to 350 degrees. Return brisket to oven and roast, uncovered, for 30 minutes to crisp the top layer of fat.

Allow meat to rest for 20 minutes. Slice across the grain into thin slices.

Serve with your favorite barbecue sauce. Makes 10 to 12 servings.

## The Old South East — Confederacy

Black-eyed peas are a traditional Southern vegetable and a good luck charm if consumed on New Year's Day. This delicious relish is great any time of year as a salad or garnish.

### LONE STAR CAVIAR

1 (16-ounce) package frozen black-eyed peas
1 cup green bell pepper, chopped into pieces about the size of black-eyed peas
1 cup red bell pepper, chopped into pieces about the size of black-eyed peas
¼ cup finely chopped jalapeno pepper, ribs and seeds removed
1 cup yellow onion, chopped into pieces about the size of black-eyed peas
1 cup finely chopped green onion, including green tops
2 cloves garlic, finely chopped
1 cup finely chopped parsley
¾ cup vegetable or olive oil
¼ cup lime or lemon juice
1 teaspoon maple syrup, optional
2 teaspoons salt, or to taste
1 teaspoon pepper, or to taste

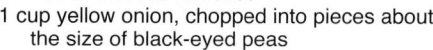

Cook black-eyed peas, according to package directions, or just until tender, 15 to 20 minutes. Drain well.

Place black-eyed peas in a large mixing bowl. Toss with peppers, onion, garlic, and parsley. Whisk together oil, lime or lemon juice, maple syrup, salt, and pepper. Adjust seasoning to taste. Pour over vegetables and refrigerate overnight to meld flavors.

Store in refrigerator up to 1 week. Makes 6 cups.

## Cowboy Country — U.S. & Lone Star

Pecans are the favorite nut of Texas. Pie made with pecan filling is one of the state's best desserts. Add a scoop of vanilla ice cream or a dollop of whipped cream if you want to make it even more special.

### PECAN PIE

½ cup sugar
¼ teaspoon salt
1 cup white or dark corn syrup
½ cup unsalted butter
3 eggs, beaten until foamy
2 teaspoons vanilla
2 cups coarsely chopped pecans or 1 cup coarsely chopped pecans and 1 cup pecan halves
1 unbaked (9-inch) pie shell, refrigerated

Preheat oven to 350 degrees F. Combine sugar, salt, and corn syrup in a small saucepan over medium-high heat. Cook until sugar dissolves and mixture is hot. Stir in butter and remove from heat. Stir until butter melts and liquid cools slightly. Add eggs, vanilla, and chopped pecans. Pour into chilled pie shell and smooth filling evenly. If using pecan halves, arrange on top of pie. Brush tops of pecans with filling from sides of saucepan.

Bake for 55 minutes to 1 hour or until tip of a sharp knife inserted in center comes out clean. Cool on wire rack. Makes 8 servings. ☆

# Texas Wine Country

*A vineyard near Fredericksburg. Photo courtesy of Traces of Texas.com.*

## The Long and Winding Trail from Grape to Wine

**By Melinda Esco**

Wine can be made from just about any fruit but most, if not all, commercial Texas wines are made from grapes. Texas winemakers are recognized in international wine competitions and the industry has grown significantly over the past couple of decades.

### HISTORY

For centuries, grapes have grown wild in Texas. Fifteen native species grow here, giving Texas the distinction of claiming more native species than anywhere in the world. In the 1600s, Spanish missionaries, with vines they brought from Mexican missions, planted grapes near the Rio Grande close to present-day El Paso, thus establishing the first vineyard at the Ysleta Mission. But for many early Texas settlers, grape growing was unfamiliar.

As Europeans from wine-producing countries began settling in Texas in the 1800s, they brought grapevine cuttings with them, and they planted the rootstock on their newly acquired land. A number of these imported grapes grew for a while, but the vines eventually died and only the native varieties survived.

Illinois native Thomas Volney Munson (1843–1913) graduated from the University of Kentucky in Lexington, earned a master of science degree from the State Agricultural and Mechanical College of Kentucky, and worked at the university as a science professor in 1870–1871. In 1873, he moved to Nebraska and began his career as a horticulturist and viticulturist. His passion for grape growing motivated him to experiment with the native wild grapes of the area, but the weather extremes in Nebraska hampered his efforts, so he moved in 1876 to the North Texas town of Denison where his brothers were already living.

Munson quickly recognized the enormous diversity of soil and climate around Texas, and he began traveling extensively throughout the state to collect native varieties of grapes. His research led him to write a number of articles on the classification and hybridization of grapes. Much of his work concentrated on improving American grapes, and his studies eventually led to the introduction of more than 300 grape varieties.

The Texas wine industry grew in the late 1800s, and by the turn of the century, as many as 25 wineries were operating in the state. But in 1919, the 18th amendment to the Constitution of the United States, the Volstead Act, was passed and Prohibition outlawed the production and sale of alcoholic beverages nationwide. Only one Texas winery survived: the Val Verde Winery that was established by Frank Qualia in 1883 near the border of Mexico in Del Rio.

Originally from Italy, Qualia moved to Mexico when he was 18 years old and eventually ended up in San Antonio. It was there that he heard that land was available through a land development program, so he moved to Del Rio and acquired some fertile property. He farmed various crops, including grapes. What began as winemaking for family and friends later turned into a commercial venture. During Prohibition, Qualia continued to grow grapes, and his vineyard was able to survive the ban on alcohol by selling table grapes.

It wasn't until 1933, when Prohibition was repealed by another amendment to the Constitution, that the wine industry got a new start.

*Thomas Volney Munson.*
*Grape Man of Texas*

But it still took years for Texas to make a comeback. Even after the repeal of Prohibition, there were still many laws on the books governing the sale and distribution of alcohol that hindered the industry. (In fact, today, there are a number of Texas counties or parts of counties that remain "dry," where the sale of alcohol is prohibited.) Vineyards in California started thriving and when their wines began winning in international competitions, people began to notice.

In 1971, Dr. Bobby Smith, an Arlington osteopathic physician, bought 50 acres of land near Springtown in Parker County and planted a vineyard that next year. A few years later, the Llano Estacado Winery just outside Lubbock began operations. Then, the Shady Lake Growers Association was formed, and a new generation of Texas wineries was born.

Texas law, however, needed changes in order to support winemaking as an industry. It was illegal for Smith to make wine in Springtown. Unable to afford a lobbyist, he spearheaded a group that eventually influenced

*The wine tasting room at the Duchman Family Winery in Hays County, southeast of Driftwood. Photo courtesy of the winery.*

*Wine-filled barrels fill a room at Llano Estacado Winery in Lubbock. USDA/Natural Resources Conservation Services photo. Grapes, below, ripen at the Dry Comal Creek Vineyards and Winery in New Braunfels. Photo courtesy of the winery.*

the Texas Legislature to pass the Texas Farm Winery Act of 1977, which enabled grape growers to produce wine in a dry county as long as the distribution of the wine itself took place where it was legal to do so. But some of the best vineyards were located in dry counties.

Smith bought property in nearby Lakeside, just inside Tarrant County, where it was legal to sell alcohol. He opened a tasting room there but had to establish it as another business so he could legally sell the wine he made in Springtown to the tasting room he ran in Lakeside. Smith later had to sell his Lakeside tasting room for the expansion of Texas 199 but continues to maintain his Springtown vineyard.

In 2001, laws changed again. Susan Combs, then-commissioner of the Texas Department of Agriculture (TDA), was instrumental in shepherding through the state legislature the successful passage of laws that paved the way for Texas wineries to profit. It finally became legal in dry counties for wineries to sell wine in their tasting rooms and to ship wine to or from

dry or wet areas.

After subsequent years of appeals and legal wrangling, customers now can place their orders with any winery in the state and pick them up at approved package stores.

## A BOOMING BUSINESS

Texas currently claims the distinction as the fifth-largest wine-producing state in the country, after California, New York, Washington, and Oregon. More than 8,000 people are employed in some aspect of the wine business, and the industry pours over a billion dollars a year into the Texas economy. There are more than 200 wineries in Texas scattered throughout the state.

Not all wineries grow grapes, and not all vineyards make and sell wine; but the ones that do both rely heavily on tourists to support their ventures. The wine business in Texas is as much about tourism as it is about the grapes on the vine or the wine in the bottle.

Wine events across the state range from intimate dinners and afternoon concerts to seasonal tours of one- to three-day road trips at various times during the year to visit regional wineries. Occasionally, winemakers work together to offer opportunities for folks to taste a number of wines from the different vineyards in a single setting. Some of the larger wineries may include a bed and breakfast (B&B), and a number of them support restaurants that prepare dishes to showcase their wines. As Gladys and Raymond Haak, owners of the Santa Fe vineyard and winery bearing their last name, put it: "We're in the entertainment business." In addition to hosting Sunday afternoon concerts during the summer, they have their

grapevines blessed by a priest and they invite the public to help them harvest. Many wineries conduct tours of their operations to share with the public how they make their wine. There are also numerous wine festivals. Grapefest—probably the state's largest one—is held annually in Grapevine over several days in September, and thousands of people attend.

The Texas Department of Agriculture supports the state's winemakers with the Go-Texan program that helps with marketing and representation on state, national, and even an international level.

Winemaking is an expensive venture.

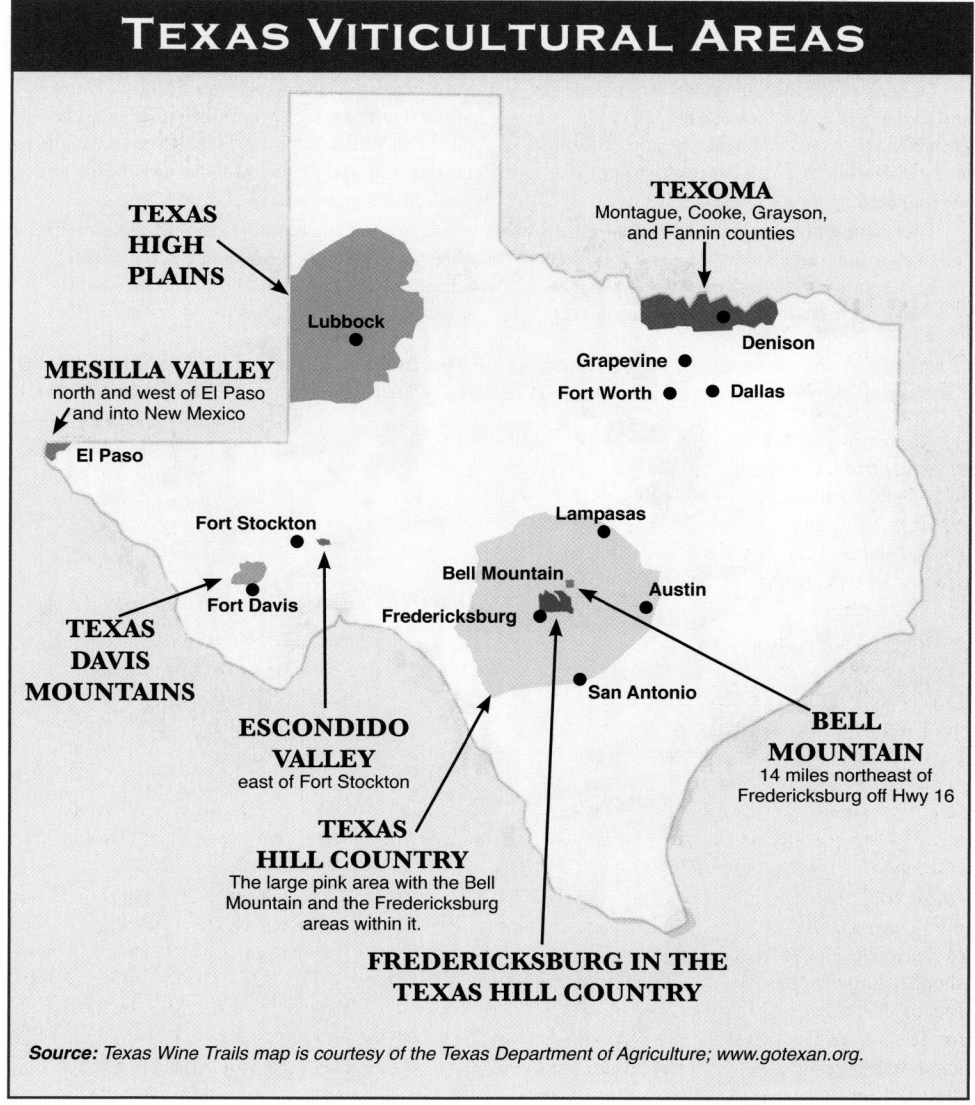

## TEXAS VITICULTURAL AREAS

**TEXAS HIGH PLAINS**

Lubbock

**MESILLA VALLEY**
north and west of El Paso and into New Mexico

El Paso

Fort Stockton

**TEXAS DAVIS MOUNTAINS**

Fort Davis

**ESCONDIDO VALLEY**
east of Fort Stockton

**TEXOMA**
Montague, Cooke, Grayson, and Fannin counties

Denison

Grapevine

Fort Worth • Dallas

Lampasas

Bell Mountain

Fredericksburg

Austin

San Antonio

**BELL MOUNTAIN**
14 miles northeast of Fredericksburg off Hwy 16

**TEXAS HILL COUNTRY**
The large pink area with the Bell Mountain and the Fredericksburg areas within it.

**FREDERICKSBURG IN THE TEXAS HILL COUNTRY**

*Source:* Texas Wine Trails map is courtesy of the Texas Department of Agriculture; www.gotexan.org.

Initially, a winemaker must decide whether to grow the grapes used to make the wine or to purchase them from other growers. This business decision affects all the rest: the location and size of the winery; what to include, such as a tasting room, an events center, a restaurant, or a B&B; which grapes to grow; which wines to make; how to market them;. It takes deep pockets to finance a winery, and there are considerable risks. Even as the number of wineries across the state continues to grow, several of them have closed. Running a winery while maintaining a vineyard requires substantial resources, including workers, and as romantic a venture as it may seem to be, it is simply a huge commitment of money, time, and effort.

## GROWING GRAPES

Despite risks, including disease, pestilence, and extreme weather conditions, growing grapes in the Lone Star State can be profitable, and the demand for Texas-grown grapes has skyrocketed.

There are a number of challenges to growing grapes that need careful consideration and the best solutions for success: how to irrigate; how to recognize disease and how to prevent it; how to control weeds and pests; and how to prune the vines. Determining which grapes to plant can be a daunting task and, consequently, has the potential to make or break a vintner. Over the past several years, however, the TDA has implemented programs to educate prospective winemakers and aid them in making such important decisions. The Texas Winegrape Network (http://winegrapes.tamu.edu), a joint effort by Texas A&M University and the Texas AgriLife Extension Service, is a valuable resource for grape farmers. There is even a grape-growing and winemaking degree offered through the Viticulture and Enology program at Grayson County College outside Sherman. Aspiring vintners can choose between an Associate of Applied Science degree or a Viticulture Certificate Program. Classes are taught at the T. V. Munson Viticulture and Enology Center located at the college, a facility that includes a library, classrooms, and labs for processing grapes to make juice and wine. It is home to the T. V. Munson Memorial.

Grapevines generally are sold as dormant, bare-rooted plants. Grapes are self-fruitful, which means they need no pollination, and most are grafted — the vine is started with a

*Festivals are a fun way to sample wines of multiple wineries. The Fredericksburg Food & Wine Fest features 25 Texas Wineries. Photo courtesy of the festival.*

*The Delaney Vineyards and Winery in Grapevine. Photo courtesy of the winery.*

cutting from one variety that is then connected to another variety by a horticultural process called grafting. The resulting rootstocks are resistant to certain pathogens. The variety of the grape determines the variety of the wine. The quality of the grape determines the quality of the wine but, additionally, every single element in the process influences the quality. The type of soil, the mineral content of the water, and the timing of the harvest all affect the outcome of the wine long before the actual fermentation process even begins.

Location is key in the grape-growing business — conditions have to be just right to grow grapes successfully and the location of a vineyard affects the amount of grapes harvested as well as the quality of the fruit.

There are eight federally approved viticulture areas in Texas and, although they are somewhat determined by region, the designation simply means that a minimum of 85 percent of a wine's grapes must be grown in that particular viticulture in order to be labeled from that area. They are the Bell Mountain Viticultural Area, established in 1986; Fredericksburg in the Texas Hill Coun-

try Viticultural Area, established in 1988; Texas Hill Country Viticultural Area, established in 1991; Escondido Valley Viticultural Area, established in 1992; Texas High Plains Viticultural Area, established in 1993; Davis Mountains Viticultural Area, established in 1999; Mesilla Valley Viticultural Area, established in 1985; and Texoma Viticultural Area, established in 1992. The viticulture area in which a vineyard

*Grape Creek Vineyards near Stonewall. Photo by Melinda Esco.*

is located has everything to do with deciding which varieties of grapes to grow. More information about these Texas grape growing regions can be found on the website http://txwineregions.tamu.edu.

Grape growing is labor intensive, and the success of a vineyard depends on the people who work in it. Currently, the single biggest threat to grape production in Texas is Pierce's disease. There is a huge effort by a number of institutions coordinating with the Texas A&M University System to understand and ultimately control this devastating disease, for which TAMU has established the Texas Pierce's Disease Research Laboratory and Vineyard at Fredericksburg.

*The annual Harvest Festival at Mitas Hill Vineyard in McKinney is open to the public. Photo courtesy of the winery. Margaret Collins, below, at La Bodega Winery, which is in DFW International Airport. Photo by Melinda Esco.*

Irrigation is critical for maintaining a vineyard. Grapes are mostly water, and with the extremes in weather, especially when it comes to rain, mechanical irrigation is a requirement. The most effective way to irrigate is by a simple drip system that supplies water to the roots, because overhead watering promotes disease. The Texas Agri-Life Extension Service offers research on best practices that consider such factors as soil composition and evapotranspiration data. If watering is the most critical component to a good crop, pruning is second. Following scientific methods of pruning during the establishment of a vineyard is important and necessary in subsequent years, as well.

## MAKING WINE

Harvested grapes, whether by machine or hand, are sorted and destemmed. Large, industrial stainless-steel crushers extract juice from the grapes. Juice from all varieties is essentially the same color; wine gets its color from how long the skins of the grapes soak in the juice during fermentation.

For white wines, the skins are removed immediately after crushing; leaving the skins in for a short amount of time results in a blush wine, while leaving them in for an extended period of time yields the reds. The crushed grapes are allowed to settle, and the sediment is removed by a process called racking, whereby juice is pumped out of one container and into another.

Next, yeast is added, which begins the fermentation process, converting sugars in the juice into alcohol and carbon dioxide. Fermentation takes place in large steel vats that are monitored closely by measuring samples for sugar content. The winemaker also checks taste and smell. White and blush wines undergo clarification, a filtration process to protect against microbial spoilage that is unnecessary for red wines. White, blush, and reds wines then undergo a fining process to remove tannins. Next come stabilization processes to prevent tartrate crystals from forming. The quality of wine is strongly affected by the stabilization process; the goal of a winemaker is to achieve stability without over-processing.

Wine is then stored and aged in oak barrels, which when full weigh about 600 pounds each. The wine can be racked again a time or two during the aging process. After aging is complete, the wine is ready to be bottled. The Texas Alcoholic Beverage Commission (TABC) enforces strict guidelines for bottling wine. The bottling area must meet state requirements, and no bottles can be reused. Corks can be either organic or manmade; screwtops are also used. Bottle labels must adhere to labeling guidelines and be approved by the TABC, as well as the U.S. Bureau of Alcohol, Tobacco, and Firearms. ☆

*Melinda Esco is a sixth-generation Texan and has lived all over the state. She has enjoyed a long career in publishing and is the production manager at TCU Press in Fort Worth. She wrote the book* Texas Wineries, *which was published by TCU Press. She and her husband, Mark, live in Azle.*

## TEXAS WINE TRAILS

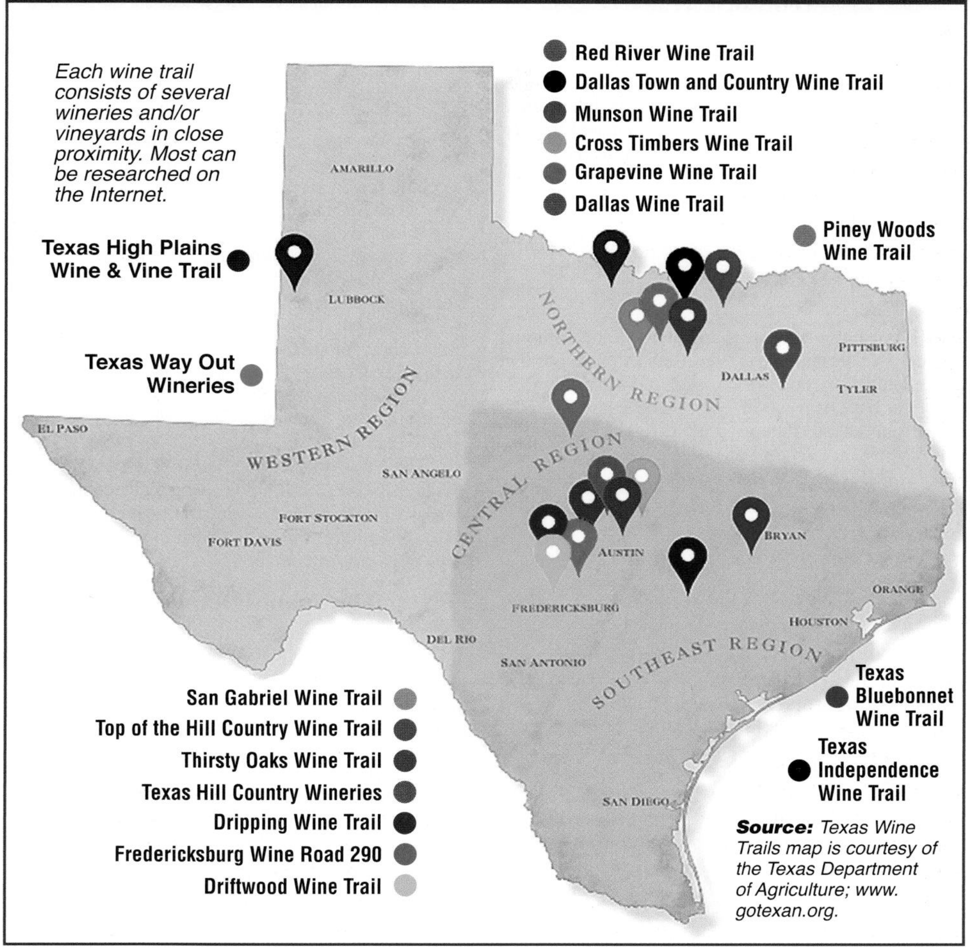

Each wine trail consists of several wineries and/or vineyards in close proximity. Most can be researched on the Internet.

- Red River Wine Trail
- Dallas Town and Country Wine Trail
- Munson Wine Trail
- Cross Timbers Wine Trail
- Grapevine Wine Trail
- Dallas Wine Trail

Piney Woods Wine Trail

Texas High Plains Wine & Vine Trail

Texas Way Out Wineries

AMARILLO

LUBBOCK

EL PASO

FORT STOCKTON

FORT DAVIS

SAN ANGELO

DEL RIO

SAN ANTONIO

FREDERICKSBURG

AUSTIN

BRYAN

DALLAS

PITTSBURG

TYLER

ORANGE

HOUSTON

SAN DIEGO

NORTHERN REGION

WESTERN REGION

CENTRAL REGION

SOUTHEAST REGION

San Gabriel Wine Trail
Top of the Hill Country Wine Trail
Thirsty Oaks Wine Trail
Texas Hill Country Wineries
Dripping Wine Trail
Fredericksburg Wine Road 290
Driftwood Wine Trail

Texas Bluebonnet Wine Trail

Texas Independence Wine Trail

**Source:** *Texas Wine Trails map is courtesy of the Texas Department of Agriculture; www.gotexan.org.*

# A Brief Sketch of
# TEXAS HISTORY

*This two-part sketch of Texas' past, from prehistoric times to 1980, is based on "A Concise History of Texas" by former Texas Almanac editor Mike Kingston. Mr. Kingston's history was published in the 1986–1987 edition of the Texas Almanac, which marked Texas' sesquicentennial. Robert Plocheck, associate editor of the Texas Almanac, edited and expanded Mr. Kingston's history.*

# Prehistory to Annexation

## Prehistoric Texas

Early Texans are believed to have been descendants of Asian groups that migrated across the Bering Strait during the Ice Ages of the past 50,000 years. At intermittent periods, enough water accumulated in massive glaciers worldwide to lower the sea level several hundred feet. During these periods, the Bering Strait became a 1,300-mile-wide land bridge between North America and Asia.

These early adventurers worked their way southward for thousands of years, eventually getting as far as Tierra del Fuego in South America about 10,000 years ago.

Biologically, they were completely modern homo sapiens. No evidence has been found to indicate that any evolutionary change occurred in the New World.

Four basic stages reflecting cultural advancement of early inhabitants are used by archeologists in classifying evidence. These stages are:

- **Paleo-Indian** (20,000 to 7,000 years ago)
- **Archaic** (7,000 years ago to about the time of Christ)
- **Woodland** (time of Christ to 800–1,000 years ago)
- **Neo-American or Late Prehistoric** (800–1,000 years ago until European contact).

Not all early people advanced through all these stages in Texas. Much cultural change occurred in adaptation to changes in climate. The Caddo tribes of East Texas, for example, reached the Neo-American stage before the Spanish and French explorers made contact in the 1500s and 1600s.

Others, such as the Karankawas of the Gulf Coast, advanced no further than the Archaic stage of civilization at the same time. Still others advanced and then regressed in the face of a changing climate.

The earliest confirmed evidence indicates that humans were in Texas sometime between 10,000 and 13,000 years ago.

**Paleo-Indians** were successful big-game hunters. Artifacts from this period are found across the state but not in great number, indicating that they were a small, nomadic population.

As Texas' climate changed at the end of the Ice Age about 7,000 years ago, inhabitants adapted. Apparently the state experienced an extended period of warming and drying, and the population during the **Archaic** period increased.

These Texans began to harvest fruits and nuts, and to exploit rivers for food, as indicated by the freshwater mussel shells in ancient garbage heaps.

The **Woodland** stage is distinguished by the development of settled societies, with crops and local wild plants providing much of their diet. The bow and arrow came into use, and the first pottery is associated with this period.

Pre-Caddoan tribes in East Texas had formed villages and were building distinctive mounds for burials and for ritual.

The **Neo-American** period is best exemplified by the highly civilized Caddoes, who had a complex culture with well-defined social stratification. They were fully agricultural and participated in trade over a wide area of North America.

## The Spanish Explorations

Spain's exploration of North America was one of the first acts of a vigorous nation that was emerging from centuries of campaigns to oust the Islamic Moors from the Iberian Peninsula.

In early **1492**, the Spanish forces retook the province of Granada, completing the reconquista or reconquest. Later in the year, the Catholic royals of the united country, Ferdinand and Isabella, took a major stride toward shaping world history by commissioning Christopher Columbus for the voyage that was to bring Europeans to America.

As early as **1519, Capt. Alonso Alvarez de Pineda**, in the service of the governor of Jamaica, mapped the coast of Texas.

Indian pictographs adorn the bluffs overlooking the Concho River, upstream from Paint Rock in Concho County. The area in West-Central Texas is one of the most remarkable rock art sites on the Edwards Plateau. There are more than 1,500 pictographs on the limestone cliff face painted in red, orange, yellow, white, and black. The American Indian creators of these pictographs portrayed human figures, buffalo, deer, and many geometric designs, and they left handprints. It is estimated the site may have been used from 1300–1650. Photo courtesy of USDA/Natural Resources Conservation Service.

The **first recorded exploration of today's Texas** was made in the 1530s by **Alvar Núñez Cabeza de Vaca**, along with two other Spaniards and a Moorish slave named Estevanico. They were members of an expedition commanded by Panfilo de Narváez that left Cuba in 1528 to explore what is now the southeastern United States. Ill-fated from the beginning, many members of the expedition lost their lives, and others, including Cabeza de Vaca, were shipwrecked on the Texas coast. Eventually the band wandered into Mexico in 1536.

In **1540**, Francisco Vázquez de Coronado was commissioned to lead an exploration of the American Southwest. The quest took him to the land of the Pueblo Indians in what is now New Mexico. Native Americans, who had learned it was best to keep Europeans away from their homes, would suggest vast riches could be found in other areas. So Coronado pursued a fruitless search for gold and silver across the **High Plains of Texas**, Oklahoma and Kansas.

While Coronado was investigating Texas from the west, Luis de Moscoso Alvarado approached from the east. He assumed leadership of Hernando de Soto's expedition when the commander died on the banks of the Mississippi River. In **1542**, Moscoso's group ventured as far west as **Central Texas** before returning to the Mississippi.

Forty years passed after the Coronado and Mos-

coso expeditions before Fray Agustín Rodríguez, a Franciscan missionary, and Francisco Sánchez Chamuscado, a soldier, led an expedition into Texas and New Mexico.

Following the Río Conchos in Mexico to its confluence with the Rio Grande near present-day **Presidio** and then turning northwestward up the great river's valley, the explorers passed through the El Paso area in **1581**.

Juan de Oñate was granted the right to develop this area populated by Pueblo Indians in 1598. He blazed a trail across the desert from Santa Barbara, Chihuahua, to intersect the Rio Grande at the Pass of the North. For the next 200 years, this was the supply route from the interior of Mexico that served the northern colonies.

Texas was attractive to the Spanish in the 1600s. Small expeditions found trade possibilities, and missionaries ventured into the territory. Frays Juan de Salas and Diego López responded to a request by the Jumano Indians for religious instruction in **1629**, and for a brief time priests lived with the Indians near present-day **San Angelo**.

The first permanent settlement in Texas was established in **1681–1682** after New Mexico's Indians rebelled and drove Spanish settlers southward. The colonists retreated to the **El Paso** area, where the missions of Corpus Christi de la Isleta and Nuestra Señora del Socorro — each named for a community in New Mexico — were established. Ysleta pueblo originally was located on the south side of the Rio Grande, but as the river changed its course, the pueblo ended up on the north bank. Now part of El Paso, the community is considered the oldest European settlement in Texas.

## French Exploration

In 1682, **René Robert Cavelier, Sieur de La Salle**, explored the Mississippi River to its mouth at the Gulf of Mexico. La Salle claimed the vast territory drained by the river for France.

Two years later, La Salle returned to the New World with four ships and enough colonists to establish his country's claim. Guided by erroneous maps, this second expedition overshot the mouth of the Mississippi by 400 miles and ended up on the Texas coast. Though short of supplies because of the loss of two of the ships, the French colonists established Fort Saint Louis on Garcitas Creek several miles inland from Lavaca Bay.

In 1687, La Salle and a group of soldiers began an overland trip to find French outposts on the Mississippi River. Somewhere west of the Trinity River, the explorer was murdered by some of his men. His grave has never been found. *(A more detailed account of La Salle's expedition can be found in the Texas Almanac 1998–1999 and on the Texas Almanac website.)*

In 1689, Spanish authorities sent **Capt. Alonso de León**, the governor of Coahuila (which at various times included Texas in its jurisdiction), into Texas to confront the French. He headed eastward from present-day **Eagle Pass** and eventually found the tattered remnants of Fort Saint Louis.

Indians had destroyed the settlement and killed many colonists. León continued tracking survivors of the ill-fated colony into East Texas.

## Spanish Rule

Father **Damián Massanet** accompanied León on this journey. The priest was fascinated with tales about the "Tejas" Indians of the region.

**Tejas** meant *friendly*, but at the time the term was considered a tribal name. Actually these Indians were members of the Caddo Confederacy that controlled parts of four present states: Texas, Louisiana, Arkansas, and Oklahoma.

The Caddo religion acknowledged one supreme god, and when a Tejas chief asked Father Massanet to stay and instruct his people in his faith, the Spaniards promised to return and establish a mission.

The pledge was redeemed in **1690** when the mission San Francisco de los Tejas was founded near present-day Weches in Houston County.

Twin disasters struck this missionary effort. Spanish government officials quickly lost interest when the French threat at colonization diminished. And as was the case with many New World Indians who had no resistance to European diseases, the Tejas soon were felled by an epidemic. The Indians blamed the new religion and resisted conversion. The mission languished, and it was difficult to supply it from other Spanish outposts in northern Mexico. In 1693, the Spanish officials finally closed the mission effort in **East Texas.**

Although Spain had not made a determined effort to settle Texas, great changes were coming to the territory. Spain introduced horses into the Southwest. By the late 1600s, Comanches were using the horses to expand their range southward across the plains, displacing the Apaches. In the **1720s,** the **Apaches** moved onto the lower Texas Plains, usurping the traditional hunting grounds of the Jumanos and others. The nomadic Coahuiltecan bands were particularly hard hit.

In 1709, Fray Antonio de San Buenaventura y Olivares had made an initial request to establish a mission at San Pedro Springs (today's San Antonio) to minister to the Coahuiltecans. Spanish officials denied the request. However, new fears over the French movement into East Texas changed that.

Another Franciscan, **Father Francisco Hidalgo**, who had earlier served at the missions in East Texas, returned to them when he and **Father Antonio Margil de Jesús** accompanied **Capt. Diego Ramón** on an expedition to the area in 1716. In that year, the mission of San Francisco de los Neches was established near the site of the old San Francisco de los Tejas mission. Nuestra Señora de Guadalupe was located at the present-day site of Nacogdoches, and Nuestra Señora de los Dolores was placed near present-day San Augustine.

The East Texas missions did little better on the second try, and supplying the frontier missions remained difficult. It became apparent that a way station between northern Mexico and East Texas was needed.

In 1718, Spanish officials consented to Fray Olivares' request to found a mission at San Pedro Springs. That mission, called **San Antonio de Valero**, was later to be known as the **Alamo**. Because the Indians of the region often did not get along with each other, other missions were established to serve each group.

These missions flourished and each became an early ranching center. But the large herds of cattle and horses attracted trouble. The San Antonio missions began to face the wrath of the Apaches. The mission system, which attempted to convert the Indians to Christianity and to "civilize" them, was partially successful in subduing minor tribes but not larger tribes like the Apaches.

The Spanish realized that more stable colonization efforts must be made. Indians from Mexico, such as the Tlascalans who fought with Cortés against the Aztecs, were brought into Texas to serve as examples of "good" Indians for the wayward natives.

In **1731**, Spanish colonists from the **Canary Islands** were brought to Texas and founded the **Villa of San Fernando de Béxar**, the first civil jurisdiction in the province and today's **San Antonio.**

In the late 1730s, Spanish officials became concerned over the vulnerability of the large area between the Sierra Madre Oriental and the Gulf Coast in northern Mexico. The area was unsettled, a haven for runaway Indian slaves and marauders, and it was a wide-open pathway for the English or French to travel from the Gulf to the rich silver mines in Durango.

For seven years, the search for the right colonizer went on before **José de Escandón** was selected in 1746. A professional military man and successful administrator, Escandón earned a high reputation by

The 84th Texas Legislature passed Senate Resolution No. 989 in May 2015 recognizing the Texas Band of Yaqui Indians. After being driven out of Mexico, the Yaqui first settled in Presidio and Fort Davis around 1870. The photo, left, was taken in 1920 in Lubbock of one of the original families of Mountain Yaqui Indians that came to Texas: Jesusa Urquides Flores, daughter Sarah Urquides Flores, and husband Bentura Flores. Sarah's three daughters are shown, above, holding her photograph. The daughters are all Yaqui Tribal Elders. The Yaqui have an exhibit at the Overland Trails Museum in Fort Davis and are based in Lubbock. Photos are courtesy of the Texas Band of Yaqui Indians; www.yaquitribetexas.com.

subduing Indians in central Mexico. On receiving the assignment, he launched a broad land survey of the area running from the mountains to the Gulf and from the Río Pánuco in Tamaulipas, Mexico, to the Nueces River in Texas.

In 1747, he began placing colonists in settlements throughout the area. **Tomás Sánchez** received a land grant on the Rio Grande in 1755 from which **Laredo** developed. And other small Texas communities along the river sprang up as a result of Escandón's well-executed plan. Many old Hispanic families in Texas hold title to their land based on grants in this period.

In the following decades, a few other Spanish colonists settled around the old missions and frontier forts. **Antonio Gil Ybarbo** led one group that settled **Nacogdoches** in the **1760s and 1770s.**

## The Demise of Spain

Spain's final 60 years of control of the province of Texas were marked with a few successes and a multitude of failures, all of which could be attributed to a breakdown in the administrative system.

Charles III, the fourth of the Bourbon line of kings, took the Spanish throne in 1759. He launched a series of reforms in the New World. The king's choice of administrators was excellent. In 1765, José de Gálvez was dispatched to New Spain (an area that then included all of modern Mexico and much of today's American West) with instructions to improve both the economy and the defense of the area.

Gálvez initially toured parts of the vast region, gaining first-hand insight into the practical problems of the colony. There were many that could be traced to

Spain's basic concepts of colonial government. Texas, in particular, suffered from the mercantilist economic system that attempted to funnel all colonial trade through ports in Mexico.

But administrative reforms by Gálvez and his nephew, Bernardo Gálvez, namesake of Galveston, were to be followed by ill-advised policies by successors.

Problems with the Comanches, Apaches and "Norteños," as the Spanish called some tribes, continued to plague the province, too.

About the same time, Spain undertook the administration of the Louisiana Territory. One of the terms of the cession by France was that the region would enjoy certain trading privileges denied to other Spanish dependencies. So although Texas and Louisiana were neighbors, trade between the two provinces was banned.

The Spanish crown further complicated matters by placing the administration of Louisiana under authorities in Cuba, while Texas remained under the authorities in Mexico City.

The death of Charles III in 1788 and the beginning of the French Revolution a year later weakened Spain's hold on the New World dominions. Charles IV was not as good a sovereign as his predecessor, and his choice of ministers was poor. The quality of frontier administrators declined, and relations with Indians soured further.

Charles IV's major blunder, however, was to side with French royalty during the revolution, earning Spain the enmity of Napoleon Bonaparte. Spain also allied with England in an effort to thwart Napoleon,

*The Durst-Taylor Historic House and Gardens is a circa 1835 wood-frame house in Nacogdoches. The historic house reflects life around 1840–1860 and is the second-oldest Nacogdoches structure still standing on its original site, which is close to the intersection of the old El Camino Real de los Tejas and La Calle de Norte. Historic leaders who lived in the house include Thomas J. Rusk, Bennet Blake, and William Ochiltree. The museum includes a fully functioning smokehouse, blacksmith shop, heirloom gardens, and a sugarcane mill. The Old-Fashioned Sweet Tooth Sugarcane event is held at the house the second Saturday in January. Nacogdoches Convention & Visitors Bureau photo.*

and in this losing cause, the Spanish were forced to cede Louisiana back to France.

In 1803, Napoleon broke a promise to retain the territory and sold it to the United States. Spain's problems in the New World thereby took on an altogether different dimension. Now, Anglo-Americans cast longing eyes on the vast undeveloped territory of Texas.

With certain exceptions for royalists who left the American colonies during the revolution, Spain had maintained a strict prohibition against Anglo or other non-Spanish settlers in their New World territories. But they were unprepared to police the eastern border of Texas after removing the presidios in the 1760s. What had been a provincial line became virtually overnight an international boundary, and an ill-defined one at that.

## American Immigrants

Around **1800, Anglo-Americans** began to probe the Spanish frontier. Some settled in East Texas and others crossed the Red River and were tolerated by authorities.

Others, however, were thought to have nefarious designs. Philip Nolan was the first of the American filibusters to test Spanish resolve. Several times he entered Texas to capture wild horses to sell in the United States.

But in 1801, the Spanish perceived an attempted insurrection by Nolan and his followers. He was killed in a battle near present-day Waco, and his company was taken captive to work in the mines in northern Mexico.

Spanish officials were beginning to realize that the economic potential of Texas must be developed if the Anglo-Americans were to be neutralized. But Spain's centuries-long role in the history of Texas was almost over.

Resistance to Spanish rule had developed in the New World colonies. Liberal ideas from the American and French revolutions had grown popular, despite the crown's attempts to prevent their dissemination.

In Spain, three sovereigns — Charles IV, Napoleon's brother Joseph Bonaparte, and Ferdinand VII — claimed the throne, often issuing different edicts simultaneously. Since the time of Philip II, Spain had been a tightly centralized monarchy with the crown making most decisions. Now, chaos reigned in the colonies.

As Spain's grip on the New World slipped between 1790 and 1820, Texas was almost forgotten, an internal province of little importance. Colonization was ignored; the Spanish government had larger problems in Europe and in Mexico.

Spain's mercantile economic policy penalized colonists in the area, charging them high prices for trade goods and paying low prices for products sent to markets in the interior of New Spain. As a result, settlers from central Mexico had no incentives to come to

Texas. Indeed, men of ambition in the province often prospered by turning to illegal trade with Louisiana or to smuggling. On the positive side, however, Indians of the province had been mollified through annual gifts and by developing a dependence on Spain for trade goods.

Ranching flourished. In **1795**, a census found **69 families** living on 45 ranches in the **San Antonio** area. A census in **1803** indicated that there were **100,000 head of cattle** in Texas. But aside from a few additional families in Nacogdoches and La Bahía (near present-day Goliad), the province was thinly populated.

The largest group of early immigrants from the United States was not Anglo, but Indian.

As early as **1818, Cherokees** of the southeastern United States came to Texas, settling north of Nacogdoches on lands between the Trinity and Sabine rivers. The Cherokees had been among the first U.S. Indians to accept the federal government's offers of resettlement. As American pioneers entered the newly acquired lands of Georgia, Alabama and other areas of the Southeast, the Indians were systematically removed, through legal means or otherwise.

Some of the displaced groups settled on land provided in Arkansas Territory, but others, such as the Cherokees, came to Texas. These Cherokees were among the "Five Civilized Tribes" that had adopted agriculture and many Anglo customs in an unsuccessful attempt to get along with their new neighbors. Alabama and Coushatta tribes had exercised squatters' rights in present-day Sabine County in the early 1800s, and soon after the Cherokees arrived, groups of Shawnee, Delaware and Kickapoo Indians came from the United States.

A **second wave of Anglo** immigrants began to arrive in Texas, larger than the first and of a different character. These Anglos were not so interested in agricultural opportunities as in other schemes to quickly recoup their fortunes.

Spain recognized the danger represented by the unregulated colonization by Americans. The Spanish Cortes' colonization law of 1813 attempted to build a buffer between the eastern frontier and northern Mexico. Special permission was required for Americans to settle within 52 miles of the international boundary, although this prohibition often was ignored.

As initially envisioned, Americans would be allowed to settle the interior of Texas. Colonists from Europe and Mexico would be placed along the eastern frontier to limit contact between the Americans and the United States. Spanish officials felt that the Americans already in Texas illegally would be stable if given a stake in the province through land ownership.

**Moses Austin**, a former Spanish subject in the vast Louisiana Territory, applied for the first empresario grant from the Spanish government. With the intercession of Baron de Bastrop, a friend of Austin's from Missouri Territory, the request was approved in January **1821**.

Austin agreed to settle **300 families** on land bounded by the Brazos and Colorado rivers on the east and west, by El Camino Real (the old military road running from San Antonio to Nacogdoches) on the north, and by the Gulf Coast.

But Austin died in June 1821, leaving the work to his son, **Stephen F. Austin**. Problems began as soon as the first authorized colonists arrived in Texas the following December when it was learned that Mexico had gained independence from Spain.

## Mexico, 1810–1836

Mexico's war for independence, 1810–1821, was savage and bloody in the interior provinces, and Texas suffered as well.

In early 1812, Mexican revolutionary **José Bernardo Gutiérrez de Lara** traveled to Natchitoches, La., where, with the help of U.S. agents, an expedition was organized. **Augustus W. Magee**, a West Point graduate, commanded the troop, which entered Texas in August 1812. This "Republican Army of the North" easily took Nacogdoches, where it gathered recruits.

After withstanding a siege at La Bahía, the army took San Antonio and proclaimed the First Republic of Texas in April 1813. A few months later, the republican forces were bloodily subdued at the Battle of Medina River.

Royalist Gen. Joaquín de Arredondo executed a staggering number of more than 300 republicans, including some Americans, at San Antonio, and a young lieutenant, **Antonio López de Santa Anna**, was recognized for valor under fire.

When the war finally ended in Mexico in 1821, little more had been achieved than separation from Spain.

Sensing that liberal reforms in Spain would reduce the authority of royalists in the New World, Mexican conservatives had led the revolt against the mother country. They also achieved early victories in the debate over the form of government the newly independent Mexico should adopt.

An independent Mexico was torn between advocates of centralist and federalist forms of government.

The former royalists won the opening debates, settling Emperor Agustín de Iturbide on the new Mexican throne. But he was overthrown and the Constitution of 1824, a federalist document, was adopted.

The Mexican election of 1828 was a turning point in the history of the country when the legally elected administration of Manuel Gómez Pedraza was overthrown by supporters of Vicente Guerrero, who in turn was ousted by his own vice president Anastasio Bustamante. Mexico's most chaotic political period followed. Between 1833 and 1855, the Mexican presidency changed hands 36 times.

## Texas, 1821–1833

Mexico's **land policy,** like Spain's, differed from the U.S. approach. Whereas the United States sold land directly to settlers or to speculators who dealt with the pioneers, the Mexicans retained tight control of the property transfer until predetermined agreements for development were fulfilled.

But a 4,428-acre *sitio* — a square league — and a 177-acre *labor* could be obtained for only surveying costs and administrative fees as low as $50. The empresario was rewarded with grants of large tracts of land, but only when he fulfilled his quota of families to be brought to the colonies.

Considering the prices the U.S. government

charged, Texas' land was indeed a bargain and a major attraction to those Americans looking for a new start.

More than 25 empresarios were commissioned to settle colonists. Empresarios included **Green DeWitt** and **Martín de León**, who in 1824 founded the city of Guadalupe Victoria (present-day Victoria).

By 1830, Texas boasted an estimated population of 15,000, with Anglo-Americans outnumbering Hispanics by a margin of four to one.

Stephen F. Austin was easily the most successful empresario. After his initial success, Austin was authorized in 1825 to bring 900 more families to Texas, and in 1831, he and his partner, **Samuel Williams**, received another concession to bring 800 Mexican and European families. Through Austin's efforts, 1,540 land titles were issued to settlers.

In the early years of colonization, the settlers busied themselves clearing land, planting crops, building homes and fending off Indian attacks. Many were successful in establishing a subsistence economy.

One weakness of the Mexican colonial policy was that it did not provide the factors for a market economy. Although towns were established, credit, banks and good roads were not provided by the government.

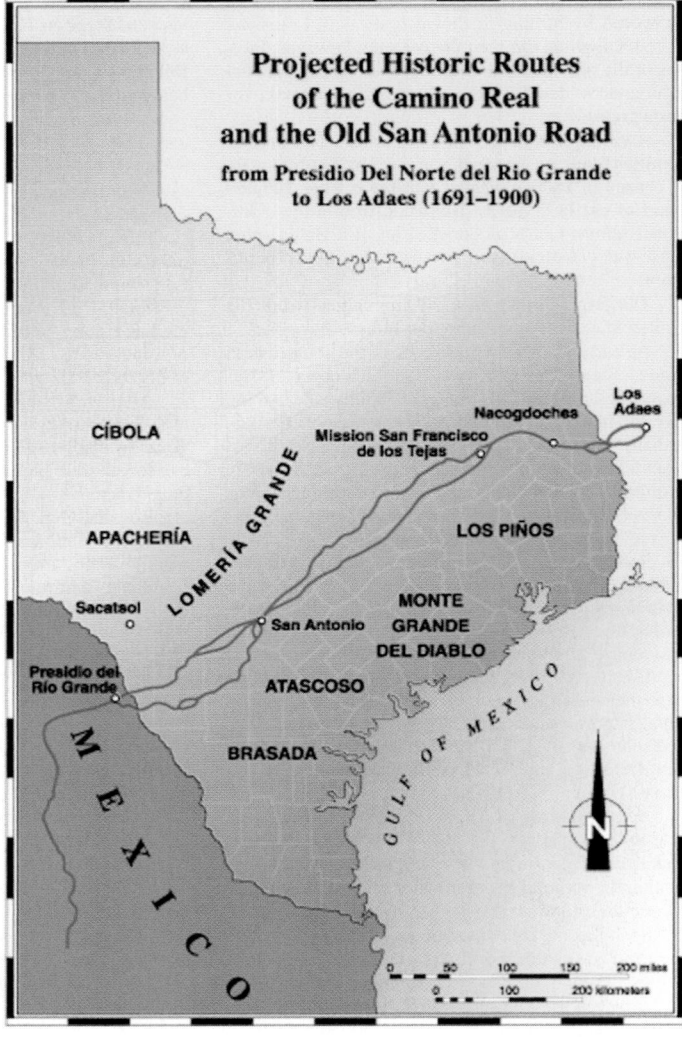

Ports were established at Galveston and Matagorda bays after Mexican independence, but the colonists felt they needed more, particularly one at the mouth of the Brazos. And foreign ships were barred from coastwise trade, which posed a particular hardship because Mexico had few merchant ships.

To settle in Texas, pioneers had to become Mexican citizens and to embrace Roman Catholicism. Most of the Americans were Protestants, if they adhered to any religion, and they were fiercely defensive of the right to **religious freedom** enjoyed in the United States.

Although no more than one-fourth of the Americans ever swore allegiance to the Catholic Church, the requirement was a long-standing irritation.

**Slavery**, too, was a point of contention. Mexico prohibited the introduction of slavery after December 1827. Nevertheless, several efforts were made to evade the government policy. Austin got the state Legislature to recognize labor contracts under which slaves were technically free but bound themselves to their masters for life. Often entire families were covered by a single contract. While many early Anglo colonists were not slaveholders, they were Southerners, and the ownership of slaves was a cultural institution that they supported. The problem was never settled during Texas' colonial period despite the tensions it generated.

Most of the early Anglo-American colonists in Texas intended to fulfill their pledge to become good Mexican citizens. But the political turmoil following the 1828 presidential election raised doubts in the Americans' minds about the ability of Mexico to make representative government function properly.

On a tour of Texas in 1827 and 1828, Gen. Manuel Mier y Terán noted that the Texans "carried their constitutions in their pockets." And he feared the Americans' desire for more rights and liberties than the government was prepared to offer would lead to rebellion. Unrest increased in Texas when Gen. Mier y Terán began reinforcing existing garrisons and establishing new ones.

But a major factor in the discontent of Americans came with the **decree of April 6, 1830**, when the Mexican government in essence banned further American immigration into Texas and tried to control slavery. (For an account of how Texans opposed this decree at Fort Anahuac, see Texas History Features on the Texas Almanac website.)

Austin protested that the prohibition against American immigration would not stop the flow of Anglos into Texas; it would stop only stable, prosperous Americans from coming.

Austin's predictions were fulfilled. Illegal immigrants continued to come. By 1836, the estimated number of people in Texas had reached 35,000.

## Prelude to Revolution

In the midst of all the turmoil, Texas was prospering. By 1834, some 7,000 bales of cotton with a value of $315,000 were shipped to New Orleans. In the middle of the decade, Texas exports, including cotton and beaver, otter and deer skins, amounted to $500,000.

Trade ratios were out of balance, however, because $630,000 in manufactured goods were imported. And, there was little currency in Texas. Ninety percent of the business transactions were conducted with barter or credit.

In 1833 and 1834, the **Coahuila y Texas** legislature was diligently trying to respond to the complaints of the Texas colonists. The English language was recognized for official purposes. Religious toleration was approved. The court system was revised, providing Texas with an appellate court and trial by jury.

In Mexico City, however, a different scenario was developing. **Santa Anna** assumed supreme authority in April 1834 and began dismantling the federalist government. Among the most offensive changes dictated by Santa Anna was the reduction of the state militias to one man per each 500 population. The intent was to eliminate possible armed opposition to the emerging centralist government.

But liberals in the state of Zacatecas in central Mexico rebelled. Santa Anna's response was particularly brutal, as he tried to make an example of the rebels. Troops were allowed to sack the state capital after the victory over the insurgents.

Trouble also was brewing closer to the Texans. In March 1833, the Coahuila y Texas legislature moved the state capital from Saltillo to Monclova. The Monclova legislature in 1834 gave the governor authority to sell 400 *sitios* — or 1.77 million acres of land — to finance the government and to provide for protection. A year later the lawmakers criticized Santa Anna's reputation on federalism. Seeing a chance to regain lost prestige, Saltillo declared for Santa Anna and set up an opposition government. In the spring of 1835, Santa Anna sent his brother-in-law, Martín Perfecto de Cos, to break up the state government at Monclova.

Texans were appalled by the breakdown in state

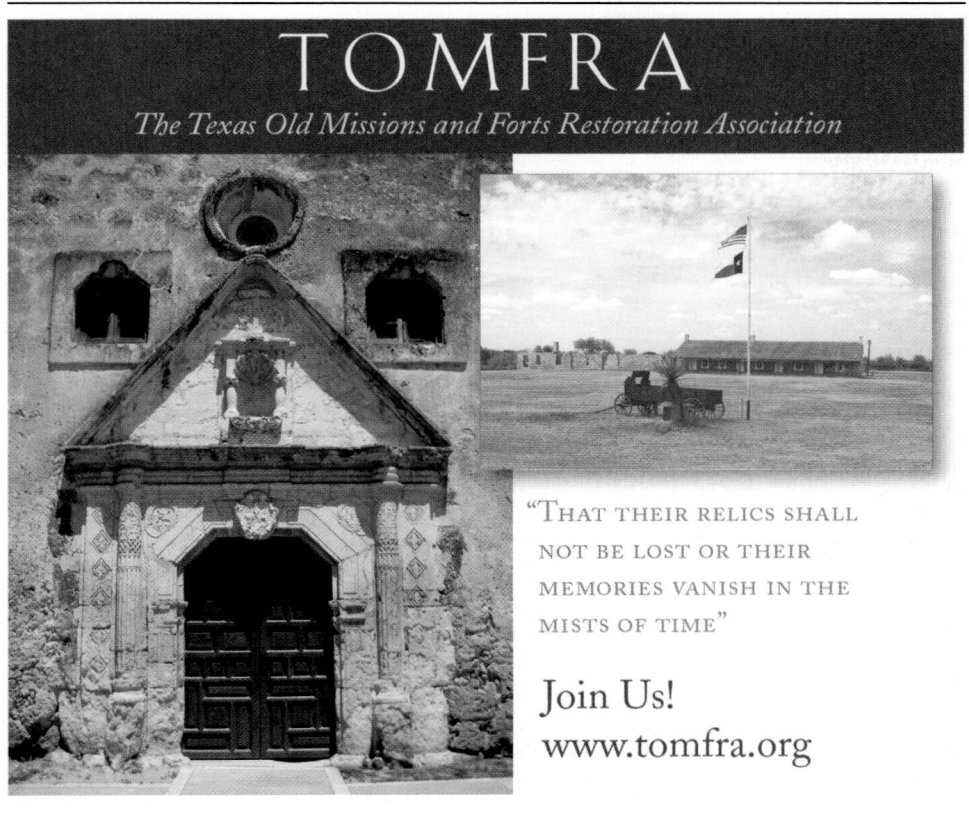

government, coming on the heels of so many assurances that the political situation was to improve.

Texas politics were polarizing. A "war party" advocated breaking away from Mexico altogether, while a "peace party" urged calm and riding out the political storm. Most of the settlers, however, aligned with neither group.

In January 1835, Santa Anna sent a detachment of soldiers to Anahuac to reinforce the customs office, but duties were being charged irregularly at various ports on the coast. William B. Travis, in an act not supported by all colonists, led a contingent of armed colonists against the Mexican soldiers, who withdrew without a fight.

Although some members of the peace party wrote Mexican Gen. **Martín Perfecto de Cos**, stationed at Matamoros, apologizing for the action, he was not compromising. Cos demanded that the group be arrested and turned over to him. The Texans refused.

The committees of correspondence, organized at the Convention of 1832 (which had asked that Texas be separated from Coahuila), began organizing another meeting. Because the term "convention" aroused visions of revolution in the eyes of Mexican officials, the gathering at Washington-on-the-Brazos in October 1835 was called a "consultation." But with the breakdown of the state government and with Santa Anna's repeal of the Constitution of 1824, the American settlers felt well within their rights to provide a new framework with which to govern Texas.

Fresh from brutally putting down the rebellion in Zacatecas, Santa Anna turned his attention to Texas. Gen. Cos was determined to regarrison the state, and the settlers were equally determined to keep soldiers out.

Col. **Domingo de Ugartechea**, headquartered at San Antonio, became concerned about armed rebellion when he heard of the incident at Anahuac. He recalled a six-pound cannon that had been given DeWitt colonists to fight Indians.

Ugartechea ordered Cpl. Casimira de León with five men to Gonzales to retrieve the weapon. No problems were expected, but officials at Gonzales refused to surrender the weapon. When the Mexicans reinforced Cpl. León's men, a call was sent out for volunteers to help the Gonzales officials. Dozens responded.

Oct. 2, 1835, the Texans challenged the Mexicans with a **"come-and-take-it" flag** over the cannon. After a brief skirmish, the Mexicans withdrew, but the first rounds in the Texas Revolution had been fired.

## Winning Independence

As 1836 opened, Texans felt in control of their destiny and secure in their land and their liberties. The Mexican army had been driven from their soil.

But tragedy loomed. Easy victories over government forces at Anahuac, Nacogdoches, Goliad, Gonzales and San Antonio in the fall of 1835 had given them a false sense of security. That independent mood was their undoing, for no government worthy of the name coordinated the defense of Texas. Consequently, as the Mexican counterattack developed, no one was in charge. Sam Houston was titular commander-in-chief of the Texas forces, but he had little authority.

Some even thought the Mexicans would not try to re-enter Texas. Few Texans counted on the energy and determination of Santa Anna, the dictator of Mexico.

The status of the strongholds along the San Antonio River was of concern to Houston. In mid-January, Houston sent **James Bowie** to San Antonio to determine if the Alamo was defensible. If not, Bowie had orders to destroy it and withdraw the men and artillery to Gonzales and Copano.

On Feb. 8, David Crockett of Tennessee, bringing 12 men with him, arrived to aid the revolutionaries.

On Feb. 12, 1836, Santa Anna's main force crossed the Rio Grande headed for San Antonio. The Mexican battle plan had been debated. But Mexico's national pride was bruised by the series of defeats the nation's army had suffered in 1835, capped by Gen. Cos's ouster from San Antonio in December.

On Feb. 11, the Consultation's "governor of the government" **Henry Smith**, sent **William B. Travis** to San Antonio. Immediately a split in command at the **Alamo** garrison arose. Most were American volunteers who looked to the Houston-appointed Bowie as their leader. Travis had only a handful of Texas army regulars. Bowie and Travis agreed to share the command of 150 men.

Arriving at the Alamo on Feb. 23, Santa Anna left no doubt regarding his attitude toward the defenders. He hoisted a blood-red flag, the traditional Mexican symbol of no quarter, no surrender, no mercy. Travis and Bowie defiantly answered the display with a cannon shot.

Immediately the Mexicans began surrounding the Alamo and bombarding it. Throughout the first night and nights to come, Santa Anna kept up a continual din to destroy the defenders' morale.

On Feb. 24, Bowie became ill and relinquished his share of command to Travis. Although the Mexican bombardment of the Alamo continued, none of the defenders was killed. In fact, they conducted several successful forays outside the fortress to burn buildings that were providing cover for the Mexican gunners and to gather firewood.

Messengers also successfully moved through the Mexican lines at will, and 32 reinforcements from Gonzales made it into the Alamo without a loss on March 1.

Historians disagree over which flag flew over the defenders of the Alamo.

Mexican sources have said that Santa Anna was outraged when he saw flying over the fortress a Mexican tricolor, identical to the ones carried by his troops except with the numbers "1 8 2 4" emblazoned upon it. Some Texas historians have accepted this version because the defenders of the Alamo could not have known that Texas' independence had been declared on March 2. To the knowledge of the Alamo's defenders, the last official position taken by Texas was in support of the Constitution of 1824, which the flag symbolized. But the only flag found after the battle, according to historian Walter Lord, was one flown by the **New Orleans Greys**.

By March 5, Santa Anna had 4,000 men in camp, a force he felt sufficient to subdue the Alamo.

Historians disagree on the date, but the story goes that on March 3 or 5, Travis called his command together and explained the bleak outlook. He then asked

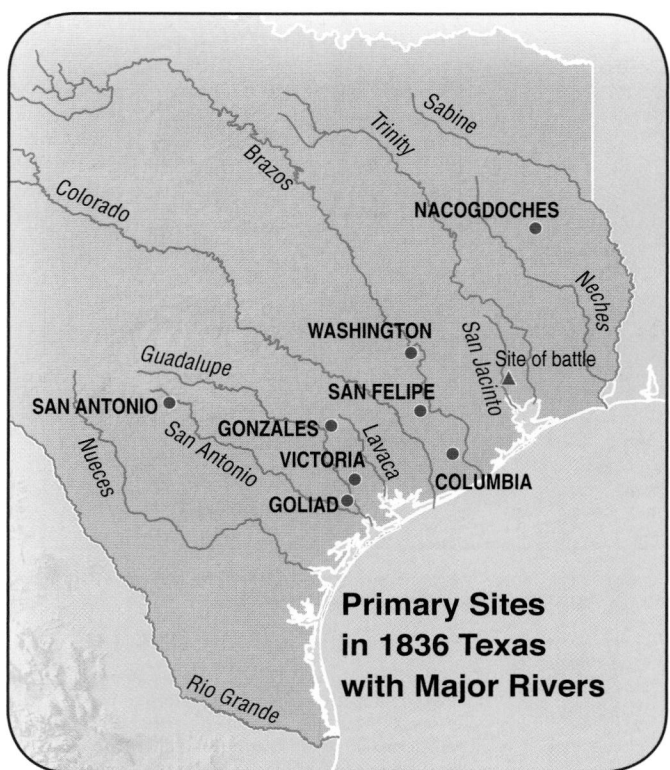

**Primary Sites in 1836 Texas with Major Rivers**

to return.

Finally, on March 19, he left, but too late. Forward elements of Gen. José de Urrea's troops caught Fannin's command on an open prairie. After a brief skirmish Fannin surrendered.

Santa Anna was furious when Gen. Urrea appealed for clemency for the captives. The Mexican leader issued orders for their execution. On March 27, a Palm Sunday, most of the prisoners were divided into groups and marched out of Goliad, thinking they were being transferred to other facilities. When the executions began, many escaped. But about 350 were killed.

On March 17, Houston reached the Colorado near the present city of La Grange and began receiving reinforcements. Within a week, the small force of several hundred had become almost respectable, with 1,200–1,400 men in camp.

By the time Houston reached the Colorado, the convention at Washington-on-the-Brazos was completing work. **David Burnet**, a New Jersey native, was named interim president of the new Texas government, and **Lorenzo de Zavala**, a Yucatán native, was named vice president.

On March 27, Houston moved his men to San Felipe on the Brazos. The Texas army was impatient for a fight, and there was talk in the ranks that, if action did not develop soon, a new commander should be elected.

As the army marched farther back toward the San Jacinto River, two Mexican couriers were captured and gave Houston the information he had hoped for. Santa Anna in his haste had led the small Mexican force in front of Houston. Now the Texans had an opportunity to win the war.

Throughout the revolt, Houston's intelligence system had operated efficiently. Scouts, commanded by **Erastus "Deaf" Smith**, kept the Texans informed of Mexican troop movements. **Hendrick Arnold,** a free black, was a valuable spy, posing as a runaway slave to enter Mexican camps to gain information.

Early on April 21, Gen. Cos reinforced Santa Anna's troops with more than 500 men. The new arrivals, who had marched all night, disrupted the camp's routine for a time, but soon all the soldiers and officers settled down for a midday rest.

About 3 p.m., Houston ordered his men to parade and the battle was launched at 4:30 p.m.

A company of Mexican-Texans, commanded by Juan Seguín, had served as the rear guard for Houston's army through much of the retreat across Texas and had fought many skirmishes with the Mexican army in the process.

those willing to die for freedom to stay and fight; those not willing could try to get through enemy lines to safety. Even the sick Jim Bowie vowed to stay. Only Louis (Moses) Rose, a veteran of Napoleon's retreat from Moscow slipped out of the Alamo that night.

At dawn March 6, Santa Anna's forces attacked. When the fighting stopped between 8:30 and 9 a.m., all the defenders were dead. Only a few women, children and black slaves survived the assault. **Davy Crockett**'s fate is still debated. Mexican officer Enrique de la Peña held that Crockett was captured with a few other defenders and was executed by Santa Anna.

Santa Anna's victory came at the cost of almost one-third his forces killed or wounded. Their deaths in such number set back Santa Anna's timetable. The fall of the Alamo also brutally shook Texans out of their lethargy.

Sam Houston, finally given command of the entire Texas army, left the convention at **Washington-on-the-Brazos** on the day of the fall of the Alamo.

On March 11, he arrived at Gonzales to begin organizing the troops. Two days later, **Susanna Dickinson**, the wife of one of the victims of the Alamo, and two slaves arrived at Houston's position at Gonzales with the news of the fall of the San Antonio fortress.

Houston then ordered **James Fannin** to abandon the old presidio **La Bahía** at Goliad and to retreat to Victoria. Fannin had arrived at the fort in late January with more than 400 men. As a former West Pointer, he had a background in military planning, but Fannin had refused Travis' pleas for help, and after receiving Houston's orders, Fannin waited for scouting parties

*Texas' revolt against Mexico pitted military leaders Santa Anna and Sam Houston against one another. Photos courtesy of the U.S. Library of Congress and the Texas State Library and Archives, respectively.*

Perhaps fearing the Mexican-Texans would be mistaken for Santa Anna's soldiers, Houston had assigned the company to guard duty as the battle approached. But after the men protested, they fought in the battle of San Jacinto.

Historians disagree widely on the number of troops on each side. Houston probably had about 900 while Santa Anna had between 1,100 and 1,300.

But the Texans had the decided psychological advantage. Two thirds of the fledging Republic's army were "old Texans" who had family and land to defend. They had an investment of years of toil in building their homes. And they were eager to avenge the massacre of men at the Alamo and Goliad.

In less than 20 minutes they set the Mexican army to rout. More than 600 Mexicans were killed and hundreds more wounded or captured. Only nine of the Texans died in the fight.

It was not until the following day that Santa Anna was captured. One Texan noticed that a grubby soldier his patrol found in the high grass had a silk shirt under his filthy jacket. Although denying he was an officer, he was taken back to camp, where he was acknowledged with cries of "El Presidente" by other prisoners. Santa Anna introduced himself when taken to the wounded Houston.

President Burnet took charge of Santa Anna, and on May 14 the dictator signed **two treaties at Velasco**, a public document and a secret one. The public agreement declared that hostilities would cease, that the Mexican army would withdraw to south of the **Rio Grande**, that prisoners would be released and Santa Anna would be shipped to Veracruz as soon as possible.

In the secret treaty, Santa Anna agreed to recognize Texas' independence, to give diplomatic recognition, to negotiate a commercial treaty and to set the Rio Grande as the new Republic's boundary.

## Republic of Texas, 1836–1845

**Sam Houston** was easily the most dominant figure throughout the nearly 10-year history of the Republic of Texas. While he was roundly criticized for the retreat across Texas during the revolution, the victory at San Jacinto endeared him to most of the new nation's inhabitants.

Houston handily defeated Henry Smith and Stephen F. Austin in the election called in September 1836 by the interim government, and he was inaugurated as president on Oct. 22.

In the same September election, voters overwhelmingly approved a proposal to request annexation to the United States.

The first cabinet appointed by the new president represented an attempt to heal old political wounds. Austin was named secretary of state and Smith was secretary of the treasury. But Texas suffered a major tragedy in late December 1836 when Austin, the acknowledged **"Father of Texas,"** died of pneumonia.

A host of problems faced the new government. Santa Anna was still in custody, and public opinion favored his execution. Texas' leadership wisely kept Santa Anna alive, first to keep from giving the Mexicans an emotional rallying point for launching another invasion. Second, the Texas leaders hoped that the dictator would keep his promise to work for recognition of Texas.

Santa Anna was released in November 1836 and made his way to Washington, D.C. Houston hoped the dictator could persuade U.S. President **Andrew Jackson** to recognize Texas. Jackson refused to see Santa Anna, who returned to Mexico, where he had fallen from power.

Another major challenge was the Texas army. The new commander, Felix Huston, favored an invasion of Mexico, and the troops, made up now mostly of American volunteers who came to Texas after the battle of

San Jacinto, were rebellious and ready to fight.

President Houston tried to replace Felix Huston with **Albert Sidney Johnston**, but Huston seriously wounded Johnston in a duel. In May 1837, Huston was asked to the capital in Columbia to discuss the invasion. While Huston was away from the troops, Houston sent **Thomas J. Rusk**, the secretary of war, to furlough the army without pay — but with generous land grants. Only 600 men were retained in the army.

The Republic's other problems were less tractable. The economy needed attention, Indians still were a threat, Mexico remained warlike, foreign relations had to be developed, and relations with the United States had to be solidified.

The greatest disappointment in Houston's first term was the failure to have the Republic annexed to the United States. Henry Morfit, President Jackson's agent, toured the new Republic in the summer of 1836. Although impressed, Morfit reported that Texas' best chance at continued independence lay in the "stupidity of the rulers of Mexico and the financial embarrassment of the Mexican government." He recommended that annexation be delayed.

Houston's foreign policy achieved initial success when **J. Pinckney Henderson** negotiated a trade treaty with Great Britain. Although the agreement was short of outright diplomatic recognition, it was progress. In the next few years, France, Belgium, The Netherlands and some German states recognized the new Republic.

Under the constitution, Houston's first term lasted only two years, and he could not succeed himself. His successor, **Mirabeau B. Lamar**, had grand visions and was a spendthrift. Houston's first term cost Texas only about $500,000, while President Lamar and the Congress spent $5 million in the next three years.

Early in 1839, Lamar gained recognition as the **"Father of Education"** in Texas when the Congress granted each of the existing 23 counties three leagues of land to be used for education. Fifty leagues of land were set aside for a university.

Despite the lip service paid to education, the government did not have the money for several years to set up a school system. Most education during the Republic was provided by private schools and churches.

**Lamar's Indian policies** differed greatly from those under Houston. Houston had lived with Cherokees as a youth, was adopted as a member of a tribe and advocated Indian rights long before coming to Texas. Lamar reflected more the frontier attitude toward American Indians. His first experience in public life was as secretary to Gov. George Troup of Georgia, who successfully opposed the federal government's policy of assimilation of Indians at the time. Indians were simply removed from Georgia.

Texans first tried to negotiate the Cherokees' removal from the region, but in July 1839, the Indians were forcibly ejected from Texas at the **Battle of the Neches River** in Van Zandt County. Houston's close friend, the aging Cherokee chief **Philip Bowles**, was killed in the battle while Houston was visiting former President Jackson in Tennessee. The Cherokees moved on to Arkansas and Indian Territory.

Houston was returned to the presidency of the

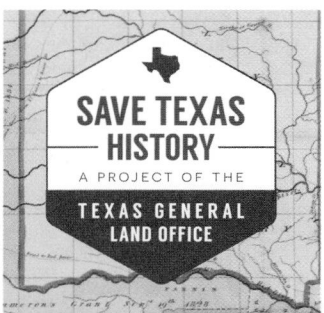

*The Brazoria Historical Militia fires a cannon during Texas Navy Day on Sept. 27, 2014, at Surfside Jetty County Park in Surfside Beach, Brazoria County. The militia is a living history organization that represents Austin's Colony during Colonial and Republic periods, around 1823–1837. Photo by Patty Brinkmeyer.*

Republic in 1841. His second administration was even more frugal than his first; soon income almost matched expenditures.

Houston re-entered negotiations with the Indians in Central Texas in an attempt to quell the raids on settlements. A number of trading posts were opened along the frontier to pacify the Indians.

War fever reached a high pitch in Texas in 1842, and Houston grew increasingly unpopular because he would not launch an offensive war against Mexico.

In March 1842, Gen. **Rafael Vásquez** staged guerrilla raids on San Antonio, Victoria and Goliad, but quickly left the Republic.

A force of 3,500 Texas volunteers gathered at San Antonio demanding that Mexico be punished. Houston urged calm, but the clamor increased when Mexican **Gen. Adrian Woll** captured San Antonio in September. He raised the Mexican flag and declared the reconquest of Texas.

Ranger Capt. **Jack Hays** was camped nearby. Within days 600 volunteers had joined him, eager to drive the Mexican invaders from Texas soil. Gen. Woll withdrew after the **Battle of Salado**.

**Alexander Somervell** was ordered by Houston to follow with 700 troops and harass the Mexican army. He reached Laredo in December and found no Mexican troops. Somervell crossed the Rio Grande to find military targets. A few days later, the commander returned home, but 300 soldiers decided to continue the raid under the command of William S. Fisher. On Christmas day, this group attacked the village of **Mier**, only to be defeated by a Mexican force that outnumbered them 10-to-1.

After attempting mass escape, the survivors of the Mier expedition were marched to Mexico City where Santa Anna, again in political power, ordered their execution. When officers refused to carry out the order, it was amended to require execution of one of every 10 Texans. The prisoners drew beans to determine who would be shot; bearers of **black beans** were executed. Texans again were outraged by the treatment of prisoners, but the war fever soon subsided.

As Houston completed his second term, the United States was becoming more interested in annexation. Texas had seriously flirted with Great Britain and France, and the Americans did not want a rival republic with close foreign ties on the North American continent. Houston orchestrated the early stages of the final steps toward annexation. It was left to his successor, **Anson Jones**, to complete the process.

The Republic of Texas' main claim to fame is simply endurance. Its settlers, unlike other Americans who had military help, had cleared a large region of Indians by themselves, had established farms and communities and had persevered through extreme economic hardship.

Adroit political leadership had gained the Republic recognition from many foreign countries. Although dreams of empire may have dimmed, Texans had established an identity on a major portion of the North American continent. The frontier had been pushed to a line running from Corpus Christi through San Antonio and Austin to the Red River.

The U.S. presidential campaign of 1844 was to make Texas a part of the Union. ☆

# Annexation to 1980

## Annexation

Annexation to the United States was far from automatic for Texas once independence from Mexico was gained in 1836. Sam Houston noted that Texas "was more coy than forward" as negotiations reached a climax in 1845.

**William H. Wharton** was Texas' first representative in Washington. His instructions were to gain diplomatic recognition of the new Republic's independence.

After some squabbles, the U.S. Congress appropriated funds for a minister to Texas, and President Andrew Jackson recognized the new country in one of his last acts in office in March 1837.

Texas President **Mirabeau B. Lamar** (1838–41) opposed annexation. He held visions of empire in which Texas would rival the United States for supremacy on the North American continent.

During his administration, Great Britain began a close relationship with Texas and made strenuous efforts to get Mexico to recognize the Republic. This relationship between Great Britain and Texas raised fears in the United States that Britain might attempt to make Texas part of its empire.

Southerners feared for the future of slavery in Texas, which had renounced the importation of slaves as a concession to get a trade treaty with Great Britain, and American newspapers noted that trade with Texas had suffered after the Republic received recognition from European countries.

In Houston's second term in the Texas presidency, he instructed **Isaac Van Zandt**, his minister in Washington, to renew the annexation negotiations. Although U.S. President **John Tyler** and his cabinet were eager to annex Texas, they were worried about ratification in the U.S. Senate. The annexation question was put off.

In January 1844, Houston again gave Van Zandt instructions to propose annexation talks. This time the United States agreed to Houston's standing stipulation that, for serious negotiations to take place, the United States must provide military protection to Texas. U.S. naval forces were ordered to the Gulf of Mexico and U.S. troops were positioned on the southwest border close to Texas.

On April 11, 1844, Texas and the United States signed a treaty for annexation. Texas would enter the Union as a territory, not a state, under terms of the treaty. The United States would assume Texas' debt up to $10 million and would negotiate Texas' southwestern boundary with Mexico.

On June 8, 1844, the U.S. Senate rejected the treaty with a vote of 35-16, with much of the opposition coming from the slavery abolition wing of the Whig Party.

But **westward expansion** became a major issue in the U.S. presidential election that year. James K. Polk, the Democratic nominee, was a supporter of expansion, and the party's platform called for adding Oregon and Texas to the Union.

After Polk won the election in November, President Tyler declared that the people had spoken on the issue of annexation, and he resubmitted the matter to Congress.

Several bills were introduced in the U.S. House of Representatives containing various proposals.

In **February 1845**, the U.S. Congress approved a resolution that would bring Texas into the Union as a state. Texas would cede its public property, such as forts and custom houses, to the United States, but it could keep its public lands and must retain its public debt. The region could be divided into four new states in addition to the original Texas. And the United States would negotiate the Rio Grande boundary claim.

British officials asked the Texas government to delay consideration of the U.S. offer for 90 days to attempt to get Mexico to recognize the Republic. The delay did no good: Texans' minds were made up.

President Anson Jones, who succeeded Houston in 1844, called a convention to write a **state constitution** in Austin on July 4, 1845.

Mexico finally recognized Texas' independence, but the recognition was rejected. **Texas voters overwhelmingly accepted** the U.S. proposal and approved the new constitution in a referendum.

On **Dec. 29, 1845**, the U.S. Congress accepted the state constitution, and Texas became the 28th state in the Union. The first meeting of the Texas Legislature took place on Feb. 16, 1846.

## 1845–1860

The entry of Texas into the Union touched off the **War with Mexico**, a war that some historians now think was planned by President James K. Polk to obtain the vast American Southwest.

Gen. **Zachary Taylor** was sent to Corpus Christi, just above the Nueces River, in July 1845. In February 1846, right after Texas formally entered the Union, the general was ordered to move troops into the disputed area south of the Nueces to the mouth of the Rio Grande. Mexican officials protested the move, claiming the status of the territory was under negotiation.

After Gen. Taylor refused to leave, Mexican President **Mariano Paredes** declared the opening of a defensive war against the United States on April 24, 1846. After initial encounters at **Palo Alto and Resaca de la Palma**, both a few miles north of today's **Brownsville**, the war was fought south of the Rio Grande.

President Polk devised a plan to raise 50,000 volunteers from every section of the United States to fight the war. About 5,000 Texans saw action in Mexico.

Steamboats provided an important supply link for U.S. forces along the Rio Grande. Historical figures such as **Richard King**, founder of the legendary King Ranch, and **Mifflin Kenedy**, another rancher and businessman, first came to the **Lower Rio Grande Valley** as steamboat operators during the war.

Much farther up the Rio Grande, the war was hardly noticed. U.S. forces moved south from Santa Fe, which had been secured in December 1846. After a minor skirmish with Mexican forces north of El Paso, the U.S. military established American jurisdiction in this part of Texas.

Gen. **Winfield Scott** brought the war to a close in March 1847 with the capture of Mexico City.

When the **Treaty of Guadalupe Hidalgo** was signed on Feb. 2, 1848, the United States had acquired the American Southwest for development. And in Texas, the Rio Grande became an international boundary.

Europeans, of whom the vast majority were **German**, rather than Anglos, were the first whites to push the Texas frontier into west Central Texas after annexation. **John O. Meusebach** became leader of the German immigration movement in Texas, and he led a wagon train of some 120 settlers to the site of **Fredericksburg** in May 1846.

Germans also migrated to the major cities, such as San Antonio and Galveston, and by 1850 there were more people of German birth or parentage in Texas than there were Mexican-Texans.

The estimated population of 150,000 at annexation grew to 212,592, including 58,161 slaves, in the first U.S. census count in Texas in 1850.

As the state's population grew, the regions developed distinct population characteristics. The southeast and eastern sections attracted immigrants from the Lower South, the principal slaveholding states. Major plantations developed in these areas.

North Texas got more Upper Southerners and Midwesterners. These immigrants were mostly small farmers and few owned slaves.

Mexican-Texans had difficulty with Anglo immigrants. The **"cart war"** broke out in 1857. Mexican teamsters controlled the transportation of goods from the Gulf coast to San Antonio and could charge lower rates than their competition.

A campaign of terror was launched by Anglo haulers, especially around Goliad, in an attempt to drive the Mexican-Texans out of business. Intervention by the U.S. and Mexican governments finally brought the situation under control, but it stands as an example of the attitudes held by Anglo-Texans toward Mexican-Texans.

**Cotton** was by far the state's largest money crop, but corn, sweet potatoes, wheat and sugar also were produced. **Saw milling** and grain milling became the major industries, employing 40 percent of the manufacturing workers.

Land disputes and the public-debt issue were settled with the **Compromise of 1850**. Texas gave up claims to territory extending to Santa Fe and beyond in exchange for $10 million from the federal government. That sum was used to pay off the debt of the Republic.

Personalities, especially Sam Houston, dominated elections during early statehood, but, for most Texans, politics were unimportant. Voter turnouts were low in

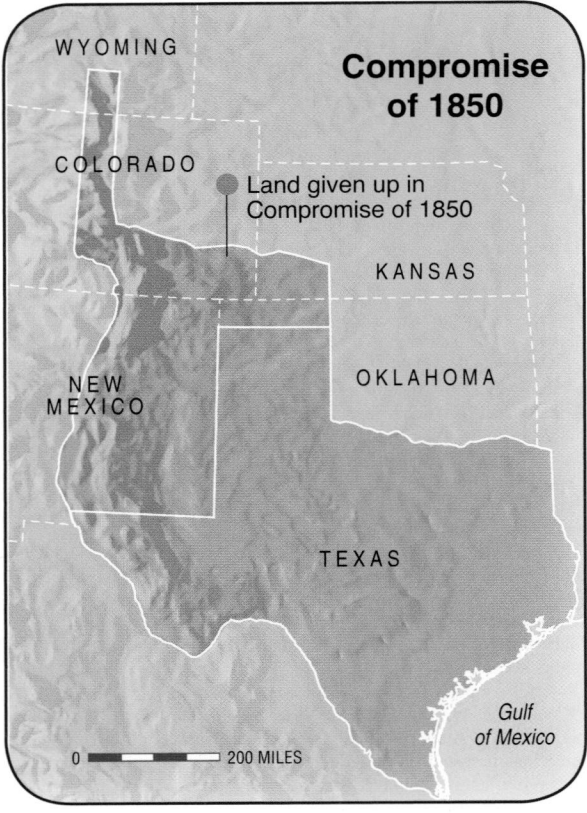

**Compromise of 1850**

WYOMING

COLORADO

Land given up in Compromise of 1850

KANSAS

NEW MEXICO

OKLAHOMA

TEXAS

Gulf of Mexico

0 ▬▬▬▬ 200 MILES

the 1850s until the movement toward secession gained strength.

## Secession

Texas' population almost tripled in the decade between 1850 and 1860, when 604,215 people were counted, including 182,921 slaves. Many of these new settlers came from the Lower South, a region familiar with slavery. Although three-quarters of the Texas population and two-thirds of the farmers did not own slaves, slaveowners controlled 60 to 70 percent of the wealth of the state and dominated the politics.

In 1850, 41 percent of the state's officeholders were from the slaveholding class; a decade later, more than 50 percent of the officeholders had slaves.

In addition to the political power of the slaveholders, they also provided role models for new immigrants to the state. After these newcomers got their first land, they saw slave ownership as another step up the economic ladder, whether they owned slaves or not. Slave ownership was an economic goal.

This attitude prevailed even in areas of Texas where slaveholding was not widespread or even practical. These factors were the wind that fanned the flames of the secessionist movement throughout the late 1850s.

The appearance of the **Know-Nothing Party**, which based its platform on a pro-American, anti-immigrant foundation, began to move Texas toward party politics. Because of the large number of foreign-born settlers, the party attracted many Anglo voters. In 1854, the Know-Nothings elected candidates to city offices in San Antonio, and a year later, the mayor of Galveston was elected with the party's backing. Also in 1855, the Know-Nothings elected 20 representatives and five senators to the Legislature.

The successes spurred the **Democrats** to serious party organization for the first time. In 1857, **Hardin Runnels** was nominated for governor at the Democratic convention held in Waco. **Sam Houston** sought the governorship as an independent, but he also got Know-Nothing backing. Democrats were organized, however, and Houston was dealt the only election defeat in his political career.

Runnels was a strong states'-rights Democrat who irritated many Texans during his administration by advocating reopening the slave trade. His popularity on the frontier also dropped when Indian raids became more severe.

Most Texans still were ambivalent about secession. The Union was seen as a protector of physical and economic stability. No threats to person or property were perceived in remaining attached to the United States.

In 1859, Houston again challenged Runnels, basing his campaign on Unionism. Combined with Houston's personal popularity, his position on the secession issue apparently satisfied most voters, for they gave him a solid victory over the more radical Runnels. In addition, Unionists **A.J. Hamilton** and **John H. Reagan** won the state's two congressional seats. Texans gave the states'-rights Democrats a sound whipping at the polls.

Within a few months, however, events were to change radically the political atmosphere of the state. On the frontier, the army could not control Indian raids, and with the later refusal of a Republican-controlled Congress to provide essential aid in fighting Indians, the federal government fell into disrepute.

**Secessionists** played on the growing distrust. Then in the summer of 1860, a series of fires in the cities around the state aroused fears that an abolitionist plot was afoot and that a slave uprising might be at hand — a traditional concern in a slaveholding society.

Vigilantes lynched blacks and Northerners across Texas, and a siege mentality developed.

When **Abraham Lincoln** was elected president (he was not on the ballot in Texas), secessionists went to work in earnest.

Pleas were made to Gov. Houston to call the Legislature into session to consider secession. Houston refused, hoping the passions would cool. They did not. Finally, **Oran M. Roberts** and other secessionist leaders issued a call to the counties to hold elections and send delegates to a convention in Austin. Ninety-two of 122 counties responded, and on Jan. 28, 1861, the meeting convened.

Only eight delegates voted against secession, while 166 supported it. An election was called for Feb. 23, 1861, and the ensuing campaign was marked by intolerance and violence. Opponents of secession were often intimidated — except the governor, who courageously stumped the state opposing withdrawal from the Union. Houston also argued that if Texas did secede it should revert to its status as an independent

republic and not join the Confederacy.

Only one-fourth of the state's population had been in Texas during the days of independence, and the argument carried no weight. On election day, 76 percent of 61,000 voters favored secession.

President Lincoln, who took office within a couple of weeks, reportedly sent the Texas governor a letter offering 50,000 federal troops to keep Texas in the Union. But after a meeting with other Unionists, Houston declined the offer. "I love Texas too well to bring strife and bloodshed upon her," the governor declared. On March 16, Houston refused to take an oath of loyalty to the Confederacy and was replaced in office by **Lt. Gov. Edward Clark.**

## Civil War

Texas did not suffer the devastation of its Southern colleagues in the Civil War. On but a few occasions did Union troops occupy territory in Texas, except in the El Paso area.

The state's cotton was important to the Confederate war effort because it could be transported from Gulf ports when other Southern shipping lanes were blockaded.

Some goods became difficult to buy, but unlike other states of the Confederacy, Texas still received consumer goods because of the trade that was carried on through Mexico during the war.

Although accurate figures are not available, historians estimate that between 70,000 and 90,000 Texans fought for the South, and between 2,000 and 3,000, including some former slaves, saw service in the Union army.

Texans became disenchanted with the Confederate government early in the war. State taxes were levied for the first time since the Compromise of 1850, and by war's end, the Confederacy had collected more than $37 million from the state.

But most of the complaints about the government centered on Brig. Gen. **Paul O. Hebert**, the Confederate commander of the Department of Texas.

In April 1862, Gen. Hebert declared martial law without notifying state officials. Opposition to the South's new conscription law, which exempted persons owning more than 15 slaves among other categories of exemptions, prompted the action.

The violence against suspected Union sympathizers reached its zenith with the **"Great Hanging at Gainesville,"** when 40 men were tried and hanged at Gainesville in October 1862. Two others were shot as they tried to escape. Although the affair reached its climax in Cooke County, men were killed in neighboring Grayson, Wise and Denton counties. Most were accused of treason or insurrection, but evidently few had actually conspired against the Confederacy, and many were innocent of the abolitionist sentiments for which they were tried.

In November 1862, Gen. Hebert prohibited the export of cotton except under government control, and this proved a disastrous policy. The final blow came when the commander failed to defend **Galveston** and it fell into Union hands in the fall of 1862.

Maj. Gen. **John B. Magruder**, who replaced Hebert, was much more popular. The new commander's first actions were to combat the Union offensive against Texas ports. Sabine Pass had been closed in September 1862 by the Union blockade, and Galveston was in Northern hands.

On Jan. 1, 1863, Magruder retook Galveston with the help of two steamboats lined with cotton bales. Sharpshooters aboard proved devastating in battles against the Union fleet. Three weeks later, Magruder used two other cotton-clad steamboats to break the Union blockade of Sabine Pass, and two of the state's major ports were reopened.

Late in 1863, the Union launched a major offensive against the Texas coast that was partly successful. On Sept. 8, however, Lt. **Dick Dowling** and 42 men fought off a 1,500-man Union invasion force at **Sabine Pass**. In a brief battle, Dowling's command sank two Union gunboats and put the other invasion ships to flight.

Federal forces were more successful at the mouth of the Rio Grande. On Nov. 1, 1863, 7,000 Union troops landed at **Brazos Santiago**, and five days later, Union forces entered Brownsville. Texas Unionists led by **E.J. Davis** were active in the Valley, moving as far upriver as Rio Grande City. Confederate Col. **John S. "Rip" Ford**, commanding state troops, finally pushed the Union soldiers out of Brownsville in July 1864, reopening the important port for the Confederacy.

Most Texans never saw a Union soldier during the war. The only ones they might have seen were in the **prisoner-of-war camps**. The largest, **Camp Ford**, near Tyler, housed 5,000 prisoners. Others operated in Kerr County and at Hempstead.

As the war dragged on, the mood of Texans changed. Those on the homefront began to feel they were sacrificing loved ones and suffering hardship so cotton speculators could profit. Public order broke down as refugees flocked to Texas. And slaves from other states were sent to Texas for safekeeping. When the war ended, there were an estimated 400,000 slaves in Texas, more than double the number counted in the 1860 census.

Morale was low in Texas in early 1865. Soldiers at Galveston and Houston began to mutiny. At Austin, Confederate soldiers raided the state treasury in March and found only $5,000 in specie. Units began breaking up, and the army was beginning to dissolve before Gen. **Robert E. Lee** surrendered at **Appomattox** in April 1865. He surrendered the Army of Northern Virginia, and while this assured Union victory, the surrender of other Confederate units was to follow until the last unit gave up in Oklahoma at the end of June.

The last land battle of the Civil War was fought at **Palmito Ranch** near Brownsville on May 13, 1865. After the Confederate's victory, they learned the governors of the Western Rebel states had authorized the disbanding of armies, and, a few days later, they accepted a truce with the Union forces.

## Reconstruction

On June 19, 1865, **Gen. Gordon Granger**, under the command of Gen. Philip M. Sheridan, arrived in Galveston with 1,800 federal troops to begin the Union occupation of Texas. Gen. Granger proclaimed the emancipation of the slaves.

**A.J. Hamilton**, a Unionist and former congressman from Texas, was named provisional governor by President Andrew Johnson.

Texas was in turmoil. Thousands of the state's men had died in the conflict. Indian raids had caused as much damage as the skirmishes with the Union army, causing the frontier to recede up to 100 miles eastward in some areas.

Even worse, confusion reigned. No one knew what to expect from the conquering forces.

Gen. Granger dispatched troops to the population centers of the state to restore civil authority. But only a handful of the 50,000 federal troops that came to Texas was stationed in the interior. Most were sent to the Rio Grande as a show of force against the French forces in Mexico, and clandestine aid was supplied to Mexican President Benito Juarez in his fight against the French and Mexican royalists.

The **frontier forts**, most of which were built during the early 1850s by the federal government to protect western settlements, had been abandoned by the U.S. Army after secession. These were not remanned, and a prohibition against a militia denied settlers a means of self-defense against Indian raids. *(For an overview of the frontier forts, see Texas Almanac 2004–2005 or www.TexasAlmanac.com.)*

Thousands of freed black slaves migrated to the cities, where they felt the federal soldiers would provide protection. Still others traveled the countryside, seeking family members and loved ones from whom they had been separated during the war.

The **Freedman's Bureau**, authorized by Congress in March 1865, began operation in September 1865 under Gen. E.M. Gregory. It had the responsibility to provide education, relief aid, labor supervision and judicial protection for the newly freed slaves.

The bureau was most successful in opening schools for blacks. Education was a priority because 95 percent of the freed slaves were illiterate.

The agency also was partially successful in getting blacks back to work on plantations under reasonable labor contracts.

Some plantation owners harbored hopes that they would be paid for their property loss when the slaves were freed. In some cases, the slaves were not released from plantations for up to a year.

To add to the confusion, some former slaves had the false notion that the federal government was going to parcel out the plantation lands to them. These blacks simply bided their time, waiting for the division of land.

Under pressure from President Johnson, Gov. Hamilton called for an election of delegates to a constitutional convention in January 1866. Hamilton told the gathering what was expected: Former slaves were to be given civil rights; the secession ordinance had to be repealed; Civil War debt had to be repudiated; and slavery was to be abolished with ratification of the Thirteenth Amendment.

Many delegates to the convention were former secessionists, and there was little support for compromise.

**J.W. Throckmorton**, a Unionist and one of eight men who had opposed secession in the convention of 1861, was elected chairman of the convention. But a coalition of conservative Unionists and Democrats

A 12-foot Civil War cannon from the doomed Union ship USS Westfield was recovered, along with the ship and many artifacts, in 2009 from the bottom of the Houston Ship Channel in Galveston Bay. Above, the restored cannon is delivered to the Texas City Museum, where it is on display. Left, the cannon, covered with nearly 150 years of sediment, is pulled from the bay. The 10,000-pound cannon was restored by the Texas A&M Conservation Research Laboratory. Bottom left, a period engraving depicts the Westfield exploding in Galveston Bay on New Year's Day 1863. The ship's commodore, William Renshaw, accidentally ran his ship aground as it and other Union vessels battled Confederate "cottonclads" (Rebel ships armored with bales of cotton). As Renshaw prepared to scuttle his ship rather than let it pass into Confederate hands, the vessel's powder magazine exploded prematurely, killing him and most of his officers and sailors.

**Photos: (top)** Marie D. De Jesus/ Houston Chronicle; **(center)** Texas A&M Conservation Research Laboratory; **(bottom)** U.S. Library of Congress.

controlled the meeting. As a consequence, Texas took limited steps toward appeasing the victorious North.

Slavery was abolished, and blacks were given some civil rights. But they still could not vote and were barred from testifying in trials against whites.

No action was taken on the Thirteenth Amendment because, the argument went, the amendment already had been ratified.

Otherwise, the constitution that was written followed closely the constitution of 1845. President Johnson in August 1866 accepted the new constitution and declared insurrection over in Texas, the last of the states of the Confederacy so accepted under **Presidential Reconstruction**.

Throckmorton was elected governor in June, along with other state and local officials. However, Texans had not learned a lesson from the war.

When the Legislature met, a series of laws limiting the rights of blacks were passed. In labor disputes, for example, the employers were to be the final arbitrators. The codes also bound an entire family's labor, not just the head of the household, to an employer.

Funding for black education would be limited to what could be provided by black taxpayers. Since few blacks owned land or had jobs, that provision effectively denied education to black children. However, the thrust of the laws and the attitude of the legislators was clear: Blacks simply were not to be considered full citizens.

Many of the laws later were overturned by the Freedman's Bureau or military authorities when, in March 1867, Congress began a **Reconstruction plan** of its own. The Southern states were declared to have no legal government and the former Confederacy was divided into districts to be administered by the military until satisfactory Reconstruction was effected. Texas and Louisiana made up the Fifth Military District under the command of Gen. Philip H. Sheridan.

Gov. Throckmorton clashed often with Gen. Sheridan. The governor thought the state had gone far enough in establishing rights for the newly freed slaves and other matters. Finally in August 1867, Throckmorton and other state officials were removed from office by Sheridan because they were considered an "impediment to the reconstruction." **E.M. Pease**, the former two-term governor and a Unionist, was named provisional governor by military authorities.

A **new constitutional convention** was called by Gen. Winfield S. Hancock, who replaced Sheridan in November 1867. For the first time, blacks were allowed to participate in the elections that selected delegates. A total of 59,633 whites and 49,497 blacks registered. The elected delegates met on June 1, 1868. Deliberations got bogged down on partisan political matters, however, and the convention spent $200,000, an astronomical sum for the time.

This constitution of 1869, as it came to be known, granted full rights of citizenship to blacks, created a system of education, delegated broad powers to the governor and generally reflected the views of the state's Unionists.

Gov. Pease, disgusted with the convention and with military authorities, resigned in September 1869. Texas had no chief executive until January 1870, when the newly elected **E.J. Davis** took office.

Meeting in February 1870, the Legislature created a **state militia** under the governor's control; created a **state police force**, also controlled by the governor; postponed the 1870 general election to 1872; enabled the governor to appoint more than 8,500 local office-holders; and granted subsidized **bonds for railroad construction** at a rate of $10,000 a mile.

For the first time, a system of public education was created. The law required compulsory attendance at school for four months a year, set aside one-quarter of the state's annual revenue for education and levied a poll tax to support education. Schools also were to be integrated, which enraged many white Texans.

The Davis administration was the most unpopular in Texas' history. In fairness, historians have noted that Davis did not feel that whites could be trusted to assure the rights of the newly freed blacks.

Violence was rampant in Texas. One study found that between the close of the Civil War and mid-1868, 1,035 people were murdered in Texas, including 486 blacks, mostly victims of white violence.

Gov. Davis argued that he needed broad police powers to restore order. Despite their unpopularity, the state police and militia — blacks made up 40 percent of the police and a majority of the militia — brought the lawlessness under control in many areas.

Democrats, aided by moderate Republicans, regained control of the Legislature in the 1872 elections, and, in 1873, the lawmakers set about stripping the governor of many of his powers.

The political turmoil ended with the gubernatorial election of 1873, when **Richard Coke** easily defeated Davis. Davis tried to get federal authorities to keep him in office, but President Grant refused to intervene.

In January of 1874, Democrats were in control of state government again. The end of Reconstruction concluded the turbulent Civil War era, although the attitudes that developed during the period lasted well into the 20th century.

## Capital and Labor

A **constitutional convention** was called in 1875 to rewrite the 1869 constitution, a hated vestige of Radical Republican rule.

Every avenue to cutting spending at any level of government was explored. Salaries of public officials were slashed. The number of offices was reduced. Judgeships, along with most other offices, were made elective rather than appointive.

The state road program was curtailed, and the immigration bureau was eliminated.

Perhaps the worst change was the destruction of the statewide school system. The new charter created a "community system" without a power of taxation, and schools were segregated by race.

Despite the basic reactionary character, the new constitution also was visionary. Following the lead of several other states, the Democrats declared railroads to be common carriers and subject to regulation.

To meet the dual challenge of lawlessness and Indian insurrection, Gov. Coke in 1874 re-established the **Texas Rangers**.

While cowboys and cattle drives are romantic subjects for movies on the Texas of this period, the fact is that the simple cotton farmer was the backbone of the

*Famed Texas rancher Charles Goodnight is credited with inventing the chuck wagon, which became a staple during the years of cattle drives, roughly 20 years from 1866–1886. This early, undated photo, titled "The Roundup," was taken in Maverick County. Photo courtesy of the Eagle Pass Chamber of Commerce.*

state's economy.

But neither the farmer nor the cattleman prospered throughout the last quarter of the 19th century. At the root of their problems was federal monetary policy and the lingering effects of the Civil War.

Although the issuance of paper money had brought about a business boom in the Union during the war, inflation also increased. Silver was demonetized in 1873. Congress passed the Specie Resumption Act in 1875 that returned the nation to the gold standard in 1879. Almost immediately a contraction in currency began. Between 1873 and 1891, the amount of national bank notes in circulation declined from $339 million to $168 million.

The reduction in the money supply was devastating in the defeated South. Land values plummeted. In 1870, Texas land was valued at an average of $2.62 an acre, compared with the national average of $18.26 an acre. With the money supply declining and the national economy growing, farm prices dropped. In 1870, a bushel of wheat brought $1. In the 1890s, wheat was 60 cents a bushel. Except for a brief spurt in the early 1880s, cattle prices followed those of crops.

Between 1880 and 1890, the number of farms in Texas doubled, but the number of tenants tripled. By 1900, almost half the state's farmers were tenants.

The much-criticized crop-lien system was developed following the war to meet credit needs of the small farmers. Merchants would extend credit to farmers through the year in exchange for liens on their crops. But the result of the crop-lien system, particularly when small farmers did not have enough acreage to operate efficiently, was a state of continual debt and despair.

The work ethic held that a man would benefit from his toil. When this apparently failed, farmers looked to the monetary system and the railroads as the causes. Their discontent hence became the source of the agrarian revolt that developed in the 1880s and 1890s.

The entry of the Texas & Pacific and the Missouri-Kansas-Texas **railroads** from the northeast changed trade patterns in the state.

Since the days of the Republic, trade generally had flowed to Gulf ports, primarily Galveston. Jefferson in Northeast Texas served as a gateway to the Mississippi River, but it never carried the volume of trade that was common at Galveston.

The earliest railroad systems in the state also were centered around Houston and Galveston, again directing trade southward. With the T&P and Katy lines, North Texas had direct access to markets in St. Louis and the East.

Problems developed with the railroads, however. In 1882, Jay Gould and Collis P. Huntington, owner of the Southern Pacific, entered into a secret agreement that amounted to creation of a monopoly of rail service in Texas. They agreed to stop competitive track extensions; to divide under a pooling arrangement freight moving from New Orleans and El Paso; to purchase all competing railroads in Texas; and to share the track between Sierra Blanca and El Paso.

The Legislature made weak attempts to regulate railroads, as provided by the state constitution. Gould thwarted an attempt to create a commission to regulate the railroads in 1881 with a visit to the state during the Legislature's debate.

The railroad tycoon subdued the lawmakers' interest with thinly disguised threats that capital would abandon Texas if the state interfered with railroad business.

As the 19th century closed, Texas remained an agricultural state. But the industrial base was growing. Between 1870 and 1900, the per capita value of manufactured goods in the United States rose from $109 to $171. In Texas, these per capita values increased from $14 to $39, but manufacturing values in Texas industry still were only one-half of annual agricultural values.

In 1886, a new breed of Texas politician appeared. **James Stephen Hogg** was not a Confederate veteran, and he was not tied to party policies of the past.

As a reform-minded attorney general, Hogg had actively enforced the state's few railroad regulatory laws. With farmers' support, Hogg was elected governor in 1890, and at the same time, a debate on the constitutionality of a **railroad commission** was settled when voters amended the constitution to provide for one. The reform mood of the state was evident. Voters returned only 22 of the 106 members of the Texas House in 1890.

Despite his reputation as a reformer, Hogg accepted the growing use of **Jim Crow laws** to limit blacks' access to public services. In 1891, the Legislature responded to public demands and required railroads to provide separate accommodations for blacks and whites.

The stage was being set for one of the major political campaigns in Texas history, however. Farmers did not think that Hogg had gone far enough in his reform program, and they were distressed that Hogg had not appointed a farmer to the railroad commission. Many began to look elsewhere for the solutions to their problems. The **People's Party** in Texas was formed in August 1891.

The 1892 general election was one of the most spirited in the state's history. Gov. Hogg's supporters shut conservative Democrats out of the convention in Houston, so the conservatives bolted and nominated railroad attorney George Clark for governor.

The People's Party, or **Populists**, for the first time had a presidential candidate, James Weaver, and a gubernatorial candidate, T.L. Nugent.

Texas Republicans also broke ranks. The party's strength centered in the black vote. After the death of former Gov. E.J. Davis in 1883, **Norris Wright Cuney**, a black, was party leader. Cuney was considered one of the most astute politicians of the period, and he controlled federal patronage.

White Republicans revolted against the black leadership, and these "Lily-whites" nominated **Andrew Jackson Houston**, son of Sam Houston, for governor.

Black Republicans recognized that alone their strength was limited, and throughout the latter part of the 19th century, they practiced fusion politics, backing candidates of third parties when they deemed it appropriate. Cuney led the Republicans into a coalition with the conservative Democrats in 1892, backing George Clark.

The election also marked the first time major Democratic candidates courted the black vote. Gov. Hogg's supporters organized black voter clubs, and the governor got about half of the black vote.

Black farmers were in a quandary. Their financial problems were the same as those small farmers who backed the Populists.

White Populists varied in their sympathy with the racial concerns of blacks. On the local level, some whites showed sympathy with black concerns about education, voting, and law enforcement. Black farmers also were reluctant to abandon the Republican Party because it was their only political base in Texas.

Hogg was re-elected in 1892 with a 43 percent plurality in a field of five candidates.

Populists continued to run well in state races until 1898. Historians have placed the beginning of the party's demise in the 1896 presidential election in which national Populists fused with the Democrats and supported **William Jennings Bryan**.

Although the Populist philosophy lived on, the party declined in importance after 1898. Farmers

remained active in politics, but most returned to the Democratic Party, which usurped many of the Populists' issues.

## Oil

Seldom can a people's history be profoundly changed by a single event on a single day. But Texas' entrance into the industrial age can be linked directly to the discovery of oil at **Spindletop**, three miles from **Beaumont**, on Jan. 10, 1901.

From that day, Texas' progress from a rural, agricultural state to a modern industrial giant was steady.

## 1900–1920

One of the greatest natural disasters ever to strike the state occurred on Sept. 8, 1900, when a **hurricane devastated Galveston**, killing 6,000 people. (For a more detailed account, see "After the Great Storm" in the *Texas Almanac 1998–1999*). In rebuilding from that disaster, Galveston's civic leaders fashioned the **commission form of municipal government**.

Amarillo later refined the system into the council-manager organization that is widely used today.

The great Galveston storm also reinforced arguments by Houston's leadership that an inland port should be built for protection against such tragedies and disruptions of trade. The **Houston Ship Channel** was soon a reality.

The reform spirit in government was not dead after the departure of Jim Hogg. In 1901, the Legislature prohibited the issuing of railroad passes to public officials. More than 270,000 passes were issued to officials that year, and farmers claimed that the free rides increased their freight rates and influenced public policy as well.

In 1903, state Sen. **A.W. Terrell** got a major **election-reform law** approved, a measure that was further modified two years later. A **primary system** was established to replace a hodgepodge of practices for nominating candidates that had led to charges of irregularities after each election.

Also in the reform spirit, the Legislature in 1903 prohibited abuse of **child labor** and set minimum ages at which children could work in certain industries. The action preceded federal child-labor laws by 13 years.

However, the state, for the first time, imposed the **poll tax** as a requirement for voting. Historians differ on whether the levy was designed to keep blacks or poor whites — or both — from voting. Certainly the poll tax cut election turnouts. Black voter participation dropped from about 100,000 in the 1890s to an estimated 5,000 in 1906.

The Democratic State Executive Committee also recommended that county committees limit participation in primaries to whites only, and most accepted the suggestion.

The election of **Thomas M. Campbell** as governor in 1906 marked the start of a progressive period in Texas politics. Interest revived in controlling corporate influence.

Under Campbell, the state's **antitrust laws** were strengthened and a **pure food and drug bill** was passed. Life insurance companies were required to invest in Texas 75 percent of their reserves on policies in the state. Less than one percent of the reserves had been invested prior to the law.

Some companies left Texas. But the law was beneficial in the capital-starved economy. In 1904, voters amended the constitution to allow the state to charter **banks** for the first time, and this eased some of the farmers' credit problems. In 1909, the Legislature approved a bank-deposit insurance plan that predated the federal program.

With corporate influence under acceptable control, attention turned to the issue of prohibition of alcohol. Progressives and prohibitionists joined forces against the conservative establishment to exert a major influence in state government for the next two decades.

**Prohibitionists** had long been active in Texas. They had the **local-option clause** written into the Constitution of 1876, which allowed counties or their subdivisions to be voted dry. But in 1887, a prohibition amendment to the state constitution had been defeated by a two-to-one margin, and public attention had turned to other problems.

In the early 20th century, the prohibition movement gathered strength. Most of Texas already was dry because of local option. When voters rejected a prohibition amendment by a slim margin in 1911, the state had 167 dry counties and 82 wet or partially wet counties. The heavily populated counties, however, were wet. Prohibition continued to be a major issue.

Problems along the U.S.-Mexico border escalated in 1911 as the decade-long **Mexican Revolution** broke out. Soon the revolutionaries controlled some northern Mexican states, including Chihuahua. Juarez and El Paso were major contact points. El Paso residents could stand on rooftops to observe the fighting between revolutionaries and government troops. Some Americans were killed.

After pleas to the federal government got no action, Gov. Oscar Colquitt sent state militia and Texas Rangers into the Valley in 1913 to protect Texans after Matamoros fell to the rebels. Unfortunately, the Rangers killed many innocent Mexican-Texans during the operation. In addition to problems caused by the fighting and raids, thousands of Mexican refugees flooded Texas border towns to escape the violence of the revolution.

In 1914, **James E. Ferguson** entered Texas politics and for the next three decades, "Farmer Jim" was one of the most dominating and colorful figures on the political stage. Ferguson, a banker from Temple, skirted the prohibition issue by pledging to veto any legislation pertaining to alcoholic beverages.

His strength was among farmers, however. Sixty-two percent of Texas' farmers were tenants, and Ferguson pledged to back legislation to limit tenant rents. Ferguson also was a dynamic orator. He easily won the primary and beat out three opponents in the general election.

Ferguson's first administration was successful. The Legislature passed the law limiting tenants' rents, although it was poorly enforced, and aid to rural schools was improved.

In 1915, the border problems heated up. A Mexican national was arrested in the Lower Rio Grande Valley carrying a document outlining plans for Mexican-Americans, Indians, Japanese and blacks in Texas and the Southwest to eliminate all Anglo males over age 16 and create a new republic. The document, whose author was never determined, started a bloodbath in the Valley. Mexican soldiers participated in raids across the Rio Grande, and Gov. Ferguson sent in the Texas Rangers.

*Judge Roy Bean, who was called "the Law West of the Pecos," tries a horse thief in 1900 at the old town of Langtry in Val Verde County. The building was both courthouse and saloon. "No other peace officers in the locality at that time," according to information with the photo, which is from the U.S. National Archives and Records Administration.*

*A crowd gathers outside of the Texas & Pacific Railroad Company building in Fort Worth on April 8, 1905, to hear President Theodore Roosevelt speak. Photo by C. L. Swartz; courtesy of the U.S. Library of Congress.*

Historians differ on the number of people who were killed, but a safe assessment would be hundreds. Gov. Ferguson and Mexican President Venustiano Carranza met at Nuevo Laredo in November 1915 in an attempt to improve relations. The raids continued.

**Pancho Villa** raided Columbus, N.M., in early 1916; two small Texas villages in the Big Bend, Glenn Springs and Boquillas, also were attacked. In July, President **Woodrow Wilson** determined that the hostilities were critical and activated the National Guard. Soon 100,000 U.S. troops were stationed along the border. **Fort Bliss** in El Paso housed 60,000 men, and **Fort Duncan** near Eagle Pass was home to 16,000.

With the exception of Gen. John J. Pershing's pursuit of Villa into Northern Mexico, few U.S. troops crossed into Mexico. But the service along the border gave soldiers basic training that was put to use when the United States entered World War I in 1917.

Ferguson was easily re-elected in 1916, and he worked well with the Legislature the following year. But after the Legislature adjourned, the governor got into a dispute with the board of regents of the **University of Texas**. The disagreement culminated in the governor's vetoing all appropriations for the school. As the controversy swirled, the Travis County grand jury indicted Ferguson for misappropriation of funds and for embezzlement. In July 1917, Speaker of the Texas House F.O. Fuller called a special session of the Legislature to consider **impeachment** of the governor.

The Texas House voted 21 articles of impeachment, and the Senate in August 1917 convicted Ferguson on 10 of the charges. The Senate's judgment not only removed Ferguson from office, but also barred him from seeking office again. Ferguson resigned the day before the Senate rendered the decision in an attempt to avoid the prohibition against seeking further office.

Texas participated actively in **World War I**. Almost 200,000 young Texans, including 31,000 blacks, volunteered for military service, and 450 Texas women served in the nurses' corps. Five thousand lost their lives overseas, either fighting or in the **influenza pandemic** that swept the globe.

Texas also was a major training ground during the conflict, with 250,000 soldiers getting basic training in the state. On the negative side, the war frenzy opened a period of intolerance and nativism in the state. German-Texans were suspect because of their ancestry. A law was passed to prohibit speaking against the war effort. Persons who failed to participate in patriotic activities often were punished. Gov. William P. Hobby even vetoed the appropriation for the German department at the University of Texas.

Ferguson's removal from office was a devastating blow to the anti-prohibitionists. Word that the former governor had received a $156,000 loan from members of the brewers' association while in office provided ammunition for the progressives. In February 1918, a special session of the Legislature prohibited saloons within a 10-mile radius of military posts and ratified the national prohibition amendment, which had been introduced in Congress by Texas Sen. **Morris Sheppard**.

Women also were given the **right to vote in state primaries** at the same session.

Although national prohibition was to become effective in early 1920, the Legislature presented a prohibition amendment to voters in May 1919, and it was approved, bringing prohibition to Texas earlier than to the rest of the nation. At the same time, a woman suffrage amendment, which would have granted women the right to vote in all elections, was defeated.

Although World War I ended in November 1918, it brought many changes to Texas. Rising prices during the war had increased the militancy of labor unions.

Blacks also became more militant after the war. Discrimination against black soldiers led in 1917 to a riot in Houston in which several people were killed.

With the election of Mexican President Alvaro Obregón in 1920, the fighting along the border subsided. In 1919, state Rep. J.T. Canales of Brownsville initiated an investigation of the **Texas Rangers**' role in the border problems. As a result of the study, the Rangers' manpower was reduced from 1,000 members to 76, and stringent limitations were placed on the agency's activities. Standards for members of the force also were upgraded.

By 1920, although still a rural state, the face of Texas was changing. Nearly one-third of the population was in the cities. **Pat M. Neff** won the gubernatorial election of 1920, beating Sen. Joseph W. Bailey in the primary. As a former prosecuting attorney in McLennan County, Neff made law and order the major thrust of his administration. During his tenure the state took full responsibility for developing a **highway system**, a **gasoline tax** was imposed, and a state **park board** was established.

In 1921, a group of West Texans threatened to form a new state because Neff vetoed the creation of a new college in their area. Two years later, **Texas Technological College** (now Texas Tech University) was authorized in Lubbock and opened its doors in 1925.

Although still predominantly a rural state, Texas cities were growing. In 1900, only 17 percent of the population lived in urban areas; by 1920, that figure had almost doubled to 32 percent. A discontent developed with the growth of the cities. Rural Texans had long seen cities as hotbeds of vice and immorality. Simple rural values were cherished, and it seemed that those values were threatened in a changing world. After World War I, this transition accelerated.

## KKK and Minorities

In addition, "foreigners" in the state became suspect; nativism reasserted itself. German-Texans were associated with the enemy in the war, and Mexican-Texans were mostly Roman Catholics and likened to the troublemakers along the border. Texas was a fertile ground for the new **Ku Klux Klan** that entered the state in late 1920. The Klan's philosophy was a mixture of patriotism, law-and-order, nativism, white supremacy and Victorian morals. Its influence spread quickly across the state, and reports of Klan violence and murder were rampant.

**Prohibition** had brought a widespread disrespect for law. Peace officers and other officials often ignored speakeasies and gambling. The Klan seemed to many Texans to be an appropriate instrument for restoring law and order and for maintaining morality in towns and cities. By 1922, many of the state's large communities were under direct Klan influence, and a Klan-backed candidate, Earle Mayfield, was elected to the U.S. Senate, giving Texas the reputation as the most powerful Klan bastion in the Union. Hiram Wesley Evans of Dallas also was elected imperial wizard of the national Klan in that year.

The Klan became more directly involved in politics and planned to elect the next governor in 1924. Judge Felix Robertson of Dallas got the organization's backing in the Democratic primary. Former governor Jim Ferguson filed to run for the office, but the Texas Supreme Court ruled that he could not because of his impeachment conviction. So Ferguson placed his wife, Miriam A. Ferguson, on the ballot. Several other prominent Democrats also entered the race.

The Fergusons made no secret that Jim would have a big influence on his wife's administration. One campaign slogan was, "Two governors for the price of one." Mrs. Ferguson easily won the runoff against Robertson when many Texans decided that "Fergusonism" was preferable to the Klan in the governor's office.

Minorities began organizing in Texas to seek their civil rights. The National Association for the Advancement of Colored People (**NAACP**) opened a Texas chapter in 1912, and by 1919, there were chapters in 31 Texas communities. Similarly, Mexican-Texans formed Orden Hijos de America in 1921, and in 1929, the **League of United Latin American Citizens** (LULAC) was organized in Corpus Christi.

The Klan dominated the Legislature in 1923, passing a law barring blacks from participation in the Democratic primary. Although blacks had in fact been barred from voting in primaries for years, this law gave **Dr. Lawrence A. Nixon**, a black dentist from El Paso, the opportunity to go to court to fight the all-white primary. In 1927, the U.S. Supreme Court overturned the statute, but that was only the beginning of several court battles, which were not resolved until 1944.

Disgruntled Democrats and Klansmen tried to beat Mrs. Ferguson in the general election in 1924, but she was too strong. Voters also sent 91 new members to the Texas House, purging it of many of the Klan-backed representatives. After that election, the Klan's power ebbed rapidly in Texas.

Mrs. Ferguson named Emma Grigsby Meharg as Texas' first woman secretary of state in 1925. The governors Ferguson administration was stormy. Jim was accused of cronyism in awarding highway contracts and in other matters. And "Ma" returned to her husband's practice of liberal clemency for prisoners. In two years, Mrs. Ferguson extended clemency to 3,595 inmates.

Although Jim Ferguson was at his bombastic best in the 1926 Democratic primary, young Attorney

General **Dan Moody** had little trouble winning the nomination and the general election.

At age 33, Moody was the youngest person ever to become governor of Texas. Like many governors during this period, he was more progressive than the Legislature, and much of his program did not pass. Moody was successful in some government reorganization. He also cleaned up the highway department, which had been criticized under the Fergusons, and abandoned the liberal clemency policy for prisoners. And Moody worked at changing Texas' image as an anti-business state. "The day of the political trust-buster is gone," he told one Eastern journalist.

Progressives and prohibitionists still had a major influence on the Democratic Party, and 1928 was a watershed year for them. Moody easily won renomination and re-election. But the state party was drifting away from the direction of national Democrats. When **Al Smith**, a wet and a Roman Catholic, won the presidential nomination at the national Democratic convention in Houston, Texans were hard-pressed to remain faithful to the "party of the fathers." Moody, who had been considered a potential national figure, ruined his political career trying to straddle the fence, angering both wets and drys, Catholics and Protestants. Former governor O.B. Colquitt led an exodus of so-called "**Hoovercrats**" from the state Democratic convention in 1928, and for the first time in its history, Texas gave its electoral votes to a Republican, Herbert Hoover, in the general election.

Through the 1920s, oil continued to increase in importance in Texas' economy. New discoveries were made at Mexia in 1920, Luling in 1922, Big Lake in Reagan Conty in 1923, in the Wortham Field in 1924 and in Borger in 1926. But oil still did not dominate the state's economic life.

As late as **1929**, meat packing, cottonseed processing and various milling operations exceeded the added value of petroleum refining. And as the 1920s ended, lumbering and food processing shared major economic roles with the petroleum industry. During the decade, Texas grew between 35 and 42 percent of U.S. cotton and 20-30 percent of the world crop. Irrigation and mechanization opened the South Plains to cotton growing. Eight years later, more than 1.1 million bales were grown in the region, mostly around Lubbock.

But Texas, with the rest of the nation, was on the threshhold of a major economic disaster that would have irreversible consequences. The **Great Depression** was at hand.

## Depression Years

Historians have noted that the state's economic collapse was not as severe as that which struck the industrialized states. Texas' economy had sputtered through the decade of the 1920s, primarily because of the fluctuation of the price of cotton and other agricultural products. But agricultural prices were improving toward the end of the decade.

The Fergusons attempted a political comeback in the gubernatorial election of 1930. But Texans elected **Ross S. Sterling**, the founder of Humble Oil Co. Early in the Depression, Texans remained optimistic that the economic problems were temporary, another of the cyclical downturns the nation experienced periodically. Indeed, some Texans even felt that the hardships would be beneficial, ridding the economy of speculators and poor businessmen. Those attitudes gave way to increasing concern as the poor business conditions dragged on.

A piece of good luck turned into a near economic disaster for the state in late 1930. **C.M. "Dad" Joiner** struck oil near Kilgore, and soon the **East Texas oil boom** was in full swing. Millions of barrrels of new oil flooded the market, making producers and small landowners wealthy. Soon the glut of new oil drove market prices down from $1.10 a barrel in 1930 to 10 cents in 1931. Many wells had to be shut in around the state because they could not produce oil profitably at the low prices.

The Texas Railroad Commission attempted in the spring of 1931 to control production through proration, which assigned production quotas to each well (called the allowable). The first proration order limited each well to about 1,000 barrels a day of production. **Proration** had two goals: to protect reserves through conservation and to maintain prices by limiting production. But, on July 28, a federal court ruled that proration was an illegal attempt to fix prices.

In August 1931, Gov. Sterling placed four counties of the East Texas field under martial law and briefly shut down oil production there altogether. A federal court later ruled the governor's actions illegal. Gov. Sterling was roundly criticized for sending troops. Opponents said the action was taken to aid the major oil companies to the disadvantage of independent producers.

In 1932, Gov. Sterling appointed **Ernest O. Thompson** to a vacancy on the railroad commission. Thompson, who had led a coalition in favor of output regulation, is credited with fashioning a compromise between independents and major oil companies. In April 1933, the railroad commission prorated production on the basis, in part, of bottom-hole pressure in each well, and the courts upheld this approach. But enforcement remained a problem.

Finally in 1935, Texas' Sen. **Tom Connally** authored the Hot Oil Act, which involved the federal government in regulation by prohibiting oil produced in violation of state law from being sold in interstate commerce. Thereafter, Texas' producers accepted the concept of proration. Since Texas was the nation's largest oil producer, the railroad commission could set the national price of oil through proration for several decades thereafter.

Despite these problems, the oil boom helped East Texas weather the Depression better than other parts of the state. Farmers were hit particularly hard in 1931. Bumper crops had produced the familiar reduction in prices. Cotton dropped from 18 cents per pound in 1928 to six cents in 1931. That year Louisiana Gov. **Huey Long** proposed a ban on growing cotton in 1932 to eliminate the surplus. The Louisiana legislature enacted the ban, but Texas was the key state to the plan since it led the nation in cotton production. Gov. Sterling was cool to the idea, but responded to public support of it by calling a special session of the Legislature. The lawmakers passed a **cotton acreage limitation** bill in 1931, but the law was declared

*A migratory laborer camps on the outskirts of Perryton in Ochiltree County in June 1938 at the opening of the wheat harvest. With his wife and growing family, he has been on the road for 13 years, migrating for work in six states. Photo by Dorothea Lange; courtesy of the U.S. Library of Congress.*

unconstitutional the following year.

One feature of the Depression had become the number of transients drifting from city to city looking for work. Local governments and private agencies tried to provide relief for the unemployed, but the effort was soon overwhelmed by the number of persons needing help. In Houston, blacks and Mexican-Texans were warned not to apply for relief because there was not enough money to take care of whites, and many Mexicans returned to Mexico voluntarily and otherwise.

To relieve the local governments, Gov. Sterling proposed a bond program to repay counties for highways they had built and to start a public-works program. Texans' long-held faith in self-reliance and rugged individualism was put to a severe test.

By **1932**, many were looking to the federal government to provide relief from the effects of the Depression.

U.S. Speaker of the House **John Nance Garner** of Texas was a presidential candidate when the Democrats held their national convention. To avoid a deadlocked convention, Garner maneuvered the Texans to change strategy. On the fourth ballot, the Texas delegation voted for the eventual nominee, New York Gov. **Franklin D. Roosevelt**. Garner got the second

place on the ticket that swept into office in the general election.

In Texas, **Miriam Ferguson** was successful in unseating Gov. Sterling in the Democratic primary, winning by about 4,000 votes. Her second administration was less turbulent than the first. State government costs were reduced, and voters approved $20 million in so-called "bread bonds" to help provide relief. In 1933, **horse racing** came to the state, authorized through a rider on an appropriations bill legalizing pari-mutuel betting. The law was repealed in 1937.

Prohibition also was repealed in 1933, although much of Texas remained dry under the **local-option** laws and the prohibition against open saloons.

State government faced a series of financial problems during Mrs. Ferguson's second term. The annual deficit climbed to $14 million, and the state had to default on the interest payments on some bonds. Voters aggravated the situation by approving a $3,000 **homestead exemption**. Many property owners were losing their homes because they could not pay taxes. And while the exemption saved their homesteads, it worsened the state's financial problems.

Many Texas banks failed during the Depression, as did banks nationally. One of Roosevelt's first actions was to declare a national bank holiday in 1933.

*Clients of the Negro Farm Security Administration listen to a farm supervisor at a mass meeting in April 1939 near Marshall. Photo by Russell Lee from the U.S. Farm Security Administration, Office of War Information Photograph Collection, U.S. Library of Congress.*

Gov. Ferguson closed state banks at the same time, although she had to "assume" authority that was not in the law.

## The New Deal

In Washington, Texans played an important role in shaping Roosevelt's **New Deal**. As vice president, Garner presided over the Senate and maneuvered legislation through the upper house. **Texans** also chaired major committees in the House: **Sam Rayburn**, Interstate and Foreign Commerce; **Hatton W. Sumners**, Judiciary; **Fritz G. Lanham**, Public Buildings and Grounds; **J.J. Mansfield**, Rivers and Harbors; and **James P. Buchanan**, Appropriations. With this influence, the Texas delegation supported the president's early social programs. In addition, **Jesse Jones** of Houston served as director of the Reconstruction Finance Corporation, the Federal Loan Administration and as Secretary of Commerce. Jones was one of the most influential men in Washington and second only to Roosevelt in wielding financial power to effect recovery.

Poor conservation practices had left many of the state's farmlands open to erosion. During the **Dust Bowl** days of the early and mid-1930s, for example, the weather bureau in Amarillo reported 192 dust storms within a three-year period. Cooperation between state and federal agencies helped improve farmers' conservation efforts and reduced the erosion problem by the end of the decade.

Mrs. Ferguson did not seek re-election in 1934, and Attorney General **James V. Allred** was elected. Under his administration, several social-welfare programs were initiated, including old-age pensions, teachers' retirement and worker's compensation. Allred was re-elected in 1936.

Some of the New Deal's luster dimmed when the nation was struck by another recession in 1937.

Although Texas' economic condition improved toward the end of the decade, a full recovery was not realized until the beginning of World War II — when the state went through another industrial revolution.

Tragedy struck the small East Texas town of **New London** in Rusk County on March 18, 1937. At 3:05 p.m., natural gas, which had seeped undetected into an enclosed area beneath a school building from a faulty pipe connection, exploded when a shop teacher turned on a sander. Approximately 298 of the 540 students and teachers in the school died, and all but 130 of the survivors were injured. The disaster prompted the Legislature to pass a law requiring that a malodorant be added to gas so leaks could be detected by smell.

In 1938, voters elected one of the most colorful figures in the state's political history to the governor's office. **W. Lee "Pappy" O'Daniel**, a flour salesman and leader of a radio hillbilly band, came from nowhere to defeat a field of much better known candidates in the Democratic primary and to easily win the general election. When re-elected two years later, O'Daniel became the first candidate to poll more than one million votes in a Texas election.

But O'Daniel's skills of state did not equal his campaigning ability, and throughout his administration, the governor and the Legislature were in conflict. In early **1941**, long-time U.S. Senator Morris Sheppard died, and O'Daniel wanted the office. He appointed Andrew Jackson Houston, Sam Houston's aged son, to fill the vacancy. Houston died after only 24 days in office. O'Daniel won the special election for the post in a close race with a young congressman, **Lyndon B. Johnson**.

Lt. Gov. **Coke R. Stevenson** succeeded O'Daniel as governor and brought a broad knowledge of government to the office. Stevenson was elected to two full terms. Thanks to frugal management and greatly increasing revenues during the war years, he left the state treasury with a surplus in 1947. Voters also solved the continuing deficit problem by approving a pay-as-you-go amendment to the constitution in 1942. It requires the state comptroller to certify that tax revenues will be available to support appropriations. Otherwise the money cannot be spent.

## World War II

As in every war after Texas entered the Union, young Texans flocked to military service when the United States entered World War II. More than 750,000 served, including 12,000 women in the auxiliary services. In December 1942, U.S. Secretary of the Navy Frank Knox said Texas contributed the largest percentage of its male population to the armed forces of any state. Thirty Texans won Congressional Medals of Honor in the fighting. **Audie Murphy**, a young farm boy from Farmersville, became one of the most decorated soldiers of the war. Dallas-born **Sam Dealey** was the most-decorated Navy man.

Important contributions also were made at home. Texas was the site of 15 training posts, at which more than one and a quarter million men were trained, and of several prisoner-of-war camps.

World War II irrevocably changed the face of Texas. During the decade of the 1940s, the state's population switched from predominantly rural to 60 percent urban. The number of **manufacturing** workers almost doubled. And as had been the dream of Texas leaders for more than a century, the state began to attract new industries.

## Conservatives vs. Liberals

The state's politics became increasingly controlled by conservative Democrats after Gov. Allred left office. In 1946, **Beauford H. Jester**, a member of the railroad commission, gained the governorship. Under Jester in 1947, the Legislature passed the state's right-to-work law, prohibiting mandatory union membership, and reorganized public education with passage of the **Gilmer-Aikin Act**.

During the Jester administration several major constitutional amendments were adopted. Also, one of Texas' greatest tragedies occurred on April 16, 1947, when the French ship SS *Grandcamp*, carrying a load of ammonium nitrate, exploded at **Texas City**. More than 500 died and 4,000 sustained injuries. Property damage exceeded $200 million.

In **1948**, Sen. W. Lee O'Daniel did not seek re-election. Congressman Lyndon Johnson and former Gov. Coke Stevenson vied for the Democratic nomination. In the runoff, Johnson won by a mere **87 votes** in the closest — and most hotly disputed — statewide election in Texas' history. Johnson quickly rose to a leadership position in the U.S. Senate, and, with House Speaker Sam Rayburn, gave Texas substantial influence in national political affairs.

Although re-elected in 1948, Jester died in July 1949, the only Texas governor to die in office, and Lt. Gov. **Allan Shivers** succeeded him. During Shivers' administration, state spending more than doubled, reaching $805.7 million in 1956, as the governor increased appropriations for public-health institutions, school salaries, retirement benefits, highways and old-age pensions.

Shivers broke with tradition, successfully winning three full terms as governor after completing Jester's unexpired term. Shivers also led a revolt by Texas Democrats against the national party in **1952**. The governor, who gained both the Democratic and Republican nominations for the office under the law that allowed cross-filing that year, supported Republican Dwight Eisenhower for the presidency. Many Texas Democrats broke with the national party over the so-called "**Tidelands issue**." Texas claimed land 12 miles out into the Gulf as state lands. The issue was important because revenue from oil and natural gas production from the area supported public education in the state.

Major oil companies also backed Texas' position because state royalties on minerals produced from the land were much lower than federal royalties. President Harry S. Truman vetoed legislation that would have given Texas title to the land. Democratic presidential nominee Adlai Stevenson was no more sympathetic to the issue, and Texas gave its electoral votes to Republican Dwight Eisenhower in an election that attracted a two million-vote turnout for the first time in Texas. President Eisenhower signed a measure into law guaranteeing Texas' tidelands.

Scandal struck state government in 1954 when irregularities were discovered in the handling of funds in the veterans' land program in the General Land Office. Land Commissioner Bascom Giles was convicted of several charges and sent to prison. Several insurance companies also went bankrupt in the mid-1950s, prompting a reorganization of the State Board of Insurance in 1957.

In 1954, the U.S. Supreme Court ruled unconstitutional the segregation of schools, and for the next quarter-century, **school integration** became a major political issue. By the late 1960s, most institutions were integrated, but the state's major cities continued to wage court battles against forced busing of students to attain racial balance. Blacks and Mexican-Texans also made gains in voting rights during the 1950s.

Shivers had easily defeated **Ralph W. Yarborough** in the Democratic primary in 1952, but the divisions between the party's loyalists and those who bolted ranks to join Republicans in presidential races were growing. Shivers barely led the first 1954 primary over Yarborough and won the nomination with 53 percent of the vote in the runoff. Yarborough ran an equally close race against **Price Daniel**, a U.S. Senator who sought the governorship in 1956. Upon election as governor, Daniel left the Senate, and Yarborough won a special election to fill the vacancy in 1957. Yarborough won re-election in 1964 before losing to **Lloyd Bentsen** in 1970 in the Democratic primary. Although a liberal, Yarborough proved to be unusually durable in Texas' conservative political climate.

The state budget topped $1 billion for the first time in 1958. The Legislature met for 205 days in regular and special sessions in 1961–62 and levied, over Gov. Daniel's opposition, the state's first broad-based **sales tax in 1962**.

# Technological Growth

Through the 1950s and 1960s, Texas' industrial base had expanded and diversified. Petroleum production and refining remained the cornerstones, but other industries grew. Attracted by cheap electricity, the aluminum industry came to Texas. Starting from the base developed during World War II, defense industries and associated high-tech firms, specializing in electronics and computers, centered on the Dallas–Fort Worth area and Houston. One of the most important scientific breakthroughs of the century came in 1958 in Dallas. **Jack Kilby**, an engineer at **Texas Instruments**, developed and patented the integrated circuit that became the central part of computers.

Sen. Lyndon Johnson unsuccessfully sought the Democratic presidential nomination in 1960, and **John F. Kennedy** subsequently selected the Texan as his running mate. Johnson is credited with keeping several Southern states, including Texas, in the Democratic column in the close election. Kennedy was a Roman Catholic and a liberal, a combination normally rejected by the Southern states. When Johnson left the Senate to assume his new office in 1961, **John Tower** won a special election that attracted more than 70 candidates. Tower became the first Republican since Reconstruction to serve as a Texas senator.

During the early 1960s, Harris County was chosen as the site for the National Aeronautics and Space Administration's manned spacecraft center. The acquisition of **NASA** further diversified Texas' industrial base.

In 1962, **John B. Connally**, a former aide to LBJ and Secretary of the Navy under Kennedy, returned to Texas to seek the governorship. Gov. Daniel sought an unprecedented fourth term and was defeated in the Democratic primary. Connally won a close Democratic runoff over liberal **Don Yarborough** and was elected easily. As governor, Connally concentrated on improving **public education, state services,** and **water development**. He was re-elected in 1964 and 1966.

# The Assassination

One of the major tragedies in the nation's history occurred in Dallas on **Nov. 22, 1963**, when President Kennedy was assassinated while riding in a motorcade. Gov. Connally also was seriously wounded. Lyndon Johnson was administered the oath of the presidency by Federal Judge Sarah T. Hughes of Dallas aboard Air Force One at Love Field. Lee Harvey Oswald was arrested for the murder of the president on the afternoon of the assassination, but Oswald was killed by Dallas nightclub operator Jack Ruby two days later.

An extensive investigation into the assassination of President Kennedy was conducted by the Warren Commission. The panel concluded that Oswald was the killer and that he acted alone. Ruby, who was convicted of killing Oswald, died of cancer in the Dallas County jail in 1967 while the case was being appealed.

The assassination damaged the Republican Party in Texas, however. Building strength in Texas' conservative political atmosphere in 1962, eight Republicans, the most in decades, had been elected to the Texas House. And two Republicans — Ed Foreman of Odessa and Bruce Alger of Dallas — served in Congress. All were defeated in the 1964 general election.

In the emotional aftermath of the tragedy, Johnson, who won the presidency outright in a **landslide election in 1964**, persuaded the Congress to pass a series of civil-rights and social-welfare programs that changed the face of the nation. Texas was particularly affected by the civil-rights legislation and a series of lawsuits challenging election practices. During the 1960s, the state constitutional limitation of urban representation in the Legislature was overturned. The poll tax was declared unconstitutional, and the practice of electing officials from at-large districts fell to the so-called "one-man, one-vote" ruling. As a result, more Republican, minority and liberal officials were elected, particularly from urban areas. In 1966, **Curtis Graves** and **Barbara Jordan** of Houston and **Joe Lockridge** of Dallas became the first blacks to serve in the Texas Legislature since 1898.

Lyndon Johnson did not seek re-election in 1968. The nation had become involved in an unpopular war in Vietnam, and Johnson bowed out of the race in the interest of national unity.

# Sharpstown Scandal

Democrats stayed firmly in control of state government. **Preston Smith** was elected governor, and **Ben Barnes** gained the lieutenant governorship. Both were re-elected in 1970. Although state spending continued to increase, particularly on education, the Legislature otherwise was quiet. A minimum-wage law was approved, and public kindergartens were authorized in 1969.

At a special session, the **Sharpstown scandal**, one of the state's major scandals developed. Gov. Smith allowed the lawmakers to consider special banking legislation supported by Houston banker Frank Sharp. Several public officials were implicated in receiving favors from the banker for seeing that the legislation passed. Texas House Speaker Gus Mutscher and Rep. Tommy Shannon were convicted of conspiracy to accept bribes in a trial held in Abilene.

Voters in **1972** demanded a new leadership in the state capital. Smith and Barnes were defeated in the Democratic primary, and **Dolph Briscoe** was elected governor. In the fall, Texans gave presidential candidate Richard Nixon the state's electoral votes. Nixon carried 246 counties over Democrat George McGovern and received more than 65 percent of the popular vote.

The Legislature in 1973 was dominated by a reform atmosphere in the wake of the Sharpstown scandal. Price Daniel Jr., son of the former governor, was selected speaker of the House, and several laws concerning ethics and disclosure of campaign donations and spending were passed. Open meetings and open records statutes also were approved.

By 1970, Texas had become an even more urban state. The census found almost 11.2 million people in the state, ranking it sixth nationally. Three Texas cities, Houston, Dallas and San Antonio, were among the 10 largest in the nation.

Through the first half of the 1970s, several major changes were made in state policy. **Liquor-by-the-drink** became legal and the age of majority was lowered from 20 to 18, giving young people the right to vote. The state's first Public Utilities Commission was created, hearing its initial case in September 1976.

## Prosperity

Texas entered a period of unparalleled prosperity in 1973 when the Organization of Petroleum Exporting Countries (OPEC) boycotted the U.S. market. Severe energy shortages resulted, and the price of oil and natural gas skyrocketed. The federal government had allowed foreign oil to be imported through the 1960s, severely reducing the incentives to find and produce domestic oil. Consequently, domestic producers could not compensate for the loss in foreign oil as a result of the boycott.

The Texas Railroad Commission had long complained about the importation of foreign oil, and in 1972, the panel had removed proration controls from wells in the state, allowing 100 percent production. For the rest of the decade, domestic producers mounted a major exploration effort, drilling thousands of wells. Nevertheless, **Texas' oil and gas production peaked in 1970** and has been declining since. Newly discovered oil and gas have not replaced the declining reserves. While Texans suffered from the inflation that followed, the state prospered. Tax revenues at all levels of government increased, and state revenues, basically derived from oil and gas taxes, spiraled, as did the state budget.

With the new revenue from inflation and petroleum taxes, state spending rose from $2.95 billion in 1970 to $8.6 billion in 1979, and education led the advance, moving from 42 percent of the budget to 51.5 percent. But there was no increase in state tax rates.

It was no surprise that **education** was one of the major beneficiaries of increased state spending. After World War II, more emphasis was placed on education across the state. **Community colleges** sprang up in many cities, and a total of 109 colleges were established between the end of the war and 1980. Quantity did not assure quality, however, and Texas' public and higher education seldom were ranked among national leaders.

In 1972, voters approved an amendment authorizing the Legislature to sit as a **constitutional convention** to rewrite the 1876 charter. The lawmakers met for several months and spent $5 million, but they failed to propose anything to be considered by voters. The public was outraged, and in 1975, the Legislature presented the work of the convention to voters in the form of eight constitutional amendments. All were defeated in a special election in November 1975.

Texas voters participated in their **first presidential primary in 1976**. Jimmy Carter of Georgia won the Democratic primary, and eventually the presidency. Ronald Reagan carried the state's Republicans, but lost the party's nomination to President Gerald Ford.

The state proved politically volatile in **1978**. First, Attorney General **John Hill** defeated Gov. Dolph Briscoe in the Democratic primary. A political newcomer, Dallas businessman **William P. Clements**, upset Hill in the general election, giving Texas its first Republican governor since Reconstruction. Also for the first time since Reconstruction, state officials were elected to **four-year terms.** ☆

Texas State Historical Association
Annual Meeting
2016

March 3 – 5, 2016 • Omni Mandalay Hotel at Las Colinas • Irving, Texas

Get more information at **TSHAonline.org/annual-meeting**

# Environment

*Enchanted Rock State Natural Area is home to one of the largest batholiths in the United States. The giant pink-granite formation covers 604 acres in the Hill Country. Photo by Mary Danz-Hitzges.*

## Physical Regions
## Geology and Soils
## Aquifers, Rivers, Lakes
## Plant Life, Forests, Grasslands
## Wildlife

# The Physical State of Texas

## The Area of Texas

Texas occupies about 7 percent of the total water and land area of the United States. Second in size among the states, **Texas has a land and water area of 268,596 square miles,** as compared with Alaska's 665,384 square miles, according to the United States Bureau of the Census. California, the third-largest state, has 163,695 square miles. Texas is as large as all of New England, New York, Delaware, Pennsylvania, Ohio, and Virginia combined.

The **state's total area** consists of 261,232 square miles of land and 7,365 square miles of water.

## Length and Breadth

The **longest straight-line distance** in a general north-south direction is 801 miles from the northwest corner of the Panhandle to the extreme southern tip of Texas on the Rio Grande southeast of Brownsville. The greatest east-west distance is 773 miles from the extreme eastward bend in the Sabine River in Newton County to the extreme western bulge of the Rio Grande just northwest of El Paso.

The **geographic center** of Texas is southwest of Mercury in north McCulloch County at approximately 99° 20' West longitude and 31° 08' North latitude.

## Texas' Boundary Lines

The boundary of Texas by segments, including only larger river bends and only the great arc of the coastline, is as follows:

| BOUNDARY | MILES |
|---|---|
| Rio Grande | 889.0 |
| Coastline | 367.0 |
| Sabine River, Lake, and Pass | 180.0 |
| Sabine River to Red River | 106.5 |
| Red River | 480.0 |
| East Panhandle line | 133.6 |
| North Panhandle line | 167.0 |
| West Panhandle line | 310.2 |
| Along 32nd parallel | 209.0 |
| TOTAL | 2,842.3 |

Following the smaller meanderings of the rivers and the tidewater coastline, the following are the boundary measurements:

| BOUNDARY | MILES |
|---|---|
| Rio Grande | 1,254.0 |
| Coastline (tidewater) | 624.0 |
| Sabine River, Lake, and Pass | 292.0 |
| Sabine River to Red River | 106.5 |
| Red River | 726.0 |
| East Panhandle line | 133.6 |
| North Panhandle line | 167.0 |
| West Panhandle line | 310.2 |
| Along 32nd parallel | 209.0 |
| TOTAL | 3,822.3 |

## Latitude and Longitude

The extremes of latitude and longitude in Texas are as follows:

★ From **25° 50' North latitude** at the extreme southern turn of the Rio Grande on the south line of Cameron County to **36° 30' North latitude** along the north line of the Panhandle, and

★ From **93° 31' West longitude** at the extreme eastern point of the Sabine River on the east line of Newton County to **106° 38' West longitude** at the extreme westward point of the Rio Grande on the western edge of El Paso.

## Named Mountain Peaks in Texas
## Above 8,000 Feet

The highest point in the state is **Guadalupe Peak** at **8,749 feet** above sea level. Its twin, **El Capitan,** stands at **8,085** feet and also is located in Culberson County near the New Mexico state line.

Both are in Guadalupe Mountains National Park, which includes the scenic McKittrick Canyon.

The elevations used on this page are from various sources, including the U.S. Geological Survey, the National Park Service, and the Texas Department of Transportation.

The named peaks above 8,000 feet and the counties in which they are located are listed below.

| NAME | COUNTY | ELEVATION |
|---|---|---|
| Guadalupe Peak | Culberson | 8,749 |
| Bush Mountain | Culberson | 8,631 |
| Shumard Peak | Culberson | 8,615 |
| Bartlett Peak | Culberson | 8,508 |
| Mount Livermore (Baldy Peak) | Jeff Davis | 8,378 |
| Hunter Peak (Pine Top Mtn.) | Culberson | 8,368 |
| El Capitan | Culberson | 8,085 |

## Elevation Highs and Lows

**HIGHEST TOWN: Fort Davis** in Jeff Davis County is the **highest town** of any size in Texas at 5,050 feet above sea level, and the county has the **highest average elevation.**

**HIGHEST HIGHWAY:** The **highest state highway point** also is in Jeff Davis County at **McDonald Observatory** on **Mount Locke,** where the road reaches 6,781 feet above sea level, as determined by the Texas Department of Transportation.

**HIGHEST RAILWAY**: The **highest railway point** is Paisano Pass, 14 miles east of Marfa in Presidio County, which is 5,074 above sea level.

**LOWEST POINT:** Sea level is the **lowest elevation** determined in Texas, and it can be found in all the coastal counties. No point in the state has been found by the geological survey to be below sea level. ☆

# Physical Regions

*This section was reviewed by Dr. David R. Butler, Texas State University System Regents' Professor of Geography.*

The principal physical regions of Texas are usually listed as follows (*see also*, the maps for Vegetational Areas and Soils):

## I. GULF COASTAL PLAINS

Texas' Gulf Coastal Plains are the western extension of the coastal plain extending from the Atlantic Ocean to beyond the Rio Grande. Its characteristic rolling to hilly surface covered with a heavy growth of pine and hardwoods extends into East Texas. In the increasingly arid west, however, its forests become secondary in nature, consisting largely of post oaks and, farther west, prairies and brushlands.

The interior limit of the Gulf Coastal Plains in Texas is the line of the **Balcones Fault and Escarpment**. This geologic fault or shearing of underground strata extends eastward from a point on the Rio Grande near Del Rio. It extends to the northwestern part of Bexar County, where it turns northeastward and extends through Comal, Hays, and Travis counties, intersecting the Colorado River immediately north of Austin. The fault line is a single, definite geologic feature, accompanied by a line of southward- and eastward-facing hills.

The resemblance of the hills to balconies when viewed from the plain below accounts for the Spanish name for this area: *balcones.*

North of Waco, features of the fault zone are sufficiently inconspicuous that the interior boundary of the Coastal Plain follows the traditional geologic contact between upper and lower Cretaceous rocks. This contact is along the eastern edge of the **Eastern Cross Timbers**.

This fault line is usually accepted as the boundary between lowland and upland Texas. Below the fault line, the surface is characteristically coastal plains. Above the Balcones Fault, the surface is characteristically interior rolling plains.

### A. Pine Belt or "Piney Woods"

The Pine Belt, called the **"Piney Woods,"** extends 75 to 125 miles into Texas from the east. From north to south, it extends from the Red River to within about 25 miles of the Gulf Coast. Interspersed among the pines are hardwood timbers, usually in valleys of rivers and creeks. This area is the source of practically all of Texas' **commercial timber production** *(see Texas Forest Resources, page 120)*. It was settled early in Texas' history and is one of the oldest farming areas in the state.

This area's soils and climate are adaptable to the production of a variety of fruit and vegetable crops. Cattle raising is widespread, along with the development of

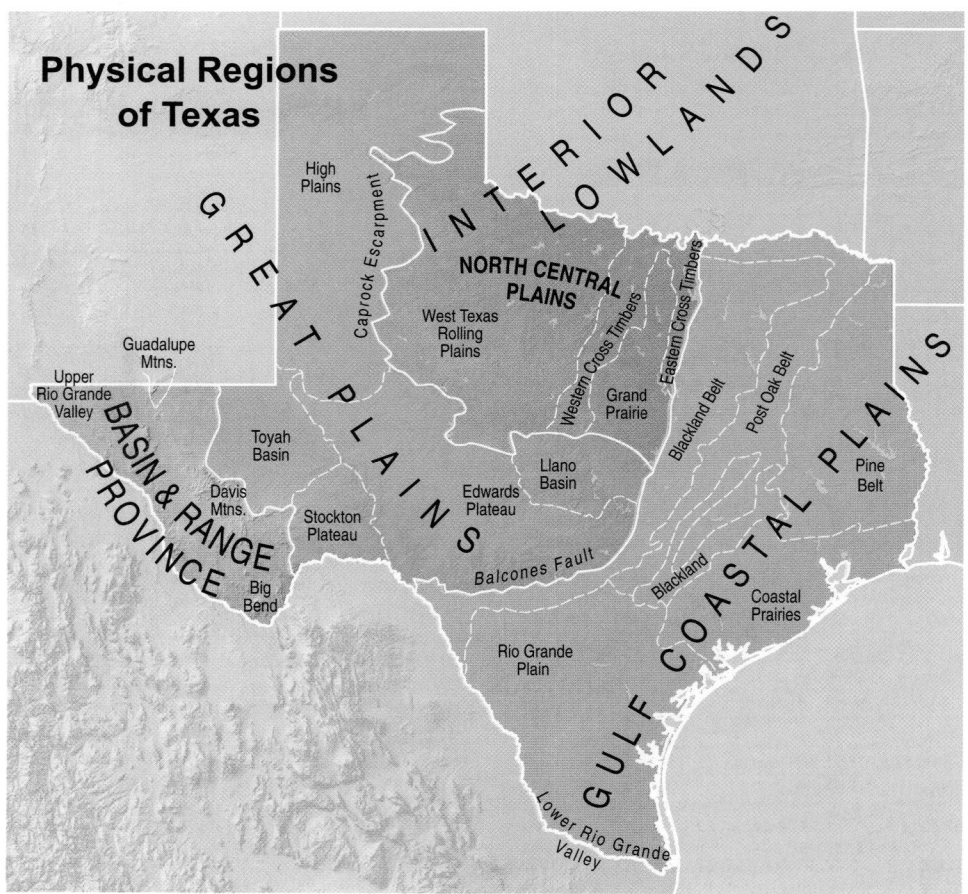

**Physical Regions of Texas**

*The wide open spaces of the Big Bend region of far West Texas lie in the Basin and Range Province. Photo courtesy of VisitBigBend.com.*

pastures planted to improved grasses. Lumber production is the principal industry. There is a large **iron-and-steel industry** near Daingerfield in Morris County based on nearby iron deposits. Iron deposits are also worked in Rusk and one or two other counties.

A **great oil field** discovered in Gregg, Rusk, and Smith counties in 1931 has done more than anything else to contribute to the economic growth of the area. This area has a variety of clays, lignite, and other minerals as potentials for development.

### B. Post Oak Belt

The main Post Oak Belt of Texas is wedged between the Pine Belt on the east, Blacklands on the west, and the Coastal Prairies on the south, covering a considerable area in East-Central Texas. The principal industry is diversified farming and livestock raising.

Throughout, it is spotty in character, with some insular areas of blackland soil and some that closely resemble those of the Pine Belt. There is a small, isolated area of loblolly pines in Bastrop, Caldwell, Fayette, and Lee counties known as the **"Lost Pines,"** the westernmost southern pines in the United States. The Post Oak Belt has lignite, commercial clays, and some other minerals.

### C. Blackland Belt

The Blackland Belt stretches from the Rio Grande to the Red River, lying just below the line of the **Balcones Fault** and varying in width from 15 to 70 miles. It is narrowest below the segment of the Balcones Fault from the Rio Grande to Bexar County and gradually widens as it runs northeast to the Red River. Its rolling prairie, easily turned by the plow, developed rapidly as a farming area until the 1930s and was the principal cotton-producing area of Texas. Now, however, other Texas areas that are irrigated and mechanized lead in farming.

Because of the early growth, the Blackland Belt is still the **most thickly populated area in the state** and contains within it and along its border more of the state's large and middle-sized cities than any other area. Primarily because of this concentration of population, this belt has the most diversified manufacturing industry of the state.

### D. Coastal Prairies

The Texas Coastal Prairies extend westward along the coast from the Sabine River, reaching inland 30 to 60 miles. Between the Sabine and Galveston Bay, the line of demarcation between the prairies and the Pine Belt forests to the north is very distinct. The Coastal Prairies extend along the Gulf of Mexico from the Sabine to the Lower Rio Grande Valley.

The eastern half is covered with a heavy growth of grass; the western half, which is more arid, is covered with short grass and, in some places, with small timber and brush. The soil is heavy clay. Grass supports the **densest cattle population in Texas,** and cattle ranching is the principal agricultural industry. Rice is a major crop, grown under irrigation from wells and rivers. Cotton, grain sorghum, and truck crops also are grown.

Coastal Prairie areas have seen the greatest industrial development in Texas history since World War II. Chief concentration has been from Orange and Beaumont to Houston, and much of the development has been in **petrochemicals and the aerospace industry**. Corpus Christi, in the Coastal Bend, and Brownsville, in the Lower Rio Grande Valley, have seaports and agricultural and industrial sections. **Cotton, grain, vegetables, and citrus fruits** are the principal crops. Cattle production is significant, with the famed King Ranch and other large ranches located here.

### E. Lower Rio Grande Valley

The deep alluvial soils and distinctive economy cause the Lower Rio Grande Valley to be classified as a subregion of the Gulf Coastal Plains. **"The Valley,"** as it is called locally, is Texas' greatest citrus and winter vegetable growing region because of the normal absence of freezing weather and the rich delta soils of the Rio Grande. Despite occasional damaging freezes, the Lower Valley ranks high among the nation's fruit and truck-farming regions. Much of the acreage is irrigated, although dry-land farming also is practiced.

### F. Rio Grande Plain

This area may be roughly defined as lying south of San Antonio between the Rio Grande and the Gulf Coast. The Rio Grande Plain shows characteristics of both the Gulf Coastal Plains and the North Mexico Plains because there is similarity of topography, climate, and plant life all the way from the Balcones Escarpment in Texas to the Sierra Madre Oriental in Mexico, which runs past Monterrey about 160 miles south of Laredo.

The Rio Grande Plain is partly prairie, but much of it is covered with a dense growth of **prickly pear, mesquite, dwarf oak, catclaw, guajillo, huisache, blackbrush, cenizo,** and other cactus and wild shrubs. It is devoted primarily to raising cattle, sheep, and goats. The **Texas Angora goat and mohair industry** centers in this area and on the Edwards Plateau, which borders it on the north. San Antonio and Laredo are its chief commercial centers, with San Antonio dominating trade.

There is some farming, and the **Winter Garden,** centering in Dimmit and Zavala counties north of Laredo, is irrigated from wells and streams to produce vegetables in late winter and early spring. Primarily, however, the central and western part of the Rio Grande Plain is devoted to **livestock raising.**

The rainfall is less than 25 inches annually, and the hot summers cause heavy evaporation, so that cultivation without irrigation is limited.

Over a large area in the central and western parts of the Rio Grande Plain, the growth of **small oaks, mesquite, prickly pear (Opuntia) cactus,** and a variety of wild shrubs is very dense, and it is often called the **Brush Country.** It is also referred to as the **chaparral** and the **monte.** (*Monte* is a Spanish word, one meaning of which is dense brush.)

## II. INTERIOR LOWLANDS

### North Central Plains

The North Central Plains of Texas are a southwestern extension into Texas of the **interior, or central, lowlands** that extend northward to the Canadian border, paralleling the Great Plains to the West. The North Central Plains of Texas extend from the **Blackland Belt** on the east to the **Caprock Escarpment** on the west. From north to south, they extend from the Red River to the Colorado River.

### A. West Texas Rolling Plains

The West Texas Rolling Plains, approximately the western two-thirds of the North Central Plains in Texas, rise from east to west in altitude from about 750 feet to 2,000 feet at the base of the **Caprock Escarpment.** Annual rainfall ranges from about 30 inches on the east to 20 inches on the west. In general, as one progresses westward in Texas, the precipitation not only declines but also becomes more variable from year to year. Temperature varies rather widely between summer's heat and winter's cold.

This area still has a **large cattle-raising industry** with many of the state's largest ranches. However, there is much level, cultivable land.

### B. Grand Prairie

Near the eastern edge of the North Central Plains is the **Grand Prairie,** extending south from the Red River in an irregular band through Cooke, Montague, Wise, Denton, Tarrant, Parker, Hood, Johnson, Bosque, Coryell, and some adjacent counties.

It is a limestone-based area, usually treeless except along the numerous streams, and adapted primarily to raising livestock and growing staple crops. Sometimes called the **Fort Worth Prairie,** it has an agricultural economy and largely rural population, with no large cities, except Fort Worth on its eastern boundary.

### C. Eastern and Western Cross Timbers

Hanging over the top of the Grand Prairie and dropping down on each side are the Eastern and Western Cross Timbers. The two southward-extending bands are connected by a narrow strip along the Red River.

The **Eastern Cross Timbers** extend southward from the Red River through eastern Denton County and along the boundary between Dallas and Tarrant counties. It then stretches through Johnson County to the Brazos River and into Hill County.

The much larger **Western Cross Timbers** extend from the Red River south through Clay, Montague, Jack, Wise, Parker, Palo Pinto, Hood, Erath, Eastland, Comanche, Brown, and Mills counties to the Colorado River, where they meet the **Llano Basin.**

Their soils are adapted to fruit and vegetable crops, which reach considerable commercial production in some areas in Parker, Erath, Eastland, and Comanche counties.

## III. GREAT PLAINS

### A. High Plains

The Great Plains, which lie to the east of the base of the Rocky Mountains, extend into northwestern Texas. This area, commonly known as the **High Plains,** is a vast, flat, high plain covered with thick layers of alluvial material. It is also known as the **Staked Plains** or the Spanish equivalent, *Llano Estacado.*

Historians differ as to the origin of this name. Some say it came from the fact that the explorer Coronado's expedition used stakes to mark its route across the trackless sea of grass so that it would be guided on its return trip. Others think that the *estacado* refers to the **palisaded appearance** of the Caprock in many places, especially the west-facing escarpment in New Mexico.

The **Caprock Escarpment** is the dividing line between the High Plains and the lower West Texas Rolling Plains. Like the Balcones Escarpment, the Caprock Escarpment is a striking physical feature, rising abruptly 200, 500, and in some places almost 1,000 feet above the plains. Unlike the **Balcones Escarpment,** the Caprock was caused by surface erosion.

Where rivers issue from the eastern face of the Caprock, there frequently are notable canyons, such as **Palo Duro Canyon** on the **Prairie Dog Town Fork of the Red River, Blanco Canyon on the White River,** as well as the breaks along the Canadian River as it crosses the Panhandle north of Amarillo.

Along the eastern edge of the Panhandle, there is a gradual descent of the land's surface from high to low plains; but at the Red River, the Caprock Escarpment becomes a striking surface feature. It continues as an east-facing wall south through Briscoe, Floyd, Motley, Dickens, Crosby, Garza, and Borden counties, gradually decreasing in elevation. South of Borden County, the escarpment is less obvious, and the boundary between the High Plains and the **Edwards Plateau** occurs where the alluvial cover of the High Plains disappears.

Stretching over the largest level plain of its kind in the United States, the High Plains rise gradually from about 2,700 feet on the east to more than 4,000 in spots along the New Mexico border.

Chiefly because of climate and the resultant agriculture, subdivisions are called the North Plains and South Plains. The **North Plains,** from Hale County north, has primarily **wheat and grain sorghum farming,** but with significant ranching and petroleum developments. Ama-

*Wildflowers blanket the landscape off Texas 41 in northwest Kerr County, the southern reach of the vast Great Plains. Photo by Ron Billings; Texas A&M Forest Service.*

rillo is the largest city, with Plainview on the south and Borger on the north as important commercial centers.

The **South Plains,** also a leading grain sorghum region, **leads Texas in cotton production.** Lubbock is the principal city, and Lubbock County is one of the state's largest cotton producers. Irrigation from underground reservoirs, centered around Lubbock and Plainview, waters much of the crop acreage.

## B. Edwards Plateau

Geographers usually consider that the Great Plains at the foot of the Rocky Mountains actually continue southward from the High Plains of Texas to the Rio Grande and the Balcones Escarpment. This southern and lower extension of the Great Plains in Texas is known as the **Edwards Plateau.**

It lies between the Rio Grande and the Colorado River. Its southeastern border is the Balcones Escarpment from the Rio Grande at Del Rio eastward to San Antonio and thence to Austin on the Colorado River. Its upper boundary is the Pecos River, though the **Stockton Plateau** is geologically and topographically classed with the Edwards Plateau.

The Edwards Plateau varies from about 750 feet high at its southern and eastern borders to about 2,700 feet in places. Almost the entire surface is a thin, limestone-based soil covered with a medium to thick growth of **cedar, small oak,** and **mesquite** and a varying growth of **prickly pear.** Grass for cattle, weeds for sheep, and tree foliage for the browsing goats support three industries — **cattle, goat,** and **sheep raising** — upon which the area's economy depends. It is the **nation's leading Angora goat and mohair producing region** and one of the nation's leading sheep and wool areas. A few crops are grown.

## Hill Country

The Hill Country is a popular name for the **eastern portion of the Edwards Plateau** south of the Llano Basin. Its notable large springs include **Barton Springs** at Austin, **San Marcos Springs** at San Marcos, **Comal Springs** at New Braunfels, several springs at San Antonio, and a number of others.

The Hill Country is characterized by rugged hills with relatively steep slopes and thin soils overlying limestone bedrock. High gradient streams combine with these steep hillslopes and occasionally heavy precipitation to produce an area with a significant flash-flood hazard.

## C. Toyah Basin

To the northwest of the Edwards and Stockton plateaus is the Toyah Basin, a broad, flat remnant of **an old sea floor** that occupied the region as recently as Quaternary time.

Located in the **Pecos River Valley,** this region, in relatively recent time, has become important for many agricultural products as a result of irrigation. Additional economic activity is afforded by **local oil fields.**

## D. Llano Basin

The Llano Basin lies at the junction of the Colorado and Llano rivers in Burnet and Llano counties. Earlier, this was known as the **"Central Mineral Region"** because of evidence there of a large number of minerals.

On the Colorado River in this area, a succession of dams impounds two large and five small reservoirs. Uppermost is **Lake Buchanan,** one of the large reservoirs, between Burnet and Llano counties. Below it in the western part of Travis County is **Lake Travis.**

Between these two large reservoirs are three smaller ones, **Inks, L.B. Johnson** (formerly Granite Shoals), and **Marble Falls** reservoirs, used primarily to produce electric power from the overflow from Lake Buchanan. **Lake Austin** is along the western part of the city of Austin. Still another small lake, **Lady Bird Lake** (formerly Town Lake), is formed by a low-water dam in Austin.

The recreational area around these lakes has been called the **Highland Lakes Country**. This is an interesting area with Precambrian and Paleozoic rocks found on the surface. Granitic domes, exemplified by **Enchanted Rock** north of Fredericksburg, form the core of this area of ancient rocks.

## IV. BASIN and RANGE PROVINCE

The Basin and Range province, with its center in Nevada, surrounds the Colorado Plateau on the west and south and enters far West Texas from southern New Mexico on the east. It consists of broad interior **drainage basins** interspersed with scattered **fault-block mountain ranges.**

Although this is the only part of Texas regarded as mountainous, these should not be confused with the Rocky Mountains. Of all the independent ranges in West Texas, only the Davis Mountains resemble the Rockies, and there is much debate about this.

Texas west of the Edwards Plateau, bounded on the north by New Mexico and on the south by the Rio Grande, is distinctive in its physical and economic conditions. Traversed from north to south by fault-block mountains, it contains all of Texas' true mountains and also is very interesting geologically.

### A. Guadalupe Mountains

Highest of the Trans-Pecos Mountains is the **Guadalupe Range,** which enters Texas from New Mexico. It abruptly ends about 20 miles south of the boundary line, where **Guadalupe Peak,** (8,749 feet, highest in Texas) and **El Capitan** (8,085 feet) are situated. El Capitan, because of perspective, appears to the observer on the plain below to be higher than Guadalupe.

Lying just west of the Guadalupe Range and extending to the **Hueco Mountains** a short distance east of El Paso is the **Diablo Plateau** or basin. It has no drainage outlet to the sea. The runoff from the scant rain that falls on its surface drains into a series of salt lakes that lie just west of the Guadalupe Mountains. These lakes are dry during periods of low rainfall, exposing bottoms of solid salt; for years they were a source of **commercial salt.** West of the Hueco Mountains are the **Franklin Mountains** in El Paso, with the Hueco Bolson (a down-dropped area approximately 4,000 feet above sea level) separating the two fault-block ranges.

### B. Davis Mountains

The Davis Mountains are principally in Jeff Davis County. The highest peak, **Mount Livermore** (8,378 feet), is **one of the highest in Texas**; there are several others more than 7,000 feet high. These mountains intercept the moisture-bearing winds and receive more precipitation than elsewhere in the Trans-Pecos, so they have **more vegetation** than the other Trans-Pecos mountains. Noteworthy are the **San Solomon Springs** at the northern base of these mountains.

### C. Big Bend

South of the Davis Mountains lies the Big Bend country, so called because it is encompassed on three sides by a great southward swing of the Rio Grande. It is a mountainous country of scant rainfall and sparse population. Its principal mountains, the **Chisos,** rise to 7,825 feet in **Mount Emory.**

Along the Rio Grande are the **Santa Elena, Mariscal,** and **Boquillas canyons** with rim elevations of 3,500 to 3,775 feet. They are among the noteworthy canyons of the North American continent.

Because of its remarkable topography and plant and animal life, the southern part of this region along the Rio Grande is home to **Big Bend National Park,** with headquarters in the Chisos Basin, a deep valley in the Chisos Mountains. It is a favorite recreation area.

### D. Upper Rio Grande Valley

The Upper Rio Grande Valley, or El Paso Valley, is a narrow strip of irrigated land running down the river from El Paso for a distance of 75 miles or more.

In this area are the historic towns and missions of **Ysleta, Socorro,** and **San Elizario,** some of the oldest in Texas. Cotton is the chief product of this valley, much of it the long-staple variety. This limited area has a dense urban and rural population, in marked contrast to the territory surrounding it. ☆

*Nacogdoches County is part of the Gulf Coastal Plains and contains many wetlands. Photo by Ron Billings; Texas A&M Forest Service.*

*Caprock Canyons State Park lies along the Caprock Escarpment, a natural transition between the Llano Estacado to the west and the lower Rolling Plains to the east. Streams flowing east from the Llano Estacado onto the lower plains have exposed geologic layers commonly called "red beds" because of the red coloration of the shales, sandstones, siltstones, and mudstones. Photo by Earl Nottingham; Texas Parks and Wildlife Department.*

# Geology of Texas

*Source: Bureau of Economic Geology, The University of Texas at Austin; www.beg.utexas.edu/*

## History in the Rocks

Mountains, seas, coastal plains, rocky plateaus, high plains, forests — all of this **physiographic variety** in Texas is controlled by the varied rocks and structures that underlie and crop out across the state. The fascinating geologic history of Texas is recorded in the rocks — both those exposed at the surface and those penetrated by holes drilled in search of oil and natural gas.

The rocks reveal a dynamic, ever-changing earth — ancient mountains, seas, volcanoes, earthquake belts, rivers, hurricanes, and winds. Today, the volcanoes and great earthquake belts are no longer active, but rivers and streams, wind and rain, and the slow, inexorable alterations of rocks at or near the surface continue to change the face of Texas.

The geologic history of Texas, as documented by the rocks, began more than a billion years ago. Its legacy is the mineral wealth and varied land forms of modern Texas.

## Geologic Time Travel

The story preserved in rocks requires an understanding of the origin of strata and how they have been deformed. **Stratigraphy** is the study of the composition, sequence, and origin of rocks: what rocks are made of, how they were formed, and the order in which the layers were formed.

**Structural geology** reveals the architecture of rocks: the locations of the mountains, volcanoes, sedimentary basins, and earthquake belts.

The **map on the following page** shows where rocks of various geologic ages are visible **on the surface** of Texas today. History concerns events through time, but geologic time is such a grandiose concept, most find it difficult to comprehend. So geologists have named the various chapters of earth history.

## Precambrian Eon

Precambrian rocks, more than 600 million years old, are exposed at the surface in the **Llano Uplift of Central Texas** and in scattered outcrops in West Texas, around and north of **Van Horn** and **near El Paso.**

These rocks, some more than a billion years old, include complexly deformed rocks that were originally formed by cooling from a liquid state, as well as rocks that were altered from pre-existing rocks.

Precambrian rocks, often called the **"basement complex,"** are thought to form the foundation of continental masses. They underlie all of Texas. The outcrop in Central Texas is only the exposed part of the **Texas Craton,** which is primarily buried by younger rocks. (A craton is a stable, almost immovable portion of the earth's crust that forms the nuclear mass of a continent.)

## Paleozoic Era

During the early part of the Paleozoic Era (approximately 600 million to 350 million years ago), broad, relatively **shallow seas** repeatedly inundated the Texas Craton and much of North and West Texas. The evidence for these events is found exposed around the Llano Uplift and in far West Texas near Van Horn and El Paso, and also in the subsurface throughout most of West and North Texas. The evidence includes early Paleozoic rocks — **sandstones, shales, and limestones,** similar to sediments that form in seas today — and the fossils of animals, similar to modern crustaceans — the **brachiopods, clams, snails, and related organisms** that live in modern marine environments.

By late Paleozoic (approximately 350 million to 240 million years ago), the Texas Craton was bordered on the east and south by a long, deep marine basin called the **Ouachita Trough.** Sediments slowly accumulated in this trough until late in the Paleozoic Era. Plate-tectonic theory postulates that the collision of the North American Plate (upon which the Texas Craton is located) with the European and African–South American plates uplifted the thick sediments that had accumulated in the trough to form the **Ouachita Mountains.**

At that time, the Ouachitas extended across Texas. Today, the Texas portion of the old mountain range is mostly buried by younger rocks. Ancient remnants can be seen in the **Marathon Basin of West Texas** due to uplift and erosion of younger sediments. The public can see the remains of this once-majestic Ouachita Mountain range at Post Park, just south of Marathon in Brewster County. Other remnants at the surface are exposed in southeastern Oklahoma and southwestern Arkansas.

During the **Pennsylvanian Period**, however, the Ouachita Mountains bordered the eastern margin of shallow inland seas that covered most of West Texas. Rivers flowed westward from the mountains to the seas bringing sediment to form deltas along an ever-changing coastline.

The sediments were then reworked by the waves and currents of the inland sea. Today, these fluvial, delta, and shallow **marine deposits** compose the late Paleozoic rocks that crop out and underlie the surface of North-Central Texas.

Broad marine shelves divided the West Texas seas into several sub-basins, or deeper areas, that received more sediments than accumulated on the limestone shelves. **Limestone reefs** rimmed the deeper basins. Today, these reef limestones are important oil reservoirs in West Texas.

These seas gradually withdrew from Texas, and by the late **Permian Period**, all that was left in West Texas were shallow basins and wide tidal flats in which salt, gypsum, and red muds accumulated in a hot, arid land. Strata deposited during the Permian Period are exposed today along the edge of the Panhandle, as far east as Wichita Falls and south to Concho County, and in the Trans-Pecos.

### Mesozoic Era

Approximately 240 million years ago, the major geologic events in Texas shifted from West Texas to East and Southeast Texas. The European and African–South American plates, which had collided with the North American plate to form the Ouachita Mountains, began to separate from North America.

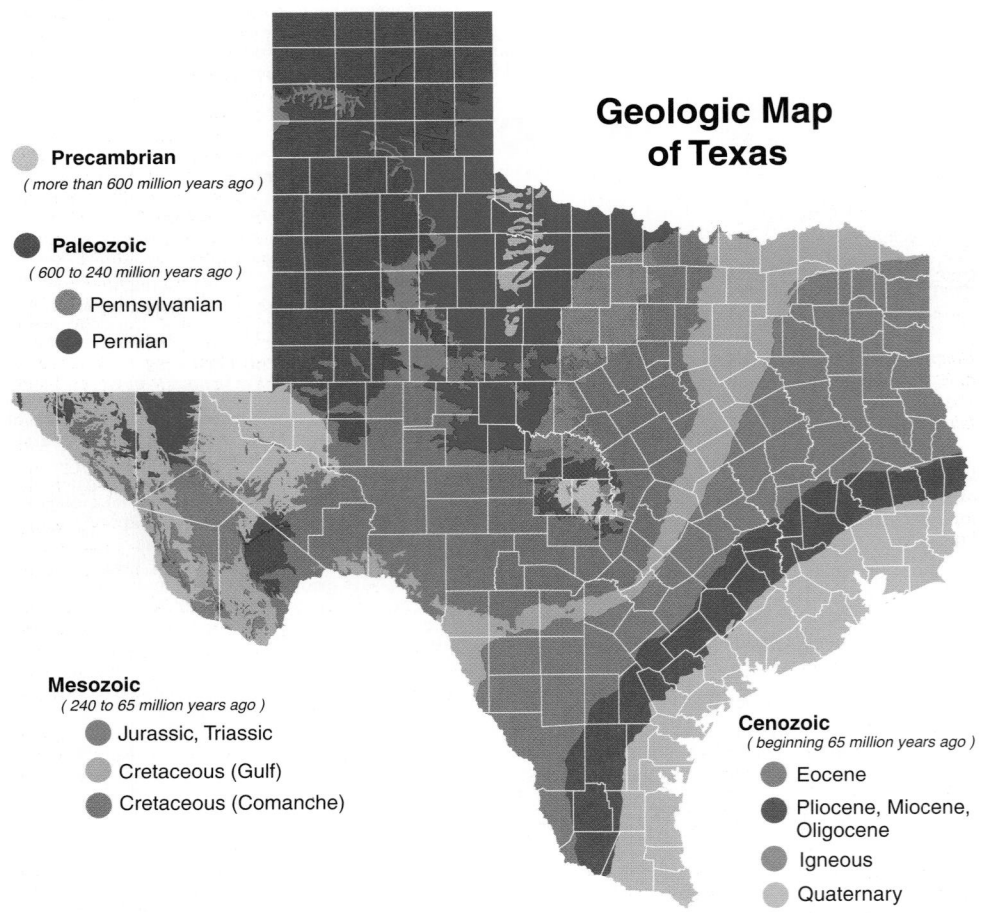

**Geologic Map of Texas**

Precambrian
( more than 600 million years ago )

Paleozoic
( 600 to 240 million years ago )

Pennsylvanian

Permian

Mesozoic
( 240 to 65 million years ago )

Jurassic, Triassic

Cretaceous (Gulf)

Cretaceous (Comanche)

Cenozoic
( beginning 65 million years ago )

Eocene

Pliocene, Miocene, Oligocene

Igneous

Quaternary

*Unique geology abounds in Hueco Tanks State Park and Historic Site northeast of El Paso. The park, which lies in the southeast portion of the Basin and Range Province, contains broad flat basins separating isolated and nearly parallel mountain ranges. Texas Parks and Wildlife Department photo.*

By the early **Cretaceous** (approximately 140 million years ago), the shallow Mesozoic seas covered a large part of Texas, eventually extending west to the Trans-Pecos area and north almost to present-day state boundaries. Today, the limestone deposited in those seas is exposed in the walls of the magnificent canyons of the Rio Grande in the **Big Bend National Park area** and in the canyons and headwaters of streams that drain the Edwards Plateau, as well as in Central Texas from San Antonio to Dallas.

Animals of many types lived in the shallow Mesozoic seas, tidal pools, and coastal swamps. Today, these lower Cretaceous rocks are some of the most fossiliferous in the state. **Tracks of dinosaurs** occur in several places, and remains of **terrestrial, aquatic, and flying reptiles** have been collected from Cretaceous rocks in many areas.

During most of the late Cretaceous, much of Texas lay beneath marine waters that were deeper than those of the early Cretaceous seas, except where rivers, deltas, and shallow marine shelves existed.

River delta and strandline sandstones are the reservoir rocks for the most prolific oil field in Texas. When discovered in 1930, this **East Texas oil field** contained recoverable reserves estimated at 5.6 billion barrels.

The chalky rock that we now call the **"Austin Chalk"** was deposited when the Texas seas became deeper. Today, the chalk (and other Upper Cretaceous rocks) crops out in a wide band that extends from near Eagle Pass on the Rio Grande, east to San Antonio, north to Dallas, and east to the Texarkana area. The Austin Chalk and other upper Cretaceous rocks dip southeastward beneath the East Texas and Gulf Coast basins.

A series of faulted basins, or rifts, extending from Mexico to Nova Scotia were formed. These **rifted basins** received sediments from adjacent uplifts. As Europe and the southern continents continued to drift away from North America, the Texas basins were eventually buried beneath **thick deposits of marine salt** within the newly formed East Texas and Gulf Coast basins.

**Jurassic and Cretaceous rocks** in East and Southeast Texas document a sequence of broad limestone shelves at the edge of the developing Gulf of Mexico. From time to time, the shelves were buried beneath **deltaic sandstones and shales,** which built the northwestern margin of the widening Gulf of Mexico to the south and southeast.

As the underlying salt was buried more deeply by dense sediments, the salt became unstable and moved toward areas of least pressure. As the salt moved, it arched or pierced overlying sediments forming, in some cases, columns known as **"salt domes."** In some cases, these salt domes moved to the surface; others remain beneath a sedimentary overburden. This mobile salt formed numerous structures that would later serve to trap oil and natural gas.

The late Cretaceous was the time of the **last major seaway across Texas,** because mountains were forming in the western United States that influenced areas as far away as Texas.

A **chain of volcanoes** formed beneath the late Cretaceous seas in an area roughly parallel to and south and east of the old, buried Ouachita Mountains. The eruptions of these volcanoes were primarily on the sea floor and great clouds of steam and ash likely accompanied them.

Between eruptions, invertebrate marine animals built reefs on the shallow volcanic cones. **Pilot Knob,** located southeast of Austin, is one of these **old volcanoes** that is now exposed at the surface.

## Cenozoic Era

At the dawn of the Cenozoic Era, approximately 65 million years ago, deltas fed by rivers were in the northern and northwestern margins of the East Texas Basin.

*Kickapoo Cavern State Park has 20 known caves, the largest being Kickapoo Cavern and Stuart Bat Cave. They serve as a migratory stopover for large numbers of Mexican free-tailed bats from mid-March to the end of October. Bat flights are often spectacular, and public observations are available with an entrance permit. Texas Parks and Wildlife Department photo.*

These streams flowed eastward, draining areas to the north and west. Although there were minor incursions of the seas, the Cenozoic rocks principally document extensive seaward building by broad deltas, marshy lagoons, sandy barrier islands, and embayments.

Thick vegetation covered the levees and areas between the streams. **Coastal plains** were taking shape under the same processes still at work today.

The Mesozoic marine salt became buried by thick sediments in the coastal plain area. The salt began to form ridges and domes in the Houston and Rio Grande areas. The heavy load of sand, silt, and mud deposited by the deltas eventually caused some areas of the coast to subside and form l**arge fault systems,** essentially parallel to the coast.

Many of these coastal faults moved slowly and probably generated little earthquake activity. However, **movement along the Balcones and Luling-Mexia-Talco zones,** a complex system of faults along the western and northern edge of the basins, likely generated large earthquakes millions of years ago.

Predecessors of modern animals roamed the Texas Cenozoic coastal plains and woodlands. Bones and teeth of **horses, camels, sloths, giant armadillos, mammoths, mastodons, bats, rats, large cats,** and other modern or extinct mammals have been excavated from coastal plain deposits.

Vegetation in the area included varieties of plants and trees both similar and dissimilar to modern ones. **Fossil palmwood,** the **Texas "state stone,"** is found in sediments of early Cenozoic age.

The Cenozoic Era in Trans-Pecos Texas was entirely different. There, **extensive volcanic eruptions** formed great calderas and produced copious lava flows. These eruptions ejected great clouds of volcanic ash and rock particles into the air — many times the amount of material ejected by the 1980 eruption of Mount St. Helens.

Ash from the eruptions drifted eastward and is found in many of the sand-and-siltstones of the Gulf Coastal Plains. **Lava** flowed over older Paleozoic and Mesozoic rocks, and igneous intrusions melted their way upward into crustal rocks. These volcanic and intrusive igneous rocks are well exposed in arid areas of the Trans-Pecos today.

In the Texas Panhandle, streams originating in the recently elevated southern Rocky Mountains brought floods of gravel and sand into Texas. As the braided streams crisscrossed the area, they formed **great alluvial fans.**

These fans, which were deposited on the older Paleozoic and Mesozoic rocks, occur from northwestern Texas into Nebraska. Between 1 million and 2 million years ago, the streams of the Panhandle were isolated from their Rocky Mountain source, and the eastern edge of this sheet of alluvial material began to retreat westward, forming the **Caprock of the modern High Plains.**

Late in the Cenozoic Era, **a great Ice Age** descended on the northern North American continent. For more than 2 million years, there were successive advances and retreats of the thick sheets of glacial ice. Four periods of extensive glaciation were separated by warmer interglacial periods. Although the glaciers never reached as far south as Texas, the state's climate and sea level underwent major changes with each period of glacial advance and retreat.

Sea level during times of glacial advance was 300 to 450 feet lower than during the warmer interglacial periods because so much sea water was captured in the ice sheets. The climate was both more humid and cooler than today, and the major Texas rivers carried more water and more sand and gravel to the sea. These deposits underlie the outer 50 miles or more of the Gulf Coastal Plain.

Approximately 3,000 years ago, sea level reached its modern position. The rivers, deltas, lagoons, beaches, and barrier islands that we know as coastal Texas today have formed since that time. ☆

*Oil and natural gas, as well as nonfuel minerals, are important to the Texas economy. For a more detailed discussion, see pages 634–643 and 644–651.*

# Soils of Texas

*Source: Natural Resources Conservation Service, U.S. Department of Agriculture, Temple, Texas; www.tx.nrcs.usda.gov/*

One of Texas' most important natural resources is its soil. Texas soils are complex because of the wide diversity of climate, vegetation, geology, and landscape. **More than 1,300 different kinds of soil** are recognized in Texas. Each has a specific set of properties that affect its use.

Soil maps and information about soils and their uses are available for all of the state's 254 counties. Texas' official soil information site is the **Web Soil Survey**: http://websoilsurvey.nrcs.usda.gov.

For more information, contact the **Natural Resources Conservation Service** at 101 S. Main, Temple 76501-7602; (254) 742-9800; or visit **www.tx.nrcs. usda.gov;** click on "Information About: Soils."

## Web Soil Survey — An Electronic Tool

For decades, soil scientists with the U.S. Department of Agriculture Natural Resources Conservation Service have been studying Texas soils and **mapping its properties, qualities, and characteristics.** Soils information that was once available only through paper maps or books is now easily accessed online through the **Web Soil Survey,** which also offers a soil survey application that can be downloaded.

As the state's population continues to move from rural to urban areas, the Web Soil Survey is a tool landowners can use to make land-use and management decisions. This free tool allows landowners to analyze soil data and maps. It is used by farmers and ranchers to find information about soil properties and qualities to optimize agricultural production, and by homeowners and commercial builders looking for information on the suitability or the limitations of a building site.

The Web Soil Survey includes downloadable soils data, archived soil surveys, and soil survey status information. In four steps, landowners can define an area of interest, view and print a soil map, explore soil information, and use a free shopping cart to collect a variety of thematic maps and reports for a printable **Custom Soil Resource report.** The site includes a glossary of words and definitions.

## Major Soil Areas

Texas can be divided into 21 **Major Land Resource Areas** that have similar or related soils, vegetation, topography, climate, and land uses. Following are brief descriptions of these areas:

### Trans-Pecos Soils

The 18.7 million acres of the Trans-Pecos, mostly west of the Pecos River, are diverse plains and valleys intermixed with mountains. Surface drainage is slow to rapid. This arid region is used mainly as **rangeland.** A small amount of irrigated cropland lies on the more fertile soils along the Rio Grande and the Pecos River. **Vineyards** are a more recent use of these soils, as is the disposal of large volumes of municipal wastes.

**Upland soils** are mostly well-drained, light reddish-brown to brown clay loams, clays, and sands (some have a large amount of gypsum or other salts). Many areas have shallow soils and rock outcrops, and sizable areas have deep sands.

**Bottomland soils** are deep, well-drained, dark grayish-brown to reddish-brown silt loams, loams, clay loams, and clays. The lack of soil moisture and wind erosion are the major soil-management problems. Only irrigated crops can be grown on these soils, and most areas lack an adequate source of good water.

*Soap weed grows on rangeland in Gray County in the Panhandle. Photo courtesy of USDA/Natural Resources Conservation Service photo.*

## Upper Pecos, Canadian Valleys, and Plains Soils

The Upper Pecos, Canadian Valleys, and Plains area occupies a little over a half-million acres and is in the northwest part of Texas near the Texas–New Mexico border. It is characterized by broad rolling plains and tablelands broken by drainageways and tributaries of the Canadian River. It includes the **Canadian Breaks**, which are rough, steep lands below the adjacent High Plains. The average annual precipitation is about 15 inches, but it fluctuates widely from year to year. Surface drainage is slow to rapid.

The soils are well drained and alkaline. The mostly reddish-brown clay loams and sandy loams were formed mostly in material weathered from sandstone and shale. Depths range from shallow to very deep.

The area is used mainly as **rangeland** and **wildlife habitat.** Native vegetation is mid- to short-grass prairie species, such as hairy grama, sideoats grama, little bluestem, alkali sacaton, vine-mesquite, and galleta in the plains and tablelands. Juniper and mesquite grow on the relatively higher breaks. Soil management problems include low soil moisture and brush control.

## High Plains Soils

The High Plains area comprises a vast high plateau of more than 19.4 million acres in northwestern Texas. It lies in the southern part of the Great Plains province that includes large, similar areas in Oklahoma and New Mexico. The flat, nearly level treeless plain has few streams to cause local relief. However, several major rivers originate in the High Plains or cross the area. The largest is the **Canadian River,** which has cut a deep valley across the Panhandle section.

**Playas,** small intermittent lakes scattered through the area, lie up to 20 feet below the surrounding plains. A 1965 survey counted more than 19,000 playas in 44 counties occupying some 340,000 acres. Most runoff from rainfall is collected in the playas, but only 10 to 40 percent of this water percolates back to the **Ogallala Aquifer.** The aquifer is virtually the exclusive water source in this area.

**Upland soils** are mostly well-drained, deep, neutral to alkaline clay loams and sandy loams in shades of brown or red. Sandy soils are in the southern part. Many soils have large amounts of lime at various depths and some are shallow over **caliche.** Soils of bottomlands are minor in extent.

The area is used mostly for **cropland,** but significant areas of rangeland are in the southwestern and extreme northern parts. **Millions of cattle** populate the many large feedlots in the area. The soils are moderately productive, and the flat surface encourages irrigation and mechanization. Limited soil moisture, constant danger of wind erosion, and irrigation water management are the major soil-management problems, but the region is Texas' leading producer of three important crops: **cotton, grain sorghums,** and **wheat.**

## Rolling Plains Soils

The Rolling Plains include 21.7 million acres east of the High Plains in northwestern Texas. The area lies west of the North Central Prairies and extends from the edge of the Edwards Plateau in Tom Green County northward into Oklahoma. The landscape is nearly level to strongly rolling, and surface drainage is moderate to rapid. Outcrops of red beds, geologic materials, and associated reddish soils have led some scientists to use the name **"Red Plains."** Limestone underlies the soils in the southeastern part. The eastern part contains large areas of badlands.

**Upland soils** are mostly deep, pale-brown through reddish-brown to dark grayish-brown, neutral to alkaline sandy loams, clay loams, and clays; some are deep sands.

Many soils have a large amount of lime in the lower part, and a few others are saline; some are shallow and stony. **Bottomland soils** are mostly reddish-brown and sandy to clayey; some are saline.

This area is used mostly for **rangeland,** but **cotton, grain sorghums,** and **wheat** are important crops. The major soil-management problems are brush control, wind erosion, low fertility, and lack of soil mosture. Salt spots are a concern in some areas.

## North Central Prairie Soils

The North Central Prairie occupies about 7 million acres in North Central Texas. Adjacent to this area on the north is the rather small area (less than 1 million acres) called **Rolling Red Prairies,** which extends into Oklahoma and is included here because the soils and land use are similar. This area lies between the Western Cross Timbers and the Rolling Plains. It is predominantly **grassland intermixed with small wooded areas.** The landscape is undulating with slow to rapid surface drainage.

**Upland soils** are mostly deep, well-drained, brown or reddish-brown, slightly acid loams over neutral to alkaline, clayey subsoils. Some soils are shallow or moderately deep to shale. **Bottomland soils** are mostly well-drained, dark-brown or gray loams and clays.

This area is used mostly as **rangeland,** but **wheat, grain sorghums,** and other crops are grown on the better soils. Brush control, wind and water erosion, and limited soil moisture are the major management concerns.

## Edwards Plateau Soils

The 22.7 million acres of the Edwards Plateau are in South Central Texas east of the Trans-Pecos and west of the Blackland Prairie. Uplands are nearly level to undulating except near large stream valleys, where the landscape is hilly with deep canyons and steep slopes. There are many **cedar brakes** in this area. Surface drainage is rapid.

**Upland soils** are mostly shallow, stony, or gravelly, dark alkaline clays and clay loams underlain by limestone. Lighter-colored soils are on steep sideslopes and deep, less-stony soils are in the valleys. **Bottomland soils** are mostly deep, dark-gray or brown, alkaline loams and clays.

Raising **beef cattle** is the main enterprise in this region, but it is also the center of Texas' and the nation's **mohair** and **wool production.** The area is a **major deer habitat,** and hunting leases produce income. Cropland is mostly in the valleys on the deeper soils and is used mainly for growing forage crops and hay. The major soil-management concerns are brush control, large stones, low fertility, excess lime, and limited soil moisture.

## Central or Llano Basin Soils

The Central Basin, also known as the Llano Basin, occupies a relatively small area in Central Texas. It includes parts or all of Llano, Mason, Gillespie, and adjoining counties. The total area is about 1.6 million acres of undulating to hilly landscape.

**Upland soils** are mostly shallow, reddish-brown to brown, mostly gravelly and stony, neutral to slightly acid sandy loams over granite, limestone, gneiss, and schist bedrock. Large boulders are on the soil surface in some areas. Deeper, less stony sandy-loam soils are in the valleys. **Bottomland soils** are minor areas of deep, dark-gray or brown loams and clays.

**Ranching** is the main enterprise, with some farms producing **peaches, grain sorghum,** and **wheat.** The area provides excellent **deer habitat,** and hunting leas-

① Trans-Pecos
② Canadian Valleys
③ High Plains
④ Rolling Plains
⑤ North Central Prairie
   ⊜ Rolling Red Prairies
⑥ Edwards Plateau
⑦ Central/Llano Basin
⑧ Northern Rio Grande Plain
⑨ Western Rio Grande Plain

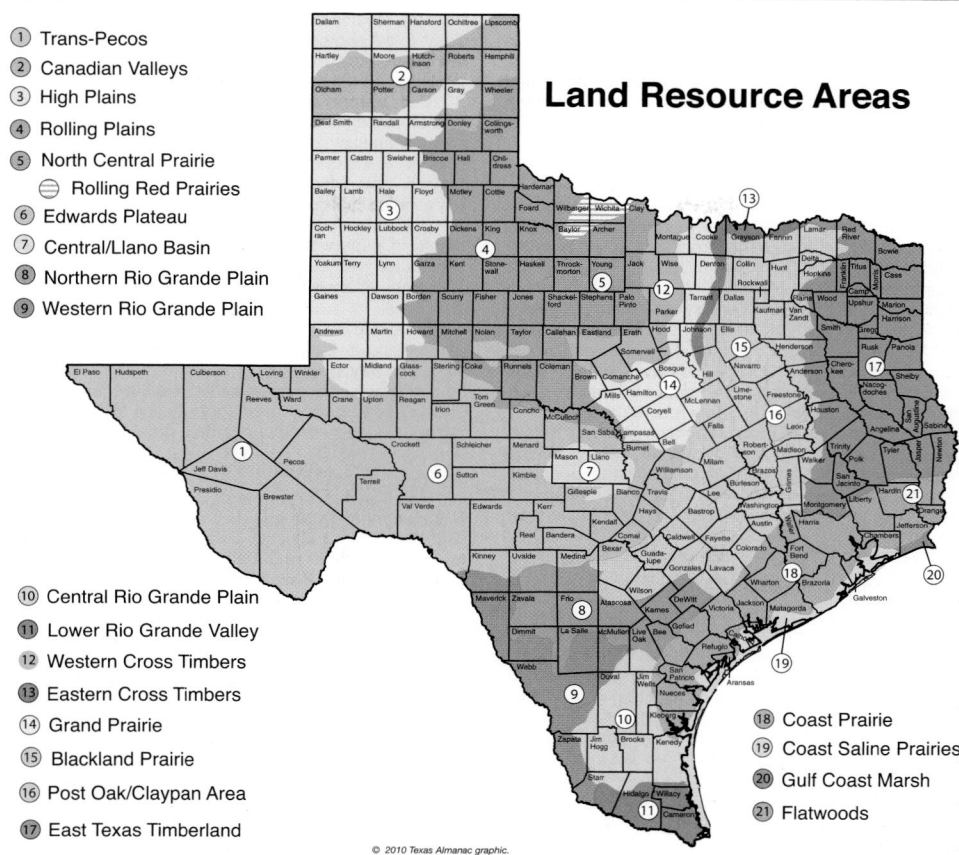

# Land Resource Areas

⑩ Central Rio Grande Plain
⑪ Lower Rio Grande Valley
⑫ Western Cross Timbers
⑬ Eastern Cross Timbers
⑭ Grand Prairie
⑮ Blackland Prairie
⑯ Post Oak/Claypan Area
⑰ East Texas Timberland

⑱ Coast Prairie
⑲ Coast Saline Prairies
⑳ Gulf Coast Marsh
㉑ Flatwoods

© 2010 Texas Almanac graphic.
Source: Natural Resources Conservation Service of the U.S. Department of Agriculture.

es are a major source of income. Brush control, large stones, and limited soil moisture are soil-management concerns.

### Northern Rio Grande Plain Soils

The Northern Rio Grande Plain comprises about 6.3 million acres in South Texas extending from Uvalde to Beeville. The landscape is nearly level to rolling, mostly brush-covered plains with slow to rapid surface drainage.

The major **upland soils** are deep, reddish-brown or dark grayish-brown, neutral to alkaline loams and clays. **Bottomland soils** are mostly dark-colored loams.

The area is mostly rangeland with significant areas of cropland. **Grain sorghums, cotton, corn, and small grains** are the major crops. Crops are irrigated in the western part, especially in the **Winter Garden** area, where vegetables such as spinach, carrots, and cabbage are grown. Much of the area is good **deer and dove habitat;** hunting leases are a major source of income. Brush control, soil fertility, and irrigation-water management are the major soil-management concerns.

### Western Rio Grande Plain Soils

The Western Rio Grande Plain comprises about 5.3 million acres in an area of southwestern Texas from Del Rio to Rio Grande City. The landscape is nearly level to undulating except near the Rio Grande where it is hilly. Surface drainage is slow to rapid.

The major soils are mostly deep, brown or gray alkaline clays and loams. Some are saline. Bottomland

Most of the soils are used for **rangeland.** Irrigated **grain sorghums** and **vegetables** are grown along the Rio Grande. **Hunting leases** are a major source of income. Brush control and limited soil moisture are the major soil-management problems.

### Central Rio Grande Plain Soils

The Central Rio Grande Plain comprises about 5.9 million acres in an area of South Texas from Live Oak County to Hidalgo County. It Includes the **South Texas Sand Sheet,** an area of deep, sandy soils and active sand dunes. The landscape is nearly level to gently undulating. Surface drainage is slow to rapid. **Upland soils** are mostly deep, light-colored, neutral to alkaline sands and loams. Many are saline or sodic. Bottomland soils are of minor extent.

Most of the area is used for raising **beef cattle.** A few areas, mostly in the northeast part, are used for growing **grain sorghums, cotton,** and small grains. **Hunting leases** are a major source of income. Brush control is the major soil-management problem on rangeland; wind erosion and limited soil moisture are major concerns on cropland.

### Lower Rio Grande Valley Soils

The Lower Rio Grande Valley comprises about 2.1 million acres in extreme southern Texas. The landscape is level to gently sloping with slow surface drainage.

**Upland soils** are mostly deep, grayish-brown, neutral to alkaline loams; coastal areas are mostly gray, silty clay loam and silty clay; some are saline. Bottomland soils are minor in extent.

Most of the soils are used for growing **irrigated vegetables** and **citrus,** along with **cotton, grain sorghums,** and **sugar cane.** Some areas are used for growing **beef cattle.** Irrigation water management and wind erosion are the major soil-management problems on cropland; brush control is the major problem on rangeland.

### Western Cross Timbers Soils

The Western Cross Timbers area comprises about 2.6 million acres. It includes the wooded section west of the Grand Prairie and extends from the Red River southward to the north edge of Brown County. The landscape is undulating and is dissected by many drainageways including the **Brazos and Red rivers.** Surface drainage is rapid.

**Upland soils** are mostly deep, grayish-brown, slightly acid loams with loamy and clayey subsoils. **Bottomland soils** along the major rivers are deep, reddish-brown, neutral to alkaline silt loams and clays.

The area is used mostly for grazing **beef and dairy cattle** on native range and improved pastures. Crops are **peanuts, grain sorghums, small grains, peaches, pecans,** and **vegetables.** The major soil-management problem on grazing lands is brush control. Waste management on dairy farms is a more recent concern. Wind and water erosion are the major problems on cropland.

### Eastern Cross Timbers Soils

The Eastern Cross Timbers area comprises about 1 million acres in a long narrow strip of wooded land that separates the northern parts of the Blackland Prairie and Grand Prairie and extends from the Red River southward to Hill County. The landscape is gently undulating to rolling and is dissected by many streams, including the **Red and Trinity rivers.** Sandstone-capped hills are prominent in some areas. Surface runoff is moderate to rapid.

The **upland soils** are mostly deep, light-colored, slightly acid sandy loams and loamy sands with reddish loamy or clayey subsoils. **Bottomland soils** are reddish-brown to dark gray, slightly acid to alkaline loams or gray clays.

**Grassland** consisting of native range and improved pastures is the major land use. **Peanuts, grain sorghums, small grains, peaches, pecans,** and **vegetables** are grown in some areas. Brush control, water erosion, and low fertility are the major soil concerns in management.

### Grand Prairie Soils

The Grand Prairie comprises about 6.3 million acres in North Central Texas. It extends from the Red River to about the Colorado River. It lies between the Eastern and Western Cross Timbers in the northern part and just west of the Blackland Prairie in the southern part. The landscape is undulating to hilly and is dissected by many streams including the **Red, Trinity, and Brazos rivers.** Surface drainage is rapid.

**Upland soils** are mostly dark-gray, alkaline clays; some are shallow over limestone and some are stony. Some areas have light-colored loamy soils over chalky limestone. **Bottomland soils** along the Red and Brazos rivers are reddish silt loams and clays. Other bottomlands have dark-gray loams and clays.

Land use is a mixture of rangeland, pastureland, and cropland. The area is mainly used for growing **beef cattle.** Some **small grain, grain sorghums, corn,** and **hay** are grown. Brush control and water erosion are the major management concerns.

### Blackland Prairie Soils

The Blackland Prairies consist of about 12.6 million acres of east-central Texas extending southwesterly from the Red River to Bexar County. There are smaller areas to the southeast. The landscape is undulating with few scattered wooded areas that are mostly in the bottomlands. Surface drainage is moderate to rapid.

Both **upland** and **bottomland** soils are deep, dark-gray to black alkaline clays. Some soils in the western part are shallow to moderately deep over chalk. Some soils on the eastern edge are neutral to slightly acid, grayish clays and loams over mottled clay subsoils (sometimes called graylands). Blackland soils are known as **"cracking clays"** because of the large, deep cracks that form in dry weather. This high shrink-swell property can cause serious damage to foundations, highways, and other structures and is a safety hazard in pits and trenches.

Land use is divided about equally between cropland and grassland. **Cotton, grain sorghums, corn, wheat, oats,** and **hay** are grown. **Grassland** is mostly improved pastures, with native range on the shallower and steeper soils. Water erosion, cotton root rot, soil tilth, and brush control are the major management problems.

### Claypan Area Soils

The Claypan Area consists of about 6.1 million acres in east-central Texas just east of the Blackland Prairie. The landscape is a gently undulating to rolling, moderately dissected woodland also known as the **Post Oak Belt** or **Post Oak Savannah.** Surface drainage is moderate.

**Upland soils** commonly have a thin, light-colored, acid sandy loam surface layer over dense, mottled red, yellow, and gray claypan subsoils. Some deep, sandy soils with less clayey subsoils exist. **Bottomlands** are deep, highly fertile, reddish-brown to dark-gray loamy to clayey soils.

Land use is mainly **rangeland.** Some areas are in improved pastures. Most cropland is in bottomlands that are protected from flooding. Major crops are **cotton, grain sorghums, corn, hay,** and **forage crops,** most of which are irrigated. Brush control on rangeland and irrigation water management on cropland are the major soil-management problems. Water erosion is a serious problem on the highly erosive claypan soils, especially where they are overgrazed.

### East Texas Timberland Soils

The East Texas Timberlands area comprises about 16.1 million acres of the forested eastern part of the state. The land is gently undulating to hilly and well dissected by many streams. Surface drainage is moderate to rapid.

This area has many kinds of **upland soils** but most are deep, light-colored, acid sands and loams over loamy and clayey subsoils. Deep sands are in scattered areas, and red clays are in areas of "redlands." **Bottomland soils** are mostly brown to dark-gray, acid loams and some clays.

The land is used mostly for growing **commercial pine timber** and for **woodland grazing.** Improved pastures are scattered throughout and are used for grazing **beef and dairy cattle** and for hay production. Some **commercial hardwoods** are in the bottomlands. Woodland management problems include seedling survival, invasion of hardwoods in pine stands, effects of logging on water quality, and control of the southern pine beetle. Lime and fertilizers are necessary for productive cropland and pastures.

### Coast Prairie Soils

The Coast Prairie includes about 8.7 million acres near the Gulf Coast. It ranges from 30 miles to 80 miles in width and parallels the coast from the Sabine River

*Range Management Specialist Preston Irwin works to execute conservation practices in the Trans Pecos. Photo courtesy of USDA/Natural Resources Conservation Service.*

in Orange County in Southeast Texas to Baffin Bay in Kleberg County in South Texas. The landscape is level to gently undulating with slow surface drainage.

**Upland soils** are mostly deep, dark-gray, neutral to slightly acid clay loams and clays. Lighter-colored and more-sandy soils are in a strip on the northwestern edge. Some soils in the southern part are alkaline; some are saline and sodic. **Bottomland soils** are mostly deep, dark-colored clays and loams along small streams but are greatly varied along the rivers.

Land use is mainly **grazing lands** and **cropland.** Some hardwood timber is in the bottomlands. Many areas are also managed for **wetland wildlife habitat.** The nearly level topography and productive soils encourage farming. **Rice, grain sorghums, cotton, corn,** and **hay** are the main crops. Brush management on grasslands and removal of excess water on cropland are the major management concerns.

## Coast Saline Prairies Soils

The Coast Saline Prairies area includes about 3.2 million acres along a narrow strip of wet lowlands adjacent to the coast; it includes the **barrier islands** that extend from Mexico to Louisiana. The surface is at or only a few feet above sea level with many areas of **saltwater marsh.** Surface drainage is very slow.

The soils are mostly deep, dark-colored clays and loams; many are saline and sodic. Light-colored sandy soils are on the barrier islands. The water table is at or near the surface of most soils.

**Cattle grazing** is the chief economic use of the various salt-tolerant cordgrasses and sedges. Many areas are managed for **wetland wildlife.** Recreation is popular on the barrier islands. Providing fresh water and access to grazing areas are the major management concerns.

## Gulf Coast Marsh Soils

This 150,000-acre area lies in the extreme southeastern corner of Texas. The area can be subdivided into four parts: **freshwater, intermediate, brackish,** and **saline (saltwater) marsh.** The degree of salinity of this

system grades landward from saltwater marshes along the coast to freshwater marshes inland. Surface drainage is very slow.

This area contains many lakes, bayous, tidal channels, and man-made canals. About one-half of the marsh is fresh; one-half is salty. Most of it is susceptible to flooding either by fresh water drained from lands adjacent to the marsh or by saltwater from the Gulf of Mexico.

Most of the soils are poorly drained, continuously saturated, soft, and can carry little weight. In general, the organic soils have a thick layer of dark gray, relatively undecomposed organic material over a gray, clayey subsoil. The mineral soils have a surface of dark gray, highly decomposed organic material over a gray, clayey subsoil.

Most of the almost treeless and uninhabited area is in marsh vegetation, such as grasses, sedges, and rushes. It is used mainly for **wildlife habitat.** Part of the fertile and productive estuarine complex supports marine life of the Gulf of Mexico. It also provides **wintering ground for waterfowl** and **habitat for many fur-bearing animals** and **alligators.** A significant acreage is firm enough to support livestock and is used for **winter grazing of cattle.** The major management problems are providing fresh water and access to grazing areas.

## Flatwoods Soils

The Flatwoods area includes about 2.5 million acres of woodland in humid Southeast Texas just north of the Coast Prairie and extending into Louisiana. The landscape is level to gently undulating. Surface drainage is slow.

**Upland soils** are mostly deep, light-colored, acid loams with gray, loamy, or clayey subsoils. **Bottomland soils** are deep, dark-colored, acid clays and loams. The water table is near the surface at least part of the year.

The land is mainly used for **forest,** although **cattle** are grazed in some areas. Woodland management problems include seedling survival, invasion of hardwoods in pine stands, effects of logging on water quality, and control of the southern pine beetle. ☆

*A blue heron watches the waters of Lake Whitney, which lies between Bosque and Hill counties and is formed by the Brazos River. Texas Parks and Wildlife Department photo.*

# Water Resources

*Sources: Texas Water Development Board, www.twdb.texas.gov; U.S. Geological Survey, http://tx.usgs.gov/*

Aquifers are water-bearing rock formations beneath the earth's surface. Texas has a wealth of fresh to slightly saline groundwater in **nine major and 21 minor aquifers,** which lie beneath more than 81 percent of the state. Groundwater provides about 60 percent of the 16.1 million acre-feet of water used yearly in Texas.

Groundwater is an important resource to every industry in Texas, from farming, ranching, and manufacturing to energy exploration and refining. It also provides water for municipal and environmental needs. Nearly 80 percent of groundwater pumped in 2013 was used for **irrigating crops,** about half of which is used in the Panhandle region. In 2013, groundwater supplied about 37 percent of the state's **municipal water** needs. The Texas Water Development Board has created videos about Texas aquifers and groundwater management at: https://www.twdb.texas.gov/groundwater/video/index.asp.

## Major Aquifers of Texas

### Ogallala

The Ogallala Aquifer extends through the majority of the Texas Panhandle. It is the southernmost extension of the largest aquifer (High Plains Aquifer) in North America. The Ogallala Formation, of late Miocene to early Pliocene age, consists of heterogeneous sequenc-es of coarse-grained sand and gravel in the lower part, grading upward into clay, silt, and fine sand. In Texas, the Panhandle is the most extensive region irrigated with groundwater. About 95 percent of the water pumped from the Ogallala Aquifer is **used for irrigation.**

Extensive pumping that exceeds the amount of recharge has resulted in **consistently declining water levels** throughout much of the aquifer. Water conservation measures promoted by agricultural and municipal users have slowed the rate of decline, and water levels have risen in a few areas. The Texas Water Development Board (TWDB) and its contractor developed computer models of the northern and southern portions of the Ogallala Aquifer to aid in managing groundwater. Several agencies are investigating playa recharge and agricultural reuse projects in the aquifer area.

### Gulf Coast Aquifer

The Gulf Coast Aquifer forms an irregularly shaped belt that parallels the Texas coastline, extending through 54 counties from the Rio Grande northeastward to the Louisiana border. The **aquifer system** is composed of Quaternary- and Tertiary-aged layers including the Catahoula, Oakville, Fleming, Goliad, Willis, Lissie, Bentley, Montgomery, and Beaumont formations.

This system has been divided into **three major water-producing components** referred to as the Chicot, Evangeline, and Jasper aquifers. These aquifers are composed of discontinuous layers of sand, silt, clay, and gravel. The Gulf Coast Aquifer is used primarily for **mu-**

**nicipal, industrial, and agricultural purposes.**
Water quality is generally good in the central and northeastern parts of the aquifer, but deteriorates to the southwest. Years of heavy pumping have caused significant water-level declines in portions of the aquifer. Some of these declines have resulted in **land subsidence,** particularly in the Houston-Galveston area.

### Edwards (Balcones Fault Zone)

The Edwards Balcones Fault Zone (BFZ) Aquifer forms a narrow belt extending through the southcentral part of the state from a groundwater divide in Kinney County through the San Antonio area northeastward to the Leon River in Bell County.

A groundwater divide in Hays County hydrologically separates the aquifer into the **San Antonio and Austin regions.** The aquifer is highly permeable, with water occurring in fractures, honeycomb-like zones (or intergranular pores), and solution channels that characterize the Edwards and associated limestone formations of Cretaceous age.

Water from the Edwards (BFZ) is primarily used for **municipal, irrigation, and recreational purposes.** The City of San Antonio meets the majority of its water needs with Edwards (BFZ) water. The aquifer also feeds several well-known recreational springs and underlies some of Texas's most environmentally sensitive areas.

In 1993, the **Edwards Aquifer Authority** (EAA) was created by the Texas Legislature to regulate pumping from the aquifer to benefit all users within the EAA's jurisdiction. The Barton Springs/Edwards Aquifer Conservation District and the Kinney County Groundwater

Conservation District also provide aquifer management in the areas of the aquifer that are not within the EAA boundaries.

The EAA has an active outreach program used to educate the public on water conservation. It also operates several active groundwater recharge sites. The San Antonio River Authority also has a number of flood-control structures that effectively recharge the aquifer.

Groundwater conservation districts that manage the Edwards (BFZ) Aquifer continually promote more efficient irrigation techniques. The EAA facilitates market-based, voluntary transfers of unused agricultural water rights to municipal uses as a water conservation and management strategy.

### Carrizo-Wilcox

The Carrizo-Wilcox Aquifer extends from south of the Rio Grande in Mexico through Texas northeastward into Arkansas and Louisiana. The aquifer consists of the Tertiary-age Wilcox Group and overlying Carrizo Sand Formation of the Claiborne Group. The aquifer is composed of a hydrologically connected system of sand locally interbedded with clay, silt, lignite, and gravel.

Throughout most of its extent in Texas, the aquifer yields fresh to slightly saline water. A little more than half of the water pumped from the aquifer is **used for irrigation;** the remaining amount pumped is used for **municipal, industrial, domestic, and livestock purposes.**

Recently, the Carrizo-Wilcox Aquifer has been considered as an alternative water supply for growing central Texas communities that have traditionally used the Edwards (BFZ) Aquifer to meet municipal needs.

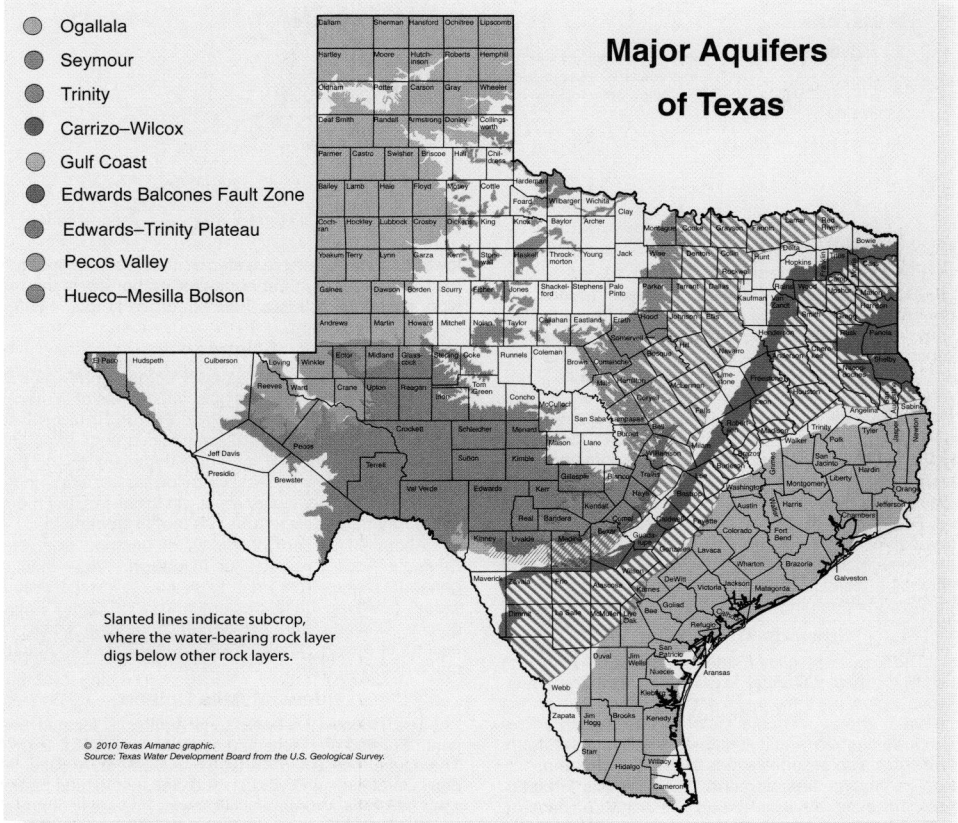

Ogallala
Seymour
Trinity
Carrizo–Wilcox
Gulf Coast
Edwards Balcones Fault Zone
Edwards–Trinity Plateau
Pecos Valley
Hueco–Mesilla Bolson

**Major Aquifers of Texas**

Slanted lines indicate subcrop, where the water-bearing rock layer digs below other rock layers.

© 2010 Texas Almanac graphic.
Source: Texas Water Development Board from the U.S. Geological Survey.

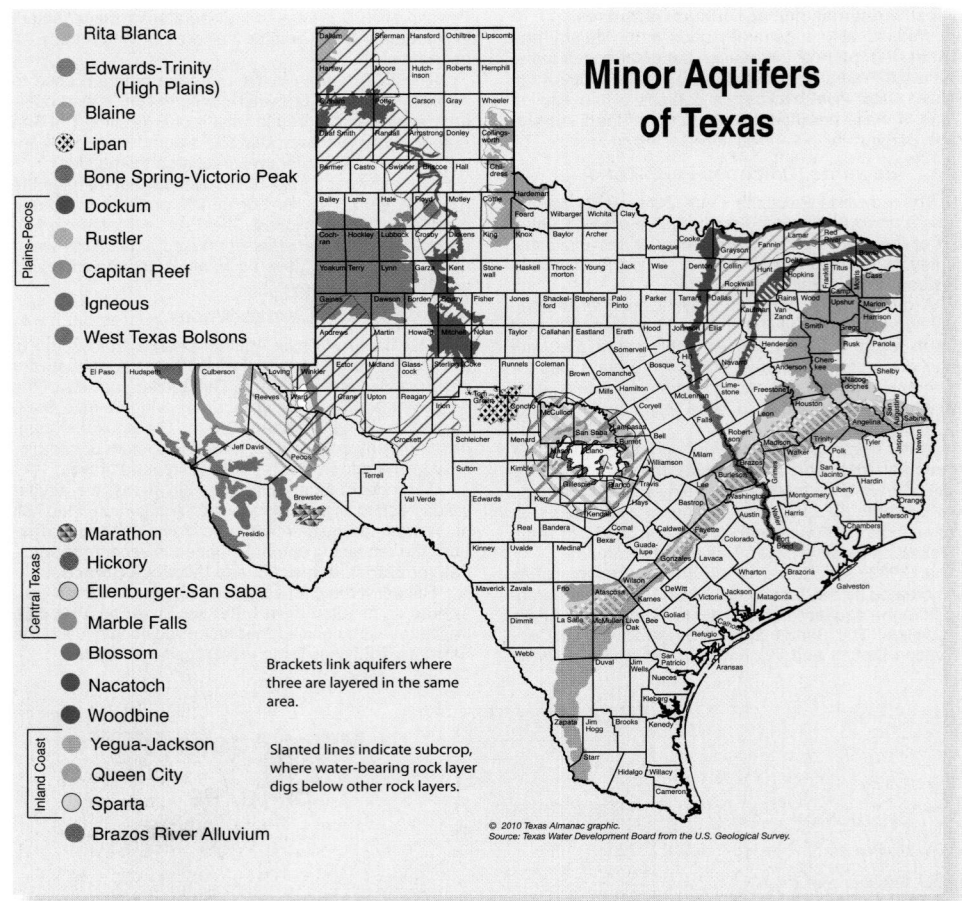

## Minor Aquifers of Texas

**Plains-Pecos**
- Rita Blanca
- Edwards-Trinity (High Plains)
- Blaine
- Lipan
- Bone Spring-Victorio Peak
- Dockum
- Rustler
- Capitan Reef
- Igneous
- West Texas Bolsons

**Central Texas**
- Marathon
- Hickory
- Ellenburger-San Saba
- Marble Falls
- Blossom
- Nacatoch
- Woodbine

**Inland Coast**
- Yegua-Jackson
- Queen City
- Sparta
- Brazos River Alluvium

Brackets link aquifers where three are layered in the same area.

Slanted lines indicate subcrop, where water-bearing rock layer digs below other rock layers.

© 2010 Texas Almanac graphic.
Source: Texas Water Development Board from the U.S. Geological Survey.

## Trinity

The Trinity Aquifer consists of basal Cretaceous-age Trinity Group formations that extend from the Red River in North Texas southward to the Hill Country of Central Texas. The aquifer is composed of the Antlers, Glen Rose, Paluxy, Twin Mountains, Travis Peak, Hensell, and Hosston aquifers. These aquifers consist of limestone, sands, clays, gravels, and conglomerates.

The Trinity Aquifer is **primarily used to meet municipal water demands,** though it also provides water for **irrigation, livestock,** and other domestic purposes. Extensive development of the Trinity Aquifer in the Dallas–Fort Worth and Waco areas has resulted in water-level declines of 350 feet to more than 1,000 feet, though these declines have slowed as a result of increasing reliance on surface water and reductions in groundwater pumping.

## Edwards-Trinity Plateau

The Edwards-Trinity (Plateau) Aquifer extends from the Hill Country of Central Texas westward to the Trans-Pecos region, covering much of the southwestern part of the state. The aquifer consists of primarily of early Cretaceous limestone and dolomites of the Edwards Group, although it also includes sands of the Trinity Group.

The aquifer **lies beneath the Edwards Plateau.** Near the plateau's edge along the northern, eastern, and southern margins of the aquifer, groundwater flows towards streams, where water discharges from springs. **Irrigation,** mainly in the northwestern portion of the region, accounts for more than two-thirds of total aquifer use.

## Seymour

The Seymour Aquifer extends across North-Central Texas. This aquifer consists of isolated areas of alluvium found in the upper Red River and Brazos River basins. It is also characterized by discontinuous beds of poorly sorted gravel, sand, silt, and clay deposited during the Quaternary Period by eastward-flowing streams. Individual accumulations vary greatly in thickness, but most of the Seymour is **less than 100 feet in thickness.**

About 90 percent of the water pumped from the Seymour Aquifer is used for **irrigation.** Water quality generally ranges from fresh to slightly saline. Localized areas, however, have moderate to very saline water quality. Chloride and nitrate concentrations occur in excess of primary drinking-water standards throughout much of the aquifer.

## Hueco-Mesilla Bolson

The Hueco-Mesilla Bolsons Aquifer is located beneath El Paso and Hudspeth counties in far West Texas. The aquifer consists of Tertiary and Quaternary basin-fill deposits of silt, sand, gravel, and clay that extend northward into New Mexico and westward into Mexico in two basins. The Hueco Bolson, located on the **eastern side** of the Franklin Mountains, has a maximum thickness of 9,000 feet and is an important source of **drinking water for both El Paso and Juarez, Mexico.** The Mesilla Bolson has a maximum thickness of 2,000 feet and contains three separate water producing zones.

Historical large-scale groundwater withdrawals, especially for the municipal uses of El Paso and Juarez, have caused major water-level declines and significantly changed the direction of flow. This pumping has also caused a deterioration of the chemical quality of the groundwater in the aquifer, according to El Paso Water Utilities and the U.S. Geological Survey (USGS).

Nearly 90 percent of the water pumped from the aquifer in the Texas extent of the bolsons is used for **public supply.** The City of El Paso has reduced its use of groundwater from the Hueco-Bolson since 1989, and observation wells indicate that water levels have stabilized from a previously declining trend. El Paso and Fort Bliss also have built the world's largest inland desalina-tion plant in El Paso County, which uses brackish groundwater from the Hueco-Bolson.

## Pecos Valley

The Pecos Valley Aquifer is located in the upper Pecos River Valley of West Texas. This aquifer, formerly called the Cenozoic Pecos Alluvium, consists of up to 1,500 feet of Tertiary and Quaternary alluvial fill and wind-blown deposits. The aquifer occupies two hydrologically separate basins: the **Pecos Trough in the west** and the **Monument Draw Trough in the east**.

More than 80 percent of groundwater pumped from the aquifer is **used for irrigation,** and the remainder is withdrawn for **industrial, power supply and municipal uses.** Water-level declines in excess of 200 feet have occurred in Reeves and Pecos counties but have slowed since the mid-1970s as irrigation pumping has decreased. Declines continue in Ward County due to increased municipal and industrial pumping. ☆

# Water Regulation in Texas

In Texas, water law historically has been different for surface water and groundwater. **Surface water** belongs to the state and, except for limited amounts of water for household and on-farm live-stock use, requires a permit for use.

The Texas Commission on Environmental Quality (TCEQ) is responsible for permitting and adjudicating surface water rights. The TCEQ is the primary regulator of surface water and polices contamination and pollution of both surface and groundwater.

In general, **groundwater** is considered the property of the surface landowner by "rule of capture," meaning the landowner may pump as much water as he wishes from beneath his land for any beneficial use and which does not harm neighboring property. This right may be limited only by groundwater conservation districts. These districts are the state's preferred method of groundwater management and provide for the conservation, preservation, protection, recharging, and prevention of waste of groundwater resources within their jurisdictions.

As of August 2015, **97 districts exist in Texas,** covering nearly 70 percent of the state. In addition, two subsidence districts cover Harris, Galveston, and Fort Bend counties. Subsidence districts regulate groundwater production to prevent land subsidence.

The Texas Water Development Board (TWDB) collects data on water quality and availability within the state; plans for future supply and use; and administers the state's funds for grants and loans to finance future water development and supply.

In January 2012, the TWDB released a comprehensive statewide water plan, which the 75th Texas Legislature (1997) required of the TWDB every five years. The TWDB divided the state into 16 regional water-planning areas. Each area's Regional Water Planning Group must adopt a water plan that addresses water management strategies for meeting future water needs, its response to future droughts, and water conservation.

# Major Rivers of Texas

There are 11,247 named Texas streams identified in the U.S. Geological Survey Geographic Names Information System. Their combined length is about 80,000 miles, and they drain 263,513 square miles within Texas. **Fourteen major rivers** are described in this section, starting with the southernmost and moving northward:

## Rio Grande

The Pueblo Indians called this river **P'osoge,** which means the "river of great water." In 1582, **Antonio de Espejo** of Nueva Vizcaya, Mexico, followed the course of the **Río Conchos** to its confluence with a great river, which Espejo named **Río del Norte (River of the North).** The name **Rio Grande** was first given the stream apparently by the explorer **Juan de Oñate,** who arrived on its banks near present-day El Paso in 1598.

Thereafter the names were often consolidated as **Río Grande del Norte.** It was shown also on early Spanish maps as **Río San Buenaventura** and **Río Ganapetuan.** In its lower course, it early acquired the name **Río Bravo,** which is its name on most Mexican maps. At times it has also been known as **Río Turbio,** probably because of its muddy appearance during its frequent rises. Some people erroneously call this watercourse the Rio Grande River.

This river **forms the boundary of Texas** and the international U.S.-Mexican border for **889** or **1,254** river miles, depending upon method of measurement. (See **Texas Boundary Lines, page 77.**)

The **U.S. Geological Survey** figure for the total length from its headwaters to its mouth on the Gulf of Mexico is **1,900** miles.

According to the USGS, the Rio Grande is tied with the St. Lawrence River (also 1,900 miles) as the **fourth-longest** North American river, exceeded only by the Missouri-Mississippi, McKenzie-Peace, and Yukon rivers. Since all of these except the Missouri-Mississippi are partly in Canada, the Rio Grande is the **second-longest river entirely within or bordering the United States.** It is **Texas' longest river.**

The snow-fed flow of the Rio Grande is used for

A canoeist paddles down Buffalo Bayou near Houston. Photo by Marina Rossow; Bayou Preservation Association.

irrigation in Colorado below the San Juan Mountains, where the river rises at the Continental Divide. Turning south, it flows through a canyon in northern New Mexico and again irrigates a broad valley of central New Mexico. Southern New Mexico impounds Rio Grande waters in Elephant Butte Reservoir for irrigation of the valley above and below El Paso.

The valley near El Paso is thought to be the **oldest irrigated area in Texas** because Indians were irrigating crops here when Spanish explorers arrived in the early 1500s.

From source to mouth, the Rio Grande drops 12,000 feet to sea level as a mountain torrent, desert stream, and meandering coastal river. Along its banks and in its valley, Europeans established some of their first North American settlements. Here are situated **three of the oldest towns in Texas — Ysleta, Socorro,** and **San Elizario.**

Because of the extensive irrigation, the Rio Grande virtually ends at the lower end of the El Paso valley, except in seasons of above-normal flow.

The river starts again as a perennially flowing stream where the Río Conchos of Mexico flows into it at Presidio-Ojinaga. Through the **Big Bend,** the Rio

Grande flows through three successive **canyons,** the **Santa Elena,** the **Mariscal,** and the **Boquillas.** The Santa Elena has a river bed elevation of 2,145 feet and a canyon-rim elevation of 3,661. Corresponding figures for Mariscal are 1,925 and 3,625, and for Boquillas, 1,850 and 3,490. The river here flows for about 100 miles around the base of the **Chisos Mountains** as the southern boundary of **Big Bend National Park.**

Below the Big Bend, the Rio Grande gradually emerges from mountains onto the Coastal Plains. A 191.2-mile strip on the U.S. side from Big Bend National Park downstream to the Terrell–Val Verde county line has federal designation as the **Rio Grande Wild and Scenic River.**

At the confluence of the Rio Grande and Devils River, the United States and Mexico have built **Amistad Dam,** to impound 3,275,532 acre-feet of water, of which Texas' share is 56.2 percent. **Falcon Reservoir,** also an international project, impounds 2,646,817 acre-feet of water, of which Texas' share in Zapata and Starr counties is 58.6 percent.

The Rio Grande, where it joins the Gulf of Mexico, has created a fertile delta called the **Lower Rio Grande Valley,** a major vegetable- and fruit-growing area. The

| AVERAGE ANNUAL FLOW | | |
|---|---|---|
| | **RIVER** | **ACRE-FEET*** |
| 1. | Brazos | 6,074,000 |
| 2. | Sabine | 5,864,000 |
| 3. | Trinity | 5,727,000 |
| 4. | Neches | 4,323,000 |
| 5. | Red | 3,464,000 |
| 6. | Colorado | 1,904,000 |

*One acre-foot equals 325,851 gallons of water.
*Source: Texas Water Development Board, 2007 State Water Plan.*

| LENGTHS OF MAJOR RIVERS | | |
|---|---|---|
| | **RIVER** | **LENGTH-MILES*** |
| 1. | Rio Grande | 1,900 |
| 2. | Red | 1,290 |
| 3. | Brazos | 1,280 |
| 4. | Pecos | 926 |
| 5. | Canadian | 906 |
| 6. | Colorado | 865 |

*Length from the original headwaters where the name defines the complete length to its outflow point. *Source: U.S. Geological Survey, 2008.*

river drains 49,387 square miles of Texas and has an average annual flow of 645,500 acre-feet.

Principal tributaries flowing from the Texas side are the **Pecos** and **Devils** rivers. On the Mexican side are **Río Conchos**, **Río Salado**, and **Río San Juan**. About three-fourths of the water running into the Rio Grande below El Paso comes from the Mexican side.

## Pecos River

The Pecos, one of the major tributaries of the Rio Grande, rises on the western slope of the Santa Fe Mountains in the **Sangre de Cristo Range** of northern New Mexico. It enters Texas as the boundary between Loving and Reeves counties and flows **350 miles** southeast as the boundary for several other counties, entering Val Verde County at its northwestern corner and angles across that county to its mouth on the **Rio Grande**, northwest of Del Rio.

According to the Handbook of Texas, the origins of the river's several names began with Antonio de Espejo, who called the river the **Río de las Vacas** ("river of the cows") because of the number of buffalo in the vicinity. Gaspar Castaño de Sosa, who followed the Pecos northward, called it the **Río Salado** because of its salty taste, which caused it to be shunned by men and animals alike.

It is believed that the name "Pecos" first appears in Juan de Oñate's reports concerning the Indian pueblo of Cicuye, now known as the **Pecos Pueblo** in New Mexico, and is of unknown origin.

Through most of its **926-mile-long** course from its headwaters, the Pecos River parallels the Rio Grande. The total drainage area of the Pecos in New Mexico and Texas is about 44,000 square miles. Most of its tributaries flow from the west; these include the **Delaware River** and **Toyah Creek**.

The topography of the river valley in Texas ranges from semi-arid irrigated farmlands, desert with sparse vegetation, and, in the lowermost reaches of the river, deep canyons.

## Nueces River

The Nueces River rises in two forks in Edwards and Real counties and flows **315 miles** to Nueces Bay on the Gulf near Corpus Christi. Draining 16,700 square miles, it is a beautiful, **spring-fed stream** flowing through **canyons** until it issues from the **Balcones Escarpment** onto the Coastal Plains in northern Uvalde County.

**Alonso de León**, in 1689, gave it its name. **Nueces**, plural of *nuez*, means nuts in Spanish. (More than a century earlier, Cabeza de Vaca had referred to a **Río de las Nueces** in this region, but that is now thought to have been the Guadalupe.)

The original Indian name for this river seems to have been **Chotilapacquen**. Crossing Texas in 1691, Terán de los Rios named the river **San Diego**.

The Nueces was the boundary line between the Spanish provinces of Texas and Nuevo Santander. After the Texas Revolution of 1836, both Texas and Mexico claimed the territory between the Nueces and the Rio Grande, a dispute that was settled in 1848 by the **Treaty of Guadalupe Hidalgo,** which fixed the international boundary at the Rio Grande.

Average runoff of the Nueces is about 496,000 acre-feet a year. Principal water conservation projects are **Lake Corpus Christi** and **Choke Canyon Reservoir**. Principal tributaries of the Nueces are the **Frio** and the **Atascosa**.

## San Antonio River

The San Antonio River has at its source **large springs** within and near the city limits of San Antonio. It flows **180 miles** across the Coastal Plains to a junction with the **Guadalupe** near the Gulf Coast. Its channel through San Antonio has been developed into a parkway known as the **River Walk.**

Its principal tributaries are the **Medina River** and **Cibolo Creek**, both spring-fed streams, and this, with its own spring origin, gives it remarkably clear water and makes it one of the steadiest of Texas rivers. Including the Medina River headwaters, it is **238 miles** in length.

The river was first named the **León** by Alonso de León in 1689; the name was not for himself, but he called it "lion" because its channel was filled with a rampaging flood.

Because of its limited and arid drainage area (4,180 square miles) the average runoff of the San Antonio River is relatively small, about 561,000 acre-feet annually.

## Guadalupe River

The Guadalupe rises in its North and South forks in western Kerr County. A **spring-fed stream,** it flows eastward through the Hill Country until it issues from the **Balcones Escarpment** near New Braunfels. It then crosses the Coastal Plains to San Antonio Bay. Its total length is **409 miles**, and its drainage area is 5,953 square miles. Its principal tributaries are the **San Marcos**, another

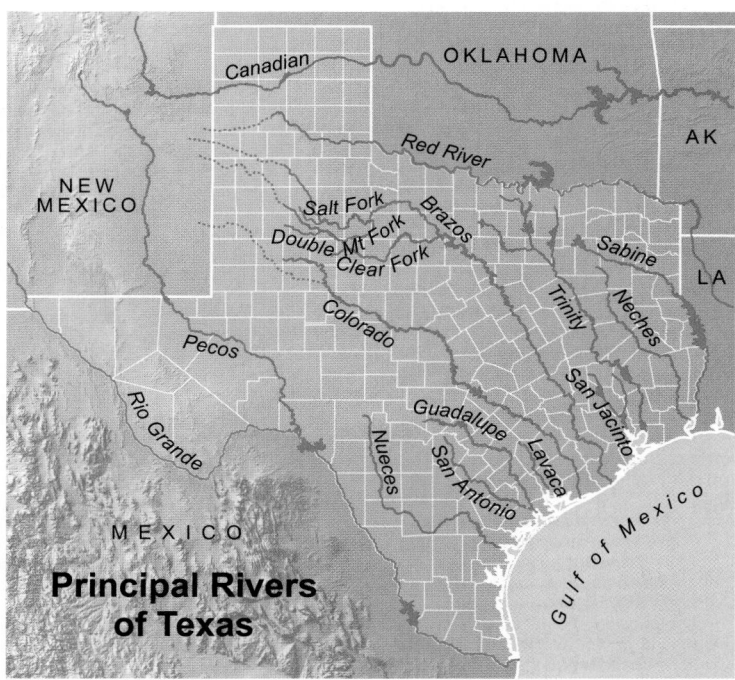

**Principal Rivers of Texas**

spring-fed stream, which joins it in Gonzales County; the **San Antonio**, which joins it just above its mouth on San Antonio Bay; and the **Comal**, which joins it at New Braunfels.

There has been power development on the Guadalupe near Gonzales and Cuero for many years, and there is also power generation at **Canyon Lake**. Because of its springs and its considerable drainage area, the Guadalupe has an average annual runoff of more than 1.38 million acre-feet.

The name Guadalupe is derived from **Nuestra Señora de Guadalupe,** the name given the stream by Alonso de León.

## Lavaca River

The Lavaca rises in extreme southeastern Fayette County and flows **117 miles** into the Gulf through Lavaca Bay. Without a spring-water source and with only a small watershed, including that of its principal tributary, the **Navidad**, its flow is intermittent. Runoff averages about 265,000 acre-feet yearly.

The Spanish called it the Lavaca (cow) because of the numerous bison found near it. It is the principal stream running to the Gulf between the Guadalupe and the Colorado, and drains 2,309 square miles. The principal lake on the **Navidad** is **Lake Texana**.

## Colorado River

Rising in east-central Dawson County, the Colorado River, which flows **865 miles** to Matagorda Bay, is the **longest river within Texas**. Its drainage area, which extends into New Mexico, is 42,318 square miles.

Its average annual runoff reaches a volume of 1.9 million acre-feet near the Gulf. Its name is a Spanish word meaning **"reddish."** There is evidence that Spanish explorers originally named the muddy Brazos "Colorado," but Spanish mapmakers later transposed the two names.

The river flows through a rolling, mostly prairie terrain to the vicinity of San Saba County, where it enters the rugged **Hill Country** and **Llano Basin**. It passes through a picturesque series of **canyons** until it issues from the **Balcones Escarpment** at Austin and flows across the Coastal Plains.

In the Hill Country, a remarkable series of reservoirs has been built to provide hydoelectric power, flood control, and water supply. The largest of these are **Lake Buchanan** in Burnet and Llano counties and **Lake Travis** in Travis County. Between the two in Burnet County are three smaller reservoirs: **Inks, Lyndon B. Johnson** (formerly Granite Shoals), and **Marble Falls**. Below Lake Travis is the older **Lake Austin**, largely filled with silt, whose dam is used to produce power from waters flowing down from the lakes above. **Lady Bird Lake** (formerly Town Lake) is in the City of Austin. This entire area is known as the **Highland Lakes Country**.

As early as the 1820s, Anglo-Americans settled on the banks of the lower Colorado, and in 1839, the **Capital Commission of the Republic of Texas** chose the picturesque area where the river flows from the **Balcones Escarpment** as the site of a new capital of the Republic — now **Austin**, capital of the state.

The early colonists encouraged navigation along the lower channel with some success. However, a **natural log raft** that formed 10 miles from the Gulf blocked river traffic after 1839, although shallow-draught vessels occasionally ventured as far upstream as Austin.

Conservation and utilization of the waters of the Colorado are under jurisdiction of three agencies created by the Legislature; the **Lower, Central,** and **Upper Colorado River Authorities**.

The principal tributaries of the Colorado River are the several prongs of the **Concho River** on its upper course, **Pecan Bayou** (farthest west "bayou" in the United States), and the **Llano, San Saba,** and **Pedernales** rivers. All except Pecan Bayou flow into the Colorado from the **Edwards Plateau** and are spring-fed, perennially flowing streams. In the numerous mussels found along these streams, **pearls** occasionally have been found. On early Spanish maps, the Middle Concho was called **Río de las Perlas**.

## Brazos River

The Brazos River proper is considered to begin where the **Double Mountain** and **Salt Forks** flow together in **northeastern Stonewall County;** it then flows **840 miles** across Texas. The **U.S. Geological Survey** puts the **total length** from the New Mexico source of its longest upper prong at **1,280 miles.**

With a drainage area of about 42,865 square miles, it is the second-largest river basin in Texas, after the Rio Grande. It flows directly into the Gulf southwest of Freeport in Brazoria County. **Its average annual flow exceeds 5.7 million acre-feet, the largest volume of any river in the state.**

The Brazos' third upper fork is the **Clear Fork**, which joins the main stream in Young County, just above **Possum Kingdom Lake**. The Brazos crosses most of the main physiographic regions of Texas — High Plains, West Texas Rolling Plains, Western Cross Timbers, Grand Prairie, and Gulf Coastal Plains.

The original name of this river was **Brazos de Dios**, meaning "Arms of God." **There are several legends as to why. One story** is that the Coronado expedition, wandering on the trackless Llano Estacado, exhausted its water and was threatened with death from thirst. Arriving at the bank of the river, they gave it the name "Brazos de Dios" in thankfulness. **Another legend** is that a ship exhausted its water supply, and its crew was saved when they found the mouth of the Brazos. **Still another story** is that miners on the San Saba were forced by drought to seek water near present-day Waco and in gratitude called it Brazos de Dios.

Much early Anglo-American colonization of Texas took place in the Brazos Valley. Along its channel were **San Felipe de Austin**, capital of Austin's colony; **Washington-on-the-Brazos**, where Texans declared independence from Mexico; and other historic settlements. There was some navigation of the **lower channel** of the Brazos in this period. Near its mouth it intersects the **Gulf Intracoastal Waterway,** which provides connection with the commerce on the Mississippi.

Most of the Brazos Valley lies within the boundaries of the **Brazos River Authority**, which conducts a multipurpose program for development. A large reservoir on the main channel of the Brazos is **Lake Whitney** (553,344 acre-feet capacity), where it is the boundary line between Hill and Bosque counties. **Lake Waco** on the Bosque and **Belton Lake** on the Leon are among the principal reservoirs on its tributaries. In addition to its three upper forks, other chief tributaries are the **Paluxy, Little,** and **Navasota** rivers.

## San Jacinto River

The San Jacinto is a short river with a drainage basin of 3,936 square miles and an average annual runoff of nearly 1.36 million acre-feet. It is formed by the junction of its East and West forks in northeastern Harris County and runs to the Gulf through Galveston Bay. Its total length, including the East Fork, is about **85 miles**.

**Lake Conroe** is on the West Fork, and **Lake Houston** is at the junction of the West Fork and the East Fork. The **Houston Ship Channel** runs through the lower course of the San Jacinto and its tributary, **Buffalo Bayou,** connecting the Port of Houston to the Gulf.

There are **two stories concerning the origin of its name.** One is that when early explorers discovered it, its channel was choked with hyacinth (**"jacinto"** is the

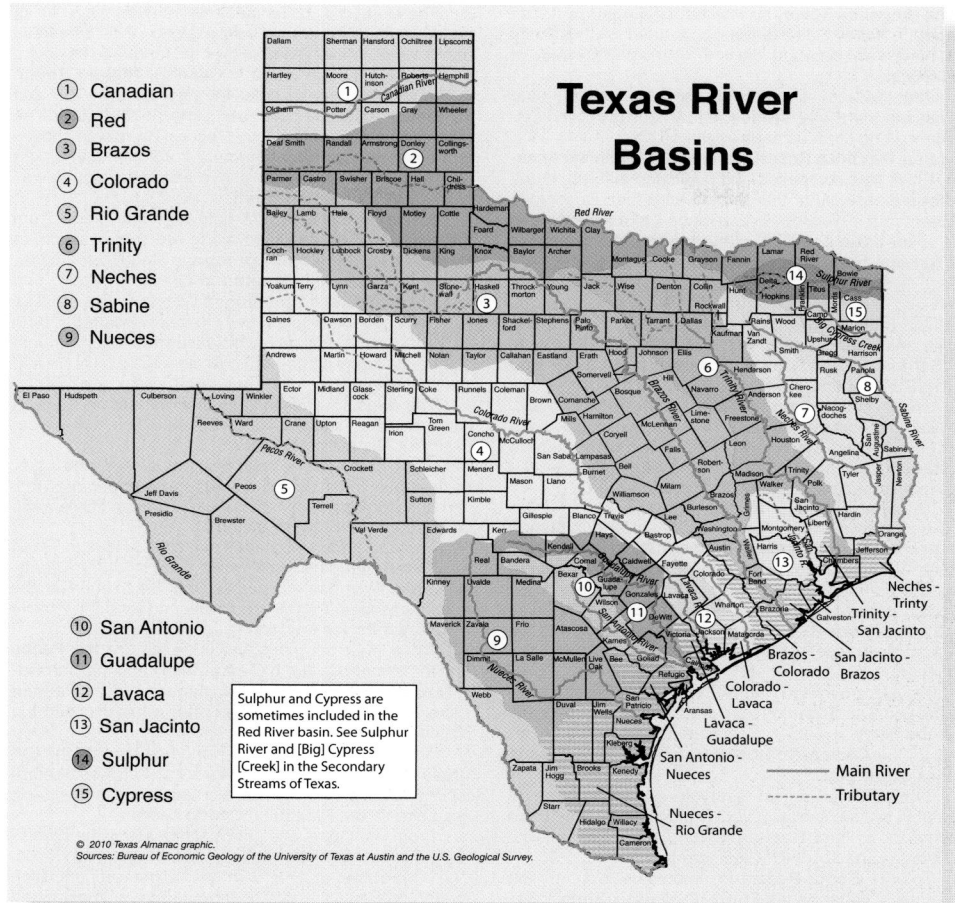

# Texas River Basins

1. Canadian
2. Red
3. Brazos
4. Colorado
5. Rio Grande
6. Trinity
7. Neches
8. Sabine
9. Nueces
10. San Antonio
11. Guadalupe
12. Lavaca
13. San Jacinto
14. Sulphur
15. Cypress

Sulphur and Cypress are sometimes included in the Red River basin. See Sulphur River and [Big] Cypress [Creek] in the Secondary Streams of Texas.

— Main River
---- Tributary

© 2010 Texas Almanac graphic.
Sources: Bureau of Economic Geology of the University of Texas at Austin and the U.S. Geological Survey.

Spanish word for hyacinth). The other is that it was discovered on Aug. 17, St. Hyacinth's Day.

The **Battle of San Jacinto** was fought on the bank of this river on April 21, 1836, when Texas won its independence from Mexico. **San Jacinto Battleground State Historic Site and monument** commemorate the battle.

## Trinity River

The Trinity rises in its East Fork, Elm Fork, West Fork, and Clear Fork in Grayson, Montague, Archer, and Parker counties, respectively. The main stream begins with the junction of the Elm and West forks at Dallas. Its length is **550 miles**, and its drainage area is 17,913 square miles. Because of moderate to heavy rainfall over its drainage area, it has a average annual flow of 5.6 million acre-feet near its mouth on Trinity Bay.

The Trinity derives its name from the Spanish **"Trinidad."** Alonso de León named it **La Santísima Trinidad** (the Most Holy Trinity).

**Navigation** was developed along its lower course with several riverport towns, such as **Sebastopol** in Trinity County. For many years, there has been a basin-wide movement for navigation, conservation, and utilization of its water. The **Trinity River Authority** is a state agency and the **Trinity Improvement Association** is a publicly supported nonprofit organization that has advocated its development.

The Trinity has in its valley **more large cities, greater population, and more industrial development** than any other river basin in Texas. On the Coastal Plains, there is large use of its waters for **rice irrigation.** Large reservoirs on the Elm Fork are **Lewisville Lake** and **Ray Roberts Lake**. There are four reservoirs above Fort Worth: **Lake Worth, Eagle Mountain Lake,** and **Lake Bridgeport** on the West Fork and **Benbrook Lake** on the Clear Fork.

**Lake Lavon** in southeast Collin County and **Lake Ray Hubbard** in Collin, Dallas, Kaufman, and Rockwall counties are on the East Fork. **Lake Livingston** is in Polk, San Jacinto, Trinity, and Walker counties. Two other reservoirs in the Trinity basin below the Dallas–Fort Worth area are **Cedar Creek Reservoir** and **Richland-Chambers Reservoir**.

## Neches River

The Neches rises in Van Zandt County in East Texas and flows **416 miles** to **Sabine Lake** near Port Arthur. It has a drainage area of 9,937 square miles. Abundant rainfall over its entire basin gives it an average annual flow near the Gulf of about 4.1 million acre-feet a year. The river takes its name from the **Neches Indians,** who the early Spanish explorers found living along its banks. Principal tributary of the Neches, and comparable with the Neches in length and flow above their confluence, is the **Angelina River,** so named for **Angelina (Little Angel),** a Hainai Indian girl who converted to Christianity and played an important role in the early development of this region.

Both the Neches and the Angelina run most of their courses in the **Piney Woods,** and there was much settlement along them as early as the 1820s.

**Sam Rayburn Reservoir,** near Jasper on the Angelina River, was completed and dedicated in 1965. It has a storage capacity of 2.86 million acre-feet. Reservoirs located on the Neches River include **Lake Palestine** in the upper basin and **B. A. Steinhagen Lake** located at the junction of the Neches and the Angelina rivers.

## Sabine River

The Sabine River is formed by three forks rising in Collin and Hunt counties. From its sources to its mouth on **Sabine Lake,** it flows approximately **360 miles** and drains 7,570 square miles.

Sabine comes from the **Spanish word** for cypress, as does the name of the **Sabinal River,** which flows into the Frio River in Southwest Texas. The Sabine has an average annual flow volume of 5.5 million acre-feet, the second-largest in the state after the Brazos.

Throughout most of Texas history, the lower Sabine has been the **eastern Texas boundary line,** although for a while there was doubt as to whether the Sabine or the Arroyo Hondo, east of the Sabine in Louisiana, was the boundary. For a number of years, the outlaw-infested **neutral ground** lay between them. There was also a **boundary dispute** in which it was alleged that the Neches River was really the Sabine and, therefore, the boundary.

Travelers over the part of the **Camino Real** known as the **Old San Antonio Road** crossed the Sabine at the **Gaines Ferry** in Sabine County, and there were crossings for the **Atascosito Road** and other travel and trade routes of that day.

Two of Texas' largest reservoirs have been created by dams on the Sabine River. The first of these is **Lake Tawakoni,** in Hunt, Rains, and Van Zandt counties, with a storage capacity of 871,685 acre-feet.

**Toledo Bend Reservoir** impounds 4.47 million acre-feet of water on the Sabine in Newton, Panola, Sabine, and Shelby counties. It is the **largest lake** lying wholly or partly in Texas and the **9th-largest reservoir (in capacity by volume) in the United States.** This is a joint project of Texas and Louisiana, through the **Sabine River Authority.**

## Red River

The Red River, with a length of **1,290 miles** from its headwaters, is exceeded in length only by the Rio Grande among rivers associated with Texas. Its original source is water in Curry County, New Mexico, near the Texas boundary, forming a definite channel as it crosses Deaf Smith County, Texas, in tributaries that flow into the **Prairie Dog Town Fork of the Red River.** These waters carve the spectacular **Palo Duro Canyon** of the High Plains before the Red River leaves the **Caprock Escarpment,** flowing eastward.

Where the Red River crosses the 100th meridian at the botton of the Panhandle, the river becomes the **Texas-Oklahoma boundary** and is soon joined by Buck Creek to form the main channel, according to the U.S. Geological Survey. Its length in Texas is **695 miles,** before it flows into Arkansas, where it swings south to flow through Louisiana.

The Red River, which drains 24,297 square miles in Texas, is a part of the **Mississippi drainage basin,** and at one time it emptied all of its water into the Mississippi. In recent years, however, part of its water, especially at flood stage, has flowed to the Gulf via the **Atchafalaya River** in Louisiana.

The Red River takes its name from the red color of the current. This caused every explorer who came to its banks to call it "red" regardless of the language he spoke — **Río Rojo** or **Río Roxo** in Spanish, **Riviere Rouge** in French. At an early date, the river became the axis for French advance from Louisiana northwestward as far as present-day Montague County. There was consistent **early navigation** of the river from its mouth on the Mississippi to Shreveport, above which navigation was blocked by a **natural log raft.**

A number of important gateways into Texas from the North were established along the stream, such as **Pecan Point** and **Jonesborough** in Red River County, **Colbert's Ferry** and **Preston** in Grayson County, and later, **Doan's Store Crossing** in Wilbarger County. The river was a menace to the early traveler because of both its variable current and its **quicksands,** which brought disaster to many a trail-herd cow, as well as ox team and covered wagon.

The largest water conservation project on the Red River is **Lake Texoma,** with a conservation storage capacity of 2.51 million acre-feet.

Red River water's high content of salt and other minerals limits its usefulness along its upper reaches. Ten **salt springs** and tributaries in Texas and Oklahoma contribute most of these minerals.

The uppermost tributaries of the Red River in Texas are **Tierra Blanca Creek,** which rises in Curry County, N.M., and flows easterly across Deaf Smith and Randall counties to meet **Palo Duro Creek** and form the **Prairie Dog Town Fork** a few miles east of Canyon.

Other principal tributaries in Texas are the **Pease** and the **Wichita** in North Central Texas and the **Sulphur** in Northeast Texas, which flows through **Wright Patman Lake,** then into the Red River after it has crossed the boundary line into Arkansas.

The last major tributary in Northeast Texas is the **Cypress Creek system,** which flows into Louisiana before joining with the Red River. Major reservoirs in this basin are **Lake O' the Pines** and **Caddo Lake.**

From Oklahoma, the principal tributary is the **Washita,** which has its headwaters in Roberts County, Texas. The **Ouachita,** a river with the same pronunciation though spelled differently, is the principal tributary to the Red River's lower course in Arkansas.

The Red River **boundary dispute,** a long-standing feud between Oklahoma and Texas, was finally settled in **2000** when the boundary was set at the vegetation line on the south bank, except for Lake Texoma, where the boundary was set within the channel of the lake.

## Canadian River

The Canadian River heads near **Raton Pass** in northern New Mexico near the Colorado boundary line and flows into Texas on the west line of Oldham County. It crosses the Texas Panhandle into Oklahoma and there flows into the Arkansas River, a total distance of **906 miles.** It drains 12,865 square miles in Texas, and much of its **213-mile course across the Panhandle** is in a deep gorge.

A tributary, the **North Canadian River,** drips briefly into the Texas Panhandle in Sherman County before it joins the main channel in Oklahoma.

One of several theories as to how the Canadian got its name is that some early explorers thought it flowed into Canada. **Lake Meredith,** formed by **Sanford Dam,** provides water for several Panhandle cities.

Because of the **deep gorge** and the **quicksand** that occurs in many places, the Canadian River has been a particularly difficult stream to bridge. It is known, especially in its lower course in Oklahoma, as outstanding among the streams of the country for the great amount of quicksand in its channel. ☆

*The old railroad trestle over Big Cypress Bayou in Jefferson, Marion County. Photo by Jerry Lentz.*

# Secondary Streams of Texas

In addition to the principal rivers just discussed, Texas has many other streams of various size. The following list gives a few of these streams as designated by the U.S. Geological Survey, with additional information from the new Handbook of Texas and previous Texas Almanacs.

**Alamito Creek** — Formed by confluence of North, South forks 3 mi. N Marfa in Presidio County. Flows SE 82 mi. to Rio Grande 5 mi. S Presidio.

**Angelina River** — Rises in central Rusk County; flows SE 120 mi. through Cherokee, Nacogdoches, Angelina, San Augustine counties into Sam Rayburn Reservoir, then into Jasper County to the Neches River 12 mi. west of Jasper. A meandering stream through forested country.

**Aransas River** — Formed 2 mi. N Skidmore in SC Bee County by union of Poesta and Aransas creeks; flows SE 40 mi. forming boundary between San Patricio and Refugio counties; then briefly into Aransas County where it empties into Copano Bay.

**Atascosa River** — Formed NW Atascosa County by confluence of North, West prongs, flows SE 92 mi. through Atascosa and Live Oak counties into Frio River 2 mi. NW Three Rivers.

**Attoyac Bayou** — Rises 2.8 mi. NE Mount Enterprise in SE Rusk County; flows SE 67 mi. through Shelby, San Augustine and Nacogdoches counties into Angelina River at Sam Rayburn Reservoir.

**Barton Creek** — Rises NE of Henly in NW Hays County; flows E 40 mi. through Travis County to Colorado River at Lady Bird Lake in Austin.

**Beals Creek** — Formed by confluence of Sulphur Springs and Mustang draws 4 mi. W Big Spring SW Howard County; flows E 55 mi. into Mitchell County to mouth on Colorado River.

**Big Cypress Creek** — Forms in SE Hopkins County E of Pickton; flows SE 60 mi. to mouth on Big Cypress Bayou 3 mi. E Jefferson in Marion County and just before the bayou flows into Caddo Lake. The creek forms the boundary lines between Camp and Titus, Camp and Morris, and Morris and Upshur counties. It passes through Lake Cypress Springs, Lake Bob Sandlin, and Lake O' the Pines, and is part of the Red River drainage basin.

**Blackwater Draw** — Rises in Curry County, N.M.; flows into Texas in extreme NW Bailey County; flows SE through Lamb, Hale, and Lubbock counties to junction with Yellow House Draw to form North Fork of the Double Mountain Fork Brazos River. Length, 100 mi.

**Blanco Creek** — Rises near the intersection of Bee, Goliad and Karnes county lines in extreme S Karnes County; flows SE 45 mi. forming boundary of Bee and Goliad counties. Joins Medio Creek in Refugio County to form Mission River.

**Blanco Creek** — Rises E of Concan in Uvalde County; flows S 44 mi. to Frio River.

**Blanco River** — Rises W Lindendale in NE Kendall County; flows SE 64 mi. through Blanco and Hay counties; joins San Marcos River, a tributary of the Guadalupe; fed by many springs.

**Bosque River** — Flows from Lake Waco in McLennan County 5 mi. into Brazos River.

**Bosque River, North** — Formed at Stephenville by the union of North, South forks in Erath County; flows generally SE 96 mi. through Hamilton, Bosque and McLennan counties into Lake Waco.

**Bosque River, South** — Rises near Coryell-McLennan county line; flows NE 24 mi. into Lake Waco.

**Brady Creek** — Rises 14 mi. SW Eden in SW Concho County; flows 90 mi. through McCulloch and San Saba counties into San Saba River 10 mi. SW of Richland Springs.

**Brazos River, Clear Fork** — Rises 8 mi. E Snyder in Scurry County; flows NE 180 mi. through Fisher, Jones, Haskell, Throckmorton, Shackelford and Stephens counties into Brazos River in S Young County; drainage area 5,728 sq. mi.

**Brazos River, Double Mountain Fork** — Rises 12 mi. SE Tahoka, Lynn County; flows E 175 mi. through Garza, Kent, Fisher and Haskell counties to confluence with Salt Fork of the Brazos, north of Old Glory in Stonewall County.

**Brazos River, North Fork Double Mountain Fork**— Formed by union of Yellow House and Blackwater draws in Lubbock; flows SE 75 miles through Crosby, Garza and Kent counties to junction with Double Mountain Fork Brazos River.

**Brazos River, Salt Fork** — Rises in SE Crosby County;

flows 150 mi. through Garza and Kent counties to confluence with Double Mountain Fork in NE Stonewall County to form the main stream of Brazos River.

**Buck Creek** — Also called Spiller Creek. Rises SE Donley County; flows SE 49 mi. through Collingsworth and Childress counties to Texas-Oklahoma boundary; then 3 mi. through Oklahoma to junction with Prairie Dog Town Fork of Red River NW Hardeman County to form main stream of the Red River.

**Buffalo Bayou** — Rises in extreme N Fort Bend County; flows E 46 mi. through Houston into San Jacinto River in Harris County. Part of Houston Ship Channel.

**California Creek** — Rises 10 mi. NE Roby in Fisher County; flows NE 70 mi. through Jones County into Paint Creek in E Haskell County.

**Caney Creek** — Rises near Wharton in Wharton County; flows 75 mi. through Matagorda County into east end of Matagorda Bay. Centuries ago, the current Caney Creek channel was the channel for the Colorado River.

**Capote/Wildhorse Draw** — Rises N of Van Horn in Culberson County; runs 86 mi. S through Jeff Davis County to SW of Marfa in Presidio County. One of a number of streams in this area with no outlet to the sea.

**Cedar Bayou** — Rises 11 mi. NW Liberty in Liberty County; flows 46 mi. S as boundary between Harris County and Liberty and Chambers counties, and into Trinity Bay.

**Chambers Creek** — Formed SW Waxahachie in Ellis County by union North, South forks; flows SE 45 mi. through Navarro County into Richland Creek at Richland-Chambers Reservoir.

**Cibolo Creek** — Rises 7 mi. W Boerne in Kendall County; flows SE through Bexar, Comal, Guadalupe and Wilson counties into San Antonio River in Karnes County; 96 mi. in length. Spring-fed, perennially flowing stream.

**Coleto Creek** — Formed SW of Mission Valley in NW Victoria County by union of Twelve Mile and Fifteen Mile creeks forming boundary between Victoria and Goliad counties. From Coleto Creek Reservoir flows to Guadalupe River in Victoria County.

**Comal River** — Rises in Comal Springs in City of New Braunfels and flows SE about 2.5 miles to Guadalupe River. Shortest river in Texas.

**Concho River** — Formed at San Angelo by conjunction North, South Concho rivers; flows E 24 mi. through Tom Green County, then 29 mi. through Concho County into Colorado River 12 m. NE Paint Rock. Drainage basin, including North and South Concho, 6,613 sq. mi. A spring-fed stream.

**Concho River, Middle** — Rises SW Sterling County; flows S, then E 66 mi. through Tom Green panhandle, Irion and Reagan counties into South Concho River at Lake Nasworthy near Tankersley in Tom Green County.

**Concho River, North** — Rises in S Howard County; flows 137 mi. through Glasscock, Sterling and Coke counties to confluence with South Concho to form Concho River in Tom Green County. Drainage basin, 1,510 sq. mi.

**Concho River, South** — Rises in C Schleicher County; flows N through Lake Nasworthy to confluence with North Concho River in Tom Green County; length, 41 mi.; drainage basin area 3, 866 sq. mi. Perennial flow from springs.

**Cowleech Fork Sabine River** — Rises 2 mi. NW Celeste NW Hunt County; flows SE 40 mi. to Lake Tawakoni.

**Deep Creek** — Rises SE Baird, Callahan County; flows N 55 mi. into Hubbard Creek in Shackelford County near McCatherine Mountain.

**Deep Creek** — Rises 4 mi. N Fluvanna NW Scurry County; flows SSE 70 mi. to mouth on Colorado River in extreme N Mitchell County.

**Delaware River** — Rises eastern slope Delaware Mountains in N Culberson County; flows in NE course; crosses Texas-New Mexico state line and enters Pecos River; length, 50 mi.

**Devils River** — Formed SW Sutton County by union Dry Devils River and Granger Draw; flows SE 95 mi. through Val Verde County into Rio Grande at Amistad Reservoir. Spring-fed, perennially flowing stream throughout most of its course.

**Elm Creek** — Rises 3 mi. SE Nolan in Nolan County; flows NE 60 mi., passes through Lake Abilene, Buffalo Gap and Abilene in Taylor County and through Lake Fort Phantom Hill into Clear Fork Brazos River near Nugent SE Jones County.

**Frio River** — Formed at Leakey in Real County by union of West and East Frio rivers; flows S 190 mi. through Uvalde, Medina, Frio, La Salle, McMullen counties (Choke Canyon Reservoir); joins Nueces River S of Three Rivers in Live Oak County. Drainage area, 7,310 sq. mi. Fed by springs in northern part, where it flows through picturesque canyon.

**Greens Bayou** — Rises 9 mi. W Aldine, C Harris County; flows ESE into Houston Ship Channel; 42 mi. long.

**Hondo Creek** — Rises 7.5 mi. NW Tarpley C Bandera County; flows SSE 67 mi. through Medina and Frio counties to Frio River 5 mi. NW Pearsall.

**Howard Draw** — Rises at Crockett-Reagan county line; flows SSW 45 mi. through Val Verde County to Pecos River near Pandale.

**Hubbard Creek** — Rises 3 mi. NW Baird N Callahan County; flows NE 62 mi. through Shackelford County; then into Stephens County (Hubbard Creek Reservoir) and joins Clear Fork of the Brazos River 10 NW Breckenridge.

**James River** — Rises SE Kimble County; flows NE 37 mi. to join Llano River in Mason County.

**Jim Ned Creek** — Rises 10 mi. NW Tuscola SC Taylor County; flows SE 71 mi. through Callahan and Coleman counties to Brown County to join Pecan Bayou, a tributary of Colorado River.

**Johnson Draw** — Rises NE Crockett County; runs SSE 66 miles to mouth on Devils River in Val Verde County.

**Lampasas River** — Rises NW Mills County; flows SE 100 miles through Hamilton, Lampasas, Burnet and Bell counties (Stillhouse Hollow Lake); unites with Leon River to form Little River.

**Leon River** — Formed by confluence North, Middle and South Forks in NC Eastland County; flows SE 185 mi. through Comanche, Hamilton and Coryell counties to junction with Lampasas River to form Little River in Bell County.

**Leona River** — Rises N Uvalde in central Uvalde County; flows SE 83 mi. through Zavala County into Frio River in Frio County.

**Limpia Creek** — Heads in the Davis Mountains on the NE slope of Mount Livermore in Jeff Davis County and flows 52 mi. E, NE and E through Limpia Canyon to disappear at the head of Barrilla Draw in Pecos County. Part of course through Limpia Canyon noted for its scenic beauty.

**Little Brazos River** — Rises 5 mi. SW Thornton, SW Limestone County; flows 72 mi. SE through Falls and Robertson counties into Brazos River in Brazos County.

**Little River** — Formed central Bell County by union Leon, Lampasas rivers; flows 75 mi. SE through Milam County into Brazos River.

**Llano River** — Formed C Kimble County by union North, South Llano rivers; flows E 100 mi. through Mason, Llano counties to Colorado River. Drainage area, including North, South Llano rivers, 4,460 sq. mi. A spring-fed stream of the Edwards Plateau, known for scenic beauty.

**Llano River, North** — Rises C Sutton County; flows E 40 mi. to union with South Llano River at Junction in Kimble County.

**Llano River, South** — Rises in NC Edwards County; flows 55 mi. NE to confluence with North Llano River at Junction in Kimble County.

**Los Olmos Creek** — Rises central Duval County; flows SE 71 mi. through Jim Wells and Brooks counties; forms boundary between Kenedy and Kleberg counties; into Baffin Bay.

**Madera Canyon** — Rises N slope Mount Livermore, Jeff Davis County, at altitude of 7,500 ft.; flows 40 mi. NE to join Aguja Creek at Reeves County line to form Toyah Creek, tributary through Pecos River to Rio Grande. Intermittent stream. Noteworthy for its beauty.

**Medina River** — Rises in North, West prongs in W Bandera County; flows SE 116 mi. through Medina and Bexar counties to San Antonio River. A spring-fed stream. Scenically beautiful along upper course.

**Medio Creek** — Rises S Karnes County; flows SE 2 mi. through Karnes County, then 7 mi. along boundary Karnes and Bee counties, then SE 37 mi. through Bee County, SE 7 mi. through Refugio County to junction with Blanco Creek to form Mission River.

**Mission River** — Formed by confluence of Blanco and Medio creeks in C Refugio County; flows SE 24 mi. to mouth on Mission Bay, an inlet of Copano Bay.

**Mulberry Creek** — Rises NW Armstrong County at Fairview; flows SE 58 mi. through Donley and Briscoe counties into Prairie Dog Town Fork Red River in NW Hall County.

**Navasota River** — Rises SE Hill County; flows SE 125 mi. through Limestone County and along boundary Leon, Madison, Robertson, Brazos and Grimes counties to Brazos River near Navasota.

**Navidad River** — Forms at juncture of East and West Navidad rivers in NE Lavaca County; flows 74 mi. through Lavaca and Jackson counties into Lake Texana near Ganado; then joins Lavaca River.

**Nolan River** — Rises in NW Johnson County; flows S 30 mi. through Lake Pat Cleburne and into Hill County where is empties into Brazos River at Lake Whitney.

**Onion Creek** — Rises 1 mi. W of Hays-Blanco county line SE Blanco County; flows SE 37 mi. through N Hays County; then 22 mi. through S Travis County into Colorado River near Garfield.

**Paint Creek** — Rises in extreme NW Jones County near Tuxedo; flows NE, then SE 53 mi. through SE corner of Stonewall County; then across S Haskell County (Lake Stamford) and into W Throckmorton County to mouth on Clear Fork Brazos River.

**Palo Blanco Creek** — Rises SE Hebbronville in N Jim Hogg County; flows SE 59 mi. through Duval and Brooks, where it passes through Laguna Salada; then into NW Kenedy County.

**Palo Duro Creek** — Rises in W Deaf Smith County; flows E 45 mi. into C Randall County to junction with Tierra Blanca Creek near Canyon to form the Prairie Dog Town Fork of the Red River. Lends its name to the notable canyon.

**Paluxy River** — Formed in E Erath County by convergence of North and South branches at Bluff Dale; flows SE 29 mi. through Hood and Somervell counties to mouth on Brazos River. Dinosaur Valley State Park at a large bend of the river in Somervell County is site of 100-million-year-old dinosaur tracks.

**Pease River** — Formed by union of North and Middle Pease rivers in NE Cottle County; flows E 100 mi. through Hardeman, Foard and Wilbarger counties into Red River 8 mi. NE of Vernon.

**Pease River, Middle** — Rises 8 mi. NW Matador in WC Motley County; flows E 63 miles into North Pease River to form the Pease River in NE Cottle County.

**Pease River, North** — Rises 9 mi. SE Cedar Hill in E Floyd County; flows E 60 mi. through Motley, Hall and Cottle counties. Joins Middle Pease to form Pease River.

**Pease River, South** — Also called Tongue River. Rises 11 mi. SW Roaring Springs in SW Motley County; flows ENE 40 mi. to mouth on Middle Pease River in W Cottle County.

**Pecan Bayou** — Formed by union of South, North prongs in SC Callahan County; flows SE 90 mi. through Coleman, Brown (Lake Brownwood) and Mills counties into Colorado River SW Goldthwaite. Westernmost bayou.

**Pedernales River** — Rises NE corner of Kerr County; flows E 106 mi. through Kimble, Gillespie, Blanco, Hays and Travis counties into Colorado River at Lake Travis. Spring-fed; a beautiful stream.

**Pine Island Bayou** — Rises near Rye NE Liberty County; flows 76 mi. SE through Hardin and Jefferson counties into Neches River.

**Red River, Prairie Dog Town Fork** — Formed by union of Palo Duro and Tierra Blanca creeks in Randall County; flows E 160 mi. through Armstrong, Briscoe, Hall, and Childress counties to junction with Buck Creek to form Red River in NW corner of Hardeman County. Palo Duro Canyon is along course of this stream as it descends from Great Plains.

**Red River, North Fork** — Rises W Gray County; flows SE 180 mi. through Wheeler County into Oklahoma to junction with the Red River NE Vernon in Wilbarger County.

**Red River, Salt Fork** — Rises N Armstrong County; flows SE 155 mi. through Donley and Collingsworth counties and into Oklahoma. It joins the Red River opposite the northernmost point of Wilbarger County.

**Richland Creek** — Rises 3.5 mi. E Itasca N Hill County; flows E 50 mi. through Ellis and Navarro counties, through Na-

*Bicyclists along the Trinity River in Fort Worth.*
*Photo by Ron Billings; Texas A&M Forest Service.*

varro Mills Lake and Richland-Chambers Reservoir; then into the Trinity River in Freestone County.

**Running Water Draw** — Rises 24 mi. WNW Clovis, N.M.; flows ESE into Texas in C Parmer County; then through Castro, Lamb, Hale and Floyd counties to join Callahan Draw 8 mi. W Floydada at head of White River, a tributary of the Brazos River.

**Sabana River** — Rises at Callahan-Eastland county line; flows SE 50 through Comanche County into Leon River at Proctor Lake.

**Sabinal River** — Rises 7 mi. N Vanderpool in NW Bandera County; flows S 60 mi. to junction with Frio River in SE Uvalde County. The West Sabinal River, which rises in Real County, joins the main stream at the Bandera-Uvalde county line.

**San Bernard River** — Rises 1 mi. S New Ulm in W Austin County; flows SE, forming boundary Austin and Colorado counties, 31 mi.; Austin and Wharton counties, 8 mi.; Wharton and Fort Bend counties, 28 mi.; approaches Gulf of Mexico in Brazoria County. Total length, 120 mi. (For more than 100 years locals have reported hearing the wail of a violin from the river. The mystery has never been solved, although some say the musical sounds are caused by escaping gas. The phenomenon has caused the stream to be called the Singing River — *Handbook of Texas.*)

**San Gabriel River** — Formed at Georgetown in C Williamson County by union of North and South forks; flows NE 50 mi. into Milam County to join Little River. Originally called San Xavier River.

**San Jacinto River, East** — Rises E Walker County; flows SE and S 69 mi. through San Jacinto, Liberty, Montgomery and Harris counties into Lake Houston and San Jacinto River.

**San Jacinto River, West** — Rises E Grimes County NE Shiro; flows SE 90 mi. through Walker County; into Lake Conroe in Montgomery County; then through Montgomery County to Lake Houston in Harris County.

**San Marcos River** — Formed near N limits City of San Marcos, Hays County, by several large springs, although watershed extends about 10 mi. NE of springs; Blanco River joins the San Marcos River 4 mi. downstream; flows SE 59 mi. as boundary between Guadalupe and Caldwell counties; then through Gonzales County to join Guadalupe River 2 mi. W Gonzales.

**Sandy Creek** — Rises SW Colorado County; flows SSE 42 mi. through Lavaca, Wharton and Jackson counties into Lake Texana.

**San Saba River** — Formed W Fort McKavett at Schleicher-Menard county line by union of North Valley and Middle Valley prongs; flows NE 140 mi. through Menard, Mason, McCulloch and San Saba counties into Colorado River 8 mi. NE San Saba. One of the picturesque streams of the Edwards Plateau.

**Spring Creek** — Rises NE Waller County near Fields Store; flows E 64 mi. forming boundary between Waller and Harris counties, and Montgomery and Harris counties to junction with West Fork San Jacinto River and Lake Houston.

**Sulphur River** — Formed E Delta County by junction North, South branches; flows E 183 miles forming boundary between Franklin and Red River counties; Titus and Red River counties; Morris and Red River and Bowie counties; then between Bowie and Cass counties, where it flows into Wright Patman Lake; continues on into Red River in S Miller County, Ark.

**Sulphur River, North** — Rises 1 mi. SW Gober S Fannin County; flows SE, E 54 mi. as boundary between Delta and Lamar counties and to union with South Sulphur River to form Sulphur River.

**Sulphur River, South** — Rises N Leonard S Fannin County; flows ESE 50 mi. through Hunt County; then as boundary between Hopkins and Delta counties (through Cooper Lake) to union with North Sulphur to form Sulphur River.

**Sulphur Springs Draw** — Rises in E Lea County, N.M.; enters Texas W Yoakum County at Bronco; flows SE 100 mi. through Terry, Gaines, Dawson, Martin, and Howard counties to confluence with Mustang Creek to form Beals Creek, a tributary of Colorado River.

**Sweetwater Creek** — Rises 2 mi. W Maryneal C Nolan County; flows NE 45 mi. through Fisher and Jones counties into Clear Fork Brazos River.

**Terlingua Creek** — Rises WC Brewster County; flows S 83 mi. into Rio Grande just E Santa Elena Canyon.

**Tierra Blanca Creek** — Rises N Curry County, N.M.; flows E across Texas state line in SW Deaf Smith County and 75 mi. through Deaf Smith, Parmer and Randall counties to junction with Palo Duro Creek where it forms Prairie Dog Town Fork Red River.

**Toyah Creek** — Forms near boundary Jeff Davis-Reeves counties; flows NE 50 mi. into Pecos River NC Reeves County.

**Trinity River, Clear Fork** — Rises NW Poolville in NW Parker County; flows SE 56 mi. through Tarrant County into West Fork Trinity River at Fort Worth.

**Trinity River, East Fork** — Rises 1.5 mi. NW Dorchester in SC Grayson County; flows S 85 mi. through Collin County (Lake Lavon and Lake Ray Hubbard); then Rockwall and Dallas counties into Trinity River in SE Kaufman County.

**Trinity River, Elm Fork** — Rises 1 mi. NW Saint Jo in E Montague County; flows 85 mi. SE through Cooke, Denton counties (Ray Roberts Lake and Lewisville Lake) to junction with West Fork to form Trinity River proper at Irving in WC Dallas County.

**Trinity River, West Fork** — Rises in SC Archer County; flows SE 145 mi. through Jack, Wise (Lake Bridgeport) and Tarrant (Eagle Mountain Lake and Lake Worth) counties to conjunction with Elm Fork to form Trinity River proper in WC Dallas County.

**Tule Creek** — Formed in Swisher County by union of North, Middle and South Tule draws; flows E 40 mi. through Mackenzie Reservoir and Briscoe County into Prairie Dog Town Fork Red River. Remarkably beautiful Tule Canyon along lower course.

**Turkey Creek** — Rises near Turkey Mountain EC Kinney County; flows SE 54 mi. through Uvalde, Zavala, Dimmit counties to Nueces River.

**Washita River** — Rises SE Roberts County; flows E 35 mi. through Hemphill County to Oklahoma state line, then SE to Red River at Lake Texhoma. Total length, 295 mi.

**West Caney Creek** — Rises 1 mi. SW Normangee in SW Leon County; flows SW 11 mi. through NW Madison County to junction with Navasota River on Brazos county line. The historic Old San Antonio Road, a thoroughfare for early Spanish and French explorers, crossed the headwaters of the stream.

**White River** — Formed 8 mi. W Floydada in WC Floyd County by union of Running Water and Callahan draws; flows SE 62 mi. through Blanco Canyon and White River Lake in Crosby County; then through Garza and Kent counties into Salt Fork Brazos River; principal tributary to Salt Fork.

**Wichita River** — Formed NE Knox County by union North, South Wichita rivers; flows NE 90 mi. through Baylor (Lake Kemp and Lake Diversion), Archer, Wichita and Clay counties to Red River N Byers.

**Wichita River, Little** — Formed in C Archer County by union of its North, Middle and South forks; flows NE 62 mi. through Clay County (Lake Arrowhead) into Red River.

**Wichita River, North** — Rises 6 mi. E East Afton in NE Dickens County; flows E through King, Cottle, Foard counties; then as boundary for Foard and Knox counties; then briefly into Baylor County to junction with South Wichita River to form Wichita River proper NE Vera in Knox County. Length, 100 mi.

**Wichita River, South** — Rises 10 mi. E Dickens in EC Dickens County; flows E 85 mi. through King and Knox counties to junction with North Wichita to form Wichita River.

**Yellow House Draw** — Rises in SE Bailey County; flows SE 80 mi. through Cochran, Hockley and Lubbock counties to confluence with Blackwater Draw at Lubbock to form the North Fork of Double Mountain Fork Brazos River. ☆

*Campers enjoy a cool setting on the shore of the 64-acre, spring-fed lake in Tyler State Park in Smith County. Visitors can boat, fish, and swim in the lake; mountain bike; picnic; and camp. The park store rents all kinds of boats year-round. A fishing license is not required to fish from shore in a state park. Texas Parks and Wildlife Department photo.*

# Artificial Lakes and Reservoirs

*Sources: U.S. Geological Survey, Texas Water Development Board, New Handbook of Texas, Texas Parks & Wildlife, U.S. Army Corps of Engineers, previous Texas Almanacs, various river basin authorities, websites of owner of reservoirs.*

The large increase in the number of reservoirs in Texas during the past half-century has greatly improved water conservation and supplies.

As late as 1913, Texas had only four major reservoirs with a total storage capacity of 288,340 acre-feet. Most of this capacity was in Medina Lake in southwest Texas, with 254,000 acre-feet* capacity, created by a dam completed in May 1913.

By January 2012, Texas had 188 major water supply reservoirs (those with a normal capacity of 5,000 acre-feet or larger) and 21 major non-water supply reservoirs (those that do not have a water supply function). The 188 water supply reservoirs have a total conservation surface area of 1.67 million acres and an original conservation storage capacity of 35 million acre-feet (only Texas' share is counted in border reservoirs). The 21 non-water supply reservoirs have a total normal surface area of 62,079 acres and an original normal storage capacity of 760,000 acre-feet.

According to the U.S. Statistical Abstract of 2008, Texas has **5,607 square miles of inland water,** ranking it first in the 48 contiguous states, followed by Florida, with 5,373 sq. mi.; Minnesota, 4,782; and Louisiana, 4,433.

There are **6,976 reservoirs** in Texas with a normal storage capacity of 10 acre-feet or larger.

## Natural Lakes in Texas

There are many natural lakes in Texas, though none is of great size. The largest designated natural lake touching the border of Texas is Sabine Lake, into which the Sabine and Neches rivers discharge. It is more properly a bay of the Gulf of Mexico.

Also near the coast, in Calhoun County, is Green Lake, which has about 10,000 acre-feet of storage capacity. It is one of the state's largest natural freshwater lakes.

Caddo Lake, on the Texas-Louisiana border, was a natural lake originally, but its present capacity and surface area are largely due to dams built to raise the surface of the original body of water.

Natural Dam Lake, in Howard County, has a similar history to Caddo Lake.

In East Texas, there are many small natural lakes formed by "horse-shoe" bends that have been eliminated from the main channel of a river. There are also a number of these "horse-shoe" lakes along the Rio Grande in the Lower Valley, where they are called *resacas*.

On the South Plains and west of San Angelo are lakes, such as Big Lake in Reagan County, that are usually dry.

# List of Lakes and Reservoirs

The table that begins below lists lakes and reservoirs in Texas having more than 5,000 acre-feet of storage capacity. Those that are normally dry are in *italics.* Some industrial cooling reservoirs are not included in this table.

Conservation storage capacity as of 2015 is used; the surface area used is that area at conservation elevation only. Because sediment deposition constantly reduces reservoir volumes over time, these are figures from the most recent surveys available.

Various methods of computing capacity area are used, and detailed information may be obtained from the Texas Water Development Board in Austin, from the U.S. Army Corps of Engineers, or from local sources. Boundary reservoir capacities include water designated for Texas and non-Texas water, as well.

Information is in the following order: **(1)** Name of lake or reservoir; **(2)** year of first impounding of water; **(3)** county or counties in which it is located; **(4)** river or creek on which it is located; **(5)** location with respect to some city or town; **(6)** purpose of reservoir; **(7)** owner of reservoir.

Some of these items, when not listed, are not available. For the larger lakes and reservoirs, the dam impounding water to form the lake bears the same name, unless otherwise indicated.

| Lakes and Reservoirs, Date of Origin | Surface Area (acres) | Storage Capacity (acre-ft.*) |
|---|---|---|
| **Abilene, L.** — (1919) Taylor Co.; Elm Cr.; 6 mi. NW Tuscola; (M-In.-R); City of Abilene . . . . . . . . . . . . | 595 | 7,900 |
| *Addicks Reservoir — (1948) Harris Co.; South Mayde Cr.; 1 mi. E of Addicks; (FC only) USAE* . . . . . . . | 16,780 | 202,128 |
| **Alan Henry, L.**— (1993) Garza Co.; Double Mountain Fork Brazos River; 10 mi. E Justiceburg; (M-In.-Ir.); City of Lubbock . . . . . . . . . . . . . . . . . . . . . . . . . . . . . . . . . . . . . . . . . . . . . . . . . . . | 2,741 | 94,808 |
| **Alcoa L.** — (1952) Milam Co.; Sandy Cr.; 7 mi. SW Rockdale; (In.-R); Alcoa Aluminum (also called Sandow L.) . . . . . . . . . . . . . . . . . . . . . . . . . . . . . . . . . . . . . . . . . . . . . . . . . . . . . . | 914 | 15,650 |
| **Amistad Reservoir, International** — (1969) Val Verde Co.; Rio Grande; an international project of the U.S. and Mexico; 12 mi. NW Del Rio; (C-R-Ir.-P-FC); International Boundary and Water Commission (Texas' share of conservation capacity is 56.2 percent.) (Formerly Diablo Reservoir) . . . . | 66,465 | 1,840,849 |
| **Amon G. Carter, L.** — (1961) Montague Co.; Big Sandy Cr.; 6 mi. S Bowie; (M-In.); City of Bowie . . . . . . | 1,489 | 19,266 |
| **Anahuac, L.** — (1936, 1954) Chambers Co.; Turtle Bayou; near Anahuac; (Ir.-In.-Mi.); Chambers-Liberty Counties Navigation District. (also called Turtle Bayou Reservoir) . . . . . . . . . . . . . . . . . . | 5,035 | 33,348 |
| **Anzalduas Channel Dam** — Hidalgo Co.; Rio Grande; 11 mi. upstream from Hidalgo; (Ir.-FC); United States and Mexico . . . . . . . . . . . . . . . . . . . . . . . . . . . . . . . . . . . . . . . . . . . . . . . . . | 1,472 | 13,910 |
| **Aquilla L.** — (1983) Hill Co.; Aquilla Cr.; 10.2 mi. W of Hillsboro; (FC-M-Ir.-In.-R); USAE–Brazos R. Auth. . . . | 3,066 | 44,460 |
| **Arlington, L.** — (1957) Tarrant Co.; Village Cr.; 7 mi. W Arlington; (M-In.); City of Arlington . . . . . . . . . . | 1,926 | 40,188 |
| **Arrowhead, L.** — (1966) Clay-Archer counties.; Little Wichita R.; 13 mi. SE Wichita Falls; (M); City of Wichita Falls . . . . . . . . . . . . . . . . . . . . . . . . . . . . . . . . . . . . . . . . . . . . . . . . . . . . . . . . | 14,506 | 230,359 |
| **Athens, L.** — (1962) Henderson Co.; 8 mi. E Athens; (M-FC-R); Athens Municipal Water Authority (formerly Flat Creek Reservoir) . . . . . . . . . . . . . . . . . . . . . . . . . . . . . . . . . . . . . . . . . . . . | 1,799 | 29,503 |
| **Austin, L.** — (1893, 1915, 1939) Travis Co.; Colorado R.; W Austin city limits; (M-In.-P); City of Austin, leased to LCRA (Imp. by Tom Miller Dam) *(In 1893, the first dam was completed. It broke in 1900. In 1915, a second dam was partially built but not completed. In 1939, the present Tom Miller Dam was completed.)* | 1,589 | 23,972 |
| **Ballinger/Moonen, L.** — (1947) Runnels Co.; Valley Creek; 5 mi. W Ballinger; (M); City of Ballinger . . . . . . | 500 | 6,850 |
| **Balmorhea, L.** — (1917) Reeves Co.; Sandia Cr.; 3 mi. SE Balmorhea; (Ir.); Reeves Co. WID No. 1 | 573 | 6,350 |
| **Bardwell L.** — (1965) Ellis Co.; Waxahachie Cr.; 3 mi. SE Bardwell; (FC-C-R); USAE. . . . . . . . . . . | 3,138 | 46,122 |
| *Barker Reservoir — (1945) Harris Co.; above Buffalo Bayou; (FC only) USAE* . . . . . . . . . . . . . . . . | 17,225 | 206,860 |
| **Bastrop, L.** — (1964) Bastrop Co.; Spicer Cr.; 3 mi. NE Bastrop; (In.); LCRA . . . . . . . . . . . . . . . . | 906 | 16,590 |
| **Baylor Creek L.** — (1950) Childress Co.; 10 mi. NW Childress; (M-R); City of Childress . . . . . . . . . . . | 610 | 9,220 |
| **Belton L.** — (1954) Bell-Coryell counties; Leon R.; 3 mi. N. Belton; (M-FC-In.-Ir.); USAE–Brazos R. Auth. . . . | 12,135 | 435,225 |
| **Benbrook L.** — (1952) Tarrant Co.; Clear Fk. Trinity R.; 10 mi. SW Fort Worth; (FC-R); USAE . . . . . . . | 3,635 | 85,648 |
| **Big Creek Reservoir** — (1987) Delta Co; Big Creek; 1 mi. N Cooper; (M); City of Cooper . . . . . . . . . . | 512 | 4,890 |
| **Bivins L.** — (1927) Randall Co.; Palo Duro Cr.; 8 mi. NW Canyon; (M); Amarillo; City of Amarillo (also called Amarillo City Lake) . . . . . . . . . . . . . . . . . . . . . . . . . . . . . . . . . . . . . . . . . . . . | 379 | 5,122 |
| **Bob Sandlin, L.** — (1977) Titus-Wood-Camp-Franklin counties; Big Cypress Cr.; 5 mi. SW Mount Pleasant; (In.-M-R); Titus Co. FWSD No. 1 (Imp. by Fort Sherman Dam) . . . . . . . . . . . . . . . . . | 8,703 | 190,822 |
| **Bonham, L.** — (1969) Fannin Co.; Timber Cr.; 5 mi. NE Bonham; (M); Bonham Municipal Water Auth. . . . . . | 1,070 | 11,027 |
| **Brady Creek Reservoir** — (1963) McCulloch Co.; Brady Cr.; 3 mi. W Brady; (M-In.); City of Brady . . . . . . | 2,020 | 28,808 |
| **Brandy Branch Reservoir** — (1983) Harrison Co.; Brandy Br.; 10 mi. SW Marshall; (In.); AEP-Southwestern Electric Power Co. . . . . . . . . . . . . . . . . . . . . . . . . . . . . . . . . . . . . . . . . . | 1,242 | 29,513 |
| **Braunig L., Victor** — (1962) Bexar Co.; Arroyo Seco; 15 mi. SE San Antonio; (In.); Pub. Svc. Bd. of San Antonio . . . . . . . . . . . . . . . . . . . . . . . . . . . . . . . . . . . . . . . . . . . . . . . . . . . . . | 1,350 | 26,500 |
| **Brazoria Reservoir** — (1954) Brazoria Co.; off-channel reservoir; 1 mi. NE Brazoria; (In.); Dow Chemical Co. | 1,865 | 21,970 |
| **Bridgeport, L.** — (1932) Wise-Jack counties; W. Fk. of Trinity R.; 4 mi. W Bridgeport; (M-In.-FC-R); Tarrant Regional Water District . . . . . . . . . . . . . . . . . . . . . . . . . . . . . . . . . . . . . . . . . . | 11,954 | 366,236 |
| **Brownwood, L.** — (1933) Brown Co.; Pecan Bayou; 8 mi. N Brownwood; (M-In.-Ir.); Brown Co. WC&ID No. 1 | 6,443 | 128,839 |
| **Bryan L.** — (1977) Brazos Co.; unnamed stream; 6 mi. NW Bryan; (R-In.); City of Bryan . . . . . . . . . . | 829 | 15,227 |

*An acre-foot is the amount of water necessary to cover an acre of surface area with water one foot deep. The **years** in the table refer to first impounding of water. **Double years** refer to later, larger dams. **Abbreviations are:** L., lake; R., river; Co., county; Cr., creek; (C) conservation; (FC) flood control; (R) recreation; (P) power; (M) municipal; (D) domestic; (Ir.) irrigation; (In.) industry; (Mi.) mining, including oil production; (FH) fish hatchery; USAE, United States Army Corps of Engineers; WC&ID, Water Control and Improvement District; WID, Water Improvement District; USBR, United States Bureau of Reclamation; Auth., Authority; LCRA, Lower Colorado River Authority; TPWD, Texas Parks & Wildlife Dept.; USDA, United States Department of Agriculture; Imp., impounded.

| Lakes and Reservoirs, Date of Origin | Surface Area (acres) | Storage Capacity (acre-ft.*) |
|---|---|---|
| **Buchanan, L.** — (1937) Burnet-Llano-San Saba counties; Colorado R.; 13 mi. W Burnet; (M-Ir.-Mi-P); LCRA | 22,137 | 816,904 |
| **Buffalo Lake** — (1938) Randall Co.; Tierra Blanca Cr.; 2 mi. S. Umbarger; (R); U.S. Fish and Wildlife Service; (Imp. by Umbarger Dam) | 1,900 | 18,150 |
| **Caddo L.** — (1873, 1914, 1971) Harrison-Marion counties, Texas, and Caddo Parish, La. An original natural lake, whose surface and capacity were increased by construction of dams. . . . . . . (In November 1873, the U.S. Army used nitroglycerin charges to remove the last portion of the Red River raft, a natural logjam. This resulted in the gradual depletion of Caddo water. In 1914, a dam was completed near Mooringsport, La. In 1971, a larger replacement dam was completed.) | 26,800 | 129,000 |
| **Calaveras L.** — (1969) Bexar Co.; Calaveras Cr.; 15 mi. SE San Antonio; (In.); Pub. Svc. Bd. of San Antonio | 3,624 | 63,200 |
| **Camp Creek L.** — (1949) Robertson Co.; 13 mi. E Franklin; (R); Camp Creek Water Co. . . . . . . . . . . | 750 | 7,000 |
| **Canyon L.** — (1964) Comal Co.; Guadalupe R.; 12 mi. NW New Braunfels; (M-In.-P-FC); Guadalupe-Blanco R. Authority & USAE . . . . . . . . . . . . . . . . . . . . . . . . . . . . . | 8,308 | 378,852 |
| **Casa Blanca L.** — (1951) Webb Co.; Chacon Cr.; 3 mi. NE Laredo; (R); Webb Co.; (Imp. by Country Club Dam) . . . . . . . . . . . . . . . . . . . . . . . . . . . . . . . . . . | 1,680 | 20,000 |
| **Cedar Creek Reservoir** — (1965) Henderson-Kaufman counties; Cedar Cr.; 3 mi. NE Trinidad; (M-R); Tarrant Regional Water District; (also called Joe B. Hogsett, L.) . . . . . . . . . . . . . . . . . . . | 32,873 | 644,691 |
| **Champion Creek Reservoir** — (1959) Mitchell Co.; 7 mi. S. Colorado City; (M-In.); City of Colorado City . . | 1,561 | 41,580 |
| **Cherokee, L.** — (1948) Gregg-Rusk counties; Cherokee Bayou; 12 mi. SE Longview; (M-In.-R); Cherokee Water Co. . . . . . . . . . . . . . . . . . . . . . . . . . . . . . . . . . . . . | 3,467 | 39,023 |
| **Choke Canyon Reservoir** — (1982) Live Oak-McMullen counties; Frio R.; 4 mi. W Three Rivers; (M-In.-R-FC); City of Corpus Christi-USBR | 25,438 | 662,820 |
| **Cisco, L.** — (1923) Eastland Co.; Sandy Cr.; 4 mi. N. Cisco; (M); City of Cisco (Imp. by Williamson Dam) . . | 10,430 | 25,895 |
| **Cleburne, L. Pat** — (1964) Johnson Co.; Nolan R.; 4 mi. S. Cleburne; (M); City of Cleburne . . . . . . . . | 1,558 | 26,008 |
| **Clyde, L.** — (1970) Callahan Co.; N. Prong Pecan Bayou; 6 mi. S. Clyde; (M); City of Clyde and USDA Soil Conservation Service . . . . . . . . . . . . . . . . . . . . . . . . . . . . . . . . . . | 449 | 5,748 |
| **Coffee Mill L.** — (1939) Fannin Co.; Coffee Mill Cr.; 12 mi. NW Honey Grove; (R); U.S. Forest Service . . . | 650 | 8,000 |
| **Coleman, L.** — (1966) Coleman Co.; Jim Ned Cr.; 14 mi. N. Coleman; (M-In.); City of Coleman . . . . . . . | 1,811 | 38,076 |
| **Coleto Creek Reservoir** — (1980) Goliad–Victoria counties; Coleto Cr.; 12 mi. SW Victoria; (In); Guadalupe-Blanco River Auth. . . . . . . . . . . . . . . . . . . . . . . . . . . . . . . . . | 3,100 | 31,040 |
| **Colorado City, L.** — (1949) Mitchell Co.; Morgan Cr.; 4 mi. SW Colorado City; (M-In.-P); TXU . . . . . . . . | 1,612 | 31,485 |
| **Conroe, L.** — (1973) Montgomery-Walker counties; W. Fk. San Jacinto R.; 7 mi. NW Conroe; (M-In.-Mi.); San Jacinto River Authority, City of Houston and Texas Water Development Board . . . . . . | 20,118 | 416,177 |
| **Cooper, L./Olney** — (1953) Archer Co.; Mesquite Crk; 8 mi. E Megargel; (W-R); City of Olney; (see L. Olney) | 446 | 6,650 |
| **Cooper Lake** — (1991) Delta-Hopkins counties; Sulphur R.; 3 mi.SE Cooper; (FC-M-R); USAE; (also called Jim Chapman Lake). | 17,958 | 298,930 |
| **Corpus Christi, L.** — (1930) Live Oak-San Patricio-Jim Wells counties; Nueces R.; 4 mi. SW Mathis; (P-M-In.-Ir.-Mi.-R.); Lower Nueces River Water Supply District (Imp. by Wesley E. Seale Dam) . . . . . . | 18,700 | 256,732 |
| **Cox Creek Reservoir** — Calhoun Co.; Cox Creek; 2 mi. E Point Comfort; (In); Alcoa Alumninum; (Also called Raw Water Lake and Recycle Lake) . . . . . . . . . . . . . . . . . . . . . . . . . . | 541 | 5,034 |
| **Crook, L.** — (1923) Lamar Co.; Pine Cr.; 5 Mi. N. Paris; (M); City of Paris . . . . . . . . . . . . . . . . | 1,060 | 9,195 |
| **Cypress Springs, L.** — (1970) Franklin Co.; Big Cypress Cr.; 8 mi. SE Mount Vernon; (In-M); Franklin Co. Water Development and Texas Water Development Board (formerly Franklin Co. L.); (Imp. by Franklin Co. Dam) . . . . . . . . . . . . . . . . . . . . . . . . . . . . . . . . | 3,252 | 66,756 |
| **Daniel, L.** — (1948) Stephens Co.; Gunsolus Cr.; 7 mi. S Breckenridge; (M-In.); City of Breckenridge; (Imp. by Gunsolus Creek Dam) . . . . . . . . . . . . . . . . . . . . . . . . . . . . . . | 924 | 9,515 |
| **Davis, L.** — Knox Co.; Double Dutchman Cr.; 5 mi. SE Benjamin; (Ir); League Ranch . . . . . . . . . | 585 | 5,454 |
| **Delta Lake Res. Units 1 and 2** — (1939) Hidalgo Co.; Rio Grande (off channel); 4 mi. N. Monte Alto; (Ir.); Hidalgo-Willacy counties WC&ID No. 1 (formerly Monte Alto Reservoir) . . . . . . . . . . . . . . . | 2,371 | 14,000 |
| **Diversion, L.** — (1924) Archer-Baylor counties; Wichita R.; 14 mi. W Holliday; (M-In.); City of Wichita Falls and Wichita Co. WID No. 2 . . . . . . . . . . . . . . . . . . . . . . . . . . . . . . . | 3,397 | 35,324 |
| **Dunlap, L.** — (1928) Guadalupe Co.; Guadalupe R.; 9 mi. NW Seguin; (P); Guadalupe-Blanco R. Auth.; (Imp. by TP-1 Dam) . . . . . . . . . . . . . . . . . . . . . . . . . . . . . . . . . . . | 410 | 5,900 |
| **Eagle L.** — (1900) Colorado Co.; Colorado R. (off channel); in Eagle Lake; (Ir.); Lakeside Irrigation Co. . | 1,200 | 9,600 |
| **Eagle Mountain Lake** — (1934) Tarrant-Wise counties; West Fork Trinity R.; 14 mi. NW Fort Worth; (M-In.-Ir.); Tarrant Regional Water District | 8,694 | 179,880 |
| **Eagle Nest Lake** — (1951) Brazoria Co.; off-channel Brazos R.; 12 mi. WNW Angleton; (Ir.); T.M. Smith, et al. (also called Manor Lake) . . . . . . . . . . . . . . . . . . . . . . . . . . . . | — | 18,000 |
| **Eastman Lakes** — 8 lakes; Harrison Co.; Sabine R. basin; NW of Longview; Texas Eastman Co. . . . . . . | — | 8,135 |
| **Electra, L.** — (1950) Wilbarger Co.; Camp Cr. and Beaver Cr.; 7 mi. SW Electra; (In.-M); City of Electra . . . | 731 | 5,626 |
| **Ellison Creek Reservoir** — (1943) Morris Co.; Ellison Cr.; 8 mi. S. Daingerfield; (P-In.); Lone Star Steel . . | 1,516 | 24,700 |
| **Fairfield L.** — (1970) Freestone Co.; Big Brown Cr.; 11 mi. NE Fairfield; (In.); TXU; (formerly Big Brown Creek Reservoir) . . . . . . . . . . . . . . . . . . . . . . . . . . . . . . . . . . . | 2,159 | 44,169 |
| **Falcon Reservoir, International** — (1954) Starr-Zapata counties; Rio Grande; (International U.S.-Mexico); 3 mi. W Falcon Heights; (M-In.-Ir.-FC-P-R); International Boundary and Water Commission; (Texas' share of total conservation capacity is 58.6 percent) . . . . . . . . . . . . . . . . . . . . | 85,195 | 1,551,031 |

*An acre-foot is the amount of water necessary to cover an acre of surface area with water one foot deep. The **years** in the table refer to first impounding of water. **Double years** refer to later, larger dams. **Abbreviations are:** L., lake; R., river; Co., county; Cr., creek; (C) conservation; (FC) flood control; (R) recreation; (P) power; (M) municipal; (D) domestic; (Ir.) irrigation; (In.) industry; (Mi.) mining, including oil production; (FH) fish hatchery; USAE, United States Army Corps of Engineers; WC&ID, Water Control and Improvement District; WID, Water Improvement District; USBR, United States Bureau of Reclamation; Auth., Authority; LCRA, Lower Colorado River Authority; TPWD, Texas Parks & Wildlife Dept.; USDA, United States Department of Agriculture; Imp., impounded.

| Lakes and Reservoirs, Date of Origin | Surface Area (acres) | Storage Capacity (acre-ft.*) |
|---|---|---|
| **Fayette Co. Reservoir** — (1958) Fayette Co.; Cedar Cr.; 8.5 mi. E. La Grange; (In.); LCRA (also called Cedar Creek Reservoir) . . . . . . . . . . . . . . . . . . . . . . . . . . . . . . | 2,400 | 71,400 |
| **Forest Grove Reservoir** — (1982) Henderson Co.; Caney Cr.; 7 mi. NW Athens; (In.); TXU, Agent . . . . . | 1,502 | 20,038 |
| **Fort Phantom Hill, Lake** — (1938) Jones Co.; Elm Cr.; 5 mi. S. Nugent; (M-R); City of Abilene . . . . . . . | 4,213 | 70,030 |
| **Georgetown, L.** — (1980) Williamson Co.; N. Fk. San Gabriel R.; 3.5 mi. W Georgetown; (FC-M-In.); USAE | 1,287 | 36,823 |
| **Gibbons Creek Reservoir** — (1981) Grimes Co.; Gibbons Cr.; 9.5 mi NW Anderson; (In.); Texas Municipal Power Agency . . . . . . . . . . . . . . . . . . . . . . . . . . . . . . . . . . . . . . | 2,770 | 27,603 |
| **Gilmer Reservoir** — (2001) Upshur Co.; Kelsey Creek; 15 mi. N of Longview; 4 mi. W of Gilmer; (M); City of Gilmer . . . . . . . . . . . . . . . . . . . . . . . . . . . . . . . . . . . . . . . . . | 1,010 | 12,720 |
| **Gladewater, L.** — (1952) Upshur Co.; Glade Cr.; in Gladewater; (M-R); City of Gladewater . . . . . . . . . | 481 | 4,637 |
| **Gonzales, Lake** — (1931) Gonzales Co.; Guadalupe R.; 4.5 mi. SE Belmont; (P); Guadalupe-Blanco R. Auth. (also called H-4 Reservoir) . . . . . . . . . . . . . . . . . . . . . . . . . . . . . . . . . | 696 | 6,500 |
| **Graham, L.** — (1929) Young Co.; Flint and Salt creeks; 2 mi. NW Graham; (M-In.); City of Graham . . . . . | 2,444 | 45,288 |
| **Granbury, L.** — (1969) Hood Co.; Brazos R.; 8 mi. SE Granbury; (M-In.-Ir.-P); Brazos River Authority (Imp. by DeCordova Bend Dam) . . . . . . . . . . . . . . . . . . . . . . . . . . . . . . . | 7,945 | 128,046 |
| **Granger L.** — (1980) Williamson Co.; San Gabriel R.; 10 mi. NE Taylor; (FC-M-In.); USAE (formerly Laneport L.) . . . . . . . . . . . . . . . . . . . . . . . . . . . . . . . . . . . . | 4,159 | 51,822 |
| **Grapevine L.** — (1952) Tarrant-Denton counties; Denton Cr.; 2 mi. NE Grapevine; (M-FC-In.-R.); USAE . . . | 6,893 | 164,703 |
| **Greenbelt L.** — (1967) Donley Co.; Salt Fork of Red R.; 5 mi. N Clarendon; (M-In.); Greenbelt Municipal and Industrial Water Auth. . . . . . . . . . . . . . . . . . . . . . . . . . . . . . . . . . | 2,025 | 59,968 |
| **Greenville City Lakes** — 6 lakes; Hunt Co.; Conleech Fork, Sabine R.; 2 mi. Greenville; (M-Other); City of Greenville . . . . . . . . . . . . . . . . . . . . . . . . . . . . . . . . . . | — | 6,864 |
| **Halbert, L.** — (1921) Navarro Co.; Elm Cr.; 4 mi. SE Corsicana; (M-In-R); City of Corsicana . . . . . . . . . | 603 | 6,033 |
| **Harris Reservoir, William** — (1947) Brazoria Co.; off-channel between Brazos R. and Oyster Cr.; 8 mi. NW Angleton; (In.); Dow Chemical Co. . . . . . . . . . . . . . . . . . . . . . . . . . . | 1,663 | 9,200 |
| **Hawkins, L.** — (1962) Wood Co.; Little Sandy Cr.; 3 mi. NW Hawkins; (FC-R); Wood County; (Imp. by Wood Co. Dam No. 3) . . . . . . . . . . . . . . . . . . . . . . . . . . . . . . . . . | 776 | 11,690 |
| **Holbrook, L.** — (1962) Wood Co.; Keys Cr.; 4 mi. NW Mineola; (FC-R); Wood County; (Imp. by Wood Co. Dam No. 2) . . . . . . . . . . . . . . . . . . . . . . . . . . . . . . . . . | 653 | 7,790 |
| **Hords Creek L.** — (1948) Coleman Co.; Hords Cr.; 5 mi. NW Valera; (M-FC); City of Coleman and USAE . . | 516 | 8,443 |
| **Houston L.** — (1954) Harris Co.; San Jacinto R.; 4 mi. N Sheldon; (M-In.-Ir.-M-R); City of Houston . . . . | 10,160 | 120,686 |
| **Houston County L.** — (1966) Houston Co.; Little Elkhart Cr.; 10 mi. NW Crockett; (M-In.); Houston Co. WC&ID No. 1 . . . . . . . . . . . . . . . . . . . . . . . . . . . . . . . . . . . . | 1,330 | 17,113 |
| **Hubbard Creek Reservoir** — (1962) Stephens Co.; 6 mi. NW Breckenridge; (M-In.-Mi.); West Central Texas Municipal Water Authority . . . . . . . . . . . . . . . . . . . . . . . . . . . | 14,922 | 322,280 |
| **Imperial Reservoir** — (1912) Reeves-Pecos counties; Pecos R.; 35 mi. N Fort Stockton; (Ir.); Pecos County WC&ID No. 2. . . . . . . . . . . . . . . . . . . . . . . . . . . . . . . . . . . | 1,530 | 6,000 |
| **Inks L.** — (1938) Burnet-Llano counties; Colorado R.; 12 mi. W Burnet; (M-Ir.-Mi.-P); LCRA . . . . . . . | 793 | 13,962 |
| **Jacksonville, L.** — (1959) Cherokee Co.; Gum Cr.; 5 mi. SW Jacksonville; (M-R); City of Jacksonville; (Imp. by Buckner Dam) . . . . . . . . . . . . . . . . . . . . . . . . . . . . . . . . . . | 1,164 | 25,670 |
| **J. B. Thomas, L.** — (1952) Scurry-Borden counties; Colorado R.; 16 mi. SW Snyder; (M- In.-R); Colorado River Municipal Water District; (Imp. by Colorado R. Dam) . . . . . . . . . . . . . . . | 7,282 | 199,931 |
| **J. D. Murphree Wildlife Management Area Impoundments** — Jefferson Co.; off-channel reservoirs between Big Hill and Taylor bayous; at Port Acres; (FH-R); TPWD (formerly Big Hill Reservoir) . . . . . . | 6,881 | 32,000 |
| **Joe Pool Lake** — (1986) Dallas-Tarrant-Ellis counties; Mountain Cr.; 14 mi. SW Dallas; (FC-M-R); USAE–Trinity River Auth. (formerly Lakeview Lake) . . . . . . . . . . . . . . . . . . . . . . . | 7,470 | 175,358 |
| **Johnson Creek Reservoir** — (1961) Marion Co.; 13 mi. NW Jefferson; (In.); AEP-Southwestern Electric Power Co. . . . . . . . . . . . . . . . . . . . . . . . . . . . . . . . . . . . . . . | 650 | 10,100 |
| **Kemp, L.** — (1923) Baylor Co.; Wichita R.; 6 mi. N Mabelle; (M-P-Ir.); City of Wichita Falls; Wichita Co. WID 2 | 15,357 | 268,811 |
| **Kickapoo, L.** — (1945) Archer Co.; N. Fk. Little Wichita R.; 10 mi. NW Archer City; (M); City of Wichita Falls . . . . . . . . . . . . . . . . . . . . . . . . . . . . . . . . . . . . . . . . | 5,864 | 86,345 |
| **Kiowa, L.** — (1969) Cooke Co.; Indian Cr.; 8 mi. SE Gainesville; (R); Lake Kiowa, Inc. . . . . . . . . . . . | 560 | 7,000 |
| **Kirby, L.** — (1928) Taylor Co.; Cedar Cr.; 5 mi. S. Abilene; (M); City of Abilene . . . . . . . . . . . . . . | 740 | 7,620 |
| **Kurth, L.** — (1950) Angelina Co.; off-channel reservoir; 8 mi. N Lufkin; (In.); Abitibi Consolidated Industries. . . . . . . . . . . . . . . . . . . . . . . . . . . . . . . . . . . . . . . | 726 | 14,769 |
| **Lady Bird Lake** (Town Lake) — (1960) Travis Co.; Colorado R.; within Austin city limits; (R); City of Austin . . | 468 | 6,409 |
| **Lake Creek L.** — (1952) McLennan Co.; Manos Cr.; 4 mi. SW Riesel; (In.); TXU . . . . . . . . . . . . . . | 550 | 8,400 |
| **Lake Fork Reservoir** — (1980) Wood-Rains counties; Lake Fork Cr.; 5 mi. W Quitman; (M-In.); Sabine River Authority. . . . . . . . . . . . . . . . . . . . . . . . . . . . . . . . . . . . . . | 27,264 | 636,133 |
| **Lake O' the Pines** — (1959) Marion-Upshur-Morris counties; Cypress Cr.; 9 mi. W Jefferson; (FC-C-R-In.-M); USAE; (Imp. by Ferrell's Bridge Dam) . . . . . . . . . . . . . . . . . . . . . . | 16,919 | 241,363 |
| **Lavon, L.** — (1953) Collin Co.; East Fk. Trinity R.; 2 mi. W Lavon; (M-FC-In.); USAE . . . . . . . . . . . | 20,559 | 406,388 |
| **Leon, Lake** — (1954) Eastland Co.; Leon R.; 7 mi. S Ranger; (M-In.); Eastland Co. Water Supply District . . | 1,590 | 26,476 |
| **Lewis Creek Reservoir** — Montgomery Co.; Lewis Cr.; 10 mi. NW Conroe; (In.); Energy . . . . . . . . . . | 1,010 | 16,400 |

*An acre-foot is the amount of water necessary to cover an acre of surface area with water one foot deep. The **years** in the table refer to first impounding of water. **Double years** refer to later, larger dams. **Abbreviations are:** L., lake; R., river; Co., county; Cr., creek; (C) conservation; (FC) flood control; (R) recreation; (P) power; (M) municipal; (D) domestic; (Ir.) irrigation; (In.) industry; (Mi.) mining, including oil production; (FH) fish hatchery; USAE, United States Army Corps of Engineers; WC&ID, Water Control and Improvement District; WID, Water Improvement District; USBR, United States Bureau of Reclamation; Auth., Authority; LCRA, Lower Colorado River Authority; TPWD, Texas Parks & Wildlife Dept.; USDA, United States Department of Agriculture; Imp., impounded.

| Lakes and Reservoirs, Date of Origin | Surface Area (acres) | Storage Capacity (acre-ft.*) |
|---|---|---|
| **Lewisville L.** — (1929, 1954) Denton Co.; Elm Fork of Trinity R.; 2 mi. NE Lewisville; (M-FC-In.-R); USAE; (also called Lake Dallas and Garza-Little Elm) . . . . . . . . . . . . . . . . . . . . . . . . . | 27,175 | 563,228 |
| **Limestone, L.** — (1978) Leon-Limestone-Robertson counties.; Navasota R.; 7 mi. NW Marquez; (M-In.-Ir.); Brazos River Authority . . . . . . . . . . . . . . . . . . . . . . . . . . . . . . . . . . . . . . | 12,486 | 203,780 |
| **Livingston, L.** — (1969) Polk-San Jacinto-Trinity-Walker counties; Trinity R.; 6 mi. SW Livingston; (M-In.-Ir.); City of Houston and Trinity River Authority . . . . . . . . . . . . . . . . . . . . . . . . . | 82,583 | 1,785,348 |
| **Loma Alta Lake** — Cameron Co.; off-channel Rio Grande; 8 mi. NE Brownsville; (M-In.); Brownsville Navigation District . . . . . . . . . . . . . . . . . . . . . . . . . . . . . . . . . . . . | 2,490 | 26,500 |
| **Lost Creek Reservoir** — (1990) Jack Co.; Lost Cr.; 4 mi. NE Jacksboro; (M); City of Jacksboro . . . . . . . | 413 | 11,950 |
| **Lyndon B. Johnson, L.** — (1951) Burnet-Llano counties; Colorado R.; 5 mi. SW Marble Falls; (P); LCRA; (Imp. by Alvin Wirtz Dam); (formerly Granite Shoals L.) . . . . . . . . . . . . . . . . . . . . . . . . | 6,024 | 111,633 |
| **Mackenzie Reservoir** — (1974) Briscoe Co.; Tule Cr.; 9 mi. NW Silverton; (M); Mackenzie Mun. Water Auth. | 896 | 46,450 |
| **Marble Falls, L.** — (1951) Burnet Co.; Colorado R.; 1.25 mi. SE Marble Falls; (P); LCRA; (Imp. by Max Starcke Dam) . . . . . . . . . . . . . . . . . . . . . . . . . . . . . . . . . . . . . . . . | 608 | 7,486 |
| **Martin Creek L.** — (1974) Rusk-Panola counties; Martin Cr.; 17 mi. NE Henderson; (P); TXU . . . . . . . . | 4,981 | 75,116 |
| **Medina L.** — (1913) Medina-Bandera counties; Medina R.; 8 mi. W Rio Medina; (Ir.); Bexar-Medina-Atascosa Co. WID No. 1 . . . . . . . . . . . . . . . . . . . . . . . . . . . . . . . . . . . . | 5,426 | 254,884 |
| **Meredith, L.** — (1965) Moore-Potter-Hutchinson counties; Canadian R.; 10 mi. NW Borger; (M-In.-FC-R); cooperative project for municipal water supply by Amarillo, Lubbock and other High Plains cities. Canadian R. Municipal Water Authority–USBR; (Imp. by Sanford Dam) . . . . . | 16,411 | 779,560 |
| **Millers Creek Reservoir** — (1990) Baylor-Throckmorton counties.; Millers Cr.; 9 mi. SE Goree; (M); North Central Texas Municipal Water Auth. and Texas Water Development Board . . . . . . . . . | 2,212 | 26,768 |
| **Mineral Wells, L.** — (1920) Parker Co.; Rock Cr.; 4 mi. E Mineral Wells; (M); Palo Pinto Co. Municipal Water District No. 1 . . . . . . . . . . . . . . . . . . . . . . . . . . . . . . . . . . . . . . | 646 | 6,760 |
| **Mitchell County Reservoir** — (1993) Mitchell Co.; branch of Beals Creek; (Mi.-In.); Colorado River Municiapl Water District . . . . . . . . . . . . . . . . . . . . . . . . . . . . . . . . . . . . . . | 1,463 | 27,266 |
| **Monticello Reservoir** — (1972) Titus Co.; Blundell Cr.; 2.5 mi. E. Monticello; (In.); TXU. . . . . . . . . . | 2,001 | 34,740 |

*An acre-foot is the amount of water necessary to cover an acre of surface area with water one foot deep. The **years** in the table refer to first impounding of water. **Double years** refer to later, larger dams. **Abbreviations are:** L., lake; R., river; Co., county; Cr., creek; (C) conservation; (FC) flood control; (R) recreation; (P) power; (M) municipal; (D) domestic; (Ir.) irrigation; (In.) industry; (Mi.) mining, including oil production; (FH) fish hatchery; USAE, United States Army Corps of Engineers; WC&ID, Water Control and Improvement District; WID, Water Improvement District; USBR, United States Bureau of Reclamation; Auth., Authority; LCRA, Lower Colorado River Authority; TPWD, Texas Parks & Wildlife Dept.; USDA, United States Department of Agriculture; Imp., impounded.

*Toledo Bend Reservoir was impounded in 1967 and touches Newton, Panola, Sabine, and Shelby counties. It is formed by the Sabine River. Photo by Ron Billings; Texas A&M Forest Service.*

| Lakes and Reservoirs, Date of Origin | Surface Area (acres) | Storage Capacity (acre-ft.*) |
|---|---|---|
| **Moss L., Hubert H.** — (1960) Cooke Co.; Fish Cr.; 10 mi. NW Gainesville; (M-In.); City of Gainesville . . . . | 1,140 | 24,155 |
| **Mountain Creek L.** — (1937) Dallas Co.; Mountain Cr.; 4 mi. SE Grand Prairie; (In.); TXU. . . . . . . . . . . | 2,696 | 22,850 |
| **Murvaul, L.** — (1958) Panola Co.; Murvaul Bayou; 10 mi. W Carthage; (M-In.-R); Panola Co. Fresh Water Supply District No. 1 . . . . . . . . . . . . . . . . . . . | 3,507 | 38,285 |
| **Mustang Lake East/West** — Brazoria Co.; Mustang Bayou; 6 mi. S Alvin; (Ir.-In.-R); Chocolate Bayou Land & Water Co. . . . . . . . . . . . . . . . | — | 6,451 |
| **Nacogdoches, L.** — (1976) Nacogdoches Co.; Bayo Loco Cr.; 10 mi. W Nacogdoches; (M); City of Nacogdoches . . . . . . . . . . . . . . . . . . . | 2,212 | 39,512 |
| **Nasworthy, L.** — (1930) Tom Green Co.; S Concho R.; 6 mi. SW San Angelo; (M-In.-Ir); City of San Angelo | 1,380 | 9,615 |
| **Natural Dam L.** — (1957, 1989) Howard Co.; Sulphur Springs Draw; 8 mi. W Big Spring; An original natural lake, whose surface and capacity were increased by construction of dams; (FC); Wilkinson Ranch & Colorado River Municipal Water District . . . . . . . . . . . . | 3,710 | 54,560 |
| **Navarro Mills L.** — (1963) Navarro-Hill counties; Richland Cr.; 16 mi. SW Corsicana; (M-FC); USAE . . . . | 4,736 | 49,827 |
| **Nocona, L.** — (1960) Montague Co.; 8 mi. NE Nocona; (M-In.-Mi.); North Montague County Water Supply District (also known as Farmers Creek Reservoir) . . . . . . . . . . . . . . . . . | 1,362 | 21,445 |
| **North Fk. Buffalo Creek Reservoir** — (1964) Wichita Co.; 5 mi. NW Iowa Park; (M); Wichita Co. WC&ID No.3 . . . . . . . . . . . . . . . . . . . . . | 1,500 | 15,400 |
| **North L.** — (1957) Dallas Co.; S. Fork Grapevine Cr.; 2 mi. SE Coppell; (In.); TXU . . . . . . . . . . | 800 | 9,400 |
| **Oak Creek Reservoir** — (1952) Coke Co.; 5 mi. SE Blackwell; (M-In.); City of Sweetwater . . . . . . . . . | 2,375 | 39,210 |
| **O. C. Fisher L.** — (1952) Tom Green Co.; N Concho R.; 3 mi. NW San Angelo; (M-FC-C- Ir.-R-In.-Mi); USAE; Upper Colorado River Auth. (formerly San Angelo L.) . . . . . . . . . . . . . . . . | 5,348 | 119,445 |
| **O. H. Ivie Reservoir** — (1990) Coleman-Concho-Runnels counties; 24 mi. SE Ballinger; (M-In.), Colorado R. Municipal Water District (formerly Stacy Reservoir) . . . . . . . . . . | 19,149 | 554,340 |
| *Olmos Reservoir* — *(1926) Bexar Co.; Olmos Cr.; in San Antonio; (FC only), City of San Antonio* . . . . . . | 1,050 | 15,500 |
| **Olney, L./Cooper**— (1935) Archer Co.; Mesquite Crk; 8 mi. E Megargel; (W-R); City of Olney; (see L. Cooper) . . . . . . . . . . . . . . . . . . . . . . | 446 | 6,650 |
| **Palestine, L.** — (1962) Anderson-Cherokee-Henderson-Smith counties; Neches R.; 4 mi. E Frankston; (M-In.-R); Upper Neches R. Municipal Water Auth.; (Imp. by Blackburn Crossing Dam) . . . . . . . | 22,656 | 373,199 |
| **Palo Duro Reservoir** — (1991) Hansford Co.; Palo Duro Cr.; 12 mi. N Spearman; (M-R); Palo Duro River Auth. . . . . . . . . . . . . . . . . . . . . . | 2,413 | 61,066 |
| **Palo Pinto, L.** — (1964) Palo Pinto Co.; 15 mi. SW Mineral Wells; (M-In.); Palo Pinto Co. Municipal Water District 1 . . . . . . . . . . . . . . . . . . . | 2,176 | 27,398 |
| **Pat Mayse L.** — (1967) Lamar Co.; Sanders Cr.; 2 mi. SW Arthur City; (M-In.-FC); USAE . . . . . . . . | 5,638 | 113,683 |
| **Pinkston Reservoir** — (1976) Shelby Co.; Sandy Cr.; 12.5 mi. SW Center; (M); City of Center; (formerly Sandy Creek Reservoir) . . . . . . . . . . . . . . . . . | 523 | 7,380 |
| **Possum Kingdom L.** — (1941) Palo Pinto-Young-Stephens-Jack counties; Brazos R.; 11 mi. SW Graford; (M-In.-Ir.-Mi.-P-R); Brazos R. Auth.; (Imp. by Morris Sheppard Dam) . . . . . . . . . | 16,716 | 540,340 |
| **Proctor L.** — (1963) Comanche Co.; Leon R.; 9 mi. NE Comanche; (M-In.-FC); USAE–Brazos River Auth. . . . . . . . . . . . . . . . . . . . . . | 4,615 | 54,762 |
| **Quitman, L.** — (1962) Wood Co.; Dry Cr.; 4 mi. N Quitman; (FC-R); Wood County; (Imp. by Wood Co. Dam No.1) . . . . . . . . . . . . . . . . . . | 814 | 7,440 |
| **Randell L.** — (1909) Grayson Co.; Shawnee Cr.; 4 mi. NW Denison; (M); City of Denison . . . . . . | 311 | 5,900 |
| **Ray Hubbard, L.** — (1968) Collin-Dallas-Kaufman-Rockwall counties; (formerly Forney Reservoir); E. Fork of Trinity R.; 15 mi. E Dallas; (M); City of Dallas . . . . . . . . . . . . . . . . | 20,963 | 452,040 |
| **Ray Roberts, L.** — (1987) Denton-Cooke-Grayson counties; Elm Fk. Trinity R.; 11 mi. NE Denton; (FC-M-D); City of Denton, Dallas, USAE; (also known as Aubrey Reservoir) . . . . . . . . . | 28,646 | 788,167 |
| **Red Bluff Reservoir** — (1937) Loving-Reeves counties, Texas; and Eddy Co.; N.M.; Pecos R.; 5 mi. N Orla; (Ir.-P); Red Bluff Water Power Control District. . . . . . . . . . | 7,495 | 152,335 |
| **Red Draw Reservoir** — (1985) Howard Co.; Red Draw; 5 mi. E Bi Spring; (Mi.-In.); Colorado River Municipal Water District . . . . . . . . . . . . . . . . . . | 374 | 8,538 |
| **Richland-Chambers Reservoir** — (1987) Freestone-Navarro counties; Richland Cr.; 20 mi. SE Corsicana; (M); Tarrant Regional Water District . . . . . . . . . . . . . . . . | 43,384 | 1,087,839 |
| **Rita Blanca, L.** — (1940) Hartley Co.; Rita Blanca Cr.; 2 mi. S Dalhart; (R) City of Dalhart . . . . . . . . | 524 | 12,050 |
| **River Crest L.** — (1953) Red River Co.; off-channel reservoir; 7 mi. SE Bogata; (In.); TXU . . . . . . . | 555 | 7,000 |
| **Sam Rayburn Reservoir** — (1965) Jasper-Angelina-Sabine-Nacogdoches-San Augustine counties; Angelina R.; (FC-P-M-In.-Ir.-R); USAE; (formerly McGee Bend Reservoir) . . . . . . . . | 112,590 | 2,857,077 |
| **San Bernard Reservoirs #1, #2, #3** — Brazoria Co.; Off-Channel San Bernard R.; 3 mi. N Sweeney; (In.); ConocoPhillips . . . . . . . . . . . . . . . . . | — | 8,610 |
| **Santa Rosa L.** — (1929) Wilbarger Co.; Beaver Cr.; 15 mi. S Vernon; (Mi.); W. T. Waggoner Estate . . . . | 1,500 | 11,570 |
| **Sheldon Reservoir** — (1943) Harris Co.; Carpenters Bayou; 2 mi. SW Sheldon; (R-FH); TPWD . . . . | 1,244 | 4,224 |
| **Smithers L.** — (1957) Fort Bend Co.; Dry Creek; 10 mi. SE Richmond; (In.); Texas Genco . . . . . . . | 2,480 | 18,700 |
| **Somerville, L.** — (1967) Burleson-Washington-Lee counties; Yegua Cr.; 2 mi. S Somerville; (M-In.-Ir.- FC); USAE–Brazos River Authority . . . . . . . . . . . . . . . . . | 10,843 | 147,104 |

*An acre-foot is the amount of water necessary to cover an acre of surface area with water one foot deep. The **years** in the table refer to first impounding of water. **Double years** refer to later, larger dams. **Abbreviations are:** L., lake; R., river; Co., county; Cr., creek; (C) conservation; (FC) flood control; (R) recreation; (P) power; (M) municipal; (D) domestic; (Ir.) irrigation; (In.) industry; (Mi.) mining, including oil production; (FH) fish hatchery; USAE, United States Army Corps of Engineers; WC&ID, Water Control and Improvement District; WID, Water Improvement District; USBR, United States Bureau of Reclamation; Auth., Authority; LCRA, Lower Colorado River Authority; TPWD, Texas Parks & Wildlife Dept.; USDA, United States Department of Agriculture; Imp., impounded.

| Lakes and Reservoirs, Date of Origin | Surface Area (acres) | Storage Capacity (acre-ft.*) |
|---|---|---|
| **South Texas Project Reservoir** — (1983) Matagorda Co.; off-channel Colorado R.; 16 mi. S Bay City; (In.); STP Nuclear Operating Co. | 7,000 | 202,600 |
| **Spence Reservoir, E. V.** — (1969) Coke Co.; Colorado R.; 2 mi. W. Robert Lee; (M-In.-Mi); Colorado R. Municipal Water District; (Imp. by Robert Lee Dam) | 14,640 | 517,272 |
| **Squaw Creek Reservoir** — (1983) Somervell-Hood counties; Squaw Cr.; 4.5 mi. N Glen Rose; (In.); TXU | 3,169 | 151,250 |
| **Stamford, L.** — (1953) Haskell Co.; Paint Cr.; 10 mi. SE Haskell; (M-In.); City of Stamford | 5,158 | 51,570 |
| **Steinhagen L., B. A.** — (1951) Tyler-Jasper counties; Neches R.; 1/2 mi. N Town Bluff; (FC-R-C); USAE; (also called Town Bluff Reservoir and Dam B. Reservoir); (Imp. by Town Bluff Dam) | 10,687 | 66,961 |
| **Stillhouse Hollow L.** — (1968) Bell Co.; Lampasas R.; 5 mi. SW Belton; (M-In.-Ir.-FC); USAE–Brazos River Authority; (also called Lampasas Reservoir) | 6,484 | 227,771 |
| **Striker Creek Reservoir** — (1957) Rusk-Cherokee counties; Striker Cr.; 18 mi. SW Henderson; (M-In.); Angelina-Nacogdoches WC&ID No. 1. | 1,920 | 22,934 |
| **Sulphur Springs, L.** — (1950) Hopkins Co.; White Oak Cr.; 2 mi. N Sulphur Springs; (M); Sulphur Springs Water District; (formerly called White Oak Creek Reservoir) | 1,340 | 17,747 |
| **Sulphur Springs Draw Reservoir** — (1992) Martin Co.; Sulphur Springs Draw; 12 mi. NE Stanton; (FC); Colorado River Municipal Water District | 970 | 7,997 |
| **Sweetwater, L.** — (1930) Nolan Co.; Bitter Creek; 6 mi. SE Sweetwater (M-R); City of Sweetwater. | 647 | 12,267 |
| **Tawakoni, L.** — (1960) Rains-Van Zandt-Hunt counties; Sabine R.; 9 mi. NE Wills Point; (M-In.-Ir-R); Sabine River Authority; (Imp. by Iron Bridge Dam) | 37,325 | 871,685 |
| **Terrell City L.** — (1955) Kaufman Co.; Muddy Cedar Cr.; 6 mi. E Terrell; (M-R); City of Terrell | 849 | 8,594 |
| **Texana, L.** — (1980) Jackson Co.; Navidad R. and Sandy Cr.; 6.8 mi. SE Edna; (M-Ir); USBR, Lavaca-Navidad R. Auth., Texas Water Dev. Bd.; (formerly Palmetto Bend Reservoir) | 9,676 | 159,640 |
| **Texoma, L.** — (1943) Grayson-Cooke counties, Texas; Bryan-Marshall-Love counties, Okla.; (Imp. by Denison Dam) on Red R. below confluence of Red and Washita rivers; (P-FC-C-R); USAE | 78,420 | 2,516,226 |
| **Toledo Bend Reservoir** — (1967) Newton-Panola-Sabine-Shelby counties; Sabine R.; 14 mi. NE Burkeville; (M-In.-Ir.-PR); Sabine River Authority (Texas' share of capacity is half amount shown) | 182,490 | 4,491,504 |
| **Tradinghouse Creek Reservoir** — (1968) McLennan Co.; Tradinghouse Cr.; 9 mi. E Waco; (In.); TXU | 2,010 | 35,110 |
| **Travis, L.** — (1942) Travis-Burnet counties; Colorado R.; 13 mi. NW Austin; (M-In.-Ir.- Mi.-P-FC-R); LCRA; (Imp. by Mansfield Dam) | 19,048 | 1,113,256 |
| **Trinidad L.** — (1923) Henderson Co.; off-channel reservoir Trinity R.; 2 mi. S. Trinidad; (P); TXU | 690 | 6,200 |
| **Truscott Brine L.** — (1987) Knox Co.; Bluff Cr.; 26 mi. NNW Knox City; (Chlorine Control); Red River Auth. | 3,146 | 111,147 |
| **Twin Buttes Reservoir** — (1963) Tom Green Co.; Concho R.; 8 mi. SW San Angelo; (M-In. -FC-Ir.-R.); City of San Angelo, USBR, Tom Green Co. WC&ID No. 1 | 8,445 | 182,454 |
| **Twin Oaks Reservoir** — (1982) Robertson Co.; Duck Cr.; 12 mi. N. Franklin; (In) TXU | 2,330 | 30,319 |
| **Tyler, L. /Lake Tyler East** — (1949/1967) Smith Co.; Prairie and Mud creeks.; 12 mi. SE Tyler; (M-In); City of Tyler; (Imp. by Whitehouse and Mud Creek dams) | 4,714 | 72,073 |
| **Upper Nueces L.** — (1926, 1948) Zavala Co.; Nueces R.; 6 mi. N Crystal City; (Ir.); Zavala-Dimmit Co. WID No. 1 | 316 | 5,200 |
| **Valley Acres Reservoir** — (1956) Hidalgo Co.; off-channel Rio Grande; 7 mi. N Mercedes; (Ir-M-FC); Valley Acres Water District | 325 | 1,950 |
| **Valley L.** — (1961) Fannin-Grayson counties; 2.5 mi. N Savoy; (P); TXU; (formerly Brushy Creek Reservoir) | 1,080 | 16,400 |
| **Waco, L.** — (1929) McLennan Co.; Bosque R.; 2 mi. W Waco; (M-FC-C-R); City of Waco, USAE, Brazos River Authority | 8,190 | 187,808 |
| **Walter E. Long, L.** — (1967) Travis Co.; Decker Cr.; 9 mi. E Austin; (M-In.-R); City of Austin; (formerly Decker Lake) | 1,269 | 33,940 |
| **Waxahachie, L.** — (1956) Ellis Co.; S Prong Waxahachie Cr.; 4 mi. SE Waxahachie; (M-In) Ellis County WC&ID No. 1; (Imp. by S. Prong Dam) | 656 | 10,779 |
| **Weatherford, L.** — (1956) Parker Co.; Clear Fork Trinity River; 7 mi. E Weatherford; (M-In.); City of Weatherford | 1,112 | 17,812 |
| **Welsh Reservoir** — (1976) Titus Co.; Swauano Cr.; 11 mi. SE Mount Pleasant; (R-In.); AEP-Southwestern Electric Power Co.; (formerly Swauano Creek Reservoir) | 1,269 | 18,431 |
| **White River L.** — (1963) Crosby Co.; 16 mi. SE Crosbyton; (M-In.-Mi.); White River Municipal Water District | 1,642 | 29,880 |
| **White Rock L.** — (1911) Dallas Co.; White Rock Cr.; within NE Dallas city limits; (R); City of Dallas | 1,088 | 9,004 |
| **Whitney, L.** — (1951) Hill-Bosque-Johnson counties; Brazos R.; 5.5 mi. SW Whitney; (FC-P); USAE | 23,220 | 553,344 |
| **Wichita, L.** — (1901) Wichita Co.; Holliday Cr.; 6 mi. SW Wichita Falls; (M-P-R); City of Wichita Falls | 2,200 | 14,000 |
| **Winnsboro, L.** — (1962) Wood Co.; Big Sandy Cr.; 6 mi. SW Winnsboro; (FC-R); Wood County; (Imp. by Wood Co. Dam No. 4) | 806 | 8,100 |
| **Winters, L.** — (1983) Runnels Co.; Elm Cr.; 4.5 mi. E Winters; (M); City of Winters (also known as Elm Creek Lake and New Lake Winters) | 638 | 7,779 |
| **Worth, L.** — (1914) Tarrant Co.; West Fork of Trinity R.; in NW Fort Worth; (M); City of Fort Worth | 3,458 | 33,495 |
| **Wright Patman L.** — (1957) Bowie-Cass-Morris-Titus-Red River counties; Sulphur R.; 8 mi. SW Texarkana; (FC-M); USAE; (formerly Texarkana Lake) | 18,247 | 310,382 |

*An acre-foot is the amount of water necessary to cover an acre of surface area with water one foot deep. The **years** in the table refer to first impounding of water. **Double years** refer to later, larger dams. **Abbreviations are:** L., lake; R., river; Co., county; Cr., creek; (C) conservation; (FC) flood control; (R) recreation; (P) power; (M) municipal; (D) domestic; (Ir.) irrigation; (In.) industry; (Mi.) mining, including oil production; (FH) fish hatchery; USAE, United States Army Corps of Engineers; WC&ID, Water Control and Improvement District; WID, Water Improvement District; USBR, United States Bureau of Reclamation; Auth., Authority; LCRA, Lower Colorado River Authority; TPWD, Texas Parks & Wildlife Dept.; USDA, United States Department of Agriculture; Imp., impounded.

*Wildflowers in the 3,200-square-foot Salehi-Olgin Butterfly Garden at the I-20 Wildlife Preserve near Midland attract more than 70 species of butterflies. Photo by Michael S. Price; I-20 Wildlife Preserve.*

# Texas Plant Life

*This article was updated for the Texas Almanac by Stephan L. Hatch, Director, S.M. Tracy Herbarium and Professor, Department of Ecosystem Science and Management, Texas A&M University.*

## Vegetational Diversity

The types of plants found in Texas vary widely from one region to the next. This is due to the amount and frequency of rainfall, diversity of soils, and the number of frost-free days. From the forests of East Texas to the deserts of West Texas, from the grassy plains of North Texas to the semi-arid brushlands of South Texas, plant species change continuously.

More than 100 million acres of Texas are devoted to **grazing,** both for domestic and wild animals. This is the **largest single use of land** in the state. More than 80 percent of the acreage is devoted to range in the Edwards Plateau, Cross Timbers and Prairies, South Texas Plains, and Trans-Pecos Mountains and Basins.

**Sideoats grama,** which occurs on more different soils in Texas than any other native grass, was officially designated as the **state grass of Texas** by the Texas Legislature in 1971.

The **10 principal plant life areas** of Texas, starting in the east, are:

### 1. Piney Woods

Most of this area of some 16 million acres ranges from about 50 to 700 feet above sea level and receives 40 to 56 inches of rain yearly. Many rivers, creeks, and bayous drain the region. Nearly all of Texas' commercial timber comes from this area. There are three native species of **pine,** the principal timber: longleaf, shortleaf, and loblolly. An introduced species, the slash pine, also is widely grown. Hardwoods include **oaks, elm, hickory,** **magnolia, sweet and black gum, tupelo,** and others.

The area is interspersed with native and improved grasslands. **Cattle** are the primary grazing animals. **Deer** and **quail** are abundant in properly managed habitats. Primary forage plants, under proper grazing management, include species of **bluestems, rossettegrass, panicums, paspalums, blackseed needlegrass, Canada and Virginia wildryes, purpletop, broadleaf and spike woodoats, switchcane, lovegrasses, indiangrass,** and numerous **legume** species.

Highly disturbed areas have understory and overstory of undesirable woody plants that suppress growth of pine and desirable grasses. The primary forage grasses have been reduced, and the grasslands have been invaded by **threeawns, annual grasses, weeds, broomsedge bluestem, red lovegrass,** and shrubby woody species.

### 2. Gulf Prairies and Marshes

The Gulf Prairies and Marshes cover approximately 10 million acres. There are two subunits: (a) the marsh and salt grasses immediately at tidewater, and (b) a little farther inland, a strip of bluestems and tall grasses, with some gramas in the western part. Many of these grasses make excellent grazing.

**Oaks, elm,** and other hardwoods grow to some extent, especially along streams, and the area has some **post oak** and brushy extensions along its borders. Much of the Gulf Prairies is fertile farmland, and the area is well suited for **cattle.**

Principal grasses of the Gulf Prairies are **tall bunchgrasses,** including **big bluestem, little bluestem, seacoast bluestem, indiangrass, eastern gamagrass,**

Texas wintergrass, switchgrass, and **gulf cordgrass**. **Saltgrass** occurs on moist saline sites.

Heavy grazing has changed the native vegetation in many cases so the predominant grasses are the less desirable **broomsedge bluestem, smutgrass, three-awns, tumblegrass,** and many other less desirable grasses. Other plants that have invaded the productive grasslands include **oak underbrush, Macartney rose, huisache, mesquite, prickly pear, ragweed, bitter sneezeweed, broomweed,** and others.

Vegetation of the Gulf Marshes consists primarily of **sedges, bullrush, flat-sedges, beakrush** and other rushes, **smooth cordgrass, marshhay cordgrass, marshmillet,** and **maidencane**. The marshes are grazed best during winter.

### 3. Post Oak Savannah

This secondary forest area, also called the **Post Oak Belt**, covers some 7 million acres. It is immediately west of the primary forest region, with less annual rainfall and a little higher elevation. Principal trees are **post oak, blackjack oak,** and **elm. Pecans, walnuts,** and other kinds of water-demanding trees grow along streams. The southwestern extension of this belt is often poorly defined, with large areas of prairie.

The upland soils are **sandy** and **sandy loam**, while the bottomlands are **sandy loams** and **clays.**

The original vegetation consisted mainly of **little bluestem, big bluestem, indiangrass, switchgrass, purpletop, silver bluestem, Texas wintergrass, woodoats, narrowleaf, post oak,** and **blackjack oak.** The area is still largely native or improved grasslands, with **small farms** located throughout. Intensive grazing has contributed to dense stands of a woody understory of **yaupon, greenbriar,** and **oak** brush.

**Mesquite** has become a serious problem. Good forage plants have been replaced by such plants as **split-beard bluestem, red lovegrass, broomsedge bluestem, broomweed, bullnettle,** and **western ragweed.**

### 4. Blackland Prairies

This area of about 12 million acres, while called a "prairie," has much timber along the streams, including a variety of **oaks, pecan, elm, bois d'arc,** and **mesquite.** In its native state, it was largely a grassy plain — the first native grassland in the westward extension of the Southern Forest Region.

Most of this fertile area has been cultivated, and only small acreages of grassland remain in original vegetation. In heavily grazed pastures, the tall bunchgrass has been replaced by **buffalograss, Texas grama,** and other less productive grasses. **Mesquite, lotebush,** and other woody plants have invaded the grasslands.

The original grass vegetation includes **big** and **little bluestem, indiangrass, switchgrass, sideoats grama, hairy grama, tall dropseed, Texas wintergrass,** and **buffalograss.** Non-grass vegetation is largely legumes and composites.

### 5. Cross Timbers and Prairies

Approximately 15 million acres of alternating woodlands and prairies, often called the **Western Cross Timbers,** constitute this region. Sharp changes in the vegetational cover are associated with different soils and topography, but the grass composition is rather uniform.

The prairie grasses are **big bluestem, little bluestem, indiangrass, switchgrass, Canada wildrye, sideoats grama, hairy grama, tall grama, tall dropseed, Texas wintergrass, blue grama,** and **buffalograss.**

On Cross Timbers soils, the vegetation is composed of **big bluestem, little bluestem, hooded windmillgrass, sand lovegrass, indiangrass, switchgrass,** and many species of legumes. The woody vegetation includes **shinnery, blackjack, post,** and **live oaks.**

The entire area has been invaded heavily by woody brush plants of oaks, mesquite, juniper, and other unpalatable plants that furnish little forage for livestock.

### 6. South Texas Plains

South of San Antonio, between the coast and the Rio Grande, are some 21 million acres of subtropical dryland vegetation, consisting of small trees, shrubs, cactus, weeds, and grasses. The area is noteworthy for extensive brushlands and is known as the **Brush Country,** or the Spanish equivalents of **chaparral** or **monte.** Principal plants are **mesquite, small live oak, post oak, prickly pear (Opuntia) cactus, catclaw, blackbrush, whitebrush, guajillo, huisache, cenizo,** and others that often grow very densely.

The original vegetation was mainly perennial warm-season **bunchgrasses** in **savannahs** of **post oak, live oak,** and **mesquite.** Other brush species form dense

*Washington County is a combination of Blackland Prairie and Post Oak Savannah. Photo by Ron Billings; Texas A&M Forest Service.*

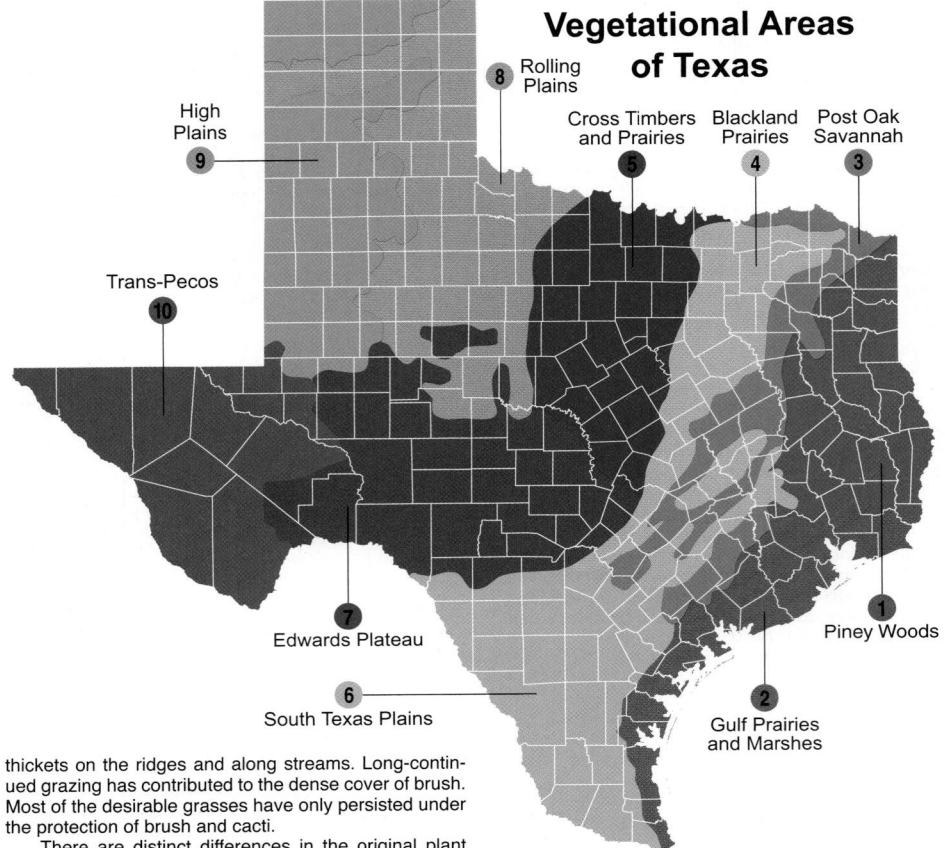

# Vegetational Areas of Texas

- **8** Rolling Plains
- **9** High Plains
- **10** Trans-Pecos
- **5** Cross Timbers and Prairies
- **4** Blackland Prairies
- **3** Post Oak Savannah
- **7** Edwards Plateau
- **6** South Texas Plains
- **1** Piney Woods
- **2** Gulf Prairies and Marshes

thickets on the ridges and along streams. Long-continued grazing has contributed to the dense cover of brush. Most of the desirable grasses have only persisted under the protection of brush and cacti.

There are distinct differences in the original plant communities on various soils. Dominant grasses on the sandy loam soils are **seacoast bluestem, bristlegrass, paspalum, windmillgrass, silver bluestem, big sandbur,** and **tanglehead.** Dominant grasses on the clay and clay loams are **silver bluestem, Arizona cottontop, buffalograss, common curlymesquite, bristlegrass, pappusgrass, gramas, plains lovegrass, Texas cupgrass, vinemesquite,** other **panicums,** and **Texas wintergrass.**

Low saline areas are characterized by **gulf cordgrass, saltgrass, alkali sacaton,** and **switchgrass.** In the post oak and live oak savannahs, the grasses are mainly **seacoast bluestem, indiangrass, switchgrass, crinkleawn, paspalums,** and **panicums.** Today much of the area has been reseeded to **buffelgrass.**

## 7. Edwards Plateau

These 25 million acres are rolling to mountainous, with woodlands in the eastern part and grassy prairies in the west. There is a good deal of brushy growth in the central and eastern areas. The combination of grasses, weeds, and small trees is ideal for **cattle, sheep, goats, deer,** and **wild turkey.**

This limestone-based area is characterized by the large number of **springfed, perennially flowing streams** that originate in its interior and flow across the **Balcones Escarpment,** which bounds it on the south and east. The soils are shallow, ranging from sands to clays, and are calcareous in reaction. This area is predominantly rangeland, with cultivation confined to the deeper soils.

In the east-central portion is the well-marked **Cen-** tral or **Llano Basin,** centering in Mason, Llano, and Burnet counties, with a mixture of granitic and sandy soils. The western portion of the area comprises the semi-arid **Stockton Plateau.**

Noteworthy is the growth of **cypress** along the perennially flowing streams. Separated by many miles from the cypress growth of the moist Southern Forest Belt, they constitute one of Texas' several **"islands" of vegetation.** These trees, which grow to stately proportions, were commercialized in the past.

The principal grasses of the clay soils are **cane bluestem, silver bluestem, little bluestem, sideoats grama, hairy grama, indiangrass, curly-mesquite, buffalograss, fall witchgrass, plains lovegrass, wildryes,** and **Texas wintergrass.**

The rocky areas support tall or mid-grasses with an overstory of **live oak, shinnery oak, juniper,** and **mesquite.** The heavy clay soils have a mixture of **tobosagrass, buffalograss, sideoats grama,** and **mesquite.**

Throughout the Edwards Plateau, **live oak, shinnery oak, mesquite,** and **juniper** dominate the woody vegetation. Woody plants have invaded to the degree that they must be controlled before range forage plants can re-establish.

## 8. Rolling Plains

This is a region of approximately 24 million acres of alternating woodlands and prairies. The area is half **mesquite woodland** and half **prairie.** Mesquite trees have steadily invaded and increased in the grasslands for many years, despite constant control efforts.

Soils range from coarse sands along outwash terraces adjacent to streams to tight or compact clays on redbed clays and shales. Rough broken lands on steep slopes are found in the western portion. About two-thirds of the area is **rangeland,** but cultivation is important in certain localities.

The original vegetation includes **big, little, sand and silver bluestems, Texas wintergrass, indiangrass, switchgrass, sideoats and blue gramas, wildryes, tobosagrass,** and **buffalograss** on the clay soils.

The sandy soils support **tall bunchgrasses,** mainly **sand bluestem. Sand shinnery oak, sand sagebrush,** and **mesquite** are the dominant woody plants.

Continued heavy grazing contributes to the increase in woody plants, low-value grasses such as **red grama, red lovegrass, tumblegrass, gummy lovegrass, Texas grama, sand dropseed,** and **sandbur,** with **western ragweed, croton,** and many other weedy forbs. **Yucca** is a problem plant on certain rangelands.

## 9. High Plains

The High Plains, some 19 million treeless acres, are an extension of the Great Plains to the north. Its level nature and porous soils prevent drainage over wide areas.

The relatively light rainfall flows into the numerous shallow **"playa" lakes** or sinks into the ground to feed the great **underground aquifer** that is the source of water for the countless wells that irrigate the surface of the plains. A large part of this area is under irrigated farming, but native grassland remains in about one-half of the High Plains.

**Blue grama** and **buffalograss** comprise the principal vegetation on the clay and clay loam "hardland" soils. Important grasses on the sandy loam "sandy land" soils are **little bluestem, western wheatgrass, indiangrass, switchgrass,** and **sand reedgrass. Sand shinnery oak, sand sagebrush, mesquite,** and **yucca** are conspicuous invading brushy plants.

## 10. Trans-Pecos Mountains and Basins

With as little as eight inches of annual rainfall, long hot summers, and usually cloudless skies to encourage evaporation, this 18-million-acre area produces only drought-resistant vegetation without irrigation. Grass is usually short and sparse.

The principal vegetation consists of **lechuguilla, ocotillo, yucca, cenizo, prickly pear,** and other arid land plants. In the more arid areas, **gyp** and **chino grama,** and **tobosagrass** prevail. There is some **mesquite.** The vegetation includes **creosote-tarbush, desert shrub, grama grassland, yucca and juniper savannahs, pine oak forest,** and **saline flats.**

The mountains are 3,000 to 8,749 feet in elevation and support **piñon pine, juniper,** and some **ponderosa pine** and other forest vegetation on a few of the higher slopes. The grass vegetation, especially on the higher mountain slopes, includes many **southwestern** and **Rocky Mountain species** not present elsewhere in Texas. On the desert flats, **black grama, burrograss,** and **fluffgrass** are frequent.

More productive sites have numerous species of **grama, muhly, Arizona cottontop, dropseed,** and **perennial threeawn grasses.** At the higher elevations, **plains bristlegrass, little bluestem, Texas bluestem, sideoats grama, chino grama, blue grama, piñon ricegrass, wolftail,** and several species of **needlegrass** are frequent.

The common invaders on all depleted ranges are **woody plants, burrograss, fluffgrass, hairy erioneuron, ear muhly, sand muhly, red grama, broom snakeweed, croton, cacti,** and several poisonous plants. ☆

### For Further Reading

Hatch, S.L., K.N. Gandhi, and L.E. Brown, *Checklist of the Vascular Plants of Texas*; MP1655, Texas Agricultural Experiment Station, College Station, 1990.

*This Texas madrone (Arbutus xalapensis) in Brewster County has a 162-inch circumference, is 46 feet tall, and has a crown spread of 61 feet. It is on the Texas Big Tree Registry and is the National Champion. The tree was nominated by Charles Stair. Photo by Ron Billings; Texas A&M Forest Service.*

*Smokey the Bear celebrates his 70th birthday at an event in College Station in 2014. The iconic bear has taught several generations about fire safety and protecting public forests. Photo by Ron Billings; Texas A&M Forest Service.*

# Public Forests and Grasslands in Texas

*Sources: U.S. Forest Service, Lufkin and Albuquerque, NM; www.fs.fed.us/r8/texas/ and the Texas Forest Service, Texas A&M University System; txforestservice.tamu.edu*

There are **four national forests** and all or part of **five national grasslands** in Texas. These federally owned lands are administered by the U.S. Department of Agriculture Forest Service and by district rangers.

The national forests cover 637,472 acres in parts of 12 Texas counties. The national grasslands cover 117,394 acres in six Texas counties. Two of these grasslands extend into Oklahoma, as well.

The four East Texas forests and two North Texas grasslands are under the supervision of the National Forests and Grasslands in Texas (2221 North Raguet St., Lufkin 75904; (936) 639-8501).

The three West Texas grasslands (Black Kettle, McClellan Creek, and Rita Blanca) are administered by the Forest Supervisor in Albuquerque, N.M., as units of the Cibola National Forest.

The following list gives the name of the forest or grassland, the administrative district(s) for each, the acreage in each county, total acreage, and named places within each forest:

## National Forests

**Angelina National Forest** — Angelina Ranger District (Zavalla); Angelina County, 58,520 acres; Jasper, 21,013; Nacogdoches, 9,238; San Augustine, 64,389. Total, 153,160 acres. Contains the Aldridge Sawmill Historic Site, and Upland Island and Turkey Hill Wilderness.

**Davy Crockett National Forest** — Davy Crockett District (Ratcliff); Houston County, 93,320 acres; Trinity, 67,313. Total, 160,633 acres. Contains the Big Slough Wilderness.

**Sabine National Forest** — Sabine District (Hemphill); Jasper County, 64 acres; Newton, 1,781; Sabine, 95,454; San Augustine, 4,287; Shelby, 59,212. Total,

160,798 acres. Contains the Indian Mounds Wilderness.

**Sam Houston National Forest** — Sam Houston District (New Waverly); Montgomery County, 47,801 acres; San Jacinto, 60,632; Walker, 54,597. Total, 163,030 acres. Contains the Little Lake Creek Wilderness.

## National Grasslands

**Lyndon B. Johnson National Grassland** and **Caddo National Grassland** — District Ranger at Decatur; Fannin County, 17,873 acres; Montague, 61; Wise, 20,252. Total, 38,186 acres.

**Black Kettle National Grassland** — Lake Marvin District Ranger in Cheyenne, Okla.; Hemphill County, 576 acres; Roger Mills County, Okla., 30,724 acres. Total, 31,300 acres.

**McClellan Creek National Grassland** — District Ranger in Cheyenne, Okla.; Gray County, 1,449 acres. Total, 1,449 acres.

**Rita Blanca National Grassland** — District Ranger at Clayton, N.M.; Dallam County, 77,183 acres; Cimarron County, Okla., 15,639 acres. Total, 92,822 acres.

## Establishment of National Forests and Grasslands

National forests in Texas were established by invitation of the Texas Legislature by an Act of 1933, authorizing the purchase of lands in Texas for the establishment of national forests. President Franklin D. Roosevelt proclaimed these purchases on Oct. 15, 1936.

The national grasslands were originally submarginal Dust Bowl project lands, purchased by the federal government primarily under the Bankhead-Jones Farm Tenant Act (1937). Today they are well covered with grasses and native shrubs.

## Forests and Grasslands Uses

The national forests are managed to achieve sustainable conditions and provide wildlife habitat, outdoor recreation, water, wood, minerals, and forage for public use while retaining the aesthetic, historic, and spiritual qualities of the land.

In 1960, the Multiple Use–Sustained Yield Act put into law what had been practiced in Texas for almost 30 years: that resources on public lands will be managed so that they are used in ways that best meet the needs of the people, that the benefits obtained will exist indefinitely, and that each natural resource will be managed in balance with other resources.

However, even the most carefully planned system of management cannot foresee factors that can cause drastic changes in a forest. Fire, storms, insects, and disease, for example, can prompt managers to deviate from land management plans and can alter the way a forest is managed.

### 1. Timber Production

About 486,000 acres of the national forests in Texas are suitable for timber production. Sales of sawtimber, pulpwood, and other forest products are initiated to implement forest plans and objectives. The estimated net growth is more than 200 million board feet per year and is valued at $40 million. A portion of this growth is normally removed by cutting.

### 2. Cattle Grazing

Permits to graze cattle on national grasslands are granted to the public for an annual fee. About 600 head of cattle are grazed on the Caddo–Lyndon B. Johnson National Grasslands annually. On the Rita Blanca National Grasslands, 5,425 head of cattle are grazed each year, most of them in Texas.

### 3. Hunting and Fishing

State hunting and fishing laws and regulations apply to all national forest land. Game law enforcement is carried out by the Texas Parks and Wildlife Department.

A wide variety of fishing opportunities are available on the Angelina, Sabine, Neches, and San Jacinto rivers; the Sam Rayburn and Toledo Bend reservoirs; Lake Conroe; and many small streams. Hunting is not permitted on the McClellan Creek National Grassland nor at the Lake Marvin Unit of the Black Kettle National Grassland.

### 4. Recreational Facilities

An estimated 3 million people visit the recreational areas in the national forests and grasslands in Texas each year, primarily for picnicking, swimming, fishing, camping, boating, and nature enjoyment.

The Sabine and Angelina National Forests are on the shores of Toledo Bend and Sam Rayburn reservoirs, two large East Texas lakes featuring fishing and other water sports. Lake Conroe and Lake Livingston offer water-related outdoor recreation opportunities on and near the Sam Houston National Forest.

*Recreational activities offered in the National Forests and Grasslands are listed in the Recreation section on pages 191–192.*

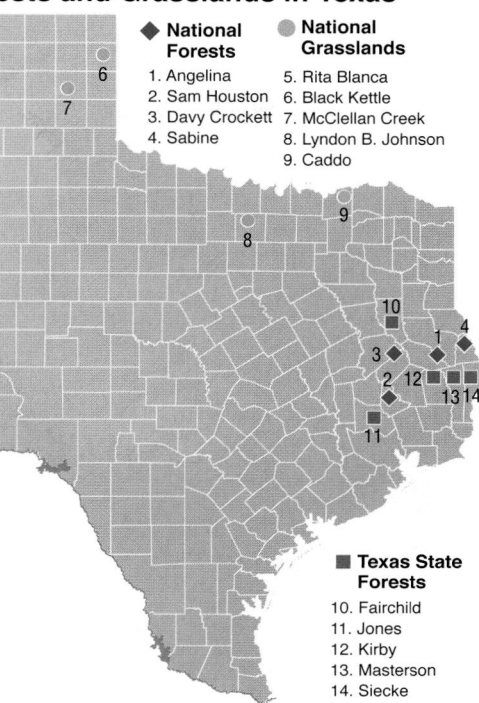

# Forests and Grasslands in Texas

◆ **National Forests**    ● **National Grasslands**

1. Angelina
2. Sam Houston
3. Davy Crockett
4. Sabine
5. Rita Blanca
6. Black Kettle
7. McClellan Creek
8. Lyndon B. Johnson
9. Caddo

■ **Texas State Forests**

10. Fairchild
11. Jones
12. Kirby
13. Masterson
14. Siecke

## State Forests

Texas has **five state forests**, all of which are used primarily for demonstration and research. They are all game sanctuaries with no firearms or hunting allowed.

Recreational opportunities, such as horseback riding, hiking, bird watching, and picnicking, are available in all but the Masterson Forest. *See page 187 for recreation information.*

**I.D. Fairchild State Forest** — Texas' largest forest is located west of Rusk in Cherokee County. This forest was transferred from the state prison system in 1925. Additional land was obtained in 1963 from the Texas State Hospitals and Special Schools for a total acreage of 2,740.

**W. Goodrich Jones State Forest** — Located south of Conroe in Montgomery County, it comprises 1,733 acres. It was purchased in 1926 and named for the founder of the Texas Forestry Association.

**John Henry Kirby Memorial State Forest** — This 600-acre forest in Tyler County was donated by lumberman John Henry Kirby in 1929, as well as later donors. Revenue from this forest is given to the Association of Former Students of Texas A&M University for student-loan purposes.

**Paul N. Masterson Memorial Forest** — Mrs. Leonora O'Neal Masterson of Beaumont donated this 519 acres in Jasper County in 1984 in honor of her husband, who was a tree farmer and an active member of the Texas Forestry Association.

**E.O. Siecke State Forest** — The first state forest, it was purchased by the state in 1924. It contains 1,722 acres of pine land in Newton County. An additional 100 acres was obtained by a 99-year lease in 1946. ☆

# Texas Forest Resources

*Source: Texas A&M Forest Service, Texas A&M University System. On the web: http://tfsweb.tamu.edu.*

Forests resources in Texas are abundant and diverse. Forest land covers roughly 38 percent of the state's land area. According to 2013 figures from the **Forest Inventory and Analysis (FIA),** there are 62.6 million acres of forests and woodlands in Texas.

## East Texas Piney Woods

The principal forest region in Texas is the East Texas pine-hardwood region, often called the **Piney Woods.** The 43-county region forms the western edge of the southern pine region, extending from Bowie and Red River counties in northeast Texas to Jefferson, Harris, and Waller counties in southeast Texas. The counties contain 12.1 million acres of forestland of which 11.9 million acres are classified as productive timberland and produce nearly all of the state's commercial timber.

Following is a summary of the findings of the Forest Inventory of East Texas, completed in 2013 by the Texas A&M Forest Service (TFS) in cooperation with the USDA Forest Service Southern Research Station.

### Timberland Acreage and Ownership

Nearly all (11.9 million of 12.1 million acres) of the East Texas forest is classified as "timberland," which is suitable for production of timber products and not reserved as parks or wilderness areas. Texas timberland acreage remained stable between 2012 and 2013. This is a result of a balance between new timberland acres coming from agricultural lands, which are either intentionally planted with trees or have naturally reverted to forest, and previous forested land that is converted to other uses, such as commercial or residential areas.

Ninety-two percent of East Texas timberland is owned by approximately 210,000 private individuals, families, partnerships, corporations, forest-products companies, and timber investment groups. The remaining 8 percent is owned by federal, state, and local governments. The following table shows acreage of timberland by ownership:

| Ownership Class | Thous. Acres |
|---|---|
| Private | 10,896.2 |
| Public: | |
| National forest | 642.1 |
| Misc. federal | 162.4 |
| State & local | 205.8 |
| **Total** | **11,906.5** |

East Texas has undergone major shifts in private ownership during the past decade, primarily a transfer of land from forest industry owners to non-industrial private owners. Information from several sources, such as the FIA, National Woodland Owner Survey, and timberland transaction records, suggests that the forest industry now accounts for no more than 50 thousand acres. Non-industrial private corporations, which include timber investment corporations, account for 3 million to 3.4 million acres, and family forest landowners account for 7.5 million to 8 million acres.

### Forest Types

Six major forest types are found in the East Texas Piney Woods. Two pine-forest types are most common. The **loblolly-shortleaf** and **longleaf-slash** forest types are dominated by the four species of southern yellow pine. In these forests, the various pine trees make up at least 50 percent of the trees.

**Oak-hickory** is the next most common forest type. These are upland hardwood forests in which oaks or hickories make up at least 50 percent of the trees, and pine species are less than 25 percent. **Oak-pine** is a mixed-forest type in which more than 50 percent of the trees are hardwoods, but pines make up 25–49 percent of the trees.

Two forest types, **oak-gum-cypress** and **elm-ash-cottonwood,** are bottomland types that are commonly found along creeks, river bottoms, swamps, and other wet areas. The oak-gum-cypress forests are typically made up of many species including blackgum, sweetgum, oaks, and southern cypress. The elm-ash-cottonwood bottomland forests are dominated by those trees but also contain many other species, such as willow, sycamore, and maple.

Other forest types found in East Texas include small acreages of **mesquite, exotic hardwoods, red cedar,** and unproductive lands that are considered forested but do not meet stocking requirements. The following table shows the breakdown in acreage by forest type:

| Forest Type Group | Thous. Acres |
|---|---|
| Southern Pine: | |
| Loblolly-shortleaf | 5,307.4 |
| Longleaf-slash | 119.9 |
| Oak-hickory | 2,824.2 |
| Oak-pine | 1,478.1 |
| Bottomland Hardwood: | |
| Oak-gum-cypress | 1,396.4 |
| Elm-ash-cottonwood | 560.5 |
| Other | 399.9 |
| **Total** | **12,086.4** |

Southern pine plantations, established by tree planting and usually managed intensively to maximize timber production, are an important source of wood fiber. Texas forests include 2.7 million acres of **pine plantations,** 63 percent of which are on industrially managed land, 34 percent on non-industrial private land, and 3 percent on public land. Genetically superior tree seedlings are usually planted to improve survival and growth.

### Timber Volume and Number of Trees

Based on 2013 Forest Inventory & Analysis Data, Texas timberland contains about **17.3 billion cubic feet of timber "growing-stock" volume.** One billion cubic feet of growing stock produces roughly enough lumber to build a 2,000-square-foot home for one out of every three Texans. Between 2012 and 2013, the **inventory of softwood remained steady** at 9.9 billion cubic feet, while the **hardwood inventory decreased slightly** from 7.9 billion cubic feet to 7.8 billion cubic feet.

There are an estimated **7.7 billion live trees in East Texas,** according to the 2013 survey. This includes 2.2 billion softwoods and 5.5 billion hardwoods. The predominant species are **loblolly and shortleaf pine;** 2 billion pine trees are found in East Texas.

### Timber Growth and Removals

Between 2008 and 2013, an annual average of 550.4 million cubic feet of growing stock timber was removed from the inventory, either through harvest or land-use changes. Meanwhile, 605.6 million cubic feet of growing stock were added to the inventory through growth each year.

For pine, an average of 420.6 million cubic feet was removed during those years, while 545.7 million cubic feet were added by growth. For hardwoods, 129.8 million cubic feet were removed, while 59.9 million cubic

# Celebrating
## 100 Years
## of Forestry
## 1914–2014

*The Texas Forestry Association (TFA) and the Texas A&M Forest Service (TFS) celebrated their 100th anniversaries in 2014 and 2015, respectively. To commemorate this centennial, the TFA published **A Century of Forestry** by Dr. Ronald F. Billings, who has worked as principal entomologist for TFS for more than 40 years. Clockwise from top left: **1.** The first steel fire towers were constructed in 1927, and by the 1940s, airplanes were used for fire detection. **2.** Two forestry workers use early labor-intensive firefighting techniques. **3.** A forest patrolman around 1926 patrols in a Model T Ford. **4.** Members of the Civilian Conservation Corps plant seedlings in 1929 at State Forest No. 1, the Siecke State Forest. **5.** W. Goodrich Jones, founder of the Texas Forestry Association, known as the father of forestry in Texas, and the namesake of Jones State Forest in Montgomery County. All photos courtesy of the TFA and TFS.*

feet were added by growth.

## The 2013 Timber Harvest

### Total Removals

Total removals of growing stock in East Texas in 2013, including both pine and hardwood, **increased 1.1 percent** from 2012. The total volume of growing stock that was removed from the 43-county timber region was 504.4 million cubic feet in 2013, compared to 498.7 million cubic feet in 2012. Included in the total growing stock removals are timber harvested for industrial use and an estimate of logging residue.

Industrial roundwood harvest in Texas in 2013, the portion of the total removal that was subsequently utilized in the **manufacture of wood products,** totaled 419.6 million cubic feet for pine and 102 million cubic feet for hardwood. The pine industrial roundwood harvest was up 2.6 percent from 2012, and the hardwood roundwood harvest was down 3.9 percent. The

## Texas Forest Products Production 2003–2013

| Year | Lumber* (thousand board feet) | | Paper (short tons) | | | Structural Panel |
|------|------|------|------|------|------|------|
| | Pine | Hardwood | Paper | Paperboard* | Total Paper Products | Pine (thousand square feet*) |
| 2003 | 1,490,311 | 287,062 | 255,462 | 2,170,185 | 2,425,647 | 2,723,225 |
| 2004 | 1,591,109 | 324,663 | 0** | 2,560,480 | 2,560,480 | 2,859,012 |
| 2005 | 1,733,314 | 230,090 | 0** | 2,512,262 | 2,512,262 | 3,249,558 |
| 2006 | 1,676,461 | 240,214 | 0** | 2,781,865 | 2,781,865 | 2,935,637 |
| 2007 | 1,550,716 | 180,713 | 0** | 2,788,308 | 2,788,308 | 2,503,941 |
| 2008 | 1,406,103 | 213,191 | 0** | 2,329,347 | 2,329,347 | 2,204,544 |
| 2009 | 1,237,801 | 171,514 | 0** | 2,007,054 | 2,007,054 | 1,958,794 |
| 2010 | 1,188,294 | 139,389 | 0** | 2,089,521 | 2,089,521 | 1,881,763 |
| 2011 | 1,308,427 | 154,593 | 0** | 2,029,405 | 2,029,405 | 1,915,605 |
| 2012 | 1,291,578 | 118,823 | 0** | 2,081,521 | 2,081,521 | 2,049,084 |
| 2013 | 1,385,043 | 140,427 | 0** | 2,168,403 | 2,168,403 | 2,017,406 |
| | *Includes tie volumes. | | *Includes fiberboard and miscellaneous products.\
**There was no paper or market pulp production due to the closure of a major paper mill. | | | *3/8-inch basis |

combined harvest increased 1.3 percent in 2013 to 521.5 million cubic feet. Top producing counties included **Polk, Nacogdoches, Hardin, Newton, and Liberty.**

### Total Harvest Value

Stumpage value of the East Texas timber harvest in 2013 was $232.2 million, a 1.3-percent decrease from 2012. The delivered value of timber was up 3.2 percent to $574.6 million. Pine timber accounted for 78.4 percent of the total stumpage value and 77.9 percent of the total delivered value.

Compared with 2012, the harvest of **sawlogs for production of lumber** increased by 5.3 percent in 2013 to 1.1 billion board feet. The pine sawlog cut totaled 976 million board feet, up 4.9 percent from 2012, and the hardwood sawlog harvest increased 8.2 percent to 132 million board feet. **Polk, Cherokee, Nacogdoches, Hardin, and Liberty counties** were the top producers of sawlogs.

Timber cut for the production of **structural panels,** including both plywood and OSB (oriented strand board) and hardwood veneer, totaled 112.3 million cubic feet, a small increase from 2012. **Nacogdoches, Polk, Houston, Cherokee, and Newton counties** were the top producers of veneer and panel roundwood.

Harvest of timber for manufacture of **pulp and paper products** decreased 3.4 percent from 2012 to 2013 to 2.8 million cords. **Cass, Hardin, Liberty, Polk, and Newton counties** were the top producers of pulpwood.

Other roundwood harvest, including posts, poles, and pilings, totaled 2.9 million cubic feet in 2013.

### Import-Export Trends

Texas was a **net importer** of timber products in 2013. Total import from other states was 97.1 million cubic feet, while the total export was 58.8 million cubic feet.

# Beyond the Piney Woods: Texas' Other Tree Regions

In addition to the 12 million acres of timberland in East Texas, there are an additional 50.5 million acres of land in the remainder of Texas that are considered forestland. These forests consist of mesquite woodlands, oak-hickory forests, juniper woodlands, and other western forest types. These forests do not have the commercial timber value of the East Texas Piney Woods but are environmentally important with benefits of wildlife habitat, improved water quality, recreation, and aesthetics.

Following is a brief description of these areas.

• **Post Oak Belt**: The Post Oak Belt forms a band of wooded savannah mixed with pasture and cropland immediately west of the Piney Woods. It extends from Lamar and Red River counties southwest as far as Bee and Atascosa counties. Predominant species include post oak, blackjack oak, and elm. An interesting area called the **"Lost Pines"** forms an isolated island of southern-pine forest in Bastrop, Caldwell, Fayette, and Lee counties just a few miles southeast of Austin.

• **Eastern and Western Cross Timbers**: The Eastern and Western Cross Timbers cover an area of about 3 million acres in North-Central Texas.

The term "cross timbers" originated with the early settlers who, in their travels from east to west, crossed alternating patches of oak forest and prairies and so affixed the name "cross timbers" to these forests.

• **Cedar Brakes**: Farther south in the Edwards Plateau region are the cedar brakes, which extend over 3.7 million acres. Cedar, live oak, and mesquite dominate these steep slopes and rolling hills. Mesquite is harvested for cooking wood, knickknacks, and woodworking. Live oak in this region is declining because of the oak wilt disease.

• **Mountain Forests**: The mountain forests of the Trans-Pecos region, including Jeff Davis County and the Big Bend, are rugged and picturesque. Several western tree species, including piñon pine, ponderosa pine, southwestern white pine, and even Douglas fir are found there, along with aspen and several species of oak.

• **Coastal Forests**: The coastal forests of the southern Gulf Coast are characterized by a mix of brush and short, scrubby trees. Common species include mesquite, live oak, and acacia. Some of these scrub forests are particularly important as migratory bird habitat.

Texas mills utilized 88.7 percent of the timber harvested in the state in 2013. The remainder was processed mainly by mills in Arkansas, Louisiana, and Oklahoma.

## Production of Forest Products

**LUMBER** — Texas sawmills produced 1.5 billion board feet of lumber in 2013, a increase of 8.2 percent over 2012. Production of pine lumber increased 7.2 percent to 1.4 billion board feet in 2013 and hardwood lumber production increased 18.2 percent to 140.4 million board feet in 2013.

**STRUCTURAL PANEL PRODUCTS** — Production of structural panels, including plywood and OSB, decreased 1.5 percent to 2 billion square feet in 2013.

**PAPER PRODUCTS** — Production of paperboard totaled 2 million tons in 2013, down 1.8 percent from a year earlier. There has not been any major paper production in Texas since 2003.

**TREATED WOOD** — There was a 11.3 percent increase in the volume of wood processed by Texas wood treaters in 2013 from 2012. The total volume treated in 2013 was 40 million cubic feet. Among major treated products, lumber accounted for 67.4 percent of the total volume; crossties accounted for 16.4 percent; utility poles and fence posts each accounted for 10.4 percent and 4.8 percent, respectively.

**PRIMARY MILL RESIDUE** — Total mill residue, including chips, sawdust, shavings and bark in primary mills, such as sawmills, panel mills and chip mills, was 5.9 million tons in 2013, an increase of 7.3 percent from 2012. Eighty-three percent of the residue was from pine species and 17 percent was from hardwood species. Chips accounted for 48.9 percent of mill residue, followed by bark (32.5 percent), sawdust (12.8 percent), and shavings (5.8 percent).

## Total Timber Production and Value by County in Texas, 2013

| County | Pine | Hardwood | Total | Stumpage Value | Delivered Value |
|---|---|---|---|---|---|
| | Cubic feet | | | Thousand dollars | |
| Anderson | 8,751,486 | 1,218,787 | 9,970,273 | $ 4,990 | $ 11,380 |
| Angelina | 14,140,109 | 3,362,494 | 17,502,603 | 8,302 | 19,715 |
| Bowie | 7,977,449 | 6,612,207 | 14,589,656 | 6,181 | 16,175 |
| Camp | 1,794,555 | 859,162 | 2,653,717 | 947 | 2,751 |
| Cass | 18,477,965 | 9,310,599 | 27,788,564 | 10,845 | 29,629 |
| Chambers | 36,326 | 66,334 | 102,660 | 63 | 135 |
| Cherokee | 19,307,159 | 5,150,208 | 24,457,367 | 14,196 | 30,017 |
| Franklin | 326,276 | 1,144,085 | 1,470,361 | 539 | 1,616 |
| Gregg | 2,158,840 | 1,627,135 | 3,785,975 | 2,169 | 4,732 |
| Grimes | 2,787,569 | 474,679 | 3,262,248 | 1,619 | 3,705 |
| Hardin | 22,294,046 | 5,968,506 | 28,262,552 | 11,433 | 30,233 |
| Harris | 3,597,181 | 1,069,987 | 4,667,168 | 2,381 | 5,405 |
| Harrison | 13,080,493 | 5,153,378 | 18,233,871 | 7,054 | 19,293 |
| Henderson | 1,129,841 | 278,144 | 1,407,985 | 560 | 1,493 |
| Houston | 14,358,390 | 532,841 | 14,891,231 | 7,131 | 16,536 |
| Jasper | 20,008,985 | 685,338 | 20,694,323 | 8,904 | 22,118 |
| Jefferson | 1,378,830 | 351,378 | 1,730,208 | 627 | 1,790 |
| Leon | 345,296 | 1,651,711 | 1,997,007 | 713 | 2,176 |
| Liberty | 21,516,744 | 6,564,605 | 28,081,349 | 12,470 | 31,061 |
| Madison | 39,319 | 0 | 39,319 | 25 | 48 |
| Marion | 8,148,483 | 2,929,057 | 11,077,540 | 5,367 | 12,613 |
| Montgomery | 5,747,937 | 1,401,356 | 7,149,293 | 3,865 | 8,456 |
| Morris | 1,896,567 | 1,160,139 | 3,056,706 | 1,078 | 3,182 |
| Nacogdoches | 24,573,311 | 4,155,181 | 28,728,492 | 13,741 | 32,235 |
| Newton | 27,461,763 | 719,264 | 28,181,027 | 9,840 | 28,145 |
| Orange | 1,618,536 | 254,871 | 1,873,407 | 678 | 1,913 |
| Panola | 16,941,549 | 3,200,517 | 20,142,066 | 8,836 | 21,932 |
| Polk | 33,695,099 | 3,353,278 | 37,048,377 | 16,986 | 40,854 |
| Red River | 4,509,199 | 5,140,016 | 9,649,215 | 3,546 | 10,366 |
| Rusk | 11,690,229 | 2,583,322 | 14,273,551 | 7,511 | 16,712 |
| Sabine | 10,916,919 | 1,541,337 | 12,458,256 | 5,348 | 13,424 |
| San Augustine | 11,590,245 | 3,460,142 | 15,050,387 | 5,984 | 15,998 |
| San Jacinto | 9,669,494 | 939,964 | 10,609,458 | 5,169 | 11,925 |
| Shelby | 18,510,678 | 3,002,603 | 21,513,281 | 10,243 | 24,044 |
| Smith | 3,607,389 | 1,978,646 | 5,586,035 | 2,799 | 6,542 |
| Titus | 1,001,683 | 1,566,883 | 2,568,566 | 1,077 | 2,891 |
| Trinity | 17,873,811 | 539,174 | 18,412,985 | 8,377 | 20,102 |
| Tyler | 23,157,665 | 1,731,528 | 24,889,193 | 10,403 | 26,571 |
| Upshur | 3,286,485 | 3,452,618 | 6,739,103 | 2,672 | 7,374 |
| Van Zandt | 174,247 | 443,024 | 617,271 | 296 | 736 |
| Walker | 7,683,771 | 876,124 | 8,559,895 | 4,631 | 10,016 |
| Waller | 220,449 | 155,262 | 375,711 | 113 | 374 |
| Wood | 1,270,271 | 3,043,971 | 4,314,242 | 1,568 | 4,681 |
| Other Counties | 815,985 | 2,253,519 | 3,069,504 | 1,329 | 3,552 |
| **Totals** | **419,568,624** | **101,963,374** | **521,531,998** | **$232,604** | **$574,648** |

## Reforestation

A total of 139,070 acres were planted during the winter 2012 and spring 2013 planting season, a 52-percent increase over the 2011–2012 season. Industrial landowners, including acres planted by Timber Investment Management Organizations and timberland Real Estate Investment Trusts, planted 101,671 acres, up 54 percent from the previous season.

The Family Forest owners planted 39,527 acres in 2012–2013, and public landowners planted 872 acres. Family forest owners received $3.1 million in cost-share assistance for reforestation through federal cost-share programs.

## Fire Protection

During the 2012 fire season, Texas A&M Forest Service (TFS) and local fire departments responded to 13,238 fires that burned 159,455 acres and destroyed 77 homes. Wildfire suppression efforts were credited with saving 3,686 homes, along with other property and improvements, valued at more than $32 million.

In 2013, TFS and local fire departments responded to 12,306 fires that burned 69,499 acres and destroyed 47 homes. Wildfire suppression efforts were credited with saving 3,350 homes, property, and improvements valued at more than $58 million.

Texas has a tiered approach to emergencies, such as wildland fires, with response coming from local, district, state, and federal levels. When a fire surpasses the capabilities of local fire departments, the TFS steps in to help. On average, TFS personnel respond to 15 percent of the wildland fires that burn across the state; however, those fires burn 70 percent of total acres lost to wildland fires each year.

More information on state wildfire response, wildfire risk assessments, fire department assistance programs, and how homeowners and communities can reduce their wildfire risk is online at: **(http://tfsweb. tamu.edu** and **http://ticc.tamu.edu).**

## Forest Pests

The **southern pine beetle** is the most destructive insect pest in the 12 million acres of commercial forests in East Texas. Typically, this bark beetle kills more timber annually than forest fires.

This destructive insect is currently at very low levels in East Texas. When outbreaks do occur, the Texas A&M Forest Service coordinates all direct control activity on state and private forestlands, including detecting infestations from the air, checking infestations on the ground to evaluate the need for control, notifying landowners, and providing technical assistance.

Recent efforts have focused on rating the susceptibility of pine stands to future southern pine beetle outbreaks, as well as prevention of infestations. Since 2003, the TFS has offered federal cost shares to private forest landowners in East Texas as an incentive to thin the young pine stands that are most susceptible to bark beetles. Thinning dense forests to promote vigorous tree growth is the preferred long-run method to reduce tree losses caused by bark beetles.

Extensive mortality of live oaks in Central Texas is caused by a vascular wilt disease called **oak wilt**. A suppression project, administered by TFS Forest Health personnel, assists affected landowners.

Invasive (non-native) insects, diseases, and plants are an increasing problem for Texas' forest landowners. The **soapberry borer,** a wood-boring beetle introduced from Mexico, has killed western soapberry trees in some 50 counties in Central Texas. Invasive plants, such as **Japanese climbing fern, Chinese tallow,** and non-native **privets,** have also spread rapidly.

In 2012 and 2013, Texas A&M Forest Service, Texas A&M AgriLife Extension Service, Sam Houston State University, and other collaborators, conducted a widespread detection survey for the emerald ash borer, a major pest of ash trees introduced from Asia. Fortunately, none were found in either years.

## Urban Forests

An estimated 86 percent of Texans live in urban areas, making urban trees and forests important.

Trees reduce urban heat island effect with shade and evaporative cooling; purify the air by absorbing pollutants, slowing chemical reactions that produce harmful ozone, and filter dust; reduce storm water runoff and soil erosion; buffer against noise, glare, and strong winds; and provide habitat for urban wildlife. ☆

*A loblolly pine plantation in East Texas. Photo by Ron Billings; Texas A&M Forest Service.*

*The nine-banded armadillo is found in most of Texas except the western Trans-Pecos. It is the official Small Mammal of Texas. Photo by Ron Billings; Texas A&M Forest Service.*

# Texas Wildlife

*Source: Texas Parks and Wildlife Department, Austin; www.nsrl.ttu.edu/tmot1/*

The wide variation of soils, climate, topography, and vegetation in Texas have resulted in an unusually rich diversity of animal life. The Texas environment supports **141 species of native terrestrial mammals,** a number exceeded in the United States only by California and New Mexico. In addition to native species, there are also 12 exotics or non-native species that have been introduced by man either accidentally (house mouse, roof rat, Norway rat) or intentionally (nutria, red fox, feral pig, axis deer, fallow deer, sika deer, nilgai, barbary sheep, and blackbuck) and have become established in the environment.

A few of the leading land mammals of Texas are described here. Those marked by an asterisk (*) are non-native species. Information was provided by the Nongame and Urban Program, Texas Parks and Wildlife Department, and updated using the online version of *The Mammals of Texas* by David J. Schmidly and the late William B. Davis: www.nsrl.ttu.edu/tmot1/. The print version was first published in 1947 and updated in 1994 by Texas Parks and Wildlife Press, Austin,. The online version is maintained by Texas Tech University. For additional wildlife information on the web: **www.tpwd.state.tx.us/huntwild/wild/species/.**

## Mammals

**Armadillo** — The **nine-banded armadillo** *(Dasypus novemcinctus)* is one of Texas' most interesting mammals. It is found in most of the state except the western Trans-Pecos. It is now common as far north and east as Oklahoma and Mississippi.

**Badger** — The **badger** *(Taxidea taxus)* is found throughout the state except the extreme eastern region. It is a fierce fighter, and it is valuable in helping control the rodent population.

**Bat** — Thirty-two species of these winged mammals have been found in Texas, more than in any other state in the United States. Of these, 27 species are known residents, though they are seldom seen by the casual observer. The **Mexican, or Brazilian, free-tailed bat** *(Tadarida brasiliensis)* and the **cave myotis** *(Myotis velifer)* constitute most of the cave-dwelling bats of Central and West Texas.

They have some economic value for their deposits of nitrogen-rich **guano.** Some commercial guano has been produced from **James River Bat Cave,** Mason County; **Beaver Creek Cavern,** Burnet County; and from large deposits in other caves including **Devil's Sinkhole,** Edwards County; **Blowout Cave,** Blanco County; and **Bandera Bat Cave,** Bandera County. The largest concentration of bats in the world is found at **Bracken Cave** in Comal County, which is thought to hold between 20 million and 40 million bats. The **big brown bat** *(Eptesicus fuscus),* the **red bat** *(Lasiurus borealis),* and the **evening bat** *(Nycticeius humeralis)* are found in East and Southeast Texas. The evening and big brown bats are forest and woodland dwelling mammals.

The rarer species of Texas bats have been found along the Rio Grande and in the Trans-Pecos. Bats can be observed at dusk near a water source, and many species may also be found foraging on insects attracted to street lights. Everywhere bats occur, they are the main predators of night-flying insects, including mosquitoes and many crop pests. On the web: **www.batcon.org/**

**Bear** — The **black bear** *(Ursus americanus),* formerly common throughout most of the state, is now surviving in remnant populations in mountainous areas of the Trans-Pecos. Some are fleeing the drought and wildfires in Mexico and moving into the Big Bend area.

**Beaver** — The **American beaver** *(Castor canadensis)* is found over most of the state except for the Llano Estacado and parts of the Trans-Pecos.

**Bighorn** — (See **Sheep.**)

*The Mexican ground squirrel is one of at least five species of ground squirrel that live in Texas, mostly in the western part of the state. Photo by Michael S. Price; I-20 Wildlife Preserve.*

**Bison** — The largest of native terrestrial wild mammals of North America, the **American bison** *(Bos bison),* commonly called **buffalo,** was formerly found in the western two-thirds of the state. Today, it is extirpated or confined on ranches. Deliberate slaughter of this majestic animal for hides and to eliminate the Plains Indians' main food source reached a peak about 1877–78, and the bison was almost eradicated by 1885. Estimates of the number of buffalo killed vary, but as many as 200,000 hides were sold in Fort Worth at a single two-day sale. Except for the interest of the late **Col. Charles Goodnight** and a few other foresighted men, the bison might be extinct.

**Cat** — The **jaguar** *(Felis onca)* is probably now extinct in Texas and, along with the **ocelot, jaguarundi,** and **margay,** is listed as endangered or threatened by both federal and state wildlife agencies. The **mountain lion** *(Felis concolor),* also known as **cougar** and **puma,** was once found statewide. It is now found in the mountainous areas of the Trans-Pecos and the dense Rio Grande Plain brushland. The **ocelot** *(Felis pardalis),* also known as the **leopard cat,** is found usually along the border. The **red-and-gray cat,** or **jaguarundi** *(Felis yagouaroundi Geoffroy)* is found, rarely, in extreme South Texas. The **margay** *(Felis wiedii)* was reported in the 1850s near Eagle Pass. The **bobcat** *(Lynx rufus)* is found throughout the state in large numbers.

**Chipmunk** — The **gray-footed chipmunk** *(Tamias canipes)* is found at high altitudes in the Guadalupe and Sierra Diablo ranges of the Trans-Pecos. (*See also,* **Ground Squirrel,** with which the chipmunk is often confused in public reference.)

**Coati** — The **white-nosed coati** *(Nasua narica),* a relative of the raccoon, is occasionally found in southern Texas from Brownsville to the Big Bend. It inhabits woodland areas and feeds both on the ground and in trees. The coati, which is on the list of threatened species, is also found occasionally in Big Bend National Park.

**Coyote** — The **coyote** *(Canis latrans)* exists in great numbers in Texas. It is the most destructive predator of Texas livestock. On the other hand, it is probably the most valuable predator in the balance of nature. It is a protection to crops and range lands by its control of rodents and rabbits. It is found throughout the state but is most numerous in the brush country of Southwest Texas. It is the second-most important fur-bearing animal in the state.

**Deer** — The **white-tailed deer** *(Odocoileus virginianus),* found throughout the state in brushy or wooded areas, is the most important Texas game animal. Its numbers in Texas are estimated at more than 3 million. The **mule deer** *(Odocoileus heminous)* is found principally in the Trans-Pecos and Panhandle areas. It has increased in number in recent years. The little **Del Carmen deer** *(white-tailed subspecies)* is found in limited numbers in the high valleys of the Chisos Mountains in the Big Bend. The only native **elk** in Texas *(Cervus merriami),* found in the southern Guadalupe Mountains, became extinct about the turn of the 20th century. The **wapiti** or **elk** *(Cervus elaphus),* was introduced into the same area about 1928. There are currently several herds totalling several hundred individuals.

A number of exotic deer species have been introduced, mostly for hunting purposes. The **axis deer**\* *(Cervus axix)* is the most numerous of the exotics. Native to India, it is found mostly in Central and South Texas, both free-ranging and confined on ranches. **Blackbuck**\* *(Antilope cervicapra),* also native to India, is the second-most numerous exotic deer in the state and is found on ranches in 86 counties. **Fallow deer**\* *(Cervus dama),* native to the Mediterranean, has been introduced to 93 counties, while the **nilgai**\* *(Boselaphus tragocamelus),* native of India and Pakistan, is found mostly on ranches in Kenedy and Willacy counties. The **sika deer**\* *(Cervus nippon),* native of southern Siberia, Japan, and China, has been introduced in 77 counties in Central and South Texas.

**Dolphin** — The **Atlantic spotted dolphin** *(Stenella frontalis)* is rather small, long-snouted, and spotted; it is purplish gray, appearing blackish at a distance, usually with numerous small white or gray spots on its sides and back. In the Gulf of Mexico, this dolphin is second in abundance only to the **bottlenose dolphin.** The bottlenose *(Tursiops truncatus)* is stout and short-beaked with sloping forehead, projecting lower jaw, and high dorsal fin. Other species, such as the Clymene, the Common dolphin, the Pantropical Spotted, Risso's, Rough-toothed, Spinner, and Striped are unusual and known in Texas only through strandings along Gulf beaches.

**Ferret** — The **black-footed ferret** *(Mustela nigripes)* was formerly found widely ranging through the West Texas country of the prairie dog on which it preyed. It is now considered extinct in Texas. It is of the same genus as the weasel and the mink.

**Fox** — The **common gray fox** *(Urocyon cinereoargenteus)* is found throughout most of the state, primarily in the woods of East Texas, in broken parts of the Edwards Plateau, and in the rough country at the foot of the High Plains. The **kit** or **Swift fox** *(Vulpes velox)* is found in the western one-third of the state. A second species of **kit fox** *(Vulpes macrotis)* is found in the Trans-Pecos and is fairly numerous in some localities. The **red fox**\* *(Vulpes vulpes)*, which ranges across Central Texas, was introduced for sport.

**Gopher** — Nine species of pocket gopher occur in Texas. The **Botta's pocket gopher** *(Thomomys bottae)* is found from the Trans-Pecos eastward across the Edwards Plateau. The **plains pocket gopher** *(Geomys bursarius)* is found from Midland and Tom Green counties east and north to McLennan, Dallas, and Grayson counties. The **desert pocket gopher** *(Geomys arenarius)* is found only in the Trans-Pecos, while the **yellow-faced pocket gopher** *(Cratogeomys castanops)* is found in the western one-third of the state, with occasional sightings along the Rio Grande in Maverick and Cameron counties. The **Texas pocket gopher** *(Geomys personatus)* is found in South Texas from San Patricio County to Val Verde County. **Attwater's pocket gopher** *(Geomys attwateri)* and **Baird's pocket gopher** *(Geomys breviceps)* are both found generally in South-Central and Coastal Texas from the Brazos River to the San Antonio River and south to Matagorda and San Patricio counties. **Jones' pocket gopher** *(Geomys knoxjonesi)* is found only in far West Texas, while the **Llano pocket gopher** *(Geomys texensis)* is found only in two isolated areas of the Hill Country.

**Ground Squirrel** — Five or more species of ground squirrel live in Texas, mostly in the western part of the state. The **rock squirrel** *(Spermophilus variegatus)* is found throughout the Edwards Plateau and Trans-Pecos. The **Mexican ground squirrel** *(Spermophilus mexicanus)* occurs throughout much of South Texas, the Trans-Pecos, and almost to the Red River just east of the Panhandle.The **spotted ground squirrel** *(Spermophilus spilosoma)* is found generally in the western half of the state. The **thirteen-lined ground squirrel** *(Spermophilus tridecemlineatus)* is found in a narrow strip from Dallas and Tarrant counties to the Gulf. The **Texas antelope squirrel** *(Ammospermophilus interpres)* is found along the Rio Grande from El Paso to Val Verde County.

**Hog, Feral** — (See **Pig, Feral.**)

**Javelina** — The **javelina** or **collared peccary** *(Tayassu tajacu)* is found in brushy semi-desert areas where prickly pear, a favorite food, is found. The javelina was hunted commercially for its hide until 1939. They are harmless to livestock and to people, though they can defend themselves ferociously when attacked by hunting dogs.

**Mink** — The **mink** *(Mustela vison)* is found in the eastern half of the state, always near streams, lakes, or other water sources. Although it is an economically important fur-bearing animal in the eastern United States, it ranked only 13th in numbers and 9th in economic value to trappers in Texas in 1988–89, according to a Texas Parks and Wildlife Department survey.

**Mole** — The **eastern mole** *(Scalopus aquaticus)* is found in the eastern two-thirds of Texas. Moles cannot see and spend most of their life in underground burrows they excavate for themselves or usurp from other mammals, such as pocket gophers. The burrowing of moles can damage lawns, row crops, and the greens of golf courses. Benefits, however, are aerating soil and eating larval insects that destroy roots of grass and crops.

**Muskrat** — The **common muskrat** *(Ondatra zibethica)* occurs in aquatic habitats in the northern, southeastern, and southwestern parts of the state. Although the muskrat was once economically valuable for its fur, its numbers have declined, mostly because of the loss of habitat.

**Nutria**\* — This introduced species *(Myocastor coypus)*, native to South America, is found in the eastern two-thirds of the state. The fur is not highly valued and, because nutria are in competition with muskrats, their spread is discouraged. They have been used widely in Texas as a cure-all for ponds choked with vegetation, with spotty results.

**Opossum** — A **marsupial**, the **Virginia opossum** *(Didelphis virginiana)* is found in nearly all parts of the state. The opossum has economic value for its pelt, and its meat is considered a delicacy by some. It is one of the chief contributors to the Texas fur crop.

**Otter** — A few **river otter** *(Lutra canadensis)* are found in the eastern quarter of the state. It has probably been extirpated from the Panhandle, North-Central, and South Texas.

**Pig, Feral**\* — Feral pigs are found throughout Texas but especially in areas of the Rio Grande and Coastal Plains, as well as in the woods of East Texas. They are descendants of escaped domestic hogs or of European wild hogs that were imported for sport. Their rooting habits can extensively destroy vegetation and soil.

**Porcupine** — The **yellow-haired porcupine** *(Erethizon dorsatum)* is found from the western half of the state east to Bosque County. It is adapted to a variety of habitats and, in recent years, has expanded into South Texas. Porcupines are expert at climbing trees but are as much at home in rocks as on the ground or in trees. They have a relatively long lifespan; one marked female lived more than 10 years under natural conditions.

**Prairie Dog** — Until recent years, probably no sight was so universal in West Texas as the **black-tailed prairie dog** *(Cynomys ludovicianus)*. Naturalists estimated its population in the hundreds of millions, and prairie-dog towns often covered many acres with thickly spaced burrows. Its destruction of range grasses and cultivated crops has caused farmers and ranchers to destroy many of them, and it is extirpated from much of its former range. It is being propagated in several public zoos, notably in the **prairie dog town in Mackenzie Park** at Lubbock. It has been honored in Texas by the naming of **Prairie Dog Town Fork** of the Red River, one segment of which is located the beautiful **Palo Duro Canyon.**

**Pronghorn** — The **Pronghorn** *(Antilocapra americana)* formerly was found in the western two-thirds of the state. It is currently found only in limited areas from the Panhandle to the Trans-Pecos. Despite management efforts, its numbers have been decreasing in recent years.

**Rabbit** — The **black-tailed jack rabbit** *(Lepus californicus)* is found throughout Texas except the Big Thicket area of East Texas. It breeds rapidly, and its long hind legs make it one of the world's faster-running animals. The **Eastern cottontail** *(Sylvilagus floridanus)* is found mostly in the eastern three-quarters of the state. The **desert cottontail** *(Sylvilagus auduboni)* is found in the western half of the state, usually on the open range. The **swamp rabbit** *(Sylvilagus aquaticus)* is found in East Texas and the coastal area.

**Raccoon** — The **raccoon** *(Procyon lotor)* is found throughout Texas, especially in woodlands and near water. It is strictly nocturnal. A raccoon makes its den in a large hollow tree or hollow log, in which its spends the daylight hours sleeping and in which it also rears its young. In western areas, dens usually are in crevices of rocky bluffs.

**Rats and Mice** — There are 40 to 50 species of rats and mice in Texas of varying characteristics, habitats, and economic destructiveness. The **Norway rat**\* *(Rattus norvegicus)* and the **roof rat**\* *(Rattus rattus),* both non-native species, are probably the most common and most destructive. They also are instrumental in the transmission of several dread diseases, including bubonic plague and typhus. The **common house mouse**\* *(Mus musculis)* is estimated in the hundreds of millions annually. The **Mexican vole** *(Microtus mexicanus guadalupensis),* also called the **Guadalupe Mountain vole,** is found only in the higher elevations of Guadalupe Mountains National Park and just over the border into New Mexico.

**Ringtail** — The **ringtail** *(Bassariscus astutus)* is a cat-sized carnivore resembling a small fox with a long raccoon-like tail. It found statewide but is rare in the Lower Valley and the Coastal Plains. Ringtails are nocturnal and live in a variety of habitats, preferring rocky areas, such as rock piles, stone fences, and canyon walls.

*A whooping crane chases a white-tailed deer fawn from its territory in the Aransas National Wildlife Refuge. The white-tailed deer is found throughout the state in brushy or wooded areas. The whooping crane is an endangered species. Photo by Steve Hillebrand; U.S. Fish and Wildlife Service.*

**Sheep** — The **mountain sheep** *(Ovis canadensis),* or **desert bighorn,** formerly was found in isolated areas of the mountainous Trans-Pecos, but the last native sheep were seen in 1959. Recently, they have been introduced into the same areas with success. The **barbary sheep**\* *(Ammotragus lervia),* or **aoudad,** first introduced to the Palo Duro Canyon area in 1957–1958, has become firmly established. A multi-partner wildlife restoration project has brought the bighorn sheep into the Edwards Plateau, Trans-Pecos, South Texas, Rolling Plains, and Post Oak Savannah regions, including Big Bend Ranch State Park.

**Shrew** — The **shrew** is one of the smallest mammals. Four species are found in Texas: the **southern short-tailed shrew** *(Blarina Carolinensis),* found in the eastern one-fourth of the state; the **least shrew** *(Cryptotis parva),* in eastern and central areas; **Elliot's short-tailed shrew** *(Blarina hylophaga),* known only in Aransas, Montague, and Bastrop counties; and the **desert shrew** *(Notiosorex crawfordi),* found in the western two-thirds of the state.

**Skunk** — There are six species of skunk in Texas. The **Eastern spotted skunk** *(Spilogale putorius)* is found in the eastern half of the state, the Gulf area, and across North-Central Texas to the Panhandle. A small skunk, it is often erroneously called civet cat. The **Western spotted skunk** *(Spilogale gracilis)* is found in the southwestern part of the state north to Garza and Howard counties and east to Bexar and Duval counties. The **striped skunk** *(Mephitis mephitis)* is found statewide, mostly in brush or wooded areas. The **hooded skunk** *(Mephitis macroura)* is found in limited numbers in the Big Bend and adjacent parts of the Trans-Pecos. The **eastern hog-nosed skunk** *(Conepatus leuconotus),* found in the Gulf Coastal Plains, ranges southward into Mexico. The **common hog-nosed skunk** *(Conepatus mesoleucus)* is found in southwestern, central, and southern Texas, north to Collin and Lubbock counties.

**Squirrel** — The **eastern fox squirrel** *(Sciurus niger)* is found in the eastern two-thirds of the state. The **eastern gray squirrel** *(Sciurus carolinensis)* is found generally in the eastern third of the state. The **flying squirrel** *(Glaucomys volans)* is found in wooded areas of East Texas. The fox and gray squirrels are important small game animals. See also, **Ground Squirrel.**

**Whale** — Some species that are found in the Gulf of Mexico include: **dwarf sperm whale** *(Kogia simus);* **pygmy sperm whale** *(Kogia breviceps),* found near the Texas coast where strandings occur relatively frequently; **short-finned pilot whale** *(Globicephala macrorhynchus),* common in the Gulf where there are numerous strandings and sightings; **sperm whale** *(Physeter macrocephalus),* an endangered species and the most numerous of the great whales in the Gulf, where sightings are relatively common. Other species are known in Texas only through strandings on Gulf beaches.

**Weasel** — The **long-tailed weasel** *(Mustela frenata),* akin to the mink, is found statewide, but is scarce in West Texas and the far north Panhandle. In general, their destruction of mice, ground squirrels, and pocket gophers benefits agriculture. But on occasion they enter poultry houses and wantonly kill chickens.

**Wolf** — The **red wolf** *(Canis rufus)* was once found throughout the eastern half of the state. It has now been extirpated from the wild, with the only known remnants of the population now in captive propagation. The **gray wolf** *(Canis lupus)* once had a wide range over the western two-thirds of the state. It is now considered extinct

in Texas. The **red wolf** and **gray wolf** are on the federal and state endangered species lists.

## Reptiles and Arachnids

Most of the more than **100 species and subspecies of snakes** found in Texas are beneficial, as also are other reptiles. There are **16 poisonous species and subspecies.**

**Poisonous reptiles** include three species of **copperheads** *(southern, broad-banded, and Trans-Pecos);* one kind of **cottonmouth** *(western);* 11 kinds of **rattlesnakes** *(canebrake, western massasauga, desert massasauga, western pigmy, western diamondback, timber, banded rock, mottled rock, northern blacktailed, Mojave, and prairie);* and the **Texas coral snake.**

Also noteworthy are the **horned lizard,** also called **horned toad,** which is on the list of threatened species; the **vinegarone,** a type of whip scorpion; **tarantula,** a hairy spider; and **alligator.** ☆

# Texas' Threatened and Endangered Species

Endangered species are those the Texas Parks and Wildlife Department (TPWD) has named as being at risk of statewide extinction. Threatened species are likely to become endangered in the future. The following species are either endangered or threatened as of July 2013. This list varies slightly from the federal list. Contact Endangered Resources Branch, Texas Parks and Wildlife, 4200 Smith School Road, Austin 78744; 800-792-1112; www.tpwd.state.tx.us/nature/endang/endang.htm.

## Endangered Species

**MAMMALS** — **Bats:** Mexican long-nosed bat. **Marine Mammals:** West Indian manatee; finback and humpback whales. **Carnivores:** jaguar; jaguarundi; ocelot; gray and red wolves.
**BIRDS** — **Waterbirds:** Whooping crane; "Eastern" brown pelican. **Raptors:** Northern aplomado falcon. **Upland Birds:** Attwater's greater prairie chicken. **Shorebirds:** Eskimo curlew; interior least tern. **Woodpeckers:** red-cockaded woodpeckers. **Songbirds:** southwestern willow flycatcher; black-capped vireo; golden-cheeked warbler.
**REPTILES** — **Turtles:** Atlantic hawksbill, Kemp's Ridley, leatherback, and sea turtles.
**AMPHIBIANS** — **Salamanders:** Barton Springs and Texas blind salamanders. **Frogs & Toads:** Houston toad.
**FISHES** — **Minnows:** Rio Grande silvery minnow. **Killifishes:** Comanche Springs and Leon Springs pupfishes. **Livebearers:** Big Bend, Clear Creek, Pecos, and San Marcos gambusias. **Perches:** Fountain darter. **Coastal Fishes:** smalltooth sawfish.
**INVERTEBRATES** — **Crustaceans:** Peck's cave amphipod. **Mollusks & Snails:** Pecos assiminea snail.
**PLANTS** — **Cacti:** Black lace, Nellie's Cory, Sneed's pincushion, star, and Tobusch fishhook cacti; Davis' green pitaya. **Trees, Shrubs, Sub-shrubs:** Texas ayenia; Johnston's frankenia; Walker's manioc; Texas snowbells. **Wildflowers:** South Texas ambrosia; Zapata and white bladderpod; Terlingua Creek cat's-eye; ashy dogweed; Texas trailing phlox; Texas poppy-mallow; Texas prairie dawn; slender rushpea; large-fruited sand-verbena. **Orchids:** Navasota ladies'-tresses. **Grasses:** little aguja pondweed; Texas wild-rice.

## Threatened Species

**MAMMALS** — **Bats:** Rafinesque's big-eared, southern yellow, and spotted bats. **Carnivores:** black and Louisiana black bears; white-nosed coati; margay. **Marine Mammals:** Atlantic spotted and rough-toothed dolphins; dwarf sperm, false killer, Gervais' beaked, goose-beaked, killer, pygmy killer, pygmy sperm, and short-finned pilot whales. **Rodents:** Palo Duro

mouse; Coues' rice rat and Texas kangaroo rat.
**BIRDS** — **Waterbirds:** reddish egret; white-faced ibis; wood stork. **Raptors:** bald eagle; American peregrine falcon; common black, gray, white-tailed, and zone-tailed hawks; swallow-tailed kite; Mexican spotted owl; cactus ferruginous pygmy-owl. **Shorebirds:** piping plover; sooty tern. **Songbirds:** rose-throated becard; tropical parula; Bachman's, Texas Botteri's, and Arizona Botteri's sparrows; northern beardless tyrannulet.
**REPTILES** — **Turtles:** loggerhead and green sea turtles; Texas tortoise; alligator snapping, Cagle's map, and Chihuahuan mud turtles. **Lizards:** reticulated gecko; mountain short-horned, reticulate collared, and Texas horned lizards. **Snakes:** speckled racer; black-striped, Brazos water, Chihuahuan desert lyre, Louisiana pine, northern cat-eyed, smooth green, scarlet, Texas indigo, and Trans-Pecos black-headed snakes; timber (canebrake) rattlesnake.
**AMPHIBIANS** — **Salamanders:** black-spotted newt; Blanco blind, Cascade Caverns, Comal blind, and San Marcos salamanders; South Texas siren (large form). **Frogs & Toads:** sheep and white-lipped frogs; Mexican treefrog; Mexican burrowing toad.
**FISHES** — **Large River Fish:** paddlefish and shovelnose sturgeon. **Minnows:** Rio Grande chub; Devils River minnow; Arkansas River, bluehead, bluntnose, Chihuahua, and proserpine shiners; Mexican stoneroller. **Suckers:** blue sucker and creek chubsucker. **Catfishes:** toothless blindcat and widemouth blindcat. **Killifishes:** Conchos and Pecos pupfishes. **Livebearers:** blotched and San Felipe gambusias. Killifishes: Conchos and Pecos pupfishes. **Perches:** blackside and Rio Grande darters. **Coastal Fishes:** opossum pipefish; river and Mexican goby.
**INVERTEBRATES** — **Mollusks & Snails:** Texas fatmucket; Mexican and Texas fawnsfoot; Texas heelsplitter; Southern hickorynut; Texas hornshell; salina mucket; golden orb; Louisiana, Texas, and triangle pigtoe; smooth and Texas pimpleback; sandbank pocketbook; false spike.
**PLANTS** — **Cacti:** Bunched cory, Chisos Mountains hedgehog, and Lloyd's mariposa cacti. **Trees, Shrubs, Sub-shrubs:** Hinckley's oak. **Wildflowers:** Pecos sunflower; earth fruit. ☆

# National Wildlife Refuges in Texas

*Source: U.S. Fish and Wildlife Service, U.S. Department of the Interior.*

Texas has more than 470,000 acres in 17 national wildlife refuges. Their descriptions, with date of acquisition in parentheses, follow.

Included in this acreage are two conservation easement refuges, which may be visited at different times of the year for bird watching and wildlife viewing, as well as hunting and fishing. Write or call before visiting to check on facilities and days and hours of operation. On the web: www.fws.gov/southwest/.

**Anahuac** (1963): The more than 34,000 acres of this refuge are located along the upper Gulf Coast in Chambers County. Fresh and saltwater marshes and miles of beautiful, sweeping coastal prairie provide wintering habitat for large flocks of waterfowl, including geese, 27 species of ducks, and six species of rails. Roseate spoonbills, great and snowy egrets, and white-faced ibis are among the other birds frequenting the refuge. Other species include alligator, muskrat, and bobcat. Fishing, bird watching, auto tours, and hunting are available. Office: Box 278, Anahuac 77514; (409) 267-3337.

**Aransas** (1937): This refuge complex comprises 115,000 acres including Blackjack Peninsula, Matagorda Island, and three satellite units in Aransas and Refugio counties. Besides providing wintering grounds for the largest wild flock of endangered whooping cranes, the refuge is home to more than 390 species of waterfowl and other migratory birds. Refuge Tour Loop is open daily, sunrise to sunset. Claude F. Lard Visitor Center is open daily, 8:30 a.m. to 4:30 p.m. Other facilities include a 40-foot observation tower and walking trails. Office: Box 100, Austwell 77950; (361) 286-3559.

**Attwater Prairie Chicken** (1972): Established in Colorado County to preserve habitat for the endangered Attwater's prairie chicken (a ground-dwelling grouse), the refuge comprises 10,528 acres of native tallgrass prairie, sandy knolls, and wooded areas. A 5-mile auto tour loop is available year-round. Two hiking trails, the Pipit and Sycamore trails, traverse the prairie, potholes, and riparian areas. The auto tour loop can also serve as

*An observation deck extends out into the Gulf at the Aransas National Wildlife Refuge. Photo by Steve Hillebrand; U.S. Fish and Wildlife Service.*

a hiking trail. Refuge open sunrise to sunset. Office: Box 519, Eagle Lake 77434; (979) 234-3021.

**Balcones Canyonlands** (1992): This 25,000-acre refuge is located in Burnet, Travis, and Williamson counties northwest of Austin. It was established to protect the nesting habitat of two endangered birds: black-capped vireo and golden-cheeked warbler. The Shin Oak Observation Deck is open almost year around (excluding a few weekends in the fall). Hunting available. Open Monday–Friday, 8:00 a.m.–4:30 p.m Office: 24518 FM-1431, Marble Falls, 78654; (512) 339-9432.

**Big Boggy** (1983): This refuge occupies 5,000 acres of coastal prairie and salt marsh along East Matagorda Bay for the benefit of wintering waterfowl. The refuge is only open to waterfowl hunting in season. Office: 6801 County Road 306, Brazoria, 77422; (979) 964-3639.

**Brazoria** (1966): The 43,388 acres of this refuge, located along the Gulf Coast in Brazoria County, serve as haven for wintering waterfowl and a wide variety of other migratory birds. The refuge also supports many marsh and water birds, from roseate spoonbills and great blue herons to white-faced ibis and sandhill cranes. Brazoria Refuge is within the Freeport Christmas Bird Count circle, which frequently achieves the highest number of species seen in a 24-hour period. Open daily sunrise to sunset. Hunting and fishing also available. Office: 24907 FM 2004, Angleton, 77515; (979) 922-1037.

**Buffalo Lake** (1958): Comprising 7,664 acres in the Central Flyway in Randall County in the Panhandle, this refuge contains some of the best remaining shortgrass prairie in the United States. Buffalo Lake is now dry; a marsh area is artificially maintained for the numerous birds, reptiles, and mammals. Available activities include picnicking, auto tour, birding, photography, and hiking. Office: Box 179, Umbarger 79091; (806) 499-3382.

**Caddo Lake** (2000): Established on portions of the 8,5000-acre Longhorn Army Ammunition Plant in Harrison County, this refuge contains a mature flooded bald cypress forest, with some trees nearly 400 years old. The wetlands support a diverse plant community. The bottomland hardwood forest ecosystem provides essential habitat for migratory and resident wildlife. The wetlands of Caddo Lake are important to migratory birds within the Central Flyway. The area supports one of the highest breeding populations of wood ducks and protho-

notary warblers. Bird watching, hunting, equestrian use, auto tour, hiking, and biking are available. Office: (903) 679-9144.

**Hagerman** (1946): Hagerman National Wildlife Refuge lies on the Big Mineral arm of Lake Texoma in Grayson County. The 4,500 acres of marsh and water and 6,900 acres of upland and farmland provide a feeding and resting place for migrating waterfowl. Bird watching, fishing, and hunting are available. Office: 6465 Refuge Road, Sherman, 75092-5817; (903) 786-2826.

**Laguna Atascosa:** (1946): This refuge is the southernmost waterfowl refuge in the Central Flyway and contains more than 45,000 acres fronting on the Laguna Madre in the Lower Rio Grande Valley in Cameron and Willacy counties. Open lagoons, coastal prairies, salt flats, and brushlands support a wide diversity of wildlife. The United States' largest concentration of redhead ducks winters here, along with many other species of waterfowl and shorebirds. White-tailed deer, javelina, and armadillo can be found, along with endangered ocelot. Bird watching and nature study are popular; auto-tour roads and nature trails are available. Camping and fishing are permitted within Adolph Thomae Jr. County Park. Hunting also available. Office: 22817 Ocelot Road, Los Fresnos, 78566; (956) 748-3607.

**Lower Rio Grande Valley** (1979): Part of the 180,000 acre South Texas Refuge Complex, this refuge lies within Cameron, Hidalgo, Starr, and Willacy counties. It comprises more than 100 separate tracts of land, some fallow farm fields connecting healthy habitat that can become travel corridors for wildlife. The refuge includes 11 different habitat types, including sabal palm forest, tidal flats, coastal brushland, mid-delta thorn forest, woodland potholes and basins, upland thorn scrub, flood forest, barretal, riparian woodland, and Chihuahuan thorn forest. Nearly 500 species of birds and over 300 butterfly species have been found there, as well as four of the five cats that occur within the United States: jaguarundi, ocelot, bobcat, and mountain lion. Seasonal hunting and canoe tours are available. Office: 3325 Green Jay Road, Alamo, 78516 ; (956) 784-7500.

**McFaddin** (1980): This refuge's 55,000 acres in Jefferson and Chambers counties are of great importance to wintering populations of migratory waterfowl. One of the densest populations of alligators in Texas is found here. Activities on the refuge include wildlife observation, hunting, fishing, and crabbing. Seven boat ramps provide access to inland lakes and waterways; limited roadways. Open daily from sunrise until sunset. Office: 7950 S. Gulfway Dr., Sabine Pass, 77655; (409) 971-2909.

**Muleshoe** (1935): Oldest of the national refuges in Texas, Muleshoe provides winter habitat for waterfowl and the continent's largest wintering population of sandhill cranes. Comprising 5,809 acres in the High Plains of Bailey County, the refuge contains playa lakes, marsh areas, caliche outcroppings, and native grasslands. A nature trail, campground, and picnic area are available. Office: Box 549, Muleshoe 79347; 806-946-3341.

**Neches River** (2013) Anderson and Cherokee counties.It was established to protect wintering and nesting habitat for migratory birds of the Central Flyway and the bottomland hardwoods for their diverse biological value. It is currently closed to the public but will eventually open for wildlife-dependent recreation.

**San Bernard** (1968): Located in Brazoria and Matagorda counties on the Gulf Coast near Freeport, this refuge's 27,414 acres attract migrating waterfowl, includ-

# National Wildlife Refuges in Texas

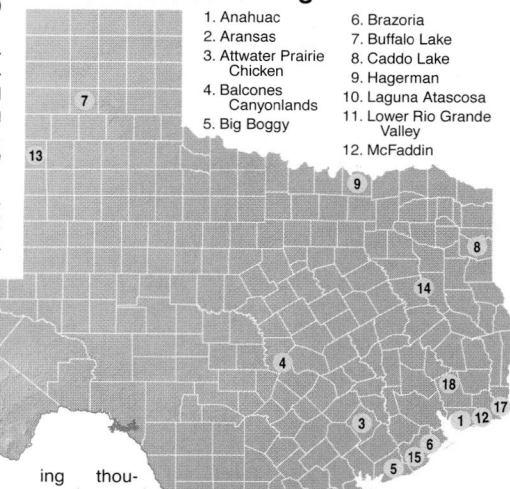

| 1. Anahuac | 6. Brazoria |
| 2. Aransas | 7. Buffalo Lake |
| 3. Attwater Prairie Chicken | 8. Caddo Lake |
| 4. Balcones Canyonlands | 9. Hagerman |
| 5. Big Boggy | 10. Laguna Atascosa |
|  | 11. Lower Rio Grande Valley |
|  | 12. McFaddin |

| 13. Muleshoe |
| 14. Neches River |
| 15. San Bernard |
| 16. Santa Ana |
| 17. Texas Point |
| 18. Trinity River |

ing thousands of white-fronted and Canada geese and several duck species, which spend the winter on the refuge. Habitats, consisting of coastal prairies, salt-mud flats, and saltwater and freshwater ponds and potholes, also attract yellow rails, roseate spoonbills, reddish egrets, and American bitterns. Visitors enjoy auto and hiking trails, photography, bird watching, fishing, and waterfowl hunting in season. Office: 6801 County Road 306, Brazoria, 77422; (979) 964-4011.

**Santa Ana** (1943): Santa Ana is located on the north bank of the Rio Grande in Hidalgo County. Santa Ana's 2,088 acres of subtropical forest and native brushland are at an ecological crossroads of subtropical, Gulf Coast, Great Plains, and Chihuahuan desert habitats. Santa Ana attracts birders from across the United States who can view many species of Mexican birds as they reach the northern edge of their ranges in South Texas. Also found at Santa Ana are ocelot and jaguarundi, endangered members of the cat family. Visitors enjoy a tram or auto drive, bicycling and hiking trails, and a tower overlook. Office: 3325 Green Jay Road, Alamo, 78516; (956) 784-7500.

**Texas Point** (1980): Texas Point's 8,900 acres are located in Jefferson County on the upper Gulf Coast, 12 miles east of McFaddin NWR, where they serve a large wintering population of waterfowl and migratory birds. The endangered southern bald eagle and peregrine falcon may occasionally be seen during peak fall and spring migrations. Alligators are commonly observed during the spring, summer, and fall months. Activities include wildlife observation, hunting, fishing, and crabbing. Access to the refuge is by boat and on foot only. Open daily from sunrise until sunset. Office: 7950 S. Gulfway Dr., Sabine Pass, 77655; (409) 971-2909.

**Trinity River** (1994): Established to protect remnant bottomland hardwood forests and associated wetlands, this refuge, located in northern Liberty County off State Highway 787 about 15 miles east of Cleveland, provides habitat for wintering, migrating, and breeding waterfowl and a variety of other wetland-dependent wildlife. A tract south of Liberty includes Champion Lake. Office: Box 10015, Liberty 77575; (936) 336-9786. ☆

# Texas Wildlife Management Areas

*Source: Texas Parks and Wildlife Department; http://www.tpwd.state.tx.us/huntwild/hunt/wma/.*

Texas Parks and Wildlife Department is responsible for managing 49 wildlife management areas (WMAs) in the state totaling 768,175 acres. Thirty of the WMAs are owned in fee title, while 19 are managed under license agreements with other agencies.

Wildlife management areas are used principally for hunting, but many are also used for research, fishing, wildlife viewing, hiking, camping, bicycling, and horseback riding, when those activities are compatible with the primary goals for which the WMA was established. See the table on the following page for activities available in Texas' WMAs.

Access to WMAs at times designated for public use is provided through various permits, depending on the activity.

Hunting permits include the drawn Special Permit ($80 or $130), Regular Daily Permit ($20), or Annual Public Hunting Permit ($48).

A Limited Public Use Permit ($12) allows access for such activities as birdwatching, hiking, camping, or picnicking.

On most WMAs, restrooms and drinking water are not provided; check with the TPWD about facilities before visiting a WMA.

For further information, contact the Texas Parks and Wildlife Department, 4200 Smith School Rd., Austin 78744; or call 1-800-792-1112 and choose menu #5, selection #1. ☆

## Texas Wildlife Management Areas

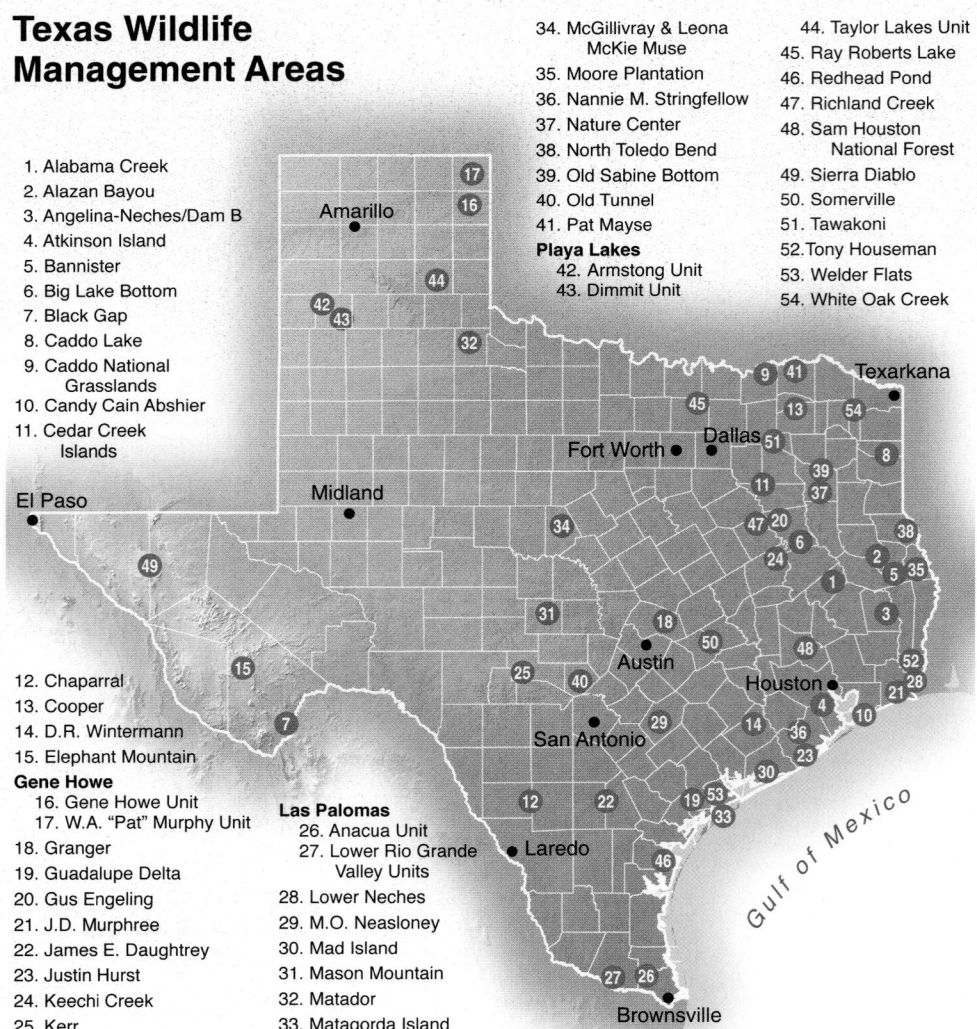

1. Alabama Creek
2. Alazan Bayou
3. Angelina-Neches/Dam B
4. Atkinson Island
5. Bannister
6. Big Lake Bottom
7. Black Gap
8. Caddo Lake
9. Caddo National Grasslands
10. Candy Cain Abshier
11. Cedar Creek Islands

12. Chaparral
13. Cooper
14. D.R. Wintermann
15. Elephant Mountain

**Gene Howe**
16. Gene Howe Unit
17. W.A. "Pat" Murphy Unit
18. Granger
19. Guadalupe Delta
20. Gus Engeling
21. J.D. Murphree
22. James E. Daughtrey
23. Justin Hurst
24. Keechi Creek
25. Kerr

**Las Palomas**
26. Anacua Unit
27. Lower Rio Grande Valley Units
28. Lower Neches
29. M.O. Neasloney
30. Mad Island
31. Mason Mountain
32. Matador
33. Matagorda Island

34. McGillivray & Leona McKie Muse
35. Moore Plantation
36. Nannie M. Stringfellow
37. Nature Center
38. North Toledo Bend
39. Old Sabine Bottom
40. Old Tunnel
41. Pat Mayse

**Playa Lakes**
42. Armstong Unit
43. Dimmit Unit

44. Taylor Lakes Unit
45. Ray Roberts Lake
46. Redhead Pond
47. Richland Creek
48. Sam Houston National Forest
49. Sierra Diablo
50. Somerville
51. Tawakoni
52. Tony Houseman
53. Welder Flats
54. White Oak Creek

## Texas Wildlife Management Areas

| | Acreage | County | Day Use Only | Hunting | Fishing | Camping | Wildlife Viewing | Hiking | Interpretive Trail | Driving | Bicycling | Equestrian | Comments |
|---|---|---|---|---|---|---|---|---|---|---|---|---|---|
| Alabama Creek | 14,561 | Trinity | | ★ | ★ | ★ | ★ | ★ | | ★ | ★ | ★ | In Davy Crockett Nat. Forest |
| Alazan Bayou | 2,063 | Nacogdoches | | ★ | ★ | ★ | ★ | | | | | ★ | |
| Angelina-Neches/Dam B | 12,636 | Jasper/Tyler | | ★ | ★ | ★ | ★ | ★ | | ★ | | | |
| Atkinson Island | 150 | Harris | ★ | | ★ | | ★ | | | | | | Boat access only |
| Bannister | 25,695 | San Augustine | | ★ | ★ | ★ | ★ | ★ | | | ★ | ★ | In Angelina National Forest |
| Big Lake Bottom | 3,894 | Anderson | ★ | ★ | ★ | | ★ | | | | | | 2,870 acres available to public |
| Black Gap | 103,000 | Brewster | ★ | ★ | ★ | ★ | ★ | ★ | | ★ | ★ | ★ | NW of Big Bend National Park |
| Caddo Lake | 8,005 | Marion/Harrison | | ★ | ★ | ★ | ★ | | | | | ★ | |
| Caddo Nat. Grasslands | 16,140 | Fannin | | ★ | ★ | ★ | ★ | ★ | | | ★ | ★ | |
| Candy Cain Abshier | 207 | Chambers | ★ | | | | ★ | | | | | | Excellent birding spring and fall |
| Cedar Creek Islands | 160 | Henderson | ★ | | | ★ | | ★ | | | | | Camp in Purvis Creek SP & Fairfield Lake SP; do not disturb rookeries in spring & summer |
| Chaparral | 15,200 | La Salle/Dimmit | | ★ | | ★ | ★ | ★ | | ★ | ★ | | |
| Cooper | 19,280 | Delta/Hopkins | ★ | ★ | ★ | | ★ | ★ | | | | | Camping at Cooper Lake SP |
| D.R. Wintermann | 246 | Wharton | ★ | | | | ★ | | | | | | Restricted access; bird refuge |
| Elephant Mountain | 23,147 | Brewster | | ★ | | ★ | ★ | ★ | | ★ | | | |
| Gene Howe | 5,887 | Hemphill | | ★ | ★ | ★ | ★ | ★ | | | ★ | ★ | Riding March–August only |
| W.A. "Pat" Murphy Unit | 432 | Hemphill | | ★ | ★ | | ★ | ★ | | | | | |
| Granger | 10,888 | Williamson | | ★ | ★ | ★ | ★ | ★ | | | ★ | | Primitive camping only |
| Guadalupe Delta | 6,593 | Calhoun/Refugio | | ★ | | ★ | ★ | ★ | | | ★ | | Freshwater marsh |
| Gus Engling | 10,958 | Anderson | | ★ | ★ | ★ | ★ | ★ | | ★ | ★ | ★ | |
| J.D. Murphree | 24,250 | Jefferson | ★ | ★ | ★ | | ★ | | | | | | Access by boat only |
| James E. Daughtrey | 4,400 | Live Oak/McMullen | ★ | ★ | | | ★ | | | | | | Primitive camping only |
| Justin Hurst | 11,938 | Brazoria | | ★ | ★ | | ★ | ★ | ★ | | ★ | | On Texas Coastal Birding Trail |
| Keechi Creek | 1,500 | Leon | | ★ | | | | | | | | | |
| Kerr | 6,493 | Kerr | | ★ | ★ | | ★ | ★ | | ★ | ★ | | On Guadalupe River |
| Las Palomas: Anacua Unit | 222 | Cameron | | ★ | | | ★ | | | | | | |
| Lower Rio Grande Valley Units | 3,311 | Cameron/Hidalgo | ★ | ★ | | | ★ | ★ | | | | | Also Starr & Willacy counties |
| Lower Neches | 7,998 | Orange | ★ | ★ | ★ | | ★ | ★ | | | | | Coastal marsh |
| M.O. Neasloney | 100 | Gonzales | ★ | | | | ★ | ★ | ★ | | | | |
| Mad Island | 7,200 | Matagorda | | ★ | | | ★ | | | | | | Coastal wetlands |
| Mason Mountain | 5,301 | Mason | | ★ | | | | | | | | | Restricted access |
| Matador | 28,183 | Cottle | | ★ | ★ | ★ | ★ | ★ | ★ | ★ | | ★ | Primitive camping; tours |
| Matagorda Island | 56,688 | Calhoun | | ★ | ★ | ★ | ★ | ★ | | ★ | | | |
| McGillivray & Leona McKie Muse | 1,972 | Brown | | ★ | | | ★ | | | | | | |
| Moore Plantation | 26,772 | Sabine/Jasper | | ★ | ★ | ★ | ★ | ★ | ★ | | ★ | ★ | In Sabine National Forest |
| Nannie M. Stringfellow | 3,664 | Brazoria | | ★ | | | ★ | | | | | | Open for special hunts only |
| Nature Center | 82 | Smith | ★ | | | | ★ | ★ | ★ | | | | Primarily for school groups |
| North Toldeo Bend | 3,650 | Shelby | | ★ | ★ | ★ | ★ | ★ | | | | ★ | Limited use of horses |
| Old Sabine Bottom | 5,158 | Smith | | ★ | ★ | ★ | ★ | ★ | | | ★ | ★ | Canoeing |
| Old Tunnel | 16 | Kendall | ★ | | | | ★ | ★ | ★ | | | | Bat viewing April–October |
| Pat Mayse | 8,925 | Lamar | | ★ | ★ | ★ | ★ | ★ | | | ★ | | |
| Playa Lakes: Armstrong Unit | 160 | Castro | ★ | | | | ★ | | | | | | |
| Dimmitt Unit | 77 | Castro | ★ | ★ | | | | | | | | | Limited access |
| Taylor Lakes Unit | 527 | Donley | ★ | ★ | | | ★ | ★ | | | | | Hunting only on Donley Co. unit |
| Ray Roberts Lake | 41,303 | Cooke/Denton | ★ | ★ | ★ | | ★ | ★ | | | | | Also Grayson County |
| Redhead Pond | 37 | Nueces | ★ | | | | ★ | | | | | | Freshwater wetland |
| Richland Creek | 13,797 | Freestone/Navarro | | ★ | ★ | ★ | ★ | ★ | | | ★ | ★ | |
| Sam Houston National Forest | 161,508 | San Jacinto/Walker | | ★ | ★ | ★ | ★ | ★ | | ★ | ★ | ★ | Also Montgomery County |
| Sierra Diablo | 11,624 | Hudspeth/Culberson | | ★ | | | | | | | | | Restricted access |
| Somerville | 11,630 | Burleson/Lee | ★ | ★ | ★ | | ★ | ★ | | | ★ | | Camping at Somerville SP |
| Tawakoni | 9,756 | Hunt/Van Zandt | | ★ | ★ | ★ | ★ | ★ | | | | ★ | |
| Tony Houseman | 3,987 | Orange | | ★ | ★ | ★ | ★ | ★ | | | | | Also called Blue Elbow Swamp |
| Welder Flats | 1,480 | Calhoun | ★ | | ★ | | ★ | | | | | | Boat access only |
| White Oak Creek | 25,777 | Bowie/Cass/Morris | ★ | ★ | ★ | | ★ | ★ | | | | ★ | Also Titus County; camp in Atlanta and Daingerfield SPs |
| **TOTAL** | **768,628** | | | | | | | | | | | | |

# Weather

*Storm clouds gather around the sunlit Guadalupe Mountains.*
*The national park in West Texas covers 86,416 acres in Hudspeth and*
*Culberson counties. Photo courtesy of Traces of Texas.com.*

## 2013 and 2014 Highlights, Summaries
## Temperatures, Precipitation
## Tornados, Droughts
## Destructive Weather 1766–2014
## Records by County

# Weather

Source: Unless otherwise noted, this information is provided by Texas State Climatologist John W. Nielsen-Gammon, graduate research assistant David Coates, and research assistant Brent McRoberts; Texas A&M University.

## Weather Highlights 2013

**February 21:** A cluster of thunderstorms moved through near Pineland in Sabine County, but no severe thunderstorm warnings or tornado warnings were issued at all for this cluster. An **EF1 tornado touched down near Pineland** and traveled 4.5 miles in its 9-minute lifespan. The estimated wind speeds in the tornado were 105 mph. A 74-year-old woman died in the tornado when her mobile home rolled over. This was the first fatal tornado in Texas since April 24, 2007. Total damages were only $250,000, but a life was lost, as well as two others were injured.

**May 15:** A massive system of severe thunderstorms spawned a deadly tornado outbreak in North Texas that killed six people and injured more than 100 others. Two violent tornadoes, an **EF4 tornado in Mambrino,** Hood County, and an **EF3 tornado in Cleburne,** Johnson County, moved through North Texas and caused well over $250 million in damages. As many as 10 tornadoes touched down, but those two were the most violent and the most deadly. School districts in the area cancelled classes for several days because some schools were damaged and also to allow time for the cleanup of debris in the towns. Many people described the damage as "homes flattened."

**Climatic Data Regions of Texas**

High Plains · Low Rolling Plains · North Central · East Texas · Trans-Pecos · Edwards Plateau · South Central · Upper Coast · South Texas · Lower Valley

**May 28:** A **massive hailstorm** moved through the Texas Panhandle and dropped hail as big as 2.75 inches in diameter — baseball size — in the heart of Amarillo. An estimated 35,000 vehicles were damaged along with thousands of homes that had windows and roofs damaged. The hailstorm caused $200 million in damages, and many residents said the damage looked worse than that sustained in the 2004 hailstorm, which was the costliest storm in Amarillo history.

**June 5:** Upslope flow across the high terrains of New Mexico caused **a band of severe thunderstorms** to develop and move through the South Plains of Texas. The storms had winds in excess of 90 mph along with hail up to the size of baseballs. There were numerous reports of downed trees and power lines along with demolished buildings in the Lubbock area. There were no deaths or injuries as a result of the severe storms, but there was $400 million in property damage.

**October 30–31:** Early autumn heavy rain caused **flash flooding** in Central Texas. There was 2–4 inches of rainfall in about eight counties; 6–10 inches of rainfall in Hays, Comal, and Travis counties; and 12–14 inches of rain from Wimberley to Driftwood. In the Oak Hill area of Travis County, there were four fatalities as a result of the flood, along with $100 million in property damage. Damage included numerous cars and homes that

## Average Temperatures 2013

| | High Plains | Low Plains | North Central | East Texas | Trans-Pecos | Edwards Plateau | South Central | Upper Coast | South Texas | Lower Valley |
|---|---|---|---|---|---|---|---|---|---|---|
| Jan. | 38.8 | 43.4 | 47.5 | 50.3 | 44.6 | 49.0 | 54.5 | 57.9 | 60.8 |
| Feb. | 41.3 | 46.5 | 50.8 | 52.7 | 49.6 | 53.3 | 59.0 | 59.4 | 63.3 | 68.3 |
| Mar. | 50.4 | 54.5 | 55.2 | 55.5 | 57.7 | 59.3 | 61.8 | 60.7 | 67.1 | 68.8 |
| April | 55.3 | 59.4 | 61.1 | 63.4 | 64.2 | 64.8 | 67.3 | 64.4 | 71.7 | 73.6 |
| May | 68.3 | 72.2 | 71.4 | 71.7 | 72.4 | 73.2 | 75.1 | 74.5 | 78.5 | 79.4 |
| June | 79.2 | 81.6 | 81.5 | 81.1 | 82.4 | 81.5 | 83.5 | 83.1 | 85.4 | 86.2 |
| July | 77.9 | 81.2 | 82.4 | 81.5 | 79.0 | 80.9 | 84.0 | 83.2 | 85.5 | 85.8 |
| Aug. | 79.1 | 82.8 | 84.9 | 84.2 | 81.3 | 83.4 | 85.4 | 84.1 | 86.9 | 86.4 |
| Sep. | 73.7 | 77.3 | 80.0 | 80.4 | 75 | 77.4 | 81.3 | 81.8 | 81.8 | 82.3 |
| Oct. | 59.5 | 64.2 | 66.2 | 67.3 | 65.2 | 66.9 | 71.7 | 71.8 | 74.9 | 77.6 |
| Nov. | 46.2 | 50.0 | 51.8 | 53.0 | 51.9 | 52.6 | 58.3 | 59.2 | 62.0 | 65.9 |
| Dec. | 37.0 | 39.7 | 42.3 | 46.5 | 45.3 | 45.3 | 50.7 | 52.1 | 53.8 | 58.0 |
| Ann. | 58.9 | 62.7 | 64.6 | 65.6 | 64.1 | 65.6 | 69.4 | 69.3 | 72.4 | 74.4 |

## Precipitation in Inches 2013

| | High Plains | Low Plains | North Central | East Texas | Trans-Pecos | Edwards Plateau | South Central | Upper Coast | South Texas | Lower Valley |
|---|---|---|---|---|---|---|---|---|---|---|
| Jan. | 0.83 | 1.31 | 3.29 | 5.33 | 1.68 | 1.99 | 3.00 | 4.65 | 1.37 | 1.37 |
| Feb. | 1.28 | 1.52 | 1.54 | 2.85 | 0.10 | 0.27 | 1.16 | 2.02 | 0.68 | 0.04 |
| Mar. | 0.25 | 0.18 | 1.66 | 1.80 | 0.01 | 0.49 | 0.57 | 0.49 | 0.11 | 0.03 |
| April | 0.08 | 0.94 | 2.56 | 3.32 | 0.28 | 1.25 | 3.51 | 4.70 | 1.90 | 2.04 |
| May | 0.71 | 1.64 | 3.60 | 4.03 | 0.62 | 3.50 | 2.88 | 2.49 | 2.68 | 2.03 |
| June | 2.60 | 3.36 | 2.28 | 3.02 | 1.18 | 1.99 | 1.76 | 2.40 | 2.80 | 0.80 |
| July | 2.09 | 3.95 | 4.08 | 3.26 | 2.65 | 2.92 | 2.31 | 3.51 | 1.83 | 1.88 |
| Aug. | 2.18 | 2.14 | 1.06 | 1.03 | 0.62 | 1.03 | 1.45 | 3.30 | 1.21 | 1.43 |
| Sep. | 1.88 | 2.44 | 3.80 | 7.00 | 2.35 | 4.13 | 5.79 | 5.58 | 5.41 | 7.14 |
| Oct. | 0.86 | 1.14 | 4.58 | 7.88 | 0.58 | 3.28 | 5.34 | 5.73 | 2.63 | 0.46 |
| Nov. | 0.64 | 0.68 | 2.26 | 4.79 | 0.75 | 1.47 | 1.99 | 4.43 | 1.72 | 4.22 |
| Dec. | 0.61 | 1.32 | 2.21 | 2.89 | 0.92 | 0.91 | 0.67 | 0.82 | 1.06 | 3.16 |
| Ann. | 14.01 | 20.62 | 32.92 | 47.20 | 11.74 | 23.23 | 30.43 | 40.12 | 23.40 | 24.60 |

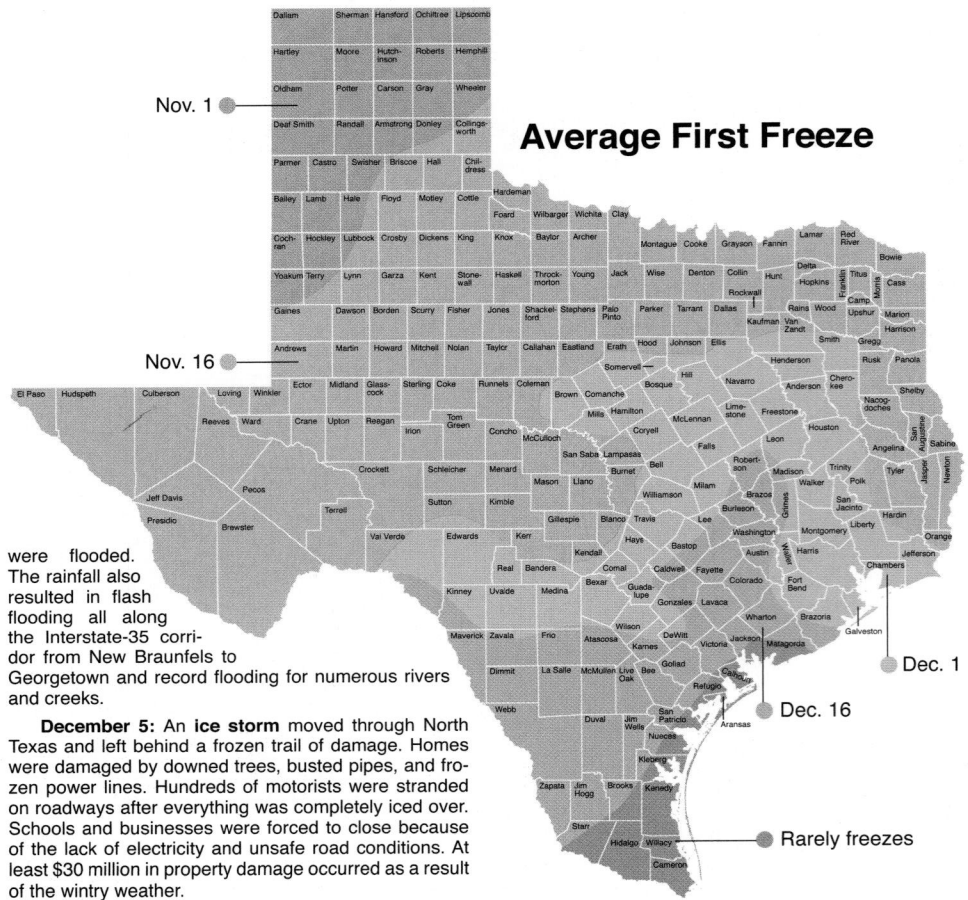

**Average First Freeze**

Nov. 1

Nov. 16

El Paso

Dec. 1

Dec. 16

Rarely freezes

were flooded. The rainfall also resulted in flash flooding all along the Interstate-35 corridor from New Braunfels to Georgetown and record flooding for numerous rivers and creeks.

**December 5:** An **ice storm** moved through North Texas and left behind a frozen trail of damage. Homes were damaged by downed trees, busted pipes, and frozen power lines. Hundreds of motorists were stranded on roadways after everything was completely iced over. Schools and businesses were forced to close because of the lack of electricity and unsafe road conditions. At least $30 million in property damage occurred as a result of the wintry weather.

## Monthly Summaries 2013

While 2012 ended with less-than-normal precipitation, **January** 2013 brought mainly above-normal precipitation and above-normal temperatures. Northeastern Texas around the Dallas–Fort Worth area averaged 1–2 degrees above normal, and that difference lessened throughout the rest of Texas. The El Paso region and the western portion of the Panhandle were the main exceptions to the warmer temperatures and experienced 1–2 degrees below normal. Most of the state received more rain than normal, with the area around El Paso receiving the most additional rain. Few areas experienced below-normal rain. The drought eased up in some areas, with the areas of exceptional drought decreasing from 11.41 percent to 6.57 percent.

Temperatures increased and precipitation decreased during **February.** During the month, temperatures were variable, as parts of the state received opposite temperature and precipitation values. Most of the precipitation came during the historic blizzard that struck the Panhandle on Feb. 25–26. The rest of the precipitation was due to cold fronts passing through the state, which also caused variable temperatures throughout the month. The Gulf of Mexico region to Central Texas experienced the warmest temperatures

| 2013 WEATHER EXTREMES | |
|---|---|
| **Lowest Temp.:** Paducah, Cottle Co., Dec. 7 | –7° F |
| **Highest Temp.:** Terlingua, Brewster Co., June 6 | 113°F |
| **24-hour Precip:** Crystal City, Zavala Co., Oct. 14 | 13.88" |
| **Monthly Precip.:** Manchaca, Travis Co., October | 20.98" |
| **Least Annual Precip.:** Pecos Municipal Airport, Reeves Co. | 5.56" |
| **Greatest Annual Precip.:** Bridge City, Orange Co. | 67.32" |

overall, with cooler-than-normal temperatures spreading from the El Paso area to the entire Panhandle. Drought conditions were stable throughout the month, although, the precipitation did bring some relief to drought areas in the Panhandle, which saw a decrease from exceptional to extreme drought conditions.

**March** brought less rain, with no areas receiving more than 75-percent of normal rainfall amounts. This caused an increase in drought coverage from 75 percent to over 88 percent. Sadly, the exceptional drought category increased from 5 percent to 11 percent during the month, and the Rio Grande Valley and the Big Country saw the largest increase of drought conditions. Parts of East Texas that were without any drought indications returned to abnormally dry conditions. A rain event from March 9–11 was the most widespread precipitation for the state, as a cold front brought rain to the majority of Texas. Fannin County received the most

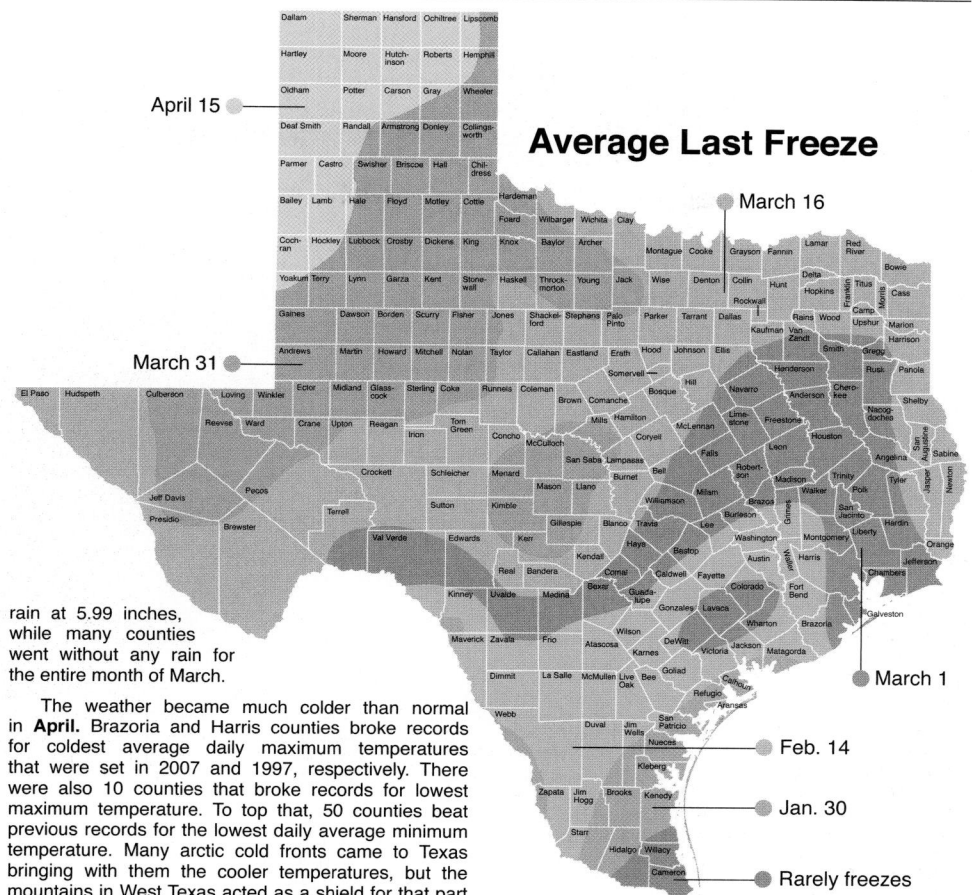

# Average Last Freeze

April 15

March 31

March 16

March 1

Feb. 14

Jan. 30

Rarely freezes

rain at 5.99 inches, while many counties went without any rain for the entire month of March.

The weather became much colder than normal in **April.** Brazoria and Harris counties broke records for coldest average daily maximum temperatures that were set in 2007 and 1997, respectively. There were also 10 counties that broke records for lowest maximum temperature. To top that, 50 counties beat previous records for the lowest daily average minimum temperature. Many arctic cold fronts came to Texas bringing with them the cooler temperatures, but the mountains in West Texas acted as a shield for that part of Texas. The Panhandle and northern far West Texas held on to below-normal precipitation, while the rest of the state received above- or near-normal precipitation. The area around the Gulf of Mexico received the most rain because of a mid-level disturbance on April 2. Despite more rain, most of Texas saw increases to the drought this month.

**May** brought unseasonably cold temperatures for all of Texas except for the Panhandle, and most of the state experienced below-average precipitation. The Austin area was the exception because it received 200 percent of its normal rain. Many storms moved through the state during the month, including supercell thunderstorms that caused a tornado outbreak on the May 15 in North Texas. Drought improved east of Interstate-35, while other areas experienced an increase to their drought.

Warm temperatures covered all of Texas in **June,** along with less rain. The state experienced temperature increases of 1–4 degrees above normal, with the warmest areas in the west. The heat was largely brought about by the lack of rain. The main form of rain was thunderstorms and showers that popped up from daytime heating. A major precipitation event even brought 10 inches of rain to Eagle Pass. Despite the lack of rain overall, the areas that received rain were the ones in need of it, which brought down drought levels for some areas of Texas. Other areas were not as lucky, as East Texas saw additional drought by the end of June. The month ended with 68 percent of Texas in severe

drought conditions.

Drought relief came somewhat during **July** due to above-normal rainfall and below-normal temperatures for most of Texas. Central Texas received the most rainfall at around 200-percent to 300-percent of normal. The month began with drought covering around 87 percent of the state and increasing in the Eastern portion of Central Texas to reach 92 percent drought coverage. By the end of July, the drought returned to 87 percent coverage.

**August** brought hot and dry conditions to the entire state. Small areas in the northeastern Panhandle and the Coastal Bend were the exception to the rule of less rainfall. These areas had been suffering from the drought but rain lessened their drought conditions. Texas overall saw a slight improvement in drought, which decreased from 88 percent coverage to 87 percent. The largest improvements were seen in the exceptional drought catagory, which decreasd from 6.24 percent to 2.74 percent during the month. The main areas to receive relief were rural Texas in the Panhandle and Permian Basin, as well as regions between Corpus Christi and Galveston, which received enough rain to decrease the drought from extreme to moderate. A strong ridge stayed over the state for most of the month, which accounted for the hot and dry temperatures. When the ridge weakened, it caused some severe storms over the eastern portions

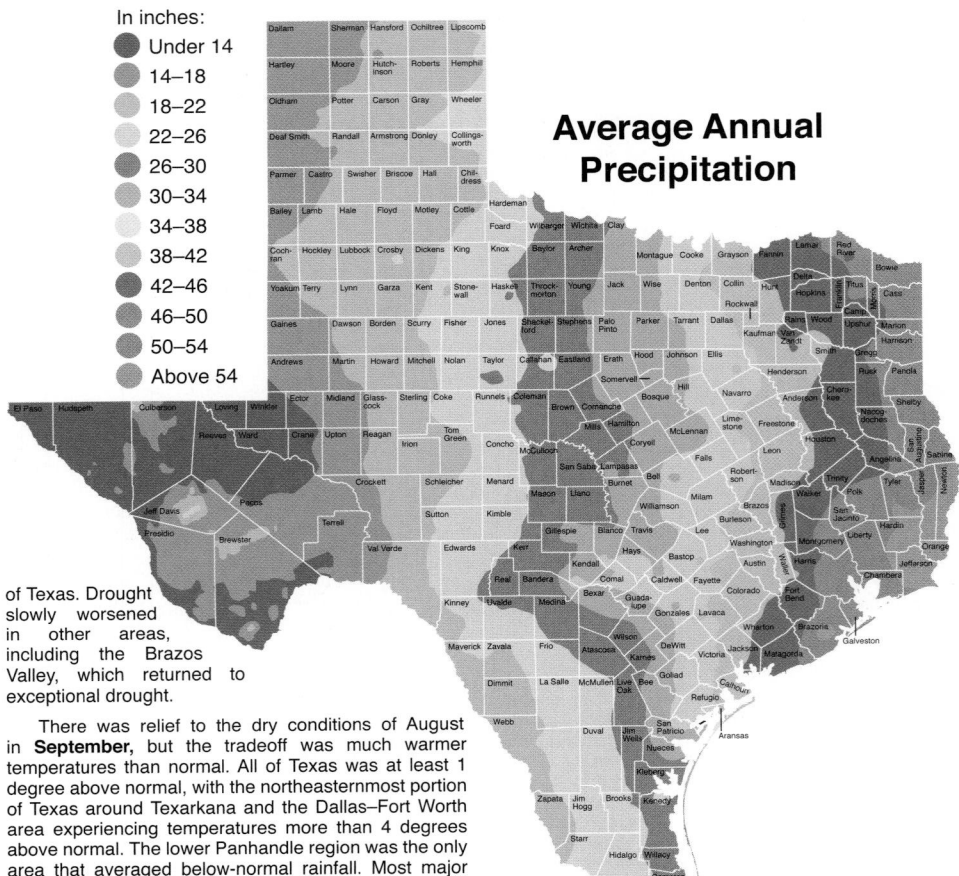

**Average Annual Precipitation**

In inches:
- Under 14
- 14–18
- 18–22
- 22–26
- 26–30
- 30–34
- 34–38
- 38–42
- 42–46
- 46–50
- 50–54
- Above 54

of Texas. Drought slowly worsened in other areas, including the Brazos Valley, which returned to exceptional drought.

There was relief to the dry conditions of August in **September,** but the tradeoff was much warmer temperatures than normal. All of Texas was at least 1 degree above normal, with the northeasternmost portion of Texas around Texarkana and the Dallas–Fort Worth area experiencing temperatures more than 4 degrees above normal. The lower Panhandle region was the only area that averaged below-normal rainfall. Most major cities recorded above-normal precipitation. Hurricane Manuel brought the most precipitation to the state on the Sept. 19–21, mainly from Abilene to Houston. Overall, drought coverage decreased from 87 percent of Texas to 80 percent. The exceptional drought category coverage went from 3 percent to nearly vanishing at 0.28 percent.

The rain and temperature variations in **October** were very sporadic. The cooler temperatures were odd considering the many prior months with higher-than-normal temperatures for most of Texas. The Panhandle and El Paso region received below-normal temperatures and below-normal rainfall. The heart of Central Texas also received slightly below-normal temperatures, and a larger portion of Central Texas, stretching from the border of Mexico to Texarkana, saw above-normal precipitation. Areas on either side of the extra rain saw below-normal precipitation. In fact, Central Texas recorded one of the wettest Octobers on record, which was in stark contrast to West Texas, which recorded one of the driest. Austin was hit hard by rain with more than a foot falling in some areas. The remnants of Tropical Storm Raymond combined with a cold front to produce "training thunderstorms," which are thunderstorms that repeatedly develop in the same area, causing flash flooding.

Cooler-than-normal temperatures developed during **November,** accompanied by below-normal precipitation. The added cooler temperatures were thanks to arctic air brought down by cold fronts. Because the cold fronts moved fast, the precipitation ahead of them also

moved swiftly across the state, leaving most of the state with below-normal precipitation. The Rio Grande and southeastern portions of the state were the exceptions, receiving normal- to above-normal rainfall. The first widespread freeze of the year occurred on Nov. 13, while the first snowfall occurred in the Panhandle, where three inches of snow fell from Amarillo to Lubbock creating dangerous ice conditions. The drought coverage improved overall from 51 percent in the beginning of the month to 47 percent by month's end.

**December** also brought below-normal temperatures, with the largest departure from normal reaching 4 degrees below normal. Precipitation was scarce over most of Texas, with the region from El Paso to the southeastern portion of the Panhandle receiving the most rain. A cold front brought most of the precipitation, including snow flurries over the Panhandle. An ice storm also hit Dallas on Dec. 5. There was a half-inch accumulation of ice over North Texas and the temperatures stayed below freezing for more than three days. Drought coverage decreased slightly during the month.

# Weather Highlights 2014

**April 3:** A severe weather outbreak in North Texas spawned **a few weak tornadoes** and brought **large hail** into the Denton area. There were several reports of hail the size of baseballs and softballs falling around the city

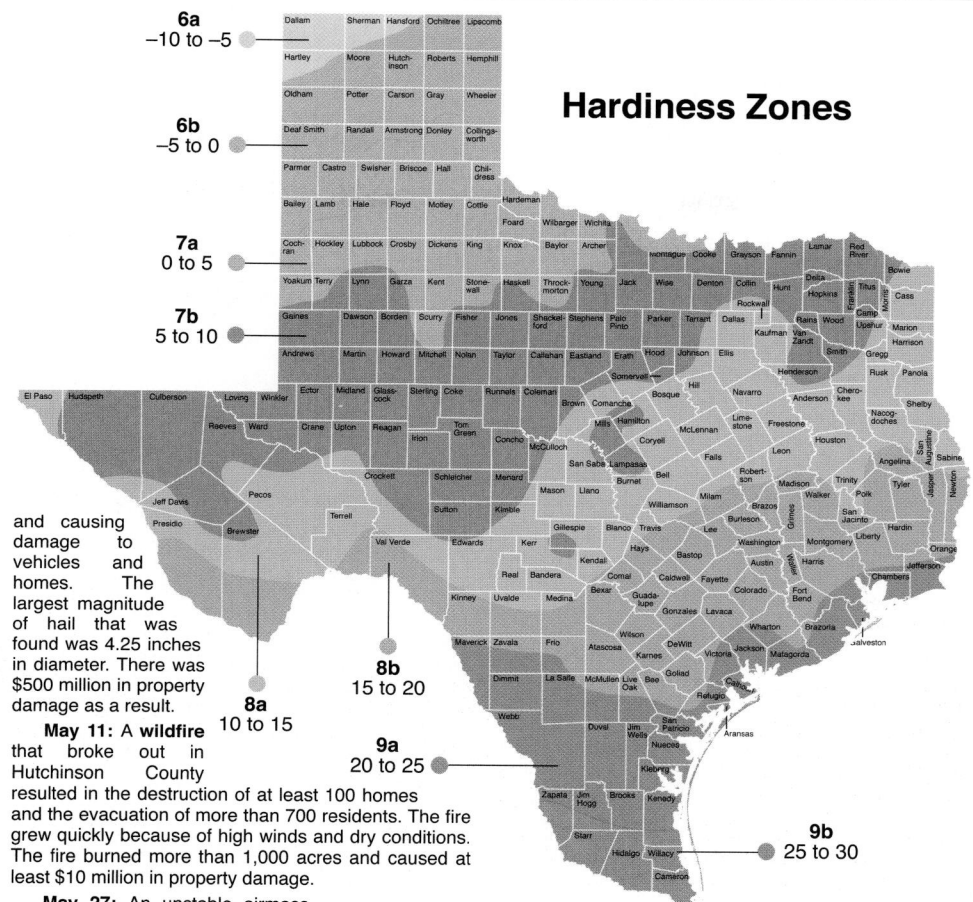

## Hardiness Zones

**6a** −10 to −5
**6b** −5 to 0
**7a** 0 to 5
**7b** 5 to 10
**8a** 10 to 15
**8b** 15 to 20
**9a** 20 to 25
**9b** 25 to 30

and causing damage to vehicles and homes. The largest magnitude of hail that was found was 4.25 inches in diameter. There was $500 million in property damage as a result.

**May 11:** A **wildfire** that broke out in Hutchinson County resulted in the destruction of at least 100 homes and the evacuation of more than 700 residents. The fire grew quickly because of high winds and dry conditions. The fire burned more than 1,000 acres and caused at least $10 million in property damage.

**May 27:** An unstable airmass combined with a surface low pressure helped to develop a **tornadic supercell** in Alice in Jim Wells County. The supercell dropped hail up to the size of golf balls and spawned two tornados, one in Alice and the other outside of Premont in the far south portion of the county. The tornado in Alice was an EF1 and caused $1.6 million in damage.

**June 12:** Heavy rainfall produced **flash flooding** that caused the death of one person when his car was swept off the road near Flat Creek in West Waco. The drainage systems for the towns of both Waco and Hewitt feed into Flat Creek, and the heavy rain caused the banks of the creek to overflow by at least a half mile. The flash flood caused the only severe-weather-related death in Texas throughout the entire year.

**June 12:** A **severe thunderstorm** near Abilene dropped large hail across the city. Numerous reports of damage to homes and vehicles came in as the thunderstorm dropped hail up to 4.5 inches in diameter. Twelve people were injured by falling hail, and $400 million in property damage occurred as a result.

## Monthly Summaries 2014

**January** was marked by both below-average temperatures and below-average rainfall. The cooler air

| 2014 WEATHER EXTREMES | |
|---|---|
| **Lowest Temp.:** Lipscomb, Lipscomb Co., March 3 | −6° F |
| **Highest Temp.:** Rio Grande Village, Brewster Co., Jun. 7 | 116°F |
| **24-hour Precip:** Kopperl, Bosque Co., June 23 | 11.87" |
| **Monthly Precip.:** Sanger, Denton Co., July | 16.21" |
| **Least Annual Precip.:** Midland Airpark, Midland Co. | 5.06" |
| **Greatest Annual Precip.:** Cloverleaf, Harris Co. | 61.09" |

came from arctic cold fronts moving across the state on a regular basis. Despite having these cold fronts, which usually bring rain, the month averaged below-normal precipitation for most of the state. West Texas had very little rain during the month, and East Texas was not much better, receiving only 75-percent of normal rainfall. A particularly strong front came from the polar regions on Jan. 6, and dozens of locations recorded record lows. The temperatures were cold enough for a Winter Storm Warning to be issued when a strong cold front arrived Jan. 23–24. Sleet and freezing rain hit College Station and places farther south, and Walker County received 4 inches of snow in some areas. Drought conditions became worse during January, with 50 percent of the state experiencing drought conditions.

**February** saw colder-than-normal temperatures for all of Texas except for the El Paso region, where it was 1–4 degrees warmer than normal. The area with the coldest temperatures stretched from slightly south of the

Dallas–Fort Worth area to Texarkana. All of Texas had below- normal precipitation, except for a small portion around Jefferson and Orange counties. A strong stationary jet stream pattern brought many strong cold fronts with arctic temperatures to Texas, and temperatues in many major cities did not rise above 65 degress throughout the month. These conditions added to the drought in Texas, particularly in the Panhandle.

The cold and dry trend persisted during **March.** Only the El Paso region experienced normal- to above- normal temperatures. Most of Texas had less-than-normal precipitation, with West-Central Texas and the Panhandle being driest. El Paso and the southernmost part of Texas were the main areas that had above-normal precipitation. Much of the rainfall came with cold fronts in the beginning of

*Most of the state's precipitation in February 2013 came during a historic blizzard that struck the Panhandle on Feb. 25–26. The blizzard walloped Amarillo and the rest of the Panhandle with 50 mph gusts and more than 11 inches of snow. Amarillo emergency personnel, above, assist a stranded motorist on the Interstate-40 service road. Photo by Michael Schumacher; Amarillo Globe-News.*

the month. Later in the month, freezing rain, snow, and sleet hit the Panhandle and North Texas, and freezing rain extended all the way to the Houston area. Despite the wintry precipitation, may areas also experienced an expansion of drought conditions. Some areas, such as the Rio Grande Valley, saw reductions in drought intensity. Overall, drought coverage in Texas increased from 57 percent to 68 percent.

**April** brought warmer-than-normal temperatures to most of the state, except for the easternmost regions, which received slightly cooler-than-normal temperatures. Across the state, the average departure from normal temperature was 1–2 degrees. Drier areas coincided with the warmer-than-normal areas, and the northeastern portion of Texas received above-normal rainfall during the month. These conditions led to an increase in the overall drought coverage to 90 percent. The Panhandle saw the largest increase in areas affected extreme and exceptional drought.

**May** brought cooler-than-normal temperatures, especially around the Rio Grande and coastal regions

of Texas. The northern portion of the Panhandle experienced above-normal temperatures again. Areas on the periphery of Texas had below-normal amounts of precipitation during the month. The area around College Station and Austin experienced the greatest amount of rain, averaging 250 percent above normal, while rainfall in the Lubbock area was 175 percent of normal. Drought coverage decreased during the month to 71 percent. The size of the exceptional drought area decreased by half from 21 percent to 10 percent of the state, and the Panhandle region saw the greatest reduction in exceptional drought.

Temperatures warmed up quickly in **June,** and most of the state saw above-normal temperatures, with the El Paso region experiencing the greatest departures from normal. South-Central Texas and areas toward the East had slightly cooler-than-normal temperatures. Precipitation was concentrated in the Plains and a small area around Val Verde County. Other portions of Texas received near-normal to slightly below-normal precipitation. The added rain in the Plains meant that drought intensity was downgraded from exceptional to

## Average Temperatures 2014     Precipitation in Inches 2014

| | High Plains | Low Plains | North Central | East Texas | Trans-Pecos | Edwards Plateau | South Central | Upper Coast | South Texas | Lower Valley | High Plains | Low Plains | North Central | East Texas | Trans-Pecos | Edwards Plateau | South Central | Upper Coast | South Texas | Lower Valley |
|---|---|---|---|---|---|---|---|---|---|---|---|---|---|---|---|---|---|---|---|---|
| Jan. | 37.8 | 41.3 | 43.1 | 43.8 | 45.6 | 44.9 | 49.4 | 49.7 | 52.1 | 55.9 | 0.03 | 0.01 | 0.28 | 1.35 | 0.00 | 0.04 | 0.80 | 1.21 | 0.24 | 0.92 |
| Feb. | 39.8 | 40.8 | 45.1 | 48.7 | 52.2 | 50.1 | 54.4 | 54.9 | 58.2 | 61.3 | 0.25 | 0.54 | 0.58 | 2.48 | 0.08 | 0.21 | 0.71 | 2.42 | 0.48 | 0.23 |
| Mar. | 48.3 | 51.3 | 53.0 | 53.9 | 56.4 | 56.3 | 59.0 | 59.0 | 62.9 | 64.9 | 0.17 | 0.36 | 1.16 | 2.97 | 0.26 | 0.24 | 2.04 | 2.69 | 1.54 | 2.00 |
| April | 58.7 | 63.6 | 64.6 | 64.4 | 65.1 | 67.0 | 69.4 | 69.0 | 73.4 | 74.9 | 0.35 | 0.68 | 1.94 | 2.48 | 0.47 | 0.55 | 0.75 | 1.03 | 0.23 | 0.09 |
| May | 67.8 | 72.1 | 71.7 | 70.9 | 72.2 | 73.1 | 73.9 | 73.5 | 77.2 | 77.7 | 2.76 | 3.47 | 4.51 | 7.13 | 0.55 | 4.45 | 6.89 | 7.08 | 2.97 | 2.12 |
| June | 76.8 | 79.4 | 79.8 | 79.5 | 82.9 | 80.2 | 82.6 | 82.1 | 85.6 | 85.6 | 3.38 | 3.61 | 4.14 | 4.49 | 1.32 | 2.38 | 2.47 | 3.62 | 1.99 | 0.61 |
| July | 78.0 | 81.5 | 81.8 | 80.3 | 81.5 | 82.4 | 84.0 | 83.2 | 86.0 | 85.9 | 2.96 | 3.05 | 3.09 | 4.64 | 1.55 | 1.26 | 1.59 | 3.68 | 1.65 | 1.00 |
| Aug. | 78.9 | 82.7 | 83.6 | 82.1 | 79.9 | 82.7 | 86.1 | 84.5 | 87.6 | 87.6 | 1.43 | 1.76 | 1.66 | 1.97 | 1.78 | 2.08 | 0.88 | 2.87 | 1.23 | 3.32 |
| Sep. | 70.6 | 74.6 | 77.6 | 78.0 | 73.7 | 76.8 | 80.5 | 80.2 | 81.5 | 81.9 | 4.33 | 3.57 | 1.60 | 2.90 | 3.77 | 3.21 | 3.89 | 5.51 | 4.92 | 10.09 |
| Oct. | 62.8 | 67.9 | 70.3 | 68.9 | 68.2 | 70.7 | 74.3 | 73.4 | 76.8 | 78.7 | 0.69 | 0.99 | 2.94 | 4.23 | 0.79 | 1.00 | 1.76 | 2.63 | 1.06 | 1.74 |
| Nov. | 44.6 | 48.2 | 50.7 | 51.9 | 50.3 | 52.2 | 56.9 | 57.9 | 59.6 | 62.9 | 1.03 | 2.16 | 3.20 | 4.38 | 1.70 | 2.80 | 4.46 | 4.39 | 3.09 | 4.20 |
| Dec. | 41.8 | 46.7 | 49.9 | 51.6 | 49.0 | 52.0 | 57.2 | 57.9 | 59.6 | 64.6 | 0.30 | 0.41 | 1.18 | 2.98 | 0.38 | 0.55 | 1.91 | 4.24 | 1.10 | 2.08 |
| Ann. | 58.8 | 62.5 | 64.3 | 64.5 | 64.8 | 65.7 | 69.0 | 68.8 | 71.7 | 73.5 | 17.68 | 20.64 | 26.28 | 42.00 | 12.65 | 18.77 | 28.15 | 41.37 | 20.50 | 28.40 |

extreme drought in some areas and to severe in others.

Below-normal temperatures came to Texas in **July**, especially in the Texarkana area, though temperatures were near- and above-normal in parts of South and West Texas. Likewise, northeast Texas received above-normal rainfall. Many areas with above-normal temperatures received below-normal rainfall. The exception to this pattern was the Dallas–Fort Worth area, which received below-normal precipitation and below-normal temperatures. Drought coverage overall decreased to 58 percent of the state.

**August** brought sporadic precipitation to Texas. Temperatures were cooler-than-normal in the Texarkana area and the El Paso region, but the Rio Grande Valley through Central Texas saw above-normal temperatures. Most of Texas had below-normal precipitation, with the greatest percentage deficits in the Austin area, while rain was above-normal in the southernmost tip of Texas as well as the Edwards Plateau region. Drought coverage increased during the month and reached 60 percent by the month's end.

**September,** much like August, brought a variety of conditions across the state. The lower High Plains area and the southernmost tip of Texas had above-normal precipitation. Lower-than-normal temperatures affected a broad region centered in the Dallas–Fort Worth area. Other portions of Texas had near-normal temperatures for the month. Areas west of DFW was drier than normal, while the rest of the state had normal- to above-normal precipitation. The El Paso region and southern High Plains regions had the greatest percentage of precipitation relative to normal. Overall, there was a significant decrease of drought coverage in Texas to 49 percent.

Warm and dry are the two words to describe **October's** weather. The entire state had temperatures 1–4 degrees above normal. Areas around Dallas–Fort Worth and the northern portions of Central Texas had the largest temperature anomalies. Only a small area around Harrison County had above-average rainfall, and barely so. There was a slight increase in areas affected by exceptional drought.

**November** brought below-average temperatures and above-normal rainfall. Most of Texas experienced temperatures more than 4 degrees cooler than normal, though El Paso and the upper Panhandle regions were only about 1 degree cooler than normal. The exceptions to the above-normal rainfall were the Dallas–Fort Worth area and the upper Panhandle region. Drought coverage decreased slightly to 43 percent.

The cooler-than-normal temperatures did not last, as **December** brought the entire state of Texas above-normal temperatures. The western Central Plains and Dallas–Fort Worth were the warmest areas, reaching 4 degrees above normal. This was coupled with below-normal precipitation values, most prominently in the middle Panhandle region. Some areas along the Gulf Coast had above-average precipitation for the month. The extent of drought increased slightly to 43 percent of Texas. ☆

# Meteorological Data

*Source: Updated as of July 2013 by the National Climatic Data Center. Additional data for these locations are listed by county in the table of Texas temperature, freeze, growing season, and precipitation records, beginning on page 153.*

| City | Temperature | | | | | | Precipitation | | | | | | Relative Humidity | | Wind | | | Sun |
|---|---|---|---|---|---|---|---|---|---|---|---|---|---|---|---|---|---|---|
| | Record High | Month & Year | Record Low | Month & Year | No. Days Max. 90° and Above | No. Days Min. 32° and Below | Maximum in 24 Hours | Month & Year | Snowfall (Mean Annual) | Max. Snowfall in 24 Hours | Month & Year | 6:00 a.m., CST | Noon, CST | Speed, MPH (Mean Annual) | Highest MPH | Month & Year | Percent Possible Sunshine |
| Abilene | 111 | 8/1943 | -9 | 1/1947 | 90 | 45 | 6.70 | 9/1961 | 5.2 | 9.3 | 4/1996 | 75 | 50 | 10.9 | 55 | 4/1998 | 70 |
| Amarillo | 111 | 6/2011 | -16 | 2/1899 | 61 | 107 | 7.25 | 7/2010 | 17.8 | 20.6 | 3/1934 | 75 | 46 | 12.8 | 68 | 6/2008 | 74 |
| Austin | 112 | 8/2011+ | -2 | 1/1949 | 111 | 12 | 15.00 | 9/1931 | 1.0 | 9.7 | 11/1937 | 84 | 57 | 7.0 | 52 | 5/1997 | 60 |
| Brownsville | 106 | 3/1984 | 16 | 12/1989 | 123 | 1 | 12.19 | 9/1967 | 0.0 | ** | 3/1993+ | 90 | 61 | 10.4 | 51 | 7/2008+ | 59 |
| Corpus Christi | 109 | 9/2000 | 13 | 12/1989 | 106 | 4 | 11.52 | 6/2006 | 0.2 | 2.3 | 12/2004 | 90 | 62 | 11.7 | 56 | 5/1999 | 60 |
| Dallas-Fort Worth | 113 | 6/1980 | -2 | 1/1949 | 95 | 29 | 5.91 | 10/1959 | 1.2 | 12.1 | 1/1964 | 82 | 56 | 10.5 | 73 | 8/1959 | 61 |
| Del Rio | 112 | 6/1988 | 10 | 12/1989 | 131 | 15 | 17.03 | 6/1948 | 0.9 | 8.6 | 1/1985 | 73 | 65 | 8.8 | 60 | 8/1970 | 84 |
| El Paso | 114 | 6/1994 | -8 | 1/1962 | 99 | 44 | 6.50 | 7/1881 | 6.9 | 16.8 | 12/1987 | 58 | 35 | 8.1 | 64 | 1/1996 | 84 |
| Galveston | 104 | 9/2000 | 8 | 2/1899 | 30 | 5 | 13.91 | 10/1901 | 0.2 | 15.4 | 2/1895 | 91 | 64 | 11.0 | *100 | 9/1900 | 62 |
| Houston † | 109 | 8/2011+ | 7 | 12/1989 | 102 | 10 | 11.02 | 6/2001 | 0.1 | 2.0 | 1/1973 | 90 | 60 | 7.5 | 51 | 8/1983 | 59 |
| Lubbock | 114 | 6/1994 | -17 | 2/1933 | 78 | 84 | 7.80 | 9/2008 | 8.2 | 16.3 | 1/1983 | 75 | 46 | 12.0 | 70 | 3/1952 | 72 |
| Midland-Odessa | 116 | 6/1994 | -11 | 2/1985+ | 101 | 58 | 5.99 | 7/1961 | 5.1 | 10.6 | 1/2012 | 74 | 43 | 10.9 | 67 | 2/1960 | 74 |
| Port Arthur-Beaumont | 108 | 8/2000 | 3 | 2/1899 | 80 | 9 | 17.16 | 9/1980 | 0.0 | 4.4 | 2/1960 | 91 | 64 | 8.6 | 105 | 8/2005 | 58 |
| San Angelo | 111 | 7/1960+ | -4 | 12/1989 | 102 | 46 | 6.25 | 9/1980 | 2.4 | 7.4 | 1/1978 | 80 | 49 | 9.7 | 75 | 4/1969 | 70 |
| San Antonio | 111 | 9/2000 | 0 | 1/1949 | 111 | 15 | 13.35 | 10/1998 | 0.7 | 13.2 | 1/1985 | 84 | 56 | 8.2 | 51 | 6/2010 | 60 |
| Victoria | 111 | 9/2000 | 9 | 12/1989 | 107 | 11 | 9.87 | 4/1991 | 0.1 | 2.1 | 1/1985 | 91 | 60 | 9.5 | 99 | 7/1963 | 49 |
| Waco | 112 | 8/1969 | -5 | 1/1949 | 104 | 31 | 7.98 | 12/1997 | 1.2 | 7.0 | 1/1949 | 86 | 57 | 10.1 | 69 | 6/1961 | 59 |
| Wichita Falls | 117 | 6/1980 | -12 | 1/1947 | 98 | 59 | 6.22 | 9/1980 | 4.2 | 9.7 | 3/1989 | 82 | 52 | 11.2 | 69 | 6/2002 | 60 |
| Shreveport, LA § | 109 | 8/2011+ | 3 | 1/1962 | 88 | 32 | 10.76 | 5/2008 | 1.0 | 5.6 | 1/1982 | 89 | 59 | 7.3 | 63 | 5/2000 | 64 |

*\*100 mph recorded at 6:15 p.m., Sept. 8, 1900, just before the anemometer blew away. Maximum velocity was estimated to be 120 mph from the northeast between 7:30 p.m. and 8:30 p.m.*

*†The official Houston station was moved from near downtown to Intercontinental Airport, 12 miles north of the old station.*

*+ Also recorded on earlier dates, months, or years.*

*§Shreveport is included because it is near the boundary line and its data can be considered representative of Texas' east border.*

*\*\*Trace is an amount too small to measure.*

# Texas Is Tornado Capital

An **average of 132 tornadoes** touch Texas soil each year. The annual total varies considerably, and certain areas are struck more often than others. Tornadoes occur most frequently in the Red River Valley.

Tornadoes may occur in any month and at any hour of the day, but they occur with greatest frequency during the late spring and early summer months, and between the hours of 4 p.m. and 8 p.m. In the period 1951–2014, 62.9 percent of all Texas tornadoes occurred within the three-month period of April, May, and June, with almost one-third of the total tornadoes occurring in May.

More tornadoes have been recorded in Texas than in any other state, which is partly due to the state's size. Between 1951 and 2014, **8,249 funnel clouds reached the ground,** thus becoming tornadoes. Texas ranks 11th among the 50 states in the density of tornadoes, with an average of 5.9 tornadoes per 10,000 square miles per year.

The greatest outbreak of tornadoes on record in Texas was associated with **Hurricane Beulah in September 1967.** Within a five-day period, Sept. 19–23, 115 known tornadoes, all in Texas, were spawned by this great hurricane. Sixty-seven occurred on Sept. 20, a Texas **record for a single day.**

The Texas **record for a single month** is September 1967 with 124 tornadoes, 115 of which were from Hurricane Beulah. The Texas **record for a single year** was 232, also in 1967. The second-highest number in a single year was in 1995, when 223 tornadoes occurred in Texas. In 1982, 123 tornadoes occurred in May, making it the worst outbreak of spring tornadoes in Texas.

On average, May has the highest number of tornadoes per month with 38.59. January has the lowest average with 2.56.

A rare winter tornado outbreak occurred on Dec. 29, 2006. There were 27 reported tornadoes on this day, which is the largest monthly total for December. The average monthly value for December is 3.12 tornadoes.

The accompanying table, compiled by the National Climatic Data Center, Environmental Data Service, and the National Oceanic and Atmospheric Administration, lists tornado occurrences in Texas by month for the period 1951–2014. ☆

## Tornadoes by Year and Month

Source: Office of the State Climatologist

| Year | Jan. | Feb. | March | April | May | June | July | Aug. | Sept. | Oct. | Nov. | Dec. | TOTAL |
|---|---|---|---|---|---|---|---|---|---|---|---|---|---|
| 1951 | 0 | 0 | 1 | 1 | 5 | 7 | 1 | 0 | 0 | 0 | 0 | 0 | 15 |
| 1952 | 0 | 1 | 3 | 4 | 2 | 1 | 0 | 1 | 0 | 0 | 0 | 1 | 13 |
| 1953 | 0 | 2 | 2 | 3 | 6 | 2 | 3 | 5 | 0 | 2 | 1 | 6 | 32 |
| 1954 | 0 | 3 | 1 | 23 | 21 | 14 | 5 | 1 | 4 | 5 | 0 | 0 | 77 |
| 1955 | 0 | 0 | 7 | 15 | 42 | 32 | 1 | 5 | 2 | 0 | 0 | 0 | 104 |
| 1956 | 0 | 3 | 5 | 3 | 17 | 5 | 6 | 4 | 2 | 9 | 2 | 0 | 56 |
| 1957 | 0 | 1 | 21 | 69 | 33 | 5 | 0 | 3 | 2 | 6 | 5 | 0 | 145 |
| 1958 | 2 | 0 | 7 | 12 | 15 | 13 | 10 | 7 | 0 | 0 | 8 | 0 | 74 |
| 1959 | 0 | 0 | 8 | 4 | 32 | 14 | 10 | 3 | 4 | 5 | 6 | 0 | 86 |
| 1960 | 4 | 1 | 0 | 8 | 29 | 14 | 3 | 4 | 2 | 11 | 1 | 0 | 77 |
| 1961 | 0 | 1 | 21 | 15 | 24 | 30 | 9 | 2 | 12 | 0 | 10 | 0 | 124 |
| 1962 | 0 | 4 | 12 | 9 | 25 | 56 | 12 | 15 | 7 | 2 | 0 | 1 | 143 |
| 1963 | 0 | 0 | 3 | 9 | 19 | 24 | 8 | 4 | 6 | 4 | 5 | 0 | 82 |
| 1964 | 0 | 1 | 6 | 22 | 15 | 11 | 9 | 7 | 3 | 1 | 3 | 0 | 78 |
| 1965 | 2 | 5 | 3 | 7 | 43 | 24 | 2 | 9 | 4 | 6 | 0 | 3 | 108 |
| 1966 | 0 | 4 | 1 | 21 | 22 | 15 | 3 | 8 | 3 | 0 | 0 | 0 | 77 |
| 1967 | 0 | 2 | 11 | 17 | 34 | 22 | 10 | 5 | 124 | 2 | 0 | 5 | 232 |
| 1968 | 2 | 1 | 3 | 13 | 47 | 21 | 4 | 8 | 5 | 8 | 11 | 16 | 139 |
| 1969 | 0 | 1 | 1 | 16 | 65 | 16 | 6 | 7 | 6 | 8 | 1 | 0 | 127 |
| 1970 | 1 | 3 | 5 | 23 | 23 | 9 | 5 | 20 | 9 | 20 | 0 | 3 | 121 |
| 1971 | 0 | 20 | 10 | 24 | 27 | 33 | 7 | 20 | 7 | 16 | 4 | 23 | 191 |
| 1972 | 1 | 0 | 19 | 13 | 43 | 12 | 19 | 13 | 8 | 9 | 7 | 0 | 144 |
| 1973 | 14 | 1 | 29 | 25 | 21 | 24 | 4 | 8 | 5 | 3 | 9 | 4 | 147 |
| 1974 | 2 | 1 | 8 | 19 | 18 | 26 | 3 | 9 | 6 | 22 | 2 | 0 | 116 |
| 1975 | 5 | 2 | 9 | 12 | 50 | 18 | 10 | 3 | 3 | 3 | 1 | 1 | 117 |
| 1976 | 1 | 1 | 8 | 53 | 63 | 11 | 16 | 6 | 13 | 4 | 0 | 0 | 176 |
| 1977 | 0 | 0 | 3 | 34 | 50 | 4 | 5 | 5 | 12 | 0 | 6 | 4 | 123 |
| 1978 | 0 | 0 | 0 | 34 | 65 | 10 | 13 | 6 | 6 | 1 | 2 | 0 | 137 |
| 1979 | 1 | 2 | 24 | 33 | 39 | 14 | 12 | 10 | 4 | 15 | 3 | 0 | 157 |
| 1980 | 0 | 2 | 7 | 26 | 44 | 21 | 2 | 34 | 10 | 5 | 0 | 2 | 153 |
| 1981 | 0 | 7 | 7 | 9 | 71 | 26 | 5 | 20 | 5 | 23 | 3 | 0 | 176 |
| 1982 | 0 | 0 | 6 | 27 | 123 | 36 | 4 | 0 | 3 | 0 | 3 | 1 | 203 |
| 1983 | 5 | 7 | 24 | 1 | 62 | 35 | 4 | 22 | 5 | 0 | 7 | 14 | 186 |
| 1984 | 0 | 13 | 9 | 18 | 19 | 19 | 0 | 4 | 1 | 5 | 2 | 5 | 95 |
| 1985 | 0 | 0 | 5 | 41 | 28 | 5 | 3 | 1 | 1 | 3 | 1 | 2 | 90 |
| 1986 | 0 | 12 | 4 | 21 | 50 | 24 | 3 | 5 | 4 | 7 | 1 | 0 | 131 |
| 1987 | 1 | 1 | 7 | 0 | 54 | 19 | 11 | 3 | 8 | 0 | 16 | 4 | 124 |
| 1988 | 0 | 0 | 0 | 11 | 7 | 7 | 6 | 2 | 42 | 4 | 10 | 0 | 89 |
| 1989 | 3 | 0 | 5 | 3 | 70 | 63 | 0 | 6 | 3 | 6 | 1 | 0 | 160 |
| 1990 | 3 | 3 | 4 | 56 | 62 | 20 | 5 | 2 | 3 | 0 | 0 | 0 | 158 |
| 1991 | 20 | 5 | 2 | 39 | 72 | 36 | 1 | 2 | 3 | 8 | 4 | 0 | 192 |
| 1992 | 0 | 5 | 13 | 22 | 43 | 66 | 4 | 4 | 4 | 7 | 21 | 0 | 189 |
| 1993 | 1 | 4 | 5 | 17 | 39 | 4 | 4 | 0 | 12 | 23 | 8 | 0 | 117 |
| 1994 | 0 | 1 | 1 | 48 | 88 | 2 | 1 | 4 | 3 | 9 | 8 | 0 | 165 |
| 1995 | 6 | 0 | 13 | 36 | 66 | 75 | 11 | 3 | 2 | 1 | 0 | 10 | 223 |
| 1996 | 7 | 1 | 2 | 21 | 33 | 9 | 3 | 8 | 33 | 8 | 4 | 1 | 130 |
| 1997 | 0 | 6 | 7 | 31 | 59 | 50 | 2 | 2 | 1 | 16 | 3 | 0 | 177 |
| 1998 | 24 | 15 | 4 | 9 | 11 | 6 | 3 | 5 | 3 | 28 | 1 | 0 | 109 |
| 1999 | 22 | 0 | 22 | 23 | 70 | 26 | 3 | 8 | 0 | 0 | 0 | 4 | 178 |
| 2000 | 0 | 7 | 49 | 33 | 23 | 8 | 3 | 0 | 0 | 10 | 20 | 1 | 154 |
| 2001 | 0 | 0 | 4 | 12 | 36 | 12 | 0 | 7 | 15 | 24 | 27 | 5 | 142 |
| 2002 | 0 | 0 | 44 | 25 | 61 | 5 | 1 | 4 | 13 | 8 | 0 | 22 | 183 |
| 2003 | 0 | 0 | 4 | 31 | 50 | 29 | 6 | 1 | 4 | 12 | 29 | 0 | 166 |
| 2004 | 1 | 1 | 27 | 25 | 29 | 34 | 1 | 5 | 0 | 4 | 55 | 2 | 184 |
| 2005 | 0 | 0 | 6 | 7 | 27 | 46 | 15 | 4 | 2 | 0 | 0 | 2 | 109 |
| 2006 | 0 | 1 | 4 | 20 | 43 | 7 | 3 | 3 | 0 | 9 | 0 | 27 | 117 |
| 2007 | 2 | 1 | 56 | 61 | 43 | 21 | 8 | 4 | 14 | 2 | 1 | 3 | 216 |
| 2008 | 0 | 3 | 15 | 48 | 33 | 9 | 5 | 1 | 2 | 3 | 1 | 3 | 123 |
| 2009 | 0 | 5 | 4 | 48 | 18 | 32 | 2 | 4 | 1 | 4 | 1 | 12 | 131 |
| 2010 | 10 | 0 | 0 | 19 | 34 | 23 | 3 | 1 | 12 | 10 | 0 | 0 | 112 |
| 2011 | 1 | 1 | 3 | 57 | 20 | 6 | 1 | 4 | 1 | 2 | 8 | 0 | 104 |
| 2012 | 22 | 3 | 9 | 36 | 31 | 3 | 0 | 1 | 2 | 3 | 0 | 5 | 115 |
| 2013 | 1 | 16 | 0 | 8 | 41 | 3 | 0 | 6 | 0 | 6 | 0 | 3 | 84 |
| 2014 | 0 | 0 | 0 | 6 | 15 | 15 | 5 | 0 | 0 | 2 | 0 | 3 | 46 |
| Total | 164 | 180 | 603 | 1436 | 2470 | 1289 | 324 | 378 | 471 | 414 | 322 | 198 | 8249 |
| Avg. | 2.56 | 2.81 | 9.42 | 22.44 | 38.59 | 20.14 | 5.06 | 5.91 | 7.36 | 6.47 | 5.03 | 3.09 | 128.89 |
| Max | 24 | 20 | 56 | 69 | 123 | 75 | 19 | 34 | 124 | 28 | 55 | 27 | 232 |

On April 10, 1979, the worst single tornado in Texas' history hit Wichita Falls. Earlier on the same day, several tornadoes hit farther west. The destruction in Wichita Falls resulted in 42 dead, 1,740 injured, more than 3,000 homes destroyed, and damage of approximately $400 million. Photo courtesy of the Texas Department of Public Safety.

# Extreme Weather Records in Texas

## TEMPERATURE

| Lowest | -23°F | Tulia | Feb. 12, 1899 |
|---|---|---|---|
| | -23°F | Seminole | Feb. 8, 1933 |
| Highest | 120°F | Seymour | Aug. 12, 1936 |
| | 120°F | Monahans | June 28, 1994 |
| Coldest Winter | | | 1898–1899 |

## WIND VELOCITY

### Highest sustained wind

| 145 mph SE | Matagorda | Sept. 11, 1961 |
|---|---|---|
| 145 mph NE | Port Lavaca | Sept. 11, 1961 |

### Highest peak gust

| 180 mph SW | Aransas Pass | Aug. 3, 1970 |
|---|---|---|
| 180 mph WSW | Robstown | Aug. 3, 1970 |

*These winds occurred during Hurricane Carla in 1961 and Hurricane Celia in 1970.*

## TORNADOES

*Since 1950, there have been six tornadoes of the F-5 category, that is, with winds between 261–318 mph.*

| Waco | McLennan County | May 11, 1953 |
|---|---|---|
| Wichita Falls | Wichita County | April 3, 1964 |
| Lubbock | Lubbock County | May 11, 1970 |
| Valley Mills | McLennan County | May 6, 1973 |
| Brownwood | Brown County | April 19, 1976 |
| Jarrell | Williamson County | May 27, 1997 |

## RAINFALL

| Wettest year statewide | | 1941 | 42.62 in. |
|---|---|---|---|
| Driest year statewide | | 1917 | 14.30 in. |
| Most annual | Clarksville | 1873 | 109.38 in. |
| Least annual | Presidio | 1956 | 1.64 in. |
| Most in 24 hours† | Alvin | July 25–26, 1979 | 43.00 in. |
| Most in 18 hours | Thrall | Sept. 9, 1921 | 36.40 in. |

*†Unofficial estimate of rainfall during Tropical Storm Claudette. Greatest 24-hour rainfall at an official site occurred at Albany, Shackelford County, on Aug. 4, 1978: 29.05 inches.*

## HAIL

*(Hailstones six inches or greater, since 1950)*

| 8.00 in. | Winkler County | May 31, 1960 |
|---|---|---|
| 7.50 in. | Young County | April 14, 1965 |
| 6.00 in. | Ward County | May 10, 1991 |
| 7.05 in. | Burleson County | Dec. 17, 1995 |

## SNOWFALL

| 65.0 in. | Season | Romero* | 1923–1924 |
|---|---|---|---|
| 61.0 in. | Month | Vega | Feb. 1956 |
| 61.0 in. | Single storm | Vega | Feb. 1–8, 1956 |
| 24.0 in. | 24 hours | Plainview | Feb. 3–4, 1956 |
| 24.2 in. | Annual average | Vega | |

*Romero was in southwestern Hartley County.*

**Source:** National Weather Service, Dallas/Fort Worth.

# Texas Droughts, 1892–2013

This table shows the extent of drought by major region, 1892–2014, by listing the **percent of normal precipitation**. *Drought here is arbitrarily defined as when there is less than 75 percent of normal precipitation.

| Year | High Plains | Low Rolling Plains | North Central | East Texas | Trans-Pecos | Edwards Plateau | South Central | Upper Coast | South Texas | Lower Valley |
|---|---|---|---|---|---|---|---|---|---|---|
| 1892 | ... | ... | ... | ... | 68 | ... | ... | ... | 73 | ... |
| 1893 | ... | ... | 67 | 70 | ... | 49 | 56 | 64 | 53 | 59 |
| 1894 | ... | ... | ... | ... | 68 | ... | ... | ... | ... | ... |
| 1897 | ... | ... | ... | ... | ... | ... | 73 | ... | 72 | ... |
| 1898 | ... | ... | ... | ... | ... | ... | ... | ... | 69 | 51 |
| 1901 | ... | 71 | 70 | ... | ... | 60 | 62 | 70 | 44 | ... |
| 1902 | ... | ... | ... | ... | ... | ... | ... | ... | 65 | 73 |
| 1907 | ... | ... | ... | ... | ... | ... | ... | ... | ... | 65 |
| 1909 | ... | ... | 72 | 68 | 67 | 74 | 70 | ... | ... | ... |
| 1910 | 59 | 59 | 64 | 69 | 43 | 65 | 69 | 74 | 59 | ... |
| 1911 | ... | ... | ... | ... | ... | ... | ... | ... | ... | 70 |
| 1916 | ... | ... | 73 | ... | 74 | 70 | ... | 73 | 69 | ... |
| 1917 | 58 | 50 | 63 | 59 | 44 | 46 | 42 | 50 | 32 | 48 |
| 1920 | ... | ... | ... | ... | ... | ... | ... | ... | ... | 71 |
| 1921 | ... | ... | ... | ... | 72 | ... | ... | ... | ... | 73 |
| 1922 | ... | ... | ... | ... | 68 | ... | ... | ... | ... | ... |
| 1924 | ... | ... | 73 | 73 | ... | 71 | ... | 72 | ... | ... |
| 1925 | ... | ... | 72 | ... | ... | ... | 72 | ... | ... | ... |
| 1927 | ... | ... | ... | ... | ... | ... | ... | 74 | ... | 74 |
| 1933 | 72 | ... | ... | ... | 62 | 68 | ... | ... | ... | ... |
| 1934 | 66 | ... | ... | ... | 46 | 69 | ... | ... | ... | ... |
| 1937 | ... | ... | ... | ... | ... | ... | ... | 72 | ... | ... |
| 1939 | ... | ... | ... | ... | ... | 69 | ... | ... | ... | 72 |
| 1943 | ... | ... | 72 | ... | ... | ... | ... | ... | ... | ... |
| 1948 | ... | ... | 73 | 74 | 62 | ... | 71 | 67 | ... | ... |
| 1950 | ... | ... | ... | ... | ... | 68 | ... | 74 | ... | 64 |
| 1951 | ... | ... | ... | ... | 61 | 53 | ... | ... | ... | ... |
| 1952 | 68 | 66 | ... | ... | 73 | ... | ... | ... | 56 | 70 |
| 1953 | 69 | ... | ... | ... | 49 | 73 | ... | ... | ... | ... |
| 1954 | 70 | 71 | 68 | 73 | ... | 50 | 50 | 57 | 71 | ... |
| 1956 | 51 | 57 | 61 | 68 | 44 | 43 | 55 | 62 | 53 | 53 |
| 1962 | ... | ... | ... | ... | ... | 68 | ... | ... | 67 | 65 |
| 1963 | ... | ... | 63 | 68 | ... | 65 | 61 | 73 | ... | ... |
| 1964 | 74 | ... | ... | ... | 69 | ... | ... | ... | ... | 63 |
| 1970 | 65 | 63 | ... | ... | ... | 72 | ... | ... | ... | ... |
| 1988 | ... | ... | ... | ... | ... | 67 | 62 | 67 | 68 | ... |
| 1989 | ... | ... | ... | ... | ... | 72 | ... | ... | 66 | 64 |
| 1990 | ... | ... | ... | ... | ... | ... | ... | ... | ... | 73 |
| 1994 | ... | ... | ... | ... | 68 | ... | ... | ... | ... | ... |
| 1996 | ... | ... | ... | ... | ... | ... | 71 | ... | 60 | 70 |
| 1998 | ... | 69 | ... | ... | 71 | ... | ... | ... | ... | ... |
| 1999 | ... | ... | 73 | ... | ... | 67 | 69 | 69 | ... | ... |
| 2000 | ... | ... | ... | ... | 74 | ... | ... | ... | ... | 67 |
| 2001 | ... | ... | ... | ... | 56 | ... | ... | ... | ... | ... |
| 2003 | 65 | 71 | ... | ... | ... | ... | ... | ... | ... | ... |
| 2005 | ... | ... | 68 | 66 | ... | ... | ... | ... | ... | 72 |
| 2006 | ... | ... | ... | ... | ... | 66 | ... | ... | ... | ... |
| 2008 | ... | ... | ... | ... | ... | 66 | 61 | ... | ... | ... |
| 2009 | ... | ... | ... | ... | ... | ... | ... | ... | ... | ... |
| 2010 | ... | ... | ... | 70 | ... | ... | ... | ... | ... | ... |
| 2011 | 40 | 43 | 65 | 63 | 29 | 49 | 47 | 47 | 46 | 52 |
| 2012 | 68 | 74 | ... | ... | ... | ... | ... | ... | 74 | 62 |
| 2013 | 74 | ... | ... | ... | ... | ... | ... | ... | ... | ... |

## Drought Frequency

This table shows the number of years of drought and the **number of separate droughts** by region. For example, the High Plains has had 10 drought years, consisting of five 1-year droughts, one 2-year drought and one 3-year drought, a total of 7 droughts.

| Years of Drought | High Plains | Low Rolling Plains | North Central | East Texas | Trans-Pecos | Edwards Plateau | South Central | Upper Coast | South Texas | Lower Valley |
|---|---|---|---|---|---|---|---|---|---|---|
| 1 | 6 | 8 | 11 | 7 | 8 | 11 | 15 | 13 | 10 | 16 |
| 2 | 1 | 2 | 2 | 3 | 5 | 5 | 2 | 1 | 4 | 3 |
| 3 | 2 | 0 | 0 | 0 | 1 | 0 | 0 | 0 | 0 | 0 |
| Total Droughts | 9 | 10 | 13 | 10 | 14 | 16 | 17 | 14 | 14 | 19 |
| Drought Years | 13 | 12 | 15 | 13 | 21 | 21 | 19 | 15 | 18 | 22 |

## Drought Definitions

*Drought has proven to be difficult to define and there is no universally accepted definition. The most commonly used drought definitions are based on meteorological, agricultural, hydrological and socioeconomic effects.

**Meteorological drought** is often defined by a period of substantially **diminished precipitation** duration and/or intensity. The commonly used definition of meteorological drought is an interval of time, generally on the order of months or years, during which the actual moisture supply at a given place consistently falls below the climatically appropriate moisture supply.

**Agricultural drought** occurs when there is **inadequate soil moisture** to meet the needs of a particular crop at a particular time. Agricultural drought usually occurs after or during meteorological drought but before hydrological drought and can also affect livestock and other dry-land agricultural operations.

**Hydrological drought** refers to **deficiencies in surface and subsurface water** supplies. It is measured as streamflow and as lake, reservoir and groundwater levels. There is usually a delay between lack of rain and less measurable water in streams, lakes and reservoirs. Therefore, hydrological measurements tend to lag other drought indicators.

**Socioeconomic drought** occurs when physical water shortages start to affect the health, well-being, and **quality of life** of the people, or when the drought starts to affect the **supply and demand** of an economic product.

*Source: New Mexico Drought Planning Team website.*

## Normal Annual Rainfall in Inches by Texas Climatic Region

Listed below is the normal annual rainfall in inches for five 30-year periods in each geographical region (See map, p. 133). Normals are given **in the same order** as the regions appear in the tables above.

| Region | HP | LRP | NC | ET | TP | EP | SC | UC | ST | LV |
|---|---|---|---|---|---|---|---|---|---|---|
| 1931–1960 | 18.51 | 22.99 | 32.93 | 45.96 | 12.03 | 25.91 | 33.24 | 46.19 | 22.33 | 24.27 |
| 1941–1970 | 18.59 | 23.18 | 32.94 | 45.37 | 11.57 | 23.94 | 33.03 | 46.43 | 21.95 | 23.44 |
| 1951–1980 | 17.73 | 22.80 | 32.14 | 44.65 | 11.65 | 23.52 | 34.03 | 45.93 | 22.91 | 24.73 |
| 1961–1990 | 18.88 | 23.77 | 33.99 | 45.67 | 13.01 | 24.00 | 34.49 | 47.63 | 23.47 | 25.31 |
| 1971–2000 | 19.64 | 24.51 | 35.23 | 48.08 | 13.19 | 24.73 | 36.21 | 50.31 | 24.08 | 25.43 |
| 1981–2010 | 20.02 | 24.85 | 36.17 | 48.21 | 13.16 | 24.86 | 35.54 | 51.14 | 24.17 | 24.67 |

# Significant and Destructive Weather

*Source: This list of significant weather events in Texas since 1766 was compiled from ESSA-Weather Bureau information, previous Texas Almanacs, the Handbook of Texas, The Dallas Morning News and other sources.*

**Sept. 4, 1766: Hurricane. Galveston Bay.** Spanish Mission Nuestra Señora de la Luz destroyed.

**Sept. 12, 1818: Hurricane. Galveston Island.** Salt water flowed four feet deep. Only six buildings remained habitable. Of the six vessels and two barges in the harbor, even the two not seriously damaged were reduced to dismasted hulks. **Pirate Jean Lafitte** moved to one hulk so his **Red House** might serve as a hospital.

**Aug. 6, 1844: Hurricane. Mouth of Rio Grande.** All houses destroyed at the mouth of the river and at **Brazos Santiago,** eight miles north; 70 lives lost.

**Sept. 19, 1854: Hurricane.** Struck near **Matagorda** and moved inland, northwestward over **Columbus.** Main impact felt in **Matagorda and Lavaca bays.** Four lives were lost in town; more lives were lost on the peninsula. Almost all buildings in Matagorda were destroyed.

**Oct. 3, 1867: Hurricane.** Moved inland south of **Galveston** but raked the entire Texas coast from the Rio Grande to the Sabine. **Bagdad** and **Clarksville,** towns at the mouth of the Rio Grande, were destroyed. Much of Galveston was flooded; property damage there was estimated at $1 million.

**Sept. 16, 1875: Hurricane.** Struck **Indianola,** Calhoun County. Three-fourths of town swept away; 176 lives lost. Flooding from the bay caused nearly all destruction.

**Aug. 13, 1880: Hurricane.** Center struck **Matamoros, Mexico; lower Texas coast** affected.

**Oct. 12–13, 1880: Hurricane. Brownsville.** City nearly destroyed, many lives lost.

**Dec. 29, 1880: Snow. Brownsville.** A rare snowstorm in the Lower Rio Grande Valley.

**Aug. 23–24, 1882: Torrential rains** caused **flooding** on the **North and South Concho and Bosque rivers** (South Concho reported 45 feet above normal level), destroying **Benficklen,** then county seat of Tom Green County, leaving only the courthouse and jail. More than 50 persons drowned in **Tom Green and Erath counties,** with property damage at $200,000 and 10,000 to 15,000 head of livestock lost.

**Aug. 19–21, 1886: Hurricane. Indianola.** Every house destroyed or damaged. Indianola was never rebuilt.

**Oct. 12, 1886: Hurricane. Sabine,** Jefferson County. Hurricane passed over Sabine. The inundation extended 20 miles inland; 150 persons drowned and nearly every house in the vicinity was moved from its foundation.

**April 28, 1893: Tornado. Cisco,** Eastland County. 23 killed, 93 injured; damage, $400,000.

**Feb. 1895: Freeze-Snow. Coastal Texas.** Probably the greatest heavy-snow anomaly in the climatic history of the U.S. resulted from a snowstorm along the Texas coast on the 14th–15th. **Houston; Orange; Stafford,** Fort Bend County; and **Columbus,** Colorado County, each reported a snowfall of 20 inches. **Galveston** had a snowfall of 15.4 inches. Snow fell as far south as the Lower Rio Grande Valley, where **Brownsville** received 5 inches. Lower Valley had lows of **22 degrees** the 14th–17th, destroying vegetable crops.

**May 15, 1896: Tornadoes. Sherman,** Grayson County; **Justin** and **Gribble Springs,** Denton County. 76 killed; damage, $225,000.

**Sept. 12, 1897: Hurricane.** Many houses in Port Arthur were demolished; 13 killed; damage, $150,000.

**May 1, 1898: Tornado. Mobeetie,** Wheeler County. Four killed; several injured; damage, $35,000.

**Feb. 11–13, 1899: Freeze.** Disastrous cold wave that newspapers described as the worst freeze ever known in the state. **Brownsville's** temperature reach 16 degrees on the 12th and remained below freezing through the 13th. Much destruction of vegetable crops.

**June 27–July 1, 1899: Rainstorm.** A storm, centered over **the Brazos River watershed,** dropped an average of 17 inches over 7,000 square miles. At **Hearne,** the gage overflowed at 24 inches and was estimated at 30 inches. At **Turnersville,** Coryell County, 33 inches were recorded in three days. The rain caused the **worst Brazos River flood on record;** 30 and 35 lives lost; property damage, $9 million.

**April 5–8, 1900: Rainstorm.** This storm began in two centers, over **Val Verde County** on the Rio Grande and over **Swisher County** on the High Plains, and converged in the vicinity of **Travis County,** causing disastrous floods in the **Colorado, Brazos, and Guadalupe rivers.** McDonald Dam on the Colorado River at Austin crumbled suddenly. A wall of water swept through the city taking at least 23 lives. Damage was estimated at $1.25 million.

**Sept. 8–9, 1900: Hurricane. Galveston.** The **Great Galveston Storm** was the **worst natural disaster in U.S. history** in terms of human life. Loss of life at Galveston has been estimated at 6,000 to 8,000, but the exact number has never been determined. The island was completely inundated; not a single structure escaped damage. Most loss of life was due to drowning by storm tides that reached 15 feet or more. The anemometer blew away when the wind reached 100 mph at 6:15 p.m. on the 8th. Wind reached an estimated maximum velocity of 120 mph between 7:30 and 8:30 p.m. Property damage was estimated at $30 million to $40 million.

**May 18, 1902: Tornado. Goliad.** The tornado cut a 250-yard-wide path through town, turning 150 buildings into rubble. Several churches were destroyed, one of which was holding services; all 40 worshippers were either killed or injured. Total deaths, 114; injured, 230; damage, $200,000.

**April 26, 1906: Tornado. Bellevue,** Clay County. Bellevue was demolished. Considerable damage done at **Stoneburg,** seven miles east in Montague County. In all, 17 killed; 20 injured; damage, $300,000.

**May 6, 1907: Tornado.** North of **Sulphur Springs,** Hopkins County. Five killed, 19 injured.

**May 13, 1908: Tornado. Linden,** Cass County. Four killed; seven injured; damage, $75,000.

**May 22–25, 1908: Rainstorm.** Unique because it originated on the Pacific Coast. It moved first into **North Texas** and southern Oklahoma and then to **Central Texas,** precipitating as much as 10 inches. Heaviest floods were in the upper Trinity basin but extended south to the Nueces. Eleven killed near Dallas; property damage, more than $5 million.

**March 23, 1909: Tornado. Slidell,** Wise County; 11 killed, 10 injured; damage, $30,000.

**May 30, 1909: Tornado. Zephyr,** Brown County; 28 killed, many injured; damage, $90,000.

**July 21, 1909: Hurricane. Velasco,** Brazoria County. Half of town destroyed; 41 lives lost; damage, $2,000,000.

**Dec. 1–5, 1913: Rainstorm.** Caused the **second major Brazos River flood** and more deaths than the 1899 storm. Formed over **Central Texas;** spread southwest and northeast, dumping 15 inches of rain at **San Marcos** and 11 inches at **Kaufman.** Floods killed 177; damage, $8.54 million.

**April 20–26, 1915: Rainstorm.** Developed over Central Texas; spread into North and East Texas. Up to 17 inches of rain caused floods in **Trinity, Brazos, Colorado and Guadalupe rivers.** More than 40 killed; damage, $2.33 million.

**Aug. 16–19, 1915: Hurricane. Galveston.** Peak wind gusts of 120 miles recorded at Galveston; tide ranged 9.5 to 14.3 feet above mean sea level in the city, and up to 16.1 feet near the causeway. Business section flooded with 5–6 feet of water. At least 275 lives lost; damage, $56 million. A new seawall prevented a repetition of the 1900 disaster.

**Aug. 18, 1916: Hurricane. Corpus Christi.** Maximum wind speed, 100 mph; 20 lives lost; damage, $1.6 million.

**Jan. 10–12, 1918: Blizzard.** The most severe since February 1899, it was accompanied by zero-degree temperatures in North Texas and temperatures from 7–12 degrees below freezing along the lower coast.

**April 9, 1919: Tornado. Leonard, Ector, and Ravenna,** Fannin County; 20 killed, 45 injured; damage, $125,000.

**April 9, 1919: Tornado. Henderson, Van Zandt, Wood, Camp, and Red River counties;** 42 killed; 150 injured; damage, $450,000.

**May 7, 1919: Windstorms. Starr, Hidalgo, Willacy, and Cameron counties.** Violent thunderstorms with high winds, hail, and rain occurred between **Rio Grande City** and the coast, killing 10 persons. Damage to property and crops was $500,000. Seven were killed at **Mission.**

**Sept. 14, 1919: Hurricane.** Near **Corpus Christi.** Center moved inland south of Corpus Christi; tides were 16 feet above normal in that area and 8.8 feet above normal at Galveston. Extreme wind at Corpus Christi measured at 110 mph; 284 lives lost; damage, $20.3 million.

**April 13, 1921: Tornado. Melissa,** Collin County, and **Petty,** Lamar County. Melissa was practically destroyed; 12 killed; 80 injured; damage, $500,000.

**April 15, 1921: Tornado. Wood, Cass, and Bowie counties;** 10 killed; 50 injured; damage, $85,000.

**Sept. 8–10, 1921: Rainstorm.** Probably the **greatest rainstorm in Texas history,** it entered Mexico as a hurricane from the Gulf. Torrential rains fell as the storm moved northeasterly across Texas. **Record floods** occurred in **Bexar, Travis, Williamson, Bell, and Milam counties,** killing 215 persons, with property losses over $19 million. Five to nine feet of water stood in downtown **San Antonio.** A total of 23.98 inches was measured at the U.S. Weather Bureau station at **Taylor** during a period of 35 hours, with a 24-hour maximum of 23.11 inches on Sept. 9–10. The **greatest rainfall recorded in U.S. history during 18 consecutive hours** (measured at an unofficial weather-monitoring site) **fell at Thrall,** Williamson County: 36.40 inches fell on Sept. 9.

**April 8, 1922: Tornado. Rowena,** Runnels County. Seven killed; 52 injured; damage, $55,000.

**April 8, 1922: Tornado. Oplin,** Callahan County. Five killed; 30 injured; damage, $15,000.

**April 23–28, 1922: Rainstorm.** An exceptional storm entered Texas from the west and moved from the **Panhandle** to **North-Central** and **East Texas.** Rains up to 12.6 inches over Parker, Tarrant, and Dallas counties caused severe floods in the Upper Trinity at **Fort Worth;** 11 lives were lost; damage was estimated at $1 million.

**May 4, 1922: Tornado. Austin,** Travis County; 12 killed; 50 injured; damage, $500,000.

**May 14, 1923: Tornado. Howard and Mitchell counties;** 23 killed; 100 injured; damage, $50,000.

**April 12, 1927: Tornado. Edwards, Real, and Uvalde counties;** 74 killed; 205 injured; damage, $1.23 million. Most damage was in **Rocksprings,** where 72 deaths occurred and the town was practically destroyed.

**May 9, 1927: Tornado. Garland;** 11 killed; damage, $100,000.

**May 9, 1927: Tornado. Nevada,** Collin County; **Wolfe City,** Hunt County; and **Tigertown,** Lamar County; 28 killed; more than 200 injured; damage, $900,000.

**Jan. 4, 1929: Tornado.** Near **Bay City,** Matagorda County. Five killed, 14 injured.

**April 24, 1929: Tornado. Slocum,** Anderson County; seven killed; 20 injured; damage, $200,000.

**May 24–31, 1929: Rainstorm.** Beginning over Caldwell County, the storm spread over much of **Central** and **Coastal Texas** with maximum rainfall of 12.9 inches, **causing floods in Colorado, Guadalupe, Brazos, Trinity, Neches, and Sabine rivers.** Much damage at **Houston** from overflow of bayous. Damage estimated at $6 million.

**May 6, 1930: Tornado. Bynum, Irene, and Mertens** in Hill County; **Ennis,** Ellis County; and **Frost,** Navarro County; 41 killed; damage, $2.1 million.

**May 6, 1930: Tornado. Kenedy** and **Runge** in Karnes County; **Nordheim,** DeWitt County; 36 killed; 34 injured; damage, $127,000.

**June 30–July 2, 1932: Rainstorm.** Torrential rains fell over the upper watersheds of the **Nueces and Guadalupe rivers,** causing destructive floods. Seven persons drowned; property losses exceeded $500,000.

**Aug. 13, 1932: Hurricane.** Near **Freeport,** Brazoria County. Wind speed at **East Columbia** estimated at 100 mph; 40 lives lost; 200 injured; damage, $7.5 million.

**March 30, 1933: Tornado. Angelina, Nacogdoches, and San Augustine counties;** 10 killed; 56 injured; damage, $200,000.

**April 26, 1933: Tornado. Bowie County** near Texarkana. Five killed, 38 injured; damage, $14,000.

**April 29, 1933: Dust storm. Panhandle, South Plains.** The dust storm extended from **Sweetwater** north to Central Kansas and from Albuquerque, N.M., to Oklahoma. Newspaper accounts described it as the worst sandstorm in years; "as dark as any night" in **Perryton.** Thousands of acres of small grain crops were blown from the soil.

**July 22–25, 1933: Tropical Storm.** One of the greatest U.S. storms in area and general rainfall. The storm reached the vicinity of **Freeport** late on the 22nd and moved slowly overland across eastern Texas through the 25th. Its center moved into northern Louisiana on the 25th. Rainfall averaged 12.50 inches over an area of about 25,000 square miles. Twenty inches or more fell in a small area of eastern Texas and western Louisiana surrounding Logansport, La. The four-day total at Logansport was 22.30 inches. Property damage was estimated at $1.12 million.

**July 30, 1933: Tornado. Oak Cliff section of Dallas,** Dallas County. Five killed; 30 injured; damage, $500,000.

**Sept. 4–5, 1933: Hurricane.** Near **Brownsville.** Center passed inland a short distance north of Brownsville, where an extreme wind of 106 mph was measured before the anemometer blew away. Peak wind gusts were estimated at 120–125 mph; 40 known dead; 500 injured; damage, $16,903,100. About 90 percent of the citrus crop in the **Lower Rio Grande Valley** was destroyed.

**July 25, 1934: Hurricane.** Near **Seadrift,** Calhoun County; 19 lives lost; many minor injuries; damage, $4.5 million. About 85 percent of damage was to crops.

**Jan.–March 1935: Dust storms. Amarillo.** Seven times, the visibility in Amarillo declined to zero from dust storms. One of these complete blackouts lasted 11 hours. One of the storms raged for 3-1/2 days.

**Sept. 15–18, 1936: Rainstorm.** Excessive rains over the **North Concho and Middle Concho rivers** caused a sharp rise in the Concho River, which overflowed **San Angelo.** Much of the business district and 500 homes were flooded. Four persons drowned and property losses were estimated at $5 million. Four-day storm rainfall at San Angelo measured 25.19 inches; 11.75 inches fell on the 15th.

**June 10, 1938: Tornado. Clyde,** Callahan County; 14 killed; 9 injured; damage, $85,000.

**Sept. 23, 1941: Hurricane.** Center moved inland near Matagorda and passed over **Houston** about midnight. Extremely high tides along coast in the **Matagorda to Galveston** area. Heaviest property and crop losses were in counties from Matagorda County to the Sabine River. Four lives lost. Damage was $6.5 million.

**April 28, 1942: Tornado. Crowell,** Foard County; 11 killed; 250 injured; damage, $1.5 million.

**Aug. 30, 1942: Hurricane. Matagorda Bay.** Highest wind estimated at 115 mph at **Seadrift.** Tide at **Matagorda** was 14.7 feet. Storm moved west-north-westward and finally diminished over the **Edwards Plateau;** eight lives lost; property damage, $11.5 million; crop damage, $15 million.

**May 10, 1943: Tornado. Laird Hill,** Rusk County, and **Kilgore,** Gregg County; four killed; 25 injured; damage, $1 million.

Debris hangs from a bridge over the swollen Blanco River, above, on May 24, 2015. Torrential rains that began Memorial Day weekend flooded much of the area around San Marcos and west of Austin. Photo by Stephen Ramirez; International Business Times. At left, members of the Texas State Guard search the banks of the Blanco River near San Marcos on June 3, 2015, looking for missing residents. At least 23 people died in the flooding, and 23 counties were declared disaster areas. Photo by Jocelyn Augustino; FEMA.

**July 27, 1943: Hurricane.** Near **Galveston.** Center moved inland across **Bolivar Peninsula and Trinity Bay.** A wind gust of 104 mph was recorded at **Texas City;** 19 lives lost; damage estimated at $16.6 million.

**Aug. 26–27, 1945: Hurricane. Aransas–San Antonio Bay** area. At **Port O'Connor,** the wind reached 105 mph when the cups were torn from the anemometer. Peak gusts of 135 mph were estimated at **Seadrift, Port O'Connor,** and **Port Lavaca;** three killed; 25 injured; damage, $20.1 million.

**Jan. 4, 1946: Tornado.** Near **Lufkin,** Angelina County, and **Nacogdoches,** Nacogdoches County; 13 killed; 250 injured; damage, $2.1 million.

**Jan. 4, 1946: Tornado.** Near **Palestine,** Anderson County; 15 killed; 60 injured; damage, $500,000.

**May 18, 1946: Tornado.** Clay, Montague, and Denton counties. Four killed; damage, $112,000.

**April 9, 1947: Tornado. White Deer,** Carson County; **Glazier,** Hemphill County; and **Higgins,** Lipscomb County; 68 killed; 201 injured; damage, $1.55 million. Glazier was destroyed. **One of the largest tornadoes on record.** Width of path, 1 mile at Higgins; length of path, 221 miles across portions of Texas, Oklahoma, and Kansas. This tornado also struck Woodward, Okla.

**May 3, 1948: Tornado. McKinney,** Collin County; three killed; 43 injured; damage, $2 million.

**May 15, 1949: Tornado. Amarillo** and vicinity; six killed, 83 injured. Total damage from tornado, wind, and hail, $5.3 million. Total destruction over one-block by three-block area in southern part of city; airport and 45 airplanes damaged; 28 railroad boxcars blown off track.

**Jan.–Feb. 1951: Freeze.** On Jan. 31.–Feb. 3 and again

on Feb. 13–17, cold waves swept over the entire state, bringing **snow and sleet.** Heavy damage was done in the **Lower Rio Grande Valley** to truck and citrus crops, notably in the earlier of these northers. During the norther of Jan. 31–Feb. 3, the temperature went to **minus 19 degrees in Dalhart.**

**Sept. 8–10, 1952: Rainstorm.** Heavy rains over the **Colorado and Guadalupe river watersheds** in southwestern Texas caused major flooding. From 23–26 inches fell between **Kerrville, Blanco, and Boerne.** Highest stages ever known occurred in the **Pedernales River; five** lives lost; three injured; 17 homes destroyed, 454 damaged. Property loss, several million dollars.

**March 13, 1953: Tornado. Jud and O'Brien,** Haskell County; and **Knox City,** Knox County; 17 killed; 25 injured; damage, $600,000.

**May 11, 1953: Tornado.** Near **San Angelo,** Tom Green County; 11 killed; 159 injured; damage, $3.24 million.

**May 11, 1953: Tornado. Waco,** McLennan County; 114 killed; 597 injured; damage, $41.15 million. **One of two most disastrous tornadoes;** 150 homes destroyed, 900 damaged; 185 other buildings destroyed, 500 damaged.

**Feb. 1–5, 1956: Blizzard. Northwestern Texas.** A major blizzard moved into the Panhandle and South Plains on the 1st. Snow and high winds continued through the 5th. Snowfall was the **heaviest on record in Texas;** 20 killed.

**April 2, 1957: Tornado. Dallas,** Dallas County; 10 killed; 200 injured; damage, $4 million. Moving through Oak Cliff and West Dallas, it damaged 574 buildings, largely homes.

**April–May, 1957: Torrential Rains.** Excessive flooding occurred in the area **east of the Pecos River to the Sabine River** during the last 10 days of April; 17 lives were lost; several hundred homes were destroyed. During May, more than 4,000 persons were evacuated from unprotected lowlands on the **West Fork of the Trinity north of Fort Worth** and along creeks in Fort Worth. Twenty-nine houses at **Christoval** were damaged or destroyed; 83 houses at **San Angelo** were damaged. Five persons drowned in **South Central Texas.**

**May 15, 1957: Tornado. Silverton,** Briscoe County; 21 killed; 80 injured; damage, $500,000.

**June 27, 1957: Hurricane Audrey.** Center crossed the Gulf Coast near the Texas-Louisiana line. **Orange** was in the western portion of the eye between 9 a.m.–10 a.m. In Texas, nine lives were lost; 450 persons injured; property damage was $8 million. Damage was extensive in **Jefferson and Orange counties,** with less in **Chambers and Galveston counties.** Maximum wind reported in Texas, 85 mph. at **Sabine Pass,** with gusts to 100 mph.

**Oct. 28, 1960: Rainstorm.** Rains of 7–10 inches fell in **South Central Texas;** 11 died from drowning in flash floods. In **Austin,** about 300 families were driven from their homes. Damage in Austin was estimated at $2.5 million.

**Sept. 8–14, 1961: Hurricane Carla. Port O'Connor.** Maximum wind gust at **Port Lavaca** estimated at 175 mph. Highest tide was 18.5 feet at Port Lavaca. Most damage was to coastal counties **between Corpus Christi and Port Arthur,** and inland, in **Jackson, Harris, and Wharton counties.** In Texas, 34 persons died, seven in a tornado that swept across **Galveston Island;** 465 persons were injured. Property and crop damage conservatively estimated at $300 million. Evacuation of an estimated 250,000 persons kept loss of life low. **Hurricane Carla was the largest hurricane of record.**

**Jan. 9–12, 1962: Freeze.** A disastrous cold wave comparable to those of 1899 and 1951. Low temperatures ranged from **minus 15 degrees in the Panhandle to 10 degrees at Rio Grande City.** Agricultural loss estimate, $50 million.

**Sept. 7, 1962: Rainstorm. Fort Worth.** Rains fell over the Big Fossil Creek and Denton Creek watersheds, ranging up to 11 inches in three hours. Extensive damage from flash flooding occurred in **Richland Hills** and **Haltom City.**

**Sept. 16–20, 1963: Hurricane Cindy.** Rains of 15 to 23.5 inches fell in portions of **Jefferson, Newton, and Orange counties** when Hurricane Cindy became stationary west of **Port Arthur.** Flooding resulted in property damage of $11.6 million and agricultural losses of $500,000.

**April 3, 1964: Tornado. Wichita Falls;** 7 killed, 111 injured; damage, $15 million; 225 homes destroyed, 50 with major damage and 200 with minor damage. Sixteen other buildings received major damage.

**Sept. 21–23, 1964: Rainstorm. Collin, Dallas, and Tarrant counties.** More than 12 inches of rain fell during the first eight hours on the 21st. Flash flooding of tributaries of the Trinity River and smaller creeks and streams resulted in two drownings and an estimated $3 million in property damage. Flooding of homes occurred in all sections of **McKinney.** In **Fort Worth,** there was considerable damage to residences along Big Fossil and White Rock creeks.

**Jan. 25, 1965: Dust Storm. West Texas.** The worst dust storm since February 1956 developed on the **southern High Plains.** Winds, gusting up to 75 mph at **Lubbock,** sent dust billowing to 31,000 feet in the area **from the Texas-New Mexico border eastward to a line from Tulia to Abilene.** Ground visibility was reduced to about 100 yards in many areas. The worst hit was the **Muleshoe, Seminole, Plains, Morton** area on the South Plains. The rain gage at Reese Air Force Base, Lubbock, contained 3 inches of fine sand.

**June 2, 1965: Tornado. Hale Center, Hale County.** Four killed, 76 injured; damage, $8 million.

**June 11, 1965: Rainstorm. Sanderson,** Terrell County. Torrential rains of up to eight inches in two hours near Sanderson caused a major flash flood that swept through the town; 26 persons drowned; property losses, $2.72 million.

**April 22–29, 1966: Flooding. Northeast Texas.** Twenty to 26 inches of rain fell in portions of Wood, Smith, Morris, Upshur, Gregg, Marion, and Harrison counties; 19 persons drowned in the rampaging rivers and creeks that swept away bridges, roads, and dams; damage, $12 million.

**April 28, 1966: Flash flooding. Dallas County.** Flash flooding from torrential rains in Dallas County resulted in 14 persons drowned and property losses at $15 million.

**Sept. 18–23, 1967: Hurricane Beulah.** Near **Brownsville.** The **third largest hurricane of record,** Hurricane Beulah moved inland near the mouth of the Rio Grande on the 20th. Wind gusts of 136 mph were reported during Beulah's passage. Rains 10–20 inches over much of the area **south of San Antonio** resulted in record-breaking floods. An unofficial gaging station at **Falfurrias** registered the highest accumulated rainfall, 36 inches. Stream overflow and surface runoff inundated 1.4 million acres. Beulah spawned 115 tornadoes, all in Texas, the **greatest number of tornadoes on record for any hurricane.** There were 13 deaths and 37 injuries (5 deaths and 34 injuries attributed to tornadoes); property losses, $100 million; crop losses, $50 million.

**April 18, 1970: Tornado.** Near **Clarendon,** Donley County; 17 killed; 42 injured; damage, $2.1 million. Fourteen persons were killed at a resort community at Green Belt Reservoir, 7 miles north of Clarendon.

**May 11, 1970: Tornado. Lubbock,** Lubbock County; 26 killed; 500 injured; damage, $135 million. Fifteen square miles, almost 1/4 of the city of Lubbock, suffered damage.

**Aug. 3–5, 1970: Hurricane Celia. Corpus Christi.** Hurricane Celia was a unique but severe storm. Measured in dollars, it was **the costliest in the state's history to that time.** Sustained wind speeds reached 130 mph, but it was great bursts of kinetic energy of short duration that appeared to cause the severe damage. Wind gusts of 161 mph were measured at the **Corpus Christi** National Weather Service Office. At **Aransas Pass,** peak wind gusts were estimated as high as 180 mph after the wind equipment blew away. In Texas, Celia caused 11 deaths, at least 466 injuries, and total property and crop damage of $453.77 million. Hurricane Celia crossed the Texas coastline midway between Corpus Christi and Aransas Pass about 3:30 p.m. CST on Aug. 3. Hardest hit was the metropolitan area of **Corpus Christi,**

*Downtown Corpus Christi bore the brunt of Hurricane Celia when it hit the Gulf Coast Aug. 3–5, 1970. Celia's sustained wind speeds reached 130 mph, with wind gusts as high as 161 mph measured at the Corpus Christi National Weather Service Office. At Aransas Pass, peak wind gusts were estimated as high as 180 mph after the wind equipment blew away. In Texas, Celia caused 11 deaths, at least 466 injuries, and total property and crop damage of more than $453 million. Texas Almanac file photo.*

including **Robstown, Aransas Pass, Port Aransas,** and small towns on the north side of Corpus Christi Bay.

**Feb. 20–22, 1971: Blizzard. Panhandle.** Paralyzing blizzard, the worst since March 22–25, 1957, transformed the Panhandle into one vast snowfield as 6–26 inches of snow were whipped by 40–60 mph winds into drifts up to 12 feet high. At **Follett,** 3-day snowfall was 26 inches. Three persons killed; property and livestock losses were $3.1 million.

**Sept. 9–13, 1971: Hurricane Fern. Coastal Bend.** Rain of 10–26 inches resulted in some of the worst flooding since Hurricane Beulah in 1967; 2 killed; damage, $30.2 million.

**May 11–12, 1972: Rainstorm. South Central Texas.** Seventeen drowned at **New Braunfels,** one at **McQueeney.** New Braunfels and **Seguin** hardest hit. Property damage, $17.5 million.

**June 12–13, 1973: Rainstorm. Southeastern Texas.** From 10–15 inches of rain recorded; 10 drowned; property and crop damage, more than $50 million.

**Nov. 23–24, 1974: Flash Flooding. Central Texas.** Thirteen killed, 10 in Travis County; damage, $1 million.

**Jan. 31–Feb. 1, 1975: Flooding. Nacogdoches County.** Widespread heavy rain caused flash flooding, resulting in three deaths; damage, more than $5.5 million.

**May 23, 1975: Rainstorm. Austin** area. Heavy rains, high winds, and hail caused 4 deaths from drowning; 40 injuries; and damage of more than $5 million.

**April 19, 1976: Tornado. Brownwood.** An F-5 tornado destroyed a few homes and airplanes; 9 people injured.

**June 15, 1976: Rainstorm. Harris County.** Rains in excess of 13 inches caused eight deaths, including three drownings; damage was nearly $25 million.

**Aug. 1–4, 1978: Heavy Rains, Flooding. Edwards Plateau, Low Rolling Plains.** Remnants of **Tropical Storm Amelia** caused some of the worst flooding of that century. As much as 30 inches of rain fell near **Albany** in Shackelford County, where six drownings were reported. In **Ban-**

dera, Kerr, Kendall, and Gillespie counties, 27 people drowned; damage was at least $50 million.

**Dec. 30–31, 1978: Ice Storm. North-Central Texas.** Possibly the **worst ice storm in 30 years** hit Dallas County particularly hard; six deaths; damage, $14 million.

**April 10, 1979: Tornado. Wichita Falls. The worst single tornado in Texas' history** hit Wichita Falls. Earlier on the same day, **several tornadoes** hit farther west. The destruction in Wichita Falls resulted in 42 dead, 1,740 injured, more than 3,000 homes destroyed, and damage of approximately $400 million. An estimated 20,000 persons were left homeless. In all, the tornadoes on April 10 killed 53 people, injured 1,812, and caused over $500 million in damages.

**May 3, 1979: Thunderstorms. Dallas County.** The county was hit by a wave of the most destructive thunderstorms in many years; 37 injuries; damages, $5 million.

**July 25–26, 1979: Tropical Storm Claudette.** This storm caused more than $750 million in property and crop damage, but fortunately only few injuries. Near **Alvin,** an estimated 43 inches of rain fell, a new state record for 24 hours.

**Aug. 24, 1979: Hailstorms. West Texas.** One of the worst hailstorms in the past 100 years; $200 million in crops, mostly cotton, were destroyed.

**Sept. 18–20, 1979: Flooding. Aransas Pass.** Coastal flooding from heavy rain: 18 inches in 24 hours at Aransas Pass, and 13 inches at **Rockport.**

**Aug. 9–11, 1980: Hurricane Allen. South Texas.** Three persons killed; property and crop damage, $650 million to $750 million; more than 250,000 coastal residents evacuated. The worst damage was along **Padre Island** and in **Corpus Christi;** 20 inches of rain fell on extreme South Texas; 29 tornadoes, one of the worst hurricane-related outbreaks.

**Summer 1980: Heat.** One of the **hottest summers** in the history of the Lone Star State.

**Sept. 5–8, 1980: Hurricane Danielle.** The storm

brought rain and flooding to southeast and Central Texas; 17 inches of rain fell at **Port Arthur;** 25 inches near **Junction.**

**May 24–25, 1981: Severe Flooding. Austin.** Thirteen killed; 100 injured; damage, $40 million. Up to 5.5 inches of rain fell in one hour west of the city.

**Oct. 11–14, 1981: Rain. North-Central Texas.** Record rain caused by the remains of **Pacific Hurricane Norma** reached more than 20 inches in some locations.

**April 2, 1982: Tornadoes. Northeast Texas.** A **tornado outbreak** with the most severe striking **Paris;** 10 people killed; 170 injured; 1,000 left homeless; damage, $50 million. In all, seven tornadoes that day left 11 dead and 174 injured.

**May 1982: Tornadoes.** Texas recorded **123 tornadoes,** the most ever in May and one less than the most recorded in any single month in the state; 1 death; 23 injuries.

**Dec. 1982: Heavy Snow. El Paso.** Snowfall recorded at 18.2 inches was the most to fall there in any month.

**Aug. 15–21, 1983: Hurricane Alicia.** This was the first hurricane to make landfall in the continental U.S. in three years (Aug. 18) and **one of the costliest in Texas history** ($3 billion). Alicia caused widespread damage to a large section of **Southeast Texas,** including coastal areas near **Galveston** and the entire **Houston** area. Alicia spawned 22 tornadoes; highest winds were estimated near 130 mph. In all, 18 people were killed and 1,800 injured.

**Jan. 12–13, 1985: Snowstorm. West and South-Central Texas.** A record-breaking snowstorm struck with up to 15 inches falling at many locations **between San Antonio and the Rio Grande.** San Antonio recorded 13.2 inches of snow on Jan. 12 (the greatest in a day) and 13.5 inches for the two-day total. Eagle Pass reported 14.5 inches of snow.

**June 26, 1986: Hurricane Bonnie.** The storm made landfall between **High Island** and **Sabine Pass** around 3:45 a.m. Highest wind measured in the area was a 97-mph gust, recorded at **Sea Rim State Park.** As much as 13 inches of rain fell in **Ace,** southern Polk County. There were several reports of funnel clouds, but no confirmed tornadoes. While the storm caused no major structural damage, there was widespread minor damage and numerous injuries.

**May 22, 1987: Tornado. Saragosa.** A strong, **multiple-vortex tornado** struck the town of Saragosa, Reeves County. Of the town's 183 inhabitants, 30 were killed and 121 were injured. Eight-five percent of the town's structures were destroyed; total damage topped $1.3 million.

**Oct. 15–19, 1994: Rain. Southeast Texas. Extreme amounts of rainfall,** up to 28.90 inches over a 4-day period, fell throughout southeastern Texas; 17 killed, mostly in flash flooding. Many rivers reached record flood levels. **Houston** was cut off as numerous roads, including Interstate 10, were under water. Damage was estimated at $700 million; 26 counties were declared disaster areas.

**May 5, 1995: Thunderstorm. Hail. Dallas–Fort Worth.** A thunderstorm moved across the area with 70 mph wind gusts and rainfall rates of almost 3 inches in 30 minutes (5 inches in one hour); 20 people killed; 109 injured by large hail, many at Fort Worth's outdoor Mayfest near the Trinity River. With more than $2 billion in damage, NOAA dubbed it the **"costliest thunderstorm event in history."**

**May 28, 1995: Supercell Thunderstorm. San Angelo.** The storm produced extreme winds and giant hail, injuring at least 80 people and causing about $120 million in damage. Sixty-one homes were destroyed; more than 9,000 were slightly damaged. In some areas, hail was 6 inches deep, with drifts to 2 feet.

**Feb. 21, 1996: Heat.** Anomalously **high temperatures** were reported over the **entire state,** breaking records in nearly every region. Temperatures near 100 degrees shattered previous records by as many as 10 degrees, and Texans experienced heat more characteristic of mid-summer than winter.

**May 10, 1996: Hail. Howard County.** Hail up to 5 inches in diameter fell; 48 injuries; property damage, $30 million.

**May 27, 1997: Tornado. Jarrell.** A half-mile-wide **F-5**

**tornado** struck Jarrell, Williamson County, leveling the Double Creek subdisivion, claiming 27 lives, injuring 12 others, and causing more than $40 million in damage.

**March–May, 1998: Drought.** According to the Climate Prediction Center, this three-month period ranks as the **seventh driest** for a region including Texas, Oklahoma, Arkansas, Louisiana, and Mississippi. May 1998 has been ranked as both the **warmest and the driest May** in this region.

**Aug. 22–25, 1998: Tropical Storm Charley. Hill Country.** The storm dumped torrential rains in the area that caused flash floods; 13 killed; more than 200 were injured.

**Oct. 17–19, 1998: Rainstorm. Hill Country.** A massive, devastating flood set all-time records for rainfall and river levels; 25 killed; more than 2,000 injured; damage, more than $500 million from the Hill Country to counties **south and east of San Antonio.**

**Jan. 22, 1999: Hail. Brazos County.** Golf ball- and softball-sized **hail** fell in the **Bryan–College Station** area; damage, $10 million to cars, homes, and offices.

**May 1999: Storms. Tornadoes. East, Central, West Texas.** Numerous severe weather outbreaks caused **damaging winds, large hail, dangerous lightning, and numerous tornadoes.** An F-3 tornado moved through downtown area and high school of **De Kalb,** Bowie County, on the 4th, injuring 22 people and causing $125 million in damage to the community. On the same day, **two F-2 tornadoes** roared through **Kilgore** simultaneously. On the 11th, an F-4 tornado moved through parts of **Loyal Valley,** Mason County, and **Castell,** Llano County, killing one and injuring six. The 25th saw storms produce **2.5-inch hail** in **Levelland** and **Amarillo.** Total damages, more than $157 million.

**August 1999: Heat. Dallas–Fort Worth.** Excessive heat throughout the month resulted in 16 fatalities. The airport reported 26 consecutive days of 100 degrees or greater.

**January–October 2000: Drought.** A **severe drought** plagued **most of Texas.** Some regions experienced little to no rain for several months during the summer. **Abilene** saw no rain for **72 consecutive days,** while **Dallas** had **no rain for 84 consecutive days** during the summer. During July, aquifers hit all-time lows, and lakes and streams fell to critical levels. Most regions had to cut back or stop agricultural activities, which resulted in $515 million in agricultural loss, according to USDA figures.

**March 28, 2000: Tornado. Fort Worth.** A supercell over Fort Worth produced an **F-3 tornado,** which injured 80 people and caused significant damage. Flooding killed two people.

**May 20, 2000: Rainstorm. Southeast Texas.** A **flash flood** in the **Liberty** and **Dayton** area was caused by 18.3 inches of rain falling in five hours. Up to 80 people were rescued from flood waters; property damage, $10 million.

**July 2000: Heat. Dallas–Fort Worth.** Excessive heat resulted from a high-pressure ridge, particularly from the 12th–21st. **DFW Airport** reported a **10-day average of 103.3 degrees. College Station** had **12 consecutive days of 100 degrees or greater.** The heat caused 34 deaths in North and Southeast Texas, primarily among the elderly.

**Aug. 2, 2000: Storm. Houston.** Lightning struck a tree at Astroworld in Houston injuring 17 teens.

**Sept. 5, 2000: Heat.** Excessive heat resulted in at least eight **all-time high temperature records** around the state, one of which was **Possum Kingdom Lake,** which reached 114 degrees. This day is regarded as the **hottest day ever in Texas,** considering the state as a whole.

**Dec. 13 and 24–25, 2000: Ice. Snow. Northeast Texas.** Two major winter storms blanketed the area with up to 6 inches of ice from each storm. Eight inches of snow fell in the **Panhandle,** while areas in North Texas received 12 inches. Thousands of motorists were stranded on Interstate 20 and had to be rescued by the National Guard; 235,000 people lost electric service from the first storm alone. Roads were treacherous, driving was halted in several counties; total cost of damages from both storms, more than $156 million.

**Jan. 1–31, 2001: Drought. South Texas.** The USDA's Farm Service Agency received a **Presidential Disaster Declaration** in December 2000 because of **persistent drought** conditions in **South Texas;** $125 million in damage was reported in the region.

**May 2001: Storms. San Antonio, High Plains.** Numerous storms caused excessive damage. **Four-inch hail** caused nearly $150 million in damage in **San Antonio** on the 6th. On the 30th, **supercell thunderstorms** in the **High Plains** produced winds over 100 mph, and golf-ball-sized hail caused more than $186 million in damage. In all, 36 injuried; property and agriculture damage, $358 million.

**June–December 2001: Drought.** Significant **drought-like** conditions occurred in Texas from early summer through December. After the yearly drought report was filed, it was determined that total crop damage across the South Plains was about $420 million. Losses occurred to crops such as cotton, wheat, grain sorghum, and corn.

**June 5–10, 2001: Tropical Storm Allison. Houston area.** The storm dumped large amounts of rain on the city and made landfall on the western end of **Galveston Island.** Over the next five days, it produced record rainfall, which led to devastating flooding across southeastern Texas. Some weather stations in the Houston area reported more than 40 inches of rain total and more than 18 inches in a 24-hour period. Twenty-two deaths; damage, $5.2 billion.

**July–August 2001: Heat.** Excessive heat plagued Texas, resulting in 17 deaths in the Houston area.

**Oct. 12, 2001: Tornado. Hondo.** An F-2 tornado caused $20 million in damage. The tornado injured 25 people and damaged the National Guard Armory, a large hangar at the Hondo Airport, and nearly two dozen aircraft. Also damaged, were some 150 homes in Hondo, 50 on its outskirts, and nearly 100 mobile homes.

**Nov. 15, 2001: Rainstorms. Central Texas.** Storms caused **flash flooding** and weak **tornadoes** in the Edwards Plateau, South-Central, and southern portions of North-Central Texas. Flash flooding caused 8 deaths and 198 injuries.

**March 2002: Storms. Central Texas.** Several **violent storms** occurred, which produced hail, tornadoes, and strong winds. Hail 1-3/4 inches in diameter caused $16 million in damage to **San Angelo** on the 19th, while 30 people where injured on the same day by an **F-2 tornado** in **Somerset,** Bexar County, that caused $2 million in damage. For the month: 3 fatalities; 64 injuries; damage, $37.5 million.

**June 30–July 7, 2002: Rainstorm. Central Texas.** Excessive rainfall occurred in the **South-Central** and **Edwards Plateau** regions, with some areas reporting more than 30 inches of rain. Damage in the South-Central region alone was nearly $250 million. In Central Texas, 29 counties were devastated by flooding and declared federal disaster areas by President George W. Bush. Total event damage, $2 billion.

**Sept. 5–7, 2002: Tropical Storm Fay. Coastal Plains.** The storm made landfall along the coast on the 6th. This system produced extremely heavy rainfall, strong damaging wind gusts, and tornadoes. Ten to 20 inches of rain fell in eastern **Wharton County. Brazoria County** was hit the hardest with about 1,500 homes flooded. The storm produced five tornadoes, flooded many areas, and caused significant wind damage; total damage, $4.5 million.

**Oct. 24, 2002: Raintorms. South Texas.** Severe **thunderstorms** in South Texas produced heavy rain, causing flooding and two tornadoes in **Corpus Christi.** The most extensive damage occurred across **Del Mar College.** The storm caused one death and 26 injuries; total damages, more then $85 million.

**Feb. 24–26, 2003: Snow. Ice. North-Central Texas.** A severe cold front brought **freezing rain, sleet,** and **snow** to the region. Snow accumulations were as high as **5 inches,** resulting in $15 million in damages. Most schools and businesses were closed for this period.

**April 8, 2003: Rainstorm. Brownsville.** A severe thunderstorm caused one of the **most destructive hail events in the history of Brownsville.** Hail exceeded 2.75 inches

in diameter and caused $50 million in damage to the city. At least 5 injuries were reported.

**July 14–16, 2003: Hurricane Claudette. Port O'Connor.** The hurricane made landfall near Port O'Connor in the late morning hours of the 14th. At landfall, wind speeds were more than 90 mph. The system then moved westward toward Big Bend and northern Mexico; 1 death; 2 injuries; damage, more than $100 million.

**September 2003: Floods. Upper Coast, South Texas.** Persistent flooding caused more than $2 million in damage. The remnants of **Tropical Storm Grace** caused flash flooding along the Upper Coast region near **Galveston** early in September, with rainfall estimates in Matagorda County ranging from 6–12 inches. During the second half of the month, **South Texas** was hit with a **deluge of rain** caused by a tropical wave combined with cold fronts. Monthly rainfall totals ranged from 7–15 inches in the deep south.

**June 1–9, 2004: Floods. North-Central Texas.** Flash flooding due to an upper air disturbance and a cold front caused damage to more than 1,000 homes. This was the first of many days in which heavy rains fell throughout the state. Estimated damage was more $7.5 million.

**June 21, 2004: Tornadoes. Panhandle.** Severe weather kicked up just ahead of a frontal boundary causing damage to **Amarillo** and the surrounding area. Eight tornadoes were reported around the Panhandle, and there were many reports of hail, topping out at 4.25 inches in diameter in Potter County. Thousands of homes were damaged, and the total damage was estimated at more than **$150 million**.

**July 28–29, 2004: Rainstorm. North-Central Texas.** A stationary front lead to torrential rainfall in **Dallas** and **Waco.** Hundreds of homes were damaged by flash flooding, as 24-hour rainfall totals for the two cities approached 5 inches. Outlying areas of the cities reported as much as 7 inches of rain in a 12-hour period on the 29th. Damage estimates topped $20 million.

**Sept. 14, 2004: Storm. Grapeland.** A lightning strike during football practice at Grapeland High School, Houston County, caused one death and injuries to 40 players and coaches.

**Dec. 24–26, 2004: Snow. Coastal Texas.** Large portions of Southeast and South Texas saw their **first white Christmas in recorded history.** A cold front past over the state a few days prior to Christmas Eve dropping temperatures below freezing. Another cold front brought snow, which accumulated Christmas Eve night and into Christmas day. Galveston and Houston recorded 4 inches of snow, while areas further south, such as **Victoria, had 12 inches. Brownsville recorded 1.5 inches of snow.**

**March 25, 2005: Hail. Austin.** In the evening, the **most destructive hailstorm in 10 years** struck the greater Austin area. The storm knocked out power to 5,000 homes in northwest Austin. Hail 2 inches in diameter was reported near the Travis County Exposition Center. Total damage was estimated at $100 million.

**May 2005–December 2006: Drought. North-Central Texas.** In May, portions of the area were upgraded from moderate to **severe drought.** By month's end, the drought had made significant agricultural and hydrological impacts on the region. In November, many Central Texas counties were added to the drought. The Texas Cooperative Extension estimated statewide drought losses at $4.1 billion, $1.9 billion in North Texas alone.

**June 9, 2005: Tornado. Petersburg.** An F-3 tornado affected an area from Petersburg in southeast Hale County to portions of southwest and south-central Floyd County. Total damage was estimated at $70 million.

**Sept. 23, 2005: Hurrican Rita. Southeast Texas.** The eye of **Hurricane Rita** moved ashore in extreme southwest Louisiana between Sabine Pass and Johnson's Bayou in Cameron Parish with maximum sustained winds of 120 mph, **category-3 strength.** On the 22nd, Rita had strengthened to a peak intensity of 175 mph winds. In Southeast Texas, Rita caused 3 fatalities, 3 injuries, and $159.5 million in property and crop damage. Total property damage, $2.1 billion.

**Dec. 27, 2005**: **Wildfire. Cross Plains,** Callahan County. The fire started just west of Cross Plains and, fanned by winds gusting near 40 mph, quickly moved east into town. Two elderly people were unable to escape the flames; 16 firefighters were also injured; property damage, $11 million.

**Jan. 1, 2006**: **Wildfires. North Texas.** Several wildfires exploded across North Texas due to low humidity, strong winds, and the ongoing drought. Fires were reported in Montague, Eastland, and Palo Pinto counties. Five injuries were reported, as well as $10.8 million in property damage.

**March 12–18, 2006: Wildfires. Borger.** A wildfire now known as the **Borger wildfire** started four miles southwest of Borger, Hutchinson County. It killed seven people and burned 479,500 acres and 28 structures; total property damage, $49.9 million; crop damage, $45.4 million. A second wildfire known as the **Interstate-40 wildfire** burned 427,696 acres. The Texas Forest Service named the two wildfires the East Amarillo Complex. In all, 12 people were killed; total property damage, $49.9 million; crop damage, $45.4 million.

**March 19, 2006: Tornado. Uvalde.** An F-2 tornado moved through the Uvalde area causing $1.5 million in property damage. It was the strongest tornado in South-Central Texas since Oct. 12, 2001.

**April 11–13, 2006: Wildfire. Canadian.** A wildfire 10 miles north of Canadian, Hemphill County, injured two; burned 18,000 acres; and destroyed $90 million of crops.

**April 18, 2006: Hail. Gillespie County.** Hailstones as large as 2.5 inches in diameter destroyed windows in homes and car windshields between Harper and Doss in Gillespie County. The hail also damaged 70 percent of the area's peach crop, an estimated loss of $5 million.

**April 20, 2006: Hail. San Marcos.** Hailstones as large at 4.25 inches in diameter (grapefruit-size) were reported south of San Marcos, damaging 10,000 vehicles on the road and another 7,000 vehicles at homes; total damage was estimated at $100 million.

**May 4, 2006: Hail. Snyder.** Lime-to-baseball-size **hail** fell across Snyder in Scurry County for a least 15 minutes. The hail was blown sideways at times by 60-to-70-mph winds. Total damage was estimated at $15 million.

**May 5, 2006: Tornado. Waco.** A tornado with peak intensity estimated at **low F-2** caused damage of $3 million.

**May 9, 2006: Tornado. Childress.** An F-2 tornado caused significant damage along a 1-1/2-mile path through the north side of Childress in the evening. An instrument at Childress High School measured a wind gust of 109 mph. Property damage was estimated at $5.7 million.

**Aug. 1, 2006: Thunderstorms. El Paso.** Storms in a saturated atmosphere repeatedly developed and moved over the northwest third of El Paso County, concentrating near the Franklin Mountains. Rainfall reports varied from 4–6 inches within 15 hours, with an isolated report of about 8 inches on the western slope of the mountain range. Four days of heavy rains, combined with the mountains' terrain, led to **excessive runoff and flooding not seen on such a large scale in the El Paso area in more than 100 years.** Property damage was estimated at $180 million.

**March 29, 2007: Floods. Corsicana.** Flash flooding along Interstate 45 submerged two cars in Navarro County, north of Corsicana, and 2 feet of water was reported on I-45 and Texas 31, east of town; damage to businesses, roads, and bridges, $19 million.

**April 13, 2007: Hail. Colleyville.** Teacup-size **hail** was reported as strong storms developed in Tarrant County. Hail damage to 5,500 cars and 3,500 homes and businesses was estimated at $10 million.

**April 24, 2007: Tornado. Eagle Pass.** A large tornado crossed the Rio Grande from Mexico around 6 p.m., striking Rosita Valley, near Eagle Pass. Ten deaths were reported, including a family of five in a mobile home. **Golf-ball-sized hail and the tornado** struck Rosita Valley Elementary School, leaving only the interior walls standing.

Damage indicated wind speeds near 140 mph and an **F-3 level,** with a path 1/4-mile wide and 4 miles long. The tornado also destroyed 59 manufactured homes and 57 houses. Total damage was estimated at $80 million.

**June 17–18, 2007: Floods. North Texas.** Torrential rain fell as an upper-level low lingered for several days. In Tarrant County, one person drowned after her rescue boat capsized. Hundreds of people were rescued from high water. In Grayson County, a woman died in floodwaters as she drove under an overpass, and another death occurred in a flooded truck. Three people in Cooke County died when a mobile home was carried away by floodwaters. Damage was estimated at $30 million in Tarrant County, $20 million in Grayson County, and $28 million in Cooke County.

**June 27, 2007: Floods. Marble Falls.** Two lines of thunderstorms produced 10–19 inches of rain in southern Burnet County. Hardest hit was Marble Falls, where two young men died in the early morning when their jeep was swept into high water east of town. Damage to more than 315 homes and businesses was $130 million.

**Sept. 13, 2007: Hurricane Humberto. Jefferson County.** The hurricane made landfall around 1 a.m. in rural southwestern Jefferson County near McFaddin National Wildlife Refuge. Minimum pressure was around 985 millibars, with maximum winds at 90 mph. **Flash flooding** occurred in urban areas between Beaumont and Orange, as 11 inches of rain fell. Coastal storm tides were 3–5 feet, with the highest **storm surge** occurring at Texas Point. Humberto caused one death, 12 injuries, and $25 million in damage.

**March 31, 2008: Hail. Northeast Texas.** Severe thunderstorms developed across the Red River valley, many producing **large hail** that damaged car windows, skylights, and roofs in Texarkana and elsewhere in Bowie County. Damage was estimated at $120 million.

**April 10, 2008: Tornadoes. Johnson County.** A lone **supercell thunderstorm** evolved in the afternoon of the 9th, producing tornadoes and large hail. A tornado touched down near Happy Hill and traveled northeast 3 miles to Pleasant Point, where it dissipated. The **F-1 tornado,** with maximum wind speeds of 90–95 mph, destroyed three homes and damaged more than 30 homes and other buildings. Damage was $25 million.

**May 14, 2008: Hail. Austin.** A severe thunderstorm southwest of Austin moved northeast across downtown, causing extensive damage from **winds and large hail.** Large trees and branches were knocked down, and baseball-sized hail and 70–80 mph winds blew out windows in apartments and office buildings, **including the State Capitol.** Total damage was estimated at $50 million.

**August 18, 2008: Floods. Wichita Falls.** An unseasonably strong upper-level storm system moved over North Texas, and several waves of heavy thunderstorms caused **heavy rain and widespread flooding** in the Iowa Park, Burkburnett, and Wichita Falls areas. In Wichita Falls, at least 118 homes were flooded, 19 of which were destroyed, and residents were evacuated by boat. Burkburnett and Iowa Park were isolated for a few hours because of street flooding. Damage was estimated at $25 million, and Gov. Rick Perry declared Wichita County a disaster area.

**Sept. 12, 2008: Hurricane Ike. Galveston.** The eye of the hurricane moved ashore near the Galveston with central pressure of 951.6 millibars and maximum sustained winds around 110 mph, which made Hurricane Ike a strong **category-2 storm.** There were 12 deaths directly related to Ike (11 occurring in Galveston County from drowning due to storm surge) and at least another 25 fatalities either due to carbon monoxide poisoning from generators, accidents while clearing debris, or house fires from candles. **Storm tide and storm surge** caused the majority of property damage at the coast. Damage in Harris, Chambers, Galveston, Liberty, Polk, Matagorda, Brazoria, Fort Bend, San Jacinto, and Montgomery counties totaled $14 billion.

**Jan. 19, 2009: Wildfire. Hidalgo County.** Aided by strong gusts, low humidity, lack of rain, and warm temperatures, a wildfire spread across 2,560 acres in Hidalgo County and consumed four buildings at Moore Air Force Base. Damage at the base was $10 million.

**March 30, 2009: Hail. Northeast Tarrant County.** A strong line of severe storms dumped **ping-pong- to baseball-sized hail** on numerous cities in northeast Tarrant County. Much of the damage was to automobiles; overall damage was $95 million.

**April 11, 2009: Hail. Midland.** Up to golf-ball-sized hail caused tremendous damage to homes and vehicles during a severe storm, with an estimated $160 million in roof damage. A woman was pelted in the stomach by a hailstone that broke through the window in her dining room.

**May 2, 2009: Thunderstorm Wind. Irving.** The National Weather Service determined that a microburst caused the **Dallas Cowboys' bubble practice facility** to collapse from winds estimated at 70 mph. Twelve people were injured, including one coach who was paralyzed from the waist down. The damage was estimated at $5 million.

**June 11, 2009: Thunderstorm Wind. Burnet.** A peak wind of 67 mph was measured at the Burnet Airport and numerous planes were flipped or blown across the tarmac. Damage in the city was $5 million.

**Sept. 16, 2009: Hail. El Paso.** A series of **supercell storms** produced golf-ball- to tennis-ball-sized hail and the **most costly hailstorm** in recorded history for the El Paso area. Estimated damage was $150 million.

**Dec. 23, 2009: Tornado. Lufkin.** An **EF-3 tornado** touched down in Lufkin, damaging structures, homes, and vehicles. The twister and heavy rains caused damage estimated at $10 million.

**June 9, 2010: Flash Flood. New Braunfels.** Storms produced rains in excess of 11 inches, which caused the **Guadalupe River to rise over 20 feet** in just two hours. Campers, vehicles, boats, homes, and businesses suffered extensive damages along the riverbanks. The flash flood resulted in one death; damage, more than $10 million.

**July 2, 2010: Tornado. Hebbronville.** An **EF-1 tornado** that developed following **Hurricane Alex** caused considerable damage in Hebbronville. Over half of the town's population lost power, and the tornado was reported to be as wide as a football field. Estimated damage, $1.5 million.

**July 4, 2010: Flood. Terry, Lubbock, Garza, and Lynn Counties.** A series of thunderstorms erupted in the early morning of the Fourth of July over the west South Texas Plains. Local flooding caused roadway closures and damage to more 100 vehicles. More than 300 homes and businesses were affected; economic losses were around $16.5 million.

**July 8, 2010: Flood. Starr County.** Another storm that formed in the aftermath of **Hurricane Alex,** dumped an estimated **50 inches or more of rain** on the lower Rio Grande Valley over 10 days leading up to the 8th. Falcon Reservoir rose during days of rain and finally spilled over on the 8th. The Rio Grande was nearly 2 miles wide at some points. Estimated damage was around $37 million.

**Oct. 24, 2010: Tornado. Rice,** Navarro County. An intense **EF-2 tornado** struck with maximum winds of 135 mph. Vehicles were overturned on Interstate 45 and 11 train cars were derailed when the tornado hit the tracks. The football, baseball, and softball fields of the local high school were damaged; the intermediate school lost the gymnasium roof and suffered a caved-in wall; damage was $1 million.

**Jan. 8, 2011: Heavy Snow. Sherman.** Between 3–7 inches of snow fell across Northeast Texas, causing hundreds of **vehicle accidents,** including more than 40 in Sherman and one fatality. Total damage, $1 million.

**Feb. 27, 2011: Wildfire. West Texas.** High winds and temperatures produced a series of wildfire complexes. The costliest was in **Tanglewood,** burning 1,659 acres and destroying 26 homes at a cost of $25 million. The biggest was in **Willow Creek,** burning 24,310 acres and 29 homes at a cost of $10 million. A combination of fires near **Lubbock, Matador, Post,** and **Levelland** burned 60,500 acres and several urban dwellings, costing $3.45 million.

**March 11, 2011: Wildfire. Aransas.** High heat, dry air, and high winds produced several fires in North-Central Texas. More than 10,000 acres burned, including **fields of hay bales in Aransas** worth $4 million. Three injuries were reported; other property losses were around $1 million.

**April 6, 2011: Wildfire. Swenson.** A wildfire near Swenson was spawned during critical fire conditions due to a cutting torch. The fire **burned for 15 days,** burning 122,500 acres of grass and ranchland; damage, $2.54 million.

**April 9–13, 2011: Wildfire. Possum Kingdom Lake.** Drought and high winds helped spark a massive fire complex that **burned for 16 days,** destroying 167 homes, 126 other buildings, and 90 percent of Possum Kingdom State Park — about 126,734 acres total. Damage was $120 million, not including the estimated $11 million needed to combat the fire, nor the loss of cattle.

**April 9, 2011: Wildfire. West Texas.** Dry conditions near the Pecos River spawned two fires near **Midland** and **Marfa.** The former burned 16,500 acres and 34 homes, causing 500 evacuations; the latter was caused by an electrical problem and burned 314,444 acres, 41 homes, and hundreds of cattle and utility poles. Total property damage was estimated at $7.7 million.

**April 15, 2011: Wildfire. Cisco.** Dry conditions caused several wildfires in North Texas. The largest was near Cisco, burning around 2,000 acres and destroying five homes. The fires burned 18,000 acres, costing $1.01 million.

**April 17, 2011: Wildfire. Oak Hill.** Dry conditions and **human negligence** combined to cause a wildfire in Travis County. Although it covered only 100 acres, it destroyed 11 homes and damage estimates reached $2 million.

**April 19, 2011: Hail. North Texas.** A series of **supercells** brought widespread hail ranging from 0.75 inches to 3.5 inches over the course of the 5-hour storm. Damage was around $1 million.

**April 25–26, 2011: Supercells. East Texas.** An upper level trough brought severe storms to East Texas for two days. On the 25th, **3 tornadoes** touched down in Cherokee and Angelina counties, including two EF-1s; moderate hail was seen and downburst winds of 90-plus mph were reported. The next day, **10 tornadoes** were reported, two of which were EF-1s near Ben Wheeler and Groesbeck, causing injuries. Total damage, $2.718 million.

**May 1, 2011: Thunderstorm Wind. Clyde.** Isolated thunderstorms popped up in the Big Country, bringing hail and strong winds. In Clyde, **straight-line winds** were reported in excess of 100 mph; damage, $2 million.

**May 11, 2011: Thunderstorm Wind. Interstate-20 Corridor.** Scattered thunderstorms from Killeen to Burns caused strong winds, hail, flash flooding, and an **EF-0 tornado** near Lake Kiowa; damage, $1 million.

**June 18, 2011: Thunderstorm Wind. Meunster.** Thunderstorms followed by a **strong microburst** in the early evening and **straight-line winds** greater than 80 mph caused widespread damage in excess of $1.36 million.

**June 20–21, 2011: Thunderstorm Wind. East Texas.** Severe thunderstorms culminated in strong downburst winds, hail, and an **EF-0 tornado.** Winds greater than 80 mph occurred in Nacogdoches and San Augustine, a tornado in Shelby County, and moderate hail; damage, $1.04 million.

**June 28, 2011: Thunderstorm Wind. Titus County.** Thunderstorms with 65 mph winds caused widespread damage at a cost of $1.6 million.

**Aug. 11, 2011: Flash Flood. Lubbock.** Scattered thunderstorms brought heavy rain, wind, and hail to the Lubbock area. Some area received 1–4 inches of rain in an hour, causing high water damage to homes and vehicles. Farm and weather equipment in Dimmit were damaged by 90 mph winds. Total damage, $1.175 million.

**September–October 2011: Wildfires. Bastrop County.** Three separate fires that began Sept. 4 merged into a single blaze east of the city of Bastrop and became

*The 10th anniversary of Hurricane Katrina, one of the deadliest disasters in U.S. history, was marked in 2015. In the early morning hours of Aug. 29, 2005, Katrina made landfall at New Orleans as a Category-3 hurricane that stretched 400 miles across. Levee breaches led to massive flooding, displacing hundreds of thousands of people in Louisiana, Mississippi, and Alabama. Above, survivors of Katrina arrive at the Houston Astrodome Red Cross Shelter on Aug. 31, 2005, after being evacuated from New Orleans. They were brought to the Astrodome after the Superdome in New Orleans became unsafe because of the levee breaks. Photo by Andrea Booher; FEMA.*

known as the **Bastrop County Complex fire.** The fire destroyed 1,691 homes and much of Bastrop State Park was burned. Declared **the most destructive wildfire in Texas history,** it was finally extinguished on Oct. 29.

**Oct. 9, 2011: Tornado. San Antonio.** An EF-1 **tornado** with winds up to 90–100 mph tore apart roofs, utility poles, and vehicles; damage, $1 million.

**Jan. 9, 2012 Supercells. South Texas.** Squall-line thunderstorms, hail, and an **EF-1 tornado** hit southeast of Alice International Airport and parts of Robstown, causing an estimated $5 million in damage. Other **straight-line winds** and hail caused total damage of $8.66 million.

**March 29, 2012: Hail. McAllen.** Strong thunderstorms, with wind gusts over 70 mph at Edinburg Airport, and **severe hail** up to 2.75 inches caused $50 million in property damage to homes and $1 million to crops. Rainfall between 4–6 inches fell in less than two hours, causing $5 million in flood damage.

**April 16, 2012: Tornadoes. Flash Floods. Gregory.** Thunderstorms along the Coastal Bend caused **four tornadoes,** including an EF-1 in Portland, two EF-0 tornadoes in Gregory, and another in Kleberg County. The Portland tornado caused $2 million in damage to homes and property. Around 80 percent of all homes in Gregory were flooded when storms dumped 2–6 inches of rain; some locations received up to 15 inches over several hours. Total damages topped $8.3 million.

**April 29, 2012: Hail. Doud.** Several severe storms blew up in West Texas near Lubbock with damaging hail and winds. **Hailstones** up to 4.5 inches fell in Whitharral, and winds gusts up to 95 mph near Wolfforth tore apart homes and cars. Damage estimates were $20 million from hail in Doud and more than $5 million from wind.

**Nov. 22, 2012: Fog. Winnie,** Chambers County. Dense fog early Thanksgiving morning caused a massive 150-car pileup on both sides of Interstate-10, causing two deaths and 80 injuries, 12 serious. Vehicular damage was $6 million.

**Dec. 19, 2012: Dust Storm. Lubbock.** A strong Pacific front kicked up winds up to 70 mph, reducing

visibility below 1/2 mile for more than 5 hours, the longest such event since 1977; property damage, $1 million.

**Dec. 25, 2012: Heavy Snow. Plano.** A moderate cold front and minor storms in North Texas produced wraparound snow between 3–6 inches that caused 89 traffic accidents and costing $1.2 million.

**May 15, 2013: Tornado Outbreak. North Texas.** A deadly tornado outbreak in North Texas claimed the lives of six people and injured more than 100 others. $250 million in damages were a result of an EF4 tornado in Mambrino and an EF3 tornado in Cleburne.

**May 28, 2013: Hailstorm. Amarillo.** A massive hailstorm moving through the Amarillo area dropped hail as big as baseballs and caused $200 million in damages. An estimated 35,000 vehicles and thousands of homes in Amarillo were damaged.

**June 5, 2013: Hailstorm. Lubbock.** Baseball-sized hail along with winds in excess of 90 mph caused more than $400 million in property damage in Lubbock. There were numerous reports of damage to homes, vehicles, as well as downed trees and power lines.

**October 30–31, 2014: Flash Flooding. Travis County.** Six to ten inches of rain fell in Travis County and more than a foot of rain fell near Wimberley and Driftwood. Near Oak Hill, four people died and the flooding caused $100 million in property damage.

**April 3, 2014: Hailstorm. Denton.** A severe thunderstorm moving through the Denton area dropped hail as big as softballs, which caused more than $500 million in damages to homes, businesses, and vehicles.

**May 11, 2014: Wildfire. Hutchinson County.** A wildfire in Hutchinson County destroyed about 100 homes and caused the evacuation of more than 700 residents. The fire burned more than 1,000 acres and caused at least $10 million in damages.

**June 12, 2014: Hailstorm. Abilene.** A severe hailstorm moving through Abilene dropped hail up to 4.5 inches in diameter across the city. There were 12 injuries and $400 million in property damage. ☆

# Texas Temperature, Freeze, Growing Season and Precipitation Records by County

Data in the table below are from the office of the Texas State Climatologist, Texas A&M University, College Station. Because of the small change in averages, data are revised only at intervals of 10 years. Data below are the latest compilations, as of Feb. 1, 2004, and reflect data compiled during 1971–2000. The table shows temperature, freeze, growing season and precipitation for each county in Texas. Data for counties where a National Weather Service Station has not been maintained long enough to establish a reliable mean are interpolated from isoline charts prepared from mean values from stations with long-established records. Mean maximum temperature for July is computed from the sum of the daily maxima. Mean minimum January is computed from the sum of the daily minima. Weather stations shown in italics do not measure all categories and some data are from the period 1961–1990. An asterisk (*) preceding a record high or low or rainfall extreme denotes a figure that also occurred on an earlier date.

| COUNTY AND STATION | Mean Max. July F. | Mean Min. January F. | Record Highest F. | Year | Record Lowest F. | Year | Last in Spring Mo. Day | First in Fall Mo. Day | Growing Season Days | January In. | February In. | March In. | April In. | May In. | June In. | July In. | August In. | September In. | October In. | November In. | December In. | Annual In. | Highest Daily Rainfall In. | Mo.-Year |
|---|---|---|---|---|---|---|---|---|---|---|---|---|---|---|---|---|---|---|---|---|---|---|---|---|
| Anderson, Palestine | 93.9 | 37.4 | 114 | 1954 | -4 | 1930 | Mar. 15 | Nov. 18 | 247 | 3.60 | 3.34 | 3.87 | 3.80 | 4.51 | 4.53 | 2.55 | 3.23 | 3.45 | 4.90 | 4.44 | 4.16 | 46.38 | 9.10 | 08-1991 |
| Andrews, Andrews | 94.5 | 30.4 | 113 | 1994 | -1 | 1985 | Mar. 29 | Nov. 10 | 226 | 0.48 | 0.51 | 0.52 | 0.85 | 1.78 | 2.12 | 2.25 | 1.77 | 2.21 | 1.43 | 0.64 | 0.59 | 15.15 | 7.60 | 07-1914 |
| Angelina, Lufkin | 93.5 | 37.9 | *110 | 2000 | *-2 | 1951 | Mar. 13 | Nov. 15 | 247 | 4.45 | 3.17 | 3.53 | 3.13 | 5.29 | 4.18 | 2.60 | 3.08 | 4.08 | 4.13 | 4.54 | 4.44 | 46.62 | 7.47 | 10-1994 |
| Aransas, Rockport | 90.1 | 44.9 | 105 | 2000 | 12 | 1983 | Feb. 2 | Dec. 20 | 318 | 2.40 | 2.18 | 2.36 | 2.07 | 3.66 | 3.50 | 2.43 | 3.13 | 5.53 | 4.23 | 2.56 | 1.91 | 35.96 | 8.15 | 09-1979 |
| Archer, Archer City | 97.0 | 26.7 | 114 | 1980 | *-10 | 1989 | Mar. 28 | Nov. 9 | 225 | 1.13 | 1.75 | 2.05 | 2.46 | 4.33 | 3.46 | 1.79 | 2.66 | 3.11 | 3.39 | 1.75 | 1.75 | 29.78 | 7.95 | 10-1981 |
| Armstrong, Claude | 90.5 | 21.2 | *108 | 1980 | -16 | 1905 | Apr. 19 | Oct. 20 | 184 | 0.51 | 0.58 | 1.23 | 1.60 | 3.34 | 3.33 | 3.08 | 3.00 | 2.37 | 1.91 | 0.82 | 0.62 | 22.39 | 10.27 | 05-1982 |
| Atascosa, Poteet | 95.9 | 39.0 | *110 | 2000 | -1 | 1949 | Feb. 25 | Dec. 2 | 279 | 1.27 | 1.83 | 1.54 | 2.50 | 4.09 | 4.06 | 1.64 | 2.69 | 2.90 | 3.04 | 1.79 | 1.65 | 29.00 | 8.75 | 07-1949 |
| Austin, Sealy | 94.9 | 40.7 | 111 | 2000 | 0 | 1989 | Feb. 18 | Dec. 8 | 291 | 3.14 | 2.81 | 2.61 | 3.22 | 4.71 | 3.85 | 1.93 | 3.06 | 4.33 | 4.44 | 3.68 | 2.90 | 40.68 | 11.00 | 08-1945 |
| Bailey, Muleshoe | 91.9 | 20.2 | *110 | 1944 | -21 | 1933 | Apr. 17 | Oct. 21 | 186 | 0.43 | 0.50 | 0.64 | 1.01 | 2.04 | 2.49 | 2.09 | 3.07 | 2.34 | 1.50 | 0.67 | 0.59 | 17.37 | 5.25 | 05-1951 |
| Bandera, Medina | 93.9 | 33.3 | 109 | 1980 | 5 | 1989 | Apr. 17 | Nov. 10 | 233 | 1.72 | 1.91 | 2.27 | 2.69 | 4.35 | 4.29 | 2.55 | 3.07 | 3.66 | 4.14 | 2.84 | 2.28 | 35.78 | 9.86 | 08-1971 |
| Bastrop, Smithville | 95.4 | 36.7 | *111 | 2000 | -1 | 1930 | Mar. 4 | Nov. 20 | 260 | 2.73 | 2.32 | 2.56 | 3.00 | 5.12 | 3.66 | 2.01 | 2.25 | 3.56 | 4.70 | 3.29 | 2.84 | 38.04 | 16.05 | 06-1940 |
| Baylor, Seymour | 96.5 | 27.7 | 120 | 1936 | -14 | 1947 | Mar. 30 | Nov. 6 | 220 | 1.05 | 1.56 | 1.88 | 1.84 | 4.13 | 3.63 | 1.86 | 2.58 | 3.51 | 2.86 | 1.48 | 1.41 | 27.79 | 6.20 | 05-1989 |
| Bee, Beeville | 94.6 | 43.1 | 111 | 1939 | 8 | 1983 | Feb. 14 | Dec. 6 | 294 | 1.94 | 1.84 | 1.90 | 2.68 | 3.49 | 4.19 | 2.69 | 3.02 | 4.30 | 3.60 | 2.00 | 1.83 | 33.48 | 10.61 | 09-1967 |
| Bell, Temple | 95.0 | 34.9 | 112 | 1947 | *-4 | 1989 | Mar. 3 | Nov. 22 | 264 | 1.91 | 2.70 | 2.65 | 2.68 | 4.56 | 3.71 | 1.82 | 2.69 | 4.00 | 3.73 | 3.04 | 2.68 | 35.81 | 9.62 | 10-1998 |
| Bexar, San Antonio | 94.6 | 38.6 | 111 | 2000 | 0 | 1949 | Feb. 28 | Nov. 25 | 270 | 1.66 | 1.75 | 1.89 | 2.60 | 4.72 | 4.30 | 2.03 | 2.57 | 3.00 | 3.86 | 2.58 | 1.96 | 32.92 | 11.26 | 10-1998 |
| Blanco, Blanco | 93.7 | 34.0 | *110 | 2000 | -6 | 1949 | Mar. 20 | Nov. 11 | 235 | 1.79 | 2.08 | 2.63 | 2.69 | 4.51 | 4.18 | 2.02 | 2.38 | 3.26 | 4.18 | 2.66 | 2.37 | 34.75 | 17.47 | 09-1952 |
| Borden, Gail | 94.6 | 29.8 | 116 | 1994 | -1 | 1989 | Mar. 27 | Nov. 8 | 226 | 0.58 | 0.73 | 0.66 | 1.20 | 2.80 | 2.81 | 2.35 | 2.52 | 2.83 | 1.77 | 0.74 | 0.69 | 19.68 | 9.13 | 10-1960 |
| Bosque, Lake Whitney | 96.2 | 32.7 | 113 | 2000 | *-3 | 1989 | Mar. 15 | Nov. 17 | 247 | 1.93 | 2.39 | 2.87 | 3.18 | 4.29 | 3.96 | 2.03 | 2.37 | 2.76 | 3.95 | 2.67 | 2.67 | 35.07 | 6.22 | 10-1971 |
| Bowie, Texarkana | 93.1 | 30.7 | 108 | 2000 | *-6 | 1989 | Mar. 20 | Nov. 14 | 238 | 3.91 | 3.80 | 4.46 | 4.23 | 4.97 | 4.82 | 3.62 | 2.41 | 3.77 | 4.61 | 5.69 | 4.95 | 51.24 | 5.45 | 03-1989 |
| Brazoria, Angleton | 91.8 | 43.7 | 107 | 2000 | *7 | 1989 | Feb. 15 | Dec. 5 | 290 | 4.76 | 3.50 | 3.76 | 3.74 | 5.20 | 6.44 | 4.24 | 4.83 | 7.49 | 4.25 | 4.86 | 4.17 | 57.24 | 14.36 | 07-1979 |
| Brazos, College Station | 95.6 | 39.8 | 112 | 2000 | 2 | 1989 | Mar. 2 | Nov. 29 | 271 | 3.32 | 2.38 | 2.84 | 3.20 | 5.05 | 3.79 | 1.92 | 2.63 | 3.91 | 4.22 | 3.18 | 3.23 | 39.67 | 6.23 | 05-1983 |
| Brewster, Alpine | 88.7 | 31.3 | 107 | 1972 | -3 | 1983 | Apr. 8 | Nov. 1 | 207 | 0.45 | 0.50 | 0.34 | 0.58 | 1.25 | 2.18 | 3.04 | 2.92 | 3.23 | 1.58 | 0.45 | 0.67 | 17.19 | 3.13 | 06-1968 |
| Brewster, Chisos Basin | 84.2 | 36.1 | 103 | 1972 | -3 | 1949 | Apr. 16 | Nov. 17 | 246 | 0.55 | 0.69 | 0.36 | 0.61 | 1.60 | 2.42 | 3.55 | 3.72 | 2.71 | 1.72 | 0.66 | 0.58 | 19.17 | 4.29 | 10-1966 |
| Briscoe, Silverton | 90.9 | 21.6 | *109 | 1994 | -9 | 1963 | Apr. 14 | Oct. 22 | 190 | 0.57 | 0.78 | 1.17 | 1.59 | 3.22 | 3.96 | 2.30 | 2.76 | 2.67 | 1.68 | 0.90 | 0.74 | 22.34 | 5.25 | 06-1979 |
| Brooks, Falfurrias | 97.0 | 43.9 | 115 | 1998 | 9 | 1962 | Feb. 6 | Dec. 13 | 311 | 1.12 | 1.56 | 0.86 | 1.48 | 2.95 | 3.25 | 1.84 | 2.91 | 3.84 | 3.22 | 1.31 | 1.08 | 25.42 | 10.00 | 09-1967 |
| Brown, Brownwood | 95.0 | 29.6 | 111 | 1964 | -6 | 1989 | Mar. 25 | Nov. 11 | 231 | 1.28 | 2.09 | 2.07 | 2.45 | 3.62 | 3.75 | 1.80 | 2.28 | 2.67 | 3.01 | 1.62 | 1.68 | 28.32 | *6.60 | 06-2000 |

| COUNTY AND STATION | Mean Max July °F | Mean Min January °F | Record Highest °F | Record Highest Year | Record Lowest °F | Record Lowest Year | Last in Spring | First in Fall | Growing Season Days | January (In.) | February (In.) | March (In.) | April (In.) | May (In.) | June (In.) | July (In.) | August (In.) | September (In.) | October (In.) | November (In.) | December (In.) | Annual (In.) | Highest Daily Rainfall (In.) | Mo.-Year |
|---|---|---|---|---|---|---|---|---|---|---|---|---|---|---|---|---|---|---|---|---|---|---|---|---|
| Burleson, Somerville | 96.7 | 36.4 | 114 | 2000 | 3 | 1989 | Mar. 3 | Nov. 23 | 264 | 2.93 | 2.53 | 2.62 | 2.92 | 4.39 | 4.21 | 1.78 | 2.43 | 3.59 | 4.33 | 3.63 | 3.14 | 38.50 | 15.25 | 10-1994 |
| Burnet, Burnet | 93.6 | 33.3 | *114 | 1917 | *-4 | 1989 | Mar. 20 | Nov. 12 | 237 | 1.61 | 2.16 | 2.33 | 2.48 | 4.58 | 4.09 | 2.04 | 2.06 | 3.15 | 3.46 | 2.32 | 2.15 | 32.43 | 9.80 | 09-1936 |
| Caldwell, Luling | 95.8 | 36.9 | *110 | 2000 | -3 | 1949 | Mar. 7 | Nov. 20 | 258 | 2.27 | 2.20 | 2.22 | 3.06 | 5.44 | 4.29 | 1.70 | 2.32 | 3.70 | 4.36 | 3.00 | 2.30 | 36.86 | 10.53 | 10-1998 |
| Calhoun, Port O'Connor | 88.2 | 47.9 | 105 | 2000 | 10 | 1989 | Jan. 29 | Dec. 31 | 338 | 3.07 | 2.20 | 1.73 | 1.55 | 3.70 | 3.25 | 3.05 | 2.94 | 4.97 | 4.45 | 2.53 | 1.82 | 34.78 | 12.50 | 07-1976 |
| Callahan, Putnam | 94.9 | 31.1 | 110 | 1964 | -8 | 1989 | Mar. 24 | Nov. 13 | 234 | 1.17 | 1.55 | 1.76 | 1.80 | 3.13 | 3.25 | 1.97 | 2.02 | 2.79 | 3.03 | 1.64 | 1.41 | 25.52 | 5.00 | 08-1978 |
| Cameron, Brownsville | 92.4 | 50.5 | 106 | 1984 | *15 | 1901 | Dec. 25 | Jan. 24 | >365 | 1.36 | 1.18 | 0.93 | 1.96 | 2.48 | 2.93 | 1.77 | 2.99 | 5.31 | 3.78 | 1.75 | 1.11 | 27.55 | 12.09 | 09-1967 |
| Camp, Pittsburg | 94.0 | 32.0 | 109 | | -3 | | Mar. 21 | Nov. 14 | 238 | 3.30 | 3.40 | 4.40 | 3.70 | 4.60 | 3.90 | 3.30 | 2.10 | 3.30 | 4.40 | 4.80 | 3.90 | 45.10 | | |
| Carson, Panhandle | 90.8 | 19.3 | 109 | 1964 | *-10 | 1963 | Apr. 18 | Oct. 22 | 186 | 0.62 | 0.73 | 1.43 | 1.80 | 3.10 | 3.54 | 2.67 | 2.78 | 2.21 | 1.71 | 0.98 | 0.64 | 22.21 | | |
| Cass, Wright Patman Dam | 91.0 | 31.0 | 111 | 1983 | 8 | | Mar. 19 | Nov. 11 | 237 | 3.70 | 3.60 | 4.40 | 3.70 | 4.50 | 4.50 | 3.30 | 2.60 | 3.50 | 5.30 | 5.30 | 4.80 | 48.20 | 8.05 | 05-1951 |
| Castro, Dimmitt | 90.1 | 20.4 | 110 | 1943 | -9 | 1986 | Apr. 25 | Oct. 16 | 172 | 0.50 | 0.51 | 0.81 | 0.99 | 2.76 | 3.12 | 2.40 | 3.06 | 2.57 | 1.58 | 0.71 | 0.70 | 19.71 | 4.38 | 10-1998 |
| Chambers, Anahuac | 91.9 | 41.7 | 110 | 2000 | 8 | 1989 | Feb. 12 | Dec. 9 | 299 | 4.84 | 2.83 | 3.33 | 3.56 | 5.22 | 5.88 | 4.59 | 4.74 | 6.42 | 4.06 | 4.31 | 4.30 | 54.08 | 15.87 | 08-1945 |
| Cherokee, Rusk | 92.8 | 36.8 | 110 | 2000 | 0 | 1982 | Mar. 10 | Nov. 21 | 255 | 4.41 | 3.64 | 4.12 | 3.86 | 4.69 | 4.34 | 2.95 | 2.38 | 4.01 | 4.94 | 4.63 | 4.53 | 48.50 | 10.00 | 06-2001 |
| Childress, Childress | 95.3 | 26.8 | 117 | 1994 | *-5 | 1989 | Apr. 1 | Nov. 6 | 218 | 0.57 | 0.95 | 1.41 | 2.01 | 3.46 | 3.51 | 1.74 | 2.19 | 2.51 | 2.07 | 1.77 | 0.86 | 22.65 | 5.32 | 10-1983 |
| Clay, Henrietta | 95.0 | 26.8 | *116 | 1994 | *-8 | 1989 | Mar. 30 | Nov. 5 | 220 | 1.53 | 2.08 | 2.45 | 2.71 | 4.39 | 3.72 | 2.40 | 2.97 | 3.35 | 3.35 | 1.77 | 2.17 | 31.66 | 6.07 | 06-1959 |
| Cochran, Morton | 91.4 | 23.1 | *110 | 1994 | -12 | 1963 | Apr. 14 | Oct. 24 | 193 | 0.50 | 0.58 | 0.64 | 0.89 | 1.92 | 2.52 | 2.61 | 2.28 | 2.66 | 1.64 | 0.79 | 0.62 | 18.34 | 4.69 | 07-1960 |
| Coke, Robert Lee | 96.4 | 29.0 | 114 | 2000 | *-2 | 1989 | Mar. 26 | Nov. 11 | 230 | 0.81 | 1.22 | 1.05 | 1.72 | 3.24 | 2.90 | 1.44 | 2.28 | 3.46 | 2.73 | 1.15 | 1.00 | 23.00 | 8.40 | 10-1957 |
| Coleman, Coleman | 93.7 | 30.0 | 114 | 1943 | -5 | 1930 | Mar. 23 | Nov. 13 | 234 | 1.03 | 1.75 | 1.84 | 2.19 | 4.11 | 4.05 | 1.77 | 2.58 | 3.25 | 3.08 | 1.57 | 1.48 | 28.70 | 8.55 | 07-1932 |
| Collin, McKinney | 92.7 | 31.1 | 118 | 1936 | -7 | 1930 | Mar. 21 | Nov. 11 | 235 | 2.43 | 2.91 | 3.37 | 3.65 | 5.68 | 4.11 | 2.25 | 2.16 | 3.15 | 4.24 | 3.71 | 3.24 | 41.01 | 12.10 | 09-1964 |
| Collingsworth, Wellington | 97.9 | 27.0 | 113 | 1994 | -6 | 1989 | Apr. 1 | Nov. 4 | 216 | 0.62 | 0.73 | 1.47 | 3.57 | 3.88 | 3.47 | 2.64 | 1.85 | 2.58 | 2.37 | 0.89 | 0.62 | 22.80 | 9.50 | 10-1986 |
| Colorado, Columbus | 96.3 | 36.8 | 116 | 2000 | *4 | 1989 | Mar. 11 | Nov. 16 | 250 | 3.61 | 2.84 | 2.93 | 2.72 | 5.75 | 5.03 | 1.99 | 3.07 | 3.92 | 4.16 | 3.99 | 3.21 | 44.72 | 10.00 | 06-1973 |
| Comal, New Braunfels | 94.7 | 35.5 | 112 | 2000 | *2 | 1989 | Mar. 4 | Nov. 21 | 261 | 1.88 | 1.98 | 2.04 | 2.81 | 5.01 | 4.81 | 1.70 | 2.32 | 3.46 | 4.38 | 2.71 | 2.44 | 35.74 | 18.35 | 10-1998 |
| Comanche, Proctor Reservoir | 95.5 | 30.6 | 113 | 2000 | -8 | 1989 | Mar. 20 | Nov. 15 | 238 | 1.34 | 2.02 | 2.13 | 2.81 | 4.75 | 3.98 | 1.70 | 2.22 | 3.01 | 3.32 | 2.07 | 1.77 | 31.12 | 8.37 | 06-1988 |
| Concho, Paint Rock | 97.4 | 31.9 | 111 | 1978 | -8 | 1985 | Mar. 31 | Nov. 6 | 219 | 1.04 | 1.52 | 1.35 | 1.56 | 3.31 | 3.77 | 1.84 | 2.40 | 3.55 | 2.81 | 1.41 | 1.29 | 25.50 | 8.25 | 09-1980 |
| Cooke, Gainesville | 95.0 | 28.0 | 112 | | -7 | | Mar. 27 | Nov. 8 | 226 | 1.80 | 2.20 | 3.40 | 3.70 | 4.60 | 3.70 | 2.00 | 2.40 | 4.50 | 4.60 | 2.60 | 1.90 | 36.90 | | |
| Coryell, Gatesville | 96.4 | 33.5 | *112 | 2000 | -6 | 1949 | Mar. 24 | Nov. 13 | 234 | 1.65 | 2.35 | 2.57 | 2.90 | 4.38 | 3.66 | 2.36 | 2.53 | 2.87 | 3.30 | 2.51 | 2.35 | 33.43 | 8.35 | 06-1964 |
| Cottle, Paducah | 96.8 | 26.2 | 118 | 1994 | *-7 | 1989 | Mar. 29 | Nov. 5 | 221 | 0.82 | 1.11 | 1.31 | 1.92 | 3.85 | 3.67 | 2.06 | 2.63 | 2.96 | 2.06 | 1.08 | 0.98 | 24.11 | 6.65 | 06-1991 |
| Crane, Crane | 95.3 | 27.7 | 115 | 1994 | -8 | 1986 | Mar. 23 | Nov. 11 | 232 | 0.57 | 0.59 | 0.34 | 0.84 | 1.86 | 1.71 | 1.57 | 2.02 | 2.95 | 1.64 | 0.68 | 0.70 | 15.38 | 5.55 | 08-1986 |
| Crockett, Ozona | 93.0 | 25.3 | *109 | 1969 | *-10 | 1930 | Apr. 1 | Nov. 2 | 215 | 0.70 | 0.78 | 1.06 | 1.86 | 2.44 | 1.94 | 1.57 | 2.02 | 2.92 | 2.25 | 0.99 | 0.67 | 18.95 | 5.80 | 10-1959 |
| Crosby, Crosbyton | 92.5 | 27.8 | 113 | 1994 | -7 | 1962 | Apr. 2 | Nov. 2 | 215 | 0.68 | 0.96 | 1.03 | 1.87 | 3.05 | 3.10 | 2.05 | 3.05 | 3.46 | 1.91 | 0.95 | 0.84 | 22.95 | 5.78 | 06-1913 |
| Culberson, Van Horn | 91.7 | 27.8 | 112 | 1969 | -7 | 1962 | Apr. 4 | Nov. 5 | 212 | 0.39 | 0.33 | 0.16 | 0.24 | 0.71 | 1.25 | 2.11 | 2.30 | 2.23 | 1.27 | 0.46 | 0.53 | 11.98 | 7.00 | 08-1966 |
| Dallam, Dalhart | 90.0 | 19.0 | *107 | 1990 | -21 | 1959 | Apr. 23 | Oct. 16 | 175 | 0.52 | 0.40 | 1.08 | 1.35 | 2.72 | 2.27 | 3.11 | 2.99 | 1.56 | 1.32 | 0.71 | 0.54 | 18.57 | 4.52 | 08-1985 |
| Dallas, Dallas | 96.1 | 36.4 | 115 | 1909 | 1 | 1989 | Mar. 3 | Nov. 25 | 267 | 1.89 | 2.31 | 3.13 | 3.46 | 5.30 | 3.92 | 2.43 | 2.17 | 2.65 | 4.65 | 2.61 | 2.53 | 37.05 | 6.02 | 03-1977 |
| Dawson, Lamesa | 92.9 | 26.0 | 114 | 1994 | -12 | 1933 | Apr. 4 | Nov. 5 | 214 | 0.57 | 0.77 | 0.73 | 0.88 | 2.35 | 2.81 | 2.19 | 2.00 | 3.42 | 1.76 | 0.82 | 0.77 | 19.07 | 6.24 | 10-1985 |

| County and Station | Mean Max. July (°F) | Mean Min. January (°F) | Record Highest (°F) | Year | Record Lowest (°F) | Year | Last in Spring | First in Fall | Growing Season (Days) | January | February | March | April | May | June | July | August | September | October | November | December | Annual | Highest Daily Rainfall (In.) | Mo.-Year |
|---|---|---|---|---|---|---|---|---|---|---|---|---|---|---|---|---|---|---|---|---|---|---|---|---|
| Deaf Smith, Hereford | 91.6 | 21.1 | 111 | 1910 | -17 | 1951 | Apr. 19 | Oct. 19 | 182 | 0.50 | 0.50 | 0.98 | 1.02 | 2.12 | 2.90 | 2.06 | 3.22 | 2.25 | 1.59 | 0.77 | 0.74 | 18.65 | *5.30 | 08-1976 |
| Delta, Cooper | 94.0 | 30.0 | 110 | | -1 | | Mar. 25 | Nov. 13 | 233 | 2.70 | 3.20 | 4.10 | 3.60 | 5.40 | 4.00 | 2.90 | 2.10 | 3.90 | 4.80 | 4.30 | 4.00 | 45.00 | 4.00 | |
| Denton, Denton | 94.1 | 32.0 | *113 | 1954 | *-3 | 1949 | Mar. 18 | Nov. 16 | 243 | 1.94 | 2.55 | 2.82 | 3.30 | 5.41 | 3.29 | 2.53 | 2.26 | 3.35 | 4.81 | 2.87 | 2.66 | 37.79 | 7.30 | 05-1982 |
| DeWitt, Cuero | 95.1 | 41.3 | 113 | 2000 | 7 | 1989 | Feb. 28 | Nov. 25 | 270 | 2.30 | 1.95 | 2.32 | 2.96 | 4.74 | 4.51 | 2.18 | 2.25 | 4.31 | 3.67 | 2.66 | 2.23 | 36.08 | 12.40 | 06-1940 |
| Dickens, Spur | 95.4 | 25.5 | 117 | 1994 | -17 | 1933 | Apr. 2 | Nov. 4 | 215 | 0.55 | 0.70 | 0.84 | 1.53 | 3.18 | 2.68 | 1.74 | 2.12 | 2.17 | 1.66 | 0.82 | 0.69 | 18.68 | 4.70 | 08-1996 |
| Dimmit, Carrizo Springs | 98.3 | 39.6 | 114 | 1942 | 10 | 1989 | Feb. 14 | Dec. 4 | 292 | 1.00 | 0.94 | 0.89 | 1.47 | 2.96 | 2.78 | 1.26 | 2.81 | 1.95 | 2.66 | 1.10 | 0.87 | 20.21 | 8.78 | 07-1990 |
| Donley, Clarendon | 94.7 | 22.4 | 117 | 1936 | -11 | 1989 | Apr. 11 | Oct. 25 | 196 | 0.64 | 0.83 | 1.43 | 2.25 | 3.60 | 3.70 | 2.37 | 2.33 | 2.69 | 1.78 | 0.94 | 0.85 | 23.89 | 9.25 | 05-2001 |
| Duval, Freer | 97.3 | 42.5 | 116 | 1998 | 12 | 1963 | Feb. 13 | Dec. 8 | 297 | 1.15 | 1.31 | 1.58 | 1.69 | 3.63 | 3.68 | 1.54 | 2.25 | 3.06 | 2.92 | 1.54 | 1.05 | 25.40 | 7.85 | 09-1971 |
| Eastland, Eastland | 94.9 | 26.7 | *115 | 1943 | *-6 | 1973 | Mar. 1 | Nov. 8 | 221 | 1.20 | 1.73 | 1.93 | 2.27 | 3.72 | 3.40 | 1.73 | 2.29 | 2.67 | 3.25 | 1.72 | 1.62 | 27.53 | 7.00 | 10-1957 |
| Ector, Penwell | 96.0 | 28.7 | 116 | 1994 | -12 | 1985 | Mar. 30 | Nov. 7 | 222 | 0.42 | 0.58 | 0.42 | 0.61 | 2.11 | 1.56 | 1.30 | 1.46 | 2.35 | 1.24 | 0.63 | 0.61 | 13.29 | 4.53 | 04-1969 |
| Edwards, Rocksprings | 91.6 | 34.3 | *108 | 1980 | *3 | 1951 | Mar. 18 | Nov. 17 | 243 | 0.77 | 1.31 | 1.36 | 1.75 | 3.23 | 3.07 | 2.05 | 2.84 | 2.44 | 3.41 | 1.50 | 1.03 | 24.76 | 9.50 | 06-1935 |
| Ellis, Waxahachie | 96.0 | 35.0 | 115 | 1909 | -4 | 1989 | Mar. 14 | Nov. 18 | 248 | 2.11 | 2.85 | 3.21 | 3.89 | 4.85 | 3.51 | 2.28 | 2.26 | 3.16 | 4.43 | 3.04 | 3.22 | 38.81 | 10.80 | 09-1958 |
| El Paso, El Paso | 94.5 | 32.9 | 114 | 1994 | -8 | 1962 | Mar. 22 | Nov. 8 | 230 | 0.45 | 0.39 | 0.26 | 0.23 | 0.38 | 0.87 | 1.49 | 1.75 | 1.61 | 0.81 | 0.42 | 0.77 | 9.43 | 2.26 | 09-1974 |
| Erath, Stephenville | 93.6 | 30.0 | 111 | 1925 | -8 | 1949 | Mar. 22 | Nov. 13 | 235 | 1.31 | 1.86 | 2.35 | 2.53 | 4.35 | 3.41 | 1.47 | 2.41 | 2.80 | 3.28 | 1.97 | 1.97 | 29.71 | 9.71 | 05-1956 |
| Falls, Marlin | 95.0 | 37.0 | *112 | 1969 | -7 | 1949 | Mar. 10 | Nov. 17 | 251 | 2.49 | 2.60 | 3.30 | 3.19 | 5.35 | 3.55 | 1.97 | 2.09 | 3.08 | 3.90 | 3.17 | 3.30 | 37.99 | 11.90 | 07-1903 |
| Fannin, Bonham | 92.6 | 30.2 | 115 | 1936 | *-5 | 1930 | Mar. 27 | Nov. 8 | 225 | 2.39 | 3.01 | 3.76 | 3.41 | 5.57 | 4.50 | 3.45 | 2.13 | 3.45 | 5.40 | 3.94 | 3.55 | 44.56 | 13.30 | 07-1903 |
| Fayette, La Grange | 95.9 | 41.4 | 110 | 2000 | 3 | 1989 | Feb. 26 | Nov. 23 | 269 | 3.05 | 2.88 | 2.55 | 2.99 | 4.82 | 4.41 | 2.25 | 2.81 | 3.68 | 4.47 | 3.36 | 3.04 | 40.31 | 9.41 | 06-1940 |
| Fisher, Rotan | 94.2 | 27.2 | 116 | 1994 | *-5 | 1989 | Mar. 29 | Nov. 9 | 225 | 0.80 | 1.35 | 1.30 | 1.72 | 3.68 | 2.74 | 1.92 | 2.76 | 3.45 | 2.30 | 1.13 | 1.07 | 24.22 | 6.85 | 08-1972 |
| Floyd, Floydada | 92.3 | 23.2 | 111 | 1994 | -9 | 1963 | Apr. 8 | Oct. 30 | 205 | 0.45 | 0.72 | 0.98 | 1.58 | 3.01 | 3.74 | 2.00 | 2.50 | 2.88 | 1.62 | 0.84 | 0.63 | 20.95 | 6.51 | 09-1942 |
| Foard, Crowell | 97.0 | 24.0 | 114 | | -7 | | Apr. 2 | Nov. 7 | 219 | 1.00 | 1.40 | 1.60 | 2.10 | 4.30 | 3.70 | 1.70 | 2.40 | 3.30 | 2.40 | 1.50 | 1.00 | 26.40 | | |
| Fort Bend, Sugar Land | 93.7 | 41.6 | 108 | 2000 | *6 | 1989 | Feb. 15 | Dec. 10 | 294 | 4.06 | 2.98 | 3.24 | 3.48 | 4.69 | 5.51 | 3.30 | 4.29 | 5.82 | 4.03 | 4.58 | 3.36 | 49.34 | 10.60 | 06-2001 |
| Franklin, Mount Vernon | 92.8 | 32.2 | *108 | 2000 | -1 | 1989 | Mar. 22 | Nov. 12 | 235 | 2.83 | 3.41 | 4.23 | 3.56 | 4.71 | 4.79 | 3.82 | 2.19 | 3.75 | 4.77 | 5.10 | 4.49 | 47.65 | 6.10 | 07-1990 |
| Freestone, Fairfield | 95.0 | 36.4 | *113 | 2000 | -2 | 1989 | Mar. 19 | Nov. 17 | 242 | 2.84 | 3.29 | 3.29 | 3.38 | 5.04 | 3.79 | 2.14 | 2.56 | 3.48 | 4.64 | 4.16 | 3.70 | 42.31 | 7.90 | 01-1999 |
| Frio, Pearsall | 97.5 | 37.9 | *113 | 2000 | *7 | 1989 | Feb. 22 | Nov. 25 | 275 | 1.30 | 1.45 | 1.30 | 2.15 | 3.33 | 3.68 | 1.58 | 2.61 | 2.29 | 1.39 | 1.60 | 1.24 | 25.73 | 7.84 | 08-1946 |
| Gaines, Seminole | 94.1 | 26.7 | 114 | 1994 | -9 | 1962 | Apr. 2 | Nov. 3 | 215 | 0.64 | 0.72 | 0.61 | 0.91 | 2.39 | 2.45 | 2.44 | 2.31 | 2.73 | 1.39 | 0.90 | 0.71 | 18.20 | 5.40 | 05-1999 |
| Galveston, Galveston | 88.7 | 49.7 | 102 | 1999 | *14 | 1989 | Jan. 19 | Jan. 9 | 358 | 4.08 | 2.61 | 2.76 | 2.56 | 3.70 | 4.04 | 3.45 | 4.22 | 5.76 | 3.49 | 3.64 | 3.53 | 43.84 | 13.63 | 07-1900 |
| Garza, Post | 97.8 | 27.8 | 115 | 1994 | *-1 | 1994 | Mar. 30 | Nov. 9 | 223 | 0.58 | 0.98 | 0.76 | 1.43 | 3.01 | 2.83 | 2.03 | 2.88 | 3.07 | 2.05 | 0.89 | 0.78 | 21.29 | 6.75 | 10-1926 |
| Gillespie, Fredericksburg | 93.1 | 36.1 | *109 | 2000 | -5 | 1949 | Mar. 18 | Nov. 12 | 238 | 1.36 | 1.91 | 1.86 | 2.40 | 4.29 | 3.97 | 2.03 | 2.88 | 3.07 | 3.72 | 2.19 | 2.14 | 31.65 | 8.03 | 07-1945 |
| Glasscock, Garden City | 94.0 | 26.7 | 114 | 1994 | -3 | 1949 | Apr. 3 | Nov. 3 | 213 | 0.73 | 0.71 | 0.70 | 1.14 | 2.18 | 1.91 | 1.86 | 2.02 | 2.97 | 1.66 | 0.69 | 0.69 | 17.32 | 8.75 | 07-1945 |
| Goliad, Goliad | 95.5 | 43.3 | *112 | 1998 | 7 | 1962 | Feb. 25 | Nov. 26 | 273 | 2.34 | 2.11 | 2.00 | 3.19 | 4.49 | 4.96 | 2.85 | 3.49 | 4.56 | 4.26 | 2.19 | 2.14 | 38.58 | 9.16 | 09-1967 |
| Gonzales, Gonzales | 93.9 | 38.7 | 111 | 2000 | *4 | 1989 | Feb. 26 | Dec. 1 | 277 | 2.36 | 2.08 | 2.22 | 3.04 | 5.43 | 4.24 | 1.60 | 2.68 | 3.20 | 3.87 | 2.84 | 2.46 | 36.02 | 16.31 | 08-1981 |
| Gray, Pampa | 92.0 | 21.9 | 111 | 1980 | -8 | 1989 | Apr. 13 | Oct. 25 | 195 | 0.57 | 0.83 | 1.50 | 1.95 | 3.37 | 3.52 | 2.85 | 2.38 | 2.29 | 1.58 | 1.20 | 0.70 | 22.74 | 3.54 | 07-1982 |
| Grayson, Sherman | 92.7 | 32.2 | 113 | 1936 | *-2 | 1989 | Mar. 22 | Nov. 14 | 236 | 2.11 | 2.63 | 3.44 | 3.49 | 5.41 | 4.37 | 2.34 | 2.25 | 4.01 | 5.15 | 3.81 | 3.03 | 42.04 | 8.40 | 08-1920 |

| County and Station | Mean Max. July (°F) | Mean Min. January (°F) | Record Highest (°F) | Highest Year | Record Lowest (°F) | Lowest Year | Last in Spring | First in Fall | Growing Season (Days) | Jan (In.) | Feb (In.) | Mar (In.) | Apr (In.) | May (In.) | June (In.) | July (In.) | Aug (In.) | Sep (In.) | Oct (In.) | Nov (In.) | Dec (In.) | Annual (In.) | Highest Daily Rainfall (In.) | Highest Daily Rainfall (Mo.-Year) |
|---|---|---|---|---|---|---|---|---|---|---|---|---|---|---|---|---|---|---|---|---|---|---|---|---|
| Gregg, Longview | 94.5 | 33.7 | 113 | 1936 | -4 | 1930 | Mar. 19 | Nov. 15 | 240 | 3.79 | 3.93 | 4.11 | 4.19 | 4.79 | 5.03 | 2.83 | 2.71 | 3.81 | 4.34 | 4.75 | 4.78 | 49.06 | 8.70 | 03-1989 |
| Grimes, Richards | 96.0 | 40.0 | 108 | | 4 | | Mar. 1 | Dec. 4 | 278 | 4.10 | 3.00 | 3.30 | 3.40 | 5.20 | 3.90 | 2.20 | 2.60 | 4.20 | 4.40 | 4.10 | 4.30 | 44.70 | | |
| Guadalupe, New Braunfels | 95.0 | 36.0 | 110 | | 0 | | Mar. 6 | Nov. 28 | 267 | 1.90 | 2.20 | 1.80 | 2.60 | 5.00 | 4.10 | 2.50 | 2.50 | 4.10 | 3.50 | 2.80 | 2.00 | 34.50 | | |
| Hale, Plainview | 91.0 | 24.4 | 111 | 1994 | -8 | 1933 | Apr. 4 | Oct. 31 | 209 | 0.59 | 0.63 | 0.80 | 1.52 | 2.91 | 3.05 | 2.45 | 2.38 | 2.28 | 1.72 | 0.84 | 0.73 | 19.90 | 7.00 | 07-1960 |
| Hall, Memphis | 95.7 | 25.5 | *117 | 1944 | -11 | 1930 | Apr. 1 | Nov. 4 | 217 | 0.57 | 0.88 | 1.52 | 2.04 | 3.93 | 3.51 | 1.88 | 2.25 | 2.45 | 1.77 | 0.96 | 0.75 | 22.51 | 8.80 | 06-1960 |
| Hamilton, Hamilton | 94.3 | 33.4 | 109 | 1964 | -3 | 1989 | Mar. 16 | Nov. 15 | 243 | 1.64 | 1.76 | 2.61 | 2.72 | 3.70 | 3.71 | 1.53 | 1.57 | 2.85 | 2.90 | 2.00 | 1.60 | 28.59 | 8.20 | 10-1959 |
| Hansford, Spearman | 95.5 | 22.4 | 111 | 1936 | -22 | 1959 | Apr. 16 | Oct. 23 | 189 | 0.53 | 0.62 | 1.52 | 1.58 | 2.83 | 2.97 | 2.77 | 2.38 | 2.08 | 1.35 | 1.01 | 0.66 | 20.30 | 5.80 | 05-1965 |
| Hardeman, Quanah | 96.5 | 24.6 | *119 | 1994 | -15 | 1989 | Apr. 4 | Nov. 2 | 211 | 0.96 | 1.17 | 1.65 | 2.08 | 3.86 | 3.73 | 2.42 | 2.57 | 3.43 | 2.37 | 1.40 | 1.12 | 26.76 | 8.03 | 08-1995 |
| Hardin, Evadale | 93.0 | 37.0 | 102 | | 12 | | Mar. 31 | Nov. 14 | 246 | 5.40 | 3.70 | 4.20 | 3.46 | 5.50 | 5.50 | 4.20 | 4.54 | 4.50 | 5.30 | 5.10 | 5.10 | 56.50 | | |
| Harris, Houston | 93.6 | 45.2 | 108 | 2000 | 9 | 1989 | Feb. 8 | Dec. 20 | 308 | 4.25 | 3.01 | 3.19 | 3.46 | 5.11 | 6.84 | 4.36 | 4.54 | 5.62 | 5.26 | 4.54 | 3.78 | 53.96 | 9.95 | 10-1949 |
| Harrison, Marshall | 92.4 | 33.4 | 112 | 1909 | -5 | 1930 | Mar. 20 | Nov. 12 | 236 | 4.38 | 4.07 | 4.33 | 4.35 | 5.07 | 5.23 | 3.02 | 2.68 | 3.89 | 4.66 | 4.59 | 4.95 | 51.22 | 8.58 | 03-1989 |
| Hartley, Channing | 90.9 | 20.0 | *108 | 1981 | -9 | 1979 | Apr. 19 | Oct. 19 | 182 | 0.35 | 0.45 | 0.76 | 1.10 | 1.88 | 2.30 | 2.59 | 3.50 | 1.66 | 1.33 | 0.61 | 0.67 | 17.20 | 8.30 | 12-1997 |
| Haskell, Haskell | 96.1 | 28.8 | *115 | 1994 | *-6 | 1989 | Mar. 27 | Nov. 12 | 235 | 0.96 | 1.47 | 1.46 | 1.99 | 3.32 | 3.26 | 2.12 | 2.74 | 2.96 | 2.53 | 1.26 | 1.37 | 24.93 | 14.29 | 08-1978 |
| Hays, San Marcos | 95.1 | 38.6 | *111 | 1994 | -2 | 1949 | Feb. 28 | Nov. 24 | 268 | 2.05 | 2.21 | 2.09 | 3.07 | 5.31 | 4.84 | 2.19 | 2.36 | 3.46 | 4.03 | 3.17 | 2.41 | 37.19 | 15.78 | 10-1998 |
| Hemphill, Canadian | 93.9 | 18.8 | *112 | 1994 | *-14 | 1942 | Apr. 10 | Oct. 16 | 188 | 0.46 | 0.71 | 1.70 | 1.72 | 3.75 | 3.33 | 2.19 | 2.36 | 2.36 | 1.47 | 0.94 | 0.69 | 21.68 | 5.15 | 10-1985 |
| Henderson, Athens | 93.4 | 35.2 | *109 | 2000 | -6 | 1985 | Apr. 10 | Nov. 14 | 239 | 2.96 | 3.37 | 3.70 | 3.47 | 4.82 | 3.95 | 1.74 | 2.43 | 3.07 | 4.70 | 3.94 | 3.88 | 42.03 | 7.19 | 04-1986 |
| Hidalgo, McAllen | 95.5 | 48.2 | 109 | 1999 | 17 | 1962 | Jan. 05 | Jan. 30 | >365 | 1.20 | 1.37 | 0.95 | 1.36 | 2.51 | 2.49 | 1.70 | 2.31 | 4.00 | 2.76 | 0.95 | 1.01 | 22.61 | 7.81 | 08-1980 |
| Hill, Hillsboro | 95.2 | 35.2 | 113 | 1917 | -6 | 1989 | Mar. 19 | Nov. 14 | 240 | 2.67 | 2.67 | 3.21 | 3.24 | 4.65 | 4.07 | 2.08 | 2.31 | 2.92 | 4.15 | 2.10 | 3.08 | 37.15 | 11.30 | 09-1936 |
| Hockley, Levelland | 92.7 | 23.7 | 115 | 1994 | -16 | 1963 | Mar. 19 | Nov. 14 | 201 | 0.27 | 0.63 | 0.58 | 1.03 | 2.35 | 2.78 | 2.22 | 2.08 | 3.24 | 1.62 | 0.85 | 0.82 | 19.58 | 4.23 | 06-1999 |
| Hood, Cresson | 97.0 | 33.0 | 110 | | -6 | | Mar. 26 | Nov. 13 | 232 | 1.60 | 2.20 | 2.60 | 2.90 | 4.70 | 3.90 | 1.70 | 2.87 | 2.60 | 3.90 | 2.30 | 2.30 | 33.10 | | |
| Hopkins, Sulphur Springs | 94.8 | 31.1 | 115 | 1969 | -4 | 1989 | Mar. 25 | Nov. 12 | 232 | 2.88 | 3.20 | 4.27 | 4.34 | 5.00 | 4.64 | 3.22 | 2.35 | 3.35 | 5.21 | 4.77 | 4.46 | 47.69 | 8.11 | 07-1994 |
| Houston, Crockett | 95.9 | 35.9 | 114 | 1909 | *0 | 1989 | Mar. 10 | Nov. 18 | 252 | 4.02 | 3.10 | 3.45 | 3.87 | 4.66 | 4.46 | 2.84 | 2.81 | 4.12 | 4.22 | 3.93 | 4.02 | 45.48 | 9.11 | 06-2001 |
| Howard, Big Spring | 94.3 | 29.6 | 114 | 1994 | *-5 | 1985 | Mar. 23 | Nov. 13 | 235 | 0.72 | 0.81 | 0.73 | 1.34 | 3.05 | 2.58 | 1.78 | 2.29 | 3.51 | 1.78 | 0.77 | 0.67 | 20.12 | 4.84 | 05-1994 |
| Hudspeth, Sierra Blanca | 92.0 | 25.1 | *109 | 1994 | -10 | 1985 | Apr. 18 | Oct. 29 | 193 | 0.49 | 0.41 | 0.26 | 0.29 | 0.53 | 1.11 | 2.11 | 2.18 | 2.19 | 1.15 | 0.44 | 0.66 | 11.93 | 3.32 | 09-1978 |
| Hunt, Greenville | 93.3 | 31.2 | 116 | 1936 | -4 | 1930 | Mar. 23 | Nov. 13 | 235 | 2.51 | 3.16 | 3.67 | 3.79 | 5.47 | 4.03 | 2.96 | 3.16 | 3.56 | 4.91 | 3.98 | 3.48 | 43.70 | 6.95 | 09-1936 |
| Hutchinson, Borger | 92.6 | 23.4 | *108 | 1998 | -12 | 1951 | Apr. 14 | Oct. 25 | 193 | 0.65 | 0.69 | 1.56 | 1.77 | 3.08 | 2.50 | 2.69 | 1.90 | 2.00 | 1.60 | 0.88 | 0.70 | 21.98 | 3.79 | 05-1959 |
| Irion, Funk Ranch | 95.0 | 32.0 | 108 | | -7 | | Mar. 27 | Nov. 11 | 229 | 0.70 | 1.10 | 1.00 | 1.60 | 2.50 | 3.18 | 1.90 | 2.26 | 3.10 | 2.10 | 1.00 | 1.83 | 19.90 | | |
| Jack, Jacksboro | 94.4 | 29.7 | *113 | 1980 | -1 | 1989 | Mar. 21 | Nov. 14 | 237 | 1.00 | 1.79 | 2.38 | 3.10 | 4.96 | 4.60 | 2.26 | 2.90 | 3.18 | 3.78 | 2.10 | 1.44 | 31.44 | 9.60 | 04-1957 |
| Jackson, Edna | 94.0 | 42.0 | 105 | | 17 | | Feb. 19 | Dec. 6 | 290 | 3.10 | 2.40 | 2.00 | 3.10 | 5.30 | 4.63 | 2.90 | 3.92 | 4.90 | 5.00 | 2.05 | 2.80 | 42.10 | | |
| Jasper, Sam Rayburn Dam | 94.5 | 35.2 | 109 | 2000 | 7 | 1989 | Mar. 17 | Nov. 14 | 241 | 5.94 | 4.55 | 5.29 | 4.51 | 5.53 | 5.81 | 4.24 | 3.92 | 3.97 | 4.84 | 5.88 | 6.09 | 60.57 | 9.04 | 03-1999 |
| Jeff Davis, Fort Davis | 89.5 | 28.4 | *107 | 1998 | *0 | 1985 | Apr. 9 | Nov. 2 | 206 | 0.43 | 0.35 | 0.34 | 0.50 | 1.46 | 1.79 | 2.95 | 2.97 | 2.76 | 1.29 | 0.49 | 0.53 | 15.86 | 5.30 | 08-1932 |
| Jeff Davis, Mount Locke | 84.5 | 32.4 | *104 | 1994 | -10 | 1962 | Apr. 17 | Oct. 26 | 191 | 0.53 | 0.49 | 0.33 | 0.60 | 1.73 | 2.56 | 3.82 | 4.02 | 3.29 | 1.71 | 0.56 | 0.73 | 20.37 | 4.13 | 05-1963 |
| Jefferson, Beaumont | 91.6 | 42.9 | 108 | 2000 | 12 | 1989 | Feb. 14 | Dec. 6 | 295 | 5.69 | 3.35 | 3.75 | 3.84 | 5.83 | 6.58 | 5.23 | 4.85 | 6.10 | 4.67 | 4.75 | 5.25 | 59.89 | 12.09 | 09-1963 |

| COUNTY AND STATION | TEMPERATURE Mean Max. July (F.) | Mean Min. January (F.) | Record Highest (F.) | Year | Record Lowest (F.) | Year | AVERAGE FREEZE DATES Last in Spring | First in Fall | Growing Season Days | MEAN PRECIPITATION January (In.) | February | March | April | May | June | July | August | September | October | November | December | Annual | EXTREMES Highest Daily Rainfall (In.) | Mo.-Year |
|---|---|---|---|---|---|---|---|---|---|---|---|---|---|---|---|---|---|---|---|---|---|---|---|---|
| Jim Hogg, Hebbronville | 97.5 | 43.8 | 111 | 1998 | *12 | 1989 | Feb. 8 | Dec. 11 | 307 | 1.12 | 1.40 | 1.14 | 1.69 | 3.33 | 3.13 | 1.44 | 2.28 | 3.68 | 2.22 | 1.22 | 1.10 | 23.75 | 9.40 | 09-1971 |
| Jim Wells, Alice | 96.1 | 44.1 | *111 | 1998 | *12 | 1989 | Jan. 29 | Dec. 15 | 320 | 1.21 | 1.51 | 1.34 | 1.65 | 3.16 | 3.41 | 1.76 | 2.70 | 4.52 | 3.55 | 1.50 | 1.21 | 27.52 | 12.14 | 09-1971 |
| Johnson, Cleburne | 97.0 | 34.0 | 114 | 1939 | -5 | 1989 | Mar. 18 | Nov. 13 | 240 | 1.90 | 2.29 | 3.07 | 3.53 | 5.11 | 3.90 | 2.18 | 2.36 | 2.88 | 3.92 | 2.54 | 2.57 | 36.25 | 9.02 | 05-1989 |
| Jones, Anson | 96.3 | 30.7 | 114 | 1994 | -12 | 1989 | Mar. 28 | Nov. 12 | 228 | 1.03 | 1.51 | 1.21 | 1.94 | 3.20 | 3.13 | 2.04 | 2.94 | 3.93 | 2.55 | 1.22 | 1.30 | 26.00 | 5.60 | 09-1988 |
| Karnes, Karnes City | 95.0 | 41.0 | 112 |  | 7 |  | Feb. 24 | Dec. 2 | 281 | 1.50 | 1.70 | 1.50 | 2.50 | 3.40 | 3.70 | 1.90 | 2.40 | 3.40 | 3.00 | 1.90 | 1.50 | 28.40 |  |  |
| Kaufman, Kaufman | 94.6 | 32.3 | 113 | 1936 | *-3 | 1989 | Mar. 19 | Nov. 14 | 240 | 2.74 | 3.04 | 3.37 | 3.06 | 4.45 | 3.31 | 2.12 | 1.98 | 2.77 | 4.81 | 3.80 | 3.45 | 38.90 | 13.66 | 08-1908 |
| Kendall, Boerne | 91.9 | 34.3 | 112 | 1925 | -4 | 1949 | Mar. 20 | Nov. 13 | 238 | 1.79 | 2.24 | 2.57 | 2.87 | 4.66 | 4.77 | 2.23 | 3.05 | 3.61 | 4.09 | 3.11 | 2.37 | 37.36 | 9.04 | 10-1913 |
| Kenedy, Sarita | 95.0 | 45.0 | 110 |  | 14 |  | Feb. 2 | Dec. 18 | 319 | 1.10 | 1.80 | 1.30 | 1.60 | 2.70 | 3.30 | 1.50 | 3.40 | 4.70 | 3.40 | 1.90 | 1.20 | 27.90 |  |  |
| Kent, Jayton | 95.7 | 24.9 | 116 | 1994 | -6 | 1985 | Apr. 2 | Nov. 7 | 218 | 0.91 | 1.14 | 1.12 | 1.73 | 3.35 | 3.21 | 1.59 | 2.81 | 3.04 | 2.17 | 0.97 | 0.90 | 22.94 | 6.50 | 06-1991 |
| Kerr, Kerrville | 92.0 | 32.0 | 110 |  | -7 |  | Apr. 6 | Nov. 6 | 216 | 1.30 | 1.80 | 2.10 | 2.30 | 4.20 | 4.00 | 2.30 | 2.20 | 3.90 | 3.80 | 2.60 | 2.10 | 32.60 |  |  |
| Kimble, Junction | 94.8 | 29.3 | *110 | 1984 | -11 | 1929 | Apr. 2 | Nov. 1 | 212 | 0.77 | 1.43 | 1.42 | 1.95 | 3.23 | 3.10 | 1.55 | 2.20 | 2.28 | 2.68 | 1.37 | 1.26 | 23.24 | 6.10 | 09-1980 |
| King, Guthrie | 96.7 | 23.9 | 119 | 1994 | -10 | 1989 | Apr. 6 | Nov. 4 | 211 | 1.03 | 1.28 | 1.26 | 1.79 | 3.90 | 3.17 | 1.94 | 2.87 | 3.25 | 2.38 | 1.12 | 1.01 | 25.00 | 8.85 | 07-1986 |
| Kinney, Brackettville | 95.5 | 37.3 | 111 | 1988 | 4 | 1962 | Mar. 5 | Nov. 15 | 255 | 0.77 | 1.16 | 1.10 | 1.99 | 2.87 | 3.18 | 1.79 | 2.29 | 2.77 | 2.49 | 1.41 | 0.97 | 22.79 | 6.20 | 05-1900 |
| Kleberg, Kingsville | 95.5 | 43.4 | *111 | 1994 | 10 | 1989 | Feb. 10 | Dec. 11 | 303 | 1.44 | 1.71 | 1.24 | 1.80 | 3.53 | 4.02 | 1.97 | 3.05 | 3.98 | 3.72 | 1.50 | 1.07 | 29.03 | 6.67 | 12-1991 |
| Knox, Munday | 96.5 | 28.1 | *117 | 1936 | *-9 | 1989 | Mar. 28 | Nov. 12 | 228 | 1.00 | 1.54 | 1.69 | 1.70 | 3.85 | 3.46 | 1.70 | 2.68 | 3.22 | 2.73 | 1.38 | 1.20 | 26.36 | 8.00 | 06-1930 |
| Lamar, Paris | 94.3 | 29.9 | 115 | 1936 | *-5 | 1930 | Mar. 18 | Nov. 14 | 240 | 2.63 | 3.00 | 4.11 | 3.56 | 5.63 | 4.25 | 3.89 | 2.39 | 4.42 | 5.04 | 4.70 | 4.20 | 47.82 | 7.61 | 06-1928 |
| Lamb, Littlefield | 92.0 | 22.7 | 112 | 1994 | -6 | 1979 | Apr. 11 | Oct. 25 | 196 | 0.55 | 0.52 | 0.75 | 1.11 | 2.24 | 3.04 | 2.44 | 2.80 | 2.26 | 1.52 | 0.77 | 0.69 | 18.69 | 5.10 | 06-1999 |
| Lampasas, Lampasas | 94.1 | 30.4 | *112 | 1917 | -12 | 1949 | Apr. 1 | Nov. 07 | 219 | 1.50 | 2.34 | 2.31 | 2.48 | 4.37 | 3.49 | 1.68 | 2.42 | 2.61 | 3.33 | 2.32 | 2.23 | 31.08 | 6.95 | 05-1957 |
| La Salle, Fowlerton | 98.9 | 39.1 | 113 | 1998 | 9 | 1962 | Feb. 27 | Nov. 26 | 271 | 0.93 | 1.08 | 1.46 | 1.84 | 2.73 | 2.61 | 1.53 | 2.19 | 2.71 | 3.15 | 1.22 | 1.11 | 22.56 | 9.50 | 10-1986 |
| Lavaca, Hallettsville | 94.4 | 41.8 | *111 | 1980 | 5 | 1989 | Feb. 25 | Nov. 29 | 277 | 2.91 | 2.50 | 2.46 | 3.44 | 5.75 | 5.02 | 2.28 | 2.95 | 4.49 | 4.07 | 2.83 | 2.57 | 42.23 | 11.30 | 07-1936 |
| Lee, Lexington | 93.6 | 37.3 | 111 | 2000 | 2 | 1989 | Mar. 1 | Nov. 22 | 265 | 2.60 | 2.13 | 2.54 | 2.48 | 4.82 | 3.78 | 1.63 | 2.06 | 3.26 | 4.69 | 3.25 | 2.78 | 36.02 | 10.13 | 10-1994 |
| Leon, Centerville | 94.7 | 34.3 | *108 | 1954 | -3 | 1949 | Mar. 17 | Nov. 14 | 242 | 3.40 | 3.18 | 3.51 | 3.29 | 4.77 | 4.12 | 2.48 | 2.62 | 3.50 | 4.79 | 3.82 | 3.60 | 43.08 | 8.50 | 10-1957 |
| Liberty, Liberty | 92.2 | 40.3 | 113 | 1913 | 7 | 1989 | Feb. 18 | Dec. 1 | 285 | 4.91 | 3.74 | 3.84 | 4.01 | 5.80 | 6.88 | 4.46 | 4.34 | 5.92 | 5.77 | 5.84 | 5.01 | 60.52 | 18.50 | 10-1994 |
| Limestone, Mexia | 95.8 | 33.7 | 112 | 1909 | -5 | 1989 | Mar. 6 | Nov. 20 | 258 | 2.44 | 3.08 | 3.45 | 3.14 | 4.91 | 3.89 | 1.99 | 2.56 | 4.16 | 4.29 | 3.64 | 3.85 | 41.40 | 11.80 | 09-1932 |
| Lipscomb, Lipscomb | 94.2 | 16.2 | 114 | 1978 | *-18 | 1974 | Apr. 23 | Oct. 11 | 170 | 0.54 | 0.81 | 1.91 | 2.00 | 3.85 | 3.28 | 2.30 | 2.52 | 1.97 | 1.46 | 1.12 | 0.81 | 22.57 | 6.62 | 05-1951 |
| Live Oak, Choke Canyon Dam | 97.0 | 42.0 | 109 |  | 12 |  | Feb. 20 | Dec. 6 | 289 | 1.20 | 1.10 | 1.80 | 2.40 | 2.80 | 2.70 | 1.60 | 1.40 | 2.10 | 2.00 | 1.70 | 1.20 | 22.00 |  |  |
| Llano, Llano | 96.0 | 32.3 | 115 | 1933 | -7 | 1929 | Mar. 18 | Nov. 12 | 238 | 1.08 | 1.80 | 0.90 | 2.19 | 3.94 | 3.40 | 1.84 | 2.03 | 2.14 | 2.88 | 2.23 | 1.90 | 27.33 | 12.53 | 09-1952 |
| Loving, Mentone | 91.9 | 28.0 | 114 |  | -14 |  | Apr. 3 | Nov. 8 | 222 | 0.30 | 0.30 | 0.30 | 0.20 | 1.10 | 0.90 | 1.80 | 1.40 | 1.20 | 1.00 | 0.30 | 0.30 | 9.10 | 5.70 | 06-1967 |
| Lubbock, Lubbock | 92.2 | 24.4 | 114 | 1994 | -17 | 1994 | Apr. 3 | Nov. 1 | 211 | 0.50 | 0.71 | 0.76 | 1.29 | 2.31 | 2.98 | 1.80 | 2.36 | 2.57 | 1.70 | 0.71 | 0.67 | 18.69 | 8.32 | 10-1913 |
| Lynn, Tahoka | 92.2 | 25.1 | 111 | 1994 | -15 | 1994 | Apr. 4 | Nov. 4 | 213 | 0.66 | 0.79 | 0.71 | 1.48 | 2.74 | 3.22 | 2.36 | 2.23 | 2.65 | 1.73 | 0.86 | 0.79 | 20.48 |  |  |
| Madison, Madisonville | 96.0 | 35.8 | 112 | 2000 | -2 | 2000 | Mar. 7 | Nov. 18 | 255 | 3.81 | 2.83 | 3.24 | 3.26 | 5.06 | 3.89 | 2.72 | 2.95 | 4.20 | 4.41 | 4.01 | 3.62 | 44.00 | 8.00 | 08-1945 |
| Marion, Jefferson | 93.1 | 31.4 | 108 | 2000 | -5 | 1989 | Mar. 25 | Nov. 6 | 225 | 4.13 | 3.96 | 4.41 | 4.07 | 4.60 | 4.84 | 2.89 | 2.93 | 3.40 | 4.64 | 4.68 | 4.71 | 49.26 | 9.10 | 04-1921 |
| Martin, Lenorah | 94.0 | 30.0 | 109 |  | -8 |  | Apr. 5 | Nov. 6 | 215 | 0.70 | 0.70 | 0.70 | 1.20 | 2.40 | 2.50 | 2.00 | 1.60 | 3.10 | 1.80 | 0.80 | 0.70 | 18.20 |  |  |

| COUNTY AND STATION | TEMPERATURE | | | | | | AVERAGE FREEZE DATES | | | MEAN PRECIPITATION | | | | | | | | | | | | | EXTREMES | |
|---|---|---|---|---|---|---|---|---|---|---|---|---|---|---|---|---|---|---|---|---|---|---|---|---|
| | Mean Max. July F. | Mean Min. January F. | Record Highest F. | Year | Record Lowest F. | Year | Last in Spring Mo. Day | First in Fall Mo. Day | Growing Season Days | January In. | February In. | March In. | April In. | May In. | June In. | July In. | August In. | September In. | October In. | November In. | December In. | Annual In. | Highest Daily Rainfall In. | Mo.-Year |
| Mason, Mason | 94.9 | 30.8 | 109 | 1962 | *3 | 1985 | Mar. 26 | Nov. 9 | 227 | 0.91 | 1.97 | 1.74 | 2.05 | 3.31 | 4.00 | 2.00 | 2.52 | 3.00 | 3.01 | 2.07 | 1.37 | 27.95 | 7.45 | 09-1952 |
| Matagorda, Bay City | 92.4 | 45.7 | *109 | 2000 | *7 | 1989 | Feb. 11 | Dec. 13 | 306 | 3.89 | 2.97 | 3.00 | 3.18 | 4.90 | 4.68 | 3.89 | 3.48 | 5.61 | 5.13 | 3.97 | 3.33 | 48.03 | 8.95 | 09-1961 |
| Maverick, Eagle Pass | 98.1 | 40.1 | *115 | 1944 | *10 | 1962 | Feb. 12 | Dec. 5 | 295 | 0.80 | 0.94 | 0.72 | 1.75 | 2.95 | 3.49 | 2.03 | 2.01 | 2.57 | 2.33 | 1.08 | 0.81 | 21.48 | 15.60 | 06-1936 |
| McCulloch, Brady | 94.5 | 32.3 | *110 | 1980 | -2 | 1989 | Mar. 21 | Nov. 11 | 235 | 1.01 | 1.68 | 1.63 | 1.92 | 3.60 | 3.26 | 2.68 | 2.57 | 3.26 | 2.68 | 1.73 | 1.61 | 27.63 | 6.51 | 07-1971 |
| McLennan, Waco | 96.7 | 35.1 | 112 | 1969 | -5 | 1949 | Mar. 13 | Nov. 19 | 250 | 1.90 | 2.43 | 2.48 | 2.96 | 4.46 | 3.08 | 2.25 | 1.85 | 2.88 | 3.67 | 2.61 | 2.76 | 33.34 | 7.98 | 12-1997 |
| McMullen, Tilden | 98.7 | 40.1 | 119 | 1910 | 5 | 1989 | Feb. 21 | Dec. 3 | 284 | 1.15 | 1.27 | 1.33 | 1.95 | 3.10 | 3.37 | 1.52 | 2.56 | 2.91 | 2.14 | 1.38 | 1.19 | 23.87 | 6.93 | 09-1967 |
| Medina, Hondo | 95.0 | 38.0 | 112 | | 4 | | Mar. 6 | Nov. 24 | 263 | 1.30 | 1.50 | 1.60 | 2.70 | 3.80 | 3.60 | 1.40 | 1.50 | 2.80 | 2.90 | 1.80 | 1.40 | 26.30 | | |
| Menard, Menard | 94.8 | 30.7 | 114 | 1927 | -6 | 1929 | Apr. 7 | Oct. 29 | 204 | 0.97 | 1.48 | 1.60 | 1.72 | 3.22 | 3.38 | 2.14 | 2.34 | 2.69 | 2.57 | 1.51 | 1.28 | 24.90 | 6.03 | 09-1936 |
| Midland, Midland | 94.3 | 29.6 | 116 | 1994 | -11 | 1985 | Mar. 30 | Nov. 12 | 226 | 0.53 | 0.58 | 0.42 | 0.73 | 1.79 | 1.71 | 1.89 | 1.77 | 2.31 | 1.77 | 0.65 | 0.65 | 14.80 | 4.75 | 05-1968 |
| Milam, Cameron | 95.7 | 39.2 | 114 | 1917 | -7 | 1930 | Mar. 7 | Nov. 22 | 260 | 2.29 | 2.53 | 2.45 | 2.88 | 5.01 | 3.22 | 1.91 | 1.95 | 3.54 | 3.73 | 3.12 | 2.86 | 35.52 | 12.45 | 09-1921 |
| Mills, Goldthwaite | 92.0 | 35.2 | 110 | 1964 | -7 | 1989 | Mar. 20 | Nov. 15 | 239 | 1.26 | 2.10 | 2.04 | 2.28 | 3.85 | 3.81 | 1.76 | 1.95 | 2.79 | 3.11 | 2.05 | 1.78 | 28.78 | 7.20 | 10-1969 |
| Mitchell, Colorado City | 95.9 | 27.0 | 115 | 1907 | -7 | 1947 | Mar. 25 | Nov. 7 | 226 | 0.44 | 0.89 | 1.07 | 1.33 | 2.49 | 2.84 | 1.23 | 2.29 | 3.09 | 2.22 | 0.90 | 0.64 | 19.43 | 8.65 | 04-1900 |
| Montague, Bowie | 94.7 | 28.3 | 115 | 1980 | -11 | 1989 | Mar. 21 | Nov. 12 | 236 | 1.47 | 2.13 | 2.62 | 2.89 | 5.04 | 3.42 | 1.81 | 2.27 | 3.67 | 4.20 | 2.18 | 2.02 | 33.72 | 10.25 | 05-1989 |
| Montgomery, Conroe | 94.3 | 40.0 | 109 | 2000 | 3 | 1989 | Feb. 27 | Nov. 25 | 270 | 4.21 | 2.97 | 2.94 | 3.85 | 5.50 | 4.58 | 3.22 | 3.73 | 4.46 | 4.70 | 4.79 | 4.37 | 49.32 | 14.35 | 10-1994 |
| Moore, Dumas | 91.7 | 20.8 | *109 | 1980 | *-18 | 1959 | Apr. 18 | Oct. 22 | 186 | 0.47 | 0.58 | 1.13 | 1.31 | 2.74 | 2.41 | 2.42 | 2.47 | 1.95 | 1.11 | 0.50 | 0.50 | 17.75 | 4.10 | 05-1988 |
| Morris, Daingerfield | 95.0 | 33.7 | 112 | 1998 | 4 | 1962 | Mar. 3 | Nov. 22 | 263 | 3.54 | 3.35 | 4.64 | 4.32 | 4.43 | 4.24 | 2.98 | 2.39 | 3.29 | 4.35 | 4.84 | 4.39 | 46.76 | 7.48 | 04-1966 |
| Motley, Matador | 94.8 | 27.3 | 116 | 1994 | -5 | 1989 | Apr. 1 | Nov. 8 | 221 | 0.67 | 0.90 | 1.21 | 1.81 | 3.16 | 3.60 | 2.10 | 2.41 | 3.11 | 2.09 | 0.99 | 0.85 | 22.90 | 5.30 | 10-1983 |
| Nacogdoches, Nacogdoches | 94.0 | 36.0 | 110 | | 0 | | Mar. 16 | Nov. 12 | 243 | 4.40 | 3.90 | 4.20 | 4.10 | 4.80 | 4.10 | 2.90 | 3.10 | 3.70 | 4.00 | 4.60 | 4.60 | 48.40 | | |
| Navarro, Corsicana | 94.5 | 34.0 | 113 | 1954 | -5 | 1949 | Mar. 9 | Nov. 23 | 259 | 2.49 | 3.08 | 3.34 | 3.39 | 4.95 | 3.40 | 2.16 | 2.37 | 3.04 | 4.33 | 3.33 | 3.60 | 39.48 | 9.96 | 05-1968 |
| Newton, Toledo Bend Dam | 94.0 | 35.0 | 107 | | 7 | | Mar. 24 | Nov. 9 | 228 | 5.70 | 4.40 | 4.80 | 4.00 | 4.90 | 5.00 | 3.60 | 2.59 | 3.90 | 4.10 | 5.00 | 6.10 | 54.90 | | |
| Nolan, Roscoe | 93.8 | 28.9 | 113 | 1994 | -11 | 1947 | Mar. 31 | Nov. 10 | 223 | 1.03 | 1.18 | 1.11 | 1.52 | 3.04 | 3.09 | 1.89 | 2.53 | 3.58 | 2.53 | 0.99 | 0.99 | 23.54 | 8.28 | 09-1980 |
| Nueces, Corpus Christi | 93.2 | 46.2 | 109 | 2000 | 13 | 1989 | Feb. 3 | Dec. 23 | 319 | 1.62 | 1.84 | 1.74 | 2.05 | 3.48 | 3.53 | 2.00 | 3.54 | 5.03 | 3.94 | 1.74 | 1.75 | 32.26 | 7.92 | 10-1995 |
| Ochiltree, Perryton | 91.4 | 18.4 | 111 | 1981 | -17 | 1988 | Apr. 25 | Oct. 17 | 174 | 0.47 | 0.62 | 1.71 | 1.80 | 3.33 | 2.97 | 2.74 | 2.22 | 1.89 | 1.38 | 1.09 | 0.66 | 20.88 | 7.11 | 05-1989 |
| Oldham, Boys Ranch | 92.3 | 20.5 | 110 | 1982 | -11 | 1983 | Apr. 13 | Oct. 11 | 186 | 0.49 | 0.28 | 0.89 | 1.13 | 2.47 | 2.18 | 2.96 | 3.20 | 1.94 | 1.48 | 0.66 | 0.50 | 18.18 | 4.50 | 09-1990 |
| Orange, Orange | 91.0 | 41.0 | 104 | | 10 | | Mar. 16 | Nov. 11 | 240 | 6.00 | 3.60 | 3.90 | 3.60 | 5.70 | 6.20 | 5.30 | 4.70 | 5.60 | 4.60 | 5.20 | 5.20 | 59.00 | | |
| Palo Pinto, Mineral Wells | 97.3 | 33.4 | *114 | 1980 | -8 | 1989 | Mar. 23 | Nov. 13 | 233 | 1.42 | 1.99 | 2.69 | 2.75 | 4.59 | 3.25 | 2.25 | 2.34 | 2.80 | 3.81 | 2.16 | 1.74 | 31.79 | 6.65 | 10-1981 |
| Panola, Carthage | 93.7 | 33.9 | *109 | 2000 | *1 | 1989 | Mar. 17 | Nov. 14 | 242 | 4.76 | 3.88 | 4.00 | 4.36 | 5.05 | 4.95 | 3.25 | 2.92 | 3.75 | 4.65 | 4.93 | 5.01 | 51.51 | 9.25 | 04-1991 |
| Parker, Weatherford | 95.2 | 33.9 | *119 | 1980 | *-10 | 1989 | Mar. 29 | Nov. 8 | 223 | 1.50 | 2.36 | 2.79 | 2.84 | 4.76 | 3.93 | 2.11 | 2.60 | 2.85 | 4.19 | 2.61 | 2.16 | 34.70 | 7.05 | 07-1962 |
| Parmer, Friona | 89.8 | 21.7 | *109 | 1994 | -15 | 1963 | Apr. 19 | Oct. 20 | 183 | 0.56 | 0.53 | 0.91 | 0.72 | 2.19 | 2.50 | 2.24 | 2.89 | 2.28 | 1.60 | 0.80 | 0.79 | 18.38 | 3.90 | 10-1998 |
| Pecos, Fort Stockton | 95.8 | 31.4 | 117 | 1994 | -6 | 1985 | Mar. 26 | Nov. 12 | 230 | 0.50 | 0.47 | 0.38 | 0.72 | 1.59 | 1.70 | 1.34 | 1.95 | 2.75 | 1.45 | 0.61 | 0.60 | 14.06 | 5.22 | 10-1986 |
| Polk, Livingston | 94.1 | 35.8 | *111 | 2000 | *3 | 1989 | Mar. 17 | Nov. 13 | 241 | 4.64 | 3.47 | 3.89 | 3.92 | 5.54 | 5.20 | 3.55 | 3.41 | 4.73 | 3.82 | 4.76 | 4.92 | 51.85 | 10.47 | 10-1994 |
| Potter, Amarillo | 91.0 | 22.6 | *108 | 1998 | -14 | 1951 | Apr. 18 | Oct. 20 | 185 | 0.63 | 0.55 | 1.13 | 1.33 | 2.50 | 3.28 | 2.68 | 2.94 | 1.88 | 1.50 | 0.68 | 0.61 | 19.71 | 4.92 | 06-1984 |
| Presidio, Marfa | 88.9 | 23.9 | *106 | 1994 | -2 | 1972 | Apr. 11 | Oct. 30 | 201 | 0.41 | 0.47 | 0.24 | 0.67 | 1.33 | 1.80 | 2.83 | 2.70 | 2.88 | 1.48 | 0.39 | 0.59 | 15.79 | 2.93 | 05-1984 |

| County and Station | TEMPERATURE Mean Max. July (F.) | Mean Min. January (F.) | Record Highest (F.) | Year | Record Lowest (F.) | Year | AVERAGE FREEZE DATES Last in Spring | First in Fall | Growing Season (Days) | MEAN PRECIPITATION January (In.) | February (In.) | March (In.) | April (In.) | May (In.) | June (In.) | July (In.) | August (In.) | September (In.) | October (In.) | November (In.) | December (In.) | Annual (In.) | EXTREMES Highest Daily Rainfall (In.) | Mo.-Year |
|---|---|---|---|---|---|---|---|---|---|---|---|---|---|---|---|---|---|---|---|---|---|---|---|---|
| Presidio, Presidio | 100.8 | 34.5 | *117 | 1960 | 4 | 1962 | Mar. 5 | Nov. 20 | 260 | 0.31 | 0.36 | 0.15 | 0.38 | 0.66 | 1.51 | 2.01 | 1.82 | 1.69 | 0.99 | 0.37 | 0.51 | 10.76 | 3.30 | 04-1979 |
| Rains, Emory | 92.4 | 31.6 | 110 | 1964 | -5 | 1989 | Mar. 22 | Nov. 12 | 234 | 3.04 | 3.34 | 3.88 | 3.72 | 5.31 | 4.19 | 2.33 | 2.23 | 2.98 | 4.66 | 3.89 | 3.93 | 43.50 | 5.65 | 06-1992 |
| Randall, Canyon | 92.6 | 23.7 | *109 | 1981 | -14 | 1951 | Apr. 13 | Oct. 22 | 191 | 0.46 | 0.52 | 0.99 | 1.08 | 2.89 | 2.96 | 2.39 | 2.84 | 1.97 | 1.78 | 0.69 | 0.62 | 19.19 | 7.87 | 08-1968 |
| Reagan, Big Lake | 93.4 | 29.1 | 110 | 1998 | *1 | 1989 | Apr. 1 | Nov. 5 | 218 | 0.68 | 0.92 | 0.81 | 1.42 | 2.39 | 1.99 | 1.79 | 2.18 | 2.97 | 1.92 | 0.88 | 0.84 | 18.79 | 4.85 | 07-1990 |
| Real, Camp Wood | 94.2 | 33.1 | *109 | 2000 | *5 | 1989 | Mar. 22 | Nov. 11 | 233 | 1.11 | 1.44 | 1.55 | 2.41 | 3.16 | 3.68 | 2.09 | 3.07 | 2.87 | 3.46 | 1.77 | 1.38 | 27.99 | 8.37 | 11-2001 |
| Red River, Clarksville | 92.2 | 29.7 | 115 | 1936 | -7 | 1930 | Mar. 28 | Nov. 9 | 226 | 2.65 | 3.17 | 4.50 | 4.02 | 5.43 | 4.00 | 3.23 | 2.07 | 3.83 | 4.99 | 5.43 | 4.51 | 47.83 | 8.30 | 05-1933 |
| Reeves, Balmorhea | 94.7 | 30.1 | 112 | 1939 | -9 | 1933 | Mar. 30 | Nov. 9 | 223 | 0.58 | 0.56 | 0.24 | 0.63 | 1.45 | 1.24 | 1.78 | 2.29 | 3.08 | 1.19 | 0.54 | 0.61 | 14.19 | 4.13 | 07-1973 |
| Reeves, Pecos | 98.5 | 28.1 | 118 | 1968 | -9 | 1962 | Mar. 26 | Nov. 7 | 225 | 0.47 | 0.45 | 0.34 | 0.47 | 1.25 | 1.24 | 1.35 | 1.62 | 2.24 | 1.10 | 0.47 | 0.61 | 11.61 | 4.38 | 05-1992 |
| Refugio, Refugio | 94.0 | 45.0 | 106 | | 8 | | Feb. 14 | Dec. 15 | 304 | 2.20 | 2.20 | 1.50 | 1.90 | 4.30 | 4.80 | 3.30 | 2.40 | 7.00 | 5.20 | 2.30 | 1.60 | 40.10 | 5.58 | 10-1985 |
| Roberts, Miami | 92.4 | 20.6 | 114 | 1917 | *-15 | 1942 | Apr. 15 | Oct. 19 | 186 | 0.68 | 0.83 | 1.74 | 2.19 | 3.77 | 3.26 | 2.39 | 2.40 | 2.38 | 1.64 | 1.12 | 0.90 | 23.30 | 7.48 | 07-1979 |
| Robertson, Franklin | 95.1 | 38.2 | 112 | 2000 | -1 | 1989 | Mar. 9 | Nov. 19 | 254 | 3.03 | 2.86 | 2.90 | 3.03 | 4.81 | 3.26 | 2.04 | 2.60 | 3.65 | 4.38 | 3.26 | 3.52 | 39.03 | | |
| Rockwall, Rockwall | 96.0 | 33.0 | 118 | | -7 | | Mar. 23 | Nov. 14 | 236 | 2.10 | 2.70 | 3.50 | 3.60 | 5.30 | 3.70 | 2.30 | 2.00 | 3.00 | 4.60 | 3.40 | 3.20 | 39.40 | | |
| Runnels, Ballinger | 94.3 | 28.5 | 116 | 1907 | -6 | 1949 | Mar. 28 | Nov. 9 | 225 | 0.94 | 1.32 | 1.27 | 1.80 | 3.38 | 3.15 | 1.39 | 2.40 | 3.08 | 2.52 | 1.31 | 1.20 | 23.76 | 7.05 | 05-1946 |
| Rusk, Henderson | 93.1 | 33.1 | *111 | 2000 | -1 | 1989 | Mar. 20 | Nov. 15 | 239 | 4.08 | 3.78 | 4.00 | 3.91 | 4.73 | 4.87 | 2.81 | 2.75 | 3.71 | 4.68 | 4.67 | 4.23 | 48.22 | 11.05 | 03-1989 |
| Sabine, Hemphill | 93.0 | 36.0 | 104 | | 8 | | Mar. 21 | Nov. 12 | 236 | 5.50 | 4.00 | 5.00 | 4.20 | 5.00 | 5.00 | 3.80 | 3.90 | 3.80 | 3.90 | 5.00 | 6.00 | 54.40 | | |
| San Augustine, Broaddus | 93.0 | 35.0 | 110 | 1998 | 9 | | Mar. 19 | Nov. 12 | 238 | 5.30 | 4.10 | 4.00 | 3.40 | 4.60 | 4.50 | 3.00 | 3.90 | 4.60 | 3.60 | 4.40 | 5.70 | 51.10 | 13.50 | 06-1973 |
| San Jacinto, Coldspring | 93.8 | 37.5 | 110 | 1998 | *3 | 1989 | Mar. 11 | Nov. 22 | 255 | 4.63 | 3.44 | 3.61 | 3.73 | 5.40 | 5.93 | 2.95 | 3.52 | 4.45 | 4.40 | 4.89 | 4.82 | 51.77 | 12.35 | 04-1930 |
| San Patricio, Sinton | 91.7 | 44.2 | 109 | 2000 | 10 | 1989 | Feb. 7 | Dec. 13 | 308 | 1.91 | 2.02 | 1.91 | 1.99 | 4.07 | 3.97 | 2.98 | 3.16 | 5.61 | 4.61 | 2.04 | 1.27 | 35.54 | 11.20 | 10-1969 |
| San Saba, San Saba | 95.8 | 33.4 | 112 | 1978 | -1 | 1989 | Mar. 20 | Nov. 11 | 236 | 1.09 | 1.94 | 1.96 | 2.13 | 3.92 | 3.62 | 1.87 | 2.29 | 2.38 | 2.82 | 2.04 | 1.66 | 27.72 | | |
| Schleicher, Eldorado | 93.0 | 28.0 | 107 | | 3 | | Mar. 28 | Nov. 12 | 229 | 0.70 | 0.90 | 0.70 | 1.70 | 2.50 | 1.90 | 1.60 | 2.10 | 3.10 | 2.10 | 1.00 | 0.60 | 19.00 | | |
| Scurry, Snyder | 94.6 | 26.7 | 115 | 1936 | -11 | 1985 | Apr. 1 | Nov. 7 | 219 | 0.69 | 1.03 | 1.09 | 1.69 | 3.01 | 3.06 | 2.04 | 2.55 | 3.30 | 2.34 | 0.91 | 0.80 | 22.51 | 5.26 | 07-1948 |
| Shackelford, Albany | 95.4 | 28.4 | 116 | 1972 | -8 | 1947 | Mar. 28 | Nov. 6 | 222 | 1.01 | 1.65 | 1.95 | 2.34 | 3.76 | 3.45 | 1.91 | 3.04 | 3.17 | 3.00 | 1.55 | 1.62 | 28.45 | 5.80 | 07-1953 |
| Shelby, Center | 93.9 | 34.9 | 112 | 2000 | 0 | 1951 | Mar. 20 | Nov. 10 | 234 | 5.04 | 4.13 | 4.21 | 4.41 | 5.04 | 4.81 | 2.31 | 3.76 | 4.20 | 4.64 | 4.68 | 5.05 | 53.01 | 9.66 | 11-1940 |
| Sherman, Stratford | 91.1 | 18.5 | *108 | 1953 | *-20 | 1933 | Apr. 26 | Oct. 15 | 171 | 0.48 | 0.44 | 1.21 | 1.46 | 2.85 | 2.26 | 2.20 | 2.67 | 1.71 | 1.15 | 0.79 | 0.56 | 17.89 | 5.60 | 08-1992 |
| Smith, Tyler | 94.0 | 38.0 | 108 | | 0 | | Mar. 7 | Nov. 21 | 259 | 3.30 | 3.70 | 4.00 | 3.70 | 4.50 | 3.70 | 2.20 | 2.60 | 3.30 | 5.10 | 4.50 | 4.80 | 45.40 | | |
| Somervell, Glen Rose | 97.3 | 28.9 | 115 | 1984 | -15 | 1989 | Apr. 11 | Oct. 29 | 200 | 1.64 | 2.28 | 2.80 | 2.91 | 5.20 | 4.02 | 2.19 | 2.18 | 3.15 | 3.83 | 2.24 | 2.38 | 34.82 | 8.48 | 07-1995 |
| Starr, Rio Grande City | 99.1 | 44.5 | 116 | 1998 | 10 | 1962 | Feb. 9 | Dec. 14 | 309 | 0.97 | 1.10 | 0.74 | 1.22 | 2.42 | 2.94 | 1.27 | 1.97 | 4.68 | 2.48 | 0.90 | 0.92 | 21.61 | 12.51 | 09-1967 |
| Stephens, Breckenridge | 96.8 | 30.9 | 114 | 1936 | -7 | 1989 | Mar. 29 | Nov. 10 | 226 | 1.30 | 1.39 | 2.05 | 1.86 | 3.53 | 3.12 | 1.40 | 2.06 | 2.93 | 3.44 | 1.56 | 1.63 | 27.04 | 15.70 | 10-1981 |
| Sterling, Sterling City | 94.7 | 27.4 | 112 | 1994 | -13 | 1985 | Apr. 4 | Nov. 3 | 212 | 0.85 | 0.91 | 0.91 | 1.43 | 2.79 | 2.33 | 1.32 | 1.87 | 3.29 | 1.84 | 0.93 | 0.93 | 19.40 | 6.53 | 07-1948 |
| Stonewall, Aspermont | 97.4 | 27.2 | 117 | 1994 | -10 | 1989 | Mar. 30 | Nov. 8 | 223 | 0.90 | 1.31 | 1.32 | 1.65 | 3.44 | 2.94 | 1.93 | 2.77 | 3.04 | 2.35 | 1.17 | 1.03 | 23.24 | 6.92 | 04-1930 |
| Sutton, Sonora | 94.7 | 27.2 | *109 | 1980 | -8 | 1951 | Apr. 4 | Nov. 3 | 213 | 0.84 | 1.16 | 1.18 | 1.57 | 2.57 | 2.54 | 1.93 | 2.93 | 3.07 | 2.53 | 1.26 | 0.82 | 22.40 | 7.92 | 09-1976 |
| Swisher, Tulia | 91.1 | 22.2 | *110 | 1994 | *-10 | 1951 | Apr. 14 | Oct. 24 | 193 | 0.59 | 0.72 | 1.05 | 1.31 | 2.99 | 3.42 | 2.32 | 2.65 | 2.40 | 1.63 | 0.87 | 0.76 | 20.71 | 5.18 | 06-1985 |
| Tarrant, Benbrook | 96.6 | 31.4 | 111 | 1954 | -6 | 1989 | Mar. 15 | Nov. 17 | 247 | 1.70 | 2.19 | 2.67 | 3.17 | 4.58 | 3.56 | 2.29 | 2.03 | 2.86 | 4.14 | 2.35 | 2.47 | 34.01 | 6.36 | 10-1991 |

| County and Station | July Mean Max. (F) | January Mean Min. (F) | Record Highest (F) | Year | Record Lowest (F) | Year | Last in Spring | First in Fall | Growing Season (Days) | Jan. (In.) | Feb. (In.) | Mar. (In.) | Apr. (In.) | May (In.) | June (In.) | July (In.) | Aug. (In.) | Sept. (In.) | Oct. (In.) | Nov. (In.) | Dec. (In.) | Annual (In.) | Highest Daily Rainfall (In.) | Mo.-Year |
|---|---|---|---|---|---|---|---|---|---|---|---|---|---|---|---|---|---|---|---|---|---|---|---|---|
| Taylor, Abilene | 94.8 | 31.8 | 110 | 1978 | *–7 | 1989 | Mar. 24 | Nov. 12 | 232 | 0.97 | 1.13 | 1.41 | 1.67 | 2.83 | 3.06 | 1.70 | 2.63 | 2.91 | 2.90 | 1.30 | 1.27 | 23.78 | 6.30 | 08-1978 |
| Terrell, Sanderson | 91.9 | 30.5 | 110 | 1969 | 3 | 1989 | Mar. 22 | Nov. 10 | 233 | 0.39 | 0.59 | 0.40 | 0.86 | 1.74 | 2.09 | 1.52 | 1.87 | 2.41 | 1.75 | 0.81 | 0.51 | 14.94 | 5.35 | 06-1965 |
| Terry, Brownfield | 92.5 | 26.1 | *111 | 1994 | *–8 | 1963 | Apr. 3 | Nov. 3 | 213 | 0.54 | 0.68 | 0.64 | 0.95 | 2.90 | 3.00 | 1.80 | 2.15 | 2.78 | 1.50 | 0.79 | 0.65 | 18.89 | 5.05 | 10-1983 |
| Throckmorton, Throckmorton | 97.0 | 28.0 | 114 | | –11 | | Mar. 31 | Nov. 6 | 220 | 1.00 | 1.50 | 1.60 | 2.10 | 3.30 | 3.50 | 1.80 | 2.60 | 3.30 | 2.90 | 1.50 | 1.50 | 26.60 | | |
| Titus, Mount Pleasant | 94.2 | 29.3 | 118 | 1936 | –12 | 1951 | Mar. 29 | Nov. 5 | 220 | 3.27 | 3.54 | 4.42 | 3.77 | 5.02 | 4.89 | 3.75 | 2.05 | 3.56 | 4.74 | 5.07 | 4.49 | 48.57 | 8.06 | 11-1994 |
| Tom Green, San Angelo | 94.4 | 31.8 | 111 | 1960 | –4 | 1989 | Mar. 28 | Nov. 13 | 230 | 0.82 | 1.18 | 0.99 | 1.60 | 3.09 | 2.52 | 1.10 | 2.05 | 2.95 | 2.57 | 1.10 | 0.94 | 20.91 | 6.24 | 09-1980 |
| Travis, Austin | 95.0 | 40.0 | 112 | 2000 | –2 | 1949 | Feb. 17 | Dec. 6 | 291 | 1.89 | 1.99 | 2.14 | 2.51 | 5.03 | 3.81 | 1.97 | 2.31 | 2.91 | 3.97 | 2.68 | 2.44 | 33.65 | 8.00 | 06-1941 |
| Trinity, Groveton | 94.8 | 37.1 | 111 | 2000 | 1 | 1989 | Mar. 14 | Nov. 14 | 244 | 4.17 | 3.21 | 3.67 | 3.13 | 5.11 | 5.01 | 3.48 | 3.25 | 4.10 | 4.07 | 4.49 | 4.41 | 48.10 | 7.12 | 10-1994 |
| Tyler, Town Bluff Dam | 92.1 | 38.3 | 109 | 2000 | 6 | 1989 | Mar. 9 | Nov. 19 | 255 | 4.17 | 4.02 | 4.56 | 4.41 | 5.61 | 5.74 | 3.46 | 2.50 | 4.17 | 3.68 | 5.56 | 5.56 | 54.79 | 7.50 | 09-1996 |
| Upshur, Gilmer | 93.4 | 31.4 | 114 | 1936 | *–4 | 1989 | Mar. 29 | Nov. 5 | 220 | 3.51 | 3.58 | 4.38 | 4.12 | 4.41 | 4.13 | 3.04 | 2.50 | 3.84 | 4.47 | 4.75 | 4.35 | 47.08 | 7.88 | 04-1966 |
| Upton, McCamey | 95.6 | 33.1 | *113 | 1994 | –2 | 1962 | Mar. 20 | Nov. 12 | 236 | 0.47 | 0.56 | 0.41 | 0.93 | 1.61 | 1.55 | 0.94 | 1.95 | 2.68 | 2.06 | 0.59 | 0.70 | 14.45 | 9.13 | 10-1986 |
| Uvalde, Uvalde | 96.0 | 37.0 | 111 | | 6 | | Mar. 10 | Nov. 21 | 255 | 1.00 | 1.10 | 1.00 | 2.00 | 3.30 | 3.50 | 1.20 | 2.60 | 2.30 | 2.40 | 1.60 | 1.30 | 23.30 | | |
| Val Verde, Del Rio | 96.2 | 39.7 | 112 | 1988 | 10 | 1989 | Feb. 19 | Dec. 1 | 284 | 0.57 | 0.96 | 0.96 | 1.71 | 2.31 | 2.34 | 2.02 | 2.26 | 2.06 | 2.00 | 0.96 | 0.75 | 18.80 | 17.03 | 08-1998 |
| Van Zandt, Wills Point | 93.3 | 31.4 | 115 | 1909 | *–2 | 1989 | Mar. 14 | Nov. 18 | 248 | 3.41 | 3.22 | 3.74 | 2.62 | 4.74 | 4.45 | 2.16 | 2.26 | 3.39 | 4.78 | 4.23 | 3.93 | 43.68 | 7.08 | 06-1945 |
| Victoria, Victoria | 93.4 | 43.6 | 111 | 2000 | 9 | 1989 | Feb. 9 | Dec. 11 | 305 | 2.44 | 2.04 | 2.25 | 2.97 | 5.12 | 4.96 | 2.90 | 3.05 | 5.00 | 4.26 | 2.64 | 2.47 | 40.10 | 9.87 | 04-1991 |
| Walker, Huntsville | 93.8 | 39.0 | 108 | 2000 | 2 | 1989 | Feb. 23 | Nov. 30 | 279 | 4.28 | 3.14 | 3.47 | 3.50 | 5.08 | 4.66 | 2.67 | 3.69 | 4.73 | 4.32 | 4.87 | 4.10 | 48.51 | 10.21 | 10-1994 |
| Waller, Hempstead | 95.0 | 38.0 | 107 | | 13 | | Feb. 28 | Dec. 4 | 283 | 2.80 | 2.90 | 2.10 | 3.90 | 4.70 | 3.60 | 3.01 | 2.40 | 4.60 | 4.00 | 3.20 | 3.00 | 38.20 | | |
| Ward, Monahans | 98.6 | 26.5 | *118 | 1994 | –9 | 1962 | Apr. 1 | Nov. 7 | 219 | 0.51 | 0.57 | 0.27 | 0.55 | 1.80 | 1.43 | 1.31 | 1.65 | 2.55 | 1.39 | 0.67 | 0.53 | 13.23 | 4.40 | 09-1980 |
| Washington, Brenham | 96.7 | 39.3 | 113 | 2000 | *–2 | 1930 | Feb. 20 | Dec. 5 | 288 | 3.41 | 2.78 | 2.93 | 2.68 | 5.14 | 4.66 | 1.93 | 2.54 | 4.83 | 4.48 | 4.17 | 3.29 | 44.15 | 10.38 | 10-1994 |
| Webb, Laredo | 101.6 | 43.7 | *114 | 1998 | 11 | 1983 | Feb. 9 | Dec. 5 | 299 | 0.76 | 0.94 | 0.92 | 1.55 | 2.73 | 2.99 | 1.79 | 2.42 | 2.73 | 2.72 | 1.13 | 0.85 | 21.53 | 6.65 | 07-1981 |
| Wharton, Pierce | 94.3 | 41.8 | 112 | 2000 | 4 | 1949 | Feb. 19 | Dec. 6 | 290 | 3.42 | 2.84 | 2.74 | 3.18 | 5.18 | 4.69 | 3.10 | 3.57 | 5.81 | 4.61 | 3.55 | 3.23 | 45.92 | 8.85 | 11-1943 |
| Wheeler, Shamrock | 93.3 | 22.9 | 113 | 1980 | –13 | 1984 | Apr. 6 | Oct. 27 | 203 | 0.56 | 0.84 | 1.88 | 2.19 | 3.92 | 3.74 | 2.17 | 2.27 | 2.83 | 1.92 | 1.17 | 0.83 | 24.32 | 8.24 | 06-1995 |
| Wichita, Wichita Falls | 97.2 | 28.9 | 117 | 1980 | –12 | 1947 | Mar. 28 | Nov. 9 | 225 | 1.12 | 1.58 | 2.27 | 2.62 | 3.92 | 3.69 | 1.58 | 2.39 | 3.19 | 3.11 | 1.68 | 1.68 | 28.83 | 6.19 | 09-1980 |
| Wilbarger, Vernon | 97.2 | 25.7 | 119 | 1943 | –9 | 1989 | Mar. 30 | Nov. 9 | 223 | 1.34 | 1.34 | 1.98 | 2.36 | 4.11 | 3.82 | 1.94 | 3.07 | 3.54 | 2.70 | 1.48 | 1.12 | 28.55 | 14.82 | 08-1995 |
| Willacy, Raymondville | 95.3 | 47.5 | 109 | 1916 | *14 | 1962 | Jan. 19 | Jan. 1 | 347 | 1.36 | 1.59 | 1.44 | 1.53 | 2.80 | 3.22 | 1.91 | 3.06 | 5.40 | 3.17 | 1.38 | 1.11 | 27.97 | 9.90 | 09-1975 |
| Williamson, Taylor | 95.3 | 35.8 | *112 | 2000 | –5 | 1949 | Mar. 5 | Nov. 20 | 259 | 2.09 | 2.38 | 2.63 | 2.68 | 5.19 | 3.78 | 1.62 | 2.09 | 3.30 | 3.83 | 2.95 | 2.57 | 35.11 | *6.00 | 06-1958 |
| Wilson, Floresville | 95.7 | 38.4 | 111 | 2000 | 5 | 1985 | Mar. 8 | Nov. 21 | 257 | 1.58 | 1.60 | 1.65 | 0.53 | 3.69 | 3.24 | 1.60 | 2.54 | 2.61 | 2.75 | 2.24 | 1.57 | 27.60 | 9.25 | 09-1967 |
| Winkler, Wink | 96.1 | 27.8 | 117 | 1994 | –14 | 1962 | Mar. 2 | Nov. 7 | 215 | 0.41 | 0.48 | 0.32 | 0.53 | 1.34 | 1.83 | 1.95 | 2.50 | 2.14 | 1.51 | 0.55 | 0.57 | 12.92 | 5.64 | 10-1940 |
| Wise, Bridgeport | 96.1 | 30.5 | *115 | 1980 | –8 | 1989 | Mar. 30 | Nov. 7 | 222 | 1.53 | 2.06 | 2.63 | 2.83 | 5.53 | 3.54 | 1.29 | 2.01 | 2.97 | 4.37 | 2.28 | 2.01 | 34.02 | 9.07 | 10-1919 |
| Wood, Mineola | 98.0 | 31.2 | *110 | 2000 | 1 | 1983 | Apr. 1 | Nov. 6 | 219 | 3.33 | 3.43 | 4.05 | 3.98 | 4.71 | 3.99 | 2.92 | 2.23 | 3.67 | 4.99 | 4.50 | 4.08 | 45.88 | 6.42 | 12-1982 |
| Yoakum, Plains | 93.1 | 25.1 | 111 | 1994 | *–12 | 1951 | Apr. 5 | Oct. 29 | 206 | 0.49 | 0.72 | 0.60 | 1.15 | 2.38 | 2.55 | 2.34 | 2.75 | 2.67 | 1.24 | 0.75 | 0.77 | 18.41 | 6.11 | 07-1960 |
| Young, Graham | 91.7 | 27.1 | 117 | 1936 | *–8 | 1989 | Apr. 2 | Nov. 6 | 217 | 1.16 | 1.79 | 2.22 | 2.45 | 4.52 | 3.60 | 2.17 | 2.32 | 3.64 | 3.79 | 1.88 | 1.81 | 31.35 | 8.22 | 10-1981 |
| Zapata, Zapata | 96.6 | 45.4 | 116 | 1998 | 11 | 1911 | Jan. 24 | Dec. 25 | 337 | 1.04 | 0.79 | 0.79 | 1.39 | 1.80 | 2.67 | 1.55 | 2.03 | 3.65 | 1.85 | 0.94 | 0.88 | 19.53 | 6.10 | 04-1966 |
| Zavala, Crystal City | 98.0 | 42.6 | 115 | 2000 | *11 | 1989 | Feb. 16 | Dec. 6 | 292 | 0.93 | 1.08 | 1.08 | 1.75 | 2.41 | 3.25 | 1.67 | 2.03 | 2.10 | 2.44 | 1.12 | 0.84 | 20.70 | 6.83 | 10-1959 |

# Calendar

*Blue sky reflects in the primary mirror of the Hobby-Eberly Telescope at McDonald Observatory atop Mount Fowlkes in the Davis Mountains. One of the world's largest optical telescopes, the HET's mirror is 36 feet and made of 91 segments. It is used for spectroscopy and the study of light from stars and galaxies. Photo by Martin Harris; McDonald Observatory.*

**Seasons**
**Morning and Evening Stars**
**Eclipses, Major Meteor Showers**
**Chronological Eras and Cycles**
**Calendars for 2016 and 2017**

# Astronomical Calendars for 2016 & 2017

## An Explanation of Texas Time

The subsequent calendars were calculated principally from data on the **U.S. Naval Observatory's website** (http://www.usno.navy.mil/USNO) and from its publications ***Astronomical Phenomena for 2016*** and ***Astronomical Phenomena for 2017.***

Times listed here are **Central Standard Time,** except for the period from 2:00 a.m. on the second Sunday in March until 2:00 a.m. on the first Sunday in November, when **Daylight Saving Time,** which is one hour later than Central Standard Time, is in effect.

All of Texas is in the Central Time Zone, except El Paso and Hudspeth counties and the northwest corner of Culberson County, which observe Mountain Time. Mountain Time is one hour earlier than Central Time.

**All times are calculated for the intersection of 99° 20' west longitude and 31° 08' north latitude,** which is closest to the **town of Mercury** and is about 15 miles northeast of Brady, McCulloch County. This point is the **approximate geographical center** of the state.

### How to Adjust Rise & Set Times

To adjust the time of sunrise or sunset, moonrise or moonset for any point in Texas, apply the following rule: **Add four minutes** to the time given in this calendar for each degree of longitude that the place lies west of the 99th meridian; **subtract four minutes** for each degree of longitude the place lies east of the 99th meridian.

At times there will be considerable variation for distances north and south of the line of 31° 08' north latitude, but the rule for calculating it is complicated. The formula given above will get sufficiently close results.

The **accompanying map** shows the intersection for which all times given here are calculated, with some major Texas cities and their longitudes. These make it convenient to calculate time at any given point.

### Planetary Configurations & Phenomena

The phenomena and planetary configurations of the heavens for 2016 and 2017 are given in the center column of the calendars on pages 164–171. Below is an explanation of the symbols used in those tables:

| | | |
|---|---|---|
| ⊙ The Sun | ● The Earth | ⛢ Uranus |
| ☾ The Moon | ♂ Mars | ♆ Neptune |
| ☿ Mercury | ♃ Jupiter | ♇ Pluto |
| ♀ Venus | ♄ Saturn | |

### Aspects: Conjunction & Opposition

☌ This symbol, appearing between symbols for heavenly bodies, means they are **"in conjunction,"** that is, having the same longitude in the sky and appearing near each other. For example, ♀ ☌ ☾ means Venus is **north** or **south** of the moon by a few degrees. Conjunctions listed in this calendar are separated by **10 degrees** or less. **Inferior** and **superior conjuctions** mean an inner plant, Venus or Mercury, is in line with the Sun, either between the Earth and the Sun **(inferior)** or on the opposite side of the Sun **(superior).**

☍ This symbol means that the heavenly body listed is in **"opposition"** to the Sun, or that they differ by 180 degrees of longitude.

### Common Astronomical Terms

★ **Aphelion** — Point at which a planet's orbit is farthest from the sun.

★ **Perihelion** — Point at which a planet's orbit is nearest the sun.

★ **Apogee** — That point of the moon's orbit farthest from the earth.

★ **Perigee** — That point of the moon's orbit nearest the earth.

## The Seasons

### 2016

**Spring** — Saturday, **March 19,** at 11:30 p.m. (CDT);
**Summer** — Monday, **June 20,** at 5:34 p.m. (CDT);
**Autumn** — Thursday, **Sept. 22,** at 9:21 a.m. (CDT);
**Winter** — Wednesday, **Dec. 21,** at 4:44 a.m. (CST).

### 2017

**Spring** — Monday, **March 20,** at 5:29 a.m. (CDT);
**Summer** — Tuesday, **June 20,** at 11:24 p.m. (CDT);
**Autumn** — Friday, **Sept. 22,** at 3:02 p.m. (CDT);
**Winter** — Thursday, **Dec. 21,** at 10:28 a.m. (CST).

## Morning & Evening Stars

### Morning Stars, 2016

**Venus** ♀ — Jan. 1 – April 30
**Mars** ♂ — Jan. 1 – May 22
**Jupiter** ♃ — Jan. 1 – March 8; Oct. 10 – Dec. 31
**Saturn** ♄ — Jan. 1 – June 3; Dec. 28 – Dec. 31

### Evening Stars, 2016

**Venus** ♀ — July 14 – Dec. 31
**Mars** ♂ — May 22 – Dec. 31
**Jupiter** ♃ — March 8 – Sept. 13
**Saturn** ♄ — June 3 – Nov. 23

### Morning Stars, 2017

**Venus** ♀ — March 30 – Nov. 28
**Mars** ♂ — Sept. 12 – Dec. 31
**Jupiter** ♃ — Jan. 1 – April 7; Nov. 9 – Dec. 31
**Saturn** ♄ — Jan. 1 – June 15

### Evening Stars, 2017

**Venus** ♀ — Jan. 1 – March 22
**Mars** ♂ — Jan. 1 – June 7
**Jupiter** ♃ — April 7 – Oct.13
**Saturn** ♄ — June 15 – Dec. 5

## Major Meteor Showers

These are **approximate dates.** Listen to local news/weather broadcasts several days beforehand to determine peak observation days and hours. Generally, viewing is best between midnight and dawn of the date listed.

*Meteor shower dates are provided by McDonald Observatory, The University of Texas at Austin.*

| Meteor Shower | Peak 2016 | Peak 2017 |
|---|---|---|
| Quadrantid | Jan. 3 | Jan. 4 |
| Lyrid | April 21 | April 22 |
| Eta Aquarid | May 5 | May 6 |
| Perseid | Aug. 12 | Aug. 13 |
| Orionid | Oct. 21 | Oct. 22 |
| Leonid | Nov. 17 | Nov. 18 |
| Geminid | Dec. 13 | Dec. 14 |

## Eclipses

### 2016

**March 8–9 — Sun, total eclipse**, visible in eastern Asia, northern and western Australasia, north Oceania.

**March 23 — Moon, penumbral eclipse**, visible in North America, west South America, Australasia, Asia.

**May 9 — Transit of Mercury,** visible in the North and South America, most of Asia, Europe, Africa, Greenland, Pacific Ocean.

**Aug. 18 — Moon, penumbral eclipse**, visible in North America, most of South America, Oceania, Australasia, easternmost Asia.

**Sept. 1 — Sun, annular eclipse**, visible in Africa, Madagascar, Antarctica.

**Sept. 16 — Moon, penumbral eclipse**, visible in Australasia, Asia, Africa, Europe, east South America.

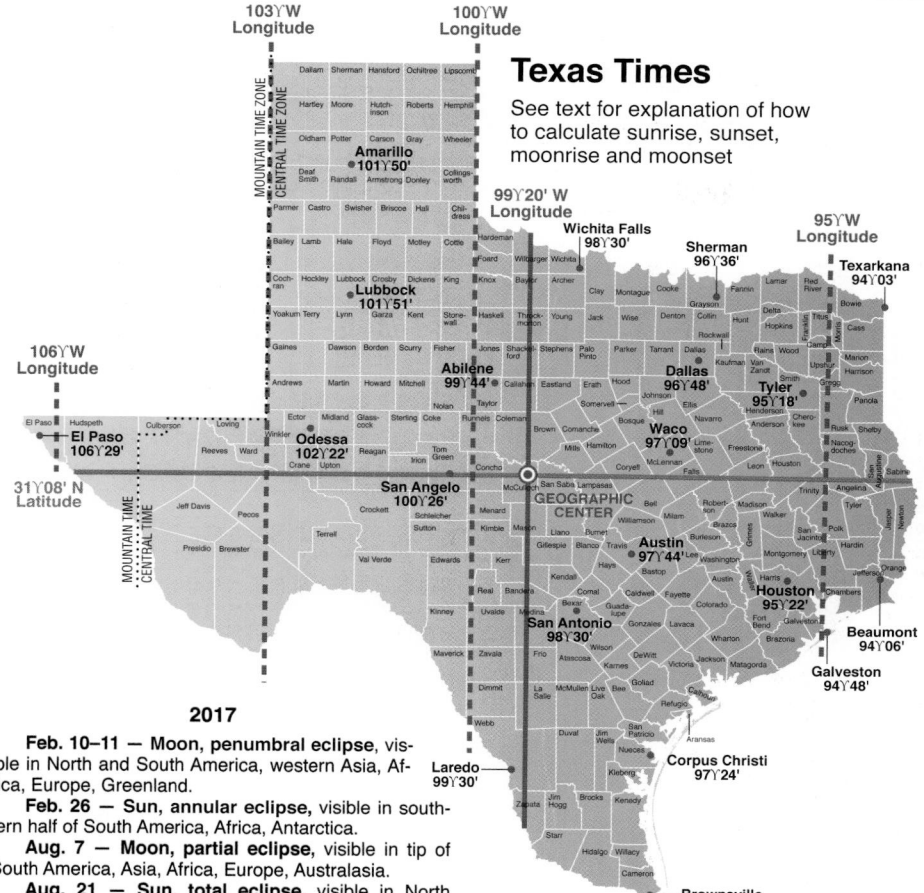

# Texas Times

See text for explanation of how to calculate sunrise, sunset, moonrise and moonset

**103ϓW Longitude**

**100ϓW Longitude**

Amarillo 101ϓ50'

**99ϓ20' W Longitude**

Wichita Falls 98ϓ30'

Sherman 96ϓ36'

**95ϓW Longitude**

Texarkana 94ϓ03'

Lubbock 101ϓ51'

**106ϓW Longitude**

Abilene 99ϓ44'

Dallas 96ϓ48'

Tyler 95ϓ18'

El Paso 106ϓ29'

Odessa 102ϓ22'

Waco 97ϓ09'

**31ϓ08' N Latitude**

San Angelo 100ϓ26'

GEOGRAPHIC CENTER

Austin 97ϓ44'

Houston 95ϓ22'

San Antonio 98ϓ30'

Beaumont 94ϓ06'

Galveston 94ϓ48'

Laredo 99ϓ30'

Corpus Christi 97ϓ24'

Brownsville 97ϓ30'

## 2017

**Feb. 10–11 — Moon, penumbral eclipse,** visible in North and South America, western Asia, Africa, Europe, Greenland.

**Feb. 26 — Sun, annular eclipse,** visible in southern half of South America, Africa, Antarctica.

**Aug. 7 — Moon, partial eclipse,** visible in tip of South America, Asia, Africa, Europe, Australasia.

**Aug. 21 — Sun, total eclipse,** visible in North America, Hawaii, Central America, north South America, western Europe and West Africa.

## Chronological Eras & Cycles

### Chronological Eras, 2016

The year 2016 of the **Christian** era comprises the latter part of the 240th and the beginning of the 241st year of the independence of the United States of America, and corresponds to the year 6729 of the Julian period. All dates, below, are given in terms of the Gregorian calendar, in which Jan. 14, 2016, corresponds to Jan. 1, 2016, of the Julian calendar:

| Era | Year | Begins |
|---|---|---|
| Byzantine | 7525 | Sept. 14 |
| Jewish (A.M.)* | 5777 | Oct. 2 |
| Chinese (bǐng shēn) | 4653 | Feb. 8 |
| Roman (A.U.C.) | 2769 | Jan. 14 |
| Nabonassar | 2765 | April 19 |
| Japanese | 2676 | Jan. 1 |
| Grecian (Seleucidæ) | 2328 | Sept. 14 or Oct. 14 |
| Indian (Saka) | 1938 | March 21 |
| Diocletian (Coptic) | 1733 | Sept. 11 |
| Islamic (Hegira)* | 1438 | Oct. 2 |

*Year begins at sunset.

### Chronological Cycles, 2016

Dominical Letter........CB  Julian Period ............ 6729
Epact .........................21 .. Roman Indiction ..................9

Golden Number or
  Lunar Cycle ..........III     Solar Cycle...................9

### Chronological Eras, 2017

The year 2017 of the **Christian** era comprises the latter part of the 241st and the beginning of the 242nd year of the independence of the United States of America, and corresponds to the year 6730 of the Julian period. All dates, below, are given in terms of the Gregorian calendar, in which Jan. 14, 2017, corresponds to Jan. 1, 2017, of the Julian calendar:

| Era | Year | Begins |
|---|---|---|
| Byzantine | 7526 | Sept. 14 |
| Jewish (A.M.)* | 5778 | Sept. 20 |
| Chinese (dīng yǒu) | 4654 | Jan. 28 |
| Roman (A.U.C.) | 2770 | Jan. 14 |
| Nabonassar | 2766 | April 19 |
| Japanese | 2677 | Jan. 1 |
| Grecian (Seleucidæ) | 2329 | Sept. 14 or Oct. 14 |
| Indian (Saka) | 1939 | March 22 |
| Diocletian (Coptic) | 1734 | Sept. 11 |
| Islamic (Hegira)* | 1439 | Sept. 21 |

*Year begins at sunset.

### Chronological Cycles, 2017

Dominical Letter........A      Julian Period ........... 6730
Epact ..........................2    Roman Indiction..............10
Golden Number or
  Lunar Cycle ......... IV      Solar Cycle...................10

# 2016

Times are **Central Standard Time**, except from **March 13 to Nov. 6,** during which **Daylight Saving Time** is observed. **Boldface times for moonrise and moonset indicate p.m.** Times are figured for the point **99° 20' West and 31° 08' North,** the approximate geographical center of the state. **See page 162** for explanation of **how to get the approximate time at any other Texas point.** (On the web: http://www.usno.navy.mil/astronomy) Please note: Not all eclipses are visible in United States. For visibility, see listing beginning on **page 162.**

## 1st Month — January 2016 — 31 Days

**Moon Phases** — *Last Qtr.,* Jan. 1, 11:30 p.m.; *New,* Jan. 9, 7:31 p.m.; *First Qtr.,* Jan. 16, 5:26 p.m.; *Full,* Jan. 23, 7:46 p.m.; *Last Qtr.,* Jan. 31, 9:28 p.m.

| Year (Month) | Month (Day) | Week | Planetary Configurations and Phenomena | Sunrise | Sunset | Moonrise | Moonset |
|---|---|---|---|---|---|---|---|
| 1 | 1 | Fr. | Last qtr. ☾ | 7:36 | 5:46 | | **12:13** |
| 2 | 2 | Sa. | ● perihelion; ☾ apogee | 7:36 | 5:47 | 12:46 | **12:46** |
| 3 | 3 | Su. | | 7:36 | 5:47 | 1:38 | **1:20** |
| 4 | 4 | Mo. | | 7:36 | 5:48 | 2:31 | **1:56** |
| 5 | 5 | Tu. | | 7:36 | 5:49 | 3:24 | **2:34** |
| 6 | 6 | We. | | 7:37 | 5:50 | 4:18 | **3:17** |
| 7 | 7 | Th. | | 7:37 | 5:50 | 5:13 | **4:05** |
| 8 | 8 | Fr. | | 7:37 | 5:51 | 6:07 | **4:57** |
| 9 | 9 | Sa. | New ☾ | 7:37 | 5:52 | 7:01 | **5:57** |
| 10 | 10 | Su. | | 7:37 | 5:53 | 7:51 | **6:53** |
| 11 | 11 | Mo. | | 7:37 | 5:54 | 8:39 | **7:53** |
| 12 | 12 | Tu. | | 7:37 | 5:55 | 9:24 | **8:59** |
| 13 | 13 | We. | | 7:37 | 5:55 | 10:07 | **10:03** |
| 14 | 14 | Th. | ☾ at perigee (8 pm) | 7:37 | 5:56 | 10:48 | **11:06** |
| 15 | 15 | Fr. | | 7:36 | 5:57 | 11:28 | |
| 16 | 16 | Sa. | First qtr. ☾; ♄ ☌ ☾ | 7:36 | 5:58 | **12:09** | 12:09 |
| 17 | 17 | Su. | | 7:36 | 5:59 | **12:51** | 1:13 |
| 18 | 18 | Mo. | | 7:36 | 6:00 | 1:36 | 2:16 |
| 19 | 19 | Tu. | Aldebaran ☌ ☾ (9 pm) | 7:36 | 6:01 | 2:24 | 3:18 |
| 20 | 20 | We. | | 7:35 | 6:02 | 3:15 | 4:19 |
| 21 | 21 | Th. | | 7:35 | 6:02 | 4:10 | 5:17 |
| 22 | 22 | Fr. | | 7:35 | 6:03 | 5:06 | **6:11** |
| 23 | 23 | Sa. | Full ☾ | 7:34 | 6:04 | 6:03 | **7:00** |
| 24 | 24 | Su. | | 7:34 | 6:05 | 7:00 | **7:45** |
| 25 | 25 | Mo. | | 7:33 | 6:06 | 7:56 | **8:26** |
| 26 | 26 | Tu. | | 7:33 | 6:08 | 8:51 | **9:03** |
| 27 | 27 | We. | ♃ ☌ ☾ (7 pm) | 7:32 | 6:09 | 9:44 | **9:38** |
| 28 | 28 | Th. | | 7:32 | 6:10 | 10:37 | **10:12** |
| 29 | 29 | Fr. | | 7:31 | 6:11 | 11:29 | **10:45** |
| 30 | 30 | Sa. | ☾ apogee (3 am) | 7:31 | 6:11 | | **11:18** |
| 31 | 31 | Su. | Last qtr. ☾ | 7:30 | 6:11 | 12:21 | **11:53** |

## 2nd Month — February 2016 — 29 Days

**Moon Phases** — *New,* Feb. 8, 8:39 a.m.; *First Qtr.,* Feb. 15, 1:46 a.m.; *Full,* Feb. 22, 12:20 p.m.

| Year (Month) | Month (Day) | Week | Planetary Configurations and Phenomena | Sunrise | Sunset | Moonrise | Moonset |
|---|---|---|---|---|---|---|---|
| 32 | 1 | Mo. | ♂ ☌ ☾ (3 am) | 7:30 | 6:12 | 1:13 | **12:30** |
| 33 | 2 | Tu. | | 7:29 | 6:13 | 2:06 | **1:10** |
| 34 | 3 | We. | | 7:28 | 6:14 | 3:00 | **1:55** |
| 35 | 4 | Th. | | 7:28 | 6:15 | 3:54 | **2:44** |
| 36 | 5 | Fr. | | 7:27 | 6:16 | 4:47 | **3:38** |
| 37 | 6 | Sa. | | 7:26 | 6:17 | 5:39 | **4:36** |
| 38 | 7 | Su. | | 7:26 | 6:18 | 6:29 | **5:38** |
| 39 | 8 | Mo. | New ☾ | 7:25 | 6:19 | 7:16 | **6:43** |
| 40 | 9 | Tu. | ♆ ☌ ☾ (6 pm) | 7:24 | 6:19 | 8:01 | **7:48** |
| 41 | 10 | We. | ☾ at perigee (9 pm) | 7:23 | 6:20 | 8:45 | **8:54** |
| 42 | 11 | Th. | | 7:22 | 6:21 | 9:27 | **10:00** |
| 43 | 12 | Fr. | | 7:22 | 6:21 | 10:08 | **11:05** |
| 44 | 13 | Sa. | | 7:21 | 6:23 | 10:51 | |
| 45 | 14 | Su. | | 7:20 | 6:24 | 11:36 | **12:09** |
| 46 | 15 | Mo. | First qtr. ☾ | 7:19 | 6:24 | **12:22** | 1:12 |
| 47 | 16 | Tu. | Aldebaran ☌ ☾ (2 am) | 7:18 | 6:25 | 1:12 | 2:13 |
| 48 | 17 | We. | | 7:17 | 6:26 | 2:05 | 3:11 |
| 49 | 18 | Th. | | 7:16 | 6:27 | 2:59 | 4:05 |
| 50 | 19 | Fr. | | 7:15 | 6:28 | 3:55 | 4:55 |
| 51 | 20 | Sa. | | 7:14 | 6:28 | 4:51 | 5:41 |
| 52 | 21 | Su. | | 7:13 | 6:29 | 5:47 | **6:23** |
| 53 | 22 | Mo. | Full ☾ | 7:12 | 6:30 | 6:42 | **7:01** |
| 54 | 23 | Tu. | ♃ ☌ ☾ (10 pm) | 7:11 | 6:31 | 7:35 | **7:37** |
| 55 | 24 | We. | | 7:10 | 6:32 | 8:28 | **8:11** |
| 56 | 25 | Th. | | 7:09 | 6:32 | 9:21 | **8:45** |
| 57 | 26 | Fr. | ☾ at apogee (9 pm) | 7:08 | 6:33 | **10:12** | 9:18 |
| 58 | 27 | Sa. | | 7:07 | 6:34 | **11:04** | 9:52 |
| 59 | 28 | Su. | | 7:06 | 6:35 | **11:57** | 10:28 |
| 60 | 29 | Mo. | | 7:04 | 6:35 | | 11:06 |

## 3rd Month — March 2016 — 31 Days

**Moon Phases** — *Last Qtr.,* March 1, 5:11 p.m.; *New,* March 8, 7:54 p.m.; *First Qtr.,* March 15, 12:03 p.m.; *Full,* March 23, 7:01 a.m.; *Last Qtr.,* March 31, 10:17 a.m.

| Year (Month) | Month (Day) | Week | Planetary Configurations and Phenomena | Sunrise | Sunset | Moonrise | Moonset |
|---|---|---|---|---|---|---|---|
| 61 | 1 | Tu. | Last qtr. ☾ | 7:03 | 6:36 | **12:49** | 11:48 |
| 62 | 2 | We. | ♄ ☌ ☾ (1 am) | 7:02 | 6:37 | 1:42 | **12:34** |
| 63 | 3 | Th. | | 7:01 | 6:38 | 2:34 | **1:24** |
| 64 | 4 | Fr. | | 7:00 | 6:39 | 3:26 | **2:19** |
| 65 | 5 | Sa. | | 6:59 | 6:39 | 4:16 | **3:18** |
| 66 | 6 | Su. | | 6:58 | 6:40 | 5:04 | **4:21** |
| 67 | 7 | Mo. | ♀ ☌ ☾ (5 am) | 6:56 | 6:40 | 5:50 | **5:26** |
| 68 | 8 | Tu. | New ☾ | 6:55 | 6:41 | 6:35 | **6:33** |
| 69 | 9 | We. | | 6:54 | 6:42 | 7:18 | **7:41** |
| 70 | 10 | Th. | ☾ at perigee. ♆ ☌ ☾ | 6:53 | 6:43 | 8:01 | **8:48** |
| 71 | 11 | Fr. | | 6:52 | 6:43 | 8:45 | **9:56** |
| 72 | 12 | Sa. | | 6:50 | 6:44 | 9:31 | **11:02** |
| 73 | †13 | Su. | DST begins | 7:49 | 7:45 | 11:18 | **12:02** |
| 74 | 14 | Mo. | | 7:48 | 7:45 | **12:09** | 1:05 |
| 75 | 15 | Tu. | First qtr. ☾ | 7:47 | 7:46 | **12:09** | 2:06 |
| 76 | 16 | We. | | 7:45 | 7:47 | 1:55 | 3:02 |
| 77 | 17 | Th. | | 7:44 | 7:47 | 2:51 | 3:53 |
| 78 | 18 | Fr. | | 7:43 | 7:48 | **3:46** | 4:40 |
| 79 | 19 | Sa. | Equinox (11:30 pm) | 7:42 | 7:49 | **4:41** | 5:22 |
| 80 | 20 | Su. | | 7:40 | 7:49 | 5:36 | 6:01 |
| 81 | 21 | Mo. | ♃ ☌ ☾ (11 pm) | 7:39 | 7:50 | **6:29** | 6:37 |
| 82 | 22 | Tu. | | 7:38 | 7:51 | **7:22** | 7:12 |
| 83 | 23 | We. | Full ☾; Eclipse ☾ | 7:37 | 7:51 | **8:14** | 7:45 |
| 84 | 24 | Th. | | 7:35 | 7:52 | **9:06** | 8:18 |
| 85 | 25 | Fr. | ☾ at apogee (9 am) | 7:34 | 7:52 | **9:58** | 8:52 |
| 86 | 26 | Sa. | | 7:33 | 7:53 | **10:51** | 9:27 |
| 87 | 27 | Su. | | 7:32 | 7:54 | **11:43** | 10:05 |
| 88 | 28 | Mo. | | 7:30 | 7:54 | | 10:45 |
| 89 | 29 | Tu. | | 7:29 | 7:55 | **12:35** | 11:28 |
| 90 | 30 | We. | | 7:28 | 7:56 | 1:26 | **12:16** |
| 91 | 31 | Th. | Last qtr. ☾ | 7:27 | 7:56 | 2:17 | **1:07** |

*† Daylight Saving Time begins at 2 a.m.*

# Astronomical Calendar for 2016

## 4th Month — April 2016 — 30 Days

Moon Phases — New, April 7, 6:24 a.m.; First Qtr., April 13, 10:59 p.m.; Full, April 22, 12:24 a.m.; Last Qtr., April 29, 10:29 p.m.

| Year | Month | Week | Planetary Configurations and Phenomena | Sunrise | Sunset | Moon-rise | Moon-set |
|---|---|---|---|---|---|---|---|
| 92 | 1 | Fr. | | 7:25 | 7:57 | 3:06 | 2:03 |
| 93 | 2 | Sa. | | 7:24 | 7:58 | 3:54 | 3:02 |
| 94 | 3 | Su. | | 7:23 | 7:58 | 4:39 | 4:04 |
| 95 | 4 | Mo. | | 7:22 | 7:59 | 5:23 | 5:09 |
| 96 | 5 | Tu. | | 7:21 | 8:00 | 6:07 | 6:16 |
| 97 | 6 | We. | | 7:19 | 8:00 | 6:50 | 7:24 |
| 98 | 7 | Th. | New ☾ at perigee | 7:18 | 8:01 | 7:34 | 8:33 |
| 99 | 8 | Fr. | | 7:17 | 8:02 | 8:20 | 9:42 |
| 100 | 9 | Sa. | | 7:16 | 8:02 | 9:08 | 10:49 |
| 101 | 10 | Su. | | 7:15 | 8:03 | 9:59 | 11:54 |
| 102 | 11 | Mo. | | 7:13 | 8:03 | 10:52 | |
| 103 | 12 | Tu. | | 7:12 | 8:04 | 11:48 | 12:54 |
| 104 | 13 | We. | First qtr. ☾ | 7:11 | 8:05 | 12:44 | 1:49 |
| 105 | 14 | Th. | | 7:10 | 8:05 | 1:41 | 2:38 |
| 106 | 15 | Fr. | | 7:09 | 8:06 | 2:37 | 3:22 |
| 107 | 16 | Sa. | | 7:08 | 8:07 | 3:31 | 4:02 |
| 108 | 17 | Su. | | 7:07 | 8:07 | 4:25 | 4:39 |
| 109 | 18 | Mo. | ♃ σ ☾ (12 am) | 7:05 | 8:08 | 5:18 | 5:14 |
| 110 | 19 | Tu. | | 7:04 | 8:09 | 6:10 | 5:47 |
| 111 | 20 | We. | | 7:03 | 8:09 | 7:02 | 6:20 |
| 112 | 21 | Th. | ☾ at apogee (11 am) | 7:02 | 8:10 | 7:54 | 6:53 |
| 113 | 22 | Fr. | Full ☾ | 7:01 | 8:11 | 8:46 | 7:28 |
| 114 | 23 | Sa. | | 7:00 | 8:11 | 9:38 | 8:04 |
| 115 | 24 | Su. | ♂ σ ☾ (11 pm) | 6:59 | 8:12 | 10:31 | 8:44 |
| 116 | 25 | Mo. | | 6:58 | 8:13 | 11:23 | 9:26 |
| 117 | 26 | Tu. | | 6:57 | 8:13 | | 10:12 |
| 118 | 27 | We. | | 6:56 | 8:14 | 12:13 | 11:02 |
| 119 | 28 | Th. | | 6:55 | 8:15 | 1:02 | 11:55 |
| 120 | 29 | Fr. | Last qtr. ☾ | 6:54 | 8:15 | 1:49 | 12:51 |
| 121 | 30 | Sa. | | 6:53 | 8:16 | 2:34 | 1:50 |

## 5th Month — May 2016 — 31 Days

Moon Phases — New, May 6, 2:30 p.m.; First Qtr., May 13, 12:02 p.m.; Full, May 21, 4:14 p.m.; Last Qtr., May 29, 7:12 a.m.

| Year | Month | Week | Planetary Configurations and Phenomena | Sunrise | Sunset | Moon-rise | Moon-set |
|---|---|---|---|---|---|---|---|
| 122 | 1 | Su. | | 6:52 | 8:17 | 3:17 | 2:52 |
| 123 | 2 | Mo. | ♆ σ ☾ (6 am) | 6:51 | 8:18 | 3:59 | 3:55 |
| 124 | 3 | Tu. | | 6:51 | 8:18 | 4:41 | 5:01 |
| 125 | 4 | We. | | 6:50 | 8:19 | 5:23 | 6:08 |
| 126 | 5 | Th. | ☾ at perigee (11 pm) | 6:49 | 8:20 | 6:07 | 7:17 |
| 127 | 6 | Fr. | New ☾ | 6:48 | 8:20 | 6:53 | 8:26 |
| 128 | 7 | Sa. | | 6:47 | 8:21 | 7:43 | 9:33 |
| 129 | 8 | Su. | | 6:46 | 8:22 | 8:37 | 10:38 |
| 130 | 9 | Mo. | Transit ☿ over ☉ | 6:46 | 8:22 | 9:33 | 11:37 |
| 131 | 10 | Tu. | | 6:45 | 8:23 | 10:32 | |
| 132 | 11 | We. | | 6:44 | 8:24 | 11:30 | 12:31 |
| 133 | 12 | Th. | | 6:43 | 8:24 | 12:28 | 1:19 |
| 134 | 13 | Fr. | First qtr. ☾ | 6:43 | 8:25 | 1:25 | 2:01 |
| 135 | 14 | Sa. | | 6:42 | 8:26 | 2:19 | 2:40 |
| 136 | 15 | Su. | | 6:41 | 8:26 | 3:13 | 3:15 |
| 137 | 16 | Mo. | | 6:41 | 8:27 | 4:05 | 3:49 |
| 138 | 17 | Tu. | | 6:40 | 8:28 | 4:57 | 4:22 |
| 139 | 18 | We. | ☾ at apogee (5 pm) | 6:40 | 8:28 | 5:49 | 4:55 |
| 140 | 19 | Th. | | 6:39 | 8:29 | 6:41 | 5:29 |
| 141 | 20 | Fr. | | 6:39 | 8:30 | 7:34 | 6:05 |
| 142 | 21 | Sa. | Full ☾ | 6:38 | 8:30 | 8:27 | 6:43 |
| 143 | 22 | Su. | | 6:38 | 8:31 | 9:19 | 7:24 |
| 144 | 23 | Mo. | | 6:37 | 8:32 | 10:11 | 8:09 |
| 145 | 24 | Tu. | | 6:37 | 8:32 | 11:01 | 8:58 |
| 146 | 25 | We. | | 6:36 | 8:33 | 11:48 | 9:50 |
| 147 | 26 | Th. | | 6:36 | 8:33 | | 10:46 |
| 148 | 27 | Fr. | | 6:35 | 8:34 | 12:33 | 11:43 |
| 149 | 28 | Sa. | | 6:35 | 8:35 | 1:16 | 12:43 |
| 150 | 29 | Su. | Last qtr. ☾ | 6:35 | 8:35 | 1:57 | 1:44 |
| 151 | 30 | Mo. | | 6:34 | 8:36 | 2:38 | 2:46 |
| 152 | 31 | Tu. | | 6:34 | 8:36 | 3:18 | 3:51 |

## 6th Month — June 2016 — 30 Days

Moon Phases — New, June 4, 10:00 p.m.; First Qtr., June 12, 3:10 a.m.; Full, June 20, 6:02 a.m.; Last Qtr., June 27, 1:19 p.m.

| Year | Month | Week | Planetary Configurations and Phenomena | Sunrise | Sunset | Moon-rise | Moon-set |
|---|---|---|---|---|---|---|---|
| 153 | 1 | We. | | 6:34 | 8:37 | 3:59 | 4:56 |
| 154 | 2 | Th. | | 6:34 | 8:37 | 4:43 | 6:03 |
| 155 | 3 | Fr. | ☾ at perigee (6 am) | 6:34 | 8:38 | 5:30 | 7:11 |
| 156 | 4 | Sa. | New ☾ | 6:33 | 8:38 | 6:21 | 8:17 |
| 157 | 5 | Su. | | 6:33 | 8:39 | 7:16 | 9:20 |
| 158 | 6 | Mo. | | 6:33 | 8:39 | 8:14 | 10:18 |
| 159 | 7 | Tu. | | 6:33 | 8:40 | 9:14 | 11:10 |
| 160 | 8 | We. | | 6:33 | 8:40 | 10:14 | 11:56 |
| 161 | 9 | Th. | | 6:33 | 8:41 | 11:13 | |
| 162 | 10 | Fr. | | 6:33 | 8:41 | 12:10 | 12:38 |
| 163 | 11 | Sa. | | 6:33 | 8:41 | 1:05 | 1:15 |
| 164 | 12 | Su. | First qtr. ☾ | 6:33 | 8:42 | 1:58 | 1:50 |
| 165 | 13 | Mo. | | 6:33 | 8:42 | 2:51 | 2:23 |
| 166 | 14 | Tu. | | 6:33 | 8:43 | 3:43 | 2:56 |
| 167 | 15 | We. | ☾ at apogee (7 am) | 6:33 | 8:43 | 4:35 | 3:30 |
| 168 | 16 | Th. | | 6:33 | 8:43 | 5:27 | 4:05 |
| 169 | 17 | Fr. | | 6:34 | 8:44 | 6:20 | 4:42 |
| 170 | 18 | Sa. | ♄ σ ☾ (7 pm) | 6:34 | 8:44 | 7:13 | 5:22 |
| 171 | 19 | Su. | | 6:34 | 8:44 | 8:06 | 6:06 |
| 172 | 20 | Mo. | Full ☾ Solstice (5:34 pm) | 6:34 | 8:44 | 8:57 | 6:53 |
| 173 | 21 | Tu. | | 6:34 | 8:45 | 9:46 | 7:45 |
| 174 | 22 | We. | | 6:34 | 8:45 | 10:33 | 8:40 |
| 175 | 23 | Th. | | 6:35 | 8:45 | 11:17 | 9:38 |
| 176 | 24 | Fr. | | 6:35 | 8:45 | 11:59 | 10:37 |
| 177 | 25 | Sa. | | 6:35 | 8:45 | | 11:38 |
| 178 | 26 | Su. | | 6:36 | 8:45 | 12:39 | 12:39 |
| 179 | 27 | Mo. | Last qtr. ☾ | 6:36 | 8:45 | 1:18 | 1:41 |
| 180 | 28 | Tu. | | 6:36 | 8:45 | 1:58 | 2:45 |
| 181 | 29 | We. | | 6:37 | 8:45 | 2:39 | 3:49 |
| 182 | 30 | Th. | | 6:37 | 8:45 | 3:23 | 4:54 |

☉ The Sun ● The Earth ☾ The Moon ☿ Mercury ♀ Venus ♂ Mars ♃ Jupiter ♄ Saturn ♅ Uranus ♆ Neptune ♇ Pluto  σ = in conjunction  ☍ = opposition to the ☉

# Astronomical Calendar for 2016

## July 2016 — 7th Month — 31 Days

Moon Phases — New, July 4, 6:01 a.m.; First Qtr., July 11, 7:52 p.m.; Full, July 19, 5:57 p.m.; Last Qtr., July 26, 6:00 p.m.

| Year | Month | Week | Planetary Configurations and Phenomena | Sunrise | Sunset | Moon-rise | Moon-set |
|---|---|---|---|---|---|---|---|
| 183 | 1 | Fr. | ☾ at perigee (2 am) | 6:37 | 8:45 | 4:10 | 6:00 |
| 184 | 2 | Sa. | | 6:38 | 8:45 | 5:02 | 7:03 |
| 185 | 3 | Su. | | 6:38 | 8:45 | 5:58 | 8:03 |
| 186 | 4 | Mo. | ● at aphelion; New ☾ | 6:39 | 8:45 | 6:57 | 8:58 |
| 187 | 5 | Tu. | | 6:39 | 8:45 | 7:57 | 9:47 |
| 188 | 6 | We. | | 6:40 | 8:45 | 8:57 | 10:32 |
| 189 | 7 | Th. | | 6:40 | 8:45 | 9:56 | 11:12 |
| 190 | 8 | Fr. | | 6:41 | 8:44 | 10:53 | 11:49 |
| 191 | 9 | Sa. | | 6:41 | 8:44 | 11:48 | |
| 192 | 10 | Su. | | 6:42 | 8:44 | 12:42 | 12:23 |
| 193 | 11 | Mo. | First qtr. ☾ | 6:42 | 8:44 | 1:34 | 12:56 |
| 194 | 12 | Tu. | | 6:43 | 8:43 | 2:26 | 1:30 |
| 195 | 13 | We. | ☾ at apogee (12 am) | 6:43 | 8:43 | 3:19 | 2:04 |
| 196 | 14 | Th. | | 6:44 | 8:43 | 4:11 | 2:40 |
| 197 | 15 | Fr. | | 6:44 | 8:42 | 5:04 | 3:18 |
| 198 | 16 | Sa. | ♄ σ ☾ (12 am) | 6:45 | 8:42 | 5:57 | 4:00 |
| 199 | 17 | Su. | | 6:45 | 8:41 | 6:49 | 4:47 |
| 200 | 18 | Mo. | | 6:46 | 8:41 | 7:40 | 5:37 |
| 201 | 19 | Tu. | Full ☾ | 6:47 | 8:40 | 8:29 | 6:31 |
| 202 | 20 | We. | | 6:47 | 8:40 | 9:15 | 7:29 |
| 203 | 21 | Th. | | 6:48 | 8:39 | 9:58 | 8:29 |
| 204 | 22 | Fr. | | 6:48 | 8:39 | 10:40 | 9:30 |
| 205 | 23 | Sa. | Ψ σ ☾ (1 am) | 6:49 | 8:38 | 11:20 | 10:33 |
| 206 | 24 | Su. | | 6:50 | 8:38 | | 11:35 |
| 207 | 25 | Mo. | | 6:50 | 8:37 | 12:00 | 12:38 |
| 208 | 26 | Tu. | Last qtr. ☾ | 6:51 | 8:36 | 12:40 | 1:42 |
| 209 | 27 | We. | ☾ at perigee (7 am) | 6:52 | 8:36 | 1:22 | 2:46 |
| 210 | 28 | Th. | | 6:52 | 8:35 | 2:07 | 3:49 |
| 211 | 29 | Fr. | Aldebaran σ ☾ (6 am) | 6:53 | 8:34 | 2:56 | 4:52 |
| 212 | 30 | Sa. | | 6:53 | 8:34 | 3:48 | 5:51 |
| 213 | 31 | Su. | | 6:54 | 8:33 | 4:45 | 6:47 |

## August 2016 — 8th Month — 31 Days

Moon Phases — New, Aug. 2, 3:45 p.m.; First Qtr., Aug. 10, 1:21 p.m.; Full, Aug. 18, 4:27 a.m.; Last Qtr., Aug. 24, 10:41 p.m.

| Year | Month | Week | Planetary Configurations and Phenomena | Sunrise | Sunset | Moon-rise | Moon-set |
|---|---|---|---|---|---|---|---|
| 214 | 1 | Mo. | | 6:55 | 8:32 | 5:43 | 7:39 |
| 215 | 2 | Tu. | New ☾ | 6:55 | 8:31 | 6:43 | 8:25 |
| 216 | 3 | We. | | 6:56 | 8:31 | 7:42 | 9:07 |
| 217 | 4 | Th. | | 6:57 | 8:30 | 8:40 | 9:45 |
| 218 | 5 | Fr. | ♃ σ ☾ (11 pm) | 6:57 | 8:29 | 9:36 | 10:21 |
| 219 | 6 | Sa. | | 6:58 | 8:28 | 10:31 | 10:55 |
| 220 | 7 | Su. | | 6:58 | 8:27 | 11:25 | 11:29 |
| 221 | 8 | Mo. | | 6:59 | 8:26 | 12:17 | |
| 222 | 9 | Tu. | ☾ at apogee (7 pm) | 7:00 | 8:25 | 1:09 | 12:03 |
| 223 | 10 | We. | First qtr. ☾ | 7:00 | 8:24 | 2:02 | 12:38 |
| 224 | 11 | Th. | ♂ σ ☾ (5 pm) | 7:01 | 8:23 | 2:54 | 1:15 |
| 225 | 12 | Fr. | | 7:02 | 8:22 | 3:46 | 1:55 |
| 226 | 13 | Sa. | | 7:02 | 8:21 | 4:39 | 2:39 |
| 227 | 14 | Su. | | 7:03 | 8:20 | 5:30 | 3:27 |
| 228 | 15 | Mo. | | 7:03 | 8:19 | 6:20 | 4:19 |
| 229 | 16 | Tu. | | 7:04 | 8:18 | 7:07 | 5:16 |
| 230 | 17 | We. | | 7:05 | 8:17 | 7:53 | 6:15 |
| 231 | 18 | Th. | Full ☾; Eclipse ☾ | 7:05 | 8:16 | 8:36 | 7:17 |
| 232 | 19 | Fr. | Ψ σ ☾ (7 am) | 7:06 | 8:15 | 9:18 | 8:21 |
| 233 | 20 | Sa. | | 7:07 | 8:14 | 9:59 | 9:25 |
| 234 | 21 | Su. | ☾ at perigee (8 pm) | 7:07 | 8:13 | 10:40 | 10:29 |
| 235 | 22 | Mo. | ♁ σ ☾ (5 am) | 7:08 | 8:12 | 11:22 | 11:34 |
| 236 | 23 | Tu. | ♂ σ Antares (11 pm) | 7:08 | 8:11 | | 12:39 |
| 237 | 24 | We. | Last qtr. ☾ | 7:09 | 8:09 | 12:06 | 1:43 |
| 238 | 25 | Th. | | 7:10 | 8:08 | 12:54 | 2:45 |
| 239 | 26 | Fr. | | 7:10 | 8:07 | 1:45 | 3:45 |
| 240 | 27 | Sa. | ☿ σ ♀ (12 am) | 7:11 | 8:06 | 2:39 | 4:41 |
| 241 | 28 | Su. | | 7:11 | 8:05 | 3:35 | 5:33 |
| 242 | 29 | Mo. | | 7:12 | 8:04 | 4:33 | 6:20 |
| 243 | 30 | Tu. | | 7:13 | 8:02 | 5:32 | 7:03 |
| 244 | 31 | We. | | 7:13 | 8:01 | 6:29 | 7:42 |

## September 2016 — 9th Month — 30 Days

Moon Phases — New, Sept. 1, 4:03 a.m.; First Qtr., Sept. 9, 6:49 a.m.; Full, Sept. 16, 2:05 p.m.; Last Qtr., Sept. 23, 4:56 a.m.; New, Sept. 30, 7:11 p.m.

| Year | Month | Week | Planetary Configurations and Phenomena | Sunrise | Sunset | Moon-rise | Moon-set |
|---|---|---|---|---|---|---|---|
| 245 | 1 | Th. | New ☾ | 7:14 | 8:00 | 7:26 | 8:19 |
| 246 | 2 | Fr. | | 7:14 | 7:59 | 8:21 | 8:54 |
| 247 | 3 | Sa. | | 7:15 | 7:57 | 9:15 | 9:28 |
| 248 | 4 | Su. | | 7:15 | 7:56 | 10:08 | 10:01 |
| 249 | 5 | Mo. | | 7:16 | 7:55 | 11:01 | 10:36 |
| 250 | 6 | Tu. | ☾ at apogee (2 pm) | 7:17 | 7:54 | 11:53 | 11:12 |
| 251 | 7 | We. | | 7:17 | 7:52 | 12:45 | 11:51 |
| 252 | 8 | Th. | | 7:18 | 7:51 | 1:37 | |
| 253 | 9 | Fr. | First qtr. ☾ | 7:18 | 7:50 | 2:28 | 12:32 |
| 254 | 10 | Sa. | | 7:19 | 7:49 | 3:19 | 1:18 |
| 255 | 11 | Su. | | 7:20 | 7:47 | 4:09 | 2:07 |
| 256 | 12 | Mo. | | 7:20 | 7:46 | 4:57 | 3:01 |
| 257 | 13 | Tu. | | 7:21 | 7:45 | 5:43 | 3:58 |
| 258 | 14 | We. | | 7:21 | 7:44 | 6:27 | 4:59 |
| 259 | 15 | Th. | | 7:22 | 7:42 | 7:10 | 6:02 |
| 260 | 16 | Fr. | Full ☾ | 7:22 | 7:41 | 7:52 | 7:07 |
| 261 | 17 | Sa. | ♀ σ Spica (6 pm) | 7:23 | 7:40 | 8:34 | 8:13 |
| 262 | 18 | Su. | ☾ at perigee (12 pm) | 7:24 | 7:38 | 9:17 | 9:20 |
| 263 | 19 | Mo. | | 7:24 | 7:37 | 10:02 | 10:27 |
| 264 | 20 | Tu. | | 7:25 | 7:36 | 10:50 | 11:33 |
| 265 | 21 | We. | | 7:25 | 7:34 | 11:41 | 12:38 |
| 266 | 22 | Th. | Equinox (9:21am) | 7:26 | 7:33 | | 1:40 |
| 267 | 23 | Fr. | Last qtr. ☾ | 7:26 | 7:32 | 12:35 | 2:38 |
| 268 | 24 | Sa. | | 7:27 | 7:31 | 1:31 | 3:31 |
| 269 | 25 | Su. | | 7:28 | 7:29 | 2:28 | 4:19 |
| 270 | 26 | Mo. | | 7:28 | 7:28 | 3:26 | 5:02 |
| 271 | 27 | Tu. | | 7:29 | 7:27 | 4:23 | 5:42 |
| 272 | 28 | We. | | 7:29 | 7:25 | 5:19 | 6:19 |
| 273 | 29 | Th. | ☿ σ ☾ (6 am) | 7:30 | 7:24 | 6:14 | 6:54 |
| 274 | 30 | Fr. | New ☾ | 7:31 | 7:23 | 7:08 | 7:28 |

**Bright stars** = Aldebaran, Antares, Spica, Pollux, Regulus. **Minor planets or asteroids** = Ceres, Pallas, Juno, Vesta.   σ = in conjunction by 10° or <   ☍ = opposition to ☉

# Astronomical Calendar for 2016

## 10th Month — October 2016 — 31 Days

**Moon Phases** — *First Qtr.*, Oct. 8, 11:33 p.m.; *Full*, Oct. 15, 11:23 p.m. *Last Qtr.*, Oct. 22, 2:14 p.m.; *New*, Oct. 30, 12:38 p.m.

| Day of Year | Day of Month | Day of Week | Planetary Configurations and Phenomena | Sunrise | Sunset | Moon-rise | Moon-set |
|---|---|---|---|---|---|---|---|
| 275 | 1 | Sa. | | 7:31 | 7:22 | 8:01 | **8:01** |
| 276 | 2 | Su. | | 7:32 | 7:20 | 8:54 | **8:35** |
| 277 | 3 | Mo. | | 7:33 | 7:19 | 9:46 | **9:11** |
| 278 | 4 | Tu. | ☾ at apogee (6 am) | 7:33 | 7:18 | 10:38 | **9:48** |
| 279 | 5 | We. | | 7:34 | 7:17 | 11:30 | **10:28** |
| 280 | 6 | Th. | | 7:34 | 7:16 | **12:21** | **11:12** |
| 281 | 7 | Fr. | | 7:35 | 7:14 | **1:12** | **11:59** |
| 282 | 8 | Sa. | First qtr. ☾ | 7:36 | 7:13 | **2:01** | |
| 283 | 9 | Su. | | 7:36 | 7:12 | **2:48** | 12:49 |
| 284 | 10 | Mo. | | 7:37 | 7:11 | **3:34** | 1:44 |
| 285 | 11 | Tu. | | 7:38 | 7:10 | **4:18** | 2:41 |
| 286 | 12 | We. | | 7:38 | 7:08 | **5:00** | 3:42 |
| 287 | 13 | Th. | ♆ ☌ ☾ (1 am) | 7:39 | 7:07 | **5:42** | 4:45 |
| 288 | 14 | Fr. | | 7:40 | 7:06 | **6:24** | 5:50 |
| 289 | 15 | Sa. | Full ☾; ⛢ ☌ ☾ (9 pm) | 7:40 | 7:05 | **7:07** | 6:57 |
| 290 | 16 | Su. | ☾at perigee (7 pm) | 7:41 | 7:04 | **7:52** | 8:05 |
| 291 | 17 | Mo. | | 7:42 | 7:03 | **8:40** | 9:14 |
| 292 | 18 | Tu. | | 7:43 | 7:02 | **9:31** | 10:22 |
| 293 | 19 | We. | Aldebaran ☌ ☾ (2 am) | 7:43 | 7:01 | **10:26** | 11:28 |
| 294 | 20 | Th. | | 7:44 | 7:00 | **11:23** | **12:30** |
| 295 | 21 | Fr. | | 7:45 | 6:59 | | **1:27** |
| 296 | 22 | Sa. | Last qtr. ☾ | 7:45 | 6:57 | 12:22 | **2:17** |
| 297 | 23 | Su. | | 7:46 | 6:56 | 1:20 | **3:03** |
| 298 | 24 | Mo. | | 7:47 | 6:55 | 2:18 | **3:43** |
| 299 | 25 | Tu. | ♀ ☌ Antares (11 pm) | 7:48 | 6:55 | 3:14 | **4:21** |
| 300 | 26 | We. | | 7:48 | 6:54 | 4:09 | **4:56** |
| 301 | 27 | Th. | | 7:49 | 6:53 | 5:03 | **5:29** |
| 302 | 28 | Fr. | ♃ ☌ ☾ (5 am) | 7:50 | 6:52 | 5:56 | **6:03** |
| 303 | 29 | Sa. | | 7:51 | 6:51 | 6:49 | **6:36** |
| 304 | 30 | Su. | New ☾; ♀ ☌ ♄ (3 am) | 7:52 | 6:50 | 7:41 | **7:11** |
| 305 | 31 | Mo. | ☾ at apogee (2 pm) | 7:52 | 6:49 | 8:33 | **7:48** |

## 11th Month — November 2016 — 30 Days

**Moon Phases** — *First Qtr.*, Nov. 7, 1:51 p.m.; *Full*, Nov. 14, 7:52 a.m.; *Last Qtr.*, Nov. 21, 2:33 a.m.; *New*, Nov. 29, 6:18 a.m.

| Day of Year | Day of Month | Day of Week | Planetary Configurations and Phenomena | Sunrise | Sunset | Moon-rise | Moon-set |
|---|---|---|---|---|---|---|---|
| 306 | 1 | Tu. | | 7:53 | 6:48 | 9:26 | **8:27** |
| 307 | 2 | We. | | 7:54 | 6:47 | 10:17 | **9:09** |
| 308 | 3 | Th. | | 7:55 | 6:47 | 11:08 | **9:54** |
| 309 | 4 | Fr. | | 7:56 | 6:46 | 11:57 | **10:43** |
| 310 | 5 | Sa. | | 7:56 | 6:45 | **12:44** | **11:35** |
| 311 | † 6 | Su. | **DST ends** | 6:57 | 5:44 | **12:29** | **11:30** |
| 312 | 7 | Mo. | First qtr. ☾ | 6:58 | 5:44 | **1:13** | |
| 313 | 8 | Tu. | | 6:59 | 5:43 | **1:54** | 12:27 |
| 314 | 9 | We. | | 7:00 | 5:42 | **2:34** | 1:27 |
| 315 | 10 | Th. | | 7:01 | 5:42 | **3:15** | 2:29 |
| 316 | 11 | Fr. | | 7:01 | 5:41 | **3:56** | 3:33 |
| 317 | 12 | Sa. | | 7:02 | 5:40 | **4:39** | 4:40 |
| 318 | 13 | Su. | | 7:03 | 5:40 | **5:25** | 5:48 |
| 319 | 14 | Mo. | Full ☾ at perigee (5 am) | 7:04 | 5:39 | **6:15** | 6:58 |
| 320 | 15 | Tu. | | 7:05 | 5:39 | **7:09** | 8:07 |
| 321 | 16 | We. | | 7:06 | 5:38 | **8:08** | 9:13 |
| 322 | 17 | Th. | | 7:07 | 5:38 | **9:08** | 10:15 |
| 323 | 18 | Fr. | | 7:07 | 5:38 | **10:09** | 11:10 |
| 324 | 19 | Sa. | | 7:08 | 5:37 | **11:09** | 11:59 |
| 325 | 20 | Su. | | 7:09 | 5:37 | | **12:43** |
| 326 | 21 | Mo. | Last qtr. ☾ | 7:10 | 5:36 | 12:08 | **1:22** |
| 327 | 22 | Tu. | | 7:11 | 5:36 | 1:04 | **1:58** |
| 328 | 23 | We. | | 7:12 | 5:36 | 1:59 | **2:32** |
| 329 | 24 | Th. | | 7:13 | 5:36 | 2:52 | **3:05** |
| 330 | 25 | Fr. | | 7:13 | 5:35 | 3:44 | **3:38** |
| 331 | 26 | Sa. | | 7:14 | 5:35 | 4:37 | **4:12** |
| 332 | 27 | Su. | ☾ at apogee (2 am) | 7:15 | 5:35 | 5:29 | **4:48** |
| 333 | 28 | Mo. | | 7:16 | 5:35 | 6:21 | **5:26** |
| 334 | 29 | Tu. | New ☾ | 7:17 | 5:35 | 7:13 | **6:07** |
| 335 | 30 | We. | | 7:18 | 5:35 | 8:05 | **6:52** |

***† Daylight Saving Time ends at 2 a.m.***

## 12th Month — December 2016 — 31 Days

**Moon Phases** — *First Qtr.*, Dec. 7, 3:03 a.m.; *Full*, Dec. 13, 6:06 p.m.; *Last Qtr.*, Dec. 20, 7:56 p.m.; *New*, Dec. 29, 12:53 a.m.

| Day of Year | Day of Month | Day of Week | Planetary Configurations and Phenomena | Sunrise | Sunset | Moon-rise | Moon-set |
|---|---|---|---|---|---|---|---|
| 336 | 1 | Th. | | 7:18 | 5:35 | 8:55 | **7:40** |
| 337 | 2 | Fr. | | 7:19 | 5:35 | 9:43 | **8:31** |
| 338 | 3 | Sa. | | 7:20 | 5:35 | 10:29 | **9:24** |
| 339 | 4 | Su. | | 7:21 | 5:35 | 11:12 | **10:20** |
| 340 | 5 | Mo. | | 7:22 | 5:35 | 11:53 | **11:18** |
| 341 | 6 | Tu. | | 7:22 | 5:35 | **12:33** | |
| 342 | 7 | We. | First qtr. ☾ | 7:23 | 5:35 | **1:11** | 12:17 |
| 343 | 8 | Th. | | 7:24 | 5:35 | **1:50** | 1:18 |
| 344 | 9 | Fr. | | 7:25 | 5:35 | **2:30** | 2:20 |
| 345 | 10 | Sa. | | 7:25 | 5:35 | **3:13** | 3:25 |
| 346 | 11 | Su. | | 7:26 | 5:36 | **4:00** | 4:32 |
| 347 | 12 | Mo. | ☾ at perigee (5 pm) | 7:27 | 5:36 | **4:51** | 5:41 |
| 348 | 13 | Tu. | Full ☾ | 7:27 | 5:36 | **5:47** | 6:49 |
| 349 | 14 | We. | | 7:28 | 5:37 | **6:47** | 7:54 |
| 350 | 15 | Th. | | 7:29 | 5:37 | **7:50** | 8:55 |
| 351 | 16 | Fr. | | 7:29 | 5:37 | **8:53** | 9:49 |
| 352 | 17 | Sa. | | 7:30 | 5:38 | **9:54** | 10:37 |
| 353 | 18 | Su. | | 7:30 | 5:38 | **10:53** | 11:19 |
| 354 | 19 | Mo. | | 7:31 | 5:39 | **11:50** | 11:58 |
| 355 | 20 | Tu. | Last qtr. ☾ | 7:31 | 5:39 | | **12:33** |
| 356 | 21 | We. | **Solstice** (4:44 am) | 7:32 | 5:40 | 12:45 | **1:07** |
| 357 | 22 | Th. | | 7:32 | 5:40 | 1:38 | **1:40** |
| 358 | 23 | Fr. | | 7:33 | 5:41 | 2:31 | **2:13** |
| 359 | 24 | Sa. | | 7:33 | 5:41 | 3:23 | **2:48** |
| 360 | 25 | Su. | ☾at apogee (12 am) | 7:34 | 5:42 | 4:15 | **3:25** |
| 361 | 26 | Mo. | | 7:34 | 5:42 | 5:07 | **4:05** |
| 362 | 27 | Tu. | | 7:35 | 5:43 | 5:59 | **4:49** |
| 363 | 28 | We. | | 7:35 | 5:44 | 6:51 | **5:36** |
| 364 | 29 | Th. | New ☾ | 7:35 | 5:44 | 7:40 | **6:26** |
| 365 | 30 | Fr. | | 7:35 | 5:45 | 8:28 | **7:20** |
| 366 | 31 | Sa. | | 7:36 | 5:46 | 9:12 | **8:15** |

☉ The Sun ● The Earth ☾ The Moon ☿ Mercury ♀ Venus ♂ Mars ♃ Jupiter ♄ Saturn ♆ Neptune ⛢ Uranus ♇ Pluto ☌ = in conjunction ☍ = opposition to the ☉

# 2017

Times are **Central Standard Time,** except from March 12 to Nov. 5, during which **Daylight Saving Time** is observed. **Boldface times for moonrise and moonset indicate p.m.** Times are figured for the point **99° 20' West and 31° 08' North,** the approximate geographical center of the state. **See page 162 for explanation of how to get the approximate time at any other Texas point.** (On the web: http://www.usno.navy.mil/astronomy) Please note: Not all eclipses are visible in United States. For visibility, see listing beginning on **page 162.**

## 1st Month — January 2017 — 31 Days

**Moon Phases** — *First Qtr.,* Jan. 5, 1:47 p.m.; *Full,* Jan. 12, 5:34 a.m.; *Last Qtr.,* Jan. 19, 4:13 p.m.; *New,* Jan. 27, 6:07 p.m.

| Day of Year | Day of Month | Day of Week | Planetary Configurations and Phenomena | Sunrise | Sunset | Moonrise | Moonset |
|---|---|---|---|---|---|---|---|
| 1 | 1 | Su. | ♂ ☌ ♆ (1 am) | 7:36 | 5:46 | 9:55 | **9:13** |
| 2 | 2 | Mo. | ♆ ☌ ☾ (10 pm) | 7:36 | 5:47 | 10:35 | **10:11** |
| 3 | 3 | Tu. | | 7:36 | 5:48 | 11:13 | **11:11** |
| 4 | 4 | We. | ● at perihelion (8 am) | 7:36 | 5:49 | 11:51 | |
| 5 | 5 | Th. | First qtr. ☾; ⛢ ☌ ☾ (8 pm) | 7:37 | 5:49 | **12:29** | 12:11 |
| 6 | 6 | Fr. | | 7:37 | 5:50 | **1:09** | 1:13 |
| 7 | 7 | Sa. | | 7:37 | 5:51 | **1:52** | 2:17 |
| 8 | 8 | Su. | | 7:37 | 5:52 | **2:39** | 3:22 |
| 9 | 9 | Mo. | | 7:37 | 5:53 | **3:31** | 4:28 |
| 10 | 10 | Tu. | ☾ at perigee (12 am) | 7:37 | 5:54 | **4:27** | 5:33 |
| 11 | 11 | We. | | 7:37 | 5:54 | **5:28** | 6:35 |
| 12 | 12 | Th. | Full ☾; ♀ ☌ ♆ (8 pm) | 7:37 | 5:55 | **6:31** | 7:33 |
| 13 | 13 | Fr. | | 7:37 | 5:56 | **7:34** | 8:25 |
| 14 | 14 | Sa. | Regulus ☌ ☾ (11 pm) | 7:36 | 5:57 | **8:36** | 9:11 |
| 15 | 15 | Su. | | 7:36 | 5:58 | **9:36** | 9:52 |
| 16 | 16 | Mo. | | 7:36 | 5:59 | **10:33** | 10:30 |
| 17 | 17 | Tu. | | 7:36 | 6:00 | **11:28** | 11:05 |
| 18 | 18 | We. | | 7:36 | 6:00 | | 11:39 |
| 19 | 19 | Th. | Last qtr. ☾ | 7:35 | 6:01 | 12:22 | **12:13** |
| 20 | 20 | Fr. | | 7:35 | 6:02 | 1:15 | **12:48** |
| 21 | 21 | Sa. | ☾ at apogee (6 pm) | 7:35 | 6:03 | 2:07 | **1:24** |
| 22 | 22 | Su. | | 7:34 | 6:04 | 2:59 | **2:02** |
| 23 | 23 | Mo. | | 7:34 | 6:05 | 3:51 | **2:44** |
| 24 | 24 | Tu. | ♄ ☌ ☾ (4 am) | 7:33 | 6:06 | 4:43 | **3:29** |
| 25 | 25 | We. | | 7:33 | 6:07 | 5:33 | **4:19** |
| 26 | 26 | Th. | | 7:33 | 6:08 | 6:22 | **5:11** |
| 27 | 27 | Fr. | New ☾ | 7:32 | 6:09 | 7:09 | **6:07** |
| 28 | 28 | Sa. | | 7:32 | 6:09 | 7:53 | **7:05** |
| 29 | 29 | Su. | | 7:31 | 6:10 | 8:34 | **8:04** |
| 30 | 30 | Mo. | | 7:30 | 6:11 | 9:14 | **9:05** |
| 31 | 31 | Tu. | ♀ ☌ ☾ (7 pm) | 7:30 | 6:12 | 9:53 | **10:05** |

## 2nd Month — February 2017 — 28 Days

**Moon Phases** — *First Qtr.,* Feb. 3, 10:19 p.m.; *Full,* Feb. 10, 6:33 p.m.; *Last Qtr.,* Feb. 18, 1:33 p.m.; *New,* Feb. 26, 8:58 a.m.

| Day of Year | Day of Month | Day of Week | Planetary Configurations and Phenomena | Sunrise | Sunset | Moonrise | Moonset |
|---|---|---|---|---|---|---|---|
| 32 | 1 | We. | | 7:29 | 6:13 | 10:31 | **11:07** |
| 33 | 2 | Th. | Ceres ☌ ☾ (8 pm) | 7:29 | 6:14 | 11:10 | |
| 34 | 3 | Fr. | First qtr. ☾ | 7:28 | 6:15 | 11:51 | 12:09 |
| 35 | 4 | Sa. | | 7:27 | 6:16 | **12:35** | 1:13 |
| 36 | 5 | Su. | | 7:26 | 6:17 | **1:24** | 2:17 |
| 37 | 6 | Mo. | ☾ at perigee (8 am) | 7:26 | 6:17 | **2:16** | 3:20 |
| 38 | 7 | Tu. | | 7:25 | 6:18 | **3:13** | 4:21 |
| 39 | 8 | We. | | 7:24 | 6:19 | **4:14** | 5:19 |
| 40 | 9 | Th. | | 7:23 | 6:20 | **5:16** | 6:13 |
| 41 | 10 | Fr. | Full ☾; **Eclipse** ☾ | 7:23 | 6:21 | **6:18** | 7:01 |
| 42 | 11 | Sa. | | 7:22 | 6:22 | **7:19** | 7:45 |
| 43 | 12 | Su. | | 7:21 | 6:23 | **8:18** | 8:24 |
| 44 | 13 | Mo. | | 7:20 | 6:23 | **9:15** | 9:01 |
| 45 | 14 | Tu. | | 7:19 | 6:24 | **10:10** | 9:36 |
| 46 | 15 | We. | | 7:18 | 6:25 | **11:04** | 10:11 |
| 47 | 16 | Th. | | 7:17 | 6:26 | **11:57** | 10:45 |
| 48 | 17 | Fr. | ♀ gr. illuminated (1 am) | 7:16 | 6:27 | | 11:21 |
| 49 | 18 | Sa. | Last qtr. ☾ at apogee | 7:15 | 6:27 | 12:50 | 11:58 |
| 50 | 19 | Su. | | 7:14 | 6:28 | 1:42 | **12:39** |
| 51 | 20 | Mo. | | 7:13 | 6:29 | 2:33 | **1:22** |
| 52 | 21 | Tu. | | 7:12 | 6:30 | 3:24 | **2:09** |
| 53 | 22 | We. | | 7:11 | 6:31 | 4:13 | **3:00** |
| 54 | 23 | Th. | | 7:10 | 6:31 | 5:01 | **3:55** |
| 55 | 24 | Fr. | | 7:09 | 6:32 | 5:46 | **4:52** |
| 56 | 25 | Sa. | | 7:08 | 6:33 | 6:29 | **5:52** |
| 57 | 26 | Su. | New ☾ | 7:07 | 6:34 | 7:10 | **6:53** |
| 58 | 27 | Mo. | ♂ ☌ ⛢ (2 am) | 7:06 | 6:34 | 7:50 | **7:55** |
| 59 | 28 | Tu. | | 7:05 | 6:35 | 8:30 | **8:58** |

† *Daylight Saving Time begins at 2 a.m.*

## 3rd Month — March 2017 — 31 Days

**Moon Phases** — *First Qtr.,* March 5, 5:32 a.m.; *Full,* March 12, 9:54 a.m.; *Last Qtr.,* March 20, 10:58 a.m.; *New,* March 27, 9:57 p.m.

| Day of Year | Day of Month | Day of Week | Planetary Configurations and Phenomena | Sunrise | Sunset | Moonrise | Moonset |
|---|---|---|---|---|---|---|---|
| 60 | 1 | We. | | 7:04 | 6:36 | 9:09 | **10:02** |
| 61 | 2 | Th. | | 7:02 | 6:37 | 9:51 | **11:06** |
| 62 | 3 | Fr. | ☾ at perigee (2 am) | 7:01 | 6:37 | 10:34 | |
| 63 | 4 | Sa. | Aldebaran ☌ ☾ (9 pm) | 7:00 | 6:38 | 11:21 | 12:10 |
| 64 | 5 | Su. | First qtr. ☾ | 6:59 | 6:39 | **12:12** | 1:14 |
| 65 | 6 | Mo. | | 6:58 | 6:40 | **1:07** | 2:15 |
| 66 | 7 | Tu. | | 6:57 | 6:40 | **2:05** | 3:13 |
| 67 | 8 | We. | | 6:55 | 6:41 | **3:05** | 4:06 |
| 68 | 9 | Th. | | 6:54 | 6:42 | **4:06** | 4:55 |
| 69 | 10 | Fr. | | 6:53 | 6:42 | **5:06** | 5:39 |
| 70 | 11 | Sa. | | 6:52 | 6:43 | **6:05** | 6:20 |
| 71 | †12 | Su. | **DST begins** Full ☾ | 7:51 | 7:44 | **8:02** | 7:58 |
| 72 | 13 | Mo. | | 7:49 | 7:44 | **8:58** | 8:33 |
| 73 | 14 | Tu. | | 7:48 | 7:45 | **9:53** | 9:08 |
| 74 | 15 | We. | | 7:47 | 7:46 | **10:47** | 9:43 |
| 75 | 16 | Th. | | 7:46 | 7:46 | **11:40** | 10:18 |
| 76 | 17 | Fr. | | 7:44 | 7:47 | | 10:55 |
| 77 | 18 | Sa. | ☾ at apogee (12 pm) | 7:43 | 7:48 | 12:33 | 11:34 |
| 78 | 19 | Su. | | 7:42 | 7:48 | 1:25 | **12:16** |
| 79 | 20 | Mo. | **Equinox** (5:29 am) | 7:41 | 7:49 | 2:15 | **1:01** |
| 80 | 21 | Tu. | | 7:39 | 7:50 | 3:04 | **1:49** |
| 81 | 22 | We. | | 7:38 | 7:50 | 3:52 | **2:42** |
| 82 | 23 | Th. | | 7:37 | 7:51 | 4:37 | **3:37** |
| 83 | 24 | Fr. | | 7:36 | 7:52 | 5:21 | **4:35** |
| 84 | 25 | Sa. | | 7:34 | 7:52 | 6:03 | **5:35** |
| 85 | 26 | Su. | | 7:33 | 7:53 | 6:43 | **6:37** |
| 86 | 27 | Mo. | New ☾ | 7:32 | 7:54 | 7:23 | **7:41** |
| 87 | 28 | Tu. | | 7:31 | 7:54 | 8:04 | **8:46** |
| 88 | 29 | We. | | 7:29 | 7:55 | 8:45 | **9:53** |
| 89 | 30 | Th. | ☾ at perigee (8 am) | 7:28 | 7:56 | 9:29 | **10:59** |
| 90 | 31 | Fr. | | 7:27 | 7:56 | 10:17 | |

# Astronomical Calendar for 2017

## 4th Month — April 2017 — 30 Days

Moon Phases — First Qtr, April 3, 1:39 p.m.; Full, April 11, 1:08 a.m.; Last Qtr, April 19, 4:57 a.m.; New, April 26, 7:16 a.m.

| Year | Month | Week | Planetary Configurations and Phenomena | Sunrise | Sunset | Moon-rise | Moon-set |
|---|---|---|---|---|---|---|---|
| 91 | 1 | Sa. | | 7:26 | 7:57 | 11:08 | 12:05 |
| 92 | 2 | Su. | | 7:25 | 7:57 | 12:02 | 1:09 |
| 93 | 3 | Mo. | First qtr. ☾ | 7:23 | 7:58 | 1:00 | 2:09 |
| 94 | 4 | Tu. | | 7:22 | 7:59 | 1:59 | 3:04 |
| 95 | 5 | We. | | 7:21 | 7:59 | 2:59 | 3:54 |
| 96 | 6 | Th. | | 7:20 | 8:00 | 3:59 | 4:39 |
| 97 | 7 | Fr. | Regulus ♂ ☾ (12 am) | 7:18 | 8:01 | 4:57 | 5:19 |
| 98 | 8 | Sa. | | 7:17 | 8:01 | 5:54 | 5:57 |
| 99 | 9 | Su. | | 7:16 | 8:02 | 6:50 | 6:33 |
| 100 | 10 | Mo. | | 7:15 | 8:03 | 7:45 | 7:07 |
| 101 | 11 | Tu. | Full ☾ | 7:14 | 8:03 | 8:39 | 7:41 |
| 102 | 12 | We. | | 7:12 | 8:04 | 9:32 | 8:16 |
| 103 | 13 | Th. | | 7:11 | 8:05 | 10:25 | 8:52 |
| 104 | 14 | Fr. | | 7:10 | 8:05 | 11:17 | 9:30 |
| 105 | 15 | Sa. | ☾ at apogee (5 am) | 7:09 | 8:06 | | 10:11 |
| 106 | 16 | Su. | | 7:08 | 8:07 | 12:09 | 10:55 |
| 107 | 17 | Mo. | | 7:07 | 8:07 | 12:58 | 11:42 |
| 108 | 18 | Tu. | | 7:06 | 8:08 | 1:46 | 12:32 |
| 109 | 19 | We. | Last qtr. ☾ | 7:05 | 8:09 | 2:31 | 1:25 |
| 110 | 20 | Th. | | 7:03 | 8:09 | 3:15 | 2:20 |
| 111 | 21 | Fr. | | 7:02 | 8:10 | 3:56 | 3:18 |
| 112 | 22 | Sa. | | 7:01 | 8:11 | 4:36 | 4:18 |
| 113 | 23 | Su. | | 7:00 | 8:11 | 5:15 | 5:21 |
| 114 | 24 | Mo. | | 6:59 | 8:12 | 5:55 | 6:25 |
| 115 | 25 | Tu. | | 6:58 | 8:13 | 6:36 | 7:31 |
| 116 | 26 | We. | New ☾ | 6:57 | 8:13 | 7:19 | 8:40 |
| 117 | 27 | Th. | ☾ at perigee (11 am) | 6:56 | 8:14 | 8:06 | 9:48 |
| 118 | 28 | Fr. | | 6:55 | 8:15 | 8:57 | 10:56 |
| 119 | 29 | Sa. | | 6:54 | 8:15 | 9:52 | 12:00 |
| 120 | 30 | Su. | | 6:53 | 8:16 | 10:51 | 12:00 |

## 5th Month — May 2017 — 31 Days

Moon Phases — First Qtr, May 2, 9:47 p.m.; Full, May 10, 4:42 p.m. Last Qtr, May 18, 7:33 p.m.; New, May 25, 2:44 p.m.

| Year | Month | Week | Planetary Configurations and Phenomena | Sunrise | Sunset | Moon-rise | Moon-set |
|---|---|---|---|---|---|---|---|
| 121 | 1 | Mo. | | 6:53 | 8:17 | 11:51 | 12:59 |
| 122 | 2 | Tu. | First qtr. ☾ | 6:52 | 8:17 | 12:53 | 1:52 |
| 123 | 3 | We. | | 6:51 | 8:18 | 1:53 | 2:39 |
| 124 | 4 | Th. | | 6:50 | 8:19 | 2:52 | 3:21 |
| 125 | 5 | Fr. | | 6:49 | 8:19 | 3:49 | 3:59 |
| 126 | 6 | Sa. | | 6:48 | 8:20 | 4:45 | 4:35 |
| 127 | 7 | Su. | ♂ ☾ Aldebaran (2 am) | 6:47 | 8:21 | 5:39 | 5:09 |
| 128 | 8 | Mo. | | 6:47 | 8:21 | 6:33 | 5:43 |
| 129 | 9 | Tu. | | 6:46 | 8:22 | 7:26 | 6:17 |
| 130 | 10 | We. | Full ☾ | 6:45 | 8:23 | 8:19 | 6:52 |
| 131 | 11 | Th. | | 6:44 | 8:23 | 9:12 | 7:29 |
| 132 | 12 | Fr. | ☾ at apogee (5 am) | 6:44 | 8:24 | 10:04 | 8:09 |
| 133 | 13 | Sa. | | 6:43 | 8:25 | 10:54 | 8:51 |
| 134 | 14 | Su. | | 6:42 | 8:25 | 11:42 | 9:37 |
| 135 | 15 | Mo. | | 6:42 | 8:26 | | 10:26 |
| 136 | 16 | Tu. | | 6:41 | 8:27 | 12:28 | 11:17 |
| 137 | 17 | We. | | 6:40 | 8:27 | 1:12 | 12:11 |
| 138 | 18 | Th. | Last qtr. ☾ | 6:40 | 8:28 | 1:53 | 1:06 |
| 139 | 19 | Fr. | | 6:39 | 8:29 | 2:33 | 2:04 |
| 140 | 20 | Sa. | | 6:39 | 8:29 | 3:11 | 3:04 |
| 141 | 21 | Su. | | 6:38 | 8:30 | 3:49 | 4:05 |
| 142 | 22 | Mo. | | 6:38 | 8:31 | 4:28 | 5:09 |
| 143 | 23 | Tu. | | 6:37 | 8:31 | 5:09 | 6:16 |
| 144 | 24 | We. | | 6:37 | 8:32 | 5:53 | 7:24 |
| 145 | 25 | Th. | New ☾ at perigee | 6:36 | 8:33 | 6:42 | 8:34 |
| 146 | 26 | Fr. | ♂ ☾ (9 pm) | 6:36 | 8:33 | 7:35 | 9:41 |
| 147 | 27 | Sa. | | 6:36 | 8:34 | 8:34 | 10:45 |
| 148 | 28 | Su. | | 6:35 | 8:34 | 9:36 | 11:43 |
| 149 | 29 | Mo. | | 6:35 | 8:35 | 10:40 | |
| 150 | 30 | Tu. | | 6:35 | 8:36 | 11:43 | 12:34 |
| 151 | 31 | We. | | 6:34 | 8:36 | 12:44 | 1:20 |

## 6th Month — June 2017 — 30 Days

Moon Phases — First Qtr, June 1, 7:42 a.m.; Full, June 9, 8:10 a.m.; Last Qtr, June 17, 6:33 a.m.; New, June 23, 9:31 p.m.; First Qtr, June 30, 7:51 p.m.

| Year | Month | Week | Planetary Configurations and Phenomena | Sunrise | Sunset | Moon-rise | Moon-set |
|---|---|---|---|---|---|---|---|
| 152 | 1 | Th. | First qtr. ☾ | 6:34 | 8:37 | 1:43 | 2:00 |
| 153 | 2 | Fr. | | 6:34 | 8:37 | 2:40 | 2:37 |
| 154 | 3 | Sa. | ♃ ♂ ☾ (9 pm) | 6:34 | 8:38 | 3:35 | 3:12 |
| 155 | 4 | Su. | | 6:33 | 8:38 | 4:29 | 3:45 |
| 156 | 5 | Mo. | | 6:33 | 8:39 | 5:22 | 4:19 |
| 157 | 6 | Tu. | | 6:33 | 8:39 | 6:15 | 4:53 |
| 158 | 7 | We. | | 6:33 | 8:40 | 7:08 | 5:29 |
| 159 | 8 | Th. | ☾ at apogee (5 pm) | 6:33 | 8:40 | 8:00 | 6:08 |
| 160 | 9 | Fr. | Full ☾; ♄ ♂ ☾ (8 pm) | 6:33 | 8:41 | 8:51 | 6:49 |
| 161 | 10 | Sa. | | 6:33 | 8:41 | 9:40 | 7:34 |
| 162 | 11 | Su. | | 6:33 | 8:41 | 10:27 | 8:22 |
| 163 | 12 | Mo. | | 6:33 | 8:42 | 11:12 | 9:12 |
| 164 | 13 | Tu. | | 6:33 | 8:42 | 11:53 | 10:05 |
| 165 | 14 | We. | | 6:33 | 8:42 | | 11:00 |
| 166 | 15 | Th. | | 6:33 | 8:42 | 12:33 | 11:56 |
| 167 | 16 | Fr. | | 6:33 | 8:43 | 1:11 | 12:54 |
| 168 | 17 | Sa. | Last qtr. ☾ | 6:33 | 8:43 | 1:47 | 1:53 |
| 169 | 18 | Su. | | 6:33 | 8:44 | 2:25 | 2:53 |
| 170 | 19 | Mo. | | 6:34 | 8:44 | 3:03 | 3:57 |
| 171 | 20 | Tu. | Solstice (11:24 pm) | 6:34 | 8:44 | 3:44 | 5:02 |
| 172 | 21 | We. | | 6:34 | 8:44 | 4:29 | 6:10 |
| 173 | 22 | Th. | | 6:34 | 8:45 | 5:19 | 7:18 |
| 174 | 23 | Fr. | New ☾ at perigee | 6:35 | 8:45 | 6:15 | 8:25 |
| 175 | 24 | Sa. | | 6:35 | 8:45 | 7:16 | 9:27 |
| 176 | 25 | Su. | | 6:35 | 8:45 | 8:20 | 10:23 |
| 177 | 26 | Mo. | | 6:35 | 8:45 | 9:25 | 11:13 |
| 178 | 27 | Tu. | Regulus ♂ ☾ (8 pm) | 6:36 | 8:45 | 10:30 | 11:57 |
| 179 | 28 | We. | | 6:36 | 8:45 | 11:31 | |
| 180 | 29 | Th. | | 6:36 | 8:45 | 12:31 | 12:36 |
| 181 | 30 | Fr. | First qtr. ☾ | 6:37 | 8:45 | 1:28 | 1:13 |

☉ The Sun   ● The Earth   ☽ The Moon   ☿ Mercury   ♀ Venus   ♂ Mars   ♃ Jupiter   ♄ Saturn   ♅ Uranus   ♆ Neptune   ♇ Pluto   ☌ = in conjunction   ☍ = opposition to the ☉

# Astronomical Calendar for 2017

## 7th Month — July 2017 — 31 Days

**Moon Phases** — *Full,* July 8, 11:07 p.m.; *Last Qtr.,* July 16, 2:26 p.m.; *New,* July 23, 4:46 a.m.; *First Qtr.,* July 30, 10:23 a.m.

| Day of Year | Day of Month | Day of Week | Planetary Configurations and Phenomena | Sunrise | Sunset | Moon-rise | Moon-set |
|---|---|---|---|---|---|---|---|
| 182 | 1 | Sa. | | 6:37 | 8:45 | **2:23** | 1:47 |
| 183 | 2 | Su. | ☿ ☌ Pollux (7 pm) | 6:38 | 8:45 | **3:17** | 2:21 |
| 184 | 3 | Mo. | ● at aphelion (3 pm) | 6:38 | 8:45 | **4:10** | 2:55 |
| 185 | 4 | Tu. | | 6:39 | 8:45 | **5:03** | 3:30 |
| 186 | 5 | We. | ☾ at apogee (11 pm) | 6:39 | 8:45 | **5:55** | 4:08 |
| 187 | 6 | Th. | ♄ ☌ ☾ (10 pm) | 6:39 | 8:45 | **6:46** | 4:48 |
| 188 | 7 | Fr. | | 6:40 | 8:45 | **7:37** | 5:31 |
| 189 | 8 | Sa. | Full ☾ | 6:40 | 8:44 | **8:25** | 6:18 |
| 190 | 9 | Su. | | 6:41 | 8:44 | **9:11** | 7:08 |
| 191 | 10 | Mo. | | 6:41 | 8:44 | **9:54** | 8:01 |
| 192 | 11 | Tu. | | 6:42 | 8:44 | **10:34** | 8:55 |
| 193 | 12 | We. | | 6:42 | 8:43 | **11:12** | 9:51 |
| 194 | 13 | Th. | | 6:43 | 8:43 | **11:49** | 10:48 |
| 195 | 14 | Fr. | ♀ ☌ Aldebaran (6 am) | 6:44 | 8:43 | | 11:46 |
| 196 | 15 | Sa. | | 6:44 | 8:42 | 12:26 | **12:45** |
| 197 | 16 | Su. | Last qtr. ☾ | 6:45 | 8:42 | 1:02 | **1:46** |
| 198 | 17 | Mo. | | 6:45 | 8:41 | 1:41 | **2:48** |
| 199 | 18 | Tu. | | 6:46 | 8:41 | 2:23 | **3:53** |
| 200 | 19 | We. | | 6:46 | 8:41 | 3:09 | **4:59** |
| 201 | 20 | Th. | ♀ ☌ ☾ (6 am) | 6:47 | 8:40 | 4:00 | **6:04** |
| 202 | 21 | Fr. | ☾ at perigee (11 am) | 6:48 | 8:40 | 4:57 | **7:08** |
| 203 | 22 | Sa. | | 6:48 | 8:39 | 5:59 | **8:07** |
| 204 | 23 | Su. | New ☾ | 6:49 | 8:38 | 7:04 | **9:00** |
| 205 | 24 | Mo. | | 6:50 | 8:38 | 8:09 | **9:48** |
| 206 | 25 | Tu. | ☿ ☌ Regulus (4 am) | 6:50 | 8:37 | 9:14 | **10:31** |
| 207 | 26 | We. | | 6:51 | 8:37 | 10:16 | **11:09** |
| 208 | 27 | Th. | | 6:51 | 8:36 | 11:15 | **11:46** |
| 209 | 28 | Fr. | | 6:52 | 8:35 | **12:13** | |
| 210 | 29 | Sa. | | 6:53 | 8:35 | **1:08** | 12:20 |
| 211 | 30 | Su. | First qtr. ☾ | 6:53 | 8:34 | **2:02** | 12:55 |
| 212 | 31 | Mo. | | 6:54 | 8:33 | **2:56** | 1:30 |

## 8th Month — August 2017 — 31 Days

**Moon Phases** — *Full,* Aug. 7, 1:11 p.m.; *Last Qtr.,* Aug. 14, 8:15 p.m.; *New,* Aug. 21, 1:30 p.m.; *First Qtr.,* Aug. 29, 3:13 a.m.

| Day of Year | Day of Month | Day of Week | Planetary Configurations and Phenomena | Sunrise | Sunset | Moon-rise | Moon-set |
|---|---|---|---|---|---|---|---|
| 213 | 1 | Tu. | | 6:55 | 8:32 | **3:48** | 2:07 |
| 214 | 2 | We. | ☾ at apogee (1 pm) | 6:55 | 8:32 | **4:40** | 2:46 |
| 215 | 3 | Th. | ♄ ☌ ☾ (2 am) | 6:56 | 8:31 | **5:31** | 3:28 |
| 216 | 4 | Fr. | | 6:56 | 8:30 | **6:20** | 4:14 |
| 217 | 5 | Sa. | | 6:57 | 8:29 | **7:07** | 5:02 |
| 218 | 6 | Su. | | 6:58 | 8:28 | **7:51** | 5:54 |
| 219 | 7 | Mo. | Full ☾ | 6:58 | 8:27 | **8:33** | 6:49 |
| 220 | 8 | Tu. | | 6:59 | 8:26 | **9:13** | 7:45 |
| 221 | 9 | We. | | 7:00 | 8:25 | **9:51** | 8:42 |
| 222 | 10 | Th. | | 7:00 | 8:25 | **10:27** | 9:41 |
| 223 | 11 | Fr. | | 7:01 | 8:24 | **11:04** | 10:40 |
| 224 | 12 | Sa. | | 7:01 | 8:23 | **11:42** | 11:40 |
| 225 | 13 | Su. | ⛢ ☌ ☾ (12 am) | 7:02 | 8:22 | | **12:41** |
| 226 | 14 | Mo. | Last qtr. ☾ | 7:03 | 8:21 | 12:22 | **1:44** |
| 227 | 15 | Tu. | | 7:03 | 8:20 | 1:05 | **2:48** |
| 228 | 16 | We. | Aldebaran ☌ ☾ (2 am) | 7:04 | 8:19 | 1:53 | **3:51** |
| 229 | 17 | Th. | | 7:05 | 8:18 | 2:46 | **4:54** |
| 230 | 18 | Fr. | ☾ at perigee (8 am) | 7:05 | 8:16 | 3:44 | **5:53** |
| 231 | 19 | Sa. | | 7:06 | 8:15 | 4:46 | **6:48** |
| 232 | 20 | Su. | | 7:06 | 8:14 | 5:50 | **7:38** |
| 233 | 21 | Mo. | New ☾; **Eclipse** ⊙ | 7:07 | 8:13 | 6:55 | **8:22** |
| 234 | 22 | Tu. | | 7:08 | 8:12 | 7:58 | **9:03** |
| 235 | 23 | We. | | 7:08 | 8:11 | 8:59 | **9:41** |
| 236 | 24 | Th. | | 7:09 | 8:10 | 9:59 | **10:17** |
| 237 | 25 | Fr. | | 7:09 | 8:09 | 10:56 | **10:52** |
| 238 | 26 | Sa. | | 7:10 | 8:07 | 11:52 | **11:27** |
| 239 | 27 | Su. | | 7:11 | 8:06 | **12:46** | |
| 240 | 28 | Mo. | | 7:11 | 8:05 | **1:40** | 12:04 |
| 241 | 29 | Tu. | First qtr. ☾ | 7:12 | 8:04 | **2:32** | 12:42 |
| 242 | 30 | We. | ☾ at apogee; ♄ ☌ ☾ | 7:12 | 8:03 | **3:23** | 1:23 |
| 243 | 31 | Th. | | 7:13 | 8:01 | **4:13** | 2:07 |

## 9th Month — September 2017 — 30 Days

**Moon Phases** — *Full,* Sept. 6, 2:03 a.m.; *Last Qtr.,* Sept. 13, 1:25 a.m.; *New,* Sept. 20, 12:30 a.m.; *First Qtr.,* Sept. 27, 9:54 p.m.

| Day of Year | Day of Month | Day of Week | Planetary Configurations and Phenomena | Sunrise | Sunset | Moon-rise | Moon-set |
|---|---|---|---|---|---|---|---|
| 244 | 1 | Fr. | | 7:14 | 8:00 | **5:01** | 2:55 |
| 245 | 2 | Sa. | | 7:14 | 7:59 | **5:46** | 3:46 |
| 246 | 3 | Su. | | 7:15 | 7:58 | **6:29** | 4:39 |
| 247 | 4 | Mo. | | 7:15 | 7:57 | **7:10** | 5:35 |
| 248 | 5 | Tu. | ♃ ☌ Spica (6 am) | 7:16 | 7:55 | **7:49** | 6:33 |
| 249 | 6 | We. | Full ☾; ♆ ☌ ☾ (12 am) | 7:17 | 7:54 | **8:27** | 7:31 |
| 250 | 7 | Th. | | 7:17 | 7:53 | **9:04** | 8:31 |
| 251 | 8 | Fr. | | 7:18 | 7:52 | **9:42** | 9:32 |
| 252 | 9 | Sa. | ⛢ ☌ ☾ (5 am) | 7:18 | 7:50 | **10:22** | 10:34 |
| 253 | 10 | Su. | | 7:19 | 7:49 | **11:04** | 11:37 |
| 254 | 11 | Mo. | | 7:19 | 7:48 | **11:50** | **12:41** |
| 255 | 12 | Tu. | | 7:20 | 7:46 | | **1:45** |
| 256 | 13 | We. | Last qtr. ☾ at perigee | 7:21 | 7:45 | 12:41 | **2:47** |
| 257 | 14 | Th. | | 7:21 | 7:44 | 1:36 | **3:46** |
| 258 | 15 | Fr. | | 7:22 | 7:43 | 2:36 | **4:41** |
| 259 | 16 | Sa. | | 7:22 | 7:41 | 3:37 | **5:31** |
| 260 | 17 | Su. | | 7:23 | 7:40 | 4:40 | **6:16** |
| 261 | 18 | Mo. | | 7:23 | 7:39 | 5:43 | **6:58** |
| 262 | 19 | Tu. | | 7:24 | 7:37 | 6:44 | **7:36** |
| 263 | 20 | We. | New ☾ | 7:25 | 7:36 | 7:44 | **8:13** |
| 264 | 21 | Th. | | 7:25 | 7:35 | 8:43 | **8:48** |
| 265 | 22 | Fr. | | 7:26 | 7:33 | 9:39 | **9:24** |
| 266 | 23 | Sa. | **Equinox** (3:02 pm) | 7:26 | 7:32 | 10:35 | **10:00** |
| 267 | 24 | Su. | | 7:27 | 7:31 | 11:30 | **10:38** |
| 268 | 25 | Mo. | | 7:28 | 7:30 | **12:23** | **11:18** |
| 269 | 26 | Tu. | ♄ ☌ ☾ (7 pm) | 7:28 | 7:28 | **1:15** | |
| 270 | 27 | We. | First qtr. ☾ at apogee | 7:29 | 7:27 | **2:05** | 12:01 |
| 271 | 28 | Th. | | 7:29 | 7:26 | **2:54** | 12:47 |
| 272 | 29 | Fr. | | 7:30 | 7:25 | **3:40** | 1:36 |
| 273 | 30 | Sa. | | 7:31 | 7:23 | **4:23** | 2:28 |

**Bright stars =** Aldebaran, Antares, Spica, Pollux, Regulus. **Minor planets or asteroids =** Ceres, Pallas, Juno, Vesta ☌ = in conjunction by 10° or < ☍ = opposition to ⊙

# Astronomical Calendar for 2017

## 10th Month — October 2017 — 31 Days

Moon Phases — *Full,* Oct. 5, 1:40 p.m.; *Last Qtr.,* Oct. 12, 7:25 a.m.; *New,* Oct. 19, 2:12 p.m.; *First Qtr.,* Oct. 27, 5:22 p.m.

| Year | Month | Week | Planetary Configurations and Phenomena | Sunrise | Sunset | Moon-rise | Moon-set |
|---|---|---|---|---|---|---|---|
| 274 | 1 | Su. |  | 7:31 | 7:22 | **5:04** | 3:22 |
| 275 | 2 | Mo. |  | 7:32 | 7:21 | **5:44** | 4:19 |
| 276 | 3 | Tu. |  | 7:32 | 7:20 | **6:22** | 5:17 |
| 277 | 4 | We. |  | 7:33 | 7:18 | **7:00** | 6:17 |
| 278 | 5 | Th. | Full ☾ | 7:34 | 7:17 | **7:38** | 7:19 |
| 279 | 6 | Fr. |  | 7:34 | 7:16 | **8:18** | 8:22 |
| 280 | 7 | Sa. |  | 7:35 | 7:15 | **9:01** | 9:26 |
| 281 | 8 | Su. |  | 7:36 | 7:13 | **9:47** | 10:32 |
| 282 | 9 | Mo. | ☾ at perigee (1 am) | 7:36 | 7:12 | **10:37** | 11:37 |
| 283 | 10 | Tu. |  | 7:37 | 7:11 | **11:31** | **12:41** |
| 284 | 11 | We. |  | 7:37 | 7:10 |  | **1:42** |
| 285 | 12 | Th. | Last qtr. ☾ | 7:38 | 7:09 | 12:30 | **2:38** |
| 286 | 13 | Fr. |  | 7:39 | 7:08 | 1:31 | **3:29** |
| 287 | 14 | Sa. |  | 7:40 | 7:06 | 2:33 | **4:15** |
| 288 | 15 | Su. | ☾ ☌ Regulus (6 am) | 7:40 | 7:05 | 3:34 | **4:56** |
| 289 | 16 | Mo. |  | 7:41 | 7:04 | 4:35 | **5:35** |
| 290 | 17 | Tu. |  | 7:42 | 7:03 | 5:34 | **6:11** |
| 291 | 18 | We. | New ☾ | 7:42 | 7:01 | 6:32 | **6:46** |
| 292 | 19 | Th. |  | 7:43 | 7:00 | 7:29 | **7:21** |
| 293 | 20 | Fr. |  | 7:44 | 7:00 | 8:25 | **7:57** |
| 294 | 21 | Sa. |  | 7:45 | 6:59 | 9:20 | **8:34** |
| 295 | 22 | Su. |  | 7:45 | 6:58 | 10:14 | **9:13** |
| 296 | 23 | Mo. |  | 7:46 | 6:57 | 11:07 | **9:55** |
| 297 | 24 | Tu. | ☾ at apogee (9 pm) | 7:47 | 6:56 | 11:58 | **10:40** |
| 298 | 25 | We. |  | 7:48 | 6:55 | **12:47** | **11:27** |
| 299 | 26 | Th. |  | 7:48 | 6:54 | **1:34** |  |
| 300 | 27 | Fr. | First qtr. ☾ | 7:49 | 6:53 | **2:18** | 12:17 |
| 301 | 28 | Sa. |  | 7:50 | 6:52 | **2:59** | 1:10 |
| 302 | 29 | Su. |  | 7:51 | 6:51 | **3:39** | 2:05 |
| 303 | 30 | Mo. |  | 7:51 | 6:50 | **4:16** | 3:01 |
| 304 | 31 | Tu. |  | 7:52 | 6:49 | **4:54** | 3:59 |

## 11th Month — November 2017 — 30 Days

Moon Phases — *Full,* Nov. 4, 12:23 a.m.; *Last Qtr.,* Nov. 10, 2:36 p.m.; *New,* Nov. 18, 5:42 a.m.; *First Qtr.,* Nov. 26, 11:03 a.m.

| Year | Month | Week | Planetary Configurations and Phenomena | Sunrise | Sunset | Moon-rise | Moon-set |
|---|---|---|---|---|---|---|---|
| 305 | 1 | We. |  | 7:53 | 6:48 | **5:31** | **5:00** |
| 306 | 2 | Th. | ☿ ☌ ☾ (8 pm) | 7:54 | 6:48 | **6:10** | **6:02** |
| 307 | 3 | Fr. |  | 7:55 | 6:47 | **6:52** | **7:07** |
| 308 | 4 | Sa. | Full ☾ | 7:55 | 6:46 | **7:37** | **8:14** |
| 309 | †5 | Su. | DST ends — ☾ at perigee | 6:56 | 5:45 | **7:27** | 8:21 |
| 310 | 6 | Mo. |  | 6:57 | 5:45 | **8:22** | 9:29 |
| 311 | 7 | Tu. |  | 6:58 | 5:44 | **9:21** | 10:33 |
| 312 | 8 | We. |  | 6:59 | 5:43 | **10:23** | 11:33 |
| 313 | 9 | Th. |  | 7:00 | 5:42 | **11:26** | **12:27** |
| 314 | 10 | Fr. | Last qtr. ☾ | 7:01 | 5:42 | 12:28 | **1:15** |
| 315 | 11 | Sa. |  | 7:01 | 5:41 | 1:29 | **1:58** |
| 316 | 12 | Su. |  | 7:02 | 5:41 | 2:28 | **2:37** |
| 317 | 13 | Mo. | ♀ ☌ ♃ (12 am) | 7:03 | 5:40 | 3:26 | **3:13** |
| 318 | 14 | Tu. |  | 7:04 | 5:40 | 4:22 | **3:48** |
| 319 | 15 | We. |  | 7:05 | 5:39 | 5:17 | **4:22** |
| 320 | 16 | Th. |  | 7:06 | 5:39 | 6:12 | **4:56** |
| 321 | 17 | Fr. |  | 7:06 | 5:38 | 7:07 | **5:32** |
| 322 | 18 | Sa. | New ☾ | 7:07 | 5:38 | 8:00 | **6:10** |
| 323 | 19 | Su. |  | 7:08 | 5:38 | 8:52 | **6:51** |
| 324 | 20 | Mo. | ☾ at apogee (1 pm) | 7:09 | 5:37 | 9:43 | **7:35** |
| 325 | 21 | Tu. |  | 7:10 | 5:37 | 10:30 | **8:21** |
| 326 | 22 | We. | ♄ ☌ ☾ (6 pm) | 7:11 | 5:36 | 11:15 | **9:10** |
| 327 | 23 | Th. |  | 7:12 | 5:36 | 11:57 | **10:02** |
| 328 | 24 | Fr. |  | 7:13 | 5:36 | **12:36** | **10:55** |
| 329 | 25 | Sa. |  | 7:14 | 5:35 | **1:13** | **11:49** |
| 330 | 26 | Su. | First qtr. ☾ | 7:15 | 5:35 | **1:50** |  |
| 331 | 27 | Mo. | ♂ ☌ Spica (6 pm) | 7:16 | 5:35 | **2:26** | 12:45 |
| 332 | 28 | Tu. | ☿ ☌ ♄ (3 am) | 7:16 | 5:35 | **3:03** | 1:43 |
| 333 | 29 | We. |  | 7:17 | 5:35 | **3:42** | 2:42 |
| 334 | 30 | Th. | ☿ ☌ ☾ (4 am) | 7:17 | 5:35 | **4:24** | 3:45 |

† Daylight Saving Time ends at 2 a.m.

## 12th Month — December 2017 — 31 Days

Moon Phases — *Full,* Dec. 3, 9:47 a.m.; *Last Qtr.,* Dec. 10, 1:51 a.m.; *New,* Dec. 18, 12:30 a.m.; *First Qtr.,* Dec. 26, 3:20 a.m.

| Year | Month | Week | Planetary Configurations and Phenomena | Sunrise | Sunset | Moon-rise | Moon-set |
|---|---|---|---|---|---|---|---|
| 335 | 1 | Fr. |  | 7:18 | 5:35 | **4:24** | 4:49 |
| 336 | 2 | Sa. |  | 7:19 | 5:35 | **5:12** | 5:57 |
| 337 | 3 | Su. | Full ☾ | 7:20 | 5:35 | **6:05** | 7:06 |
| 338 | 4 | Mo. | ☾ at perigee (3 am) | 7:21 | 5:35 | **7:04** | 8:14 |
| 339 | 5 | Tu. |  | 7:21 | 5:35 | **8:07** | 9:19 |
| 340 | 6 | We. |  | 7:22 | 5:35 | **9:12** | 10:18 |
| 341 | 7 | Th. |  | 7:23 | 5:35 | **10:18** | 11:11 |
| 342 | 8 | Fr. |  | 7:24 | 5:35 | **11:21** | 11:57 |
| 343 | 9 | Sa. |  | 7:24 | 5:35 |  | **12:38** |
| 344 | 10 | Su. | Last qtr. ☾ | 7:25 | 5:35 | 12:22 | **1:16** |
| 345 | 11 | Mo. |  | 7:26 | 5:36 | 1:21 | **1:51** |
| 346 | 12 | Tu. |  | 7:27 | 5:36 | 2:17 | **2:25** |
| 347 | 13 | We. |  | 7:27 | 5:36 | 3:13 | **2:59** |
| 348 | 14 | Th. |  | 7:28 | 5:37 | 4:07 | **3:34** |
| 349 | 15 | Fr. |  | 7:28 | 5:37 | 5:02 | **4:10** |
| 350 | 16 | Sa. |  | 7:29 | 5:37 | 5:55 | **4:50** |
| 351 | 17 | Su. |  | 7:30 | 5:38 | 6:48 | **5:32** |
| 352 | 18 | Mo. | New ☾ at apogee | 7:30 | 5:38 | 7:39 | **6:17** |
| 353 | 19 | Tu. |  | 7:31 | 5:38 | 8:27 | **7:06** |
| 354 | 20 | We. |  | 7:31 | 5:39 | 9:13 | **7:56** |
| 355 | 21 | Th. | Solstice (10:28 am) | 7:32 | 5:39 | 9:56 | **8:49** |
| 356 | 22 | Fr. |  | 7:32 | 5:40 | 10:36 | **9:43** |
| 357 | 23 | Sa. |  | 7:33 | 5:41 | 11:14 | **10:37** |
| 358 | 24 | Su. |  | 7:33 | 5:41 | 11:49 | **11:33** |
| 359 | 25 | Mo. |  | 7:34 | 5:42 | **12:24** |  |
| 360 | 26 | Tu. | First qtr. ☾ | 7:34 | 5:42 | **12:59** | 12:30 |
| 361 | 27 | We. |  | 7:34 | 5:43 | **1:36** | 1:28 |
| 362 | 28 | Th. |  | 7:35 | 5:44 | **2:15** | 2:29 |
| 363 | 29 | Fr. |  | 7:35 | 5:44 | **2:58** | 3:33 |
| 364 | 30 | Sa. | Aldebaran ☌ ☾ (7 pm) | 7:35 | 5:45 | **3:47** | 4:40 |
| 365 | 31 | Su. |  | 7:36 | 5:46 | **4:42** | 5:48 |

☉ The Sun   ● The Earth   ☾ The Moon   ☿ Mercury   ♀ Venus   ♂ Mars   ♃ Jupiter   ♄ Saturn   ♆ Neptune   ⛢ Uranus   ♇ Pluto   ☌ = in conjunction   ☍ = opposition to the ☉

# Recreation

*Colorful catamarans glide across the Gulf of Mexico off South Padre.
Photo courtesy of the City of South Padre Island.*

**Texas State Parks and Historic Sites**
**Texas State Forests**
**National Parks and Recreation Areas**
**Birding, Fishing, Hunting**
**Fairs and Festivals**

*Gage Hotel Sponsors the Recreation Section*

# Texas State Parks and Historic Sites

Texas' diverse system of state parks and historic sites offers contrasting attractions — mountains and canyons, arid deserts and lush forests, spring-fed streams, sandy dunes, saltwater surf and fascinating historic sites.

The state park information was provided by **Texas Parks and Wildlife** (TPW) and the historic site information was provided by the **Texas Historical Commission**. Additional information and brochures on individual parks are available from the TPW's Austin headquarters, 4200 Smith School Rd., Austin 78744; 1-800-792-1112; **http://tpwd.texas.gov**, and the historical commission, **www.thc.state.tx.us/**.

The TPW's **Central Reservation Center** can take reservations for almost all state parks. Exceptions are Indian Lodge, the Texas State Railroad, and facilities not operated by the TPW. Call the center during usual business hours at 512-389-8900. The TDD line is 512-389-8915.

The **Texas State Parks Pass**, currently costing $60 per year, waives entrance fees for all members and all passengers in member's vehicle to all state parks when entrance fees are required, as well as other benefits. For further information, contact TPW 512-389-8900.

**Texas State Parklands Passport** is a windshield decal granting discounted entrance to state parks for Texas residents who are senior citizens or are collecting Social Security disability payments and free entrance for disabled U.S. veterans. Available at state parks with proper identification. Details can be obtained at numbers or addresses above.

The following information is a brief glimpse of what each park has to offer. Refer to the **chart on pages 178–179** for a more complete list of available activities and facilities. Entrance fees to state parks range from $1 to $5 per person. There are also fees for tours and some activities. For up-to-date information, call the information number listed above before you go. Road abbreviations used in this list are: IH – interstate highway, US – U.S. Highway, TX – state highway, FM – farm-to-market road, PR – park road.

## List of State Parks and Historic Sites

**Abilene State Park**, 16 miles southwest of Abilene on FM 89 and PR 32 in Taylor County, consists of 529.4 acres that were deeded by the City of Abilene in 1933. A part of the **official Texas longhorn herd** and bison are located in the park. Large groves of pecan trees that once shaded bands of Comanches now shade visitors at picnic tables. Activities include camping, hiking, picnicking, nature study, biking, lake swimming and fishing. In addition to **Lake Abilene, Buffalo Gap**, the original Taylor County seat (1878) and one of the early frontier settlements, is nearby. Buffalo Gap was on the **Western**, or **Goodnight-Loving, Trail**, over which pioneer Texas cattlemen drove herds to railheads in Kansas.

**Acton State Historic Site** is a .01-acre cemetery plot in Hood County where **Davy Crockett's** second wife, Elizabeth, was buried in 1860. It is 4.5 miles east of Granbury on US 377 to FM 167 south, then 2.4 miles south to Acton. Nearby attractions include **Cleburne, Dinosaur Valley** and **Lake Whitney state parks**.

**Admiral Nimitz State Historic Site** (see **National Museum of the Pacific War**).

**Atlanta State Park** is 1,475 acres located 11 miles northwest of Atlanta on FM 1154 in Cass County; adjacent to **Wright Patman Dam** and **Reservoir**. Land acquired from the U.S. Army in 1954 by license to 2004 with option to renew to 2054. Camping, biking and hiking in pine forests, as well as water activities, such as boating, fishing, lake swimming. Nearby are historic town of **Jefferson** and the **Caddo Lake** and **Daingerfield state parks**.

---

### More Travel Information

Call the **Texas Department of Transportation**'s toll-free number: **1-800-888-8TEX** for:

• The **Texas State Travel Guide**, a free, full-color publication with information about attractions, activities, history and historic sites.

• The official **Texas state highway map**.

On the Internet: **www.traveltex.com**

---

**Balmorhea State Park** is 45.9 acres four miles southwest of Balmorhea on TX 17 between Balmorhea and Toyahvale in Reeves County. Deeded in 1934-35 by private owners and Reeves Co. Water Imp. Dist. No. 1 and built by the Civilian Conservation Corps (CCC). Swimming pool (1-3/4 acres) fed by artesian **San Solomon Springs**; also provides water to **aquatic refuge** in park. Activities include swimming, picnicking, camping, scuba and skin diving. Motel rooms available at **San Solomon Springs Courts**. Nearby are city of Pecos, **Fort Davis National Historic Site, Davis Mountains State Park** and **McDonald Observatory**.

**Barton Warnock Environmental Education Center** consists of 99.9 acres in Brewster County. Originally built by the Lajitas Foundation in 1982 as the Lajitas Museum Desert Gardens, the TPW purchased it in 1990 and renamed it for Texas botanist Dr. Barton Warnock. The center is also the eastern entrance station to **Big Bend Ranch State Park**. Self-guiding botanical and museum tours. On FM 170 one mile east of Lajitas.

**Bastrop State Park** is 3,503.7 acres one mile east of Bastrop on TX 21 or from TX 71. The park was acquired by deeds from the City of Bastrop and private owners in 1933-35; additional acreage acquired in 1979. Site of famous "Lost Pines," isolated region of loblolly pine and hardwoods. **Swimming pool, cabins** and **lodge** are among facilities. Fishing at Lake Bastrop, backpacking, picnicking, canoeing, bicycling, hiking. Golf course adjacent to park. **State capitol** at Austin 32 miles away; 13-mile drive through forest leads to **Buescher State Park**.

**Battleship** *Texas* **State Historic Site** (see **San Jacinto Battleground State Historic Site** and **Battleship Texas**)

**Bentsen-Rio Grande Valley State Park**, a scenic park, is along the Rio Grande five miles southwest of Mission off FM 2062 in Hidalgo County. The 760 acres of **subtropical resaca woodlands and brushlands** were acquired from private owners in 1944. Park is excellent base from which to tour **Lower Rio Grande Valley** of Texas and adjacent **Mexico**; most attractions within an hour's drive. Hiking trails provide chance to study unique plants and animals of park. Many birds unique to southern United States found here, including **pauraque, groove-billed ani, green kingfisher, rose-throated becard** and **tropical parula**. Birdwatching tours guided by park naturalists offered daily December–March. Park is one of last natural refuges in Texas for **ocelot** and **jaguarundi**. Trees include **cedar elm, anaqua, ebony** and **Mexican ash**. Camping, hiking, picnicking, boating, fishing also available. Nearby are **Santa Ana National Wildlife Refuge, Falcon State Park** and **Sabal Palm Sanctuary**.

**Big Bend Ranch State Park**, more than 299,008 acres of **Chihuahuan Desert wilderness** in Brewster and Presidio counties along the Rio Grande, was purchased from private owners in 1988. The purchase more than doubled the size of the state park system, which comprised at that time 220,000 acres. Eastern entrance at Barton Warnock Environmental Education Center one mile east of Lajitas on FM 170; western entrance is at **Fort Leaton State Historic Park** four miles east of Presidio on FM 170. The area includes **extinct volcanoes**, several **waterfalls**, two

*Devil's River State Natural Area preserves one of the best remaining examples of an ecologically intact river system in Texas. Unspoiled waters tumble over limestone and past rugged ridges, canyons, and grassy banks. All camping and pictograph tours are by reservation only. Photo by Laurence Parent; Texas Parks and Wildlife Department.*

mountain ranges, at least **11 rare species of plants and animals**, and **90 major archaeological sites**. There is little development. Vehicular access limited; wilderness backpacking, hiking, scenic drive, picnicking, fishing and swimming. There are longhorns in the park, although they are not part of the official **state longhorn herd**.

**Big Spring State Park** is 382 acres located on FM 700 within the city limits of Big Spring in Howard County. Both city and park were named for a natural spring that was replaced by an artificial one. The park was deeded by the City of Big Spring in 1934 and 1935. Drive to top of **Scenic Mountain** provides panoramic view of surrounding country and look at **prairie dog colony**. The "big spring," nearby in a city park, provided watering place for herds of bison, antelope and wild horses. Used extensively also as campsite for early Indians, explorers and settlers.

**Blanco State Park** is 104.6 acres along the Blanco River four blocks south of Blanco's town square in Blanco County. The land was deeded by private owners in 1933. Park area was used as campsite by early explorers and settlers. Fishing, camping, swimming, picnicking, boating. **LBJ Ranch** and **LBJ State Historic Site, Pedernales Falls** and **Guadalupe River state parks** are nearby.

**Bonham State Park** is a 261-acre park located two miles southeast of Bonham on TX 78, then two miles southeast on FM 271 in Fannin County. It includes a 65-acre lake, **rolling prairies** and **woodlands**. The land was acquired in 1933 from the City of Bonham. Swimming, camping, mountain-bike trail, lighted fishing pier, boating. **Sam Rayburn Memorial Library** in Bonham. **Sam Rayburn Home** and **Valley Lake** nearby.

**Brazos Bend State Park** in Fort Bend County, eight miles east of Damon off FM 1462 on FM 762, approximately 28 miles south of Houston. The 4,897-acre park was purchased from private owners in 1976–77. **George Observatory** in park. **Observation platform** for spotting and photographing the **270 species of birds, 23 species of mammals, and 21 species of reptiles and amphibians, including American alligator**, that frequent the park. Interpretive and educational programs every weekend.

Backpacking, camping, hiking, biking, fishing. Creekfield Lake Nature Trail.

**Buescher State Park**, a scenic area, is 1,016.7 acres 2 miles northwest of Smithville off TX 71 to FM 153 in Bastrop County. Acquired between 1933 and 1936, about one-third deeded by private owner; heirs donated a third; balance from City of Smithville. **El Camino Real** once ran near park, connecting **San Antonio de Béxar** with **Spanish missions in East Texas**. Park land was part of **Stephen F. Austin's colonial grant.** Some **250 species of birds** can be seen. Camping, fishing, hiking, boating. Scenic park road connects with **Bastrop State Park** through **Lost Pines** area.

**Caddo Lake State Park**, north of Karnack one mile off TX 43 to FM 2198 in Harrison County, consists of 483.85 acres along **Cypress Bayou**, which runs into Caddo Lake. A scenic area, it was acquired from private owners in 1933. Nearby Karnack is childhood home of Lady Bird Johnson. Close by is old city of **Jefferson**, famous as commercial center of Northeast Texas during last half of 19th century. Caddo Indian legend attributes formation of Caddo Lake to **a huge flood**. Cypress trees, **American lotus** and **lily pads**, as well as **71 species of fish**, predominate in lake. **Nutria, beaver, mink, squirrel, armadillo, alligator** and **turtle** abound. Activities include camping, hiking, swimming, fishing, canoeing. Screened shelters, cabins.

**Caddo Mounds State Historic Site** in Cherokee County six miles southwest of Alto on TX 21. Total of 93.8 acres acquired in 1975. Open for day visits only, park offers exhibits and interpretive trails through reconstructed **Caddo dwellings and ceremonial areas**, including two temple mounds, a burial mound and a village area typical of people who lived in region for 500 years beginning about A.D. 800. Open Tuesday–Sunday. Nearby are **Jim Hogg** and **Mission Tejas State historic sites** and **Texas State Railroad**.

**Caprock Canyons State Park and Trailway**, 100 miles southeast of Amarillo and 3.5 miles north of Quitaque off FM 1065 and TX 86 in Briscoe, Floyd, and Hall counties, has 15,313 acres. Purchased in 1975. Scenic escarpment's canyons provided camping areas for **Indians of Folsom culture** more than 10,000 years ago. **Mesquite** and **cacti** in the **badlands** give way to **tall grasses, cottonwood** and **plum thickets** in the bottomlands. Wildlife includes **aoudad sheep, coyote, bobcat, porcupine** and **fox**. Activities include scenic drive, camping, hiking, mountain-bike riding, horse riding and horse camping. A **64.25-mile trailway** (hike, bike, and equestrian trail) extends from South Plains to Estelline.

**Casa Navarro State Historic Site**, on .7 acre at corner of S. Laredo and W. Nueva streets in downtown San Antonio, was acquired by donation from San Antonio Conservation Society Foundation in 1975. The furnished **Navarro House** three-building complex, built about 1848, was home of statesman, rancher and Texas patriot **José Antonio Navarro**. Guided tours; exhibits. Open Wednesday through Sunday.

**Cedar Hill State Park**, an urban park on 1,826 acres 10 miles southwest of Dallas via US 67 and FM 1382 on **Joe Pool Lake**, was acquired by long-term lease from the Army Corp of Engineers in 1982. Camping mostly in wooded areas. Fishing from two lighted jetties and a perch pond for children. Swimming, boating, bicycling, birdwatching and picnicking. Vegetation includes several sections of **tall-grass prairie**. Penn Farm Agricultural History Center includes reconstructed buildings of the **19th-century Penn Farm** and exhibits; self-guided tours.

**Choke Canyon State Park** consists of two units, South Shore and Calliham, located on 26,000-acre **Choke Canyon Reservoir**. Park acquired in 1981 in a 50-year agreement among Bureau of Reclamation, City of Corpus Christi and Nueces River Authority. Thickets of **mesquite** and **blackbrush acacia** predominate, supporting populations of **javelina, coyote, skunk** and **alligator**, as well as the **crested caracara**. The 385-acre **South Shore Unit** is located 3.5 miles west of Three Rivers on TX 72 in Live Oak County; the 1,100-acre **Calliham Unit** is located 12 miles west of Three Rivers, on TX 72, in McMullen County. Both units offer camping, picnicking, boating, fishing, lake swimming, and baseball and volleyball areas. The Calliham Unit also has a hiking trail, wildlife educational center, screened shelters, rentable **gym and kitchen**. **Sports complex** includes swimming pool and tennis, volleyball, shuffleboard and basketball courts. Across dam from South Shore is North Shore Equestrian and Camping Area; 18 miles of horseback riding trails.

**Cleburne State Park** is a 528-acre park located 10 miles southwest of Cleburne via US 67 and PR 21 in Johnson County with 116-acre spring-fed lake; acquired from the City of Cleburne and private owners in 1935 and 1936. **Oak, elm, mesquite, cedar** and **redbud** cover white rocky hills. Bluebonnets in spring. Activities include camping, picnicking, hiking, bicycling, canoeing, swimming, boating, fishing. Nearby are **Fossil Rim Wildlife Center** and **dinosaur tracks** in Paluxy River at **Dinosaur Valley State Park**.

**Colorado Bend State Park**, a 5,328.3-acre facility, is 28 miles west of Lampasas in Lampasas and San Saba counties. Access is from Lampasas to Bend on FM 580 west, then follow signs (access road subject to flooding). Park site was purchased partly in 1984, with balance acquired in 1987. Primitive camping, fishing, swimming, hiking, biking and picnicking; guided tours to Gorman Falls; crawling cave tours require reservations. Rare and endangered species here include **golden-cheeked warbler, black-capped vireo** and **bald eagle**.

**Confederate Reunion Grounds State Historic Site**, located in Limestone County on the Navasota River, is 77.1 acres in size. Acquired 1983 by deed from Joseph E. Johnston Camp No. 94 CSA. Entrance is 6 miles south of Mexia on TX 14, then 2.5 miles west on FM 2705. **Historic buildings**, two **scenic footbridges** span creek; hiking trail. Nearby are **Fort Parker State Park** and **Old Fort Parker**.

**Cooper Lake State Park**, comprises 3,026 acres three miles southeast of Cooper in Delta and Hopkins counties acquired in 1991 by 25-year lease from Army Corps of Engineers. Two units, **Doctors Creek** and **South Sulphur**, adjoin 19,300-surface-acre Cooper Lake. Fishing, boating, camping, picnicking, swimming. Screened shelters and cabins. South Sulphur offers equestrian camping and horseback riding trails. Access to Doctors Creek Unit is via TX 24 east from Commerce to Cooper, then east on TX 154 to FM 1529 to park. To South Sulphur Unit, take IH 30 to Exit 122 west of Sulphur Springs to TX 19, then TX 71, then FM 3505.

**Copper Breaks State Park**, 12 miles south of Quanah on TX 6 in Hardeman County, was acquired by purchase from private owner in 1970. Park features rugged scenic beauty on 1,898.8 acres, two lakes, **grass-covered mesas** and juniper breaks. Nearby **medicine mounds** were important ceremonial sites of Comanche Indians. Nearby **Pease River** was site of 1860 battle in which **Cynthia Ann Parker** was recovered from Comanches. Part of **state longhorn herd** lives at park. Abundant wildlife. Nature, hiking and equestrian trails; natural and historical exhibits; summer programs; horseback riding; camping, equestrian camping.

*Picnickers enjoy a spring day at the South Shore Unit at Choke Canyon State Park on the McMullen and Live Oak county line in South Texas. The South Shore Unit is a day-use park, while the Calliham Unit has additional activities, such as camping and a beach on the Choke Canyon Reservoir. Texas Parks and Wildlife Department photo.*

*Lake Livingston State Park in the Pineywoods offers several camping options including screened shelters on the lake. Texas Parks and Wildlife photo.*

**Daingerfield State Park**, off TX 49 and PR 17 southeast of Daingerfield in Morris County, is a 550.9-acre recreational area that includes an 80-surface-acre lake; deeded in 1935 by private owners. This area is center of iron industry in Texas; nearby is Lone Star Steel Co. In spring, **dogwood, redbuds** and **wisteria** bloom; in fall, brilliant foliage of **sweetgum, oaks** and **maples** contrast with dark green pines. Campsites, lodge and cabins.

**Davis Mountains State Park** is 2,709 acres in Jeff Davis County, 4 miles northwest of Fort Davis via TX 118 and PR 3. The scenic area was deeded in 1933-1937 by private owners. First European, **Antonio de Espejo**, came to area in 1583. Extremes of altitude produce both **plains grasslands** and **piñon-juniper-oak woodlands. Montezuma quail**, rare in Texas, visit park. Scenic drives, camping and hiking. **Indian Lodge**, built by the Civilian Conservation Corps during the early 1930s, has 39 rooms, restaurant and swimming pool (reservations: 432-426-3254). Four-mile hiking trail leads to **Fort Davis National Historic Site**. Other nearby points of interest include **McDonald Observatory** and 74-mile scenic loop through **Davis Mountains**. Nearby are scenic

Limpia, Madera, Musquiz and Keesey canyons; Camino del Rio; ghost town of Shafter; Big Bend National Park; Big Bend Ranch State Park; Fort Davis National Historic Site; and **Fort Leaton State Historic Site**.

**Devil's River State Natural Area** comprises 37,000 acres in Val Verde County, 22 miles off US 277, about 65 miles north of Del Rio on graded road. It is an **ecological and archaeological crossroads**. Ecologically, it is in a **transitional area** between the **Edwards Plateau**, the **Trans-Pecos desert** and the **South Texas brush country**. Archaeological studies suggest occupation and use by cultures from both east and west. Camping, hiking, and mountain biking. All camping, facility stays, canyon, and pictograph-site tours are by reservation only. **Dolan Falls** is nearby and is accessible only through The Nature Conservancy of Texas.

**Devil's Sinkhole State Natural Area**, comprising 1,859.7 acres about 6 miles northeast of Rocksprings on US 377 in Edwards County, is a **vertical cavern**. The sinkhole, discovered by Anglo settlers in 1867, is a registered **National Natural Landmark**; it was purchased in 1985 from private owners. The cavern opening is about 40 by 60 feet, with a vertical drop of about 140 feet. Access by prearranged tour with Devil's Sinkhole Society (830-683-BATS). Bats can be viewed in summer leaving cave at dusk; no access to cave itself. Contact **Kickapoo Cavern State Park** to arrange a tour.

**Dinosaur Valley State Park**, located off US 67 four miles west of Glen Rose in Somervell County, is a 1,524.72-acre scenic park. Land was acquired from private owners in 1968. **Dinosaur tracks** in bed of Paluxy River and two full-scale dinosaur models, originally created for New York World's Fair in 1964–65, on display. Part of state **longhorn herd** is in park. Camping, picnicking, hiking, mountain biking, swimming, fishing.

**Eisenhower Birthplace State Historic Site** is 6 acres off US 75 at 609 S. Lamar, Denison, Grayson County. The property was acquired in 1958 from the Eisenhower Birthplace Foundation. Restoration of home of President Dwight Eisenhower includes furnishings of period and some personal effects of Gen. Eisenhower. Guided tour; call for schedule. Park open daily, except Christmas Day and New Year's Day; call for hours. Town of Denison established on **Butterfield Overland Mail** Route in 1858.

**Eisenhower State Park**, 423.1 acres five miles northwest of Denison via US 75 to TX 91N to FM 1310 on the shores of **Lake Texoma** in Grayson County, was acquired by an Army lease in 1954. Named for the 34th U.S. president, **Dwight D. Eisenhower**. First Anglo settlers came to area in 1835; **Fort Johnson** was established in area in 1840;

*Parks text continues on page 180*

# ★ Texas State Parks & State Historic Sites ★

| Park / †Type of Park / Special Features | Nearest Town | Day Use Only | Historic Site/Museum | Exhibit/Interp. Center | Restrooms | Showers | Trailer Dump Stn. | Camping †† | Screened Shelters | Cabins | Group Facilities | Nature Trail | Hiking Trail | Picnicking | Boat Ramp | Fishing | Swimming | Canoe Rentals | Miscellaneous |
|---|---|---|---|---|---|---|---|---|---|---|---|---|---|---|---|---|---|---|---|
| Abilene SP | BUFFALO GAP | | | | ★ | ★ | ★ | 15 | ★ | | BG | ★ | | ★ | | ☆ | ★ | | L |
| Acton SHS ▲   Grave of Davy Crockett's Wife | GRANBURY | ★ | ★ | | | | | | | | | | | | | | | | |
| Atlanta SP | ATLANTA | | | | ★ | ★ | ★ | 14 | | | DG | ★ | ★ | ★ | ★ | ☆ | ☆ | ★ | |
| Balmorhea SP   San Solomon Springs Courts | BALMORHEA | | | ★ | ★ | ★ | ★ | 14 | | | DG | | | ★ | | | ★ | | I |
| Barton Warnock Environmental Ed. Center | LAJITAS | ★ | | ★ | ★ | | | ★ | | | | | | ★ | | | | | |
| Bastrop SP | BASTROP | | | | ★ | ★ | ★ | 10 | | ★ | BG | ★ | | ★ | | ☆ | ★ | ★ | G |
| Battleship *Texas* SHS   San Jacinto Battleground | DEER PARK | ★ | ★ | ★ | | | | | | | | | | | | | | | |
| Bentsen–Rio Grande Valley SP | MISSION | | | | ★ | ★ | | 10 | | | BG | ★ | ★ | ★ | ★ | ☆ | | | |
| Big Bend Ranch SP | PRESIDIO | | | | ★ | ★ | ★ | 1 | | | NG | ★ | ★ | ★ | | ☆ | ☆ | | B1, L, E |
| Big Spring SP | BIG SPRING | | | | ★ | ★ | | 13 | | | BG | ★ | ★ | ★ | | | | | |
| Blanco SP | BLANCO | | | | ★ | ★ | ★ | 16 | ★ | | DG | ★ | | ★ | | ☆ | ☆ | | |
| Bonham SP | BONHAM | | | | ★ | ★ | ★ | 14 | | | BG | ★ | ★ | ★ | ★ | ☆ | | | B1 |
| Brazos Bend SP   George Observatory | RICHMOND | | | ★ | ★ | ★ | ★ | 4 | ★ | | BG | ★ | ★ | ★ | | ★ | | | B1, B2 |
| Buescher SP | SMITHVILLE | | | | ★ | ★ | ★ | 14 | ★ | | BG | ★ | | ★ | | ★ | ☆ | | B2 |
| Caddo Lake SP | KARNACK | | | | ★ | ★ | ★ | 15 | ★ | ★ | BG | ★ | ★ | ★ | ★ | ★ | ☆ | ★ | |
| Caddo Mounds SHS ▲ | ALTO | ★ | ★ | ★ | ★ | | | | | | | ★ | | | | | | | |
| Caprock Canyons SP & TW | QUITAQUE | | | | ★ | ★ | ★ | 8 | | | BG | ★ | ★ | ★ | ★ | ★ | ★ | | B1, E |
| Casa Navarro SHS ▲ | SAN ANTONIO | ★ | ★ | ★ | ★ | | | | | | | | | | | | | | |
| Cedar Hill SP | CEDAR HILL | | | | ★ | ★ | ★ | 12 | | | DG | ★ | ★ | ★ | ★ | ★ | ☆ | | B1 |
| Choke Canyon SP, Calliham Unit | CALLIHAM | | | | ★ | ★ | ★ | 10 | ★ | | BG | ★ | ★ | ★ | ★ | ★ | ☆ | | |
|     South Shore Unit | THREE RIVERS | | | | ★ | ★ | ★ | 8 | | | DG | ★ | | ★ | ★ | ★ | ☆ | | B1, E |
| Cleburne SP | CLEBURNE | | | | ★ | ★ | ★ | 16 | ★ | | BG | ★ | ★ | ★ | ★ | ★ | ☆ | ☆ | |
| Colorado Bend SP   Cave Tours | BEND | | | | ★ | | | 1 | | | | ★ | ★ | ★ | ★ | ★ | ☆ | ★ | B1 |
| Confederate Reunion Grounds SHS ▲ | MEXIA | | ★ | ★ | ★ | | | 1 | | | BG | ★ | ★ | ★ | | ☆ | | | |
| Cooper Lake SP, Doctors Creek Unit | COOPER | | | | ★ | ★ | ★ | 4 | ★ | | DG | ★ | ★ | ★ | ★ | ★ | ★ | | |
|     South Sulphur Unit | SULPHUR SPRINGS | | | | ★ | ★ | ★ | 14 | ★ | ★ | DG | ★ | ★ | ★ | ★ | ★ | ★ | | B1, E |
| Copper Breaks SP | QUANAH | | | ★ | ★ | ★ | | 10 | | | BG | ★ | ★ | ★ | ★ | ★ | ☆ | | B1, E, L |
| Daingerfield SP | DAINGERFIELD | | | | ★ | ★ | ★ | 15 | | ★ | BG | ★ | ★ | ★ | ★ | ★ | ★ | | I, E |
| Davis Mountains SP   Indian Lodge | FORT DAVIS | | | ★ | ★ | ★ | ★ | 11 | | | DG | ★ | ★ | | | | | | I, E |
| Devils River SNA   Reservations Required | DEL RIO | | | | | | | 1 | | | BG | | | | | | | | B1, E |
| Devil's Sinkhole SNA | ROCKSPRINGS | | | | | (No access to cavern. Tours of SNA by special request only.) | | | | | | | | | | | | | |
| Dinosaur Valley SP   Dinosaur Footprints | GLEN ROSE | | | ★ | ★ | ★ | ★ | 12 | | | DG | ★ | ★ | ★ | | ☆ | ☆ | | B1, E, L |
| Eisenhower SP   Marina | DENISON | | | | ★ | ★ | ★ | 15 | ★ | | BG | ★ | ★ | ★ | ★ | ★ | ☆ | | B1 |
| Eisenhower Birthplace SHS ▲ | DENISON | ★ | ★ | ★ | ★ | | | | | | DG | | | | | | | | |
| Enchanted Rock SNA | FREDERICKSBURG | | | | ★ | ★ | | 9 | | | DG | ★ | ★ | ★ | | | | | R |
| Estero Llano Grande SP | WESLACO | | | | | | | | | | | | | | | | | | |
| Fairfield Lake SP | FAIRFIELD | | | | ★ | ★ | ★ | 11 | | | DG | | ★ | ★ | ★ | ★ | ☆ | | B1 |
| Falcon SP   Airstrip | ZAPATA | | | | ★ | ★ | ★ | 15 | ★ | | BG | ★ | | ★ | ★ | ☆ | ☆ | | B1 |
| Fannin Battleground SHS ▲ | GOLIAD | ★ | ★ | ★ | ★ | | | | | | DG | | | ★ | | | | | |
| Fanthorp Inn SHS | ANDERSON | ★ | ★ | ★ | ★ | | | | | | | | | ★ | | | | | |
| Fort Boggy SP | CENTERVILLE | ★ | | | ★ | | | | | | DG | ★ | ★ | ★ | ☆ | ☆ | | | |
| Fort Griffin SHS ▲ | ALBANY | ★ | | ★ | ★ | ★ | ★ | 10 | | | BG | ★ | ★ | ★ | | ☆ | | | L, E |
| Fort Lancaster SHS ▲ | OZONA | ★ | ★ | ★ | ★ | | | | | | | | | | | ☆ | | | |
| Fort Leaton SHS | PRESIDIO | ★ | ★ | ★ | ★ | | | | | | | ★ | | ★ | | | | | |
| Fort McKavett SHS ▲ | FORT McKAVETT | ★ | ★ | ★ | ★ | | | | | | | ★ | | ★ | | | | | |
| Fort Parker SP | MEXIA | | | | ★ | ★ | ★ | 14 | ★ | | BG | ★ | ★ | ★ | ★ | ★ | ☆ | ★ | B1 |
| Fort Richardson SP & Lost Creek Res. TW | JACKSBORO | | ★ | | ★ | ★ | ★ | 10 | ★ | | DG | ★ | ★ | ★ | | ★ | ★ | | E |
| Franklin Mountains SP   Wyler Aerial Tramway | EL PASO | ★ | | | ★ | | | 6 | | | DG | ★ | ★ | | | | | | B1, E, R |
| Fulton Mansion SHS ▲ | FULTON | ★ | ★ | ★ | ★ | | | | | | | | | ★ | | | | | |
| Galveston Island SP   Summer Theater | GALVESTON | | | | ★ | ★ | ★ | 4 | ★ | | BG | | | ★ | | ☆ | ☆ | | B1 |
| Garner SP | CONCAN | | | | ★ | ★ | ★ | 14 | ★ | ★ | BG | ★ | | ★ | | ☆ | ☆ | ★ | B2 |
| Goliad SP & Mission Espiritu Santo HS | GOLIAD | ★ | ★ | ★ | ★ | ★ | ★ | 11 | | | DG | ★ | | ★ | | ☆ | ☆ | | B1 |
| Goose Island SP | ROCKPORT | | | | ★ | ★ | ★ | 14 | | | BG | | | ★ | ★ | ★ | | | |
| Government Canyon SNA | SAN ANTONIO | | | | | | | | | | | | | | | | | | |
| Gov. Hogg Shrine | QUITMAN | ★ | ★ | ★ | ★ | | | | | | DG | ★ | | ★ | | | | | |
| Guadalupe River SP & Honey Creek SNA | BOERNE | | | | ★ | ★ | ★ | 13 | | | | | ★ | ★ | | ☆ | ☆ | | E |
| Hill Country SNA | BANDERA | | | | | | | 6 | | | NG | ★ | | | | ☆ | ☆ | | B1, E |
| Hueco Tanks SP & HS   Indian Pictographs | EL PASO | ★ | | ★ | ★ | ★ | ★ | 14 | | | DG | ★ | | ★ | | | | | R |
| Huntsville SP | HUNTSVILLE | | | | ★ | ★ | ★ | 14 | ★ | | DG | ★ | ★ | ★ | ★ | ★ | ☆ | ★ | B1, B2 |
| Inks Lake SP | BURNET | | | | ★ | ★ | ★ | 10 | ★ | | BG | | ★ | ★ | ★ | ★ | ☆ | ★ | G |
| Jim Hogg HS ▲ | RUSK | ★ | ★ | ★ | ★ | | | | | | | ★ | | ★ | | | | | |
| Kickapoo Cavern SP   Reservations Required | BRACKETTVILLE | | | | ★ | ★ | | 6 | | | NG | ★ | ★ | | | | | | B1 |
| Lake Arrowhead SP | WICHITA FALLS | | | | ★ | ★ | ★ | 10 | | | DG | ★ | ★ | ★ | ★ | ★ | ☆ | | E |

## † — TYPES OF PARKS

| SP | State Park | HS | Historic Site |
|---|---|---|---|
| SHS | State Historic Site | TW | Trailway |
| SNA | State Natural Area | | |

## †† — TYPES OF CAMPING

1–Primitive/Backpacking; 2–Walk-in Tent; 3–Tent; 4–Water & Electric; 5–Water, Electric & Sewer; 6–1 & 2; 7–1, 2 & 4; 8–1, 2, 3 & 4; 9–1 & 3; 10–1, 2, 3 & 4; 11–1, 3, 4 & 5; 12–1 & 4; 13–2, 3 & 4; 14–3 & 4; 15–3, 4 & 5; 16–4 & 5; 17–1, 3, 5.

# ★ Texas State Parks & State Historic Sites ★

| Park / †Type of Park / Special Features | NEAREST TOWN | Day Use Only | Historic Site/Museum | Exhibit/Interpretive Center | Restrooms | Showers | Trailer Dump Stn. | Camping †† | Screened Shelters | Cabins | Group Facilities | Nature Trail | Hiking Trail | Picnicking | Boat Ramp | Fishing | Swimming | Canoe Rentals | Miscellaneous |
|---|---|---|---|---|---|---|---|---|---|---|---|---|---|---|---|---|---|---|---|
| Lake Bob Sandlin SP | MOUNT PLEASANT | | | | ★ | ★ | ★ | 10 | ★ | | DG | ★ | ★ | ★ | ★ | ☆ | | | B1 |
| Lake Brownwood SP | BROWNWOOD | | | | ★ | ★ | ★ | 15 | ★ | ★ | BG | ★ | ★ | ★ | ★ | ★ | ☆ | | |
| Lake Casa Blanca International SP | LAREDO | | | | ★ | ★ | ★ | 14 | | | DG | | | ★ | ★ | ☆ | ☆ | | B1 |
| Lake Colorado City SP | COLORADO CITY | | | | ★ | ★ | ★ | 14 | | ★ | BG | ★ | ★ | ★ | ★ | ★ | ☆ | | |
| Lake Corpus Christi SP | MATHIS | | | | ★ | ★ | ★ | 15 | | | DG | | | ★ | ★ | ★ | ★ | | |
| Lake Livingston SP | LIVINGSTON | | | | ★ | ★ | ★ | 15 | ★ | | DG | ★ | ★ | ★ | ★ | ★ | ☆ | | B1, B2, E |
| Lake Mineral Wells SP & TW | MINERAL WELLS | | | | ★ | ★ | ★ | 10 | ★ | | DG | ★ | ★ | ★ | ★ | ★ | ☆ | ★ | B1, E, R |
| Lake Somerville SP & TW, Birch Creek Unit | SOMERVILLE | | | ★ | ★ | ★ | ★ | 10 | | | BG | ★ | ★ | ★ | ★ | ★ | ☆ | ★ | B1, E |
|    Nails Creek Unit | LEDBETTER | | | | ★ | ★ | ★ | 10 | | | DG | ★ | ★ | ★ | ★ | ★ | ☆ | ★ | B1, E |
| Lake Tawakoni SP | WILLS POINT | | | | ★ | ★ | ★ | 4 | | | | | ★ | ★ | ★ | ★ | ☆ | ☆ | |
| Lake Texana SP | EDNA | | | | ★ | ★ | ★ | 14 | | | DG | ★ | | ★ | ★ | ★ | ☆ | | B1 |
| Lake Whitney SP    Airstrip | WHITNEY | | | | ★ | ★ | ★ | 15 | ★ | | BG | ★ | | ★ | ★ | ★ | ☆ | | B1 |
| Landmark Inn SHS ▲    Hotel Rooms | CASTROVILLE | ★ | ★ | ★ | | | | | | | DG | ★ | | ★ | | | ☆ | | I |
| Lipantitlan SHS | SAN PATRICIO | ★ | | | | | | | | | | | | ★ | | | | | |
| Lockhart SP | LOCKHART | | | | ★ | ★ | | 16 | | | BG | | | ★ | | | ★ | | G |
| Longhorn Cavern SP ▲    Cavern Tours | BURNET | ★ | ★ | ★ | ★ | | | | | | | ★ | ★ | ★ | | | | | |
| Lost Maples SNA | VANDERPOOL | | | ★ | ★ | ★ | ★ | 12 | | | | ★ | ★ | ★ | | ☆ | ☆ | | |
| Lyndon B. Johnson SP & HS | STONEWALL | ★ | ★ | ★ | ★ | | | | | | DG | ★ | | ★ | | ☆ | ★ | | L |
| Magoffin Home SHS ▲ | EL PASO | ★ | ★ | ★ | ★ | | | | | | | | | | | | | | |
| Martin Creek Lake SP | TATUM | | | | ★ | ★ | ★ | 12 | ★ | ★ | DG | ★ | ★ | ★ | ★ | ★ | ☆ | | B1 |
| Martin Dies Jr. SP | JASPER | | | | ★ | ★ | ★ | 14 | ★ | | BG | ★ | ★ | ★ | ★ | ★ | ☆ | ★ | B1 |
| McKinney Falls SP | AUSTIN | ★ | | ★ | ★ | ★ | ★ | 13 | ★ | | BG | ★ | ★ | ★ | | ☆ | ☆ | | B1, B2 |
| Meridian SP | MERIDIAN | | | | ★ | ★ | ★ | 13 | ★ | | BG | ★ | ★ | ★ | ★ | ☆ | ☆ | | |
| Mission Tejas SP | WECHES | | ★ | | ★ | ★ | ★ | 15 | | | BG | ★ | ★ | ★ | | | ☆ | | |
| Monahans Sandhills SP | MONAHANS | | | ★ | ★ | ★ | ★ | 14 | | | DG | ★ | | ★ | | | | | E |
| Monument Hill & Kreische Brewery SHS | LA GRANGE | ★ | ★ | ★ | ★ | | | | | | | ★ | | ★ | | | | | |
| Mother Neff SP | MOODY | | | | ★ | ★ | ★ | 10 | | | BG | ★ | ★ | ★ | | | ☆ | | |
| Mustang Island SP | PORT ARANSAS | | | | ★ | ★ | ★ | 12 | | | | | | ★ | | ☆ | ☆ | | B1 |
| National Museum of the Pacific War ▲ | FREDERICKSBURG | ★ | ★ | ★ | ★ | | | | | | ★ | | | | | | | | |
| Old Fort Parker ▲ | GROESBECK | ★ | ★ | ★ | | | | 1 | | | | | | | | | | | E |
| Palmetto SP | LULING | | | | ★ | ★ | ★ | 15 | | | BC | ★ | ★ | ★ | | ★ | ☆ | ★ | B1, E, L |
| Palo Duro Canyon SP    Summer Drama: "Texas" | CANYON | | | ★ | ★ | ★ | ★ | 8 | | ★ | | ★ | ★ | ★ | | ★ | | | B1, E, L |
| Pedernales Falls SP | JOHNSON CITY | | | | ★ | ★ | ★ | 9 | | | NG | ★ | ★ | ★ | | ☆ | ☆ | | B1, E |
| Port Isabel Lighthouse SHS ▲ | PORT ISABEL | ★ | ★ | | ★ | | | | | | | | | | | | | | |
| Possum Kingdom SP | CADDO | | | | ★ | ★ | ★ | 10 | | ★ | | ★ | ★ | ★ | ★ | ★ | ☆ | ★ | |
| Purtis Creek SP | EUSTACE | | | | ★ | ★ | ★ | 10 | | | ★ | ★ | ★ | ★ | ★ | ☆ | ☆ | ★ | P |
| Ray Roberts Lake SP, Isle du Bois Unit | PILOT POINT | | | | ★ | ★ | ★ | 13 | | | DG | ★ | ★ | ★ | ★ | ★ | ☆ | ★ | B1, B2, E |
|    Johnson Branch Unit | VALLEY VIEW | | | | ★ | ★ | ★ | 7 | | | DG | ★ | ★ | ★ | ★ | ★ | ☆ | ★ | B1, B2 |
|    Jordan Unit    Lantana Resort | PILOT POINT | | | | | | | | | | | | | | | | | | |
| Resaca de la Palma SP | BROWNSVILLE | | | | | | | | | | | | | | | | | | |
| Sabine Pass Battleground SHS ▲ | SABINE PASS | ★ | ★ | ★ | | | | ★ | 12 | | | | | ★ | ★ | ☆ | | | |
| Sam Bell Maxey House SHS ▲ | PARIS | ★ | ★ | ★ | | | | | | | | | | | | | | | |
| Sam Rayburn House SHS ▲ | BONHAM | ★ | ★ | ★ | | | | | | | | | | | | | | | |
| San Angelo SP | SAN ANGELO | | | | ★ | ★ | ★ | 8 | | ★ | BG | ★ | ★ | ★ | ★ | ☆ | | | B1, E, L |
| San Felipe de Austin SHS ▲ | SAN FELIPE | | | | | | | | | | | | | | | | | | |
| San Jacinto Battleground SHS   Battleship Texas | HOUSTON | ★ | ★ | ★ | | | | | | | DG | ★ | | ★ | | ☆ | | | |
| Sea Rim SP | PORT ARTHUR | | | ★ | ★ | ★ | ★ | 10 | | | | ★ | ★ | ★ | ☆ | ★ | | | B1 |
| Sebastopol House SHS | SEGUIN | ★ | ★ | ★ | | | | | | | | | | | | | | | |
| Seminole Canyon SP & HS   Indian Pictographs | LANGTRY | | ★ | ★ | ★ | ★ | ★ | 14 | | | | ★ | ★ | ★ | | | | | B1 |
| Sheldon Lake SP   Environmental Learning Center | HOUSTON | ★ | | | | | | | | | | ★ | ☆ | ★ | ★ | | | | |
| South Llano River SP | JUNCTION | | | ★ | | ★ | ★ | ★ | 10 | | | | ★ | ★ | ★ | | ☆ | ☆ | | B1 |
| Starr Family Home SHS ▲ | MARSHALL | ★ | ★ | ★ | ★ | | | | | | | | | | | | | | |
| Stephen F. Austin SP | SAN FELIPE | | | ★ | | ★ | ★ | ★ | 15 | ★ | | BG | ★ | ★ | ★ | | | ☆ | | G |
| Texas State Railroad ▲ | PALESTINE & RUSK | ★ | ★ | ★ | ★ | | | | | | | | | | | | | | |
| Tyler SP | TYLER | | | | ★ | ★ | ★ | 15 | ★ | | BG | ★ | ★ | ★ | ★ | ★ | ☆ | ★ | B1 |
| Varner-Hogg Plantation SHS ▲ | WEST COLUMBIA | ★ | ★ | ★ | ★ | | | | | | | | ★ | ★ | | ☆ | | | |
| Village Creek SP | LUMBERTON | | | | ★ | ★ | ★ | 13 | | | BG | ★ | ★ | ★ | | ☆ | ☆ | | B1 |
| Walter Umphrey SP ▲ | PORT ARTHUR | *(Managed by Jefferson County)* | | | | | | | | | | | | | | | | | |
| Washington-on-the-Brazos SHS   Barrington Living History Farm (Anson Jones Home) | WASHINGTON | ★ | ★ | ★ | ★ | | | | | | DG | ★ | ★ | | | | | | |
| Wyler Aerial Tramway at Franklin Mts. SP | EL PASO | ★ | | ★ | ★ | | | | | | | | | | | | | | |

## Facilities

▲ Facilities not operated by Parks & Wildlife Department.

★ Facilities or services available for activity.

☆ Permitted but facilities not provided.

## Miscellaneous Codes

   Some handicap accessible facilities

**B1** Mountain Biking

**B2** Surfaced Bike Trail

**DG** Day-Use Group Facilities

**NG** Overnight Group Facilities

**BG** Both Day & Night Group Facilities

**E** Equestrian Facilities and/or Trails

**G** Golf

**I** Hotel-Type Facilities

**L** Texas Longhorn Herd

**R** Rock Climbing

**Colbert's Ferry** established on Red River in 1853 and operated until 1931. Areas of **tall-grass prairie** exist. Hiking, camping, picnicking, fishing, swimming.

**Enchanted Rock State Natural Area** is 1,643.5 acres on Big Sandy Creek 18 miles north of Fredericksburg on FM 965 on the line between Gillespie and Llano counties. Acquired in 1978 by The Nature Conservancy of Texas; state acquired from TNCT in 1984. Enchanted Rock is huge **pink granite boulder** rising 425 feet above ground and covering 640 acres. It is **second-largest batholith** (underground rock formation uncovered by erosion) in the United States. Indians believed **ghost fires** flickered at top and were awed by weird creaking and groaning, which geologists say resulted from rock's heating and expanding by day, cooling and contracting at night. Enchanted Rock is a **National Natural Landmark** and is on the **National Register of Historic Places**. Activities include hiking, geological study, camping, **rock climbing** and star gazing.

**Estero Llano Grande State Park,** part of the World Birding Center network, is a 176-acre wetlands refuge 3.2 miles southeast of Weslaco off FM 1015. Birds seen here include **waders, shorebirds** and **migrating waterfowl**, as well as coastal species such as **Roseate spoonbill** and **Ibis**. Rare spottings include r**ed-crowned parrots** and **green parakeets**. Opened daily. Guided tours offered.

**Fairfield Lake State Park** is 1,460 acres adjacent to Lake Fairfield, 6 miles northeast of the city of Fairfield off FM 2570 and FM 3285 in Freestone County. It was leased from Texas Utilities in 1971-72. Surrounding woods offer sanctuary for many species of birds and wildlife. Camping, hiking, backpacking, nature study, water-related activities available. Extensive schedule of tours, seminars and other activities.

**Falcon State Park** is 572.6 acres located 15 miles north of Roma off US 83 and FM 2098 at southern end of Falcon Reservoir in Starr and Zapata counties. Park leased from International Boundary and Water Commission in 1949. Gently rolling hills covered by **mesquite, huisache, wild olive, ebony, cactus**. Excellent **birding** and **fishing**. Camping and water activities also. Nearby are **Mexico, Fort Ringgold** in Rio Grande City and historic city of **Roma. Bentsen-Rio Grande Valley State Park** is 65 miles away.

**Fannin Battleground State Historic Site**, 9 miles east of Goliad in Goliad County off US 59 to PR 27. The 13.6-acre park site was acquired by the state in 1914; transferred to TPW by legislative enactment in 1965. At this site on March 20, 1836, **Col. James Fannin** surrendered to Mexican **Gen. José Urrea** after **Battle of Coleto**; 342 massacred and 28 escaped near what is now **Goliad State Park**. Near Fannin site is **Gen. Ignacio Zaragoza's Birthplace** and partially restored **Mission Nuestra Señora del Espíritu Santo de Zúñiga** (see also **Goliad State Park** in this list).

**Fanthorp Inn State Historic Site** includes a historic double-pen cedar-log dogtrot house and 1.4 acres in Anderson, county seat of Grimes County, south of TX 90. Acquired by purchase in 1977 from a Fanthorp descendant and opened to the public in 1987. Inn records report visits from many prominent civic and military leaders, including **Sam Houston, Anson Jones,** and generals **Ulysses S. Grant, Robert E. Lee** and **Stonewall Jackson**. Originally built in 1834, it has been restored to its 1850 use as a family home and travelers' hotel. Tours available Friday, Saturday, Sunday. Call TPW for stagecoach-ride schedule. No dining or overnight facilities.

**Fort Boggy State Park** is 1,847 acres of wooded, rolling hills in Leon County near Boggy Creek, about 4 miles south of Centerville on TX 75. Land donated to TPWD in 1985 by Eileen Crain Sullivan. Area once home to Keechi and Kickapoo tribes. Log fort was built by settlers in 1840s; first settlement north of the Old San Antonio Road and between the Navasota and Trinity rivers. Swimming beach, fishing, picnicking, nature trails for hiking and mountain biking. Fifteen-acre lake open to small craft.

Open-air group pavilion overlooking lake can be reserved ($50 per day). Nearby attractions include **Rusk/Palestine, Fort Parker,** and **Texas State Railroad state parks,** and **Old Fort Parker Historic Site.** Open Wed.–Sun. for day use only; entrance fee. For reservations, call 512-389-8900.

**Fort Griffin State Historic Site** is 506.2 acres 15 miles north of Albany off US 283 in Shackelford County. The state was deeded the land by the county in 1935. Portion of **state longhorn herd** resides in park. On bluff overlooking townsite of **Fort Griffin** and **Clear Fork of Brazos River** valley are partially restored ruins of **Old Fort Griffin**, restored bakery, replicas of enlisted men's huts. Fort constructed in 1867, deactivated 1881. Camping, equestrian camping, hiking. Nearby are **Albany** with restored courthouse square, **Abilene** and **Possum Kingdom** state parks. Albany annually holds **"Fandangle"** musical show in commemoration of frontier times.

**Fort Lancaster State Historic Site**, 81.6-acres located about 8 miles east of Sheffield on TX 290 in Crockett County. Acquired in 1968 by deed from Crockett County; Henry Meadows donated 41 acres in 1975. **Fort Lancaster** established Aug. 20, 1855, to guard San Antonio-El Paso Road and protect movement of supplies and immigrants from Indian hostilities. Site of part of Camel Corps experiment. Fort abandoned March 19, 1861, after Texas seceded from Union. Exhibits on history, natural history and archaeology; nature trail, picnicking. Open daily; day use only.

**Fort Leaton State Historic Site**, 4 miles southeast of Presidio in Presidio County on FM 170, was acquired in 1967 from private owners. Consists of 23.4 acres, 5 of which are on site of **trading post**. In 1848, **Ben Leaton** built fortified adobe trading post known as Fort Leaton near present Presidio. Ben Leaton died in 1851. Guided tours; exhibits trace history, natural history and archaeological history of area. Serves as western entrance to **Big Bend Ranch State Park**. Day use only.

**Fort McKavett State Historic Site**, 79.5 acres acquired from 1967 through the mid-1970s from Fort McKavett Restoration, Inc., Menard County and private individuals, is located 23 miles west of Menard off US 190 and FM 864. Originally called **Camp San Saba**, the fort was built by War Department in 1852 to protect frontier settlers and travelers on Upper El Paso Road from Indians. Camp later renamed for **Capt. Henry McKavett**, killed at Battle of Monterrey, Sept. 21, 1846. Fort abandoned March 1859; reoccupied April 1868. A **Buffalo Soldier post**. Abandoned again June 30, 1883. Once called by Gen. Wm. T. Sherman, "the prettiest post in Texas." More than 25 restored buildings, ruins of many others. Interpretive exhibits. Day use only.

**Fort Parker State Park** includes 1,458.8 acres, including 758.78 land acres and 700-acre lake between Mexia and Groesbeck off TX 14 in Limestone County. Named for the former private fort built near present park in 1836, the site was acquired from private owners and the City of Mexia 1935-1937. Camping, fishing, swimming, canoeing, picnicking. Nearby is **Old Fort Parker Historic Site**, which is operated by the City of Groesbeck.

**Fort Richardson State Park, Historic Site, and Lost Creek Reservoir Trailway,** located one-half mile south of Jacksboro off US 281 in Jack County, contains 454 acres. Acquired in 1968 from City of Jacksboro. Fort founded in 1867, northernmost of line of federal forts established after Civil War for protection from Indians; originally named **Fort Jacksboro**. In April 1867, fort was moved to its present location from 20 miles farther south; on Nov. 19, 1867, made permanent post at Jacksboro and named for **Israel Richardson**, who was fatally wounded at Battle of Antietam. Expeditions sent from Fort Richardson arrested Indians responsible for **Warren Wagon Train Massacre** in 1871 and fought Comanches in **Palo Duro Canyon**. Fort abandoned in May 1878. Park contains seven restored buildings and two replicas. Interpretive center, picnicking, camping, fishing; **ten-mile trailway**.

**Franklin Mountains State Park**, created by an act of the

*High water makes for exciting rafting through Colorado Canyon on the Rio Grande upstream from Lajitas in Big Bend Ranch State Park. Photo courtesy of VisitBigBend.com.*

legislature in 1979 to protect the mountain range as a wilderness preserve and acquired by TPW in 1981, comprises 24,247.56 acres, all within El Paso city limits. **Largest urban park in the nation**. It includes virtually an entire **Chihuahuan Desert mountain range**, with an elevation of 7,192 feet at the summit. The park is habitat for many Chihuahuan Desert plants including **sotol, lechuguilla, ocotillo, cholla** and **barrel cactus**, and such animals as **mule deer, fox** and an occasional **cougar**. Camping, mountain biking, nature study, hiking, picnicking, rock-climbing. **Wyler Aerial Tramway,** an aerial cable-car tramway on 195 acres of rugged mountain on east side of Franklin Mountains. Purchase tickets at tramway station on McKinley Ave. Check with park for fees and hours; 915-566-6622. Other area attractions include **Hueco Tanks State Historic Site and Magoffin Home State Historic Site.**

**Fulton Mansion State Historic Site** in Fulton is 3.5 miles north of Rockport off TX Business 35 on South Fulton Beach Rd. in Aransas County. The 2.3 acre-property was acquired by purchase from private owner in 1976. Three-story wooden structure, built in 1874-1877, was home of **George W. Fulton**, prominent in South Texas for economic and commercial influence; mansion derives significance from its innovative construction and Victorian design. Call ahead for days and hours of guided tours; open Wednesday–Sunday; 800-792-1112.

**Galveston Island State Park**, on the west end of Galveston Island on FM 3005, is a 2,013.1-acre site acquired in 1969 from private owners. Camping, birding, nature study, swimming, bicycling and fishing amid **sand dunes and grassland**. Musical productions in **amphitheater** during summer.

**Garner State Park** is 1,419.8 acres of recreational facilities on US 83 on the Frio River in Uvalde County 9 miles south of Leakey. Named for **John Nance Garner**, U.S. Vice President, 1933-1941, the park was deeded in 1934-36 by private owners. Camping, hiking, picnicking, river recreation, miniature golf, biking, boat rentals. Cabins available. Nearby is **John Nance "Cactus Jack" Gar-**

**ner Museum** in Uvalde. Nearby also are ruins of historic **Mission Nuestra Señora de la Candelaria del Cañon**, founded in 1749; **Camp Sabinal** (a U.S. Cavalry post and later Texas Ranger camp) established 1856; **Fort Inge**, established 1849.

**Goliad State Park** and **Mission Espíritu Santo Historic Site** are 188.3 acres one-fourth mile south of Goliad on US 183 and 77A, along the San Antonio River in Goliad County. The land was deeded to the state in 1931 by the City and County of Goliad; transferred to TPW 1949. Nearby are the sites of several battles in the Texas fight for independence from Mexico. The park includes a replica of **Mission Nuestra Señora del Espíritu Santo de Zúñiga**, originally established 1722 and settled at its present site in 1749. **Gen. Ignacio Zaragoza Birthplace State Historic Site**, which is located near **Presidio la Bahía**, across the river. Gen. Zaragoza was the Mexican national hero who led troops against the French at historic **Battle of Puebla** on May 5, 1862. The restored presidio and chapel, **Nuestra Señora de Loreto de la Bahía**, dates to 1749. Adjacent is a memorial shaft marking the common burial site of **Fannin** and victims of Goliad massacre (1836). Located four miles west of Goliad on US 59 is the **Mission Rosario State Historic Site** which contains ruins of **Nuestra Señora del Rosario** mission, established 1754. At Goliad State Park are camping, picnicking, historical exhibits, nature trail. (See also **Fannin Battleground State Historic Site**.)

**Goose Island State Park,** 321.4 acres 10 miles northeast of Rockport on TX 35 and PR 13 on St. Charles and Aransas bays in Aransas County, was deeded by private owners in 1931-1935 plus an additional seven acres donated in the early 1990s by Sun Oil Co. Located here is "Big Tree" estimated to be a 1,000-year-old **live oak**. Fishing, picnicking and camping, plus excellent birding; no swimming. Rare and endangered **whooping cranes** can be viewed during winter just across St. Charles Bay in **Aransas National Wildlife Refuge**.

**Government Canyon State Natural Area** is an 8,622-acre area in Bexar County, northwest of San Antonio, 3.5 miles northwest of Loop 1604 and FM 471, then 1.6 miles north on Galm Road. Day use only. No camping. Open Friday–Monday. Trees such as **mounatin laurel, Ashe juniper, Mexican buckeye** and **Escarpment black cherry.**

**Gov. Hogg Shrine Historic Site** is a 26.7-acre tract on TX 37 about six blocks south of the Wood County Courthouse in Quitman. Named for **James Stephen Hogg,** first native-born governor of Texas, the park includes museums housing items that belonged to the Hogg and Stinson families. Seventeen acres deeded by the Wood County Old Settlers Reunion Association in 1946; 4.74 acres gift of Miss Ima Hogg in 1970; 3 acres purchased **Gov. James Stephen Hogg Memorial Shrine** created in 1941. Three museums: Gov. Hogg's wedding held in **Stinson Home; Honeymoon Cottage; Miss Ima Hogg Museum** houses both park headquarters and display of representative history of entire Northeast Texas area. Operated by City of Quitman.

**Guadalupe River State Park** comprises 1,938.7 acres on cypress-shaded Guadalupe River in Kendall and Comal counties, 13 miles east of Boerne on TX 46. Acquired by deed from private owners in 1974. Park has four miles of river frontage with several **white-water rapids** and is located in a stretch of **Guadalupe River** noted for canoeing, tubing. Picnicking, camping, hiking, nature study. Trees include **sycamore, elm, basswood, pecan, walnut, persimmon, willow** and **hackberry** (see also **Honey Creek State Natural Area**).

**Hill Country State Natural Area** in Bandera and Medina counties, 9 miles west of Bandera on FM 1077. The 5,369.8-acre site acquired by gift from Merrick Bar-O-Ranch and purchased in 1976. Park is located in typical Texas Hill Country on West Verde Creek and contains several **spring-fed streams.** Primitive and equestrian camping, hiking, horseback riding, mountain biking, fishing. Group lodge.

**Honey Creek State Natural Area** consists of 2,293.7 acres adjacent to **Guadalupe River State Park** (above); entrance is in the park. Acquired from The Nature Conservancy of Texas in 1985 with an addition from private individual in 1988. Diverse plant life includes **agarita, Texas persimmon** and **Ashe juniper** in hills, and **cedar elm, Spanish oak, pecan, walnut** and **Mexican buckeye** in bottomlands. Abundant wildlife includes **ringtail, leopard frog, green kingfisher, golden-cheeked warbler** and **canyon wren.** Schedule varies; call 830-796-4413 for details.

**Hueco Tanks State Park and Historic Site,** located 32 miles northeast of El Paso in El Paso County on FM 2775 just north of US 62-180, was obtained from the county in 1969, with additional 121 acres purchased in 1970. Featured in this 860.3-acre park are large **natural rock basins** that provided water for archaic hunters, Plains Indians, Butterfield Overland Mail coach horses and passengers, and other travelers in this arid region. In park are **Indian pictographs, old ranch house** and relocated **ruins of stage station.** Rock climbing, picnicking, camping, hiking. Wildlife includes **gray fox, bobcat, prairie falcons, golden eagles.** Visitation is limited. Pictograph tours are by advanced request. Call 1-800-792-112, (Option 3).

**Huntsville State Park** is 2,083.2-acre recreational area off IH 45 and PR 40 six miles south of Huntsville in Walker County, acquired by deeds from private owners in 1937. Heavily wooded park adjoins **Sam Houston National Forest** and encloses **Lake Raven.** Hiking, camping, fishing, biking, paddle boats, canoeing. At nearby Huntsville are **Sam Houston's old homestead (Steamboat House),** containing some of his personal effects, and **his grave.** Approximately 50 miles away is **Alabama-Coushatta Indian Reservation** in Polk County.

**Inks Lake State Park** is 1,201 acres of recreational facilities along Inks Lake, 9 miles west of Burnet on the Colorado River off TX 29 on PR 4 in Burnet County. Acquired by deeds from the Lower Colorado River Authority and private owners in 1940. Camping, hiking, fishing, swimming, boating, golf. **Deer, turkey** and other wildlife abundant.

Nearby are **Longhorn Cavern State Park, LBJ Ranch, LBJ State Historic Site, Pedernales Falls State Park** and **Enchanted Rock State Natural Area. Granite Mountain** quarry at nearby Marble Falls furnished red granite for **Texas state capitol. Buchanan Dam,** considered the largest multi-arch dam in the nation, located 4 miles from park.

**Jim Hogg Historic Site** is 178.4 acres of East Texas Pineywoods in Cherokee County, 2 miles east of Rusk off U.S. 84 E. and Fire Tower Road. Memorial to Texas' first native-born governor, James Stephen Hogg, 1891–1895. Remnants of 1880s iron ore mining. Scale replica of Hogg birthplace. Picnicking, historical study, nature study, hiking and bird watching. Self-guided and guided museum tours and nature trail tours. Operated by the City of Rusk; 903-683-4850. Area attractions: **Caddoan Mounds** and **Mission Tejas State historic sites, Rusk/Palestine, Texas State Railroad** and **Tyler state parks** and historic Nacogdoches. Day use only; entrance fee.

**Kickapoo Cavern State Park** is located about 22 miles north of Brackettville on RM 674 on the Kinney/Edwards county line in the southern Edwards Plateau. The park (6,368.4 acres) contains **20 known caves,** two of which are large enough to be significant: **Kickapoo Cavern,** about 1/4 mile in length, has impressive formations, and **Stuart Bat Cave** (formally Green Cave), slightly shorter, supports a nursery colony of **Mexican freetail bats** in summer. Public observations of bat flights are available with an entrance permit. Birds include rare species such as **black-capped vireo, varied bunting** and **Montezuma quail.** Reptiles and amphibians include **barking frog, mottled rock rattlesnake** and **Texas alligator lizard.** Open Friday–Monday. Cavern tours on Saturday by reservation. Group lodge; primitive camping; hiking and mountain-biking trails.

**Kreische Brewery State Historic Site (see Monument Hill and Kreische Brewery State Historic Sites).**

**Lake Arrowhead State Park** consists of 524 acres in Clay County, about 14 miles south of Wichita Falls on US 281 to FM 1954, then 8 miles to park. Acquired in 1970 from the City of Wichita Falls. **Lake Arrowhead** is a reservoir on the Little Wichita River with 106 miles of shoreline. The land surrounding the lake is generally semiarid, gently rolling prairie, much of which has been invaded by mesquite in recent decades. Fishing, camping, lake swimming, picnicking, horseback-riding area.

**Lake Bob Sandlin State Park,** on the wooded shoreline of 9,400-acre Lake Bob Sandlin, is located 12 miles southwest of Mount Pleasant off FM 21 in Titus County. Activities in the 639.8-acre park include picnicking, camping, mountain biking, hiking, swimming, fishing and boating. **Oak, hickory, dogwood, redbud, maple** and **pine** produce spectacular fall color. Eagles can sometimes be spotted in winter months.

**Lake Brownwood State Park** in Brown County is 537.5 acres acquired from Brown County Water Improvement District No. 1 in 1934. Park reached from TX 279 to PR 15, 16 miles northwest of Brownwood on Lake Brownwood near **geographical center of Texas.** Water sports, hiking, camping. Cabins available.

**Lake Casa Blanca International State Park,** located one mile east of Laredo off US 59 on Loop 20, was formerly operated by the City of Laredo and Webb County and was acquired by TPW in 1990. Park includes 371 acres on Lake Casa Blanca. **Recreation hall** can be reserved. Camping, picnicking, fishing, ball fields, playgrounds, amphitheater, and tennis courts. County-operated golf course nearby.

**Lake Colorado City State Park,** 500 acres leased for 99 years from a utility company. It is located in Mitchell County 11 miles southwest of Colorado City off IH 20 on FM 2836. Water sports, picnicking, camping, hiking. Part of **state longhorn herd** can be seen in park.

**Lake Corpus Christi State Park,** a 14,112-acre park in San Patricio, Jim Wells and Live Oak counties. Located 35

Tubing on the Blanco River in Blanco State Park. The park lies four blocks south of the town of Blanco. Texas Parks and Wildlife Department photo.

use.

**Lake Somerville State Park**, northwest of Brenham in Lee and Burleson counties, was leased from the federal government in 1969. **Birch Creek Unit** (2,365 acres reached from TX 60 and PR 57) and **Nails Creek Unit** (3,155 acres reached from US 290 and FM 180), are connected by a **13-mile trailway system**, with **equestrian and primitive camp sites**, rest benches, shelters and drinking water. Also camping, birding, picnicking, volleyball and water sports. **Somerville Wildlife Management Area**, 3,180 acres is nearby.

**Lake Tawakoni State Park** is a 376.3-acre park in Hunt County along the shore of its namesake reservoir. It was acquired in 1984 through a 50-year lease agreement with the Sabine River Authority and opened in 2001. Includes a swimming beach, half-mile trail, picnic sites, boat ramp and campsites. A **40-acre tallgrass prairie** managed in the post-oak woodlands. The park is reached from IH 20 on TX 47 north to FM 2475 about 20 miles past Wills Point.

**Lake Texana State Park** is 575 acres, 6.5 miles east of Edna on TX 111, halfway between Houston and Corpus Christi in Jackson County, with camping, boating, fishing and picnicking facilities. It was acquired by a 50-year lease agreement with the Bureau of Reclamation in 1977. Good birding in the **oak/pecan woodlands**. **Alligators** are often found in park coves.

**Lake Whitney State Park** is 1,280.7 acres along the east shore of Lake Whitney west of Hillsboro via TX 22 and FM 1244 in Hill County. Acquired in 1954 by a Department of the Army lease. Located near ruins of **Towash**, early Texas settlement inundated by the lake. Towash Village named for chief of Hainai Indians. Park noted for **bluebonnets** in spring. Camping, hiking, birding, picnicking, water activities.

miles northwest of Corpus Christi and four miles southwest of Mathis off TX 359 and Park Road 25. Was leased from City of Corpus Christi in 1934. Camping, picnicking, birding, water sports. Nearby are **Padre Island National Seashore; Mustang Island, Choke Canyon, Goliad and Goose Island state parks; Aransas National Wildlife Refuge, and Fulton Mansion State Historic Site.**

**Lake Livingston State Park**, in Polk County, about one mile southwest of Livingston on FM 3126 and PR 65, contains 635.5 acres along Lake Livingston. Acquired by deed from private landowners in 1971. Near ghost town of **Swartwout**, steamboat landing on Trinity River in 1830s and 1850s. Camping, picnicking, swimming pool, fishing, mountain biking and stables.

**Lake Mineral Wells State Park and Trailway**, located 4 miles east of Mineral Wells on US 180 in Parker County, consists of 3,282.5 acres encompassing Lake Mineral Wells. In 1975, the City of Mineral Wells donated 1,095 land acres and the lake to TPW; the federal government transferred additional land from Fort Wolters army post. Popular for **rock-climbing/rappelling**. Swimming, fishing, boating, camping; the 20-mile **Lake Mineral Wells State Trailway** avaiable for hiking, bicycling, equestrian

**Landmark Inn State Historic Site**, 4.7 acres in Castroville, Medina County, about 15 miles west of San Antonio, was acquired through donation by Miss Ruth Lawler in 1974. Castroville, settled in the 1840s by Alsatian farmers, is called **Little Alsace of Texas**. Landmark Inn built about 1844 as residence and store for **Cesar Monod**, mayor of Castroville 1851-1864. Special workshops, tours and events held at inn; grounds may be rented for receptions, family reunions and weddings. Overnight lodging; all rooms air-conditioned and nonsmoking.

**Lipantitlan State Historic Site** is 5 acres 9 miles east of Orange Grove in Nueces County off Texas 359, FM 624 and FM 70. The property was deeded by private owners in 1937. Fort constructed here in 1833 by Mexican government fell to Texas forces in 1835. Only facilities are picnic tables. **Lake Corpus Christi State Park** is nearby.

**Lockhart State Park** is 263.7 acres 4 miles south of Lockhart via US 183, FM 20 and PR 10 in Caldwell County. The land was deeded by private owners between 1934 and 1937. Camping, picnicking, hiking, fishing, 9-hole golf course. After Comanche raid at Linnville, **Battle of Plum**

Creek (1840) was fought in area.

**Longhorn Cavern State Park**, off US 281 and PR 4 about 6 miles west and 6 miles south of Burnet in Burnet County, is 645.62 acres dedicated as a natural landmark in 1971. It was acquired in 1932-1937 from private owners. The cave has been used as a shelter since prehistoric times. Among legends about the cave is that the outlaw **Sam Bass** hid stolen money there. Confederates made gunpowder in the cave during the Civil War. Nature trail; guided tours of cave; picnicking, hiking. Cavern operated by concession agreement. **Inks Lake State Park** and **Lyndon B. Johnson Ranch** located nearby.

**Lost Maples State Natural Area** consists of 2,174.2 scenic acres on the Sabinal River in Bandera and Real counties, 5 miles north of Vanderpool on FM 187. Acquired by purchase from private owners in 1973-1974. Outstanding example of Edwards Plateau flora and fauna, features isolated stand of uncommon **Uvalde bigtooth maple**. Rare **golden-cheeked warbler, black-capped vireo** and **green kingfisher** nest and feed in park. Fall foliage can be spectacular (late Oct. through early Nov.). Hiking trails, camping, fishing, picnicking, birding.

**Lyndon B. Johnson State Park & Historic Site**, off US 290 in Gillespie County 14 miles west of Johnson City near Stonewall, contains 717.9 acres. Acquired in 1965 with private donations. **Home of Lyndon B. Johnson** located north bank of **Pedernales River** across Ranch Road 1 from park; portion of **official Texas longhorn herd** maintained at park. Wildlife exhibit includes **turkey, deer and bison. Living-history demonstrations** at restored **Sauer-Beckmann house**. Reconstruction of **Johnson birthplace** is open to public. Historic structures, swimming pool, tennis courts, baseball field, picnicking. Day use only. Nearby is family cemetery where former president and relatives are buried. In Johnson City is **boyhood home of President Johnson**. (See **National Parks**.)

**Magoffin Home State Historic Site**, in El Paso, is a 19-room territorial-style adobe on a 1.5-acre site. Purchased by the state and City of El Paso in 1976, it is operated by TPW. Home was built in 1875 by El Pasoan **Joseph Magoffin**. Furnished with original family artifacts. Guided tours; call for schedule. Day use only.

**Martin Creek Lake State Park**, 286.9 acres, is located 4 miles south of Tatum off TX 43 and CR 2183 in Rusk County. It was deeded to the TPW by Texas Utilities in 1976. Water activities; also cabins, camping, picnicking. Roadbed of **Trammel's Trace**, old Indian trail that became major route for settlers moving to Texas from Arkansas, can be seen. **Hardwood and pine** forest shelters abundant wildlife including **swamp rabbits, gophers, nutria** and numerous species of land birds and waterfowl. Annual perch fishing contest for children ages 4–12 the first Saturday in September.

**Martin Dies Jr. State Park** is 705 acres in Jasper and Tyler counties on B. A. Steinhagen Reservoir between Woodville and Jasper via US 190. Land leased for 50 years from Corps of Engineers in 1964. Located at edge of **Big Thicket**. Plant and animal life varied and abundant. Winter **bald eagle census** conducted at nearby Sam Rayburn Reservoir. Camping, hiking, mountain biking, water activities. Wildscape/herb garden. Park is approximately 30 miles from **Alabama and Coushatta Indian Reservation**.

**McKinney Falls State Park** is 744.4 acres 13 miles southeast of the state Capitol in Austin off US 183. Acquired in 1970 by gift from private owners. Named for Thomas F. McKinney, **one of Stephen F. Austin's first 300 colonists**, who built his home here in the mid-1800s on Onion Creek. Ruins of his homestead can be viewed. Swimming, hiking, biking, camping, picnicking, fishing, guided tours.

**Meridian State Park** in Bosque County is a 505.4-acre park. The heavily wooded land, on TX 22 three miles southwest of Meridian, was acquired from private owners in 1933-1935. **Texas-Santa Fe expedition** of 1841 passed through Bosque County near present site of park

on Bee Creek. **Endangered golden-cheeked warbler** nests here. Camping, picnicking, hiking, fishing, lake swimming, birding, bicycling.

**Mission Tejas State Park** is a 363.5-acre park in Houston County. Situated 12 miles west of Alto via TX 21 and PR 44, the park was acquired from the Texas Forest Service in 1957. In the park is a representation of **Mission San Francisco de los Tejas**, the first mission in East Texas (1690). It was abandoned, then re-established 1716; abandoned again 1719; re-established again 1721; abandoned for last time in 1730 when the mission was moved to San Antonio. Also in park is restored **Rice Family Log Home**, built about 1828. Camping, hiking, fishing, picnicking.

**Monahans Sandhills State Park** consists of 3,840 acres of sand dunes, some up to 70 feet high, in Ward and Winkler counties 5 miles northeast of Monahans on IH 20 to PR 41. Land leased by state from private foundation until 2056. Dunes used as meeting place by raiding Indians. Camping, hiking, picnicking, sand-surfing. Scheduled tours. **Odessa meteor crater** is nearby, as is **Balmorhea State Park**.

**Monument Hill State Historic Site** and **Kreische Brewery State Historic Site** are operated as one park unit. Monument Hill consists of 40.4 acres one mile south of La Grange on US 77 to Spur Road 92 in Fayette County. Monument and tomb area acquired by state in 1907; additional acreage acquired from the Archdiocese of San Antonio in 1956. Brewery and home purchased from private owners in 1977. Monument is dedicated to **Capt. Nicholas Dawson** and his men, who fought at **Salado Creek** in 1842, in Mexican **Gen. Adrián Woll**'s invasion of Texas, and to the men of the **"black bean lottery"** (1843) of the **Mier Expedition**. Remains were brought to **Monument Hill** for reburial in 1848. Kreische Complex, on 36 acres, is linked to Monument Hill through interpretive trail. **Kreische Brewery State Historic Site** includes the brewery and stone-and-wood house built between 1850–1855 on Colorado River. One of **first commercial breweries** in state, it closed in 1884. Smokehouse and barn also in complex. Guided tours of brewery and house; call for schedule. Also picnicking, nature study.

**Mother Neff State Park** was the **first official state park** in Texas. It originated with 6 acres donated by Mrs. I. E. Neff, mother of **Pat M. Neff**, governor of Texas from 1921 to 1925. Gov. Neff and Frank Smith donated remainder in 1934. The park, located 8 miles west of Moody on FM 107 and TX 236, now contains 259 acres along the Leon River in Coryell County. Heavily wooded. Camping, picnicking, fishing, hiking.

**Mustang Island State Park**, 3,954 acres on Gulf of Mexico in Nueces County, 14 miles south of Port Aransas on TX 361, was acquired from private owners in 1972. Mustang Island is a barrier island with a complicated ecosystem, dependent upon the sand dune. The foundation plants of the dunes are **sea oats, beach panic grass and soil-bind morning glory**. Beach camping, picnicking; sun, sand and water activities. Excellent birding. **Padre Island National Seashore** 14 miles south.

**National Museum of the Pacific War** and **Admiral Nimitz State Historic Site** is on 7 acres in downtown Fredericksburg. First established as a state agency in 1969 by Texas Legislature; transferred to TPW in 1981. George Bush Gallery opened in 1999. Named for **Adm. Chester W. Nimitz** of World War II fame, it includes the **Pacific War Museum** in the **Nimitz Steamboat Hotel**; the **Japanese Garden of Peace**, donated by the people of Japan; the **History Walk of the Pacific War**, featuring planes, boats and other equipment from World War II; and other special exhibits. Nearby is **Kerrville State Park**.

**Old Fort Parker** is a 37.5-acre park 4 miles north of Groesbeck on TX 14 in Limestone County. Deeded by private owners in 1936 and originally constructed by the Civilian Conservation Corps (CCC); rebuilt in 1967. Reconstructed fort is pioneer memorial and site of Cynthia Ann Parker abduction on May 19, 1836, by Comanche Indians.

Nearby Fort Parker Cemetery has graves of those killed at the fort in the 1836 raid. Historical study and picnicking. Living History events throughout year. Primitive skills classes/campouts by appointment. Groups welcome. Operated by the City of Groesbeck, 254-729-5253.

**Palmetto State Park**, a scenic park, is 270.3 acres 8 miles southeast of Luling on US 183 and PR 11 along the San Marcos River in Gonzales County. Land deeded in 1934-1936 by private owners and City of Gonzales. Named for **tropical dwarf palmetto** found there. Diverse plant and animal life; excellent birding. Also picnicking, fishing, hiking, pedal boats, swimming. Nearby **Gonzales** and **Ottine** important in early Texas history. Gonzales settled 1825 as center of **Green DeWitt's colonies**.

**Palo Duro Canyon State Park** consists of 16,402 acres 12 miles east of Canyon on TX 217 in Armstrong and Randall counties. The land was deeded by private owners in 1933 and is the scene of the annual summer production of the musical drama, "**Texas**." Spectacular one-million-year-old **scenic canyon** exposes rocks spanning about 200 million years of geological time. **Coronado** may have visited canyon in 1541. Canyon officially discovered by **Capt. R. B. Marcy** in 1852. Scene of decisive battle in 1874 between Comanche and Kiowa Indians and U.S. Army troops under **Gen. Ranald Mackenzie**. Also scene of ranching enterprise started by **Charles Goodnight** in 1876. Part of **state longhorn herd** is kept here. Camping, mountain biking, scenic drives, horseback and hiking trails, horse rentals.

**Pedernales Falls State Park**, 5,211.7 acres in Blanco County on US 281 9 miles east of Johnson City on FM 2766 along Pedernales River, was acquired from private owners in 1970. Typical **Edwards Plateau** terrain, with **live oaks**, **deer**, **turkey** and **stone hills**. Camping, picnicking, hiking, swimming, tubing. Falls main scenic attraction.

**Port Isabel Lighthouse State Historic Site** consists of 0.9 acre in Port Isabel, Cameron County. Acquired by purchase from private owners in 1950, site includes **lighthouse** constructed in 1852; visitors can climb to top. Park is near sites of Civil War battle of **Palmito Ranch** (1865),

and Mexican War battles of **Palo Alto** and **Resaca de la Palma** (1846). Operated by City of Port Isabel.

**Possum Kingdom State Park**, west of Mineral Wells via US 180 and PR 33 in Palo Pinto County, is 1,528.7 acres adjacent to **Possum Kingdom Lake**, in **Palo Pinto Mountains** and **Brazos River Valley**. Rugged canyons home to **deer**, other wildlife. Acquired from the Brazos River Authority in 1940. Camping, picnicking, swimming, fishing, boating. Cabins available.

**Purtis Creek State Park** is 1,582.4 acres in Henderson and Van Zandt counties 3.5 miles north of Eustace on FM 316. Acquired in 1977 from private owners. Fishing, camping, hiking, picnicking, paddle boats and canoes.

**Ray Roberts Lake State Park (Isle du Bois Unit)**, consists of 2,263 acres on the south side of Ray Roberts Lake on FM 455 in Denton County. **Johnson Branch Unit** contains 1,514 acres on north side of lake in Denton and Cooke counties 7 miles east of IH 30 on FM 3002. There are also six satellite parks. Land acquired in 1984 by lease from Department of the Army. Abundant and varied plant and animal life. Fishing, camping, picnicking, swimming, hiking, biking; tours of 19-century farm buildings at Johnson Branch. Includes Lantana Ridge Lodge on the east side of the lake. It is a full-service lodging facility with restaurant.

**Resaca de la Palma State Park**, part of the World Birding Center network, is 1,700 semi-tropical acres off US 281, four miles west of Brownsville in Cameron County. Park grounds are open 7 days a week year-round from sunrise to sunset. Birding and natural history tours offered. Colorful neo-tropical and nearctic migrant birds have been seen.

**Sabine Pass Battleground State Historic Site** in Jefferson County 1.5 miles south of Sabine Pass on Dick Dowling Road, contains 57.6 acres acquired from Kountze County Trust in 1972. **Lt. Richard W. Dowling**, with small Confederate force, repelled an attempted 1863 invasion of Texas by Union gunboats. **Monument, World War II ammunition bunkers**. Fishing, picnicking, camping.

**Sam Bell Maxey House State Historic Site**, at the corner of South Church and Washington streets in Paris, Lamar

*The Starr Family Home State Historic Site in Marshall comprises several elegant structures that map the 150-year history of the Starr family in Texas. It is operated by the Texas Historical Commission. Photo by Jim Hoffheins.*

County, was donated by City of Paris in 1976. Consists of .4 acre with 1868 Victorian Italianate-style frame house, plus outbuildings. Most of furnishings accumulated by Maxey family. Maxey served in Mexican and Civil wars and was two-term U.S. Senator. House is on the **National Register of Historic Places**. Open for tours Friday through Sunday.

**San Angelo State Park**, on **O.C. Fisher Reservoir** adjacent to the city of San Angelo in Tom Green County, contains 7,677 acres of land, most of which will remain undeveloped. Leased from U.S. Corps of Engineers in 1995. Access is from US 87 or 67, then FM 2288. Highly diversified plant and animal life. Activities include boating, water activities, hiking, mountain biking, horseback riding, camping, picnicking. Part of **state longhorn herd** in park. Nearby is **Fort Concho**.

**San Jacinto Battleground State Historic Site** and **Battleship *Texas* State Historic Site** are located 20 miles east of downtown Houston off TX 225 east to TX 134 to PR 1836 in east Harris County. The park is 1,200 acres with 570-foot-tall monument erected in 1936-1939 in honor of Texans who defeated Mexican **Gen. Antonio López de Santa Anna** on April 21, 1836, to win Texas' independence from Mexico. The park is original site of Texans' camp acquired in 1883. Subsequent acquisitions made in 1897, 1899 and 1985. Park transferred to TPW in 1965. Park registered as **National Historic Landmark**. Elevator ride to observation tower near top of monument; museum. Monument known as **tallest free-standing concrete structure in the world** at the time it was erected. Interpretive trail around battleground. Adjacent to park is the **U.S.S. Texas**, commissioned in 1914. The battleship, the only survivor of the dreadnought class and the only surviving veteran of two world wars, was donated to people of Texas by U.S. Navy. Ship was moored in the Houston Ship Channel at the **San Jacinto Battleground** on San Jacinto Day, 1948. Extensive repairs were done 1988-1990. Some renovation is on-going, but ship is open for tours. Ship closed Christmas Eve and Christmas Day.

**Sea Rim State Park** in Jefferson County, 20 miles south of Port Arthur, off TX 87, contains 4,141 acres of marshland and 5.2 miles of **Gulf beach** shoreline, acquired from private owners in 1972. It is prime wintering area for **waterfowl**. Wetlands also shelter such wildlife as river otter, nutria, alligator, mink, muskrat. Camping, fishing, swimming; wildlife observation; nature trail; boating. **Airboat tours of marsh**. Near **McFaddin National Wildlife Refuge**.

**Sebastopol House State Historic Site** at 704 Zorn Street in Seguin, Guadalupe County, was acquired by purchase in 1976 from Seguin Conservation Society; approximately 2.2 acres. Built about 1856 by **Col. Joshua W. Young** of **limecrete**, concrete made from local gravel and lime, the Greek Revival-style house, which was restored to its 1880 appearance by the TPW, is on National Register of Historic Places. Tours available Friday and Sunday. Also of interest in the area is historic **Seguin**, founded 1838.

**Seminole Canyon State Historic Site** in Val Verde County, 9 miles west of Comstock off US 90, contains 2,172.5 acres; acquired by purchase from private owners 1973-1977. **Fate Bell Shelter** in canyon contains several important **prehistoric Indian pictographs**. Historic interpretive center. Tours of rock-art sites Wednesday-Sunday; also hiking, mountain biking, camping.

**Sheldon Lake State Park and Environmental Learning Center**, 2,800 acres in Harris County on Garrett Road 20 miles east of Beltway 8. Acquired by purchase in 1952 from the City of Houston. Freshwater marsh habitat. Activities include nature study, birding, fishing. Wildscape gardens of native plants.

**South Llano River State Park**, 5 miles south of Junction in Kimble County off US 377, is a 524-acre site. Land donated to the TPW by private owner in 1977. Wooded bottomland along the winding South Llano River is **largest and oldest winter roosting site for the Rio Grande turkey** in Central Texas. Roosting area closed to visitors October-March. Other animals include **wood ducks, javelina, fox, beaver, bobcat** and **armadillo**. Camping,

picnicking, tubing, swimming and fishing, hiking, mountain biking.

**Starr Family Home State Historic Site**, 3.1 acres at 407 W. Travis in Marshall, Harrison County. Greek Revival-style mansion, **Maplecroft**, built 1870-1871, was home to four generations of Starr family, powerful and economically influential Texans. Two other family homes also in park. Acquired by gift in 1976; additional land donated in 1982. Maplecroft is on National Register of Historic Places. Tours Friday–Sunday or by appointment. Special events during year.

**Stephen F. Austin State Park** is 663.3 acres along the Brazos River in San Felipe, Austin County, named for the **"Father of Texas."** The area was deeded by the San Felipe de Austin Corporation and the **San Felipe** Park Association in 1940. Site of township of San Felipe was seat of government where conventions of 1832 and 1833 and Consultation of 1835 held. These led to **Texas Declaration of Independence**. San Felipe was home of **Stephen F. Austin** and other famous early Texans; home of **Texas' first Anglo newspaper (the Texas Gazette)** founded in 1829; postal system of Texas originated here. Area called "Cradle of Texas Liberty." Museum. Camping, picnicking, golf, fishing, hiking.

**Texas State Railroad**, in Anderson and Cherokee counties between the cities of Palestine and Rusk, adjacent to US 84, contains 499 acres. Operated by American Heritage Railways since 2007. Trains run seasonal schedules on 25.5 miles of track. Call for information and reservations: 1-888-987-2461. Railroad built by the State of Texas to support the **state-owned iron works** at Rusk. Begun in 1893, and built largely by inmates from the state prison system, the railroad was gradually extended until it reached Palestine in 1909 and established regular rail service between the towns. **Rusk and Palestine Parks** are adjacent to the two **Texas State Railroad Depot**s. Fishing, picnicking, camping, tennis courts, playground. **Train rides** in restored passenger cars.

**Tyler State Park** is 985.5 acres two miles north of IH 20 on FM 14 north of Tyler in Smith County. Includes 64-acre lake. The land was deeded by private owners in 1934–1935. Heavily wooded. Camping, hiking, fishing, boating, lake swimming. Nearby Tyler called **Rose Capital of Nation**, with **Tyler Rose Garden** and annual **Tyler Rose Festival**. Also in Tyler are **Caldwell Children's Zoo** and **Goodman Museum**.

**Varner-Hogg Plantation State Historic Site** is 66 acres in Brazoria County two miles north of West Columbia on FM 2852. Land originally owned by Martin Varner, a member of Stephen F. Austin's **"Old Three Hundred"** colony; later was home of Texas governor **James Stephen Hogg**. Property was deeded to the state in 1957 by Miss Ima Hogg, Gov. Hogg's daughter. **First rum distillery** in Texas established in 1829 by Varner. Mansion tours Tuesday through Saturday. Also picnicking, fishing.

**Village Creek State Park**, comprising 1,004 heavily forested acres, is located in Lumberton, Hardin County, 10 miles north of Beaumont off US 69 and FM 3513. Purchased in 1979 from private owner, the park contains abundant flora and fauna typical of the Big Thicket area. The **200 species of birds** found here include wood ducks, egrets and herons. Activities include fishing, camping, canoeing, swimming, hiking and picnicking. Nearby is the **Big Thicket National Preserve**.

**Walter Umphrey State Park** is operated by Jefferson County on the south end of Please Island off TX 82. For RV site reservations, contact SGS Causeway Bait & Tackle, 409-985-4811.

**Washington-on-the-Brazos State Historic Site** consists of 293.1 acres 7 miles southwest of Navasota in Washington County on TX 105 and FM 1155. Land acquired by deed from private owners in 1916, 1976 and 1996. Park includes the site of the signing on March 2, 1836, of the **Texas Declaration of Independence** from Mexico, as well as the site of the later **signing of the Constitution**

*Riding the horse trails is a popular activity in Jones State Forest in Montgomery County. Photo by Ron Billings; Texas A&M Forest Service.*

of the Republic of Texas. In 1842 and 1845, the land included the **capitol of the Republic. Star of the Republic Museum**. Activities include picnicking and birding. **Barrington Living History Farm** is the home of **Anson Jones, the last president of the Republic of Texas.** Activities are guided by entries that Jones made in his daybook while living there. For more information: call 916-878-2214 or link to barrington.farm@tpwd.state.tx.us**.**

# Recreation in State Forests

All Texas State Forests are game sanctuaries with no firearms or hunting allowed. For general information about the Texas State Forests, *see page 117 in the Environment section.*

## I.D. Fairchild State Forest

Located in Cherokee County, recreation includes hiking, horseback riding, picnicking, wildlife viewing and biking. Special attractions are a **historical fire tower** site with plaque, Red Cockaded Woodpecker Management Area and a pond with picnic area. Forest management demonstration sites throughout the forest. There are no restroom facilities in this forest.

Open year-round during daylight hours. Obtain information and maps at the Palestine District Office, 2203 West Spring St. (US-287 West) or call (903) 729-7738 weekdays.

## W. Goodrich Jones State Forest

Recreational opportunities in this forest, located in Montgomery County, include bird watching, hiking, horseback riding, picnicking, wildlife viewing and biking.

Special attractions include **Sweetleaf Nature Trail** with State Champion Sweetleaf Tree, Red Cockaded Woodpecker Management Area, two small lakes with limited fishing and picnicking. Forest management demonstration sites throughout the forest.

Open year-round during daylight hours. Information, maps, permits and restrooms available at the Conroe

District Office on FM 1488, 1.5 miles west of I-45. Call (936) 273-2261 for information.

### John Henry Kirby Memorial State Forest

Located in Tyler County, forest resource educational opportunities at this forest include demonstrations and nature study. Group education tours available by appointment. Recreational opportunities include hiking, picnicking, bird and wildlife watching. Special attractions are forest management demonstration sites, small picnic area and **John Henry Kirby Monument.**

Open year-round to foot traffic during daylight hours. Contact the district office prior to entry. Special arrangements are needed for vehicle access. Information and maps can be obtained at the Woodville District Office on Hwy. 69 south or by calling (409) 283-3785 weekdays. No restroom facilities are available in this forest.

### Masterson State Forest

All use of this forest in Jasper County is by reservation only. Group resource education tours are available by appointment. No public facilities are available. Information and maps can be obtained at the Kirbyville District Office, FM 82, 4.5 miles southeast of Kirbyville; call weekdays at (409) 423-2890.

### E.O. Siecke State Forest

Recreational opportunities in this Newton County forest include hiking, bird watching, nature study, horseback riding, picnicking and wildlife viewing.

Special attractions are a **historic fire tower,** the **oldest slash pine stand in Texas** and a **trout creek.** Forest management demonstration sites throughout.

Open year-round during daylight hours. Limited access by vehicle. Information, maps and restrooms are available at the Kirbyville District Office, located at the state forest on FM 82, 4.5 miles southeast of Kirbyville. Call (409) 423-2890 weekdays for information. ☆

# National Parks, Historic Sites, Recreation Areas

Below are listed the facilities in and the activities that can be enjoyed at the two national parks, a national seashore, a biological preserve, several historic sites, memorials and recreation areas in Texas. They are under supervision of the **U.S. Department of Interior**. On the web: **http://www.nps.gov/findapark/index.htm**; under "Select State," choose "Texas." In addition, the recreational opportunities in the national forests and national grasslands in Texas, under the jurisdiction of the **U.S. Department of Agriculture**, are listed at the end of the article.

**Alibates Flint Quarries National Monument** consists of 1,371 acres in Potter County. For more than 10,000 years, **pre-Columbian Indians** dug agatized limestone from the quarries to make projectile points, knives, scrapers and other tools. The area is presently undeveloped. You may visit the flint quarries on guided walking tours with a park ranger. Tours are at 10:00 a.m. and 2:00 p.m. from Memorial Day to Labor Day. Off-season tours can be arranged by writing to Lake Meredith National Recreation Area, Box 1460, Fritch 79036, or by calling 806-857-3151.

**Amistad National Recreation Area** is located on the U.S. side of Amistad Reservoir, an international reservoir on the Texas-Mexico border. The 57,292-acre park's attractions include boating, water skiing, swimming, fishing, camping and archaeological sites. If lake level is normal, visitors can see 4000-year-old prehistoric pictographs in Panther and Parida caves, which are accessible only by boat. Check with park before visiting. The area is one of the densest concentrations of **Archaic rock art** in North America — more than 300 sites. Commercial campgrounds, motels and restaurants nearby. Marinas located at Diablo East and Rough Canyon. Open year round. NPS Administration, 4121 Hwy. 90 W, Del Rio 78840; 830-775-7491.

**Big Bend National Park**, established in 1944, has spectacular mountain and **desert scenery** and a variety of unusual geological structures. It is the nation's largest protected area of Chihuahuan Desert. Located in the great bend of the Rio Grande, the 801,000-acre park, which is part of the international boundary between the United States and Mexico, was designated a U.S. Biosphere Reserve in 1976. Hiking, birding and float trips are popular. Numerous campsites are located in park, and the Chisos Mountain Lodge has accommodations for approximately 345 guests. Write for reservations

Muralist Carlos Flores, right, stands in front of the mural *Nuestra Herencia (Our Heritage)* that he created at Chamizal National Memorial in El Paso. In 2015, Flores and his son Marcos finished a restoration of the mural as part of the Memorial's 50th Anniversary and the National Park Service's Centennial Legacy projects. The 18-x-120 foot mural was a gift to the National Park Service by the Junior League of El Paso as part of the Los Murales Project in 1992. The mural features such figures as Hernán Cortés and Miguel de Cervantes, author of Don Quixote. Flores is accompanied, above, by friend Bob Gourdoux. Photo by Mary Gourdoux.

to National Park Concessions, Inc., Big Bend National Park, Texas 79834; 915-477-2291; www.chisosmountainslodge.com. Park open year round; facilities most crowded during spring break. PO Box 129, Big Bend National Park 79834; 915-477-2251.

**Big Thicket National Preserve**, established in 1974, consists of 15 separate units totalling 97,000 acres of diverse flora and fauna, often nicknamed the "biological crossroads of North America." The preserve, which includes parts of seven East Texas counties, has been designated an "International Biosphere Reserve" by the United Nations Educational, Scientific and Cultural Organization (UNESCO). The preserve includes **four different ecological systems:** Southeastern swamps, Eastern forests, Central Plains and Southwestern deserts. The visitor information station is located on FM 420, seven miles north of Kountze; phone 409-951-6725. Open daily from 9 a.m. to 5 p.m. Naturalist activities are available by reservation only; reservations are made through the station. Eight trails, ranging in length from one-half mile to 18 miles, visit a variety of forest com-

munities. The two shortest trails are handicapped accessible. Trails are open year round, but flooding may occur after heavy rains. Horses permitted on the Big Sandy Horse Trail only. Boating and canoeing are popular on preserve corridor units. Park headquarters are at 3785 Milam, Beaumont 77701; 409-246-2337.

**Chamizal National Memorial**, established in 1963 and opened to the public in 1973, stands as a monument to Mexican-American friendship and goodwill. The memorial, on 52 acres in El Paso, commemorates the peaceful settlement on Aug. 29, 1963, of a 99-year-old boundary dispute between the United States and Mexico. Chamizal uses the **visual and performing arts** as a medium of interchange, helping people better understand not only other cultures but their own, as well. It hosts a variety of programs throughout the year, including: the fall Chamizal Festival musical event; the Siglo de Oro drama festival (early March); the Oñate Historical Festival celebrating the First Thanksgiving (April); and Music Under the Stars (Sundays, June-August). The park has a 1.8-mile walking trail and picnic areas.

*Waco Mammoth National Monument became part of the National Park Service on July 10, 2015. It is the only recorded discovery of a nursery herd of Columbian mammoths in the United States. Visitors, above, view the exhibit, which includes the original paleontological site. Below, the NPS sign goes up at the monument's entrance in Waco. National Park Service photos.*

Phone: 915-532-7273.

**Fort Davis National Historic Site** in Jeff Davis County was a key post in the West Texas defense system, guarding immigrants and tradesmen on the San Antonio-El Paso road from 1854 to 1891. At one time, Fort Davis was manned by black troops, called **"Buffalo Soldiers"** (because of their curly hair) who fought with great distinction in the Indian Wars. Henry O. Flipper, the first black graduate of West Point, served at Fort Davis in the early 1880s. The 474-acre historic site is located on the north edge of the town of Fort Davis in the Davis Mountains, the second-highest mountain range in the state. The site includes a museum, an auditorium with daily audio-visual programs, restored and refurnished buildings, picnic area and hiking trails. Open year round except Christmas Day. PO Box 1379, Fort Davis 79734; 915-426-3224.

**Guadalupe Mountains National Park**, established in 1972, includes 86,416 acres in Hudspeth and Culberson counties. The Park contains one of the most extensive fossil reefs on record. Deep canyons cut through this reef and provide a rare opportunity for geological study. Special points of interest are **McKittrick Canyon**, a fragile riparian environment, and **Guadalupe Peak**, the highest in Texas. Camping, hiking on 80 miles of trails, Frijole Ranch Museum, summer amphitheater programs. Orientation, free information and natural history exhibits available at Visitor Center. Open year round. Lodging at Van Horn, Texas, and White's City or Carlsbad, NM. HC 60, Box 400, Salt Flat 79847; 915-828-3251.

**Lake Meredith National Recreation Area**, 30 miles northeast of Amarillo, centers on a reservoir on the Canadian River, in Moore, Hutchinson and Potter counties. The 50,000-acre recreational area is popular for **water-based activities.** Boat ramps, picnic areas, unimproved campsites. Commercial lodging and trailer hookups available in nearby towns. Open year round. PO Box 1460, Fritch 79036; 806-857-3151.

**Lyndon B. Johnson National Historic Park** includes two separate districts 14 miles apart. The Johnson City District comprises the boyhood home of the 36th President of United States and the Johnson Settlement, where his grandparents resided during the late 1800s. The LBJ Ranch District can be visited only by taking the National Park Service bus tour starting at the LBJ State Historic Site. The tour includes the reconstructed **LBJ Birthplace**, old school, family cemetery, show barn and a view of the **Texas White House.** Site in Blanco and Gillespie counties was established in 1969, and contains 1,570 acres, 674 of which are federal. Open year round except Thanksgiving, Christmas Day, and New Year's Day. No camping on site; commercial campgrounds, motels in area. PO Box 329, Johnson City 78636; 830-868-7128.

**Padre Island National Seashore** consists of a 67.5-mile stretch of a barrier island along the Gulf Coast; noted for **white-sand beaches,** excellent fishing and abundant bird and marine life. Contains 133,000 acres in Kleberg, Willacy and Kenedy counties. Open year round. One paved campground (fee charged) located north of Malaquite Beach; unpaved (primitive) campground area south on beach. Five miles of beach are accessible by regular vehicles; 55 miles are accessible only by 4x4 vehicles. Off-road vehicles prohibited. Camping permitted in two designated areas. Commercial lodging available on the island outside the National Seashore boundaries. PO Box 181300, Corpus Christi 78480; 361-949-8068.

**Palo Alto Battlefield National Historic Site**, Brownsville, preserves the site of the first major battle in the Mexican-American War. Fought on May 8, 1846, it is recognized for the innovative use of light or "flying" artillery. Participating in the battle were **three future presidents:** General Zachary Taylor and Ulysses S. Grant on the U.S. side, and Gen. Mariano Arista on the Mexican. Historical markers are located at the junction of Farm-to-Market roads 1847 and 511. Access to the 3,400-acre site is currently limited. Exhibits at the visitors center interpret the battle as well as the causes and consequences of the war. Phone 956-541-2785.

**Rio Grande Wild and Scenic River** is a 196-mile strip on the U.S. shore of the Rio Grande in the Chihuahuan Desert, beginning in Big Bend National Park and continuing downstream to the Terrell-Val Verde County line. There are federal facilities in Big Bend National Park only. Contact Big Bend National Park for more information.

**San Antonio Missions National Historical Park** preserves four Spanish Colonial Missions — **Concepción, San José, San Juan** and **Espada** — as well as the Espada dam and aqueduct, which are two of the best-preserved remains in the United States of the Spanish Colonial irrigation system, and **Rancho de las Cabras,** the colonial ranch of Mission Espada. All were crucial elements to Spanish settlement on the Texas frontier. When Franciscan attempts to establish a chain of missions in East Texas in the late 1600s failed, the Spanish Crown ordered three missions transferred to the San Antonio River valley in 1731.

The missions are located within the city limits of San Antonio, while Rancho de las Cabras is located 25 miles south in Wilson County near Floresville. The four missions, which are **still in use as active parishes,** are open to the public from 9 a.m. to 5 p.m. daily except Thanksgiving, Christmas and New Year's. Public roadways connect the sites; a hike-bike trail is being developed. The visitor center for the mission complex is at San José. For more information, write to 2202 Roosevelt Ave., San Antonio 78210; 210-534-8833 or 210-932-1001.

**Waco Mammoth National Monument** was designated in 2015 and is the newest Texas unit of the National Park System. This paleontological site represents the nation's only recorded discovery of a nursery herd

## Recreational Facilities, Corps of Engineers Lakes, 2014

*Source: Fort Worth District, Corps of Engineers*

| Reservoir | Swim Beaches | Boat Ramps | Picnic Sites | Camp Sites | Rental Cabins | Visitor Hours, 2012[6] |
|---|---|---|---|---|---|---|
| Aquilla | 0 | 3 | 0 | 0 | 0 | 427,858 |
| Bardwell | 1 | 3 | 30 | 49 | 0 | 452,907 |
| Belton | 3 | 18 | 120 | 194 | 0 | 10,792,949 |
| Benbrook | 3 | 12 | 116 | 117 | 0 | 2,452,987 |
| Buffalo Bayou[1,3] | 0 | 0 | 849 | 0 | 0 | 12,579,750 |
| Canyon | 6 | 24 | 212 | 588 | 81 | 2,330,305 |
| Cooper | 2 | 5 | 110 | 184 | 20 | 3,584,508 |
| Georgetown | 1 | 3 | 82 | 251 | 0 | 3,821,266 |
| Granger | 2 | 5 | 129 | 134 | 0 | 911,174 |
| Grapevine | 2 | 20 | 286 | 212 | 13 | 8,139,531 |
| Hords Creek | 3 | 5 | 8 | 83 | 0 | 122,629 |
| Joe Pool | 3 | 7 | 315 | 576 | 8 | 7,947,574 |
| Lake O' the Pines | 7 | 31 | 164 | 443 | 0 | 10,274,929 |
| Lavon | 2 | 15 | 223 | 235 | 0 | 4,122,596 |
| Lewisville | 7 | 25 | 454 | 449 | 38 | 14,603,735 |
| Navarro Mills | 3 | 6 | 24 | 255 | 0 | 5,126,680 |
| O.C. Fisher | 0 | 13 | 75 | 71 | 0 | 484,342 |
| Pat Mayse[2] | 2 | 11 | 0 | 282 | 3 | 1,181,120 |
| Proctor | 6 | 7 | 75 | 193 | 0 | 1,925,515 |
| Ray Roberts | 2 | 11 | 309 | 356 | 0 | 20,438,511 |
| Sam Rayburn | 7 | 23 | 26 | 643 | 50 | 12,311,846 |
| Somerville | 2 | 12 | 112 | 753 | 21 | 10,638,077 |
| Stillhouse Hollow | 3 | 5 | 83 | 73 | 0 | 2,434,943 |
| Texoma[2,4] | 4 | 41 | 107 | 937 | 285 | 55,820,257 |
| Town Bluff[5] | 1 | 15 | 83 | 362 | 9 | 4,132,876 |
| Waco | 3 | 12 | 170 | 235 | 2 | 1,895,636 |
| Wallisville[1] | 0 | 3 | 60 | 0 | 0 | 1,247,916 |
| Whitney | 6 | 31 | 106 | 780 | 14 | 7,421,591 |
| Wright Patman | 4 | 22 | 186 | 543 | 0 | 13,533,363 |
| **Totals** | **85** | **388** | **4,514** | **8,998** | **544** | **221,157,371** |

*All of the lakes in this table are managed by the Fort Worth District, U.S. Army Corps of Engineers, with the following exceptions:*
[1] *Managed by Galveston District, USACE.*
[2] *Managed by Tulsa District, USACE.*
[3] *Includes both Addicks Dam and Barker Dam.*
[4] *Figures for facilities are for Texas side of lake. Visitation is for entire lake.*
[5] *Also called B.A. Steinhagen Lake and Dam B. Reservoir.*
[6] *Visitor hours are from October 2011–September 2012.*

of Columbian mammoths. Visitors can view "in situ" fossils including female mammoths, a bull mammoth, and a camel that lived approximately 67,000 years ago. The park is managed in partnership by the National Park Service, the City of Waco, and Baylor University. Welcome Center located at 6220 Steinbeck Bend Road. It is open Tuesday through Saturday, except Thanksgiving, Christmas Day, and New Year's Day.

## Recreation in National Forests

For general information about the National Forests and National Grasslands, **see page 116 in the Environment section.**

An estimated 3 million people visit the National Forests in Texas for recreation annually. These visitors use established recreation areas primarily for hiking, picnicking, swimming, fishing, camping, boating and nature enjoyment. In the following list of some of these areas, Forest Service Road is abbreviated FSR:

### Angelina National Forest

Boykin Springs, 14 miles southeast of Zavalla, has a 6-acre lake and facilities for hiking, swimming, picnicking, fishing, and camping. Bouton Lake, 14 miles southeast of Zavalla off Texas 63 and FSR 303, has a 9-acre natural lake with primitive facilities for camping, picnicking, and fishing.

Caney Creek on Sam Rayburn Reservoir, 10 miles southeast of Zavalla off FM 2743, offers fishing, boating, and camping. Sandy Creek, 15.5 miles east of Zavalla on Sam Rayburn, offers fishing, boating, and camping.

The Sawmill Hiking Trail is 2.5 miles long and winds from Aldridge Sawmill trail head to Boykin Springs Recreation Area.

### Davy Crockett National Forest

Ratcliff Lake, 25 miles west of Lufkin on Texas 7, is a 45-acre lake with facilities for picnicking, hiking, swimming, boating, fishing, and camping. There is also an amphitheater.

The 20-mile-long 4C National Recreation Trail connects Ratcliff Recreation Area to the Neches Bluff overlook. The Piney Creek Horse Trail is 54 miles long and can be entered approximately 5.5 miles south of Kennard off County Road 4625. There are two horse camps along this trail system.

### Sabine National Forest

Indian Mounds Recreation Area, located 12 miles southeast of Hemphill off FM 83 about, has camping facilities and a boat ramp. Lakeview, on Toledo Bend Reservoir, 21 miles from Pineland, offers camping, hiking, and fishing and can be reached via Texas 87, FM 2928, and FSR 120.

Ragtown, 26 miles southeast of Center and accessible by Texas 87 and Texas 139, County Road 3184, and FSR 132, is also on Toledo Bend and has facilities for hiking, camping, and boating. Red Hill Lake, 3 miles north of Milam on Texas 87, has facilities for fishing, swimming, camping, and picnicking. Willow Oak Recreation Area on Toledo Bend, 13 miles south of Hemphill off Texas 87, offers fishing, picnicking, camping, and boating.

Trail Between the Lakes is 28 miles long from Lakeview Recreation Area on Toledo Bend to U.S. 96 near Sam Rayburn Reservoir.

### Sam Houston National Forest

Cagle Recreation Area is located on the shores of Lake Conroe, 50 miles north of Houston and 5 miles west of I-45 at FM 1375. Cagle offers camping, fishing,

hiking, birding, and other recreational opportunities in a forested lakeside setting.

Double Lake, 3 miles south of Coldspring on FM 2025, has facilities for picnicking, hiking, camping, swimming, and fishing.

Stubblefield Lake, 15 miles west-northwest of New Waverly off Texas 1375 on the shores of Lake Conroe, has facilities for camping, hiking, picnicking, and fishing.

The Lone Star Hiking Trail, approximately 128 miles long, is located in Sam Houston National Forest in Montgomery, Walker, and San Jacinto counties.

## Recreation on National Grasslands

### North Texas

Lake Davy Crockett Recreation Area **(Caddo National Grassland)**, 12 miles north of Honey Grove (Fannin County) on FM 409, just off FM 100, has a boat-launch ramp and camping sites on a 450-acre lake.

Coffee Mill Lake Recreation Area has camping and picnicking facilities on a 650-acre lake. This area is 4 miles west of Lake Davy Crockett Recreation Area.

The Caddo Multi-Use Trail system, also 4 miles west of Lake Crockett, offers camping, hiking, and horseback riding on 35 miles of trails.

Black Creek Lake Recreation Area **(Lyndon B. Johnson National Grassland)** is 8 miles north of Decatur (Wise County) and has camping, picnic facilities, and a boat-launch ramp on a 35-acre lake.

Cottonwood Lake, 13 miles north of Decatur, is around 40 acres and offers hiking, boating, and fishing.

The Cottonwood-Black Creek Hiking Trail is 4 miles long and connects the two lakes. It is rated moderately difficult. There are nearly 75 miles of multipurpose trails that run in the Cottonwood Lake vicinity.

TADRA Horse Trail, 10 miles north of Decatur, has camping and 75 miles of horse trails. Restrooms and and parking facilities are available.

### West Texas

Lake McClellan **(McClellan Creek National Grassland)** in Gray County and Lake Marvin, which is part of the **Black Kettle National Grassland** in Hemphill County, receive more than 28,000 recreation visitors annually.

These areas provide camping, picnicking, fishing, birdwatching, and boating facilities. Concessionaires operate facilities at Lake McClellan, and a nominal fee is charged for use of the areas.

At the **Rita Blanca National Grassland** (Dallam County), about 4,500 visitors a year enjoy picnicking and hunting. Thompson Grove Picnic Area is 14 miles northeast of Texline. ☆

# National Natural Landmarks in Texas

Twenty Texas natural areas have been listed on the **National Registry of Natural Landmarks**.

The registry was established by the Secretary of the Interior in 1962 to identify and encourage the preservation of geological and ecological features that represent nationally significant examples of the nation's natural heritage.

The registry currently lists a total of 587 national natural landmarks. Texas areas on the list, as of August 2001, and their characteristics, are these (year of listing in parentheses):

**Attwater Prairie Chicken Preserve**, Colorado

County, 55 miles west of Houston in the national wildlife refuge, is rejuvenated Gulf Coastal Prairie, which is habitat for Attwater's prairie chickens. (1968)

**Bayside Resaca Area**, Cameron County, Laguna Atascosa National Wildlife Refuge, 28 miles north of Brownsville. Excellent example of a resaca, supporting coastal salt-marsh vegetation and rare birds. (1980)

**Catfish Creek**, Anderson County, 20 miles northwest of Palestine, is undisturbed riparian habitat. (1983)

**Cave Without a Name**, Kendall County, 12 miles northeast of Boerne, is a cave of several rooms that are filled with spectacular formations. (2009)

**Caverns of Sonora**, Sutton County, 16 miles south-

*The Cave Without a Name near Boerne in Kendall County is the latest National Natural Landmark designated in Texas. The cave is filled with spectacular formations in six major rooms and is 66 degrees year-round. Photo courtesy of the Edwards Aquifer Website.*

west of Sonora, has unusual geological formations. (1965)

**Devil's Sink Hole**, Edwards County, 9 miles northeast of Rocksprings, is a deep, bell-shaped, collapsed limestone sink with cave passages extending below the regional water table. (1972)

**Dinosaur Valley**, Somervell County, in Dinosaur Valley State Park, four miles west of Glen Rose, contains fossil footprints exposed in bed of Paluxy River. (1968)

**Enchanted Rock**, Gillespie and Llano counties, 12 miles southwest of Oxford, is a classic batholith, composed of coarse-grained pink granite. (1971)

**Ezell's Cave**, Hays County, within the city limits of San Marcos, houses at least 36 species of cave creatures. (1971)

**Fort Worth Nature Center and Refuge**, Tarrant County, within the Fort Worth city limits. Contains remnants of the Grand Prairie and a portion of the Cross Timbers, with limestone ledges and marshes. Refuge for migratory birds and other wildlife, and home to 11 buffalo raised by the center's staff. Educational programs offered for youth and adults. Self-guided hiking. (1980)

**Greenwood Canyon**, Montague County, along a tributary of Braden Branch, is a rich source of Cretaceous fossils. (1975)

**High Plains Natural Area**, Randall County, Buffalo Lake National Wildlife Refuge, 26 miles southwest of Amarillo, is a grama-buffalo shortgrass area. (1980)

**Little Blanco River Bluff**, Blanco County, compris-

es an Edwards Plateau limestone-bluff plant community. (1982)

**Longhorn Cavern**, Burnet County, 11 miles southwest of Burnet. Formed at least 450 million years ago, cave contains several unusual geologic features. (1971)

**Lost Maples State Natural Area**, Bandera and Real counties, 61 miles northwest of San Antonio, contains Edwards Plateau fauna and flora, including unusual bigtooth maple. Largest known nesting population of golden-cheeked warbler. (1980)

**Muleshoe National Wildlife Refuge**, Bailey County, 59 miles northwest of Lubbock, contains playa lakes and typical High Plains shortgrass grama grasslands. (1980)

**Natural Bridge Caverns**, Comal County, 16 miles west of New Braunfels, is a multilevel cavern system, with beautiful and unusual geological formations. (1971)

**Odessa Meteor Crater**, Ector County, 10 miles southwest of Odessa, is one of only two known meteor sites in the country. (1965)

**Palo Duro Canyon State Park**, Armstrong and Randall counties, 22 miles south-southwest of Amarillo. Cut by waters of the Red River, it contains cross-sectional views of sedimentary rocks representing four geological periods. (1976)

**Santa Ana National Wildlife Refuge**, Hidalgo County, 7 miles south of Alamo, is a lowland forested area with jungle-like vegetation. It is habitat for more than 300 species of birds and some rare mammals. (1966) ☆

*An angler casts his line into the Pedernales River, a beautiful, spring-fed river that rises in Kerr County and flows through the Hill Country. Photo by Ron Billings; Texas A&M Forest Service.*

# Recreational Fishing in Texas

*Source: Texas Parks and Wildlife Department; http://tpwd.texas.gov/fishboat/fish/*

## Freshwater Fishing

Freshwater fishing in Texas is an activity enjoyed by an estimated 1.21 million recreational anglers. In 2013, these anglers contributed an economic output of approximately $96 million to the Texas economy.

Among the 268 species of freshwater fish in Texas, the most popular fish for recreational fishing are:

- **largemouth bass**
- **catfish**
- **crappie**
- **striped, white, and hybrid striped bass**

Texas anglers can fish in approximately 1,100 public reservoirs and about 191,000 miles of rivers and streams, together totaling 1.7 million acres.

The Texas Parks and Wildlife Department operates field stations, fish hatcheries, and research facilities to support the conservation and management of fishery resources. The hatcheries operated by TPWD raise largemouth and smallmouth bass, as well as catfish, striped and hybrid striped bass, and sunfish.

TPWD has continued its programs of stocking fish in public waters to increase angling opportunities. Many conservation-minded anglers who desire continued quality fishing practice **catch-and-release fishing.**

## Texas Freshwater Fisheries Center

The Texas Freshwater Fisheries Center in Athens, about 75 miles southeast of Dallas, is an $18-million hatchery and educational center, where visitors can learn about the underwater life.

The interactive Visitors Center includes aquarium displays of fish in their natural environment. Visitors get an "eye-to-eye" view of three authentically designed Texas freshwater habitats: a **Hill Country stream,** an **East Texas pond,** and a **reservoir.** A **marsh exhibit** features live American alligators.

A **casting pond** stocked with rainbow trout in the winter and catfish year-around provides a place for visitors to learn how to bait a hook, cast a line, and land a fish. The center has conference facilities and hosts groups by appointment.

The Texas Freshwater Fisheries Center is open Tuesday through Saturday, 9 a.m. to 4 p.m., and Sunday, 1 p.m. to 4 p.m. It is closed on Monday. Admission is charged. The center is located 4.5 miles east of Athens on FM 2495 at Lake Athens. Address: 5550 FM 2495, Athens 75752, or call (903) 676-2277. Download the free **Texas Freshwater Fisheries Center smartphone app** from the Apple app store or Google Play. For more information, visit:

**http://tpwd.texas.gov/spdest/visitorcenters/tffc/** or visit us on Facebook.

## Saltwater Fishing

There are about 672,000 saltwater anglers in Texas (16 years old and older) who spend an estimated $1.1 billion annually on fishing-related expenditures. In 2013, anglers harvested 1.74 million fish from both Texas bays and the Gulf of Mexico off Texas.

The most popular saltwater sport fish in Texas bays are spotted seatrout, sand seatrout, Atlantic croaker, red drum, southern flounder, black drum, sheepshead, and gafftopsail catfish.

Offshore, some of the fish that anglers target are red snapper, king mackerel, Spanish mackerel, dolphin (fish), cobia, tarpon, and yellowfin tuna. ☆

***For Commercial Fishing data, see page 627 in the Business section.***

# Licenses and Game Harvests

*Source: Texas Parks and Wildlife Department; http://tpwd.texas.gov/huntwild/hunt/.*

## Licenses and Revenue

Texas Parks and Wildlife Department reported the following totals for hunting and fishing licenses, stamps, and permits for the 2012–2013 and the 2013–2014 seasons, which begin Sept. 1 and end Aug. 31:

| 2012–2013 Season | Volume | Revenue |
|---|---|---|
| Hunting Licenses | 532,127 | $23,892,386 |
| Fishing Licenses | 1,346,022 | $36,505,584 |
| Combined Licenses | 647,525 | $32,890,905 |
| **TOTALS** | **2,525,674** | **$93,288,875** |
| **2013–2014 Season** | **Volume** | **Revenue** |
| Hunting Licenses | 554,233 | $25,156,994 |
| Fishing Licenses | 1,345,388 | $36,459,588 |
| Combined Licenses | 678,297 | $34,484,623 |
| **TOTALS** | **2,577,918** | **$96,101,206** |

*A multi-pronged white-tailed deer in Choke Canyon State Park. Texas Parks and Wildlife Department photo.*

## Game Harvest Estimates

During the **2012–2013 license year,** TPWD estimated that hunters harvested:

- 636,325 – white-tailed deer
- 18,976 – mule deer
- 18,763 – wild turkey in the fall
- 20,514 – wild turkey in the spring
- 6,452,323 – mourning dove
- 141,010 – bobwhite quail
- 22,912 – javelina

During the **2013–2014 license year,** TPWD estimated that hunters harvested:

- 700,449 – white-tailed deer
- 22,418 – mule deer
- 19,066 – wild turkey in the fall
- 19,941 – wild turkey in the spring
- 7,446,300 – mourning dove
- 220,502 – bobwhite quail
- 22,590 – javelina

*As of the 2005–2006 hunting year, rabbits and squirrels are no longer surveyed.* ☆

## Fishing Licenses

All **fishing licenses and endorsements** are valid only from Sept. 1 through the following Aug. 31, except licenses issued for a specific number of days or time periods. If you own any valid **freshwater fishing package,** you will be able to purchase a saltwater stamp and also fish saltwater.

If you own any valid **saltwater fishing package,** you will be able to purchase a freshwater stamp and also fish freshwater. An all-water fishing package is available that enables anglers to fish both fresh- and saltwater.

Detailed information concerning licenses, endorsements, seasons, and regulations can be obtained from Texas Parks and Wildlife Department, 4200 Smith School Road, Austin 78744, (800) 792-1112 or (512) 389-4820; or at: **http://tpwd.texas.gov/business/licenses/**

This website includes a full digital copy of the TPWD Outdoor Annual that lists all rules and regulations.

## Hunting Licenses

A hunting license is required of Texas residents and non-residents who hunt any legal bird or animal. Hunting licenses and endorsements are valid during the period Sept. 1 through the following Aug. 31 of each year, except licenses issued for a specific number of days or time periods.

A hunting license (except the non-resident special hunting license and non-resident 5-day special hunting license) is valid for taking all legal species of wildlife in Texas including deer, turkey, javelina, antelope, aoudad (sheep), alligator, and all small game and migratory game birds. Endorsement and tag requirements apply.

A trapper's license is required for all persons to hunt, shoot, or take for sale those species classified as fur-bearing animals or their pelts.

In addition to a valid hunting license:

★ An Archery Endorsement is required to hunt deer or turkey during Archery-Only open season.

★ An Upland Game Bird Endorsement is required to hunt turkey, pheasant, quail, or chachalaca. Non-residents who purchase the non-resident spring turkey license are exempt from this endorsement requirement.

★ A Migratory Game Bird Endorsement and HIP (Harvest Information Program) Certification is required to hunt any migratory game birds, including waterfowl, coot, rail, gallinule, snipe, dove, sandhill crane, and woodcock.

★ A valid Federal Duck Stamp is required of waterfowl hunters age 16 or older.

On the web, information from TPWD on hunting: **http://tpwd.texas.gov/huntwild/hunt/.**

## Hunting Leases

Hunting leases are important to the economies of many Texas towns. The Texas Parks and Wildlife Department hosts Hunt Texas, a free online connection between landowners and hunters, at: **http://tpwd.texas.gov/exptexas/programs/hunt-texas/.**

Through the website, landowners can register their leases, and hunters can search by county, game type, length of lease terms, costs, and weapons allowed. ☆

*A boardwalk gives birding enthusiasts a great view to observe some of the more than 220 species of birds that have been sighted at the I-20 Wildlife Preserve in Midland. Photo by Michael S. Price; I-20 Wildlife Preserve.*

# Birding in Texas

## World Birding Center

The World Birding Center comprises nine birding education centers and observation sites in the Lower Rio Grande Valley designed to protect wildlife habitat and offer visitors a view of more than 500 species of birds. The center has partnered with the Texas Parks and Wildlife Department, the U.S. Fish and Wildlife Service and nine communities to turn 10,000 acres back into natural areas for birds, butterflies and other wildlife.

This area in Cameron, Hidalgo and Starr counties is a natural migratory path for millions of birds that move between the Americas. The nine WBC sites are situated along the border with Mexico:

### Bentsen–Rio Grande
### Valley State Park

This is the World Birding Center Headquarters and comprises the 760-acre Bentsen-RGV State Park and 1,700 acres of adjoining federal refuge land near **Mission.** The site offers: daily tram service; 4 nature trails ranging in length from 1/4 mile to 2 miles; 2-story high Hawk Observation Tower with a 210-foot-long handicapped access ramp; 2 observation decks; 2 accessible bird blinds; primitive camping sites (by reservation); rest areas; picnic sites with tables; exhibit hall; park store; coffee bar; meeting room (available for rental); catering kitchen; bike rentals (1 and 2 seat bikes). Access within the park is by foot, bike and tram only; (956) 585-1107. **Hours:** 6 a.m. to 10 p.m., seven days a week.

### Edinburg Scenic Wetlands

This 40-acre wetlands in **Edinburg** is an oasis for water-loving birds, butterflies and other wildlife. The site is currently offering:walking trails, nature tours and classes; (956) 381-9922. **Hours:** 8 a.m. – 5 p.m., Monday through Wednesday; 8 a.m.–6 p.m., Thursday through Saturday. Closed Sunday.

### Estero Llano Grande State Park

This 176-acre refuge in **Weslaco** attracts a wide array of South Texas wildlife with its varied landscape of shallow lake, woodlands and thorn forest; 956-565-3919. **Hours:** 8 a.m.–5 p.m., Monday through Friday; 8 a.m.–7:30 p.m., Saturday and Sunday through August.

### Harlingen Arroyo Colorado

This site in **Harlingen** is connected by an arroyo waterway, as well as hike-and-bike trails meandering through the city, Hugh Ramsey Nature Park to the east and the Harlingen Thicket to the west; (956) 427-8873. **Hours:** Office, 8 a.m.–5:00 p.m., Monday through Friday. Nature trails are open seven days a week, sunrise to sunset.

### Old Hidalgo Pumphouse

Visitors to this museum in **Hidalgo** on the Rio Grande can learn about the steam-driven irrigation pumps that transformed Hidalgo County into a year-round farming area. The museum's grounds feature hummingbird gardens, walking trails and historic tours; (956) 843-8686. **Hours:** 10 a.m.–5 p.m., Monday through Friday; 1 p.m.–5 p.m., Sunday. Closed Saturday.

### Quinta Mazatlan

This 1930s country estate in **McAllen** is a historic Spanish Revival adobe hacienda surrounded by lush tropical landscaping and native woodland. It is also an urban oasis, where quiet trails wind through more than

15 acres of birding habitat; (956) 688-3370. **Hours:** 8 a.m.–5 p.m., Tuesday through Saturday. Open until sunset on Thursdays. Closed Mondays and holidays.

### Resaca de la Palma State Park

More than 1,700 acres of newly opened wilderness near **Brownsville**, this site comprises the largest tract of native habitat in the World Birding Center network. The park offers birding tours and natural history tours. Admission is by appointment and reservation only; (956) 565-3919.

### Roma Bluffs

History and nature meet on scenic bluffs above the Rio Grande, where the World Birding Center in **Roma** is located on the old plaza of a once-thriving steamboat port. Part of a national historic district, the WBC Roma Bluffs includes a riverside nature area of three acres in Starr County. The site offers: walking trails, canoe trips, birding tours, natural history tours and classes; (956) 849-4930. **Hours:** 8 a.m.–4:00 p.m. Tuesday through Saturday, although trails are open seven days a week and are free to the public.

### South Padre Island Birding and Nature Center

At the southern tip of the world's longest barrier island, **South Padre Island** Birding and Nature Center is a slender thread of land between the shallow Laguna Madre and the Gulf of Mexico. This site offers: a nature trail boardwalk and birding tours; 1-800-SOPADRE. **Hours:** 9 a.m.–5 p.m., seven days a week.

*An osprey flies with his catch near the Laguna Atascosa National Wildlife Refuge in the Lower Rio Grande Valley. Photo by Robert Burton; U.S. Fish and Wildlife Service.*

# Great Texas Coastal Birding Trail

The Great Texas Coastal Birding Trail winds its way through 43 Texas counties along the entire Texas coastal region. The trail was completed in April 2000 and is divided into upper, central, and lower coastal regions. It includes 308 wildlife-viewing sites and such amenities as boardwalks, parking pullouts, kiosks, observation platforms, and landscaping to attract native wildlife.

Color-coded maps are available, and signs mark each site. Trail maps contain information about the birds and habitats likely to be found at each site, the best season to visit, and food and lodging.

For information, contact: Nature Tourism Coordinator, Texas Parks and Wildlife Department, 4200 Smith School Road, Austin, TX 78744; (512) 389-4396. On the web: **http://tpwd.texas.gov/huntwild/wildlife/wildlife-trails/coastal.**

# West Texas

### I-20 Wildlife Preserve and Jenna Welch Nature Study Center

The 1-20 Wildlife Preserve is an 87-acre urban playa lake in its natural state in southwest Midland that opened in 2013. It was maintained for many years by the Midland Naturalists and other volunteers, including Jenna Welch, a birding enthusiast and a member of the group.

It comprises 3.4 miles of hiking trails, including 1.45 miles of ADA-accessible trails, seven bird observation blinds, four teaching platforms, the 24-foot tall Hawk Observation Platform, and the Merritt Pavilion.

Jenna Welch Nature Study Center operates an educational outreach program to local schools and area colleges and universities. Land was acquired to build a facility to house the nature study center.

The preserve, at 2201 S. Midland Dr., Midland, TX 79701, is open to the public daily from dawn until dusk. For more information, call (432) 853-9453. On the web: **www.i20wildlifepreserve.org.** ☆

**Bird Sighting Regions**

Panhandle-Plains

North Central

East Texas Timberlands

Trans-Pecos

Central Plateau

Central Prairie

Coastal Prairie

Rio Grande Brushlands

Source: Texas Ornithological Society

# Texas State Aquarium

The Texas State Aquarium, 7.3 acres on the southernmost tip of Corpus Christi Beach in Corpus Christi, is operated by the Texas State Aquarium Association, a nonprofit, self-supporting organization established in 1978. Efforts to fund a public aquarium in South Texas began in 1952, and several nonprofit organizations founded over the years eventually grew into the Texas State Aquarium Association.

Since 1978, the association has raised more than $28 million in private and public funding to build and operate of the aquarium. Corpus Christi provided $14.5 million, including $4 million from a bond issue.

In 1985, the 69th Texas Legislature declared the project the "Official Aquarium of the State of Texas."

The Jesse H. and Mary Gibbs Jones Gulf of Mexico Exhibit Building was completed in July 1990. In 2003, Dolphin Bay opened for Atlantic bottlenose dolphins and the Environmental Discovery Center opened, featuring a library, a Family Learning Center, and the Flint Hills Resources Distance Learning Studio.

The aquarium's exhibits and research focus on the plants and animals of the Gulf of Mexico and the Caribbean. It is the first U.S. facility to do so.

The aquarium is open daily 9 a.m. to 5 p.m., Labor Day through March 1, and until 6 p.m. March 1 through Labor Day. There are admission and parking fees. For more information, call 1-800-477-GULF; www.texasstateaquarium.org. — *New Handbook of Texas and Texas State Aquarium.* ☆

# Sea Center Texas

*Source: Texas Parks and Wildlife Department; http://tpwd.texas.gov/spdest/visitorcenters/seacenter/*

The Texas Parks and Wildlife Department operates Sea Center Texas — a marine aquarium, fish hatchery, and nature center that educates and entertains visitors. It is located in Lake Jackson, 50 miles south of Houston, off of Texas 288.

The visitor center opened in 1996 and has interpretive displays, a "touch tank," and native Texas habitat exhibits depicting a salt marsh, bay, jetty, reef, and open Gulf waters. The Gulf aquarium features "Cooper," a 50-pound grouper; a green moray eel; a nurse shark; and other offshore species.

Sea Center is said to be the world's largest redfish hatchery and is one of three marine hatcheries on the Texas coast that produces juvenile red drum and spotted seatrout for enhancing natural populations in Texas bays. The hatchery can produce 15 million juvenile fish yearly and is a testing ground for production of other marine species, such as flounder. Hatchery tours and educational programs are available by reservation.

A half-acre youth fishing pond introduces youngsters to saltwater fishing through scheduled activities. The pond is handicap accessible, and stocked with a variety of marine fish.

The center's wetland area is part of the Great Texas Coastal Birding Trail, where more than 150 species of birds have been identified. They include one-acre of salt marsh and a three-acres of freshwater marsh. Damselflies, dragonflies, butterflies, turtles, and frogs can be sited off the boardwalk, and an outdoor pavilion is adjacent to butterfly and hummingbird gardens.

Sea Center Texas is operated in partnership with The Dow Chemical Company and the Coastal Conservation Association. Admission and parking are free. Hours are 9 a.m. to 4 p.m. Tuesday through Saturday, and 1 p.m. to 4 p.m. Sunday, except some holidays. Reservations are required for group tours, nature tours, and hatchery tours. For more information; 979-292-0100 or email: Seacenter@tpwd.texas.gov. ☆

Sea Center features a 50,000-gallon aquarium that allows visitors to view large Gulf of Mexico marine animals. Texas Parks and Wildlife photo.

*Sisters Martie Maguire and Emily Robison of Dixie Chicks fame perform as the Court Yard Hounds at the Continental Club in Austin. Photo courtesy of the Austin Convention and Visitors Bureau.*

# Fairs, Festivals, and Special Events

Fairs, festivals, and other special events provide year-round recreation in Texas. Some are of national interest, while many attract visitors from across the state. Each county profile in the Counties section also lists events in the Recreation paragraph and following town names. Information here was furnished by event coordinators.

**Abilene** — West Texas Fair & Rodeo; September; 1700 Hwy. 36, 79602; www.taylorcountyexpocenter.com. *Since 1897.*

**Albany** — Fort Griffin Fandangle; June; PO Box 155, 76430; www.fortgriffinfandangle.org. *Since 1938.*

**Alvarado** — Johnson County Pioneers & Old Settlers Reunion; August; PO Box 217, 76009. *Since 1893.*

**Amarillo** — Tri-State Fair; September; PO Box 31087, 79120.

**Anderson** — Grimes County Fair; June; PO Box 435, 77830.

**Angleton** — Brazoria County Fair; October; PO Box 818, 77516; www.bcfa.org. *Since 1939.*

**Aransas Pass** — Shrimporee; June, 130 W. Goodnight, 78336; www.aransaspass.org. *Since 1949.*

**Arlington** — Texas Scottish Festival; June; PO Box 511, 76634; www.texasscottishfestival.com. *Since 1986.*

**Athens** — Cinco de Mayo Celebration; May; Texas Freshwater Fisheries Center, 5550 FM 2495; 75752. www.athenstx.org; (903) 670-2266.

**Athens** — Texas Fiddlers' Asso. Reunion; May (last Fri.); PO Box 1441, 75751. *Since 1932.*

**Austin** — Star of Texas Fair & Rodeo; March; 9100 Decker Lake Rd. 78724; www.rodeoaustin.com. *Since 1937.*

**Austin** — Austin Fine Arts Festival; April; PO Box 5705, 78763; www.austinfineartsfestival.org.

**Bay City** — Matagorda County Fair & Livestock Show; February; PO Box 1803, 77404; www.matagordacountyfair.com. *Since 1945.*

**Bay City** — Bay City Rice Festival; October; PO Box 867; 77404; www.baycitylions.org.

**Beaumont** — South Texas State Fair; October; 7250 Wespark Cr., 77705; www.ymbl.org. *Since 1943.*

**Bellville** — Austin County Fair; October; PO Box 141, 77418; www.austincountyfair.com.

**Belton** — 4th of July Celebration & PRCA Rodeo; July; PO Box 659, 76513; www.beltonchamber.com.

**Belton** — Central Texas State Fair; Aug.-Sept.; PO Box 206, 76513; www.centraltexasstatefair.com.

**Big Spring** — Howard County Fair; September; PO Box 2356, 79721. *Since 1973*

**Boerne** — Boerne Berges Fest; June; PO Box 748, 78006; www.bergesfest.com.

**Boerne** — Kendall County Fair; September (Labor Day Wknd.); PO Box 954, 78006; www.kcfa.org. *Since 1906.*

**Brackettville** — Gunfighter Competition; July; PO Box 528, 78832; www.alamovillage.com.

**Brackettville** — Western Horse Races & BBQ; September (Labor Day); PO Box 528, 78832; www.alamovillage.com.

**Brenham** — Washington County Fair; September; 1305 E. Blue Bell Rd., 77833; www.washingtoncofair.com. *Since 1870.*

**Brownsville** — Charro Days Fiesta; February; PO Box 3247, 78523-3247; www.charrodaysfiesta.com. *Since 1938.*

**Burnet** — Burnet Bluebonnet Festival; April; 229 S. Pierce; 78611. 222.burnetchamber.org. *Since 1986.*

**Burton** — Cotton Gin Festival; April (3rd wknd.); PO Box 98; 77835; www.cottonginmuseum.org. *Since 1990.*

**Caldwell** — Kolache Festival; September; 301 N. Main Street; 77836; (979) 567-0000.

**Caldwell** — Burleson County Fair; September; PO Box 634, 77836; (979) 567-9319.

**Canyon** — TEXAS! Musical Drama; June–August; 1514 5th Ave., 79015; www.texas-show.com. *Since 1966.*

**Chappell Hill** — Bluebonnet Festival; April; 152 Cnty. Rd. 4145, 76634; http://clifton.centraltx.com/heritage.htm.

**Clifton** — Norse Smorgasbord; November; 152 Cnty. Rd. 4145, 76634; http://clifton.centraltx.com/heritage.htm.

**Clute** — Great Texas Mosquito Festival; July; PO Box 997, 77531; www.mosquitofestival.com. *Since 1981.*

**Columbus** — Colorado County Fair; September; PO Box 506, 78933; www.coloradocountyfair.org.

**Conroe** — Montgomery County Fair; March–April; PO Box 869, 77305-0869; www.mcfa.org. *Since 1957.*

**Corpus Christi** — Bayfest; September–October; PO Box 1858, 78403-1858; www.bayfesttexas.com.

**Corpus Christi** — Buc Days; April–May; PO Box 30404, 78463; www.bucdays.com.

**Corsicana** — Derrick Days; April; 120 N. 12th St., 75110; www.corsicana.org. *Since 1976.*

**Crowell** — Cynthia Ann Parker Festival; May; PO Box 452, 79227; www.crowelltex.com/CAP/cappage1.html.

**Dalhart** — XIT Rodeo & Reunion; August (1st full wknd.); PO Box 967, 79022. *Since 1937.*

**Dallas** — State Fair of Texas; September–October; PO Box 150009, 75315; www.bigtex.com. *Since 1886.*

**Decatur** — Wise County Old Settlers Reunion; July (last full week); PO Box 203, 76234.

*The GrapeStomp competition is a highlight of GrapeFest, which takes place each September in the historic town of Grapevine in Tarrant County. Photo courtesy of the Grapevine Convention & Visitors Bureau.*

**De Leon** — De Leon Peach & Melon Festival; August; PO Box 44, 76444-0044; www.cctc.net/~pmdeleon/index.htm. *Since 1917.*

**Denton** — North Texas State Fair & Rodeo; August; PO Box 1695, 76202; www.ntfair.com. *Since 1929.*

**Edna** — Jackson County Youth Fair; October; PO Box 457, 77957; www.jcyf.org. *Since 1949.*

**Ennis** — National Polka Festival; May; PO Box 1177, 75120-1237; www.visitennis.org/festivals.html.

**Fairfield** — Freestone County Fair; June; PO Box 196; 75840.

**Flatonia** — Czhilispiel; October (4th full wknd.); PO Box 610, 78941; www.flatoniachamber.com. *Since 1973.*

**Fort Worth** — Pioneer Days; September; 131 E. Exchange Ave., Ste 100B, 76106; www.fortworthstockyards.org.

**Fort Worth** — Southwestern Exposition & Livestock Show; January-February; PO Box 150, 76101; www.fwssr.com. *Since 1896.*

**Fredericksburg** — Food and Wine Fest; October (4th Sat.); 703 North Llano Street, 78624; www.fbgfoodandwinefest.com. *Since 1990.*

**Fredericksburg** — Night in Old Fredericksburg; July; 302 E. Austin, 78624; www.fredericksburg-texas.com. *Since 1963.*

**Fredericksburg** — Oktoberfest; October (1st wknd.); PO Box 222, 78624; www.Oktoberfestinfbg.com. *Since 1980.*

**Freer** — Freer Rattlesnake Roundup; May; PO Box 717, 78357; www.freerrattlesnake.com. *Since 1966.*

**Galveston** — Dickens on The Strand; December; 502 20th St., 77550; www.dickensonthestrand.org. *Since 1973.*

**Galveston** — Galveston Historic Homes Tour; May; 502 20th St., 77550-2014; www.galvestonhistory.org. *Since 1974.*

**Gilmer** — East Texas Yamboree; October; PO Box 854, 75644; www.yamboree.com. *Since 1937.*

**Glen Flora** — Wharton County Youth Fair; April; PO Box 167, 77443; www.whartoncountyyouthfair.org. *Since 1976.*

**Graham** — Art Splash on the Square; May; PO Box 1684, 76450; www.art-splash.com.

**Graham** — Red, White & You Parade & Festivities; July; PO Box 299; 76450; www.visitgraham.com.

**Granbury** — Annual July 4th Celebration; July; 116 W. Bridge St., 76048; www.granburychamber.com.

**Granbury** — Harvest Moon Festival; October; 116 W. Bridge St., 76048; www.hgma.com. *Since 1977.*

**Grand Prairie** — National Championship Pow-Wow; September; 2602 Mayfield Rd, 75052; www.tradersvillage.com. *Since 1963.*

**Grapevine** — GrapeFest; September; 636 S. Main St., 76051; www.grapevinetexasusa.com. *Since 1986.*

**Greenville** — Hunt County Fair; June; PO Box 1071, 75403; www.huntcountyfair.com. *Since 1970.*

**Groesbeck** — Limestone County Fair; March–April; PO Box 965, 76642.

**Hallettsville** — Hallettsville Kolache Fest; September; PO Box 313, 77964; www.hallettsville.com. *Since 1995.*

**Helotes** — Helotes Cornyval; May (1st wknd.); PO Box 376, 78023; www.cornyval.com. *Since 1967.*

**Hempstead** — Waller County Fair; September–October; PO Box 911, 77445. www.wallercountyfair.com. *Since 1946.*

**Hico** — Hico Old Settler Reunion; July; PO Box 93, 76457; www.hico-tx.com. *Since 1887.*

**Hidalgo** — BorderFest; March; PO Box 722; 78557; www.borderfest.com.

**Hondo** — Medina County Fair; September (3rd wknd.); PO Box 4, 78861. *Since 1980.*

**Houston** — Harris County Fair; October; 1 Abercrombie Dr, 77084-4233; www.harriscountyfair.net. *Since 1977.*

**Houston** — Houston International Festival; April–May; 1111 Bagby St., Ste. 2550, 77002; www.ifest.org.

**Houston** — Houston Livestock Show and Rodeo; March; PO Box 20070; 77225-0070; www.hlsr.com.

**Hughes Springs** — Wildflower Trails of Texas; April; PO Box 805, 75656. *Since 1970.*

**Huntsville** — Walker County Fair & Rodeo; March–April; PO Box 1817, 77342; www.walkercountyfair.com. *Since 1979.*

**Jefferson** — Historical Pilgrimage and Spring Festival; May (1st wknd.); PO Box 301, 75657-0301; www.theexcelsiorhouse.com. *Since 1947.*

**Johnson City** — Blanco County Fair; August; PO Box 261, 78636-0261; www.lbjcountry.com/

**Kenedy** — Bluebonnet Days; April; 205 South 2nd St., 78119-2729.

**Kerrville** — Kerr County Fair; October; PO Box 290842, 78029; www.kerrcountyfair.com. *Since 1980.*

**Kerrville** — Kerrville Folk Festival; May–June; PO Box 291466, 78029; www.kerrvillefolkfestival.com. *Since 1972.*

**Kerrville** — The Official Texas State Arts & Crafts Fair; May (Memorial wknd.); 4000 Riverside Dr., 78028, www.tacef.org. *Since 1972.*

**Kerrville** — Kerrville Wine and Music Festival; September (Labor Day wknd.); PO Box 291466; 78029; www.kerrvillefolkfestival.com. *Since 1991.*

**Killeen** — Take 190 West: Killeen Salutes the Arts; February; www.take190west.com.

**LaGrange** — Fayette County Fair; September (Labor Day wknd.); PO Box 544, 78945; www.fayettecountyfair.net. *Since 1926.*

**Laredo** — Border Olympics; January–March; PO Box 450037, 78044-0037; http://borderolympics.net. *Since 1947.*

**Laredo** — Laredo International Fair & Expo; March; PO Box 1770, 78043; www.laredofair.com. *Since 1963.*

**Laredo** — Washington's Birthday Celebration; January–February; 1819 E. Hillside Rd., 78041-3383; www.wbcalaredo.com. *Since 1898.*

**Longview** — Gregg County Fair & Exposition; September; 1511 Judson Rd., Ste. F, 75601; www.greggcountyfair.com. *Since 1951.*

**Lubbock** — 4th on Broadway Festival; July; PO Box 1643, 79408; www.broadwayfestivals.com. *Since 1991.*

**Lubbock** — Lights on Broadway Celebration; December; PO Box 1643, 79408; www.broadwayfestivals.com.

**Lubbock** — Panhandle-South Plains Fair; September; PO Box 208, 79408; www.southplainsfair.com. *Since 1914.*

**Lufkin** — Texas Forest Festival; September; 1615 S. Chestnut St., 75901; www.texasforestfestival.com.

**Luling** — Luling Watermelon Thump; June (last full wknd); PO Box 710, 78648-0710; www.watermelonthump.com. *Since 1953.*

**Marshall** — Fire Ant Festival; October; PO Box 520, 75671; www.marshall-chamber.com. *Since 1984.*

**Marshall** — Stagecoach Days Festival; May; PO Box 520, 75671; www.marshall-chamber.com. Since 1973.

**Marshall** — Wonderland of Lights; November–December; PO Box 520, 75671; www.marshalltxchamber.com.

**Mercedes** — Rio Grande Valley Livestock Show; March; 1000 N. Texas; www.rgvlivestockshow.com. *Since 1940.*

**Mesquite** — Mesquite Championship Rodeo; April–September (each Fri. & Sat.); 1818 Rodeo Dr, 75149-3800; www.mesquiterodeo.com. *Since 1958.*

**Monahans** — Butterfield-Overland Stage Coach and Wagon Festival; July; 401 S. Dwight Ave., 79756 www.butterfield.ws/. *Since 1994.*

**Mount Pleasant** — Titus County Fair; September; PO Box 1232, 75456-1232; www.tituscountyfair.com.

**Nacogdoches** — Piney Woods Fair; October; 3805 NW Stallings Dr., 75964; www.nacexpo.net. *Since 1978.*

**Nederland** — Nederland Heritage Festival; March; PO Box 1176, 77627; www.nederlandhf.org. *Since 1973.*

**New Braunfels** — Comal County Fair; September; PO Box 310223, 78131-0223; www.comalcountyfair.org. *Since 1894.*

**New Braunfels** — Wurstfest; October–November; PO Box 310309, 78131-0309; www.wurstfest.com.

**Odessa** — Permian Basin Fair & Expo; September; 218 W. 46th St., 79764; www.permianbasinfair.com.

**Palestine** — Dogwood Trails Festival; March–April; PO Box 2828, 75802-2828; www.visitpalestine.com.

**Paris** — Red River Valley Fair; August–September; 570 E. Center St., 75460; www.rrvfair.org. *Since 1911.*

**Pasadena** — Pasadena Livestock Show & Rodeo; September–October; 7601 Red Bluff Rd., 77507-1035; www.pasadenarodeo.com.

**Port Aransas** — Whooping Crane Festival; February (last weekend); 403 West Cotter, 78373; www.whoopingcranefestival.org. *Since 1996.*

**Port Arthur** — CalOILcade; October; PO Box 2336, 77643; www.portarthur.com/cavoilcade. *Since 1953.*

**Port Lavaca** — Calhoun County Fair; October (3rd wknd.); PO Box 42, 77979-0042. *Since 1963.*

**Poteet** — Poteet Strawberry Festival; April; PO Box 227, 78065; www.strawberryfestival.com. *Since 1948.*

**Refugio** — Refugio County Fair & Rodeo & Livestock Show; March; PO Box 88, 78377. *Since 1961.*

**Rio Grande City** — Starr County Fair; March (1st full wknd.); PO Box 841, 78582. *Since 1961.*

**Rosenberg** — Fort Bend County Fair; September–October; PO Box 428, 77471; www.fbcfa.org. *Since 1937.*

**Salado** — Salado Scottish Games and Competitions; November (2nd wknd); PO Box 36, 76571-0036; www.ctam-salado.org.

**San Angelo** — San Angelo Stock Show & Rodeo; February; 200 W 43rd St., 76903; www.sanangelorodeo.com. *Since 1932.*

**San Antonio** — Fiesta San Antonio; April; 2611 Broadway St.; 78215; www.fiesta-sa.org. *Since 1891.*

**San Antonio** — Texas Folklife Festival; June; 801 S. Bowie, 78205; www.texasfolklifefestival.org. *Since 1972.*

Two moods of Galveston: The Victorian festival Dickens on The Strand, above, during a December snow, and a sunny car show near the Galvez Hotel, below. Photos by Raul Reyes.

**Sanderson** — Cinco de Mayo Celebration; May (1st Sat.); PO Box 598, 79848.

**Sanderson** — 4th of July Celebration; July; PO Box 4810, 79848-4810; www.sandersontx.info. *Since 1908.*

**Sanderson** — Prickly Pear Pachanga; October; PO Box 410, 79848; www.sandersontx.info. *Since 2001.*

**Santa Fe** — Galveston County Fair & Rodeo; April; PO Box 889, 77510; www.galvestoncountyfair.com.

**Schulenburg** — Schulenburg Festival; August (1st full wknd.); PO Box 115; 78956; www.schulenburgfestival.com. *Since 1976.*

**Seguin** — Guadalupe Agricultural & Livestock Fair; October (2nd wknd); PO Box 334, 78155; www.guadalupecountyfairandrodeo.com. *Since 1885.*

**Shamrock** — St. Patrick's Day Celebration; March; PO Box 588, 79079. www.shamrocktx.net/site/index-2.html. *Since 1947.*

**Stamford** — Texas Cowboy Reunion; July; PO Box 948, 79553; www.tcrrodeo.com. *Since 1933.*

**Sulphur Springs** — Hopkins County Fall Festival; September (3rd Sat.); PO Box 177, 75483. **Sweetwater** — Rattlesnake Roundup; March; PO Box 416, 79556-0416; www.rattlesnakeroundup.net. *Since 1958.*

**Terlingua** — Terlingua International Chili Championship; November; PO Box 39, 79852; www.chili.org. *Since 1947.*

**Texarkana** — Four States Fair; September; 3700 E. 50th St., Texarkana AR, 75504; www.fourstatesfair.com.

**Todd Mission** — Texas Renaissance Festival; October–November (8 weekends); 21778 FM 1774, 77363; www.texrenfest.com. *Since 1975.*

**Tyler** — East Texas State Fair; September; 2112 W. Front St., 75702; www.etstatefair.com. *Since 1914.*

**Tyler** — Texas Rose Festival; Ocober (3rd wknd.); PO Box 8224, 75711; www.texasrosefestival.com. *Since 1933.*

**Waco** — Heart O' Texas Fair & Rodeo; October; 4601 Bosque Blvd.; 76710; www.hotfair.com. *Since 1954.*

**Waxahachie** — Gingerbread Trail Tour of Homes; June (1st full wknd); PO Box 706, 75168; www.-rootsweb.com/~txecm/ginger.htm. *Since 1969.*

**Waxahachie** — Scarborough Renaissance Festival; April–May; PO Box 538, 75168-0538; www.scarboroughrenfest.com. *Since 1980.*

**Weatherford** — Parker County Peach Festival; July (2nd Sat.); PO Box 310, 76086; www.weatherford-chamber.com. *Since 1985.*

**Weatherford** — Christmas on the Square; December; PO Box 310, 76086; www.weatherford-chamber.com. *Since 1988.*

**West** — Westfest; September (Labor Day wknd.); PO Box 123, 76691; www.westfest.com. *Since 1976.*

**Winnsboro** — Autumn Trails Festival; October (every wknd.); PO Box 464; 75494.

**Woodville** — Tyler County Dogwood Festival; March–April; PO Box 2151, 75979-2151; www.tylercountydogwoodfestival.org. *Since 1944.*

**Yorktown** — Yorktown's Fiesta En La Calle Festival; April (1st Sat.); PO Box 488, 78164-0488; www.yorktowntx.com.

**Yorktown** — Yorktown's Annual Western Days Celebration; October (3rd full wknd.); PO Box 488, 78164-0488; www.yorktowntx.com. *Since 1959.* ☆

# Sports

*Texan Jordan Spieth won the U.S. Open in 2015, along with other major tournaments. Adrian Dennis/AFP, Getty Images; jordanspiethgolf.com.*

## The State of Texas Sports
## Assault: 1946 Triple Crown Winner
## High School Champions
## College Champions
## Professional Sports Teams
## Hall of Fame, Olympic Medalists

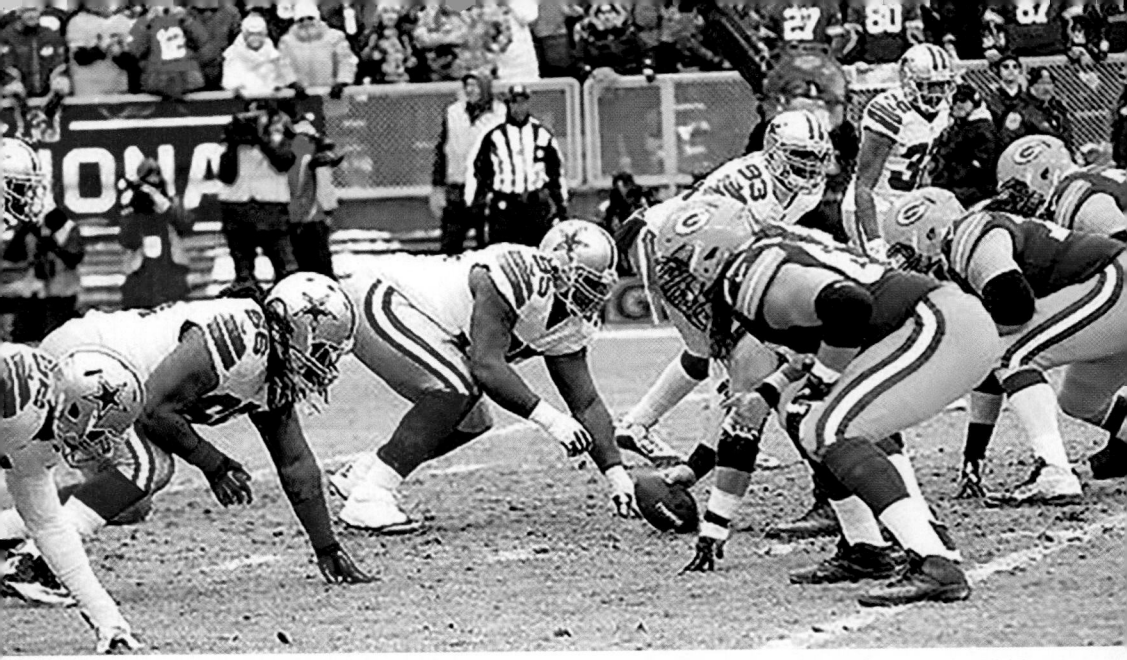

*The Dallas Cowboys faced the Green Bay Packers in the Divisional Round on Jan. 11, 2015. The Cowboys lost 26–21 amid a controversial play. Photo courtesy of the Dallas Cowboys.*

# The State of Texas Sports

## *Lone Star Fans Ride the Wild Winds of Change*

### By Norm Hitzges

An oft-repeated adage about Texas weather suggests that if you don't like the weather around here, just wait a minute and it'll change. Well, the Texas sports fan can certainly understand the wisdom of that thinking.

In 1964, iconic singer-songwriter Bob Dylan penned the folk rock classic "The Times They Are A-Changin'." Some 50 years later, as Texas entered the 2000-and-teens, Lone Star fans rode a wild roller coaster of change in virtually every major sports arena except one, where the more things change, the more they seem to stay the same.

## NFL Football

For decades, the Dallas Cowboys had carried the hopes of possible NFL championships for this state. And they'd produce *five* of them. The Houston Texans? Uh, well, "How 'Bout Those Cowboys."

But the pendulum appeared to have swung dramatically entering 2013. Houston had become the new darling of the state. The Texans' building program appeared to have reached the verge of remarkable success. They'd cast off their identity as an annual NFL also-ran to win 10 games in 2011, make the playoffs for the first time in years, and actually advance to the second round before losing a rugged game to Baltimore. They came right back in 2012 to win a dozen regular-season games and again won in the first round of the playoffs before being eliminated by traditional playoff bully New England.

Texan fans seemed certain they saw the light at the end of the NFL tunnel. How could they ever imagine that light was actually from an on-coming train that would splatter their hopes and create massive turnover in their organization? And "turnover" IS the most appropriate word to use without question. Buried by an avalanche of interceptions and fumbles, the 2013 Texans, who had become a chic choice to win that year's Super Bowl, instead experienced a free fall that never stopped until they hit rock bottom. After winning their first two games, Houston almost unthinkably managed to lose 14 straight games in what was truly a journey from the NFL penthouse to the outhouse. Veteran quarterback Matt Schaub's inexplicably miserable year resulted in him being released. Coach Gary Kubiak, who patiently built a roster and a philosophy for eight years, also got his walking papers.

That chic choice to perhaps win it all had lost it all, finishing dead last at 2–14. The winds of change that had swept out so many, swept in new coach Bill O'Brien, who had a much-better-that-expected 2014, going 9–7 and barely missing the playoffs. He relied on a stout defense and excellent pass rush headed by perhaps the league's best defensive lineman, J. J. Watt. But as the calendar turned to 2015, one huge question loomed for a franchise hoping to step forward off that surprisingly good 2014 season: Who's the quarterback capable of taking the club to the next level? Hoyer, Mallett, and Savage seemed like the name of an intriguing law firm. But those three — veteran backup Brian Hoyer, former Patriots reserve Ryan Mallet, and 2014 mid-round draft choice Tom Savage — represented the hopes at this oh-so-critical position approaching 2015. Most observers were of the opinion that this lack of proven ability at QB would mean the Texans hopes would be limited. But, when it comes to this franchise, those trying to predict what would happen have been wrong, and sometimes *very* wrong, before.

Meanwhile, as Houston seemed to be ascending, the proud Cowboys had descended into NFL mediocrity. As 2014 arrived, Dallas had gone 8–8, 8–8, and 8–8 the three previous seasons. They'd come close to the playoffs but seemed equally close to disintegrating. As 2014 approached, coach Jason Garrett was the consensus choice of experts to be the coach mostly likely to be fired first. He had only one season left on his contract and everyone understood that owner-GM Jerry Jones longed to be back in the spotlight of Super Bowl contention. Unthinkably, the club had won only one playoff game since its last Super Bowl in 1995. But the fingers of blame for Dallas' fall from grace pointed much more at Jones than Garrett. Poor drafts, bad trades, and often terrible contract decisions all got placed at the feet of Jones and his "I-do-it-all" franchise management policy.

Adding to the Cowboys woes in '14 was the shaky physical condition of the club's star quarterback Tony Romo, who'd also taken his share of blame for the Cowboys failure to step forward over the years. But suddenly Romo fans and critics alike in Dallas hung on every word about his physical situation. Romo had undergone *three* back operations in the past year-plus. His status was so tenuous that he never practiced two consecutive days at training camp as the team treated his worrisome back problems with kid gloves.

All this resulted in ominous predictions about those 2014 Cowboys. Virtually no one picked them to get as high as nine wins. Many

*Houston Texans quarterback Brian Hoyer attempts a pass in a 2015 preseason game against the New Orleans Saints. Photo courtesy of the Houston Texans.*

suggested they'd slip all the way to four or five. And if Romo disappeared because of injury? Well, you get the picture. "Bleak" would have been a good, descriptive word.

So, what actually happened? Dallas, with a healthy Romo, surged out of the gate going 6–1. A minor injury *did* keep him out for one game — but one game only. The Dallas offense became one of the finest in the league centered on runner Demarco Murray, who would lead the NFL in rushing by nearly 500 yards! Dallas glided into the playoffs at 12–4, beat the Detroit Lions in round one, and could have beaten Green Bay next, if not for a still-controversial non-catch call against wide receiver Dez Bryant. Romo topped the league in quarterback rating. Coach Garrett got a new mega-contract, and the often-maligned Jones picked up the league's Executive of the Year Award.

As the 2015 season approached, Dallas again wore the mantle of enormous expectation. They pulled together perhaps the NFL's best offensive line and boasted a now-healthy Romo, a mega-star in Bryant, and a vastly improved pass rush. Leading rusher Murray's gone to free agency. But otherwise, these Cowboys entered 2015 off of a 12-win season, a playoff victory, and with real hope everywhere. Sort of like the 2012 Texans. But with fingers crossed that, unlike the Texans, their Super Bowl dreams become reality.

# College Football

Perhaps no where have the winds of change created more of a sports upheaval in this state than in college football. Forever (or at least it seemed that way) Texas and Oklahoma had controlled and often dominated the Big 12. Each school has a national championship this century. No other Big 12 team can claim that. Oh, occasionally another large state school like Oklahoma State or Kansas State would rise to the top, as had Texas A&M, Nebraska, Colorado, and Missouri. But those latter four all left the conference as part of the flurry of moves that engulfed major college football just a handful of years ago. Their exits only seemed to buttress the belief that UT and OU would roll on at the top. How wrong that thinking proved to be!

In '13 and '14, national banner of the Big 12 was carried by none other than former bottom-feeders TCU and Baylor. The Frogs resurgence actually began several years before under vastly under-rated coach Gary Patterson. But the Frogs ascent began outside the Big 12. Back in the 90s when the Southwest Conference and Big 8 merged, they asked the Frogs to politely go away, along with other schools like SMU and Rice. Many folks wondered at that time why they didn't send Baylor packing also. But under Patterson, the Frogs began beating up on competition in lesser conferences, securing bowl bids every year from 2005 to 2011, while winning a whopping 77 games over those seven seasons. When some of those bigger Big 12 schools left for either greener or more friendly pastures, the conference suddenly wanted these Frogs-who'd-turned-into-princes back in the fold.

TCU's return to glory culminated when the Frogs finished the regular season 11–1 in 2014, sharing the regular-season title with, who else, the Baylor Bears. TCU capped that glorious '14 season by routing Ole Miss in a bowl game and securing a spot in the nation's top 5 final rankings.

Baylor's rise was more sudden than that of the Frogs. But it was none-the-less stunning. The mighty schools of the Big 12 had been wiping their feet on the Waco Bears for years until Art Briles and his rapid-fire offense arrived in 2008. In Briles' first year, the Green and Gold Bears won four, then five, then seven, ending 2010 with a loss in a minor bowl. All along, though, the base of a sound foundation was being built. Suddenly Baylor began producing double-digit-win seasons and piled up 40 victories over the four seasons from '11 through '14. Like the Frogs, they've pushed their way into the top handful of teams in the country, seemingly just a few years after being one of the least-productive programs in America.

The meteoric rise of these two church-based private schools reached its peak in the months leading up to the 2015 season. *Both* took places in the top-five preseason national rankings (TCU No. 2 and Baylor No. 4), and the Frogs boasted of having one of the favorites to win the Heisman Trophy in quarterback Trevone Boykin.

And what has become of those two formerly dominant conference goliaths — Texas and Oklahoma?

Texas took one of the most dramatic falls in the country. As late as 2009, the Longhorns entered the postseason unbeaten only to lose

*TCU Horned Frogs running back Aaron Green (22) runs past Texas Longhorns safety Mykkele Thompson (2) during the Nov. 27, 2014, game at Darrell K Royal–Texas Memorial Stadium. Photo by Brendan Maloney-USA TODAY Sports.*

to powerful Alabama in a bowl game. From that point, the unraveling began quickly! Those Horns, who'd lost only nine games in six years from 2004 to 2009, suddenly dropped *seven* in just 2010. Things didn't get much better the next three years as the Horns simply seemed unable to find a quarterback to lead them. The unrest grew and Mack Brown, who'd had a legendary coaching run for more than a decade and a half, eventually got pushed out of his job after the 2013 season, having posted just a 30–22 record for the previous four years. Some schools would love such a four-year run (like TCU or Baylor at points in the '80s or '90s). But at Texas, 22 losses in four years represents failure, and Brown paid for it with his job. Three-decade Athletic Director DeLoss Dodds also exited, despite having overseen one of the most successful on and off the field departments in America for 30 years.

To replace Brown, the Horns brought in Charlie Strong, who'd been fabulously successful at Louisville. But as Strong revamped the program both on the field and culturally off of it, the Horns did no better in 2014, winding up with a 6–7 record, including a bad beating by Arkansas in a bowl game. That 2014 season

could well be viewed as Strong's "honeymoon period" in Austin. But UT fans, never noted for their patience, will be expecting more very, very soon in Austin.

And what of the Sooners? The OU decline hasn't been nearly as dramatic as that of their Orange and White brethren in Austin. But fans of the Crimson and Cream surely don't like looking up at teams like TCU and Baylor. Coach Bob Stoops' Sooners shared a conference title in 2012 with Kansas State. That's their only trophy for football in the Big 12 in the last four years. Like Texas, they've had some trouble locating the proper triggerman for their offense, and by 2014 had sunk into an unacceptable-in-Sooner-land tie for fourth in the conference with none other than Texas, causing historians to search for the last time neither UT nor OU had been in the top three in the region. It was a very long search.

Elsewhere in the state, after flourishing under Heisman Trophy winner Johnny Manziel's two years at the school, Texas A&M fell back to 8–5 in the rugged SEC. A defense that allowed 34 points or more six times in '14 proved to be the culprit. That D had also been a problem to some extent while Manziel was guiding the Aggies, but during those seasons, the offense was generally producing so many points that it covered for most of the shortcomings on the other side of the ball. The Aggies settled nicely into the ridiculously good SEC West, where powerhouses like Alabama, LSU, and Auburn hang out along with vastly improved programs at Ole Miss, Mississippi State, and Arkansas. That incredible strength of schedule and the respect the SEC gets nationally make the Aggies mark of 17–9 the last two years look more than acceptable for Coach Kevin Sumlin's troops.

Texas Tech seemed to have found a local-boy-makes-good story when the Red Raiders leaped out to a 7–0 start in 2013 under new coach and former Tech QB Kliff Kingsbury. But the joy soon melted away as the Raiders lost five of their last six that season and followed that up with a 4–8 mark in 2014, meaning that they'd gone 5–13 since that auspicious Kingsbury beginning. As with other programs around the state, stopping the other team has proven problematic for the club from Lubbock. Of those last 13 losses, eight came by margins of between 18 and 55 points.

Texas teams from lesser conferences had mixed results. After a handful of encouraging years under Coach June Jones (four consecutive bowls from 2009 through 2012 after not having been to a bowl since the Ronald Reagan presidency), the SMU Mustangs completely cratered in 2014. Jones quit. Interim coach Tom Mason replaced him. But the losing continued. At year's end, the bottom line read 1–11 and the Ponies will start all over in 2015 under respected new headman Chad Morris, who'd posted a terrific career in Texas high school coaching and then rose to become the highest-paid college offensive coordinator at Clemson.

Rice continued to out-perform predictions going 48–53 under David Baliff, who's been the head Owl since 2007. In that time, the feisty birds have won three of the four bowls they've been invited to — an admirable record at a place where academics are so emphasized.

Meanwhile, out in the West Texas town of El Paso (to quote an old Marty Robbins country and western hit song) the Miners of UTEP have taken a bit of a step back from the years of Mike Price, who won 47 percent of his games as the Miners head coach from 2004–2012. Price's replacement, Sean Kugler, has gone 9–15 through two seasons, though there was optimism that the arrow would point upward in 2015.

Finally, North Texas appears to have found a coach they're comfortable with. Former Iowa State mentor Dan McCarney took over the program in 2011 and by 2013, he'd guided the Mean Green to their first bowl in nine years — a 36–14 pounding of the University of Nevada-Las Vegas in the Heart of Dallas bowl, which capped off a nine-win season. Unfortunately, the Mean Green fell back to 4–8 in 2014, but the fans in Denton felt their team would be poised for a bounce back campaign in 2015.

# Major League Baseball

As baseball moved into 2013, Texas' two major league teams, the Texas Rangers and Houston Astros, had taken up places at the opposite ends of the sport's spectrum.

Texas, which had never in its 40-year history experienced anything that could be termed a "streak of success," had exploded into baseball's upper echelon, reaching the World Series in both 2010 and in 2011. Those Ranger teams GM Jon Daniels had assembled for manager Ron Washington came oh-so-close but never could close the deal in either playoff, losing the championships to first San Francisco and then a year later to St. Louis. But they still bounced right back to make it to the postseason again in 2013 and '14 before falling short again as a wild card team.

The Rangers future, however, still appeared bright. They'd won at least 90 games in all four of those contending years, something the franchise had never come close to achieving before. Their roster core certainly wasn't old. They'd covered for the loss to free agency of star outfielder Josh Hamilton to the Angels prior to the '13 season, and their farm system annually ranked amongst baseball's best.

Then the roof fell in! Everything that could go wrong *did* go wrong in 2014. Texas suffered so many injuries, they broke the all-time major league records for both pitchers used and total players used during a single season. Despite the injuries, they managed to stay afloat for a while, posting a 35–35 record through 70 games. But what followed qualified as one of the ugliest stretches of ball the franchise had ever seen. With injuries tearing open holes everywhere, the Rangers proceeded to go 18–52 over the next 70. Then things got even worse. On Sept. 5, 2013, manager Ron Washington,

*Houston Astros' shortstop Carlos Correa is mobbed by teammates after hitting a walk-off single in the 13th inning versus the Tampa Bay Rays on Aug. 19, 2015. Photo by Pat Sullivan/AP.*

the winningest manager in team history, abruptly resigned. Reports from several media outlets (which surfaced after his resignation) suggested he'd been having an extramarital affair with one of the female reporters who'd covered the club. Without any notice, Washington revealed his indiscretions at a hastily called press conference that day and, with little other explanation, announced he was quitting to concentrate on reconciling with his wife, Gerry. Just like that, he was gone! In just one year, Texas tumbled from what had been a lofty perch into the dregs of baseball.

When that bottom did fall out of the Rangers, they crashed into a neighborhood the Astros had been living in for some time. Since late in the 2009 season through 2014, Dave Clark, Brad Mills, Tony DeFrancesco, Bo Porter, and Tom Lawless had all taken shots at managing what had become a confirmed loser. Of that group, interim '14 manager Lawless was the only one to win as much as 40 percent of the games he managed (11–13 for 45.8 percent). The "Dis-Astros" lost 107 games in 2012, and then managed to get even worse in

'13, stumbling to a 111-loss season. The year Texas collapsed, Houston actually had started to plant some seeds of hope. With the franchise under the guidance of new President Reid Ryan and GM Jeff Luhnow, Houston improved modestly to a still-poor 70–92 mark which, sadly for major league fans in the state, made them the state's *best* team, with the Rangers tumbling to 67–95 that same season.

Little did we know that Houston's improvement in 2014 signaled the start of something big. During their cellar-dwelling years, the Astros had begun collecting an impressive set of young players through the draft. José Altuve, Carlos Correa, George Springer, Dallas Keuchel, and others suddenly provided long-suffering 'Stros fans hope for better days somewhere down the road. Still more talent came in trades as the club was totally torn down, started over, and begun to rise. The 2015 season opened with many observers suggesting these same recently down-trodden Astros had the look of a "team of the future." Those evaluations proved incorrect. All at once Houston, under new manager A. J. Hinch, became a

*Prince Fielder congratulates Delino DeShields after driving in Bobby Wilson and scoring during the Aug. 27, 2015, game against the Toronto Blue Jays. Photo by Kelly Gavin/Texas Rangers.*

"team of the present!" The Astros surged from the gate, established a strong hold atop the AL West, then slumped a bit before surging again to lead the division into the home stretch.

To the north and west of Houston, the Rangers had also circled the wagons. Again, injuries had shredded the team with their three best starting pitchers — Yu Darvish, Derek Holland, and Martin Perez — all failing to make any significant contribution.

But the Rangers seemed to buy into new manager Jeff Banister's slogan of "NeverEver-Quit." Texas weathered a slow start, rallied to push back past the .500 mark, and retained playoff hopes as the last third of the season arrived. Even banished former Ranger star Josh Hamilton returned. Having performed dreadfully in the two-plus years he was a Los Angeles Angel, Texas swung a deal to get the often-troubled but sometimes terrific Hamilton back to the place he'd experienced the most success of his career.

With the happenings of the 2015 season, and with each franchise still possessing very highly regarded farm systems, there was hope that perhaps, for the first time ever in the history of major league baseball in this state, Texas might be approaching a period in which *both* of the state's teams might be considered significant contenders.

## NBA Basketball

While change had been the theme of the other major sports in the state in recent years, in the NBA, one could argue for the wisdom of the adage "the more things change, the more they stay the same."

The San Antonio Spurs remained one of the constants of the league. In fact, they remained one of the constants in all of sports. When the "we all thought them too old" Spurs failed to take down Miami in the NBA finals of 2013, most felt that near miss signaled the swan song for this proud group of champions. Under mega-successful coach Greg Popovich, SA had taken home titles in 1999, 2003, 2005, and 2007. But as the 2000-teens arrived and the Spurs couldn't handle LeBron James and the Heat, the consensus of the NBA's best minds was that "father time" had finally caught up with the stars of the team — Tim Duncan, Manu Ginobili, and Tony Parker. But again, San Antonio surprised the league. The Spurs rebounded from that painful loss to Miami to capture their fifth NBA title in a 15-year period in 2014, led not by one of those brilliant veterans but by young, emerging star Kawhi Leonard.

Those five titles in 15 seasons made them the most dominant champion in any of America's four major sports. No other basketball, football, baseball, or hockey team could boast of such a run of rings in that decade and a half. And the Spurs still may not be finished. Just when the roundball world seemed certain (again) that age would catch up with the Spurs, the team from the river city went out in the summer of 2015 and landed one of the league's very best free agents, signing 30-year-old Texas native LaMarcus Aldridge, who averaged 19 points and 8½ rebounds a game during a stellar nine-year career in Portland.

With that revered threesome of Duncan, Ginobili, and Parker still around and aging ever so gracefully and with Aldridge joining Leonard to form perhaps the best forward pairing in the league, the Spurs again figured as one of the teams to beat in the NBA in a city where winning never seems to grow old.

While the Spurs continued their amazing run, the state's other two teams still proved plenty good enough to make the trip into the "Texas Triangle," one of the most daunting road trips in any sport.

The Houston Rockets have slowly but steadily gotten better and better in recent seasons. The addition of all-star guard James Harden and then star center Dwight "Superman" Howard have turned the Kevin McHale–coached Rockets into a formidable team whose 56 regular season victories in the 2014–15 year tied them for the third-best record in the league. Houston then reached the NBA West finals before bowing out to Golden State, which went on to capture its first NBA title in 40 years.

The third stop in that Texas Triangle, the Dallas Mavericks, remained competitive but not on the same level as the Spurs and Rockets. Dallas opted to significantly change its roster after upsetting the Miami Heat for their first ever title in 2010–11. But omnipresent owner Mark Cuban's Mavs haven't in the succeeding years assembled the

*Dwight Howard is a key to the rapidly improving Houston Rockets. NBA/Getty photo.*

*Forward Kawhi Leonard, left, won a championship with the Spurs in 2014 and was named the NBA Finals MVP. Photo courtesy of the San Antonio Spurs.*

right pieces around now-aging superstar and future Hall of Famer Dirk Nowitzki. The Rick Carlisle–coached Mavericks continued to post solid regular seasons. But in the rugged NBA West, teams like the Mavs, who put up around 50 wins per year, get rewarded only with low seeds in the playoffs and tough match-ups that lead to early postseason exits.

## PGA Golf

Of all the sports that have underdone significant shake-ups over the last couple of years, none has witnessed a more significant flip flop than the American pro golf scene — and Texas is right in the middle of it.

As the 2015 PGA tour swung into its final tournaments, the No. 1 American player for the year hadn't ever won a pro tournament as late as mid-2013. And the No. 1 player in the world in mid-2013 had fallen well out of the top 200 in just two years. The remarkable ascent of Dallasite Jordan Spieth and the rapid descent of Tiger Woods created golf headlines virtually every week.

Spieth turned pro after a year and a half playing for the University of Texas golf team. Everyone knew he'd be a very good pro some day — but this good? He broke through by winning a playoff in the John Deere Classic in July 2013. And he just kept going. In virtually a *half a year* of golf that season, he wound up No. 20 in the world for the year! In '14, he took the Valspar Championship in a three-way playoff. Then, he won the Australian Open and the next week the Hero World Challenge in Florida. At barely 21 years old, he made the U.S. Ryder Cup team and was one of its best players for our country while facing the best from Europe in golf's most highly pressured international competition.

But the best, the very best, was yet to come. Spieth ran away from the 2015 Masters field, capturing his first major title and in the process tying Tiger Woods for the all-time lowest 72-hole score in the history of golf's most prestigious tournament. Weeks later, he hoisted yet another major trophy, winning the U.S. Open. Next, he barely missed making it three majors in a row (previously done only by Texan Ben Hogan) when he finished just short in the British Open.

As Spieth ascended, Tiger collapsed! The man who'd ruled the world rankings for nearly a decade and a half looked like he'd put injuries, surgeries, scandal, and a highly publicized divorce totally behind him when he won five tournaments in 2013. Albeit, none of them was a highly coveted major title, but Tiger was back. Or so we thought.

He hadn't won again since. He hardly even was a contender in majors these days. Scores in the 80s began popping up in his rounds. One day he'd spray drives all over the course. The next day, his short game would desert him. Then the putting touch failed. And with each failure, he slipped further and further down the rankings, at one point falling to an unthinkable No. 266 in the world. That same week, Spieth's meteoric rise carried him up to No. 2!

At 22, Speith looked poised to be a central figure on the tour for years and years and years — like Tiger used to be. And, approaching 40, Tiger's surrounded by nothing but questions.

## The Future

In general, the future of major sports in Texas looks good or even very good. Both NFL teams, both baseball franchises, and all three NBA squads seem poised for good days head. The Big 12 boasts two of the nation's top-four rated football schools entering the 2015 schedule. Finally, there seemed almost no end to the gigantic golf promise of Jordan Spieth. But will such projections turn into reality?

Perhaps it's best to go back to that iconic song written by Bob Dylan and slightly alter its title as we look forward because history teaches us that "These Times They Will Keep A-Changin'."

*In August 2015, Norm Hitzges celebrated his 40th continuous year of doing sports talk in Dallas — the longest current streak of any major market sports talk show in the country. He also spent 15 years as a color commentator for major league baseball with the Texas Rangers and*  *ESPN, did TV analysis of Dallas Mavericks NBA games for six years, and has authored four books. He and his wife, Mary, live in north Dallas and his talk show on Sports Radio 1310 AM and 96.7 FM "The Ticket" can be heard every weekday from 10 a.m. to noon.* ☆

*Assault with Warren Mehrtens up enters the Kentucky Derby winner's circle on May 4, 1946. Photo courtesy of Keeneland-Morgan.*

# Assault: King of the Turf

## Despite a Near-Fatal Injury, King Ranch Colt Raced to the 1946 Triple Crown

### By Elizabeth Cruce Alvarez

It is fitting that the most coveted prize of the "Sport of Kings" — the Triple Crown of Thoroughbred Racing — was won 70 years ago by a King Ranch horse. Assault, the feisty chestnut colt who was the seventh Triple Crown Champion, is the only horse from Texas to claim this crown.

But Assault's victory in 1946 is not just remarkable because he was born and bred in the *brasada*, the brush country of South Texas, instead of the lush bluegrass of Kentucky.

Rather, Assault's championship is remarkable because he was technically lame. As a foal, he had injured his right forefoot so severely that he was nearly put down, never to run on the turf or stand in the winner's circle.

Since 1919, there have been 12 Triple Crown winners, and all of these horses are extraordinary in some way or another. But Assault's story is unique.

He was born on March 26, 1943, on Robert J. Kleberg Jr.'s King Ranch, and his pedigree is impressive. His sire, Bold Venture, won two Triple Crown races in 1936, the Kentucky Derby and the Preakness Stakes, but bowed a tendon before the Belmont Stakes and did not start. He was subsequently retired and purchased by Kleberg in 1939 for the ranch's breeding program. Bold Venture is the only Kentucky Derby Champion to sire two Derby winners: Assault (1946) and Middleground (1950), both out of King Ranch mares. Interestingly, Middleground is listed among Triple Crown near misses: He

*Assault won the Kentucky Derby on May 4, 1946, by eight lengths, a Derby record he shares with Whirlaway and that still stands today. Photo courtesy of Keeneland-Morgan.*

finished second in the Preakness but went on to win the Belmont. His main rival in each race was Prince Hill, who was ridden by two-time Triple Crown jockey Eddie Arcaro (1941, 1948) and was owned by C.T. Chenery, whose Meadow Stable later bred the 1973 Triple Crown winner, Secretariat.

Assault's dam, Igual, although sickly and unraced, was by Equipoise, a two-time horse of the year who won 29 races during his career from 1930–1935. Igual's dam, Incandescent, was out of Masda, a full sister of Man o' War, one of the greatest racehorses of all time.

Assault's injury came when he was not even a year old. The frisky colt was running in the rugged King Ranch pastures and stepped on a surveyor's stake that was inadvertently left behind. The stake punctured the front wall of his right-front hoof. Kleberg, seeing the extreme pain the colt was suffering, felt that he should be destroyed. But Dr. J. K. Northway, the ranch's veterinarian, doctored on it constantly with the help of some of the ranch hands' children.

Once Assault recovered enough to get back to ranch life, he limped and often stumbled, but eventually regained his confidence. The hoof, however, was deformed and the wall was too

thin for a shoe nail. Ranch blacksmith John Dern devised a shoe with a metal tip that turned up, clung to the hoof's front, holding it in place.

Assault loved to run and earned his right to train for the big races by winning trials on the ranch. Always considered a feisty, clever horse with a big personality, Assault could sense if his rider was not paying attention. At such times, he knew if he made a sudden turn, he could leave his rider in the dirt while he ran off at full gallop.

When trainer and Fredericksburg, Texas, native Max Hirsch was hired by King Ranch in 1944, he was surprised that Kleberg wanted to include Assault among the yearlings shipped out East to train. Years later, Hirsch would say, "I've never trained a better horse."

When Assault began racing on eastern tracks, spectators and journalists, too, where stunned to see a racehorse with such an odd, stumbling gait. Some racing fans said it looked as if Assault would fall over. But when he reached a full gallop, all signs of awkwardness were gone, and he was fast. At that time, people began calling him "The Club-Footed Comet." Hirsch reckoned that Assault had gotten into the habit of limping to protect his foot and continued even after the hoof had healed.

# Assault's Pedigree

| | | | |
|---|---|---|---|
| **BOLD VENTURE** chestnut 1933 | **ST. GERMANS** bay 1921 | **SWYNFORD** brown, 1907 | JOHN O'GAUNT bay, 1901 |
| | | | CANTERBURY PILGRIM chestnut, 1893 |
| | | **HAMOAZE** bay, 1911 | TORPOINT bay, 1900 |
| | | | MAID OF THE MIST bay, 1906 |
| | **POSSIBLE** chestnut 1920 | **ULTIMUS** chestnut, 1906 | COMMANDO black/brown, 1898 |
| | | | RUNNING STREAM chestnut, 1898 |
| | | **LIDA FLUSH** chestnut, 1910 | ROYAL FLUSH III chestnut, 1893 |
| | | | LIDA H chestnut, 1888 |
| **IGUAL** chestnut 1937 | **EQUIPOISE** chestnut 1928 | **PENNANT** chestnut, 1911 | PETER PAN bay, 1904 |
| | | | ROYAL ROSE bay, 1894 |
| | | **SWINGING** chestnut, 1922 | BROOMSTICK bay, 1901 |
| | | | BALANCOIRE II bay, 1911 |
| | **INCANDESCENT** bay 1931 | **CHICLE** bay, 1913 | SPEARMINT bay, 1903 |
| | | | LADY HAMBURG II brown, 1908 |
| | | **MASDA** chestnut, 1915 | FAIR PLAY chestnut 1905 |
| | | | MAHUBAH bay, 1910 |

*The Derby Winner's Circle with trainer Max Hirsch, far left. Keeneland-Morgan photo.*

*Assault beat Lord Boswell in the Preakness by a neck. Keeneland-Morgan photo.*

Assault's two-year-old season was marked by a few racing victories, but when he turned three, he blossomed.

## The 1946 Season

When Assault began his championship season, he was ridden by a 25-year-old Brooklyn-born jockey named Warren Mehrtens. They won the Experimental Free Handicap at Jamaica by four lengths and then the Wood Memorial. But they lost the Derby Trial at Churchill Downs on a muddy track.

On May 4, the 72nd running of the Kentucky Derby in front of a record 100,000 spectators, the favorites were Lord Boswell, ridden by Eddie Arcaro, and Spy Song, with Johnny Longden as jockey. For most of the race, Assault trailed both competitors. But when they entered the stretch, Assault and Mehrtens found an opening on the inside rail, took the lead, and pulled away. Assault won the Kentucky Derby by 8 lengths, which is a record he shares with three other horses, one of which was a fellow Triple Crown champion (Whirlaway, 1941).

On May 11 at the Preakness, Assault fell to the back of the pack but broke out and gained the lead. The surge for the lead cost Assault, and he began to tire as Lord Boswell closed in. It was down to the wire, but Assault hung on and won by a neck.

The Belmont Stakes, the final leg of the Triple Crown quest, was run June 1 with a field of seven horses. Assault stumbled out of the gate, and Mehrtens was nearly thrown. Although they recovered, Assault stayed to the rear. When he entered the homestretch of the mile-and-a-half track, Assault had moved up to third. Then in a burst of speed, he passed the leader, Natchez, and won by three lengths.

Assault was voted "Horse of the Year" in 1946 and continued to win races throughout 1946 and 1947. His last major career win was the 1949 Brooklyn Handicap at Aqueduct. He was ridden by Dave Gorman, and Mehrtens rode another horse. He continued to race until age 7, retiring twice for breeding. Assault never sired a thoroughbred offspring, although it is recorded with the American Quarter Horse Association

## TRIPLE CROWN WINNERS

| DATE | HORSE | JOCKEY | TRAINER | OWNER |
|---|---|---|---|---|
| 1919 | Sir Barton | John Loftus | H. G. Bedwell | J. K. L. Ross |
| 1930 | Gallant Fox | Earl Sande | James Fitzsimmons | Belair Stud |
| 1935 | Omaha | William Saunders | James Fitzsimmons | Belair Stud |
| 1937 | War Admiral | Charley Kurtsinger | George Conway | Samuel D. Riddle |
| 1941 | Whirlaway | Eddie Arcaro | Ben A. Jones | Calumet Farm |
| 1943 | Count Fleet | John Longden | Don Cameron | Mrs. J. D. Hertz |
| 1946 | Assault | Warren Mehrtens | Max Hirsch | King Ranch |
| 1948 | Citation | Eddie Arcaro | Ben A. Jones | Calumet Farm |
| 1973 | Secretariat | Ron Turcotte | Lucien Laurin | Meadow Stable |
| 1977 | Seattle Slew | Jean Cruguet | William Turner, Jr. | Karen L. Taylor |
| 1978 | Affirmed | Steve Cauthen | Lazaro S. Barrera | Harbor View Farm |
| 2015 | American Pharoah | Victor Espinoza | Bob Baffert | Zayat Stables |

that he sired two quarter horse fillies.

Assault was finally retired for good in 1950, and lived a life of ease on King Ranch. He injured a leg in a paddock accident and was euthanized on Sept. 1, 1971, at age 28. He is buried at the ranch. With the perpetual interest in the Triple Crown, Assault will live on as "The Club-Footed Comet" who surprised horse-racing fans with his limp, his small size, his big heart, and his extraordinary speed and will to win.

*Elizabeth Cruce Alvarez is the editor of the Texas Almanac.*

### SOURCES

Boyd, Eva Jolene. *Assault*. Lexington, KY: Eclipse Press, 2004.

Drager, Marvin. *The Most Glorious Crown*. Chicago: Triumph Books, 1975.

Drape, Joe. *To the Swift: Classic Triple Crown Horses and Their Race for Glory*. New York: St. Martin's Press, 2008.

Handbook of Texas Online. Texas State Historical Association: https://tshaonline.org/handbook/online/articles/tca04.

Shoop, Robert. *Down to the Wire: The Lives of the Triple Crown Champions*. Everson, WA: Russell Dean and Company, 2004. ☆

---

## ASSAULT FAST FACTS

**NAME:** Assault was named by Robert Kleberg's wife, Helen; a name that possibly reflected the nation's mood of war and patriotism in the mid-1940s. In those days, there also was a penchant for one-word names.

**NICKNAMES:** "The Club-Footed Comet," "The Horse with Three Legs and a Heart," "Texas Flier," and "Texas Terror."

**RACE EARNINGS:** $675,470.

**RACE RECORD:** 42 starts, 18 wins, 6 seconds, 7 thirds.

**RANKING:** No. 33 out of the top 100 U.S. racehorses of the 20th century, as ranked by *Blood-Horse* magazine.

**SILKS:** King Ranch racing silks are brown and white with the Running W.

**SIZE:** 15.1–15.2 hands and around 1,000 pounds or less.

---

*Hall of Fame jockey Eddie Arcaro began racing Assault in November 1946. They are shown, below, after winning the Butler Handicap on July 12, 1947, at the now-defunct Jamaica Race Course in Queens, New York. Photo courtesy of Keeneland-Morgan.*

*"Assault was fun to ride. He moved up on you quick, then exploded."*
*— Eddie Arcaro*

# STATE: High School Championships

**UIL**: The University Interscholastic League, which governs literary and athletic competition among public schools in Texas, was organized in 1910 as a division of the University of Texas extension service. Initially, it sponsored forensic competition. By 1920, the UIL organized the structure of the high school football game in response to the growing popularity of the sport in Texas.

**TAPPS**: The Texas Association of Private and Parochial Schools is the largest group of private schools in the state with more than 225 member institutions.

The interscholastic competition began in 1978 and was significantly expanded when the Texas Christian Interscholastic League ceased to exist in 2000 and many of those schools moved into TAPPS.

Listed are state champions and the game scores.
*Sources: The University Interscholastic League at www.uil.utexas.edu; the Texas Association of Private and Parochial Schools.*

## 2014 1A Division II

*The Throckmorton Greyhounds take the field at AT&T Stadium in Arlington. They went on to defeat Groom 66–20.*

*Photo by Jeffrey Bishop, 1stphototexas.*

## Football

| Year | Division | Champion | Runner Up |
|------|----------|----------|-----------|
| UIL 2014 | 1A Division I | Crowell 62 | May 14 |
| | 1A Division II | Throckmorton 66 | Groom 20 |
| | 2A Division I | Canadian 34 | Mason 7 |
| | 2A Division II | Bremond 28 | Albany 21 |
| | 3A Division I | Cameron Yoe 70 | Mineola 40 |
| | 3A Division II | Waskom 41 | Newton 22 |
| | 4A Division I | Navasota 42 | Argyle 35 |
| | 4A Division II | Gilmer 35 | West Orange-Stark 25 |
| | 5A Division I | Aledo 49 | Temple 45 |
| | 5A Division II | Ennis 38 | Cedar Park 35 |
| | 6A Division I | Allen 47 | Cypress Ranch 16 |
| | 6A Division II | Cedar Hill 23 | Katy 20 |
| TAPPS 2014 | 6-Man Div. I | Boerne Geneva 59 | Watauga Harvest Christian 14 |
| | 6-Man Div. II | SA Castle Hills Baptist 80 | Waco Live Oak Classical 46 |
| | 6-Man Dev. III | Fredericksburg Heritage 46 | Longview Trinity 16 |
| | Division III | Cedar Hill Trinity Christian 54 | League City Bay Aria Christian 18 |
| | Division II | Dallas Parish Episcopal 56 | Dallas Christian 14 |
| | Division I | Dallas Bishop Dunne 41 | Plano Prestonwood Christian 10 |

# Football

| Year | Division | Champion | Runner Up |
|---|---|---|---|
| UIL 2013 | 6-Man Div. I | Crowell 78 | May 52 |
| | 6-Man Div. II | Grandfalls-Royalty 73 | Milford 28 |
| | 1A Division I | Stamford 41 | Shiner 28 |
| | 1A Division II | Wellington 42 | Falls City 20 |
| | 2A Division I | Cameron Yoe 35 | Wall 14 |
| | 2A Division II | Cisco 56 | Refugio 36 |
| | 3A Division I | Carthage 34 | Kilgore 23 |
| | 3A Division II | Argyle 38 | Fairfield 33 |
| | 4A Division I | Denton Guyer 31 | San Antonio Brennan 14 |
| | 4A Division II | Aledo 38 | Brenham 10 |
| | 5A Division I | Allen 63 | Pearland 28 |
| | 5A Division II | Cedar Hill 34 | Katy 24 |
| TAPPS 2013 | 6-Man Div. I | Dallas Covenant 60 | Boerne Geneva 12 |
| | 6-Man Div. II | SA Castle Hills Baptist 65 | Fredericksburg Heritage 44 |
| | Division III | Dallas First Baptist 35 | Bryan Brazos Christian 21 |
| | Division II | Midland Christian 28 | Katy Pope John XXIII 20 |
| | Division I | Fort Worth Nolan 24 | Plano Prestonwood Christian 21 |

# Baseball

| Year | Division | Champion | Runner Up |
|---|---|---|---|
| UIL 2015 | 2A | Flatonia 4 | Crawford 3 |
| | 3A | West 4 | Bishop 3 |
| | 4A | Argyle 7 | West Orange-Stark 3 |
| | 5A | Prosper 8 | Georgetown 2 |
| | 6A | Cypress Ranch (Houston) 3 | Arlington Martin 2 |
| TAPPS 2015 | 1A and 2A | Pasadena First Baptist 8 | Muenster Sacred Heart 7 |
| | 3A | Lubbock Christian 4 | Sugar Land Logos 1 |
| | 4A | Houston Lutheran South 8 | Austin Hyde Park 5 |
| | 5A | Tomball Concordia 7 | Beaumont Kelly 6 |
| UIL 2014 | 1A | Douglass 10 | Flatonia 0 |
| | 2A | Sunnyvale 13 | Troy 3 |
| | 3A | College Station 5 | Argyle 2 |
| | 4A | Aledo 4 | Victoria East 0 |
| | 5A | Flower Mound 10 | San Antonio Reagan 0 |
| TAPPS 2014 | 1A and 2A | Brazosport Christian 8 | DeSoto Canterbury 2 |
| | 3A | Houston Cypress Christian 3 | Lubbock Christian 1 |
| | 4A | Houston Second Baptist 12 | Forth Worth Christian 1 |
| | 5A | Houston St. Thomas 2 | Tomball Concordia 1 |
| UIL 2013 | 1A | Price Carlisle 6 | Stamford 1 |
| | 2A | Hallettsville 4 | Hughes Springs 2 |
| | 3A | La Grange 10 | Pleasant Grove (Texarkana) 2 |
| | 4A | Tomball 6 | Corpus Christi Moody 1 |
| | 5A | Conroe The Woodlands 9 | Fort Bend Dulles 5 |
| TAPPS 2013 | 1A and 2A | Shiner St. Paul 9 | Tyler East Texas 2 |
| | 3A | Bullard Brook Hill 7 | Bryan Brazos Christian 5 |
| | 4A | Sugar Land Fort Bend 12 | Midland Christian 11 |
| | 5A | Argyle Liberty Christian 6 | Houston St. Pius 1 |

# Girls Basketball

| Year | Division | Champion | Runner Up |
|------|----------|----------|-----------|
| UIL 2015 | 1A | Nazareth 56 | Lipan 40 |
| | 2A | Martins Mill 49 | Gruver 36 |
| | 3A | Sunnyvale 52 | Shallowater 37 |
| | 4A | Argyle 46 | Wylie (Abilene) 25 |
| | 5A | Canyon 48 | Dallas Adams 41 |
| | 6A | Cypress Woods (Houston) 57 | Dallas Skyline 49 |
| TAPPS 2015 | 1A | Granbury North Central Texas 57 | Brownsville First Baptist 34 |
| | 2A | Sherman Texoma Christian 59 | Tomball Rosehill 34 |
| | 3A | Lubbock Christian 56 | Houston Lutheran North 44 |
| | 4A | Lubbock Trinity 87 | Houston Westbury Christian 55 |
| | 5A | Argyle Liberty Christian 45 | Plano Prestonwood 38 |
| UIL 2014 | 1A Division I | Plains 57 | Kerens 44 |
| | 1A Division II | Nazareth 82 | Calvert 41 |
| | 2A | Wall 48 | Brock 44 |
| | 3A | Waco La Vega 47 | Argyle 42 |
| | 4A | Canyon 49 | McKinney North 42 |
| | 5A | Manvel 58 | Duncanville 53 |
| TAPPS 2014 | 1A | Granbury Happy Hill 61 | Fredericksburg Heritage 43 |
| | 2A | Marble Falls Faith 47 | New Braunfels Christian 45 |
| | 3A | Midland Classical 54 | Austin Brentwood 41 |
| | 4A | Lubbock Trinity 47 | Houston Second Baptist 40 |
| | 5A | Plano Prestonwood 53 | Tomball Concordia 43 |
| UIL 2013 | 1A Division I | Martins Mill 49 | Smyer 46 |
| | 1A Division II | Whitharral 45 | Saltillo 36 |
| | 2A | Brock 40 | Merkel 32 |
| | 3A | Mexia 69 | Kennedale 62 |
| | 4A | Georgetown 65 | Dallas Lincoln 60 |
| | 5A | Duncanville 59 | Cibolo Steele 36 |
| TAPPS 2013 | 1A | Granbury Happy Hill 35 | Selma River City Believers 28 |
| | 2A | Sherman Texoma Chrisitan 45 | Boerne Geneva 39 |
| | 3A | Lubbock Chrisitan 56 | Austin Brentwood 38 |
| | 4A | Lubbock Trinity 75 | Sugar Land Fort Bend Christian 34 |
| | 5A | Plano John Paul II 46 | Argyle Liberty Chrisitian 39 |

# Boys Basketball

| Year | Division | Champion | Runner Up |
|------|----------|----------|-----------|
| UIL 2015 | 1A | Texline 76 | Lenorah Grady 55 |
| | 2A | Canadian 68 | Dallardsville Big Sandy 60 |
| | 3A | Brock 37 | Universal City Randolph 32 |
| | 4A | Bridgeport 83 | Houston Sterling 57 |
| | 5A | Lancaster 59 | Beaumont Ozen 47 |
| | 6A | Plano West 56 | Clear Lake (Houston) 54 |
| TAPPS 2015 | 1A | Granbury North Central Texas 67 | Kingwood Northeast 65 |
| | 2A | Dallas Cambridge 52 | San Antonio Christian Academy 37 |
| | 3A | Cedar Hill Trinity Christian 74 | Houston St. Thomas Episcopal 48 |
| | 4A | Houston Westbury Christian 73 | Tyler All Saints 52 |
| | 5A | Plano Prestonwood 49 | Addison Trinity Christian 32 |

## Boys Basketball

| Year | Division | Champion | Runner Up |
|------|----------|----------|-----------|
| UIL 2014 | 1A Division I | Mumford 64 | Muenster 57 |
| | 1A Division II | Water Valley 68 | Laneville 44 |
| | 2A | Ponder 66 | Tatum 56 |
| | 3A | Houston Yates 1 (by forfeit) | Dallas Madison 0 |
| | 4A | Dallas Kimball 52 | Amarillo 37 |
| | 5A | Houston North Shore 57 | Converse Judson 45 |
| TAPPS 2014 | 1A | Granbury Happy Hill 56 | SA Castle Hills First Baptist 48 |
| | 2A | Abilene Christian 63 | Boerne Geneva 47 |
| | 3A | Houston St. Thomas Episcopal 70 | Lubbock Christian 59 |
| | 4A | Houston Westbury Christian 70 | Cedar Hill Trinity Christian 54 |
| | 5A | Plano Prestonwood 46 | Plano John Paul II 45 |
| UIL 2013 | 1A Division I | Dallas Triple A Academy 80 | Mumford 54 |
| | 1A Division II | Roxton 60 | Douglass 54 |
| | 2A | White Oak 56 | Brock 54 |
| | 3A | Dallas Madison 85 | Houston Yates 72 |
| | 4A | Rosenberg Terry 55 | Dallas Kimball 47 |
| | 5A | Fort Bend Travis 46 | South Grand Prairie 38 |
| TAPPS 2013 | 1A | Plainview Christian 65 | Orange Community Christian 44 |
| | 2A | Boerne Geneva 59 | Waco Vanguard Prep 49 |
| | 3A | Lubbock Christian 53 | The Woodlands Christian 52 |
| | 4A | Houston Westbury Christian 58 | Dallas Christian 48 |
| | 5A | Plano Prestonwood Christian 71 | Fort Worth Nolan Catholic 66 |

*Houston North Shore celebrates its championship victory in 2014 over Converse Judson. Photo by Jeffrey Bishop/1stphototexas.*

# Volleyball

| Year | Division | Champion | Runner Up |
|---|---|---|---|
| UIL 2014 | 1A | Schulenburg 3 | Lindsay 1 |
| | 2A | Poth 3 | Brock 0 |
| | 3A | Decatur 3 | Argyle 0 |
| | 4A | Lucas Lovejoy 3 | Dripping Springs 0 |
| | 5A | Conroe The Woodlands 3 | League City Clear Falls 1 |
| TAPPS 2014 | 1A | Waxahachie Prep 3 | San Antonio Gateway 0 |
| | 2A | Bryan Brazos Christian 3 | Waco Live Oak Classical 0 |
| | 3A | Arlington Grace Prep 3 | Austin Brentwood 1 |
| | 4A | Lubbock Trinity Christian 3 | Sugar Land Fort Bend Baptist 1 |
| | 5A | Dallas Bishop Lynch 3 | Dallas Ursuline 1 |
| UIL 2013 | 1A | Round Top – Carmine 3 | Windthorst 0 |
| | 2A | Bushland 3 | Schulenburg 2 |
| | 3A | Decatur 3 | Bellville 0 |
| | 4A | Amarillo 3 | Prosper 1 |
| | 5A | Conroe The Woodlands 3 | San Antonio Churchill 0 |
| TAPPS 2013 | 1A | Wichita Falls Christian 3 | Bellville Faith 2 |
| | 2A | Denton Calvary 3 | Boerne Geneva 2 |
| | 3A | Amarillo San Jacinto 3 | Austin Brentwood 2 |
| | 4A | Carrollton Prince of Peace 3 | Victoria St. Joseph 1 |
| | 5A | Dallas Bishop Lynch 3 | Dallas Ursuline 0 |

# Boys Soccer

| Year | Division | Champion | Runner Up |
|---|---|---|---|
| UIL 2015 | 4A | San Elizario 4 | Liberty Hill 2 |
| | 5A | Lufkin 3 | Gerogetown East View 1 |
| | 6A | Brownsville Rivera 2 | Katy Cinco Ranch 0 |
| TAPPS 2015 | Fall 2014 | Longview Christian Heritage 6 | Austin Brentwood 4 |
| | Division III | Pharr Oratory 2 | Austin Hill Country Christian 0 |
| | Division II | Houston Village School 3 | Bullard Brook Hill 2 |
| | Division I | El Paso Cathedral 3 | Houston Awty 1 |
| UIL 2014 | 4A | San Antonio Northwest Nelson 2 | Pharr Valley View 1 |
| | 5A | Fort Bend Clements 3 | Coppell 0 |
| TAPPS 2014 | Fall 2013 | Houston British School 8 | Sherman Texoma Christian 1 |
| | Division III | Colleyville Covenant Christian 2 | Houston Cypress 1 |
| | Division II | Grapvince Faith Christian 2 | Houston Awtry Internaltion 1 |
| | Division I | San Antonio Central Catholic 2 | Addison Trinity Christian 1 (SO) |
| UIL 2013 | 4A | Waco University 1 | El Paso Del Valle 0 |
| | 5A | Coppell 3 (OT) | Brownsville Hanna 2 |
| TAPPS 2013 | Fall 2012 | Longview Christian Heritage 2 | Kingsville Pan American 1 |
| | Division III | Colleyville Covenant 4 | Houston Cypress Christian 0 |
| | Division II | Grapevine Faith Christian 2 | Houston Awty International 1 |
| | Division I | Fort Worth Nolan 2 | Dallas Bishop Lynch 1 |

**For track, tennis, and other high school sports champions, see page 597 in the Education section.**

# Softball

| Year | Division | Champion | Runner Up |
|------|----------|----------|-----------|
| UIL 2015 | 2A | Shiner 3 | Harelton 0 |
| | 3A | East Bernard 8 | Hallettsville 1 |
| | 4A | Huffman Hargrave 6 | Needville 4 |
| | 5A | Aledo 3 | Cedar Park Vista Ridge 2 |
| | 6A | Katy 3 | Lewisville 2 |
| TAPPS 2015 | 1A and 2A | Brazosport Christian 13 | Richardson Canyon Creek 3 |
| | 3A | Schertz John Paul II 8 | Waco Vanguard 2 |
| | 4A | Houston Lutheran South 3 | Waco Reicher 0 |
| | 5A | San Antonio Incarnate Word 5 | San Antonio Antonian 4 |
| UIL 2014 | 1A | Weimar 4 | Harleton 3 |
| | 2A | Crawford 5 | East Bernard 3 |
| | 3A | La Grange 7 | Van 3 |
| | 4A | Aledo 10 | Ennis 3 |
| | 5A | Deer Park 8 | Conroe The Woodlands 2 |
| TAPPS 2014 | 1A and 2A | Waco Vanguard 6 (14 innings) | Hallettsville Sacred Heart 4 |
| | 3A | Lubbock Christian 10 | League City Bay Area Christian 0 |
| | 4A | Waco Reicher 9 | Sugar Land Fort Bend Baptist 1 |
| | 5A | Dallas Bishop Lynch 10 | San Antonio Antonian 4 |
| UIL 2013 | 1A | Weimar 2 | Ivanhoe Rayburn 0 |
| | 2A | Pilot Point 1 | Santa Gertrudis Academy 0 |
| | 3A | Lufkin Hudson 12 | Mineola 9 |
| | 4A | Buda Hays 11 | Lucas Lovejoy 8 |
| | 5A | Lewisville 3 | Humble Kingwood 2 |
| TAPPS 2013 | A and AA | Bellville Faith Academy 15 | Sherman Texoma Chrisitan 8 |
| | AAA | League City Bay Area 8 | Dallas First Baptist 2 |
| | AAAA | Sugar Land Fort Bend 4 | Fort Worth Chrisitan 0 |
| | AAAAA | San Antonio Incarnate Word 6 | Houston St. Agnes 3 |

# Girls Soccer

| Year | Division | Champion | Runner Up |
|------|----------|----------|-----------|
| UIL 2015 | 4A | Kennedale 4 | Princeton 3 |
| | 5A | Wylie East 1 | Austin Vandgrift 0 |
| | 6A | Coppell 3 | Highland Park (Dallas) 0 |
| TAPPS 2015 | Division III | Austin Veritas 7 | Dallas Covenant 1 |
| | Division II | San Antonio Christian 2 | Colleyville Covenant 0 |
| | Division I | Dallas Bishop Lynch 2 | Dallas Ursuline 1 |
| UIL 2014 | 4A | Austin Vandergrift 1 | Wylie East 0 |
| | 5A | Lewisville Hebron 1 | Plano West 0 (SO) |
| TAPPS 2014 | Division III | Bullard Brook Hill 1 | Austin Veritas 0 |
| | Division II | Dallas Parish Episcopal 5 | Houston Awty International 0 |
| | Division I | Dallas Ursuline 1 | Dallas Bishop Lynch 0 (SO) |
| UIL 2013 | 4A | Denton Guyer 2 | Highland Park (Dallas) 1 |
| | 5A | Plano West 4 | Southlake Carroll 1 |
| TAPPS 2013 | Division III | Bullard Brook Hill 3 | Colleyville Covenant 0 |
| | Division II | Dallas Parish Episcopal 5 | Houston Awty International 0 |
| | Division I | Dallas Ursuline 2 | Houston St. Agnes 0 |

# Texas College Sports — Division I

## Big 12 champions

In 1994, Texas, Texas A&M, Texas Tech, and Baylor accepted an invitation to join the Big Eight Conference to form the Big 12 Conference.

Texas A&M left the conference in 2012 to join the Southeastern Conference.

Also in 2012, TCU joined the Big 12, along with West Virginia University.

In 2014, the Texas schools in the **Big 12** were:
**University of Texas at Austin**
**Texas Tech University**
**Texas Christian University**
**Baylor University**
Other schools in the Big 12 are the University of Kansas, Kansas State University, the University of Oklahoma, Oklahoma State University, Iowa State University, and West Virginia University.

| 2014-2015 | Season | Tournament | National Playoffs |
|---|---|---|---|
| Football | Baylor, TCU | | TCU won Peach Bowl, Baylor lost Cotton |
| Men's Basketball | Kansas | Iowa State | Kansas lost regional to Wichita State 78-65 |
| Women's Basketball | Baylor | Baylor | lost in Elite 8 to Ntore Dame  77-68 |
| Baseball | TCU | Texas | TCU lost in semifinals to Vanderbilt |
| Softball | Oklahoma | – | lost super regional to Alabama |

| 2013-2014 | Season | Tournament | National Playoffs |
|---|---|---|---|
| Football | Baylor | | lost Fiesta Bowl to UCF 52-42 |
| Men's Basketball | Kansas | Iowa State | Iowa State lost in regional to UConn. 81-76 |
| Women's Basketball | Baylor | Baylor | lost regional to Notre Dame  88-69 |
| Baseball | Oklahoma St. | TCU | Texas lost in semifinals to Vanderbilt |
| Softball | Oklahoma | – | Baylor lost in semifinals to Florida |

| 2012-2013 | Season | Tournament | National Playoffs |
|---|---|---|---|
| Football | Kansas State | | lost Fiesta Bowl to Oregon  35-17 |
| Men's Basketball | Kansas | Kansas | lost in Elite 8 to Michigan 87-85 |
| Women's Basketball | Baylor | Baylor | lost 3rd round to Louisville 82-81 |
| Baseball | Kansas State | Oklahoma | Texas lost semifinal to Vanderbilt |
| Softball | Oklahoma | – | **National champs**, beating Tennessee  2-0 |

*The 2012 Holiday Bowl in which Baylor defeated UCLA, 49-26. Photo by Polupharmakos (CC).*

# SEC champions

**Texas A&M University** joined the **Southeastern Conference** in 2012 and competed in the West Divi- sion against LSU, Arkansas, Ole Miss, Mississippi State, Alabama, and Auburn. Schools in the East Division are Missouri, Kentucky, Vanderbilt, Tennessee, Georgia, South Carolina, and Florida.

| 2014-2015 | Season | Tournament | National Playoffs |
|---|---|---|---|
| Football | Alabama | | lost Sugar Bowl to Ohio State  42-35 |
| Men's Basketball | Kentucky | Kentucky | lost in Final Four to Wisconsin 71-64 |
| Women's Basketball | South Carolina | S. Carolina | lost in Final Four to Notre Dame  66-65 |
| Baseball | LSU | Florida | Florida lost semifinals to Virginia |
| Softball | Florida | Auburn | **National champ** Florida over Michigan |

| 2013-2014 | Season | Tournament | National Playoffs |
|---|---|---|---|
| Football | Auburn | | lost BCS to Florida State  34-31 |
| Men's Basketball | Florida | Florida | in Final Four, lost to UConn. 63-53 |
| Women's Basketball | South Carolina | Tennessee | S. Carolina lost regional semifinal |
| Baseball | Florida | LSU | Vanderbilt **national champs** |
| Softball | Alabama | Georgia | **National champ** Florida over Alabama |

| 2012-2013 | Season | Tournament | National Playoffs |
|---|---|---|---|
| Football | Alabama | | **BCS champion** over Notre Dame  42-14 |
| Men's Basketball | Florida | Ole Miss | Florida in Final 4 |
| Women's Basketball | Tennessee | Texas A&M | A&M lost 2nd round; Tech lost 1st round |
| Baseball | Vanderbilt | LSU | Miss. State lost final to UCLA |
| Softball | Florida | Florida | double-elimination at CWS |

# C-USA champions

Texas schools in **Conference USA** in 2014 were:
**Rice University**
**University of Texas at San Antonio**
**Univeristy of Texas at El Paso**
**University of North Texas**
**Rice** and **UTEP** joined in 2005. In 2013, the **University of North Texas** and the **University of Texas at San Antonio** joined the conference. The U of H joined in 1996 and left in 2013. Other teams in Conference USA are University of Alabama-Birmingham, Florida Atlantic University, Florida International University, Louisiana Tech University, Marshall University, Middle Tennessee State University, University of North Carolina at Charlotte, Old Dominion University, University of Southern Mississippi, and Western Kentucky University.

| 2014-2015 | Champion | Runner-up | National Playoffs |
|---|---|---|---|
| Football | Marshall | La. Tech | Marshall won Boca Rotan, LT won Dallas |
| Men's Basketball | UAB | Mid. Tenn. | UAB lost in regional to UCLA 92-75 |
| Women's Basketball | W. Kentucky | Sou. Miss. | |
| Baseball | Florida Int. | UAB | |
| Softball | W. Kentucky | FAU | |

| 2013-2014 | Champion | Runner-up | National Playoffs |
|---|---|---|---|
| Football | Rice | Marshall | Rice lost Liberty Bowl to Miss. State 44-7 |
| Men's Basketball tie | La.Tech, Tulsa, M.Tenn. S.Miss. | | Tulsa lost Round of 64 to UCLA  76-59 |
| Women's Basketball | Tulsa | UCF | |
| Baseball | Rice | UTSA | Rice lost 2nd round regional to Texas |
| Softball | Tulsa | Marshall | Tulsa lost regional final to Baylor |

| 2012-2013 | Champion | Runner-up | National Playoffs |
|---|---|---|---|
| Football | Tulsa | UCF | won Liberty Bowl over Iowa State  31-17 |
| Men's Basketball | Memphis | S. Miss | Memphis lost in Sweet 16 to Michigan 70-48 |
| Women's Basketball | Tulsa | UCF | Tulsa lost 1st round to Stanford |
| Baseball | Rice | S. Miss | |
| Softball | Marshall | U of H | both teams lost in regionals |

# Sun Belt champions

In 2013, **Texas State University–San Marcos** and the **University of Texas at Arlington** joined the Sun Belt Conference. Other schools in the conference are University of Louisiana-Monroe, University of Lou-isiana-Lafayette, University of Arkansas-Little Rock, Arkansas State University, Troy University, University of South Alabama, Middle Tennessee State University, Appalachian State University, Georgia Southern University and Georgia State University.

| 2014-2015 | Season | Tournament | National Playoffs |
|---|---|---|---|
| Football | Georgia Southern | | |
| Men's Basketball | Ga. State | Ga. State | lost regional to Xavier  75-67 |
| Women's Basketball | UA-Little Rock | Little Rock | lost in regional to Arizona State  57-54 |
| Baseball | Sou. Alabama | La,-Lafayette | La.-Lafayette lost super regional to LSU |
| Softball | La.-Lafayette | Sou. Ala. | La.-Lafayette lost super regional to Auburn |

| 2013-2014 | Season | Tournament | National Playoffs |
|---|---|---|---|
| Football | Ark. State, La.-Lafayette | | Ark. St. won GoDaddy over Ball State  23-20 |
| Men's Basketball | Ga. State | La.-Lafayette | |
| Women's Basketball | Arkansas State | W.Kentucky | |
| Baseball | La.-Lafayette | La.-Lafayette | lost regional final to Ole Miss |
| Softball | La.-Lafayette | La.-Lafayette | lost in 1st round to Oklahoma |

| 2012-2013 | Season | Tournament | National Playoffs |
|---|---|---|---|
| Football | Arkansas State | | won GoDaddy Bowl over Kent State  17-13 |
| Men's Basketball | Ark.State/MTenn | W. Kentucky | W. Kent. lost in second round to Kansas |
| Women's Basketball | UALR / MTenn | MTenn | MTenn. lost 1st round to Louisville 74-49 |
| Baseball | S. Ala/Troy | Florida Atlan. | |
| Softball | W. Kentucky | S. Alabama | W. Kentucky lost at regionals |

# American Athlethic Conference champions

The 2013-14 season was the first for the AAC after the breakup of the Big East Conference. **Southern Methodist University** and the **University of Hous-**ton are in the Amercian Athletic Conference. Other schools in the conference are the University of Memphis, University of Cincinnati, University of Central Florida, East Carolina University, Temple University, University of South Florida, Tulane University, University of Tulsa and the University of Connecticut.

| 2014-2015 | Season | Tournament | National Playoffs |
|---|---|---|---|
| Football | UCF, Cincinnati, Memphis | | Cincinnati lost Military, UCF lost St. Pete |
| Men's Basketball | SMU | SMU | |
| Women's Basketball | U.Conn. | U.Conn. | won **champtionship** over Notre Dame 63-53 |
| Baseball | U. of H. | E. Carolina | |
| Softball | UCF | UCF | |

| 2013-2014 | Season | Tournament | National Playoffs |
|---|---|---|---|
| Football | U. of Central Florida | | won Fiesta Bowl over Baylor, 52-42 |
| Men's Basketball | Louisville, Cin. | Louisville* | U.Conn. went on to .**Natiional Champions** |
| Women's Basketball | U.Conn. | U.Conn | **NCAA Champion** |
| Baseball | Louisville | U. of H. | |
| Softball | UCF | Louisville | |

*Louisville left The AAC after the season for the ACC.*

## For records of previous years in all Sports categories, see www.texasalmanac.com

# SWAC champions

Texas schools in **Southwestern Athletic Conference** in 2012 were:
**Prairie View A&M University**
**Texas Southern University**
The Prairie View A&M Panthers have been in the conference since its founding in 1920 and the Texas Southern Tigers joined the conference in 1954. Other teams in the SWAC Western Division are Grambling State University, Southern University, and University of Arkansas at Pine Bluff. Schools in the Eastern Division are Jackson State University, Mississippi Valley State University, Alcorn State University, Alabama State Univserity, and Alabama A&M University.

| 2014-2015 | Season | Tournament | National Playoffs |
|---|---|---|---|
| Football | Alcorn Sate | | |
| Men's Basketball | Texas Southern | Texas Southern | lost second round to Arizona  93-72 |
| Women's Basketball | Texas Southern | Alabama State | Ala. State lost to Florida State 91-49 |
| Baseball | Texas Southern | | |
| Softball | Texas Southern | | |

| 2013-2014 | Season | Tournament | National Playoffs |
|---|---|---|---|
| Football | Southern | | |
| Men's Basketball | Southern | Texas Southern | |
| Women's Basketball | Southern | Prairie View | |
| Baseball | Jackson State | | lost regional 2nd round  to Miss. State |
| Softball | Texas Southern | | lost regional 1st round to La.-Lafayette |

| 2012-2013 | Season | Tournament | National Playoffs |
|---|---|---|---|
| Football | Arkansas-Pine Bluff | | |
| Men's Basketball | Texas Southern | Southern | Southern lost 2nd round to Gonzaga |
| Women's Basketball | Texas Southern | Prairie View | lost to Baylor in NCAA tourney |
| Baseball | Jackson State | | |
| Softball | Mississippi Valley State | | lost at regionals |

# Southland champions

Texas schools in the **Southland Conference** in 2014:
**Abilene Christian Universtiy**
**Houston Baptist University**
**Texas A&M University–Corpus Christi**
**Stephen F. Austin State University**
**Sam Houston State University**
**Lamar University**
**Univserity of the Incarnate Word**
Oral Roberts left in 2014. Other schools are Central Arkansas, McNeese State, Nicholls State, and Southeastern Louisiana.

| 2014-2015 | Champion | Runner-up | National Playoffs |
|---|---|---|---|
| Football | Sam Houston State | | won quarterfinal over Villianova |
| Men's Basketball | Stephen F. Austin | Sam Houston | SFA lost second round to Utah  57-50 |
| Women's Basketball | NW State | Houston Baptist | NW State lost to Baylor 77-36 |
| Baseball | Houston Baptist | Sam Houston | |
| Softball | Central Arkansas | NW State | |

| 2013-2014 | Champion | Runner-up | National Playoffs |
|---|---|---|---|
| Football | Southeastern Louisiana | | |
| Men's Basketball | Stephen F. Austin | Sam Houston St | |
| Women's Basketball | NW State | S. F. Austin | NW Sate lost regional 1st round |
| Baseball | SE Louisiana | Central Ark. | SE La. lost regional 2nd round |
| Softball | NW State | McNeese | NW State lost regional 1st round |

| 2012-2013 | Champion | Runner-up | National Playoffs |
|---|---|---|---|
| Football | Sam Houston/Central Ark. co-champs | | lost final to North Dakota State  29-3 |
| Men's Basketball | NW State | SFA | NW lost 2nd round to Florida 79-47 |
| Women's Basketball | Oral Roberts | Sam Houston | ORU lost 1st to Tennessee 83-62 |
| Baseball | Central Ark. | SE Lou. | |
| Softball | NW State | Sam Houston | lost at regionals |

*Cotton Bowl stadium is now the home of the annual Heart of Dallas Bowl.*

*Photo by Adam (CC).*

# Football Bowl Games 2014-2015

Following are the college football bowl games involving Texas schools, as well as bowl games held in the state.

| Bowl | Winner | Opponent | Date, Place |
|---|---|---|---|
| Peach Bowl | TCU 42 | Ole Miss 3 | Dec. 31, Atlanta, Georgia Dome |
| New Mexico Bowl | Utah State 21 | UTEP 6 | Dec. 20, Albuquerque, U. Stadium |
| Hawaii Bowl | Rice 30 | Fresno State 6 | Dec. 24, Honolulu, Aloha Stadium |
| Alamo Bowl | UCLA 40 | Kansas State 35 | Jan. 2, San Antonio, Alamodome |
| Texas Bowl | Arkansas 31 | Texas 7 | Dec. 29, Houston, NRG Stadium |
| Heart of Dallas Bowl | La. Tech 35 | Illinois 18 | Dec. 26, Dallas, Cotton Bowl |
| Cotton Bowl | Michigan State 42 | Baylor 41 | Jan. 1, Arlington, AT&T Stadium |
| Sun Bowl | Airzona State 36 | Duke 31 | Dec. 27, El Paso, Sun Bowl |
| Liberty Bowl | Texas A&M 45 | West Virginia 37 | Dec. 29, Memphis, Liberty Bowl |
| Armed Forces Bowl | Houston 35 | Pittsburgh 34 | Jan. 2, Fort Worth, Armon G. Carter |

# Football Bowl Games 2013-2014

| Bowl | Winner | Opponent | Date, Place |
|---|---|---|---|
| Cotton Bowl | Missouri 41 | Oklahoma State 31 | Jan. 3, Arlington, AT&T Stadium |
| Texas Bowl | Syracuse 21 | Minnesota 17 | Dec. 27, Houston, Reliant Stadium |
| Alamo Bowl | Oregon 30 | Texas 7 | Dec. 30, San Antonio, Alamodome |
| Chick-fil-A Bowl | Texas A&M 52 | Duke 48 | Dec. 31, Atlanta, Georgia Dome |
| Holiday Bowl | Texas Tech 37 | Arizona State 23 | Dec. 30, San Diego, Qualcomm |
| Fiesta Bowl | UCF 52 | Baylor 42 | Jan. 1, Gendale, AZ., U of Phoenix |
| Sun Bowl | UCLA 42 | Va. Tech 12 | Dec. 31, El Paso, Sun Bowl |
| Armed Forces Bowl | Navy 24 | Middle Tenn. 6 | Dec. 30, Ft. Worth, Amon Carter |
| BBVACompass Bowl | Vanderbilt 41 | Houston 24 | Jan. 4, Birmingham, Legion Field |
| Heart of Dallas Bowl | North Texas 36 | UNLV 14 | Jan. 1, Dallas, Cotton Bowl |
| Liberty Bowl | Miss. State 44 | Rice 7 | Dec. 31, Memphis, Liberty Bowl |

# Football Bowl Games 2012-2013

| Bowl | Winner | Opponent | Date, Place |
|---|---|---|---|
| Holiday Bowl | Baylor 49 | UCLA 26 | Dec. 27, San Diego, Qualcomm |
| Hawaii Bowl | SMU 43 | Fresno State 10 | Dec. 24, Honolulu, Aloha Stadium |
| Buffalo Wild Wings | Michigan State 17 | TCU 16 | Dec. 29, Tempe, Sun Devil Stadium |
| Alamo Bowl | Texas 31 | Oregon State 27 | Dec. 29, San Antonio, Alamodome |
| Texas Bowl | Texas Tech 34 | Minnesota 31 | Dec. 28, Houston, Reliant Stadium |
| Heart of Dallas Bowl | Oklahoma State 58 | Purdue 14 | Jan. 1, Dallas, Cotton Bowl |
| Cotton Bowl | Texas A&M 41 | Oklahoma 13 | Jan. 4, Arlington, Cowboys Stadium |
| Sun Bowl | Georgia Tech 21 | USC 7 | Dec. 31, El Paso, Sun Bowl |
| Armed Forces Bowl | Rice 33 | Air Force 14 | Dec. 29, Fort Worth, Amon Carter |

# Texas College Sports — Division II

## Lone Star champions

The **Lone Star Conference**, founded in 1931, has long been the athletic conference for Texas schools in the NCAA second tier of schools, Division II.

Texas schools in the conference in 2014 were:
**Angelo State University**
**Midwestern State University**
**Tarleton State University**
**Texas A&M University—Commerce**
**Texas A&M University—Kingsville**
**Texas Woman's University**
**West Texas A&M University**

In 2013, the University of the Incarnate Word and Abilene Christian University moved up to Division I, joining the Southland Conference.

Other teams in conference are Cameron University (Okla.) and Eastern New Mexico State University.

| 2014-2015 | Season | Tournament | National Playoffs |
|---|---|---|---|
| Football | A&M–Commerce | Angelo State | Angelo State lost in second round |
| Men's Basketball | Tarleton | Tarleton | lost Final Four to Mt. Olive 77-59 |
| Women's Basketball | West Texas A&M | W.Tex. A&M | lost in Elite 8 to Emporia State |
| Baseball | W.Tex. A&M, Kingsville | Angelo State | |
| Softball | West Texas A&M | W.Tex. A&M | |

| 2013-2014 | Season | Tournament | National Playoffs |
|---|---|---|---|
| Football | Eastern New Mexico and Tarleton | | |
| Men's Basketball | Tarleton, Midwestern | Tarleton | Tarleton lost in round 2 |
| Women's Basketball | West Texas A&M | West Texas A&M | lost in final to Bentley 73-65 |
| Baseball | Texas A&M-Kingsville | Tarleton | |
| Softball | West Texas A&M | Angelo State | W.Tex. A&M national champions |

| 2012-2013 | Season | Tournament | National Playoffs |
|---|---|---|---|
| Football | Midwestern and West Texas A&M | | W.Tex A&M lost semifinal |
| Men's Basketball | Midwestern State | Tarleton | Tarleton lost 1st to Metro State |
| Women's Basketball | Midwestern/ Abilene C. | Midwestern | Midw. lost quarterf. to Colo.Mesa |
| Baseball | Tarleton State | A&M Kingsville | |
| Softball | Texas Women's | Texas Women's | lost in quarterfinals |

## Heartland champions

The **Heartland Conference** was formed in 1999. Texas schools in the conference in 2014 were:
**Texas A&M International University**
**St. Mary's University**
**St. Edward's University**
**Dallas Baptist University**
**University of Texas of the Permian Basin**
**Lubbock Christian University**.

Other members are: University of Arkansas-Fort Smith, Oklahoma Christian University, Newman University (Kansas), Oklahoma Panhandle State University and Rogers State University (Oklahoma). The conference does not have football competition.

| 2014-2015 | Season | Tournament | National Playoffs |
|---|---|---|---|
| Men's Basketball | St. Mary's | St. Mary's | lost first round to Tarleton  71-52 |
| Women's Basketball | LCU, UA-Ft. Smith | UA-Fort Smith | lost round 2 to W. Tex. A&M  70-57 |
| Baseball | St. Ed, St Mary's | St. Mary's | |
| Softball | LCU, St. Mary's | St. Mary's | St. Mary's lost first round to Shorter |

| 2013-2014 | Season | Tournament | National Playoffs |
|---|---|---|---|
| Men's Basketball | UA-Fort Smith | A&M International | A&M Inter., St.Mary's lost 1st round |
| Women's Basketball | A&M International | St. Edward's | A&M Inter., St. Mary's lost 1st round |
| Baseball | St. Edward's | St. Edward's | lost in regionals |
| Softball | St. Mary's | St. Mary's | lost to W.Tex A&M in regionals |

| 2012-2013 | Season | Tournament | National Playoffs |
|---|---|---|---|
| Men's Basketball | UA-Fort Smith | St. Mary's | St.Mary lost quarterfinals to Metro |
| Women's Basketball | UT-Permian | St. Mary's | St.Mary lost 1st to Metro |
| Baseball | St. Mary's | St. Edward's | |
| Softball | St. Mary's | St. Mary's | lost in regionals |

# Texas Olympic Medalists

This is a list of athletes with Texas connections who have won medals in Olympic Games. This includes those born here or have lived in Texas, as well as U.S. team members who spent their collegiate careers at Texas universities.

Information included is: the athlete's name, the sport and the year, as well as the types of medals (G-Gold, S-Silver, B-Bronze).

If the athlete won more than one of the same kind of medal in any one year, the number is noted before the letter code; i.e., 2G indicates that the athlete won two gold medals in the games indicated.

The symbol (†) following the medal code indicates that the athlete participated in preliminary contests only; the medal was awarded because of membership on a winning team. Years in which the athlete participated in the Games but did not win a medal are not included.

Track indicates all track and field events except those noted separately.

*Source: United States Olympic Committee.*

| Olympian | Sport | Year | Medal |
|---|---|---|---|
| Abdallah, Nia Nicole | Taekwondo | 2004 | S |
| Allen, Chad | Baseball | 1996 | B |
| *Armstrong, Lance* | *Cycling* | *2000* | *B\** |
| Arnette, Jay Hoyland | Basketball | 1960 | G |
| Austin, Charles | Track | 1996 | G |
| Baker, Walter Thane | Track | 1956 | G,S,B |
| | | 1952 | S |
| Baptiste, Kirk | Track | 1984 | S |
| Barr, Beth | Swimming | 1988 | S |
| Bassham, Lanny Robert | Shooting | 1976 | G |
| | | 1972 | S |
| Bates, Michael D. | Track | 1992 | B |
| Beck, Robert Lee | Pentathlon | 1960 | 2B |
| Bedforth, B.J. | Swimming | 2000 | G |
| Berens, Ricky | Swimming | 2012 | G, S |
| | | 2008 | G |
| Berube, Ryan Thomas | Swimming | 1996 | G |
| Boudia, David | Diving | 2012 | G, B |
| Brew, Derrick K. | Track | 2004 | G, B |
| Brown, Earlene Dennis | Track | 1960 | B |
| Browning, David (Skippy) | Diving | 1952 | G |
| Buckner, William Quinn | Basketball | 1976 | G |
| Buford-Bailey, Tonja | Track | 1996 | B |
| Burrell, Leroy Russel | Track | 1992 | G |
| Carey, Rick | Swimming | 1984 | 3G |
| Carlisle, Daniel T. | Shooting | 1984 | B |
| Carter, Michael D. | Shotput | 1984 | S |
| Catchings, Tamika | Basketball | 2012 | G |
| Clay, Bryan E. | Decathlon | 2008 | G |
| | | 2004 | S |
| Cline, Nancy Lieberman | Basketball | 1976 | S |
| Cohen, Tiffany | Swimming | 1984 | G |
| Corbelli, Laurie Flachmeier | Volleyball | 1984 | S |
| Cotton, John | Baseball | 2000 | G |
| Crocker, Ian | Swimming | 2008 | G |
| | | 2004 | G,S,B |
| | | 2000 | G |
| Cross-Battle, Tara | Volleyball | 1992 | B |
| Davis, Clarissa G. | Basketball | 1992 | B |
| Davis, Jack Wells | Track | 1956 | S |
| | | 1952 | S |
| Davis, Josh C. | Swimming | 2000 | 2S |
| | | 1996 | 3G |
| Davis, W.F. (Buddy) | High Jump | 1952 | G |
| DeLoach, Joseph N. Jr. | Track | 1988 | G |

| Olympian | Sport | Year | Medal |
|---|---|---|---|
| Dersch, Hans | Swimming | 1992 | G |
| Didrikson, Mildred (Babe) | Track | 1932 | 2G, S |
| Donie, Scott R. | Diving | 1992 | S |
| Drexler, Clyde | Basketball | 1992 | G |
| Dumais, Troy | Diving | 2012 | B |
| Durant, Kevin | Basketball | 2012 | G |
| Dusing, Nate | Swimming | 2004 | B |
| | | 2000 | S |
| Eller, Glenn | Shooting | 2008 | G |
| Ethridge, Mary (Kamie) | Basketball | 1988 | G |
| Farmer-Patrick, Sandra | Track | 1992 | S |
| Feigen, Jimmy | Swimming | 2012 | S† |
| Finn-Burrell, Michelle Bonae | Track | 1992 | G |
| Forbes, James Ricardo | Basketball | 1972 | S |
| Ford, Gilbert (Gib) | Basketball | 1956 | G |
| Foreman, George | Boxing | 1968 | G |
| Fortenberry, Joe Cephis | Basketball | 1936 | G |
| Garrison, Zina | Tennis | 1988 | G, B |
| George, Chris | Baseball | 2000 | G |
| Gjertson, Doug | Swimming | 1992 | G, B |
| | | 1988 | G |
| Glenesk, Dean William | Pentathlon | 1984 | S |
| Goldblatt, Scott | Swimming | 2004 | G |
| | | 2000 | B |
| Gonzáles, Paul G. Jr. | Boxing | 1984 | G |
| Guidry, Carlette D. | Track | 1996 | G† |
| | | 1992 | G |
| Hall, Gary Jr. | Swimming | 2004 | G, B |
| | | 2000 | 2G,S,B |
| | | 1996 | 2G, 2S |
| Hamm, Mia | Soccer | 2004 | G |
| | | 2000 | S |
| | | 1996 | G |
| Hannan, Tommy | Swimming | 2000 | G |
| Hansen, Brendan | Swimming | 2012 | G, B |
| | | 2008 | G |
| | | 2004 | G,S,B |
| Hansen, Fred Morgan | Track | 1964 | G |
| Hardee, Trey | Track | 2012 | S |
| Harkrider, Kiplan P. | Baseball | 1996 | B |

| Olympian | Sport | Year | Medal |
|---|---|---|---|
| Hartwell, Erin Wesley | Cycling | 1996 | S |
| | | 1992 | B |
| Hays, Todd | Bobsled | 2002 | S |
| Heath, Michael Steward | Swimming | 1984 | 2G, S |
| Hedgepeth, Whitney L. | Swimming | 1996 | G, 2S |
| Hedrick, Chad | Speed Skating | 2010 | S,B |
| | | 2006 | G,S,B |
| Heidenreich, Jerry | Swimming | 1972 | 2G,S,B |
| Henry, James Edward | Diving | 1968 | B |
| Hill, Denean E. | Track | 1992 | S |
| | | 1988 | S |
| | | 1984 | G |
| Hill, Grant Henry | Basketball | 1996 | G |
| Homfeld, Conrad E. | Equestrian | 1984 | G, S |
| Hooker, Destinee | Volleyball | 2012 | S |
| Hooper, Darrow | Shotput | 1952 | S |
| Horton, Jonathan | Gymnastics | 2008 | S |
| Howard, Sherri Francis | Track | 1988 | S |
| | | 1984 | G |
| Jackson, Lucious Brown | Basketball | 1964 | G |
| Jacobs, Chris | Swimming | 1988 | 2G, S |
| Johnson, Michael | Track | 2000 | 2G |
| | | 1996 | 2G |
| | | 1992 | G |
| Johnson, Rafer L. | Decathlon | 1960 | G |
| | | 1956 | S |
| Jones, John Wesley (Lam) | Track | 1976 | G |
| Jordan, Shaun | Swimming | 1992 | G |
| | | 1988 | G |
| Juarez, Ricardo Rocky | Boxing | 2000 | S |
| Julich, Robert William | Cycling | 2004 | B |
| Keeler, Kathryn Elliott | Rowing | 1984 | G |
| Kern, Douglas James | Sailing | 1992 | S |
| Kiefer, Adolph | Swimming | 1936 | G |
| Kimmons, Trell | Track | 2012 | S |
| King, Judith Brown | Track | 1984 | S |
| Kleine, Megan | Swimming | 1992 | G† |
| Knight, Bianca | Track | 2012 | G |
| Kolius, John Waldrip | Sailing | 1976 | S |
| Lane, Colleen | Swimming | 2004 | S |
| Langkop, Dorothy Franey | Speed Skating | 1932 | B |
| Leetch, Brian Joseph | Ice Hockey | 2002 | S |
| Lewis, F. (Carl) Carlton | Track | 1996 | G |
| | | 1992 | 2G |
| | | 1988 | 2G, S |
| | | 1984 | 4G |
| Lienhard, William Barner | Basketball | 1952 | G |
| Lipinski, Tara K. | Figure Skating | 1998 | G |
| Liukin, Nastia | Gymnastics | 2008 | G,3S,B |
| Lloyd, Andrea | Basketball | 1988 | G |
| Losey, Robert G. (Greg) | Pentathlon | 1984 | S |
| Lopez, Diana | Taekwondo | 2008 | B |
| Lopez, Mark | Taekwondo | 2008 | S |
| Lopez, Steve | Taekwondo | 2008 | B |
| Lowe, Sara Elizabeth | Swimming | 2004 | B |
| Magers, Rose Mary | Volleyball | 1984 | S |

| Olympian | Sport | Year | Medal |
|---|---|---|---|
| Malone, Jordan | Speed Skating | 2014 | S |
| | | 2010 | B |
| Manzano, Leo | Track | 2012 | S |
| Marsh, Michael L. | Track | 1996 | S |
| | | 1992 | 2G |
| Marshall, Christine | Swimming | 2008 | B |
| Matson, James Randel (Randy) | Shotput | 1968 | G |
| | | 1964 | G |
| Matson, Ollie G. | Track | 1952 | S, B |
| McFalls, Jennifer Yvonne | Softball | 2000 | G |
| McFarlane, Tracey | Swimming | 1988 | S |
| McKenzie, Kim | Track | 1984 | B |
| Meadows, Earle | Track | 1936 | G |
| Mills, Ronald P. | Swimming | 1968 | B |
| Mitchell, Betsy | Swimming | 1988 | S |
| | | 1984 | G, S |
| Moceanu, Dominique H. | Gymnastics | 1996 | G |
| Montgomery, James P. | Swimming | 1976 | 3G, B |
| Moore, James Warren | Pentathlon | 1964 | S |
| Morrow, Bobby Joe | Track | 1956 | 3G |
| Munoz, Felipe | Swimming | 1968 | G |
| Neilson-Bell, Sandy | Swimming | 1972 | 3G |
| Nelson, Lianne Bennion | Rowing | 2004 | S |
| Newhouse, Frederick V. | Track | 1976 | G, S |
| Nott/Cunningham, Tara Lee | Weightlifting | 2004 | G |
| Okafor, Emeka | Basketball | 2004 | B |
| Olajuwon, Hakeem | Basketball | 1996 | G |
| Olsen, Justin | Bobsled | 2010 | G |
| Osterman, Catherine (Cat) | Softball | 2008 | S |
| | | 2004 | G |
| Paddock, Charles W. | Track | 1924 | S |
| | | 1920 | 2G, S |
| Patterson, Carly | Gymnastics | 2004 | G, 2S |
| Patton, Darvis | Track | 2004 | S |
| Peirsol, Aaron | Swimming | 2008 | 2G, S |
| | | 2004 | 3G |
| | | 2000 | S |
| Perry, Nanceen L. | Track | 2000 | B |
| Pesthy, Paul Karoly | Fencing | 1964 | S |
| Phenix, Erin | Swimming | 2000 | G |
| Pinder, Demetrius | Track | 2012 | G |
| Postma, Joan Spillane | Swimming | 1960 | G |
| Potter, Cynthia Ann | Diving | 1976 | B |
| Rambo, John Barnett | Track | 1964 | B |
| Rauch, Jamie | Swimming | 2000 | S |
| Retton, Mary Lou | Gymnastics | 1984 | G,2S,2B |
| Richards, Robert E. | Track | 1956 | G |
| | | 1952 | G |
| | | 1948 | B |
| Richards-Ross, Sanya | Track | 2012 | 2G |
| | | 2008 | G, B |
| | | 2004 | G |
| Ritter, Louise | Track | 1988 | G |
| Robertson, Alvin Cyrrale | Basketball | 1984 | G |
| Robinson, David M. | Basketball | 1996 | G |
| | | 1992 | G |
| | | 1988 | B |
| Robinson, Moushaumi | Track | 2004 | G |
| Robinson, Robert J. | Basketball | 1948 | G |

| Olympian | Sport | Year | Medal |
|---|---|---|---|
| Robinzine, Kevin B. | Track | 1988 | G |
| Roe, Frederick | Polo | 1924 | S |
| Russell, Douglas Albert | Swimming | 1968 | 2G |
| Russell, John William | Equestrian | 1952 | B |
| Schneider, Marcus B. | Rowing | 1996 | B |
| Slay, Brandon Douglas | Wrestling | 2000 | G |
| Smith, Dean | Track | 1952 | G |
| Smith, Lamont | Track | 1996 | G |
| Smith, Owen Guinn | Track | 1948 | G |
| Smith, Tommie C. | Track | 1968 | G |
| Southern, S. Edward | Track | 1956 | S |
| Steinseifer, Carrie | Swimming | 1984 | 2G |
| Sterkle, Jill Ann | Swimming | 1988 | 2B |
| | | 1984 | G |
| | | 1976 | G |
| Stevenson, Toby | Pole Vault | 2004 | S |
| Stulce, Michael S. | Shotput | 1992 | G |
| Swoopes, Sheryl Denise | Basketball | 2004 | G |
| | | 2000 | G |
| | | 1996 | G |
| Sykora, Stacy | Volleyball | 2008 | S |
| Tarmoh, Jeneba | Track | 2012 | G |
| Taylor, Robert | Track | 1972 | G, S |
| Teagarden, Taylor | Baseball | 2008 | B |
| Tinsley, Michael | Track | 2012 | S |
| Tisdale, Wayman L. | Basketball | 1984 | G |
| Valdez, Jesse | Boxing | 1972 | B |
| Van, Allen | Ice Hockey | 1952 | S |
| Vollmer, Dana | Swimming | 2012 | 3G |
| | | 2004 | G |

| Olympian | Sport | Year | Medal |
|---|---|---|---|
| Walker, Laura Anne | Swimming | 1988 | B |
| Walker, Neil | Swimming | 2004 | G, B |
| | | 2000 | G, S |
| Walters, Dave | Swimming | 2008 | G |
| Wariner, Jeremy | Track | 2008 | G, S |
| | | 2004 | 2G |
| Weatherspoon, Teresa G. | Basketball | 1992 | B |
| | | 1988 | G |
| Weber-Gale, Garrett | Swimming | 2008 | 2G |
| Wells, Rhoshii S. | Boxing | 1996 | B |
| Wells, Wayne A. | Wrestling | 1972 | G |
| Whitfield, Malvin G. | Track | 1952 | G, S |
| | | 1948 | G, S |
| Wilkinson, Laura A. | Diving | 2000 | G |
| Williams, Christa L. | Softball | 2000 | G |
| | | 1996 | G |
| Williamson, Darold | Track | 2004 | G |
| Wilson, Craig Martin | Water Polo | 1988 | S |
| | | 1984 | S |
| Wolfe, Rowland (Flip) | Gymnastics | 1932 | G |
| Wrightson, Bernard C. | Diving | 1968 | G |
| Wylie, Paul Stanton | Figure Skating | 1992 | S |
| Young, Earl Verdelle | Track | 1960 | 2G |
| Zmeskal, Kim | Gymnastics | 1992 | B |

• In January 2013, the International Olympic Committee disqualified Lance Armstrong from the 2000 events he competed in after he was found to have used drugs to enhance his performance.

Demetrius Pinder leads in his competition at the 2012 Olympics when he competed for his native Bahamas. He attended Texas A&M University and has a residence in College Station. Photo by Anthony (CC).

# Major Professional Sports

*San Antonio Spurs Boris Diaw and Tim Duncan playing against the Washington Wizards in February 2014. The Spurs went on to win their fifth NBA championship that season.*

*Photo by Keith Allison (CC).*

## National Basketball Association (NBA)
### San Antonio Spurs (Southwest)

| Year | Win | Loss | % | Finish |
|------|-----|------|------|--------|
| 2011-12 | 50 | 16 | .758 | lost Western conference finals to Oklahoma City Thunder 4-2 |
| 2012-13 | 58 | 24 | .707 | Western conference champions; lost finals to Miami 4-3 |
| 2013-14 | 62 | 20 | .756 | won **NBA championship** over Miami Heat 4–1 |
| 2014-15 | 55 | 27 | .671 | lost first round to Los Angeles Clippers 4–3 |

### Houston Rockets (Southwest)

| Year | Win | Loss | % | Finish |
|------|-----|------|------|--------|
| 2011-12 | 34 | 32 | .515 | |
| 2012-13 | 45 | 27 | .549 | lost first round to Oklahoma City Thunder 4-2 |
| 2013-14 | 54 | 28 | .659 | lost first round to Portland Trail Blazers 4-2 |
| 2014-15 | 56 | 26 | .683 | lost conference finals to Golden State Warriors 4–1 |

### Dallas Mavericks (Southwest)

| Year | Win | Loss | % | Finish |
|------|-----|------|------|--------|
| 2011-12 | 36 | 30 | .541 | lost first round to Oklahoma City Thunder 0-4 |
| 2012-13 | 41 | 41 | .500 | |
| 2013-14 | 49 | 33 | .598 | lost first round to San Antonio Spurs 4-3 |
| 2014-15 | 50 | 32 | .610 | lost first round to Houston Rockets 4–1 |

## National Hockey League (NHL)
### Dallas Stars

| Year | Win | Loss | Overtime loss | Finish |
|------|-----|------|---------------|--------|
| **(Pacific Div.)** | | | | |
| 2011-12 | 42 | 35 | 5 | |
| 2013 | 22 | 22 | 4 | Lockout forced abbreviated season |
| **(Central Div.)** | | | | |
| 2013-14 | 40 | 30 | 11 | lost conference quarterfinals to Ducks 4-2 |
| 2014-15 | 41 | 31 | 10 | |

# National Football League (NFL)
## Houston Texans (AFC South)

| Year | Win | Loss | Finish |
|------|-----|------|--------|
| 2011 | 10 | 6 | 1st AFC South: lost division playoff to Baltimore Ravens 20-13 |
| 2012 | 12 | 4 | 1st AFC South: lost division playoff to New Englland Patriots 41-28 |
| 2013 | 2 | 14 | |
| 2014 | 9 | 7 | |

## Dallas Cowboys (NFC East)

| Year | Win | Loss | Finish |
|------|-----|------|--------|
| 2011 | 8 | 8 | |
| 2012 | 8 | 8 | |
| 2013 | 8 | 8 | |
| 2014 | 12 | 4 | 1st NFC East; lost divisional playoff to Green Bay Packers 26-21 |

# Major League Baseball
## Texas Rangers (American League West)

| Year | Win | Loss | % | Finish |
|------|-----|------|---|--------|
| 2011 | 96 | 66 | .593 | 1st in division; lost **World Series** to St. Louis Cardinals 4-3 |
| 2012 | 93 | 69 | .574 | 2nd in division; lost wild card to Baltimore Orioles 5-1 |
| 2013 | 91 | 72 | .562 | 2nd in division |
| 2014 | 67 | 95 | .414 | 5th in division |

## Houston Astros (National League Central / American League West)

| Year | Win | Loss | % | Finish |
|------|-----|------|---|--------|
| 2011 | 56 | 106 | .346 | 6th in Central Divison |
| 2012 | 55 | 107 | .340 | 6th in Central Division |
| **Realignment** to American League, West Division | | | | |
| 2013 | 51 | 111 | .315 | 5th in division |
| 2014 | 70 | 92 | .432 | 4th in division |

# Major League Soccer (MLS)
## Houston Dynamo (Eastern)

| Year | Win | Loss | Draw | Finish |
|------|-----|------|------|--------|
| 2011 | 12 | 9 | 13 | 2nd in conference; lost final to Los Angeles Galaxy 1-0 |
| 2012 | 16 | 9 | 9 | 5th in conference; lost final to Los Angeles Galaxy 3-1 |
| 2013 | 14 | 11 | 9 | 4th in conference; lost confernce final to Kansas City 2-1 |
| 2014 | 11 | 17 | 6 | 8th in conference |

## FC Dallas (Western)

| Year | Win | Loss | Draw | Finish |
|------|-----|------|------|--------|
| 2011 | 15 | 12 | 7 | 4th in conference; lost wild-card game to New York Red Bulls 0-2 |
| 2012 | 9 | 13 | 12 | 6th in conference |
| 2013 | 11 | 12 | 11 | 8th in conference |
| 2014 | 16 | 12 | 6 | 4th in confernce; lost semifinals to Seattle Sounders |

# Texas Sports Hall of Fame

The Texas Sports Hall of Fame was organized in 1951 by the Texas Sports Writers Association. Each year the honorees are inducted into the Hall of Fame at a gala dinner.

(The second such fete in 1952 was headlined by, "That filmland athlete, Ronald Reagan, and his actress wife, Nancy Davis," *The Dallas Morning News*, June 9, 1952.)

The hall was originally in Grand Prairie in the Dallas-Fort Worth area.

The Hall of Fame was closed in 1986 for financial reasons, but in 1991 it was reopened in Waco.

In addition to memorabilia, the new location also houses archives.

Under the current selection process, dues-paying members of the Texas Sports Hall of Fame can nominate any number of individuals. (Anyone can become a member.)

The selection committee, chaired by Dave Campbell, founder of *Texas Football Magazine*, reviews all nominees and creates the "Official Voting Membership" ballot.

Ballots are then mailed to the voting membership, former Texas Sports Hall of Fame inductees, and the media selection committee.

The results of the balloting are announced in the autumn with the induction banquet following in the winter.

The hall of fame website is at www.tshof.org.

*Sanya Richards-Ross ran track at the University of Texas at Austin beginning in 2003. Photo by Citizen59 (CC).*

| Year | Inductee | Sport | Texas connection, career |
|------|----------|-------|--------------------------|
| \*Designation changed from year the inductees were selected to the year the award was presented. Sources: From the Texas Sports Hall of Fame, The Handbook of Texas, The Dallas Morning News, and other sources. | | | |
| 2015 | Zelmo Beaty | Basketball | Hillister, Woodville, Prairie View A&M, NBA-ABA 1962-75 |
| | Gil Brandt | Football | Dallas Cowboys personnel executive 1960-88 |
| | Ty Detmer | Football | Laredo, SA Southwest quarterback, 1990 Heisman at BYU |
| | Cliff Harris | Football | Dallas Cowboys safety 1970-79 |
| | Richard Quick | Swimming | Highland Park, SMU, UT coach, Olympics coach 1984-2004 |
| | Nolan Richardson | Basketball | El Paso, Texas Western 1961-64, Western Texas coach |
| | Everson Walls | Football | Richardson Berkner, Cowboys defensive back 1981-89 |
| | Jeremy Wariner | Track | Arlington Lamar, Baylor, Olympic medalist 2004-08 |
| 2014\* | Doug English | Football | Dallas Adams, UT tackle, Detroit Lions 1975-85 |
| | Larry Johnson | Basketball | Dallas Skyline, Odessa College, UNLV, NBA 1991-2001 |
| | Charlie Krueger | Football | Caldwell, A&M All-American under Bear Bryant, 49ers 1959-73 |
| | Dat Nguyen | Football | Rockport-Fulton, A&M linebacker 1995-98, Dallas 1999-2005 |
| | Pudge Rodriguez | Baseball | Texas Ranger starting in 1991, All-Star catcher 14 times |
| | Thurman Thomas | Football | Houston, Oklahoma State, NFL running back 1988-2000 |
| | Sanya Richards-Ross | Track | Austin, UT track, Olympic medalist 2004, 2008, 2012 |
| | Don Trull | Football | All-American quarterback Baylor 1960s, AFL-NFL 1963-74 |

**Go to the Sports page at www.texasalmanac.com for a complete list of inductees beginning with 1951.**

| Year | Inductee | Sport | Texas connection, career |
|------|----------|-------|--------------------------|
| 2012* | Drew Brees | Football | Austin Westlake quarterback 1993-96, New Orleans Saints |
| | Walt Garrison | Football | Lewisville, fullback Dallas Cowboys 1966-74 |
| | Eddie Mathews | Baseball | Texarkana, Boston/Milwaukee/Atlanta Braves 1952-66 |
| | Bobby Moegle | Baseball | winningest high school coach, Lubbock Monterey 1960-99 |
| | Shaquille O'Neal | Basketball | San Antonio Cole, 19 years NBA, Lakers, Heat |
| | Cat Osterman | Softball | Houston, Cypress Springs, UT pitcher, Olympics |
| | Ricky Williams | Football | UT running back 1995-98, Heisman, NFL 1999-2011 |
| 2011 | Shawn Andaya | Softball | A&M pitcher 1984-87, 3 national championships |
| | Gary Blair | Basketball | Dallas, women's coach, A&M, SFA, South Oak Cliff |
| | Mack Brown | Football | UT Longhorn coach 1998- 2013 |
| | Fred Couples | Golf | U of Houston 1977-80, PGA |
| | G.A. Moore Jr. | Football | Winningest HS coach, PIlot Point, Celina, Aubrey 2004- |
| | Dave Parks | Football | Abilene, Texas Tech 1962-63, NFL 1964-73 |
| | Tobin Rote | Football | San Antonio, Rice, Green Bay QB 1950-56, other NFL teams |
| | Bubba Smith | Football | Beaumont, Michigan State, Baltimore, Raiders, Oilers 1967-76 |
| | Lovie Smith | Football | Big Sandy, U of Tulsa, coach Chicago Bears 2004- |
| | Andre Ware | Football | Dickinson, U of Houston, Detroit Lions QB 1990-93 |
| 2010 | Charley Johnson | Football | Big Spring, NFL quarterback 1961-75, Houston Oilers |
| | Donna Lopiano | Women's Sports | Softball All-American, UT women's athletic director 1975-92 |
| | Clint Murchison | Football | initial owner of Dallas Cowboys 1960-1984 |
| | Drew Pearson | Football | Dallas Cowboy receiver 1973-1983 |
| | John Randle | Football | Hearne, Texas A&I lineman, NFL 1990-03, Minnesota Vikings |
| | Jim Sundberg | Baseball | MLB catcher 1974-89, executive, Texas Rangers |
| | Emmitt Thomas | Football | Angleton, Bishop College, Kansas City Chiefs 1966-78 |
| | Willie Willis | Baseball | Austin, Negro League shortstop 1920s-30s |
| | Laura Wilkinson | Swimming | Spring, Olympic Gold in diving 2000, UT All-American |
| 2009 | Bud Adams | Football | Houston Oilers owner, co-founder AFL 1960 |
| | Lance Berkman | Baseball | Waco, New Braunfels Canyon, Rice, Houston Astros |
| | Lawrence Elkins | Football | Brownwood, Baylor receiver, Houston Oilers 1965-68 |
| | Burt Hooton | Baseball | UT, Cubs, Dodgers, Texas Rangers 1985, Astros coach |
| | Chuck Howley | Football | Dallas Cowboys linebacker 1961-73 |
| | Tommy Kramer | Football | San Antonio, Rice quarterback, Minnesota Vikings 1977-89 |
| | Harvey Martin | Football | East Texas State, Dallas Cowboys defensive end 1973-83 |
| | Kim Mulkey | Basketball | Baylor women's coach 2000- |
| | Dan Reeves | Football | Dallas Cowboys running back/QB 1965-72, NFL coach |
| | Max Williams | Basketball | Avoca, SMU, coach Dallas Chaparrals 1969-70 |
| 2008 | Rolando Blackman | Basketball | Olympics 1980, Dallas Mavericks 1981-92 |
| | Bill Bradley | Football | Palestine, UT, Philadelphia Eagles defensive back 1969-76 |
| | Lee Roy Jordan | Football | Dallas Cowboys linebacker 1963-76 |
| | Abe Lemons | Basketball | UT coach 1977-82 |
| | Kyle Rote Jr. | Soccer | Dallas Tornado 1973-78, Houston Hurricane 1979 |
| | LaDainian Tomlinson | Football | Waco, TCU, San Diego Chargers running back 2001- |
| | Steve Worster | Football | Bridge City, UT fullback 1968-70 |
| 2007 | Leta Andrews | Basketball | Granbury 1954-55, coach 1962- at Calallen, Granbury, others |
| | Ray Childress | Football | Richardson, A&M tackle, Houston Oilers 1985-95 |
| | Spike Dykes | Basketball | coach at Coahoma, Midland Lee, others, Texas Tech 1986-99 |
| | Mia Hamm | Soccer | Wichita Falls, college/national/Olympics 1989-2004 |
| | Abner Haynes | Football | North Texas, Dallas Texans running back, AFL 1960-67 |
| | Michael Irvin | Football | Dallas Cowboys receiver 1988-99 |
| | Mike Modano | Hockey | Dallas Stars 1993-2010 |
| | Jim Ray Smith | Football | West Columbia, Baylor, Cleveland 1956-62, Cowboys 1962-64 |

# Counties

*The Henderson County Courthouse in Athens was built in the Classical Revival style and completed in 1913. Photo by Jim Hoffheins.*

**History**

**Maps**

**Vital Statistics**

**Cities and Towns**

**Climate**

# Counties of Texas

These pages describe Texas' 254 counties and hundreds of towns. Descriptions are based on reports from chambers of commerce, the Texas AgriLife Extension agents, federal and state agencies, the *New Handbook of Texas* and other sources. Consult the index for other county information.

County maps are based on those of the Texas Department of Transportation and are copyrighted, 2015, as are the entire contents.

**Physical Features**: Descriptions are from U.S. Geological Survey and local sources.

**Economy**: From information provided by local chambers of commerce and county extension agents.

**History**: From Texas statutes, *Fulmore's History and Geography of Texas as Told in County Names*, WPA Historical Records Survey, Texas Centennial Commission Report and the *New Handbook of Texas*.

**Race/Ethnicity**: Percentage estimates of 2013 from the Texas State Data Center, University of Texas at San Antonio. Anglo refers to non-Hispanic whites; Asian refers to persons having origins in the Far East, Southeast Asia or the Indian subcontinent. Other refers to some other race alone or in combination.

**Vital Statistics**: From the Texas Department of State Health Services Annual Report 2012.

**Recreation**: From information provided by local chambers of commerce and county extension agents. Attempts were made to note activities unique to the area or that point to ethnic or cultural heritage.

**Minerals**: From county extension agents.

**Agriculture**: Condensed from information provided to the Texas Almanac by county extension agents in 2015. Market value (total cash receipts) of agricultural products sold is from the last **Census of Agriculture** of the U.S. Department of Agriculture that was conducted in 2012.

**Cities**: Towns listed include the county seat, incorporated cities and towns with post offices, as well as certain census designated places (CDP). Population figures for incorporated towns and CDPs are estiamtes for Jan. 1, 2014, from the Texas State Data Center. Population estimates for other towns are from local officials received through a Texas Almanac survey. When figures for small portions of major cities are given, they are in brackets, such as **part [46,885] of Dallas** in Collin County.

### Sources of DATA LISTS

**Population (of county)**: The county population estimate of July 1, 2014, U.S. Census Bureau. The line following gives the percentage of increase or decrease from the 2010 U.S. census count.

**Area**: Total area in square miles, including water surfaces, as determined in the 2010 U.S. census.

**Land Area**: The land area in square miles as determined by the U.S. Census Bureau in 2010.

**Altitude** (ft.): Principally from U.S. Geological Survey topographic maps, including revisions available in 2008. Not all of the surface of Texas has been precisely surveyed for elevation; in some cases data are from the Texas Railroad Commission or the Texas Department of Transportation.

**Climate**: Provided by the National Oceanic and Atmospheric Administration state climatologist, College Station. Data are revised at 10-year intervals to cover the previous three decades. Listed are the latest compilations, as of Feb. 1, 2013, and pertain to a particular site within the county (usually the county seat). The data include: **Rainfall** (annual mean in inches); **Temperature** (in degrees Fahrenheit); January mean minimum and July mean maximum.

**Workforce/Wages**: Prepared by the Texas Workforce Commission, Austin, in cooperation with the Bureau of Labor Statistics of the U.S. Department of Labor. The data are computed from reports by all establishments subject to the Texas Unemployment Compensation Act.

(Agricultural employers are subject to the act if they employ as many as three workers for 20 weeks or pay cash wages of $6,250 in a quarter. Employers who pay $1,000 in wages in a quarter for domestic services are subject also. Still not mandatorily covered are self-employed, unpaid family workers, and those employed by churches and some small nonprofit organizations.)

The work/wage data include (state total, lowest county and highest county included here):

**Civilian labor force** as of July 2014. Texas, 13,079,296; Loving County, 40; Harris County, 2,197,938.

**Unemployed**: The unemployment rate (percentage of workforce) as of July 2014. Texas, 5.6; McMullen County, 1.9; Starr County, 14.2.

**Total Wages** paid in the third quarter of 2013. Texas, $136,686,322,365; Loving County $950,546; Harris County, $33,768,162,528.

**Per Capita Income** is for 2013, as reported by the U.S. Bureau of Economic Analysis. Texas, $43,862; Midland County, $87,897; Starr County, $20,811.

**Property Values**: Appraised gross market value of real and personal property in each county appraisal district in 2013 as reported to the State Property Tax Board.

**Retail Sales**: Figures for 2013 as reported to the state Comptroller of Public Accounts.

# Anderson County

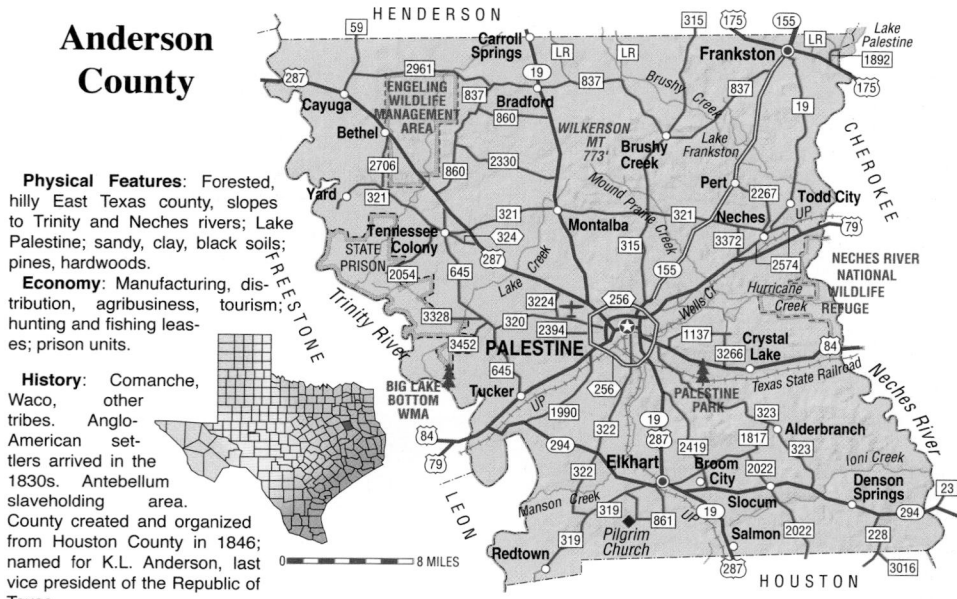

**Physical Features**: Forested, hilly East Texas county, slopes to Trinity and Neches rivers; Lake Palestine; sandy, clay, black soils; pines, hardwoods.

**Economy**: Manufacturing, distribution, agribusiness, tourism; hunting and fishing leases; prison units.

**History**: Comanche, Waco, other tribes. Anglo-American settlers arrived in the 1830s. Antebellum slaveholding area. County created and organized from Houston County in 1846; named for K.L. Anderson, last vice president of the Republic of Texas.

**Race/Ethnicity**: (In percent) Anglo, 60.2; Black, 21.5; Hispanic, 16.9; Asian, 0.8; Other, 2.3.

**Vital Statistics**, annual: Births, 564; deaths, 618; marriages, 370; divorces, 96.

**Recreation**: Fishing, hunting, streams, lakes; dogwood trails; national wildlife refuge; historic sites; railroad park; museums.

**Minerals**: Oil and gas.

**Agriculture**: Cattle, hay, truck vegetables, melons, pecans, peaches. Market value $44.6 million. Timber sold.

**PALESTINE** (18,922), county seat; clothing, metal, wood products; transportation and agribusiness center; scientific balloon station; historic bakery; library; vocational-technical facilities; hospitals; community college; dulcimer festival in March, hot pepper festival in October.

Other towns include: **Cayuga** (137); **Elkhart** (1,382); **Frankston** (1,196), tourism, packaging industry, oil and gas, commuters to Tyler; depot museum, Square Fair in October; **Montalba** (110); **Neches** (175); and **Tennessee Colony** (300) site of state prisons.

Population ............................ **57,627**
Change fm 2010 ........................ – 1.4
Area (sq. mi.) ......................... 1,078.0
Land Area (sq. mi.) ................... 1,062.6
Altitude (ft.) ........................... 174-773
Rainfall (in.) .............................. 46.60
Jan. mean min. .......................... 34.5
July mean max. .......................... 92.3
Civ. Labor ............................... 21,902
Unemployment ........................... 6.5
Wages ......................... $179,554,183
Per Capita Income ................. $30,065
Prop. Value ................. $3,826,323,353
Retail Sales ................. $516,118,936

## Railroad Abbreviations

| | |
|---|---|
| AAT | Austin Area Terminal Railroad |
| AGC | Alamo Gulf Coast Railway |
| ATK | AMTRAK |
| ANR | Angelina & Neches River Railroad |
| ATCX | Austin & Texas Central Railroad |
| BLR | Blacklands Railroad |
| BNSF | BNSF Railroad |
| BOP | Border Pacific Railroad |
| BRG | Brownsville & Rio Grande Int'l Railroad |
| CMC | CMC Railroad |
| DART | Dallas Area Rapid Transit |
| DGNO | Dallas, Garland & Northeastern Railroad |
| FWWR | Fort Worth & Western Railroad/Tarantula |
| GCSR | Gulf, Colorado & San Saba RailwayCorp. |
| GRR | Georgetown Railroad |
| GVSR | Galveston Railroad |
| KCS | Kansas City Southern Railway |
| KRR | Kiamichi Railroad Company |
| MCSA | Moscow, Camden & San Augustine RR |
| PCN | Point Comfort & Northern Railway |
| PNR | Panhandle Northern Railroad Company |
| PTRA | Port Terminal Railroad Association |
| PVS | Pecos Valley Southern Railway |
| RC | Rusk County Rural Rail Transportation District |
| RSS | Rockdale, Sandow & Southern Railroad |
| RVSC | Rio Valley Switching |
| SAW | South Plains Switching LTD |
| SRN | Sabine River & Northern Railroad Company |
| SSC | Southern Switching (Lone Star Railroad) |
| SW | Southwestern Shortline Railroad |
| TCT | Texas City Terminal Railway |
| TIBR | Timber Rock Railroad |
| TM | The Texas Mexican Railway Company |
| TN | Texas & Northern Railway |
| TNER | Texas Northeastern Railroad |
| TNMR | Texas & New Mexico Railroad |
| TNW | Texas North Western Railway |
| TP | Texas Pacifico Transportation |
| TSE | Texas South-Eastern Railroad Company |
| TXGN | Texas, Gonzales & Northern Railway |
| TXR | Texas Rock Crusher Railway |
| TSSR | Texas State Railroad |
| UP | Union Pacific Railroad Company |
| WTJR | Wichita, Tillman & Jackson Railway |
| WTLR | West Texas & Lubbock Railroad |

# Andrews County

**Physical Features**: South Plains, drain to playas; grass, mesquite, shin oak; red clay, sandy soils.

**Economy**: Natural resources/mining; manufacturing; trade, construction; government/services; agribusiness.

**History**: Apache, Comanche area until U.S. Army campaigns of 1875. Ranching developed around 1900. Oil boom in 1940s. County created 1876 from Bexar Territory; organized 1910; named for Texas Revolutionary soldier Richard Andrews.

**Race/Ethnicity**: (In percent) Anglo, 42.9; Black, 2.1; Hispanic, 53.4; Asian, 0.8; Other, 2.9.

**Vital Statistics**, annual: Births, 317; deaths, 139; marriages, 141; divorces, 66.

**Recreation**: Prairie dog town, wetlands, bird viewing; museum; camper facilities; Fall Fiesta in September.

**Minerals**: Oil and gas.

**Agriculture**: Beef, cotton, sorghums, grains, corn, hay; significant irrigation. Market value $12.6 million.

**ANDREWS** (12,736) county seat; trade center, amphitheatre, hospital.

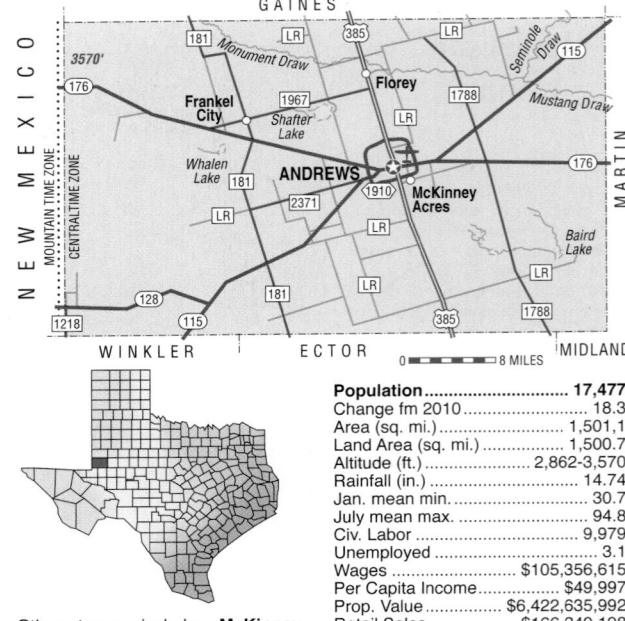

Other towns include, **McKinney Acres** (927).

| | |
|---|---|
| Population | **17,477** |
| Change fm 2010 | 18.3 |
| Area (sq. mi.) | 1,501,1 |
| Land Area (sq. mi.) | 1,500.7 |
| Altitude (ft.) | 2,862-3,570 |
| Rainfall (in.) | 14.74 |
| Jan. mean min. | 30.7 |
| July mean max. | 94.8 |
| Civ. Labor | 9,979 |
| Unemployed | 3.1 |
| Wages | $105,356,615 |
| Per Capita Income | $49,997 |
| Prop. Value | $6,422,635,992 |
| Retail Sales | $166,249,198 |

# Angelina County

**Physical Features**: Rolling, hilly East Texas county; black, red, gray soils; Angelina National Forest.

**Economy**: Timber; manufacturers of iron and steel castings, truck trailers, mobile homes; government/services; wood and paper products.

**History**: Caddoan area. First land deed to Vicente Micheli 1801. Anglo-American settlers arrived in 1820s. County created and organized in 1846 from Nacogdoches County; named for legendary Indian maiden Angelina.

**Race/Ethnicity**: (In percent) Anglo, 62.0; Black, 15.6; Hispanic, 20.8; Asian, 1.1; Other, 2.0.

**Vital Statistics**, annual: Births, 1,193; deaths, 866; marriages, 752; divorces, 402.

**Recreation**: Sam Rayburn Reservoir; national, state forests, parks; locomotive exhibit in Lufkin; Texas State Forest Festival and bike ride in September/October.

**Minerals**: Limited output of natural gas and oil.

**Agriculture**: Poultry, beef, horticulture, limited fruits and vegetables. Market value $46.4 million. A leading timber-producing county.

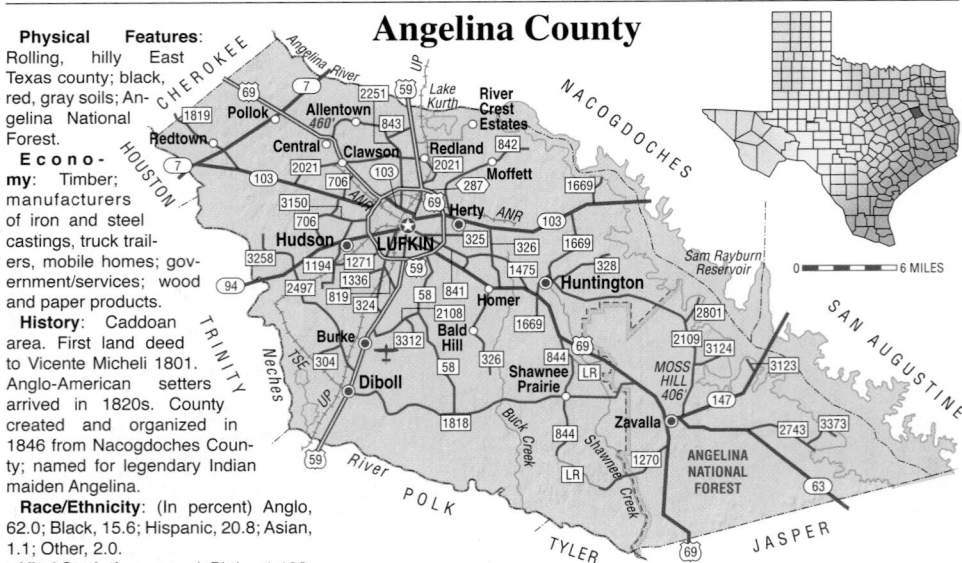

**LUFKIN** (36,656) county seat; manufacturing; Angelina College; hospitals; U.S., Texas Forest centers; zoo; Expo Center and Texas Forestry Museum.

Other towns include: **Burke** (734); **Diboll** (5,446); **Hudson** (4,779); **Huntington** (2,148); **Pollok** (400); **Zavalla** (726).

*For explanation of sources, abbreviations and symbols, see p. 238, and foldout map.*

| | |
|---|---|
| Population | **87,750** |
| Change from 2010 | 1.1 |
| Area (sq. mi.) | 864.7 |
| Land Area (sq. mi.) | 797.8 |
| Altitude (ft.) | 102-460 |
| Rainfall (in.) | 48.95 |
| Jan. mean min. | 38.3 |
| July mean max. | 93.3 |
| Civ. Labor | 40,378 |
| Unemployed | 5.5 |
| Wages | $331,586,318 |
| Per Capita Income | $36,112 |
| Prop. Value | $5,075,925,179 |
| Retail Sales | $1,232,975,333 |

# Mileage between T

| | Abilene | Amarillo | Austin | Beaumont | Big Bend | Big Spring | Brownsville | Brownwood | Bryan | Childress | Corpus Christi | Dalhart | Dallas | Del Rio | El Paso | Fort Stockton | Fort Worth |
|---|---|---|---|---|---|---|---|---|---|---|---|---|---|---|---|---|---|
| **Amarillo** | 266 | | | | | | | | | | | | | | | | |
| **Austin** | 213 | 478 | | | | | | | | | | | | | | | |
| **Beaumont** | 412 | 637 | 238 | | | | | | | | | | | | | | |
| **Big Bend** | 392 | 484 | 462 | 699 | | | | | | | | | | | | | |
| **Big Spring** | 107 | 222 | 289 | 519 | 281 | | | | | | | | | | | | |
| **Brownsville** | 516 | 765 | 325 | 437 | 636 | 567 | | | | | | | | | | | |
| **Brownwood** | 77 | 342 | 137 | 350 | 398 | 174 | 471 | | | | | | | | | | |
| **Bryan** | 253 | 503 | 100 | 158 | 559 | 360 | 382 | 191 | | | | | | | | | |
| **Childress** | 154 | 116 | 367 | 521 | 483 | 204 | 671 | 231 | 388 | | | | | | | | |
| **Corpus Christi** | 387 | 636 | 192 | 288 | 524 | 438 | 159 | 329 | 237 | 542 | | | | | | | |
| **Dalhart** | 343 | 82 | 556 | 719 | 525 | 294 | 842 | 420 | 637 | 197 | 713 | | | | | | |
| **Dallas** | 180 | 361 | 192 | 276 | 559 | 287 | 517 | 157 | 165 | 245 | 377 | 443 | | | | | |
| **Del Rio** | 246 | 450 | 232 | 434 | 253 | 231 | 378 | 231 | 318 | 382 | 268 | 520 | 388 | | | | |
| **El Paso** | 439 | 418 | 573 | 810 | 329 | 332 | 801 | 493 | 660 | 482 | 691 | 617 | 424 | | | | |
| **Fort Stockton** | 250 | 338 | 335 | 572 | 136 | 143 | 563 | 260 | 422 | 347 | 453 | 398 | 416 | 185 | 238 | | |
| **Fort Worth** | 150 | 337 | 187 | 301 | 529 | 257 | 512 | 127 | 167 | 222 | 372 | 419 | 30 | 358 | 587 | 385 | |
| **Gainesville** | 195 | 309 | 252 | 345 | 584 | 301 | 577 | 185 | 232 | 193 | 437 | 391 | 69 | 416 | 625 | 439 | 65 |
| **Galveston** | 398 | 646 | 206 | 78 | 651 | 493 | 374 | 336 | 145 | 531 | 219 | 728 | 288 | 393 | 774 | 536 | 309 |
| **Houston** | 348 | 596 | 162 | 86 | 603 | 449 | 352 | 286 | 95 | 480 | 207 | 678 | 238 | 349 | 730 | 492 | 259 |
| **Huntsville** | 304 | 528 | 153 | 113 | 602 | 411 | 414 | 241 | 54 | 412 | 269 | 610 | 170 | 369 | 714 | 475 | 191 |
| **Laredo** | 373 | 609 | 232 | 396 | 434 | 406 | 199 | 330 | 318 | 528 | 141 | 686 | 424 | 179 | 602 | 364 | 416 |
| **Longview** | 305 | 482 | 256 | 194 | 649 | 412 | 557 | 278 | 177 | 366 | 411 | 564 | 125 | 488 | 742 | 535 | 155 |
| **Lubbock** | 162 | 119 | 368 | 574 | 360 | 104 | 655 | 232 | 415 | 139 | 526 | 196 | 322 | 332 | 344 | 220 | 292 |
| **Lufkin** | 336 | 529 | 219 | 108 | 675 | 443 | 470 | 274 | 121 | 414 | 325 | 611 | 168 | 439 | 761 | 523 | 199 |
| **McAllen** | 480 | 728 | 300 | 430 | 578 | 531 | 56 | 423 | 364 | 634 | 152 | 806 | 491 | 322 | 745 | 507 | 486 |
| **Odessa** | 167 | 255 | 334 | 567 | 222 | 60 | 609 | 219 | 408 | 263 | 480 | 315 | 347 | 247 | 274 | 83 | 317 |
| **Paris** | 281 | 403 | 294 | 292 | 665 | 388 | 615 | 257 | 234 | 287 | 470 | 485 | 103 | 488 | 717 | 516 | 131 |
| **Pecos** | 240 | 320 | 388 | 625 | 190 | 133 | 616 | 293 | 475 | 337 | 506 | 374 | 420 | 238 | 207 | 53 | 390 |
| **San Angelo** | 89 | 293 | 203 | 436 | 300 | 87 | 481 | 96 | 277 | 225 | 352 | 371 | 252 | 158 | 402 | 164 | 222 |
| **San Antonio** | 244 | 493 | 79 | 281 | 406 | 295 | 272 | 187 | 165 | 398 | 143 | 570 | 271 | 154 | 548 | 310 | 262 |
| **South Padre** | 530 | 779 | 339 | 451 | 644 | 251 | 27 | 473 | 396 | 684 | 172 | 856 | 531 | 392 | 815 | 577 | 526 |
| **Texarkana** | 359 | 495 | 340 | 256 | 744 | 466 | 634 | 335 | 261 | 379 | 489 | 576 | 178 | 566 | 795 | 594 | 209 |
| **Tyler** | 277 | 457 | 224 | 192 | 647 | 384 | 526 | 242 | 145 | 342 | 381 | 539 | 97 | 455 | 714 | 500 | 127 |
| **Van Horn** | 328 | 401 | 454 | 690 | 199 | 221 | 682 | 378 | 540 | 425 | 571 | 447 | 508 | 304 | 119 | 119 | 478 |
| **Victoria** | 334 | 600 | 122 | 209 | 522 | 402 | 230 | 259 | 152 | 489 | 85 | 677 | 292 | 264 | 661 | 423 | 287 |
| **Waco** | 183 | 423 | 102 | 242 | 518 | 290 | 427 | 123 | 85 | 307 | 287 | 504 | 91 | 334 | 610 | 372 | 86 |
| **Wichita Falls** | 141 | 225 | 283 | 412 | 513 | 234 | 608 | 169 | 270 | 109 | 474 | 307 | 136 | 388 | 552 | 376 | 112 |

*Wil*

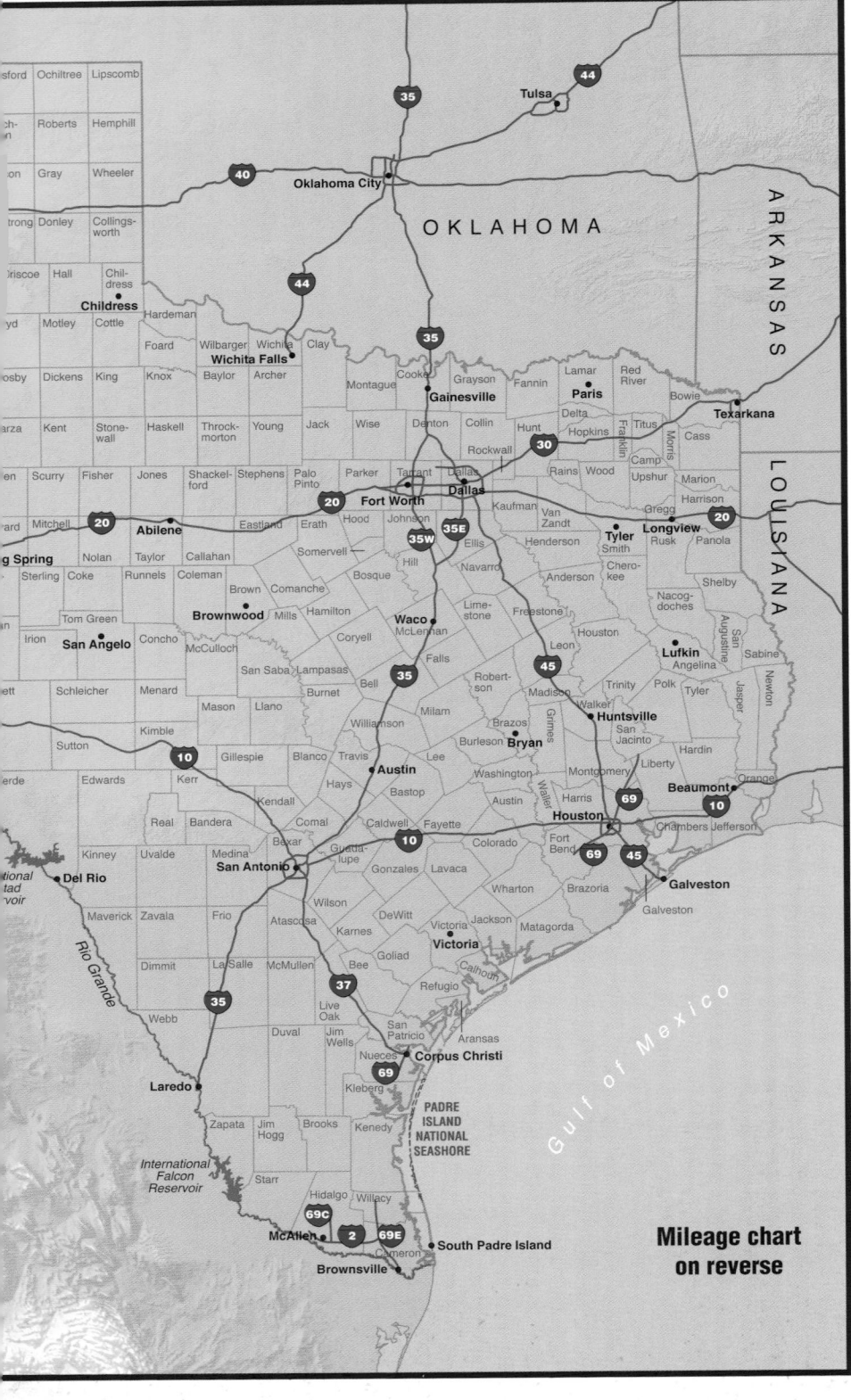

**Mileage chart on reverse**

| Worth | Gainesville | Galveston | Houston | Huntsville | Laredo | Longview | Lubbock | Lufkin | McAllen | Odessa | Paris | Pecos | San Angelo | San Antonio | South Padre Island | Texarkana | Tyler | Van Horn | Victoria |
|---|---|---|---|---|---|---|---|---|---|---|---|---|---|---|---|---|---|---|---|
| 458 | | | | | | | | | | | | | | | | | | | |
| 307 | 50 | | | | | | | | | | | | | | | | | | |
| 239 | 119 | 69 | | | | | | | | | | | | | | | | | |
| 480 | 341 | 311 | 365 | | | | | | | | | | | | | | | | |
| 78 | 253 | 206 | 151 | 488 | | | | | | | | | | | | | | | |
| 90 | 560 | 510 | 466 | 498 | 447 | | | | | | | | | | | | | | |
| 38 | 166 | 119 | 72 | 429 | 87 | 490 | | | | | | | | | | | | | |
| 51 | 367 | 345 | 398 | 143 | 541 | 618 | 463 | | | | | | | | | | | | |
| 60 | 538 | 494 | 458 | 422 | 472 | 137 | 491 | 565 | | | | | | | | | | | |
| 96 | 342 | 291 | 224 | 527 | 102 | 383 | 184 | 594 | 447 | | | | | | | | | | |
| 34 | 589 | 545 | 528 | 417 | 546 | 203 | 565 | 560 | 74 | 521 | | | | | | | | | |
| 75 | 407 | 363 | 327 | 321 | 372 | 183 | 360 | 444 | 131 | 352 | 205 | | | | | | | | |
| 26 | 241 | 197 | 217 | 154 | 334 | 382 | 285 | 236 | 336 | 373 | 363 | 209 | | | | | | | |
| 91 | 387 | 366 | 428 | 216 | 570 | 668 | 484 | 73 | 622 | 629 | 630 | 495 | 286 | | | | | | |
| 88 | 328 | 283 | 235 | 572 | 88 | 475 | 165 | 624 | 525 | 92 | 599 | 430 | 418 | 648 | | | | | |
| 59 | 247 | 197 | 130 | 456 | 36 | 419 | 84 | 508 | 444 | 101 | 517 | 336 | 302 | 540 | 116 | | | | |
| 22 | 654 | 610 | 594 | 483 | 633 | 291 | 642 | 626 | 161 | 608 | 88 | 282 | 428 | 696 | 686 | 605 | | | |
| 52 | 154 | 124 | 186 | 187 | 328 | 489 | 242 | 220 | 447 | 385 | 476 | 316 | 114 | 244 | 407 | 296 | 542 | | |
| 51 | 230 | 180 | 130 | 334 | 163 | 345 | 157 | 401 | 340 | 194 | 413 | 209 | 181 | 441 | 244 | 128 | 490 | 202 | |
| 84 | 421 | 371 | 303 | 490 | 257 | 208 | 304 | 572 | 293 | 178 | 366 | 230 | 336 | 621 | 270 | 232 | 454 | 399 | 198 |

*flowers near Highway 21 in Houston County. Photo by Ron Billings; Texas A&M Forest Service.*

# Counties
# of Texas

A close-up map of each
county is included with
each county article on
pages 239–415.

Below is the legend to the
symbols used on those maps:

## Legend to counties

| | |
|---|---|
| ———— | Principal road |
| ———— | Secondary road |
| ———— | Local road |
| ═══ | Divided highway |
| (10) | Interstate highway |
| (377) | U.S. highway |
| (81) | State highway |
| [308] | Farm-to-market road |
| [LR] | Local roads |
| (28) | Loop |
| +++++ | Railway |
| *BNSF* | Railway name |
| ∿ | River or creek |
| ⬭ | Lake |
| ⬭ | Intermittent water source |
| ———— | Intracoastal Waterway |
| ✪ | County seat |
| ◉ | Incorporated town |
| ○ | Unincorporated town |
| ----- | County boundary |
| PECOS | Name of neighboring county |
| *400'* | Elevation |
| *880'* | Highest point in county |
| ✈ | Major airport with scheduled jet service |
| ✟ | Municipal airport |
| ✦ | Military airport |
| 🌲 | National park or wildlife management area |
| ▭ | Federal land |
| 🌲 | State park or wildlife management area |
| ▭ | State land |
| ◆ | Ranger station |
| ········ | Time zone line |
| ▭ | Boundary of prison or military installation |

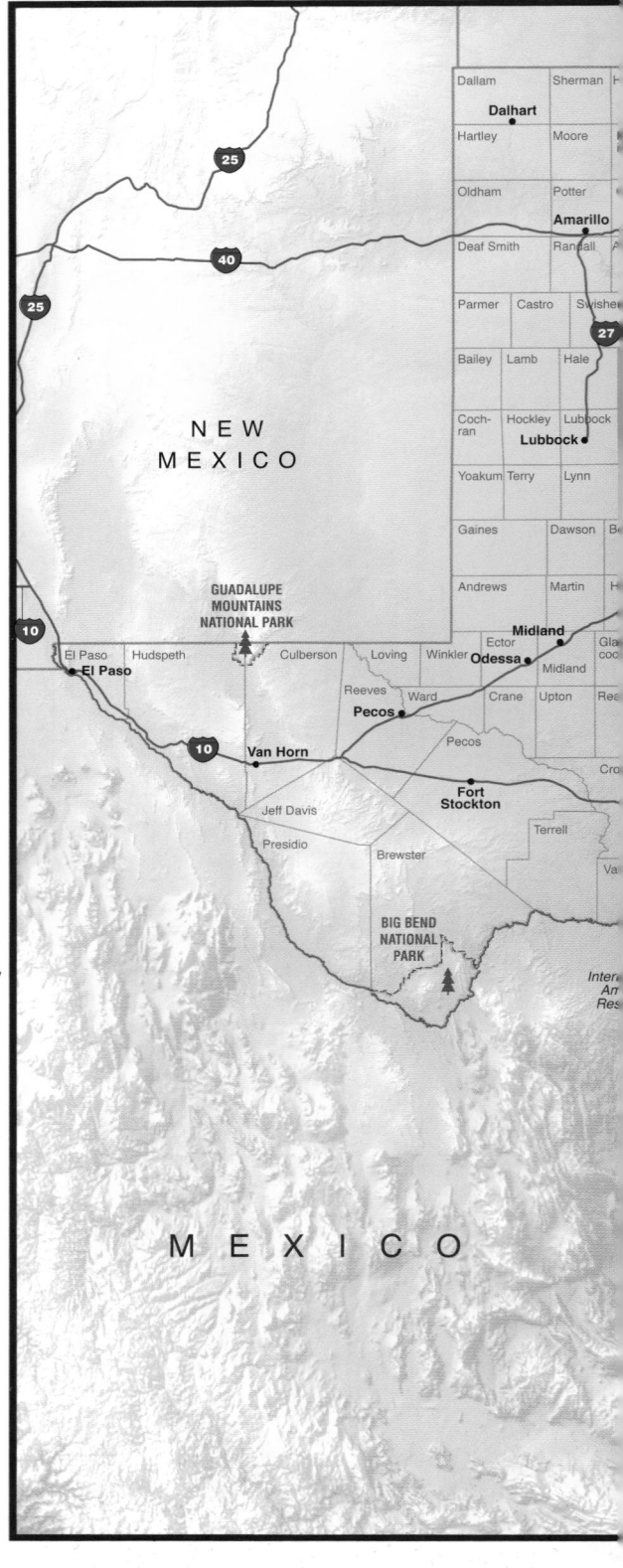

# Aransas County

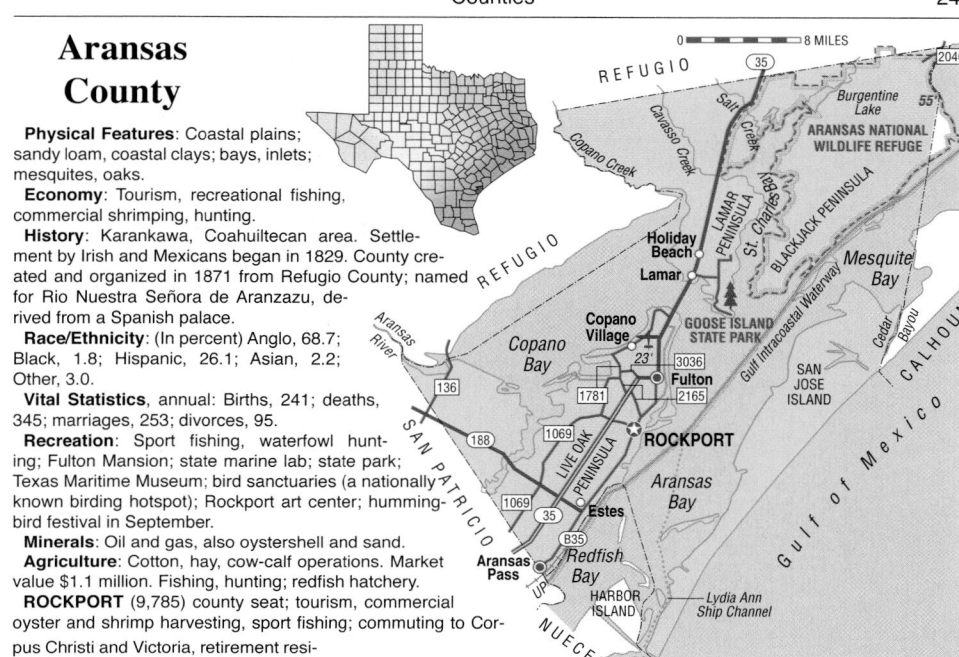

**Physical Features**: Coastal plains; sandy loam, coastal clays; bays, inlets; mesquites, oaks.

**Economy**: Tourism, recreational fishing, commercial shrimping, hunting.

**History**: Karankawa, Coahuiltecan area. Settlement by Irish and Mexicans began in 1829. County created and organized in 1871 from Refugio County; named for Rio Nuestra Señora de Aranzazu, derived from a Spanish palace.

**Race/Ethnicity**: (In percent) Anglo, 68.7; Black, 1.8; Hispanic, 26.1; Asian, 2.2; Other, 3.0.

**Vital Statistics**, annual: Births, 241; deaths, 345; marriages, 253; divorces, 95.

**Recreation**: Sport fishing, waterfowl hunting; Fulton Mansion; state marine lab; state park; Texas Maritime Museum; bird sanctuaries (a nationally known birding hotspot); Rockport art center; humming-bird festival in September.

**Minerals**: Oil and gas, also oystershell and sand.

**Agriculture**: Cotton, hay, cow-calf operations. Market value $1.1 million. Fishing, hunting; redfish hatchery.

**ROCKPORT** (9,785) county seat; tourism, commercial oyster and shrimp harvesting, sport fishing; commuting to Corpus Christi and Victoria, retirement residences; Festival of Wines in May.

**Fulton** (1,501) tourism, oyster and shrimp harvesting, Oysterfest in March; **Holiday Beach** (557); and **Lamar** (685).

Also, part [724] of **Aransas Pass**.

| | |
|---|---|
| **Population** | **24,972** |
| Change fm 2010 | 7.8 |
| Area (sq. mi.) | 528.0 |
| Land Area (sq. mi.) | 252.1 |
| Altitude (ft.) | sea level-26 |
| Rainfall (in.) | 34.59 |
| Jan. mean min. | 47.9 |
| July mean max. | 91.5 |
| Civ. Labor | 11,208 |
| Unemployed | 5.4 |
| Wages | $55,549,150 |
| Per Capita Income | $47,075 |
| Prop. Value | $3,046,990,029 |
| Retail Sales | $279,882,297 |

*Seagulls and fishing boats at Fulton. Photo by Robert Plocheck.*

# Archer County

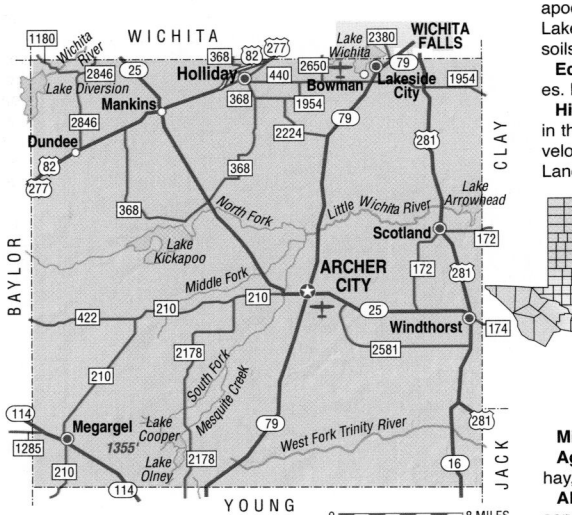

**Population** .................................**8,811**
Change fm 2010 ....................... − 2.7
Area (sq. mi.) ........................ 925.4
Land Area (sq. mi.) ................. 903,1
Altitude (ft.) ..................... 900-1,355
Rainfall (in.) ............................. 30.72
Jan. mean min. ........................ 29.0

July mean max. ......................... 96.5
Civ. Labor ................................ 4,712
Unemployed .............................. 4.4
Wages ........................... $17,736,483
Per Capita Income ............... $53,578
Prop. Value ................$1,767,253,811
Retail Sales ...................$63,211,466

**Physical Features**: Northwestern county, rolling to hilly, drained by Wichita, Trinity River forks; Lake Kickapoo, Lake Diversion, Lake Wichita, Lake Arrowhead, Lake Cooper and Lake Olney; black, red loams, sandy soils; mesquites, post oaks.

**Economy**: Cattle, milk production, oil, hunting leases. Part of Wichita Falls metropolitan area.

**History**: Caddo, Comanche, Kiowas and other tribes in the area until 1875; Anglo-American settlement developed soon afterward. County created from Fannin Land District in 1858; organized in 1880. Named for Dr. B.T. Archer, Republic commissioner to United States.

**Race/Ethnicity**: (In percent) Anglo, 88.6; Black, 0.8; Hispanic, 8.5; Asian, 0.3; Other, 2.8.

**Vital Statistics**, annual: Births, 75; deaths, 72; marriages, 42; divorces, 37.

**Recreation**: Hunting of deer, turkey, dove, feral hog, coyote; fishing in area lakes, county rodeo in June.

**Minerals**: Oil and natural gas.

**Agriculture**: Cow/calf, stocker cattle, dairy, wheat, hay, silage and horses. Market value $76.8 million.

**ARCHER CITY** (1,828) county seat; cattle, oil field service center; museum; book center; Royal Theatre productions; some manufacturing.

Other towns include: **Holliday** (1,798) Mayfest in spring; **Lakeside City** (1,039); **Megargel** (201); **Scotland** (513); **Windthorst** (425), biannual German sausage festival (also in Scotland).

# Armstrong County

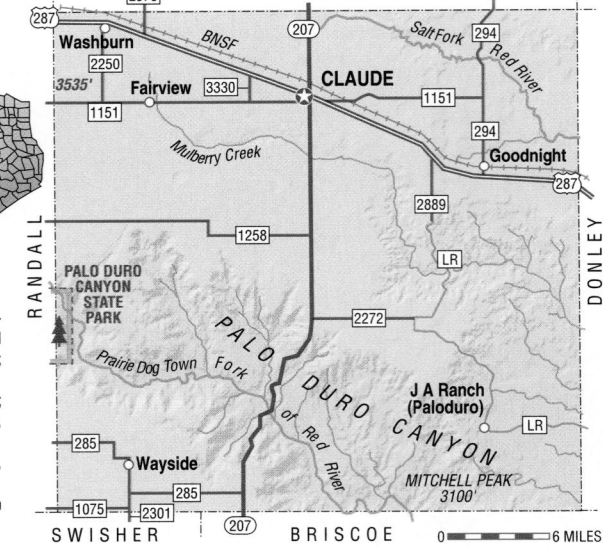

**Physical Features**: Partly on High Plains, broken by Palo Duro Canyon. Chocolate loam, gray soils.

**Economy**: Agribusiness, tourism, commuting to Amarillo.

**History**: Apache, then Comanche territory until U.S. Army campaigns of 1874-75. Anglo-Americans began ranching soon afterward. County created from Bexar District, 1876; organized 1890; name honors pioneer Texas family.

**Race/Ethnicity**: (In percent) Anglo, 87.1; Black, 1.4; Hispanic, 9.5; Asian, 0.0; Other, 2.5.

**Vital Statistics**, annual: Births, 30; deaths, 39; marriages, 9; divorces, 13.

**Recreation**: State park; Goodnight Ranch Home.

**Minerals**: Sand, gravel.

**Agriculture**: Stocker cattle, cow-calf operations; wheat, sorghum, cotton and hay; some irrigation. Market value $19.2 million.

**CLAUDE** (1,219) county seat; farm, ranch supplies; glass company; medical center; Caprock Roundup in July.

**Population** ............................... **1,955**
Change fm 2010 ........................... 2.8
Area (sq. mi.) ........................... 913.8
Land Area (sq. mi.) .................. 909.1
Altitude (ft.) .................... 2,300-3,535
Rainfall (in.) ............................. 22.25
Jan. mean min. .......................... 22.4
July mean max. .......................... 90.6
Civ. Labor ................................. 986

Unemployed ................................ 3.6
Wages .............................. $2,710,651
Per Capita Income ............... $46,513
Prop. Value ................ $538,268,750
Retail Sales .................... $7,556,676

*For explanation of sources, abbreviations and symbols, see p. 238, and foldout map.*

# Atascosa County

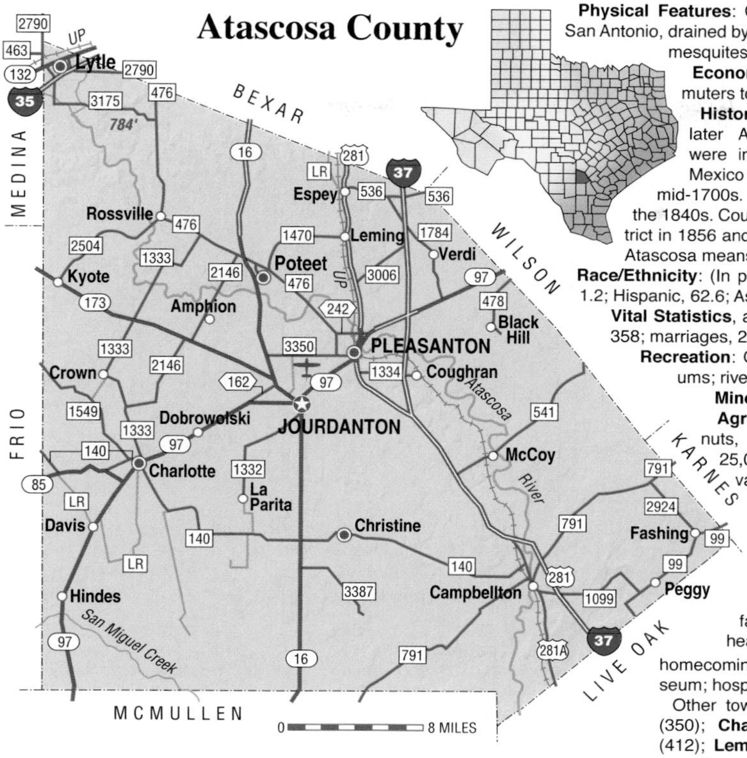

For explanation of sources, abbreviations and symbols, see p. 238, and foldout map.

**Physical Features**: On grassy prairie south of San Antonio, drained by Atascosa River, tributaries; mesquites, other brush.

**Economy**: Coal plant, oil, commuters to San Antonio.

**History**: Coahuiltecan Indians; later Apaches and Comanches were in the area. Families from Mexico established ranches in the mid-1700s. Anglo-Americans arrived in the 1840s. County created from Bexar District in 1856 and organized that same year. Atascosa means boggy in Spanish.

**Race/Ethnicity**: (In percent) Anglo, 35.3; Black, 1.2; Hispanic, 62.6; Asian, 0.6; Other, 2.4.

**Vital Statistics**, annual: Births, 644; deaths, 358; marriages, 292; divorces, 0.

**Recreation**: Quail, deer hunting; museums; river park; theater group.

**Minerals**: Lignite, oil, gas.

**Agriculture**: Beef cattle, peanuts, vegetable farming. Some 25,000 acres irrigated. Market value $85 million.

**JOURDANTON** (4,135) county seat; coal mining; hospital; park, walking trail; chili cookoff in May, Czech Day in July. **PLEASANTON** (9,524) farming, oil-field drilling, health services; cowboy homecoming in August, Longhorn museum; hospital.

Other towns include: **Campbellton** (350); **Charlotte** (1,803); **Christine** (412); **Leming** (1,011); **Lytle** (2,762) greenhouse, peanuts processed; **Peggy** (22); **Poteet** (3,414) government/services, library, strawberry festival in April.

| | |
|---|---|
| Population .............................. **47,774** | July mean max. .......................... 95.4 |
| Change frm 2010 ......................... 6.4 | Civ. Labor ................................. 20,543 |
| Area (sq. mi.) ......................... 1,221.5 | Unemployed ................................. 5.4 |
| Land Area (sq. mi.) ................. 1,219.5 | Wages ........................ $139,763,164 |
| Altitude (ft.) ............................ 180-784 | Per Capita Income ................. $36,060 |
| Rainfall (in.) ............................... 32.07 | Prop. Value ............... $4,560,122,104 |
| Jan. mean min. ........................... 39.3 | Retail Sales ................. $634,254,083 |

*The general store in Windthorst, Archer County. Photo by Robert Plocheck.*

# Austin County

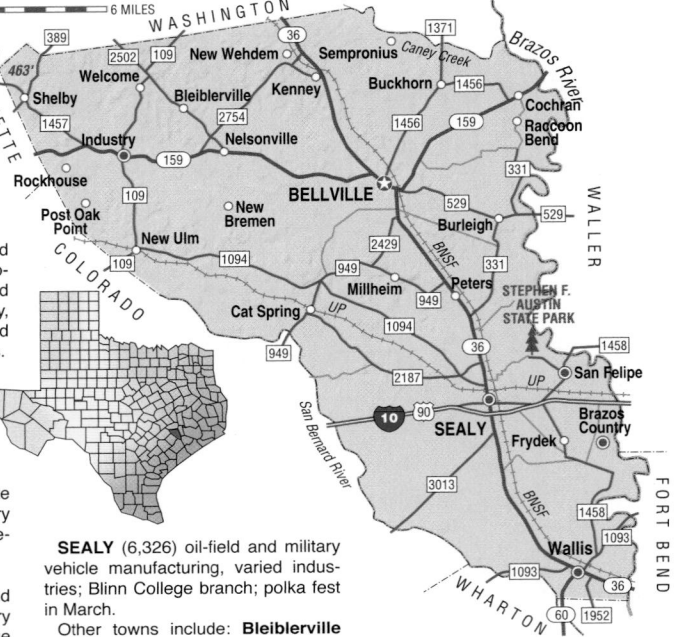

**Physical Features**: Level to hilly, drained by San Bernard, Brazos rivers; black prairie to sandy upland soils.

**Economy**: Agribusiness; tourism, government/services; metal, other manufacturing; commuting to Houston.

**History**: Tonkawa Indians; reduced by diseases. Birthplace of Anglo-American colonization, 1821, and German mother colony at Industry, 1831. County created 1837; named for Stephen F. Austin, father of Texas.

**Race/Ethnicity**: (In percent) Anglo, 63.8; Black, 9.6; Hispanic, 25.5; Asian, 0.5; Other, 2.2.

**Vital Statistics**, annual: Births, 348; deaths, 258; marriages, 198; divorces, 105.

**Recreation**: Fishing, hunting; state park, Pioneer Trail; Bellville Country Livin' festival in April; Lone Star Raceway Park.

**Minerals**: Oil and natural gas.

**Agriculture**: Beef production and hay. Also rice, corn, sorghum, nursery crops, grapes, pecans. Market value $43.5 million.

**BELLVILLE** (4,232) county seat; varied manufacturing; hospital; oil.

**SEALY** (6,326) oil-field and military vehicle manufacturing, varied industries; Blinn College branch; polka fest in March.

Other towns include: **Bleiblerville** (125); **Brazos Country** (488); **Cat Spring** (200); **Frydek** (900) Grotto celebration in April; **Industry** (315); **Kenney** (957); **New Ulm** (974) retail, art festival in April; **San Felipe** (788) colonial capital of Texas; **Wallis** (1,290) autofest in October.

| | |
|---|---|
| Population | **29,144** |
| Change fm 2010 | 2.5 |
| Area (sq. mi.) | 656.4 |
| Land Area (sq. mi.) | 646.5 |
| Altitude (ft.) | 70-463 |

| | |
|---|---|
| Rainfall (in.) | 41.75 |
| Jan. mean min. | 39.7 |
| July mean max. | 93.2 |
| Civ. Labor | 14,775 |
| Unemployed | 5.0 |

| | |
|---|---|
| Wages | $109,288,864 |
| Per Capita Income | $43,550 |
| Prop. Value | $4,537,088,108 |
| Retail Sales | $2,018,688,182 |

# Bailey County

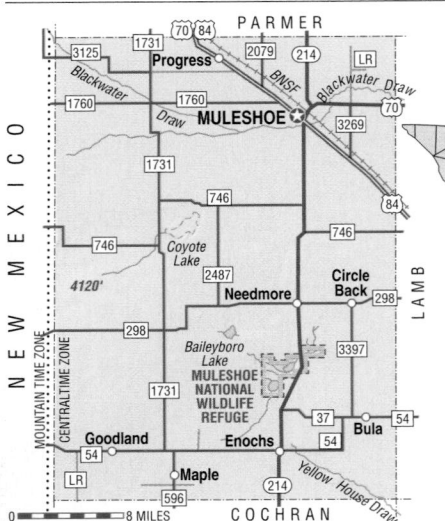

**Physical Features**: High Plains county, sandy loam soils; mesquite brush; drains to draws forming upper watershed of Brazos River, playas.

**Economy**: Farm supply manufacturing; electric generating plant; food-processing plants.

**History**: Settlement began after 1900. County created from Bexar District 1876, organized 1917. Named for Alamo hero Peter J. Bailey.

**Race/Ethnicity**: (In percent) Anglo, 36.6; Black, 1.6; Hispanic, 61.1; Asian, 0.7; Other, 3.7.

**Vital Statistics**, annual: Births, 116; deaths, 65; marriages, 44; divorces, 20.

**Recreation**: Muleshoe National Wildlife Refuge; "Old Pete," the national mule memorial; historical building park; museum; motorcycle rally; mule deer, sandhill crane, pheasant hunting.

**Minerals**: Insignificant.

**Agriculture**: Feedlot, dairy cattle; cotton, wheat, sorghum, corn, vegetables; some 50,000 acres irrigated. Market value $292 million.

**MULESHOE** (5,078) county seat; agribusiness center; feed-corn milling; hospital; livestock show.

Other towns include: **Enochs** (80); **Maple** (40).

| | |
|---|---|
| Population | **6,910** |
| Change fm 2010 | – 3.6 |
| Area (sq. mi.) | 827.5 |
| Land Area (sq. mi.) | 826.8 |
| Altitude (ft.) | 3,660-4,120 |
| Rainfall (in.) | 18.38 |

| | |
|---|---|
| Jan. mean min. | 19.4 |
| July mean max. | 92.0 |
| Civ. Labor | 3,172 |
| Unemployed | 5.5 |

| | |
|---|---|
| Wages | $21,004,948 |
| Per Capita Income | $37,877 |
| Prop. Value | $444,807,224 |
| Retail Sales | $38,182,898 |

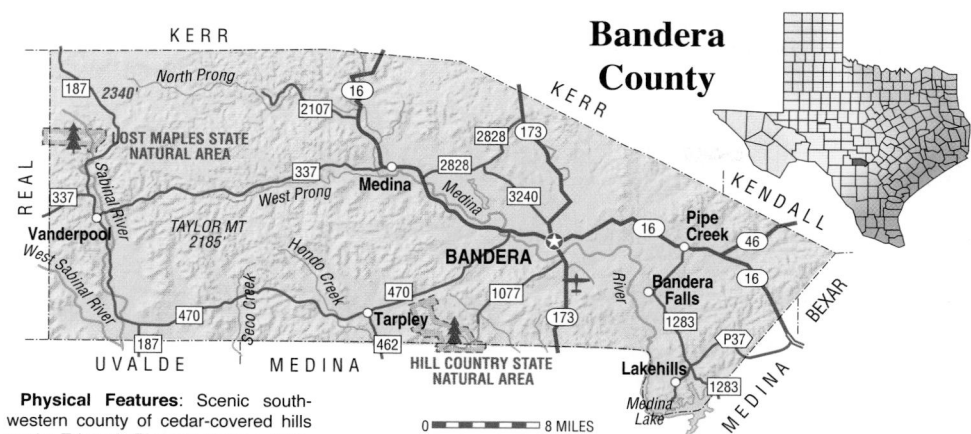

# Bandera County

**Physical Features**: Scenic southwestern county of cedar-covered hills on the Edwards Plateau; Medina, Sabinal Rivers; limestone, sandy soils; species of oaks, walnuts, native cherry and Uvalde maple.

**Economy**: Tourism, hunting, fishing, ranching supplies, forest products.

**History**: Apache, then Comanche territory. White settlement began in the early 1850s, including Mormons and Poles. County, created, organized, from Bexar, Uvalde counties in 1856; named for Bandera (flag) Mountains.

**Race/Ethnicity**: (In percent) Anglo, 79.7; Black, 0.7; Hispanic, 17.4; Asian, 0.5, Other, 2.6.

**Vital Statistics**, annual: Births, 164; deaths, 181; marriages, 121; divorces, 77.

**Recreation**: RV parks, resort ranches; Lost Maples and Hill Country State Natural Areas; rodeo on Memorial Day weekend; Medina Lake.

**Minerals**: Not significant.

**Agriculture**: Beef cattle, sheep, goats, horses, deer (first in numbers in captivity), apples. Market value $11.2 million. Hunting and nature tourism important.

**BANDERA** (883) county seat; "cowboy capital of the world"; tourism, ranching, furniture making; Frontier Times Museum.

Other towns include: **Medina** (850) apple growing; **Pipe Creek** (130); **Tarpley** (30); **Vanderpool** (20).

Also, the community of **Lakehills** (5,285) on Medina Lake, Cajun Fest in September, and **Lake Medina Shores** (1,273).

| Population | 20,892 |
|---|---|
| Change fm 2010 | 2.0 |
| Area (sq. mi.) | 797.6 |
| Land Area (sq. mi.) | 791.0 |
| Altitude (ft.) | 1,064-2,340 |
| Rainfall (in.) | 37.37 |
| Jan. mean min. | 34.5 |
| July mean max. | 93.0 |
| Civ. Labor | 10,012 |
| Unemployed | 4.9 |
| Wages | $23,408,817 |
| Per Capita Income | $42,262 |
| Prop. Value | $3,484,904,813 |
| Retail Sales | $99,545,258 |

*For explanation of sources, abbreviations and symbols, see p. 238, and foldout map.*

*Campers at Lost Maples State Natural Area in Bandera County. Photo by Robert Plocheck.*

# Bastrop County

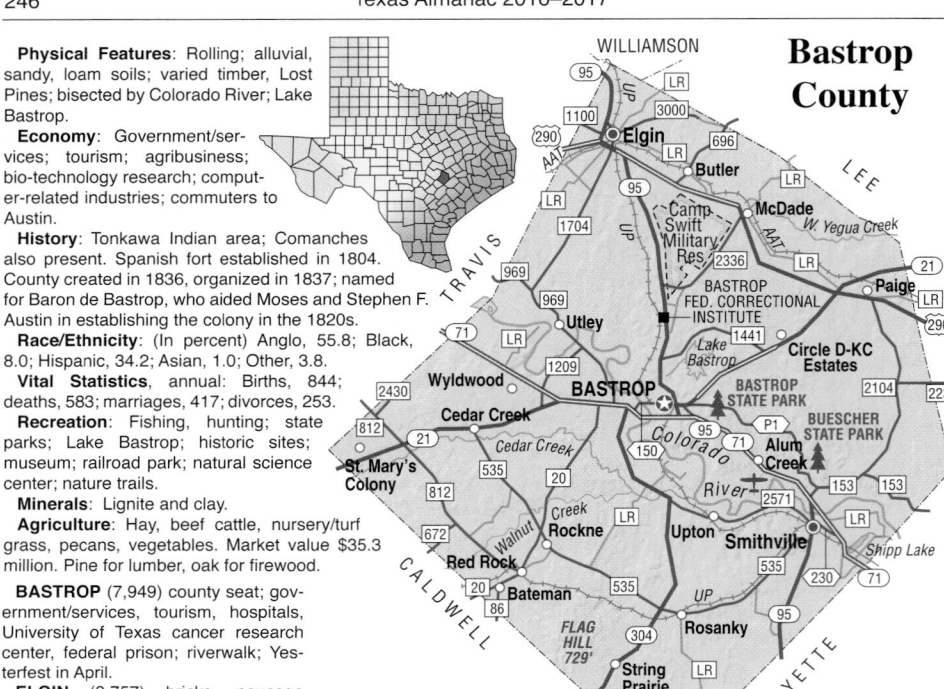

**Physical Features**: Rolling; alluvial, sandy, loam soils; varied timber, Lost Pines; bisected by Colorado River; Lake Bastrop.

**Economy**: Government/services; tourism; agribusiness; bio-technology research; computer-related industries; commuters to Austin.

**History**: Tonkawa Indian area; Comanches also present. Spanish fort established in 1804. County created in 1836, organized in 1837; named for Baron de Bastrop, who aided Moses and Stephen F. Austin in establishing the colony in the 1820s.

**Race/Ethnicity**: (In percent) Anglo, 55.8; Black, 8.0; Hispanic, 34.2; Asian, 1.0; Other, 3.8.

**Vital Statistics**, annual: Births, 844; deaths, 583; marriages, 417; divorces, 253.

**Recreation**: Fishing, hunting; state parks; Lake Bastrop; historic sites; museum; railroad park; natural science center; nature trails.

**Minerals**: Lignite and clay.

**Agriculture**: Hay, beef cattle, nursery/turf grass, pecans, vegetables. Market value $35.3 million. Pine for lumber, oak for firewood.

**BASTROP** (7,949) county seat; government/services, tourism, hospitals, University of Texas cancer research center, federal prison; riverwalk; Yesterfest in April.

**ELGIN** (8,757) bricks, sausage manufacturing; horse, cattle breeding; medical research; depot museum; Western Days in June, Hogeye festival in October.

**Smithville** (4,125) government/services, hospital, railroad; parks, hike & bike trails, museums; jamboree on weekend after Easter, Reel Film Expo in May.

Other towns: **Cedar Creek** (145); **Circle D-KC Estates** (2,622); **Mc-Dade** (731) watermelon festival in July; **Paige** (275); **Red Rock** (40); **Rosanky** (210) automotive museum; **Wyldwood** (2,695). Also, **Camp Swift** (6,714).

| | |
|---|---|
| Population | 78,069 |
| Change fm 2010 | 5.3 |
| Area (sq. mi.) | 895.6 |
| Land Area (sq. mi.) | 888.2 |
| Altitude (ft.) | 300-729 |
| Rainfall (in.) | 37.62 |
| Jan. mean min. | 37.6 |
| July mean max. | 95.4 |
| Civ. Labor | 37,042 |
| Unemployed | 5.6 |
| Wages | $126,980,737 |
| Per Capita Income | $31,552 |
| Prop. Value | $6,313,367,932 |
| Retail Sales | $1,007,452,241 |

*For explanation of sources, abbreviations and symbols, see p. 238, and foldout map.*

*Bicyclers in Bastrop State Park. The area was hit by a wildfire in 2010. Photo by Ron Billings, Texas A&M Forest Service.*

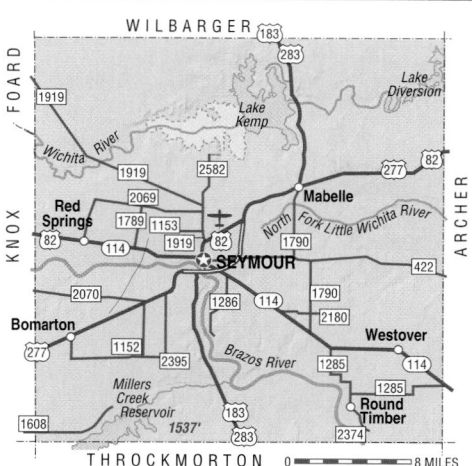

# Baylor County

**Physical Features**: Northwest county; level to hilly; drains to Brazos, Wichita rivers; Lake Kemp, Lake Diversion, Millers Creek Reservoir; sandy, loam, red soils; grassy, mesquites, cedars.

**Economy**: Agribusiness; retail/service; health services.

**History**: Comanches, with Wichitas and other tribes; removed in 1874-75. Anglo-Americans settled in the 1870s. County created from Fannin County 1858; organized 1879. Named for H.W. Baylor, Texas Ranger surgeon.

**Race/Ethnicity**: (In percent) Anglo, 83.2; Black, 3.0; Hispanic, 12.4; Asian, 0.1; Other, 2.1.

**Vital Statistics**, annual: Births, 48; deaths, 72; marriages, 20; divorces, 18.

**Recreation**: Lakes; hunting; settlers reunion, rodeo, go-cart races in July.

**Minerals**: Oil, gas produced.

**Agriculture**: Wheat, cattle, cow-calf operations, grain sorghum, cotton, hay. Market value $44.7 million.

SEYMOUR (2,610) county seat; agribusiness; hospital; dove hunters' breakfast in September.

| | |
|---|---|
| Population | 3,592 |
| Change fm 2010 | − 3.6 |
| Area (sq. mi.) | 901.1 |
| Land Area (sq. mi.) | 867.5 |
| Altitude (ft.) | 1,053-1,537 |
| Rainfall (in.) | 28.95 |
| Jan. mean min. | 28.1 |
| July mean max. | 96.5 |
| Civ. Labor | 1,895 |
| Unemployed | 4.3 |
| Wages | $9,170,252 |
| Per Capita Income | $40,331 |
| Prop. Value | $723,283,030 |
| Retail Sales | $28,731,868 |

# Bee County

**Physical Features**: South Coastal Plain, level to rolling; black clay, sandy, loam soils; brushy.

**Economy**: Agriculture, government/services; hunting leases; oil and gas business.

**History**: Karankawa, Apache, Pawnee territory. First Spanish land grant, 1789. Irish settlers arrived 1826-29. County created from Karnes, Live Oak, Goliad, Refugio, San Patricio, 1857; organized 1858; named for Barnard Bee Sr., secretary of state and diplomat for the Republic.

**Race/Ethnicity**: (In percent) Anglo, 33.1; Black, 8.5; Hispanic, 57.4; Asian, 0.6; Other, 2.0.

**Vital Statistics**, annual: Births, 360; deaths, 221; marriages, 216; divorces, 74.

**Recreation**: Hunting, birding, camping; historical sites, antiques; rodeo/roping events.

**Minerals**: Oil, gas produced.

**Agriculture**: Beef cattle, corn, cotton and grain sorghum. Market value $26 million. Hunting leases.

BEEVILLE (13,061) county seat; aircraft maintenance, waste-bind manufacturing, retail center; Costal Bend College; hospital; art museum; Diez y Seis festival in September.

Other towns and places include: **Blueberry Hill** (880); **Mineral** (65); **Normanna** (117); **Pawnee** (165); **Pettus** (560); **Skidmore** (918); **Tuleta** (296); **Tynan** (282).

| | |
|---|---|
| Population | 32,863 |
| Change fm 2010 | 3.1 |
| Area (sq. mi.) | 880.3 |
| Land Area (sq. mi.) | 880.2 |
| Altitude (ft.) | 39-540 |
| Rainfall (in.) | 31.95 |
| Jan. mean min. | 43.7 |
| July mean max. | 93.9 |
| Civ. Labor | 13,618 |
| Unemployed | 6.2 |
| Wages | $103,221,354 |
| Per Capita Income | $31,135 |
| Prop. Value | $2,216,607,550 |
| Retail Sales | $340,495,807 |

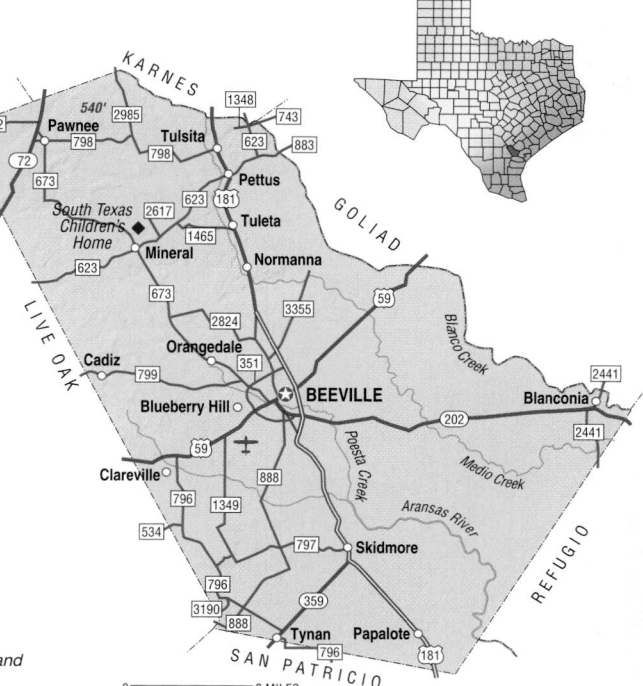

For explanation of sources, abbreviations and symbols, see p. 238, and foldout map.

# Bell County

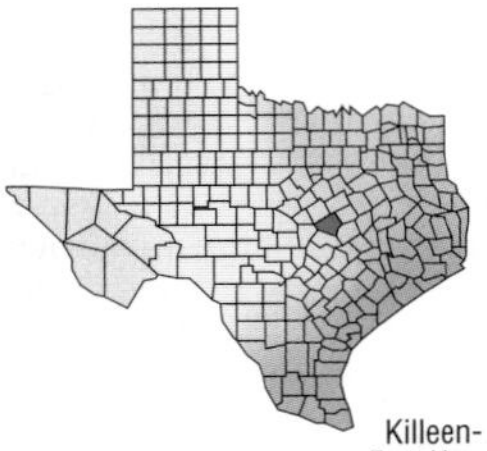

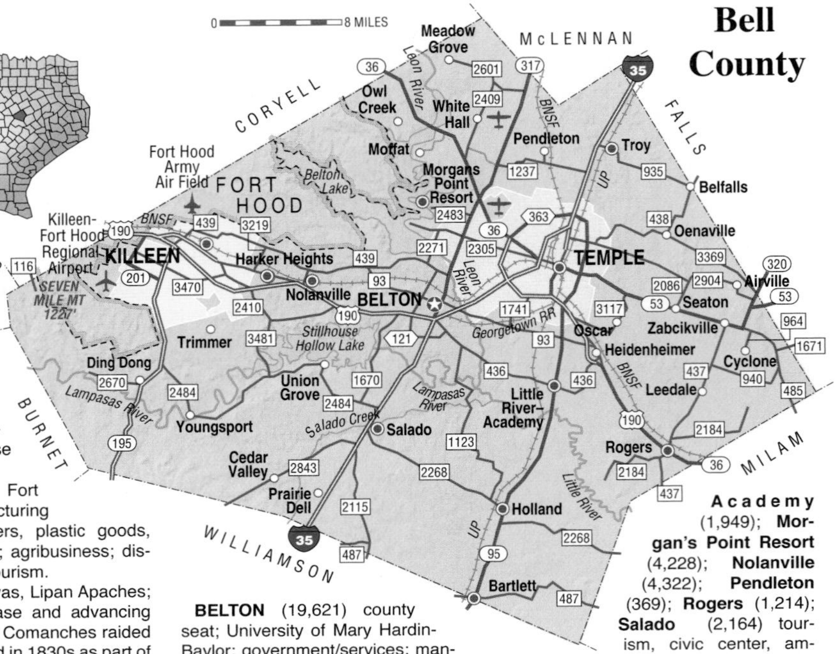

0 ▬▬▬▬ 8 MILES

**Physical Features**: Central Texas Blackland, level to hilly; black to light soils in west; mixed timber; Belton Lake, Stillhouse Hollow Lake.

**Economy**: Fort Hood; manufacturing includes computers, plastic goods, furniture, clothing; agribusiness; distribution center; tourism.

**History**: Tonkawas, Lipan Apaches; reduced by disease and advancing frontier by 1840s. Comanches raided into 1870s. Settled in 1830s as part of Robertson's colony. A few slaveholders in 1850s. County created from Milam County in 1850; named for Gov. P.H. Bell.

**Race/Ethnicity**: (In percent) Anglo, 48.9; Black, 22.4; Hispanic, 23.2; Asian, 3.2; Other, 6.2.

**Vital Statistics**, annual: Births, 6,215; deaths, 1,881; marriages, 4,209; divorces, 2,510.

**Recreation**: Fishing, hunting; lakes; historic sites; exposition center; Salado gathering of Scottish clans in November.

**Minerals**: Gravel.

**Agriculture**: Beef, corn, sorghum, wheat, cotton. Market value $84.9 million.

**BELTON** (19,621) county seat; University of Mary Hardin-Baylor; government/services; manufacturing; museum, nature center.

**KILLEEN** (138,241) Fort Hood; colleges; regional airport; retail center, varied manufacturing; hospital; museums, planetarium; Four Winds Powwow in September.

**TEMPLE** (70,730) Major medical center with two hospitals and VA hospital; diversified industries; rail, wholesale distribution center; retail center; Temple College, Texas A&M College of Medicine; Azalee Marshall Cultural Activities Center; Czech museum; early-day tractor, engine show in October.

Other towns include: **Harker Heights** (28,233) Founder's Day in October; **Heidenheimer** (224); **Holland** (1,126) corn festival in June; **Little River-Academy** (1,949); **Morgan's Point Resort** (4,228); **Nolanville** (4,322); **Pendleton** (369); **Rogers** (1,214); **Salado** (2,164) tourism, civic center, amphitheathre, art fair in August; **Troy** (1,738). Also, part [690] of **Bartlett**.

**Fort Hood** has a population of 30,633.

| | |
|---|---|
| Population | 329,140 |
| Change fm 2010 | 6.1 |
| Area (sq. mi.) | 1,087.8 |
| Land Area (sq. mi.) | 1,051.0 |
| Altitude (ft.) | 390-1,227 |
| Rainfall (in.) | 36.11 |
| Jan. mean min. | 35.6 |
| July mean max. | 94.6 |
| Civ. Labor | 138,784 |
| Unemployed | 6.3 |
| Wages | $1,112,147,472 |
| Per Capita Income | $39,298 |
| Prop. Value | $16,348,947,444 |
| Retail Sales | $4,066,258,503 |

*Mission San Jose in San Antonio. Photo by Robert Plocheck.*

**Physical Features**: On edge of Balcones Escarpment, Coastal Plain; heavy black to thin limestone soils; spring-fed streams; underground water; mesquite, other brush; Braunig Lake, Calaveras Lake.

**Economy**: Medical/biomedical research and services; government center with large federal payroll, military bases; tourism; education center.

**History**: Coahuiltecan Indian area; also Lipan Apaches and Tonkawas present. Mission San Antonio de Valero (Alamo) founded in 1718. Canary Islanders arrived in 1731. Anglo-American settlers began arriving in the late 1820s. County created in 1836 from Spanish municipality named to honor the duke of Bexar; a colonial capital of Texas.

**Race/Ethnicity**: (In percent) Anglo, 29.5; Black, 8.2; Hispanic, 59.1; Asian, 2.8; Other, 3.5.

**Vital Statistics**, annual: Births, 26,277; deaths, 11,888; marriages, 12,741; divorces, 3,756.

**Recreation**: Historic sites include the Alamo, other missions, Casa Na-

# Bexar County

varro, La Villita; River Walk, El Mercado (market), Tower of the Americas, Brackenridge Park, zoo, SeaWorld, HemisFair Park, Institute of Texan Cultures; museums, symphony orchestra; hunting, fishing; NBA Spurs; Fiesta in April, Folklife Festival in June.

**Minerals**: Gravel, sand, limestone.

**Agriculture**: Nursery crops, beef cattle, grain sorghum, hay, corn. Market value $72.4 million.

**Education**: Fourteen colleges including Our Lady of the Lake University, St. Mary's University, Texas A&M University–San Antonio, Trinity University, the University of Texas at San Antonio.

**SAN ANTONIO** (1,393,875) county seat; Texas' second largest city; healthcare/biosciences, government/ services, manufacturing, tourism, information technology, aerospace, education, energy; Alamodome.

**Leon Springs** is now part of San Antonio.

Other towns include: **Alamo Heights** (7,570); **Balcones Heights** (2,996); **Castle Hills** (4,332); **China Grove** (1,263); **Converse** (20,739); **Elmendorf** (1,602); **Fair Oaks Ranch** (6,794); **Grey Forest** (499) Helotes (8,325) government/services, retail trade, Cornyval Festival in May, Highland games in April, John T. Floore Country Store, Gugger Homestead; **Hill Country Village** (1,036); **Hollywood Park** (3,182).

Also, **Kirby** (8,345); **Leon Valley** (10,893); **Live Oak** (14,974); **Macdona** (613); **Olmos Park** (2,337); **St. Hedwig** (2,277); **Selma** (7,431, parts in Guadalupe and Comal counties); **Shavano Park** (3,363); **Somerset** (1,734); **Terrell Hills** (5,199); **Universal City** (19,540); **Von Ormy** (1,111); **Windcrest** (5,700).

Part [1,157] of **Schertz** (35,510).

**Lackland** Air Force Base (10,837); **Randolph** Air Force Base (1,283).

| | |
|---|---|
| Population | 1,855,866 |
| Change fm 2010 | 8.2 |
| Area (sq. mi.) | 1,256.1 |
| Land Area (sq. mi.) | 1,239.8 |
| Altitude (ft.) | 400-1,896 |
| Rainfall (in.) | 32.27 |
| Jan. mean min. | 40.7 |
| July mean max. | 94.6 |
| Civ. Labor | 845,178 |
| Unemployed | 5.3 |
| Wages | $8,276,910,700 |
| Per Capita Income | $39,005 |
| Prop. Value | $114,700,600,900 |
| Retail Sales | $29,792,063,098 |

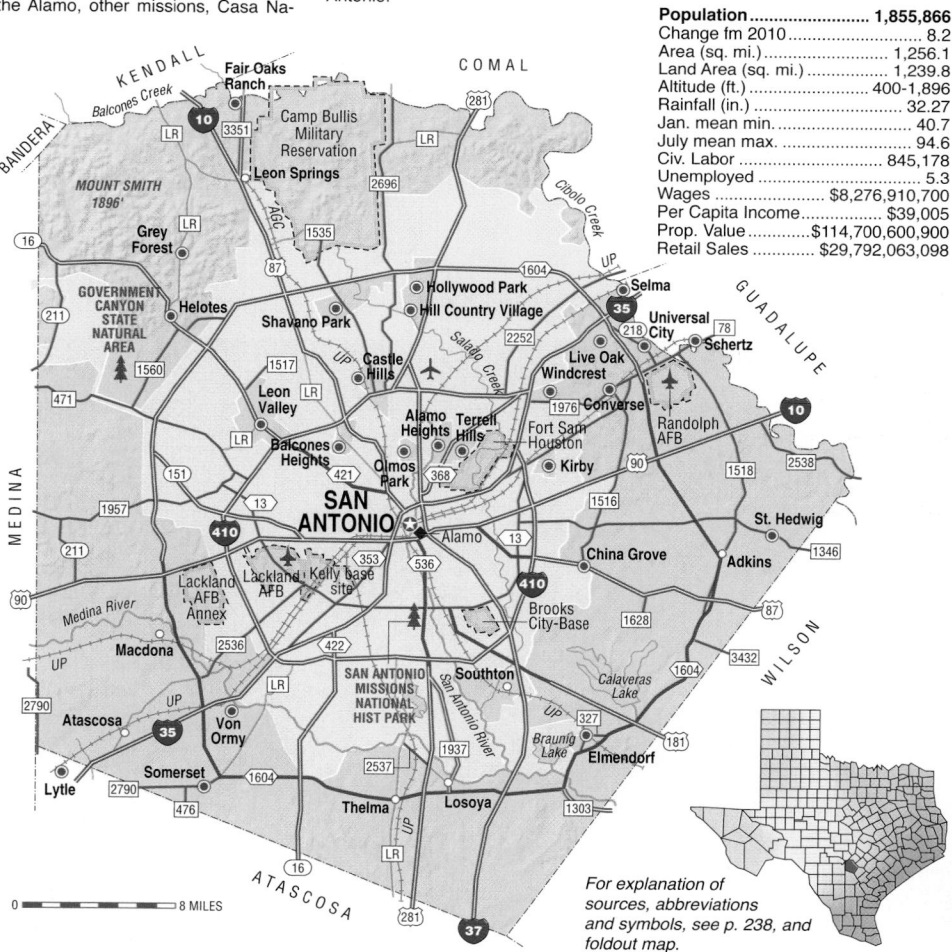

*For explanation of sources, abbreviations and symbols, see p. 238, and foldout map.*

# Blanco County

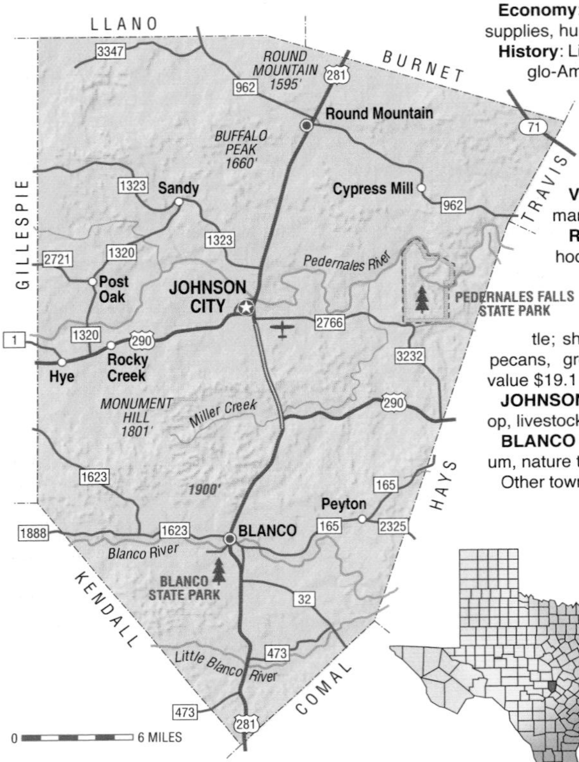

**Physical Features**: Hill Country county; Blanco, Pedernales rivers; cedars, pecans, live oaks, other trees.

**Economy**: Tourism, agribusiness/wholesale nursery, ranch supplies, hunting/fishing.

**History**: Lipan Apache area. Comanches present when Anglo-Americans settled in the 1850s. County created, organized, 1858 from Burnet, Comal, Gillespie, Hays counties; named for Blanco (white) River.

**Race/Ethnicity**: (In percent), Anglo, 77.1; Black, 1.3; Hispanic, 19.7; Asian, 0.5; Other, 4.0.

**Vital Statistics**, annual: Births, 90; deaths, 107; marriages, 72; divorces, 37.

**Recreation**: President Lyndon B. Johnson's boyhood home; state parks; hunting, fishing; scenic drives, wineries/vineyards.

**Minerals**: Insignificant.

**Agriculture**: Cow-calf operation, stocker cattle; sheep, goats; hay, vegetables, peaches, grapes, pecans, greenhouse nurseries; limited irrigation. Market value $19.1 million.

**JOHNSON CITY** (1,724) county seat; tourism, electric co-op, livestock center.

**BLANCO** (1,764) tourism, old courthouse, Pioneer museum, nature trail; lavender festival in June.

Other towns include: **Hye** (72) and **Round Mountain** (180).

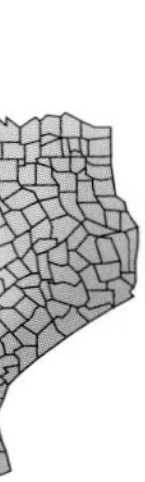

| | |
|---|---:|
| Population | 10,812 |
| Change fm 2010 | 3.0 |
| Area (sq. mi.) | 713.4 |
| Land Area (sq. mi.) | 709.3 |
| Altitude (ft.) | 741-1,900 |
| Rainfall (in.) | 34.87 |
| Jan. mean min. | 34.8 |
| July mean max. | 92.8 |
| Civ. Labor | 5,383 |
| Unemployed | 4.3 |
| Wages | $27,989,447 |
| Per Capita Income | $54,051 |
| Prop. Value | $3,974,506,587 |
| Retail Sales | $66,068,727 |

*Swimmers at Blanco State Park. Photo from Texas Parks & Wildlife.*

# Borden County

**Physical Features**: Rolling surface, broken by Caprock Escarpment; drains to Colorado River; sandy loam, clay soils.

**Economy**: Agriculture and hunting leases; oil; wind turbines.

**History**: Comanche area. Anglo-Americans settled in 1870s. County created 1876 from Bexar District, organized 1891; named for Gail Borden, patriot, inventor, editor.

**Race/Ethnicity**: (In percent) Anglo, 82.1; Black, 0.6; Hispanic, 15.5; Asian, 0.2; Other, 3.6.

**Vital Statistics**, annual: Births, 6; deaths, 3; marriages, 5; divorce, 1.

**Recreation**: Fishing; quail and deer hunting; Lake J.B. Thomas; museum; Coyote Opry in September; junior livestock show in January; ranch horse competition in September.

**Minerals**: Oil, gas, caliche, sand, gravel.

**Agriculture**: Beef cattle, cotton, wheat, hay, pecans, oats; some irrigation. Market value $9.4 million.

**GAIL** (256) county seat; museum, antique shop, ambulance service; "star" construction atop Gail Mountain.

*For explanation of sources, abbreviations and symbols, see p. 238, and foldout map.*

| | | |
|---|---|---|
| **Population** | 652 | |
| Change fm 2010 | 1.7 | |
| Area (sq. mi.) | 906.1 | |
| Land Area (sq. mi.) | 897.4 | |
| Altitude (ft.) | 2,258-2,990 | |
| Rainfall (in.) | 19.06 | |
| Jan. mean min. | 33.1 | |

| | |
|---|---|
| July mean max. | 94.8 |
| Civ. Labor | 544 |
| Unemployed | 2.6 |
| Wages | $1,543,259 |
| Per Capita Income | $61,289 |
| Prop. Value | $1,162,696,670 |
| Retail Sales | $193,631 |

# Bosque County

**Physical Features**: Hilly, broken by Brazos, Bosque rivers; limestone to alluvial soils; cedars, oaks, mesquites.

**Economy**: Agribusiness, government/services, small industries, tourism.

**History**: Tonkawa, Waco and Tawakoni Indians. Settlers from England and Norway arrived in 1850s. County created, organized, 1854 from Milam District, McLennan County; named for Bosque (woods) River.

**Race/Ethnicity**: (In percent) Anglo, 79.5; Black, 2.0; Hispanic, 16.7; Asian, 0.5; Other, 2.4.

**Vital Statistics**, annual: Births, 185; deaths, 247; marriages, 101; divorces, 54.

**Recreation**: Lake Whitney, state park, museum at Clifton, fine art conservatory; fishing, hunting; scenic routes, Norwegian smorgasbord at Norse in November.

**Minerals**: Limestone, gas & oil.

**Agriculture**: Beef cattle, forages, small grains, turkeys. Market value $78.3 million. Hunting leases.

**MERIDIAN** (1,498) county seat; food processing, government/services, tourism; retirement home, community college; national championship barbecue cookoff in October.

**CLIFTON** (3,416) retirement/health care, limestone sales, light manufacturing; hospital, nursing school; library; Norwegian historic district; Norwegian Country Christmas.

Other towns include: **Cranfills Gap** (285) Lutefisk dinner in December; **Iredell** (332); **Kopperl** (225); **Laguna Park** (1,338); **Morgan** (516); **Valley Mills** (1,223); **Walnut Springs** (843).

| | | |
|---|---|---|
| **Population** | 17,780 | |
| Change fm 2010 | - 2.4 | |
| Area (sq. mi.) | 1,002.5 | |
| Land Area (sq. mi.) | 983.0 | |
| Altitude (ft.) | 410-1,284 | |

| | |
|---|---|
| Rainfall (in.) | 36.04 |
| Jan. mean min. | 34.8 |
| July mean max. | 96.4 |
| Civ. Labor | 8,209 |
| Unemployed | 6.0 |
| Wages | $29,911,135 |
| Per Capita Income | $36,838 |
| Prop. Value | $2,809,448,149 |
| Retail Sales | $91,335,334 |

# Bowie County

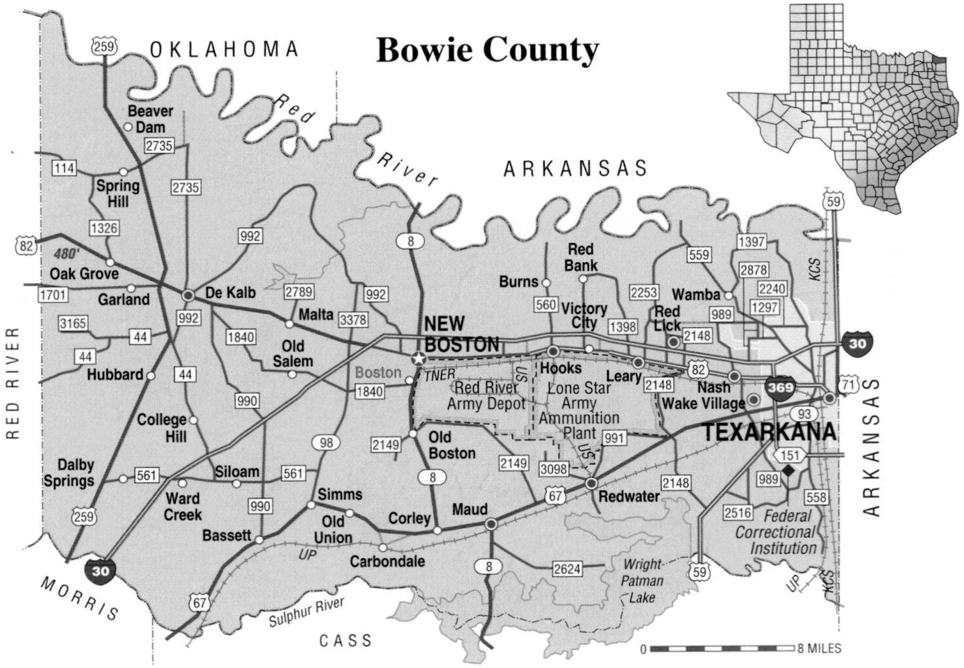

*[Map of Bowie County showing major roads, towns, rivers, and neighboring states/counties including OKLAHOMA, ARKANSAS, RED RIVER, MORRIS, CASS. Towns shown include Beaver Dam, Spring Hill, Oak Grove, Garland, De Kalb, Hubbard, College Hill, Dalby Springs, Ward Creek, Bassett, Old Union, Carbondale, Malta, Old Salem, Old Boston, Boston, NEW BOSTON, Simms, Corley, Maud, Burns, Victory City, Red Bank, Wamba, Red Lick, Hooks, Leary, Nash, Wake Village, Redwater, TEXARKANA, Red River Army Depot, Lone Star Army Ammunition Plant, Federal Correctional Institution, Wright-Patman Lake. Inset map of Texas with Bowie County located in the northeast corner.]*

0 [scale bar] 8 MILES

**Physical Features**: Forested hills at northeast corner of the state; clay, sandy, alluvial soils; drained by Red and Sulphur rivers; Wright Patman Lake.

**Economy**: Government/services, lumber, manufacturing, agribusiness.

**History**: Caddo area, abandoned in 1790s after trouble with Osage tribe. Anglo-Americans began arriving 1815-20. County created, organized, 1840 from Red River County; named for Alamo hero James Bowie.

**Race/Ethnicity**: (In percent) Anglo, 65.4; Black, 24.5; Hispanic, 7.2; Asian, 0.9; Other, 3.2.

**Vital Statistics**, annual: Births, 1,256; deaths, 994; marriages, 585; divorces, 505.

**Recreation**: Lake activities, Crystal Springs beach; hunting, fishing; his- toric sites; Four-States Fair in Septem- ber, Octoberfest.

**Minerals**: Oil, gas, sand, gravel.

**Agriculture**: Beef cattle, pecans, hay, corn, poultry, soybeans, dairy, nurseries, wheat, rice, horses, milo. Market value $66 million. Pine timber, hardwoods, pulpwood harvested.

**NEW BOSTON** (4,523) site of coun- ty courthouse; army depot, lumber mill, steel manufacture, agribusiness, state prison; Pioneer Days in August. The area of Boston, officially desig- nated as the county seat, has been annexed by New Boston.

**TEXARKANA** (38,073 in Texas, 30,049 in Arkansas) rubber company, paper manufacturing, distribution; hospitals; tourism; colleges; federal prison; Perot Theatre; Quadrangle Festival in September.

Other towns include: **De Kalb** (1,694) agriculture, government/ services, commuting to Texarkana, Oktoberfest; **Hooks** (2,817); **Leary** (509); **Maud** (1,071); **Nash** (3,085); **Red Lick** (1,021); **Redwater** (1,047); **Simms** (300); **Wake Village** (5,555).

| | |
|---|---|
| **Population** | **93,275** |
| Change fm 2010 | 0.8 |
| Area (sq. mi.) | 922.77 |
| Land Area (sq. mi.) | 887.87 |
| Altitude (ft.) | 200-480 |
| Rainfall (in.) | 51.24 |
| Jan. mean min. | 30.7 |
| July mean max. | 93.1 |
| Civ. Labor | 43,918 |
| Unemployed | 6.7 |
| Wages | $386,562,269 |
| Per Capita Income | $35,360 |
| Prop. Value | $5,386,011,537 |
| Retail Sales | $1,488,127,162 |

*Oyster boats in the Gulf of Mexico. Texas Parks & Wildlife photo.*

# Brazoria County

**Physical Features**: Flat Coastal Plain, coastal soils, drained by Brazos and San Bernard rivers; Brazoria Reservoir, Eagle Nest Lake, Harris Reservoir, Mustang Lake East/West, San Bernard Reservoirs.

**Economy**: Petroleum and chemical industry, fishing, tourism, agribusiness. Part of Houston metropolitan area.

**History**: Karankawa area. Part of Austin's "Old Three Hundred" colony of families arriving in early 1820s. County created 1836 from Municipality of Brazoria, organized in 1837; name derived from Brazos River.

**Race/Ethnicity**: (In percent) Anglo, 50.7; Black, 13.3; Hispanic, 28.9; Asian, 6.0; Other, 2.7.

**Vital Statistics**, annual: Births, 4,610; deaths, 2,041; marriages, 1,897; divorces, 1,305.

**Recreation**: Beaches, water sports; fishing, hunting; wildlife refuges, historic sites, plantations; state and county parks; replica of the first capitol of the Republic of Texas at West Columbia.

**Minerals**: Oil, gas, sand, gravel.

**Agriculture**: Cattle, hay, rice, soybeans, sorghum, nurseries, corn, cotton, aquaculture, bees. Some 20,000 acres of rice irrigated. Market value $118.2 million.

**ANGLETON** (19,296) county seat; banking and distribution center for oil, chemical, agricultural area; fish-processing plant; hospital.

**BRAZOSPORT** (58,597) is a community of eight cities; chemical complex, deepwater seaport, commercial fishing, tourism; college; hospital; Brazosport cities include: **Clute** (11,184) mosquito festival in July, **Freeport** (12,272) blues festival in August, **Jones Creek** (2,088), **Lake Jackson** (27,587) museum, sea center, Gulf Coast Bird Observatory, **Oyster Creek** (1,146), **Quintana** (65); Neotropical Bird Sanctuary, **Richwood** (3,727), **Surfside Beach** (528).

**ALVIN** (25,320) petrochemical processing, agribusiness, rail, trucking; junior college; hospital; Crawfest and Shrimp Boil in April.

**PEARLAND** (103,841, parts in Harris, Fort Bend counties) trucking, metal fabrication, oilfield, chemical production; commuting to Houston, NASA; community college; Hindu temple; Winter Fest in January.

Other towns include: **Bailey's Prairie** (733); **Bonney** (328); **Brazoria** (3,090) government/services, retail, manufacturing; library; No-Name Festival in June, Santa Anna Ball in July;

**Brookside Village** (1,570).

Also, **Damon** (579); **Danbury** (1,755); **Danciger** (90); **Hillcrest Village** (731); **Holiday Lakes** (1,183); **Iowa Colony** (1,188); **Liverpool** (493); **Manvel** (6,530); **Old Ocean** (150); **Rosharon** (1,261); **Sandy Point** (210); **Sweeny** (3,725) petrochemicals, government/services, hospital, library, Pride Day in May, Levi Jordan Plantation; **West Columbia** (3,969) chemical industry, retail, cattle, rice farming, museum, historic sites, plantation, San Jacinto Festival in April, Stephen F. Austin funeral procession reenactment in October.

| | |
|---|---|
| **Population** | **338,124** |
| Change fm 2010 | 8.0 |
| Area (sq. mi.) | 1,608.6 |
| Land Area (sq. mi.) | 1,357.7 |
| Altitude (ft.) | sea level-146 |
| Rainfall (in.) | 57.47 |
| Jan. mean min. | 45.6 |
| July mean max. | 90.3 |
| Civ. Labor | 163,183 |
| Unemployed | 5.7 |
| Wages | $1,130,215,074 |
| Per Capita Income | $41,751 |
| Prop. Value | $25,150,494,638 |
| Retail Sales | $3,850,675,773 |

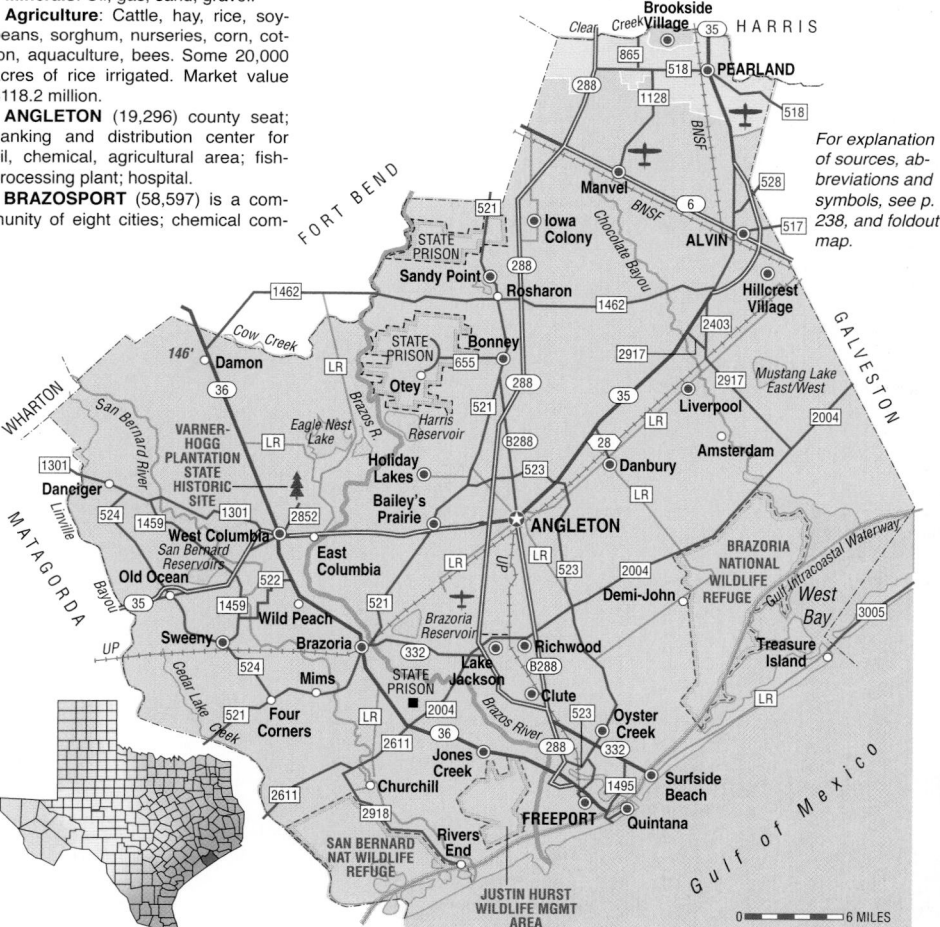

*For explanation of sources, abbreviations and symbols, see p. 238, and foldout map.*

# Brazos County

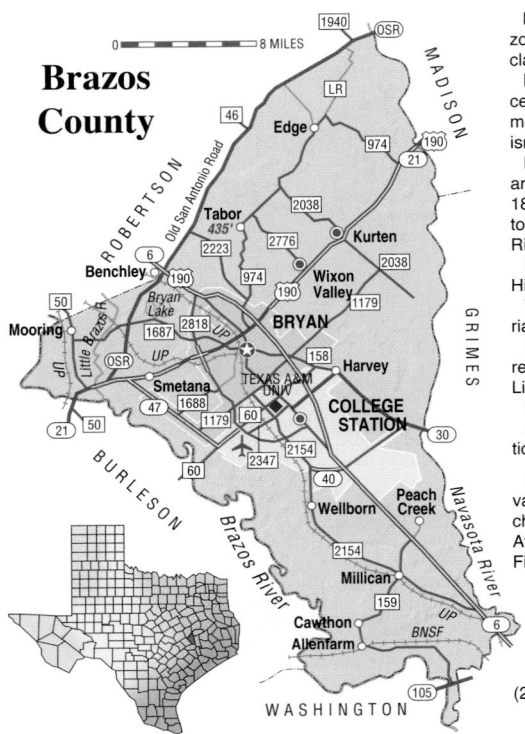

**Physical Features**: South central county between Brazos, Navasota rivers; Bryan Lake; rich bottom soils, sandy, clays on rolling uplands; oak trees.

**Economy**: Texas A&M University; market and medical center; agribusiness; computers, research and development; government/services; winery; industrial parks; tourism.

**History**: Bidais and Tonkawas; Comanches hunted in the area. Part of Stephen F. Austin's second colony of the late 1820s. County created in 1841 from Robertson, Washington counties and named Navasota; renamed for Brazos River in 1842, organized in 1843.

**Race/Ethnicity**: (In percent) Anglo, 57.7; Black, 11.3; Hispanic, 24.5; Asian, 5.5; Other, 2.5.

**Vital Statistics**, annual: Births, 2,596; deaths, 851; marriages, 1,330; divorces, 353.

**Recreation**: Fishing, hunting; raceway; many events related to Texas A&M activities; George Bush Presidential Library and Museum; winery harvest weekends in August.

**Minerals**: Sand and gravel, lignite, gas, oil.

**Agriculture**: Cattle, poultry, cotton, hay, horses and horticulture. Market value $95 million.

**BRYAN** (79,417) county seat; defense electronics, other varied manufacturing, agribusiness center; hospitals, psychiatric facilities; Blinn College extension; Brazos Valley African American Museum; steak & grape festival in June, Fiestas Patrias in September.

**COLLEGE STATION** (100,091) home of Texas A&M University, varied high-tech manufacturing, research; hospital.

Other towns include: **Kurten** (400); **Lake Bryan** (1,809); **Millican** (239); **Wellborn** (400); **Wixon Valley** (252).

| | |
|---|---|
| Population | 209,152 |
| Change fm 2010 | 7.3 |
| Area (sq. mi.) | 591.2 |
| Land Area (sq. mi.) | 585.5 |
| Altitude (ft.) | 157-435 |
| Rainfall (in.) | 40.06 |
| Jan. mean min. | 41.2 |
| July mean max. | 94.8 |
| Civ. Labor | 104,412 |
| Unemployed | 4.7 |
| Wages | $834,672,686 |
| Per Capita Income | $32,241 |
| Prop. Value | $14,302,531,781 |
| Retail Sales | $3,720,158,212 |

*Terlingua Creek near the Rio Grande, in Brewster County. Photo by Robert Plocheck.*

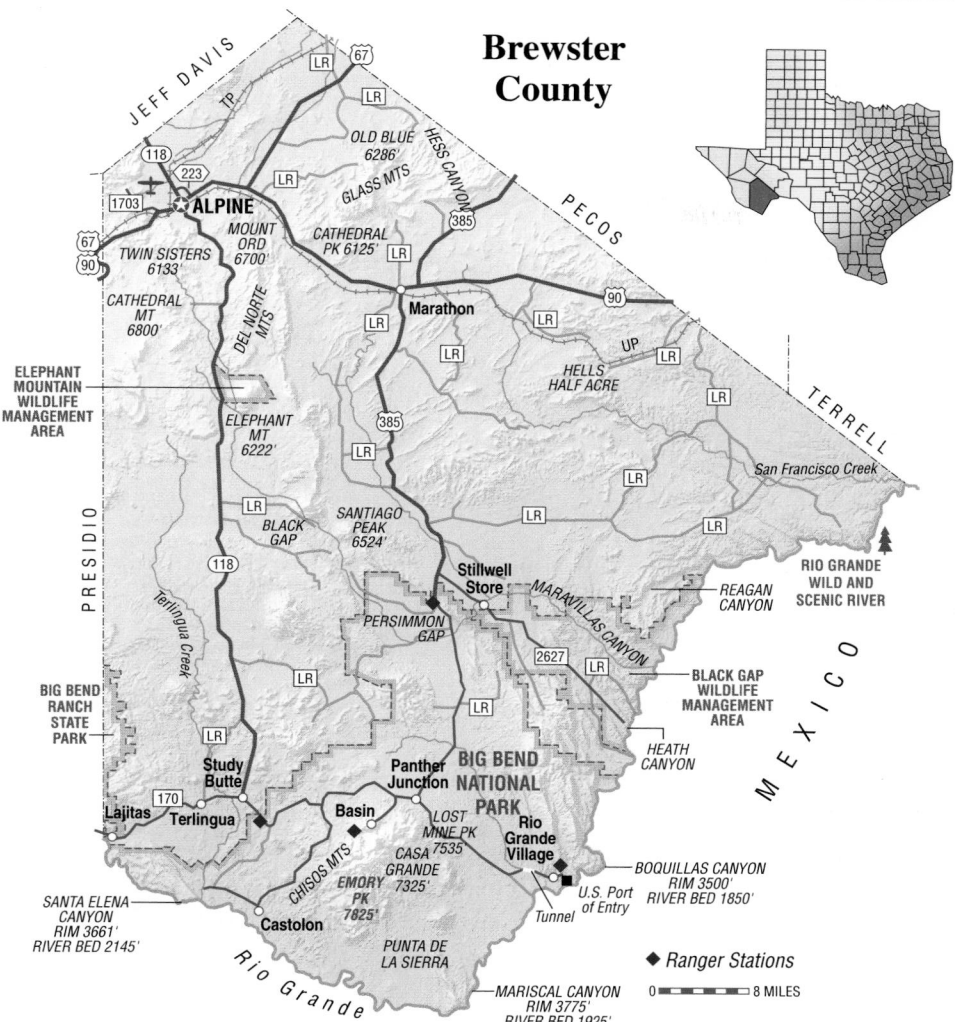

# Brewster County

**Physical Features**: Largest county, with area slightly less than that of Connecticut plus Rhode Island; mountains, canyons, distinctive geology, plant life, animals.

**Economy**: Agriculture, tourism, government/services, Sul Ross State University, mining.

**History**: Pueblo culture had begun when Spanish explored in 1500s. Mescalero Apaches in Chisos; Comanches raided in area. Ranching developed in northern part 1880s, with Mexican agricultural communities along river. County created, organized, 1887 from Presidio County; named for Henry P. Brewster, Republic secretary of war.

**Race/Ethnicity**: (In percent) Anglo, 52.8; Black, 1.5; Hispanic, 43.5; Asian, 1.0; Other, 3.7.

**Vital Statistics**, annual: Births, 114; deaths, 63; marriages, 68; divorces, 0.

**Recreation**: Big Bend National Park, Big Bend Ranch State Park, Rio Grande Wild and Scenic River; ghost towns, scenic drives; hunting; museum; rockhound areas; cavalry post, Barton Warnock Environmental Education Center at Lajitas; cowboy poetry and Western art show in Feburary; Terlingua chili cookoff in November.

**Minerals**: Bentonite.

**Agriculture**: Beef cattle, meat goats, horses. Market value $9.9 million. Hunting leases important.

**ALPINE** (5,951) county seat; ranch trade center, tourism, varied manufacturing; Sul Ross State University; hospital.

**Marathon** (451) tourism, ranching center, Gage Hotel, Marathon Basin quilt show in October.

Also, **Basin** (30); **Study Butte** (241), and **Terlingua** (59).

| Population | 9,173 |
|---|---|
| Change fm 2010 | − 0.6 |
| Area (sq. mi.) | 6,192.3 |
| Land Area (sq. mi.) | 6,183.7 |
| Altitude (ft.) | 1,400-7,825 |
| Rainfall (in.) Alpine | 17.00 |
| Rainfall (in.) Big Bend | 19.17 |
| Jan. mean min. Alpine | 30.3 |
| Jan. mean min. Big Bend | 36.1 |
| July mean max. Alpine | 88.5 |
| July mean max. Big Bend | 84.2 |
| Civ. Labor | 4,369 |
| Unemployed | 5.2 |
| Wages | $36,122,374 |
| Per Capita Income | $40,558 |
| Prop. Value | $908,958,763 |
| Retail Sales | $85,055,508 |

*For explanation of sources, abbreviations and symbols, see p. 238, and foldout map.*

# Briscoe County

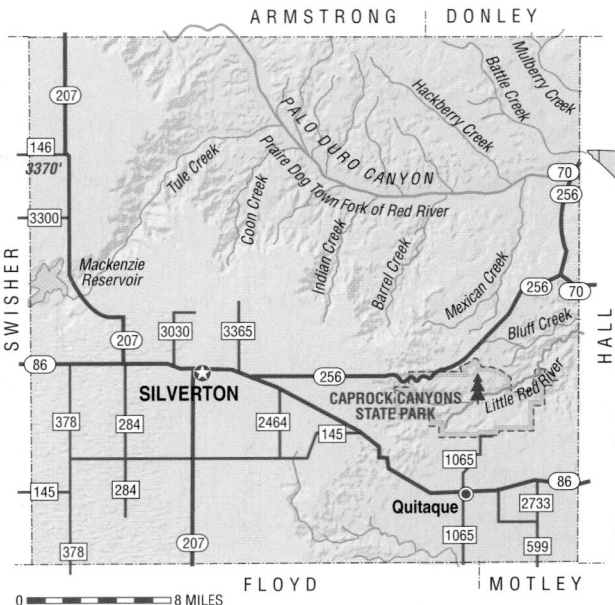

**Physical Features**: Partly on High Plains, broken by Caprock Escarpment, fork of Red River; sandy, loam soils.

**Economy**: Agriculture, government/services.

**History**: Apaches, displaced by Comanches around 1700. Ranchers settled in 1880s. County created from Bexar District, 1876, organized 1892; named for Andrew Briscoe, Republic of Texas soldier.

**Race/Ethnicity**: (In percent) Anglo, 69.1; Black, 2.6; Hispanic, 27.0; Asian, 0.1; Other, 2.2.

**Vital Statistics**, annual: Births, 9; deaths, 17; marriages, 11; divorces, 3.

**Recreation**: Hunting, fishing; scenic drives; museum; state park, trailway, Clarity tunnel, Mackenzie Reservoir; Briscoe County Celebration in August.

**Minerals**: Insignificant.

**Agriculture**: Cotton, beef, grain sorghum, wheat, hay. Some 23,000 acres irrigated. Market value $20.4 million.

**SILVERTON** (661) county seat; agribusiness center, irrigation supplies manufactured; clinics.

**Quitaque** (378) trade center, agribusiness, nature tourism.

| | | |
|---|---|---|
| Population | | 1,536 |
| Change fm 2010 | | – 6.2 |
| Area (sq. mi.) | | 901.6 |
| Land Area (sq. mi.) | | 900.0 |
| Altitude (ft.) | | 2,064-3,370 |
| Rainfall (in.) | | 22.41 |
| Jan. mean min. | | 23.2 |
| July mean max. | | 90.9 |
| Civ. Labor | | 606 |
| Unemployed | | 5.5 |
| Wages | | $2,134,818 |
| Per Capita Income | | $43,606 |
| Prop. Value | | $295,219,465 |
| Retail Sales | | $5,712,691 |

# Brooks County

**Physical Features**: On Rio Grande plain; level to rolling; brushy; light to dark sandy loam soils.

**Economy**: Oil, gas, hunting leases, cattle, watermelons and hay.

**History**: Coahuiltecan Indians in area. Spanish land grants date to around 1800. County created from Hidalgo, Starr and Zapata counties in 1911; organized in 1912. Named for J.A. Brooks, Texas Ranger and legislator.

**Race/Ethnicity**: (In percent) Anglo, 8.4; Black, 1.0; Hispanic, 89.9; Asian, 1.0; Other, 1.1.

**Vital Statistics**, annual: Births, 112; deaths, 73; marriages, 62; divorces, 22.

**Recreation**: Hunting, fishing; Heritage Museum, Don Pedrito shrine; Fiesta del Campo in October.

**Minerals**: Oil, gas production; uranium.

**Agriculture**: Beef cow-calf operations, stocker; crops include hay, squash, watermelons, habanero peppers. Market value $50.8 million.

**FALFURRIAS** (5,021) county seat; oil and gas, agricultural, government/services.

Other town includes: **Encino** (145).

*For explanation of sources, abbreviations and symbols, see p. 238, and foldout map.*

| | | |
|---|---|---|
| Population | | 7,194 |
| Change fm 2010 | | – 0.4 |
| Area (sq. mi.) | | 943.7 |
| Land Area (sq. mi.) | | 943.4 |
| Altitude (ft.) | | 46-431 |
| Rainfall (in.) | | 26.47 |
| Jan. mean min. | | 42.5 |
| July mean max. | | 97.0 |
| Civ. Labor | | 3,426 |
| Unemployed | | 7.5 |
| Wages | | $26,144,537 |
| Per Capita Income | | $33,003 |
| Prop. Value | | $1,280,083,161 |
| Retail Sales | | $75,688,185 |

# Brown County

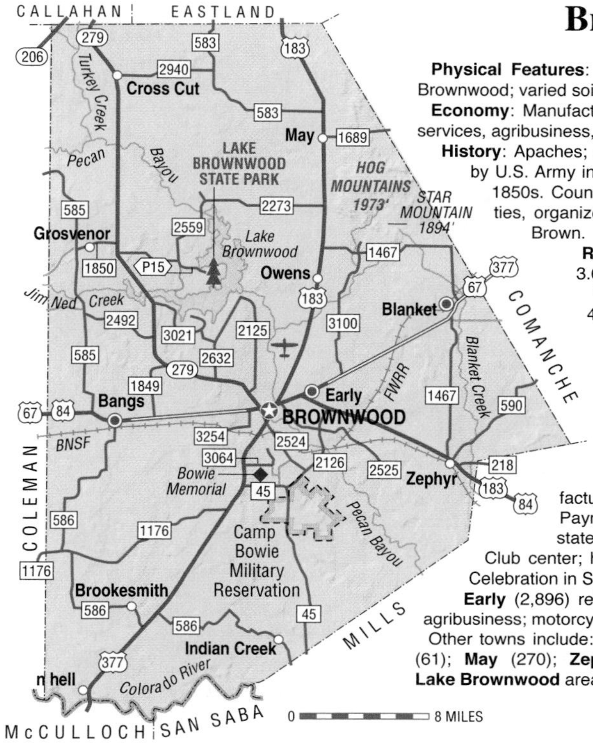

**Physical Features**: Rolling, hilly; drains to Colorado River; Lake Brownwood; varied soils, timber.

**Economy**: Manufacturing plants, distribution centers, government/services, agribusiness, medical, education.

**History**: Apaches; displaced by Comanches who were removed by U.S. Army in 1874-75. Anglo-Americans first settled in mid-1850s. County created 1856 from Comanche, Travis counties, organized in 1857. Named for frontiersman Henry S. Brown.

**Race/Ethnicity**: (In percent) Anglo, 73.5; Black, 3.6; Hispanic, 20.8; Asian; 0.6; Other, 2.5.

**Vital Statistics**, annual: Births, 422; deaths, 448; marriages, 325; divorces, 110.

**Recreation**: State park; museums; fishing, hunting; wildflowers, walking trails.

**Minerals**: Oil, gas, paving materials, gravel, clays.

**Agriculture**: Cattle, hay, peanuts, pecans, meat goats, wheat, hogs. Market value $40.7 million.

**BROWNWOOD** (19,694) county seat; manufacturing, retail trade, distribution center; Howard Payne University, MacArthur Academy of Freedom; state substance abuse treatment center; state 4-H Club center; hospital; train museum, aquatic park; Reunion Celebration in September.

**Early** (2,896) retail, light manufacturing, government/services, agribusiness; motorcycle rally in October.

Other towns include: **Bangs** (1,593); **Blanket** (405); **Brookesmith** (61); **May** (270); **Zephyr** (201).

**Lake Brownwood** area has 1,619.

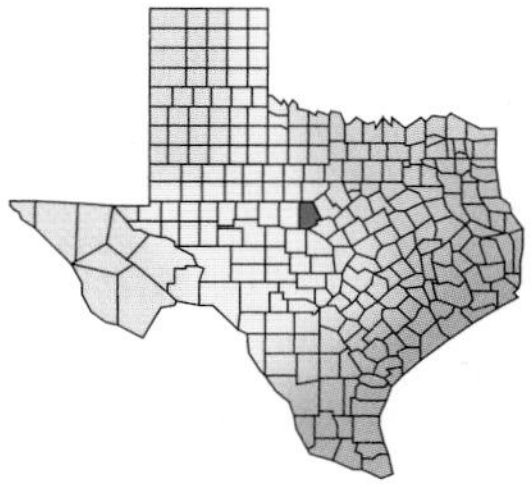

| | |
|---|---|
| Population | **37,653** |
| Change fm 2010 | – 1.2 |
| Area (sq. mi.) | 957.0 |
| Land Area (sq. mi.) | 944.4 |
| Altitude (ft.) | 1,230-1,973 |
| Rainfall (in.) | 30.43 |
| Jan. mean min. | 30.1 |
| July mean max. | 95.7 |
| Civ. Labor | 18,849 |
| Unemployed | 6.2 |
| Wages | $123,155,966 |
| Per Capita Income | $33,760 |
| Prop. Value | $3,430,155,929 |
| Retail Sales | $466,672,578 |

*A South Texas ranch on FM 755, Brooks County. Photo by Robert Plocheck.*

# Burleson County

**Physical Features**: Rolling to hilly; drains to Brazos, Yegua Creek, Somerville Lake; loam and heavy bottom soils; oaks, other trees.

**Economy**: Oil and gas, tourism, commuters to Texas A&M University, agribusiness.

**History**: Tonkawas and Caddoes roamed the area. Mexicans and Anglo-Americans settled around fort in 1830. Black freedmen migration increased until 1910. Germans, Czechs, Italians migrated in 1870s-80s. County created, organized, 1846 from Milam, Washington counties; named for Edward Burleson, a hero of the Texas Revolution.

**Race/Ethnicity**: (In percent) Anglo, 66.3; Black, 12.7; Hispanic, 19.6; Asian, 0.3; Other, 2.4.

**Vital Statistics**, annual: Births, 200; deaths, 216; marriages, 111; divorces, 43.

**Recreation**: Fishing, hunting; lake recreation; historic sites; Czech heritage museum.

**Minerals**: Oil, gas, sand, gravel.

**Agriculture**: Cattle, cotton, corn, hay, sorghum, broiler production, soybeans; some irrigation. Market value $90.1 million.

**CALDWELL** (4,210) county seat; agribusiness, oil and gas, manufacturing, distribution center, tourism; hospital; civic center, museum; Kolache Festival in September.

**Somerville** (1,313) tourism, railroad center, some manufacturing; museum; Country Cajun festival in March.

Other towns include: **Chriesman** (30); **Deanville** (130); **Lyons** (360); **Snook** (505) Snookfest in June.

| | |
|---|---|
| Population | 17,253 |
| Change fm 2010 | 0.4 |
| Area (sq. mi.) | 676.8 |
| Land Area (sq. mi.) | 659.0 |
| Altitude (ft.) | 177-566 |
| Rainfall (in.) | 38.67 |
| Jan. mean min. | 36.8 |
| July mean max. | 95.2 |
| Civ. Labor | 8,115 |
| Unemployed | 4.7 |
| Wages | $47,438,606 |
| Per Capita Income | $40,348 |
| Prop. Value | $2,340,908,952 |

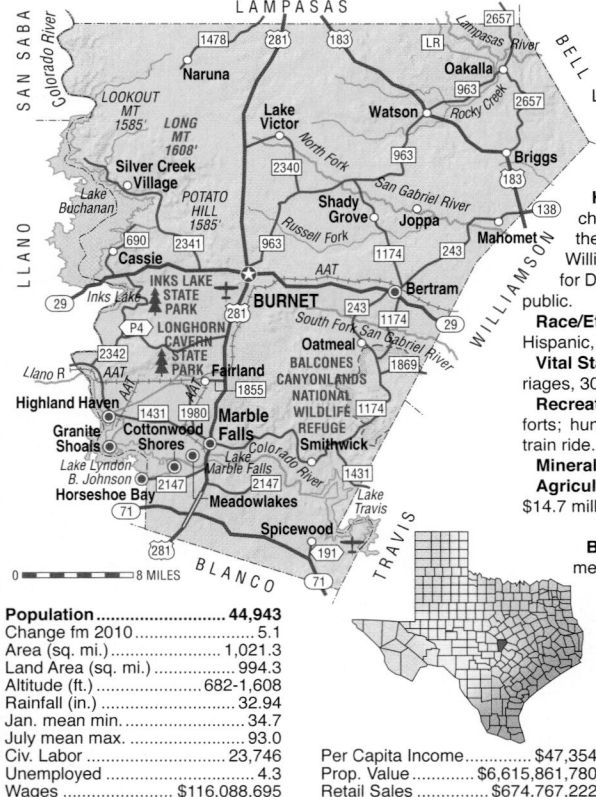

# Burnet County

**Physical Features**: Scenic Hill Country county with Lake Buchanan, Inks Lake, Lake Lyndon B. Johnson, Lake Travis, Lake Marble Falls; caves; sandy, red, black waxy soils; cedars, other trees.

**Economy**: Tourism, stone processing, hunting leases.

**History**: Tonkawas, Lipan Apaches. Comanches raided in area. Frontier settlers arrived in the late 1840s. County created from Bell, Travis, Williamson counties, 1852; organized 1854; named for David G. Burnet, provisional president of the Republic.

**Race/Ethnicity**: (In percent) Anglo, 74.6; Black, 2.2; Hispanic, 21.4; Asian, 0.6; Other, 2.5.

**Vital Statistics**, annual: Births, 449; deaths, 433; marriages, 308; divorces, 172.

**Recreation**: Water sports on lakes; sites of historic forts; hunting; state parks; wildflowers; birding; scenic train ride.

**Minerals**: Granite, limestone.

**Agriculture**: Cattle, goats, grapes, hay. Market value $14.7 million. Deer, wild hog and turkey hunting leases.

**BURNET** (6,144) county seat; tourism, government/services, varied industries, ranching; hospital; museums; vineyards; Bluebonnet festival in April.

**MARBLE FALLS** (6,208) tourism, retail, manufacturing; granite, limestone quarries; August drag boat race.

Other towns include: **Bertram** (1,398) Oatmeal festival on Labor Day; **Briggs** (172); **Cottonwood Shores** (1,148); **Granite Shoals** (5,042); **Highland Haven** (347); **Meadowlakes** (1,848); **Spicewood** (4,000). Also, part of **Horseshoe Bay** (3,458).

| | |
|---|---|
| Population | 44,943 |
| Change fm 2010 | 5.1 |
| Area (sq. mi.) | 1,021.3 |
| Land Area (sq. mi.) | 994.3 |
| Altitude (ft.) | 682-1,608 |
| Rainfall (in.) | 32.94 |
| Jan. mean min. | 34.7 |
| July mean max. | 93.0 |
| Civ. Labor | 23,746 |
| Unemployed | 4.3 |
| Wages | $116,088,695 |
| Per Capita Income | $47,354 |
| Prop. Value | $6,615,861,780 |
| Retail Sales | $674,767,222 |

# Caldwell County

**Physical Features:** Varied soils ranging from black clay to waxy; level, draining to San Marcos River.

**Economy:** Petroleum, varied manufacturing, government/services; part of Austin metro area, also near San Antonio.

**History:** Tonkawa area. Part of the DeWitt colony, Anglo-Americans settled in the 1830s. Mexican migration increased after 1890. County created from Bastrop and Gonzales counties and organized in 1848; named for frontiersman Mathew Caldwell.

**Race/Ethnicity:** (In percent) Anglo, 42.6; Black, 7.1; Hispanic, 48.9; Asian, 1.0; Other, 3.2.

**Vital Statistics,** annual: Births, 466; deaths, 282; marriages, 171; divorces, 50.

**Recreation:** Fishing, state park, nature trails, museums, barbecue havens; Luling Watermelon Thump and Lockhart Chisholm Trail roundup in June.

**Minerals:** Oil, gas, sand, gravel.

**Agriculture:** Eggs, beef cattle, hay, broilers. Market value $62.9 million.

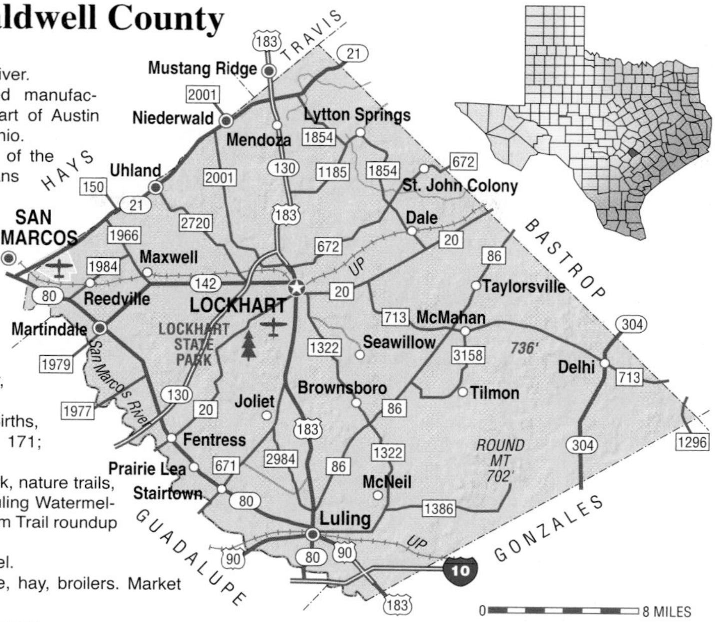

**LOCKHART** (13,098) county seat; agribusiness center, government/services, tourism, light manufacturing, prison; renowned barbecue at Kruez, Smitty's, Blacks.

**Luling** (5,626) oil, tourism, agriculture; oil museum; hospital, barbecue cook-off in April.

Other towns include: **Dale** (300); **Fentress** (380); **Martindale** (1,166); **Maxwell** (500); part of **Mustang Ridge** (930, mostly in Travis County),

and **Prairie Lea** (320).

Also, part of **Niederwald** (577), part of **Uhland** (1,022) and a small part of **San Marcos** (55,527), all mostly in Hays County.

| Population | 39,810 |
|---|---|
| Change fm 2010 | 4.6 |
| Area (sq. mi.) | 547.2 |
| Land Area (sq. mi.) | 545.3 |
| Altitude (ft.) | 315-736 |
| Rainfall (in.) | 35.93 |

| Jan. mean min. | 37.8 |
|---|---|
| July mean max. | 94.8 |
| Civ. Labor | 17,488 |
| Unemployed | 6.1 |
| Wages | $69,519,516 |
| Per Capita Income | $29,485 |
| Prop. Value | $2,614,834,909 |
| Retail Sales | $369,056,093 |

*For explanation of sources, abbreviations and symbols, see p. 238, and foldout map.*

*Campers at Boca Chica Beach at the southern tip of Texas, Cameron County. Photo by Robert Plocheck.*

# Calhoun County

**Physical Features**: Sandy, broken by bays; Green Lake, Powderhorn Lake, Cox Creek Reservoir; partly on Matagorda Island.

**Economy**: Aluminum, plastics plants; marine construction; agribusinesses; petroleum; tourism; fish processing.

**History**: Karankawa area. Empresario Martín De León brought 41 families in 1825. County created and organized from Jackson, Matagorda, and Victoria counties in 1846. Named for John C. Calhoun, U.S. statesman.

**Race/Ethnicity**: (In percent) Anglo, 44.1; Black, 3.0; Hispanic, 47.6; Asian, 4.9; Other, 1.9.

**Vital Statistics**, annual: Births, 261; deaths, 213; marriages, 180; divorces, 47.

**Recreation**: Beaches, fishing, water sports, duck, goose hunting; historic sites, county park; La Salle Days in April.

**Minerals**: Oil, gas.

**Agriculture**: Cotton, cattle, corn, grain sorghum. Market value $42.1 million. Commercial fishing.

**PORT LAVACA** (12,281) county seat; commercial seafood operations, offshore drilling, tourist center; some manufacturing; convention center; hospital.

Other towns include: **Long Mott** (76); **Point Comfort** (743) aluminum, plastic plants, deepwater port; **Port O'Connor** (1,287) tourist center, seafood processing, manufacturing, lighted boat parade in December; **Seadrift** (1,425) commercial fishing, processing plants, Bayfront Park, Shrimpfest in June.

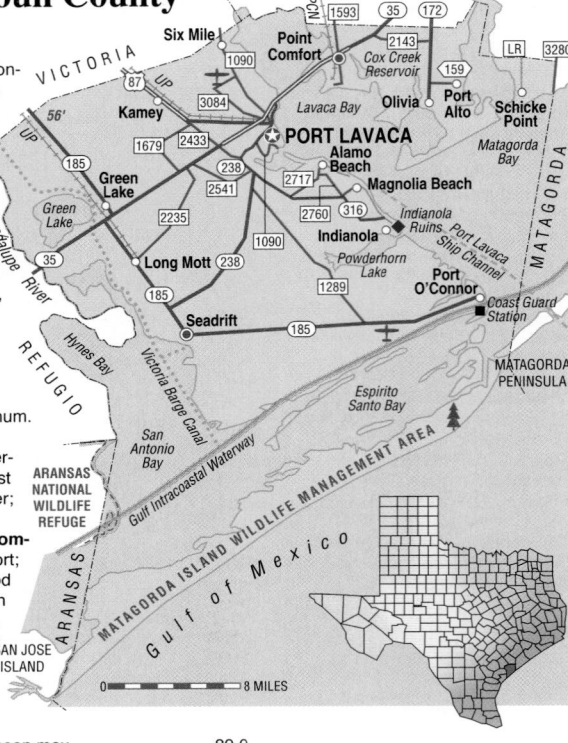

| | |
|---|---|
| Population | 21,797 |
| Change fm 2010 | 1.9 |
| Area (sq. mi.) | 1,032.7 |
| Land Area (sq. mi.) | 506.8 |
| Altitude (ft.) | sea level-56 |
| Rainfall (in.) | 35.93 |
| Jan. mean min. | 46.5 |
| July mean max. | 89.0 |
| Civ. Labor | 10,702 |
| Unemployed | 5.4 |
| Wages | $154,517,401 |
| Per Capita Income | $35,858 |
| Prop. Value | $4,266,280,759 |
| Retail Sales | $220,247,436 |

# Callahan County

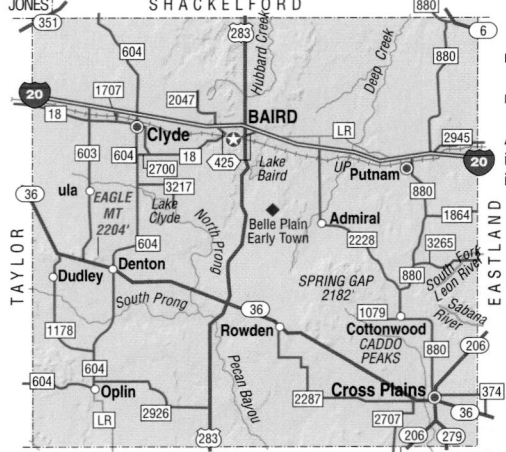

**Physical Features**: On divide between Brazos, Colorado rivers; Lake Clyde, Lake Baird; level to rolling.

**Economy**: Ranching; feed and fertilizer business; commuting to Abilene; 200,000 acres in hunting leases.

**History**: Comanche territory until the 1870s. Anglo-American settlement began around 1860. County created in 1858 from Bexar, Bosque and Travis counties; organized in 1877. Named for Texas Ranger J.H. Callahan.

**Race/Ethnicity**: (In percent) Anglo, 87.4; Black, 1.5; Hispanic, 8.8; Asian, 0.6; Other, 2.5.

**Vital Statistics**, annual: Births, 137; deaths, 171; marriages, 61; divorces, 55.

**Recreation**: Hunting, lakes; museums; Cross Plains Hunters' Feed at deer season.

**Minerals**: Oil and gas.

**Agriculture**: Cattle, wheat, sorghum, oats. Market value $29.9 million. Hunting leases.

**BAIRD** (1,582) county seat; agricultural trade center, antiques shops, some manufacturing, shipping; historic sites; Railhead Day in May.

**Clyde** (3,754) steel water systems manufacturing, government/services; library; Pecan Festival in October.

Other towns include: **Cross Plains** (1,028) oil and gas, agriculture, government/services, home of creator of Conan the Barbarian, museum, Barbarian Festival in June; **Putnam** (98).

| | |
|---|---|
| Population | 13,513 |
| Change fm 2010 | – 0.2 |
| Area (sq. mi.) | 901.3 |
| Land Area (sq. mi.) | 899.4 |
| Altitude (ft.) | 1,350-2,204 |
| Rainfall (in.) | 27.42 |
| Jan. mean min. | 31.4 |
| July mean max. | 94.8 |
| Civ. Labor | 6,914 |
| Unemployed | 4.1 |
| Wages | $18,003,158 |
| Per Capita Income | $36,892 |
| Prop. Value | $1,530,273,450 |
| Retail Sales | $131,441,812 |

# Cameron County

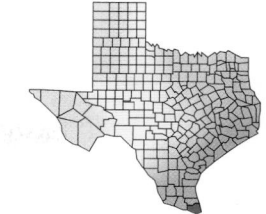

**Physical Features**: Southernmost county in rich Rio Grande Valley soils; flat landscape; semitropical climate; Loma Alta Lake.

**Economy**: Agribusiness, tourism, seafood processing, shipping, manufacturing, government/services.

**History**: Coahuiltecan Indian area. Spanish land grants date to 1781. County created from Nueces County, 1848; named for Capt. Ewen Cameron of Mier Expedition.

**Race/Ethnicity**: (In percent) Anglo, 10.1; Black, 0.8; Hispanic, 88.5; Asian, 0.8; Other, 1.2.

**Vital Statistics**, annual: Births, 7,358; deaths, 2,423; marriages, 2,637; divorces, 1,024.

**Recreation**: South Padre Island: year-round resort; fishing, hunting, water sports; historical sites, Palo Alto visitors center; gateway to Mexico, state parks; wildlife refuge; recreational vehicle center.

**Minerals**: Natural gas, oil.

**Agriculture**: Cotton, grain sorghums, vegetables. Ranked second in sugar cane acreage. Wholesale nursery plants raised. Small feedlot and cow-calf operations. Some 112,000 acres irrigated, mostly cotton and grain sorghums. Market value $160.4 million. Ranked third in value of aquaculture.

**BROWNSVILLE** (185,058) county seat; international trade, varied industries, shipping, tourism; college, hospitals, crippled children health center; Gladys Porter Zoo, historic Fort Brown; University of Texas at Brownsville.

**Harlingen** (66,415) health care, government/services, tourism; hospitals; college extension campuses; nature center; birding festival in November.

**San Benito** (24,704) retail center, tourism, agriculture; hospital; museums, arts center, historic buildings; recreation facilities, including walking/jogging trail; ResacaFest on July 4.

**South Padre Island** (2,962) beaches, tourism/convention center, real estate and construction; birding/nature center, Sandcastle Days in October, Spring Break in March.

Other towns include: **Bayview** (404); **Bluetown** (366); **Cameron Park** (7,245); **Combes** (3,081); **Encantada-Ranchito El Calaboz** (2,305); **Indian Lake** (670); **La Feria** (7,830); **Laguna Heights** (3,765); **Laguna Vista** (3,262); **Laureles** (3,839); **Los Fresnos** (6,317) Little Graceland Museum, Butterfly Farm, library; **Los Indios** (1,117); **Olmito** (1,248); **Palm Valley** (1,330).

Also, **Port Isabel** (5,066) tourist center, fishing, museums, old lighthouse, Shrimp Cook-Off in November; **Primera** (4,216); **Rancho Viejo** (2,531); **Rangerville** (299); **Rio Hondo** (2,463); **Santa Maria** (754); **Santa Rosa** (2,939).

| | |
|---|---:|
| Population | 420,392 |
| Change fm 2010 | 3.5 |
| Area (sq. mi.) | 1,276.5 |
| Land Area (sq. mi.) | 890.9 |
| Altitude (ft.) | sea level-67 |
| Rainfall (in.) | 27.44 |
| Jan. mean min. | 51.6 |
| July mean max. | 93.6 |
| Civ. Labor | 166,428 |
| Unemployed | 8.9 |
| Wages | $1,006,706,160 |
| Per Capita Income | $24,802 |
| Prop. Value | $17,863,512,863 |
| Retail Sales | $4,045,679,030 |

*For explanation of sources, abbreviations and symbols, see p. 238, and foldout map.*

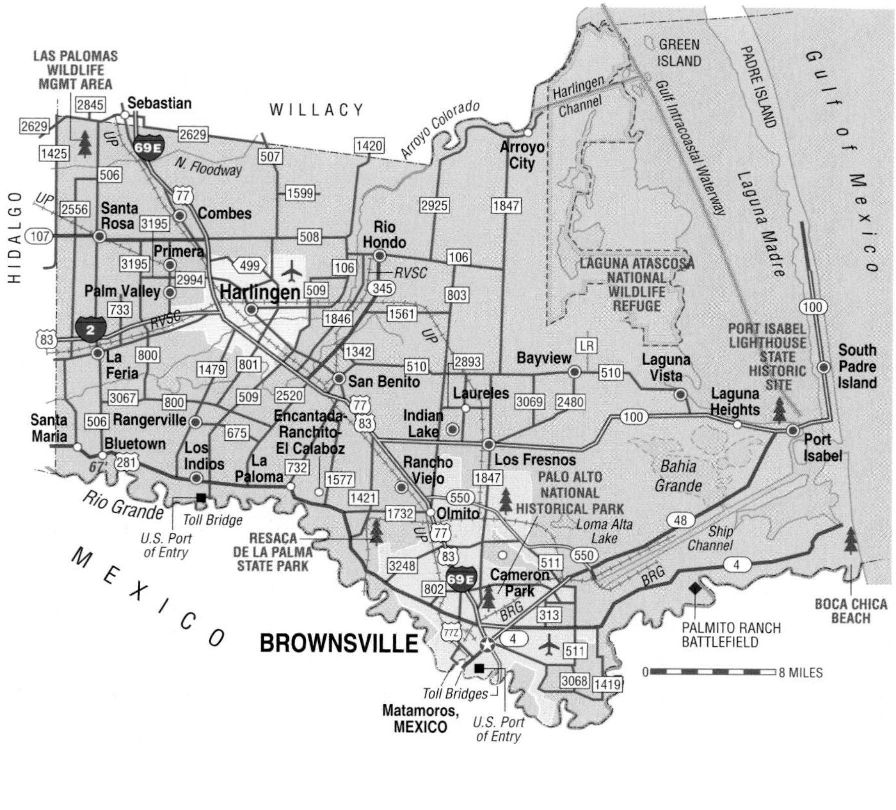

# Camp County

Population .............................. **12,621**
Change fm 2010 ........................... 1.8
Area (sq. mi.) .......................... 203.2
Land Area (sq. mi.) ................... 195.8
Altitude (ft.) .......................... 236-538
Rainfall (in.) ............................. 45.10
Jan. mean min. ........................... 33.1
July mean max. .......................... 95.2
Civ. Labor ................................. 5,621
Unemployed ................................. 6.3
Wages .......................... $34,944,069
Per Capita Income............... $35,458
Prop. Value ................. $929,349,791
Retail Sales ................. $120,145,604

**Physical Features**: East Texas county with forested hills; drains to Big Cypress Creek on the north; Lake Bob Sandlin; third smallest county in Texas.

**Economy**: Agribusiness, chicken processing, timber industries, light manufacturing, retirement center.

**History**: Caddo area. Anglo-American settlers arrived in late 1830s. Antebellum slaveholding area. County created, organized, from Upshur County 1874; named for jurist J.L. Camp.

**Race/Ethnicity**: (In percent) Anglo, 57.6; Black, 16.9; Hispanic, 23.0; Asian, 0.9; Other, 3.6.

**Vital Statistics**, annual: Births, 189; deaths, 145; marriages, 106; divorces, 31.

**Recreation**: Water sports, fishing on lakes; farmstead and airship museum; Pittsburg hot links; Chickfest in September.

**Minerals**: Oil, gas, clays, coal.

**Agriculture**: Poultry and products important; beef, dairy cattle, horses; peaches, hay, blueberries, vegetables. Market value $137.7 million. Forestry.

**PITTSBURG** (4,586) county seat; agribusiness, timber, tourism, food processing, light manufacturing, commuting to Longview, Tyler; hospital; community college; Prayer Tower.

Other towns include: **Leesburg** (128) and **Rocky Mound** (71).

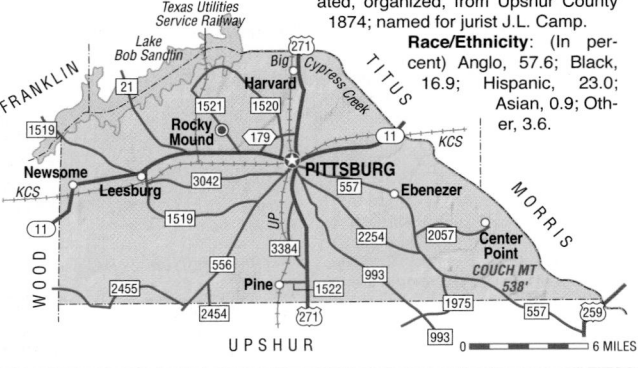

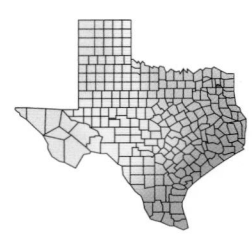

---

# Carson County

**Physical Features**: In center of Panhandle on level, some broken land; loam soils.

**Economy**: Pantex nuclear weapons assembly/disassembly facility (U.S. Department of Energy), commuting to Amarillo, petrochemical plants, agribusiness.

**History**: Apaches, displaced by Comanches. Anglo-American ranchers settled in the 1880s. German, Polish farmers arrived around 1910. County created from Bexar District, 1876; organized 1888. Named for Republic secretary of state S.P. Carson.

**Race/Ethnicity**: (In percent) Anglo, 87.0; Black, 0.8; Hispanic, 9.5; Asian, 0.5; Other, 2.7.

**Vital Statistics**, annual: Births, 65; deaths, 73; marriages, 39; divorces, 14.

**Recreation**: Museum, The Cross at Groom; Square House Barbecue in fall.

**Minerals**: Oil and natural gas production.

**Agriculture**: Cattle, cotton, wheat, sorghum, corn, hay, soybeans. Market value $83 million.

**PANHANDLE** (2,348) county seat; government/services, agribusiness, petroleum center, commuters to Amarillo; Veterans Day celebration, car show in June.

Other towns include: **Groom** (558) farming center, government/services, Groom Day festival in August; **Skellytown** (459); **White Deer** (976) Polish Sausage festival in November.

Population ....................................**6,013**
Change fm 2010 ............................– 2.7
Area (sq. mi.) ..........................924.1
Land Area (sq. mi.) ........................920.2
Altitude (ft.) .....................2,926-3,595
Rainfall (in.) ..............................21.78
Jan. mean min. ...............................20.3
July mean max. ..............................92.2
Civ. Labor .....................................3,188
Unemployed .......................................3.4
Wages ................................$75,986,926
Per Capita Income....................$47,640
Prop. Value ...............$1,382,836,100
Retail Sales ......................$167,793,523

*For explanation of sources, abbreviations and symbols, see p. 238, and foldout map.*

# Cass County

**Physical Features**: Forested Northeast county rolling to hilly; drained by Cypress Bayou, Sulphur River; Wright Patman Lake.

**Economy**: Timber, paper industries; varied manufacturing; agribusiness; government/services.

**History**: Caddoes, who were displaced by other tribes in the 1790s. Anglo-Americans arrived in the 1830s. Antebellum slaveholding area. County created and organized in 1846 from Bowie County; named for U.S. Sen. Lewis Cass.

**Race/Ethnicity**: (In percent) Anglo, 76.4; Black, 17.4; Hispanic, 4.3; Asian, 0.4; Other, 2.1.

**Vital Statistics**, annual: Births, 348; deaths, 402; marriages, 183; divorces, 155.

**Recreation**: Fishing, hunting, water sports; state, county parks; lake, wildflower trails.

**Minerals**: Oil, iron ore.

**Agriculture**: Poultry, cattle, nurseries, forage, watermelons. Market value $67.6 million. Timber important.

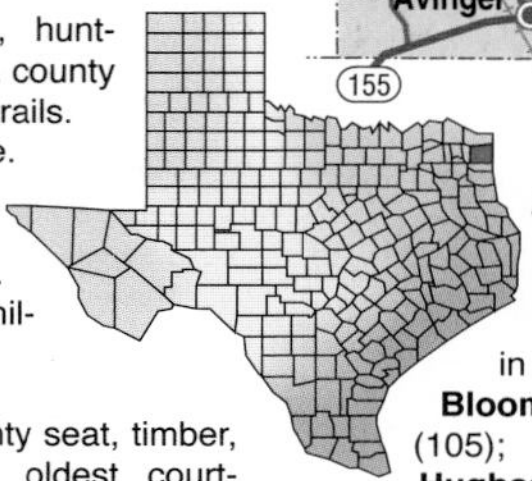

**LINDEN** (2,022) county seat, timber, agribusiness; tourism; oldest courthouse still in use as courthouse, hospital; Rock and Roll Hall of Fame.

**ATLANTA** (5,742) Paper and timber industries, government/services, varied manufacturing, hospital, library; Forest Festival in August.

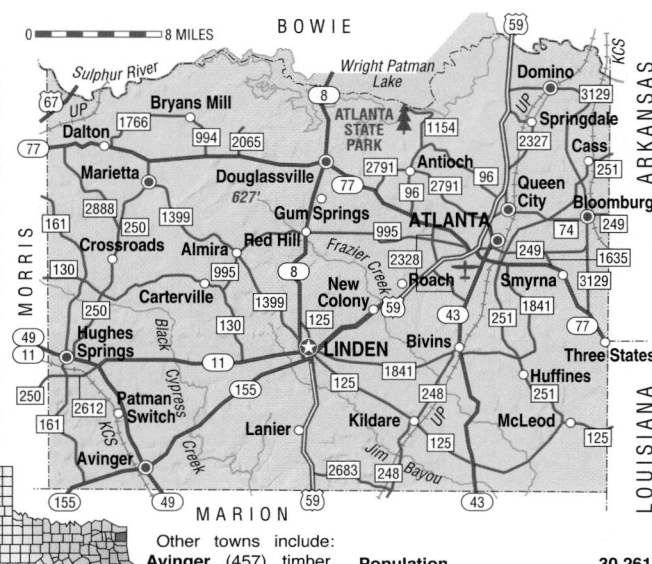

Other towns include: **Avinger** (457) timber, paper industry, steel plant, early cemetery, Glory Days celebration in October; **Bivins** (215); **Bloomburg** (407); **Domino** (105); **Douglassville** (237); **Hughes Springs** (1,809) varied manufacturing, warehousing, trucking school, Pumpkin Glow in October; **Kildare** (104); **Marietta** (137); **McLeod** (600); **Queen City** (1,511) paper industry, commuters to Texarkana, government/services, historic sites.

| | |
|---|---|
| Population | **30,261** |
| Change fm 2010 | − 0.7 |
| Area (sq. mi.) | 960.3 |
| Land Area (sq. mi.) | 937.0 |
| Altitude (ft.) | 167-627 |
| Rainfall (in.) | 49.17 |
| Jan. mean min. | 34.6 |
| July mean max. | 92.1 |
| Civ. Labor | 12,628 |
| Unemployed | 7.9 |
| Wages | $66,237,558 |
| Per Capita Income | $33,946 |
| Prop. Value | $2,661,127,842 |
| Retail Sales | $275,303,754 |

*The Castro County Courthouse in Dimmitt. Photo by Robert Plocheck.*

# Castro County

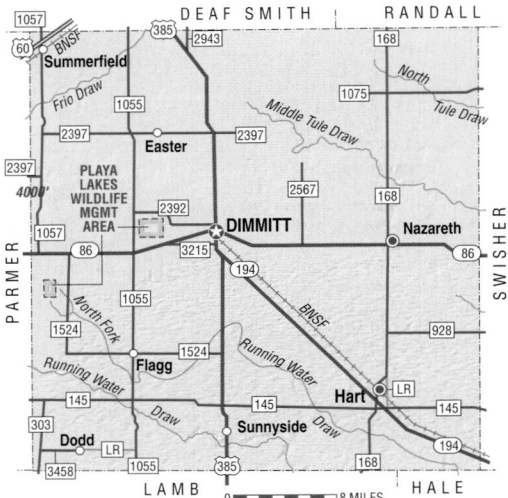

**Physical Features:** Flat Panhandle county, drains to creeks, draws and playas; underground water.

**Economy:** Agribusiness.

**History:** Apaches, who were displaced by Comanches in the 1720s. Anglo-American ranchers began settling in the 1880s. Germans settled after 1900. Mexican migration increased after 1950. County created in 1876 from Bexar District, organized in 1891. Named for Henri Castro, Texas colonizer.

**Race/Ethnicity:** (In percent) Anglo, 34.6; Black, 2.6; Hispanic, 62.3; Asian, 0.6; Other, 2.6.

**Vital Statistics,** annual: Births, 138; deaths, 68; marriages, 54; divorces, 15.

**Recreation:** Pheasant hunting; Italian POW camp site; Dimmitt Harvest Days celebrated in August.

**Minerals:** Insignificant.

**Agriculture:** Beef cattle, dairies (first in number of milk cows), corn, cotton, wheat, sheep. Market value $1.31 billion; third in state.

| | |
|---|---|
| Population | 7,781 |
| Change fm 2010 | – 3.5 |
| Area (sq. mi.) | 899.3 |
| Land Area (sq. mi.) | 894.4 |
| Altitude (ft.) | 3,565-4,000 |
| Rainfall (in.) | 21.22 |
| Jan. mean min. | 21.3 |
| July mean max. | 91.0 |
| Civ. Labor | 3,271 |
| Unemployed | 5.5 |
| Wages | $20,237,333 |
| Per Capita Income | $41,188 |
| Prop. Value | $1,046,486,290 |
| Retail Sales | $58,904,131 |

**DIMMITT** (4,375) county seat; agribusiness center; library, hospital; quilt festival in April.

Other towns include: **Hart** (1,088) and **Nazareth** (303).

# Chambers County

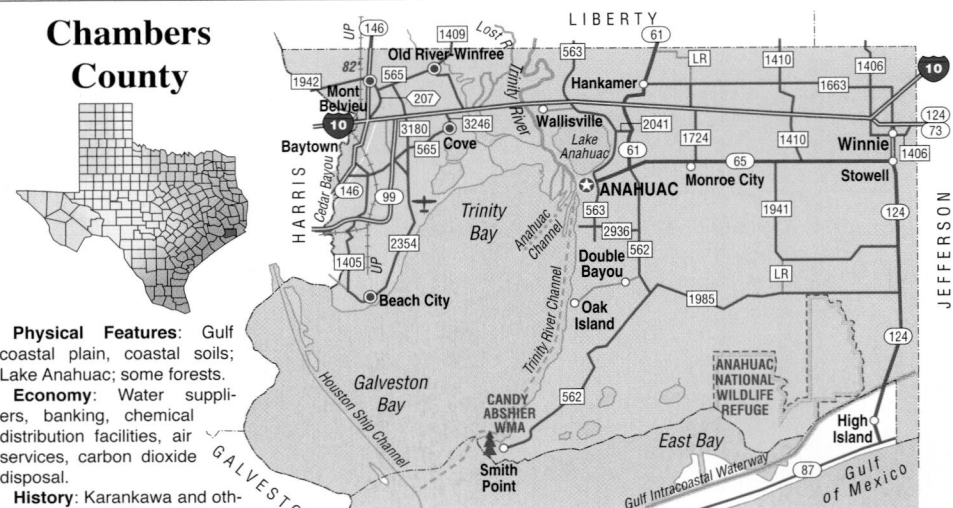

**Physical Features:** Gulf coastal plain, coastal soils; Lake Anahuac; some forests.

**Economy:** Water suppliers, banking, chemical distribution facilities, air services, carbon dioxide disposal.

**History:** Karankawa and other coastal tribes. Nuestra Señora de la Luz Mission established near present Wallisville in 1756. County created and organized in 1858 from Liberty, Jefferson counties. Named for Gen. T. J. Chambers, surveyor.

**Race/Ethnicity:** (In percent) Anglo, 69.0; Black, 8.3; Hispanic, 20.6; Asian, 1.1; Other, 2.6.

**Vital Statistics,** annual: Births, 459; deaths, 258; marriages, 197; divorces, 201.

**Recreation:** Fishing, hunting; water sports; camping; county parks; wildlife refuge; historic sites; Wallisville Heritage Museum; Texas Gatorfest in September.

**Minerals:** Oil, gas.

**Agriculture:** Beef cattle, rice, hay, aquaculture; significant irrigation. Market value $25.6 million. Hunting, fishing important.

**ANAHUAC** (2,288) county seat; canal connects with Houston Ship Channel; agribusiness; hospital, library.

**WINNIE** (3,423) oil and gas; hospital; depot museum; Texas Rice Festival in October.

Other towns include: **Beach City** (2,365), **Cove** (505), **Hankamer** (226), **Mont Belvieu** (4,418), **Old River-**Winfree (1,248), **Stowell** (1,839) and **Wallisville** (300).

Part [4,116] of **Baytown**.

| | |
|---|---|
| Population | 38,145 |
| Change fm 2010 | 8.7 |
| Area (sq. mi.) | 871.2 |
| Land Area (sq. mi.) | 597.1 |
| Altitude (ft.) | sea level-82 |
| Rainfall (in.) | 57.11 |
| Jan. mean min. | 42.2 |
| July mean max. | 90.6 |
| Civ. Labor | 18,664 |
| Unemployed | 6.1 |
| Wages | $184,297,180 |
| Per Capita Income | $54,496 |
| Prop. Value | $9,036,152,385 |
| Retail Sales | $2,276,462,884 |

# Cherokee County

**Physical Features**: East Texas county; hilly, partly forested; drains to Angelina, Neches rivers; many streams; Lake Palestine, Lake Striker, Lake Jacksonville; sandy, clay soils.

**Economy**: Government/services, varied manufacturing, agribusiness.

**History**: Caddo tribes attracted Spanish missionaries around 1720. Cherokees began settling area around 1820, and soon afterward Anglo-Americans began to arrive. Cherokees forced to Indian Territory 1839. Named for Indian tribe; created 1846 from Nacogdoches County.

**Race/Ethnicity**: (In percent) Anglo, 61.8; Black, 14.9; Hispanic, 21.7; Asian, 0.6; Other, 3.4.

**Vital Statistics**, annual: Births, 722; deaths, 526; marriages, 332; divorces, 184.

**Recreation**: Water sports; fishing, hunting; historic sites and parks, national wildlife refuge; Texas State Railroad; nature trails through forests; lakes.

**Minerals**: Gas, oil.

**Agriculture**: Nurseries (second in the state in value of sales), hay, beef cattle, dairies, poultry. Market value $134 million. Timber, hunting income significant.

**RUSK** (5,638) county seat; agribusiness, tourism, state mental hospital, prison unit; historic footbridge, heritage festival in October.

**JACKSONVILLE** (15,236) varied manufacturing, plastics, agribusiness, tourism, retail center; hospitals, junior colleges; Love's Lookout; Tomato Fest in June.

Other towns include: **Alto** (1,243) farming, timber, light manufacturing, pecan festival in November; **Cuney** (140); **Gallatin** (439); **Maydelle** (250); **New Summerfield** (1,154); **Reklaw** (389, partly in Rusk County); **Wells** (825).

Part [47] of **Bullard** and part [61] of **Troup**.

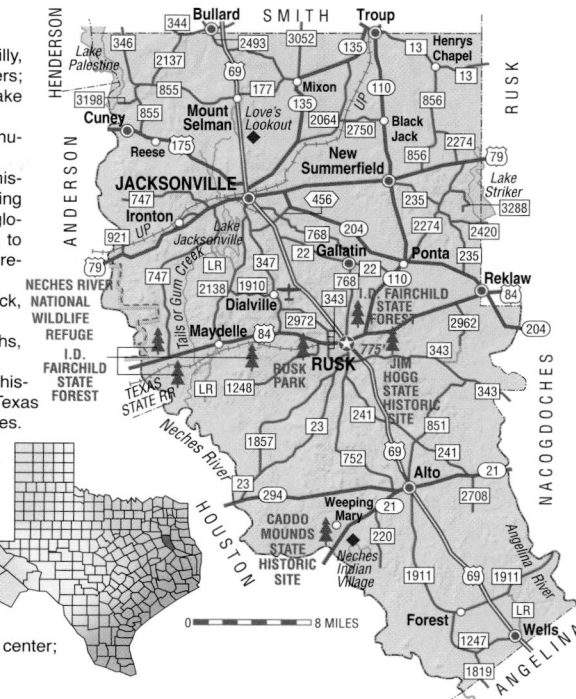

| Population | 50,902 |
|---|---|
| Change fm 2010 | 0.1 |
| Area (sq. mi.) | 1,062.2 |
| Land Area (sq. mi.) | 1,052.9 |
| Altitude (ft.) | 187-775 |
| Rainfall (in.) | 49.54 |
| Jan. mean min. | 36.3 |
| uly mean max. | 91.2 |
| Civ. Labor | 20,572 |

| | |
|---|---|
| Unemployed | 6.8 |
| Wages | $118,297,180 |
| Per Capita Income | $31,893 |
| Prop. Value | $3,324,209,472 |
| Retail Sales | $431,072,102 |

*For explanation of sources, abbreviations and symbols, see p. 238, and foldout map.*

---

*The Fred Hartman Bridge over the Houston Ship Channel at Baytown. Photo by Robert Plocheck.*

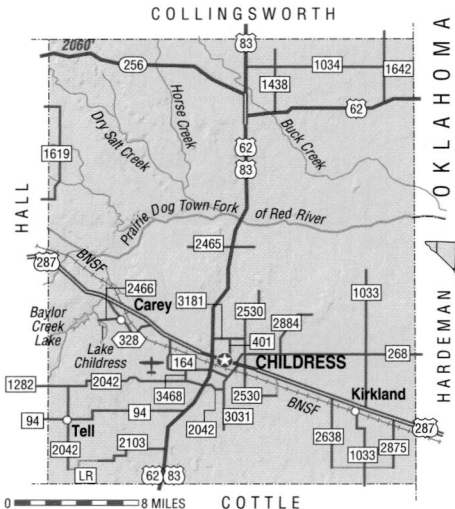

# Childress County

**Physical Features**: Rolling prairie, at corner of Panhandle, draining to fork of Red River; Baylor Creek Lake, Lake Childress; mixed soils.

**Economy**: Government/services, retail trade, tourism, agriculture.

**History**: Apaches, displaced by Comanches. Ranchers arrived around 1880. County created 1876 from Bexar, Young districts; organized 1887; named for writer of Texas Declaration of Independence, George C. Childress.

**Race/Ethnicity**: (In percent) Anglo, 58.7; Black, 10.2; Hispanic, 29.3; Asian, 0.8; Other, 1.9.

**Vital Statistics**, annual: Births, 69; deaths, 79; marriages, 54; divorces, 12.

**Recreation**: Recreation on lakes and creeks, fishing; hunting of deer, turkey, wild hog, quail, dove; parks; county museum.

**Minerals**: Insignificant.

**Agriculture**: Cotton, beef cattle, wheat, hay, sorghum, peanuts; some 9,000 acres irrigated. Market value $19.9 million. Hunting leases.

**CHILDRESS** (6,016) county seat; agribusiness, hospital, prison unit; settlers reunion and rodeo in July.

Other towns include: **Tell** (20).

| | | |
|---|---|---|
| Population | | 7,089 |
| Change fm 2010 | | 0.7 |
| Area (sq. mi.) | | 713.7 |
| Land Area (sq. mi.) | | 696.4 |
| Altitude (ft.) | | 1,560-2,060 |
| Rainfall (in.) | | 26.43 |
| Jan. mean min. | | 26.8 |

| | | |
|---|---|---|
| July mean max. | | 95.7 |
| Civ. Labor | | 3,036 |
| Unemployed | | 4.7 |
| Wages | | $18,344,760 |

| | | |
|---|---|---|
| Per Capita Income | | $28,561 |
| Prop. Value | | $577,566,698 |
| Retail Sales | | $91,768,695 |

# Clay County

**Physical Features**: Hilly, rolling; Northwest county drains to Red, Trinity rivers; Lake Arrowhead; sandy loam, chocolate soils; mesquites, post oaks.

**Economy**: Oil, agribusiness.

**History**: Wichitas arrived from the north-central plains in the mid-1700s, followed by Apaches and Comanches. Ranching attempts began in the 1850s. County created from Cooke County, 1857; Indians forced disorganization in 1862; reorganized in 1873; named for Henry Clay, U.S. statesman.

**Race/Ethnicity**: (In percent) Anglo, 91.0; Black, 1.0; Hispanic, 5.2; Asian, 0.2; Other, 3.4.

**Vital Statistics**, annual: Births, 95; deaths, 127; marriages, 62; divorces, 40.

**Recreation**: Fishing, hunting, water sports; state park; pioneer reunion in September.

**Minerals**: Oil and gas, stone.

**Agriculture**: Beef cattle, wheat, pecans. Market value $79.8 million. Oaks, cedar, elms sold to nurseries, mesquite cut for firewood.

**HENRIETTA** (3,175) county seat; agribusiness, government/services, manufacturing; hospital; museum; Turkey Fest in April.

Other towns include: **Bellevue** (360), **Bluegrove** (135), **Byers** (481), **Dean** (498), **Jolly** (184), **Petrolia** (675).

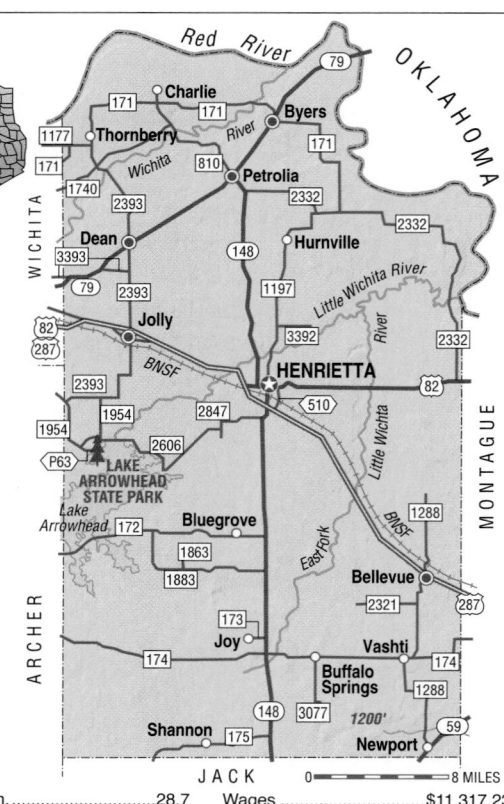

| | | |
|---|---|---|
| Population | | 10,370 |
| Change fm 2010 | | – 3.6 |
| Area (sq. mi.) | | 1,116.8 |
| Land Area (sq. mi.) | | 1,088.7 |
| Altitude (ft.) | | 791-1,200 |
| Rainfall (in.) | | 32.68 |

| | | |
|---|---|---|
| Jan. mean min. | | 28.7 |
| July mean max. | | 96.6 |
| Civ. Labor | | 5,585 |
| Unemployed | | 4.3 |

| | | |
|---|---|---|
| Wages | | $11,317,239 |
| Per Capita Income | | $51,237 |
| Prop. Value | | $1,708,283,100 |
| Retail Sales | | $81,142,155 |

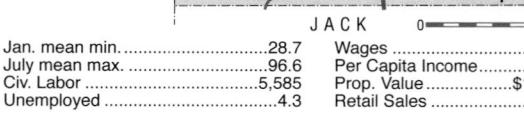

# Cochran County

**Physical Features**: South Plains bordering New Mexico with small lakes (playas); underground water; loam, sandy loam soils.

**Economy**: Farming, government/services, retail.

**History**: Hunting area for various Indian tribes. Ranches operated in the 1880s but population in 1900 was still only 25. Farming began in the 1920s. County created from Bexar and Young districts in 1876; organized in 1924; named for Robert Cochran, who died at the Alamo.

**Race/Ethnicity**: (In percent) Anglo, 38.2; Black, 4.8; Hispanic, 56.3; Asian, 0.3; Other, 3.7.

**Vital Statistics**, annual: Births, 49; deaths, 31; marriages, 27; divorces, 6.

**Recreation**: Museum; Last Frontier Trail Drive and Buffalo Soldier Day in June.

**Minerals**: Insignificant.

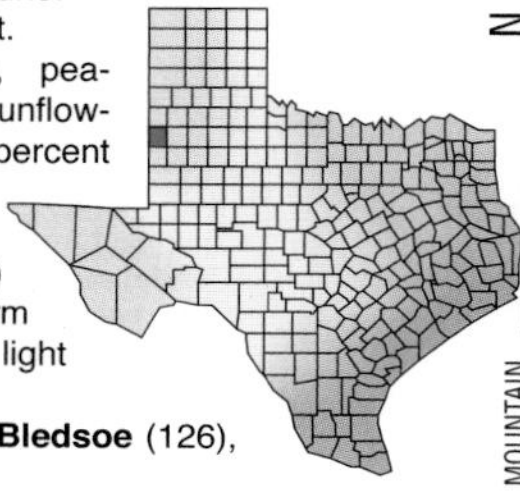

**Agriculture**: Cotton, peanuts, sorghum, peas, sunflowers, wheat. Crops 60 percent irrigated. Market value $100.8 million.

**MORTON** (1,885) county seat; oil, farm center, meat packing, light manufacture; hospital.

Other towns include: **Bledsoe** (126), **Whiteface** (420).

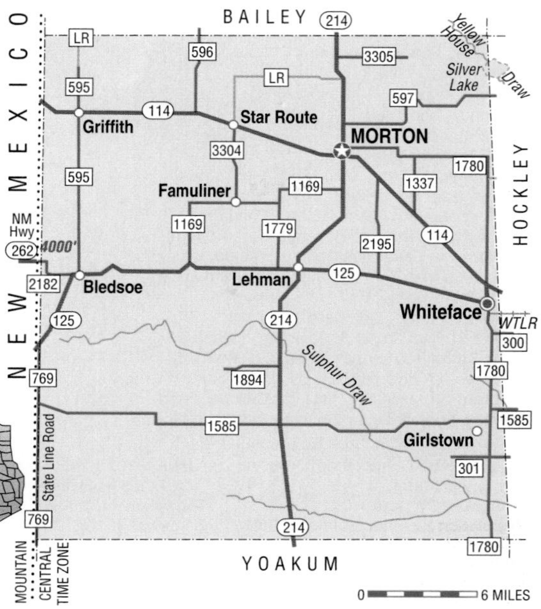

| | | |
|---|---|---|
| Population | | **2,935** |
| Change fm 2010 | | – 6.1 |
| Area (sq. mi.) | | 775.2 |
| Land Area (sq. mi.) | | 775.2 |
| Altitude (ft.) | | 3,565-4,000 |
| Rainfall (in.) | | 18.93 |
| Jan. temp. min. | | 24.4 |
| July temp. max. | | 91.5 |
| Civ. Labor | | 1,331 |
| Unemployed | | 6.3 |
| Wages | | $6,645,326 |
| Per Capita Income | | $42,759 |
| Prop. Value | | $919,057,318 |
| Retail Sales | | $24,616,970 |

*For explanation of sources, abbreviations and symbols, see p. 238, and foldout map.*

*A tractor working in a field in Clay County off FM 2393. Photo by Robert Plocheck.*

# Coke County

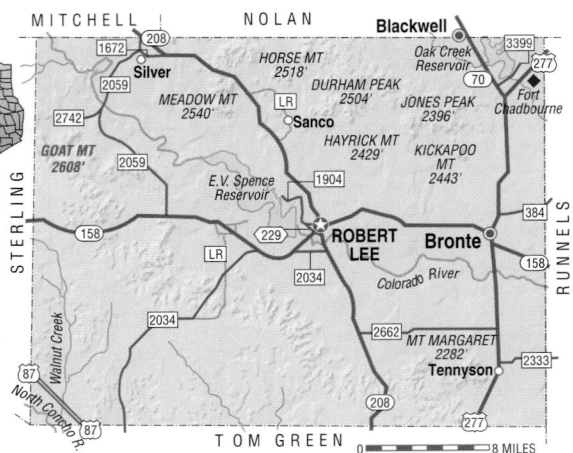

**Physical Features**: West Texas prairie, hills, Colorado River valley; sandy loam, red soils; E.V. Spence Reservoir, Oak Creek Reservoir.

**Economy**: Oil and gas, government/services, agriculture.

**History**: From 1700 to 1870s, Comanches roamed the area. Ranches began operating after the Civil War. County created, organized, 1889 from Tom Green County; named for Gov. Richard Coke.

**Race/Ethnicity**: (In percent) Anglo, 75.6; Black, 1.1; Hispanic, 21.5; Asian, 0.3; Other, 3.3.

**Vital Statistics**, annual: Births, 29; deaths, 51; marriages, 17; divorces, 6.

**Recreation**: Hunting, fishing, Caliche Loop birdwatching trail; lakes; Sumac hiking trail; historic sites, Fort Chadbourne, county museum, Fort Chadbourne Days in May; amphitheater.

**Minerals**: Oil, gas.

**Agriculture**: Beef cattle, small grains, sheep and goats, hay. Market value $7 million.

**ROBERT LEE** (1,009) county seat; oil, gas, wind farms, ranching, government/services; old jail museum.

**Bronte** (978) ranching, oil.

Other towns include: **Silver** (34) and **Tennyson** (46). Also, a small part of **Blackwell** (310).

| | |
|---|---|
| Population | **3,254** |
| Change from 2010 | – 2.0 |
| Area (sq. mi.) | 928.0 |
| Land Area (sq. mi.) | 911.5 |

| | |
|---|---|
| Altitude (ft.) | 1,700-2,608 |
| Rainfall (in.) | 22.75 |
| Jan. mean min. | 28.4 |
| July mean max. | 96.7 |
| Civ. Labor | 1,242 |
| Unemployed | 5.4 |
| Wages | $4,925,460 |
| Per Capita Income | $36,991 |
| Prop. Value | $946,034,410 |
| Retail Sales | $23,133,724 |

# Coleman County

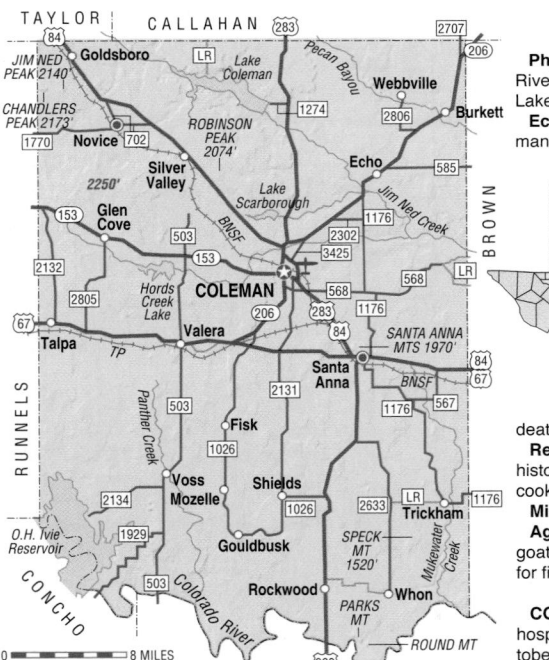

**Physical Features**: Hilly, rolling; drains to Colorado River, Pecan Bayou; O.H. Ivie Reservoir Hords Creek Lake, Lake Coleman; mesquite, oaks.

**Economy**: Agribusiness, petroleum, ecotourism, varied manufacturing.

**History**: Presence of Apaches and Comanches brought military outpost, Camp Colorado, before the Civil War. Settlers arrived after organization. County created in 1858 from Brown, Travis counties; organized in 1864; named for Houston's aide, R.M. Coleman.

**Race/Ethnicity**: (In percent), Anglo, 77.9; Black, 2.8; Hispanic, 17.3; Asian, 0.5; Other, 2.8.

**Vital Statistics**, annual: Births, 97; deaths, 126; marriages, 81; divorces, 36.

**Recreation**: Fishing, hunting; water sports; city park, historic sites; lakes; Santa Anna Peak; Santa Anna bison cook-off in May.

**Minerals**: Oil, gas, stone, clays.

**Agriculture**: Cattle, wheat, sheep, hay, grain sorghum, goats, oats, cotton. Market value $28.4 million. Mesquite for firewood and furniture.

**COLEMAN** (4,600) county seat; varied manufacturing; hospital, library, museums: Fiesta de la Paloma in October.

**Santa Anna** (1,100) agribusiness, oil, tourism; museum; Funtier days in May.

Other towns include: **Burkett** (90), **Goldsboro** (15), **Gouldbusk** (70), **Novice** (137), **Rockwood** (53), **Talpa** (127), and **Valera** (80).

| | |
|---|---|
| Population | 8,430 |
| Change from 2000 | – 5.2 |
| Area (sq. mi.) | 1,281.4 |
| Land Area (sq. mi.) | 1,262.0 |
| Altitude (ft.) | 1,289-2,250 |
| Rainfall (in.) | 28.74 |
| Jan. mean min. | 33.7 |

| | |
|---|---|
| July mean max. | 95.7 |
| Civ. Labor | 4,000 |
| Unemployed | 5.6 |
| Wages | $13,926,079 |
| Per Capita Income | $36,322 |
| Prop. Value | $1,310,366,662 |
| Retail Sales | $66,248,504 |

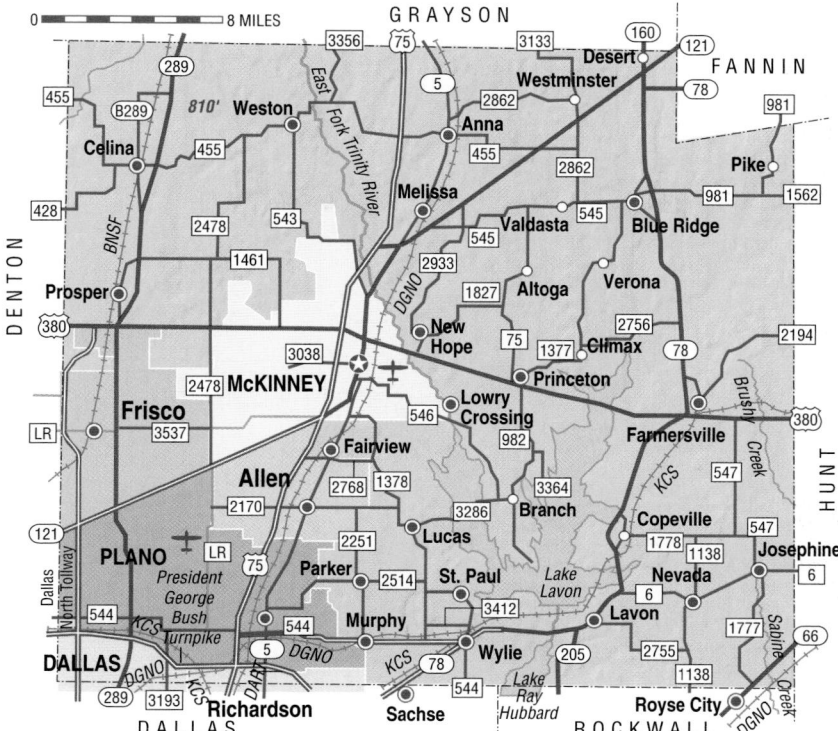

# Collin County

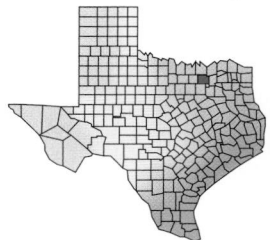

**Physical Features**: Heavy, black clay soil; level to rolling; drains to Trinity River; Lake Lavon, Lake Ray Hubbard.

**Economy**: Government/services, manufacturing plants, retail and wholesale center, many residents work in Dallas.

**History**: Caddo tribal area until 1850s. Settlers of Peters colony arrived in early 1840s. County created, organized, from Fannin County 1846. Named for pioneer settler Collin McKinney.

**Race/Ethnicity**: (In percent) Anglo, 61.2; Black, 9.4; Hispanic, 15.0; Asian, 12.3; Other, 3.2.

**Vital Statistics**, annual: Births, 10,342; deaths, 3,385; marriages, 5,107; divorces, 2,528.

**Recreation**: Fishing, water sports; historic sites; old homes restorations, tours; natural science museum.

**Minerals**: Insignificant.

**Agriculture**: Landscape nurseries, corn, wheat, cattle, hay, grain sorghum. Market value $77.8 million.

**McKINNEY** (150,033) county seat; agribusiness, trade center, varied industry; hospital, community college; museums.

*For explanation of sources, abbreviations and symbols, see p. 238, and foldout map.*

**PLANO** (278,495) corporate headquarters for telecommunications, manufacturing; medical services, research; community college; hospitals; museums, nature preserves; balloon festival in September, AsiaFest in May.

**Frisco** (139,355) technical, aerospace industry, hospital, community college.

Other towns include: **Allen** (93,642) retail, manufacturing, wholesale trade, hospital, community college, nature conservatory, natatorium, historic stone dam, Stampede rodeo in October; **Anna** (9,719); **Blue Ridge** (825).

Also, **Celina** (6,744) museum, historic town square, Fun Day in September; **Copeville** (243); **Fairview** (8,223) government/services, retail center, commuters, museum, old mill site, wildlife sanctuary, veterans cel-

ebration in November; **Farmersville** (3,402) agriculture, light industries, Audie Murphy Day in June.

Also, **Josephine** (1,029); **Lavon** (2,470); **Lowry Crossing** (1,702); **Lucas** (6,120); **Melissa** (6,245) industrial plants, library, old town; **Murphy** (19,816); **Nevada** (907); **New Hope** (636); **Parker** (4,194); **Princeton** (7,832) manufacturing, commuters, Spring Onion festival in April; **Prosper** (12,980); **St. Paul** (1,063); **Westminster** (964); **Weston** (570); **Wylie** (45,032) manufacturing, retail, hospital, historic sites, big cat sanctuary, July Jubilee.

Also, part [46,885] of **Dallas**, part [28,569] of **Richardson** and part [6,301] of **Sachse**.

| | |
|---|---|
| Population | **885,241** |
| Change fm 2010 | 13.2 |
| Area (sq. mi.) | 886.1 |
| Land Area (sq. mi.) | 841.2 |
| Altitude (ft.) | 434-810 |
| Rainfall (in.) | 42.32 |
| Jan. mean min. | 30.1 |
| July mean max. | 91.5 |
| Civ. Labor | 474,749 |
| Unemployed | 5.0 |
| Wages | $4,579,158,004 |
| Per Capita Income | $55,520 |
| Prop. Value | $90,306,686,328 |
| Retail Sales | $16,041,940,997 |

# Collingsworth County

**Physical Features**: Panhandle county of rolling, broken terrain, draining to Red River forks; sandy and loam soils.

**Economy**: Agribusiness.

**History**: Apaches, displaced by Comanches. Ranchers from England arrived in the late 1870s. County created in 1876, from Bexar and Young districts, organized in 1890. Named for Republic of Texas' first chief justice, James Collinsworth (name misspelled in law).

**Race/Ethnicity**: (In percent) Anglo, 60.5; Black, 6.0; Hispanic, 32.0; Asian, 0.5; Other, 3.9.

**Vital Statistics**, annual: Births, 41; deaths, 45; marriages, 30; divorces, 17.

**Recreation**: Deer, quail hunting; children's camp, county museum, pioneer park; Wellington peanut festival in September.

**Minerals**: Gas, oil production.

**Agriculture**: Cotton, peanuts, cow-calf operations, wheat, stocker cattle; 22,000 acres irrigated. Market value $43.1 million.

**WELLINGTON** (2,077) county seat; peanut-processing plants, varied manufacturing, agriculture; hospital, library; restored Ritz Theatre.

Other towns include: **Dodson** (106), **Quail** (17), **Samnorwood** (51).

| | |
|---|---|
| Population | 3,017 |
| Change fm 2010 | – 1.3 |
| Area (sq. mi.) | 919.3 |
| Land Area (sq. mi.) | 918.4 |
| Altitude (ft.) | 1,750-2,840 |
| Rainfall (in.) | 22.59 |
| Jan. mean min. | 27.4 |
| July mean max. | 97.6 |
| Civ. Labor | 1,319 |
| Unemployed | 4.5 |
| Wages | $6,915,728 |
| Per Capita Income | $44,534 |
| Prop. Value | $558,042,980 |
| Retail Sales | $12,721,681 |

# Colorado County

**Physical Features**: Located in three soil areas; level to rolling; bisected by Colorado River; Eagle Lake; oaks.

**Economy**: Agribusiness, oil and gas services, gravel mining.

**History**: Karankawa and other tribes. Anglo settlers among Stephen F. Austin's Old Three Hundred families. First German settlers arrived around 1840. Antebellum slaveholding area. County created 1836, organized 1837; named for river.

**Race/Ethnicity**: (In percent) Anglo, 58.3; Black, 13.3; Hispanic, 27.9; Asian, 0.7; Other, 2.3.

**Vital Statistics**, annual: Births, 237; deaths, 292; marriages, 123; divorces, 59.

**Recreation**: Hunting of duck, geese, deer, exotics; canoeing, bicycling; historic sites; prairie chicken refuge; opera house in Columbus.

**Minerals**: Gas, oil, gravel.

**Agriculture**: Rice (third in state in acres), cattle, corn, cotton, soybeans, sesame, hay, pecans, nurseries; significant irrigation for rice. Market value $68 million.

**COLUMBUS** (3,842) county seat; mining, agribusiness center, tourism, oil-field servicing, timber-treating center; hospital; historical sites, homes, walking tour; Live Oak festival in May.

**Eagle Lake** (3,868) rice drying center; hospital; goose hunting; Prairie Edge museum.

**Weimar** (2,223) agriculture, light industry, meat processing, retail; hospital, library; "Gedenke" (remember) celebration on Mother's Day weekend.

Other towns include: **Altair** (30), **Garwood** (600), **Glidden** (698), **Nada** (165), **Oakland** (80), **Rock Island** (160), **Sheridan** (300).

| | |
|---|---|
| Population | 20,719 |
| Change fm 2010 | – 0.7 |
| Area (sq. mi.) | 973.7 |
| Land Area (sq. mi.) | 960.3 |
| Altitude (ft.) | 125-450 |
| Rainfall (in.) | 43.93 |
| Jan. mean min. | 40.8 |
| July mean max. | 94.3 |
| Civ. Labor | 11,683 |
| Unemployed | 4.3 |
| Wages | $63,836,721 |
| Per Capita Income | $44,021 |
| Prop. Value | $3,958,675,637 |
| Retail Sales | $322,757,586 |

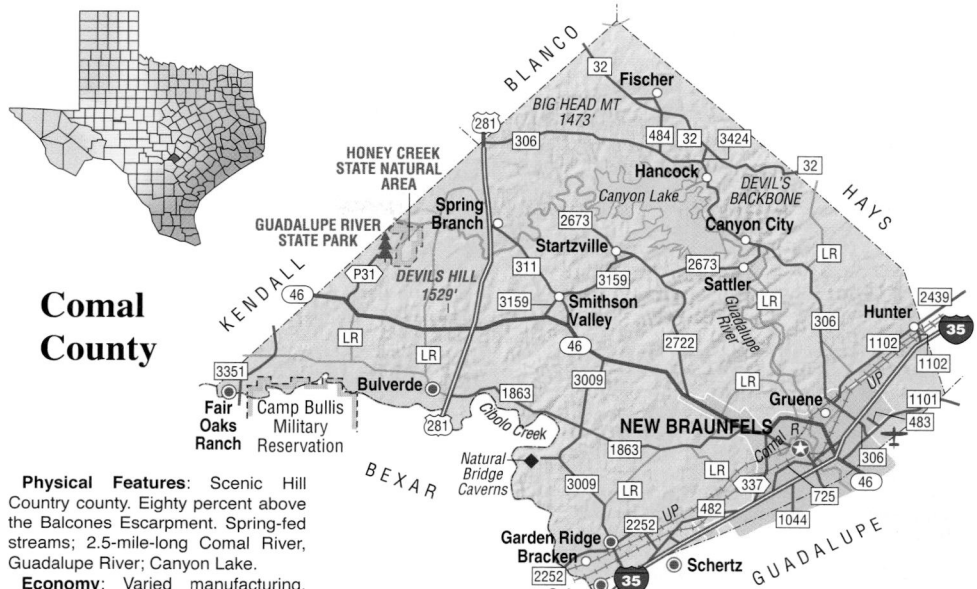

# Comal County

**Physical Features**: Scenic Hill Country county. Eighty percent above the Balcones Escarpment. Spring-fed streams; 2.5-mile-long Comal River, Guadalupe River; Canyon Lake.

**Economy**: Varied manufacturing, tourism, government/services, agriculture; county is in the San Antonio metropolitan area.

**History**: Tonkawa, Waco Indian tribes. A pioneer German settlement in 1845. Mexican migration peaked during the Mexican Revolution of the 1910s. County created from Bexar, Gonzales, Travis counties and organized in 1846; named for river, a name for Spanish earthenware or metal pan used for cooking tortillas.

**Race/Ethnicity**: (In percent) Anglo, 69.5; Black, 2.1; Hispanic, 26.2; Asian, 1.0; Other, 3.5.

**Vital Statistics**, annual: Births, 1,309; deaths, 1,080; marriages, 1,012; divorces, 328.

**Recreation**: Fishing, hunting; historic sites; scenic drives; lake facilities; Prince Solms Park, other county parks; Landa Park with 76 species of trees; Gruene historic area; caverns; river resorts; river tubing; Schlitterbahn water park; Wurstfest in November, Wasselfest in December.

**Minerals**: Stone, lime, sand and gravel.

| | |
|---|---|
| Population | **123,694** |
| Change fm 2010 | 14.0 |
| Area (sq. mi.) | 574.9 |
| Land Area (sq. mi.) | 559.5 |
| Altitude (ft.) | 560-1,529 |
| Rainfall (in.) | 33.97 |
| Jan. mean min. | 38.1 |
| July mean max. | 93.3 |
| Civ. Labor | 58,780 |
| Unemployed | 5.1 |
| Wages | $397,675,810 |
| Per Capita Income | $48,466 |
| Prop. Value | $14,720,144,743 |
| Retail Sales | $1,903,834,770 |

*For explanation of sources, abbreviations and symbols, see p. 238, and foldout map.*

**Agriculture**: Cattle, goats, sheep, hogs, horses; nursery, hay, corn, sorghum, wheat.

**NEW BRAUNFELS** (63,675) county seat; manufacturing, retail, distribution center; picturesque city, making it a tourist center; Conservation Plaza; rose garden; hospital; library; mental health and retardation center. **Gruene** is now part of New Braunfels.

Other towns include: **Bulverde** (4,868); **Garden Ridge** (3,551); the retirement and recreation community around **Canyon Lake** (22,679), which includes **Startzville**, **Sattler**, **Smithson Valley**, **Canyon City**, **Hancock**, **Fischer** and **Spring Branch**.

Also in the county, parts of **Fair Oaks Ranch** (6,794), **Selma** (7,431) and **Schertz** (35,510).

*The Gruene Family Home in Gruene. © 2007 Larry D. Moore (CC).*

# Comanche County

**Physical Features**: Rolling, hilly terrain; sandy, loam, waxy soils; drains to Leon River, Proctor Lake; pecans, oaks, mesquites, cedars.

**Economy**: Dairies, peanut-, pecan-shelling plants, manufacturing.

**History**: Comanche area. Anglo-American settlers arrived in 1854 on land granted earlier to Stephen F. Austin and Samuel May Williams. County created and organized in 1856 from Bosque and Coryell counties; named for the Indian tribe.

**Race/Ethnicity**: (In percent) Anglo, 71.4; Black, 0.9; Hispanic, 26.8; Asian, 0.3; Other, 2.1.

**Vital Statistics**, annual: Births, 155; deaths, 156; marriages, 106; divorces, 38.

**Recreation**: Hunting, fishing, water sports, nature tourism; parks, community center, museums; Comanche Pow-Wow in September, rodeo in July.

**Minerals**: Limited gas, oil, stone, clay.

**Agriculture**: Dairies, beef cattle, pecans (first in state in acreage), hay, wildlife, melons. Market value $158.1 million.

**COMANCHE** (4,338) county seat; plants process feed, food; varied manufacturing; agribusiness; winery; hospital; Ranger College branch; library; state's oldest courthouse, "Old Cora," on display on town square.

**De Leon** (2,240) pecans, light manufacturing; hospital; car museum, Peach and Melon Festival in August.

Other towns include: **Energy** (70), **Gustine** (479), **Proctor** (228) and **Sidney** (148).

| | |
|---|---|
| Population | 13,550 |
| Change fm 2010 | – 3.0 |
| Area (sq. mi.) | 947.7 |
| Land Area (sq. mi.) | 937.8 |
| Altitude (ft.) | 1,020-1,847 |
| Rainfall (in.) | 32.38 |
| Jan. mean min. | 31.4 |
| July mean max. | 95.7 |
| Civ. Labor | 6,350 |
| Unemployed | 5.2 |
| Wages | $26,379,965 |
| Per Capita Income | $37,013 |
| Prop. Value | $1,839,228,476 |
| Retail Sales | $125,886,338 |

# Concho County

**Physical Features**: On Edwards Plateau; rough, broken to south; level in north; sandy, loam and dark soils; drains to creeks and Colorado River.

**Economy**: Agribusiness, manufacturing.

**History**: Athabascan-speaking Plains Indians, then Jumanos in the 1600s, absorbed by Lipan Apaches in the 1700s. Comanches raided after 1800. Anglo-Americans began ranching around 1850; farming began after the Civil War. Mexican-Americans employed on sheep ranches in 1920s-30s. County created from Bexar District in 1858, organized in 1879; named for river.

**Race/Ethnicity**: (In percent) Anglo, 42.6; Black, 2.5; Hispanic, 54.5; Asian, 0.4; Other, 2.1.

**Vital Statistics**, annual: Births, 23; deaths, 31; marriages, 8; divorces, 10.

**Recreation**: Famed for 1,500 Indian pictographs; O.H. Ivie Reservoir.

**Minerals**: Oil, gas, stone.

**Agriculture**: Sheep, cattle, and goats; wheat, feed grains; 2,000 acres irrigated for cotton. Market value $22.8 million.

**PAINT ROCK** (262) county seat; named for Indian pictographs nearby; farming, ranching center.

**EDEN** (2,725) steel fabrication, detention center; hospital; fall fest.

Other towns include: **Eola** (215), **Lowake** (40) and **Millersview** (80).

| | |
|---|---|
| Population | 4,050 |
| Change fm 2010 | – 0.9 |
| Area (sq. mi.) | 993.7 |
| Land Area (sq. mi.) | 983.8 |
| Altitude (ft.) | 1,421-2,413 |
| Rainfall (in.) | 24.96 |
| Jan. mean min. | 29.5 |
| July mean max. | 95.2 |
| Civ. Labor | 1,328 |
| Unemployed | 5.4 |
| Wages | $7,571,181 |
| Per Capita Income | $28,814 |
| Prop. Value | $783,850,883 |
| Retail Sales | $16,650,201 |

*For explanation of sources, abbreviations and symbols, see p. 238, and foldout map.*

# Cooke County

**Physical Features**: North Texas county; drains to Red, Trinity rivers; Ray Roberts Lake, Lake Texoma, Lake Kiowa, Hubert H. Moss Lake; sandy, red, loam soils.

**Economy**: Oil and gas, varied manufacturing, commuting to northern DFW metroplex.

**History**: Frontier between Caddoes and Comanches. Anglo-Americans arrived in the late 1840s. Germans settled western part of county around 1890. County created and organized in 1848 from Fannin County; named for Capt. W.G. Cooke of the Texas Revolution.

**Race/Ethnicity**: (In percent) Anglo, 77.2; Black, 3.2; Hispanic, 16.7; Asian, 1.0; Other, 3.0.

**Vital Statistics**, annual: Births, 564; deaths, 431; marriages, 532; divorces, 157.

**Recreation**: Water sports; hunting, fishing; zoo; museum; park; historic buildings, Gainesville Depot Day/car show in October.

**Minerals**: Oil, natural gas, sand, gravel.

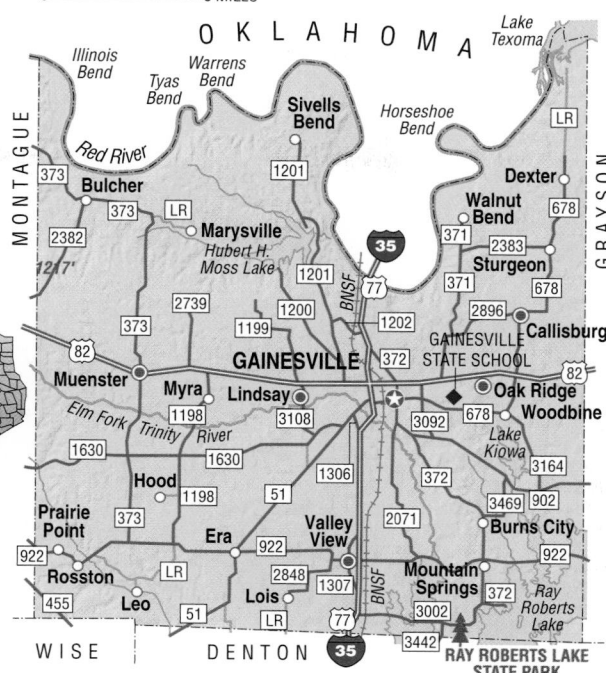

**Agriculture**: Beef cattle, horses, forages, wheat. Market value $63.3 million. Hunting leases important.

**GAINESVILLE** (16,502) county seat; tourism, plastics, agribusiness, aircraft and steel fabrication; Victorian homes, walking tours; hospital; community college, juvenile correction unit; Camp Sweeney for diabetic children.

**Muenster** (1,620) varied manufacturing, food processing, oil and gas, agriculture; hospital, Germanfest in April.

Other towns include: **Callisburg** (371), **Era** (150), **Lindsay** (1,082) 1919 Romanesque-style St. Peter Church, **Myra** (150), **Oak Ridge** (158), **Rosston** (75), **Valley View** (780) and the residential community around **Lake Kiowa** (2,011).

| | |
|---|---|
| Population | **38,761** |
| Change fm 2010 | 0.8 |
| Area (sq. mi.) | 898.4 |
| Land Area (sq. mi.) | 874.8 |
| Altitude (ft.) | 617-1,217 |
| Rainfall (in.) | 42.70 |
| Jan. mean min. | 31.3 |
| July mean max. | 93.4 |
| Civ. Labor | 23,632 |
| Unemployed | 3.9 |
| Wages | $181,319,938 |
| Per Capita Income | $58,815 |
| Prop. Value | $5,195,070,959 |
| Retail Sales | $869,630,289 |

*For explanation of sources, abbreviations and symbols, see p. 238, and foldout map.*

*St. Peter Church in Lindsay. Photo by Robert Plocheck.*

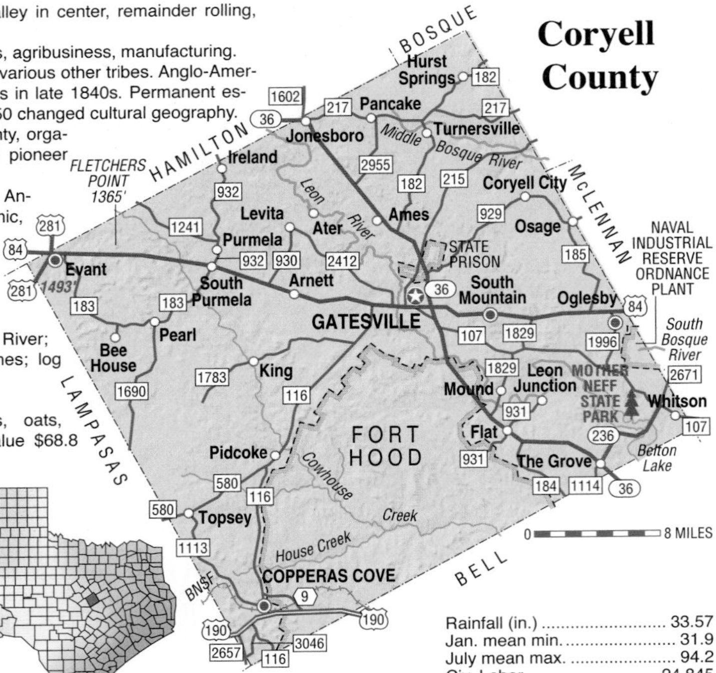

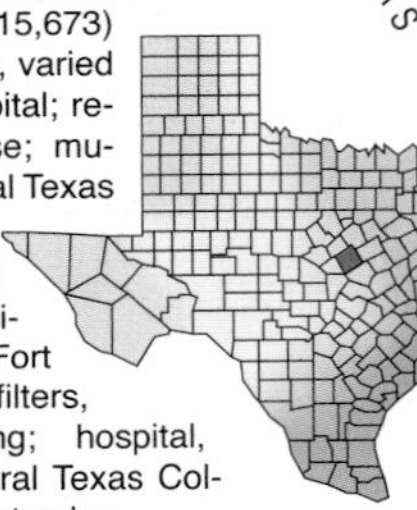

**Physical Features**: Leon Valley in center, remainder rolling, hilly; Belton Lake.

**Economy**: Fort Hood, prisons, agribusiness, manufacturing.

**History**: Tonkawa area, later various other tribes. Anglo-Americans settled around Fort Gates in late 1840s. Permanent establishment of Fort Hood in 1950 changed cultural geography. County created from Bell County, organized, 1854; named for local pioneer James Coryell.

**Race/Ethnicity**: (In percent) Anglo, 60.2; Black, 17.2; Hispanic, 17.2; Asian, 2.2; Other, 6.1.

**Vital Statistics**, annual: Births, 918; deaths, 394; marriages, 519; divorces, 345.

**Recreation**: State park; deer hunting; fishing; lake, Leon River; bluebonnet area; historic homes; log jail; Shivaree in June.

**Minerals**: Oil and gas.

**Agriculture**: Beef, forages, oats, wildlife, row crops. Market value $68.8 million. Hunting leases, timber.

**GATESVILLE** (15,673) county seat; prisons, varied manufacturing; hospital; refurbished courthouse; museum; branch Central Texas College.

**C O P P E R A S COVE** (33,064) business center for Fort Hood; industrial filters, other manufacturing; hospital; library; branch Central Texas College; Spurfest in September.

Other towns include: **Evant** (414, partly in Hamilton County), **Flat** (210), **Jonesboro** (125), **Mound** (125), **Oglesby** (467), **Purmela** (50), **South Mountain** (381). Part [14, 415] of **Fort Hood**.

# Coryell County

| | |
|---|---|
| Population | 75,562 |
| Change fm 2010 | 0.2 |
| Area (sq. mi.) | 1,056.8 |
| Land Area (sq. mi.) | 1,052.1 |
| Altitude (ft.) | 600-1,493 |

| | |
|---|---|
| Rainfall (in.) | 33.57 |
| Jan. mean min. | 31.9 |
| July mean max. | 94.2 |
| Civ. Labor | 24,845 |
| Unemployed | 7.5 |
| Wages | $114,726,079 |
| Per Capita Income | $36,900 |
| Prop. Value | $3,437,014,938 |
| Retail Sales | $497,766,336 |

*For explanation of sources, abbreviations and symbols, see p. 238, and foldout map.*

---

*A truck passes a roadside park planted with trees, a rare sight in Crane County. Photo by Robert Plocheck.*

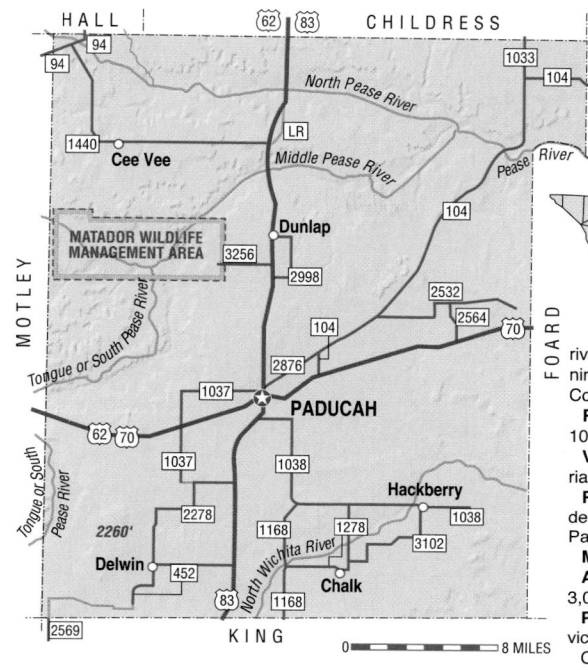

## Cottle County

**Physical Features**: Northwest county below Caprock, rough in west, level in east; gray, black, sandy and loam soils; drains to Pease River.

**Economy**: Agribusiness, government/services.

**History**: Around 1700, Apaches were displaced by Comanches, who in turn were driven out by U.S. Army in the 1870s. Anglo-American settlers arrived in the 1880s. County created 1876 from Fannin County; organized 1892; named for George W. Cottle, Alamo hero.

**Race/Ethnicity**: (In percent) Anglo, 65.6; Black, 10.1; Hispanic, 23.8; Asian, 0.1; Other, 2.0.

**Vital Statistics**, annual: Births, 9; deaths, 29; marriages, 12; divorces, 0.

**Recreation**: Hunting of quail, dove, wild hogs, deer; wildlife management area; museum, Fiestas Patrias in September, horse and colt show in April.

**Minerals**: Oil, natural gas.

**Agriculture**: Beef cattle, cotton, peanuts, wheat. 3,000 acres irrigated. Market value $15.9 million.

**PADUCAH** (1,143) county seat; government/services, library.

Other towns include: **Cee Vee** (45).

| | | |
|---|---|---|
| Population ................................. 1,415 | Rainfall (in.) ............................. 24.94 | Unemployed ................................. 5.4 |
| Change fm 2010 ......................... − 6.0 | Jan. mean min. ......................... 27.9 | Wages ............................. $3,513.775 |
| Area (sq. mi.) ............................. 901.6 | July mean max. .......................... 97.2 | Per Capita Income................... $41,652 |
| Land Area (sq. mi.) .................... 900.6 | Civ. Labor ..................................... 737 | Prop. Value .................... $428,307,060 |
| Altitude (ft.) ...................... 1,470-2,260 | | Retail Sales ................... $10,357,983 |

**Physical Features**: Rolling prairie, Pecos Valley, some hills; sandy, loam soils; Juan Cordona Lake (intermittent).

**Economy**: Oil and gas; agriculture; government/services.

**History**: Lipan Apache area. Ranching developed in 1890s. Oil discovered in 1926. County created from Tom Green County 1887, organized 1927; named for Baylor University president W. C. Crane.

**Race/Ethnicity**: (In percent) Anglo, 35.3; Black, 3.6; Hispanic, 60.1; Asian, 0.6; Other, 2.5.

**Vital Statistics**, annual: Births, 81; deaths, 43; marriages, 32; divorces, 2.

**Recreation**: Museum of the Desert Southwest; sites of pioneer trails and historic Horsehead Crossing on Pecos River; hunting of mule deer, quail; camping park; rodeo in May.

**Minerals**: Oil, gas production.

**Agriculture**: Cattle ranching, goats. Market value $1.4 million.

**CRANE** (3,756) county seat; oil-well servicing and production, foundry, steel, surfboard manufacturing; hospital.

## Crane County

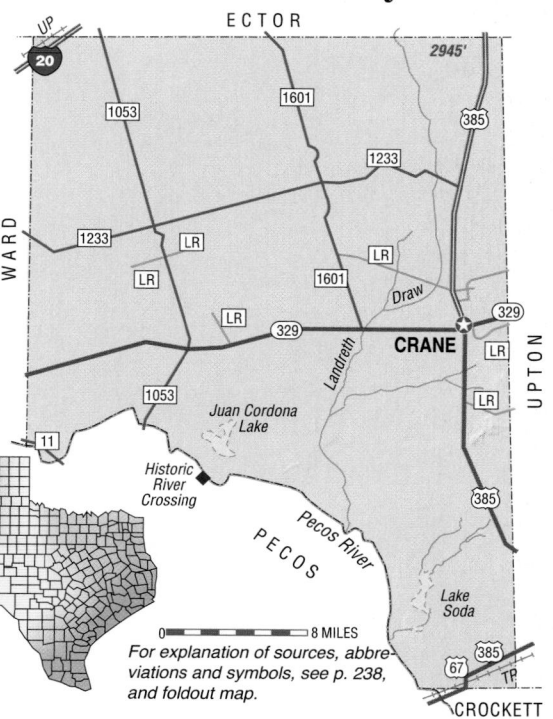

*For explanation of sources, abbreviations and symbols, see p. 238, and foldout map.*

| | |
|---|---|
| Population ................................... 4,950 | |
| Change fm 2010 ........................... 13.1 | |
| Area (sq. mi.) .............................. 785.7 | |
| Land Area (sq. mi.) ...................... 785.1 | |
| Altitude (ft.) ........................ 2,290-2,945 | |
| Rainfall (in.) ................................. 15.60 | |
| Jan. mean min. ............................. 31.9 | |
| July mean max. ............................. 93.3 | |
| Civ. Labor .................................... 2,048 | |
| Unemployed ..................................... 4.8 | |
| Wages ............................. $27,345,878 | |
| Per Capita Income................... $45,803 | |
| Prop. Value ................. $2,618,190,090 | |
| Retail Sales ..................... $27,745,490 | |

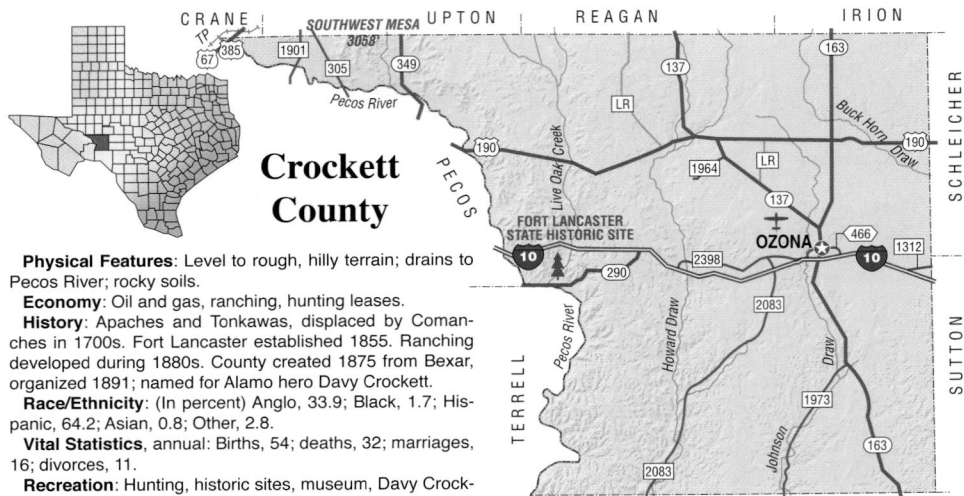

# Crockett County

**Physical Features**: Level to rough, hilly terrain; drains to Pecos River; rocky soils.

**Economy**: Oil and gas, ranching, hunting leases.

**History**: Apaches and Tonkawas, displaced by Comanches in 1700s. Fort Lancaster established 1855. Ranching developed during 1880s. County created 1875 from Bexar, organized 1891; named for Alamo hero Davy Crockett.

**Race/Ethnicity**: (In percent) Anglo, 33.9; Black, 1.7; Hispanic, 64.2; Asian, 0.8; Other, 2.8.

**Vital Statistics**, annual: Births, 54; deaths, 32; marriages, 16; divorces, 11.

**Recreation**: Hunting, historic sites, museum, Davy Crockett statue in park; Davy Crockett festival in August, Deerfest in December.

**Minerals**: Oil, gas production.

**Agriculture**: Sheep (first in numbers), goats; also beef cattle. Market value $13.9 million.

**OZONA** (3,237) county seat; trade center for ranching, hunting leases, tourism.

| | | | |
|---|---|---|---|
| Population | 3,812 | July mean max. | 93.4 |
| Change fm 2010 | 2.5 | Civ. Labor | 2,461 |
| Area (sq. mi.) | 2,807.4 | Unemployed | 3.0 |
| Land Area (sq. mi.) | 2,807.3 | Wages | $15,460,462 |
| Altitude (ft.) | 1,720-3,058 | Per Capita Income | $40,585 |
| Rainfall (in.) | 18.86 | Prop. Value | $2,248,039,300 |
| Jan. mean min. | 30.2 | Retail Sales | $62,598,638 |

# Crosby County

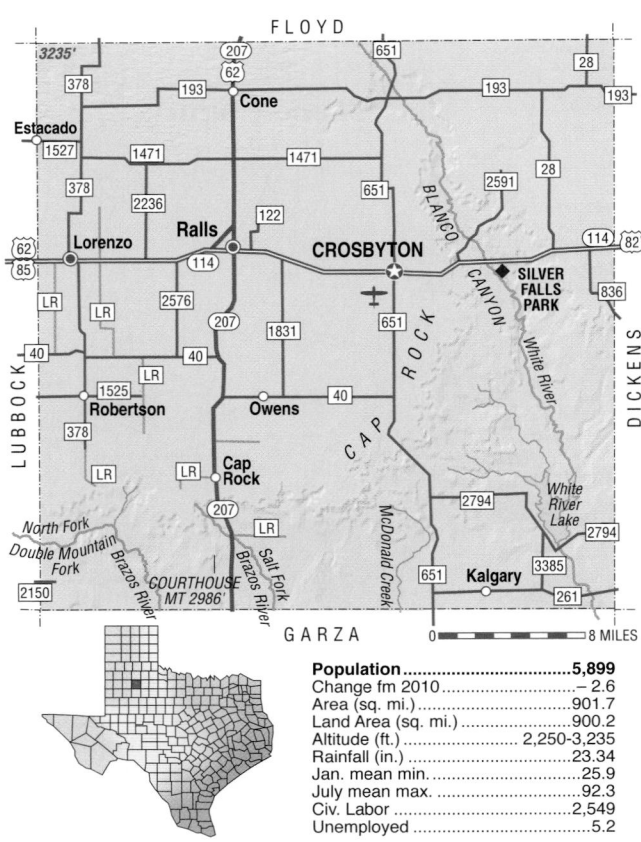

**Physical Features**: Flat, rich soil above Caprock, broken below; drains into Brazos River forks and playas.

**Economy**: Agribusiness, tourism, commuters to Lubbock.

History: Comanches, driven out by U.S. Army in 1870s; ranching developed soon afterward. Quaker colony founded in 1879. County created from Bexar District 1876, organized 1886; named for Texas Land Commissioner Stephen Crosby.

**Race/Ethnicity**: (In percent) Anglo, 41.2; Black, 4.4; Hispanic, 53.8; Asian, 0.1; Other, 2.9.

**Vital Statistics**, annual: Births, 71; deaths, 68; marriages, 26; divorces, 13.

**Recreation**: White River Lake; Silver Falls Park; hunting.

**Minerals**: Sand, gravel, oil, gas.

**Agriculture**: Cotton, beef cattle, sorghum; about 112,000 acres irrigated. Market value $71.6 million.

**CROSBYTON** (1,678) county seat; agribusiness center; hospital, Pioneer Museum, Prairie Ladies Multi-Cultural Center, library; Cowboy Gathering in October.

Other towns include: **Lorenzo** (1,149); **Ralls** (1,891) government/services, agribusiness, museums, Cotton Boll Fest in September.

| | |
|---|---|
| Population | 5,899 |
| Change fm 2010 | – 2.6 |
| Area (sq. mi.) | 901.7 |
| Land Area (sq. mi.) | 900.2 |
| Altitude (ft.) | 2,250-3,235 |
| Rainfall (in.) | 23.34 |
| Jan. mean min. | 25.9 |
| July mean max. | 92.3 |
| Civ. Labor | 2,549 |
| Unemployed | 5.2 |

| | |
|---|---|
| Wages | $11,672,025 |
| Per Capita Income | $49,814 |
| Prop. Value | $790,849,371 |
| Retail Sales | $37,064,519 |

*Vegetation along the trail in McKittrick Canyon, Guadalupe Mountains National Park. Photo by Robert Plocheck.*

# Culberson County

**Physical Features**: Contains Texas' highest mountain; slopes toward Pecos Valley on east, Diablo Bolson on west; salt lakes; unique vegetation in canyons.

**Economy**: Tourism, government/services, talc mining and processing, agribusiness, sulfur mining.

**History**: Apaches arrived about 600 years ago. U.S. military frontier after Civil War. Ranching developed after 1880. Mexican migration increased after 1920. County created from El Paso County 1911, organized 1912; named for D.B. Culberson, Texas congressman.

**Race/Ethnicity**: (In percent) Anglo, 22.5; Black, 1.1; Hispanic, 73.4; Asian, 1.3; Other, 5.1.

**Vital Statistics**, annual: Births, 30; deaths, 14; marriages, 0; divorces, 4.

**Recreation**: National park; Guadalupe and El Capitan, twin peaks; scenic canyons and mountains; classic car museum, antique saloon bar; frontier days in June, big buck tournament.

**Minerals**: Sulfur, talc, marble, oil.

**Agriculture**: Beef cattle; crops include cotton, vegetables, melons, pecans; 6,000 acres in irrigation. Market value $13.7 million.

**VAN HORN** (2,040) county seat; agribusiness, tourism, rock crushing, government/services; hospital.

Other towns: **Kent** (30).

| | |
|---|---|
| Population | 2,266 |
| Change fm 2010 | – 5.5 |
| Area (sq. mi.) | 3,813.0 |
| Land Area (sq. mi.) | 3,812.8 |
| Altitude (ft.) | 2,900-8,749 |
| Rainfall (in.) | 11.58 |
| Jan. mean min. | 28.3 |
| July mean max. | 92.3 |
| Civ. Labor | 1,829 |
| Unemployed | 2.7 |
| Wages | $8,792,389 |
| Per Capita Income | $37,359 |
| Prop. Value | $542,969,770 |
| Retail Sales | $120,348,281 |

*For explanation of sources, abbreviations and symbols, see p. 238, and foldout map.*

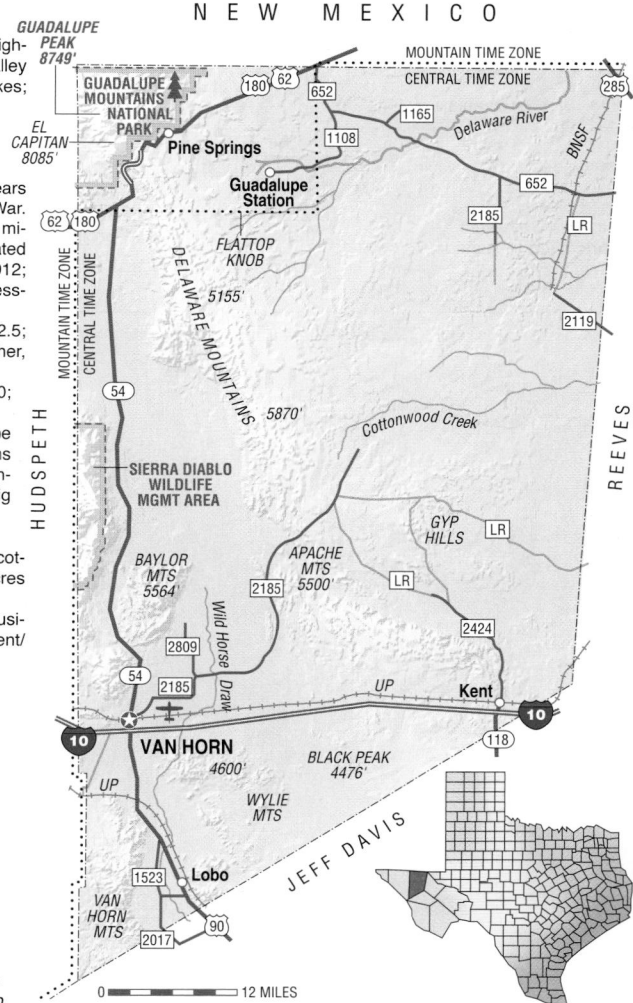

# Dallam County

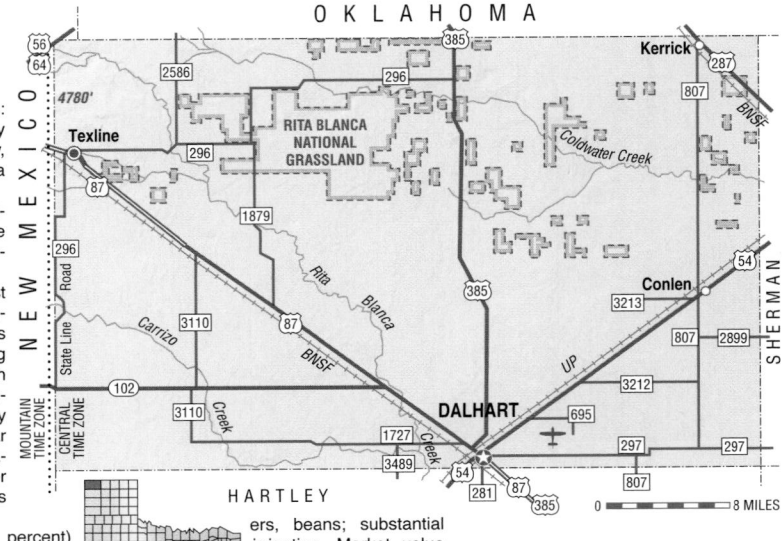

**Physical Features**: Prairie, broken by creeks; playas; sandy, loam soils; Rita Blanca National Grassland.

**Economy**: Agribusiness, dairies, cheese manufacturing, tourism.

**History**: Earliest Plains Apaches; displaced by Comanches and Kiowas. Ranching developed in late 19th century. Farming began after 1900. County created from Bexar District, 1876, organized 1891. Named for lawyer-editor James W. Dallam.

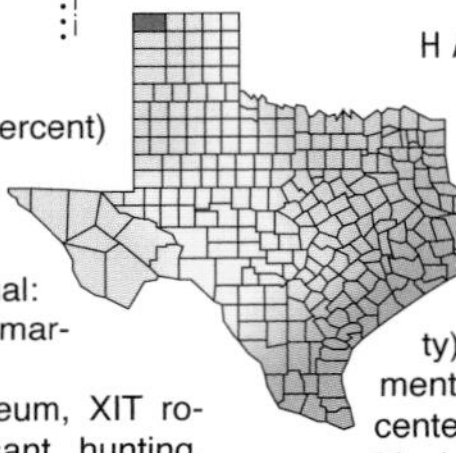

**Race/Ethnicity**: (In percent) Anglo, 53.2; Black, 1.9; Hispanic, 42.5; Asian, 0.8; Other, 3.9.

**Vital Statistics**, annual: Births, 147; deaths, 54; marriages, 98; divorces, 30.

**Recreation**: XIT museum, XIT rodeo in August, pheasant hunting, wildlife, grasslands.

**Minerals**: Petroleum.

**Agriculture**: A leader in production of grain (corn, wheat, sorghum). Cattle, hogs, dairies, potatoes, sunflowers, beans; substantial irrigation. Market value $651.7 million.

**DALHART** (8,147, partly in Hartley County) county seat; government/services; agribusiness center for parts of Texas, New Mexico, Oklahoma; railroad; cheese plant; grain operations; junior college branch; hospital; prison.

Other towns include: **Kerrick** (35) and **Texline** (519).

| | |
|---|---|
| Population | 7,135 |
| Change fm 2010 | 6.4 |
| Area (sq. mi.) | 1,505.3 |
| Land Area (sq. mi.) | 1,503.3 |
| Altitude (ft.) | 3,655-4,780 |
| Rainfall (in.) | 17.59 |
| Jan. mean min. | 18.3 |
| July mean max. | 91.1 |
| Civ. Labor | 3,691 |
| Unemployed | 3.6 |
| Wages | $39,823,005 |
| Per Capita Income | $49,518 |
| Prop. Value | $1,383,829,267 |
| Retail Sales | $86,366,143 |

*A jogger on the park road at Cedar Hill State Park, with Joe Pool Lake in the background. Photo by Robert Plocheck.*

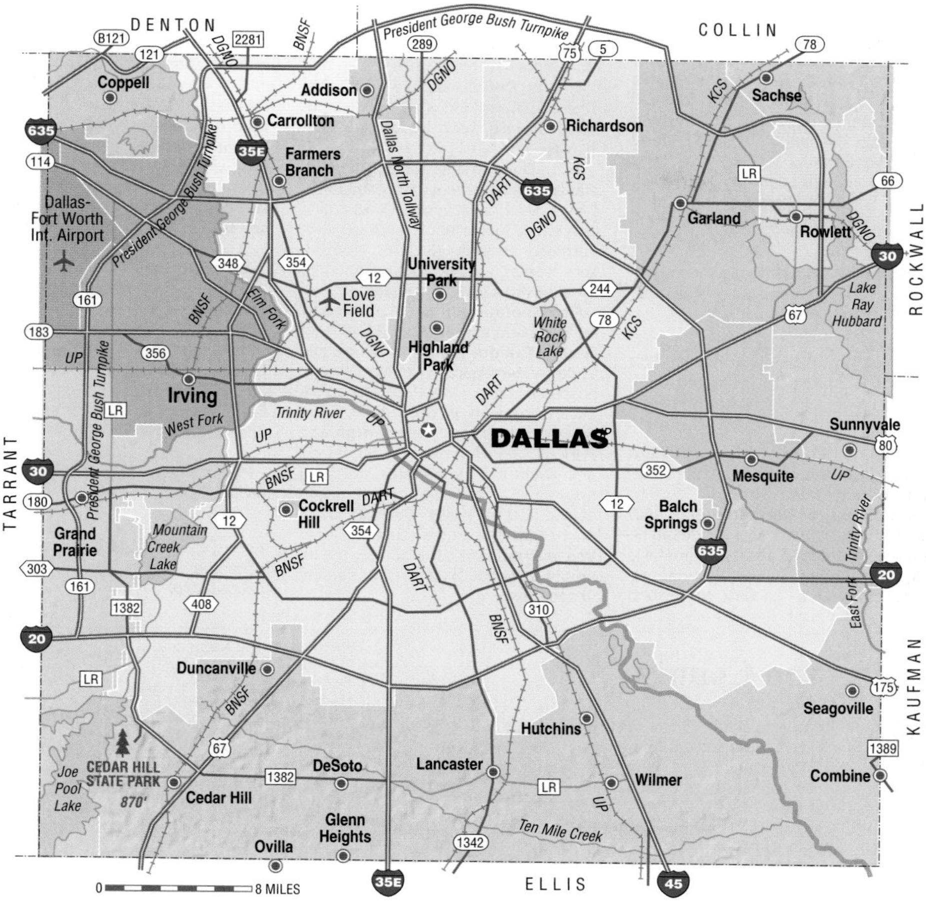

## Map

D E N T O N — COLLIN

B121 — 2281 — BNSF — President George Bush Turnpike — 289 — 75 — 5 — 78

121 — DGNO

Coppell — Addison — Richardson — Sachse — KCS

635 — Carrollton — Dallas North Tollway — DART — 635 — LR — 66

114 — 35E — Farmers Branch — KCS — Garland — Rowlett — DGNO

Dallas-Fort Worth Int. Airport — 348 — 354 — University Park — DGNO — 30

Love Field — 161 — BNSF — 244 — Lake Ray Hubbard — ROCKWALL

183 — White Rock Lake — 78 — KCS — 67

356 — Highland Park — DART

Irving — Trinity River — UP — DALLAS — Sunnyvale — 80

West Fork — LR — UP — 352 — Mesquite — UP

30 — BNSF — LR — DART — Balch Springs

180 — Cockrell Hill — 12 — 635

Grand Prairie — Mountain Creek Lake — 354 — BNSF — 20

303 — 161 — BNSF — DART — BNSF — 310

1382 — 408 — East Fork Trinity River

20 — KAUFMAN

Duncanville — 175 — Seagoville

LR — BNSF — Hutchins

67 — 1389

Joe Pool Lake — CEDAR HILL STATE PARK 870' — 1382 — DeSoto — Lancaster — LR — Wilmer — Combine

Cedar Hill — Glenn Heights

Ovilla — 1342 — Ten Mile Creek

0 — 8 MILES — 35E — ELLIS — 45

TARRANT

---

## Physical Features

**Physical Features**: Mostly flat, heavy blackland soils, sandy clays in west; drains to Trinity River; Joe Pool Lake, White Rock Lake, Mountain Creek Lake, Lake Ray Hubbard, North Lake.

**Economy**: A national center for telecommunications, transportation, electronics manufacturing, data processing, conventions and trade shows; foreign-trade zone located at D/FW International Airport, U.S. Customs port of entry; government/services.

**History**: Caddoan area. Anglo-Americans began arriving in 1840. Antebellum slaveholding area. County created 1846 from Nacogdoches, Robertson counties; named for U.S. Vice President George Mifflin Dallas.

**Race/Ethnicity**: (In percent) Anglo, 31.7; Black, 23.1; Hispanic, 39.0; Asian, 5.7; Other, 2.9.

**Vital Statistics**, annual: Births,

*For explanation of sources, abbreviations and symbols, see p. 238, and foldout map.*

# Dallas County

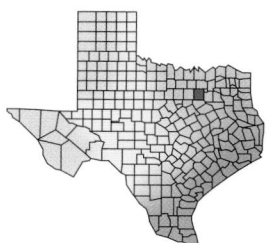

38,769; deaths, 14,506; marriages, 15,627; divorces, 8,239.

**Recreation**: One of the state's top tourist destinations and one of the nation's most popular convention centers; State Fair, museums, zoo, West End shopping and tourist district, historical sites, including Sixth Floor museum in the old Texas School Book Depository, site of the assassination of President Kennedy.

| | |
|---|---|
| Population | 2,518,638 |
| Change fm 2010 | 6.4 |
| Area (sq. mi.) | 908.6 |
| Land Area (sq. mi.) | 871.3 |
| Altitude (ft.) | 350-870 |
| Rainfall (in.) | 37.57 |
| Jan. mean min. | 37.3 |
| July mean max. | 96.0 |
| Civ. Labor | 1,238,466 |
| Unemployed | 5.8 |
| Wages | $21,786,341,497 |
| Per Capita Income | $48,638 |
| Prop. Value | $195,297,321,560 |
| Retail Sales | $46,373,958,271 |

Also, the Morton H. Meyerson Symphony Center; performing arts; professional sports; Texas broadcast museum; lakes, state park, Audubon center; theme and amusement parks.

**Minerals**: Sand, gravel, oil and gas.

**Agriculture**: Horticultural crops, wheat, hay, corn, soybeans, horses. Market value $44.5 million.

**Education**: Southern Methodist University, University of Dallas, Dallas Baptist University, University of Texas at Dallas, University of Texas Southwestern Medical Center and many other education centers.

**DALLAS** (1,255,343) county seat; center of state's largest consolidated metropolitan area and third-largest city in Texas; D/FW International Airport is one of the world's busiest; headquarters for the U.S. Army and Air Force Exchange Service; Federal Reserve Bank; a leader in fashions and in computer operations; hospitals; many hotels in downtown area offer adequate accommodations for most conventions.

**Garland** (235,508) varied manufacturing, community college branch, hospitals, performing arts center.

**Irving** (230,662) finance, technology, tourism, distribution center; Boy Scout headquarters and museum; North Lake College; hospitals; parks; Dragon Boat Festival in May.

Other cities include: **Addison** (16,185) general aviation airport, theater center; **Balch Springs** (25,201); part [49,392] of **Carrollton** (126,466) residential community, distribution center, hospital; **Cedar Hill** (46,041) residential, light manufacturing, retail, distribution center, Northwood

University, community college, state park, Penn Farm, Country Day on the Hill in October; **Cockrell Hill** (4,295); **Coppell** (40,041) distribution, varied manufacturing, office center, hike and bike trails; **DeSoto** (52,035) residential community, light industry and distribution, hospitals; Toad Holler Creekfest in June.

Also, **Duncanville** (39,695) varied manufacturing, many commuters to Dallas; Sandra Meadows Classic girls basketball tournament in December; **Farmers Branch** (31,378) distribution center, varied manufacturing, Brookhaven College, hospital.

Also, **Glenn Heights** (11,782, partly in Ellis County); most [123,487] of **Grand Prairie** (184,144) wholesale trade, aerospace, entertainment, hospital, library, Joe Pool Reservoir, Indian pow-wow in September, Lone Star horse-racing track; **Highland Park** (8,732); **Hutchins** (5,283) varied manufacturing; **Lancaster** (37,314) residential, industrial, distribution center, Cedar Valley College, Commemorative Air Force museum, Cold War air museum, Bear Creek nature preserve, depot, historic town square, Oktoberfest.

Also, **Mesquite** (144,330) varied industries, shipping, rail port hub, retail; hospitals; championship rodeo, rodeo parade in spring, Real Texas Festival in April; community college, historical parks; most [70,654] of **Richardson** (104,037) telecommunications, software development, financial services, hospital, library, Wildflower Music Festival in May; **Rowlett** (59,203) residential, manufacturing, government/services, hospital, library, park, hike and bike trails.

Also, **Sachse** (22,385, partly in Collin County) commuting to Dallas, government/services, Fallfest in October; **Seagoville** (15,408) rural/suburban setting, federal prison, Seagofest in October; **Sunnyvale** (5,829) tile manufacturing, hospital, Samuell Farm, Sunnyfest on July 4; **University Park** (23,739); **Wilmer** (3,739).

Part of **Combine** (2,033) and part of **Ovilla** (3,557).

*For explanation of sources, abbreviations and symbols, see p. 238, and foldout map.*

# Dawson County

**Physical Features**: South Plains county, broken on the east; loam and sandy soils.

**Economy**: Agriculture, farm and gin equipment manufacturing, peanut plant, government/services.

**History**: Comanche, Kiowa tribes in area. Ranching developed in 1880s. Farming began after 1900. Hispanic population increased after 1940. County created from Bexar District, 1876, organized 1905; named for Nicholas M. Dawson, San Jacinto veteran.

**Race/Ethnicity**: (In percent) Anglo, 37.4; Black, 7.1; Hispanic, 54.9; Asian, 0.7; Other, 2.6.

**Vital Statistics**, annual: Births, 190; deaths, 126; marriages, 78; divorces, 29.

**Recreation**: Parks, museum, campground; Lamesa poetry and music fest in May.

**Minerals**: Oil, natural gas.

**Agriculture**: Cotton, peanuts, sorghums, watermelons, alfalfa, grapes. 60,000 acres irrigated. Market value $73.1 million.

**LAMESA** (9,383) county seat; agribusiness, food processing, oil-field services, some manufacturing, computerized cotton-classing office; hospital, library; Howard College branch; prison unit; chicken-fried steak festival in April.

Other towns include: **Ackerly** (232, partly in Martin County), **Los Ybanez** (20) and **Welch** (229).

Also, **O'Donnell** (792, mostly in Lynn County) bust of Dan Blocker.

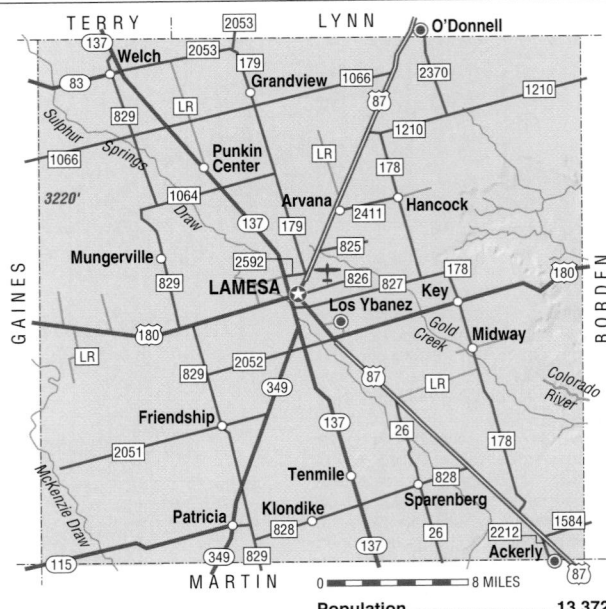

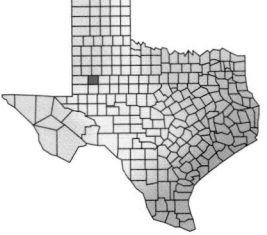

| Population | 13,372 |
|---|---|
| Change fm 2010 | – 3.3 |
| Area (sq. mi.) | 902.1 |
| Land Area (sq. mi.) | 900.3 |
| Altitude (ft.) | 2,580-3,220 |
| Rainfall (in.) | 19.14 |
| Jan. mean min. | 26.0 |
| July mean max. | 93.1 |
| Civ. Labor | 5,164 |
| Unemployed | 5.9 |
| Wages | $47,666,802 |
| Per Capita Income | $34,782 |
| Prop. Value | $1,419,069,200 |
| Retail Sales | $161,442,753 |

# Deaf Smith County

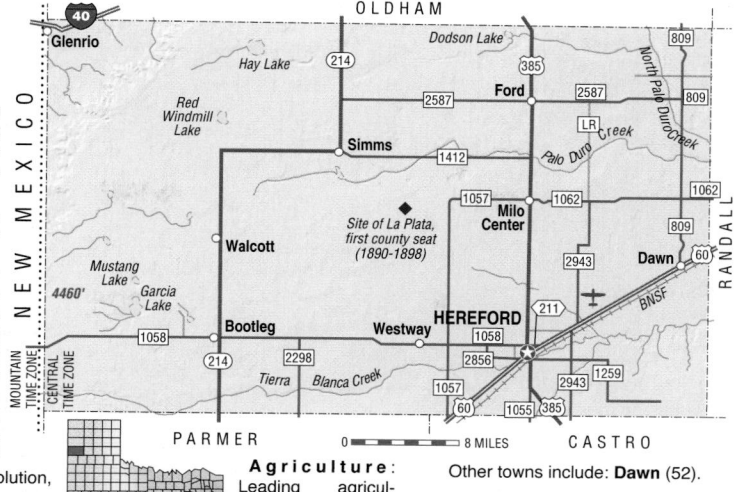

**Physical Features**: High Plains county, partly broken; chocolate and sandy loam soils; drains to Palo Duro and Tierra Blanca creeks.

**Economy**: Agriculture, varied industries, meat packing, offset printing.

**History**: Apaches, displaced by Comanches, Kiowas. Ranching developed after U.S. Army drove out Indians 1874-75. Farming began after 1900. Hispanic settlement increased after 1950. County created 1876, from Bexar District; organized 1890. Named for famed scout in Texas Revolution, Erastus (Deaf) Smith.

**Race/Ethnicity**: (In percent) Anglo, 27.7; Black, 1.9; Hispanic, 69.9; Asian, 0.5; Other, 2.8.

**Vital Statistics**, annual: Births, 355; deaths, 145; marriages, 168; divorces, 33.

**Recreation**: Museum, tours, POW camp chapel; Cinco de Mayo, Pioneer Days in May.

**Minerals**: Insignificant.

**Agriculture**: Leading agricultural county, dairies (second in number of milk cows), feedlot operations, cotton, wheat, sorghum, corn; 50 percent irrigated. Market value $1.38 billion, first in state.

**HEREFORD** (15,211) county seat; cattle feeding, agriculture, trucking; hospital; Amarillo College branch; aquatic center.

Other towns include: **Dawn** (52).

Population .............................. **19,195**
Change fm 2010 ......................... – 0.9
Area (sq. mi.) ......................... 1,498.4
Land Area (sq. mi.) .................. 1,496.9
Altitude (ft.) ....................... 3,650-4,460
Rainfall (in.) ............................. 20.05
Jan. mean min. ........................... 22.5
July mean max. ........................... 91.4
Civ. Labor ................................ 9,130
Unemployed ................................. 4.2
Wages ............................. $66,284,380
Per Capita Income................. $36,401
Prop. Value ............... $1,728,667,701
Retail Sales ................. $338,781,692

---

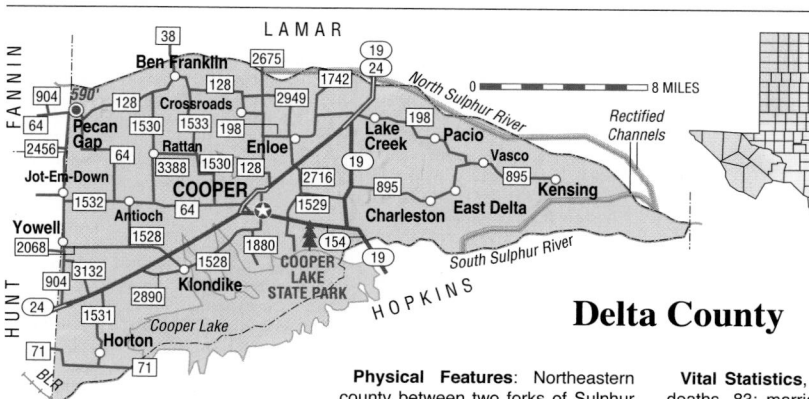

# Delta County

Population .............................. **5,238**
Change fm 2010 ........................... 0.1
Area (sq. mi.) ........................... 277.9
Land Area (sq. mi.) .................... 256.8
Altitude (ft.) .......................... 322-590
Rainfall (in.) ............................ 44,80
Jan. mean min. ........................... 30.0
July mean max. ........................... 94.0
Civ. Labor ................................ 2,443
Unemployed ................................. 7.7
Wages ............................. $6,901,606
Per Capita Income................. $31,172
Prop. Value ................. $391,048,666
Retail Sales ................. $14,135,173

**Physical Features**: Northeastern county between two forks of Sulphur River; Cooper Lake (also designated Jim Chapman Lake); black, sandy loam soils.

**Economy**: Agriculture, government/services, retirement location.

**History**: Caddo area, but disease, other tribes caused displacement around 1790. Anglo-Americans arrived in 1820s. County created from Lamar, Hopkins counties 1870. Greek letter delta origin of name, because of shape of the county.

**Race/Ethnicity**: (In percent) Anglo, 81.3; Black, 7.5; Hispanic, 6.9; Asian, 0.8; Other, 4.6.

**Vital Statistics**, annual: Births, 61; deaths, 83; marriages, 27; divorces, 24.

**Recreation**: Fishing, hunting; lake, state park; Cooper Chiggerfest in October.

**Minerals**: Insignificant.

**Agriculture**: Beef, hay, soybeans, wheat, corn, sorghum, cotton. Market value $29.3 million.

**COOPER** (1,987) county seat; commuters, industrial park, some manufacturing, agribusiness; museum, library; post office mural.

Other towns include: **Ben Franklin** (60), **Enloe** (90), **Klondike** (175), **Lake Creek** (55) and **Pecan Gap** (195).

*For explanation of sources, abbreviations and symbols, see p. 238, and foldout map.*

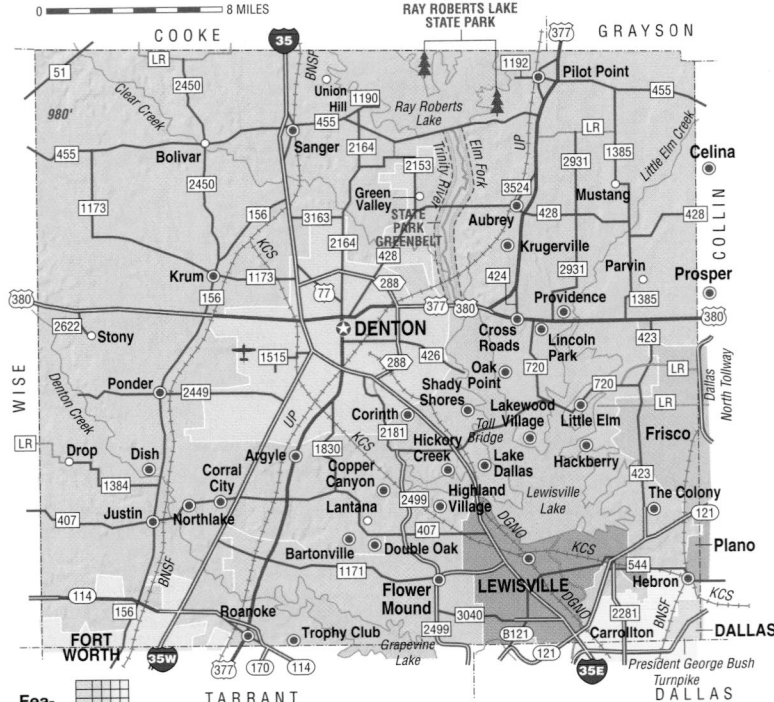

**Physical Features**: North Texas county; partly hilly, draining to Elm Fork of Trinity River, Lewisville Lake, Ray Roberts Lake, Grapevine Lake; Blackland and Grand Prairie soils and terrain.

**Economy**: Varied industries, colleges, horse industry, tourism, government/services; part of Dallas-Fort Worth metropolitan area.

**History**: Land grant from Texas Congress 1841 for Peters colony. County created out of Fannin County 1846; named for John B. Denton, pioneer Methodist minister.

**Race/Ethnicity**: (In percent) Anglo, 62.5; Black, 9.4; Hispanic, 18.9; Asian, 7.3; Other, 3.4.

**Vital Statistics**, annual: Births, 9,330; deaths, 2,947; marriages, 4,300; divorces, 2,828.

**Recreation**: Lake activities, parks; universities' cultural, athletic activities, including "Texas Women; A Celebration of History"; "First Ladies of Texas" collection of memorabilia; Little Chapel in the Woods; Texas Motor Speedway; Denton Jazz Festival in April.

**Minerals**: Natural gas.

**Education**: University of North Texas and Texas Woman's University.

**Agriculture**: Second in number of horses. Eggs, nurseries, turf, cattle; also, hay, sorghum, wheat, peanuts grown. Market value $137 million.

# Denton County

**DENTON** (121,122) county seat; universities, manufacturers of trucks (Peterbilt), medical, aviation; hospitals; historic courthouse square; storytelling festival in March.

**LEWISVILLE** (100,237) commuting to Dallas-Fort Worth, retail center, electronics and varied industries; hospital, library; Celtic Feis & Scottish Highland Games in March.

**Flower Mound** (67,796) residential community, library, mound of native grasses, bike classic in spring.

**Carrollton** (126,466, also in Dallas County), hospital.

Other towns include: **Argyle** (3,548) horse farms/training, bluegrass festival in March; **Aubrey** (2,634) horse farms/training, cabinet production, peanut festival in October; **Bartonville** (1,572); **Copper Canyon** (1,379); **Corinth** (20,007); **Corral City** (28); **Cross Roads** (1,623); **Dish** (294); **Double Oak** (2,937); **Hackberry** (955); **Hebron** (409); **Hickory Creek** (3,963); **Highland Village** (15,703); **Justin** (3,277); **Krugerville** (1,667); **Krum** (4,622) commuters, old grain mill, heritage museum, North Pole Days in December; **Lake Dallas**

(7,139) light manufacturing, marina, historic downtown, Mardi Gras.

Also, **Lakewood Village** (555); **Lantana** (7,263); **Lincoln Park** (332); **Little Elm** (34,145) light manufacturing, lake activities, summer concert series; Northlake (1,878); **Oak Point** (3,048); **Pilot Point** (3,975) light manufacturing, horse ranches, Fireman's Fest in April; **Ponder** (1,413); **Providence** (4,992); **Roanoke** (6,626).

Also, **Sanger** (7,315) distribution center, commuters, government/services, lakes, Sellabration in September; **Shady Shores** (2,705); **The Colony** (39,640) retail, business offices, industrial firms; parks, nature trails, salute to veterans on Veterans Day; and **Trophy Club** (9,960) commuters, retail.

Part [26,579] of **Dallas**, part [7,813] **Fort Worth**, part [44,500] **Frisco**, part [5,316] **Plano**, and small parts of **Coppell, Celina, Prosper, Southlake, Westlake**.

*County adopted in honor of:*
**Dr. Phyllis Bridges, beloved, long-time professor of English at Texas Woman's University**

| Population | 753,363 |
|---|---|
| Change fm 2010 | 13.7 |
| Area (sq. mi.) | 953.0 |
| Land Area (sq. mi.) | 878.4 |
| Altitude (ft.) | 433-980 |
| Rainfall (in.) | 38.09 |
| Jan. mean min. | 33.0 |
| July mean max. | 95.3 |
| Civ. Labor | 409,263 |
| Unemployed | 5.0 |
| Wages | $2,112,319,928 |
| Per Capita Income | $45,602 |
| Prop. Value | $65,299,859,281 |
| Retail Sales | $10,563,303,979 |

# DeWitt County

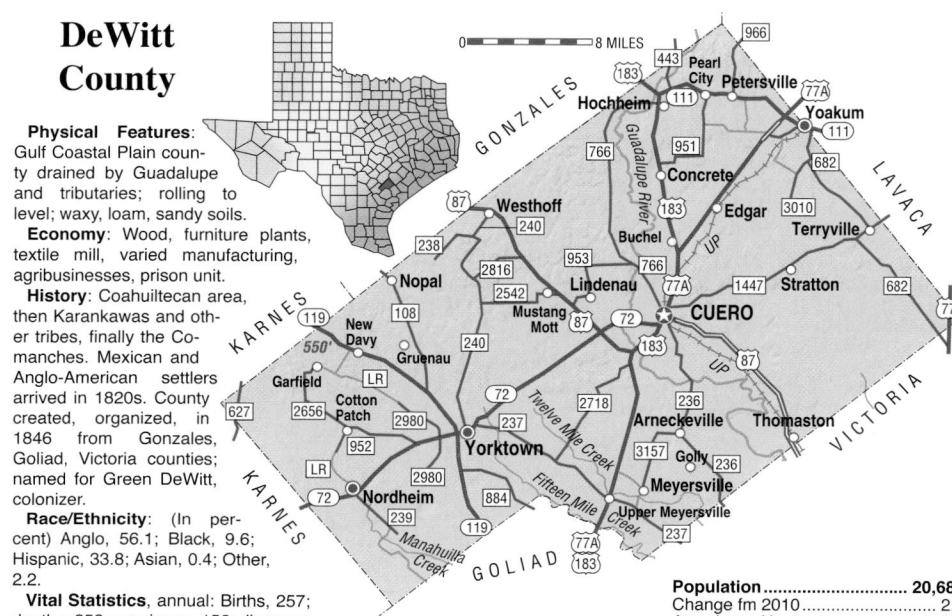

**Physical Features**: Gulf Coastal Plain county drained by Guadalupe and tributaries; rolling to level; waxy, loam, sandy soils.

**Economy**: Wood, furniture plants, textile mill, varied manufacturing, agribusinesses, prison unit.

**History**: Coahuiltecan area, then Karankawas and other tribes, finally the Comanches. Mexican and Anglo-American settlers arrived in 1820s. County created, organized, in 1846 from Gonzales, Goliad, Victoria counties; named for Green DeWitt, colonizer.

**Race/Ethnicity**: (In percent) Anglo, 56.1; Black, 9.6; Hispanic, 33.8; Asian, 0.4; Other, 2.2.

**Vital Statistics**, annual: Births, 257; deaths, 252; marriages, 156; divorces, 69.

**Recreation**: Hunting, fishing, historic homes, museums, wildflowers, German dance halls.

**Minerals**: Oil and natural gas.

**Agriculture**: Cattle, dairy products, poultry, swine, corn, sorghum, cotton, hay, pecans. Market value $61.4 million.

**CUERO** (7,017) county seat; agribusiness, leather products, food processing; hospital; Turkeyfest in October.

**Yorktown** (2,086) agribusiness, oil and gas; library, museum, park, hike/bike trail; Western Days in October; German feasts, spring and fall.

Other towns include: **Hochheim** (70), **Meyersville** (110), **Nordheim** (311), **Thomaston** (45), **Westhoff** (410).

Part [2,138] of **Yoakum** (5,928 total) cattle, leather, meat processing, hospital, museum, Tom Tom festival in June.

| | |
|---|---|
| Population | 20,684 |
| Change fm 2010 | 2.9 |
| Area (sq. mi.) | 910.5 |
| Land Area (sq. mi.) | 909.0 |
| Altitude (ft.) | 100-550 |
| Rainfall (in.) | 35.67 |
| Jan. mean min. | 39.1 |
| July mean max. | 96.5 |
| Civ. Labor | 10,111 |
| Unemployed | 4.6 |
| Wages | $68,287,082 |
| Per Capita Income | $45,919 |
| Prop. Value | $7,02,250,050 |
| Retail Sales | $260,170,817 |

*For explanation of sources, abbreviations and symbols, see p. 238, and foldout map.*

---

*The towers of Texas Woman's University in Denton. Photo by Robert Plocheck.*

# Dickens County

**Physical Features**: West Texas county; broken land, Caprock in northwest; sandy, chocolate, red soils; drains to Croton, Duck creeks.

**Economy**: Agriculture, government services/prison unit, hunting leases, wind farms.

**History**: Comanches driven out by U.S. Army 1874-75. Ranching and some farming began in late 1880s. County created 1876, from Bexar District; organized 1891; named for Alamo hero who is variously listed as James R. Demkins or Dimpkins and J. Dickens.

**Race/Ethnicity**: (In percent) Anglo, 63.2; Black, 5.7; Hispanic, 29.6; Asian, 1.0; Other, 4.1.

**Vital Statistics**, annual: Births, 18; deaths, 24; marriages, 15; divorces, 7.

**Recreation**: Hunting, fishing; Soldiers Mound site, Dickens Springs; downtown Spur.

**Minerals**: Oil, gas.

**Agriculture**: Cattle, horses, cotton, hay, small grains. Some irrigation. Market value $18.5 million.

Hunting leases important.

**DICKENS** (265) county seat, market for ranching country.

**SPUR** (1,247) farming, ranching, hunting, government/services; museum; homecoming in October.

Other towns include: **Afton** (15) and **McAdoo** (75).

| | |
|---|---|
| Population | **2,218** |
| Change fm 2010 | − 9.2 |
| Area (sq. mi.) | 905.2 |
| Land Area (sq. mi.) | 901.7 |
| Altitude (ft.) | 1,800-3,037 |
| Rainfall (in.) | 22.75 |
| Jan. mean min. | 26.6 |
| July mean max. | 94.7 |
| Civ. Labor | 892 |
| Unemployed | 6.1 |
| Wages | $3,314,379 |
| Per Capita Income | $33,780 |
| Prop. Value | $773,051,450 |
| Retail Sales | $13,924,369 |

# Dimmit County

**Physical Features**: Southwest county; level to rolling; much brush; sandy, loam, red soils; drained by Nueces River.

**Economy**: Government/services, agribusiness, petroleum products, tourism.

**History**: Coahuiltecan area, later Comanches. John Townsend, a black man from Nacogdoches, led the first attempt at settlement before the Civil War. Texas Rangers forced out the Comanches in 1877. Mexican migration increased after 1910. County created 1858 from Bexar, Maverick, Uvalde, Webb counties; organized 1880. Named for Philip Dimmitt of the Texas Revolution; law misspelled name.

**Race/Ethnicity**: (In percent) Anglo, 12.6; Black, 1.7; Hispanic, 85.4; Asian, 0.6; Other, 1.5.

**Vital Statistics**, annual: Births, 196; deaths, 85; marriages, 68; divorces, 4.

**Recreation**: Hunting, fishing, campsites, wildlife area; winter haven for tourists.

**Minerals**: Oil, natural gas.

**Agriculture**: Onions, pecans, cantaloupes, olives, tomatoes, tangerines, cattle, goats, horses, hay. Market value $35.2 million.

**CARRIZO SPRINGS** (6,085) county seat; agribusiness center, feedlot, food processing, oil, gas processing, hunting center; hospital; historic Baptist church; Brush Country Day in October.

Other towns include: **Asherton** (1,162), **Big Wells** (806) Cinco de Mayo, and **Catarina** (138) Camino Real festival in April.

| | |
|---|---|
| Population | 11,089 |
| Change fm 2010 | 10.9 |
| Area (sq. mi.) | 1,334.5 |
| Land Area (sq. mi.) | 1,328.9 |
| Altitude (ft.) | 410-871 |
| Rainfall (in.) | 19.77 |
| Jan. mean min. | 40.5 |
| July mean max. | 97.8 |
| Civ. Labor | 8,180 |
| Unemployed | 4.0 |
| Wages | $67,944,182 |
| Per Capita Income | $43,890 |
| Prop. Value | $6,217,834,435 |
| Retail Sales | $190,457,576 |

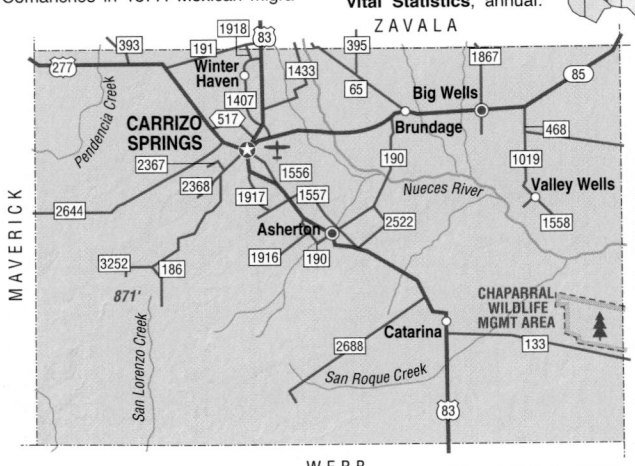

# Donley County

**Physical Features**: Panhandle county bisected by Red River Salt Fork; Greenbelt Lake, Lelia Lake; rolling to level; clay, loam, sandy soils.

**Economy**: Agribusiness, government/services, tourism.

**History**: Apaches displaced by Kiowas and Comanches, who were driven out in 1874–1875 by U.S. Army. Methodist colony from New York settled in 1878. County created in 1876, organized 1882, out of Bexar District; named for Texas Supreme Court Justice S.P. Donley.

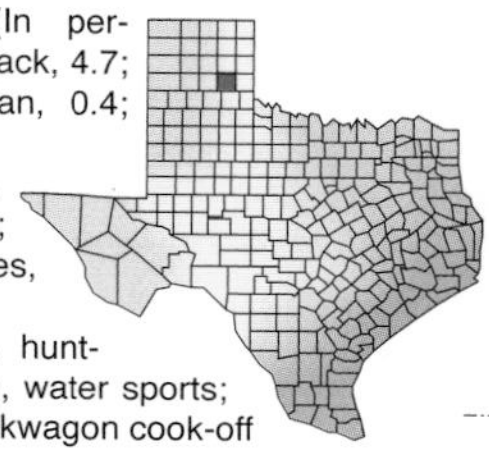

**Race/Ethnicity**: (In percent) Anglo, 82.6; Black, 4.7; Hispanic, 10.5; Asian, 0.4; Other, 2.2.

**Vital Statistics**, annual: Births, 39; deaths, 51; marriages, 31; divorces, 14.

**Recreation**: Lake, hunting, fishing, camping, water sports; Col. Goodnight Chuckwagon cook-off in September.

**Minerals**: Small amount of natural gas.

**Agriculture**: Cattle top revenue source; cotton, peanuts, alfalfa, wheat, hay, melons; 15,000 acres irrigated. Market value $95.1 million.

**CLARENDON** (1,944) county seat; higher education, agribusiness, tourism, medical center clinic; Saints Roost museum, library, junior college; restored historic buildings.

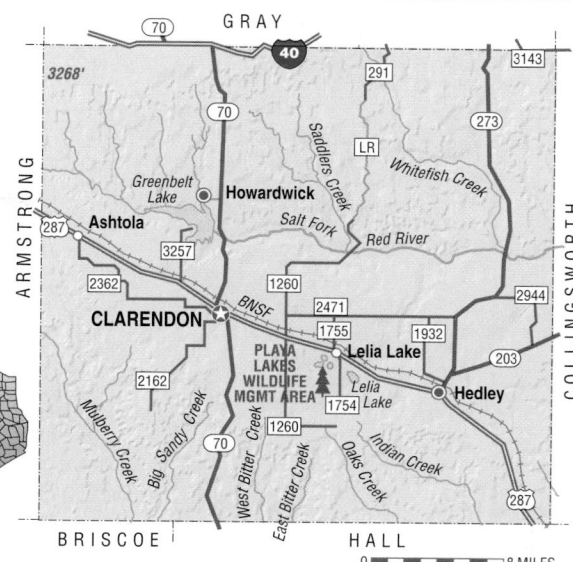

Other towns include: **Hedley** (318) cotton festival in October, **Howardwick** (393) and **Lelia Lake** (70).

| | |
|---|---|
| **Population** | **3,543** |
| Change fm 2010 | – 3.6 |
| Area (sq. mi.) | 933.1 |
| Land Area (sq. mi.) | 929.9 |
| Altitude (ft.) | 2,080-3,268 |
| Rainfall (in.) | 24.02 |
| Jan. mean min. | 23.8 |
| July mean max. | 94.7 |
| Civ. Labor | 1,863 |
| Unemployed | 5.2 |
| Wages | $12,159,712 |
| Per Capita Income | $43,555 |
| Prop. Value | $569,780,614 |
| Retail Sales | $35,426,766 |

*For explanation of sources, abbreviations and symbols, see p. 238, and foldout map.*

---

*A wind farm amid the cotton fields near McAdoo, Dickens County. Photo by Robert Plocheck.*

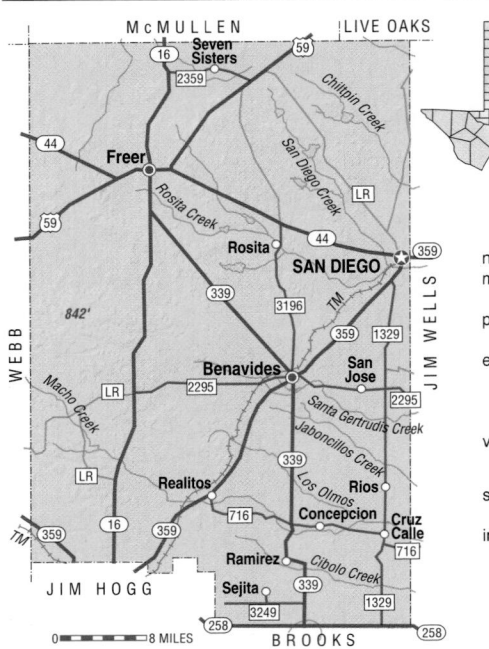

# Duval County

**Physical Features**: South Texas county; level to hilly, brushy in most areas; varied soils.

**Economy**: Ranching, petroleum, tourism, government/services.

**History**: Coahuiltecans, displaced by Comanche bands. Mexican settlement began in 1812. County created from Live Oak, Nueces, and Starr counties in 1858, organized in 1876; named for Burr H. Duval, a victim of Goliad massacre.

**Race/Ethnicity**: (In percent) Anglo, 10.0; Black, 1.4; Hispanic, 88.5; Asian, 0.3; Other, 1.2.

**Vital Statistics**, annual: Births, 177; deaths, 126; marriages, 50; divorces, 18.

**Recreation**: Hunting, tourist crossroads.

**Minerals**: Oil, gas, salt, sand, gravel, uranium.

**Agriculture**: Most income from beef cattle; grains, cotton, vegetables, hay, dairy. Market value $14.8 million.

**SAN DIEGO** (4,417, part [900] in Jim Wells County) county seat; ranching, oil field, tourist center; hospital.

**Freer** (2,791) oil and gas, construction, ranching and hunting; rattlesnake roundup in May.

**Benavides** (1,341) serves truck-farming area.

Other towns include: **Concepcion** (80) and **Realitos** (192).

| | |
|---|---|
| Population | **11,533** |
| Change fm 2010 | – 2.1 |
| Area (sq. mi.) | 1,795.6 |
| Land Area (sq. mi.) | 1,793.5 |
| Altitude (ft.) | 180-842 |
| Rainfall (in.) | 25.99 |
| Jan. mean min. | 43.1 |
| July mean max. | 97.0 |
| Civ. Labor | 6,112 |
| Unemployed | 5.6 |
| Wages | $41,310,413 |
| Per Capita Income | $40,347 |
| Prop. Value | $2,126,294,221 |
| Retail Sales | $173,466,114 |

# Eastland County

| | |
|---|---|
| Population | **18,176** |
| Change fm 2010 | – 2.2 |
| Area (sq. mi.) | 931.9 |
| Land Area (sq. mi.) | 926.5 |
| Altitude (ft.) | 960-1,980 |
| Rainfall (in.) | 29.02 |
| Jan. mean min. | 28.8 |
| July mean max. | 94.6 |
| Civ. Labor | 9,277 |
| Unemployed | 5.1 |
| Wages | $81,652,117 |
| Per Capita Income | $70,322 |
| Prop. Value | $2,457,482,390 |
| Retail Sales | $323,627,010 |

**Physical Features**: Hilly, rolling; sandy, loam soils; drains to Leon River forks; Lake Cisco, Lake Leon.

**Economy**: Agribusiness, education, petroleum industries, varied manufacturing.

**History**: Plains Indian area. Frank Sánchez among first settlers in 1850s. County created from Bosque, Coryell, Travis counties, 1858, organized 1873; named for W.M. Eastland, Mier Expedition casualty.

**Race/Ethnicity**: (In percent) Anglo, 80.0; Black, 2.3; Hispanic, 15.8; Asian, 0.5; Other, 2.4.

**Vital Statistics**, annual: Births, 160; deaths, 233; marriages, 145; divorces, 81.

**Recreation**: Lakes, water sports; fishing, hunting; museums; historic sites and displays.

**Minerals**: Oil, natural gas.

**Agriculture**: Beef cattle, forage and hay. Some 9,000 acres irrigated. Market value $27.9 million.

**EASTLAND** (3,968) county seat; tourism, government/services, petroleum industries, varied manufacturing; hospital, library; Old Ripfest in September.

**CISCO** (3,866) manufacturing, oilfield services; Conrad Hilton's first hotel restored, museums; community college; folklife festival in April.

**RANGER** (2,547) oil center, varied manufacturing, junior college.

Other towns include: **Carbon** (275) livestock equipment manufacturing; **Desdemona** (180); **Gorman** (1,092) peanut processing, agribusiness, hospital; **Olden** (113), and **Rising Star** (858) cap manufacturing, plant nursery; Octoberfest.

# Ector County

**Physical Features**: West Texas county; level to rolling, some sand dunes; meteor crater; desert vegetation.

**Economy**: Center for Permian Basin oil field operations, plastics, electric generation plants.

**History**: First settlers in late 1880s. Oil boom in 1926. County created from Tom Green County, 1887; organized 1891; named for jurist M.D. Ector.

**Race/Ethnicity**: (In percent) Anglo, 37.3; Black, 4.8; Hispanic, 56.4; Asian, 1.0; Other, 2.9.

**Vital Statistics**, annual: Births, 2,755; deaths, 1,152; marriages, 1,316; divorces, 523.

**Recreation**: Globe Theatre replica; presidential museum and Bush childhood home; art institute; second-largest U.S. meteor crater; Stonehenge replica.

**Minerals**: More than 3 billion barrels of oil produced since 1926; gas, cement, stone.

**Agriculture**: Beef cattle, horses are chief producers; pecans, hay, poultry; minor irrigation. Market value $2.2 million.

**Education**: University of Texas of Permian Basin, Texas Tech University Health Sciences Center, Odessa (junior) College.

**ODESSA** (113,534, part [1,670] in Midland County) county seat; oil and gas, manufacturing, ranching; hospitals; cultural center; Permian Basin Fair and Expo in September.

Other towns include: **Gardendale** (1,670), **Goldsmith** (280), **Notrees** (20), **Penwell** (41), and **West Odessa** (24,288).

| | |
|---|---|
| Population | 153,904 |
| Change fm 2010 | 12.2 |
| Area (sq. mi.) | 901.8 |
| Land Area (sq. mi.) | 897.7 |
| Altitude (ft.) | 2,780-3,360 |
| Rainfall (in.) | 13.45 |
| Jan. mean min. | 31.8 |
| July mean max. | 94.8 |
| Civ. Labor | 87,540 |
| Unemployed | 3.6 |
| Wages | $981,403,769 |
| Per Capita Income | $44,168 |
| Prop. Value | $15,293,231,282 |
| Retail Sales | $3,462,088,353 |

# Edwards County

**Physical Features**: Rolling, hilly, with caves and spring-fed streams; rocky, thin soils; drained by Llano, Nueces rivers; varied timber.

**Economy**: Hunting leases, tourism, oil, gas production, ranching.

History: Apache area. First land sold in 1876. County created from Bexar District, 1858; organized 1883; named for Nacogdoches empresario Hayden Edwards.

**Race/Ethnicity**: (In percent) Anglo, 43.7; Black, 0.8; Hispanic, 54.6; Asian, 0.7; Other, 2.6.

**Vital Statistics**, annual: Births, 20; deaths, 19; marriages, 11; divorces, 1.

**Recreation**: Hunting, fishing; scenic drives; Devil's Sinkhole, Kickapoo Cavern state parks.

**Minerals**: Gas.

**Agriculture**: Second in number of goats. Mohair-wool production, Angora goats (first in numbers), sheep, cattle, some pecans. Market value $8.2 million. Cedar for oil.

**ROCKSPRINGS** (1,055) county seat; government/services, hunting, ranching, oil and gas, hunters' barbecue in November.

Other towns include: **Barksdale** (100).

| | |
|---|---|
| Population | 1,879 |
| Change fm 2010 | – 6.1 |
| Area (sq. mi.) | 2,119.9 |
| Land Area (sq. mi.) | 2,117.9 |
| Altitude (ft.) | 1,480-2,415 |
| Rainfall (in.) | 26.56 |
| Jan. mean min. | 36.6 |
| July mean max. | 90.4 |
| Civ. Labor | 851 |
| Unemployed | 4.7 |
| Wages | $3,062,318 |
| Per Capita Income | $35,384 |
| Prop. Value | $1,480,354,993 |
| Retail Sales | $17,390,221 |

*For explanation of sources, abbreviations and symbols, see p. 238, and foldout map.*

# Ellis County

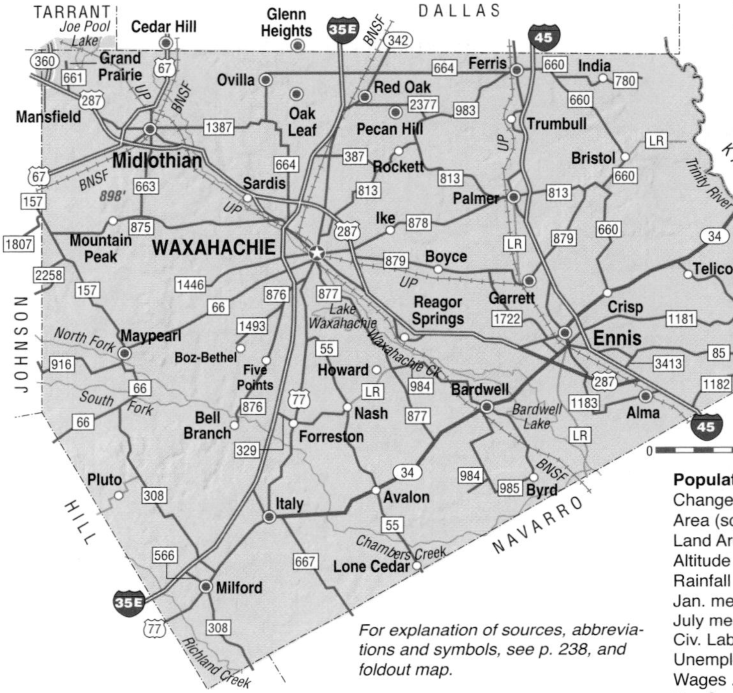

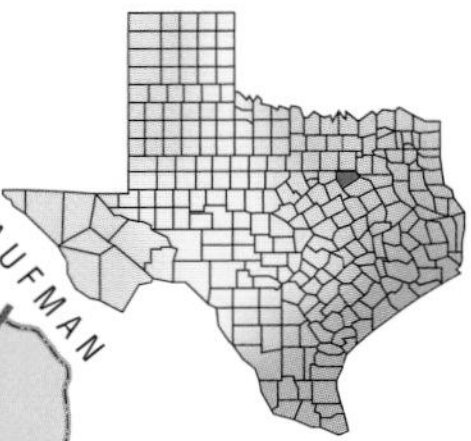

### Map

TARRANT
Joe Pool Lake
Cedar Hill
Grand Prairie
Glenn Heights
DALLAS
342
45
360
661
67
Ovilla
664
Ferris
660
India
780
Mansfield
287
1387
Oak Leaf
Red Oak
2377
983
660
Trumbull
Pecan Hill
Bristol
LR
Midlothian
664
387
Rockett
813
813
660
67
BNSF
898'
663
Sardis
813
Palmer
813
157
875
Ike
878
287
879
660
Mountain Peak
WAXAHACHIE
Boyce
LR
34
1807
879
Telico
2258
157
1446
UP
Reagor Springs
Garrett
Crisp
1181
66
876
877
1722
Ennis
North Fork
Maypearl
1493
Lake Waxahachie
85
85
916
Boz-Bethel
55
3413
South Fork
Five Points
Howard
LR
984
Bardwell
287
1182
66
876
Nash
877
Bardwell Lake
1183
Alma
66
Bell Branch
77
Forreston
LR
45
329
0    8 MILES
Pluto
308
34
984
985
Byrd
HILL
Italy
Avalon
55
NAVARRO
566
Chambers Creek
Lone Cedar
667
35E
Milford
77
308
Richland Creek

*For explanation of sources, abbreviations and symbols, see p. 238, and foldout map.*

KAUFMAN
HENDERSON
JOHNSON

| Population | 159,317 |
|---|---|
| Change fm 2010 | 6.5 |
| Area (sq. mi.) | 951.8 |
| Land Area (sq. mi.) | 935.5 |
| Altitude (ft.) | 300-898 |
| Rainfall (in.) | 39.12 |
| Jan. mean min. | 33.8 |
| July mean max. | 93.9 |
| Civ. Labor | 77,947 |
| Unemployed | 5.5 |
| Wages | $402,497,576 |
| Per Capita Income | $37,616 |
| Prop. Value | $12,406,934,913 |
| Retail Sales | $1,595,283,449 |

**Physical Features**: Blackland soils; level to rolling; Chambers Creek, Trinity River; Bardwell Lake, Lake Waxahachie.

**Economy**: Cement, steel production, warehousing and distribution, government/services; many residents work in Dallas.

**History**: Tonkawa area. Part of Peters colony settled in 1843. County created 1849, organized 1850, from Navarro County. Named for Richard Ellis, president of convention that declared Texas' independence.

**Race/Ethnicity**: (In percent) Anglo, 64.2; Black, 9.4; Hispanic, 24.6; Asian, 0.7; Other, 2.5.

**Vital Statistics**, annual: Births, 1,839; deaths, 1,059; marriages, 1,152; divorces, 172.

**Recreation**: Lakes, fishing, hunting; bluebonnet trails, historic homes, courthouse; Medieval-theme Scarborough Faire in spring.

**Minerals**: Cement, gas, sand, gravel.

**Agriculture**: Cattle, cotton, corn, hay, nurseries. Market value $91.4 million.

**WAXAHACHIE** (31,621) county seat; manufacturing, steel, aluminum, tourism; hospital; colleges, museums; hike/bike trail; Crape Myrtle festival in July.

**Ennis** (18,707) manufacturing, distribution, agribusiness, tourism; hospital; bluebonnet trails, National Polka Festival in May.

**Midlothian** (20,183) cement plants, steel plant, distribution center, manufacturing; heritage park, cabin; spring fling in April.

Other towns include: **Alma** (337); **Avalon** (400); **Bardwell** (668); **Bristol** (679); **Ferris** (2,492); **Forreston** (400); **Garrett** (802); **Howard** (60); **Italy** (1,890); **Maypearl** (1,322); **Milford** (737); **Oak Leaf** (1,323); **Ovilla** (3,557); **Palmer** (2,015); **Pecan Hill** (628); and **Red Oak** (11,315) manufacturing, Founders Day in September.

Also, **Glenn Heights** (11,782, mostly in Dallas County). Part of **Grand Prairie** and **Mansfield**.

*The approach to Hueco Tanks State Historic Site, El Paso County. Photo by Robert Plocheck.*

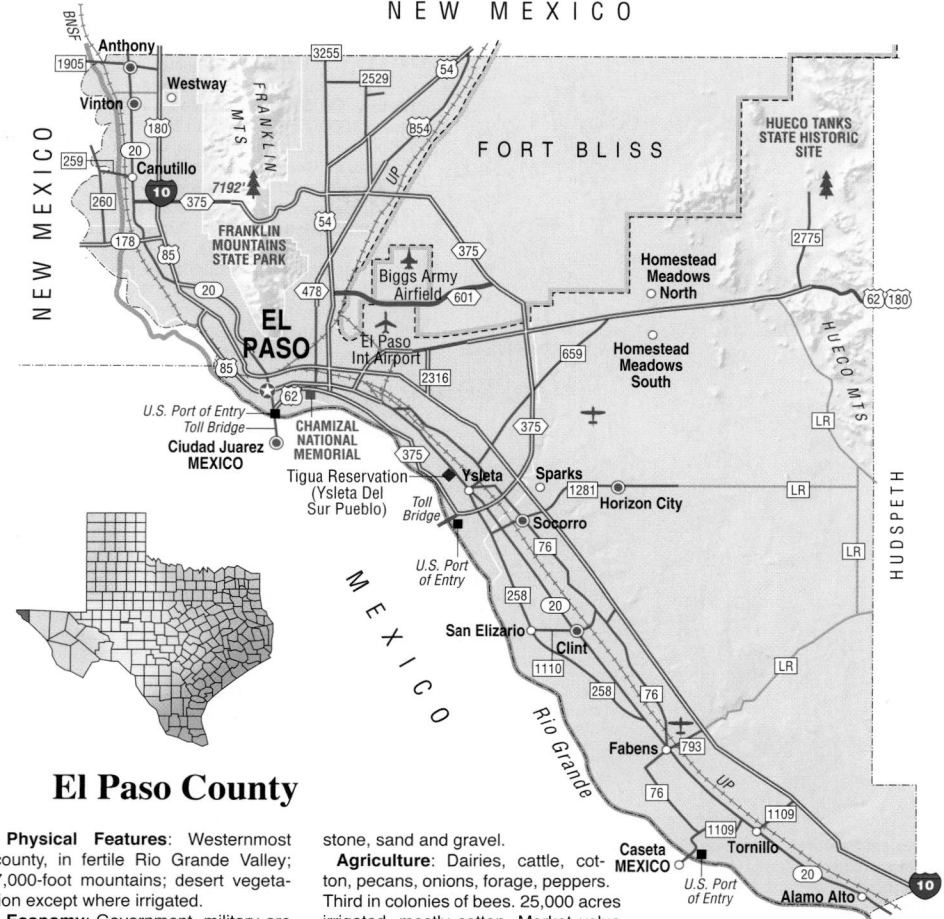

# El Paso County

**Physical Features**: Westernmost county, in fertile Rio Grande Valley; 7,000-foot mountains; desert vegetation except where irrigated.

**Economy**: Government, military are major economic factors; wholesale and retail distribution center, education, tourism, maquiladora plants, varied manufacturing, oil refining, cotton, food processing.

**History**: Various Indian tribes inhabited the valley before Spanish civilization arrived in late 1650s. Agriculture in area dates to at least 100 A.D. Spanish along with Tigua and Piro tribes fleeing Santa Fe uprising of 1680 sought refuge in area. County created from Bexar District, 1849; organized 1850; named for historic pass (Paso del Norte), lowest all-weather pass through Rocky Mountains.

**Race/Ethnicity**: (In percent) Anglo, 13.5; Black, 4.0; Hispanic, 81.1; Asian, 1.3; Other, 2.5.

**Vital Statistics**, annual: Births, 13,871; deaths, 4,882; marriages, 7,547; divorces, 37.

**Recreation**: Gateway to Mexico; Chamizal Museum; major tourist center; December Sun Carnival with football game; state parks, mountain tramway, missions and other historic sites.

**Minerals**: Production of cement,

stone, sand and gravel.

**Agriculture**: Dairies, cattle, cotton, pecans, onions, forage, peppers. Third in colonies of bees. 25,000 acres irrigated, mostly cotton. Market value $45.5 million.

**Education**: University of Texas at El Paso, UT School of Nursing at El Paso, Texas Tech University Health Sciences Center, El Paso Community College.

**EL PASO** (669,882) county seat; Texas' sixth-largest city, fifth-largest metro area, largest U.S. city on Mexican border.

A center for government operations. Federal installations include Fort Bliss, home of the U.S. Army 1st Armored Division, William Beaumont General Hospital, and La Tuna federal prison.

Manufactured products include clothing, electronics, auto equipment, plastics; trade and distribution; refining; processing oil, food, cotton and other farm products.

Hospitals; museums; convention center; theater, symphony orchestra.

Other towns include: **Anthony** (5,262 in Texas, 9,360 in New Mexico); **Canutillo** (6,714); **Clint** (961); **Fabens** (8,387); **Homestead Meadows North**

(5,399); **Homestead Meadows South** (7,427); **Horizon City** (19,266); **Prado Verde** (253); **San Elizario** (14,230), red & green chile war festival in September; **Socorro** (32,468) settled in 1680; **Sparks** (4,874); **Tornillo** (1,572); **Vinton** (1,948); **Westway** (4,262), and **Ysleta** (now within El Paso) settled in 1680, called the oldest town in Texas.

And, **Fort Bliss** (9,075).

| | |
|---|---|
| Population | **833,487** |
| Change fm 2010 | 4.1 |
| Area (sq. mi.) | 1,015.0 |
| Land Area (sq. mi.) | 1,012.7 |
| Altitude (ft.) | 3,520-7,192 |
| Rainfall (in.) | 9.71 |
| Jan. mean min. | 32.5 |
| July mean max. | 94.7 |
| Civ. Labor | 322,916 |
| Unemployed | 7.7 |
| Wages | $2,417,040,483 |
| Per Capita Income | $31,156 |
| Prop. Value | $41,124,745,900 |
| Retail Sales | $9,684,273,129 |

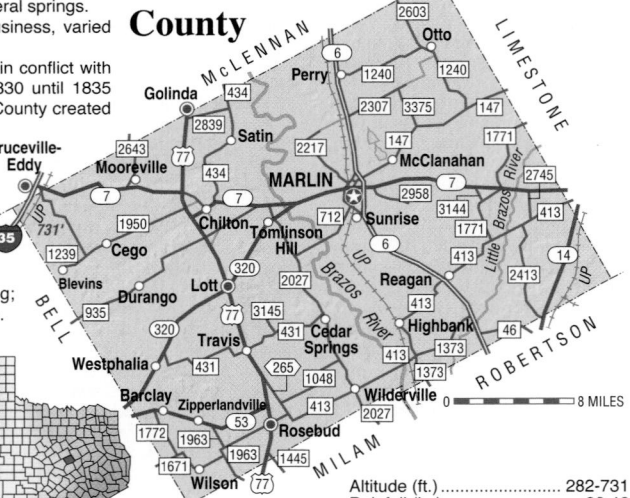

# Erath County

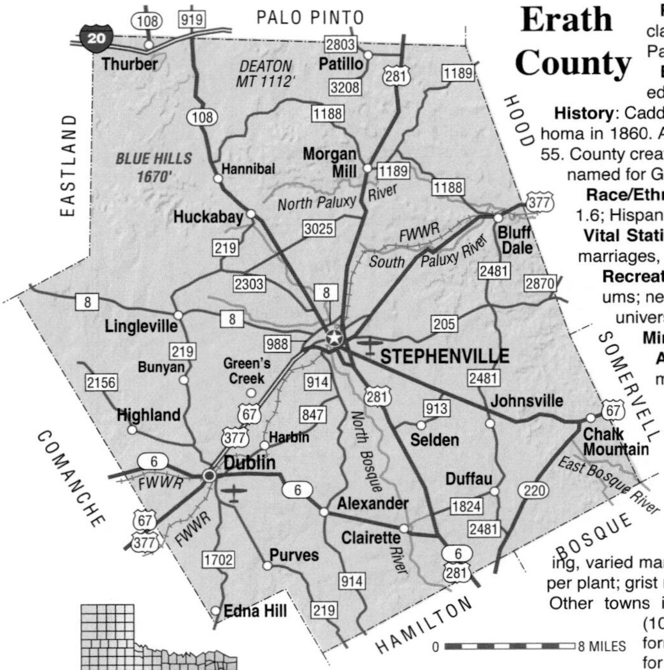

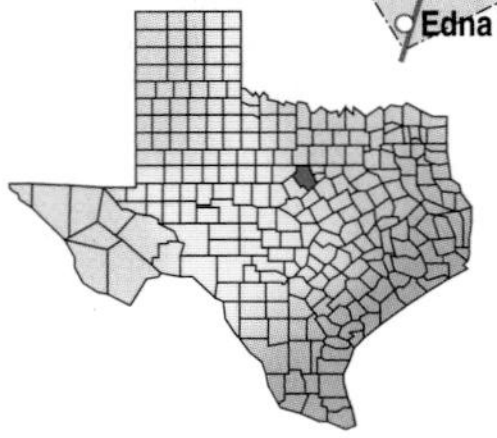

**Physical Features**: On Rolling Plains; clay loam, sandy soils; drains to Bosque, Paluxy rivers.

**Economy**: Agricultural, industrial and educational enterprises.

**History**: Caddo and Anadarko Indians moved to Oklahoma in 1860. Anglo-American settlement began 1854-55. County created from Bosque, Coryell counties 1856; named for George B. Erath, Texas Revolution figure.

**Race/Ethnicity**: (In percent) Anglo, 76.0; Black, 1.6; Hispanic, 20.2; Asian, 0.8; Other, 2.9.

**Vital Statistics**, annual: Births, 491; deaths, 289; marriages, 289; divorces, 125.

**Recreation**: Old courthouse, log cabins, museums; nearby lakes, hunting, Bosque River Park; university fine arts center; Dairy Fest in June.

**Minerals**: Gas, oil.

**Agriculture**: Dairies (first in number of milk cows). Beef cattle, horticulture industry, horses raised. Market value $256.4 million.

**STEPHENVILLE** (18,715) county seat; Tarleton State University, varied manufacturing; hospital, mental health center; Texas A&M research and extension center.

**Dublin** (3,773) dairies, food processing, varied manufacturing, tourism; library; old Dr Pepper plant; grist mill; St. Patrick's Day celebration.

Other towns include: **Bluff Dale** (400); **Lingleville** (100); **Morgan Mill** (206); **Thurber** (48) former coal-mining town; Gordon Center for Industrial History of Texas.

| | | | |
|---|---|---|---|
| Population | 40,147 | July mean max. | 94.2 |
| Change fm 2010 | 6.0 | Civ. Labor | 18,688 |
| Area (sq. mi.) | 1,089.8 | Unemployed | 5.3 |
| Land Area (sq. mi.) | 1,083.1 | Wages | $115,392,852 |
| Altitude (ft.) | 820-1,670 | Per Capita Income | $32,800 |
| Rainfall (in.) | 31.54 | Prop. Value | $4,223,449,660 |
| Jan. mean min. | 31.0 | Retail Sales | $521,230,900 |

---

# Falls County

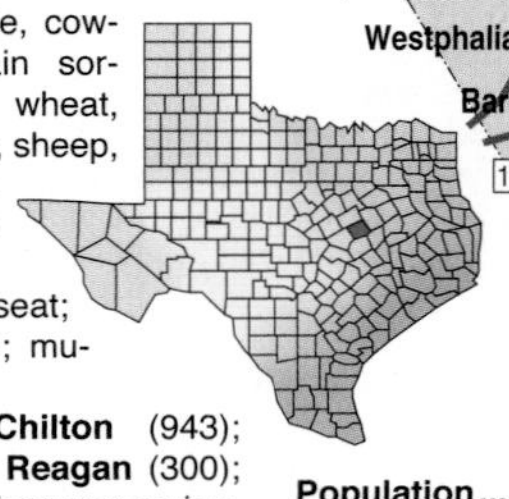

**Physical Features**: On rolling prairie; bisected by Brazos; blackland, red, sandy loam soils; mineral springs.

**Economy**: Government/services, agribusiness, varied manufacturing.

**History**: Wacos, Tawokanis, Anadarkos in conflict with Comanches. Cherokees alone in area 1830 until 1835 when Anglo-American settlement began. County created 1850 from Limestone, Milam counties; named for Brazos River falls.

**Race/Ethnicity**: (In percent) Anglo, 51.7; Black, 25.2; Hispanic, 22.2; Asian, 0.5; Other, 2.6.

**Vital Statistics**, annual: Births, 202; deaths, 182; marriages, 53; divorces, 11.

**Recreation**: Fishing, hunting, camping; Highland Mansion and Falls on the Brazos.

**Minerals**: Gravel, sand, oil.

**Agriculture**: Stocker cattle, cow-calf operations, corn, grain sorghum, soybeans, cotton, wheat, oats (first in acreage), goats, sheep, horses. Some cotton irrigated. Market value $135.3 million.

**MARLIN** (5,740) county seat; agriculture, prison; hospital; museum.

Other towns include: **Chilton** (943); **Golinda** (561); **Lott** (740); **Reagan** (300); **Rosebud** (1,360) feed, fertilizer processing, clothing manufactured; **Satin** (86).

Part of **Bruceville-Eddy** (1,771).

| | | | |
|---|---|---|---|
| Population | 16,989 | Altitude (ft.) | 282-731 |
| Change fm 2010 | – 4.9 | Rainfall (in.) | 38.46 |
| Area (sq. mi.) | 773.8 | Jan. mean min. | 35.4 |
| Land Area (sq. mi.) | 765.5 | July mean max. | 94.2 |
| | | Civ. Labor | 6,486 |
| | | Unemployed | 6.9 |
| | | Wages | $24,861,518 |
| | | Per Capita Income | $32,019 |
| | | Prop. Value | $1,169,506,390 |
| | | Retail Sales | $107,315,112 |

# Fannin County

**Physical Features**: North Texas county of rolling prairie, drained by Red River, Bois d'Arc Creek; Coffe Mill Lake, Lake Bonham, Valley Lake; mostly blackland soils; national grasslands.

**Economy**: Commuting to DFW metroplex, agribusiness.

**History**: Caddoes who joined with Cherokees. Anglo-American settlement began in 1836. County created from Red River County, 1837, organized 1838; named for James W. Fannin, a victim of Goliad massacre.

**Race/Ethnicity**: (In percent) Anglo, 79.7; Black, 7.0; Hispanic, 10.1; Asian, 0.6; Other, 3.4.

**Vital Statistics**, annual: Births, 323; deaths, 408; marriages, 215; divorces, 128.

**Recreation**: Water activities on lakes; hunting; state park, fossil beds, winery; Sam Rayburn home, library; Bois D'Arc festival in May.

**Minerals**: Sand.

**Agriculture**: Beef cattle, wheat, corn. Market value $71.1 million. Hunting leases important.

**BONHAM** (10,266) county seat; varied manufacturing, veterans hospital and private hospital, state jail; Sam Rayburn birthday celebration in January.

Other towns include: **Bailey** (301); **Dodd City** (386); **Ector** (709); **Gober** (146); **Honey Grove** (1,746) agribusiness center, varied manufacturing,

tourism, historic buildings, library, Davy Crockett Festival in October; **Ivanhoe** (110).

Also, **Ladonia** (640) restored historical downtown, tourism, varied manufacturing, commuters, rodeo; **Leonard** (2,063) government/services, power plant, retail, light industry, museums, community picnic in July; **Randolph** (600); **Ravenna** (213); **Savoy** (867); **Telephone** (210); **Trenton** (660); **Windom** (207).

Also, part of **Pecan Gap** (195) and part of **Whitewright** (1,625).

| | |
|---|---|
| Population | **33,752** |
| Change fm 2010 | − 0.5 |
| Area (sq. mi.) | 898.9 |
| Land Area (sq. mi.) | 890.8 |
| Altitude (ft.) | 450-800 |
| Rainfall (in.) | 46.13 |
| Jan. mean min. | 30.9 |
| July mean max. | 92.3 |
| Civ. Labor | 13,905 |
| Unemployed | 6.9 |
| Wages | $60,753,680 |
| Per Capita Income | $32,728 |
| Prop. Value | $2,485,841,437 |
| Retail Sales | $206,788,821 |

*For explanation of sources, abbreviations and symbols, see p. 238, and foldout map.*

*Campers at Bonham State Park, Fannin County. Photo by Robert Plocheck.*

**Physical Features**: South central county bisected by Colorado River; Fayette County Reservoir; rolling to level; sandy loam, black waxy soils.

**Economy**: Agribusiness, electricity, mineral production, government/services, small manufacturing, tourism.

**History**: Lipan Apaches and Tonkawas. Austin's colonists arrived in 1822. Germans and Czechs began arriving in 1840s. County created from Bastrop, Colorado counties, 1837; organized, 1838; named for hero of American Revolution, Marquis de Lafayette.

**Race/Ethnicity**: (In percent) Anglo, 72.7; Black, 6.8; Hispanic, 19.6; Asian, 0.4; Other, 2.3.

**Vital Statistics**, annual: Births, 218; deaths, 315; marriages, 140; divorces, 87.

**Recreation**: Monument Hill, Kreische brewery, Faison Home Museum, other historic sites including "Painted Churches"; hunting, fishing, lake; German and Czech ethnic foods; Prazska Pout in August, Octoberfests.

**Minerals**: Oil, gas, sand, gravel, bentonite clay.

**Agriculture**: Beef cattle, corn, hay, sorghum, pecans, dairies. Market value $66.4 million. Firewood sold.

**LA GRANGE** (4,622) county seat; electric-power generation, varied manufacturing, food processing, retail trade, tourism; hospital, library, quilt museum, polka museum, archives; Czech heritage center; Best Little Cowboy Gathering in March.

**Schulenburg** (2,860) varied manufacturing, food processing; festival in August.

**Round Top** (88) music center, tourism; old Lutheran church, heritage museum; antiques shows, April/October; International Festival Institute, July-August; Shakespeare festival in April, Schuetzenfest in September, and **Winedale** (67), historic restorations including Winedale Inn.

Other towns include: **Carmine** (259); **Ellinger** (386) Tomato Festival in May; **Fayetteville** (255) tourism, antiques, old precinct courthouse, Lickskillet festival in October; **Flatonia** (1,365) food production, manufacturing, cattle ranching; rail history museum, Czhilispiel in

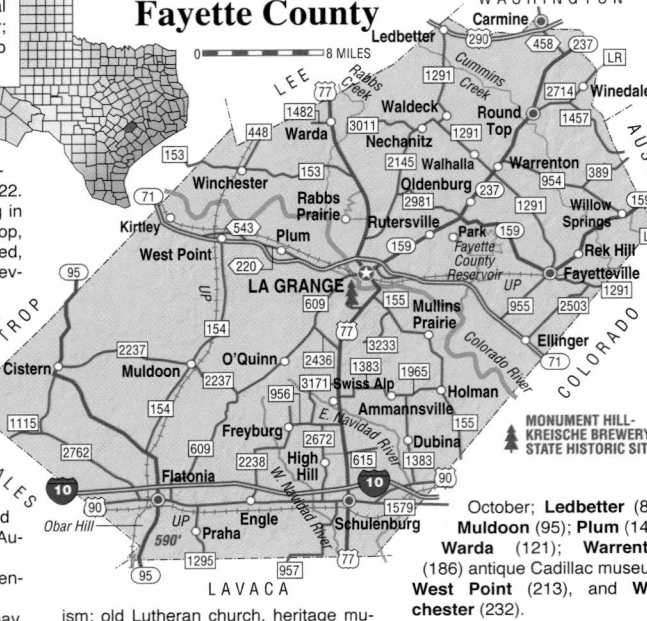

# Fayette County

October; **Ledbetter** (83); **Muldoon** (95); **Plum** (145); **Warda** (121); **Warrenton** (186) antique Cadillac museum; **West Point** (213), and **Winchester** (232).

Population ...................... 24,833
Change fm 2010 .................... 1.1
Area (sq. mi.) .................... 959.8
Land Area (sq. mi.) ............. 950.0
Altitude (ft.) .................... 200-590
Rainfall (in.) .................... 40.46
Jan. mean min. .................... 39.2
July mean max. .................... 95.5
Civ. Labor ........................ 13,434
Unemployed ........................ 3.9
Wages ..................... $84,646,117
Per Capita Income.......... $45,338
Prop. Value ......... $4,843,484,643
Retail Sales .......... $356,339,866

# Fisher County

**Physical Features**: On rolling prairie; mesquite; red, sandy loam soils; drains to forks of Brazos River.

**Economy**: Agribusiness, hunting, gypsum.

**History**: Lipan Apaches, disrupted by Comanches and other tribes around 1700. Ranching began in 1876. County created from Bexar District, 1876; organized 1886; named for S.R. Fisher, Republic of Texas secretary of navy.

**Race/Ethnicity**: (In percent) Anglo, 67.6; Black, 3.8 Hispanic, 27.5; Asian, 0.3; Other, 2.7.

**Vital Statistics**, annual: Births, 32; deaths, 52; marriages, 24; divorces, 9.

**Recreation**: Quail, dove, turkey hunting; wildlife viewing; county fair, rodeo in August in Roby.

**Minerals**: Gypsum, oil.

**Agriculture**: Cattle, cotton, hay, wheat, sorghum, horses, sheep, goats. Irrigation for cotton and alfalfa. Market value $31.1 million.

**ROBY** (645) county seat; agribusiness, cotton gin; hospital between Roby and Rotan.

**ROTAN** (1,501) gypsum plant, oil mill, agribusiness.

Other towns include: **McCaulley** (96) and **Sylvester** (79).

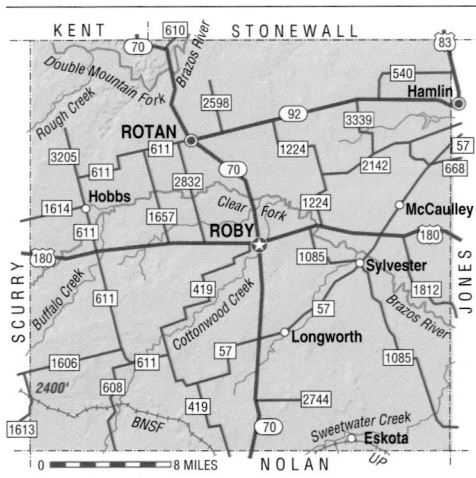

Population ........................ 3,831
Change fm 2010 ................. – 3.6
Area (sq. mi.) ...................... 901.8
Land Area (sq. mi.) ............. 898.9
Altitude (ft.) .......... 1,720-2,405
Rainfall (in.) ........................ 24.76
Jan. mean min. .................... 30.5
July mean max. .................... 94.6
Civ. Labor ........................... 1,959
Unemployed ........................ 5.0
Wages ..................... $7,627,685
Per Capita Income.......... $48,096
Prop. Value ............. $787,398,744
Retail Sales ............. $16,376,822

# Floyd County

**Physical Features**: Flat High Plains, broken by Caprock on east, by White River on south; many playas; red, black loam soils.

**Economy**: Cotton, wind farm, varied manufacturing, government/services.

**History**: Plains Apaches and later Comanches. First white settlers arrived in 1884. County created from Bexar District, 1876; organized 1890. Named for Dolphin Ward Floyd, who died at the Alamo.

**Race/Ethnicity**: (In percent) Anglo, 40.3; Black, 3.9; Hispanic, 55.7; Asian, 0.3; Other, 1.9.

**Vital Statistics**, annual: Births, 90; deaths, 73; marriages, 31; divorces, 16.

**Recreation**: Hunting of pheasant, deer, quail; fishing; Blanco Canyon; Floydada Punkin Day in October; museum.

**Minerals**: Not significant.

**Agriculture**: Cotton, wheat, sorghum, corn; pumpkins. Some 260,000 acres irrigated. Market value $282.7 million.

**FLOYDADA** (2,898) county seat; agriculture, varied manufacturing; Texas A&M engineering extension.

**Lockney** (1,752) agriculture center; manufacturing; hospital.

Other towns include: **Aiken** (52), **Dougherty** (91), and **South Plains** (67).

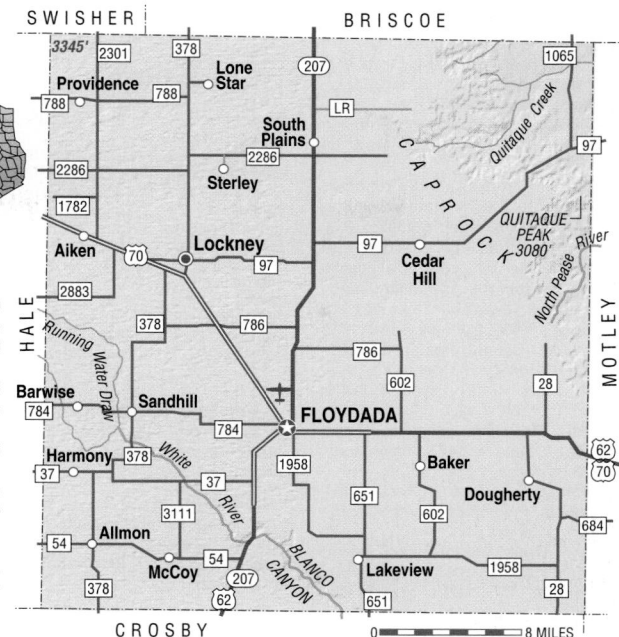

| | |
|---|---|
| Population | 5,949 |
| Change fm 2010 | – 7.7 |
| Area (sq. mi.) | 992.5 |
| Land Area (sq. mi.) | 992.1 |
| Altitude (ft.) | 2,440-3,345 |
| Rainfall (in.) | 21.60 |
| Jan. mean min. | 25.1 |
| July mean max. | 92.4 |
| Civ. Labor | 2,870 |
| Unemployed | 7.6 |
| Wages | $13,952,068 |
| Per Capita Income | $44,677 |
| Prop. Value | $580,853,920 |
| Retail Sales | $45,584,690 |

---

# Foard County

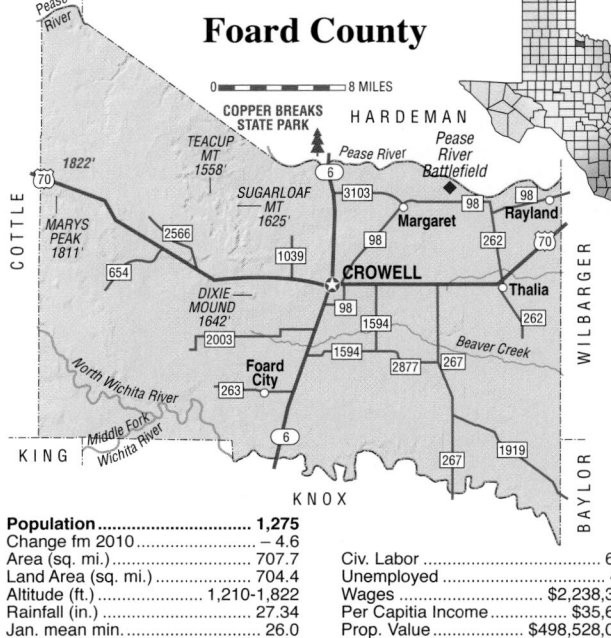

**Physical Features**: Northwest county drains to North Wichita, Pease rivers; sandy, loam soils, rolling surface.

**Economy**: Agribusiness, clothes manufacturing, government/service.

**History**: Comanches, Kiowas ranged the area until driven away in 1870s. Ranching began in 1880. County created out of Cottle, Hardeman, King, Knox counties, 1891, organized the same year; named for Maj. Robert L. Foard of the Confederate army.

**Race/Ethnicity**: (In percent) Anglo, 76.0; Black, 4.9; Hispanic, 17.4; Asian, 0.7; Other, 1.5.

**Vital Statistics**, annual: Births, 18; deaths, 17; marriages, 2; divorces, 0.

**Recreation**: Three museums; hunting; astronomy and ecotourism foundation; wild hog cook-off in November.

**Minerals**: Natural gas, some oil.

**Agriculture**: Wheat, cattle, alfalfa, cotton, sorghum, dairies. Market value $13.8 million. Hunting leases important.

**CROWELL** (880) county seat; retail center, clothing manufacturing; library, Fire Hall museum.

*For explanation of sources, abbreviations and symbols, see p. 238, and foldout map.*

| | |
|---|---|
| Population | 1,275 |
| Change fm 2010 | – 4.6 |
| Area (sq. mi.) | 707.7 |
| Land Area (sq. mi.) | 704.4 |
| Altitude (ft.) | 1,210-1,822 |
| Rainfall (in.) | 27.34 |
| Jan. mean min. | 26.0 |
| July mean max. | 98.0 |
| Civ. Labor | 631 |
| Unemployed | 4.4 |
| Wages | $2,238,310 |
| Per Capitia Income | $35,656 |
| Prop. Value | $498,528,060 |
| Retail Sales | $6,602,151 |

**Physical Features**: On Gulf Coastal Plain; drained by Brazos, San Bernard rivers; Smithers Lake; level to rolling; rich alluvial soils.

**Economy**: Agribusiness, petrochemicals, technology, government/services; many residents work in Houston.

**History**: Karankawa tribes retreated to Mexico by 1850s. Named for Brazos River bend where some of Austin's colonists settled in 1824 and built a blockhouse for protection against Indians. Antebellum plantations made it one of six Texas counties with black majority in 1850. County created 1837 from Austin County; organized 1838.

**Race/Ethnicity**: (In percent) Anglo, 35.6; Black, 21.2; Hispanic, 24.0; Asian, 18.4; Other, 2.7.

**Vital Statistics**, annual: Births, 8,136; deaths, 2,473; marriages, 3,015; divorces, 1,738.

**Recreation**: Many historic sites, museums, memorials, parks; George Ranch historical park; state park with George Observatory; fishing, waterfowl hunting.

**Minerals**: Oil, natural gas, sulfur, salt, clays, sand and gravel.

# Fort Bend County

| | |
|---|---|
| Population | **685,345** |
| Change fm 2010 | 17.1 |
| Area (sq. mi.) | 885.3 |
| Land Area (sq. mi.) | 861.5 |
| Altitude (ft.) | 46-158 |
| Rainfall (in.) | 50.35 |
| Jan. mean min. | 44.1 |
| July mean max. | 94.9 |
| Civ. Labor | 332,865 |
| Unemployed | 5.1 |
| Wages | $1,980,293,238 |
| Per Capita Income | $53,717 |
| Prop. Value | $56,033,531,961 |
| Retail Sales | $7,376,864,189 |

**Agriculture**: Nursery crops, cotton, sorghum, corn, hay, cattle, horses; irrigation for rice. Market value $103.8 million.

**RICHMOND** (11,372) county seat; foundry; University of Houston branch, Wharton County Junior College branch; Richmond State supported-living center, hospital.

**SUGAR LAND** (81,898) government/services, prisons, commuting to Houston; hospitals; University of Houston branch; Museum of Southern History.

**MISSOURI CITY** (68,473, part [5,603] in Harris County) hospital.

**ROSENBERG** (32,571) varied industry, railroad museum.

Other towns include: **Arcola** (1,592); **Beasley** (652); **Cinco Ranch** (18,749); **Fairchilds** (840); **Fresno** (20,309); **Fulshear** (3,342); **Guy** (239); **Katy** (15,094, mostly in Harris County) hospital; **Kendleton** (371); **Meadows Place** (4,669); **Mission Bend** (37,824).

Also, **Needville** (2,962); **New Territory** (15,465); **Orchard** (360); **Pecan Grove** (16,508); **Pleak** (1,140); **Simonton** (807); **Stafford** (17,899, partly in Harris County); **Thompsons** (267); **Weston Lakes** (2,452).

Also, part [38,124] of **Houston**.

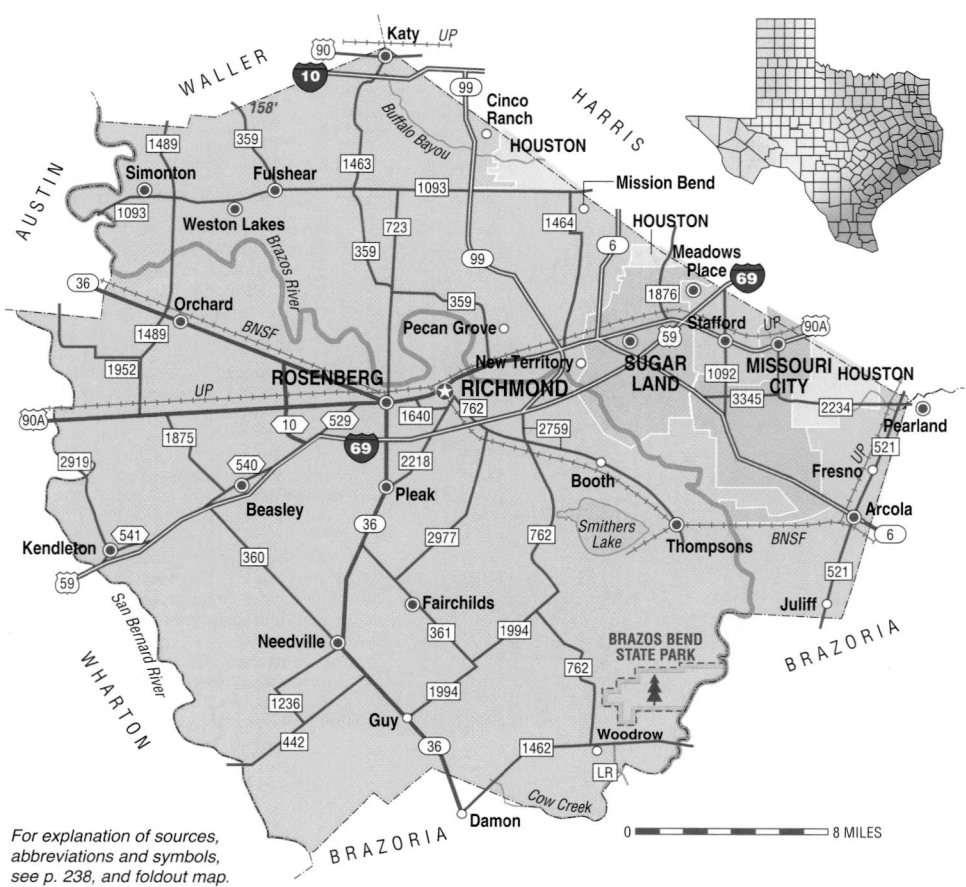

*For explanation of sources, abbreviations and symbols, see p. 238, and foldout map.*

# Franklin County

**Physical Features**: Small Northeast county with many wooded hills; drained by numerous streams; alluvial to sandy clay soils; Lake Bob Sandlin, Lake Cypress Springs.

**Economy**: Agribusiness, government/services, retirement area, distribution.

**History**: Caddoes abandoned the area in the 1790s because of disease and other tribes. First white settlers arrived around 1818. County created in 1875 from Titus County, organized the same year; named for jurist B.C. Franklin.

| | |
|---|---|
| Population | **10,600** |
| Change fm 2010 | 0.0 |
| Area (sq. mi.) | 294.8 |
| Land Area (sq. mi.) | 284.4 |
| Altitude (ft.) | 300-600 |
| Rainfall (in.) | 47.42 |
| Jan. mean min. | 31.9 |
| July mean max. | 92.0 |
| Civ. Labor | 5,268 |
| Unemployed | 5.0 |
| Wages | $25,071,572 |
| Per Capita Income | $36,679 |
| Prop. Value | $1,468,059,570 |
| Retail Sales | $116,158,051 |

**Race/Ethnicity**: (In percent) Anglo, 79.8; Black, 4.5; Hispanic, 13.4; Asian, 0.7; Other, 2.6.

**Vital Statistics**, annual: Births, 95; deaths, 106; marriages, 69; divorces, 40.

**Recreation**: Fishing, water sports; historic homes; wild hog hunting, horse stables; stew cook-off in October.

**Minerals**: Lignite coal, oil and natural gas.

**Agriculture**: Beef cattle, milk production, poultry, hay. Market value $86 million. Timber marketed.

**MOUNT VERNON** (2,633) county seat; distribution center, manufacturing, tourism, antiques; hospital; nature preserves, museum with Don Meredith exhibit; wine festivals in May and October.

Other towns include: **Scroggins** (150), and **Winnsboro** (3,458, mostly in Wood County) commercial center, Autumn Trails.

*For explanation of sources, abbreviations and symbols, see p. 238, and foldout map.*

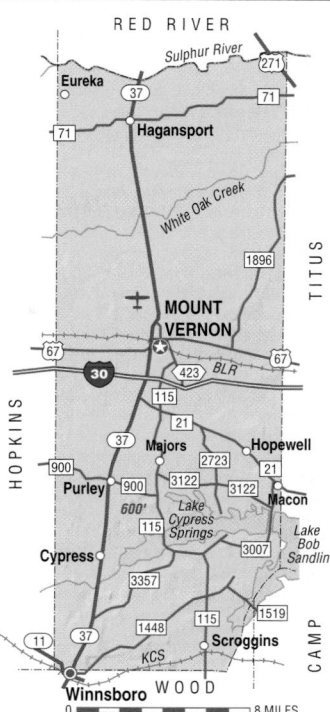

---

**Physical Features**: East central county bounded by the Trinity River; Richland-Chambers Reservoir, Fairfield Lake; rolling Blackland, sandy, loam soils.

**Economy**: Natural gas, mining, electricity generating plants, agriculture.

**History**: Caddo and Tawakoni area. David G. Burnet received land grant in 1825. Seven Mexican citizens received grants in 1833. In 1860, more than half the population was black. County created in 1850 from Limestone County; organized in 1851. Named for the indigenous stone.

# Freestone County

**Race/Ethnicity**: (In percent) Anglo, 67.2; Black, 16.8; Hispanic, 14.6; Asian, 0.8; Other, 3.0.

**Vital Statistics**, annual: Births, 235; deaths, 234; marriages, 151; divorces, 58.

**Recreation**: Fishing, hunting; lakes; historic sites; state park; Teague amateur rodeo in July.

**Minerals**: Gas, oil and lignite coal.

**Agriculture**: Beef cattle, peaches (second in acreage), hay, blueberries, horticulture. Market value $44.1 million. Hunting leases.

**FAIRFIELD** (2,951) county seat; lignite mining, government/services, trade center; hospital, museum; wild game supper in July.

**TEAGUE** (3,697) railroad terminal, oil and gas, government/services, electric generating plant, agriculture; library, museum; Parkfest in October.

Other towns include: **Donie** (250), **Kirvin** (129), **Streetman** (260), **Wortham** (1,048) agribusiness, blues festivals in September, Blind Lemon Jefferson gravesite.

| | |
|---|---|
| Altitude (ft.) | 200-608 |
| Rainfall (in.) | 43.12 |
| Jan. mean min. | 35.3 |
| July mean max. | 93.5 |
| Civ. Labor | 10,176 |
| Unemployed | 4.9 |
| Wages | $60,713,240 |
| Per Capita Income | $36,516 |
| Prop. Value | $4,075,949,910 |
| Retail Sales | $188,428,660 |

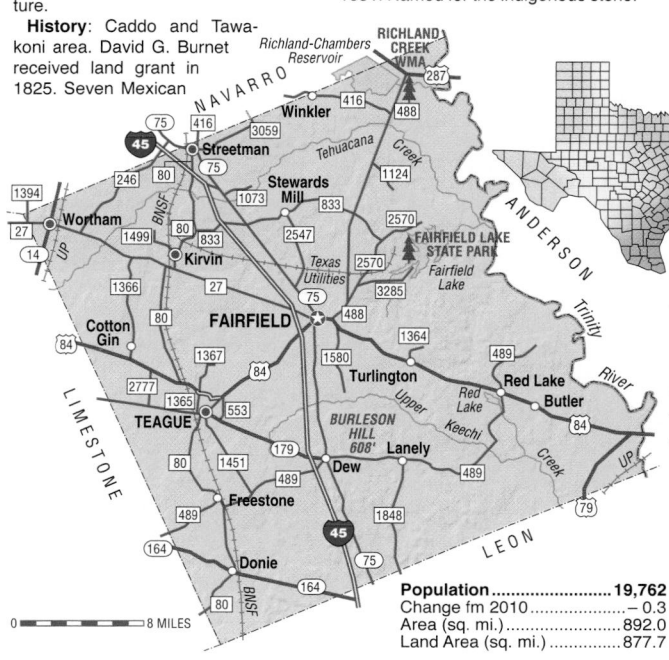

| | |
|---|---|
| Population | **19,762** |
| Change fm 2010 | − 0.3 |
| Area (sq. mi.) | 892.0 |
| Land Area (sq. mi.) | 877.7 |

# Frio County

**Physical Features**: South Texas county of rolling terrain with much brush; bisected by Frio River; sandy, red sandy loam soils.

**Economy**: Agribusiness, oil-field services, hunting leases.

**History**: Coahuiltecans; many taken into the San Antonio missions. Comanche hunters kept settlers out until after the Civil War. Mexican citizens recruited for labor after 1900. County created in 1858 from Atascosa, Bexar, Uvalde counties, organized in 1871; named for the Frio (cold) River.

**Race/Ethnicity**: (In percent) Anglo, 16.1; Black, 3.9; Hispanic, 78.0; Asian, 2.3; Other, 1.6.

**Vital Statistics**, annual: Births, 256; deaths, 129; marriages, 94; divorces, 28.

**Recreation**: Hunting, Big Foot Wallace Museum, Winter Garden area, Pearsall potato fest in May.

**Minerals**: Oil, natural gas, stone.

**Agriculture**: Peanuts, potatoes, sorghum, cotton, corn, spinach, cucumbers, watermelons, bees (second in number of colonies). Second in vegetables harvested. Market value $183.7 million. Hunting leases.

**PEARSALL** (9,681) county seat; agriculture center, oil and natural gas, food processing, shipping; old jail museum; hospital; Pioneer Days in April.

**Dilley** (4,075) shipping center for melons and peanuts; hospital.

Other towns include: **Bigfoot** (496), **Hilltop** (311); **Moore** (509) and **North Pearsall** (673).

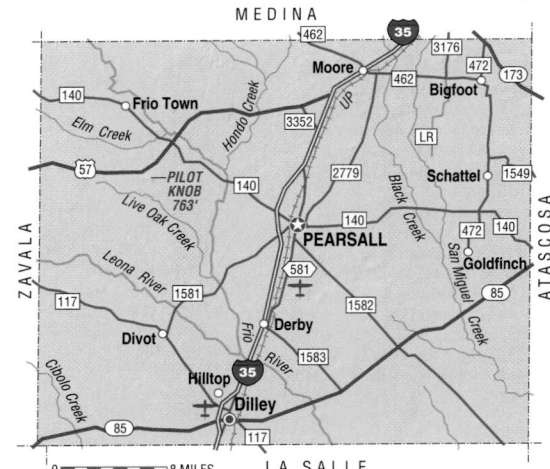

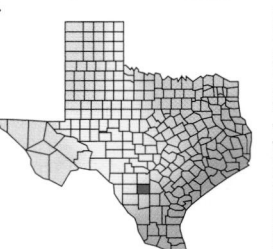

| | |
|---|---|
| Population | 18,531 |
| Change fm 2010 | 7.6 |
| Area (sq. mi.) | 1,134.4 |
| Land Area (sq. mi.) | 1,133.5 |
| Altitude (ft.) | 400-763 |
| Rainfall (in.) | 24.73 |
| Jan. mean min. | 35.0 |
| July mean max. | 97.4 |
| Civ. Labor | 10,117 |
| Unemployed | 4.6 |
| Wages | $65,769,658 |
| Per Capita Income | $32,501 |
| Prop. Value | $2,877,622,000 |
| Retail Sales | $216,995,202 |

# Gaines County

| | |
|---|---|
| Population | 19,425 |
| Change fm 2010 | 10.8 |
| Area (sq. mi.) | 1,502.9 |
| Land Area (sq. mi.) | 1,502.4 |
| Altitude (ft.) | 2,935-3,695 |
| Rainfall (in.) | 18.36 |
| Jan. mean min. | 27.7 |
| July mean max. | 93.4 |
| Civ. Labor | 8,317 |
| Unemployed | 4.1 |
| Wages | $62,727,686 |
| Per Capita Income | $36,911 |
| Prop. Value | $6,743,698,532 |
| Retail Sales | $212,328,247 |

**Physical Features**: On South Plains, drains to draws; playas; underground water.

**Economy**: Oil and gas, cotton, peanuts.

**History**: Comanche country until the U.S. Army campaigns of 1875. Ranchers arrived in the 1880s; farming began around 1900. County created from Bexar District, 1876; organized 1905; named for James Gaines, signer of the Texas Declaration of Independence.

**Race/Ethnicity**: (In percent) Anglo, 58.3; Black, 2.1; Hispanic, 38.7; Asian, 0.5; Other, 2.3.

**Vital Statistics**, annual: Births, 348; deaths, 121; marriages, 181; divorces, 34.

**Recreation**: Cedar Lake one of largest alkali lakes on Texas plains.

**Minerals**: Oil, gas.

**Agriculture**: Cotton (first in bales produced), peanuts (first in acreage), small grains, pecans, paprika, rosemary; cattle, sheep, hogs; substantial irrigation. Market value $180.5 million.

**SEMINOLE** (7,110) county seat; farming, oil and gas, ranching, market center; hospital, library, museum; county airport; Go Nuts produce fair in September.

**Seagraves** (2,609) market for three-county area; cotton, peanut farming; library, museum; Celebrate Seagraves in July.

Other towns include: **Loop** (235). Also, part of **Denver City** (4,705).

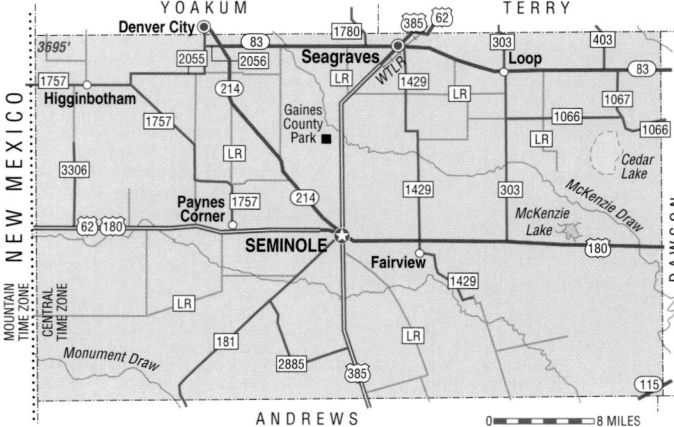

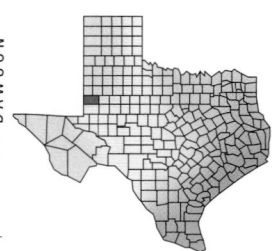

# Galveston County

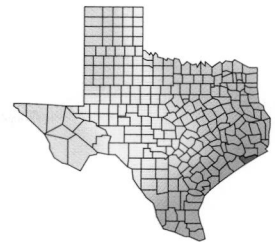

**Physical Features**: Partly island, partly coastal; flat, artificial drainage; sandy, loam, clay soils; broken by bays.

**Economy**: Port activities dominate economy; insurance and finance center, petrochemical plants, varied manufacturing, tourism, medical education, oceanographic research, ship building, commercial fishing.

**History**: Karankawa and other tribes roamed the area until 1850. French, Spanish and American settlement began in 1815 and reached 1,000 by 1817. County created from Brazoria County in 1838; organized in 1839; named for the Spanish governor of Louisiana Count Bernardo de Gálvez.

**Race/Ethnicity**: (In percent) Anglo, 58.3; Black, 13.7; Hispanic, 23.5; Asian, 3.3; Other, 2.8.

**Vital Statistics**, annual: Births, 3,895; deaths, 2,317; marriages, 2,123; divorces, 1,123.

**Recreation**: One of Texas' most historic cities; popular tourist and convention center; fishing, surfing, boating, sailing and other water sports; state park; historic homes tour in spring, Moody Gardens; Mardi Gras celebration; Rosenberg Library; museums; restored sailing ship, "Elissa," railroad museum; Dickens on the Strand in early December.

**Minerals**: Oil, gas, clays, sand and gravel.

**Agriculture**: Cattle, aquaculture, nursery crops, rice, hay, horses, soybeans, grain sorghum.

**GALVESTON** (48,686) county seat; tourist center, shipyard, other industries, insurance, port container facility; University of Texas Medical Branch; National Maritime Research Center; Texas A&M University at Galveston; Galveston College; hospitals.

**League City** (92,669, part [1,562] in Harris County) residential community, commuters to Houston, hospital.

**Texas City** (45,823) refining, petrochemical plants, port, rail shipping; College of the Mainland; hospital, library; dike; Cinco de Mayo, Shrimp Boil in August.

**Bolivar Peninsula** (2,452) includes: **Port Bolivar** (700) lighthouse, free ferry; **Crystal Beach** (800) seafood industry, sport fishing, tourism, Fort Travis Seashore Park, shorebird sanctuary, Crab Festival in May; **Gilchrist** (400) and **High Island** (300).

Other towns include: **Bacliff** (8,876); **Bayou Vista** (1,549); **Clear Lake Shores** (1,121).

Also, **Dickinson** (19,260) manufacturing, commuters, strawberry festival in May; **Friendswood** (37,855, part [10,295] in Harris County); **Hitchcock** (7,326) residential community, tourism, fishing and shrimping, Good Ole Days in August, WWII blimp base, museum.

Also, **Jamaica Beach** (1,014); **Kemah** (1,923) tourism, boating, commuters, museum, Blessing of Fleet in August; **La Marque** (15,210) refining, greyhound racing, farming, hospital, library, Gulf Coast Grill-off in October; **San Leon** (5,199); **Santa Fe** (12,553); **Tiki Island** (993).

| | |
|---|---|
| Population | 314,198 |
| Change fm 2010 | 7.9 |
| Area (sq. mi.) | 873.8 |
| Land Area (sq. mi.) | 378.4 |
| Altitude (ft.) | sea level-40 |
| Rainfall (in.) | 50.76 |
| Jan. mean min. | 48.6 |
| July mean max. | 89.6 |
| Civ. Labor | 157,026 |
| Unemployed | 6.2 |
| Wages | $1,031,426,378 |
| Per Capita Income | $47,186 |
| Prop. Value | $26,462,905,165 |
| Retail Sales | $3,532,621,191 |

*For explanation of sources, abbreviations and symbols, see p. 238, and foldout map.*

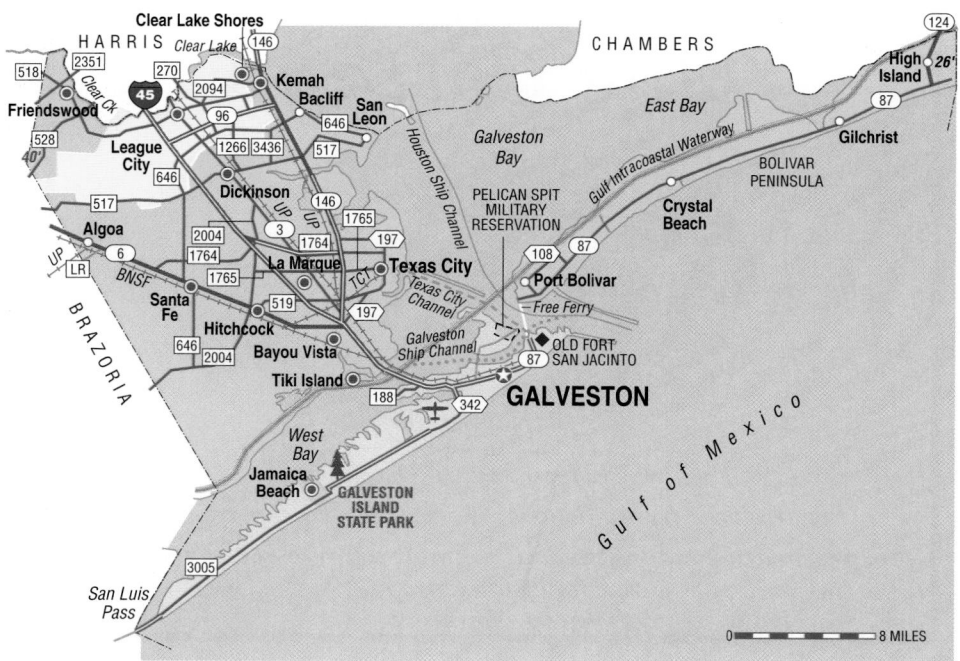

## Garza County

**Physical Features**: On edge of Caprock; rough, broken land, with playas, gullies, canyons, Brazos River forks, Lake Alan Henry; sandy, loam, clay soils.

**Economy**: Agriculture, oil and gas, trade, government/services, hunting leases.

**History**: Kiowas and Comanches yielded to the U.S. Army in 1875. Ranching began in the 1870s, farming in the 1890s. C.W. Post, the cereal millionaire, established enterprises in 1906. County created from Bexar District, 1876; organized 1907; named for a pioneer Bexar County family.

**Race/Ethnicity**: (In percent) Anglo, 44.2; Black, 7.3; Hispanic, 48.3; Asian, 0.2; Other, 1.5.

**Vital Statistics**, annual: Births, 50; deaths, 42; marriages, 36; divorces, 22.

**Recreation**: Scenic areas, lake activities, Post-Garza Museum, trade days monthly.

**Minerals**: Oil, gas, sand, gravel.

**Agriculture**: Cotton, beef cattle, hay. Some 8,000 acres irrigated. Market value $12.4 million. Hunting leases.

**POST** (5,470) county seat; founded by C.W. Post; agriculture, tourism, government/services, prisons; gospel theater.

| | |
|---|---|
| Population | 6,435 |
| Change fm 2010 | – 0.4 |
| Area (sq. mi.) | 896.2 |
| Land Area (sq. mi.) | 893.4 |
| Altitude (ft.) | 2,140-3,030 |
| Rainfall (in.) | 21.99 |
| Jan. mean min. | 29.0 |
| July mean max. | 94.4 |
| Civ. Labor | 2,787 |

| | |
|---|---|
| Unemployed | 4.7 |
| Wages | $18,943,637 |
| Per Capita Income | $61,667 |
| Prop. Value | $1,229,014,112 |
| Retail Sales | $45,418,314 |

*For explanation of sources, abbreviations and symbols, see p. 238, and foldout map.*

# Gillespie County

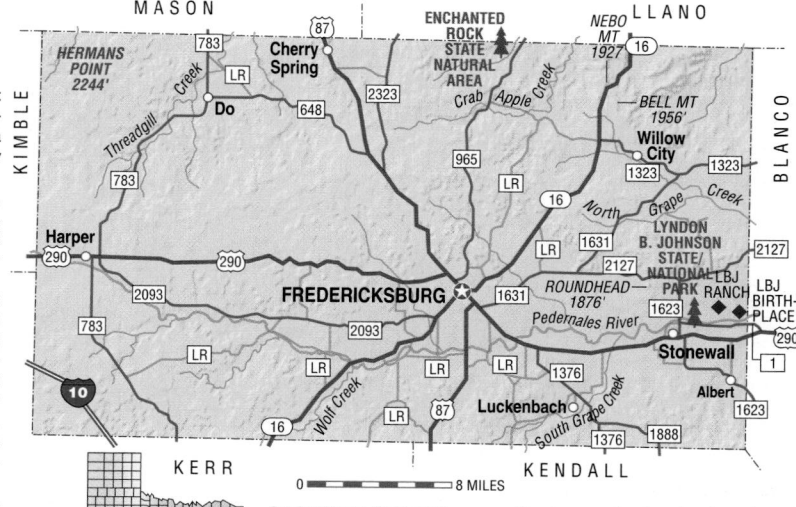

**Physical Features**: Picturesque Edwards Plateau area with hills, broken by spring-fed streams.

**Economy**: Tourism, government/services, agriculture, wine and specialty foods, hunting leases.

**History**: German settlement founded in 1846 in the heart of Comanche country. County created in 1848 from Bexar and Travis counties, organized the same year; named for Texas Ranger Capt. R.A. Gillespie. The birthplace of President Lyndon B. Johnson and World War II Fleet Admiral Chester W. Nimitz.

**Race/Ethnicity**: (In percent) Anglo, 76.9; Black, 0.6; Hispanic, 21.3; Asian, 0.5; Other, 2.1.

**Vital Statistics**, annual: Births, 245; deaths, 342; marriages, 189; divorces, 71.

**Recreation**: Among leading deer-hunting areas; numerous historic sites and tourist attractions include LBJ Ranch, Nimitz Hotel and Pacific war museum; Pioneer Museum Complex, Enchanted Rock, wineries, produce stands.

**Minerals**: Sand, gravel.

**Agriculture**: Beef cattle, wine, hay, peaches (first in acreage). Market value $46.1 million. Hunting leases important.

**FREDERICKSBURG** (11,031) county seat; agribusiness, tourism, wineries, food processing; museum; tourist attractions; hospital; Easter Fires, Oktoberfest.

**Harper** (1,283) ranching, deer hunting, Dachshund Hounds Downs race and Trades Day in October.

Other towns include: **Doss** (100); **Luckenbach** (25) saloon, general store and dance hall; **Stonewall** (526)

agribusiness, wineries, tourism, hunting, Peach Jamboree in June, and **Willow City** (22) scenic drive.

| | |
|---|---|
| Population | **25,520** |
| Change fm 2010 | 2.7 |
| Area (sq. mi.) | 1,061.7 |
| Land Area (sq. mi.) | 1,058.2 |
| Altitude (ft.) | 1,040-2,244 |
| Rainfall (in.) | 31.53 |
| Jan. mean min. | 34.3 |
| July mean max. | 92.7 |
| Civ. Labor | 14,533 |
| Unemployed | 3.5 |
| Wages | $77,706,648 |
| Per Capita Income | $54,527 |
| Prop. Value | $6,645,683,786 |
| Retail Sales | $491,219,787 |

*For explanation of sources, abbreviations and symbols, see p. 238, and foldout map.*

# Glasscock County

**Physical Features**: Western county on rolling plains, broken by small streams; sandy, loam soils.

**Economy**: Farming, ranching, hunting leases, oil and gas.

**History**: Hunting area for Kickapoos and Lipan Apaches. Anglo-American sheep ranchers and Mexican-American shepherds or pastores moved into the area in the 1880s. County created in 1887 from Tom Green County; organized in 1893; named for Texas pioneer George W. Glasscock.

**Race/Ethnicity**: (In percent) Anglo, 64.9; Black, 1.8; Hispanic, 32.5; Asian, 0.1; Other, 1.4.

**Vital Statistics**, annual: Births, 12; deaths, 6; marriages, 13; divorces, 1.

**Recreation**: Hunting of deer, quail, turkey, fox, bobcat, coyote; St. Lawrence Fall Festival in October.

**Minerals**: Oil, gas, stone/rock.

**Agriculture**: Cotton, watermelons, wheat, sorghum, hay; 25,000 acres irrigated. Cattle, goats, sheep, hogs raised. Market value $25.9 million.

**GARDEN CITY** (355), county seat; serves sparsely settled ranching, oil area.

Also, **St. Lawrence** (90), farming.

| | |
|---|---|
| Population | **1,291** |
| Change fm 2010 | 5.3 |
| Area (sq. mi.) | 901.1 |
| Land Area (sq. mi.) | 900.2 |
| Altitude (ft.) | 2,470-2,785 |
| Rainfall (in.) | 17.57 |
| Jan. mean min. | 28.3 |

| | |
|---|---|
| July mean max. | 92.6 |
| Civ. Labor | 711 |
| Unemployed | 3.5 |
| Wages | $3,551,944 |
| Per Capita Income | $78,569 |
| Prop. Value | $3,280,255,274 |
| Retail Sales | $15,070,598 |

# Goliad County

**Physical Features**: Coastal Plain county; rolling, brushy; bisected by San Antonio River; Coleto Creek Reservoir; sandy, loam, alluvial soils.

**Economy**: Government/services, oil and gas, agriculture, electricity-generating plant, tourism.

**History**: Karankawas, Comanches and other tribes in area in historic period. La Bahía presidio/mission established in 1749. County created in 1836 from Spanish municipality; organized in 1837; name is anagram of (H)idalgo. Birthplace of Gen. Ignacio Zaragoza, hero of Battle of Puebla (Mexico).

**Race/Ethnicity**: (In percent) Anglo, 58.4; Black, 5.5; Hispanic, 35.4; Asian, 0.4; Other, 2.1.

**Vital Statistics**, annual: Births, 68; deaths, 76; marriages, 35; divorces, 17.

**Recreation**: Missions, restored Presidio La Bahía, Fannin Battleground; Old Market House museum; lake, fishing, hunting (deer, quail, dove, hogs), camping, canoeing, birding.

**Minerals**: Production of oil, gas.

**Agriculture**: Beef cattle, stocker operations and fed cattle are top revenue producers; corn, grain sorghum, cotton, hay; minor irrigation for pasture. Market value $19.4 million. Hunting leases.

**GOLIAD** (1,943) county seat; one of state's oldest towns; oil, gas center; agriculture; tourism; library; Zaragoza Birthplace State Historic Site, statue; Goliad Massacre re-enactment in March, Diez y Seis in September.

Other towns include: **Berclair** (253), **Fannin** (359) and **Weesatche** (411).

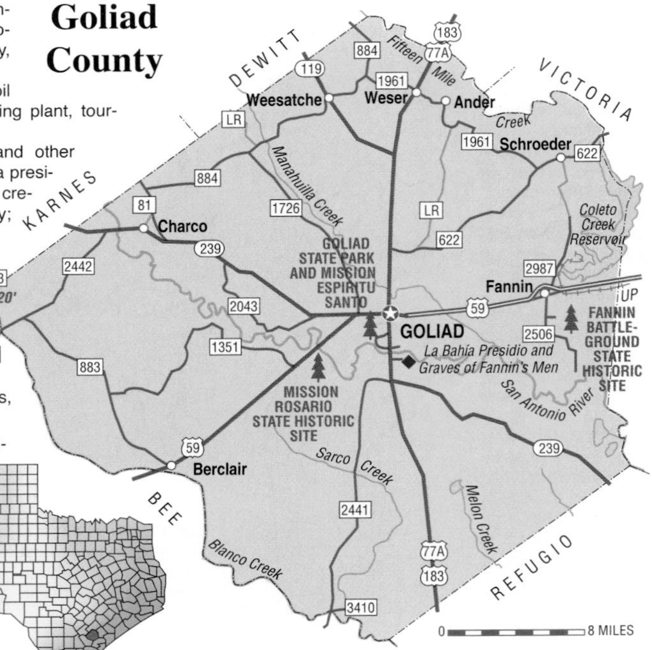

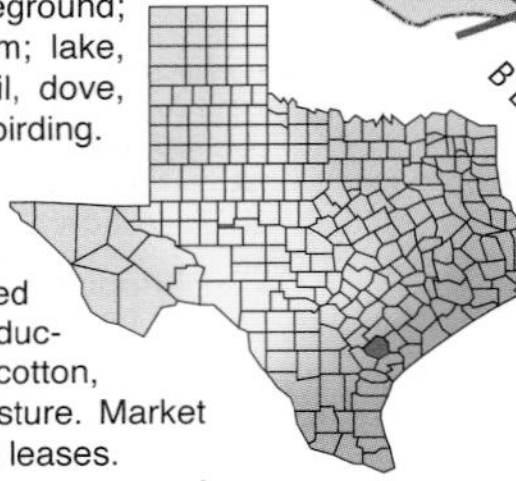

| | |
|---|---|
| Population | 7,549 |
| Change fm 2010 | 4.7 |
| Area (sq. mi.) | 859.4 |
| Land Area (sq. mi.) | 852.0 |
| Altitude (ft.) | 50-420 |
| Rainfall (in.) | 36.78 |
| Jan. mean min. | 42.5 |
| July mean max. | 93.8 |

| | |
|---|---|
| Civ. Labor | 3,839 |
| Unemployed | 4.4 |
| Wages | $13,907,374 |
| Per Capita Income | $36,019 |
| Prop. Value | $1,977,616,600 |
| Retail Sales | $36,690,028 |

*For explanation of sources, abbreviations and symbols, see p. 238, and foldout map.*

*The interior of the Presidio chapel at Goliad. Photo by Robert Plocheck.*

# Gonzales County

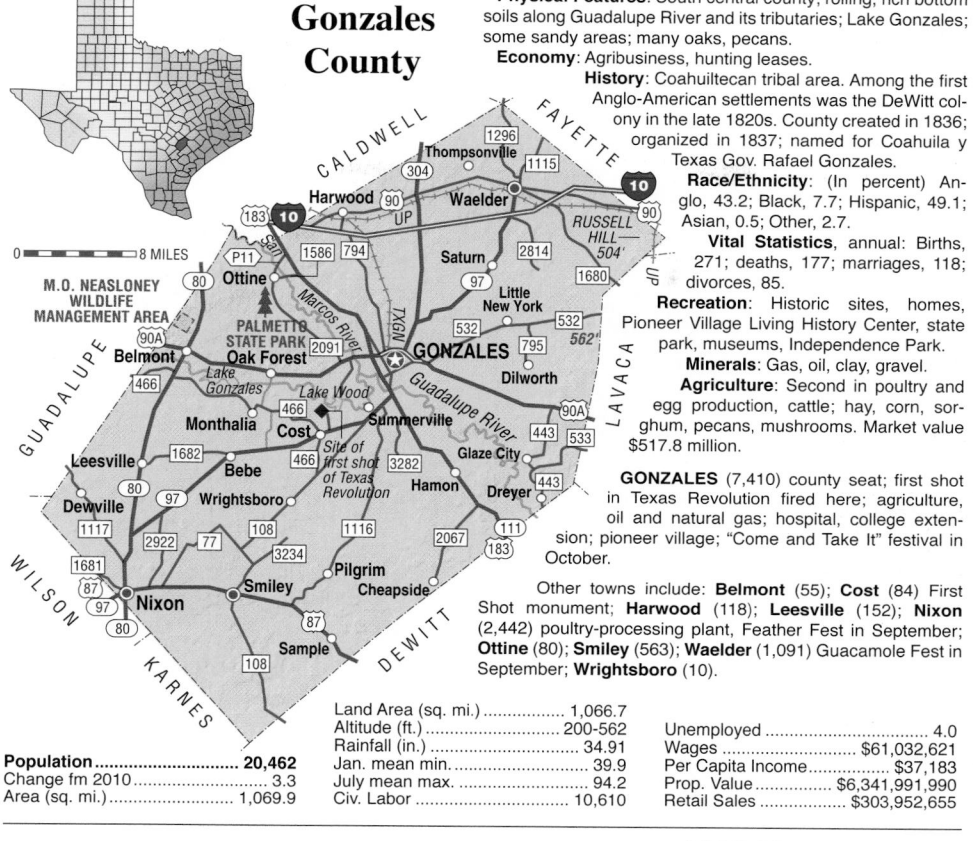

**Physical Features**: South central county; rolling, rich bottom soils along Guadalupe River and its tributaries; Lake Gonzales; some sandy areas; many oaks, pecans.

**Economy**: Agribusiness, hunting leases.

**History**: Coahuiltecan tribal area. Among the first Anglo-American settlements was the DeWitt colony in the late 1820s. County created in 1836; organized in 1837; named for Coahuila y Texas Gov. Rafael Gonzales.

**Race/Ethnicity**: (In percent) Anglo, 43.2; Black, 7.7; Hispanic, 49.1; Asian, 0.5; Other, 2.7.

**Vital Statistics**, annual: Births, 271; deaths, 177; marriages, 118; divorces, 85.

**Recreation**: Historic sites, homes, Pioneer Village Living History Center, state park, museums, Independence Park.

**Minerals**: Gas, oil, clay, gravel.

**Agriculture**: Second in poultry and egg production, cattle; hay, corn, sorghum, pecans, mushrooms. Market value $517.8 million.

**GONZALES** (7,410) county seat; first shot in Texas Revolution fired here; agriculture, oil and natural gas; hospital; college extension; pioneer village; "Come and Take It" festival in October.

Other towns include: **Belmont** (55); **Cost** (84) First Shot monument; **Harwood** (118); **Leesville** (152); **Nixon** (2,442) poultry-processing plant, Feather Fest in September; **Ottine** (80); **Smiley** (563); **Waelder** (1,091) Guacamole Fest in September; **Wrightsboro** (10).

| | | |
|---|---|---|
| Population ............................ **20,462** | Land Area (sq. mi.) ................ 1,066.7 | Unemployed ................................. 4.0 |
| Change fm 2010 ............................ 3.3 | Altitude (ft.) ............................ 200-562 | Wages ............................ $61,032,621 |
| Area (sq. mi.) ........................... 1,069.9 | Rainfall (in.) ............................... 34.91 | Per Capita Income ................ $37,183 |
| | Jan. mean min. ........................... 39.9 | Prop. Value ................ $6,341,991,990 |
| | July mean max. .......................... 94.2 | Retail Sales ................. $303,952,655 |
| | Civ. Labor ............................... 10,610 | |

# Gray County

**Physical Features**: High Plains, broken by Red River forks, tributaries; sandy loam, waxy soils.

**Economy**: Petroleum, agriculture, government/services.

**History**: Apaches, displaced by Comanches and Kiowas. Ranching began in the late 1870s. Farmers arrived around 1900. Oil discovered in 1926. County created in 1876, from Bexar District; organized in 1902; named for Peter W. Gray, member of first Legislature.

**Race/Ethnicity**: (In percent) Anglo, 66.1; Black, 5.3; Hispanic, 26.3; Asian, 0.6; Other, 3.3.

**Vital Statistics**, annual: Births, 346; deaths, 271; marriages, 189; divorces, 76.

**Recreation**: Water sports, Lake McClellan and grassland; White Deer Land Museum, barbed-wire museum; Top of Texas livestock show in January.

**Minerals**: Natural gas, oil.

**Agriculture**: Cattle, hogs, wheat, cotton, corn, sorghum, hay, milk. Market value $207.7 million.

**PAMPA** (18,566) county seat; petroleum, agriculture; hospital; college; prison; Woody Guthrie museum; Mud Bog car show in June.

Other towns include: Alanreed (48); Lefors (508); McLean (794) commercial center for southern part of county.

| | | |
|---|---|---|
| Population ............................ **23,044** | July mean max. .......................... 91.4 |
| Change fm 2010 ............................ 2.3 | Civ. Labor ............................... 12,027 |
| Area (sq. mi.) .............................. 929.3 | Unemployed ................................. 3.8 |
| Land Area (sq. mi.) ................ 926.0 | Wages .......................... $101,236,498 |
| Altitude (ft.) ..................... 2,450-3,320 | Per Capita Income ................ $45,733 |
| Rainfall (in.) ............................... 23.19 | Prop. Value ............ $2,270,750,760 |
| Jan. mean min. ........................... 23.3 | Retail Sales ............. $304,125,729 |

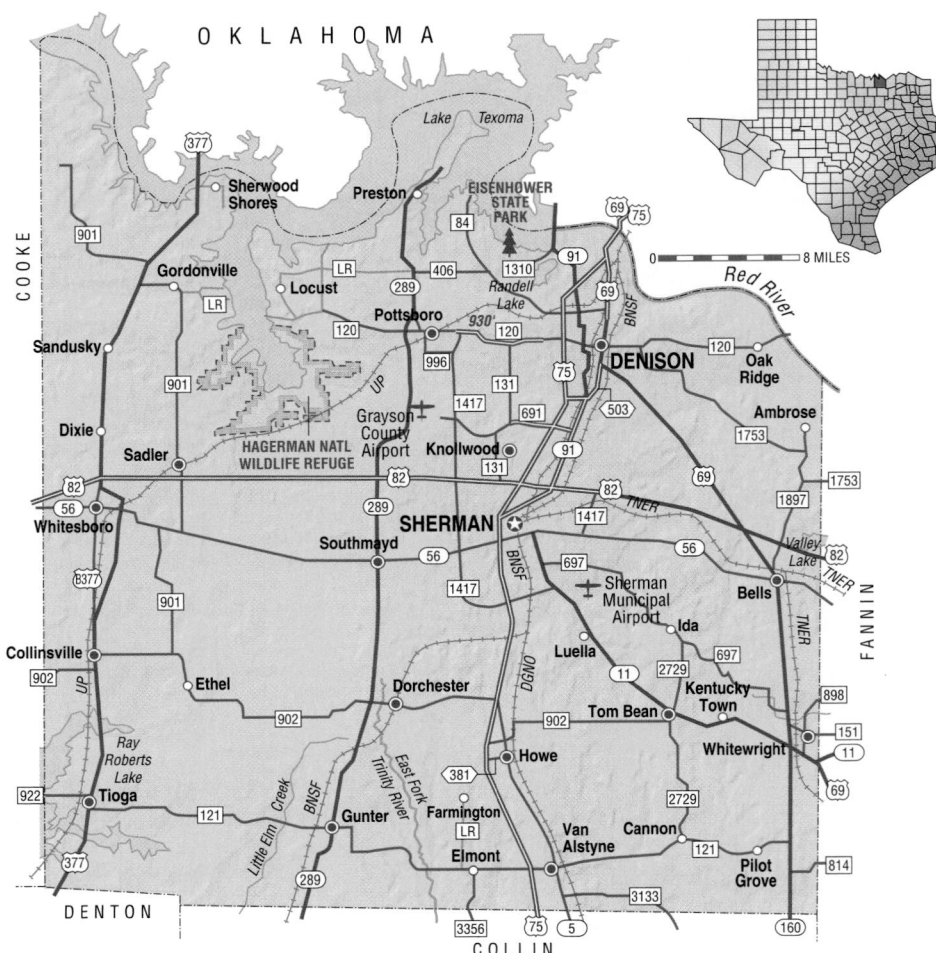

## Grayson County

**Physical Features**: North Texas county; level, some low hills; sandy loam, blackland soils; drains to Red River and tributaries of Trinity River; Lake Texoma, Ray Roberts Lake, Valley Lake, Randell Lake.

**Economy**: A manufacturing, distribution and trade center for northern Texas and southern Oklahoma; nature tourism, mineral production.

**History**: Caddo and Tonkawa area. Preston Bend trading post established 1836-37. Peters colony settlers arrived in the 1840s. County created in 1846 from Fannin County; named for Republic Attorney General Peter W. Grayson.

**Race/Ethnicity**: (In percent) Anglo, 77.3; Black, 6.1; Hispanic, 12.2; Asian, 1.1; Other, 4.3.

**Vital Statistics**, annual: Births, 1,500; deaths, 1,348; marriages, 919; divorces, 396.

**Recreation**: Lakes, fishing, hunting, water sports, state park, cultural activities, wildlife refuge, Pioneer Village, railroad museum.

**Minerals**: Oil, gas, gravel, sand.

**Agriculture**: Wheat, corn, hay, beef cattle, horses. Market value $92 million.

**Education**: Austin College in Sherman and Grayson County College located between Sherman and Denison.

**SHERMAN** (39,464) county seat; varied manufacturing, processors and distributors for major companies; Austin College; hospital.

**DENISON** (22,979) health care, manufacturing, retail center; hospital; Eisenhower birthplace, air force base museum; Main Street Fall festival in October.

Other towns include: **Bells** (1,407); **Collinsville** (1,618); **Dorchester** (149); **Gordonville** (165); **Gunter** (1,455); **Howe** (2,585) distribution, varied manufacturing, museum, Founders' Day in May; **Knollwood** (427); **Pottsboro** (2,215) lake activities, marinas, Frontier Days in Sep-

tember; **Sadler** (349), **Sherwood Shores** (1,174).

Also, **Southmayd** (1,002); **Tioga** (820) Gene Autry museum, festival in September; **Tom Bean** (1,043); **Van Alstyne** (3,137) real estate/financial services, electronic refurbishing, manufacturing, museum, Fall Der All in October; **Whitesboro** (3,853) agribusiness, tourism, manufacturing, library, Peanut Festival in October; **Whitewright** (1,625) manufacturing, retail, farming, museum, skydiving, Wine & Rose tour in May.

| | |
|---|---|
| Population | 123,534 |
| Change fm 2010 | 2.2 |
| Area (sq. mi.) | 979.2 |
| Land Area (sq. mi.) | 932,8 |
| Altitude (ft.) | 500-930 |
| Rainfall (in.) | 43.60 |
| Jan. mean min. | 33.1 |
| July mean max. | 92.1 |
| Civ. Labor | 59,061 |
| Unemployed | 5.4 |
| Wages | $425,672,662 |
| Per Capita Income | $36,098 |
| Prop. Value | $9,810,923,741 |
| Retail Sales | $1,655,867,201 |

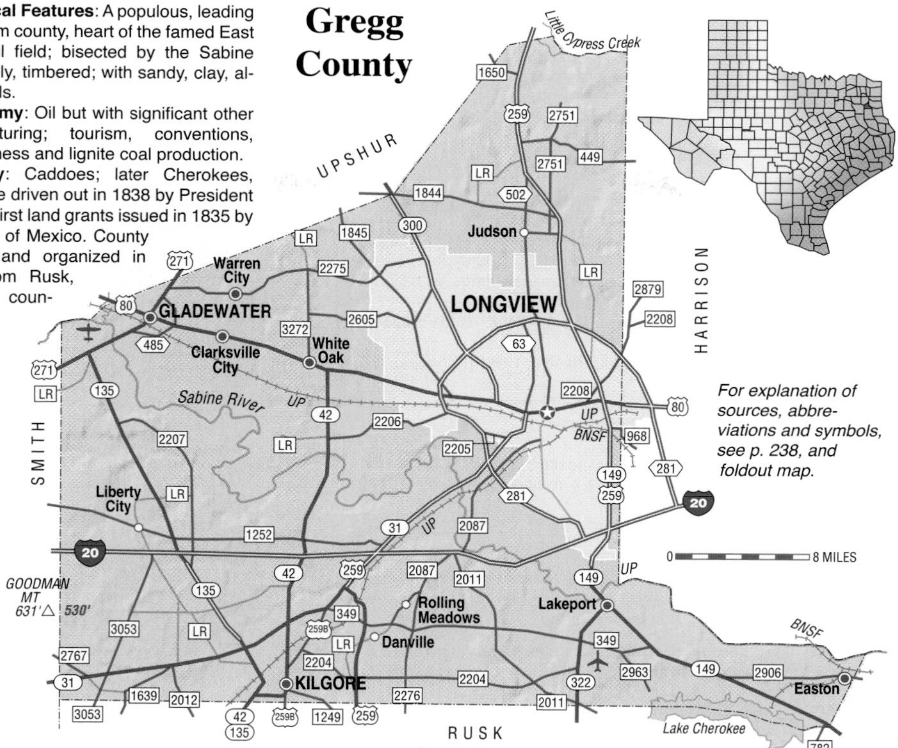

# Gregg County

**Physical Features**: A populous, leading petroleum county, heart of the famed East Texas oil field; bisected by the Sabine River; hilly, timbered; with sandy, clay, alluvial soils.

**Economy**: Oil but with significant other manufacturing; tourism, conventions, agribusiness and lignite coal production.

**History**: Caddoes; later Cherokees, who were driven out in 1838 by President Lamar. First land grants issued in 1835 by Republic of Mexico. County created and organized in 1873 from Rusk, Upshur coun-

ties; named for Confederate Gen. John Gregg. In U.S. censuses 1880-1910, blacks were more numerous than whites. Oil discovered in 1931.

**Race/Ethnicity**: (In percent) Anglo, 59.6; Black, 20.3; Hispanic, 17.5; Asian, 1.3; Other, 2.8.

**Vital Statistics**, annual: Births, 1,939; deaths, 1,202; marriages, 1,363; divorces, 401.

**Recreation**: Water activities on Lake Cherokee, hunting, varied cultural events, East Texas Oil Museum in Kilgore.

**Minerals**: Leading oil-producing county with more than 3 billion barrels produced since 1931; also, sand, gravel and natural gas.

**Agriculture**: Cattle, horses, hay, nursery crops. Market value $3.6 million. Timber sales.

**LONGVIEW** (82,314, small part [1,870] in Harrison County) county seat; chemical manufacturing, oil industry, distribution and retail center; hospitals; LeTourneau University, UT-Tyler Longview center; convention center; balloon race in July.

**Kilgore** (14,793, part [3,013] in Rusk County), oil, distribution center; Kilgore College, Rangerette museum; Shakespeare festival in summer.

**Gladewater** (6,563, part [2,447] in Upshur County) oil, manufacturing, tourism, antiques; library, airport, skydiving; Gusher Days in April; daffodils in February-March.

Other towns include: **Clarksville City** (886); **Easton** (505, partly in Rusk County); **Judson** (1,057); **Lakeport** (998); **Liberty City** (2,397) oil,

tourism, government/services, Honor America Night in November; **Warren City** (460); **White Oak** (6,511) oil and gas, commuting to Longview, Tyler; park, Roughneck Days in spring every three years.

| | |
|---|---|
| Population | **123,204** |
| Change fm 2010 | 1.2 |
| Area (sq. mi.) | 275.8 |
| Land Area (sq. mi.) | 273.3 |
| Altitude (ft.) | 240-530 |
| Rainfall (in.) | 48.09 |
| Jan. mean min. | 34.2 |
| July mean max. | 93.8 |
| Civ. Labor | 68,317 |
| Unemployed | 4.8 |
| Wages | $844,803,032 |
| Per Capita Income | $47,934 |
| Prop. Value | $9,761,380,773 |
| Retail Sales | $4,884,559,996 |

*For explanation of sources, abbreviations and symbols, see p. 238, and foldout map.*

*Eisenhower State Park at Lake Texoma, Grayson County. Texas Parks & Wildlife photo.*

# Grimes County

**Physical Features:** Rich bottom soils along Brazos, Navasota rivers; remainder hilly, partly forested; Gibbons Creek Reservoir.

**Economy:** Varied manufacturing, agribusiness, tourism.

**History:** Bidais (customs similar to the Caddoes) lived peacefully with Anglo-American settlers who arrived in 1820s, but tribe was removed to Indian Territory. Planter agriculture reflected in 1860 census, which listed 77 persons owning 20 or more slaves. County created from Montgomery County in 1846, organized the same year; named for Jesse Grimes, who signed Texas Declaration of Independence.

**Race/Ethnicity:** (In percent) Anglo, 59.5; Black, 16.5; Hispanic, 22.6; Asian, 0.5; Other, 2.3.

**Vital Statistics,** annual: Births, 292; deaths, 256; marriages, 138; divorces, 86.

**Recreation:** Hunting, fishing; Gibbons Creek Reservoir; historic sites; fall Renaissance Festival at Plantersville.

**Minerals:** Lignite coal, natural gas.

**Agriculture:** Cattle, forage, horses, poultry; berries, pecans, honey sales significant. Market value $48.1 million. Some timber sold, Christmas tree farms.

**ANDERSON** (232) county seat; rural center; Fanthorp Inn historic site; Go-Texan weekend in February.

**NAVASOTA** (7,586) agribusiness center for parts of three counties; varied manufacturing; food, wood processing; hospital; prisons; La Salle statue; Blues Fest in August.

Other towns include: **Bedias** (468); **Iola** (430); **Plantersville** (260); **Richards** (300); **Roans Prairie** (64); **Shiro** (210); **Todd Mission** (114).

| | |
|---|---|
| Population | 27,172 |
| Change fm 2010 | 2.1 |
| Area (sq. mi.) | 801.6 |
| Land Area (sq. mi.) | 787.5 |
| Altitude (ft.) | 150-470 |
| Rainfall (in.) | 43.51 |

| | |
|---|---|
| Jan. mean min. | 40.0 |
| July mean max. | 96.0 |
| Civ. Labor | 12,561 |
| Unemployed | 5.5 |
| Wages | $88,798,871 |
| Per Capita Income | $34,808 |

| | |
|---|---|
| Prop. Value | $4,314,395,249 |
| Retail Sales | $218,617,375 |

*For explanation of sources, abbreviations and symbols, see p. xxx and foldout map.*

*Anderson, county seat of Grimes County, has many homes dating to the 1850s. Photo by Robert Plocheck.*

# Guadalupe County

**Physical Features**: South central county bisected by Guadalupe River, Lake Dunlap, Lake McQueeney; level to rolling surface; sandy, loam, black-land soils.

**Economy**: Varied manufacturing, commuting to San Antonio, agribusiness.

**History**: Karankawas, Comanches, and other tribes until the 1850s. The first Spanish land grant was in 1806 to José de la Baume. DeWitt colonists arrived in 1827. County created, organized, in 1846 from Bexar, Gonzales counties; named for the river.

**Race/Ethnicity**: (In percent) Anglo, 52.8; Black, 7.7; Hispanic, 36.6; Asian, 1.7; Other, 3.6.

**Vital Statistics**, annual: Births, 1,763; deaths, 910; marriages, 304; divorces, 515.

**Recreation**: Fishing, hunting, river floating; Sebastopol House, other historic sites; river drive; Fiestas Juan Seguin in June, Diez y Seis in September in Seguin.

**Minerals**: Oil, gas, gravel, clays.

**Agriculture**: Cattle, corn, milo, wheat, cotton, hay, nursery crops, pecans. Market value $61.6 million.

**SEGUIN** (25,757) county seat; steel production, varied manufacturing, government/services; hospital, museums; Texas Lutheran University; Pecan Fest in early fall.

Other towns include: **Cibolo** (23,656), **Geronimo** (1,076), **Kingsbury** (823), **Marion** (1,072), **Mc-** **Queeney** (2,588), **New Berlin** (514), **Redwood** (4,471), **Santa Clara** (743), **Schertz** (35,510, parts in Bexar and Comal counties), **Staples** (263).

Also, part [10,154] of **New Braunfels**, part [1,377] of **Selma** and a small part of **San Marcos**.

**Population** ............................ 147,250
Change fm 2010 .......................... 11.9

| | |
|---|---|
| Area (sq. mi.) | 714.8 |
| Land Area (sq. mi.) | 711.3 |
| Altitude (ft.) | 350-952 |
| Rainfall (in.) | 34.62 |
| Jan. mean min. | 40.5 |
| July mean max. | 95.2 |
| Civ. Labor | 70,661 |
| Unemployed | 4.9 |
| Wages | $298,763,762 |
| Per Capita Income | $40,399 |
| Prop. Value | $11,976,383,782 |
| Retail Sales | $1,395,917,699 |

# Hale County

**Physical Features**: High Plains; fertile sandy, loam soils; playas; large underground water supply.

**Economy**: Agribusiness, food processing/ distribution, manufacturing, government/services.

**History**: Comanche hunters driven out by U.S. Army in 1875. Ranching began in the 1880s. First motor-driven irrigation well drilled in 1911. County created from Bexar District in 1876; organized in 1888; named for Lt. J.C. Hale, who died at San Jacinto.

**Race/Ethnicity**: (In percent), Anglo, 35.5; Black, 5.9; Hispanic, 58.0; Asian, 0.5; Other, 2.9.

**Vital Statistics**, annual: Births, 537; deaths, 277; marriages, 274; divorces, 50.

**Recreation**: Llano Estacado Museum; art gallery, antiques stores; pheasant hunting; Cowboy Days in September at Plainview.

**Minerals**: Some oil.

**Agriculture**: Cotton, fed beef, sorghum, dairies, corn, vegetables, wheat. Market value $409.9 million. Irrigation of 200,000 acres.

**PLAINVIEW** (21,305) county seat; agriculture, distribution, corn milling; Wayland Baptist University, South Plains College branch; hospital, library, mental health center; state prisons.

**Hale Center** (2,156) trade center; farm museum, library, parks, murals, cacti gardens.

**Abernathy** (2,816, part [697] in Lubbock County) government/services, farm supplies, textile plant, gins.

Other towns include: **Cotton Center** (300), **Edmonson** (106), **Petersburg** (1,169), **Seth Ward** (2,068).

**Population** ............................ 34,720
Change fm 2010 ....................... – 4.3
Area (sq. mi.) ........................ 1,004.8
Land Area (sq. mi.) ................ 1,004.7

| | |
|---|---|
| Altitude (ft.) | 3,180-3,620 |
| Rainfall (in.) | 20.45 |
| Jan. mean min. | 25.8 |
| July mean max. | 91.0 |
| Civ. Labor | 14,520 |
| Unemployed | 9.7 |
| Wages | $96,983,301 |
| Per Capita Income | $29,606 |
| Prop. Value | $2,463,220,568 |
| Retail Sales | $323,320,255 |

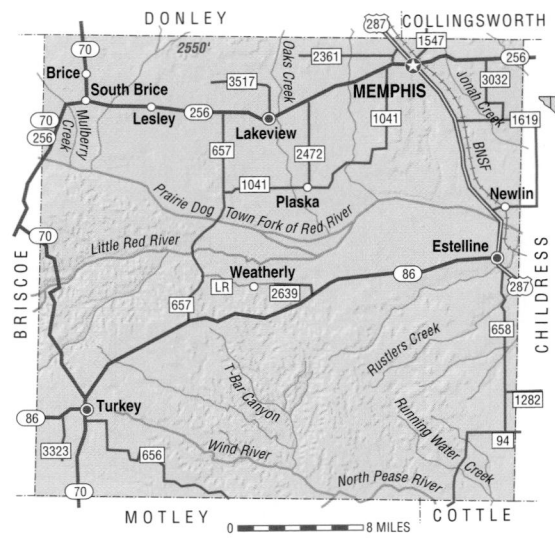

# Hall County

**Physical Features**: Rolling to hilly, broken by Red River forks, tributaries; red and black sandy loam.

**Economy**: Agriculture, farm, ranch supplies, marketing for large rural area.

**History**: Apaches displaced by Comanches, who were removed to Indian Territory in 1875. Ranching began in the 1880s. Farming expanded after 1910. County created in 1876 from Bexar, Young districts; organized in 1890; named for Republic of Texas secretary of war W.D.C. Hall.

**Race/Ethnicity**: (In percent) Anglo, 56.9; Black, 7.8; Hispanic, 34.6; Asian, 0.4; Other, 2.5.

**Vital Statistics**, annual: Births, 33; deaths, 56; marriages, 11; divorces, 7.

**Recreation**: Hunting of deer, wild hog, turkey, quail, dove; Rails to Trails system; Bob Wills museum; Memphis Picnic festival in September.

**Minerals**: None.

**Agriculture**: Cotton, cattle, peanuts, wheat, sorghum, alfalfa hay. Market value $24.8 million. Hunting leases.

**MEMPHIS** (2,252) county seat; agriculture, retail; historic buildings.

Other towns include: **Estelline** (140), motorcycle rally/chili cookoff in August, **Lakeview** (104), **Turkey** (409) Bob Wills Day in April.

| | |
|---|---|
| Population | 3,147 |
| Change fm 2010 | – 6.1 |
| Area (sq. mi.) | 904.1 |
| Land Area (sq. mi.) | 883.5 |
| Altitude (ft.) | 1,750-2,550 |
| Rainfall (in.) | 22.59 |
| Jan. mean min. | 26.0 |
| July mean max. | 95.7 |
| Civ. Labor | 1,280 |
| Unemployed | 6.6 |
| Wages | $6,453,315 |
| Per Capita Income | $41,184 |
| Prop. Value | $491,295,560 |
| Retail Sales | $47,966,876 |

# Hamilton County

**Physical Features**: Hilly north central county broken by scenic valleys; loam soils.

**Economy**: Varied manufacturing, agribusiness, hunting leases, tourism.

**History**: Waco and Tawakoni Indian area. Anglo-American settlers arrived in the mid-1850s. County created and organized in 1858, from Bosque, Comanche, Lampasas counties; named for South Carolina Gov. James Hamilton, who aided the Texas Revolution and Republic.

**Race/Ethnicity**: (In percent) Anglo, 86.3; Black, 0.9; Hispanic, 11.2; Asian, 0.5; Other, 2.6.

**Vital Statistics**, annual: Births, 96; deaths, 112; marriages, 76; divorces, 33.

**Recreation**: Deer, quail, duck hunting; Linear Pecan Creek park in Hamilton; Hamilton dove festival in October.

**Minerals**: Natural gas.

**Agriculture**: Beef, milk, hay. Market value $55.8 million. Hunting leases important.

**HAMILTON** (2,977) county seat; medical services, farming, varied manufacturing; hospital; museum, historical homes, winery, 4-acre rodeo arena.

**Hico** (1,356) tourism, agriculture, varied manufacturing; antiques shops, Billy the Kid museum; steak cookoff in May.

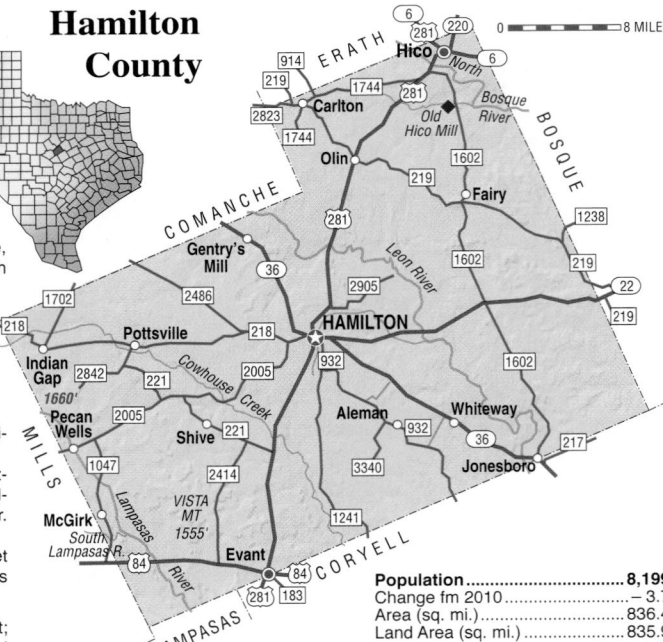

Other towns include: **Carlton** (75), **Evant** (414, partly in Coryell County), **Jonesboro** (125, partly in Coryell County); **Pottsville** (105).

*For explanation of sources, abbreviations and symbols, see p. 238, and foldout map.*

| | |
|---|---|
| Population | 8,199 |
| Change fm 2010 | – 3.7 |
| Area (sq. mi.) | 836.4 |
| Land Area (sq. mi.) | 835.9 |
| Altitude (ft.) | 860-1,660 |
| Rainfall (in.) | 35.28 |
| Jan. mean min. | 30.8 |
| July mean max. | 94.0 |
| Civ. Labor | 3,967 |
| Unemployed | 4.7 |
| Wages | $20,203,869 |
| Per Capita Income | $37,972 |
| Prop. Value | $1,786,583,145 |
| Retail Sales | $79,827,561 |

# Hansford County

**Physical Features**: High Plains, many playas, creeks, draws; sandy, loam, black soils; underground water; Palo Duro Reservoir.

**Economy**: Agribusinesses; oil, gas operations; wind energy.

**History**: Apaches, pushed out by Comanches around 1700. U.S. Army removed Comanches in 1874-75, and ranching began soon afterward. Farmers, including Norwegians, moved in around 1900. County created in 1876, from Bexar, Young districts; organized in 1889; named for jurist J.M. Hansford.

**Race/Ethnicity**: (In percent) Anglo, 52.7; Black, 0.9; Hispanic, 45.5; Asian, 0.4; Other, 2.7.

**Vital Statistics**, annual: Births, 76; deaths, 55; marriages, 45; divorces, 10.

**Recreation**: Stationmasters House Museum, hunting, lake activities, ecotourism, Lindbergh landing site.

**Minerals**: Production of gas, oil.

**Agriculture**: Large cattle-feeding operations; corn, wheat (first in acreage), sorghum; hogs. Substantial irrigation. Market value $783.2 million.

**SPEARMAN** (3,274) county seat; farming, cattle production, oil and gas, wind energy, biofuels; hospital, library, windmill collection; Heritage Days in May with rib cookoff.

Other towns include: **Gruver** (1,157) farm-ranch market, natural gas production, Fourth of July barbecue; **Morse** (148).

*For explanation of sources, abbreviations and symbols, see p. 238, and foldout map.*

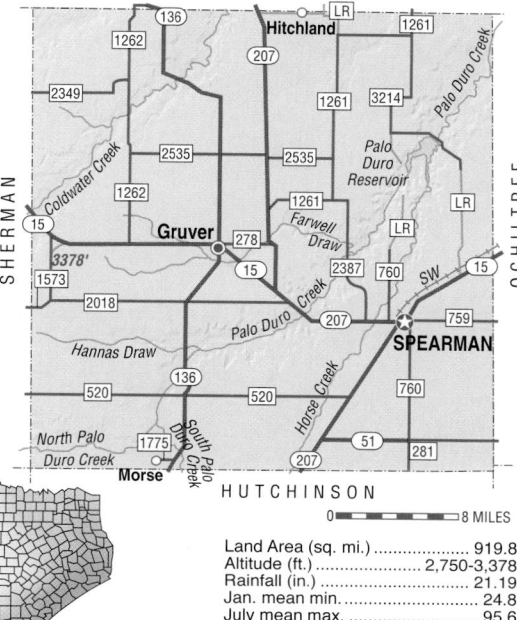

Population ............................... **5,509**
Change fm 2010 ......................... − 1.9
Area (sq. mi.) ............................. 920.4

| | |
|---|---|
| Land Area (sq. mi.) | 919.8 |
| Altitude (ft.) | 2,750-3,378 |
| Rainfall (in.) | 21.19 |
| Jan. mean min. | 24.8 |
| July mean max. | 95.6 |
| Civ. Labor | 2,955 |
| Unemployed | 3.4 |
| Wages | $24,354,305 |
| Per Capita Income | $55,742 |
| Prop. Value | $1,076,198,790 |
| Retail Sales | $48,623,448 |

*Big sky, field and farm on the High Plains of Hansford County in the Panhandle. Photo by Robert Plocheck.*

The Quanah railroad depot, built in 1908, now houses a museum. Photo by Ron Billings, Texas A&M Forest Service.

# Hardeman County

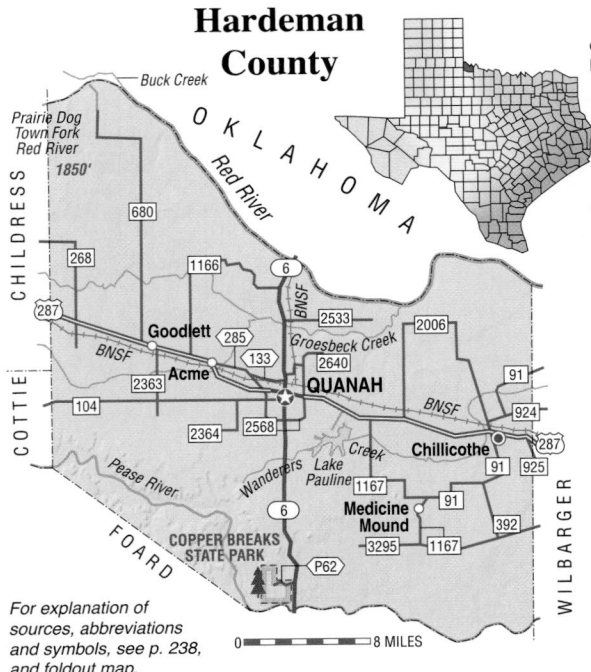

Buck Creek

Prairie Dog Town Fork Red River — 1850'

OKLAHOMA

Red River

CHILDRESS

COTTLE

FOARD

WILBARGER

680
268
287
1166
6
2533
2006
BNSF
Goodlett 285
Groesbeck Creek
2640
91
133
BNSF
Acme
QUANAH
BNSF
104
2363
2364
2568
924
Creek
Chillicothe
287
91
925
Wanderers Lake Pauline
1167
91
Medicine Mound
392
6
3295
1167
COPPER BREAKS STATE PARK
P62

0 ———— 8 MILES

For explanation of sources, abbreviations and symbols, see p. 238, and foldout map.

**Physical Features**: Rolling, broken area on divide between Pease, Red rivers; Lake Pauline; sandy, loam soils.

**Economy**: Agriculture, gypsum production, oil and natural gas.

**History**: Apaches, later the semi-sedentary Wichitas and Comanche hunters. Ranching began in the late 1870s. Farming expanded after 1900. County created in 1858 from Fannin County; re-created in 1876, organized in 1884; named for pioneer brothers Bailey and T.J. Hardeman.

**Race/Ethnicity**: (In percent) Anglo, 70.2; Black, 6.3; Hispanic, 21.5; Asian, 0.4; Other, 3.3.

**Vital Statistics**, annual: Births, 40; deaths, 39; marriages, 32; divorces, 17.

**Recreation**: Copper Breaks State Park; lake activities; Medicine Mound aborigine gathering site; Quanah Parker monument; hunting of deer, quail, wild hogs.

**Minerals**: Oil, natural gas, gypsum.

**Agriculture**: Wheat, cattle, cotton. Market value $25.4 million. Hunting leases.

**QUANAH** (2,531) county seat; manufacturing, farming, ranching, oil and gas; state hospital, general hospital; historical sites; Fall Festival in September.

Other towns include: **Chillicothe** (678) farm market center, hospital.

| | |
|---|---|
| Land Area (sq. mi.) | 695.1 |
| Altitude (ft.) | 1,250-1,850 |
| Rainfall (in.) | 26.85 |
| Jan. mean min. | 26.2 |
| July mean max. | 95.7 |
| Civ. Labor | 2,009 |

| | |
|---|---|
| **Population** | **3,982** |
| Change fm 2010 | – 5.1 |
| Area (sq. mi.) | 696.9 |

| | |
|---|---|
| Unemployed | 4.8 |
| Wages | $8,836,414 |
| Per Capita Income | $37,303 |
| Prop. Value | $685,221,990 |
| Retail Sales | $33,013,978 |

# Hardin County

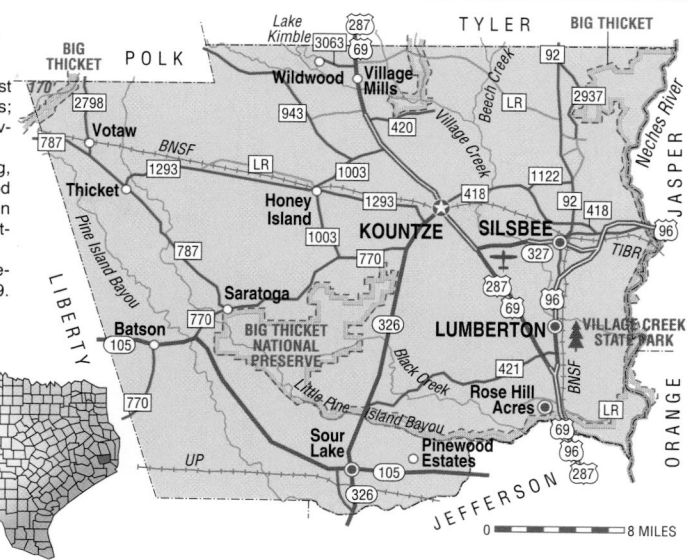

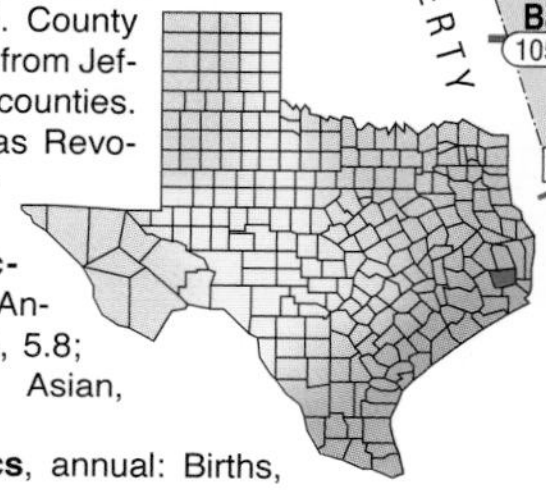

**Physical Features**: Southeast county; timbered; many streams; sandy, loam soils; Big Thicket covers much of area.

**Economy**: Paper manufacturing, wood processing, minerals, food processing, oil and gas; county in Beaumont-Port Arthur-Orange metropolitan area.

**History**: Lorenzo de Zavala received first land grant in 1829. Anglo-American settlers arrived in 1830. County created in 1858 from Jefferson, Liberty counties. Named for Texas Revolutionary leader William Hardin.

**Race/Ethnicity**: (In percent) Anglo, 87.1; Black, 5.8; Hispanic, 5.2; Asian, 0.7; Other, 1.6.

**Vital Statistics**, annual: Births, 700; deaths, 537; marriages, 420; divorces, 311.

**Recreation**: Big Thicket with rare plant, animal life; national preserve; Red Cloud Water Park in Silsbee; hunting, fishing; state park; Cajun Country Music Festival in October in Kountze.

**Minerals**: Oil, gas, sand, gravel.

**Agriculture**: Beef cattle, hay, blueberries, bees and rice. Timber provides most income; more than 85 percent of county forested. Hunting leases.

**KOUNTZE** (2,204) county seat; government/services, retail center, commuting to Beaumont; library, museum.

**SILSBEE** (7,038) forest products, rail center, oil, gas; library, Ice House museum; Dulcimer Festival in fall.

**LUMBERTON** (12,743) construction, government/services, tourism; library; Village Creek Festival in October.

Other towns and places include: **Batson** (140); **Pinewood Estates** (1,769); **Rose Hill Acres** (467); **Saratoga** (1,000) Big Thicket Museum; **Sour Lake** (1,899) oil, lumbering; Old Timer's Day in September; **Thicket** (306); **Village Mills** (200); **Votaw** (160), and **Wildwood** (1,305).

| | |
|---|---|
| Population | 55,621 |
| Change fm 2010 | 1.8 |
| Area (sq. mi.) | 897.6 |
| Land Area (sq. mi.) | 890.6 |
| Altitude (ft.) | 7-170 |
| Rainfall (in.) | 61.06 |
| Jan. mean min. | 37.5 |
| July mean max. | 93.6 |
| Civ. Labor | 26,762 |
| Unemployed | 7.1 |
| Wages | $119,249,783 |
| Per Capita Income | $40,638 |
| Prop. Value | $3,635,689,890 |
| Retail Sales | $700,826,717 |

*For explanation of sources, abbreviations and symbols, see p. 238, and foldout map.*

*A basketball game at a downtown park in Houston, Harris County. Photo by Robert Plocheck.*

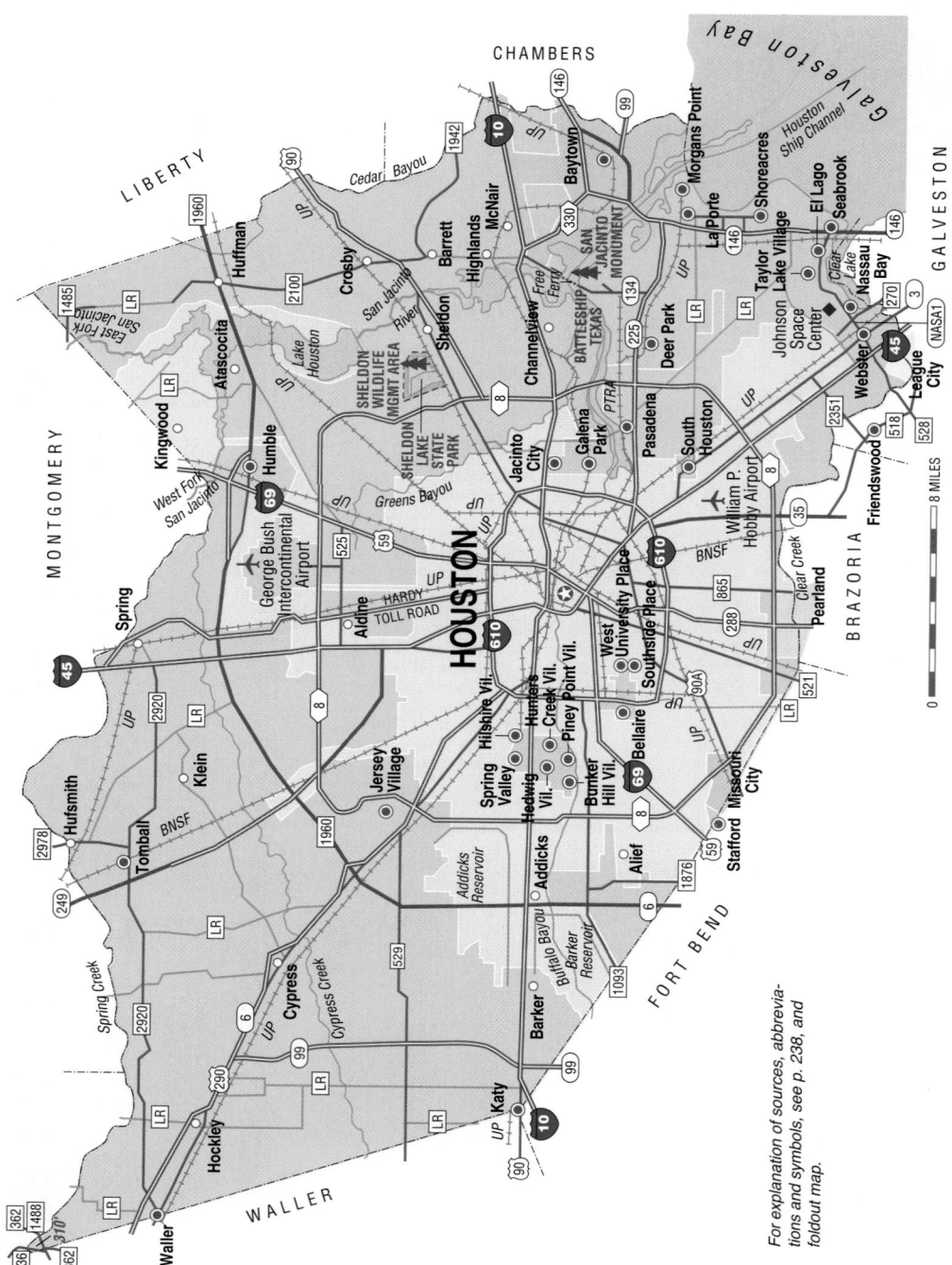

For explanation of sources, abbreviations and symbols, see p. 238, and foldout map.

**Physical Features**: Largest county in eastern half of state; level; typically coastal surface and soils; many bayous, canals for artificial drainage; Lake Houston, Sheldon Reservoir; partly forested.

**Economy**: Highly industrialized county with largest population; more than 92 foreign governments maintain offices in Houston; corporate management center; nation's largest concentration of petrochemical plants; largest U.S wheat-exporting port, among top U.S. ports in the value of foreign trade and total tonnage.

Petroleum refining, chemicals, food, fabricated metal products, non-electrical machinery, primary metals, scientific instruments; paper and allied products, printing and publishing; center for energy, space and medical research; center of international business.

**History**: Orcoquiza villages visited by Spanish authorities in 1746. Pioneer settlers arrived by boat from Louisiana in 1822. Antebellum planters brought black slaves. Mexican migration increased after Mexican Revolution. County created in 1836, organized in 1837; named for John R. Harris, founder of Harrisburg (now part of Houston).

**Race/Ethnicity**: (In percent) Anglo, 31.9; Black, 19.5; Hispanic, 41.6; Asian, 6.8; Other, 2.9.

**Vital Statistics**, annual: Births, 67,354; deaths, 23,409; marriages, 31,125; divorces, 14,030.

**Recreation**: Professional baseball, basketball, football, soccer; rodeo and livestock show; Jones Hall for the Performing Arts; Nina Vance Alley Theatre; Convention Center; Toyota Center, a 19,000-seat sports and entertainment center; Reliant Stadium and downtown ballpark.

Sam Houston Park, with restored early Houston homes, church, stores; Museum of Fine Arts, Contemporary Arts Museum, Rice Museum; Wortham Theater; Hobby Center for Performing Arts; museum of natural science, planetarium, zoo in Hermann Park.

San Jacinto Battleground, Battleship Texas; Johnson Space Center.

Fishing, boating, other freshwater and saltwater activities.

**Minerals**: Among leading oil, gas, petrochemical areas; production of petroleum, cement, natural gas, salt, lime, sulfur, sand and gravel, clays, stone.

**Agriculture**: Nursery crops, grass (third in acreage of sod), cattle, hay, horses, vegetables, Christmas trees (first in acreage), goats, rice, corn. Market value $65.2 million. Substantial income from forest products.

**Education**: Houston is a major center of higher education, with more than 300,000 students enrolled in 28 colleges and universities in the county. Among these are Rice University, the University of Houston, Texas Southern

# Harris County

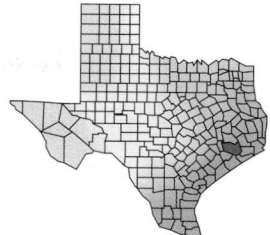

University, University of St. Thomas, Houston Baptist University.

Medical schools include Houston Baptist University School of Nursing, University of Texas Health Science Center, Baylor College of Medicine, Institute of Religion and Human Development, Texas Chiropractic College, Texas Woman's University-Houston Center.

**HOUSTON** (2,201,974, small parts in Fort Bend, Montgomery counties) county seat; largest Texas city; fourth-largest in nation.

A leading center for manufacture of petroleum equipment, agricultural chemicals, fertilizers, pesticides, oil and gas pipeline transmission; a leading scientific center; manufacture of machinery, fabricated metals; a major distribution, shipping center; engineering and research center; food processing; 85 hospitals.

Plants make apparel, lumber and wood products; furniture, paper, chemical, petroleum and coal products; publishing center; one of the nation's largest public school systems; prominent corporate center; Go Texan Days (rodeo) in February/March, international festival in March/April.

**Pasadena** (152,868) residential city with large industrial area manufacturing petrochemicals and other petroleum-related products; civic center; San Jacinto College, Texas Chiropractic College; hospitals; historical museum; Strawberry Festival in May.

**Baytown** (75,764, part [4,116] in Chambers County) refining, petrochemical center; commuters to Houston; Lee College; hospital, museum, library; historical homes; Chili When It's Chilly cookoff and the Great Bull Run in January.

The **Clear Lake** Area — which includes **El Lago** (2,772); **Nassau Bay**

*For explanation of sources, abbreviations and symbols, see p. 238, and foldout map.*

(4,095); **Seabrook** (12,735); **Taylor Lake Village** (3,627); **Webster** (11,035) — tourism, Johnson Space Center, University of Houston-Clear Lake, commuting to Houston; Bayport Industrial Complex includes Port of Bayport; 12 major marinas; hospitals; Christmas lighted boat parade.

Other towns include: **Aldine** (16,684); **Atascocita** (70,516); **Barrett** (3,293); **Bellaire** (17,655) residential city with several major office buildings; **Bunker Hill Village** (3,834); **Channelview** (40,830) hospital; **Crosby** (2,398) government/services, chemical plant, Czech Fest in October; **Cypress** (120,000); **Deer Park** (33,667) ship-channel industries, Totally Texas celebration in April.

Also, **Galena Park** (11,072); **Hedwig Village** (2,664); **Highlands** (7,695) commuters, heritage museum, Jamboree in October; **Hilshire Village** (779); **Hockley** (400); **Huffman** (15,000); **Humble** (15,480) oil-field equipment manufactured, retail center, hospital; **Hunters Creek Village** (4,523); Jacinto City (10,817); **Jersey Village** (7,890).

Also, **Katy** (15,094, partly in Fort Bend, Waller counties) corporate headquarters, distribution center, hospitals; museums, park; Rice Harvest festival in October; **Klein** (45,000); **La Porte** (34,839) petrochemical industry; depot museum; Sylvan Beach Festival in April; Galveston Bay; **Morgan's Point** (353); **Piney Point Village** (3,204); **Sheldon** (2,065); **Shoreacres** (1,577); **South Houston** (17,443).

Also, **Southside Place** (1,793); **Spring** (58,156); **Spring Valley** (4,083); **Tomball** (11,162) computers, oil equipment, retail center, antiques, hospital, sports medical center, museum, junior college, parks, Germanfest in March; **West University Place** (15,506).

Parts of **Friendswood, League City, Missouri City, Pearland, Stafford** and **Waller**.

**Addicks, Alief** and **Kingwood** are now within the city limits of Houston.

| | |
|---|---|
| Population | 4,441,370 |
| Change fm 2010 | 8.5 |
| Area (sq. mi.) | 1,777.5 |
| Land Area (sq. mi.) | 1,703.5 |
| Altitude (ft.) | sea level-310 |
| Rainfall (in.) | 56.81 |
| Jan. mean min. | 43.4 |
| July mean max. | 90.7 |
| Civ. Labor | 2,197,938 |
| Unemployed | 5.5 |
| Wages | $33,768,162,528 |
| Per Capita Income | $53,141 |
| Prop. Value | $369,657,943,752 |
| Retail Sales | $84,925,305,382 |

# Harrison County

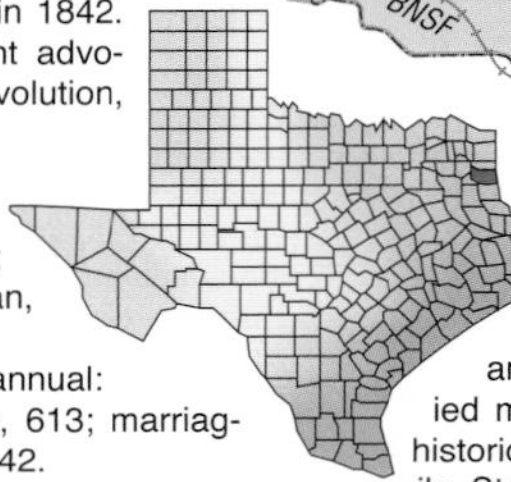

**Physical Features**: East Texas county; hilly, rolling; over half forested; Sabine River; Caddo Lake, Brandy Branch Reservoir.

**Economy**: Oil, gas processing, lumbering, pottery, other varied manufacturing.

**History**: Agriculturist Caddo Indians whose numbers were reduced by disease. Anglo-Americans arrived in 1830s. In 1850, the county had more slaves than any other in the state. County created in 1839 from Shelby County; organized in 1842. Named for eloquent advocate of Texas Revolution, Jonas Harrison.

**Race/Ethnicity**: (In percent) Anglo, 63.7; Black, 22.4; Hispanic, 12.1; Asian, 0.7; Other, 2.9.

**Vital Statistics**, annual: Births, 823; deaths, 613; marriages, 438; divorces, 142.

**Recreation**: Fishing, other water activities on Caddo and other lakes; hunting; plantation homes, historic sites; Stagecoach Days in May; Old Courthouse Museum; Old World Store; state park, performing arts; Fire Ant festival in October.

**Minerals**: Oil, gas, lignite coal, clays, sand and gravel.

**Agriculture**: Cattle, hay. Also, poultry, nursery plants, horses, vegetables, watermelons. Market value $19 million. Hunting leases important. Substantial timber industry.

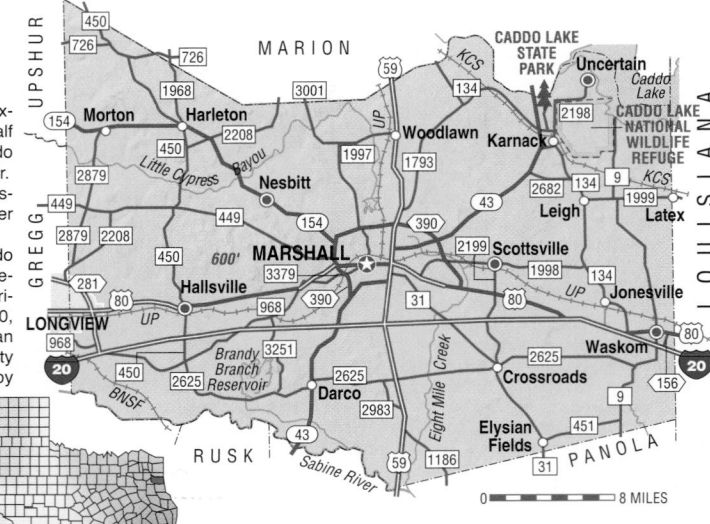

**MARSHALL** (24,036) county seat; petroleum and lumber processing, varied manufacturing; civic center; historic sites, including Starr Family State Historic Site; hospital; Wiley College, East Texas Baptist University; Wonderland of Lights in December.

Other towns include: **Elysian Fields** (500); **Hallsville** (3,894) government/services, utilities, Western Days in October, museum; **Harleton** (390); **Jonesville** (70); **Karnack** (350); **Nesbitt** (278); **Scottsville** (366); **Uncertain** (94) tourism, fishing, hunting, Mayhaw Festival in May; **Waskom** (2,155) oil, gas, ranching, Armadillo Daze in April; **Woodlawn** (560).

Also, part [1,870] of **Longview**.

| | |
|---|---|
| Population | 67,336 |
| Change fm 2010 | 2.6 |
| Area (sq. mi.) | 915.8 |
| Land Area (sq. mi.) | 900.0 |
| Altitude (ft.) | 168-600 |
| Rainfall (in.) | 50.18 |
| Jan. mean min. | 35.3 |
| July mean max. | 92.3 |
| Civ. Labor | 35,390 |
| Unemployed | 5.6 |
| Wages | $299,331,288 |
| Per Capita Income | $47,391 |
| Prop. Value | $7,497,725,398 |
| Retail Sales | $662,740,161 |

*For explanation of sources, abbreviations and symbols, see p. 238, and foldout map.*

*Caddo Lake. Photo by Chase Fountain/Texas Parks & Wildlife.*

# Hartley County

**Physical Features**: Panhandle High Plains; drains to Canadian River tributaries, playas; sandy, loam, chocolate soils; lake.

**Economy**: Agriculture, dairies, gas production.

**History**: Apaches, pushed out by Comanches around 1700. U.S. Army removed Indians in 1875. Pastores(sheepmen) in area until the 1880s when cattle ranching began. Farming expanded after 1900. County created in 1876 from Bexar, Young districts; organized in 1891; named for Texas pioneers O.C. and R.K. Hartley.

**Race/Ethnicity**: (In percent) Anglo, 66.1; Black, 7.5; Hispanic, 24.9; Asian, 0.7; Other, 1.5.

**Vital Statistics**, annual: Births, 64; deaths, 32; marriages, 6; divorces, 12.

**Recreation**: Lake Rita Blanca activities; ranch museum; XIT Rodeo and Reunion at Dalhart in August.

**Minerals**: Sand, gravel, natural gas.

**Agriculture**: Cattle, corn (second in acreage), wheat, hay, dairy cows, vegetables. 155,000 acres irrigated. Market value $1.18 billion. Hunting leases.

**CHANNING** (379) county seat, old XIT Ranch general headquarters, Round-up in July.

**DALHART** (8,147, mostly in Dallam County), government/services; agribusiness center for parts of Texas, New Mexico, Oklahoma; railroad; cheese plant; grain operations; junior college branch; hospital; prison.

Also, **Hartley** (553).

| | |
|---|---|
| Population | **6,089** |
| Change fm 2010 | 0.4 |
| Area (sq. mi.) | 1,463.2 |
| Land Area (sq. mi.) | 1,462.0 |
| Altitude (ft.) | 3,340-4,465 |
| Rainfall (in.) | 21.02 |
| Jan. mean min. | 21.4 |
| July mean max. | 91.6 |
| Civ. Labor | 2,712 |
| Unemployed | 4.1 |
| Wages | $18,409,426 |
| Per Capita Income | $50,931 |
| Prop. Value | $1,170,293,268 |
| Retail Sales | $34,555,761 |

# Haskell County

**Physical Features**: Northwest county; rolling; broken areas; drained by Brazos tributaries; lake; sandy loam, gray, black soils.

**Economy**: Agribusiness, oil-field operations.

**History**: Apaches until 1700, then a Comanche area. Ranching began in the late 1870s after the Indians were removed. Farming expanded after 1900. County created in 1858, from Milam and Fannin counties; re-created in 1876 and organized in 1885; named for Goliad victim C.R. Haskell.

**Race/Ethnicity**: (In percent) Anglo, 68.8; Black, 4.5; Hispanic, 25.0; Asian, 0.6; Other, 2.8.

**Vital Statistics**, annual: Births, 45; deaths, 104; marriages, 35; divorces, 23.

**Recreation**: Lake Stamford activities, bass tournament in August; Haskell arts & crafts show in November; hunting of deer, geese, wild hog.

**Minerals**: Oil and gas.

**Agriculture**: Wheat, cotton, peanuts; 28,000 acres irrigated. Beef cattle raised. Market value $38.7 million.

**HASKELL** (3,266) county seat; farming center; hospital; city park; Wild Horse Prairie Days in June.

Other towns include: **O'Brien** (103), **Rochester** (320), **Rule** (627) farming, cotton gins/warehouses, oil, mural, park, Trunk or Treat in Octiber, **Weinert** (169).

Also, **Stamford** (2,964, mostly in Jones County).

| | |
|---|---|
| Population | 5,769 |
| Change fm 2010 | - 2.2 |
| Area (sq. mi.) | 910.3 |
| Land Area (sq. mi.) | 903.1 |
| Altitude (ft.) | 1,340-1,795 |
| Rainfall (in.) | 26.40 |
| Jan. mean min. | 29.1 |
| July mean max. | 94.9 |
| Civ. Labor | 2,786 |
| Unemployed | 4.6 |
| Wages | $12,803,005 |
| Per Capita Income | $39,164 |
| Prop. Value | $666,324,540 |
| Retail Sales | $86,630,842 |

*For explanation of sources, abbreviations and symbols, see p. 238, and foldout map.*

**Physical Features**: Hilly in west, blackland in east; bisected by Blanco River; on edge of Balcones Escarpment.

**Economy**: Education, tourism, retirement area, some manufacturing; part of Austin metropolitan area.

**History**: Tonkawa area, also some Apache and Comanche presence. Spanish authorities attempted the first permanent settlement in 1807. Mexican land grants in early 1830s to Juan Martín Veramendi, Juan Vicente Campos and Thomas Jefferson Chambers. County created in 1843 from Travis County; named for Capt. Jack Hays, a famous Texas Ranger.

**Race/Ethnicity**: (In percent) Anglo, 56.8; Black, 4.0; Hispanic, 36.7; Asian, 1.4; Other, 3.4.

**Vital Statistics**, annual: Births, 2,050; deaths, 844; marriages, 957; divorces, 482.

**Recreation**: Fishing, hunting; college cultural, athletic events; African-American museum, LBJ museum; Cypress Creek and Blanco River resorts, guest ranches, Wonder World park, Aquarena center.

**Minerals**: Sand, gravel, cement produced.

**Agriculture**: Beef cattle, goats, exotic wildlife; greenhouse nurseries; hay, corn, sorghum, wheat and cotton. Market value $15 million.

**SAN MARCOS** (55,527) county seat; manufacturing, education, tourism; Texas State University, government/services, outlet center; hospital; San Marcos River; Cinco de Mayo festival, Juneteenth.

**Kyle** (32,673) medical, education, retail center, Claiborne Kyle Log House, Katherine Anne Porter House, 5k Kyle-O-Meter in October.

Other towns include: **Bear Creek** (384); **Buda** (10,822) construction, manufacturing, retail, government/

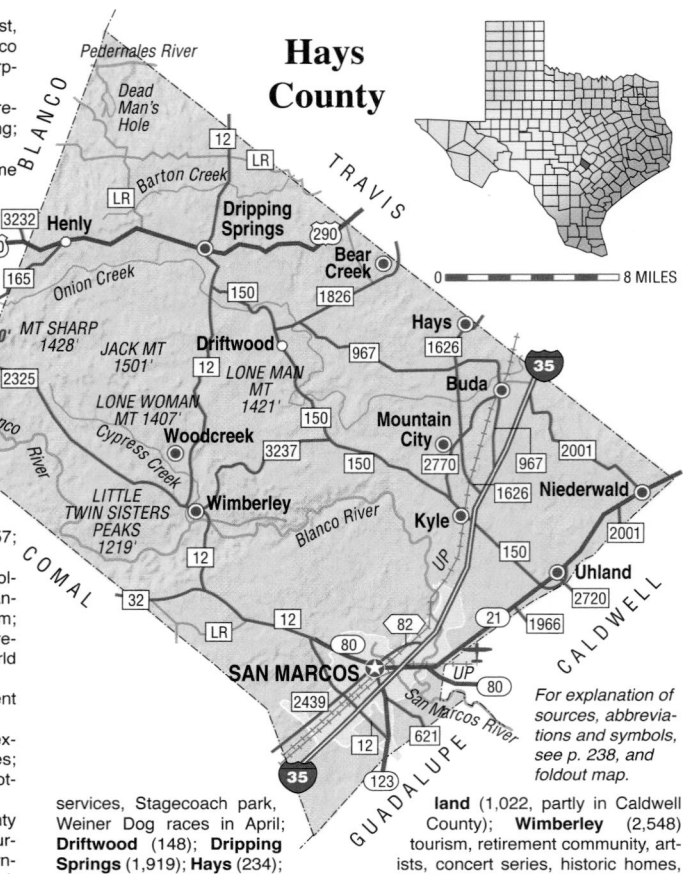

## Hays County

services, Stagecoach park, Weiner Dog races in April; **Driftwood** (148); **Dripping Springs** (1,919); **Hays** (234); **Mountain City** (646); **Niederwald** (577, partly in Caldwell County); **Uh**-

land (1,022, partly in Caldwell County); **Wimberley** (2,548) tourism, retirement community, artists, concert series, historic homes, arts and butterfly festivals in April; **Woodcreek** (1,461).

| | |
|---|---|
| Population | 185,025 |
| Change fm 2010 | 17.8 |
| Area (sq. mi.) | 679.9 |
| Land Area (sq. mi.) | 678.0 |
| Altitude (ft.) | 550-1,620 |
| Rainfall (in.) | 35.73 |
| Jan. mean min. | 38.7 |
| July mean max. | 94.3 |
| Civ. Labor | 93,266 |
| Unemployed | 4.6 |
| Wages | $470,193,602 |
| Av. Weekly Wage | $34,927 |
| Prop. Value | $15,152,403,147 |
| Retail Sales | $2,836,210,569 |

*Downtown Canadian with the tower of the Hemphill County Courthouse at the top of the hill. Photo by Robert Plocheck.*

# Hemphill County

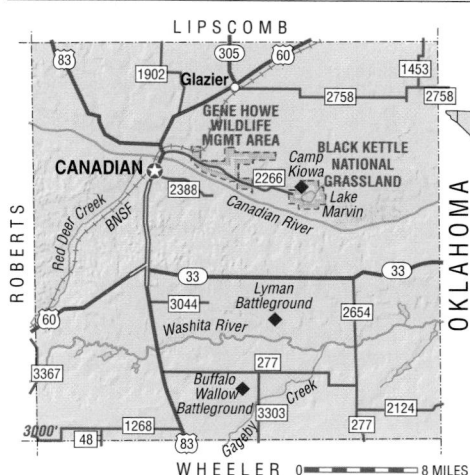

**Physical Features**: Panhandle county; sloping surface, broken by Canadian, Washita rivers; sandy, red, dark soils.

**Economy**: Oil and gas, agriculture, tourism and hunting, government/services.

**History**: Apaches, who were pushed out by Comanches, Kiowas. Tribes removed to Indian Territory in 1875. Ranching began in the late 1870s. Farmers began to arrive after 1900. County created from Bexar and Young districts in 1876; organized in 1887; named for Republic of Texas Justice John Hemphill.

**Race/Ethnicity**: (in percent) Anglo, 65.8; Black, 0.7; Hispanic, 31.6; Asian, 0.9; Other, 2.0.

**Vital Statistics**, annual: Births, 67; deaths, 35; marriages, 42; divorces, 13.

**Recreation**: Lake Marvin; fall foliage tour; hunting, fishing; Indian Battleground, wildlife management area; museum; 4th of July rodeo; prairie chicken viewing in April.

**Minerals**: Oil, natural gas, caliche.

**Agriculture**: Beef cattle, wheat, horses, hay, alfalfa; some irrigation. Market value $110.6 million. Hunting leases, nature tourism.

**CANADIAN** (2,814) county seat; oil, gas production; hospital; art foundation.

| | |
|---|---|
| Population | 4,180 |
| Change fm 2010 | 9.8 |
| Area (sq. mi.) | 912.2 |
| Land Area (sq. mi.) | 906.3 |
| Altitude (ft.) | 2,170-3,000 |
| Rainfall (in.) | 21.77 |
| Jan. mean min. | 21.2 |
| July mean max. | 93.2 |
| Civ. Labor | 3,120 |
| Unemployed | 2.3 |
| Wages | $29,462,423 |
| Per Capita Income | $77,681 |
| Prop. Value | $2,349,190,990 |
| Retail Sales | $51,235,828 |

# Henderson County

**Physical Features**: East Texas county bounded by Neches and Trinity rivers; hilly, rolling; one-third forested; sandy, loam, clay soils; commercial timber; lakes.

**Economy**: Agribusiness, retail trade, varied manufacturing, minerals, recreation, tourism.

**History**: Caddo area. Cherokee, other tribes migrated into the area in 1819-20 ahead of white settlement. Cherokees forced into Indian Territory in 1839. Anglo-American settlers arrived in 1840s. County created in 1846 from Nacogdoches, Houston counties and named for Gov. J. Pinckney Henderson.

**Race/Ethnicity**: (In percent) Anglo, 79.4; Black, 6.6; Hispanic, 11.8; Asian, 0.6; Other, 2.5.

**Vital Statistics**, annual: Births, 886; deaths, 1,004; marriages, 525; divorces, 41.

**Recreation**: Cedar Creek Reservoir, Lake Palestine, other lakes; Purtis Creek State Park; hunting, fishing, bird-watching; Zip Line (aerial ropeslide) at New York; East Texas Arboretum.

**Minerals**: Oil, gas, clays, lignite, sulfur, sand and gravel.

**Agriculture**: Beef cattle, forages, nurseries/horticulture, rodeo stock. Market value $49.5 million. Hunting leases and fishing. Timber important.

**ATHENS** (12,872) county seat; agribusiness center, varied manufacturing, tourism, state fish hatchery and museum, hospital, mental health center; Trinity Valley Community College; Texas Fiddlers' Contest in May.

**Gun Barrel City** (6,023) recreation, retirement, retail center.

**Malakoff** (2,313) brick factory, varied industry, tourism, library, Cornbread Festival in April.

Other towns include: **Berryville** (1,013); **Brownsboro** (1,033); **Caney City** (223); **Chandler** (2,842) commuting to Tyler, retail trade, tourism, Pow Wow Festival in October; **Coffee City** (290); **Enchanted Oaks** (332); **Eustace** (992); **Larue** (250); **Log Cabin** (710); **Moore Station** (200); **Murchison** (604); **Payne Springs** (757); **Poynor** (310); **Seven Points** (1,409) agribusiness, retail trade, recreation, Monte Carlo celebration in November; **Star Harbor** (448); **Tool** (2,265), and **Trinidad** (885).

Also, **Mabank** (3,108, mostly in Kaufman County).

| | |
|---|---|
| Population | 79,290 |
| Change fm 2010 | 1.0 |
| Area (sq. mi.) | 949.3 |
| Land Area (sq. mi.) | 873.8 |
| Altitude (ft.) | 256-763 |
| Rainfall (in.) | 42.94 |
| Jan. mean min. | 34.5 |
| July mean max. | 92.6 |
| Civ. Labor | 36,480 |
| Unemployed | 5.8 |
| Wages | $127,472,908 |
| Per Capita Income | $35,429 |
| Prop. Value | $6,903,065,244 |
| Retail Sales | $752,591,193 |

# Hidalgo County

**Physical Features**: Rich alluvial soils along Rio Grande; sandy, loam soils in north; semitropical vegetation; Anzalduas Channel Dam, Delta Lake, Valley Acres Reservoir.

**Economy**: Food processing and shipping, other agribusinesses, tourism, mineral operations.

**History**: Coahuiltecan and Karankawa area. Comanches forced Apaches southward into valley in the 1700s; Comanches arrived in valley in the 1800s. Spanish settlement occurred 1750-1800. County created in 1852 from Cameron and Starr counties, organized the same year; named for leader of Mexico's independence movement of 1810, Father Miguel Hidalgo y Costillo.

**Race/Ethnicity**: (In percent) Anglo, 7.3; Black, 0.8; Hispanic, 91.0; Asian, 1.1; Other, 0.9.

**Vital Statistics**, annual: Births, 16,301; deaths, 3,817; marriages, 4,856; divorces, 3.

**Recreation**: Winter resort, retirement area; fishing, hunting; gateway to Mexico; historical sites; Bentsen-Rio Grande Valley State Park; museums; All-Valley Winter Vegetable Show at Pharr.

**Minerals**: Oil, gas, stone, sand and gravel.

**Agriculture**: Ninety percent of farm cash receipts from crops (ranked first in state), principally from sugar cane (first in acreage), grain sorghum (first in acreage), vegetables (first in acreage), citrus, cotton; livestock includes cattle; 184,000 acres irrigated. Market value $452.8 million.

**EDINBURG** (85,456) county seat; vegetable processing and packing, petroleum operations, tourism, clothing; planetarium; the University of Texas-Pan American; hospitals; behavioral, health

| Population | 831,073 |
| --- | --- |
| Change fm 2010 | 7.3 |
| Area (sq. mi.) | 1,582.9 |
| Land Area (sq. mi.) | 1,570.9 |
| Altitude (ft.) | 28–376 |
| Rainfall (in.) | 22.20 |
| Jan. mean min. | 49.3 |
| July mean max. | 96.2 |
| Civ. Labor | 314,257 |
| Unemployed | 9.9 |
| Wages | $1,773,840,360 |
| Per Capita Income | $23,073 |
| Prop. Value | $32,608,029,618 |
| Retail Sales | $9,399,973,895 |

center; museum; Texas Cook'em High Steaks July 4 weekend, Fiesta Edinburg in February.

**McALLEN** (138,356) government/services; food processing and shipping, varied manufacturing, tourism; community college; hospitals; Palmfest in October.

**Mission** (81,581) citrus groves, agricultural processing and distribution; hospital; community college; international butterfly park; Citrus Fiesta in January.

**Pharr** (74,334) agriculture, trading center; trucking; tourism; old clock, juke box museums; folklife festival in February.

Other towns include: **Abram** (2,193); **Alamo** (19,225) live steam museum; **Alton** (13,943); **Doffing** (5,355); **Donna** (17,446) citrus center, varied manufacturing; **Edcouch** (3,243); **Elsa** (6,354); **Granjeno** (296); **Hargill** (900); **Hidalgo** (12,679) trade zone, shipping, winter resort, agribusiness, historical sites, library, Borderfest in March; **La Blanca** (2,558); **La Homa** (12,602); **La Joya** (4,238); **La Villa** (1,952); **Los Ebanos** (346).

Also, **Mercedes** (16,556) "boot capital," citrus, and vegetable center, food processing, tourism, recreation vehicle show in January, Hispanic Fest July 4; **Mila Doce** (6,659); **Monte Alto** (2,036); **North Alamo** (3,598); **Nurillo** (7,838); **Palmhurst** (2,665); **Palmview** (6,798); **Palmview South** (5,843); **Peñitas** (4,505); **Perezville** (5,660; **Progreso** (5,868); **Progreso Lakes** (249); **San Carlos** (3,299); **San Juan** (36,120) retirement area, trucking, Shrine of Our Lady of San Juan, Spring Fiesta in February; **San Manuel-Linn** (831); **South Alamo** (3,517); **Sullivan City** (4,253); **Weslaco** (37,515) agriculture, nature tourism, South Texas College, hospital, Dragonfly Days in May.

# Hill County

**Physical Features**: North central county; level to rolling; blackland soils, some sandy loams; drains to Brazos; Lake Whitney, Aquilla Lake.

**Economy**: Agri-business, tourism, varied manufacturing.

**History**: Waco and Tawakoni area, later Comanches. Believed to be Indian "council spot," a place of safe passage without evidence of raids. Anglo-Americans of the Robertson colony arrived in early 1830s. Fort Graham established in 1849. County created from Navarro County 1853, organized the same year; named for G.W. Hill, Republic of Texas official.

**Race/Ethnicity**: (In percent) Anglo, 72.0; Black, 7.0; Hispanic, 19.4; Asian, 0.5; Other, 2.5.

**Vital Statistics**, annual: Births, 413; deaths, 408; marriages, 212; divorces, 115.

**Recreation**: Lake activities; excursion boat on Lake Whitney; Texas Heritage Museum including Confederate and Audie Murphy exhibits, historic structures, rebuilt frontier fort barracks; motorcycle track.

**Minerals**: Gas, limestone.

**Agriculture**: Corn, cattle, sorghum, wheat, cotton, dairies, turkeys. Market value $119.9 million. Some firewood marketed.

**HILLSBORO** (8,235) county seat; agribusiness, varied manufacturing, retail, outlet center, tourism, antiques malls; Hill College; hospital; Cell Block

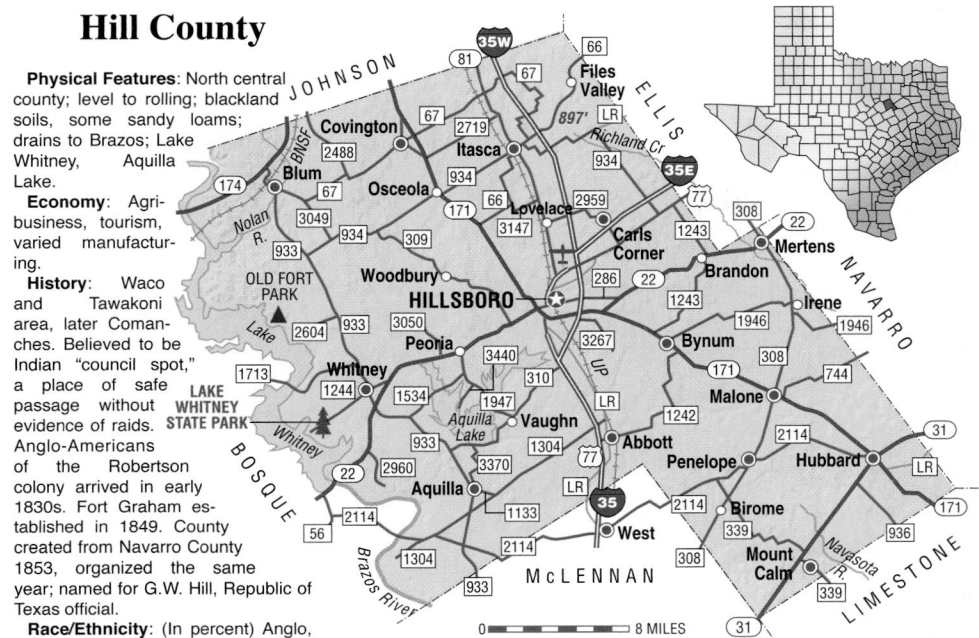

museum, restored courthouse; Cotton Pickin Fair in September.

**Whitney** (2,058) healthcare, manufacturing, stone works, tourist resorts; hospital; museum; Pioneer Days in October, lawn mower races in April.

Other towns include: **Abbott** (361); **Aquilla** (107); **Blum** (437); **Brandon** (75); **Bynum** (196); **Carl's Corner** (174); **Covington** (268); **Hubbard** (1,374) agriculture, machine shop, antiques, museum, library, Magnolias & Mistletoe Victorian Christmas celebration; **Irene** (170); **Itasca** (1,597); **Malone** (240); **Mertens** (129); **Mount Calm** (317); **Penelope** (196).

| | |
|---|---|
| Population | **34,848** |
| Change fm 2010 | – 0.7 |
| Area (sq. mi.) | 985.7 |
| Land Area (sq. mi.) | 958.9 |
| Altitude (ft.) | 417-897 |
| Rainfall (in.) | 37.93 |
| Jan. mean min. | 34.8 |
| July mean max. | 95.0 |
| Civ. Labor | 16,653 |
| Unemployed | 5.8 |
| Wages | $83,012,123 |
| Per Capita Income | $35,572 |
| Prop. Value | $3,038,274,299 |

*For explanation of sources, abbreviations and symbols, see p. 238, and foldout map.*

*Irrigated fields along U.S. 281 in Hidalgo County. Photo by Robert Plocheck.*

# Hockley County

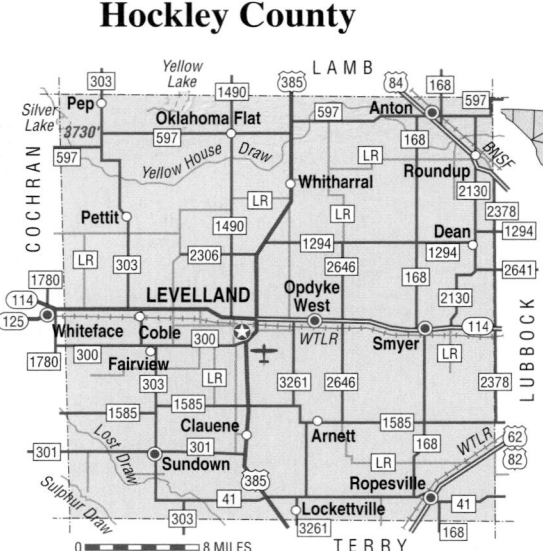

**Physical Features**: South Plains, numerous playas, drains to Yellow House Draw; loam, sandy loam soils.

**Economy**: Extensive oil, gas production and services; manufacturing; varied agribusiness.

**History**: Comanches displaced the Apaches in the early 1700s. Large ranches of the 1880s brought few residents. Homesteaders arrived after 1900. County created in 1876, from Bexar and Young districts; organized in 1921. Named for the Republic of Texas secretary of war Gen. G.W. Hockley.

**Race/Ethnicity** (in percent):Anglo, 48.7; Black, 4.1; Hispanic, 46.2; Asian, 0.4; Other, 2.6.

**Vital Statistics**, annual: Births, 368; deaths, 190; marriages, 161; divorces, 90.

**Recreation**: Early Settlers' Day in July; Marigolds Arts, Crafts Festival in November.

**Minerals**: Oil, gas, stone; one of leading oil counties with more than 1 billion barrels produced.

**Agriculture**: Cotton, grain sorghum; cattle, hogs raised; substantial irrigation. Market value $78.7 million.

**LEVELLAND** (14,017) county seat; oil, cotton, cattle center; government/services; hospital; South Plains College; Hot Burrito & Bluegrass Music Festival in July.

Other towns include: **Anton** (1,158); **Opdyke West** (180); **Pep** (3); **Ropesville** (441); **Smyer** (497); **Sundown** (1,439); **Whitharral** (158).

| | |
|---|---|
| Population...................... **23,577** | July mean max. ................... 91.6 |
| Change fm 2010.................... 2.8 | Civ. Labor ....................... 13,421 |
| Area (sq. mi.).................... 908.8 | Unemployed ......................... 4.1 |
| Land Area (sq. mi.)............ 908.4 | Wages ................... $121,219,034 |
| Altitude (ft.).............3,300-3,730 | Per Capita Income.......... $50,312 |
| Rainfall (in.) ...................... 19.84 | Prop. Value ........ $4,410,942,265 |
| Jan. mean min.................... 26.1 | Retail Sales ......... $254,133,093 |

---

# Hood County

**Physical Features**: Hilly; broken by Paluxy, Brazos rivers; sandy loam soils; Lake Granbury, Squaw Creek Reservoir.

**Economy**: Tourism, commuting to Fort Worth, nuclear power plant, agriculture.

**History**: Lipan Apache and Comanche area. Anglo-American settlers arrived in the late 1840s. County created in 1866 from Johnson and Erath counties, organized the same year; named for Confederate Gen. John B. Hood.

**Race/Ethnicity**: (In percent) Anglo, 85.8; Black, 0.8; Hispanic, 11.2; Asian, 0.7; Other, 2.3.

**Vital Statistics**, annual: Births, 570; deaths, 615; marriages, 402; divorces, 208.

**Recreation**: Lakes, fishing, scenic areas; summer theater; Gen. Granbury's Bean & Rib cookoff in March; Acton historic site.

**Minerals**: Oil, gas, stone.

**Agriculture**: Hay, turfgrass, beef cattle, nursery crops, pecans, peaches; some irrigation. Market value $18.7 million.

**GRANBURY** (9,059) county seat; tourism, real estate, power plants; historic downtown area, opera house; hospital; library; Civil War re-enact-

ment in October.

Other towns include: **Acton** (1,129) grave of Elizabeth Crockett, wife of Davy; **Brazos Bend** (321); **Cresson** (765); **DeCordova** (2,732); **Lipan** (442); **Oak Trail Shores** (2,888); **Pecan Plantation** (5,400); **Tolar** (724).

| | |
|---|---|
| Population.............................. **52,921** | |
| Change fm 2010........................... 5.4 | |
| Area (sq. mi.)............................. 436.8 | |

| | |
|---|---|
| Land Area (sq. mi.) ................... 420,6 | |
| Altitude (ft.) ........................ 600-1,230 | |
| Rainfall (in.) ............................. 35.08 | |
| Jan. mean min............................ 30.1 | |
| July mean max. ........................... 95.1 | |
| Civ. Labor ................................ 29,700 | |
| Unemployed .................................. 4.4 | |
| Wages ........................ $165,514,901 | |
| Per Capita Income................ $45,061 | |
| Prop. Value ............... $12,692,498,630 | |
| Retail Sales ................. $722,011,107 | |

*For explanation of sources, abbreviations and symbols, see p. 238, and foldout map.*

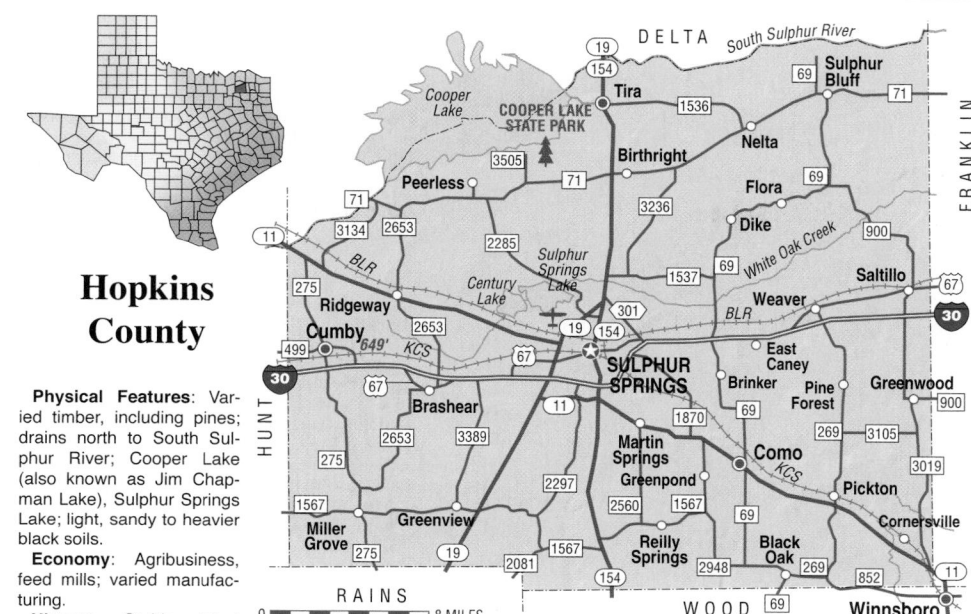

# Hopkins County

**Physical Features**: Varied timber, including pines; drains north to South Sulphur River; Cooper Lake (also known as Jim Chapman Lake), Sulphur Springs Lake; light, sandy to heavier black soils.

**Economy**: Agribusiness, feed mills; varied manufacturing.

**History**: Caddo tribal area, displaced by Cherokees, who in turn were forced out by President Lamar in 1839. First Anglo-American settlement in 1837. County created in 1846 from Lamar and Nacogdoches counties, organized the same year; named for pioneer Hopkins family.

**Race/Ethnicity**: (In percent) Anglo, 74.4; Black, 7.4; Hispanic, 16.1; Asian, 0.6; Other, 3.0.

**Vital Statistics**, annual: Births, 458; deaths, 377; marriages, 288; divorces, 176.

**Recreation**: Fishing, hunting; Cooper Lake State Park, lake activities; dairy museum; dairy festival in June;

stew contest in September.

**Minerals**: Lignite coal.

**Agriculture**: Dairies, beef cattle, hay (first in acreage). Market value $205.9 million. Firewood and hardwood lumber marketed.

**SULPHUR SPRINGS** (15,690) county seat; dairy farming, equine center, food processing and distribution, varied manufacturing, tourism; hospital; library, heritage park, music box gallery, civic center.

Other towns include: **Brashear** (280), **Como** (697), **Cumby** (771), **Dike** (170), **Pickton** (300), **Saltillo** (200), **Sulphur Bluff** (280), **Tira** (301).

| | |
|---|---|
| Population | 35,921 |
| Change fm 2010 | 5.4 |
| Area (sq. mi.) | 792.8 |
| Land Area (sq. mi.) | 767.2 |
| Altitude (ft.) | 340-649 |
| Rainfall (in.) | 47.18 |
| Jan. mean min. | 32.9 |
| July mean max. | 93,1 |
| Civ. Labor | 19,208 |
| Unemployed | 4.7 |
| Wages | $109,637,111 |
| Per Capita Income | $35,172 |
| Prop. Value | $2,499,268,516 |
| Retail Sales | $542,432,377 |

*For explanation of sources, abbreviations and symbols, see p. 238, and foldout map.*

---

*Students on the campus of South Plains College in Levelland. Photo by Robert Plocheck.*

# Houston County

**Physical Features**: East Texas county over half forested; rolling terrain, draining to Neches, Trinity rivers; timber production.

**Economy**: Livestock, timber, government/services, manufacturing, tourism.

**History**: Caddo group attracted mission San Francisco de los Tejas in 1690. Spanish town of Bucareli established in 1774. Both lasted only a few years. Anglo-American settlers arrived in the 1820s. County created in 1837 from Nacogdoches County by Republic, organized the same year; named for Sam Houston. Cotton plantations before the Civil War had many slaves.

**Race/Ethnicity**: (In percent) Anglo, 61.7; Black, 26.1; Hispanic, 10.9; Asian, 0.6; Other, 1.7.

**Vital Statistics**, annual: Births, 254; deaths, 310; marriages, 159; divorces, 102.

**Recreation**: Fishing, hunting; national forest; Mission Tejas State Park; 75 historical markers; county lake.

**Minerals**: Oil, gas, gravel.

**Agriculture**: Cattle, hay, watermelons, cotton. Market value $49.6 million. Hunting leases. Timber principal income source.

**CROCKETT** (6,766), county seat; timber, steel and plastic products, clothing manufacturing, Crockett State School; hospital; historic sites; Black Expo in February; fiddlers festival in June.

Other towns include: **Grapeland** (1,489) steel, agribusiness, oil and gas, Peanut Festival in October; **Kennard** (334); **Latexo** (334); **Lovelady** (652) Lovefest in February; **Ratcliff** (106).

| | |
|---|---|
| Population | 22.741 |
| Change fm 2010 | – 4.2 |
| Area (sq. mi.) | 1,236.6 |
| Land Area (sq. mi.) | 1,230.9 |
| Altitude (ft.) | 150-552 |
| Rainfall (in.) | 45.18 |
| Jan. mean min. | 36.8 |
| July mean max. | 93.4 |

| | |
|---|---|
| Civ. Labor | 8,167 |
| Unemployed | 7.7 |
| Wages | $65,703,419 |
| Per Capita Income | $32,863 |
| Prop. Value | $2,758,197,630 |
| Retail Sales | $172,938,093 |

---

# Howard County

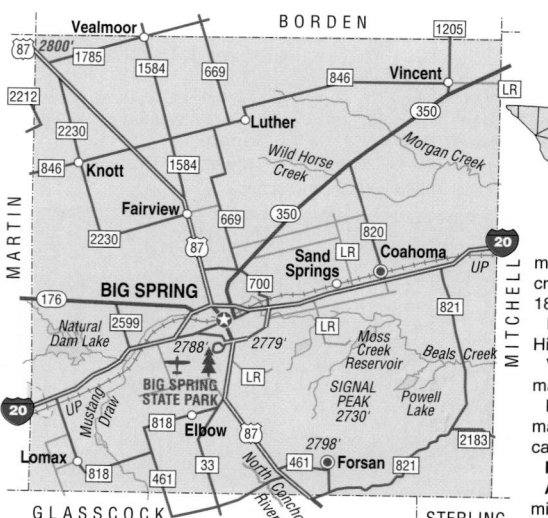

**Physical Features**: On edge of Llano Estacado; sandy loam soils; Natural Dam Lake.

**Economy**: Agriculture, petrochemicals, government/services.

**History**: Pawnee and Comanche area. Anglo-American settlement began in 1870. Oil boom in mid-1920s. County named for V.E. Howard, legislator; created 1876 from Bexar, Young districts; organized 1882.

**Race/Ethnicity**: (In percent), Anglo, 52.0; Black, 7.0; Hispanic, 39.4; Asian, 1.1; Other, 3.2.

**Vital Statistics**, annual: Births, 460; deaths, 378; marriages, 258; divorces, 12.

**Recreation**: Lakes, state park; campground in Comanche Trail Park, Native Plant Trail, museum, historical sites, Pow Wow in April, Pops in the Park in July.

**Minerals**: Oil, gas, sand, gravel and stone.

**Agriculture**: Cotton, beef, hay. Market value $13.9 million.

**BIG SPRING** (28,339) county seat; agriculture, petrochemicals, varied manufacturing; hospitals including a state institution and Veterans Administration hospital; federal prison; Howard College; railroad plaza.

Other towns include: **Coahoma** (846), **Forsan** (223), **Knott** (200), and **Sand Springs** (851).

| | |
|---|---|
| Population | 35,651 |
| Change fm 2010 | 4.7 |
| Area (sq. mi.) | 904.2 |
| Land Area (sq. mi.) | 900.8 |
| Altitude (ft.) | 2,180-2,800 |
| Rainfall (in.) | 19.50 |
| Jan. mean min. | 31.3 |
| July mean max. | 94.6 |

| | |
|---|---|
| Civ. Labor | 14,912 |
| Unemployed | 5.2 |
| Wages | $134,904,787 |
| Per Capita Income | $37,092 |
| Prop. Value | $3,768,867,333 |
| Retail Sales | $478,366,050 |

*The Hudspeth County Courthouse is an adobe structure built in 1922. Photo by Robert Plocheck.*

# Hudspeth County

**Physical Features**: Plateau, basin terrain, draining to salt lakes; Rio Grande; mostly rocky, alkaline, clay soils and sandy loam soils, except alluvial along Rio Grande; desert, mountain vegetation. Fertile agricultural valley.

**Economy**: Agribusiness, mining, tourism, hunting leases.

**History**: Mescalero Apache area. Fort Quitman established in 1858 to protect routes to west. Railroad in 1881 brought Anglo-American settlers. Political turmoil in Mexico (1912–1929) brought more settlers from Mexico. County named for Texas political leader Claude B. Hudspeth; created 1917 from El Paso County, organized the same year.

**Race/Ethnicity**: (In percent) Anglo, 19.7; Black, 1.6; Hispanic, 77.9; Asian, 0.8; Other, 2.5.

**Vital Statistics**, annual: Births, 44; deaths, 18; marriages, 5; divorces, 0.

**Recreation**: Scenic drives; fort sites; hot springs; salt basin; white sands; hunting; birding; part of Guadalupe Mountains National Park, containing unique plant life, canyons.

**Minerals**: Talc, stone, gypsum.

**Agriculture**: Most income from cotton, vegetables, hay, alfalfa; beef cattle raised; 18,000 acres irrigated. Market value $34.5 million.

**SIERRA BLANCA** (567) county seat; ranching center, tourist stop on interstate highway; adobe courthouse; 4th of July fair, livestock show in January.

Other towns include: **Dell City** (337) feedlots, vegetable packing, gypsum processing, trade center, airport, some of largest water wells in state, Wild West Chili Fest in September; and **Fort Hancock** (1,731).

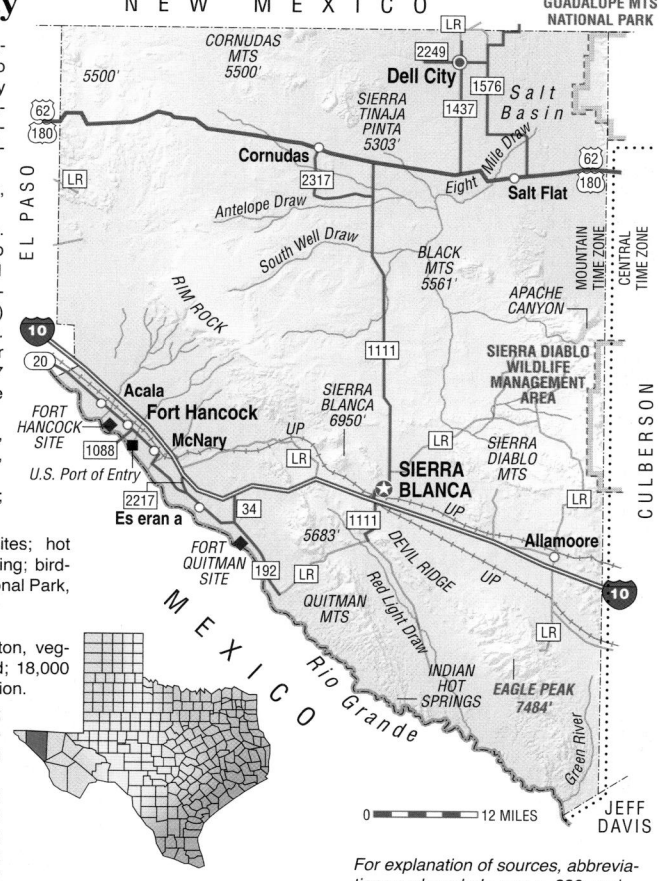

For explanation of sources, abbreviations and symbols, see p. 238, and foldout map.

| | | |
|---|---|---|
| Population .................................. 3,211 | Rainfall (in.) .................................. 11.24 | Wages ............................ $14,775,315 |
| Change fm 2010 ......................... − 7.6 | Jan. mean min. .............................. 25.7 | Per Capita Income .................. $31,118 |
| Area (sq. mi.) ........................... 4,571.8 | July mean max. .............................. 92.5 | Prop. Value .................... $621,228,664 |
| Land Area (sq. mi.) .................. 4,571.0 | Civ. Labor .................................... 1,657 | Retail Sales ...................... $9,020,426 |
| Altitude (ft.) ....................... 3,117–7,484 | Unemployed ..................................... 5.1 | |

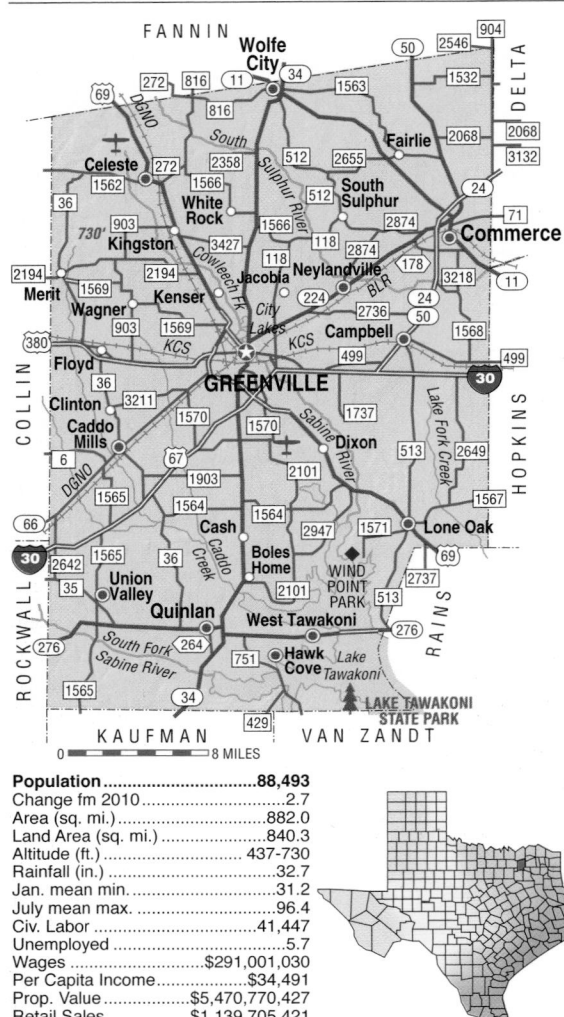

# Hunt County

**Physical Features**: Level to rolling surface; Sabine, Sulphur rivers; Lake Tawakoni, Greenville City Lakes; mostly heavy Blackland soil, some loam, sandy loams.

**Economy**: Education, varied manufacturing, agribusiness; several Fortune 500 companies in county; many residents employed in Dallas area.

**History**: Caddo Indians were gone by the 1790s. Kiowa bands were in the area when Anglo-American settlers arrived in 1839. County named for Memucan Hunt, Republic secretary of navy; created 1846 from Fannin, Nacogdoches counties, organized the same year.

**Race/Ethnicity**: (In percent) Anglo, 73.9; Black, 8.4; Hispanic, 14.6; Asian, 1.2; Other, 3.3.

**Vital Statistics**, annual: Births, 1,060; deaths, 784; marriages, 533; divorces, 300.

**Recreation**: Lake Tawakoni sports, catfish tournament in August; Texas A&M University-Commerce events.

**Minerals**: Sand and white rock, gas, oil.

**Agriculture**: Cattle, forage, greenhouse crops, top revenue sources; horses, wheat, oats, cotton, grain sorghum. Market value $69.3 million. Some firewood sold.

**GREENVILLE** (26,643) county seat; varied manufacturing, government/services, commuters to Dallas; hospital; branch of Paris Junior College; cotton museum, Audie Murphy exhibit; Native American Pow-wow in January.

**Commerce** (8,359) Texas A&M University-Commerce, government/services, varied manufacturing; emergency medical center; planetarium, children's museum; Bois d'Arc Bash in September.

Other towns include: **Caddo Mills** (1,436); **Campbell** (669); **Celeste** (846); **Hawk Cove** (496); **Lone Oak** (632); **Merit** (225); **Neylandville** (99); **Quinlan** (1,414); **Union Valley** (322); **West Tawakoni** (1,629) tourist center, light industry, Lakefest in October; **Wolfe City** (1,430) manufacturing, antiques shops, commuters to Dallas, museum, library, car and truck show in October.

*For explanation of sources, abbreviations and symbols, see p. 238, and foldout map.*

| | |
|---|---|
| Population | **88,493** |
| Change fm 2010 | 2.7 |
| Area (sq. mi.) | 882.0 |
| Land Area (sq. mi.) | 840.3 |
| Altitude (ft.) | 437-730 |
| Rainfall (in.) | 32.7 |
| Jan. mean min. | 31.2 |
| July mean max. | 96.4 |
| Civ. Labor | 41,447 |
| Unemployed | 5.7 |
| Wages | $291,001,030 |
| Per Capita Income | $34,491 |
| Prop. Value | $5,470,770,427 |
| Retail Sales | $1,139,705,421 |

*Downtown Greenville, Hunt County. Photo by Robert Plocheck.*

# Hutchinson County

**Physical Features**: High Plains, broken by Canadian River and tributaries, Lake Meredith; fertile valleys along streams.

**Economy**: Oil, gas, petrochemicals, agribusiness, varied manufacturing, tourism.

**History**: Antelope Creek Indian area. Later Comanches were driven out in U.S. cavalry campaigns of 1874-75. Adobe Walls site of two Indian attacks, 1864 and 1874. Ranching began in late 1870s. Oil boom in early 1920s. County created 1876 from Bexar Territory; organized 1901; named for pioneer jurist Anderson Hutchinson.

**Race/Ethnicity**: (In percent) Anglo, 71.9; Black, 2.8; Hispanic, 22.0; Asian, 0.5; Other, 4.4.

**Vital Statistics**, annual: Births, 311; deaths, 242; marriages, 154; divorces, 114.

**Recreation**: Lake activities, fishing, camping; Adobe Walls, historic Indian battle site.

**Minerals**: Gas, oil, sand, gravel.

**Agriculture**: Cattle, corn, wheat, grain sorghum; about 35,000 acres irrigated. Market value $55.9 million.

**STINNETT** (1,842) county seat; petroleum refining, farm center.

**BORGER** (12,775) petroleum refining, petrochemicals, carbon-black production, oil-field servicing, varied manufacturing, retail center; Frank Phillips College; museum; hospital; downtown beach bash in June.

Other cities include: **Fritch** (2,039), **Sanford** (165).

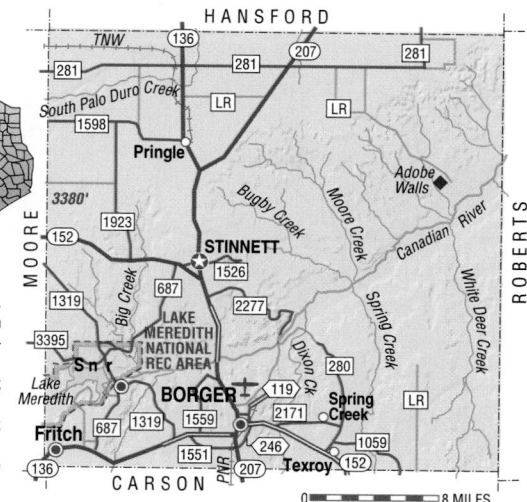

| | |
|---|---|
| Population | 21,773 |
| Change fm 2010 | – 1.7 |
| Area (sq. mi.) | 895.0 |
| Land Area (sq. mi.) | 887.4 |
| Altitude (ft.) | 2,600-3,380 |
| Rainfall (in.) | 21.72 |
| Jan. mean min. | 25.2 |
| July mean max. | 93.8 |
| Civ. Labor | 11,890 |
| Unemployed | 4.4 |
| Wages | $112,484,748 |
| Per Capita Income | $41,967 |
| Prop. Value | $3,204,132,950 |
| Retail Sales | $188,837,600 |

---

# Irion County

**Physical Features**: West Texas county with hilly surface, broken by Middle Concho, tributaries; clay, sandy soils.

**Economy**: Ranching, oil, gas production, wildlife recreation.

**History**: Tonkawa Indian area. Anglo-American settlement began in the late 1870s. County named for Republic leader R.A. Irion; created in 1889 from Tom Green County and organized the same year.

**Race/Ethnicity**: (In percent) Anglo, 69.4; Black, 1.9; Hispanic, 26.9; Asian, 0.3; Other, 2.3.

**Vital Statistics**, annual: Births 16; deaths, 13; marriages, 2; divorces, 1.

**Recreation**: Hunting; historic sites, including Dove Creek battlefield and stagecoach stops, old Sherwood courthouse built 1900; hunters appreciation dinner in November.

**Minerals**: Oil, gas.

**Agriculture**: Beef cattle, sheep, goats; hay, wheat. Market value $7.5 million.

**MERTZON** (852) county seat; farm center, wool warehousing.

Other towns include: **Barnhart** (110).

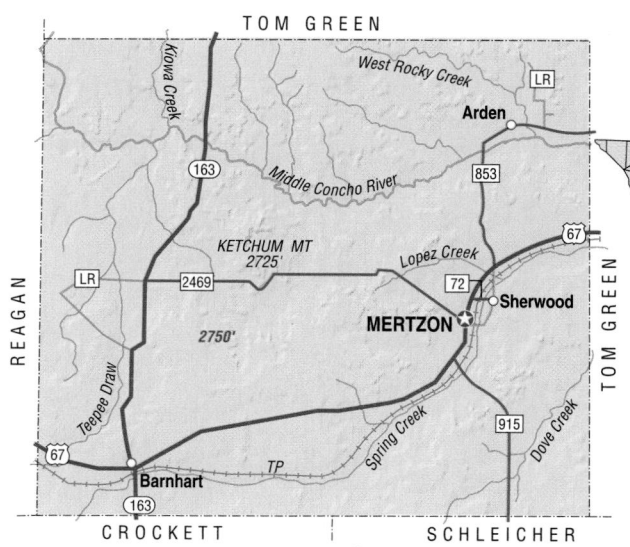

| | |
|---|---|
| Population | 1,574 |
| Change fm 2010 | – 1.6 |
| Area (sq. mi.) | 1,051.6 |
| Land Area (sq. mi.) | 1,051.6 |
| Altitude (ft.) | 2,000-2,750 |
| Rainfall (in.) | 20.15 |
| Jan. mean min. | 32.0 |
| July mean max. | 95.0 |
| Civ. Labor | 857 |
| Unemployed | 3.9 |
| Wages | $9,915,302 |
| Per Capita Income | $54,776 |
| Prop. Value | $1,494,958,080 |
| Retail Sales | $7,059,677 |

*For explanation of sources, abbreviations and symbols, see p. 238, and foldout map.*

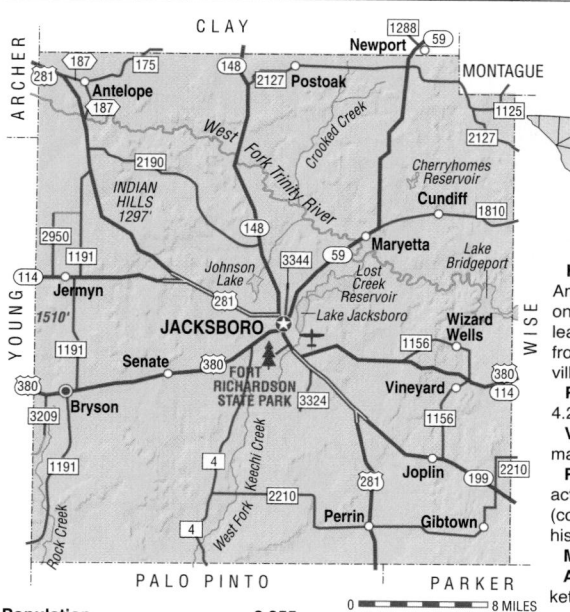

# Jack County

**Physical Features**: Rolling Cross Timbers, broken by West Fork of Trinity, other streams; sandy, dark brown, loam soils; lakes.

**Economy**: Petroleum production, oil-field services, livestock, manufacturing, tourism.

**History**: Caddo and Comanche borderland. Anglo-American settlers arrived in 1855, part of Peters Colony. County named for brothers P.C. and W.H. Jack, leaders in Texas' independence effort; created 1856 from Cooke County; organized 1857 with Mesquite-ville (original name of Jacksboro) as county seat.

**Race/Ethnicity**: (In percent) Anglo, 78.5; Black, 4.2; Hispanic, 15.8; Asian, 0.5; Other, 2.0.

**Vital Statistics**, annual: Births, 89; deaths, 80; marriages, 62; divorces, 35.

**Recreation**: Hunting, wildlife leases; fishing; lake activities; Fort Richardson, Texas 4-H Museum (county is birthplace of 4-H clubs in Texas), other historic sites; Lost Creek Reservoir State Trailway.

**Minerals**: Oil, gas.

**Agriculture**: Cattle, hay, wheat, goats, sheep. Market value $22.5 million. Firewood sold.

**JACKSBORO** (4,565) county seat; agribusiness, petroleum production and services, tourism; hospital; library; Fort Richardson Living History Days in April.

Other towns include: **Bryson** (526), **Jermyn** (75), Perrin (405).

| | |
|---|---|
| Population | 8,855 |
| Change fm 2010 | − 2.1 |
| Area (sq. mi.) | 920.1 |
| Land Area (sq. mi.) | 910.7 |
| Altitude (ft.) | 836-1,510 |
| Rainfall (in.) | 32.92 |
| Jan. mean min. | 29.7 |
| July mean max. | 94.4 |
| Civ. Labor | 6,256 |
| Unemployed | 3.3 |
| Wages | $40,830,743 |
| Per Capita Income | $48,985 |
| Prop. Value | $2,631,604,240 |
| Retail Sales | $41,288,450 |

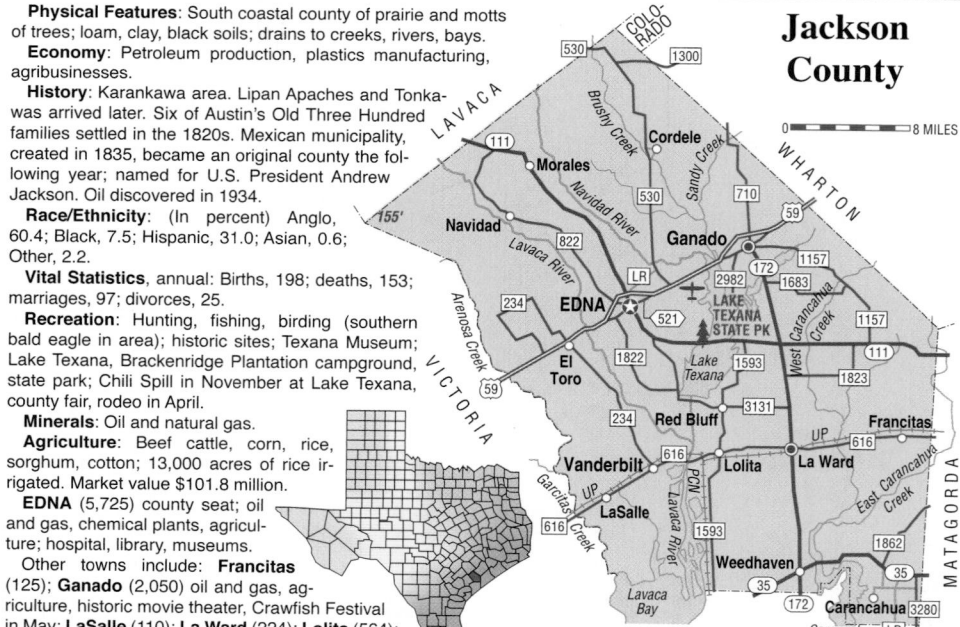

# Jackson County

**Physical Features**: South coastal county of prairie and motts of trees; loam, clay, black soils; drains to creeks, rivers, bays.

**Economy**: Petroleum production, plastics manufacturing, agribusinesses.

**History**: Karankawa area. Lipan Apaches and Tonkawas arrived later. Six of Austin's Old Three Hundred families settled in the 1820s. Mexican municipality, created in 1835, became an original county the following year; named for U.S. President Andrew Jackson. Oil discovered in 1934.

**Race/Ethnicity**: (In percent) Anglo, 60.4; Black, 7.5; Hispanic, 31.0; Asian, 0.6; Other, 2.2.

**Vital Statistics**, annual: Births, 198; deaths, 153; marriages, 97; divorces, 25.

**Recreation**: Hunting, fishing, birding (southern bald eagle in area); historic sites; Texana Museum; Lake Texana, Brackenridge Plantation campground, state park; Chili Spill in November at Lake Texana, county fair, rodeo in April.

**Minerals**: Oil and natural gas.

**Agriculture**: Beef cattle, corn, rice, sorghum, cotton; 13,000 acres of rice irrigated. Market value $101.8 million.

**EDNA** (5,725) county seat; oil and gas, chemical plants, agriculture; hospital, library, museums.

Other towns include: **Francitas** (125); **Ganado** (2,050) oil and gas, agriculture, historic movie theater, Crawfish Festival in May; **LaSalle** (110); **La Ward** (224); **Lolita** (564); **Vanderbilt** (401).

| | |
|---|---|
| Population | 14,739 |
| Change fm 2010 | 4.7 |
| Area (sq. mi.) | 856.9 |
| Land Area (sq. mi.) | 829.4 |
| Altitude (ft.) | sea level-155 |
| Rainfall (in.) | 43.25 |
| Jan. mean min. | 42.0 |
| July mean max. | 94.0 |
| Civ. Labor | 7,439 |
| Unemployed | 4.6 |
| Wages | $54,536,655 |
| Per Capita Income | $37,136 |
| Prop. Value | $2,459,407,498 |
| Retail Sales | $200,346,091 |

# Jasper County

**Physical Features**: East Texas county; hilly to level; national forest; Sam Rayburn Reservoir, B.A. Steinhagen Lake; Neches River.

**Economy**: Timber industries; nature tourism, government/services.

**History**: Caddo and Atakapa Indian area. Land grants to John R. Bevil and Lorenzo de Zavala in 1829. County created in 1836, organized in 1837, from Mexican municipality; named for Sgt. William Jasper of American Revolution.

**Race/Ethnicity**: (In percent) Anglo, 75.0; Black, 16.5; Hispanic, 6.4; Asian, 0.7; Other, 2.2.

**Vital Statistics**, annual: Births, 430; deaths, 430; marriages, 309; divorces, 171.

**Recreation**: Lake activities; hunting, fishing; state park, Big Thicket; Butterfly Festival in October.

**Minerals**: Oil, gas produced.

**Agriculture**: Cattle, plant nurseries, fruits, vegetables. Market value $10.1 million. Timber is major income producer. Hunting leases and fishing tournaments are major income producers.

**JASPER** (7,595) county seat; tourism, government/services; hospital; Angelina College extension; museum; arboretum and outdoor learning center; Azalea Festival in March.

Other towns include: **Browndell** (215); **Buna** (2,149) timber, oil, polka dot house, redbud festival in March; **Evadale** (1,531); **Kirbyville** (2,114) government/services, retail, commuters, museum, Calaboose museum, Magnolia Festival in April; **Sam Rayburn** (600).

| | |
|---|---|
| Population.............................. **35,552** | July mean max. .......................... 91.4 |
| Change fm 2010 ........................ – 0.4 | Civ. Labor ............................... 15,481 |
| Area (sq. mi.)............................ 969.7 | Unemployed ................................. 8.3 |
| Land Area (sq. mi.) ................... 938.9 | Wages ........................... $92,708,071 |
| Altitude (ft.) ............................ 10–580 | Per Capita Income................ $34,573 |
| Rainfall (in.) ............................. 59.75 | Prop. Value ............... $2,934,459,197 |
| Jan. mean min. ........................... 38.7 | Retail Sales ................. $357,888,964 |

*For explanation of sources, abbreviations and symbols, see p. 238, and foldout map.*

*Ranch land in Jack County along FM 4. Photo by Robert Plocheck.*

*The restored Fort Davis, which was established in 1854. Photo by Robert Plocheck.*

# Jeff Davis County

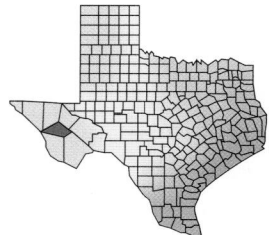

**Physical Features**: Highest average elevation in Texas; peaks (Mt. Livermore, 8,378 ft.), canyons, plateaus; intermountain wash, clay, loam soils; cedars, oaks in highlands.

**Economy**: Tourism, agriculture, McDonald Observatory.

**History**: Mescalero Apaches in area when Antonio de Espejo explored in 1583. U.S. Army established Fort Davis in 1854 to protect routes to west. Civilian settlers followed, including Manuel Músquiz, a political refugee from Mexico. County named for Jefferson Davis, U.S. Secretary of War, Confederate president; created 1887 from Presidio County, organized the same year.

**Race/Ethnicity**: (In percent) Anglo, 62.2; Black, 1.6; Hispanic, 34.5; Asian, 0.4; Other, 2.7.

**Vital Statistics**, annual: Births, 11; deaths, 11; marriages, 1; divorces, 0.

**Recreation**: Scenic drives including loop along Limpia Creek, Mt. Livermore, Blue Mountain; hunting; Fort Davis National Historic Site; state park; McDonald Observatory on Mt. Locke; solar power park; Chihuahuan Desert Research Institute; hummingbird festival in August.

**Minerals**: Not significant.

**Agriculture**: Greenhouse tomatoes, beef cattle, horses, meat goats. Hunting leases important.

**FORT DAVIS** (1,168), county seat; ranch center, trade, tourism, government/services; library; "Coolest July 4th in Texas."

Other town: **Valentine** (124).

| | |
|---|---|
| Population | 2,204 |
| Change fm 2010 | – 5.9 |
| Area (sq. mi.) | 2,264.6 |
| Land Area (sq. mi.) | 2,264.6 |
| Altitude (ft.) | 3,162-8,378 |
| Rainfall (in.) Fort Davis | 17.47 |
| Rainfall (in.) Mt. Locke | 20.37 |
| Jan. mean min. Fort Davis | 28.9 |
| Jan. mean min. Mt. Locke | 32.4 |
| July mean max. Fort Davis | 88.7 |
| July mean max. Mt. Locke | 84.5 |
| Civ. Labor | 1,149 |
| Unemployed | 4.4 |
| Wages | $7,088,584 |
| Per Capita Income | $39,670 |
| Prop. Value | $499,272,400 |
| Retail Sales | $8,475,279 |

*For explanation of sources, abbreviations and symbols, see p. 238, and foldout map.*

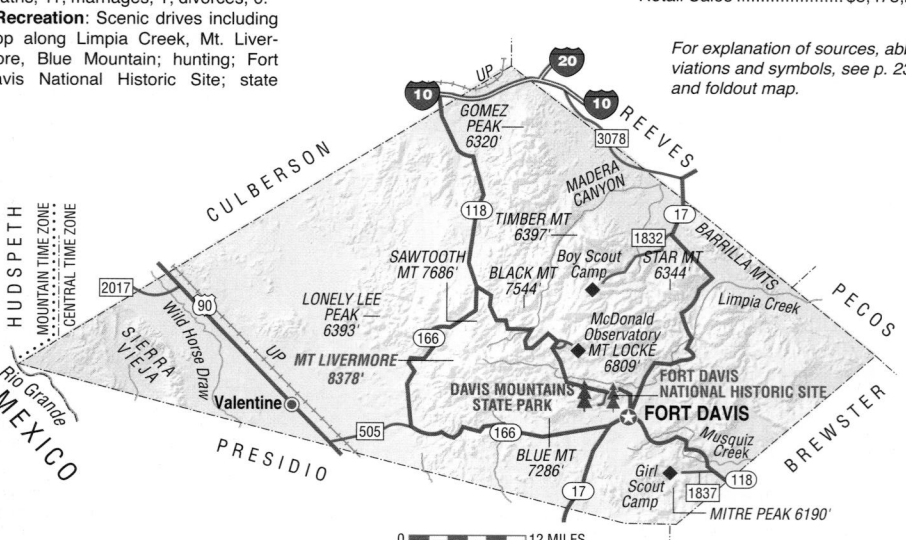

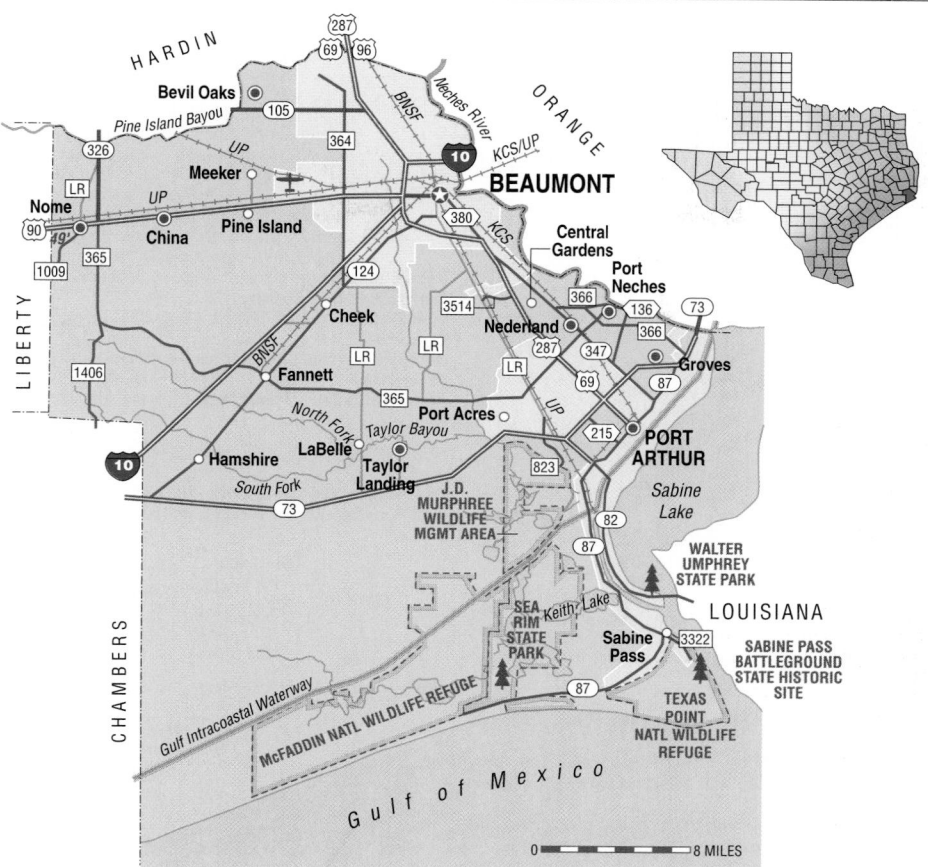

**Physical Features**: Gulf Coast grassy plain, with timber in northwest; beach sands, sandy loams, black clay soils; drains to Neches River, Gulf of Mexico.

**Economy**: Government/services, petrochemical and other chemical plants, shipbuilding, steel mill, port activity, oil-field supplies.

**History**: Atakapas and Orcoquizas, whose numbers were reduced by epidemics or migration before Anglo-American settlers arrived in 1820s. Cajuns arrived in 1840s; Europeans in 1850s. Antebellum slaveholding area. County created in 1836 from Mexican municipality; organized in 1837; named for U.S. President Thomas Jefferson.

**Race/Ethnicity**: (In percent) Anglo, 42.9; Black, 34.4; Hispanic, 18.5; Asian, 3.8; Other, 2.6.

**Vital Statistics**, annual: Births, 3,430; deaths, 2,390; marriages, 1,969; divorces, 747.

**Recreation**: Beaches, fresh and saltwater fishing; duck, goose hunting; water activities; Dick Dowling Monument and Park; Spindletop site, energy, fire museums; saltwater lake;

# Jefferson County

J.D. Murphree WMA, McFaddin wildlife refuge, Texas Point wildlife refuge; Lamar University events; historic sites; South Texas Fair in March-April.

**Minerals**: Large producer of oil, gas, sulfur, salt, sand and gravel.

**Agriculture**: Rice, hay, beef cattle, crawfish; considerable rice irrigated. Market value $38 million. Timber sales significant.

**BEAUMONT** (118,180) county seat; oil and gas production, government/services, engineering and industrial services, port; Lamar University, Institute of Technology; hospitals; entertainment district; Neches River Festival in April.

**PORT ARTHUR** (54,597) oil, chemical activities, shrimping and crawfishing, shipping, offshore marine, tourism; hospitals; museum; prison; Asian New Year Tet, Janis Joplin Birthday Bash in January. Sabine Pass and Port Acres are now within the city limits of Port Arthur.

Other towns include: **Bevil Oaks** (1,289); **Central Gardens** (4,361); **China** (1,160); **Fannett** (2,262);

**Groves** (15,800) retail center, some manufacturing, government/services, tourism; hospital, pecan festival in September; **Hamshire** (759).

Also, **Nederland** (17,483) manufacturing, transportation, petrochemical refining; Windmill and French museum; hospital; Tex Ritter memorial and park, heritage festival in March (city founded by Dutch immigrants in 1898).

Also, **Nome** (587); **Port Neches** (12,919) chemical and synthetic rubber industry, manufacturing, library, riverfront park with La Maison Beausoleil, RiverFest in May; **Taylor Landing** (229).

| Population | 252,235 |
|---|---|
| Change fm 2010 | 0.0 |
| Area (sq. mi.) | 1,112.7 |
| Land Area (sq. mi.) | 876.3 |
| Altitude (ft.) | sea level-49 |
| Rainfall (in.) | 60.42 |
| Jan. mean min. | 41.7 |
| July mean max. | 92.0 |
| Civ. Labor | 114,307 |
| Unemployed | 8.6 |
| Wages | $1,399,771,755 |
| Per Capita Income | $39,958 |
| Prop. Value | $31,713,218,439 |
| Retail Sales | $3,714,246,078 |

# Jim Hogg County

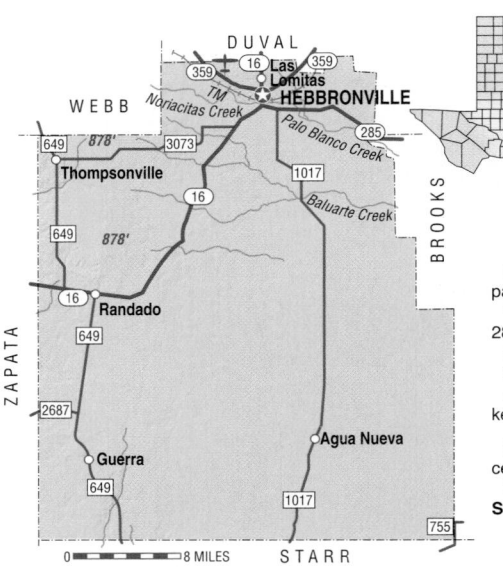

**Physical Features**: South Texas county on rolling plain, with heavy brush cover; white blow sand and sandy loam; hilly, broken.

**Economy**: Oil, cattle operations.

**History**: Coahuiltecan tribal area, then Lipan Apache. Spanish land grant in 1805 to Xavier Vela. County named for Gov. James Stephen Hogg; created and organized in 1913 from Brooks and Duval counties.

**Race/Ethnicity**: (In percent) Anglo, 6.3; Black, 0.6; Hispanic, 92.1; Asian, 0.6; Other, 1.2.

**Vital Statistics**, annual: Births, 93; deaths, 48; marriages, 28; divorces, 1.

**Recreation**: White-tailed deer and bobwhite hunting.

**Minerals**: Oil and gas.

**Agriculture**: Cattle, hay, milk goats; some irrigation. Market value $11.1 million.

**HEBBRONVILLE** (4,468) county seat; ranching, oil-field center.

Other towns include: **Guerra** (6), **Las Lomitas** (232), **South Fork Estates** (74), and **Thompsonville** (45).

| | |
|---|---|
| Population | 5,255 |
| Change fm 2010 | – 0.8 |
| Area (sq. mi.) | 1,136.2 |
| Land Area (sq. mi.) | 1,136.1 |
| Altitude (ft.) | 230-878 |
| Rainfall (in.) | 23.79 |
| Jan. mean min. | 44.8 |
| July mean max. | 96.7 |
| Civ. Labor | 3,124 |
| Unemployed | 4.5 |
| Wages | $19,811,560 |
| Per Capita Income | $39,276 |
| Prop. Value | $637,572,360 |
| Retail Sales | $37,288,677 |

# Jim Wells County

**Physical Features**: South Coastal Plains; level to rolling; sandy to dark soils; grassy with mesquite brush; Lake Corpus Christi.

**Economy**: Oil and gas production, agriculture, nature tourism.

**History**: Coahuiltecans, driven out by Lipan Apaches in 1775. Tomás Sánchez established settlement in 1754. Anglo-American settlement began in 1878. County created 1911 from Nueces County; organized 1912; named for developer J.B. Wells Jr.

**Race/Ethnicity**: (In percent) Anglo, 19.2; Black, 0.9; Hispanic, 79.3; Asian, 0.6; Other, 1.7.

**Vital Statistics**, annual: Births, 619; deaths, 439; marriages, 255; divorces, 147.

**Recreation**: Hunting; fiestas; Tejano Roots hall of fame; South Texas museum.

**Minerals**: Oil, gas, caliche.

**Agriculture**: Cattle, sorghum, corn, cotton, dairies, goats, wheat, watermelons, sunflowers, peas, hay. Market value $82.9 million.

**ALICE** (19,682) county seat; oil-field service center, agribusiness, government/services; hospital; Bee County College extension; Fiesta Bandana (from original name of city) in May.

Other towns include: **Alfred** (95); **Ben Bolt** (1,600); **Orange Grove** (1,366); **Pernitas Point** (274, partly in Live Oak County); **Premont** (2,710) wildflower tour in spring; **Rancho Alegre** (1,747); **Sandia** (382).

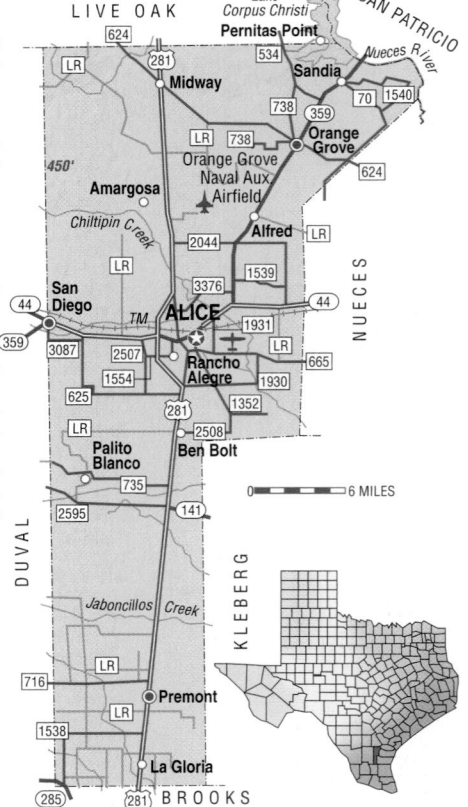

| | |
|---|---|
| Population | 41,353 |
| Change fm 2010 | 1.3 |
| Area (sq. mi.) | 868.3 |
| Land Area (sq. mi.) | 865.0 |
| Altitude (ft.) | 50-450 |
| Rainfall (in.) | 28.43 |
| Jan. mean min. | 44.9 |
| July mean max. | 97.2 |
| Civ. Labor | 24,743 |
| Unemployed | 4.8 |
| Wages | $234,029,566 |
| Per Capita Income | $44,885 |
| Prop. Value | $3,006,949,784 |
| Retail Sales | $555,106,884 |

*For explanation of sources, abbreviations and symbols, see p. 238, and foldout map.*

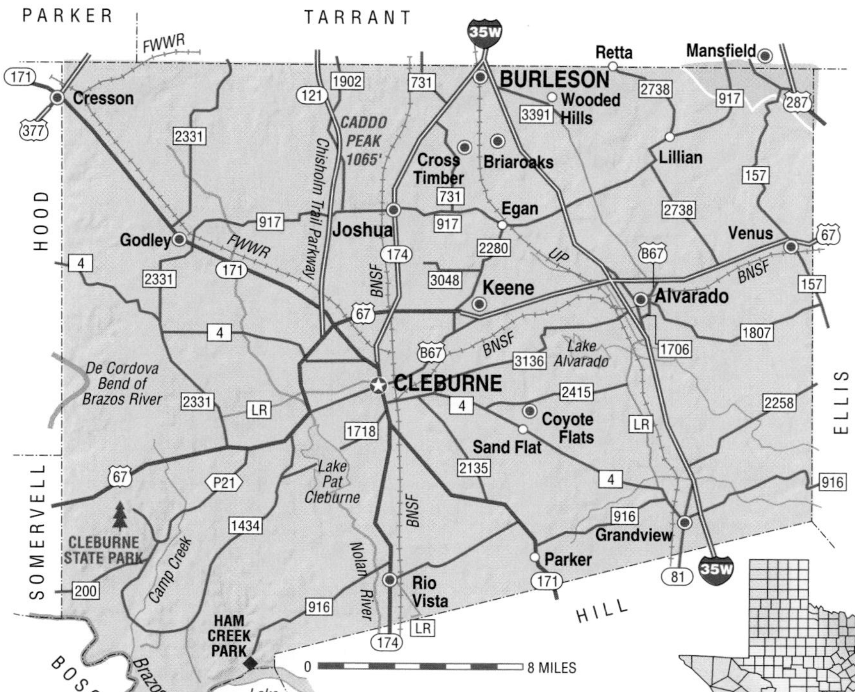

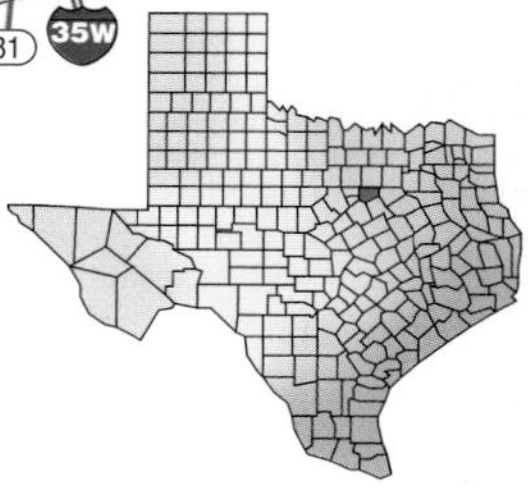

Map labels (Johnson County):

PARKER · TARRANT
FWWR
171
Cresson
377
2331
HOOD
121
1902
731
CADDO PEAK 1065'
Chisholm Trail Parkway
Cross Timber
731
Briaroaks
BURLESON
Wooded Hills
3391
Retta
Mansfield
2738
917
287
Lillian
157
Godley
917
FWWR
171
2331
Joshua
174
917
2280
Egan
2738
Venus
67
BNSF
67
3048
Keene
B67
Alvarado
BNSF
157
De Cordova Bend of Brazos River
2331
LR
B67
BNSF
3136
Lake Alvarado
1706
1807
CLEBURNE
4
2415
2258
ELLIS
1718
Coyote Flats
LR
Lake Pat Cleburne
2135
Sand Flat
4
916
67
P21
1434
BNSF
Nolan River
916
Grandview
SOMERVELL
CLEBURNE STATE PARK
200
Camp Creek
916
Rio Vista
LR
174
Parker
171
81
35W
HILL
BOSQUE
Brazos River
HAM CREEK PARK
Lake Whitney
0 --------- 8 MILES

# Johnson County

**Physical Features**: North central county drained by tributaries of Trinity, Brazos rivers; lakes; hilly, rolling, many soil types.

**Economy**: Agribusiness, railroad shops; manufacturing, distribution, lake activities, many residents employed in Fort Worth; part of Fort Worth-Arlington metropolitan area.

**History**: No permanent Indian tribal villages existed in area. Anglo-American settlers arrived in the 1840s. County named for Col. M.T. Johnson of the Mexican War, Confederacy; created and organized in 1854. Formed from McLennan, Hill, and Navarro counties.

**Race/Ethnicity**: (In percent) Anglo, 74.8; Black, 3.1; Hispanic, 19.4; Asian, 0.8; Other, 3.2.

**Vital Statistics**, annual: Births, 1,944; deaths, 1,246; marriages, 1,252; divorces, 563.

**Recreation**: Bird, deer hunting; wa-ter activities on Lake Pat Cleburne, Lake Whitney; state park; sports complex; museum; Chisholm Trail; Goatneck bike ride in July

**Minerals**: Limestone, sand, gravel.

**Agriculture**: Cattle, hay, horses, dairies, cotton, sorghum, wheat, oats, hogs. Market value $78.9 million.

**CLEBURNE** (29,569) county seat; manufacturing, oil and gas; hospital, library, museum; Hill College campus; Whistle Stop Christmas.

**BURLESON** (41,828, part in Tarrant County) agriculture, retail center; hospital.

Other towns include: **Alvarado** (3,934) County Pioneer Days; **Briaroaks** (592); **Coyote Flats** (320); **Cross Timber** (278); **Godley** (1,038); **Grandview** (1,603); **Joshua** (6,090) many residents work in Fort Worth; **Keene** (6,176) Southwestern Adventist University; **Lillian** (1,160); **Rio Vista** (944), and **Venus** (3,174).

Also, part of **Cresson** (765), and part [1,652] of **Mansfield** (62,022, mostly in Tarrant County).

| Population | 157,456 |
|---|---|
| Change fm 2010 | 4.3 |
| Area (sq. mi.) | 734.5 |
| Land Area (sq. mi.) | 724.7 |
| Altitude (ft.) | 500-1,065 |
| Rainfall (in.) | 37.61 |
| Jan. mean min. | 32.6 |
| July mean max. | 95.7 |
| Civ. Labor | 76,634 |
| Unemployed | 5.5 |
| Wages | $419,094,342 |
| Per Capita Income | $36,336 |
| Prop. Value | $12,334,519,796 |
| Retail Sales | $3,375,889,060 |

*The bridge at Cleburne State Park that was built by the Civilian Conservation Corps in the 1930s. Photo by Bryan Frazier/Texas Parks and Wildlife.*

# Jones County

**Physical Features**: West Texas Rolling Plains; drained by Brazos River fork, tributaries; Lake Fort Phantom Hill.

**Economy**: Agribusiness; government/services; varied manufacturing.

**History**: Comanches and other tribes hunted in the area. U.S. military presence began in 1851. Ranching established in the 1870s. County named for the last president of the Republic, Anson Jones; created in 1858 from Bexar and Bosque counties; re-created in 1876; organized in 1881.

**Race/Ethnicity**: (In percent) Anglo, 60.2; Black, 13.0; Hispanic, 26.3; Asian, 0.7; Other, 2.6.

**Vital Statistics**, annual: Births, 185; deaths, 181; marriages, 75; divorces, 67.

**Recreation**: Lake activities, hunting, Fort Phantom Hill, Cowboy Reunion July 4 in Stamford.

**Minerals**: Oil, gas, sand and gravel, stone.

**Agriculture**: Cotton, wheat, sesame and peanuts; cattle. Some 3,500 acres irrigated for peanuts and hay. Market value $43.3 million.

**ANSON** (2,293) county seat; farming center, government/services; hospital; old courthouse, opera house, museums; Mesquite Daze festivals in April and October.

**STAMFORD** (2,964) trade center for three counties, hospital, historic homes, cowboy museum.

**HAMLIN** (1,992) farm and ranching, feed mill, oil/gas, electricity/steam plant using mesquite trees; hospital; museums; dove cookoff in October.

Other towns include: **Hawley** (602), **Lueders** (333) limestone quarries. Part [5,145] of **Abilene**.

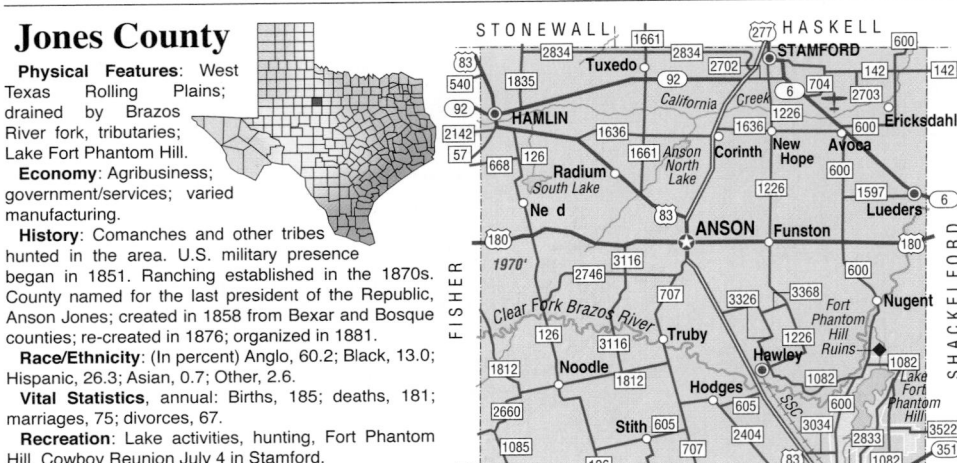

| | |
|---|---|
| Population | 19,936 |
| Change fm 2010 | – 1.3 |
| Area (sq. mi.) | 937.1 |

| | |
|---|---|
| Land Area (sq. mi.) | 928.6 |
| Altitude (ft.) | 1,480-1,970 |
| Rainfall (in.) | 26.06 |
| Jan. mean min. | 31.1 |
| July mean max. | 96.2 |
| Civ. Labor | 7,879 |
| Unemployed | 5.5 |
| Wages | $35,073,328 |
| Per Capita Income | $32,145 |
| Prop. Value | $1,060,066,880 |
| Retail Sales | $191,726,519 |

# Karnes County

**Physical Features**: Sandy loam, dark clay, alluvial soils in rolling terrain; traversed by San Antonio River; mesquite, oak trees.

**Economy**: Oil, gas, agribusiness.

**History**: Coahuiltecan Indian area. Spanish ranching began around 1750. Anglo-Americans arrived in the 1840s; Polish in the 1850s. County created in 1854 from Bexar, Goliad, and San Patricio counties, organized the same year; named for Texas Revolutionary figure Henry W. Karnes.

**Race/Ethnicity:** (In percent) Anglo, 39.1; Black, 9.3; Hispanic, 51.2; Asian, 0.3; Other, 1.9.

**Vital Statistics**, annual: Births, 166; deaths, 159; marriages, 95; divorces, 30.

**Recreation**: Panna Maria, nation's oldest Polish settlement, founded 1854; Old Helena restored courthouse, museum; hunting, nature tourism, guest ranches.

**Minerals**: Oil, gas, uranium.

**Agriculture**: Beef cattle, grain, cotton, hay. Market value $27.6 million.

**KARNES CITY** (3,183) county seat; oil and gas, agribusiness, tourism, processing center, oil-field servicing, manufacturing; library; Lonesome Dove Fest in September.

**KENEDY** (3,285) farm and oil center, library, dove/quail hunting, prison, hospital; Bluebonnet Days in April.

Other towns include: **Falls City** (657) ranching, sausage making, library, city park on river; **Gillett** (120); **Hobson** (135); **Panna Maria** (45); **Runge** (1,005) oil and gas services, farming, museum, library; cowboy breakfast in December.

| | |
|---|---|
| Population | 14,906 |
| Change fm 2010 | 0.6 |
| Area (sq. mi.) | 753.6 |
| Land Area (sq. mi.) | 747.6 |

| | |
|---|---|
| Altitude (ft.) | 180-580 |
| Rainfall (in.) | 30.14 |

| | |
|---|---|
| Jan. mean min. | 41.8 |
| July mean max. | 95.1 |
| Civ. Labor | 6,920 |
| Unemployed | 4.7 |
| Wages | $47,505,806 |
| Per Capita Income | $38,597 |
| Prop. Value | $7,539,850,530 |
| Retail Sales | $209,388,594 |

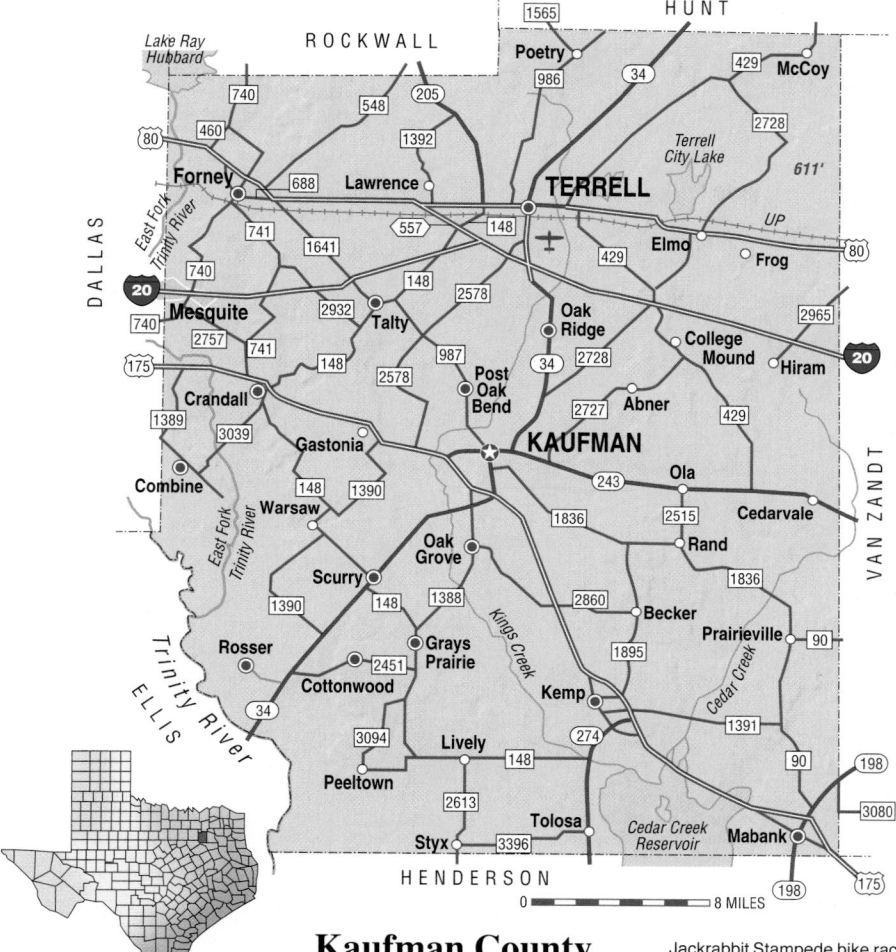

# Kaufman County

**Physical Features**: North Blackland prairie, draining to the Trinity River; Cedar Creek Reservoir, Lake Ray Hubbard and Terrell City Lake.

**Economy**: Varied manufacturing, a retail trade center, government/services, antiques center, commuting to Dallas.

**History**: Caddo and Cherokee Indians; removed by 1840 when Anglo-American settlement began. County created from Henderson County and organized, 1848; named for member of Texas and U.S. congresses D.S. Kaufman.

**Race/Ethnicity**: (In percent) Anglo, 68.0; Black, 10.7; Hispanic, 18.8; Asian, 1.1; Other, 2.9.

**Vital Statistics**, annual: Births, 1,453; deaths, 823; marriages, 661; divorces, 382.

**Recreation**: Lake activities; Porter Farm near Terrell is site of origin of U.S.-Texas Agricultural Extension pro-

gram; antique centers near Forney; historic homes at Terrell.

**Minerals**: Gravel, sand, oil, gas.

**Agriculture**: Cattle, forages, nursery crops, horses, soybeans, corn. Market value $59 million.

**KAUFMAN** (6,829) county seat; government/services, manufacturing and distribution, commuters to Dallas; hospital; Octoberfest.

**TERRELL** (16,287) agribusiness, varied manufacturing, outlet center; private hospital, state hospital; community college, Southwestern Christian College; British flying school museum, Heritage Jubilee in April.

Other towns include: **Combine** (2,033, partly in Dallas County); **Cottonwood** (170); **Crandall** (2,968) Cotton Festival in September; **Elmo** (802); **Forney** (16,943) an important antiques center, light industrial, commuters to Dallas, historic homes, the

Jackrabbit Stampede bike race in September.

Also, **Grays Prairie** (347); **Kemp** (1,197); **Lawrence** (259); **Mabank** (3,108, partly in Henderson County) varied manufacturing, tourism, retail trade, Western Week in June; **Oak Grove** (639); **Oak Ridge** (516); **Post Oak Bend** (628); **Rosser** (342); **Scurry** (715); **Talty** (1,793).

| | |
|---|---|
| Population | **111,236** |
| Change fm 2010 | 7.6 |
| Area (sq. mi.) | 807.7 |
| Land Area (sq. mi.) | 780.7 |
| Altitude (ft.) | 300-611 |
| Rainfall (in.) | 39.92 |
| Jan. mean min. | 33.1 |
| July mean max. | 94.3 |
| Civ. Labor | 52.521 |
| Unemployed | 5.7 |
| Wages | $248,440,546 |
| Per Capita Income | $36,325 |
| Prop. Value | $7,840,249,192 |
| Retail Sales | $1,156,598,479 |

*For explanation of sources, abbreviations and symbols, see p. 238, and foldout map.*

# Kendall County

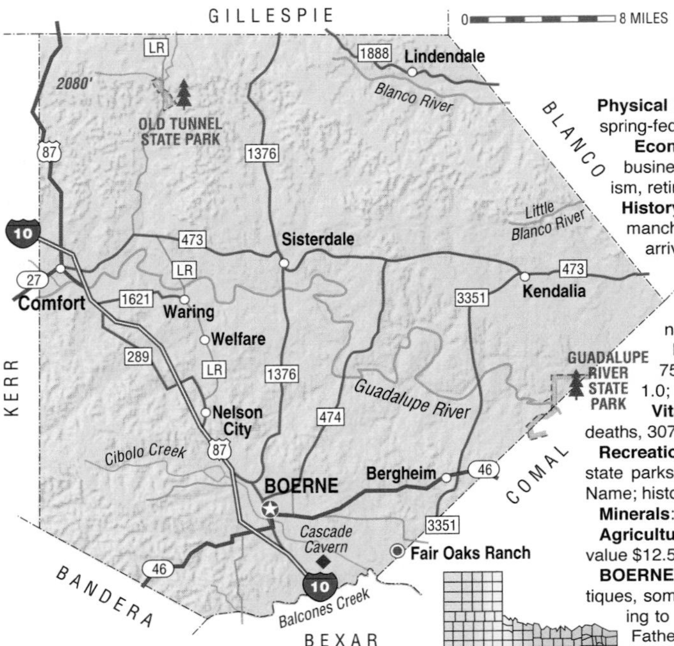

**Physical Features**: Hill Country, plateau, with spring-fed streams; caves; scenic drives.

**Economy**: Government/services, agribusiness, commuters to San Antonio, tourism, retirement area, some manufacturing.

**History**: Lipan Apaches, Kiowas and Comanches in area when German settlers arrived in 1840s. County created from Blanco, Kerr counties 1862; named for pioneer journalist-sheepman and early contributor to Texas Almanac, George W. Kendall.

**Race/Ethnicity**: (In percent) Anglo, 75.2; Black, 1.0; Hispanic, 21.7; Asian, 1.0; Other, 2.3.

**Vital Statistics**, annual: Births, 341; deaths, 307; marriages, 421; divorces, 115

**Recreation**: Hunting, fishing, exotic wildlife, state parks; Cascade Cavern, Cave Without a Name; historic sites.

**Minerals**: Limestone rock, caliche.

**Agriculture**: Cattle, goats, sheep, hay. Market value $12.5 million. Cedar posts, firewood sold.

**BOERNE** (12,314) county seat; tourism, antiques, some manufacturing, ranching, commuting to San Antonio; library; Berges Fest on Father's Day weekend.

Other towns include: **Comfort** (2,2,537) tourism, ranching, Civil War monument honoring Unionists, library, mountain bike trail; **Kendalia** (149); **Sisterdale** (110); **Waring** (73).

Part of **Fair Oaks Ranch** (6,794).

| | |
|---|---|
| Population | 38,880 |
| Change fm 2010 | 16.4 |
| Area (sq. mi.) | 663.0 |
| Land Area (sq. mi.) | 662.5 |
| Altitude (ft.) | 1,000-2,080 |
| Rainfall (in.) | 38,10 |
| Jan. mean min. | 35.4 |
| July mean max. | 92.5 |
| Civ. Labor | 18,113 |
| Unemployed | 4.5 |
| Wages | $122,269,214 |
| Per Capita Income | $64,797 |
| Prop. Value | $6,664,634,693 |
| Retail Sales | $996,939,089 |

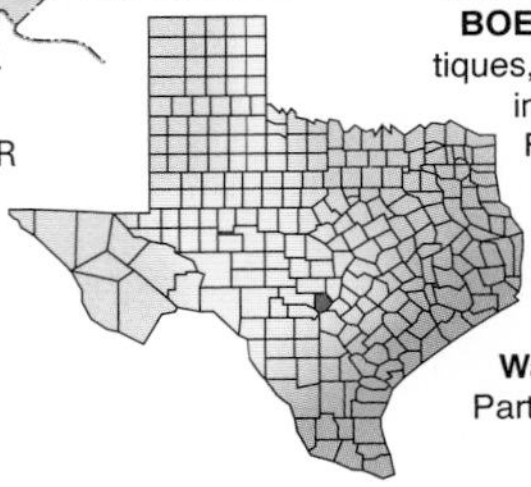

*For explanation of sources, abbreviations and symbols, see p. xxx and foldout map.*

*Boerne's old St. Peter's Catholic Church, built in 1923 in the Spanish mission style. Photo by Robert Plocheck.*

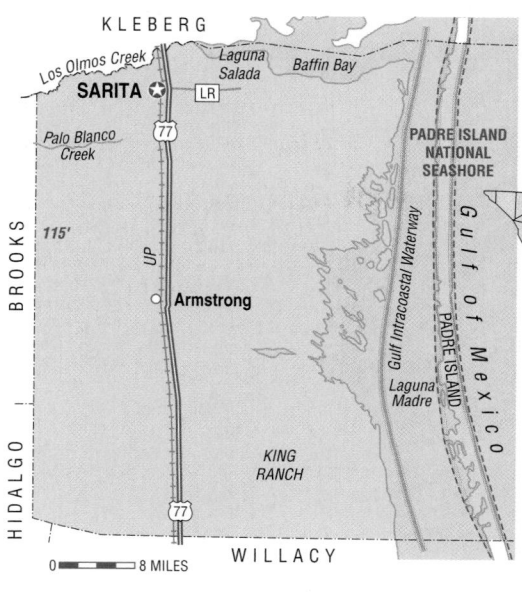

# Kenedy County

**Physical Features**: Gulf coastal county; flat, sandy terrain, some loam soils; motts of live oaks.

**Economy**: Oil, ranching, nature tourism, hunting leases, wind farm.

**History**: Coahuiltecan Indians who assimilated or were driven out by Lipan Apaches. Spanish ranching began in the 1790s. Anglo-Americans arrived after the Mexican War. Among last counties created and organized in 1921, from Cameron, Hidalgo, Willacy counties; named for pioneer steamboat operator and cattleman, Capt. Mifflin Kenedy.

**Race/Ethnicity**: (In percent) Anglo, 20.4; Black, 4.1; Hispanic, 75.2; Asian, 0.5; Other, 1.7.

**Vital Statistics**, annual: Births, 6; deaths, 3; marriages, 2; divorces, 0.

**Recreation**: Hunting, fishing, nature tourism.

**Minerals**: Oil, gas.

**Agriculture**: Beef cattle. Market value $23.7 million. Hunting leases, nature tourism important.

**SARITA** (246) county seat; cattle-shipping point, ranch headquarters, gas processing; one of state's least populous counties.

Also, **Armstrong** (4).

| | | |
|---|---|---|
| Population ...................................400 | Jan. mean min. ...........................44.4 | Wages ..............................$9,018,408 |
| Change fm 2010 .........................− 3.8 | July mean max. ..........................94.6 | Per Capita Income.................$65,500 |
| Area (sq. mi.)..........................1,945.8 | Civ. Labor ...................................278 | Prop. Value ................$1,852,482,203 |
| Land Area (sq. mi.) .................1,458.3 | Unemployed .................................2.9 | Retail Sales ...................................NA |
| Altitude (ft.) ................... sea level-115 | | |
| Rainfall (in.) ..............................29.17 | | |

---

# Kent County

**Physical Features**: Rolling, broken terrain; lake; drains to Salt and Double Mountain forks of Brazos River; sandy, loam soils.

**Economy**: Agribusiness, oil and gas operations, government/services, hunting leases.

**History**: Comanches driven out by the U.S. Army in the 1870s. Ranching developed in the 1880s. County created in 1876 from Bexar and Young territories; organized in 1892. Name honors Andrew Kent, one of 32 volunteers from Gonzales who died at the Alamo.

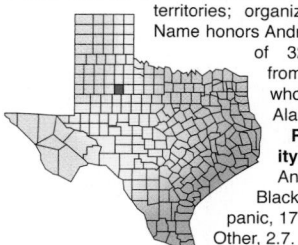

**Race/Ethnicity**: (In percent) Anglo, 79.9; Black, 1.2; Hispanic, 17.0; Asian, 0.0; Other, 2.7.

**Vital Statistics**, annual: Births, 9; deaths, 16; marriages, 12; divorces, 3.

**Recreation**: Hunting and fishing; scenic croton breaks and salt flat; Winterfest in December.

**Minerals**: Oil, gas.

**Agriculture**: Cattle, cotton, wheat, sorghum.

**JAYTON** (516) county seat; oil-field services, farming center; Summerfest in August.

Other towns include: **Girard** (54).

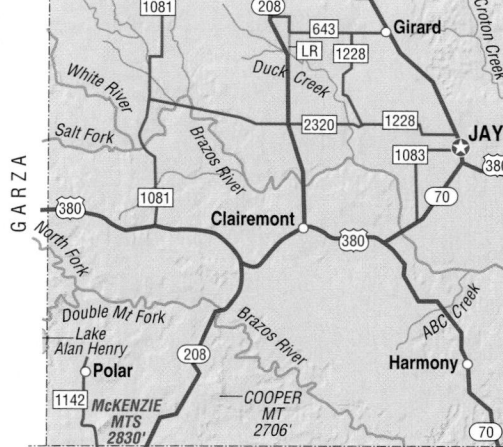

| | | |
|---|---|---|
| Population ................................. 785 | Unemployed ..................................4.7 | |
| Change fm 2010 .......................− 2.8 | Wages ............................$2,343,857 | |
| Area (sq. mi.)...........................902.9 | Per Capita Income................$40,164 | |
| Land Area (sq. mi.) ...................902.5 | Prop. Value ...............$1,281,642,480 | |
| Altitude (ft.) .....................1,740-2,830 | Retail Sales ...................$11,699,563 | |
| Rainfall (in.) ..............................23.51 | | |
| Jan. mean min. ...........................27.2 | *For explanation of sources, abbreviations and symbols, see p. 238, and foldout map.* | |
| July mean max. ..........................94.6 | | |
| Civ. Labor ...................................430 | | |

## Kerr County

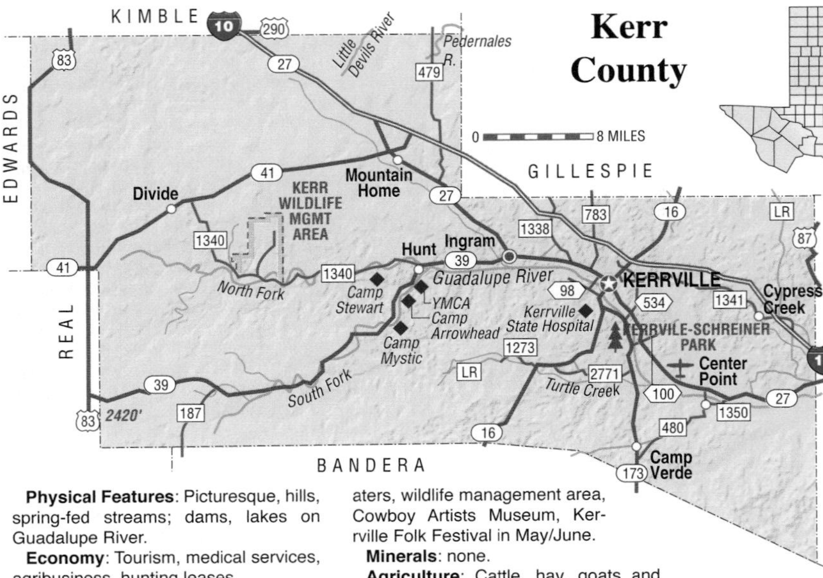

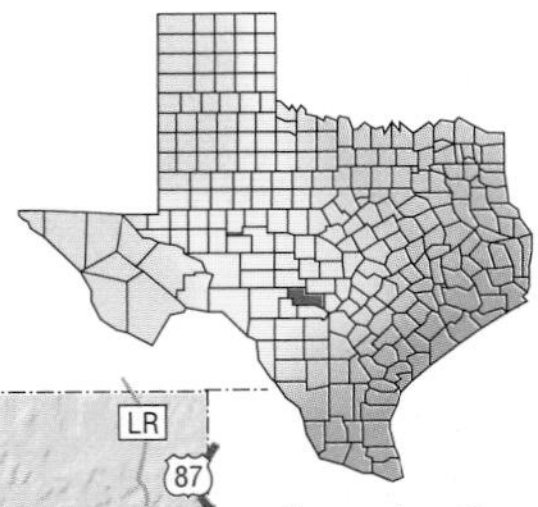

For explanation of sources, abbreviations and symbols, see p. 238, and foldout map.

**Physical Features**: Picturesque, hills, spring-fed streams; dams, lakes on Guadalupe River.

**Economy**: Tourism, medical services, agribusiness, hunting leases.

**History**: Lipan Apaches, Kiowas and Comanches in area. Anglo-American settlers arrived in the late 1840s. County created in 1856 from Bexar County; named for a member of Austin's Colony, James Kerr.

**Race/Ethnicity**: (In percent) Anglo, 70.7; Black, 2.1; Hispanic, 25.2; Asian, 1.0; Other, 2.9.

**Vital Statistics**, annual: Births, 494; deaths, 719; marriages, 362; divorces, 172.

**Recreation**: Youth camps, dude ranches, park, Cailloux and Point the-aters, wildlife management area, Cowboy Artists Museum, Kerrville Folk Festival in May/June.

**Minerals**: none.

**Agriculture**: Cattle, hay, goats and horses; deer (second in numbers as livestock). Market value $10.8 million. Hunting leases important.

**KERRVILLE** (23,177) county seat; tourist center, youth camps, agribusiness, aircraft and parts, varied manufacturing; Schreiner University; state hospital, veterans hospital, private hospital; retirement center; retail trade; state arts, crafts show in May.

Other towns include: **Camp Verde** (41); **Center Point** (800); **Hunt** (708) youth camps, hospital; **Ingram** (1,846) camps, cabins; **Mountain Home** (96).

| | |
|---|---|
| Population | **50,562** |
| Change fm 2010 | 1.9 |
| Area (sq. mi.) | 1,107.3 |
| Land Area (sq. mi.) | 1,103.3 |
| Altitude (ft.) | 1,400–2,420 |
| Rainfall (in.) | 32.05 |
| Jan. mean min. | 33.8 |
| July mean max. | 92.2 |
| Civ. Labor | 22,466 |
| Unemployed | 4.5 |
| Wages | $154,978,430 |
| Per Capita Income | $46,898 |
| Prop. Value | $6,097,680,101 |
| Retail Sales | $833,897,006 |

*Fishing at South Llano River State Park, Kimble County. Photo by Earl Nottingham/Texas Parks & Wildlife.*

# Kimble County

**Population** .......................... **4,438**
Change fm 2010 ................... − 3.7
Area (sq. mi.) .................... 1,251.2
Land Area (sq. mi.) .......... 1,251.0
Altitude (ft.) ............... 1,476-2,460
Rainfall (in.) ......................... 26.98
Jan. mean min. ..................... 27.8
July mean max. .................... 94.3
Civ. Labor ........................... 1,987
Unemployed .......................... 4.6
Wages ..................... $10,989,249
Per Capita Income .......... $39,572
Prop. Value ......... $2,111,642,007
Retail Sales ............. $67,105,255

**Physical Features**: Picturesque Edwards Plateau; rugged, broken by numerous streams; drains to Llano River; sandy, gray, chocolate loam soils.

**Economy**: Livestock production and market, tourism, cedar oil and wood products, metal building materials.

**History**: Apache, Kiowa and Comanche stronghold until the 1870s. U.S. military outposts protected the first Anglo-American settlers in the 1850s. County created from Bexar County in 1858 and organized in 1876. Named for George C. Kimble, a Gonzales volunteer who died at the Alamo.

**Race/Ethnicity**: (In percent) Anglo, 72.1; Black, 0.5; Hispanic, 25.6; Asian, 0.8; Other, 2.0.

**Vital Statistics**, annual: Births, 43; deaths, 49; marriages, 29; divorces, 30.

**Recreation**: Hunting, fishing in spring-fed streams, nature tourism; among leading deer counties; state park; Kimble Kounty Kow Kick on Labor Day, Wild Game dinner on Thanksgiving Saturday.

**Minerals**: gravel.

**Agriculture**: Beef cattle, meat goats, sheep, Angora goats, pecans. Hunting leases are important. Also, firewood, cedar sold.

**JUNCTION** (2,667) county seat; tourism, varied manufacturing, livestock production; two museums; Texas Tech University center; hospital; library; airport.

Other towns include: **London** (180); **Roosevelt** (14).

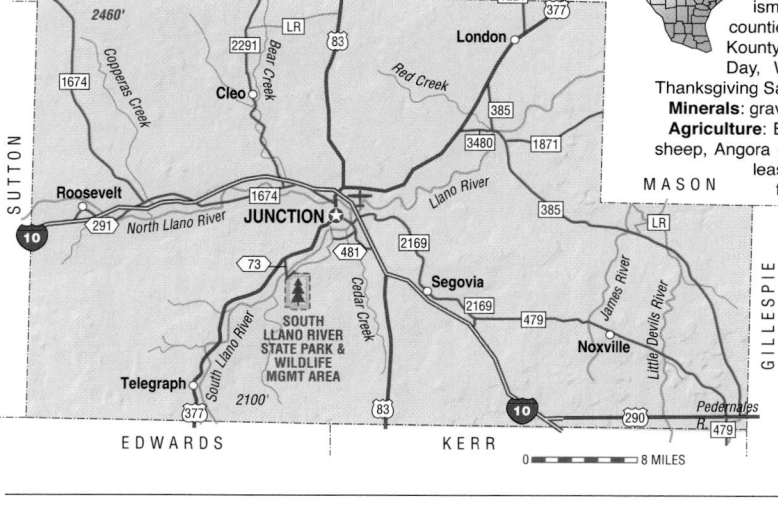

# King County

**Physical Features**: Hilly, broken by Wichita, Brazos tributaries; extensive grassland; dark loam to red soils.

**Economy**: Oil and gas, ranching, government/services, horse sales, hunting leases.

**History**: Apache area until Comanches moved in about 1700. The Comanches were removed by the U.S. Army in 1874-75 after which ranching began. County created in 1876 from Bexar District; organized in 1891; named for William P. King, a volunteer from Gonzales who died at the Alamo.

**Race/Ethnicity**: (In percent) Anglo, 79.3; Black, 0.0; Hispanic, 16.5; Asian, 0.0; Other, 4.9.

**Vital Statistics**, annual: Births, 1; deaths, 3; marriages, 1; divorces, 0.

**Recreation**: 6666 Ranch visits, hunting, roping and ranch horse competitions.

**Minerals**: Oil, gas.

**Agriculture**: Cattle, horses, wheat, hay, cotton. Market value $6.6 million. Hunting leases important.

**GUTHRIE** (160) county seat; ranch-supply center, government/services; community center complex, library; Thanksgiving community supper.

**Population** ............................. **262**
Change fm 2010 ...................... − 8.4
Area (sq. mi.) .......................... 913.3
Land Area (sq. mi.) ................. 910.9
Altitude (ft.) .................... 1,450-2,250
Rainfall (in.) ........................... 25.53
Jan. mean min. .......................... 27.0
July mean max. .......................... 95.9
Civ. Labor ................................... 165
Unemployed ................................ 5.5
Wages ........................... $1,705,600
Per Capita Income ............... $52,095
Prop. Value ................. $711,458,790
Retail Sales ................................ NA

# Kinney County

**Physical Features**: Hilly, broken by Rio Grande tributaries; Anacacho Mountains; Nueces Canyon.

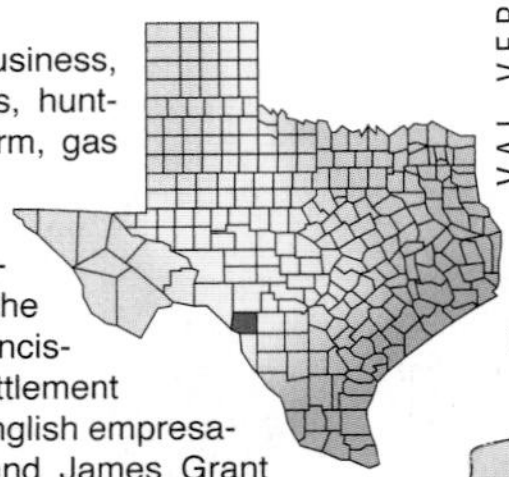

**Economy**: Agribusiness, government/services, hunting leases, wind farm, gas pipelines.

**History**: Coahuiltecans, Apaches, Comanches in the area. Spanish Franciscans established settlement in the late 1700s. English empresarios John Beales and James Grant established English-speaking colony in 1834. Black Seminoles served as army scouts in the 1870s. County created from Bexar County in 1850; organized in 1874; named for H.L. Kinney, founder of Corpus Christi.

**Race/Ethnicity**: (In percent) Anglo, 40.0; Black, 2.0; Hispanic, 57.0; Asian, 0.7; Other, 2.6.

**Vital Statistics**, annual: Births, 35; deaths, 31; marriages, 19; divorces, 0.

**Recreation**: Hunting; old Fort Clark Springs; state park; Seminole Indian cemetery; Cinco de Mayo, Juneteenth.

**Minerals**: Not significant.

**Agriculture**: Cattle, sheep, goats, hay, sorghum, cotton, corn oats, wheat, pecans. Market value $4.7 million. Hunting important.

**BRACKETTVILLE** (1,683) county seat; agriculture, tourism; museum.

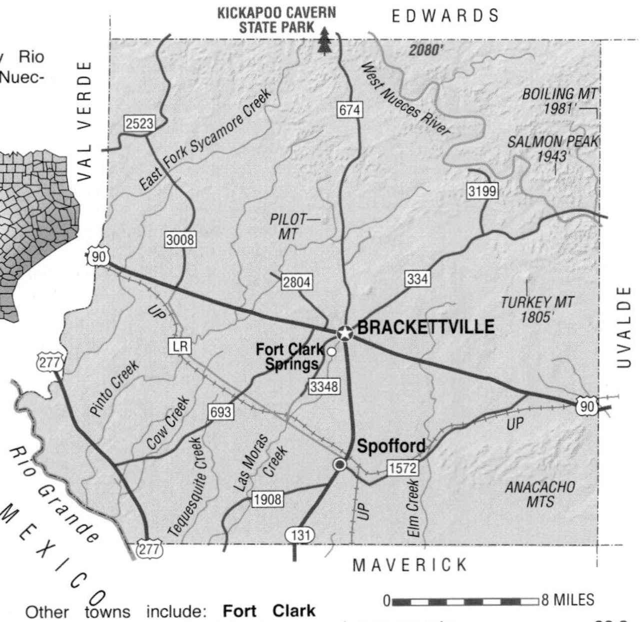

Other towns include: **Fort Clark Springs** (1,260); **Spofford** (103).

| | |
|---|---|
| Population | **3,526** |
| Change fm 2010 | – 2.0 |
| Area (sq. mi.) | 1,365.1 |
| Land Area (sq. mi.) | 1,363.1 |
| Altitude (ft.) | 790-2,080 |
| Rainfall (in.) | 23.56 |
| Jan. mean min. | 38.8 |
| July mean max. | 93.9 |
| Civ. Labor | 1,465 |
| Unemployed | 6.6 |
| Wages | $8,100,473 |
| Per Capita Income | $32,329 |
| Prop. Value | $1,315,422,430 |
| Retail Sales | $11,457,299 |

0 ▬▬▬▬ 8 MILES

# Kleberg County

**Physical Features**: Coastal plain, broken by bays; sandy, loam, clay soils; tree motts.

**Economy**: Oil and gas, Naval air station, chemicals and plastics, Texas A&M University – Kingsville, agriculture.

**History**: Coahuiltecan and Karankawa area. Span-ish land grants date to 1750s. In 1853 Richard King purchased Santa Gertrudis land grant. County created 1913 from Nueces County, organized the same year; named for San Jacinto veteran and rancher Robert Kleberg.

**Race/Ethnicity**: (In percent) Anglo, 21.9; Black, 4.4; Hispanic, 71.4; Asian, 2.4; Other, 2.5.

**Vital Statistics**, annual: Births, 481; deaths, 225; marriages, 227; divorces, 110.

**Recreation**: Fishing, hunting, water sports, park at Baffin Bay; wildlife sanctuary; winter bird watching; university events, museum; King Ranch headquarters, tours; La Posada celebration in November.

**Minerals**: Oil, gas, uranium.

**Agriculture**: Cattle, sorghum, cotton. Market value $61.8 million. Hunting/ecotourism.

**KINGSVILLE** (26,074) county seat; government/services, oil, gas, agribusiness, tourism, chemical plant, university, Coastal Bend College branch; hospital; ranching heritage festival in February, King Ranch Breakfast in November.

Other towns include: **Ricardo** (1,081), **Riviera** (696).

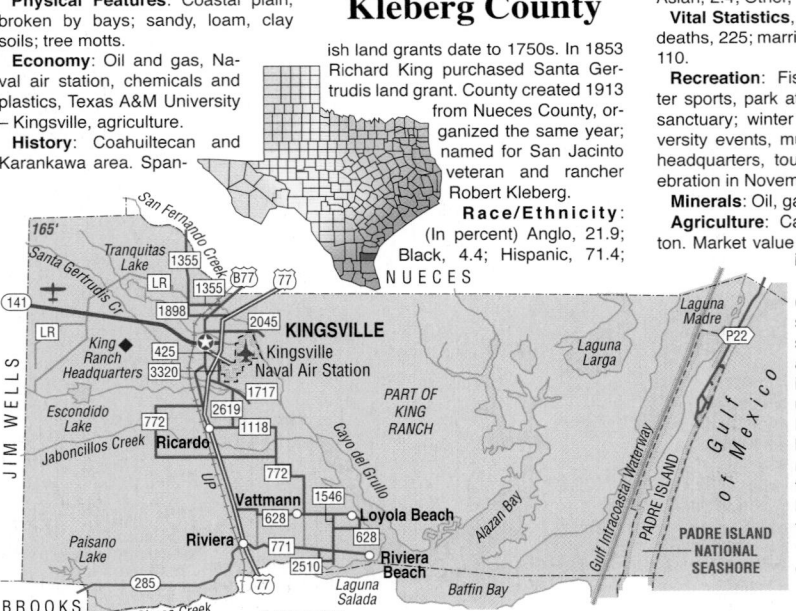

| | |
|---|---|
| Population | **32,190** |
| Change fm 2010 | 0.4 |
| Area (sq. mi.) | 1,090.2 |
| Land Area (sq. mi.) | 881.3 |
| Altitude (ft.) | sea level-165 |
| Rainfall (in.) | 30.38 |
| Jan. mean min. | 45.8 |
| July mean max. | 95.1 |
| Civ. Labor | 18,345 |
| Unemployed | 5.1 |
| Wages | $112,817,294 |
| Per Capita Income | $37,334 |
| Prop. Value | $1,921,096,773 |
| Retail Sales | $544,559,910 |

# Knox County

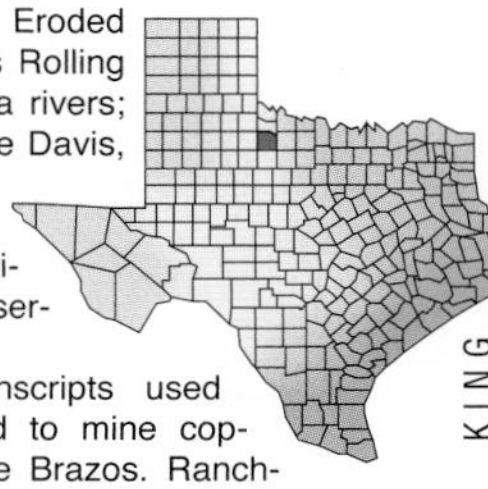

**Physical Features**: Eroded breaks on West Texas Rolling Plains; Brazos, Wichita rivers; sandy, loam soils; Lake Davis, Lake Catherine and Truscott Brine Lake.

**Economy**: Oil, agriculture, government/services.

**History**: Indian conscripts used during Spanish period to mine copper deposits along the Brazos. Ranching, farming developed in 1880s. German colony settled in 1895. County created from Bexar, Young territories 1858; re-created 1876; organized 1886; named for U.S. Secretary of War Henry Knox.

**Race/Ethnicity**: (In percent) Anglo, 60.1; Black, 6.0; Hispanic, 32.8; Asian, 0.2; Other, 3.3.

**Vital Statistics**, annual: Births, 53; deaths, 53; marriages, 20; divorces, 8.

**Recreation**: Lake activities, fishing, hunting; Knox City seedless watermelon festival in July.

**Minerals**: Oil, gas.

**Agriculture**: Wheat, cattle, cotton. Some cotton irrigated. Market value $59 million.

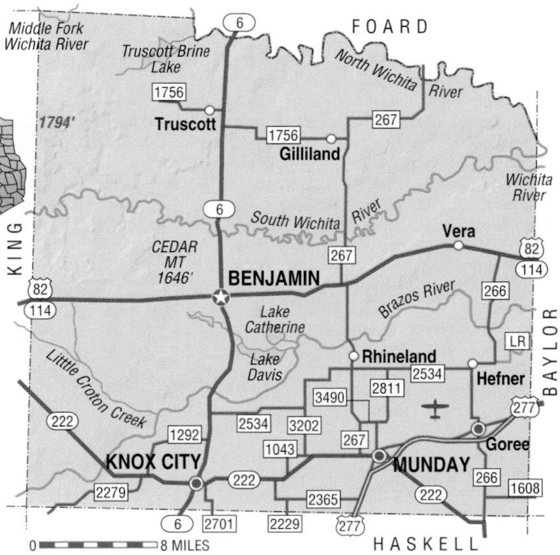

**BENJAMIN** (247) county seat; ranching, farm center; veterans memorial.

**MUNDAY** (1,191) portable buildings, other manufacturing; A&M vegetable research station.

**KNOX CITY** (1,040) agribusiness, petroleum center; USDA plant materials research center; hospital.

Other towns include: **Goree** (192); **Rhineland** (120) old church established by German immigrants.

| | |
|---|---|
| Population | 3,858 |
| Change fm 2010 | 3.7 |
| Area (sq. mi.) | 855.5 |
| Land Area (sq. mi.) | 850.6 |
| Altitude (ft.) | 1,200-1,794 |
| Rainfall (in.) | 26.43 |

| | |
|---|---|
| Jan. mean min. | 29.1 |
| July mean max. | 96.3 |
| Civ. Labor | 1,634 |
| Unemployed | 4.8 |
| Wages | $12,453,171 |
| Per Capita Income | $39,505 |
| Prop. Value | $548,158,890 |
| Retail Sales | $27,026,017 |

*For explanation of sources, abbreviations and symbols, see p. 238, and foldout map.*

*Texas A&M University – Kingsville, Kleberg County. Photo by Robert Plocheck.*

# Lamar County

**Physical Features**: North Texas county on divide between Red, Sulphur rivers; soils chiefly blackland, except along Red; pines, hardwoods; Pat Mayse Lake and Lake Crook.

**Economy**: Varied manufacturing, agri-business, medical, government/services.

**History**: Caddo Indian area. First Anglo-American settlers arrived about 1815. County created 1840 from Red River County; organized 1841; named for second president of Republic, Mirabeau B. Lamar.

**Race/Ethnicity**: (In percent) Anglo, 75.3; Black, 13.5; Hispanic, 7.1; Asian, 0.7; Other, 4.2.

**Vital Statistics**, annual: Births, 647; deaths, 613; marriages, 396; divorces, 268.

**Recreation**: Lake activities; Gambill goose refuge; hunting, fishing; state park; Trail de Paris rail-to-trail; Sam Bell Maxey Home; State Sen. A.M. Aikin Archives, other museums.

**Minerals**: Negligible.

**Agriculture**: Beef, hay, dairy, soybeans (first in acreage), wheat, corn, sorghum, cotton. Market value $84.9 million.

**PARIS** (25,092) county seat; varied manufacturing, food processing, govern-ment/services; hospitals; junior college; museums; Tour de Paris bicycle rally in July; archery pro-am tournament in March.

Other towns include: **Arthur City** (180), **Blossom** (1,582), **Brookston** (130), **Chicota** (150), **Cunningham** (110), **Deport** (568, partly in Red River County), **Pattonville** (180), **Petty** (130), **Powderly** (1,215), **Reno** (3,293), **Roxton** (651), **Sumner** (95), **Sun Valley** (73), **Toco** (75).

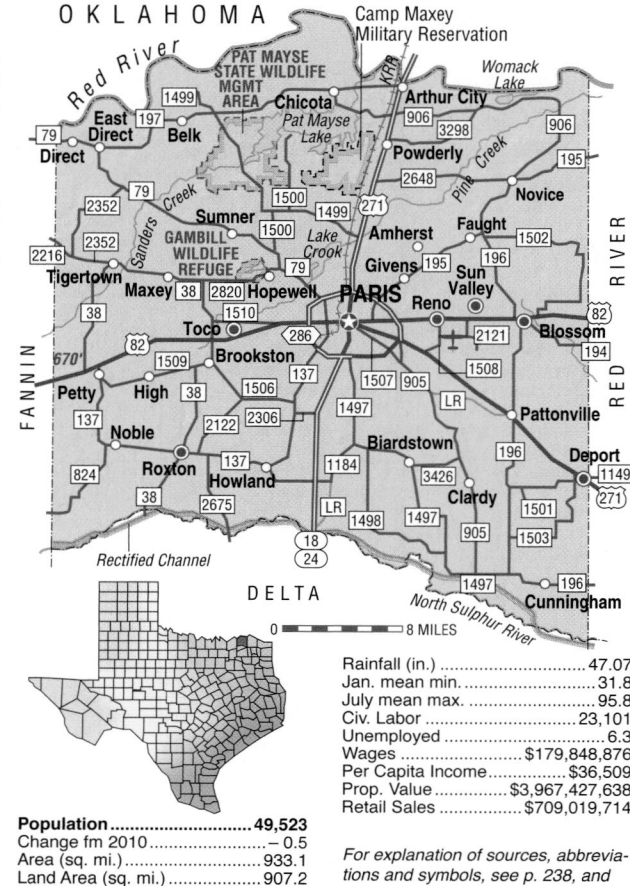

| | |
|---|---|
| Rainfall (in.) | 47.07 |
| Jan. mean min. | 31.8 |
| July mean max. | 95.8 |
| Civ. Labor | 23,101 |
| Unemployed | 6.3 |
| Wages | $179,848,876 |
| Per Capita Income | $36,509 |
| Prop. Value | $3,967,427,638 |
| Retail Sales | $709,019,714 |

| | |
|---|---|
| Population | 49,523 |
| Change fm 2010 | − 0.5 |
| Area (sq. mi.) | 933.1 |
| Land Area (sq. mi.) | 907.2 |
| Altitude (ft.) | 335-670 |

*For explanation of sources, abbreviations and symbols, see p. 238, and foldout map.*

*Plant X, a steam-electric plant, south of U.S. 70 near Earth, Lamb County. Photo by Robert Plocheck.*

# Lamb County

**Physical Features**: Rich, red, brown soils on the High Plains; some hills; drains to upper Brazos River tributaries; numerous playas.

**Economy**: Agribusiness; distribution center; denim textiles.

**History**: Apaches, who were displaced by Comanches around 1700. U.S. Army pushed Comanches into Indian Territory in 1875. Ranching began in 1880s; farming after 1900. County created in 1876 from Bexar District and organized in 1908; named for Lt. G.A. Lamb, who died in battle of San Jacinto.

**Race/Ethnicity**: (In percent) Anglo, 40.6; Black, 5.1; Hispanic, 53.8; Asian, 0.3; Other, 3.5.

**Vital Statistics**, annual: Births, 179; deaths, 129; marriages, 69; divorces, 20.

**Recreation**: Waylon Jennings Birthday Bash in June at Littlefield, museums, Earth Day in April.

**Minerals**: Oil, stone, gas.

**Agriculture**: Fed cattle; cotton, corn, wheat, grain sorghum, vegetables, soybeans, hay; sheep. 179,500 acres irrigated. Market value $575.3 million.

**LITTLEFIELD** (6,238) county seat; textile mill, agribusiness, manufacturing; hospital, prison.

**Olton** (2,124) agribusiness, retail center; Sandcrawl museum; pheasant hunt in winter; Sandhills Celebration in August.

Other towns include: **Amherst** (697); **Earth** (1,032) farming center, dairies, feed lot, supplies; **Fieldton** (20); **Spade** (72); **Springlake** (106); **Sudan** (935) farming center, government/services, Homecoming Day in fall.

| | |
|---|---|
| Population | 13,574 |
| Change fm 2010 | – 2.9 |
| Area (sq. mi.) | 1,017.7 |
| Land Area (sq. mi.) | 1,016.2 |
| Altitude (ft.) | 3,390-3,870 |
| Rainfall (in.) | 18.87 |
| Jan. mean min. | 24.5 |
| July mean max. | 92.0 |
| Civ. Labor | 6,648 |
| Unemployed | 10.7 |
| Wages | $36,115,204 |
| Per Capita Income | $32,489 |
| Prop. Value | $1,113,821,431 |
| Retail Sales | $106,984,843 |

# Lampasas County

**Physical Features**: Central Texas on edge of Hill Country; Colorado, Lampasas rivers; cedars, oaks, pecans.

**Economy**: Many employed at Fort Hood, several industrial plants, agribusinesses, tourism.

**History**: Mineral springs attracted first Anglo-Americans in 1853. Frontier confrontations between settlers, Comanches continued into 1870s. County created, organized, 1856 from Bell, Travis counties. Named for river. Some have speculated that an early expedition named river for city of Lampazos in Mexico.

**Race/Ethnicity**: (In percent) Anglo, 73.6; Black, 4.0; Hispanic, 18.7; Asian, 1.3; Other, 4.3.

**Vital Statistics**, annual: Births, 216; deaths, 206; marriages, 136; divorces, 128.

**Recreation**: Scenic drives; state park; deer hunting, fishing; Hancock Springs free-flow swim area at Lampasas.

**Minerals**: Sand, gravel, building stone.

**Agriculture**: Beef cattle, hay, goats, exotic animals. Market value $16.1 million. Hunting leases, ecotourism.

**LAMPASAS** (6,829) county seat; commuters to Ft. Hood, industrial plants, agriculture, tourism; historic downtown; hospital, college extensions; museum; Spring Ho in July.

Other towns include: **Bend** (115, partly in San Saba County); **Izoro** (17); **Kempner** (1,159); **Lometa** (909) market and shipping point; Diamondback Jubilee in March.

| | |
|---|---|
| Population | 20,156 |
| Change fm 2010 | 2.4 |
| Area (sq. mi.) | 713.9 |
| Land Area (sq. mi.) | 712.8 |
| Altitude (ft.) | 800-1,669 |
| Rainfall (in.) | 32.23 |
| Jan. mean min. | 33.4 |
| July mean max. | 95.6 |
| Civ. Labor | 9,722 |
| Unemployed | 5.1 |
| Wages | $33,587,417 |
| Per Capita Income | $52,983 |
| Prop. Value | $2,234,328,950 |
| Retail Sales | $203,369,992 |

# La Salle County

**Physical Features**: Brushy plain, broken by Nueces, Frio rivers and their tributaries; chocolate, dark gray, sandy loam soils.

**Economy**: Agribusiness, hunting leases, tourism, government services.

**History**: Coahuiltecans, squeezed out by migrating Apaches. U.S. military outpost in 1850s; settlers of Mexican descent established nearby village. Anglo-American ranching developed in 1870s. County created from Bexar District 1858; organized 1880; named for Robert Cavelier Sieur de La Salle, French explorer who died in Texas.

**Race/Ethnicity**: (In percent) Anglo, 13.8; Black, 1.0; Hispanic, 84.8; Asian, 0.2; Other, 1.4.

**Vital Statistics**, annual: Births, 103; deaths, 43; marriages, 39; divorces, 0.

**Recreation**: Nature trails; school where Lyndon B. Johnson taught; wildlife management area; deer, bird, javelina hunting; fishing; wild hog cookoff in March.

**Minerals**: Oil, gas.

**Agriculture**: Beef cattle, peanuts, watermelons, grain sorghum. Market value $18.7 million.

**COTULLA** (4,183) county seat; livestock, state prison; hunting center; Brush Country museum; Cinco de Mayo celebration.

Other towns include: **Encinal** (592), **Fowlerton** (62).

| | |
|---|---|
| Population | **7,474** |
| Change fm 2010 | 8.5 |
| Area (sq. mi.) | 1,494.2 |
| Land Area (sq. mi.) | 1,486.7 |
| Altitude (ft.) | 255-650 |
| Rainfall (in.) | 24.70 |
| Jan. mean min. | 38.9 |
| July mean max. | 96.9 |
| Civ. Labor | 5,722 |
| Unemployed | 3.1 |
| Wages | $44,371,506 |
| Per Capita Income | $40,858 |
| Prop. Value | $5,802029,567 |
| Retail Sales | $186,411,765 |

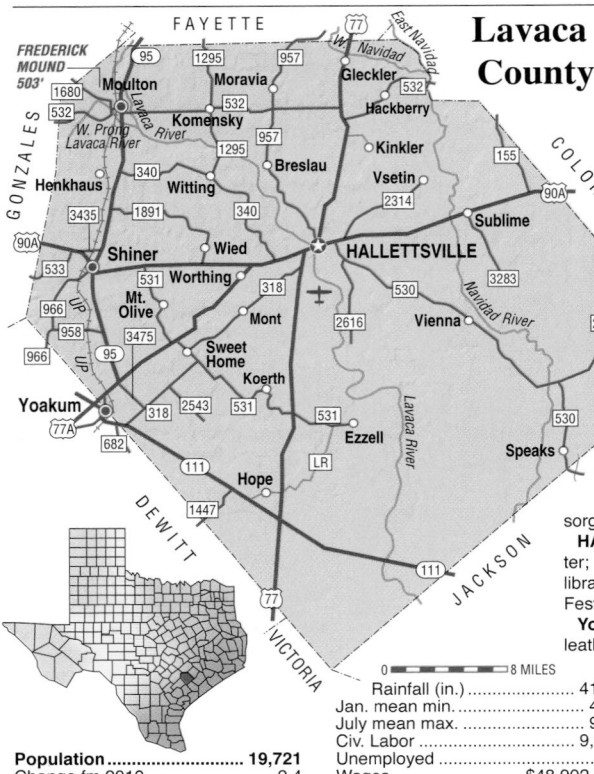

# Lavaca County

**Physical Features**: Coastal Plains county; north rolling; sandy loam, black waxy soils; drains to Lavaca, Navidad rivers.

**Economy**: Varied manufacturing, oil and gas production, agribusinesses, tourism.

**History**: Coahuiltecan area; later a Comanche area until the 1850s. Anglo-Americans first settled in 1831. Germans and Czechs arrived 1880–1900. County created in 1846 from Colorado, Jackson, Gonzales, and Victoria counties. Name is the Spanish word for cow, la vaca, from name of river.

**Race/Ethnicity**: (In percent) Anglo, 74.5; Black, 7.2; Hispanic, 17.4; Asian, 0.4; Other, 1.9.

**Vital Statistics**, annual: Births, 237; deaths, 245; marriages, 125; divorces, 51.

**Recreation**: Deer, other hunting, fishing; wildflower trails, historic sites, churches; Hallettsville fiddlers frolics in April.

**Minerals**: Some oil, gas.

**Agriculture**: Cattle, forage, poultry, rice, corn, sorghum. Market value $61.9 million. Hunting leases.

**HALLETTSVILLE** (2,605) county seat; retail center; varied manufacturing; agribusiness; museum, library, hospital; domino, "42" tournaments; Kolache Fest in September.

**Yoakum** (5,928, partly in DeWitt County); cattle, leather, meat processing; hospital; museum; Tom Tom festival in June.

**Shiner** (2,061) Spoetzl brewery, varied manufacturing; museum; clinic; Half Moon Holidays in July.

Other towns include: **Moulton** (877) agribusiness, Town & Country Jamboree in July; **Sublime** (75); **Sweet Home** (360).

| | |
|---|---|
| Population | **19,721** |
| Change fm 2010 | 2.4 |
| Area (sq. mi.) | 970.4 |
| Land Area (sq. mi.) | 969.7 |
| Altitude (ft.) | 85-503 |
| Rainfall (in.) | 41.06 |
| Jan. mean min. | 41.3 |
| July mean max. | 93.4 |
| Civ. Labor | 9,816 |
| Unemployed | 4.1 |
| Wages | $48,902,647 |
| Per Capita Income | $43,525 |
| Prop. Value | $4,209,668,856 |
| Retail Sales | $235,084,073 |

# Lee County

**Physical Features**: Rolling terrain, broken by Yegua and its tributaries; red to black soils, sandy to heavy loams; lake.

**Economy**: Varied manufacturing, agribusiness, lignite coal operations, government/services.

**History**: Tonkawas; removed in 1855 to Brazos Reservation. Most Anglo-American settlement occurred after Texas Revolution. Slaveholding area. Germans, Wends, other Europeans began arriving in the 1850s. County created from Bastrop, Burleson, Fayette, and Washington counties and organized in 1874; named for Confederate Gen. Robert E. Lee.

**Race/Ethnicity**: (In percent) Anglo, 64.1; Black, 11.2; Hispanic, 23.2; Asian, 0.5; Other, 2.7.

**Vital Statistics**, annual: Births, 197; deaths, 138; marriages, 104; divorces, 46.

**Recreation**: Fishing, hunting, lake activities, state park; pioneer village; historic sites.

**Minerals**: Lignite coal, iron ore, gravel.

**Agriculture**: Beef cattle, hay, nurseries, poultry, peanuts, goats, horses, aquaculture, corn; some irrigation. Market value $38.6 million. Firewood.

**GIDDINGS** (5,155) county seat; agriculture, government/services, oil-field services, light manufacturing; hospital; Charcoal Challenge barbecue cookoff in May.

Other towns include: **Dime Box** (381); **Lexington** (1,149) livestock-marketing center, log cabins heritage center, Chocolate Lovers festival in October; **Lincoln** (336); **Serbin** (109) Wendish museum.

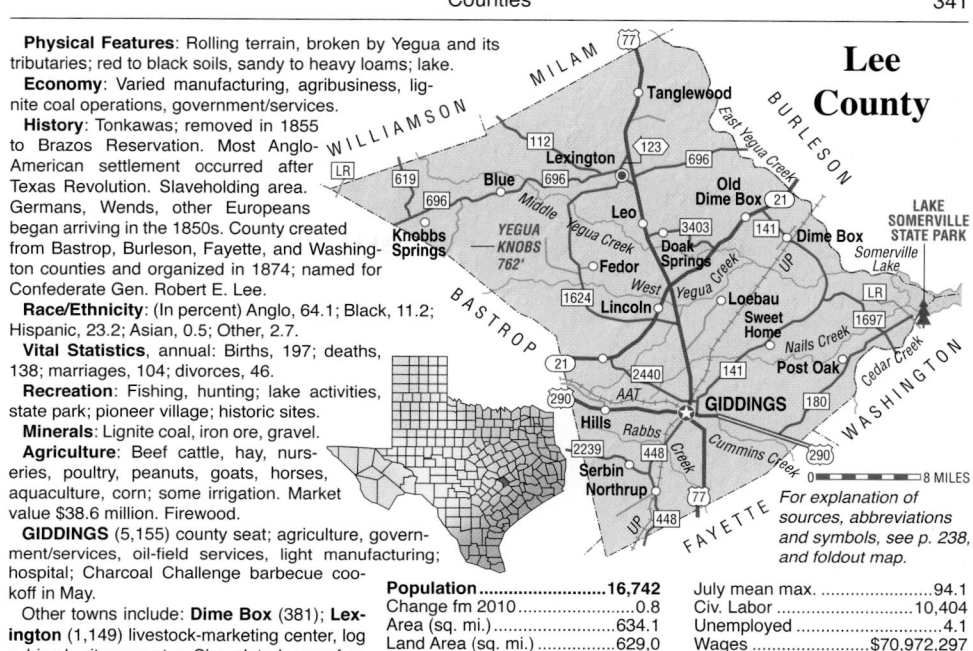

For explanation of sources, abbreviations and symbols, see p. 238, and foldout map.

| | |
|---|---|
| Population | 16,742 |
| Change fm 2010 | 0.8 |
| Area (sq. mi.) | 634.1 |
| Land Area (sq. mi.) | 629,0 |
| Altitude (ft.) | 238-762 |
| Rainfall (in.) | 36.61 |
| Jan. mean min. | 37.2 |
| July mean max. | 94.1 |
| Civ. Labor | 10,404 |
| Unemployed | 4.1 |
| Wages | $70,972,297 |
| Per Capita Income | $44,324 |
| Prop. Value | $2,598,369,382 |
| Retail Sales | $427,087,203 |

# Leon County

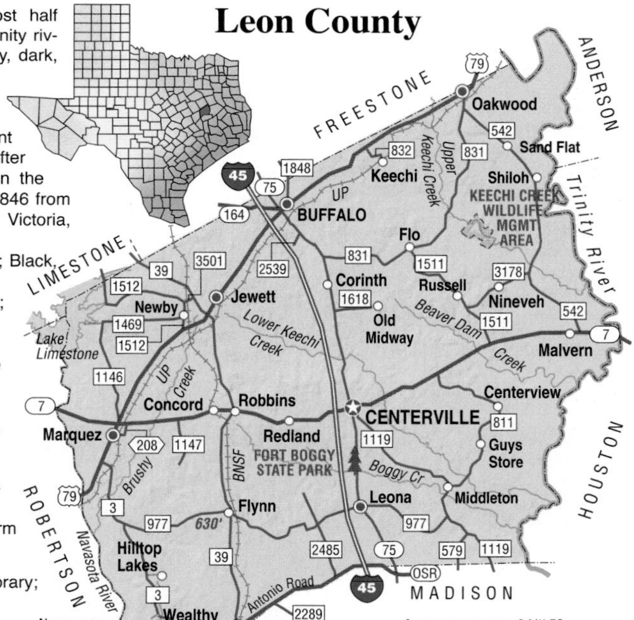

**Physical Features**: Hilly, rolling, almost half covered by timber; drains to Navasota, Trinity rivers and tributaries; Lake Limestone; sandy, dark, alluvial soils.

**Economy**: Oil, gas, agribusiness.

**History**: Bidais band, absorbed into Kickapoos and other groups. Permanent settlement by Anglo-Americans occurred after the Texas Revolution; Germans arrived in the 1870s. County created and organized in 1846 from Robertson County; named for founder of Victoria, Martín de León.

**Race/Ethnicity**: (In percent) Anglo, 76.7; Black, 7.5; Hispanic, 14.0; Asian, 0.8; Other, 2.0.

**Vital Statistics**, annual: Births, 238; deaths, 178; marriages, 95; divorces, 86.

**Recreation**: Hilltop Lakes resort area; sites of Camino Real, Fort Boggy State Park; deer hunting.

**Minerals**: Oil, natural gas, lignite coal.

**Agriculture**: Cow-calf production, hogs, poultry. Hay, watermelons, vegetables, small grains. Christmas trees. Market value $148.7 million. Hardwoods, pine marketed.

**CENTERVILLE** (889) county seat; farm center, hunting, tourism, oil, gas, timber.

**BUFFALO** (1,869) coal mining, oil/gas; library; May Spring Fest with fiddlers' contest.

Other towns include: **Concord** (28); **Flynn** (81); **Hilltop Lakes** (1,109) resort, retirement center; **Jewett** (1,147) electricity-generating plant, steel mill, strip mining, civic center, museum, library, Classic Coon Hunt in January; **Leona** (171) candle factory; **Marquez** (259); **Normangee** (668, partly in Madison County) farming, tourism; library, museum, city park; **Oakwood** (501).

| | |
|---|---|
| Population | 16,861 |
| Change fm 2010 | 0.4 |
| Area (sq. mi.) | 1,080.6 |
| Land Area (sq. mi.) | 1,073,2 |
| Altitude (ft.) | 150-630 |
| Rainfall (in.) | 42.29 |
| Jan. mean min. | 34.9 |
| July mean max. | 93.7 |
| Civ. Labor | 8,089 |
| Unemployed | 5.2 |
| Wages | $58,297,061 |
| Per Capita Income | $39,468 |
| Prop. Value | $3,149,134,650 |
| Retail Sales | $184,756,009 |

# Liberty County

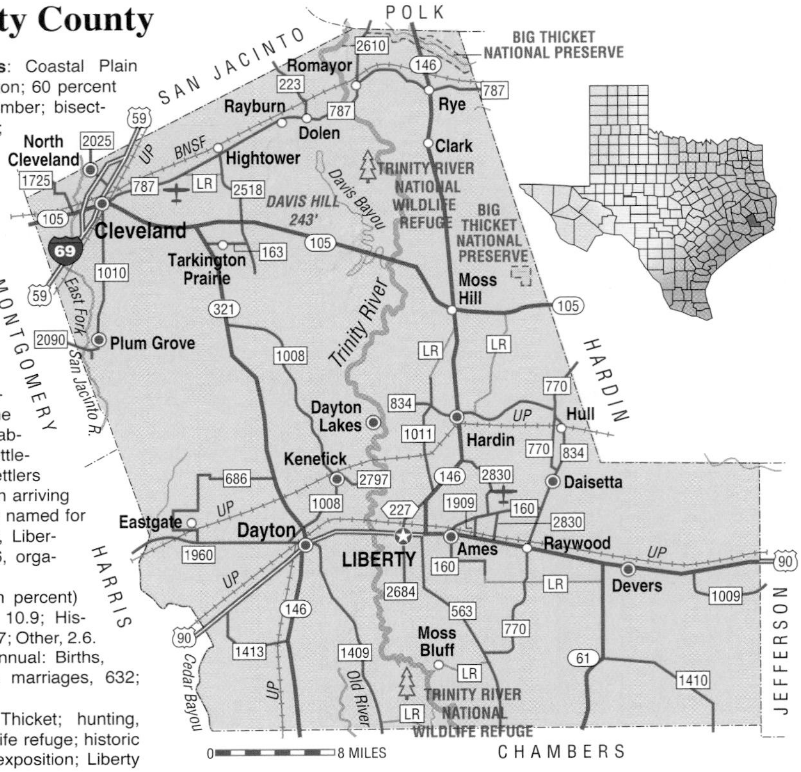

**Physical Features:** Coastal Plain county east of Houston; 60 percent in pine, hardwood timber; bisected by Trinity River; sandy, loam, black soils; Big Thicket.

**Economy:** Agribusiness; chemical plants; varied manufacturing; tourism; forest industries; prisons; many residents work in Houston; part of Houston metropolitan area.

**History:** Karankawa area until the 1740s. Spanish established Atascosito settlement in 1756. Settlers from Louisiana began arriving in the 1810s. County named for Spanish municipality, Libertad; created in 1836, organized in 1837.

**Race/Ethnicity:** (In percent) Anglo, 67.5; Black, 10.9; Hispanic, 19.7; Asian, 0.7; Other, 2.6.

**Vital Statistics,** annual: Births, 1,052; deaths, 683; marriages, 632; divorces, 271.

**Recreation:** Big Thicket; hunting, fishing; national wildlife refuge; historic sites; Trinity Valley exposition; Liberty Opry.

**Minerals:** Oil, gas.

**Agriculture:** Beef cattle; rice is principal crop. Also nursery crops, corn, hay, sorghum, bees (first in number of colonies). Market value $34.9 million. Some lumbering.

**LIBERTY** (9,028) county seat; petroleum-related industry, agribusiness; library, museum, regional historical resource depository; Liberty Bell, Price Daniel House; hospital; Jubilee in March.

**Cleveland** (8,010) forest products processed, shipped; tourism; library; museum; hospital.

**Dayton** (7,642) rice, oil center.

Other towns include: **Ames** (1,078); **Daisetta** (1,008); **Dayton Lakes** (98); **Devers** (466); **Hardin** (869); **Hull** (693); **Kenefick** (605); **North Cleveland** (249); **Plum Grove** (628); **Raywood** (231); **Romayor** (135); **Rye** (150).

*For explanation of sources, abbreviations and symbols, see p. 238, and foldout map.*

| | |
|---|---|
| Population | **78,117** |
| Change fm 2010 | 3.3 |
| Area (sq. mi.) | 1,176.3 |
| Land Area (sq. mi.) | 1,158.4 |
| Altitude (ft.) | 3-243 |
| Rainfall (in.) | 61.25 |
| Jan. mean min. | 41.2 |
| July mean max. | 92.1 |
| Civ. Labor | 33,544 |
| Unemployed | 7.1 |
| Wages | $164,201,566 |
| Per Capita Income | $36,799 |
| Prop. Value | $5,562,047,386 |
| Retail Sales | $856,215,888 |

*Canoeing at Fort Parker State Park, Limestone County. Texas Parks & Wildlife photo.*

# Limestone County

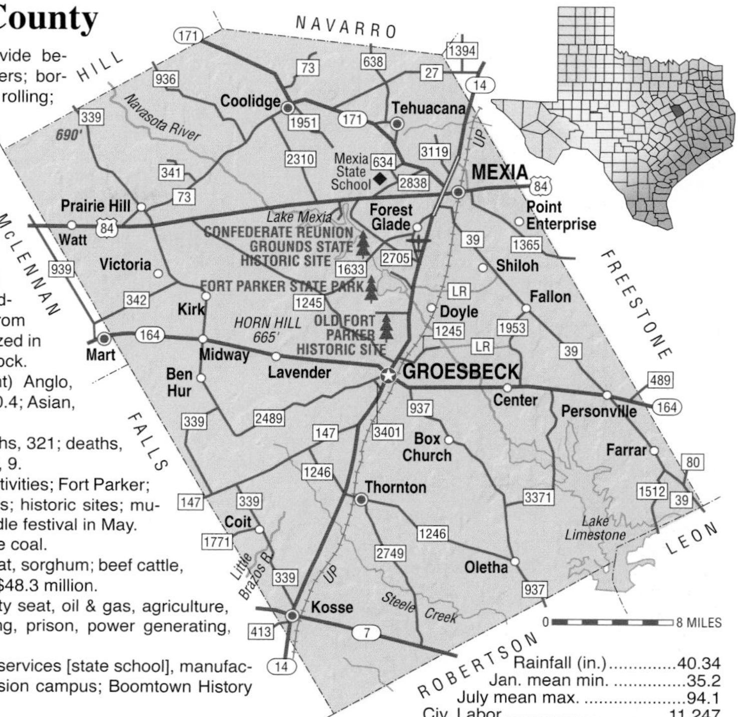

**Physical Features**: On divide between Brazos and Trinity rivers; borders Blacklands, level to rolling; drained by Navasota and tributaries; lake.

**Economy**: Government/services, electricity-generating plant.

**History**: Tawakoni (Tehuacana) and Waco area, later Comanche raiders. First Anglo-Americans arrived in 1833. Antebellum slaveholding area. County created from Robertson County and organized in 1846; named for indigenous rock.

**Race/Ethnicity**: (In percent) Anglo, 60.5; Black, 18.0; Hispanic, 20.4; Asian, 0.5; Other, 2.6.

**Vital Statistics**, annual: Births, 321; deaths, 256; marriages, 184; divorces, 9.

**Recreation**: Fishing, lake activities; Fort Parker; Confederate Reunion Grounds; historic sites; museum; hunting; Groesbeck fiddle festival in May.

**Minerals**: Natural gas, lignite coal.

**Agriculture**: Hay, corn, wheat, sorghum; beef cattle, horses, poultry. Market value $48.3 million.

**GROESBECK** (4,223) county seat; oil & gas, agriculture, manufacturing, hunting, mining, prison, power generating, hospital, museum.

**MEXIA** (7,313) government/services [state school], manufacturing; hospital, college extension campus; Boomtown History Day in April.

Other towns include: **Coolidge** (931), **Kosse** (460), **Prairie Hill** (150), **Tehuacana** (272), **Thornton** (517).

| | |
|---|---|
| Population | **23,524** |
| Change fm 2010 | 0.6 |
| Area (sq. mi.) | 933.2 |
| Land Area (sq. mi.) | 905.3 |
| Altitude (ft.) | 363-690 |

| | |
|---|---|
| Rainfall (in.) | 40.34 |
| Jan. mean min. | 35.2 |
| July mean max. | 94.1 |
| Civ. Labor | 11,247 |
| Unemployed | 5.5 |
| Wages | $74,614,367 |
| Per Capita Income | $34,746 |
| Prop. Value | $3,411,550,657 |
| Retail Sales | $265,497,613 |

---

# Lipscomb County

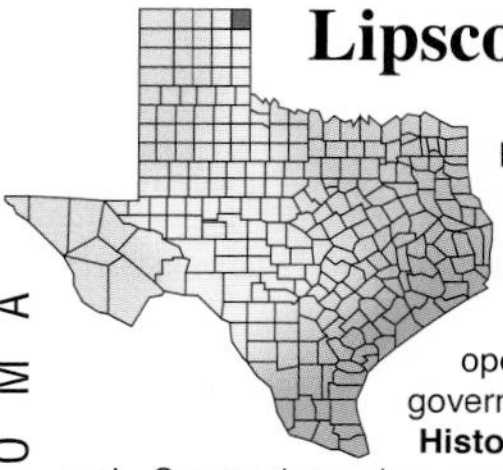

**Physical Features**: High Plains, broken in east; drains to tributaries of Canadian, Wolf Creek; sandy loam, black soils.

**Economy**: Oil, gas operations, agribusinesses, government/services.

**History**: Apaches, later Kiowas and Comanches who were driven into Indian Territory in 1875. Ranching began in the late 1870s. County created in 1876 from Bexar District; organized in 1887; named for A.S. Lipscomb, Republic of Texas leader.

**Race/Ethnicity**: (In percent) Anglo, 65.0; Black, 1.8; Hispanic, 31.6; Asian, 0.4; Other, 4.5.

**Vital Statistics**, annual: Births, 35; deaths, 32; marriages, 32; divorces, 12.

**Recreation**: Hunting; Wolf Creek museum, prairie chicken booming grounds.

**Minerals**: Oil, natural gas.

**Agriculture**: Cattle, corn, wheat, grain sorghum, hay, sunflowers. Some 23,000 acres irrigated. Market value $52.7 million.

**LIPSCOMB** (38), county seat; livestock center.

**BOOKER** (1,595, partly in Ochiltree County) trade center, library.

Other towns include: **Darrouzett** (376) Deutsches Fest in July; **Follett** (489); **Higgins** (428) library, Will Rogers Day in August.

| | |
|---|---|
| Population | **3,553** |
| Change fm 2010 | 7.6 |
| Area (sq. mi.) | 932.3 |
| Land Area (sq. mi.) | 932.2 |
| Altitude (ft.) | 2,220-2,892 |
| Rainfall (in.) | 22.25 |
| Jan. mean min. | 18.1 |

| | |
|---|---|
| July mean max. | 94.0 |
| Civ. Labor | 1,755 |
| Unemployed | 3.6 |
| Wages | $12,040,450 |
| Per Capita Income | $51,805 |
| Prop. Value | $1,386,188,081 |
| Retail Sales | $27,139,891 |

# Live Oak County

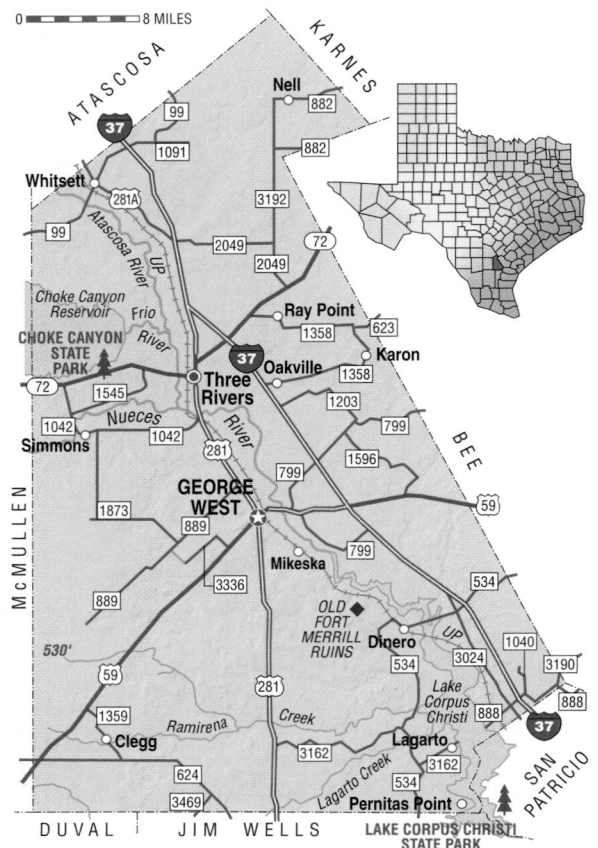

0 ▭▭▭ 8 MILES

**Physical Features**: Brushy plains between San Antonio and Corpus Christi, partly broken by Nueces and tributaries; black waxy, gray sandy, other soils; Lake Corpus Christi, Choke Canyon Reservoir.

**Economy**: Oil, government/services, tourism, agribusinesses.

**History**: Coahuiltecans squeezed out by Lipan Apaches and Spanish. Spanish ranching started in the 1810s. Settlers from Ireland arrived in 1835. County named for predominant tree; created and organized in 1856 from Nueces and San Patricio counties.

**Race/Ethnicity**: (In percent) Anglo, 57.0; Black, 4.8; Hispanic, 36.9; Asian, 0.7; Other, 2.1.

**Vital Statistics**, annual: Births, 130; deaths, 119; marriages, 60; divorces, 40.

**Recreation**: Lakes; water activities; state park; hunting; historic sites.

**Minerals**: Oil, gas, sand, gravel.

**Agriculture**: Cow-calf operations; hogs; corn, grain sorghum, cotton; some irrigation for hay, coastal Bermuda pastures. Market value $17.9 million.

**GEORGE WEST** (2,459) county seat, oil and gas operations, museum, Storyfest in November.

**Three Rivers** (1,939) oil and gas, hunting and fishing, agriculture, federal prison, salsa festival in April.

Other towns include: **Dinero** (344); **Lagarto** (735), **Pernitas Point** (274, partly in Jim Wells County), **Whitsett** (200).

| | |
|---|---|
| Altitude (ft.) | 94-530 |
| Rainfall (in.) | 26.36 |
| Jan. mean min. | 42.4 |
| July mean max. | 95.5 |
| Civ. Labor | 7,246 |
| Unemployed | 3.6 |
| Wages | $43,004,855 |
| Per Capita Income | $45,926 |
| Prop. Value | $4,003,352,805 |
| Retail Sales | $244,129,728 |

*For explanation of sources, abbreviations and symbols, see p. 238, and foldout map.*

| | |
|---|---|
| **Population** | **12,091** |
| Change fm 2010 | 4.9 |
| Area (sq. mi.) | 1,078.9 |
| Land Area (sq. mi.) | 1,039.7 |

*Llano County, along Texas 29. Photo by Ron Billings/Texas A&M Forest Service.*

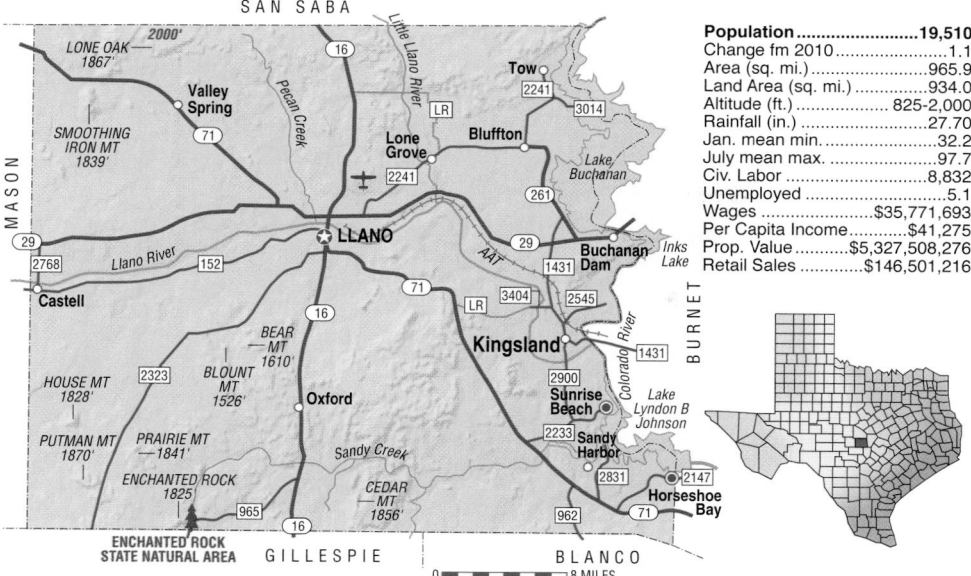

| Population | 19,510 |
|---|---|
| Change fm 2010 | 1.1 |
| Area (sq. mi.) | 965.9 |
| Land Area (sq. mi.) | 934.0 |
| Altitude (ft.) | 825-2,000 |
| Rainfall (in.) | 27.70 |
| Jan. mean min. | 32.2 |
| July mean max. | 97.7 |
| Civ. Labor | 8,832 |
| Unemployed | 5.1 |
| Wages | $35,771,693 |
| Per Capita Income | $41,275 |
| Prop. Value | $5,327,508,276 |
| Retail Sales | $146,501,216 |

## Llano County

**Physical Features**: Central county drains to Colorado, Llano rivers; rolling to hilly; Lake Buchanan, Inks Lake, Lake Lyndon B. Johnson.

**Economy**: Tourism, retirement, ranch trading center, vineyards.

**History**: Tonkawa tribal area, later Comanches. Anglo-American and German settlers arrived in the 1840s. County name is Spanish for plains; created, organized 1856 from Bexar District, Gillespie County.

**Race/Ethnicity**: (In percent) Anglo, 87.7; Black, 1.2; Hispanic, 9.3; Asian, 0.6; Other, 2.1.

**Vital Statistics**, annual: Births, 161; deaths, 309; marriages, 95; divorces, 70.

**Recreation**: Leading deer-hunting county; fishing, lake activities, major tourist area, Enchanted Rock, eagles' nest on Highway 29, bluebonnet festival, Hill Country Wine Trail in spring.

**Minerals**: Granite, vermiculite, llanite.

**Agriculture**: Beef cattle, sheep, goats. Market value $13.8 million. Deer-hunting, wildlife leases.

**LLANO** (3,306) county seat; agriculture, hunting, tourism; hospital; historic district; museum; Texas gold panning championship in September.

**Kingsland** (6,380) tourism, retirement community, recreation, vineyards; library; archaeological center; AquaBoom on July 4.

Other towns include: **Bluffton** (75); **Buchanan Dam** (1,524) hydroelectric industry, tourism, fishing, water sports; **Castell** (72); **Horseshoe Bay** (3,458, partly in Burnet County); **Sunrise Beach** (710); **Tow** (305); **Valley Spring** (50).

## Loving County

**Physical Features**: Flat desert terrain with a few low-rolling hills; slopes to Pecos River; Red Bluff Reservoir; sandy, loam, clay soils.

**Economy**: Petroleum operations; cattle.

**History**: Land developers began operations in the late 19th century. Oil discovered in 1925. County created in 1887 from Tom Green County; organized in 1893, deorganized in 1897, again organized in 1931, the last county organized. Named for Oliver Loving, trail driver. Loving is Texas' least populous county.

**Race/Ethnicity**: (In percent) Anglo, 78.9; Black, 0.0; Hispanic, 17.9; Asian, 0.0; Other, 3.2.

**Vital Statistics**, annual: Births, 0; deaths, 1; marriages, 2; divorces, 0.

**Recreation**: NA.

**Minerals**: Oil, gas.

**Agriculture**: Some cattle. Market value $912,000.

**MENTONE** (20) county seat; oil-field supply center; the only town.

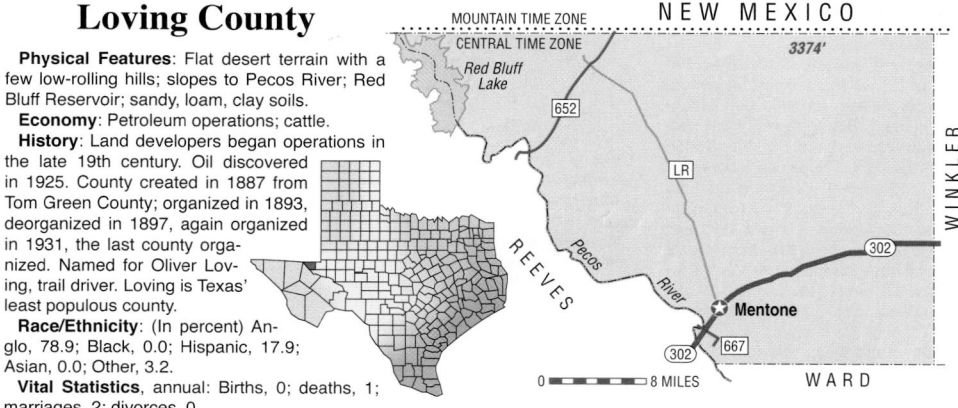

| Population | 86 |
|---|---|
| Change fm 2010 | 4.9 |
| Area (sq. mi.) | 676.7 |
| Land Area (sq. mi.) | 668.9 |
| Altitude (ft.) | 2,660-3,374 |
| Rainfall (in.) | 12.57 |
| Jan. mean min. | 29.7 |
| July mean max. | 99.3 |
| Civ. Labor | 40 |
| Unemployed | 10.0 |
| Wages | $950,546 |
| Per Capita Income | $40,358 |
| Prop. Value | $623,236,390 |
| Retail Sales | NA |

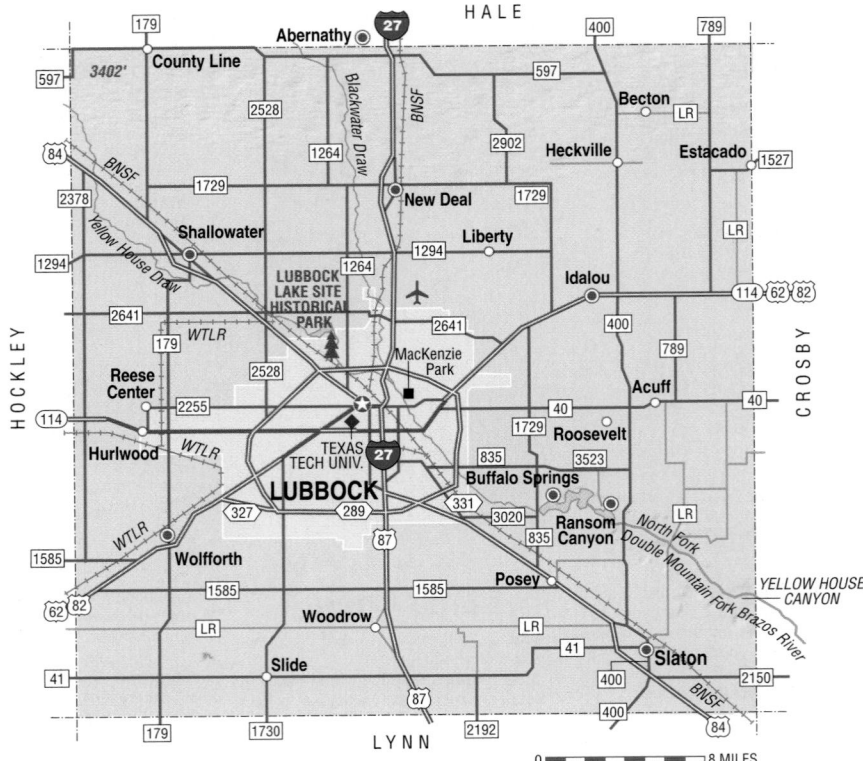

# Lubbock County

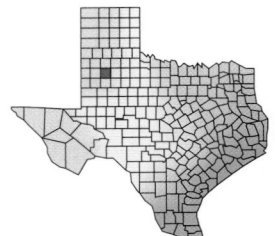

**Physical Features**: South Plains, broken by 1,500 playas, upper Brazos River tributaries; rich soils with underground water.

**Economy**: Among world's largest cottonseed processing centers, a leading agribusiness center, cattle feedlots, varied manufacturing, higher education center, medical center, government/services.

**History**: Evidence of human habitation for 12,000 years. In historic period, Apache Indians, followed by Comanche hunters. Sheep raisers from Midwest arrived in the late 1870s. Cotton farms brought in Mexican laborers in the 1940s-1960s. County named for Col. Tom S. Lubbock, an organizer of the Confederate Terry's Rangers; county created in 1876 from Bexar District; organized in 1891.

**Race/Ethnicity**: (In percent) Anglo, 55.8; Black, 7.8; Hispanic, 33.4; Asian, 2.3; Other, 2.8.

**Vital Statistics**, annual: Births, 3,927; deaths, 2,308; marriages, 2,017; divorces, 1,201.

**Recreation**: Lubbock Lake archaeological site; Texas Tech events; civic center; Buddy Holly statue, Walk of Fame, Lubbock Music Fest in fall; planetarium.

Also, Ranching Heritage Center; Panhandle-South Plains Fair, National

Cowboy symposium in September; wine festivals; Buffalo Springs Lake.

**Minerals**: Oil, gas, stone, sand and gravel.

**Agriculture**: Second in bales of cotton produced. Fed beef, cow-calf operations; poultry, eggs; hogs. Other crops, nursery, grain sorghum, wheat, sunflowers, soybeans, hay, vegetables; more than 155,000 acres irrigated, mostly cotton. Market value $174.8 million.

**Education**: Texas Tech University with law and medical schools; Lubbock Christian University; South Plains College branch; Wayland Baptist Univer-

*For explanation of sources, abbreviations and symbols, see p. 238, and foldout map.*

sity off-campus center.

**LUBBOCK** (243,994) county seat; center for large agricultural area; manufacturing includes electronics, earth-moving equipment, food containers, fire-protection equipment, clothing, other products; distribution center for South Plains; feedlots; museum; government/services; hospitals, psychiatric hospital; wind power center.

Other towns include: **Buffalo Springs** (457); **Idalou** (2,365); **New Deal** (770); **Ransom Canyon** (1,145); **Shallowater** (2,497); **Slaton** (6,180) agriculture, railroad, government/services, Harvey House, air museum, sausagefest in October; **Wolfforth** (4,082) retail, government/services.

Also, part of **Abernathy** (2,816).

| Population | 293,974 |
|---|---|
| Change fm 2010 | 5.4 |
| Area (sq. mi.) | 900.7 |
| Land Area (sq. mi.) | 895.6 |
| Altitude (ft.) | 2,821-3,402 |
| Rainfall (in.) | 19.12 |
| Jan. mean min. | 26.4 |
| July mean max. | 92.8 |
| Civ. Labor | 149,212 |
| Unemployed | 4.7 |
| Wages | $1,230,924,961 |
| Per Capita Income | $38,311 |
| Prop. Value | $17,361,897,568 |
| Retail Sales | $5,185,629,227 |

# Lynn County

**Physical Features**: South Plains, broken by Caprock Escarpment, playas, draws; sandy loam, black, gray soils.

**Economy**: Agribusiness.

**History**: Apaches, ousted by Comanches who were removed to Indian Territory in 1875. Ranching began in 1880s. Farming developed after 1900. County created 1876 from Bexar District; organized 1903; named for Alamo victim W. Lynn.

**Race/Ethnicity**: (In percent) Anglo, 49.4; Black, 2.5; Hispanic, 47.0; Asian, 0.3; Other, 3.4.

**Vital Statistics**, annual: Births, 80; deaths, 68; marriages, 27; divorces, 6.

**Recreation**: Pioneer museum in Tahoka; Dan Blocker museum in O'Donnell; sandhill crane migration in winter.

**Minerals**: Oil, natural gas.

**Agriculture**: Cotton produces largest income (first in acreage); 72,000 acres irrigated. Also, ranching, grain sorghum. Market value $67.6 million.

**TAHOKA** (2,548) county seat; agricultural center, electric/telephone cooperatives; hospital; museum; Harvest Festival in the fall.

**O'Donnell** (792, partly in Dawson County) commercial center.

Other towns include: **New Home** (342); **Wilson** (469).

| | |
|---|---|
| Population | 5,771 |
| Change fm 2010 | – 2.4 |
| Area (sq. mi.) | 893.5 |
| Land Area (sq. mi.) | 891.9 |
| Altitude (ft.) | 2,660-3,300 |
| Rainfall (in.) | 21.21 |
| Jan. mean min. | 28.0 |
| July mean max. | 91.9 |
| Civ. Labor | 2,644 |
| Unemployed | 5.5 |
| Wages | $11,323,330 |
| Per Capita Income | $46,496 |
| Prop. Value | $706,642,080 |
| Retail Sales | $44,208,812 |

# Madison County

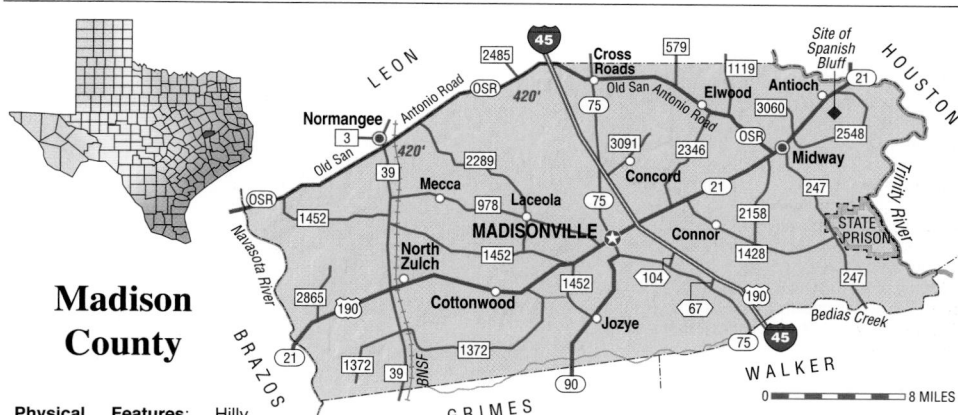

**Physical Features**: Hilly, draining to Trinity, Navasota rivers, Bedias Creek; one-fifth of area timbered; alluvial, loam, sandy soils.

**Economy**: Prison, government/services, varied manufacturing, agribusiness, oil production.

**History**: Caddo, Bidai Indian area; Kickapoos migrated from the east. Spanish settlements established in 1774 and 1805. Anglo-Americans arrived in 1829. Census of 1860 showed 30 percent of population was black. County named for U.S. President James Madison; created from Grimes, Leon, Walker counties 1853; organized 1854.

**Race/Ethnicity**: (In percent) Anglo, 56.5; Black, 20.3; Hispanic, 21.8; Asian, 0.8; Other, 2.8.

**Vital Statistics**, annual: Births, 160; deaths, 117; marriages, 117; divorces, 57.

**Recreation**: Fishing, hunting; Spanish Bluff where survivors of the Gutiérrez-Magee expedition were executed in 1813; other historic sites.

**Minerals**: sand, oil.

**Agriculture**: Nursery crops, cattle, horses, poultry raised; forage for livestock. Market value $82.9 million.

**MADISONVILLE** (4,708) county seat; farm-trade center, varied manufacturing; hospital, library; Spring Fling in April.

Other towns, **Midway** (236); **Normangee** (668, mostly in Leon County); **North Zulch** (600).

| | |
|---|---|
| Population | 13,861 |
| Change fm 2010 | 1.4 |
| Area (sq. mi.) | 472.4 |
| Land Area (sq. mi.) | 466.1 |
| Altitude (ft.) | 131-420 |
| Rainfall (in.) | 45.12 |
| Jan. mean min. | 36.9 |
| July mean max. | 94.4 |
| Civ. Labor | 5,881 |
| Unemployed | 5.6 |
| Wages | $38,010,731 |
| Per Capita Income | $30,731 |
| Prop. Value | $1,875,416,821 |
| Retail Sales | $246,182,772 |

# Marion County

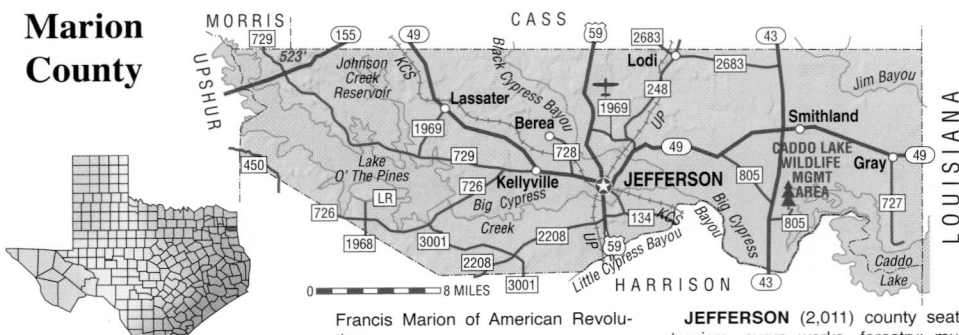

**Physical Features**: Northeastern county; hilly, three-quarters forested with pines, hardwoods; drains to Caddo Lake, Lake O' the Pines, Big Cypress Bayou; Johnson Creek Reservoir.

**Economy**: Agriculture, tourism, forestry, food processing.

**History**: Caddoes forced out in 1790s. Kickapoo in area when settlers arrived from Deep South around 1840. Antebellum slaveholding area. County created 1860 from Cass County, organized the same year; named for Gen.

Francis Marion of American Revolution.

**Race/Ethnicity**: (In percent) Anglo, 71.0; Black, 22.0; Hispanic, 3.8; Asian, 0.6; Other, 3.3.

**Vital Statistics**, annual: Births, 110; deaths, 154; marriages, 79; divorces, 43.

**Recreation**: Lake activities, hunting, Excelsior Hotel, 84 medallions on historic sites including Jay Gould railroad car, museum, historical homes tour in May, Spring Festival.

**Minerals**: Iron ore, natural gas, oil.

**Agriculture**: Beef cattle, hay. Market value $3.4 million. Forestry is most important industry.

**JEFFERSON** (2,011) county seat; tourism, syrup works, forestry; museum, library; historical sites.

Other towns include: **Lodi** (175).

| | |
|---|---|
| Population | 10,149 |
| Change fm 2010 | – 3.8 |
| Area (sq. mi.) | 420.3 |
| Land Area (sq. mi.) | 380.9 |
| Altitude (ft.) | 168-523 |
| Rainfall (in.) | 48.23 |
| Jan. mean min. | 32.7 |
| July mean max. | 92.6 |
| Civ. Labor | 5,362 |
| Unemployed | 5.8 |
| Wages | $14,573,312 |
| Per Capita Income | $35,216 |
| Prop. Value | $964,759,750 |
| Retail Sales | $63,122,954 |

# Martin County

**Physical Features**: South Plains; sandy, loam soils, broken by playas, creeks; Sulphur Springs Draw Reservoir.

**Economy**: Oil, gas production, agribusiness.

**History**: Apaches, ousted by Comanches who in turn were forced out by the U.S. Army in 1875. Farming began in 1881. County created from Bexar District in 1876; organized in 1884; named for Wylie Martin, senator of Republic of Texas.

**Race/Ethnicity**: (In percent) Anglo, 52.0; Black, 2.1; Hispanic, 44.7; Asian, 0.7; Other, 2.3.

**Vital Statistics**, annual: Births, 87; deaths, 39; marriages, 34; divorces, 14.

**Recreation**: Museum, settlers reunion in July at Stanton.

**Minerals**: Oil, gas.

**Agriculture**: Cotton, beef cattle, milo, wheat, horses, meat goats. Market value $20.3 million.

**STANTON** (2,847) county seat; oil and gas production, agribusiness; commuting to Midland, Big Spring; hospital; historic monastery, other historic buildings; Old Sorehead trade days April, June, October.

Other towns include: **Ackerly** (232, partly in Dawson County); **Lenorah** (83); **Tarzan** (30).

A small part of **Midland**.

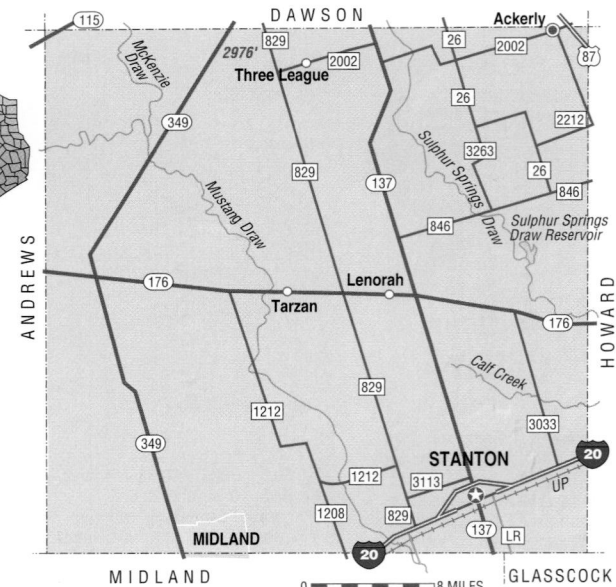

| | |
|---|---|
| Population | 5,460 |
| Change fm 2010 | 13.6 |
| Area (sq. mi.) | 915.7 |
| Land Area (sq. mi.) | 914.9 |
| Altitude (ft.) | 2,470-2,976 |
| Rainfall (in.) | 17.56 |
| Jan. mean min. | 30.0 |
| July mean max. | 94.0 |
| Civ. Labor | 2,796 |
| Unemployed | 3.7 |
| Wages | $17,456,891 |
| Per Capita Income | $48,843 |
| Prop. Value | $5,668,450,260 |
| Retail Sales | $102,706,263 |

*For explanation of sources, abbreviations and symbols, see p. 238, and foldout map.*

# Mason County

**Physical Features**: Central county; hilly, draining to Llano and San Saba rivers and their tributaries; limestone, red soils; varied timber.

**Economy**: Sand plants, agriculture, tourism, hunting.

**History**: Lipan Apaches, driven south by Comanches around 1790. German settlers arrived in mid-1840s, followed by Anglo-Americans. Mexican immigration increased after 1930. County created from Bexar, Gillespie counties in 1858, organized the same year; named for Mexican War victim U.S. Army Lt. G.T. Mason.

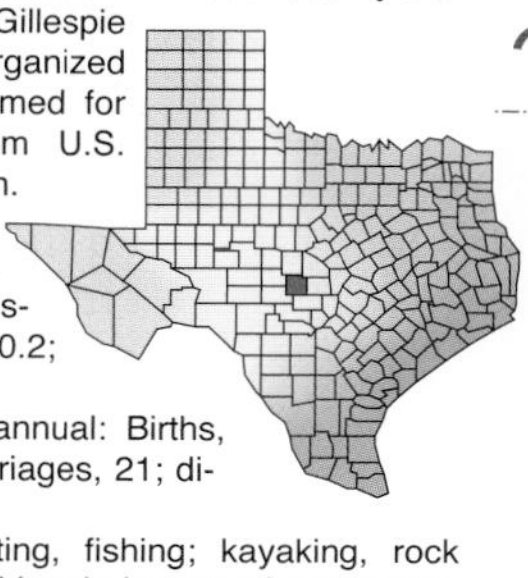

**Race/Ethnicity**: (In percent) Anglo, 75.1; Black, 1.0; Hispanic, 23.1; Asian, 0.2; Other, 1.6.

**Vital Statistics**, annual: Births, 41; deaths, 40; marriages, 21; divorces, 13.

**Recreation**: Hunting, fishing; kayaking, rock crawling, camping; historic homes of stone; prehistoric Indian artifacts exhibit; Fort Mason, where Robert E. Lee served; bat cave; wildflower drives in spring, Roundup rodeo in July.

**Minerals**: Sand, topaz, granite.

**Agriculture**: Beef cattle, hay, meat goats. Market value $51.4 million. Hunting leases important.

**MASON** (2,234) county seat; agriculture, hunting, nature tourism; museums, historical district, homes, rock fences built by German settlers; wild game dinner in November.

Other towns include: **Art** (14), **Fredonia** (55), **Pontotoc** (125).

**Population** ................................ **4,071**
Change fm 2010 ........................... 1.5
Area (sq. mi.) ............................. 932.2

Land Area (sq. mi.) ................... 928.8
Altitude (ft.) ...................... 1,180-2,217
Rainfall (in.) ............................. 29.19
Jan. mean min. ........................... 32.1
July mean max. .......................... 92.3
Civ. Labor ................................. 2,341
Unemployed ................................. 4.0
Wages ............................. $7,957,565
Per Capita Income................ $37,500
Prop. Value .............. $1,755,968,030
Retail Sales ................... $24,669,210

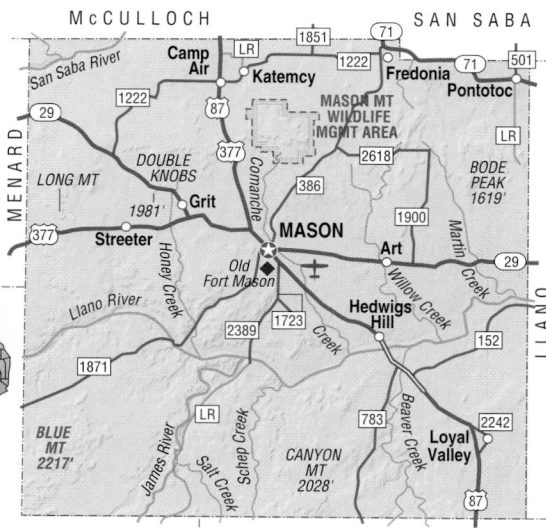

*The Hilda Methodist Church, Mason County, was built in 1902 near Beaver Creek. Photo by Robert Plocheck.*

# Matagorda County

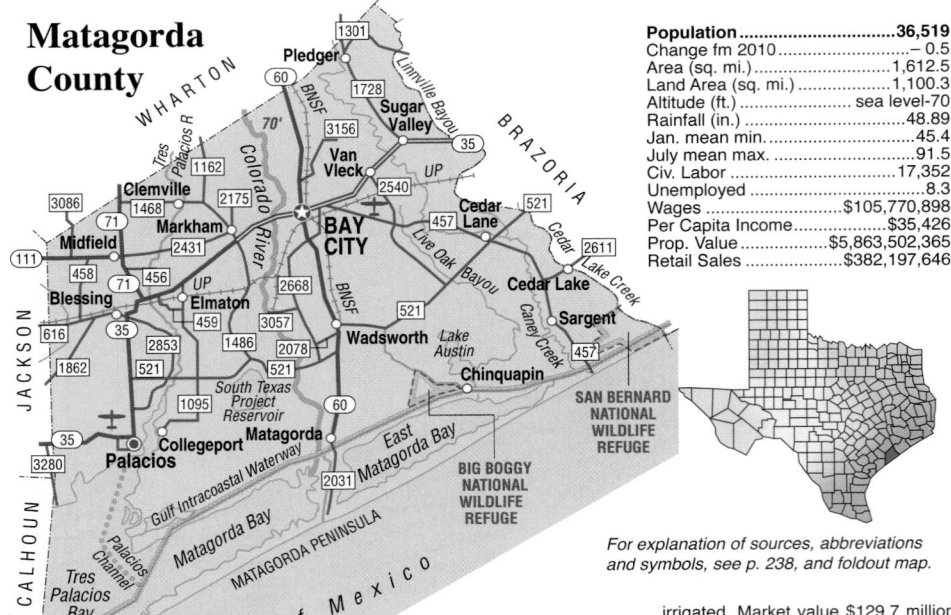

| | |
|---|---|
| Population | **36,519** |
| Change fm 2010 | – 0.5 |
| Area (sq. mi.) | 1,612.5 |
| Land Area (sq. mi.) | 1,100.3 |
| Altitude (ft.) | sea level-70 |
| Rainfall (in.) | 48.89 |
| Jan. mean min. | 45.4 |
| July mean max. | 91.5 |
| Civ. Labor | 17,352 |
| Unemployed | 8.3 |
| Wages | $105,770,898 |
| Per Capita Income | $35,426 |
| Prop. Value | $5,863,502,365 |
| Retail Sales | $382,197,646 |

*For explanation of sources, abbreviations and symbols, see p. 238, and foldout map.*

**Physical Features**: Gulf Coastal Plain; flat, broken by bays; many different soils; drains to Colorado River, creeks, coast; South Texas Project Reservoir.

**Economy**: Nuclear power plant, petrochemicals, agribusiness.

**History**: Karankawa tribal area, Tonkawas in the area later. Anglo-Americans arrived in 1822. Mexican immigration increased after 1920. An original county, created 1836 from a Spanish municipality, named for canebrake; organized in 1837; settled by Austin colonists.

**Race/Ethnicity**: (In percent) Anglo, 46.2; Black, 11.4; Hispanic, 40.0; Asian, 2.2; Other, 2.6.

**Vital Statistics**, annual: Births, 498; deaths, 365; marriages, 313; divorces, 144.

**Recreation**: Fishing, water sports, hunting, birding; historic sites, museums; Bay City rice festival in September.

**Minerals**: Oil and gas.

**Agriculture**: Cattle, rice, cotton, sorghum, soybeans; Some 33,000 acres irrigated. Market value $129.7 million. First in value of aquaculture.

**BAY CITY** (17,342) county seat; government/services, education, nuclear power plant; petrochemicals; agribusiness; hospital, junior college branch.

**Palacios** (4,574) tourism, seafood industry; hospital; Marine Education Center; public fishing piers; Bay Festival on Labor Day.

Other towns include: **Blessing** (941) historic sites; **Cedar Lane** (300); **Collegeport** (80); **Elmaton** (160); **Markham** (1,082); **Matagorda** (520); **Midfield** (305); **Pledger** (265); **Sargent** (900) retirement community, fishing, birding, commercial fishing, barbecue cookoff in April; **Van Vleck** (1,912); **Wadsworth** (160).

*A baseball game beneath the International Bridge at Eagle Pass, Maverick County. Photo by Robert Plocheck.*

# Maverick County

**Physical Features**: Southwestern county on Rio Grande; broken, rolling surface, with dense brush; clay, sandy, alluvial soils.

**Economy**: Oil, government/services, agribusiness, tourism.

**History**: Coahuiltecan Indian area; later Comanches in the area. Spanish ranching began in the 1760s. First Anglo-Americans arrived in 1834. County named for Sam A. Maverick, whose name is now a synonym for unbranded cattle; created in 1856 from Kinney County and organized in 1871.

**Race/Ethnicity**: (In percent) Anglo, 3.2; Black, 0.6; Hispanic, 95.1; Asian, 0.5; Other, 1.9.

**Vital Statistics**, annual: Births, 1,101; deaths, 340; marriages, 543; divorces, 118.

**Recreation**: Tourist gateway to Mexico; white-tailed deer, bird hunting; fishing; historic sites, Fort Duncan museum.

**Minerals**: Oil, gas, sand, gravel.

**Agriculture**: Cattle feedlots; pecans, vegetables, sorghum, wheat; goats, sheep. Some irrigation from Rio Grande. Market value $32.6 million.

**EAGLE PASS** (27,479) county seat; government/services, retail center, tourism; hospital; junior college, Sul Ross college branch; entry point to Piedras Negras, Mex., Nacho Festival in Piedras Negras in October.

Other communities include: **Chula Vista** (3,927), **Eidson Road** (9,158), **El Indio** (187), **Las Quintas Fronterizas** (3,436), and **Rosita** (2,744), all immediately south of Eagle Pass.

Also, **Elm Creek** (2,593) and **Quemado** (234).

| | | |
|---|---|---|
| Population ............................ 57,023 | Rainfall (in.) .............................. 20.41 | Wages ......................... $125,540,859 |
| Change fm 2010 ........................... 5.1 | Jan. mean min. .......................... 41.5 | Per Capita Income................. $23,440 |
| Area (sq. mi.) ........................ 1,291.8 | July mean max. ......................... 98.1 | Prop. Value ............... $3,575,709,620 |
| Land Area (sq. mi.) ............... 1,279.3 | Civ. Labor .............................. 23,196 | Retail Sales ................. $646,406,947 |
| Altitude (ft.) ........................... 550-975 | Unemployed .............................. 10.6 | |

# McCulloch County

**Physical Features**: Hilly and rolling; drains to Colorado River, Brady Creek and Brady Creek Reservoir, San Saba River; black loams to sandy soils.

**Economy**: Agribusiness, manufacturing, tourism, hunting leases.

**History**: Apache area. First Anglo-American settlers arrived in the late 1850s, but Comanche raids delayed further settlement until 1870s. County created from Bexar District 1856; organized 1876; named for San Jacinto veteran Gen. Ben McCulloch.

**Race/Ethnicity**: (In percent) Anglo, 65.2; Black, 2.6; Hispanic, 31.3; Asian, 0.5; Other, 2.2.

**Vital Statistics**, annual: Births, 97; deaths, 98; marriages, 59; divorces, 30.

**Recreation**: Hunting; lake activities; museum, restored Santa Fe depot, goat cookoff on Labor Day, muzzle-loading rifle association state championship; rodeos; golf, tennis tournaments.

**Minerals**: Sand, gravel, gas and oil.

**Agriculture**: Beef cattle provide most income; wheat, sheep, goats, hay, cotton, sorghum, hogs, dairy cattle; some irrigation for peanuts. Market value $22.6 million.

**BRADY** (5,540) county seat; silica sand, oilfield equipment, ranching, tourism, other manufacturing; hospital; Heart of Texas car show in April, Cinco de Mayo.

Other towns: **Doole** (74), **Lohn** (149), **Melvin** (181), **Mercury** (166), **Rochelle** (163) and **Voca** (56).

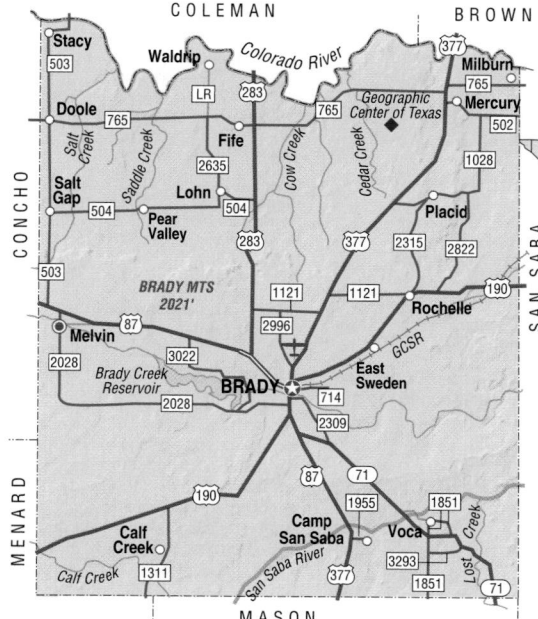

| | |
|---|---|
| Population ........................... 8,199 | July mean max. ..................... 94.2 |
| Change fm 2010 ................. – 1.0 | Civ. Labor ........................... 4,084 |
| Area (sq. mi.) .................... 1,073.4 | Unemployed ........................... 4.7 |
| Land Area (sq. mi.) .......... 1,065.6 | Wages ..................... $31,538,210 |
| Altitude (ft.) ............... 1,280-2,021 | Per Capita Income......... $43,200 |
| Rainfall (in.) ........................ 27.60 | Prop. Value ......... $1,507,423,780 |
| Jan. mean min. ..................... 32.2 | Retail Sales ........... $101,766,568 |

# McLennan County

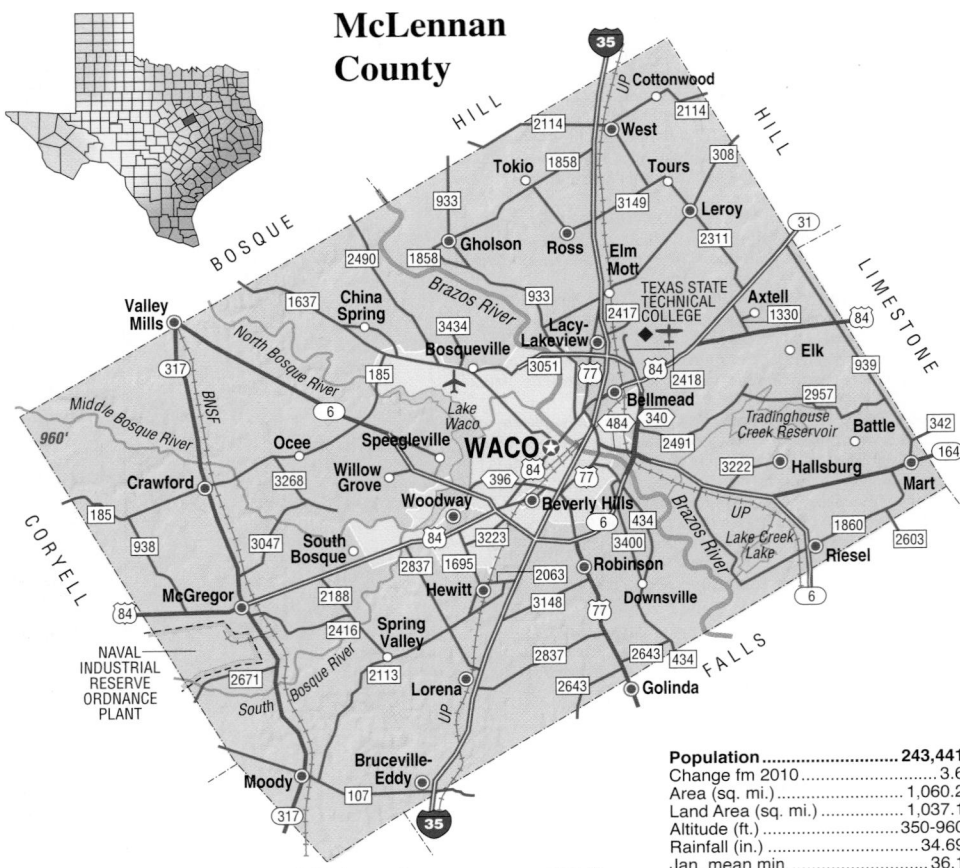

Population .......................... 243,441
Change fm 2010 .......................... 3.6
Area (sq. mi.) ........................ 1,060.2
Land Area (sq. mi.) ................. 1,037.1
Altitude (ft.) ............................ 350-960
Rainfall (in.) .............................. 34.69
Jan. mean min. .......................... 36.1
July mean max. .......................... 96.3
Civ. Labor ............................ 116,542
Unemployed ................................. 5.8
Wages ...................... $1,000,825,933
Per Capita Income ................. $36,205
Prop. Value ............. $15,835,702,960
Retail Sales .............. $3,503,375,768

**Physical Features**: Central Texas county of mostly Blackland prairie, but rolling hills in west; drains to Bosque and Brazos rivers and Lake Waco, Tradinghouse Creek Reservoir abd Lake Creek Lake; heavy, loam, sandy soils.

**Economy**: Diversified manufacturing, agriculture, aerospace and education.

**History**: Tonkawas, Wichitas and Wacos in area. Anglo-American settlers arrived in the =1840s. Indians removed to Brazos reservations in 1854. County created from Milam County in 1850; named for settler, Neil McLennan Sr.

**Race/Ethnicity**: (In percent) Anglo, 57.8; Black, 15.0; Hispanic, 24.8; Asian, 1.6; Other, 3.0.

**Vital Statistics**, annual: Births, 3,398; deaths, 2,049; marriages, 1,766; divorces, 998.

**Recreation**: Texas Ranger Hall of Fame; Texas Sports Hall of Fame; Dr Pepper Museum; Cameron Park; drag boat races April and May; zoo; historic sites, homes; museums; libraries, art center; symphony; civic theater; Baylor University events; Heart o' Texas Fair in October.

**Minerals**: Sand and gravel.

**Agriculture**: Beef cattle, corn, wheat, milk/dairy, hay. Market value $183 million.

**Education**: Baylor University; McLennan Community College; Texas State Technical College.

**WACO** (129,179) county seat; aerospace/aviation, manufacturing, higher education, medical services/hospitals, government/services; riverside park, zoo.

**Hewitt** (14,118) iron works, other manufacturing; hamburger cookoff in September.

**West** (2,851) famous for Czech foods; varied manufacturing; Westfest Labor Day weekend.

Other towns include: **Axtell** (300); **Bellmead** (10,241); **Beverly Hills** (2,011); **Bruceville-Eddy** (1,771, partly in Falls County); **China Spring** (1,312); **Crawford** (742); **Elm Mott** (300).

Also, **Gholson** (1,092); **Hallsburg**
(528); **Lacy-Lakeview** (6,661); **Leroy** (347); **Lorena** (1,740); **Mart** (1,912) agricultural center, some manufacturing, museum, juvenile correction facility.

Also, **McGregor** (5,063) agriculture, manufacturing, distribution; private telephone museum; Frontier Founders Day in September; **Moody** (1,400) agriculture, commuting to Waco, Temple; library; Cotton Harvest fest in September; **Riesel** (1,018); **Robinson** (11,507); **Ross** (293); **Woodway** (8,764).

Part of **Golinda** (561, mostly in Falls County) and part of **Valley Mills** (1,223, mostly in Bosque County).

*For explanation of sources, abbreviations and symbols, see p. 238, and foldout map.*

# McMullen County

**Physical Features**: Southern county of brushy plain, sloping to Frio, Nueces rivers and tributaries, Choke Canyon Reservoir; saline clay soils.

**Economy**: Government/services, retail, agriculture, oil and gas services.

**History**: Coahuiltecans, squeezed out by Lipan Apaches and other tribes. Anglo-American settlers arrived in 1858. Sheep ranching of 1870s attracted Mexican laborers. County created from Atascosa, Bexar, Live Oak counties 1858; organized 1862, reorganized 1877; named for Nueces River pioneer-empresario John McMullen.

**Race/Ethnicity**: (In percent) Anglo, 60.5; Black, 1.0; Hispanic, 36.6; Asian, 0.5; Other, 3.5.

**Vital Statistics**, annual: Births, 7; deaths, 10; marriages, 6; divorces, 3.

**Recreation**: Hunting, wildlife viewing; lake activities, state park; Labor Day rodeo.

**Minerals**: Gas, oil, lignite coal, caliche, kaolinite.

**Agriculture**: Beef cattle. Market value $8.3 million. Wildlife enterprises important.

**TILDEN** (321), county seat; oil, gas, lignite mining, ranch center, government/services. Other towns include: **Calliham** (100).

| | | |
|---|---|---|
| Population.....................................805 | | |
| Change fm 2010.........................13.9 | | |
| Area (sq. mi.).......................1,156.8 | Jan. mean min. ...........................42.6 | Wages ..............................$6,618,389 |
| Land Area (sq. mi.) .................1,139.4 | July mean max. ...........................96.4 | Per Capita Income.................$71,840 |
| Altitude (ft.) ...........................150-642 | Civ. Labor .....................................933 | Prop. Value ...............$3,675,852,577 |
| Rainfall (in.) ...............................23.99 | Unemployed .................................1.9 | Retail Sales ...................$47,299,459 |

# Medina County

**Physical Features**: Scenic hills in north; south has fertile valleys, rolling surface; Medina River, lake.

**Economy**: Agribusiness, tourism, commuters to San Antonio.

**History**: Lipan Apaches and Comanches in area. Settled by Alsatians led by Henri Castro in 1844. Mexican immigration increased after 1900. County created and organized in 1848 from Bexar; named for river, probably for Spanish engineer Pedro Medina.

**Race/Ethnicity**: (In percent) Anglo, 45.3; Black, 2.9; Hispanic, 50.6; Asian, 0.9; Other, 2.1.

**Vital Statistics**, annual: Births, 503; deaths, 371; marriages, 280; divorces, 117.

**Recreation**: A leading deer area; scenic drives, camping, fishing, historic buildings, museum, market trail days most months.

**Minerals**: Oil and natural gas.

**Agriculture**: Cattle, corn, grains, cotton, hay, vegetables; 50,000 acres irrigated. Market value $115.5 million.

**HONDO** (9,080) county seat; flight training center, aerospace industry, agribusiness, varied manufacturing, hunting leases; hospital; prisons; wild game festival in January.

**Castroville** (2,925) farming; tourism; commuting to San Antonio; Landmark Inn, museum; St. Louis Day celebration in August.

**Devine** (4,622) commuters, shipping for truck crop-livestock; fall festival in October.

Other towns: **D'Hanis** (870), **La Coste** (1,179), **Natalia** (1,506), **Riomedina** (60), **Yancey** (209). Also, **Lytle** (2,762, mostly in Atascosa County).

| | | |
|---|---|---|
| Population ...................... 47,894 | July mean max. ................... 94.9 | |
| Change fm 2010................... 4.1 | Civ. Labor ........................ 21,261 | |
| Area (sq. mi.)................. 1,334.4 | Unemployed .......................... 5.2 | |
| Land Area (sq. mi.) ........ 1,325.4 | Wages ................... $72,078,041 | |
| Altitude (ft.) ............... 570-1,995 | Per Capita Income......... $36,259 | |
| Rainfall (in.) ...................... 30.32 | Prop. Value ........ $4,813,063,491 | |
| Jan. mean min. ................... 39.1 | Retail Sales .......... $449,445,381 | |

# Menard County

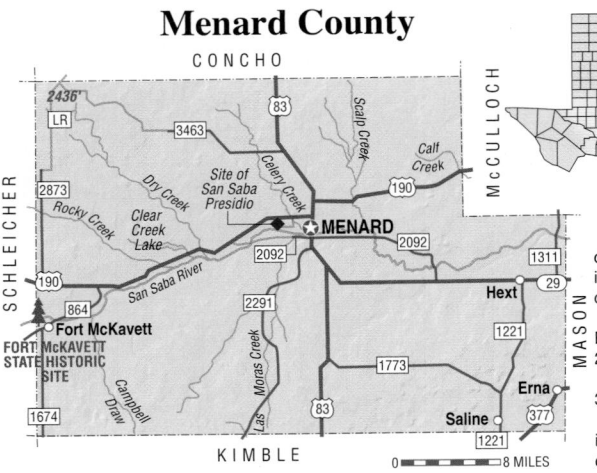

**Physical Features**: Rolling topography, draining to San Saba River and tributaries; limestone soils.

**Economy**: Agriculture, tourism, oil, gas.

**History**: Apaches, followed by Comanches in the 18th century. Mission Santa Cruz de San Sabá established in 1757. A few Anglo-American and German settlers arrived in 1840s. County created from Bexar County in 1858, organized in 1871; named for Galveston's founder, Michel B. Menard.

**Race/Ethnicity**: (In percent) Anglo, 62.6; Black, 1.4; Hispanic, 35.4; Asian, 0.2; Other, 2.1.

**Vital Statistics**, annual: Births, 21; deaths, 37; marriages, 16; divorces, 8.

**Recreation**: Hunting, fishing; historic sites, including Spanish presidio, mission, irrigation ditches; U.S. fort; railroad museum; Jim Bowie day in September.

**Minerals**: Oil, gas.

**Agriculture**: Cattle, sheep, goats, pecans, hay. Market value $9.6 million. Hunting leases, ecotourism important.

**MENARD** (1,461) county seat; agribusiness, government/services. Other towns include: **Fort McKavett** (50); **Hext** (75).

| | |
|---|---|
| Population | 2,147 |
| Change fm 2010 | – 4.2 |
| Area (sq. mi.) | 902.3 |
| Land Area (sq. mi.) | 902.0 |
| Altitude (ft.) | 1,690-2,436 |
| Rainfall (in.) | 23.32 |
| Jan. mean min. | 29.3 |
| July mean max. | 93.1 |
| Civ. Labor | 936 |
| Unemployed | 5.2 |
| Wages | $2,631,751 |
| Per Capita Income | $30,524 |
| Prop. Value | $1,079,662,680 |
| Retail Sales | $14,609,154 |

---

# Midland County

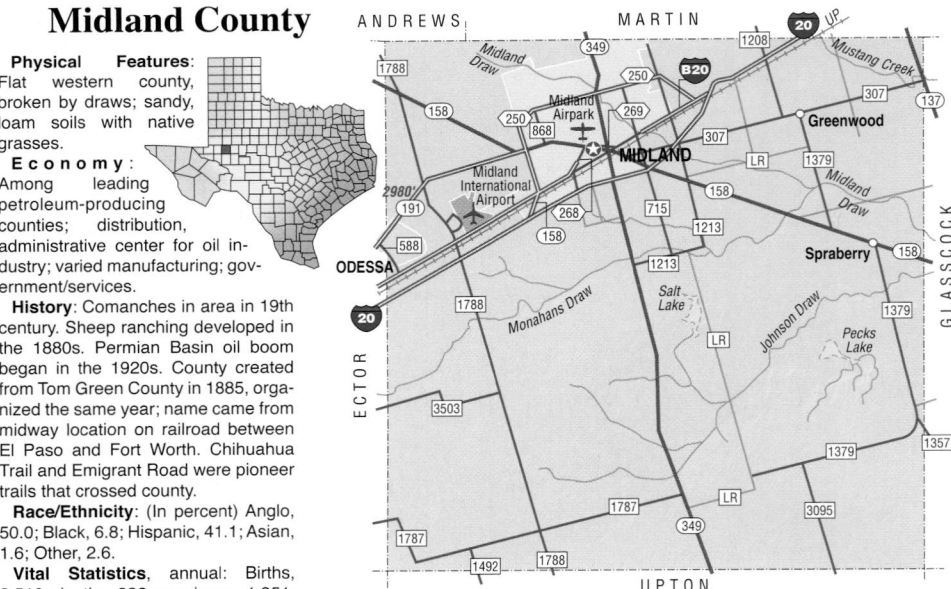

**Physical Features**: Flat western county, broken by draws; sandy, loam soils with native grasses.

**Economy**: Among leading petroleum-producing counties; distribution, administrative center for oil industry; varied manufacturing; government/services.

**History**: Comanches in area in 19th century. Sheep ranching developed in the 1880s. Permian Basin oil boom began in the 1920s. County created from Tom Green County in 1885, organized the same year; name came from midway location on railroad between El Paso and Fort Worth. Chihuahua Trail and Emigrant Road were pioneer trails that crossed county.

**Race/Ethnicity**: (In percent) Anglo, 50.0; Black, 6.8; Hispanic, 41.1; Asian, 1.6; Other, 2.6.

**Vital Statistics**, annual: Births, 2,510; deaths, 986; marriages, 1,351; divorces, 641.

**Recreation**: Permian Basin Petroleum Museum, Library, Hall of Fame; Museum of Southwest; Commemorative Air Force and Museum; community theater; metropolitan events; homes of Presidents Bush.

**Minerals**: Oil, natural gas.

**Agriculture**: Beef cattle, horses, sheep and goats; cotton, hay, pecans; some 11,000 acres irrigated. Market value $17.2 million.

**MIDLAND** (127,598) county seat; petroleum, petrochemical center; varied manufacturing; livestock sale center; hospitals; cultural activities; community college; polo club, Texas League baseball; Celebration of the Arts in May.

| | |
|---|---|
| Population | 155,830 |
| Change fm 2010 | 13.9 |
| Area (sq. mi.) | 902.1 |
| Land Area (sq. mi.) | 900.3 |
| Altitude (ft.) | 2,550-2,980 |
| Rainfall (in.) | 14.80 |
| Jan. mean min. | 31.5 |
| July mean max. | 96.2 |
| Civ. Labor | 100,153 |
| Unemployed | 2.9 |
| Wages | $1,269,992,010 |
| Per Capita Income | $87,897 |
| Prop. Value | $19,838,123,509 |
| Retail Sales | $4,137,804,077 |

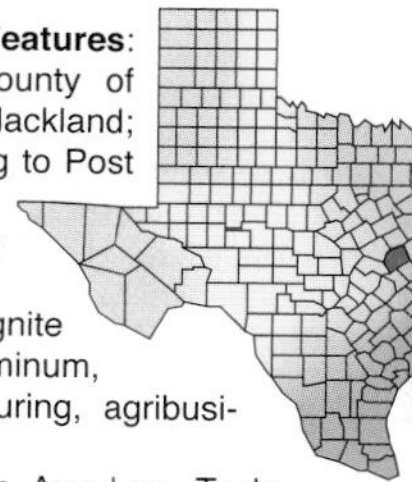

# Milam County

**Physical Features**: East central county of partly level Blackland; southeast rolling to Post Oak Belt; Brazos, Little rivers; Alcoa Lake.

**Economy**: Lignite mining, aluminum, other manufacturing, agribusiness.

**History**: Lipan Apaches, Tonkawas and Comanches in area. Mission San Francisco Xavier established 1745–1748. Anglo-American settlers arrived in 1834 and a private fort was established in 1840 at Bryant Station to help protect the settlers from Indian raids. County created in 1836 from municipality named for Ben Milam, a leader who died at the battle for San Antonio in December 1835; organized in 1837.

**Race/Ethnicity**: (In percent) Anglo, 64.1; Black, 10.1; Hispanic, 24.8; Asian, 0.6; Other, 2.5.

**Vital Statistics**, annual: Births, 312; deaths, 292; marriages, 125; divorces, 92.

**Recreation**: Fishing, hunting; historic sites include Fort Sullivan, Indian battlegrounds, mission sites; museum in old jail at Cameron, El Camino Real.

**Minerals**: Large lignite deposits, barite, limited oil and gas production.

**Agriculture**: Cattle, poultry (first in number of turkeys), corn. Market value $144.7 million.

**CAMERON** (5,349) county seat; government/services, manufacturing; hospital, library; dewberry festival in April.

**ROCKDALE** (5,325) aluminum plant, government/services; hospital,

juvenile detention center.

Other towns include: **Buckholts** (508); **Burlington** (100); **Davilla** (191); **Gause** (425); **Milano** (409); **Thorndale** (1,331) agribusiness, farming, ranching, antiques, barbecue cook-off in June.

*For explanation of sources, abbreviations and symbols, see p. 238, and foldout map.*

| Population | 24,256 |
|---|---|
| Change fm 2010 | –2.0 |
| Area (sq. mi.) | 1,021.8 |
| Land Area (sq. mi.) | 1,016.9 |
| Altitude (ft.) | 250-648 |
| Rainfall (in.) | 36.97 |
| Jan. mean min. | 33.8 |
| July mean max. | 88.7 |
| Civ. Labor | 10,994 |
| Unemployed | 6.4 |
| Wages | $59,115,153 |
| Per Capita Income | $37,727 |
| Prop. Value | $3,060,543,336 |
| Retail Sales | $179,074,621 |

*The Veterans Memorial at the airport in Midland. Photo by Robert Plocheck.*

# Mills County

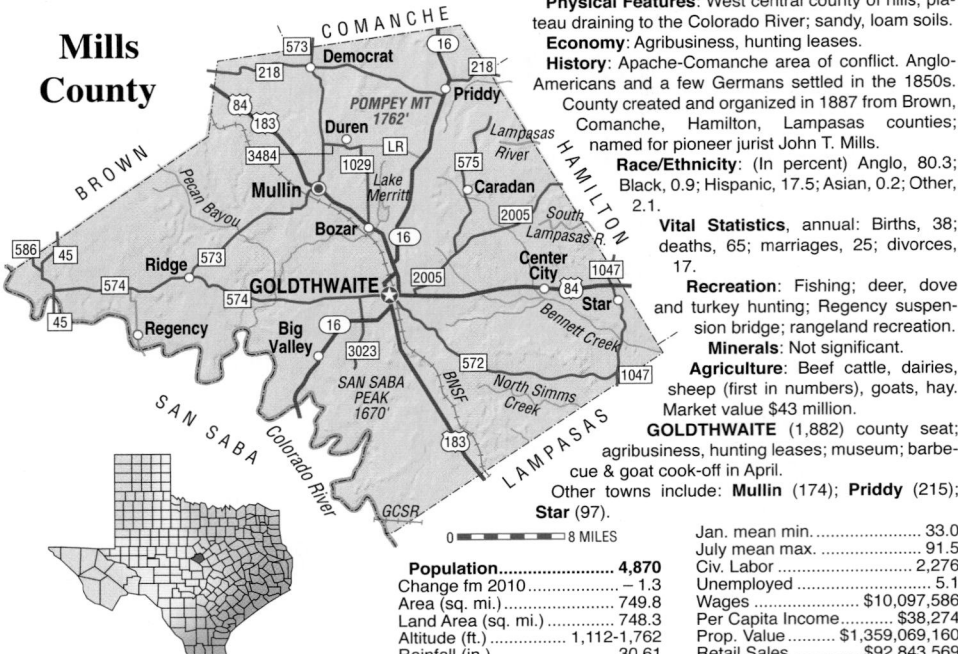

**Physical Features:** West central county of hills, plateau draining to the Colorado River; sandy, loam soils.

**Economy:** Agribusiness, hunting leases.

**History:** Apache-Comanche area of conflict. Anglo-Americans and a few Germans settled in the 1850s. County created and organized in 1887 from Brown, Comanche, Hamilton, Lampasas counties; named for pioneer jurist John T. Mills.

**Race/Ethnicity:** (In percent) Anglo, 80.3; Black, 0.9; Hispanic, 17.5; Asian, 0.2; Other, 2.1.

**Vital Statistics,** annual: Births, 38; deaths, 65; marriages, 25; divorces, 17.

**Recreation:** Fishing; deer, dove and turkey hunting; Regency suspension bridge; rangeland recreation.

**Minerals:** Not significant.

**Agriculture:** Beef cattle, dairies, sheep (first in numbers), goats, hay. Market value $43 million.

**GOLDTHWAITE** (1,882) county seat; agribusiness, hunting leases; museum; barbecue & goat cook-off in April.

Other towns include: **Mullin** (174); **Priddy** (215); **Star** (97).

| | |
|---|---|
| Population | **4,870** |
| Change fm 2010 | – 1.3 |
| Area (sq. mi.) | 749.8 |
| Land Area (sq. mi.) | 748.3 |
| Altitude (ft.) | 1,112-1,762 |
| Rainfall (in.) | 30.61 |

| | |
|---|---|
| Jan. mean min. | 33.0 |
| July mean max. | 91.5 |
| Civ. Labor | 2,276 |
| Unemployed | 5.1 |
| Wages | $10,097,586 |
| Per Capita Income | $38,274 |
| Prop. Value | $1,359,069,160 |
| Retail Sales | $92,843,569 |

# Mitchell County

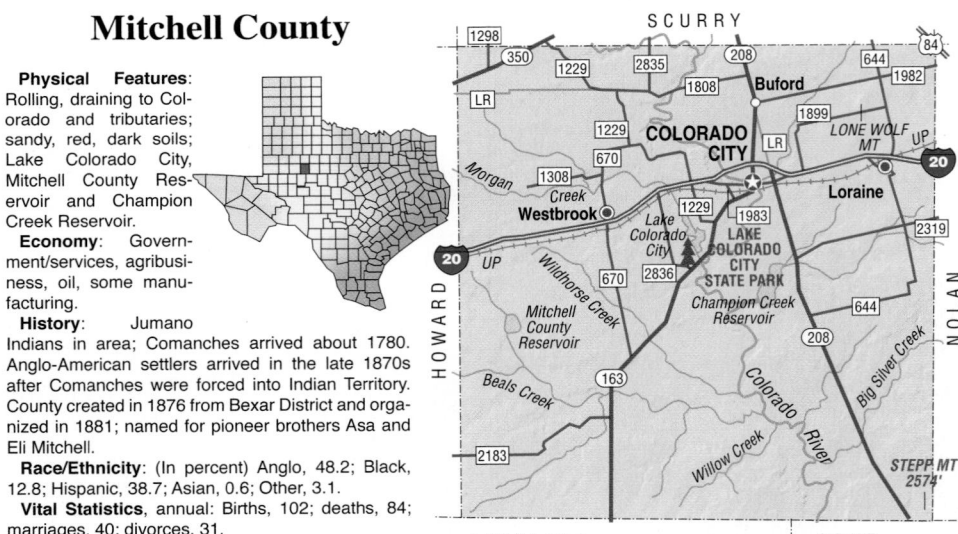

**Physical Features:** Rolling, draining to Colorado and tributaries; sandy, red, dark soils; Lake Colorado City, Mitchell County Reservoir and Champion Creek Reservoir.

**Economy:** Government/services, agribusiness, oil, some manufacturing.

**History:** Jumano Indians in area; Comanches arrived about 1780. Anglo-American settlers arrived in the late 1870s after Comanches were forced into Indian Territory. County created in 1876 from Bexar District and organized in 1881; named for pioneer brothers Asa and Eli Mitchell.

**Race/Ethnicity:** (In percent) Anglo, 48.2; Black, 12.8; Hispanic, 38.7; Asian, 0.6; Other, 3.1.

**Vital Statistics,** annual: Births, 102; deaths, 84; marriages, 40; divorces, 31.

**Recreation:** Lake activities, state park, museums, hunting, Colorado City playhouse.

**Minerals:** Oil.

**Agriculture:** Cotton principal crop, grains also produced. Cattle, sheep, goats, hogs raised. Market value $21.2 million.

**COLORADO CITY** (4,025) county seat; government/services, agriculture, oil, manufacturing; hospital; boar goat cook-off in October.

Other towns include: **Loraine** (592) and **Westbrook** (245), trade centers.

The community around **Lake Colorado City** (593).

| | |
|---|---|
| Population | 9,076 |
| Change fm 2010 | – 3.5 |
| Area (sq. mi.) | 915.9 |
| Land Area (sq. mi.) | 911.1 |
| Altitude (ft.) | 1,930-2,574 |
| Rainfall (in.) | 20.42 |

| | |
|---|---|
| Jan. mean min. | 28.3 |
| July mean max. | 95.0 |
| Civ. Labor | 3,447 |
| Unemployed | 5.8 |
| Wages | $23,000,019 |
| Per Capita Income | $30,950 |
| Prop. Value | $1,871,336,111 |
| Retail Sales | $54,150,782 |

*For explanation of sources, abbreviations and symbols, see p. 238, and foldout map.*

# Montague County

**Physical Features**: Rolling, draining to tributaries of Trinity, Red rivers; sandy loams, red, black soils; Lake Nocona, Lake Amon G. Carter.

**Economy**: Agribusiness, oil, varied manufacturing, government/services.

**History**: Kiowas and Wichitas who allied with Comanches. Anglo-American settlements developed in 1850s. County created from Cooke County 1857, organized 1858; named for pioneer Daniel Montague.

**Race/Ethnicity**: (In percent) Anglo, 86.6; Black, 0.6; Hispanic, 10.4; Asian, 0.6; Other, 2.7.

**Vital Statistics**, annual: Births, 233; deaths, 249; marriages, 160; divorces, 94.

**Recreation**: Lake activities; quail, turkey, deer hunting; scenic drives; museums; historical sites, motorcycle dirt track.

**Minerals**: Oil, rock, limestone, sand.

**Agriculture**: Beef, hay, wheat, dairies, pecans, peaches, melons. Market value $44.9 million.

**MONTAGUE** (316) county seat.

**BOWIE** (5,236) varied manufacturing, oil and gas operations; hospital; library; Jim Bowie Days in June.

**NOCONA** (3,040) athletic goods, boot manufacturing; hospital; Fun Day each May, Chisholm Trail rodeo in September.

Other towns include: **Forestburg** (50); **Ringgold** (100); **Saint Jo** (1,024) ranching, oil and gas, machine shops, rodeo in August; **Sunset** (504).

| | |
|---|---|
| Population | 19,416 |
| Change fm 2010 | – 1.5 |
| Area (sq. mi.) | 938.3 |
| Land Area (sq. mi.) | 930.9 |
| Altitude (ft.) | 715-1,318 |
| Rainfall (in.) | 35.06 |
| Jan. mean min. | 29.2 |
| July mean max. | 93.3 |
| Civ. Labor | 11,694 |
| Unemployed | 3.8 |

| | |
|---|---|
| Wages | $55,122,077 |
| Per Capita Income | $50,047 |
| Prop. Value | $3,341,962,030 |
| Retail Sales | $200,015,276 |

*For explanation of sources, abbreviations and symbols, see p. 238, and foldout map.*

*Texas proud, Nocona, Montague County. Photo by Robert Plocheck.*

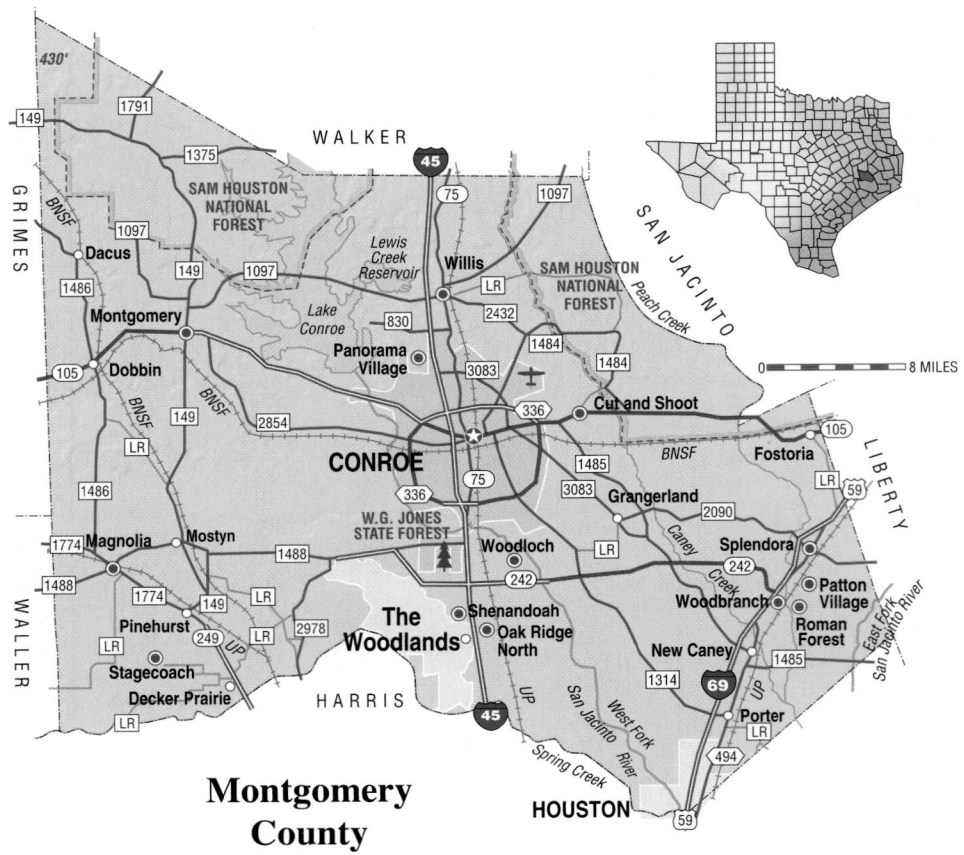

# Montgomery County

**Physical Features**: Rolling, half of the area is timbered; Sam Houston National Forest; loam, sandy, alluvial soils; Lake Conroe and Lewis Creek Reservoir.

**Economy**: Varied manufacturing, oil production, medical research, government/services, many residents work in Houston.

**History**: Orcoquisac and Bidais tribes, removed from the area by the 1850s. Anglo-Americans arrived in the 1820s as part of Austin's colony. County created and organized in 1837 from Washington County; named for Richard Montgomery, American Revolution general.

**Race/Ethnicity**: (In percent) Anglo, 69.4; Black, 4.7; Hispanic, 21.9; Asian, 2.6; Other, 2.8.

**Vital Statistics**, annual: Births, 6,382; deaths, 2,994; marriages, 3,176; divorces, 1,946.

**Recreation**: Hunting, fishing; Lake Conroe activities; national and state forests; hiking, boating, horseback riding; historic sites.

**Minerals**: Natural gas.

**Agriculture**: Greenhouse crops, hay, beef cattle, horses. Market value $23.8 million. Timber important.

**CONROE** (63,322) county seat; retail/wholesale center, government/services, manufacturing, commuters to Houston; hospitals, community college, museum; Cajun catfish festival in October.

**The Woodlands** (99,040) commuters to Houston, energy, tourism; college branches, hospitals, museums, parks, concerts, festivals at Mitchell Pavilion.

Other towns include: **Cut and Shoot** (1,075); **Dobbin** (310); **Grangerland** (300); **Magnolia** (1,584) government/services, drilling technology, construction, depot museum, Love Bug Fest in June.

Also, **Montgomery** (682) commuters to Houston and Conroe, antiques stores, pioneer museum, historic homes tour in April; **New Caney** (6,800); **Oak Ridge North** (3,184); **Panorama Village** (2,263); **Patton Village** (1,585).

Also, **Pinehurst** (4,922); **Porter** (4,200); **Porter Heights** (1,754); **Roman Forest** (1,781); **Shenandoah** (2,681); **Splendora** (1,624); **Stagecoach** (569); **Willis** (5,964) commuters to Conroe and Houston; **Woodbranch** (1,357); **Woodloch** (218).

Also, part [4,047] of **Houston [Kingwood]**, hospital.

| | |
|---|---|
| Population | 518,947 |
| Change fm 2010 | 13.9 |
| Area (sq. mi.) | 1,076.9 |
| Land Area (sq. mi.) | 1,041.9 |
| Altitude (ft.) | 50-430 |
| Rainfall (in.) | 48.77 |
| Jan. mean min. | 40.4 |
| July mean max. | 93.5 |
| Civ. Labor | 254,405 |
| Unemployed | 4.8 |
| Wages | $1,769,306,796 |
| Per Capita Income | $53,192 |
| Prop. Value | $42,691,931,564 |
| Retail Sales | $9,136,831,855 |

*For explanation of sources, abbreviations and symbols, see p. 238, and foldout map.*

# Moore County

**Physical Features**: Flat to rolling, broken by creeks; sandy loams; Lake Meredith.

**Economy**: Varied agribusiness, petroleum, natural gas.

**History**: Comanches, removed to Indian Territory in 1874–1875; ranching began soon afterward. Farming developed after 1910. Oil boom in the 1920s. County created in 1876 from Bexar District; organized in 1892; named for Republic of Texas navy commander E.W. Moore.

**Race/Ethnicity**: (In percent) Anglo, 35.9; Black, 2.7; Hispanic, 52.9; Asian, 7.8; Other, 2.9.

**Vital Statistics**, annual: Births, 414; deaths, 127; marriages, 172; divorces, 93.

**Recreation**: Lake Meredith activities; pheasant, deer, quail hunting; historical museum; arts center; free overnight RV park; Dogie Days in June.

**Minerals**: Oil and gas.

**Agriculture**: Fed beef, corn, wheat, stocker cattle, sorghum, cotton, soybeans, sunflowers. Market value $605 million. Irrigation of 122,000 acres.

**DUMAS** (14,926) county seat; tourism, retail trade, varied agribusiness; hospital, hospice, retirement complex.

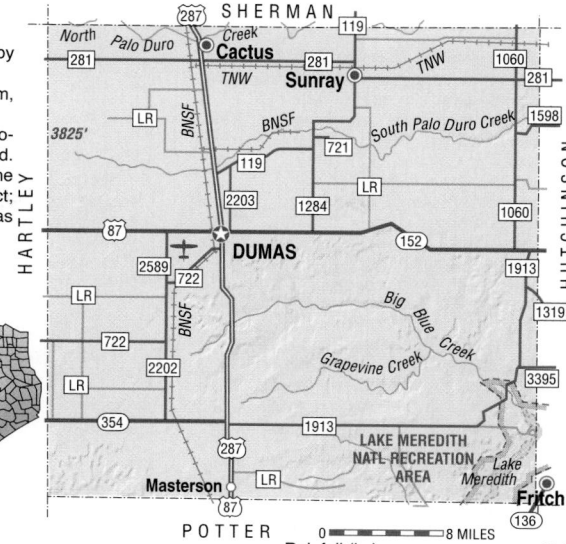

Other towns include: **Cactus** (3,169), **Sunray** (1,916). Small part of **Fritch**.

| | |
|---|---|
| Population | **22,148** |
| Change fm 2010 | 1.1 |
| Area (sq. mi.) | 909.6 |
| Land Area (sq. mi.) | 899.7 |
| Altitude (ft.) | 2,915-3,825 |
| Rainfall (in.) | 18.37 |
| Jan. mean min. | 22.1 |
| July mean max. | 91.6 |
| Civ. Labor | 11,985 |
| Unemployed | 3.9 |
| Wages | $102,310,358 |
| Per Capita Income | $35,924 |
| Prop. Value | $2,930,351,849 |
| Retail Sales | $431,900,481 |

# Morris County

**Physical Features**: East Texas county of forested hills; drains to streams, Lake O' the Pines, Ellison Creek Reservoir, Barnes Creek Reservoir.

**Economy**: Steel manufacturing, agriculture, timber, government/services.

**History**: Caddo Indians until 1790s. Kickapoo and other tribes in area 1820s-30s. Anglo-American settlement began in mid-1830s. Antebellum slaveholding area. County named for legislator-jurist W.W. Morris; created from Titus County and organized in 1875.

**Race/Ethnicity**: (In percent) Anglo, 65.8; Black, 22.8; Hispanic, 8.8; Asian, 0.5; Other, 3.1.

**Vital Statistics**, annual: Births, 165; deaths, 171; marriages, 85; divorces, 59.

**Recreation**: Activities on Lake O' the Pines, small lakes; fishing, hunting; state park.

**Minerals**: Iron ore.

**Agriculture**: Beef cattle, broiler production, hay. Market value $46.9 million. Timber industry significant.

**DAINGERFIELD** (2,608) county seat; varied manufacturing; library, museum, city park, historic theater; Northeast Texas Community College; Daingerfield Days in October.

Other towns include: **Cason** (173); **Lone Star** (1,657) oil-field equipment manufactured, catfish farming, Starfest in September; **Naples** (1,431) trailer manufacturing, livestock, watermelon festival in July; **Omaha** (1,054), retail center, government/services, commuters.

| | |
|---|---|
| Population | **12,743** |
| Change fm 2010 | – 1.5 |
| Area (sq. mi.) | 258.7 |
| Land Area (sq. mi.) | 252.0 |
| Altitude (ft.) | 228-614 |
| Rainfall (in.) | 46.79 |
| Jan. mean min. | 35.1 |
| July mean max. | 94.1 |
| Civ. Labor | 6,322 |
| Unemployed | 7.2 |
| Wages | $56,022,383 |
| Per Capita Income | $37,281 |
| Prop. Value | $1,061,929,820 |
| Retail Sales | $72,990,397 |

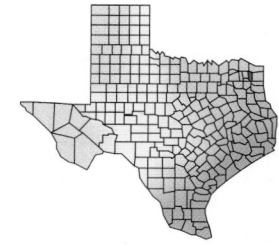

*For explanation of sources, abbreviations and symbols, see p. 238, and foldout map.*

# Motley County

**Physical Features**: Western county just below Caprock; rough terrain, broken by Pease tributaries; sandy to red clay soils.

**Economy**: Agriculture, government/services, light manufacturing.

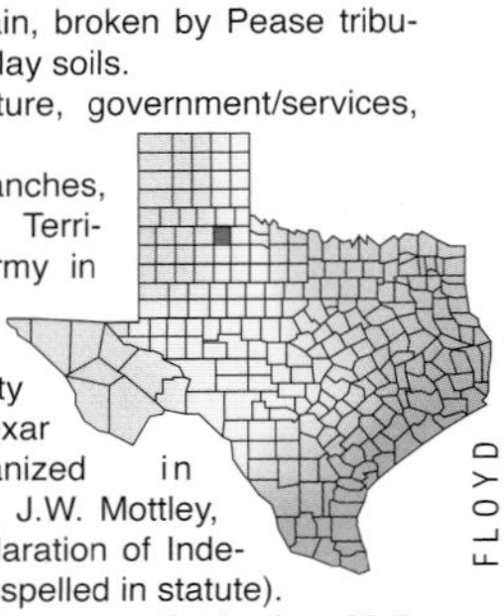

**History**: Comanches, removed to Indian Territory by the U.S. Army in 1874–1875. Ranching began in the late 1870s. County created out of Bexar District in 1876; organized in 1891; named for Dr. J.W. Mottley, signer of Texas Declaration of Independence (name misspelled in statute).

**Race/Ethnicity**: (In percent) Anglo, 80.7; Black, 2.1; Hispanic, 15.7; Asian, 0.8; Other, 1.7.

**Vital Statistics**, annual: Births, 11; deaths, 16; marriages, 4; divorces, 4.

**Recreation**: Quail, dove, turkey, deer, feral hog hunting; Matador Ranch headquarters; spring-fed pool at Roaring Springs; Motley-Dickens settlers reunion in August at Roaring Springs.

**Minerals**: Minimal.

**Agriculture**: Beef cattle, cotton, wheat, sorghum, hay. Some irrigation. Market value $12.8 million. Hunting leases important.

**MATADOR** (592) county seat; ranching, farming, government/services; museum, historic oil-derrick gas station; motorcycles race in April.

Other towns include: **Flomot** (181)

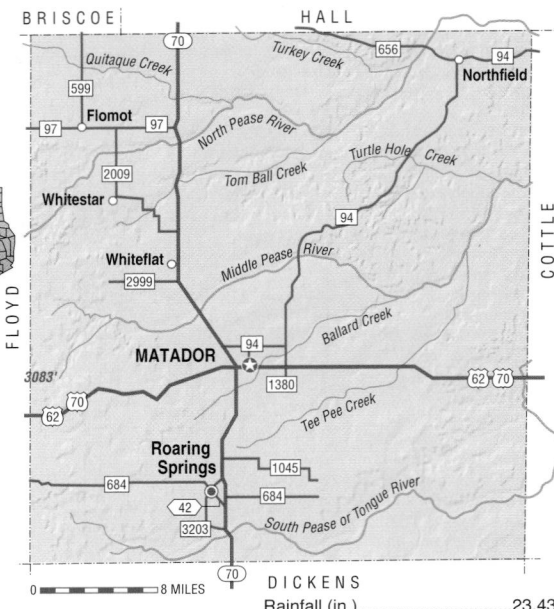

bluegrass festival in May, and **Roaring Springs** (222).

| | |
|---|---:|
| Population | 1,153 |
| Change fm 2010 | – 4.7 |
| Area (sq. mi.) | 989.8 |
| Land Area (sq. mi.) | 989.6 |
| Altitude (ft.) | 1,800-3,083 |

| | |
|---|---:|
| Rainfall (in.) | 23.43 |
| Jan. mean min. | 29.6 |
| July mean max. | 94.2 |
| Civ. Labor | 557 |
| Unemployed | 4.3 |
| Wages | $1,993,836 |
| Per Capita Income | $38,574 |
| Prop. Value | $3238,205,530 |
| Retail Sales | $8,185,558 |

*Redbuds in bloom in Nacogdoches County. Photo by Ron Billings/Texas A&M Forest Service.*

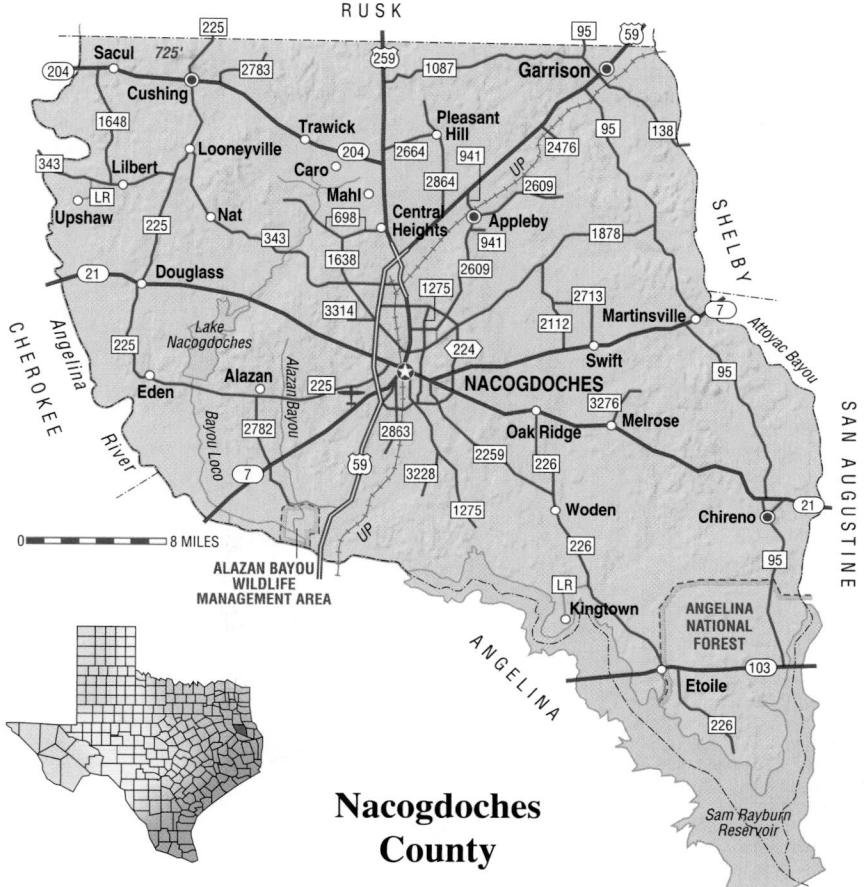

RUSK

SHELBY

CHEROKEE

SAN AUGUSTINE

ANGELINA

Attoyac Bayou

Angelina River

Bayou Loco

Alazan Bayou

0 ━━━━━ 8 MILES

**ALAZAN BAYOU
WILDLIFE
MANAGEMENT AREA**

ANGELINA
NATIONAL
FOREST

Sam Rayburn
Reservoir

Sacul   725'
Cushing
Garrison
Trawick
Pleasant
Hill
Looneyville
Caro
Lilbert
Upshaw
Nat
Mahl
Central
Heights
Appleby
Douglass
Lake
Nacogdoches
Martinsville
Swift
Eden
Alazan
**NACOGDOCHES**
Melrose
Oak Ridge
Woden
Chireno
Kingtown
Etoile

# Nacogdoches
County

**Physical Features**: East Texas county on divide between streams; hilly; two-thirds forested; red, gray, sandy soils; Sam Rayburn Reservoir, Lake Nacogdoches.

**Economy**: Agribusiness, timber, manufacturing, education, and tourism.

**History**: Caddo tribes, joined by displaced Cherokees in the 1820s. Indian tribes moved west of the Brazos River by 1840. Spanish missions were es-tablished in 1716.

Spanish settlers arrived in the mid-1700s. Anglo-Americans arrived in the 1820s. An original county of the Republic in 1836, organized in 1837. Name comes from Caddo tribe that was in the area.

**Race/Ethnicity**: (In percent) Anglo, 60.4; Black, 18.4; Hispanic, 18.5; Asian, 1.5; Other, 2.6.

**Vital Statistics**, annual: Births, 897; deaths, 579; marriages, 570; divorces, 75.

**Recreation**: Lake, river activities; Stephen F. Austin State University events; Angelina National Forest; historic sites; tourist attractions include the Old Stone Fort, pioneer homes, museums.

Also, Millard's Crossing Historic Village, Piney Woods Native Plant Center; Azalea Trail in March, Blueberry Festival in June.

**Minerals**: First Texas oil discovered here, 1866; gas, oil, clay, stone.

**Agriculture**: A leading poultry-producing county (third in number of broilers); beef cattle raised. Market value $322.3 million. Also, Substantial timber sold.

**NACOGDOCHES** (33,103) county seat; varied manufacturing, lumber mills, wood products, trade center; hospitals; Stephen F. Austin State University; Nine Flags Festival in November/December.

Other towns include: **Appleby** (482), **Chireno** (382), **Cushing** (606), **Douglass** (380), **Etoile** (700), **Garrison** (880), **Martinsville** (350), **Sacul** (150), **Woden** (400).

| Population | 65,301 |
|---|---|
| Change fm 2010 | 1.2 |
| Area (sq. mi.) | 981.2 |
| Land Area (sq. mi.) | 946.5 |
| Altitude (ft.) | 164-725 |
| Rainfall (in.) | 49.28 |
| Jan. mean min. | 35.8 |
| July mean max. | 93.2 |
| Civ. Labor | 30,644 |
| Unemployed | 6.0 |
| Wages | $180,428,519 |
| Per Capita Income | $31,592 |
| Prop. Value | $5,082,902,610 |
| Retail Sales | $883,971,428 |

*For explanation of sources, abbreviations and symbols, see p. 238, and foldout map.*

# Navarro County

ELLIS

Trinity River

HENDERSON

Rice
Chatfield
Bazette
Emhouse
Roane
Black Hills
Powell
Kerens
Frost
CORSICANA
Samaria
Blooming Grove
Barry
Goodlow
Lake Halbert
Dresden
Rural Shade
Oak Valley
Mustang
Mildred
Brushie Prairie
Eureka
Emmett
Silver City
Corbet
Retreat
Navarro
Pelham
Angus
Navarro Mills Lake
Purdon
Richland-Chambers Reservoir
Navarro Mills
Cheneyboro
Spring Hill
Richland Creek
Winkler
Dawson
Pursley
Richland
HILL
LIMESTONE
Union High
Streetman
FREESTONE

0 ————— 8 MI

**Physical Features:** Level Blackland, some rolling; drains to creeks, Trinity River; Navarro Mills Lake, Richland-Chambers Reservoir, Lake Halbert.

**Economy:** Diversified manufacturing, agribusinesses, oil-field operations, distribution.

**History:** Kickapoo and Comanche area. Anglo-Americans settled in late 1830s. Antebellum slaveholding area. County created from Robertson County, organized in 1846; named for Republic of Texas leader José Antonio Navarro.

**Race/Ethnicity:** (In percent) Anglo, 58.4; Black, 14.0; Hispanic, 25.2; Asian, 0.8; Other, 3.5.

**Vital Statistics,** annual: Births, 706; deaths, 492; marriages, 392; divorces, 213.

**Recreation:** Lake activities; Pioneer Village; historic buildings; youth exposition, Derrick Days in April.

**Minerals:** Longest continuous Texas oil flow; more than 200 million barrels produced since 1895; natural gas, sand and gravel also produced.

**Agriculture:** Beef cattle, cotton, sorghum, corn, wheat, sunflowers, herbs, horses, dairies. Market value $66.4 million.

**CORSICANA** (24,769) county seat; major distribution center, pecans, candy, fruitcakes; varied manufacturing; agribusiness; hospital; Navarro College; Texas Youth Commission facility.

Other towns include: **Angus** (433); **Barry** (249); **Blooming Grove** (836); **Chatfield** (40); **Dawson** (825); **Emhouse** (138); **Eureka** (317); **Frost** (675); **Goodlow** (201).

Also, **Kerens** (1,607) commuting, nature tourism, Cotton Harvest Festival in October; **Mildred** (388); **Mustang** (22); **Navarro** (215); **Oak Valley** (372); **Powell** (143); **Purdon** (133); **Retreat** (402); **Rice** (965); **Richland** (278).

| | |
|---|---|
| **Population** | **48,195** |
| Change fm 2010 | 1.0 |
| Area (sq. mi.) | 1,085.9 |
| Land Area (sq. mi.) | 1,009.6 |
| Altitude (ft.) | 250-623 |
| Rainfall (in.) | 39.78 |
| Jan. mean min. | 34.7 |
| July mean max. | 94.1 |
| Civ. Labor | 22,526 |
| Unemployed | 6.0 |
| Wages | $140,445,459 |
| Per Capita Income | $36,985 |
| Prop. Value | $3,701,531,754 |
| Retail Sales | $615,383,653 |

*For explanation of sources, symbols and abbreviations, see p. xxx and foldout map.*

*The easternmost point of all highways in the state is on Texas 63 in Newton County. Photo by Robert Plocheck.*

# Newton County

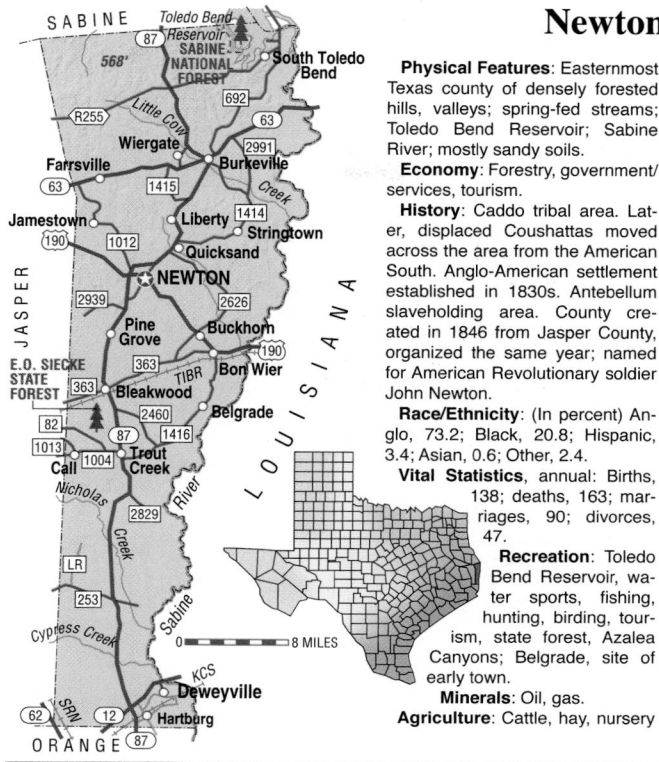

**Physical Features**: Easternmost Texas county of densely forested hills, valleys; spring-fed streams; Toledo Bend Reservoir; Sabine River; mostly sandy soils.

**Economy**: Forestry, government/services, tourism.

**History**: Caddo tribal area. Later, displaced Coushattas moved across the area from the American South. Anglo-American settlement established in 1830s. Antebellum slaveholding area. County created in 1846 from Jasper County, organized the same year; named for American Revolutionary soldier John Newton.

**Race/Ethnicity**: (In percent) Anglo, 73.2; Black, 20.8; Hispanic, 3.4; Asian, 0.6; Other, 2.4.

**Vital Statistics**, annual: Births, 138; deaths, 163; marriages, 90; divorces, 47.

**Recreation**: Toledo Bend Reservoir, water sports, fishing, hunting, birding, tourism, state forest, Azalea Canyons; Belgrade, site of early town.

**Minerals**: Oil, gas.

**Agriculture**: Cattle, hay, nursery crops, vegetables, goats, hogs. Market value $2.9 million. Hunting leases. Major forestry area.

**NEWTON** (2,449) county seat; lumber manufacturing, plywood mill, private prison unit, tourist center; genealogical library, museum; Wild Azalea festival in March.

**Deweyville** (1,035) power plant, commercial center for forestry, farming area.

Other towns include: **Bon Wier** (375); **Burkeville** (603); **Call** (493); **South Toledo Bend** (518); **Wiergate** (350).

| | |
|---|---|
| Population | **14,138** |
| Change fm 2010 | – 2.1 |
| Area (sq. mi.) | 939.7 |
| Land Area (sq. mi.) | 933.7 |
| Altitude (ft.) | 10-568 |
| Rainfall (in.) | 54.92 |
| Jan. mean min. | 36.5 |
| July mean max. | 93.1 |
| Civ. Labor | 5,294 |
| Unemployed | 9.7 |
| Wages | $11,954,111 |
| Per Capita Income | $30,049 |
| Prop. Value | $2,218,770,879 |
| Retail Sales | $39,776,198 |

# Nolan County

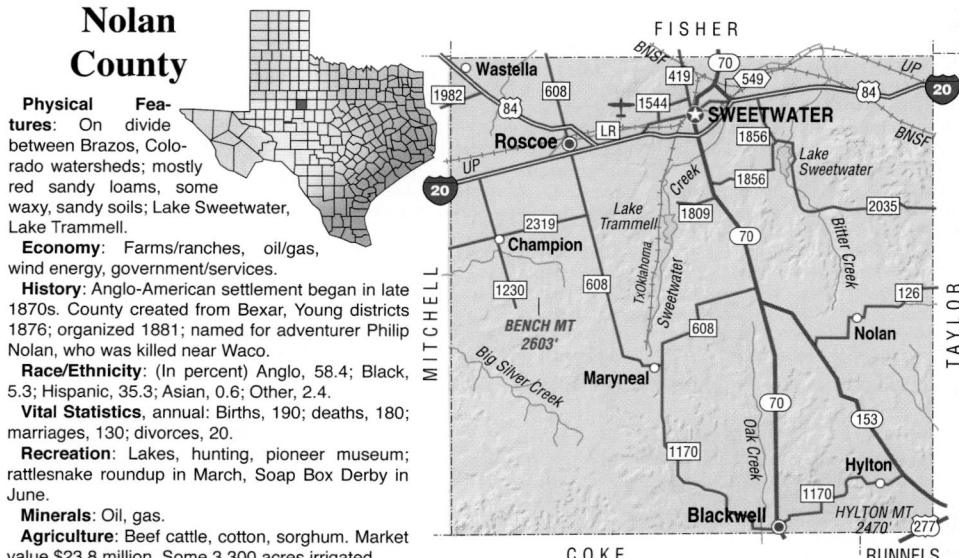

**Physical Features**: On divide between Brazos, Colorado watersheds; mostly red sandy loams, some waxy, sandy soils; Lake Sweetwater, Lake Trammell.

**Economy**: Farms/ranches, oil/gas, wind energy, government/services.

**History**: Anglo-American settlement began in late 1870s. County created from Bexar, Young districts 1876; organized 1881; named for adventurer Philip Nolan, who was killed near Waco.

**Race/Ethnicity**: (In percent) Anglo, 58.4; Black, 5.3; Hispanic, 35.3; Asian, 0.6; Other, 2.4.

**Vital Statistics**, annual: Births, 190; deaths, 180; marriages, 130; divorces, 20.

**Recreation**: Lakes, hunting, pioneer museum; rattlesnake roundup in March, Soap Box Derby in June.

**Minerals**: Oil, gas.

**Agriculture**: Beef cattle, cotton, sorghum. Market value $23.8 million. Some 3,300 acres irrigated.

**SWEETWATER** (10,652) county seat; wind energy, varied manufacturing, gypsum; hospital; Texas State Technical College; WWII museum.

Other towns include: **Blackwell** (310, partly in Coke County), Oak Creek Reservoir to south; **Maryneal** (50); **Nolan** (60); **Roscoe** (1,304).

| | |
|---|---|
| Population | 15,093 |
| Change fm 2010 | – 0.8 |
| Area (sq. mi.) | 914.0 |
| Land Area (sq. mi.) | 912.0 |
| Altitude (ft.) | 1,896-2,603 |
| Rainfall (in.) | 22.42 |
| Jan. mean min. | 29.0 |
| July mean max. | 93.9 |
| Civ. Labor | 7,728 |
| Unemployed | 4.4 |
| Wages | $54,917,400 |
| Per Capita Income | $38,072 |
| Prop. Value | $3,202,220,370 |
| Retail Sales | $267,886,012 |

# Nueces County

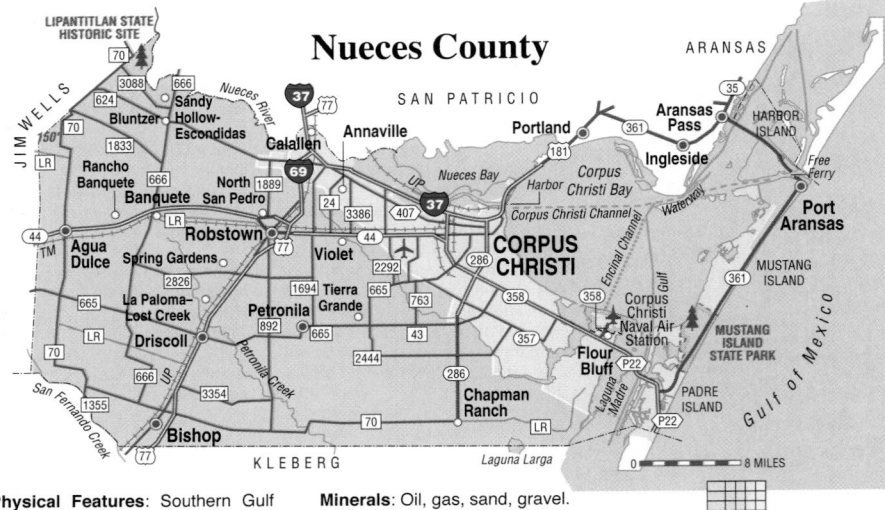

**Physical Features**: Southern Gulf Coast county; flat, rich soils, broken by bays, Nueces River, Petronila Creek; includes Mustang Island, north tip of Padre Island.

**Economy**: Petroleum processing, deepwater port facility, agriculture, tourism.

**History**: Coahuiltecan, Karankawa and other tribes who succumbed to disease or fled by the 1840s. Spanish settlers arrived in the 1760s. Settlers from Ireland arrived around 1830. County name is Spanish for nuts; county named for river; created and organized in 1846 out of San Patricio County.

**Race/Ethnicity**: (In percent) Anglo, 31.4; Black, 4.4; Hispanic, 62.0; Asian, 1.9; Other, 2.3.

**Vital Statistics**, annual: Births, 4,810; deaths, 2,797; marriages, 2,264; divorces, 1,239.

**Recreation**: Major resort area; beaches, fishing, water sports, birding; Padre Island National Seashore, Mustang Island State Park, Lipantitlan State Historic Site; Art Museum of South Texas, Corpus Christi Museum of Science and History; Texas State Aquarium; professional baseball, hockey; greyhound race track.

**Minerals**: Oil, gas, sand, gravel.

**Agriculture**: Grain sorghum (second in acreage), cotton, cattle, wheat, hay, nurseries/turfgrass. Market value $84.9 million.

**CORPUS CHRISTI** (317,004) county seat; seaport, naval bases, varied manufacturing, petroleum processing, tourism; hospitals; museums; Army depot; Texas A&M University-Corpus Christi, Del Mar College; replica of Columbus' ship on display, USS Lexington museum, Harbor Lights; Buccaneer Days in late April.

**Port Aransas** (3,772) deepwater port, tourism, marine research, Coast Guard base, fishing industry; University of Texas Marine Science Institute; museum, beach; Celebration of Whooping Cranes in February; Texas Sand Fest in April.

**Robstown** (11,730) agriculture, transportation, tourism, petroleum processing; regional fairgrounds; Cottonfest in October, Fiesta Mexicana in March.

Other towns include: **Agua Dulce** (830); **Banquete** (762); **Bishop** (3,179) petrochemicals, agriculture, pharmaceuticals, plastics, nature trail, Old Tyme Faire in April; **Chapman Ranch** (200); **Driscoll** (753); **La**

**Paloma-Lost Creek** (407); **North San Pedro** (906); **Petronila** (114); **Rancho Banquete** (426); **Sandy Hollow-Escondidas** (308); **Spring Gardens** (592); **Tierra Grande** (421), and **Tierra Verde** (295).

**Annaville, Calallen** and **Flour Bluff** are now part of Corpus Christi.

| | |
|---|---|
| **Population** | **356,221** |
| Change fm 2010 | 4.7 |
| Area (sq. mi.) | 1,165,6 |
| Land Area (sq. mi.) | 835.5 |
| Altitude (ft.) | sea level-150 |
| Rainfall (in.) | 32.49 |
| Jan. mean min. | 46.6 |
| July mean max. | 93.1 |
| Civ. Labor | 179,832 |
| Unemployed | 5.2 |
| Wages | $1,687,688,709 |
| Per Capita Income | $42,151 |
| Prop. Value | $26,519,426,985 |
| Retail Sales | $5,293,233,871 |

*The Corpus Christi skyline. Photo by Robert Plocheck.*

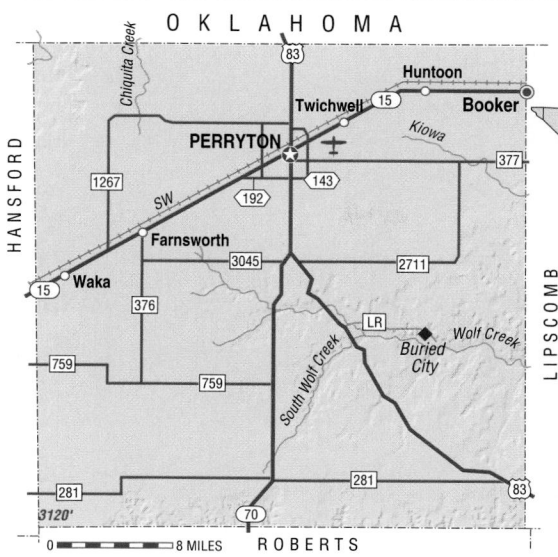

# Ochiltree County

**Physical Features**: Panhandle county bordering Oklahoma; level, broken by creeks; deep loam, clay soils.

**Economy**: Oil/gas, agribusiness, center of large feedlot and swine operations.

**History**: Apaches, pushed out by Comanches in the late 1700s. Comanches removed to Indian Territory in 1874–1875. Ranching developed in the 1880s; farming began after 1900. Created from Bexar District in 1876 and organized in 1889; named for Republic of Texas leader W.B. Ochiltree.

**Race/Ethnicity**: (In percent) Anglo, 46.4; Black, 0.9; Hispanic, 51.2; Asian, 0.7; Other, 2.7.

**Vital Statistics**, annual: Births, 168; deaths, 92; marriages, 93; divorces, 23.

**Recreation**: Wolf Creek park; Museum of the Plains; Prehistoric settlement site of "Buried City"; pheasant hunting, also deer and dove; Wheatheart of the Nation celebration in August.

**Minerals**: Oil, natural gas, caliche.

**Agriculture**: Cattle, swine, wheat (second in acreage), corn, sorghum, cotton; some 50,000 acres irrigated. Market value $424.6 million.

**PERRYTON** (9,349) county seat; oil/gas, cattle feeding, grain center; hospital; college.

Other towns include: **Farnsworth** (130); **Waka** (65). Also, **Booker** (1,595, mostly in Lipscomb County).

| | |
|---|---|
| Population | 10,758 |
| Change fm 2010 | 5.2 |
| Area (sq. mi.) | 918.1 |
| Land Area (sq. mi.) | 917.6 |
| Altitude (ft.) | 2,550-3,120 |
| Rainfall (in.) | 22.10 |
| Jan. mean min. | 19.0 |
| July mean max. | 92.4 |
| Civ. Labor | 6,633 |
| Unemployed | 2.9 |
| Wages | $61,534,727 |
| Per Capita Income | $54,671 |
| Prop. Value | $2,109,913,059 |
| Retail Sales | $138,385,860 |

*For explanation of sources, symbols and abbreviations, see p. 238, and foldout map.*

# Oldham County

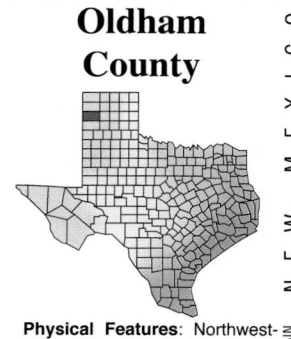

**Physical Features**: Northwestern Panhandle county; level, broken by Canadian River and tributaries.

**Economy**: Agriculture, wind energy, sand and gravel.

**History**: Apaches; followed later by Comanches, Kiowas. U.S. Army removed Indians in 1875. Anglo ranchers and Spanish pastores (sheep men) from New Mexico were in area in 1870s. County created 1876 from Bexar District; organized 1880; named for editor-Confederate senator W.S. Oldham.

**Race/Ethnicity**: (In percent) Anglo, 78.8; Black, 3.7; Hispanic, 14.9; Asian, 1.0; Other, 2.5.

**Vital Statistics**, annual: Births, 18; deaths, 18; marriages, 17; divorces, 2.

**Recreation**: Old Tascosa, Cal Far-ley's Boys Ranch, Boot Hill Cemetery, museums; midway point on old Route 66; County Roundup in August, Boys Ranch rodeo Labor Day weekend.

**Minerals**: Sand and gravel, oil, natural gas, stone.

**Agriculture**: Beef cattle; crops include wheat, grain sorghum. Market value $113 million.

**VEGA** (902) county seat; ranch trade center; museums.

Other towns include: **Adrian** (159); **Wildorado** (210). Also, Cal Farley's **Boys Ranch** (290).

| | |
|---|---|
| Population | 2,070 |
| Change fm 2010 | 0.9 |
| Area (sq. mi.) | 1,501.4 |
| Land Area (sq. mi.) | 1,500.5 |
| Altitude (ft.) | 3,140-4,360 |
| Rainfall (in.) | 19.16 |
| Jan. mean min. | 20.7 |
| July mean max. | 92.3 |
| Civ. Labor | 1,112 |
| Unemployed | 4.0 |
| Wages | $9,474,066 |
| Per Capita Income | $52,776 |
| Prop. Value | $1,006,179,097 |
| Retail Sales | $13,043,696 |

# Orange County

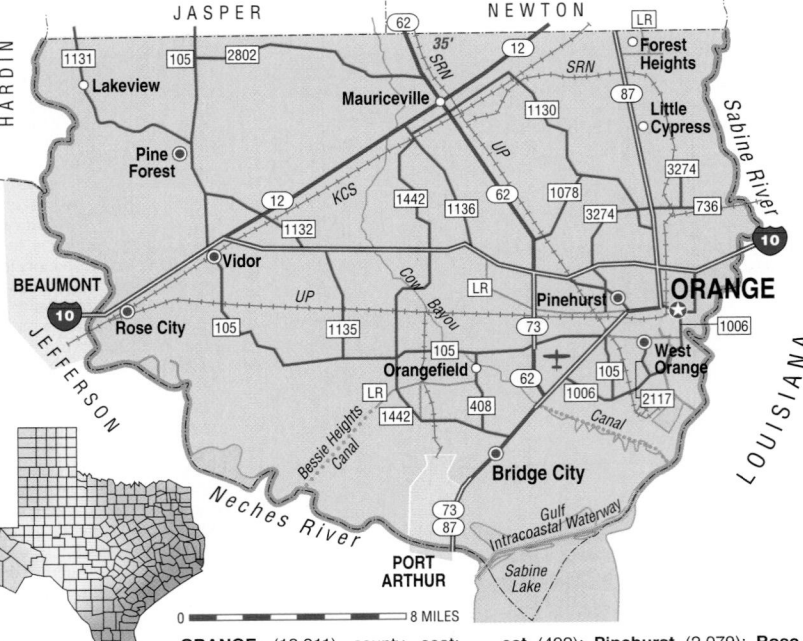

**Physical Features**: In southeastern corner of the state; bounded by Sabine, Neches rivers, Sabine Lake; coastal soils; two-thirds timbered.

**Economy**: Petrochemicals, varied manufacturing, agri-business, tourism, lumber processing.

**History**: Atakapan Indian area. French traders in area by 1720. Anglo-American settlement began in 1820s. County created from Jefferson County in 1852, organized the same year; named for early orange grove.

**Race/Ethnicity**: (In percent) Anglo, 82.0; Black, 8.6; Hispanic, 6.7; Asian, 1.4; Other, 2.2.

**Vital Statistics**, annual: Births, 1,103; deaths, 945; marriages, 649; divorces, 201.

**Recreation**: Fishing, hunting, water sports, birding, county park, museums; historical homes, crawfish and crab festivals in spring.

**Minerals**: Salt, oil, gas, clays, sand and gravel.

**Agriculture**: Cattle, hay, Christmas trees and rice are top revenue sources; honey a significant revenue producer; fruits, berries, vegetables. Also, crawfishing. Market value $4.3 million. Hunting leases. Timber important.

**ORANGE** (18,911) county seat; seaport, petrochemical plants, varied manufacturing, food and timber processing shipping; hospital, theater, museums; Lamar State College-Orange; Mardi Gras/gumbo festival in February.

**Bridge City** (7,941) varied manufacturing, ship repair yard, steel fabrication, fish farming, government/services; library; tall bridge and newer suspension bridge over Neches; stop for Monarch butterfly in fall during its migration to Mexico.

**Vidor** (10,746) steel processing, railroad-car refinishing; library; barbecue festival in April.

Other towns include: **Mauriceville** (3,384); **Orangefield** (725); **Pine Forest** (492); **Pinehurst** (2,079); **Rose City** (506); **West Orange** (3,454).

| Population | 83,433 |
|---|---|
| Change fm 2010 | 2.0 |
| Area (sq. mi.) | 379.5 |
| Land Area (sq. mi.) | 333.7 |
| Altitude (ft.) | sea level-35 |
| Rainfall (in.) | 64.21 |
| Jan. mean min. | 39.6 |
| July mean max. | 91.2 |
| Civ. Labor | 39,881 |
| Unemployed | 8.3 |
| Wages | $261,492,058 |
| Per Capita Income | $39,941 |
| Prop. Value | $6,217,801,621 |
| Retail Sales | $956,507,646 |

*For explanation of sources, symbols and abbreviations, see p. 238, and foldout map.*

---

*Sunset in Palo Pinto County. Photo by Ron Billings/Texas A&M Forest Service.*

# Palo Pinto County

**Physical Features**: North central county; broken, hilly, wooded in parts; Possum Kingdom Lake, Lake Palo Pinto; sandy, gray, black soils.

**Economy**: Varied manufacturing, tourism, petroleum, agribusiness.

**History**: Anglo-American ranchers arrived in 1850s. Conflicts between settlers and numerous Indian tribes who had sought refuge on Brazos resulted in Texas Rangers removing Indians in 1856. County created 1856 from Bosque, Navarro counties; organized 1857; named for creek (in Spanish name means painted stick).

**Race/Ethnicity**: (In percent) Anglo, 76.0; Black, 2.4; Hispanic, 19.6; Asian, 0.7; Other, 2.4.

**Vital Statistics**, annual: Births, 378; deaths, 297; marriages, 212; divorces, 127.

**Recreation**: Lake activities, hunting, fishing, state park, hiking, biking, fossil park.

**Minerals**: Oil, gas, clays.

**Agriculture**: Cattle, dairy products, nursery crops, hay, wheat. Market value $53.8 million. Cedar posts marketed.

**PALO PINTO** (243) county seat.

**MINERAL WELLS** (17,123, part [2,144] in Parker County) oil and gas, manufacturing, tourism; hospital, Weatherford College branch; art center; state park east of city in Parker County; Crazy Water Festival in October.

Other towns include: **Gordon** (486); **Graford** (602) retirement/recreation area, Pos-

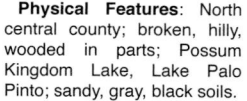

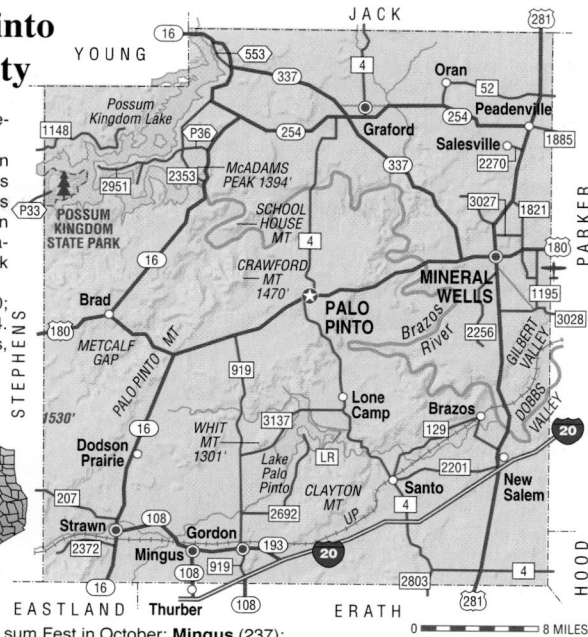

sum Fest in October; **Mingus** (237); **Santo** (445), and **Strawn** (644).

| | |
|---|---|
| Population | 28,096 |
| Change fm 2010 | – 0.1 |
| Area (sq. mi.) | 985.5 |
| Land Area (sq. mi.) | 951.8 |
| Altitude (ft.) | 782-1,530 |
| Rainfall (in.) | 32.05 |
| Jan. mean min. | 32.2 |
| July mean max. | 95.5 |
| Civ. Labor | 14,859 |
| Unemployed | 4.9 |
| Wages | $80,394,117 |
| Per Capita Income | $38,820 |
| Prop. Value | $4,000,031,780 |
| Retail Sales | $383,394,403 |

# Panola County

**Physical Features**: East Texas county; sixty percent forested, rolling plain; broken by Sabine, Murvaul Creek; Toledo Bend Reservoir, Lake Murvaul, Martin Creek Lake.

**Economy**: Gas, oil-field operations, food processing, agribusiness.

**History**: Caddo tribal area. Anglo-American settlement established in 1833. Antebellum slaveholding area. County name is Indian word for cotton; created from Harrison, Shelby counties 1846.

**Race/Ethnicity**: (In percent) Anglo, 73.3; Black, 16.0; Hispanic, 8.8; Asian, 0.5; Other, 2.6.

**Vital Statistics**, annual: Births, 279; deaths, 237; marriages, 182; divorces, 79.

**Recreation**: Lake fishing, water activities, hunting; Jim Reeves memorial, Tex Ritter museum and Texas Country Music Hall of Fame.

**Minerals**: Oil, gas, coal.

**Agriculture**: Broilers, cattle, forages. Market value $93.3 million. Timber sales significant.

**CARTHAGE** (6,959) county seat; petroleum processing, poultry, sawmills; hospital, junior college; Oil & Gas Blast in October.

Other towns include: **Beckville** (856), **Clayton** (125), **DeBerry** (200), **Gary** (315), **Long Branch** (150), **Panola** (305). Also, **Tatum** (1,412, mostly in Rusk County).

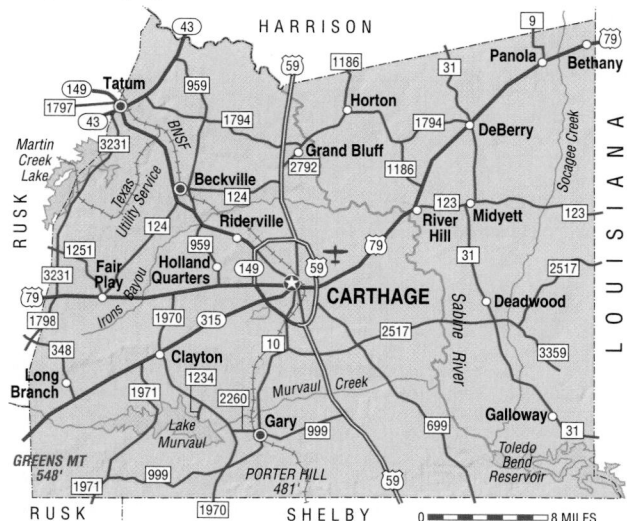

| | |
|---|---|
| Population | 23,769 |
| Change fm 2010 | – 0.1 |
| Area (sq. mi.) | 821.3 |
| Land Area (sq. mi.) | 801.8 |
| Altitude (ft.) | 172-548 |
| Rainfall (in.) | 51.43 |
| Jan. mean min. | 35.2 |
| July mean max. | 93.0 |
| Civ. Labor | 16,115 |
| Unemployed | 4.2 |
| Wages | $117,404,884 |
| Per Capita Income | $45,738 |
| Prop. Value | $4,902,880,340 |
| Retail Sales | $252,093,089 |

# Parker County

**Physical Features**: Hilly, broken by Brazos, Trinity tributaries, Lake Mineral Wells, Lake Weatherford; varied soils.

**Economy**: Agriculture, varied manufacturing, government/services, commuting to Fort Worth; part of Dallas-Fort Worth metropolitan area.

**History**: Comanche and Kiowa area in late 1840s when Anglo-American settlers arrived. County named for pioneer legislator Isaac Parker; created 1855 from Bosque, Navarro counties, organized the same year.

**Race/Ethnicity**: (In percent) Anglo, 84.2; Black, 2.0; Hispanic, 11.2; Asian, 0.7; Other, 2.6.

**Vital Statistics**, annual: Births, 1,345; deaths, 904; marriages, 745; divorces, 403.

**Recreation**: Water sports; state park and trailway; trails; hunting; Peach Festival in July, frontier rodeo days in June; first Monday trade days monthly.

**Minerals**: Gas, oil, stone, sand and gravel, clays.

**Agriculture**: Cattle, greenhouses, hay, horses (first in number), peaches, pecans. Market value $74.3 million.

**WEATHERFORD** (26,879) county seat; retail center, manufacturing, warehousing, tourism, commuting to Fort Worth, government/services, equine industry; hospital, Weatherford College; museums, public gardens, historic buildings.

Other towns include: **Aledo** (2,928); **Annetta** (1,340), **Annetta North** (541) and **Annetta South** (538); **Cool** (157); **Dennis** (300); **Hudson Oaks** (1,917); **Millsap** (419); **Peaster** (1,000); **Poolville** (520); **Reno** (2,552); **Sanctuary** (334); **Springtown** (2,690) commuters, government/services, Wild West Festival in September; **Whitt** (38); **Willow Park** (4,376).

Also, parts of **Azle** (11,413); **Briar** (5,832), and **Cresson** (765); part [2,144] of **Mineral Wells**. Also, a small part of **Fort Worth**.

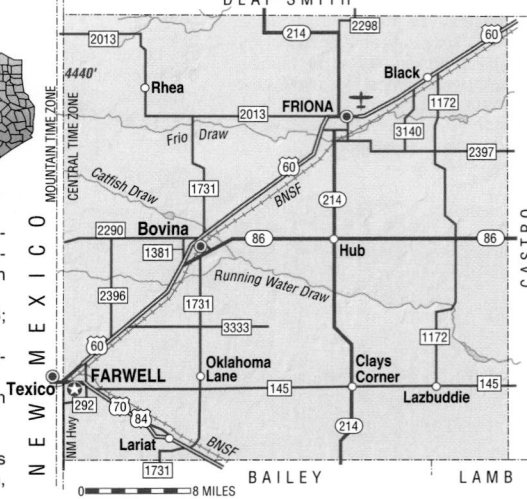

| | |
|---|---|
| Population | **123,164** |
| Change fm 2010 | 5.3 |
| Area (sq. mi.) | 910.1 |
| Land Area (sq. mi.) | 903.5 |
| Altitude (ft.) | 700-1,362 |
| Rainfall (in.) | 35.77 |
| Jan. mean min. | 30.1 |
| July mean max. | 93.2 |
| Civ. Labor | 59,723 |
| Unemployed | 5.1 |
| Wages | $312,337,859 |
| Per Capita Income | $45,856 |
| Prop. Value | $12,399,699,050 |
| Retail Sales | $2,075,798,166 |

# Parmer County

**Physical Features**: Western High Plains, broken by draws, playas; sandy, clay, loam soils.

**Economy**: Cattle feeding, grain elevators, meatpacking plant, other agribusiness.

**History**: Apaches, pushed out in late 1700s by Comanches and Kiowas. U.S. Army removed Indians in 1874–1875. Anglo-Americans arrived in the 1880s. Mexican migration increased after 1950. County named for Republic figure Martin Parmer; created from Bexar District in 1876, organized in 1907.

**Race/Ethnicity**: (In percent) Anglo, 36.6; Black, 1.6; Hispanic, 61.4; Asian, 0.6; Other, 3.1.

**Vital Statistics**, annual: Births, 150; deaths, 69; marriages, 32; divorces, 24.

**Recreation**: Hunting, playa lake, Border Town Days in July at Farwell.

**Minerals**: Not significant.

**Agriculture**: Beef cattle (second in numbers), dairies (third in number of milk cows); crops include wheat, corn, cotton, grain sorghum, alfalfa; apples and potatoes also raised; 163,000 acres irrigated. Market value $1.33 billion, second in state.

**FARWELL** (1,287) county seat; agribusiness center, grain storage, plants make farm equipment.

**FRIONA** (3,911) farming, cattle feeding, feed mill; hospital; museum; Cheeseburger Festival in July.

Other towns include: **Bovina** (1,761) farm trade center; **Lazbuddie** (248).

| | |
|---|---|
| Population | **9,908** |
| Change fm 2010 | – 3.5 |
| Area (sq. mi.) | 885.2 |
| Land Area (sq. mi.) | 880.8 |
| Altitude (ft.) | 3,785-4,440 |
| Rainfall (in.) | 20.14 |
| Jan. mean min. | 22.5 |
| July mean max. | 89.8 |
| Civ. Labor | 4,584 |
| Unemployed | 4.3 |
| Wages | $50,709,822 |
| Per Capita Income | $38,530 |
| Prop. Value | $1,047,398,101 |
| Retail Sales | $62,296,218 |

# Pecos County

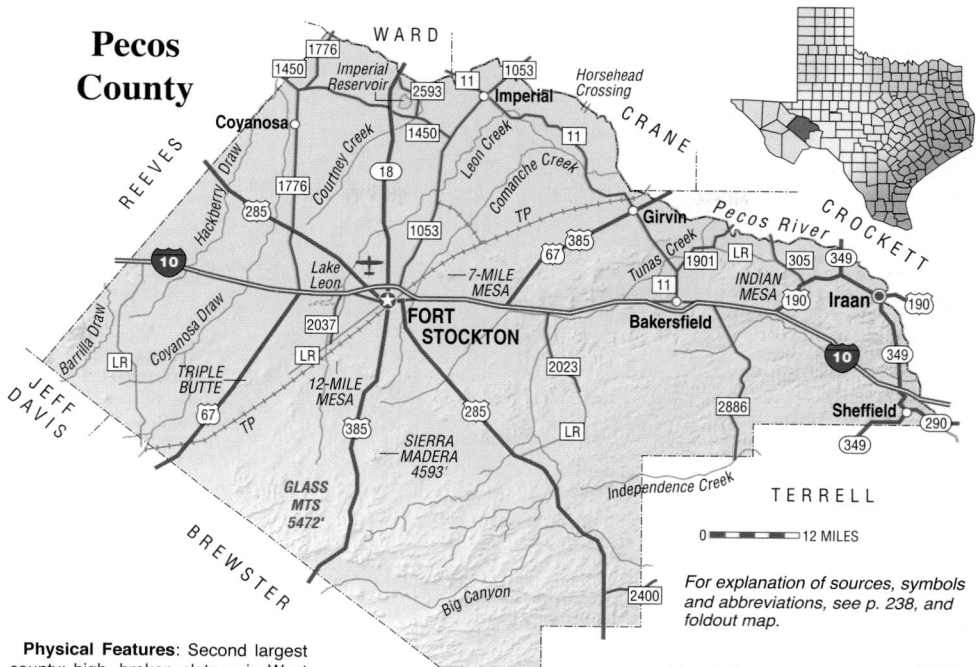

**Physical Features**: Second largest county; high, broken plateau in West Texas; draining to Pecos and tributaries; Imperial Reservoir, Lake Leon; sandy, clay, loam soils.

**Economy**: Oil, gas, agriculture, government/services, wind turbines.

**History**: Comanches in area when military outpost established in 1859. Settlement began after Civil War. Created from Presidio County 1871; organized 1872; named for Pecos River, name origin uncertain.

**Race/Ethnicity**: (In percent) Anglo, 27.0; Black, 4.3; Hispanic, 67.5; Asian, 1.1; Other, 2.1.

**Vital Statistics**, annual: Births, 207; deaths, 122; marriages, 71; divorces, 11.

**Recreation**: Old Fort Stockton, Annie Riggs Museum, stagecoach stop, scenic drives, Dinosaur Track Roadside Park, cattle-trail sites, archaeo-

logical museum with oil and ranch-heritage collections; Comanche Springs Water Carnival in summer.

**Minerals**: Natural gas, oil, gravel, caliche.

**Agriculture**: Cattle, alfalfa, pecans, sheep, goats, onions, peppers, melons. Market value $47.5 million. Aquaculture firm producing shrimp. Hunting leases.

**FORT STOCKTON** (8,547) county seat, distribution center for petroleum industry, government/services, agriculture, tourism, varied manufacturing, winery, prison units, spaceport launching small satellites; hospital; historical tours.

| Population | 15,893 |
|---|---|
| Change fm 2010 | 2.5 |
| Area (sq. mi.) | 4,764.8 |
| Land Area (sq. mi.) | 4,763.9 |
| Altitude (ft.) | 2,040-5,472 |
| Rainfall (in.) | 15.15 |
| Jan. mean min. | 33.2 |
| July mean max. | 94.3 |
| Civ. Labor | 8,565 |
| Unemployed | 4.1 |
| Wages | $59,326,937 |
| Per Capita Income | $31,723 |
| Prop. Value | $4,365,242,3900 |
| Retail Sales | $219,797,410 |

**Iraan** (1,273) oil and gas center, wind energy, ranching; hospital, museum; Alley Oop park; Holiday bazaar/celebration in November.

Other towns include: **Coyanosa** (174); **Girvin** (20); Imperial (280) center for irrigated farming; **Sheffield** (322) oil, gas center.

*Texas 349 through Sheffield, Pecos County. Photo by Robert Plocheck.*

# Polk County

Population ........................ 46,079
Change fm 2010 ...................... 1.5
Area (sq. mi.) .................... 1,109.7
Land Area (sq. mi.) ............ 1,057.1
Altitude (ft.) ...................... 68-484
Rainfall (in.) ........................ 51.53
Jan. mean min. ...................... 39.6
July mean max. ..................... 93.7
Civ. Labor .......................... 18,187
Unemployed ............................ 7.0
Wages ...................... $91,000,497
Per Capita Income ........... $41,659
Prop. Value ........... $4,269,201,644
Retail Sales ............ $480,572,680

**Physical Features**: Rolling; densely forested, with Big Thicket, unique plant, animal life; Neches, Trinity rivers, tributaries; Lake Livingston.

**Economy**: Timber, lumber production, tourism, manufacturing.

**History**: Caddo area; Alabama and Coushatta Indians arrived from Louisiana in the late 1700s. Anglo-American and Hispanic families received land grants in the early 1830s. County named for U.S. President James K. Polk; created from Liberty County and organized 1846.

**Race/Ethnicity**: (In percent) Anglo, 71.5; Black, 11.4; Hispanic, 14.0; Asian, 0.7; Other, 3.7.

**Vital Statistics**, annual: Births, 495; deaths, 643; marriages, 341; divorces, 168.

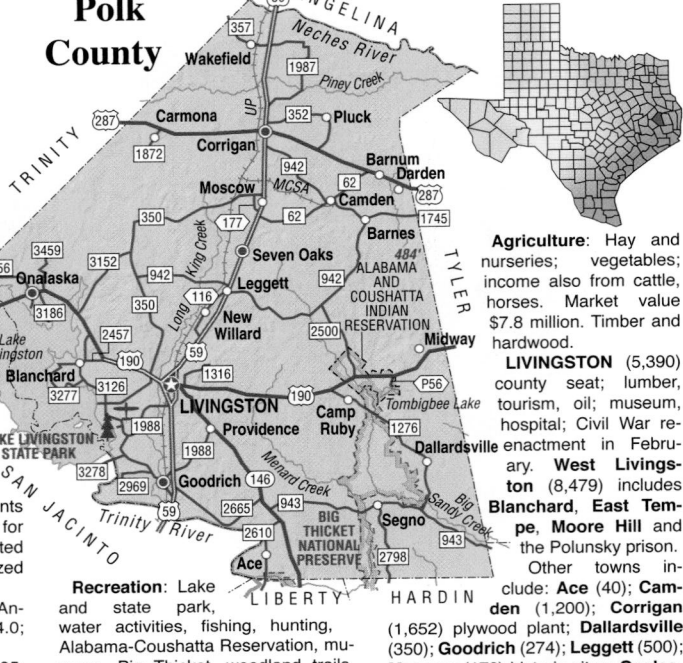

**Recreation**: Lake and state park, water activities, fishing, hunting, Alabama-Coushatta Reservation, museum, Big Thicket, woodland trails, champion trees, historic homes.

**Minerals**: Oil, gas, sand, gravel.

**Agriculture**: Hay and nurseries; vegetables; income also from cattle, horses. Market value $7.8 million. Timber and hardwood.

**LIVINGSTON** (5,390) county seat; lumber, tourism, oil; museum, hospital; Civil War reary. **West Livingston** (8,479) includes **Blanchard**, **East Tempe**, **Moore Hill** and the Polunsky prison.

Other towns include: **Ace** (40); **Camden** (1,200); **Corrigan** (1,652) plywood plant; **Dallardsville** (350); **Goodrich** (274); **Leggett** (500); **Moscow** (170) historic sites; **Onalaska** (1,829); **Seven Oaks** (115).

---

# Potter County

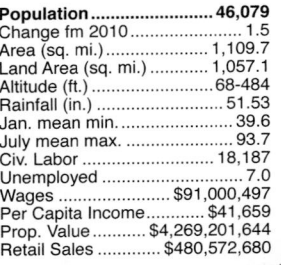

**Physical Features**: Panhandle; mostly level, part rolling; broken by Canadian River and tributaries; sandy, sandy loam, chocolate loam, clay soils; Lake Meredith.

**Economy**: Transportation and distribution hub for large area, manufacturing, agribusiness, tourism, government/services, petrochemicals, gas processing.

**History**: Apaches, pushed out by Comanches in the 1700s. Comanches removed to Indian Territory in 1874–1875. Ranching began in the late 1870s. Oil boom in the 1920s. County named for Robert Potter, Republic leader; created in 1876 from Bexar District; organized in 1887.

**Race/Ethnicity**: (In percent) Anglo, 47.1; Black, 10.8; Hispanic, 36.7; Asian, 4.6; Other, 3.4.

**Vital Statistics**, annual: Births, 2,101; deaths, 1,194; marriages, 1,448; divorces, 435.

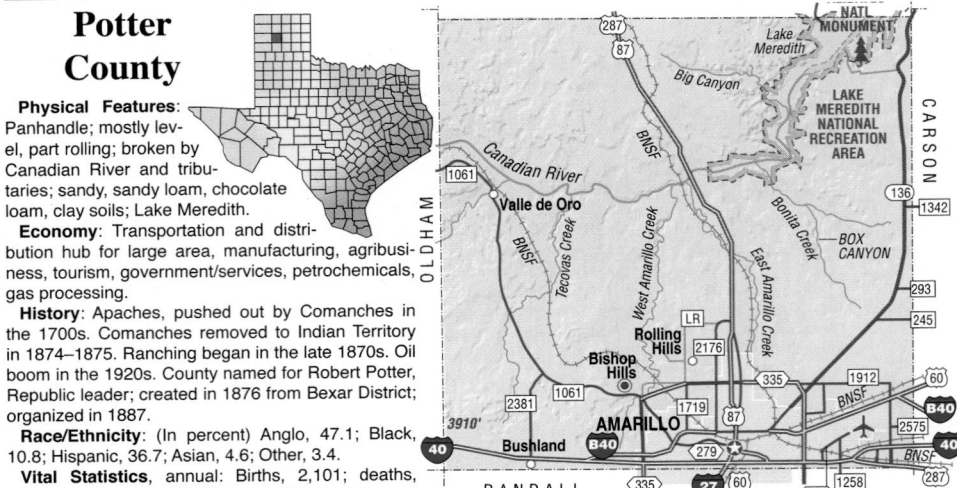

**Recreation**: Lake activities, Alibates Flint Quarries National Monument, hunting, fishing, Wildcat Bluff nature center, Cadillac Ranch, professional sports events, Tri-State Fair in September.

**Minerals**: Natural gas, oil, helium.

**Agriculture**: Beef cattle production and processing; wheat, sorghum, cotton. Market value $21 million.

**AMARILLO** (200,526 total, part [85,209] in Randall County) county seat; hub for northern Panhandle oil and ranching, distribution and marketing center, tourism, manufacturing, food processing, prison; hospitals; Amarillo College, Texas Tech University medical, engineering, pharmacy schools; Quarter Horse Hall of Fame, museum.

Other towns include: **Bishop Hills** (195) and **Bushland** (1,485).

Population ........................ 121,627

Change fm 2010 ........................... 0.5
Area (sq. mi.) .......................... 922.0
Land Area (sq. mi.) ................. 908.4
Altitude (ft.) .................... 2,915-3,910
Rainfall (in.) ......................... 20.36
Jan. mean min. ....................... 23.4
July mean max. ........................ 91.4
Civ. Labor ............................ 56,865
Unemployed .............................. 4.8
Wages ...................... $777,993,226
Per Capita Income ........... $35,712
Prop. Value ........... $7,406,883,335
Retail Sales ............. $2,714,925,989

An old-style wagon at Fort Leaton State Historic Site, Presidio County. Photo by Robert Plocheck.

# Presidio County

**Physical Features**: Rugged, some of Texas' tallest mountains; clays, loams, sandy loams on uplands; intermountain wash; timber sparse; Capote Falls, state's highest.

**Economy**: Government/services, ranching, hunting leases, tourism.

**History**: Presidio area has been cultivated farmland since at least 1200 A.D. Spanish explorers of the 1500s encountered permanent villages along Rio Grande. Jumanos, Apaches and Comanches in the area when Spanish missions began in 1680s. Anglo-Americans arrived in the 1840s. County created in 1850 from Bexar District; organized in 1875; named for Spanish Presidio del Norte (fort of the north).

**Race/Ethnicity**: (In percent) Anglo, 14.9; Black, 1.4; Hispanic, 82.0; Asian, 1.5; Other, 2.3.

**Vital Statistics**, annual: Births, 106; deaths, 34; marriages, 21; divorces, 0.

**Recreation**: Hunting; scenic drives along Rio Grande, in mountains; ghost towns, mysterious Marfa Lights; Fort D.A. Russell; Big Bend Ranch State Park; hot springs; Cibolo Creek Ranch Resort; Chinati Foundation art festival in fall. (Chinati Mountains State Natural Area not yet open to public.)

**Minerals**: Sand, gravel, silver, zeolite.

**Agriculture**: Cattle, tomatoes, hay, onions, melons. Some irrigation near Rio Grande.

**MARFA** (1,976) county seat; ranching supply center, Border Patrol headquarters, tourism, art center, gateway to mountainous area; Paisano Hotel, headquarters for 1950s classic movie, *Giant*; Old Timers Roping on Memorial Day weekend.

**PRESIDIO** (4,462) international bridge to Ojinaga, Mex., gateway to Mexico's West Coast by rail; Fort Leaton historic site; asado cook-off in February.

Other towns include: **Redford** (92); **Shafter** (57) old mining town.

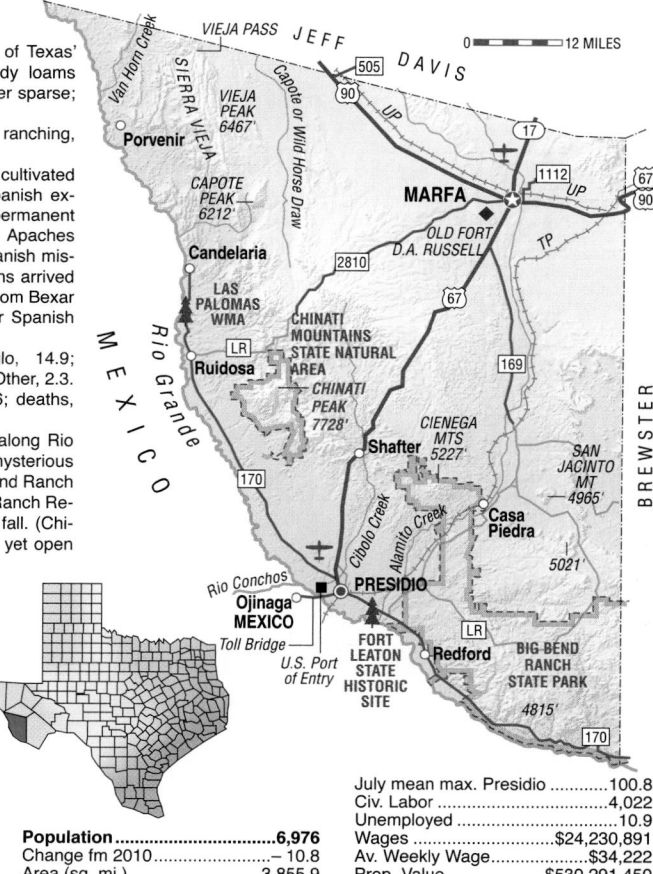

| Population | 6,976 |
|---|---|
| Change fm 2010 | – 10.8 |
| Area (sq. mi.) | 3,855.9 |
| Land Area (sq. mi.) | 3,855.2 |
| Altitude (ft.) | 2,400-7,728 |
| Rainfall (in.) Marfa | 15.38 |
| Rainfall (in.) Presidio | 10.76 |
| Jan. mean min. Marfa | 23.2 |
| Jan. mean min. Presidio | 34.5 |
| July mean max. Marfa | 88.5 |
| July mean max. Presidio | 100.8 |
| Civ. Labor | 4,022 |
| Unemployed | 10.9 |
| Wages | $24,230,891 |
| Av. Weekly Wage | $34,222 |
| Prop. Value | $530,291,450 |
| Retail Sales | $53,698,064 |

*For explanation of sources, symbols and abbreviations, see p. 238, and foldout map.*

# Rains County

**Physical Features**: Northeastern county; rolling; partly Blackland, sandy loams, sandy soils; Sabine River, Lake Tawakoni, Lake Fork Reservoir.

**Economy**: Agribusiness, some manufacturing.

**History**: Caddo area. In the 1700s, Tawakoni Indians entered the area. Anglo-Americans arrived in the 1840s. County, county seat named for Emory Rains, Republic leader; created in 1870 from Hopkins, Hunt and Wood counties, organized the same year; birthplace of National Farmers Union, 1902.

**Race/Ethnicity**: (In percent) Anglo, 86.3; Black, 2.9; Hispanic, 8.2; Asian, 0.7; Other, 2.6.

**Vital Statistics**, annual: Births, 112; deaths, 124; marriages, 85; divorces, 60.

**Recreation**: Lake Tawakoni and Lake Fork Reservoir activities; birding, Eagle Fest in February.

**Minerals**: Gas, oil.

**Agriculture**: Beef, forages, dairies, vegetables (second in sweet potato acreage), fruits, nurseries. Market value $15.3 million.

**EMORY** (1,226) county seat; local trade, tourism, government/services, commuting to Greenville and Dallas; African-American museum.

Other towns include: **East Tawakoni** (876) and **Point** (811), manufacturing, tourism, tamale fest on July 4. Part of **Alba** (528), mostly in Wood County.

| | |
|---|---|
| Population | 11,032 |
| Change fm 2010 | 1.1 |
| Area (sq. mi.) | 258.8 |
| Land Area (sq. mi.) | 229.5 |
| Altitude (ft.) | 340-570 |
| Rainfall (in.) | 44.47 |
| Jan. mean min. | 31.4 |
| July mean max. | 91.4 |
| Civ. Labor | 5,237 |
| Unemployed | 5.5 |
| Wages | $11,803,400 |
| Per Capita Income | $32,531 |
| Prop. Value | $886,340,268 |
| Retail Sales | $104,136,467 |

# Randall County

**Physical Features**: Panhandle county; level, but broken by scenic Palo Duro Canyon, Buffalo Lake; Bivins Lake; silty clay, loam soils.

**Economy**: Agribusiness, education, tourism, part of Amarillo metropolitan area.

**History**: Comanche Indians removed in mid-1870s; ranching began soon afterward. County created 1876 from Bexar District; organized 1889; named for Confederate Gen. Horace Randal (name misspelled in statute).

**Race/Ethnicity**: (In percent) Anglo, 75.3; Black, 3.0; Hispanic, 18.7; Asian, 1.7; Other, 2.6.

**Vital Statistics**, annual: Births, 1,618; deaths, 984; marriages, 472; divorces, 505.

**Recreation**: State park, with Texas outdoor musical drama each summer; Panhandle-Plains Historical Museum; West Texas A&M University events; aoudad sheep, migratory waterfowl hunting in season; Buffalo Lake National Wildlife Refuge; cowboy breakfasts at ranches.

**Minerals**: Not significant.

**Agriculture**: Grain sorghum, beef cattle, wheat, silage, cotton, dairies, hay. Market value $540.3 million.

**CANYON** (13,908) county seat; West Texas A&M University, tourism, commuting to Amarillo, ranching, farm center, light manufacturing, gateway to state park.

**AMARILLO** (200,526 total, part [105,486] in Potter County) hub for northern Panhandle oil and ranching, distribution and marketing center, manufacturing; hospitals.

Other towns include: **Lake Tanglewood** (825); **Palisades** (324); **Timbercreek Canyon** (434); **Umbarger** (327) German sausage festival in November. Part of **Happy** (668, mostly in Swisher County).

| | |
|---|---|
| Population | 128,220 |
| Change fm 2010 | 6.2 |
| Area (sq. mi.) | 922.4 |
| Land Area (sq. mi.) | 911.5 |
| Altitude (ft.) | 2,700-3,890 |
| Rainfall (in.) | 20.15 |
| Jan. mean min. | 21.5 |
| July mean max. | 91.7 |
| Civ. Labor | 73,247 |
| Unemployed | 3.7 |
| Wages | $259,499,588 |
| Per Capita Income | $43,444 |
| Prop. Value | $8,637,671,108 |
| Retail Sales | $1,596,683,410 |

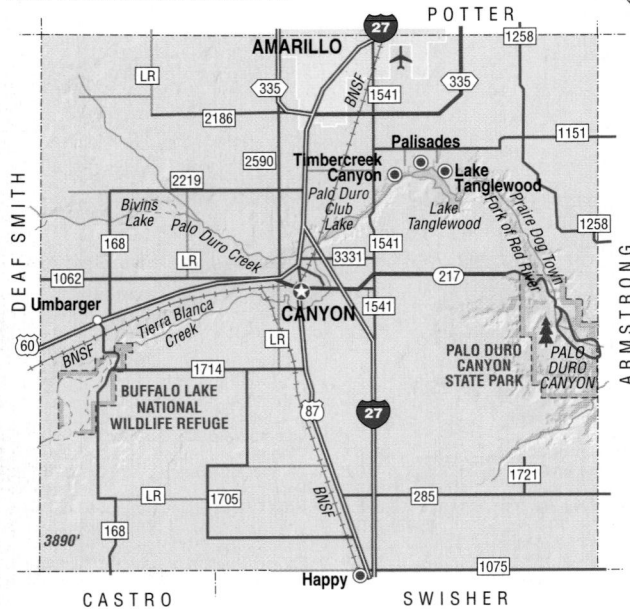

# Reagan County

**Physical Features**: Western county; level to hilly, broken by draws, Big Lake (intermittent); sandy, loam, clay soils.

**Economy**: Oil and gas production, hunting, ranching.

**History**: Comanches in the area until the mid-1870s. Ranching began in the 1880s. Hispanic migration increased after 1950. County named for Texas' U.S. Sen. John H. Reagan, first chairman of the Texas Railroad Commission; county created and organized in 1903 from Tom Green County.

**Race/Ethnicity**: (In percent) Anglo, 31.3; Black, 3.4; Hispanic, 65.3; Asian, 0.6; Other, 3.1.

**Vital Statistics**, annual: Births, 51; deaths, 35; marriages, 24; divorces, 15.

**Recreation**: Site of 1923 discovery well Santa Rita No. 1 on University of Texas land, Texon reunion in June.

**Minerals**: Gas, oil.

**Agriculture**: Cotton, cattle, sheep, goats. Market value $11.1 million. Hunting leases important.

**BIG LAKE** (3,219) county seat; center for oil activities, agriculture, government/services; hospital; Spring bluegrass festival, St. Rita festival in August.

*For explanation of sources, symbols and abbreviations, see p. 238, and foldout map.*

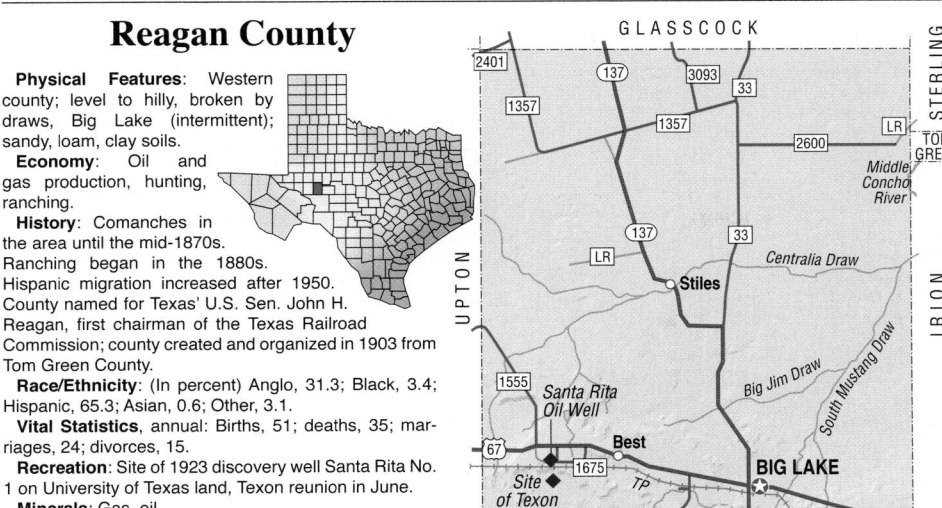

| | |
|---|---|
| Population | 3,755 |
| Change fm 2010 | 11.5 |
| Area (sq. mi.) | 1,176.0 |
| Land Area (sq. mi.) | 1,175.3 |
| Altitude (ft.) | 2,370-2,960 |
| Rainfall (in.) | 19.29 |
| Jan. mean min. | 30.8 |
| July mean max. | 93.5 |
| Civ. Labor | 2,751 |
| Unemployed | 2.6 |
| Wages | $24,918,787 |
| Per Capita Income | $47,777 |
| Prop. Value | $3,032,277,200 |
| Retail Sales | $32,466,362 |

*Old Main, on the campus of West Texas A&M University in Canyon, Randall County. Photo by Robert Plocheck.*

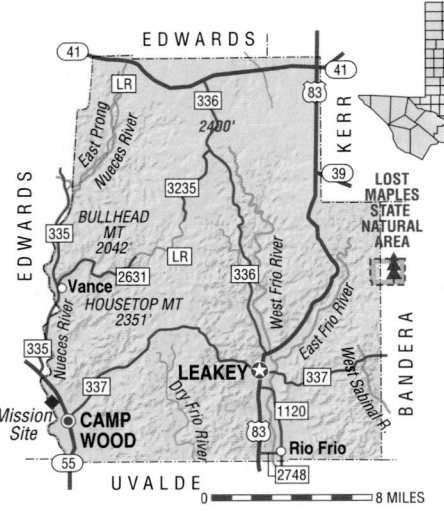

# Real County

**Physical Features**: Hill Country, spring-fed streams, scenic canyons; Frio, Nueces rivers; cedars, pecans, walnuts, many live oaks.

**Economy**: Ranching, tourism, government/services, cedar cutting.

**History**: Tonkawa area; Lipan Apaches arrived in the early 1700s; later, Comanche hunters arrived in the area. Spanish mission established in 1762. Anglo-Americans arrived in the 1850s. County created and organized in 1913 from Bandera, Edwards and Kerr counties; named for legislator-ranchman Julius Real.

**Race/Ethnicity**: (In percent) Anglo, 69.6; Black, 1.0; Hispanic, 26.9; Asian, 0.2; Other, 3.9.

**Vital Statistics**, annual: Births, 31; deaths, 66; marriages, 5; divorces, 1.

**Recreation**: Tourist and hunting center, birding, fishing, camping, scenic drives, state natural area.

**Minerals**: Not significant.

**Agriculture**: Goats, sheep, beef cattle produce most income. Market value $1.6 million. Cedar posts processed.

**LEAKEY** (430) county seat; tourism, ranching; museums; July Jubilee.

**CAMP WOOD** (703) tourism, hunting, ranching; medical clinic; San Lorenzo de la Santa Cruz mission site; museum; Lindbergh Park, settlers reunion in August.

Other towns include: **Rio Frio** (50).

| | |
|---|---|
| Population | 3,371 |
| Change fm 2010 | 1.9 |
| Area (sq. mi.) | 700.1 |
| Land Area (sq. mi.) | 699.2 |
| Altitude (ft.) | 1,400-2,400 |
| Rainfall (in.) | 27.38 |
| Jan. mean min. | 33.6 |
| July mean max. | 93.0 |
| Civ. Labor | 1,625 |
| Unemployed | 4.4 |
| Wages | $4,262,700 |
| Per Capita Income | $33,319 |
| Prop. Value | $1,110,199,505 |
| Retail Sales | $18,372,530 |

# Red River County

**Physical Features**: On Red-Sulphur rivers' divide; 39 different soil types; half timbered; River Crest Reservoir.

**Economy**: Manufacturing, government/services, agriculture.

**History**: Caddo Indians abandoned area in 1790s. One of the oldest counties; settlers were moving in from the United States in 1810s. Kickapoo and other tribes arrived in 1820s. Antebellum slaveholding area. County created 1836 as original county of the Republic; organized 1837; named for Red River, its northern boundary.

**Race/Ethnicity**: (In percent) Anglo, 73.4; Black, 17.4; Hispanic, 7.0; Asian, 0.3; Other, 3.2.

**Vital Statistics**, annual: Births, 130; deaths, 200; marriages, 59; divorces, 68.

**Recreation**: Historical sites include pioneer homes, birthplace of John Nance Garner; fall foliage; water activities; hunting of deer, turkey, duck, small game.

**Minerals**: Small oil flow.

**Agriculture**: Beef cattle, corn, soybeans, wheat, sorghum, hay. Market value $53.5 million. Timber sales substantial.

**CLARKSVILLE** (3,096) county seat; varied manufacturing; hospital, library; Historical Society bazaar in October

Other towns include: **Annona** (300); **Avery** (463); **Bagwell** (150); **Bogata** (1,094); **Detroit** (687) commercial center in west. Part of **Deport** (568).

| | |
|---|---|
| Population | 12,446 |
| Change fm 2010 | – 3.2 |
| Area (sq. mi.) | 1,056.7 |
| Land Area (sq. mi.) | 1,036.6 |
| Altitude (ft.) | 260-560 |
| Rainfall (in.) | 48.77 |
| Jan. mean min. | 30.8 |
| July mean max. | 91.9 |
| Civ. Labor | 5,360 |
| Unemployed | 7.7 |
| Wages | $17,741,592 |
| Per Capita Income | $34,111 |
| Prop. Value | $1,297,902,040 |
| Retail Sales | $49,379,990 |

*A desert storm approaches Balmorhea, Reeves County. Photo by Robert Plocheck.*

# Reeves County

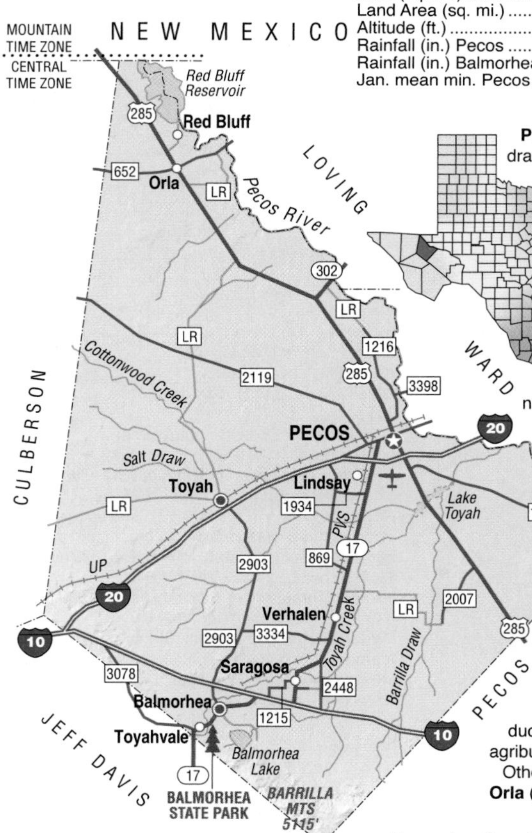

| | |
|---|---|
| Population | **14,349** |
| Change fm 2010 | 4.1 |
| Area (sq. mi.) | 2,642.1 |
| Land Area (sq. mi.) | 2,635.4 |
| Altitude (ft.) | 2,460-5,115 |
| Rainfall (in.) Pecos | 11.61 |
| Rainfall (in.) Balmorhea | 13.54 |
| Jan. mean min. Pecos | 28.1 |
| Jan. mean min. Balmorhea | 30.3 |
| July mean max. Pecos | 98.5 |
| July mean max. Balmorhea | 94.4 |
| Civ. Labor | 4,933 |
| Unemployed | 6.6 |
| Wages | $40,031,544 |
| Per Capita Income | $25,630 |
| Prop. Value | $1,722,675,290 |
| Retail Sales | $223,206,625 |

**Physical Features**: Rolling plains, broken by many draws, Pecos River, Balmorhea Lake, Lake Toyah, Red Bluff Reservoir; Barrilla Mountains on the south; chocolate loam, clay, sandy, mountain wash soils.

**Economy**: Agriculture, tourism, food processing, government/services, gravel.

**History**: Jumanos were irrigating crops from springs (Balmorhea) when Spanish explored in 1583. Mexican farmers supplied nearby Fort Davis in mid-19th century. Anglo-Americans arrived in the 1870s. County created in 1883 from Pecos County; organized in 1884; named for Confederate Col. George R. Reeves.

**Race/Ethnicity**: (In percent) Anglo, 19.2; Black, 5.4; Hispanic, 74.5; Asian, 1.0; Other, 1.7.

**Vital Statistics**, annual: Births, 164; deaths, 95; marriages, 53; divorces, 30.

**Recreation**: Replica of Judge Roy Bean store, West of Pecos museum; park with javelina, prairie dogs; scenic drives; water activities; state park; night in old Pecos, cantaloupe festival in July.

**Minerals**: Oil, gas, gravel.

**Agriculture**: Ranching, dairies, hay, cotton, cantaloupes, pecans, pistachios. Some 11,000 acres irrigated. Market value $54.2 million.

**PECOS** (8,870) county seat; food processing, produce shipping, government/services, prison, tourism, agribusiness; hospital; 16th of September fiesta.

Other towns include: **Balmorhea** (504), **Lindsay** (267); **Orla** (80), **Saragosa** (185), **Toyah** (92), **Toyahvale** (60).

For explanation of sources, symbols and abbreviations, see p. 238, and foldout map.

# Refugio County

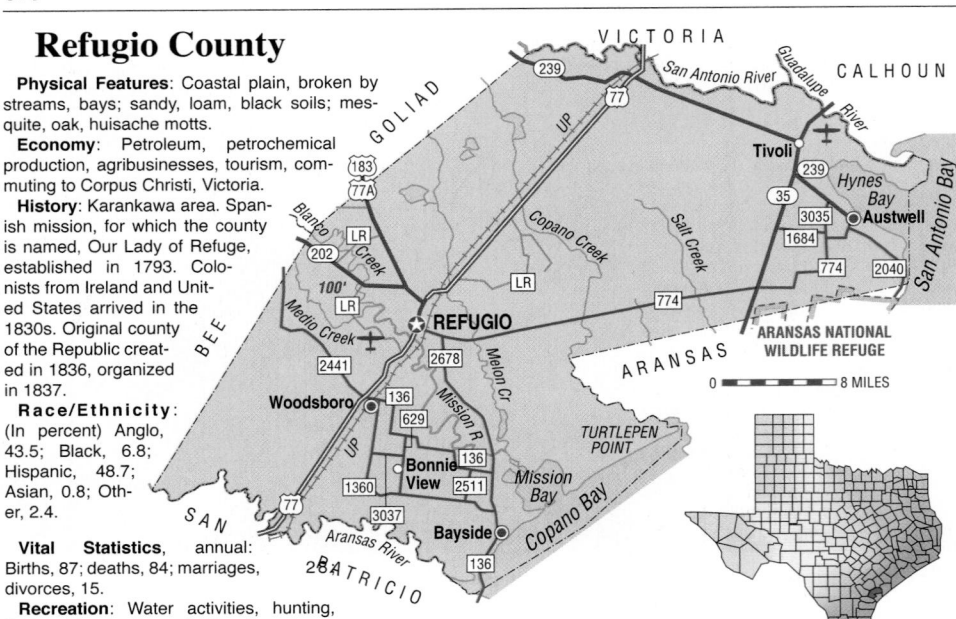

**Physical Features**: Coastal plain, broken by streams, bays; sandy, loam, black soils; mesquite, oak, huisache motts.

**Economy**: Petroleum, petrochemical production, agribusinesses, tourism, commuting to Corpus Christi, Victoria.

**History**: Karankawa area. Spanish mission, for which the county is named, Our Lady of Refuge, established in 1793. Colonists from Ireland and United States arrived in the 1830s. Original county of the Republic created in 1836, organized in 1837.

**Race/Ethnicity**: (In percent) Anglo, 43.5; Black, 6.8; Hispanic, 48.7; Asian, 0.8; Other, 2.4.

**Vital Statistics**, annual: Births, 87; deaths, 84; marriages, divorces, 15.

**Recreation**: Water activities, hunting, fishing, historic sites, wildlife refuge, home of the whooping crane; chili cook-off in August, Festival of Flags in October.

**Minerals**: Oil, natural gas.

**Agriculture**: Cotton, beef cattle, sorghum, corn, soybeans, horses. Market value $43 million. Hunting leases.

**REFUGIO** (2,812) county seat; petroleum, agribusiness center; hospital; museum, historic homes.

Other towns include: **Austwell** (147); **Bayside** (329) resorts; **Tivoli** (482); **Woodsboro** (1,469) commercial center.

| | |
|---|---|
| Population | 7,302 |
| Change fm 2010 | − 1.1 |
| Area (sq. mi.) | 818.2 |
| Land Area (sq. mi.) | 770.4 |
| Altitude (ft.) | sea level-100 |
| Rainfall (in.) | 36.89 |
| Jan. mean min. | 44.3 |
| July mean max. | 92.0 |
| Civ. Labor | 4,827 |
| Unemployed | 3.6 |
| Wages | $25,537,135 |
| Per Capita Income | $46,429 |
| Prop. Value | $1,846,542,700 |
| Retail Sales | $71,377,220 |

# Roberts County

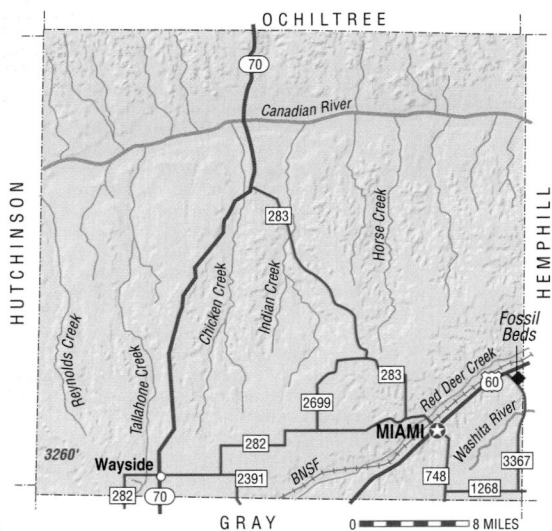

**Physical Features**: Rolling, broken by the Canadian River and tributaries; Red Deer Creek; black, sandy loam, alluvial soils.

**Economy**: Oil-field operations, agribusiness.

**History**: Apaches; pushed out by Comanches who were removed in 1874–1875 by U.S. Army. Ranching began in the late 1870s. County created in 1876 from Bexar District; organized in 1889; named for Texas leaders John S. Roberts and Gov. O.M. Roberts.

**Race/Ethnicity**: (In percent) Anglo, 82.9; Black, 0.7; Hispanic, 13.4; Asian, 0.2; Other, 3.6.

**Vital Statistics**, annual: Births, 8; deaths, 10; marriages, 5; divorces, 6.

**Recreation**: Scenic drives, hunting, museum; national cow-calling contest in June.

**Minerals**: Production of gas, oil.

**Agriculture**: Beef cattle; wheat, sorghum, corn, soybeans, hay; 6,300 acres irrigated. Market value $16.4 million.

**MIAMI** (584) county seat; ranching, oil center, some manufacturing.

| | |
|---|---|
| Population | 928 |
| Change fm 2010 | − 0.1 |
| Area (sq. mi.) | 924.2 |
| Land Area (sq. mi.) | 924.1 |
| Altitude (ft.) | 2,380-3,260 |
| Rainfall (in.) | 24.08 |
| Jan. mean min. | 22.1 |
| July mean max. | 92.1 |
| Civ. Labor | 594 |
| Unemployed | 2.4 |
| Wages | $1,889,554 |
| Per Capita Income | $53,953 |
| Prop. Value | $995,873,119 |
| Retail Sales | $2,625,384 |

**Physical Features**: Rolling in north and east, draining to bottoms along Brazos, Navasota rivers; sandy soils, heavy in bottoms; Lake Limestone, Twin Oaks Reservoir, Camp Creek Reservoir.

**Economy**: Agribusiness, government/services, oil and gas.

**History**: Tawakoni, Waco, Comanche and other tribes. Anglo-Americans arrived in the 1820s. Antebellum slaveholding area. County created in 1837, organized in 1838, subdivided into many others later; named for pioneer Sterling Clack Robertson.

**Race/Ethnicity**: (In percent) Anglo, 58.3; Black, 21.3; Hispanic, 19.2; Asian, 0.8; Other, 2.4.

**Vital Statistics**, annual: Births, 194; deaths, 185; marriages, 104; divorces, 39.

**Recreation**: Hunting, fishing; historic sites; dogwood trails, wildlife preserves.

**Minerals**: Gas, oil, lignite coal.

**Agriculture**: Poultry, beef cattle, cotton, hay, corn; 20,000 acres of cropland irrigated. Market value $136.4 million.

**FRANKLIN** (1,617) county seat; oil and gas, power plants, mining, agriculture; Carnegie library.

**HEARNE** (4,486) agribusiness, varied manufacturing; depot museum, World War II POW camp.

Other towns include: **Bremond** (915) power plant, coal mining, library, museum, Polish Days in June; **Calvert** (1,149) agriculture, tourism, antiques, Maypole festival, tour of homes; **Mumford** (170); **New Baden** (150); **Wheelock** (225).

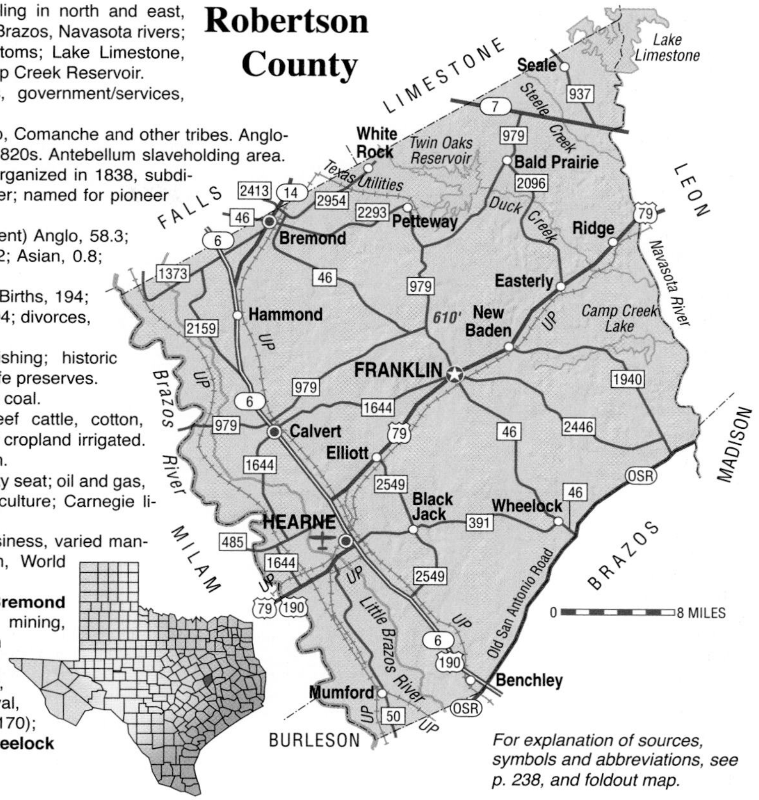

## Robertson County

For explanation of sources, symbols and abbreviations, see p. 238, and foldout map.

| | | |
|---|---|---|
| Population | 16,500 | |
| Change fm 2010 | − 0.7 | |
| Area (sq. mi.) | 865.4 | |
| Land Area (sq. mi.) | 855.7 | |
| Altitude (ft.) | 230-610 | |

| | |
|---|---|
| Rainfall (in.) | 39.50 |
| Jan. mean min. | 38.8 |
| July mean max. | 94.9 |
| Civ. Labor | 7,260 |

| | |
|---|---|
| Unemployed | 5.7 |
| Wages | $37,685,894 |
| Per Capita Income | $41,656 |
| Prop. Value | $4,935,060,784 |
| Retail Sales | $142,821,110 |

*The prairie land at Aransas National Wildlife Refuge, Refugio-Aransas counties. NERR photo.*

# Rockwall County

**Physical Features**: Rolling prairie, mostly Blackland soil; Lake Ray Hubbard. Texas' smallest county.

**Economy**: Industrial employment in local plants and in Dallas; in Dallas metropolitan area; residential development around Lake Ray Hubbard.

**History**: Caddo area. Cherokees arrived in 1820s. Anglo-American settlers arrived in 1840s. County created 1873 from Kaufman, organized the same year; named for wall-like rock formation.

**Race/Ethnicity**: (In percent) Anglo, 72.8; Black, 6.1; Hispanic, 16.7; Asian, 2.7; Other, 2.6.

**Vital Statistics**, annual: Births, 966; deaths, 529; marriages, 1,351; divorces, 358.

**Recreation**: Lake activities; proximity to Dallas; unusual rock outcrop.

**Minerals**: Not significant.

**Agriculture**: Small grains, cattle, horticulture, horses. Market value $4.1 million.

**ROCKWALL** (41,147) county seat; commuters, varied manufacturing, government/services; hospital; harbor retail and enterainment district; Founders Day in April.

Other towns include: **Fate** (8,267); **Heath** (7,704); **McLendon-Chisholm** (1,672) chili cookoff in October; Mo-

bile City (185); **Royse City** (10,338) government/services, varied manufacturing, agribusiness, museum, library, Funfest in October.

Part [7,011] of **Rowlett**, hospital, and a small part [1,055] of **Wylie**.

| | |
|---|---|
| Population | 87,809 |
| Change fm 2010 | 12.1 |
| Area (sq. mi.) | 148.7 |
| Land Area (sq. mi.) | 127.0 |
| Altitude (ft.) | 430-624 |
| Rainfall (in.) | 38,58 |
| Jan. mean min. | 33.0 |
| July mean max. | 96.0 |
| Civ. Labor | 43,567 |
| Unemployed | 5.0 |
| Wages | $211,595,781 |
| Per Capita Income | $53,379 |
| Prop. Value | $7,921,927,688 |
| Retail Sales | $1,604,111,808 |

# Runnels County

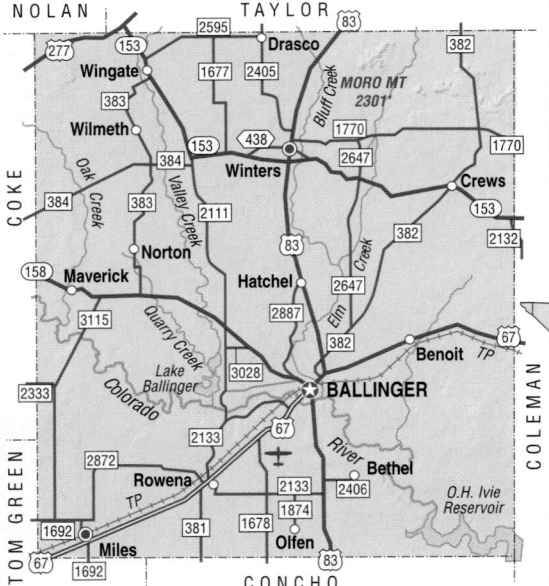

**Physical Features**: Level to rolling; bisected by Colorado and tributaries; sandy loam, black waxy soils; O.H. Ivie Reservoir, Lake Ballinger.

**Economy**: Agribusiness, oil, government/services, manufacturing.

**History**: Spanish explorers found Jumanos Indians in the area in 1650s; later, Apaches and Comanches were driven out in 1870s by U.S. military. First Anglo-Americans arrived in the 1850s; Germans, Czechs began arriving around 1900. County named for planter-legislator H.G. Runnels; created 1858 from Bexar, Travis counties; not organized until 1880.

**Race/Ethnicity**: (In percent) Anglo, 62.8; Black, 2.6; Hispanic, 33.6; Asian, 0.6; Other, 2.5.

**Vital Statistics**, annual: Births, 99; deaths, 133; marriages, 64; divorces, 25.

**Recreation**: Deer, dove and turkey hunting; lakes; fishing; antique car museum; historical markers in county.

**Minerals**: Oil, gas, sand.

**Agriculture**: Beef cattle, cotton, wheat, sorghum, some dairies, sheep and goats. Market value $47.4 million.

**BALLINGER** (3,612) county seat; varied manufacturing, oil-field services, meat processing; Carnegie Library, hospital, Western Texas College extension; the Cross, 100-ft. tall atop hill south of city; Festival of Ethnic Cultures in April.

Other towns include: **Miles** (827); **Norton** (50); **Rowena** (349); **Wingate** (100); **Winters** (2,452) manufacturing, museum, hospital.

| | |
|---|---|
| Population | 10,416 |
| Change fm 2010 | – 0.8 |
| Area (sq. mi.) | 1,057.1 |
| Land Area (sq. mi.) | 1,050.9 |
| Altitude (ft.) | 1,915-2,301 |
| Rainfall (in.) | 24,04 |
| Jan. mean min. | 31.2 |
| July mean max. | 94.4 |
| Civ. Labor | 4,459 |
| Unemployed | 5.5 |
| Wages | $23,715,779 |
| Per Capita Income | $34,548 |
| Prop. Value | $1,206,290,170 |
| Retail Sales | $78,948,287 |

# Rusk County

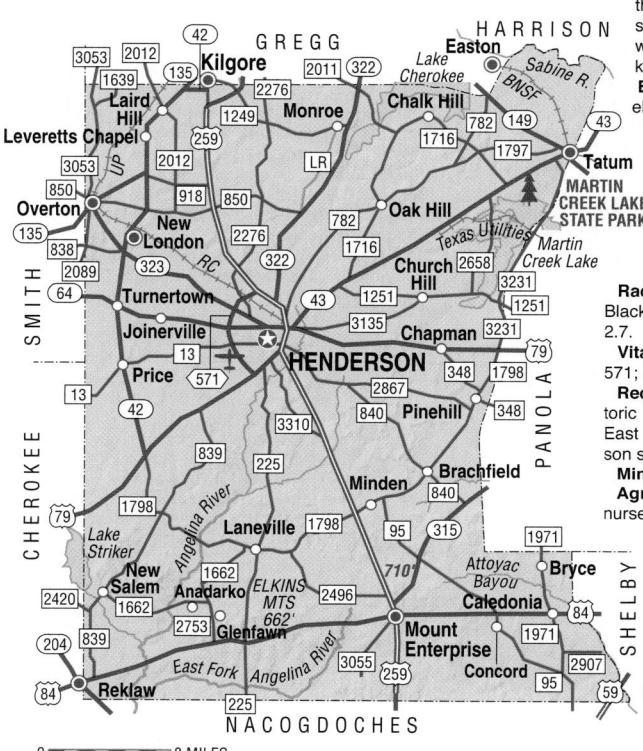

**Physical Features**: East Texas county on the Sabine-Angelina divide; varied deep, sandy soils; over half area in pines, hardwoods; Martin Creek Lake, Lake Cherokee, Lake Striker.

**Economy**: Oil and gas, lignite mining, electricity generation, agriculture.

**History**: Caddo tribal area. Cherokees settled in the 1820s; removed in 1839. First Anglo-Americans arrived in 1829. Antebellum slaveholding area. County named for Republic, state leader Thomas J. Rusk; created and organized from Nacogdoches County in 1843.

**Race/Ethnicity**: (In percent) Anglo, 64.9; Black, 17.6; Hispanic, 15.7; Asian, 0.6; Other, 2.7.

**Vital Statistics**, annual: Births, 700; deaths, 571; marriages, 317; divorces, 242.

**Recreation**: Water sports, state park, historic homes and sites, scenic drives, site of East Texas Field discovery oil well; Henderson syrup festival in November.

**Minerals**: Oil, natural gas, lignite.

**Agriculture**: Beef cattle, forage, poultry, nursery plants. Market value $75.3 million. Timber income substantial.

**HENDERSON** (13,637) county seat; power plant, mining, lumber, state jails; hospital, museum.

Other towns include: **Joinerville** (140); **Laird Hill** (300); **Laneville** (169); **Minden** (150); **Mount Enterprise** (449); **New London** (996) site of 1937 school explosion that killed 293 students and faculty.

Also, **Overton** (2,557, partly in Smith County) oil, lumbering center, petroleum processing, prison, A&M research center, blue grass festival in July; **Price** (275); **Tatum** (1,412, partly in Panola County); **Turnertown-Selman City** (271).

Also, part of **Easton** (505, mostly in Gregg County), part of **Reklaw** (389, mostly in Cherokee County) and part [3,013] of **Kilgore** (14,793 total).

| Population | 53.923 |
| --- | --- |
| Change fm 2010 | 1.1 |
| Area (sq. mi.) | 938.4 |
| Land Area (sq. mi.) | 924.0 |
| Altitude (ft.) | 250-710 |
| Rainfall (in.) | 49.36 |
| Jan. mean min. | 34.9 |
| July mean max. | 92.7 |
| Civ. Labor | 27,232 |
| Unemployed | 5.1 |
| Wages | $146,956,738 |
| Per Capita Income | $34,541 |
| Prop. Value | $5,920,819,590 |
| Retail Sales | $413,965,444 |

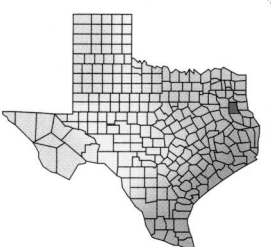

*For explanation of sources, symbols and abbreviations, see p. 238, and foldout*

*The intersection of FM 1798 and FM 225 in Laneville, Rusk County. Photo by Robert Plocheck.*

# Sabine County

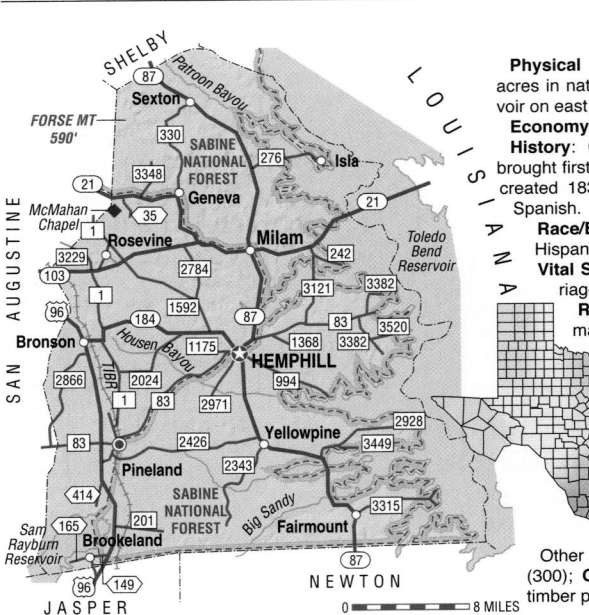

**Physical Features**: Eighty percent forested; 114,498 acres in national forest; Sabine River, Toledo Bend Reservoir on east; Sam Rayburn Reservoir on southwest.

**Economy**: Timber, government/services, tourism.

**History**: Caddo area. Spanish land grants in 1790s brought first Spanish and Anglo settlers. An original county, created 1836; organized 1837. Name means cypress in Spanish.

**Race/Ethnicity**: (In percent) Anglo, 86.7; Black, 7.5; Hispanic, 3.8; Asian, 0.4; Other, 2.1.

**Vital Statistics**, annual: Births, 83; deaths, 170; marriages, 88; divorces, 7.

**Recreation**: Lake activities, hunting, campsites, marinas, historic homes; McMahan's Chapel, pioneer Protestant church; Sabine National Forest.

**Minerals**: Glauconite, oil.

**Agriculture**: Beef cattle; forage, fruit raised. Market value $14.7 million. Significant timber industry.

**HEMPHILL** (1,215) county seat; timber, livestock center, retail trade, tourism, manufacturing; jail museum, library; Deerfest in September.

Other towns include: **Bronson** (377); **Brookeland** (300); **Geneva** (200); **Milam** (1,535); **Pineland** (839) timber processing.

| | | |
|---|---|---|
| Population | | 10,350 |
| Change fm 2010 | | – 4.5 |
| Area (sq. mi.) | | 576.7 |
| Land Area (sq. mi.) | | 491.4 |
| Altitude (ft.) | | 164-590 |
| Rainfall (in.) | | 54.60 |
| Jan. mean min. | | 36.5 |
| July mean max. | | 93.1 |
| Civ. Labor | | 3,519 |
| Unemployed | | 11.0 |
| Wages | | $17,700,401 |
| Per Capita Income | | $34,370 |
| Prop. Value | | $987,475,851 |
| Retail Sales | | $63,417,397 |

# San Augustine County

**Physical Features**: Hilly East Texas county, 80 percent forested with 66,799 acres in Angelina National Forest, 4,317 in Sabine National Forest; Sam Rayburn Reservoir; varied soils, sandy to black alluvial.

**Economy**: Lumbering, poultry, varied manufacturing.

**History**: Presence of Ais Indians attracted Spanish mission in 1717. First Anglos and Indians from U.S. southern states arrived around 1800. Antebellum slaveholding area. County created and named for Mexican municipality in 1836; an original county; organized 1837.

**Race/Ethnicity**: (In percent) Anglo, 68.8; Black, 22.6; Hispanic, 7.0; Asian, 0.4; Other, 2.0.

**Vital Statistics**, annual: Births, 113; deaths, 137; marriages, 66; divorces, 3.

**Recreation**: Lake activities, historic homes, tourist facilities in national forests; sassafras festival in October.

**Minerals**: Small amount of oil.

**Agriculture**: Poultry, cattle, horses; watermelons, peas, corn, truck crops. Market value $63.2 million. Timber sales significant.

**SAN AUGUSTINE** (2,089) county seat; oil and gas, poultry farms, logging, tourism; hospital; Mission Dolores museum.

Other towns include: **Broaddus** (208).

| | | |
|---|---|---|
| Population | | 8,610 |
| Change fm 2010 | | – 02.9 |
| Area (sq. mi.) | | 592.3 |
| Land Area (sq. mi.) | | 530.7 |
| Altitude (ft.) | | 164-590 |
| Rainfall (in.) | | 51.89 |
| Jan. mean min. | | 35.6 |
| July mean max. | | 92.7 |
| Civ. Labor | | 3,459 |
| Unemployed | | 8.2 |
| Wages | | $12,683,808 |
| Per Capita Income | | $31,590 |
| Prop. Value | | $1,074,387,600 |
| Retail Sales | | $60,355,005 |

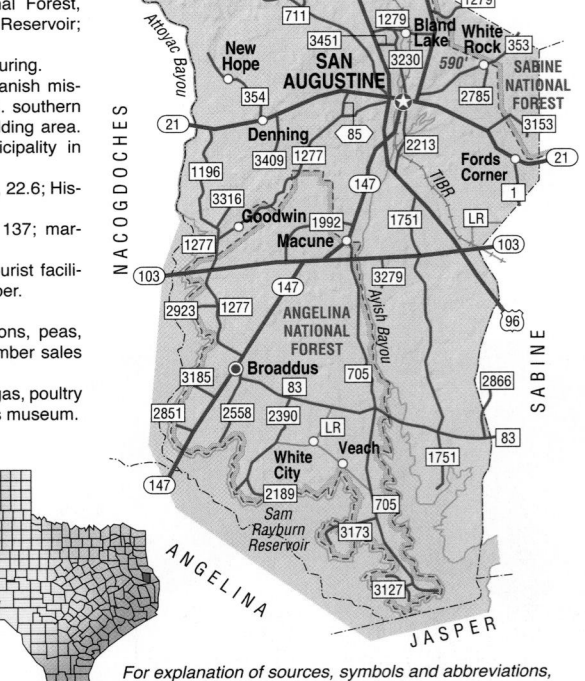

*For explanation of sources, symbols and abbreviations, see p. 238, and foldout map.*

# San Jacinto County

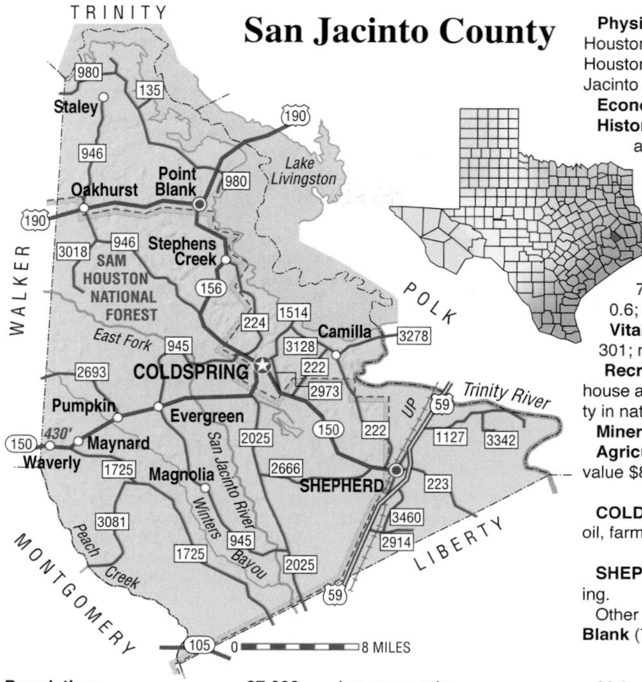

**Physical Features**: East Texas county north of Houston; rolling hills; 80 percent forested; Sam Houston National Forest; Trinity, East Fork San Jacinto rivers; Lake Livingston.

**Economy**: Timber and oil.

**History**: Atakapa Indian area. Anglo-Americans arrived in the 1820s. Land grants issued to Mexican families in the early 1830s. County created from Liberty, Montgomery, Polk, and Walker counties in 1869; organized in 1870; named for the battle.

**Race/Ethnicity**: (In percent) Anglo, 75.4; Black, 10.5; Hispanic, 12.0; Asian, 0.6; Other, 2.8.

**Vital Statistics**, annual: Births, 273; deaths, 301; marriages, 150; divorces, 131.

**Recreation**: Lake activities, hunting, old courthouse and jail. Approximately 60 percent of county in national forest.

**Minerals**: Oil, rock, gravel and iron ore.

**Agriculture**: Beef cattle and forages. Market value $8.5 million. Timber principal product.

**COLDSPRING** (922) county seat; lumbering, oil, farming center, tourism; historic sites.

**SHEPHERD** (2,444) lumbering, tourism, ranching.

Other towns include: **Oakhurst** (245); **Point Blank** (733) logging, agribusiness, construction.

| | | |
|---|---|---|
| Population | 27,099 | |
| Change fm 2010 | 2.7 | |
| Area (sq. mi.) | 627.9 | |
| Land Area (sq. mi.) | 569.2 | |
| Altitude (ft.) | 62-430 | |
| Rainfall (in.) | 50.68 | |
| Jan. mean min. | 38.2 | |
| July mean max. | 92.4 | |
| Civ. Labor | 11,627 | |
| Unemployed | 6.0 | |
| Wages | $16,214,208 | |
| Per Capita Income | $34,441 | |
| Prop. Value | $2,173,118,834 | |
| Retail Sales | $52,794,449 | |

For explanation of sources, symbols and abbreviations, see p. 238, and foldout map.

*A hardwood swamp in Sam Houston National Forest. Photo by Chris M./Commons.*

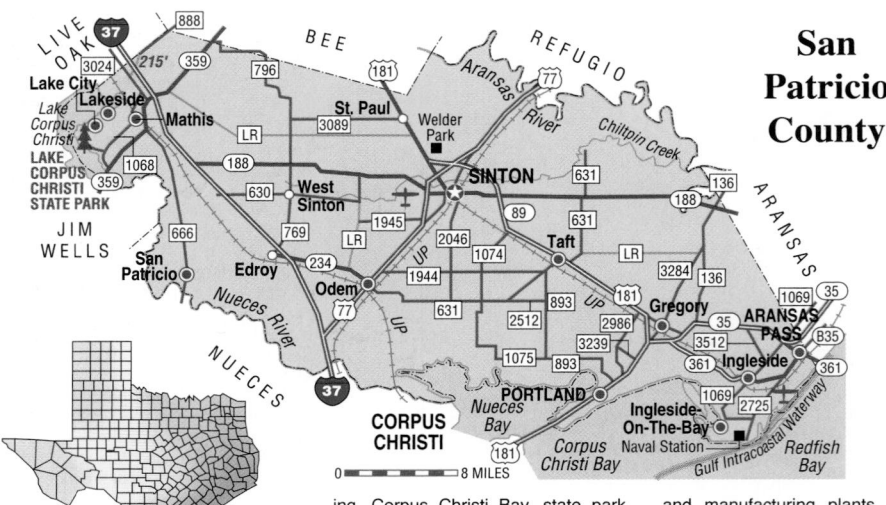

# San Patricio County

**Physical Features**: Grassy, coastal prairie draining to Aransas, Nueces rivers and to bays; sandy loam, clay, black loam soils; Lake Corpus Christi.

**Economy**: Oil, petrochemicals, agribusiness, manufacturing, tourism, in Corpus Christi metropolitan area.

**History**: Karankawa area. Mexican sheep herders in area before colonization. Settled by Irish families in 1830 (name is Spanish for St. Patrick). Created, named for municipality 1836; organized 1837, reorganized 1847.

**Race/Ethnicity**: (In percent) Anglo, 40.8; Black, 2.1; Hispanic, 55.4; Asian, 1.1; Other, 2.4.

**Vital Statistics**, annual: Births, 926; deaths, 614; marriages, 299; divorces, 223.

**Recreation**: Water activities, hunting, Corpus Christi Bay, state park, Welder Wildlife Foundation and Park, birdwatching.

**Minerals**: Oil, gas, gravel, caliche.

**Agriculture**: Cotton, grain sorghum, beef cattle, corn. Market value $86.2 million. Fisheries income significant.

**SINTON** (5,712) county seat; oil, agribusiness, tourism; Go Texan Days in October.

**ARANSAS PASS** (8,305, part [724] in Aransas County) deepwater port, shrimping, tourism, offshore oil-well servicing, aluminum and chemical plants; hospital; Shrimporee in May.

**PORTLAND** (15,553) retail center, petrochemicals, commuters to Corpus Christi; Indian Point pier; Windfest in April.

Other towns include: **Edroy** (336); **Gregory** (1,926); **Ingleside** (9,605) offshore well servicing, chemical and manufacturing plants, commuters, birding, Round Up Days in April; **Ingleside-on-the-Bay** (625); **Lake City** (512); **Lakeside** (309); **Mathis** (4,973); **Odem** (2,415); **St. Paul** (597); **San Patricio** (387); **Taft** (3,056) agriculture, drug rehabilitation center, commuters, wind farm, blackland museum, barbecue, tamale and hot sauce cook-off in December; **Taft Southwest** (1,483).

| Population | 66,915 |
|---|---|
| Change fm 2010 | 3.3 |
| Area (sq. mi.) | 707.8 |
| Land Area (sq. mi.) | 693,5 |
| Altitude (ft.) | sea level-215 |
| Rainfall (in.) | 35.28 |
| Jan. mean min. | 44.2 |
| July mean max. | 93.4 |
| Civ. Labor | 29,648 |
| Unemployed | 6.9 |
| Wages | $202,779,486 |
| Per Capita Income | $41,545 |
| Prop. Value | $6,226,524,166 |
| Retail Sales | $860,172,394 |

*Wildflowers in Union Band Cemetery in San Saba County. Photo by Ron Billings/Texas A&M Forest Service.*

# San Saba County

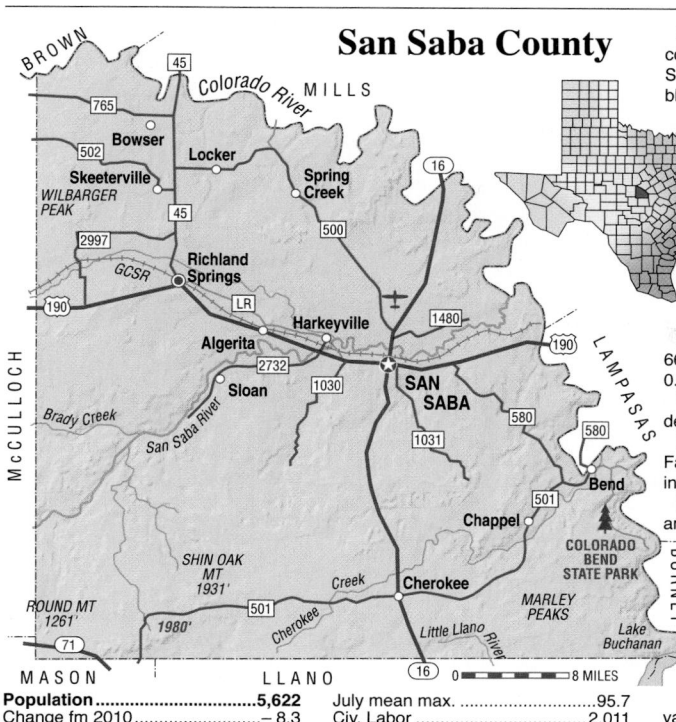

**Physical Features**: West central county; hilly, rolling; bisected by San Saba River; Colorado River on east; black, gray sandy loam, alluvial soils; northern tip of Lake Buchanan.

**Economy**: Pecan processing plants, tourism, hunting leases.

**History**: Apaches and Comanches in area when Spanish explored. Anglo-American settlers arrived in 1850s. County created from Bexar District 1856, organized the same year; named for river.

**Race/Ethnicity**: (In percent) Anglo, 66.1; Black, 3.6; Hispanic, 29.0; Asian, 0.3; Other, 2.7.

**Vital Statistics**, annual: Births, 75; deaths, 74; marriages, 35; divorces, 4.

**Recreation**: State park with Gorman Falls; deer hunting; historic sites; fishing; scenic drives; wildflower trail.

**Minerals**: Rock quarry, limestone and sand stone.

**Agriculture**: Cattle, pecans (second in acreage), wheat, hay, some sheep/goats. Market value $30 million. Hunting, wildlife leases.

**SAN SABA** (3,075) county seat; claims title "Pecan Capital of the World"; stone processing, varied manufacturing, prison; Cow Camp cookoff in May.

Other towns include: **Bend** (115, partly in Lampasas County); **Cherokee** (175); **Richland Springs** (333).

| | |
|---|---|
| Population | 5,622 |
| Change fm 2010 | – 8.3 |
| Area (sq. mi.) | 1,138.4 |
| Land Area (sq. mi.) | 1,135.3 |
| Altitude (ft.) | 1,020-1,980 |
| Rainfall (in.) | 28.50 |
| Jan. mean min. | 34.6 |
| July mean max. | 95.7 |
| Civ. Labor | 2,011 |
| Unemployed | 6.8 |
| Wages | $10,172,764 |
| Per Capita Income | $32,590 |
| Prop. Value | $1,4276,029,730 |
| Retail Sales | $35,325,478 |

# Schleicher County

**Physical Features**: West central county on edge of Edwards Plateau, broken by Devils, Concho, San Saba river tributaries; part hilly; black soils.

**Economy**: Oil, ranching, hunting.

**History**: Jumanos in the area in the 1630s. Later, Apaches and Comanches arrived; removed in the 1870s. Ranching began in the 1870s. Census of 1890 showed third of population from Mexico. County named for Gustav Schleicher, founder of German colony; county created from Crockett County 1887, organized 1901.

**Race/Ethnicity**: (In percent) Anglo, 46.6; Black, 1.8; Hispanic, 50.9; Asian, 0.4; Other, 2.3.

**Vital Statistics**, annual: Births, 40; deaths, 24; marriages, 11; divorces, 8.

**Recreation**: Hunting, livestock show in January, youth and open rodeos, mountain bike events.

**Minerals**: Oil, natural gas.

**Agriculture**: Beef cattle, sheep, goats, and cotton, hay. Market value $13.6 million. Hunting leases important.

**ELDORADO** (1,881) county seat; oil activities, center for livestock, mohair marketing, woolen mill, government/services; hospital.

*For explanation of sources, symbols and abbreviations, see p. 238, and foldout map.*

| | |
|---|---|
| Population | 3,162 |
| Change fm 2010 | – 8.6 |
| Area (sq. mi.) | 1,310.7 |
| Land Area (sq. mi.) | 1,310.6 |
| Altitude (ft.) | 2,070-2,600 |
| Rainfall (in.) | 23.21 |
| Jan. mean min. | 31.1 |
| July mean max. | 92.1 |
| Civ. Labor | 1,709 |
| Unemployed | 3.5 |
| Wages | $10,567,136 |
| Per Capita Income | $38,755 |
| Prop. Value | $970,786,817 |
| Retail Sales | $11,138,244 |

# Scurry County

**Physical Features**: Plains county below Caprock, some hills; drained by Colorado, Brazos tributaries; Lake J.B. Thomas; sandy, loam soils.

**Economy**: Oil, government/services, agribusiness, manufacturing.

**History**: Apaches; displaced later by Comanches who were relocated to Indian Territory in 1875. Ranching began in late 1870s. County created from Bexar District 1876; organized 1884; named for Confederate Gen. W.R. Scurry.

**Race/Ethnicity**: (In percent) Anglo, 55.2; Black, 5.2; Hispanic, 38.5; Asian, 0.8; Other, 2.6.

**Vital Statistics**, annual: Births, 270; deaths, 173; marriages, 126; divorces, 70.

**Recreation**: Lake J.B. Thomas water recreation; Towle Memorial Park; museums, community theater, White Buffalo Days and Bikefest in October.

**Minerals**: Oil, gas.

**Agriculture**: Cotton, wheat, cattle, hay. Market value $29 million.

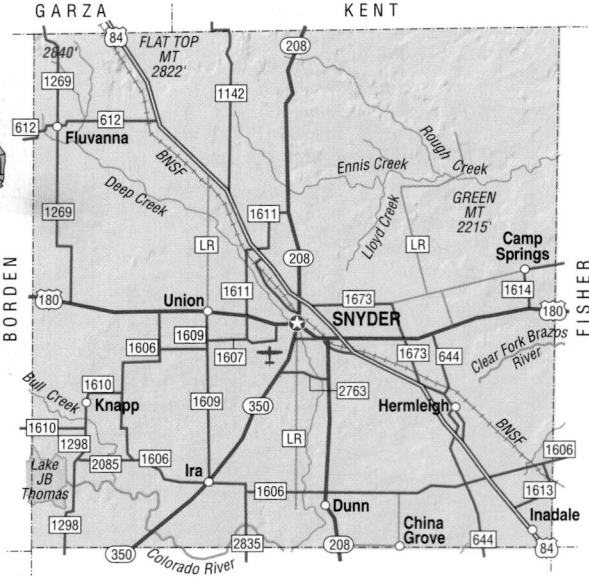

**SNYDER** (11,839) county seat; oil, wind energy, agriculture; Western Texas College, hospital, museum; Western Swing days in June.

Other towns include: **Dunn** (75); **Fluvanna** (180); **Hermleigh** (360); **Ira** (250).

| | | | |
|---|---|---|---|
| Population | 17,328 | July mean max. | 93.9 |
| Change fm 2010 | 2.4 | Civ. Labor | 9,853 |
| Area (sq. mi.) | 907.5 | Unemployed | 3.8 |
| Land Area (sq. mi.) | 905.4 | Wages | $103,997,969 |
| Altitude (ft.) | 1,800-2,840 | Per Capita Income | $56,643 |
| Rainfall (in.) | 22.68 | Prop. Value | $4,264,813,439 |
| Jan. mean min. | 28.2 | Retail Sales | $225,515,899 |

---

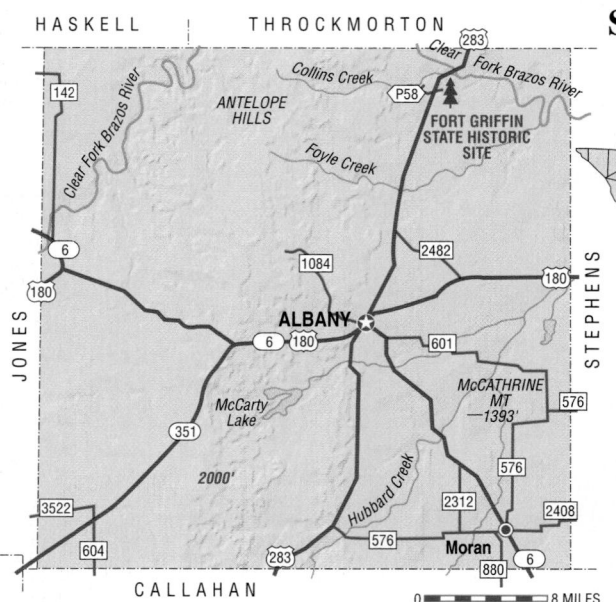

# Shackelford County

**Physical Features**: Rolling, hilly, drained by tributaries of Brazos; sandy and chocolate loam soils; lake.

**Economy**: Oil and ranching, some manufacturing, hunting.

**History**: Apaches; driven out by Comanches. First Anglo-American settlers arrived soon after establishment of military outpost in 1850s. County created from Bosque County 1858; organized 1874; named for Dr. Jack (or John) Shackelford, Texas Revolutionary hero.

**Race/Ethnicity**: (In percent) Anglo, 86.3; Black, 1.3; Hispanic, 10.8; Asian, 0.3; Other, 2.2.

**Vital Statistics**, annual: Births, 42; deaths, 32; marriages, 27; divorces, 18.

**Recreation**: Fort Griffin historic site, courthouse historical district, hunting, lake, outdoor activities, June Fandangle musical about area history.

**Minerals**: Oil, natural gas.

**Agriculture**: Beef cattle, wheat, hay, cotton. Market value $22.3 million. Hunting leases.

**ALBANY** (2,038) county seat; tourism, hunting, oil, ranching; historical district, Old Jail art center.

Other town: **Moran** (271).

| | | | |
|---|---|---|---|
| Population | 3,343 | July mean max. | 94.4 |
| Change fm 2010 | – 1.0 | Civ. Labor | 3,087 |
| Area (sq. mi.) | 915.6 | Unemployed | 2.4 |
| Land Area (sq. mi.) | 914.3 | Wages | $26,124,115 |
| Altitude (ft.) | 1,150-2,000 | Per Capita Income | $87,115 |
| Rainfall (in.) | 28.36 | Prop. Value | $1,477,940,239 |
| Jan. mean min. | 30.2 | Retail Sales | $16,614,207 |

# Shelby County

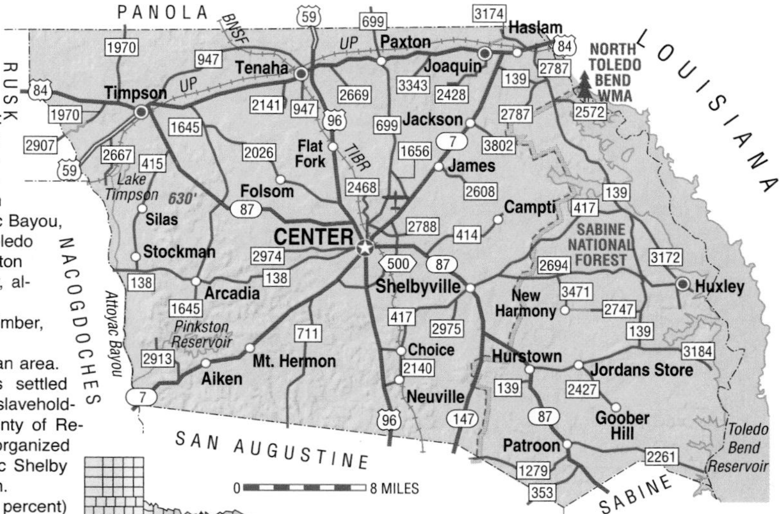

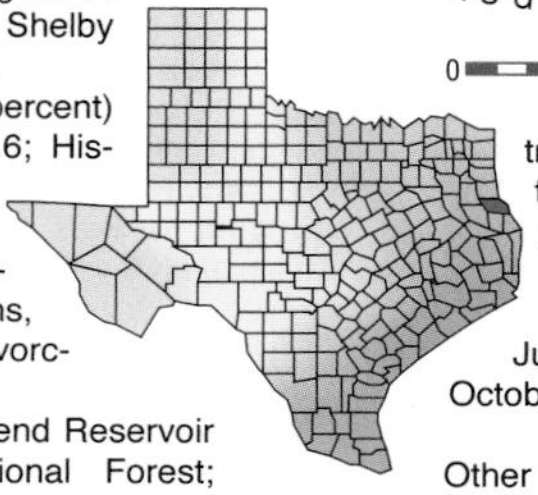

**Physical Features**: East Texas county; partly hills, much bottomland; well-timbered, 67,762 acres in national forest; Attoyac Bayou, other streams; Toledo Bend Reservoir, Pinkston Reservoir; sandy, clay, alluvial soils.

**Economy**: Poultry, timber, cattle, tourism.

**History**: Caddo Indian area. First Anglo-Americans settled in 1810s. Antebellum slaveholding area. Original county of Republic, created 1836; organized 1837; named for Isaac Shelby of American Revolution.

**Race/Ethnicity**: (In percent) Anglo, 63.5; Black, 17.6; Hispanic, 17.6; Asian, 0.7; Other, 2.1.

**Vital Statistics**, annual: Births, 370; deaths, 249; marriages, 177; divorces, 61.

**Recreation**: Toledo Bend Reservoir activities; Sabine National Forest; hunting, fishing; camping; historic sites, restored 1885 courthouse.

**Minerals**: Natural gas, oil.

**Agriculture**: First in poultry and egg production. Beef cattle. Hay. Market value $473.2 million. Timber sales significant.

**CENTER** (5,453) county seat; poultry, timber, oil and gas, tourism; hospital, Panola College extension, museum; What-A-Melon festival in July, poultry festival in October.

Other towns: **Huxley** (390); **Joaquin** (851); **Shelbyville** (600); **Tenaha** (1,203); **Timpson** (1,169) livestock, timber, farming, commuters, genealogy library, Frontier Days in July.

| | |
|---|---|
| Population | 25,515 |
| Change fm 2010 | 0.3 |
| Area (sq. mi.) | 834.6 |
| Land Area (sq. mi.) | 795.6 |
| Altitude (ft.) | 174-630 |
| Rainfall (in.) | 54.20 |
| Jan. mean min. | 35.1 |
| July mean max. | 94.4 |
| Civ. Labor | 12,705 |
| Unemployed | 5.9 |
| Wages | $68,398,481 |
| Per Capita Income | $35,812 |
| Prop. Value | $2,229,448,139 |
| Retail Sales | $303,075,065 |

*For explanation of sources, symbols and abbreviations, see p. 238, and foldout map.*

---

*The old administration building at Fort Griffin, Shackelford County. Photo by Mark Fisher (CC).*

# Sherman County

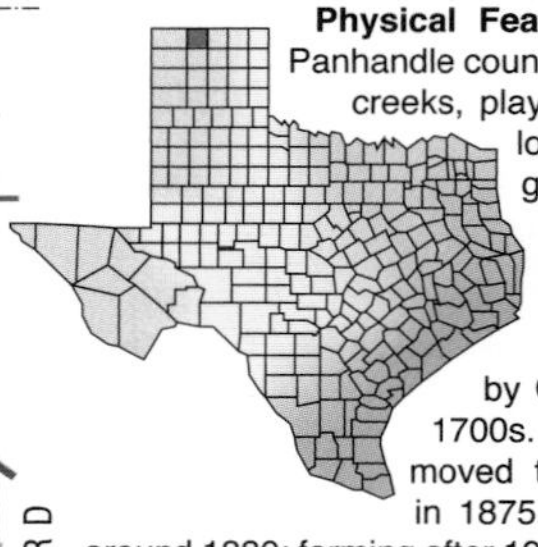

O K L A H O M A

Texhoma

North Canadian River

3805'  2677

UP

Frisco Creek

BNSF 287

STRATFORD

15

15

54

2014  2232  LR

2899

LR

1573

1573

LR

BNSF

119

297

287

MOORE

Coldwater Creek

North Palo Duro Creek

1573

1573

520

1060

DALLAM

HANSFORD

0 ▬▬▬▬ 8 MILES

**Physical Features**: A northern Panhandle county; level, broken by creeks, playas; sandy to dark loam soils; underground water.

**Economy**: Agri-business, tourism.

**History**: Apaches; pushed out by Comanches in the 1700s. Comanches removed to Indian Territory in 1875. Ranching began around 1880; farming after 1900. County named for Republic of Texas Gen. Sidney Sherman; created from Bexar District in 1876; organized in 1889.

**Race/Ethnicity**: (In percent) Anglo, 55.5; Black, 0.9; Hispanic, 42.3; Asian, 0.5; Other, 2.5.

**Vital Statistics**, annual: Births, 35; deaths, 29; marriages, 22; divorces, 1.

**Recreation**: Depot museum; pheasant, pronghorn hunting, jamboree and rodeo in July, carriage driving event in September.

**Minerals**: Natural gas, oil.

**Agriculture**: Beef and stocker cattle, wheat, corn, milo, cotton; 127,000 acres irrigated. Market value $590.4 million.

| | |
|---|---|
| Population | 3,084 |
| Change fm 2010 | 1.6 |
| Area (sq. mi.) | 923.2 |
| Land Area (sq. mi.) | 923.0 |
| Altitude (ft.) | 3,200-3,805 |
| Rainfall (in.) | 17.77 |
| Jan. mean min. | 19.5 |
| July mean max. | 91.5 |
| Civ. Labor | 1,394 |
| Unemployed | 4.3 |

| | |
|---|---|
| Wages | $9,455,320 |
| Per Capita Income | $48,489 |
| Prop. Value | $874,572,210 |
| Retail Sales | $15,789,542 |

*For explanation of sources, symbols and abbreviations, see p. 238, and foldout map.*

**STRATFORD** (2,050) county seat; agribusiness, petroleum, tourism, birdseed packaging; VA clinic; science and art museum.

**Texhoma** (1,295 [with 352 in Texas]) other principal town.

A campsite at Tyler State Park, Smith County. Texas Parks & Wildlife photo.

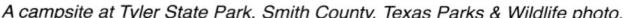

# Smith County

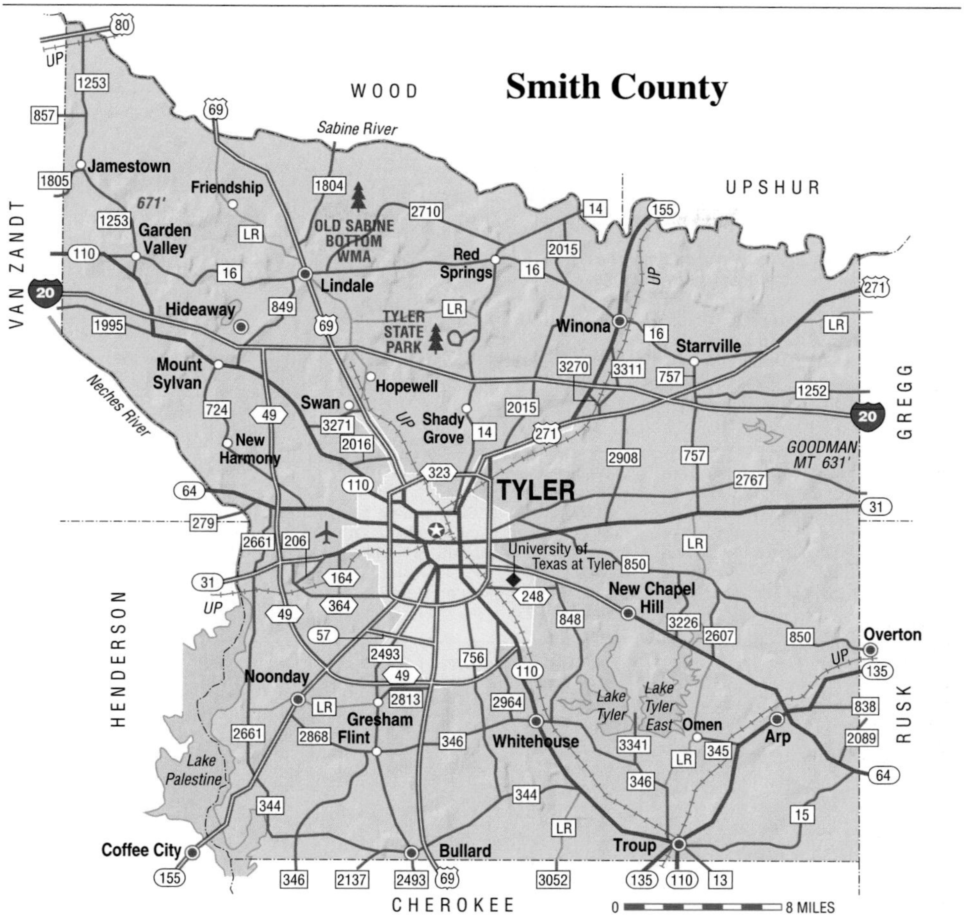

WOOD

Sabine River

UPSHUR

VAN ZANDT

HENDERSON

CHEROKEE

GREGG

RUSK

80
UP
1253
857
1253
69
Jamestown
1805
671'
Friendship
1804
Garden
Valley
LR
110
16
Lindale
Hideaway
849
69
Mount
Sylvan
724
49
New
Harmony
2016
3271
64
279
31
UP
49
364
57
2661 206
164
OLD SABINE
BOTTOM
WMA
2710
Red
Springs
16
TYLER
STATE
PARK
LR
Swan
Hopewell
Shady
Grove
110
323
248
2493
49
Noonday
LR
2813
2661
2868 Flint
Gresham
346
756
2964
110
14
2015
16
2015
271
14
2908
TYLER
University of
Texas at Tyler
848
Whitehouse
344
344
155
271
1995
16
155
UP
3270 3311
757
757
3226
Winona
Starrville
850
New Chapel
Hill
2607
Lake
Tyler
Lake
Tyler
East
3341
3341
LR
Omen
345
346
LR
271
1252
GOODMAN
MT 631'
2767
LR
31
850
271
20
Overton
135
838
Arp
2089
64
15
LR
Coffee City
Lake
Palestine
344
Bullard
346 2137 2493 69
3052
Troup
135 110 13
0 ■■■■ 8 MILES

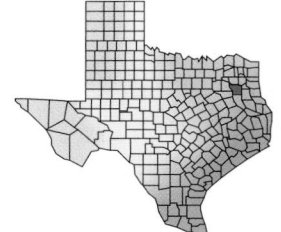

**Physical Features:** Populous East Texas county of rolling hills, many timbered; Sabine, Neches rivers, other streams; Lake Palestine, Lake Tyler, Lake Tyler East; alluvial, gray, sandy loam, clay soils.

**Economy:** Medical facilities, education, government/services, agribusiness, petroleum production, manufacturing, distribution center, tourism.

**History:** Caddoes of area reduced by disease and other tribes in the 1790s. Cherokees settled in the 1820s; removed in 1839. In the late 1820s, first Anglo-American settlers arrived. Antebellum slaveholding area. County named for Texas Revolutionary Gen. James Smith; county created and organized in 1846 from Nacogdoches County.

**Race/Ethnicity:** (In percent) Anglo, 61.3; Black, 17.9; Hispanic, 18.3; Asian, 1.4; Other, 2.4.

**Vital Statistics,** annual: Births, 2,992; deaths, 1,903; marriages, 1,813; divorces, 751.

**Recreation:** Activities on Palestine, Tyler lakes; Rose Garden; state park; Goodman Museum; Caldwell Zoo; collegiate events; Juneteenth celebration,

Rose Festival in October, Azalea Trail, East Texas Fair in September/October.

**Minerals:** Oil, gas.

**Agriculture:** Horticultural crops and nurseries, beef cattle, forages, fruits and vegetables, horses, Christmas trees. Market value $76.8 million. Timber sales substantial.

**TYLER** (98,987) county seat; health services, education, retail center, varied manufacturing; University of Texas at Tyler, Tyler Junior College, Texas College, University of Texas Health Center; hospitals, nursing school; museums, Camp Ford historic park; claims title, "Rose Capital of the Nation."

Other towns include: **Arp** (983) Strawberry Festival in April; **Bullard** (2,679, part in Cherokee County); **Flint** (2,500); **Hideaway** (3,135); **Lindale** (5,365) distribution center, foundry, varied manufacturing, Country Fest in October; **New Chapel Hill** (599); **Noonday** (806) Sweet Onion festival in June; **Troup** (1,884, part in Cherokee County) plastic manufacturing, motorcycle customization, Crawfish Boil in May; **Whitehouse** (7,908) commuters to Tyler, government/services, Yesteryear festival in June; **Winona** (588).

Part of **Overton** (2,557, mostly in Rusk County).

| | |
|---|---|
| **Population** | **218,842** |
| Change fm 2010 | 4.4 |
| Area (sq. mi.) | 949.7 |
| Land Area (sq. mi.) | 921.5 |
| Altitude (ft.) | 275-671 |
| Rainfall (in.) | 46.63 |
| Jan. mean min. | 36.4 |
| July mean max. | 92.7 |
| Civ. Labor | 103,429 |
| Unemployed | 5.5 |
| Wages | $972,093,405 |
| Per Capita Income | $42,573 |
| Prop. Value | $16,419,476,569 |
| Retail Sales | $3,656,364,711 |

# Somervell County

**Physical Features**: Hilly terrain southwest of Fort Worth; Brazos, Paluxy rivers; Squaw Creek Reservoir; gray, dark, alluvial soils; second-smallest county.

**Economy**: Tourism, nuclear power plant, government/services, commuters, natural gas.

**History**: Wichita, Tonkawa area; Comanches later. Anglo-Americans arrived in the 1850s. County created as Somerville County from Hood County, organized 1875. Spelling was changed in 1876; named for Republic of Texas Gen. Alexander Somervell.

**Race/Ethnicity**: (In percent) Anglo, 77.1; Black, 1.2; Hispanic, 19.1; Asian, 0.9; Other, 3.5.

**Vital Statistics**, annual: Births, 94; deaths, 80; marriages, 67; divorces, 39.

**Recreation**: Fishing, hunting; unique geological formations; dinosaur tracks in state park; Glen Rose Big Rocks Park; Fossil Rim Wildlife Center; nature trails, museums; exposition center; Paluxy Pedal bicycle ride in October.

**Minerals**: Sand, gravel, silica, natural gas.

**Agriculture**: Cattle, hay, horses, nurseries. Market value $4.3 million. Hunting leases important.

**GLEN ROSE** (2,529) county seat: nuclear power plant, tourism, farm trade center; hospital; Hill College branch.

Other towns include: **Nemo** (56); **Rainbow** (121).

| | |
|---|---|
| Population | **8,694** |
| Change fm 2010 | 2.4 |
| Area (sq. mi.) | 192.0 |
| Land Area (sq. mi.) | 186.5 |
| Altitude (ft.) | 550-1,310 |
| Rainfall (in.) | 36.87 |
| Jan. mean min. | 27.4 |
| July mean max. | 97.0 |
| Civ. Labor | 5,104 |
| Unemployed | 5.0 |
| Wages | $51,873,232 |
| Per Capita Income | $41,667 |
| Prop. Value | $3,363,419,963 |
| Retail Sales | $53,032,250 |

# Starr County

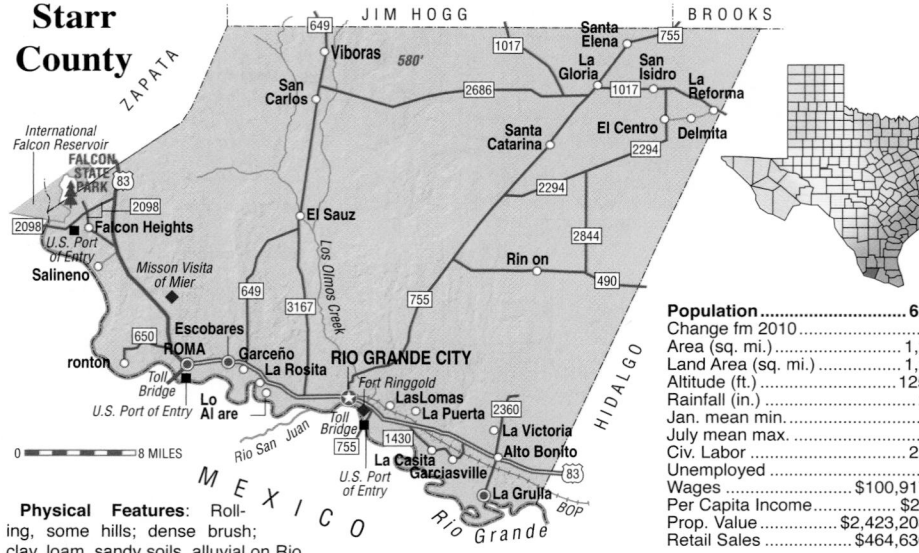

**Physical Features**: Rolling, some hills; dense brush; clay, loam, sandy soils, alluvial on Rio Grande; Falcon Reservoir.

**Economy**: Vegetable packing, other agribusiness, oil processing, tourism, government/services.

**History**: Coahuiltecan Indian area. Settlers from Spanish villages that were established in 1749 on south bank began to move across river soon afterward. Fort Ringgold established in 1848. County named for Dr. J.H. Starr, secretary of treasury of the Republic; county created from Nueces County and organized in 1848.

**Race/Ethnicity**: (In percent) Anglo, 3.9; Black, 0.4; Hispanic, 95.7; Asian, 0.3; Other, 0.5.

**Vital Statistics**, annual: Births, 1,346; deaths, 356; marriages, 408; divorces, 0.

**Recreation**: Falcon Reservoir activities; deer, white-wing dove hunting; access to Mexico; historic houses, Lee House at Fort Ringgold; grotto at Rio Grande City; Roma Fest in November.

**Minerals**: Oil, gas, sand, gravel.

**Agriculture**: Beef and fed cattle; vegetables, cotton, sorghum; 8,500 acres irrigated for vegetables. Market value $108.5 million.

**RIO GRANDE CITY** (14,132) county seat; government/services, tourism, agriculture; hospital, college branches;

trolley tours; Vaquero Days in February.

**ROMA**-Los Saenz (9,830) agriculture center; La Purísima Concepcíon Visita.

Other towns include: **Delmita** (225); **Escobares** (2,753); **Falcon Heights** (54); **Fronton** (194); **Garceño** (435); **Garciasville** (47); **La Casita** (127); **La Grulla** (1,612); **La Puerta** (642); **La Rosita** (89); **Las Lomas** (3,189); **La Victoria** (175); **Los Alvarez** (299); **North Escobares** (126); **Salineño** (193); **San Isidro** (241); **Santa Elena** (35).

| | |
|---|---|
| Population | **62,955** |
| Change fm 2010 | 3.3 |
| Area (sq. mi.) | 1,229.1 |
| Land Area (sq. mi.) | 1,223.2 |
| Altitude (ft.) | 125-580 |
| Rainfall (in.) | 22.65 |
| Jan. mean min. | 45.9 |
| July mean max. | 98.4 |
| Civ. Labor | 25,127 |
| Unemployed | 14.2 |
| Wages | $100,917,768 |
| Per Capita Income | $20,811 |
| Prop. Value | $2,423,208,940 |
| Retail Sales | $464,630,495 |

# Stephens County

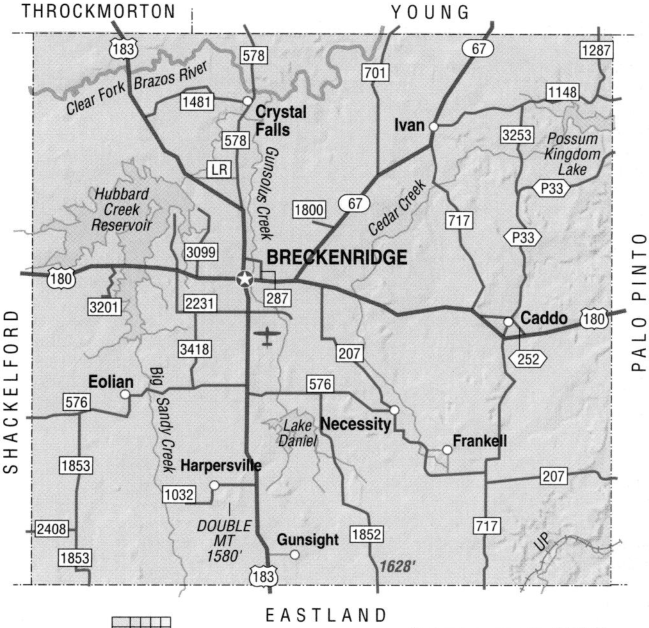

**Physical Features**: West central county; broken, hilly; Hubbard Creek Reservoir, Possum Kingdom Lake, Lake Daniel; Brazos River; loam, sandy soils.

**Economy**: Oil, agribusiness, manufacturing, recreation.

**History**: Comanches, Tonkawas in area when Anglo-American settlement began in 1850s. County created as Buchanan 1858 from Bosque; renamed 1861 for Confederate Vice President Alexander H. Stephens; organized 1876.

**Race/Ethnicity**: (In percent) Anglo, 73.7; Black, 2.5; Hispanic, 22.4; Asian, 0.4; Other, 2.0.

**Vital Statistics**, annual: Births, 99; deaths, 114; marriages, 61; divorces, 54.

**Recreation**: Lakes activities, hunting, campsites, historical points, Swenson Museum, Sandefer Oil Museum, aviation museum, festival and car show in fall.

**Minerals**: Oil, natural gas, stone.

**Agriculture**: Beef cattle, hogs, goats, sheep; wheat, oats, hay, peanuts, grain sorghum, cotton, pecans. Market value $9.2 million.

**BRECKENRIDGE** (5,581) county seat; oil, agriculture, oil-field equipment, aircraft parts; hospital, prison, Texas State Technical College branch, library.

Other towns include: **Caddo** (70) gateway to Possum Kingdom State Park.

*For explanation of sources, symbols and abbreviations, see p. 238, and foldout map.*

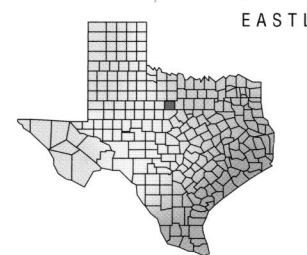

| Population | 9,405 |
|---|---|
| Change fm 2010 | – 2.3 |
| Area (sq. mi.) | 921.5 |
| Land Area (sq. mi.) | 896.7 |
| Altitude (ft.) | 995-1,628 |
| Rainfall (in.) | 29.98 |
| Jan. mean min. | 30.3 |
| July mean max. | 95.8 |
| Civ. Labor | 4,678 |
| Unemployed | 4.6 |
| Wages | $30,225,744 |
| Per Capita Inc. | $54,430 |
| Prop. Value | $1,712,818,186 |
| Retail Sales | $99,579,586 |

*The dinosaur models at Dinosaur Valley State Park, Somervell County. Photo by Gary S. Hickinbotham.*

# Sterling County

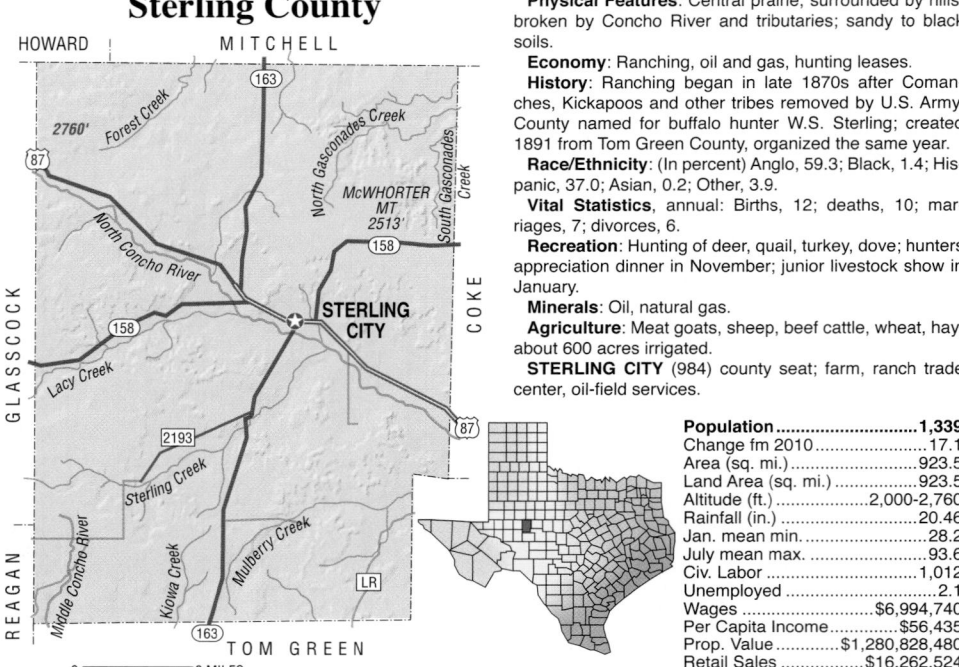

**Physical Features**: Central prairie, surrounded by hills, broken by Concho River and tributaries; sandy to black soils.

**Economy**: Ranching, oil and gas, hunting leases.

**History**: Ranching began in late 1870s after Comanches, Kickapoos and other tribes removed by U.S. Army. County named for buffalo hunter W.S. Sterling; created 1891 from Tom Green County, organized the same year.

**Race/Ethnicity**: (In percent) Anglo, 59.3; Black, 1.4; Hispanic, 37.0; Asian, 0.2; Other, 3.9.

**Vital Statistics**, annual: Births, 12; deaths, 10; marriages, 7; divorces, 6.

**Recreation**: Hunting of deer, quail, turkey, dove; hunters appreciation dinner in November; junior livestock show in January.

**Minerals**: Oil, natural gas.

**Agriculture**: Meat goats, sheep, beef cattle, wheat, hay; about 600 acres irrigated.

**STERLING CITY** (984) county seat; farm, ranch trade center, oil-field services.

| | |
|---|---|
| Population | **1,339** |
| Change fm 2010 | 17.1 |
| Area (sq. mi.) | 923.5 |
| Land Area (sq. mi.) | 923.5 |
| Altitude (ft.) | 2,000-2,760 |
| Rainfall (in.) | 20.46 |
| Jan. mean min. | 28.2 |
| July mean max. | 93.6 |
| Civ. Labor | 1,012 |
| Unemployed | 2.1 |
| Wages | $6,994,740 |
| Per Capita Income | $56,435 |
| Prop. Value | $1,280,828,480 |
| Retail Sales | $16,262,524 |

# Stonewall County

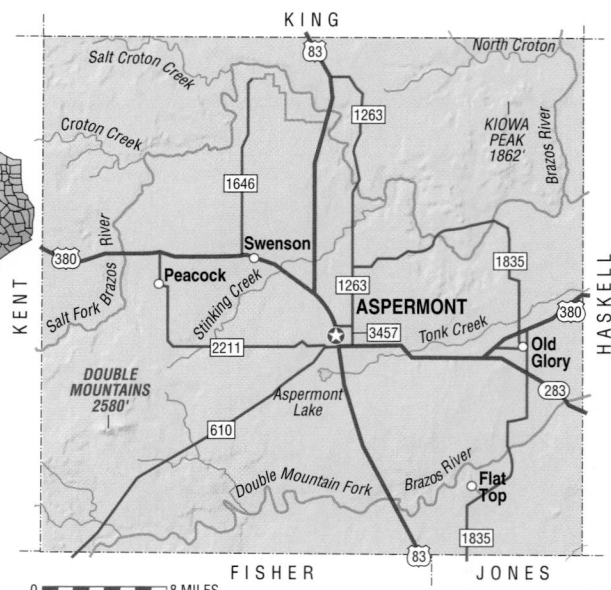

**Physical Features**: Western county on Rolling Plains below Caprock, bisected by Brazos forks; sandy loam, sandy, other soils; some hills.

**Economy**: Agribusiness, light fabrication, government/services.

**History**: Anglo-American ranchers arrived in 1870s after Comanches and other tribes removed by U.S. Army. German farmers settled after 1900. County named for Confederate Gen. T.J. (Stonewall) Jackson; created from Bexar District 1876, organized 1888.

**Race/Ethnicity**: (In percent) Anglo, 78.5; Black, 4.1; Hispanic, 15.6; Asian, 0.8; Other, 2.9.

**Vital Statistics**, annual: Births, 12; deaths, 28; marriages, 9; divorces, 12.

**Recreation**: Deer, quail, feral hog, turkey hunting; rodeos in June, September.

**Minerals**: Gypsum, gravel, oil.

**Agriculture**: Beef cattle, wheat, cotton, peanuts, hay. Also, grain sorghum, meat goats and swine. Market value $47.4 million.

**ASPERMONT** (835) county seat; oil field and ranching center, light fabrication; hospital; livestock show in February, Springfest.

Other towns include: **Old Glory** (100) farming center.

*For explanation of sources, symbols and abbreviations, see p. 238, and foldout map.*

| | | | |
|---|---|---|---|
| Population | **1,403** | July mean max. | 97.0 |
| Change fm 2010 | – 5.8 | Civ. Labor | 825 |
| Area (sq. mi.) | 920.2 | Unemployed | 3.6 |
| Land Area (sq. mi.) | 916.3 | Wages | $5,074,218 |
| Altitude (ft.) | 1,450-2,580 | Per Capita Income | $53,240 |
| Rainfall (in.) | 23.77 | Prop. Value | $890,314,107 |
| Jan. mean min. | 28.5 | Retail Sales | $10,805,090 |

# Sutton County

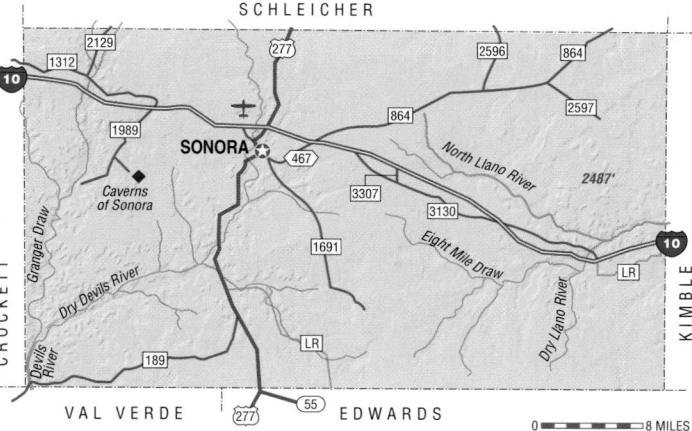

**Physical Features**: Southwestern county; level in west, rugged terrain in east, broken by tributaries of Devils, Llano rivers; black, red loam soils.

**Economy**: Natural gas, hunting, tourism, agriculture.

**History**: Lipan Apaches drove out Tonkawas in 1600s. Comanches, military outpost and disease forced Apaches south. Anglo-Americans settled in 1870s. Mexican immigration increased after 1890. County created from Crockett 1887; organized 1890; named for Confederate Col. John S. Sutton.

**Race/Ethnicity**: (In percent) Anglo, 37.8; Black, 0.9; Hispanic, 61`.1; Asian, 0.4; Other, 1.6.

**Vital Statistics**, annual: Births, 54; deaths, 38; marriages, 23; divorces, 12.

**Recreation**: Hunting, Meirs Museum, ranch museum, Caverns of Sonora, wildlife sanctuary, Cinco de Mayo.

**Minerals**: Oil, natural gas.

**Agriculture**: Meat goats (first in numbers), sheep, cattle, Angora goats (second in numbers). Exotic wildlife. Wheat and oats raised for grazing, hay; minor irrigation. Market value $10.9 million. Hunting leases important.

**SONORA** (2,999) county seat; oil and gas production, ranching, tourism; hospital; wool, mohair show in June.

| | |
|---|---|
| **Population** | **3,972** |
| Change fm 2010 | – 3.8 |
| Area (sq. mi.) | 1,454.4 |
| Land Area (sq. mi.) | 1,453.9 |
| Altitude (ft.) | 1,840-2,487 |
| Rainfall (in.) | 23.03 |
| Jan. mean min. | 29.2 |
| July mean max. | 94.4 |
| Civ. Labor | 3,293 |
| Unemployed | 2.5 |
| Wages | $39,23,623 |
| Per Capita Income | $69,100 |
| Prop. Value | $1,296,501,576 |
| Retail Sales | $35,613,880 |

# Swisher County

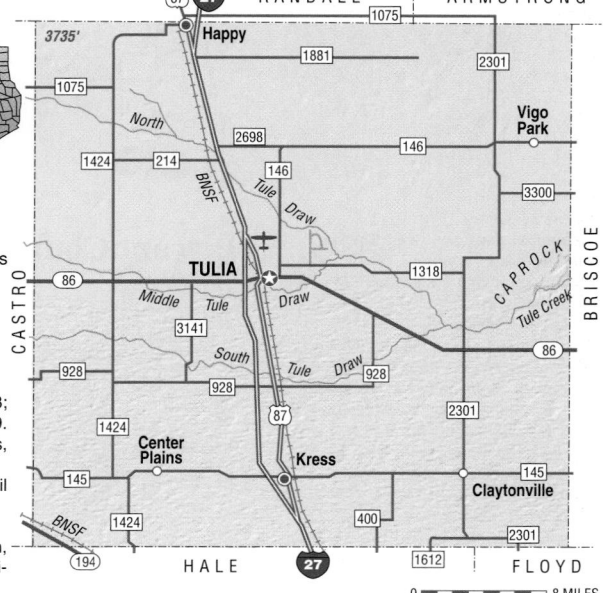

**Physical Features**: High Plains; level, broken by Tule Canyon and Creek; playas; large underground water supply; rich soils.

**Economy**: Feedlots, grain storage, manufacturing, tourism, prison.

**History**: Apaches; displaced by Comanches around 1700. U.S. Army removed Comanches in 1874. Ranching began in the late 1870s. Farming developed after 1900. County named for J.G. Swisher of Texas Revolution; county created from Bexar, Young territories in 1876; organized in 1890.

**Race/Ethnicity**: (In percent) Anglo, 49.3; Black, 7.7; Hispanic, 42.1; Asian, 0.4; Other, 2.9.

**Vital Statistics**, annual: Births, 96; deaths, 82; marriages, 49; divorces, 24.

**Recreation**: Mackenzie battle site, Ozark Trail marker festival in May.

**Minerals**: Not significant.

**Agriculture**: Stocker cattle, feedlots. Cotton, corn, wheat, sorghum. Some 65,000 acres irrigated. Market value $586.8 million.

**TULIA** (4,771) county seat; wind energy, feedlots, manufacturing, cotton storage, prison; hospital, library, museum; stock show in January.

Other towns include: **Happy** (668, partly in Randall County); **Kress** (703); **Vigo Park** (36).

| | |
|---|---|
| **Population** | **7,581** |
| Change fm 2010 | – 3.5 |
| Area (sq. mi.) | 900.7 |
| Land Area (sq. mi.) | 890.2 |
| Altitude (ft.) | 3,160-3,735 |
| Rainfall (in.) | 21.57 |
| Jan. mean min. | 22.0 |
| July mean max. | 91.9 |
| Civ. Labor | 3,153 |
| Unemployed | 6.5 |
| Wages | $14,458,810 |
| Per Capita Income | $34,329 |
| Prop. Value | $570,979,063 |
| Retail Sales | $61,932,303 |

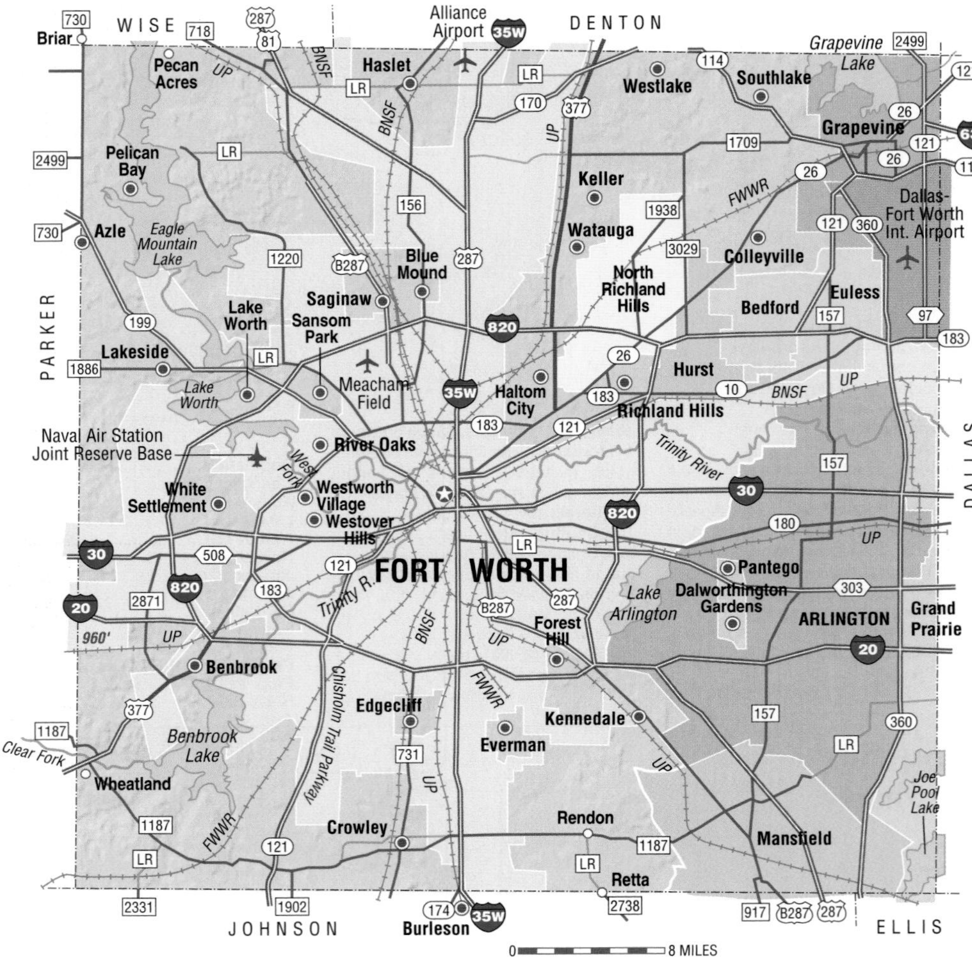

## Map of Tarrant County and surrounding area

WISE | DENTON

Briar, Pecan Acres, Haslet, Alliance Airport, Westlake, Southlake, Grapevine Lake, Grapevine

Pelican Bay, Keller, Watauga, Colleyville, Dallas-Fort Worth Int. Airport

Azle, Eagle Mountain Lake, Blue Mound, North Richland Hills, Bedford, Euless

Lakeside, Lake Worth, Saginaw, Sansom Park, Haltom City, Richland Hills, Hurst

Naval Air Station Joint Reserve Base, Meacham Field, River Oaks

White Settlement, Westworth Village, Westover Hills, FORT WORTH, Pantego, Dalworthington Gardens, ARLINGTON, Grand Prairie

Benbrook, Edgecliff, Forest Hill, Lake Arlington

Wheatland, Benbrook Lake, Everman, Kennedale, Joe Pool Lake

Crowley, Rendon, Mansfield

Retta

JOHNSON | Burleson | ELLIS

0 — 8 MILES

## Tarrant County

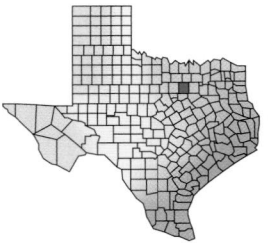

**Physical Features**: Part Blackland, level to rolling; drains to Trinity; Lake Worth, Grapevine Lake, Eagle Mountain Lake, Benbrook Lake, Joe Pool Lake, Lake Arlington.

**Economy**: Tourism, planes, helicopters, foods, mobile homes, electronic equipment, chemicals, plastics among products of more than 1,000 factories, large federal expenditure, D/FW International Airport, economy closely associated with Dallas urban area.

**History**: Caddoes in area. Comanches, other tribes arrived about 1700. Anglo-Americans settled in 1840s. Named for Republic of Texas Gen. Edward H. Tarrant, who helped drive Indian tribes from area. County created 1849 from Navarro County; organized 1850.

**Race/Ethnicity**: (In percent) Anglo, 50.1; Black, 15.9; Hispanic, 27.6; Asian, 5.0; Other, 3.3.

**Vital Statistics**, annual: Births, 27,671; deaths, 11,474; marriages, 13,318; divorces, 7,462.

**Recreation**: Scott Theatre; Amon G. Carter Museum; Kimbell Art Museum; Modern Art Museum; Museum of Science and History; Casa Mañana; Botanic Gardens; Fort Worth Zoo; Log Cabin Village, all in Fort Worth.

Also, Six Flags Over Texas at Arlington; Southwestern Exposition, Stock Show; Convention Center; Stockyards Historical District; Texas Rangers and Dallas Cowboys at Arlington, other athletic events.

**Minerals**: Production of cement, sand, gravel, stone, gas.

**Agriculture**: Hay, beef cattle, wheat, horses, horticulture. Market value $34.6 million. Firewood marketed.

**Education**: Texas Christian University, University of Texas at Arlington, Texas Wesleyan University, Southwestern Baptist Theological Seminary and several other academic centers including a junior college system with five campus and various centers.

**FORT WORTH** (798,382, small parts in Denton, Parker and Wise counties) county seat; a major mercantile, commercial and financial center; airplane, helicopter and other manufacturing plants.

A cultural center with renowned art museums, Bass Performance Hall;

many conventions held in downtown center; agribusiness center for wide area with grain-storage and feed-mill operations; adjacent to D/FW International Airport; hospitals.

**ARLINGTON** (380,698) University of Texas-Arlington, General Motors plant, tourism, the Texas Rangers baseball team, AT&T Stadium, retail, hospitals, bowling museum, art museum; Scottish festival in June.

Other towns include: **Hurst** (38,598); **Euless** (53,355); **Bedford** (49,084) helicopter plant, hospital, Celtic festival in fal. These three cities in the northeast part of the county are sometimes referred to as **HEB**.

**North Richland Hills** (68,670) hospital.

**Azle** (11,413, partly in Parker County) government/services, varied industries, natural gas, hospital, commuters to Fort Worth, Jumpin' Jack Jamboree in September; **Benbrook** (22,524) varied manufacturing, hospitals; **Blue Mound** (2,476); **Briar** (5,832, parts in Wise and Parker counties).

Also, **Colleyville** (25,256) medical services, commuters, government/ services, barbecue cook-off in April; **Crowley** (14,437) varied manufacturing, government/services, hospital; **Dalworthington Gardens** (2,347);

*For explanation of sources, symbols and abbreviations, see p. xxx and foldout map.*

### Largest U.S. Media Markets

| Rank | TV Homes |
|---|---|
| 1. New York | 7.44 million |
| 2. Los Angeles | 5.52 million |
| 3. Chicago | 3.48 million |
| 4. Philadelphia | 2.95 million |
| 5. Dallas/Fort Worth | 2.60 million |
| 6. San Francisco | 2.48 million |
| 7. Boston | 2.42 million |
| 8. Washington, D.C. | 2.41 million |
| 9. Atlanta | 2.33 million |
| 10. Houston | 2.30 million |

*Source: Nielsen Media Research, 2015.*

**Edgecliff** (2,928); **Everman** (6,272); **Forest Hill** (12,744).

Also, **Grapevine** (51,330) manufacturing, distribution, near the D/FW International Airport, tourist center, hospital, Grapefest in September; **Haltom City** (43,735) light manufacturing, food processing, medical center; library; **Haslet** (1,667) commuters, government/services, chili fest and rodeo in May; **Keller** (43,572) Bear Creek Park, Wild West Fest.

Also, **Kennedale** (7,305) commuters, printing, manufacturing, library, drag strip, custom car show in May; **Lakeside** (1,370); **Lake Worth** (4,679) retail, tourism, museum, nature center; **Mansfield** (62,022, partly in Johnson, Ellis counties) varied manufacturing,

retail, government/services, commuters, hospital, community college, library, museum, parks, Pecan festival in September; **Pantego** (2,494); **Pelican Bay** (1,564); **Rendon** (13,185); **Richland Hills** (8,001).

Also, **River Oaks** (7,645); **Saginaw** (21,493) grain milling, manufacturing, distribution, library, aquatic center; **Sansom Park** (4,781); **Southlake** (28,864) technology, financial, retail center, hospital, parks, Oktoberfest; **Watauga** (24,418); **Westlake** (1,130); **Westover Hills** (715); **Westworth Village** (2,623).

Also, **White Settlement** (16,790) aircraft manufacturing, drilling equipment, technological services, museums including Civil War museum, parks, historic sites; industrial park; settlers day festival in fall.

Also, part [7,579] of **Burleson** (41,828); part [51,864] of **Grand Prairie** (184,144), and part of **Pecan Acres** (4,239).

| | |
|---|---|
| Population | 1,945,360 |
| Change fm 2010 | 7.5 |
| Area (sq. mi.) | 902.3 |
| Land Area (sq. mi.) | 863.6 |
| Altitude (ft.) | 420-960 |
| Rainfall (in.) | 35.50 |
| Jan. mean min. | 32.4 |
| July mean max. | 95.5 |
| Civ. Labor | 990,288 |
| Unemployed | 5.4 |
| Wages | $9,600,260,658 |
| Per Capita Income | $44,417 |
| Prop. Value | $140,913,903,632 |
| Retail Sales | $29,844,336,396 |

*The river-rafting ride at Six Flags over Texas in Arlington. Photo by David R. Tribble / Commons.*

# Taylor County

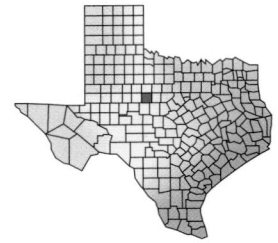

**Physical Features**: Prairies, with Callahan Divide in the middle of the county, draining to Colorado tributaries, Brazos forks; Lake Abilene, Lake Kirby; mostly loam soils.

**Economy**: Agribusiness, oil and gas, education, Dyess Air Force Base.

**History**: Comanches in area about 1700. Anglo-American settlers arrived in the 1870s. Named for Alamo heroes Edward, James and George Taylor, brothers; county created from Bexar and Travis counties 1858; organized 1878.

**Race/Ethnicity**: (In percent) Anglo, 65.8; Black, 7.8; Hispanic, 23.1; Asian, 1.8; Other, 3.6.

**Vital Statistics**, annual: Births, 2,089; deaths, 1,306; marriages, 1,196; divorces, 710.

**Recreation**: Abilene State Park, lake activities, Nelson Park Zoo, college events, Buffalo Gap historical tour and arts festival in April, Western Heritage ranch rodeo in May and West Texas Fair in September at Abilene.

**Minerals**: Oil, natural gas.

**Agriculture**: Beef cattle, small grain, cotton, milo. Market value $37.6 million.

**Education**: Abilene Christian University, Hardin-Simmons University, McMurry University, Texas Tech University pharmacy, nursing schools and branch campus, Cisco Junior College branch.

**ABILENE** (121,495, a small part in Jones County) county seat; retail center, oil and gas, military, colleges; hospitals, Abilene State School; Fort Phantom Hill (in Jones County). **Wylie** is now part of Abilene.

Other communities include: **Buffalo Gap** (455) historic sites; **Impact** (34); **Lawn** (321); **Merkel** (2,637) agribusiness center, clothing manufacturing, oil-field services; **Ovalo** (225); **Potosi** (3,070); **Trent** (339); **Tuscola** (750); **Tye** (1,254).

| | |
|---|---:|
| Population | 135,143 |
| Change fm 2010 | 2.8 |
| Area (sq. mi.) | 919.3 |
| Land Area (sq. mi.) | 915.6 |
| Altitude (ft.) | 1,640-2,490 |
| Rainfall (in.) | 24.82 |
| Jan. mean min. | 30.2 |
| July mean max. | 94.2 |
| Civ. Labor | 69,088 |
| Unemployed | 4.5 |
| Wages | $543,830,663 |
| Per Capita Income | $41,800 |
| Prop. Value | $8,018,565,849 |
| Retail Sales | $2,348,092,437 |

*For explanation of sources, symbols and abbreviations, see p. 238, and foldout map.*

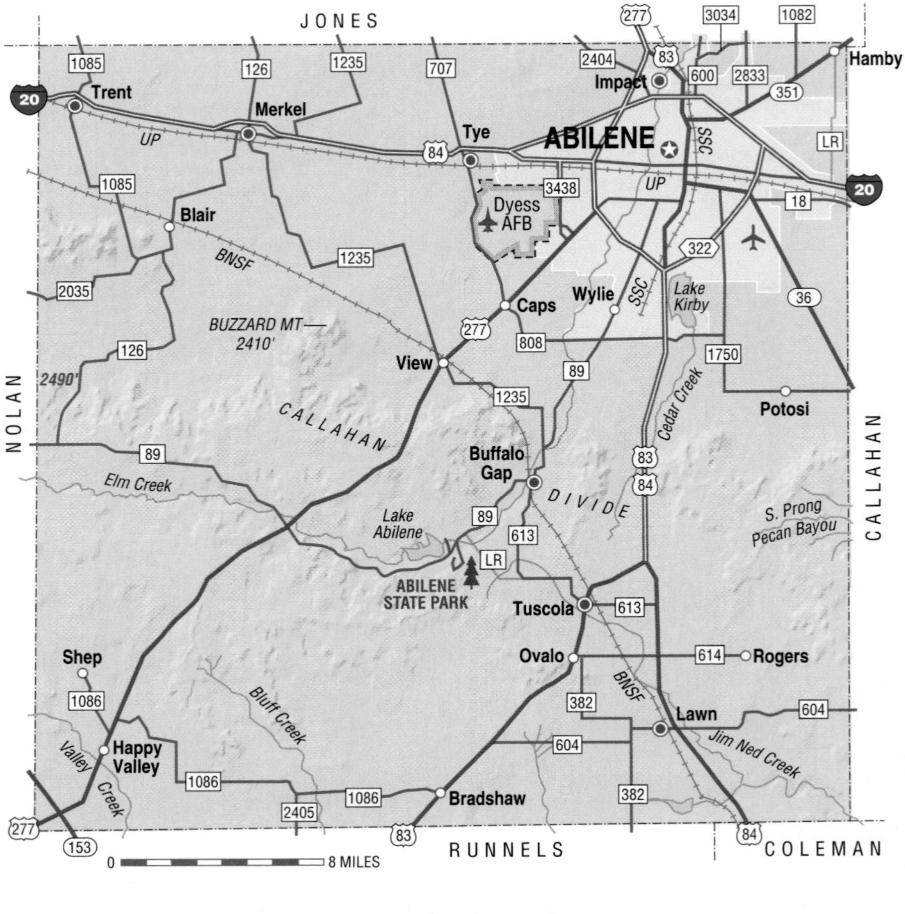

JONES

Trent · 20 · 1085 · 126 · 1235 · 707 · Merkel · UP · Tye · 84 · ABILENE · 277 · 3034 · 1082 · 2404 · 83 · Impact · 600 · 2833 · 351 · Hamby · LR · SSC

1085 · Blair · BNSF · 1235 · Dyess AFB · 3438 · UP · 18 · 20 · 322

2035 · BUZZARD MT— 2410' · 126 · Caps · Wylie · SSC · Lake Kirby · 36 · 277 · 808 · 1750

NOLAN · 2490' · 89 · View · 1235 · 89 · Potosi · CALLAHAN · Cedar Creek

Elm Creek · Buffalo Gap · 83 · 84 · DIVIDE · S. Prong · Pecan Bayou

Lake Abilene · 89 · 613 · LR · ABILENE STATE PARK · Tuscola · 613

Shep · 1086 · Ovalo · 614 · Rogers · BNSF

Bluff Creek · 382 · Lawn · 604 · Happy Valley · 1086 · 604 · Jim Ned Creek

Valley Creek · 1086 · Bradshaw · 382 · 2405

277 · 153 · 0 _____ 8 MILES · 83 · RUNNELS · 84 · COLEMAN

# Terrell County

**Physical Features**: Trans-Pecos southwestern county; semi-mountainous, many canyons; rocky, limestone soils.

**Economy**: Ranching, hunting leases, oil and gas exploration, tourism.

**History**: Coahuiltecans, Jumanos and other tribes left many pictographs in area caves. Sheep ranching began in 1880s. Named for Confederate Gen. A.W. Terrell; county created 1905 from Pecos County, organized the same year.

**Race/Ethnicity**: (In percent) Anglo, 45.8; Black, 1.2; Hispanic, 47.8; Asian, 3.7; Other, 4.3.

**Vital Statistics**, annual: Births, 12; deaths, 12; marriages, 7; divorces, 3.

**Recreation**: Nature tourism, hunting, especially white-tailed and mule deer, Rio Grande Wild and Scenic River, varied wildlife, hiking trail; Snake Days in June, Cactus Pachanga in October.

**Minerals**: Gas, oil, limestone.

**Agriculture**: Goats (meat, Angora); sheep (meat, wool); some beef cattle. Market value $3.1 million. Wildlife leases important.

**SANDERSON** (806) county seat; ranching, hunting, tourism, government/services; museum.

Other town: **Dryden** (13).

| | |
|---|---|
| **Population** | **927** |
| Change fm 2010 | – 5.8 |
| Area (sq. mi.) | 2,358.1 |
| Land Area (sq. mi.) | 2,358.0 |
| Altitude (ft.) | 1,180-3,765 |
| Rainfall (in.) | 14.72 |

| | |
|---|---|
| Jan. mean min. | 31.5 |
| July mean max. | 92.2 |
| Civ. Labor | 395 |
| Unemployed | 4.8 |

| | |
|---|---|
| Wages | $4,204,811 |
| Per Capita Income | $48,375 |
| Prop. Value | $764,710,456 |
| Retail Sales | $2,246,507 |

# Terry County

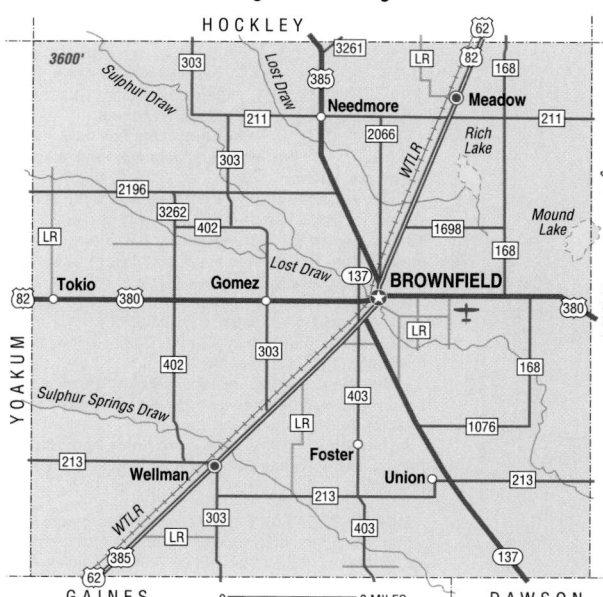

**Physical Features**: South Plains, broken by draws, playas; sandy, sandy loam, loam soils.

**Economy**: Government/services, oil-field services, agribusiness.

**History**: Comanches removed in 1870s by U.S. Army. Ranching developed in 1890s; farming after 1900. Oil discovered in 1940. County named for Confederate Col. B.F. Terry, head of the Eighth Texas Cavalry (Terry's Texas Rangers). Created from Bexar District 1876; organized 1904.

**Race/Ethnicity**: (In percent), Anglo, 41.6; Black, 5.0; Hispanic, 53.0; Asian, 0.6; Other, 2.3.

**Vital Statistics**, annual: Births, 197; deaths, 121; marriages, 85; divorces, 49.

**Recreation**: Museum, aquatic center, quilt show in April, harvest festival in October.

**Minerals**: Oil, gas, salt mining.

**Agriculture**: Cotton is principal crop; peanuts (third in acreage), grain sorghum, guar, wheat, melons, cucumbers, sesame. 98,000 acres irrigated. Market value $125.8 million.

**BROWNFIELD** (9,572) county seat; oil-field services, wind energy, agribusiness, minerals and peanut processing; hospital; prison.

Other towns include: **Meadow** (590); **Tokio** (6); **Wellman** (203).

| | |
|---|---|
| **Population** | **12,739** |
| Change fm 2010 | 0.7 |
| Area (sq. mi.) | 890.9 |
| Land Area (sq. mi.) | 888.8 |
| Altitude (ft.) | 3,080-3,600 |
| Rainfall (in.) | 19.58 |
| Jan. mean min. | 26.9 |

| | |
|---|---|
| July mean max. | 92.4 |
| Civ. Labor | 5,685 |
| Unemployed | 5.0 |
| Wages | $36,102,140 |
| Per Capita Income | $37,535 |
| Prop. Value | $1,518,471,337 |
| Retail Sales | $168,889,870 |

# Throckmorton County

**Physical Features**: Northwest county southwest of Wichita Falls; rolling, between Brazos forks; red to black soils.

**Economy**: Oil, agribusiness, hunting.

**History**: Site of Comanche Reservation 1854-59. Ranching developed after Civil War. County named for Dr. W.E. Throckmorton, father of Gov. J.W. Throckmorton; county created from Fannin 1858; organized 1879.

**Race/Ethnicity**: (In percent) Anglo, 86.2; Black, 0.9; Hispanic, 11.2; Asian, 0.4; Other, 1.7.

**Vital Statistics**, annual: Births, 16; deaths, 24; marriages, 7; divorces, 3.

**Recreation**: Hunting, fishing; historic sites include Camp Cooper, site of former Comanche reservation, restored ranch home; Millers Creek Reservoir; wild game dinner in January.

**Minerals**: Natural gas, oil.

**Agriculture**: Cattle, horses, wheat, hay. Market value $24.8 million. Mesquite sold. Hunting important.

**THROCKMORTON** (802) county seat; varied manufacturing, oil-field services; hospital; Old Jail museum.

Other towns include: **Elbert** (29), **Woodson** (259).

| | |
|---|---|
| Population | 1,608 |
| Change fm 2010 | – 2.0 |
| Area (sq. mi.) | 915.5 |
| Land Area (sq. mi.) | 912.6 |
| Altitude (ft.) | 1,100-1,730 |
| Rainfall (in.) | 29.78 |
| Jan. mean min. | 29.6 |
| July mean max. | 95.8 |
| Civ. Labor | 900 |
| Unemployed | 4.4 |
| Wages | $3,354,809 |
| Per Capita Income | $51,733 |
| Prop. Value | $829,885,843 |
| Retail Sales | $9,726,689 |

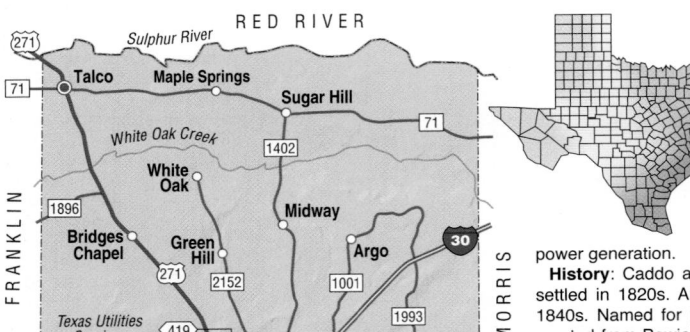

# Titus County

**Physical Features**: Northeast Texas county; hilly, timbered; drains to Big Cypress Creek, and Sulphur River; Lake Bob Sandlin, Welsh Reservoir, Monticello Reservoir.

**Economy**: Agribusiness, varied manufacturing, and electric power generation.

**History**: Caddo area. Cherokees and other tribes settled in 1820s. Anglo-American settlers arrived in 1840s. Named for pioneer settler A.J. Titus; county created from Bowie, Red River counties in 1846, organized the same year.

**Race/Ethnicity**: (In percent) Anglo, 47.5; Black, 10.3; Hispanic, 40.9; Asian, 0.9; Other, 3.8.

**Vital Statistics**, annual: Births, 502; deaths, 268; marriages, 240; divorces, 76.

**Recreation**: Fishing, hunting, lake activities, state park, rodeo, railroad museum, flower gardens.

**Minerals**: Lignite coal, oil, gas.

**Agriculture**: Poultry, beef cattle, hay, horticulture, horses. Market value $81.2 million. Timber sales significant.

**MOUNT PLEASANT** (16,150) county seat; tourism, varied manufacturing, food-processing plants; hospital; Northeast Texas Community College; jubilee and outhouse races in May.

Other towns include: **Cookville** (105), **Millers Cove** (154), **Talco** (523), **Winfield** (535).

| | |
|---|---|
| Population | 32,506 |
| Change fm 2010 | 0.5 |
| Area (sq. mi.) | 425.6 |
| Land Area (sq. mi.) | 406.1 |
| Altitude (ft.) | 250-530 |
| Rainfall (in.) | 47.70 |
| Jan. mean min. | 31.1 |
| July mean max. | 92.9 |
| Civ. Labor | 13,524 |
| Unemployed | 6.8 |
| Wages | $124,152,868 |
| Per Capita Income | $29,680 |
| Prop. Value | $3,052,560,281 |
| Retail Sales | $605,482,233 |

*For explanation of sources, symbols and abbreviations, see p. 238, and foldout map.*

# Tom Green County

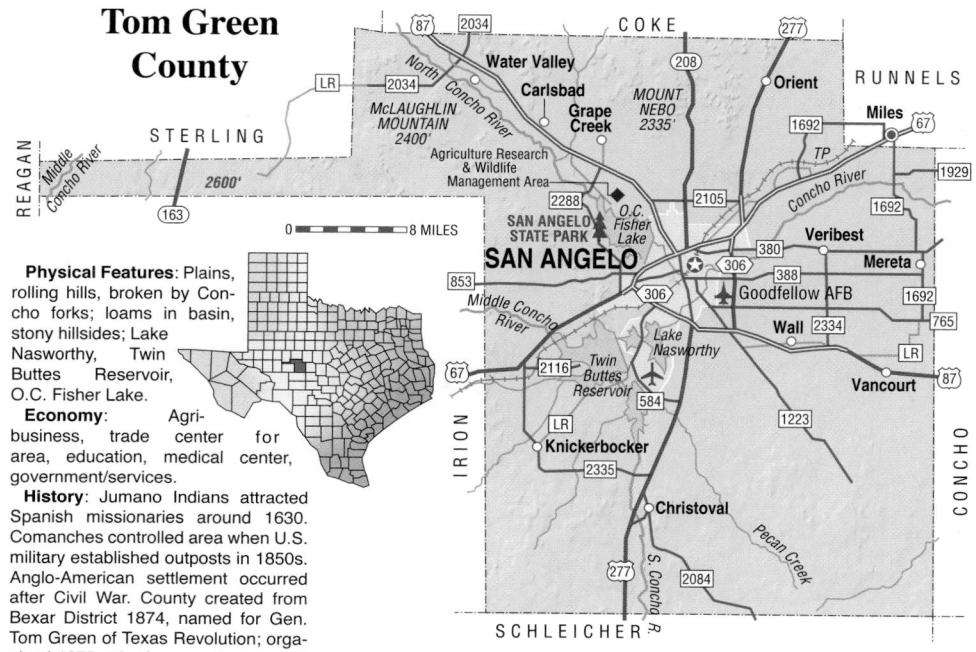

**Physical Features**: Plains, rolling hills, broken by Concho forks; loams in basin, stony hillsides; Lake Nasworthy, Twin Buttes Reservoir, O.C. Fisher Lake.

**Economy**: Agribusiness, trade center for area, education, medical center, government/services.

**History**: Jumano Indians attracted Spanish missionaries around 1630. Comanches controlled area when U.S. military established outposts in 1850s. Anglo-American settlement occurred after Civil War. County created from Bexar District 1874, named for Gen. Tom Green of Texas Revolution; organized 1875; 12 other counties created from original.

**Race/Ethnicity**: (In percent) Anglo, 55.9; Black, 4.7; Hispanic, 37.3; Asian, 1.3; Other, 3.1.

**Vital Statistics**, annual: Births, 1,491; deaths, 947; marriages, 1,117; divorces, 426.

**Recreation**: Water sports, hunting, Fort Concho museum, symphony, baseball team, Christmas at Old Fort Concho, February rodeo.

**Minerals**: Oil, natural gas.

**Agriculture**: Cotton, cattle, goats, sheep (third in number), small grains, milo. About 30,000 acres irrigated.

Market value $131.4 million.

**SAN ANGELO** (98,040) county seat; government/services, retail, transportation, education; hospitals, Angelo State University, Howard Junior College branch; riverwalk; Museum of Fine Arts, drag boat races in June.

Other towns include: **Carlsbad** (725); **Christoval** (547); **Grape Creek** (3,174); **Knickerbocker** (94); **Mereta** (131); **Vancourt** (131); **Veribest** (115); **Wall** (329); **Water Valley** (203).

*For explanation of sources, symbols and abbreviations, see p. 238, and foldout map.*

| | |
|---|---|
| **Population** | **116,608** |
| Change fm 2010 | 5.8 |
| Area (sq. mi.) | 1,540.6 |
| Land Area (sq. mi.) | 1,522.0 |
| Altitude (ft.) | 1,675-2,600 |
| Rainfall (in.) | 23.03 |
| Jan. mean min. | 29.6 |
| July mean max. | 94.5 |
| Civ. Labor | 56,585 |
| Unemployed | 4.5 |
| Wages | $423,782,289 |
| Per Capita Income | $41,329 |
| Prop. Value | $7,010,436,584 |
| Retail Sales | $1,899,913,953 |

*The state Capitol viewed from the campus of the University of Texas at Austin. Photo by Robert Plocheck.*

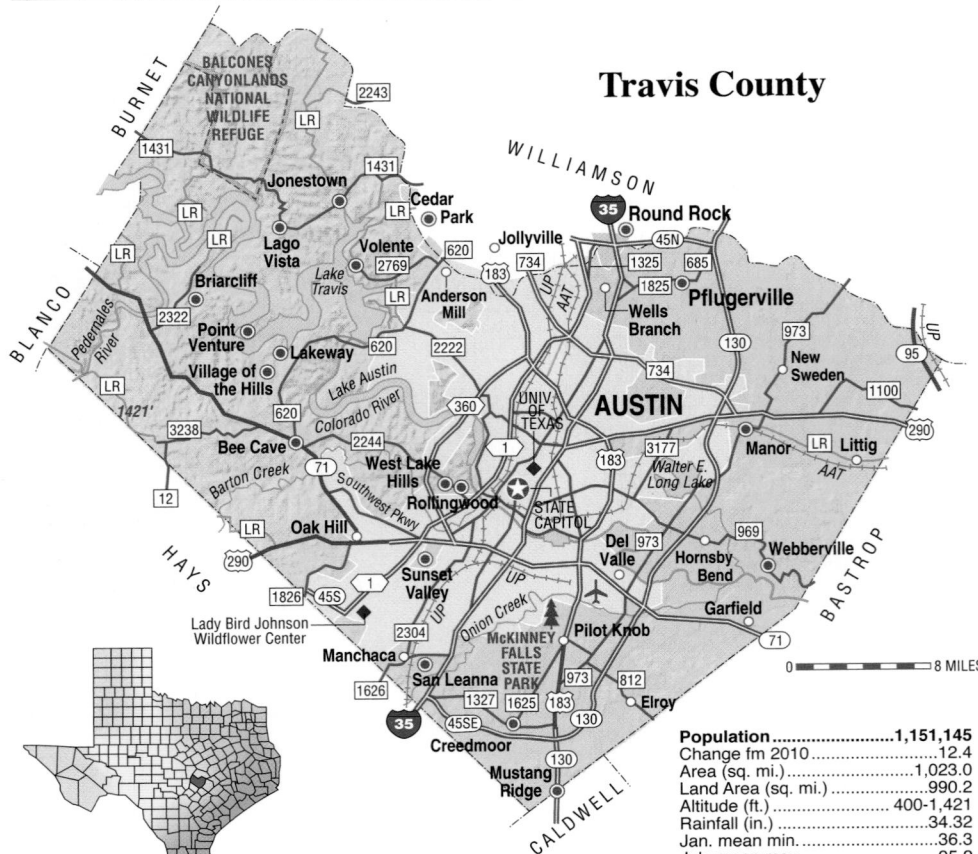

# Travis County

| | |
|---|---|
| Population | 1,151,145 |
| Change fm 2010 | 12.4 |
| Area (sq. mi.) | 1,023.0 |
| Land Area (sq. mi.) | 990.2 |
| Altitude (ft.) | 400-1,421 |
| Rainfall (in.) | 34.32 |
| Jan. mean min. | 36.3 |
| July mean max. | 95.2 |
| Civ. Labor | 633,933 |
| Unemployed | 4.4 |
| Wages | $8,483,358,344 |
| Per Capita Income | $48,562 |
| Prop. Value | $127,144,392,234 |
| Retail Sales | $18,519,915,109 |

**Physical Features**: Central county of scenic hills, broken by Colorado River; Lake Travis, Lake Austin, Lady Bird Lake, Walter E. Long Lake; cedars, pecans, other trees; diverse soils, mineral deposits.

**Economy**: Government/services, education, technology, research and industry.

**History**: Tonkawa and Lipan Apache area; Comanches, Kiowas arrived about 1700. Spanish missions from East Texas temporarily relocated near Barton Springs in 1730 before removing to San Antonio. Anglo-Americans arrived in the early 1830s. County created in 1840, when Austin became Republic's capital, from Bastrop County; organized in 1843; named for Alamo commander Col. William B. Travis; many other counties created from its original area.

**Race/Ethnicity**: (In percent) Anglo, 50.0; Black, 8.9; Hispanic, 33.8; Asian, 6.2; Other, 3.9.

**Vital Statistics**, annual: Births, 15,826; deaths, 5,063; marriages, 8,637; divorces, 2,771.

**Recreation**: Colorado River lakes, hunting, fishing; McKinney Falls State Park; LBJ Presidential Library, Lady Bird Johnson Wildflower Center; collegiate, metropolitan, governmental events; official buildings and historic sites; museums, including Bullock state history museum; Sixth St. restoration area; scenic drives; many city parks; South by Southwest film, music festival in March.

**Minerals**: Production of lime, stone, sand, gravel, oil and gas.

**Agriculture**: Cattle, nursery crops, hogs; sorghum, corn, cotton, small grains, pecans. Market value $41.7 million.

**Education**: University of Texas, St. Edward's University, Concordia Lutheran University, Huston-Tillotson College, Austin Community College, Episcopal and Presbyterian seminaries.

**AUSTIN** (877,210, part [35,697] in Williamson County) county seat and state capital; state and federal payrolls, IRS center, high-tech industries, healthcare/hospitals, including state institutions for blind, deaf, mental illnesses; popular retirement area. **Anderson Mill, Del Valle** and **Oak Hill** are now part of Austin.

Other towns include: **Bee Cave** (5,448) retail, tourism, SpringFest in April; **Briarcliff** (1,516); **Creedmoor** (221); **Garfield** (1,748); **Jonestown** (2,050) tourism, retail, commuters, Chili Pod chili cook-off in April; **Lago Vista** (6,577); **Lakeway** (14,059) residential real estate, retail, tourism, lake activities; **Manchaca** (1,194); **Manor** (6,443); **Mustang Ridge** (930, partly in Caldwell County).

Also, **Pflugerville** (54,235) high-tech industries, agriculture, government/services, Deutchenfest in May; **Point Venture** (887); **Rollingwood** (1,512); **San Leanna** (529); **Sunset Valley** (683); **The Hills** (2,599) residential community; **Volente** (554); **Webberville** (417); **Wells Branch** (12,783); **West Lake Hills** (3,319).

Also, part [489] of **Cedar Park**, part [882] of **Jollyville** and part [1,362] of **Round Rock**, all mostly in Williamson County.

*For explanation of sources, symbols and abbreviations, see p. 238, and foldout map.*

# Trinity County

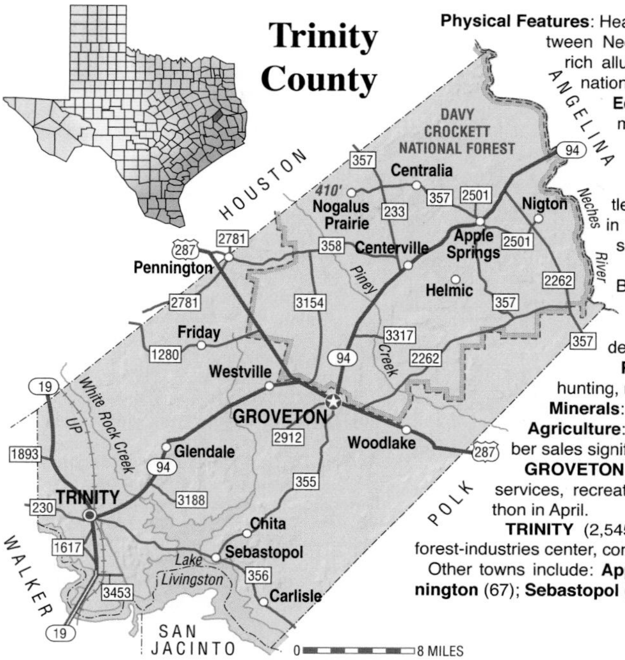

**Physical Features**: Heavily forested East Texas county of hills, between Neches and Trinity (Lake Livingston) rivers; rich alluvial soils, sandy upland; 67,910 acres in national forest.

**Economy**: Forestry, cattle, tourism, government/services.

**History**: Caddoes, reduced by disease in late 1700s. Kickapoo, Alabama, Coushatta in area when Anglo-Americans settled in 1840s. Named for river; county created in 1850 out of Houston County, organized the same year.

**Race/Ethnicity**: (In percent) Anglo, 78.9; Black, 9.6; Hispanic, 9.2; Asian, 0.7; Other, 2.3.

**Vital Statistics**, annual: Births, 110; deaths, 225; marriages, 70; divorces, 58.

**Recreation**: Lake activities, fishing, hiking, hunting, national forest, historic site.

**Minerals**: Limited oil, gas, sand and gravel.

**Agriculture**: Beef cattle. Market value $7.1 million. Timber sales significant. Hunting leases, fishing.

**GROVETON** (985) county seat; logging, government/services, recreation; museum, library; Bear Chase marathon in April.

**TRINITY** (2,545) government/services, steel fabrication, forest-industries center, commuters; hospital.

Other towns include: **Apple Springs** (350); **Centralia** (190); **Pennington** (67); **Sebastopol** (300) historic town; **Woodlake** (180).

| | |
|---|---|
| Population | 14,224 |
| Change fm 2010 | − 2.5 |
| Area (sq. mi.) | 714.0 |
| Land Area (sq. mi.) | 693.6 |
| Altitude (ft.) | 131-410 |
| Rainfall (in.) | 49.31 |
| Jan. mean min. | 35.1 |
| July mean max. | 92.9 |
| Civ. Labor | 5,775 |
| Unemployed | 6.3 |
| Wages | $17,352,722 |
| Per Capita Income | $31,502 |
| Prop. Value | $1,365,920,024 |
| Retail Sales | $77,530,098 |

# Tyler County

**Physical Features**: Hilly East Texas county; densely timbered; drains to Neches River; B.A. Steinhagen Lake; Big Thicket is unique plant and animal area.

**Economy**: Lumbering, government/services, some manufacturing, tourism, hunting leases.

**History**: Caddoan area. Cherokees, Alabama and Coushatta pushed into area from U.S. South in 1820s. Anglo-Americans settled in 1830s. Named for U.S. President John Tyler; county created in 1846 from Liberty County, organized the same year.

**Race/Ethnicity**: (In percent) Anglo, 79.4; Black, 11.6; Hispanic, 7.4; Asian, 0.3; Other, 2.1.

**Vital Statistics**, annual: Births, 240; deaths, 256; marriages, 145; divorces, 127.

**Recreation**: Big Thicket National Preserve; Heritage Village; lake activities; Allan Shivers Museum; state forest; historic sites; dogwood festival in spring; rodeo, frontier frolics in September; gospel music fest in June.

**Minerals**: Oil, natural gas.

**Agriculture**: Cattle, hay, nursery crops, blueberries, horses. Market value $19.1 million. Timber sales significant.

**WOODVILLE** (2,636) county seat; lumber, cattle market, varied manufacturing, tourism; hospital, prison.

Other towns include: **Chester** (324) **Colmesneil** (611), **Doucette** (160), **Fred** (300), **Hillister** (250), **Ivanhoe** (1,455), **Spurger** (590), **Warren** (833).

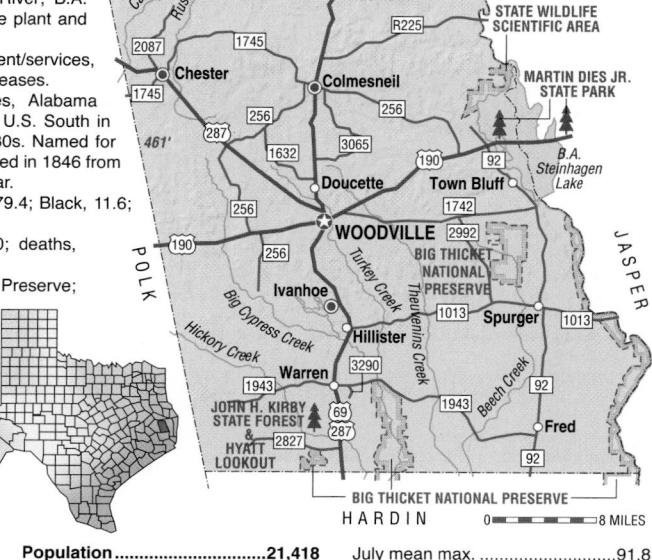

| | |
|---|---|
| Population | 21,418 |
| Change fm 2010 | − 1.6 |
| Area (sq. mi.) | 935.6 |
| Land Area (sq. mi.) | 924.5 |
| Altitude (ft.) | 50-461 |
| Rainfall (in.) | 56.18 |
| Jan. mean min. | 37.5 |
| July mean max. | 91.8 |
| Civ. Labor | 8,268 |
| Unemployed | 8.1 |
| Wages | $30,328,491 |
| Per Capita Income | $30,602 |
| Prop. Value | $2,125,869,217 |
| Retail Sales | $114,891,061 |

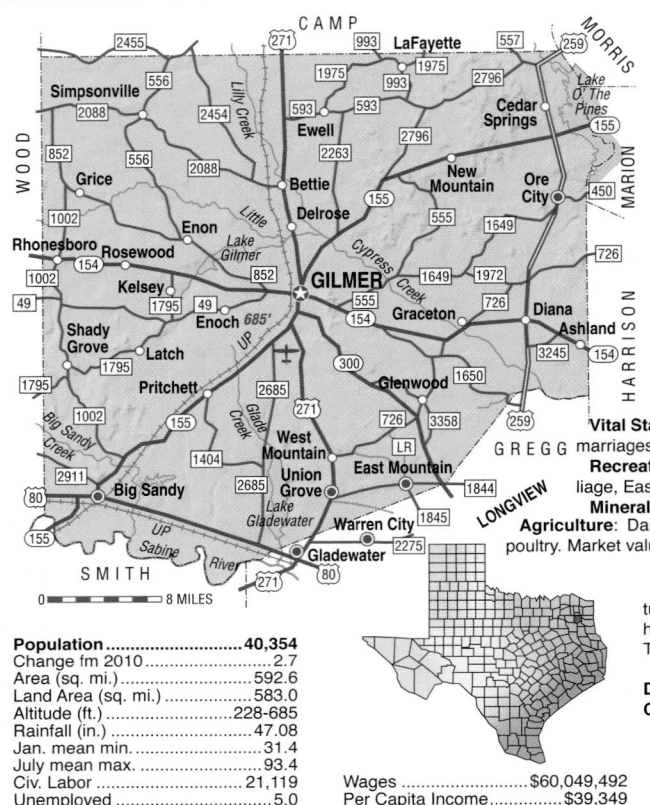

# Upshur County

**Physical Features**: East Texas county; rolling to hilly, over half forested; drains to Sabine River, Little Cypress Creek, Lake O' the Pines, Lake Gilmer, Lake Gladewater.

**Economy**: Manufacturing, oil, gas, agribusiness, timber.

**History**: Caddoes; reduced by epidemics in 1700s. Cherokees in area in 1820s. Anglo-American settlement in mid-1830s. County created from Harrison, Nacogdoches counties in 1846, organized the same year; named for U.S. Secretary of State A.P. Upshur.

**Race/Ethnicity**: (In percent) Anglo, 81.1; Black, 8.7; Hispanic, 7.4; Asian, 0.5; Other, 3.0.

**Vital Statistics**, annual: Births, 463; deaths, 431; marriages, 239; divorces, 233.

**Recreation**: Scenic trails, hunting, fishing, fall foliage, East Texas Yamboree in October.

**Minerals**: Oil, gas, sand, gravel.

**Agriculture**: Dairies, beef cattle, hay, vegetable crops, poultry. Market value $60.6 million. Timber a major product.

**GILMER** (5,127) county seat; manufacturing, communications, electric power; hospital; museums; Texas Motorized Trails.

Other towns include: **Big Sandy** (1,359); **Diana** (585); **East Mountain** (804); **Ore City** (1,160); **Union Grove** (365).

Part [2,447] of **Gladewater** (6,583).

| | |
|---|---|
| Population | 40,354 |
| Change fm 2010 | 2.7 |
| Area (sq. mi.) | 592.6 |
| Land Area (sq. mi.) | 583.0 |
| Altitude (ft.) | 228-685 |
| Rainfall (in.) | 47.08 |
| Jan. mean min. | 31.4 |
| July mean max. | 93.4 |
| Civ. Labor | 21,119 |
| Unemployed | 5.0 |

| | | | |
|---|---|---|---|
| Wages | $60,049,492 | Prop. Value | $2,730,614,183 |
| Per Capita Income | $39,349 | Retail Sales | $303,692,627 |

# Upton County

**Physical Features**: Western county; north flat, south rolling, hilly; limestone, sandy loam soils, drains to creeks.

**Economy**: Oil, wind turbines, farming, ranching.

**History**: Apache and Comanche area until tribes removed by U.S. Army in the 1870s. Sheep, cattle ranching developed in the 1880s. Oil discovered in 1925. County created in 1887 from Tom Green County; organized in 1910; name honors brothers John and William Upton, Confederate colonels.

**Race/Ethnicity**: (In percent) Anglo, 44.5; Black, 2.6; Hispanic, 51.6; Asian, 0.3; Other, 4.7.

**Vital Statistics**, annual: Births, 52; deaths, 36; marriages, 26; divorces, 13.

**Recreation**: Historic sites, Mendoza Trail museum, scenic areas; McCamey chili cookoff in October, pecan show in November.

**Minerals**: Oil, natural gas.

**Agriculture**: Cotton, sheep, goats, cattle, watermelons, pecans. Extensive irrigation. Market value $12.7 million.

**RANKIN** (754) county seat, oil, ranching, farming; hospital; Barbados cookoff in May, All Kid rodeo in June.

**McCAMEY** (1,860) oil, gas, wind; hospital; Wind Energy bluegrass festival in September.

Other town: **Midkiff** (182).

| | |
|---|---|
| Population | 3,454 |
| Change fm 2010 | 3.0 |
| Area (sq. mi.) | 1,241.5 |
| Land Area (sq. mi.) | 1,241.3 |
| Altitude (ft.) | 2,310-3,141 |
| Rainfall (in.) | 15.14 |
| Jan. mean min. | 31.9 |
| July mean max. | 95.3 |
| Civ. Labor | 2,408 |

| | | | |
|---|---|---|---|
| | | Unemployed | 2.7 |
| | | Wages | $21,875,137 |
| | | Per Capita Income | $61,179 |
| | | Prop. Value | $4,912,693,971 |
| | | Retail Sales | $37,338,064 |

# Uvalde County

**Physical Features**: Edwards Plateau, rolling hills below escarpment; spring-fed Sabinal, Frio, Leona, Nueces rivers; cypress, cedar, other trees, including maple groves.

**Economy**: Agribusinesses, hunting leases, light manufacturing, tourism.

**History**: Spanish mission Nuestra Señora de la Candelaria founded in 1762 for Lipan Apaches near present-day Montell; Comanches harassed mission. U.S. military outpost established in 1849. County created from Bexar 1850; re-created, organized 1856; named for 1778 governor of Coahuila, Juan de Ugalde, with name Anglicized.

**Race/Ethnicity**: (In percent) Anglo, 28.2; Black, 1.2; Hispanic, 69.9; Asian, 0.6; Other, 2.0.

**Vital Statistics**, annual: Births, 372; deaths, 259; marriages, 166; divorces, 32.

**Recreation**: Deer, turkey hunting; Garner State Park; water activities on rivers; John Nance Garner museum; Uvalde Memorial Park; scenic trails, historic sites.

**Minerals**: Asphalt, stone, sand, gravel.

**Agriculture**: Cattle, vegetables, corn, cotton, sorghum, sheep, goats, hay, wheat. Substantial irrigation. Market value $112.5 million.

**UVALDE** (16,201) county seat; veg-

etable, wool, mohair processing, tourism; opera house; junior college, A&M research center; hospital; Fort Inge Day in April.

**Sabinal** (1,710) farm, ranch center, tourism, retirement area.

Other towns include: **Concan** (500); **Knippa** (688); **Utopia** (228) resort; **Uvalde Estates** (2,228).

| | |
|---|---|
| **Population** | **27,117** |
| Change fm 2010 | 2.7 |
| Area (sq. mi.) | 1,558.6 |
| Land Area (sq. mi.) | 1,552.0 |
| Altitude (ft.) | 650-2,200 |
| Rainfall (in.) | 24,60 |
| Jan. mean min. | 38.6 |
| July mean max. | 96.1 |
| Civ. Labor | 11,986 |
| Unemployed | 6.3 |
| Wages | $75,317,843 |
| Per Capita Income | $39,286 |
| Prop. Value | $2,855,706,700 |
| Retail Sales | $495,787,360 |

# Val Verde County

**Physical Features**: Southwestern county bordering Mexico, rolling, hilly; brushy; Devils, Pecos rivers, Rio Grande and Amistad Reservoir; limestone, alluvial soils.

**Economy**: Agribusiness, tourism, trade center, military, Border Patrol, hunting leases, fishing.

**History**: Apaches, Coahuiltecans, Jumanos present when Spanish came through in late 1500s. Comanches arrived later. U.S. military outposts established in 1850s to protect settlers. Only county named for Civil War battle; Val Verde means green valley. Created 1885 from Crockett, Kinney, Pecos counties, organized the same year.

**Race/Ethnicity**: (In percent) Anglo, 17.2; Black, 1.8; Hispanic, 80.2; Asian, 0.7; Other, 2.0.

**Vital Statistics**, annual: Births, 865; deaths, 340; marriages, 376; divorces, 141.

**Recreation**: Gateway to Mexico; deer hunting, fishing; Amistad lake activities; two state parks; Langtry restoration of Judge Roy Bean's saloon; ancient pictographs; San Felipe Springs; winery.

**Minerals**: Production sand, gravel, gas, oil.

**Agriculture**: Sheep, Angora goats, meat goats (second in numbers); cattle; minor irrigation. Market value $10.7 million.

**DEL RIO** (34,651) county seat; government/services including federal agencies and military, agribusiness, tourism; hospital, extension colleges; Fiesta de Amistad in October.

**Laughlin Air Force Base** (1,648).

Other towns and places include: **Cienegas Terrace** (3,459); **Comstock** (344); **Langtry** (30); **Val Verde Park** (2,439).

| | |
|---|---|
| **Population** | **48,974** |
| Change fm 2010 | 0.2 |
| Area (sq. mi.) | 3,232.7 |
| Land Area (sq. mi.) | 3,144.8 |
| Altitude (ft.) | 845-2,343 |
| Rainfall (in.) | 20.19 |
| Jan. mean min. | 38.7 |
| July mean max. | 96.4 |
| Civ. Labor | 20,137 |
| Unemployed | 6.2 |
| Wages | $140,243,671 |
| Per Capita Income | $32,137 |
| Prop. Value | $3,067,844,592 |
| Retail Sales | $555,349,291 |

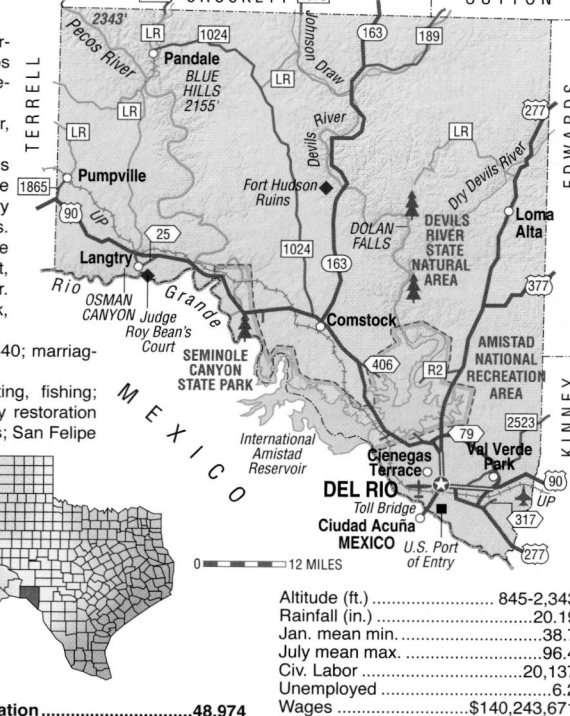

# Van Zandt County

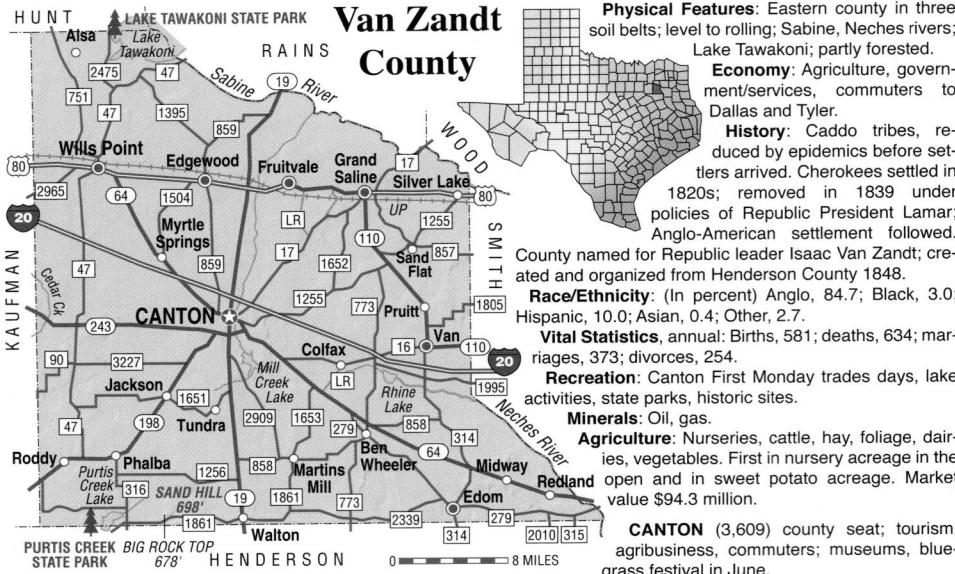

**Physical Features**: Eastern county in three soil belts; level to rolling; Sabine, Neches rivers; Lake Tawakoni; partly forested.

**Economy**: Agriculture, government/services, commuters to Dallas and Tyler.

**History**: Caddo tribes, reduced by epidemics before settlers arrived. Cherokees settled in 1820s; removed in 1839 under policies of Republic President Lamar; Anglo-American settlement followed. County named for Republic leader Isaac Van Zandt; created and organized from Henderson County 1848.

**Race/Ethnicity**: (In percent) Anglo, 84.7; Black, 3.0; Hispanic, 10.0; Asian, 0.4; Other, 2.7.

**Vital Statistics**, annual: Births, 581; deaths, 634; marriages, 373; divorces, 254.

**Recreation**: Canton First Monday trades days, lake activities, state parks, historic sites.

**Minerals**: Oil, gas.

**Agriculture**: Nurseries, cattle, hay, foliage, dairies, vegetables. First in nursery acreage in the open and in sweet potato acreage. Market value $94.3 million.

**CANTON** (3,609) county seat; tourism, agribusiness, commuters; museums, bluegrass festival in June.

| | |
|---|---|
| Population | 52,910 |
| Change fm 2010 | 0.6 |
| Area (sq. mi.) | 859.6 |
| Land Area (sq. mi.) | 842.6 |
| Altitude (ft.) | 330-698 |
| Rainfall (in.) | 44.15 |
| Jan. mean min. | 33.7 |
| July mean max. | 93.7 |
| Civ. Labor | 26,802 |
| Unemployed | 5.1 |

| | |
|---|---|
| Wages | $78,946,365 |
| Per Capita Income | $36,878 |
| Prop. Value | $3,868,049,551 |
| Retail Sales | $445,048,819 |

**Wills Point** (3,594) government/services, retail, tourism, commuters to Dallas and Tyler; depot museum, bluebird festival in April.

Other towns include: **Ben Wheeler** (504); **Edgewood** (1,473) commuters, heritage park, antiques; **Edom** (388) arts and crafts; **Fruitvale** (424); **Grand Saline** (3,147) salt plant, agriculture, medical services/hospital, Salt Palace museum, salt prairie marsh, birding, Salt Festival in June; **Van** (2,720) oil center, hay, cattle, oil festival in October.

# Victoria County

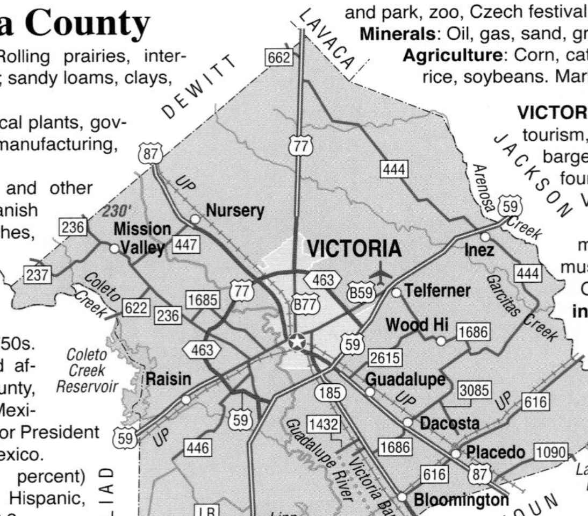

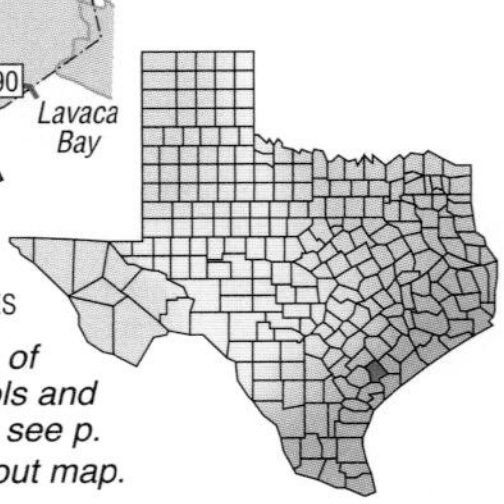

**Physical Features**: Rolling prairies, intersected by many streams; sandy loams, clays, alluvial soils.

**Economy**: Petrochemical plants, government/services, oil, manufacturing, agribusiness, tourism.

**History**: Karankawas and other tribes in area when Spanish arrived in 1528. Comanches, Tawakonis arrived later. La Salle's camp on Garcitas Creek 1685–1687. Spanish ranching developed in the 1750s. Anglo-Americans arrived after 1836. An original county, created in 1836 from Mexican municipality named for President Guadalupe Victoria of Mexico.

**Race/Ethnicity**: (In percent) Anglo, 46.7; Black, 6.8; Hispanic, 44.9; Asian, 1.3; Other, 2.3.

**Vital Statistics**, annual: Births, 1,292; deaths, 801; marriages, 719; divorces, 376.

**Recreation**: Fishing, hunting; saltwater activities, historic homes, sites, riverside park, Coleto Creek Reservoir

and park, zoo, Czech festival in September at Victoria.

**Minerals**: Oil, gas, sand, gravel.

**Agriculture**: Corn, cattle, grain sorghums, cotton, rice, soybeans. Market value $47.6 million.

**VICTORIA** (64,834) county seat; tourism, agribusiness center, on barge canal, petrochemicals, foundry equipment; hospitals; Victoria College, University of Houston at Victoria; community theater, symphony, museums.

Other towns include: **Bloomington** (2,540), **Inez** (2,196), **McFaddin** (50), **Nursery** (600), **Placedo** (720), **Telferner** (700).

| | |
|---|---|
| Population | 91,081 |
| Change fm 2010 | 4.9 |
| Area (sq. mi.) | 888.8 |
| Land Area (sq. mi.) | 882.1 |
| Altitude (ft.) | sea level-230 |

| | |
|---|---|
| Rainfall (in.) | 41.08 |
| Jan. mean min. | 40.7 |
| July mean max. | 94.1 |
| Civ. Labor | 50,041 |
| Unemployed | 4.4 |

| | |
|---|---|
| Wages | $434,035,520 |
| Per Capita Income | $47,041 |
| Prop. Value | $7,826,845,727 |
| Retail Sales | $2,115,976,294 |

*For explanation of sources, symbols and abbreviations, see p. 238, and foldout map.*

# Walker County

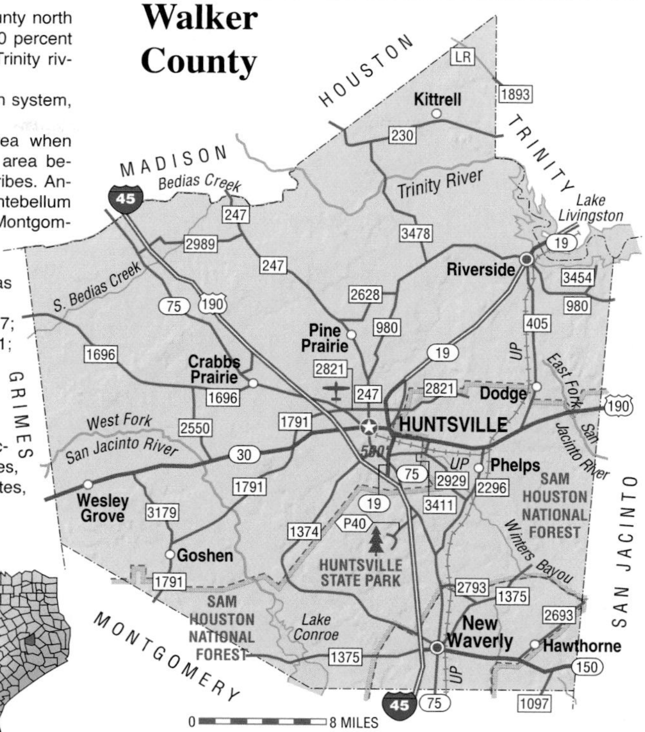

**Physical Features**: South central county north of Houston of rolling hills; more than 70 percent forested; national forest; San Jacinto, Trinity rivers; Lake Livingston, Lake Conroe.

**Economy**: State employment in prison system, education.

**History**: Coahuiltecans, Bidais in area when Spanish explored around 1690. Later, area became trading ground for many Indian tribes. Anglo-Americans settled in the 1830s. Antebellum slaveholding area. County created from Montgomery County and organized in 1846; first named for U.S. Secretary of the Treasury R.J. Walker; renamed 1863 for Texas Ranger Capt. S.H. Walker.

**Race/Ethnicity**: (In percent) Anglo, 57.7; Black, 22.8; Hispanic, 17.5; Asian, 1.1; Other, 2.3.

**Vital Statistics**, annual: Births, 597; deaths, 511; marriages, 415; divorces, 203.

**Recreation**: Fishing, hunting, lake activities; Sam Houston museum, homes, grave; prison museum; other historic sites, state park, Sam Houston National Forest; Sam Houston folk festival in spring.

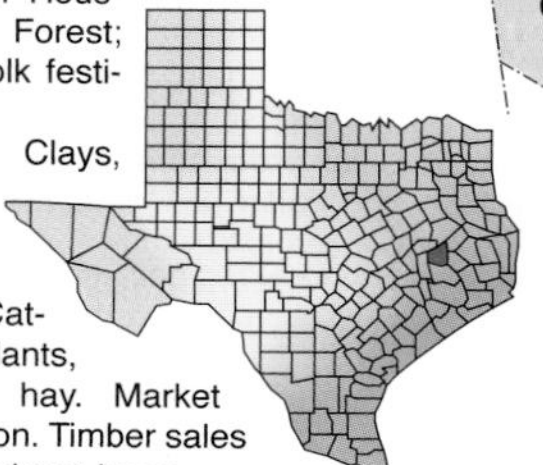

**Minerals**: Clays, natural gas, oil, sand and gravel, stone.

**Agriculture**: Cattle, nursery plants, poultry, cotton, hay. Market value $34.5 million. Timber sales substantial; Christmas trees.

**HUNTSVILLE** (40,125) county seat; state prison system, Sam Houston State University, forest products, varied manufacturing; hospital; museums, arts center.

Other towns include: **Dodge** (150), **New Waverly** (1,027), **Riverside** (489).

| | |
|---|---|
| **Population** | **69,789** |
| Change fm 2010 | 2.8 |
| Area (sq. mi.) | 801.5 |
| Land Area (sq. mi.) | 784.2 |
| Altitude (ft.) | 131-500 |
| Rainfall (in.) | 49.08 |
| Jan. mean min. | 39.7 |
| July mean max. | 93.3 |
| Civ. Labor | 27,974 |
| Unemployed | 6.1 |
| Wages | $203,039,416 |
| Per Capita Income | $25,508 |
| Prop. Value | $3,774,049,650 |
| Retail Sales | $958,983,201 |

*For explanation of sources, symbols and abbreviations, see p. 238, and foldout map.*

---

*Blooming dogwoods in Purtis Creek State Park, Van Zandt-Henderson counties. Photo by Earl Nottingham/Texas Parks & Wildlife.*

# Waller County

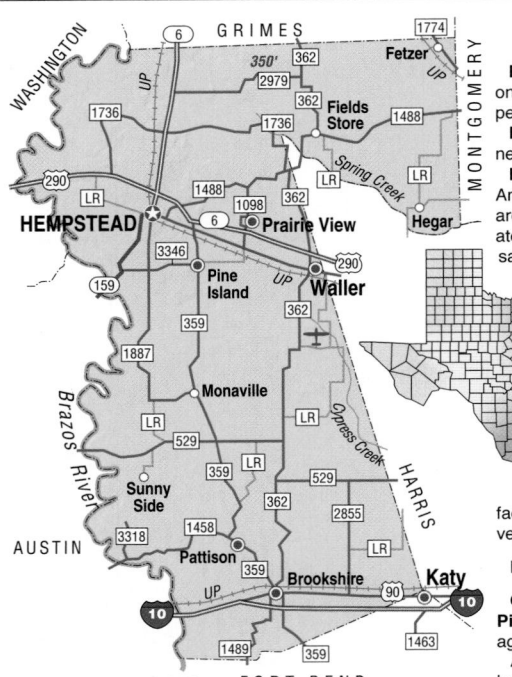

**Physical Features**: South central county near Houston on rolling prairie; drains to Brazos; alluvial soils; about 20 percent forested.

**Economy**: Agribusiness, education, equine-related businesses, part of Houston metropolitan area.

**History**: Bidais Indians reduced to about 100 when Anglo-Americans settled in the 1820s. Antebellum slaveholding area. County named for Edwin Waller, Republic leader; created in 1873 from Austin, Grimes counties, organized the same year.

**Race/Ethnicity**: (In percent), Anglo, 43.6; Black, 25.8; Hispanic, 29.5; Asian, 0.7; Other, 3.0.

**Vital Statistics**, annual: Births, 579; deaths, 281; marriages, 248; divorces, 138.

**Recreation**: Fishing, hunting; historic sites; museum.

**Minerals**: Oil, gas.

**Agriculture**: Cattle, hay, rice, greenhouse nurseries, turf grass. 10,000 acres irrigated. Market value $91.7 million. Some timber marketed.

**HEMPSTEAD** (6,476) county seat; varied manufacturing, commuting to Houston, agribusiness center, large vegetable market; watermelon fest in July.

**Prairie View** (5,809) home of Prairie View A&M University.

Other towns include: **Brookshire** (4,831), **Pattison** (513), **Pine Island** (1,012), **Waller** (2,445, partly in Harris County) agriculture, education, construction.

Also, part [1,156] of **Katy** (15,094, mostly in Harris County) hospitals.

| | | |
|---|---|---|
| Population.............................46,820 | Altitude (ft.) ...........................100-350 | Unemployed ....................................5.7 |
| Change fm 2010.............................8.4 | Rainfall (in.) ...............................45.53 | Wages .............................$164,808,502 |
| Area (sq. mi.).............................517.8 | Jan. mean min. ............................38.0 | Per Capita Income.................$31,605 |
| Land Area (sq. mi.) .....................513.4 | July mean max. ...........................95.0 | Prop. Value ...............$4,987,952,845 |
| | Civ. Labor ................................21,195 | Retail Sales .................$505,234,025 |

# Ward County

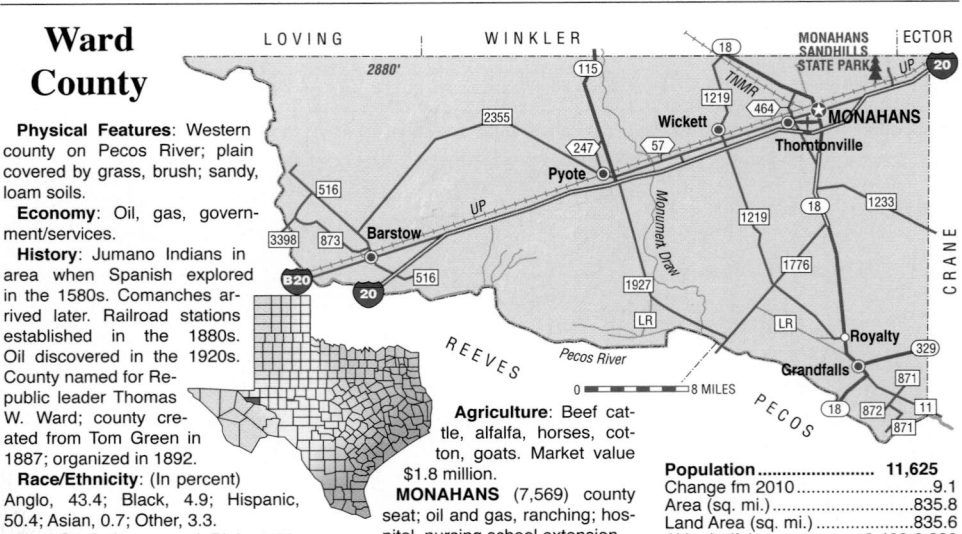

**Physical Features**: Western county on Pecos River; plain covered by grass, brush; sandy, loam soils.

**Economy**: Oil, gas, government/services.

**History**: Jumano Indians in area when Spanish explored in the 1580s. Comanches arrived later. Railroad stations established in the 1880s. Oil discovered in the 1920s. County named for Republic leader Thomas W. Ward; county created from Tom Green in 1887; organized in 1892.

**Race/Ethnicity**: (In percent) Anglo, 43.4; Black, 4.9; Hispanic, 50.4; Asian, 0.7; Other, 3.3.

**Vital Statistics**, annual: Births, 170; deaths, 122; marriages, 109; divorces, 30.

**Recreation**: Sandhills state park, camel treks, Million Barrel museum in Monahans, county park, Butterfield stagecoach festival in July.

**Minerals**: Oil, gas, caliche, sand, gravel.

**Agriculture**: Beef cattle, alfalfa, horses, cotton, goats. Market value $1.8 million.

**MONAHANS** (7,569) county seat; oil and gas, ranching; hospital, nursing school extension.

Other towns: **Barstow** (370); **Grandfalls** (393); **Pyote** (122) Rattlesnake bomber base museum; **Thorntonville** (514); **Wickett** (525).

*For explanation of sources, symbols and abbreviations, see p. 238, and foldout map.*

| | |
|---|---|
| Population ...................... 11,625 | |
| Change fm 2010.............................9.1 | |
| Area (sq. mi.) .............................835.8 | |
| Land Area (sq. mi.) ....................835.6 | |
| Altitude (ft.) .....................2,400-2,880 | |
| Rainfall (in.) ...............................13.87 | |
| Jan. mean min. ............................30.9 | |
| July mean max. ...........................94.9 | |
| Civ. Labor ..................................6,457 | |
| Unemployed ...................................3.6 | |
| Wages ...........................$59,521,924 | |
| Per Capita Income.................$46,347 | |
| Prop. Value ...............$2,941,682,460 | |
| Retail Sales .................$196,737,570 | |

# Washington County

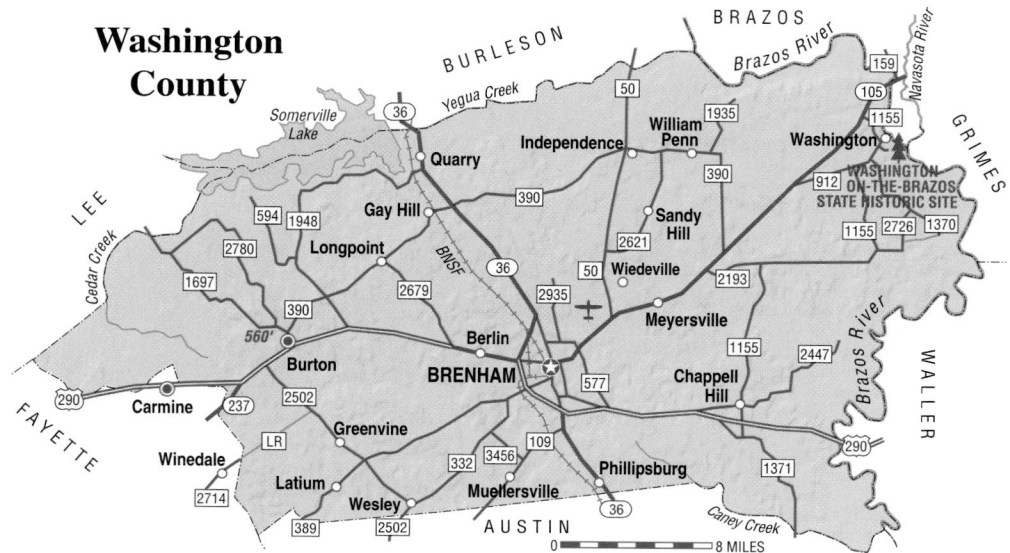

## Physical Features
South central county in Brazos valley; rolling prairie of sandy loam, alluvial soils; Brazos River, Somvervville Lake.

## Economy
Agribusiness, oil, tourism, manufacturing, government/services.

## History
Coahuiltecan and Tonkawa tribes were in the area when Anglo-American settlers began arriving in 1821. Antebellum slaveholding area. Germans arrived around 1870. County named for George Washington; an original county, created 1836, organized 1837.

## Race/Ethnicity
(In percent), Anglo, 65.1; Black, 18.0; Hispanic, 14.9; Asian, 1.7; Other, 1.6.

## Vital Statistics
annual: Births, 396; deaths, 375; marriages, 227; divorces, 96.

## Recreation
Many historic sites, including Washington-on-the-Brazos,

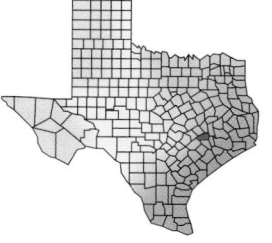

Texas Baptist Historical Museum, Star of Republic Museum; wildflowers, Somerville Lake, fishing, hunting, birding; antique rose nursery.

## Minerals
Oil, gas and stone.

## Agriculture
Cattle, poultry, dairy products, hogs, horses; hay, corn, sorghum, cotton, small grains, nursery crops. Market value $45.7 million.

**BRENHAM** (16,212) county seat; Blue Bell creamery, retail, tourism;

hospital; Blinn College; Maifest.

Other towns include: **Burton** (305) agriculture, tourism, national landmark cotton gin, festival in April; **Chappell Hill** (750) sausage production, tourism, historic homes, Scarecrow festival in October; **Washington** (100) site of signing of Texas Declaration of Independence.

| | |
|---|---|
| **Population** | **34,438** |
| Change fm 2010 | 2.1 |
| Area (sq. mi.) | 621.8 |
| Land Area (sq. mi.) | 604.0 |
| Altitude (ft.) | 150-560 |
| Rainfall (in.) | 45.14 |
| Jan. mean min. | 39.0 |
| July mean max. | 94.2 |
| Civ. Labor | 18,068 |
| Unemployed | 4.8 |
| Wages | $134,533,114 |
| Per Capita Income | $50,396 |
| Prop. Value | $5,219,928,938 |
| Retail Sales | $504,347,549 |

*The house in Independence where the wife of Sam Houston lived while he served in the U.S. Senate. Photo by Robert Plocheck.*

# Webb County

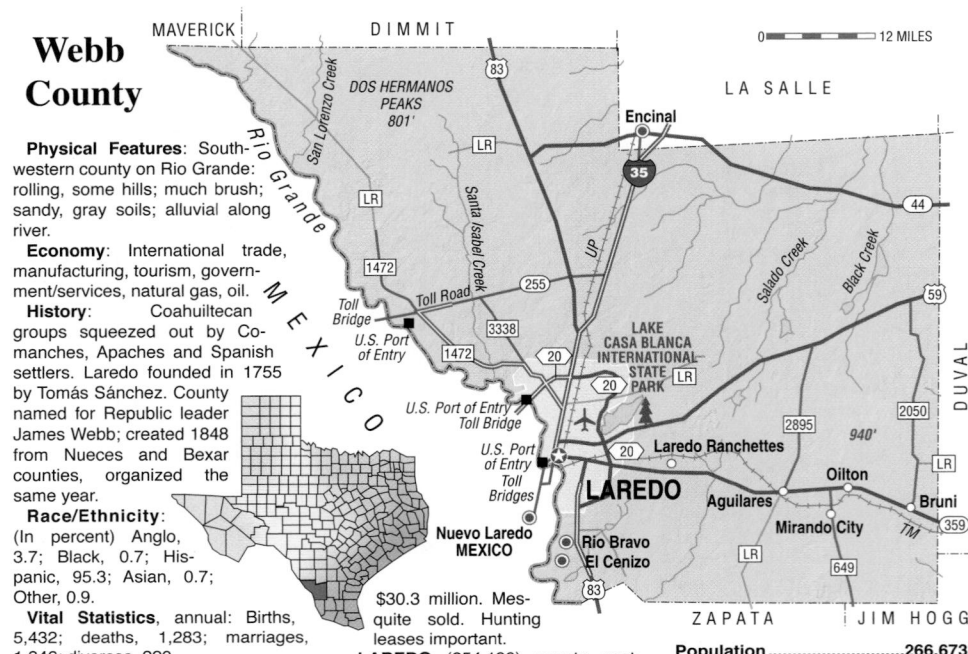

**Physical Features**: Southwestern county on Rio Grande; rolling, some hills; much brush; sandy, gray soils; alluvial along river.

**Economy**: International trade, manufacturing, tourism, government/services, natural gas, oil.

**History**: Coahuiltecan groups squeezed out by Comanches, Apaches and Spanish settlers. Laredo founded in 1755 by Tomás Sánchez. County named for Republic leader James Webb; created 1848 from Nueces and Bexar counties, organized the same year.

**Race/Ethnicity**: (In percent) Anglo, 3.7; Black, 0.7; Hispanic, 95.3; Asian, 0.7; Other, 0.9.

**Vital Statistics**, annual: Births, 5,432; deaths, 1,283; marriages, 1,846; divorces, 220.

**Recreation**: Tourist gateway to Mexico; hunting, fishing; Lake Casa Blanca park, water recreation; historic sites; Museum of Republic of the Rio Grande; Fort McIntosh; minor league baseball, hockey; Washington's Birthday celebration.

**Minerals**: Natural gas, oil, coal.

**Agriculture**: Onions, melons, nursery crops, cattle, horses, goats. About 2,500 acres irrigated. Market value $30.3 million. Mesquite sold. Hunting leases important.

**LAREDO** (254,190) county seat; international trade, retail center, government/services; rail, highway gateway to Mexico; junior college, Texas A&M International University, community college; hospitals; entertainment/sports arena; "El Grito" on Sept. 15; Jalapeño festival in February.

Other towns and places include: **Bruni** (390); **El Cenizo** (3,319); **Mirando City** (392); **Oilton** (367); **Rio Bravo** (4,833).

| | |
|---|---|
| Population | 266,673 |
| Change fm 2010 | 6.5 |
| Area (sq. mi.) | 3,375.6 |
| Land Area (sq. mi.) | 3,361.5 |
| Altitude (ft.) | 310-940 |
| Rainfall (in.) | 20.20 |
| Jan. mean min. | 46.1 |
| July mean max. | 99.3 |
| Civ. Labor | 102,112 |
| Unemployed | 6.3 |
| Wages | $766,857,229 |
| Per Capita Income | $27,102 |
| Prop. Value | $18,998,316,902 |
| Retail Sales | $3,606,333,182 |

*Sculpture "Among Friends There Are No Borders" by Armando Hinojosa at the Laredo airport. Photo by Robert Plocheck.*

# Wharton County

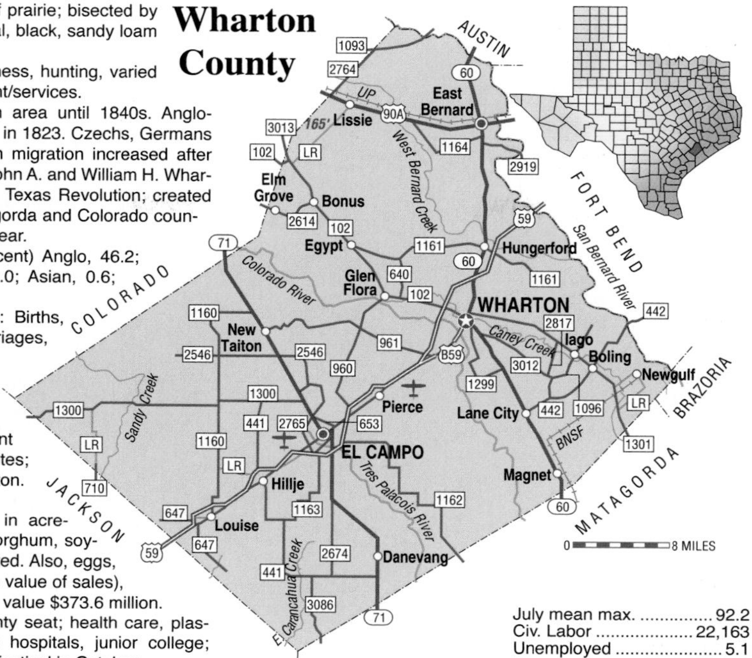

**Physical Features**: Gulf prairie; bisected by the Colorado River; alluvial, black, sandy loam soils.

**Economy**: Oil, agribusiness, hunting, varied manufacturing, government/services.

**History**: Karankawas in area until 1840s. Anglo-American colonists settled in 1823. Czechs, Germans arrived in 1880s. Mexican migration increased after 1950. County named for John A. and William H. Wharton, brothers active in the Texas Revolution; created 1846 from Jackson, Matagorda and Colorado counties, organized the same year.

**Race/Ethnicity**: (In percent) Anglo, 46.2; Black, 14.4; Hispanic, 39.0; Asian, 0.6; Other, 1.6.

**Vital Statistics**, annual: Births, 540; deaths, 418; marriages, 209; divorces, 117.

**Recreation**: Waterfowl hunting, fishing, big-game, birding; art, historical museums; river-front park at Wharton; historic sites; old Plaza Theater at Wharton.

**Minerals**: Oil, gas.

**Agriculture**: Rice (first in acreage); cotton, milo, corn, sorghum, soybeans; 72,000 acres irrigated. Also, eggs, nurseries/turf grass (first in value of sales), cattle, aquaculture. Market value $373.6 million.

**WHARTON** (8,664) county seat; health care, plastics, government/services; hospitals, junior college; Juneteenth, wine and arts festival in October.

**EL CAMPO** (11,515) rice processing, plastic, styrofoam processing; hospital; Polka Expo in November.

Other towns include: **Boling** (1,131); **Danevang** (61); **East Bernard** (2,318) commuters, agribusiness, retail, klobase-kolache festival in June; **Egypt** (26); **Glen Flora** (210); **Hungerford** (335); **Lane City** (111); **Lissie** (72); **Louise** (1,011); **Pierce** (51).

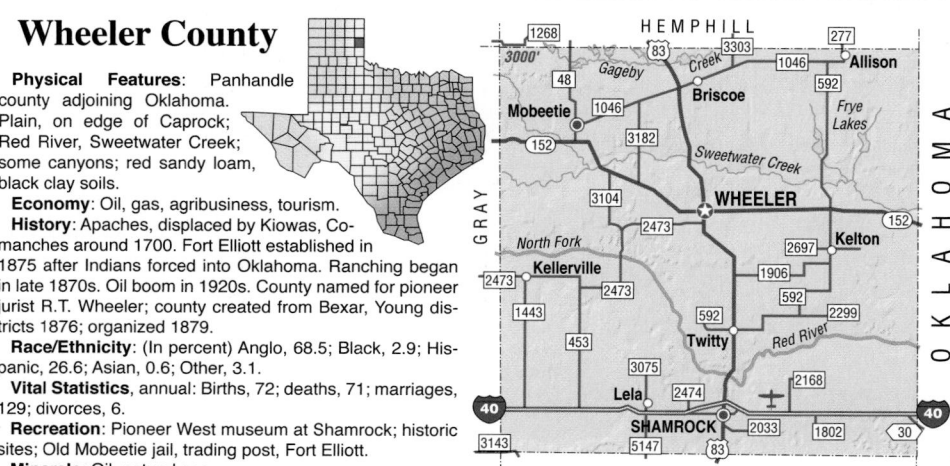

| Population | 41,168 |
|---|---|
| Change fm 2010 | – 0.3 |
| Area (sq. mi.) | 1,094.4 |
| Land Area (sq. mi.) | 1,086.2 |
| Altitude (ft.) | 50-165 |
| Rainfall (in.) | 47.47 |
| Jan. mean min. | 43.0 |

| July mean max. | 92.2 |
|---|---|
| Civ. Labor | 22,163 |
| Unemployed | 5.1 |
| Wages | $136,849,551 |
| Per Capita Income | $40,559 |
| Prop. Value | $4,532,539,863 |
| Retail Sales | $812,255,024 |

*For explanation of sources, symbols and abbreviations, see p. 238, and foldout map.*

---

# Wheeler County

**Physical Features**: Panhandle county adjoining Oklahoma. Plain, on edge of Caprock; Red River, Sweetwater Creek; some canyons; red sandy loam, black clay soils.

**Economy**: Oil, gas, agribusiness, tourism.

**History**: Apaches, displaced by Kiowas, Comanches around 1700. Fort Elliott established in 1875 after Indians forced into Oklahoma. Ranching began in late 1870s. Oil boom in 1920s. County named for pioneer jurist R.T. Wheeler; county created from Bexar, Young districts 1876; organized 1879.

**Race/Ethnicity**: (In percent) Anglo, 68.5; Black, 2.9; Hispanic, 26.6; Asian, 0.6; Other, 3.1.

**Vital Statistics**, annual: Births, 72; deaths, 71; marriages, 129; divorces, 6.

**Recreation**: Pioneer West museum at Shamrock; historic sites; Old Mobeetie jail, trading post, Fort Elliott.

**Minerals**: Oil, natural gas.

**Agriculture**: Fed beef, cow-calf and stocker cattle, swine, horses; wheat, rye, grain sorghum, cotton. Market value $111.2 million.

**WHEELER** (1,750) county seat; agribusiness, petroleum center, tourism; slaughter plant; hospital, library.

**SHAMROCK** (2,087) tourism, agribusiness antiques shops; hospital, library, old Route 66 sites; St. Patrick's Day event.

Other towns include: **Allison** (135); **Briscoe** (135); **Mobeetie** (112).

| Population | 5,714 |
|---|---|
| Change fm 2010 | 5.6 |
| Area (sq. mi.) | 915.5 |
| Land Area (sq. mi.) | 914.5 |

| Altitude (ft.) | 2,005-3,000 |
|---|---|
| Rainfall (in.) | 25.16 |
| Jan. mean min. | 24.0 |
| July mean max. | 93.3 |
| Civ. Labor | 4,134 |
| Unemployed | 3.1 |
| Wages | $26,202,382 |
| Per Capita Income | $54,538 |
| Prop. Value | $3,259,535,890 |
| Retail Sales | $84,520,324 |

# Wichita County

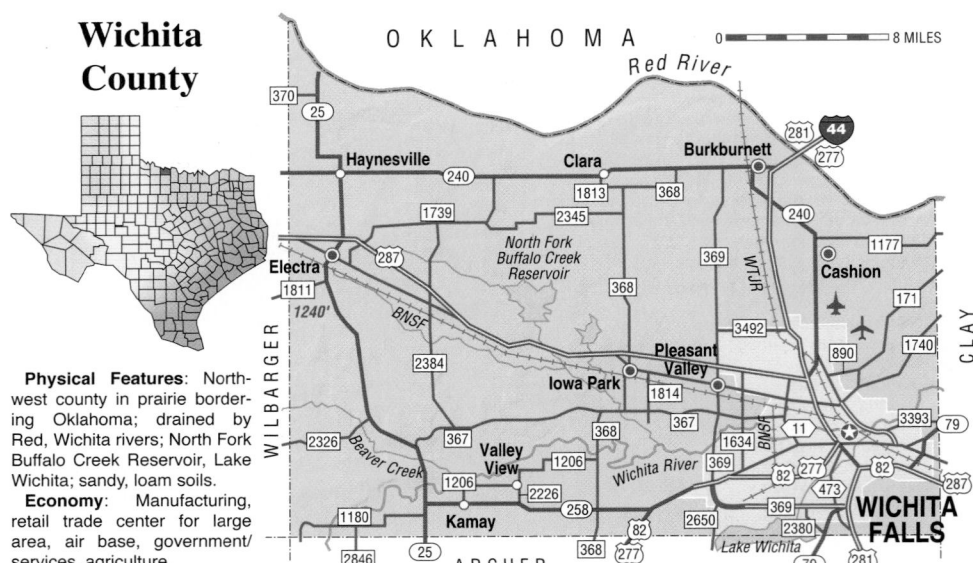

**Physical Features:** Northwest county in prairie bordering Oklahoma; drained by Red, Wichita rivers; North Fork Buffalo Creek Reservoir, Lake Wichita; sandy, loam soils.

**Economy:** Manufacturing, retail trade center for large area, air base, government/services, agriculture.

**History:** Wichitas and other Caddoan tribes in area in 1700s; Comanches, Apaches also present until 1850s. Anglo-American settlement increased after 1870. County named for tribe; created from Young Territory 1858; organized 1882.

**Race/Ethnicity:** (In percent) Anglo, 67.2; Black, 10.7; Hispanic, 17.9; Asian, 2.2; Other, 3.8.

**Vital Statistics,** annual: Births, 1,766; deaths, 1,285; marriages, 1,502; divorces, 629.

**Recreation:** Museums; historic sites; Texas-Oklahoma High School Oil Bowl football game; collegiate activities; water sports on lakes; Fiestas Patrias parade, Ranch Round-up in August.

**Minerals:** Oil.

**Agriculture:** Beef cattle, horticulture, wheat, hay. Seventy-five percent of hay irrigated; 10 percent of wheat/cotton. Market value $37.9 million.

**WICHITA FALLS** (105,984) county seat; distribution center for large area of Texas and Oklahoma, government/services, varied manufacturing, oil-field services; hospitals, including North Texas state hospital; Midwestern State University, vocational-technical training center; hiking trails; Hotter'n Hell bicycle race in August; Sheppard Air Force Base.

Other cities include: **Burkburnett** (11,270) some manufacturing, Trails and Tales of Boomtown USA display and tours; **Cashion** (352); **Electra** (2,787) oil, agriculture, manufacturing, commuters to Wichita Falls; hospital; goat barbecue in May; **Iowa Park** (6,501) manufacturing, prison, Parkfest in May; **Kamay** (640); **Pleasant Valley** (337).

| | |
|---|---|
| **Population** | **132,355** |
| Change fm 2010 | 0.7 |
| Area (sq. mi.) | 633.1 |
| Land Area (sq. mi.) | 627.8 |
| Altitude (ft.) | 912-1,240 |
| Rainfall (in.) | 28.92 |
| Jan. mean min. | 29.8 |
| July mean max. | 96.9 |
| Civ. Labor | 60,663 |
| Unemployed | 5.8 |
| Wages | $476,853,312 |
| Per Capita Income | $40,066 |
| Prop. Value | $7,020,715,901 |
| Retail Sales | $1,788,367,531 |

*For explanation of sources, symbols and abbreviations, see p. 238, and foldout map.*

*Cattle graze in a pasture in Wilbarger County near the Red River. Photo by Robert Plocheck.*

# Wilbarger County

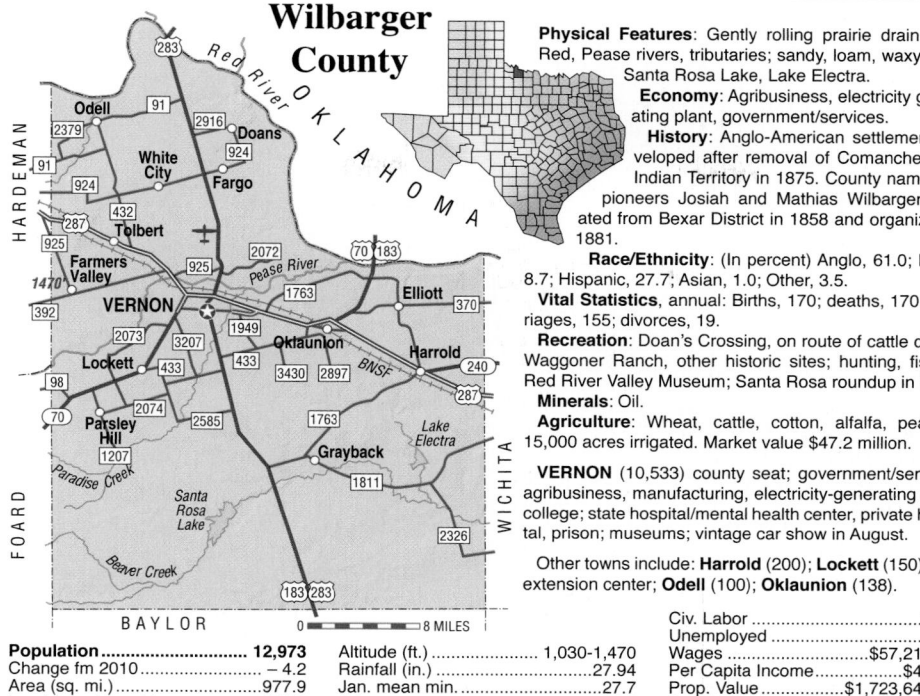

**Physical Features**: Gently rolling prairie draining to Red, Pease rivers, tributaries; sandy, loam, waxy soils; Santa Rosa Lake, Lake Electra.

**Economy**: Agribusiness, electricity generating plant, government/services.

**History**: Anglo-American settlement developed after removal of Comanches into Indian Territory in 1875. County named for pioneers Josiah and Mathias Wilbarger; created from Bexar District in 1858 and organized in 1881.

**Race/Ethnicity**: (In percent) Anglo, 61.0; Black, 8.7; Hispanic, 27.7; Asian, 1.0; Other, 3.5.

**Vital Statistics**, annual: Births, 170; deaths, 170; marriages, 155; divorces, 19.

**Recreation**: Doan's Crossing, on route of cattle drives; Waggoner Ranch, other historic sites; hunting, fishing; Red River Valley Museum; Santa Rosa roundup in May.

**Minerals**: Oil.

**Agriculture**: Wheat, cattle, cotton, alfalfa, peanuts; 15,000 acres irrigated. Market value $47.2 million.

**VERNON** (10,533) county seat; government/services, agribusiness, manufacturing, electricity-generating plant; college; state hospital/mental health center, private hospital, prison; museums; vintage car show in August.

Other towns include: **Harrold** (200); **Lockett** (150) A&M extension center; **Odell** (100); **Oklaunion** (138).

| | |
|---|---|
| Population | **12,973** |
| Change fm 2010 | – 4.2 |
| Area (sq. mi.) | 977.9 |
| Land Area (sq. mi.) | 970.8 |
| Altitude (ft.) | 1,030-1,470 |
| Rainfall (in.) | 27.94 |
| Jan. mean min. | 27.7 |
| July mean max. | 96.6 |
| Civ. Labor | 7,317 |
| Unemployed | 4.1 |
| Wages | $57,212,520 |
| Per Capita Income | $40,628 |
| Prop. Value | $1,723,648,660 |
| Retail Sales | $128,048,114 |

# Willacy County

**Physical Features:** Flat coastal prairie sloping toward Gulf; alluvial, sandy, marshy soils; Padre Island; La Sal Vieja, salt lake; wildlife refuge.

**Economy:** Agribusiness, oil, government/services.

**History:** Coahuiltecan area when Spanish explored in 1500s. Spanish ranching began in 1790s. County named for Texas legislator John G. Willacy; created 1911 from Cameron, Hidalgo counties, organized in 1912; reorganized 1921 after most of its territory was given over to the newly created Kenedy County.

**Race/Ethnicity:** (In percent) Anglo, 9.6; Black, 2.6; Hispanic, 87.4; Asian, 0.8; Other, 1.2.

**Vital Statistics**, annual: Births, 328; deaths, 167; marriages, 98; divorces, 48.

**Recreation:** Fresh and saltwater fishing, hunting of deer, turkey, dove; mild climate attracts many winter tourists.

**Minerals**: Oil, natural gas.

**Agriculture:** Cotton, sorghum, corn, vegetables, sugar cane; 20 percent of cropland irrigated. Livestock includes cattle, horses, goats, hogs. Market value $82.6 million.

**RAYMONDVILLE** (11,030) county seat; agribusiness, oil center, food processing, tourism, enterprise zone, prison; museum; Boot Fest in October.

Other towns include: **Lasara** (1,048); **Lyford** (2,579); **Port Mansfield** (222) sport-fishing, birding, tourism, fishing tournament in July; **San Perlita** (564); **Sebastian** (1,956).

| | |
|---|---|
| Population | **21,903** |
| Change fm 2010 | – 1.0 |
| Area (sq. mi.) | 784.3 |
| Land Area (sq. mi.) | 590.6 |
| Altitude (ft.) | sea level-94 |
| Rainfall (in.) | 26.08 |
| Jan. mean min. | 47.6 |
| July mean max. | 96.7 |
| Civ. Labor | 8,639 |
| Unemployed | 11.4 |
| Wages | $33,147,638 |
| Per Capita Income | $27,196 |
| Prop. Value | $1,800,969,597 |
| Retail Sales | $150,643,094 |

*For explanation of sources, symbols and abbreviations, see p. 238, and foldout map.*

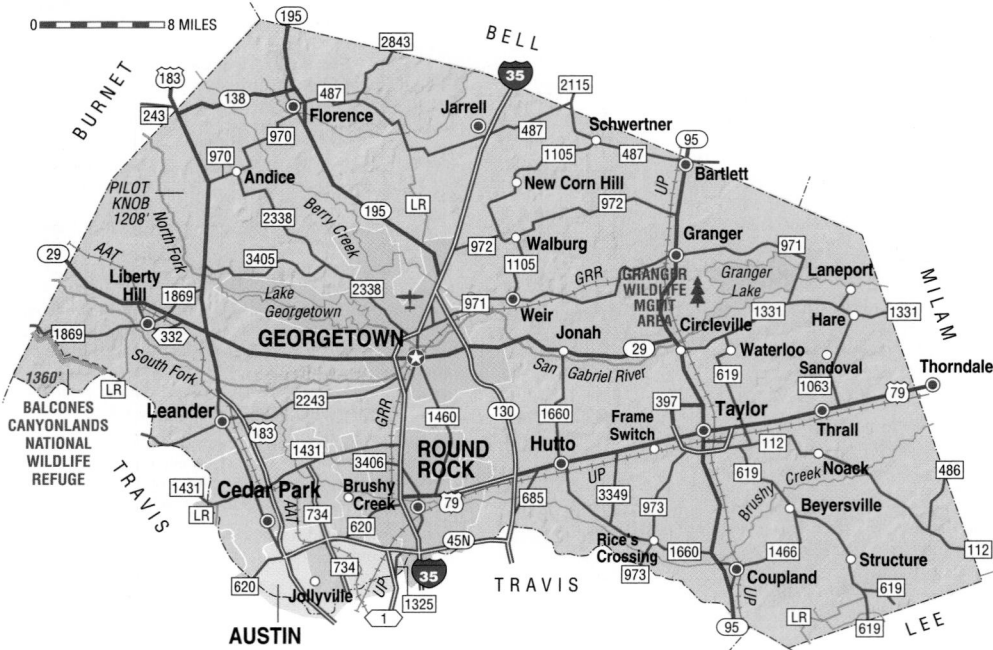

# Williamson County

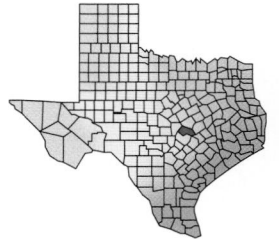

**Physical Features**: Central county near Austin. Level to rolling; mostly Blackland soil, some loam, sand; drained by San Gabriel River and tributaries; Granger Lake, Lake Georgetown.

**Economy**: Agribusinesses, varied manufacturing, education center, government/services; the county is part of Austin metropolitan area.

**History**: Tonkawa area; later, there were other tribes. Comanches raided until 1860s. Anglo-American settlement began in late 1830s. County named for Robert M. Williamson, pioneer leader; created from Milam and organized in 1848.

**Race/Ethnicity**: (In percent) Anglo, 62.3; Black, 6.7; Hispanic, 23.8; Asian, 5.6; Other, 3.5.

**Vital Statistics**, annual: Births, 6,135; deaths, 2,132; marriages, 2,421; divorces, 776.

**Recreation**: Lake recreation; Inner Space Cavern; historic sites; deer hunting, fishing; Gov. Dan Moody Museum at Taylor; San Gabriel Park; old settlers park; walking tours, rattlesnake sacking, barbecue cookoff, frontier days in summer.

Also, the Round Rock Express AAA minor league baseball; Cedar Park Center, home of the Austin Spurs NBA developmental basketball team and the Texas Stars AHL hockey team.

**Minerals**: Building stone, sand and gravel.

**Agriculture**: Corn, cattle, sorghum, cotton, wheat, hay, nursery crops. Market value $129.6 million.

**GEORGETOWN** (56,536) county seat; education, health, government/services, manufacturing, retail; hospital; Southwestern University; Red Poppy festival in April.

**ROUND ROCK** (110,326, part [1,362] in Travis County) semiconductor, varied manufacturing, tourism and distribution center; hospital; Texas Baptist Children's Home.

**Cedar Park** (57,504, part [489] in Travis County) energy equipment manufacturing, millwork, concrete production, and commuting to Austin; hospital, community college extension; steam-engine train; Cedar Fest in the spring.

**Taylor** (16,178) varied manufacturing, wholesale, transportation, government/services; hospital; college extension campuses, museum, parks; Blackland Prairie Day in May.

Other towns include: **Andice** (300); **Bartlett** (2,700, partly in Bell County) cotton, corn production, commuters, prison, first rural electrification in nation in 1933, clinic, library, Friendship Fest in September; **Brushy Creek** (23,072); **Coupland** (280); **Florence** (1,169).

Also, **Granger** (1,443); **Hutto** (18,371) agriculture, manufacturing, government/services, commuters to Austin, museum, Olde Tyme Days in October; **Jarrell** (1,022); **Jollyville** (16,852, partly in Travis County); **Leander** (32,276); **Liberty Hill** (1,053) artisans center; **Schwertner** (175); **Thrall** (896); **Walburg** (277); **Weir** (462).

Also, part [35,697] of **Austin**.

| Population | 489,250 |
|---|---|
| Change fm 2010 | 15.7 |
| Area (sq. mi.) | 1,134.4 |
| Land Area (sq. mi.) | 1,118.3 |
| Altitude (ft.) | 400-1,360 |
| Rainfall (in.) | 35.73 |
| Jan. mean min. | 36.5 |
| July mean max. | 94.9 |
| Civ. Labor | 251,877 |
| Unemployed | 4.7 |
| Wages | $1,672,165,073 |
| Per Capita Income | $42,786 |
| Prop. Value | $41,951,463,782 |
| Retail Sales | $8,317,927,555 |

*For explanation of sources, symbols and abbreviations, see p. 238, and foldout map.*

# Wilson County

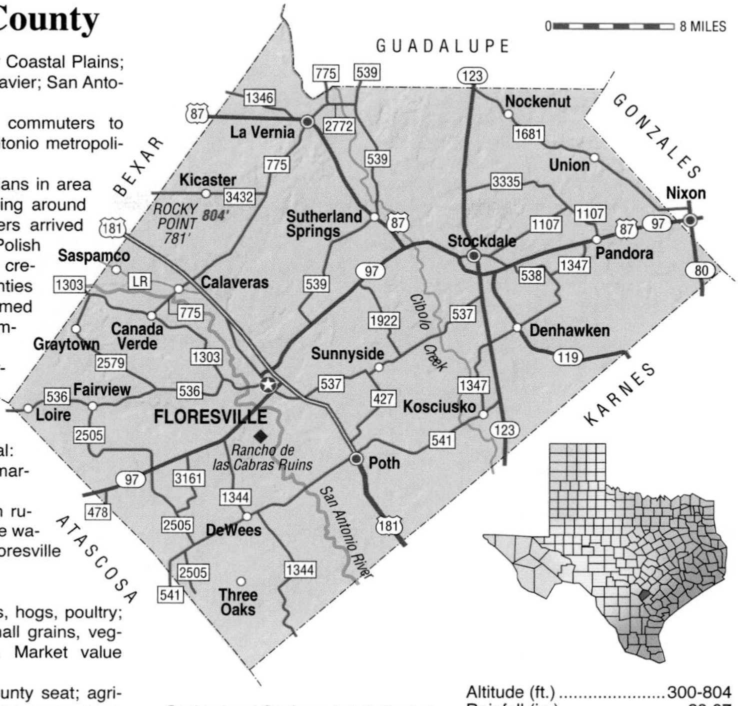

**Physical Features**: Upper Coastal Plains; mostly sandy soils, some heavier; San Antonio River, Cibolo Creek.

**Economy**: Agribusiness, commuters to San Antonio; part of San Antonio metropolitan area.

**History**: Coahuiltecan Indians in area when Spanish began ranching around 1750. Anglo-American settlers arrived in the 1840s. Germans, Polish settled in the 1850s. County created from Bexar, Karnes counties and organized in 1860; named for James C. Wilson, a member of the Mier Expedition.

**Race/Ethnicity**: (In percent) Anglo, 58.0; Black, 1.8; Hispanic, 38.8; Asian, 0.5; Other, 2.3.

**Vital Statistics**, annual: Births, 497; deaths, 335; marriages, 253; divorces, 135.

**Recreation**: Mission ranch ruins, historic homes; Stockdale watermelon jubilee in June; Floresville peanut festival in October.

**Minerals**: Oil, gas, clays.

**Agriculture**: Cattle, dairies, hogs, poultry; peanuts, sorghum, corn, small grains, vegetables, watermelons, fruit. Market value $102.1 million.

**FLORESVILLE** (7,100) county seat; agribusiness; hospital, veterans home; Heritage Days in spring.

Other towns include: **La Vernia** (1,200); **Pandora** (110); **Poth** (2,098) agriculture, commuting to San Antonio; bicycle ride in September; **Stockdale** (1,560) agriculture, commuting to San Antonio, museum, nature center, watermelon jubilee in June;

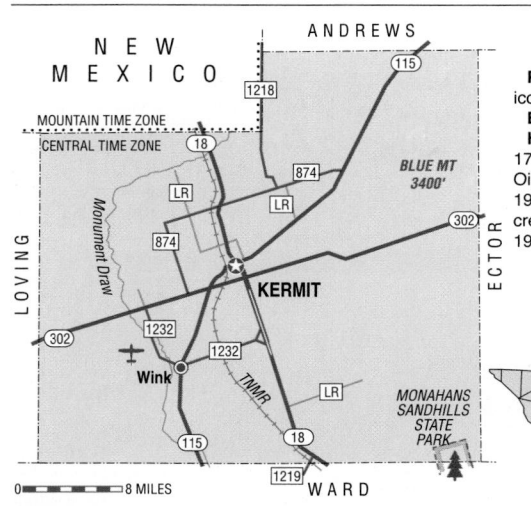

**Sutherland Springs** (420). Part of **Nixon** (2,442, mostly in Gonzales County).

| Population | 46,402 |
| --- | --- |
| Change fm 2010 | 8.1 |
| Area (sq. mi.) | 808.4 |
| Land Area (sq. mi.) | 803.7 |

| Altitude (ft.) | 300-804 |
| --- | --- |
| Rainfall (in.) | 29.07 |
| Jan. mean min. | 37.2 |
| July mean max. | 95.5 |
| Civ. Labor | 21,010 |
| Unemployed | 4.8 |
| Wages | $57,288,894 |
| Per Capita Income | $40,351 |
| Prop. Value | $3,944,482,972 |
| Retail Sales | $534,276,837 |

---

# Winkler County

**Physical Features**: Western county adjoining New Mexico on plains, partly sandy hills.

**Economy**: Oil, gas, ranching, prison, some farming.

**History**: Apache area until arrival of Comanches in the 1700s. Anglo-Americans began ranching in the 1880s. Oil discovered in 1926. Mexican migration increased after 1960. County named for Confederate Col. C.M. Winkler; created from Tom Green County in 1887; organized in 1910.

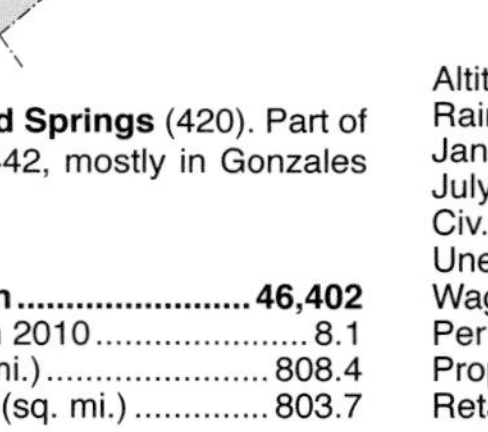

**Race/Ethnicity**: (In percent) Anglo, 39.2; Black, 2.9; Hispanic, 57.3; Asian, 0.5; Other, 2.9.

**Vital Statistics**, annual: Births, 132; deaths, 82; marriages, 43; divorces, 29.

**Recreation**: Monahans Sandhills State Park; museum; zoo; wooden oil derrick; Roy Orbison festival in June at Wink; Wink Sink, large sinkhole.

**Minerals**: Oil, gas.

**Agriculture**: Beef cattle. Market value $3.4 million.

**KERMIT** (6,187) county seat; oil, gas, ranching, some farming; hospital; Celebration Days in August.

**Wink** (1,028) oil, gas, ranching.

| Population | 7,821 |
| --- | --- |
| Change fm 2010 | 10.0 |
| Area (sq. mi.) | 841.3 |
| Land Area (sq. mi.) | 841.1 |
| Altitude (ft.) | 2,665-3,400 |
| Rainfall (in.) | 13.09 |
| Jan. mean min. | 28.9 |

| July mean max. | 96.9 |
| --- | --- |
| Civ. Labor | 4,158 |
| Unemployed | 3.7 |
| Wages | $39,649,702 |
| Per Capita Income | $43,004 |
| Prop. Value | $1,473,846,885 |
| Retail Sales | $85,949,657 |

# Wise County

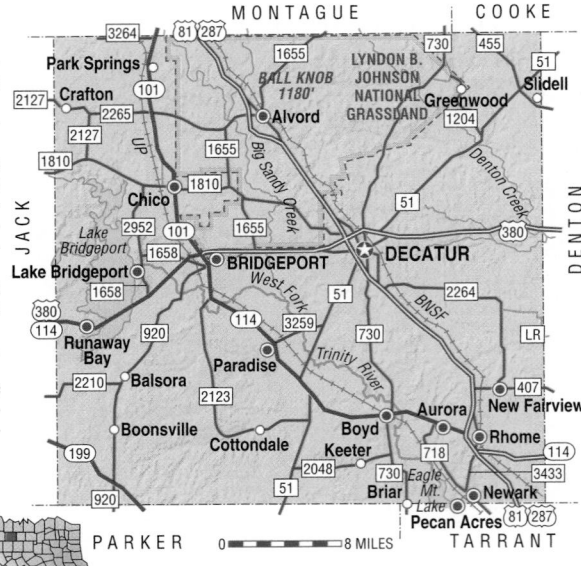

**Physical Features**: Northwest county of rolling prairie, some oaks; clay, loam, sandy soils; Lake Bridgeport, Eagle Mountain Lake.

**Economy**: Petroleum, sand and gravel, agribusiness, many residents work in Fort Worth.

**History**: Caddo Indian groups. Delaware tribe present when Anglo-Americans arrived in 1850s. County created 1856 from Cooke County, organized the same year; named for Virginian, U.S. Sen. Henry A. Wise, who favored annexation of Texas.

**Race/Ethnicity**: (In percent) Anglo, 78.3; Black, 1.5; Hispanic, 18.2; Asian, 0.5; Other, 2.5.

**Vital Statistics**, annual: Births, 763; deaths, 498; marriages, 495; divorces, 323.

**Recreation**: Lake activities, hunting, exotic deer preserve, historical sites, Lyndon B. Johnson National Grassland, heritage museum; Decatur Chisholm trail days in June, Bridgeport Butterfield stage days in July.

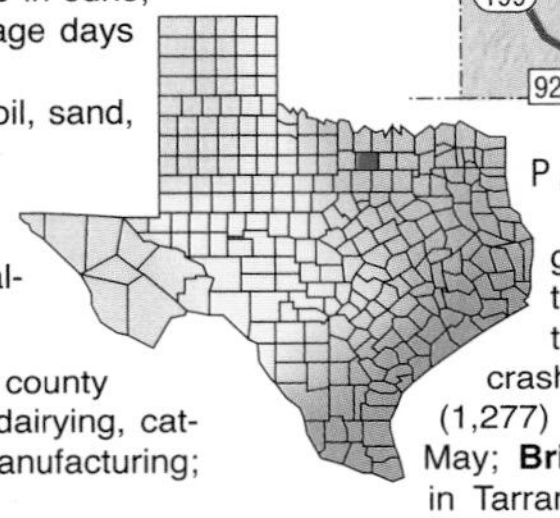

**Minerals**: Natural as, oil, sand, gravel.

**Agriculture**: Beef cattle, hay, dairies, horses, wheat, goats. Market value $49.9 million.

**DECATUR** (6,336) county seat; petroleum center, dairying, cattle marketing, some manufacturing; hospital.

**BRIDGEPORT** (6,227) trade center for lake resort, oil and natural gas production, manufacturing, prison release facility; time-share housing, art community.

Other towns include: **Alvord** (1,380); **Aurora** (1,268) sand and gravel, manufacturing, equestrian center, "alien crash" site; **Boyd** (1,277) chili cookoff in May; **Briar** (5,832, mostly in Tarrant County); **Chico** (1,072); **Greenwood** (76); **Lake Bridgeport** (354); **Newark** (1,044); **New Fairview** (1,253); **Paradise** (455); **Pecan Acres** (4,239, partly in Tarrant County); **Rhome** (1,580); **Runaway Bay** (1,366) tourism, fishing, boating, Spring Fest at Easter; **Slidell** (175).

| Population | 61,638 |
| --- | --- |
| Change fm 2010 | 4.2 |
| Area (sq. mi.) | 922.6 |
| Land Area (sq. mi.) | 904.4 |
| Altitude (ft.) | 649-1,180 |
| Rainfall (in.) | 34.71 |
| Jan. mean min. | 29.7 |
| July mean max. | 94.2 |
| Civ. Labor | 29,889 |
| Unemployed | 5.4 |
| Wages | $251,865,759 |
| Per Capita Income | $41,019 |
| Prop. Value | $9,433,239,436 |
| Retail Sales | $683,408,008 |

*For explanation of sources, symbols and abbreviations, see p. 238, and foldout map.*

*Lake Bridgeport at Runaway Bay, Wise County. Photo by Robert Plocheck.*

# Wood County

**Physical Features**: Hilly northeastern county almost half forested; sandy to alluvial soils; drained by Sabine and tributaries; Lake Fork Reservoir, Lake Quitman, Lake Winnsboro, Lake Hawkins, Holbrook Lake.

**Economy**: Agribusiness, oil, gas, tourism.

**History**: Caddo Indians, reduced by disease. Anglo-American settlement developed in 1840s. County created from Van Zandt County in 1850, organized the same year; named for Gov. George T. Wood.

**Race/Ethnicity**: (In percent) Anglo, 83.7; Black, 4.9; Hispanic, 9.3; Asian, 0.6; Other, 2.4.

**Vital Statistics**, annual: Births, 415; deaths, 627; marriages, 259; divorces, 166.

**Recreation**: Autumn trails; lake activities; hunting, fishing, birding; Gov. Hogg shrine and museum; historic sites; scenic drives; Mineola depot.

**Minerals**: Gas, oil, sand, gravel.

**Agriculture**: Cattle, dairies, poultry, forages, vegetables, nurseries. Market value $105.9 million. Timber production significant.

**QUITMAN** (1,883) county seat; tourism, food processing, some manufacturing; hospital; botanical gardens; Dogwood Fiesta.

**MINEOLA** (4,721) agriculture, railroad center (Amtrak), oil and gas, heritage and nature tourism; museum, library; nature preserve; Ironhorse Festival in November.

**Winnsboro** (3,458, partly in Franklin County) poultry production, dairies, distribution, prison; hospital.

Other towns include: **Alba** (628, partly in Rains County); **Golden** (398) Sweet Potato festival in October; **Hawkins** (1,393) petroleum, water bottling, Jarvis Christian College; oil festival in October; **Holly Lake Ranch** (2,973); **Yantis** (399).

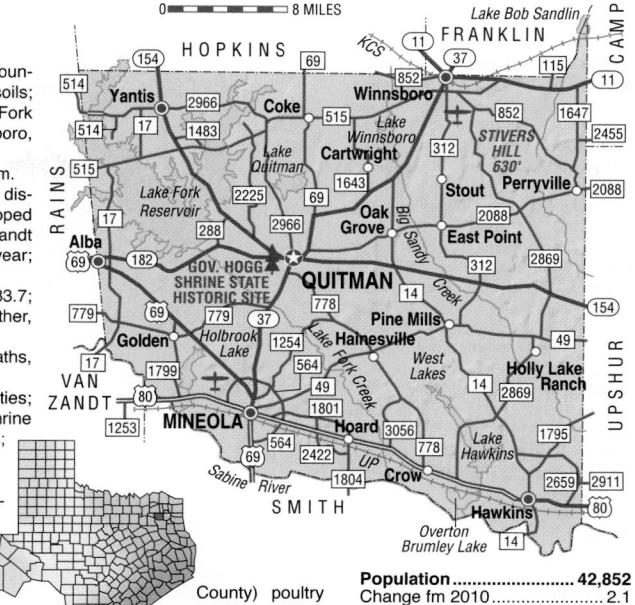

| | |
|---|---|
| Population | 42,852 |
| Change fm 2010 | 2.1 |
| Area (sq. mi.) | 695.7 |
| Land Area (sq. mi.) | 645.2 |
| Altitude (ft.) | 270-630 |
| Rainfall (in.) | 43.02 |
| Jan. mean min. | 32.5 |
| July mean max. | 94.4 |
| Civ. Labor | 18,256 |
| Unemployed | 5.9 |
| Wages | $75,304,426 |
| Per Capita Income | $34,231 |
| Prop. Value | $4,132,894,466 |
| Retail Sales | $386,796,495 |

---

# Yoakum County

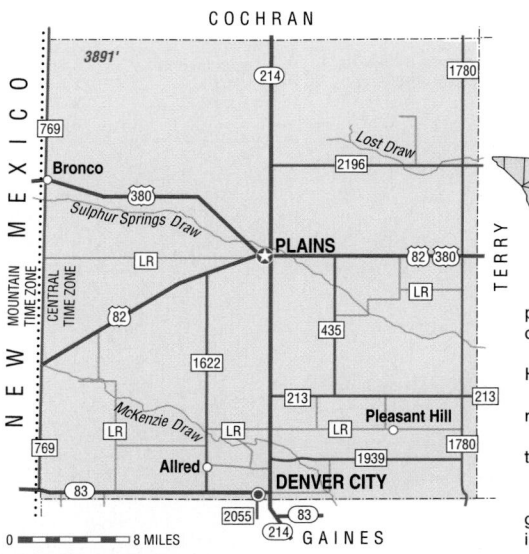

**Physical Features**: Western county is level to rolling; playas, draws; sandy, loam, chocolate soils.

**Economy**: Oil, gas, agriculture.

**History**: Comanche hunting area. Anglo-Americans began ranching in the 1890s. Oil was discovered 1936. Mexican migration increased in the 1950s. County named for Henderson Yoakum, pioneer historian; created from Bexar District in 1876; organized in 1907.

**Race/Ethnicity**: (In percent) Anglo, 35.2; Black, 1.5; Hispanic, 62.4; Asian, 0.5; Other, 2.9.

**Vital Statistics**, annual: Births, 128; deaths, 74; marriages, 57; divorces, 22.

**Recreation**: Tsa Mo Ga museum at Plains; Plains watermelon roundup on Labor Day weekend.

**Minerals**: Oil, natural gas.

**Agriculture**: Cotton, peanuts (third in acreage), sorghum, wheat, watermelons, cattle. Some 90,000 acres irrigated. Market value $80 million.

**PLAINS** (1,556) county seat; oil, agribusiness center.

**DENVER CITY** (4,705) center for oil, agriculture activities in two counties; hospital, library, museum; Fly-In Breakfast at airport in June.

| | |
|---|---|
| Population | 8,286 |
| Change fm 2010 | 5.2 |
| Area (sq. mi.) | 799.7 |
| Land Area (sq. mi.) | 799.7 |
| Altitude (ft.) | 3,400-3,891 |
| Rainfall (in.) | 18.20 |
| Jan. mean min. | 25.7 |
| July mean max. | 91.7 |
| Civ. Labor | 4,888 |
| Unemployed | 3.0 |
| Wages | $54,264,533 |
| Per Capita Income | $55,226 |
| Prop. Value | $4,478,603,503 |
| Retail Sales | $89,391,097 |

# Young County

**Physical Features**: Hilly, broken; drained by Brazos and tributaries; Possum Kingdom Lake, Lake Graham.

**Economy**: Oil, agribusiness, tourism, hunting leases.

**History**: U.S. military outpost established in 1851. Site of the Brazos Indian Reservation 1854–1859 with Caddoes, Wacos, other tribes. Anglo-American settlers arrived in the 1850s. County named for early Texan, Col. W.C. Young; created from Bosque and Fannin counties, and organized in 1856; reorganized 1874.

**Race/Ethnicity**: (In percent) Anglo, 79.3; Black, 1.7; Hispanic, 17.4; Asian, 0.6; Other, 2.6.

**Vital Statistics**, annual: Births, 246; deaths, 239; marriages, 150; divorces, 65.

**Recreation**: Lake activities; hunting; old Fort Belknap; marker at oak tree in Graham where ranchers formed forerunner of the Texas and Southwestern Cattle Raisers Association.

**Minerals**: Oil, natural gas, sand, gravel.

**Agriculture**: Beef cattle; wheat is the chief crop, also grown are hay, cotton, pecans, nursery plants. Market value $23.7 million.

**GRAHAM** (9,317) county seat; oil, gas, agriculture, tourism, government/services; hospital; old post office museum/art center; Western heritage days in September.

Other towns include: **Loving** (300), named for the Loving Ranch; **Newcastle** (593) an old coal-mining town; **Olney** (3,406) aluminum, varied manufacturing, hospital; the One-Arm Dove Hunt in September; **South Bend** (100).

*For explanation of sources, symbols and abbreviations, see p. 238, and foldout map.*

| Population | 18,350 |
|---|---|
| Change fm 2010 | – 1.1 |
| Area (sq. mi.) | 930.9 |
| Land Area (sq. mi.) | 914.5 |
| Altitude (ft.) | 995-1,522 |
| Rainfall (in.) | 31.51 |
| Jan. mean min. | 28.3 |
| July mean max. | 96.2 |
| Civ. Labor | 9,839 |
| Unemployed | 4.0 |
| Wages | $65,349,780 |
| Per Capita Income | $51,282 |
| Prop. Value | $2,073,815,540 |
| Retail Sales | $234,062,669 |

*U.S. 83 into Zapata, county seat of Zapata County. Photo by Robert Plocheck.*

# Zapata County

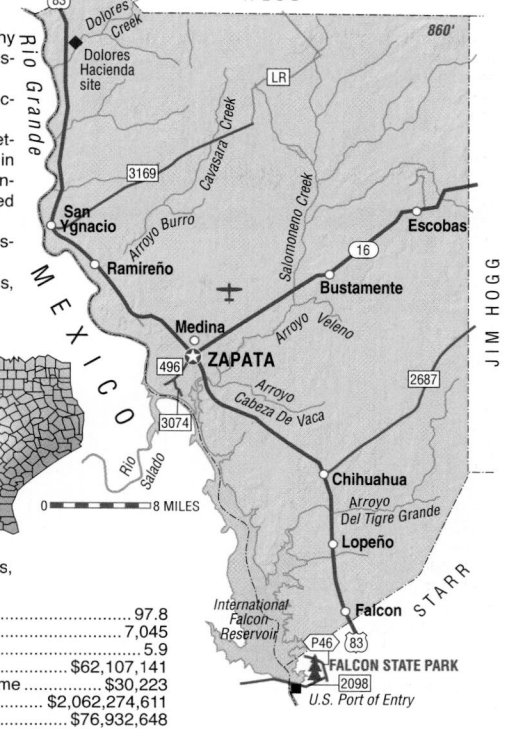

**Physical Features**: South Texas county of rolling, brushy topography; broken by tributaries of Rio Grande; Falcon Reservoir.

**Economy**: Natural gas, oil, ranching, Falcon Reservoir activities, government/services.

**History**: Coahuiltecan Indians in area when the ranch settlement of Nuestra Señora de los Dolores was established in 1750. Anglo-American migration increased after 1980. County named for Col. Antonio Zapata, pioneer rancher; created and organized in 1858 from Starr, Webb counties.

**Race/Ethnicity**: (In percent) Anglo, 5.8; Black, 0.5; Hispanic, 93.5; Asian, 0.2; Other, 0.6.

**Vital Statistics**, annual: Births, 283; deaths, 71; marriages, 88; divorces, 1.

**Recreation**: Lake, state park, Dolores Hacienda site, rock hunting, hang gliding encampment June/July.

**Minerals**: Natural gas, oil, caliche.

**Agriculture**: Cattle; onions, cantaloupes, melons, goats. Market value $11.8 million. Hunting/wildlife leases.

**ZAPATA** (5,091) county seat; tourism, agribusiness, oil, retirement center; clinic; fajita cook-off in November.

Other towns include: **Falcon** (185); **Lopeño** (180); **Medina** (4,150), and **San Ygnacio** (659) historic buildings, museum.

| | |
|---|---|
| Population .............................. 14,319 | July mean max. .......................... 97.8 |
| Change fm 2010 ......................... 2.1 | Civ. Labor ................................ 7,045 |
| Area (sq. mi.) ......................... 1,058.0 | Unemployed ................................. 5.9 |
| Land Area (sq. mi.) .................... 998.4 | Wages ........................... $62,107,141 |
| Altitude (ft.) ........................... 301-860 | Per Capita INcome .............. $30,223 |
| Rainfall (in.) ............................. 19.77 | Prop. Value .............. $2,062,274,611 |
| Jan. mean min. ........................... 46.3 | Retail Sales .................. $76,932,648 |

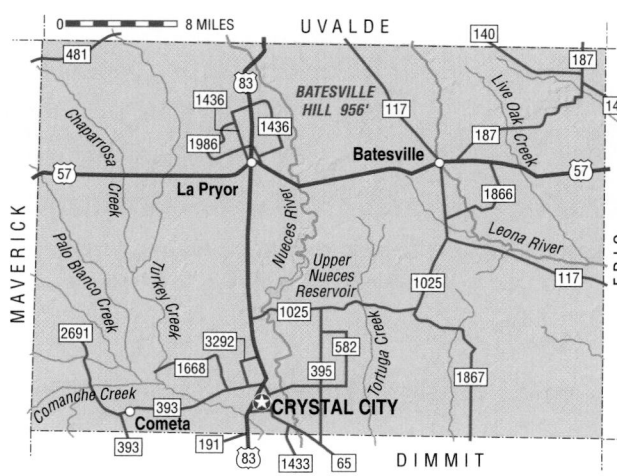

# Zavala County

**Physical Features**: Southwestern county near Mexican border; rolling plains broken by much brush; Nueces, Leona, other streams; Upper Nueces Reservoir.

**Economy**: Agribusiness, food packaging, leading county in Winter Garden truck-farming area, government/services.

**History**: Coahuiltecan area; Apaches, Comanches arrived later. Ranching developed in late 1860s. County created from Maverick, Uvalde counties 1858; organized 1884; named for Texas Revolutionary leader Lorenzo de Zavala.

**Race/Ethnicity**: (In percent) Anglo, 6.4; Black, 1.2; Hispanic, 92.9; Asian, 0.1; Other, 1.7.

**Vital Statistics**, annual: Births, 215; deaths, 90; marriages, 44; divorces, 0.

**Recreation**: Hunting, fishing; spinach festival in November.

**Minerals**: Oil, natural gas.

**Agriculture**: Cattle, grains, vegetables, cotton, pecans. About 30,000 acres irrigated. Market value $72.7 million. Hunting leases important.

**CRYSTAL CITY** (7,454) county seat; agribusiness, food processing, oil-field services; site of Japanese detention center. Home of Popeye statue.

Other towns include: **Batesville** (1,115) and **La Pryor** (1,747).

| | |
|---|---|
| Population ........................... 12,267 | |
| Change fm 2010 ......................... 5.1 | |
| Area (sq. mi.) ...................... 1,301.7 | |
| Land Area (sq. mi.) .............. 1,297.4 | |
| Altitude (ft.) ....................... 540-956 | |
| Rainfall (in.) ........................... 19.58 | |
| Jan. mean min. ........................... 43.6 | |
| July mean max. ........................ 97.2 | |
| Civ. Labor ............................. 3,906 | |
| Unemployed ............................. 13.3 | |
| Wages ........................ $16,152,145 | |
| Per Capita Income ............. $21,747 | |
| Prop. Value ............. $1,761,632,063 | |
| Retail Sales ................ $61,594,255 | |

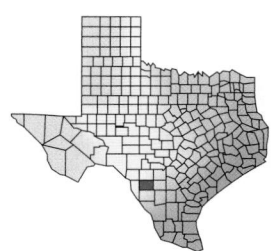

# Population

*Music Under the Star concerts draw a crowd of music lovers to the Bullock Museum in Austin. Photo courtesy of the Bullock Museum.*

**U.S. Census of Towns**
**State Growth Analysis**
**Metro Areas**
**Center of Population by Decades**

# Recent Population Growth in Texas

The estimated population of Texas on July 1, 2014, was 26,956,958, according to the U.S. Census, an increase of 1,810,854 persons from the 2010 census count. Texas is the second largest state after California, which has a 2014 estimated population of 38,802,500.

Texas' estimated rate of population increase over the four years, 7.2 percent, outpaced that of the nation as a whole, 3.3 percent.

Several counties of the state were among the 50 fastest-growing in the nation from 2010 to 2014 for counties with populations of 10,000 or more. Andrews County was the 6th fastest-growing with a 18.2 percent population increase.

Others, with national rank and increase rate:

9. Hays County, up 17.8 percent
10. Fort Bend County, up 17.2 percent
13. Kendall County, up 16.4 percent
15. Williamson County, up 15.8 percent
19. Comal County, up 14.0 percent
20. Montgomery County, up 13.9 percent
21. Midland County, up 13.8 percent
22. Denton County, up 13.7 percent
23. Collin County, up 13.2 percent
27. Travis County, up 12.4 percent
30. Ector County, up 12.2 percent
33. Rockwall County, up 12.1 percent
35. Guadalupe County, up 11.9 percent
47. Gaines County, up 10.8 percent

The growth of Andrews, Midland and Gaines counties reflects the oil and gas boom in the Permian Basin, and the other fast-growing counties are suburban parts of the major metro areas of the state.

While there was a population increase in these places, contributing to the 1.8 million person increase statewide, many of the smaller rural counties of the state continued to decline in population.

From 2010 to 2014, a total of 102 of the state's 254 counties had declining populations. That continues a trend of decline for most of them from the decade of 2000 to 2010, when 79 of the counties had population decreases.

The population growth in Texas between 2000 and 2010 was the largest of any state in raw numbers, and was the third largest in percentage terms, exceeded only by Arizona and Nevada.

According to the Texas State Data Center, the population of Texas grows rapidly through both natural increase (the excess of births over deaths) and in-migration.

The Hispanic population of Texas grew by 41.9 percent between 2000 and 2010, while the non-Hispanic white population grew by only 4.2 percent. So, the racial and ethnic composition has changed. In 2000, non-Hispanic whites made up 53 percent of the population, Hispanics made up 32 percent, blacks were 11 percent, while 4 percent were classified as "other," mainly Asian descent.

In 2010, non-Hispanic whites made up 45 percent of the population, blacks remained at 11 percent, "other" was at 6 percent, while the Hispanic portion increased to 38 percent of the state's population.

A large majority of growth in the state occurs in its four largest metropolitan areas: Dallas-Fort Worth, Houston, San Antonio and Austin. With Dallas-Fort Worth ranked 4th and Houston ranked 5th, this gives Texas two of the top five metro areas in the nation.

Other statistics from the Office of the State Demographer:

— Rural: Texas is the second largest state in terms of square miles and approximately 17 percent of the population lives in rural areas.

— Family: Texas ranks third among states for the percent of households that are married-couple families with children. ☆

*Sources: U.S. Bureau of the Census and the Texas State Data Center.*

## Population change, 1850–2014

| Year | Total Population | | Percent change | |
|------|--------|--------|--------|--------|
| | **Texas** | **U.S.** | **Texas** | **U.S.** |
| 1850 | 212,592 | 23,191,876 | ... | ... |
| 1860 | 604,215 | 31,443,321 | 184.2 | 35.6 |
| 1870 | 818,579 | 39,181,449 | 35.5 | 26.6 |
| 1880 | 1,591,749 | 50,155,783 | 94.5 | 26.0 |
| 1890 | 2,235,527 | 62,947,714 | 40.4 | 25.5 |
| 1900 | 3,048,710 | 75,994,575 | 36.4 | 20.7 |
| 1910 | 3,896,542 | 91,972,266 | 27.8 | 21.0 |
| 1920 | 4,663,228 | 105,710,620 | 19.7 | 14.9 |
| 1930 | 5,824,715 | 122,775,046 | 24.9 | 16.1 |
| 1940 | 6,414,824 | 131,669,275 | 10.1 | 7.2 |
| 1950 | 7,711,194 | 150,697,361 | 20.2 | 14.5 |
| 1960 | 9,579,677 | 179,323,175 | 24.2 | 19.0 |
| 1970 | 11,196,730 | 203,302,031 | 16.9 | 13.4 |
| 1980 | 14,229,191 | 226,545,805 | 27.1 | 11.4 |
| 1990 | 16,986,510 | 248,709,873 | 19.4 | 9.8 |
| 2000 | 20,851,820 | 281,421,906 | 22.8 | 13.2 |
| **2010** | **25,145,561** | **308,745,538** | **20.6** | **9.7** |
| *2014* | *26,956,958* | *318,857,056* | *7.2* | *3.3* |
| Source: U.S. Census, 2014 is an estimate. | | | | |

| Ten Largest U.S. Metro Areas | | |
|------|------|------|
| **Rank** | **Metro Area** | **2014 Estimates** |
| 1. | New York | 20,092,883 |
| 2. | Los Angeles | 13,262,220 |
| 3. | Chicago | 9,554,598 |
| **4.** | **Dallas-Fort Worth** | **6,954,330** |
| **5.** | **Houston** | **6,490,180** |
| 6. | Philadelphia | 6,051,170 |
| 7. | Washington, D.C. | 6,033,737 |
| 8. | Miami | 5,929,819 |
| 9. | Atlanta | 5,614,323 |
| 10. | Boston | 4,732,161 |
| | | Source: U.S. Census. |

# Counties of Significant Population Change: 2010 to 2014

| Fastest Growing by Percent Gain | | | Fastest Growing by Most Persons Gained | | |
|---|---|---|---|---|---|
| Rank, County | Major cities | Percent | Rank, County | Major cities | Number |
| 1. Andrews | Andrews | 18.2 | 1. Harris | Houston | 348,359 |
| 2. Hays | San Marcos | 17.8 | 2. Dallas | Dallas | 151,002 |
| 3. Fort Bend | Sugar Land | 17.2 | 3. Bexar | San Antonio | 141,092 |
| 4. Sterling | Sterling City | 17.1 | 4. Tarrant | Fort Worth | 135,823 |
| 5. Kendall | Boerne | 16.4 | 5. Travis | Austin | 126,844 |
| 6. Williamson | Round Rock-Georgetown | 15.8 | 6. Collin | Plano-Frisco-McKinney | 102,890 |
| 7. Comal | New Braunfels | 14.0 | 7. Fort Bend | Sugar Land | 100,448 |
| 8. Montgomery | Woodlands-Conroe | 13.9 | 8. Denton | Denton-Lewisville | 90,759 |
| 9. McMullen | Tilden | 13.9 | 9. Williamson | Round Rock-Georgetown | 66,601 |
| 10. Midland | Midland | 13.8 | 10. Montgomery | Woodlands-Conroe | 63,183 |

*Chart shows Andrews County increased in population by 18.2 percent since 2010, while Harris County (Houston) gained 348,359 people, etc. Source: U.S. Bureau of the Census.*

| Fastest Declining by Percent Loss | | | Fasting Declining by Most Persons Lost | | |
|---|---|---|---|---|---|
| Rank, County | Major cities | Percent | Rank, County | Major cities | Number |
| 1. Presidio | Marfa-Presidio | – 10.8 | 1. Hale | Plainview | – 1,553 |
| 2. Dickens | Dickens-Spur | – 9.1 | 2. Houston | Crockett | – 991 |
| 3. Schleicher | Eldorado | – 8.6 | 3. Falls | Marlin | – 877 |
| 4. King | Guthrie | – 8.4 | 4. Presidio | Marfa=Presidio | – 841 |
| 5. San Saba | San Saba | – 8.3 | 5. Anderson | Palestine | – 831 |
| 6. Floyd | Floydada | – 7.7 | 6. Wilbarger | Vernon | – 562 |
| 7. Hudspeth | Sierra Blanca | – 7.6 | 7. San Saba | San Saba | – 509 |
| 8. Briscoe | Silverton-Quitaque | – 6.2 | 8. Milam | Cameron-Rockdale | – 502 |
| 9. Edwards | Rocksprings | – 6.1 | 9. Floyd | Floydada | – 497 |
| 10. Hall | Memphis | – 6.1 | 10. Sabine | Hemphill | – 485 |

*Chart shows Presidio County declined in population by 10.8 percent since the 2010 census, while Hale County declined by 1,553\ people, etc. Source: U.S. Bureau of the Census.*

## Largest Counties by Population 2014

| Rank, County | Major cities | Population | Rank, County | Major cities | Population |
|---|---|---|---|---|---|
| 1. Harris | Houston | 4,441,370 | 16. Bell | Temple-Killeen | 329,140 |
| 2. Dallas | Dallas | 2,518,638 | 17. Galveston | Galveston | 314,198 |
| 3. Tarrant | Fort Worth | 1,945,360 | 18. Lubbock | Lubbock | 293,974 |
| 4. Bexar | San Antonio | 1,855,866 | 19. Webb | Laredo | 266,673 |
| 5. Travis | Austin | 1,151,145 | 20. Jefferson | Beaumont | 252,235 |
| 6. Collin | Plano-Frisco-McKinney | 885,241 | 21. McLennan | Waco | 243,441 |
| 7. El Paso | El Paso | 833,487 | 22. Smith | Tyler | 218,842 |
| 8. Hidalgo | McAllen | 831,073 | 23. Brazos | Bryan-College Station | 209,152 |
| 9. Denton | Denton-Lewisville | 753,363 | 24. Hays | San Marcos | 185,025 |
| 10. Fort Bend | Sugar Land | 685,345 | 25. Ellis | Waxahachie | 159,317 |
| 11. Montgomery | Woodlands-Conroe | 518,947 | 26. Johnson | Cleburne-Burleson | 157,456 |
| 12. Williamson | Round Rock | 489,250 | 27. Midland | Midland | 155,830 |
| 13. Cameron | Brownsville | 420,392 | 28. Ector | Odessa | 153,904 |
| 14. Nueces | Corpus Christi | 356,221 | 29. Guadalupe | Seguin | 147,250 |
| 15. Brazoria | Brazosport | 338,124 | 30. Taylor | Abilene | 135,143 |

*Source: U.S. Bureau of the Census.*

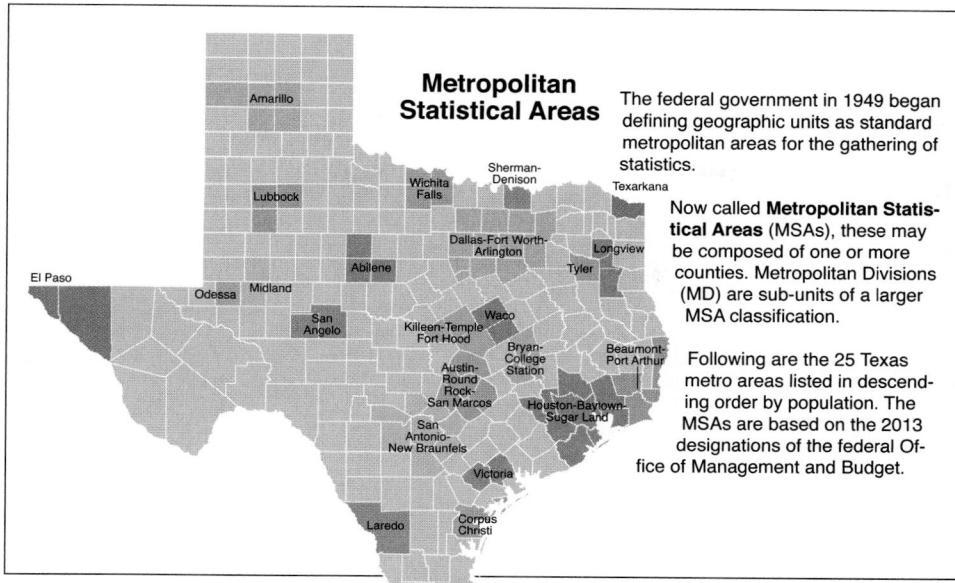

**Metropolitan Statistical Areas**

The federal government in 1949 began defining geographic units as standard metropolitan areas for the gathering of statistics.

Now called **Metropolitan Statistical Areas** (MSAs), these may be composed of one or more counties. Metropolitan Divisions (MD) are sub-units of a larger MSA classification.

Following are the 25 Texas metro areas listed in descending order by population. The MSAs are based on the 2013 designations of the federal Office of Management and Budget.

| Metropolitan Statistical Areas | 2014 Population | Percent change 2010-2014 |
|---|---|---|
| 1. **Dallas-Fort Worth-Arlington** (Dallas-Plano-Irving MD and Fort Worth-Arlington MD) Dallas-Plano-Irving (Collin, Dallas, Denton, Ellis, Hunt, Kaufman, Rockwall counties) Fort Worth-Arlington (Hood, Johnson, Parker, Somervell, Tarrant, Wise counties) | 6,954,330 | 8.2 |
| 2. **Houston-The Woodlands-Sugar Land** (Austin, Brazoria, Chambers, Fort Bend, Galveston, Harris, Liberty, Montgomery, Waller counties) | 6,490,180 | 9.6 |
| 3. **San Antonio-New Braunfels** (Atascosa, Bandera, Bexar, Comal, Guadalupe, Kendall, Medina, Wilson counties) | 2,328,652 | 8.7 |
| 4. **Austin-Round Rock** (Bastrop, Caldwell, Hays, Travis, Williamson counties) | 1,943,299 | 13.2 |
| 5. **El Paso** (El Paso, Hudspeth counties) | 836,698 | 4.1 |
| 6. **McAllen-Edinburg-Mission** (Hidalgo County) | 831,073 | 7.3 |
| 7. **Corpus Christi** (Aransas, Nueces, San Patricio counties) | 448,108 | 4.7 |
| 8. **Killeen-Temple** (Bell, Coryell, Lampasas counties) | 424,858 | 4.8 |
| 9. **Brownsville-Harlingen** (Cameron County) | 420,392 | 3.5 |
| 10. **Beaumont-Port Arthur** (Hardin, Jefferson, Newton, Orange counties) | 405,427 | 0.6 |
| 11. **Lubbock** (Crosby, Lubbock, Lynn counties) | 305,644 | 5.1 |
| 12. **Laredo** (Webb County) | 266,673 | 6.5 |
| 13. **Waco** (Falls, McLennan County) | 260,430 | 3.0 |
| 14. **Amarillo** (Armstrong, Carson, Oldham, Potter, Randall counties) | 259,885 | 3.2 |
| 15. **Bryan-College Station** (Brazos, Burleson, Robertson counties) | 242,905 | 6.2 |
| 16. **Tyler** (Smith County) | 218,842 | 4.4 |
| 17. **Longview** (Gregg, Rusk, Upshur counties) | 217,481 | 1.4 |
| 18. **Abilene** (Callahan, Jones, Taylor counties) | 168,592 | 2.0 |
| 19. **Midland** (Martin, Midland counties) | 161,290 | 13.8 |
| 20. **Odessa** (Ector County) | 153,904 | 12.2 |
| 21. **Wichita Falls** (Archer, Clay, Wichita counties) | 151,536 | 0.0 |
| 22. **Texarkana** (Bowie County, TX, and Miller, LIttle River counties, AR) | 149,235 | 0.0 |
| 23. **Sherman-Denison** (Grayson County) | 123,534 | 2.2 |
| 24. **San Angelo** (Irion, Tom Green counties) | 118,182 | 5.7 |
| 25. **Victoria** (Goliad, Victoria counties) | 98,630 | 4.9 |

# Population 2010 and 2014

**Population**: Numbers in parentheses are from the 2010 U.S. census. The Census Bureau counts only incorporated cities and a few unincorporated towns called Census Designated Places.

Population figures at the far right for incorporated cities and CDPs are the Texas State Data Center estimates for Jan. 1, 2014. Names of the incorporated cities are in capital letters, e.g., "ABBOTT".

The population figure given for all other towns is an estimate received from local officials through a Texas Almanac survey.

When no 2010 census was conducted for a newly incorporated city, these places show "(nc)" for "not counted" in place of a 2010 population figure.

**Location**: The county in which the town is located follows the name of town. If more than one county is listed, the town is principally in the first-named county, e.g., "ABERNATHY, Hale-Lubbock".

**Businesses**: For incorporated cities, the number following the county name indicates the number of business in the city as of January 2014 as reported by the state comptroller. For unincorporated towns, it is the number of businesses within the postal zip code as reported by the U.S. Bureau of the Census for 2011.

For example, "ABBOTT, Hill, 27" means Abbott in Hill County had 28 businesses.

**Post Offices**: Places with post offices, as of Nov. 2010, are marked with an asterisk (*), e.g., "*Afton".

| Town, County ............. Pop. 2014 | Town, County ............. Pop. 2014 | Town, County ............. Pop. 2014 |
|---|---|---|
| *ABBOTT, Hill, 27, (356)............... 361 | *ALAMO, Hidalgo, 550, | Altoga, Collin ...................... 137 |
| *ABERNATHY, Hale-Lubbock, 76, | (18,353) ........................ 19,225 | *ALTON, Hidalgo, 315, |
| (2,805) .............................. 2,816 | Alamo Alto, El Paso ...................... 19 | (12,341) ....................... 13,943 |
| *ABILENE, Taylor-Jones, 3,960, | Alamo Beach, Calhoun............... 100 | Alum Creek, Bastrop ..................... 70 |
| (117,063) ..................... 121,495 | ALAMO HEIGHTS, Bexar, 353, | *ALVARADO, Johnson, 217, |
| Ables Springs, Kaufman ................ 20 | (7,031) .......................... 7,570 | (3,785) .......................... 3,934 |
| Abner, Kaufman............................. 75 | *Alanreed, Gray, 2 ....................... 48 | *ALVIN, Brazoria, 973, |
| Abram, Hidalgo, (2,067) .......... 2,193 | Alazan, Nacogdoches................... 100 | (24,236) ...................... 25,320 |
| *ACADEMY [Little River-], Bell, 35, | *ALBA, Wood-Rains, 65, (504)..... 528 | *ALVORD, Wise, 56, (1,334) ..... 1,380 |
| (1,961) .............................. 1,949 | *ALBANY, Shackelford, 111, | Amada Acres, Starr, (92) ............... 87 |
| Acala, Hudspeth ........................... 25 | (2,034) .......................... 2,038 | Amargosa, Jim Wells, (291) ......... 310 |
| *Ace, Polk, 1 ............................... 40 | Albert, Gillespie ........................... 25 | *AMARILLO, Potter-Randall, |
| *ACKERLY, Dawson-Martin, 15, | Albion, Red River........................... 52 | 6,737, (190,695) ............. 200,526 |
| (220) ................................. 232 | Alderbranch, Anderson ................... 3 | Amaya, Zavala, (93) ...................... 92 |
| Acme, Hardeman............................. 7 | Aldine, Harris,(15,869)............. 16,684 | Ambia, Lamar ............................... 16 |
| Acton, Hood............................ 1,129 | *ALEDO, Parker, 277, (2,716) ... 2,928 | Ambrose, Grayson.......................... 90 |
| Acuff, Lubbock............................ 152 | Aleman, Hamilton ......................... 50 | Ames, Coryell ............................... 10 |
| Acworth, Red River........................ 50 | Alexander, Erath ........................... 40 | AMES, Liberty, 11, (1,003)......... 1,078 |
| Adams Gardens, Cameron........... 350 | Aley, Henderson ........................... 45 | Amherst, Lamar .......................... 125 |
| Adams Store, Panola..................... 12 | Alfred, Jim Wells, (91) .................. 95 | *AMHERST, Lamb, 15, (721)....... 697 |
| Adamsville, Lampasas.................... 75 | Algerita, San Saba......................... 10 | Amistad, Val Verde, (53)................ 51 |
| Addicks, Harris ........ [part of Houston] | Algoa, Galveston ........................ 135 | Ammannsville, Fayette ................ 137 |
| Addielou, Red River........................ 31 | *ALICE, Jim Wells, 798, | Amphion, Atascosa........................ 26 |
| *ADDISON, Dallas, 1,853, | (19,104) ........................ 19,682 | Amsterdam, Brazoria ................... 193 |
| (13,056) ......................... 16,185 | Alice Acres, Jim Wells, (490) ........ 502 | Anacua, Starr, (12) ........................ 12 |
| Adell, Parker................................ 100 | *Alief, Harris............ [part of Houston] | Anadarko, Rusk............................. 30 |
| *Adkins, Bexar, 76 ...................... 400 | Allamoore, Hudspeth .................... 10 | *ANAHUAC, Chambers, 70, |
| Admiral, Callahan .......................... 18 | *ALLEN, Collin, 2,807, | (2,243) .......................... 2,288 |
| Adobes, Presidio ............................. 5 | (84,246) ......................... 93,642 | Anchor, Brazoria .......................... 150 |
| *ADRIAN, Oldham, 8, (166)......... 159 | Allenfarm, Brazos ........................... 35 | *ANDERSON, Grimes, 52, |
| Advance, Parker.......................... 100 | Allenhurst, Matagorda ................... 72 | (222) ................................. 232 |
| *Afton, Dickens, 1 ........................ 15 | Allen's Chapel, Fannin................... 30 | Anderson Mill, Williamson-Travis, |
| Agnes, Parker................................ 60 | Allen's Point, Fannin,.................... 40 | ................ [part of Austin] |
| *AGUA DULCE, Nueces, 25, | Allentown, Angelina ..................... 800 | Ander-Weser-Kilgore, Goliad........ 322 |
| (812) ................................. 830 | Alleyton, Colorado, 14 ................. 165 | Andice, Williamson ...................... 300 |
| Agua Dulce, El Paso, (3,014) .... 3,251 | *Allison, Wheeler, 4 ................... 135 | *ANDREWS, Andrews, 456, |
| Agua Nueva, Jim Hogg.................... 5 | Allmon, Floyd................................ 24 | (11,088) ....................... 12,736 |
| Aguilares, Webb, (21).................... 23 | Allred, Yoakum.............................. 90 | *ANGLETON, Brazoria, 629, |
| *Aiken, Floyd, 1 ........................... 52 | ALMA, Ellis, 9, (331)................... 337 | (18,862) ....................... 19,296 |
| Aiken, Shelby.............................. 150 | Almira, Cass ................................. 30 | ANGUS, Navarro, 19, (414).......... 433 |
| Aikin Grove, Red River.................. 15 | *ALPINE, Brewster, 375, | *ANNA, Collin, 218, (8,249)....... 9,719 |
| Airport Heights, Starr, (161)......... 166 | (5,905) .......................... 5,951 | Annaville, Nueces, |
| Airport Road Addition, Brooks, | Alsa, Van Zandt ............................ 30 | ................ [part of Corpus Christi] |
| (93) ................................... 91 | *Altair, Colorado, 6......................... 30 | ANNETTA, Parker, 29, (1,288) .. 1,340 |
| Airville, Bell .................................. 65 | *ALTO, Cherokee, 66, (1,225) ... 1,243 | ANNETTA NORTH, Parker, 12, |
| Alabama-Coushatta, Polk,(572) ... 572 | Alto Bonito Heights, Starr, (342)... 348 | (518) .............................. 541 |

| Town, County ...............Pop. 2014 | Town, County ...............Pop. 2014 | Town, County ...............Pop. 2014 |
|---|---|---|

ANNETTA SOUTH, Parker, 11,
(526) ....................................... 538
*ANNONA, Red River, 9, (315)..... 300
*ANSON, Jones, 98, (2,430) ..... 2,293
Antelope, Jack ............................... 65
*ANTHONY, El Paso, 123,
(5,011) ................................. 5,262
Antioch, Cass ................................ 45
Antioch, Delta ............................... 10
Antioch, Madison ........................... 15
Antioch Colony, Hays .................... 25
*ANTON, Hockley, 13, (1,126)... 1,158
APPLEBY, Nacogdoches,
(474) ....................................... 482
*Apple Springs, Trinity, 11 ............ 350
*AQUILLA, Hill, 10, (109)............. 107
*ARANSAS PASS, San Patricio-
Aransas, 344, (8,204)......... 8,305
Arbala, Hopkins ............................. 41
Arcadia, Shelby ............................. 35
*ARCHER CITY, Archer, 76,
(1,834) ................................. 1,828
ARCOLA, Fort Bend, 56,
(1,642) ................................. 1,592
Arden, Irion ..................................... 7
Argo, Titus ..................................... 90
*ARGYLE, Denton, 230,
(3,282), .............................. 3,548
*ARLINGTON, Tarrant, 10,955,
(365,438) ...................... 380,698
Armstrong, Bell .............................. 25
*Armstrong, Kenedy, 1...................... 4
Arneckeville, DeWitt ...................... 50
Arnett, Coryell................................ 15
Arnett, Hockley ................................ 5
*ARP, Smith, 61, (970)................. 983
Arroyo City, Cameron, ................. 600
Arroyo Colorado Estates, Cameron,
(997) .................................... 1,062
Arroyo Gardens, Cameron,
(456) ....................................... 485
*Art, Mason, 1................................ 14
Artesia Wells, La Salle, 2............... 35
*Arthur City, Lamar, 7 ................... 180
Arvana, Dawson ............................... 8
Asa, McLennan.............................. 46
Ash, Houston ................................. 19
Ashby, Matagorda.......................... 60
*ASHERTON, Dimmit, 16,
(1,084) ............................... 1,162
Ashland, Upshur ............................ 45
Ashtola, Donley ............................. 20
Ashwood, Matagorda.................... 132
Asia, Polk....................................... 83
*ASPERMONT, Stonewall, 60,
(919) ....................................... 835
Atascocita, Harris, (65,844)..... 70,516
*Atascosa, Bexar, 34 ................... 600
Ater, Coryell.................................. 12
*ATHENS, Henderson, 627,
(12,710) ............................ 12,872
*ATLANTA, Cass, 237,
(5,675) ................................. 5,742
Atlas, Lamar .................................. 28
Atoy, Cherokee .............................. 50
*AUBREY, Denton, 122,
(2,595) ................................. 2,634
Augusta, Houston .......................... 40
AURORA, Wise, 23, (1,220)...... 1,268
*AUSTIN, Travis-Williamson,
34,397, (790,390) .......... 877,210

Austonio, Houston ......................... 37
*AUSTWELL, Refugio, 5, (147).... 147
Authon, Parker................................ 15
*Avalon, Ellis, 4............................ 400
*AVERY, Red River, 16, (482)....... 463
*AVINGER, Cass, 27, (444).......... 457
*Avoca, Jones, 4........................... 121
*Axtell, McLennan, 22.................. 300
*AZLE, Tarrant-Parker, 567,
(10,947) ........................... 11,413

**B**

Back, Gray....................................... 6
*Bacliff, Galveston, 86,
(8,619) ................................. 8,876
*Bagwell, Red River, 1................. 150
*BAILEY, Fannin, 11,
(289) ....................................... 301
BAILEY'S PRAIRIE, Brazoria, 12,
(727) ....................................... 733
Baileyville, Milam ........................... 32
Bainer, Lamb ................................. 10
Bainville, Karnes.............................. 8
*BAIRD, Callahan, 63,
(1,496) ............................... 1,562
Baker, Floyd................................... 28
Bakersfield, Pecos........................... 9
*BALCH SPRINGS, Dallas, 575,
(23,728) ........................... 25,201

BALCONES HEIGHTS, Bexar,
144, (2,941) ....................... 2,996
Bald Hill, Angelina........................ 100
Bald Prairie, Robertson ................. 40
*BALLINGER, Runnels, 201,
(3,767) ............................... 3,612
*BALMORHEA, Reeves, 16,
(479) ....................................... 504
Balsora, Wise ................................ 50
B and E, Starr, (518)................... 545
*BANDERA, Bandera, 266,
(857) ....................................... 883
Bandera Falls, Bandera................. 90
*BANGS, Brown, 38, (1,603)..... 1,593
*Banquete, Nueces, 7, (726)........ 762
Barbarosa, Guadalupe .................. 46
Barclay, Falls ................................ 58
*BARDWELL, Ellis, 9, (649) ........ 668
*Barker, Harris, 8, ..................... 2,500
*Barksdale, Edwards, 3 ............... 100
Barnes, Harris ............................... 75
*Barnhart, Irion, 8 ....................... 110
Barnum, Polk................................. 50
Barrera, Starr,(108) .................... 116
*Barrett, Harris, (3,199) ........... 3,293
*BARRY, Navarro, 11, (242) ........ 249
*BARSTOW, Ward, 2, (349) ......... 370
*BARTLETT, Williamson-Bell, 55,
(2,684) ............................... 2,700

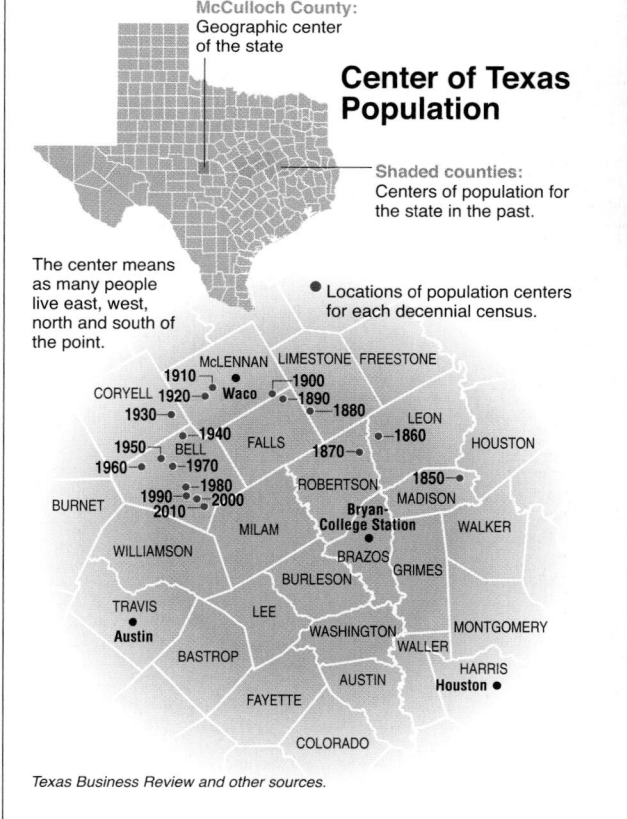

McCulloch County:
Geographic center
of the state

**Center of Texas Population**

Shaded counties:
Centers of population for
the state in the past.

The center means
as many people
live east, west,
north and south of
the point.

● Locations of population centers
for each decennial census.

*Texas Business Review and other sources.*

| Town, County ..............Pop. 2014 | Town, County ...............Pop. 2014 | Town, County ...............Pop. 2014 |
|---|---|---|

Barton Corners, Lipscomb,............... 4
Barton Creek, Travis, (3,077) .... 3,156
BARTONVILLE, Denton, 94,
    (1,469)................................... 1,572
Barwise, Floyd ............................ 16
*Basin, Brewster, 3 ......................... 30
Bassett, Bowie ............................ 100
*BASTROP, Bastrop, 703,
    (7,218)................................7,949
Bateman, Bastrop......................... 12
Batesville, Red River .................... 14
*Batesville, Zavala, 14,
    (1,068)................................. 1,115
*Batson, Hardin, 18 .................... 140
Battle, McLennan......................... 100
Baxter, Henderson....................... 150
*BAY CITY, Matagorda, 587,
    (17,614)............................ 17,342
Baylor Lake, Childress.................. 50
BAYOU VISTA, Galveston, 32,
    (1,537)................................. 1,549
*BAYSIDE, Refugio, 10, (325)...... 329
*BAYTOWN, Harris-Chambers,
    1,859, (71,802)................ 75,764
BAYVIEW, Cameron, 6, (383) ...... 404
Bazette, Navarro........................... 30
BEACH CITY, Chambers,
    (2,198)................................ 2,365
BEAR CREEK, Hays, (382)........... 384
*BEASLEY, Fort Bend, 18,
    (641)...................................... 652
Beattie, Comanche........................ 48
*BEAUMONT, Jefferson, 4,029,
    (118,296) ......................... 118,180
Beaver Dam, Bowie....................... 10
Bebe, Gonzales ............................ 42
Becker, Kaufman .......................... 300
*BECKVILLE, Panola, 25, (847)... 856
Becton, Lubbock............................ 62
*BEDFORD, Tarrant, 1,446,
    (46,979) ............................ 49,084
*BEDIAS, Grimes, 36, (443)......... 468
BEE CAVE, Travis, 381,
    (3,925)................................ 5,448
Bee House, Coryell........................ 15
*BEEVILLE, Bee, 499,
    (12,863) ............................ 13,061
Belcherville, Montague .................. 25
Belfalls, Bell.................................. 30
Belgrade, Newton .......................... 20
Belk, Lamar .................................. 58
*BELLAIRE, Harris, 786,
    (16,855) ............................ 17,655
Bell Branch, Ellis........................... 125
*BELLEVUE, Clay, 8, (362) ......... 360
*BELLMEAD, McLennan, 255,
    (9,901) .............................. 10,241
*BELLS, Grayson, 38,
    (1,392)................................. 1,407
*BELLVILLE, Austin, 313,
    (4,097)................................ 4,232
Belmena, Milam............................ 15
*Belmont, Gonzales, 4.................. 55
Belott, Houston............................. 101
*BELTON, Bell, 761,
    (18,216)............................ 19,621
Ben Arnold, Milam ....................... 100
*BENAVIDES, Duval, 18,
    (1,362)................................. 1,341
*Ben Bolt, Jim Wells, 4 ............. 1,600
*BENBROOK, Tarrant, 701,
    (21,234) ............................ 22,524

Benchley, Robertson-Brazos ........ 110
*Bend, San Saba-Lampasas, 1 .... 115
*Ben Franklin, Delta....................... 60
Ben Hur, Limestone....................... 42
*BENJAMIN, Knox, 15, (258) ...... 247
Benjamin Perez, Starr, (34) ........... 34
Bennett, Parker............................. 120
Benoit, Runnels ............................ 10
Bentonville, Jim Wells.................... 15
*Ben Wheeler, Van Zandt, 60 ....... 504
*Berclair, Goliad, 1 ...................... 253
Berea, Houston.............................. 41
Berea, Marion ............................. 200
Bergheim, Kendall, 17 ............... 1,213
Berlin, Washington ........................ 40
Bernardo, Colorado ...................... 155
BERRYVILLE, Henderson, 9,
    (975).................................. 1,013
*BERTRAM, Burnet-Williamson,
    77, (1,353) ......................... 1,398
Bessmay, Jasper .......................... 400
Best, Reagan................................. 2
Bethany, Panola............................ 50
Bethel, Anderson .......................... 75
Bethel, Henderson ........................ 125
Bethel, Runnels ............................ 20
Bethlehem, Upshur........................ 75
Bettie, Upshur............................... 110
Beulah, Limestone ........................ 12
BEVERLY HILLS, McLennan, 104,
    (1,995)................................ 2,011
BEVIL OAKS, Jefferson, 30,
    (1,274)................................. 1,289
Bevilport, Jasper............................ 12
Beyersville, Williamson.................. 80
Biardstown, Lamar......................... 75
*Bigfoot, Frio, 4, (450) ................. 496
Big Hill, Limestone.......................... 9
*BIG LAKE, Reagan, 151,
    (2,936)................................ 3,219
*BIG SANDY, Upshur, 98,
    (1,343)................................. 1,359
*BIG SPRING, Howard, 669,
    (27,282) ............................ 28,339
Big Thicket Estates, Liberty-Polk,
    (742).................................... 788
Big Valley, Mills............................ 35
*BIG WELLS, Dimmit, 14, (697) ... 806
Biloxi, Newton............................... 75
Birch, Burleson ............................ 200
Birome, Hill .................................. 30
Birthright, Hopkins ....................... 100
Biry, Medina ................................. 24
*BISHOP, Nueces, 63,
    (3,134)................................ 3,179
BISHOP HILLS, Potter, (193) ....... 195
*Bivins, Cass, 9 ........................... 215
Bixby, Cameron, (504)................. 543
Black, Parmer................................ 100
Blackfoot, Anderson...................... 50
Black Hill, Atascosa ...................... 60
Black Hills, Navarro ...................... 80
Black Jack, Cherokee.................... 47
Black Jack, Robertson................... 45
Black Oak, Hopkins ..................... 150
*BLACKWELL, Nolan-Coke, 19,
    (311) ................................... 310
Blair, Taylor................................... 25
Blanchard, Polk ............................ 500
*BLANCO, Blanco, 243,
    (1,739)................................. 1,764
Blanconia, Bee ............................. 100

Bland Lake, San Augustine ........... 80
*BLANKET, Brown, 21, (390)........ 405
Blanton, Hill.................................... 5
Bleakwood, Newton....................... 450
*Bledsoe, Cochran, 1.................... 126
*Bleiblerville, Austin, 4 ................. 125
*Blessing, Matagorda, 22,
    (927).................................... 941
Blevins, Falls................................. 36
Blewett, Uvalde............................... 7
Blodgett, Titus............................... 60
*BLOOMBURG, Cass, 9, (404) .... 407
*BLOOMING GROVE, Navarro,
    18, (821)............................. 836
*Bloomington, Victoria, 10,
    (2,459)................................ 2,540
*BLOSSOM, Lamar, 38,
    (1,494)................................. 1,582
Blue, Lee ...................................... 75
Blueberry Hill, Bee, (866) ............. 880
*Bluegrove, Clay, 1 ...................... 135
BLUE MOUND, Tarrant, 37,
    (2,394)................................ 2,476
*BLUE RIDGE, Collin, 32,
    (822) ................................... 825
Bluetown, Cameron, (356)............ 366
*Bluff Dale, Erath, 21 ................... 400
*Bluffton, Llano, 3 ......................... 75
*BLUM, Hill, 16, (444)................... 437
Bluntzer, Nueces .......................... 150
Boca Chica Village, Cameron......... 34
*BOERNE, Kendall, 1,353,
    (10,471) ............................ 12,314
*BOGATA, Red River, 29,
    (1,153)................................. 1,094
Bois d'Arc, Anderson .................... 25
Bois d'Arc, Rains ........................... 6
Bold Springs, Polk ....................... 100
Boles Home, Hunt ........................ 100
*Boling, Wharton, 23, (1,122) .... 1,131
Bolivar, Denton ............................. 140
Bolivar Peninsula, Galveston,
    (2,417)................................ 2,452
Bomarton, Baylor........................... 15
Bonami, Jasper.............................. 12
Bonanza, Hopkins ......................... 26
Bonanza Hills, Webb, (37).............. 38
*BONHAM, Fannin, 364,
    (10,127) ............................ 10,266
Bonita, Montague .......................... 25
BONNEY, Brazoria, (310),............ 328
Bonnie View, Refugio .................... 97
Bonus, Wharton............................. 44
*Bon Wier, Newton, 8 ................... 375
*BOOKER, Lipscomb-Ochiltree,
    58, (1,516) ......................... 1,595
Boonsville, Wise ........................... 52
Booth, Fort Bend............................ 50
Bootleg, Deaf Smith...................... 10
Borden, Colorado .......................... 20
*BORGER, Hutchinson, 470,
    (13,251) ............................ 12,775
Bosqueville, McLennan ................ 200
Boston, Bowie,... [part of New Boston]
Botines, Webb, (117) .................... 121
*BOVINA, Parmer, 29,
    (1,868)................................. 1,761
Bowers City, Gray.......................... 10
*BOWIE, Montague, 338,
    (5,218)................................ 5,236
Bowman, Archer ........................... 300
Bowser, San Saba......................... 20

| Town, County ...............Pop. 2014 | Town, County ...............Pop. 2014 | Town, County ...............Pop. 2014 |
|---|---|---|
| Box Canyon, Val Verde, (34) ......... 24 | *Brookston, Lamar, 11 ................. 130 | *Burkeville, Newton, 16 ............... 603 |
| Box Church, Limestone ................. 45 | Broom City, Anderson .................... 20 | Burleigh, Austin ......................... 150 |
| Boxelder, Red River ..................... 100 | BROWNDELL, Jasper, 2, | *BURLESON, Johnson-Tarrant, |
| Boxwood, Upshur, ......................... 20 | (197) ....................................... 215 | 1,361, (36,690) ............... 41,828 |
| Boyce, Ellis ................................. 125 | *BROWNFIELD, Terry, 282, | *Burlington, Milam, 7 ................. 100 |
| Boyd, Fannin ............................... 105 | (9,657) .................................. 9,572 | *BURNET, Burnet, 424, |
| *BOYD, Wise, 111, (1,207) ........ 1,277 | Browning, Smith ........................... 25 | (5,987) ................................. 6,144 |
| *Boys Ranch, Oldham, 3, | Brownsboro, Caldwell .................... 50 | Burns, Bowie .............................. 400 |
| (282) ....................................... 290 | *BROWNSBORO, Henderson, | Burns City, Cooke ......................... 45 |
| Boz-Bethel, Ellis ......................... 100 | 656, (1,039) ......................... 1,033 | Burrantown, Houston ..................... 70 |
| Bozar, Mills ................................... 9 | *BROWNSVILLE, Cameron, | *BURTON, Washington, 55, |
| Brachfield, Rusk ........................... 40 | 4,872, (175,023) ............. 185,058 | (300) ....................................... 305 |
| Bracken, Comal ............................ 95 | *BROWNWOOD, Brown, 749, | *Bushland, Potter, 13 ................. 1,485 |
| *BRACKETTVILLE, Kinney, 65, | (19,288) .............................. 19,694 | Bustamante, Zapata ..................... 10 |
| (1,688) .................................. 1,683 | Broyles Chapel, Anderson ............. 60 | Busterville, Hockley ........................ 6 |
| Brad, Palo Pinto ........................... 16 | *BRUCEVILLE-EDDY, McLennan- | Butler, Bastrop ............................. 40 |
| Bradford, Anderson ....................... 60 | Falls, 24, (1,475) ................ 1,771 | Butler, Freestone .......................... 67 |
| Bradshaw, Taylor .......................... 61 | Brumley, Upshur .......................... 75 | Butterfield, El Paso, (114) ............. 125 |
| *BRADY, McCulloch, 265, | Brundage, Dimmit, (27) ................. 32 | *BYERS, Clay, 17, (496) ............... 481 |
| (5,528) ................................. 5,540 | *Bruni, Webb, 5, (379) ................ 390 | *BYNUM, Hill, 4, (199) ................. 196 |
| Branch, Collin ............................. 530 | Brushie Prairie, Navarro ................. 35 | Byrd, Ellis .................................... 30 |
| Branchville, Milam ....................... 127 | Brushy Creek, Anderson ............... 125 | Byrdtown, Lamar ........................... 22 |
| *Brandon, Hill, 1 ........................... 75 | Brushy Creek, Williamson, | |
| *Brashear, Hopkins, 10 ................ 280 | (21,764) .............................. 23,072 | **C** |
| *BRAZORIA, Brazoria, 223, | *BRYAN, Brazos, 2,415, | *CACTUS, Moore, 36, |
| (3,019) .................................. 3,090 | (76,201) .............................. 79,417 | (3,179) ................................. 3,169 |
| Brazos, Palo Pinto ........................ 97 | Bryans Mill, Cass ........................ 150 | *Caddo, Stephens, 3 ..................... 70 |
| BRAZOS BEND, Hood, (305) ....... 321 | Bryarly, Red River .......................... 3 | *CADDO MILLS, Hunt, 101, |
| BRAZOS COUNTRY, Austin, 13, | Bryce, Rusk ................................. 15 | (1,338) ................................. 1,436 |
| (469) ....................................... 488 | *BRYSON, Jack, 18, (539) ........... 526 | Cade Chapel, Navarro-Freestone .. 25 |
| Brazos Point, Bosque ..................... 20 | *Buchanan Dam, Llano, 41, | Cadiz, Bee ................................... 15 |
| Brazosport, Brazoria, | (1,519) ................................. 1,524 | Calallen, Nueces, |
| (57,288) .............................. 58,597 | Buchanan Lake Village, Llano, | ............... [part of Corpus Christi] |
| *BRECKENRIDGE, Stephens, | (692) ....................................... 684 | Calaveras, Wilson ....................... 100 |
| 295, (5,780) ......................... 5,581 | Buchel, DeWitt ............................. 45 | *CALDWELL, Burleson, 322, |
| *BREMOND, Robertson, 47, | Buckeye, Matagorda ...................... 16 | (4,104) ................................. 4,210 |
| (929) ....................................... 915 | *BUCKHOLTS, Milam, 16, | Caledonia, Rusk ........................... 75 |
| *BRENHAM, Washington, 997, | (515) ....................................... 508 | Calf Creek, McCulloch ................... 23 |
| (15,716) .............................. 16,212 | Buckhorn, Austin .......................... 50 | Calina, Limestone ......................... 10 |
| Breslau, Lavaca ............................ 65 | Buckhorn, Newton ......................... 80 | *Call, Newton, 5 .......................... 493 |
| Briar, Tarrant-Wise-Parker, | Buckner, Parker ............................ 10 | Callender Lake, Van Zandt, |
| (5,665) ................................. 5,832 | *BUDA, Hays, 533, | (1,039) ................................. 1,081 |
| BRIARCLIFF, Travis, 36, | (7,295) .............................. 10,822 | *Calliham, McMullen, 1 ............... 100 |
| (1,438) ................................. 1,516 | Buena Vista, Shelby ...................... 20 | CALLISBURG, Cooke, (353) ........ 371 |
| BRIAROAKS, Johnson, 9, (495)... 502 | Buena Vista, Starr, (102) ............. 107 | Call Junction, Jasper ..................... 50 |
| Brice, Hall, Briscoe ....................... 20 | *BUFFALO, Leon, 163, | *CALVERT, Robertson, 70, |
| *BRIDGE CITY, Orange, 213, | (1,856) ................................. 1,869 | (1,192) ................................. 1,149 |
| (7,840) ................................. 7,941 | *BUFFALO GAP, Taylor, 39, | Camargito, Starr, (388) ................ 400 |
| *BRIDGEPORT, Wise, 305, | (464) ....................................... 455 | *Camden, Polk, 5 ....................... 1,200 |
| (5,976) ................................. 6,227 | Buffalo Mop, Limestone ................. 21 | *CAMERON, Milam, 204, |
| Bridges Chapel, Titus ..................... 60 | Buffalo Springs, Clay ..................... 45 | (5,552) ................................. 5,349 |
| *Briggs, Burnet, 8 ........................ 172 | BUFFALO SPRINGS, Lubbock, | Cameron Park, Cameron, |
| Bright Star, Rains .......................... 25 | (453) ....................................... 457 | (6,963) ................................. 7,245 |
| Brinker, Hopkins .......................... 100 | Buford, Mitchell ........................... 30 | Camilla, San Jacinto .................... 200 |
| *Briscoe, Wheeler, 5 ................... 135 | Bugscuffle, Rusk .......................... 12 | Camp Air, Mason .......................... 12 |
| Bristol, Ellis, (668) ...................... 679 | Bula, Bailey ................................. 35 | *CAMPBELL, Hunt, 47, (638) ....... 669 |
| *BROADDUS, San Augustine, 27, | Bulcher, Cooke .............................. 3 | *Campbellton, Atascosa, 3 ........... 350 |
| (207) ....................................... 208 | *BULLARD, Smith-Cherokee, 148, | Camp Creek Lake, Robertson ........ 350 |
| Broadway, Lamar ........................... 25 | (2,463) ................................. 2,679 | Campo Verde, Starr, (132) ........... 139 |
| Brock, Parker ............................. 2,000 | Bull Run, Newton .......................... 90 | Camp Ruby, Polk .......................... 35 |
| Brock Junction, Parker ................. 100 | *BULVERDE, Comal, 424, | Camp San Saba, McCulloch .......... 36 |
| Bronco, Yoakum ............................ 30 | (4,630) ................................. 4,868 | Camp Seale, Polk .......................... 53 |
| *Bronson, Sabine, 10 ................... 377 | *Buna, Jasper, 76, (2,142) ......... 2,149 | Camp Springs, Scurry, .................. 10 |
| *BRONTE, Coke, 48, (999) ......... 978 | Buncombe, Panola ........................ 95 | Camp Swift, Bastrop, (6,383) .... 6,714 |
| *Brookeland, Sabine, 29 .............. 300 | Bunger, Young .............................. 24 | Camp Switch, Gregg ...................... 70 |
| *Brookesmith, Brown, 3 ................. 61 | BUNKER HILL VILLAGE, Harris, | Campti, Shelby ............................. 25 |
| Brooks, Panola ............................. 40 | 58, (3,633) ........................... 3,834 | *Camp Verde, Kerr ........................ 41 |
| Brookshier, Runnels ...................... 15 | Bunyan, Erath .............................. 20 | *CAMP WOOD, Real, 33, |
| *BROOKSHIRE, Waller, 190, | *BURKBURNETT, Wichita, 271, | (706) ....................................... 703 |
| (4,702) ................................. 4,821 | (10,811) .............................. 11,270 | Canada Verde, Wilson ................... 40 |
| BROOKSIDE VILLAGE, Brazoria, | BURKE, Angelina, (737) .............. 734 | *CANADIAN, Hemphill, 162, |
| 33, (1,523) ........................... 1,570 | *Burkett, Coleman, 1 ..................... 90 | (2,649) ................................. 2,814 |

| Town, County ............... Pop. 2014 | Town, County ............... Pop. 2014 | Town, County ............... Pop. 2014 |
|---|---|---|
| Candelaria, Presidio ....................... 55 | *CEDAR HILL, Dallas-Ellis, | Cherry Spring, Gillespie ................... 75 |
| CANEY CITY, Henderson, 10, | 1,188, (45,028) ................ 46,041 | *CHESTER, Tyler, 10, (312) ......... 324 |
| (217) ........................................ 223 | Cedar Hill, Floyd ........................... 24 | Chesterville, Colorado ................... 30 |
| Cannon, Grayson ......................... 50 | Cedar Lake, Matagorda .............. 160 | *CHICO, Wise, 66, (1,002) ....... 1,072 |
| *CANTON, Van Zandt, 845, | *Cedar Lane, Matagorda, 3 ......... 300 | *Chicota, Lamar, 2 ...................... 150 |
| (3,581) ................................... 3,609 | *CEDAR PARK, Williamson-Travis, | Chihuahua, Zapata, (84) ................ 81 |
| Cantu Addition, Brooks, (188) ...... 197 | 2,071, (48,937) ................ 57,504 | *CHILDRESS, Childress, 201, |
| *Canutillo, El Paso, 174, | Cedar Point, Polk, (630) ............. 664 | (6,105) ................................... 6,016 |
| (6,321) ................................... 6,714 | Cedar Shores, Bosque ................ 270 | *CHILLICOTHE, Hardeman, 21, |
| *CANYON, Randall, 413, | Cedar Springs, Falls ..................... 90 | (707) ........................................ 678 |
| (13,303) ............................... 13,908 | Cedar Springs, Upshur ................ 100 | *Chilton, Falls, 8, (911) ................ 943 |
| Canyon City, Comal ..................... 600 | Cedarvale, Kaufman ...................... 50 | *CHINA, Jefferson, 49, |
| Canyon Creek, Hood, (916) ......... 963 | Cedar Valley, Bell ......................... 14 | (1,160) ................................... 1,160 |
| *Canyon Lake, Comal, 228, | Cee Vee, Cottle, .......................... 45 | CHINA GROVE, Bexar, 52, |
| (21,262) ............................... 22,679 | Cego, Falls ................................... 42 | (1,179) ................................... 1,263 |
| Cape Royale, San Jacinto, (670).. 744 | Cele, Travis ................................... 20 | China Grove, Scurry ...................... 15 |
| Caplen, Galveston, ....................... 60 | *CELESTE, Hunt, 34, (814) ......... 846 | *China Spring, McLennan, 57, |
| Capps Corner, Montague ............. 30 | *CELINA, Collin-Denton, | (1,281) ................................... 1,312 |
| Cap Rock, Crosby ........................... 6 | 224, (6,028) ...................... 6,744 | Chinati, Presidio ............................. 8 |
| Caps, Taylor ............................... 300 | Center, Limestone ......................... 76 | Chinquapin, Matagorda .................... 6 |
| Caradan, Mills ............................... 20 | *CENTER, Shelby, 364, | *CHIRENO, Nacogdoches, 18, |
| Carancahua, Jackson ................... 375 | (5,193) ................................... 5,453 | (386) ........................................ 382 |
| *CARBON, Eastland, 8, (272) ...... 275 | Center City, Mills ......................... 27 | CHISHOLM [McLendon-], |
| Carbondale, Bowie ....................... 10 | Center Grove, Houston ................ 39 | Rockwall, 3, (1,373) ........... 1,672 |
| Carey, Childress .......................... 25 | Center Grove, Titus ...................... 35 | Chita, Trinity ................................. 81 |
| Carlisle, Trinity ............................ 110 | Center Hill, Houston ................... 105 | Choate, Karnes ............................. 30 |
| Carlos, Grimes .............................. 60 | Center Plains, Swisher ................. 20 | Chocolate Bayou, Brazoria ............. 60 |
| *Carlsbad, Tom Green, 11, | Center Point, Camp ...................... 41 | Choice, Shelby ............................. 35 |
| (719) ........................................ 725 | *Center Point, Kerr, 41 ................ 800 | *Chriesman, Burleson, 1 ................ 30 |
| CARL'S CORNER, Hill, 3, (173) ... 174 | Center Point, Upshur .................... 50 | *CHRISTINE, Atascosa, 4, |
| Carlson, Travis .............................. 20 | Centerview, Leon ........................... 20 | (390) ........................................ 412 |
| *Carlton, Hamilton, 2 .................... 75 | *CENTERVILLE, Leon, 87, | *Christoval, Tom Green, 19, |
| *CARMINE, Fayette, 57, (250) ..... 259 | (892) ........................................ 889 | (504) ........................................ 547 |
| Carmona, Polk .............................. 50 | Centerville, Trinity, ....................... 60 | Chula Vista, Zavala, (450) ........... 464 |
| Caro, Nacogdoches ...................... 70 | Central, Angelina ...................... 1,400 | Chula Vista, Cameron, (288) ........ 302 |
| Carrizo Hill, Dimmit, (582) ........... 694 | Central Gardens, Jefferson, | Chula Vista, Maverick, (3,818) .. 3,927 |
| *CARRIZO SPRINGS, Dimmit, | (4,347) ................................... 4,361 | Church Hill, Rusk .......................... 20 |
| 171, (5,368) ...................... 6,085 | Central Heights, Nacogdoches ..... 300 | Churchill, Brazoria ........................ 90 |
| Carroll, Smith ............................... 60 | Central High, Cherokee ................ 30 | *CIBOLO, Guadalupe, 397, |
| Carroll Springs, Anderson- | *Centralia, Trinity ........................ 190 | (15,349) ............................... 23,656 |
| Henderson .............................. 20 | Cesar Chavez, Hidalgo, | Cienegas Terrace, Val Verde, |
| *CARROLLTON, Dallas-Denton, | (1,929) ................................... 2,120 | (3,424) ................................... 3,459 |
| 5,005, (119,907) ............. 126,466 | Cestohowa, Karnes ..................... 110 | Cinco Ranch, Fort Bend-Harris, |
| Carson, Fannin ............................. 22 | Chalk, Cottle ............................... 17 | (18,274) ............................... 18,749 |
| Carta Valley, Edwards .................. 12 | Chalk Hill, Rusk .......................... 200 | Cipres, Hidalgo ............................. 20 |
| Carterville, Cass ........................... 39 | Chalk Mountain, Erath ................... 25 | Circle, Lamb ................................... 6 |
| *CARTHAGE, Panola, 363, | Chambliss, Collin .......................... 29 | Circle Back, Bailey .......................... 8 |
| (6,779) ................................... 6,959 | Champion, Nolan .......................... 10 | Circle D-KC Estates, Bastrop, |
| Cartwright, Wood ........................ 144 | Champions, Harris ................... 21,250 | (2,393) ................................... 2,622 |
| Casa Blanca, Starr, (54) ............... 57 | Chances Store, Burleson ............... 15 | Circleville, Williamson ................... 50 |
| Casa Piedra, Presidio ..................... 8 | *CHANDLER, Henderson, 143, | *CISCO, Eastland, 155, |
| Casas, Starr, (39) ......................... 42 | (2,734) ................................... 2,842 | (3,899) ................................... 3,866 |
| Cash, Hunt ................................... 56 | Chaney, Eastland .......................... 35 | Cistern, Fayette .......................... 137 |
| CASHION, Wichita, (348) ............ 352 | *Channelview, Harris, 398, | Citrus City, Hidalgo, (2,321) ....... 2,496 |
| *Cason, Morris, 3 ........................ 173 | (38,289) ............................... 40,830 | Citrus Grove, Matagorda ............... 30 |
| Cass, Cass ................................. 100 | *CHANNING, Hartley, 12, (363) ... 379 | Clairemont, Kent .......................... 12 |
| Cassie, Burnet ............................ 496 | Chaparrito, Starr, (114) .............. 114 | Clairette, Erath ............................. 55 |
| Cassin, Bexar ............................. 200 | Chapeno, Starr, (47) .................... 50 | Clara, Wichita ............................. 100 |
| *Castell, Llano, 3 .......................... 72 | Chapman, Rusk ............................ 20 | Clardy, Lamar ............................. 160 |
| CASTLE HILLS, Bexar, 339, | *Chapman Ranch, Nueces ........... 200 | *CLARENDON, Donley, 94, |
| (4,116) ................................... 4,332 | Chappel, San Saba ....................... 25 | (2,026) ................................... 1,944 |
| Castolon, Brewster ......................... 8 | *Chappell Hill, Washington, 37 ..... 750 | Clareville, Bee .............................. 25 |
| *CASTROVILLE, Medina, 242, | Charco, Goliad .............................. 96 | Clark, Liberty ............................... 75 |
| (2,680) ................................... 2,925 | Charleston, Delta-Hopkins ........... 150 | Clarkson, Milam ............................ 10 |
| *Catarina, Dimmit, 7, (118) ......... 138 | Charlie, Clay ................................. 70 | *CLARKSVILLE, Red River, 165, |
| *Cat Spring, Austin, 18 ............... 200 | *CHARLOTTE, Atascosa, 33, | (3,285) ................................... 3,096 |
| Caviness, Lamar ........................... 90 | (1,715) ................................... 1,803 | CLARKSVILLE CITY, Gregg-Upshur, |
| Cawthon, Brazos .......................... 75 | *Chatfield, Navarro, 1 ................... 40 | 19, (865) ................................ 886 |
| Cayote, Bosque ............................ 75 | Cheapside, Gonzales ...................... 5 | *CLAUDE, Armstrong, 45, |
| *Cayuga, Anderson, 3 .................. 137 | Cheek, Jefferson ..................... 1,096 | (1,196) ................................... 1,219 |
| Cedar Bayou, Harris ................. 1,555 | Cheneyboro, Navarro .................. 100 | Clauene, Hockley .......................... 10 |
| *Cedar Creek, Bastrop, 116 ......... 145 | *Cherokee, San Saba, 9 .............. 175 | Clawson, Angelina .................... 1,500 |

| Town, County ...............Pop. 2014 | Town, County ...............Pop. 2014 | Town, County ...............Pop. 2014 |
|---|---|---|
| Clay, Burleson ................................. 61 | Cochran, Austin ........................... 200 | Colton, Travis.................................. 50 |
| Clays Corner, Parmer..................... 15 | COCKRELL HILL, Dallas, 97, | *COLUMBUS, Colorado, 311, |
| *Clayton, Panola, 3....................... 125 | (4,193) ................................. 4,295 | (3,655) .............................. 3,842 |
| Claytonville, Swisher ...................... 85 | COFFEE CITY, Henderson, 26, | *COMANCHE, Comanche, 213, |
| Clear Creek, Burnet......................... 78 | (278) ....................................... 290 | (4,335) .............................. 4,338 |
| CLEAR LAKE SHORES, Galveston, | Coffeeville, Upshur ......................... 50 | *COMBES, Cameron, 41, |
| 94, (1,063) ......................... 1,121 | Cofferville, Lamb.............................. 4 | (2,895) .............................. 3,081 |
| *CLEBURNE, Johnson, 1,136, | Coit, Limestone.............................. 25 | COMBINE, Kaufman-Dallas, 53, |
| (29,337) ............................ 29,569 | Coke, Wood .................................... 53 | (1,942) .............................. 2,033 |
| Clegg, Live Oak............................ 125 | *COLDSPRING, San Jacinto, 114, | Cometa, Zavala ............................. 10 |
| Clemville, Matagorda...................... 25 | (853) ....................................... 922 | *Comfort, Kendall, 139, |
| Cleo, Kimble ....................................3 | *COLEMAN, Coleman, 209, | (2,363) .............................. 2,537 |
| Cleveland, Austin.......................... 125 | (4,709) .............................. 4,600 | *COMMERCE, Hunt, 221, |
| *CLEVELAND, Liberty, 460, | Colfax, Van Zandt .......................... 94 | (8,078) .............................. 8,359 |
| (7,675) ................................ 8,010 | Colita, Polk .................................... 50 | *COMO, Hopkins, 25, (702).......... 697 |
| Cliffside, Potter ............................ 206 | College Hill, Bowie ......................... 40 | *Comstock, Val Verde................... 344 |
| *CLIFTON, Bosque, 242, | College Mound, Kaufman............. 500 | Comyn, Comanche.......................... 30 |
| (3,442) ................................ 3,416 | *Collegeport, Matagorda, 1............ 80 | *Concan, Uvalde, 25.................... 500 |
| Climax, Collin................................. 82 | *COLLEGE STATION, Brazos, | *Concepcion, Duval, 1, (62)........... 80 |
| Cline, Uvalde ................................. 15 | 2,268, (93,857) ............... 100,091 | Concord, Cherokee ........................ 50 |
| *CLINT, El Paso, 55, | *COLLEYVILLE, Tarrant, | *Concord, Leon............................. 28 |
| (926) ....................................... 961 | 1,102, (22,807) ................ 25,256 | Concord, Madison .......................... 50 |
| Clinton, Hunt................................ 150 | *COLLINSVILLE, Grayson, 44, | Concord, Rusk............................... 23 |
| Close City, Garza............................ 65 | (1,624) .............................. 1,618 | Concrete, DeWitt ........................... 46 |
| Cloverleaf, Harris, (22,942) ..... 23,707 | *COLMESNEIL, Tyler, 30, | Cone, Crosby................................. 50 |
| *CLUTE, Brazoria, 366, | (596) ....................................... 611 | Conlen, Dallam .............................. 14 |
| (11,211)............................ 11,184 | Colony, Rains ................................ 35 | Connor, Madison ........................... 20 |
| *CLYDE, Callahan, 155, | Colorado Acres, Webb, | *CONROE, Montgomery, 2,911, |
| (3,713) ................................ 3,893 | (296) ....................................... 317 | (56,207) ............................ 63,322 |
| *COAHOMA, Howard, 28, | *COLORADO CITY, Mitchell, | Content, Bell................................. 25 |
| (817) ....................................... 846 | 186, (4,146) ........................ 4,025 | *CONVERSE, Bexar, 446, |
| Coble, Hockley .............................. 11 | Coltharp, Houston........................... 40 | (18,198) ............................ 20,739 |

*The Landmark Inn in Castroville. Photo by Robert Plocheck.*

| Town, County ............... Pop. 2014 | Town, County ............... Pop. 2014 | Town, County ............... Pop. 2014 |
|---|---|---|
| Conway, Carson ............................. 20 | *CRANDALL, Kaufman, 118, | Cypress Creek, Kerr .................... 200 |
| Cooks Point, Burleson ................... 60 | (2,858) .............................. 2,968 | *Cypress [-Fairbanks], Harris, |
| *Cookville, Titus, 11 ...................... 105 | *CRANE, Crane, 103, | 1,236 ...................... 120,000 |
| COOL, Parker, 7, (157) ............... 160 | (3,353) .............................. 3,756 | Cypress Mill, Blanco .................... 200 |
| *COOLIDGE, Limestone, 12, | *CRANFILLS GAP, Bosque, 14, | |
| (955) .............................. 931 | (281) .............................. 285 | **D** |
| *COOPER, Delta, 77, | *CRAWFORD, McLennan, 37, | Dacosta, Victoria ............................ 89 |
| (1,969) .............................. 1,987 | (717) .............................. 742 | Dacus, Montgomery .................... 190 |
| Cooper, Houston ............................ 27 | Creath, Houston ............................ 20 | Daffan, Travis .............................. 500 |
| Copano Village, Aransas .............. 210 | Crecy, Trinity ................................ 15 | *DAINGERFIELD, Morris, 93, |
| *Copeville, Collin, 2 ...................... 243 | CREEDMOOR, Travis, 31, | (2,560) .............................. 2,608 |
| *COPPELL, Dallas-Denton, | (202) .............................. 221 | *DAISETTA, Liberty, 18, |
| 1,361, (38,659) ............ 40,142 | Crescent Heights, Henderson ...... 180 | (966) .............................. 1,008 |
| *COPPERAS COVE, Coryell, | *CRESSON, Hood-Johnson-Parker, | Dalby Springs, Bowie ..................... 75 |
| 582, (32,032) .................. 33,064 | 88, (741) ........................ 765 | *Dale, Caldwell, 22 ...................... 300 |
| COPPER CANYON, Denton, 42, | Crews, Runnels .............................. 30 | *DALHART, Dallam-Hartley, 303, |
| (1,334) .............................. 1,379 | Crisp, Ellis .................................. 115 | (7,930) .............................. 8,147 |
| Corbet, Navarro ............................ 80 | *CROCKETT, Houston, 312, | *Dallardsville, Polk, ...................... 350 |
| Cordele, Jackson ............................ 51 | (6,950) .............................. 6,766 | *DALLAS, Dallas-Collin-Denton, |
| CORINTH, Denton, 529, | *Crosby, Harris, 343, (2,299) ..... 2,398 | 42,505, (1,197,816) ..... 1,255,343 |
| (19,935) .......................... 20,007 | *CROSBYTON, Crosby, 46, | Dalton, Cass .................................. 50 |
| Corinth, Jones ................................ 10 | (1,741) .............................. 1,678 | DALWORTHINGTON GARDENS, |
| Corinth, Leon ................................ 50 | Cross, Grimes ................................ 53 | Tarrant, 155, (2,259) ........... 2,347 |
| Corley, Bowie ................................ 35 | Cross, McMullen ............................ 25 | *Damon, Brazoria, 23, (552) ......... 579 |
| Cornersville, Hopkins .................... 200 | Cross Cut, Brown ............................ 22 | *DANBURY, Brazoria, 46, |
| Cornett, Cass ................................ 30 | Cross Mountain, Bexar, | (1,715) .............................. 1,755 |
| Cornudas, Hudspeth ......................... 5 | (3,124) .............................. 3,377 | *Danciger, Brazoria, 1 .................... 90 |
| *CORPUS CHRISTI, Nueces, | *CROSS PLAINS, Callahan, 69, | *Danevang, Wharton, 6 .................. 61 |
| 9,354, (305,215) ............ 317,004 | (982) .............................. 1,028 | Daniels, Panola ............................ 75 |
| CORRAL CITY, Denton, 3, (27) ...... 28 | Crossroads, Cass .......................... 60 | Danville, Gregg ............................ 200 |
| *CORRIGAN, Polk, 68, | Crossroads, Delta .......................... 20 | Darby Hill, San Jacinto .................. 25 |
| (1,595) .............................. 1,652 | CROSS ROADS, Denton, 50, | Darco, Harrison ............................ 10 |
| *CORSICANA, Navarro, 984, | (1,563) .............................. 1,623 | Darden, Polk ................................ 320 |
| (23,770) .......................... 24,769 | Crossroads, Harrison .................... 100 | *DARROUZETT, Lipscomb, 14, |
| Coryell City, Coryell ...................... 70 | Cross Roads, Henderson ............. 160 | (350) .............................. 376 |
| *Cost, Gonzales, 5 .......................... 84 | Crossroads, Hopkins ...................... 50 | Datura, Limestone ........................... 2 |
| Cotton Center, Fannin .................... 33 | Cross Roads, Madison .................... 75 | *Davilla, Milam, 1 .......................... 191 |
| *Cotton Center, Hale, 6 ................ 300 | Cross Roads, Milam ........................ 35 | Davis, Atascosa ............................... 8 |
| Cottondale, Wise ........................... 300 | CROSS TIMBER, Johnson, | Davis Prairie, Limestone ................ 17 |
| Cotton Gin, Freestone .................... 28 | (268) .............................. 278 | *Dawn, Deaf Smith, 5 .................... 52 |
| Cotton Patch, DeWitt ...................... 11 | Croton, Dickens ............................... 7 | *DAWSON, Navarro, 27, (807) ..... 825 |
| Cottonwood, Callahan .................... 55 | Crow, Wood ................................ 178 | *DAYTON, Liberty, 368, |
| COTTONWOOD, Kaufman, | *CROWELL, Foard, 46, (948) ....... 880 | (7,242) .............................. 7,642 |
| (185) .............................. 170 | *CROWLEY, Tarrant, 357, | DAYTON LAKES, Liberty, (93) ....... 98 |
| Cottonwood, Madison ...................... 40 | (12,838) .......................... 14,437 | Deadwood, Panola ........................ 106 |
| Cottonwood, McLennan ................ 150 | Crown, Atascosa ............................ 10 | DEAN, Clay, 2, (493) .................... 498 |
| Cottonwood, Somervell .................. 24 | Cruz Calle, Duval .......................... 12 | Dean, Hockley .............................. 20 |
| COTTONWOOD SHORES, Burnet, | Cryer Creek, Navarro ...................... 15 | *Deanville, Burleson, 5 .................. 130 |
| 36, (1,123) ........................ 1,148 | Crystal Beach, Galveston ............. 800 | *DeBerry, Panola, 26 .................... 200 |
| *COTULLA, La Salle, 104, | *CRYSTAL CITY, Zavala, 101, | *DECATUR, Wise, 436, |
| (3,603) .............................. 4,183 | (7,136) .............................. 7,454 | (6,042) .............................. 6,336 |
| Couch, Karnes ................................ 10 | Crystal Falls, Stephens .................. 10 | Decker Prairie, Montgomery ...... 2,000 |
| Coughran, Atascosa ...................... 20 | Crystal Lake, Anderson .................. 12 | DeCORDOVA, Hood, (2,683) ..... 2,732 |
| Country Acres, San Patricio, | Cuadrilla, El Paso .......................... 67 | *DEER PARK, Harris, 1,032, |
| (185) .............................. 191 | *CUERO, DeWitt, 296, | (32,010) .......................... 33,667 |
| County Line, Lubbock .................... 59 | (6,841) .............................. 7,017 | *DE KALB, Bowie, 90, |
| County Line, Rains ........................ 40 | Cuevitas, Hidalgo, (40) .................. 48 | (1,699) .............................. 1,694 |
| *COUPLAND, Williamson, 19 ....... 280 | *CUMBY, Hopkins, 52, (777) ........ 771 | *DE LEON, Comanche, 113, |
| Courtney, Grimes ............................ 60 | Cumings, Fort Bend, (981) ........ 1,067 | (2,246) .............................. 2,240 |
| COVE, Chambers, 15, | Cundiff, Jack ................................ 45 | Delhi, Caldwell ............................ 150 |
| (510) .............................. 505 | *CUNEY, Cherokee, 7, (140) ........ 145 | Delia, Limestone ............................ 20 |
| Cove Springs, Cherokee ................ 40 | *Cunningham, Lamar .................... 110 | *DELL CITY, Hudspeth, 18, |
| *COVINGTON, Hill, 18, (269) ....... 268 | Currie, Navarro .............................. 25 | (365) .............................. 337 |
| Cox, Upshur ................................ 30 | Curtis, Jasper .............................. 150 | Del Mar Heights, Cameron, (113). 115 |
| *Coyanosa, Pecos, 8, (163) .......... 174 | *CUSHING, Nacogdoches, 35, | *Delmita, Starr, 4, (216) ................ 225 |
| Coy City, Karnes ............................ 30 | (612) .............................. 606 | Delray, Panola ............................... 45 |
| Coyote Acres, Jim Wells, (508) .... 566 | Cusseta, Cass ................................ 30 | *DEL RIO, Val Verde, 935, |
| COYOTE FLATS, Johnson, | *CUT AND SHOOT, Montgomery, | (35,591) .......................... 34,651 |
| (312) .............................. 320 | 56, (1,070) ........................ 1,075 | Delrose, Upshur ............................ 35 |
| Crabbs Prairie, Walker ................ 240 | Cuthand, Red River .................... 116 | Del Sol, San Patricio, (239) ........ 248 |
| Craft, Cherokee ............................ 21 | Cyclone, Bell ................................ 47 | *Del Valle, Travis, 99, .. [part of Austin] |
| Crafton, Wise .............................. 100 | Cypress, Franklin .......................... 20 | Delwin, Cottle .............................. 12 |

| Town, County ...............Pop. 2014 | Town, County ...............Pop. 2014 | Town, County ...............Pop. 2014 |
|---|---|---|
| Demi-John, Brazoria.....................300 | Dog Ridge, Bell............................215 | *EARTH, Lamb, 31, (1,065).......1,032 |
| Democrat, Mills.................................8 | Dogwood City, Smith ...................800 | East Afton, Dickens .........................13 |
| Denhawken, Wilson........................52 | Dolen, Liberty ..................................75 | East Alto Bonito, Starr, (824)........875 |
| *DENISON, Grayson, 942, | DOMINO, Cass, 4, (93) ................105 | *EAST BERNARD, Wharton, 95, |
| (22,682)................................22,979 | *Donie, Freestone, 8.....................250 | (2,272)..................................2,318 |
| Denning, San Augustine..............100 | *DONNA, Hidalgo, 414, | East Caney, Hopkins ....................100 |
| *Dennis, Parker, 4.........................300 | (15,798)...........................17,446 | East Columbia, Brazoria.................95 |
| Denson Springs, Anderson............60 | *Doole, McCulloch..........................74 | East Delta, Delta.............................60 |
| Denton, Callahan..............................6 | Doolittle, Hidalgo, (2,769)..........2,910 | East Direct, Lamar...........................48 |
| *DENTON, Denton, 3,367, | DORCHESTER, Grayson, | Easter, Castro.................................26 |
| (113,383) ........................121,122 | (148) ................................149 | Easterly, Robertson ........................61 |
| *DENVER CITY, Yoakum, 179, | Dorras, Stonewall ...........................20 | Eastgate, Liberty...........................200 |
| (4,479)..................................4,705 | Doss, Cass .....................................15 | East Hamilton, Shelby .....................25 |
| *DEPORT, Lamar-Red River, 13, | *Doss, Gillespie, 7 ........................100 | *EASTLAND, Eastland, 230, |
| (578).......................................568 | Dot, Falls ........................................17 | (3,960)..................................3,968 |
| Derby, Frio .......................................50 | Dotson, Panola ...............................35 | East Lopez, Starr, (166)................171 |
| *Desdemona, Eastland, 3.............180 | Double Bayou, Chambers ............200 | EAST MOUNTAIN, Upshur, 17, |
| Desert, Collin..................................35 | DOUBLE OAK, Denton, 136, | (797)................................804 |
| *DeSOTO, Dallas, 1,091, | (2,867).................................2,937 | *EASTON, Gregg-Rusk, 4, |
| (49,047)..............................52,035 | *Doucette, Tyler, 3 ........................160 | (510)................................505 |
| *DETROIT, Red River, 31, | *Dougherty, Floyd, 1 .......................91 | East Point, Wood.............................40 |
| (732).......................................687 | Dougherty, Rains............................40 | East Sweden, McCulloch................40 |
| *DEVERS, Liberty, 17, (447) ........466 | *Douglass, Nacogdoches, 20 .......380 | EAST TAWAKONI, Rains, 19, |
| *DEVINE, Medina, 234, | *DOUGLASSVILLE, Cass, 7, | (883)................................876 |
| (4,350)..................................4,622 | (229) ................................237 | Ebenezer, Camp..............................55 |
| Dew, Freestone ............................150 | Downing, Comanche ......................30 | Ebenezer, Jasper............................50 |
| DeWees, Wilson .............................60 | Downsville, McLennan..................150 | Echo, Coleman..................................6 |
| Deweesville, Karnes.......................12 | Downtown Texas, Milam.................34 | Ecleto, Karnes.................................22 |
| *Deweyville, Newton, 9, | Doyle, Limestone............................50 | *ECTOR, Fannin, 21, (695) ..........709 |
| (1,023)..................................1,035 | Doyle, San Patricio, (254).............255 | *EDCOUCH, Hidalgo, 48, |
| Dewville, Gonzales.........................30 | Dozier, Collingsworth........................4 | (3,161)..................................3,243 |
| Dexter, Cooke.................................12 | Drane, Navarro................................16 | *EDDY [Bruceville-], McLennan- |
| *D'Hanis, Medina, 19, (847) ........870 | Drasco, Runnels..............................15 | Falls, 24, (1,475) ...............1,771 |
| Dial, Fannin.....................................76 | Draw, Lynn......................................18 | *EDEN, Concho, 48, (2,766) .....2,725 |
| Dialville, Cherokee........................200 | Dreka, Shelby..................................30 | Eden, Nacogdoches ......................100 |
| *Diana, Upshur, 37 .......................585 | Dresden, Navarro ...........................25 | Edgar, DeWitt....................................8 |
| *DIBOLL, Angelina, 118, | Dreyer, Gonzales............................20 | Edge, Brazos....................................10 |
| (5,359)..................................5,446 | *Driftwood, Hays, 61, (144) .........148 | EDGECLIFF, Tarrant, |
| Dicey, Parker ..................................40 | *DRIPPING SPRINGS, Hays, | (2,776)..................................2,928 |
| *DICKENS, Dickens, 15, (286).....265 | 489, (1,788) ......................1,919 | Edgewater Estates, San Patricio, |
| *DICKINSON, Galveston, 549, | *DRISCOLL, Nueces, 19, (739)....753 | (72)................................77 |
| (18,680)..............................19,260 | Drop, Denton ..................................90 | *EDGEWOOD, Van Zandt, 93, |
| *Dike, Hopkins, 4 ..........................170 | *Dryden, Terrell, 2............................13 | (1,441)..................................1,473 |
| *DILLEY, Frio, 68, (3,894)..........4,075 | Dubina, Fayette ............................272 | Edgeworth, Bell ..............................15 |
| Dilworth, Gonzales.........................18 | *DUBLIN, Erath, 154, (3,654)....3,773 | Edhube, Fannin ..............................40 |
| Dilworth, Red River.........................25 | Dudley, Callahan ............................25 | *EDINBURG, Hidalgo, 1,643, |
| *Dime Box, Lee, 18.......................381 | Duffau, Erath ..................................76 | (74,588)............................85,456 |
| *DIMMITT, Castro, 142, | *DUMAS, Moore, 407, | *EDMONSON, Hale, 3, (111)........106 |
| (4,393)..................................4,375 | (14,691)...........................14,926 | *EDNA, Jackson, 270, |
| Dimple, Red River...........................60 | Dumont, King..................................19 | (5,499)..................................5,725 |
| *Dinero, Live Oak ...................3,344 | Dunbar, Rains..................................40 | Edna Hill, Erath...............................32 |
| Ding Dong, Bell.............................301 | *DUNCANVILLE, Dallas, 1,155, | EDOM, Van Zandt, 14, (375)........388 |
| Direct, Lamar..................................85 | (38,524)...........................39,695 | *Edroy, San Patricio, 2, |
| Dirgin, Rusk....................................50 | Dundee, Archer...............................12 | (331)................................336 |
| DISH, Denton, (201).....................294 | Dunlap, Cottle.................................10 | Egan, Johnson...............................133 |
| Divide, Kerr.....................................50 | Dunlap, Travis.................................80 | *Egypt, Wharton, 1 .........................26 |
| Divot, Frio .......................................30 | Dunlay, Medina.............................145 | Eidson Road, Maverick, |
| Dixie, Grayson................................17 | *Dunn, Scurry..................................75 | (8,960)..................................9,158 |
| Dixon, Hunt.....................................31 | Duplex, Fannin ...............................25 | Elam Springs, Upshur.....................50 |
| Dixon-Hopewell, Houston .............10 | Durango, Falls ................................54 | Elbert, Throckmorton, (30).............29 |
| Doak Springs, Lee..........................50 | Duren, Mills.....................................15 | Elbow, Howard.................................10 |
| Doans, Wilbarger............................20 | Duster, Comanche..........................25 | El Brazil, Starr, (47)........................49 |
| *Dobbin, Montgomery, 3...............310 | Dye, Montague ...............................30 | El Camino Angosto, Cameron, |
| Dobrowolski, Atascosa ..................10 | | (253)................................269 |
| Dodd, Castro..................................12 | **E** | *EL CAMPO, Wharton, 630, |
| *DODD CITY, Fannin, 25, | Eagle, Chambers............................30 | (11,602) ...........................11,515 |
| (369) ................................386 | *EAGLE LAKE, Colorado, 130, | El Castillo, Starr, (188).................201 |
| *Dodge, Walker, 2.........................150 | (3,639)..................................3,868 | EL CENIZO, Webb, 35, |
| *DODSON, Collingsworth, 2, | *EAGLE PASS, Maverick, 901, | (3,273)..................................3,319 |
| (109)................................106 | (26,248)...........................27,479 | El Cenizo, Starr, (249) .................264 |
| Dodson Prairie, Palo Pinto ............18 | *EARLY, Brown, 175, | El Centro, Starr...............................50 |
| Doffing, Hidalgo, (5,091)..........5,355 | (2,762)..................................2,896 | El Chaparral, Starr, (464)............482 |

| Town, County | Pop. 2014 |
| --- | --- |

*ELDORADO, Schleicher, 77,
(1,951) .................................. 1,881
Eldorado Center, Navarro .............. 20
Eldridge, Colorado ......................... 10
*ELECTRA, Wichita, 81,
(2,791) .................................. 2,787
Elevation, Milam ............................ 12
*ELGIN, Bastrop, 376,
(8,135) .................................. 8,757
Elias-Fela Solis, Starr, (30) ............. 31
Eliasville, Young ........................... 100
*El Indio, Maverick, 1, (190) ........ 187
Elk, McLennan ............................. 150
*ELKHART, Anderson, 68,
(1,371) .................................. 1,382
EL LAGO, Harris, 81, (2,706) .... 2,772
*Ellinger, Fayette, 8 ..................... 386
Elliott, Robertson .......................... 55
Elliott, Wilbarger .......................... 50
*Elmaton, Matagorda, 4 .............. 160
Elm Creek, Maverick, (2,469) .... 2,593
*ELMENDORF, Bexar, 60,
(1,488) .................................. 1,602
El Mesquite, Starr, (38) .................. 40
Elm Grove, Cherokee ..................... 50
Elm Grove, San Saba ..................... 15
Elm Grove, Wharton ...................... 76
Elm Grove Camp, Guadalupe ........ 88
*Elm Mott, McLennan, 69 ........... 300
*Elmo, Kaufman, 1, (768) ............ 819
Elmont, Grayson ........................... 15
Elm Ridge, Milam .......................... 25
Elmwood, Anderson ...................... 15
Eloise, Falls .................................. 19
El Oso, Karnes .............................. 35
*EL PASO, El Paso, 15,965,
(649,121) ......................... 669,882
El Quiote, Starr, (208) ................. 212
El Rancho Vela, Starr, (274) ......... 283
El Refugio, Starr, (331) ............... 355
Elroy, Travis ............................... 125
*ELSA, Hidalgo, 134, (5,660) .... 6,354
El Sauz, Starr .............................. 50
El Socio, Starr, (130) ................... 129
Elton, Dickens ............................... 4
El Toro, Jackson .......................... 136
Elwood, Fannin ............................. 31
Elwood, Madison ........................... 50
*Elysian Fields, Harrison, 6 .......... 500
Emberson, Lamar .......................... 80
Emerald Bay, Smith, (1,047) ...... 1,076
EMHOUSE, Navarro, 3, (133) ...... 138
Emmett, Navarro ......................... 100
*EMORY, Rains, 184, (1,239) .... 1,226
Encantada-Ranchito El Calaboz,
Cameron, (2,255) .............. 2,305
ENCHANTED OAKS, Henderson,
(326) .................................. 332
*ENCINAL, La Salle, 23, (559) ..... 592
*Encino, Brooks, 6, (143) ............ 145
*Energy, Comanche, 2 .................. 70
Engle, Fayette ............................. 141
English, Red River ....................... 100
*Enloe, Delta, 1 ............................ 90
*ENNIS, Ellis, 713,
(18,513) ........................... 18,707
Enoch, Upshur .............................. 25
*Enochs, Bailey ............................ 80
Enon, Upshur .............................. 204
*Eola, Concho, 3 ......................... 215
Eolian, Stephens ............................ 9
*Era, Cooke, 6 ............................ 150

Ericksdahl, Jones .......................... 35
Erin, Jasper ................................... 70
Erna, Menard ................................ 27
Erwin, Grimes ............................... 52
Escobares, Starr, 25, (1,188) .... 2,753
Escobar I, Starr, (324) ................. 352
Escobas, Zapata .............................. 2
Escondidas [Sandy Hollow-],
Nueces, (296) ....................... 308
Eskota, Fisher ................................ 32
Esperanza, Hudspeth ..................... 75
Espey, Atascosa ............................ 55
Estacado, Lubbock-Crosby ............ 32
*ESTELLINE, Hall, 7, (145) .......... 140
Estes, Aransas ............................. 300
Ethel, Grayson ............................... 40
*Etoile, Nacogdoches, 10 ............ 700
Eugenio Saenz, Starr, (159) ......... 164
Eula, Callahan ............................. 125
*EULESS, Tarrant, 1,433,
(51,277) ........................... 53,355
Eulogy, Bosque ............................. 10
Eureka, Franklin ............................ 18
EUREKA, Navarro, 11, (307) ........ 317
*EUSTACE, Henderson, 43,
(991) .................................. 992
*Evadale, Jasper, 17, (1,483) .... 1,531
*EVANT, Coryell-Hamilton, 30,
(426) .................................. 414
Evergreen, San Jacinto ................. 100
Evergreen, Starr, (73) .................... 76
EVERMAN, Tarrant, 119,
(6,108) .................................. 6,272
Ewell, Upshur ............................... 20
Ezzell, Lavaca ............................... 55

**F**

*Fabens, El Paso, 58,
(8,257) .................................. 8,387
Fabrica, Maverick (923) ............... 940
FAIRCHILDS, Fort Bend (763) ..... 840
*FAIRFIELD, Freestone, 243,
(2,951) .................................. 2,951
Fairland, Burnet ........................... 340
Fairlie, Hunt ................................. 80
Fairmount, Sabine .................... 1,500
Fair Oaks, Limestone ..................... 15
*FAIR OAKS RANCH, Bexar-Comal-
Kendall, 131, (5,986) ......... 6,794
Fair Play, Panola ........................... 80
Fairview, Armstrong ....................... 10
Fairview, Cass ............................... 20
FAIRVIEW, Collin, 257,
(7,248) .................................. 8,223
Fairview, Gaines ........................... 160
Fairview, Hockley ........................... 20
Fairview, Hood .............................. 30
Fairview, Howard ............................ 5
Fairview, Wilson ............................ 95
Fairy, Hamilton .............................. 40
Falcon, Zapata (191) ................... 185
Falconaire, Starr (132) ................. 132
*Falcon Heights, Starr (53) ............ 54
Falcon Lake Estates, Zapata
(1,036) .................................. 1,083
Falcon Mesa, Zapata (405) .......... 399
Falcon Village, Starr (47) ............... 50
*FALFURRIAS, Brooks, 137,
(4,981) .................................. 5,021
Fallon, Limestone ........................ 100
*FALLS CITY, Karnes, 38,
(611) .................................. 657

Falman, San Patricio (76) .............. 79
Famuliner, Cochran .......................... 5
Fannett, Jefferson (2,252) ........ 2,262
*Fannin, Goliad, 6 ........................ 359
Fargo, Wilbarger ......................... 169
Farmers Academy, Titus ................ 75
*FARMERS BRANCH, Dallas,
1,884, (28,616) ............... 31,378
Farmers Valley, Wilbarger .............. 30
*FARMERSVILLE, Collin, 179,
(3,301) .................................. 3,402
Farmington, Grayson ..................... 40
*Farnsworth, Ochiltree, 7 ............ 130
Farrar, Limestone .......................... 51
Farrsville, Newton ....................... 152
*FARWELL, Parmer, 46,
(1,363) .................................. 1,287
Fashing, Atascosa ......................... 35
*FATE, Rockwall, 146,
(6,357) .................................. 8,267
Faught, Lamar ............................... 25
Faulkner, Lamar ............................ 10
Fawil, Newton ............................. 183
*FAYETTEVILLE, Fayette, 56,
(258) .................................. 255
Faysville, Hidalgo (439) ............... 464
Fedor, Lee ................................... 92
*Fentress, Caldwell, 7 .................. 380
Fernando Salinas, Starr (15) ......... 15
*FERRIS, Ellis, 96, (2,436) ....... 2,492
Fetzer, Waller ............................. 150
Fields Store, Waller ..................... 500
*Fieldton, Lamb, 1 ........................ 20
Fife, McCulloch ............................ 32
Fifth Street, Fort Bend (2,486) ... 2,665
Files Valley, Hill ........................... 60
Fincastle, Henderson ..................... 75
Finney, Hale ................................. 18
*Fischer, Comal, 8 ....................... 200
Fisk, Coleman ............................... 40
Five Points, Ellis ............................ 25
Flaccus, Karnes ............................. 15
Flagg, Castro ................................ 26
*Flat, Coryell, 2 ........................... 210
Flat Fork, Shelby ........................... 10
*FLATONIA, Fayette, 102,
(1,383) .................................. 1,365
Flat Prairie, Trinity ......................... 33
Flats, Rains .................................. 40
Flat Top, Stonewall ......................... 5
*Flint, Smith, 163, ..................... 2,500
Flo, Leon ..................................... 12
*Flomot, Motley, 1 ...................... 181
Flora, Hopkins .............................. 20
Flor de Rio, Starr (122) ............... 132
*FLORENCE, Williamson, 82,
(1,136) .................................. 1,169
*FLORESVILLE, Wilson, 317,
(6,448) .................................. 7,100
Florey, Andrews ............................ 25
Flour Bluff, Nueces,
.............. [part of Corpus Christi]
Flowella, Brooks (118) ................. 121
Flower Hill, Colorado ..................... 20
*FLOWER MOUND, Denton,
2,342, (64,669) ............... 67,796
Floyd, Hunt .................................. 90
*FLOYDADA, Floyd, 114,
(3,038) .................................. 2,898
*Fluvanna, Scurry, 5 .................... 180
*Flynn, Leon, 2 ............................ 81
Foard City, Foard .......................... 10

CITIES & TOWNS

| Town, County ............ Pop. 2014 | Town, County ............ Pop. 2014 | Town, County ............ Pop. 2014 |
|---|---|---|
| Goodland, Bailey ............................ 10 | *GRAPELAND, Houston, 94, | Grow, Kin............................................. 9 |
| Goodlett, Hardeman ...................... 80 |   (1,489) ............................... 1,489 | Gruenau, DeWitt................................ 18 |
| GOODLOW, Navarro, 4, (200) ..... 201 | *GRAPEVINE, Tarrant, 2,761, | Gruene, Comal, |
| Good Neighbor, Hopkins ............... 40 |   (46,334) ........................... 51,330 | ............... [part of New Braunfels] |
| Goodnight, Armstrong..................... 20 | Grassland, Lynn ............................. 40 | *GRUVER, Hansford, 45, |
| *GOODRICH, Polk, 28, (271) ....... 274 | Gray, Marion .................................... 12 |   (1,194) ............................... 1,157 |
| Goodsprings, Rusk......................... 40 | Grayback, Wilbarger....................... 10 | Guadalupe, Victoria ......................... 70 |
| Goodwill, Burleson.......................... 12 | GRAYS PRAIRIE, Kaufman, 4, | Guadalupe-Guerra, Starr, (37)........ 40 |
| Goodwin, San Augustine ............... 70 |   (337) ..................................... 347 | Guadalupe Station, Culberson ....... 10 |
| *GORDON, Palo Pinto, 27, | Graytown, Wilson ............................ 85 | *Guerra, Jim Hogg, 1, (6) ................. 6 |
|   (478) ....................................... 486 | Greatwood, Fort Bend, | Gum Springs, Cass ......................... 50 |
| *Gordonville, Grayson, 22 ............ 165 |   (11,538) ........................... 12,141 | *GUN BARREL CITY, Henderson, |
| *GOREE, Knox, 4, (203)............... 192 | Green, Karnes ................................. 50 |   318, (5,672) ....................... 6,023 |
| *GORMAN, Eastland, 38, | Green Hill, Titus .............................. 80 | Gunsight, Stephens ........................... 6 |
|   (1,083) ............................... 1,092 | Green Lake, Calhoun .................... 51 | *GUNTER, Grayson, 63, |
| Goshen, Walker.............................. 250 | Greenpond, Hopkins..................... 150 |   (1,498) ............................... 1,455 |
| Gould, Cherokee ............................ 20 | Green's Creek, Erath...................... 75 | Gus, Burleson.................................... 50 |
| *Gouldbusk, Coleman, 2................ 70 | Green Valley, Denton.................... 100 | *GUSTINE, Comanche, 18, |
| Graceton, Upshur ......................... 100 | Green Valley Farms, Cameron, |   (476) ..................................... 479 |
| *GRAFORD, Palo Pinto, 27, |   (1,272) ............................... 1,380 | *Guthrie, King, 1, (160)................... 160 |
|   (584) ....................................... 602 | Greenview, Hopkins......................... 25 | Gutierrez, Starr, (79)........................ 81 |
| Graham, Garza................................ 60 | *GREENVILLE, Hunt, 945, | *Guy, Fort Bend, 11 ....................... 239 |
| *GRAHAM, Young, 571, |   (25,557) ........................... 26,643 | Guys Store, Leon.............................. 20 |
|   (8,903) ............................... 9,317 | Greenvine, Washington ................. 35 | |
| *GRANBURY, Hood, 1,158, | Greenwood, Hopkins.................... 100 | **H** |
|   (7,978) ............................... 9,059 | Greenwood, Midland ................. 2,000 | Haciendito, Presidio......................... 10 |
| Grand Acres, Cameron, (49) ......... 54 | Greenwood, Red River................... 20 | Hackberry, Cottle ............................. 30 |
| Grand Bluff, Panola ...................... 115 | *Greenwood, Wise, 6...................... 76 | HACKBERRY, Denton, 20, |
| *GRANDFALLS, Ward, 5, | *GREGORY, San Patricio, 35, |   (968) ..................................... 955 |
|   (360) ....................................... 393 |   (1,907) ............................... 1,926 | Hackberry, Edwards .......................... 3 |
| *GRAND PRAIRIE, Dallas-Tarrant- | Gresham, Smith............................ 1,000 | Hackberry, Garza............................... 5 |
|   Ellis, 4,448, | GREY FOREST, Bexar, 22, | Hackberry, Lavaca........................... 40 |
|   (175,396) ...................... 184,144 |   (483) ..................................... 499 | Hagansport, Franklin ...................... 40 |
| *GRAND SALINE, Van Zandt, | Gribble Springs, Denton ................. 55 | Hagerville, Houston ........................ 70 |
|   140, (3,136) ....................... 3,147 | Grice, Upshur .................................. 20 | Hail, Fannin ..................................... 30 |
| Grandview, Dawson.......................... 8 | Griffith, Cochran ............................. 12 | Hainesville, Wood............................ 95 |
| Grandview, Gray............................. 13 | Grigsby, Shelby ............................... 15 | *HALE CENTER, Hale, 47, |
| *GRANDVIEW, Johnson, 103, | Grit, Mason ..................................... 15 |   (2,252) ............................... 2,156 |
|   (1,561) ............................... 1,603 | *GROESBECK, Limestone, 164, | Halfway, Hale................................. 165 |
| *GRANGER, Williamson, 43, |   (4,328) ............................... 4,223 | Hall, San Saba................................. 25 |
|   (1,419) ............................... 1,443 | *GROOM, Carson, 32, | *HALLETTSVILLE, Lavaca, 204, |
| Grangerland, Montgomery............ 300 |   (574) ..................................... 558 |   (2,550) ............................... 2,605 |
| *GRANITE SHOALS, Burnet, 72, | Grosvenor, Brown........................... 24 | Halls Bluff, Houston ........................ 67 |
|   (4,910) ............................... 5,042 | *GROVES, Jefferson, 349, | HALLSBURG, McLennan, 8, |
| GRANJENO, Hidalgo, 3, (293) ..... 296 |   (16,144) ........................... 15,800 |   (507) ..................................... 528 |
| Grape Creek, Tom Green, | *GROVETON, Trinity, 47, | *HALLSVILLE, Harrison, 110, |
|   (3,154) ............................... 3,174 |   (1,057) ..................................... 985 |   (3,577) ............................... 3,894 |

*The skyline of Hereford across the grain fields. Photo by Robert Plocheck.*

| Town, County ...............Pop. 2014 | Town, County ...............Pop. 2014 | Town, County ...............Pop. 2014 |
|---|---|---|
| *HALTOM CITY, Tarrant, 1,334, (42,409) ..............................43,735 | HEBRON, Denton, 50, (415) ........409 | Hilltop, Frio, (287) .........................311 |
| Hamby, Taylor...............................100 | Heckville, Lubbock.........................91 | Hilltop, Starr, (77)..........................81 |
| *HAMILTON, Hamilton, 186, (3,095) ................................2,977 | *HEDLEY, Donley, 7, (329)...........318 | *Hilltop Lakes, Leon, (1,101) .....1,109 |
| *HAMLIN, Jones-Fisher, 76, (2,124) ................................1,992 | Hedwigs Hill, Mason ......................12 | HILSHIRE VILLAGE, Harris, 25, (746) .................................779 |
| Hammond, Robertson ...................44 | HEDWIG VILLAGE, Harris, 256, (2,557) ................................2,664 | Hinckley, Lamar ..............................40 |
| Hamon, Gonzales ..........................20 | Hefner, Knox....................................3 | Hindes, Atascosa ...........................14 |
| *Hamshire, Jefferson, 15..............759 | Hegar, Waller................................100 | Hinkles Ferry, Brazoria ................100 |
| Hancock, Comal ..........................400 | Heidelberg, Hidalgo, (1,725)......1,851 | Hiram, Kaufman..............................75 |
| Hancock, Dawson ..........................20 | *Heidenheimer, Bell, 6 .................224 | *HITCHCOCK, Galveston, 192, (6,961) ................................7,326 |
| *Hankamer, Chambers, 8 .............226 | Helena, Karnes ..............................35 | Hitchland, Hansford .......................15 |
| Hannibal, Erath..............................25 | Helmic, Trinity ...............................86 | Hix, Burleson ..................................35 |
| Hanover, Milam...............................25 | *HELOTES, Bexar, 531, (7,341) ................................8,325 | Hoard, Wood ...................................45 |
| *HAPPY, Swisher-Randall, 18, (678) ...................................668 | *HEMPHILL, Sabine, 135, (1,198) ................................1,215 | Hobbs, Fisher .................................32 |
| Happy Union, Hale .........................25 | *HEMPSTEAD, Waller, 245, (5,770) ................................6,476 | *Hobson, Karnes, 7 ......................135 |
| Happy Valley, Taylor ......................12 | *HENDERSON, Rusk, 591, (13,712) ..............................13,637 | *Hochheim, DeWitt..........................70 |
| Harbin, Erath..................................21 | Henkhaus, Lavaca..........................88 | *Hockley, Harris, 107 ...................400 |
| *HARDIN, Liberty, 11, (819)..........869 | Henly, Hays ..................................140 | Hodges, Jones...............................150 |
| Hare, Williamson ...........................60 | *HENRIETTA, Clay, 126, (3,141) ................................3,175 | Hogansville, Rains.........................300 |
| *Hargill, Hidalgo, 3, (877) ...........900 | Henry's Chapel, Cherokee .............75 | Hogg, Burleson ...............................20 |
| *HARKER HEIGHTS, Bell, 616, (26,700) ............................28,233 | *HEREFORD, Deaf Smith, 463, (15,370) ..............................15,211 | Holiday Beach, Aransas, (514) .....557 |
| Harkeyville, San Saba ...................12 | Hermits Cove, Rains.......................40 | HOLIDAY LAKES, Brazoria, 6, (1,107) ................................1,183 |
| *Harleton, Harrison, 20 ...............390 | *Hermleigh, Scurry, 11, (345) .......360 | *HOLLAND, Bell, 55, (1,121).....1,126 |
| *HARLINGEN, Cameron, 2,176, (64,849) ............................66,415 | Hester, Navarro ..............................35 | Holland Quarters, Panola ...............40 |
| Harmon, Lamar ..............................12 | *HEWITT, McLennan, 357, (13,549) ..............................14,118 | *HOLLIDAY, Archer, 67, (1,758) ................................1,798 |
| Harmony, Floyd ..............................42 | *Hext, Menard................................75 | Holly, Houston ................................95 |
| Harmony, Grimes............................12 | HICKORY CREEK, Denton, 114, (3,247) ................................3,963 | Holly Grove, Polk ............................20 |
| Harmony, Kent................................10 | Hickory Creek, Houston..................31 | Holly Lake Ranch, Wood, (2,774) ................................2,973 |
| Harmony, Nacogdoches .................50 | Hickory Creek, Hunt .......................40 | Holly Springs, Jasper......................50 |
| *Harper, Gillespie, 35, (1,192) ................................1,283 | *HICO, Hamilton, 123, (1,379) ................................1,356 | HOLLYWOOD PARK, Bexar, 117, (3,062) ........................3,182 |
| Harpersville, Stephens ...................5 | *HIDALGO, Hidalgo, 476, (11,198) ..............................12,671 | Holman, Fayette ...........................101 |
| Harrison, McLennan .....................100 | Hidden Acres [Lakeshore Gardens-], San Patricio, (504)................520 | Homer, Angelina ...........................475 |
| *Harrold, Wilbarger, 4 .................200 | HIDEAWAY, Smith, (3,083)........3,135 | Homestead Meadows North, El Paso, (5,247).................5,399 |
| *HART, Castro, 35, (1,114) ................................1,088 | Higginbotham, Gaines ...................21 | Homestead Meadows South, El Paso, (7,247).................7,427 |
| Hartburg, Newton .........................893 | *HIGGINS, Lipscomb, 14, (397) ...................................428 | *HONDO, Medina, 296, (8,803) ................................9,080 |
| Hart Camp, Lamb .............................4 | High, Lamar ....................................14 | *HONEY GROVE, Fannin, 66, (1,668) ................................1,746 |
| *Hartley, Hartley, 20, (540) ...........553 | Highbank, Falls ..............................20 | Honey Island, Hardin ....................200 |
| Harvard, Camp ...............................48 | High Hill, Fayette ..........................176 | Hood, Cooke...................................13 |
| Harvey, Brazos ...........................1,000 | *High Island, Galveston, 7............300 | Hooker Ridge, Rains ....................250 |
| Harwell Point, Burnet....................138 | Highland, Erath..............................60 | *HOOKS, Bowie, 70, (2,769).....2,817 |
| *Harwood, Gonzales, 8.................118 | HIGHLAND HAVEN, Burnet, (431) ...................................437 | Hoover, Gray ....................................5 |
| *HASKELL, Haskell, 110, (3,322) ................................3,266 | HIGHLAND PARK, Dallas, 427, (8,564) ................................8,732 | Hoover, Lamar .................................20 |
| Haslam, Shelby ...........................100 | *Highlands, Harris, 106, (7,522) ................................7,695 | Hope, Lavaca ..................................45 |
| *HASLET, Tarrant, 191, (1,517) ................................1,667 | HIGHLAND VILLAGE, Denton, 508, (15,056) ..................15,703 | Hopewell, Franklin ..........................50 |
| Hasse, Comanche ..........................50 | Hightower, Liberty ........................225 | Hopewell, Houston ..........................22 |
| Hatchel, Runnels .............................6 | HILL COUNTRY VILLAGE, Bexar, 88, (985) ........................1,038 | Hopewell, Lamar..............................90 |
| Hatchettville, Hopkins ....................20 | Hillcrest, Colorado .........................25 | Hopewell, Red River .....................152 |
| Havana, Hidalgo, (407)..................417 | HILLCREST VILLAGE, Brazoria, (730) ...................................731 | Hopewell, Smith..............................45 |
| HAWK COVE, Hunt, 4, (483) ........496 | *Hillister, Tyler, 9 .........................250 | Hopewell [Dixon-], Houston............10 |
| *HAWKINS, Wood, 88, (1,278) ................................1,393 | Hillje, Wharton ...............................51 | HORIZON CITY, El Paso, 200, (16,735) ..............................19,266 |
| *HAWLEY, Jones, 34, (634)..........602 | Hills, Lee .........................................20 | Hornsby Bend, Travis, (6,791)...7,145 |
| Hawthorne, Walker .......................100 | *HILLSBORO, Hill, 378, (8,456) ................................8,235 | HORSESHOE BAY, Llano-Burnet, 163, (3,418) ........................3,458 |
| Haynesville, Wichita .......................65 | Hillside Acres, Webb, (30 .............34 | Hortense, Polk ................................20 |
| HAYS, Hays, 6, (217) ...................234 | | Horton, Delta ...................................40 |
| Hazeldell, Comanche .....................12 | | Horton, Panola ..............................200 |
| H. Cuellar Estates, Starr, (20).........19 | | *HOUSTON, Harris-Fort Bend-Montgomery, 86,437, (2,100,263) ................2,201,974 |
| *HEARNE, Robertson, 154, (4,459) ................................4,486 | | Howard, Ellis...................................60 |
| HEATH, Rockwall-Kaufman, 249, (6,921) ................................7,704 | | HOWARDWICK, Donley, 10, (402) ...................................393 |
| *Hebbronville, Jim Hogg, 97, (4,558) ................................4,468 | | |

| Town, County ............... Pop. 2014 | Town, County ............... Pop. 2014 | Town, County ............... Pop. 2014 |
|---|---|---|
| *HOWE, Grayson, 74, (2,600) ................................ 2,585 | Indio, Starr, (50) .............................. 54 | JOLLY, Clay, 6, (172) ................... 184 |
| Howland, Lamar ............................ 65 | *INDUSTRY, Austin, 38, (304) ...... 315 | Jollyville, Williamson-Travis, (16,151) .......................... 16,852 |
| Hoxie, Williamson .......................... 60 | *Inez, Victoria, 37, (2,098) ......... 2,196 | Jonah, Williamson .......................... 60 |
| Hoyte, Milam.................................. 20 | *INGLESIDE, San Patricio, 244, (9,387) .............................. 9,605 | *Jonesboro, Coryell-Hamilton, 5... 125 |
| Hub, Parmer .................................. 25 | INGLESIDE-ON-THE-BAY, San Patricio, 18, (615).......... 625 | JONES CREEK, Brazoria, 25, (2,020) .............................. 2,088 |
| Hubbard, Bowie ............................ 350 | *INGRAM, Kerr, 158, (1,804)..... 1,846 | Jones Prairie, Milam ...................... 20 |
| *HUBBARD, Hill, 56, (1,423) ..... 1,374 | *IOLA, Grimes, 11, (401) ............ 430 | JONESTOWN, Travis, 95, (1,834) .............................. 2,050 |
| Huber, Shelby ................................ 15 | IOWA COLONY, Brazoria, 22, (1,170) .............................. 1,188 | *Jonesville, Harrison, 3................... 70 |
| Huckabay, Erath ........................... 150 | *IOWA PARK, Wichita, 174, (6,355) .............................. 6,501 | Joplin, Jack ................................... 15 |
| HUDSON, Angelina, 74, (4,731) .............................. 4,779 | *Ira, Scurry, 12............................. 250 | Joppa, Burnet ................................ 84 |
| Hudson Bend, Travis, (2,981)... 3,082 | *IRAAN, Pecos, 60, (1,229)....... 1,273 | Jordans Store, Shelby .................... 20 |
| HUDSON OAKS, Parker, 121, (1,662) .............................. 1,917 | *IREDELL, Bosque, 14, (339)...... 332 | *JOSEPHINE, Collin, 21, (812) .............................. 1,029 |
| Huffines, Cass ............................. 140 | Ireland, Coryell ............................. 60 | *JOSHUA, Johnson, 273, (5,910) .............................. 6,090 |
| *Huffman, Harris, 131 ............. 15,000 | Irene, Hill .................................... 170 | Josserand, Trinity .......................... 29 |
| Hufsmith, Harris........................... 500 | Ironton, Cherokee....................... 110 | Jot-Em-Down, Delta ........................ 8 |
| *HUGHES SPRINGS, Cass, 61, (1,760) .............................. 1,809 | *IRVING, Dallas, 6,590, (216,290) ...................... 230,662 | *JOURDANTON, Atascosa, 132, (3,871) ....................... 4,135 |
| *Hull, Liberty, 16, (669) ............. 693 | Isla, Sabine................................. 350 | Joy, Clay ..................................... 110 |
| *HUMBLE, Harris, 1,843, (15,133) ........................... 15,480 | Israel, Polk.................................... 25 | Jozye, Madison.............................. 36 |
| *Hungerford, Wharton, 15, (347) .............................. 335 | *ITALY, Ellis, 54, (1,863) ........... 1,890 | Juarez, Cameron, (1,017)......... 1,084 |
| *Hunt, Kerr, 40 ............................. 708 | *ITASCA, Hill, 54, (1,644) ......... 1,597 | Jud, Haskell .................................. 60 |
| Hunter, Comal................................ 40 | Ivan, Stephens.............................. 15 | *Judson, Gregg, 4.................... 1,057 |
| HUNTERS CREEK VILLAGE, Harris, 113, (4,367) ...................... 4,523 | *Ivanhoe, Fannin, 8 .................... 110 | Juliff, Fort Bend ........................... 100 |
| *HUNTINGTON, Angelina, 110, (2,118) .............................. 2,148 | IVANHOE, Tyler, (887)............... 1,455 | Jumbo, Panola................................ 60 |
| Huntoon, Ochiltree........................ 22 | Izoro, Lampasas............................ 17 | *JUNCTION, Kimble, 174, (2,574) .............................. 2,667 |
| *HUNTSVILLE, Walker, 1,066, (38,548) ........................... 40,125 | **J** | Justiceburg, Garza, 3 ..................... 45 |
| Hurley, Wood ................................ 30 | *JACINTO CITY, Harris, 198, (10,553) ........................... 10,760 | *JUSTIN, Denton, 182, (3,246) .............................. 3,277 |
| Hurlwood, Lubbock ....................... 152 | *JACKSBORO, Jack, 171, (4,511) .............................. 4,565 | |
| Hurnville, Clay ............................... 10 | Jackson, Shelby ............................ 50 | **K** |
| *HURST, Tarrant, 1,625, (37,337) ........................... 38,598 | Jackson, Van Zandt....................... 25 | Kalgary, Crosby ............................... 2 |
| Hurstown, Shelby .......................... 20 | *JACKSONVILLE, Cherokee, 716, (14,544) ........................... 15,236 | *Kamay, Wichita, 8 ...................... 640 |
| Hurst Springs, Coryell..................... 10 | Jacobia, Hunt................................ 60 | Kamey, Calhoun.............................. 25 |
| *HUTCHINS, Dallas, 116, (5,338) .............................. 5,283 | Jakes Colony, Guadalupe.............. 95 | Kanawha, Red River ....................... 90 |
| *HUTTO, Williamson, 383, (14,698) ........................... 18,371 | JAMAICA BEACH, Galveston, 39, (983) .............................. 1,014 | *Karnack, Harrison, 24 ................. 350 |
| HUXLEY, Shelby, 4, (385) ............. 390 | James, Shelby ............................... 75 | *KARNES CITY, Karnes, 87, (3,042) .............................. 3,183 |
| *Hye, Blanco, 9............................. 72 | Jamestown, Newton ..................... 196 | Karon, Live Oak............................. 25 |
| Hylton, Nolan ................................... 6 | Jamestown, Smith ......................... 75 | Katemcy, Mason............................. 80 |
| | Jardin de San Juan, Starr, (22)....... 22 | *KATY, Harris-Waller-Fort Bend, 2,438, (14,102) .......... 15,094 |
| **I** | *JARRELL, Williamson, 89, (984) .............................. 1,022 | *KAUFMAN, Kaufman, 343, (6,703) .............................. 6,829 |
| Iago, Wharton, (161)..................... 159 | *JASPER, Jasper, 469, (7,590) .............................. 7,595 | K-Bar Ranch, Jim Wells (358) ...... 370 |
| Ida, Grayson .................................. 30 | *JAYTON, Kent, 20, (534) ............ 516 | Keechi, Leon.................................. 15 |
| *IDALOU, Lubbock, 81, (2,250) .............................. 2,365 | Jean, Young ................................. 110 | *KEENE, Johnson, 120, (6,106) .............................. 6,176 |
| Iglesia Antigua, Cameron, (413)... 442 | *JEFFERSON, Marion, 239, (2,106) .............................. 2,011 | Keeter, Wise ................................ 250 |
| Ike, Ellis ....................................... 50 | Jenkins, Morris ............................ 350 | Keith, Grimes.................................. 50 |
| Illinois Bend, Montague ................. 40 | Jennings, Lamar ............................ 85 | *KELLER, Tarrant, 1,481, (39,627) ........................... 43,572 |
| IMPACT, Taylor, (35)...................... 34 | *Jermyn, Jack, 3 ........................... 75 | Kellerville, Wheeler ........................ 15 |
| *Imperial, Pecos, 5, (278)............. 287 | JERSEY VILLAGE, Harris, 257, (7,620) .............................. 7,890 | Kellogg, Hunt ................................ 20 |
| Inadale, Scurry ............................. 12 | *JEWETT, Leon, 66, (1,167) .............................. 1,147 | Kellyville, Marion ........................... 75 |
| Independence, Washington.......... 140 | JF Villarreal, Starr, (104)............... 105 | Kelsey, Upshur .............................. 50 |
| India, Ellis .................................... 30 | Jiba, Kaufman................................ 50 | Kelton, Wheeler ............................ 34 |
| Indian Creek, Brown....................... 28 | *JOAQUIN, Shelby, 52, (824)....... 851 | *KEMAH, Galveston, 308, (1,773) .............................. 1,923 |
| Indian Creek, Smith ..................... 300 | Joe Lee, Bell................................... 8 | *KEMP, Kaufman, 104, (1,154) .............................. 1,197 |
| Indian Gap, Hamilton..................... 35 | *JOHNSON CITY, Blanco, 143, (1,656) .............................. 1,724 | Kemper City, Victoria ..................... 16 |
| Indian Hill, Newton.......................... 7 | Johnsville, Erath ............................ 45 | *KEMPNER, Lampasas, 70, (1,089) .............................. 1,159 |
| Indian Hills, Hidalgo, (2,591) ..... 2,782 | Johntown, Red River ................... 175 | *Kendalia, Kendall, 8 ................... 149 |
| INDIAN LAKE, Cameron, (640)... 670 | *Joinerville, Rusk .......................... 140 | *KENDLETON, Fort Bend, 10, (380) .............................. 371 |
| Indianola, Calhoun ....................... 200 | Joliet, Caldwell.............................. 70 | |
| Indian Rock, Upshur....................... 45 | | |
| Indian Springs, Polk, (785) .......... 828 | | |
| Indio, Presidio................................. 5 | | |

| Town, County ................ Pop. 2014 | Town, County ................ Pop. 2014 | Town, County ................ Pop. 2014 |
|---|---|---|
| La Paloma-Lost Creek, Nueces, (408) ........................ 407 | Laureles, Cameron, (3,692) ....... 3,839 | *LEON VALLEY, Bexar, 489, (10,151) ............................ 10,893 |
| La Paloma Ranchettes, Starr, (239) ...................................... 250 | Lavender, Limestone ...................... 30 | *LEROY, McLennan, 11, (337) ..... 347 |
| La Parita, Atascosa ........................ 48 | *LA VERNIA, Wilson, 151, (1,034) ................................ 1,200 | Lesley, Hall ...................................... 25 |
| *LA PORTE, Harris, 912, (33,800) ............................ 34,839 | La Victoria, Starr, (171) ................ 175 | *LEVELLAND, Hockley, 482, (13,542) ............................ 14,017 |
| La Presa, Webb, (319) ................. 329 | *LA VILLA, Hidalgo, 18, (1,957) ................................ 1,952 | Leverett's Chapel, Rusk ............... 400 |
| *La Pryor, Zavala, 15, (1,643)... 1,747 | *LAVON, Collin, 88, (2,219) ....... 2,470 | Levi, McLennan ............................... 50 |
| La Puerta, Starr, (632) ................. 642 | *LA WARD, Jackson, 7, (213) ...... 224 | Levita, Coryell ................................. 70 |
| *LAREDO, Webb, 6,235, (236,091) ........................ 254,190 | *LAWN, Taylor, 6, (314) ............... 321 | *LEWISVILLE, Denton, 3,625, (95,290) ...................... 100,237 |
| Laredo Ranchettes, Webb, (22) ..... 20 | Lawrence, Kaufman ...................... 259 | *LEXINGTON, Lee, 79, (1,177) ................................ 1,149 |
| La Reforma, Starr ........................... 20 | *Lazbuddie, Parmer, 9 ................. 248 | *LIBERTY, Liberty, 443, (8,397) ................................ 9,028 |
| Lariat, Parmer ............................... 100 | *LEAGUE CITY, Galveston-Harris, 2,409, (83,560) ................ 92,669 | Liberty, Lubbock ........................... 228 |
| La Rosita, Starr, (85) ..................... 89 | Leagueville, Henderson ................. 50 | Liberty, Milam ................................. 40 |
| *Larue, Henderson, 17 ................. 250 | *LEAKEY, Real, 65, (425) ............. 430 | Liberty, Newton ............................. 128 |
| *LaSalle, Jackson ......................... 110 | *LEANDER, Williamson, 909, (26,521) ............................ 32,276 | Liberty City, Gregg, (2,351) ....... 2,397 |
| Lasana, Cameron, (84) ................... 85 | LEARY, Bowie, 8, (495) ............... 509 | Liberty Hill, Houston ...................... 73 |
| *Lasara, Willacy, 3, (1,039) ....... 1,046 | *Ledbetter, Fayette, 13 .................. 83 | Liberty Hill, Milam .......................... 25 |
| Las Escobas, Starr ........................... 5 | Leedale, Bell .................................. 24 | *LIBERTY HILL, Williamson, 278, (967) ........................ 1,053 |
| Las Haciendas, Webb, (7) ............... 7 | *Leesburg, Camp, 13 .................... 128 | Lilbert, Nacogdoches ................... 100 |
| Las Lomas, Starr, (3,147) .......... 3,189 | *Leesville, Gonzales, 3 ................. 152 | *Lillian, Johnson, 12 ................... 1,160 |
| Las Lomitas, Jim Hogg, (244) ....... 232 | *LEFORS, Gray, 18, (497) ............. 520 | *Lincoln, Lee, 11 ........................... 336 |
| Las Palmas, Zapata, (67) ............... 66 | *Leggett, Polk, 6 ........................... 500 | LINCOLN PARK, Denton, 9, (308) .............................. 332 |
| Las Palmas II, Cameron, (1,605) ............................... 1,722 | Lehman, Cochran ............................. 6 | *LINDALE, Smith, 406, (4,818) ................................ 5,365 |
| Las Pilas, Webb, (28) ..................... 32 | Leigh, Harrison ............................... 60 | *LINDEN, Cass, 94, (1,988) ....... 2,022 |
| Las Quintas Fronterizas, Maverick, (3,290) ................ 3,436 | Lela, Wheeler ............................... 135 | Lindenau, DeWitt ............................ 50 |
| Lassater, Marion ............................. 60 | *Lelia Lake, Donley, 1 .................... 70 | Lindendale, Kendall ........................ 70 |
| Las Yescas, Cameron ................... 221 | *Leming, Atascosa, 4, (946) ...... 1,011 | *LINDSAY, Cooke, 22, (1,018) ................................ 1,082 |
| Latch, Upshur ................................. 50 | *Lenorah, Martin, 5 ........................ 83 | Lindsay, Reeves, (271) ................ 267 |
| Latex, Harrison ............................... 75 | Lenz, Karnes ................................... 50 | *Lingleville, Erath, 1 ..................... 100 |
| *LATEXO, Houston, 7, (322) ........ 334 | Leo, Cooke ..................................... 20 | Linn Flat, Nacogdoches ................. 60 |
| La Tina Ranch, Cameron, (618) ... 656 | Leo, Lee .......................................... 10 | *Linn [San Manuel-], Hidalgo, 7, (801) ...................................... 831 |
| Latium, Washington ........................ 30 | *LEONA, Leon, 13, (175) ............. 171 | |
| Laughlin Air Force Base, Val Verde, (1,569) .............. 1,648 | *LEONARD, Fannin, 104, (1,990) ................................ 2,063 | |
| Laurel, Newton ............................. 357 | Leon Junction, Coryell ................... 50 | |
| | Leon Springs, Bexar, ................. [part of San Antonio] | |

*Signs on the approach to the liquor store in Los Ybañez warn of the troubles from alcohol. Photo by Robert Plocheck.*

| Town, County ...............Pop. 2014 | Town, County ...............Pop. 2014 | Town, County ...............Pop. 2014 |
|---|---|---|
| Linwood, Cherokee...................... 40 | Longpoint, Washington .................. 30 | Luther, Howard ............................... 3 |
| *LIPAN, Hood, 42, (430).............. 442 | *LONGVIEW, Gregg-Harrison, | Lutie, Collingsworth ....................... 10 |
| *Lipscomb, Lipscomb, 1, (37)......... 38 | 3,705, (80,455)................... 82.314 | Lydia, Red River ........................... 109 |
| *Lissie, Wharton, 4 ...................... 72 | Longworth, Fisher........................... 47 | *LYFORD, Willacy, 34, |
| Littig, Travis ................................ 35 | Looneyville, Nacogdoches............. 50 | (2,611) .............................. 2,579 |
| Little Cypress, Orange................. 900 | *Loop, Gaines, 8, (225) ............... 235 | Lynn Grove, Grimes ...................... 25 |
| *LITTLE ELM, Denton, 578, | *Lopeño, Zapata, (174)................ 180 | *Lyons, Burleson, 5 .................... 360 |
| (25,898) ............................ 34,145 | Lopezville, Hidalgo, (4,333)....... 4,466 | *LYTLE, Atascosa-Medina-Bexar, |
| *LITTLEFIELD, Lamb, 200, | *LORAINE, Mitchell, 13, | 148, (2,492) ..................... 2,762 |
| (6,372) .............................. 6,238 | (602) ................................... 592 | Lytton Springs, Caldwell .............. 300 |
| Little Hope, Wood ......................... 25 | *LORENA, McLennan, 140, | |
| Little Midland, Burnet................... 82 | (1,691) .............................. 1,740 | **M** |
| Little New York, Gonzales ............. 15 | *LORENZO, Crosby, 27, | *MABANK, Kaufman-Henderson, |
| *LITTLE RIVER-ACADEMY, Bell, | (1,147) .............................. 1,149 | 208, (3,035).................... 3,108 |
| 35, (1,961) ......................... 1,949 | Los Altos, Webb, (140) ................ 147 | Mabelle, Baylor.............................. 9 |
| Lively, Kaufman ........................... 50 | Los Alvarez, Starr, (303).............. 299 | Mabry, Red River ........................... 60 |
| LIVE OAK, Bexar, 380, | Los Angeles, La Salle ................... 15 | *Macdona, Bexar, 2, (559)........... 613 |
| (13,131) ............................ 14,974 | Los Angeles Subdivision, Willacy, | Macon, Franklin ............................ 21 |
| *LIVERPOOL, Brazoria, 16, | (121) ................................... 127 | Macune, San Augustine................ 50 |
| (482) ................................... 493 | Los Arcos, Webb, (127) .................... | *MADISONVILLE, Madison, 198, |
| *LIVINGSTON, Polk, 584, | Los Arrieros, Starr, (91) ................ 94 | (4,396) .............................. 4,708 |
| (5,335) .............................. 5,390 | Los Barreras, Starr, (288)............. 289 | Madras, Red River......................... 61 |
| *LLANO, Llano, 264, | Los Centenarios, Webb, (87).........91 | Magnet, Wharton .......................... 42 |
| (3,232) .............................. 3,306 | Los Corralitos, Webb, (35)............. 36 | *MAGNOLIA, Montgomery, 531, |
| Llano Grande, Hidalgo, | *Los Ebanos, Hidalgo, 1, | (1,393) .............................. 1,584 |
| (3,008) .............................. 3,090 | (335) ................................... 346 | Magnolia, San Jacinto ................. 150 |
| Lobo, Culberson ........................... 15 | Los Ebanos, Starr, (280).............. 285 | Magnolia Beach, Calhoun ........... 250 |
| Locker, San Saba ......................... 16 | Los Escondidos, Burnet................ 80 | Magnolia Springs, Jasper ............. 20 |
| Lockett, Wilbarger....................... 150 | *LOS FRESNOS, Cameron, | Maha, Travis ............................... 200 |
| Lockettville, Hockley .................... 20 | 159, (5,542) ...................... 6,317 | Mahl, Nacogdoches ..................... 150 |
| *LOCKHART, Caldwell, 446, | Los Fresnos, Webb, (67).............. 71 | Mahomet, Burnet........................... 97 |
| (12,698) ............................ 13,098 | Los Huisaches, Webb, (17)........... 17 | Majors, Franklin ........................... 13 |
| *LOCKNEY, Floyd, 56, | *LOS INDIOS, Cameron, 20, | *MALAKOFF, Henderson, 110, |
| (1,842) .............................. 1,752 | (1,083) .............................. 1,117 | (2,324) .............................. 2,313 |
| Locust, Grayson .......................... 118 | Los Lobos, Zapata, (9) ................... 8 | Mallard, Montague ....................... 12 |
| *Lodi, Marion ............................. 175 | Los Minerales, Webb, (20) ............ 20 | *MALONE, Hill, 19, (269)............. 270 |
| Loebau, Lee.................................. 35 | Los Nopalitos, Webb, (62)............. 64 | Malta, Bowie ............................... 350 |
| Logan, Panola .............................. 40 | Losoya, Bexar.............................. 500 | Malvern, Leon ............................... 12 |
| LOG CABIN, Henderson, 6, | LOS SAENZ [Roma-], Starr, 218, | Mambrino, Hood ........................... 74 |
| (714) ................................... 710 | (9,765) .............................. 9,830 | *Manchaca, Travis, 96, |
| *Lohn, McCulloch, 3 .................... 149 | Lost Creek, Travis, (4,509) ........ 4,646 | (1,133) .............................. 1,194 |
| Loire, Wilson................................ 50 | Lost Creek [La Paloma-], Nueces, | Manchester, Red River ................ 185 |
| Lois, Cooke................................. 10 | (408) ................................... 407 | Mangum, Eastland........................ 15 |
| *Lolita, Jackson, 9, (555).............. 564 | Lost Prairie, Limestone.................... 2 | Manheim, Lee............................... 50 |
| Loma Alta, McMullen .................... 25 | Los Veteranos I, Webb, (24).......... 25 | Mankin, Henderson ...................... 30 |
| Loma Alta, Val Verde .................... 30 | Los Veteranos II, Webb, (24)......... 28 | Mankins, Archer ........................... 10 |
| Loma Grande, Zavala, (107) ........ 110 | LOS YBANEZ, Dawson, 2, (19)..... 20 | *MANOR, Travis, 187, |
| Loma Linda, San Patricio, (122)... 122 | *LOTT, Falls, 42, (759) ................ 740 | (5,037) .............................. 6,443 |
| Loma Linda East, Jim Wells, | *Louise, Wharton, 31, (995)....... 1,011 | *MANSFIELD, Tarrant-Johnson- |
| (254) ................................... 268 | Lovelace, Hill ................................ 30 | Ellis, 1,861, (56,368)...... 62,022 |
| Loma Linda East, Starr, (44).......... 45 | *LOVELADY, Houston, 28, | Manuel Garcia, Starr, (203) ........ 212 |
| Loma Linda West, Starr, (114)..... 123 | (649) ................................... 652 | Manuel Garcia II, Starr, (77) ......... 76 |
| Loma Vista, Starr, (160)................ 161 | *Loving, Young, 2........................ 300 | *MANVEL, Brazoria, 226, |
| Lomax, Howard ............................ 25 | *Lowake, Concho, 1 ..................... 40 | (5,179) .............................. 6,530 |
| *LOMETA, Lampasas, 47, | LOWRY CROSSING, Collin, 52, | *Maple, Bailey.............................. 40 |
| (856) ................................... 909 | (1,711) .............................. 1,702 | Maple, Red River........................... 30 |
| *London, Kimble, 4 ..................... 180 | Loyal Valley, Mason...................... 52 | Maple Springs, Titus .................... 25 |
| Lone Camp, Palo Pinto ............... 110 | Loyola Beach, Kleberg ................. 195 | Mapleton, Houston ....................... 32 |
| Lone Cedar, Ellis ......................... 18 | *Lozano, Cameron, 2, (404) ........ 429 | *Marathon, Brewster, 17, |
| Lone Grove, Llano ........................ 50 | *LUBBOCK, Lubbock, 7,908, | (430) .................................. 451 |
| Lone Oak, Colorado ...................... 50 | (229,573) ........................ 243,994 | *MARBLE FALLS, Burnet, 683, |
| *LONE OAK, Hunt, 51, (598)........ 632 | LUCAS, Collin, 156, (5,166) ...... 6,120 | (6,077).............................. 6,208 |
| Lone Pine, Houston ...................... 81 | Luckenbach, Gillespie .................. 25 | *MARFA, Presidio, 145, |
| Lone Star, Cherokee..................... 20 | *LUEDERS, Jones, 17, (346) ....... 333 | (1,981) .............................. 1,976 |
| Lone Star, Floyd .......................... 42 | Luella, Grayson ........................... 639 | Margaret, Foard............................ 50 |
| Lone Star, Lamar.......................... 35 | *LUFKIN, Angelina, 1,715, | Marie, Runnels ............................ 10 |
| *LONE STAR, Morris, 44, | (35,067) .......................... 36,656 | *MARIETTA, Cass, 2, (134)......... 137 |
| (1,581) .............................. 1,657 | *LULING, Caldwell, 257, | *MARION, Guadalupe, 106, |
| *Long Branch, Panola, 2.............. 150 | (5,411) .............................. 5,626 | (1,066) .............................. 1,072 |
| Long Lake, Anderson.................... 30 | *LUMBERTON, Hardin, 460, | *Markham, Matagorda, 16, |
| Long Mott, Calhoun ...................... 76 | (11,943) .......................... 12,743 | (1,082) .............................. 1,082 |
| Longoria, Starr, (92)..................... 93 | Lums Chapel, Lamb ....................... 6 | Markley, Young ............................. 25 |

CITIES & TOWNS

| Town, County .............. Pop. 2014 | Town, County .............. Pop. 2014 | Town, County .............. Pop. 2014 |
|---|---|---|
| *MARLIN, Falls, 177, (5,967)..... 5,740 | McMilln, San Saba......................... 15 | Midway, Polk, 525 |
| Marlow, Milam................................. 45 | McNair, Harris.......................... 2,039 | Midway North, Hidalgo, |
| *MARQUEZ, Leon, 27, (263)........ 259 | McNary, Hudspeth ..................... 100 | (4,752) ............................... 4,951 |
| Mars, Van Zandt, Henderson.......... 20 | McNeil, Caldwell ......................... 50 | Midway South, Hidalgo, |
| *MARSHALL, Harrison, 927, | *McQueeney, Guadalupe, 43, | (2,239) ............................... 2,354 |
| (23,523) ............................ 24,036 | (2,545).............................. 2,588 | Midyett, Panola............................ 150 |
| Marston, Polk................................. 25 | *MEADOW, Terry, 11, (593).......... 590 | Miguel Barrera, Starr, (128).......... 136 |
| *MART, McLennan, 58, | Meadow Grove, Bell ...................... 22 | MIkes, Starr, (910)...................... 956 |
| (1,897).............................. 1,912 | MEADOWLAKES, Burnet, 18, | Mikeska, Live Oak ........................ 10 |
| *MARTINDALE, Caldwell, 50, | (1,777).............................. 1,848 | Mila Doce, Hidalgo, (6,222)...... 6,659 |
| (1,116) ............................... 1,166 | MEADOWS PLACE, Fort Bend, | *Milam, Sabine, 11, (1,480) ....... 1,535 |
| Martinez, Starr, (69)....................... 70 | 105, (4,660) ..................... 4,669 | *MILANO, Milam, 29, (428) ....... 409 |
| Martins Mill, Van Zandt................ 158 | Mecca, Madison ........................... 48 | Milburn, McCulloch ........................ 8 |
| Martin Springs, Hopkins ............. 200 | Medicine Mound, Hardeman .......... 25 | MILDRED, Navarro, 6, (368)........ 388 |
| *Martinsville, Nacogdoches, 1 ...... 350 | Medill, Lamar................................ 50 | *MILES, Runnels, 43, (829)........ 827 |
| Marvin, Lamar................................ 48 | *Medina, Bandera, 24.................. 850 | *MILFORD, Ellis, 23, (728)........ 737 |
| Maryetta, Jack................................. 7 | Medina, Zapata, (3,935) ........... 4,150 | Mill Creek, Washington.................. 40 |
| *Maryneal, Nolan, 5 ....................... 50 | Meeker, Jefferson ..................... 2,280 | Miller Grove, Hopkins ................. 115 |
| Marysville, Cooke .......................... 12 | Meeks, Bell..................................... 6 | MILLERS COVE, Titus, 4, |
| *MASON, Mason, 208, | *MEGARGEL, Archer, 11, | (149)................................. 154 |
| (2,114) ............................... 2,234 | (203) ................................. 201 | *Millersview, Concho, 3 ................ 80 |
| Massey Lake, Anderson ................ 30 | *MELISSA, Collin, 153, | Millett, La Salle ........................... 60 |
| Masterson, Moore, 2......................... 2 | (4,695) .............................. 6,245 | Millheim, Austin.......................... 170 |
| *MATADOR, Motley, 36, (607)...... 592 | Melrose, Nacogdoches............... 400 | *Millican, Brazos, 6, (240)......... 239 |
| *Matagorda, Matagorda, 22, | *MELVIN, McCulloch, 5, (178)...... 181 | *MILLSAP, Parker, 43, |
| (503) ................................. 520 | *MEMPHIS, Hall, 84, | (403)................................. 419 |
| *MATHIS, San Patricio, 132, | (2,290) .............................. 2,252 | Milo Center, Deaf Smith.................. 5 |
| (4,942) ............................... 4,973 | *MENARD, Menard, 73, | Milton, Lamar................................ 50 |
| Matthews, Colorado........................ 20 | (1,471) .............................. 1,461 | Mims, Brazoria............................ 160 |
| *MAUD, Bowie, 35, (1,056) ....... 1,071 | Mendoza, Caldwell ..................... 100 | *Minden, Rusk, 4 ........................ 150 |
| *Mauriceville, Orange, 15, | Menlow, Hill ................................. 12 | *MINEOLA, Wood, 404, |
| (3,252)............................... 3,384 | *Mentone, Loving, 2, (19) ............. 20 | (4,515) ............................... 4,721 |
| Maverick, Runnels .......................... 35 | Mentz, Colorado ......................... 100 | Mineral, Bee ................................. 65 |
| Maxdale, Bell ................................. 25 | *MERCEDES, Hidalgo, 484, | *MINERAL WELLS, Palo Pinto- |
| Maxey, Lamar.................................. 70 | (15,570).......................... 16,556 | Parker, 642, (16,788)........ 17,123 |
| *Maxwell, Caldwell, 22................. 500 | Mercury, McCulloch ..................... 166 | Minerva, Milam............................ 100 |
| *May, Brown, 17 ........................... 270 | *Mereta, Tom Green .................... 131 | Mings Chapel, Upshur.................... 50 |
| *Maydelle, Cherokee ................... 250 | *MERIDIAN, Bosque, 75, | *MINGUS, Palo Pinto, 22, |
| Mayfield, Hale................................ 26 | (1,493) .............................. 1,498 | (235)................................. 237 |
| Mayfield, Hill ................................. 25 | *Merit, Hunt, 2............................. 225 | Minter, Lamar................................ 78 |
| Mayflower, Newton ........................ 50 | *MERKEL, Taylor, 97, (2,590).... 2,637 | Mi Ranchito Estate, Starr, (281) ... 275 |
| Maynard, San Jacinto..................... 90 | Merle, Burleson ............................ 10 | *Mirando City, Webb, 13, (375) .... 392 |
| *MAYPEARL, Ellis, 49, (934)..... 1,322 | Merriman, Eastland ....................... 14 | *MISSION, Hidalgo, 1,753, |
| Maysfield, Milam.......................... 140 | *MERTENS, Hill, 4, (125) ............ 129 | (77,058) ........................... 81,581 |
| *McAdoo, Dickens, 2 ..................... 75 | *MERTZON, Irion, 49, (781)......... 852 | Mission Bend, Fort Bend-Harris, |
| *McALLEN, Hidalgo, 5,182, | *MESQUITE, Dallas-Kaufman, | (36,501) ........................... 37,824 |
| (129,877) ......................... 138,356 | 3,262, (139,824) ........... 144,330 | Mission Valley, Victoria ................ 225 |
| McBeth, Brazoria............................ 20 | Mesquite, Starr, (505)................. 523 | *MISSOURI CITY, Fort Bend-Harris, |
| *McCAMEY, Upton, 53, | Metcalf Gap, Palo Pinto.................... 6 | 1,784, (67,358) ................ 68,473 |
| (1,887).............................. 1,860 | *MEXIA, Limestone, 314, | Mixon, Cherokee .......................... 50 |
| *McCaulley, Fisher, 1 ..................... 96 | (7,459).............................. 7,313 | *MOBEETIE, Wheeler, 6, |
| McClanahan, Falls.......................... 30 | *Meyersville, DeWitt, 8 ............... 110 | (101) ................................. 112 |
| McCook, Hidalgo ............................ 50 | Meyersville, Washington............... 15 | MOBILE CITY, Rockwall, 3, |
| McCoy, Atascosa ............................ 30 | *MIAMI, Roberts, 25, (597).......... 584 | (188) ................................. 185 |
| McCoy, Floyd ................................. 20 | Mico, Medina .............................. 107 | Moffat, Bell............................... 1,406 |
| McCoy, Kaufman ............................ 20 | Midcity, Lamar .............................. 50 | Moffett, Angelina ........................ 100 |
| McCoy, Panola ............................... 30 | Middleton, Leon ........................... 26 | Moline, Lampasas ......................... 32 |
| McCoy, Red River......................... 175 | *Midfield, Matagorda, 1............... 305 | *MONAHANS, Ward, 280, |
| *McDade, Bastrop, 16, (685)........ 731 | *Midkiff, Upton, 13 ...................... 182 | (6,953) ............................... 7,569 |
| *McFaddin, Victoria ....................... 50 | *MIDLAND, Midland-Martin, | Monaville, Waller ........................ 180 |
| McGirk, Hamilton ........................... 18 | 4,640, (111,147)............. 127,598 | Monkstown, Fannin ....................... 35 |
| *McGREGOR, McLennan, 210, | *MIDLOTHIAN, Ellis, 639, | Monroe, Rusk ............................... 96 |
| (4,987).............................. 5,063 | (18,037) ........................... 20,183 | Monroe City, Chambers.................... 5 |
| *McKINNEY, Collin, 3,960, | Midway, Dawson............................ 12 | Mont, Lavaca ................................ 30 |
| (131,117) ......................... 150,033 | Midway, Fannin............................. 51 | *Montague, Montague, 13, |
| McKinney Acres, Andrews, | Midway, Jim Wells ........................ 24 | (304)................................. 316 |
| (815) ................................. 927 | Midway, Limestone .......................... 9 | *Montalba, Anderson, 14 ............. 110 |
| *McLEAN, Gray, 28, (778)........... 814 | *MIDWAY, Madison, 15, (228) ...... 236 | *MONT BELVIEU, Chambers, 161, |
| McLENDON-CHISHOLM, Rockwall, | Midway, Red River......................... 40 | (3,835) ............................... 4,418 |
| 3, (1,373) ......................... 1,672 | Midway, Titus ............................. 110 | Monte Alto, Hidalgo, (1,924)...... 2,036 |
| *McLeod, Cass, 6 ........................ 600 | Midway, Upshur ............................ 20 | Monte Grande, Cameron................ 97 |
| McMahan, Caldwell ....................... 90 | Midway, Van Zandt ........................ 31 | Montell, Uvalde............................. 20 |

CITIES & TOWNS

| Town, County ............... Pop. 2014 | Town, County ............... Pop. 2014 | Town, County ............... Pop. 2014 |
|---|---|---|
| *MONTGOMERY, Montgomery, 470, (621) .............................. 682 | *Mumford, Robertson, 2 ............... 170 | Newburg, Comanche ..................... 32 |
| Monthalia, Gonzales ..................... 32 | *MUNDAY, Knox, 37, (1,300) ..... 1,191 | Newby, Leon .................................. 40 |
| Monticello, Titus ............................. 20 | Munger, Limestone ........................... 5 | *New Caney, Montgomery, 195 ..................................... 6,800 |
| *MOODY, McLennan, 73, (1,371) ............................... 1,400 | Mungerville, Dawson ..................... 20 | *NEWCASTLE, Young, 25, (585) ................................. 593 |
| *Moore, Frio, 17, (475) ................. 509 | Muniz, Hidalgo, (1,370) ............. 1,474 | NEW CHAPEL HILL, Smith, 7, (594) ................................. 599 |
| Moore's Crossing, Travis ............... 25 | *MURCHISON, Henderson, 51, (594) ................................. 604 | New Colony, Bell ............................ 12 |
| MOORE STATION, Henderson, (201) ..................................... 200 | MURPHY, Collin, 480, (17,708) ........................... 19,816 | New Colony, Cass .......................... 65 |
| Mooreville, Falls ............................. 96 | Murray, Young ................................ 29 | New Corn Hill, Williamson ............ 475 |
| Mooring, Brazos ............................ 80 | Murvaul, Panola ........................... 150 | New Davy, DeWitt ........................... 20 |
| Moraida, Starr, (212) .................... 224 | Mustang, Denton ........................... 25 | *NEW DEAL, Lubbock, 17, (794) ................................. 770 |
| Morales, Jackson .......................... 72 | MUSTANG, Navarro, 1, (21) .......... 22 | NEW FAIRVIEW, Wise, 12, (1,258) ............................. 1,253 |
| *MORAN, Shackelford, 8, (270) ..................................... 271 | Mustang Mott, DeWitt .................... 20 | Newgulf, Wharton .......................... 10 |
| Moravia, Lavaca ........................... 165 | MUSTANG RIDGE, Travis-Caldwell, 26, (861) ............................... 930 | New Harmony, Shelby .................... 40 |
| *MORGAN, Bosque, 12, (490) ..... 516 | *Myra, Cooke, 2 ........................... 150 | New Harmony, Smith .................... 350 |
| Morgan Creek, Burnet ................. 126 | Myrtle Springs, Van Zandt, (828) ................................. 883 | *NEW HOME, Lynn, 5, (334) ........ 342 |
| Morgan Farm Area, San Patricio, (463) ..................................... 466 | | New Hope, Cherokee ..................... 50 |
| *Morgan Mill, Erath, 1 .................. 206 | **N** | NEW HOPE, Collin, 15, (614) ....... 636 |
| MORGAN'S POINT, Harris, 18, (339) ..................................... 353 | *NACOGDOCHES, Nacogdoches, 1,364, (32,996) ................ 33,103 | New Hope, Jones ............................. 9 |
| MORGAN'S POINT RESORT, Bell, 59, (4,170) ........................ 4,228 | *Nada, Colorado, 14 ..................... 165 | New Hope, San Augustine ............. 75 |
| Morning Glory, El Paso, (651) ...... 648 | *NAPLES, Morris, 52, (1,378) ............................. 1,431 | New Hope, Smith ........................... 75 |
| *Morse, Hansford, 3, (147) .......... 148 | Narciso Pena, Starr, (30) ............... 34 | New Hope, Wood ........................... 15 |
| *MORTON, Cochran, 46, (2,006) ............................. 1,885 | Naruna, Burnet .............................. 95 | Newlin, Hall .................................... 27 |
| Morton, Harrison ............................ 75 | *NASH, Bowie, 88, (2,960) ........ 3,085 | *NEW LONDON, Rusk, 14, (998) ................................. 996 |
| Morton Valley, Eastland ................. 46 | Nash, Ellis ..................................... 40 | New Lynn, Lynn ............................... 4 |
| *Moscow, Polk, 10 ....................... 170 | NASSAU BAY, Harris, 170, (4,002) ............................. 4,095 | New Moore, Lynn ........................... 10 |
| Mosheim, Bosque .......................... 75 | Nat, Nacogdoches .......................... 50 | New Mountain, Upshur ................... 20 |
| Moss Bluff, Liberty ......................... 65 | *NATALIA, Medina, 60, (1,431) ............................. 1,506 | Newport, Clay-Jack ........................ 75 |
| Moss Hill, Liberty ......................... 180 | NAVARRO, Navarro, (210) .......... 215 | New Salem, Palo Pinto ................... 89 |
| Mostyn, Montgomery ...................... 90 | Navarro Mills, Navarro ................... 90 | New Salem, Rusk ........................... 55 |
| *MOULTON, Lavaca, 71, (886) ..................................... 877 | *NAVASOTA, Grimes, 362, (7,049) ............................. 7,586 | Newsome, Camp .......................... 113 |
| *Mound, Coryell, 2 ....................... 125 | Navidad, Jackson ......................... 227 | *NEW SUMMERFIELD, Cherokee, 18, (1,111) ...................... 1,154 |
| Mound City, Anderson-Houston ...... 25 | *NAZARETH, Castro, 11, (311) .... 303 | New Sweden, Travis ...................... 60 |
| MOUNTAIN CITY, Hays, 24, (648) ..................................... 646 | Necessity, Stephens ...................... 10 | New Taiton, Wharton ...................... 10 |
| *Mountain Home, Kerr, 17 ............. 96 | Nechanitz, Fayette ......................... 57 | New Territory, Fort Bend, (15,186) ....................... 15,465 |
| Mountain Peak, Ellis .................... 300 | *Neches, Anderson, 4 .................. 175 | *NEWTON, Newton, 72, (2,478) ............................. 2,449 |
| Mountain Springs, Cooke ............ 600 | *NEDERLAND, Jefferson, 686, (17,547) ........................ 17,483 | *New Ulm, Austin, 43 ................... 974 |
| Mount Bethel, Panola ..................... 65 | Needmore, Bailey ........................... 20 | *NEW WAVERLY, Walker, 92, (1,032) ............................. 1,027 |
| *MOUNT CALM, Hill, 14, (320) ..................................... 317 | Needmore, Terry .............................. 7 | New Wehdem, Austin ................... 414 |
| *MOUNT ENTERPRISE, Rusk, 54, (447) ............................... 449 | *NEEDVILLE, Fort Bend, 144, (2,823) ............................. 2,962 | New Willard, Polk ......................... 160 |
| Mount Haven, Cherokee ................ 30 | Negley, Red River ......................... 136 | New York, Henderson ..................... 60 |
| Mount Hermon, Shelby ................... 80 | Neinda, Jones ................................ 21 | NEYLANDVILLE, Hunt, 2, (97) ....... 99 |
| Mount Olive, Lavaca ...................... 50 | Nell, Live Oak ................................ 60 | NIEDERWALD, Hays-Caldwell, 14, (565) ............................. 577 |
| *MOUNT PLEASANT, Titus, 715, (15,564) ........................ 16,150 | Nelson City, Kendall ...................... 50 | Nigton, Trinity ................................ 87 |
| Mount Rose, Falls ......................... 15 | Nelsonville, Austin ....................... 200 | Nimrod, Eastland ........................... 45 |
| Mount Selman, Cherokee ............. 325 | Nelta, Hopkins ............................... 36 | Nina, Starr, (141) ......................... 146 |
| Mount Sylvan, Smith .................... 181 | *Nemo, Somervell, 11 .................... 56 | Nineveh, Leon ............................... 50 |
| *MOUNT VERNON, Franklin, 150, (2,662) ..................... 2,633 | Nesbitt, Harrison, (281) ............... 278 | Nix, Lampasas ............................... 14 |
| Mount Vernon, Houston .................. 43 | Netos, Starr, (31) ........................... 32 | *NIXON, Gonzales-Wilson, 55, (2,385) ............................. 2,442 |
| Mozelle, Coleman .......................... 15 | Neuville, Shelby ............................. 65 | Noack, Williamson ......................... 70 |
| Muellersville, Washington .............. 20 | *NEVADA, Collin, 44, (822) ......... 907 | Nobility, Fannin ............................ 100 |
| *MUENSTER, Cooke, 134, (1,544) ............................. 1,620 | *NEWARK, Wise, 52, (1,005) ..... 1,044 | Noble, Lamar ................................ 14 |
| Mulberry, Fannin .......................... 141 | *New Baden, Robertson, 5 ........... 150 | Nockernut, Wilson .......................... 20 |
| *Muldoon, Fayette, 5 ...................... 95 | NEW BERLIN, Guadalupe, 15, (511) ................................. 514 | *NOCONA, Montague, 135, (3,033) ............................. 3,040 |
| *MULESHOE, Bailey, 175, (5,158) ............................. 5,078 | New Bielau, Colorado .................... 30 | Nocona Hills, Montague, (675) ..... 696 |
| *MULLIN, Mills, 4, (179) .............. 174 | *NEW BOSTON, Bowie, 172, (4,550) ............................. 4,523 | Nogalus Prairie, Trinity ................ 109 |
| Mullins Prairie, Fayette ................ 107 | *NEW BRAUNFELS, Comal-Guadalupe, 2,939, (57,740) ...................... 63,675 | *Nolan, Nolan ................................ 60 |
| | New Bremen, Austin ..................... 125 | *NOLANVILLE, Bell, 52, (4,259) ............................. 4,322 |
| | | *NOME, Jefferson, 23, (588) ........ 587 |

| Town, County ............... Pop. 2014 | Town, County ............... Pop. 2014 | Town, County ............... Pop. 2014 |
|---|---|---|
| Noodle, Jones.................................. 40 | *ODEM, San Patricio, 63, | *Orla, Reeves, 2 ............................. 80 |
| NOONDAY, Smith, 56, (777) ........ 806 | (2,389) ............................... 2,415 | Osage, Colorado ........................... 10 |
| Nopal, DeWitt ................................. 25 | *ODESSA, Ector-Midland, | Osage, Coryell............................... 30 |
| *NORDHEIM, DeWitt, 17, (307) ... 311 | 3,962, (99,940) .............. 113,534 | Oscar, Bell .................................... 58 |
| Norman, Williamson ..................... 40 | *O'DONNELL, Lynn-Dawson, | Osceola, Hill .................................. 95 |
| Normandy, Maverick .................... 114 | 14, (831) .............................. 792 | Otey, Brazoria ............................... 31 |
| *NORMANGEE, Leon-Madison, | Oenaville, Bell............................... 108 | Ottine, Gonzales ........................... 80 |
| 55, (685) ................................ 668 | O'Farrell, Cass.............................. 20 | Otto, Falls .................................... 48 |
| *Normanna, Bee, 1, (113)............. 117 | Ogburn, Wood ............................. 10 | *Ovalo, Taylor, 1 ......................... 225 |
| Norse, Bosque ............................. 110 | *OGLESBY, Coryell, 21, | *OVERTON, Rusk-Smith, 99, |
| North Alamo, Hidalgo, (3,235) ... 3,598 | (484) ................................... 467 | (2,554) ............................... 2,557 |
| NORTH CLEVELAND, Liberty, | *Oilton, Webb, 2, (353) ................ 367 | *OVILLA, Ellis-Dallas, 126, |
| 4, (247) ................................ 249 | Oklahoma, Montgomery .............. 800 | (3,492) ............................... 3,557 |
| North Escobares, Starr, (118) ....... 126 | Oklahoma Flat, Hockley ................. 4 | Owens, Brown .............................. 16 |
| NORTHLAKE, Denton, 53, | Oklahoma Lane, Parmer ............... 25 | Owens, Crosby ............................... 4 |
| (1,724) ............................... 1,864 | *Oklaunion, Wilbarger, 3............. 138 | Owentown, Smith ........................ 100 |
| North Pearsall, Frio, (614) ........... 673 | Okra, Eastland .............................. 20 | Owl Creek, Bell ........................... 130 |
| *NORTH RICHLAND HILLS, Tarrant, | Ola, Kaufman................................ 65 | Owl Ranch, Jim Wells, (225) ........ 224 |
| 1,923, (63,343) ................. 68,670 | Old Boston, Bowie ...................... 100 | Oxford, Llano ................................ 18 |
| Northridge, Starr, (78).................... 82 | Old Center, Panola ....................... 83 | OYSTER CREEK, Brazoria, 36, |
| Northrup, Lee................................. 86 | Old Dime Box, Lee ...................... 225 | (1,111)............................... 1,146 |
| North San Pedro, Nueces, (895) .. 906 | *Olden, Eastland, 4..................... 113 | *Ozona, Crockett, 131, |
| North Star, Archer......................... 10 | Oldenburg, Fayette........................ 92 | (3,225) ............................... 3,237 |
| *North Zulch, Madison, 16............ 600 | Old Escobares, Starr, (97) ............. 97 | |
| Norton, Runnels............................ 50 | *Old Glory, Stonewall, 1.............. 100 | **P** |
| *Notrees, Ector, 1 ......................... 20 | Old Midway, Leon ......................... 12 | Pablo Pena, Starr, (63) ................. 64 |
| *NOVICE, Coleman, 5, (139)....... 137 | *Old Ocean, Brazoria, 17............. 150 | Pacio, Delta .................................. 35 |
| Novice, Lamar ............................... 35 | OLD RIVER-WINFREE, Chambers, | Padgett, Young .............................. 18 |
| Noxville, Kimble .............................. 3 | 17, (1,245) ........................ 1,248 | *PADUCAH, Cottle, 51, |
| Nugent, Jones ............................... 50 | Old Salem, Bowie ......................... 50 | (1,186) ............................... 1,143 |
| Nunelee, Fannin ............................ 90 | Old Union, Bowie ........................ 100 | *Paige, Bastrop, 25...................... 275 |
| Nurillo, Hidalgo, (7,344)............. 7,838 | Old Union, Limestone .................... 25 | Paint Creek, Haskell .................... 150 |
| *Nursery, Victoria, 3...................... 600 | Oletha, Limestone ......................... 53 | *PAINT ROCK, Concho, 12, |
| | Olfen, Runnels .............................. 35 | (273) ................................... 262 |
| **O** | Olin, Hamilton ............................... 15 | Paisano Park, San Patricio, |
| Oakalla, Burnet .............................. 99 | Olivarez, Hidalgo, (3,827).......... 4,119 | (130) ................................... 128 |
| Oakdale, Polk ................................ 25 | Olivia, Calhoun ............................ 215 | *PALACIOS, Matagorda, 147, |
| Oak Forest, Gonzales.................... 24 | Olivia Lopez de Gutierrez, Starr, | (4,718) ............................... 4,574 |
| Oak Grove, Bowie ......................... 90 | (93) ....................................... 92 | *PALESTINE, Anderson, 792, |
| Oak Grove, Colorado..................... 40 | Ollie, Polk ...................................... 5 | (18,712) ........................... 18,922 |
| OAK GROVE, Kaufman, (603) ..... 639 | *Olmito, Cameron, 55, | PALISADES, Randall, |
| Oak Grove, Wood......................... 140 | (1,210) ............................... 1,248 | (325) ................................... 324 |
| Oak Hill, Rusk.............................. 200 | Olmito and Olmito, Starr, (271)..... 285 | Palito Blanco, Jim Wells .............. 750 |
| Oak Hill, Travis, .......... [part of Austin] | Olmos, Guadalupe......................... 65 | *PALMER, Ellis, 76, (2,000)....... 2,015 |
| *Oakhurst, San Jacinto, 7, | OLMOS PARK, Bexar, 114, | PALMHURST, Hidalgo, 83, |
| (233) ................................... 245 | (2,237) ............................... 2,337 | (2,607) ............................... 2,665 |
| Oak Island, Chambers, (363) ....... 372 | *OLNEY, Young, 125, | PALM VALLEY, Cameron, 20, |
| Oakland, Cherokee........................ 50 | (3,285) ............................... 3,406 | (1,304) ............................... 1,330 |
| *Oakland, Colorado ....................... 80 | *OLTON, Lamb, 64, (2,215)....... 2,124 | PALMVIEW, Hidalgo, 219, |
| Oakland, Van Zandt....................... 26 | *OMAHA, Morris, 38, (1,021)..... 1,054 | (5,460) ............................... 6,798 |
| OAK LEAF, Ellis, 45, | Omen, Smith................................ 150 | Palmview South, Hidalgo, |
| (1,298) ............................... 1,323 | *ONALASKA, Polk, 116, | (5,575) ............................... 5,843 |
| OAK POINT, Denton, 94, | (1,764) ............................... 1,829 | Palo Blanco, Starr, (204) ............. 214 |
| (2,786) ............................... 3,048 | Opdyke, Hockley ........................... 50 | Paloduro, Armstrong...................... 10 |
| OAK RIDGE, Cooke, 10, (141)..... 158 | OPDYKE WEST, Hockley, 3, | Paloma Creek, Denton, |
| Oak Ridge, Grayson ..................... 161 | (174) ................................... 180 | (2,501) ............................... 2,682 |
| OAK RIDGE, Kaufman, 10, | Oplin, Callahan .............................. 75 | Paloma Creek South, Denton, |
| (495) ................................... 516 | O'Quinn, Fayette .......................... 191 | (2,753) ............................... 2,892 |
| Oak Ridge, Nacogdoches............. 225 | Oran, Palo Pinto ............................ 61 | *Palo Pinto, Palo Pinto, 11, |
| OAK RIDGE NORTH, Montgomery, | *ORANGE, Orange, 669, | (333) ................................... 343 |
| 198, (3,049)..................... 3,184 | (18,595) ........................... 18,911 | Paluxy, Hood ................................ 36 |
| Oak Trail Shores, Hood, | Orangedale, Bee ........................... 40 | *PAMPA, Gray, 642, |
| (2,755) ............................... 2,888 | *Orangefield, Orange, 6............... 725 | (17,994) ........................... 18,566 |
| OAK VALLEY, Navarro, 1, | *ORANGE GROVE, Jim Wells, | Pancake, Coryell ........................... 11 |
| (368) ................................... 372 | 99, (1,318) ........................ 1,366 | Pandale, Val Verde ....................... 25 |
| Oakville, Live Oak, 4.................... 260 | Orangeville, Fannin ....................... 60 | *Pandora, Wilson, 1 .................... 110 |
| *OAKWOOD, Leon, 29, (510)....... 501 | Orason, Cameron, (129).............. 130 | *PANHANDLE, Carson, 64, |
| Oatmeal, Burnet ............................ 74 | *ORCHARD, Fort Bend, 15, | (2,452) ............................... 2,348 |
| *O'BRIEN, Haskell, 1, (106) ........ 103 | (352) ................................... 360 | *Panna Maria, Karnes, 7 .............. 45 |
| Ocee, McLennan ........................... 84 | *ORE CITY, Upshur, 64, | *Panola, Panola, 2........................ 305 |
| Odds, Limestone ........................... 24 | (1,144) ............................... 1,160 | PANORAMA VILLAGE, Montgomery, |
| Odell, Wilbarger........................... 100 | Orient, Tom Green ......................... 57 | 30, (2,170) ........................ 2,263 |

| Town, County ...............Pop. 2014 | Town, County ...............Pop. 2014 | Town, County ...............Pop. 2014 |
|---|---|---|
| *PORT LAVACA, Calhoun, 463, (12,248) ............................ 12,281 | Pruitt, Cass.................................... 25 | RANCHO VIEJO, Cameron, 44, (2,437)................................... 2,531 |
| *Port Mansfield, Willacy, 9, (226)...................................... 222 | Pruitt, Van Zandt........................... 45 | Rancho Viejo, Starr, (228) ............ 241 |
| *PORT NECHES, Jefferson, 347, (13,040)........................... 12,919 | Pueblo Nuevo, Webb, (521) ......... 541 | Rand, Kaufman............................... 70 |
| *Port O'Connor , Calhoun, 34, (1,253)............................... 1,287 | Puerto Rico, Hidalgo..................... 50 | Randado, Jim Hogg.......................... 6 |
| Port Sullivan, Milam........................ 15 | Pullman, Potter.............................. 31 | *Randolph, Fannin, 1.................... 600 |
| Porvenir, Presidio ............................ 3 | Pumphrey, Runnels ...................... 15 | Randolph Air Force Base, Bexar, (1,241) ............................... 1,283 |
| Posey, Hopkins............................... 12 | Pumpkin, San Jacinto .................. 100 | *RANGER, Eastland, 92, (2,468)................................... 2,547 |
| Posey, Lubbock ............................ 225 | Pumpville, Val Verde...................... 25 | RANGERVILLE, Cameron, (289)...................................... 299 |
| *POST, Garza, 163, (5,376)................................... 5,470 | Punkin Center, Dawson................... 8 | Rankin, Ellis ................................... 10 |
| Post Oak, Blanco............................ 10 | Punkin Center, Eastland ............... 12 | *RANKIN, Upton, 46, (778).......... 754 |
| Postoak, Jack ................................. 20 | *Purdon, Navarro, 8...................... 133 | RANSOM CANYON, Lubbock, 37, (1,096) ......................... 1,145 |
| Postoak, Lamar ............................... 65 | Purley, Franklin ........................... 100 | Ratamosa, Cameron, (254).......... 267 |
| Post Oak, Lee ............................... 100 | *Purmela, Coryell, 2....................... 50 | *Ratcliff, Houston, 3.................... 106 |
| POST OAK BEND, Kaufman, 14, (595)...................................... 628 | Pursley, Navarro ........................... 40 | Ratibor, Bell .................................. 22 |
| Post Oak Point, Austin.................... 60 | Purves, Erath.................................. 50 | Rattan, Delta .................................. 10 |
| *POTEET, Atascosa, 119, (3,260)................................... 3,414 | *PUTNAM, Callahan, 7, (94)...................................... 98 | *RAVENNA, Fannin, 11, (209)..... 213 |
| *POTH, Wilson, 50, (1,908)....... 2,098 | *PYOTE, Ward, 5, (114) ............... 122 | Rayburn, Liberty ........................... 60 |
| Potosi, Taylor, (2,991)................ 3,070 | | Rayland, Foard............................... 30 |
| *POTTSBORO, Grayson, 122, (2,160)................................... 2,217 | **Q** | *RAYMONDVILLE, Willacy, 198, (11,284)........................... 11,030 |
| Pottsville, Hamilton ...................... 105 | *Quail, Collingsworth, 1, (19).......... 17 | Ray Point, Live Oak...................... 200 |
| *Powderly, Lamar, 48, (1,178)............................... 1,215 | Quail Creek, Victoria, (1,628) .... 1,685 | *Raywood, Liberty, 11................. 231 |
| *POWELL, Navarro, 13, (136)..... 143 | *QUANAH, Hardeman, 107, (2,641)................................... 2,531 | Razor, Lamar ................................. 20 |
| *POYNOR, Henderson, 15, (305)...................................... 310 | Quarry, Washington........................ 60 | *Reagan, Falls, 4.......................... 300 |
| Prado Verde, El Paso, (246)......... 253 | Quarterway, Hale........................... 24 | Reagan Wells, Uvalde ................... 30 |
| Praesel, Milam.............................. 115 | *QUEEN CITY, Cass, 70, (1,476)................................... 1,511 | Reagor Springs, Ellis.................... 250 |
| Praha, Fayette................................ 90 | *Quemado, Maverick, 9, (230)...... 234 | *Realitos, Duval, 5, (184)............. 192 |
| Prairie Chapel, McLennan............. 35 | Quesada, Starr, (25).................... 26 | Red Bank, Bowie ......................... 125 |
| Prairie Dell, Bell............................. 34 | Quicksand, Newton ........................ 50 | Red Bluff, Jackson......................... 45 |
| *Prairie Hill, Limestone, 2 ............. 150 | Quihi, Medina .............................. 125 | Red Bluff, Reeves.......................... 40 |
| Prairie Hill, Washington ................. 20 | *QUINLAN, Hunt, 202, (1,394)................................... 1,414 | Redfield, Nacogdoches, (441)..... 453 |
| *Prairie Lea, Caldwell, 10 ............. 320 | QUINTANA, Brazoria, 4, (56) ......... 65 | Redford, Presidio, (90)................... 92 |
| Prairie Point, Cooke........................ 22 | *QUITAQUE, Briscoe, 18, (411)...................................... 378 | Red Hill, Cass ................................ 28 |
| *PRAIRIE VIEW, Waller, 32, (5,576)................................... 5,809 | *QUITMAN, Wood, 172, (1,809)................................... 1,883 | Red Hill, Limestone ....................... 20 |
| Prairieville, Kaufman....................... 75 | | Red Lake, Freestone ..................... 50 |
| *PREMONT, Jim Wells, 61, (2,653)................................... 2,710 | **R** | Redland, Angelina, (1,047)........ 1,090 |
| *PRESIDIO, Presidio, 88, (4,426)................................... 4,462 | Rabbs Prairie, Fayette................... 79 | Redland, Leon ................................ 35 |
| Preston, Grayson, (2,096) ......... 2,149 | Raccoon Bend, Austin ................. 775 | Redland, Van Zandt........................ 45 |
| *Price, Rusk, 4.............................. 275 | Rachal, Brooks .............................. 36 | RED LICK, Bowie, (1,008)......... 1,021 |
| *Priddy, Mills, 12.......................... 215 | Radar Base, Maverick, (762)........ 789 | *RED OAK, Ellis, 465, (10,769) ........................... 11,315 |
| PRIMERA, Cameron, 25, (4,070)................................... 4,216 | Radium, Jones ............................... 10 | Red Ranger, Bell ........................... 30 |
| Primrose, Van Zandt....................... 26 | Rafael Pena, Starr, (17)................. 15 | *Red Rock, Bastrop, 17 ................. 40 |
| *PRINCETON, Collin, 197, (6,807)................................... 7,832 | Ragtown, Lamar ............................. 30 | Red Springs, Baylor........................ 42 |
| Pringle, Hutchinson ....................... 20 | *Rainbow, Somervell, 15 ............. 121 | Red Springs, Smith...................... 350 |
| Pritchett, Upshur........................... 125 | Raisin, Victoria............................... 85 | Redtown, Anderson ........................ 30 |
| *Proctor, Comanche, 3 ................. 228 | Raleigh, Navarro............................. 40 | Redtown, Angelina........................ 500 |
| *PROGRESO, Hidalgo, 56, (5,507)................................... 5,868 | *RALLS, Crosby, 53, (1,944) ..... 1,891 | *REDWATER, Bowie, 16, (1,057)................................... 1,047 |
| PROGRESO LAKES, Hidalgo, 9, (240)...................................... 249 | Ramireno, Zapata, (35) ................. 34 | Redwood, Guadalupe, (4,338) .. 4,471 |
| Progress, Bailey ............................. 49 | Ramirez, Duval ............................... 42 | Reeds Settlement, Red River......... 50 |
| Prospect, Rains .............................. 40 | Ramirez-Perez, Starr, (78)............. 76 | Reedville, Caldwell ...................... 520 |
| *PROSPER, Collin-Denton, 328, (9,423)............................. 12,980 | Ramos, Starr, (116) ..................... 117 | Reese, Cherokee............................ 75 |
| Providence, Floyd........................... 78 | Ranchette Estates, Willacy, (152)...................................... 151 | Refuge, Houston ............................ 20 |
| Providence, Polk........................... 350 | Ranchito El Calaboz [Encantada-], Cameron, (2,284) ............... 2,269 | *REFUGIO, Refugio, 124, (2,890)................................... 2,812 |
| PROVIDENCE, Denton, (4,786)................................... 4,992 | Ranchitos Del Norte, Starr, (112).. 118 | Regency, Mills ................................ 25 |
| | Ranchitos East, Webb, (212)....... 215 | Regino Ramirez, Starr, (85)........... 91 |
| | Ranchitos Las Lomas, Webb, (266)...................................... 284 | Rehburg, Washington ..................... 20 |
| | Rancho Alegre, Jim Wells, (1,704)................................... 1,747 | Reid Hope King, Cameron, (786)...................................... 850 |
| | Rancho Banquete, Nueces, (424)...................................... 426 | Reilly Springs, Hopkins................... 75 |
| | Rancho Chico, San Patricio, (396)...................................... 417 | Rek Hill, Fayette ........................... 168 |
| | Ranchos Penitas West, Webb, (573)...................................... 601 | *REKLAW, Cherokee-Rusk, 4, (379)...................................... 389 |
| | | Relampago, Hidalgo, (132).......... 142 |
| | | Rendon, Tarrant, (12,552) ....... 13,185 |

| Town, County ...............Pop. 2014 | Town, County ...............Pop. 2014 | Town, County ...............Pop. 2014 |
|---|---|---|

*RENO, Lamar, 94, (3,166) ....... 3,293
RENO, Parker-Tarrant, 28,
   (2,494) ............................... 2,552
Retreat, Grimes ........................... 25
RETREAT, Navarro, (377) ........... 402
Retta, Tarrant-Johnson ............... 780
Reynard, Houston.......................... 75
Rhea, Parmer ............................... 98
Rhineland, Knox .......................... 120
*RHOME, Wise, 88, (1,522) ..... 1,580
Rhonesboro, Upshur ..................... 40
Ricardo, Kleberg, (1,048) .......... 1,081
*RICE, Navarro, 44, (923) ........... 965
Rice's Crossing, Williamson ........ 130
*Richards, Grimes, 15 ................. 300
*RICHARDSON, Dallas-Collin,
   4,711, (99,223) ............... 104,037
*RICHLAND, Navarro, 8, (264)..... 278
Richland, Rains ............................. 50
*RICHLAND HILLS, Tarrant,
   387, (7,801) ...................... 8,001
*RICHLAND SPRINGS, San Saba,
   8, (338) ................................ 333
*RICHMOND, Fort Bend, 776,
   (11,679) ......................... 11,372
RICHWOOD, Brazoria, 76,
   (3,510) ............................. 3,727
Riderville, Panola.......................... 50
Ridge, Mills ................................... 25
Ridge, Robertson.......................... 67
Ridgeway, Hopkins ....................... 54
Ridings, Fannin ........................... 200
*RIESEL, McLennan, 46,
   (1,007) ............................. 1,018
Rincon, Starr................................... 5
*Ringgold, Montague, 3 ............... 100
RIO BRAVO, Webb, 47,
   (4,794) ............................. 4,833
*Rio Frio, Real, 5 .......................... 50
*RIO GRANDE CITY, Starr, 387,
   (13,834) ......................... 14,132
Rio Grande Village, Brewster ........ 12
*RIO HONDO, Cameron, 59,
   (2,356) ............................. 2,463

*Riomedina, Medina, 11 ................ 60
Rios, Duval ................................... 75
*RIO VISTA, Johnson, 48,
   (873) ................................. 944
*RISING STAR, Eastland, 33,
   (835) ................................. 858
Rita, Burleson ............................... 50
Rivera, Starr, (162) ..................... 169
Riverby, Fannin.............................. 8
River Crest Estates, Angelina....... 150
Rivereno, Starr, (61) ..................... 62
River Hill, Panola ........................ 125
RIVER OAKS, Tarrant, 130,
   (7,427) ............................. 7,645
Rivers End, Brazoria...................... 90
*RIVERSIDE, Walker, 30,
   (510) ................................. 489
*Riviera, Kleberg, 28, (689) ......... 696
Riviera Beach, Kleberg................ 155
Roach, Cass ................................. 50
Roane, Navarro ........................... 120
*ROANOKE, Denton, 365,
   (5,962) ............................. 6,626
*Roans Prairie, Grimes, 3 ............. 64
*ROARING SPRINGS, Motley,
   11, (234) ............................ 222
Robbins, Leon ............................... 20
*ROBERT LEE, Coke, 42,
   (1,049) ............................. 1,009
Robertson, Crosby........................ 10
ROBINSON, McLennan, 343,
   (10,509) ......................... 11,507
*ROBSTOWN, Nueces, 351,
   (11,487) ......................... 11,730
*ROBY, Fisher, 26, (643) ............. 621
*Rochelle, McCulloch, 4 .............. 163
*ROCHESTER, Haskell, 12,
   (324) ................................. 320
Rock Bluff, Burnet.......................... 90
Rock Creek, Somervell.................. 70
*ROCKDALE, Milam, 265,
   (5,595) ............................. 5,325
Rockett, Ellis............................... 300
Rockford, Lamar ........................... 30

Rockhouse, Austin....................... 100
*Rock Island, Colorado, 2............ 160
Rockland, Tyler............................. 98
Rockne, Bastrop ......................... 190
*ROCKPORT, Aransas, 705,
   (8,766) ............................. 9,785
*ROCKSPRINGS, Edwards, 58,
   (1,182) ............................. 1,055
*ROCKWALL, Rockwall, 1,845,
   (37,490) ......................... 41,147
*Rockwood, Coleman, 3................ 53
Rocky Branch, Morris .................. 135
Rocky Creek, Blanco ..................... 20
ROCKY MOUND, Camp, 1,
   (75) ................................... 71
Rocky Point, Burnet..................... 152
Roddy, Van Zandt.......................... 29
Rodney, Navarro............................ 15
Roeder, Titus ................................ 75
Roganville, Jasper ........................ 70
*ROGERS, Bell, 54, (1,218) ...... 1,214
Rogers, Taylor ............................. 151
Rolling Hills, Potter ................... 1,000
Rolling Meadows, Gregg ............. 362
ROLLINGWOOD, Travis, 127,
   (1,412) ............................. 1,512
Roma Creek, Starr, (350) ............ 359
*ROMA-Los Saenz, Starr, 209,
   (9,765) ............................. 9,830
ROMAN FOREST, Montgomery,
   (1,538) ............................. 1,781
*Romayor, Liberty, 3 .................... 135
*Roosevelt, Kimble, 1 .................... 14
Roosevelt, Lubbock ..................... 362
*ROPESVILLE, Hockley, 16,
   (434) ................................. 441
Rosalie, Red River....................... 100
*Rosanky, Bastrop, 10 ................. 210
*ROSCOE, Nolan, 47,
   (1,322) ............................. 1,304
*ROSEBUD, Falls, 60,
   (1,412) ............................. 1,360
ROSE CITY, Orange, 31, (502) .... 506
Rose Hill, Harris.......................... 3,500

*Folks at the spring antiques fair in Round Top. Photo by Robert Plocheck.*

| Town, County ...............Pop. 2014 | Town, County ...............Pop. 2014 | Town, County ...............Pop. 2014 |
|---|---|---|
| Rose Hill, San Jacinto ................... 30 | St. Mary's Colony, Bastrop ............. 50 | San Gabriel, Milam-Williamson ...... 70 |
| ROSE HILL ACRES, Hardin, | ST. PAUL, Collin, 31, | *SANGER, Denton, 253, |
| (441) ...................................... 467 | (1,066) ............................... 1,063 | (6,916) ............................... 7,315 |
| *ROSENBERG, Fort Bend, 977, | St. Paul, San Patricio, (584) ........ 597 | *San Isidro, Starr, 9, (240) ........... 241 |
| (30,618) ............................. 32,571 | *SALADO, Bell, 305, | San Jose, Duval ............................ 15 |
| Rosevine, Sabine ........................... 50 | (2,126) ............................... 2,164 | *SAN JUAN, Hidalgo, 558, |
| Rosewood, Upshur ..................... 100 | Salem, Cherokee ........................... 20 | (33,856) ............................ 36,120 |
| *Rosharon, Brazoria, 135, | Salem, Grimes .............................. 54 | San Juan, Starr, (129) ................. 136 |
| (1,152) ............................... 1,261 | Salem, Newton ............................ 218 | SAN LEANNA, Travis, (497) ........ 529 |
| Rosita, Duval ................................ 25 | Salesville, Palo Pinto .................... 88 | San Leon, Galveston, (4,970)... .5,199 |
| Rosita, Maverick, (2,704)........... 2,744 | Saline, Menard .............................. 70 | *San Manuel-Linn, Hidalgo, 7, |
| *ROSS, McLennan, 10, (283) ...... 293 | *Salineño, Starr, 1, (201) ............. 193 | (801) ...................................... 831 |
| *ROSSER, Kaufman, 12, (332) .... 342 | Salineño North, Starr, (115) .......... 119 | *SAN MARCOS, Hays-Caldwell- |
| *Rosston, Cooke, 2........................ 75 | Salmon, Anderson ......................... 20 | Guadalupe, 1,821, |
| Rossville, Atascosa ..................... 200 | Salt Flat, Hudspeth ......................... 8 | (44,894) ............................ 55,527 |
| *ROTAN, Fisher, 43, (1,508)...... 1,437 | Salt Gap, McCulloch ...................... 25 | SAN PATRICIO, San Patricio, |
| Rough Creek, San Saba.................. 8 | *Saltillo, Hopkins, 5..................... 200 | (395) ...................................... 387 |
| Round House, Navarro .................. 40 | Samaria, Starr ............................... 90 | San Pedro, Cameron, (530) ......... 544 |
| *ROUND MOUNTAIN, Blanco, 8, | Sammy Martinez, Starr, (110) ....... 112 | *SAN PERLITA, Willacy, 2, |
| (181) ...................................... 180 | *Samnorwood, Collingsworth, | (573) ...................................... 564 |
| Round Mountain, Travis................. 59 | (51) .......................................... 51 | San Roman, Starr ............................ 5 |
| Round Prairie, Navarro .................. 40 | Sample, Gonzales .......................... 16 | *SAN SABA, San Saba, 156, |
| *ROUND ROCK, Williamson-Travis, | *SAN ANGELO, Tom Green, | (3,099) ............................... 3,075 |
| 3,706, (99,887) ............... 110,326 | 3,460, (93,200) ............... 98,040 | SANSOM PARK, Tarrant, 98, |
| Round Timber, Baylor ...................... 2 | *SAN ANTONIO, Bexar, | (4,686) ............................... 4,781 |
| *ROUND TOP, Fayette, 67, (90)..... 88 | 39,837, (1,327,407) ..... 1,419,762 | *SANTA ANNA, Coleman, 55, |
| Roundup, Hockley .......................... 20 | San Antonio Prairie, Burleson......... 20 | (1,099) ............................... 1,100 |
| Rowden, Callahan ......................... 15 | *SAN AUGUSTINE, San Augustine, | Santa Anna, Starr, (13) ................. 14 |
| *Rowena, Runnels, 11 ................. 349 | 120, (2,108) ...................... 2,089 | Santa Catarina, Starr ..................... 15 |
| *ROWLETT, Dallas-Rockwall, | *SAN BENITO, Cameron, 601, | SANTA CLARA, Guadalupe, |
| 1,663, (56,199) ................ 59,203 | (24,250) ............................ 24,704 | 20, (725) ............................... 743 |
| *ROXTON, Lamar, 17, (650) ........ 651 | San Carlos, Hidalgo, (3,130) .....3,299 | Santa Cruz, Starr, (54)................... 51 |
| Royalty, Ward ............................... 27 | San Carlos, Starr ........................... 10 | *Santa Elena, Starr, 2................... 35 |
| *ROYSE CITY, Rockwall-Collin, | San Carlos I, Webb, (316) ............ 331 | *SANTA FE, Galveston, 416, |
| 385, (9,349) ...................... 10,338 | San Carlos II, Webb, (261) ........... 271 | (12,222) ............................ 12,553 |
| Rucker, Comanche ........................ 28 | Sanco, Coke ................................. 15 | *Santa Maria, Cameron, 2, |
| Rugby, Red River .......................... 24 | SANCTUARY, Parker, 22, | (733) ...................................... 754 |
| Ruidosa, Presidio .......................... 18 | (329) ...................................... 334 | Santa Monica, Willacy, (83) ........... 86 |
| *RULE, Haskell, 13, (636) ........... 627 | Sand Branch, Dallas .................... 400 | *SANTA ROSA, Cameron, 37, |
| Rumley, Lampasas ........................ 30 | *Sanderson, Terrell, 15, | (2,873) ............................... 2,939 |
| RUNAWAY BAY, Wise, 31, | (837) ...................................... 806 | Santa Rosa, Starr, (241)............... 240 |
| (1,286) ............................... 1,366 | Sand Flat, Johnson ...................... 133 | Santel, Starr, (44) ......................... 48 |
| *RUNGE, Karnes, 25, | Sand Flat, Rains ............................ 45 | *Santo, Palo Pinto, 20 ................. 445 |
| (1,031) ............................... 1,005 | Sand Flat, Smith .......................... 100 | *San Ygnacio, Zapata, 2, |
| Rural Shade, Navarro ..................... 30 | Sand Flat, Van Zandt ..................... 25 | (667) ...................................... 659 |
| *RUSK, Cherokee, 177, | Sand Flat, Leon ............................. 32 | *Saragosa, Reeves, 1................. 185 |
| (5,551) ............................... 5,767 | Sandhill, Floyd .............................. 33 | *Saratoga, Hardin, 12 ............... 1,000 |
| Russell, Leon ................................ 27 | Sand Hill, Upshur .......................... 75 | Sardis, Ellis .................................. 60 |
| Rutersville, Fayette ..................... 137 | *Sandia, Jim Wells, 34, (379) ....... 382 | Sargent, Matagorda ..................... 900 |
| Ruth Springs, Henderson ............. 120 | *SAN DIEGO, Duval-Jim Wells, | *Sarita, Kenedy, 11, (238)............ 246 |
| *Rye, Liberty, 5 ........................... 150 | 87, (4,488) ........................ 4,417 | Saron, Trinity .................................. 5 |
| | Sandlin, Stonewall .......................... 3 | Saspamco, Wilson ....................... 300 |
| **S** | Sandoval, Williamson ..................... 60 | *Satin, Falls, 1 .............................. 86 |
| Sabanno, Eastland ........................ 12 | Sandoval, Starr, (32) ..................... 36 | Sattler, Comal ........................... 1,000 |
| *SABINAL, Uvalde, 60, | Sand Springs, Howard, (835) ....... 851 | Saturn, Gonzales .......................... 15 |
| (1,695) ............................... 1,710 | Sandusky, Grayson ....................... 15 | Savannah, Denton, |
| *Sabine Pass, Jefferson, 16, | Sandy, Blanco .............................. 150 | (3,318) ............................... 3,501 |
| ....................[part of Port Arthur] | Sandy, Limestone ............................ 5 | *SAVOY, Fannin, 26, (831) ........... 867 |
| *SACHSE, Dallas-Collin, 509, | Sandy Harbor, Llano ...................... 85 | Scenic Oaks, Bexar, (4,957)... .5,285 |
| (20,229) ............................ 22,385 | Sandy Hill, Washington .................. 50 | Schattel, Frio ................................ 30 |
| *Sacul, Nacogdoches ................. 150 | Sandy Hollow-Escondidas, Nueces, | *SCHERTZ, Guadalupe-Comal- |
| *SADLER, Grayson, 17, (343)...... 349 | (296) ...................................... 308 | Bexar, 959, (31,465).........35,510 |
| Sagerton, Haskell ....................... 171 | SANDY POINT, Brazoria, | Schicke Point, Calhoun .................. 70 |
| *SAGINAW, Tarrant, 492, | (250) ...................................... 210 | Schroeder, Goliad ....................... 347 |
| (19,806) ............................ 21,493 | *SAN ELIZARIO, El Paso, 48, | *SCHULENBURG, Fayette, 234, |
| St. Francis, Potter ......................... 30 | (13,603) ............................ 14,230 | (2,852) ............................... 2,860 |
| *ST. HEDWIG, Bexar, 97, | *SAN FELIPE, Austin, 26, | Schumansville, Guadalupe .......... 678 |
| (2,094) ............................... 2,277 | (747) ...................................... 788 | Schwab City, Polk ....................... 120 |
| *SAINT JO, Montague, 49, | San Fernando, Starr, (68) .............. 69 | *Schwertner, Williamson, 4........... 175 |
| (1,043) ............................... 1,024 | *SANFORD, Hutchinson, 8, | Scissors, Hidalgo, (3,186) .........3,343 |
| St. John Colony, Caldwell............. 150 | (164) ...................................... 165 | *SCOTLAND, Archer, 10, |
| St. Lawrence, Glasscock ............... 90 | | (501) ...................................... 513 |

| Town, County ...............Pop. 2014 | Town, County ...............Pop. 2014 | Town, County ...............Pop. 2014 |
|---|---|---|
| *SCOTTSVILLE, Harrison, 7, (376) .................................... 366 | SHAVANO PARK, Bexar, 113, (3,035) ................................. 3,363 | *SKELLYTOWN, Carson, 14, (473) .................................... 459 |
| Scranton, Eastland ........................ 40 | Shawnee Prairie, Angelina ............ 20 | *Skidmore, Bee, 11, (925) ........... 918 |
| Scrappin Valley, Newton ............... 25 | Shaws Bend, Colorado ................. 100 | Slate Shoals, Lamar ..................... 10 |
| *Scroggins, Franklin, 12 .............. 150 | *Sheffield, Pecos, 9 ..................... 322 | *SLATON, Lubbock, 172, |
| *SCURRY, Kaufman, 37, (681) ..... 715 | Shelby, Austin ............................. 300 | (6,121) .............................. 6,180 |
| *SEABROOK, Harris, 483, (11,952) .......................... 12,735 | *Shelbyville, Shelby, 32 .............. 600 | Slayden, Gonzales ....................... 10 |
| | Sheldon, Harris, (1,990) ........... 2,065 | Slide, Lubbock ........................... 245 |
| *SEADRIFT, Calhoun, 55, (1,364) .............................. 1,425 | SHENANDOAH, Montgomery, 248, (2,134) ...................... 2,681 | *Slidell, Wise, 5........................... 175 |
| *SEAGOVILLE, Dallas, 374, (14,835) .......................... 15,408 | Shep, Taylor.................................. 25 | Sloan, San Saba ......................... 30 |
| *SEAGRAVES, Gaines, 53, (2,417) .............................. 2,609 | *SHEPHERD, San Jacinto, 81, (2,319) .............................. 2,444 | Slocum, Anderson ..................... 150 |
| Seale, Robertson.......................... 60 | *Sheridan, Colorado, 14 ............. 300 | Smetana, Brazos .......................... 80 |
| *SEALY, Austin, 349, (6,019) ..... 6,326 | *SHERMAN, Grayson, 1,600, (38,521) .......................... 39,464 | *SMILEY, Gonzales, 15, (549) ...... 563 |
| Seaton, Bell ................................. 60 | Sherry, Red River .......................... 15 | Smithland, Marion....................... 179 |
| Seawillow, Caldwell ...................... 75 | Sherwood, Irion .......................... 170 | Smith Point, Chambers................ 180 |
| *Sebastian, Willacy, 14, (1,917) .............................. 1,956 | Sherwood Shores, Bell ................ 774 | Smithson Valley, Comal............... 400 |
| Sebastopol, Trinity ..................... 300 | Sherwood Shores, Burnet ........... 920 | *SMITHVILLE, Bastrop, 259, (3,817) .............................. 4,125 |
| Seco Mines, Maverick, (560) ....... 582 | Sherwood Shores, Grayson, (1,190) .............................. 1,179 | Smithwick, Burnet ...................... 102 |
| Security, Montgomery.................. 200 | Shields, Coleman ........................... 8 | *SMYER, Hockley, 6, (474) .......... 497 |
| Sedalia, Collin.............................. 24 | Shiloh, Leon................................. 30 | Smyrna, Cass ............................ 215 |
| Segno, Polk .................................. 80 | Shiloh, Limestone ...................... 250 | Smyrna, Rains .............................. 25 |
| Segovia, Kimble............................ 12 | *SHINER, Lavaca, 149, (2,069) .............................. 2,061 | *SNOOK, Burleson, 27, (511)....... 505 |
| *SEGUIN, Guadalupe, 1,210, (25,175) .......................... 25,757 | Shirley, Hopkins ........................... 20 | Snow Hill, Collin........................... 23 |
| Sejita, Duval ................................ 24 | *Shiro, Grimes, 3 ....................... 210 | Snow Hill, Upshur ........................ 75 |
| Selden, Erath............................... 55 | Shive, Hamilton ........................... 60 | *SNYDER, Scurry, 524, (11,202) .......................... 11,839 |
| Selfs, Fannin................................ 30 | SHOREACRES, Harris, 19, (1,493) .............................. 1,577 | *SOCORRO, El Paso, 596, (32,013) .......................... 32,468 |
| SELMA, Bexar-Guadalupe-Comal, 278, (5,540) .................... 7,431 | Short, Shelby ............................... 15 | Soldier Mound, Dickens................ 10 |
| *Selman City [Turnertown-], Rusk, 6 .......................................... 271 | Shovel Mountain, Burnet ............. 148 | Solis, Cameron, (512)................. 524 |
| *SEMINOLE, Gaines, 307, (6,430) .............................. 7,110 | *Sidney, Comanche, 2 ................ 148 | *SOMERSET, Bexar, 60, (1,631) .............................. 1,734 |
| Sempronius, Austin....................... 25 | Sienna Plantation, Fort Bend, (13,721) .......................... 14,841 | *SOMERVILLE, Burleson, 79, (1,376) .............................. 1,313 |
| Senate, Jack................................ 20 | *Sierra Blanca, Hudspeth, 12, (553) .............................. 567 | Sommer's Mill, Bell ...................... 27 |
| Serbin, Lee ................................ 109 | Siesta Acres, Maverick, (1,885) .............................. 1,936 | *SONORA, Sutton, 153, (3,027) .............................. 2,999 |
| Serenada, Williamson, (1,641) .............................. 1,719 | Siesta Shores, Zapata, (1,382) .............................. 1,446 | *SOUR LAKE, Hardin, 103, (1,813) .............................. 1,899 |
| Seth Ward, Hale, (2,025).......... 2,068 | Silas, Shelby ................................ 75 | South Alamo, Hidalgo, (3,361)... 3,517 |
| SEVEN OAKS, Polk, 1, (111) ....... 115 | Siloam, Bowie .............................. 50 | *South Bend, Young, 2 ................ 100 |
| Seven Pines, Gregg-Upshur.......... 50 | *SILSBEE, Hardin, 288, (6,611) .............................. 7,038 | South Bosque, McLennan ........ 1,523 |
| *SEVEN POINTS, Henderson, 85, (1,455) ...................... 1,409 | *Silver, Coke, 1 ........................... 34 | South Brice, Hall .......................... 10 |
| Seven Sisters, Duval .................... 25 | Silver City, Milam ......................... 25 | South Fork Estates, Jim Hogg, (70) .................................... 74 |
| Sexton, Sabine ............................ 29 | Silver City, Navarro .................... 100 | *SOUTH HOUSTON, Harris, 611, (16,983) .................. 17,443 |
| *SEYMOUR, Baylor, 121, (2,704) .............................. 2,610 | Silver City, Red River .................... 25 | *SOUTHLAKE, Tarrant-Denton, 1,620, (26,575) ................ 28,864 |
| Shadybrook, Cherokee, (1,967) .............................. 2,112 | Silver Creek Village, Burnet.......... 300 | Southland, Garza........................ 157 |
| Shady Grove , Burnet................. 114 | Silver Lake, Van Zandt .................. 42 | South La Paloma , Jim Wells, (345) .................................... 350 |
| Shady Grove, Cherokee ................ 30 | *SILVERTON, Briscoe, 31, (731) .................................... 661 | *SOUTHMAYD, Grayson, 24, (992) ................................ 1,002 |
| Shady Grove, Houston .................. 83 | Silver Valley, Coleman .................. 15 | SOUTH MOUNTAIN, Coryell, (384) .................................... 381 |
| Shady Grove, Panola .................... 45 | Simmons, Live Oak ....................... 65 | *SOUTH PADRE ISLAND, Cameron, 330, (2,816) ....... 2.962 |
| Shady Grove, Smith .................... 250 | *Simms, Bowie, 7 ....................... 300 | *South Plains, Floyd, 1 .................. 67 |
| Shady Grove, Upshur .................... 40 | Simms, Deaf Smith ......................... 6 | South Point, Cameron, (1,376).. 1,437 |
| Shady Hollow, Travis, (5,004)... 5,073 | *SIMONTON, Fort Bend, 37, (814) .................................... 807 | South Purmela, Coryell.................. 10 |
| Shady Oaks, Henderson ............. 300 | Simpsonville, Matagorda ................ 6 | South Shore, Bell ......................... 80 |
| SHADY SHORES, Denton, 63, (2,612) .............................. 2,705 | Simpsonville, Upshur .................. 100 | SOUTHSIDE PLACE, Harris, 61, (1,715) .............................. 1,793 |
| Shafter, Presidio .......................... 57 | Sinclair City, Smith....................... 50 | South Sulphur, Hunt ..................... 60 |
| *SHALLOWATER, Lubbock, 88, (2,484) .............................. 2,497 | Singleton, Grimes ........................ 47 | South Toledo Bend, Newton, (524) .................................... 518 |
| *SHAMROCK, Wheeler, 104, (1,910) .............................. 2,087 | *SINTON, San Patricio, 192, (5,665) .............................. 5,712 | Southton, Bexar.......................... 113 |
| Shangri La, Burnet...................... 108 | Sipe Springs, Comanche............... 70 | *Spade, Lamb, 3, (73) .................. 72 |
| Shankleville, Newton ................... 35 | Sisterdale, Kendall...................... 110 | Spanish Fort, Montague ............... 50 |
| Shannon, Clay ............................. 20 | Sivells Bend, Cooke ..................... 36 | Sparenberg, Dawson.................... 40 |
| Sharp, Milam ............................... 52 | Six Mile, Calhoun........................ 300 | |
| | Skeeterville, San Saba ................. 10 | |

| Town, County ............... Pop. 2014 | Town, County ............... Pop. 2014 | Town, County ............... Pop. 2014 |
|---|---|---|
| Sparks, Bell ...................... 40 | *STAMFORD, Jones-Haskell, | Stratton, DeWitt .............................. 25 |
| Sparks, El Paso, (4,529)............ 4,874 | 126, (3,124) ........................ 2,964 | *STRAWN, Palo Pinto, 26, |
| Speaks, Lavaca............................. 60 | Stampede, Bell ............................... 6 | (653) ................................. 644 |
| *SPEARMAN, Hansford, 121, | Stamps, Upshur.............................. 45 | Streeter, Mason .............................. 85 |
| (3,368) ............................... 3,274 | *STANTON, Martin, 84, | *STREETMAN, Freestone, 22, |
| Speegleville, McLennan ............ 1,655 | (2,492) ............................... 2,847 | (247) ................................ 260 |
| *Spicewood, Burnet, 209 ........... 4,000 | *Staples, Guadalupe, 5, (267) ...... 263 | String Prairie, Bastrop ................ 40 |
| Spider Mountain, Burnet................. 92 | *Star, Mills, 1................................... 97 | Stringtown, Newton ...................... 20 |
| *SPLENDORA, Montgomery, 148, | STAR HARBOR, Henderson, 7, | Structure, Williamson..................... 50 |
| (1,615) ............................... 1,624 | (444) .................................. 448 | Stubblefield, Houston ................... 15 |
| SPOFFORD, Kinney, (95) ........... 103 | Star Route, Cochran...................... 15 | Stubbs, Kaufman ........................ 50 |
| Spraberry, Midland ........................ 46 | Starrville, Smith .............................. 75 | *Study Butte, Brewster, 27, |
| *Spring, Harris, 480, | Startzville, Comal...................... 5,000 | (233) ................................ 241 |
| (54,298) ........................... 58,156 | Steele Hill, Dickens......................... 4 | Sturgeon, Cooke............................ 10 |
| *Spring Branch, Comal, 269 ...... 2,000 | Stephens Creek, San Jacinto ....... 385 | Styx, Kaufman............................... 50 |
| Spring Creek, Hutchinson.............. 20 | *STEPHENVILLE, Erath, 845, | *Sublime, Lavaca............................ 75 |
| Spring Creek, San Saba................ 20 | (17,123) ............................ 18,715 | *SUDAN, Lamb, 20, (958) ........... 935 |
| Springdale, Cass ........................... 55 | Sterley, Floyd ................................. 31 | Sugar Hill, Titus ............................ 90 |
| Springfield, Anderson .................... 30 | *STERLING CITY, Sterling, 39, | *SUGAR LAND, Fort Bend, |
| Spring Gardens, Nueces, (563).... 592 | (888) .................................. 984 | 3,466, (78,817) ................. 81,898 |
| Spring Hill, Bowie ........................ 100 | Stewards Mill, Freestone .............. 22 | Sugar Valley, Matagorda ............. 45 |
| Spring Hill, Navarro ....................... 60 | Stewart, Rusk ................................. 15 | *SULLIVAN CITY, Hidalgo, 69, |
| Spring Hill, San Jacinto ................ 38 | Stiles, Reagan ................................. 4 | (4,002) ............................. 4,253 |
| *SPRINGLAKE, Lamb, 8, | Stillwell Store, Brewster................... 2 | *Sulphur Bluff, Hopkins, 4............. 280 |
| (108) ................................. 106 | *STINNETT, Hutchinson, 53, | *SULPHUR SPRINGS, Hopkins, |
| *SPRINGTOWN, Parker, 275, | (1,881) ............................... 1,842 | 796, (15,449) ................... 15,690 |
| (2,658) ............................... 2,690 | Stith, Jones..................................... 50 | Summerfield, Castro....................... 48 |
| SPRING VALLEY, Harris, 120, | *STOCKDALE, Wilson, 59, | Summerville, Gonzales.................... 45 |
| (3,715) ............................... 4,083 | (1,442) ............................... 1,560 | *Sumner, Lamar, 29....................... 95 |
| Spring Valley, McLennan .............. 400 | Stockman, Shelby........................... 55 | *SUNDOWN, Hockley, 57, |
| *SPUR, Dickens, 55, (1,318)..... 1,247 | Stoneburg, Montague ..................... 51 | (1,397) ............................. 1,439 |
| *Spurger, Tyler, 10 ........................ 590 | Stoneham, Grimes.......................... 15 | Sunnyside, Castro ......................... 64 |
| Stacy, McCulloch ............................ 20 | *Stonewall, Gillespie, 27, | Sunny Side, Waller ....................... 250 |
| Staff, Eastland ............................... 65 | (505) .................................. 526 | Sunnyside, Wilson ....................... 100 |
| *STAFFORD, Fort Bend-Harris, | Stony, Denton ................................. 25 | SUNNYVALE, Dallas, 222, |
| 1,439, (17,693) ................. 17,899 | Stout, Wood .................................. 302 | (5,130) ............................. 5,829 |
| Stag Creek, Comanche ................ 45 | *Stowell, Chambers, 9, | *SUNRAY, Moore, 55, |
| STAGECOACH, Montgomery, 28, | (1,756) ............................... 1,839 | (1,926) ............................. 1,916 |
| (538) ................................. 569 | Stranger, Falls ................................ 12 | Sunrise, Falls................................ 200 |
| Stairtown, Caldwell ........................ 35 | *STRATFORD, Sherman, 70, | *SUNRISE BEACH, Llano, 34, |
| Staley, San Jacinto ........................ 30 | (2,017) ............................... 2,050 | (713) ................................ 710 |

*La Junta general store in Ruidosa. Photo by Robert Plocheck.*

| Town, County ...............Pop. 2014 | Town, County ...............Pop. 2014 | Town, County ...............Pop. 2014 |
|---|---|---|
| *SUNSET, Montague, 20, (497) .................................... 504 | *TENAHA, Shelby, 26, (1,150) ................................ 1,203 | *TIMPSON, Shelby, 70, (1,155) ................................ 1,169 |
| Sunset, Starr, (47) .......................... 49 | Tenmile, Dawson ........................... 30 | Tin Top, Parker ........................... 500 |
| Sunset Acres, Webb, (23).............. 26 | *Tennessee Colony, Anderson, 11.............................................. 300 | *TIOGA, Grayson, 39, (803)........ 820 |
| Sunset Oaks, Burnet ................... 198 | | TIRA, Hopkins, (297).................... 301 |
| SUNSET VALLEY, Travis, 133, (648) .................................... 683 | *Tennyson, Coke, 1 ...................... 46 | *Tivoli, Refugio, 7, (479) ............ 482 |
| SUN VALLEY, Lamar, 3, (69).......... 73 | *Terlingua, Brewster, (58) .............. 59 | TOCO, Lamar, 2, (75).................... 75 |
| SURFSIDE BEACH, Brazoria, 24, (482) ................................ 528 | *TERRELL, Kaufman, 734, (15,816) ........................... 16,287 | Todd City, Anderson...................... 10 |
| *Sutherland Springs, Wilson, 8..... 420 | TERRELL HILLS, Bexar, 122, (4,878) .............................. 5,199 | TODD MISSION, Grimes, 83, (107) .................................... 114 |
| Swamp City, Gregg.......................... 8 | Terry Chapel, Falls......................... 30 | Tokio, McLennan .......................... 250 |
| Swan, Smith ................................. 150 | Terryville, DeWitt............................ 40 | Tokio, Terry .................................... 6 |
| *SWEENY, Brazoria, 115, (3,684) ................................ 3,725 | *TEXARKANA, Bowie, (Miller Co., Ark.), 2,673, (66,035) ....... 67,697 | *TOLAR, Hood, 40, (681) ............ 724 |
| Sweet Home, Guadalupe ............. 294 | *TEXAS CITY, Galveston, 971, (45,099) ........................... 45,823 | Tolbert, Wilbarger ......................... 15 |
| *Sweet Home, Lavaca, 5.............. 360 | | Tolette, Lamar................................ 40 |
| Sweet Home, Lee .......................... 30 | TEXHOMA, Sherman, (Texas Co., Okla.), 25, (1,295) .............. 1,295 | Tolosa, Kaufman............................ 65 |
| Sweet Union, Cherokee................. 40 | *TEXLINE, Dallam, 23, (507)........ 519 | *TOMBALL, Harris, 1,348, (10,753) ........................... 11,162 |
| *SWEETWATER, Nolan, 404, (10,906) ........................... 10,652 | Texroy, Hutchinson ........................ 50 | *TOM BEAN, Grayson, 21, (1,045) ................................ 1,043 |
| Swenson, Stonewall ...................... 80 | Thalia, Foard ................................. 50 | |
| Swift, Nacogdoches...................... 210 | *THE COLONY, Denton, 885, (36,328) ........................... 39,640 | Tomlinson Hill, Falls...................... 64 |
| Swiss Alp, Fayette ........................ 17 | Thedford, Smith ............................ 65 | TOOL, Henderson, 58, (2,240) ................................ 2,265 |
| Sylvan, Lamar................................ 68 | The Grove, Coryell ....................... 100 | Topsey, Coryell ............................. 35 |
| *Sylvester, Fisher, 1....................... 79 | THE HILLS, Travis, (2,472) ....... 2,599 | *Tornillo, El Paso, 17, (1,568).... 1,572 |
| | Thelma, Bexar ............................. 150 | Tours, McLennan ......................... 130 |
| **T** | Thelma, Limestone ........................ 20 | *Tow, Llano, 7 .............................. 305 |
| Tabor, Brazos .............................. 150 | Theon, Williamson ......................... 30 | Town Bluff, Tyler .......................... 429 |
| Tadmor, Houston ........................... 67 | Thermo, Hopkins ........................... 56 | *TOYAH, Reeves, 1, (90) .............. 92 |
| *TAFT, San Patricio, 78, (3,048) ................................ 3,056 | *The Woodlands, Montgomery, 591, (93,847)................... 99,040 | *Toyahvale, Reeves, 1.................... 60 |
| Taft Southwest, San Patricio, (1,460) ................................ 1,483 | *Thicket, Hardin, 6........................ 306 | Tradewinds, San Patricio, (180) ... 184 |
| | *Thomaston, DeWitt, 2 ................. 45 | Travis, Falls .................................. 48 |
| *TAHOKA, Lynn, 74, (2,673) ................................ 2,548 | *THOMPSONS, Fort Bend, 4, (246) .................................... 267 | Travis Ranch, Kaufman, (2,556) ................................ 2,680 |
| *TALCO, Titus, 18, (516) .............. 523 | Thompsonville, Gonzales .............. 30 | Trawick, Nacogdoches ................. 375 |
| *Talpa, Coleman, 7 ...................... 127 | Thompsonville, Jim Hogg, (46)....... 45 | Treasure Island, Guadalupe ......... 172 |
| TALTY, Kaufman, 27, (1,535)..... 1,793 | Thornberry, Clay ........................... 75 | Treasure Island, Brazoria ............ 152 |
| Tamina, Montgomery.................... 900 | *THORNDALE, Milam, 72, (1,336) ................................ 1,311 | *TRENT, Taylor, 6, (337)............. 339 |
| Tanglewood, Lee ........................... 60 | *THORNTON, Limestone, 22, (526) .................................... 517 | *TRENTON, Fannin, 57, (635) .................................... 660 |
| Tanquecitos South Acres, Webb, (233) .................................... 240 | THORNTONVILLE, Ward, 7, (476) .................................... 514 | Trickham, Coleman ........................ 29 |
| Tanquecitos South Acres II, Webb, (50) ...................................... 52 | Thorp Spring, Hood .................... 222 | Trimmer, Bell ............................... 390 |
| Tarkington Prairie, Liberty............. 300 | *THRALL, Williamson, 31, (839) .................................... 896 | *TRINIDAD, Henderson, 30, (886) .................................... 885 |
| *Tarpley, Bandera, 2 ...................... 30 | Three League, Martin ..................... 20 | *TRINITY, Trinity, 153, (2,697) ................................ 2,545 |
| *Tarzan, Martin, 8 .......................... 30 | Three Oaks, Wilson ..................... 150 | TROPHY CLUB, Denton, 241, (8,024) ................................ 9,960 |
| Tascosa Hills, Potter...................... 90 | *THREE RIVERS, Live Oak, 115, (1,848) ................................ 1,939 | *TROUP, Smith-Cherokee, 115, (1,869) ................................ 1,884 |
| *TATUM, Rusk-Panola, 70, (1,385) ................................ 1,412 | Three States, Cass........................ 45 | Trout Creek, Newton ...................... 70 |
| *TAYLOR, Williamson, 528, (15,191) ........................... 16,178 | *THROCKMORTON, Throckmorton, 50, (828) ................................ 802 | *TROY, Bell, 90, (1,645) ............ 1,752 |
| TAYLOR LAKE VILLAGE, Harris, 80, (3,544) ........................ 3,621 | Thunderbird Bay, Brown, (663)..... 708 | Truby, Jones .................................. 26 |
| TAYLOR LANDING, Jefferson, (228) .................................... 229 | Thurber, Erath................................ 48 | Trumbull, Ellis ............................. 100 |
| Taylorsville, Caldwell ..................... 35 | Tidwell, Hunt ................................. 50 | Truscott, Knox ............................... 50 |
| Taylor Town, Lamar ....................... 40 | Tierra Bonita, Cameron, (141)...... 139 | Tucker, Anderson ........................ 175 |
| Tazewell, Hopkins.......................... 20 | Tierra Dorada, Starr, (28) ............. 30 | *Tuleta, Bee, 10, (288) ................ 296 |
| *TEAGUE, Freestone, 119, (3,560) ................................ 3,697 | Tierra Grande, Nueces, (356)...... 421 | *TULIA, Swisher, 148, (4,967) ................................ 4,771 |
| Teaselville, Smith......................... 150 | Tierra Verde, Nueces, (277) ........ 295 | Tulip, Fannin ................................. 10 |
| *TEHUACANA, Limestone, 2, (283) .................................... 272 | Tigertown, Lamar.......................... 400 | Tulsita, Bee, (14) ........................... 12 |
| Telegraph, Kimble............................ 3 | TIKI ISLAND, Galveston, 29, (968) .................................... 993 | Tundra, Van Zandt.......................... 34 |
| *Telephone, Fannin, 10................. 210 | *Tilden, McMullen, 16, (261) .................................... 321 | Tunis, Burleson ........................... 150 |
| *Telferner, Victoria, 7 ................... 700 | Tilmon, Caldwell ............................ 60 | *TURKEY, Hall, 13, (421) ............. 409 |
| Telico, Ellis ................................. 115 | TIMBERCREEK CANYON, Randall, (418)........................ 434 | Turlington, Freestone ..................... 27 |
| *Tell, Childress............................... 20 | Timberwood, Bexar, (13,447) .. 14,625 | Turnersville, Coryell ..................... 125 |
| *TEMPLE, Bell, 2,043, (66,102) ........................... 70,730 | | Turnersville, Travis ........................ 90 |
| | | *Turnertown-Selman City, Rusk, 6 ................................... 271 |
| | | Turtle Bayou, Chambers................. 55 |
| | | *TUSCOLA, Taylor, 58, (742) ....... 750 |
| | | Tuxedo, Jones ............................... 42 |

| Town, County ...............Pop. 2014 | Town, County ...............Pop. 2014 | Town, County ...............Pop. 2014 |
|---|---|---|
| Twichell, Ochiltree ........................... 22 | Vasco, Delta ..................................... 20 | *WALNUT SPRINGS, Bosque, |
| Twitty, Wheeler ............................... 12 | Vashti, Clay...................................... 70 |    21, (827) .................................. 843 |
| *TYE, Taylor, 55, (1,242) .......... 1,254 | Vattmann, Kleberg ........................... 25 | Walton, Van Zandt ........................... 60 |
| *TYLER, Smith, 4,510, | Vaughan, Hill ................................... 75 | Wamba, Bowie ............................... 430 |
|    (96,900) .................................98,987 | Veach, San Augustine .................... 12 | Waneta, Houston ............................. 19 |
| *Tynan, Bee, 7, (278)..................... 282 | Vealmoor, Howard ............................. 5 | Waples, Hood ................................ 155 |
| Type, Williamson-Bastrop............... 40 | *VEGA, Oldham, 36, (884) .......... 902 | *Warda, Fayette, 6........................ 121 |
| | *VENUS, Johnson, 63, | Ward Creek, Bowie .......................... 10 |
| **U** |    (2,960) ................................3,174 | *Waring, Kendall, 9......................... 73 |
| UHLAND, Hays-Caldwell, 15, | Vera, Knox....................................... 30 | *Warren, Tyler, 22, (757).............. 833 |
|    (1,014) .................................. 1,022 | Verdi, Atascosa ............................. 110 | WARREN CITY, Gregg-Upshur, |
| Umbarger, Randall, 1.................... 327 | Verhalen, Reeves ............................ 12 |    8, (298) .................................. 460 |
| UNCERTAIN, Harrison, 7, (94) ....... 94 | *Veribest, Tom Green, 3 .............. 115 | Warrenton, Fayette ....................... 186 |
| Union, Scurry.................................. 20 | *VERNON, Wilbarger, 361, | Warsaw, Kaufman ......................... 100 |
| Union, Terry ...................................... 8 |    (11,002) ...........................10,533 | Washburn, Armstrong .................... 120 |
| Union, Wilson .................................. 52 | Verona, Collin .................................. 34 | *Washington, Washington, 19 ...... 100 |
| Union Grove, Bell ........................... 12 | Vessey, Red River .......................... 15 | *WASKOM, Harrison, 76, |
| UNION GROVE, Upshur, 4, | Viboras, Starr................................... 15 |    (2,160) .................................. 2,155 |
|    (357) ........................................ 365 | Vick, Concho .................................... 20 | Wastella, Nolan .............................. 12 |
| Union High, Navarro ...................... 30 | Victoria, Limestone ......................... 25 | *WATAUGA, Tarrant, 578, |
| Union Hill, Denton.......................... 25 | *VICTORIA, Victoria, 2,750, |    (23,497) ...........................24,418 |
| UNION VALLEY, Hunt, (307) ........ 322 |    (62,592) ...........................64,834 | Waterloo, Williamson...................... 70 |
| Unity, Lamar ................................... 60 | Victoria Vera, Starr, (110) ............111 | Waterman, Shelby ........................... 40 |
| UNIVERSAL CITY, Bexar, 591, | Victory City, Bowie......................... 350 | *Water Valley, Tom Green, 3......... 203 |
|    (18,530) ............................ 19,540 | *VIDOR, Orange, 481, | Watson, Burnet................................ 50 |
| UNIVERSITY PARK, Dallas, 848, |    (10,579) ...........................10,746 | Watt, Limestone .............................. 25 |
|    (23,068) ............................ 23,739 | Vienna, Lavaca ............................... 40 | Waverly, San Jacinto .................... 200 |
| Upper Meyersville, DeWitt............. 33 | View, Taylor ................................... 350 | *WAXAHACHIE, Ellis, 1,122, |
| Upshaw, Nacogdoches.................. 400 | Vigo Park, Swisher ......................... 36 |    (29,621) ...........................31,621 |
| Upton, Bastrop ................................ 25 | Villa del Sol, Cameron, (175)........ 194 | Wayne, Cass .................................... 15 |
| Urbana, San Jacinto ....................... 15 | *Village Mills, Hardin, 11 .............. 200 | Wayside, Armstrong, 2 ................... 25 |
| Utley, Bastrop ................................. 30 | Villa Pancho, Cameron, (788) ..... 835 | Wayside, Roberts ............................ 40 |
| Utopia, Uvalde, 33, (227)............. 228 | Villarreal, Starr, (131)................... 135 | Wealthy, Leon ................................. 12 |
| UVALDE, Uvalde, 561, | Villa Verde, Hidalgo, (874)........... 895 | *WEATHERFORD, Parker, |
|    (15,751) ............................ 16,201 | Vincent, Howard ............................. 10 |    1,590, (25,250) ...................26,879 |
| Uvalde Estates, Uvalde, | Vineyard, Jack ................................. 19 | Weatherly, Hall ................................. 8 |
|    (2,171) .................................. 2,228 | VINTON, El Paso, 90, (1,971) .. 1,948 | Weaver, Hopkins ............................. 35 |
| | Violet, Nueces .............................. 160 | WEBBERVILLE, Travis, 12, |
| **V** | Vistula, Houston ............................. 21 |    (392) ........................................ 417 |
| Valdasta, Collin .............................. 82 | *Voca, McCulloch, 4 ....................... 56 | Webbville, Coleman......................... 15 |
| *VALENTINE, Jeff Davis, 1, | VOLENTE, Travis, 31, (520)........ 554 | *WEBSTER, Harris, 791, |
|    (134)......................................... 124 | Volga, Houston .................................. 9 |    (10,400) ...........................11,035 |
| *Valera, Coleman, 3........................ 80 | *VON ORMY, Bexar, 70, | Weches, Houston ............................ 46 |
| Valle de Oro, Potter ..................... 250 |    (1,085)..................................1,111 | Weedhaven, Jackson ...................... 35 |
| Valle Vista, Starr, (469)................ 488 | Voss, Coleman, 2 ............................ 20 | Weeping Mary, Cherokee ............... 85 |
| Valley Creek, Fannin .................... 110 | *Votaw, Hardin, 4........................... 160 | *Weesatche, Goliad, 2.................. 411 |
| *VALLEY MILLS, Bosque- | Vsetin, Lavaca ................................ 45 | *WEIMAR, Colorado, 180, |
|    McLennan, 76, (1,203) ....... 1,223 | |    (2,151) .................................. 2,223 |
| *Valley Spring, Llano, 1 ................. 50 | **W** | *WEINERT, Haskell, 7, (172)........ 169 |
| *VALLEY VIEW, Cooke, 63, | *WACO, McLennan, 4,397, | *WEIR, Williamson, 14, (450)....... 462 |
|    (757) ........................................ 780 |    (124,805) ........................129,179 | Wiess Bluff, Jasper......................... 60 |
| Valley View, Runnels ...................... 10 | *Wadsworth, Matagorda, 12......... 160 | *Welch, Dawson, 6, (222)............ 229 |
| Valley View, Upshur........................ 75 | *WAELDER, Gonzales, 27, | Welcome, Austin ........................... 300 |
| Valley View, Wichita...................... 210 |    (1,065) .................................. 1,091 | Weldon, Houston ........................... 131 |
| Valley Wells, Dimmit ....................... 21 | Wagner, Hunt ................................... 75 | Welfare, Kendall ............................. 10 |
| Val Verde, Milam ............................ 25 | *Waka, Ochiltree, 2......................... 65 | *Wellborn, Brazos, 4..................... 400 |
| Val Verde Park, Val Verde, | Wakefield, Polk ............................... 25 | *WELLINGTON, Collingsworth, |
|    (2,384) .................................. 2,439 | *WAKE VILLAGE, Bowie, 106, |    79, (2,189) .......................... 2,077 |
| *Van, Van Zandt, 111, |    (5,492) .................................. 5,555 | *WELLMAN, Terry, 2, (203) ......... 203 |
|    (2,632) .................................. 2,720 | *Walburg, Williamson, 5 .............. 277 | *WELLS, Cherokee, 20, (790)...... 825 |
| *VAN ALSTYNE, Grayson, 155, | Walcott, Deaf Smith.......................... 5 | Wells, Lynn ..................................... 10 |
|    (3,046) .................................. 3,137 | Waldeck, Fayette ............................. 34 | Wells Branch, Travis, |
| Vance, Real ..................................... 20 | Waldrip, McCulloch.......................... 15 |    (12,120) ...........................12,783 |
| *Vancourt, Tom Green, 1 .............. 131 | Walhalla, Fayette ............................ 38 | *WESLACO, Hidalgo, 988, |
| Vandalia, Red River........................ 35 | *Wall, Tom Green, 11..................... 329 |    (35,670) ...........................37,515 |
| *Vanderbilt, Jackson, 6, (395)....... 401 | Wallace, Van Zandt.......................... 70 | Wesley, Washington-Austin ........... 65 |
| *Vanderpool, Bandera, 3 ............... 20 | *WALLER, Waller-Harris, 251, | Wesley Grove, Walker .................... 25 |
| Vandyke, Comanche ....................... 20 |    (2,326) .................................. 2,445 | *WEST, McLennan, 180, |
| *VAN HORN, Culberson, 83, | *WALLIS, Austin, 71, (1,252) ... 1,290 |    (2,807) .................................. 2,851 |
|    (2,063) .................................. 2,040 | *Wallisville, Chambers, 15............ 300 | West Alto Bonito, Starr, (696) ...... 718 |
| *Van Vleck, Matagorda, 29, | Walnut Bend, Cooke....................... 45 | *WESTBROOK, Mitchell, 13, |
|    (1,844) .................................. 1,912 | Walnut Grove, Panola ................... 125 |    (253)......................................... 245 |

| Town, County .............. Pop. 2014 | Town, County .............. Pop. 2014 | Town, County .............. Pop. 2014 |
|---|---|---|

*WEST COLUMBIA, Brazoria,
182, (3,905) ...................... 3,969
Westcott, San Jacinto ................... 55
Westdale, Jim Wells, (372) .......... 406
Western Lake, Parker, (1,525)... 1,573
*Westhoff, DeWitt, 3 ................... 410
WESTLAKE, Tarrant-Denton,
78, (992) .............................. 1,130
*WEST LAKE HILLS, Travis, 473,
(3,063) ............................... 3,319
West Livingston, Polk, (8,071)... 8,479
West Mineola, Wood .................... 20
*Westminster, Collin, (861) .......... 964
West Mountain, Upshur ................ 325
West Odessa, Ector,
(22,707) .......................... 24,288
*WESTON, Collin, 14, (563) ......... 570
WESTON LAKES, Fort Bend,
(2,482) .............................. 2,452
WEST ORANGE, Orange, 97,
(3,443) ............................... 3,454
Westover, Baylor .......................... 18
WESTOVER HILLS, Tarrant,
(682) ...................................... 715
Westphalia, Falls ......................... 186
*West Point, Fayette, 10 .............. 213
West Sharyland, Hidalgo,
(2,309) .............................. 2,414
West Sinton, San Patricio ............ 150
WEST TAWAKONI, Hunt, 46,
(1,576) .............................. 1,629
WEST UNIVERSITY PLACE,
Harris, 309, (14,787) ........ 15,506
Westville, Trinity .......................... 46
Westway, Deaf Smith ................... 15
Westway, El Paso, (4,188) ........ 4,262
Westwood Shores, Trinity,
(1,162) .............................. 1,170
WESTWORTH VILLAGE, Tarrant,
46, (2,472) ......................... 2,623
*WHARTON, Wharton, 360,
(8,832) .............................. 8,664
Wheatland, Tarrant ...................... 175
*WHEELER, Wheeler, 73,
(1,592) .............................. 1,750
Wheeler Springs, Houston ............. 89
*Wheelock, Robertson, 6 .............. 225
White City, San Augustine ............. 20
White City, Wilbarger .................... 40
*WHITE DEER, Carson, 34,
(1,000) .................................. 976
*WHITEFACE, Cochran, 16,
(449) ...................................... 420
Whiteflat, Motley ............................ 4
White Hall, Bell ........................... 262
Whitehall, Grimes .......................... 30
*WHITEHOUSE, Smith, 294,
(7,660) .............................. 7,908
*WHITE OAK, Gregg, 252,
(6,489) .............................. 6,511
White Oak, Titus ........................... 60
White River Lake, Crosby .............. 83
White Rock, Hunt .......................... 60
White Rock, Red River .................. 90
White Rock, Robertson .................. 80
White Rock, San Augustine ........... 60
*WHITESBORO, Grayson, 178,
(3,793) ............................... 3,853
*WHITE SETTLEMENT, Tarrant,
301, (16,116) ................... 16,790
White Star, Motley .......................... 6
Whiteway, Hamilton ........................ 8

*WHITEWRIGHT, Grayson-Fannin,
87, (1,604) ......................... 1,625
*Whitharral, Hockley, 2 ................ 158
Whitman, Washington .................... 25
*WHITNEY, Hill, 187, (2,087) ..... 2,058
*Whitsett, Live Oak, 4 .................. 200
Whitson, Coryell ............................ 50
*Whitt, Parker ................................ 38
Whon, Coleman .............................. 35
*WICHITA FALLS, Wichita,
3,116, (104,553) ............ 105,984
*WICKETT, Ward, 29, (498) ......... 525
Wied, Lavaca ................................. 65
Wiedeville, Washington .................. 35
*Wiergate, Newton, 2 .................. 350
Wigginsville, Montgomery ............. 100
Wilcox, Burleson ............................ 39
Wilderville, Falls ............................ 45
*Wildorado, Oldham, 6 ................. 210
Wild Peach, Brazoria, (2,452).... 2,546
Wildwood, Hardin, (1,235) ......... 1,305
Wilkins, Upshur .............................. 75
Willamar, Willacy, (15) .................. 15
William Penn, Washington .............. 40
*WILLIS, Montgomery, 410,
(5,662) .............................. 5,964
*Willow City, Gillespie, 4 ............... 22
Willow Grove, McLennan .............. 100
WILLOW PARK, Parker, 155,
(3,982) .............................. 4,376
Willow Springs, Fayette ................. 74
Willow Springs, Rains .................... 25
*WILLS POINT, Van Zandt, 222,
(3,524) .............................. 3,594
*WILMER, Dallas, 55, (3,682) ... 3,742
Wilmeth, Runnels ........................... 15
Wilson, Falls ................................. 42
*WILSON, Lynn, 12, (489) ........... 469
*WIMBERLEY, Hays, 636,
(2,626) .............................. 2,548
Winchell, Brown ............................. 20
Winchester, Fayette ...................... 232
WINDCREST, Bexar, 250,
(5,364) .............................. 5,700
Windemere, Travis, (1,037) ....... 1,086
*WINDOM, Fannin, 13, (199) ....... 207
*WINDTHORST, Archer, 37,
(409) ...................................... 425
Winedale, Fayette .......................... 67
*WINFIELD, Titus, 23, (524) ......... 535
WINFREE [Old River-], Chambers,
17, (1,245) ......................... 1,248
*Wingate, Runnels, 4 ................... 100
*WINK, Winkler, 24, (940) .......... 1,028
Winkler, Navarro-Freestone ........... 26
*Winnie, Chambers, 131,
(3,254) .............................. 3,423
*WINNSBORO, Wood-Franklin,
301, (3,252) ....................... 3,458
*WINONA, Smith, 56, (576) .......... 588
Winter Haven, Dimmit ................... 123
*WINTERS, Runnels, 86,
(2,562) .............................. 2,452
Witting, Lavaca .............................. 90
WIXON VALLEY, Brazos, 17,
(254) ...................................... 252
Wizard Wells, Jack ........................ 69
*Woden, Nacogdoches, 3 ............. 400
*WOLFE CITY, Hunt, 51,
(1,412) .............................. 1,430
*WOLFFORTH, Lubbock, 158,
(3,670) .............................. 4,082

Womack, Bosque ........................... 25
Woodbine, Cooke ......................... 250
WOODBRANCH, Montgomery,
(1,282) .............................. 1,357
Woodbury, Hill ............................... 45
WOODCREEK, Hays, 43,
(1,457) .............................. 1,461
Wooded Hills, Johnson ................. 580
Wood Hi, Victoria .......................... 35
*Woodlake, Trinity, 2 ................... 180
Woodland, Red River .................... 128
*Woodlawn, Harrison, 7 ............... 550
WOODLOCH, Montgomery,
(207) ...................................... 218
Woodrow, Fort Bend ..................... 190
Woodrow, Lubbock .................... 2,034
Woods, Panola ............................... 65
*WOODSBORO, Refugio, 55,
(1,512) .............................. 1,469
*WOODSON, Throckmorton, 14,
(264) ...................................... 259
Wood Springs, Smith .................... 200
Woodville, Cherokee ...................... 20
*WOODVILLE, Tyler, 187,
(2,586) .............................. 2,636
Woodward, La Salle ......................... 6
WOODWAY, McLennan, 317,
(8,452) .............................. 8,764
Woosley, Rains .............................. 47
*WORTHAM, Freestone, 41,
(1,073) .............................. 1,048
Worthing, Lavaca ........................... 55
Wright City, Smith ........................ 172
Wrightsboro, Gonzales .................. 10
Wyldwood, Bastrop, (2,505) ...... 2,695
*WYLIE, Collin-Rockwall-Dallas,
1,029, (41,427) ................ 45,032
Wylie, Taylor, ........... [part of Abilene]

**Y**

*Yancey, Medina, 6 ...................... 209
*YANTIS, Wood, 54, (388) ........... 399
Yard, Anderson .............................. 50
Yarrellton, Milam ........................... 35
Yellowpine, Sabine ........................ 97
*YOAKUM, Lavaca-DeWitt, 223,
(5,815) .............................. 5,928
*YORKTOWN, DeWitt, 113,
(2,092) .............................. 2,086
Youngsport, Bell ............................ 49
Yowell, Delta-Hunt ........................ 30
Ysleta del Sur Pueblo, El Paso,
(350) ...................................... 350
Yznaga, Cameron, (91) .................. 99

**Z**

Zabcikville, Bell .............................. 76
*Zapata, Zapata, 160,
(5,089) .............................. 5,091
Zapata Ranch, Willacy, (108) ........ 111
Zarate, Starr, (59) .......................... 60
*ZAVALLA, Angelina, 37,
(713) ...................................... 726
*Zephyr, Brown, 13 ...................... 201
Zimmerscheidt, Colorado .............. 50
Zion Hill, Guadalupe .................... 595
Zipperlandville, Falls ...................... 22
Zorn, Guadalupe .......................... 287
Zuehl, Guadalupe, (376) .............. 384
Zunkerville, Karnes ........................ 15

# Elections

*Gov. Greg Abbott, First Lady Cecilia Abbott, and daughter Audrey on a large screen at the Inaugural Ball in Austin. Photo by Lamberto Alvarez.*

**2014 Governor's Race**
**Results by County**
**General Election**
**Party Primary Elections**

# 2014 Election Results for Governor, Lt. Governor

Below are the results by county in the races for governor and lieutenant governor. The Democratic Party candidate for governor was state Sen. Wendy Davis of Fort Worth. The Republican Party candidate was state Attorney Gen. Greg Abbott.

The Republican candidate for lieutenant governor was state Sen. Dan Patrick of Houston. The Demo-cratic candidate was state Sen. Leticia Van der Putte of San Antonio.

The voting age population in 2014 was estimated at 18,915,297.

The statewide turnout in the previous gubernatorial election in 2010 was 38 percent of the registered voters. *Source: Texas Secretary of State.*

| COUNTY | Registered Voters | Turn-out % | GOVERNOR | | | | LT. GOVERNOR | | | |
|---|---|---|---|---|---|---|---|---|---|---|
| | | | Abbott | % | Davis | % | Patrick | % | Van der Putte | % |
| **Statewide** | **14,025,441** | **33.70** | **2,796,547** | **59.15** | **1,835,596** | **38.83** | **2,724,493** | **58.14** | **1,813,974** | **38.71** |
| Anderson | 26,938 | 37.91 | 7,732 | 75.70 | 2,286 | 22.38 | 7,659 | 75.27 | 2,215 | 21.76 |
| Andrews | 8,521 | 26.06 | 1,988 | 93.28 | 203 | 9.14 | 1,950 | 88.67 | 205 | 9.32 |
| Angelina | 49,862 | 33.69 | 12,940 | 77.01 | 3,686 | 21.93 | 12,749 | 76.22 | 3,625 | 21.67 |
| Aransas | 15,804 | 37.99 | 4,460 | 73.55 | 1,480 | 24.29 | 4,364 | 72.67 | 1,455 | 24.22 |
| Archer | 6,290 | 41.90 | 2,297 | 87.13 | 302 | 11.45 | 2,261 | 86.96 | 287 | 11.03 |
| Armstrong | 1,329 | 42.96 | 502 | 87.91 | 59 | 10.33 | 507 | 89.57 | 40 | 7.06 |
| Atascosa | 24,575 | 30.37 | 4,760 | 63.76 | 2,589 | 34.68 | 4,535 | 61.01 | 2,764 | 37.18 |
| Austin | 18,562 | 38.69 | 5,813 | 80.93 | 1,252 | 17.43 | 5,739 | 80.17 | 1,238 | 17.29 |
| Bailey | 3,527 | 28.46 | 868 | 86.45 | 130 | 12.94 | 834 | 83.65 | 151 | 15.14 |
| Bandera | 14,845 | 42.74 | 4,911 | 77.38 | 1,257 | 19.80 | 4,853 | 76.46 | 1,261 | 19.86 |
| Bastrop | 42,505 | 39.90 | 9,803 | 57.79 | 6,566 | 38.71 | 9,635 | 57.31 | 6,289 | 37.40 |
| Baylor | 2,511 | 33.61 | 700 | 82.93 | 134 | 15.87 | 667 | 81.14 | 128 | 15.57 |
| Bee | 15,113 | 34.57 | 2,972 | 56.86 | 2,128 | 40.71 | 2,719 | 53.09 | 2,267 | 44.26 |
| Bell | 168,877 | 26.04 | 28,778 | 65.42 | 14,412 | 32.76 | 28,595 | 65.39 | 13,864 | 31.70 |
| Bexar | 957,110 | 31.44 | 149,697 | 49.74 | 145,711 | 48.41 | 139,505 | 46.55 | 153,105 | 51.09 |
| Blanco | 7,390 | 48.82 | 2,622 | 72.67 | 874 | 24.22 | 2,606 | 72.50 | 831 | 23.12 |
| Borden | 439 | 59.22 | 240 | 92.30 | 18 | 6.92 | 229 | 90.51 | 16 | 6.32 |
| Bosque | 11,824 | 41.50 | 3,881 | 79.07 | 933 | 19.00 | 3,840 | 79.11 | 862 | 17.75 |
| Bowie | 57,235 | 37.62 | 15,583 | 72.37 | 5,564 | 25.84 | 15,484 | 73.23 | 5,024 | 23.76 |
| Brazoria | 183,488 | 33.94 | 41,373 | 66.43 | 19,703 | 31.63 | 40,876 | 65.91 | 19,087 | 30.78 |
| Brazos | 92,928 | 34.01 | 21.859 | 69.15 | 9,125 | 28.86 | 20,929 | 66.79 | 9,148 | 29.19 |
| Brewster | 7,032 | 41.35 | 1,499 | 51.54 | 1,311 | 45.08 | 1,395 | 48.98 | 1,279 | 44.90 |
| Briscoe | 1,132 | 45.05 | 431 | 84.50 | 75 | 14.70 | 430 | 84.64 | 65 | 12.79 |
| Brooks | 6,433 | 33.35 | 588 | 27.39 | 1,478 | 68.87 | 427 | 20.74 | 1,556 | 75.60 |
| Brown | 22,744 | 36.05 | 7,176 | 87.50 | 901 | 10.98 | 7,042 | 86.38 | 883 | 10.83 |
| Burleson | 11,050 | 38.08 | 3,199 | 76.02 | 959 | 22.78 | 3,140 | 75.28 | 938 | 22.48 |
| Burnet | 27,384 | 43.39 | 8,995 | 75.69 | 2,571 | 21.63 | 9,007 | 75.86 | 2,360 | 19.87 |
| Caldwell | 21,175 | 42.05 | 5,037 | 56.55 | 3,578 | 40.17 | 5,042 | 57.08 | 3,441 | 38.95 |
| Calhoun | 12,700 | 32.71 | 2,737 | 65.87 | 1,326 | 31.91 | 2,666 | 64.89 | 1,308 | 31.84 |
| Callahan | 8,838 | 33.59 | 2,636 | 88.78 | 285 | 9.59 | 2,582 | 87.14 | 291 | 9.82 |
| Cameron | 186,563 | 21.12 | 16,556 | 42.01 | 21,859 | 55.46 | 14,527 | 37.46 | 23,094 | 59.55 |
| Camp | 7,218 | 36.20 | 1,862 | 71.25 | 718 | 27.47 | 1,808 | 69.72 | 721 | 27.80 |
| Carson | 4,248 | 43.71 | 1,634 | 87.99 | 193 | 10.39 | 1,613 | 87.99 | 167 | 9.11 |
| Cass | 19,251 | 36.08 | 5,185 | 74.63 | 1,687 | 24.28 | 5,137 | 74.63 | 1,593 | 23.14 |
| Castro | 3,963 | 29.06 | 917 | 79.60 | 217 | 18.83 | 901 | 79.24 | 204 | 17.94 |
| Chambers | 25,104 | 33.52 | 6,778 | 80.54 | 1,490 | 17.70 | 6,717 | 80.23 | 1,420 | 16.96 |
| Cherokee | 26,944 | 35.92 | 7,709 | 79.57 | 1,862 | 19.21 | 7,600 | 78.96 | 1,821 | 18.91 |
| Childress | 3,569 | 30.68 | 944 | 86.21 | 134 | 12.23 | 942 | 86.50 | 129 | 11.84 |
| Clay | 7,610 | 37.34 | 2,436 | 85.71 | 363 | 12.77 | 2,393 | 85.55 | 339 | 12.12 |
| Cochran | 1,772 | 27.93 | 423 | 85.45 | 65 | 13.13 | 407 | 83.40 | 65 | 13.31 |
| Coke | 2,135 | 36.06 | 696 | 90.38 | 67 | 8.70 | 663 | 86.66 | 82 | 10.71 |
| Coleman | 5,902 | 37.95 | 1,974 | 88.12 | 234 | 10.44 | 1,922 | 87.16 | 225 | 10.20 |
| Collin | 485,406 | 36.49 | 116,365 | 65.69 | 57,757 | 32.60 | 113,844 | 64.76 | 56,379 | 32.07 |
| Collingsworth | 1,890 | 42.43 | 651 | 81.17 | 132 | 16.45 | 651 | 84.32 | 98 | 12.69 |
| Colorado | 13,414 | 38.44 | 3,881 | 75.25 | 1,192 | 23.11 | 3,825 | 74.85 | 1,166 | 22.81 |
| Comal | 82,137 | 42.27 | 26,642 | 76.73 | 7,428 | 21.39 | 25,939 | 74.89 | 7,703 | 22.23 |
| Comanche | 8,593 | 35.71 | 2,447 | 79.73 | 544 | 17.72 | 2,415 | 78.84 | 523 | 17.07 |
| Concho | 1,645 | 36.35 | 511 | 85.45 | 77 | 12.87 | 491 | 83.93 | 76 | 12.99 |
| Cooke | 23,970 | 36.79 | 7,402 | 83.93 | 1,273 | 14.43 | 7,311 | 83.32 | 1,241 | 14.14 |

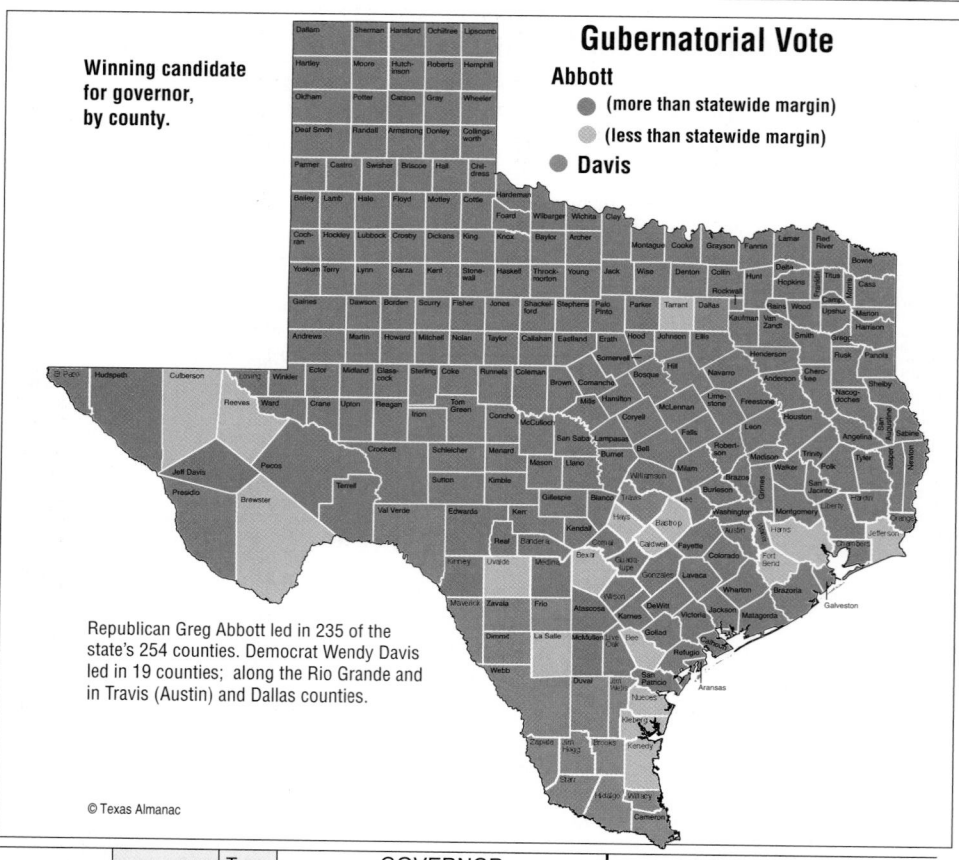

# Gubernatorial Vote

**Winning candidate for governor, by county.**

**Abbott**
- ● (more than statewide margin)
- ◌ (less than statewide margin)

**Davis**
- ● 

Republican Greg Abbott led in 235 of the state's 254 counties. Democrat Wendy Davis led in 19 counties; along the Rio Grande and in Travis (Austin) and Dallas counties.

© Texas Almanac

| COUNTY | Registered Voters | Turn-out % | GOVERNOR | | | | LT. GOVERNOR | | | |
|---|---|---|---|---|---|---|---|---|---|---|
| | | | Abbott | % | Davis | % | Patrick | % | Van der Putte | % |
| Coryell | 35,232 | 24.65 | 6,465 | 74.43 | 2,017 | 23.22 | 6,459 | 74.86 | 1,885 | 21.84 |
| Cottle | 1,091 | 33.18 | 310 | 85.63 | 48 | 13.25 | 295 | 85.26 | 46 | 13.29 |
| Crane | 2,519 | 33.78 | 713 | 83.78 | 127 | 14.92 | 673 | 81.28 | 127 | 15.33 |
| Crockett | 2,543 | 32.83 | 624 | 74.73 | 203 | 24.31 | 565 | 70.89 | 208 | 26.09 |
| Crosby | 3,600 | 29.77 | 813 | 75.83 | 239 | 22.29 | 773 | 74.47 | 231 | 22.25 |
| Culberson | 1,759 | 18.64 | 172 | 52.43 | 146 | 44.51 | 154 | 44.67 | 143 | 46.12 |
| Dallam | 3,088 | 27.33 | 727 | 86.12 | 100 | 11.84 | 720 | 86.95 | 81 | 9.78 |
| Dallas | 1,203,513 | 33.83 | 178,273 | 43.77 | 223,136 | 54.78 | 172,311 | 42.62 | 220,550 | 54.55 |
| Dawson | 7,495 | 27.59 | 1,687 | 82.53 | 335 | 16.38 | 1,589 | 79.56 | 363 | 18.17 |
| Deaf Smith | 8,439 | 32.32 | 2,182 | 79.98 | 503 | 18.43 | 2,147 | 79.34 | 497 | 18.36 |
| Delta | 3,575 | 38.54 | 984 | 71.40 | 351 | 25.47 | 1,024 | 75.34 | 277 | 20.38 |
| Denton | 407,040 | 35.37 | 93,683 | 65.05 | 47,238 | 32.80 | 92,468 | 64.55 | 45,116 | 31.49 |
| DeWitt | 11,932 | 33.67 | 3,269 | 81.35 | 695 | 17.29 | 3,208 | 80.36 | 704 | 17.63 |
| Dickens | 1,314 | 39.34 | 452 | 87.42 | 60 | 11.60 | 440 | 86.44 | 57 | 11.19 |
| Dimmit | 7,301 | 25.70 | 599 | 31.91 | 1,245 | 66.32 | 524 | 28.32 | 1,283 | 69.35 |
| Donley | 2,410 | 39.12 | 803 | 85.15 | 120 | 12.72 | 797 | 85.88 | 102 | 10.99 |
| Duval | 8,381 | 36.79 | 750 | 24.31 | 2,271 | 72.98 | 569 | 18.91 | 2,337 | 77.69 |
| Eastland | 10,858 | 36.20 | 3,503 | 89.11 | 372 | 9.46 | 3,439 | 87.70 | 359 | 9.15 |
| Ector | 68,480 | 21.65 | 12,139 | 81.87 | 2,478 | 16.71 | 12,000 | 81.05 | 2,429 | 16.40 |
| Edwards | 1,504 | 52.26 | 540 | 68.70 | 222 | 28.24 | 512 | 66.84 | 210 | 28.07 |
| Ellis | 93,126 | 34.54 | 23,604 | 73.36 | 7,963 | 24.74 | 23,386 | 73.14 | 7,589 | 23.73 |
| El Paso | 403,979 | 19.90 | 29,953 | 37.25 | 48,506 | 60.32 | 29,025 | 36.41 | 47,665 | 59.79 |
| Erath | 20,456 | 36.14 | 5,953 | 80.52 | 1,301 | 17.59 | 5,924 | 80.56 | 1,194 | 16.23 |
| Falls | 9,854 | 31.09 | 2,147 | 70.07 | 877 | 28.62 | 2,106 | 69.48 | 842 | 27.77 |
| Fannin | 19,872 | 32.65 | 4,897 | 75.45 | 1,449 | 22.32 | 4,900 | 76.21 | 1,291 | 20.08 |

| COUNTY | Registered Voters | Turn-out % | GOVERNOR | | | | LT. GOVERNOR | | | |
|---|---|---|---|---|---|---|---|---|---|---|
| | | | Abbott | % | Davis | % | Patrick | % | Van der Putte | % |
| Fayette | 15,850 | 47.57 | 5,885 | 78.05 | 1,547 | 20.51 | 5,831 | 78.48 | 1,402 | 18.87 |
| Fisher | 2,764 | 45.04 | 891 | 71.56 | 334 | 26.82 | 798 | 66.83 | 349 | 29.22 |
| Floyd | 4,079 | 26,84 | 955 | 87.21 | 133 | 12.14 | 925 | 85.33 | 135 | 12.45 |
| Foard | 1,069 | 28.99 | 205 | 66.12 | 102 | 32.90 | 213 | 71.00 | 81 | 27.00 |
| Fort Bend | 363,147 | 36.47 | 73,749 | 55.67 | 56,825 | 42.89 | 75,120 | 54.73 | 56,204 | 42.65 |
| Franklin | 6,657 | 38.96 | 2,197 | 84.69 | 353 | 13.60 | 2,161 | 84.02 | 353 | 13.72 |
| Freestone | 11,419 | 38.97 | 3,473 | 78.04 | 902 | 20.26 | 3,427 | 77.46 | 898 | 20.29 |
| Frio | 9,966 | 18.49 | 863 | 46.82 | 953 | 51.70 | 841 | 45.73 | 970 | 52.74 |
| Gaines | 8,078 | 31.09 | 2,235 | 88.97 | 235 | 9.35 | 2,161 | 86.85 | 254 | 10.20 |
| Galveston | 191,961 | 33.78 | 40,422 | 62.32 | 23,201 | 35.77 | 39,864 | 61.68 | 22,577 | 34.93 |
| Garza | 2,727 | 30.80 | 752 | 89.52 | 80 | 9.52 | 729 | 87.72 | 86 | 10.34 |
| Gillespie | 18,149 | 48.75 | 7,168 | 81.01 | 1,502 | 16.97 | 7,078 | 80.37 | 1,455 | 16.52 |
| Glasscock | 756 | 52.91 | 377 | 94.25 | 15 | 3.75 | 367 | 93.62 | 18 | 4.59 |
| Goliad | 5,522 | 50.48 | 1,873 | 67.18 | 873 | 31.31 | 1,791 | 65.94 | 865 | 31.84 |
| Gonzales | 12,104 | 30.66 | 2,789 | 75.13 | 840 | 22.62 | 2,698 | 73.55 | 883 | 24.07 |
| Gray | 12,997 | 28.66 | 3,358 | 90.14 | 302 | 8.10 | 3,375 | 90.94 | 248 | 6.68 |
| Grayson | 74,580 | 31.52 | 18,103 | 77.00 | 5,067 | 21.55 | 17,832 | 76.13 | 4,922 | 21.01 |
| Gregg | 67,904 | 34.22 | 17,210 | 74.05 | 5,808 | 24.99 | 16,786 | 72.57 | 5,824 | 25.18 |
| Grimes | 15,275 | 32.43 | 3,716 | 74.99 | 1,125 | 22.70 | 3,670 | 74.24 | 1,110 | 22.45 |
| Guadalupe | 84,076 | 36.37 | 21,235 | 69.44 | 8,788 | 28.73 | 20,776 | 68.12 | 8,955 | 29.36 |
| Hale | 19,341 | 22.33 | 3,703 | 85.71 | 567 | 13.12 | 3,643 | 84.48 | 593 | 13.75 |
| Hall | 2,034 | 28.02 | 485 | 85.08 | 74 | 12.98 | 493 | 86.79 | 68 | 11.97 |
| Hamilton | 5,378 | 45.18 | 1,891 | 77.81 | 491 | 20.20 | 1,890 | 79.04 | 435 | 18.19 |
| Hansford | 3,072 | 38.28 | 1,105 | 93.96 | 55 | 4.67 | 1,124 | 93.66 | 55 | 4.58 |
| Hardeman | 2,565 | 25.96 | 523 | 78.52 | 130 | 19.51 | 514 | 77.99 | 121 | 18.36 |
| Hardin | 35,997 | 32.15 | 9,923 | 85.72 | 1,494 | 12.90 | 9,735 | 84.91 | 1,456 | 12.69 |
| Harris | 2,062,792 | 32.96 | 349,639 | 51.41 | 320,160 | 47.07 | 340,808 | 50.32 | 317,241 | 46.84 |
| Harrison | 42,742 | 34.29 | 10,384 | 70.83 | 4,086 | 27.87 | 10,269 | 70.63 | 3,929 | 27.02 |
| Hartley | 2,855 | 38.80 | 1,006 | 90.79 | 87 | 7.85 | 1,004 | 90.94 | 75 | 6.79 |
| Haskell | 3,502 | 30.41 | 821 | 77.08 | 230 | 21.59 | 787 | 75.81 | 223 | 21.48 |
| Hays | 106,581 | 36.90 | 21,002 | 53.39 | 17,300 | 43.98 | 20,456 | 52.35 | 16,713 | 42.77 |
| Hemphill | 2,281 | 36.38 | 715 | 86.14 | 100 | 12.04 | 708 | 86.34 | 88 | 10.73 |
| Henderson | 49,175 | 34.82 | 13,118 | 76.60 | 3,689 | 21.54 | 13,097 | 76.84 | 3,456 | 20.27 |
| Hidalgo | 318,772 | 25.16 | 27,909 | 34.79 | 50,303 | 62.70 | 23,376 | 29.77 | 53,040 | 67.57 |
| Hill | 22,021 | 40.50 | 6,855 | 76.85 | 1,887 | 21.15 | 6,880 | 77.56 | 1,763 | 19.87 |
| Hockley | 13,517 | 27.35 | 3,222 | 87.15 | 425 | 11.49 | 3,137 | 85.45 | 450 | 12.25 |
| Hood | 35,899 | 37.99 | 10,784 | 79.06 | 2,577 | 18.89 | 10,700 | 78.72 | 2,451 | 18.03 |
| Hopkins | 21,475 | 35.56 | 5,745 | 75.22 | 1,759 | 23.03 | 5,720 | 76.00 | 1,602 | 21.28 |
| Houston | 12,915 | 36.00 | 3,696 | 79.48 | 901 | 19.37 | 3,657 | 79.20 | 867 | 18.77 |
| Howard | 16,785 | 25.49 | 3.492 | 81.60 | 664 | 15.51 | 3,422 | 80.65 | 691 | 16.28 |
| Hudspeth | 1,739 | 25.12 | 267 | 61.09 | 151 | 34.55 | 245 | 59.46 | 142 | 34.46 |
| Hunt | 49,123 | 33.23 | 12,294 | 75.31 | 3,688 | 22.59 | 12,325 | 75.84 | 3,384 | 20.82 |
| Hutchinson | 13,432 | 33.45 | 3,956 | 88.02 | 462 | 10.28 | 3,966 | 88.42 | 409 | 9.11 |
| Irion | 1,313 | 33.13 | 383 | 88.04 | 43 | 9.88 | 371 | 86.07 | 45 | 10.44 |
| Jack | 4,783 | 36.10 | 1,473 | 85.29 | 225 | 13.02 | 1,447 | 84.57 | 218 | 12.74 |
| Jackson | 8,796 | 33.48 | 2,420 | 82.17 | 488 | 16.57 | 2,356 | 80.85 | 497 | 17.05 |
| Jasper | 22,331 | 31.95 | 5,644 | 79.10 | 1,415 | 19.83 | 5,502 | 78.05 | 1,406 | 19.94 |
| Jeff Davis | 1,684 | 61.10 | 623 | 60.54 | 366 | 35.56 | 560 | 56.62 | 375 | 37.91 |
| Jefferson | 146,020 | 36.44 | 26,876 | 50.50 | 25,799 | 48.48 | 26,122 | 49.79 | 25,405 | 48.43 |
| Jim Hogg | 3,853 | 18.68 | 190 | 26.38 | 521 | 72.36 | 149 | 20.86 | 557 | 78.01 |
| Jim Wells | 25,634 | 22.27 | 2,589 | 45.33 | 3,016 | 52.81 | 2,398 | 42.77 | 3,084 | 55.01 |
| Johnson | 84,067 | 34.81 | 22,715 | 77.59 | 5,978 | 20.42 | 22,658 | 77.78 | 5,462 | 18.74 |
| Jones | 9,887 | 33.79 | 2,745 | 82.16 | 534 | 15.98 | 2,651 | 80.23 | 556 | 16.82 |
| Karnes | 7,802 | 32.31 | 1,770 | 70.21 | 715 | 28.36 | 1,679 | 67.48 | 748 | 30.06 |
| Kaufman | 61,580 | 33.05 | 14,590 | 71.68 | 5,449 | 26.77 | 14,547 | 71.69 | 5,162 | 25.44 |
| Kendall | 26,699 | 44.46 | 9,713 | 81.79 | 1,989 | 16.74 | 9,396 | 79.41 | 2,132 | 18.01 |
| Kenedy | 346 | 36.12 | 64 | 51.20 | 59 | 47.20 | 53 | 44.91 | 61 | 51.69 |
| Kent | 610 | 50.81 | 251 | 80.96 | 49 | 15.80 | 243 | 81.81 | 45 | 15.15 |
| Kerr | 32,627 | 45.76 | 11,740 | 78.61 | 2,901 | 19.43 | 11,437 | 76.89 | 2,976 | 20.00 |
| Kimble | 2,877 | 42.54 | 1,096 | 89.54 | 113 | 9.23 | 1,072 | 88.23 | 121 | 9.95 |

| COUNTY | Registered Voters | Turn-out % | GOVERNOR | | | | LT. GOVERNOR | | | |
|---|---|---|---|---|---|---|---|---|---|---|
| | | | Abbott | % | Davis | % | Patrick | % | Van der Putte | % |
| King | 186 | 50.00 | 90 | 96.77 | 1 | 1.07 | 84 | 94.38 | 1 | 1.12 |
| Kinney | 2,290 | 50.13 | 747 | 65.06 | 375 | 32.66 | 708 | 63.27 | 371 | 33.15 |
| Kleberg | 17,357 | 33.17 | 2,836 | 49.24 | 2,804 | 48.68 | 2,562 | 45.28 | 2,948 | 52.10 |
| Knox | 2,372 | 37.90 | 726 | 80.75 | 159 | 17.68 | 687 | 79.14 | 155 | 17.85 |
| Lamar | 29,729 | 36.66 | 7,785 | 71.42 | 2,869 | 26.32 | 7,847 | 72.96 | 2,588 | 24.06 |
| Lamb | 8,317 | 25.39 | 1,841 | 87.16 | 251 | 11.88 | 1,780 | 85.00 | 272 | 12.98 |
| Lampasas | 13,114 | 35.41 | 3,745 | 80.92 | 787 | 17.00 | 3,678 | 80.33 | 755 | 16.40 |
| La Salle | 4,094 | 21.12 | 434 | 50.17 | 422 | 48.78 | 396 | 46.20 | 448 | 52.27 |
| Lavaca | 13,114 | 38.32 | 4,180 | 83.16 | 784 | 15.59 | 4,109 | 82.42 | 791 | 15.86 |
| Lee | 9,859 | 43.45 | 3,199 | 74.67 | 963 | 22.47 | 3,166 | 75.13 | 877 | 20.81 |
| Leon | 10,887 | 39.04 | 3,694 | 86.89 | 511 | 12.02 | 3,675 | 86.81 | 488 | 11.52 |
| Liberty | 42,265 | 29.58 | 9,576 | 76.59 | 2,681 | 21.44 | 9,554 | 76.81 | 2,523 | 20.28 |
| Limestone | 13,405 | 32.12 | 3,278 | 76.12 | 979 | 22.73 | 3,255 | 75.87 | 943 | 21.98 |
| Lipscomb | 1,980 | 43.08 | 740 | 86.75 | 93 | 10.90 | 749 | 88.32 | 83 | 9.78 |
| Live Oak | 7,083 | 34.60 | 2,007 | 81.75 | 400 | 16.29 | 1,956 | 80.06 | 433 | 17.72 |
| Llano | 14,426 | 48.89 | 5,552 | 78.71 | 1,363 | 19.32 | 5,500 | 78.15 | 1,273 | 18.09 |
| Loving | 122 | 33.60 | 35 | 85.36 | 4 | 9.75 | 32 | 82.05 | 6 | 15.38 |
| Lubbock | 157,054 | 30.04 | 36,038 | 76.36 | 10,438 | 22.11 | 35,357 | 75.22 | 10,187 | 21.67 |
| Lynn | 3,861 | 31.31 | 1,013 | 83.78 | 180 | 14.88 | 962 | 81.31 | 193 | 16.31 |
| Madison | 6,943 | 34.98 | 1,941 | 79.90 | 462 | 19.02 | 1,928 | 79.63 | 437 | 18,05 |
| Marion | 7,019 | 31.52 | 1,480 | 66.87 | 705 | 31.85 | 1,484 | 66.99 | 687 | 31.01 |
| Martin | 3,084 | 37.45 | 1,016 | 87.96 | 116 | 10.04 | 932 | 82.77 | 155 | 13.76 |
| Mason | 2,866 | 47.83 | 1,104 | 80.52 | 243 | 17.73 | 1,075 | 79.10 | 236 | 17.36 |
| Matagorda | 20,945 | 33.19 | 4,691 | 67.47 | 2,115 | 30.42 | 4,654 | 67.23 | 2,045 | 29.54 |
| Maverick | 28,852 | 18.36 | 1,392 | 26.27 | 3,723 | 70.27 | 1,109 | 21.05 | 4,002 | 75.99 |
| McCulloch | 5,222 | 33.47 | 1,456 | 83.29 | 258 | 14.75 | 1,423 | 82.68 | 248 | 14.41 |
| McLennan | 128,501 | 34.47 | 30,507 | 68.86 | 13,092 | 29.55 | 30,090 | 68.29 | 12,679 | 28.77 |
| McMullen | 695 | 37.84 | 222 | 84.41 | 34 | 12.92 | 204 | 80.00 | 45 | 17.64 |
| Medina | 28,406 | 34.68 | 7,194 | 73.01 | 2,506 | 25.43 | 6,955 | 70.71 | 2,694 | 27.39 |
| Menard | 1,530 | 31.50 | 411 | 85.26 | 65 | 13.48 | 398 | 84.14 | 61 | 12.89 |
| Midland | 75,348 | 31.29 | 20,204 | 85.69 | 3,012 | 12.77 | 19,885 | 84.71 | 2,979 | 12.69 |
| Milam | 14,411 | 34.44 | 3,576 | 72.03 | 1,293 | 26.04 | 3,535 | 72.02 | 1,206 | 24.57 |
| Mills | 3,368 | 40.17 | 1,194 | 88.24 | 134 | 9.90 | 1,183 | 87.82 | 127 | 9.42 |
| Mitchell | 4,564 | 26.53 | 1,020 | 84.22 | 176 | 14.53 | 964 | 81.21 | 188 | 15.83 |
| Montague | 12,930 | 52.15 | 5,691 | 84.39 | 916 | 13.58 | 5,699 | 85.08 | 806 | 12.03 |
| Montgomery | 281,496 | 37.26 | 83,938 | 80.02 | 19,179 | 18.28 | 82,650 | 78.97 | 18,775 | 17.94 |
| Moore | 9,336 | 29.62 | 2,421 | 87.52 | 301 | 10.88 | 2,424 | 87.88 | 275 | 9.97 |
| Morris | 8,525 | 36.45 | 2,033 | 65.41 | 1,031 | 33.17 | 1,953 | 64.43 | 1,003 | 33.09 |
| Motley | 791 | 47.02 | 344 | 92.47 | 20 | 5.37 | 336 | 92.30 | 18 | 4.94 |
| Nacogdoches | 30,741 | 39.17 | 9,021 | 74.91 | 2,845 | 23.62 | 8,906 | 74.56 | 2,723 | 22.79 |
| Navarro | 27,357 | 34.84 | 6,983 | 73.25 | 2,376 | 24.92 | 6,954 | 73.57 | 2,235 | 23.64 |
| Newton | 8,955 | 32.43 | 2,161 | 74.38 | 703 | 24.19 | 2,085 | 73.02 | 701 | 24.55 |
| Nolan | 8,554 | 30.92 | 2,117 | 80.03 | 474 | 17.92 | 2,011 | 77.46 | 488 | 18.79 |
| Nueces | 190,191 | 29.97 | 30,854 | 54.12 | 24,746 | 43.41 | 28,914 | 51.23 | 25,555 | 45.28 |
| Ochiltree | 5,223 | 30.44 | 1,500 | 94.33 | 70 | 4.40 | 1,467 | 92.90 | 87 | 5.50 |
| Oldham | 1,350 | 41.40 | 519 | 92.84 | 33 | 5.90 | 516 | 92.63 | 31 | 5.56 |
| Orange | 50,528 | 34.17 | 13,400 | 77.60 | 3,600 | 20.85 | 13,111 | 76.86 | 3,541 | 20.75 |
| Palo Pinto | 17,022 | 33.31 | 4,410 | 77.76 | 1,141 | 20.11 | 4,385 | 77.88 | 1,071 | 19.02 |
| Panola | 15,763 | 36.49 | 4,614 | 80.21 | 1,069 | 18.58 | 4,580 | 80.04 | 1,048 | 18.31 |
| Parker | 78,345 | 40.66 | 25,683 | 80.61 | 5,540 | 17.38 | 25,593 | 80.62 | 5,069 | 15.96 |
| Parmer | 4,387 | 31.91 | 1,234 | 88.14 | 153 | 10.92 | 1,238 | 88.68 | 137 | 9.81 |
| Pecos | 8,146 | 37.20 | 2,146 | 70.80 | 817 | 26.95 | 1,868 | 63.79 | 957 | 32.68 |
| Polk | 37,149 | 28.25 | 7,858 | 74.86 | 2,410 | 22.96 | 7,856 | 75.40 | 2,214 | 21.24 |
| Potter | 52,747 | 26.07 | 10,584 | 76.94 | 2,925 | 21.26 | 10,590 | 77.10 | 2,764 | 20.12 |
| Presidio | 5,288 | 18.98 | 364 | 36.25 | 613 | 61.05 | 306 | 32.93 | 579 | 62.32 |
| Rains | 6,819 | 35.94 | 1,976 | 80.62 | 440 | 17.95 | 1,991 | 81.53 | 389 | 15.92 |
| Randall | 80,151 | 35.20 | 24,134 | 85.52 | 3,650 | 12.93 | 24,059 | 85.51 | 3,318 | 11.79 |
| Reagan | 1,774 | 28.52 | 425 | 83.99 | 68 | 13.43 | 410 | 83.50 | 64 | 13.03 |
| Real | 2,437 | 43.29 | 862 | 81.70 | 175 | 16.58 | 833 | 79.71 | 182 | 17.41 |
| Red River | 7,927 | 34.91 | 1,993 | 72.00 | 730 | 26.37 | 1,983 | 72.82 | 674 | 24.75 |

| COUNTY | Registered Voters | Turn-out % | GOVERNOR | | | | LT. GOVERNOR | | | |
|---|---|---|---|---|---|---|---|---|---|---|
| | | | Abbott | % | Davis | % | Patrick | % | Van der Putte | % |
| Reeves | 6,549 | 18.65 | 695 | 56.87 | 510 | 41.73 | 599 | 50.50 | 559 | 47.13 |
| Refugio | 5,033 | 40.53 | 1,238 | 60.68 | 750 | 36.76 | 1,173 | 58.91 | 759 | 38.12 |
| Roberts | 678 | 50.88 | 324 | 93.91 | 15 | 4.34 | 320 | 93.29 | 12 | 3.49 |
| Robertson | 11,362 | 44.93 | 3,270 | 64.05 | 1,768 | 34.63 | 3,137 | 63.08 | 1,707 | 34.32 |
| Rockwall | 51,787 | 40.71 | 16,100 | 76.35 | 4,670 | 22.14 | 15,797 | 75.40 | 4,574 | 21.83 |
| Runnels | 6,595 | 35.05 | 2,057 | 88.97 | 230 | 9.94 | 1,986 | 86.61 | 237 | 10.33 |
| Rusk | 30,326 | 34.71 | 8,517 | 80.89 | 1,906 | 18.10 | 8,403 | 80.38 | 1,853 | 17.72 |
| Sabine | 7,453 | 37.05 | 2,372 | 85.87 | 355 | 12.85 | 2,328 | 85.46 | 341 | 12.51 |
| SanAugustine | 6,130 | 44.43 | 1,920 | 70.48 | 756 | 27.75 | 1,851 | 69.77 | 716 | 26.98 |
| San Jacinto | 16,510 | 38.97 | 4,641 | 72.13 | 1,632 | 25.36 | 4,644 | 73.04 | 1,479 | 23.26 |
| San Patricio | 39,941 | 28.87 | 7,202 | 62.45 | 4,071 | 35.30 | 6,906 | 60.42 | 4,175 | 36.52 |
| San Saba | 3,693 | 39.12 | 1,280 | 88.58 | 145 | 10.03 | 1,253 | 87.56 | 147 | 10.27 |
| Schleicher | 1,827 | 47.01 | 635 | 73.92 | 213 | 24.79 | 579 | 69.42 | 229 | 27.45 |
| Scurry | 9,381 | 30.50 | 2,518 | 87.98 | 298 | 10.41 | 2,456 | 86.72 | 310 | 10.94 |
| Shackelford | 2,312 | 35.03 | 751 | 92.71 | 50 | 6.17 | 749 | 93.27 | 43 | 5.35 |
| Shelby | 14,592 | 37.71 | 4,330 | 78.67 | 1,116 | 20.27 | 4,226 | 78.38 | 1,058 | 19.62 |
| Sherman | 1,515 | 39.60 | 538 | 89.66 | 52 | 8.66 | 518 | 88.39 | 50 | 8.53 |
| Smith | 126,425 | 38.62 | 37,360 | 76.50 | 10,846 | 22.20 | 36,889 | 75.89 | 10,661 | 21.93 |
| Somervell | 5,809 | 38.64 | 1,796 | 80.00 | 405 | 18.04 | 1,786 | 80.48 | 359 | 16.17 |
| Starr | 30,198 | 17.17 | 1,104 | 21.29 | 4,008 | 77.29 | 759 | 14.94 | 4,253 | 83.76 |
| Stephens | 5,590 | 34.61 | 1,737 | 89.76 | 169 | 8.73 | 1,726 | 89.66 | 165 | 8.57 |
| Sterling | 842 | 55.81 | 429 | 91.27 | 33 | 7.02 | 421 | 90.92 | 33 | 7.12 |
| Stonewall | 1,011 | 37.68 | 297 | 77.95 | 76 | 19.94 | 281 | 77.19 | 70 | 19.23 |
| Sutton | 2,491 | 29.82 | 619 | 83.31 | 113 | 15.20 | 610 | 82.65 | 113 | 15.31 |
| Swisher | 4,113 | 34.62 | 1,029 | 72.26 | 362 | 25.42 | 1,025 | 73.42 | 331 | 23.71 |
| Tarrant | 999,687 | 37.30 | 213,120 | 57.14 | 153,214 | 41.07 | 211,586 | 57.06 | 146,548 | 39.52 |
| Taylor | 75,743 | 30.89 | 19,100 | 81.62 | 3,876 | 16.56 | 18,785 | 80.78 | 3,738 | 16.07 |
| Terrell | 822 | 48.41 | 273 | 68.59 | 108 | 27.13 | 247 | 63.98 | 123 | 31.86 |
| Terry | 7,127 | 32.17 | 1,896 | 82.68 | 366 | 15.96 | 1,826 | 81.37 | 367 | 16.35 |
| Throckmorton | 1,293 | 41.37 | 456 | 85.23 | 66 | 12.33 | 451 | 85.25 | 65 | 12.28 |
| Titus | 15,981 | 32.30 | 3,802 | 73.65 | 1,288 | 24.95 | 3,732 | 73.63 | 1,211 | 23.89 |
| Tom Green | 61,759 | 30.00 | 14,670 | 79.15 | 3,559 | 19.20 | 14,220 | 77.28 | 3,613 | 19.63 |
| Travis | 655,056 | 40.88 | 91,301 | 34.09 | 169,141 | 63.16 | 86,674 | 32.60 | 164,173 | 61.76 |
| Trinity | 11,041 | 35.59 | 2,837 | 72.18 | 996 | 25.34 | 2,799 | 72.51 | 937 | 24.27 |
| Tyler | 13,241 | 36.01 | 3,788 | 79.42 | 885 | 18.55 | 3,670 | 78.83 | 841 | 18.04 |
| Upshur | 26,395 | 33.52 | 7,294 | 82.43 | 1,426 | 16.11 | 7,163 | 81.57 | 1,396 | 15.89 |
| Upton | 2,189 | 30.60 | 555 | 82.83 | 106 | 15.82 | 515 | 80.72 | 102 | 15.98 |
| Uvalde | 16,278 | 31.59 | 2,967 | 57.69 | 2,101 | 40.85 | 2,862 | 56.00 | 2,152 | 42.11 |
| Val Verde | 26,447 | 26.77 | 3,306 | 46.68 | 3,608 | 50.94 | 3,049 | 43.19 | 3,825 | 54.18 |
| Van Zandt | 34,522 | 34.53 | 9,751 | 81.79 | 1,938 | 16.25 | 9,744 | 82.37 | 1,770 | 14.96 |
| Victoria | 51,878 | 33.05 | 12,657 | 73.81 | 4,233 | 24.68 | 12,267 | 72.26 | 4,278 | 25.20 |
| Walker | 30,160 | 37.75 | 7,669 | 67.34 | 3,476 | 30.52 | 7,543 | 66.84 | 3,379 | 29.94 |
| Waller | 29,871 | 30.78 | 6,329 | 68.83 | 2,741 | 29.80 | 6,302 | 68.80 | 2,634 | 28.75 |
| Ward | 6,310 | 31.37 | 1,535 | 77.52 | 411 | 20.75 | 1,447 | 74.43 | 452 | 23.25 |
| Washington | 22,242 | 40.42 | 6,886 | 76.58 | 1,952 | 21.71 | 6,776 | 75.75 | 1,919 | 21.45 |
| Webb | 115,638 | 22,83 | 7,622 | 28.86 | 17,963 | 68.03 | 6,018 | 23.19 | 18,820 | 72.54 |
| Wharton | 24,663 | 34.05 | 6,215 | 73.99 | 2,075 | 24.70 | 6,130 | 73.41 | 2,064 | 24.71 |
| Wheeler | 3,475 | 38.04 | 1,185 | 89.63 | 120 | 9.07 | 1,179 | 90.13 | 101 | 7.72 |
| Wichita | 72,256 | 29.41 | 16,130 | 75.88 | 4,822 | 22.68 | 16,070 | 75.98 | 4,516 | 21.35 |
| Wilbarger | 7,946 | 34.62 | 2,141 | 77.82 | 574 | 20.86 | 2,099 | 78.43 | 508 | 18.98 |
| Willacy | 11,529 | 18.95 | 854 | 39.08 | 1,274 | 58.30 | 702 | 32.95 | 1,357 | 63.70 |
| Williamson | 271,612 | 38.25 | 61,496 | 59.18 | 39,516 | 38.02 | 60,179 | 58.31 | 37,711 | 36.53 |
| Wilson | 28,787 | 36.22 | 7,506 | 71.97 | 2,707 | 25.95 | 7,263 | 69.95 | 2,867 | 27.61 |
| Winkler | 3,691 | 26.68 | 829 | 84.16 | 136 | 13.80 | 786 | 81.87 | 151 | 15.72 |
| Wise | 36,321 | 34.79 | 10,181 | 80.55 | 2,178 | 17.23 | 10,171 | 80.67 | 1,985 | 15.74 |
| Wood | 27,625 | 40.94 | 9,778 | 86.45 | 1,403 | 12.40 | 9,713 | 86.23 | 1,342 | 11.91 |
| Yoakum | 3,969 | 28.94 | 1,046 | 91.03 | 93 | 8.09 | 997 | 88.70 | 105 | 9.34 |
| Young | 11,659 | 45.48 | 4,497 | 84.80 | 679 | 12.80 | 4,468 | 85.08 | 588 | 11.19 |
| Zapata | 7,438 | 15.82 | 372 | 31.60 | 788 | 66.94 | 292 | 25.30 | 845 | 73.22 |
| Zavala | 8,736 | 16.98 | 350 | 23.58 | 1,110 | 74.79 | 311 | 21.40 | 1,123 | 77.28 |

# General Election, 2014

Below are the voting results for the general election held November 4, 2014, for all statewide races and for contested congressional, state senate, courts of appeals and state board of education races. These are official returns as canvassed by the State Canvassing Board. Abbreviations used are (Dem.) Democrat, (Rep.) Republican, (Lib.) Libertarian, (Ind.) Independent and (W-I) Write-in.

### Govenor

| | | |
|---|---|---|
| Greg Abbott (Rep.) | 2,796,547 | 59.15% |
| Wendy R. Davis (Dem.) | 1,835,596 | 38.83% |
| Kathie Glass (Lib.) | 75,488 | 1.59% |
| Brandon Parmer (Green) | 18,490 | 0.39% |
| Sarah M. Pavitt (W-I) | 1,060 | 0.02% |
| Total vote | 4,727,181 | |

### U.S. Senator

| | | |
|---|---|---|
| John Cornyn (Rep.) | 2,862,531 | 61.56% |
| David M. Alameel (Dem.) | 1,597,387 | 34.36% |
| Rebecca Paddock (Lib.) | 133,751 | 2.87% |
| Emily "Spicybrown" Sanchez (Green) | 54,701 | 1.17% |
| Mohammed Tahiro (W-I) | 988 | 0.02% |
| Total Vote | 4,648,358 | |

### Lieutenant Governor

| | | |
|---|---|---|
| Dan Patrick (Rep.) | 2,724,493 | 58.14% |
| Leticia Van de Putte (Dem.) | 1,813,974 | 38.71% |
| Robert D. Butler (Lib.) | 119,833 | 2.55% |
| Chandrakantha Courtney (Green) | 27,719 | 0.59% |
| Total vote | 4,686,019 | |

### Attorney General

| | | |
|---|---|---|
| Ken Paxton (Rep.) | 2,743,473 | 58.81% |
| Sam Houston (Dem.) | 1,773,250 | 38.01% |
| Jamie Balagia (Lib.) | 118,197 | 2.53% |
| Jamar Osborne (Green) | 29,591 | 0.63% |
| Total vote | 4,664,511 | |

### Comptroller of Public Accouts

| | | |
|---|---|---|
| Glenn Hegar (Rep.) | 2,698,682 | 58.37% |
| Mike Collier (Dem.) | 1,742,050 | 37.68% |
| Ben Sanders (Lib.) | 136,884 | 2.96% |
| Deb Shafto (Green) | 44,985 | 0.97% |
| Total vote | 4,622,801 | |

### Commissioner of General Land Office

| | | |
|---|---|---|
| George P. Bush (Rep.) | 2,827,584 | 60.67% |
| John Cook (Dem.) | 1,645,828 | 35.31% |
| Justin Knight (Lib.) | 126,422 | 2.71% |
| Valerie Alessi (Green) | 60,116 | 1.29% |
| Total vote | 4,659,950 | |

### Commissioner of Agriculture

| | | |
|---|---|---|
| Sid Miller (Rep.) | 2,699,508 | 58.59% |
| Jim Hogan (Dem.) | 1,697,227 | 36.48% |
| David "Rocky" Palmquist (Lib.) | 132,518 | 2.87% |
| Kenneth Kendrick (Green) | 77,557 | 1.68% |
| Total vote | 4,606,810 | |

### Railroad Commissioner

| | | |
|---|---|---|
| Ryan Sitton (Rep.) | 2,691,417 | 58.33% |
| Steve Brown (Dem.) | 1,682,796 | 36.48% |
| Mark A. Miller (Lib.) | 145,381 | 3.15% |
| Martina Salinas (Green) | 93,813 | 2.03% |
| Total vote | 4,613,407 | |

### U.S. HOUSE OF REPRESENTATIVES

*(See map of districts on p. xxx.)*

### District 1

| | | |
|---|---|---|
| Louie Gohmert (Rep.) | 115,084 | 77.46% |
| Shirley J. McKellar (Dem.) | 33,476 | 22.53% |
| Total Vote | 148,560 | |

### District 2

| | | |
|---|---|---|
| Ted Poe (Rep.) | 101,936 | 67.94% |

| | | |
|---|---|---|
| Niko Letsos (Dem.) | 44,462 | 29.63% |
| James B. Veasaw (Lib.) | 2,316 | 1.54% |
| Mark Roberts (Green) | 1,312 | 0.87% |
| Total Vote | 150,026 | |

### District 3

| | | |
|---|---|---|
| Sam Johnson (Rep.) | 113,404 | 82.01% |
| Paul Blair (Green) | 24,876 | 17.98% |
| Total Vote | 138,280 | |

### District 5

| | | |
|---|---|---|
| Jeb Hensarling (Rep.) | 88.998 | 85.35% |
| Ken Ashby (Lib.) | 15,264 | 14.64% |
| Total Vote | 104,262 | |

### District 6

| | | |
|---|---|---|
| Joe Barton (Rep.) | 92,334 | 61.14% |
| David E. Cozad (Dem.) | 55,027 | 36.44% |
| Hugh Chauvin (Lib.) | 3,635 | 2.40% |
| Total Vote | 150,996 | |

### District 7

| | | |
|---|---|---|
| John Culberson (Rep.) | 90,606 | 63.26% |
| James Cargas (Dem.) | 49,478 | 34.54% |
| Gerald Fowler (Lib.) | 3,135 | 2.18% |
| Total Vote | 143,219 | |

### District 8

| | | |
|---|---|---|
| Kevin Brady (Rep.) | 125,066 | 89.32% |
| Ken Petty (Lib.) | 14,947 | 10,67% |
| Total Vote | 140,013 | |

### District 9

| | | |
|---|---|---|
| Al Green (Dem.) | 78,109 | 90.82% |
| Johnny Johnson (Lib.) | 7,894 | 9.17% |
| Total Vote | 86,003 | |

### District 10

| | | |
|---|---|---|
| Michael McCaul (Rep.) | 109,726 | 62.18% |
| Tawana Walter-Cadien (Dem.) | 60,243 | 34.13% |
| Bill Kelsey (Lib.) | 6,491 | 3.67% |
| Total Vote | 176,460 | |

### District 11

| | | |
|---|---|---|
| Mike Conaway (Rep.) | 107,939 | 90.26% |
| Ryan T. Lange (Lib.) | 11,635 | 9.73% |
| Total Vote | 119,574 | |

### District 12

| | | |
|---|---|---|
| Kay Granger (Rep.) | 113,186 | 71.30% |
| Mark Greene (Dem.) | 41,757 | 26.30% |
| Ed Colliver (Lib.) | 3,787 | 2.38% |
| Total Vote | 158,730 | |

### District 13

| | | |
|---|---|---|
| Mac Thornberry (Rep.) | 110,842 | 84.32% |
| Mike Minter (Dem.) | 16,822 | 12.79% |
| Emily Pivoda (Lib.) | 2,863 | 2.17% |
| Don Cook (Green) | 924 | 0.70% |
| Total Vote | 131,451 | |

### District 14

| | | |
|---|---|---|
| Randy Weber (Rep.) | 90,116 | 61.85% |
| Donald G. Brown (Dem.) | 52,545 | 36.06% |
| John Wieder (Lib.) | 3,037 | 2.08% |
| Total Vote | 145,698 | |

### District 15

| | | |
|---|---|---|
| Rubén Hinojosa (Dem.) | 48,708 | 54.00% |
| Eddie Zamora (Rep.) | 39,016 | 43.26% |
| Johnny Partain (Lib.) | 2,460 | 2.72% |
| Total Vote | 90,184 | |

### District 16
| | | |
|---|---|---|
| Beto O'Rourke (Dem.) | 49,338 | 67.48% |
| Corey Roen (Rep.) | 21,324 | 29.16% |
| Jaime O. Perez (Lib..) | 2,443 | 3.34% |
| Total Vote | 73,105 | |

### District 17
| | | |
|---|---|---|
| Bill Flores (Rep.) | 85,807 | 64.58% |
| Nick Haynes (Dem.) | 43,049 | 32.40% |
| Shawn Michael Hamilton (Lib.) | 4,009 | 3.01% |
| Total Vote | 132,865 | |

### District 18
| | | |
|---|---|---|
| Sheila Jackson Lee (Dem.) | 76,097 | 71.78% |
| Sean Seibert (Rep.) | 26,249 | 24.76% |
| Remington Alessi (Green) | 1,302 | 1.22% |
| Vince Duncan (Ind.) | 2,362 | 2.22% |
| Total Vote | 106,010 | |

### District 19
| | | |
|---|---|---|
| Randy Neugebauer (Rep.) | 89,326 | 77.12% |
| Neal Marchbanks (Dem.) | 21,325 | 18.41% |
| Richard "Chip" Peterson (Lib.) | 5,120 | 4.42% |
| Donald L. Vance (W-I) | 54 | 0.04% |
| Total Vote | 115,825 | |

### District 20
| | | |
|---|---|---|
| Joaquin Castro (Dem.) | 66,554 | 75.66% |
| Jeffrey C. Blunt (Lib.) | 21,410 | 24.33% |
| Total Vote | 87,964 | |

### District 21
| | | |
|---|---|---|
| Lamar Smith (Rep.) | 135,660 | 71.77% |
| Ryan Shields (Lib.) | 25,505 | 13.49% |
| Antonio Diaz (Green) | 27,831 | 14.72% |
| Total Vote | 188,996 | |

### District 22
| | | |
|---|---|---|
| Pete Olson (Rep.) | 100,861 | 66.54% |
| Frnak Briscoe (Dem.) | 47,844 | 31.56% |
| Rob Lapham (Lib.) | 2,861 | 1.88% |
| Total Vote | 151,566 | |

### District 23
| | | |
|---|---|---|
| Will Hurd (Rep.) | 57,459 | 49.77% |
| Pete P. Gallego (Dem.) | 55,037 | 47.68% |
| Ruben Corvalan (Lib.) | 2,933 | 2.54% |
| Total Vote | 115,429 | |

### District 24
| | | |
|---|---|---|
| Kenny E. Marchant (Rep.) | 93,712 | 65.04% |
| Patrick McGehearty (Dem.) | 46,548 | 32.30% |
| Mike Kolls (Lib.) | 3,813 | 2.64% |
| Total Vote | 144,073 | |

### District 25
| | | |
|---|---|---|
| Roger Williams (Rep.) | 107,120 | 60.21% |
| Marco Montoya (Dem.) | 64,463 | 36.23% |
| John Betz (Lib.) | 6,300 | 3.54% |
| Total Vote | 177,883 | |

### District 26
| | | |
|---|---|---|
| Michael Burgess (Rep.) | 116,944 | 82.66% |
| Mark Boler (Lib.) | 24,526 | 17.33% |
| Total Vote | 141,470 | |

### District 27
| | | |
|---|---|---|
| Blake Farenthold (Rep.) | 83,342 | 63.59% |
| Wesley Reed (Dem.) | 44,152 | 33.69% |
| Roxanne Simonson (Lib.) | 3,553 | 2.71% |
| Total Vote | 131,047 | |

### District 28
| | | |
|---|---|---|
| Henry Cuellar (Dem.) | 62,508 | 82.10% |
| William Aikens (Lib.) | 10,153 | 13.33% |
| Michael D. Cary (Green) | 3,475 | 4.56% |
| Total Vote | 76,136 | |

### District 29
| | | |
|---|---|---|
| Gene Green (Dem.) | 41,321 | 89.54% |
| James Stanczak (Lib.) | 4,822 | 10.45% |
| Total Vote | 46,143 | |

### District 30
| | | |
|---|---|---|
| Eddie Bernice Johnson (Dem.) | 93,041 | 87.94% |
| Max W. Koch III (Lib.) | 7,154 | 6.76% |
| Eric LeMonte Williams (Ind.) | 5,598 | 5.29% |
| Total Vote | 105,793 | |

### District 31
| | | |
|---|---|---|
| John Carter (Rep.) | 91,607 | 64.04% |
| Louie Minor (Dem.) | 45,715 | 31.96% |
| Scott J. Ballard (Lib.) | 5,706 | 3.98% |
| Total Vote | 143,028 | |

### District 32
| | | |
|---|---|---|
| Pete Sessions (Rep.) | 96,495 | 61.81% |
| Frank Perez (Dem.) | 55,325 | 35.44% |
| Ed Rankin (Lib.) | 4,276 | 2.73% |
| Total Vote | 156,096 | |

### District 33
| | | |
|---|---|---|
| Marc Veasey (Dem.) | 43,769 | 86.51% |
| Jason Reeves (Lib.) | 6,823 | 13.48% |
| Total Vote | 50,592 | |

### District 34
| | | |
|---|---|---|
| Filemon Vela (Dem.) | 47,503 | 59.47% |
| Larry S. Smith (Rep.) | 30,811 | 38.57% |
| Ryan Rowley (Lib.) | 1,563 | 1.95% |
| Total Vote | 79,877 | |

### District 35
| | | |
|---|---|---|
| Lloyd Doggett (Dem.) | 60,124 | 62.48% |
| Susan Narvaiz (Rep.) | 32,040 | 33.29% |
| Cory W. Bruner (Lib.) | 2,767 | 2.87% |
| Kat Swift (Green) | 1,294 | 1.34% |
| Total Vote | 96,225 | |

### District 36
| | | |
|---|---|---|
| Brian Babin (Rep.) | 101,663 | 75.95% |
| Michael K. Cole (Dem.) | 29,543 | 22.07% |
| Rodney Veach (Lib.) | 1,951 | 1.45% |
| Hal J. Ridley Jr. (Green) | 685 | 0.51% |
| Total Vote | 133,842 | |

## OTHER STATE RACES
### Chief Justice, Supreme Court
| | | |
|---|---|---|
| Nathan Hecht (Rep.) | 2,757,218 | 59.69% |
| William Moody (Dem.) | 1,720,343 | 37.24% |
| Tom Oxford (Lib.) | 146,338 | 3.05% |
| Total Vote | 4,618,899 | |

### Justice, Supreme Court, Place 6 (unexpired term)
| | | |
|---|---|---|
| Jeff Brown (Rep.) | 2,772,824 | 60.32% |
| Lawrence Edward Meyers (Dem.) | 1,677,478 | 36.49% |
| Mark Ash (Lib.) | 146,530 | 3.18% |
| Total Vote | 4,596,832 | |

### Justice, Supreme Court, Place 7
| | | |
|---|---|---|
| Jeff Boyd (Rep.) | 2,711,363 | 58.89% |
| Gina Benavides (Dem.) | 1,731,031 | 37.60% |
| Don Fulton (Lib.) | 126,725 | 2.75% |
| Charles E. Waterbury (Green) | 34,493 | 0.74% |
| Total Vote | 4,603,612 | |

### Justice, Supreme Court, Place 8
| | | |
|---|---|---|
| Phil Johnson (Rep.) | 2,948,052 | 78.79% |
| RS Roberto Koelsch (Lib.) | 447,522 | 11.96% |
| Jim Chisolm (Green) | 345,675 | 9.23% |
| Total Vote | 3,741,249 | |

### Judge, Court of Criminal Appeals, Place 3
| | | |
|---|---|---|
| Bert Richardson (Rep.) | 2,738,412 | 59.84% |
| John Granberg (Dem.) | 1,671,921 | 36.53% |
| Mark W. Bennett (Lib.) | 165,327 | 3.61% |
| Total Vote | 4,575,660 | |

### Judge, Court of Criminal Appeals, Place 4
| | | |
|---|---|---|
| Kevin Patrick Yeary (Rep.) | 2,876,256 | 76.21% |
| Quanah Parker (Lib.) | 503,492 | 13.34% |
| Judith Sanders-Castro (Green) | 394,015 | 10.44% |
| Total Vote | 3,773,763 | |

### Judge, Court of Criminal Appeals, Place 9

David Newell (Rep.)...........................2,929,963 ...... 78.28%
William Bryan Strange III (Lib.)............492,026 ...... 13.14%
George Joseph Altgelt (Green)...........320,520 ........ 8.56%
    Total Vote ...................................3,742,509

## STATE BOARD OF EDUCATION
### District 3

Marisa B. Perez (Dem.) ...................... 129,840 ....... 59.57%
Dave Mundy (Rep.) .............................81,295 ...... 37.29%
Josh Morales (Lib.)................................. 6,827 ......... 3.13%
    Total Vote ..................................... 217,962

### District 4

Lawrence A. Allen Jr. (Dem.) .............. 158,506 ....... 76.45%
Dorothy Olmos (Rep.)........................... 48,804 ...... 23.54%
    Total Vote ..................................... 207,310

### District 7

David Bradley (Rep.) ........................... 226,856 ....... 63.88%
Kathy King (Dem.) .............................. 120,212 ...... 33.85%
Megan DaGata (Lib.).............................. 8,021 ......... 2.25%
    Total Vote ..................................... 355,089

### District 11

Patricia "Pat" Hardy (Rep.) ................. 242,165 ....... 65.11%
Nancy Bean (Dem.)............................. 116,674 ...... 31.37%
Craig Sanders (Lib.) ............................. 13,044 ......... 3.50%
    Total Vote ..................................... 371,883

### District 12

Geraldine "Tincy" Miller (Rep.) ........... 222,347 ....... 61.39%
Lois Parrott (Dem.) ............................. 127,616 ...... 35.23%
Mark Wester (Lib.) ................................ 12,210 ......... 3.37%
    Total Vote ..................................... 362,173

### District 13

Erika Beltran (Dem.) ........................... 172,404 ....... 89.82%
Junart Sodoy (Lib.) .............................. 19,520 ...... 10.17%
    Total Vote ..................................... 191,924

## STATE SENATE
### District 2

Bob Hall (Rep.)..................................... 99,925 ....... 83.58%
Don Bates (Lib.)..................................... 19,626 ....... 16.41%
    Total Vote ..................................... 119,551

### District 3

Robert Nichols (Rep.) ......................... 140,069 ....... 90.55%
J. Tyler Lindsey (Lib.) .......................... 14,605 ......... 9.44%
    Total Vote ..................................... 154,674

### District 5

Charles Schwertner (Rep.) ................. 112,930 ....... 64.97%
Joel Shapiro (Dem.).............................. 54,286 ...... 31.23%
Matthew Whittington (Lib.)...................... 6,595 ......... 3.79%
    Total Vote ..................................... 173,811

### District 7

Paul Bettencourt (Rep.) ...................... 123,551 ....... 71.82%
Jim Davis (Dem.).................................. 45,230 ...... 26.29%
Whitney Bilyeu (Lib.).............................. 3,244 ......... 1.88%
    Total Vote ..................................... 172,025

### District 8

Van Taylor (Rep.) ................................ 114,498 ....... 79.06%
Scott Jameson (Lib.)............................. 30,312 ...... 20.93%
    Total Vote ..................................... 144,810

### District 9

Kelly Hancock (Rep..)........................... 89,331 ....... 65.06%
Gregory R. Perry (Dem.) ..................... 47,965 ...... 34.93%
    Total Vote ..................................... 137,296

### District 10

Konni Burton (Rep.)............................. 95,532 ....... 52.82%
Libby Willis (Dem.)................................ 80,872 ...... 44.72%
Gene Lord (Lib.) ................................... 3,340 ......... 1.84%
John Tunmire (Green) .......................... 1,094 ......... 0.60%
    Total Vote ..................................... 180,838

### District 14

Kirk Watson (Dem.) ............................. 154,391 ....... 79.97%
James Arthur Strohm (Lib.)................... 38,648 ...... 20,02%
    Total Vote ..................................... 193,039

### District 15

John Whitmire (Dem.)........................... 74,192 ....... 59.16%
Ron Hale (Rep.) ................................... 48,249 ...... 38.47%
Gilberto Valesquez Jr. (Lib.) ................... 2,947 ......... 2.35%
    Total Vote ..................................... 125,388

### District 17

Joan Huffman (Rep.) ........................... 113,817 ....... 63.33%
Rita Lucido (Dem.)............................... 60,934 ...... 33.90%
George Hardy (Lib.) .............................. 3,642 ......... 2.02%
David Courtney (Green) ......................... 1,303 ......... 0.72%
    Total Vote ..................................... 179,696

### District 23

Royce West (Dem.) ............................. 99,102 ....... 79.39%
John Lawson (Rep.) ............................. 23,520 ...... 18.84%
Jonathan F. Erhardt (Lib.) ...................... 2,204 ......... 1.76%
    Total Vote ..................................... 124,826

### District 25

Donna Campbell (Rep.)........................ 153,536 ....... 65.15%
Daniel Boone (Dem.)............................ 75,012 ...... 31.83%
Brandin P. Lea (Lib..) ............................. 7,106 ......... 3.01%
    Total Vote ..................................... 235,654

### District 30

Craig Estes (Rep.)............................... 140,240 ....... 86.65%
Cory Lane (Lib..).................................... 21,599 ...... 13.34%
    Total Vote ..................................... 161,839

### District 31

Kel Seliger (Rep.) ............................... 107,030 ...... 90.40%
Steven Gibson (Lib.)............................. 11,355 ......... 9.59%
    Total Vote ..................................... 118,385

## COURTS OF APPEALS
### Chief Justice, Third District

Jeff Rose (Rep.) ..................................307,589 ... 54.12%
Diane Henson (Dem.)..........................260,661 ...... 45.87%
    Total Vote ....................................568,250

### Chief Justice, Fourth District

Sandee Bryan Marion (Rep.)...............258,379 ...... 55.52%
Irene Rios (Dem.)................................206,982 ...... 44.47%
    Total Vote ....................................465,361

### Chief Justice, Fourteenth District

Kem Thompson Frost (Rep.)...............551,558 ...... 57.63%
Kyle Carter (Dem.)...............................405,415 ...... 42.36%
    Total Vote ....................................956,973

### Justice, First District, Place 3

Russell Lloyd (Rep.) ...........................547,589 ...... 57.13%
Jim Sharp (Dem.) ...............................410,857 ...... 42.86%
    Total Vote ....................................958,446

### Justice, Fifth District, Place 5 (unexpired)

Craig Stoddart (Rep.) ..........................354,978 ...... 55.61%
Ken Molberg (Dem.) ...........................283,306 ...... 44.38%
    Total Vote ....................................638,284

### Justice, Thirteenth District, Place 6

Dori Contreras Garza (Dem.) ..............130,724 ...... 50.85%
Doug Norman (Rep.) ...........................126,332 ...... 49.14%
    Total Vote ....................................257,056

### Justice, Fourteenth District, Place 7

Ken Wise (Rep.) ..................................556,600 ...... 58.23%
Gordon Goodman (Dem.).....................399,103 ...... 41.76%
    Total Vote ....................................955,703

# Republican Primary Election, 2014

Following are the official results for the contested races in the Republican Party primary held March 4, 2014. Included are statewide races and selected district races. Runoffs were held on May 27, 2014.

### Governor
| | | |
|---|---|---|
| Greg Abbott | 1,222,596 | 91.48% |
| Lisa Fritsch | 59,172 | 4.42% |
| Miriam Martinez | 35,567 | 2.66% |
| Secede Kilgore | 19,039 | 1.42% |
| Total Vote | 1,336,374 | |

### U.S. Senator
| | | |
|---|---|---|
| John Cornyn | 780,454 | 59.43% |
| Steve Stockman | 251,273 | 19.13% |
| Chris Mapp | 23,514 | 1.79% |
| Dwayne Stovall | 140,545 | 10.70% |
| Linda Vega | 50,025 | 3.80% |
| Curt Cleaver | 12,319 | 0.93% |
| Reid Reasor | 20,587 | 1.56% |
| Ken Cope | 34,362 | 2.61% |
| Total Vote | 1,313,079 | |

### Lieutenant Governor
| | | |
|---|---|---|
| Dan Patrick | 552,243 | 41.44% |
| David Dewhurst | 377,521 | 28.33% |
| Todd Staples | 236,364 | 17.73% |
| Jerry Patterson | 166,261 | 12.47% |
| Total Vote | 1,332,389 | |

### Attorney General
| | | |
|---|---|---|
| Ken Paxton | 568,446 | 44.45% |
| Dan Branch | 427,764 | 33.45% |
| Barry Smitherman | 282,419 | 22.08% |
| Total Vote | 1,278,629 | |

### Comptroller of Public Accounts
| | | |
|---|---|---|
| Glenn Hegar | 611,681 | 50.00% |
| Harvey Hilderbran | 318,474 | 26.03% |
| Debra Medina | 236,220 | 19.31% |
| Raul Torres | 56,903 | 4.65% |
| Total Vote | 1,223,278 | |

### Land Commissioner
| | | |
|---|---|---|
| George P. Bush | 936,937 | 72.99% |
| David Watts | 346,582 | 27.00% |
| Total Vote | 1,283,519 | |

### Agriculture Commissioner
| | | |
|---|---|---|
| Sid Miller | 411,187 | 34.56% |
| Tommy Merritt | 249,179 | 20.94% |
| Eric Opiela | 207,050 | 17.40% |
| Joe Cotten | 174,075 | 14.63% |
| J. Allen Carnes | 147,973 | 12.44% |
| Total Vote | 1,189,464 | |

### Railroad Commissioner
| | | |
|---|---|---|
| Wayne Christian | 502,893 | 42.66% |
| Ryan Sitton | 359,827 | 30.52% |
| Malachi Boyuls | 117,397 | 9.96% |
| Becky Berger | 198,507 | 16.84% |
| Total Vote | 1,178,624 | |

## U.S. HOUSE OF REPRESENTATIVES

### District 3
| | | |
|---|---|---|
| Sam Johnson | 31,178 | 80.55% |
| Harry Pierce | 3,004 | 7.76% |
| Cami Dean | 2,435 | 6.29% |
| Josh Loveless | 2,086 | 5.38% |
| Total Vote | 38,703 | |

### District 4
| | | |
|---|---|---|
| Ralph M. Hall | 29,848 | 45.41% |
| John Ratcliffe | 18,917 | 28.78% |
| Lou Gigliotti | 10,601 | 16.13% |
| Brent Lawson | 2,290 | 3.48% |

| | | |
|---|---|---|
| Tony Arterburn | 1,252 | 1.90% |
| John Stacy | 2,812 | 4.27% |
| Total Vote | 65,720 | |

### District 6
| | | |
|---|---|---|
| Joe L. Barton | 32,618 | 72.66% |
| Frank C. Kuchar | 12,272 | 27.33% |
| Total Vote | 44,890 | |

### District 8
| | | |
|---|---|---|
| Kevin Brady | 41,590 | 68.12% |
| Craig McMichael | 19,459 | 31.87% |
| Total Vote | 61,049 | |

### District 11
| | | |
|---|---|---|
| Mike Conaway | 53,272 | 73.70% |
| Wade Brown | 19,010 | 26.29% |
| Total Vote | 72,282 | |

### District 13
| | | |
|---|---|---|
| Mac Thornberry | 45,168 | 68,20% |
| Elaine Hays | 12,330 | 18.61% |
| Pam Barlow | 8,723 | 13.17% |
| Total Vote | 66,221 | |

### District 15
| | | |
|---|---|---|
| Eddie Zamora | 7,810 | 54.93% |
| Doug Carlile | 6,407 | 45.06% |
| Total Vote | 14,217 | |

### District 19
| | | |
|---|---|---|
| Randy Neugebauer | 39,611 | 64.36% |
| Donald R. May | 14,498 | 23.55% |
| Chris Winn | 7,429 | 12.07% |
| Total Vote | 61,538 | |

### District 21
| | | |
|---|---|---|
| Lamar Smith | 40,441 | 60.43% |
| Matt McCall | 22,681 | 33.89% |
| Michael J. Smith | 3,796 | 5.67% |
| Total Vote | 66,918 | |

### District 23
| | | |
|---|---|---|
| Will Hurd | 10,496 | 40.96% |
| Francisco "Quico" Canseco | 10,332 | 40.32% |
| Robert Lowry | 4,796 | 18.71% |
| Total Vote | 25,624 | |

### District 26
| | | |
|---|---|---|
| Michael Burgess | 33,909 | 82.62% |
| Joel A. Krause | 6,433 | 15.67% |
| Divency Watrous | 698 | 1.70% |
| Total Vote | 41,040 | |

### District 32
| | | |
|---|---|---|
| Pete Sessions | 28,981 | 63.61% |
| Katrina Pierson | 16,574 | 36.38% |
| Total Vote | 45,555 | |

### District 36
| | | |
|---|---|---|
| Brian Babin | 17,194 | 33.36% |
| Ben Streusand | 12,024 | 23.33% |
| John Manlove | 3,556 | 6.90% |
| Jim Engstrand | 1,288 | 2.49% |
| Chuck Meyer | 1,574 | 3.05% |
| Kim I. Morrell | 1,444 | 2.80% |
| John Amdur | 1,470 | 2.85% |
| Dave Norman | 2,325 | 4.51% |
| Pat Kasprzak | 1,116 | 2.16% |
| Robin Riley | 2,648 | 5,13% |
| Phil Fitzgerald | 3,388 | 6.57% |
| Doug Centilli | 3,506 | 6.80% |
| Total Vote | 51,533 | |

## STATE COURTS

### Chief Justice, Supreme Court
Nathan Hecht............................................. 709,674 ...... 60.48%
Robert Talton ............................................ 463,701 ...... 39.51%
Total Vote.................................. 1,173,375

### Justice, Supreme Court, Place 6 (unexpired)
Jeff Brown................................................. 822,482 ...... 71.89%
Joe Pool.................................................... 321,506 ...... 28.10%
Total Vote.................................. 1,143,988

### Justice, Supreme Court, Place 8
Phil Johnson ............................................. 733,032 ...... 64.01%
Sharon McCally. ........................................ 412,025 ...... 35.98%
Total Vote.................................. 1,145,057

### Judge, Court of Criminal Appeals, Place 3
Bert Richardson......................................... 667,729 ...... 60.33%
Barbara Walther ........................................ 438,936 ...... 39.66%
Total Vote.................................. 1,106,665

### Judge, Court of Criminal Appeals, Place 4
Keven Patrick Yeary .......................... 558,290 ...... 50.89%
Jani Jo Wood............................................. 232,068 ...... 21.15%
Richard Dean Davis.................................. 306,683 ...... 27.95%
Total Vote.................................. 1,097,041

### Judge, Court of Criminal Appeals, Place 9
David Newell.............................................. 571,277 ...... 52.23%
W.C. "Bud" Kirkendall ......................... 522,404 ...... 47.76%
Total Vote.................................. 1,093,681

## STATE SENATE

### District 2
Bob Deuell................................................. 23,863 ...... 48.49%
Bob Hall.................................................... 19,102 ...... 38.81%
Mark Thompson......................................... 6,244 ...... 12.68%
Total Vote.................................. 49,209

### District 7
Paul Bettencourt. ....................................... 39,461 ...... 89.17%
James Wilson. ............................................ 4,792 ...... 10.82%
Total Vote.................................. 44,253

### District 10
Konni Burton.............................................. 19,288 ...... 43.23%
Mark M. Shelton ........................................ 15,689 ...... 35.16%
Tony Pompa................................................ 5,595 ...... 12.54%
Jon Schweitzer ........................................... 1,368 ...... 3.06%
Mark Skinner .............................................. 2,677 ...... 5.99%
Total Vote.................................. 44,617

### District 16
Don Huffines.............................................. 25,141 ...... 50.63%
John Carona .............................................. 24,509 ...... 49.36%
Total Vote.................................. 49,650

### District 17
Joan Huffman. ............................................ 33,011 ...... 81.08%
Derek A. Anthony. ....................................... 7,699 ...... 18.91%
Total Vote.................................. 40,710

### District 25
Donna Campbell.......................................... 40,867 ...... 55.40%
Mike Novak................................................. 14,943 ...... 20.30%
Elisa Chan................................................. 17,916 ...... 24.29%
Total Vote.................................. 73,596

### District 31
Kel Seliger ................................................. 36,777 ...... 52.51%
Mike Canon ............................................... 33,252 ...... 47.48%
Total Vote.................................. 70,029

## STATE BOARD OF EDUCATION

### District 7
David Bradley ............................................ 50,434 ...... 55.28%
Rita Ashley................................................. 40,788 ...... 44.71%
Total Vote.................................. 91,222

### District 11
Patricia "Pat" Hardy .............................. 43,113 ...... 49.57%
Eric Mahroum ............................................ 37,843 ...... 43.51%
Lady Theresa Thombs. ............................... 6,011 ......... 6.91%
Total Vote.................................. 86,967

## PROPOSITIONS

### Prop. 1 – Allow prayer in public places
In Favor ................................................. 1,314,296 ...... 97.24%
Against.................................................. 37,238 ......... 2.75%
Total Vote.................................. 1,351,534

### Prop. 2 – Expand concealed hangun liberties
In Favor ................................................. 1,163,645 ...... 86.91%
Against.................................................. 175,254 ...... 13.08%
Total Vote.................................. 1,338,899

### Prop. 3 – Abolish state franchise tax
In Favor ................................................. 1,153,228 ...... 88.48%
Against.................................................. 150,089 ...... 11.51%
Total Vote.................................. 1,303,317

### Prop. 4 – Drug testing for welfare recepients
In Favor ................................................. 1,284,271 ...... 94.88%
Against.................................................. 69,200 ......... 5.11%
Total Vote.................................. 1,353,471

### Prop. 5 – Elected officals and staff subject to same laws as constituents
In Favor ................................................. 1,347,967 ...... 99.36%
Against.................................................. 8,609 ......... 0.63%
Total Vote.................................. 1,356,576

### Prop. 6 – Repeal Affordable Care Act (Obamacare)
In Favor ................................................. 1,255,323 ...... 92,93%
Against.................................................. 95,428 ......... 7.06%
Total Vote.................................. 1,350,751

## COURTS OF APPEALS

### Justice, First District, Place 3
Russell Lloyd ............................................ 87,435 ...... 50.40%
Chad Bridges............................................. 37,641 ...... 21.69%
Dan Linebaugh ......................................... 48,404 ...... 27.90%
Total Vote.................................. 173,480

### Justice, Nineth District, Place 3 (unexpired)
Leanne Johnson ....................................... 41,900 ...... 56.14%
Earl B. Stover III. ...................................... 32,724 ...... 43.85%
Total Vote.................................. 74,624

### Justice, Eleventh District, Place 3 (unexpired)
John Bailey ............................................... 33,383 ...... 56.36%
Cade W. Browning. .................................... 25,842 ...... 43.63%
Total Vote.................................. 59,225

### Justice, Thirteenth District, Place 6
Doug Norman. ........................................... 25,558 ...... 64.58%
Bradford M. Condit .................................... 14,012 ...... 35.41%
Total Vote.................................. 39,570

## REPUBLICAN RUNOFF

### Lieutenant Governor
Dan Patrick............................................... 489,586 ...... 65.03%
David Dewhurst ......................................... 263,194 ...... 34.96%
Total Vote.................................. 752,780

### Attorney General
Ken Paxton................................................ 466,407 ...... 63.41%
Dan Branch................................................ 269,098 ...... 36.58%
Total Vote.................................. 735,505

### Agriculture Commissioner
Sid Miller................................................... 364,756 ...... 53.20%
Tommy Merritt............................................ 320,835 ...... 46.79%
Total Vote.................................. 685,591

### Railroad Commissioner
Ryan Sitton ............................................... 400,259 ...... 57.26%
Wayne Christian ........................................ 298,659 ...... 42.73%
Total Vote.................................. 698,918

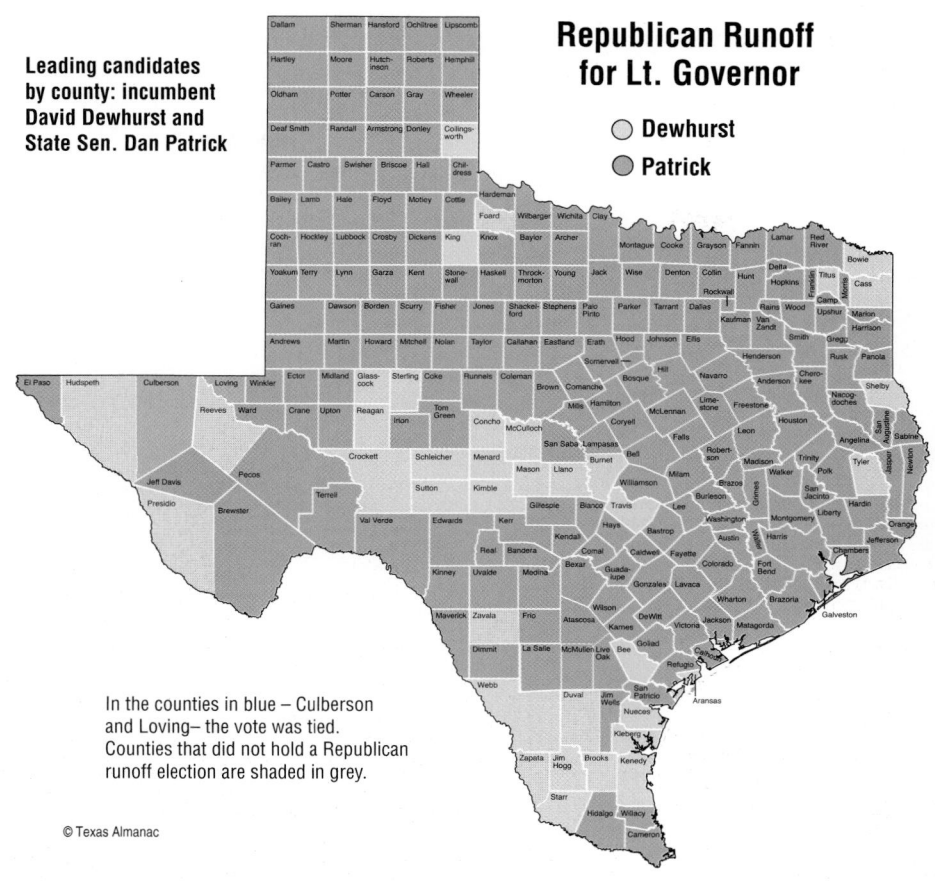

**Leading candidates by county: incumbent David Dewhurst and State Sen. Dan Patrick**

# Republican Runoff for Lt. Governor

○ Dewhurst
● Patrick

In the counties in blue – Culberson and Loving– the vote was tied. Counties that did not hold a Republican runoff election are shaded in grey.

© Texas Almanac

---

## U.S. HOUSE OF REPRESENTATIVES
### District 4
| | | |
|---|---|---|
| John Ratcliffe | 22,271 | 52.81% |
| Ralph M. Hall | 19,899 | 47.18% |
| Total Vote | 42,170 | |

### District 23
| | | |
|---|---|---|
| Will Hurd | 8,699 | 59.46% |
| Francisco "Quico" Canseco | 5,930 | 40.53% |
| Total Vote | 14,629 | |

### District 36
| | | |
|---|---|---|
| Brian Babin | 19,301 | 57.83% |
| Ben Streusand | 14,069 | 42.16% |
| Total Vote | 33,370 | |

## STATE SENATE
### District 2
| | | |
|---|---|---|
| Bob Hall | 18,233 | 50.41% |
| Bob Deuell | 17,933 | 49.58% |
| Total Vote | 36,166 | |

### District 10
| | | |
|---|---|---|
| Konni Burton | 17,435 | 60.22% |
| Mark M. Shelton | 11,515 | 39.77% |
| Total Vote | 28,950 | |

## STATE BOARD OF EDUCATION
### District 11
| | | |
|---|---|---|
| Patricia "Pat" Hardy | 32,973 | 58.68% |
| Eric Mahroum | 23,211 | 41.31% |
| Total Vote | 56,184 | |

## Special Elections
### State Senate
### District 4
#### Runoff held Aug. 5, 2014
| | | |
|---|---|---|
| Brandon Creighton (Rep.) | 15,232 | 67,38% |
| Steve Toth (Rep.) | 7,373 | 32.61% |
| Total Vote | 22,605 | |

### District 28
#### Held Sept. 9, 2014
| | | |
|---|---|---|
| Charles Perry (Rep.) | 22,860 | 53.39% |
| Jodey Arrington (Rep.) | 12,958 | 30.26% |
| Greg Wortham (Dem.) | 5,616 | 13.11% |
| Delwin Jones (Rep.) | 677 | 1.58% |
| Kerry Douglas McKennon (Lib.) | 358 | 0.83% |
| E.M. Garza (Rep.) | 347 | 0.81% |
| Total Vote | 42,816 | |

### District 18
#### Held Dec. 6, 2014
| | | |
|---|---|---|
| Cindy Drabek (Dem.) | 1,893 | 4.81% |
| Gary Gates (Rep.) | 13,439 | 34.15% |
| Charles Gregory (Rep.) | 779 | 1.98% |
| Christian E. Hawkins (Dem.) | 1,280 | 3.25% |
| Lois W. Kolkhorst (Rep.) | 21,961 | 55.81% |
| Total Vote | 39,352 | |

### District 26
#### Runoff held Feb. 17, 2015
| | | |
|---|---|---|
| Trey Maretinez Fischer (Dem.) | 9,635 | 40.95% |
| Jose Menendez (Dem.) | 13,891 | 59.05% |
| Total Vote | 23,526 | |

# Democratic Primary Election, 2014

Following are the official results for the contested races in the Democratic Party primary held March 4, 2014. Included are statewide races and selected district races.

### Governor
| | | |
|---|---|---|
| Wendy R. Davis | 432,595 | 78.08% |
| Reynaldo "Ray" Madrigal | 121,419 | 21.91% |
| Total vote | 554,014 | |

### U.S. Senator
| | | |
|---|---|---|
| David M. Alameel | 239,914 | 47.04% |
| Kesha Rogers | 110,146 | 21.59% |
| Maxey Marie Scherr | 90,359 | 17.71% |
| Michael "Fjet" Fjetland | 24,383 | 4.78% |
| Harry Kim | 45,207 | 8.86% |
| Total Vote | 510,009 | |

### Agriculture Commissioner
| | | |
|---|---|---|
| Jim Hogan | 190,090 | 38.74% |
| Richard "Kinky" Friedman | 185,180 | 37.74% |
| Hugh Asa Fitzsimmons III | 115,395 | 23.51% |
| Total Vote | 490,665 | |

### Railroad Commissioner
| | | |
|---|---|---|
| Steve Brown | 299,009 | 64.02% |
| Dale Henry | 168,036 | 35.97% |
| Total Vote | 467,045 | |

### U.S. HOUSE OF REPRESENTATIVES
#### District 7
| | | |
|---|---|---|
| James Cargas | 4,098 | 62.19% |
| Lissa Squiers | 2,491 | 37.80% |
| Total Vote | 6,589 | |

#### District 14
| | | |
|---|---|---|
| Donald G. Brown | 9,780 | 68.23% |
| Buck Willis | 3,699 | 25.80% |
| Gagan Panjhazari | 853 | 5.95% |
| Total Vote | 14,332 | |

#### District 22
| | | |
|---|---|---|
| Frank Briscoe | 3,378 | 53.18% |
| Mark Gibson | 2,973 | 46.81% |
| Total Vote | 6,351 | |

#### District 25
| | | |
|---|---|---|
| Marco Montoya | 11,691 | 75.16% |
| Sruart Gourd | 3,863 | 24.83% |
| Total Vote | 15,554 | |

#### District 30
| | | |
|---|---|---|
| Eddie Bernice Johnson | 23,756 | 69.92% |
| Barbara Mallory Caraway | 10,216 | 30.07% |
| Total Vote | 33,972 | |

#### District 33
| | | |
|---|---|---|
| Marc Veasey | 13,292 | 73.47% |
| Tom Sanchez | 4,798 | 26.52% |
| Total Vote | 18,090 | |

### STATE SENATE
#### District 10
| | | |
|---|---|---|
| Libby Willis | 13,041 | 56.48% |
| Mike Martinez | 10,047 | 43.51% |
| George Boll | 0 | 0.00% |
| Total Vote | 23,088 | |

#### District 15
| | | |
|---|---|---|
| John Whitmire | 9,766 | 75.09% |
| Damien LaCroix | 3,239 | 24.90% |
| Total Vote | 13,005 | |

### STATE BOARD OF EDUCATION
#### District 13
| | | |
|---|---|---|
| Erika Beltran | 23,570 | 47.02% |
| Andrea Hilburn | 13,733 | 27.39% |
| A. Denise Russell | 12,819 | 25.57% |
| Total Vote | 50,122 | |

### PROPOSITIONS

#### Prop. 1 – Immigration reform with path to citizenship
| | | |
|---|---|---|
| In Favor | 476,761 | 86.46% |
| Against | 74,605 | 13.53% |
| Total Vote | 551,366 | |

#### Prop. 2 – Raise minimum wage to 110% of poverty level
| | | |
|---|---|---|
| In Favor | 499,724 | 89.23% |
| Against | 60,309 | 10.76% |
| Total Vote | 560,033 | |

#### Prop. 3 – Expand Medicaid
| | | |
|---|---|---|
| In Favor | 497,413 | 89.05% |
| Against | 61,116 | 10.94% |
| Total Vote | 558,529 | |

#### Prop. 4 – Expand non-discrimination laws to cover sexual orientation and gender identity
| | | |
|---|---|---|
| In Favor | 487,785 | 88.12% |
| Against | 65,714 | 11.87% |
| Total Vote | 553,499 | |

### COURTS OF APPEALS
#### Chief Justice, Eighth District
| | | |
|---|---|---|
| Ann Crawford McClure | 18,339 | 52.61% |
| Mario Alberto Gonzalez | 16,517 | 47.38% |
| Total Vote | 34,856 | |

### DEMOCRATIC RUNOFF
#### U.S. Senator
| | | |
|---|---|---|
| David M. Alameel | 145,227 | 72.15% |
| Kesha Rogers | 56,056 | 27.84% |
| Total Vote | 201,283 | |

#### Agriculture Commissioner
| | | |
|---|---|---|
| Jim Hogan | 105,887 | 53.70% |
| Richard "Kinky" Friedman | 91,282 | 46.29% |
| Total Vote | 197,169 | |

#### STATE BOARD OF EDUCATION
#### District 13
| | | |
|---|---|---|
| Erika Beltran | 13,159 | 66.52% |
| Andrea Hilburn | 6,622 | 33.47% |
| Total Vote | 19,781 | |

## Political Party Organizations

**DEMOCRATIC State Executive Committee**
www.txdemocrats.org
**Chairman**, Gilberto Hinojosa, 4818 E. Ben White Blvd., Ste. 104, Austin 78741.

**REPUBLICAN State Executive Committee**
www.texasgop.org
**Chairman**, Tom Mechler, 1108 Lavaca, Ste. 500, Austin 78701.

**LIBERTARIAN State Executive Committee**
www.lptexas.org
**Chair**, Kurt Hildebrand, 111 Congress Ave. Ste. 400, Austin 78701.

**GREEN State Executive Committee**
txgreens.org
**Co-Chairs**, Aaron Renaud and Laura Palmer, P.O. Box 271080, Houston 77277-1080.

# Government

*Festivities filled the Capitol grounds on a sunny Inauguration Day, Jan. 20, 2015. Photo by Lamberto Alvarez.*

## Historical Documents
## Constitutional Amendments
## Chief Officials, 1691–2015
## State, Local, Federal Government
## Crime in Texas

The Texas House of Representatives conducts business with a full house of spectators during the 84th Legislature. Texas House of Representatives photo.

# Budget Increase, Tax Cuts, Gun Rights Highlight
# Mostly Harmonious 84th Legislative Session

### By Carolyn Barta

The 84th Texas Legislature convened for its 140-day regular session in January 2015 with an infusion of tea-party backed members and the first change in top state political leadership in more than a decade. Texans could easily claim one of the most conservative and Republican-dominated governments in the country. Legislators cut taxes, beefed up border security, and passed more permissive gun laws.

But for some in the GOP, it wasn't conservative enough. Bills that failed included measures that would reinforce the state's ban on gay marriage, provide new school-choice options, end in-state college tuition for illegal immigrants, and prohibit "sanctuary cities" where police can't ask those they stop about immigration status.

Legislators easily crafted a record $209.4 billion biennial state budget, a 3.6-percent increase, made easier by a robust economy that produced a forecast of $17 billion in uncommitted funds.

Candidates who promised tax cuts were able to deliver. Lawmakers cut the business franchise tax by 25 percent, or $2.56 billion over two years, and increased property tax homestead exemptions that, if approved by voters, would save the average homeowner about $125 annually. Besides covering the $3.8 billion in tax cuts, the budget stockpiled funds for an economic downturn, or other unforeseen events, with $6.4 billion in unspent revenues and $11 billion in the oil-and-gas-production fed Rainy Day Fund.

Democrats argued that the conservative approach to spending left such priorities as public schools and health care underfunded, including failure to address long-standing school finance inequities.

A Travis County District Court judge ruled the state's school finance system unconstitutional in August 2014 because of inadequate funding, distribution flaws, and because it imposed a de facto state property tax. Some 600 school districts — more than two-thirds of the districts in Texas — had filed a massive lawsuit against the state after lawmakers slashed public school funding in 2011. The state appealed the district court ruling to the Texas Supreme Court, and the higher court wasn't expected to render judgement until late 2015 or even 2016. Most legislators wanted to hear that ruling before attempting a school finance overhaul, even if it meant a special session might have to be called by the governor before the next regular session in 2017.

As for spending, legislators found a way to boost the state's long insufficient budget for roads and highways, without raising tolls, fees, debt, or taxes. The transportation package would require voter approval of a revenue shift from the general sales tax and motor vehicle sales tax. The Texas Department of Transportation had said it needed another $5 billion a year to keep congestion from getting worse and to maintain roads, and leaders estimated the package, beginning in 2018, would ultimately give TxDOT an additional $4 billion a year.

Republicans were overwhelmingly in control. They held all statewide offices, had their largest majority (20–11) in the Texas Senate, and held roughly two-thirds of the 150 House seats.

New leadership came in the top three political offices — governor, lieutenant governor, and attorney general. After 14 years as governor, Rick Perry, longest-serving governor in Texas history, relinquished the office to make a second run for president, joining fellow Texan, U.S. Sen. Ted Cruz, in a crowded GOP presidential primary field.

Greg Abbott, former attorney general, became governor after easily defeating the Democratic nominee, State Sen. Wendy Davis. Abbott's style was more low-key than Perry's, working mostly behind the scenes to deliver a largely harmonious session, one marked by its lack of theatrics and acrimony.

It was a far cry from two years before, when the Legislature was forced into special sessions to finish business. The first special session in 2013 will long be remembered for Wendy Davis' abortion-bill filibuster that hamstrung Senate action in the final hours. It was the climax of a session torn asunder by stringent anti-abortion bills, and it launched Davis' unsuccessful run for governor. It also spelled future defeat for Lt. Gov. David Dewhurst, who lost control in hours of pre-adjournment mayhem.

Dewhurst, Senate presiding officer for 12 years, was defeated in a Republican primary runoff by Dan Patrick, a state senator from Houston and one-time talk show host considered the most conservative candidate in the four-man primary. In the attorney general's slot, Abbott was succeeded by Ken Paxton, a former legislator from Collin County who had strong tea-party support. Other new statewide office faces included Land Commissioner George P. Bush, nephew of former governor and President George W. Bush.

Abbott claimed among his successes the authorization of:

• An additional $800 million for border security to be used for public safety personnel, technology, and local resources.

• More than $400 million to elevate university research programs and $40 million for the Governor's University Research Initiative to attract top-notch researchers.

• $130 million to enable school districts in the state's half-day pre-kindergarten programs to receive extra funds if they adopt new standards.

Contentious gun bills that passed were a "campus carry" law that will allow licensed Texans who are 21 years and older to carry concealed handguns in most state university buildings and an "open carry" law that will allow licensed Texans to openly carry handguns in hip or shoulder holsters.

After Texas passed the country's most sweeping anti-abortion measures in 2013, the 2015 Legislature approved only one major abortion bill, one that made it more difficult for minors to obtain court approval for an abortion without parental permission.

Some Republicans wanted to repeal a law in effect since 2001 that allows in-state college tuition for unauthorized immigrants who graduate from public high schools. Others saw it as detrimental to the job pool for Texas employers, and the law was preserved. Another conservative-backed measure that failed was a $100 million school voucher plan that would allow lower-income public school children to transfer to private or religious schools.

In other action, the Legislature: moved the investigation of state officials out of Travis County and into their home counties; banned cities, such as Denton, from restricting within city limits the oil and gas drilling practice known as fracking; decriminalized most aspects of truancy; and legalized access to low-THC marijuana extracts to treat people with symptoms of intractable seizures. Other marijuana bills were snubbed, and a bill outlawing texting while driving failed to pass the Senate.

The session was notable for its orderly work, and a House that often moderated positions of the Senate. Speaker Joe Straus, R-San Antonio, who presided over his fourth regular House session, commended members for working at a slow and steady pace. He termed it a "cautious, conservative session."

*Carolyn Barta, a retired Dallas Morning News political writer, is a journalism professor at Southern Methodist University.* ☆

*The Texas Senate in session during the 84th Legislature in 2015. Texas Senate photo.*

# Declaration of Independence of the Republic of Texas

The Declaration of Independence of the Republic of Texas was adopted in general convention at Washington-on-the-Brazos, March 2, 1836.

Richard Ellis, president of the convention, appointed a committee of five to write the declaration for submission to the convention. However, there is much evidence that George C. Childress, one of the members, wrote the document with lit-tle or no help from the other members. Childress is therefore generally accepted as the author.

The text of the declaration is followed by the names of the signers of the document. The names are presented here as the signers actually signed the document.

Our thanks to the staff of the Texas State Archives for furnishing a photocopy of the signatures.

---

UNANIMOUS

## *Declaration of Independence,*

BY THE

DELEGATES OF THE PEOPLE OF TEXAS,

**IN GENERAL CONVENTION,**

AT THE TOWN OF WASHINGTON,

ON THE SECOND DAY OF MARCH, 1836.

When a government has ceased to protect the lives, liberty and property of the people from whom its legitimate powers are derived, and for the advancement of whose happiness it was instituted; and so far from being a guarantee for the enjoyment of those inestimable and inalienable rights, becomes an instrument in the hands of evil rulers for their oppression; when the Federal Republican Constitution of their country, which they have sworn to support, no longer has a substantial existence, and the whole nature of their government has been forcibly changed without their consent, from a restricted federative republic, composed of sovereign states, to a consolidated central military despotism, in which every interest is disregarded but that of the army and the priesthood — both the eternal enemies of civil liberty, and the ever-ready minions of power, and the usual instruments of tyrants; When long after the spirit of the Constitution has departed, moderation is at length, so far lost, by those in power that even the semblance of freedom is removed, and the forms, themselves, of the constitution discontinued; and so far from their petitions and remonstrances being regarded, the agents who bear them are thrown into dungeons; and mercenary armies sent forth to force a new government upon them at the point of the bayonet. When in consequence of such acts of malfeasance and abdication, on the part of the government, anarchy prevails, and civil society is dissolved into its original elements: In such a crisis, the first law of nature, the right of self-preservation — the inherent and inalienable right of the people to appeal to first principles and take their political affairs into their own hands in extreme cases — enjoins it as a right towards themselves and a sacred obligation to their posterity, to abolish such government and create another in its stead, calculated to rescue them from impending dangers, and to secure their future welfare and happiness.

Nations, as well as individuals, are amenable for their acts to the public opinion of mankind. A statement of a part of our grievances is, therefore, submitted to an impartial world, in justification of the hazardous but unavoidable step now taken of severing our political connection with the Mexican people, and assuming an independent attitude among the nations of the earth.

The Mexican government, by its colonization laws, invited and induced the Anglo-American population of Texas to colonize its wilderness under the pledged faith of a written constitution, that they should continue to enjoy that constitutional liberty and republican government to which they had been habituated in the land of their birth, the United States of America. In this expectation they have been cruelly disappointed, inasmuch as the Mexican nation has acquiesced in the late changes made in the government by General Antonio Lopez de Santa Anna, who, having overturned the constitution of his country, now offers us the cruel alternative either to abandon our homes, acquired by so many privations, or submit to the most intolerable of all tyranny, the combined despotism of the sword and the priesthood.

It has sacrificed our welfare to the state of Coahuila, by which our interests have been continually depressed, through a jealous and partial course of legislation carried on at a far distant seat of government, by a hostile majority, in an unknown tongue; and this too, notwithstanding we have petitioned in the humblest terms, for the establishment of a separate state government, and have, in accordance with the provisions of the national constitution, presented the general Congress, a republican constitution which was without just cause contemptuously rejected.

It incarcerated in a dungeon, for a long time, one of our citizens, for no other cause but a zealous endeavor to procure the acceptance of our constitution and the establishment of a state government.

It has failed and refused to secure on a firm basis, the right of trial by jury; that palladium of civil liberty, and only safe guarantee for the life, liberty, and property of the citizen.

It has failed to establish any public system of education, although possessed of almost boundless resources (the public domain) and, although, it is an axiom, in political science, that unless a people are educated and enlightened it is idle to expect the continuance of civil liberty, or the capacity for self-government.

It has suffered the military commandants stationed among us to exercise arbitrary acts of oppression and tyranny; thus trampling upon the most sacred rights of the citizen and rendering the military superior to the civil power.

It has dissolved by force of arms, the state Congress of Coahuila and Texas, and obliged our representatives to fly for their lives from the seat of government; thus depriving us of the fundamental political right of representation.

It has demanded the surrender of a number of our citizens, and ordered military detachments to seize and carry them into the Interior for trial; in contempt of the civil authorities, and in defiance of the laws and constitution.

It has made piratical attacks upon our commerce; by commissioning foreign desperadoes, and authorizing them to seize our vessels, and convey the property of our citizens to far distant ports of confiscation.

It denies us the right of worshipping the Almighty according to the dictates of our own consciences, by the support of a national religion calculated to promote the temporal interests of its human functionaries rather than the glory of the true and living God.

It has demanded us to deliver up our arms; which are essential to our defense, the rightful property of freemen, and formidable only to tyrannical governments.

It has invaded our country, both by sea and by land, with intent to lay waste our territory and drive us from our homes; and has now a large mercenary army advancing to carry on against us a war of extermination.

It has, through its emissaries, incited the merciless savage, with the tomahawk and scalping knife, to massacre the inhabitants of our defenseless frontiers.

It hath been, during the whole time of our connection with it, the contemptible sport and victim of successive military revolutions and hath continually exhibited every characteristic of a weak, corrupt and tyrannical government.

These, and other grievances, were patiently borne by the people of Texas until they reached that point at which forbearance ceases to be a virtue. We then took up arms in defense of the national constitution. We appealed to our Mexican brethren for assistance. Our appeal has been made in vain. Though months have elapsed, no sympathetic response has yet been heard from the Interior. We are, therefore, forced to the melancholy conclusion that the Mexican people have acquiesced in the destruction of their liberty, and the substitution therefor of a military government — that they are unfit to be free and incapable of self-government.

The necessity of self-preservation, therefore, now decrees our eternal political separation.

*We, therefore, the delegates, with plenary powers, of the people of Texas, in solemn convention assembled, appealing to a candid world for the necessities of our condition, do hereby resolve and DECLARE that our political connection with the Mexican nation has forever ended; and that the people of Texas do now constitute a FREE, SOVEREIGN and INDEPENDENT REPUBLIC, and are fully invested with all the rights and attributes which properly belong to the independent nations; and, conscious of the rectitude of our intentions, we fearlessly and confidently commit the issue to the decision of the Supreme Arbiter of the destinies of nations.*

RICHARD ELLIS, president of the convention and Delegate from Red River.

Charles B Stewart

Tho⁵ Barnett
John S.D. Byrom

Fran^co Ruiz
J. Antonio Navarro
Jesse B. Badgett
W^m D. Lacey
William Menefee
Jn° Fisher
Mathew Caldwell
William Mottley
Lorenzo de Zavala
Stephen H. Everitt
Geo W Smyth

Elijah Stapp
Claiborne West

W^m B Scates

M.B. Menard
A.B. Hardin
J.W. Bunton
Tho⁵ J. Gasley
R. M. Coleman
Sterling C. Robertson
Benj Briggs Goodrich
G.W. Barnett
James G. Swisher
Jesse Grimes
S. Rhoads Fisher
John W. Moore
John W. Bower
Sam^l A Maverick from Bejar
Sam P. Carson
A. Briscoe
J.B. Woods
Jas Collinsworth
Edwin Waller
Asa Brigham
Geo. C. Childress
Bailey Hardeman
Rob. Potter

Thomas Jefferson Rusk
Chas. S. Taylor
John S. Roberts

Robert Hamilton
Collin McKinney
Albert H Latimer
James Power

Sam Houston
David Thomas

Edw^d Conrad
Martin Parmer
Edwin O. LeGrand
Stephen W. Blount
Ja⁵ Gaines
W^m Clark, Jr
Sydney O. Penington
W^m Carrol Crawford
Jn° Turner

Test. H.S. Kimble, Secretary

# Documents Concerning the Annexation of Texas to the United States

For an overview of the subject, please see these discussions: The New Handbook of Texas, Texas State Historical Association, Austin, 1996; Vol. 1, pages 192–193. On the web: www.tshaonline.org/handbook/online/articles/AA/mga2.html. Also see, the Texas State Library and Archives website: www.tsl.state.tx.us/ref/abouttx/annexation/index.html and the Texas Almanac website: www.texasalmanac.com/history/timeline/annexation/.

## Joint Resolution for Annexing Texas to the United States

### Resolved

by the Senate and House of Representatives of the United States of America in Congress assembled,

That Congress doth consent that the territory properly included within and rightfully belonging to the Republic of Texas, may be erected into a new State to be called the State of Texas, with a republican form of government adopted by the people of said Republic, by deputies in convention assembled, with the consent of the existing Government in order that the same may by admitted as one of the States of this Union.

2. And be it further resolved, That the foregoing consent of Congress is given upon the following conditions, to wit:

First, said state to be formed, subject to the adjustment by this government of all questions of boundary that may arise with other government,

—and the Constitution thereof, with the proper evidence of its adoption by the people of said Republic of Texas, shall be transmitted to the President of the United States, to be laid before Congress for its final action on, or before the first day of January, one thousand eight hundred and forty-six.

Second, said state when admitted into the Union, after ceding to the United States all public edifices, fortifications, barracks, ports and harbors, navy and navy yards, docks, magazines and armaments, and all other means pertaining to the public defense, belonging to the said Republic of Texas, shall retain funds, debts, taxes and dues of every kind which may belong to, or be due and owing to the said Republic;

and shall also retain all the vacant and unappropriated lands lying within its limits, to be applied to the payment of the debts and liabilities of said Republic of Texas, and the residue of said lands, after discharging said debts and liabilities, to be disposed of as said State may direct; but in no event are said debts and liabilities to become a charge upon the Government of the United States.

Third — New States of convenient size not exceeding four in number, in addition to said State of Texas and having sufficient population, may, hereafter by the consent of said State, be formed out of the territory thereof, which shall be entitled to admission under the provisions of the Federal Constitution;

and such states as may be formed out of the territory lying south of thirty-six degrees thirty minutes north latitude, commonly known as the Missouri Compromise Line, shall be admitted into the Union, with or without slavery, as the people of each State, asking admission shall desire;

and in such State or States as shall be formed out of said territory, north of said Missouri Compromise Line, slavery, or involuntary servitude (except for crime) shall be prohibited.

3. And be it further resolved, That if the President of the United States shall in his judgment and discretion deem it most advisable, instead of proceeding to submit the foregoing resolution of the Republic of Texas, as an overture on the part of the United States for admission, to negotiate with the Republic; then,

Be it resolved, That a State, to be formed out of the present Republic of Texas, with suitable extent and boundaries, and with two representatives in Congress, until the next appointment of representation, shall be admitted into the Union, by virtue of this act, on an equal footing with the existing States, as soon as the terms and conditions of such admission, and the cession of the remaining Texian territory to the United States shall be agreed upon by the governments of Texas and the United States:

And that the sum of one hundred thousand dollars be, and the same is hereby, appropriated to defray the expenses of missions and negotiations, to agree upon the terms of said admission and cession, either by treaty to be submitted to the Senate, or by articles to be submitted to the two houses of Congress, as the President may direct.

### Approved, March 1, 1845.

Source: Peters, Richard, ed., The Public Statutes at Large of the United States of America, v.5, pp. 797–798, Boston, Chas. C. Little and Jas. Brown, 1850.

# [No. 1.] Joint Resolution for the Admission of the State of Texas into the Union

## Whereas

the Congress of the United States, by a joint resolution approved March the first, eighteen hundred and forty-five, did consent that the territory properly included within, and rightfully belonging to, the Republic of Texas, might be erected into a new State, to be called _The State of Texas,_ with a republican form of government, to be adopted by the people of said republic, by deputies in convention assembled, with the consent of the existing government, in order that the same might be admitted as one of the States of the Union;

which consent of Congress was given upon certain conditions specified in the first and second sections of said joint resolution;

and whereas the people of the said Republic of Texas, by deputies in convention assembled, with the consent of the existing government, did adopt a constitution, and erect a new State with a republican form of government, and, in the name of the people of Texas, and by their authority, did ordain and declare that they assented to and accepted the proposals, conditions, and guaranties contained in said first and second sections of said resolution:

and whereas the said constitution, with the proper evidence of its adoption by the people of the Republic of Texas, has been transmitted to the President of the United States and laid before Congress, in conformity to the provisions of said joint resolution:

## Therefore —

Resolved by the Senate and House of Representatives of the United States of America in Congress assembled, That the State of Texas shall be one, and is hereby declared to be one, of the United States of America, and admitted into the Union on an equal footing with the original States in all respects whatever.

Sec. 2. And be it further resolved, That until the representatives in Congress shall be apportioned according to an actual enumeration of the inhabitants of the United States, the State of Texas shall be entitled to choose two representatives.

## Approved, December 29, 1845.

SOURCE: Minot, Geo., ed., Statutes at Large and Treaties of the United States of America from Dec. 1, 1845, to March 3, 1851, V. IX, p. 108

# Constitution of Texas

The complete official text of the Constitution of Texas, including the original document, which was adopted Feb. 15, 1876, plus all amendments approved since then, is available on the State of Texas website:

**http://www.constitution.legis.state.tx.us**

An index and search features at that website allow exploration of the 17 Articles and subsequent Sections of the Constitution, along with other Texas Statues.

For election information, upcoming elections, amendment or other election votes, and voter registration information, go to:

**www.sos.state.tx.us/elections/index.shtml**

According to the **Legislative Reference Library of Texas**, "The Texas Constitution is one of the longest in the nation and is still growing. As of 2013 (83rd Legislature), the Texas Legislature has proposed a total of 666 amendments. Of these, 484 have been adopted and 179 have been defeated by Texas voters. Thus, the Texas Constitution has been amended 484 times since its adoption in 1876."

Amending the Texas Constitution requires a two-thirds favorable vote by both the Texas House of Representatives and the Texas Senate, followed by a majority vote of approval by voters in a statewide election.

Prior to 1973, amendments to the constitution could not be submitted by a special session of the Legislature. But the constitution was amended in 1972

| Constitutional Amendments Submitted to Voters by the Texas Legislature | | |
|---|---|---|
| Year . . . . . . No. | Year . . . . . . No. | Year . . . . . No. |
| 1879............1 | 1929............7 | 1977.........15 |
| 1881............2 | 1931............9 | 1978............1 |
| 1883............5 | 1933............12 | 1979.........12 |
| 1887............6 | 1935............13 | 1981.........10 |
| 1889............2 | 1937............7 | 1982............3 |
| 1891............5 | 1939............4 | 1983.........19 |
| 1893............2 | 1941............5 | 1985.........17 |
| 1895............2 | 1943............3 | 1986............1 |
| 1897............5 | 1945............8 | 1987.........28 |
| 1899............1 | 1947............9 | 1989.........21 |
| 1901............1 | 1949.........10 | 1990............1 |
| 1903............3 | 1951............7 | 1991.........15 |
| 1905............3 | 1953.........11 | 1993.........18 |
| 1907............9 | 1955............9 | 1995.........14 |
| 1909............4 | 1957.........12 | 1997.........15 |
| 1911............5 | 1959............4 | 1999.........17 |
| 1913............7 | 1961.........14 | 2001.........20 |
| 1915............7 | 1963............7 | 2003.........22 |
| 1917............3 | 1965.........27 | 2005............9 |
| 1919.........13 | 1967.........20 | 2007.........17 |
| 1921............5 | 1969.........16 | 2009.........11 |
| 1923............2 | 1971.........18 | 2011.........10 |
| 1925............4 | 1973............9 | 2013.........11 |
| 1927............8 | 1975.........12 | 2015............7 |

to allow submission of amendments if the special session was opened to the subject by the governor.

Constitutional amendments are not subject to a gubernatorial veto. Once submitted, voters have the final decision on whether to change the constitution as proposed.

The table on page 467 lists the total number of amendments submitted to voters by the Texas Legislature and shows the year in which the Legislature approved them for submission to voters; e.g., the 70th Legislature in 1987 approved 28 bills proposing amendments to be submitted to voters — 25 in 1987 and 3 in 1988.

For more information on bills and constitutional amendments, see the Legislative Reference Library of Texas website:

**http://www.lrl.state.tx.us/legis/index.cfm**

## Amendments, 2013

*The following 10 amendments were submitted to the voters by the 83rd Legislature in an election on **Nov. 5, 2013:***

**SJR 1** — Providing for the creation of the State Water Implementation Fund for Texas and the State Water Implementation Revenue Fund for Texas to assist in the financing of priority projects in the state water plan to ensure the availability of adequate water resources. **Passed:** 839,369 for; 304,981 against.

**SJR 18** — Authorizing the making of a reverse mortgage loan for the purchase of homestead property and to amend lender disclosures and other requirements in connection with a reverse mortgage loan. **Passed:** 683,402 for; 408,197 against.

**HJR 24** — Authorizing the legislature to provide for an exemption from ad valorem taxation of part of the market value of the residence homestead of a partially disabled veteran or the surviving spouse of a partially disabled veteran if the residence homestead was donated to the disabled veteran by a charitable organization. **Passed:** 965,377 for; 168,435 against.

**SJR 42** — Relating to expanding the types of sanctions that may be assessed against a judge or justice following a formal proceeding instituted by the State Commission on Judicial Conduct. **Passed:** 925,509 for; 167,825 against.

**SJR 54** — Repealing the constitutional provision Section 7, Article IX, authorizing the creation of a hospital district in Hidalgo County. **Passed:** 743,510 for; 283,933 against.

**HJR 62** — Authorizing the legislature to provide for an exemption from ad valorem taxation of all or part of the market value of the residence homestead of the surviving spouse of a member of the armed services of the United States who is killed in action. **Passed:** 999,724 for; 149,613 against.

**HJR 79** — Eliminating an obsolete requirement for a State Medical Education Board and a State Medical Education Fund, neither of which is operational. **Passed:** 950,046 for; 171,666 against.

**HJR 87** — Authorizing a home-rule municipality to provide in its charter the procedure to fill a vacancy on its governing body for which the unexpired term is 12 months or less. **Passed:** 809,844 for; 278,878 against.

**HJR 133** — Authorizing a political subdivision of this state to extend the number of days that aircraft parts that are exempt from ad valorem taxation due to their location in this state for a temporary period may be located in this state for purposes of qualifying for the tax exemption. **Passed:** 626,602 for; 458,767 against.

**HJR 147** — Repealing the constitutional provision Section 7, Article IX, authorizing the creation of a hospital district in Hidalgo County. **Passed:** 743,510 for; 283,933 against.

*The following amendment, proposed in the 83rd Leislature's 3rd Called Session, was submitted to the voters in an election on **Nov. 4, 2014:***

**SJR 1** — Providing for the use and dedication of certain money transferred to the state highway fund to assist in the completion of transportation construction, maintenance, and rehabilitation projects, not to include toll roads. **Passed:** 1,799,703 for; 420,923 against.

## Amendments, 2015

*The following 7 amendments were submitted to the voters by the 84th Legislature in an election on **Nov. 3, 2015:***

**SJR 1** — Increasing the amount of the residence homestead exemption from ad valorem taxation for public school purposes from $15,000 to $25,000, providing for a reduction of the limitation on the total amount of ad valorem taxes that may be imposed for those purposes on the homestead of an elderly or disabled person to reflect the increased exemption amount, authorizing the legislature to prohibit a political subdivision that has adopted an optional residence homestead exemption from ad valorem taxation from reducing the amount of or repealing the exemption, and prohibiting the enactment of a law that imposes a transfer tax on a transaction that conveys fee simple title to real property.

**SJR 5** — Dedicating certain sales and use tax revenue and motor vehicle sales, use, and rental tax revenue to the state highway fund to provide funding for nontolled roads and the reduction of certain transportation-related debt.

**SJR 17** — The constitutional amendment to authorize counties with a population of 7,500 or less to perform private road construction and maintenance.

**SJR 22** — The constitutional amendment recognizing the right of the people to hunt, fish, and harvest wildlife subject to laws that promote wildlife conservation.

**SJR 52** — The constitutional amendment repealing the requirement that state officers elected by voters statewide reside in the state capital.

**HJR 73** — The constitutional amendment authorizing the legislature to permit professional sports team charitable foundations to conduct charitable raffles.

**HJR 75** — The constitutional amendment authorizing the legislature to provide for an exemption from ad valorem taxation of all or part of the market value of the residence homestead of the surviving spouse of a 100 percent or totally disabled veteran who died before the law authorizing a residence homestead exemption for such a veteran took effect. ☆

# Texas' Chief Governmental Officials

On this and the following pages are lists of the principal administrative officials who have served the Republic and State of Texas with dates of their tenures of office. In a few instances, there are disputes as to the exact dates of tenures. Dates listed here are those that appear the most authentic.

★ ★ ★ ★ ★ ★ ★

## Governors and Presidents

### *Spanish Royal Governors

| | |
|---|---|
| Domingo Terán de los Rios | 1691–1692 |
| Gregorio de Salinas Varona | 1692–1697 |
| Francisco Cuerbo y Valdés | 1698–1702 |
| Mathías de Aguirre | 1703–1705 |
| Martín de Alarcón | 1705–1708 |
| Simón Padilla y Córdova | 1708–1712 |
| Pedro Fermin de Echevers y Subisa | 1712–1714 |
| Juan Valdéz | 1714–1716 |
| Martín de Alarcón | 1716–1719 |
| José de Azlor y Virto de Vera, Marqués de San Miguel de Aguayo | 1719–1722 |
| Fernando Pérez de Almazán | 1722–1727 |
| Melchor de Mediavilla y Azcona | 1727–1731 |
| Juan Antonio Bustillo y Ceballos | 1731–1734 |
| Manuel de Sandoval | 1734–1736 |
| Carlos Benites Franquis de Lugo | 1736–1737 |
| Joseph Fernández de Jáuregui y Urrutia | 1737–1737 |
| Prudencio de Orobio y Basterra | 1737–1741 |
| Tomás Felipe Winthuisen (or Winthuysen) | 1741–1743 |
| Justo Boneo y Morales | 1743–1744 |
| Francisco García Larios | 1744–1748 |
| Pedro del Barrio Junco y Espriella | 1748–1750 |
| Jacinto de Barrios y Jáuregui | 1751–1759 |
| Angel de Martos y Navarrete | 1759–1767 |
| Hugo Oconór | 1767–1770 |
| Juan María Vicencio, Barón de Ripperdá | 1770–1778 |
| Domingo Cabello y Robles | 1778–1786 |
| Rafael Martínez Pacheco | 1787–1790 |
| Manuel Muñoz | 1790–1799 |
| Juan Bautista de Elguezábal | 1799–1805 |
| Antonio Cordero y Bustamante | 1805–1808 |
| Manuel María de Salcedo | 1808–1813 |

*(Mexico's War of Independence 1810–1812 created governmental instability.)*

| | |
|---|---|
| Juan Bautista de las Casas *(Revolutionary governor)* | 1811–1811 |
| Cristóbal Domínguez, Benito de Armiñan, Mariano Varela, Juan Ignacio Pérez, Manuel Pardo *(ad interim)* | 1813–1817 |
| Antonio María Martínez | 1817–1821 |

*\*Some authorities would include Texas under administrations of several earlier Spanish governors. The late Dr. C.E. Castañeda, Latin-American librarian of The University of Texas and authority on the history of Texas and the Southwest, would include the following four: Francisco de Garay, 1523–1526; Pánfilo de Narváez, 1526–28; Nuño de Guzmán, 1528–1530; Hernando de Soto, 1538–1543.*

### Governors Under Mexican Rule

The first two governors under Mexican rule, Trespalacios and García, were of Texas only as Texas was then constituted. Beginning with Gonzáles, 1824, the governors were for the joint State of Coahuila y Texas.

| | |
|---|---|
| José Felix Trespalacios | 1822–1823 |
| Luciano García | 1823–1824 |
| Rafael Gonzáles | 1824–1826 |
| Victor Blanco | 1826–1827 |
| José María Viesca | 1827–1830 |
| Ramón Eca y Músquiz | 1830–1831 |
| José María Letona | 1831–1832 |
| Ramón Eca y Músquiz | 1832–1832 |
| Juan Martín de Veramendi | 1832–1833 |
| Juan José de Vidáurri y Villasenor | 1833–1834 |
| Juan José Elguezábal | 1834–1835 |
| José María Cantú | 1835–1835 |
| Agustín M. Viesca | 1835–1835 |
| Marciel Borrego | 1835–1835 |
| Ramón Eca y Músquiz | 1835–1835 |

### Provisional Colonial Governor, Before Independence

| | |
|---|---|
| Henry Smith (Impeached) | 1835–Jan. 1836 |

*(James W. Robinson served as acting governor after Smith was impeached.)*

### Presidents of the Republic of Texas

| | |
|---|---|
| David G. Burnet *(provisional)* | Mar. 16, 1836–Oct. 22, 1836 |
| Sam Houston | Oct. 22, 1836–Dec. 10, 1838 |
| Mirabeau B. Lamar | Dec. 10, 1838–Dec. 13, 1841 |
| Sam Houston | Dec. 13, 1841–Dec. 9, 1844 |
| Anson Jones | Dec. 9, 1844–Feb. 19, 1846 |

### Governors Since Annexation

*(Abbreviations: (D) Democrat, (R) Republican, (I) Independent.)*

| | |
|---|---|
| J. Pinckney Henderson | Feb. 19, 1846–Dec. 21, 1847 |

*(Albert C. Horton served as acting governor while Henderson was away in the Mexican War.)*

| | |
|---|---|
| George T. Wood | Dec. 21, 1847–Dec. 21, 1849 |
| Peter Hansbrough Bell | Dec. 21, 1849–Nov. 23, 1853 |

*(Resigned to enter U.S. House of Representatives.)*

| | |
|---|---|
| J. W. Henderson | Nov. 23, 1853–Dec. 21, 1853 |
| Elisha M. Pease | Dec. 21, 1853–Dec. 21, 1857 |
| Hardin R. Runnels (D) | Dec. 21, 1857–Dec. 21, 1859 |
| Sam Houston | Dec. 21, 1859–Mar. 16, 1861 |

*(Resigned because of state's secession from the Union.)*

| | |
|---|---|
| Edward Clark | Mar. 16, 1861–Nov. 7, 1861 |
| Francis R. Lubbock | Nov. 7, 1861–Nov. 5, 1863 |

*(Resigned to enter Confederate Army.)*

| | |
|---|---|
| Pendleton Murrah | Nov. 5, 1863–June 17, 1865 |

*(Fled to Mexico upon the fall of Confederacy. Lt. Gov. Fletcher S. Stockdale briefly acted as governor after Murrah's departure.)*

| | |
|---|---|
| Andrew J. Hamilton | June 17, 1865–Aug. 9, 1866 |

*(Hamilton received a commission as "military governor of Texas" from President Abraham Lincoln on Nov. 14, 1862. He appears to have served in that capacity continuously until his "reappointment" as "provisional governor" by President Andrew Johnson on June 17, 1865. Apparently Johnson used the term "reappointment" because Hamilton was already serving as military governor.)*

| | |
|---|---|
| James W. Throckmorton | Aug. 9, 1866–Aug. 8, 1867 |
| Elisha M. Pease (R) | Aug. 8, 1867–Sept. 30, 1869 |

*(Appointed under martial law after Throckmorton was removed on July 30, 1867, by Gen. Philip Sheridan. Pease formally took possession of the office on Aug. 8. He resigned and vacated the office Sept. 30, 1869, but no successor was named until Jan. 8, 1870. Some historians extend Pease's term to that date, but in reality Texas was without a head of governemnt for that period.)*

Edmund J. Davis (R) .......... Jan. 8, 1870–Jan. 15, 1874
*(Appointed provisional governor after being elected.)*

Richard Coke (D) ................Jan. 15, 1874–Dec. 1, 1876
*(Resigned to enter U.S. Senate.)*

Richard B. Hubbard (D) ......Dec. 1, 1876–Jan. 21, 1879
Oran M. Roberts (D) ......... Jan. 21, 1879–Jan. 16, 1883
John Ireland (D) ................ Jan. 16, 1883–Jan. 18, 1887
Lawrence Sullivan Ross (D) ................... Jan. 18, 1887–
........................................................................ Jan. 20, 1891
James Stephen Hogg (D) . Jan. 20, 1891–Jan. 15, 1895
Charles A. Culberson (D).. Jan. 15, 1895–Jan. 17, 1899
Joseph D. Sayers (D) ....... Jan. 17, 1899–Jan. 20, 1903
S. W. T. Lanham (D) ......... Jan. 20, 1903–Jan. 15, 1907
Thos. Mitchell Campbell (D) ................... Jan. 15, 1907–
........................................................................ Jan. 17, 1911
Oscar Branch Colquitt (D) .Jan. 17, 1911–Jan. 19, 1915
James E. Ferguson (D) ...Jan. 19, 1915–Sept. 25, 1917
*(Impeached in August 1917. Lt. Gov. Hobby served as acting governor during the impeachment proceedings. Ferguson was removed from office Sept. 25.)*

William Pettus Hobby (D) .Aug. 25, 1917–Jan. 18, 1921
Pat Morris Neff (D)............ Jan. 18, 1921–Jan. 20, 1925
Miriam A. Ferguson (D) .... Jan. 20, 1925–Jan. 17, 1927
Dan Moody (D) ................. Jan. 17, 1927–Jan. 20, 1931
Ross S. Sterling (D).......... Jan. 20, 1931–Jan. 17, 1933
Miriam A. Ferguson (D) .... Jan. 17, 1933–Jan. 15, 1935
James V. Allred (D)........... Jan. 15, 1935–Jan. 17, 1939
W. Lee O'Daniel (D)...........Jan. 17, 1939–Aug. 4, 1941
*(Resigned to enter U.S. Senate.)*

Coke R. Stevenson (D).......Aug. 4, 1941–Jan. 21, 1947
Beauford H. Jester (D).......Jan. 21, 1947–July 11, 1949
*(Died in office. Succeeded by Lt. Gov. Shivers.)*

Allan Shivers (D)................July 11, 1949–Jan. 15, 1957
Price Daniel (D) ................ Jan. 15, 1957–Jan. 15, 1963
John Connally (D).............. Jan. 15, 1963–Jan. 21, 1969
Preston Smith (D) ............. Jan. 21, 1969–Jan. 16, 1973
Dolph Briscoe (D) ............ Jan. 16, 1973–Jan. 16, 1979
*(Effective in 1975, the term of office was increased from 2 to 4 years.)*

William P. Clements (R).... Jan. 16, 1979–Jan. 18, 1983
Mark White (D) ................ Jan. 18, 1983–Jan. 20, 1987
William P. Clements (R).... Jan. 20, 1987–Jan. 15, 1991
Ann W. Richards (D)......... Jan. 15, 1991–Jan. 17, 1995
George W. Bush (R) .........Jan. 17, 1995–Dec. 21, 2000
*(Resigned to become U.S. president.)*

Rick Perry (R) ...................Dec. 21, 2000–Jan. 20, 2015
**Greg Abbott** (R)........................ Jan. 20, 2015–present

★ ★ ★ ★ ★ ★ ★

# Vice Presidents and Lieutenant Governors

## Vice Presidents of the Republic

Lorenzo de Zavala      March 16, 1836–Oct, 17, 1836
*(Provisional.)*

Mirabeau B. Lamar............Oct. 22, 1836–Dec.10, 1838
David G. Burnet................ Dec. 10, 1838–Dec.13, 1841
Edward Burleson .............. Dec. 13, 1841–Dec. 9, 1844
Kenneth L. Anderson............ Dec. 9, 1844–July 3, 1845
*(Died in office.)*

## Lieutenant Governors

Albert C. Horton (D)............May 2, 1846–Dec. 21, 1847
John A. Greer (D) ............ Dec. 21, 1847–Dec. 22, 1851
J. W. Henderson (D)........ Dec. 22, 1851–Nov. 23, 1853
*(Briefly succeeded to governorship when Gov. Bell resigned to enter U.S. House of Representatives.)*

D. C. Dickson (D)............. Dec. 21, 1853–Dec. 21, 1855
H. R. Runnels (D) ............ Dec. 21, 1855–Dec. 21, 1857
F. R. Lubbock (D)............. Dec. 21, 1857–Dec. 21, 1859
Edward Clark (I).............Dec. 21, 1859–March 16, 1861
*(Succeeded Gov. Sam Houston when Houston refused to take oath to Confederacy.)*

John M. Crockett (D) ............Nov. 7, 1861–Nov. 5, 1863
Fletcher S. Stockdale (D) ..Nov. 7, 1863–June 17, 1865
*(Fall of Confederacy.)*

George W. Jones (D).......... Aug. 9, 1866–July 30, 1867
*(Jones was removed by Gen. Philip Sheridan.)*

J. W. Flanagan (R)................................................1869
*(Elected in 1869, Flanagan was appointed U.S. senator and was never inaugurated as lt. governor.)*

R. B. Hubbard (D)...............Jan. 15, 1873–Dec. 1, 1876

### Early Leaders of Texas

*The presidents of the Republic of Texas and the state's first Governor, from far left: David G. Burnet, provisional president; Sam Houston, second and fourth presidents; Mirabeau B. Lamar, third president; Anson Jones, the Republic's last president; and J. Pinckney Henderson, the Lone Star State's first governor.*

*(Succeeded Gov. Richard Coke when he resigned to become U.S. senator.)*

J. D. Sayers (D) ............... Jan. 21, 1879–Jan. 18, 1881
L. J. Storey (D) ................ Jan. 18, 1881–Jan. 16, 1883
Marion Martin (D) ............. Jan. 16, 1883–Jan. 20, 1885
Barnett Gibbs (D) ............. Jan. 20, 1885–Jan. 19, 1887
T. B. Wheeler (D) ............ Jan. 19, 1887– Jan. 21, 1891
George C. Pendleton (D).. Jan. 21, 1891–Jan. 17, 1893
M. M. Crane (D) ............... Jan. 17, 1893–Jan. 15, 1895
George T. Jester (D) ........ Jan. 15, 1895–Jan. 17, 1899
J. N. Browning (D) ........... Jan. 17, 1899– Jan. 20, 1903
George D. Neal (D) .......... Jan. 20, 1903–Jan. 15, 1907
A. B. Davidson (D) ........... Jan. 15, 1907–Jan. 21, 1913
Will H. Mayes (D) .............Jan. 21, 1913–Aug. 14, 1914
*(resigned)*
William P. Hobby (D) .........Jan. 19, 1915–Aug. 25, 1917
*(Served as acting governor during the impeachment of Gov. Jim Ferguson. Took oath as governor after Ferguson was removed from office Sept. 25.)*
W. A. Johnson (D) ............Sept. 29, 1917–Jan. 18, 1921
*(Selected as president of the state Senate and acting lt. governor, serving Hobby's unexpired term. He was then elected statewide to the office in 1918.)*
Lynch Davidson (D) .......... Jan. 18, 1921–Jan. 16, 1923
T. W. Davidson (D) ........... Jan. 16, 1923–Jan. 20, 1925
Barry Miller (D) ............... Jan. 20, 1925–Jan. 20, 1931
Edgar E. Witt (D) ............. Jan. 20, 1931–Jan. 15, 1935
Walter Woodul (D) ........... Jan. 15, 1935–Jan. 17, 1939
Coke R. Stevenson (D).......Jan. 17, 1939–Aug. 4, 1941
*(Became governor upon resignation of Gov. W. Lee O'Daniel to become U.S. senator.)*
John Lee Smith (D)........... Jan. 19, 1943–Jan. 21, 1947
Allan Shivers (D)................Jan. 21, 1947–July 11, 1949
*(Shivers succeeded to the governorship on death of Gov. Beauford H. Jester.)*
Ben Ramsey (D) ..............Jan. 16, 1951–Sept. 18, 1961
*(Ramsey resigned to become a member of the Texas Railroad Commission.)*
Preston Smith (D) ............ Jan. 15, 1963–Jan. 21, 1969
Ben Barnes (D)................. Jan. 21, 1969–Jan. 16, 1973
William P. Hobby Jr. (D).... Jan. 16, 1973–Jan. 19, 1991
Robert D. Bullock (D)........ Jan. 15, 1991–Jan. 19, 1999
Rick Perry (R) ...................Jan. 19, 1999–Dec. 21, 2000
Bill Ratliff (R)....................Dec. 28, 2000–Jan. 14, 2003
*(Elected by state Senate when Perry succeeded to governorship.)*
David Dewhurst ............... Jan. 21, 2003–Jan. 20, 2015
**Dan Patrick**................................ Jan. 20, 2015–present

★ ★ ★ ★ ★ ★ ★

## Secretaries of State
### Of the Republic

*Raines Yearbook for Texas, 1901, gives the following record of Secretaries of State during the era of the Republic of Texas:*

**Under David G. Burnet** — Samuel P. Carson, James Collingsworth, and W. H. Jack.

**Under Sam Houston** (first term) — Stephen F. Austin, 1836. J. Pinckney Henderson and Dr. Robert A. Irion, 1837–1838.

**Under Mirabeau B. Lamar** — Bernard Bee appointed Dec. 16, 1838; James Webb appointed Feb. 6, 1839; D. G. Burnet appointed Acting Secretary of State, May 31, 1839; N. Amory appointed Acting Secretary of State, July 23, 1839; D. G. Burnet appointed Acting Secretary of State, Aug. 5, 1839; Abner S. Lipscomb appointed Secretary of State, Jan. 31, 1840, and resigned Jan. 22, 1841; Joseph Waples appointed Acting Secretary of State, Jan. 23, 1841, and served until Feb. 8, 1841; James S. Mayfield appointed Feb. 8, 1841; Joseph Waples appointed April 30, 1841, and served until May 25, 1841; Samuel A. Roberts appointed May 25, 1841; reappointed Sept. 7, 1841.

**Under Sam Houston** (second term) — E. Lawrence Stickney, Acting Secretary of State until Anson Jones was appointed Dec. 13, 1841. Jones served as Secretary of State throughout this term except during the summer and part of this term of 1842, when Joseph Waples filled the position as Acting Secretary of State.

**Under Anson Jones** — Ebenezer Allen served from Dec. 10, 1844, until Feb. 5, 1845, when Ashbel Smith became Secretary of State. Allen was again named Acting Secretary of State, March 31, 1845, and later named Secretary of State.

(In addition to the above, documents in the Texas State Archives indicate that Joseph C. Eldredge, Chief Clerk of the State Department during much of the Republic's existence, signed a number of documents in the absence of the office-holder in the capacity of "Acting Secretary of State.")

### State Secretaries of State

Charles Mariner.................. Feb. 20, 1846–May 4, 1846
David G. Burnet................... May 4, 1846–Jan. 1, 1848
Washington D. Miller ........... Jan. 1, 1848–Jan. 2, 1850

James Webb....................... Jan. 2, 1850–Nov. 14, 1851
Thomas H. Duval............ Nov. 14, 1851–Dec. 22, 1853
Edward Clark......................... Dec. 22, 1853–Dec. 1857
T. S. Anderson ...................... Dec. 1857–Dec. 27, 1859
E. W. Cave.........................Dec. 27, 1859–Mar. 16, 1861
Bird Holland............................Mar. 16, 1861–Nov. 1861
Charles West............................ Nov. 1861–Sept. 1862
Robert J. Townes...................Sept. 1862–May 2, 1865
Charles R. Pryor.....................May 2, 1865–Aug, 1865
James H. Bell ........................... Aug. 1865–Aug. 1866
John A. Green............................. Aug. 1866–Aug. 1867
D. W. C. Phillips.........................Aug. 1867–Jan. 1870
J. P. Newcomb................... Jan. 1, 1870–Jan. 17, 1874
George Clark ................. Jan. 17, 1874–Jan. 27, 1874
A. W. DeBerry...................Jan. 27, 1874–Dec. 1, 1876
Isham G. Searcy................Dec. 1, 1876–Jan. 23, 1879
J. D. Templeton................ Jan. 23, 1879–Jan. 22, 1881
T. H. Bowman ................... Jan. 22, 1881–Jan. 18, 1883
J. W. Baines ..................... Jan. 18, 1883–Jan. 21, 1887
John M. Moore................. Jan. 21, 1887–Jan. 22, 1891
George W. Smith ............. Jan. 22, 1891–Jan. 17, 1895
Allison Mayfield.................. Jan. 17, 1895–Jan. 5, 1897
J. W. Madden ..................... Jan. 5, 1897–Jan. 18, 1899
D. H. Hardy....................... Jan. 18, 1899–Jan. 19, 1901
John G. Tod ......................... Jan. 19, 1901–Jan., 1903
J. R. Curl.....................................Jan. 1903–April 1905
O. K. Shannon .............................. April 1905–Jan. 1907
L. T. Dashiel.................................Jan. 1907–Feb. 1908
W. R. Davie.................................. Feb. 1908–Jan. 1909
W. B. Townsend...........................Jan. 1909–Jan. 1911
C. C. McDonald ........................... Jan. 1911–Dec. 1912
J. T. Bowman ................................Dec. 1912–Jan. 1913
John L. Wortham ....................... Jan. 1913–June 1913
F. C. Weinert................................June 1913–Nov. 1914
D. A. Gregg.................................Nov. 1914–Jan. 1915
John G. McKay.............................Jan. 1915–Dec. 1916
C. J. Bartlett................................. Dec. 1916–Nov. 1917
George F. Howard .......................Nov. 1917–Nov. 1920
C. D. Mims...................................Nov. 1920–Jan. 1921
S. L. Staples................................Jan. 1921–Aug. 1924
J. D. Strickland ........................Sept. 1924–Jan. 1, 1925
Henry Hutchings................. Jan. 1, 1925–Jan. 20, 1925
Mrs. Emma G. Meharg .......... Jan. 20, 1925–Jan. 1927
Mrs. Jane Y. McCallum................ Jan. 1927–Jan. 1933
W. W. Heath .................................. Jan. 1933–Jan. 1935
Gerald C. Mann .....................Jan. 1935–Aug. 31, 1935
R. B. Stanford ................. Aug. 31, 1935–Aug. 25, 1936
B. P. Matocha ..................Aug. 25, 1936–Jan. 18, 1937
Edward Clark .................... Jan. 18, 1937–Jan. 1939
Tom L. Beauchamp.......................Jan. 1939–Oct. 1939
M. O. Flowers ................. Oct. 26, 1939–Feb. 25, 1941
William J. Lawson...................Feb. 25, 1941–Jan. 1943
Sidney Latham..............................Jan. 1943–Feb. 1945
Claude Isbell .................................Feb. 1945–Jan. 1947
Paul H. Brown........................ Jan. 1947–Jan. 19, 1949
Ben Ramsey .......................Jan. 19, 1949–Feb. 9, 1950
John Ben Shepperd............Feb. 9, 1950–April 30, 1952
Jack Ross ........................ April 30, 1952–Jan. 9, 1953
Howard A. Carney ..............Jan. 9, 1953–Apr. 30, 1954
C. E. Fulgham....................... May 1, 1954–Feb. 15, 1955
Al Muldrow..........................Feb. 16, 1955–Nov. 1, 1955
Tom Reavley.......................Nov. 1, 1955–Jan. 16, 1957
Zollie Steakley ................... Jan. 16, 1957–Jan. 2, 1962
P. Frank Lake...................... Jan. 2, 1962–Jan. 15, 1963
Crawford C. Martin ........ Jan. 15, 1963–March 12, 1966
John L. Hill.................... March 12, 1966–Jan. 22, 1968
Roy Barrera ..................... March 7, 1968–Jan. 23, 1969
Martin Dies Jr....................Jan. 23, 1969–Sept. 1, 1971
Robert D. (Bob) Bullock.......Sept. 1, 1971–Jan. 2, 1973
V. Larry Teaver Jr............... Jan. 2, 1973–Jan. 19, 1973

## The Capitals of Texas

The Capitals of the six nations that have
ruled Texas have been:

**SPAIN**: Valladolid (before 1551) and
   Madrid;

**FRANCE**: Paris;

**MEXICO**: Mexico City, D.F.;

**REPUBLIC OF TEXAS**:
   San Felipe de Austin,
   Washington-on-the-Brazos,
   Harrisburg,
   Galveston Island,
   Velasco,
   Columbia,
   Houston,
   Austin;

**UNITED STATES**: Washington, D.C.;

**CONFEDERATE STATES
OF AMERICA**:
   Montgomery, Ala., and
   Richmond, Va.

*From "The Capitals of Texas," on the Texas
Almanac website. Full article at:*

*www.texasalmanac.com/topics/history/
capitals-texas*

Mark W. White Jr. ..............Jan. 19, 1973–Oct. 27,1977
Steven C. Oaks ................Oct. 27, 1977–Jan. 16, 1979
George W. Strake Jr. ...........Jan. 16, 1979–Oct. 6, 1981
David A. Dean....................Oct. 22, 1981–Jan. 18, 1983
John Fainter........................Jan. 18, 1983–July 31, 1984
Myra A. McDaniel ..............Sept. 6, 1984–Jan. 26, 1987
Jack Rains ...................... Jan. 26, 1987–June 15, 1989
George Bayoud Jr.......... June 19, 1989–Jan. 15, 1991
John Hannah Jr. ............ Jan. 17, 1991–March 11, 1994
Ronald Kirk ......................... April 4, 1994–Jan. 10, 1995
Antonio O. "Tony" Garza Jr. Jan. 18, 1995–Dec. 2, 1997
Alberto R. Gonzales ...........Dec. 2, 1997–Jan. 10, 1999
Elton Bomer.......................Jan. 11, 1999–Dec. 31, 2000
Henry Cuellar.........................Jan. 2, 2001–Oct. 5, 2001
Gwyn Shea ..........................Jan. 2, 2002–Aug. 4, 2003
Geoff Connor ....................Sept. 26, 2003–Jan. 1, 2005
J. Roger Williams.................Jan. 1, 2005–July 1, 2007
Phil Wilson............................. July 1, 2007–July 6, 2008
Esperanza (Hope) Andrade July 23, 2008–Nov. 23, 2012
John T. Steen Jr..................Nov. 27, 2012–Jan. 7, 2014
Nandita Berry....................... Jan. 7, 2014–Jan 21, 2015
**Carlos H. Cascos** ...................... Jan 21, 2015–present

### ★ ★ ★ ★ ★ ★ ★

### Attorneys General
#### Of the Republic

David Thomas and
   Peter W. Grayson ................. Mar. 2–Oct. 22, 1836
J. Pinckney Henderson, Peter W. Grayson,
   John Birdsall, A. S. Thurston.................. 1836–1838

J. C. Watrous ............................Dec. 1838–June 1, 1840
Joseph Webb and F. A. Morris.....................1840–1841
George W. Terrell, Ebenezer Allen ..............1841–1844
Ebenezer Allen ...........................................1844–1846

## *Of the State

Volney E. Howard (D)........Feb. 21, 1846–May 7, 1846
John W. Harris (D)..............May 7, 1846–Oct. 31, 1849
Henry P. Brewster.............Oct. 31, 1849–Jan. 15, 1850
A. J. Hamilton .....................Jan. 15, 1850–Aug. 5, 1850

*(The first few attorneys general held office by appointment of the governor. The office was made elective in 1850 by constitutional amendment. Ebenezer Allen was the first elected attorney general.)*

Ebenezer Allen .................... Aug. 5, 1850–Aug. 2, 1852
Thomas J. Jennings ........... Aug. 2, 1852–Aug. 4, 1856
James Willie ....................... Aug. 4, 1856–Aug. 2, 1858
Malcolm D. Graham (D)....... Aug. 2, 1858–Aug. 6, 1860

*(Confederacy)*
George M. Flournoy (D)......Aug. 6, 1860–Jan. 15, 1862
N. G. Shelley (D) ............... Feb. 3, 1862–Aug. 1, 1864
B. E. Tarver (D)................. Aug. 1, 1864–Dec. 11, 1865

*(Reconstruction)*
Wm. Alexander (Unionist) Dec. 11, 1865–June 25, 1866
W. M. Walton (D) .............June 25, 1866–Aug. 27, 1867
Wm. Alexander (R) ........... Aug. 27, 1867–Nov. 5, 1867
Ezekiel B. Turner (I)............Nov. 5, 1867–July 11, 1870
Wm. Alexander (R) ............July 11, 1870–Jan. 27, 1874

*(Reconstruction ends.)*
George Clark (D) ...............Jan. 27, 1874–Apr. 25, 1876
H. H. Boone (D) ................. Apr. 25, 1876–Nov. 5, 1878
George McCormick...............Nov. 5, 1878–Nov. 2, 1880
J. H. McLeary (D) ...............Nov. 2, 1880–Nov. 7, 1882
John D. Templeton (D)........Nov. 7, 1882–Nov. 2, 1886
James S. Hogg (D) ..............Nov. 2, 1886–Nov. 4, 1890
C. A. Culberson (D) .............Nov. 4, 1890–Nov. 6, 1894
M. M. Crane (D) ................Nov. 6, 1894–Nov. 8,1898
Thomas S. Smith (D) ...........Nov. 8, 1898–Mar. 15,1901
C. K. Bell (D).........................Mar. 20, 1901–Jan., 1904
R. V. Davidson (D)..................Jan. 1904–Dec. 31, 1909
Jewel P. Lightfoot (D)..........Jan. 1, 1910–Aug. 31, 1912
James D. Walthall (D)..........Sept. 1, 1912–Jan. 1, 1913
B. F. Looney (D)...................... Jan. 1, 1913–Jan., 1919
C. M. Cureton (D) ........................Jan. 1919–Dec. 1921
W. A. Keeling (D) .........................Dec. 1921–Jan. 1925
Dan Moody (D) ............................. Jan. 1925–Jan. 1927
Claude Pollard (D)........................Jan. 1927–Sept. 1929
R. L. Bobbitt (D) .........................Sept. 1929–Jan. 1931
    *(Appointed.)*

James V. Allred (D)........................ Jan. 1931–Jan. 1935
William McCraw (D)....................... Jan. 1935–Jan. 1939
Gerald C. Mann (D) ...................... Jan. 1939–Jan. 1944
    *(Resigned.)*

Grover Sellers (D)......................... Jan. 1944–Jan. 1947
Price Daniel (D) ............................ Jan. 1947–Jan. 1953
John Ben Shepperd (D)............ Jan. 1953–Jan. 1, 1957
Will Wilson (D) ................... Jan. 1, 1957–Jan. 15, 1963
Waggoner Carr (D) ............. Jan. 15, 1963–Jan. 1, 1967
Crawford C. Martin (D) .......Jan. 1, 1967–Dec. 29, 1972
John Hill (D).......................... Jan. 1, 1973–Jan. 16, 1979
Mark White (D) ................. Jan. 16, 1979–Jan. 18, 1983
Jim Mattox (D) ................. Jan. 18, 1983–Jan. 15, 1991
Dan Morales (D) ............... Jan. 15, 1991–Jan. 13, 1999
John Cornyn (R) ............... Jan. 13, 1999–Dec. 2, 2002
Greg Abbott (R) .................Dec. 2, 2002–Jan. 20, 2015
**Ken Paxton** (R)...........................Jan. 20, 2015–present

★ ★ ★ ★ ★ ★ ★

## Treasurers
### Of the Republic

Asa Brigham................................................1838–1840
James W. Simmons.....................................1840–1841
Asa Brigham................................................1841–1844
Moses Johnson ...........................................1844–1846

### Of the State

James H. Raymond........... Feb. 24, 1846–Aug. 2, 1858
C. H. Randolph ........................Aug. 2, 1858–June 1865
    *(Randolph fled to Mexico upon collapse of Confederacy. No exact date is available for his departure from office or for Harris' succession to the post. It is believed Harris took office Oct. 2, 1865.)*

Samuel Harris.....................Oct. 2, 1865–June 25, 1866
W. M. Royston ..................June 25, 1866–Sept. 1, 1867
John Y. Allen ............................Sept. 1, 1867–Jan. 1869
George W. Honey ........................ Jan. 1869–Jan. 1874
    *(Honey was removed from office for a short period in 1872 and B. Graham served in his place.)*
B. Graham *(short term)* ...........beginning May 27, 1872
A. J. Dorn.................................... Jan. 1874–Jan. 1879
F. R. Lubbock................................ Jan. 1879–Jan. 1891
W. B. Wortham ............................ Jan. 1891–Jan. 1899
John W. Robbins ......................... Jan. 1899–Jan. 1907
Sam Sparks ................................. Jan. 1907–Jan. 1912
J. M. Edwards.............................. Jan. 1912–Jan. 1919
John W. Baker ............................. Jan. 1919–Jan. 1921
G. N. Holton............................ July 1921–Nov. 21, 1921
C. V. Terrell ..................... Nov. 21, 1921–Aug. 15, 1924
S. L. Staples .....................Aug. 16, 1924–Jan. 15, 1925
W. Gregory Hatcher............ Jan. 16, 1925–Jan. 1, 1931
Charley Lockhart .................Jan. 1, 1931–Oct. 25, 1941
Jesse James......................Oct. 25, 1941–Sept. 29, 1977
Warren G. Harding ...............Oct. 7, 1977–Jan. 3, 1983
Ann Richards........................ Jan. 3, 1983–Jan. 2, 1991
Kay Bailey Hutchison............... Jan. 2, 1991–June 1993
Martha Whitehead ....................June 1993–Aug. 1996
    *(The office of treasurer was eliminated by constitutional amendment in an election Nov. 7, 1995, effective the last day of August 1996.)*

★ ★ ★ ★ ★ ★ ★

## Railroad Commission of Texas

*After the first three names in the following list, each commissioner's name is followed by a surname in parentheses. The name in parentheses is the name of the commissioner whom that commissioner succeeded.*

John H. Reagan.............. June 10, 1891–Jan. 20, 1903
L. L. Foster ......................June 10, 1891–April 30, 1895
W. P. McLean...................June 10, 1891–Nov. 20, 1894
L. J. Storey (McLean) ........Nov. 21, 1894–Mar. 28,1909
N. A. Stedman (Foster).... May 1, 1895–Jan. 4, 1897
Allison Mayfield (Stedman). Jan. 5, 1897–Jan. 23, 1923
O. B. Colquitt (Reagan) .....Jan. 21, 1903–Jan. 17, 1911
William D. Williams (Storey)April 28, 1909–Oct. 1, 1916
John L. Wortham (Colquitt)..Jan. 21, 1911–Jan. 1, 1913
Earle B. Mayfield (Wortham)
    ....................................Jan. 2, 1913–March 1, 1923
Charles Hurdleston (Williams)
    ..................................Oct. 10, 1916–Dec. 31,1918
Clarence Gilmore (Hurdleston)
    ...................................... Jan. 1, 1919–Jan. 1, 1929
N. A. Nabors (A. Mayfield) .. Mar. 1, 1923–Jan. 18, 1925

William Splawn (E. Mayfield)
..................................Mar. 1, 1923–Aug. 1, 1924
C. V. Terrell (Splawn) ..........Aug. 15, 1924–Jan. 1, 1939
Lon A. Smith ( Nabors) .......Jan. 29, 1925–Jan. 1, 1941
Pat M. Neff (Gilmore)............. Jan. 1, 1929–Jan. 1, 1933
Ernest O. Thompson (Neff) .. Jan. 1, 1933–Jan. 8, 1965
G. A. (Jerry) Sadler (Terrell).. Jan. 1, 1939–Jan. 1, 1943
Olin Culberson (Smith) ...... Jan. 1, 1941–June 22, 1961
Beauford Jester (Sadler) .... Jan. 1, 1943–Jan. 21, 1947
William J. Murray Jr. (Jester)
..................................Jan. 21, 1947–Apr. 10, 1963
Ben Ramsey (Culberson)Sept. 18, 1961–Dec. 31, 1976
Jim C. Langdon (Murray)..May 28, 1963–Dec. 31, 1977
Byron Tunnell (Thompson)
..................................Jan. 11, 1965–Sept. 15, 1973
Mack Wallace (Tunnell) . Sept. 18, 1973–Sept. 22, 1987
Jon Newton (Ramsey) ........ Jan. 10, 1977–Jan. 4, 1979
John H. Poerner (Langdon).. Jan. 2, 1978–Jan. 1, 1981
James E. Nugent (Newton) ... Jan. 4, 1979–Jan. 3,1995
Buddy Temple (Poerner).... Jan. 2, 1981–March 2, 1986
Clark Jobe (Temple) ............. Mar. 3, 1986–Jan. 5, 1987
John Sharp (Jobe ................ Jan. 6, 1987–Jan. 2, 1991
Kent Hance (Wallace)........Sept. 23, 1987–Jan. 2, 1991
Robert Krueger (Hance) ..... Jan. 3, 1991–Jan. 22, 1993
(Krueger resigned when Gov. Ann Richards appoint-
ed him interim U.S. senator on the resignation of Sen.
Lloyd Bentsen.)
Lena Guerrero (Sharp) ....Jan. 23, 1991–Sept. 25, 1992
James Wallace (Guerrero) ....Oct. 2, 1992–Jan. 4, 1993
Barry Williamson (Wallace) .. Jan. 5, 1993–Jan. 4, 1999
Mary Scott Nabers (Krueger)Feb. 9, 1993–Dec. 9, 1994
Carole K. Rylander (Nabers)
..................................Dec. 10, 1994–Jan. 4, 1999
Charles Matthews (Nugent) Jan. 3, 1995–Jan. 31, 2005
Antonio Garza (Williamson) Jan. 4, 1999–Nov. 18, 2002
Michael Williams (Rylander)Jan. 4, 1999–Mar. 31, 2011
Victor G. Carrillo (Garza) .... Feb. 19, 2003–Jan. 3, 2011
Elizabeth A. Jones (Matthews)
..................................Feb. 2, 2005–Feb. 28, 2012
**David Porter** (Carrillo) ................. Jan. 5, 2011–
Barry T. Smitherman (Williams) ................July 8, 2011–
..................................Jan. 2, 2015
Buddy Garcia (Jones)........ April 16, 2012–Dec. 7, 2012
(Appointed by Gov. Perry.)
**Christi Craddick** (Garcia)..........Dec. 17, 2012–present
**Ryan Sitton** (Smitherman)..........Jan 5, 2015–present

★ ★ ★ ★ ★ ★ ★

# Comptroller of Public Accounts
## Of the Republic

John H. Money .....................Dec. 30, 1835–Jan. 17, 1836
H. C. Hudson .....................Jan. 17, 1836–Oct. 22, 1836
E. M. Pease.................................June 1837–Dec. 1837
F. R. Lubbock...............................Dec. 1837–Jan. 1839
Jas. W. Simmons.............Jan. 15, 1839–Sept. 30, 1840
Jas. B. Shaw................... Sept. 30, 1840–Dec. 24, 1841
F. R. Lubbock.....................Dec. 24, 1841–Jan. 1, 1842
Jas. B. Shaw....................... Jan. 1, 1842–Jan. 1, 1846

## Of the State

Jas. B. Shaw..................... Feb. 24, 1846–Aug. 2, 1858
Clement R. Johns................ Aug. 2, 1858–Aug. 1, 1864
Willis L. Robards.............Aug. 1, 1864–Oct. 12, 1865
Albert H. Latimer.............. Oct. 12, 1865–Mar. 27, 1866
Robert H. Taylor............... Mar. 27, 1866–June 25, 1866
Willis L. Robards.............June 25, 1866–Aug. 27, 1867
Morgan C. Hamilton............Aug. 27, 1867–Jan. 8, 1870
A. Bledsoe ......................... Jan. 8, 1870–Jan. 20, 1874
Stephen H. Darden.............Jan. 20, 1974–Nov. 2, 1880

W. M. Brown ......................Nov. 2, 1880–Jan. 16, 1883
W. J. Swain......................Jan. 16, 1883–Jan. 18, 1887
John D. McCall ................ Jan. 18, 1887–Jan. 15, 1895
R. W. Finley ....................Jan. 15, 1895–Jan. 15, 1901
R. M. Love ............................Jan. 15, 1901–Jan. 1903
J. W. Stephen ...............................Jan. 1903–Jan. 1911
W. P. Lane ..................................Jan. 1911–Jan. 1915
H. B. Terrell...............................Jan. 1915–Jan. 1920
M. L. Wiginton.............................Jan. 1920–Jan. 1921
Lon A. Smith ...............................Jan. 1921–Jan. 1925
S. H. Terrell...............................Jan. 1925–Jan. 1931
Geo. H. Sheppard................. Jan., 1931–Jan. 17, 1949
Robert S. Calvert ............. Jan. 17, 1949–Jan., 1975
Robert D. (Bob) Bullock............ Jan. 1975–Jan. 3, 1991
John Sharp .......................... Jan. 3, 1991–Jan. 2, 1999
Carole Keeton Strayhorn...... Jan. 2, 1999–Jan. 1, 2007
Susan Combs ...................... Jan. 1, 2007–Jan. 1, 2015
**Glenn Hegar** .......................... Jan. 2, 2015–present

★ ★ ★ ★ ★ ★ ★

# U.S. Senators from Texas

*U.S. Senators were selected by the legislatures
of the states until the U.S. Constitution was amended
in 1913 to require popular elections. In Texas, the first
senator chosen by the voters in a general election was
Charles A. Culberson in 1916. Because of political pres-
sures, however, the rules of the Democratic Party of
Texas were changed in 1904 to require that all candidates for office stand before voters in the primary. Consequently, Texas' senators faced voters in 1906, 1910
and 1912 before the U.S. Constitution was changed.*

*Following is the succession of Texas representa-
tives in the United States Senate since the annexation
of Texas to the Union in 1845:*

## Houston Succession

Sam Houston (I) ................Feb. 21, 1846–Mar. 4, 1859
John Hemphill (D)...............Mar. 4, 1859–July 11, 1861

*Louis T. Wigfall and W. S. Oldham took their seats in
the Confederate Senate, Nov. 16, 1861, and served until
the Confederacy collapsed. After that event, the State
Legislature on Aug. 21, 1866, elected David G. Burnet
and Oran M. Roberts to the U.S. Senate, anticipating
immediate readmission to the Union, but they were not
allowed to take their seats.*

Morgan C. Hamilton (R)......Feb. 22, 1870–Mar. 3, 1877
Richard Coke (D)..................Mar. 4, 1877–Mar. 3, 1895
Horace Chilton (D)................Mar. 3, 1895–Mar. 3, 1901
Joseph W. Bailey (D) ........... Mar. 3, 1901–Jan. 8, 1913
(Resigned.)
Rienzi Melville Johnston (D). Jan. 8, 1913–Feb. 3, 1913
(Appointed to fill vacancy.)
Morris Sheppard (D)........... Feb. 13, 1913–Apr. 9, 1941
(Died in office.)
Andrew J. Houston (D) ........................ June 2–26, 1941
(Appointed to fill vacancy.)
W. Lee O'Daniel (D)...............Aug. 4, 1941–Jan. 3, 1949
Lyndon B. Johnson (D)....... Jan. 3, 1949–Jan. 20, 1961
(Resigned to become U.S. vice president.)
William A. Blakley (D) ...... Jan. 20, 1961–June 15, 1961
(Appointed to fill vacancy.)
John G. Tower (R) .......... June 15, 1961–Jan. 21, 1985
Phil Gramm (R)...................Jan. 21, 1985–Dec. 2, 2002
**John Cornyn** (R) ........................Dec. 2, 2002–present

## Rusk Succession

Thomas J. Rusk (D)........... Feb 21, 1846–July 29, 1857
(Died in office.)

J. Pinckney Henderson (D).. Nov. 9, 1857–June 4, 1858
(*Died in office.*)
Matthias Ward (D) ............ Sept. 29, 1858–Dec. 5, 1859
(*Appointed to fill vacancy.*)
Louis T. Wigfall (D) ..........Dec. 5, 1859–March 23, 1861
(*Succession was broken by secession. See note above under Houston Succession.*)
James W. Flanagan (R)......Feb. 22, 1870–Mar. 3, 1875
Samuel B. Maxey (D) ........... Mar. 3, 1875–Mar. 3, 1887
John H. Reagan (D)........... Mar. 3, 1887–June 10, 1891
(*Resigned to head Texas Railroad Commission.*)
Horace Chilton (D)...............Dec. 7, 1891–Mar. 30,1892
(*Appointed to fill vacancy.*)
Roger Q. Mills (D)............... Mar. 30, 1892–Mar. 3, 1899
Charles A. Culberson (D)...... Mar. 3, 1899–Mar. 4, 1923
Earle B. Mayfield (D) ............ Mar. 4, 1923–Mar. 4, 1929
Tom Connally (D)................. Mar. 4, 1929–Jan. 3, 1953
Price Daniel (D) .................. Jan. 3, 1953–Jan. 15, 1957
(*Resigned to become governor.*)
William A. Blakley (D) ........Jan. 15, 1957–Apr. 27, 1957
(*Appointed to fill vacancy.*)
Ralph W. Yarborough (D) ..Apr. 27, 1957–Jan. 12, 1971
Lloyd Bentsen (D)............. Jan. 12, 1971–Jan. 20, 1993
(*Resigned to become U.S. Secretary of Treasury.*)
Robert Krueger (D).......... Jan. 20, 1993–June 14, 1993
(*Appointed to fill vacancy.*)
Kay Bailey Hutchison (R) June 14, 1993–Jan. 20, 2013
**Ted Cruz** (R) .............................. Jan. 20, 2013–present

★ ★ ★ ★ ★ ★ ★

# Commissioners of the General Land Office

## Of the Republic

John P. Borden ............... Aug. 23, 1837–Dec. 12, 1840
H. W. Raglin ...................... Dec. 12, 1840–Jan. 4, 1841
Thomas William Ward ...... Jan. 4, 1841–Mar. 20, 1848
(*Part of term after annexation.*)

## Of the State

George W. Smyth ...............Mar. 20, 1848–Aug. 4, 1851
Stephen Crosby...................Aug. 4, 1851–Mar. 1, 1858
Francis M. White.................. Mar. 1, 1858–Mar. 1, 1862
Stephen Crosby...................Mar. 1, 1862–Sept. 1, 1865
Francis M. White................ Sept. 1, 1865–Aug. 7, 1866
Stephen Crosby................. Aug. 7, 1866–Aug. 27, 1867
Joseph Spence..................Aug. 27, 1867–Jan. 19, 1870
Jacob Kuechler................. Jan. 19, 1870–Jan. 20, 1874
J. J. Groos ...................... Jan. 20, 1874–June 15, 1878
W. C. Walsh.....................July 30, 1878–Jan. 10, 1887
R. M. Hall ...................... Jan. 10, 1887–Jan. 16, 1891
W. L. McGaughey............. Jan. 16, 1891–Jan. 26, 1895
A. J. Baker...................... Jan. 26, 1895–Jan. 16, 1899
George W. Finger .............. Jan. 16, 1899–May 4, 1899
Charles Rogan..................May 11, 1899–Jan. 10, 1903
John J. Terrell.................Jan. 10, 1903–Jan. 11, 1909
J. T. Robison..........................Jan, 1909–Sept. 11, 1929
J. H. Walker .......................... Sept. 11, 1929–Jan., 1937
William H. McDonald .................... Jan 1937–Jan. 1939
Bascom Giles .......................... Jan. 1939–Jan. 5, 1955
J. Earl Rudder.....................Jan. 5, 1955–Feb. 1, 1958
Bill Allcorn ............................ Feb. 1, 1958–Jan. 1, 1961
Jerry Sadler ......................... Jan. 1, 1961–Jan. 1, 1971
Bob Armstrong...................... Jan. 1, 1971–Jan. 1, 1983
Garry Mauro ........................ Jan. 1, 1983–Jan. 7, 1999
David Dewhurst ................... Jan. 7, 1999–Jan. 3, 2003
Jerry Patterson .................... Jan. 3, 2003–Jan. 2, 2015
**George P. Bush** ............................ Jan. 2, 2015–present

★ ★ ★ ★ ★ ★ ★

# Speaker of the House

*The Speaker of the Texas House of Representatives is the presiding officer of the lower chamber of the Legislature. The official is elected at the beginning of each regular session by a vote of the members of the House.*

## Of the Republic

| Speaker | Term | Congress |
|---|---|---|
| Ira Ingram | 1836–37 | 1st |
| Branch Tanner Archer | 1837 | 2nd |
| Joseph Rowe | 1838 | 2nd |
| John M. Hansford | 1838–39 | 3rd |
| David Spangler Kaufman | 1840–41 | 4th, 5th |
| Kenneth L. Anderson | 1841–42 | 6th |
| Nicholas H. Darnell | 1842–43 | 7th |
| Richardson A. Scurry | 1843–44 | 8th |
| John M. Lewis | 1844–45 | 9th |

## Of the State

| Speaker, Residence | Term | Legislature |
|---|---|---|
| William E. Crump (D), Bellville | 1846 | 1st |
| John Brown (D), Brownsboro | 1846 | 1st |
| Edward T. Branch (D), Liberty | 1846 | 1st |
| William H. Bourland (D), Paris | 1846 | 1st |
| Stephen W. Perkins (D), Columbia | 1846 | 1st |
| James W. Henderson (D), Houston | 1847–48 | 2nd |
| Charles G. Keenan (D), Huntsville | 1849–51 | 3rd |
| David C. Dickson (D), Anderson | 1851–53 | 4th |
| Hardin R. Runnels (D), Boston | 1853–55 | 5th |
| Hamilton P. Bee (D), Laredo | 1855–57 | 6th |
| William S. Taylor (D), Larissa | 1857–58 | 7th |
| Matt F. Locke (D), Lafayette | 1858–59 | 7th |
| Marion DeKalb Taylor (D), Jefferson | 1859–61 | 8th |
| Constantine W. Buckley (D), Richmond | 1861 | 9th |
| Nicholas H. Darnell (D), Dallas | 1861–62 | 9th |
| Constantine W. Buckley (D), Richmond | 1863 | 9th |
| Marion DeKalb Taylor (D), Jefferson | 1863–65 | 10th |
| Nathaniel M. Burford (Unionist), Dallas | 1866 | 11th |

*(Vacant, under Congressional Reconstruction and military administration.)*

| | | |
|---|---|---|
| Ira H. Evans (R), Corpus Christi | 1870–71 | 12th |
| William H. Sinclair (R), Galveston | 1871–73 | 12th |
| Marion DeKalb Taylor (D), Jefferson | 1873–74 | 13th |
| Guy M. Bryan (D), Galveston | 1874–76 | 14th |
| Thomas R. Bonner (D), Tyler | 1876–79 | 15th |
| John H. Cochran (D), Dallas | 1879–81 | 16th |
| George R. Reeves (D), Pottsboro | 1881–83 | 17th |
| Charles R. Gibson (D), Waxahachie | 1883–85 | 18th |
| Lafayette L. Foster (D), Groesbeck | 1885–87 | 19th |
| George C. Pendleton (D), Belton | 1887–89 | 20th |
| Frank P. Alexander (D), Greenville | 1889–91 | 21st |
| Robert T. Milner (D), Henderson | 1891–93 | 22nd |
| John H. Cochran (D), Dallas | 1893–95 | 23rd |
| Thomas Slater Smith (D), Hillsboro | 1895–97 | 24th |
| L. Travis Dashiell (D), Jewett | 1897–99 | 25th |
| J. S. Sherrill (D), Greenville | 1899–1901 | 26th |
| Robert E. Prince (D), Corsicana | 1901–03 | 27th |
| Pat M. Neff (D), Waco | 1903–05 | 28th |
| Francis W. Seabury (D), Rio Grande City | 1905–07 | 29th |
| Thomas B. Love (D), Lancaster | 1907–09 | 30th |
| Austin M. Kennedy (D), Waco | 1909 | 31st |

*(Resigned.)*

| | | |
|---|---|---|
| John W. Marshall (D), Whitesboro | 1909–11 | 31st |
| Sam Rayburn (D), Bonham | 1911–13 | 32nd |

| | | | |
|---|---|---|---|
| Chester H. Terrell (D), San Antonio | 1913–15 | 33rd | |
| John W. Woods (D), Rotan | 1915–17 | 34th | |
| Franklin O. Fuller (D), Coldspring | 1917–19 | 35th | |
| R. Ewing Thomason (D), El Paso | 1919–21 | 36th | |
| Charles G. Thomas (D), Lewisville | 1921–23 | 37th | |
| Richard E. Seagler (D), Palestine | 1923–25 | 38th | |
| R. Lee Satterwhite (D), Amarillo | 1925–27 | 39th | |
| Robert L. Bobbitt (D), Laredo | 1927–29 | 40th | |
| W. S. Barron (D), Bryan | 1929–31 | 41st | |
| Fred H. Minor (D), Denton | 1931–33 | 42nd | |
| Coke R. Stevenson (D), Junction | 1933–35 | 43rd | |
| '' | 1935–37 | 44th | |
| Robert W. Calvert (D), Hillsboro | 1937–39 | 45th | |
| R. Emmett Morse (D), Houston | 1939–41 | 46th | |
| Homer L. Leonard (D), McAllen | 1941–43 | 47th | |
| Price Daniel (D), Liberty | 1943–45 | 48th | |
| Claud H. Gilmer (D), Rocksprings | 1945–47 | 49th | |
| William O. Reed (D), Dallas | 1947–49 | 50th | |
| Durwood Manford (D), Smiley | 1949–51 | 51st | |
| Reuben Senterfitt (D), San Saba | 1951–53 | 52nd | |
| '' | 1953–55 | 53rd | |
| Jim T. Lindsey (D), Texarkana | 1955–57 | 54th | |
| Waggoner Carr (D), Lubbock | 1957–59 | 55th | |
| '' | 1959–61 | 56th | |
| James A. Turman (D), Gober | 1961–63 | 57th | |
| Byron M. Tunnell (D), Tyler | 1963–65 | 58th | |
| Ben Barnes (D), De Leon | 1965–67 | 59th | |
| '' | 1967–69 | 60th | |
| Gus F. Mutscher (D), Brenham | 1969–71 | 61st | |
| '' | 1971–72 | 62nd | |
| *(Resigned)* | | | |
| Rayford Price (D), Palestine | 1972–73 | 62nd | |
| Price Daniel Jr. (D), Liberty | 1973–75 | 63rd | |
| Bill Clayton (D), Springlake | 1975–77 | 64th | |
| '' | 1977–79 | 65th | |
| '' | 1979–81 | 66th | |
| '' | 1981–83 | 67th | |
| Gib Lewis (D), Fort Worth | 1983–85 | 68th | |
| '' | 1985–87 | 69th | |
| '' | 1987–89 | 70th | |
| '' | 1989–91 | 71st | |
| '' | 1991–93 | 72nd | |
| Pete Laney (D), Hale Center | 1993–95 | 73rd | |
| '' | 1995–97 | 74th | |
| '' | 1997–99 | 75th | |
| '' | 1999–2001 | 76th | |
| '' | 2001–03 | 77th | |
| Tom Craddick (R), Midland | 2003–05 | 78th | |
| '' | 2005–07 | 79th | |
| '' | 2007–09 | 80th | |
| **Joe Straus** (R), San Antonio | 2009–11 | 81st | |
| '' | 2011–13 | 82nd | |
| '' | 2013–15 | 83rd | |
| '' | 2015–present | 84th | |

★ ★ ★ ★ ★ ★ ★

## Chief Justice of the Supreme Court

### Republic of Texas

James Collinsworth .......... Dec. 16, 1836–July 23, 1838
John Birdsall .............................. Nov. 19–Dec. 12, 1838
Thomas J. Rusk ................. Dec. 12, 1838–Dec. 5, 1840
John Hemphill .................... Dec. 5, 1840–Dec. 29, 1845

### Under the Constitutions of 1845 and 1861

John Hemphill .................... Mar. 2, 1846–Oct. 10, 1858
Royall T. Wheeler .................. Oct. 11, 1858–April 1864

Oran M. Roberts ................ Nov. 1, 1864–June 30, 1866

### Under the Constitution of 1866
#### (Presidential Reconstruction)

George F. Moore ............ Aug. 16, 1866–Sept. 10, 1867
*(Removed under Congressional Reconstruction by military authorities who appointed members of the next court.)*

### Under the Constitution of 1866
#### (Congressional Reconstruction)

Amos Morrill ...................... Sept. 10, 1867–July 5, 1870

### Under the Constitution of 1869

Lemuel D. Evans ................ July 5, 1870–Aug. 31, 1873
Wesley Ogden .................. Aug. 31, 1873–Jan. 29, 1874
Oran M. Roberts ................ Jan. 29, 1874–Apr. 18, 1876

### Under the Constitution of 1876

Oran M. Roberts .................. Apr. 18, 1876–Oct. 1, 1878
George F. Moore .................. Nov. 1, 1878–Nov. 1, 1881
Robert S. Gould ................. Nov. 1, 1881–Dec. 23, 1882
Asa H. Willie ...................... Dec. 23, 1882–Mar. 3, 1888
John W. Stayton ................... Mar. 3, 1888–July 5, 1894
Reuben R. Gaines .............. July 10, 1894–Jan. 5, 1911
Thomas J. Brown ................. Jan. 7, 1911–May 26, 1915
Nelson Phillips .................. June 1, 1915–Nov. 16, 1921
C. M. Cureton ...................... Dec. 2, 1921–Apr. 8, 1940
Hortense Sparks Ward ....... Jan. 8, 1925–May 23, 1925
*(Mrs. Ward headed a special Supreme Court to hear one case in 1925.)*
W. F. Moore ........................ Apr. 17, 1940–Jan. 1, 1941
James P. Alexander ............. Jan. 1, 1941–Jan. 1, 1948
J. E. Hickman ...................... Jan. 5, 1948–Jan. 3, 1961
Robert W. Calvert ................ Jan. 3, 1961–Oct. 4, 1972
Joe R. Greenhill .................. Oct. 4, 1972–Oct. 25, 1982
Jack Pope ........................... Nov. 29, 1982–Oct. 5, 1985
John L. Hill Jr. ...................... Jan. 5, 1985–Jan. 4, 1988
Thomas R. Phillips .............. Jan. 4, 1988–Sept. 3 2004
Wallace B. Jefferson .......... Sept. 14, 2004–Oct. 1, 2013
**Nathan L. Hecht** ...................... Oct. 1, 2013–present

★ ★ ★ ★ ★ ★ ★

## Presiding Judges, Court of Appeals (1876–1891)
## and Court of Criminal Appeals (1891–present)

Mat D. Ector ........................ May 6, 1876–Oct. 29, 1879
John P. White ..................... Nov. 9, 1879–Apr. 26, 1892
James M. Hurt ................... May 4, 1892–Dec. 31, 1898
W. L. Davidson ................. Jan. 2, 1899–June 27, 1913
A. C. Prendergast ........... June 27, 1913–Dec. 31, 1916
W. L. Davidson .................. Jan. 1, 1917–Jan. 25, 1921
Wright C. Morrow ............... Feb. 8, 1921–Oct. 16, 1939
Frank Lee Hawkins ............. Oct. 16, 1939–Jan. 2, 1951
Harry N. Graves ............... Jan. 2, 1951–Dec. 31, 1954
W. A. Morrison ..................... Jan. 1, 1955–Jan. 2, 1961
Kenneth K. Woodley ............ Jan. 3, 1961–Jan. 4, 1965
W. T. McDonald ................. Jan. 4, 1965–June 25, 1966
W. A. Morrison ................. June 25, 1966–Jan. 1, 1967
Kenneth K. Woodley ............ Jan. 1, 1967–Jan. 1, 1971
John F. Onion Jr. .................. Jan. 1, 1971–Jan. 1, 1989
Michael J. McCormick ......... Jan. 1, 1989–Jan. 1, 2001
**Sharon Keller** .............................. Jan. 1, 2001–present

★ ★ ★ ★ ★ ★ ★

## Administrators of Public Education

### Superintendents of Public Instruction

Pryor Lea ........................ Nov. 10, 1866–Sept. 12, 1867
Edwin M. Wheelock ........... Sept. 12, 1867–May 6, 1871
Jacob C. DeGress .............. May 6, 1871–Jan. 20, 1874
O. H. Hollingsworth ............. Jan. 20, 1874–May 6, 1884
B. M. Baker ......................... May 6, 1884–Jan. 18, 1887
O. H. Cooper ..................... Jan 18, 1887–Sept. 1, 1890
H. C. Pritchett ................. Sept. 1, 1890–Sept. 15, 1891
J. M. Carlisle ................... Sept. 15, 1891–Jan. 10, 1899
J. S. Kendall ........................ Jan. 10, 1899–July 2, 1901
Arthur Lefevre ...................... July 2, 1901–Jan. 12, 1905
R. B. Cousins ...................... Jan. 12, 1905–Jan. 1, 1910
F. M. Bralley ......................... Jan. 1, 1910–Sept. 1, 1913
W. F. Doughty ...................... Sept. 1, 1913–Jan. 1, 1919
Annie Webb Blanton ........... Jan. 1, 1919–Jan. 16, 1923
S. M. N. Marrs ................. Jan. 16, 1923–April 28, 1932
C. N. Shaver ...................... April 28, 1932–Oct. 1, 1932

L. W. Rogers ....................... Oct. 1, 1932–Jan. 16, 1933
L. A. Woods .................................... Jan. 16, 1933–1951

*(The office of State Superintendent of Public Instruction was abolished by the Gilmer-Aikin act of 1949 and the office of Commissioner of Education created, appointed by a new State Board of Education elected by the people.)*

### State Commissioner of Education

J. W. Edgar ...................... May 31, 1951–June 30, 1974
Marlin L. Brockette.............. July 1, 1974–Sept. 1, 1979
Alton O. Bowen.................. Sept. 1, 1979–June 1, 1981
Raymon Bynum ................. June 1, 1981–Oct. 31, 1984
W. N. Kirby.......................... April 13, 1985–July 1, 1991
Lionel R. Meno ................. July 1, 1991–March 1, 1995
Michael A. Moses ............ March 9, 1995–Aug. 18, 1999
Jim Nelson .................... Aug. 18, 1999–March 25, 2002
Felipe Alanis ................... March 25, 2002–July 31, 2003
Shirley J. Neeley................. Jan. 12, 2004–July 1, 2007
Robert Scott........................... July 1, 2007–July 2, 2012
**Michael Williams** ...................... Sept. 1, 2012–present

## First Ladies of Texas

Martha Evans Gindratt Wood.................. 1847–1849
Bell Administration .................................. 1849–1853
*(Gov. Peter Hansbrough Bell was not married while in office.)*
Lucadia Christiana Niles Pease 1853–57; 1867–1869
Runnels Administration ........................... 1857–1859
*(Gov. Hardin R. Runnels never married.)*
Margaret Moffette Lea Houston .............. 1859–1861
Martha Evans Clark .......................................... 1861
Adele Barron Lubbock .......................... 1861–1863
Susie Ellen Taylor Murrah ...................... 1863–1865
Mary Jane Bowen Hamilton .................... 1865–1866
Annie Rattan Throckmorton .................... 1866–1867
Ann Elizabeth Britton Davis .................... 1870–1874
Mary Home Coke .................................... 1874–1876
Janie Roberts Hubbard .......................... 1876–1879
Frances Wickliff Edwards Roberts .......... 1879–1883
Anne Maria Penn Ireland ........................ 1883–1887
Elizabeth Dorothy Tinsley Ross .............. 1887–1891
Sarah Stinson Hogg................................ 1891–1895
Sally Harrison Culberson ........................ 1895–1899
Orlene Walton Sayers ............................ 1899–1903
Sarah Beona Meng Lanham .................... 1903–1907
Fannie Brunner Campbell ....................... 1907–1911
Alice Fuller Murrell Colquitt .................... 1911–1915
Miriam A. Wallace Ferguson ................... 1915–1917
*(Miriam A. Wallace Ferguson was Mistress of the Mansion while her husband, James E. Ferguson, was governor, 1915–1917. She served as both Governor and Mistress of the Mansion, 1925–1927 and 1933–1935.)*
Willie Cooper Hobby ............................... 1917–1921
Myrtle Mainer Neff.................................. 1921–1925
Mildred Paxton Moody ............................ 1927–1931
Maud Gage Sterling................................ 1931–1933
Jo Betsy Miller Allred.............................. 1935–1939
Merle Estella Butcher O'Daniel ............... 1939–1941
Fay Wright Stevenson............................. 1941–1942
*(Died in the Governor's Mansion on Jan. 3, 1942.)*
Edith Will Scott Stevenson ..................... 1942–1946
*(Mother of Gov. Coke R. Stevenson and Mistress of the Mansion upon the death of the governor's wife.)*

*Cecilia Abbott. Photo courtesy of the Office of the First Lady.*

Mabel Buchanan Jester .......................... 1946–1949
Marialice Shary Shivers .......................... 1949–1957
Jean Houston Baldwin Daniel................. 1957–1963
Idanell Brill Connally ............................... 1963–1969
Ima Mae Smith........................................ 1969–1973
Betty Jane Slaughter Briscoe.................. 1973–1979
Rita Crocker Bass Clements................... 1979–1983
Linda Gale Thompson White .................. 1983–1987
Rita Crocker Bass Clements................... 1987–1991
Richards Administration .......................... 1991–1995
*(Gov. Ann Richards' was not married while in office.)*
Laura Welch Bush................................... 1995–2000
Anita Thigpen Perry ............................... 2000–2015
**Cecilia Abbott .................................... 2015–present**

# State Government

Texas state government is divided into executive, legislative and judicial branches under the Texas Constitution adopted in 1876.

The chief executive is the Governor, whose term is for four years. Other elected state officials with executive responsibilities include the Lieutenant Governor, Attorney General, Comptroller of Public Accounts, Commissioner of the General Land Office and Commissioner of Agriculture. The terms of those officials are also four years.

The Secretary of State and the Commissioner of Education are appointed by the Governor.

Except for making numerous appointments and calling special sessions of the Legislature, the Governor's powers are limited in comparison with those in most states.

Current state executives "not-to-exceed" salaries are for the 2012–2013 biennium (maximum possible salaries; actual salaries can be lower); salaries for the 2014–2015 biennium were not available from the State Auditor at press time.

The Governor's office welcomes comments and concerns, which are relayed to government officials who may offer assistance. Send a message at: http://www2.governor.state.tx.us/contact/ or call the **Citizen's Opinion Hotline (1-800-252-9600).**

**Governor Greg Abbott**
P.O. Box 12428, Austin 78711
(512) 463-2000
www.governor.state.tx.us
**Salary:** $150,000

**Lt. Governor Dan Patrick**
P.O. Box 12068, Austin 78711
(512) 463-0001
www.senate.state.tx.us
**Salary:** Same as Senator when serving as
President of the Senate; same as Governor
when serving as Governor

**Attorney General**
**Ken Paxton**
P.O. Box 12548, Austin 78711
(512) 463-2100
www.oag.state.tx.us
**Salary:** $150,000

**Comptroller of Public**
**Accounts Glenn Hegar**
P.O. Box 13528, Austin 78711
(512) 463-4600
www.window.state.tx.us
**Salary:** $150,000

**Texas Land Commissioner**
**George P. Bush**
P.O. Box 12873, Austin 78711
(512) 463-5256
www.glo.texas.gov
**Salary:** $137,500

| **Agriculture Commissioner** | **Secretary of State** | **Education Commissioner** |
|:---:|:---:|:---:|
| **Sid Miller** | **Carlos H. Cascos** | **Michael Williams** |
| P.O. Box 12847, Austin 78711 | P.O. Box 12697, Austin 78711 | 1701 N. Congress Ave. |
| (512) 463-7476 | (512) 463-5770 | Austin 78701 |
| www.texasagriculture.gov | www.sos.state.tx.us | (512) 463-8985 |
| **Salary:** $137,500 | **Salary:** $125,880 | www.tea.state.tx.us |
| | | **Salary:** $215,000 |

# State Government Income and Expenditures

Taxes are the state government's primary source of income. On this and the following pages are summaries of state income and expenditures, percent change from previous year, tax collections, tax revenue by type of tax, a summary of the state budgets for the 2014–2015 and 2016–2017 bienniums, Texas Lottery income and expenditures, and the amount of federal payments to state agencies. Totals may not sum due to rounding.

## State Revenues by Source and Expenditures by Function
### Amounts (in Millions) and Percent Change from Previous Year

| **Revenues by Source** | **2014** | **%** | **2013** | **%** | **2012** | **%** | **2011** | **%** | **2010** | **%** |
|---|---|---|---|---|---|---|---|---|---|---|
| Tax Collections | $50,993 | 6.7 | 47,781 | 8.4 | $44,079 | 13.4 | $38,856 | 9.9 | $35,369 | −6.5 |
| Federal Income | 34,266 | 5.3 | 32,530 | −1.2 | 32,922 | −14.3 | 38,431 | 4.3 | 36,857 | 19.4 |
| Licenses, Fees, Permits, Fines, Penalties | 8,497 | 7.3 | 7,920 | 4.1 | 7,608 | −3.4 | 7,877 | 14.8 | 6,863 | −4.7 |
| Interest & Other Investment Income | 1,463 | 23.7 | 1,183 | 7.6 | 1,099 | 6.2 | 1,035 | −2.3 | 1,059 | −21.4 |
| Net Lottery Proceeds | 1,878 | −0.8 | 1,893 | 3.4 | 1,831 | 9.3 | 1,676 | 2.5 | 1,634 | 3.3 |
| Sales of Goods & Services | 262 | 16.1 | 225 | −37.7 | 363 | 28.1 | 283 | −30.6 | 408 | −4.6 |
| Settlements of Claims | 575 | −5.7 | 610 | 9.0 | 560 | −4.8 | 588 | 5.5 | 557 | −1.3 |
| Land Income | 1,863 | 40.6 | 1,326 | −3.4 | 1,372 | −6.1 | 1,462 | 92.2 | 761 | −3.5 |
| Contributions to Employee Benefits | 87 | 0.5 | 86 | −31.6 | 0.13 | −19.9 | 0.16 | −6.6 | 0.17 | −37.5 |
| Other Revenues | 5,144 | −7.7 | 5,574 | 15.5 | 4,828 | 18.8 | 4,065 | 5.6 | 3,850 | 4.2 |
| **Total Net Revenues** | **$104,942** | **6.0** | **$99,043** | **4.6** | **$94,661** | **0.4** | **$94,271** | **7.9** | **$87,357** | **3.6** |
| **Expenditures by Function** | **2014** | **%** | **2013** | **%** | **2012** | **%** | **2011** | **%** | **2010** | **%** |
| General Government – Total | 2,831 | 4.5 | 2,709 | −10.5 | $3,026 | −30.3 | $4,342 | 20.0 | $3,618 | 25.9 |
| Executive | 2,386 | 3.6 | 2,303 | −12.2 | 2,622 | −33.2 | 3,925 | 22.2 | 3,212 | 29.7 |
| Legislative | 129 | −4.7 | 135 | 11.3 | 122 | −12.4 | 139 | 5.9 | 131 | −7.5 |
| Judicial | 315 | 16.7 | 270 | −4.1 | 282 | 0.9 | 279 | 1.4 | 275 | 7.9 |
| Education | 32,760 | 3.9 | 31,531 | −6.4 | 33,703 | 0.4 | 33,558 | 3.5 | 32,418 | −2.1 |
| Employee Benefits | 3,816 | 9.7 | 3,478 | 4.7 | 3,321 | −2.6 | 3,411 | 2.0 | 3,342 | 14.1 |
| Health and Human Services | 41,701 | 7.7 | 38,736 | 1.6 | 38,127 | −1.5 | 38,718 | 6.7 | 36,301 | 8.4 |
| Public Safety and Corrections | 4,360 | 1.5 | 4,296 | 0 | 4,295 | −5.6 | 4,549 | −3.3 | 4,704 | −6.7 |
| Transportation | 8,841 | 16.3 | 7,604 | 10.4 | 6,890 | 2.7 | 6,706 | 12.3 | 5,972 | −11.2 |
| Natural Resources/Recreational Services | 2,342 | 1.7 | 2,304 | 6.5 | 2,163 | 19.6 | 1,808 | −0.3 | 1,813 | −12.4 |
| Regulatory Agencies | 614 | 71.7 | 358 | 6.5 | 336 | 7.5 | 312 | −6.1 | 333 | −6.7 |
| Lottery Winnings Paid* | 603 | −8.8 | 661 | 6.8 | 619 | 14.3 | 541 | 11.2 | 487 | −0.9 |
| Debt Service – Interest | 1,293 | −3.1 | 1,335 | 3.8 | 1,286 | 31.3 | 980 | 11.2 | 881 | −12.4 |
| Capital Outlay | 495 | −11.1 | 556 | 13.0 | 492 | −7.6 | 532 | −5.9 | 566 | 19.4 |
| **Total Net Expenditures** | **$99,655** | **6.5** | **$93,567** | **−0.7** | **$94,257** | **−1.3** | **$95,459** | **5.6** | **$90,434** | **2.1** |

*\* Does not include payments made by retailers. All amounts rounded. Revenue and expenditures exclude trust funds. Fiscal years end August 31. Source: 2014 State of Texas Annual Cash Report, Revenue and Expenditures of State Funds for the Year Ending August 31, 2014, Comptroller of Public Accounts' Office.*

# State Government Budget Summary
# 2016–2017 Biennium

Source: Legislative Budget Board; www.lbb.state.tx.us.

The Legislative Budget Board's (LBB) baseline appropriations for state government operations for the 2016–2017 biennium total $209.4 billion from All Funds functions of state government. The funding is a $7.35 billion, or 3.6 percent, increase from the 2014–2015 biennial level.

General Revenue Funds, including funds dedicated within the General Revenue Fund, total $106.6 billion for the 2016–2017 biennium, an increase of $11.4 billion, or 12 percent, from the estimated/budgeted 2014–2015 biennial spending level.

The LBB recommended appropriations for the 2016–2017 biennium are within the Comptroller's 2016–2017 Biennial Revenue Estimate. ☆

| Article (Governmental Division) (all funds in millions) | Estimated/ Budgeted for 2014–2015* | Recommended 2016–2017 Budget | Biennial Change | Percentage Change |
|---|---|---|---|---|
| Art. I — General Government | $ 5,218.8 | $ 6,385.6 | $ 1,166.8 | 22.4% |
| Art. II — Health and Human Services | 74,513.4 | 77,168.3 | 2,655.0 | 3.6% |
| Art. III — Agencies of Education | 73,941.8 | 78,360.4 | 4,418.5 | 6.0% |
| *Public Education* | *55,403.8* | *58,429.8* | *3,026.0* | *5.5%* |
| *Higher Education* | *18,538.1* | *19,930.6* | *1,392.5* | *7.5%* |
| Art. IV — The Judiciary | 764.0 | 796.8 | 32.8 | 4.3% |
| Art. V — Public Safety & Criminal Justice | 11,765.2 | 12,391.0 | 625.8 | 5.3% |
| Art. VI — Natural Resources | 6,931.1 | 4,354.4 | −$2,576.7 | −37.2% |
| Art. VII — Business & Economic Dev. | 27,447.6 | 27,745.0 | 297.4 | 1.1% |
| Art. VIII — Regulatory | 1,127.3 | 920.4 | −$206.8 | −18.3% |
| Art. IX — General Provisions | $0.0 | 924.0 | 924.0 | N/A |
| Art. X — The Legislature | 374.0 | 385.5 | 11.5 | 3.1% |
| **Total** | **$ 202,083.1** | **$ $209,431.6** | **$ 7,348.5** | **3.6%** |

**Notes:** (1) Includes certain anticipated supplemental spending adjustments. (2) Excludes interagency contracts. (3) Biennial change and percentage change are calculated on actual amounts before rounding. Therefore, figure totals may not sum due to rounding. (4) All funds are in millions.

**Source:** Summary of 2016–17 Conference Committee Report For House Bill 1: Appropriations for the 2016–17 Biennium May 2015; Figure 2 – Funding By Article, All Funds.

# State Tax Collections 1998–2014

| FY* | State Tax Collections | Resident Population | Per Capita Tax Collec-tions | Taxes as % of Per-sonal Income |
|---|---|---|---|---|
| 2014 | 50,992,561,539 | 26,788,600 | 1,904 | 4.3 |
| 2013 | 47,781,045,666 | 26,399,510 | 1,810 | 4.2 |
| 2012 | 44,079,118,749 | 26,005,770 | 1,695 | 4.0 |
| 2011 | 38,856,175,733 | 25,592,790 | 1,518 | 3.8 |
| 2010 | 35,368,901,064 | 25,191,450 | 1,404 | 3.7 |
| 2009 | 37,822,453,013 | 24,737,000 | 1,529 | 4.1 |
| 2008 | 41,357,928,953 | 24,250,000 | 1,705 | 4.3 |
| 2007 | 36,955,629,884 | 23,778,000 | 1,554 | 4.3 |
| 2006 | 33,544,497,547 | 23,339,000 | 1,437 | 4.1 |
| 2005 | 29,838,277,614 | 22,808,000 | 1,308 | 4.0 |
| 2004 | 27,913,001,645 | 22,409,000 | 1,246 | 4.1 |
| 2003 | 26,126,675,424 | 22,052,000 | 1,185 | 4.1 |
| 2002 | 26,279,146,493 | 21,673,000 | 1,213 | 4.2 |
| 2001 | 27,230,212,416 | 21,317,000 | 1,277 | 4.5 |
| 2000 | 25,283,768,842 | 20,904,000 | 1,210 | 4.4 |
| 1999 | 23,614,611,235 | 20,507,000 | 1,152 | 4.4 |
| 1998 | 22,634,019,740 | 20,104,000 | 1,126 | 4.4 |

* Fiscal years end on August 31.

**Sources:** *Tax collection data* were compiled by the Texas Comptroller of Public Accounts from the Annual Cash Reports. **Population estimates and personal income figures** are from the Comptroller's Fall 2014 state economic forecast data bank.

# Tax Revenues, 2013–2014

Below are the major taxes for fiscal years 2013 and 2014, the amounts each contributed to the state, and the percent change from the previous year.

| Type of Tax | FY 2013 | % | FY 2014 | % |
|---|---|---|---|---|
| Sales | $25,943,807,086 | 7.2 | $27,385,709,242 | 5.6 |
| Motor Vehicle Sales and Rentals* | 3,878,379,684 | 9.0 | 4,209,952,925 | 8.5 |
| Motor Fuels | 3,221,502,038 | 1.6 | 3,315,952,089 | 2.9 |
| Franchise | 4,798,699,188 | 5.1 | 4,732,261,872 | −1.4 |
| Insurance | 1,764,153,450 | 17.9 | 1,947,908,252 | 10.4 |
| Natural Gas Production | 1,495,202,962 | −2.6 | 1,899,581,526 | 27.0 |
| Cigarette &Tobacco | 1,598,089,091 | 11.9 | 1,342,454,822 | −16 |
| Alcoholic Beverages | 976,893,685 | 5.1 | 1,053,231,009 | 7.8 |
| Oil Production | 2,990,890,113 | 42.2 | 3,874,070,862 | 29.5 |
| Inheritance | −10,293,450 | 2,028 | 11,543 | 100 |
| Utility | 434,870,937 | −3.6 | 478,188,876 | 10 |
| Hotel | 441,131,849 | 9.9 | 485,384,563 | 10 |
| Other Taxes | 247,719,032 | −1.3 | 267,853,959 | 8.1 |
| **Totals** | **$47,781,045,666** | **8.4** | **$50,992,561,539** | **6.7** |

*Includes tax on manufactured housing sales.
**Source:** 2014 State of Texas Annual Cash Report, Net Revenue by Source – All Funds Excluding Trust for the Year Ending August 31, 2014, Texas Comptroller of Public Accounts.

# Federal Revenue by State Agency

*Source: Texas Comptroller of Public Accounts, 2014 State of Texas Annual Cash Report, Revenue and Expenditures of State Funds for the Year Ending Aug. 31, 2014.*

Texas received $34.3 billion in federal funds during fiscal 2014, a increase of $1.74 billion, or 5.3 percent from fiscal 2013. Federal funds accounted for 32.7 percent of total net revenue, the second largest source of revenue in fiscal 2014.

| State Agency | 2014 | 2013 | 2012 | 2011 |
|---|---|---|---|---|
| Health and Human Services Commission | $21,056,130,946 | $19,454,754,015 | $18,665,829,591 | $21,571,516,119 |
| Texas Education Agency | 4,944,487,430 | 5,107,598,232 | 5,911,025,809 | 7,222,053,401 |
| Texas Department of Transportation | 3,383,800,362 | 2,860,010,862 | 2,882,935,626 | 3,012,762,271 |
| Department of State Health Services | 9 58,029,437 | 994,671,003 | 1,016,007,645 | 1,070,932,556 |
| Texas Workforce Commission | 898,702,380 | 879,534,482 | 880,657,818 | 1,075,003,324 |
| Department of Agriculture | 504,076,040 | 514,126,922 | 407,287,580 | 399,546,594 |
| General Land Office | 455,031,363 | 418,772,299 | 503,411,602 | 55,388,820 |
| Department of Assistive and Rehabilitative Services | 412,327,532 | 411,321,506 | 429,026,031 | 469,657,631 |
| TDepartment of Family and Protective Services | 388,758,860 | 427,236,384 | 398,471,624 | 436,253,662 |
| Department of Public Safety | 315,574,922 | 430,037,245 | 421,370,878 | 554,804,844 |
| Texas Department of Housing and Community Affairs | 269,240,040 | 289,839,464 | 475,784,041 | 1,136,349,138 |
| Attorney General | 214,357,352 | 201,899,841 | 227,582,828 | 236,753,250 |
| Department of Aging and Disability Services | 114,963,350 | 126,128,411 | 128,606,831 | 131,739,810 |
| Texas Military Department | 66,408,489 | 69,959,344 | 98,177,094 | 108,677,566 |
| Governor – Fiscal | 60,743,306 | 48,805,837 | 83,584,266 | 54,002,498 |
| Parks and Wildlife Department | 54,082,909 | 52,899,169 | 58,785,101 | 63,350,002 |
| All Other Agencies | 1 69,328,167 | 242,731,013 | 333,496,091 | 831,684,340 |
| **Total All Agencies** | **$34,266,042,884** | **$32,530,326,029** | **$32,922,040,458** | **$38,430,475,826** |

*Totals may not sum due to rounding.*

# Texas Lottery

*Source: Texas Lottery Commission; www.txlottery.org/*

The State Lottery Act was passed by the Texas Legislature in July 1991. Texas voters approved a constitutional amendment authorizing a state lottery in an election on Nov. 5, 1991, by a vote of 1,326,154 to 728,994. Since the first ticket was sold on May 29, 1992, the Texas Lottery® has generated more than $75 billion in total sales and more than $22 billion in revenue for the state. More than $44 billion in prizes have been distributed to players through fiscal year 2014.

Since 1997, the Texas Lottery has contributed more than $17 billion to the Foundation School Fund, which supports public education. Before September 1997, revenues were deposited in the General Revenue Fund.

As authorized by the state Legislature, certain Texas Lottery revenues benefit state programs, including the Fund for Veterans Assistance, which is administered by the Texas Veterans Commission. Sales and unclaimed prizes from the veterans' designated scratch-off games have funded more than $39 million in aid for Texas veterans since the first veterans scratch-off game was launched in November 2009.

Other Texas Lottery funds, such as unclaimed prizes, contribute to other causes and programs as authorized by the Texas Legislature.

**Distribution** of Texas Lottery proceeds for fiscal year 2014:

- 62.5 percent to prizes paid
- 27.5 percent to the Foundation School Fund
- 5.4 percent to retailer commissions
- 4.2 percent for lottery administration
- 0.4 percent to veterans' assistance and other state programs

The Texas Lottery offers players a wide range of games: around 90 scratch-off games per year and nine draw games, including the two multi-state games Mega Millions and Powerball and their add-on features.

**Scratch-off tickets** amounted to 74.8 percent of total lottery sales in Fiscal Year 2014.

The approximate **percentage of sales for draw games** for 2014 were: Lotto Texas (3.1%), Lotto Texas Extra! add-on feature (0.4%), Pick 3 (5.8%), Pick 3 Sum It Up! add-on feature (0.1%) Daily 4 (1.9%), Daily 4 Sum It Up! add-on feature (0.1%), Cash Five (1.2%), Texas Two Step (1.3%), Mega Millions (4.2%), Megaplier add-

## Texas Lottery Financial Data

Start-up to Aug. 31, 2014. All dollar amounts in millions.

| Period | Sales | Value of Prizes Won | Retailer Comm- issions | Admin- istration | Revenue to State of Texas* |
|---|---|---|---|---|---|
| Start-up– FY 1993 | $2,448 | $1,251 | $122 | $170 | $907 |
| FY 1994 | 2,760 | 1,529 | 138 | 167 | 928 |
| FY 1995 | 3,037 | 1,689 | 152 | 188 | 1,015 |
| FY 1996 | 3,432 | 1,951 | 172 | 217 | 1,098 |
| FY 1997 | 3,745 | 2,152 | 187 | 236 | 1,189 |
| FY 1998 | 3,090 | 1,648 | 155 | 198 | 1,098 |
| FY 1999 | 2,572 | 1,329 | 129 | 169 | 953 |
| FY 2000 | 2,657 | 1,509 | 133 | 172 | 863 |
| FY 2001 | 2,825 | 1,643 | 141 | 173 | 864 |
| FY 2002 | 2,966 | 1,715 | 148 | 167 | 929 |
| FY 2003 | 3,131 | 1,845 | 157 | 158 | 949 |
| FY 2004 | 3,488 | 2,069 | 174 | 181 | 1,051 |
| FY 2005 | 3,662 | 2,228 | 183 | 179 | 1,070 |
| FY 2006 | 3,775 | 2,311 | 189 | 185 | 1,090 |
| FY 2007 | 3,774 | 2,315 | 189 | 183 | 1,093 |
| FY 2008 | 3,671 | 2,281 | 184 | 168 | 1,035 |
| FY 2009 | 3,720 | 2,300 | 186 | 192 | 1,062 |
| FY 2010 | 3,738 | 2,300 | 187 | 185 | 1,063 |
| FY 2011 | 3,811 | 2,387 | 191 | 184 | 1,024 |
| FY 2012 | 4,191 | 2,633 | 210 | 169 | 1,156 |
| FY 2013 | 4,376 | 2,767 | 219 | 182 | 1,214 |
| FY 2014 | 4,385 | 2,741 | 220 | 185 | 1,221 |

*Revenue to the state presented on an accrual basis.*

on feature (0.9%), Powerball (4.5%) Power Play add-on feature (0.6%), All or Nothing (1.1%). *Percentages may not total 100 due to rounding.*

The **approximate odds** for winning the jackpot or top prize for each draw game are:

| | |
|---|---|
| Lotto Texas (jackpot) | 1 : 25,827,165 |
| Cash Five (top prize) | 1 : 435,897 |
| All or Nothing (top prize) | 1 : 2,704,156 |
| Texas Two Step (jackpot) | 1 : 1,832,600 |
| Mega Millions (jackpot) | 1 : 258,890,850 |
| Powerball (jackpot) | 1 : 175,223,510 |
| Pick 3 | 1 : 167 – 1 : 1,000 |
| Daily 4 | 1 : 100 – 1 : 10,000 |
| Texas Triple Chance (top prize) | 1 : 1,691,064 ☆ |

*\*\*Texas Triple Chance was introduced in Fiscal Year 2016.*

*Lt. Gov. Dan Patrick presides over the Texas Senate during the May 14, 2015, session. Photo courtesy of the Office of the Lieutenant Governor.*

# Texas Legislature

The Texas Legislature has **181 members: 31 in the Senate** and **150 in the House of Representatives**. Regular sessions convene on the second Tuesday of January in odd-numbered years, but the governor may call special sessions. Article III of the Texas Constitution deals with the legislative branch. On the web: **www.capitol.state.tx.us**.

The following lists are of members of the **84th Legislature**, which convened for its Regular Session on Jan. 13, 2015, and adjourned on June 1, 2015. The **85th Legislature** is scheduled to convene on Jan. 10, 2017, and adjourn May 29, 2017.

## State Senate

**Thirty-one members of the State Senate** are elected to four-year, overlapping terms. Salary: The salary of all members of the Legislature, both Senators and Representatives, is $7,200 per year and $124 per diem during legislative sessions; mileage allowance at same rate provided by law for state employees. The per diem payment applies during each regular and special session of the Legislature.

**Senatorial Districts** include one or more whole counties; some counties have more than one Senator.

The **address of Senators** is Texas Senate, P.O. Box 12068, Austin 78711-2068; phone (512) 463-0200; Fax: 512-463-0326. On the web: **www.senate.state.tx.us**.

**President of the Senate:** Lt. Gov. Dan Patrick; **President Pro Tempore:** Juan (Chuy) Hinojosa; **Secretary of the Senate:** Patsy Spaw; **Sergeant-at-Arms:** Rick DeLeon.

### Texas State Senators

District, Member, Party-Hometown, Occupation

1. Kevin P. Eltife, R-Tyler; businessman.
2. Bob Hall, R-Edgewood; retired military, management.
3. Robert Nichols, R-Jacksonville; engineer.
4. Brandon Creighton, R-Conroe; attorney.
5. Charles Schwertner, R-Georgetown; surgeon.
6. Sylvia R. Garcia, D-Houston; attorney.
7. Paul Bettencourt, R-Houston; tax advisor.
8. Van Taylor, R-Plano; businessman.
9. Kelly G. Hancock, R-North Richland Hills; business owner.
10. Konni Burton, R-Colleyville; small business owner.
11. Larry Taylor, R-Friendswood; insurance agent.
12. Jane Nelson, R-Flower Mound; businesswoman.
13. Rodney Ellis, D-Houston; attorney, investment banker.
14. Kirk Watson, D-Austin; attorney.
15. John Whitmire, D-Houston; attorney (**Dean of the Senate**).
16. Don Huffines, R-Dallas; real estate, finance.
17. Joan Huffman, R-Houston; attorney.
18. Lois W. Kolkhorst, R-Brenham.
19. Carlos I. Uresti, D-San Antonio; attorney.
20. Juan (Chuy) Hinojosa, D-McAllen; attorney.
21. Judith Zaffirini, D-Laredo; communications specialist, former educator.
22. Brian Birdwell, R-Granbury; retired military.
23. Royce West, D-Dallas; attorney.
24. Troy Fraser, R-Horseshoe Bay; businessman.
25. Donna Campbell, R-New Braunfels; physician.
26. José Menéndez, D-San Antonio; businessman.
27. Eddie Lucio Jr., D-Brownsville; advertising executive.
28. Charles Perry, R-Lubbock; land developer.
29. José R. Rodriguez, D-El Paso; former El Paso County attorney.
30. Craig Estes, R-Wichita Falls; state senator.
31. Kel Seliger, R-Amarillo; business owner.

# House of Representatives

This is a list of the 150 members of the House of Representatives in the 84th Legislature. They were elected for two-year terms from the districts shown below. Representatives and senators receive the same salary (see State Senate).

The **address of all Representatives** is House of Representatives, P.O. Box 2910, Austin, 78768-2910; phone: (512) 463-1000; Fax: (512) 463-5896. On the web: **www.house.state.tx.us/**

**Speaker,** Joe Straus III (R-San Antonio). **Speaker Pro Tempore,** Dennis H. Bonnen (R-Angleton). **Chief Clerk,** Robert Haney. **Sergeant-at-Arms,** Rod Welsh.

## Texas State Representatives

### District, Member, Party-Hometown, Occupation

1. Gary VanDeaver, R-New Boston; educator.
2. Dan Flynn, R-Van; attorney, businessman.
3. Cecil Bell Jr., R-Magnolia; general contractor.
4. Stuart Spitzer, R-Kaufman; surgeon.
5. Bryan Hughes, R-Mineola; attorney.
6. Matt Schaefer, R-Tyler; attorney.
7. David Simpson, R-Longview; businessman.
8. Byron Cook, R-Corsicana; businessman, rancher.
9. Chris Paddie, R-Marshall; broadcasting.
10. John Wray, R-Waxahachie; attorney.
11. Travis Clardy, R-Nacogdoches; attorney.
12. Kyle J. Kacal, R-College Station; rancher.
13. Leighton Schubert, R-Caldwell; attorney.
14. John Raney, R-Bryan; small business owner.
15. Mark Keough, R-The Woodlands; pastor, radio host, salesman.
16. Will Metcalf, R-Conroe; bank executive.
17. John Cyrier, R-Lockhart; Sabre Commercial CEO.
18. John C. Otto, R-Dayton; CPA.
19. James White, R-Hillister; educator.
20. Marsha Farney, R-Geogetown; educator.
21. Dade Phelan, R-Beaumont; real estate.
22. Joe Deshotel, D-Beaumont; attorney, businessman.
23. Wayne Faircloth, R-Galveston; insurance.
24. Greg Bonnen, R-Friendswood; neurosurgeon, businessman.
25. Dennis H. Bonnen, R-Angleton; banking.
26. Rick Miller, R-Sugar Land; business.
27. Ron Reynolds, D-Missouri City; attorney.
28. John Zerwas, R-Richmond; physician.
29. Ed Thompson, R-Pearland; business.
30. Geanie W. Morrison, R-Victoria; state representative.
31. Ryan Guillen, D-Rio Grande City; Investor.
32. Todd Hunter, R-Corpus Christi; attorney.
33. Scott Turner, R-Frisco; business.
34. Abel Herrero, D-Corpus Christi; attorney.
35. Oscar Longoria, D-La Joya; attorney.
36. Sergio Muñoz Jr., D-Palmview; attorney.
37. Rene O. Oliveira, D-Brownsville; attorney.
38. Eddie Lucio III, D-Brownsville; attorney.
39. Armando (Mando) Martinez, D-Weslaco; firefighter, paramedic.
40. Terry Canales, D-Edinburg; attorney.
41. Robert (Bobby) Guerra, D-Edinburg; attorney.
42. Richard Peña Raymond, D-Laredo; businessman.
43. J.M. Lozano, D-Kingsville; restauranteur.
44. John Kuempel, R-Seguin; salesman.
45. Jason A. Isaac, R-Dripping Springs; small business owner.
46. Dawnna M. Dukes, D-Austin; business consultant, marketing.

*Speaker Joe Straus of San Antonio has served as speaker since 2009. He represents District 121.*

47. Paul Daniel Workman, R-Austin; commercial contractor.
48. Donna Howard, D-Austin; nursing, public health.
49. Elliott Naishtat, D-Austin; attorney.
50. Celia Israel, D-Austin; real estate.
51. Eddie Rodriguez, D-Austin; state representative.
52. Larry Gonzales, R-Round Rock; owner of graphic design company.
53. Andrew S. Murr, R-Junction; attorney.
54. Jimmie Don Aycock, R-Killeen; veterinarian, rancher.
55. Molly S. White, R-Belton; activist.
56. Charles (Doc) Anderson, R-Waco; veterinarian.
57. Trent Ashby, R-Lufkin; business.
58. DeWayne Burns, R-Cleburne; investment manager.
59. J.D. Sheffield, R-Gatesville; physician.
60. James L. (Jim) Keffer, R-Eastland; businessman.
61. Phil S. King, R-Weatherford; attorney.
62. Larry Phillips, R-Sherman; attorney.
63. Tan Parker, R-Flower Mound; businessman.
64. Myra Crownover, R-Denton; ranching, businesswoman.
65. Ron Simmons, R-Carrollton; business.
66. Matt Shaheen, R-Plano; management consultant.
67. Jeff Leach, R-Plano; attorney.
68. Drew Springer, R-Muenster; financial services.
69. James Frank, R-Wichita Falls; business.
70. Scott Sanford, R-McKinney; CPA.
71. Susan Lewis King, R-Abilene; surgical nurse.
72. Drew Darby, R-San Angelo; attorney, businessman.
73. Doug Miller, R-New Braunfels; insurance agent.
74. Alfonso (Poncho) Nevárez, D-Eagle Pass.
75. Mary E. Gonzalez, D-El Paso; community work; educator.
76. Cesar Blanco, D-El Paso; military service, congressional staffer.
77. Marisa Marquez, D-El Paso; community relations manager.
78. Joe Moody, D-El Paso; attorney.
79. Joseph C. (Joe) Pickett, D-El Paso; real estate.
80. Tracy O. King, D-Batesville; businessman.
81. Brooks Landgraf, R-Odessa; attorney.
82. Tom Craddick, R-Midland; investor, sales representative.

83. Dustin Burrows, R-Lubbock; attorney.
84. John Frullo, R-Lubbock; small business owner.
85. Phil Stephenson, R-Wharton; CPA.
86. John T. Smithee, R-Amarillo; attorney.
87. Four Price, R-Amarillo; attorney.
88. Ken King, R-Canadian; business.
89. Jodie Laubenberg, R-Parker; state representative.
90. Ramon Romero Jr., D-Fort Worth; construction.
91. Stephanie Klick, R-Fort Worth; nurse, health-care consultant.
92. Jonathan Stickland, R-Bedford; business consultant.
93. Matt Krause, R-Fort Worth; attorney.
94 Tony Tinderholt, R-Arlington; educator.
95. Nicole Collier, D-Fort Worth; attorney, business.
96. William (Bill) Zedler, R-Arlington; consultant.
97. Craig Goldman, R-Fort Worth; real estate.
98. Giovanni Capriglione, R-Southlake; finance.
99. Charlie L. Geren, R-Fort Worth; restaurant owner, real estate broker, rancher.
100. Eric Johnson, D-Dallas; attorney.
101. Chris Turner, D-Arlington; public relations consultant.
102. Linda Koop, R-Dallas; retired.
103. Rafael Anchia, D-Dallas; attorney.
104. Roberto R. Alonzo, D-Dallas; attorney.
105. Rodney Anderson, R-Grand Prairie; title insurance company vice president.
106. Pat Fallon, R-Frisco; business.
107. Kenneth Sheets, R-Dallas; attorney.
108. Morgan Meyer, R-Dallas; attorney.
109. Helen Giddings, D-Dallas; small business owner.
110. Toni Rose, D-Dallas; mental health professional.
111. Yvonne Davis, D-Dallas; small business owner.
112. Angie Chen Button, R-Garland; CPA, marketing executive.
113. Cindy Burkett, R-Mesquite; small business owner.
114. Jason Villalba, R-Dallas; probate attorney, businessman.
115. Matt Rinaldi, R-Irving; attorney.
116. Trey Martinez Fischer, D-San Antonio; attorney.
117. Rick Galindo, R-San Antonio; investment management.
118. Joe Farias, D-San Antonio; retired.
119. Roland Gutierrez, D-San Antonio; attorney.
120. Ruth Jones McClendon, D-San Antonio; businesswoman.
121. Joe Straus, R-San Antonio; insurance, investments; Speaker.
122. Lyle Larson, R-San Antonio; small business owner.
123. Diego Bernal, D-San Antonio; attorney.
124. Ina Minjarez , D-San Antonio; former Bexar County prosecutor.
125. Justin Rodriquez, D-San Antonio; attorney, small business owner.
126. Patricia F. Harless, R-Spring; automobile dealer.
127. Dan Huberty, R-Houston; company vice president.
128. Wayne Smith, R-Baytown; civil engineer.
129. Dennis Paul, R-Houston; engineer, businessman.
130. Allen Fletcher, R-Tomball; small business owner.
131. Alma A. Allen, D-Houston; educator.
132. Mike Schofield, R-Katy; attorney.
133. Jim Murphy, R-Houston; commercial real estate.
134. Sarah Davis, R-West University Place; attorney.
135. Gary Elkins, R-Houston; business consultant.
136. Tony Dale, R-Cedar Park; energy consultant.
137. Gene Wu, D-Houston; attorney.
138. Dwayne Bohac, R-Houston; businessman.
139. Sylvester Turner, D-Houston; attorney.
140. Armando Lucio Walle, D-Houston; consultant.
141. Senfronia Thompson, D-Houston; attorney.
142. Harold V. Dutton Jr., D-Houston; attorney.
143. Ana E. Hernandez, D-Houston; attorney.
144. Gilbert Pena, R-Pasadena; retired.
145. Carol Alvarado, D-Houston; small business consultant.
146. Borris L. Miles, D-Houston; insurance agent.
147. Garnet Coleman, D-Houston; business consultant.
148. Jessica Cristina Farrar, D-Houston; architect.
149. Hubert Vo, D-Houston; Realtor, developer.
150. Debbie Riddle, R-Tomball; horse breeder. ☆

*One of many statues on the grounds of the state Capitol. Photo by Ron Billings; Texas A&M Forest Service.*

The Supreme Court of Texas: (seated, left to right) Justice Paul W. Green, Chief Justice Nathan L. Hecht, and Justice Phil Johnson; (standing, left to right) Justice John Phillip Devine, Justice Debra Lehrmann, Justice Don R. Willett, Justice Eva Guzman, Justice Jeffrey S. Boyd, and Justice Jeff Brown. Photo by Osler McCarthy; Texas Supreme Court.

# Texas State Judiciary

The judiciary of the state consists of 9 justices of the Supreme Court of Texas; 9 judges of the Court of Criminal Appeals; 80 justices of the 14 Courts of Appeals; 445 judges of the State District Courts; 13 judges of the Criminal District Courts; 510 County Court judges; 817 Justice Court judges; and 1,288 Municipal Courts judges in 926 cities.

Since 1876, judges at all levels are elected by voters in partisan elections. The **Judicial Campaign Fairness Act** was added to the Texas Election Code in 1995 by the 74th Legislature and limits individual campaign contributions to $5,000 for a statewide judicial office and $1,000–$5,000 for other judicial offices, depending on judicial district population. The exception is law firms, for which a $50 limit is set.

In addition to its system of formal courts, the State of Texas has established 18 **Alternative Dispute Resolution Centers.** The centers are headed by a director and help ease the caseload of Texas courts by using mediation, arbitration, negotiation, and moderated settlement conferences to handle disputes.

Centers are located in Amarillo, Austin, Beaumont, Bryan–College Station, Conroe, Corpus Christi, Dallas, Denton, El Paso, Fort Worth, Houston, Kerrville, Lubbock, Paris, Richmond, San Antonio, San Marcos, and Waco.

(The list of U.S. District Courts in Texas can be found in the Federal Government section, page 551.)

## State Higher Courts

The state's higher courts are listed below and are current as of July 2015. Notations in parentheses are term of office expiration dates. Justices of the Supreme Court, Court of Criminal Appeals, and Courts of Appeals are elected to 6-year, overlapping terms. District Court judges are elected to 4-year terms.

Judicial salaries paid by the state for fiscal year 2013–2014 were: Supreme Court and Court of Criminal Appeals chief justices, $170,500, justices, $168,000; Court of Appeals chief justices, $156,500; justices, $154,000. Court of Appeals justices also may receive additional compensation paid by counties for extra judicial service, not to exceed $9,000 per year.

District Court judges receive $140,000 from the state. They may receive additional compensation paid by counties, not to exceed $18.000 per year.

Below is information on the Supreme Court, Court of Criminal Appeals, and Courts of Appeals, as it appeared on each court's website and in the Texas State Directory, as of July 2015. Elsewhere in this section are lists of District Court judges by district number, district court numbers in each county, and county court judges.

## Supreme Court

**Chief Justice**, Nathan L. Hecht (12/31/20). **Justices**: Paul W. Green (12/31/16); Phil Johnson (12/31/20); Don R. Willett (12/31/18); Eva Guzman (12/31/16); Debra H. Lehrmann (12/31/16); Jeffrey S. Boyd (12/31/20); John Phillip Devine (12/31/18); and Jeff Brown (12/31/16).

**Clerk of Court**, Blake A. Hawthorne. Location of court, Austin. Web: **http://www.txcourts.gov/supreme.**

## Court of Criminal Appeals

**Presiding Judge**, Sharon Keller (12/31/18). **Judges**: Lawrence E. Meyers (12/31/16); Cheryl Johnson (12/31/16); Michael E. Keasler (12/31/18); Elsa Alcala (12/31/18); Barbara Parker Hervey (12/31/18); Bert Richardson (12/31/20); Kevin Patrick Yeary (12/31/20); and David Newell (12/31/20). State Prosecuting Attorney, Lisa C. McMinn.

**Clerk of Court**, Abel Acosta. Location of court, Austin. Web: **http://www.txcourts.gov/cca.**

# Courts of Appeals

These courts have jurisdiction within their respective supreme judicial districts. A constitutional amendment approved in 1978 raised the number of associate justices for Courts of Appeals where needed. Judges are elected from the district for 6-year terms. An amendment adopted in 1980 changed the name of the old Courts of Civil Appeals to the Courts of Appeals and changed the jurisdiction of the courts. Web: **www.courts.state.tx.us/courts/coa.asp.**

**First District — Houston:\*** Chief Justice Sherry Radack (12/31/16). **Justices**: Jane Nenninger Bland (12/31/18); Harvey G. Brown (12/31/18); Laura Carter Higley (12/31/14); Rebeca Huddle (12/31/18); Terry Jennings (12/31/18); Evelyn Keyes (12/31/16); Michael C. Massengale (12/31/18); and Jim Sharp (12/31/14). **Clerk of Court**, Christopher A. Prine. Counties in the First District: Austin, Brazoria, Chambers, Colorado, Fort Bend, Galveston, Grimes, Harris, Waller, Washington.

**Second District — Fort Worth: Chief Justice.** Terrie Livingston (12/31/18). **Justices**: Lee Ann Dauphinot (12/31/18); Lee Gabriel (12/31/14); Anne L. Gardner (12/31/16); Bob McCoy (12/31/18); Bill Meier (12/31/14); and Sue Walker (12/31/18). **Clerk of Court**, Debra Spisak. Counties in Second District: Archer, Clay, Cooke, Denton, Hood, Jack, Montague, Parker, Tarrant, Wichita, Wise, Young.

**Third District — Austin: Chief Justice** J. Woodfin (Woodie) Jones (12/31/14). **Justices**: Scott Field (12/31/18); Melissa Goodwin (12/31/16); Robert H. Pemberton (12/31/18); David Puryear (12/31/18); Jeff L. Rose (12/31/18). **Clerk of Court**, Jeffrey D. Kyle. Counties in the Third District: Bastrop, Bell, Blanco, Burnet, Caldwell, Coke, Comal, Concho, Fayette, Hays, Irion, Lampasas, Lee, Llano, McCulloch, Milam, Mills, Runnels, San Saba, Schleicher, Sterling, Tom Green, Travis, Williamson.

**Fourth District — San Antonio: Chief Justice** Catherine M. Stone (12/31/14). **Justices**: Patricia Alvarez (12/31/18); Karen Angelini (12/31/18); Marialyn Price Barnard (12/31/18); Luz Elena Chapa (12/31/18); Sandee Bryan Marion (12/31/16); and Rebeca C. Martinez (12/31/18). **Clerk of Court**, Keith E. Hottle. Counties in the Fourth District: Atascosa, Bandera, Bexar, Brooks, Dimmit, Duval, Edwards, Frio, Gillespie, Guadalupe, Jim Hogg, Jim Wells, Karnes, Kendall, Kerr, Kimble, Kinney, La Salle, Mason, Maverick, McMullen, Medina, Menard, Real, Starr, Sutton, Uvalde, Val Verde, Webb, Wilson, Zapata, Zavala.

**Fifth District — Dallas: Chief Justice** Carolyn I. Wright (12/31/18). **Justices**: David L. Bridges (12/31/14); David Evans (12/31/18); Molly Meredith Francis (12/31/18); Douglas S. Lang (11/4/18); Elizabeth Lang-Miers (12/31/12); Robert M. Fillmore (12/31/18); David Lewis (12/31/18); Jim A. Moseley (12/31/18); Mary Murphy (12/31/14); Lana R. Myers (12/31/18); Michael J. O'Neill (12/31/18); Martin E. Richter (12/31/12). **Clerk of Court**, Lisa Matz. Counties in the Fifth District: Collin, Dallas, Grayson, Hunt, Kaufman, Rockwall.

**Sixth District — Texarkana: Chief Justice** Josh R. Morris III (12/31/16). **Justices**: Jack Carter (12/31/14); and Bailey C. Moseley (12/31/18). **Clerk of Court**, Debbie Autrey. Counties in the Sixth District: Bowie, Camp, Cass, Delta, Fannin, Franklin, Gregg, Harrison, Hopkins, Hunt, Lamar, Marion, Morris, Panola, Red River, Rusk, Titus, Upshur, Wood.

**Seventh District — Amarillo: Chief Justice** Brian P. Quinn (12/31/14). **Justices**: James T. Campbell (12/31/16); Mackey Hancock (12/31/18); and Patrick A. Pirtle (12/31/18). **Clerk of Court**, Peggy Culp. Counties in the Seventh District: Armstrong, Bailey, Briscoe, Carson, Castro, Childress, Cochran, Collingsworth, Cottle,

Crosby, Dallam, Deaf Smith, Dickens, Donley, Floyd, Foard, Garza, Gray, Hale, Hall, Hansford, Hardeman, Hartley, Hemphill, Hockley, Hutchinson, Kent, King, Lamb, Lipscomb, Lubbock, Lynn, Moore, Motley, Ochiltree, Oldham, Parmer, Potter, Randall, Roberts, Sherman, Swisher, Terry, Wheeler, Wilbarger, Yoakum.

**Eighth District — El Paso: Chief Justice** Ann Crawford McClure (12/31/18). **Justices**: Guadalupe Rivera (12/31/18) and Yvonne Rodriguez (12/31/18). **Clerk of Court**, Denise Pacheco. Counties in the Eighth District: Andrews, Brewster, Crane, Crockett, Culberson, El Paso, Hudspeth, Jeff Davis, Loving, Pecos, Presidio, Reagan, Reeves, Terrell, Upton, Ward, Winkler.

**Ninth District — Beaumont: Chief Justice** Steve McKeithen (12/31/14). **Justices**: David B. Gaultney (12/31/18); Henry Hollis Horton (12/31/18); and Charles Kreger (12/31/16). **Clerk of Court**, Carol Anne Flores. Counties in the Ninth District: Hardin, Jasper, Jefferson, Liberty, Montgomery, Newton, Orange, Polk, San Jacinto, Tyler.

**Tenth District — Waco: Chief Justice** Thomas W. Gray (12/31/18). **Justices**: Rex D. Davis (12/31/14) and Al Scoggins Jr. (12/31/16). **Clerk of Court**, Sharri Roessler. Counties in the Tenth District: Bosque, Brazos, Burleson, Coryell, Ellis, Falls, Freestone, Hamilton, Hill, Johnson, Leon, Limestone, Madison, McLennan, Navarro, Robertson, Somervell, Walker.

**Eleventh District — Eastland: Chief Justice** Jim R. Wright (12/31/18). **Justices**: Terry McCall (12/31/16) and Mike Willson (12/31/18). **Clerk of Court**, Sherry Williamson. Counties in the Eleventh District: Baylor, Borden, Brown, Callahan, Coleman, Comanche, Dawson, Eastland, Ector, Erath, Fisher, Gaines, Glasscock, Haskell, Howard, Jones, Knox, Martin, Midland, Mitchell, Nolan, Palo Pinto, Scurry, Shackelford, Stephens, Stonewall, Taylor, Throckmorton.

**Twelfth District — Tyler: Chief Justice** James T. Worthen (12/31/20). **Justices**: Sam Griffith (12/31/18) and Brian T. Hoyle (12/31/16). **Clerk of Court**, Cathy S. Lusk. Counties in the Twelfth District: Anderson, Angelina, Cherokee, Gregg, Henderson, Houston, Nacogdoches, Rains, Rusk, Sabine, San Augustine, Shelby, Smith, Trinity, Upshur, Van Zandt, Wood.

**Thirteenth District — Corpus Christi**: Chief Justice Rogelio Valdez (12/31/18). **Justices**: Gina M. Benavides (12/31/18); Dori Contreras Garza (12/31/16); Nora Longoria (12/31/18); Greg Perkes (12/31/14); Nelda V. Rodriguez (12/31/18). **Clerk of Court**, Dorian E. Ramirez. Counties in the Thirteenth District: Aransas, Bee, Calhoun, Cameron, DeWitt, Goliad, Gonzales, Hidalgo, Jackson, Kenedy, Kleberg, Lavaca, Live Oak, Matagorda, Nueces, Refugio, San Patricio, Victoria, Wharton, Willacy.

**Fourteenth District—Houston†**: Chief Justice Adele Hedges (12/31/14). **Justices**: William J. Boyce (12/31/18); Jeff Brown (12/31/18); Brett Busby (12/31/18); Tracy E. Christopher (12/31/18); John Donovan (12/31/18); Kem Thompson Frost (12/31/14); Martha Hill Jamison (12/31/18); and Sharon McCally (12/31/16). **Clerk of Court**, Christopher A. Prine. Counties in the Fourteenth District: Austin, Brazoria, Chambers, Colorado, Fort Bend, Galveston, Grimes, Harris, Waller, Washington. ☆

\*The location of the First Court of Appeals was changed from Galveston to Houston by the 55th Legislature, with the provision that all cases originated in Galveston County be tried in that city and with the further provision that any case may, at the discretion of the court, be tried in either city.

†Because of the heavy workload of the Houston area Court of Appeals, the 60th Legislature in 1967 provided for the establishment of a Fourteenth Appeals Court in Houston.

# District Judges in Texas

Below are the names of all district judges in Texas, as of July 2015, listed in district court order. To determine which judges have jurisdiction in specific counties, refer to the table on pages 490–491.

*Sources: Texas Judicial System Directory 2015, Office of Court Administration, and Texas State Directory.*

| Court | Judge | Court | Judge | Court | Judge |
|---|---|---|---|---|---|
| 1 | Craig M. Mixson (R) | 61 | Erin Lunceford | 123 | Charles (Brick) Dickerson (R) |
| 1A | Delinda Gibbs-Walker (R) | 62 | John William (Will) Biard (R) | 124 | F. Alfonso Charles (R) |
| 2 | Dwight L. Phifer (D) | 63 | Enrique Fernandez (D) | 125 | Kyle Carter (D) |
| 3 | Mark A. Calhoon (R) | 64 | Robert W. Kinkaid Jr. (R) | 126 | Darlene Byrne (D) |
| 4 | J. Clay Gossett (D) | 65 | Yahara Lisa Gutierrez (D) | 127 | R.K. Sandill (D) |
| 5 | Bill Miller (R) | 66 | A. Lee Harris (R) | 128 | Courtney Burch-Arkeen (R) |
| 6 | Eric S. Clifford (R) | 67 | Donald J. Cosby (R) | 129 | Michael Paul Gomez (D) |
| 7 | Kerry L. Russell (R) | 68 | Martin J. Hoffman (D) | 130 | Craig Estlinbaum (D) |
| 8 | Eddie Northcutt (R) | 69 | Ronald E. Enns (R) | 131 | John D. Gabriel Jr. (D) |
| 9 | Kelly W. Case (R) | 70 | W. Denn Whalen (R) | 132 | Ernie B. Armstrong (R) |
| 10 | Kerry Lane Neves (R) | 71 | Brad Morin (R) | 133 | Jaclanel McFarland (D) |
| 11 | Mike Miller (D) | 72 | Reuben Gonzales Reyes (R) | 134 | Dale B. Tillery (D) |
| 12 | Donald L. Kraemer (R) | 73 | David A. Canales (D) | 135 | K. Stephen Williams (R) |
| 13 | James E. Lagomarsino (R) | 74 | Gary Coley Jr. (R) | 136 | Milton G. Shuffield (D) |
| 14 | Eric V. Moyé (D) | 75 | Mark A. Morefield (R) | 137 | John (Trey) McClendon (R) |
| 15 | Jim Patrick Fallon (R) | 76 | Kerry (Danny) Woodson (R) | 138 | Arturo Cisneros Nelson (D) |
| 16 | Sherry Shipman (R) | 77 | Patrick (Pat) Simmons (D) | 139 | Jose Roberto Flores (D) |
| 17 | Melody Wilkinson (R) | 78 | W. Bernard Fudge (R) | 140 | Jim Bob Darnell (R) |
| 18 | John Edward Neill (R) | 79 | Richard Clark Terrell (D) | 141 | John Parrish Chupp (R) |
| 19 | Ralph T. Strother (R) | 80 | Larry Weiman (D) | 142 | George (Jody) Gilles (R) |
| 20 | John W. Youngblood (R) | 81 | Donna S. Rayes (D) | 143 | John M. (Mike) Swanson (R) |
| 21 | Carson T. Campbell (R) | 82 | Robert Miller Stem (D) | 144 | Lorina Rummel (R) |
| 22 | Bruce Boyer (R) | 83 | Robert Cadena (D) | 145 | Campbell Cox II (R) |
| 23 | Ben Hardin (R) | 84 | William D. (Bill) Smith (R) | 146 | Jack Jones (R) |
| 24 | Jack W. Marr (R) | 85 | Kyle Hawthorne (R) | 147 | Clifford A. Brown (D) |
| 25 | William D. Old III (R) | 86 | Casey Blaire (R) | 148 | Guy Williams (D) |
| 25A | W.C. (Bud) Kirkendall (R) | 87 | Deborah Oakes Evans (R) | 149 | Terri Tipton Holder (R) |
| 26 | Donna King (R) | 88 | Earl B. Stover III (D) | 150 | Renee Yanta (R) |
| 27 | John Gauntt (R) | 89 | Charles M. Barnard | 151 | Mike Engelhart (D) |
| 28 | Nanette Hasette (D) | 90 | Stephen E. Bristow (R) | 152 | Robert K. Schaffer (D) |
| 29 | Mike Moore (R) | 91 | Steven R. Herod (R) | 153 | Susan McCoy (R) |
| 30 | Robert P. Brotherton (R) | 92 | Luis M. Singleterry (D) | 154 | Felix Klein (R) |
| 31 | Steven R. Emmert (R) | 93 | Rodolfo (Rudy) Delgado (D) | 155 | Jeff Steinhauser (R) |
| 32 | Glen N. Harrison (R) | 94 | Bobby M. Galvan (D) | 156 | Patrick L. Flanigan (R) |
| 33 | J. Allan Garrett (R) | 95 | Ken Molberg (D) | 157 | Randall William Wilson (R) |
| 34 | William E. Moody (D) | 96 | R.H. Wallace Jr. (R) | 158 | Steve Burgess (R) |
| 35 | William Stephen Ellis (D) | 97 | Jack A. McGaughey (R) | 159 | Paul E. White (R) |
| 36 | Starr Bauer (R) | 98 | Rhonda Hurley (D) | 160 | Jim Jordan (D) |
| 37 | Michael Mery (D) | 99 | William Charles Sowder (R) | 161 | John W. Smith (R) |
| 38 | Camile L. DuBose (R) | 100 | Stuart M. Messer (R) | 162 | Phyllis Lister Brown (D) |
| 39 | Shane Hadaway (D) | 101 | Staci Williams (D) | 163 | Dennis Robert Powell (R) |
| 40 | Robert (Bob) J. Carroll (R) | 102 | Bobby Lynn Lockhart (D) | 164 | Alexandra Smoots-Hogan (D) |
| 41 | Anna Perez (D) | 103 | Janet L. Leal (D) | 165 | Debra Ibarra Mayfield (R) |
| 42 | John Wilson Weeks (R) | 104 | Lee Hamilton (R) | 166 | Laura Salinas (D) |
| 43 | Craig Towson (R) | 105 | Jack W. Pulcher (R) | 167 | David Wahlberg (D) |
| 44 | Bonnie Lee Goldstein (D) | 106 | Carter T. Schildknecht (R) | 168 | Marcos A. Lizarraga (D) |
| 45 | Stephani Walsh (R) | 107 | Benjamin Euresti Jr. (D) | 169 | Gordon G. Adams (R) |
| 46 | Dan Mike Bird (D) | 108 | Douglas Woodburn (R) | 170 | Jim Meyer (R) |
| 47 | Daniel Leon Schaap (R) | 109 | Martin B. Muncy (R) | 171 | Bonnie Rangel (D) |
| 48 | David L. Evans (R) | 110 | William Paul Smith (R) | 172 | Donald J. Floyd (D) |
| 49 | Jose A. (Joe) Lopez (D) | 111 | Monica Zapata Notzon (D) | 173 | Willis Daniel Moore (R) |
| 50 | Bobby Burnett | 112 | Pedro (Pete) Gomez Jr. (D) | 174 | Ruben Guerrero (D) |
| 51 | Barbara Lane Walther (R) | 113 | Michael Landrum (R) | 175 | Mary D. Roman (D) |
| 52 | Trent D. Farrell (R) | 114 | Christi Kennedy (R) | 176 | Stacey Bond (D) |
| 53 | Scott H. Jenkins (D) | 115 | Lauren L. Parish (D) | 177 | Ryan Kelly Patrick (R) |
| 54 | Matt Johnson (R) | 116 | Tonya Parker (D) | 178 | David Mendoza (D) |
| 55 | Jeff Shadwick (R) | 117 | Sandra L. Watts (D) | 179 | Kristin M. Guiney (R) |
| 56 | Lonnie Cox (R) | 118 | Timothy D. Yeats (R) | 180 | Catherine V. Evans (R) |
| 57 | Antonia (Toni) Arteaga (D) | 119 | Garland (Ben) Woodward (R) | 181 | John Boyd Board (R) |
| 58 | Kent Walston (D) | 120 | Maria A. Salas-Mendoza (D) | 182 | Jeannine S. Barr (R) |
| 59 | Rayburn (Rim) M. Nall Jr. (R) | 121 | Kelly Glen Moore (R) | 183 | Vanessa Velasquez (R) |
| 60 | James Gary Sanderson (D) | 122 | John A. Ellisor (R) | 184 | Jan Krocker (R) |

| Court | Judge | Court | Judge | Court | Judge |
|---|---|---|---|---|---|
| 185 | Susan Brown (R) | 253 | Chap B. Cain III (R) | 321 | Carole W. Clark (R) |
| 186 | Jefferson Moore (R) | 254 | Susan Rankin | 322 | Nancy L. Berger (R) |
| 187 | Steve Hilbig (R) | 255 | Kim Cooks (D) | 323 | Timothy A. Menikos (R) |
| 188 | David Scott Brabham (R) | 256 | Davis Lopez (D) | 324 | Jerome Scott Hennigan (R) |
| 189 | William R. Burke Jr. (R) | 257 | Judy Lynn Warne (R) | 325 | Judith G. Wells (R) |
| 190 | Patricia J. Kerrigan (R) | 258 | Ernie McClendon (R) | 326 | Paul Rotenberry (R) |
| 191 | Gena Slaughter (D) | 259 | Brooks H. Hagler (R) | 327 | Linda Yee Chew (D) |
| 192 | Craig Smith (D) | 260 | Buddie J. Hahn (D) | 328 | Ronald R. Pope (R) |
| 193 | Carl H. Ginsberg (D) | 261 | Lora J. Livingston (D) | 329 | Randy M. Clapp (D) |
| 194 | Ernest B. White (D) | 262 | Denise Dryer Bradley (R) | 330 | Andrea D. Plumlee (D) |
| 195 | Fred Tinsley (D) | 263 | Jim Wallace (R) | 331 | David F. Crain (D) |
| 196 | Andrew Bench (R) | 264 | Martha Jane Trudo (R) | 332 | Mario E. Ramirez Jr. (D) |
| 197 | Migdalia Lopez (D) | 265 | Jennifer Bennett (D) | 333 | Joseph (Tad) Halbach Jr. (R) |
| 198 | Melvin (Rex) Emerson (R) | 266 | Jason Cameron Cashon (R) | 334 | Grant Dorfman (R) |
| 199 | Angela Michelle Tucker (R) | 267 | Juergen (Skipper) Koetter (R) | 335 | Reva L. Towslee-Corbett (R) |
| 200 | Gisela D. Triana (D) | 268 | Brady Gifford Elliott (R) | 336 | Laurine Jean Blake (R) |
| 201 | Amy Clark-Meachum (D) | 269 | Daniel E. Hinde (R) | 337 | Reneé H. Magee (R) |
| 202 | Leon F. Pesek Jr. (D) | 270 | Brent C. Gamble (R) | 338 | Brock Thomas (R) |
| 203 | Teresa Hawthorne (D) | 271 | John H. Fostel (D) | 339 | Maria T. (Terri) Jackson (D) |
| 204 | Tammy Kemp (D) | 272 | Travis B. Bryan III (R) | 340 | Jay Weatherby (D) |
| 205 | Francisco X. Dominguez (D) | 273 | Charles Ramsey Mitchell (D) | 341 | Rebecca Palomo (D) |
| 206 | Rose Guerra Reyna (D) | 274 | Gary L. Steel (R) | 342 | James Wade Birdwell (R) |
| 207 | Jack Hollis Robison (R) | 275 | Juan R. Partida (D) | 343 | Janna K. Whatley (R) |
| 208 | Denise M. Collins (R) | 276 | Robert M. Rolston (D) | 344 | Randy McDonald (R) |
| 209 | Michael T. McSpadden (R) | 277 | Stacey Mathews (R) | 345 | Stephen A. Yelenosky (D) |
| 210 | Gonzalo Garcia (D) | 278 | Hal R. Ridley (R) | 346 | Angie Juarez Barill (D) |
| 211 | Brody Shanklin (R) | 279 | Jeffrey Randall Shelton (D) | 347 | Mary (Missy) Medary (R) |
| 212 | Patricia V. Grady (R) | 280 | Lynn M. Bradshaw-Hull (R) | 348 | Dana Michelle Womack (R) |
| 213 | Louis E. Sturns (R) | 281 | Sylvia A. Matthews (R) | 349 | Pamela Foster Fletcher (R) |
| 214 | José Longoria (D) | 282 | Amber Givens (D) | 350 | Thomas Michael Wheeler (R) |
| 215 | Elaine H. Palmer (D) | 283 | Rick Magnis (D) | 351 | Mark Kent Ellis (R) |
| 216 | N. Keith Williams (R) | 284 | Cara Cordell Wood (R) | 352 | Grant Dorfman (R) |
| 217 | Robert K. Inselman (R) | 285 | Richard E. Price (R) | 353 | Tim M. Sulak (D) |
| 218 | Russell Wilson (R) | 286 | Jay Michael (Pat) Phelan (R) | 354 | Richard (Rick) Beacom (R) |
| 219 | Scott J. Becker (R) | 287 | Gordon Houston Green (D) | 355 | Ralph H. Walton Jr. (R) |
| 220 | George Philip Robertson (R) | 288 | Solomon (Sol) Casseb III (R) | 356 | Steven Ray Thomas (R) |
| 221 | Lisa Benge Michalk (R) | 289 | Daphne P. Austin (R) | 357 | Juan A. Magallanes (D) |
| 222 | Roland Saul (R) | 290 | Melisa C. Skinner (R) | 358 | Stacy Trotter (R) |
| 223 | Philip N. Vanderpool (R) | 291 | Stephanie Mitchell (D) | 359 | Kathleen A. Hamilton (R) |
| 224 | Cathy Stryker (R) | 292 | Brandon Birmingham (D) | 360 | Michael K. Sinha (R) |
| 225 | Peter Sakai (D) | 293 | Cynthia L. Muniz (D) | 361 | Steven Lee Smith (R) |
| 226 | Sid L. Harle (R) | 294 | Teresa Drum (R) | 362 | R. Bruce McFarling (R) |
| 227 | Kevin M. O'Connell (R) | 295 | Caroline E. Baker (R) | 363 | Tracy F. Holmes (D) |
| 228 | Marc Christopher Carter (R) | 296 | John R. Roach Jr. (R) | 364 | Billy Eichman (R) |
| 229 | Ana Lisa Garza (D) | 297 | David Hagerman (R) | 365 | Amado Jose Abascal III (D) |
| 230 | Bradley (Brad) S. Hart (R) | 298 | Emily G. Tobolowsky (D) | 366 | Raymond (Ray) Wheless (R) |
| 231 | Jesus Nevarez Jr. (R) | 299 | Karen Sage (D) | 367 | Margaret Ellens Barnes (R) |
| 232 | Mary Lou Keel (R) | 300 | K. Randall Hufstetler (R) | 368 | Rick J. Kennon (R) |
| 233 | William Wren Harris (R) | 301 | Mary Brown (D) | 369 | Bascom W. Bentley III (R) |
| 234 | Wesley R. Ward (R) | 302 | Tena T. Callahan (D) | 370 | Noe Gonzalez (D) |
| 235 | Janelle M. Haverkamp (R) | 303 | Dennise Garcia (D) | 371 | Mollee Bennett Westfall (R) |
| 236 | Thomas Wilson Lowe III (R) | 304 | Andrea Martin (D) | 372 | David Scott Wisch (R) |
| 237 | Leslie (Les) F. Hatch (R) | 305 | Cheryl Lee Shannon (D) | 377 | Eli Garza (R) |
| 238 | Elizabeth Byer Leonard (R) | 306 | Anne Darring (R) | 378 | Joe F. Grubbs (R) |
| 239 | Patrick Edward Sebesta (R) | 307 | Tim Womack (D) | 379 | Ron Rangel (D) |
| 240 | Chad Bridges | 308 | James T. Lombardino (R) | 380 | Benjamin N. Smith (R) |
| 241 | Jack M. Skeen Jr. (R) | 309 | Sherill Dean (R) | 381 | Jose Luis Garza (D) |
| 242 | Lowell (Kregg) Hukill (R) | 310 | Lisa Ann Millard (R) | 382 | Brett Hall (R) |
| 243 | Luis Aguilar (D) | 311 | Alicia Franklin (R) | 383 | Mike Herrera (D) |
| 244 | James M. Rush | 312 | David D. Farr (R) | 384 | Patrick Michael Garcia (D) |
| 245 | Roy L. Moore (R) | 313 | Glenn Devlin (R) | 385 | Robin Malone Darr (R) |
| 246 | Charley Prine (R) | 314 | John Franklin Phillips (R) | 386 | Laura Lee Parker (R) |
| 247 | John Schmude (R) | 315 | Michael H. Schneider Jr. (R) | 387 | Brenda Mullinix (R) |
| 248 | Katherine Cabaniss (R) | 316 | James Mosley (R) | 388 | Laura Strathmann (D) |
| 249 | Dennis Wayne Bridewell (R) | 317 | Larry Edward Thorne III (D) | 389 | Leticia (Letty) Lopez (D) |
| 250 | Karin Crump (D) | 318 | David W. Lindemood (R) | 390 | Julie Harris Kocurek (D) |
| 251 | Ana E. Estevez (R) | 319 | David Stith (R) | 391 | Thomas J. Gossett (R) |
| 252 | Raquel West (D) | 320 | Don R. Emerson (R) | 392 | Carter William Tarrance (R) |

| Court | Judge |
|-------|-------|
| 393 | Doug Robison (R) |
| 394 | Roy B. Ferguson (D) |
| 395 | Michael Paul Jergins (R) |
| 396 | George W. Gallagher (R) |
| 397 | Brian Keith Gary (R) |
| 398 | Aida Salinas Flores (D) |
| 399 | Ray J. Olivarri (R) |
| 400 | Maggie Jaramillo (D) |
| 401 | Mark Joseph Rusch (R) |
| 402 | George Timothy Boswell (R) |
| 403 | Brenda P. Kennedy (D) |
| 404 | Elia Cornejo Lopez (D) |
| 405 | Michelle Slaughter (R) |
| 406 | Oscar (O.J.) Hale Jr. (D) |
| 407 | Karen Pozza (D) |
| 408 | Larry E. Noll (D) |
| 409 | Sam Medrano Jr. (D) |
| 410 | K. Michael Mayes (R) |
| 411 | Kaycee L. Jones (R) |
| 412 | W. Edwin Denman (R) |
| 413 | William C. Bosworth Jr. (R) |
| 414 | Vicki Lynn Menard (R) |
| 415 | Graham Quisenberry (R) |
| 416 | John Christopher Oldner (R) |
| 417 | Cynthia M. Wheless (R) |
| 418 | Tracy A. Gilbert (R) |

| Court | Judge |
|-------|-------|
| 419 | Orlinda L. Naranjo (D) |
| 420 | Edwin Allen Klein (R) |
| 421 | Todd Alexander Blomerth (R) |
| 422 | B. Michael Chitty (R) |
| 423 | Chris Duggan (D) |
| 424 | Evan Stubbs (R) |
| 425 | Betsy Lambeth (R) |
| 426 | Fancy H. Jezek (R) |
| 427 | Jim Coronado (D) |
| 428 | William R. (Bill) Henry (R) |
| 429 | Jill R. Willis (R) |
| 430 | Israel Ramon Jr. (D) |
| 431 | Jonathan Mark Bailey (R) |
| 432 | Ruben Gonzalez Jr. (R) |
| 433 | Dibrell (Dib) Waldrip (R) |
| 434 | James H. Shoemake (R) |
| 435 | Michael Thomas Seiler (R) |
| 436 | Lisa Jarrett (R) |
| 437 | Lori I. Valenzuela (R) |
| 438 | Gloria Saldaña (D) |
| 439 | David Rakow (R) |
| 440 | (Effective 1/1/17.) |
| 441 | Rodney W. Satterwhite (R) |
| 442 | Tiffany Haertling (R) |
| 443 | Cindy Ermatinger (R) |
| 444 | David A. Sanchez (D) |

| Court | Judge |
|-------|-------|
| 445 | J. Rolando Olvera (D) |
| 448 | Sergio H. Enriquez (D) |
| 449 | Jesse Contreras (D) |
| 452 | Robert Hofmann (R) |
| 505 | David Perwin |
| 506 | Albert (Buddy) McCaig Jr. (R) |
| 507 | (Effective 1/1/16.) |

| Criminal District Courts | |
|--------------------------|--------------------------|
| Dallas 1 | Robert D. Burns III (D) |
| Dallas 2 | Don Adams (D) |
| Dallas 3 | Gracie Lewis (D) |
| Dallas 4 | Dominique Collins (D) |
| Dallas 5 | Carter Thompson (D) |
| Dallas 6 | Jeanine L. Howard (D) |
| Dallas 7 | Elizabeth Davis Frizell (D) |
| El Paso | Diane Navarette (D) |
| Jefferson | John B. Stevens Jr. (D) |
| Tarrant 1 | Elizabeth Beach (R) |
| Tarrant 2 | Wayne Francis Salvant (R) |
| Tarrant 3 | Robb Caralano (R) |
| Tarrant 4 | Michael R. Thomas (R) |

## Administrative Judicial Districts of Texas

There are **nine administrative judicial districts** in the state for administrative purposes. Presiding Judges are appointed by the Governor and must be active or retired district judges or active or retired appellate judges with judicial experience in a district court. They receive extra compensation of $5,000, paid by counties in the that administrative district.

The Presiding Judge convenes an annual conference of judges in the administrative district to consult on business in the courts and to adopt rules for administering cases in the district.

The Presiding Judge may assign active or retired district judges residing within the administrative district to any of its district courts. The Presiding Judge of one administrative district may request the Presiding Judge of another administrative district to assign a judge from that district to sit in a district court in the requesting Judge's administrative district.

The Chief Justice of the Supreme Court of Texas convenes an annual conference of the nine Presiding Judges to determine the need for assignment of judges and to promote the uniform administration of the assignments. The Chief Justice can assign judges of one administrative district for service in another district.

**First District** — John David Ovard, Dallas (2/1/13): Anderson, Bowie, Camp, Cass, Cherokee, Collin, Dallas, Delta, Ellis, Fannin, Franklin, Grayson, Gregg, Harrison, Henderson, Hopkins, Houston, Hunt, Kaufman, Lamar, Marion, Morris, Nacogdoches, Panola, Rains, Red River, Rockwall, Rusk, Shelby, Smith, Titus, Upshur, Van Zandt, and Wood.

**Second District** — Olen Underwood, Willis (4/3/17): Angelina, Bastrop, Brazoria, Brazos, Burleson, Chambers, Fort Bend, Freestone, Galveston, Grimes, Hardin, Harris, Jasper, Jefferson, Lee, Leon, Liberty, Limestone, Madison, Matagorda, Montgomery, Newton, Orange, Polk, Robertson, Sabine, San Augustine, San Jacinto, Trinity, Tyler, Walker, Waller, Washington, and Wharton.

**Third District** — Billy Ray Stubblefield, Georgetown (2/3/14): Austin, Bell, Blanco, Bosque, Burnet, Caldwell, Colorado, Comal, Comanche, Coryell, Falls, Fayette, Gonzales, Guadalupe, Hamilton, Hays, Hill, Johnson, Lampasas, Lavaca, Llano, McLennan, Mason, Milam, Navarro, San Saba, Travis, and Williamson.

**Fourth District** — David Peeples, San Antonio (10/8/16): Aransas, Atascosa, Bee, Bexar, Calhoun, DeWitt, Dimmit, Frio, Goliad, Jackson, Karnes, LaSalle, Live Oak, Maverick, McMullen, Refugio, San Patricio, Victoria, Webb, Wilson, Zapata, and Zavala.

**Fifth District** — J. Rolando Olvera, Brownsville (12/31/14): Brooks, Cameron, Duval, Hidalgo, Jim Hogg, Jim Wells, Kenedy, Kleberg, Nueces, Starr and Willacy.

**Sixth District** — Stephen Ables, Kerrville (12/31/16): Bandera, Brewster, Crockett, Culberson, Edwards, El Paso, Gillespie, Hudspeth, Jeff Davis, Kendall, Kerr, Kimble, Kinney, Mason, Medina, Pecos, Presidio, Reagan, Real, Sutton, Terrell, Upton, Uvalde, and Val Verde.

**Seventh District** — Dean Rucker, Midland (12/31/14): Andrews, Borden, Brown, Callahan, Coke, Coleman, Concho, Crane, Dawson, Ector, Fisher, Gaines, Garza, Glasscock, Haskell, Howard, Irion, Jones, Kent, Loving, Lynn, Martin, McCulloch, Menard, Midland, Mills, Mitchell, Nolan, Reeves, Runnels, Schleicher, Scurry, Shackelford, Sterling, Stonewall, Taylor, Throckmorton, Tom Green, Ward, and Winkler.

**Eighth District** — Roger Walker, Fort Worth (12/31/14): Archer, Clay, Cooke, Denton, Eastland, Erath, Hood, Jack, Johnson, Montague, Palo Pinto, Parker, Somervell, Stephens, Tarrant, Wichita, Wise, and Young.

**Ninth District** — Kelly G. Moore, Brownfield (12/31/16): Armstrong, Bailey, Baylor, Briscoe, Carson, Castro, Childress, Cochran, Collingsworth, Cottle, Crosby, Dallam, Deaf Smith, Dickens, Donley, Floyd, Foard, Gray, Hale, Hall, Hansford, Hardeman, Hartley, Hemphill, Hockley, Hutchinson, King, Knox, Lamb, Lipscomb, Lubbock, Moore, Motley, Ochiltree, Oldham, Parmer, Potter, Randall, Roberts, Sherman, Swisher, Terry, Wheeler, Wilbarger and Yoakum. ☆

# Texas Courts by County

Below are listed the state district court or courts, court of appeals district, administrative judicial district, and U.S. judicial district for each county in Texas as of July 2015. For the names of the district court judges, see table by district number on page 487. Lists of other judges in the Texas court system begin on page 485.

| County | State Dist. Court(s) | Ct. of App'ls Dist | Adm. Jud. Dist | U.S. Jud. Dist. |
|---|---|---|---|---|
| Anderson | 3, 87, 349, 369 | 12 | 1 | E-Tyler |
| Andrews | 109 | 8 | 7 | W-Midland |
| Angelina | 159, 217 | 12 | 2 | E-Lufkin |
| Aransas | 36, 156, 343 | 13 | 4 | S-C.Christi |
| Archer | 97 | 2 | 8 | N-W. Falls |
| Armstrong | 47 | 7 | 9 | N-Amarilllo |
| Atascosa | 81, 218 | 4 | 4 | W-San Ant. |
| Austin | 155 | 1, 14 | 3 | S-Houston |
| Bailey | 287 | 7 | 9 | N-Lubbock |
| Bandera | 216 | 4 | 6 | W-San Ant. |
| Bastrop | 21, 335, 423 | 3 | 2 | W-Austin |
| Baylor | 50 | 11 | 9 | N-W. Falls |
| Bee | 36, 156, 343 | 13 | 4 | S-C.Christi |
| Bell | 27, 146, 169, 264, 426 | 3 | 3 | W-Waco |
| Bexar | 37, 45, 57, 73, 131, 144, 150, 166, 175, 186, 187, 224, 225, 226, 227, 285, 288, 289, 290, 379, 386, 399, 407, 408, 436, 437, 438 | 4 | 4 | W-San Ant. |
| Blanco | 33, 424 | 3 | 3 | W-Austin |
| Borden | 132 | 11 | 7 | N-Lubbock |
| Bosque | 220 | 10 | 3 | W-Waco |
| Bowie | 5, 102, 202 | 6 | 1 | E-Texark. |
| Brazoria | 23, 149, 239, 300, 412 | 1, 14 | 2 | S-Galves. |
| Brazos | 85, 272, 361 | 10 | 2 | S-Houston |
| Brewster | 394 | 8 | 6 | W-Pecos |
| Briscoe | 110 | 7 | 9 | N-Amarilllo |
| Brooks | 79 | 4 | 5 | S-C.Christi |
| Brown | 35 | 11 | 7 | N-S. Angelo |
| Burleson | 21, 335 | 10 | 2 | W-Austin |
| Burnet | 33, 424 | 3 | 3 | W-Austin |
| Caldwell | 22, 207, 421 | 3 | 3 | W-Austin |
| Calhoun | 24, 135, 267 | 13 | 4 | S-Victoria |
| Callahan | 42 | 11 | 7 | N-Abilene |
| Cameron | 103, 107, 138, 197, 357, 404, 444, 445 | 13 | 5 | S-Brownsville |
| Camp | 76, 276 | 6 | 1 | E-Marshall |
| Carson | 100 | 7 | 9 | N-Amarilllo |
| Cass | 5 | 6 | 1 | E-Marshall |
| Castro | 64, 242 | 7 | 9 | N-Amarilllo |
| Chambers | 253, 344 | 1, 14 | 2 | S-Galves. |
| Cherokee | 2, 369 | 12 | 1 | E-Tyler |
| Childress | 100 | 7 | 9 | N-Amarilllo |
| Clay | 97 | 2 | 8 | N-W. Falls |
| Cochran | 286 | 7 | 9 | N-Lubbock |
| Coke | 51 | 3 | 7 | N-S. Angelo |
| Coleman | 42 | 11 | 7 | N-S. Angelo |
| Collin | 199, 219, 296, 366, 380, 401, 416, 417, 429 | 5 | 1 | E-Sherman |
| Collingsworth | 100 | 7 | 9 | N-Amarilllo |
| Colorado | 25, 25-A | 1, 14 | 3 | S-Houston |
| Comal | 22, 207, 274, 433 | 3 | 3 | W-San Ant. |
| Comanche | 220 | 11 | 3 | N-Ft. Worth |
| Concho | 119 | 3 | 7 | N-S. Angelo |
| Cooke | 235 | 2 | 8 | E-Sherman |
| Coryell | 52, 440 | 10 | 3 | W-Waco |
| Cottle | 50 | 7 | 9 | N-W. Falls |
| Crane | 109 | 8 | 7 | W-Midland |
| Crockett | 112 | 8 | 6 | N-S. Angelo |
| Crosby | 72 | 7 | 9 | N-Lubbock |
| Culberson | 205, 394 | 8 | 6 | W-Pecos |
| Dallam | 69 | 7 | 9 | N-Amarilllo |
| Dallas | 14, 44, 68, 95, 101, 116, 134, 160, 162, 191, 192, 193, 194,195, 203, 204, 254, 255, 256, 265, 282, 283, 291, 292, 298, 301, 302, 303 304, 305, 330, 363, Cr. 1, Cr. 2, Cr. 3, Cr. 4, Cr. 5, Cr. 6, Cr. 7, | 5 | 1 | N-Dallas |
| Dawson | 106 | 11 | 7 | N-Lubbock |
| Deaf Smith | 222 | 7 | 9 | N-Amarillo |
| Delta | 8, 62 | 6 | 1 | E-Sherman |
| Denton | 16, 158, 211, 362, 367, 393, 431 | 2 | 8 | E-Sherman |
| DeWitt | 24, 135, 267 | 13 | 4 | S-Victoria |
| Dickens | 110 | 7 | 9 | N-Lubbock |
| Dimmit | 293, 365 | 4 | 4 | W-San Ant. |
| Donley | 100 | 7 | 9 | N-Amarilllo |
| Duval | 229 | 4 | 5 | S-C.Christi |
| Eastland | 91 | 11 | 8 | N-Abilene |
| Ector | 70, 161, 244, 358 | 11 | 7 | W-Midland |
| Edwards | 63 | 4 | 6 | W-Del Rio |
| Ellis | 40, 378 | 10 | 1 | N-Dallas |
| El Paso | 34, 41, 65, 120, 168, 171, 205, 210, 243, 327, 346, 383, 384, 388, 409, 448, Cr. 1 | 8 | 6 | W-El Paso |
| Erath | 266 | 11 | 8 | N-Ft. Worth |
| Falls | 82 | 10 | 3 | W-Waco |
| Fannin | 336 | 6 | 1 | E-Sherman |
| Fayette | 155 | 3 | 3 | S-Houston |
| Fisher | 32 | 11 | 7 | N-Abilene |
| Floyd | 110 | 7 | 9 | N-Lubbock |
| Foard | 46 | 7 | 9 | N-W. Falls |
| Fort Bend | 240, 268, 328, 387, 400, 434 | 1, 14 | 2 | S-Houston |
| Franklin | 8, 62 | 6 | 1 | E-Texark. |
| Freestone | 77, 87 | 10 | 2 | W-Waco |
| Frio | 81, 218 | 4 | 4 | W-San Ant. |
| Gaines | 106 | 11 | 7 | N-Lubbock |
| Galveston | 10, 56, 122, 212, 306, 405 | 1, 14 | 2 | S-Galves. |
| Garza | 106 | 7 | 7 | N-Lubbock |
| Gillespie | 216 | 4 | 6 | W-Austin |
| Glasscock | 118 | 11 | 7 | N-S. Angelo |
| Goliad | 24, 135, 267 | 13 | 4 | S-Victoria |
| Gonzales | 25, 25-A | 13 | 3 | W-San Ant. |
| Gray | 31, 223 | 7 | 9 | N-Amarilllo |
| Grayson | 15, 59, 397 | 5 | 1 | E-Sherman |
| Gregg | 124, 188, 307 | 6, 12 | 1 | E-Tyler |
| Grimes | 12, 506 | 1, 14 | 2 | S-Houston |
| Guadalupe | 25, 25-A, 274 | 4 | 3 | W-San Ant. |
| Hale | 64, 242 | 7 | 9 | N-Lubbock |
| Hall | 100 | 7 | 9 | N-Amarilllo |
| Hamilton | 220 | 10 | 3 | W-Waco |
| Hansford | 84 | 7 | 9 | N-Amarilllo |
| Hardeman | 46 | 7 | 9 | N-W. Falls |
| Hardin | 88, 356 | 9 | 2 | E-B'mont. |
| Harris | 11, 55, 61, 80, 113, 125, 127, 129, 133, 151, 152, 157, 164, 165, 174, 176, 177, 178, 179, 180, 182, 183, 184, 185, 189, 190, 208, 209, 215, 228, 230, 232, 234, 245, 246, 247, 248, 257, 262, 263, 269, 270, 280, 281, 295, 308, 309, 310, 311, 312, 313, 314, 315, 333, 334, 337, 338, 339, 351 | 1, 14 | 2 | S-Houston |
| Harrison | 71 | 6 | 1 | E-Marshall |
| Hartley | 69 | 7 | 9 | N-Amarilllo |
| Haskell | 39 | 11 | 7 | N-Abilene |
| Hays | 22, 207, 274, 428 | 3 | 3 | W-Austin |
| Hemphill | 31 | 7 | 9 | N-Amarilllo |
| Henderson | 3, 173, 392 | 12 | 1 | E-Tyler |
| Hidalgo | 92, 93, 139, 206, 275, 332, 370, 389, 398, 430, 449 | 13 | 5 | S-McAllen |
| Hill | 66 | 10 | 3 | W-Waco |
| Hockley | 286 | 7 | 9 | N-Lubbock |
| Hood | 355 | 2 | 8 | N-Ft. Worth |
| Hopkins | 8, 62 | 6 | 1 | E-Sherman |

| County | State Dist. Court(s) | Ct. of App'ls Dist | Adm. Jud. Dist | U.S. Jud. Dist. |
|---|---|---|---|---|
| Houston | 3, 349 | 12 | 1 | E-Lufkin |
| Howard | 118 | 11 | 7 | N-Abilene |
| Hudspeth | 205, 394 | 8 | 6 | W-Pecos |
| Hunt | 196, 354 | 5, 6 | 1 | N-Dallas |
| Hutchinson | 84, 316 | 7 | 9 | N-Amarilllo |
| Irion | 51 | 3 | 7 | N-S. Angelo |
| Jack | 271 | 2 | 8 | N-Ft. Worth |
| Jackson | 24, 135, 267 | 13 | 4 | S-Victoria |
| Jasper | 1, 1-A | 9 | 2 | E-B'mont. |
| Jeff Davis | 394 | 8 | 6 | W-Pecos |
| Jefferson | 58, 60, 136, 172, 252, 279, 317, Cr. 1 | 9 | 2 | E-B'mont. |
| Jim Hogg | 229 | 4 | 5 | S-Laredo |
| Jim Wells | 79 | 4 | 5 | S-C.Christi |
| Johnson | 18, 249, 413 | 10 | 8 | N-Dallas |
| Jones | 259 | 11 | 7 | N-Abilene |
| Karnes | 81, 218 | 4 | 4 | W-San Ant. |
| Kaufman | 86, 422 | 5 | 1 | N-Dallas |
| Kendall | 216 | 4 | 6 | W-San Ant. |
| Kenedy | 105 | 13 | 5 | S-C.Christi |
| Kent | 39 | 7 | 7 | N-Lubbock |
| Kerr | 198, 216 | 4 | 6 | W-San Ant. |
| Kimble | 198 | 4 | 6 | W-Austin |
| King | 50 | 7 | 9 | N-W. Falls |
| Kinney | 63 | 4 | 6 | W-Del Rio |
| Kleberg | 105 | 13 | 5 | S-C.Christi |
| Knox | 50 | 11 | 9 | N-W. Falls |
| Lamar | 6, 62 | 6 | 1 | E-Sherman |
| Lamb | 154 | 7 | 9 | N-Lubbock |
| Lampasas | 27 | 3 | 3 | W-Austin |
| La Salle | 81, 218 | 4 | 4 | S-Laredo |
| Lavaca | 25, 25-A | 13 | 3 | S-Victoria |
| Lee | 21, 335 | 3 | 2 | W-Austin |
| Leon | 12, 87, 278 | 10 | 2 | W-Waco |
| Liberty | 75, 253 | 9 | 2 | E-B'mont. |
| Limestone | 77, 87 | 10 | 2 | W-Waco |
| Lipscomb | 31 | 7 | 9 | N-Amarilllo |
| Live Oak | 36, 156, 343 | 13 | 4 | S-C.Christi |
| Llano | 33, 424 | 3 | 3 | W-Austin |
| Loving | 143 | 8 | 7 | W-Pecos |
| Lubbock | 72, 99, 137, 140, 237, 364 | 7 | 9 | N-Lubbock |
| Lynn | 106 | 7 | 7 | N-Lubbock |
| Madison | 12, 278 | 10 | 2 | S-Houston |
| Marion | 115, 276 | 6 | 1 | E-Marshall |
| Martin | 118 | 11 | 7 | W-Midland |
| Mason | 198 | 4 | 6 | W-Austin |
| Matagorda | 23, 130 | 13 | 2 | S-Galves. |
| Maverick | 293, 365 | 4 | 4 | W-Del Rio |
| McCulloch | 198 | 3 | 7 | W-Austin |
| McLennan | 19, 54, 74, 170, 414 | 10 | 3 | W-Waco |
| McMullen | 36, 156, 343 | 4 | 4 | S-Laredo |
| Medina | 38 | 4 | 6 | W-San Ant. |
| Menard | 198 | 4 | 7 | N-S. Angelo |
| Midland | 142, 238, 318, 385, 441 | 11 | 7 | W-Midland |
| Milam | 20 | 3 | 3 | W-Waco |
| Mills | 35 | 3 | 7 | N-S. Angelo |
| Mitchell | 32 | 11 | 7 | N-Abilene |
| Montague | 97 | 2 | 8 | N-W. Falls |
| Montgomery | 9, 221, 284, 359, 410, 418, 435 | 9 | 2 | S-Houston |
| Moore | 69 | 7 | 9 | N-Amarillo |
| Morris | 76, 276 | 6 | 1 | E-Marshall |
| Motley | 110 | 7 | 9 | N-Lubbock |
| Nacogdoches | 145, 420 | 12 | 1 | E-Lufkin |
| Navarro | 13 | 10 | 3 | N-Dallas |
| Newton | 1, 1-A | 9 | 2 | E-B'mont. |
| Nolan | 32 | 11 | 7 | N-Abilene |
| Nueces | 28, 94, 105, 117, 148, 214, 319, 347 | 13 | 5 | S-C.Christi |
| Ochiltree | 84 | 7 | 9 | N-Amarillo |
| Oldham | 222 | 7 | 9 | N-Amarillo |
| Orange | 128, 163, 260 | 9 | 2 | E-B'mont. |
| Palo Pinto | 29 | 11 | 8 | N-Ft. Worth |
| Panola | 123 | 6 | 1 | E-Tyler |
| Parker | 43, 415 | 2 | 8 | N-Ft. Worth |
| Parmer | 287 | 7 | 9 | N-Amarillo |
| Pecos | 83, 112 | 8 | 6 | W-Pecos |
| Polk | 258, 411 | 9 | 2 | E-Lufkin |

| County | State Dist. Court(s) | Ct. of App'ls Dist | Adm. Jud. Dist | U.S. Jud. Dist. |
|---|---|---|---|---|
| Potter | 47, 108, 181, 251, 320 | 7 | 9 | N-Amarilllo |
| Presidio | 394 | 8 | 6 | W-Pecos |
| Rains | 8, 354 | 12 | 1 | E-Tyler |
| Randall | 47, 181, 251 | 7 | 9 | N-Amarillo |
| Reagan | 112 | 8 | 6 | N-S. Angelo |
| Real | 38 | 4 | 6 | W-San Ant. |
| Red River | 6, 102 | 6 | 1 | E-Texark. |
| Reeves | 143 | 8 | 7 | W-Pecos |
| Refugio | 24, 135, 267 | 13 | 4 | S-Victoria |
| Roberts | 31 | 7 | 9 | N-Amarilllo |
| Robertson | 82 | 10 | 2 | W-Waco |
| Rockwall | 382, 439 | 5 | 1 | N-Dallas |
| Runnels | 119 | 3 | 7 | N-S. Angelo |
| Rusk | 4 | 6, 12 | 1 | E-Tyler |
| Sabine | 1, 273 | 12 | 2 | E-Lufkin |
| San Augustine | 1, 273 | 12 | 2 | E-Lufkin |
| San Jacinto | 258, 411 | 9 | 2 | S-Houston |
| San Patricio | 36, 156, 343 | 13 | 4 | S-C.Christi |
| San Saba | 33, 424 | 3 | 3 | W-Austin |
| Schleicher | 51 | 3 | 7 | N-S. Angelo |
| Scurry | 132 | 11 | 7 | N-Lubbock |
| Shackelford | 259 | 11 | 7 | N-Abilene |
| Shelby | 123, 273 | 12 | 1 | E-Lufkin |
| Sherman | 69 | 7 | 9 | N-Amarilllo |
| Smith | 7, 114, 241, 321 | 12 | 1 | E-Tyler |
| Somervell | 18, 249 | 10 | 8 | W-Waco |
| Starr | 229, 381 | 4 | 5 | S-McAllen |
| Stephens | 90 | 11 | 8 | N-Abilene |
| Sterling | 51 | 3 | 7 | N-S. Angelo |
| Stonewall | 39 | 11 | 7 | N-Abilene |
| Sutton | 112 | 4 | 6 | N-S. Angelo |
| Swisher | 64, 242 | 7 | 9 | N-Amarilllo |
| Tarrant | 17, 48, 67, 96, 141, 153, 213, 231, 233, 236, 297, 322, 323, 324, 325, 342, 348, 352, 360, 371, 372, 396, 432, Cr. 1, Cr. 2, Cr. 3, Cr. 4 | 2 | 8 | N-Ft. Worth |
| Taylor | 42, 104, 326, 350 | 11 | 7 | N-Abilene |
| Terrell | 63, 83 | 8 | 6 | W-Del Rio |
| Terry | 121 | 7 | 9 | N-Lubbock |
| Throckmorton | 39 | 11 | 7 | N-Abilene |
| Titus | 76, 276 | 6 | 1 | E-Texark. |
| Tom Green | 51, 119, 340, 391 | 3 | 7 | N-S. Angelo |
| Travis | 53, 98, 126, 147, 167, 200, 201, 250, 261, 299, 331, 345, 353, 390, 403, 419, 427 | 3 | 3 | W-Austin |
| Trinity | 258, 411 | 12 | 2 | E-Lufkin |
| Tyler | 1-A, 88 | 9 | 2 | E-Lufkin |
| Upshur | 115 | 6, 12 | 1 | E-Marshall |
| Upton | 112 | 8 | 6 | W-Midland |
| Uvalde | 38 | 4 | 6 | W-Del Rio |
| Val Verde | 63, 83 | 4 | 6 | W-Del Rio |
| Van Zandt | 294 | 12 | 1 | E-Tyler |
| Victoria | 24, 135, 267, 377 | 13 | 4 | S-Victoria |
| Walker | 12, 278 | 10 | 2 | S-Houston |
| Waller | 155, 506 | 1, 14 | 2 | S-Houston |
| Ward | 143 | 8 | 7 | W-Pecos |
| Washington | 21, 335 | 1, 14 | 2 | W-Austin |
| Webb | 49, 111, 341, 406 | 4 | 4 | S-Laredo |
| Wharton | 23, 329 | 13 | 2 | S-Houston |
| Wheeler | 31 | 7 | 9 | N-Amarilllo |
| Wichita | 30, 78, 89 | 2 | 8 | N-W. Falls |
| Wilbarger | 46 | 7 | 9 | N-W. Falls |
| Willacy | 197 | 13 | 5 | S-Brownsville |
| Williamson | 26, 277, 368, 395, 425 | 3 | 3 | W-Austin |
| Wilson | 81, 218 | 4 | 4 | W-San Ant. |
| Winkler | 109 | 8 | 7 | W-Pecos |
| Wise | 271 | 2 | 8 | N-Ft. Worth |
| Wood | 402 | 6, 12 | 1 | E-Tyler |
| Yoakum | 121 | 7 | 9 | N-Lubbock |
| Young | 90 | 2 | 8 | N-W. Falls |
| Zapata | 49 | 4 | 4 | S-Laredo |
| Zavala | 293, 365 | 4 | 4 | W-Del Rio |

# Texas State Agencies

On the following pages is information about several of the many state agencies in Texas. Information was supplied to the Texas Almanac by the agencies, their websites, and from news reports. The web address for more information about state agencies, boards, and commissions is: www.tsl.state.tx.us/apps/lrs/agencies/.

## Texas Commission on Environmental Quality

*Source: Texas Commission on Environmental Quality; www.tceq.texas.gov*

The Texas Commission on Environmental Quality (TCEQ) is the state's leading environmental agency. Known as the Texas Natural Resource Conservation Commission until September 2002, it works to protect Texas' human and natural resources in a manner consistent with sustainable economic development.

The TCEQ has about 2,700 employees; of those, about 800 work in the 16 regional offices. The **operating budget** for the 2014 fiscal year was $379.1 million, of which 84 percent ($317.7 million) was generated by program fees. The remaining revenues came from federal funds ($41.3 million or 11 percent); state general revenue ($11.5 million or 3 percent); and other sources ($9.2 million or 2 percent).

One of the TCEQ's major functions is issuing permits and other authorizations for the control of **air pollution**, the safe operation of **water and wastewater utilities,** and the management of **hazardous and nonhazardous waste.** More than 120,000 environmental permit applications are received annually.

The agency promotes voluntary compliance with environmental laws through pollution prevention programs, regulatory workshops, and assistance to businesses and local governments. But when environmental laws are violated, the TCEQ has the authority to levy penalties as much as $25,000 a day per violation for administrative cases. In a typical year, the agency conducts more than 100,000 investigations at regulated entities for compliance with state and federal laws, and receives about 6,500 complaints.

In fiscal year 2014, the TCEQ issued 1,708 administrative orders and collected stipulated penalties for two additional orders, which yielded $10.1 million in fines, and directed another $2.6 million to supplemental environmental projects benefiting some of the communities in which the environmental violations occurred. Divisions of the TCEQ include:

### Air Quality

Texas is home to some of the largest U.S. cities, with several metropolitan populations of greater than 1 million people. With these concentrated populations, vehicular traffic and other emissions can create air quality among the most challenging in the country.

The state has a fast-growing population, a large industrial base concentrated along the Gulf Coast, and a rapidly growing oil and gas industry expanding throughout much of the state. The TCEQ conducts survey activities along with targeted and/or specialized monitoring activities to **evaluate changing air quality conditions** across the state.

The TCEQ measures air quality across the state for compliance with federal standards, as well as for localized compounds of concern. Texas' air toxic monitoring network is the most comprehensive in the country with over 80 monitoring sites located across the state.

The TCEQ is responsible for developing a state implementation plan to bring metropolitan areas into compliance with federal air quality standards, such as the ozone standard. The leading areas of concern for ozone issues are the areas og Houston-Galveston-Brazoria and Dallas–Fort Worth.

### Water Quality

The TCEQ preserves and improves the quality of the state's **surface waters** by establishing surface water quality standards; monitoring, assessing, and reporting conditions; and implementing plans to reduce pollution and improve water quality. It protects surface water users through the water rights permitting process and the Watermaster programs.

The TCEQ is responsible for most state and federal regulatory programs that protect **groundwater,** administers permits for the discharge of **wastewater** and **stormwater,** and conducts 401 federal permit certifications.

The agency enforces the federal Safe Drinking Water Act, oversees the protection of the state's approximately 7,000 public water systems that provide drinking water to roughly 27 million customers, and has general supervision of water districts.

### Waste Management

Waste management projects at the TCEQ include **Superfund projects, pesticide collections, and waste tire recycling.** In 2014, there were 113 Superfund sites in the state and federal Superfund programs. Another major clean-up program focuses on **leaking petroleum storage tanks.** As of 2014, more than 25,332 such sites were corrected, and work continues at another 1,600 sites.

The TCEQ also issues permits and other authorizations for municipal and industrial waste management, including **landfills and storage, processing, and recycling operations.** In addition, the safe recycling of both municipal and industrial waste streams is encouraged.

The TCEQ also regulates the **disposal of radioactive material,** with the exception of naturally occurring radioactive material (NORM) generated as a result of oil and gas exploration. This includes the regulation of the receipt, processing, storage, and disposal of by-product and low-level radioactive waste, the licensing of uranium and thorium recovery facilities, permitting for underground injection control, and legacy radioactive material disposal sites.

### Help With Understanding Environmental Rules

The TCEQ offers services to anyone interested in environmental stewardship and navigating TCEQ's programs and regulatory requirements. Staff members host workshops on recycling and disposal opportunities, and on regulatory and pollution prevention topics. The TCEQ also offers free compliance assistance to thousands of small businesses and local governments each year. Contact the TCEQ at PO Box 13087, Austin, 78711; (512) 239-1000; www.tceq.texas.gov. ☆

# Health and Human Services Commission

Source: Texas Health and Human Services Commission; www.hhs.state.tx.us

The Texas Health and Human Services Commission (HHSC) is the oversight agency for the state's health and human services system. HHSC also administers state and federal programs that provide financial, health, and social services to Texans.

In 2003, the 78th Texas Legislature mandated an unprecedented transformation of the state's health and human services system to create an integrated, effective, and accessible health and human services enterprise that protects public health and brings high-quality services and support to Texans in need. The transformation blended 12 agencies into five, creating a system that is client-centered, efficient in its use of public resources, and focused on accountability.

The Health and Human Services Commission coordinates administrative functions across the system, determines eligibility for its programs, and administers Medicaid, the Children's Health Insurance Program, Temporary Assistance for Needy Families, SNAP food benefits (formerly know as food stamps), and family violence, disaster assistance, and refugee resettlement programs.

The HHSC executive commissioner is Chris Traylor. The executive commissioner is appointed by the governor and confirmed by the Senate.

The state's health and human services agencies spend more than $25 billion per year to administer more than 200 programs, employ more than 55,000 state workers, and operate from more than 1,000 locations. The four agencies under the oversight of HHSC are:

**The Department of Family and Protective Services** includes child and adult protective services, childcare licensing, and child abuse prevention, and early intervention services.

**The Department of Assistive and Rehabilitative Services** provides rehabilitation services, including vocational rehabilitation and independent living programs; disability determination services; services for the blind, visually impaired, deaf and hard of hearing; and early childhood intervention services.

**The Department of Aging and Disability Services** is responsible for aging services; community-based services and state-supported living centers for people with cognitive and development disabilities; community care programs for people with disabilities; and inspection of nursing homes and other long-term care facilities.

**The Department of State Health Services** includes public health programs, such as immunizations, bioterrorism preparedness, and state laboratory services; Kidney Health Care program; Children with Special Health Care Needs; Women, Infants & Children (WIC); mental health services; substance abuse services; and regulatory services for a variety of health care professionals, facilities, and consumer health protection.

| AGENCY BUDGETS FOR THE 2016–2017 BIENNIUM | |
|---|---|
| Department of Aging and Disability Services | $8.8 billion |
| Department of Assistive and Rehabilitative Services | $1 billion |
| Department of Family and Protective Services | $3.5 billion |
| Department of State Health Services | $6.4 billion |
| Health and Human Services Commission | $56.6 billion |

## Other HHSC programs

**The Family Violence program** offers emergency shelter and services to victims and their children.

**The Disaster Assistance program** processes grant applications for victims of presidentially declared disasters, such as tornados, floods, and hurricanes.

**The Refugee Resettlement program** is federally funded and provides cash, health care, and social services to eligible refugees to help them quickly become self-sufficient after arriving in the United States. ☆

## Major HHSC Programs at a Glance

The **Medicaid** program provides healthcare coverage for one out of every three children in Texas, pays for half of all births and accounts for 25 percent of the state's total budget. In 2010, an average of 3.3 million Texans received healthcare coverage through Medicaid.

The **Children's Health Insurance Program (CHIP)** is designed for families who earn too much money to qualify for Medicaid, yet cannot afford private insurance.

The **Temporary Assistance for Needy Families (TANF)** program provides basic financial assistance for needy children and the parents or caretakers with whom they live. As a condition of eligibility, caretakers must sign and abide by a personal-responsibility agreement. Time limits for benefits have been set by both state and federal welfare-reform legislation.

**SNAP food benefits,** formerly known as food stamps, is a federally funded program that assists low-income families, the elderly, and single adults obtain a nutritionally adequate diet. Those eligible for food benefits include households receiving TANF or federal Supplemental Security Income benefits, and non-public assistance households having incomes below 130 percent of the poverty level. In 2011, more than 3.5 million Texans received SNAP food benefits, and the average monthly benefit amount was about $300.

Both SNAP and TANF benefits are delivered via the electronic benefit transfer (EBT) system, through which clients access benefits at about 12,000 retail locations statewide with the Lone Star card.

Information about Medicaid, CHIP, and other health and human services programs can be found at www.hhsc.state.tx.us, www.211texas.org, or by calling 2-1-1, a toll-free local resource for information on health and human service programs.

# The General Land Office

Source: General Land Office of Texas.  On the Web: www.glo.state.tx.us

## History of the General Land Office

The Texas General Land Office (GLO) is one of the oldest governmental entities in the state, dating back to the Republic of Texas. The first General Land Office was **established in 1836 by the Republic's constitution,** and the first Texas Congress enacted the provision into law in 1837. The GLO was established to oversee distribution of public lands, register titles, issue patents on land, and maintain records of land granted.

In the early years of statehood, beginning in 1845, Texas established the precedent of using its vast public domain for public benefit. The first use was to sell or trade land to **eliminate the huge debt** remaining from Texas' War for Independence and the early years of the Republic.

Texas also gave away land to **settlers** as homesteads; to **veterans** as compensation for service; for internal **improvements,** including building railroads, shipbuilding, and improving rivers for navigation; and to build the state **Capitol.**

The **public domain was closed in 1898** when the Texas Supreme Court declared there was no more vacant and unappropriated land in Texas. In 1900, all remaining unappropriated land was set aside by the Legislature to benefit public schools.

Today, 19.9 million acres of land and minerals, owned by the **Permanent School Fund,** the **Permanent University Fund,** various other state agencies, and the **Veterans Land Board,** are managed by the General Land Office and the Commissioner of the Texas General Land Office. This includes over 4 million acres of **submerged coastal lands,** which consist of bays, inlets, and the area from the Texas shoreline to the three-marine-league line (10.36 miles) in the Gulf of Mexico. It is estimated that more than 1 million acres make up the public domain of the state's riverbeds and another 1.7 million acres as excess lands belonging to the Permanent School Fund.

The General Land Office is the **steward of the Texas Gulf Coast,** serving as the premier state agency for protecting and renourishing the coast and fighting coastal erosion. In 1999, the Legislature created the Coastal Erosion Planning and Response Act and put the GLO in charge of facilitating restoration and preservation of eroding beaches, dunes, wetlands, and other bay shorelines along the Texas coast.

The Permanent University Fund holds title to 2.1 million fee acres, and other state agencies and special schools hold title to another 2.3 million acres. The Permanent School Fund owns mineral rights alone in almost 7.4 million acres covered under the Relinquishment Act, the Free Royalty Act, and the various sales acts, and it has outright ownership to about 747,522 upland acres, mostly west of the Pecos River.

## Texas Veterans Land Board Programs

The Veterans Land Board (VLB) was formally established by the Legislature to administer benefits for Texas Veterans in 1946 with the first loan made in 1949. Since then, the programs have evolved to include low-interest

| Historic Distribution of the Public Lands of Texas | |
| --- | --- |
| **PURPOSE** | **ACRES** |
| Settlers | **68,027,108** |
| Spain and Mexico | 24,583,923 |
| Spanish and Mexican Grants south of the Nueces River, recognized by Act of Feb. 10, 1852 | 3,741,241 |
| Headrights | 30,360,002 |
| Republic colonies | 4,494,806 |
| Preemption land | 4,847,136 |
| **Military** | **9,874,262** |
| Bounty | 5,354,250 |
| Battle donations | 1,162,240 |
| Veterans donations | 1,377,920 |
| Confederate | 1,979,852 |
| **Improvements** | **37,155,714** |
| Road | 27,716 |
| Navigation | 4,261,760 |
| Irrigation | 584,000 |
| Ships | 17,000 |
| Manufacturing | 111,360 |
| Railroads | 32,153,878 |
| **Education** | **52,329,168** |
| University, public school and eleemosynary institutions | 52,329,168 |
| **Total of distributed lands.** | **167,386,252** |

land, housing, and home improvement loans. VLB has funded more than 220,000 loans amounting to more than $11 billion in for Texas Veterans, military members, and their families since its inception.

VLB strives to offer the best benefits program in the nation and is works to ensure that Texas veterans are aware of these benefits. VLB equips veterans with opportunities to build wealth through land and home ownership, while also serving the needs of veterans through VLB State Veterans Homes and Cemeteries.

In a joint effort with the Texas Veterans Commission, the VLB operates the Texas Veterans Call Service Center to connect veterans, military members, and their families with the benefits and services they need. For more information, contact VLB at 1-800-252-VETS (8387) or www.TexasVeterans.com.

### Texas State Veterans Homes

In 1997, the 75th Legislature approved legislation authorizing the Veterans Land Board to construct and operate Texas State Veterans Homes under a cost-sharing program with the U.S. Department of Veterans Affairs. The homes provide affordable, quality, long-term care for Texas' veterans.

### Texas State Veterans Cemeteries

The Veterans Land Board owns and operates several cemeteries under USDVA guidelines. The USDVA funds the design and construction of the cemeteries, but the land must be donated.

For more information on any of these veterans programs, call 1-800-252-VETS (8387), or visit the Texas Veterans Land Board Web site at www.glo.texas.gov/vlb/index.html.

### Voices of Veterans Oral History Program

The Voices of Veterans oral history program seeks to record the stories of Texas veterans and archive the transcripts in the Office of Veterans Records for future researchers and historians. Any veteran interested in including his or her story in the Voices of Veterans program should contact the Veterans Land Board at 1-800-252-VETS. ☆

## Texas Historical Commission

The Texas Historical Commission protects and preserves the state's historic and prehistoric resources. The Texas State Legislature established the Texas State Historical Survey Committee in 1953 to identify important historic sites across the state.

The Texas Legislature changed the agency's name to the Texas Historical Commission in 1973 and increased its mission and its protective powers. Today the agency's concerns include archaeology, architecture, community heritage development, historic sites, history programs, education. The commission:

• Works with communities and individuals to help identify important historic resources and develop a plan to preserve them.

• Provides leadership and training to county historical commissions, heritage organizations, and museums in Texas' 254 counties.

• Helps protect Texas' diverse architectural heritage, including historic county courthouses.

• Partners with communities to stimulate tourism and economic development.

• Assists Texas cities in the revitalization of their historic downtowns through the Texas Main Street Program.

• Administers the state's historical marker program, which has around 15,000 markers across the state.

• Consults with citizens and groups to nominate properties as Recorded Texas Historic Landmarks, State Archeological Landmarks, and to the National Register of Historic Places.

• Operates 20 state historic sites including house museums, military forts, and archeological sites.

• Works with property owners to save archeological sites on private land and ensures archeological sites are protected as land is developed for highways and other public construction projects.

Mailing address: PO Box 12276, Austin 78711-2276; (512) 463-6100; www.thc.state.tx.us.

## Railroad Commission of Texas

The Railroad Commission of Texas has primary regulatory jurisdiction over the oil and natural gas industry, pipeline transporters, the natural gas and hazardous liquid pipeline industry, natural gas utilities, the liquefied petroleum gas (LP-gas) industry, rail industry, and coal and uranium surface mining operations. It also promotes the use of LP-gas as an alternative fuel in Texas through research and education.

The commission exercises its statutory responsibilities under provisions of the Texas Constitution, the Texas Natural Resources Code, the Texas Water Code, the Texas Utilities Code, the Coal and Uranium Surface Mining and Reclamation Acts, the Pipeline Safety Acts, and the Railroad Safety Act.

The commission has regulatory and enforcement responsibilities under federal law, including the Federal Railroad Safety Act, the Local Rail Freight Assistance Act, the Surface Coal Mining Control and Reclamation Act, Safe Drinking Water Act, the Pipeline Safety Acts, the Resource Conservation Recovery Act, and the Clean Water Act.

The Railroad Commission was established by the Texas Legislature in 1891 and given jurisdiction over rates and operations of railroads, terminals, wharves and express companies. In 1917, the legislature declared pipelines to be common carriers and gave the commission regulatory authority over them. It was also given the responsibility to administer conservation laws relating to oil and natural gas production.

The Railroad Commission exists to protect the environment, public safety, and the rights of mineral interest owners; to prevent waste of natural resources, and to assure fair and equitable utility rates in those industries over which it has authority. Mailing address: PO Box 12967, Austin 78711-2967; (512) 463-7288; www.rrc.state.tx.us.

## Texas Department of Juvenile Justice

The Texas Department of Juvenile Justice was created on Dec. 1, 2011, by Senate Bill 653, 82nd Legislature. Its creation abolished both the Texas Youth Commission and the Texas Juvenile Probation Commission.

The agency's executive director is Mike Griffiths, and it has a 13-member commission who are appointed to six-year terms. It is chaired by Scott Fisher of Bedford.

The Texas Youth Commission had operated correctional facilities and halfway houses for serious youth offenders. In 2007, widespread sexual and physical abuse was uncovered at many of its facilities. After a number of supervisors were dismissed, the entire TYC board resigned on March 15, 2007, and their powers were transferred to a conservator. The 80th Texas Legislature approved a bill to overhaul the troubled agency.

The Texas Department of Juvenile Justice is a unified state juvenile justice agency that works in partnership with local county governments, courts, and communities to promote public safety by providing services to youth from initial contact through end of supervision. Its expressed goals are to:

• Support development of county-based programs and services for youth and families that reduce the need for out-of-home placement;

• Seek alternatives to placing youthful offenders in secure state facilities, while also addressing treatment of youth and protecting the public;

• Locate facilities as geographically close as possible to workforce and other services, and support youths' connection to their families;

• Encourage regional and county collaboration;

• Enhance the continuity of care throughout the juvenile justice system; and

• Use secure facilities of a size that supports effective youth rehabilitation and public safety.

The agency is located at Braker H Complex, 11209 Metric Blvd., Austin 78758. Mailing Address: PO Box 12757, Austin 78711-2757; (512) 490-7717; www.tjjd.texas.gov.

## Texas Workforce Commission

The Texas Workforce Commission (TWC) is the state government agency charged with overseeing and providing workforce development services to employers and job seekers of Texas.

For employers, TWC offers recruiting, retention, training and retraining, outplacement services and information on labor law and labor market statistics.

For job seekers, TWC offers career development information, job search resources, training programs, and, as appropriate, unemployment benefits. While targeted populations receive intensive assistance to overcome barriers to employment, all Texans can benefit from the services offered by TWC and our network of workforce partners.

The Texas Workforce Commission is part of a local and state network dedicated to developing the workforce of Texas. The network is composed of the statewide efforts of the commission coupled with planning and service provision on a regional level by 28 local workforce boards. This network gives customers access to local workforce solutions and statewide services in a single location—Texas Workforce Centers.

Primary services of the Texas Workforce Commission and our network partners are funded by federal tax revenue and are generally free to all Texans. Mailing address: 101 E. 15th Street, Austin 78778; (512) 463-2222; www.twc.state.tx.us. ☆

# Texas Department of Criminal Justice

Source: Texas Department of Criminal Justice. On the Web: www.tdcj.state.tx.us

The Texas Board of Criminal Justice is composed of nine non-salaried members who are appointed by the governor for staggered six-year terms. The board employs the Texas Department of Criminal Justice (TDCJ) executive director, sets rules and policies that guide the agency, and considers other agency actions at its meetings.

Board members serve in a separate capacity as the Board of Trustees for the **Windham School District** by hiring a superintendent and providing similar oversight. The Windham School District is a separate entity primarily funded through the Texas Education Agency (TEA).

In addition to hiring the TDCJ executive director, the board appoints an inspector general, a director of internal audits, a director of state counsel for offenders, and a prison rape elimination act ombudsman.

The TDCJ executive director is responsible for the administration and enforcement of statutes relative to the criminal justice system.

The Correctional Institutions Division, Private Facility Contract Monitoring and Oversight Division, Parole Division, and Community Justice Assistance Division are most involved in the everyday confinement and supervision of convicted felons.

The actual supervision of probationers is the responsibility of local community supervision and corrections departments. Victim Services coordinates a central mechanism for crime victims to participate in the criminal justice process.

Below is a description of the primary divisions of the TDCJ:

**The Correctional Institutions Division (CID)** is responsible for the confinement of adult felony and state jail offenders who are sentenced to incarceration in a secure state-operated correctional facility.

**Private Facility Contract Monitoring and Oversight Division** is responsible for oversight and monitoring contracts for privately operated secure facilities, as well as community-based facilities, which include substance abuse treatment services.

The **Parole Division** supervises all offenders released on parole or mandatory supervision; conducts release and transition planning; and verifies compliance with statutory provisions of release.

In addition, this division contracts for electronic monitoring and processing responses to violations, administers programs and services through District Resource Centers and Parole Offices, and coordinates the Interstate Compact for Adult Offender Supervision.

**The Community Justice Assistance Division (CJAD)** administers community supervision, also known as adult probation in Texas. CJAD is responsible for the distribution of formula and grant funds; the development of standards, including best-practice treatment standards; approval of Community Justice Plans and budgets; conducting program and fiscal audits; and providing training and certification of community supervision officers.

## INMATE PROFILE
### As of Fiscal Year 2014

| SEX – ETHNICITY – AGE | |
|---|---|
| Male: 91.9% | Hispanic: 33.1% |
| Black: 34.7% | Other: 0.5% |
| White: 31.7% | Average age: 38.3 |

| AVERAGE SENTENCES | |
|---|---|
| Prison: 19.2 years | State jail: 1 year |

| AVERAGE PART OF SENTENCE SERVED | |
|---|---|
| Prison: 58.1% | State jail: 99.4% |

Based on offenders released in Fiscal Year 2014.

| EDUCATION | |
|---|---|
| Average IQ | 90.9 |
| Average education achievement score | 7.99 |
| Percent lacking high school diploma or GED: | 40.9% |

## ON-HAND POPULATION
### As of Aug. 31, 2014

| PRISONERS | |
|---|---|
| Prison | 136,460 |
| State Jails | 10,524 |
| SAFP (Substance Abuse) | 3,377 |
| **TOTAL:** | **150,361** |

Includes 10,509 housed in privately operated facilities.

| PAROLE | |
|---|---|
| Mandatory Supervision Population | 87,455 |

| PROBATION | |
|---|---|
| Felony and Misdemeanor | 391,479 |

Total Adults on Direct, Indirect, and Pretrial Supvervision, minus transfers

The remaining divisions support the overall operation of the TDCJ. These include:

Office of the General Counsel
Administrative Review and Risk Management
Business and Finance
Information Technology
Manufacturing and Logistics
Facilities
Rehabilitation Programs
Re-entry and Integration Programs
Health Services and Human Resources ☆

# Correctional Institutions Division

The town listed is the nearest one to the facility, although the unit may actually be in another county. For instance, the Middleton Transfer Facility is in Jones County, but the nearest city is Abilene, which is in Taylor County. Data is current as of Aug. 31, 2014. **SAFPF** = Substance Abuse Felony Punishment Facilities; **DDP** = Developmentally Disabled Program.

| COUNTY | UNIT | NEAREST TOWN | INMATES | GENDER | EMPLOYEES | TYPE |
|---|---|---|---|---|---|---|
| Anderson | Beto | Tennessee Colony | 3,422 | Male | 552 | Prison |
| Anderson | Coffield | Tennessee Colony | 4,106 | Male | 785 | Prison |
| Anderson | Gurney | Tennessee Colony | 1,944 | Male | 365 | Transfer Facility |
| Anderson | Michael | Tennessee Colony | 3,254 | Male | 715 | Prison |
| Anderson | Powledge | Palestine | 1,125 | Male | 247 | Prison |
| Angelina | Diboll | Diboll | 431 | Male | 120 | Private Prison |
| Angelina | Duncan | Diboll | 541 | Male | 129 | Geriatric |
| Bee | Garza East | Beeville | 2,306 | Male | 388 | Transfer Facility |
| Bee | Garza West | Beeville | 2,109 | Male | 426 | Transfer Facility |
| Bee | McConnell | Beeville | 2,732 | Male | 524 | Prison |
| Bexar | Dominguez | San Antonio | 2,128 | Male | 329 | State Jail |
| Bowie | Telford | New Boston | 2,790 | Male | 616 | Prison |
| Brazoria | C.T. Terrell | Rosharon | 1,582 | Male | 391 | Prison |
| Brazoria | Clemens | Brazoria | 1,127 | Male | 289 | Prison |
| Brazoria | Darrington | Rosharon | 1,867 | Male | 495 | Prison |
| Brazoria | Ramsey | Rosharon | 1,698 | Male | 384 | Prison |
| Brazoria | Scott | Angleton | 1,062 | Male | 275 | Prison |
| Brazoria | Stringfellow | Rosharon | 1,148 | Male | 285 | Prison |
| Brazos | Hamilton | Bryan | 1,080 | Male | 236 | Pre-Release |
| Brown | Havins | Brownwood | 577 | Male | 148 | Pre-Release |
| Burnet | Halbert | Burnet | 584 | Female | 126 | SAFPF |
| Caldwell | Lockhart | Lockhart | 498 | Female | 79 | Private Prison/ Work Program |
| Caldwell | Lockhart PPT | Lockhart | 500 | Male | 79 | Private Pre-Parole Transfer |
| Cherokee | Hodge | Rusk | 930 | Male | 304 | DDP |
| Cherokee | Skyview | Rusk | 65 425 | Female Male | 295 | Psychiatric |
| Childress | Roach | Childress | 1,440 | Male | 341 | Prison |
| Coryell | Crain | Gatesville | 1,990 | Female | 653 | Prison |
| Coryell | Hilltop | Gatesville | 519 | Female | 241 | Prison |
| Coryell | Hughes | Gatesville | 1 2,792 | Female Male | 676 | Prison |
| Coryell | Mountain View | Gatesville | 626 | Female | 279 | Prison |
| Coryell | Murray | Gatesville | 1,307 | Female | 326 | Prison |
| Coryell | Woodman | Gatesville | 875 | Female | 227 | State Jail |
| Dallas | Hutchins | Dallas | 2,200 | Male | 349 | State Jail |
| Dawson | Smith | Lamesa | 1,711 | Male | 351 | Prison |
| DeWitt | Stevenson | Cuero | 1,382 | Male | 249 | Prison |
| Duvall | Glossbrenner | San Diego | 420 | Male | 116 | SAFPF |
| El Paso | Sanchez | El Paso | 970 | Male | 261 | State Jail |
| Falls | Hobby | Marlin | 1,363 | Female | 238 | Prison |
| Falls | Marlin | Marlin | 552 | Female | 111 | Transfer Facility |
| Fannin | C. Moore | Bonham | 1,178 | Male | 223 | Transfer Facility |
| Fannin | Cole | Bonham | 849 | Male | 202 | State Jail |
| Fort Bend | Jester I | Richmond | 301 | Male | 101 | SAFPF |
| Fort Bend | Jester III | Richmond | 1,085 | Male | 252 | Prison |
| Fort Bend | Jester IV | Richmond | 5 493 | Female Male | 339 | Psychiatric |
| Fort Bend | Vance | Richmond | 328 | Male | 101 | Prison |
| Freestone | Boyd | Fairfield | 1,336 | Male | 253 | Prison |
| Frio | Briscoe | Dilley | 1,369 | Male | 255 | Prison |

The Milam County Jail opened in 1895. It is now a museum operated by the Milam County Historical Commission. Photo by Ron Billings; Texas A&M Forest Service.

| COUNTY | UNIT | NEAREST TOWN | INMATES | GENDER | EMPLOYEES | TYPE |
|---|---|---|---|---|---|---|
| Galveston | Hospital Galveston | Galveston | 17<br>120 | Female<br>Male | 323 | Medical |
| Galveston | Young | Galveston | 315<br>109 | Female<br>Male | 200 | Medical |
| Gray | Jordan | Pampa | 1.397 | Male | 267 | Prison |
| Grimes | Luther | Navasota | 1,247 | Male | 270 | Prison |
| Grimes | Pack | Navasota | 1,459 | Male | 291 | Prison |
| Hale | Formby | Plainview | 1,008 | Male | 245 | State Jail |
| Hale | Wheeler | Plainview | 520 | Male | 118 | State Jail |
| Harris | Kegans | Houston | 595 | Male | 148 | State Jail |
| Harris | Lychner | Humble | 2,145 | Male | 358 | State Jail |
| Hartley | Dalhart | Dalhart | 1,385 | Male | 219 | Prison |
| Hays | Kyle | Kyle | 519 | Male | 103 | Private Prison |
| Henderson | East Texas Treatment | Henderson | 43<br>687 | Female<br>Male | 447 | Multi-Use |
| Hidalgo | Lopez | Edinburg | 1,026 | Male | 227 | State Jail |
| Hidalgo | Segovia | Edinburg | 1,177 | Male | 210 | Pre-Release |
| Houston | Eastham | Lovelady | 2,427 | Male | 617 | Prison |
| Jack | Lindsey | Jacksboro | 979 | Male | 161 | Private State Jail |
| Jasper | Goodman | Jasper | 577 | Male | 140 | Transfer Facility |
| Jefferson | Gist | Beaumont | 2,094 | Male | 298 | State Jail |
| Jefferson | Leblanc | Beaumont | 1,197 | Male | 228 | Pre-Release |
| Jefferson | Stiles | Beaumont | 2,925 | Male | 651 | Prison |
| Johnson | Estes | Venus | 1,040 | Male | 200 | Private Prison |
| Jones | Middleton | Abilene | 2,100 | Male | 436 | Transfer Facility |
| Jones | Robertson | Abilene | 2,966 | Male | 669 | Prison |
| Karnes | Connally | Kenedy | 2,113 | Male | 524 | Prison |
| La Salle | Cotulla | Cotulla | 583 | Male | 100 | Transfer Facility |
| Liberty | Cleveland | Cleveland | 516 | Male | 116 | Private Prison |
| Liberty | Henley | Dayton | 509 | Female | 105 | State Jail |
| Liberty | Hightower | Dayton | 1,371 | Male | 292 | Prison |

| COUNTY | UNIT | NEAREST TOWN | INMATES | GENDER | EMPLOYEES | TYPE |
|--------|------|--------------|---------|--------|-----------|------|
| Liberty | Plane | Dayton | 2,149 | Female | 345 | State Jail |
| Lubbock | Montford | Lubbock | 945 | Male | 455 | Psychiatric |
| Madison | Ferguson | Midway | 2,357 | Male | 591 | Prison |
| Medina | Ney | Hondo | 544 | Male | 122 | State Jail |
| Medina | Torres | Hondo | 1,371 | Male | 250 | Prison |
| Mitchell | Wallace | Colorado City | 1,414 | Male | 229 | Prison |
| Mitchell | Ware | Colorado City | 479 | Male | 131 | Transfer Facility |
| Pecos | Fort Stockton | Fort Stockson | 581 | Male | 108 | Transfer Facility |
| Pecos | Lynaugh | Fort Stockton | 1,410 | Male | 263 | Prison |
| Polk | Polunsky | Livingston | 2,965 | Male | 657 | Prison |
| Potter | Clements | Amarillo | 3,748 | Male | 948 | Prison |
| Potter | Neal | Amarillo | 1,712 | Male | 328 | Prison |
| Rusk | B. Moore | Overton | 500 | Male | 94 | Private Prison |
| Rusk | Bradshaw | Henderson | 1,963 | Male | 221 | Private State Jail |
| San Saba | San Saba | San Saba | 550 | Male | 119 | Transfer Facility |
| Scurry | Daniel | Snyder | 1,344 | Male | 258 | Prison |
| Stephens | Sayle | Breckenridge | 562 | Male | 133 | SAFPF |
| Swisher | Tulia | Tulia | 579 | Male | 125 | Transfer Facility |
| Terry | Rudd | Brownfield | 579 | Male | 125 | Transfer Facility |
| Travis | Travis County | Austin | 1,017 | Male | 240 | State Jail |
| Tyler | Lewis | Woodville | 2,179 | Male | 513 | Prison |
| Walker | Byrd | Huntsville | 1,235 | Male | 261 | Prison |
| Walker | Ellis | Huntsville | 2,431 | Male | 536 | Prison |
| Walker | Estelle | Huntsville | 3,107 | Male | 830 | Prison |
| Walker | Goree | Huntsville | 47 953 | Female Male | 316 | Prison |
| Walker | Holliday | Huntsville | 2,116 | Male | 389 | Transfer Facility |
| Walker | Huntsville | Huntsville | 1,573 | Male | 388 | Prison |
| Walker | Wynne | Huntsville | 2,596 | Male | 547 | Prison |
| Wichita | Allred | Iowa Park | 3,648 | Male | 815 | Prison |
| Willacy | Willacy County | Raymondville | 1,069 | Male | 134 | Private State Jail |
| Williamson | Bartlett | Bartlett | 1,045 | Male | 161 | Private State Jail |
| Wise | Bridgeport | Bridgeport | 520 | Male | 103 | Private Prison |
| Wise | Bridgeport PPT | Bridgeport | 199 | Female | 54 | Private Pre-Parole Transfer |
| Wood | Johnston | Winnsboro | 585 | Male | 156 | SAFPF |

## TEXAS' 12 OLDEST PRISONS

| UNIT | COUNTY | DATE ESTABLISHED | TYPE |
|------|--------|------------------|------|
| Huntsville | Walker | 1849 | Prison |
| Wynne | Walker | 1883 | Prison |
| Jester I | Fort Bend | 1885 | SAFPF |
| Vance | Fort Bend | 1885 | Prison |
| Clemens | Brazoria | 1893 | Prison |
| Goree | Walker | 1907 | Prison |
| Ramsey | Brazoria | 1908 | Prison |
| Stringfellow | Brazoria | 1908 | Prison |
| Darrington | Brazoria | 1917 | Prison |
| Eastham | Houston | 1917 | Prison |
| Scott | Brazoria | 1919 | Prison |
| Ferguson | Madison | 1962 | Prison |

*In 2011, the state closed the Central Unit in Fort Bend County, which had opened in 1909.*

# Texas State Boards and Commissions

Following is a list of appointees to state boards and commissions, as well as names of other state officials, revised to **July 15, 2015**. Information includes, where available, (1) date of creation; (2) whether the position is elective or appointive; (3) length of term; (4) compensation, if any; (5) number of members; (6) names of appointees, their hometowns, and expiration of terms. In some instances the date of term expiration has passed; in such cases, no new appointment had been made by press time, and the official is continuing to fill the position until a successor is named. Most positions marked "apptv." are appointed by the Governor. Where otherwise, appointing authority is given. Most advisory boards are not listed. Salaries for commissioners and administrators are those that were authorized by the appropriations bill passed by the 83rd Legislature for the 2014–2015 biennium. They are "not-to-exceed" salaries: maximum authorized salaries for the positions. Actual salaries may be less than those stated here.

**Accountancy, Texas State Board of Public** – (1945 with 2-yr. terms; reorganized 1959 as 9-member board with 6-yr. overlapping terms; number of members increased to 12 in 1979; increased to 15 in 1989; per diem and expenses: Chair Thomas G. Prothro, Tyler (1/31/15); J. Coalter Baker, Austin (1/31/17); John R. Broaddus, El Paso (1/31/17); Jonathan B. Cluck, Fair Oaks Ranch (1/31/17); Rocky L. Duckworth, Houston (1/31/17); Everett R. Ferguson, Abilene (1/31/15); James C. Flagg, College Station (1/31/15); Susan Fletcher, Fisco (1/31/19); Donna J. Hugly, Addison (1/31/19); William Lawrence, Highland Village (1/31/19); Robert M. McAdams, San Antonio (1/31/19); Maribess L. Miller, Dallas (1/31/15); Steve D. Peña, Georgetown (1/31/19); Phillip W. Worley, Hebbronville (1/31/17). Exec. Dir. William Treacy ($127,308), 333 Guadalupe, Ste. 3-900, Austin 78701-3900; (512) 305-7800.

**Acupuncture Examiners, Texas State Board of** – (1993); apptv.; 6-yr.; per diem; 9 members: Chair Allen Cline, Austin (1/31/19); Rodrigo Ceballos, El Paso (1/31/19); Suehing (Sue) Chiang, Sugar Land (1/31/19); Linda Wynn Drain, Lucas (1/31/15); Raymond J. Graham, Dallas (1/31/17); KarenJingyu Gu, Austin (1/31/15); Karen Siegel, Houston (1/31/17); Rachelle Webb, Austin (1/31/19); Rey Ximenes, Austin (1/31/15). Exec. Dir. Mari Robinson, 333 Guadalupe, Tower III, #610, Austin 78768; (512) 305-7010. *Consumer Complaints: (800) 201-9353.*

**Ad Valorem Tax Rate, Board to Calculate the** – Est. 1907 with 3 ex-officio members: Governor, State Comptroller of Public Accounts, and State Treasurer; consolidated in 1973 with State Tax Board; abolished by 66th Legislature (SB 621, which created the Property Tax Code, effective 1/1/82, and replaced by the Texas State Property Tax Board.

**Adjutant General's Dept.** – (1836 by Republic of Texas; present office established 1905); apptv.; 2-yr.; 3 members: Adjutant General, Major Gen. John F. Nichols, Spring Branch (2/1/16); ($139,140); Assistant for Army, William (Len) Smith, Austin; Assistant for Air, Brig. Gen. Kenneth Wisian, Weatherford. Assistants each serve a term at the pleasure of the Gov.; c/o Camp Mabry, PO Box 5218, Austin 78763-5218; (512) 782-5001.

**Administrative Hearings, State Office of** – Created in 1991 by 72nd Leg.; apptv.; 2-yr.; 1 member: Chief Admin. Law Judge Cathleen Parsley ($122,500). William P. Clements Building, 300 W. 15th St., Ste. 504, Austin 78701; (512) 475-4993.

**Administrative Judicial Districts of Texas, Presiding Judges** – Apptv.; term served concurrent with term as District Judge, subject to reappointment if re-elected to bench. No additional compensation. For names of judges, *see* Administrative Judicial Districts in index.

**Aging and Disability Services Council, Department of (DADS)** – (2004); apptv.; 6-yr.; 9 members: Chair Sharon Swift Butterworth, El Paso (2/1/17); Barry L. Anderson, Grand Prairie (2/1/19); Glyn S. Crane, Longview (2/1/15); John A. Cuellar, Dallas (2/1/17); Judy Foster, San Antonio (2/01/17); Carolyn Harvey, Tyler (2/1/15); Ann Schneider, Austin (2/1/15); J. Russell Shannon, Andrews (2/1/19); Donna Stauber, Waco, (2/1/19). Commissioner Jon Weizenbaum ($163,200), John H. Winters Human Services Complex, 701 W. 51st St., PO Box 149030, Austin 78714-9030; (512) 438-3011.

**Agricultural Finance Authority, Texas** – (1987); apptv.; 2-yr.; expenses; 2 ex-officio members: Agriculture Commissioner and Director for Institute for International Agribusiness Studies at Prairie View A&M Univeristy; 7 apptd. members: Lisa Birkman, Round Rock (1/1/10); Ted Conover, Tyler (1/1/11); Dal DeWees, San Angelo (2/1/11); Mike Golden, Lake Jackson (1/1/10); Stanley Ray, Georgetown (1/1/11); Victoria Salin, College Station (1/1/10); Larry Shafer, Granbury (1/1/10). Robert Wood, PO Box 12847, Austin 78711; (512) 936-0273.

**Alcohol and Drug Abuse, Texas Commission on** – (1953 as Texas Commission on Alcoholism); abolished by House Bill 2292 and functions merged into Department of State Health Services in January 2004.

**Alcoholic Beverage Commission, Texas** – (1935 as Liquor Control Board; name changed in 1970); apptv.; 6-yr; per diem and expenses; administrator apptd. by commission; 3 members: Chair Jose Cuevas Jr., Midland (11/15/15); Ida Louise (Weisie) Steen, San Antonio (11/15/19); Steven M. Weinberg, Colleyville (11/15/17). Administrator Sherry Cook ($122,500), PO Box 13127, Austin 78711-3127; (512) 206-3333.

**Alzheimer's Disease & Related Disorders, Texas Council on** – (1999); apptv.; 2-yr.; 19 members: Chair Debbie Hanna, Austin (8/31/15); Ronald Devere, Austin (8/31/15); Leon Douglas, Bertram; Carlos Escobar, San Angelo (8/31/15); Carolyn Frazier, Huffman (8/31/13); Grayson Hankins, Odessa (8/31/13); Clint Hackney, Austin; Rita Hortenstine, Dallas (8/31/13); Mary M. Kenan, Houston; Jack C. Kern, Austin; Margaret Krasovec, Austin; Ray Lewis, Arlington; Audrey Deckinga, Austin; Sam Shore, Austin; Jennifer Smith, Austin; Winnie Rutledge, Austin; Michael Wilson, Austin; Bobby D. Schmidt, Austin; Mary Somerville, Austin. Project Coor. Jim Hinds; (512) 263-1943.

**Angelina and Neches River Authority** – (1935 as Sabine-Neches Conservation Dist.; reorganized in 1950 and name changed to Neches River Conservation Dist.; changed to present name in 1977); apptv.; expenses; 6-yr.; 9 members: Chair Jody Anderson, Lufkin (9/5/19); Louis A. Bronaugh, Lufkin (9/5/17); Dominick B. (Nick) Bruno, Jacksonville (9/5/15); Patricia E. Dickey, Crockett (9/5/17); Julie Dowell, Bullard, (9/5/19); Keith Drewery, Nacogdoches (9/5/15); James Hughes Jr., Jasper (9/5/15); David King, Nacogdoches (9/5/19); Thomas R. Murphy, Crockett (9/5/13). Gen. Mgr. Kelley Holcomb, PO Box 387, Lufkin 75902-0387; (936) 632-7795.

**Animal Health Commission, Texas** – (1893 as Texas Livestock Sanitary Commission; name changed in 1959; members increased to 9 in 1973; raised to 12 in 1983); apptv.; per diem and expenses; 6-yr.; 13 members: Chair Ernesto A. Morales, Devine (9/6/17); Brandon Bouma, Plainview (9/6/17); William F. Edmiston Jr., Eldorado (9/6/19); Ken Jordan, San Saba (9/6/19); Thomas George Kezar, Dripping Springs (9/6/17); Joe Lynn Leathers, Guthrie (9/6/19); Coleman Hudgins Locke, Wharton (9/6/15); Thomas Eugene Oates, Huntsville (9/6/19); Ralph Simmons, Center (9/6/19); Michael Louis Vickers, Falfurrias, (9/6/17); Beau White, Rosanky (9/6/15); Eric Dean White, Mason (9/6/19); R.W. (Dick) Winters Jr., Eden (9/6/19). Exec. Dir. Dee B. Ellis ($120,000), PO Box 12966, Austin 78711-2966; (512) 719-0700.

**Appraiser Licensing and Certification Board, Texas** – (1991); 2-yr.; apptv.; per diem on duty; 9 members; 1 ex officio: Texas General Land Office; 8 app'td.: Chair Jamie Wickliffe, Midlothian (1/31/15); Walker Beard, El Paso (1/31/15); Clayton Black, Stanton (1/31/15); Laurie Fontana, Houston (1/31/16); Keith W. Kidd, Reno (1/31/14); Shannon McClendon, Dripping Springs (1/31/14); Sheryl R. Swift, Galveston (1/31/14). Commissioner Douglas E. Oldmixon ($106,500), PO Box 12188, Austin 78711-2188; (512) 936-3001.

**Architectural Examiners, Texas Board of** – (1937 as 3-member board; raised to 6 members in 1951 and to 9 in 1977); apptv.; 6-yr.; per diem and expenses; 9 members: Chair Alfred Vidaurri Jr., Aledo (1/31/15); Charles H. Anastos, Corpus Christi (1/31/19); Corbett (Chase) Bearden, Austin (1/31/15); Chad Davis, Lubbock (1/31/19); Debra Dockery, San Antonio (1/31/17); Davey Edwards, Decatur (1/31/19); H.L. (Bert) Mijares Jr., El Paso (1/31/15); Paula A. Miller, The Woodlands (1/31/17); Sonya Odell, Dallas (1/31/17). Exec. Dir. Cathy L. Hendricks ($114,801), 333 Guadalupe St., Ste. 2-350, PO Box 12337, Austin 78711-

The Jefferson Historical Museum stands on the corner of historic Jefferson in Marion County. Built in 1888, it served as the Federal Court House and U.S. Post Office until 1965. The building now houses the collections of the Jefferson Historical Society, including art, antiquities, Civil War collections, Caddo Indian artifacts, early pioneer implements, early Texas textiles, children's toys and dolls, genealogy archives. Photo by Ron Billings; Texas A&M Forest Service.

2337; (512) 305-9000.

**Arts, Texas Commission on the** – (1965 as Texas Fine Arts Commission; name changed to Texas Commission on the Arts and Humanities and members increased to 18 in 1971; name changed to present form in 1979); apptv.; 6-yr.; expenses; 17 members: Chair Patty A. Bryant, Amarillo (8/31/17); Rita E. Baca, El Paso (8/31/17); Andrew Barlow, Austin (8/31/17); Dale W. Brock, Fort Worth (8/31/13); Alphonse A. Dotson, Voca (8/31/13); David C. Garza, Brownsville (8/31/17); Mila Gibson, Sweetwater (8/31/15); Linda Lowes Hatchel, Woodway (8/31/15); Molly Hipp Hubbard, Houston (8/31/13); Patty Hayes Huffines, Austin (8/31/15); Liza B. Lewis, San Antonio (8/31/15); Paul Kellam McCash Jr., Texarkana (8/31/13); Jeanne Parker, Austin (8/31/13); Marsha Wilson Rappaport, Galveston (8/31/13); Ronald (Ronnie) Sanders, San Antonio (8/31/17); S. Shawn Stephens, Houston (8/31/15); 1 vacancy. Exec. Dir. Gary Gibbs ($85,250), 920 Colorado St., PO Box 13406, Austin 78711-3406; (512) 463-5535.

**Assistive and Rehabilitative Services Council, Department of (DARS)** – (2004) apptv.; 6-yr.; 9 members: Chair Lee Chayes, El Paso (2/1/19); Jon Arnold, San Antonio (2/1/17); Amanda Davis, Buffalo (2/1/19); Diego Demaya, Houston (2/1/15); Berkley Dyer, Austin (2/1/17); Tom Fordyce, Huntsville (2/1/17); Thomas W. Grahm, Tyler (2/1/17); Donald D. Roy, Mount Pleasant (2/1/19); Judy Scott, Dallas (2/1/15). Commissioner Debra Wanser ($145,860), 4800 N. Lamar Blvd., PO Box 12866, Austin 78711-2866; (512) 377-0800.

**Athletic Trainers, Advisory Board of** – (1971 as Texas Board of Athletic Trainers; name changed in 1975); expenses; 6-yr.; 5 members: Chair David J. Weir, College Station (1/31/17); Marty Akins, Austin (1/31/15); David R. Schmidt, San Antonio (1/31/19); Rebecca Spurlock, Keller (1/31/15); Cathy Supak, Houston (1/31/19). Program Director Stewart Myrick, PO Box 149347, MC 1982, Austin 78714-9347; (512) 834-6615.

**Attorney, State Prosecuting** – (1923) apptd. by Court of Criminal Appeals: Lisa C. McMinn ($125,000), 209 W. 14th St., Ste. 203, PO Box 13046, Austin 78711; (512) 463-1660.

**Auditor's Office, State** – (1929); 2-yr.; apptd. by Legislative Audit Committee, a joint Senate-House committee: State Auditor John Keel ($198,000), Robert E. Johnson Bldg., 1501 N. Congress, P.O. Box 12067, Austin 78711-2067; (512) 936-9500.

**Autism and Pervasive Developmental Disorders, Texas Council on** – (1987); 2-yr.; expenses; 13 members: 7 ex officio; 6 apptd. by Gov.: Chair Frank McCamant, Austin; Daniel Durany, Austin; Tammy Lemoine, Center; Nyria Melchor, Austin; Pamela Rollins, Dallas; Stephanie Sokolosky, Harlingen; Callie M. Vivion-Matthews, Austin; c/o Texas Dept. of Aging and Disability Services; Texas Council on Autism and PDD; Mail Code W-578, PO Box 149030, Austin 78714-9030; (512) 438-3512.

**Banking Commissioner, State** – (1923); 2-yr.; apptd. by State Finance Commission: Charles G. Cooper ($205,200), 2601 N. Lamar Blvd., Austin 78705-4294; (512) 475-1300. (See also Finance Commission of Texas.)

**Bar of Texas, State** – (1939 as administrative arm of Supreme Court); 30 directors elected by membership; 3-yr. terms; expenses paid from dues collected from membership. Executive director, general counsel and immediate past chair serve as ex-officio members. Exec. Dir. Michelle Hunter; Texas Law Center, 1414 Colorado, P.O. Box 12487, Austin 78711; (512) 427-1463.

**Barbering Advisory Board, State** – (1929 as 3-member Texas Board of Barber Examiners; members increased in 1975; named changed to current in 2005 and functions transferred to Texas Dept. of Licensing and Regulation); 6-yr.; apptd. by dept. commissioners; 5 members: Chair Linda G. Connor, Austin (9/29/11); Ronald Brown, Austin (9/29/15); Michael Funk, Dumas (9/29/13); Jennifer Grisham, Alpine (9/29/15); Jimmy Johnson, Manor (9/29/13). c/o Texas Dept. of Licensing and Regulation, 920 Colorado St., PO Box 12884, Austin 78711; (512) 463-6599.

**Blind and Severely Disabled Persons, Committee on Purchases of Products of** – (See Disabilities, Texas Council on Purchasing from People with.)

**Blind, Texas Commission for the** – Now the Division for Blind Services within the Department of Assistive and Rehabilitative Services (DARS) of the Health and Human Services Commission as of 3/1/04.

**Blind and Visually Impaired Governing Board, Texas School for the** – (1979); apptv.; 6-yr.; expenses; 9 members: Mary K. Alexander, Valley View (1/31/15); Gene I. Brooks, Austin (1/31/15); Anne Corn, Austin (1/31/17); Caroline K. Daley, Kingwood (1/31/17); Bobby Druesedow, Aledo (1/31/19); Cynthia Finley, Lubbock (1/31/17); Michael E. Garrett, Missouri City (1/31/19); Joseph Muñoz, Harlingen (1/31/15); B. Lee Sonnenberg, Lubbock (1/31/19). Superintendent William Daugherty ($115,000), 1100 W. 45th St., Austin 78756-3494; (512) 454-8631.

**Board of** (Note: In most instances, state boards are alphabetized under key word, as **Accountancy, Texas State Board of Public.**)

**Bond Review Board** – (1987); composed of Governor, Lieutenant Governor, House Speaker, and Comptroller of Public Accounts; oversees debt financing for Texas' infrastructure and other public purposes, debt issuance, and debt management functions of state and local entities, and the state's private activity bond allocation; Exec. Dir. Robert C. Kline ($99,000); 300 W. 15th St., Ste. 409, PO Box 13292, Austin 78711-3292; (512) 463-1741.

**Brazos River Authority** – (1929 as Brazos River Conservation and Reclamation District; name changed to present form in 1953); apptv.; 6-yr; expenses; 21 members: Chair G. Dave Scott, Richmond (2/1/19); Christopher Steve Adams Jr., Granbury (2/1/17); Richard L. Ball, Mineral Wells (2/1/19); F. LeRoy Bell, Tuscola (2/1/19); Kari Belt, Gatesville (2/1/15); Peter G. Bennis, Fort Worth (2/1/19); Cynthia Olson Bourland, Round Rock (2/1/17); Michel (Todd) Brashears, Wolfforth (2/1/15); Paul J. Christensen, Crawford (2/1/17); Col. Robert M. Christian, Jewett (2/1/17); Chet D. Creel, Olney (2/1/15); Carolyn H. Johnson, Freeport (2/1/17); Roberta Jean Killgore, Somerville (2/1/17); Sara Lowrey Mackie-Shull, Salado (2/1/15); William Masterson, Guthrie (2/1/19); Henry Munson, Angleton (2/1/17); William J. Rankin, Brenham (2/1/15); Jeffery S. Tallas, Sugar Land (2/1/15); Robert E. Tesch, Georgetown (2/1/15); Raleigh White IV, Temple (2/1/19); Salvatore A. Zaccagnino, Caldwell (2/1/19). Gen. Mgr./CEO Phillip J. Ford, 4600 Cobbs Drive, PO Box 7555, Waco 76714-7555; (254) 761-3100.

**Building and Procurement Commission, Texas** – (1919; renamed Texas Facilities Commission in 2007 and some procurement duties transferred to the Comptroller of Public Accounts); *see* **Facilities Commission, Texas.**

**Canadian River Compact Commissioner** – (1951); apptv.; salary and expenses; (negotiates with New Mexico and Oklahoma regarding waters of the Canadian): James E. Herring. Interstate Compacts Coordinator Suzy Valentine, TCEQ, PO Box 13087, Austin 78711-3087; (512) 239-4730.

**Canadian River Municipal Water Authority** – (1953); 2-yr; 17 members apptd. by member cities: Pres. Steve Tucker, Slaton; Glenn Bickel, Plainview; Bill Carder, Borger; Jerry Carlson, Pampa; James O. Collins, Lubbock; Richard Ellis, Levelland; William Hallerberg, Amarillo; Shannon Himango, Levelland; Jay Dee House, O'Donnell; Glendon Jett, Borger; Robert Keys, Amarillo; Dwight McDonald, Lubbock; Rex McKay, Pampa; Dale Newberry, Lamesa; L.J. Richardson, Brownfield; Bruce Vaughn, Tahoka; Norman Wright, Plainview. Gen. Mgr. Kent Satterwhite, PO Box 9, Sanford 79078-0009; (806) 865-3325.

**Cancer Prevention & Research Institute of Texas** – (1985 as Texas Cancer Council; named changed in 2007); apptv.; 4-yr.; expenses; 11 members; 2 ex officio: Attorney General and Comptroller of Public Accounts; 9 apptd.: Chair James M. Mansour, Austin (12/4/15); Joseph S. Bailes, Austin (12/4/19); Pete Geren, Fort Worth (12/4/17); Faith S. Johnson, DeSoto (12/4/17); Alejandro G. (Alex) Meade III, Mission (1/31/15); Walker Moody, Houston (12/4/13); Charles Tate, Houston (12/4/17); Mark E. Watson, Jr., San Antonio (12/4/17); 1 vacancy. Interim Exec. Dir. Wayne Roberts ($214,000 plus supplement) 211 E. 7th St., Ste. 300, PO Box 12097, Austin 78711-2097; (512) 463-3190.

**Cardiovascular Disease and Stroke, Texas Council on** – (1999); apptv.; 6-yr.; 15 members: 4 ex officio: Department of Assistive and Rehabilitative Services, Department of Aging and Disability Services, Texas Education Agency, Texas Department of State Health Services; 11 apptd.: Chair Thomas E. Tenner Jr., Lubbock (2/1/15); Pamela R.W. Akins, Austin (2/1/15); Paula Gomez, Brownsville (2/1/19); Michael Hawkins, Temple (2/1/19); Suzanne Hildebrand, Live Oak (2/1/19); Melbert (Bob) C. Hillert Jr., Dallas (2/1/15); Floristene Johnson, DeSoto (2/1/17); Cheryle Locke, Austin (2/1/19); Howard R. Marcus, Austin (2/1/17); J. Neal Rutledge, Austin (2/1/17); Ann Quinn Todd, Houston (2/1/15); c/o Texas Dept. of State Health Services, PO Box 149347, Austin 78714-9347; (512) 458-7111.

**Cemetery Committee, Texas State** – (1997); apptv.; 6-yr.; 3 members: Chair Scott P. Sayers Jr., Austin (2/1/15); Jim Bayless, Austin (2/1/17); 1 vacancy. Superintendent Harry Bradley, 909 Navasota, Austin 78702; (512) 463-6023.

**Central Colorado River Authority** (*See* **Colorado River Authority, Central.**)

**Chemist, Office of State** – (1911); ex officio, indefinite term: State Chemist Timothy J. Herrman, PO Box 3160, College Station

77841-3160; (979) 845-1121.

**Childhood Intervention, Interagency Council on Early** – Combined 3/1/04 into Department of Assistive and Rehabilitative Services (DARS) of the Health and Human Services Commission.

**Chiropractic Examiners, Texas Board of** – (1949); apptv.; 6-yr.; expenses; 9 members: Chair Cynthia Tays, Austin (2/1/19); Anne Boatright, Smithville (2/1/15); Karen Campion, Bryan (2/1/17); Tim McCullough, Friendswood (2/1/17); Larry R. Montgomery, Belton (2/1/15); John H. Riggs III, Midland (2/1/19); Patrick J. Thomas, Corpus Christi (2/1/15); John Steinberg, Marion (2/1/19); Kenya Scott Woodruff, Dallas (2/1/17). Exec. Dir. Yvette Yarbrough ($70,000), 333 Guadalupe, Ste. 3-825, Austin 78701; (512) 305-6700.

**Coastal Water Authority** – (1967 as Coastal Industrial Water Authority; name changed in 1985); 2-yr.; per diem and expenses; 7 members; 4 apptd. by Houston mayor; 3 apptd. by Gov.: Pres. D. Wayne Klotz, Houston (3/31/13); John Odis Cobb, Houston (3/31/14); Alan D. Conner, Dayton (3/31/14); Tony L. Council, Houston (3/31/13); Zebulun Nash, Houston (4/1/15); Douglas Walker, Beach City (4/1/15); Giti Zarinkelk, Houston (4/1/14). Exec. Dir. Donald R. Ripley, 1801 Main, Ste. 800, Houston 77002; (713) 658-9020.

**Colorado River Authority, Central** – (1935); apptv.; 6-yr.; per diem on duty; 5 members: Mathew K. Gaines, Coleman (2/1/19); Patrick S. Justiss, Coleman (2/1/17); Herman Law, Burkett (2/1/19); Bruce N. Pittard, Novice (2/1/19); Andrew Mark Young, Coleman (2/1/19). Operations Mgr. Lynn W. Cardinas, PO Box 964, Coleman 76834-0964; (325) 625-9001.

**Colorado River Authority, Lower** – (1934 as 9-member board; members increased in 1951 and 1975); apptv.; 6-yr.; per diem on duty; 15 members: Chair Timothy Timmerman, Austin (2/1/19); J. Scott Arbuckle, El Campo (2/1/17); Steve K. Balas, Eagle Lake (2/1/17); Lori A. Berger, Flatonia (2/1/15); John C. Dickerson III, Matagorda (2/1/15); Pamela Jo (PJ) Ellison, Brenham, (2/1/19); John M. Franklin, Burnet (2/1/17); Raymond A. (Ray) Gill Jr., Horseshoe Bay (2/1/17); Jett J. Johnson, Goldthwaite (2/1/15); Sandra Wright Kibby, New Braunfels (2/1/17); Robert (Bobby) Lewis, Elgin, (2/1/19); Thomas Michael Martine, Cypress Mill (2/1/19); Michael G. McHenry, San Saba (2/1/15); Vernon E. (Buddy) Schrader, Horseshoe Bay (2/1/19); Franklin (Scott) Spears Jr., Austin (2/1/19). Gen. Man. Becky Motal, 3700 Lake Austin Blvd., PO Box 220, Austin 78767-0220; (512) 473-3200.

**Colorado River Authority, Upper,** – (1935 as 9-member board; reorganized in 1965); apptv.; 6-yr.; per diem and expenses; 9 members: Chair Jeffie Harmon Roberts, Robert Lee (2/1/17); Ronny Alexander, Paint Rock (2/1/15); Bill Holland, San Angelo (2/1/13); William R. Hood, Robert Lee (2/1/15); Eva Horton, San Angelo (2/1/15); Martin Lee, Bronte (2/1/17); John Nikolauk, Eldorado (2/1/13); Hyman D. Sauer, Eldorado (2/1/17); Hugh Stone, San Angelo (2/1/17). Director Chuck Brown, 512 Orient, San Angelo 76903; (325) 655-0565.

**Commissioner of** (*See keyword,* as **Agriculture, Commissioner of.**)

**Concho River Water and Soil Conservation Authority, Lower** – Established in 1939; abolished by the 81st Texas Legislature on 9/1/09.

**Consumer Credit Commissioner** – Leslie L. Pettijohn ($170,500), 2601 N. Lamar, Austin 78705-4207; (512) 936-7600. *Consumer Help Line: (800) 538-1579.*

**Cosmetology Advisory Board, Texas** – (1935 as 3-member State Board of Hairdressers and Cosmetologists; name changed and members increased in 1971; named changed to current in 2005 and functions transferred to Texas Dept. of Licensing and Regulation); apptv.; per diem and expenses; 6-yr.; 8 members: Chair Daired Ogle, Arlington (9/29/13); Rojean S. Brewer, Lubbock (9/29/15); Pamela Gold, Plano (9/29/15); Marisela Higgins, Laredo (9/29/17); Glenda Jemison, Houston (9/29/15); Gordon Logan, Georgetown (9/29/13); Ron Robinson, Waco (9/29/15); ex officio, Diane Salazar, Austin; c/o Texas Dept. of Licensing and Regulation, 920 Colorado, PO Box 12157, Austin 78711; (512) 463-6599.

**Counselors, Texas State Board of Examiners of Professional** – (1981); apptv.; 6-yr.; expenses; 9 members: Chair Glenda Corley, Round Rock (2/1/17); Sarah Abraham, Sugar Land (2/1/19); Brenda (Brandi) Buckner, Weatherford (2/1/15); Karen R. Burke, Austin (2/1/15); Steven D. Christopherson, Pasadena (2/1/19); Brenda S. Compagnone, Carrizo Springs (2/1/15); Lauren Polunsky Dreszer, San Antonio (2/1/17); Etienne Nguyen, Houston (2/1/17); Leslie F. Pohl, Austin (2/1/19). Exec. Dir. Bobbe Alexander, c/o Texas Dept. of State Health Services, 1100 W. 49th St., PO Box 149347, Austin 78714-9347; (512) 834-6658.

**Texas County and District Retirement System** – (*See* **Retirement System, Texas County and District**.

**Court Administration, State Office of** – (1985); apptd. by State Supreme Court chief justice; 1 member who also serves as executive director of the Texas Judicial Council: Admin. Dir. David Slayton ($130,000); Tom C. Clark State Courts Bldg., 205 W. 14th, 6th Flr., PO Box 12066, Austin 78711; (512) 463-1625.

**Court Reporters Certification Board** – (1977 as 9-member Texas Reporters Committee; name changed to present form and members increased in 1983); 6-yr.; expenses; 13 members (6 apptd. by State Supreme Court): Chair Lee Hamilton, Abilene (12/31/18); Attorney members: Charles Noteboom, Hurst (12/31/14); Adam Poncio, San Antonio (12/31/13). Official reporters: Velma Arellano, Corpus Christi (12/31/16); Paula Frederick, Bryan (12/31/17). Freelance reporters: Judy Hobart, Bedford (12/31/15); Donald Riley, Fort Worth (12/31/16); Firm reps.: Donna Collins, Dallas (12/31/15); Amy Cummings, Dallas (12/31/18); Lay members: Julie Hopkins, Cross Plains (12/31/17); Esther Kelly, Dallas (12/31/13); Richard Neely, University Park (12/31/15); Krista M. Saeger, Austin (12/31/14). Dir. Michele L. Henricks, 205 W. 14th St., Ste. 101, PO Box 13131, Austin 78711; (512) 463-1630.

**Credit Union Commission** – (1949 as 3-member Credit Union Advisory Commission; name changed and members increased to 6 in 1969; increased to 9 in 1981); apptv.; 6-yr.; expenses; 9 members: Chair Manuel Cavazos IV, Austin (2/15/17); Gary L. Janacek, Belton (2/15/15); Robert Kyker, Richardson (2/15/15); Sherrie Merket, Midland (2/15/17); Allyson (Missy) Morrow, San Benito (2/15/19); Barbara Stewart, Daingerfield (2/15/15); Gary Tuma, Sugar Land (2/15/17); Vik Vad, Austin (2/15/19); A. John Yoggerst, San Antonio (2/15/15). Commissioner Harold E. Feeney ($142,400), 914 E. Anderson Ln., Austin 78752-1699; (512) 837-9236.

**Crime Stoppers Advisory Council** – (1981); apptv.; 4-yr.; per diem and expenses; 5 members: Chair Jorge E. Gaytan, Houston (9/1/16); Emerson F. Lane Jr., Beaumont (9/1/16); William Randy McDaniel, Montgomery (9/1/13); Ernesto (Ernie) Rodriguez, Jr., McAllen (9/1/16); Susan Rogers, Odessa (9/1/13); Texas State University San Marcos, 601 University Dr., San Marcos 78666-4610; (866) 220-4357.

**Crime Victims' Institute Advisory Council** – (1995 as function of attorney general's office; transferred to Sam Houston State University in 2003); apptv.; 2-yr.; 3 ex-officio: Attorney General, 1 member of House, 1 member of Senate; 14 apptd. members: Dallas Barrington, Kountz (1/31/13); Victoria Camp, Austin (1/31/14); Stefani Carter, Dallas (1/31/13); Ben M. Crouch, College Station (1/31/14); Nancy Ghigna, Conroe (1/31/14); Rodman Goode, Dallas (1/31/14); Henry Porretto, Galveston (1/31/14); Richard L. Reynolds, Austin (1/31/14); Stephanie Schulte, El Paso (1/31/14); Kel Seliger, Amarillo (1/31/13); Jane Shafer, San Antonio (1/31/13); Debbie Unruh, Amarillo (1/31/14); Mary Anne Wiley, Austin (1/31/14); Mark Wilson, Fort Worth (1/31/13). Director Leana Bouffard, Crime Victims' Institute, 816 17th St., Sam Houston State University, Huntsville 77340; (936) 294-3100.

**Criminal Justice, Texas Board of** – (1989: assumed duties of former Board of Corrections, Adult Probation Commission and Board of Pardons and Paroles); apptv; 6-yr.; expenses; 9 members: Chair Oliver J. Bell, Austin (2/1/15); John (Eric) Gambrell, Dallas (2/1/19); Larry Gist, Beaumont (2/1/17); Janice Harris Lord, Arlington (2/1/17); R. Terrell McCombs, San Antonio (2/1/19); Tom Mechler, Amarillo (2/1/17); Leopoldo R. Vasquez III, Houston (2/1/17); Carmen Villanueva-Hiles, Palmhurst (2/1/15); Thomas Wingate, Mission (2/1/19). Exec. Dir. Dept. of Criminal Justice: Brad Livingston ($186,300), 209 West 14th St., Ste. 500, Price Daniel Bldg., PO Box 13084, Austin 78711-3084; (512) 475-3250.

**Deaf, Texas School for the, Governing Board** – (1979) apptv.; 6-yr.; expenses; 9 members: Chair Walter Camenisch III, Austin (1/31/15); Jean Andrews, Beaumont (1/31/17); Beatrice M. Burke, Temple (1/31/13); Shalia Cowan, Dripping Springs (1/31/17); Eric Hogue, Wylie (1/31/15); Tyran Lee, Humble (1/31/13); Susan K. Ridley, Sugar Land (1/31/13); Connie F. Sefcik-Kennedy, Austin (1/31/17); Angela O. Wolf, Austin (1/31/15). Superintendent Claire Bugen ($115,000), 1102 S. Congress, Austin 78704; (512) 462-5353.

**Deaf and Hard of Hearing, Texas Commission for the** – Combined into Department of Assistive and Rehabilitative Services (DARS) of the Health and Human Services Commission as of 3/1/04.

**Demographer, Office of the State** – (2001); created by 77th Legislature: Lloyd Potter, 1700 N. Congress Ave., Ste. 220W, PO Box 13455, Austin 78711; (512) 463-8390.

**Dental Examiners, State Board of** – (1919 as 6-member board; increased to 9 members in 1971; increased to 12 in 1981; increased to 15 in 1991; sunsetted in 1994; reconstituted with 18 members in 1995; reduced to 15 in 2005); apptv.; 6-yr.; per diem and expenses; 15 members: Chair Rodolfo G. (Rudy) Ramos Jr., Houston (2/1/15); Steven J. Austin, Amarillo (2/1/19); William R. Birdwell, Bryan (2/1/15); Kirby Bunel Jr., Texarkana (2/1/19); James W. Chancellor, Garden Ridge (2/1/15); Renee Cornett, Austin (2/1/15); D. Bradley Dean, Frisco (2/1/17);Tamela L. Gough, Allen (2/1/17); Christie Leedy, Abilene (2/1/17); Whitney Hyde, Midland (2/1/15); Evangelia (Lia) Mote, Cedar Park (2/1/17); Jim O'Hare, Famers Branch (2/1/19); Lois Palermo, League City (2/1/19); Lewis White, Humble (2/1/19); Emily Willeford, San Antonio (2/1/17). Exec. Dir. Glenn Parker ($82,500), 333 Guadalupe, Tower III, #800, Austin 78701-3942; (512) 463-6400.

**Depository Board, State** – Abolished in May 1997.

**Diabetes Council, Texas** – (1983; with 5 ex officio and 6 public members serving 2-yr. terms; changed in 1987 to 3 ex officio and 8 public members; changed to present in 1991; term length changed from 4 to 6 years in 1997); 6-yr.; 14 members: 11 apptv.: Chair Victor Hugo Gonzalez, McAllen (2/1/15); Gene Fulton Bell, Lubbock (2/1/15); Maria Duarte-Gardea, El Paso (2/1/17); Carley Gomez-Meade, Austin (2/1/19); Alicia Gracia, Brownsville (2/1/19); John Griffin Jr., Victoria (2/1/17); Arthur E. Hernandez, Corpus Christi (2/1/15); Dora Rivas, Dallas (2/1/15); Jason Michael Ryan, Houston (2/1/19); Curtis Triplitt, San Antonio (2/1/19); Don Yarbrough, Garland (2/1/17); 3 ex officio: reps. from Dept. of Assistive and Rehabilitative Services; Dept. of State Health Services; Health and Human Services Commission. Dir. Roger Faske, c/o Texas Dept. of State Health Services, PO Box 149347 Austin 78714-9347; (512) 458-7490.

**Dietitians, State Board of Examiners of** – (1983); apptv.; 6-yr.; per diem and expenses; 9 members: Chair Janet S. Hall, Georgetown (9/1/13); Belinda Bazan-Lara, San Antonio (9/1/17); Brian Irons, Lubbock (9/1/13); Amy N. McLeod, Houston (9/1/13); Aida (Letty) Moreno-Brown, El Paso (9/1/17); D.A. Sharpe, Aurora (9/1/17); Christina Sterling, Brownsville (9/1/15); Elizabeth J. Tindall, Odessa (9/1/15); Mary Kate (Suzy) Weems, Waco (9/1/15). Exec. Dir. Bobbe Alexander, c/o Texas Dept. of State Health Services, 1100 W. 49th, PO Box 149347, MC 1982 Austin 78714-9347; (512) 834-6601.

**Disabilities, Governor's Committee on People with** – (1949 as Gov.'s Committee on Employment of the Handicapped; recreated in 1983 as Gov.'s Committee for Disabled Persons; in 1991, given current name and expanded duties); apptv.; 2-yr. and at pleasure of Gov.; 12 members: Chair Joe Bontke, Houston (2/1/11); Aaron Bangor, Austin (2/1/14); Rodolfo (Rudy) Becerra Jr., Nacogdoches (2/1/14); Daphne Brookins, Fort Worth (2/1/11); David A. Fowler, Katy (2/1/11); Connie Sue Kelley, Humble (2/1/13); Mackenzie Kelly, Austin (2/1/14); Margaret Larson, Austin (2/1/14); Maureen F. McClain, Mercedes (2/1/12); David G. Ondich, Burleson (2/1/13); Shawn P. Saladin, Edinburg (2/1/13); Patty Watson, Flower Mound (2/1/14). Exec. Dir. Angi English, 1100 San Jacinto, PO Box 12428, Austin 78711-2428; (512) 463-5739; 7-1-1 TDD.

**Disabilities, Texas Council for Developmental** – (1971); apptv.; 6-yr.; 27 members: 19 apptv.: Chair Mary M. Durheim, McAllen (2/1/11); Rebecca Hunter Adkins, Lakeway (2/1/15); Kimberley A. Blackmon, Fort Worth (2/1/15); Kristine Clark, San Antonio (2/1/17); Gladys Cortez, McAllen (2/1/17); Kristen L. Cox, El Paso (2/1/15); Andrew D. Crim, Fort Worth (2/1/13); Mateo Delgado, El Paso (2/1/13); Stephen Gersuk, Plano (2/1/13); Cindy Johnston, Dallas (2/1/13); Diana Kern, Cedar Creek (2/1/15); Scott McAvoy, Cedar Park (2/1/15); John C. Morris, Leander (2/1/13); Dana S. Perry, Brownwood (2/1/15); Joe Rivas, Denton (2/1/17); David Taylor, El Paso (2/1/17); Lora T. Taylor, Houston (2/1/13); Richard A. Tisch, Spring (2/1/15); Susan Vardell, Sherman (2/1/13); 8 ex offico members from various state agencies. Exec. Dir. Roger A. Webb, 6201 E. Oltorf, Ste. 600, Austin 78741; (512) 437-5432.

**Disabilities, Texas Council on Purchasing from People**

with – (1979 as 10-member Committee on Purchases of Products and Services of Blind and Severely Disabled Persons; name changed and members reduced to 9 in 1995); apptv.: expenses; 5-yr.; 9 members: Chair John W. Luna, Euless (1/31/15); Jack (Dan) Bremer, New Braunfels (1/31/19); Kevin Cloud, Austin (1/31/17); Glenn Hagler, Georgetown (1/31/17); Kevin M. Jackson, Austin (1/31/19); Beverly Jackson Loss, Wolfe City (1/31/15); Alfred (Al) Manson, Tyler (1/31/19); Dietrich M. von Biedenfeld, West Columia (1/31/17); Wanda White Stovall, Fort Worth (1/31/15). Exec. Dir. Kelvin Moore, 111 E. 17th St., PO Box 13528, Austin 78711; (512) 463-3244.

**Disabilities, Texas Office for Prevention of Developmental** – (1991) 6-yr.; apptv.; 9 members: Chair Richard Garnett, Fort Worth; Angelo Giardino, Houston; Ashley C. Givens, Dallas (2/1/15); Rep. Jim L. Jackson, Carrollton; Valerie Kiper, Amarillo (2/1/19); Joan Roberts-Scott, Austin; Marian Sokol, San Antonio (2/1/17); Mary S. Tijerina, San Marcos; 1 vacancy. Exec. Dir. Janet Sharkis, 909 West 45th St., PO Box 12668, Austin 78711; (512) 206-4544.

**Disaster Recovery and Renewal, Governor's Commission for** – (2008); apptv.; terms at pleasure of Gov.; 23 ex-officio members: County judges from the coastal counties of Aransas, Brazoria, Calhoun, Cameron, Chambers, Galveston, Harris, Hidalgo, Jackson, Jefferson, Kenedy, Kleberg, Liberty, Matagorda, Nueces, Orange, Refugio, San Patricio, Starr, Victoria, and Willacy along with the General Land Office Commissioner and the Agriculture Commissioner; 24 apptd. members: Chair Robert Eckels, Houston; Ronnie Acosta, Pearland; William B. Claybar, Orange; Irma Diaz-Gonzalez, Houston; George (Trey) H. Henderson III, Lufkin; Gary L. Hockstra, Lake Jackson; Jo Ann Howard, Austin; Jerry Kane, Corpus Christi; Mary E. Kelly, Austin; William E. King, Houston; H. Thomas Kornegay, Houston; David L. Lakey, Austin; David S. Lopez, Houston; Ross D. Margraves Jr., Houston; Scott McClelland, Houston; Tracye McDaniel, Houston; Allan B. Polunsky, San Antonio; Penny Redington, Austin; Regina Rogers, Beaumont; Rolando Rubiano, Harlingen; Karen A. Sexton, Galveston; Wade E. Upton, Houston; Daniel J. Wolterman, Houston; H. Edwin Young, Houston. c/o Office of the Governor, PO Box 12428, Austin, 78711; (512) 463-2000.

**Education Board, Southern Regional** – (1969); apptv.; 4-yr.; 5 members: Gov. ex officio, 4 apptv.: Rep. Dan Branch, Dallas (6/30/15); Rep. Rob Eissler, The Woodlands (6/30/16); Sen. Florence Shapiro, Plano (6/30/13); Michael L. Williams, Austin (6/30/14). President Daivd Spence, 592 10th St. N.W., Atlanta, GA 30318-5776; (404) 875-9211.

**Education, Commissioner of** – (1866 as Superintendent of Public Instruction; 1949 changed to present name by Gilmer-Aiken Act); apptd. by Gov. since 1995; 4-yr.: Michael L. Williams ($186,300 plus supplement), 1701 N. Congress Ave., Austin 78701-1494; (512) 463-9734.

**Education, State Board of** – (1866; re-created in 1928 and re-formed in 1949 by Gilmer-Aikin Act to consist of 21 elective members from districts co-extensive with 21 congressional districts at that time; increased to 24 with congressional redistricting in 1971; increased to 27 with congressional redistricting in 1981; reorganized by special legislative session as 15-member apptv. board in 1984; became elective board again in 1988); expenses; 4-yr.; 15 members: **Dist. 1:** Martha M. Dominguez (D), El Paso (1/1/17); **Dist. 2:** Ruben Cortez Jr. (D), Brownsville (1/1/19); **Dist. 3:** Marisa B. Perez (D), San Antonio (1/1/19); **Dist. 4:** Lawrence A. Allen Jr. (D), Fresno (1/1/19); **Dist. 5:** Ken Mercer (R), San Antonio (1/1/17); **Dist. 6:** Donna Bahorich (R), Houston (1/1/17); **Dist. 7:** David Bradley (R), Beaumont (1/1/19); **Dist. 8:** Chair Barbara Cargill (R), The Woodlands (1/1/17); **Dist. 9:** Thomas Ratliff (R), Mount Pleasant (1/1/17); **Dist. 10:** Tom Maynard (R), Florence (1/1/17); **Dist. 11:** Patricia Hardy (R), Weatherford (1/1/19); **Dist. 12:** Geraldine (Tincy) Miller (R), Dallas (1/1/19); **Dist. 13:** Erika Beltran (D), Fort Worth (1/1/19); **Dist. 14:** Sue Melton-Malone (R), Waco (1/1/17); **Dist. 15:** Marty Rowley (R), Amarillo (1/1/17). c/o Texas Education Agency, 1701 N. Congress Ave., Austin 78701-1494; (512) 463-9007.

**Educator Certification, State Board for** – (1995); apptv.; 6-yr.; expenses; 14 members; 3 ex officio: rep. of Comm. of Education; rep. of Comm. of Higher Education; 1 dean of a college of education; 11 apptv.: Chair Bonny L. Cain, Waco (2/1/15); Brad W. Allard, Burleson (2/1/15); Dawn Buckingham, Lakeway (2/1/19); Laurie Bricker, Houston (2/1/19); Sandra D. Bridges, Rockwall (2/1/19); Curtis Culwell, Garland (2/1/17); Jill Druesedow, Haskell (2/1/19); Kathryn Everest, Arlington (2/1/15); Suzanne McCall,

Lubbock (2/1/17); Christie Pogue, Buda (2/1/17); Judy Robison, El Paso (2/1/15); Grant W. Simpson, Gainesville (2/1/17); 1701 N. Congress Ave., 5th floor, Austin 78701-1494; (512) 936-8400.

**Edwards Aquifer Authority** – (1993); 4-yr.; expenses; 17 members (2 apptv. and 15 elected from single-member districts). Elected members: **Dist. 1:** Carol Patterson, Bexar Co. (12/1/14); **Dist. 2:** Byron Miller, Bexar Co. (12/1/16); **Dist. 3:** Lauro A. Bustamante, Bexar County (12/1/14); **Dist. 4:** Benjamin F. Youngblood, Bexar Co. (12/1/16); **Dist. 5:** Ron Ellis, Bexar Co. (12/1/14); **Dist. 6:** Susan Hughes, Bexar Co. (12/1/16); **Dist. 7:** Enrique Valdivia, Bexar Co. (12/1/14); **Dist. 8:** Craig Massouh, Comal Co. (12/1/16); **Dist. 9:** Ronald J. Walton Sr., Comal & Guadalupe Cos. (12/1/14); **Dist. 10:** Patrick Stroka, Hays Co. (12/1/16); **Dist. 11:** Peggy Jones, Hays & Caldwell Cos. (12/1/14); **Dist. 12:** Adam Yablonski, Medina Co. (12/1/16); **Dist. 13:** Chair Luana Buckner, Medina & Atascosa Cos. (12/1/14); **Dist. 14:** Juan O. Sanchez, Uvalde Co. (12/1/16); **Dist. 15:** Joe Parker, Uvalde Co. (12/1/14). Apptv. members: Fohn Bendele, Medina & Uvalde Cos. (12/1/16); Jerry James, South Central Texas Water Advisory Committee (12/1/16). Gen. Mgr. Roland Ruiz, 1615 N. St. Mary's St., San Antonio 78215; (210) 222-2204.

**Egg Marketing Advisory Board** – Abolished May 1997.

**Election Commission, State** – (1973); 9 members; 4 ex officio: Chmn. of Democratic State Executive Committee; Chmn. of Republican State Executive Committee; Chief Justice of Supreme Court; Court of Criminal Appeals Presiding Judge; 5 apptv.: 1 justice of the Court of Appeals apptd. by Chief Justice of Supreme Court, 1 District Judge apptd. by presiding judge of Court of Criminal Appeals; 2 county chairmen (1 Democrat, 1 Republican, named by their parties); Secretary of State.

**Emergency Communications, Commission on State** – (1985 as 17-member Advisory Commission on State Emergency Communications; name changed and members reduced to 12 in 2000); apptv.; 4-yr.; expenses; 12 members: 3 ex offico: reps. of Dept. of State Health Services, Public Utilities Comm., and Dept. of Information Resources; 9 apptd.: Chair William Buchholtz, San Antonio (9/1/15); Kay Alexander, Abilene (8/31/13); James Beauchamp, Midland (8/31/13); Sue Brannon, Midland (9/1/17); Richard Campbell, Center (9/1/17) Mitchell Fuller II, Cedar Park (9/1/15); Terry Henley, Meadows Place (9/1/13); Laura Gibbs Maczka, Richardson (9/1/17); Jack D. Miller, Denton (9/1/15). Exec. Dir. Kelli Merriweather ($90,750), 333 Guadalupe St., Ste. 2-212, Austin 78701-3942; (512) 305-6911.

**Emergency Management Council, State** – 32 members from state agencies and volunteer organizations. Texas Division of Emergency Management Chief W. Kim Kidd, 5805 N. Lamar Blvd., P.O. Box 4087, Austin 78773; (512) 424-2138.

**Emergency Services Retirement System, Texas** – (See Retirement System, Texas Emergency Services.)

**Employment Commission, Texas** – (See Workforce Commission, Texas.)

**Engineers, Texas Board of Professional** – (1937 as 6-member Texas State Board of Registration for Professional Engineers; members increased to 9 in 1981; name changed to present in 1997); apptv.; per diem and expenses; 6-yr.; 9 members: Chair Daniel O. Wong, Houston (9/26/13); Carry A. Baker, Amarillo (9/26/15); Lamberto (Bobby) Balli, San Antonio (9/26/15); James Alan Greer, Dallas (9/26/15); Sam Kannappan, Baytown (9/26/17); Sina K. Nejad, Beaumont (9/26/13); Elvira Reyna, Little Elm (9/26/13); Edward L. Summers, Austin (9/26/17); Kyle Womack, Horseshoe Bay (9/26/17). Exec. Dir. Lance Kinney ($107,625), 1917 IH-35 S, Austin 78741; (512) 440-7723.

**Environmental Quality, Texas Commission on** – (1913 as State Board of Water Engineers; name changed in 1962 to Texas Water Commission; reorganized and name changed in 1965 to Water Rights Commission; reorganized and name changed back to Texas Water Commission in 1977 to perform judicial function for the Texas Dept. of Water Resources; name changed to Texas Natural Resource Conservation Commission in 1993; changed to present form in 2002); apptv.; 6-yr.; 3 members full-time ($150,000): Chair Bryan W. Shaw, Bryan (8/31/13); Toby Baker, Austin (8/31/17); Zak Covar, Round Rock (8/31/15). Exec. Dir. Richard A. Hyde ($145,200), PO Box 13087, Austin 78711-3087; (512) 239-3900.

**Ethics Commission, Texas** – (1991); apptv.; 4-yr.; 8 members: 2 apptd. by House Speaker, 2 apptd. by Lt. Gov, 4 apptd. by Gov.: Chair Paul W. Hobby, Houston (11/19/15); Hugh C. Akin, Dallas (11/19/17); James Clancy, Portland (11/19/17); Wilhelmina Delco, Austin (11/19/15); Tom Harrison, Farmers Branch (11/19/11); Robert (Bob) Long, Bastrop (11/19/15); Thomas Ramsey, Mount Vernon (11/19/17); Chase Untermeyer, Houston (11/19/17). Exec. Dir. Natalia Luna Ashley ($115,000), 201 E. 14th St., 10th Floor, PO Box 12070, Austin 78711; (512) 463-5800. *Disclosure Filing Fax:* (512) 463-8808.

**Facilities Commission, Texas** – (2007; formerly Texas Building and Procurement Commission); apptv.; 6-yr.; 7 members: Chair Betty Reinbeck, Sealy (1/31/17); William Derek Darby, Austin (1/31/15); Douglas M. Hartman, Austin (1/31/13); Virginia I. Hermosa, Austin (1/31/15); Brant C. Ince, Dallas (1/31/15); Mike Novak, San Antonio (1/31/19); Alvin Shaw, Round Rock (1/31/17). Exec. Dir. Terry Keel ($126,500) 1711 San Jacinto, PO Box 13047, Austin 78711; (512) 463-3446.

**Family and Protective Services Advisory Council, Department of** – (1991 as Dept. of Protective and Regulatory Services; reorganized to present form in 2004); apptv.; 6-yr.; 9 members: Chair Gigi Edwards Bryant, Austin (2/1/13); Patricia Cole, Fort Worth (2/1/17); Debbie Epperson, Austin (1/31/13); Anna Jimenez, Corpus Christi (2/1/17); Christina R. Martin, Mission (2/1/15); Imogen Papadopoulos, Houston (2/1/15); Benny Morris, Cleveland (2/1/17); Linda Bell Robinson, Houston (2/1/13); Scott Rosenbach, Amarillo (2/1/15). Commissioner John J. Specia ($168,000), 701 West 51st St., PO Box 149030, Austin 78714; (512) 438-4800. *Abuse Hotline:* (800) 252-5400. *Ombudsman Hotline:* (800) 720-7777.

**Finance Commission of Texas** – (1923 as Banking Commission; reorganized as Finance Commission in 1943 with 9 members; members increased to 12 in 1983; changed back to 9 members in 1989; increased to 11 in 2009); apptv.; 6-yr.; per diem and traveling expenses; 11 members: Chair William James White, Georgetown (2/1/16); Susan Burton, Addison (2/1/16); Darby Ray Byrd Sr., Orange (2/1/18); Victor Leal, Amarillo (2/1/18); Stacy G. London, Houston (2/1/14); Cindy F. Lyons, El Paso (2/1/16); Lori B. McCool, Boerne (2/1/14); Jonathan B. Newton, Houston (2/1/16); Larry Patton, El Paso (2/1/14); Paul Plunket, Dallas (2/1/14); H.J. (Jay) Shands III, Lufkin (2/1/18). Banking Commissioner, Charles Cooper ($136,191), 2601 N. Lamar Blvd., Austin 78705; (512) 936-6222; appointee of Finance Commission. (*See also* Banking Commissioner, State.)

**Fire Fighters' Pension Commissioner** – (1937); apptv.; 4-yr.: Sherri Barr Walker, Pflugerville (7/1/15) ($77,000), 920 Colorado St., 11th Floor, PO Box 12577, Austin 78711; (512) 936-3372. (*See also* Retirement System, Texas Emergency Services.)

**Fire Protection, Texas Commission on** – (1991; formed by consolidation of Fire Dept. Emergency Board and Commission on Fire Protection Personnel Standards and Education); apptv.; 6-yrs.; expenses; 13 members: Chair Steven C. Tull, Valley Mills (2/1/15); Elroy Carson, Ransom Canyon (2/1/17); Pat Ekiss, Taylor (2/1/17); Yusuf Elias Farran, El Paso (2/1/15); Carl (Gene) Giles, Carthage (2/1/15); John Kelly Gillette III, Frisco (2/1/17); Joseph (Jody) Gonzalez, Krugerville (2/1/19); John W. Green, San Leon (2/1/17); Joseph Gutheinz, Pearland (2/1/19); John T. McMakin, LaRue (2/1/19); Robert Moore, Bryan (2/1/15); Lenny Perez, Brownsville (2/1/19); Ronald Poynter, McKinney (2/1/15). Exec. Dir. Don Wilson ($92,600), 1701 N. Congress, Ste. 1-105, PO Box 2286, Austin 78768; (512) 936-3838.

**Food and Fibers Commission, Texas** – Abolished Jan. 1, 2006, and duties transferred to the Texas Dept. of Agriculture Food and Fibers Research Council; PO Box 12847, Austin 78711; (512) 936-2450.

**Forensic Science Commission, Texas** – (2005); apptv.: 2-yr.; 9 members: 4 apptd. by Gov., 3 apptd. by Lt. Gov., and 2 apptd. by Atty. Gen.: Chair Vincent J.M. Di Maio, San Antonio (9/1/13); Richard B. Alpert, Fort Worth (9/1/13); Jeffrey J. Barnard, Dallas (9/1/13); Arthur Jay Eisenberg, Fort Worth (9/1/12); Jean Hampton, Houston (9/1/13); Brent Hutson, Dallas (9/1/13); Sarah Kerrigan, Huntsville (9/1/12); Robert J. Lerma, Brownsville, (9/1/13); Nizam Peerwani, Fort Worth (9/1/13). Coor. Leigh M. Tomlin, 1700 N. Congress Ave., Ste. 445, Austin, TX 78701; (888) 296-4232.

**Funeral Service Commission, Texas** – (1903 as State Board of Embalming; 1935 as State Board of Funeral Directors and Embalmers; name changed to present form in 1987); apptv.; per diem and expenses; 6-yr.; 7 members: Chair Gene Allen, Kerrville (2/1/15); Sue Evenwel, Mt. Pleasant (2/1/15); Joyce M. Odom, San Antonio (2/1/17); Jean (Jeanne) Olinger, Wichita Falls (9/1/19); Patrick Robertson, Clarendon (2/1/17); Jonathan Scepanski, McAllen (2/1/19); Gary Shaffer, San Angelo (2/1/19). Exec.

Dir. Kevin Heyburn ($70,000), 333 Guadalupe St., Ste. 2-110, Austin 78701; (512) 936-2474.

**General Services Commission** – Abolished in February 2002, with most functions taken over by the newly created Texas Building and Procurement Commission, which was renamed Texas Facilities Commission in 2007.

**Geoscientists, Texas Board of Professional** – (2001); apptv.; expenses; 3-yr.; 9 members (6 professional geoscientists, 3 public members): Chair Charles S. Knobloch, Houston (2/1/15); Joseph P. DeWoody, Fort Worth (2/1/19); Charles T. (Tom) Hallmark, Hearne (2/1/19); Becky L. Johnson, Fort Worth (2/1/17); Kelly Krenz-Doe, Houston (2/1/15); Christopher C. Mathewson, College Station (2/1/17); Justin McNamee, Rowlett (2/1/15); W. David Prescott II, Amarillo (2/1/19); Gregory C. Ulmer, Houston (2/1/17). Exec. Dir. Charles Horton ($70,000), 333 Guadalupe St., Tower 1, Ste. 530; PO Box 13225, Austin 78711; (512) 936-4400.

**Guadalupe-Blanco River Authority** – (1935); apptv.; per diem and expenses on duty; 6-yr.; 9 members: Chair Oscar H. Fogle, Lockhart (2/1/17); Robert (Rusty) Brockman, New Braunfels (2/1/17); William R. Carbonara, Tivoli (2/1/19); Grace G. Kunde, Seguin (2/1/15); Thomas (Tommy) Mathews, Boerne (2/1/15); Darrell McLain, Gonzales (2/1/19); Don B. Meador, Dripping Springs (2/1/19); Kenneth Motl, Port Lavaca (2/1/17); Dennis Patillo, Victoria (2/1/15). Gen. Mgr. William E. West, 933 E. Court St., Seguin 78155; (830) 379-5822.

**Guadalupe River Authority Board of Directors, Upper** – (1939); apptv.; 6-yr.; 9 members: Pres. Stan R. Kubenka, Kerrville (2/1/15); Mike L. Allen, Kerrville (2/1/19); Harold Danford, Kerrville (2/1/17); Lester C. Ferguson, Kerrville (2/1/15); D. Michael (Mike) Hughes, Ingram (2/1/17); Hugh Jons, Kerrville (2/1/17); Claudell Kercheville, Kerrville (2/1/19); Lucy Wilke, Kerrville (2/1/15); Brian Wright, Center Point (2/1/19). Gen. Mgr. Ray Buck Jr., 125 Lehman Dr., Ste. 100, Kerrville 78028-5908; (830) 896-5445.

**Guaranteed Student Loan Corporation, Texas** – (1979 as non-profit corp.); apptv.; 6-yr.; 1 ex-officio member (Comptroller of Public Accounts); 9 apptv.: Ivan A. Andarza, Austin (1/31/13); Yvonne Batts, Abilene (1/31/17); Frank (Skip) Landis, College Station (1/31/17); Richard M. Rhodes, Austin (1/31/15); Connie S. Sitterly, Fort Worth (1/31/13); Dora Ann Verde, San Antonio (1/31/15); 2 vacancies; student apptee.: Fernando Trevino, Jr., Del Rio (1/31/17). Pres. and CEO Sue McMillin, 301 Sundance Parkway, PO Box 83100, Round Rock 78683; (800) 252-5700.

**Guardianship Certification Board** – (2006); apptd. by the Texas Supreme Court; 6-yr.; 15 members: Chair Judge Gladys Burwell, Friendswood (2/1/17); Barry Anderson, Arlington (2/1/13); Jason Armstrong, Lufkin (2/1/13); Leah Cohen, Austin (2/1/15); Patricia Blair, Houston (2/1/15); Garth Corbett, Austin (2/1/17); Carol Patrice Dabner, Dallas (2/1/15); Don D. Ford III, Houston (2/1/17); Toni Rhodes Glover, Fort Worth (2/1/17); Philip A. Grant, Conroe (2/1/15); Jamie MacLean, Austin (2/1/17); Marlane Meyer, McAllen (2/1/13); Amy R. Parsons, Houston (2/1/13); Robert Warach, El Paso (2/1/15); Bob Jones, Lubbock (2/1/13). Dir. Lesley Martin Ondrechen, 205 W. 14th St., 6th Floor, PO Box 12066, Austin 78711; (512) 463-1635.

**Gulf Coast Waste Disposal Authority** – (1969); apptv.; 2-yr.; per diem, expenses on duty; 9 members: 3 apptd. by Gov., 3 by County Commissioners Courts of counties in district, 3 by Mayors Council of cities in district. Chair Mark Schultz, Chambers Co. (8/31/13); Zoe Milian Barinaga, Harris Co. (8/31/13); Stan Cromartie, Galveston Co. (8/31/14); Ron Crowder, Galveston Co. (8/31/13); Franklin Jones Jr., Harris Co. (8/31/13); Lamont Meaux, Chambers Co. (8/31/14); Irvin Osborne-Lee, Harris Co. (8/31/14); Chris Peden, Galveston Co. (8/31/15); Rita Standridge, Chambers Co. (8/31/14). Gen. Mgr. Ricky Clifton, 910 Bay Area Blvd., Houston 77058; (281) 488-4115.

**Gulf States Marine Fisheries Commission** – (1949 with members from Texas, Alabama, Florida, Louisiana and Mississippi); apptv.; 3-yr.; 3 Texas members: 2 ex officio: Texas Parks and Wildlife Dept. exec. dir. and 1 member of Legislature; 1 apptd. by Gov.: Troy B. Williamson II, Portland (3/17/14). Interim Exec. Dir. David M. Donaldson, PO Box 726, Ocean Springs, MS 39566-0726; (228) 875-5912.

**Health Coordinating Council, Statewide** – (1977); apptv.; 6-yr.; 17 members (4 ex officio; 13 apptd. by Gov.): Chair Mike Ragain, Lubbock (8/1/15); James L. Alexander, College Station (8/1/13); Abigail Blackburn, Austin (8/1/15); Richard Beard, Mesquite (8/1/15); Davidica Blum, Georgetown (8/1/13); Fred S. Brinkley Jr., Austin (8/1/15); Lourdes M. Cuellar, Houston

(8/1/17); Mabrie Jackson, Plano (8/1/17); Ayeez A. Lalji, Sugar Land (8/1/13); Elva C. LeBlanc, Fort Worth (8/1/13); Danny K. Mc-Coy, Corsicana (8/1/17); Elizabeth Protas, League City (8/1/17); Bob Yancy, College Station (8/1/15). Ex-officio members include 1 each from Texas Dept. of State Health Services, Texas Dept. of Aging and Disability Services, Texas Higher Education Coordinating Board, and Texas Health and Human Services Commission. Interim Proj. Dir. Ann Barnett, PO Box 149347, Austin, TX 78714-9347; (512) 776-7261.

**Health and Human Services Commission Council** – (1991); apptv.; 4-yr.; 9 members: Chair Jerry Kane, Corpus Christi (2/1/15); Kathleen O. Angel, Georgetown (2/1/17); James (Richard) Barajas, Fort Worth (2/1/19); Maryann Choi, Georgetown (2/1/17); Karen Harris, Lakehills (2/1/17); Rev. Manson B. Johnson, Houston (2/1/15); Leon J. Leach, Houston (2/1/17); Thomas Craig Wheat, Dallas (2/1/19); Teresa (Terry) Wilkinson, Midland (2/1/15). Commissioner Chris Traylor ($230,000; 2/1/15), 4900 North Lamar, PO Box 13247, Austin 78711; (512) 424-6500.

**Health and Human Services, Commissioner of** – (1879 as State Health Officer; 1955 changed to Commissioner of Health; 1975 changed to Director, Texas Department of Health Resources; 1977 changed to Commissioner, Texas Dept. of Health; changed to present name in 2004); apptv.; 2-yr.: Chris Traylor ($230,000; 2/1/15), PO Box 13247, Austin 78711-3247; (512) 424-6603.

**Health Professions Council** – (1993); ex officio; 14 members: 1 from Gov.'s office and 1 each from the following 13 regulating agencies: Texas Board of Chiropractic Examiners, Texas State Board of Dental Examiners, Texas Medical Board, Texas Board of Nursing, Texas Optometry Board, Texas State Board of Pharmacy, Physical Therapy Examiners Board, Texas State Board of Podiatric Medical Examiners, Texas Board of Examiners of Psychologists, Occupational Therapy Examiners Board, Texas Board of Veterinary Medical Examiners, Texas Funeral Service Commission, Texas Department of State Health Services Professional Licensing and Certification Unit. Admin. Officer John Monk, 333 Guadalupe St., Ste. 2-220, Austin 78701; (512) 305-8550.

**Health Services Authority, Texas** – (2007); apptv.; 2-yr.; expenses; 2 ex officio plus 11 apptd. members: Chair Edward W. Marx, Colleyville (6/15/13); Fred Buckwold, Houston (6/15/13); David C. Fleeger, Austin (6/15/13); Matthew J. Hamlin, Argyle (6/15/13); James Martin, Austin (6/15/13); Kathleen K. Mechler, Fredericksburg (6/15/13); William Phillips Jr., San Antonio (6/15/13); Judy Powell, The Woodlands (6/15/13); Jennifer Rangel, Austin (6/15/13); J. Darren Rodgers, Dallas (6/15/13); Stephen Yurco, Austin (6/15/13). CEO Tony Gilman, Texas Health Services Authority, San Jacinto Building, 221 E. 9th, Ste. 201, Austin 78701; (512) 814-0321.

**Health Services Council, Texas Department of State** – (1975); apptv.; 4-yr.; 9 members: Chair Glenda R. Kane, Corpus Christi (2/1/15); Kirk Aquilla Calhoun, Tyler (2/1/17); Lewis E. Foxhall, Houston (2/1/15); Jacinto P. Juarez, Laredo (2/1/19); Rev. William Lovell, Dallas (2/1/17); Jeffrey A. Ross, Bellaire, (2/1/19); Nasruddin Rupani, Sugar Land (2/1/15); Maria Teran, El Paso (2/1/19); David Woolweaver, Harlingen (2/1/17). Commissioner David L. Lakey ($183,750), 1100 West 49th St., PO Box 149347, Austin 78714; (512) 458-7111.

**Hearing Instruments, State Committee of Examiners in the Fitting and Dispensing of** – (1969); apptv.; 6-yr.; expenses; 9 members: Chair William McCrae, San Antonio (12/31/17); Gary A. Haun, San Angelo (12/31/15); Carla Hoffman, Corpus Christi (12/31/15); James Leffingwell, Arlington (12/31/13); Benjamin Norris, Elm Mott (12/31/13); Jesus Rangel, Longview (12/31/17); Cindy M. Steinbart, Round Rock (12/31/15); Amy Trost, Seguin (12/31/13); Barbara Willy, Sugar Land (12/31/17). Exec. Dir. Joyce N. Parsons, c/o Texas Dept. of State Health Services, PO Box 149347, MC 1982, Austin 78714-9347; (512) 834-6784.

**Higher Education Coordinating Board, Texas** – (1953 as temporary board; 1955 as permanent 15-member Texas Commission on Higher Education; 1965 as Texas College and University Systems Coordinating Board; name and membership changed to present form in 1987); apptv.; 6-yr.; expenses; 9 members plus 1 student rep.: Chair Harold W. Hahn, El Paso (8/31/19); Dora G. Alcala, Del Rio (8/31/15); S. Javaid Anwar, Midland (8/31/15); Sada Cumber, Sugar Land (8/31/15); Janelle Shepard, Weatherford (8/31/17); John Steen, San Antonio (8/31/19); David D. Teuscher, Beaumont (8/31/17); one vacancy. Commissioner of Higher Education, Raymund A. Paredes, ($186,300 plus supplement) 1200 E. Anderson Lane, PO Box 12788, Austin 78711; (512) 427-6101.

**Higher Education Tuition Board, Texas Prepaid** – (1995); apptv.; expenses; term at pleasure of Gov.; 6 members, plus 1 ex officio: State Comptroller; 2 apptd. by Gov. and 4 apptd. by Lt. Gov. Gov. appointments: Joe Colonnetta, Dallas (2/1/17); Stephen N. Mueller, Cypress (2/1/15); c/o Educational Opportunities & Investments Division, Comptroller of Public Accounts, PO Box 13407, Austin 78711-3407; (800) 445-4723.

**Historian, Texas State** – (2005); apptv.; 2-yr.; Bill O'Neal, Carthage (8/22/14).

**Historical Commission, Texas** – (1953); apptv.; expenses; 6-yr.; 17 members: Chair John L. Nau III, Houston (2/1/21); Earl P. Broussard Jr., Austin (2/1/17); John Crain, Dallas (1/31/19); Deanna Benavides Galo, Laredo (2/1/21); Thomas M. Hatfield, Austin (2/1/17); Wallace B. Jefferson, Austin (2/1/19); Tom Perini, Buffalo Gap (2/1/17); Gilbert E. Peterson III, Alpine (1/31/19); Judy Richardson, Caldwell (2/1/17); Robert K. Shepard, Weatherford (2/1/17); Daisy Sloan White, Houston (2/1/17); 1 vacancy. Exec. Dir. Mark Wolfe ($128,775), 1511 Colorado St., PO Box 12276, Austin 78711; (512) 463-6100.

**Holocaust and Genocide Commission, Texas** – (2009); created by 81st Legislature. apptv.; 4-yr.; 18 members: 3 ex officio,15 apptv.: Chair Peter N. Berkowitz, Houston (2/1/15); Fran Berg, Dallas (2/1/15); Martin Fein, Houston (2/1/15); Ian F. Hancock, Buda (2/1/15); Frank Kasman, Midland (2/1/15); Zsuzsanna Ozsvath, Richardson (2/1/15); Gregg Philipson, Austin (2/1/15); Suzanne Ransleben, Rockport (2/1/15); Stanley Rosenberg, San Antonio (2/1/15); David Alex Schulz, San Antonio (2/1/15); Ambassador Sichan Siv, San Antonio (2/1/15); Anna Steinberger, Houston (2/1/15); Gilbert Tuhabonye, Austin (2/1/15); LaSalle R. Vaughn, Helotes (2/1/15); Chaja Verveer, Friendswoodn (2/1/15). Exec. Dir. Mark Wolfe 1511 Colorado St., PO Box 12276, Austin 78711; (512) 463-8815.

**Housing and Community Affairs, Texas Dept. of** – (1979 as Texas Housing Agency; merged with Department of Community Affairs and name changed in 1991); apptv.; expenses; 6-yr.; 7 members: Chair John Paul (J. Paul) Oxer, Sugar Land (1/31/17); Leslie Bingham-Escareño, Brownsville (1/31/19); Tom H. Gann, Lufkin (1/31/15); Lowell Keig, Austin (1/31/19); John (Mark) McWatters, Dallas (1/31/15); Juan Sanchez Muñoz, Lubbock (1/31/17); 1 vacancy. Exec. Dir. Tim Irvine ($129,250), 221 East 11th St., PO Box 13941, Austin 78711; (512) 475-3800.

**Housing Corp., Texas State Affordable** – (1994); 6 yrs.; 5 members: Chair Robert Jones, Corpus Christi (2/1/17); William H. Dietz Jr., Waco (2/1/19); Gerry Evenwel, Mt. Pleasant (2/1/17); Alex Meade III, Mission (2/1/19); Jerry Romero, El Paso (2/1/15). Pres. David Long, PO Box 12637, Austin 78711-2637; (512) 477-3555.

**Human Rights, Texas Commission on** – (2004 as part of the Texas Workforce Commission's Civil Rights Division); apptv.; 6-yr.; 7 members: Chair Thomas M. Anderson, Richmond (2/1/19); Michelle H. Diggs, Cedar Park (2/1/15); Toni Rhodes Glover, Fort Worth (2/1/17); Shara Michalka, Dallas (2/1/17); Danny L. Osterhout, Andrews (2/1/19); Veronica Vargas Stidvent, Austin (2/1/15); Sharon Breckenridge Thomas, San Antonio (2/1/15). Dir. Jonathan Babiak, 101 E. 15th St., Rm. 144, Austin 78778-0001; (512) 463-2642.

**Industrialized Building Code Council, Texas** – (1973); apptv.; 2-yr.; 12 members: Chair Rolando R. Rubiano, Harlingen (2/1/15); Roland L. Brown, Mansfield (2/1/15); Joe D. Campos, Dallas (2/1/14); Randy Childers, Waco (2/1/14); Steven Fitzpatrick, Tyler, (2/1/14); Edward Martin Jr., Austin (2/1/15); Scott A. McDonald, Amarillo (2/1/15); Mark Remmert, Round Rock (2/1/14); Jesse Rider, Tyler (2/01/14); Douglas O. Robinson, Fort Worth (2/1/15); William F. Smith III, Dripping Springs (2/1/14); Larry E. Wilkinson, League City (2/1/15); c/o Texas Dept. of Licensing and Regulation, PO Box 12157, Austin 78711; (512) 463-6599.

**Information Resources, Department of** – (1981 as Automated Information and Telecommunications Council; name changed to current in 1990); 6-yr.; expenses; 10 members: 3 ex officio, 7 apptv.: Chair Charles Bacarisse, Houston (2/1/19); Richard Moore, Goliad (2/1/15); Phillip (Keith) Morrow, Southlake (2/1/17); Robert E. Pickering Jr., Houston (2/1/15); Wanda Rohm, San Antonio (2/1/17); Arthur Troilo III, Lakeway (2/1/15); Cynthia Villa, El Paso (2/1/19); ex-officio members are from Health and Human Services Commission, Texas Dept. of Insurance and Texas Dept. of Transportation. Chief Information Officer, Karen Robinson ($175,000), 300 W.15th, #1300, PO Box 13564, Austin 78711; (512) 475-4700.

**Insurance Commissioner, Texas Dept. of** – (1876 as Dept. of Insurance; 1887 as Dept. of Agriculture, Insurance, Statistics and History; 1907 as Dept. of Insurance and Banking; 1923 as Dept. of Insurance); apptv.; 2-yr.; Commissioner David Mattax, Austin (2/1/15), ($175,000), 333 Guadalupe, PO Box 149104, Austin 78714; (512) 463-6169.

**Insurance Counsel, Office of Public** – (*See* Public Insurance Counsel, Office of.)

**Interstate Commission for Adult Offender Supervision** – (1937 as Interstate Compact for the Supervision of Parolees and Probationers; 2000 as present name); 50 member states; apptv.: Kathie Winckler, Houston (2/1/17). Compact Admin. for Texas Stuart Jenkins, 8712 Shoal Creek Blvd., Ste. 290, Austin 78757; (512) 406-5990.

**Interstate Mining Compact Commission** – (1970); 19 member states, plus 5 associate member states; ex officio or apptv., according to Gov's. choice; Texas reps. are appointed from the Texas Railroad Commission: David J. Porter. Exec. Dir. Gregory E. Conrad, 445-A Carlisle Dr., Herndon, VA 22170-4802; (703) 709-8654.

**Interstate Oil and Gas Compact Commission** – (1935); 30 member states, plus 8 associate member states; ex officio or apptv., according to Gov's. choice; per diem and expenses. Official rep. for Texas:David J. Porter, Austin. Exec. Dir. Mike Smith, PO Box 53127, Oklahoma City, OK 73152; (405) 525-3556.

**Jail Standards, Texas Commission on** – (1975); apptv.; 6-yr.; expenses; 9 members: Chair Donna S. Klaeger, Burnet (1/31/19); Irene A. Armendariz, El Paso (1/31/15); Albert Cain, Carthage (1/31/17); Stanley D. Egger, Abilene (1/31/17); Jerry W. Lowry, New Caney (1/31/19); Larry S. May, Sweetwater (1/31/19); Gary Painter, Midland (2/1/15); Michael M. Seale, Houston (1/31/17); Tam Terry, White Deer (1/31/15). Exec. Dir. Brandon Wood Jr. ($75,350), 300 W. 15th St., Ste. 503, PO Box 12985, Austin 78711-2985; (512) 463-5505.

**Judicial Compensation Commission** – (2007); apptv.; 6-yr.; expenses; 9 members: Chair William Strawn, Austin (2/1/15); Bill Brod, Jr., Pasadena (2/1/17); Conrith Warren Davis, Sugar Land (2/1/17); Tommy Harwell, El Paso (2/1/13); Cruz G. Hernandez, Burleson (2/1/15); Patrick Mizell, Houston (2/1/19); Paul Bane Phillippi, Austin (2/1/15); Linda Russell, Houston (2/1/19); Michael Slack, Austin (2/1/17); c/o Office of Court Administration, Tom C. Clark Building, 205 W. 14th St., Ste. 600, Austin 78701; (512) 463-1625.

**Judicial Conduct, State Commission on** – (1965 as 9-member Judicial Qualifications Commission; name changed to present in 1977); expenses; 6-yr.; 13 members: 6 apptd. by Supreme Court; 2 apptd. by State Bar; 5 apptd. by Gov.: Chair Steven L. Seider, Dallas (11/19/15); Joel Baker, Tyler (11/19/17); Valerie Ertz, Dallas (11/19/17); Demetrius Bivins, Houston (11/19/19); Douglas S. Lang, Dallas, (11/19/19); M. Sue Kurita, El Paso (11/19/15); Orlinda Naranjo, Austin (11/19/19); Ricky Raven, Houston (11/19/17); Edward J. Spillaine III, College Station (11/19/15). *Public Members:* Martha Morales Hernandez, Diboll (11/19/15); Patti H. Johnson, Canyon Lake (11/19/17); David M. Russell, Dripping Springs (11/19/19); Diane De La Torre Threadgill, Midlothian (11/19/15). Exec. Dir. Seana B. Willing ($110,000), PO Box 12265, Austin 78711-2265; (512) 463-5533.

**Judicial Council, Texas** – (1929 as Texas Civil Judicial Council; name changed in 1975); 6-yr.; expenses; 22 members: 16 ex officio and 6 apptd. from general public. *Citizen Members:* Richard Battle, Lakeway (6/30/15); Richard S. Figueroa, Houston (6/30/19); Allyson Ho, Dallas (6/30/19); Ashley Johnson, Dallas (6/30/17); Henry (Hank) Nuss, Corpus Christi (6/30/15). Exec. Dir. David Slayton ($121,847), PO Box 12066, Austin 78711; (512) 463-1625.

**Judicial Districts Board** – (1985); 12 ex-officio members (term in other office); 1 apptv. (4 yrs.); ex officio: Chief Justice of Texas Supreme Court; Presiding Judge, Court of Criminal Appeals; Presiding Judge of each of 9 Administrative Judicial Districts; Gov. apptee.: Craig Enoch, Austin (12/12/14).

**Judicial Districts of Texas, Administrative, Presiding Judges of** – (*See* Administrative Judicial Districts, Presiding Judges.)

**Juneteenth Cultural and Historical Commission, Texas Emancipation** – (1997); apptv.; 6 yr.; expenses; 11 members; 5 ex officio, 6 apptd by Gov.: Chair Rep. Al Edwards, Houston; Vicki D. Blanton, Dallas (2/1/11); Willie Belle Boone, Houston (2/1/15);

Carmen Francis, Georgetown (2/1/11); Clarence E. Glover Jr., Dallas (2/1/13); Rev. William H. Watson, Lubbock (2/1/13); PO Box 2910, Austin 78768-2910; (512) 463-0518.

**Juvenile Probation Commission, Texas** – (1981); abolished on Dec. 1, 2011, pursuant to Senate Bill 653, passed by the 82nd Texas Legislature and signed by the Gov.; its operations and those of the Texas Youth Commission were transferred to the Texas Juvenile Justice Department.

**Juvenile Justice, Texas Department of** – (2011) created by Senate Bill 653, 82nd Legislature; combines the Texas Youth Commission and Texas Juvenile Probation Commission; apptv.; 6-yr.; expenses; 13 members: Chair Scott Fisher, Bedford (2/1/19); John Brieden, Brenham (2/1/17); Joseph Brown, Sherman (2/1/17); Carol Bush, Waxahachie (2/1/19); Becky Gregory, Dallas (2/1/19); Jane Anderson King, Canyon (2/1/17); David (Scott) Matthew, Georgetown (2/1/19); MaryLou Mendoza, San Antonio (2/1/19); Rene Olvera, San Antonio (2/1/17); Laura Lee Parker, San Antonio (2/1/15); Jimmy Smith, Midland (2/1/15); Calvin Stephens, Dallas (2/1/15); Melissa Weiss, Bellville (2/1/15). Exec. Dir. Mike Griffiths ($172,000), 11209 Metric Boulevard, P.O. Box 12757, Austin 78711-2757; (512) 424-6130.

**Land Board, School** – (1939); 2-yr.; per diem and expenses; 3 members: 1 ex officio: Comm. of General Land Office; 2 apptd.: 1 by Atty. Gen. and 1 by Gov.: Tommy Orr, Houston (8/29/11); David S. Herrmann, San Antonio (8/31/11); c/o General Land Office, SFA Office Bldg., 1700 N. Congress Ave., Austin 78701-1495; (512) 463-5001.

**Land Board, Veterans'** – (Est. 1949 as 3-member ex-officio board; reorganized 1956); 4-yr.; per diem and expenses; 3 members: 1 ex officio: Comm. of General Land Office; 2 apptd.: Alan L. Johnson, Harlingen (12/29/16); Alan K. Sandersen, Missouri City (12/29/14). Exec. Sec. Paul E. Moore, PO Box 12873, Austin 78711-2873; (800) 252-8387.

**Land Surveying, Texas Board of Professional** – (1979; formed from consolidation of Board of Examiners of Licensed Land Surveyors, est. 1977, and State Board of Registration for Public Surveyors, est. 1955); apptv.; 6-yr.; 9 members: 1 ex officio: Comm. of General Land Office; 8 apptd.: Chair David G. (Greg) Smyth, Uvalde (1/31/13); James Allen Childress, San Saba (1/31/15); Mary Chruszczak, The Woodlands (1/31/17); Nedra J. Foster, Silsbee (1/31/15); Gerardo M. (Jerry) Garcia, Corpus Christi (1/21/17); Jon Hodde, Brenham (1/31/13); Paul P. Kwan, Houston (1/31/17); Robert H. (Bob) Price, Euless (1/31/15). Exec. Dir. Frank DiTucci ($65,000), 12100 Park 35 Circle, Bldg. A, Ste. 156, MC 230, Austin 78753; (512) 239-5263.

**Lands, Board for Lease of University** – (1929 as 3-member board; members increased to 4 in 1985); ex officio; term in other office; 4 members: Comm. of General Land Office, 2 members of Board of Regents of The University of Texas, 1 member Board of Regents of Texas A&M University. Sec. Sharon Burks, The University of Texas System; (432) 684-4404.

**Lavaca-Navidad River Authority, Board of Directors** – (1954 as 7-member Jackson County Flood Control District; reorganized as 9-member board in 1959; name changed to present form in 1969); apptv.; 6-yr.; per diem and expenses; 9 members: Jerry Adelman, Palacios (5/1/17); Jon Bradford, Edna (5/1/13); John Alcus Cotten Jr., Ganado (5/1/15); Sherry Kay Frels, Edna (5/1/13); Olivia R. Jarratt, Edna (5/1/13); Ronald Edwin Kubecka, Palacios (5/1/15); Nils P. Mauritz, Ganado (5/1/15); David Martin Muegge, Edna (5/1/17); Terri Parker, Ganado (5/1/17). Gen. Mgr. Patrick Brzozowski, PO Box 429, Edna 77957; (361) 782-5229.

**Law Enforcement Officer Standards & Education, Texas Commission on** – (1965); expenses; 14 members; 5 ex officio: Atty. Gen., Dir. of Public Safety, Comm. of Education, Exec. Dir. of Gov.'s Office Criminal Justice Division, and Comm. of Higher Education; 9 apptv. members: Chair Charles R. Hall, Midland (8/30/11); Stephen M. Griffith, Sugar Land (8/10/13); Johnny E. Lovejoy II, San Antonio (8/30/13); James Oakley, Spicewood (8/30/11); Joseph B. Pennington, Jersey Village (8/10/15); Joel W. Richardson, Canyon (8/30/13); Pat Scheckel-Hollingsworth, Arlington (8/30/13); Ruben Villescas, Pharr (8/30/15); John Randall (Randy) Watson, Burleson (8/30/15). Exec. Dir. Timothy Braaten ($88,000), 6330 U.S. Hwy. 290 E, Ste. 200, Austin 78723-1035; (512) 936-7700.

**Law Examiners, Texas Board of** – (1919); 9 attorneys apptd. by Supreme Court biennially for 2-year terms expiring Sept. 30 of odd-numbered years. Compensation set by Supreme Court not to exceed $20,000 per annum: Chair John Simpson, Lubbock;

Jerry Grissom, Dallas; Jerry Nugent, Austin; Al Odom, Houston; Cynthia Olsen, Houston; E. Lee Parsley, Austin; Dan Pozza, San Antonio; Michael Sokolow, Houston; Sandra Zamora. Exec. Dir. Julia Vaughan, PO Box 13486, Austin 78711-3486; (512) 463-1621.

**Law Library Board, Texas State** – (1971); ex officio; expenses; 3 members: Atty. Gen., Chief Justice State Supreme Court, Presiding Judge Court of Criminal Appeals. Dir. Dale Propp ($70,180), PO Box 12367, Austin 78711-2367; (512) 463-1722.

**Legislative Budget Board** – (1949); 10 members; 5 ex-officio: Lt. Gov.; House Speaker; Chmn., Senate Finance Comm.; Chmn., House Appropriations Comm.; Chmn., House Ways and Means Comm.; plus 5 other members of Legislature. Dir. John O'Brian, PO Box 12666, Austin 78711-2666; (512) 463-1200.

**Legislative Council, Texas** – (1949); 14 ex-officio members: Lt. Gov.; House Speaker; 6 senators apptd. by Lt. Gov.; 5 representatives apptd. by Speaker; Chmn., House Administration Committee. Exec. Dir. Debbie Irvine, PO Box 12128, Austin 78711-2128; (512) 463-1155.

**Legislative Redistricting Board** – (1951); 5 ex-officio members: Lt. Gov., House Speaker, Atty. Gen., Comptroller of Public Accounts and Comm. of General Land Office; PO Box 12128, Austin 78711-2128; (512) 463-1155.

**Legislative Reference Library** – See Library, Legislative Reference.

**Librarian, State** – (Originally est. in 1839; present office est. 1909); apptv., indefinite term: Peggy D. Rudd ($104,500), PO Box 12927, Austin 78711-2927; (512) 463-5455.

**Library and Archives Commission, Texas State** – (1909 as 5-member Library and State Historical Commission; name changed to present form in 1979); apptv.; per diem and expenses on duty; 6-yr.; 7 members: Chair Sandra J. Pickett, Liberty (9/28/15); Sharon T. Carr, El Paso (9/28/11); Martha Doty Freeman, Austin (9/28/15); Larry G. Holt, College Station (9/28/15); Wm. Scott McAfee, Dripping Springs (9/28/13); Sally Reynolds, Rockport (9/28/11); Michael C. Waters, Dallas (9/28/13). Dir. and Librarian Peggy D. Rudd ($104,500), PO Box 12927, Austin 78711-2927; (512) 463-5455.

**Library, Legislative Reference** – (1909); 3 ex-officio members: Lt. Gov., House Speaker, Chrm., House Appropriations Committee; 3 Legislative members; indefinite term. Dir. Mary Camp, Box 12488, Austin 78711-2488; (512) 463-1252.

**Licensing and Regulation, Texas Department on** – (1989); apptv.; 6-yr.; expenses; 7 members: Chair Frank S. Denton, Conroe (2/1/13); Mike Arismendez Jr., Shallowater (2/1/15); LuAnn Roberts Morgan, Midland (2/1/15); Fred N. Moses, Plano (2/1/15); Lillian Norman-Keeney, Taylor Lake Village (2/1/17); Ravi Shah, The Colony (2/1/17); Deborah A. Yurco, Austin (2/1/13). Exec. Dir. Willliam H. Kuntz Jr. ($145,000); PO Box 12157, Austin 78711-2157; (800) 803-9202.

**Licensing Standards, Committee on**– (2007); apptv.; 2-yr.; expenses; 7 members: Chair Karyn Purvis, Fort Worth (2/1/11); Dan Adams, Amarillo (2/1/11); Adriene J. Driggers, San Antonio (2/1/11); Kimberly B. Kofron, Round Rock (2/1/11); Sasha Rasco, Austin (2/1/11); Ann Stanley, Austin (2/1/11); Tivy Whitlock, Mico (2/1/11). Dept. of Family and Protective Services, PO Box 149030, Austin 78714-9030; (512) 438-4800.

**Lottery Commission, Texas** – (1993); 6-yrs.; apptv.; expenses; 5 members: Chair J. Winston Krause, Austin (2/1/19); Carmen Arrieta-Candelaria, El Paso (2/1/17); Peggy Heeg, Houston (2/1/19); Doug Lowe, Houston (2/1/17); Robert Rivera, Arlington (2/1/21). Exec. Dir. Gary Grief ($185,319), PO Box 16630, Austin 78761-6630; (512) 344-5000.

**Lower Colorado River Authority** – (See Colorado River Authority, Lower).

**Lower Concho River Water and Soil Conservation Authority** – (See Concho River Water and Soil Conservation, Lower).

**Lower Neches Valley Authority** – (See Neches Valley Authority, Lower).

**Manufactured Housing Governing Board** – (1995); apptv.; 6 yrs.; 5 members: Chair Michael H. Bray, El Paso (1/31/17); Anthony Burks, Fort Worth (1/31/17); Pablo Schneider, Richardson (1/31/13); Sheila M. Vallés-Pankratz, Mission (1/31/15); Donnie W. Wisenbaker, Sulphur Springs (1/31/13). Exec. Dir. Joe Garcia, PO Box 12489, Austin 78711-2489; (512) 475-2200.

**Marriage & Family Therapists, Texas State Board of Examiners of** – (1991); apptv.; 6 yrs.; per diem and transportation expenses; 9 members: Chair Sandra L. DeSobe, Houston (2/1/13); Rick Bruhn, Huntsville (2/1/17); Joe Ann Clack, Missouri City (2/1/15); George Francis IV, Georgetown (2/1/17); Michael Miller, Belton (2/1/13); Michael R. Puhl, McKinney (2/1/15); Jennifer Smothermon, Abilene (2/1/13); Sean Stokes, Denton (2/1/17); Beverly Walker Womack, Jacksonville (2/1/15). Exec. Dir. Carol Miller, Texas Dept. of Health Services, PO Box 149347, MC 1982, Austin 78714-9347; (512) 834-6657.

**Medical Board, Texas** – (1907 as 11-member Texas State Board of Medical Examiners; members increased to 12 in 1931, 15 in 1981,18 in 1993 and 19 in 2003; changed to present name in 2005 by Senate Bill 419); apptv.; 6-yr.; per diem on duty; 19 members: Chair Michael Arambula, M.D., Pharm.D., San Antonio (4/13/19); Manuel G. Guajardo, M.D., Brownsville (4/13/15); John Guerra, D.O., Mission (4/13/17); J. Scott Holliday, University Park (4/13/19); Margaret C. McNeese, M.D., Houston (4/13/19); Allan N. Shulkin, M.D., Dallas (4/13/15); Robert Simonson, D.O., Duncanville (4/13/15); Wynne M. Snoots M.D., Dallas (4/13/15); Karl W. Swann, M.D., Belton (4/13/19); Surendra K. Varma, M.D., Lubbock (4/13/19); Stanley Wang, M.D., Austin (4/13/17); George Willeford III, M.D., Austin (4/13/17). *Public Members:* Julie Attebury, Amarillo (4/13/17); David Baucom, Sulphur Springs (4/13/15); Frank S. Denton, Conroe (4/13/19); John D. Ellis Jr., Houston (4/13/15); Carlos L. Gallardo, Frisco (4/13/17); Paulette B. Southard, Alice (4/13/15); Timothy Webb, Houston (4/13/19); Exec. Dir. Mari Robinson ($121,000 plus supplement), PO Box 2018, Austin 78768-2018; (512) 305-7010. *Consumer Complaint Hotline: (800) 201-9353.*

**Medical Physicists, Texas Board of Licensure for Professional** – (1991); apptv.; 6-yrs.; 9 members: Chair Richard E. Wendt III, Houston (2/1/13); Charles Beasley, Bellaire (2/1/17); Valerie Foreman, Frisco (2/1/15); Douglas A. Johnson, College Station (2/1/13); John R. Leahy, Austin (2/1/13); James Marbach, San Antonio (2/1/17); Pamela M. Otto, San Antonio (2/1/15); Kiran Shah, Houston (2/1/17); Alvin (Lee) Schlichtemeier (2/1/15). Exec. Sec. Ann Hammer, PO Box 149347, Austin 78714-9347; (512) 834-6655.

**Midwestern State University, Board of Regents** – (1959); apptv.; 6-yr.; 9 members: Chair Carol Carlson Gunn, Graford (2/25/12); Michael Bernhardt, Wichita Falls (2/25/16); J. Kenneth Bryant, Wichita Falls (2/25/16); Tiffany D. Burks, Grand Prairie (2/25/16); Charles Engleman, Wichita Falls (2/25/14); Fenton Lynwood Givens, Plano (2/25/12); Shawn G. Hessing, Fort Worth (2/25/14); Samuel M. Sanchez, Fort Worth (2/25/12); Jane W. Spears, Wichita Falls (2/25/14). Pres. Dr. Jesse W. Rogers, 3410 Taft Blvd., Wichita Falls 76308; (940) 397-4010.

**Midwifery Board, Texas** – (1999); apptv. by Health and Human Services Comm.; 6-yr.; travel expenses; 9 members: Chair Meredith Rentz-Cook (1/31/15); Janet Dirmeyer (1/31/17); Laurie Fremgen (1/31/19); Charleta Guillory, M.D. (1/31/13); Sylyna Kennedy (1/31/17); Helen Jolly Nelson (1/31/17); Michael Nix M.D. (1/31/15); James Shue (1/31/19); one vacancy. c/o Texas Dept. of Health Services, PO Box 149347, Austin 78714-9347; (512) 834-4523.

**Military Facilities Commission, Texas** – (1935 as 3-member Texas National Guard Armory Board; reorganized in 1981 as 6-member board; abolished in 2007 by the 80th Legislature.

**Military Preparedness Commission, Texas**– (2003); apptv.; some terms at pleasure of Gov.; 2 ex-officio members (1 Senator, 1 House Representative); 13 apptv.: Chair Paul F. Paine, Fort Worth; Anna Chapman, Del Rio; Tom Duncavage, League City; Arthur Emerson, San Antonio; Woody Gilliland, Abilene; Alvin W. Jones, College Station; Dennis Lewis, Texarkana; Charles E. Powell, San Angelo; Karen Rankin, San Antonio; William Shine, Killeen; Connie Scott, Corpus Christi; A.F. (Tom) Thomas, El Paso; Thomas Whaylen, Wichita Falls; PO Box 12428, Austin, 78711; (512) 463-8800.

**Motor Vehicles Board, Texas Dept. of** – (2009); 9 members; 6-yr.: Chair John Walker III, Houston (2/1/17); Robert Barnwell III, Magnolia (2/1/19); Luanne Caraway, Kyle (2/1/19); Laura Ryan-Heizer, Cyress (2/1/15); Blake Ingram, Sunnyvale (2/1/17); Raymond Palacios, Jr. El Paso (2/1/19); Victor Rodriguez, McAllen (2/1/15); Marvin Rush, Seguin (2/1/17). Exec. Dir. Whitney Brewster, 4000 Jackson Ave., Austin, TX 78731; (888) 368-4689.

**Municipal Retirement System, Texas** (See Retirement System, Texas Municipal).

**National Guard Armory Board, Texas** – (*See* Military Facilities Commission, Texas).

**Natural Resource Conservation Commission, Texas** (*See* Environmental Quality, Texas Commission on).

**Neches River Municipal Water Authority, Upper** – (1953 as 9-member board; members decreased to 3 in 1959); apptv.; 6-yr.; 3 members: Jesse D. Hickman, Palestine (2/1/15); William Barry James, Palestine (2/1/13); Robert E. McKelvey, Palestine (2/1/11). Gen. Mgr. Monty D. Shank, PO Box 1965, Palestine 75802; (903) 876-2237.

**Neches Valley Authority, Lower** – (1933); apptv.; per diem and expenses on duty; 6-yr.; 9 members: Lonnie Arrington, Beaumont (7/28/13); Brian Babin, Woodville (7/28/13); Sue Cleveland, Lumberton (7/28/15); Jimmie Ruth Cooley, Woodville (7/28/15); Kathleen Thea Jackson, Beaumont (7/28/15); Steven M. McReynolds, Groves (7/28/13); Dade Phelan, Beaumont (7/28/11); Jordan Reese IV, Beaumont (7/28/11); James Olan Webb, Silsbee (7/28/11). Gen. Mgr. Robert Stroder, PO Box 5117, Beaumont 77726-5117; (409) 892-4011.

**Nueces River Authority** – (1953 as Nueces River Conservation and Reclamation District; name changed to present in 1971); apptv.; 6-yr.; per diem and expenses; 22 members: President Dan S. Leyendecker, Corpus Christi (2/1/13); W. Scott Bledsoe III, Oakville (2/1/11); Karen Bonner, Corpus Christi (2/1/11); Rebecca Bradford, Corpus Christi (2/1/13); Fernando Camarillo, Boerne (2/1/15); Manuel D. Cano, Corpus Christi (2/1/13); Joe M. Cantu, Pipe Creek (2/1/13); James T. Clancy, Portland (2/1/15); William I. Dillard, Uvalde (2/1/15); Robert M. Dullnig, San Antonio (2/1/13); John Galloway, Beeville (2/1/09); Gary Jones, Beeville (2/1/11); Yale Leland Kerby, Uvalde (2/1/11); Lindsey Alfred Koenig, Orange Grove (2/1/15); James Richard Marmion III, Carrizo Springs (2/1/11); Betty Ann Peden, Hondo (2/1/09); Scott James Petty, Hondo (2/1/13); Curtis Raabe, Poth (2/1/15); Thomas M. Reding Jr., Portland (2/1/15); Fidel R. Rul Jr., Alice (2/1/11); Roxana P. Tom, Campbellton (2/1/11); 1 vacancy. Exec. Dir. Con Mims, PO Box 349, Uvalde 78802-0349; (830) 278-6810.

**Nursing, Texas Board of** – (1909 as 5-member Texas Board of Nurse Examiners; members increased to 6 in 1931 and to 9 in 1981; name changed to present and members increased to 13 in 2007); apptv.; per diem and expenses; 6-yr.; 13 members: President Linda Rounds, Galveston (1/31/11); Deborah Hughes Bell, Abilene (1/31/11); Kristin K. Benton, Austin (1/31/13); Patricia Clapp, Dallas (1/31/13); Tamara Cowen, Harlingen (2/1/15); Sheri Crosby, Mesquite (2/1/15); Marilyn Davis, Sugar Land (1/31/13); Blanca Rosa (Rosie) Garcia, Corpus Christi (1/31/11); Richard Gibbs, Mesquite (1/31/13); Kathy Leader-Horn, Granbury (2/1/15); Josefina Lujan, El Paso (2/1/15); Beverly Jean Nutall, Bryan (1/31/11); Mary Jane Salgado, Eagle Pass (2/1/15). Exec. Dir. Katherine A. Thomas ($92,600), 333 Guadalupe, Ste. 3-460, Austin 78701; (512) 305-7400.

**Nursing Facility Administrators, Texas Board of** – Abolished Sept. 1997 and responsibilities transferred to Texas Dept. of Human Services, which itself was abolished in 2004 and responsibilities transferred to Texas Dept. of Aging and Disability Services.

**Occupational Therapy Examiners, Texas Board of** – (1983 as 6-member board; increased to 9 in 1999); apptv.; 6-yr.; per diem and expenses; 9 members: Catherine Benavidez, Carrollton (2/1/15); Judith Ann Chambers, Austin (2/1/13); Dely De Guia Cruz, Houston (2/1/09); Kathleen Hill, Hutto (2/1/13); Stephanie Johnston, Houston (2/1/11); Pamela D. Nelon, Fort Worth (2/1/11); Todd Novosad, Austin (2/1/13); Angela Sieffert, Dallas (2/1/15); Bobby James Vasquez, Frisco (2/1/11). Exec. Dir. John Maline ($70,000), 333 Guadalupe St., Ste. 2-510, Austin 78701-3942; (512) 305-6900.

**Offenders with Medical or Mental Impairments, Texas Correctional Office on** – Apptv.; 6-yr.; 21 members: 11 ex officio from various state agencies; 10 apptd. by Gov.: Chair John Bradley, Georgetown (2/1/13); Ellen Cokinos, Houston (7/20/08); Joseph Gutheinz, Houston (7/20/08); Kevin E. Haynes, Ennis (2/1/11); Gabriel Holguin, San Antonio (2/1/11); Christopher C. Kirk, Bryan (10/21/11); Kathryn J. Kotria, Georgetown (2/1/13); Jan Krocker, Houston (7/20/08); John L. Moore, Denison (2/1/13); Eulon Ross Taylor, Austin (2/1/13). Dir. Dee Wilson, 8610 Shoal Creek Blvd., Austin 78757; (512) 406-5406.

**Office of Injured Employee Counsel** – (2005; represents the interests of workers' compensation claimants); apptv.; 2-yr.; 1 member: Public Counsel Norman Darwin ($115,500), 7551 Metro Center Dr., Ste. 100, Austin 78744-1609; (866) 393-6432.

**One-Call Board of Texas** – (1997; created by the Underground Facility Damage Prevention and Safety Act and serves as the board for the Texas Underground Facility Notification Corp.); apptv.; 3-yr.; 12 members: Chair Joseph F. Berry, Houston (8/31/10); Christian A. Alvarado, Austin (8/31/11); Dean D. Bernal, Austin (8/31/12); Barry Calhoun, Grapevine (8/31/09); Julio Cerda, Mission (8/31/12); Bill Daugette Jr., Huntsville (8/31/09); Judith H. Devenport, Midland (8/31/07); Jason Hartgraves, Frisco (8/31/12); John Linton, Fort Worth (8/31/10); Barbara J. Mathis, Lufkin (8/31/11); John A. Menchaca II, Austin (8/31/09); Christopher J. Rourk, Dallas (8/31/09); Rodney J. Unruh, Spring Branch (8/31/11); Janie Walenta, Quitman (8/31/12); James Wynn, Midland (8/31/11). Exec. Dir. Donald M. Ward, PO Box 9764, Austin 78766-9764; (512) 467-9764.

**Optometry Board, Texas** – (1921 as 6-member State Board of Examiners in Optometry; name changed to present in 1981 and members increased to 9); apptv.; per diem; 6-yr.; 9 members: Chair D. Dixon Golden, Center (1/31/15); Carolyn Carmen-Merrifield, Mansfield (1/31/11); Melvin Cleveland, Arlington (1/31/13); John Coble, Rockwall (1/31/11); James Dyess, Austin (1/31/13); Larry Fields, Carthage (1/31/11); Cynthia T. Jenkins, Irving (1/31/15); Randall N. Reichle, Houston (1/31/15); Virginia Sosa, Uvalde (1/31/13). Exec. Dir. Chris Kloeris ($70,000), 333 Guadalupe St., Ste. 2-420, Austin 78701; (512) 305-8501.

**Orthotics and Prosthetics, Texas Board of** – (1998 with 6 members; increased to 7 in 2003); apptv.; per diem and travel expenses; 6-yr.; 7 members: Chair Richard Michael Neider, Lubbock (2/1/13); Erin Elizabeth Berling, Coppell (2/1/13); Rebecca Hill Brou, Rockport (2/1/11); Leah F. Esparza, Austin (2/1/15); Roy McCoy, Round Rock (2/1/15); Miguel Mojica, Coppell (2/1/15); James C. Wendlandt, Austin (2/1/11). Exec. Dir. David D. Olvera, Texas Dept. of Health Services, PO Box 149347, Austin 78714-9347; (512) 834-4520.

**Pardons and Paroles, Texas Board of** – (1893 as Board of Pardon Advisers; changed in 1936 to Board of Pardons and Paroles with 3 members; members increased to 6 in 1983; made a division of the Texas Dept. of Criminal Justice in 1990); apptv.; 6-yr.; 7 members (chairman, $99,500; members, $93,500 each): Chair Rissie L. Owens, Huntsville (2/1/15); Conrith Davis, Sugar Land (2/1/13); Juanita M. Gonzalez, Round Rock (2/1/15); David Gutierrez, Lubbock (2/1/15); James LaFavers, Amarillo (2/1/17); Thomas A. Leeper, Huntsville (2/1/13); Michelle Skyrme, Flint (2/1/17). *Parole Commissioners:* Pamela Freeman, Angleton; Roy Garcia, Huntsville; James Hensarling, Palestine; Elvis Hightower, Gatesville; Billy Humphrey, Huntsville; Paul Kiel, Palestine; Edgar Morales, San Antonio; Lynn Ruzicka, Angleton; Charles A. Shipman, Amarillo; Charles Speier, San Antonio; Howard Thrasher, Gatesville. Gen. Counsel Bettie L. Wells, PO Box 13401, Austin 78711-3401; (512) 406-5852.

**Parks and Wildlife Commission, Texas** – (1963 as 3-member board; members increased to 6 in 1971 and to 9 in 1983); apptv.; expenses; 6-yr.; 9 members: Chair T. Dan Friedkin, Houston (2/1/17); Ralph H. Duggins, Fort Worth (2/1/19); Antonio Falcon, Rio Grande City (2/1/13); Karen J. Hixon, San Antonio (2/1/13); Dan Allen Hughes, Jr., Beeville (2/1/15); Bill Jones, Austin (2/1/17); James H. "Jim" Lee, Houston (2/1/19); Margaret Martin, Boerne (2/1/15); S. Reed Morian, Houston (2/1/17); Dick Scott, Wimberly (2/1/17). Chairman-Emeritus Lee Marshall Bass, Fort Worth. Exec. Dir. Carter Smith ($143,000), 4200 Smith School Rd., Austin 78744; (512) 389-4800.

**Pecos River Compact Commissioner** – (1942); apptv.; 6-yr.; salary and expenses; (negotiates with New Mexico regarding waters of the Pecos): Julian W. Thrasher Jr. ($32,247), Monahans (1/23/11), PO Box 340, Monahans 79756; (432) 940-1753.

**Pension Boards** – For old age, blind and dependent children's assistance, *see* Health and Human Services Commission Council. *Also see,* listings under Retirement for state and municipal employee and teacher retirement systems.

**Pension Review Board, State** – (1979); apptv.; 6-yr.; 9 members (1 senator apptd. by Lt. Gov., 1 representative apptd. by Speaker, 7 apptd. by Gov.): Chair Richard Earl McElreath, Amarillo (1/31/13); Paul A. Braden, Dallas (1/31/15); Andrew Cable, Wimberly (1/31/13); Jerry R. Massengale, Lubbock (1/31/11); Norman W. Parrish, The Woodlands (1/31/13); Wayne R. Roberts, Austin (1/31/15); Scott D. Smith, Cedar Park (1/31/15). Exec. Dir. Paul Janssen Nicholson ($80,000), PO Box 13498, Austin 78711-3498; (512) 463-1736.

**Perfusionists, Texas State Board of Examiners of** – Abolished September 2005; responsibilities transferred to the Texas

Dept. of Human Services, now part of the Health and Human Services Commission.

**Pest Control Board, Texas Structural** – Abolished August 2007; responsibilities transferred to the Texas Dept. of Agriculture, Structural Pest Control Service, Pesticide Program.

**Pharmacy, Texas State Board of** – (1907 as 6-member board; members increased to 9 in 1981; apptv.; 6-yr.; 9 members: Chair Jeanne D. Waggener, Waco (8/31/11); Buford T. Abeldt Sr., Lufkin (8/31/13); Rosemary F. Combs, El Paso (8/31/11); Wilson Benjamin Fry, San Benito (8/31/15); Suzan Kedron, Dallas (8/31/13); Alice G. Mendoza, Kingsville (8/31/11); Joyce Tipton, Houston (8/31/15); Charles Wetherbee, Boerne (8/31/15); Dennis Wiesner, Austin (8/31/13). Exec. Dir. Gay Dodson ($106,500), 333 Guadalupe St., Ste. 3-600, Austin 78701-3903; (512) 305-8000. *Consumer complaints: (800) 821-3205.*

**Physical Therapy Examiners, Texas Board of** – (1971); apptv.; 6-yr.; expenses; 9 members: Chair Karen Gordon, Port O'Connor (1/31/13); Frank Bryan Jr., Austin (1/31/13); Gary Gray, Midland (1/31/11); Kevin Lindsey, Mission (1/31/15); Phillip B. Palmer, Abilene (1/31/11); Rene Peña, El Paso (1/31/15); Daniel Reyna, Waco (1/31/11); Melinda A. Rodriguez, San Antonio (1/31/15); Shari Waldie, Fredericksburg (1/31/13). Exec. Dir. John Maline ($70,000), 333 Guadalupe St., Ste. 2-510, Austin 78701-3942; (512) 305-6900.

**Physical Therapy and Occupational Therapy Examiners, Executive Council of** – (1971); apptv.; 2-yr.; expenses; 5 members: Chair Arthur Roger Matson, Georgetown (2/1/11); Stephanie Johnston, Houston (2/1/11); Pamela D. Nelon, Fort Worth (2/1/11); Daniel Reyna, Waco (2/1/11); Melinda Rodriguez, San Antonio (2/1/09). Exec. Dir. John Maline ($62,000), 333 Guadalupe St., Ste. 2-510, Austin 78701-3942; (512) 305-6900.

**Physician Assistant Board, Texas** – (1993 as Physician Assistant Advisory Council; changed to present name in 1995); apptv.; 6-yr.; 9 members: Chair Margaret K. Bentley, DeSoto (2/1/15); Ron Bryce, Red Oak (2/1/15); Anna Arredondo Chapman, Del Rio (2/1/11); Teralea Davis Jones, Beeville (2/1/13); Felix Koo, McAllen (2/1/11); Michael Allen Mitchell, Wichita Falls (2/1/13); Richard R. Rahr, Galveston (2/1/11); Abelino (Abel) Reyna, Waco (2/1/13); Edward W. Zwanziger, Eustace (2/1/15). Exec. Dir. Mari Robinson ($110,000), 333 Guadalupe, Tower III, #610, TX 78768; (512) 305-7010. *Consumer Complaints: (800) 201-9353.*

**Plumbing Examiners, State Board of** – (1947 as 6-member board; members increased to 9 in 1981; apptv.; expenses; 6-yr.; Chair Tammy Betancourt, Houston (9/05/09); Enrique Castro, El Paso (9/05/11); Ricardo Jose Guerra, Austin (9/05/11); Robert Franklin Jalnos, San Antonio (9/05/09); Dave Lilley, Wichita Falls (9/05/09); Richard Allen Lord, Pasadena (9/05/09); Carol Lynne McLemore, La Marque (9/05/11); Alex Meade III, Brownsville (9/05/13); Ed Thompson, Tyler (9/05/13). Exec. Dir. Robert L. Maxwell ($77,000), PO Box 4200, Austin 78765-4200; (800) 845-6584.

**Podiatric Medical Examiners, Texas State Board of** – (1923 as 6-member State Board of Chiropody Examiners; name changed to State Board of Podiatry Examiners in 1967; made 9-member board in 1981; name changed to present in 1996); apptv.; 6-yr.; expenses; 9 members: Pres. Doris A. Couch, Burleson (7/10/11); Charles Jason Hubbard, Austin (7/10/15); H. Ashley Ledger, Midland (7/10/15); James Michael Lunsford, Katy (7/10/13); Joe E. Martin Jr., College Station (7/10/13); James Michael Miller, Aledo (7/10/13); Travis Motley, Colleyville (7/10/11); Morgan Talbot, McAllen (7/10/15); Ana Urukalo, Austin (7/10/11). Exec. Dir. Hemant Makan ($69,000), PO Box 12216, Austin 78711-2216; (512) 305-7000. *Consumer Complaint Hotline: (800) 821-3205.*

**Polygraph Examiners Board** – (1965); apptv.; 6-yr.; 7 members: Chair Andy Sheppard, Fate (6/18/09); Elizabeth P. Bellegarde, El Paso (6/18/07); Priscilla Jane Kleinpeter, Amarillo (6/18/09); Gory Dean Loveday, Tyler (6/18/11); Lawrence D. Mann, Plano (6/18/09); Horacio Ortiz, Corpus Christi (6/18/07); Donald K. Schutte, Texarkana (6/18/11). Exec. Officer Frank Di Tucci ($49,080), PO Box 4087, Austin 78765-4087; (512) 424-2058.

**Port Freeport Commission** – Apptv.; 6-yr.; 6 members: James F. Brown, Lake Jackson (5/31/11); John W. Damon, West Columbia (5/31/09); J.M Lowrey, Brazosport (5/31/11); Thomas S. Perryman, Angleton (5/31/09); Ravi K. Singhania, Brazoria (5/31/13); Bill Terry, Brazosport (5/31/13). Exec. Dir. A.J. Reixach Jr., PO Box 615, Freeport 77542-0615; (800) 362-5743.

**Preservation Board, State** – (1983); 2-yr.; 6 members (3 ex officio: Gov., Lt. Gov., House Speaker); 3 apptv.: 1 apptd. by Gov.: Iris Moore, San Antonio (2/1/17); 1 senator apptd. by Lt. Gov.; 1 representative apptd. by Speaker. Exec. Dir. John Sneed ($160,000), PO Box 13286, Austin 78711-3286; (512) 463-5495.

**Prison Board** – (*See* Criminal Justice, Texas Dept. of)

**Prison Industries Oversight Authority, Private Sector** – (1997); 6-yr.; expenses; 6 ex officio: Senate member, House member, Dept. of Criminal Justice, Texas Youth Comm., Texas Work Force Comm., employer liaison; 8 apptd.: Chair Jeffery R. LaBroski, Richmond (2/1/13); Sarah Abraham, Sugar Land (2/1/13); Elaine (Anne) Boatright, Smithville (2/1/15); Burnis Brazil, Richmond (2/1/15); William B. Brod, Granbury (2/1/11); S. Roxanne Carter, Canyon (2/1/15); Suzanne C. Hart, San Antonio (2/1/11); Rigoberto Villarreal, Mission (2/1/13); Employer Liaison: Randall Henderson, Austin. Admin. Robert Carter, 8610 Shoal Creek, Austin 78757; (512) 406-5310.

**Private Security Bureau, Texas** – (1969 as Board of Private Investigators and Private Security Agencies; reorganized in 1998 as Texas Comm. on Private Security; reestablished in 2004 as a bureau of the Texas Dept. of Public Safety); apptv.; expenses; 6-yr.; 8 members (1 ex officio: Dir., Dept. of Public Safety); 7 apptd. members: Chair John E. Chism, Irving (1/31/15); Stella Caldera, Houston (1/31/11); Charles E. Crenshaw, Austin (1/31/13); Howard H. Johnsen, Dallas (1/31/11); Patrick A. Patterson, Boerne (1/31/15); Mark L. Smith, Dallas (1/31/11); Doris F. Washington, Arlington (1/31/13). Man. Capt. Leonard Hinojosa, PO Box 4087, Austin 78773-0001; (512) 424-7710.

**Process Server Review Board** – Apptv. by Texas Supreme Court; staggered terms; 9 members: Chair Carl Weeks, Austin (7/1/11); Mark P. Blenden, Bedford (7/1/11); Joe F. Brown Jr., San Antonio (7/1/09); Ron Hickman, Houston (7/1/09); Tony Lindsay, Houston (7/1/11); Connie Mayfield, Corsicana (7/1/09); Justiss Rasberry, El Paso (7/1/10); Lois Rogers, Tyler (7/1/10); Lee H. Russell, Dallas (7/1/10). Clerk Meredith Musick, PO Box 12248, Austin 78711-2248; (512) 463-2713.

**Produce Recovery Fund Board** – (1977 as 3-member board; members increased to 5 in 1981); apptv.; expenses; 6-yr.; 5 members: Chair Doyle (Neal) Newson III, Plains (1/31/15); Ralph Diaz, Corpus Christi (1/31/05); Steven Dexter Jones, Lubbock (1/31/01); Ly H. Nguyen, Lake Jackson (1/31/15); Byron Edward White, Arlington (1/31/01). Coor. Rick Garza, c/o Texas Dept. of Agriculture, PO Box 12847, Austin 78711-2847; (512) 936-2430.

**Psychologists, Texas Board of Examiners of** – (1969 as 6-member board; members increased to 9 in 1981); apptv.; 6-yr.; per diem and expenses; 9 members: Chair Timothy Branaman, Dallas (10/31/13); Donna L. Black, Houston (10/31/11); Jo Ann Campbell, Abilene (10/31/11); Carlos R. Chacón, El Paso (10/31/15); Angela A. Downes, Irving (10/31/13); Gary R. Elkins, Temple (10/31/09); Lou Ann Todd Mock, Bellaire (10/31/13); Leslie Rosenstein, Austin (10/31/15); Carl E. Settles, Killeen (10/31/09). Exec. Dir. Sherry L. Lee ($75,075), 333 Guadalupe St., Ste. 2-450, Austin 78701; (512) 305-7700.

**Public Finance Authority, Texas** – (1984, assumed duties of Texas Building Authority); apptv.; per diem and expenses; 6-yr.; 7 members: Chair Gary E. Wood, Austin (2/1/15); Gerald Byron Alley, Arlington (2/1/13); D. Joseph Meister, Dallas (2/1/11); Rodney K. Moore, Lufkin (2/1/15); Robert Thomas Roddy, San Antonio (2/1/11); Ruth Schiermeyer, Lubbock (2/1/13); Macedonio (Massey) Villarreal, Missouri City (2/1/11). Exec. Dir. Dwight D. Burns ($120,000), PO Box 12906, Austin 78711-2906; (512) 463-5544.

**Public Insurance Counsel, Office of** – (1995); apptv.; 2-yr.; 1 member: Deeia Beck (2/1/11) ($106,500), 333 Guadalupe St., Ste. 3-120; Austin 78701; (512) 322-4143.

**Public Safety Commission** – (1935 with 3 members; members increased to 5 in 2007); apptv.; expenses; 5 members: Chair A. Cynthia Leon, Mission (1/1/16); Manny Flores, Jr., Austin (12/31/17); Faith S. Johnson, Cedar Hill (12/31/19); Steven Mach, Houston (1/1/15); Randy Watson, Burleson (1/1/18). Dir. of Texas Dept. of Public Safety, Steven McCraw ($162,000), PO Box 4087, Austin 78773-0001; (512) 424-2000.

**Public Utility Commission** – (1975); apptv.; 6-yr., 3 members (chairman, $111,800; members, $109,200): Chair Donna L. Nelson, Austin (9/1/15); Kenneth W. Anderson, Dallas (9/1/17); Brandy Marty, Austin (9/1/19). Exec. Dir. Brian H. Lloyd ($120,000), PO Box 13326, Austin 78711-3326; (512) 936-7120.

**Public Utility Counsel, Office of** – (1983); apptv.; 2-yr.; 1 member: Tonya Baer, Austin (2/1/17); ($115,000), PO Box 12397, Austin 78711-2397; (512) 936-7500.

**Racing Commission, Texas** – (1986); apptv.; 6-yr.; per diem and expenses; 9 members; 2 ex officio: Chmn., Public Safety Commission and Comptroller of Public Accounts; 7 apptv.: Chair Robert Schmidt, Fort Worth (2/1/17); Gary Aber, D.V.M, Simonton (2/01/15); Ronald F. Ederer, Fair Oaks Ranch (2/1/19); Gloria Hicks, Corpus Christi (2/1/17); Michael F. Martin, D.V.M, San Antonio (2/1/15); John T. Steen III, Houston (2/1/19); Vicki Smith Weinberg, Colleyville (2/1/15). Exec. Dir. Charla Ann King ($88,000), PO Box 12080, Austin 78711-2080; (512) 833-6699.

**Radiation Advisory Board, Texas** – (1961); apptv.; 6-yr.; 18 members: Jesse Ray Adams, Longview (4/16/13); Bradley Bunn, Andrews (4/16/13); Bill Campbell, Fort Worth (4/16/13); Amy Clark, Floresville (4/16/15); Ana Cleveland, Denton (4/16/11); John Hageman, San Antonio (4/16/11); Bobby J. Haley, Denton (4/16/11); Ian Hamilton, Cypress (4/16/15); L.R. (Rick) Jacobi Jr., Austin (4/16/15); Nora Anita Janjan, Navasota (4/16/15); Mitch Lucas, Glen Rose (4/16/13); Melanie Marshall, Mansfield (4/16/15); Darlene Metter, San Antonio (4/16/13); Rosana G. Moreira, College Station (4/16/11); Jay Murphy, Houston (4/16/13); David Nichols, Austin (4/16/15); Kevin Raabe, Austin (4/16/11); Mark Silberman, Austin (4/16/11). Program Dir. Richard A. Ratliff, Radiation Control MC 2835, Texas Dept. of State Health Services, PO Box 149347, Austin 78714-9347; (512) 834-6679.

**Radioactive Waste Disposal Compact, Texas Low-Level** – (1993); apptv.; 6-yr.; expenses; 6 Texas members, plus one member each from Maine and Vermont; Texas apptees.: Chair Michael Ford, Amarillo (11/25/14); Richard Dolgener, Andrews (11/25/14); Bob Gregory, Austin (11/25/14); Kenneth L. Peddicord, College Station (11/25/14); John White, Plano (11/25/14); Robert C. Wilson, Lockhart (11/25/14). Radioactive Materials Division MC-233, Texas Commission on Environmental Quality, PO Box 13087, Austin 78711-3087; (512) 239-6466.

**Railroad Commission of Texas** – (1891); elective; 6-yr.; 3 members, $137,500 each: Elizabeth Ames Jones (12/31/12); David Porter (12/31/16); Barry Thomas Smitherman (12/31/12). Dir. John Tintera ($106,381), PO Box 12967, Austin 78711-2967; (512) 463-7288.

**Real Estate Commission, Texas** – (1949 as 6-member board; members increased to 9 in 1979); apptv.; per diem and expenses; 6-yr.; 9 members: Chair John D. Eckstrum, Conroe (1/31/11); Troy C. Alley Jr., Arlington (1/31/11); Adrian A. Arriaga, McAllen (1/31/13); Robert C. (Chris) Day, Jacksonville (1/31/13); Jaime Blevins Hensley, Lufkin (1/31/15); Joanne Justice, Arlington (1/31/15); Tom C. Mesa Jr., Houston (1/31/11); Dona Scurry, El Paso (1/31/13); Avis Wukasch, Goergetown (1/31/13). Admin. Douglas E. Oldmixon ($116,700), PO Box 12188, Austin 78711-2188; (512) 459-6544.

**Real Estate Research Center Advisory Committee** – (1971); apptv.; 6-yr.; 10 members; 1 ex officio: rep. of Texas Real Estate Commission; 9 apptv.: Chair D. Marc McDougal, Lubbock (1/31/11); Mona R. Bailey, North Richland Hills (1/31/13); James M. Boyd, Houston (1/31/15); Louis A. (Tony) Cortes, San Antonio (1/31/15); Jacquelyn K. Hawkins, Austin (1/31/11); Joe Bob McCartt, Amarillo (1/31/13); Kathleen McKenzie Owen, Pipe Creek (1/31/13); Barbara A. Russell, Denton (1/31/13); Ronald C. Wakefield, San Antonio (1/31/15). Dir. Gary Maler, Texas A&M University Real Estate Center, 2115 TAMU, College Station 77843-2115; (979) 845-0460.

**Red River Authority of Texas** – (1959); apptv.; 6-yr.; per diem and expenses; 9 members: Nathan J. (Jim) Bell IV, Paris (8/11/11); Lisa Caldwell Brent, Amarillo (8/11/11); Cole Camp, Amarillo (8/11/13); Penny Cogdell Carpenter, Silverton (8/11/13); Jerry B. Daniel, Truscott (8/11/15); Mayfield McCraw Jr., Telephone (8/11/11); George (Wilson) Scaling II, Henrietta (8/11/15); Clyde Siebman, Pottsboro (8/11/13); Cliff A. Skiles Jr., Hereford (8/11/15). Gen. Mgr. Curtis W. Campbell, PO Box 240, Wichita Falls 76307-0240; (940) 723-8697.

**Red River Compact Commissioner** – (1949); apptv.; 4-yr.; salary and expenses; (negotiates with Oklahoma, Arkansas and Louisiana regarding waters of the Red): William A. Abney ($24,225), El Paso (2/1/11); PO Box 1386, Marshall 75671; (903) 938-4572.

**Redistricting Board, Legislative** – (*See* Legislative Redistricting Board.)

**Rehabilitation Commission, Texas** – Combined into Department of Assistive and Rehabilitative Services (DARS) of the Health and Human Services Commission as of 3/1/04.

**Residential Construction Commission, Texas** – apptv.; 6-yr.; expenses; 9 members: Chair J. Paulo Flores, Dallas (2/1/11); Lewis Brown, Trinity (2/1/11); Art Cuevas, Lubbock (2/1/11); Kenneth L. Davis, Weatherford (2/1/09); Gerardo M. (Jerry) Garcia, Corpus Christi (2/1/13); John R. Krugh, Houston (2/1/09); Steven Leipsner, Lakeway (2/1/09); Glenda C. Mariott, Bryan (2/1/13); Mickey R. Redwine, Ben Wheeler (2/1/13). Exec. Dir. A. Duane Waddill ($98,000), PO Box 13509, Austin 78711-3509; (512) 463-1040.

**Retirement System of Texas, Employees** – (1949); apptv.; 6-yr.; 6 members: 1 apptd. by Gov., 1 by Chief Justice of State Supreme Court, 1 by House Speaker; 3 elected by ERS members: Chair Cheryl MacBride, Austin (8/31/19); Gov.'s apptee: Cydney Donnell, College Station (8/31/18); Chief Justice's apptee: I. Craig Hester, Austin (8/31/16); Speaker's apptee: Frederick E. Rowe Jr., Dallas (8/31/14). Elected members: Yolanda (Yoly) Griego, El Paso (8/31/15); Brian Ragland, Austin (8/31/17). Exec. Dir. Ann S. Bishop ($312,000 plus bonus), 200 East 18th St., PO Box 13207, Austin 78711; (512) 867-7711.

**Retirement System of Texas, Teacher** – (1937 as 6-member board; members increased to 9 in 1973); 6-yr.; expenses; 9 members; 2 apptd. by State Board of Education, 3 apptd. by Gov., 4 apptd. by Gov. after being nominated by popular ballot of retirement system members: Chair R. David Kelly, Plano (8/31/11); Todd Barth, Houston (8/31/15); Charlotte Renee Clifton, Snyder (8/31/13); Robert P. Gauntt, Houston (8/31/13); Eric C. McDonald, Lubbock (8/31/13); Christopher Moss, Lufkin (8/31/15); Phillip M. Mullins, Austin (8/31/11); Nanette Sissney, Whitesboro (8/31/13); Linus D. Wright, Dallas (8/31/11). Exec. Dir. Ronnie Jung ($270,000), 1000 Red River, Austin 78701; (512) 542-6400.

**Retirement System, Texas County and District** – (1967); apptv.; 6-yr.; 9 members: Chair Robert Eckels, Houston (12/31/13); Jerry Bigham, Canyon (12/31/15); H.C. (Chuck) Cazalas, Corpus Christi (12/31/17); Daniel R. Haggerty, El Paso (12/31/15); Jan Kennady, New Braunfels (12/31/15); Bridget McDowell, Baird (12/31/13); Kristeen Roe, Bryan (12/31/17); Robert C. Willis, Livingston (12/31/13); 1 vacancy. Exec. Dir. Gene Glass, 901 MoPac Expwy. S., Bldg. IV, Ste. 500, PO Box 2034, Austin 78768-2034; (512) 328-8889.

**Retirement System, Texas Municipal,** – (1947); apptv.; 6-yr.; expenses; 6 members: Ben Gorzell Jr., San Antonio (2/1/13); Patricia Hernandez, Plainview (2/1/11); Carolyn M. Linér, San Marcos (2/1/13); April Nixon, Arlington (2/1/09); Roel Rodriguez, McAllen (2/1/11); H. Frank Simpson, Missouri City (2/1/09). Exec. Dir. (vacant), PO Box 149153, Austin 78714-9153; (512) 476-7577.

**Retirement System, Texas Emergency Services** – (1977; formerly the Fire Fighters' Relief and Retirement Fund); apptv.; expenses; 6-yr.; 9 members: Chair Francisco R. Torres, Raymondville (9/1/17); Graciela G. Flores, Corpus Christi (9/1/15); Dan Key, Friendswood (9/1/13); Ronald V. Larson, Horizon City (9/1/13); Jenny Moore, Lake Jackson (9/1/15); Maxie L. Patterson, Houston (9/1/13); Dennis Rice, Canyon (9/1/15); Don R. Shipman, Colleyville (9/1/17); Stephen Williams, Carthage (9/1/17). Commissioner Sherri Barr Walker ($77,000), c/o Office of the Fire Fighters' Pension, 920 Colorado, 11th Floor, PO Box 12577, Austin 78711; (512) 936-3372. (*See also* Fire Fighters' Pension Commissioner.)

**Rio Grande Compact Commissioner of Texas** – (1929); apptv.; 6-yr.; salary and expenses; (negotiates with Colorado and New Mexico regarding waters of the Rio Grande): Patrick R. Gordon ($41,195), El Paso (6/9/13); PO Box 1917, El Paso 79950-1917; (915) 834-7075.

**Rio Grande Regional Water Authority** – (2003); apptv.; 4-yr.; 18 members: 12 apptd. by Gov.; 6 apptd. by member counties. Gov.'s apptees.: Joe A. Barrera III, Brownsville (2/1/13); Dario (D.V.) Guerra Jr., Edinburg (2/1/13); Wayne Halbert, Harlingen (2/1/09); Paul Glenn Heller, Mission (2/1/11); Sonny Hinojosa, Edinburg (2/1/13); Sonia Kaniger, San Benito (2/1/13); Brian Macmanus, Rio Hondo (2/1/09); Joe Pennington, Raymondville (2/1/13); Roel Rodriguez, McAllen (2/1/11); Bobby Sparks, Valley Acres (2/1/09); Jimmie Steidinger, Donna (2/1/13); Frank Torres, Willacy Co.; Karran Westerman, Zapata Co. Exec. Dir. Kenneth N. Jones Jr., 311 N. 15th St., McAllen 78501-4705; (956) 682-3481. **County apptees.:** John Bruciak, Cameron Co.; Jim Darling, Hidalgo Co.; Ricardo Gutierrez, Starr Co.; Fitzgerald G. Sanchez, Webb Co.; Frank Torres, Willacy Co.; White, Progreso Lakes (2/1/13).

**Risk Management, State Office of** – apptv.; 2-yr.; 5 members: Chair Ernest C. Garcia, Austin (2/1/09); Lloyd M. Garland, Lubbock (2/1/13); Ruben W. Hope, Montgomery (2/1/13); Kenneth N. Mitchell, El Paso (2/1/09); Ronald James Walenta, Quitman (2/1/11). Exec. Dir. Jonathan D. Bow ($104,500), PO Box 13777 Austin 78711-3777; (512) 475-1440.

**Rural Affairs, Texas Department of** – (2001 as Office of Rural Community Affairs; named changed to present in 2009); apptv.; 6-yr.; 11 members: 1 ex officio, Agriculture Commissioner; 10 apptd.: Chair Wallace Klussmann, Fredericksburg (2/1/13); Dora G. Alcala, Del Rio (2/1/15); David Alders, Nacogdoches (2/1/13); Woodrow Anderson, Colorado City (2/1/15); Mackie Bobo, Bedias (2/1/13); Charles N. Butts Sr., Lampasas (2/1/13); Remelle Farrar, Crowell (2/1/11); Charles W. Graham, Elgin (2/1/15); Bryan Tucker, Childress (2/1/11); Patrick Wallace, Athens (2/1/11). Exec. Dir. Charles S. (Charlie) Stone ($99,000), 1700 N. Congress Ave., Ste. 220, PO Box 12877, Austin 78711-2877; (512) 936-6701.

**Sabine River Authority of Texas** – (1949); apptv.; per diem and expenses; 6-yr.; 9 members: Cary (Mac) Abney, Marshall (7/06/15); Don O. Covington, Orange (7/06/11); J.D. Jacobs Jr., Rockwall (7/06/13); David W. Koonce, Center (7/06/13); Stanley N. Mathews, Orange (7/6/11); Cliff R. Todd, Carthage (7/6/11); Connie J. Wade, Longview (7/06/15); Connie Moore Ware, Marshall (7/06/15); Clarence Earl Williams, Orange (7/06/13). Gen. Mgr. Jerry L. Clark, PO Box 579, Orange 77630; (409) 746-2192.

**Sabine River Compact Commission** – (1953); apptv.; 6-yr.; salary ($8,487) and expenses; (negotiates with Louisiana regarding the waters of the Sabine); 5 members — the chairman, who does not vote, is appointed by the President of United States; Texas and Louisiana each have 2 members. Texas members: Jerry F. Gipson, Longview (7/12/16); Michael H. Lewis, Newton (7/12/19); c/o P.O. Box 13087, Austin 78711; (512) 239-4707.

**San Antonio River Authority** – (1937); apptv., 6 yr., 12 members: Sara (Sally) Buchanan, Bexar Co. (11/1/17); Terry E. Baiamonte, Goliad Co. (11/1/15); Darrell T. Brownlow, Wilson Co. (11/1/19); John Flieller, Wilson Co. (11/1/15); James Fuller, Goliad Co. (11/1/19); Lourdes Galvan, Bexar Co. (11/1/19); Jerry G. Gonzales, Bexar Co. (11/1/19); Michael W. Lackey, Bexar Co. (11/1/15); Hector Morales, Bexar Co. (11/1/17); Gaylon J. Oehlke, Karnes Co. (11/1/19); H.B. (Trip) Ruckman III, Karnes Co. (11/1/15); Thomas G. Weaver, Bexar Co. (11/1/15). Gen. Mgr. Suzanne B. Scott, PO Box 839980, San Antonio 78283-9980; (210) 227-1373.

**San Jacinto River Authority, Board of Directors** – (1937); apptv.; expenses while on duty; 6-yr.; 6 members: Pres. R. Gary Montgomery, The Woodlands (10/16/13); David Kleimann, Willis (10/16/13); Mary L. Rummell, Spring (10/16/09); John H. Stibbs, The Woodlands (10/16/09); Lloyd B. Tisdale, Conroe (10/16/11); Joseph V. Turner, Conroe (10/16/11). Gen. Mgr. H. Reed Eichelberger, PO Box 329, Conroe 77305; (936) 588-1111.

**Savings and Mortgage Lending Commissioner** – (1961); apptd. by State Finance Commission: Douglas B. Foster ($176,700), 2601 N. Lamar, Ste. 201, Austin 78705; (512) 475-1350. *Consumer Complaint Hotline: 877-276-5550.*

**School Land Board** – (*See* Land Board, School).

**School Safety Center, Texas** – (2001); apptv.; 2-yr.; 6 ex-officio members from the Texas Commissioner of Higher Education, Texas Youth Commission, Texas Education Agency, Dept. of State Health Services, Attorney General's office, and the Texas Juvenile Probation Commission; 10 apptd. members: Chair James R. Pendell, James R. Pendell, Barbara Ann Beto, Mike D. Cox, Dr. Dawn DuBose-Randle, Garry E. Eoff, Judge Daniel F. Gilliam, Evan Gonzales, Cpl. Dan Griffith, Kirk Cole, Dr. Tracy Levins, Robert Martinez, Dr. Carl A. Montoya, Adelaida Olivares, Dr. Raymund Paredes, Candace Stoltz. Director Kathy Martinez-Prather, 415 N. Guadalupe, Ste. 164, San Marcos 78666; (877) 304-2727.

**Securities Board, State** – (Est. 1957, the outgrowth of several amendments to the Texas Securities Act, originally passed in 1913); act is administered by the Securities Commissioner, who is appointed by the board members; expenses; 6-yr.; 5 members: Chair Beth Ann Blackwood, Dallas (1/20/19); David Appleby, El Paso (1/20/17); E. Wally Kinney, Dripping Springs (1/20/19); Miguel Romano Jr., Austin (1/20/21); Alan Waldrop, Austin (1/20/17). Commissioner John Morgan ($130,000), PO Box 13167, Austin 78711-3167; (512) 305-8300.

**Seed and Plant Board, State** – (1959); apptv.; 2-yr.; 6 members: Chair David Baltensperger, College Station (10/6/16); Dr. Eric Hequet, Lubbock (10/6/16); Mike Mann, Austin (10/6/15); Dr.

Roy Martens, Alvin (10/6/16); Jim Massey IV, Robstown (10/6/16); Andrew Watley, Spearman (10/6/15). Regulatory Branch Chief Ed Price, Texas Dept. of Agriculture, PO Box 12847, Austin 78711; (512) 463-7607.

**Sex Offender Treatment, Council on** – (1983); apptv.; expenses; 6-yr.; 7 members: Chair Frederick Liles Arnold, Plano (2/1/15); Ronnie Fanning, Woodway (2/1/11); Joseph Gutheinz, Houston (2/1/15); Alida S. Hernandez, McAllen (2/1/13); Holly A. Miller, The Woodlands (2/1/15); Aaron Paul Pierce, Rockdale (2/1/11); Dan Powers, Carrollton (2/1/13). Exec. Dir. Allison Taylor, c/o Texas Dept. of State Health Services, c/o Texas Dept. of State Health Services, PO Box 149347, Austin 78714-9347; (512) 834-4530

**Skill Standards Board, Texas** – (1995); apptv.; terms at pleasure of Gov.; 11 members: Chair Wayne J. Oswald, Freeport; Bruce Aumack, Austin; Gary Forrest Blagg, Grapevine; Carlos Chacón, El Paso; Andy Ellard, Dallas; Edward C. Foster Jr., Mansfield; Iria Ganious, Dallas; Erma Palmer, Houston; Linda Stegall, Houston; Whitney Wolf, San Antonio; 1 vacancy; PO Box 2241, Austin 78768-2241; (512) 936-8100.

**Social Worker Examiners, Texas State Board of** – (1993); apptv.; 6-yr.; per diem and travel expenses; 9 members: Chair Timothy M. Brown, Bryan (2/1/13); Jody Anne Armstrong, Abilene (2/1/15); Stewart Geise, Austin (2/1/15); Candace Guillen, La Feria (2/1/13); Kimberly Hernandez, El Paso (2/1/11); Dorinda N. Noble, San Marcos (2/1/11); Denise Pratt, Baytown (2/1/11); Nary Spears, Houston (2/1/15); Mark Talbot, McAllen (2/1/13). Exec. Dir. Charles Horton, c/o Texas Dept. of State Health Services, PO Box 149347 Austin 78714-9347; (512) 719-3521.

**Soil and Water Conservation Board, Texas State** – (1939); 2-yr.; 7 members: 2 apptd. by Gov.; 5 elected by district directors; **Gov.'s apptees:** Larry D. Jacobs, Montgomery (2/1/12); Joe L. Ward, Telephone (2/1/11); elected members: **Dist. 1:** Aubrey Russell, Panhandle (5/1/09); **Dist. 2:** Marty H. Graham, Rocksprings (5/1/10); **Dist. 3:** José Dodier Jr., Zapata (5/1/10); **Dist. 4:** Jerry D. Nichols, Nacogdoches (5/2/10); **Dist. 5:** Barry Mahler, Iowa Park (5/1/09). Exec. Dir. Rex Isom ($92,600), 4311 S. 31st St., Ste. 125, PO Box 658, Temple 76503; (254) 773-2250.

**Special Education Continuing Education Advisory Committee, Texas** – (1997); apptv.; 4 yr.; 17 members: Lené Al-Rashid, Austin (2/1/11); Ismael (Mel) Capelo, Pasadena (2/1/13); Rose Marie Cruz, Laredo (2/1/13); Debra B. Emerson, Austin (2/1/13); Julia W. Erwin, Montgomery (2/1/13); Kathy L. Grant, Houston (2/1/11); Sherri Hammack, Austin (2/1/13); Marjie Haynes, Huntsville (2/1/11); Candance L. Hawks, Belton (2/1/13); Teresa Hernandez, San Marcos (2/1/11); Drusilla Knight-Villarreal, Corpus Christi (2/1/11); Marnie L. Mast, Austin (2/1/11); Diane Taylor, Stephenville (2/1/13); Jennifer L. Taylor, Houston (2/1/13); Paul Watson, Flower Mound (2/1/13); Shewanda Williams, Houston (2/1/11); Pam Willson, Brookesmith (2/1/13); c/o Texas Education Agency, Division of IDEA Coordination, 1701 N. Congress Ave., Austin 78701-1494; (512) 463-9414; *Parent Information Line: 1-800-252-9668.*

**Speech-Language Pathology and Audiology, State Board of Examiners for** – (1983); apptv.; 6-yr.; per diem and expenses; 9 members: Chair Vickie B. Dionne, Nederland (8/31/11); Patricia Elaine Brannon, San Antonio (8/31/11); Tammy Camp, Lubbock (8/31/13); Kimberly M. Carlisle, Plano (8/31/15); Kerry Ormson, Amarillo (8/31/15); Christopher Rourk, Dallas (8/31/15); Sonya Salinas, Mission (8/31/11); Leila Ramirez Salmons, Houston (8/31/13); Phillip Lee Wilson, Dallas (8/31/13). Exec. Dir. Joyce Parsons, c/o Texas Dept. of State Health Services, PO Box 149347, MC 1982, Austin 78714-9347; (512) 834-6627.

**Stephen F. Austin State University, Board of Regents** – (1969); apptv.; expenses; 6-yr.; 9 members: Chair Scott Coleman, Houston (1/31/21); David Alders, Nacogdoches (1/31/19); Nelda Luce Blair, Houston (1/31/21); Alton Frailey, Katy (1/31/21); John R. (Bob) Garrett, Tyler (1/31/19); Brigettee Carnes Henderson, Lufkin (1/31/17); Barry Nelson, Dallas (1/31/19); Kenton E. Schaefer, Brownsville (1/31/17); Ralph C. Todd, Plano (1/31/17). Pres. Baker Pattillo, PO Box 13026, SFA Station, Nacogdoches 75962-3026; (936) 468-4048.

**Sulphur River Basin Authority** – (1985); 7 members; 6-yr.; **Region I:** Borden E. Bell Jr., Texarkana (2/1/15); Richard (Doug) Smith, Clarksville (2/1/11); **Region 2:** David T. Neeley, Mount Pleasant (2/1/15); Patricia A. Wommack, Lone Star (2/1/11); **Region 3:** Mike Russell, Powderly (2/1/13); Brad Drake, Paris (2/1/13); Kirby Hollingsworth, Mount Vernon (6/15/15); 911 N. Bishop St., Ste. C 104, Wake Village 75501; (903) 223-7887.

**Sunset Advisory Commission** – (1977); 12 members: 5 members of House of Representatives, 5 members of Senate, 1 public member apptd. by Speaker, 1 public member apptd. by Lt. Gov.; 2-yr.; expenses. Public members: Dawn Buckingham, Lakeway (9/1/17); Tom Luce, Dallas (9/1/17). Dir. Joey Longley, PO Box 13066, Austin 78711-3066; (512) 463-1300.

**Tax Board, State** – Est. 1905; 3 ex-officio members: Comptroller, Secretary of State and State Treasurer; abolished by the 66th Legislature, effective 1/1/82, and replaced by the Texas State Property Tax Board.

**Tax Professional Examiners, Texas Board of** – (1977 as Board of Tax Assessor Examiners; name changed to present form 1983); apptv.; expenses; 6-yr.; 5 members: Chair Dorye Kristeen Roe, Bryan (3/1/13) James E. Childers, Canyon (3/1/11); P.H. (Fourth) Coates, Medina (3/1/11); Linda Lowes Hatchel, Woodway (3/1/15); Steve Mossman, Flower Mound (3/1/11). Exec. Dir. David E. Montoya ($60,000), 333 Guadalupe, Ste. 2-520 Austin 78701-3942; (512) 305-7300.

**Teacher Retirement System** – See, Retirement System, Teacher.

**Texas A&M University System Board of Regents** – (1875); apptv.; 6-yr.; expenses; 9 members: Chair Cliff Thomas, Victoria (2/1/17); Phil Adams, Bryan-College Station (2/1/21); Robert L. Albritton, Fort Worth (2/1/19); Anthony G. Buzbee, Houston (2/1/19); Morris E. Foster, Austin (2/1/19); William Mahomes, Jr., Dallas (2/1/21); Elaine Mendoza, San Antonio (2/1/17); Judy Morgan, Texarkana (2/1/17); Charles W. Schwartz, Houston (2/1/19). Chancellor John Sharp, PO Box 15812, College Station 77841-5013; (979) 845-9600.

**Texas Southern University Board of Regents** – (1947); expenses; 6-yr.; 9 members: Chair Glenn O. Lewis, Fort Worth (2/1/19); Gary Bledsoe, Austin (2/1/17); Samuel Lee Bryant, Austin (2/1/17); Richard Knight Jr., Dallas (2/1/17); Derrick Mitchell, Houston (2/1/21); Sarah Monty-Arnoni, Houston (2/1/19); Marilyn A. Rose, Houston (2/1/21); Erik Salwen, Houston (2/1/19); Wesley Terrell, Dallas (2/1/21). Pres. Dr. John M. Rudley. Exec. Dir. Karen A. Griffin 3100 Cleburne St., Hannah Hall, Rm. 104, Houston 77004; (713) 313-7992.

**Texas State Technical College System Board of Regents** – (1960 as Board of the Texas State Technical Institute; changed to present name in 1991); apptv.; expenses; 6-yr.; 9 members: Chair Ellis M. Skinner II, Dallas (8/31/19); Ivan Andarza, Austin (8/31/19); Penny Forrest, Waco (8/31/15); Joe M. Gurecky, Rosenberg (8/31/17); John Hatchel, Woodway (8/31/17); Joe K. Hearne, Richardson, (8/31/17); Keith Honey, Longview (8/31/19); James Virgil (J.V.) Martin, Sweetwater (8/31/17); Linda McKenna, Harlingen (8/31/15). Chancellor Michael L. Reeser, TSTC System, 3801 Campus Dr., Waco 76705; (254) 867-4891.

**Texas State University System Board of Regents** – (1911 as Board of Regents of State Teachers Colleges; name changed in 1965 to Board of Regents of State Senior Colleges; changed to present form in 1975); apptv.; per diem and expenses; 6-yr.; 9 members: Chair Jaime Garza, San Antonio (2/1/17); Charlie Amato, San Antonio (2/1/19); Veronica M. Edwards, San Antonio (2/1/21); J. David Montagne, Beaumont (2/1/21); Vernon Reaser III, Bellaire (2/1/19); Rossanna Salazar, Austin (2/1/17); William Scott, Nederland (2/1/19); Alan L. Tinsley, Madisonville (2/1/17); Donna N. Williams, Arlington (2/1/17). Chancellor Brian McCall, Thomas J. Rusk Bldg., 200 E. 10th St., Ste. 600, Austin, 78701; (512) 463-1808.

**Texas Tech University Board of Regents** – (1923); apptv.; expenses; 6-yr.; 9 members: Larry Keith Anders, Dallas (1/31/17); John D. Esparza, Austin (1/31/19); L. Frederick (Rick) Francis, El Paso (1/31/19); Ronnie Hammonds, Houston (1/31/21); Christopher M. Huckabee, Fort Worth (1/31/21); Tim Lancaster, Abilene (1/31/19); Mickey L. Long, Midland (1/31/21); Debbie Montford, San Antonio (1/31/17); John D. Steinmetz, Lubbock (1/31/17); John B. Walker, Houston (1/31/15). Chancellor Robert L. Duncan, P.O. Box 42011, Lubbock 79409-2011; (806) 742-2161.

**Texas Woman's University Board of Regents** – (1901); apptv.; expenses; 6-yr.; 9 members: Anna Maria Farias, Corpus Christi (2/1/19); Debbie Gibson, Houston (2/1/17); John V. Lattimore Jr., McKinney (2/1/21); Ann Scanlon McGinity, Pearland (2/1/21); Nancy P. Paup, Fort Worth (2/1/19); Nolan Perez, Harlingen (2/1/21); George R. Schrader, Dallas (2/1/19); Melissa Tonn, Dallas (2/1/17); Mary Pincoffs Wilson, Austin (2/1/17). Chancellor Dr. Carine M. Feyten, PO Box 425587, TWU Station, Denton 76204-5587; (940) 898-3250.

**Transportation Commission, Texas** – (1917 as State Highway Commission; merged with Mass Transportation Commission and name changed to State Board of Highways and Public Transportation in 1975; merged with Texas Dept. of Aviation and Texas Motor Vehicle Commission and name changed to present form in 1991); apptv.; 6-yr.; 5 members ($15,914 each): Chair Tryon D. Lewis., Odessa (2/1/21); Jeff Austin III, Tyler (2/1/19); Bruce Bugg Jr., San Antonio (2/1/21); Jeff Moseley, Houston (2/1/17); Victor Vandergriff, Arlington (2/1/19). Exec. Dir. General Joe Weber ($292,500), 125 E. 11th St., Austin 78701-2483; (512) 463-8585.

**Trinity River Authority Board of Directors** – (1955); apptv.; per diem and expenses; 6-yr.; 25 members (3 from Tarrant County, 4 from Dallas County, 3 from area-at-large and 1 each from 15 other districts): Chair Kim C. Wyatt, Corsicana (3/15/15); Henry Borbolla III, Fort Worth (3/15/19); William W. Collins Jr., Fort Worth (3/15/15); Christina Melton Crain, Dallas (3/15/17); Michael Cronin, Terrell (3/15/17); Steve Cronin, Shepherd (3/15/17); Amanda B. Davis, Buffalo (3/15/17); Valerie Ertz, Dallas (3/15/15); Tommy G. Fordyce, Huntsville (3/15/19); Ronald J. Goldman, Fort Worth (3/15/15); Martha Hernandez, Burleson (3/15/19); Harold Jenkins, Irving (3/15/15); Jess A. Laird, Athens (3/15/19); David Leonard, Liberty (3/15/19); Kevin Maxwell, Crockett (3/15/15); Dennis (Joe) McCleskey, Apple Springs (3/15/17); James W. Neale, Dallas (3/15/19); Manny Rachal, Livingston (3/15/15); Amir A. Rupani, Dallas (3/15/19); Ana Laura Saucedo, Dallas (3/15/19); Shirley K. Seale, Anahuac (3/15/15); Dudley Skyrme, Palestine (3/15/19); C. Dwayne Somerville, Mexia (3/15/19); J. Carol Spillars, Madisonville (3/15/17). Gen. Mgr. J. Kevin Ward, 5300 S. Collins, PO Box 60, Arlington 76004-0060; (817) 467-4343.

**Tuition Board, Prepaid Higher Education** – (See Higher Education Tuition Board, Texas Prepaid).

**Uniform State Laws, Commission on** – (1941 as 5-member Commissioners to the National Conference on Uniform State Laws; name changed to present form, members increased to 6 and term of office raised to 6 years in 1977; members increased to 9 in 2001); apptv.; 6-yr.; 9 members: Levi J. Benton, Houston (9/30/16); Eric Hougland, Austin (9/30/14); Debra H. Lehrmann, Colleyville (9/30/16); Peter K. Munson, Sherman (9/30/20); Frank E. Perez, Brownsville (9/30/16); Marilyn Phelan, Lubbock (9/30/18); Harry L. Tindall, Houston (9/30/18); Karen R. Washington, Dallas (9/30/16); Earl L. Yeakel III, Austin (9/30/18); one vacancy. Life members: Patrick Guillot, Dallas; Leonard Reece, Austin; Rodney Wayne Satterwhite, Midland. Exec. Dir. John Sebert, 111 N. Washington Ave., Ste. 1010, Chicago, IL, 60602; (312) 450-6600.

**University of Houston System Board of Regents** – (1963); apptv.; expenses; 6-yr.; 9 members: Chair Tilman J. Fertitta, Houston (8/31/15); Durga D. Agrawal, Houston (8/31/15); Spencer D. Armour III, Midland (8/31/17); Jarvis V. Hollingsworth, Houston (8/31/15); Beth Madison, Houston (8/31/15); Paula M. Mendoza, Houston (8/31/19); Peter K. Taaffe, Austin (8/31/19); Welcome W. Wilson Jr., Houston (8/31/17); Roger F. Welder, Victoria (8/31/17). Chancellor Dr. Renu Khator; Exec. Admin. Gerry Mathisen, 4800 Calhoun, 128 E. Cullen Bldg., Houston 77204-6001; (832) 842-3444.

**University of North Texas System Board of Regents** – (1949); apptv.; 6-yr.; expenses; 9 members: Chair George (Brint) Ryan, Dallas (5/22/15); Michael R. Bradford, Midland (5/22/15); Milton B. Lee II, San Antonio (5/22/17); Steve Mitchell, Richardson (5/22/15); Donald Potts, Dallas (5/22/17); Rusty Reid, Fort Worth (5/22/19); Gwyn Shea, Irving (5/22/19); Alfredo (Al) Silva, San Antonio (5/22/17); B. Glen Whitley, Hurst (5/22/19). Chancellor Lee F. Jackson; Brd. Sec. Julia A. Boyce, 1901 Main St., Dallas, 75201; (214) 752-5533.

**University of Texas System Board of Regents** – (1881); apptv.; expenses; 6-yr.; 9 members: Chair Paul L. Foster, El Paso (2/1/19); Ernest Aliseda, McAllen (2/1/19); David Beck, Houston (2/1/21); Alex M. Cranberg, Houston (2/1/17); Wallace L. Hall Jr., Dallas (2/1/17); R. Steven Hicks, Austin (2/1/21); Jeff Hildebrand, Houston (2/1/21); Brenda Pejovich, Dallas (2/1/17); Sara Martinez Tucker, Dallas (2/1/21). Chancellor Admiral William H. McRaven USN (Ret.), 201 W. Seventh St., Ste. 820, Austin, 78701-2981; (512) 499-4402.

**Utility Commission, Public** – (See Public Utility Commission).

**Veterans Commission, Texas** – (1927 as Veterans State Service Office; reorganized as Veterans Affairs Commission in 1947 with 5 members; name changed to present in 1985); apptv.; 6-yr.; per diem while on duty and expenses; 5 members: Chair

Eliseo Cantu Jr., Corpus Christi (12/31/19); Jake Ellzey, Midlothian (12/31/17); Richard A. McLeon IV, Henderson (12/31/17); Daniel P. Moran, Cypress (12/31/19); James H. Scott, San Antonio (12/31/15). Exec. Dir. Thomas P. Palladino ($115,000), PO Box 12277, Austin 78711-2277; (512) 463-6564.

**Veterans' Land Board** – (*See* Land Board, Veterans').

**Veterinary Medical Examiners, Texas State Board of** – (1911; revised 1953; made 9-member board in 1981); apptv.; expenses on duty; 6-yr.; 9 members: Chair Bud E. Alldrege Jr., Sweetwater (8/26/15); Dan Lee Craven, Crockett (8/26/19); Janie Allen Carpenter, Dallas (8/26/17); Todd Henry, Wimberly (8/26/15); Joe Mac King, Dallas (8/26/17); Roland Lenarduzzi, Alvin (8/26/19). Public Members: James (Jim) McAdams, Seguin (8/26/19); Keith Pardue, Austin (8/26/15); Chad Upham, Boerne (8/26/17). Exec. Dir. Nicole Oria ($80,500), 333 Guadalupe St., Ste. 3-810, Austin 78701-3942; (512) 305-7555.

**Wastewater Treatment Research Council, Texas On-Site** – Formed in 1987 as an apptv., 2-yr., 11-member council. Abolished on Sept. 1, 2011, by House Bill 2694.

**Water Development Board, Texas** – (1957; legislative function for the Texas Dept. of Water Resources, 1977); apptv.; per diem and expenses; 6-yr.; 3 members: Chair Bech K. Bruun, Austin (2/1/15); Kathleen Jackson, Beaumont (12/31/15); Carlos Rubinstein, Austin (12/31/17). Exec. Admin. Kevin Patteson($135,000), 1700 N. Congress Ave., Ste. 690, PO Box 13231, Austin 78711-3231; (512) 463-7847.

**Women, Governor's Commission for** – (1967); apptv.; 2-yr. term or at pleasure of Gov.; 12 members: Chair Carol Foxhall Peterson, Alpine (12/31/13); Gina Bridwell, Abilene (12/31/13); Stephanie Cavender, San Antonio (12/31/13); Julie Crosswell, Houston (12/31/13); Cynthia Tyson Jenkins, Irving (12/31/13); Claudia Kreisle, Houston (12/31/13); Elisa (Lisa) Gonzales Lucero, Austin (12/31/13); Becky McKinley, Amarillo (12/31/13); Carmen Pagan, McAllen (12/31/13); Ivy Pate, Beaumont (12/31/13); Teresa Rockwell, Austin (12/31/13); Connie Weeks, Austin (12/31/13). Exec. Dir. Lesley Guthrie, 1100 San Jacinto Blvd., Rm. 2.256, PO Box 12428, Austin 78711; (512)

475-2615.

**Workers' Compensation Commissioner, Texas** – (1991); functions transferred to the Texas Dept. of Insurance Division of Workers' Compensation in 2005; apptv.; 2-yr.; Commissioner Ryan Brannan ($140,000) Austin, (2/1/15), PO Box 149104, Austin 78714-9104; (800) 839-5323.

**Workforce Commission, Texas** – (1936 as Texas Employment Commission; name changed 1995); apptv.; chairman, $125,000; commissioners, $115,000; 6-yr.; 3 members: Chair Andres Alcantar, Austin (2/1/19), representing the public; Ruth Ruggero Hughs, Austin (9/1/15); Mark Dunn, representing employers; Ronald G. Congleton, Rockwall (2/1/17), representing labor. Exec. Dir. Larry Temple ($140,000), 101 E. 15th St., Austin 78778-0001; (512) 463-2222.

**Workforce Investment Council, Texas** – (1993); apptv.; 19 members: 5 ex officio (directors from Economic Development and Tourism, Higher Education Coordinating Board, Texas Education Agency, Texas Health and Human Services Comm., Texas Workforce Comm.); 14 apptd.: Chair Wes Jurey, Arlington (9/1/13); James M. Brookes, Amarillo (9/1/17); Blas Castaneda, Laredo (9/1/13); Robert Cross, Houston (9/1/13); Mark Dunn, Lufkin (9/1/13); Carmen Olivas Graham, El Paso (9/1/17); Richard Hatfield, Austin (9/1/15); Robert Hawkins, Bellmead (9/1/17); Sharla E. Hotchkiss, Midland (9/1/17); Larry Jeffus, Garland (9/1/15); Matthew Maxfield, Brownwood (9/1/15); Paul Mayer, Garland (9/1/13); Danny Prosperie, Bridge City (9/1/13); Joyce Delores Taylor, Houston (9/1/15). Dir. Lee Rector, 1100 San Jacinto, Ste. 1.100 PO Box 2241, Austin 78768; (512) 936-8100.

**Youth Commission, Texas** – (1949 as 9-member advisory board; reorganized in 1957 and again in 1975; in March 2007, all board members resigned and the commission was placed under conservatorship; in October 2008, the Gov. removed TYC from conservatorship); abolished on Dec. 1, 2011, pursuant to Senate Bill 653, passed by the 82nd Texas Legislature and signed by the Gov.; operations of TYC and the Texas Juvenile Probation Commission were transferred to the Texas Juvenile Justice Department. ☆

**Texas State Historical Association**
**2017 Annual Meeting**

March 2 – 4, 2017 • Hyatt Regency Houston • Houston, Texas

Get more information at **TSHAonline.org/annual-meeting**

*The Dallas skyline. Photo by Ron Billings: Texas A&M Forest Service.*

# Local Government

Texas has **254 counties,** a number that has not changed since 1931 when Loving County was organized. Loving has a population of 86, according to the Jan. 1, 2014, Texas State Data Center estimate, compared with 164 in 1970 and a peak of 285 in 1940. It is the **least-populous county** in Texas. In contrast, Harris County has the **most residents** in Texas, with a 2014 population estimate of 4,441,370.

Counties range in area from Rockwall's 148.7 square miles to the 6,192.78 square miles in Brewster, which is equal to the combined area of the states of Connecticut and Rhode Island.

The Texas Constitution makes a county a legal subdivision of the state. Each county has a commissioners court. It consists of four commissioners, each elected from a commissioner's precinct, and a county judge elected from the entire county. In smaller counties, the county judge retains judicial responsibilities in probate and insanity cases. For names of county and district officials, see tables on pages 533–544.

There are **1,215 incorporated municipalities** in Texas that range in size from 20 residents in Los Ybañez to Houston's 2,201,974, according to the Jan. 1, 2014, Texas State Data Center estimates. More than 80 percent of the state's population lives in cities and towns, meeting the U.S. Census Bureau definition of urban areas.

Texas had 345 incorporated towns with more than 5,000 population, according to the 2014 State Data Center estimates. Under law, these cities may adopt their own charters (called **home rule**) by a majority vote. Cities of less than 5,000 may be chartered only under the **general law.**

Some home-rule cities may show fewer than 5,000 residents because population has declined since adopting home-rule charters. **Home-rule cities are marked in this list by a single-dagger symbol (†) after the name.** ☆

## Mayors and City Managers of Texas Cities

This list was compiled from questionnaires sent out after the May 10, 2015, municipal elections. It includes the name of each city's mayor, as well as the name of the city manager, city administrator, city coordinator, or other managing executive for municipalities having that form of government. If a town's mail goes to a post office in a different town, the mailing address is included. If the Texas Almanac received no response to the questionnaire, the information is from other official sources.

### — A —

**Abbott** ............... Anthony R. Pustejovsky
**Abernathy** ........................ Lindsey Webb
   City Mgr., Mike Cypert
**Abilene (†)** ...................... Norm Archibald
   City Mgr., Larry D. Gilley
**Ackerly** .................................. Scott Ragle
**Addison (†)** ........................... Todd Meier
   City Mgr., Ron Whitehead
**Adrian** .................................. Finis Brown
**Agua Dulce** .......................... Carl Vajdos
**Alamo (†)** ........................ Rudy Villarreal

   City Mgr., Luciano Ozuna Jr.
**Alamo Heights (†)** (6116 Broadway, San Antonio 78209) ........... Louis R. Cooper
   City Mgr., J. Mark Browne
**Alba** ..................................... Orvin Carroll
**Albany** ...................... Rodney Alexander
   City Mgr., (vacant)
**Aledo** ................................. Kit Marshall
   City Admin., Ken Pfeifer
**Alice (†)** ............................... Ike Ornelas
   City Mgr., Jesus (Chuy) Garcia
**Allen (†)** ........................ Stephen Terrell
   City Mgr., Peter H. Vargas
**Alma** ................................ Mark Stephens

**Alpine (†)** ........... Avinash K. (Avi) Rangra
   City Mgr., Erik Zimmer
**Alto,** City of .......................... Jimmy Allen
**Alton** ................................. Salvador Vela
   City Mgr., Jorge Arcaute
**Alvarado** ................. E. Dewayne Richters
   City Mgr., Clint Davis
**Alvin (†)** .............................. Paul A. Horn
   City Mgr., Sereniah Breland
**Alvord** ........................................ Roy King
   City Admin., (vacant)
**Amarillo (†)** ....................... Paul Harpole
   City Mgr., Jarrett Atkinson
**Ames** ..................................... John White

Amherst.................Joe A. Miller
Anahuac ........................ Cheryl Sanders
   City Admin., Ken Bays
Anderson...................... Gail M. Sowell
Andrews (†)...........................Flora Braly
   City Mgr., Glen E. Hackler
Angleton (†) ................. Randy Rhyne
   City Mgr., Michael Stoldt
Angus .......... (6008 S. I-45 W, Corsicana
   75109) ..................... Julie Humphries
Anna (†) ................................... Mike Crist
   City Mgr., Philip Sanders
Annetta ......(PO Box 1150, Aledo 76008)
   ........................Bruce M. Pinckard
Annetta North.........(PO Box 1238, Aledo
   76008) ...................... Robert Schmidt
Annetta South........... (PO Box 61, Aledo
   76008) ...............Gerhard Kleinschmidt
Annona ................ George H. English Sr.
   City Mgr., (vacant)
Anson (†) ......................Michael Herndon
   City Mgr., Sonny Campbell
Anthony ...............................Martin Lerma
Anton .................................Blake Cate
   City Mgr., Mike Sea
Appleby (15485 N. Hwy. 59, Garrison
   75946) ....................Gerald Herbert Sr.
Aquilla .................... James Hamner Sr.
Aransas Pass (†)................. Adan Chapa
   City Mgr., Sylvia Carrillo
Archer City ........................ Kelvin Green
   City Mgr., George Huffman
Arcola .......................Mary Etta Anderson
Argyle .......................Peggy R. Krueger
   City Mgr., Paul Frederiksen
Arlington (†) ....................W. Jeff Williams
   City Mgr., Trey Yelverton
Arp ..................................... Penny Wilson
Asherton ...................... Enrique Jasso
   City Mgr., Adrian Zamora
Aspermont.................Kathy Castaneda
   City Admin., Lorenzo Calamaco
Athens (†)..................... Jerry Don Vaught
   City Mgr., Philip Rodriguez
Atlanta (†).......................Keith Crow
   City Mgr., David Cockrell
Aubrey ...........................Janet Meyers
   City Admin., Matt McCombs
Aurora............................. Terry Solomon
   City Admin., Toni Wheeler
Austin (†)......................Steve Adler
   City Mgr., Marc A. Ott
Austwell........................... David Cann
Avery ..................................Dan Halley
Avinger ........................Marvin E. Parvino
Azle (†)............................. Alan Brundrett
   City Mgr., (vacant)

**— B —**

Bailey ................... John Robert Stephens
Bailey's Prairie..... (PO Box 71, Angleton
   77516) ..............................Jo Mapel
Baird .......................................Jeff Barton
Balch Springs (†)........Carrie J. Marshall
   City Mgr., Susan Cluse
Balcones Heights .......Suzanne de Leon
   City Admin., David Harris
Ballinger (†)................... Sam Mallory
   City Mgr., Bryan Grimes
Balmorhea .......................John L. Davis
Bandera .................John Hegemier
   City Admin., Lamar Schulz
Bangs............................Eric Bishop
   City Admin., Leo Smith
Bardwell..............................Clinton Ivy
Barry ........................... Charles Worsham
Barstow ............................Olga Abila
Bartlett ................................Norris L. Ivy
   City Admin., Christopher Hill
Bartonville ...........................Bill Scherer
   Town Admin., Stacey Almond

Bastrop (†)........................ Ken Kesselus
   City Mgr., Michael H. Talbot
Bay City (†)....................... Mark Bricker
Bayou Vista ................ Daniel S. Konyha
Bayside....................Tom Van Buren
Baytown (†) ......... Stephen H. DonCarlos
   City Mgr., Richard L. Davis
Bayview ........................Thomas Rodino
Beach City ....................... Billy Combs
Bear Creek (13012 S. Madrone Trail, Aus-
   tin 78737) ................... Bruce Upham
Beasley ........................ Kenneth Reid
Beaumont (†)...................... Becky Ames
   City Mgr., Kyle Hayes
Beckville ..................... Gene Mothershed
Bedford (†) .......................Jim Griffen
   City Mgr., Roger Gibson
Bedias .............. Mackie Bobo-White
Bee Cave (†) .............Caroline L. Murphy
   City Mgr., Travis Askey
Beeville (†)....................David Carabajal
   City Mgr., Jack S. Hamlett
Bellaire (†) ......................... Phil Nauert
   City Mgr., Paul Hoffman
Bellevue......................... Robert Ratliff
Bellmead (†) .............. Doss Youngblood
   City Mgr., Everett (Bo) Thomas
Bells .............................Angela LeBlanc
Bellville ........................Joe Ed Lynn
   City Admin., Shawn Jackson
Belton (†) .......................Marion Grayson
   City Mgr., Sam A. Listi
Benavides ......... Ernestina C. Gonzalez
Benbrook (†) ...................Jerry B. Dittrich
   City Mgr., Andy Wayman
Benjamin ........................Ronnie White
   City Mgr., Kim Sealy
Berryville ..........(PO Box 908, Frankston
   75763) ..............................Roy Brown
Bertram...........................Dickie Allen
Beverly Hills (3418 Memorial Dr., Waco
   76711) ....................David Gonzales
Bevil Oaks ...... Rebecca M. (Becky) Ford
Big Lake...........................Kyle Roekwell
   City Admin., Evelyn Ammons
Big Sandy ........................ Nancy Church
Big Spring (†).............Larry McLellan
   City Mgr., Todd Darden Todd Darden
Big Wells ............................Jesus Ponce
   City Admin., (vacant)
Bishop ............................Joe H. Morales
Bishop Hills (#6 Manchester Rd., Ama-
   rillo 79124)....................Betty Benham
Blackwell ....................... Laura Rozzlle
Blanco............................M. Bruce Peele
Blanket .............................Judy Eoff
Bloomburg ................... Melvin Timmons
Blooming Grove..... Gary (Yig) Pattersoh
Blossom ........................Charlotte Burge
Blue Mound .....(301 S. Blue Mound Rd.,
   Fort Worth 76131) .............Alan Hooks
   City Admin., Kathryn Sanchez
Blue Ridge................... Rhonda Williams
Blum................................Chryle Hackler
Boerne (†).................. Michael D. Schultz
   City Mgr., Ronald C. Bowman
Bogata ............................. Vincent Lum
Bonham (†) ....................Roy V. Floyd
   City Mgr., Sean Pate
Bonney ........................ Raymond Cantu
Booker ...........................C.J. Skipper
Borger (†) ......................... Robert Vinyard
   City Mgr., Eddie Edwards
Bovina..........................Frank Gonzalez
   City Mgr., Cesar Marquiz
Bowie (†)..................... Larry Slack
   City Mgr., Ricky Tow
Boyd..................Rodney (Bill) Scroggins
   City Admin., Greg Arrington
Brackettville .............. Andres Rodriguez
Brady (†) ................... Anthony Groves
   City Mgr., Kim Lenoir

Brazoria ...................... Ken Corley
   City Mgr., Teresa Borders
Brazos Bend............. Vernon E. Oechsle
Brazos Country (316 Pecan Grove Rd.,
   Sealy 77474) .......Charles A. Kalkomey
Breckenridge (†)............. Jimmy McKay
   City Mgr., Andy McCuistion
Bremond............................Ricky Swick
Brenham (†)............. Milton Y. Tate Jr.
   City Mgr., Terry K. Roberts
Briarcliff..........................Al Hostetler
   City Admin., Aaron Johnson
Briaroaks .........(PO Box 816, Burleson
   76097).......................James Dunn
Bridge City (†) ...........Kirk Roccaforte
   City Mgr., Jerry D. Jones
Bridgeport........................Corey Lane
Broaddus.......................Shirley J. Parker
Bronte...........................Gerald Sandusky
   City Mgr., Ricky Royall
Brookshire..............................Eric Scott
Brookside Village ...............Craig Bailey
Browndell    (Box 430, Brookeland
   75931) ...................David Sanderson
Brownfield ......................... Tom Hesse
   City Mgr., Eldon Jobe
Brownsboro ........................ Terry Mills
Brownsville ......................Tony Martinez
   City Mgr., Charlie Cabler
Brownwood (†).........Stephen E. Haynes
   City Mgr., Emily Crawford
Bruceville-Eddy ...... (143 Wilcox Dr., #A,
   Eddy 76524) ..................Rick Eaton
   City Admin., Koni Billings
Bryan (†)....................Jason P. Bienski
   City Mgr., Kean Register
Bryson ...............................Sheila Birdwell
Buckholts ........................ Kathy Mayes
Buda....................................Todd Ruge
   City Mgr., Kenneth Williams
Buffalo ....................... Royce Dawkins
Buffalo Gap ..................... David L. Perry
Buffalo Springs (99-B Pony Express Trl.,
   Lubbock 79404)........ Dennis Wardroup
Bullard ........................Pam Frederick
   City Mgr., Larry Morgan
Bulverde ...........................Bill Krawietz
   City Admin., E.A. Hoppe IV
Bunker Hill Village (11977 Memorial Dr.,
   Houston 77024)............. Jay Williams
   City Admin., Karen Glynn
Burkburnett (†).........................Carl Law
   City Mgr., Mike Whaley
Burke ... (3770 Tidwell Rd., Diboll 75941)
   ........................John Thomas Jones
Burleson (†)...................... Ken Shetter
   City Mgr., Dale Cheatham
Burnet (†).......................... Gary Wideman
   City Mgr., David Vaughn
Burton.........................Peggy A. Felder
Byers...............................Carl Barnhill
Bynum ............................Thomas Hanson

**— C —**

Cactus.......................Socorro Marquez
   City Mgr., Aldo Gallegos
Caddo Mills ................. Dwayne Pattison
   City Mgr., Matt McMahan
Caldwell.....................Norris L. McManus
   City Admin., Johnny L. Price
Callisburg.........................Frances West
Calvert .................... Marcus D. Greaves
   City Admin., Kevin O'Carroll
Cameron (†)....................Connie Anderle
   City Mgr., J. Rhett Parker
Campbell .............................Ken Padilla
Camp Wood ......................Jesse Chevez
Canadian ............................ Rob Talley
   City Mgr., Hoyt Manning
Caney City ...........................Joe Barron
Canton .........................Lou Ann Everett
   City Mgr., Lonny Cluck

**Canyon (†)** .....................Quinn Alexander
City Mgr., Randy Criswell
**Carbon** ..................................... Corey Hull
**Carl's Corner** ..............Carl W. Cornelius
**Carmine** ........................................Jerry Knox
**Carrizo Springs (†)** ..........Dina Balderas
City Mgr., (vacant)
**Carrollton (†)** ..............Matthew Marchant
City Mgr., Leonard Martin
**Carthage (†)** ....................... Lunn Vincent
City Mgr., Brenda Samford
**Cashion** (354 Baker Rd., Wichita Falls
76305) ................................ Debra Carr
**Castle Hills** (209 Lemonwood Dr., San
Antonio 78213) ................... Tim Howell
City Mgr., Diane Pfeil
**Castroville** ............................ Jeff Gardner
City Admin., Mark B. Roath
**Cedar Hill (†)** ............... Rob Franke
City Mgr., Greg Porter
**Cedar Park (†)** ...............Matthew Powell
City Mgr., Brenda Eivens
**Celeste**...................................Larry Godwin
**Celina (†)** ...............................Sean Terry
City Mgr., Mike Foreman
**Center (†)** ....................... David Chadwick
City Mgr., Chad D. Nehring
**Centerville** ........Noal Ray (N.R.) Goolsby
**Chandler** ..........................Libby Fulgham
City Admin., John Taylor
**Channing** ........................... Brent Loudder
**Charlotte**..... Augustine (PeeWee) Munoz
**Chester** ..........................C.E. Lawrence
**Chico**..........................Karen M. Garrison
**Childress** ..................................Brett Parr
City Mgr., Bryan Tucker
**Chillicothe** ..........................Cathy Young
**China**..................................... John Walker
**China Grove** ................. Dennis A. Dunk
**Chireno** ................Susan Higginbothan
City Admin., Steven Spencer
**Christine** ............................Odel Vasquez
**Cibolo** ............................. Lisa M. Jackson
**Cisco (†)** ..........................James Maples
City Mgr., Johnny T. Carson
**Clarendon** ........................... Larry Hicks
City Admin., David Dockery
**Clarksville**................................Ann Rushing
City Mgr., Wayne Dial
**Clarksville City**......(Box 1111, White Oak
75693) ..........................Larry G. Allen
City Mgr., John Whitsell
**Claude**...................................Jim Hubbard
**Clear Lake Shores** ...........Vern Johnson
City Admin., George K. Jones
**Cleburne (†)**............................Scott Cain
City Mgr., Dan O'Leary
**Cleveland (†)** ........................Niki Coats
City Mgr., Kelly McDonald
**Clifton** ...........................Richard Spitzer
City Admin., Pamela K. Harvey
**Clint**............................. Dale T. Reinhardt
**Clute (†)** ............................Calvin Shiflet
City Mgr., Gary Beverly
**Clyde**................................. Matthew Howard
City Admin., Keith Selman
**Coahoma** .....................Warren Wallace
**Cockrell Hill**....................Luis D. Carrera
City Admin., Bret Haney
**Coffee City**.............................. Pam Drost
**Coldspring**..........................Pat Eversole
**Coleman (†)**....................Kay R. Joffrion
City Mgr., Paul Catoe
**College Station (†)** .............. Nancy Berry
City Mgr., Kelly Templin
**Colleyville (†)** ...................... David Kelly
City Mgr., Jennifer Fadden
**Collinsville**..................Brandon R. White
City Admin., Troy Vannoy
**Colmesneil** ........................ Donald Baird

**Colorado City (†)** .................... Jim Baum
City Mgr., David Hoover
**Columbus** ...........................Dwain Dungen
City Mgr., Donald Warschak
**Comanche** ........................Ronnie Clifton
City Admin., Robert Evans
**Combes** ......................... Marco Sanchez
City Mgr., Lonnie Bearden
**Combine** ......................... Tim M. Ratcliff
**Commerce (†)**...........R. John Ballotti, Sr.
City Mgr., Marc Clayton
**Como** .................................... Ron Walker
City Admin., Sue Jones
**Conroe (†)**...................... Webb K. Melder
City Admin., Paul Virgadamo
**Converse (†)**............................Al Suarez
City Mgr., Lanny S. Lambert
**Cool** ....... (150 FM 113 S., Millsap 76066)
.................................. Dorothy Hall
**Coolidge** .............................Jesse Ashmore
**Cooper** ..............Thomas Scott Stegall
**Coppell (†)** ...................Karen Selbo Hunt
City Mgr., Clay Phillips
**Copperas Cove (†)** .............. John Hull
City Mgr., Andrea M. Gardner
**Copper Canyon** ...................... Sue Tejml
Town Admin., Donna Welsh
**Corinth (†)** ...................Bill Heidemann
City Mgr., Rick Chaffin
**Corpus Christi (†)** .....Nelda Martinez
City Mgr., Ron Olson
**Corral City** (14007 Corral City Dr., Argyle
76226) ........................Jamie S. Harris
**Corrigan**........................Jonathan Clark
City Mgr., Darrian Hudman
**Corsicana (†)**...........Chuck McClanahan
City Mgr., Connie Standridge
**Cottonwood**...... (Box 293, Scurry 75158)
.........................................Jeff Gray
**Cottonwood Shores** ..............Donald Orr
City Admin., Sheila C. Moore
**Cotulla** .............................Joe R. Lozano
City Admin., Larry Dovalina
**Coupland** ........................ Jack Piper
**Cove**.......................................Judy Leggitt
**Covington**.....................George Burnett
**Coyote Flats** (1800 County Rd. 415, Cle-
burne 76031) ................ Doug Peterson
**Crandall** ............................Cody Frazier
City Mgr., L. Scott Wall
**Crane** .................................. Mark Pahl
City Admin., Dru Gravens
**Cranfills Gap** ................... David D. Witte
**Crawford**........................ Brent W. Meyer
**Creedmoor** ..................Robert L. Wilhite
City Admin. Richard L. Crandal Jr.
**Cresson** ..................W.R. (Bob) Cornett
**Crockett (†)**..................Robert Meadows
City Admin., Sean Hutchison
**Crosbyton**......................Dusty Cornelius
City Admin., Margot Hardin
**Cross Plains**..........................Ray Purvis
City Admin., Debbie Gosnell
**Cross Roads** ......................Steve Smith
**Cross Timber** ............. Wava McCullough
**Crowell**............................Gayle Simpson
**Crowley (†)** ......................Billy P. Davis
City Mgr., Robert Loftin
**Crystal City (†)** ..................Ricardo Lopez
City Mgr., W. James Jonas III
**Cuero (†)**...................... Sara Post Meyer
City Mgr., Raymond Zella
**Cumby** ...........................Kathy Hall-Carter
**Cuney** ........................... Charles Cross
**Cushing** ...........................Mahesh Desai
**Cut and Shoot** ..................Nyla Dalhaus

**— D —**

**Daingerfield (†)** ........................ Lou Irvin
City Mgr., Marty Byers

**Daisetta**........................Debra Kay Fregia
**Dalhart (†)**............................. Phillip Hass
City Mgr., James Stroud
**Dallas (†)**........................... Mike Rawlings
City Mgr., A.C. Gonzalez
**Dalworthington Gardens**..Michel Tedder
City Admin., Melinda G. Brittain
**Danbury** ........................... Richard Stone
**Darrouzett**....................... Sandra Woods
Town Mgr., Melanie Davis
**Dawson**...................... Stephen Sanders
**Dayton (†)** ....................Jeff K. Lambright
City Mgr., David Douglas
**Dayton Lakes** ........... (Box 1476, Dayton
77535) ...................... Daniel Norris
**Dean** (6913 State Hwy. 79 N., Wichita
Falls 76035)............... Steve L. Sicking
**Decatur (†)** ..................Martin Woodruff
City Mgr., Brett Shannon
**DeCordova** (PO Box 5905, Granbury
76049) .................................Pat Revill
**Deer Park (†)** ............. Jerry L. Mouton Jr.
City Mgr., James J. Stokes
**De Kalb**..........................Dennis Wandrey
City Admin., Abbi Capps
**De Leon (†)** .......................... Toby Hight
City Admin., Karen Wilkerson
**Dell City** ........................... Marcie Guillen
**Del Rio (†)**..........................Robert Garza
City Mgr., Harold Bean
**Denison (†)** ......................Jared Johnson
City Mgr., Jud Rex
**Denton (†)**.............................Chris Watts
City Mgr., George Campbell
**Denver City (†)** ....................Tommy Hicks
City Mgr., Stan David
**Deport**................................Mike Francies
**DeSoto (†)** ...................Carl O. Sherman
City Mgr., Tarron Richardson
**Detroit**................... Kenneth Snodgrassr
**Devers**...........................Donna Traywick
**Devine**......................William L. Herring
City Admin., Gary Pelech
**Diboll (†)** ............................. John McClain
City Mgr., Dennis McDuffie
**Dickens**........................... David Warren
**Dickinson (†)**..........Julie Dues Masters
City Admin., Julie Robinson
**Dilley, City of**.............Mary Ann Obregon
City Admin., Noel Perez
**Dimmitt (†)**......................Roger Malone
City Mgr., B.J. Potts
**Dish**.................................William Sciscoe
**Dodd City**..........................Jackie Lackey
**Dodson** ................................Steve Kane
**Domino** ......................Alfred Campbell
**Donna (†)** ........................... Irene Munozs
City Mgr., Fernando Flores
**Dorchester**.........................David Smith
**Double Oak** ...................Mike Donnelly
**Douglassville** ...........Douglass B. Heath
**Dripping Springs** ............. Todd Purcell
City Admin., Michelle Fischer
**Driscoll** .......................... John A. Aguilar
**Dublin** ....................David Leatherwood
City Mgr., Nancy Wooldridge
**Dumas (†)** ............................Pat L. Sims
City Mgr., Vince DiPiazza
**Duncanville (†)** ....................David Green
City Mgr., Kevin Hugman

**— E —**

**Eagle Lake**................Mary Chaney Parr
City Mgr., Sylvia Rucka
**Eagle Pass (†)** .....Ramsey English Cantu
City Mgr., Gloria M. Barrientos
**Early**........................ Robert G. Mangrum
City Admin., Tony Aaron
**Earth** ..............................J. Allen Gover
**East Bernard** ................ Marvin R. Holub
**Eastland (†)** ........................Larry Vernon

City Mgr., Ron Duncan
**East Mountain** (103 Municipal Dr., Gilmer 75645) .............................. Neal Coulter
**Easton** ..............................Shannon Brown
**East Tawakoni**.............Johnnie LaPrade
**Ector** ........................... Brett J. Stone
**Edcouch** .............Robert T. Schmalzried
City Mgr., Noe Cavazos
**Eden** ..........................Eddy Markham
**Edgecliff Village**............. Tony Dauphinot
**Edgewood** ........................Charles Prater
**Edinburg (†)**..............Richard H. Garcia
City Mgr., Ramiro Garza Jr.
**Edmonson** ...................Sammy Shannon
**Edna (†)** ......................Joe D. Hermes
City Mgr., Don Doering
**Edom**...............................Barbara Crow
**El Campo (†)** .................Randy Collins
City Mgr., Mindi Snyder
**El Cenizo** ..........................Raul L. Reyes
**Eldorado** ..........................John Nikolauk
City Admin., Theogene Melancon
**Electra (†)** ............................ Pam Ward
Interim City Admin., Mike Price
**Elgin (†)** .................................Marc Holm
City Mgr., Kerry Lacy
**Elkhart** ..................................Erroll Tatum
**El Lago**...........................Robert K. White
**Elmendorf**.........................Evelyn Lykins
City Admin., Cody D. Dailey
**El Paso (†)** .........................Oscar Leeser
City Mgr., Tommy Gonzalez
**Elsa (†)**...............Alonzo R. (Al) Perez Jr.
City Mgr., Jose Cantu
**Emhouse** (3825 Joe Johnson Dr., Corsicana 75110)................Johnny Pattison
**Emory** ......................Carolyn Hill
City Admin., Michael Dunn
**Enchanted Oaks** (PO Box 5019, Gun Barrel City 75147) Donald G. Warner III
**Encinal**......................Sylvano Sanchez
City Mgr., Velma Davila
**Ennis (†)** ...................Russell R. Thomas
City Mgr., Charles Ewings
**Escobares** ........................Noel Escobar
**Estelline**................................Rick Manley
**Euless (†)**.......................Linda Martin
City Mgr., Loretta Getchell
**Eureka**...........(1305 FM 2859, Corsicana 75109) .............. R.B. (Barney) Thomas
**Eustace** ..........................Elicia Sanders
**Evant**..............................Sterling Manning
**Everman (†)**.......................Ray Richardson
City Mgr., Michael Box

**— F —**

**Fairchilds** (8713 Fairchilds Rd., Richmond 77469) .................... Bob Haenel
**Fairfield**.............................Roy W. Hill
City Admin., Jeff Looney
**Fair Oaks Ranch** ...........Cheryl Landman
City Admin., Marcus Jahns
**Fairview (†)**................ Darion Culbertson
Town Mgr., Julie Couch, Interim
**Falfurrias** ..............ALetty Garza, pro-tem
City Admin., Sammy Maldonado
**Falls City**.........................Brent Houdmann
**Farmers Branch (†)**............Bob Phelps
City Mgr., Gary D. Greer
**Farmersville** ........ Joseph E. Helmberger
City Mgr., Benjamin L. White
**Farwell** ..............................Joe Stanton
**Fate (†)**...........................Lorne Megyesi
**Fayetteville**...............Ronald Pflughaupt
City Mgr., Billy J. Wasut
**Ferris**........................ Micheal L. Driggars
City Mgr., R. Scott Dixon
**Flatonia**.............................. Bryan Milson
**Florence**.......................Mary Condon
**Floresville (†)** ...................Diana Garza
City Mgr., Henrietta Turner

**Flower Mound (†)**..... Thomas E. Hayden
Town Mgr., Jimmy Stathatos
**Floydada** ..................... Bobby Gilliland
City Mgr., Jeff Johnston
**Follett**......................................Kevin Wynn
City Mgr., Robert Williamson
**Forest Hill (†)**.................. Gerald Joubert
City Mgr., Sheyi I. Ipaye
**Forney (†)** ........................ Rick Wilson
City Mgr., Brian Brooks
**Forsan** .................................Steve Park
**Fort Stockton**................Chris Alexander
City Mgr., Raul Rodriguez
**Fort Worth (†)** .......................Betsy Price
City Mgr., Tom Higgins
**Franklin**...............................Molly Hedrick
**Frankston** ........................Johnny Wheeler
**Fredericksburg (†)** ..... Linda Langerhans
City Mgr., Kent Myers
**Freeport (†)**.........Norma Moreno Garcia
**Freer**...................... Andrea Bierstedt
**Friendswood (†)** ...........Kevin M. Holland
City Mgr., Roger Roecker
**Friona**.....................................Ricky White
City Mgr., Patricia Phipps
**Frisco (†)** ..........................Maher Maso
City Mgr., George Purefoy
**Fritch**........................W. Kelly Henderson
City Mgr., Steve McKay
**Frost**.............................Jimmy Alexander
**Fruitvale**............................Carl Waddell
**Fulshear**......... Thomas C. Kuykendall Jr.
City Admin., Christopher J. Snipes
**Fulton**.............................Jimmy Kendrick

**— G —**

**Gainesville (†)** .............Jim Goldsworthy
City Mgr., Barry L. Sullivan
**Galena Park (†)** ........... Esmeralda Moya
City Admin., Robert Pruett
**Gallatin** ..........................Juanita Cotton
**Galveston (†)**.......... James D. Yarbrough
City Mgr., Brian Maxwell
**Ganado** ......................Clinton W. Tegeler
**Garden Ridge** ................Nadine L. Knaus
City Admin., Nancy Cain
**Garland (†)**........................ Douglas Athas
City Mgr., Bryan Bradford
**Garrett**................................ Matt Newsom
**Garrison**................................Robert Cook
**Gary** ..................................Maxie Lake
**Gatesville (†)** ..............Gary M. Chumley
City Mgr., William H. Parry III
**Georgetown (†)** .......................Dale Ross
City Mgr., David Morgan
**George West (†)** ........Dickie Lee Person
City Mgr., (vacant)
**Gholson** (155 Wesley Chapel Rd., Waco 76705) ...................Larry Binnion
**Giddings (†)**...........................John Dowell
City Mgr., Ricky Jorgensen
**Gilmer (†)** ..........................Tim Marshall
City Mgr., Jeff Ellington
**Gladewater (†)**...............Harold R. Wells
City Mgr., (vacant)
**Glenn Heights (†)** ........Leon Payton Tate
City Mgr., Aretha Ferrell-Benavides
**Glen Rose**............Onda (Sam) Moody
City Admin., (vacant)
**Godley**.........................David J. Wallis
**Goldsmith**............................Todd Hiner
City Mgr., Bennie Coper
**Goldthwaite** ..................Mike McMahan
City Mgr., Rob Lindsey III
**Goliad** ...........................Anna Machacek
**Golinda**.........................Doyle W. Parks
**Gonzales (†)** .....Robert A. (Bobby) Logan
City Mgr., Allen Barnes
**Goodlow**...............Willie Washington Jr.
**Goodrich**...........................Jeremy Harper
**Gordon**.............................. Jack Coleman

**Goree** .............................. Glenna Decker
**Gorman (†)** ...........................Robert Ervin
**Graford** ...........................Carl J. Walston
**Graham (†)**.........................Jack Graham
City Mgr., Brandon Anderson
**Granbury (†)**.............................. Nin Hulett
City Mgr., Criss Coffman
**Grandfalls**.............................Jim Cahill
City Admin., Geraldine F. Bookmiller
**Grand Prairie (†)** .................Ron Jensen
City Mgr., Tom Hart
**Grand Saline** .................Don Yarbrough
City Admin., Rex White
**Grandview** ........................... Bart Clark
City Admin., Travis Buck
**Granger**.................................Jerry Lalla
City Admin., Sabra Davis
**Granite Shoals (†)**...........Carl J. Brugger
City Mgr., Ken Nickel
**Granjeno** (6603 S. FM 494, Mission 78572) ........................ Yvette Cabrera
**Grapeland**.................. George R. Pierson
**Grapevine (†)**...............William D. Tate
City Mgr., Bruno Rumbelow
**Grays Prairie** (Box 116, Scurry 75158)
....................................Lorenzo Garza Jr.
**Greenville (†)** .......................David Dreiling
City Mgr., Massoud Ebrahim
**Gregory**.........................Freddy R. Garcia
**Grey Forest** ........................ Ron Reinhard
**Groesbeck**.....................Ray O'Docharty
City Admin., Jim Cox
**Groom**.................................Joe L. Homer
**Groves (†)**.........................Brad P. Bailey
City Mgr., D.E. Sosa
**Groveton**........................Byron Richards
**Gruver**................................Steven Davis
City Mgr., (vacant)
**Gun Barrel City (†)** ................... (vacant)
City Mgr., Gerry Boren
**Gunter**................................. Tim Slattery
**Gustine** ............................... Ken Huey

**— H —**

**Hackberry** (119 Maxwell Rd., #B-7, Frisco 75034) ..........................Ronald Austin
City Admin., Brenda Lewallen
**Hale Center**......................Eugene Carter
**Hallettsville**.............Warren Grindeland
City Admin., Jason Cozza
**Hallsburg** .........................Mike Glockzin
**Hallsville** ..........................Steve Eitelman
**Haltom City (†)** ..................David Averitt
City Mgr., Tom Muir
**Hamilton** ......................Michael R. Collett
City Admin., Bill Funderburk
**Hamlin**..................................Tom Hartley
**Happy**.......................................Sara Tirey
**Hardin**............................Stephanie Blume
**Harker Heights (†)**........ Robert Robinson
City Mgr., David Mitchell
**Harlingen (†)** ..................... Chris Boswell
City Mgr., Carlos Yerena
**Hart** .............................. Eliazar Castillo
**Haskell** ...........................John Gannaway
City Admin., Edward Hansen
**Haslet**...................................Bob Golden
City Admin., Jim Quin
**Hawk Cove** ................ Anthony Cuciniello
**Hawkins** ..........................William Rogers
**Hawley** ..........................Billy Richardson
**Hays** ..................(Box 1285, Buda 78610)
.......................................Harvey Davis
**Hearne (†)** .......................Ruben Gomez
City Mgr., (vacant)
**Heath (†)**........................Lorne O. Liechty
City Mgr., Edward Thatcher
**Hebron** ... (Box 118916, Carrollton 75011)
.......................................Kelly Clem
**Hedley**...............................Leon Ward

**Hedwig Village** .............. Brian T. Muecke
**Helotes**................. Thomas A. Schoolcraft
City Admin., Rick Schroder
**Hemphill** ....................... Robert Hamilton
City Mgr., Donald P. Iles
**Hempstead** .................... Michael S. Wolfe Sr.
**Henderson (†)** .............. Patricia L. Brack
City Mgr., Tim Kelty
**Henrietta** ......................... Howard Raeke
City Admin., Kelley Bloodworth
**Hereford (†)** ........... Robert D. Josserand
City Mgr., Rick L. Hanna
**Hewitt (†)** .... Wilbert (Walky) Wachtendorf
City Mgr., Adam Miles
**Hickory Creek** ................. Lynn C. Clark
Town Admin., John M. Smith, Jr.
**Hico**.................................Michael Price
City Admin., Michael Leamons
**Hidalgo (†)** ........................ Martin Cepeda
City Mgr., Julian J. Gonzalez
**Hideaway** ................................Pat Bonds
**Higgins** ............................. Gary Duncan
City Mgr., Randy Immel
**Highland Haven**....................Olan Kelley
**Highland Park (†)** ....... Joel T. Williams III
Town Admin., Bill Lindley
**Highland Village (†)** .. Charlotte J. Wilcox
City Mgr., Michael Leavitt
**Hill Country Village**
..............................Gabriel Durand-Hollis
City Admin., Frank Morales, Jr.
**Hillcrest Village** (Box 1172, Alvin 77512)
..........................................Tom Wilson
**Hillsboro (†)**...........Edith Turner Omberg
City Mgr., Frank Johnson
**Hilshire Village** (8301 Westview Dr.,
Houston 77055).... Shannon S. Whiting
**Hitchcock (†)**...............Anthony Matranga
**Holiday Lakes** (RR 4, Box 747, Angleton
77515) ............... Norman C. Schroeder
**Holland** .............................. Mae Smith
**Holliday** ........................... Allen Moore
**Hollywood Park**..................... Chris Fails
**Hondo (†)** ............... James W. Danner Sr.
City Mgr., Kim Davis
**Honey Grove** ................... Claude Caffee
**Hooks** ......................... Michael W. Babb
**Horizon City (†)** ............ Walter Miller
**Horseshoe Bay** .......... Stephen T. Jordan
City Mgr., Stan R. Farmer
**Houston (†)**.................... Annise D. Parker
**Howardwick** ......................Mike Rowland
**Howe** ........................... Jeffrey Stanley
City Admin., Joe Shephard
**Hubbard**...............................Nancy Smith
City Mgr., Dorothy Jackson
**Hudson** ............................ Robert Smith
City Admin., James M. Freeman
**Hudson Oaks** ...................... Par Deen
City Admin., Patrick Lawler
**Hughes Springs**...............Reba Simpson
City Admin., George K. Fite
**Humble (†)** ........................Merle Aaron
City Mgr., Darrell Boeske
**Hunters Creek Village** (1 Hunters Creek
Pl., Houston 77024)... David A. Wegner
City Admin., Tom Fullen
**Huntington** ......................... Frank Harris
City Admin., Greg Lowe
**Huntsville (†)** ................. Mac Woodward
City Mgr., Matt Benoit
**Hurst (†)** ........................ Richard Ward
City Mgr., Allan Weegar
**Hutchins** ........................ Mario Vasquez
**Hutto**...........................Debbie Holland
City Mgr., Karen Daly
**Huxley** (11798 FM 2694, Shelbyville
75973) ............................Larry Vaughn

— I —

**Idalou**................................David W. Riley

City Admin., Suzette Williams
**Impact** .................................... Jack Sharp
**Indian Lake** (62 S. Aztec Cove Dr., Los
Fresnos 78566) ....... Barbara J. Collum
**Industry** ............................Mable Meyers
**Ingleside (†)**.......................Pete Perkins
City Mgr., Jim Gray
**Ingleside on the Bay** (PO Box 309, Ingle-
side 78362)............... Howard Gillespie
**Ingram** ............................... James Salter
City Admin., John Washbum
**Iola** ................................Christina Stover
**Iowa Colony** (12003 County Rd. 65, Ro-
sharon 77583) ............. Michael Holton
**Iowa Park (†)** .................. Ray Schultz
City Admin., Jerry Flemming
**Iraan**............................. Kevin Allen
**Iredell** ........................... Royce P. Heath
**Irving (†)** ...................... Beth Van Duyne
City Mgr., Chris Hillman
**Italy** ............................... Steven Farmer
**Itasca** ............................James Bouldin
City Admin., Mark Gropp
**Ivanhoe** (880 Charmaine Dr. E, Ste. A
Woodville 75979).......... Cathy Bennett
**Ivanhoe North** ....................Joe McIntyre

— J —

**Jacinto City (†)** ........................Ana Diaz
City Mgr., Lon D. Sqruyes
**Jacksboro**..................... Alton Morris, Jr.
City Admin., Shawna Dowell
**Jacksonville (†)**.....................Dick Stone
City Mgr., Mo Raissi
**Jamaica Beach** ...................Steve Spicer
City Admin., John Brick
**Jarrell**..............................Larry Bush
City Mgr., Mel Yantis
**Jasper (†)**.....................Randy Sayers
Interim City Mgr., Denise Kelley
**Jayton**.......................................Doyle Lee
**Jefferson** ....................Carey B. Heaster, Jr.
**Jersey Village (†)** ....................Justin Ray
City Mgr., Mike Castro
**Jewett** ................................John D. Sitton
City Admin., Virginia S. Sitton-Powell
**Joaquin**.......................................Bill Baker
**Johnson City**.....................Dawn Capra
**Jolly** .......... (194 Milton St., Wichita Falls
76310) ....................D. LeAnn Skinner
**Jones Creek** ................. Michael Hobbs
**Jonestown** ................ Deane Armstrong
City Admin., Ron Wilde
**Josephine**...........................Keith Koop
**Joshua (†)**......................Joe M. Hollarn
City Mgr., Joshua Jones
**Jourdanton**............... Susan B. Netardus
City Mgr., Daniel G. Nick
**Junction**...................Russell Hammonds
**Justin** .....................................Greg Scott
City Admin., Ashley Stathatos

— K —

**Karnes City**......................Leroy J. Skloss
City Mgr., Don Tymrak
**Katy (†)** ........................ Fabol R. Hughes
City Admin., Byron J. Hebert
**Kaufman (†)**...................... Jeff Jordan
City Mgr., Michael T. Slye
**Keene (†)** ...................... James Chapline
City Admin., William Guinn
**Keller (†)** ..........................Mark Mathews
City Mgr., Mark Hafner
**Kemah**............ Robert M (Bob) Cummins
City Admin., (vacant)
**Kemp**.......................Laura Hanna Peace
City Admin., Regina Kiser
**Kempner**..........................Carolyn Crane
**Kendleton** .......... Darryl K. Humphrey Sr.
**Kenedy** ........................Randy Garza
City Mgr., Ford Patton

**Kenefick** (3564 FM 1008, Dayton 77535)
..............................Martin Wells
**Kennard** ........................Jesse Stephens
City Admin., Mike Deckard
**Kennedale (†)**.................. Brian Johnson
City Mgr., Bob Hart
**Kerens**.......................Jeffrey Saunders
City Admin., Cindy Scott
**Kermit (†)**......................Jerry L. Phillips
City Mgr., Gloria Saenz
**Kerrville (†)**.............................Jack Pratt
City Mgr., Todd Parton
**Kilgore (†)** .................Ronnie Spradlin
City Mgr., Joshua Selleck
**Killeen (†)** ...................... Scott Cosper
City Mgr., Glenn Morrison
**Kingsville (†)** ................... Sam R. Fugate
City Mgr., Courtney Alvarez
**Kirby (†)** .......................Timothy Wilson
City Mgr., Monique L. Vernon
**Kirbyville** ........................ Frank George
**Kirvin** ............................ J. W. Walthall
**Knollwood** (100 Collins Dr., Sherman
75090) .................... Richard R. Roelke
**Knox City**............................. (vacant)
City Admin., Sam Watson
**Kosse**.............................Jarrod Eno
**Kountze** .........................Fred E. Williams
City Mgr., Roderick Hutto
**Kress**.........................Jeromy Bechtold
**Krugerville**...............................Dave Hill
City Admin., Sheila J. Martin
**Krum** .......................Ronald G. Harris, Jr.
**Kurten** ....................... Ronnie Vitulli
**Kyle (†)**.............................Todd Webster
City Mgr., Scott Sellers

— L —

**La Coste** ................................Andy Keller
City Admin., George Salzman
**Lacy-Lakeview (†)**...........Calvin Hodde
City Mgr., Keith Bond
**Ladonia** .......................... Chris Burch
**La Feria (†)** ............. Victor Gonzalez, Jr.
City Mgr., Sunny K. Philip
**Lago Vista (†)** ................... Randy Kruger
City Mgr., Melissa Byrne Vossmer
**La Grange (†)** .................... Janet Moerbe
City Mgr., Shawn Raborn
**La Grulla**..........................Pedro Flores
**Laguna Vista** ..........................Stan Hulse
City Mgr., Iris Hill
**La Joya**.................Jose A. (Fito) Salinas
City Admin., Mike Alaniz
**Lake Bridgeport** ............... Maude Smith
**Lake City** ................... A.G. (Jake) Hoskins
**Lake Dallas (†)** ........................ (vacant)
City Mgr., Nick Ristagno
**Lake Jackson (†)**.................Joe Rinehart
City Mgr., William P. Yenne
**Lakeport** (207 Milam Rd., Longview
75603) ................. Johnny Sammons
**Lakeside** (San Patricio Co.; Box 787,
Mathis 78368)...................Scott Knight
**Lakeside** (Tarrant Co.) .......Patrick Jacob
Town Admin., Norman Craven
**Lakeside City** (Box 4287, Wichita Falls
76308) .................. James M. Henson
City Admin., Sam Bownds
**Lake Tanglewood** (100 N. Shore Dr.,
Amarillo 79118) .........Ruben McGilvary
**Lakeview**.................................Kelly Clark
**Lakeway (†)**.....................David DeOme
City Mgr., Steve Jones
**Lakewood Village** ..........Mark E. Vargus
City Mgr., Linda Asbell
**Lake Worth (†)**............. Walter Bowen
City Mgr., Brett McGuire
**La Marque (†)**.................Bobby Hocking
City Mgr., Carol Jo Buttler
**Lamesa (†)**..............................Dave Nix

City Mgr., Shawna D. Burkhart
**Lampasas (†)**................. Christian Toups
    City Mgr., Finley deGraffenried
**Lancaster (†)** ...............Marcus E. Knight
    City Mgr., Opal Mauldin Robertson
**La Porte (†)**.......................Louis R. Rigby
    City Mgr., Corby D. Alexander
**Laredo (†)** ...........................Pete Saenz
    City Mgr., Jesus Olivaresa
**Latexo** ........................Robert Hernandez
**La Vernia**....................... Robert Gregory
**La Villa** ...........................Hector Elizondo
**Lavon** ................................Chuck Teske
**La Ward** ...........................Richard Koch
**Lawn** ........................ Veronica Burleson
**League City (†)**................Tim Paulissen
    City Admin., R. Mark Rohr
**Leakey** ..................... Harry Schneemann
**Leander (†)** ...............Christopher Fielder
    City Mgr., Kent Cagle
**Leary** ........ (PO Box 1799, Hooks 75561)
...............................................Keith Storey
    City Admin., Randy Mansfield
**Lefors**................................Jeanne Swires
**Leona** ............... Ernest (Bubba) Oden
**Leonard** ....................... Willie F. Johnson
**Leon Valley**..........................Chris Riley
    City Mgr., Manuel Longoria Jr.
**Leroy**................................David Williams
**Levelland (†)**......................Barbra Pinner
    City Mgr., Richard A. Osburn
**Lewisville (†)** .................... Rudy Durham
    City Mgr., Donna Barron
**Lexington** ...................Charlotte Hooper
**Liberty (†)** ...........................Carl Pickett
    City Mgr., Gary Broz
**Liberty Hill**........................Connie Fuller
    City Mgr., Greg Boatright
**Lincoln Park** (110 Parker Pkwy., Aubrey
76227) .................................Loretta Ray
    City Mgr., Nat Parker III
**Lindale (†)** ...............Robert L. Nelson Sr.
    City Mgr., Craig Lindholm
**Linden**............................ Clarence Burns
    City Admin., (vacant)
**Lindsay** ....................Donald L. Metzler
**Lipan** ................................Mike Stowe
**Little Elm (†)** ................ David Hillock
    City Mgr., Matt Mueller
**Littlefield (†)** .........................Eric Turpen
    City Mgr., (vacant)
**Little River-Academy**... Ronnie W. White
**Live Oak (†)** ................... Mary M. Dennis
    City Mgr., Scott Wayman
**Liverpool** ..............W.A. (Bill) Strickland
**Livingston** ..........................Clarke Evans
    City Mgr., Marilyn Sutton
**Llano**...................................Mike Reagor
    City Mgr., Brenton Lewis
**Lockhart (†)**...................... Lew White
    City Mgr., Vance Rodgers
**Lockney** ...............................Tina Graves
    City Admin., Shad Schlueter
**Log Cabin** ..........................Judy Bearden
**Lometa**..............................Cynthia Kirby
**Lone Oak** ......................... Doug Williams
**Lone Star** ....................Karl W. Stoermer
**Longview (†)**......................... Andy Mack
    City Mgr., David Willard
**Loraine**...........................Richard Alvarez
**Lorena**................................. Chuck Roper
    City Mgr., Billy Clemons
**Lorenzo**.......................Lester C. Bownds
    City Admin., Rusty Forbes
**Los Fresnos (†)**..................Polo Narvaez
    City Mgr., Mark W. Milum
**Los Indios**......................... Rick Cavazos
    City Admin., Jared Hockema
**Los Ybañez**....................Mary A. Ybañez
    City Mgr., John Henry Castillo
**Lott** .................................... Annita Tindle
**Lovelady** .....................Byron Shoemaker

**Lowry Crossing** (1405 S. Bridgefarmer
Rd., McKinney 75069) Derek Stephens
**Lubbock (†)** ...............Glen C. Robertson
    City Mgr., James W. Loomis
**Lucas (†)** ........................Rebecca Mark
    City Mgr., Joni Clarke
**Lueders**.......................Danny J. Dillard
**Lufkin (†)** ..............................Bob Brown
    City Mgr., Keith N. Wright
**Luling (†)** ........................Mike Hendricks
    City Mgr., Mark Mayo
**Lumberton (†)** ....................Don Surratt
    City Mgr., Steve Clark
**Lyford** ...........................Henry de la Paz
**Lytle** ........................... Mark L. Bowen

### — M —

**Mabank** ................................Jeff Norman
**Madisonville**............William (Bill) Parten
    City Mgr., Danny Singletary
**Magnolia**............................... Todd Kana
    City Mgr., Paul Mendes
**Malakoff**............................Delois Pagitt
    City Admin., Ann Baker
**Malone**.......................James A. Lucko
**Manor (†)** ........................ Rita G. Jonse
    City Mgr., Tom Bolt
**Mansfield (†)**....................David L. Cook
    City Mgr., Clayton W. Chandler
**Manvel (†)** ...................Delores M. Martin
    City Mgr., Kyle Jung
**Marble Falls (†)** ................... John Packer
    City Mgr., Mike Hodge
**Marfa**..........................Daniel P. Dunlap
    City Admin., James R. Mustard Jr.
**Marietta**............................. Frances Elliott
**Marion** ...........................Glenn A. Hild
**Marlin (†)**................... Elizabeth J. Nelson
    City Mgr., Deck Shaver Jr.
**Marquez**............................Stynette Clary
    City Mgr., Lauren Powers
**Marshall (†)**..............................Eric Neal
    City Mgr., Lisa Agnor
**Mart** ....................................Len Williams
**Martindale**..........................Doyle Mosier
**Mason** ..........................Brent Hinckley
    City Admin., John Palacio
**Matador** ......................... Alvin Alexander
**Mathis (†)**............ Ciriaco (Ciri) Villarreal
    City Admin., Michael Barrera
**Maud** ....................................Robert Wells
**Maypearl** ......................... Adele Mooney
**McAllen (†)** ........................... Jim Darling
    City Mgr., Roel (Roy) Rodriguez
**McCamey** ......................... Sherry Phillips
**McGregor (†)** ................James S. Hering
    City Mgr., Kevin P. Evans
**McKinney (†)** ...........Brian S. Loughmiller
    City Mgr., Tom Muehlenbeck
**McLean** ................................Tanner Hess
**McLendon-Chisholm** ......Gary L. Moody
    City Admin., David O. Butler
**Meadow**...........................Natalie Howard
    City Admin., Terri McClanahan
**Meadowlakes** .......... Mary Ann Raesener
    City Mgr., Johnnie Thompson
**Meadows Place** ..... Charles D. Jessup IV
**Megargel**..........................Chris Bearmon
**Melissa**............................... Reed Greer
    City Admin., Jason Little
**Melvin** ............................ Chad Holubec
**Memphis**....................Robert C. Maddox
    City Admin., Nelwyn Ward
**Menard**............................Barbara Hooten
    City Admin., Don Kerns
**Mercedes (†)** ...............Henry Hinojosa
    City Mgr., Ricardo Garcia
**Meridian**...................Johnnie Hauerland
    City Admin., Marie Garland
**Merkel** ..........................Marie Schrampfer

City Mgr., Steve Campbell
**Mertens**............................ Travis Kaddatz
**Mertzon**...............................Carol Shaw
**Mesquite (†)**.........................Stan Pickett
    City Mgr., Ted Barron
**Mexia (†)** .........................Troy A. Miller
    City Mgr., Larry Brown
**Miami** ............................ Chad Breeding
**Midland (†)**........................ Jerry Morales
    City Mgr., Courtney B. Sharp
**Midlothian (†)** .....................Bill Houston
    City Mgr., Chris Dick
**Midway** ...............................Tony Leago
**Milano** ..............................Billy Barnett
**Mildred**............(5417 FM 637, Corsicana
75109) ..............................Kyle Carrigan
**Miles**...................... Sylvester Schwertner
**Milford** ......................... Bruce Perryman
**Miller's Cove** (PO Box 300 Winfield
75493) .........................Willie B. Garrett
**Millsap** ............................. Jamie French
    City Mgr., Mark Barnes
**Mineola** ...........................Rodney Watkins
    City Admin., David Stevenson
**Mineral Wells (†)** ...................Mike Allen
    City Mgr., Lance Howerton
**Mingus**...................................Milo Moffit
**Mission (†)**.................... Norberto Salinas
    City Mgr., Martin Garza
**Missouri City (†)**...................Allen Owen
    City Mgr., Bill Atkinson
**Mobeetie**............................. Gordon Estes
**Mobile City** ..(824 Lilac, Rockwall 75087)
.............................................. Dana Lawson
**Monahans (†)** ...............David B. Cutbirth
    City Mgr., David Mills
**Mont Belvieu** ......................... Nick Dixon
    City Admin., Bryan Easum
**Montgomery** ........................ Kirk Jones
    City Admin., Jack Yates
**Moody**...................................Ken Brown
    City Admin., William Sterling
**Moore Station** (4720 County Rd. 4319,
LaRue 75770)......Charles R. Anderson
**Moran** ............................ Mike Whitt
**Morgan**.................. Jonathan W. Croom II
**Morgan's Point** ...............Michel Bechtel
    City Admin., Brian Schneider
**Morgan's Point Resort** ........ Ken Steger
    City Mgr., David Huseman
**Morton** ........................Eric Charles Silhan
    City Mgr., Brenda Shaw
**Moulton**.................................Ervin Patek
**Mountain City** .............. (Box 1494, Buda
78610) ............................Tiffany Curnutt
    City Mgr., Thomas Brown
**Mount Calm** ......................Jimmy Tucker
**Mount Enterprise**........ Harvey L. Graves
    City Admin., Rosena J. Becker-Ross
**Mount Pleasant (†)**... Paul O. Meriwether
    City Mgr., Michael K. Ahrens
**Mount Vernon** .............. Margaret Sears
    City Admin., Darrek Ferrell
**Muenster**..........................Tim Felderhoff
    City Admin., Stan Endres
**Muleshoe (†)**......................... Cliff Black
    City Mgr., David Brunson
**Mullin** ...................................Jean Smith
**Munday** ...........................Robert Bowen
    City Admin., (vacant)
**Murchison** ....................Deanna Benson
**Murphy (†)** ........................... Eric Barna
    City Mgr., James Fisher
**Mustang**...................(Box 325, Corsicana
75151).............................Jackie Bounds
**Mustang Ridge** .............. Alfred Vallejo II

### — N —

**Nacogdoches (†)**.......... Roger Van Horn
    City Mgr., Jim Jeffers
**Naples**.............................Dennis Chastier

The Camp Tonkawa Springs, northeast of Nacogdoches, is a clear, spring-fed swimming hole that stays a cool 65 degrees year round. Photo by Shannon Pate.

**Nash**..............................Robert H. Bunch
  City Admin., Doug Bowers
**Nassau Bay (†)** ............ Mark A. Denman
  City Mgr., Chris Reed
**Natalia (†)** ..................... Ruberta C. Vera
  City Mgr., Lisa Hernandez
**Navarro** (222 S. Harvard Ave., Corsicana
  75109) ................... Vickie Lynn Farmer
**Navasota (†)** ...........................Bert Miller
  City Mgr., Brad Stafford
**Nazareth** .............................Marlin Dubin
**Nederland (†)**............. R.A. (Dick) Nugent
  City Mgr., Christopher Duque
**Needville**...........................Delbert Wendt
**Nevada**................................Joe Poovey
**Newark**...........................Gary L. Wagner
  City Admin., Diane Rasor
**New Berlin**.............(275 FM 2538 Seguin
  78155) ...................... Gilbert R. Merkle
**New Boston** ................Johnny L. Branson
**New Braunfels (†)** ....... Barron Casteel
  City Mgr., Robert Camareno
**Newcastle**...........................Gina Maxwell
**New Chapel Hill** (PO Box 132717, Tyler
  75713) ...........................Riley Harris
**New Deal**.............. Leta Owens-Maxfield
**New Fairview** .................Joe Max Wilson
**New Home** .........................David Gandy
**New Hope** (Box 562, McKinney 75070)
  ...................................Johnny Hamm
**New London** ......................Dale McNeel
**New Summerfield** ..............Jane Barrow
**Newton**.................................Mark Bean
  City Admin., Donald H. Meek
**New Waverly** ................Dan Underwood
**Neylandville** (2469 County Rd. 4311,
  Greenville 75401)...........Kathy Wilson
**Niederwald** .......................Reynell Smith
**Nixon** ..........................Hector Dominguez
**Nocona** .....................Robert H. Fenoglio
  City Mgr., Lynn Henley
**Nolanville**..........................Dennis Biggs
  City Mgr., Kara Escajeda
**Nome**..................................Kerry Abney
**Noonday** ..........(Box 6425, Tyler 75711)
  ...................................J. Mike Turman

**Nordheim**......................Katherine Payne
**Normangee**...................Ronnie Meadors
**North Cleveland** (Box 1266, Cleveland
  77327) .........................Robert Bartlett
**Northlake** ........................Peter Dewing
  Town Admin., Drew Corn
**North Richland Hills (†)**....Oscar Treviño
  City Mgr., Mark Hindman
**Novice**................................ Wanda Motley

— O —

**Oak Grove** ... (Box 309, Kaufman 75142)
  ...............................David P. Dunlap
**Oak Leaf** ...........................Craig Wilson
**Oak Point**...........................Duane Olson
  City Mgr., Luke Olson
**Oak Ridge** (Cooke Co.; 129 Oak Ridge
  Dr., Gainesville 76240).. Chad Ramsey
**Oak Ridge** (Kaufman Co.; Box 458,
  Kaufman 75142)....................Al Rudin
**Oak Ridge North** .......James Kuykendall
  City Mgr., Vicky Rudy
**Oak Valley** (2211 Oak Valley, Corsicana
  75110) ...........................Linda Bennett
**Oakwood** ..........................Vicki Stroud
**O'Brien**............................ Richard Garcia
**Odem** .....................................Billy Huerta
**Odessa (†)** .....................David R. Turner
  City Mgr., Richard N. Morton
**O'Donnell**.........................Scott Martinez
**Oglesby** ...................................(vacant)
**Old River-Winfree** (PO Box 1169, Mont
  Belvieu 77580) ...................Joe Landry
**Olmos Park** ............. Kenneth Farrimond
  City Mgr., Celia M. Deleon
**Olney (†)** ........................ Phil B. Jeske IIt
  City Admin., Danny C. Parker
**Olton** ............................ Mark McFadden
  City Mgr., Marvin Tillman
**Omaha** .............................Ernest Pewitt
**Onalaska**............................ Roy Newport
**Opdyke West** (Box 1527, Levelland
  79336) ......................... Wayne Riggins
**Orange (†)**...........................Jimmy Sims
  City Mgr., Shawn Oubre
**Orange Grove**............................Carl Srp

  City Admin., Rick Lopez
**Orchard**..............................Rod Pavlock
**Ore City** .......................Glenn Breazeale
**Overton**...........................C.R. Evans Jr.
  City Mgr., Charles L. Cunningham
**Ovilla**.........................Richard A. Dormier
  City Admin., Dennis Burn
**Oyster Creek** ..........Clifford Louis Guidry

— P —

**Paducah**......................Gordon B. Melton
**Paint Rock** ...................Debrorah Brown
**Palacios (†)**..................John C. Sardelich
  City Mgr., David Korvrek
**Palestine (†)** ...................Bob Herrington
  City Mgr., Wendy Ellis
**Palisades** (115 Brentwood Rd., Amarillo
  79118) .............................Dale Conner
**Palmer**....................... Kenneth Bateman
  City Admin., Doug Young
**Palmhurst**.......Ramiro J. Rodriguez Jr.
  City Mgr., Lori A. Lopez
**Palm Valley** (1313 Stuart Place Rd., Har-
  lingen 78552).................George Rivera
**Palmview** ...........................Jerry Perez
  City Mgr., Ramon Segovia
**Pampa (†)** .............................Brad Pingel
  City Mgr., Shane Stokes
**Panhandle** .....................Doyle Robinson
  City Mgr., Terry Coffee
**Panorama Village** ......Howard L. Kravetz
**Pantego** ................... Melody L. Paradise
  City Mgr., Matthew Fielder
**Paradise**............................Sam E. Starr
**Paris (†)** ............ Arjumand (A.J.) Hashmi
  City Mgr., John Godwin
**Parker** ................................. Z Marshall
  City Admin., Jeff Flanigan
**Pasadena (†)** ..................Johnny Isbell
**Pattison** ............................Bill Matthews
**Patton Village** ....................Leah Tarrant
**Payne Springs** ............Rodney Renberg
**Pearland (†)**...............................Tom Reid
  City Mgr., Clay Pearson
**Pearsall (†)** ........................Mary Moore
  City Mgr., José G. Treviño

**Pecan Gap** ..................... Warner Cheney
**Pecan Hill** .................. Stephanie Starrett
**Pecos (†)** .......................... Venetta Seals
City Mgr., Eric Honeyfield
**Pelican Bay** ........................... Bill Morley
**Penelope** ................................. Ben Neal
**Peñitas** ............................... Rigo Lopez
City Mgr., Oscar Cuellar Jr.
**Perryton** ........................... Charles Kelly
City Mgr., David Landis
**Petersburg** ......................... Darin Greene
City Mgr., Ronald Heggemeier
**Petrolia** ............... William (Bill) Holmberg
**Petronila** (2475 County Rd. 69, Robstown
78380) ...................... Kartina Burkhart
**Pflugerville (†)** ................... Jeff Coleman
City Mgr., Brandon Wade
**Pharr (†)** ................. Ambrosio Hernandez
City Mgr., Juan G. Guerra
**Pilot Point (†)** ........Shea Dane-Patterson
City Mgr., John R. Dean Jr.
**Pine Forest** ............(305 Nagel Dr., Vidor
77662) ............................... Joey Peno
**Pinehurst** (2497 Martin Luther King Jr.
Dr., Orange 77630)
................Joseph L. (Pete) Runnels
City Admin., Robbie L. Hood
**Pine Island** (36722 Brumlow Rd., Hemp-
stead 77445) ................... Debra Ferris
**Pineland**............................. Randy Burch
City Admin., Chuck Corley
**Piney Point Village** (7676 Woodway Dr.,
#300, Houston 77063)..........Lee Butler
City Admin., Ben Griffin
**Pittsburg (†)** ............. Shawn Kennington
City Mgr., Clint Hardeman
**Plains**......................... Pamela K. Redman
City Admin., Terry B. Howard
**Plainview (†)**.................. Wendell Dunlap
City Mgr., Jeffrey Snyder
**Plano (†)** ..................... Harry LaRosiliere
City Mgr., Bruce D. Glasscock
**Pleak Village** (6621 FM 2218 S., Rich-
mond 77469) ...............Larry J. Bittner
**Pleasanton (†)**............Clinton J. Powell
City Mgr., Bruce Pearson
**Pleasant Valley** (4006 U.S. 287 E, Iowa
Park 76367)...........Raymond Haynes
City Mgr., Norm Hodges
**Plum Grove** (Box 1358, Splendora
77372) ............................... T.W. Garrett
**Point**.................................John Ellsworth
**Point Blank**............... Clyde L. Chandler
**Point Comfort**.................. Pam Lambden
**Point Venture** .................Cristin Cecala
**Ponder** ............................. John Bassler
**Port Aransas (†)**............Keith McMullen
City Mgr., David Parsons
**Port Arthur (†)** .... Deloris (Bobbie) Prince
City Mgr., Brian McDougal
**Port Isabel (†)**.....................Joe E. Vega
City Mgr., Edward Meza
**Portland (†)**..................David R. Krebs
City Mgr., Randy L. Wright
**Port Lavaca (†)**.................. Jack Whitlow
City Mgr., Bob Turner
**Port Neches (†)** ......... R. Glenn Johnson
City Mgr., André Wimer
**Post**....................................Archie Gill
City Mgr., Deana Watson
**Post Oak Bend** (1175 County Rd. 278,
Kaufman 75142).......Raymond Bedrick
**Poteet**...................... Richard E. Tuttle Sr.
City Admin., Scott Moore
**Poth**.............................. Anthony Smolka
**Pottsboro**......................... Frank Budra
City Mgr., Kevin M. Farley
**Powell** ....................... Dennis Bancroft
**Poynor**...........................Dannie Smith
**Prairie View** ................ Frank D. Jackson
**Premont**........................... Norma Tallos
**Presidio** ......................... John Ferguson

City Admin., Marco Baeza
**Primera** ........................... Pat Patterson
City Admin., Javier Mendez
**Princeton** ........................Ken Bowers
City Mgr., Derek Borg
**Progreso** .......................... Arturo Aleman
City Admin., Alfredo (Fred) Espinosa
**Progreso Lakes**........O.D. (Butch) Emery
**Prosper (†)** ..........................Ray Smith
Town Mgr., Harlan Jefferson
**Providence Village**...............Dave Shuck
Town Mgr., Brian Robertson
**Putnam** ........................ Hubert Donaway
**Pyote**...................................... Glen West

## — Q —

**Quanah (†)**..................... Dale Eaton
City Admin., Paula Wilson
**Queen City**.....................Harold Martin
**Quinlan** ......................... Jacky Goleman
City Admin., John Adel
**Quintana** ......................... Harold Doty
**Quitaque** ..................... Janice Henson
City Mgr., Maria Cruz Merrell
**Quitman** ...............................J.R. Evans

## — R —

**Ralls**................................ Heath Verett
City Admin., Gloria Velasquez
**Rancho Viejo** .............. Cyndie Rathbun
Town Admin.,  Fred Blanco
**Ranger (†)** ........................ Joe Pilgrim
City Admin., Penny Cate
**Rangerville** (31850 Rangerville Rd., San
Benito 78586) .............. Wayne Halbert
**Rankin**...................... Timothy J. Potter
**Ransom Canyon** ....... Robert G. Englund
City Admin., Elena Quintanilla
**Ravenna**.....................Claude L. Lewis
**Raymondville (†)** ......... Gilbert Gonzales
**Red Lick** ........(3193 Old Redlick Rd.,
Texarkana 75503).......Sheila K. Kegley
**Red Oak (†)**.......................Alan Hugley
City Mgr., Todd Fuller
**Redwater** ................... Robert Lorance
**Refugio** ............................Joey Heard
**Reklaw** ..................... Harlan Crawford
**Reno** (Lamar Co.) ...................Bart Jetton
**Reno** (Parker Co.; 195 W. Reno Rd., Azle
76020) .................... Lynda Stokes
City Admin., Joseph Polino
**Retreat** (621 N. Spikes Rd., Corsicana
75110) ....................Janice Barfknecht
**Rhome** ........................Michelle Pitman
**Rice** ................................ Jim Fortson
City Admin., Tonya Roberts
**Richardson (†)** ....................Paul Voelker
City Mgr., Daniel Johnson
**Richland** ...................... Dolores Baldwin
**Richland Hills (†)** ...................... Bill Agan
City Mgr., Eric Strong
**Richland Springs**..........Douglas Gibson
**Richmond (†)** .................... Evalyn Moore
City Mgr., Terri Vela
**Richwood** ......................Clint Kocurek
City Mgr., Glenn Patton
**Riesel** ...........................Roger Fitzpatrick
**Rio Bravo** ..................... Manuel Vela
**Rio Grande City (†)**...........Joel Villarreal
City Mgr., (vacant)
**Rio Hondo** .........Gustavo (Gus) Olivares
City Admin., Ben Medina
**Rio Vista** ................................. (vacant)
**Rising Star**.....................Debbie Winfrey
City Admin., Darwin Archer
**River Oaks (†)** ........Herman D. Earwood
City Admin., Marvin Gregory
**Riverside** .............................Frank Rich
City Mgr., Joan C. Harvey
**Roanoke** .... Carl E. (Scooter) Gierisch Jr.
City Mgr., H. Scott Campbell

**Roaring Springs**............. Corky Marshall
City Mgr., Robert Osborn
**Robert Lee**..........................Leroy Casey
**Robinson (†)**.................Bryan Ferguson
City Mgr., Robert E. Cervenka
**Robstown (†)** ................. Mandy Barrera
**Roby** ................................Eli Sepeda
City Mgr., Jack W. Brown
**Rochester** ............... Marvin Stegemoeller
City Mgr., Gail Nunn
**Rockdale (†)** ......................... John King
City Mgr., Chris Whittaker
**Rockport (†)** ..........Charles J. (CJ) Wax
City Mgr., Kevin Carruth
**Rocksprings**.................. Pauline Gonzales
City Admin., Romana Bienek
**Rockwall (†)**........................... Jim Pruitt
City Mgr., Richard R. Crowley
**Rocky Mound**..........(Box 795, Pittsburg
75686)..........................Noble T. Smith
**Rogers** ....................... Tammy Cockrum
**Rollingwood** ..................... Thom Farrell
City Admin., Charles R. Winfield
**Roma (†)** ...........Jose Alfredo Guerra, Jr.
City Mgr., Crisanto Salinas
**Roman Forest** .................. Ray Ricks Jr.
City Admin., Liz Mullane
**Ropesville**..................... Kenny Greenlee
**Roscoe**................. Frank S. (Pete) Porter
City Mgr., Cody Thompson
**Rosebud**.........................Larry G. Boone
City Admin., Keith Whitfield
**Rose City** ....................Bonnie Stephenson
**Rose Hill Acres** (100 Jordan Rd., Lum-
berton 77657) ........... Rick L. Thomisee
**Rosenberg (†)** .........Cynthia A. McConathy
City Mgr., Robert Gracia
**Ross**............................James L. Jaska Sr.
**Rosser** ................... Shannon Rex Corder
**Rotan** ..........................Marissa Nowlin
City Admin., Carla Thornton
**Round Mountain** .............Alvin Gutierrez
**Round Rock (†)**.................Alan McGraw
City Mgr., Laurie Hadley
**Round Top**................... Barnell Albers
City Admin., Dwight M. Nittsche
**Rowlett (†)** ......................Todd W. Gottel
City Mgr., Brian Funderburk
**Roxton** .........................Phillip Rutherford
**Royse City (†)**..................... Janet Nichol
City Mgr., Carl Alsabrook
**Rule**...............................Jerry Cannon
**Runaway Bay** ....................... Robert Ryan
City Admin., Oneta Berghoefer
**Runge** ...........................Homer Lott Jr.
**Rusk (†)** .......................... Angela Raiborn
City Mgr., Mike Murray

## — S —

**Sabinal**.................... Louis A. Landeros Jr.
**Sachse (†)** ...................... Mike J. Felix
City Mgr., Gina Nash
**Sadler**...............................Jaime Vannoy
**Saginaw (†)**...................Gary Brinkley
City Mgr., Nan Stanford
**Saint Hedwig** ..................... Dee Grimm
**Saint Jo** ............................. Brad Bugg
**Saint Paul** .......................... Opie Walter
**Salado** ......................... Skip Blancett
City Admin., Kim Foutz
**San Angelo (†)** ............. Dwain Morrison
City Mgr., Daniel Valenzuela
**San Antonio (†)** ...................... Ivy Taylor
City Mgr., Sheryl L. Sculley
**San Augustine** .................. Leroy Hughes
City Mgr., (vacant)
**San Benito (†)** .............Celeste Sanchez
City Mgr., Arturo Rodriguez
**Sanctuary** ..........(Box 125, Azle 76098)
........................................... Cliff Scallan
**San Diego**................. Rupert Canales, III

City Mgr., Rupert Canales, III
**Sandy Point**........................Curt Mowery
**San Elizario**.....................Maya Sanchez
**San Felipe**............................Bobby Byars
**Sanford**...................Bernard V. Pacheco
**Sanger (†)**............................Thomas Muir
City Mgr., Michael Brice
**San Juan (†)**..........San Juanita Sanchez
City Mgr., Juan Gonzalez
**San Leanna** (Box 1107, Manchaca 78652).....................Elizabeth A. Korts
City Admin., Kathleen Lessing
**San Marcos (†)**..............Daniel Guerrero
City Mgr., Jared Miller
**San Patricio**.........(4615 Main St., Mathis 78368)....................Lonnie Glasscock III
**San Perlita**.......................Oscar de Luna
**San Saba**.............Kenneth G. Jordan
City Mgr., Stan Weik
**Sansom Park** (5500 Buchanan St., Fort Worth 76114).................Jim Barnett Jr.
City Admin., Karen Bolyard
**Santa Anna**.................Harold Fahrlender
**Santa Clara** ......(Box 429, Marion 78124)
..........................................Jeff Hunt
**Santa Fe (†)**.......................Jeff Tambrella
City Mgr., Joe Dickson
**Santa Rosa**...................Ruben Ochoa Jr.
City Mgr., Chris Lopez
**Savoy**...................................Denise Pugh
**Schertz (†)**.............Michael R. Carpenter
City Mgr., John C. Kessel
**Schulenburg**..........Roger Moellenberndt
City Admin., Tami Blaschke-Walker
**Scotland** ...............................Brian Vieth
**Scottsville**.........................Kerry L. Cade
**Scurry**................................Johnny Blazek
**Seabrook (†)**....................Glenn R. Royal
City Mgr., Gayle Cook
**Seadrift** ........................Elmer DeForest
**Seagoville (†)**..........Dennis K. Childress
City Mgr., Pat Stallings
**Seagraves**............................Brace Huse
**Sealy (†)**........................Mark A. Stolarski
City Mgr., Larry Kuciemba
**Seguin (†)**................................Don Keil
City Mgr., Douglas G. Faseler
**Selma** ............................ Tom Daly
City Admin., Ken Roberts
**Seminole (†)**......................Wayne Mixon
City Admin., Tommy Phillips
**Seven Oaks** ....(Box 334, Leggett 77350)
.....................................Anna Wallace
**Seven Points**............................Bill Hash
**Seymour** ....................Nan Gilbert-Mathis
City Admin., Steve Bieclermann
**Shady Shores** (Box 362, Lake Dallas 75065).............................Cindy Spencer
**Shallowater** ..........Robert W. Olmsted Jr.
City Admin., Michael Neighbors
**Shamrock** ....Howard F. (Buc) Weatherby
City Mgr., David Rushing
**Shavano Park** ......................Bob Werner
City Mgr., Bill Hill
**Shenandoah** ......................Garry Watts
City Admin., Greg Smith
**Shepherd**.............................Glenn Dillon
**Sherman (†)**..............Carolyn S. Wacker
**Shiner** .....................Fred Henry Hilscher
**Shoreacres**...........................Rick Moses
City Admin., David K. Stall
**Silsbee (†)**.............Herbert C. Muckleroy
City Mgr., Charles T. (Tommy) Bartosh
**Silverton** ........................Lane B. Garvin
City Admin., Wade Willson
**Simonton**....................Daniel McJunkin
**Sinton (†)**........................Edward Adams
City Mgr., John Hobson.
**Skellytown**.............................Ralph Tice
**Slaton (†)**............................D.W. Englund
City Admin., Mike Lamberson

*Anglers compete in a fishing tournament at Spring Lake Park in Texarkana. Photo courtesy of the City of Texarkana.*

**Smiley** .............................Ellis Villanueva
**Smithville**........................Mark A. Bunte
City Mgr., Robert Tamble
**Smyer**...........................Mary Beth Sims
**Snook**........................John W. See III
**Snyder (†)**.....................Anthony Wofford
City Mgr., Merle Taylor
**Socorro (†)**..........................Jesus Ruiz
City Mgr., (vacant)
**Somerset** .........................Paul G. Cuellar
**Somerville**..........................James Hare
City Admin., Martin Mangum
**Sonora** ...........................Wanda Shurley
City Mgr. Edward Carrasco
**Sour Lake (†)**.................Bruce Robinson
City Mgr., Larry Saurage
**South Houston**.........................Joe Soto
**Southlake (†)**...........................Laura Hill
City Mgr., Shana Yelverton
**Southmayd** .......................Thomas Byler
**South Mountain** (107 Barton Ln., Gatesville 76528)....................Billy Mayhew
**South Padre Island**..........Bharat R. Patel
City Mgr., William DiLebero
**Southside Place** (6309 Edloe Ave., Houston 77005)..........Glen (Pat) Patterson
City Mgr., David N. Moss
**Spearman** ..........................Brian Gillispie
**Splendora**.......................Dorothy Welch
**Spofford** (P.O. Box 1541 Brackettville, 78832) ..............................Alex Solis
City Mgr., Sarah Terrazas
**Springlake** .......................Gaylon Conner
**Springtown**.....................Tom W. Clayton
City Admin., Doug Hughes
**Spring Valley Village** (1025 Campbell Rd., Houston 77055) .......Tom Ramsey
City Admin., Stephen Ashley
**Spur** ...................................Stephen Bland
**Stafford (†)**.................Leonard Scarcella
**Stagecoach** .....................Galen Mansee
**Stamford (†)**...............John E. Anders Jr.
City Mgr., Alan L. Plumlee
**Stanton** ...............................Justin Burch
City Mgr., Michael Adams
**Staples**..............................Eddie Daffern
**Star Harbor** ...(Box 949, Malakoff 75148)
...................................Bobby Howell
**Stephenville (†)**..........Jerry K. Weldon II
City Admin., Pat Bridges
**Sterling City** .....Enrique (Henry) Estrada

**Stinnett**...................................Colin Locke
City Mgr., (vacant)
**Stockdale**.....................Ernest Ray Wolff
City Mgr., Alton Banks Akin
**Stratford**................................Ricky Reed
City Admin., Tommy R. Bogart
**Strawn**..................................Tye Jackson
**Streetman**...............Johnny A. Robinson
**Sudan**..................................Sam Miller
**Sugar Land (†)**.......James A. Thompson
City Mgr., Allen Bogard
**Sullivan City (†)**.......Rosendo Benavides
City Mgr., Judy Davila
**Sulphur Springs (†)**.............Kayla Price
City Mgr., Marc Maxwell
**Sundown** ...................................Jim Winn
City Admin., Curtis Schrader
**Sunnyvale**...............................Jim Phaup
Town Mgr., Sean Fox
**Sunray** ............................Brenda Emmert
City Mgr., Greg Smith
**Sunrise Beach Village**.......Patricia Frain
**Sunset Valley** ..................Rose Cardona
**Sun Valley** (800 Shady Grove Rd., Paris 75462) ............................Tom Wagnon
**Surfside Beach** ...............Larry Davidson
**Sweeny (†)**...........................Dale Lemon
City Mgr., Cindy King
**Sweetwater (†)**.................Jim McKenzie
City Mgr., Edward P. Brown

— **T** —

**Taft** .................................. Robert Vega Jr.
City Mgr., (vacant)
**Tahoka** ...............................John B. Baker
City Mgr., Jerry W. Webster
**Talco** .............................K.M. (Mike) Sloan
**Talty** (9550 Helms Trail, Ste. 500, Forney 75126) ..........................Larry Farthing
Town Admin., James Stroman
**Tatum** ...................................Phil Cory
**Taylor (†)**.............................Jesse Ancira
City Mgr., Isaac D. Turner
**Taylor Lake Village** .........Jon R. Keeney
**Taylor Landing** ................John J. Durkay
**Teague** ..........................Earnest G. Pack
City Admin., Judith A. Keally
**Tehuacana** .......Herman Douglas East Jr.
**Temple (†)**.......................Daniel A. Dunn

City Mgr., Jonathan Graham
**Tenaha** ..........................Orinthia Johnson
**Terrell (†)** ..............................Hal Richards
  City Mgr., Torry L. Edwards
**Terrell Hills (†)**..........Anne M. Ballantyne
  City Mgr., Columbus Stutes III
**Texarkana (†)**...................Bob Bruggeman
  City Mgr., John Whitson
**Texas City (†)** ..............Matthew T. Doyle
**Texhoma** ...........................Daniel Bogart
**Texline** ................................ Leo Martinez
  City Mgr., Jon Rose
**The Colony (†)**....................Joe McCourry
  City Mgr., Troy Powell
**Thompsons** ..........Freddie Newsome Jr.
**Thorndale** ..................................Allen Hejl
  City Admin., Keith Kiesling
**Thornton**....................Joe W. Neason Sr.
**Thorntonville** (Box 740, Monahans 79756).................David Mitchell
**Thrall**..........................................Troy Marx
**Three Rivers**.......................Sam Garcia
  City Admin., M.R. (Rosie) Forehand.....
**Throckmorton** ........................Will Carroll
**Tiki Island** ......................Vernon Teltschick
**Timbercreek Canyon** (101 S. Timbercreek Dr., Amarillo 79118) ... Kyle Black
  City Mgr., Joe Price
**Timpson**...........................Debra P. Smith
**Tioga** ...................................Craig Jezek
**Tira** (801 County Rd. 4612, Sulphur Springs 75482)................ Floyd Payton
**Toco** (2103 Chestnut Dr., Brookston 75421) ...................John Jason Waller
**Todd Mission** (21718 FM 1774, Plantersville 77363).................George Coulam
  City Mgr., Kay Conroy
**Tolar**...............................Terry R. Johnson
**Tomball (†)**...................Gretchen Fagan
  City Mgr., George Shackelford
**Tom Bean** ....................Sherry E. Howard
**Tool** ......................................Donny Daniel
**Toyah** ...................... Karen Hornberger
**Trent**......................................Leanna West
**Trenton** ......................Rodney Alexander
**Trinidad**...........................Larry D. Estes
  City Admin., Terri R. Newhouse
**Trinity** ......................Billy Joe Slaughter
  City Mgr., Jo Bitner
**Trophy Club (†)** ..................Nick Sanders
  Town Mgr., Stephen Seidel
**Troup**.......................................Joe Carlyle
  City Admin., Gene Cottle
**Troy** ................................Michael Morgan
  City Admin., Jeff Straub
**Tulia (†)**........................ Ross W. James
  City Mgr., Dion Miller
**Turkey** ...................................Pat Carson
  City Mgr., Lynn Gray
**Tuscola** .................................Dale Martin
**Tye**.......................................Nancy Moore
**Tyler (†)**.............................Martin Heines
  City Mgr., Edward Broussard

**– U –**

**Uhland** ........................................ (vacant)
  City Admin., Karen Gallaher
**Uncertain** ...........................Sam Canup
**Union Grove** (10648 US Hwy. 271 S., Gladewater 75647). Randy Lee Simcox
**Union Valley** ........................Chris Elliott
**Universal City (†)** ..............John Williams
  City Mgr., Ken Taylor
**University Park (†)**.............Olin Lane, Jr.
  City Mgr., Robbie Corder
**Uvalde (†)** ................ Don McLaughlin, Jr.
  City Mgr., Vince DiPiazza

**– V –**

**Valentine (†)** ....... Jesús (Chuy) Calderon

**Valley Mills** ....................Ray Bickerstaff
**Valley View** ......................Donald Bryant
**Van** ........................................Dean Stone
**Van Alstyne** ..................... Larry O. Cooper
  City Mgr., Frank Baker
**Van Horn**.....................Glenn Humphries
  City Admin., Fran Malafronte
**Vega** ...........................Mark J. Groneman
**Venus** ...........................James Burgess
  City Admin., April Stoll
**Vernon (†)**............................Joe Rogers
  City Mgr., Joe Jarosek
**Victoria (†)** ......................Paul Polasek
  City Mgr., Charmelle Garrett
**Vidor (†)**........................Robert Viator Jr.
  City Mgr., Mike Kunst
**Village of the Hills** .................Ron Dodd
  City Admin., Dan Roark
**Vinton** ..........................Madeleine Praino
  City Admin., Jessica Garza
**Volente** .....................................Ken Beck
  City Admin., Barbara Wilson
**Von Ormy**............... Art Martinez de Vara

**– W –**

**Waco (†)**....................Malcolm Duncan Jr.
  City Mgr., Dale Fisseler
**Waelder** .........................Rebecca Ayala
**Wake Village (†)** .................Jim Roberts
  City Admin., Mike Burke
**Waller** .........................Danny Marburger
**Wallis** ....................................Jerry Delso
**Walnut Springs** ....................Kay Moore
**Warren City** (3004 George Richey Rd., Gladewater 75647).....Ricky J. Wallace
**Waskom**..............................Jesse Moore
**Watauga (†)** ...................Hector F. Garcia
  City Mgr., Greg T. Vick
**Waxahachie (†)**............Kevin Strength
  City Mgr., Paul Stevens
**Weatherford (†)**.................Dennis Hooks
  City Mgr., Sharon Hayes
**Webberville** .................Hector Gonzales
**Webster (†)** .......................Donna Rogers
  City Mgr., Wayne J. Sabo
**Weimar**................................. Milton Koller
  City Mgr., Mike Barrow
**Weinert** ...................................Ed Murphy
**Weir**...................................Mervin Walker
**Wellington** .............................Durk Green
  City Mgr., Jon Sessions
**Wellman** ...........................Karl Spuhler
**Wells** ................................C.W. Williams
**Weslaco (†)**.......................David Suarez
  City Mgr., Mike R. Perez
**West** .................................Tommy Muska
**Westbrook** .........................Lynn Gaston
**West Columbia**....Laurie Beal Kincannon
  City Mgr., Debbie Sutherland
**Westlake** ..............................Laura Wheat
  Town Mgr., Thomas Brymer
**West Lake Hills** .................Dave Claunch
  City Admin., Robert Wood
**Weston**..........................Patti Harrington
**Weston Lakes** (PO Box 1082, Fulshear 77441) ............Mary Rose Zdunkewicz
**West Orange (†)** ..................Roy McDonald
**Westover Hills** (5824 Merrymount, Fort Worth 76107)................ Steven Tatum
  City Admin., Lyle H. Dresher
**West Tawakoni** ................Calvin Travers
  City Admin., Susan Roberts
**West University Place (†)**Susan Sample
  City Mgr., Michael Ross
**Westworth Village**..........Anthony Yeager
  City Admin., Roger Unger
**Wharton (†)**.........Domingo Montalvo, Jr.
  City Mgr., Andres Garza Jr.
**Wheeler**.................................Bob McCain
**White Deer**................................Kent Kelp

**Whiteface**.................................Jack Seay
  City Mgr., Belinda Terrell
**Whitehouse (†)**...............Charles Parker
  City Mgr., Kevin Huckabee
**White Oak**...........................Richard May
  City Coordinator, Charles Smith
**Whitesboro**................ W.D. (Dee) Welch
  City Admin., Michael Marter
**White Settlement (†)** ..... Ronald A. White
  City Mgr., James Ryan
**Whitewright** ......................Allen D. West
**Whitney**.................... Kristen Sims-Miller
  City Admin., Christopher Bentley
**Wichita Falls (†)** ...............Glenn Barham
  City Mgr., Darron Leiker
**Wickett**...........................Harold Ferguson
**Willis** ...............................Leonard Reed
  City Mgr., Hector Forestier
**Willow Park** ..........Richard Neverdousky
  City Admin., Matt Shaffstall
**Wills Point**............................Mark Turner
  City Mgr., Mike Ohrt
**Wilmer**................................Casey Burgess
  City Admin., William McDonald
**Wilson** .............................Donald Klaus
**Wimberley** ...................... Steve Thurber
  City Admin., Don Ferguson
**Windcrest** ...........................Alan Baxter
  City Admin., Rafael Castillo Jr.
**Windom** ...............................Donny Cobb
**Windthorst**.........................Greg P. Vieth
**Winfield** .............................Brett Webster
**Wink** ....................................Eric Hawkins
**Winnsboro**......................Richard Parrish
  City Admin., Jeffrey Howell
**Winona** ...........................Lisa LaFrance
**Winters** ..........................Lewis Bergman
**Wixon Valley** (9500 E. State Hwy. 21, Bryan 77808)......... James (Jim) Soefje
**Wolfe City** ......................Barbara Woodruff
**Wolfforth**.................Charles Addington II
  City Mgr., Darrell G. Newson
**Woodbranch Village** (58-A Woodbranch, New Caney 77357)............. Vera Craig
**Woodcreek** ..................Michael T. Steinert
  City Mgr., John W. Sone
**Woodloch** .....(Box 1379, Conroe 77305) ................................ Diane L. Lincoln
**Woodsboro**...................Larry D. Jochetz
**Woodson** ......................Bobby Mathiews
**Woodville**...........Thomas D. Fortenberry
  City Admin., Mandy K. Risinger
**Woodway (†)** ..................Donald J. Baker
  City Mgr., Yousry (Yost) A. Zakhary
**Wortham** ...............................Rodney Price
**Wylie (†)**............................... Eric Hogue
  City Mgr., Mindy Manson

**– Y –**

**Yantis** ..............................Jerry E. Miller
**Yoakum (†)** ...............Anita R. Rodriguez
  City Mgr., Kevin M. Coleman
**Yorktown** ......................Rene Hernandez
  City Admin., Robert Mendez

**– Z –**

**Zavalla** .........................Kelly Dickinson ☆

# County Courts

*Each Texas county has one county court created by the Texas Constitution — a **constitutional county court** — which is presided over by the county judge (see table beginning on **page 533** for a list of county judges). In more populated counties, the Legislature has created **statutory county courts,** including courts at law, probate courts, juvenile courts, domestic relations courts, and criminal courts at law. **Following is a list of statutory county courts and judges,** as reported in the Texas Judicial Directory as of February 2015. Other courts with jurisdiction in each county can be found on **pages 485–489. Other county and district officials can be found on pages 533–544.***

**Anderson** — *Court at Law:* Brendan Jeffrey Doran.

**Angelina** — *Court at Law No. 1:* Robert Inselmann; *No. 2:* Derek Flournoy.

**Aransas** — *Court at Law:* William Adams.

**Austin** — *Court at Law:* Daniel W. Leedy.

**Bastrop** — *Court at Law:* M. Benton Eskew.

**Bell** — *Court at Law No. 1, Probate & Juvenile courts:* Edward S. Johnson. *Court at Law No. 2, Domestic Relations & Criminal Court at Law:* John Mischtian. *Court at Law No. 3, Domestic Relations & Criminal Court at Law:* Rebecca DePew.

**Bexar** — *Court at Law No. 1:* John D. Fleming; *No. 2:* Jason W. Wolff; *No. 3:* David J. Rodriguez; *No. 4:* Sarah E. Garrahan-Moulder; *No. 5:* Jason Pulliam; *No. 6:* Wayne A. Christian; *No. 7:* Eugenia (Genie) Jenkins Wright; *No. 8:* Liza A. Rodriguez; *No. 9:* Walden Shelton; *No. 10:* Irene Alarcon Rios; *No. 11:* Carlo R. Key; *No. 12:* Scott Roberts; *No. 13:* Monica A. Gonzalez; *No. 14:* Bill C. White; *No. 15:* Michael T. LaHood. *Probate Court No. 1:* Polly Jackson Spencer; *No. 2:* Tom Rickhoff. *Probate Court No. 1:* Polly Jackson Spencer; *No. 2:* Tom Rickhoff.

**Bosque** — *Court at Law:* David Barham Christian.

**Bowie** — *Court at Law:* Jeff M. Addison.

**Brazoria** — *Court at Law No. 1 & Probate:* Jerri Lee Mills; *No. 2 & Probate:* Marc W. Holder; *No. 3 & Probate:* Jeremy E. Warren; *No. 4 & Probate:* Lori L.

Rickert.

**Brazos** — *Court at Law No. 1:* Amanda Matzke; *No. 2:* James (Jim) White Locke. *Juvenile Court:* Glynis Gore.

**Brown** — *Court at Law & Criminal Court at Law:* Frank E. Griffin.

**Burnet** — *Court at Law:* William Randolph Savage.

**Caldwell** — *Court at Law, Juvenile Court, and Criminal Court at Law:* Edward L. Jarrett. *Probate Court:* Tom Bonn and Edward L. Jarrett. *Domestic Relations Court:* Todd Blomerth.

**Calhoun** — *Court at Law:* Alex R. Hernandez.

**Cameron** — *Court at Law No. 1:* Arturo McDonald Jr.; *No. 2:* Laura Betancourt; *No. 3:* David Gonzales III; *No. 4:* (Effective 1/1/17); *No. 5:* (Effective 1/1/18).

**Cass** — *Court at Law & Criminal Court at Law:* Donald W. Dowd.

**Cherokee** — *Court at Law:* Craig A. Fletcher.

**Collin** — *Court at Law No. 1:* Corinne Ann Mason; *No. 2:* Barnett Walker; *No. 3:* Lance S. Baxter; *No. 4:* David D. Rippel; *No. 5:* Dan K. Wilson; *No. 6:* Jay A. Bender. *Probate Court:* Weldon S. Copeland Jr.

**Comal** — *Court at Law No. 1:* Randy C. Gray; No. 2 Charles A. Stephens II.

**Cooke** — *Court at Law:* John H. Morris.

**Coryell** — *Court at Law:* John R. Lee.

**Dallas** — *Court at Law No. 1:* DeMetria Benson; *No.*

*Val Verde County has had only one courthouse, which was built in 1887 in Del Rio. It was constructed in the Second Empire style with Classical details. Photo by Ron Billings; Texas A&M Forest Service.*

2: T. King Fifer; *No. 3:* Sally L. Montgomery; *No. 4:* William K. (Ken) Tapscott Jr.; *No. 5:* Mark Greenberg. *County Criminal Court No. 1:* Dan Patterson; *No. 2:* Julia Hayes; *No. 3:* Douglas W. Skemp; *No. 4:* Teresa Tolle; *No. 5:* Etta J. Mullin; *No. 6:* Angela M. King; *No. 7:* Elizabeth Hampton Crowder; *No. 8:* Tina Yoo; *No. 9:* Peggy Hoffman; *No. 10:* Roberto Canas; *No. 11:* Elizabeth Frizell. *Probate Court No. 1:* Brenda Hull-Thompson; *No. 2:* Chris Wilmoth; *No. 3:* Michael E. Miller. *County Criminal Court of Appeals No. 1:* Kristin Swanson Wade; *No. 2:* Jeffrey L. Rosenfield.

**Denton** — *Court at Law No. 1:* Kimberly McCary; *No. 2:* Robert Ramirez. *Probate Court:* Bonnie Robison; *Juvenile Court:* Kimberly McCary. *Criminal Court at Law No. 1:* Jim E. Crouch; *No. 2:* Virgil L. Vahlenkamp; *No. 3:* David D. Garcia; *No. 4:* Joe D. Bridges; *No. 5:* Richard S. Podgorski.

**Ector** — *Court at Law No. 1 & Juvenile Court:* J.A. (Jim) Bobo; *No. 2:* Mark D. Owens.

**Ellis** — *Court at Law No. 1:* Jim Chapman; *Court at Law No. 2:* A. Gene Calvert Jr.

**El Paso** — *Court at Law No. 1:* Ricardo Herrera; *No. 2:* Julie Gonzalez; *No. 3:* Javier Alvarez; *No. 4:* Alejandro Gonzalez; *No. 5:* Carlos Villa; *No. 6:* M. Sue Kurita; *No. 7:* Thomas A. Spieczny. *Probate Court No. 1:* Patricia B. Chew; *No. 2:* Eduardo Gamboa. *Domestic Relations Court:* Jim Fashing. *Juvenile Court No. 1:* Richard Anise; *No. 2:* Maria T. Leyva-Ligon. *Criminal Court at Law No. 1:* Alma R. Trejo; *No. 2:* Robert S. Anchondo; *No. 3:* Carlos Carrasco; *No. 4:* Jesus M. Herrera.

**Erath** — *Court at Law:* Ernest Bart McDougal.

**Fannin** — *Court at Law:* Charles Butler.

**Fort Bend** — *Court at Law No. 1:* Ben W. Childers; *No. 2:* Jeffery A. McMeans; *No. 3:* Susan Griffin Lowery; *No. 4:* R.H. (Sandy) Bielstein; *No. 5:* (Effective 1/1/16).

**Galveston** — *Court at Law No. 1:* John Grady; *No. 2:* Barbara E. Roberts; *No. 3:* Christopher Dupuy. *Probate Court:* Kimberly A. Sullivan.

**Grayson** — *Court at Law & Criminal Court at Law No. 1:* James C. Henderson; *No. 2:* Carol M. Siebman.

**Gregg** — *Court at Law No. 1:* Rebecca Lynn Simpson. *No. 2:* Vincent L. Dulweber.

**Guadalupe** — *Court at Law No. 1:* Linda Z. Jones; *No. 2:* Frank Follis. *Juvenile Court:* Linda Z. Jones.

**Harris** — *Court at Law No. 1:* Debra Ibarra Mayfield; *No. 2:* Theresa W. Chang; *No. 3:* Linda Storey; *No. 4:* Roberta Anne Lloyd. *County Criminal Court at Law No. 1:* Paula Goodhart; *No. 2:* William (Bill) Harmon; *No. 3:* Natalie C. Fleming; *No. 4:* John Clinton; *No. 5:* Margaret Stewart Harris; *No. 6:* Larry Standley; *No. 7:* Pam Derbyshire; *No. 8:* Jay Karahan; *No. 9:* Analia H. Wilkerson; *No. 10:* Sherman A. Ross; *No. 11:* Diane Bull; *No. 12:* Robin Brown; *No. 13:* Donald Alan Smyth; *No. 14:* Michael R. Fields; *No. 15:* Jean Spradling Hughes; *No. 16:* (Effective 1/1/16). *Probate Court No. 1:* Lloyd H. Wright; *No. 2:* Mike Wood; *No. 3:* Rory Robert Olsen; *No. 4:* Christine Riddle Butts.

**Harrison** — *Court at Law:* James Harry Ammerman II.

**Hays** — *Court at Law No. 1:* Robert E. Updegrove; *No. 2:* Linda A. Rodriguez. *Probate Court:* Robert Updegrove, Linda A. Rodriguez. *Domestic Relations Court:* Brenda Smith. *Juvenile Court:* Linda A. Rodriguez. *Criminal Court at Law:* Robert Updegrove, Linda A. Rodriguez.

**Henderson** — *Court at Law No 1:* D. Matt Livingston; *No 2:* Nancy Adams Perryman.

**Hidalgo** — *Court at Law No. 1:* Rodolfo (Rudy) Gon-

zalez; *No. 2:* Jaime (Jay) Palacios; *No. 4:* Federico (Fred) Garza Jr.; *No. 5:* Arnoldo Cantu; Jr. *No. 6:* Albert Garcia; *No. 7:* Sergio Valdez; *No. 7:* Rolando Cantu.

**Hill** — *Court at Law:* A. Lee Harris.

**Hood** — *Court at Law:* Vincent Messina. *Probate and Juvenile courts:* Darrell Cockerham. *Domestic Relations Court:* Ralph Walton.

**Hopkins** — *Court at Law:* Amy McCorkle Smith.

**Houston** — *Court at Law:* Sarah Tunnell Clark.

**Hunt** — *Court at Law No. 1:* J. Andrew Bench; *No. 2:* F. Duncan Thomas.

**Jefferson** — *Court at Law No. 1:* Gerald Eddins; *No. 2:* G.R. (Lupe) Flores; *No. 3:* John Paul Davis.

**Johnson** — *Court at Law No. 1:* Robert B. Mayfield III; *No. 2:* Jerry D. Webber.

**Kaufman** — *Court at Law No. 1, Criminal Court at Law & Juvenile Court:* Erleigh Norville Wiley. *Court at Law No. 2:* David A. Lewis. *Probate Court:* James Bruce Wood and David A. Lewis.

**Kerr** — *Court at Law:* Spencer W. Brown.

**Kleberg** — *Court at Law:* Guadalupe O. Mendoza.

**Lamar** — Court at Law: Bill H. Harris.

**Liberty** — *Court at Law:* Thomas A. Chambers.

**Lubbock** — *Court at Law No. 1:* Mark J. Hocker; *No. 2:* Drue A. Farmer; *No. 3:* Judy C. Parker.

**McLennan** — *Court at Law No. 1:* Mike Freeman; *No. 2:* T. Bradley Cates.

**Medina** — *Court at Law:* Vivian Torres.

**Midland** — *Court at Law No. 1 & Juvenile:* Kyle Peeler. *Court at Law No. 2 & Criminal Court at Law:* Marvin L. Moore. *Probate Court:* Mike Bradford. *Domestic Relations Court:* Dean Rucker.

**Montgomery** — *Court at Law No. 1:* Dennis D. Watson; *No. 2:* Claudia L. Laird; *No. 3:* Patrice McDonald; *No. 4:* Mary Ann Turner; *No. 5:* Keith M. Stewart.

**Moore** — *Court at Law:* Delwin T. McGee.

**Nacogdoches** — *Court at Law:* John A. (Jack) Sinz.

**Navarro** — *Court at Law, Juvenile & Criminal Court at Law:* Amanda D. Putman. *Probate Court:* H.M. Davenport. *Juvenile Court & Criminal Court at Law:* James Lagomarsino.

**Nolan** — *Court at Law:* David C. Hall.

**Nueces** — *Court at Law No. 1:* Robert J. Vargas; *No. 2:* Anna (Lisa) Elisabet Gonzales; *No. 3:* Deeanne Scoboda Galvan; *No. 4:* James E. Klager; *No. 5:* Brent Jackson Chesney.

**Orange** — *Court at Law No. 1:* Mandy White-Rogers; *No 2:* Troy Johnson.

**Panola** — *Court at Law:* Terry D. Bailey.

**Parker** — *Court at Law No. 1:* Jerry D. Buckner; *No. 2:* Charles (Ben) Benjamin Akers.

**Polk** — *Court at Law:* J. Stephen Phillips.

**Potter** — *Court at Law No. 1:* W.F. (Corky) Roberts; *No. 2:* Pamela Cook Sirmon.

**Randall** — *Court at Law No. 1:* James W. Anderson. *No. 2:* Ronnie Walker.

**Reeves** — *Court at Law:* Walter M. Holcombe.

**Rockwall** — *Court at Law:* Brian Williams.

**Rusk** — *Court at Law:* Chad W. Dean.

**San Patricio** — *Court at Law:* Patrick L. Flanigan.

**Smith** — *Court at Law No. 1:* Thomas A. Dunn; *No. 2:* Randall L. Rogers. *No. 3:* Floyd Thomas Getz.

**Starr** — *Court at Law:* Romero Molina.

**Tarrant** — *Court at Law No. 1:* Donald R. Pierson; *No. 2:* Jennifer Rymell; *No. 3:* Mike Hrabal. *Criminal Court at Law No. 1:* Sherry L. Hill; *No. 2:* Mike Mitchell; *No. 3:* Billy D. Mills; *No. 4:* Deborah L. Nekhom; *No. 5:* Jamie Cummings; *No. 6:* Molly S. Jones; *No. 7:*

The T.C. Lindsey & Co. Jonesville General Store comes into view around the bend of Farm Road 134 in Jonesville. The iconic Harrison County country store has been in business since 1847, when it was the Jones Trading Post. Owned by the Miller family, the store sells everything from food to antiques. Long-time employee Syble Elliott (in red, below, and age 93 in 2015) has worked at the store since 1957. Top photo by Jerry Lentz; bottom photo by Bill A. Belt.

Cheril S. Hardy; *No. 8:* Daryl Russell Coffey; *No. 9:* Brent A. Carr; *No. 10:* Phil A. Sorrels. *Probate Court No. 1:* Steve M. King; *No. 2:* Patrick W. Ferchill. *Juvenile Court:* Jean Boyd.

**Taylor** — *Court at Law No. 1:* Robert Harper; *No. 2:* Samuel (Sam) J. Carroll.

**Tom Green** — *Court at Law No. 1:* Charles (Ben) Nolan; *No. 2:* Penny Anne Roberts.

**Travis** — *Court at Law No. 1:* J. David Phillips; *No. 2:* Eric Shepperd; *No. 3:* John Lipscombe; *No. 4:* Mike E. Denton; *No. 5:* Nancy Hohengarten; *No. 6:* Brandy Mueller; *No. 7:* Elisabeth A. Earle; *No. 8:* Carlos H. Barrera. *Probate Court:* Guy Herman.

**Val Verde** — *Court at Law:* Sergio J. Gonzalez.

**Van Zandt** — *Court at Law :* Randal L. McDonald.

**Victoria** — *Court at Law No. 1:* Travis H. Ernst; *No. 2:* Daniel F. Gilliam.

**Walker** — *Court at Law:* Barbara Wade Hale.

**Waller** — *Court at Law:* June Jackson.

**Washington** — *Court at Law:* Matthew A. Reue.

**Webb** — *Court at Law No. 1:* Alvino (Ben) Morales; *No. 2:* Jesús (Chuy) Garza.

**Wichita** — *Court at Law No. 1:* Gary Wayne Butler; *No. 2:* Greg King.

**Williamson** — *Court at Law No. 1:* Suzanne S. Brooks; *No. 2:* Tim L. Wright; *No. 3:* Doug Arnold; *No. 4:* John B. McMaster.

**Wise** — *Court at Law No. 1 & Criminal Court at Law:* Melton D. Cude. *Court at Law No. 2 & Probate:* Stephen J. Wren. ☆

# Wet-Dry Counties

Source: Texas Alcoholic Beverage Commission; www.tabc.state.tx.us//

The sale of alcohol in Texas varies from one county to another. The list below shows the wet-or-dry status of counties in Texas as of July 2013.

An asterisk (*) indicates counties in which the sale of mixed beverages (liquor by the drink) is legal in all or part of the county.

In seven counties marked with a dagger (†), the sale of mixed beverages in restaurants is permitted, but the sale of distilled spirits for off-premise consumption is not permitted.

When approved in local-option elections in "wet" precincts of counties, sale of liquor by the drink is permitted in Texas. This resulted from adoption of an amendment to the Texas Constitution in 1970 and subsequent legislation, followed by local-option elections. This amendment marked the first time in 50 years that the sale of liquor by the drink was legal in Texas.

In 2013, there were 13 counties wholly dry. In 1986, there were 62 counties wholly dry.

## Wet / Dry Counties 2013

- ● Wet: Including distilled spirits
- ● Part wet: Including distilled spirits
- ● Wine/beer permitted in part or all
- ● Beer permitted in part or all
- ● Dry: No alcohol sales permitted

© Texas Almanac

**Counties (in part or all) in Which Distilled Spirits Are Legal (222):** *Anderson, *†Angelina, *Aransas, Archer, *Armstrong, *Atascosa, *Austin, *Bandera, *Bastrop, *Bee, *Bell, *Bexar, *Blanco, *Bosque, *†Bowie, *Brazoria, *Brewster, *Briscoe, *Brooks, *Brown, Burleson, *Burnet, *Caldwell, *Calhoun, *Callahan, *Cameron, *Camp, Carson, Cass, Castro, *Chambers, *Cherokee, *Childress, †Clay, Coleman, *Collin, *Colorado, *Comal, *Comanche, *Cooke, *Coryell, *Cottle, Crane, Crockett, *†Crosby, Culberson.

Dallam, *Dallas, *Dawson, Deaf Smith, *Denton, *DeWitt, Dickens, *Dimmit, *Donley, *Duval, Eastland, *Ector, Edwards, *Ellis, *El Paso, Erath, Falls, Fannin, *Fayette, *Floyd, *Foard, *Fort Bend, †Franklin, Freestone, *Frio, *Galveston, *Garza, *Gillespie, *Goliad, *Gonzales, Gray, *Grayson, *Gregg, *Grimes, *Guadalupe, *Hale, Hall, Hamilton, †Hansford, *Hardeman, *Hardin, *Harris, Harrison, Hartley, *Haskell, *Hays, *Henderson, *Hidalgo, *Hill, *Hockley, *Hood, Hopkins, *†Houston, *Howard, *Hudspeth, *Hunt, Hutchinson, Jack, *Jackson, *Jasper, *Jeff Davis, *Jefferson, *Jim Hogg, *Jim Wells, *Johnson, *Jones.

*Karnes, *Kaufman, *Kendall, *Kenedy, *Kerr, Kimble, King, *Kinney, *Kleberg, Knox, *Lamar, Lamb, *Lampasas, *La Salle, *Lavaca, *Lee, *Leon, *Liberty, Live Oak, *Llano, *Lubbock, Lynn, *†Madison, *Marion, *Matagorda, *Maverick, *McCulloch, *McLennan, *Medina, Menard, *Midland, *Milam, Mills, *Mitchell, *Montague, *Montgomery, *Moore, *Morris, *Motley, Nacogdoches, *Navarro, Newton, *Nolan, *Nueces.

*†Ochiltree,*†Oldham, *Orange, Palo Pinto, *Parker, *Pecos, *Polk, *Potter, *Presidio, *Rains, *Randall, Reagan, Red River, *Reeves, Refugio, *Robertson, *Rockwall, Runnels, †Rusk, Sabine, San Augustine, San Jacinto, *San Patricio, *San Saba, Schleicher, *Scurry, Shackelford, Shelby, *†Sherman,*Smith, *Starr, Stonewall, *Sutton, Swisher, *Tarrant, *Taylor, Terrell, Titus, *Tom Green, *Travis, Trinity, *†Tyler, Upshur, Upton, *Uvalde, *Val Verde, *Victoria, *Walker, Waller, Ward, *Washington, *Webb, *Wharton, *Wheeler, *Wichita, *Wilbarger, *Willacy, *Williamson, *Wilson, Winkler, *Wise, *†Wood, Young, *Zapata, *Zavala.

**Counties in Which Only Beer Is Legal (4):** Baylor, Irion, Mason, Stephens.

**Counties in Which Beer and Wine Up to 14 Percent Alcohol by Volume Are Legal (15):** Cochran, Coke, Concho, Gaines, Glasscock, Limestone, Lipscomb, Loving, McMullen, Panola, Real, Somervell, Terry, Van Zandt, Yoakum.

**Counties Wholly Dry (13):** Andrews, Bailey, Borden, Collingsworth, Delta, Fisher, Hemphill, Kent, Martin, Parmer, Roberts, Sterling, Throckmorton. ☆

# Regional Councils of Government

*Source: Texas Association of Regional Councils; www.txregionalcouncil.org/*

The concept of regional planning and cooperation, fostered by enabling legislation in 1965, has spread across Texas since organization of the North Central Texas Council of Governments in 1966.

Regional councils are voluntary associations of local governments that deal with problems and planning needs that cross the boundaries of individual local governments or that require regional attention.

These concerns include criminal justice, emergency communications, job-training programs, solid-waste management, transportation, and water-quality management. The councils make recommendations to member governments and may assist in implementing the plans. Financing is provided by local, state, and federal governments.

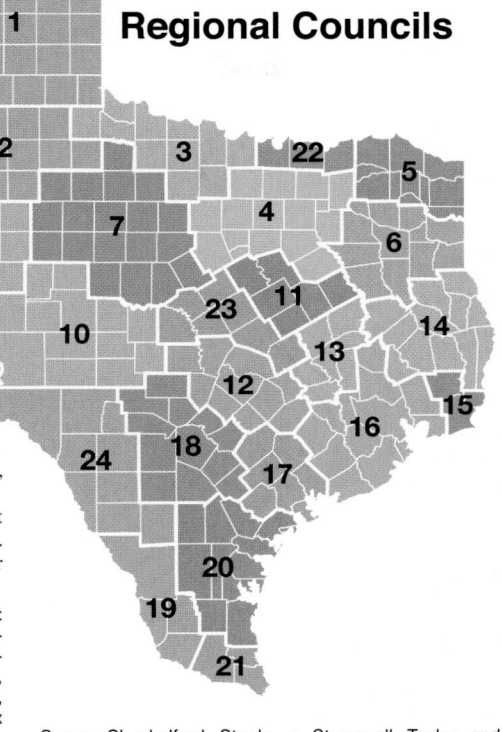

Regional Councils

The Texas Association of Regional Councils is at 701 Brazos, Ste. 780, Austin 78701; (512) 478-4715. Following is a list of the 24 regional councils, member counties, executive director, and contact information:

**1. Panhandle Regional Planning Commission:** Armstrong, Briscoe, Carson, Castro, Childress, Collingsworth, Dallam, Deaf Smith, Donley, Gray, Hall, Hansford, Hartley, Hemphill, Hutchinson, Lipscomb, Moore, Ochiltree, Oldham, Parmer, Potter, Randall, Roberts, Sherman, Swisher, and Wheeler. **Gary Pitner,** PO Box 9257, Amarillo 79105-9257; (806) 372-3381; www.prpc.cog.tx.us.

**2. South Plains Association of Governments:** Bailey, Cochran, Crosby, Dickens, Floyd, Garza, Hale, Hockley, King, Lamb, Lubbock, Lynn, Motley, Terry, and Yoakum. **Tim Pierce,** PO Box 3730, Lubbock 79452-3730; (806) 762-8721; www.spag.org.

**3. Nortex Regional Planning Commission:** Archer, Baylor, Clay, Cottle, Foard, Hardeman, Jack, Montague, Wichita, Wilbarger, and Young. **Dennis Wilde,** PO Box 5144, Wichita Falls 76307-5144; (940) 322-5281; www.nortexrpc.org.

**4. North Central Texas Council of Governments:** Collin, Dallas, Denton, Ellis, Erath, Hood, Hunt, Johnson, Kaufman, Navarro, Palo Pinto, Parker, Rockwall, Somervell, Tarrant, and Wise. **R. Michael Eastland,** PO Box 5888, Arlington 76005-5888; (817) 640-3300; www.nctcog.org.

**5. Ark-Tex Council of Governments:** Bowie, Cass, Delta, Franklin, Hopkins, Lamar, Morris, Red River, Titus, and Miller County, Ark. **L.D. Williamson,** PO Box 5307, Texarkana, Texas 75505-5307; (903) 832-8636; www.atcog.org.

**6. East Texas Council of Governments:** Anderson, Camp, Cherokee, Gregg, Harrison, Henderson, Marion, Panola, Rains, Rusk, Smith, Upshur, Van Zandt, and Wood. **David Cleveland,** 3800 Stone Rd., Kilgore 75662-6297; (903) 984-8641; www.etcog.org.

**7. West Central Texas Council of Governments:** Brown, Callahan, Coleman, Comanche, Eastland, Fisher, Haskell, Jones, Kent, Knox, Mitchell, Nolan, Runnels, Scurry, Shackelford, Stephens, Stonewall, Taylor, and Throckmorton. **Tom Smith,** 3702 Loop 322, Abilene 79602-7300; (325) 672-8544; www.wctcog.org.

**8. Rio Grande Council of Governments:** Brewster, Culberson, El Paso, Hudspeth, Jeff Davis, Presidio, and Doña Ana County, N.M. **Annette Gutierrez,** 1100 N. Stanton, Ste. 610, El Paso 79902; (915) 533-0998; www.riocog.org.

**9. Permian Basin Regional Planning Commission:** Andrews, Borden, Crane, Dawson, Ector, Gaines, Glasscock, Howard, Loving, Martin, Midland, Pecos, Reeves, Terrell, Upton, Ward, and Winkler. **Terri Moore,** PO Box 60660, Midland 79711-0660; (432) 563-1061; www.pbrpc.org.

**10. Concho Valley Council of Governments:** Coke, Concho, Crockett, Irion, Kimble, Mason, McCulloch, Menard, Reagan, Schleicher, Sterling, Sutton, and Tom Green. **Jeffrey Sutton,** Box 60050, San Angelo 76906-0050; (325) 944-9666; www.cvcog.org.

**11. Heart of Texas Council of Governments:** Bosque, Falls, Freestone, Hill, Limestone, and McLennan. **Kenneth Simons,** PO Box 20847, Waco 76712; (254) 292-1800; www.hotcog.org.

**12. Capital Area Council of Governments:** Bastrop, Blanco, Burnet, Caldwell, Fayette, Hays, Lee, Llano, Travis, and Williamson. **Betty Voights,** 6800 Burleson Rd., Bldg. 310, Ste. 165, Austin 78744; (512) 916-6000; www.capcog.org.

**13. Brazos Valley Council of Governments:** Brazos, Burleson, Grimes, Leon, Madison, Robertson, and Washington. **Tom Wilkinson Jr.,** 3991 E. 29th St., Bryan 77803; (979) 595-2800; www.bvcog.org.

**14. Deep East Texas Council of Governments**: Angelina, Houston, Jasper, Nacogdoches, Newton, Polk, Sabine, San Augustine, San Jacinto, Shelby, Trinity, and Tyler. **Walter G. Diggles,** 210 Premier Dr., Jasper 75951; (409) 384-5704; www.detcog.org.

**15. South East Texas Regional Planning Commission**: Hardin, Jefferson, and Orange. **Shaun P. Davis,** 2210 Eastex Fwy., Beaumont 77703; (409) 899-8444; www.setrpc.org.

**16. Houston-Galveston Area Council**: Austin, Brazoria, Chambers, Colorado, Fort Bend, Galveston, Harris, Liberty, Matagorda, Montgomery, Walker, Waller, and Wharton. **Jack Steele,** PO Box 22777, Houston 77227-2777; (713) 627-3200; www.h-gac.com.

**17. Golden Crescent Regional Planning Commission**: Calhoun, DeWitt, Goliad, Gonzales, Jackson, Lavaca, and Victoria. **Joe Brannan,** 120 S. Main, Ste. 210, Victoria 77901; (361) 578-1587; www.gcrpc.org.

**18. Alamo Area Council of Governments**: Atascosa, Bandera, Bexar, Comal, Frio, Gillespie, Guadalupe, Karnes, Kendall, Kerr, Medina, and Wilson. **Gloria C. Arriaga,** 8700 Tesoro Dr., Ste. 700, San Antonio 78217; (210) 362-5200; www.aacog.com.

**19. South Texas Development Council**: Jim Hogg, Starr, Webb, and Zapata. **Amando Garza Jr.,** 1002 Dicky Lane, Laredo 78044-2187; (956) 722-3995; www.stdc.cog.tx.us.

**20. Coastal Bend Council of Governments**: Aransas, Bee, Brooks, Duval, Jim Wells, Kenedy, Kleberg, Live Oak, McMullen, Nueces, Refugio, and San Patricio. **John P. Buckner,** PO Box 9909, Corpus Christi 78469-9909; (361) 883-5743; cbcog98.org.

**21. Lower Rio Grande Valley Development Council**: Cameron, Hidalgo, and Willacy. **Kenneth N. Jones Jr.,** 311 N. 15th, McAllen 78501-4705; (956) 682-3481; www.lrgvdc.org.

**22. Texoma Council of Governments**: Cooke, Fannin, and Grayson. **Susan B. Thomas,** 1117 Gallagher Dr., Ste. 100, Sherman 75090; (903) 813-3512; www.texoma.cog.tx.us.

**23. Central Texas Council of Governments**: Bell, Coryell, Hamilton, Lampasas, Milam, Mills, and San Saba. **James Reed,** PO Box 729, Belton 76513-0729; (254) 770-2200; www.ctcog.org.

**24. Middle Rio Grande Development Council**: Dimmit, Edwards, Kinney, La Salle, Maverick, Real, Uvalde, Val Verde, and Zavala. **Leodoro Martinez Jr.,** PO Box 1199, Carrizo Springs 78834-1199; (830) 876-3533; www.mrgdc.org. ☆

# County Tax Appraisers

*The following list of Chief Appraisers for Texas counties was furnished by the State Property Tax Division of the State Comptroller's office. It includes the mailing address for each appraiser and is current to July 2015.*

**Anderson** — Carson Wages, PO Box 279, Palestine 75802

**Andrews** — Jackie Martin, 600 N. Main St., Andrews 79714

**Angelina** — Tim Chambers, PO Box 2357, Lufkin 75902

**Aransas** — Kevin Jamison, 601 S. Church St., Rockport 78382

**Archer** — Kimbra York, PO Box 1141, Archer City 76351

**Armstrong** — Joe Reck, PO Box 835, Claude 79019

**Atascosa** — Michelle Cardenas, PO Box 139, Poteet 78065

**Austin** — Carmen Ottmer, 906 E. Amelia St., Bellville 77418

**Bailey** — Kaye Elliott, 302 Main St., Muleshoe 79347

**Bandera** — Wendy Grams, PO Box 1119, Bandera 78003

**Bastrop** — Mark Boehnke, PO Drawer 578, Bastrop 78602

**Baylor** — Beth Hrncirik, 211 N. Washington, Seymour 76380

**Bee** — Domingo Palomo, 401 N. Washington, Beeville 78102

**Bell** — Marvin Hahn, PO Box 390, Belton 76513

**Bexar** — Michael Amezquita, PO Box 830248, San Antonio 78283

**Blanco** — Hollis Boatright, PO Box 338, Johnson City 78636

**Borden** — Judy Harris, PO Box 298, Gail 79738

**Bosque** — Marlee Greenwood, PO Box 393, Meridian 76665

**Bowie** — Mike Brower, PO Box 6527, Texarkana 75505

**Brazoria** — Cheryl Evans, 500 N. Chenango, Angleton 77515

**Brazos** — Mark Price, 1673 Briarcrest Dr., #A-101, Bryan 77802

**Brewster** — Matt White, 107 W. Avenue E, #2, Alpine 79830

**Briscoe** — Pat McWaters, PO Box 728, Silverton 79257

**Brooks** — Mary Lou Cantu, PO Drawer A, Falfurrias 78355

**Brown** — Brett McKibben, 403 Fisk Ave., Brownwood 76801

**Burleson** — Kim Orr, PO Box 1000, Caldwell 77836

**Burnet** — Stan Hemphill, PO Box 908, Burnet 78611

**Caldwell** — Mary LaPoint, PO Box 900, Lockhart 78644

**Calhoun** — Jesse Hubbell, PO Box 49, Port Lavaca 77979

**Callahan** — Don Jones, 132 W. 4th St., Baird 79504

**Cameron** — Frutoso Gomez Jr., PO Box 1010, San Benito 78586

**Camp** — Jan Tinsley, 143 Quitman St., Pittsburg 75686

**Carson** — Donita Davis, PO Box 970, Panhandle 79068

**Cass** — Jordan Klein, 502 N. Main St., Linden 75563

**Castro** — Jerry Heller, 204 S.E. 3rd (Rear), Dimmitt 79027

**Chambers** — Mitchell McCullough, PO Box 1520, Anahuac 77514

**Cherokee** — Lee Flowers, PO Box 494, Rusk 75785

**Childress** — Terry Holley, 1710 Ave. F NW, Childress 79201

**Clay** — Gerald Holland, PO Box 108, Henrietta 76365

**Cochran** — David Greener, 109 S.E. First St., Morton 79346

**Coke** — Gayle Sisemore, PO Box 2, Robert Lee 76945

**Coleman** — Bill W. Jones, PO Box 914, Coleman 76834

**Collin** — Bo Daffin, 250 W. Eldorado, McKinney 75069

**Collingsworth** — Dwight Bowen, 800 West Ave., Rm. 104, Wellington, 79095

**Colorado** — Billie Mitchell Jr., PO Box 10, Columbus 78934

**Comal** — Curtis Koehler, PO 900 S. Seguin Ave., New Braunfels 78130

**Comanche** — JoAnn Hohertz, PO Box 6, Comanche 76442

**Concho** — Scott Sutton, PO Box 68, Paint Rock 76866

**Cooke** — Doug Smithson, 201 N. Dixon, Gainesville 76240

**Coryell** — Mitch Fast, 705 E. Main St., Gatesville 76528

**Cottle** — Nakia Hargrave, PO Box 459, Paducah 79248

**Crane** — Byron Bitner, 511 W. 8th St., Crane 79731

**Crockett** — Rhonda Shaw, PO Drawer H, Ozona 76943

**Crosby** — Kathy Lowrie, PO Box 505, Crosbyton 79322

**Culberson** — Maricel Gonzalez, PO Box 550, Van Horn 79855

**Dallam** — Holly McCauley, PO Box 579, Dalhart 79022

**Dallas** — Ken Nolan, 2949 N. Stemmons Fwy., Dallas 75247

**Dawson** — Norma J. Brock, PO Box 797, Lamesa 79331

**Deaf Smith** — Danny Jones, PO Box 2298, Hereford 79045

**Delta** — Kim Gregory, PO Box 47, Cooper 75432

**Denton** — Rudy Durham, PO Box 2816, Denton 76202

**DeWitt** — Beverly Malone, 103 E. Bailey St., Cuero 77954

**Dickens** — Patti Abbott, PO Box 180, Dickens 79229

**Dimmit** — Norma Carrillo, 404 W. Peña St., Carrizo Springs 78834

**Donley** — Paula Lowrie, PO Box 1220, Clarendon 79226

**Duval** — Gary Zeitler, PO Box 809, San Diego 78384

**Eastland** — Randy Clark, PO Box 914, Eastland 76448

**Ector** — Anita Campbell, 1301 E. 8th St., Odessa 79761

**Edwards** — Nelia McNeal, PO Box 858, Rocksprings 78880

**Ellis** — Kathy Rodrigue, PO Box 878, Waxahachie 75168

**El Paso** — Dinah Kilgore, 5801 Trowbridge Dr., El Paso 79925

**Erath** — Jerry Lee, 1390 N. Harbin Dr., Stephenville 76401

**Falls** — Allen McKinley, 403 Craik St., Marlin 76661

**Fannin** — Michael Jones, 831 W. State Hwy. 56, Bonham 75418

**Fayette** — Richard Moring, PO Box 836, La Grange 78945

**Fisher** — Twila Butler, PO Box 516, Roby 79543

**Floyd** — Jim Finley, PO Box 249, Floydada 79235

**Foard** — Jo Ann Vecera, PO Box 419, Crowell 79227

**Fort Bend** — Glen Whitehead, 2801 B.F. Terry Blvd., Rosenberg 77471

**Franklin** — Genea Burnaman, PO Box 720, Mount Vernon 75457

**Freestone** — Bud Black, 218 N. Mount St., Fairfield 75840

**Frio** — Luciano R. Gonzales, PO Box 1129, Pearsall 78061

**Gaines** — Gayla Harridge, PO Box 490, Seminole 79360

**Galveston** — Tommy Watson, 9850 Emmet F Lowry Exp, Ste. A, Texas City 77591

**Garza** — Irene Fry, PO Drawer F, Post 79356

**Gillespie** — David Oehler, 101 W. Main St., Unit 11, Fredericksburg 78624

**Glasscock** — Priscilla A. Ginnetti, PO Box 155, Garden City 79739

**Goliad** — Richard Miller, PO Box 34, Goliad 77963

**Gonzales** — John Liford, PO Box 867, Gonzales 78629

**Gray** — Tyson Paronto, PO Box 836, Pampa 79066

**Grayson** — Shawn Coker, 205 N. Travis, Sherman 75090

**Gregg** — Thomas Hays, 4367 W. Loop 281, Longview 75604

**Grimes** — Bill Sullivan, PO Box 489, Anderson 77830

**Guadalupe** — Jamie Osborne, 3000 N. Austin St., Seguin 78155

**Hale** — Nikki Branscum, PO Box 29, Plainview 79073

**Hall** — Gina Chavira, 512 W. Main St., Ste. 14, Memphis 79245

**Hamilton** — Doyle Roberts, 119 E. Henry St., Hamilton 76531

**Hansford** — Brandi Thompson, 709 W. 7th Ave., Spearman 79081

**Hardeman** — Jan Evans, PO Box 388, Quanah 79252

**Hardin** — Alex Stephens, PO Box 670, Kountze 77625

**Harris** — Sands Stiefer, PO Box 920975, Houston 77292

**Harrison** — Robert Lisman, PO Box 818, Marshall 75671

**Hartley** — Patsy Jan Lowry, PO Box 405, Hartley 79044

**Haskell** — Leah Robertson, PO Box 467, Haskell 79521

**Hays** — David G. Valle, 21001 N. IH-35, Kyle 78640

**Hemphill** — Jason Caron, 223 Main St., Canadian 79014

**Henderson** — Bill Jackson, PO Box 430, Athens 75751

**Hidalgo** — Rolando Garza, PO Box 208, Edinburg 78540

**Hill** — Mike McKibben, PO Box 416, Hillsboro 76645

**Hockley** — Greg Kelley, PO Box 1090, Levelland 79336

**Hood** — Greg Stewart, PO Box 819, Granbury 76048

**Hopkins** — Cathy Singleton, PO Box 753, Sulphur Springs 75483

**Houston** — Carey Minter, PO Box 112, Crockett 75835

**Howard** — Ronny Babcock, PO Box 1151, Big Spring 79721

**Hudspeth** — Zedoch Pridgeon, PO Box 429, Sierra Blanca 79851

**Hunt** — Brent South, PO Box 1339, Greenville 75403

**Hutchinson** — Joe Raper, PO Box 5065, Borger 79008

**Irion** — Byron Bitner, PO Box 980, Mertzon 76941

**Jack** — Kathy Conner, PO Box 958, Jacksboro 76458

**Jackson** — Damon Moore, 404 N. Allen St., Edna 77957

**Jasper** — David Luther, PO Box 1300, Jasper 75951

**Jeff Davis** — Zedoch Pridgeon, PO Box 373, Fort Davis 79734

**Jefferson** — Angela Bellard, PO Box 21337, Beaumont 77720

**Jim Hogg** — Jorge Arellano, PO Box 459, Hebbronville 78361

**Jim Wells** — Sidney Vela, PO Box 607, Alice 78333

**Johnson** — Jim Hudspeth, 109 N. Main, Cleburne 76033

**Jones** — Kim McLemore, PO Box 348, Anson 79501

**Karnes** — Brian Stahl, 915 S. Panna Maria Ave., Karnes City 78118

**Kaufman** — Chris Peace, PO Box 819, Kaufman 75142

**Kendall** — Shelby Presley, PO Box 788, Boerne 78006

**Kenedy** — Thomas G. Denney, PO Box 39, Sarita 78385

**Kent** — Kay Byrd, PO Box 68, Jayton 79528

**Kerr** — P.H. Coates IV, PO Box 294387, Kerrville 78029

**Kimble** — Kandy Dick, PO Box 307, Junction 76849

**King** — Kala Briggs, PO Box 117, Guthrie 79236

**Kinney** — Gene C. Slate, PO Box 1377, Brackettville 78832

**Kleberg** — Tina Flores, PO Box 1027, Kingsville 78364

**Knox** — Mitzi Welch, PO Box 47, Benjamin 79505

**Lamar** — Jerry Patton, PO Box 400, Paris 75461

**Lamb** — Lesa Kloiber, PO Box 950, Littlefield 79339

**Lampasas** — Melissa Gonzales, Box 175, Lampasas 76550

**La Salle** — Annie Garcia, PO Box 1530, Cotulla 78014

**Lavaca** — Greg Cook, PO Box 386, Hallettsville 77964

**Lee** — James Orr, 898 E. Richmond, Ste. 100, Giddings 78942

**Leon** — Jeff Beshears, PO Box 536, Centerville 75833

**Liberty** — Alan Conner, PO Box 10016, Liberty 77575

**Limestone** — Karen Wietzikoski, PO Drawer 831, Groesbeck 76642

**Lipscomb** — Pam Scates, PO Box 128, Darrouzett 79024

**Live Oak** — Debra Morin, PO Box 2370, George West 78022

**Llano** — Gary Eldridge, 103 E. Sandstone, Llano 78643

**Loving** — Sherlene Burrows, PO Box 352, Mentone 79754

**Lubbock** — Tim Radloff, PO Box 10542, Lubbock 79408

**Lynn** — Marquita Scott, PO Box 789, Tahoka 79373

**Madison** — Matt Newton, PO Box 1328, Madisonville 77864

**Marion** — Coy Johnson, PO Box 690, Jefferson 75657

**Martin** — Marsha Graves, PO Box 1349, Stanton 79782

**Mason** — Ted H. Smith, PO Box 1119, Mason 76856

**Matagorda** — Vince Maloney, 2225 Ave. G, Bay City 77414

**Maverick** — Maggie Duran, PO Box 2628, Eagle Pass 78852

**McCulloch** — Zane Brandenberger, 306 W. Lockhart, Brady 76825

**McLennan** — Andrew Hahn, PO Box 2297, Waco 76703

**McMullen** — Juan Saucedo, PO Box 38, Tilden 78072

**Medina** — Johnette Dixon, 1410 Ave. K, Hondo 78861

**Menard** — Kayla Wagner, PO Box 1008, Menard 76859

**Midland** — Jerry Bundick, PO Box 908002, Midland 79708

**Milam** — Dyann White, PO Box 769, Cameron 76520

**Mills** — Dori Blesh, PO Box 565, Goldthwaite 76844

**Mitchell** — Linda McSpadden, 2112 Hickory St., Colorado City 79512

**Montague** — Kim Haralson, PO Box 121, Montague 76251

**Montgomery** — Mark Castleschouldt, PO Box 2233, Conroe 77305

**Moore** — Jackie Hayhurst, PO Box 717, Dumas 79029

**Morris** — Summer Golden, PO Box 563, Daingerfield 75638

**Motley** — Jim Finley, PO Box 249, Floydada 79235

**Nacogdoches** — Gary Woods, 216 W. Hospital St., Nacogdoches 75961

**Navarro** — Karen Morris, PO Box 3118, Corsicana 75110

**Newton** — Margie L. Herrin, 109 Court St., Newton 75966

**Nolan** — Brenda Klepper, PO Box 1256, Sweetwater 79556

**Nueces** — Ronnie Canales, 201 N. Chaparral, Ste. 206, Corpus Christi 78401

**Ochiltree** — Burton Jones, 825 S. Main, Ste. 100, Perryton 79070

**Oldham** — Brenda Perkins, PO Box 310, Vega 79092

**Orange** — Michael Cedars, PO Box 457, Orange 77631

**Palo Pinto** — Donna Rhoades, PO Box 250, Palo Pinto 76484

**Panola** — Michael Douglas, 1736 Ballpark Dr., Carthage 75633

**Parker** — Larry Hammonds, 1108 Santa Fe Dr., Weatherford 76086

**Parmer** — Jill Timms, PO Box 56, Bovina 79009

**Pecos** — Sam Calderon, PO Box 237, Fort Stockton 79735

*Music and dancing draw Austinites and visitors to Guero's Taco Bar in South Austin. Photo courtesy of the Austin Convention and Visitor's Bureau.*

**Polk** — Chad Hill, 114 Matthews St., Livingston 77351

**Potter** — Jim Childers, PO Box 7190, Amarillo 79114

**Presidio** — Cynthia Ramirez, PO Box 879, Marfa 79843

**Rains** — Carrol Houllis, PO Box 70, Emory 75440

**Randall** — Jim Childers, PO Box 7190, Amarillo 79114

**Reagan** — Rhonda Shaw, PO Box 8, Big Lake 76932

**Real** — Kelley V. Shults, PO Box 158, Leakey 78873

**Red River** — Christie Ussery, PO Box 461, Clarksville 75426

**Reeves** — John Huddleston, PO Box 1229, Pecos 79772

**Refugio** — Connie Raymond, PO Box 156, Refugio 78377

**Roberts** — DeAnn Williams, PO Box 458, Miami 79059

**Robertson** — Nancy Commander, PO Box 998, Franklin 77856

**Rockwall** — Patricia Davis, 841 Justin Rd., Rockwall 75087

**Runnels** — Larry Reagan, PO Box 524, Ballinger 76821

**Rusk** — Terry Decker, PO Box 7, Henderson 75653

**Sabine** — Tom Ince, PO Box 137, Hemphill 75948

**San Augustine** — Evelyn Biggers, 122 N. Harrison, San Augustine 75972

**San Jacinto** — Kelly Foxworth, PO Box 1170, Coldspring 77331

**San Patricio** — Rufino Lozano, PO Box 938, Sinton 78387

**San Saba** — Jan Vanderburg, 423 E. Wallace St., San Saba 76877

**Schleicher** — Jani Coffey, PO Box 936, Eldorado 76936

**Scurry** — Larry Crooks, 2612 College Ave., Snyder 79549

**Shackelford** — Richard Petree, PO Box 2247, Albany 76430

**Shelby** — Robert N. Pigg, 724 Shelbyville St., Center 75935

**Sherman** — Teresa Edmond, PO Box 239, Stratford 79084

**Smith** — Michael D. Barnett, 245 South S.E. Loop 323, Tyler 75702

**Somervell** — Wes Rollen, 112 Allen Dr., Glen Rose 76043

**Starr** — Rosalva Guerra, 100 N. FM 3167, Ste. 300, Rio Grande City 78582

**Stephens** — Terri Sullivan, PO Box 351, Breckenridge 76424

**Sterling** — Ronnie Krejci, PO Box 28, Sterling City 76951

**Stonewall** — Debra Daniels, PO Box 308, Aspermont 79502

**Sutton** — Mary Bustamante, 300 E. Oak St., Ste. 2, Sonora 76950

**Swisher** — Cindy McDowell, PO Box 8, Tulia 79088

**Tarrant** — Jeff Law, 2500 Handley-Ederville Rd., Fort Worth 76118

**Taylor** — Gary Earnest, PO Box 1800, Abilene 79604

**Terrell** — Blain Chriesman, PO Box 747, Sanderson 79848

**Terry** — Ronny Burran, PO Box 426, Brownfield 79316

**Throckmorton** — Gary Zeitler, Box 788, Throckmorton 76483

**Titus** — Geraldine Hull, PO Box 528, Mount Pleasant 75456

**Tom Green** — Bill Benson, PO Box 3307, San Angelo 76902

**Travis** — Marya Crigler, PO Box 149012, Austin 78714

**Trinity** — Greg Gallant, PO Box 950, Groveton 75845

**Tyler** — David Luther, PO Drawer 9, Woodville 75979

**Upshur** — Sarah Curtis, 105 Diamond Loch, Gilmer 75644

**Upton** — Sheri Stephens, PO Box 1110, McCamey 79752

**Uvalde** — Alberto M. Mireles, 209 N. High St., Uvalde 78801

**Val Verde** — Cherry Sheedy, 417 W. Cantu Rd., Del Rio 78842

**Van Zandt** — Scott Hyde, PO Box 926, Canton 75103

**Victoria** — John Haliburton, 2805 N. Navarro, Ste. 300, Victoria 77901

**Walker** — Raymond Kiser, PO Box 1798, Huntsville 77342

**Waller** — Chris Barzilla, PO Box 887, Hempstead 77445

**Ward** — Arlice Wittie, PO Box 905, Monahans 79756

**Washington** — Willy Dilworth, PO Box 681, Brenham 77834

**Webb** — Martin Villarreal, 3302 Clark Blvd., Laredo 78043

**Wharton** — Tylene Gamble, 308 E. Milam, Wharton 77488

**Wheeler** — Kimberly Morgan, PO Box 1200, Wheeler 79096

**Wichita** — Edward Trigg, PO Box 5172, Wichita Falls 76307

**Wilbarger** — Sandy Burkett, PO Box 1519, Vernon 76385

**Willacy** — Agustin Lopez, Rt. 2, Box 256, Raymondville 78580

**Williamson** — Alvin Lankford, 625 FM 1460, Georgetown 78626

**Wilson** — Jennifer Coldewey, 1611 Railroad St., Floresville 78114

**Winkler** — Connie Carpenter, PO Box 1219, Kermit 79745

**Wise** — Michael Hand, 400 E. Business 380, Decatur 76234

**Wood** — Tracy Nichols, PO Box 1706, Quitman 75783

**Yoakum** — JoAnn Dobson, PO Box 748, Plains 79355

**Young** — Luke Robbins, PO Box 337, Graham 76450

**Zapata** — Amada Gonzalez, PO Box 2315, Zapata 78076

**Zavala** — Yolanda Cervera, 323 W. Zavala, Crystal City 78839 ☆

# Texas County and District Officials – Table No. 1

**County Seats, County Judges, County Clerks, County Attorneys, County Treasurers, Tax Assessors-Collectors, and Sheriffs.**

*See Table No. 2 on pages following this table for District Clerks, District Attorneys, and County Commissioners. Judges in county courts at law, as well as probate courts, juvenile/domestic relations courts, county criminal courts, and county criminal courts of appeal, can be found beginning on page 525. The officials listed here are elected by popular vote. Officials listed in this table are from county clerks who returned our questionnaire or from most the recent Texas State Directory.*

| County | County Seat | County Judge | County Clerk | County Attorney | County Treasurer | Assessor-Collector | Sheriff |
|---|---|---|---|---|---|---|---|
| Anderson | Palestine | Robert D. Johnston | Mark C. Johnston | Tim Mason | Tara Holiday | Teri Garvey | Greg Taylor |
| Andrews | Andrews | Richard H. Dolgener | Kenda Heckler | Ed C. Jones | Office abolished 11-5-1985. | Robin Harper | Sam H. Jones |
| Angelina | Lufkin | Wes Suiter | Amy Fincher | Kristen Barnebey | Deborah D. Huffman | Thelma Sherman | Greg Sanches |
| Aransas | Rockport | C.H. (Burt) Mills Jr. | Valerie K. Amason | David A. Levy | Alma Tamburin Cartwright | Jeri D. Cox | William (Bill) Mills |
| Archer | Archer City | Randall C. Jackson | Karren Winter | | Patricia Vieth | Teresa K. Martin | Staci Williams Beesinger |
| Armstrong | Claude | Hugh Reed | Patricia Sherrill | Scott Sherwood | Sara Messer | Joe Reck | J.R. Walker |
| Atascosa | Jourdanton | Robert Hurley | Diane Gonzales | Lucinda A. Vickers | Laura Pawelek | Loretta Holley | David Soward |
| Austin | Bellville | Carolyn Bilski | Carrie Gregor | | Laura Kaye | Marcus A. Peña | Jack W. Brandes |
| Bailey | Muleshoe | Sherri Harrison | Robin Dickerson | Jackie Claborn | Shonda Black | Maria Gonzalez | Richard Wills |
| Bandera | Bandera | Richard A. Evans | Candy Wheeler | Janna I. Lindig | Billie J. Reeves | Gwenda Tschirhart | Daniel R. Butts |
| Bastrop | Bastrop | Paul Pape | Rose Pietsch | | Laurie Ingram | Linda Harmon | Terry Pickering |
| Baylor | Seymour | Rusty Stafford | Chris Jakubicek | Jennifer Habert Dick | Kevin Hostas | Jeanette Holub | Bob Elliott |
| Bee | Beeville | Stephanie Silvas | Mirella Escamilla Davis | Michael J. Knight | Office abolished 11-2-1982. | Linda G. Bridge | Carlos Carrizales Jr. |
| Bell | Belton | Jon H. Burrows | Shelley Coston | James E. Nichols | Charles Jones | Sharon Long | Eddy Lange |
| Bexar | San Antonio | Nelson W. Wolff | Gerald Rickhoff | Office abolished. | Office abolished 11-5-1985. | Albert Uresti | Susan L. Pamerleau |
| Blanco | Johnson City | Brett Bray | Laura Walla | David Allen Hall | Camille Swift | Hollis Boatright | Robert (Bob) Morgan |
| Borden | Gail | Ross Sharp | Jana Underwood | Marlo Holbrooks | Shawna Gass | Benny Allison | Benny Allison |
| Bosque | Meridian | Dewey Ratliff | Tabatha Ferguson | Natalie Cobb Koehler | Cheryl Niemeier | Arlene Swiney | Anthony Malott |
| Bowie | New Boston | James Carlow | Tina Petty | | Donna Burns | Treva Braley | James Prince |
| Brazoria | Angleton | E.J. (Joe) King | Joyce Hudman | | Sharon L. Reynolds | RoVin Garrett | Charles S. Wagner |
| Brazos | Bryan | Duane Peters | Karen McQueen | Rodney Anderson | Laura Taylor-Davis | Kristeen (Kristy) Roe | Christopher C. (Chris) Kirk |
| Brewster | Alpine | Val Clark Beard | Berta Rios-Martinez | Steve Houston | Carol Ofenstein | Betty Jo Rooney | Ronny D. Dodson |
| Briscoe | Silverton | Wayne Nance | Bena Hester | Emily Teegardin | Mary Jo Brannon | Jon Etta Ziegler | Garrett Davis |
| Brooks | Falfurrias | Raul M. Ramirez | Frutoso (Pepe) Garza | Homer Mora | Horacio Villarreal III | Rey Rodriguez | Rey Rodriguez |
| Brown | Brownwood | E. Ray West III | Sharon Ferguson | Shane Britton | Ann Krpoun | Christine Pentecost | Bobby Grubbs |
| Burleson | Caldwell | Mike Sutherland | Anna L. Schielack | Joseph J. Skrivanek III | Beth Andrews Bills | Curtis Doss | Alfred Dale Stroud |
| Burnet | Burnet | James Oakley | Janet F. Parker | Eduardo Arredondo | Karrie Crownover | Sherri Frazier | W.T. Smith |
| Caldwell | Lockhart | Ken Schawe | Carol Holcomb | Jordan Powell | Lori D. Rangel-Pompa | Darla Law | Daniel C. Law |
| Calhoun | Port Lavaca | Michael J. Pfeifer | Anna Goodman | | Rhonda Sikes Kokena | Gloria Ann Ochoa | George Aleman |
| Callahan | Baird | Roger Corn | Donna Bell | Shane Deel | Dianne Gunter | Tammy T. Walker | Terry Joy |
| Cameron | Brownsville | Carlos H. Cascos | Joe G. Rivera | | David A. Betancourt | Antonio Yzaguirre Jr. | Omar Lucio |
| Camp | Pittsburg | Thomas Cravey | Elaine Young | Angela L. Hammonds | Kim Pittman | Gale Burns | Alan D. McCandless |
| Carson | Panhandle | Lewis Powers | Celeste Bichsel | Scott Sherwood | Denise Salzbrenner | Jackie Moore | Tam Terry |
| Cass | Linden | Becky Wilbanks | Jamie A. O'Rand | | Donna Early | Becky Watson-Fant | Larry Rowe |
| Castro | Dimmitt | Carroll Gerber | JoAnna Blanco | Shalyn Hamlin | Kristen M. Yorton | Pamala Rickert | Salvadore (Sal) Rivera Jr. |
| Chambers | Anahuac | Jimmy Sylvia | Heather Hawthorne | Scott Peal | Nicole (Nikki) Whittington | Denise Hutter | Brian Hawthorne |

| County | County Seat | County Judge | County Clerk | County Attorney | County Treasurer | Assessor-Collector | Sheriff |
|---|---|---|---|---|---|---|---|
| Cherokee | Rusk | Chris Davis | Laverne Lusk | Dana Norris Young | Patsy J. Lassiter | Linda Little | James E. Campbell |
| Childress | Childress | Jay Mayden | Barbara Spitzer | Greg Buckley | Brenda Overstreet | Kathy Dobbs | Michael Pigg |
| Clay | Henrietta | Kenneth Liggett | Sasha Kelton | Seth Slagle | Debra Alexander | Linda Overstreet Sellers | K.R. (Kenny) Lemons Jr. |
| Cochran | Morton | Pat S. Henry | Shanna Dewbre | James Collier Adams Jr. | Doris Sealy | Treva Jackson | Raymond Daniel Weber |
| Coke | Robert Lee | Roy Blair | Mary Grim | Nancy Arthur | Hal Spain | Josie Dean | Wayne McCutchen |
| Coleman | Coleman | Billy Bledsoe | Stacey Mendoza | Joe L. Rose | Jerri Ann Chambers | Jamie Trammell | Robert Wade Turner |
| Collin | McKinney | Keith Self | Stacey Kemp | | Stacey Kemp | Kenneth L. Maun | Terry G. Box |
| Collingsworth | Wellington | John A. James | Jackie Johnson | G. Keith Davis | Gina Harris | Generah Manuel | Alan Kent Riley |
| Colorado | Columbus | Ty Prause | Kimberly Menke | Jay Johannes | Joyce Stancik | Mary Jane Poenitzsch | R.H. (Curly) Wied |
| Comal | New Braunfels | Sherman Krause | Joy Streater | | Renee Couch | Cathy Talcott | James R. (Bob) Holder |
| Comanche | Comanche | James R. (Bob) Arthur | Ruby Lesley | Craig Willingham | Sue Brown | Gay Horton Green | Jeff D. Lambert |
| Concho | Paint Rock | David Dillard | Phyllis F. Lovell | Bill Campbell | Shawn L. Walston | Chad Miller | Chad Miller |
| Cooke | Gainesville | John O. Roane | Rebecca Lawson | Edmund Zielinski | Patty Brennan | Billie Jean Knight | Terry Gilbert |
| Coryell | Gatesville | John E. Firth | Barbara Simpson | Brandon Belt | Donna Medford | Justin Carothers | Johnny Burks |
| Cottle | Paducah | Karl Holloway | Elissa Love Smith | John H. Richards | Crystal Tucker | Nakia Hargrave | Mark Box |
| Crane | Crane | John Farmer | Judy Crawford | Susan Loyless | Cristy Tarin | Judy Crumrine | Robert DeLeon |
| Crockett | Ozona | Fred Deaton | Debbi Puckett | Jody K. Upham | Karen Webb | Rhonda Shaw | Roy Glenn Sutton |
| Crosby | Crosbyton | David Wigley | Tammy Marshall | Michael Sales | Debra Riley | Anna R. Rodriguez | Ethan Villanueva |
| Culberson | Van Horn | Carlos G. Urias | Linda McDonald | Stephen L. Mitchell | Susana R. Hinojos | Amalia Y. Hernandez | Oscar E. Carrillo |
| Dallam | Dalhart | Wes Ritchey | Terri Banks | Jon King | Kenda McKay | Kay Howell | Bruce Scott |
| Dallas | Dallas | Clay Jenkins | John F. Warren | | Pauline Medrano | John R. Ames | Lupe Valdez |
| Dawson | Lamesa | Foy O'Brien | Gloria Vera | Steven B. Payson | Julie Frizzell | Sylvia Ortiz | Kent Parchman |
| Deaf Smith | Hereford | D.J. Wagner | Imelda DeLaCerda | Jim English | Karen Smith | Teresa Garth | J. Dale Butler |
| Delta | Cooper | Jason Murray | Jane Jones | Jay Garrett | Bonnie Hobbs | Dawn Stewart | Ricky Smith |
| Denton | Denton | Mary Horn | Juli Luke | | Cindy Yeatts Brown | Michelle French | William B. Travis |
| DeWitt | Cuero | Daryl L. Fowler | Natalie Carson | Raymond H. Reese | Carol Ann Martin | Susie Dreyer | Joe C. (Jode) Zavesky |
| Dickens | Dickens | Lesa Arnold | Winona Humphreys | Trey Poage | Sandy Vickrey | Sherry Hill | Jimmie Land |
| Dimmit | Carrizo Springs | Francisco G. Ponce | Mario Z. Garcia | Daniel M. Gonzalez | Estanislado Z. Martinez | Mary Ellen Sandoval | Marion M. Boyd |
| Donley | Clarendon | Jack Hall | Fay Vargas | Landon Lambert | Wanda Smith | Linda Crump | Charles (Butch) Blackburn |
| Duval | San Diego | Ricardo O. Carrillo | Elodia M. Garza | Baldemar F. Gutierrez | Sylvia Lazo | Carlos J. Montemayor Jr. | Romeo R. Ramirez |
| Eastland | Eastland | Rex Fields | Cathy Jentho | | Christina Dodrill | Sandra Cagle | Wayne Bradford |
| Ector | Odessa | Susan M. Redford | Linda Haney | Dusty Gallivan | Cleopatra Anderson | Barbara Horn | Mark Donaldson |
| Edwards | Rocksprings | Souli Asa Shanklin | Olga Lydia Reyes | Allen Ray Moody | Lupe Sifuentes-Enriquez | Mark Bean | Pamela Elliott |
| Ellis | Waxahachie | Carol Bush | Cindy Polley | Patrick Wilson | Cheryl Chambers | John Bridges | Johnny Brown |
| El Paso | El Paso | Veronica Escobar | Delia Briones | Jo Anne Bernal | Office abolished 1989. | Ruben P. Gonzalez | Richard D. Wiles |
| Erath | Stephenville | Tab Thompson | Gwinda Jones | Lisa Pence | Donna Kelly | Jennifer Carey | Tommy Bryant |
| Falls | Marlin | Jay T. Elliott | Linda Watkins | Jody Gilliam | Molly Downes | Diane Michalk | Ben Kirk |
| Fannin | Bonham | Creta L. Carter II | Tammy Biggar | Richard Glaser | David Woodson | Gail Young | Donnie Foster |
| Fayette | La Grange | Edward F. Janecka | Julie Karstedt | Peggy S. Supak | Office abolished 11-3-87. | Rosalinda Adamcik | Keith K. Korenek |
| Fisher | Roby | Ken Holt | Pat Thomson | Rudy V. Hamric | Kathy Davenport | Jonnye Lu Gibson | J.A. Robinson |
| Floyd | Floydada | Marty Lucke | Ginger Morgan | Lex S. Herrington | Lori Morales | Delia G. Suarez | Paul Raissez |
| Foard | Crowell | Mark Christopher | Debra Hopkins | Daryl Halencak | Darcy Moore | Mike Brown | Mike Brown |
| Fort Bend | Richmond | Robert E. Hebert | Laura Richard | Roy L. Cordes Jr. | Jeff Council | Patsy Schultz | Troy Nehls |
| Franklin | Mount Vernon | Scott Lee | Betty Crane | Gene Stump | Betty Sue Allen | Sue Ann Harper | Ricky Jones |

| County | County Seat | County Judge | County Clerk | County Attorney | County Treasurer | Assessor-Collector | Sheriff |
|---|---|---|---|---|---|---|---|
| Freestone | Fairfield | Linda K. Grant | Linda Jarvis | Chris Martin | Kay Barger | Lisa Foree | Thomas Don Anderson |
| Frio | Pearsall | Arnulfo C. Luna | Angie Tullis | Hector M. Lozano | Anna Luna Hernández | Anna Alaniz | Lionel G. Treviño |
| Gaines | Seminole | Tom N. Keyes | Vicki Phillips | Joe H. Nagy Jr. | Michael Lord | Susan Shaw | Ronny Pipkin |
| Galveston | Galveston | Mark Henry | Dwight D. Sullivan | Bob Boemer | Kevin C. Walsh | Cheryl E. Johnson | Henry Trochessett |
| Garza | Post | John Lee Norman | Jim Plummer | Ted Weems | LuAnne Terry | Nancy Wallace | Terry L. Morgan |
| Gillespie | Fredericksburg | Mark Stroeher | Mary Lynn Rusche | Chris Nevins | Laura Lundquist | Marissa Weinheimer | Buddy Mills |
| Glasscock | Garden City | Kim Halfmann | Rebecca Batla | Hardy L. Wilkerson | Alan J. Dierschke | Nancy Hillger | Keith Burnett |
| Goliad | Goliad | P.T. (Pat) Calhoun | Mary Ellen Flores | Rob Baiamonte | Daphne Buelter | Michelle D. Garcia | Kirby J. Brumby |
| Gonzales | Gonzales | David Bird | Lee Riedel | Paul Watkins | Sheryl Barborak | Crystal Cedillo | Glen A. Sachtleben |
| Gray | Pampa | Richard Peet | Susan Winborne | Joshua Seabourn | Scott Hahn | Gaye Whitehead | Don Copeland |
| Grayson | Sherman | Drue Bynum | Wilma Blackshear Bush | | Trent Bass | John W. Ramsey | J. Keith Gary |
| Gregg | Longview | Bill Stoudt | Connie J. Wade | | Office abolished 1-1-88. | William Kirk Shields | Maxey Cerliano |
| Grimes | Anderson | Ben Leman | David Pasket | Jon C. Fultz | Janice Trant | Connie Perry | Donald G. Sowell |
| Guadalupe | Seguin | Kyle Kutscher | Teresa Kiel | David Willborn | Linda Douglass | Tavie Murphy | Arnold S. Zwicke |
| Hale | Plainview | Bill A. Coleman | Latrice Kemp | James (Jim) Tirey | Ida A. Tyler | Roland Nash | David B. Mull |
| Hall | Memphis | Ray Powell | Raye Bailey | John M. Deaver II | Janet Bridges | Teresa Altman | Tom Heck |
| Hamilton | Hamilton | W. Mark Tynes | Debbie Rudolph | Mark C. Henkes | Shawna Sherry | Terry Payne Short | Gregg Bewley |
| Hansford | Spearman | Benny D. Wilson | Kim V. Vera | John L. Hutchison | Wanda Wagner | Linda Cummings | Tim Glass |
| Hardeman | Quanah | Ronald Ingram | Ellen London | Stanley R. Watson | Mary Ann Naylor | Darlene Gamble | Charles Mance Nelson |
| Hardin | Kountze | Wayne McDaniel | Glenda Alston | Rebecca R. Walton | Deborah McWilliams | Shirley Stephens | Ed J. Cain |
| Harris | Houston | Ed Emmett | Stan Stanart | Vince Ryan | Orlando Sanchez | Mike Sullivan | Ron Hickman |
| Harrison | Marshall | Hugh Taylor | Patsy Cox | | Jamie Noland | Veronica King | William T. (Tom) McCool |
| Hartley | Channing | Ronnie Gordon | Melissa Mead | Robert Elliott | Dinkie Parman | Franky Scott | Franky Scott |
| Haskell | Haskell | David C. Davis | Belia Abila | Kristen L. Fouts | Janis McDaniel | Connie Benton | Winston Stephens |
| Hays | San Marcos | Bert Cobb | Liz Q. Gonzalez | | Michele Tuttle | Luanne Caraway | Gary Cutler |
| Hemphill | Canadian | George Bryant | Lisa Johnson | Ty M. Sparks | Kay Smallwood | Debra L. Ford | James Pearson |
| Henderson | Athens | Richard Sanders | Mary Margaret Wright | Clint Davis | Michael Bynum | Peggy Goodall | Ray Nutt |
| Hidalgo | Edinburg | Ramon Garcia | Arturo Guajardo Jr. | | Norma G. Garcia | Pablo (Paul) Villarreal Jr. | J.E. (Eddie) Guerra |
| Hill | Hillsboro | Justin Lewis | Nicole Tanner | David Holmes | Rhonda Burkhart | Marchel Eubank | Wes Collins |
| Hockley | Levelland | Larry D. Sprowls | Irene Gumula | Anna Hord | Denise Bohannon | Debra (Debbie) Bramlett | R.C. Cheek |
| Hood | Granbury | Darrell Cockerham | Katie Lang | Lori Kaspar | Kathy Davis | Teresa McCoy | Roger Deeds |
| Hopkins | Sulphur Springs | Robert Newsom | Debbie Shirley | Dusty Hyde Rabe | Jim Thompson | Debbie Jenkins | Charles (Butch) Adams |
| Houston | Crockett | Erin Ford | Bridget Lamb | Daphne Session | Dina Herrera | Danette Millican | Darrel E. Bobbitt |
| Howard | Big Spring | Kathryn Wiseman | Donna Wright | Joshua Hamby | Teresa Thomas | Diane Carter | Stan Parker |
| Hudspeth | Sierra Blanca | Charles Michael Doyal | Virginia Doyal | C.R. (Kit) Bramblett | Jennifer Canaba | Kay Scarbrough | Arvin West |
| Hunt | Greenville | John Horn | Jennifer Lindenzweig | Joel Littlefield | Delores Shelton | Randy Wineinger | Randy Meeks |
| Hutchinson | Stinnett | Faye Blanks | Jan Barnes | Michael D. Milner | Kathy Sargent | Carrie Kimmell | Don Johnson |
| Irion | Mertzon | Tom Aiken | Molly Criner | Kenneth Greer Jr. | Carolyn Huelster | Joyce Gray | W.A. Estes |
| Jack | Jacksboro | Mitchell G. Davenport | Janice C. Robinson | Michael Brad Dixon | Kim Gibby | Sharon S. Robinson | Melvin F. Mayo Jr. |
| Jackson | Edna | Dennis Simons | Barbara Williams | | Mary Horton | Donna Atzenhoffer | A.J. (Andy) Louderback |
| Jasper | Jasper | Mark Allen | Debbie Newman | | Rene Kelley | Bobby Biscamp | Mitchell Newman |
| Jeff Davis | Fort Davis | Jeannette Duer | Jennifer Wright | Teresa Todd | Cecilia G. Davis | Rick McIvor | Rick McIvor |
| Jefferson | Beaumont | Jeff Branick | Carolyn L. Guidry | | Tim Funchess | J. Shane Howard | G. Mitch Woods |
| Jim Hogg | Hebbronville | Humberto Gonzalez | Zonia Garza Morales | Rodolfo V. Gutierrez | Gloria (Gigi) Benavides | Norma Liza S. Hinojosa | Erasmo (Kiko) Alarcon Jr. |

| County | County Seat | County Judge | County Clerk | County Attorney | County Treasurer | Assessor-Collector | Sheriff |
|---|---|---|---|---|---|---|---|
| Jim Wells | Alice | Pedro (Pete) Trevino Jr. | J.C. Perez III | Jesusa Sánchez-Vera | Becky Dominguez | Mary Lozano | Oscar Lopez |
| Johnson | Cleburne | Roger Harmon | Becky Ivey | Bill Moore | Debbie Rice | Scott Porter | Bob L. Alford |
| Jones | Anson | Dale Spurgin | LeeAnn Jennings | Chad Cowan | Amber Thompson | Mary Ann Lovelady | Larry Moore |
| Karnes | Karnes City | Barbara Najrar Shaw | Carol Swize | Robert L. Busselman | Vida Swierc Malone | Ann Franke | David A. Jalufka |
| Kaufman | Kaufman | James Bruce Wood | Laura Hughes | | Ronnie Oldfield | Tonya Ratcliff | David Byrnes |
| Kendall | Boerne | Darrel L. Lux | Darlene Herrin | Don Allee | Sheryl D'Spain | James A. Hudson Jr. | Al Auxier |
| Kenedy | Sarita | Louis E. Turcotte III | Veronica Vela | Allison Strauss | Cynthia M. Salinas | Eleuteria (Susie) Gonzalez | Ramon Salinas III |
| Kent | Jayton | Jim White | Craig Harrison | Bill Ballard | Linda McCurry | Brenda Long | William D. (Billy) Scogin |
| Kerr | Kerrville | Tom Pollard | Rebecca Bolin | Heather Stebbins | Tracy Soldan | Diane Bolin | Wm. R. (Rusty) Hierholzer |
| Kimble | Junction | Andrew S. Murr | Haydee Torres | Allen J. Ahlschwede | Jolene Williams | Hilario Cantu | Hilario Cantu |
| King | Guthrie | Duane Daniel | Jammye D. Timmons | Marshall Capps | Traci Butler | Sadie Spitzer | Gilbert Lee (Cotton) Elliott |
| Kinney | Brackettville | James Tully Shahan | Dora Elia Sandoval | Robert Adams | Diane Gutierrez | Martha Peña Padron | Leland K. Burgess |
| Kleberg | Kingsville | Rudy Madrid | Stephanie G. Garza | Kira Talip | Priscilla Alaniz Cantu | Melissa T. De La Garza | Edward M. (Ed) Mata Sr. |
| Knox | Benjamin | Travis Floyd | Lisa Cypert | Lina Trevino | Rosie Ake | Mitzi Welch | Dean W. Homstad |
| Lamar | Paris | Maurice C. Superville Jr. | Russ Towers | Gary Young | Shirley Fults | Haskell Maroney | Scott Cass |
| Lamb | Littlefield | James M. DeLoach | Tonya Ritchie | Scott A. Say | Jerry Yarbrough | Brenda Goheen | Gary Maddox |
| Lampasas | Lampasas | Wayne L. Boultinghouse | Connie Hartmann | Larry W. Allison | Nelda DeRiso | Linda Crawford | David Whitis |
| La Salle | Cotulla | Joel Rodriguez Jr. | Margarita A. Esqueda | Elizabeth Martinez | Thelma R. Treviño | Dora A. Gonzales | Miguel A. Rodriguez |
| Lavaca | Hallettsville | Tramer J. Woytek | Elizabeth A. Kouba | John Stuart Fryer | Karen Bludau | Deborah A. Sevcik | Micah C. Harmon |
| Lee | Giddings | Paul E. Fischer | Sharon Blasig | Martin Placke | Melinda (Lyndy) Krause | David Matthijetz | Rodney W. Meyer |
| Leon | Centerville | Byron Ryder | Christie Wakefield | James R. Witt Jr. | Brandi S. Hill | Brandi S. Hill | Kevin Ellis |
| Liberty | Liberty | Jay Knight | Paulette Shivers Williams | Wesley Hinch | Kim Harris | Richard L. Brown | Bobby Rader |
| Limestone | Groesbeck | Daniel Burkeen | Peggy Beck | William Roy DeFriend | Carol Pickens | Stacy Hall | Dennis D. Wilson |
| Lipscomb | Lipscomb | Willis V. Smith | Kim Blau | Matthew D. Bartosiewicz | Diana Schoenhals | (vacant) | James Robertson |
| Live Oak | George West | Jim Huff | Ida Vasquez | Gene Chapline | Nancy Coquat | Mari Gonzales | Larry R. Busby |
| Llano | Llano | Mary Cunningham | Marci Hadeler | Rebecca Lange | Teresa Kassell | Dexter Sagebiel | William (Bill) Blackburn |
| Loving | Mentone | Skeet Lee Jones | Mozelle Carr | Roddy Harrison | Domino Banwart | Chris H. Busse | Chris H. Busse |
| Lubbock | Lubbock | Thomas V. Head | Kelly J. Pinion | | Sharon Gossett | Ronnie Keister | Kelly Rowe |
| Lynn | Tahoka | Mike Braddock | Susan Tipton | Rebekah Filley | Amy Schuknecht | Donna Willis | Jerry D. Franklin |
| Madison | Madisonville | Arthur M. Henson | Charlotte Barrett | | Judy Weathers | Karen Lane | Travis Neeley |
| Marion | Jefferson | Lex Jones | Vickie Wray Smith | Angela Smoak | Terrie S. Neuville | Karen Jones | Morgan David McKnight |
| Martin | Stanton | Bryan Cox | Sharon Jones | James Napper | Cynthia O'Donnell | Kathy Hull | Brad Ingram |
| Mason | Mason | Jerry M. Bearden | Pam Beam | Shain V.H. Chapman | Polly McMillan | James (Buster) Nixon | James (Buster) Nixon |
| Matagorda | Bay City | Nate McDonald | Janet Hickl | Denise Fortenberry | Tammy McDonald | Cristyn Hallmark | Frank (Skipper) Osborne |
| Maverick | Eagle Pass | David R. Saucedo | Sara Montemayor | Ricardo Ramos | Manuel Reyes Jr. | Isamari Villarreal | Tom Schmerber |
| McCulloch | Brady | Danny Neal | Tina A. Smith | Mark Marshall | Steven Estes | Silvia B. Campos | John Stafford |
| McLennan | Waco | Scott Felton | J.A. (Andy) Harwell | | Bill Helton | Randy Riggs | Parnell McNamara |
| McMullen | Tilden | James E. Teal | Mattie Sadovsky | Kimberly Kreider Dusek | Judy Wyatt | Bessilia Guerrero | Emmitt Shelton |
| Medina | Hondo | Chris Schuchart | Lisa J. Wernette | Kim Havel | Debra Southwell | Melissa Lutz | Randy R. Brown |
| Menard | Menard | Richard Cordes | Ann Kothmann | Tom Roberson | Robert Bean | Tim Powell | Buck Miller |
| Midland | Midland | Michael R. Bradford | Alison Haley | Russell Malm | Mitzi Baker | Karen Hood | Gary Painter |
| Milam | Cameron | David Barkemeyer | Barbara Vansa | W.W. (Bill) Torrey | Donna Orsag | Kolette Morgan | David Greene |
| Mills | Goldthwaite | Kirkland A. Fulk | Carolyn Foster | Gerald Hale | Terrena Busby | Clint Hammonds | Clint Hammonds |
| Mitchell | Colorado City | Ray Mayo | Debby Carlock | Ty Wood | Jennifer Rivera | Sylvia Clanton | Patrick Toombs |

| County | County Seat | County Judge | County Clerk | County Attorney | County Treasurer | Assessor-Collector | Sheriff |
|---|---|---|---|---|---|---|---|
| Montague | Montague | Rick Lewis | Glenda Henson | Clay Riddle | Linda McGaughey | Sydney Nowell | Paul Cunningham |
| Montgomery | Conroe | Craig Doyal | Mark Turnbull | J.D. Lambright | Stephanie Davenport | Tammy J. McRae | Tommy Gage |
| Moore | Dumas | J.D. (Rowdy) Rhoades | Brenda McKanna | Scott Higginbotham | Pam Cox | Nikki McDonald | J.E. (Bo) DeArmond |
| Morris | Daingerfield | Lynda Munkres | Scott Sartain | J. Stephen Cowan | Nita Beth Traylor | Kim Thomasson | Jack. D. Martin |
| Motley | Matador | James B. (Jim) Meador | Jamie Martin | Tom Edwards | Misty Jones | Jo Elaine Hart | Chris O. Spence |
| Nacogdoches | Nacogdoches | Mike Perry | June Clifton | John Fleming | Denise Baublet | Kim Morton | Jason Bridges |
| Navarro | Corsicana | H.M. Davenport Jr. | Sherry Dowd | | Ryan Douglas | Russell P. Hudson | Elmer Tanner |
| Newton | Newton | Truman Dougharty | Sandra K. Duckworth | Lisa W. Peterson | Ginger Siau | Melissa J. Burks | Edward L. Shannon Jr. |
| Nolan | Sweetwater | Whitley May | Patricia (Pat) McGowan | | Jeanne Wells | Kathy Bowen | David Warren |
| Nueces | Corpus Christi | Samuel L. (Loyd) Neal | Diana T. Barrera | Laura Garza Jimenez | Office abolished 11-3-87. | Ramiro (Ronnie) Canales | Jim Kaelin |
| Ochiltree | Perryton | Earl J. McKinley | Stacey Brown | Barrett Dye | Janet Reynolds | Linda Womble | Terry L. Bouchard |
| Oldham | Vega | Don R. Allred | Darla Lookingbill | Kent Birdsong | Sherri Johnson | Linda Brown | David T. Medlin |
| Orange | Orange | Stephen Brint Carlton | Brandy Robertson | John D. Kimbrough | Christy Khoury | Lynda Gunstream | Keith Merritt |
| Palo Pinto | Palo Pinto | David C. Nicklas | Janette K. Green | Phil Garrett | Tanya Fallin | Linda G. Tuggle | Ira Mercer |
| Panola | Carthage | David L. Anderson | Clara Jones | | Gloria Portman | Margaret Dyer | Jack Ellett |
| Parker | Weatherford | Mark Riley | Jeane Brunson | John Forrest | Jenny Barnwell | Margorie King | Larry Fowler |
| Parmer | Farwell | Trey Ellis | Gerri Bowers | Jeff Actkinson | Altha Herington | Bobbie Pierson | Randy Geries |
| Pecos | Fort Stockton | Joe Shuster | Liz Chapman | Ori T. White | Barry McCallister | Santa Acosta | Cliff Harris |
| Polk | Livingston | Sydney Murphy | Schelana Hock | | Terri Williams | Leslie Jones Burks | Kenneth Hammack |
| Potter | Amarillo | Nancy Tanner | Julie Smith | C. Scott Brumley | Leann Renee Jennings | Sherri Aylor | Brian Thomas |
| Presidio | Marfa | Cinderla Guevara | Virginia Pallarez | John Fowlkes | Frances Garcia | Norma Arroyo | Danny C. Dominguez |
| Rains | Emory | Wayne Wolfe | Linda Wallace | Robert F. Vititow | Teresa Northcutt | Sheila Floyd | David Traylor |
| Randall | Canyon | Ernie Houdashell | Renee Calhoun | | Glenna Canada | Sharon Hollingsworth | Joel W. Richardson |
| Reagan | Big Lake | Larry Isom | Terri Curry | J. Russell Ash | Ginna Hruska | Cynthia Aguilar | Jeff N. Garner |
| Real | Leakey | Garry A. Merritt | Bella A. Rubio | Bobby Jack Rushing | Mairi Gray | Donna Brice | James Earl Brice |
| Red River | Clarksville | L.D. Williamson | Shawn Weemes | Val J. Varley | Sandra Embrey | Tonya R. Martin | Robert Bridges |
| Reeves | Pecos | Won Joo Bang | Dianne O. Florez | Alva E. Alvarez | Zulema Rodriguez | Rosemary Chabarria | Arthur (Art) Granado |
| Refugio | Refugio | Robert Blaschke | Ida Ramirez | Todd P. Steele | Rita Trojcak | Robin M. Burgess | Robert Bolcik |
| Roberts | Miami | Rick Tennant | Toni Rankin | William P. Weiman | Amy Tennant | DeAnn Williams | Dana Miller |
| Robertson | Franklin | Charles Ellison | Kathryn N. Brimhall | William Coty Siegert | Mindy Turner | Carol D. Bielamowicz | Gerald Yezak |
| Rockwall | Rockwall | David Sweet | Shelli Miller | | David Peek | Kim Sweet | Harold Eavenson |
| Runnels | Ballinger | Barry Hilliard | Julia Miller | Kenneth Slimp | Ann Strube | Lanita Whitehead | William A. Baird |
| Rusk | Henderson | Joel B. Hale | Trudy McGill | Michael E. Jimerson | Andy Vinson | Martha Stone | Jeff Price |
| Sabine | Hemphill | Daryl Melton | Janice McDaniel | Robert G. Neal Jr. | Tricia Woods Jacks | Regina A. Barthol | Thomas N. Maddox |
| San Augustine | San Augustine | Samye Johnson | Margo Noble | Wesley E. Hoyt | Pamela Smith | Kelly Selmer | David Smith |
| San Jacinto | Coldspring | John Lovett | Dawn Wright | | Amanda Washburn | Dalia Sanchez | Greg Capers |
| San Patricio | Sinton | Terry Simpson | Gracie Alaniz-Gonzales | David Aken | Courtenay Dugat | Stephen L. Boyd | Leroy Moody |
| San Saba | San Saba | Byron Theodosis | Kim Wells | Randall Robinson | Lois H. VanBeck | Jeanne Snelson | Stephen L. Boyd |
| Schleicher | Eldorado | Charlie Bradley | Mary Ann Gonzalez | Clint T. Griffin | Jennifer Henderson | | David R. Doran |
| Scurry | Snyder | Ricky Fritz | Melody Appleton | Michael W. Hartman | Nelda Colvin | Jana Young | Trey Wilson |
| Shackelford | Albany | Ross Montgomery | Cheri Hawkins | Colton P. Johnson | Tammy Brown | Edward Miller | Edward Miller |
| Shelby | Center | Allison Harbison | Jennifer Fountain | Gary W. Rholes | Ann Blackwell | Debora Riley | Willis Blackwell |
| Sherman | Stratford | Terri Beth Carter | Gina Gray | Kimberly Allen | Doris Parsons | Valerie McAlister | Joe Powell |
| Smith | Tyler | Joel Baker | Karen Phillips | | Kelli White | Gary Barber | Larry R. Smith |

| County | County Seat | County Judge | County Clerk | County Attorney | County Treasurer | Assessor-Collector | Sheriff |
|---|---|---|---|---|---|---|---|
| Somervell | Glen Rose | Danny L. Chambers | Michelle Reynolds | Andrew Lucas | Suzanne (Susie) Graves | Darlene Chambers | Greg Doyle |
| Starr | Rio Grande City | Eloy Vera | Dennis D. Gonzalez | Victor Canales | Fernando Pena | Rosalinda Guerra | Rene Fuentes |
| Stephens | Breckenridge | Gary L. Fuller | Jackie Ensey | Gary D. Trammel | Sharon Trigg | Christie Latham | George W. (Billy) Wade III |
| Sterling | Sterling City | Leslie Mackie | Jerri McCutchen | | Rhea McGinnis | Julie Thomason | Timothy A. Sanders |
| Stonewall | Aspermont | Ronnie Moorhead | Holly McLaury | Kollin Shadle | Anya Mullen | Jim B. Ward | William (Bill) M. Mullen |
| Sutton | Sonora | Carla Garner | Rachel Chavez Duran | David W. Wallace | Janalyn Jones | Erica Berry | Joe M. Fincher |
| Swisher | Tulia | Harold Keeter | C.J. Chasco | J. Michael Criswell | Tricia Speed | Deborah Lemons | Jim McCaslin |
| Tarrant | Fort Worth | B. Glen Whitley | Mary Louise Garcia | | Office abolished 4-2-83. | Ron Wright | Dee B. Anderson |
| Taylor | Abilene | Downing A. Bolls Jr. | Larry G. Bevill | | Lesa Hart Crosswhite | Janet Dukes | Ricky Bishop |
| Terrell | Sanderson | Santiago Flores | Martha Allen | Marsha Monroe | Ana Barron | Clint McDonald | Clint McDonald |
| Terry | Brownfield | J.D. Wagner | Kim Carter | Jo'Shae Ferguson-Worley | Karen Grigsby | Rexann Turrentine | Larry Gilbreath |
| Throckmorton | Throckmorton | Trey Carrington | Dianna Moore | Jeff Mathiews | Brenda Rankin | John V. Riley | John V. Riley |
| Titus | Mount Pleasant | Brian Lee | Joan Newman | John Mark Cobern | Sheryl Preddy | Judy Cook | Tim Ingram |
| Tom Green | San Angelo | Stephen C. Floyd | Elizabeth (Liz) McGill | Chris Taylor | Dianna Spieker | Becky Robles | David Jones |
| Travis | Austin | Samuel T. Biscoe | Dana DeBeauvoir | David Escamilla | Dolores Ortega-Carter | Bruce Elfant | Greg Hamilton |
| Trinity | Groveton | Doug Page | Shasta Bergman | Joe Warner Bell | Bob Dockens | Lindy Warren | Woody Wallace |
| Tyler | Woodville | Jacques L. Blanchette | Donece Gregory | | Sue Saunders | Lynette Cruse | Bryan Weatherford |
| Upshur | Gilmer | Dean Fowler | Terri Ross | | Brandy Vick | Sherron Laminack | Anthony Betterton |
| Upton | Rankin | Bill Eyler | LaWanda McMurray | Melanie Spratt-Anderson | Sharon Harper | Monica Zarate | Dan W. Brown |
| Uvalde | Uvalde | William R. Mitchell | Donna M. Williams | John P. Dodson | Joni Deorsam | Margarita (Maggie) Del Toro | Charles Mendeke |
| Val Verde | Del Rio | Laura Allen | Generosa Gracia-Ramon | Ana Markowski-Smith | Morris L. Taylor | Beatriz I. (Bea) Muñoz | Joe Frank Martinez |
| Van Zandt | Canton | Rhita Koches | Charlotte Bledsoe | | Teri Pruitt | Shirley Chisham | Michael (Lindsey) Ray |
| Victoria | Victoria | Ben Zeller | Heidi Easley | | Sean K. Kennedy | Rena Scherer | T. Michael O'Connor |
| Walker | Huntsville | R.D. (Danny) Pierce | Kari A. French | | Sharon Duke | Diana McRae | Clint McRae |
| Waller | Hempstead | Carbett (Trey) J. Duhon III | Debbie Hollan | | Joan Sargent | Ellen C. Shelburne | R. Glenn Smith |
| Ward | Monahans | Greg M. Holly | Natrell Cain | Hal Upchurch | Teresa Perry-Stoner | Vicki Heflin | Mikel Strickland |
| Washington | Brenham | John Brieden | Beth A. Rothermel | Renee Mueller | Peggy Kramer | Dot Borchgardt | Otto Hanak |
| Webb | Laredo | Tano E. Tijerina | Margie Ramirez Ibarra | Marco Montemayor | Delia Perales | Patricia Barrera | Martin Cuellar |
| Wharton | Wharton | Phillip S. Spenrath | Sandra K. Sanders | G.A. (Trey) Maffett III | Donna Thornton | Patrick L. Kubala | Jess Howell |
| Wheeler | Wheeler | Jerry Dan Hefley | Margaret Dorman | Leslie Standerfer | Renee Warren | Lewis Scott Porter | Wes Crites |
| Wichita | Wichita Falls | Woodrow (Woody) Gossom Jr. | Lori Bohannon | Meredith Kennedy | Robert J. (Bob) Hampton | Thomas (Tommy) Smyth | David Duke |
| Wilbarger | Vernon | Greg Tyra | Jana Kennon | Cory Curtis | Joann Carter | Chris Quisenberry | Larry Lee |
| Willacy | Raymondville | Aurelio (Keeter) Guerra Jr. | Terry Flores | Bernard Ammerman | Ruben Cavazos | Elizabeth Barnhart | Larry G. Spence |
| Williamson | Georgetown | Dan A. Gattis | Nancy E. Rister | Doyle E. Hobbs | Vivian Wood | Deborah Hunt | James R. Wilson |
| Wilson | Floresville | Richard L. Jackson | Eva S. Martinez | Daynah J. Fallwell | Jan Hartl | Olga M. Marrero | Joe D. Tackitt Jr. |
| Winkler | Kermit | Charles M. Wolf | Shethelia Reed | Thomas Duckworth Jr. | Eulonda Everest | Minerva Soltero | George Keely |
| Wise | Decatur | Bill McElhaney | Sherry Lemon | James Stainton | Katherine Hudson | Monte Shaw | David Walker |
| Wood | Quitman | Bryan Jeanes | Kelley Price | Jim Wheeler | Becky Burford | Carol Taylor | Jim Brown |
| Yoakum | Plains | Jim Barron | Deborah L. Rushing | Bill Helwig | Barbara Wright | Jan Parrish | Don Corzine |
| Young | Graham | John C. Bullock | Debra J. Taylor | Louis Dayne Miller | Ann Daily | Nancy Thomas | Bryan Walls |
| Zapata | Zapata | Joe Rathmell | Mary J. Villarreal-Bonoan | Said Alfonso Figueroa | Romeo Salinas | Luis Lauro Gonzalez | Sigifredo Gonzalez Jr. |
| Zavala | Crystal City | Joe Luna | Oralia G. Treviño | Eduardo Serna | Janie Z. Rodriguez | Cynthia M. Rivera | Eusevio E. Salinas Jr. |

# Texas County and District Officials — Table No. 2

## District Clerks, District Attorneys, and County Commissioners

*See Table No. 1 on preceding pages for County Seats, County Judges, County Clerks, County Attorneys, County Treasurers, Tax Assessors-Collectors, and Sheriffs. Judges in county courts at law, as well as probate courts, juvenile/domestic relations courts, county criminal courts, and county criminal courts of appeal, can be found beginning on page 525. Officials listed in this table are from county clerks who returned our questionnaire or from most the recent Texas State Directory. If more than one district attorney is listed for a county, the district court number is noted in parentheses after each attorney's name. If no district attorney is listed, the county attorney, whose name is listed in Table No. 1, assumes the duties of that office.*

| County | District Clerk | District Attorney | Comm. Precinct 1 | Comm. Precinct 2 | Comm. Precinct 3 | Comm. Precinct 4 |
|---|---|---|---|---|---|---|
| Anderson | Janice Staples | Allyson Mitchell | Greg Chapin | Rashad Q. Mims | Kenneth Dickson | Joey Hill |
| Andrews | Cynthia Jones | | Barney Fowler | Brad Young | Jeneane Anderegg | Jim Waldrop |
| Angelina | Reba Squyres | Art Bauereiss | Greg Harrison | Kenneth Timmons | Robert Louis Loggins | Bobby Cheshire |
| Aransas | Pam Heard | Michael Welborn | Jack Chaney | L.E. (Bubba) Casterline Jr. | Charles Smith | Betty Stiles |
| Archer | Lori Rutledge | Paige Williams | Richard Shelley | Darin Wolf | Pat Martin III | Darryl Lightfoot |
| Armstrong | Patricia Sherrill | Randall C. Sims | John Britten | Parker Stewart | Tom Ferris | Bruce Ferguson |
| Atascosa | Margaret Littleton | Rene Peña | Lonnie (Lon) Gillespie | William (Bill) Torans | Freddie Ogden | Bill Carroll |
| Austin | Sue Murphy | Travis J. Koehn | Reese Turner | Robert Wayne (Bobby) Rinn | Randy Reichardt | Douglas King |
| Bailey | Elaine Parker | Kathryn Gurley | Floyd J. (Butch) Vandiver | Mike Slayden | Joey Kindle | Juan Chavez |
| Bandera | Tammy Kneuper | E. Bruce Curry | Robert H. Grimes | Robert A. Harris | Andy L. Wilkerson Sr. | Jordan Rutherford |
| Bastrop | Sarah Loucks | Bryan Goertz | William M. Piña | Clara Beckett | John Klaus | Gary (Bubba) Snowden |
| Baylor | Chris Jakubicek | David Hajek | Rick Gillispie | John Edd Nelson | Don Emsoff | Larry Burnett |
| Bee | Zenaida Silva | Jose Luis Aliseda Jr. | Carlos Salazar Jr. | Dennis DeWitt | Eloy Rodriguez | Ken Haggard |
| Bell | Joanna Staton | Henry L. Garza | Richard Cortese | Tim Brown | Bill Schumann | John Fisher |
| Bexar | Donna Kay McKinney | Nicholas LaHood | Sergio (Chico) Rodriguez | Paul Elizondo | Kevin A. Wolff | Tommy Calvert |
| Blanco | Debby Elsbury | Wiley (Sonny) McAfee | John F. Wood | James Sultemeier | Chris Liesmann | Paul Granberg |
| Borden | Jana Underwood | Ben smith | Monte Smith | Randy L. Adcock | Ernest Reyes | Joe T. Belew |
| Bosque | Juanita Miller | B.J. Shepherd | Doug Day | Durwood Koonsman | Sammy Leach | Ronny Liardon |
| Bowie | Billy Fox | Jerry Rochelle | Sammy Stone | Tom Whitten | Kelly Blackburn | Mike Carter |
| Brazoria | Rhonda Barchak | Jeri Yenne | Donald W. (Dude) Payne | L.M. (Matt) Sebesta | Stacy L. Adams | L.L. (Larry) Stanley |
| Brazos | Marc Hamlin | Jarvis Parsons | Lloyd Wassermann | Sammy Catalena | G. Kenny Mallard Jr. | Irma Cauley |
| Brewster | JoAnn Salgado | Jesse Gonzales Jr. | Asa (Cookie) Stone | Kathy Killingsworth | Ruben Ortega | Matilde Pallanez |
| Briscoe | Bena Hester | Becky B. McPherson | Jimmy Burson | Wade Proctor | Dewey Estes | John Burson |
| Brooks | Noe Guerra | Armando Berrera | Gloria Garza | Luis Arevalo | Carlos Villarreal | Jose A. (Tony) Martinez |
| Brown | Cheryl Jones | Michael B. Murray | Gary Worley | Joel Kelton | Wayne Shaw | Larry Traweek |
| Burleson | Joy Brymer | Julie Renken | Dwayne Beran | Keith Schroeder | David Hildebrand | John B. Landolt Jr. |
| Burnet | Casie Walker | Wiley B. (Sonny) McAfee | Bill Neve | Russell Graeter | Ronny Hibler | Joe Don Dockery |
| Caldwell | Tina Morgan | Fred Weber | Alfredo Munoz | Eddie Moses | Neto Madrigal | Joe Ivan Roland |
| Calhoun | Pamela Martin Hartgrove | Dan W. Heard | Roger C. Galvan | Vernon Lyssy | Neil E. Fritsch | Kenneth W. Finster |
| Callahan | Amber Tinsley | | Harold Hicks | Bryan Farmer | Tom Windham | Cliff Kirkham |
| Cameron | Aurora De La Garza | Armando Villalobos | Sofia C. Benavides | Ernie Hernandez | David A. Garza | Dan Sanchez |
| Camp | Teresa Bockmon | Charles C. Bailey | Bart Townsend | Steven D. Hudnall | L.H. Henderson | Steve Lindley |
| Carson | Celeste Bichsel | Luke Inman | Mike Britten | James Martin | Paul Dethen | Kevin Howell |
| Cass | Jamie Albertson | Randal Lee | Brett Fitts | Jon Borseth | Paul Cothren | Darrell Godwin |
| Castro | JoAnna Blanco | Shalyn Hamlin | Tom McLain | Tim Elliott | Steve Smith | Ralph Brockman |

| County | District Clerk | District Attorney | Comm. Precinct 1 | Comm. Precinct 2 | Comm. Precinct 3 | Comm. Precinct 4 |
|---|---|---|---|---|---|---|
| Chambers | Patti L. Henry | Cheryl S. Lieck | Mark Huddleston | Larry George | Gary R. Nelson | Rusty Senac |
| Cherokee | Janet Gates | Rachel Patton | Kelly Traylor | Steven Norton | Katherine Pinotti | Byron Underwood |
| Childress | Barbara Spitzer | Luke Inman | Richard Decker | Mark Ross | Lyall Foster | Richard Elliott |
| Clay | Dan Slagle | Jack McGaughey | R.L. (Lindy) Choate | Johnny Gee | John McGregor | A.J. Peek |
| Cochran | Shanna Dewbre | Christopher Dennis | Donnie B. Simpson | Bruce Heflin | Stacey Dunn | Reynaldo Morin |
| Coke | Mary Grim | Allison Palmer | Troy Gene Montgomery | Paul Williams | Gaylon L. Pitcock | Joe Sefcik |
| Coleman | Margie Mayo | Heath Hemphill | Mark Williams | Rick Beal | Mike Stephenson | Alan Davis |
| Collin | Andrea Stroh Thompson | Greg Willis | Susan Fletcher | Cheryl Williams | Chris Hill | Duncan Webb |
| Collingsworth | Jackie Johnson | Luke Inman | Elmer Keller | Mike Hughs | Eddie Orr | Kirby Campbell |
| Colorado | Linda Holman | Jay Johannes | Doug Wessels | Darrell Kubesch | Tommy Hahn | Darrell Gertson |
| Comal | Katherine H. Faulkner | Jennifer Anne Tharp | Donna Eccleston | Scott Haag | Gregory Parker | Jan Kennady |
| Comanche | Brenda Dickey | B.J. Shepard | Gary D. (Corky) Underwood | Russell Gillette | Sherman Sides | Jimmy Dale Johnson |
| Concho | Phyllis F. Lovell | George E. McCrea | Trey Bradshaw | Ralph Willberg | Gary Gierisch | Aaron (Sonny) Browning Jr. |
| Cooke | Susan Hughes | Janice Warder | Gary Hollowell | B.C. Lemons | Alan Smith | Leon Klement |
| Coryell | Janice M. Gray | Dusty Boyd | Jack Wall | Daren Moore | Don Jones | Wyllis Ament |
| Cottle | Elissa Love Smith | David W. Hajek | Jimmy W. Sweeney | Vance Thompson | Manuel Cruz Jr. | Marvin Powe |
| Crane | Judy Crawford | Dorothy Holguin | Tom Brown | Dennis Young | Domingo Escobedo | Ruby Martinez |
| Crockett | Ninfa Preddy | Laurie K. English | Frank Tambunga | Pleas Childress III | Randy Branch | Eligio Martinez |
| Crosby | Shari Smith | Michael Sales | Gary Jordan | Frank Mullins | Larry Wampler | James Caddell |
| Culberson | Linda McDonald | Jaime Esparza | Cornelio Garibay | Raul Rodriguez | Gilda Morales | Adrian Norman |
| Dallam | Terri Banks | David M. Green | Carl McCarty | Corey Crabtree | Don J. Bowers | Floyd French |
| Dallas | Felicia Pitre | Susan Hawk | Theresa Daniel | Mike Cantrell | John Wiley Price | Elba Garcia |
| Dawson | Pam Huse | Michael Munk | Ricky Minjarez | Joe Raines | Nicky Goode | Russell Cox |
| Deaf Smith | Elaine Gerber | Jim English | Pat Smith | Jerry O'Connor | Mike Brumley | Dale Artho |
| Delta | Jane Jones | Will Ramsay | B.V. (Rip) Templeton | Gary C. Anderson | Loyd Vandygriff | Mark Brantley |
| Denton | Sherri Adelstein | Paul Johnson | Hugh Coleman | Ron Marchant | Bobbie J. Mitchell | Andrew (Andy) Eads |
| DeWitt | Tabeth Gardner | Michael A. Sheppard | Curtis G. Afflerbach | James B. Plichiek Sr. | James Kaiser | Richard Randle |
| Dickens | Winona Humphreys | Becky B. McPherson | Wayne Smith | Ricky West | Doc Edwards | Sheldon Parsons |
| Dimmit | Maricela G. Gonzalez | Roberto Serna | Mike Uriegas | Alonso G. Carmona | Juan R. Carmona | Valerie Rubulcaba |
| Donley | Fay Vargas | Luke Inman | Mark White | Don Hall | Andy Wheatly | Dan Sawyer |
| Duval | Richard M. Barton | Omar Escobar | Alejo C. Garcia | Rene M. Perez | DAvid Orlando Garza | Gilberto Uribe Jr. |
| Eastland | Tessa K. Culverhouse | Russell D. Thomason | Cindy Maxwell | John (Buzzy) Rutledge | Ronnie Wilson | Robert Rains |
| Ector | Clarissa Webster | Robert Newton Bland IV | Eddy Shelton | Greg Simmons | Dale Childers | Armando S. Rodriguez |
| Edwards | Olga Lydia Reyes | Scott Monroe | William Epperson | Lee Sweeten | Matt Fry | Mike Grooms |
| Ellis | Melanie P. Reed | Patrick Wilson | Dennis Robinson | Bill Dodson | Paul Perry | Ron Brown |
| El Paso | Norma L. Favela | Jaime E. Esparza | Carlos Leon | David Stout | Vincent Perez | Andrew Haggerty |
| Erath | Wanda Pringle | Jason Cashon | Dee Stephens | Herbert Brown | Joe Brown | Scot Jackson |
| Falls | Christi Wideman | Kathryn (Jodi) Gilliam-Morris | Milton Albright | F.A. Green | Nelson Coker | Nita Wuebker |
| Fannin | Nancy Young | Richard Glaser | Gary Whitlock | Stanley Barker | Gary Whitlock | Dean Lackey |
| Fayette | Virginia Wied | Peggy S. Supak | Jason B. McBroom | Gary Weishuhn | Harvey Berckenhoff | Tom Muras |
| Fisher | Tammy Haley | Ann Reed | Gordon Pippin | Billy Henderson | Preston Martin | Scott Feagan |
| Floyd | Patty Davenport | Becky B. McPherson | Mike Anderson | Lindan Morris | Nathan Johnson | Amado Morales |
| Foard | Debra Hopkins | Staley Heatly | Rick Hammonds | Rockne Wisdom | Larry Wright | Anthony Hinsley |
| Fort Bend | Annie Rebecca Elliott | John Healey Jr. | Richard Morrison | Grady Prestage | W.A. (Andy) Meyers | James Patterson |

| County | District Clerk | District Attorney | Comm. Precinct 1 | Comm. Precinct 2 | Comm. Precinct 3 | Comm. Precinct 4 |
|---|---|---|---|---|---|---|
| Franklin | Ellen Jaggers | Will Ramsay | Danny Chitsey | Larkin Jumper | Deryl Carr | Sam Young |
| Freestone | Teresa Black | Chris Martin | Luke Ward | Craig Oakes | Bodie Emmons | Clyde E. Ridge Jr. |
| Frio | Ramona B. Rodriguez | Rene M. Peña | Jesus G. Salinas | Richard Graf | Ruben Maldonado | Jose (Pepe) Flores |
| Gaines | Sharon Taylor | Michael Munk | Danny Yocom | Craig Belt | Blair Tharp | Biz Houston |
| Galveston | John Kinard | Jack Roady | Ryan Dennard | Kevin O'Brien | Stephen W. Holmes | Kenneth F. Clark |
| Garza | Jim Plummer | Michael Munk | Gary McDaniel | Charles Morris | Ted Brannon | Jerry Benham |
| Gillespie | Jan Davis | E. Bruce Curry | Curtis Cameron | William A. Roeder | Calvin Ransleben | Donnie Schuch |
| Glasscock | Rebecca Batla | Hardy L. Wilkerson | Jimmy Strube | Mark L. Halfmann | Gary Jones | Michael Hoch |
| Goliad | Mary Ellen Flores | Michael A. Sheppard | Julian Flores | Alonzo Morales | Ronald W. Bailey | David Bruns |
| Gonzales | Janice Sutton | Franklin McDonough | Kenneth O. (Dell) Whiddon | Donnie R. Brzozowski | Kevin T. La Fleur | Otis S. (Bud) Wuest |
| Gray | Jo Mays | Franklin McDonough | Joe Wheeley | Gary Willoughby | Neil Fulton | Jeff Haley |
| Grayson | Kelly Ashmore | Joseph D. Brown | Johnny Waldrip | David Whitlock | Jackie Crisp | Bart Lawrence |
| Gregg | Barbara Duncan | Carl Dorrough | Charles W. Davis | R. Darryl Primo | Gary W. Boyd | John Mathis |
| Grimes | Gay Wells | Tuck Moody McLain | vacant | David Dobyanski | Barbara Henley Walker | Gary Hunsfeld |
| Guadalupe | Debra Crow | Heather McMinn | Greg Seidenberger | Jack Shanafelt | Jim O. Wolverton | Judy Cope |
| Hale | Carla Cannon | Wally Hatch | Harold King | Mario Martinez | Kenny Kernell | Benny Cantwell |
| Hall | Raye Bailey | Luke Inman | Winfred McQueen | Terry Lindsey | Gary Proffitt | James Fuston |
| Hamilton | Leoma Larance | B.J. Shepherd | Johnny Wagner | Keith Allen Curry | Lloyd Huggins | Dickie Clary |
| Hansford | Kim V. Vera | Mark Snider | Ira G. (Butch) Reed | David Thomas | Tim Stedje | Danny Henson |
| Hardeman | Ellen London | Staley Heatly | Christopher Call | Rodger Tabor | Barry Haynes | Rodney Foster |
| Hardin | Dana Hogg | David Sheffield | L.W. Cooper Jr. | Chris Kirkendall | Ken Pelt | Alvin Roberts |
| Harris | Chris Daniel | Devon Anderson | El Franco Lee | Jack Morman | Steve Radack | R. Jack Cagle |
| Harrison | Sherry Griffis | Coke Solomon | William Hatfield | Zephaniah Timmins | James Greer | Jay Ebarb |
| Hartley | Melissa Mead | David M. Green | David Vincent | David Ford | Chad Hicks | Robert (Butch) Owens |
| Haskell | Penny Anderson | Michael E. Fouts | Billy Wayne Hester | Tiffen Mayfield | Kenny Thompson | Neal Kreger |
| Hays | Beverly Crumley | Wes Mau | Debbie Gonzales Ingalsbe | Mark Jones | Will Conley | Ray Whisenant |
| Hemphill | Lisa Johnson | Franklin McDonough | Coleman Bartlett | Ed Culver | Mark Meek | Nicholas Thomas |
| Henderson | Betty Herriage | Scott McKee | Scotty Thomas | Wade McKinney | Ronny Lawrence | Ken Geeslin |
| Hidalgo | Laura L. Hinojosa | Ricardo Rodriguez | A.C. Cuellar Jr. | Eduardo (Eddie) Cantu | Joe M. Flores | Joseph Palacios |
| Hill | Angelia Orr | Mark Pratt | Danny Bodeker | Larry Crumpton | Larry Wright | Harley Davis |
| Hockley | Dennis Price | Christopher E. Dennis | Curtis D. Thrash | Larry R. Carter | J.L. (Whitey) Barnett | Thomas R. Clevenger |
| Hood | Tonna Hitt | Robert Christian | James Deaver | Butch Barton | Jeff Tout | Steve Berry |
| Hopkins | Cheryl Fulcher | Will Ramsay | Beth B. Wisenbaker | Mike Odell | Wade Bartley | Danny Evans |
| Houston | Carolyn Rains | Donna Gordon Kaspar | Roger Dickey | Willie Kitchen | Pat Perry | Kennon Kellum |
| Howard | Colleen Barton | Hardy L. Wilkerson | Oscar Garcia | Craig Bailey | Jimmie Long | John Cline |
| Hudspeth | Virginia Doyal | Jaime Esparza | Wayne West | Manuel Galindo | Jim Ed Miller | Larry Brewton |
| Hunt | Stacey Landrum | Noble Walker | Eric Evans | Tod McMahan | Phillip Martin | Jim Latham |
| Hutchinson | Robin Stroud | Mark Snider | Larry Coffman | Jerry D. Hefner | S.T. (Red) Isbell Jr. | Eddie Whittington |
| Irion | Molly Criner | Allison Palmer | Tia Paxton | Jeff Davidson | John Nanny | Bill (Beaver) McManus |
| Jack | Tracie J. Pippin | Greg Lowery | Keith Umphress | James L. Brock | James L. Cozart | Terry D. Ward |
| Jackson | Sharon Mathis | Robert E. (Bobby) Bell | Wayne Hunt | Wayne Bubela | Johnny E. Belicek | Dennis Karl |
| Jasper | Kathy Kent | Steve Hollis | Charles Shofner Jr. | Roy Parker | Willie Stark | Vance Moss |
| Jeff Davis | Jennifer Wright | Rod Ponton | Larry Francell | Kerith Sproul | Curtis Evans | Albert Miller |
| Jefferson | Lolita Ramos | Tom Maness | Eddie Arnold | Brent Weaver | Michael (Shane) Sinegal | Everette (Bo) Alfred |

| County | District Clerk | District Attorney | Comm. Precinct 1 | Comm. Precinct 2 | Comm. Precinct 3 | Comm. Precinct 4 |
|---|---|---|---|---|---|---|
| Jim Hogg | Zonia G. Morales | Omar Escobar | Linda Jo G. Soliz | Abelardo (Valo) Alaniz | Sandalio (Sandy) Ruiz | Cynthia Guerra Betancourt |
| Jim Wells | R. David Guerrero | Carlos Omar Garcia | Margie H. Gonzalez | Ventura Garcia Jr. | Richard Miller | Emede Garcia |
| Johnson | David Lloyd | Dale Hanna | Rick Bailey | Kenny Howell | Jerry D. Stringer | Larry Woolley |
| Jones | Lacey Hansen | Joe Edd Boaz | James Clawson | Mike Polk | Ross Davis | Greg Pinkston |
| Karnes | Robbie Shortner | Stella Saxon | Carl Hummel | Pete Jauer | James Rosales | Tracey Schendel |
| Kaufman | Rhonda Hughey | Erleigh Norville Wiley | Jimmy Joe Vrzalik | Skeet Phillips | Kenneth Schoen | Jakie Allen |
| Kendall | Susan Jackson | E. Bruce Curry | Mike Fincke | Richard Elkins | Tommy Pfeiffer | Royce Steubing |
| Kenedy | Veronica Vela | John T. Hubert | Joe L. Recio | Roberto Salazar Jr. | Sarita Armstrong-Hixon | Gumecinda Gonzales |
| Kent | Craig Harrison | Michael E. Fouts | Roy W. Chisum | Don Long | Harold Parker | Robert Graham |
| Kerr | Robbin Burlew | Scott Monroe (198th) E. Bruce Curry (216th) | H.A. (Buster) Baldwin | Tom Moser | Jonathan A. Letz | Bob Reeves |
| Kimble | Haydee Torres | Tonya Ahlschwede | Billy Braswell | Charles McGuire | Wylie Taff | Chad Gipson |
| King | Jammye D. Timmons | David W. Hajek | Reggie J. Hatfield | Larry Rush | Bobby J. Tidmore | Jay Hurt |
| Kinney | Dora Elia Sandoval | Fred Hernandez | Mark Frerich | Joe Montalvo | Dennis Dodson | Pat Melancon |
| Kleberg | Jennifer Whittington | John T. Hubert | David Rosse | Joe Hinojosa | Roy Cantu | Romeo L. Lomas |
| Knox | Lisa Cypert | David W. Hajek | Johnny McCowan | Dan Godsey | Jimmy Urbanczyk | Nathan Urbanczyk |
| Lamar | Shawntel Golden | Scott A. Say | Lawrence Malone | Lonnie Layton | Rodney Pollard | Keith Mitchell |
| Lamb | Stephanie Chester | Scott A. Say | Cory DeBerry | Kent Lewis | Danny Short | Jimmy Young |
| Lampasas | Terri Cox | Larry W. Allison | Robert L. Vincent Jr. | Alex Wittenburg | Lowell B. Ivey | Jack B. Cox |
| La Salle | Margarita A. Esqueda | René M. Peña | Abel B. Gonzalez | Ricardo Garza | Rene Benavidez | Raul Ayala |
| Lavaca | Sherry T. Henke | Heather McMinn | Edward Pustka | Ronald Berkenhoff | Richard W. Brown | Dennis W. Kocian |
| Lee | Lisa Teinert | Martin Placke | Maurice Pitts Jr. | Charles Murray | Alan Turner | Steven Knobloch |
| Leon | Beverly Wilson | Hope L. Knight | Joey Sullivan | David Ferguson | Dean Stanford | David Grimes |
| Liberty | Donna G. Brown | Logan Pickett | Mike McCarty | Greg Arthur | Eddie Lowery | Leon Wilson |
| Limestone | Carol Sue Jenkins | William Roy DeFriend | John McCarver | W.A. (Sonny) Baker | Jerry Allen | Bobby Forrest |
| Lipscomb | Kim Blau | Franklin McDonough | Juan Cantu | Merle Miller | Scotty Schilling | Johnie Steele |
| Live Oak | Melanie Matkin | José Aliseda | Richard Lee | Donna Kopplin Mills | Willie James | Emilio Garza |
| Llano | Joyce Gillow | Wylie B. McAfee | Peter Jones | Linda Raschke | Ron Wilson | Jerry Don Moss |
| Loving | Mozelle Carr | Randall W. Reynolds | Harlan Hopper | Ysidro Renteria | Thomas Elgin Jones | William (Bill) Wilkinson |
| Lubbock | Barbara Sucsy | Matthew D. Powell | Bill McCay | Mark E. Heinrich | Gilbert Flores | Patti Jones |
| Lynn | Sandra Laws | Michael Munk | Keith Wied | John Hawthorne | Don Blair | Larry Durham |
| Madison | Joyce Batson | Brian Risinger | Ricky Driskell | Phillip Grisham | Carl Cannon | Sam Cole |
| Marion | Susan Anderson | Angela Smoak | John Ross (J.R.) Ashley | Joe McKnight | Glenn Dorough | C.W. (Charlie) Treadwell |
| Martin | Sharon Jones | Hardy L. Wilkerson | Kenny Stewart | Robin Barnes | Bobby Holland | Koy Blocker |
| Mason | Pam Beam | Tonya Spaeth Ahlschwede | Wayne Hofmann | Will Frey | Stanley Toeppich | Stephen Mutschink |
| Matagorda | Jamie Bludau | Steven E. Reis | Daniel Pustka | Kent Pollard | James Gibson | Charles R. (Bubba) Frick |
| Maverick | Leopoldo Vielma | Roberto Serna | Gerardo Morales | Rosy Cantu | Jose Luis Rosales | Roberto Ruiz |
| McCulloch | Michelle Pitcox | Robert (Bob) Hofmann | Jim Quinn | Gene Edmiston | Jim Ross | Brent C. Deeds |
| McLennan | Jon Gimble | Abel Reyna | Kelly Snell | Lester Gibson | Will Jones | Ben Perry |
| McMullen | Mattie Sadovsky | Jose Aliseda | Larry Garcia | Murray Swaim | Scotty McClaugherty | Maximo G. Quintanilla Jr. |
| Medina | Cindy Fowler | Daniel J. Kindred | Richard C. Saathoff | Larry Sittre | David Lynch | Jerry Beck |
| Menard | Ann Kothmann | Tonya Ahlschwede | Boyd Murchison | Jay Cunningham | Ed Keith | Larry Burch |
| Midland | Ross Bush | Teresa Clingman | Jimmy Smith | Robert R. (Robin) Donnelly | Luis D. Sanchez | Randy Prude |
| Milam | Karen Berry | W.W. (Bill) Torrey | Richard (Opey) Watkins | Donald Shuffield | John Fisher | Jeff Muegge |
| Mills | Carolyn Foster | Michael B. Murray | Mike Wright | Jed Garren | Robert Hall | Jason Williams |

| County | District Clerk | District Attorney | Comm. Precinct 1 | Comm. Precinct 2 | Comm. Precinct 3 | Comm. Precinct 4 |
|---|---|---|---|---|---|---|
| Mitchell | Belinda Blassingame | Ann Reed | Randy Anderson | Jeremy Strain | Jesse Munoz | Billy H. Preston |
| Montague | Lesia Darden | Jack McGaughey | Herman Conway | Mike Mayfield | Mark Murphey | Bob Langford |
| Montgomery | Barbara Gladden Adamick | Brett W. Ligon | Mike Meador | Charlie Riley | James Noack | Jim Clark |
| Moore | Diane Hoefling | David M. Green | J. Daniel Garcia | Len Sheets | Milton Pax | Lynn Cartrite |
| Morris | Gwen Oney | J. Stephen Cowan | Dennis Allen | Weldon Lilley | Michael Clair | Todd Freeman |
| Motley | Jamie Martin | Becky B. McPherson | Guy Campbell | Donnie L. Turner | Franklin Jameson | David Stafford |
| Nacogdoches | Loretta Cammack | Nicole Lostracco | Jerry Don Williamson | Jerry Stone | Jim Elder | Elton Milstead Jr. |
| Navarro | Josh Tackett | R. Lowell Thompson | Jason Grant | Dick Martin | David (Butch) Warren | James Olsen |
| Newton | Bree Allen | Courtney Ponthier | William L. (Bill) Fuller | Thomas Gill | Prentiss L. Hopson | Leonard Powell |
| Nolan | Jamie Clem | Ann Reed | Terry Willman | Doug Alexander | Tommy White | Tony Lara |
| Nueces | Patsy Perez | Mark Skurka | Mike Pusley | Joe A. Gonzalez | Oscar O. Ortiz | Joe McComb |
| Ochiltree | Shawn Bogard | Barrett Dye | Duane Pshigoda | David Peckenpaugh | Richard Burger | Dempsey Malaney |
| Oldham | Darla Lookingbill | | Quincy Taylor | Larry Groneman | Roger Morris III | Billy Don Brown |
| Orange | Vickie Edgerly | John D. Kimbrough | David Dubose | Barry Burton | John Banken | Jody Crump |
| Palo Pinto | Janie Glover | Michael K. Burns | Curtis Henderson | Louis Ragle | Mike Pierce | Jeff Fryer |
| Panola | Debra Johnson | Danny Buck Davidson | Ronnie LaGrone | John Gradberg | Hermon E. Reed Jr. | Dale LaGrone |
| Parker | Sharena Gilliland | Don Schnebly | George Conley | Craig Peacock | Larry Walden | Steve Dugan |
| Parmer | Sandra Warren | Gordon Green | Kirk Frye | Steve Cockerham | Kenny White | Lloyd Bradshaw |
| Pecos | Gayle Henderson | Rod Ponton (83rd) / Laurie English (112th) | George Riggs | Lupe Dominguez | J.H. (Jay) Kent | Santiago Cantu Jr. |
| Polk | Bobbye Richards | William (Lee) Hon | Robert C. (Bob) Willis | Ronnie Vincent | Milton (Milt) Byrd Purvis | C.T. (Tommy) Overstreet |
| Potter | Caroline Woodburn | Randall C. Sims | H.R. Kelly | Mercy Murguia | Leon Church | Alphonso S. Vaughn |
| Presidio | Virginia Pallarez | Rod Ponton | Jim White III | Eloy Aranda | Lorenzo Hernandez | Loretto Vasquez |
| Rains | Deborah Traylor | Robert Vittitow | Patsy Marshall | Mike Willis | Michael Godwin | Joe Humphrey |
| Randall | Jo Carter | James A. Farren | Christy Dyer | Mark Benton | Bob Robinson | Buddy DeFord |
| Reagan | Terri Curry | Laurie English | Jim O'Bryan | Tim Sellman | Tommy Holt | Thomas Strube |
| Real | Bella A. Rubio | Daniel J. Kindred | Manuel Rubio | Bryan Shackelford | Gene Buckner | Joe W. Connell Sr. |
| Red River | Janice Gentry | Val J. Varley | Donnie Gentry | David Hutson | Joe DePriest | Wayne Johnson |
| Reeves | Patricia Tarin | Randall W. Reynolds | Rojelio (Roy) Alvarado | Louise C. Moore | Paul Hinojos | Tony Trujillo |
| Refugio | Ruby Garcia | Michael A. Sheppard | Ann Lopez | David Joe Vega | Gary D. Bourland | Rodrigo Bernal |
| Roberts | Toni Rankin | Franklin McDonough | Cleve Wheeler | Ken R. Gill | Kelly V. Flowers | James F. Duvall Jr. |
| Robertson | Barbara Axtell | William Coty Siegert | Keith Petitt | Donald Threadgill | Keith Nickelson | Robert Bielamowicz |
| Rockwall | Kay McDaniel | Kenda Culpepper | Cliff Sevier | Lee Gilbert | Dennis Bailey | David Magness |
| Runnels | Tammy Burleson | George McCrea | Robert H. (Bobby) Moore | Ronald Presley | Sam Scott | Richard W. (Ricky) Strube |
| Rusk | Terrie Willard | Micheal E. Jimerson | W.D. (Bill) Hale | Tammy Pepper | Freddy Swann | Harold Howell |
| Sabine | Tanya Walker | J. Kevin Dutton | Keith C. Clark | Jimmy McDaniel | Doyle Dickerson | Fayne Warner |
| San Augustine | Jean Steptoe | J. Kevin Dutton | Stanley Jackson | Edward Wilson | Joey Holloway | David McEachern |
| San Jacinto | Rebecca Capers | Robert H. Trapp | Bay McCoppin | Donnie Marrs | Thomas Bonds | Mark Nettuno |
| San Patricio | Laura Miller | Michael E. Welborn | Nina G. Treviño | Fred P. Nardini | Alma V. Moreno | Jim Price Jr. |
| San Saba | Kim Wells | Sonny McAfee | Otis Judkins | Rickey Lusty | Kenley Kroll | Pat S. Pool |
| Schleicher | Mary Ann Gonzalez | Allison Palmer | Johnny F. Mayo Jr. | Lynn Meador | Kirk Griffin | Matt Brown |
| Scurry | Candace Jones | Ben Smith | Terry D. Williams | Marianne Randals | David Harrell | Jim Robinson |
| Shackelford | Cheri Hawkins | Joe Edd Boaz | Steve Riley | Shawn Askew | Lanham Martin | Cody Jordan |
| Shelby | Lori Oliver | Kenneth Florence | Roscoe McSwain | Jimmy Lout | Travis Rodgers | Bradley Allen |
| Sherman | Gina Gray | David M. Green | Dana Buckles | Randy Williams | Jeff Crippen | David Davis |

| County | District Clerk | District Attorney | Comm. Precinct 1 | Comm. Precinct 2 | Comm. Precinct 3 | Comm. Precinct 4 |
|---|---|---|---|---|---|---|
| Smith | Lois Rogers | D. Matt Bingham III | Jeff Warr | Cary Nix | Terry Phillips | JoAnn Hampton |
| Somervell | Michelle Reynolds | Dale Hanna | Larry Hulsey | John Curtis | Kenneth Wood | Don Kranz |
| Starr | Eloy R. Garcia | Omar Escobar Jr. | Jaime M. Alvarez | Raul (Roy) Peña Jr. | Eloy Garza | Ruben D. Saenz |
| Stephens | Christie Coapland | Dee Peavy | Ed Russell | D.C. (Button) Sikes | Joe F. High | Rickie Ray Carr |
| Sterling | Jerri McCutchen | Allison Palmer | John Ross Copeland | Edward J. Michulka Jr. | Deborah H. Horwood | Reed Stewart |
| Stonewall | Holly McLaury | Michael E. Fouts | David Hoy | Janice Harris | Billy Kirk Meador | Gary Myers |
| Sutton | Rachel Chavez Duran | Laurie K. English | Miguel (Mike) Villanueva | John Wade | Carl Teaff | Fred Perez |
| Swisher | C.J. Chasco | J. Michael Criswell | Lloyd Rahlfs | Joe Bob Thompson | Harvey N. Foster | Larry Buske |
| Tarrant | Thomas A. Wilder | Sharen Wilson | Roy C. Brooks | Andy H. Nguyen | Gary Fickes | J.D. Johnson |
| Taylor | Patricia Henderson | James M. Eidson | Randall Williams | Kyle Kendrick | Stan D. Egger | Charles (Chuck) Statler |
| Terrell | Martha Allen | Fred Hernandez | Yolanda G. Lopez | Michelle Marquez | Charles Stegall | Jon Tom Lowrance |
| Terry | Paige Lindsey | Kelly Moore | Mike Swain | Kirby Keesee | Sisilio Castilleja | John R. Franks |
| Throckmorton | Mary (Susie) Walraven | Michael E. Fouts | Casey Wells | John Jones | Teddy Clark | Wilton Cantrell |
| Titus | Debra Abston | Charles C. (Chuck) Bailey | Albert Riddle | Mike Fields | Phillip Hinton | Jimmy Parker |
| Tom Green | Sheri Woodfin | Allison Palmer (51st) George McCrea (119th) | Ralph Hoelscher | Aubrey de Cordova | Steve Floyd | Bill A. Ford |
| Travis | Amalia Rodriguez-Mendoza | Rosemary Lehmberg | Ron Davis | Sarah Eckhardt | Gerald Daugherty | Margaret Gómez |
| Trinity | Kristen Raiford | Benny Schiro | Grover Worsham | Richard Chamberlin | Neal Smith | Jimmy Brown |
| Tyler | Chynt Pounds | Lou Ann Cloy | Martin Nash | James (Rusty) Hughes | Mike Marshall | Jack Walston |
| Upshur | Karen Bunn | William (Billy) Byrd | Paula Gentry | Don Gross | Frank Berka | Mike Spencer |
| Upton | Pedro (Pete) Gomez Jr. | Laurie English | Dean Titsworth | Tommy Owens | David Mooney | Leon Patrick |
| Uvalde | Christina Ovalle | Daniel J. Kindred | Randy Scheide | Mariano Pargas Jr. | Jerry W. Bates | Raul R. Flores |
| Val Verde | Luz Clara Balderas | Fred Hernandez | Ramiro V. Ramon | Lewis Owens | Robert Beau Nettleton | Gustavo Flores |
| Van Zandt | Karen Wilson | Chris Martin | Brandon Brown | Virgil Melton Jr. | Bobby Chaney | Ronald G. Carroll |
| Victoria | Cathy Stuart | Stephen B. Tyler | Danny Garcia Jr. | Kevin M. Janak | Gary E. Burns | Clint C. Ives |
| Walker | Robyn Flowers | David P. Weeks | B.J. Gaines Jr. | Ronnie White | Bobby Warren | Tim Paulsel |
| Waller | Liz Pirkle | Elton Mathis | John A. Amsler | Russell Klecka | Jeron Barnett | Justin Beckendorff |
| Ward | Patricia Oyerbides | Randall W. Reynolds | Julian Florez | Larry Hanna | Dexter Nichols | Eddie Nelms |
| Washington | Tammy Brauner | Julie Renken | Zeb Heckmann | Luther Hueske | Kirk Hanath | Joy Fuchs |
| Webb | Esther Degollado | Isidro R. Alaniz | Frank J. Sciaraffa | Rosaura (Wawi) Tijerina | John C. Galo | Jaime A. Canales |
| Wharton | Kendra Charbula | Ross Kurtz | Leroy Dettling | D.C. (Chris) King | Steven Goetsch | Doug Mathews |
| Wheeler | Sherri Jones | Franklin McDonough | Daryl G. Snelgrooes | Bob Hink | Richard Kincannon | John Walker |
| Wichita | Patti Flores | Maureen Shelton | Ray Gonzalez | Lee Harvey | Barry Mahler | Jeff Watts |
| Wilbarger | Brenda Peterson | Staley Heatly | Richard Jacobs | Philip Graf | Rodney Johnston | Josh Patterson |
| Willacy | Gilbert Lozano | Bernard Ammerman | Eliberto Guerra | Oscar De Luna | Alfredo Serrato | Edward (Eddie) Gonzales |
| Williamson | Lisa David | Jana Duty Hunsicker | Lisa Birkman | Cynthia Long | Valerie Covey | Ron Morrison |
| Wilson | Deborah Bryan | René M. Peña | Albert Gamez Jr. | Paul W. Pfeil | Ricky R. Morales | Larry A. Wiley |
| Winkler | Sherry Terry | Dorothy Holguin | Billy J. Stevens | James R. (Robbie) Wolf | Randy Neal | Billy Ray Thompson |
| Wise | Brenda Rowe | Greg Lowery | Danny White | Kevin Burns | Harry Lamance | Glenn Hughes |
| Wood | Jenica Turner | Jim Wheeler | Virgil Holland | Jerry Gaskill | Roger W. Pace | Russell Acker |
| Yoakum | Sandra Roblez | Dee Peavy | Woody Lindsey | Ray Marion | Ty Powell | Tim Addison |
| Young | Jamye Rogers | Isidro (Chilo) Alaniz | Mike Sipes | Matthew Pruitt | Stacey Rogers | Jimmy R. Wiley |
| Zapata | Dora M. Ramos | Roberto Serna | Jose Emilio Vela | Gabriel Villarreal Jr. | Eddie Martinez | Norberto Garza |
| Zavala | Rachel P. Ramirez | | Isidro Cantu | Miguel Acosta | Jesse Gonzalez | Fred Enriquez |

# Texans in Congress

Besides the two members of the U.S. Senate allocated to each state, Texas was allocated 36 members in the U.S. House of Representatives for the 114th Congress. The term of office for members of the House is two years; the terms of all members will expire on Jan. 3, 2017. Senators serve six-year terms. Sen. John Cornyn's term will end in 2021. Sen. Ted Cruz's term will end in 2019.

Addresses and phone numbers of the lawmakers' Washington and district offices are below, as well as the committees on which they serve. Washington zip codes are 20515 for members of the House and 20510 for senators. The telephone area code for Washington is 202. On the Internet, House members can be reached through www.house.gov/writerep.

In 2015, members of Congress received a salary of $174,000. Members in leadership positions received $193,400.

## U.S. SENATE

**CORNYN, John. Republican (Home: Austin); Washington Office:** 517 HSOB, Washington, D.C. 20510; (202) 224-2934, Fax 228-2856. www.cornyn.senate.gov.

**Texas Offices:** 221 W. 6th Ste. 1530, **Austin** 78701, (512) 469-6034; 5001 Spring Valley Ste. 1125 E, **Dallas** 75244, (972) 239-1310; 222 E. Van Buren Ste. 404, **Harlingen** *John Cornyn.* 78550, (956) 423-0162; 5300 Memorial Dr. Ste. 980, **Houston** 77007, (713) 572-3337; 1500 Broadway Ste. 1230, **Lubbock** 79401, (806) 472-7533; 600 Navarro Ste. 210, **San Antonio** 78205, (210) 224-7485; 100 E. Ferguson Ste. 1004, **Tyler** 75702, (903) 593-0905.

**Committees:** Finance; Judiciary. Majority Whip of the U.S. Senate.

**CRUZ, Ted. Republican (Home: Houston); Washington Office:** 185 DSOB, Washington, D.C. 20510; (202) 224-5922. www.cruz.senate.gov.

**Texas Offices:** 300 E. 8th, Ste. 961, **Austin** 78701, (512) 916-5834; 3626 N. Hall, Ste. 410, **Dallas** 75219, (214) 599-8749; 806 Travis St. Ste. 1420, *Ted Cruz.* **Houston** 77002, (713) 718-3057; 200 S. 10th, Ste. 1603, **McAllen** 78501, (956) 686-7339; 9901 IH-10W, Ste. 950, **San Antonio** 78230, (210) 340-2885 305 S. Broadway, Ste. 501, **Tyler** 75702, (903) 593-5130.

**Committees:** Armed Services; Commerce, Science and Transportation; Judiciary; Rules and Administration; Joint Economic Committee.

## U.S. HOUSE of REPRESENTATIVES

**District 1 — GOHMERT, Louie, R-Tyler;** Washington Office: 2243 RHOB; (202) 225-3035, Fax 226-1230; District Offices: 1121 ESE Loop 323 Ste. 206, Tyler 75701, (903) 561-6349; 101 E. Methvin Ste. 302, Longview 75601, (903) 236-8597; 300 E. Shepherd Ste. 210, Lufkin 75901, (936) 632-3180; 102 W. Houston, Marshall 75670, (866) 535-6302; 101 W.

Main Ste. 160, Nacogdoches 75961, (866) 535-6302. Committees: Judiciary; Natural Resources.

**District 2 — POE, Ted, R-Humble;** Washington Office: 2412 RHOB; (202) 225-6565, Fax 225-5547. District Offices: 505 Orleans Ste. 100, Beaumont 77701, (409) 212-1997; 1801 Kingwood Ste 340, Kingwood 77339 (281) 446-0242. Committees: Foreign Affairs; Judiciary.

**District 3 — JOHNSON, Sam, R-Plano;** Washington Office: 2304 RHOB; (202) 225-4201, Fax 225-1485; District Office: 2929 N. Central Expressway, Ste. 240, Richardson 75080, (972) 470-0892. Committee: Ways and Means, Joint Taxation.

**District 4 — RATCLIFFE, John, R-Heath;** Washington Office, 325 CHOB; (202) 225-6673, Fax 225-3332: District Offices: 6531 Horizon Ste. A, Rockwall 75032, (972) 771-0100; 100 W. Houston, 2nd Floor, Sherman 75090, (903) 813-5270; 26i00 N. Robison Ste. 190, Texarkana 75599, (903) 823-3173. Committees: Judiciary, Homeland Security.

**District 5 — HENSARLING, Jeb, R-Dallas;** Washington Office: 2228 RHOB; (202) 225-3484, Fax 226-4888. District Offices: 6510 Abrams Rd. Ste. 243, Dallas 75231, (214) 349-9996; 702 E. Corsicana St., Athens 77571, (903) 675-8288. Committees: Financial Services.

**District 6 — BARTON, Joe, R-Ennis;** Washington Office: 2107 RHOB; (202) 225-2002;District Offices: 6001 West I-20 Ste. 200, Arlington 76017, (817) 543-1000; 303 N. 6th, Crockett 75835, (936) 544-8488; 2106A W. Ennis Ave. Ennis 75119, (972) 875-8488. Committee: Energy and Commerce (chairman).

**District 7 — CULBERSON, John Abney, R-Houston;** Washington Office: 2372 RHOB; (202) 225-2571, Fax 225-4381; District Office: 10000 Memorial Dr. Ste. 620, Houston 77024, (713) 682-8828. Committee: Appropriations.

**District 8 — BRADY, Kevin, R-The Woodlands;** Washington Office: 301 CHOB; (202) 225-4901, Fax 225-5524. District Offices: 200 River Pointe Ste. 304, Conroe 77304, (936) 441-5700; 1202 Sam Houston Ave. Ste. 8, Huntsville 77340, (936) 439-9542; 420 Green Ave., Orange 77630, (409) 883-4197. Committees: Ways and Means; Joint Taxation.

**District 9 — GREEN, Al, D-Houston;** Washington Office: 2347 RHOB; (202) 225-7508;District Office: 3003 South Loop West Ste. 460, Houston 77054, (713) 383-9234.Committee: Financial Services.

**District 10 — McCAUL, Michael, R-Austin;**

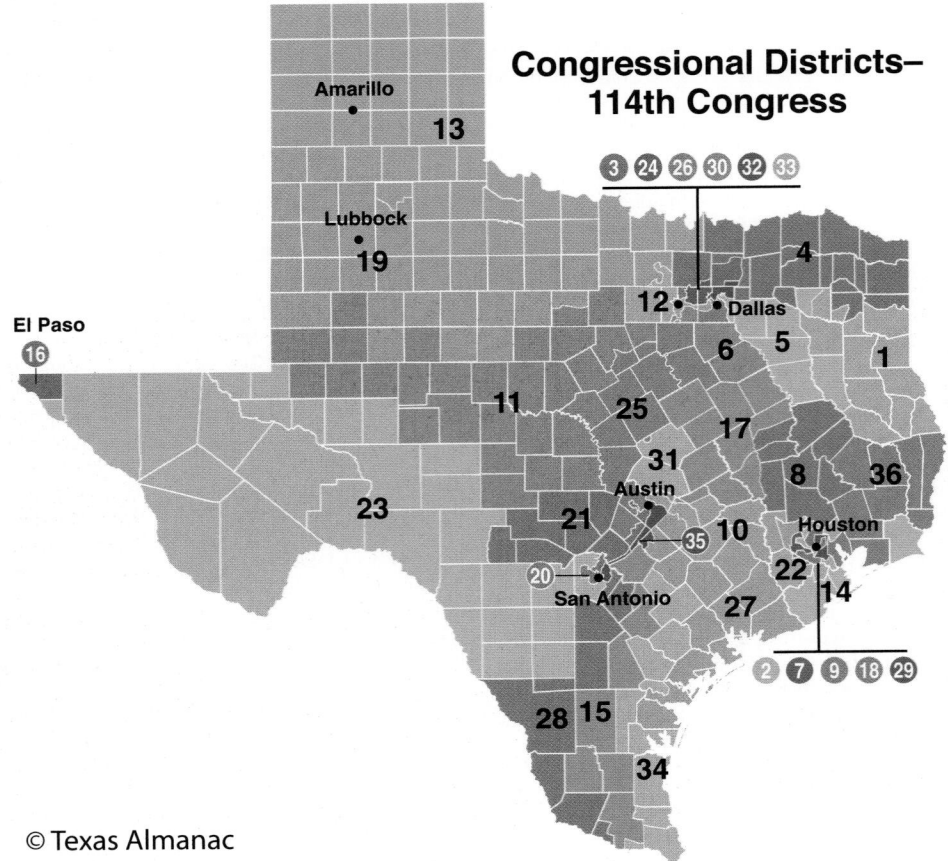

# Congressional Districts–
# 114th Congress

© Texas Almanac

Washington Office: 131 CHOB; (202) 225-2401, Fax 225-5955. District Offices: 5929 Balcones Dr. Ste. 305, Austin 78731, (512) 473-2357; 2000 S. Market Ste. 303, Brenham 77833, (979) 830-8497; [Katy] 1550 Foxlake Ste. 120, Houston 77084, (281) 398-1247; 990 Village Sq. Ste. B, Tomball 77375. Committees: Foreign Affairs, Homeland Security, also Science, Space and Technology.

**District 12 — GRANGER, Kay, R-Fort Worth;** Washington Office: 1026 LHOB; (202) 225-5071, Fax 225-5683; District Office: 1701 River Run Rd. Ste. 407, Fort Worth 76107, (817) 338-0909. Committee: Appropriations.

**District 13 — THORNBERRY, William M. (Mac), R-Clarendon;** Washington Office: 2208 RHOB; (202) 225-3706, Fax 225-3486; District Of-

fices: 905 S. Fillmore Ste. 520, Amarillo 79101, (806) 371-8844; 4245 Kemp Ste. 506, Wichita Falls 76308, (940) 692-1700. Committees: Armed Services.

**District 14 — WEBER, Randy, R-Alvin;** Washington Office: 510 CHOB; (202) 225-2831. District Offices: 505 Orleans Ste. 103, Beaumont 77701, (409) 835-0108; 122 West Way Ste. 301, Lake Jackson 77566, (979) 285-0231. Committees: Science, Space and Technology; Foreign Affairs.

**District 15 — HINOJOSA, Rubén, D-Mercedes;** Washington Office: 2262 RHOB; (202) 225-2531, Fax 225-5688; District Offices: 2864 W. Trenton Rd., Edinburg 78539, (956) 682-5545; 107 S. St. Mary's St., Beeville 78102, (361) 358-8400. Committees: Education and Workforce; Financial Services.

**District 16 — O'ROURKE, Beto, D-El Paso;** Washington Office: 1330 LHOB; (202) 225-4831. District Offices; 310 N. Mesa Ste. 300, El Paso 79901, (915) 534-4400; 303 N. Oregon Ste. 210, El Paso 79901. Committees: Armed Services, Veterans Affairs.

**District 17 — FLORES, Bill, R-Bryan;** Washington Office: 1030 LHOB; (202) 225-6105; District Offices: 400 Austin Ave. Ste. 302, Waco 76701, (254) 732-0748; 1 N. Walnut Ste. 145, Cleburne 76033, (817) 774-2551; 2800 S. Texas Ave. Ste. 403, Bryan

77802, (979) 703-403. Committee: Energy and Commerce.

**District 18 — JACKSON LEE, Sheila, D-Houston;** Washington Office: 2160 RHOB; (202) 225-3816, Fax 225-3317; District Offices: 1919 Smith Ste. 1180, Houston 77002, (713) 655-0050; 420 W. 19th St., Houston 77008, (713) 861-4070; 6719 W. Montgomery Ste. 204, Houston 77091; 3300 Lyons Ave. Ste. 301, Houston 77020, (713) 227-7740.Committees: Homeland Security; Judiciary.

**District 19 — NEUGEBAUER, Randy, R-Lubbock;** Washington Office: 1424 LHOB; (202) 225-4005, Fax 225-9615. District Offices: 500 Chestnut Rm. 819, Abilene 79602, (325) 675-9779; 1510 Scurry Ste. B, Big Spring 79720, (432) 264-7592; 611 University Ave. Ste. 220, Lubbock 79401, (806) 763-1611. Committees: Agriculture; Financial Services; Science, Space and Technology.

**District 20 — CASTRO, Joaquin, D-San Antonio;** Washington Office: 212 CHOB; (202) 225-3236. District Office: 4715 Fredericksburg Rd. Ste. 512, San Antonio 78229, (210) 348-8216. Committees: Armed Services; Foreign Affairs.

**District 21 — SMITH, Lamar S., R-San Antonio;** Washington Office: 2409 RHOB; (202) 225-4236, Fax 225-8628; District Offices: 1100 NE Loop 410 Ste. 640, San Antonio 78209, (210) 821-5024; 3536 Bee Cave Rd. Ste. 212, Austin 78746, (512) 306-0439; 301 Junction Hwy. Ste. 346C, Kerrville 78028, (830) 896-0154. Committees: Homeland Security; Judiciary (chairman); Science, Space and Technology.

**District 22 — OLSON, Pete, R-Sugar Land;** Washington Office: 2133 RHOB; (202) 225-5951, Fax 225-5241. District Offices: 1650 Hwy 6 Ste. 150, Sugar Land 77478, (281) 494-2690; 6302 W. Broadway Ste. 220, Pearland 77581, (281) 485-4855. Committee: Energy and Commerce.

**District 23 — HURD, Will, R-San Antonio;** Washington Office: 317 CHOB; (202) 225-6625, Fax 225-4511.. District Office; 1714 SW Millitary Ste. 110, San Antonio 78221, (210) 921-3130. Committees: Homeland Security, Oversight and Government, Small Business.

**District 24 — MARCHANT, Kenny, R-Coppell;** Washington Office: 2313 RHOB; (202) 225-6605, Fax 225-0074. District Office: 9901 E. Valley Ranch Parkway Ste. 3035, Irving 75063, (972) 556-0162. Committees: Ways and Means; Ethics

**District 25 — WILLIAMS, Roger, R-Austin;** Washington Office: 1323 LHOB; (202) 225-4865. District Office: 1005 Congress Ave. Ste. 928, Austin 78701; 1 Walnut Ste. 145, Cleburne 76033. Committee: Financial Services.

**District 26 — BURGESS, Michael, R-Lewisville;** Washington Office: 2336 RHOB; (202) 225-7772, Fax 225-2919. District Offices: 1660 S. Stemmons Fwy. Ste. 230, Lewisville 75067, (972) 434-9700; 1100 Circle Dr. Ste. 200, Fort Worth 76119, (817) 531-8454. Committees: Energy and Commerce; Rules.

**District 27 — FARENTHOLD, Blake, R-Corpus Christi;** Washington Office: 1027 LHOB; (202) 225-7742; District Offices; 101 N. Shoreline Blvd. Ste. 300, Corpus Christi 78401, (361) 884-2222; 1805 Ruben Torres Ste. B-27, Brownsville 78521, (956) 544-8800. Committees: Homeland Security; Oversight and Government; Transportation; Judiciary.

**District 28 — CUELLAR, Henry, D-Laredo;** Washington Office: 2209 RHOB; (202) 225-1640. District Offices: 602 E. Calton Rd., Laredo 78041, (956) 725-0639; 615 E. Houston Ste. 451, San Antonio 78205, (210) 271-2851; 117 E. Tom Landry, Mission 78572, (956) 424-3942; 100 S. Austin, Seguin 78155, (830) 401-0457; 100 N. FM 3167, Rio Grande City 78582, (956) 488-0952. Committee: Appropriations.

**District 29 — GREEN, Gene, D-Houston;** Washington Office: 2470 RHOB; (202) 225-1688, Fax 225-9903; District Offices: 256 N. Sam Houston Pkwy. E. Ste. 29, Houston 77060, (281) 999-5879; 11811 I-10 East Ste. 430, Houston 77029, (713) 330-0761; 909 Decker Dr. Ste. 124, Baytown 77520, (281) 420-0502. Committee: Energy and Commerce.

**District 30 — JOHNSON, Eddie Bernice, D-Dallas;** Washington Office: 2468 RHOB; (202) 225-8885, Fax 225-1477; District Office: 3102 Maple Ave. Ste. 600, Dallas 75201, (214) 922-8885. Committees: Scienc, Space and Technology; Transportation.

**District 31 — CARTER, John, R-Round Rock;** Washington Office: 2110 RHOB; (202) 225-3864. District Offices: 1717 N. I-35 Ste. 303, Round Rock 78664, (512) 246-1600; 6544B S. General Bruce Dr., Temple 76502, (254) 933-1392. Committee: Appropriations.

**District 32 — SESSIONS, Pete, R-Dallas;** Washington Office: 2233 RHOB; (202) 225-2231, Fax 225-5878; District Office: 12750 Merit Dr. Ste. 1434, Dallas 75251, (972) 392-0505. Committee: Rules, (chairman).

**District 33 — VEASEY, Marc, D-Fort Worth;** Washington Office: 414 CHOB; (202) 225-1688. District Office: JP Morgan Chase Bldg. 1881 Sylvan Ave. Ste 108, Dallas 75028; 420 South Fwy. Ste. 412, Fort Worth 76115. Committee: Armed Services; Science, Space and Technology.

**District 34 — VELA, Filemon, D-Brownsville;** Washington Office: 437 CHOB; (202) 225-9901. District Offices: 500 E. Main, Alice 78332; 333 Ebony Ave., Brownsville 78520; 1390 W. Expressway 83, San Benito 78586. Committee: Agriculture, Homeland Security.

**District 35 — DOGGETT, Lloyd, D-Austin;** Washington Office: 2307 RHOB; (202) 225-4865. District Offices: 300 E. 8th Ste. 763, Austin 78701, (512) 916-5921; 217 W. Travis St., San Antonio 78205, (210) 704-1080. Committee: Ways and Means.

**District 36 — BABIN, Brian, R-The Woodlands;** Washington Office: 316 CHOB; (202) 225-1555, Fax 226-0396. District Office: 203 Ivy Ave. Ste 600, Deer Park 77536, (832) 780-0966; 420 Green Ave., Orange 77630, (409) 883-8075; Woodville, (844) 303-8934. Committee: Transportation, also Science, Space and Technology. ☆

# U.S. Tax Collections in Texas

| Fiscal Year | Individual Income and Employment Taxes | Corporation Income Taxes | Estate Taxes | Gift Taxes | Excise Taxes | TOTAL U.S. Taxes Collected in Texas |
|---|---|---|---|---|---|---|
| | **(1,000 of dollars)** *Information for fiscal years, furnished by the Internal Revenue Service.* | | | | | |
| 2013 | $ 195,542,035 | $ 33,933,242 | $ 890,069 | $ 596,861 | $ 18,950,003 | $ 249,912,209 |
| 2012 | 171,880,127 | 27,984,282 | 796,227 | 180,060 | 18,619,137 | 219,459,878 |
| 2011 | 160,086,749 | 21,880,905 | 117,936 | 359,987 | 15,850,240 | 198,295,817 |
| 2010 | 147,748,859 | 24,991,374 | 1,210,600 | 287,181 | 14,904,099 | 189,142,112 |
| 2009 | 158,798,111 | 24,235,172 | 1,780,030 | 242,918 | 15,465,279 | 200,521,512 |
| 2008 | 178,761,539 | 39,971,658 | 1,549,767 | 243,043 | 15,150,053 | 235,676,058 |
| 2007 | 160,306,445 | 41,823,425 | 1,473,490 | 218,194 | 21,569,350 | 225,390,904 |
| 2006 | 145,758,275 | 37,004,514 | 1,135,160 | 136,377 | 20,702,545 | 204,736,871 |
| 2005 | 125,816,805 | 29,186,478 | 1,196,362 | 118,231 | 13,074,838 | 169,392,715 |
| 2004 | 118,410,514 | 17,127,574 | 1,109,558 | 104,214 | 15,939,329 | 152,691,189 |
| 2003 | 116,353,959 | 11,487,059 | 958,791 | 147,351 | 12,987,394 | 141,934,554 |
| 2002 | 117,685,965 | 13,702,495 | 1,287,937 | 109,064 | 13,654,721 | 146,440,182 |
| 2001 | 127,738,858 | 17,598,181 | 1,242,130 | 248,892 | 14,350,268 | 161,178,329 |
| 2000 | 116,094,820 | 20,310,672 | 1,176,278 | 269,109 | 14,732,513 | 152,583,349 |
| 1995 | 69,706,333 | 10,677,881 | 869,528 | 152,683 | 11,135,857 | 92,342,282 |
| 1990 | 52,795,489 | 6,983,762 | 521,811 | 196,003 | 5,694,006 | 66,191,071 |
| 1985 | 41,497,114 | 5,637,148 | 528,106 | 41,560 | 6,058,110 | 53,762,038 |
| 1980 | 25,707,514 | 7,232,486 | 453,830 | 23,722 | 4,122,538 | 37,540,089 |
| 1970 | 6,096,961 | 1,184,342 | 135,694 | 20,667 | 843,724 | 8,281,389 |
| 1960 | 2,059,075 | 622,822 | 70,578 | 10,583 | 209,653 | 2,972,712 |

# Federal Funds Distribution in Texas

| | 2010 | 2011 | 2012 | 2013 |
|---|---|---|---|---|
| **(1,000 of dollars)** *Information for fiscal years, furnished by the U.S. Census Bureau and other sources.* | | | | |
| Social Security to individuals | $ 43,234,584 | $ 44,988,770 | $ 48,359,227 | $ 50,975,226 |
| Medicare benefits | $ 36,035,272 | $ 37,892,501 | $ 39,479,456 | $ 41,204,288 |
| Federal employees / military | $ 29,926,435 | NA | NA | $ 38,800,000 |
| Direct to local governments | $ 4,411,478 | $ 4,373,508 | $ 4,258,589 | $ 4,500,000 |
| Direct to state goverment | $ 41,450,202 | $ 42,858,907 | $ 37,310,756 | $ 38,844,736 |
| Federal contracts | $ 40,594,474 | $ 38,842,000 | $ 38,176,000 | $ 39,042,000 |
| All other / including farm subsidies | $ 29,072,481 | NA | NA | $ 25,875,750 |
| **TOTAL** | $ 225,724,926 | NA | NA | $ 239,242,000 |

*NA: not available.*

# Federal Funds Distribution to State Governments

| | 2013 | | | | 2013 | | |
|---|---|---|---|---|---|---|---|
| Rank | State | % General Revenue from Federal Goverment | Total Revenue from Federal Government | Rank | State | % General Revenue from Federal Goverment | Total Revenue from Federal Government |
| | **(Thousands of dollars, 000)** | | | | **(Thousands of dollars, 000)** | | |
| 1 | Mississippi | 42.89% | $ 7,509,589 | 15 | Idaho | 34.37% | $ 2,522,766 |
| 2 | Louisiana | 41.94% | $ 10,592,657 | 16 | West Virgina | 34.14% | $ 4,230,663 |
| 3 | Tennessee | 39.49% | $ 10,819,977 | 17 | Oklahoma | 33.79% | $ 7,028,696 |
| 4 | South Dakota | 39.03% | $ 1,575,212 | 18 | Rhode Island | 33.26% | $ 2,331,473 |
| 5 | Missouri | 38.21% | $ 10,188,272 | 19 | Ohio | 33.61% | $ 20,482,575 |
| 6 | Montana | 37.42% | $ 2,158,227 | 20 | Vermont | 33.18% | $ 1,869,831 |
| 7 | Georgia | 37.31% | $ 14,323,163 | 21 | Indiana | 33.41% | $ 11,192,452 |
| 8 | New Mexico | 36.57% | $ 5,228,141 | 22 | Arkansas | 32.87% | $ 5,689,390 |
| 9 | Alabama | 36.15% | $ 8,226,967 | 23 | Michigan | 32.81% | $ 17,829,882 |
| 10 | Maine | 35.30% | $ 2,821,145 | 24 | **Texas** | **32.62%** | **$ 36,844,736** |
| 11 | Wyoming | 35.18% | $ 2,085,931 | 25 | North Carolina | 32.52% | $ 15,470,808 |
| 12 | Kentucky | 35.10% | $ 8,047,093 | *Source: U.S. Census Bureau 2015. Some discrepancies result from differing starts of fiscal years.* | | | |
| 13 | Oregon | 34.98% | $ 7,987,139 | | | | |
| 14 | Arizona | 34.85% | $ 10,166,478 | | | | |

# Major Military Installations

Below are listed the major military installations in Texas in 2015. Data are taken from the U.S. Department of Defense *Base Structure Report 2014* and other sources. "Civilian" refers to Department of Defense personnel, and "other" refers to employees such as contractor personnel. *In October 2010, Fort Sam Houston, Lackland AFB and Randolph AFB were merged into Joint Base San Antonio under the jurisdiction of the U.S. Air Force 502nd Air Base Wing.*

## U.S. NAVY

**Naval Air Station Corpus Christi**

Location: Corpus Christi (est. 1941).

Address: NAS Corpus Christi, 11001 D St., Corpus Christi 78418

Main phone number: (361) 961-2811.

Personnel: 1,249 active-duty; 472 reserve; 705 civilians.

Major units: Naval Air Training Command Headquarters; Training Air Wing 4; Marine Aviation Training Support Group; Coast Guard Air Group; Corpus Christi Army Depot (est. 1961).

**Naval Air Station-Joint Reserve Base Fort Worth**

Location: westside Fort Worth (est. 1994) [Carswell, est. 1942 as Fort Worth Army Air Field, closed 1993].

Address: NAS-JRB, 1510 Chennault Ave., Fort Worth 76113

Main phone number: (817) 782-3058

Personnel: Active-duty — 4 Army, 236 Navy, 418 Marines, 156 Air Force; Reserve — 509 Army, 2,095 Navy, 1,345 Marines, 1,656 Air Force, 892 Air National Guard; 705 civilians.

Major units: Navy Fleet Logistics Support Squadrons 59 and 46; 8th Marine Corps District; Marine Air Group 41; 14th Marine Regiment; Marine Aviation Logistics Squadron 41; Marine Fighter Attach Squadron 112; 36th Airlift Wing, Texas Air National Guard; 90th Aviation Support Battalion; 10th Air Force, 301st Fighter Wing, Air Force Reserve.

**Naval Air Station Kingsville**

Location: Kingsville (est. 1942).

Address: NAS Kingsville, Texas 78363

Main phone number: (361) 516-6136

Personnel: 364 active-duty; 212 reserve; 129 civilians.

Major units: Training Air Wing Two; Training Squadrons 21 and 22; Naval Auxiliary Landing Field Orange Grove; McMullen Target Range, Escondido Ranch.

## U.S. ARMY

**Fort Bliss**

Location: El Paso (est. 1849).

Address: Fort Bliss, Texas 79916

Main phone number: (915) 568-2121

Personnel: 27,577 active-duty; 200 reserve; 4,125 civilians.

Major units: 1st Armored Division; 32nd Air and Missile Defense Command; 15th Sustainment Brigade; 5th Armored Brigade; Air Defense Artillery School; 11th Air Defense Artillery Brigades; Joint Task Force North; 204th Military Intelligence Battalion; 212th Fires Brigade; 402nd Field Artillery Brigade; Biggs Army Airfield (est. 1916).

**Fort Hood**

Location: Killeen (est. 1942).

Address: Fort Hood, Texas 76544

Main phone number: (254) 286-5139

Personnel: 42,001 active-duty; 803 reserve; 5,337 civilians.

Major units: III Corps, Headquarters Command; First Army Division West; 1st Cavalry Division; 13th Sustainment Command; 89th Military Police Brigade; 3rd Armored Cavalry Regiment; 41st Fires Brigade; 504th Battlefield Surveillance Brigade; Army Operational Test Command; Darnell Army Medical Center.

**Fort Sam Houston***

Location: San Antonio (est. 1878).

Address: Fort Sam Houston, Texas 78234

Main phone number: (210) 221-1211

Personnel: 11,623 active-duty; 946 reserve; 8,687 civilians.

Major units: U.S. Army North; U.S. Army South; Brooke Army Medical Center; Institute of Surgical Research; Army Medical Command; Army Medical Dept. Center and School; 5th Recruiting Brigade; 12th Brigade, Western Region (ROTC); Camp Bullis (est. 1917), training area.

**Red River Army Depot**

Location: 18 miles west of Texarkana (est. 1941).

Address: Red River Army Depot, Texarkana 75507

Main phone number: (903) 334-2141

Personnel: 14 active-duty; 111 reserve; 2,992 civilians.

Major unit: Defense Distribution Center; U.S. Army Tank-Automotive and Armaments Command.

## U.S. AIR FORCE

**Brooks City-Base**

Location: San Antonio (est. 1917) In 2002, the property of Brooks AFB was conveyed to the Brooks Development Authority for mainly commercial use, and in 2011 the U.S. Air Force School of Aerospace Medicine, the last unit, left the location.

**Dyess Air Force Base**

Location: Abilene (est. 1942 as Tye Army Airfield, closed at end of World War II, re-established in 1956).

Address: Dyess Air Force Base, Texas 79607

Main phone number: (325) 696-3113

Personnel: 4,402 active-duty; 329 reserve; 396 civilians.

Major units: 7th Bomb Wing (Air Combat Command); 317th Airlift Group.

**Goodfellow Air Force Base**

Location: San Angelo (est. 1940).

Address: Goodfellow AFB, San Angelo 76908

Main phone number: (325) 654-3876

Personnel: 3,108 active-duty; 55 reserve; 613 civilians.

Major units: 17th Training Group; 517th Training Group; 17th Medical Group. 17th Mission Support Group.

**Lackland Air Force Base\***

Location: San Antonio (est. 1942 when separated from Kelly Field).

Address: Lackland Air Force Base, Texas 78236

Main phone number: (210) 671-1110

Personnel: 19,403 active-duty; 3,126 reserve; 8,491 civilians.

Major units: 37th Training Wing; 737th Training Group; 340th Flying Training Group; Defense Language Institute; Inter-American Air Force Academy; Kelly Field Annex (was Kelly Air Force Base, est. 1916).

**Laughlin Air Force Base**

Location: Del Rio (est. 1942).

Address: Laughlin Air Force Base, Texas 78843

Main phone number: (830) 298-3511

Personnel: 1,434 active-duty; 166 reserve; 853 civilians.

Major unit: 47th Flying Training Wing.

**Randolph Air Force Base\***

Location: San Antonio (est. 1930).

Address: Randolph Air Force Base, Texas 78150

Main phone number: (210) 652-1110

Personnel: 2,440 active-duty; 350 reserve; 4,543 civilians.

Major units: 12th Flying Training Wing; 359th Medical Group; Air Education and Training Command; 902nd Mission Support Group; Air Force Recruiting Command; Air Force Manpower Agency.

**Sheppard Air Force Base**

Location: Wichita Falls (est. 1941).

Address: Sheppard Air Force Base, Texas 76311

Main phone number: (940) 676-2511

Personnel: 4,617 active-duty; 138 reserve; 1,129 civilians.

Major units: 82nd Training Wing; 80th Flying Training Wing; NCO Academy.

### TEXAS MILITARY FORCES

**Camp Mabry**

Location: Austin. Just west of MoPac Blvd.

Address: Box 5218, Austin, Texas 78763

Main phone number: (512) 465-5101

Web site: www.txmf.us

**Adjutant General of Texas:**

Maj. General John F. Nichols.

Major units: Joint Force Headquarters, the Standing Joint Interagency Task Force, the 36th Infantry Division, the 147th Reconnaissance

Wing, 149th Fighter Wing, and the 136th Airlift Wing. Texas Air National Guard.

**Texas Military Forces Museum,** open Wednesday–Sunday, 10 a.m. - 4 p.m.

Tracing their history to early frontier days, the Texas Military Forces are organized into the Army and Air National Guard and the Texas State Guard.

The governor is commander-in-chief of the Texas Military Forces. This command function is exercised through the adjutant general appointed by the governor and approved by both federal and state legislative authority.

When not in active federal service, Camp Mabry, in west Austin, serves as the administative and storage headquarters. Camp Mabry was established in the early 1890s as a summer encampment of the Texas Volunteer Guard, a forerunner of the Texas National Guard. The name honors Woodford Haywood Mabry, adjutant general from 1891–1898.

The State Guard, an all-volunteer backup force, was created by the Legislature in 1941. It became an active element of the state military forces in 1965 with a mission of reinforcing the National Guard in emergencies, and replacing National Guard units called into federal service. The State Guard had a membership of approximately 2,232 personnel in 2014.

The Army National Guard is available for state and national emergencies and has been used extensively during hurricanes, tornadoes and floods. There were 19,146 Texans serving in the Texas Army National Guard in 2014.

When the military forces were reorganized following World War II, the Texas Air National Guard was added. Its units augment major Air Force commands. Approximately 3,006 men and women currently make up the Air Guard in the state.

Since 2003, some 31,000 National Guard troops from Texas have served in Iraq and Afghanistan.

In 2014, Adjutant General John F. Nichols commanded a total of some 25,000 soldiers, airmen and civilians.

When called into active federal service, National Guard units come within the chain of command of the Army and Air Force units. ☆

# Medal of Freedom

Dallas native Ernie Banks, famed baseball player for the Chicago Cubs, was among 16 Presidential Medal of Freedom honorees in August 2013.

Ernie Banks, born in Dallas in 1931, attended Booker T. Washington High School where he played football and ran track. He went of to be "Mr. Cub" and play in 11 All-Star games and hit more than 500 home runs.

Others honored by President Obama in 2013 included Loretta Lynn, Oprah Winfrey and Bill Clinton.

President Kenedy established the nation's highest civilian award to honor those who make outstanding contributions in public and private endeavors. ☆

# Federal Courts in Texas

*Source: The following list of U.S. appeals and district court judges and officials was compiled from court Web sites.*

Texas is divided into four federal judicial districts, each of which is comprised of several divisions. Appeal from all Texas federal courts is to the **U.S. Fifth Circuit Court of Appeals** in New Orleans.

## U.S. COURT OF APPEALS, FIFTH CIRCUIT

The Fifth Circuit is composed of Louisiana, Mississippi and Texas. Sessions are held in each of the states at least once a year and may be scheduled at any location having adequate facilities. U.S. circuit judges are appointed for life and received a salary of $211,200 in 2015.

**Circuit Judges — Chief Judge**, Carl E. Stewart, Shreveport. **Judges**: Priscilla R. Owen, Austin; Catharina Haynes, Dallas; Edith H. Jones, Jerry E. Smith and Jennifer Walker Elrod, Greg J. Costa, Houston; James E. Graves Jr., Leslie H. Southwick and E. Grady Jolly, Jackson, Miss.; W. Eugene Davis, Lafayette, La.; James L. Dennis, Stephen A. Higginson and Edith Brown Clement, New Orleans; Edward C. Prado, San Antonio. **Senior Judges**: Harold R. DeMoss Jr., Carolyn Dineen King and Thomas M. Reavley, Houston; Fortunato P. Benavides and Patrick E. Higginbotham, Austin; Rhesa H. Barksdale, Jackson, Miss.; Jacques L. Wiener Jr., New Orleans. **Clerk of Court**: Lyle W. Cayce, New Orleans.

## U.S. DISTRICT COURTS

U.S. district judges are appointed for life and received a salary in 2015 of $199,100.

### Northern Texas District
www.txnd.uscourts.gov
**District Judges — Chief Judge**, Jorge Solis, Dallas. **Judges**: Mary Lou Robinson, Amarillo; Sam A. Lindsay, Barbara M.G. Lynn, Sidney A. Fitzwater, David C. Godbey, Ed Kinkeade, Jane J. Boyle, Reed O'Connor, Dallas; John H. McBryde, Fort Worth. **Senior Judges**: A. Joe Fish, Robert B. Maloney, Dallas; Terry R. Means, Fort Worth; Sam R. Cummings, Lubbock. **Clerk of District Court**: Karen Mitchell, Dallas. **U.S. Attorney**: (acting) John R. Parker, Dallas. **Federal Public Defender**: Jason Hawkins. **U.S. Marshal**: (acting) Benjamin E. Kates, Dallas. **Bankruptcy Judges**: Harlan D. Hale, Barbara J. Houser and Stacey G.C. Jernigan, Dallas; D. Michael Lynn and Russell F. Nelms, Fort Worth; Robert Jones, Lubbock. Court is in continuous session in each division of the Northern Texas District.

Following are the different divisions of the Northern District and the counties in each division:

#### Abilene Division
Callahan, Eastland, Fisher, Haskell, Howard, Jones, Mitchell, Nolan, Shackelford, Stephens, Stonewall, Taylor and Throckmorton. **Magistrate**: E. Scott Frost, Abilene. **Deputy-in-charge**: Marsha Elliott.

#### Amarillo Division
Armstrong, Briscoe, Carson, Castro, Childress, Collingsworth, Dallam, Deaf Smith, Donley, Gray, Hall, Hansford, Hartley, Hemphill, Hutchinson, Lipscomb, Moore, Ochiltree, Oldham, Parmer, Potter, Randall, Roberts, Sherman, Swisher and Wheeler. **Magistrate**: Clinton E. Averitte. **Deputy-in-charge**: Jeanetta Hetrick.

#### Dallas Division
Dallas, Ellis, Hunt, Johnson, Kaufman, Navarro and Rockwall. **Magistrates**: Paul Stickney, Irma C. Ramirez, Renee H. Toliver, David L. Horan. **Deputy-in-charge**: Jundy Hendrick.

## Medal of Honor to Texans

The Medal of Honor for conspicuous gallantry was awarded in March 2014 to 24 Hispanic and Jewish veterans of World War II, the Korean War and the Vietnam War.

In 2002, Congress called for a review of war records to ensure those deserving were not denied because of prejudice.

Among those recognized were several Texans, including (with site of mission action):

Santiago J. Erevia of San Antonio and Nordheim, Vietnam 1969.

Jose Rodela of San Antonio and Corpus Christi, Vietnam 1969.

*Santiago J. Erevia of San Antonio salutes at the presentation ceremony. White House photo.*

Candelario Garcia of Corsicana, Vietnam 1969.
Victor H. Espinoza of El Paso, Korea 1952.
Mike C. Pena of Corpus Christi and Newgulf, Korea 1950.
Pedro Cano of Edinburg, Germany 1944.
Felix Conde-Falcon of Rogers, Vietnam 1969.

# Federal Judicial Districts

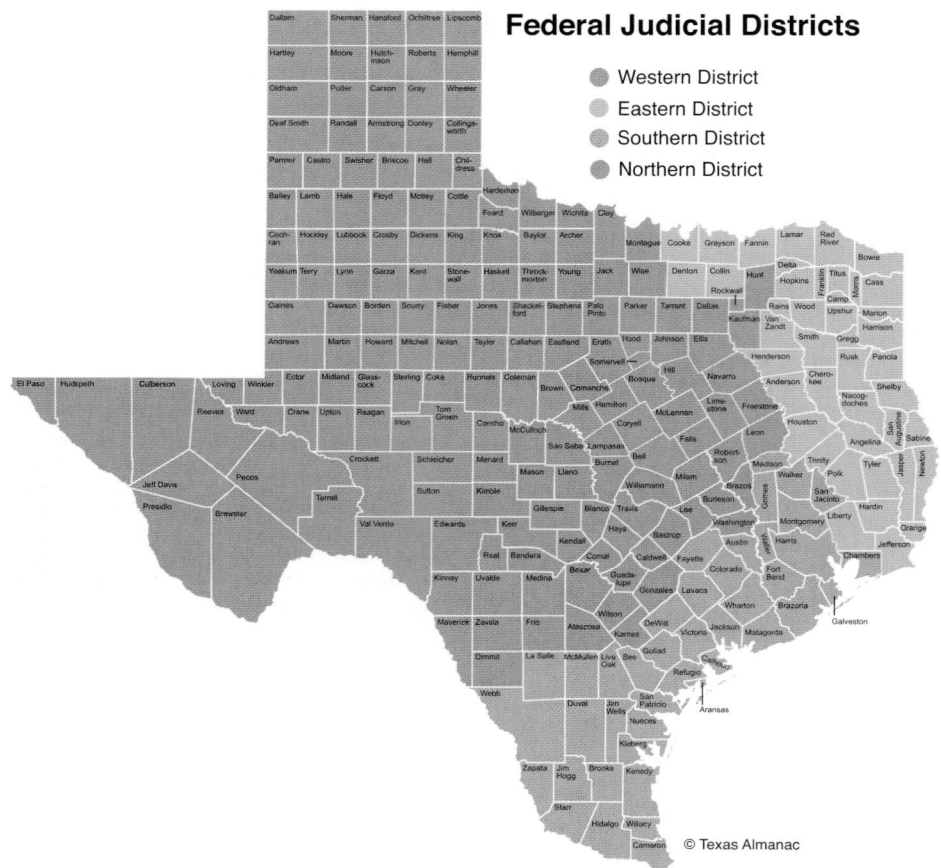

- ● Western District
- ● Eastern District
- ● Southern District
- ● Northern District

© Texas Almanac

### Fort Worth Division
Comanche, Erath, Hood, Jack, Palo Pinto, Parker, Tarrant and Wise. **Magistrate**: Jeffrey L. Cureton. **Deputy-in-charge**: Lynn Sherman.

### Lubbock Division
Bailey, Borden, Cochran, Crosby, Dawson, Dickens, Floyd, Gaines, Garza, Hale, Hockley, Kent, Lamb, Lubbock, Lynn, Motley, Scurry, Terry and Yoakum. **Magistrate**: Nancy M. Koenig. **Deputy-in-charge**: Kristy Weinheimer.

### San Angelo Division
Brown, Coke, Coleman, Concho, Crockett, Glasscock, Irion, Menard, Mills, Reagan, Runnels, Schleicher, Sterling, Sutton and Tom Green. **Magistrate**: E. Scott Frost. **Deputy-in-charge**: Joyce Lowe.

### Wichita Falls Division
Archer, Baylor, Clay, Cottle, Foard, Hardeman, King, Knox, Montague, Wichita, Wilbarger and Young. **Magistrate**: Robert K. Roach. **Deputy-in-Charge**: Teena McNeely.

### Western Texas District
www.txwd.uscourts.gov
**District Judges — Chief Judge**, Fred Biery, San Antonio. **Judges**: Xavier Rodriguez, Orlando Garcia, Robert L. Pitman, San Antonio; Kathleen Cardone, Frank J. Montalvo, Philip R. Martinez, David C. Guaderrama, El Paso; Sam Sparks and Lee Yeakel, Austin; Alia Moses, Del Rio; Robert A. Junell, Midland-Odessa; Walter S. Smith Jr., Waco. **Senior Judges**: David A. Erza and Royce C. Lamberth, San Antonio; Harry Lee Hudspeth, James R. Nowlin, Austin; David Briones, El Paso. **Clerk of District Court**: Jeannette Clack, San Antonio. **U.S. Attorney**: (acting) Richard L. Durbin Jr. **Federal Public Defender**: Maureen Scott Franco. **U.S. Marshal**: Robert R. Almonte, San Antonio. **Bankruptcy Judges**: Chief Judge, Ronald B. King. Judges; Craig A. Gargotta, H. Christopher Mott and Tony M. Davis, Austin.

Following are the different divisions of the Western District, and the counties in each division.
### Austin Division
Bastrop, Blanco, Burleson, Burnet, Caldwell, Gillespie, Hays, Kimble, Lampasas, Lee, Llano, Mason, McCulloch, San Saba, Travis, Washington and Williamson. **Magistrates**: Andrew W. Austin and Mark Lane, Austin. **Divisional Office Manager**: David O'Toole. **Bankruptcy Court Deputy-in-charge**: Theresa Mills.

### Del Rio Division
Edwards, Kinney, Maverick, Terrell, Uvalde, Val Verde and Zavala. **Magistrate**: Roberto Garcia and

Collis White. **Divisional Office Manager**: Rebecca Moore.

## El Paso Division

El Paso County only. **Magistrates**: Ann T. Benton, Robert F. Castañeda, Norbert J. Garney, Miguel A. Torres. **Divisional Office Manager**: Tom Hilburger. **Bankruptcy Court Deputy-in-charge**: Julie Herrera.

## Midland-Odessa Division

Andrews, Crane, Ector, Martin, Midland and Upton. Court for the Midland-Odessa Division is held at Midland, but may, at the discretion of the court, be held in Odessa. **Magistrate**: David Counts. **Divisional Office Manager**: Laura Fowler-Gonzales, Midland. **Bankruptcy Court Deputy-in-charge**: Christy Carouth.

## Pecos Division

Brewster, Culberson, Hudspeth, Jeff Davis, Loving, Pecos, Presidio, Reeves, Ward and Winkler. **Magistrate**: David Counts, Midland; B. Dwight Goains, Alpine. **Pecos Divisional Office Manager**: Karen J. White. **Alpine Magistrate Deputy**: Rebecca Hart.

## San Antonio Division

Atascosa, Bandera, Bexar, Comal, Dimmit, Frio, Gonzales, Guadalupe, Karnes, Kendall, Kerr, Medina, Real and Wilson. **Magistrates**: Pamela A. Mathy, John W. Primomo, Henry J. Bemporad. **Divisional Office Manager**: Michael F. Oakes. **Bankruptcy Court Deputy-in-Charge**: Mary Croy.

## Waco Division

Bell, Bosque, Coryell, Falls, Freestone, Hamilton, Hill, Leon, Limestone, McLennan, Milam, Robertson and Somervell. **Magistrate**: Jeffrey C. Manske. **Divisional Office Manager**: Mark G. Borchardt. **Bankruptcy Court Deputy-in-charge**: Bridget Hardage.

## Eastern Texas District
### www.txed.uscourts.gov

**District Judges — Chief Judge**, Ron Clark, Beaumont. **Judges**: Marcia A. Crone and Thad Heartfield, Beaumont; Leonard Davis, Michael H. Schneider, Tyler; Rodney Gilstrap, Marshall; Richard A. Schell, Plano; Amos L. Mazzant, Sherman; Robert W. Schroeder III, Texarkana. **Clerk of District Court**: David Maland. **U.S. Attorney**: John Malcolm Bales. **Federal Public Defender**: G. Patrick Black. **U.S. Marshal**: Robert L. Hobbs. **Bankruptcy Judges**: Chief Judge, Brenda T. Roades, Plano and William Parker, Tyler.

Following are the divisions of the Eastern District and the counties in each division:

## Beaumont Division

Hardin, Jasper, Jefferson, Liberty, Newton, Orange. **Magistrates**: Zach Hawthorn and Keith F. Giblin.

## Lufkin Division

Angelina, Houston, Nacogdoches, Polk, Sabine, San Augustine, Shelby, Trinity, Tyler. **Magistrates**: Keith F. Giblin and Zach Hawthorn.

## Marshall Division

Camp, Cass, Harrison, Hopkins, Marion, Morris, Upshur. **Magistrate**: Roy Payne.

## Sherman Division

Collin, Cooke, Delta, Denton, Fannin, Grayson, Hopkins and Lamar. **Magistrates**: Don D. Bush, Plano.

## Texarkana Division

Bowie, Franklin, Red River and Titus. **Magistrate**: Caroline M. Craven.

## Tyler Division

Anderson, Cherokee, Gregg, Henderson, Panola, Rains, Rusk, Smith, Van Zandt and Wood. **Magistrates**: John Love and K. Nicole Mitchell.

## Southern Texas District
### www.txs.uscourts.gov

**District Judges — Chief Judge**, Ricardo H. Hinojosa, McAllen. **Judges**: Nancy F. Atlas, Keith Ellison, Vanessa Gilmore, Melinda Harmon, Kenneth M. Hoyt, Lynn N. Hughes, Sim Lake, Gray Miller, Lee H. Rosenthal, Houston; Hayden Head, Janis Graham Jack, Nelva Gonzales Ramos, Corpus Christi; Hilda G. Tagle and Andrew S. Hanen, Brownsville; Gregg Costa, Galveston; Micaela Alvarez, Randy Crane, McAllen; George P. Kazen, Marina Garcia Marmolejo, Diana Saldaña, Laredo; John D. Rainey, Victoria. **Senior Judges**: David Hittner and Ewing Werlein Jr., Houston. **Clerk of Court**: David J. Bradley, Houston. **U. S. Attorney**: Kenneth Magidson, Houston. **Federal Public Defender**: Marjorie A. Meyers. **U.S. Marshal**: Elizabeth Saenz. **Bankruptcy Judges**: Chief, Jeff Bohm, Houston; Karen K. Brown, Marvin Isgur, David Jones, Letitia Z. Paul, Houston; Richard S. Schmidt, Corpus Christi.

Following are the different divisions of the Southern District and the counties in each division:

## Brownsville Division

Cameron and Willacy. **Magistrates**: Ronald G. Morgan, Ignacio Torteya III. **Deputy-in-charge**: Rosalina D'Venturi.

## Corpus Christi Division

Aransas, Bee, Brooks, Duval, Jim Wells, Kenedy, Kleberg, Live Oak, Nueces and San Patricio. **Magistrates**: B. Janice Ellington and Jason B. Libby. **Deputy-in-charge**: Marianne Serpa.

## Galveston Division

Brazoria, Chambers, Galveston and Matagorda. **Magistrate**: John R. Froeschner. **Deputy-in-charge**: Cathy Carnew.

## Houston Division

Austin, Brazos, Colorado, Fayette, Fort Bend, Grimes, Harris, Madison, Montgomery, San Jacinto, Walker, Waller and Wharton. **Magistrates**: George Hanks, Frances H. Stacy, Nancy Johnson, Mary Milloy and Stephen Wm. Smith. **Deputy-in-charge**: Darlene Hansen.

## Laredo Division

Jim Hogg, La Salle, McMullen, Webb and Zapata. **Magistrates**: J. Scott Hacker, Diana Song Quiroga, Guillermo R. Garcia.

## McAllen Division

Hidalgo and Starr. **Magistrates**: Dorina Ramos, Peter Ormsby.

## Victoria Division

Calhoun, DeWitt, Goliad, Jackson, Lavaca, Refugio and Victoria. **Magistrate**: Nancy K. Johnson. **Deputy-in-charge**: Lana Tesch. ☆

*The Peace Officer Memorial Service in Abilene is held in May during National Police Week. Photo by John Cummins.*

# Crime in Texas — 2013

*Source: Texas Department of Public Safety, Austin; www.txdps.state.tx.us*

During 2013, there was a reported total of 966,340 index offenses in Texas. This represents a crime-volume decrease of 1.6 percent when compared to 981,582 reported offenses in 2012.

In 2013, there were 3,653.7 crimes per 100,000 people, compared with 3,811.8 in 2012, according to data compiled by the Department of Public Safety's Uniform Crime Reporting (UCR) program. The crime rate is based on a 2013 population of 26,448,193, compared with a 2012 population of 26,059,203.

Monthly crime variations show that, in general, crime occurrences peaked in the month of July.

The 2013 **violent crime rate** decreased 2 percent from 2012, and the **nonviolent, or property, crime rate** decreased 4.4 percent from 2012. Of the seven major crime categories, the UCR defines **violent crime** as murder, rape, robbery, and aggravated assault; **property crime** is defined as burglary, larceny-theft, and motor vehicle theft.

In 2013, the murder rate remained unchanged from 2012 at 4.4-percent, although the number of murders increased, 1,151 in 2013, compared with 1,145 in 2012.

Both the crime rate and the volume of both rape and aggravated assault decreased in 2013 by 4.7 and 4.1 percent, respectively. Robbery, however, showed a 3.3-percent increase over 2012, with the actual number of robberies increasing from 30,375 in 2012 to 31,852 in 2013.

The crime rate of all property crimes showed a decrease from 2012 rates. The rate of burglaries was down 8.4 percent, larceny-theft decreased by 1.6 percent, and motor vehicle theft dropped 15.7 percent from 2012. The volume of in these categories decreased, as well, with the exception of motor vehicle theft, which increased 1.1 percent.

The value of property stolen during the commission of index crimes in 2013 was more than $1.9 billion, and about 25 percent of that property was recovered.

During 2013, Texas law enforcement officers made 936,358 arrests, a decrease from the 1,056,215 arrests made in 2012. Of the 2013 arrested, 7.5 percent were 16 years of age and under.

In Texas, the Department of Public Safety collects data for the national UCR program from police, sheriff's offices, and it's own officers. Data are estimated for non-reporting agencies and those that did not have 12 months of data.

### Family Violence in Texas in 2013

Family violence decreased by 1.9 percent in 2013 over 2012. In 2013, there were 185,453 reported incidents of family violence involving 199,752 victims and 194,756 offenders. In 2012, there were 188,992 reported incidents of family violence involving 198,504 victims and 194,317 offenders.

In 38.4 percent of the 2013 reports, the relationship of victim to offender was marital. Of those victims, 14.94 percent were wives, and 12.3 percent were common-law wives.

Of the remaining offenses, 16.2 percent involved parents against children or children against parents; and 45.4 involved other family or household relationships, such as grandparents, grandchildren, siblings, stepsiblings, roommates, or in-laws. The 77th Legislature amended the Texas Family Code to include violence in a "dating relationship."

There are six general categories of family violence: assault, homicide, kidnapping, robbery, forcible sex offenses, and nonforcible sex offenses. Assaults (including aggravated, simple, and intimidation) accounted for 97 percent of all family violence in 2013.

### Hate Crimes in Texas in 2013

In 2013, there were 135 hate crime incidents reported with 176 victims, 175 offenders, and 136 offenses. This is an decrease of 21 percent from the 171 incidents in 2012. The 2012 hate crimes involved 198 victims and 198 offenders.

### Arson in 2013

The reported number of arsons committed in Texas in 2013 was 4,159, a decrease of 5.7 percent compared with 4,411 in 2012. In 2013, arson victims suffered losses totaling $75 million, an 18-percent decrease when compared with 2012 total arson losses of more than $91 million.

### Law Enforcement Deaths, Injuries

A total of 12 law enforcement officers were killed in 2013; six were feloniously killed in the line of duty and six died in duty-related accidents. ☆

## Texas Crime History 1993–2013

| Year | Murder | Rape | Robbery | Aggravated Assault | Burglary | Larceny-Theft | Motor Vehicle Theft | Rate per 100,000 Population |
|------|--------|------|---------|--------------------|----------|---------------|---------------------|------------------------------|
| 1993 | 2,149 | 9,923 | 40,464 | 84,892 | 233,944 | 664,738 | 124,822 | 6,438.5 |
| 1994 | 2,023 | 9,101 | 37,639 | 81,079 | 214,698 | 624,048 | 110,772 | 5,873.1 |
| 1995 | 1,694 | 8,526 | 33,666 | 80,377 | 202,637 | 632,523 | 104,939 | 5,684.5 |
| 1996 | 1,476 | 8,374 | 32,796 | 80,572 | 204,335 | 659,397 | 104,928 | 5,708.3 |
| 1997 | 1,328 | 8,007 | 30,513 | 77,239 | 200,966 | 645,174 | 101,687 | 5,478.2 |
| 1998 | 1,343 | 7,914 | 28,672 | 73,648 | 194,872 | 606,805 | 96,614 | 5,110.7 |
| 1999 | 1,218 | 7,629 | 29,424 | 74,165 | 190,347 | 614,478 | 91,992 | 5,035.2 |
| 2000 | 1,236 | 7,821 | 30,186 | 73,987 | 188,205 | 634,575 | 92,878 | 4,952.4 |
| 2001 | 1,331 | 8,191 | 35,330 | 77,221 | 204,240 | 669,587 | 102,838 | 5,152.3 |
| 2002 | 1,305 | 8,541 | 37,599 | 78,713 | 212,702 | 690,028 | 102,943 | 5,196.7 |
| 2003 | 1,417 | 7,986 | 37,000 | 75,706 | 219,733 | 697,790 | 98,174 | 5,144.1 |
| 2004 | 1,360 | 8,401 | 35,811 | 75,983 | 220,079 | 696,220 | 93,844 | 5,032.0 |
| 2005 | 1,405 | 8,505 | 35,781 | 75,409 | 219,733 | 676,022 | 93,471 | 4,857.1 |
| 2006 | 1,385 | 8,407 | 37,271 | 74,624 | 215,754 | 648,083 | 95,750 | 4,599.6 |
| 2007 | 1,415 | 8,430 | 38,777 | 73,570 | 228,325 | 662,481 | 94,026 | 4,631.1 |
| 2008 | 1,373 | 8.004 | 37,757 | 76,487 | 230,263 | 654,133 | 85,411 | 4,494.7 |
| 2009 | 1,327 | 8,286 | 38,041 | 74,135 | 240,193 | 678,340 | 76,617 | 4,507.0 |
| 2010 | 1,247 | 7,626 | 32,865 | 71,561 | 229,269 | 654,484 | 68,220 | 4,236.4 |
| 2011 | 1,089 | 7,445 | 28,399 | 68,028 | 215,512 | 613,528 | 63,379 | 3,884.7 |
| 2012 | 1,145 | 7,692 | 30,375 | 67,050 | 204,976 | 605,362 | 64,982 | 3,811.8 |
| 2013 | 1,151 | 7,443 | 31,852 | 65,267 | 190,567 | 604,389 | 65,671 | 3,653.7 |

Sources: Texas Department of Public Safety, Austin, and the Federal Bureau of Investigation, Washington. The crime rate is based on the 2013 Texas population of 26,448,193.

## Crime Profile of Texas Counties for 2013

| County | Agencies | Commissioned Personnel † | Murder | Rape | Robbery | Assault | Burglary | Larceny-Theft | Auto Theft | Total Index Crimes (see page 554 for definition) | Crime Rate per 100,000 |
|--------|----------|--------------------------|--------|------|---------|---------|----------|---------------|------------|---------------------------------------------------|------------------------|
| Anderson | 3 | 68 | 1 | 20 | 36 | 114 | 443 | 1080 | 93 | 1,787 | 3,061.6 |
| Andrews | 2 | 33 | 0 | 22 | 2 | 78 | 112 | 274 | 33 | 521 | 3,130.1 |
| Angelina | 5 | 141 | 5 | 22 | 35 | 217 | 805 | 2045 | 106 | 3,235 | 3,668.0 |
| Aransas | 3 | 70 | 3 | 10 | 11 | 35 | 332 | 639 | 41 | 1,071 | 4,577.5 |
| Archer ‡ | 2 | 12 | 0 | 0 | 1 | 6 | 19 | 42 | 9 | 77 | 1,112.2 |
| Armstrong | 1 | 4 | 0 | 0 | 0 | 4 | 4 | 30 | 1 | 39 | 1,981.7 |
| Atascosa ‡ | 5 | 117 | 1 | 2 | 11 | 53 | 212 | 820 | 53 | 1,152 | 2,416.7 |
| Austin ‡ | 6 | 75 | 0 | 4 | 6 | 63 | 126 | 296 | 25 | 520 | 1,805.4 |
| Bailey ‡ | 2 | 13 | 0 | 1 | 0 | 8 | 19 | 56 | 6 | 90 | 1,258.6 |
| Bandera | 1 | 31 | 0 | 8 | 1 | 15 | 82 | 147 | 30 | 283 | 1,372.5 |
| Bastrop | 4 | 119 | 6 | 30 | 21 | 184 | 362 | 1,004 | 125 | 1,732 | 2,273.4 |
| Baylor | 2 | 8 | 0 | 3 | 0 | 15 | 48 | 50 | 4 | 120 | 3,326.9 |
| Bee | 2 | 42 | 2 | 2 | 2 | 52 | 95 | 350 | 21 | 524 | 1,593.5 |
| Bell ‡ | 13 | 590 | 14 | 126 | 269 | 780 | 2,518 | 6,952 | 355 | 11,014 | 3,371.2 |
| Bexar ‡ | 29 | 3,376 | 97 | 761 | 2,340 | 6,463 | 17,355 | 66,728 | 7,261 | 101,005 | 5,559.4 |
| Blanco | 3 | 19 | 0 | 5 | 1 | 18 | 40 | 82 | 11 | 157 | 1,460.9 |
| Borden | 1 | 2 | 0 | 0 | 0 | 2 | 5 | 8 | 3 | 18 | 2,955.7 |
| Bosque | 4 | 25 | 0 | 2 | 1 | 4 | 77 | 116 | 6 | 206 | 1,133.9 |
| Bowie | 7 | 132 | 4 | 41 | 75 | 339 | 930 | 2,530 | 191 | 4,110 | 4,386.6 |
| Brazoria | 21 | 573 | 7 | 87 | 114 | 409 | 1,523 | 4,569 | 292 | 7,001 | 2,090.9 |
| Brazos | 4 | 429 | 2 | 71 | 116 | 597 | 1,133 | 4,062 | 175 | 6,156 | 3,029.8 |
| Brewster | 3 | 29 | 0 | 0 | 1 | 13 | 32 | 91 | 3 | 140 | 1,494.4 |
| Briscoe | 1 | 2 | 0 | 0 | 0 | 1 | 8 | 9 | 1 | 19 | 1,229.0 |
| Brooks | 2 | 23 | 1 | 3 | 2 | 9 | 64 | 70 | 0 | 149 | 2,075.2 |
| Brown | 4 | 71 | 0 | 14 | 8 | 79 | 253 | 805 | 32 | 1191 | 3,143.8 |
| Burleson | 3 | 29 | 2 | 5 | 2 | 20 | 87 | 99 | 8 | 223 | 1,282.1 |
| Burnet | 6 | 107 | 5 | 22 | 6 | 64 | 187 | 676 | 58 | 1,018 | 2,246.9 |
| Caldwell | 4 | 71 | 2 | 12 | 12 | 97 | 177 | 526 | 38 | 864 | 2,234.3 |

# Crime Profile of Texas Counties for 2013

| County | Agencies | Commissioned Personnel † | Murder | Rape | Robbery | Assault | Burglary | Larceny-Theft | Auto Theft | Total Index Crimes (see page 554 for definition) | Crime Rate per 100,000 |
|---|---|---|---|---|---|---|---|---|---|---|---|
| Calhoun ‡ | 2 | 44 | 0 | 8 | 2 | 59 | 109 | 202 | 18 | 396 | 2,027.8 |
| Callahan | 3 | 16 | 0 | 1 | 0 | 6 | 63 | 84 | 10 | 164 | 1,208.5 |
| Cameron ‡ | 19 | 696 | 6 | 126 | 242 | 630 | 2,739 | 11,511 | 492 | 15,746 | 3,749.5 |
| Camp | 2 | 17 | 0 | 5 | 3 | 32 | 153 | 217 | 16 | 426 | 3,404.2 |
| Carson | 2 | 11 | 0 | 1 | 0 | 9 | 14 | 24 | 6 | 54 | 873.8 |
| Cass ‡ | 6 | 48 | 1 | 11 | 12 | 65 | 329 | 494 | 57 | 969 | 3,207.9 |
| Castro ‡ | 3 | 15 | 0 | 0 | 2 | 14 | 68 | 114 | 13 | 211 | 2,567.8 |
| Chambers | 3 | 59 | 1 | 5 | 8 | 52 | 205 | 435 | 89 | 795 | 2,437.0 |
| Cherokee ‡ | 5 | 69 | 0 | 25 | 21 | 146 | 337 | 773 | 75 | 1,377 | 2,685.0 |
| Childress | 1 | 5 | 0 | 0 | 0 | 3 | 1 | 7 | 0 | 11 | 1,124.7 |
| Clay | 1 | 11 | 0 | 2 | 0 | 4 | 52 | 31 | 13 | 102 | 969.9 |
| Cochran | 1 | 7 | 0 | 2 | 0 | 6 | 37 | 70 | 4 | 119 | 3,927.4 |
| Coke | 1 | 5 | 0 | 0 | 0 | 1 | 15 | 2 | 3 | 21 | 653.2 |
| Coleman ‡ | 3 | 16 | 0 | 2 | 0 | 13 | 103 | 111 | 5 | 234 | 2,708.0 |
| Collin | 16 | 1,085 | 9 | 131 | 197 | 522 | 2,603 | 11,489 | 545 | 15,496 | 1,862.0 |
| Collingsworth | 1 | 5 | 0 | 0 | 0 | 0 | 0 | 0 | 0 | 0 | 0.0 |
| Colorado ‡ | 4 | 47 | 2 | 5 | 5 | 22 | 75 | 206 | 22 | 337 | 1,626.4 |
| Comal | 4 | 250 | 0 | 35 | 30 | 231 | 645 | 2,251 | 182 | 3,379 | 2,678.5 |
| Comanche | 3 | 23 | 1 | 1 | 0 | 23 | 82 | 193 | 8 | 308 | 2,239.5 |
| Concho ‡ | 2 | 7 | 1 | 0 | 0 | 3 | 3 | 4 | 3 | 14 | 349.7 |
| Cooke ‡ | 3 | 44 | 2 | 9 | 14 | 68 | 197 | 642 | 59 | 991 | 5,820.9 |
| Coryell | 3 | 94 | 0 | 18 | 21 | 80 | 329 | 1,033 | 41 | 1,522 | 1933.7 |
| Cottle | 2 | 3 | 0 | 1 | 0 | 1 | 2 | 1 | 0 | 5 | 336.5 |
| Crane | 2 | 14 | 0 | 2 | 0 | 3 | 8 | 23 | 4 | 40 | 861.1 |
| Crockett ‡ | 1 | 8 | – | – | – | – | – | – | – | – | NA |
| Crosby | 4 | 12 | 1 | 2 | 0 | 5 | 21 | 27 | 0 | 56 | 906.3 |
| Culberson | 1 | 6 | 0 | 0 | 0 | 3 | 7 | 4 | 1 | 15 | 662.3 |
| Dallam | 2 | 20 | 2 | 2 | 0 | 51 | 54 | 128 | 6 | 241 | 2,425.0 |
| Dallas | 36 | 5,682 | 185 | 829 | 5,508 | 5254 | 24,604 | 62,834 | 11,373 | 110,587 | 4,023.3 |
| Dawson | 2 | 24 | 1 | 5 | 2 | 38 | 104 | 330 | 20 | 458 | 5,013.0 |
| Deaf Smith | 2 | 34 | 0 | 7 | 9 | 46 | 211 | 312 | 26 | 611 | 3,147.1 |
| Delta | 1 | 11 | 0 | 0 | 1 | 0 | 44 | 33 | 5 | 83 | 1,542.2 |
| Denton ‡ | 22 | 903 | 7 | 155 | 180 | 554 | 1,746 | 6,898 | 653 | 10,193 | 1,829.0 |
| DeWitt | 3 | 39 | 0 | 15 | 1 | 94 | 139 | 299 | 18 | 566 | 3,060.8 |
| Dickens | 2 | 5 | 0 | 0 | 0 | 3 | 3 | 4 | 2 | 12 | 523.6 |
| Dimmit | 1 | 29 | 0 | 0 | 1 | 44 | 130 | 262 | 21 | 458 | 4,298.9 |
| Donley | 1 | 6 | 0 | 0 | 1 | 4 | 20 | 18 | 1 | 44 | 1,226.7 |
| Duval | 3 | 29 | 0 | 1 | 7 | 84 | 127 | 224 | 20 | 463 | 3,648.5 |
| Eastland ‡ | 6 | 35 | 0 | 4 | 2 | 22 | 151 | 314 | 21 | 514 | 2,787.1 |
| Ector | 4 | 272 | 3 | 59 | 179 | 966 | 1,178 | 4,551 | 652 | 7,588 | 5,081.3 |
| Edwards | 1 | 5 | 0 | 0 | 0 | 4 | 14 | 27 | 2 | 47 | 2,387.0 |
| Ellis ‡ | 9 | 233 | 7 | 11 | 40 | 130 | 639 | 2,365 | 141 | 3,333 | 2,236.5 |
| El Paso | 10 | 1,509 | 12 | 235 | 496 | 2,114 | 2,347 | 14,931 | 961 | 21,096 | 2,514.5 |
| Erath | 4 | 83 | 4 | 3 | 6 | 35 | 188 | 574 | 31 | 841 | 2,104.1 |
| Falls ‡ | 4 | 18 | 0 | 2 | 2 | 15 | 40 | 47 | 6 | 112 | 636.6 |
| Fannin | 2 | 37 | 0 | 21 | 2 | 23 | 113 | 281 | 16 | 456 | 1,445.4 |
| Fayette | 4 | 48 | 2 | 5 | 1 | 25 | 91 | 171 | 18 | 313 | 1,259.3 |
| Fisher | 1 | 5 | 0 | 0 | 0 | 17 | 34 | 50 | 9 | 110 | 2,873.6 |
| Floyd | 3 | 13 | 0 | 3 | 2 | 11 | 60 | 67 | 4 | 147 | 2,304.1 |
| Foard | 2 | 3 | 0 | 0 | 0 | 3 | 1 | 3 | 0 | 7 | 537.6 |
| Fort Bend | 10 | 880 | 11 | 71 | 311 | 867 | 2,079 | 6,290 | 487 | 10,116 | 1,668.2 |
| Franklin | 1 | 9 | 0 | 8 | 0 | 5 | 45 | 45 | 9 | 112 | 1,120.4 |
| Freestone | 4 | 34 | 0 | 1 | 5 | 26 | 141 | 163 | 17 | 353 | 1,810.7 |
| Frio | 3 | 40 | 0 | 1 | 3 | 15 | 117 | 263 | 12 | 411 | 2,290.2 |
| Gaines | 3 | 27 | 3 | 7 | 2 | 15 | 71 | 180 | 18 | 293 | 1,576.6 |
| Galveston | 16 | 575 | 14 | 104 | 244 | 356 | 2,130 | 7,097 | 559 | 10,504 | 3,313.8 |
| Garza | 1 | 8 | 0 | 0 | 0 | 3 | 17 | 31 | 0 | 51 | 794.0 |
| Gillespie | 2 | 59 | 1 | 2 | 3 | 9 | 86 | 270 | 5 | 376 | 1,483.4 |
| Glasscock | 1 | 4 | 0 | 0 | 0 | 0 | 6 | 2 | 1 | 9 | 705.9 |

# Crime Profile of Texas Counties for 2013

| County | Agencies | Commissioned Personnel † | Murder | Rape | Robbery | Assault | Burglary | Larceny-Theft | Auto Theft | Total Index Crimes (see page 554 for definition) | Crime Rate per 100,000 |
|---|---|---|---|---|---|---|---|---|---|---|---|
| Goliad | 1 | 13 | 1 | 0 | 0 | 10 | 69 | 80 | 5 | 165 | 2,222.2 |
| Gonzales ‡ | 4 | 49 | 1 | 18 | 7 | 98 | 127 | 418 | 12 | 681 | 3,369.1 |
| Gray | 2 | 40 | 2 | 0 | 7 | 182 | 148 | 605 | 51 | 995 | 4,279.4 |
| Grayson | 13 | 209 | 7 | 24 | 42 | 252 | 726 | 2,171 | 170 | 3,392 | 2,787.2 |
| Gregg | 5 | 335 | 11 | 67 | 183 | 417 | 1,157 | 4,125 | 335 | 6,295 | 4,801.4 |
| Grimes | 2 | 48 | 0 | 4 | 8 | 90 | 141 | 283 | 45 | 571 | 2,118.7 |
| Guadalupe ‡ | 5 | 216 | 1 | 57 | 36 | 136 | 576 | 1,899 | 71 | 2,776 | 2,090.2 |
| Hale | 4 | 60 | 1 | 7 | 5 | 57 | 234 | 785 | 26 | 1,115 | 2,993.8 |
| Hall | 2 | 8 | 0 | 1 | 0 | 7 | 10 | 21 | 2 | 31 | 1,388.8 |
| Hamilton | 1 | 10 | 0 | 0 | 2 | 13 | 56 | 88 | 6 | 165 | 2,376.8 |
| Hansford ‡ | 3 | 11 | 1 | 2 | 0 | 1 | 13 | 33 | 2 | 52 | 942.5 |
| Hardeman | 2 | 8 | 0 | 0 | 1 | 0 | 66 | 60 | 4 | 131 | 3,213.9 |
| Hardin | 5 | 77 | 2 | 8 | 7 | 65 | 221 | 627 | 54 | 984 | 1,771.3 |
| Harris ‡ | 42 | ** 3,856 | 333 | 1,058 | 13,737 | 16,048 | 40,564 | 119,329 | 20,944 | 212,013 | 4,874.3 |
| Harrison ‡ | 4 | 116 | 3 | 18 | 16 | 167 | 420 | 1,082 | 61 | 1,767 | 2,661.4 |
| Hartley | 1 | 5 | 0 | 0 | 0 | 0 | 5 | 11 | 0 | 16 | 475.1 |
| Haskell | 2 | 6 | 0 | 0 | 0 | 6 | 18 | 23 | 10 | 57 | 966.1 |
| Hays | 5 | 317 | 4 | 54 | 72 | 353 | 727 | 2,490 | 226 | 3,926 | 2,263.5 |
| Hemphill | 1 | 9 | 0 | 1 | 0 | 4 | 17 | 56 | 3 | 81 | 1,929.9 |
| Henderson ‡ | 7 | 138 | 1 | 35 | 14 | 202 | 710 | 1,055 | 172 | 2,189 | 2,757.3 |
| Hidalgo | 23 | 1,379 | 22 | 197 | 469 | 1,658 | 6,412 | 22,242 | 1,562 | 32,562 | 3,974.6 |
| Hill ‡ | 5 | 71 | 1 | 5 | 10 | 54 | 217 | 551 | 27 | 865 | 2,453.0 |
| Hockley ‡ | 4 | 42 | 0 | 14 | 9 | 68 | 194 | 443 | 33 | 761 | 3,274.0 |
| Hood ‡ | 3 | 84 | 2 | 8 | 1 | 60 | 189 | 815 | 44 | 1,119 | 2,131.6 |
| Hopkins | 3 | 58 | 1 | 8 | 5 | 30 | 105 | 244 | 25 | 418 | 1,170.9 |
| Houston | 3 | 37 | 0 | 2 | 3 | 31 | 148 | 362 | 26 | 572 | 2,478.8 |
| Howard | 2 | 58 | 3 | 10 | 19 | 147 | 365 | 934 | 67 | 1,545 | 4,328.7 |
| Hudspeth | 1 | 16 | 0 | 0 | 0 | 1 | 7 | 18 | 0 | 26 | 786.7 |
| Hunt ‡ | 7 | 141 | 0 | 28 | 67 | 238 | 707 | 1,659 | 182 | 2,881 | 3,351.8 |
| Hutchinson | 2 | 54 | 0 | 4 | 3 | 150 | 186 | 411 | 47 | 801 | 3,987.1 |
| Irion | 1 | 4 | 0 | 0 | 0 | 1 | 7 | 27 | 1 | 36 | 2,297.4 |
| Jack | 2 | 20 | 0 | 0 | 1 | 20 | 88 | 96 | 7 | 212 | 2,353.7 |
| Jackson | 3 | 25 | 3 | 2 | 1 | 16 | 41 | 175 | 10 | 248 | 1,724.6 |
| Jasper | 3 | 42 | 1 | 30 | 4 | 82 | 246 | 691 | 14 | 1,068 | 2,958.0 |
| Jeff Davis | 1 | 4 | 0 | 0 | 0 | 3 | 9 | 7 | 1 | 20 | 868.1 |
| Jefferson | 7 | 681 | 28 | 92 | 572 | 1,101 | 3,137 | 6,718 | 525 | 12,173 | 4,818.0 |
| Jim Hogg | 1 | 16 | 0 | 0 | 0 | 3 | 13 | 9 | 1 | 26 | 494.8 |
| Jim Wells | 4 | 82 | 3 | 17 | 14 | 207 | 479 | 1,140 | 78 | 1,938 | 4,693.4 |
| Johnson | 8 | 251 | 0 | 42 | 29 | 201 | 814 | 2,527 | 189 | 3,802 | 2,352.9 |
| Jones | 5 | 25 | 0 | 0 | 1 | 39 | 103 | 166 | 14 | 323 | 2,180.2 |
| Karnes | 3 | 36 | 1 | 0 | 0 | 15 | 126 | 299 | 12 | 453 | 2,935.5 |
| Kaufman ‡ | 6 | 176 | 9 | 31 | 32 | 160 | 742 | 1,189 | 184 | 2,347 | 2,174.1 |
| Kendall | 2 | 80 | 0 | 6 | 1 | 23 | 93 | 455 | 34 | 612 | 1,735.8 |
| Kenedy | 1 | 11 | 0 | 4 | 0 | 0 | 4 | 3 | 2 | 13 | 2,968.0 |
| Kent | 1 | 3 | 0 | 1 | 0 | 2 | 5 | 6 | 0 | 14 | 1,643.2 |
| Kerr | 3 | 101 | 4 | 17 | 8 | 48 | 207 | 781 | 43 | 1,108 | 2,214.5 |
| Kimble | 2 | 14 | 0 | 2 | 0 | 6 | 20 | 31 | 0 | 59 | 1,290.7 |
| King | 1 | 2 | 0 | 0 | 0 | 0 | 0 | 2 | 0 | 2 | 732.6 |
| Kinney | 1 | 17 | 0 | 0 | 0 | 1 | 0 | 2 | 1 | 4 | 206.7 |
| Kleberg | 3 | 86 | 1 | 8 | 20 | 92 | 323 | 791 | 28 | 1,263 | 3,929.9 |
| Knox ‡ | 3 | 5 | 0 | 0 | 0 | 2 | 11 | 20 | 4 | 37 | 967.1 |
| Lamar | 4 | 94 | 6 | 5 | 30 | 161 | 473 | 1,121 | 53 | 1,849 | 3,697.4 |
| Lamb ‡ | 4 | 23 | 0 | 0 | 7 | 34 | 140 | 225 | 11 | 417 | 3,183.4 |
| Lampasas | 3 | 38 | 1 | 3 | 3 | 17 | 84 | 322 | 11 | 441 | 2,372.4 |
| La Salle | 1 | 24 | 0 | 0 | 0 | 6 | 3 | 41 | 0 | 50 | 692.9 |
| Lavaca | 4 | 32 | 0 | 2 | 5 | 24 | 161 | 164 | 15 | 371 | 1,700.3 |
| Lee | 3 | 28 | 0 | 13 | 2 | 19 | 98 | 250 | 12 | 394 | 2,364.1 |
| Leon ‡ | 2 | 23 | 1 | 2 | 0 | 21 | 81 | 142 | 20 | 267 | 1,487.9 |
| Liberty | 4 | 104 | 1 | 27 | 27 | 264 | 566 | 1,685 | 225 | 2,795 | 3,623.2 |

## Crime Profile of Texas Counties for 2013

| County | Agencies | Commissioned Personnel † | Murder | Rape | Robbery | Assault | Burglary | Larceny-Theft | Auto Theft | Total Index Crimes (see page 554 for definition) | Crime Rate per 100,000 |
|---|---|---|---|---|---|---|---|---|---|---|---|
| Limestone | 4 | 47 | 1 | 4 | 8 | 44 | 205 | 449 | 16 | 727 | 3,063.4 |
| Lipscomb | 1 | 7 | 0 | 0 | 0 | 6 | 8 | 15 | 0 | 29 | 813.9 |
| Live Oak | 2 | 22 | 1 | 2 | 0 | 34 | 77 | 152 | 12 | 278 | 2,365.8 |
| Llano | 3 | 44 | 0 | 3 | 2 | 11 | 130 | 232 | 11 | 389 | 2,359.0 |
| Loving | 1 | 3 | 0 | 0 | 0 | 3 | 1 | 6 | 0 | 10 | 1,4705.9 |
| Lubbock ‡ | 9 | 674 | 9 | 116 | 394 | 1,481 | 2,901 | 8,906 | 955 | 14,762 | 5,123.6 |
| Lynn | 3 | 12 | 0 | 2 | 0 | 10 | 34 | 32 | 3 | 81 | 1,376.4 |
| Madison | 2 | 23 | 0 | 0 | 3 | 29 | 56 | 145 | 16 | 249 | 1,815.8 |
| Marion | 2 | 16 | 0 | 4 | 6 | 51 | 149 | 188 | 18 | 416 | 4,037.7 |
| Martin | 2 | 9 | 0 | 1 | 1 | 2 | 16 | 68 | 8 | 96 | 1,879.8 |
| Mason | 1 | 5 | 0 | 0 | 0 | 1 | 8 | 32 | 1 | 42 | 1,045.8 |
| Matagorda | 4 | 89 | 1 | 14 | 13 | 90 | 372 | 737 | 37 | 1,264 | 3,449.9 |
| Maverick | 2 | 31 | 2 | 5 | 6 | 85 | 308 | 982 | 22 | 1,410 | 2,522.5 |
| McCulloch | 2 | 16 | 0 | 0 | 0 | 9 | 51 | 114 | 3 | 177 | 2,113.2 |
| McLennan | 15 | 558 | 7 | 106 | 178 | 561 | 2,089 | 5,995 | 314 | 9,250 | 3,899.2 |
| McMullen | 1 | 11 | 0 | 0 | 0 | 6 | 7 | 27 | 0 | 40 | 5,449.6 |
| Medina | 4 | 60 | 0 | 18 | 3 | 33 | 106 | 367 | 18 | 545 | 1,197.1 |
| Menard | 1 | 5 | 0 | 0 | 0 | 0 | 0 | 4 | 1 | 5 | 222.3 |
| Midland | 3 | 260 | 6 | 23 | 67 | 319 | 759 | 2,935 | 250 | 4,359 | 2,929.7 |
| Milam | 4 | 41 | 1 | 2 | 4 | 37 | 158 | 365 | 14 | 581 | 2,412.9 |
| Mills | 1 | 7 | 0 | 0 | 0 | 7 | 6 | 16 | 3 | 32 | 665.6 |
| Mitchell | 2 | 11 | 0 | 0 | 1 | 36 | 52 | 99 | 8 | 196 | 2,096.3 |
| Montague ‡ | 4 | 34 | 0 | 6 | 1 | 23 | 134 | 364 | 21 | 549 | 2,802.0 |
| Montgomery | 12 | 648 | 6 | 20 | 188 | 505 | 2,184 | 5,877 | 603 | 9,383 | 1,908.0 |
| Moore ‡ | 4 | 45 | 1 | 12 | 5 | 60 | 90 | 324 | 26 | 518 | 2,300.4 |
| Morris | 5 | 24 | 0 | 4 | 7 | 34 | 134 | 213 | 12 | 404 | 3,158.7 |
| Motley | 1 | 4 | 0 | 0 | 0 | 1 | 3 | 7 | 1 | 12 | 995.9 |
| Nacogdoches | 3 | 131 | 1 | 8 | 32 | 125 | 494 | 1,221 | 100 | 1,981 | 2,966.1 |
| Navarro ‡ | 3 | 101 | 6 | 27 | 25 | 102 | 504 | 1,136 | 35 | 1,835 | 3,803.2 |
| Newton | 1 | 12 | 1 | 1 | 1 | 11 | 47 | 34 | 6 | 101 | 711.7 |
| Nolan | 4 | 40 | 0 | 10 | 10 | 63 | 156 | 374 | 31 | 644 | 4,326.8 |
| Nueces | 7 | 588 | 19 | 156 | 403 | 1,474 | 2,877 | 12,350 | 563 | 17,842 | 5,074.4 |
| Ochiltree ‡ | 2 | 21 | 0 | 0 | 1 | 14 | 21 | 57 | 13 | 106 | 967.0 |
| Oldham | 1 | 6 | 0 | 0 | 1 | 0 | 8 | 16 | 2 | 27 | 1,303.7 |
| Orange ‡ | 7 | 95 | 4 | 13 | 49 | 219 | 663 | 1,431 | 166 | 2,545 | 3,042.5 |
| Palo Pinto | 2 | 54 | 0 | 5 | 16 | 44 | 303 | 682 | 59 | 1,109 | 3,690.9 |
| Panola | 2 | 44 | 0 | 11 | 7 | 51 | 209 | 460 | 42 | 780 | 3,260.2 |
| Parker ‡ | 5 | 166 | 4 | 7 | 3 | 75 | 442 | 1,285 | 111 | 1,924 | 1,646.2 |
| Parmer | 4 | 16 | 0 | 1 | 1 | 7 | 26 | 58 | 2 | 95 | 932.5 |
| Pecos | 2 | 45 | 0 | 15 | 4 | 40 | 91 | 293 | 8 | 451 | 2,870.8 |
| Polk | 4 | 85 | 1 | 31 | 19 | 97 | 329 | 701 | 64 | 1,242 | 2,705.1 |
| Potter | 4 | 464 | 10 | 114 | 279 | 918 | 2,174 | 6,853 | 819 | 11,167 | 5,250.9 |
| Presidio ‡ | 3 | 12 | 0 | 0 | 0 | 4 | 9 | 9 | 1 | 23 | 309.0 |
| Rains | 1 | 10 | 0 | 5 | 0 | 18 | 76 | 111 | 10 | 220 | 2,001.5 |
| Randall | 3 | 112 | 0 | 5 | 6 | 38 | 99 | 285 | 26 | 459 | 1,226.7 |
| Reagan | 1 | 12 | 0 | 0 | 0 | 0 | 1 | 1 | 0 | 2 | 56.6 |
| Real | 1 | 4 | 0 | 0 | 0 | 0 | 1 | 1 | 2 | 16 | 470.3 |
| Red River | 3 | 33 | 0 | 3 | 5 | 44 | 83 | 145 | 13 | 293 | 2,307.6 |
| Reeves | 2 | 37 | 0 | 0 | 6 | 19 | 38 | 181 | 19 | 263 | 1,897.7 |
| Refugio | 2 | 26 | 1 | 1 | 1 | 12 | 25 | 68 | 1 | 109 | 1,501.4 |
| Roberts | 1 | 4 | 0 | 0 | 0 | 0 | 4 | 14 | 1 | 19 | 2,272.7 |
| Robertson | 4 | 50 | 1 | 2 | 3 | 54 | 84 | 208 | 16 | 368 | 2,216.9 |
| Rockwall | 4 | 143 | 1 | 15 | 7 | 48 | 173 | 849 | 80 | 1,173 | 1,504.1 |
| Runnels ‡ | 4 | 13 | 0 | 1 | 2 | 10 | 69 | 100 | 3 | 185 | 1,766.8 |
| Rusk | 4 | 75 | 2 | 12 | 15 | 168 | 419 | 996 | 79 | 1,691 | 3,272.6 |
| Sabine | 2 | 11 | 0 | 2 | 0 | 26 | 71 | 85 | 10 | 194 | 2,036.5 |
| San Augustine | 2 | 15 | 0 | 2 | 1 | 12 | 39 | 70 | 8 | 132 | 1,491.4 |
| San Jacinto | 1 | 23 | 2 | 5 | 11 | 52 | 237 | 346 | 74 | 727 | 2,646.2 |
| San Patricio | 9 | 125 | 2 | 32 | 18 | 151 | 541 | 1,393 | 96 | 2,233 | 3,334.0 |

# Crime Profile of Texas Counties for 2013

| County | Agencies | Commissioned Personnel † | Murder | Rape | Robbery | Assault | Burglary | Larceny-Theft | Auto Theft | Total Index Crimes (see page 554 for definition) | Crime Rate per 100,000 |
|---|---|---|---|---|---|---|---|---|---|---|---|
| San Saba | 2 | 6 | 0 | 3 | 0 | 6 | 38 | 50 | 5 | 102 | 1,704.8 |
| Schleicher | 1 | 5 | 0 | 0 | 0 | 0 | 8 | 6 | 1 | 15 | 468.3 |
| Scurry ‡ | 3 | 28 | 2 | 11 | 2 | 76 | 147 | 422 | 30 | 690 | 3,999.3 |
| Shackelford | 1 | 5 | 0 | 1 | 1 | 3 | 5 | 11 | 2 | 23 | 682.9 |
| Shelby ‡ | 3 | 38 | 1 | 11 | 5 | 80 | 150 | 334 | 30 | 611 | 2,320.8 |
| Sherman | 2 | 8 | 0 | 1 | 0 | 4 | 6 | 14 | 1 | 26 | 838.4 |
| Smith ‡ | 10 | 451 | 9 | 48 | 100 | 481 | 1,575 | 4,523 | 336 | 7,072 | 3,257.1 |
| Somervell | 1 | 20 | 0 | 0 | 1 | 9 | 30 | 56 | 5 | 101 | 1,165.7 |
| Starr | 5 | 126 | 1 | 5 | 22 | 167 | 231 | 643 | 107 | 1,176 | 1,896.0 |
| Stephens | 2 | 18 | 0 | 6 | 0 | 9 | 32 | 87 | 7 | 141 | 1,490.0 |
| Sterling | 1 | 5 | 0 | 0 | 0 | 3 | 0 | 9 | 0 | 12 | 988.5 |
| Stonewall | 1 | 3 | 0 | 0 | 0 | 2 | 7 | 5 | 4 | 18 | 1,221.2 |
| Sutton | 2 | 9 | 0 | 0 | 0 | 9 | 3 | 9 | 2 | 23 | 585.2 |
| Swisher | 3 | 10 | 1 | 2 | 1 | 10 | 27 | 64 | 0 | 105 | 1,324.8 |
| Tarrant | 37 | 2,313 | 83 | 630 | 2175 | 4736 | 14906 | 48697 | 4,298 | 75,525 | 4066.1 |
| Taylor | 6 | 262 | 1 | 42 | 127 | 343 | 1,157 | 3,658 | 268 | 5,596 | 4,003.9 |
| Terrell | 1 | 7 | 0 | 0 | 0 | 0 | 2 | 7 | 0 | 9 | 1,007.8 |
| Terry | 2 | 29 | 2 | 1 | 3 | 37 | 96 | 149 | 10 | 298 | 2,355.2 |
| Throckmorton | 1 | 2 | 0 | 0 | 0 | 2 | 8 | 10 | 2 | 22 | 1,376.7 |
| Titus | 2 | 52 | 0 | 0 | 8 | 63 | 259 | 604 | 31 | 965 | 2,934.6 |
| Tom Green | 3 | 240 | 5 | 53 | 30 | 215 | 809 | 2,956 | 191 | 4,259 | 3,714.8 |
| Travis ‡ | 16 | 2,312 | 36 | 257 | 821 | 2,646 | 7,768 | 37,551 | 2,396 | 51,475 | 4,453.7 |
| Trinity | 2 | 17 | 0 | 8 | 2 | 30 | 138 | 132 | 16 | 326 | 2,284.7 |
| Tyler ‡ | 2 | ** 9 | 0 | 0 | 6 | 41 | 158 | 106 | 14 | 325 | 1,515.1 |
| Upshur ‡ | 4 | ** 21 | 3 | 7 | 6 | 70 | 314 | 505 | 32 | 937 | 2,552.9 |
| Upton | 1 | 9 | 0 | 0 | 0 | 0 | 1 | 16 | 2 | 19 | 580.7 |
| Uvalde | 3 | 55 | 1 | 7 | 9 | 103 | 208 | 907 | 27 | 1,262 | 4,680.3 |
| Val Verde | 2 | 89 | 0 | 0 | 16 | 67 | 155 | 712 | 18 | 968 | 1,983.1 |
| Van Zandt ‡ | 6 | ** 55 | 2 | 0 | 3 | 89 | 345 | 478 | 42 | 959 | 1,824.2 |
| Victoria | 2 | 210 | 2 | 37 | 63 | 356 | 674 | 2,269 | 105 | 3,506 | 3,875.2 |
| Walker | 2 | 86 | 3 | 37 | 27 | 194 | 386 | 962 | 72 | 1,681 | 2,444.2 |
| Waller | 5 | 112 | 1 | 22 | 19 | 59 | 231 | 487 | 57 | 876 | 1,986.3 |
| Ward | 2 | 26 | 0 | 6 | 1 | 54 | 92 | 272 | 16 | 441 | 4,003.6 |
| Washington | 2 | ** 65 | 1 | 14 | 14 | 76 | 146 | 432 | 24 | 707 | 2,058.1 |
| Webb | 5 | ** 338 | 4 | 80 | 211 | 838 | 1,536 | 8,952 | 391 | 12,012 | 4,568.4 |
| Wharton | 3 | 92 | 1 | 12 | 15 | 131 | 247 | 710 | 38 | 1,154 | 2,784.7 |
| Wheeler | 2 | 13 | 1 | 0 | 0 | 6 | 29 | 62 | 15 | 113 | 1,973.1 |
| Wichita | 6 | 295 | 7 | 39 | 131 | 319 | 1,179 | 3,695 | 311 | 5,681 | 4,301.4 |
| Wilbarger | 2 | 28 | 0 | 6 | 2 | 31 | 103 | 258 | 22 | 422 | 3188.8 |
| Willacy | 5 | 39 | 0 | 20 | 5 | 191 | 199 | 474 | 19 | 908 | 4,106.7 |
| Williamson | 12 | 460 | 4 | 82 | 73 | 332 | 985 | 5,099 | 190 | 6,765 | 1,554.6 |
| Wilson | 5 | 55 | 0 | 1 | 1 | 47 | 133 | 405 | 43 | 630 | 1,400.5 |
| Winkler | 3 | 23 | 0 | 0 | 1 | 23 | 11 | 64 | 11 | 110 | 1,477.1 |
| Wise | 4 | 100 | 1 | 5 | 9 | 81 | 175 | 586 | 57 | 914 | 1,495.2 |
| Wood | 5 | 52 | 1 | 0 | 5 | 54 | 449 | 590 | 38 | 1,137 | 2,650.3 |
| Yoakum | 2 | 15 | 1 | 5 | 0 | 5 | 39 | 65 | 11 | 126 | 1539.2 |
| Young | 3 | 40 | 0 | 2 | 2 | 22 | 122 | 371 | 20 | 539 | 2,938.0 |
| Zapata | 1 | 36 | 0 | 6 | 2 | 79 | 217 | 188 | 33 | 525 | 3,639.8 |
| Zavala ‡ | 2 | 25 | 0 | 0 | 2 | 9 | 94 | 91 | 13 | 209 | 1,728.0 |
| **TOTAL** | **1,048** | **45,990** | **1,151** | **7,443** | **31,852** | **65,267** | **190,567** | **604,389** | **65,671** | **966,340** | **3,653.7** |

* County population figures used for calculation of crime rate are the U.S. Census Bureau revised figures for 2013.
† The commissioned officers listed here are fulltime sworn officers employed as of Oct. 31, 2013, by sheriffs' offices and police departments of municipalities; universities, colleges, and public-school districts; transit systems; park departments; and medical facilities. The Texas Department of Public Safety has 3,494 commissioned personnel stationed statewide. There are a total of 37,881 civilian personnel employed by all agencies.
** Counties with at least one agency that did not report its commissioned personnel.
‡ County in which one or more law-enforcement agencies did not report data for all of 2013 to the DPS. The numbers of index crimes for the county includes estimates for nonreporting agencies to enable the DPS to provide comparable data. Commissioned personnel for nonreporting agencies my be omitted from the personnel total.

# THE BRYAN MUSEUM

### GALVESTON, TX

## MUSEUM HOURS

| | |
|---|---|
| FRIDAY | 11 AM - 4 PM |
| SATURDAY | 11 AM - 4 PM |
| SUNDAY | 11 AM - 4 PM |
| MONDAY | 11 AM - 4 PM |
| TUES. - THURS. | CLOSED |

## ADMISSION

| | |
|---|---|
| ADULT | $10.00 |
| SENIOR | $8.00 |
| MILITARY | $8.00 |
| STUDENT (WITH ID) | $8.00 |
| AGE 6 - 12 | $4.00 |

GROUP RATES AND MEMBERSHIPS ARE NOW AVAILABLE. SEE WEBSITE FOR DETAILS.

WWW.THEBRYANMUSEUM.ORG    THE BRYAN MUSEUM    409.632.7685
1315 21ST ST. GALVESTON, TX 77550

# Culture & Arts

*The Austin City Limits Music Festival takes place the first two weekends in September. Photo by Nick Simonite.*

## Museums, Texas Medal of the Arts
## Texas Institute of Letters
## State Artists, Poets, Historians
## Film and Television
## Holidays and Religion

*The Bryan Museum Sponsors the Culture Section*

# Texas Museums of Arts, Science, History

*Listed below are links to the websites of Texas museums. Where required some have indication of the area of emphasis of the exhibits.*

### Abilene
Frontier Texas! (history)
www.frontiertexas.com
Grace Museum (art, history)
www.thegracemuseum.org
National Center for Children's Illustrated Literature
www.nccil.org

### Addison
Cavanaugh Flight Museum
www.cavanaughflightmuseum.com

### Albany
Old Jail Art Center
www.theoldjailartcenter.org

### Alpine
Museum of the Big Bend (history)
www.sulross.edu/museum

### Amarillo
Amarillo Museum of Art
www.amarilloart.org
American Quarter Horse Hall of Fame & Museum
www.aqha.com/foundation/museum
Don Harrington Discovery Center (science, children's)
www.dhdc.org
Texas Pharmacy Museum
www.ttuhsc.edu/sop/prospective/visitors/museum.aspx

### Angleton
Brazoria County Historical Museum
www.bchm.org

### Austin
Austin Children's Museum
www.austinkids.org
Austin Museum of Art
www.amoa.org
Bob Bullock Texas State History Museum
www.thestoryoftexas.com
Capitol Visitors Center (history)
www.tspb.state.tx.us/CVC/home/home.html
Elisabet Ney Museum (art, history)
www.austintexas.gov/department/elisabet-ney-museum
French Legation Museum (history)
www.frenchlegationmuseum.org
Harry Ransom Humanities Research Center (history, literature)
www.hrc.utexas.edu
Jack S. Blanton Museum of Art
www.blantonmuseum.org
Jacob Fontaine Religious Museum
www.cornbread.com/~jfrm
Jourdan-Bachman Pioneer Farms
www.pioneerfarms.org
Lady Bird Johnson Wildflower Center
www.wildflower.org
Lyndon B. Johnson Library
www.lbjlibrary.org
Mexic-Arte Museum (Art)
www.mexic-artemuseum.org

O. Henry Museum (history)
www.austintexas.gov/department/o-henry-museum
Texas Memorial Museum (history, natural history)
www.utexas.edu/tmm
Texas Military Forces Museum
www.texasmilitaryforcesmuseum.org
Texas Music Museum
www.texasmusicmuseum.org
Umlauf Sculpture Garden & Museum
www.umlaufsculpture.org
Wild Basin Wilderness Preserve
www.wildbasin.org
Women and Their Work
www.womenandtheirwork.org

### Bay City
Matagorda County Museum
www.matagordacountymuseum.org

### Beaumont
Art Museum of Southeast Texas
www.amset.org
Edison Museum (science)
www.edisonmuseum.org
Fire Museum of Texas
www.firemuseumoftexas.org
Spindletop/Gladys City Boomtown Museum (history)
www.spindletop.org
Texas Energy Museum (history)
www.texasenergymuseum.org

### Beeville
Beeville Art Museum
www.bamtexas.org

### Belton
Bell County Museum
www.bellcountymuseum.org

### Big Spring
Heritage of Big Spring
www.heritagebigspring.com

### Bonham
Sam Rayburn Library/Museum
www.cah.utexas.edu/museums/rayburn.php

### Borger
Hutchinson County Historical Museum
www.hutchinsoncountymuseum.org

### Brownsville
Brownsville Museum of Fine Art
www.brownsvillemfa.org
Children's Museum of Brownsville
www.cmofbrownsville.org
Historic Brownsville Museum
www.brownsvillemuseum.org

### Brownwood
Brown County Museum of History
http://browncountyhistory.org/bcmoh.html

### Bryan
Brazos Valley Museum of Natural History
www.brazosvalleymuseum.org

### Buffalo Gap
Buffalo Gap Historic Village
www.tfhcc.com/buff/index.html

### Burton
Burton Cotton Gin and Museum
www.cottonginmuseum.org

### Canadian
River Valley Pioneer Museum
www.rivervalleymuseum.org
The Citadelle Art Foundation
www.thecitadelle.org

### Canyon
Panhandle-Plains Historical Museum
www.panhandleplains.org

### Carthage
Texas Country Music Hall of Fame & Tex Ritter Museum
www.carthagetexas.com/HallofFame/index.html

### Clarendon
Saints' Roost Museum (history)
www.saintsroost.org

### Clifton
Bosque Museum (history)
www.bosquemuseum.org

### College Station
George Bush Presidential Library
www.georgebushfoundation.org
Stark University Center Galleries
http://uart.tamu.edu/permanent-collection
Virtual Museum of Nautical Archaeology
www.ina.tamu.edu/vm.htm

### Conroe
Heritage Museum of Montgomery County
www.heritagemuseum.us

### Corpus Christi
Art Museum of South Texas
www.stia.org
Corpus Christi Museum of Science and History
www.ccmuseum.com/museum/index.cfm
Texas State Aquarium
www.texasstateaquarium.org
Texas State Museum of Asian Cultures
www.asianculturesmuseum.org
USS Lexington Museum
www.usslexington.com

### Corsicana
Pearce Western Art/Civil War Museum
www.pearcecollections.us

### Cotulla
Brush Country Historical Museum
www.historicdistrict.com/museum

### Dalhart
XIT Museum (history)
www.xitmuseum.com

*Fun at the Children's Museum of Brownsville. Photo courtesy of the museum.*

### Dallas
African American Museum
www.aamdallas.org
Museum of the American Railroad
www.dallasrailwaymuseum.com
Crow Collection of Asian Art
www.crowcollection.org
Dallas Historical Society (Fair Park)
www.dallashistory.org
Dallas Museum of Art
www.dallasmuseumofart.org
Dallas Museum of Natural History
www.natureandscience.org
Frontiers of Flight Museum
www.flightmuseum.com
George W. Bush Presidential Center
www.bushcenter.com
International Museum of Cultures
www.internationalmuseumofcultures.org
Perot Museum of Nature and Science
www.perotmuseum.org
Nash Sculpture Center
www.nashersculpturecenter.org
Meadows Museum (art)
www.smu.edu/meadows/museum
Dallas Heritage Village
www.dallasheritagevillage.org
The Sixth Floor Museum (history)
www.jfk.org

### Denison
Red River Railroad Museum
www.redriverrailmuseum.org

### Denton
Courthouse-on-the-Square Museum (history)
www.dentoncounty.com/dept/main.asp?Dept=72
University of North Texas Art Galleries

www.gallery.unt.edu
Denton County Historical Museum
www.dentoncountyhistoricalmuseum.com

### Dublin
Dr Pepper Bottling Company Museum
www.dublindrpepper.com

### Dumas
Window on the Plains Museum
www.dumasmuseumandartcenter.org

### Edgewood
Edgewood Heritage Park and Historical Village
www.vzinet.com/heritage

### Edinburg
Museum of South Texas History
www.mosthistory.org

### El Campo
El Campo Museum of Natural History
www.elcampomuseum.com

### El Paso
Centennial Museum / Chihuahuan Desert Gardens
www.museum.utep.edu
El Paso Museum of Archaeology
www.elpasotexas.gov/arch_museum
El Paso Museum of Art
www.elpasoartmuseum.org
El Paso Museum of History
www.elpasotexas.gov/history

### Fort Davis
Chihuahuan Desert Research
http://cdri.org

### Fort Stockton

Annie Riggs Museum (history)
www.tourtexas.com/fortstockton/ftstockriggs.html

### Fort Worth
Amon Carter Museum (art)
www.cartermuseum.org
Cattle Raisers Museum
www.cattleraisersmuseum.org
Fort Worth Museum of Science and History
www.fwmuseum.org
Kimbell Art Museum
www.kimbellart.org
Log Cabin Village (history)
www.logcabinvillage.org
Modern Art Museum of Fort Worth
http://themodern.org
National Cowgirl Museum and Hall of Fame
www.cowgirl.net
Sid Richardson Collection of Western Art
www.sidrmuseum.org
Texas Civil War Museum
www.texascivilwarmuseum.com

### Fredericksburg
Gillespie County Historical Society
www.pioneermuseum.com
National Museum of the Pacific War
www.nimitz-museum.org

### Galveston
The Bryan Museum
www.thebryanmuseum.org
Lone Star Flight Museum
www.lsfm.org
Moody Mansion
www.moodymansion.org
Offshore Energy Center / Ocean Star

(science, industry)
www.oceanstaroec.com
Texas Seaport Museum and Tallship "Elissa"
www.tsm-elissa.org

### Gilmer
Flight of Phoenix Aviation Museum
www.flightofthephoenix.org

### Greenville
Audie Murphy / American Cotton Museum
www.cottonmuseum.com

### Henderson
The Depot Museum (history)
www.depotmuseum.com

### Houston
Blaffer Gallery, University of Houston
www.class.uh.edu/blaffer
Children's Museum of Houston
www.cmhouston.org
(**Houston**, continued)

Contemporary Arts Museum
www.camh.org
Houston Center for Contemporary Craft
www.crafthouston.org
Houston Center for Photography
www.hcponline.org
Houston Fire Museum (history)
www.houstonfiremuseum.org
Houston Museum of Natural Science
www.hmns.org
Lawndale Art Center
www.lawndaleartcenter.org
The Menil Collection (art)
www.menil.org
Museum of Fine Arts
www.mfah.org
Museum of Health and Medical Science
www.mhms.org
Museum of Printing History
www.printingmuseum.org
Rice University Art Gallery
www.ricegallery.org
San Jacinto Museum of History
www.sanjacinto-museum.org
Space Center Houston
www.spacecenter.org

### Huntsville
Sam Houston Memorial Museum
http://samhoustonmemorialmuseum.com
Texas Prison Museum
www.txprisonmuseum.org

### Kerrville
Museum of Western Art
www.museumofwesternart.org

### Kilgore
East Texas Oil Museum
www.easttexasoilmuseum.com

### Lake Jackson
Lake Jackson Historical Museum
www.lakejacksonmuseum.org

### Laredo
Republic of the Rio Grande Museum
www.webbheritage.org/index_files/21RRG.htm

Texas A&M International University Planetarium
www.tamiu.edu/coas/planetarium

### League City
West Bay Common School Children's Museum (history)
www.oneroomschoolhouse.org

### Longview
Longview Museum of Fine Arts
www.lmfa.org

### Lubbock
American Museum of Agriculture
www.agriculturehistory.org
Buddy Holly Center (history)
www.buddyhollycenter.org
Museum of Texas Tech University (art, humanities, science)
www.depts.ttu.edu/museumttu
National Ranching Heritage Center
www.depts.ttu.edu/ranchhc/home.htm
Science Spectrum
www.sciencespectrum.org/new/home.shtml

### Lufkin
Texas Forestry Museum
www.treetexas.com

### Marfa
Chinati Foundation (art)
www.chinati.org

### Marshall
Harrison County Historical Museum
http://harrisoncountymuseum.org
Michelson Museum of Art
www.michelsonmuseum.org

### McAllen
International Museum of Art & Science
www.imasonline.org

### McKinney
Heard Natural Science Museum
www.heardmuseum.org

### Midland
American Airpower Heritage Museum / Commerative Air Force
www.airpowermuseum.org
Museum of the Southwest (art, science, children's)
www.museumsw.org
Petroleum Museum
www.petroleummuseum.org

### Mineral Wells
National Vietnam War Museum
www.nationalvnwarmuseum.org

### Mobeetie
Old Mobeetie Texas Association
www.mobeetie.com

### Nacogdoches
Millard's Crossing Historic Village
www.millardscrossing.org

### New Braunfels
Sophienburg Museum of History and Culture
www.sophienburg.org

### Odessa
Ellen Noel Art Museum
www.noelartmuseum.org
Presidential Museum
http://thepresidentialmuseum.org

### Orange
Stark Museum of Art
www.starkmuseum.org

### Panhandle
Square House Museum
www.squarehousemuseum.org

### Perryton
Museum of the Plains
www.museumoftheplains.com
### Plano
Heritage Farmstead Museum
www.heritagefarmstead.org
### Port Arthur
Museum of the Gulf Coast (history)
www.museumofthegulfcoast.org

### Port Lavaca
Calhoun County Museum (history)
www.calhouncountymuseum.org
### Richmond
George Ranch Historical Park
www.georgeranch.org
### Rockport
Texas Maritime Museum
www.texasmaritimemuseum.org
### Rosenberg
Rosenberg Railroad Museum
www.rosenbergrrmuseum.org

### Round Top
Henkel Square (history)
www.henkelsquareroundtop.com
Winedale Historical Center
www.cah.utexas.edu/museums/winedale_intro.php
### San Angelo
San Angelo Museum of Fine Arts and Children's Art Museum
www.samfa.org
### San Antonio
The Alamo
www.thealamo.org
Briscoe Western Art Museum
www.briscoemuseum.org
Hertzberg Circus Collection
www.wittemuseum.org
Institute of Texan Cultures
www.texancultures.com
Kleberg South Texas Heritage Center
www.wittemuseum.org/index.php/plan/140-stheritage
Magic Lantern Castle Museum
www.magiclanterns.org
Museo Alameda
www.thealameda.org
The McNay Art Museum
www.mcnayart.org
San Antonio Art League Museum
www.saalm.org
San Antonio Museum of Art
www.samuseum.org/main
Stieren Center for Exhibitions
www.mcnayart.org/index.php?option=com_content&view=article&id=134&Itemid=158
Witte Museum (science, history)
www.wittemuseum.org

**San Marcos**
Southwestern Writers Collection and Wittliff Gallery of Southwestern & Mexican Photography
www.thewittliffcollections.txstate.edu

**Sarita**
Kenedy Ranch Museum of South Texas
www.kenedymuseum.org

**Schulenburg**
Stanzel Model Aircraft Museum
www.stanzelmuseum.org

**Serbin**
Texas Wendish Heritage Museum
http://wendish.concordia.edu

**Sherman**
Red River Historical Museum
http://hosting.texoma.net/rrhms/frames.htm

**Snyder**
Scurry County Museum
http://scurrycountymuseum.org

**Sulphur Springs**
Southwest Dairy Center/Museum
www.southwestdairyfarmers.com

**Teague**
The B-RI Railroad Museum
www.therailroadmuseum.com

**Temple**
Czech Heritage Museum
www.czechmuseum.org
Railroad and Heritage Museum
www.rrhm.org

**Texarkana**
Museum of Regional History
www.texarkanamuseums.org

**Thurber**
W.K. Gordon Center for Industrial History of Texas
www.tarleton.edu/~gordoncenter

**Tyler**
Discovery Science Place
www.discoveryscienceplace.com
Historic Aviation Memorial Musuem
www.tylerhamm.com
Smith County Historical Museum
www.smithcountyhistoricalsociety.org/index.php
Tyler Museum of Art
www.tylermuseum.org

**Victoria**
Museum of the Coastal Bend (history)
www.museumofthecoastalbend.org

**Waco**
Dr Pepper Museum (history)
www.drpeppermuseum.com
Mayborn Museum Complex (history, science)

www.baylor.edu/mayborn
Texas Ranger Hall of Fame / Museum
www.texasranger.org
Texas Sports Hall of Fame
www.tshof.org

**Washington**
Star of the Republic Museum (history)
www.starmuseum.org

**Weatherford**
Museum of the Americas
www.museumoftheamericas.com

**Wharton**
20th Century Technology Museum
www.20thcenturytech.com

**White Settlement**
White Settlement Historical Museum
www.wsmuseum.com

**Wichita Falls**
Kell House Museum (history)
www.wichita-heritage.org/Kellhousemain.htm
Museum of Art
www.mwsu.edu/wfma

**Yoakum**
Yoakum Heritage Museum
www.yoakumareachamber.com/pages/yoakumheritagemuseum.html ☆

# Philosophical Society of Texas Book Award

The Philosophical Society of Texas established the Award of Merit in 2000 and expanded it in 2012 to separate categories, one for fiction and one for non-fiction. The book must be about Texas or the author must have been born in or have resided within the boundaries claimed by the Republic of Texas in 1836. Award of Merit winners are listed below.

| | | |
|---|---|---|
| 2000 | | Gregg Cantrell, *Stephen F. Austin, Empresario*, Yale University Press, 1999. |
| 2001 | | Frank D. Welch, *Philip Johnson & Texas*, University of Texas Press, 2000. |
| 2002 | | Hal K. Rothman, *LBJ's Texas White House: "Our Heart's Home,"* Texas A&M University Press, 2001. |
| 2003 | | James L. Haley, *Sam Houston*, University of Oklahoma Press, 2002. |
| 2004 | | Randolph B. Campbell, *Gone to Texas: A History of the Lone Star State*, Oxford University Press, 2003. |
| 2005 | | David La Vere, *The Texas Indians*, Texas A&M University Press, 2004. |
| 2006 | | Mavis P. Kelsey Sr. and Robin Brandt Hutchinon, *Engraved Prints of Texas, 1554–1900*, Texas A&M University Press, 2005 |
| 2007 | | Richard B. McCaslin, *At the Heart of Texas, 100 Years of the Texas State Historical Association, 1897–1997*, Texas State Historical Association Press, 2006. |
| 2008 | | Stephen Fox, *The Country Houses of John F. Staub*, Texas A&M University Press, 2007. |
| 2009 | | Pekka Hämäläinen, *The Comanche Empire*, Yale University Press, 2008. |
| 2010 | | Emilio Zamora, *Claiming Rights and Righting Wrongs in Texas: Mexican Workers and Job Politics During World War II*, Texas A&M University Press, 2009. |
| 2011 | | Dan K. Utley and Cynthia J. Beeman, *History Ahead: Stories beyond the Texas Roadside Markers*, Texas A&M University Press, 2011. |
| 2012 | Fiction | Gerald Duff, *Blue Sabine*, Moon City Press, 2011. |
| | Non-fiction | Michael Berryhill, *The Trails of Eroy Brown: The Murder Case that Shook the Texas Prison System*, University of Texas Press, 2011. |
| 2013 | Fiction | Ben Rehder, *The Chicken Hanger: A Novel*, Texas Christian University Press, 2012. |
| | Non-fiction | Jan Reid, *Let the People In: The Life and Times of Ann Richards*, University of Texas Press, 2012. |
| 2014 | Fiction | Thomas Zigal, *Many Rivers to Cross*, Texas Christian University Press, 2013. |
| | Non-fiction | Raúl Coronado, *A World Not to Come: A History of Latino Writing and Print Culture*, Harvard University Press, 2013. |

# State Cultural Agencies Assist the Arts

*Source: Principally, the Texas Commission on the Arts, along with other state cultural agencies.*

Culture in Texas, as in any market, is a mixture of activity generated by both the commercial and the nonprofit sectors.

The commercial sector encompasses Texas-based profit-making businesses including commercial recording artists, nightclubs, record companies, private galleries, assorted boutiques that carry fine art collectibles and private dance and music halls. Texas also has extensive cultural resources offered by nonprofit organizations that are engaged in charitable, educational and humanitarian activities.

The Legislature has authorized five state agencies to administer cultural services and funds for the public good. The agencies are:

Texas Commission on the Arts; Texas Film Commission; Texas Historical Commission; Texas State Library and Archives Commission, and the State Preservation Board.

Although not a state agency, another organization that provides cultural services to the citizens of Texas is Humanities Texas.

The Commission on the Arts was established in 1965 to develop a receptive climate for the arts through the conservation and advancement of Texas' rich and diverse arts and cultural industries.

The Texas Commission on the Arts' primary goals are:

• provide grants for the arts and cultural industries in Texas.

• provide the financial, human, and technical resources necessary to ensure viable arts and cultural communities

• promote widespread attendance at arts and cultural performances and exhibitions in Texas.

• ensure access to arts in Texas through marketing, fund raising, and cultural tourism.

The arts commission is responsible for several initiatives including:

• Arts Education – programs that serve the curricular and training needs of the state's school districts, private schools, and home schools.

• Marketing and Public Relations – marketing and fund-raising expertise to generate funds for agency operations and increase visibility of the arts in Texas.

• Cultural Tourism – programs that develop and promote tourism destinations featuring the arts.

Information on programs is available on the Texas Commission on the Arts at www.arts.state.tx.us. ☆

*The Hobby Center in Houston. Photo by Ed Schipul (CC).*

## Performing Arts Organizations

The Texas Commission on the Arts provides a complete listing of performing arts organizations in Texas at www.arts.state.tx.us. There are links arranged by category; dance, theater, music, etc.

# Public Libraries in Texas

*The following information furnished by the Library Development Division of the Texas State Library and Archives in Austin.*

Texas public libraries continue to strive to meet the education and information needs of Texans by providing library services of high quality with oftentimes-limited resources.

Each year, services provided by public libraries increase, with more visits to public libraries and higher attendance in library programs.

The challenges facing the public libraries in Texas are many and varied. The costs for providing electronic and on-line sources, in addition to traditional library services, are growing faster than library budgets.

Urban libraries are trying to serve growing populations, while libraries in rural areas are trying to serve remote populations and provide distance learning where possible.

National rankings of public libraries are published by the National Center for Education Statistics. These rankings may be found at:

**www.imis.gov/research/default.aspx.**

When comparing Texas statistics to those nationally, Texas continues to rank below most of the other states in most categories, with the exception of Reference Transactions and Public Use Internet Terminals.

Complete statistical information on public libraries is available on the Texas State Library's website: **www.tsl.texas.gov**. There is also a listing of libraries at: **www.tsl.texas.gov/texshare/libsearch/index.php.**

# Texas Medal of the Arts Awards

*Source: Texas Commission on the Arts.*

The Texas Medals of the Arts were presented to artists and arts patrons with Texas ties in February 2015.

The awards are administered by the Texas Cultural Trust Council. The council was established to raise money and awareness for the Texas Cultural Trust Fund, which was created by the Legislature in 1993 to support cultural arts in Texas (www.txculturaltrust. org).

The medals, awarded every two years, were first presented in 2001. A concurrent proclamation by the state Senate and House of Representatives honors the recipients, and the governor presents the awards in Austin.

## 2015

**Lifetime Achievement Award:** The Gatlin Brothers of Seminole, Abilene and Odessa.

**Multimedia:** Emilio Nicolas Sr. of San Antonio, for work as broadcaster.

**Music:** T Bone Burnett of Fort Worth.

**Visual arts:** Rick Lowe of Houston, artist.

**Dance:** Kilgore Rangerettes.

**Literary:** Lawrence Wright, Austin and Dallas.

**Film:** Jamie Foxx, Terrell, actor.

**Television:** Dan Rather, Wharton, news broadcaster.

**Television:** Chandra Wilson, Houston, actor.

**Theater:** Robert Schenkkan, Austin.

**Arts education:** Booker T. Washington High School for the Performing and Visual Arts, Dallas.

**Architecture:** Charles Renfro, Houston.

**Individual arts patron:** Margaret McDermott, Dallas.

**Corporate arts patron:** Dr Pepper Snapple Group, Plano.

**Standing Ovation Award:** Ruth Altshuler of Dallas.

## 2013

**Multimedia:** Eva Longoria of Corpus Christi, for work as actress, author and philanthropist.

**Music:** Steve Miller of Dallas.

**Visual arts:** James Surls, Splendora, artist.

**Dance:** Houston Ballet.

**Television/Film:** Ricardo Chavira, San Antonio, actor.

**Theater arts:** Joe Sears and Jaston Williams, Austin, (Greater Tuna fame).

**Arts education:** Big Thought / Gigi Antoni, Dallas.

**Individual arts patron:** Gene Jones and Charlotte Jones Anderson, Dallas.

**Foundation arts patron:** Kimbell Arts Foundation, Fort Worth.

**Corporate arts patron:** Texas Monthly.

## 2011

**Lifetime Achievement Award:** Barbara Smith Conrad from Center Point near Pittsburg, operatic mezzo-soprano and civil rights icon.

**Music:** ZZ Top of Houston, legendary band that sold over 50 million albums.

**Literary:** Robert M. Edsel, Dallas, author and founder/president of the Monuments Men Foundation for the Preservation of Art.

**Visual arts:** James Drake, Lubbock, artist.

**Television:** Bob Schieffer, Fort Worth, CBS news anchor.

**Theater arts:** Alley Theatre, Houston.

**Multimedia:** Ray Benson, Austin, front man for Asleep at the Wheel and co-writer of the play *A Ride with Bob* based on the life of Bob Wills.

**Film:** Marcia Gay Harden, UT-Austin graduate, Oscar-winning actress.

**Film:** Bill Paxton, Fort Worth, four-time Golden Globe nominee.

**Arts education:** Tom Staley, director of the Harry Ransom Center at UT-Austin.

**Individual arts patron:** Ernest and Sarah Butler of Austin, major donors to Austin arts groups.

**Corporate arts patron:** H-E-B, grocer with a long history of supporting the arts throughout Texas.

## 2009

**A Standing Ovation Award** was presented to former First Lady Laura Bush of Midland and Dallas.

**Lifetime Achievement Award:** posthumously to artist Robert Rauschenberg, born in Port Arthur.

**Music:** Clint Black of Katy, country music singer/songwriter.

**Literary:** T.R. Fehrenbach of San Antonio. Mr. Fehrenbach, born in San Benito, is the author of 18 nonfiction books, including *Lone Star: A History of Texas and Texans.*

**Visual arts:** Keith Carter of Beaumont, photographer.

**Theater arts:** Betty Buckley of Fort Worth, Tony Award winner and film actress.

**Multimedia:** Austin City Limits, the 30-year television series.

**Film:** Robert Rodriguez of Austin. Mr. Rodriguez, born in San Antonio, is a film director and writer.

**Architecture:** David Lake of Austin and Ted Flato of Corpus Christi, both now working in San Antonio.

**Arts education:** Pianist James Dick of Round Top, founder of the International Festival-Institute there.

**Individual arts patron:** Edith O'Donnell of Dallas.

**Corporate arts patron:** Anheuser-Busch of St. Louis and Houston.

## 2007

**Lifetime Achievement Award:** Broadcast newsman Walter Cronkite of Houston.

**Music:** Ornette Coleman of Fort Worth, jazz saxophonist.

**Dance:** Alvin Ailey American Dance Theater. The late Alvin Ailey, born in Rogers, was a creator of African American dance works.

**Literary:** writer Sandra Brown of Waco.

**Visual arts:** Jesús Moroles of Corpus Christi/Rockport, sculptor.

**Theater arts:** actress Judith Ivey of El Paso.

**Multimedia:** Bill Wittliff of Taft and Austin, publisher, writer, photographer, director, producer.

**Arts education:** Paul Baker of Hereford/Waelder. Headed drama departments at Baylor and Trinity universities.

**Individual arts patron:** Diana and Bill Hobby of Houston.

**Corporate arts patron:** Neiman Marcus, Dallas.

**Foundation arts patron:** Sid W. Richardson Foundation of Fort Worth.

## 2005

**Lifetime Achievement Award:** singer Vikki Carr of El Paso.

**Television/theater:** actress Phylicia Rashad of Houston.

**Music:** singer/songwriter Lyle Lovett of Klein.

**Dance:** Ben Stevenson of Houston and Fort Worth.

**Literary arts:** Naomi Shihab Nye of San Antonio.

**Visual arts:** Jose Cisneros of El Paso.

**Theater:** Robert Wilson of Waco.

**Arts education:** Ginger Head-Gearheart of Fort Worth, advocate of arts education in public schools.

**Individual arts patrons:** Joe R. and Teresa Lozano Long of Austin, philanthropists.

**Foundation arts patron:** Nasher Foundation/Dallas.

## 2003

**Lifetime Achievement:** John Graves of Glen Rose, author of *Goodbye to A River.*

**Media-film/television acting:** Fess Parker of Fort Worth.

**Music:** country singer Charley Pride of Dallas.

**Dance:** Tommy Tune of Wichita Falls and Houston.

**Theater:** Enid Holm of Odessa, actress and former executive director of Texas Nonprofit Theatres.

**Literary arts:** Sandra Cisneros of San Antonio.

**Visual arts:** sculptor Glenna Goodacre of Dallas.

**Folk arts:** Tejano singer Lydia Mendoza of San Antonio.

**Architecture:** State Capitol Preservation Project of Austin, headed by Dealey Herndon.

**Arts education:** theater teacher Marca Lee Bircher, Dallas.

**Individual arts patron**: philanthropist Nancy B. Hamon of Dallas.
**Corporate arts patron**: Exxon/Mobil based in Irving.
**Foundation arts patron**: Houston Endowment Inc.

### 2001
**Lifetime Achievement**: Van Cliburn of Fort Worth.
**Film**: actor Tommy Lee Jones of San Saba.
**Music**: singer-songwriter Willie Nelson of Austin.
**Dance**: Debbie Allen of Houston, choreographer, director, actress and composer.
**Theater**: *Texas* musical-drama producer Neil Hess of Amarillo.

**Literary arts**: playwright Horton Foote of Wharton.
**Visual arts**: muralist John Biggers of Houston.
**Folk arts**: musician brothers Santiago Jimenez Jr. and Flaco Jimenez of San Antonio.
**Architecture**: restoration architect Wayne Bell of Austin.
**Arts education**: theater arts director Gilberto Zepeda Jr. of Pharr.
**Individual arts patron**: philanthropist Jack Blanton of Houston.
**Corporate arts patron**: SBC Communications Inc. of San Antonio.
**Foundation arts patron**: Meadows Foundation of Dallas. ☆

# Texas Institute of Letters Awards

Each year since 1939, the **Texas Institute of Letters** (texasinstituteofletters.org/) has honored outstanding literature and journalism that is either by Texans or about Texas subjects.

Awards have been made for fiction, nonfiction, Southwest history, general information, magazine and newspaper journalism, children's books, translation, poetry, and book design. The awards of recent years are listed below:

**Writer/Designer: Title**

### 2015
Elizabeth Crook: *Monday, Monday*
Michael Morton: *Getting Life: An Innocent Man's 25-Year Journey from Prison to Peace*
Merritt Tierce: *Love Me Back*
Lawrence T. Jones: *Lens on the Texas Frontier*
Katherine Hoerth: *Goddess Wears Cowboy Boots*
Brian Van Reet: "Eat The Spoil," in *Missouri Review*
Chloe Honum: *The Tulip-Flame*
Pamela Colloff: "The Witness," *Texas Monthly*
Bill Wittliff and Ellen McKie: *The Devil's Backbone*, written by Bill Wittliff, illustrated by Jack Unruh
Nikki Lofton, *Nightingale's Nest*
Glaudia Guadalupe Martinez: *Pig Park*
Pat Mora and Lilbby Martinez: *I Pledge Allegiance*
**Lon Tinkle Award (for career): Lawrence Wright**

### 2014
Tom Zigal: *Many Rivers to Cross*
John Taliaferro: *All The Great Prizes: The Life of John Hay from Lincoln to Roosevelt*
Lawrence Wright: *Going Clear: Scientology, Hollywood, and the Prison of Belief*
Nan Cuba: *Body and Bread*
Raúl Coronado: *A World Not to Come: A History of Latino Writing and Print Culture*
Pattiann Rogers: *Holy Heathen Rhapsody*
Bret Anthony Johnston: "To A Good Home," *Virginia Quarterly Review*
Sasha West: *Failure And I Bury The Body*
John MacCormack: "Life On The Shale," *San Antonio Express-News*, series
Lindsay Starr, *Two Prospectors: The Letters of Sam Shepard and Johnny Dark*
Xavier Garza, *Maximilian and the Mystery of the Bingo Rematch*
Kathi Appelt: *The True Blue Scouts of Sugar Man Swamp*
David Bowles: *Flower, Song, Dance: Aztec and Mayan Poetry*
**Lon Tinkle Award (for career): Jan Reid**

### 2013
Ben Fountain: *Billy Lynn's Long Halftime Walk*
Margie Crisp: *River of Contrasts*
Kevin Grauke: *Shadows of Men*

Kate Sayen Kirkland: *Captain James A. Baker of Houston: 1857–1941*
Ken Fontenot: *Kingdom of Birds*
James Sanderson: "Bankers," in *Descant*
Kathleen Winter: *Nostalgia for the Criminal Past*
Mellissa Del Bosque: "The Deadliest Place in Mexico," *The Texas Observer*, February, 12, 2012
Kristina Kachele: *In the Country of Empty Crosses*, written by Arturo Madrid
Donna Rubin, *Log Cabin Kitty*
Melodie Cuate: *Journey to Plum Creek*
**Lon Tinkle Award (for career): Stephen Harrigan**

### 2012
Stephen Harrigan: *Remember Ben Clayton*
Steven Fenberg: *Unprecedented Power: Jesse Jones, Capitalism, and the Common Good*
Siobhan Fallon: *You Know When the Men Are Gone*
Christopher Long: *The Looshaus*
Jennifer Grotz: *The Needle*
Bret Anthony Johnston: "Paradeability," *American Short Fiction*
Jose Antonio Rodriguez: *The Shallow End of Sleep*
Skip Hollandsworth: "The Lost Boys," *Texas Monthly,* April 2011
Jordan Smith: "The Science of Injustice," *Austin Chronicle*, August 19, 2011
Barbara Werden and Lindsay Starr, *Lone Star Law*, written by Michael Ariens
Dave Oliphant, *After-Dinner Declarations* by Nicanor Parra
Elaine Scott: *Space, Stars and the Beginning of Time*
J.L. Powers: *This Thing Called the Future*
**Lon Tinkle Award (for career): Gary Cartwright**

### 2011[1]
Jan Reid: *Comanche Sundown*
Gary Lavergne: *Before Brown: Heman Marion Sweatt, Thurgood Marshall and the Long Road to Justice*
Neil Foley: *Quest for Equality: The Failed Promise of Black-Brown Solidarity*
Bruce Machart: *The Wake of Forgiveness*
Barbara Ras: *The Last Skin*
Elyse Fenton: *Clamor*
Pamela Colloff: "Innocence Lost," *Texas Monthly*, October 2010
C.W. Smith: "Caustic," *Southwest Review*, Summer 2010
Tim Madigan: series on the surgery of a child, *Fort Worth Star-Telegram*
Julie Savasky and DJ Stout: *The Gernsheim Collection*
Diane Gonzales Bertrand: T*he Party for Papa Luis/La Fiesta Para Papa Luis*
Dotti Enderle: *Crosswire*
**Lon Tinkle Award (for career): C.W. Smith**

### 2009
Scott Blackwood: *We Agreed to Meet Just Here*
Bryan Burrough: *The Big Rich: The Rise and Fall of the*

[1] *Beginning in 2011 the award date reflects the actual date of the presentation. For instance, Larry King's 2009 award was actually presented in 2010.*

*Greatest Texas Oil Fortunes*

John Pipkin: *Woodsburner*

Emilio Zamoro: *Claiming Rights and Righting Wrongs in Texas: Mexican Workers and Job Politics During World War II*

William Virgil Davis: *Landscape and Journey*

John Spong: "Holding Garmsir," *Texas Monthly*, January 2009.

Gwendolyn Zepeda: *Sunflowers/Girasoles*

Marjorie Kempner: "Discovered America," *Southwest Review*, Fall 2009

Lindsay Starr: *"I Do Not Apologize for the Length of This Letter": The Mari Sandoz Letters on Native American Rights, 1940–1965*

**Lon Tinkle Award (for career): Larry L. King**

### 2008

Brendan M. Greeley Jr.: *The Two Thousand Yard Stare: Tom Lea's World War II Paintings, Drawings, and Eyewitness Accounts*

Thomas Cobb: *Shavetail*

Ann Weisgarber: *The Personal History of Rachel DuPree*

Rick Bass: "Mary Katherine's First Deer" in *Gray's Sporting Journal*

Todd Benson and Guillermo Contreras: "Texas' Deadliest Export" in the *San Antonio Express-News*

Benjamin Alire Saenz: *The Perfect Season for Dreaming*

Claudia Guadalupe Martinez: *The Smell of Old Lady Perfume*

James Allen Hall: *Now You're the Enemy*

Kerry Neville Bakken: "Indignity" in *Gettysburg Review*

James M. Smallwood: *The Feud that Wasn't: The Taylor Ring, Bill Sutton, John Wesley Hardin, and Violence in Texas*

Barbara Whitehead: *Traces of Forgotten Places*

Reginald Gibbons: translator of *Sophocles, Selected Poems: Odes and Fragments*

**Lon Tinkle Award (for career): Carolyn Osborn**

### 2007

Robert Krueger and Kathleen Tobin Krueger: *From Bloodshed to Hope in Burundi: Our Embassy Years During Genocide*

John J. McLaughlin: *Run in the Fam'ly*

Todd Benson: "Breaching America" in the *San Antonio Express-News*

DJ Stout and Julie Savasky: *Reflections of a Man: The Photographs of Stanley Marcus*

Rick Bass: "The Lives of the Browns" in *Southern Review*

Rick Bass: "The Elephant"

Arturo O. Martinez: *Perdito's Way*

Naomi Shihab Nye: *I'll Ask You Three Times, Are You OK?*

Jerry Thompson: *Cortina: Defending the Mexican Name in Texas*

Cate Marvin: *Fragment of the Head of a Queen*

**Lon Tinkle Award (for career): David J. Weber**

### 2006

Lawrence Wright: *The Looming Tower: Al-Qaeda and the Road to 9/11*

Cormac McCarthy: *The Road*

Dominic Smith: *The Mercury Visions of Louis Daguerre*

Marian Schwartz: translator of *White on Black* by Ruben Gallego

Tony Freemantle: "The Gulf Coast Revisited" in the *Houston Chronicle*

Mary Ann Jacob: *Timeless Texas*

John Sprong: "The Good Book and the Bad Book" in *Texas Monthly*

Mark Wisniewski: "Prisoners of War"

Tim Tingle: *Crossing Bok Chitto: A Choctaw Tale of Friendship and Freedom*

Heather Hepler: *Scrambled Eggs at Midnight*

Jerry Thompson: *Civil War to the Bloody End: The Life and Times of Major Samuel P. Heintzelman*

Christopher Bakken: *Goat Funeral*

**Lon Tinkle Award (for career): William D. Wittliff**

Special Citation: Allen Maxwell ☆

# SXSW

*An animation presentation at the 2015 SXSW in Austin. Event photo.*

Those four letters above have become internationally recognized for the annual South by Southwest Music, Film, and Interactive Festival held each March in Austin. The festival began in 1987 to promote the Austin music scene. That first event had about 200 musical acts, mostly local, and some 700 registrants.

In 2015, there were more than 2,000 performing acts – music and comedy – from all over the world and more than 85,000 registrants.

The festival has evolved to include film, video and gaming. The festival's Interactive portion, which includes all aspects of the Internet, web design and new technologies has become the biggest draw in terms of registrants attending; more than 33,000 in 2015.

The film portion attracts celebrities to promote new projects and over the last few years television talk shows have relocated to Austin to share some of the spotlight.

The music portion includes acts just developing as well as legends such as Bruce Springsteen, Lou Reed and Stevie Nicks.

# State Artists of Texas

Since 2001, a committee of seven members appointed by the governor, lieutenant governor, and speaker of the House of Representatives selects the poet laureate, state artists and state musician based on recommendations from the Texas Commission on the Arts. Earlier, the Legislature made the nominations.

The state historian is appointed by the governor and is recommended by both the Texas State Historical Association and the Texas Historical Commission.

*Sources: Texas State Library and Archives; Texas Commission on the Arts; The Dallas Morning News.*

| Years | Artist, Hometown/Residence |
|---|---|
| 1971-72 | Joe Ruiz Grandee, Arlington |
| 1972-73 | Melvin C. Warren, Clifton |
| 1973-74 | Ronald Thomason, Weatherford<br>A.C. Gentry Jr., Tyler, alternate |
| 1974-75 | Joe Rader Roberts, Dripping Springs<br>Bette Lou Voorhis, Austin, alternate |
| 1975-76 | Jack White, New Braunfels |
| July 4, 1975 –July 4, 1976 | Robert Summers, Glen Rose<br>Bicentennial Artist |
| 1976-77 | James Boren, Clifton<br>Kenneth Wyatt, Lubbock, alternate |
| 1977-78 | Edward "Buck" Schiwetz, DeWitt County<br>Renne Hughes, Tarrant County, alternate |
| 1978-79 | Jack Cowan, Rockport<br>Gary Henry, Palo Pinto County, alternate<br>Joyce Tally, Caldwell County, alternate |
| 1979-80 | Dalhart Windberg, Travis County<br>Grant Lathe, Canyon Lake, alternate |
| 1980-81 | Harry Ahysen, Huntsville<br>Jim Reno, Simonton, alternate |
| 1981-82 | Jerry Newman, Beaumont<br>Raul Guiterrez, San Antonio, alternate |
| 1982-83 | Dr. James H. Johnson, Bryan<br>Armando Hinojosa, Laredo, alternate |
| 1983-84 | Raul Gutierrez, San Antonio<br>James Eddleman, Lubbock, alternate |
| 1984-85 | Covelle Jones, Lubbock<br>Ragan Gennusa, Austin, alternate |
| 1986-87 | Chuck DeHaan, Graford |
| 1987-88 | Neil Caldwell, Angleton<br>Rey Gaytan, Austin, alternate |
| 1988-89 | George Hallmark, Walnut Springs<br>Tony Eubanks, Grapevine, alternate |

| Years | Two-dimensional | Three-dimensional |
|---|---|---|
| 1990-91 | Mondel Rogers, Sweetwater | Ron Wells, Cleveland |
| 1991-92 | Woodrow Foster, Center | Kent Ullberg, Corpus Christi |
| | Harold Phenix, Houston, alternate | Mark Clapham, Conroe, alternate |

| Years | Two-dimensional | Three-dimensional |
|---|---|---|
| 1993-94 | Roy Lee Ward, Hunt | James Eddleman, Lubbock |
| 1994-95 | Frederick Carter, El Paso | Garland A. Weeks, Wichita Falls |
| 1998-99 | Carl Rice Embrey, San Antonio | Edd Hayes, Humble |
| *2000-02* | *none designated* | |
| 2003 | Ralph White, Austin | Dixie Friend Gay, Houston |
| 2004 | Sam Caldwell, Houston | David Hickman, Dallas |

| | Two-dimensional | Three-dimensional |
|---|---|---|
| 2005 | Kathy Vargas, San Antonio | Sharon Kopriva, Houston |
| 2006 | George Boutwell, Bosque | James Surls, Athens |
| 2007 | Lee Herring, Rockwall | David Keens, Arlington |
| 2008 | Janet Eager Krueger, Encinal | Damian Priour, Austin |
| 2009 | René Alvarado, San Angelo | Eliseo Garcia, Farmers Branch |
| 2010 | Marc Burckhardt, Austin | John Bennett, Fredericksburg |
| 2011 | Melissa Miller, Austin | Jesús Moroles, Rockport |
| 2012 | Karl Umlauf, Waco | Bill FitzGibbons, San Antonio |
| 2013 | Jim Woodson, Waco, Fort Worth | Joseph Havel, Houston |
| 2014 | Julie Speed, Austin, Marfa | Ken Little, Canyon, San Antonio |
| 2015 | Vincent Valdez, San Antonio | Margo Sawyer, Houston, Elgin |
| 2016 | Dornith Doherty, Houston, Southlake | Dario Robleto, San Antonio, Houston |

# Poets Laureate of Texas

| Years | Poet, Hometown/Residence |
|---|---|
| 1932-34 | Judd Mortimer Lewis, Houston |
| 1934-36 | Aline T. Michaelis, Austin |
| 1936-39 | Grace Noll Crowell, Dallas |
| 1939-41 | Lexie Dean Robertson, Rising Star |
| 1941-43 | Nancy Richey Ranson, Dallas |
| 1943-45 | Dollilee Davis Smith, Cleburne |
| 1945-47 | DavidRiley Russell, Dallas |
| 1947-49 | Aline B. Carter, San Antonio |
| 1949-51 | Carlos Ashley, Llano |
| 1951-53 | Arthur M. Sampley, Denton |
| 1953-55 | Mildred Lindsey Raiborn, San Angelo<br>Dee Walker, Texas City, alternate |
| 1955-57 | Pierre Bernard Hill, Hunt |
| 1957-59 | Margaret Royalty Edwards, Waco |
| 1959-61 | J.V. Chandler, Kingsville<br>Edna Coe Majors, Colorado City, alternate |
| 1961 | Lorena Simon, Port Arthur |
| 1962 | Marvin Davis Winsett, Dallas |
| 1963 | Gwendolyn Bennett Pappas, Houston<br>Vassar Miller, Houston, alternate |

| Years | Poet, Hometown/Residence |
|---|---|
| 1964-65 | Jenny Lind Porter, Austin<br>Edith Rayzor Canant, Texas City, alternate |
| 1966 | Bessie Maas Rowe, Port Arthur<br>Grace Marie Scott, Abilene, alternate |
| 1967 | William E. Bard, Dallas<br>Bessie Maas Rowe, Port Arthur, alternate |
| 1968 | Kathryn Henry Harris, Waco<br>Sybil Leonard Armes, El Paso, alternate |
| 1969-70 | Anne B. Marely, Austin<br>Rose Davidson Speer, Brady, alternate |
| 1970-71 | Mrs. Robby K. Mitchell, McKinney<br>Faye Carr Adams, Dallas, alternate |
| 1971-72 | Terry Fontenot, Port Arthur<br>Faye Carr Adams, Dallas, alternate |
| 1972-73 | Mrs. Clark Gresham, Burkburnett<br>Marion McDaniel, Sidney, alternate |
| 1973-74 | Violette Newton, Beaumont<br>Stella Woodall, San Antonio, alternate |
| 1974-75 | Lila Todd O'Neil, Port Arthur<br>C.W. Miller, San Antonio, alternate |
| 1975-76 | Ethel Osborn Hill, Port Arthur<br>Gene Shuford, Denton, alternate |
| 1976-77 | Florice Stripling Jeffers, Burkburnett<br>Vera L. Eckert, San Angelo, alternate |
| 1977-78 | Ruth Carruth, Vernon<br>Joy Gresham Hagstrom, Burkburnett,<br>alternate |
| 1978-79 | Patsy Stodghill, Dallas<br>Dorothy B. Elfstroman, Galveston, alternate |
| 1979-80 | Dorothy B. Elfstroman, Galveston<br>Ruth Carruth, Vernon, alternate |
| 1980-81 | Weems S. Dykes, McCamey<br>Mildred Crabree Speer, Amarillo, alternate |
| 1981-82 | none designated |
| 1982-83 | William D. Barney, Fort Worth<br>Vassar Miller, Houston, alternate |
| 1983-87 | none designated |
| 1987-88 | Ruth E. Reuther, Wichita Falls |
| 1988-89 | Vassar Miller, Houston |
| 1989-93 | none designated |
| 1993-94 | Mildred Baass, Victoria |

| Years | Poet, Hometown/Residence |
|---|---|
| 1994-99 | none designated |
| 2000 | James Hoggard, Wichita Falls |
| 2001 | Walter McDonald, Lubbock |

| Years | Poet, Hometown/Residence |
|---|---|
| 2002 | none designated |
| 2003 | Jack Myers, Mesquite |
| 2004 | Cleatus Rattan, Cisco |
| 2005 | Alan Birkelbach, Plano |
| 2006 | Red Steagall, Fort Worth |
| 2007 | Steven Fromholz, Kopperl, Sugar Land |
| 2008 | Larry Thomas, Houston |
| 2009 | Paul Ruffin, Huntsville |
| 2010 | Karla K. Morton, Denton, Fort Worth |
| 2011 | David M. Parsons, Conroe |
| 2012 | Jan Seale, McAllen |
| 2013 | Rosemary Catacalos, San Antonio |
| 2014 | Dean Young, Austin |
| 2015 | Carmen Tafolla, San Antonio |
| 2016 | Laurie Ann Guerrero, San Antonio |

# State Musicians of Texas

| Year | Artist, Hometown/Residence |
|---|---|
| 2003 | James Dick, Round Top |
| 2004 | Ray Benson, Austin |
| 2005 | Johnny Gimble, Tyler |
| 2006 | Billy Joe Shaver, Waco |
| 2007 | Dale Watson, Pasadena, Austin |
| 2008 | Shelley King, Austin |
| 2009 | Willie Nelson, Abbott, Austin |
| 2010 | Sara Hickman, Austin |
| 2011 | Lyle Lovett, Klein |
| 2012 | Billy Gibbons (ZZ Top), Houston |
| 2013 | Craig Hella Johnson, Austin |
| 2014 | Flaco Jiménez, San Antonio |
| 2015 | Jimmie Vaughn, Dallas, Austin |
| 2016 | Joe Ely, Lubbock, Austin |

# State Historians of Texas

| Years | Historian, Hometown/Residence |
|---|---|
| 2007-09 | Jesús de la Teja, San Marcos |
| 2009-12 | Light Cummins, Sherman |
| 2012-16 | Bill O'Neal, Carthage |

*Cast and crew in the Big Bend on the set of* Boyhood. *Photo by Matt Lankes, from his book,* Boyhood: Twelve Years on Film.

# Film and Television Work in Texas

*Source: Texas Film Commission at governor.state.tx.us/film*

For almost a century, Texas has been one of the nation's top film-making states, after California and New York.

More than 1,300 projects have been made in Texas since 1910, including **Wings**, the first film to win an Academy Award for Best Picture, which was made in San Antonio in 1927.

Texas' attractions to filmmakers are its diverse locations, abundant sunshine and moderate winter weather, and a variety of support services. The economic benefits of hosting on-location filming over the past decade are estimated at more than $2.79 billion.

Besides salaries paid to locally hired technicians and actors, as well as fees paid to location owners, the production companies do business with hotels, car rental agencies, lumberyards, restaurants, grocery stores, utilities, office furniture suppliers, gas stations, security services and florists.

All types of projects come to Texas besides films, including television specials, commercials, corporate films and game videos.

Many projects made in Texas originate in California studios, but Texas is also the home of many independent filmmakers who make films outside the studio system.

Some films and television shows made in Texas have become icons. **Giant**, John Wayne's **The Alamo**, and the long-running TV series **Dallas** all made their mark on the world's perception of Texas.

The Texas Film Commission, a division of the Office of the Governor, markets to Hollywood Texas' locations, support services and workforce availablity. The commission awarded incentive grants to production companies, amounting to $74.8 million between 2007 and 2012 (see chart on following page.)

The commission's free services include location research, employment referrals, red-tape-cutting, and information on laws, weather, travel and other topics affecting filmmakers. ☆

---

## Regional Commissions

**Amarillo Film Office**
1000 S. Polk, Amarillo 79101
(806) 374-1497
amarillofilm.org

**Austin Film Office**
301 Congress Ave. Ste. 200
Austin 78701, (800) 926-2282
austintexas.org

**Brownsville Border Film Comm.**
P.O. Box 911, City Hall
Brownsville 78520, (956) 548-6176
filmbrownsville.com

**Dallas Film Commission**
325 N. St. Paul Ste. 700
Dallas 75201, (214) 571-1050
filmdfw.com

**El Paso Film Commission**
One Civic Center Plaza
El Paso 79901, (800) 351-6024
elpasocvb.com

**Houston Film Commission**
901 Bagby Ste. 100
Houston 77002, (800) 365-7575
filmhouston.texaswebhost.com

**Northeast Texas Film Commission**
P.O. Box 247

Jefferson 75657, (903) 214-1144
netexasmovies.com

**San Antonio Film Commission**
203 S. St. Mary's, 2nd Floor
San Antonio 78205, (800)447-3372
filmsanantonio.com

**South Padre Island Film Comm.**
7355 Padre Blvd.
South Padre Island 78597
(800) 657-2373, sopadre.com

**Texas Panhandle Film Commission**
P.O. Box 3293, Amarillo 79116
(806) 679-1116
txpanhandlefilm.com

# Recent Movies Made in Texas

Following is a partial list of recent major productions filmed in Texas, in descending order by date. The date is for the year of release of the film, while actual location shots occurred earlier.

Location information is from the Texas Film Commission and other sources.

When only a small portion of the movie is known to have been filmed in Texas, "(part)" is listed next to the movie title.

Some of the major artists who worked on the project are listed in the column at far right.

*Sources: Texas Film Commission, and online.*

| YEAR | MOVIE | LOCATIONS | ARTISTS |
|------|-------|-----------|---------|
| 2013 | Boyhood | Alpine, Austin, Houston, San Marcos, Big Bend, Webster, Pedernales State Park | Ethan Hawke, Patricia Arquette, Richard Linklater (director) |
| 2013 | Parkland | Dallas, Austin | Billy Bob Thornton, Zac Efron |
| 2011 | Bernie | Carthage, Smithville, Georgetown, Bastrop, Lockhart, Austin | Jack Black, Shirley MacLaine, Matthew McConaughey, Richard Linklater (director) |
| 2011 | The Tree of Life | Bastrop, Austin, Dallas, Houston, La Grange, Matagorda, San Marcos, Smithville, Waco | Brad Pitt, Sean Penn |
| 2009 | Friday the 13th | Ausitn, Bastrop, La Grange, Marshall, Wimberley | Marcus Nispel (director) |
| 2006 | No Country for Old Men (part) | Marfa | Daniel Day-Lewis |
| 2006 | There Will Be Blood (part) | Marfa, Big Bend National Park | Ethan and Joel Coen, Tommy Lee Jones |
| 2005 | The Three Burials of Melquiades Estrada | Van Horn, Monahans, Santa Elena Canyon, Lajitas, Shafter, Midland/Odessa | Tommy Lee Jones, Julio Cedillo |
| 2004 | The Alamo | Dripping Springs, Wimberley, Pedernales Falls State Park, Bastrop, Austin | Dennis Quaid, Jason Patric |
| 2004 | Friday Night Lights | Odessa, Notrees, Austin, Houston | Billy Bob Thornton |
| 2003 | Texas Chainsaw Massacre | Martindale, Taylor, Austin | |
| 2002 | The Rookie | Thorndale, Taylor, Arlington, Big Lake | Dennis Quaid |
| 2000 | All the Pretty Horses | Boerne, Helotes, Pipe Creek, Big Bend | Matt Damon, Sam Shepard |
| 2000 | Miss Congeniality | Austin, San Antonio | Sandra Bullock, Michael Caine |
| 1999 | Where the Heart Is | Austin, Baylor University, Lockhart, Taylor, Kyle, Driftwood, Bastrop, Georgetown | Natalie Portman, Ashley Judd |
| 1999 | Boys Don't Cry | Greenville, Dallas area | Hilary Swank |
| 1999 | Office Space | Austin, Dallas | Jennifer Aniston, Ron Livingston |
| 1999 | Varsity Blues | Elgin, Coupland, Taylor, Georgetown | John Van Der Beek, Jon Voight |
| 1998 | Dancer, Texas Pop. 81 | Fort Davis, Alpine | Breckin Meyer, Peter Facinelli |
| 1998 | Home Fries | Coupland, Taylor, Bastrop, Austin, El Paso | Drew Barrymore, Luke Wilson |
| 1998 | Hope Floats | Smithville, Austin | Sandra Bullock, Harry Connick Jr. |
| 1998 | The Newton Boys | Bertram, Martindale, Bartlett, Lockhart, Austin, San Antonio | Matthew McConaughey, Ethan Hawke |
| 1996 | Bottle Rocket | Hillsboro, Grand Prairie, Dallas | Luke and Owen Wilson, James Caan |
| 1996 | Courage Under Fire | Bertram, Bastrop, San Marcos, Austin, El Paso | Denzel Washington, Meg Ryan |
| 1996 | Lone Star | Eagle Pass, Del Rio, Laredo | Matthew McConaughey, Kris Kristofferson |
| 1996 | Michael | Gruene, Muldoon, Granger, New Corn Hill | John Travolta, William Hurt |
| 1995 | Apollo 13 | Houston area | Tom Hanks, Kevin Bacon |
| 1993 | Dazed and Confused | Austin, Georgetown, Seguin | Richard Linklater (director), Matthew McConaughey |
| 1993 | What's Eating Gilbert Grape | Manor, Lockhart, Austin | Johnny Depp, Leonardo DiCaprio |

# Total Production in Texas by Year

| Year | Jobs | Labor | Expenditures | Total Texas Spending | Incentive Grants |
|------|------|-------|--------------|----------------------|------------------|
| | | | (in $ millions) | | |
| 2007 | 1,102 | 28.8 | 16.3 | 45.1 | 2.4 |
| 2008 | 1,150 | 46.6 | 33.1 | 79.8 | 4.2 |
| 2009 | 1,086 | 48.9 | 15.5 | 64.4 | 5.6 |
| 2010 | 3,314 | 138.5 | 56.4 | 194.9 | 31.1 |
| 2011 | 1,934 | 110.0 | 57.1 | 167.1 | 19.6 |
| 2012 | 1,103 | 58.9 | 30.6 | 89.5 | 12.0 |

*TV programs received 46.2 % of grants, followed by feature films at 25%. Source: Texas Film Commission.*

# Holidays, Anniversaries, and Festivals, 2016 – 2017

Below are listed the principal federal and state government holidays; Christian, Jewish, and Islamic holidays and festivals; and special recognition days for 2016 and 2017. Technically, the United States does not observe national holidays. Each state has jurisdiction over its holidays, which are usually designated by its legislature. This list was compiled partially from the Texas Government Code, the U.S. Office of Personnel Management, and *Astronomical Phenomena 2016* and *Astronomical Phenomena 2017,* which are published jointly by the U.S. Naval Observatory and the United Kingdom Hydrographic Office. See the footnotes for explanations of the symbols.

| 2016 | | 2017 | |
|---|---|---|---|
| New Year's Day § † | Fri., Jan. 1 | New Year's Day § † | Sun., Jan. 1 |
| Epiphany | Wed., Jan. 6 | Epiphany | Fri., Jan. 6 |
| Sam Rayburn Day ‡ | Wed., Jan. 6 | Sam Rayburn Day ‡ | Fri., Jan. 6 |
| Martin Luther King Jr. Day § † | Mon., Jan. 18 | Martin Luther King Jr. Day § † | Mon., Jan. 16 |
| Confederate Heroes Day † * | Tues., Jan. 19 | Confederate Heroes Day † * | Thurs., Jan. 19 |
| Ash Wednesday | Wed., Feb 10 | Valentine's Day | Tues., Feb. 14 |
| Valentine's Day | Sun., Feb. 14 | Presidents' Day § † ** | Mon., Feb. 20 |
| Presidents' Day § † ** | Mon., Feb. 15 | Ash Wednesday | Wed., March 1 |
| Primary Election Day | Tues., March 1 | Texas Independence Day † | Thurs., March 2 |
| Texas Independence Day † | Wed., March 2 | Texas Flag Day ‡ | Thurs., March 2 |
| Texas Flag Day ‡ | Wed., March 2 | César Chávez Day † | Fri., March 31 |
| Palm Sunday | Sun., March 20 | Palm Sunday | Sun., April 9 |
| Good Friday † | Fri., March 25 | Former Prisoners of War Day ‡ | Sun., April 9 |
| Easter Day | Sun., March 27 | Passover (Pesach), first day of ¶ | Tues., April 11 |
| César Chávez Day † | Thur., March 31 | Good Friday † | Fri., April 14 |
| Former Prisoners of War Day ‡ | Sat., April 9 | Easter Day | Sun., April 16 |
| San Jacinto Day † | Thurs., April 21 | San Jacinto Day † | Fri., April 21 |
| Passover (Pesach), first day of ¶ | Sat., April 23 | Mother's Day | Sun., May 14 |
| Ascension Day | Thurs., May 5 | Armed Forces Day | Sat., May 20 |
| Mother's Day | Sun., May 8 | Ascension Day | Thurs., May 25 |
| Whit Sunday — Pentecost | Sun., May 15 | Ramadan, first day of §§ | Sat. May 27 |
| Armed Forces Day | Sat., May 21 | Memorial Day § † | Mon., May 29 |
| Trinity Sunday | Sun., May 22 | Shavuot (Feast of Weeks) ¶ | Wed., May 31 |
| Memorial Day § † | Mon., May 30 | Whit Sunday — Pentecost | Sun., June 4 |
| Ramadan, first day of §§ | Tues., June 7 | Trinity Sunday | Sun., June 11 |
| Shavuot (Feast of Weeks) ¶ | Sun., June 12 | Flag Day (U.S.) | Wed., June 14 |
| Flag Day (U.S.) | Tues., June 14 | Father's Day | Sun., June 18 |
| Father's Day | Sun., June 19 | Emancipation Day in Texas (Juneteenth) † | Mon., June 19 |
| Emancipation Day in Texas (Juneteenth) † | Sun., June 19 | Independence Day § † | Tues., July 4 |
| Independence Day § † | Mon., July 4 | Lyndon Baines Johnson Day † | Sun., Aug. 27 |
| Lyndon Baines Johnson Day † | Sat., Aug. 27 | Labor Day § † | Mon., Sept. 4 |
| Labor Day § † | Mon., Sept. 5 | Grandparents Day | Sun., Sept. 10 |
| Grandparents Day | Sun., Sept. 11 | Rosh Hashanah (Jewish New Year) ¶ | Thurs., Sept. 21 |
| Rosh Hashanah (Jewish New Year) ¶ | Mon., Oct. 3 | Islamic New Year §§ | Fri., Sept. 22 |
| Islamic New Year §§ | Mon., Oct. 3 | Yom Kippur (Day of Atonement) ¶ | Sat., Sept. 30 |
| Columbus Day § ‡ | Mon., Oct. 10 | Sukkot (Tabernacles), first day of ¶ | Thurs., Oct. 5 |
| Yom Kippur (Day of Atonement) ¶ | Wed., Oct. 12 | Columbus Day § ‡ | Mon., Oct. 9 |
| Sukkot (Tabernacles), first day of ¶ | Mon., Oct. 17 | Halloween | Tues., Oct. 31 |
| Halloween | Mon., Oct. 31 | Father of Texas (Stephen F. Austin) Day ‡ | Fri., Nov. 3 |
| Father of Texas (Stephen F. Austin) Day ‡ | Thurs., Nov. 3 | Veterans Day § † | Sat., Nov. 11 |
| General Election Day † | Tues., Nov. 8 | Thanksgiving Day § † †† | Thurs., Nov. 23 |
| Veterans Day § † | Fri., Nov. 11 | First Sunday in Advent | Sun., Dec. 3 |
| Thanksgiving Day § † †† | Thurs., Nov. 24 | Hanukkah, first day of ¶ | Wed., Dec. 13 |
| First Sunday in Advent | Sun., Nov. 27 | Christmas Day § † | Mon. Dec. 25 |
| Hanukkah, first day of ¶ | Sun., Dec. 25 | | |
| Christmas Day § † | Sun., Dec. 25 | | |

**§ Federal legal public holiday.** If the holiday falls on a Sunday, the following Monday may be treated as a holiday. If the holiday falls on a Saturday, the preceding Friday may be treated as a holiday.

**† State holiday in Texas.** For state employees, the Friday after Thanksgiving Day, Dec. 24, and Dec. 26 are also holidays. *Optional holidays* are César Chávez Day, Good Friday, Rosh Hashanah, and Yom Kippur. *Partial-staffing holidays* are Confederate Heroes Day, Texas Independence Day, San Jacinto Day, Emancipation Day in Texas, and Lyndon Baines Johnson Day. State offices will be open on optional holidays and partial-staffing holidays.

**‡ State Recognition Days,** as designated by the Texas Legislature.

**\* Confederate Heroes Day** combines the birthdays of Robert E. Lee (Jan. 19) and Jefferson Davis (June 3).

**\*\* Presidents' Day** combines the birthdays of George Washington (Feb. 22) and Abraham Lincoln (Feb. 12).

**¶ §§ Jewish (¶) and Islamic (§§) holidays** are tabular, meaning they begin at sunset on the previous evening.

**†† Between 1939 and 1957,** Texas observed **Thanksgiving Day** on the last Thursday in November. As a result, in a November having five Thursdays, Texas celebrated national Thanksgiving on the fourth Thursday and Texas Thanksgiving on the fifth Thursday. In 1957, Texas changed the state observance to coincide with the national holiday. ☆

# Religious Affiliation Change: 2000 to 2010

Texas remains one of the nation's more "religious" states, even though a smaller portion of Texans is affiliated with a congregation than ten years ago.

At the same time, the estimated number of Muslims in the state increased to 421,972, making it the fifth largest religious group in the state and making Texas first in the nation in number of Muslims.

Texas ranks in the upper half among the states in percentage of the population belonging to a denomination. According to the *2010 U.S. Religion Census*, at least **56.0 percent** of Texans are adherents to a religion. The national average is 48.8 percent.

The census, sponsored by the Association of Statisticians of American Religious Bodies, is the only U.S. survey to report religious membership down to the county level, as well as at the state level. The census relies on self-reports from congregations for membership numbers.

But in the past, the African-American churches did not participate in the study, and in 2010 less than half of those congregations participated.

Only 345,998 black Protestants were counted in Texas in 2010. According to the U.S. Census of 2010, there were 2,782,876 blacks in Texas, which would mean 87.6 percent of black Texans, who are predominately Protestant, were designated as unaffiliated to any church. This probably leaves out some one million Texas church members.

In 1990, it was estimated that there were 815,000 black Baptists in Texas. An estimate of the membership in black Pentecostal churches was about 300,000. And, an estimate for black Methodists in Texas was approximately 200,000.

According to the *2010 U.S. Religion Census*, **Texas ranks**:

— **First** in number of evangelical Protestants, with 6,457,044.
— **First** in number that belong to non-denominational Christian churches, with 1,546,542.
— **First** in number of Muslims, with 421,972 estimated. New York is second with 392,9053 estimated.
— **Second**, behind Pennsylvania, in number of Mainline Protestants at 1,641,527.
— **Second**, behind California, in number of Hindus.
— **Third** in number of Buddhists.
— **Third** in number of Catholics.
— **Fifth** in number of Mormons.

Carrying over those estimates into 2010 and adjusting for these additions, then the percentage of Texans that are adherents* of a religion would be closer to **59.8 percent** in 2010.

[In addition, the religion census includes denominations that provide numbers of congregations, but who have not enumerated the numbers of adherents in each congregation. Even with factoring in an average congregation size of 100 persons for Protestant congregations, (a figure used by the census study) the total percentage would vary less than a one percent, to **60.7 percent**.]

Although that is higher than the 56.0 percent figure compiled from the reporting churches, still, it would be down from **67.1 percent** twenty years ago, indicating a move away from religious affiliation in Texas.

However, with the total state population booming, the churches still reported an **increase of 2.17 million** members, while the total population of Texas increased by 4.29 million from 2000 to 2010.

During the same period, the number of Texans not attached to a religion rose by **2.13 million.**

Thus, according to the Texas Almanac analysis from a variety of sources, there are **10.1 million** persons in the state who are not claimed by a religious group and about 15 million who are congregation members. (The U.S. census counted **25,145,561** persons in Texas in 2010.) — RP.

| Largest Religious Bodies | Adherents* | Percent of Texas Population |
|---|---|---|
| 1. Catholic Church | 4,673,500 | 18.59 % |
| 2. Southern Baptist Convention | 3,722,194 | 14.80 % |
| 3. Non-Denominational Christian | 1,546,542 | 6.15 % |
| 4. United Methodist Church | 1,122,736 | 4.46 % |
| 5. Muslim estimate | 421,972 | 1.68 % |
| 6. Church of Christ | 351,129 | 1.40 % |
| 7. Latter-Day Saints (Mormons) | 296,141 | 1.18 % |
| 8. Assembly of God | 275,565 | 1.10 % |
| 9. Presbyterian Church (U.S.A.) | 155,046 | 0.62 % |
| 10. Episcopal Church | 148,439 | 0.59 % |
| 11. Lutheran (Missouri Synod) | 132,508 | 0.53 % |
| 12. Lutheran (E.L.C.A.) | 111,647 | 0.44 % |
| Unclaimed by any faith | 10,103,455 | 40.20 % |

*__Adherents__ include all full members, their children, and others who regularly attend services. All figures used here by the Texas Almanac refer to these adherents.*

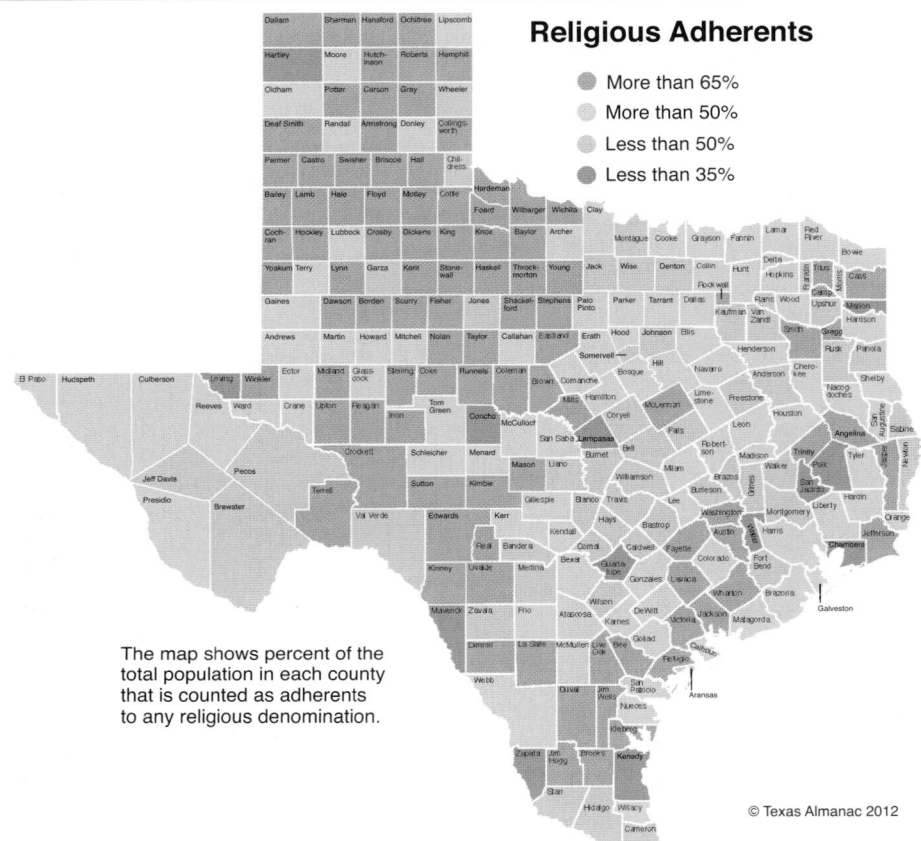

## Religious Adherents

- More than 65%
- More than 50%
- Less than 50%
- Less than 35%

The map shows percent of the total population in each county that is counted as adherents to any religious denomination.

© Texas Almanac 2012

# Numbers of Members Statewide by Denomination

| Religious Groups in Texas | 2000 | Change | 2010 |
|---|---|---|---|
| **Adventists** | **46,323** | **+ 27,797** | **74,120** |
| Church of God (Seventh Day) (70 congregations) | — | | — |
| Church of God General Conference | 55 | | 65 |
| Seventh-Day Adventists | 46,268 | | 74,055 |
| **Baha'i** | **10,777** | **+ 2,458** | **13,253** |
| **Baptist** | **4,537,918** | **+ 52,228** | **4,590,143** |
| Alliance of Baptists (9 congregations) | | | — |
| American Baptist Association | 61,272 | | 39,354 |
| American Baptist Churches in the USA | 7,057 | | 7,172 |
| Baptist General Conference | 340 | | 1,320 |
| Baptist Missionary Association of America | 123,198 | | — |
| Conservative Baptist Association of America (1 congregation) | | | — |
| Free Will Baptist, National Association of, Inc. | 2,822 | | 3,111 |
| Independent Baptist Fellowship International (258 cong.) | | | — |
| Interstate & Foreign Landmark Missionary Baptists Association | 93 | | — |
| Landmark Baptist, Indep. Assns. & Unaffil. Churches | 964 | | — |
| National Primitive Baptist Convention, USA | 4,463 | | — |
| North American Baptist Conference | 1,569 | | 1,157 |
| Primitive Baptists Associations | | | — |
| Primitive Baptist Church — Old Line (118 congregations) | | | — |
| Progressive Primitive Baptists | 197 | | — |
| Reformed Baptist Churches of America (27 congregations) | | | — |

| Religious Groups in Texas | 2000 | Change | 2010 |
|---|---|---|---|
| Regular Baptist Churches, General Assn. of (6 congregations) | 684 | | — |
| Seventh Day Baptist General Conference | | | 67 |
| Southern Baptist Convention | 3,519,459 | | 3,722,194 |
| Southwide Baptist Fellowship (13 congregations) | | | — |
| Two-Seed-in-the-Spirit Predestinarian Baptists | 29 | | — |
| Black Baptists (Estimate)* | (815,771)* | | (815,771)* |
|     National Baptist Convention of America, Inc. | | | 89,050 |
|     National Baptist Convention, USA, Inc. | | | 59,529 |
|     National Missionary Bapist Convention, Inc. | | | 34,039 |
|     Progressive National Baptist Convention, Inc. | | | 2,683 |
|     Full Gospel Baptist Church Fellowship (52 congregations) | | | — |
| **Buddhist** (95 congregations) | **—** | | **66,116** |
|   Mahayana | | | 49,874 |
|   Theravada | | | 13,461 |
|   Vajrayana | | | 2,781 |
| **Catholic Church** | **4,368,969** | **+ 304,531** | **4,673,500** |
| **(Christian Scientists) Church of Christ, Scientist** (64 cong.) | **—** | | **—** |
| **Churches of Christ** | **424,907** | **– 30,843** | **394,064** |
|   Church of Christ | 377,264 | | 351,129 |
|   Independent Christian Churches and Churches of Christ | 43,602 | | 40,078 |
|   International Churches of Christ | 4,041 | | 2,857 |
| **(Disciples of Christ) Christian Church** | **111,288** | **– 36,471** | **74,817** |
| **Episcopal** | **177,910** | **– 29,471** | **148,439** |
|   Episcopal Church, The | 177,910 | | 148,439 |
|   Reformed Episcopal Church | | | — |
|   Anglican Church in North America (111 congregations) | | | — |
| **Hindu** (34 congregations in 2000) | **—** | | **60,725** |
|   Indian-American HIndu Temple Assn. | | | 36,550 |
|   Post-Renaissance | | | 968 |
|   Renaissance | | | 98 |
|   Traditional Temples | | | 23,109 |
| **Holiness** | **86,942** | **– 1,738** | **85,204** |
|   Christian & Missionary Alliance, The | 3,858 | | 5,465 |
|   Church of Christ (Holiness), U.S.A. (4 congregations) | | | — |
|   Church of God (Anderson, Ind.) | 4,669 | | 3,990 |
|   Churches of Christ in Christian Union (2 congregations) | | | — |
|   Free Methodist Church of North America | 874 | | 1,864 |
|   Missionary Church, The | 403 | | 3,119 |
|   Nazarene, Church of the | 50,528 | | 44,836 |
|   Salvation Army | 25,070 | | 23,761 |
|   Wesleyan Church, The | 1,540 | | 2,169 |
| **Jain** (6 congregations) | **—** | | **—** |
| **Jehovah's Witnesses** (426 congregations) | **—** | | **—** |
| **Judaism, (estimate)** * | **(128,000)*** | **– 67,355** | **60,645** |
|   Conservative | | | **17,889** |
|   Orthodox | | | **8,410** |
|   Reconstructionist | | | **356** |
|   Reform | | | **33,990** |
| **Lutheran** | **301,518** | **– 29,452** | **272,066** |
|   Church of the Lutheran Brethren of America | — | | 72 |
|   Church of the Lutheran Confession (4 congregations) | — | | — |
|   Evangelical Lutheran Church in America | 155,019 | | 111,647 |
|   Evangelical Lutheran Synod | — | | — |
|   Free Lutheran Congregations, The Assoc. of | 368 | | 75 |
|   Lutheran Church–Missouri Synod, The | 140,106 | | 132,508 |
|   Lutheran Congregations in Mission for Christ | — | | 20,936 |
|   North American Lutheran Church (26 congregations) | — | | — |
|   Wisconsin Evangelical Lutheran Synod | 6,025 | | 6,828 |

| Religious Groups in Texas | 2000 | Change | 2010 |
|---|---|---|---|
| **Mennonite/Amish** | **4,930** | **– 1,330** | **3,600** |
| Amish, Old Order or Conservative Unaffiliated | 24 | | 309 |
| Amish, undifferentiated | 68 | | 52 |
| Apostolic Christian Church of America, Inc. | 27 | | 46 |
| Beachy Amish Mennonite Churches | 127 | | 265 |
| Brethren in Christ Church (1 congregation) | | | — |
| Church of God in Christ (Mennonite) | 849 | | 1,068 |
| Church of the Brethren | 284 | | 118 |
| Conservative Mennonite Conference | 191 | | 106 |
| Evangelical Bible Churches, Fellowship of (was Ev. Menn. Bre.) | | | — |
| Eastern Pennsylvania Mennonite Church | 65 | | — |
| Grace Brethren Churches, Fellowship of (3 congregations) | | | — |
| Mennonite Brethren Churches, U.S. Conference of | 425 | | 403 |
| Mennonite, other | 1,655 | | — |
| Mennonite Church USA | 1,215 | | 1,233 |
| **Messianic Judaism** | **—** | | **—** |
| Association of Messianic Congregations (1 congregation) | — | | — |
| Union of Messianic Jewish Congregations (5 congregations) | — | | — |
| **Methodist** | **1,219,533** | **+ 94,912** | **1,314,445** |
| Black Methodists (estimate)* | (197,191)* | | (150,000)* |
| African Methodist Episcopal Zion | (2,191)* | | 1,327 |
| African Methodist Episcopal | (150,000)* | | 43,839 |
| Christian Methodist Episcopal | (45,000)* | | 37,986 |
| Congregational Methodist Church | — | | 2,396 |
| Evangelical Methodist Church (11 congregations) | | | — |
| Southern Methodist Church (2 congregations) | | | — |
| United Methodist Church, The | 1,022,342 | | 1,122,736 |
| **(Mormons)** | **158,268** | **+ 142,323** | **300,591** |
| Church of Jesus Christ of Latter-day Saints, The | 155,451 | | 296,141 |
| Community of Christ | 2,817 | | 4,450 |
| **Muslim, estimate** | **114,999** | **+ 306,973** | **421,972** |
| **Non-denominational** (Evangelical Protestant) | **—** | | **1,546,542** |
| Independent Non-Charismatic Churches | 145,249 | | — |
| Independent Charismatic Churches | 159,449 | | — |
| **Orthodox** (Eastern Christian) | **22,755** | **+ 9,695** | **32,450** |
| Antiochian Orthodox of North America | 4,642 | | 5,348 |
| Armenian Apostolic Church/Cilicia | 80 | | — |
| Armenian Apostolic Church/Etchmiadzin | 1,275 | | 515 |
| Assyrian Apostolic Church | | | — |
| Coptic Orthodox Church (8 congregations) | — | | 3,866 |
| Eritrean Orthodox | — | | 1,000 |
| Ethiopian Orthodox  (4 congregations) | | | — |
| Greek Orthodox Archdiocese of America | 9,444 | | 12,167 |
| Greek Orthodox Archdiocese of Vasiloupulis | 135 | | — |
| Malankara Archdiocese/Syrian Orthodox Church in North Amer. | 825 | | 1,260 |
| Malankara Orthodox Syrian Church, American Diocese of the | 2,675 | | 2,433 |
| Romanian Orthodox Archdiocese in Americas) | 413 | | 600 |
| Orthodox Church in America (Territorial Dioceses) | 2,096 | | 2,657 |
| Russian Orthodox Church Outside of Russia (4 congregations) | — | | 1,022 |
| Serbian Orthodox Church in North America | 1,110 | | 1,372 |
| Syrian Orthodox Church of Antioch | 60 | | 210 |
| **Pentecostal/Charismatic** | **615,258** | **+ 61,825** | **677,083** |
| Apostolic Faith Mission of Portland, Ore. | — | | 135 |
| Assemblies of God | 228,098 | | 275,565 |
| Assemblies of God International Fellowship (3 congregations) | — | | — |
| Black Pentecostals (estimate)* | (300,000)* | | (300,000)* |
| Church of God in Christ (estimate)* | (300,000)* | | 77,545 |
| Church of Our Lord Jesus Christ of Apostolic Faith (22 cong.) | — | | — |
| Calvary Chapel Fellowship Churches (57 congregations) | — | | — |
| Church of God (Cleveland, Tenn.) | 38,259 | | 47,709 |
| Church of God of Prophecy | 2,906 | | 3,610 |

| Religious Groups in Texas | 2000 | Change | 2010 |
|---|---|---|---|
| Church of God of the Apostolic Faith, Inc. (18 congregations) | — | | — |
| Church of Our Lord Jesus Christ of Apostolic Faith (22 cong.) | — | | |
| Congregational Holiness Church | — | | 1,280 |
| International Church of the Foursquare Gospel | 12,501 | | 11,047 |
| Open Bible Standard Churches, Inc. | — | | 148 |
| Pentecostal Church of God | 11,592 | | 13,486 |
| Pentecostal Holiness Church, International | 10,265 | | 15,576 |
| Pentecostal Church International, United (656 congregations) | — | | — |
| Vineyard USA | 11,637 | | 8,527 |
| **Presbyterian** | **204,804** | **– 21,514** | **183,290** |
| Associate Reformed Presbyterian Church | 28 | | 223 |
| Cumberland Presbyterian Church | 8,422 | | 6,355 |
| Cumberland Presbyterian Church in America (19 cong.) | — | | |
| Evangelical Presbyterian Church | 1,449 | | 2,883 |
| Korean Presbyterian Church Abroad (2 congregations) | — | | |
| Korean Presbyterian Church in America (8 congregations) | — | | |
| Korean-American Presbyterian Church (4 congregations) | — | | — |
| Orthodox Presbyterian Church, The | 644 | | 824 |
| Presbyterian Church (USA) | 180,315 | | 155,046 |
| Presbyterian Church in America | 13,946 | | 17,959 |
| Reformed Presbyterian Church General Assembly (1 cong.) | — | | — |
| Reformed Presbyterian Church Hanover Presbytery (1 cong) | — | | — |
| Reformed Presbyterian Church in the United States (1 cong.) | — | | — |
| **(Quakers)** | **1,074** | **+ 1,700** | **2,774** |
| Evangelical Friends Church International | — | | 1,845 |
| Friends General Conference | — | | 929 |
| Unaffiliated Friends Meetings (2 congregations) | — | | — |
| **Reformed/Congregational** | **30,308** | **+ 2,599** | **32,907** |
| Communion of Reformed Evangelical Churches (5 cong.) | — | | — |
| Christian Reformed Church in North America | 1,936 | | 1,416 |
| Conservative Congregational Christian Conference | 25 | | 29 |
| Evangelical Assn. of Reformed, and Congregational (5 cong.) | — | | |
| Evangelical Free Church of America, The | 9,720 | | 13,486 |
| Hungarian Reformed Churches (2 congregations) | — | | |
| Reformed Church in America | 2,040 | | 512 |
| United Church of Christ | 16,587 | | 17,464 |
| **Sikh (24 congregations)** | **—** | | **—** |
| **Tao (1 congregation)** | **—** | | **—** |
| **Unitarian Universalist Association** | **6,872** | **+ 1,235** | **8,107** |
| **Unity Churches, Association of (43 congregations)** | **—** | | **—** |
| **Zoroastrian (3 congregations)** | **NR** | | **1,095** |
| OTHERS | | | |
| Christian Brethren (4 congregations) | — | | — |
| Evangelical Covenant Church, The | 1,022 | | 1,393 |
| Grace Gospel Fellowship (4 congregations) | — | | — |
| Independent Fundamentalist Churches of America (1 cong.) | — | | — |
| Metropolitan Community Churches, Universal Fellowship of | 5,570 | | 2,765 |
| National Spiritualist Association of Churches (4 congregations) | — | | — |
| New Apostolic Church of North America (13 congregations) | — | | — |
| Polish National Catholic Church  (3 congregations) | — | | — |
| **Statewide Totals**\*\* | **12,875,018** | **+ 2,167,088** | **15,042,106** |
| Unclaimed (not counted as adherent to religion) | 7,976,802 | + 2,126,653 | 10,103,455 |

*Texas Almanac estimates. **2000 statewide totals include smaller denominations not reported in 2010 and not listed here.

Compiled from the 2010 suvery sponsored by the Association of Statisticians of American Religious Bodies, also other sources, including: Churches and Church Membership in the United States 2000, Glenmary Research Center, Nashville, Tenn., 2002. National Council of Churches of Christ in the USA, New York, Yearbook of American and Canadian Churches, annual. New Handbook of Texas, 1996, various: "Christian Methodist Episcopal Church," by Charles E. Tatum; "African-American Churches," "African Methodist Episcopal Church," and "African Methodist Episcopal Zion Church," by William E. Montgomery; "Religion," by John W. Storey.

# Health & Science

*Edinburg Children's Hospital is a freestanding pediatric hospital in the Rio Grande Valley that opened in 2006. Photo by LaCasse Photography.*

**Honored Scientists**

**Research Funding in Texas**

**Vital Statistics**

**Hospitals**

**Drug Treatment, Mental Health Care**

# Texans in the National Academy of Sciences

Source: National Academy of Sciences

The National Academy of Sciences is a private organization of scientists and engineers dedicated to the furtherance of science and its use for the general welfare. A total of 121 scientists affiliated with Texas institutions have been named members or associates.

Established by congressional acts of incorporation, which were signed by President Abraham Lincoln in 1863, the academy acts as official adviser to the federal government in matters of science or technology.

Election to the academy is one of the highest honors that can be accorded a scientist. As of July 2015, the number of active members was 2,250.

Elected from Texas in 2014 was; Dora E. Angelaki

and Martin M. Matzuk of Baylor College of Medicine in Houston, and Zhijian (James) Chen of UT Southwestern Medical Center in Dallas.

Elected from Texas in 2015 was; Lora Virginia Hooper and Steven A. Kliewer of UTSWMC in Dallas, and Rebecca R. Richards-Kortum and Moshe Y. Vardi of Rice University in Houston.

Three foreign associates with ties to Texas institution have been elected to the academy. In 1970, D.H.R. Barton from Texas A&M University, in 1997, Johann Deisenhofer of UTSWMC in Dallas, and, in 2002, Jan-Ake Gustafsson of the University of Houston.

In 1946, Robert J. Williams of UT-Austin became the first from Texas elected to the science academy. ☆

| Academy Member | Affiliation* | Year Elected | Academy Member | Affiliation* | Year Elected |
|---|---|---|---|---|---|
| Perry L. Adkisson | A&M | 1979 | Verne E. Grant † | UT-Austin | 1968 |
| Richard W. Aldrich | UT-Austin | 2008 | Norman Hackerman † | Welch | 1971 |
| James P. Allison | UT-MD Anderson | 1997 | Namoi J. Halas | Rice | 2013 |
| Abram Amsel † | UT-Austin | 1992 | Dudley Herschbach | A&M | 1967 |
| Neal R. Amundson † | U of H | 1992 | David M. Hillis | UT-Austin | 2008 |
| Dora E. Angelaki | Baylor Medical | 2014 | Helen H. Hobbs | UTSWMC | 2007 |
| Charles J. Arntzen | A&M | 1983 | Lora Virginia Hooper | UTSWMC | 2015 |
| David H. Auston | Rice | 1991 | A. James Hudspeth | UTSWMC | 1991 |
| Paul F. Barbara † | UT-Austin | 2006 | Thomas J.R. Hughes | UT-Austin | 2009 |
| Frederic C. Bartter † | UTHSC-SanAntonio | 1979 | Nancy A. Jenkins | MHRI | 2008 |
| Allen J. Bard | UT-Austin | 1982 | James L. Kinsey † | Rice | 1991 |
| John D. Baxter † | HMRI | 2003 | Steven A. Kliewver | UTSWMC | 2015 |
| Arthur L. Beaudet | Baylor Medical | 2011 | Ernst Knobil † | UTHSC-Houston | 1986 |
| Brian J.L. Berry | UT-Dallas | 1975 | Jay K. Kochi † | U of H | 1982 |
| Bruce Beutler | UTSWMC | 2008 | P. Kusch † | UT-Dallas | 1956 |
| Lewis R. Binford | SMU | 2001 | Alan M. Lambowitz | UT-Austin | 2004 |
| R.H. Bing † | UT-Austin | 1965 | David M. Lee | A&M | 1991 |
| Harold C. Bold † | UT-Austin | 1973 | Beth Levine | UTSWMC | 2013 |
| Norman E. Borlaug | A&M | 1968 | Herbert Levine | Rice | 2011 |
| Michael S. Brown | UTSWMC | 1980 | Alan G. MacDiarmid † | UT-Dallas | 2002 |
| Karl W. Butzer | UT-Austin | 1996 | David J. Mangelsdorf | UT-Austin | 2008 |
| Luis A. Caffarelli | UT-Austin | 1991 | John L. Margrave † | Rice | 1974 |
| C. Thomas Caskey | Baylor Medical | 1993 | Martin M. Matzuk | Baylor Medical | 2014 |
| Joseph W. Chamberlain † | Rice | 1965 | S.M. McCann † | UTSWMC | 1983 |
| Zhijian (James) Chen | UTSWMC | 2014 | Allan H. MacDonald | UT-Austin | 2010 |
| Wah Chiu | Baylor Medical | 2012 | Steven L. McKnight | UTSWMC | 1992 |
| C.W. Chu | U of H | 1989 | David J. Meltzer | SMU | 2009 |
| Melanie H. Cobb | UTSWMC | 2006 | Nancy A. Moran | UT-Austin | 2004 |
| Neal G. Copeland | HMRI | 2009 | Hans J. Muller-Eberhard † | UTHSC-Houston | 1974 |
| F. Albert Cotton † | A&M | 1967 | Ferid Murad | UTHSC-Houston | 1997 |
| Robert F. Curl Jr. | Rice | 1997 | Jack Myers † | UT-Austin | 1975 |
| Ronald A. DePinho | UT-MD Anderson | 2012 | Kyriacos C. Nicolaou | Rice | 1996 |
| Gerard H. de Vaucouleurs † | UT-Austin | 1986 | Robert N. Noyce † | Sematech/Austin | 1980 |
| Bryce DeWitt † | UT-Austin | 1990 | David R. Nygren | UT-Arlington | 2000 |
| Robert E. Dickinson | UT-Austin | 1988 | Eric N. Olson | UTSWMC | 2000 |
| Richard A. Dixon | UNT | 2007 | Bert W. O'Malley | Baylor Medical | 1992 |
| Stephen J. Elledge | Baylor Medical | 2003 | Jose N. Onuchic | Rice | 2006 |
| Ronald W. Estabrook † | UTSWMC | 1979 | Luis F. Parada | UTSWMC | 2011 |
| Mary K. Estes | Baylor Medical | 2007 | Kenneth L. Pike † | SIL | 1985 |
| Karl Folkers † | UT-Austin | 1948 | William H. Press | UT-Austin | 1994 |
| Marye Anne Fox | UT-Austin | 1994 | Darwin J. Prockop | A&M | 1991 |
| David L. Garbers † | UTSWMC | 1993 | Lester J. Reed | UT-Austin | 1973 |
| Wilson S. Geisler | UT-Austin | 2008 | Peter M. Rentzepis | A&M | 1978 |
| Quentin H. Gibson | Rice | 1982 | Rebecca Richards-Kortum | Rice | 2015 |
| Alfred G. Gilman | UTSWMC | 1985 | Peter J. Rossky | UT-Austin | 2011 |
| Joseph L. Goldstein | UTSWMC | 1980 | David W. Russell | UTSWMC | 2006 |
| John B. Goodenough | UT-Austin | 2012 | Marlan O. Scully | A&M | 2001 |
| William E. Gordon | Rice | 1968 | Richard E. Smalley † | Rice | 1990 |

| Academy Member | Affiliation* | Year Elected |
|---|---|---|
| Esmond E. Snell † | UT-Austin | 1955 |
| Richard C. Starr † | UT-Austin | 1976 |
| Thomas Südhof | UTSWMC | 2002 |
| Max D. Summers | A&M | 1989 |
| Harry L. Swinney | UT-Austin | 1992 |
| Joseph S. Takahashi | UTSWMC | 2003 |
| John T. Tate | UT-Austin | 1969 |
| Karen K. Uhlenbeck | UT-Austin | 1986 |
| Jonathan W. Uhr | UTSWMC | 1984 |
| Roger H. Unger | UTSWMC | 1986 |
| Moshe Y. Vardi | Rice | 2015 |
| Ellen S. Vitetta | UTSWMC | 1994 |
| Salih J. Wakil | Baylor Medical | 1990 |
| Xiaodong Wang | UTSWMC | 2004 |
| Steven Weinberg | UT-Austin | 1972 |
| D. Fred Wendorf | SMU | 1987 |
| Roger J. Williams † | UT-Austin | 1946 |
| Jean D. Wilson | UTSWMC | 1983 |
| Peter G. Wolynes | Rice | 1991 |

| Academy Member | Affiliation* | Year Elected |
|---|---|---|
| James E. Womack | A&M | 1999 |
| Masahi Yanagisawa | UTSWMC | 2003 |
| Huda Y. Zoghbi | Baylor Medical | 2004 |

† Deceased

*A&M - Texas A&M University
Baylor Medical - Baylor College of Medicine, Houston
HMRI - Houston Methodist Research Institute
Rice - Rice University
SIL - Summer Institute of Linguistics
SMU - Southern Methodist University
U of H - University of Houston
UNT – Universtiy of North Texas
UT-Austin - The University of Texas at Austin
UT-Dallas - The University of Texas at Dallas
UTHSC - Houston - The University of Texas Health Science Center at Houston
UTHSC - The Univeristy of Texas Health Science Center at San Antonio
UT-MD Anderson Cancer Center - Houston
UTSWMC - The University of Texas Southwestern Medical Center at Dallas
Welch - Robert A. Welch Foundation

# Science Research Funding at Universities

The following chart shows funding for research and development by source at universities in Texas, in order of total R&D funding. The figures are from the National Science Foundation and are for fiscal year 2012.

| (Thousands of dollars, $ 000) | All R&D expenditures | Federal gov. | State/local gov. | Business | Nonprofit Org. | Institutional funds |
|---|---|---|---|---|---|---|
| United States | $65,774,524* | $ 40,130,460 | $3,704,365 | $3,281,809 | $4,033,233 | $13,673,539 |
| Texas (statewide) | 4,651,322 | 2,172,856 | 726,823 | 303,073 | 416,253 | 985,361 |
| 1. Texas A&M University | 693,421 | 269,460 | 128,819 | 49,392 | 52,378 | 193,012 |
| 2. U. Texas M.D. Anderson Cancer Ctr. | 685,814 | 196,753 | 246,988 | 68,414 | 100,795 | 72,864 |
| 3. University of Texas-Austin | 621,538 | 354,873 | 36,018 | 67,890 | 32,202 | 125,732 |
| 4. Baylor College of Medicine | 474,700 | 268,753 | 23,278 | 14,673 | 45,304 | 122,687 |
| 5. U. Texas Southwestern Med. Dallas | 435,085 | 207,513 | 64,958 | 18,464 | 44,437 | 64,679 |
| 6. U. Texas Health Sci. Houston | 236,250 | 146,424 | 28,554 | 11,214 | 30,251 | 19,807 |
| 7. U. Texas Health Sci. San Antonio | 184,298 | 106,177 | 7,040 | 10,833 | 22,316 | 37,932 |
| 8. U. Texas Medical Branch Galveston | 180,888 | 109,867 | 5,455 | 2,885 | 13,719 | 48,962 |
| 9. Texas Tech University | 138,026 | 29,969 | 17,602 | 11,274 | 9,950 | 69,231 |
| 10. Rice University | 117,233 | 76,964 | 3,961 | 4,848 | 9,933 | 21,617 |
| 11. University of Houston | 116,288 | 55,812 | 21,527 | 8,822 | 6,153 | 23,974 |
| 12. University of Texas-Dallas | 90,700 | 35,297 | 16,349 | 11,375 | 5,968 | 21,711 |
| 13. Texas A&M Health Sci. Ctr. | 82,833 | 30,739 | 15,400 | 1,204 | 4,219 | 25,979 |
| 14. University of Texas-El Paso | 79,649 | 40,024 | 13,861 | 1,792 | 8,940 | 15,032 |
| 15. University of Texas-Arlington | 78,556 | 33,150 | 10,890 | 4,853 | 3,110 | 26,553 |
| 16. Texas Tech Health Science Center | 61,219 | 13,944 | 33,740 | 925 | 3,894 | 8,716 |
| 17. University of Texas-San Antonio | 57,233 | 32,672 | 10,481 | 621 | 3,827 | 9,632 |
| 18. University of North Texas | 46,943 | 18,043 | 895 | 1,408 | 1,829 | 24,539 |
| 19. U. North Texas Health Sci. Ft.Worth | 46,865 | 26,627 | 6,680 | 2,370 | 1,303 | 9,741 |
| 20. Texas State University | 36,664 | 11,950 | 7,011 | 855 | 2,800 | 14,048 |
| 21. Southern Methodist University | 24,397 | 16,640 | 506 | 1,340 | 382 | 4,763 |
| 22. Texas A&M University-Kingsville | 17,419 | 6,480 | 3,072 | 676 | 4,046 | 3,145 |
| 23. Texas A&M U.-Corpus Christi | 15,776 | 5,446 | 3,809 | 1,449 | 2,599 | 2,470 |
| 24. Prairie View A&M University | 14,552 | 10,569 | 2,489 | 53 | 78 | 1,363 |
| 25. Baylor University | 10,161 | 3,513 | 278 | 612 | 732 | 4,978 |
| 26. Tarleton State University | 9,393 | 5,086 | 2,589 | 765 | 104 | 849 |
| 27. University of Texas-Pan American | 9,062 | 5,622 | 1,460 | 446 | 625 | 909 |
| 28. University of Texas-Tyler | 8,520 | 6,535 | 1,782 | 25 | 178 | 0 |
| 29. University of Texas-Brownsville | 8,318 | 7,098 | 578 | 0 | 15 | 627 |
| 30. Texas Christian University | 7,775 | 4,998 | 1,028 | 1,621 | na | 128 |

**Colleges and universities not listed received less.** 'na' information not available. *Total includes some $1 billion nationally from other sources. Source: National Science Foundation, 2014.

# Death, Birth Rates Continue Trends in Texas Vital Statistics

Heart disease and cancer remained the major causes of death in 2012, the latest year for which statistical breakdowns were available from the Bureau of Vital Statistics, Department of State Health Services.

Of the 173,935 deaths, heart disease claimed 39,026 lives, and cancer claimed 38,116 lives. These two diseases have been the leading causes of death in Texas and the nation since 1950. Cerebrovascular diseases (strokes) ranked third with 8,779 deaths.

These three diseases accounted for nearly half, 49.4 percent, of all Texas resident deaths in 2012.

The number of babies born in 2012 (382,438) to Texas mothers increased from 377,274 in 2011. But, the state's birth rate remained at an all-time low of 14.7 per 1,000 population. In 1960, the figure was 25.7.

In 2012, the number induced abortions continued to decline to 65,574 from a high in 2008 of 81,591.

## Health Care and Deaths in Texas Counties

| County | 2013 Physicians | 2012 Hospital Beds | Total Deaths 2012 | 2012 Pregnancy rate* | 2012 Abortions | County | 2013 Physicians | 2012 Hospital Beds | Total Deaths 2012 | 2012 Pregnancy rate* | 2012 Abortions |
|---|---|---|---|---|---|---|---|---|---|---|---|
| **Statewide Total** | **45,650** | **64,587** | **173,935** | **82.1** | **65,574*** | Comal | 169 | 80 | 1,080 | 74.3 | 150 |
| Anderson | 76 | 113 | 618 | 75.0 | 55 | Comanche | 11 | 25 | 156 | 75.0 | 12 |
| Andrews | 11 | 44 | 139 | 105.1 | 14 | Concho | 3 | 16 | 31 | 63.8 | 1 |
| Angelina | 156 | 358 | 866 | 75.8 | 116 | Cooke | 30 | 66 | 431 | 89.0 | 40 |
| Aransas | 15 | 0 | 345 | 83.6 | 38 | Coryell | 24 | 25 | 394 | 56.2 | 134 |
| Archer | 1 | 0 | 72 | 53.5 | 3 | Cottle | 0 | 0 | 29 | 51.7 | 3 |
| Armstrong | 0 | 0 | 39 | 103.1 | 2 | Crane | 2 | 25 | 43 | 97.8 | 2 |
| Atascosa | 37 | 67 | 358 | 79.9 | 63 | Crockett | 1 | 0 | 32 | 92.6 | 7 |
| Austin | 9 | 23 | 258 | 77.0 | 36 | Crosby | 1 | 25 | 68 | 79.7 | 17 |
| Bailey | 5 | 25 | 65 | 88.5 | 3 | Culberson | 3 | 14 | 14 | 79.0 | 5 |
| Bandera | 9 | 0 | 181 | 64.6 | 19 | Dallam | 0 | 0 | 54 | 108.8 | 2 |
| Bastrop | 35 | 10 | 583 | 72.0 | 134 | Dallas | 5,972 | 6,653 | 14,506 | 91.2 | 9,899 |
| Baylor | 7 | 38 | 72 | 93.2 | 4 | Dawson | 8 | 22 | 126 | 94.2 | 10 |
| Bee | 25 | 49 | 221 | 84.5 | 44 | Deaf Smith | 9 | 42 | 145 | 96.4 | 10 |
| Bell | 731 | 948 | 1,881 | 100.2 | 1,044 | Delta | 1 | 0 | 83 | 71.5 | 4 |
| Bexar | 3,857 | 5,470 | 11,888 | 82.7 | 5,531 | Denton | 810 | 1,113 | 2,947 | 65.1 | 1,234 |
| Blanco | 4 | 0 | 107 | 64.9 | 11 | DeWitt | 11 | 35 | 252 | 87.1 | 23 |
| Borden | 0 | 0 | 3 | 95.7 | 3 | Dickens | 0 | 0 | 24 | 81.9 | 6 |
| Bosque | 8 | 33 | 247 | 70.2 | 18 | Dimmit | 9 | 35 | 85 | 109.2 | 17 |
| Bowie | 251 | 648 | 994 | 74.5 | 16 | Donley | 1 | 0 | 51 | 69.9 | 7 |
| Brazoria | 272 | 168 | 2,041 | 81.0 | 617 | Duval | 0 | 0 | 126 | 99.1 | 27 |
| Brazos | 438 | 445 | 851 | 55.9 | 534 | Eastland | 11 | 36 | 233 | 55.1 | 11 |
| Brewster | 13 | 25 | 63 | 75.8 | 12 | Ector | 224 | 606 | 1,152 | 100.1 | 214 |
| Briscoe | 0 | 0 | 17 | 104.8 | 17 | Edwards | 1 | 0 | 19 | 83.9 | 5 |
| Brooks | 3 | 0 | 73 | 110.3 | 20 | Ellis | 114 | 112 | 1,059 | 64.8 | 200 |
| Brown | 65 | 168 | 448 | 65.2 | 27 | El Paso | 1,025 | 1,952 | 4,882 | 89.0 | 2,115 |
| Burleson | 6 | 25 | 216 | 75.0 | 18 | Erath | 42 | 54 | 289 | 60.6 | 66 |
| Burnet | 71 | 25 | 433 | 69.6 | 53 | Falls | 8 | 32 | 182 | 60.1 | 19 |
| Caldwell | 44 | 59 | 282 | 69.4 | 75 | Fannin | 14 | 25 | 408 | 63.7 | 21 |
| Calhoun | 19 | 25 | 213 | 72.7 | 22 | Fayette | 29 | 44 | 315 | 62.4 | 22 |
| Callahan | 4 | 0 | 171 | 65.4 | 12 | Fisher | 3 | 10 | 52 | 56.8 | 4 |
| Cameron | 504 | 1,081 | 2,423 | 89.9 | 543 | Floyd | 6 | 25 | 73 | 83.8 | 3 |
| Camp | 14 | 24 | 145 | 91.0 | 10 | Foard | 0 | 0 | 17 | 88.8 | 1 |
| Carson | 0 | 0 | 73 | 66.0 | 4 | Fort Bend | 752 | 867 | 2,473 | 72.6 | 1,365 |
| Cass | 12 | 54 | 402 | 68.6 | 5 | Franklin | 6 | 30 | 106 | 61.7 | 12 |
| Castro | 4 | 25 | 68 | 98.8 | 9 | Freestone | 8 | 20 | 234 | 82.1 | 29 |
| Chambers | 7 | 39 | 258 | 74.3 | 92 | Frio | 9 | 22 | 129 | 107.7 | 31 |
| Cherokee | 70 | 59 | 526 | 83.5 | 44 | Gaines | 7 | 25 | 121 | 97.9 | 6 |
| Childress | 8 | 39 | 79 | 77.1 | 6 | Galveston | 373 | 395 | 2,317 | 79.0 | 741 |
| Clay | 4 | 25 | 127 | 59.0 | 10 | Garza | 0 | 0 | 42 | 57.7 | 2 |
| Cochran | 1 | 13 | 31 | 86.4 | 2 | Gillespie | 72 | 57 | 342 | 74.8 | 21 |
| Coke | 0 | 0 | 51 | 72.8 | 4 | Glasscock | 0 | 0 | 6 | 56.3 | 0 |
| Coleman | 3 | 25 | 126 | 75.7 | 7 | Goliad | 3 | 0 | 76 | 66.1 | 6 |
| Collin | 1,763 | 1,682 | 3,385 | 66.1 | 1,434 | Gonzales | 18 | 32 | 177 | 84.8 | 27 |
| Collingswrth | 3 | 13 | 45 | 82.0 | 1 | Gray | 22 | 52 | 271 | 93.0 | 13 |
| Colorado | 29 | 55 | 292 | 76.1 | 18 | Grayson | 259 | 518 | 1,348 | 73.2 | 140 |
| | | | | | | Gregg | 347 | 585 | 1,202 | 81.3 | 59 |

| County | Physicians 2013 | Hospital Beds 2012 | Total Deaths 2012 | Pregnancy rate* 2012 | Abortions 2012 | County | Physicians 2013 | Hospital Beds 2012 | Total Deaths 2012 | Pregnancy rate* 2012 | Abortions 2012 |
|---|---|---|---|---|---|---|---|---|---|---|---|
| Grimes | 14 | 18 | 256 | 73.8 | 25 | Madison | 8 | 25 | 117 | 80.0 | 5 |
| Guadalupe | 94 | 90 | 910 | 68.7 | 154 | Marion | 2 | 0 | 154 | 76.5 | 8 |
| Hale | 29 | 68 | 277 | 80.6 | 16 | Martin | 3 | 20 | 39 | 94.0 | 3 |
| Hall | 1 | 0 | 56 | 60.3 | 0 | Mason | 0 | 0 | 40 | 80.3 | 2 |
| Hamilton | 11 | 42 | 112 | 77.0 | 3 | Matagorda | 41 | 69 | 365 | 80.1 | 37 |
| Hansford | 3 | 14 | 55 | 74.2 | 1 | Maverick | 33 | 101 | 340 | 100.5 | 59 |
| Hardeman | 6 | 31 | 39 | 66.9 | 4 | McCulloch | 5 | 25 | 98 | 87.5 | 18 |
| Hardin | 13 | 0 | 537 | 69.7 | 30 | McLennan | 462 | 567 | 2,049 | 74.4 | 470 |
| Harris | 9,424 | 12,878 | 23,409 | 90.6 | 16,869 | McMullen | 0 | 0 | 10 | 111.1 | 6 |
| Harrison | 55 | 142 | 613 | 66.1 | 13 | Medina | 18 | 25 | 371 | 68.1 | 45 |
| Hartley | 6 | 21 | 32 | 77.0 | 1 | Menard | 1 | 0 | 37 | 76.7 | 2 |
| Haskell | 2 | 15 | 104 | 55.0 | 0 | Midland | 220 | 306 | 986 | 91.8 | 194 |
| Hays | 196 | 223 | 844 | 63.4 | 456 | Milam | 11 | 21 | 292 | 80.8 | 32 |
| Hemphill | 5 | 19 | 35 | 103.1 | 2 | Mills | 2 | 0 | 65 | 62.2 | 8 |
| Henderson | 75 | 127 | 1,004 | 71.8 | 72 | Mitchell | 4 | 17 | 84 | 93.9 | 13 |
| Hidalgo | 868 | 2,256 | 3,817 | 98.3 | 1,380 | Montague | 12 | 69 | 249 | 77.1 | 18 |
| Hill | 26 | 66 | 408 | 72.5 | 36 | Montgomery | 842 | 1,264 | 2,994 | 73.7 | 614 |
| Hockley | 15 | 22 | 190 | 85.5 | 19 | Moore | 15 | 47 | 127 | 97.6 | 12 |
| Hood | 65 | 83 | 615 | 78.5 | 56 | Morris | 2 | 0 | 171 | 72.8 | 4 |
| Hopkins | 35 | 50 | 377 | 74.4 | 28 | Motley | 1 | 0 | 16 | 80.5 | 1 |
| Houston | 12 | 46 | 310 | 76.0 | 6 | Nacgdoches | 138 | 227 | 579 | 61.8 | 79 |
| Howard | 39 | 75 | 378 | 84.0 | 21 | Navarro | 49 | 148 | 492 | 85.0 | 53 |
| Hudspeth | 0 | 0 | 18 | 69.8 | 1 | Newton | 5 | 0 | 163 | 59.8 | 6 |
| Hunt | 91 | 163 | 784 | 69.0 | 101 | Nolan | 12 | 52 | 180 | 78.2 | 14 |
| Hutchinson | 17 | 25 | 242 | 79.4 | 8 | Nueces | 770 | 1,476 | 2,797 | 79.4 | 782 |
| Irion | 0 | 0 | 13 | 61.4 | 1 | Ochiltree | 6 | 25 | 92 | 89.0 | 10 |
| Jack | 6 | 17 | 80 | 68.8 | 6 | Oldham | 0 | 0 | 18 | 45.7 | 1 |
| Jackson | 6 | 25 | 153 | 88.7 | 18 | Orange | 33 | 40 | 945 | 82.2 | 149 |
| Jasper | 31 | 48 | 430 | 82.2 | 75 | Palo Pinto | 27 | 42 | 297 | 84.2 | 36 |
| Jeff Davis | 1 | 0 | 11 | 36.8 | 0 | Panola | 20 | 23 | 237 | 65.0 | 3 |
| Jefferson | 551 | 1,232 | 2,390 | 85.3 | 705 | Parker | 102 | 86 | 904 | 67.7 | 144 |
| Jim Hogg | 1 | 0 | 48 | 103.0 | 6 | Parmer | 3 | 15 | 69 | 78.1 | 4 |
| Jim Wells | 30 | 115 | 439 | 87.8 | 88 | Pecos | 9 | 40 | 122 | 85.2 | 13 |
| Johnson | 110 | 85 | 1,246 | 71.6 | 196 | Polk | 43 | 66 | 643 | 80.4 | 45 |
| Jones | 12 | 65 | 181 | 74.6 | 9 | Potter | 438 | 918 | 1,194 | 92.1 | 133 |
| Karnes | 5 | 25 | 159 | 90.3 | 20 | Presidio | 5 | 0 | 34 | 78.0 | 8 |
| Kaufman | 81 | 68 | 823 | 75.0 | 164 | Rains | 2 | 0 | 124 | 69.1 | 7 |
| Kendall | 54 | 0 | 307 | 64.5 | 25 | Randall | 65 | 4 | 984 | 66.2 | 101 |
| Kenedy | 0 | 0 | 3 | 72.3 | 0 | Reagan | 2 | 7 | 35 | 83.2 | 4 |
| Kent | 1 | 0 | 16 | 86.2 | 1 | Real | 0 | 0 | 66 | 71.6 | 3 |
| Kerr | 128 | 124 | 719 | 74.1 | 70 | Red River | 5 | 36 | 200 | 67.2 | 12 |
| Kimble | 3 | 15 | 49 | 72.5 | 6 | Reeves | 8 | 25 | 95 | 83.5 | 6 |
| King | 0 | 0 | 3 | 87.0 | 3 | Refugio | 4 | 20 | 84 | 78.2 | 6 |
| Kinney | 1 | 0 | 31 | 81.6 | 4 | Roberts | 0 | 0 | 10 | 47.9 | 0 |
| Kleberg | 23 | 79 | 225 | 79.8 | 81 | Robertson | 2 | 0 | 185 | 70.5 | 18 |
| Knox | 3 | 14 | 53 | 73.3 | 5 | Rockwall | 153 | 162 | 529 | 64.0 | 85 |
| Lamar | 116 | 217 | 613 | 74.9 | 58 | Runnels | 9 | 37 | 133 | 60.3 | 6 |
| Lamb | 3 | 41 | 129 | 76.3 | 6 | Rusk | 33 | 47 | 571 | 78.5 | 24 |
| Lampasas | 14 | 35 | 206 | 69.4 | 30 | Sabine | 2 | 25 | 170 | 58.3 | 6 |
| La Salle | 2 | 0 | 43 | 115.6 | 21 | S. Augustine | 3 | 18 | 137 | 87.8 | 5 |
| Lavaca | 16 | 50 | 245 | 87.0 | 18 | San Jacinto | 3 | 0 | 301 | 66.8 | 25 |
| Lee | 5 | 0 | 138 | 83.2 | 40 | San Patricio | 29 | 54 | 614 | 83.2 | 85 |
| Leon | 7 | 0 | 178 | 97.5 | 15 | San Saba | 1 | 0 | 74 | 92.0 | 3 |
| Liberty | 50 | 112 | 683 | 71.2 | 81 | Schleicher | 3 | 14 | 24 | 65.0 | 2 |
| Limestone | 25 | 78 | 256 | 93.3 | 47 | Scurry | 10 | 49 | 173 | 98.5 | 17 |
| Lipscomb | 1 | 0 | 32 | 63.8 | 1 | Shackelford | 0 | 0 | 32 | 81.2 | 3 |
| Live Oak | 0 | 0 | 119 | 83.5 | 14 | Shelby | 6 | 0 | 249 | 80.1 | 5 |
| Llano | 19 | 20 | 309 | 78.5 | 16 | Sherman | 0 | 0 | 29 | 69.3 | 4 |
| Loving | 0 | 0 | 1 | — | 0 | Smith | 757 | 1,172 | 1,903 | 75.3 | 303 |
| Lubbock | 656 | 1,429 | 2,308 | 68.4 | 496 | Somervell | 14 | 16 | 80 | 66.0 | 11 |
| Lynn | 5 | 24 | 68 | 83.2 | 3 | Starr | 20 | 47 | 356 | 105.3 | 75 |

| County | Physicians 2013 | Hospital Beds 2012 | Total Deaths 2012 | Pregnancy rate* 2012 | Abortions 2012 |
|---|---|---|---|---|---|
| Stephens | 6 | 21 | 114 | 70.1 | 8 |
| Sterling | 0 | 0 | 10 | 67.7 | 1 |
| Stonewall | 2 | 12 | 28 | 62.5 | 2 |
| Sutton | 5 | 12 | 38 | 80.3 | 6 |
| Swisher | 3 | 20 | 82 | 81.1 | 3 |
| Tarrant | 3,568 | 4,852 | 11,474 | 79.5 | 4,551 |
| Taylor | 311 | 623 | 1,306 | 79.3 | 148 |
| Terrell | 0 | 0 | 12 | 177.3 | 13 |
| Terry | 5 | 26 | 121 | 100.5 | 11 |
| Throckmortn | 1 | 0 | 24 | 70.8 | 1 |
| Titus | 48 | 91 | 268 | 79.7 | 26 |
| Tom Green | 282 | 413 | 947 | 73.4 | 179 |
| Travis | 2,940 | 2,517 | 5,063 | 779.9 | 4,032 |
| Trinity | 4 | 22 | 225 | 55.1 | 15 |
| Tyler | 10 | 25 | 256 | 90.7 | 41 |
| Upshur | 13 | 35 | 431 | 67.6 | 8 |
| Upton | 1 | 24 | 36 | 87.7 | 1 |
| Uvalde | 29 | 48 | 259 | 80.7 | 40 |
| Val Verde | 37 | 80 | 340 | 94.7 | 55 |
| Van Zandt | 11 | 0 | 634 | 69.9 | 50 |
| Victoria | 221 | 567 | 801 | 82.9 | 119 |
| Walker | 74 | 97 | 511 | 53.4 | 145 |
| Waller | 5 | 0 | 281 | 68.4 | 93 |
| Ward | 4 | 0 | 122 | 90.7 | 14 |
| Washington | 48 | 54 | 375 | 74.3 | 54 |
| Webb | 220 | 569 | 1,283 | 96.1 | 225 |

| County | Physicians 2013 | Hospital Beds 2012 | Total Deaths 2012 | Pregnancy rate* 2012 | Abortions 2012 |
|---|---|---|---|---|---|
| Wharton | 41 | 129 | 418 | 80.8 | 65 |
| Wheeler | 6 | 29 | 71 | 76.1 | 2 |
| Wichita | 281 | 457 | 1,285 | 76.0 | 178 |
| Wilbarger | 21 | 27 | 170 | 75.1 | 14 |
| Willacy | 10 | 0 | 167 | 88.6 | 23 |
| Williamson | 727 | 566 | 2,132 | 72.2 | 880 |
| Wilson | 20 | 17 | 335 | 66.6 | 47 |
| Winkler | 1 | 19 | 82 | 106.6 | 12 |
| Wise | 72 | 154 | 498 | 75.4 | 77 |
| Wood | 34 | 60 | 627 | 69.7 | 20 |
| Yoakum | 5 | 22 | 74 | 87.7 | 7 |
| Young | 23 | 64 | 239 | 82.6 | 9 |
| Zapata | 4 | 0 | 71 | 104.0 | 27 |
| Zavala | 4 | 0 | 90 | 103.6 | 24 |

**Sources: Texas Department of State Health Services: Vital Statistics, 2012** (by county of residence) and **Center for Health Statistics, 2013**.
Physicians - All M.D.s and D.O.s in direct patient care. (Previous lists included researchers, administrators and teachers.)
Hospital Beds - Staffed beds not including military and veteran's hospitals, nor beds in hospitals that were not in compliance with state regulations.
*Pregnancy Rate figured per 1,000 women age 15-44.
*Abortion total statewide includes abortions performed in Texas but county of residence unknown, plus abortions obtained outside the state by Texas residents.

# Marriage and Divorce

These charts are for certain years, including 1946 when there was a significant increase in marriages after World War II as well as a significant increase in divorces. Also included are the years 1979-81 when the marriage and divorce rates reached another peak. *Source: Statistical Abstracts of the United States, National Vital Statistics System.*

## Texas

| Year | Total marriages | Marriage rate* | Total divorces | Divorce rate* |
|---|---|---|---|---|
| 1940 | 86,500 | 13.5 | 27,500 | 4.3 |
| 1946 | 143,092 | 20.5 | 57,112 | 8.4 |
| 1950 | 89,155 | 11.6 | 37,400 | 4.9 |
| 1955 | 91,210 | 10.4 | 34,921 | 4.0 |
| 1960 | 91,700 | 9.6 | 34,732 | 3.6 |
| 1965 | 111,500 | 10.5 | 41,300 | 3.9 |
| 1970 | 139,500 | 12.5 | 51,500 | 4.6 |
| 1975 | 153,200 | 12.5 | 76,700 | 6.3 |
| 1979 | 172,800 | 12.9 | 92,400 | 6.9 |
| 1980 | 181,800 | 12.8 | 96,800 | 6.8 |
| 1981 | 194,800 | 13.2 | 101,900 | 6.9 |
| 1985 | 213,800 | 13.1 | 101,200 | 6.2 |
| 1990 | 182,800 | 10.5 | 94,000 | 5.5 |
| 1995 | 188,500 | 10.1 | 98,400 | 5.3 |
| 2000 | 196,400 | 9.6 | 85,200 | 4.2 |
| 2005 | 169,300 | 7.4 | 74,000 | 3.2 |
| 2009 | 172,395 | 7.0 | 81,822 | 3.3 |
| 2010 | 174,171 | 6.9 | 82,098 | 3.3 |
| 2011 | 177,219 | 6.9 | 79,024 | 3.1 |
| 2012 | 184,690 | 7.1 | 80,030 | 3.1 |

*Rate per 1,000 population.

## United States

| Year | Total marriages | Marriage rate* | Total divorces | Divorce rate* |
|---|---|---|---|---|
| 1940 | 1,595,879 | 12.1 | 264,000 | 2.0 |
| 1946 | 2,291,045 | 16.4 | 610,000 | 4.3 |
| 1950 | 1,667,231 | 11.1 | 385,144 | 2.6 |
| 1955 | 1,531,000 | 9.3 | 377,000 | 2.3 |
| 1960 | 1,523,381 | 8.5 | 393,000 | 2.2 |
| 1965 | 1,800,200 | 9.3 | 479,000 | 2.5 |
| 1970 | 2,159,000 | 10.6 | 708,000 | 3.5 |
| 1975 | 2,152,700 | 10.1 | 1,036,000 | 4.9 |
| 1979 | 2,331,300 | 10.6 | 1,181,000 | 5.4 |
| 1980 | 2,390,300 | 10.6 | 1,189,000 | 5.2 |
| 1981 | 2,422,100 | 10.6 | 1,213,000 | 5.3 |
| 1985 | 2,425,000 | 10.2 | 1,187,000 | 5.0 |
| 1990 | 2,443,000 | 9.8 | 1,182,000 | 4.7 |
| 1995 | 2,336,000 | 8.9 | 1,169,000 | 4.4 |
| 2000 | 2,329,000 | 8.2 | **944,000 | 4.0 |
| 2005 | 2,230,000 | 7.5 | 847,000 | 3.6 |
| 2009 | 2,080,000 | 6.8 | 840,000 | 3.5 |
| 2010 | 2,096,000 | 6.8 | 872,000 | 3.6 |
| 2011 | 2,118,000 | 6.8 | 877,000 | 3.6 |
| 2012 | 2,131,000 | 6.8 | 851.000 | 3.4 |

**Since 2000, the total number of divorces does not include four to six states, including California.

# National Health Expenditures

| GDP and Expenditures ($ billions) | 1970 | 1980 | 1990 | 2000 | 2010 | 2013 |
|---|---|---|---|---|---|---|
| Total Health Expenditures | $74.9 | $ 255.8 | $ 724.3 | $ 1,377.2 | $ 2,593.6 | $ 2,919.1 |
| Percent of GDP | 7.2 | 9.2 | 12.5 | 13.8 | 17.4 | 17.4 |
| Per capita amount in dollars | $ 356 | $ 1,110 | $2,854 | $ 4,878 | $ 8,402 | $ 9,255 |
| Personal health care expenditure | $ 300 | $ 943 | $ 2,430 | $ 4,128 | $ 7,082 | $ 7,826 |
| Cost of private insurance | $ 12 | $ 52 | $ 153 | $ 288 | $ 570 | $ 668 |
| Price deflator for GDP (2009=100) | – | – | – | – | 102.7 | 108.3 |
| Gross Domestic Product (GDP) | $ 1,038 | $ 2,788 | $ 5,801 | $ 9,952 | $ 14,527 | $ 16,768 |

Source: U.S. Centers for Medicare and Medicaid Services, 2013.

## Comparison of Vital Statistics

The most current data available, with selected states; those bordering Texas and other large states. **Lowest and highest with number in bold.**

| State/ Country | BIRTH rate* | DEATH rate* | LIFE expec- tancy |
|---|---|---|---|
| Texas | 14.6 | 6.8 | 78.3 |
| Alaska | 15.6 | **5.4** | - |
| Arkansas | 12.8 | 10.3 | - |
| California | 12.9 | 6.5 | - |
| Florida | 11.0 | 9.3 | - |
| Georgia | 12.9 | 7.5 | - |
| Illinois | 12.2 | 8.0 | - |
| Louisiana | 13.7 | 9.4 | - |
| Michigan | 11.5 | 9.3 | - |
| New Mexico | 12.6 | 8.1 | - |
| New York | 12.1 | 7.7 | - |
| Ohio | 12.0 | 9.8 | - |
| Oklahoma | 13.9 | 10.0 | - |
| Utah | **17.6** | 5.6 | - |
| New Hampshire | **9.4** | 8.2 | - |
| West Virginia | 12.1 | **11.8** | - |
| United States | 13.4 | 8.2 | 79.6 |
| Afghanistan | 38.8 | 14.1 | 50.1 |
| Angola | 39.0 | 11.7 | 55.3 |
| Brazil | 14.7 | 6.5 | 73.3 |
| Canada | 10.3 | 8.3 | 81.7 |
| Germany | 8.4 | 11.3 | 80.4 |
| Italy | 8.8 | 10.1 | 82.0 |
| Japan | **8.2** | 9.4 | **84.5** |
| Mexico | 19.0 | 5.2 | 75.4 |
| Niger | **46.1** | 12.7 | 54.7 |
| Russia | 11.9 | 13.8 | 70.2 |
| South Africa | 18.9 | **17.5** | **49.6** |
| United Arab Em. | 15.5 | **2.0** | 77.1 |
| United Kingdom | 12.2 | 9.3 | 80.4 |
| World | 18.7 | 7.9 | 68.4 |

*Rates are number during 1 year per 1,000 persons. Sources: National Vital Statistics System 2015; CIA World Factbook, 2013; Texas Vital Statistics Annual Report 2013.

## Life Expectancy for Texans by Group

| | All | Whites | Blacks | Hispanics |
|---|---|---|---|---|
| Total population | 78.3 | 78.3 | 74.7 | 79.5 |
| Males | 75.8 | 75.9 | 71.8 | 77.0 |
| Females | 80.7 | 80.6 | 77.3 | 81.9 |

Source: Texas Department of State Health Services, for 2012.

## Texas Births by Race/Ethnicity and Sex

| | 2012 | 2000 | 1990 | 1980 |
|---|---|---|---|---|
| All Races | 382,438 | 363,325 | 316,257 | 273,433 |
| All Male | 195,525 | 185,591 | 161,522 | 139,999 |
| All Female | 186,913 | 177,734 | 154,735 | 133,434 |
| White Total | 132,288 | 142,553 | 150,461 | 151,725 |
| White Male | 67,687 | 72,972 | 77,134 | 78,086 |
| White Female | 64,601 | 69,581 | 73,327 | 73,639 |
| Black Total | 43,100 | 41,180 | 43,342 | 38,544 |
| Black Male | 22,071 | 21,128 | 21,951 | 19,501 |
| Black Female | 21,029 | 20,052 | 21,391 | 19,043 |
| Hispanic Total | 182,855 | 166,440 | 115,576 | 79,324 |
| Hispanic Male | 93,288 | 84,750 | 58,846 | 40,475 |
| Hispanic Female | 89,336 | 81,690 | 56,730 | 38,849 |
| Other* Total | 24,195 | 13,152 | 6,687 | 3,840 |
| Other Male | 12,479 | 6,741 | 3,591 | 1,937 |
| Other Female | 11,716 | 6,411 | 3,287 | 1,903 |

*Other includes births of unknown race/ethnicity.
Source: Texas Department of State Health Services, 2015.

## Disposition of Bodies in Texas by Percent of Deaths

| Year | Burial | Cremation | Donation of body | Removal from state/other |
|---|---|---|---|---|
| 1989 | 83.7 | 7.1 | 0.7 | 8.5 |
| 1991 | 83.6 | 8.5 | 1.0 | 7.1 |
| 1993 | 82.8 | 10.1 | 0.9 | 6.2 |
| 1995 | 81.7 | 11.6 | 0.8 | 5.8 |
| 1997 | 79.9 | 12.9 | 1.0 | 6.2 |
| 1999 | 78.0 | 14.9 | 0.9 | 6.2 |
| 2001 | 75.5 | 17.3 | 0.8 | 6.3 |
| 2003 | 73.1 | 19.7 | 0.9 | 6.2 |

Source: Texas Department of State Health Services, 2013.

# Nobel Prizes to Texans

*Südhof.*

*Moerner.*

Two scientists with Texas connections were awarded the Nobel Prize in 2013 and 2014.

Thomas C. Südhof received the prize in medicine in 2013. He was chair of neuroscience at the University of Texas Southwestern Medical Center in Dallas where he worked for 25 years starting in 1983. The award recognized his and others' research in cellular transport systems.

William Moerner received the prize in chemistry in 2014 for his work with others in improving microscopes. He grew up in San Antonio where he attended Longfellow Junior High School and graduated from Thomas Jefferson High School in 1971.

Moerner is a professor at Stanford University in California, and so is Südhof, who continued his research there since 2008.

# Community Hospitals in Texas

*Source: The Texas Hospital Association.*

– Of the 590 reporting hospitals in Texas in 2013, 424 were considered community hospitals.

(A community hospital is defined as either a non-federal, short-term general hospital or a special hospital whose facilities and services are available to the public. A hospital may include a nursing home-type unit and still be classified as short-term, provided that the majority of its patients are admitted to units where the average length-of-stay is less than 30 days.)

– The 424 hospitals employed 313,500 full-time equivalent people (FTEs) with a payroll, including benefits, of more than $24.7 billion.

– These hospitals contained some 61,600 beds.

– The average length-of-stay was 5.2 days in 2013, compared to 6.8 days in 1975. This was less than the U.S. average of 5.4 days.

– The average cost per adjusted admission in Texas was $11,200 or $2,240 per day. This was 3.8 percent less than the U.S. average of $11,650.

– There were 2.5 million admissions in Texas, which accounted for 13,.1 million inpatient days.

– There were 40.1 million outpatient visits in 2013, of which 10.4 million were emergency room visits.

– Of the FTEs working in community hospitals within Texas, there were 99,200 registered nurses and 8,000 licensed vocational nurses. ☆

*The West Texas Medical Center in Denver City. Photo by Robert Plocheck.*

# Substance Abuse and Mental Health Admissions

## Drug Treatment in State-Funded Programs: 2012

| Primary Drug | Total Admissions | White | Black | Hispanic* | Percent that use daily | Average age | Percent male |
|---|---|---|---|---|---|---|---|
| | | (percent of clients) | | | | | |
| All Drugs | 75,103 | 45.6 | 18.2 | 31.4 | 40.9 | 32.7 | 59.9 |
| Heroin | 9,416 | 42.6 | 7.0 | 43.9 | 76.2 | 32.8 | 61.4 |
| Opiates/Synthetics | 1,826 | 73.9 | 5.6 | 17.7 | 64.5 | 33.2 | 51.4 |
| Alcohol | 22,117 | 52.2 | 12.5 | 30.4 | 42.6 | 38.6 | 67.3 |
| Vicodin | 3,277 | 72.6 | 8.1 | 15.9 | 69.4 | 33.9 | 35.1 |
| Amphetamines or Methamphetamine | 7,649 | 52.2 | 12.5 | 30.4 | 30.8 | 32.4 | 41.4 |
| Cocaine/Crack | 9,735 | 24.8 | 44.3 | 46.8 | 29.3 | 38.3 | 50.8 |
| Marijuana/Hashish | 17,241 | 25.1 | 25.6 | 43.3 | 22.2 | 22.6 | 72.0 |
| Xanax | 1,144 | 52.4 | 19.1 | 24.0 | 39.2 | 27.2 | 37.7 |
| PCP | 730 | 5.6 | 88.2 | 4.1 | 27.7 | 30.7 | 38.4 |

*Used as cultural term, can be of any race. Source: Texas Department of State Health Services, 2013.

## Estimated Use of Drugs in Texas and Bordering States: 2011-2012

| State | Any illicit drug | Marijuana | Other than marijuana[1] | Cigarettes | Binge alcohol[2] |
|---|---|---|---|---|---|
| | Current users[3] as **percent of population, age 12+ years**. Selected states. | | | | |
| U.S. total | 8.95 | 7.13 | 3.27 | 26.60 | 22.80 |
| **Texas** | **7.05** | **5.11** | **3.15** | **24.44** | **23.55** |
| Arkansas | 7.55 | 5.30 | 3.83 | 31.62 | 20.42 |
| Louisana | 4.62 | 4.84 | 3.48 | 32.95 | 25.06 |
| Oklahoma | 8.36 | 6.04 | 3.70 | 35.11 | 21.78 |
| New Mexico | 11.28 | 9.14 | 3.85 | 26.07 | 21.38 |

[1]Marijuana users who have also used another drug are included. [2]Binge use is defined as drinking five or more drinks on the same occasion on a least one day in the past 30 days. [3]Used drugs at least once within month. *Source: U.S. Substance Abuse and Mental Health Services Administration,* National Household Survey on Drug Use and Health, 2012.

## Primary Diagnosis of Clients in Texas and Bordering States: 2013

| State | Schizophrenia | Bipolar and Mood Disorders | Other Psychoses | All Other Diagnosis | No Diagnosis |
|---|---|---|---|---|---|
| | In percent of clients. | | | | |
| U.S. total | 13.2 | 45.3 | 3.4 | 25.6 | 12.5 |
| **Texas** | **23.8** | **67.6** | **0.3** | **1.0** | **7.3** |
| Arkansas | 14.1 | 51.4 | 2.5 | 28.7 | 3.4 |
| Louisana | 17.4 | 67.2 | 4.0 | 8.3 | 3.1 |
| New Mexico | 6.8 | 43.6 | 1.6 | 47.8 | 0.2 |
| Oklahoma | 7.2 | 40.3 | 1.6 | 21.3 | 29.7 |

*Source: U.S. Department of Health and Human Services, Center for Mental Health Services,* Uniform Reporting System, 2013.

## Readmission within 180 Days of Treatment: 2013

| Age | Civil* Texas | Civil U.S. | States/Terr. reporting | Forensic* Texas | Forensic U.S. |
|---|---|---|---|---|---|
| | In percent of clients. | | | | |
| 0 to 12 | 13.6 % | 15.2 % | 18 | – | – |
| 13 to 17 | 13.9 % | 13.4 % | 25 | 2.7 % | 8.3 % |
| 18 to 20 | 17.3 % | 17.9 % | 46 | 18.0 % | 12.1 % |
| 21 to 64 | 21.2 % | 20.8 % | 49 | 15.1 % | 15.2 % |
| 65 to 74 | 17.6 % | 15.1 % | 39 | 22.7 % | 14.3 % |
| 75 and over | 9.1 % | 7.2 % | 21 | – | 8.8 % |
| age not available | – | 5.1 % | 2 | – | – |
| Total | 20.3 % | 20.5 % | 49 | 14.1 % | 14.9 % |

*Forensic services are mental health services provided to persons directed into treatment by the criminal justice system, others are listed as "Civil". *Source: U.S. Department of Health and Human Services, Center for Mental Health Services,* Uniform Reporting System, 2013.

# State Institutions for Mental Health Services

*Source: Texas Department of State Health Services.*

Mental health services are provided to some 100,000 Texans each year in various institutions. In fiscal year 2014, the Texas Department of State Health Services (TDSHS) budget was $558 million for mental health centers and substance-abuse treatment.

On Sept. 1, 2004, the TDSHS was created, bringing together:
— the Texas Department of Health,
— the Texas Department of Mental Health and Mental Retardation (MHMR),
— Commission on Alcohol and Drug Abuse,
— the Texas Health Care Information Council.

With the consolidation of the four agencies, TDSHS, with more than 11,500 employees, now includes treatment and prevention for mental illness and substance abuse in its public health framework. The web address is: www.dshs.state.tx.us

*Following is a list of state hospitals, the year each was founded and average daily census in fiscal year 2015.*

### Hospitals for Persons with Mental Illness

**Austin** State Hospital — Austin; 1857; 253 patients.
**Big Spring** State Hospital — Big Spring; 1937; 187 patients.
**El Paso** Psychiatric Center — El Paso; 1974; 66 patients.
**Kerrville** State Hospital — Kerrville; 1950; 196 patients.
**North Texas** State Hospital — Wichita Falls (1922) and Vernon (1969); 559 patients.
**Rio Grande** State Center — Harlingen; 1962; 53 patients.
**Rusk** State Hospital — Rusk; 1919; 317 patients.
**San Antonio** State Hospital — San Antonio; 1892; 241 patients.
**Terrell** State Hospital — Terrell; 1885; 250 patients.
**Waco** Center for Youth — Waco; 1979; 68 patients.

*Following is a list of community mental health centers, the year each was founded, and the counties each serves.*

### Community Mental Health Centers

**Abilene** — Betty Hardwick Center; 1971; Callahan, Jones, Shackleford, Stephens and Taylor.
**Amarillo** — Texas Panhandle MHMR; 1968; Armstrong, Carson, Collingsworth, Dallam, Deaf Smith, Donley, Gray, Hall, Hansford, Hartley, Hemphill, Hutchinson, Lipscomb, Moore, Ochiltree, Oldham, Potter, Randall, Roberts, Sherman and Wheeler.
**Austin** — Austin-Travis County Center; 1967; Travis.
**Beaumont** — Spindletop MHMR Services; 1967; Chambers, Hardin, Jefferson and Orange.
**Big Spring** — West Texas Centers; 1997; Andrews, Borden, Crane, Dawson, Fisher, Gaines, Garza, Glasscock, Howard, Kent, Loving, Martin, Mitchell, Nolan, Reeves, Runnels, Scurry, Terrell, Terry, Upton, Ward, Winkler and Yoakum.
**Brownwood** — Center for Life Resources; 1969; Brown, Coleman, Comanche, Eastland, McCulloch, Mills and San Saba.
**Bryan-College Station** — MHMR Authority of Brazos Valley; 1972; Brazos, Burleson, Grimes, Leon, Madison, Robertson and Washington.
**Cleburne** — Johnson-Ellis-Navarro County Center; 1985; Ellis, Johnson, Navarro.
**Conroe** — Tri-County Services; 1983; Liberty, Montgomery and Walker.

**Corpus Christi** — Nueces County Community Center; 1970; Nueces.
**Dallas** — Dallas MetroCare; 1967; Dallas.
**Denton** — Denton County Center; 1987; Denton.
**Edinburg** — Tropical Texas Center; 1967; Cameron, Hidalgo and Willacy.
**El Paso** — Community Center; 1968; El Paso.
**Fort Worth** — MHMR of Tarrant County; 1969; Tarrant.
**Galveston** — Gulf Coast Center; 1969; Brazoria and Galveston.
**Houston** — MHMR Authority/Harris County; 1965; Harris.
**Jacksonville** — Anderson-Cherokee Community Enrichment Services; 1995; Anderson, Cherokee.
**Kerrville** — Hill Country Community Center; 1997; Bandera, Blanco, Comal, Edwards, Gillespie, Hays, Kendall, Kerr, Kimble, Kinney, Llano, Mason, Medina, Menard, Real, Schleicher, Sutton, Uvalde and Val Verde.
**Laredo** — Border Region Community Center; 1969; Jim Hogg, Starr, Webb and Zapata.
**Longview** — Sabine Valley Center; 1970; Gregg, Harrison, Marion, Panola, Rusk and Upshur.
**Lubbock** — Lubbock Regional Center; 1969; Cochran, Crosby, Hockley, Lubbock and Lynn.
**Lufkin** — Burke Center; 1975; Angelina, Houston, Jasper, Nacogdoches, Newton, Polk, Sabine, San Augustine, San Jacinto, Shelby, Trinity and Tyler.
**Lytle** — Camino Real Community Center; 1996; Atascosa, Dimmit, Frio, La Salle, Karnes, Maverick, McMullen, Wilson and Zavala.
**McKinney** — LifePath Systems; 1986; Collin.
**Midland** — Permian Basin Community Centers; 1969; Brewster, Culberson, Ector, Hudspeth, Jeff Davis, Midland, Pecos and Presidio.
**Plainview** — Central Plains Center; 1969; Bailey, Briscoe, Castro, Floyd, Hale, Lamb, Motley, Parmer and Swisher.
**Portland** — Coastal Plains Community; 1996; Aransas, Bee, Brooks, Duval, Jim Wells, Kenedy, Kleberg, Live Oak and San Patricio.
**Rosenberg** — Texana Center; 1996; Austin, Colorado, Fort Bend, Matagorda, Waller and Wharton.
**Round Rock** — Bluebonnet Trails Community Center; 1997; Bastroop, Burnet, Caldwell, Fayette, Gonzales, Guadalupe, Lee and Williamson.
**San Angelo** — MHMR Services for the Concho Valley; 1969; Coke, Concho, Crockett, Irion, Reagan, Sterling and Tom Green.
**San Antonio** — The Center for Health Care Services; 1966; Bexar.
**Sherman** — MHMR Services of Texoma; 1974; Cooke, Fannin and Grayson.
**Stephenville** — Pecan Valley Region; 1977; Erath, Hood, palo Pinto, Parker and Somervell.
**Temple** — Central Counties Center; 1967; Bell, Coryell, Hamilton, Lampasas and Milam.
**Terrell** — Lakes Regional Center; 1996; Camp, Delta, Franklin, Hopkins, Hunt, Kaufman, Lamar, Morris, Rockwall and Titus.
**Texarkana** — Northeast Texas Center; 1974; Bowie, Cass and Red River.
**Tyler** — Andrews Center; 1970; Henderson, Rains, Smith, Van Zandt and Wood.
**Victoria** — Gulf Bend Center; 1970; Calhoun, DeWitt, Jackson, Lavaca, Refugio and Victoria.
**Waco** — Heart of Texas Region Center; 1969; Bosque, Falls, Freestone, Hill, Limestone and McLennan.
**Wichita Falls** — Helen Farabee Regional Centers; 1969; Archer, Bayor, Childress, Clay, Cottle, Dickens, Foard, Hardeman, Haskell, Jack, King, Knox, Montague, Stonewall, Throckmorton, Wichita, Wilbarger and Young. ☆

# Education

*Sul Ross State University in Alpine sits in the foothills of the Davis Mountains in northwest Brewster County. Photo courtesy of Sul Ross.*

**Texas Public Schools**
**UIL Winning Schools, 2013–2014, 2014–2015**
**Higher Education in Texas**
**Universities and Colleges**

# Texas Public Schools

*Source: Texas Education Agency; http://tea.texas.gov.*

Enrollment in Texas public schools reached a peak of 5,151,925 students in the 2013–2014 school year, according to the Texas Education Agency. That is an increase of 92,986 students, or 1.8-percent, over 2012–2013, when enrollment was 5,058,939.

The seven largest school districts in Texas (listed in descending order by average daily attendance) are:

| School District | County | Enrollment |
|---|---|---|
| Houston | Harris | 215,225 |
| Dallas | Dallas | 160,253 |
| Cypress-Fairbanks | Harris | 113,023 |
| Northside | Bexar | 103,606 |
| Fort Worth | Tarrant | 85,975 |
| Austin | Travis | 84,564 |
| Fort Bend | Fort Bend | 72,152 |

In Texas, there are 1,025 independent and common school districts and 202 charter operators. Independent school districts are administered by an elected board of trustees and deal directly with the Texas Education Agency. Common districts are supervised by elected county school superintendents and county trustees. Charter schools are discussed later in this article.

## Brief History of Public Education

Public education was one of the primary goals of the early settlers of Texas, who listed in the Texas Declaration of Independence the failure to provide education as one of their grievances against Mexico.

As early as 1838, President Mirabeau B. Lamar's message to the Republic of Texas Congress advocated setting aside public domain for public schools. His interest caused him to be called the "Father of Education in Texas." In 1839, Congress designated three leagues of land to support public schools for each Texas county and 50 leagues for a state university. In 1840, each county was allocated one more league of land.

The Republic, however, did not establish a public school system or a university. After Texas was admitted into the Union, the 1845 Texas State Constitution advocated public education, instructing the Legislature to designate at least 10 percent of the tax revenue for schools. Further delay occurred until Gov. Elisha M. Pease, on Jan. 31, 1854, signed the bill setting up the Texas public school system.

The public school system was made possible by setting aside $2 million out of $10 million Texas received for relinquishing its claim to land north and west of its present boundaries in the Compromise of 1850 (see map on page 53).

During 1854, legislation provided for state apportionment of funds based upon an annual census. Also, railroads receiving grants were required to survey alternate sections to be set aside for public-school financing. The first school census that year showed 65,463 students; state fund apportionment was 62 cents per student.

When adopted in 1876, the present Texas Constitution provided: "All funds, lands, and other property heretofore set apart and appropriated for the support

## Texas School Enrollment and Expenditures per Student

| School Year | Enrollment | Spending per student |
|---|---|---|
| 2013–2014 | 5,151,925 | $9,903 |
| 2012–2013 | 5,058,939 | $9,969 |
| 2011–2012 | 4,978,120 | $10,335 |
| 2010–2011 | 4,912,385 | $11,142 |
| 2009–2010 | 4,824,778 | $11,543 |
| 2008–2009 | 4,728,204 | $11,567 |
| 2007–2008 | 4,651,516 | $10,162 |
| 2006–2007 | 4,576,933 | $ 9,629 |
| 2005–2006 | 4,505,572 | $ 9,269 |
| 2004–2005 | 4,383,871 | $ 8,916 |
| 2003–2004 | 4,311,502 | $ 7,708 |

## Graduates and Dropouts

| School Year | Graduates | *Dropouts |
|---|---|---|
| 2012–2013 | 301,418 | 34,696 |
| 2011–2012 | 292,636 | 36,276 |
| 2010–2011 | 290,581 | 34,363 |
| 2009–2010 | 280,520 | 33,235 |
| 2008–2009 | 264,275 | 40,923 |
| 2007–2008 | 252,121 | 45,796 |
| 2006–2007 | 241,193 | 55,306 |
| 2005–2006 | 240,485 | 51,841 |
| 2004–2005 | 239,716 | 18,290 |
| 2003–2004 | 244,165 | 16,434 |
| 2002–2003 | 238,109 | 15,117 |

*Grades 7–12.

## Personnel and Salaries

| Year/ Personnel Type | Personnel (Full-Time Equivalent) | Average Base Salaries |
|---|---|---|
| **2013–2014 Personnel** | | |
| Teachers | 334,511 | $49,692 |
| Campus Administrators | 19,207 | $72,764 |
| Central Administrators | 6,785 | $94,630 |
| Professional Support* | 61,075 | $58,551 |
| *Total Professionals* | *421,578* | *$68,909* |
| Educational Aides | 62,010 | $19,389 |
| Auxiliary Staff | 172,954 | $23,576 |
| *Total Staff* | *656,542* | *$53,100* |
| **2012–2013 Personnel** | | |
| Teachers | 327,420 | $48,821 |
| Campus Administrators | 18,711 | $71,259 |
| Central Administrators | 6,553 | $91,993 |
| Professional Support* | 57,943 | $57,253 |
| *Total Professionals* | *$410,627* | *$67,332* |
| Educational Aides | 60,039 | $18,886 |
| Auxiliary Staff | 171,518 | $23,056 |
| *Total Staff* | *$642,184* | *$51,878* |

*Support staff includes supervisors, counselors, educational diagnosticians, librarians, nurses/physicians, therapists, and psychologists.*

The Rockwall High School Class of 2015 celebrates as its graduation ceremony concludes on June 10, 2015, at the Curtis Culwell Center in Garland. Rockwall ISD photo.

of public schools; all the alternate sections of land reserved by the state of grants heretofore made or that may hereafter be made to railroads, or other corporations, of any nature whatsoever; one half of the public domain of the state, and all sums of money that may come to the state from the sale of any portion of the same shall constitute a perpetual public school fund."

More than 52 million acres of the Texas public domain were allotted for school purposes. (See table, Distribution of the Public Lands of Texas on page 498.)

The Constitution also provided for one-fourth of occupation taxes and a poll tax of one dollar for school support, and it made provisions for local taxation.

No provision was made for direct ad valorem taxation for maintenance of an available school fund, but a maximum 20-cent state ad valorem school tax was adopted in 1883 and raised to 35 cents in connection with provision of free textbooks in the amendment of 1918.

In 1949, the Gilmer-Aikin Laws reorganized the state system of public schools by making sweeping changes in administration and financing. The Texas Education Agency, headed by the governor-appointed Commissioner of Education, administers the public-school system.

The policy-making body for public education is the 15-member State Board of Education, which is elected from separate districts for overlapping four-year terms. Current membership of the board is listed in the State Government section of this Almanac.

## Significant Changes in Public Education

The 68th Legislature passed one of the most historic education-reform bill of the past 50 years when lawmakers met in special session in the summer of 1984. House Bill 72 came in response to growing concern over deteriorating literacy among Texas' schoolchildren over two decades, reflected in students' scores on standardized tests.

Provisions of HB 72 raised teachers' salaries, but tied those raises to teacher performance. It also introduced more stringent teacher certification and initiated competency testing for teachers.

Academic achievement was set as a priority in public education with stricter attendance rules. A no-pass, no-play rule prohibited students who are failing courses from participating in sports and other extracurricular activities for a six-week period. Lawmakers also created the 22:1 class size ration for kindergarten through fourth-grade classes.

Many HB 72 reforms have been modified in subsequent years. For example, the high-profile no-pass, no-play rule now requires only a three-week suspension for a failing course grade, during which time the student can continue to practice, but not participate in extracurricular activities.

In 1995, the 74th Legislature took on a monumental task and completely rewrote all the state's public education laws. The Public Schools Reform Act of 1995 increased local control of public schools by limiting the Texas Education Agency to recommending and reporting on educational goals; overseeing charter schools; managing the permanent, foundation, and available school funds; administering an accountability system; creating and implementing the student testing program; recommending educator appraisal and counselor evaluation instruments; and developing plans for special, bilingual, compensatory, gifted and talented, vocational, and technology education. It also reduced the authority of the State Board of Education. The goal was to return as much authority as possible to the local level. However, each subsequent legislature has reinstated some state-level control.

Another substantial change in recent decades involves requiring students to show that they have mastered certain knowledge and skills in order to receive a high school diploma. Texas students, beginning with the Class of 1987, have been required to pass an exit-level exam, along with their courses, in order to receive a diploma from a Texas public high school. Starting with the Class of 2015, Texas students must pass the State of Texas Assessments of Academic Readiness (STAAR) end-of-course exams to meet graduation requirements.

Test results and graduation rates have been used to rate schools since the creation of the Texas accountability system in 1993.

## Actions of the 84th Legislature Affecting Public Schools

The public backlash against student testing continued in 2015 with the 84th Texas Legislature reducing the focus on exit-level testing. Although 92 percent of the Class of 2015 had passed all five end-of-course exams by May of their senior year, lawmakers passed a bill that allowed students, who had passed their required classes but had failed up to two of the five end-of-course exams, to receive a diploma if approved by an individual graduation committee. Lawmakers also made changes to the state's school rating system. Beginning with the 2017-2018 school year, districts and schools will receive a ratings of A, B, C, D or F, rather than a rating label such as Met Standard or Improvement Required.

Legislators repealed the criminal offense associated with failing to attend school. Truancy will now carry a civil penalty. It is still a Class C misdemeanor for a parent to contribute to their child's truancy.

At the request of Gov. Greg Abbott, lawmakers worked to strengthen high-quality prekindergarten programs. They also reinstated funding for math and reading academies, providing training for teachers.

## Charter Schools

Charter-school legislation in Texas provides for four types of charter schools: the home-rule school district charter, the campus or campus-program charter, the open-enrollment charter and a university-sponsored charter.

As of July 2015, no district has created a home-rule charter, although citizens in Dallas ISD discussed it. Houston, Dallas, Nacogdoches, San Antonio, Clear Creek, Colorado, Corpus Christi, and Spring Branch school districts have created campus charter schools, which are overseen by each school district's board of trustees.

The most popular form of charter schools is called open-enrollment charter schools. These are public schools released from some Texas education laws and regulations. Many charter schools have focused efforts on educating young people who are at risk of dropping out of school or who have dropped out and then returned to school.

The state also approves university-sponsored charters.

Since the inception of the charter school movement in Texas, the charter contracts have been granted by the State Board of Education (SBOE). However, SB2 passed during the 2013 legislative session shifted the authority to grant a charter to the commissioner of education. The State Board of Education, however, may veto any of his selections.

A charter contract is typically granted for five years and can be revoked if the school violates its charter. By 2015, about four percent of the state's public school students attend charter schools. ☆

## Permanent School Fund

The Texas public school system was established and the Permanent School Fund (PSF) set up by the Fifth Legislature, Jan. 31, 1854.

The 158-year-old PSF is managed by the State Board of Education and is the second-largest educational endowment in the United States. It is invested in global markets and broadly diversified.

Every year, a distribution is made from PSF to pay a portion of educational costs in each public school district. During the 2012–2013 biennium, which ended Aug. 31, 2013, more than $2 billion was distributed. Since 1960, the PSF has distributed more than $22 billion.

The PSF balance, as of Aug. 31, 2012, was $28.8 billion, an increase of $1.86 billion from the prior year.

The PSF also provides a guarantee for bonds issued by local school districts, allowing districts to pay lower interest rates. As of Aug. 31, 2012, PSF assets guaranteed $53.6 billion in school district bonds to 800 public school districts in the state.

### Permanent School Fund

| Year | Total Investment Fund* | Total Income Earned by P.S.F. | Amount of P.S.F. Distributed to Schools |
|---|---|---|---|
| 1854 | $ 2,000,000 | . . . | $ 40,587 |
| 1880 | 3,542,126 | . . . | 679,317 |
| 1900 | 9,102,873 | $ 783,142 | 3,002,820 |
| 1910 | 16,752,407 | 1,970,527 | 5,931,287 |
| 1920 | 25,698,282 | 2,888,555 | 18,431,716 |
| 1930 | 38,718,106 | 2,769,547 | 27,342,473 |
| 1940 | 68,299,082 | 3,331,874 | 34,580,475 |
| 1950 | 161,179,979 | 3,985,974 | 93,996,600 |
| 1960 | 425,821,601 | 12,594,000 | 164,188,461 |
| 1970 | 842,217,721 | 34,762,955 | 287,159,758 |
| 1980 | 2,464,579,397 | 166,475,426 | 3,042,476 |
| 1985 | 5,095,802,979 | 417,080,383 | 807,680,617 |
| 1988 | 6,493,070,622 | 572,665,253 | 882,999,623 |
| 1989 | 6,873,610,771 | 614,786,823 | 917,608,395 |
| 1990 | 7,328,172,096 | 674,634,994 | 700,276,846 |
| 1991 | 10,227,777,535 | 661,744,804 | 739,200,044 |
| 1992 | 10,944,944,872 | 704,993,826 | 739,494,967 |
| 1993 | 11,822,465,497 | 714,021,754 | 737,677,545 |
| 1994 | 11,330,590,652 | 716,972,115 | 737,008,244 |
| 1995 | 12,273,168,900 | 737,008,244 | 739,996,574 |
| 1996 | 12,995,820,070 | 739,996,574 | 692,678,412 |
| 1997 | 15,496,646,498 | 692,678,412 | 690,802,024 |
| 1998 | 16,296,199,389 | 690,802,024 | 661,892 '466 |
| 1999 | 19,615,730,341 | 661,892,466 | 698,487,305 |
| 2000 | 22,275,586,452 | 698,487,305 | NA |
| 2001 | 19,021,750,040 | 794,284,231 | NA |
| 2002 | 17,047,245,212 | 764,554,567 | NA |
| 2003 | 18,037,320,374 | 896,810,915 | NA |
| 2004 | 19,261,799,285 | 54,922,310 | 825,059,655 |
| 2005 | 21,354,333,727 | NA | 879,981,967 |
| 2006 | 22,802,708,177 | NA | 841,878,709 |
| 2007 | 25,311,835,346 | NA | 843,136,949 |
| 2008 | 23,142,393,002 | NA | 716,534,543 |
| 2009 | 20,545,271,679 | NA | 716,533,764 |
| 2010 | 22,107,795,468 | NA | 60,700,000 |
| 2011 | 24,091,592,601 | NA | 1,092,809,024 |
| 2012 | 25,502,953,268 | NA | 1,020,886,905 |

*For years before 1991, includes cash, bonds at par and stocks at book value. For years beginning with 1991, includes cash, bonds and stocks at fair value.

# University Interscholastic League Winning Schools for the 2013–2014 and 2014–2015 School Years

The **UIL Lone Star Cup** is awarded annually to six high schools, one in each of the six UIL classifications, based on their team performance in district and state championships. The winning schools receive the UIL Lone Star Cup trophy and a $1,000 scholarship. The 6A classification was created for the 2014–2015 school year.

| YEAR | 1A | 2A | 3A | 4A | 5A | 6A |
|------|-----|-----|-----|-----|-----|-----|
| **Lone Star Cup Champions** | | | | | | |
| 2014–15 | Cross Plains | Shiner | Brock | Argyle | Austin Vandegrift | — |
| 2013–14 | Weimar | Salado | Argyle | Friendswood | Southlake Carroll | — |

*Winners in the academic, music, and the arts categories are listed first, then winners in some sports categories.* **For other sports results, see page 218.** *A dash (—) in the box means there was no competition in that conference in that category for that year. Source: University Interscholastic League. www.uiltexas.org/*

## Academics

| YEAR | 1A | 2A | 3A | 4A | 5A | 6A |
|------|-----|-----|-----|-----|-----|-----|
| **Overall State Meet Academic Champions** | | | | | | |
| 2014–15 | Slidell | Sabine | Holliday | Argyle | Austin Johnson | Dulles |
| 2013–14 | Sabine Pass | Salado | Argyle | Hallsville | Clements | — |
| **Accounting** | | | | | | |
| 2014–15 | Happy | Sabine Pass | Lexington | Giddings | Magnolia | Kingwood |
| 2013–14 | Sabine Pass | Caddo Mills | Giddings | Magnolia | Sugar Land Dulles | — |
| **Accounting Team** | | | | | | |
| 2014–15 | Happy | Gladewater | Jim Ned Tuscola | Giddings | Magnolia | Kingwood |
| 2013–14 | Sabine Pass | Caddo Mills | Giddings | Cleburne | Sugar Land Dulles | — |
| **Calculator Applications** | | | | | | |
| 2014–15 | Garden City | San Augustine | George West | Abilene Wylie | Frisco Liberty | Dallas Science-Eng Magnet |
| 2013–14 | Pettus | Daingerfield | Argyle | Frisco Liberty | Dallas Science-Eng Magnet | — |
| **Calculator Applications Team** | | | | | | |
| 2014–15 | Whitharral | Pettus | Gainesville Callisburg | Abilene Wylie | Edinburg Vela | Dallas Science-Eng Magnet |
| 2013–14 | Whitharral | Daingerfield | Argyle | Hallsville | Edinburg Vela | — |
| **Computer Applications** | | | | | | |
| 2014–15 | Slidell | Goldthwaite | Mt Pleasant | Argyle | Livingston | Houston North Shore |
| 2013–14 | Chireno | Sunnyvale | Needville | Livingston | Cypress Cypress Woods | — |
| **Computer Science** | | | | | | |
| 2014–15 | Bynum | Booker | Blanco | Kennedale | Frisco Heritage | Plano West Sr |
| 2013–14 | Sudan | Jim Ned Tuscola | Needville | Austin Johnson | Sugar Land Clements | — |
| **Computer Science Team** | | | | | | |
| 2014–15 | Slidell | Booker | Blanco | Needville | Austin Johnson | Sugar Land Clements |
| 2013–14 | Fort Worth Harmony | Mount Vernon | Needville | Austin Johnson | Sugar Land Clements | — |
| **Number Sense** | | | | | | |
| 2014–15 | Garden City | Lindsay | Wichita Falls City View | Argyle | Mission Veterans Memorial | Klein |
| 2013–14 | Lovelady | Abernathy | Argyle | Mission Veterans Memorial | Sugar Land Clements | — |
| **Number Sense Team** | | | | | | |
| 2014–15 | Garden City | Lindsay | Paris Chisum | Argyle | Frisco Liberty | Edinburg Edinburg North |
| 2013–14 | Lindsay | Salado | Argyle | Dallas Highland Park | Sugar Land Clements | — |
| **Mathematics** | | | | | | |
| 2014–15 | Savoy | Latexo | Kirbyville | Abilene Wylie | Grapevine | San Antonio Jay |
| 2013–14 | Latexo | Abernathy | Liberty Hill | Frisco Liberty | Carrollton Hebron | — |
| **Mathematics Team** | | | | | | |
| 2014–15 | Savoy | Latexo | Queen City | Abilene Wylie | Grapevine | Sugar Land Dulles |
| 2013–14 | Latexo | Salado | Argyle | Hallsville | Sugar Land Clements | — |
| **Science** | | | | | | |
| 2014–15 | Comstock | Lockney | Whitney | Irving Uplift North Hills Prep | San Antonio Alamo Heights | Sugar Land Dulles |
| 2013–14 | Lockney | San Antonio Cole | College Station | Pearland Dawson | Sugar Land Dulles | — |

| YEAR | 1A | 2A | 3A | 4A | 5A | 6A |
|------|-----|-----|-----|-----|-----|-----|
| **Science Team** | | | | | | |
| 2014–15 | Knippa | Valley View | Frontier College Prep Brownsville | Argyle | College Station | Sugar Land Dulles |
| 2013–14 | Fort Worth Harmony | Lago Vista | Argyle | Pearland Dawson | Sugar Land Dulles | — |
| **Social Studies** | | | | | | |
| 2014–15 | Crosbyton | Weimar | Jim Ned Tuscola | Fischer Canyon Lake | N Richland Hills Birdville | Irving MacArthur |
| 2013–14 | Weimar | Gainesville Callisburg | Fischer Canyon Lake | Hereford | Southlake Carroll | — |
| **Social Studies Team** | | | | | | |
| 2014–15 | Hartley | Sabine Pass | Paris Chisum | Wimberley | N Richland Hills Birdville | Irving MacArthur |
| 2013–14 | Sabine Pass | Gainesville Callisburg | Liberty Hill | N Richland Hill Birdville | Southlake Carroll | — |
| **Current Issues** | | | | | | |
| 2014–15 | Hartley | Sabine Pass | Sadler S&S Consol. | Wimberley | Hereford | Katy Taylor |
| 2013–14 | Latexo | Holliday | Lufkin Hudson | The Colony | Grapevine | — |
| **Current Issues Team** | | | | | | |
| 2014–15 | Comstock | Sabine Pass | **TIE:** Fort Worth Harmony Sadler S&S Consol. | Wimberley | College Station A&M Cons | Irving MacArthur |
| 2013–14 | Latexo | Sadler S&S Consol. | Orangefield | Friendswood | College Station A&M Cons | — |
| **Literary Criticism** | | | | | | |
| 2014–15 | Whiteface | Lockney | Holliday | Rockport-Fulton | Sulphur Springs | Los Fresnos |
| 2013–14 | Martin's Mill | Elkhart | Bridge City | Denton | Southlake Carroll | — |
| **Literary Criticism Team** | | | | | | |
| 2014–15 | Whiteface | Martin's Mill | Holliday | Liberty | Sulphur Springs | Katy Seven Lakes |
| 2013–14 | Martin's Mill | Elkhart | Liberty | Hallsville | Los Fresnos | — |
| **Poetry Interpretation** | | | | | | |
| 2014–15 | Gail | Sundown | Little River Academy | Melissa | Prosper | Converse Judson |
| 2013–14 | Sundown | New Boston | Seminole | Denton Guyer | Houston Hastings | — |
| **Prose Interpretation** | | | | | | |
| 2014–15 | Douglass | Tolar | Corsicana Mildred | Van | Arlington Timberview | San Angelo Central |
| 2013–14 | Martin's Mill | Tolar | Seminole | Denton Guyer | San Angelo Central | — |
| **Ready Writing** | | | | | | |
| 2014–15 | Slidell | Sulphur Springs | Brownsville Frontier College Prep | Orange Little Cypress-Mauriceville | Whitehouse | Katy Seven Lakes |
| 2013–14 | Ira | Wichita Falls City View | Gilmer | Lucas Lovejoy | Coppell | — |
| **Speech Team** | | | | | | |
| 2014–15 | Lometa | Abernathy | Mt Pleasant Chapel Hill | Seminole | Lindale | Sugar Land Dulles |
| 2013–14 | Lometa | Salado | Paris North Lamar | Trophy Club Nelson | Klein | — |
| **Informative Speaking** | | | | | | |
| 2014–15 | Lometa | Latexo | Blanco | Crandall | Richmond Foster | Trophy Club Nelson |
| 2013–14 | Sudan | Salado | Paris North Lamar | Trophy Club Nelson | Plano Sr. | — |
| **Persuasive Speaking** | | | | | | |
| 2014–15 | Cross Plains | Tolar | Holliday | Salado | Prosper | San Antonio Johnson |
| 2013–14 | Gail Borden | Salado | Van | Georgetown East View | Houston Cypress Creek | — |
| **Lincoln-Douglas Debate** | | | | | | |
| 2014–15 | Chireno | Stratford | Hooks | Big Spring | Richmond Foster | Sugar Land Dulles |
| 2013–14 | Three Rivers | Mt Pleasant Chapel Hill | Van | Trophy Club Nelson | Klein | — |
| **Cross Examination Team Debate** | | | | | | |
| 2014–15 | Lometa Team 1 | Abernathy Team 1 | Whitesboro Team 2 | Athens Team 1 | Lindale Team 2 | Katy Taylor Team 1 |
| 2013–14 | Gail Borden | Salado | Athens | Crosby | Houston Clear Lake | |
| **Spelling & Vocabulary** | | | | | | |
| 2014–15 | Knippa | Sulphur Springs | McGregor | Salado | Port Lavaca Calhoun | Katy Seven Lakes |
| 2013–14 | Kennard | Henrietta | Port Isabel | Sulphur Springs | Del Rio | — |
| **Spelling & Vocabulary Team** | | | | | | |
| 2014–15 | Savoy | Sabine Pass | Holliday | Port Isabel | Port Lavaca Calhoun | Katy Seven Lakes |
| 2013–14 | Sabine Pass | Henrietta | Groesbeck | Sulphur Springs | Katy Seven Lakes | — |

| YEAR | 1A | 2A | 3A | 4A | 5A | 6A |
|------|----|----|----|----|----|----|
| **Journalism Team** | | | | | | |
| 2014–15 | Channing | Thrall | White Oak | Atlanta | Austin Johnson | — |
| 2013–14 | Archer City | White Oak | Carthage | Lindale | Longview | — |
| **Editorial Writing** | | | | | | |
| 2014–15 | Channing | Archer City | White Oak | Lampasas | Hallsville | Sugar Land Dulles |
| 2013–14 | Archer City | Little River Academy | Orangefield | Mont Belvieu Barbers Hill | Lufkin | |
| **Feature Writing** | | | | | | |
| 2014–15 | Channing | Claude | Comanche | Salado | Port Neches Port Neches-Groves | San Antonio Reagan |
| 2013–14 | Douglass | White Oak | Carthage | Lindale | Longview | |
| **Headline Writing** | | | | | | |
| 2014–15 | Channing | Plains | Ballinger | Snyder | Grapevine | Katy Seven Lakes |
| 2013–14 | Harper | Bangs | Orange West Orange-Stark | N Richland Hills Birdville | Keller Central | |
| **News Writing** | | | | | | |
| 2014–15 | Channing | Thrall | White Oak | Bandera | Magnolia | San Antonio Stevens |
| 2013–14 | Archer City | White Oak | Atlanta | Canyon | Longview | — |

## Publications

| Year | Yearbooks (Gold Awards) | Newspapers (Gold Awards) |
|------|-------------------------|--------------------------|
| 2014–15 | McKinney, Pleasant Grove, St. Mark's School of Texas, Stony Point, Texas, The Hockaday School, Austin Westlake. | Albany, Episcopal School of Dallas, Pleasant Grove, St. Mark's School of Texas, Texas, Austin Westlake. |
| 2013–14 | Burges, McKinney Pleasant Grove, St. Mark's School of Texas, Thrall, Austin Westlake. | Albany, Liberal Arts and Science Academy, Pleasant Grove, St. Mark's School of Texas, Texas, Austin Westlake. |

## Music and Theater

| YEAR | 1A | 2A | 3A | 4A | 5A | 6A |
|------|----|----|----|----|----|----|
| **One-Act Play** | | | | | | |
| 2014–15 | Abbott | Mason | Lago Vista | Seminole | Lewisville The Colony | Lewisville |
| 2013–14 | Mason | Mount Vernon | Seminole | Pearland Dawson | Houston Carnegie Vanguard | — |
| **State Marching Band Contest** | | | | | | |
| 2014–15 | — | — | — | Argyle | — | Flower Mound Marcus |
| 2013–14 | Shiner | Whitesboro | — | Vandegrift | — | — |

# Athletics

| YEAR | 1A | 2A | 3A | 4A | 5A | 6A |
|------|----|----|----|----|----|----|
| **Cross Country Team, Boys** | | | | | | |
| 2014–15 | Cumby Miller Grove | Valley View | Luling | San Elizario | Houston Stratford | Southlake Carroll |
| 2013–14 | Ozona | Luling | Lytle | Houston Stratford | Southlake Carroll | — |
| **Cross Country Individual, Boys** | | | | | | |
| 2014–15 | Sanderson | Ozona | Bruceville-Eddy | Burkburnett | Frisco Independence | Colleyville Heritage |
| 2013–14 | Forsan | Van Alstyne | Decatur | Frisco Heritage | Houston Strake Jesuit | — |
| **Cross Country Team, Girls** | | | | | | |
| 2014–15 | Hartley | Sundown | Eustace | Bandera | Canyon Randall | Lewisville Hebron |
| 2013–14 | Harper | Eustace | College Station | Canyon Randall | Southlake Carroll | |
| **Cross Country Individual, Girls** | | | | | | |
| 2014–15 | O'Donnell | Sundown | Holliday | Levelland | Grapevine | Comal Smithson Valley |
| 2013–14 | Sundown | Crawford | College Station | Dallas Highland Park | New Braunfels | — |
| **Golf Team, Boys** | | | | | | |
| 2014–15 | Throckmorton | Normangee | Brock | Argyle | Austin Vandegrift | Southlake Carroll |
| 2013–14 | Weimar | Salado | Andrews | Austin Vandegrift | Austin Westlake | — |
| **Golf Individual, Boys** | | | | | | |
| 2014–15 | Throckmorton | Normangee | San Antonio Cole | Fredericksburg | Huntsville | Southlake Carroll |
| 2013–14 | Olney | Whitesboro | Andrews | Dallas Highland Park | Austin Westlake | |

| YEAR | 1A | 2A | 3A | 4A | 5A | 6A |
|------|----|----|----|----|----|----|
| **Golf Team, Girls** | | | | | | |
| 2014–15 | Wink | Memphis | Sonora | Andrews | Humble Kingwood Park | Austin Lake Travis |
| 2013–14 | Weimar | Sonora | Andrews | Huntsville | Allen | — |
| **Golf Individual, Girls** | | | | | | |
| 2014–15 | Briscoe Fort Elliott | Miles | Sonora | La Vernia | Aledo | Montgomery |
| 2013–14 | Petrolia | East Bernard | La Vernia | Aledo | Allen | — |
| **Tennis, Team** | | | | | | |
| 2014–15 | — | — | — | Abilene Wylie | Grapevine | Dallas Highland Park |
| 2013–14 | — | — | — | Dallas Highland Park | New Braunfels | — |
| **Tennis, Boys Singles** | | | | | | |
| 2014–15 | Rocksprings | Corpus Christi London | Tuscola Jim Ned | Longview Spring Hill | Houston Stratford | El Paso Coronado |
| 2013–14 | Corpus Christi London | Tuscola Jim Ned | College Station | Wichita Falls Rider | Katy Taylor | — |
| **Tennis, Boys Doubles** | | | | | | |
| 2014–15 | Crowell | Mason | Tulia | Abilene Wylie | Grapevine | Houston Memorial |
| 2013–14 | Mason | Kountze | Abilene Wylie | Dallas Highland Park | Houston Memorial | — |
| **Tennis, Girls Singles** | | | | | | |
| 2014–15 | Paint Rock | Junction | Brock | Fredericksburg | Saginaw | Austin Westlake |
| 2013–14 | Junction | Franklin | Fredericksburg | Dallas Highland Park | Houston Clear Lake | — |
| **Tennis, Girls Doubles** | | | | | | |
| 2014–15 | Fort Davis | Mason | Lago Vista | Vernon | San Antonio Alamo Heights | Dallas Highland Park |
| 2013–14 | Mason | Lago Vista | Vernon | Dallas Highland Park | Plano West | — |
| **Tennis, Mixed Doubles** | | | | | | |
| 2014–15 | Leakey | Mason | Tulia | Kaufman | Grapevine | New Braunfels |
| 2013–14 | Menard | Brock | Abilene Wylie | Dallas Highland Park | Austin Westlake | — |
| **Track & Field, Boys Team** | | | | | | |
| 2014–15 | Water Valley | New Deal | Coleman | Gilmer | Fort Bend Marshall | Manvel |
| 2013–14 | Div 1: Alto Div 1: Bronte | Rosebud-Lott | Kennedale | Texarkana | Humble Kingwood | — |
| **Track & Field, Girls Team** | | | | | | |
| 2014–15 | Burton | Rosebud-Lott | Leonard | Uplift Hampton Prep | Arlington Seguin | Converse Judson |
| 2013–14 | Div 1: Van Horn Div 1: Cross Plains | Dallas Hampton Prep | West Oso | Lancaster | Converse Judson | — |

### Swimming & Diving, Team

| | GIRLS | | BOYS | |
|------|-------|------|------|------|
| YEAR | 5A | 6A | 5A | 6A |
| 2014–15 | Austin Vandegrift | Austin Westlake | Humble Kingwood Park | Southlake Carroll |
| YEAR | 4A | 5A | 4A | 5A |
| 2013–14 | SA Alamo Heights | Austin Westlake | Frisco Wakeland | Southlake Carroll |

### Wrestling, Boys

| 2014–15 | **TEAM: 5A:** Frisco Centennial; **6A:** Allen. **Weight Class 5A 106:** Dumas; **113:** Canyon Randall; **120:** Austin Vandergrift; **126:** Dumas; **132:** Argyle; **138:** El Paso Chapin; **145:** Frisco Centennial; **152:** Frisco Centennial; **160:** Boys Ranch; **170:** The Colony; **182:** Dripping Springs; **195:** Grapevine; **220:** Wylie; **285:** Azle. **Weight Class 6A 106:** Arlington Martin; **113:** El Paso Franklin; **120:** Arlington Martin; **126:** Arlington Martin; **132:** El Dorado; **138:** Allen; **145:** Allen; **152:** Arlington; **160:** Cinco Ranch; **170:** Allen; **182:** Allen; **195:** El Paso Franklin; **220:** Klein; **285:** Hebron. |
|------|------|
| 2013–14 | **TEAM: 4A:** Frisco Centennial; **5A** Allen. **4A Weight Class 106:** Carrollton Creekview; **113:** Canyon Randall; **120:** Amarillo; **126:** Frisco Centennial; **132:** El Paso Chapin; **138:** Canyon Randall; **145:** Dallas Highland Parkn; **152:** Frisco Centennial; **160:** Dallas Highland Park; **170:** Friendswood; **182:** Amarillo Caprock; **195:** Canyon Randall; **220:** Georgetown; **285:** Hereford. **5A Weight Class 106:** Austin Westlake; **113:** Lewisville Hebron; **120:** El Paso Coronado; **126:** Katy Morton Ranch; **132:** Katy; **138:** Arlington Martin; **145:** Arlington; **152:** Amarillo Tascosa; **160:** Southlake Carroll; **170:** Allen; **182:** Katy Cinco Ranch; **195:** Conroe The Woodlands; **220:** Grapevine; **285:** Coppell. |

### Wrestling, Girls

| 2014–15 | **TEAM: 5A:** El Paso Hanks; **6A** Houston Cypress Ridge. **5A Weight Class 95:** Amarillo Caprock; **102:** El Paso Andress; **110:** Canyon Randall; **119:** Carrollton Creekview; **128:** El Paso Hanks; **138:** Azle; **148:** El Paso Hanks; **165:** Frisco Lone Star; **185:** El Paso Jefferson; **215:** North Dallas. **6A Weight Class 95:** Arlington; **102:** Klein; **110:** San Antonio Wagner; **119:** Plano East; **128:** Allen; **138:** Amarillo Tascosa; **148:** Klein Oak; **165:** Klein; **185:** Lewisville; **215:** Keller Timber Creek. |
|------|------|
| 2013–14 | **TEAM: 4A:** El Paso Hanks; **5A** Amarillo Tascosa. **4A Weight Class 95:** Amarillo Caprock; **102:** Amarillo Caprock; **110:** Carrollton Creekview; **119:** Bushland; **128:** El Paso Hanks; **138:** Hereford; **148:** El Paso Hanks; **165:** Frisco; **185:** Azle; **215:** Saginaw. **5A Weight Class 95:** Klein; **102:** Arlington Houston; **110:** San Antonio Wagner; **119:** League City Clear Springs; **128:** Houston Cypress Woods; **138:** Houston Cypress Falls; **148:** Conroe Oak Ridge; **165:** Lewisville; **185:** Conroe; **215:** Conroe. |

*The University of Texas at Austin was established in 1881. Photo © 2014 by Larry D. Moore (CC).*

# Brief History of Higher Education in Texas

The first permanent institutions of higher education established in Texas were church-supported schools, although there were some earlier efforts:

• **Rutersville University** was established in 1840 by Methodist minister Martin Ruter in Fayette County and was the predecessor of Southwestern University in Georgetown, which was established in 1843;

• **Baylor University,** now at Waco, was established in 1845 at Independence, Washington County, by the Texas Union Baptist Association; and

• **Austin College,** now at Sherman, was founded in 1849 at Huntsville by the Brazos Presbytery of the Old School Presbyterian Church.

Other historic Texas schools of collegiate rank included:

**Larissa College,** 1848, at Larissa, Cherokee County; **McKenzie College,** 1841, Clarksville, Red River County; **Chappell Hill Male and Female Institute,** 1850, Chappell Hill, Washington County; **Soule University,** 1855, Chappell Hill; **Johnson Institute,** 1852, Driftwood, Hays County; **Nacogdoches University,** 1845, Nacogdoches; **Salado College,** 1859, Salado, Bell County.

**Add-Ran College,** established in 1873 at Thorp Spring, Hood County, was the predecessor of present-day **Texas Christian University,** Fort Worth.

## Texas A&M University and The University of Texas

The Agricultural and Mechanical College of Texas (now **Texas A&M University**), authorized by the Legislature in 1871, opened its doors in 1876 to become the first publicly supported institution of higher education in Texas.

In 1881, Texans established **The University of Texas in Austin,** with a medical branch in Galveston. The Austin institution opened Sept. 15, 1883, and the Galveston school opened in 1891.

## First College for Women

In 1901, the 27th Legislature established the **Girls Industrial College,** which began classes at its campus in Denton in 1903. A campaign to establish a state industrial college for women was led by the State Grange and Patrons of Husbandry.

A bill was signed into law on April 6, 1901, creating the college. It was charged with a dual mission, which continues to guide the university today, to provide a liberal arts education and to prepare young women with a specialized education "for the practical industries of the age."

In 1905, the name of the college was changed to the College of Industrial Arts; in 1934, it was changed to Texas State College for Women.

Since 1957, the institution, which is now the largest university principally for women in the United States, has been the **Texas Woman's University.**

### Historic, Primarily Black Colleges

A number of Texas schools were established primarily for blacks, although collegiate racial integration has long been the status quo.

The black-oriented institutions include state-supported **Prairie View A&M University** (originally established as Alta Vista Agricultural College in 1876) Prairie View; **Texas Southern University,** Houston; privately supported **Huston-Tillotson University,** Austin; **Jarvis Christian College,** Hawkins; **Wiley College,** Marshall; **Paul Quinn College,** originally located in Waco, now in Dallas; and **Texas College,** Tyler.

Predominantly black colleges that are important in the history of higher education in Texas, but which have ceased operations, include **Bishop College,** established in Marshall in 1881, then moved to Dallas; **Mary Allen College,** established in Crockett in 1886; and **Butler College,** originally named the Texas Baptist Academy, in 1905 in Tyler.

# Recent Developments in Texas Higher Education

*Source: Texas Higher Education Coordinating Board; www.thecb.state.tx.us/*

## State Appropriations

The total All Funds appropriation for higher education in Texas for the **2016–2017 biennium is $19.9 billion,** an increase of $1.4 billion over the 2014–2015 biennium. General Revenue and General Revenue-Dedicated funds (GR and GR-D) increased by $1.5 billion (9.1 percent) to $17.4 billion.

Fiscal Year 16–17 runs from Sept. 1, 2015, through Aug. 31, 2017.

The FY 16–17 All Funds appropriation for **general academic institutions** is $6.82 billion, an increase of $398.8 million (or 6.2 percent) over FY 14–15. **Health-related institutions** All Funds appropriation increased by about $178.4 million to $3.04 billion, a 6.2-percent increase. All funding for **public two-year institutions** decreased by $11.5 million (or 0.6 percent) due to a decline in contact hours.

The total All Funds appropriation for the entire state for FY 16–17 is $209.4 billion, an increase of $7.3 billion, or 3.6 percent, over 14–15 funding levels. GR and GR-D statewide increased 11.3 percent to $114.1 billion for the new biennium.

In the FY 16–17 budget, **higher education will represent 9.5 percent** of the entire All Funds budget and 15.2 percent of the GR and GR-D budget.

*Source: Summary Tables for Senate Bill 1 Conference Committee Report, Legislative Budget Board.*

## Enrollment

Enrollment in Texas public, independent, career, and private colleges and universities in fall 2014 totaled 1,621,725 students, an increase of 5,807 from fall 2013.

Enrollment in the 39 **public universities** and **all health-related institutions** increased by 19,657 students to 628,127 students. Thirty-two universities reported enrollment increases, while seven reported decreases.

The state's **public community college districts, Lamar State Colleges,** and **Texas State Technical College System,** which offer two-year degree programs, reported fall 2014 enrollments totaling 712,478 students, a decrease of 7,363 over fall 2013.

Enrollments for fall 2014 at **independent and career colleges and universities** decreased to 229,639 students, down 11,569 students from fall 2013.

## Actions of the 84th Legislature

Below are bills passed by the 84th Legislature that affect higher education in Texas.

★ **HB 3348** creates a pilot program to offer a community college **baccalaureate in dental hygiene** at Tyler Junior College. It was signed by the governor.

★ **HB 100** authorizes $3.1 billion in tuition revenue bonds for **64 projects** at public universities, health-related institutions, and state and technical colleges. It was signed by the governor.

★ **SB 11** regarding **firearms on college campuses** was signed by the governor. The final language states that institutions may not adopt a general rule to prohibit licensed holders from carrying handguns on the campus, except that they may establish "reasonable" restrictions on where firearms may be permitted on campus and how they may be stored.

★ **HB 700** repeals the **B-On-Time Loan Repayment Program (BOT)** from statute. It was signed by the governor. The legislation limits BOT to renewal students only, beginning in academic year 2015–2016, and abolishes the program entirely in 2020.

★ **SB 18** makes key revisions to streamline and improve the efficiency of existing **Graduate Medical Education (GME) programs** and sets up a Permanent Fund Supporting GME from funds transferred from the Texas Medical Liability Insurance Underwriting Association. Funds from the permanent fund would be used to support GME programs established by SB 18.

★ **HB 2628** directs the Texas Higher Education Coordinating Board to periodically review each **Field of Study curriculum.** Approved Fields of Study curricula provide a statewide guarantee of transfer of course credits to any public college or university in Texas, and further promises that the courses in the approved Field of Study will apply to a student's relevant degree program. The legislation also directs the agency to develop Programs of Study by assembling advisory committees to identify the knowledge, skills, and abilities required to prepare students for high-skill, high-wage jobs in high-demand occupations.

★ **SB 632** creates a **"Governor's University Research Initiative Fund" (GURIF)** as a dedicated account in the general revenue fund. Monies placed in the GURIF are to be allocated by the Texas Economic Development and Tourism Office within the Office of the Governor. The Office will award matching grants to assist eligible institutions in recruiting distinguished researchers, preferentially but not exclusively in science, technology, engineering, and mathematics (STEM). ☆

# Universities and Colleges

Sources: Texas Higher Education Coordinating Board and individual institutions. Dates of establishment may differ from Brief History on page 599 because schools use the date when authorization was given rather than date of first classes. For explanation of type of institution and other symbols, see notes at end of table. www.thecb.state.tx.us

| Name of Institution — Location; (*type or ownership, if private sectarian institution); date of founding; president (unless otherwise noted) | Number of Faculty † 2012 | Enrollment | | |
|---|---|---|---|---|
| | | Fall Term 2014 | Summer Sessions 2012 § | Extesion or Contining Education 2012 |
| **Abilene Christian University** — Abilene; (3–Church of Christ); 1906 (as Childers Classical Institute; as Abilene Christian College, 1914; as university, 1976); Dr. Phil Schubert. | 346 | 4,259 | 2,181 | NA |
| **ALAMO COLLEGES (9)** — **Dr. Bruce H. Leslie, chancellor.** 1978 (as San Antonio Community College District; 1982, as Alamo Community College District; current name, 2009). System consists of following colleges and presidents: | 2,567 | 58,292 | 26,957 | 2,256 |
| **Northeast Lakeview College** — San Antonio; (7); 2007; Dr. Craig T. Follins. | 73 | 2,325 | 144 | 321 |
| **Northwest Vista College** — San Antonio; (7); 1995; Dr. Ric Baser. | 680 | 15,797 | 7,084 | 356 |
| **Palo Alto College** — San Antonio; (7); 1983; Dr. Michael Flores. | 315 | 8,376 | 4,110 | 551 |
| **San Antonio College** — San Antonio; (7); 1925; Dr. Robert Vela. | 1,044 | 21,280 | 11,119 | 567 |
| **St. Philip's College** — San Antonio; (7); 1898; Dr. Adena Williams Loston. | 455 | 10,514 | 4,500 | 461 |
| **Alvin Community College** — Alvin; (7); 1949; Dr. Christal Albrecht. | 238 | 4,914 | 2,547 | 0 |
| **Amarillo College** — Amarillo; (7); 1929; Dr. Russell Lowery-Hart. | 384 | 9,948 | 3,393 | 25,000 |
| **Amberton University** — Garland; (3); 1971 (as Amber University; current name, 2001); Dr. Melinda H. Reagan. | 40 | 1,381 | 1,378 | NA |
| **Angelina College** — Lufkin; (7); 1968; Dr. Michael Simon. | 110 | 5,145 | 2,613 | 2,574 |
| **Angelo State University** — San Angelo (*See* **Texas Tech University**) | | | | |
| **Arlington Baptist College** — Arlington; (3–Baptist); 1939 (as Bible Baptist Seminary; name changed to current in 1965); Dr. D. L. Moody. | 22 | 260 | 65 | 60 |
| **Austin College** — Sherman; (3–Presbyterian USA); 1849; Dr. Marjorie Hass. | 106 | 1,301 | ** | ** |
| **Austin Community College** — Austin; (7); 1972; Dr. Richard M. Rhodes. | 1,842 | 37,900 | 24,407 | 16,002 |
| **Austin Presbyterian Theological Seminary** — Austin; (3–Presbyterian U.S.A.); 1902 (successor of Austin School of Theology, est. 1884); Dr. Theodore J. Wardlaw. | 17 | 195 | | |
| **Baptist Missionary Association Theological Seminary** — Jacksonville; (3–Baptist Missionary); 1955; Dr. Charley Holmes. | 15 | 145 | NA | 30 |
| **Baylor College of Medicine** — Houston; (5); 1903 (in Dallas; moved to Houston, 1943; Baptist until 1969); Dr. Paul Klotman. | 3,696 | 1,576 | NA | 17,901 |
| **Baylor University** — Waco; (3–Southern Baptist); 1845 (in Independence; merged with Waco University and moved to Waco, 1887); Kenneth W. Starr. | 823 | 16,263 | 4,789 | NA |
| **Bee County College** — Beeville (*See* **Coastal Bend College**) | | | | |
| **Blinn College** — Brenham; (7); 1883 (as academy; jr. college, 1927); Dr. Mary Hensley. | 1,420 | 18,769 | 10,926 | ** |
| **Brazosport College** — Lake Jackson; (7); 1967; Dr. Millicent M. Valek. | 86 | 4,131 | 2,434 | 1,088 |
| **Brookhaven College** — Farmers Branch (*See* **Dallas County Community College**) | | | | |
| **Cedar Valley College** — Lancaster (*See* **Dallas County Community College District**) | | | | |
| **Central Texas College** — Killeen; (7); 1965; Dr. Jim Yeonopolus, interim chancellor. | 658 | 10,657 | 9,047 | 3,511 |
| **Cisco College** — Cisco; (7); 1909 (as Cisco Junior College, a private institution; became state school in 1939; name changed to current in 2009); Dr. Bobby Smith. | 195 | 3,564 | 1,435 | 67 |
| **Clarendon College** — Clarendon; (7); 1898 (as church school; became state school in 1927); Dr. Robert Keith Riza. | 77 | 1,199 | 483 | 220 |
| **Coastal Bend College** — Beeville; (7); (1966 as Bee County College, name changed in 1999); Dr. Beatriz T. Espinoza. | 219 | 3,751 | 1,607 | 651 |
| **College of the Mainland** — Texas City; (7); 1967; Dr. Elizabeth Lewis. | 175 | 3,858 | § 2,095 | 2,514 |
| **College of Saints John Fisher & Thomas More, The** — Fort Worth; (3–Roman Catholic); 1981 (as St. Thomas More Institute; as The College of St. Thomas More, 1991; name changed in 2012; closed in 2014. last president, Michael G. King. | Closed in 2014. | | | |
| **Collin College** — McKinney; (7); 1985 (as Collin County Community College); Dr. H. Neil Matkin. | 1,186 | 27,525 | 17,747 | 5,114 |
| **Concordia University Texas**— Austin; (3–Lutheran Church–Missouri Synod); 1926 (as Concordia Lutheran College; current name, 1995); part of Concordia University System. Dr. Thomas Cedel. | 358 | 2,521 | 1,256 | 314 |
| **Cooke County College** — Gainesville (*See* **North Central Texas College**) | | | | |
| **Corpus Christi State University** — (*See* **Texas A&M University System**) | | | | |
| **Cy-Fair College** — Houston (*See* **Lone Star College System**) | | | | |
| **Dallas Baptist University** — Dallas; (3–Baptist); 1898 (as Decatur Baptist College; moved to Dallas, name changed to Dallas Baptist College, 1965; became university, 1985); Dr. Gary R. Cook. | 568 | 5,445 | 2,279 | NA |
| **Dallas Christian College** — Dallas; (3–Christian); 1950; Dr. Brian D. Smith. | 60 | 354 | 116 | NA |
| **DALLAS COUNTY COMMUNITY COLLEGE DISTRICT (9)** — **Dr. Joe May, chancellor.** System consists of following colleges and presidents: | 3,323 | 71,433 | 48,188 | 20,262 |
| **Brookhaven College** — Farmers Branch; (7); 1978; Dr. Thom D. Chesney. | 565 | 9,763 | 7,777 | 2,633 |
| **Cedar Valley College** — Lancaster; (7); 1977; Dr. Jennifer B. Wimbish. | 249 | 6,016 | 3,376 | 685 |
| **Eastfield College** — Mesquite; (7); 1970; Dr. Jean Conway. | 474 | 12,739 | 8,250 | 1,959 |
| **El Centro College** — Dallas; (7); 1966; Dr. José Adames. | 471 | 9,474 | 5,541 | 6,240 |
| **Mountain View College** — Dallas; (7); 1970; Dr. Robert Garza. | 325 | 8,080 | 5,008 | 1,299 |
| **North Lake College** — Irving; (7); 1977; Christa Slejko. | 463 | 9,210 | 6,365 | 2,876 |
| **Richland College** — Dallas; (7); 1972; Dr. Kay Eggleston. | 776 | 16,151 | 11,871 | 4,570 |

| Name of Institution — Location; (*type or ownership, if private sectarian institution); date of founding; president (unless otherwise noted) | Number of Faculty † 2012 | Enrollment | | |
|---|---|---|---|---|
| | | Fall Term 2014 | Summer Sessions 2012 § | Extesion or Contining Education 2012 |
| Dallas Theological Seminary — Dallas; (3–Christian); 1924 (as Evangelical Theological College; current name, 1936); Dr. Mark L. Bailey. | 119 | 2,036 | 1,144 | 493 |
| Del Mar College — Corpus Christi; (7); 1935; Dr. Mark Escamilla. | 314 | 10,439 | 7,256 | 2,188 |
| Eastfield College — Mesquite (See Dallas County Community College District) | | | | |
| East Texas Baptist University — Marshall; (3–Baptist); 1913 (as College of Marshall; as East Texas Baptist College, 1944; as university, 1984); Lawrence Ressler, interim. | 64 | 1,349 | NA | NA |
| East Texas State University — Commerce (See Texas A&M University System) | | | | |
| East Texas State University at Texarkana — Texarkana (See Texas A&M University–Texarkana under Texas A&M University System) | | | | |
| El Centro College — Dallas (See Dallas County Community College District) | | | | |
| El Paso Community College — El Paso; (7); 1969; five campuses: Mission del Paso, Northwest, Rio Grande, Transmountain, and Valle Verde; Dr. William Serrata. | # 1,337 | 27,330 | 15,586 | ** |
| Episcopal Theological Seminary of the Southwest — Austin; (3–Episcopal); 1952; Rev. Cynthia Briggs Kittredge. | 38 | 109 | 55 | NA |
| Frank Phillips College — Borger; (7); 1948; includes campus in Perryton; Dr. Jud Hicks. | 73 | 1,342 | 594 | 994 |
| Galveston College — Galveston; (7); 1967; Dr. W. Myles Shelton. | 70 | 2,048 | 1,643 | 154 |
| Grayson College — Denison; (7); 1963; Dr. Jeremy McMillen. | 259 | 4511 | 1,770 | 1,735 |
| Hardin-Simmons University — Abilene; (3–Southern Baptist); 1891 (as Simmons College; as Simmons University, 1925; current name, 1934); Dr. Lanny Hall. | 157 | 2,084 | 1,123 | NA |
| Hill College — Hillsboro; (7); 1923 (as Hillsboro Junior College; name changed to current, 1962); Dr. Pamela Boehm. | 195 | 4,022 | 1,512 | 161 |
| Houston Baptist University — Houston; (3–Baptist); 1960; Dr. Robert B. Sloan Jr. | 225 | 3,128 | 968 | NA |
| HOUSTON COMMUNITY COLLEGE (9) — Cesar Maldonado, chancellor. Houston; 1971. System consists of following colleges and presidents: | 2,504 | 47,415 | 45,107 | 12,130 |
| Central Campus — Houston; (7); Dr. William W. Harmon. | | | | |
| Coleman College for Health Sciences — Houston; (7); 2004; Dr. Phil Nicotera. | | | | |
| Northeast Campus — Houston; (7); Dr. Margaret Ford Fisher. | | | | |
| Northwest Campus — Houston; (7); Dr. Zachary R. Hodges. | | | | |
| Southeast Campus — Houston; (7); Dr. Irene M. Porcarello. | | | | |
| Southwest Campus — Houston; (7); Dr. Orfelina (Fena) Garza. | | | | |
| Howard College — Big Spring; (7); 1945; Dr. Cheryl T. Sparks; (three campuses: Big Spring, Lamesa and San Angelo, and the Southwest Collegiate Institute for the Deaf, Mark J. Myers, provost. | 309 | 3,920 | ** | ** |
| Howard Payne University — Brownwood; (3–Baptist); 1889; Dr. William N. Ellis. | 120 | 1,140 | 162 | 44 |
| Huston-Tillotson University — Austin; (3–United Church of Christ and United Methodist); 1952 (as Huston-Tillotson College, the merger of Tillotson College, 1875, and Samuel Huston College, 1876; current name, 2005); Dr. Larry L. Earvin. | 71 | 1,031 | 146 | NA |
| International Bible College — San Antonio; (3–Christian); 1944; Closed in 2010. Last president, Rev. David W. Cook. | Closed in 2010. | | | |
| Jacksonville College — Jacksonville; (8–Missionary Baptist); 1899; Dr. William Michael Smith. | 33 | 555 | 144 | NA |
| Jarvis Christian College — Hawkins; (3); 1912; Dr. Lester Newman. | ** | 716 | ** | ** |
| Kilgore College — Kilgore; (7); 1935; Dr. William M. Holda. | 293 | 5,740 | 2,897 | 3,838 |
| Kingwood College — Kingwood (See Lone Star College System) | | | | |
| Lamar University and all branches (See Texas State University System) | | | | |
| Laredo Community College — Laredo; (7); 1946; Dr. Juan L. Maldonado. | 337 | 8,277 | 4,480 | 3,545 |
| Lee College — Baytown; (7); 1934; Dr. Dennis Brown. | 364 | 6,481 | 4,615 | 2,616 |
| LeTourneau University — Longview; (3); 1946 (as LeTourneau Technical Institute; became 4-yr. college, 1961); Dr. Dale A. Lunsford. | 213 | 2,555 | NA | NA |
| Lon Morris College — Jacksonville; (8–Methodist); 1854 (as Danville Academy; changed name in 1873 to Alexander Institution; name changed to present, 1923; filed for bankruptcy and was closed in 2012); last president: Dr. Miles McCall. | Closed in 2012. | | | |
| LONE STAR COLLEGE SYSTEM (9) — Dr. Richard Carpenter, chancellor. 1973; formerly North Harris Montgomery Community College District. System consists of following colleges and presidents: | 3,323 | 73,559 | 39,270 | 5,104 |
| Lone Star College–Cy-Fair — Houston; (7); 2003; Dr. Audre Levy. | 875 | 18,488 | 9,516 | 747 |
| Lone Star College–Kingwood — Humble; (7); 1984; Dr. Katherine Persson. | 537 | 11,820 | 6,232 | 1,201 |
| Lone Star College–Montgomery — Conroe; (7); 1995; Dr. Rebecca L. Riley. | 582 | 11,904 | 6,919 | 1,268 |
| Lone Star College–North Harris — Houston; (7); 1973; Dr. Penny Westerfeld. | 790 | 15,644 | 8,651 | 901 |
| Lone Star College–Tomball — Tomball; (7); 1986; Dr. Lee Ann Nutt. | 345 | 7,612 | 4,674 | 667 |
| Lone Star College–University Park — Houston; (7); 2012; Shah Ardalan. | 194 | 8,091 | 3,278 | 320 |
| Lubbock Christian University — Lubbock; (3–Church of Christ); 1957; Dr. L. Tim Perrin. | 172 | 1,909 | 588 | NA |
| McLennan Community College — Waco; (7); 1965; Dr. Johnette McKown. | 386 | 8,291 | 6,743 | 900 |
| McMurry University — Abilene; (3–Methodist); 1923; Dr. Sandra Harper. | 104 | 1,007 | 612 | NA |
| Midland College — Midland; (7); 1972; Dr. Steve Thomas. | 284 | 4,617 | 6,136 | 15,000 |
| Midwestern State University — Wichita Falls; (2); 1922; Dr. Jesse W. Rogers. | 342 | 5,589 | 3,837 | 261 |
| Montgomery College — Conroe (See Lone Star College System) | | | | |
| Mountain View College — Dallas (See Dallas County Community College District) | | | | |
| Navarro College — Corsicana; (7); 1946; four campuses: Corsicana, Mexia, Midlothian and Waxahachie; Dr. Barbara Kavalier. | 738 | 9,825 | 4,720 | 658 |
| North Central Texas College — Gainesville; (7); 1924 (as Gainesville Jr. College; Cooke County College, 1960; present name, 1994); five campuses: Bowie, Corinth, Flower Mound, Gainesville, and Graham. Dr. Brent Wallace. | 437 | 10,112 | 4,106 | 2,491 |

| Name of Institution — Location; (*type or ownership, if private sectarian institution); date of founding; president (unless otherwise noted) | Number of Faculty † 2012 | Fall Term 2014 | Summer Sessions 2012 § | Extesion or Contining Education 2012 |
|---|---|---|---|---|
| **Northeast Lakeview College** — San Antonio (*See **Alamo Colleges**) | | | | |
| **Northeast Texas Community College** — Mount Pleasant; (7); 1984; Dr. Bradley W. Johnson. | 182 | 3,193 | 1,100 | 685 |
| **North Harris College** — Houston (*See **Lone Star College System**) | | | | |
| **North Lake College** — Irving (*See **Dallas County Community College District**) | | | | |
| **Northwest Vista College** — San Antonio (*See **Alamo Colleges**) | | | | |
| **Northwood University** — Cedar Hill; (3); 1966; Dr. Kevin Fegan, pres. Texas Campus. | 26 | 839 | 100 | NA |
| **Oblate School of Theology** — San Antonio; (3–Roman Catholic); 1903 (formerly Scholasticate); the Rev. Ronald Rolheiser. | 24 | 166 | 78 | ** |
| **Odessa College** — Odessa; (7); 1946; Dr. Gregory Williams. | 191 | 5,019 | 2,858 | 1,934 |
| **Our Lady of the Lake University of San Antonio** — San Antonio; (3–Roman Catholic); 1895 (as school for girls; as senior college, 1911; as university, 1975); *two campuses:* San Antonio and Houston; Dr. Jane Ann Slater. | 256 | 3,173 | | |
| **Palo Alto College** — San Antonio (*See **Alamo Colleges**) | | | | |
| **Panola College** — Carthage; (7); 1947 (as Panola Junior College; name changed, 1988); Dr. Gregory S. Powell. | 148 | 2,563 | 879 | 313 |
| **Paris Junior College** — Paris; (7); 1924; Dr. Pamela Anglin. | 95 | 5,086 | 2,582 | 773 |
| **Parker University** — Dallas; (5); 1982 as Parker College of Chiropractic; name changed to present in 2011. Dr. Brian McAulay. | 92 | 1,030 | 981 | 424 |
| **Paul Quinn College** — Dallas; (3–African Methodist Episcopal Church); 1872 (in Waco; moved to Dallas, 1990); Dr. Michael J. Sorrell. | 55 | 273 | | NA |
| **Prairie View A&M University** — Prairie View (*See **Texas A&M University System**) | | | | |
| **Ranger College** — Ranger; (7); 1926; Dr. William Campion. | 23 | 2,011 | 398 | NA |
| **Rice University** — Houston; (3); chartered, 1891; opened, 1912 (as Rice Institute; as William Marsh Rice University, 1960); Dr. David W. Leebron. | 741 | 6,621 | NA | 5,432 |
| **Richland College** — Dallas (*See **Dallas County Community College District**) | | | | |
| **St. Edward's University** — Austin; (3–Catholic); 1885; Dr. George E. Martin. | 522 | 4,686 | | 1,886 |
| **St. Mary's University of San Antonio** — San Antonio; (3–Roman Catholic); 1852; Dr. Tom Mengler. | 351 | 3,694 | 1,153 | ** |
| **St. Philip's College** — San Antonio (*See **Alamo Colleges**) | | | | |
| **Sam Houston State University** — Huntsville (*See **Texas State University System**) | | | | |
| **San Antonio College** — San Antonio (*See **Alamo Colleges**) | | | | |
| **SAN JACINTO COLLEGE DISTRICT (9) — Dr. Brenda Lang Hellyer, chancellor.** System consists of following colleges and provosts | 1,296 | 31,967 | 15,953 | 1,499 |
| **Central** — Pasadena; (7); Dr. Van Wigginton. | 581 | 13,592 | 7,366 | 971 |
| **North** — Houston; (7); Dr. William Raffetto. | 316 | 7,496 | 3,010 | 173 |
| **South** — Houston; (7); Dr. Brenda Jones. | 399 | 10,879 | 5,577 | 355 |
| | | | | |
| **Schreiner University** — Kerrville; (3–Presbyterian); 1923; Dr. Tim Summerlin. | 100 | 1,126 | 297 | NA |
| **South Plains College** — Levelland; (7); 1957; Dr. Kevin Sharp. | 289 | 9,661 | 2,500 | ** |
| **South Texas College** — McAllen; (7); NA; Dr. Shirley A. Reed. | 760 | 30,849 | 10,775 | 1,678 |
| **South Texas College of Law** — Houston; (3); 1923; Dr. Donald J. Guter. | 94 | 1,091 | 538 | NA |
| **Southern Methodist University** — Dallas; (3–Methodist); 1911; Dr. R. Gerald Turner. | 1,155 | 11,272 | 4,257 | 1,160 |
| **Southwest Collegiate Institute for the Deaf** — Big Spring (*See **Howard College**) | 20 | 120 | NA | NA |
| **Southwest Texas Junior College** — Uvalde; (7); 1946; Dr. Hector Gonzales. | ** | 5,572 | ** | ** |
| **Southwest Texas State University** — San Marcos (*See **Texas State University System**) | | | | |
| **Southwestern Adventist University** — Keene; (3–Seventh-Day Adventist); 1893 (as Keene Industrial Academy; as Southwestern Junior College, 1916; as Southwestern Union College, 1963; as Southwestern Adventist College,1980; as university, 1996); Dr. Ken Shaw. | 75 | 822 | 260 | 289 |
| **Southwestern Assemblies of God University** — Waxahachie; (3–Assemblies of God); 1927 (in Enid, Okla., as Southwestern Bible School; moved to Fort Worth and merged with South Central Bible Institute, 1941; moved to Waxahachie as Southwestern Bible Institute, 1943; as Southwestern Assemblies of God College,1963; as university, 1996); Dr. Kermit S. Bridges. | 96 | 1,984 | ** | NA |
| **Southwestern Baptist Theological Seminary** — Fort Worth; (3–Southern Baptist); 1908; Dr. L. Paige Patterson. | 91 | 3,579 | 1,179 | 26 |
| **Southwestern Christian College** — Terrell; (3–Church of Christ); 1948 (as Southern Bible Institute in Fort Worth; moved to Terrell and changed name, 1950); Dr. Jack Evans Sr. | 20 | 164 | NA | NA |
| **Southwestern University** — Georgetown; (3–United Methodist); 1840 (merger of Rutersville College, 1840; McKenzie College, 1841; Wesleyan College, 1846; and Soule University, 1855; first named Texas University; current name, 1875); Dr. Edward B. Burger. | 165 | 1,533 | NA | NA |
| **Stephen F. Austin State University** — Nacogdoches; (2); 1921; Dr. Baker Pattillo. | 728 | 12,644 | 5,684 | NA |
| **Sul Ross State University** — Alpine (*See **Texas State University System**) | | | | |
| **Sul Ross State University–Rio Grande College** — Uvalde (*See **Texas State University System**) | | | | |
| **Tarleton State University** — Stephenville (*See **Texas A&M University System**) | | | | |
| **TARRANT COUNTY COLLEGE DISTRICT (9) — Erma Johnson Hadley, chancellor.** Fort Worth; 1965 (as Tarrant County Junior College; name changed, 1999). System consists of following colleges and presidents: | 1,925 | 57,424 | 33,715 | 10,356 |
| **Northeast Campus** — Hurst; (7); Dr. Allen Goben. | 510 | 12,103 | 8,292 | 2,825 |
| **Northwest Campus** — Fort Worth; (7); Dr. Elva Concha LeBlanc. | 381 | 8,687 | 6,784 | 3,769 |
| **South Campus** — Fort Worth; (7); Dr. Peter Jordan. | 352 | 8,540 | 6,788 | 1,421 |
| **Southeast Campus** — Arlington; (7); Dr. William Coppola. | 397 | 11,151 | 8,261 | 1,306 |
| **Trinity River Campus** — Fort Worth, (7); Dr. Tahita Fulkerson. | 285 | 16,943 | 4,089 | 1,035 |

| Name of Institution — Location; (*type or ownership, if private sectarian institution); date of founding; president (unless otherwise noted) | Number of Faculty † 2012 | Enrollment | | |
|---|---|---|---|---|
| | | Fall Term 2014 | Summer Sessions 2012 § | Extesion or Contining Education 2012 |
| **Temple College** — Temple; (7); 1926; Dr. Glenda O. Barron. | 261 | 5,197 | 2,065 | 1,163 |
| **Texarkana College** — Texarkana; (7); 1927; Dr. James Russell. | 215 | 4,009 | 1,812 | 4,000 |
| **Texas A&I University** — Kingsville (See **Texas A&M University–Kingsville** under **Texas A&M University System**) | | | | |
| **TEXAS A&M UNIVERSITY SYSTEM (1) — Dr. John Sharp, chancellor.** System consists of following colleges and presidents: | 7,016 | 137,948 | 49,508 | NA |
| **Texas A&M University** — College Station; (2); 1876 (as Agricultural and Mechanical of Texas; current name,1963); includes College of Veterinary Medicine and College of Medicine at College Station; Dr. Michael K. Young. | 2,507 | 56,507 | 17,270 | NA |
| **Texas A&M University at Galveston** — Galveston; (2); 1962 (as Texas Maritime Academy; as 4-yr. Moody College of Marine Sciences and Maritime Resources, 1971); Rear Admiral Robert Smith III, USN (Ret.). | 160 | 2,305 | 751 | NA |
| **Prairie View A&M University** — Prairie View; (2); 1876 (as Alta Vista Agricultural College; as Prairie View State Normal Institute, 1879; as Prairie View Normal and Industrial College; as Prairie View A&M College, 1947, as branch of Texas A&M University System; current name, 1973); Dr. George C. Wright. | 440 | 8,343 | 2,841 | NA |
| **Tarleton State University** — Stephenville; (2); 1899 (as John Tarleton College; as state-run John Tarleton Agricultural College,1917; as Tarleton State College, 1949; current name, 1973); includes campus in Killeen; Dr. F. Dominic Dottavio. | 560 | 11,681 | 4,522 | NA |
| **Texas A&M International University** — Laredo; (2); 1970 (as Laredo State University; current name, 1993); Dr. Ray M. Keck III. | 303 | 7,554 | 2,878 | NA |
| **Texas A&M University–Corpus Christi** — Corpus Christi; (2); 1973 (as upper-level Corpus Christi State University; current name, 1993; 4-year in 1994); Dr. Flavius C. Killebrew. | 568 | 11,234 | 5,080 | NA |
| **Texas A&M University–Kingsville** — Kingsville; (2); 1925 (as South Texas Teachers College; as Texas College of Arts and Industries, 1929; as Texas A&I University, 1967; joined University of South Texas System, 1977; joined Texas A&M University System, 1993); Dr. Steven H. Tallant. | 410 | 8,728 | 2,615 | NA |
| **West Texas A&M University** — Canyon; (2); 1910 (as West Texas State Normal College; as West Texas State Teachers College, 1923; as West Texas State College, 1949; as West Texas State Univ., 1963; currentt name, 1993); Dr. J. Patrick O'Brien. | 386 | 8,970 | 3,107 | NA |
| **Texas A&M University–Commerce** — Commerce; (2); 1889 (as East Texas Normal College; as East Texas State Teachers College, 1923; as East Texas State College, 1957; university status conferred and named changed to East Texas State University, 1965; transferred to Texas A&M System, 1995); includes ETSU Metroplex Commuter Facility, Mesquite; Dr. Dan R. Jones. | 649 | 11,490 | 5,379 | NA |
| **Texas A&M University–Texarkana** — Texarkana; (2); 1971 (as East Texas State University at Texarkana; transferred to Texas A&M System and name changed, 1996); Dr. Emily Fourmy Cutrer. | 140 | 1,812 | 833 | NA |
| **Texas A&M University–Central Texas** — Killeen; (2); Dr. Marc A. Nigliazzo. | 147 | 2,316 | 1,519 | NA |
| **Texas A&M University–San Antonio** — San Antonio; (2); Dr. Cynthia Teniente-Matson. | 206 | 4,521 | 1,610 | NA |
| **Texas A&M University Health Science Center** — (4); Includes Baylor College of Dentistry, College of Medicine, Graduate School of Biomedical Sciences, Institute of Biosciences and Technology, School of Rural Public Health, and HSC Statellite locations; Dr. Brett P. Giroir, Exec. Vice President and CEO. | 540 | 2,487 | 1,103 | NA |
| **Texas Baptist Institute-Seminary** — Henderson; (3–Calvary Baptist); 1948; Dr. Ray O. Brooks. | 16 | 50 | NA | 20 |
| **Texas Christian University** — Fort Worth; (3–Disciples of Christ); 1873 (as AddRan Male and Female College at Thorp Spring; moved to Waco, 1895; as AddRan Christian University, 1889; current name,1902; moved to Fort Worth, 1910); Dr. Victor J. Boschini Jr., chancellor. | 1,984 | 10,012 | **2,604 | **2,050 |
| **Texas Chiropractic College** — Pasadena; (5); 1908; Dr. Brad McKechnie. | 36 | 260 | 243 | NA |
| **Texas College** — Tyler; (3–C.M.E.); 1894; Dr. Dwight Fennell. | 42 | 826 | 109 | NA |
| **Texas College of Osteopathic Medicine** — Fort Worth (See **University of North Texas Health Science Center at Fort Worth**) | | | | |
| **Texas Lutheran University** — Seguin; (3–Evangelical Lutheran); 1891 (as Evangelical Lutheran College in Brenham; as Lutheran College of Seguin, 1912; as Texas Lutheran College,1932; as university, 1996); Dr. Stuart Dorsey. | 128 | 1,319 | 221 | NA |
| **Texas Southern University** — Houston; (2); 1926 (as Houston Colored Junior College; as 4-yr. Houston College for Negroes, mid-1930s; as Texas State University for Negroes, 1947; present name, 1951); Dr. John M. Rudley. | 578 | 9,233 | 2,818 | 50 |
| **Texas Southmost College** — Brownsville; (7); 1926 (as The Junior College of the Lower Rio Grande Valley; 1931 as Brownsville Junior College; current name, 1949); Dr. Lily F. Tercero. | | 3,895 | | |
| **TEXAS STATE TECHNICAL COLLEGE SYSTEM (6) — Dr. Michael L. Reeser, chancellor.** System consists of following colleges and presidents: | 580 | 11,642 | 6,826 | 743 |
| **Texas State Technical College–Harlingen** — Harlingen; 1967; Dr. Stella Garcia, interim. | 182 | 5,225 | 2,797 | 617 |
| **Texas State Technical College–Marshall** — Marshall; 1991 (as extension center; as independent college, 1999); Dr. Barton Day, interim president. | 48 | 858 | 492 | 60 |
| **Texas State Technical College–Waco** — Waco; 1965 (as James Connally Technical Institute; current name, 1969); Dr. Rob Wolaver, interim president. | 261 | 4,112 | 2,951 | NA |
| **Texas State Technical College–West Texas** — Abilene, Breckenridge, Brownwood and Sweetwater; 1970; Dr. Kyle Smith, interim president. | 89 | 1,447 | 586 | 66 |
| **TEXAS STATE UNIVERSITY SYSTEM (1) — Dr. Brian McCall, chancellor.** System consists of following colleges and presidents: | | | | |
| **Lamar University** — Beaumont; (2); 1923 (as South Park Junior College; as Lamar College, 1932; as Lamar State College of Technology, 1951; present name, 1971; transferred from Lamar University System, 1995); Dr. Kenneth Evans. | 561 | 14,452 | 6,836 | 4,263 |

| Name of Institution — Location; (*type or ownership, if private sectarian institution); date of founding; president (unless otherwise noted) | Number of Faculty† 2012 | Enrollment Fall Term 2014 | Summer Sessions 2012 § | Extesion or Contining Education 2012 |
|---|---|---|---|---|
| **Lamar State College–Orange** — Orange; (10); 1969 (transferred from Lamar University System, 1995; current name, 2000); Dr. J. Michael Shahan. | 97 | 2,259 | 694 | 97 |
| **Lamar State College–Port Arthur** — Port Arthur; (10); 1909 (as Port Arthur College; joined Lamar University System, 1975; joined TSU System, 1995; current name, 2000); Dr. Betty J. Reynard. | 115 | 2,078 | 1,772 | 485 |
| **Lamar Institute of Technology** — Beaumont; (10); (joined TSU System, 1995); Dr. Paul Szuch. | 162 | 2,708 | 889 | 650 |
| **Sam Houston State University** — Huntsville; (2); 1879; Dr. Dana G. Hoyt. | 669 | 19,573 | 10,722 | NA |
| **Sul Ross State University** — Alpine; (2); 1917 (as Sul Ross State Normal College; as Sul Ross State Teachers College, 1923; as Sul Ross State College, 1949; current name, 1969); Dr. William (Bill) Kibler. | 148 | 1,897 | 1,024 | NA |
| **Sul Ross State University – Rio Grande College** — Uvalde, Eagle Pass, Del Rio (2); 1973 (current name, 1995); Dr. William (Bill) Kibler. | 30 | 1,009 | 1,020 | NA |
| **Texas State University** — San Marcos; (2); 1903 (as Southwest Texas Normal School; as Southwest Texas State Normal College, 1918; as Southwest Texas State Teachers College, 1923; as Southwest Texas State College, 1959; as Southwest Texas State University, 1969; current name, 2003); Dr. Denise M. Trauth. | 1,300 | 36,739 | 17,011 | 1,759 |
| **TEXAS TECH UNIVERSITY SYSTEM (1) —Robert L. Duncan, chancellor.** System consists of following colleges and presidents: | | | | |
| **Angelo State University** — San Angelo; (2); 1928 (was part of Texas State University System; joined Texas Tech system, 2007); Dr. Brian J. May. | 356 | 6,389 | 3,719 | NA |
| **Texas Tech University** — Lubbock; (2); 1923 (as Texas Technological College; current name, 1969); Dr. Duane Nellis. | 2,488 | 34,843 | 16,990 | ** |
| **Texas Tech University Health Sciences Center** — Lubbock; (4); 1972; Dr.Tedd Mitchell. | 596 | 2,487 | ** | NA |
| **Texas Tech University Health Sciences Center** — El Paso; (4); 2013; Dr. Richard Lange. | | 468 | | |
| **Texas Wesleyan University** — Fort Worth; (3–United Methodist); 1891 (as college; current name, 1989); Dr. Frederick G. Slabach. | 274 | 2,606 | 1,207 | NA |
| **Texas Woman's University** — Denton; (2); 1901 (as College of Industrial Arts; as Texas State College for Women, 1934; current name, 1957); Dr. Carine M. Feyten, chancellor and president. | 1,074 | 14,889 | 7,571 | NA |
| **Tomball College** — Tomball (*See* **Lone Star College System**) | | | | |
| **Trinity University** — San Antonio; (3–Presbyterian U.S.A.); 1869 (at Tehuacana; moved to Waxahachie, 1902; to San Antonio, 1942); Dr. Danny J. Anderson. | 326 | 2,432 | 160 | NA |
| **Trinity Valley Community College** — Athens; (7); 1946 (as Henderson County Junior College); includes campus at Terrell; Dr. Glendon S. Forgey. | 124 | 6,755 | 2,500 | 1,400 |
| **Tyler Junior College** — Tyler; (7); 1926; Dr. Mike Metke. | 492 | 9,630 | 3,951 | 1,782 |
| **University of Central Texas** — Killeen (*See* **Tarleton State University** under **Texas A&M University System**) | | | | |
| **University of Dallas** — Irving; (3–Roman Catholic); 1956; Dr. Thomas Keefe. | 249 | 2,548 | 1,153 | 735 |
| **UNIVERSITY OF HOUSTON SYSTEM (1) — Dr. Renu Khator, chancellor.** System consists of following colleges and presidents: | 3,615 | 68,422 | 27,261 | |
| **University of Houston** — Houston; (2); 1927; Dr. Renu Khator. | 2,221 | 40,914 | 15,101 | NA |
| **University of Houston–Clear Lake** — Houston; (2); 1974; Dr. William A. Staples. | 511 | 8,665 | 4,346 | NA |
| **University of Houston–Downtown** — Houston; (2); 1948 (as South Texas College; joined University of Houston System, 1974); Dr. William V. Flores. | 673 | 14,436 | 5,475 | NA |
| **University of Houston–Victoria** — Victoria; (2); 1973; Dr. Vic Morgan. | 210 | 4,407 | 2,339 | NA |
| **University of the Incarnate Word** — San Antonio; (3–Roman Catholic); 1881 (as Incarnate Word College; current name, 1996); Dr. Louis J. Agnese Jr. | 581 | 8,701 | 3,275 | NA |
| **University of Mary Hardin–Baylor** — Belton; (3–Baptist); 1845; Dr. Randy O'Rear. | 286 | 3,740 | 1,068 | NA |
| **UNIVERSITY OF NORTH TEXAS SYSTEM (1) — Lee F. Jackson, chancellor.** System consists of following colleges and presidents: | | 40,966 | | |
| **University of North Texas** — Denton; (2); 1890 (as North Texas Normal College; as North Texas State Teachers College, 1923; as North Texas State College, 1949; as university, 1961; current name, 1988); Dr. Neal J. Smatresk. | 1,998 | 36,164 | 15,025 | 18,075 |
| **University of North Texas Dallas Campus** — Dallas; (2); (2000); Robert Mong. | | 2,575 | | |
| **University of North Texas Health Science Center at Fort Worth** — Fort Worth; (4);1966 (as private college; part of North Texas State University, 1975; current name, 1993); Dr. Michael R. Williams. | | 2,227 | 1,021 | 777 |
| **University of St. Thomas** — Houston; (3–Roman Catholic); 1947; Dr. Robert Ivany. | 336 | 3,420 | 2,055 | NA |
| **THE UNIVERSITY OF TEXAS SYSTEM (1) — Admiral William H. McRaven (Ret.) chancellor.** System consists of following colleges and presidents: | 18,371 | 217,112 | ** | ** |
| **University of Texas at Austin, The** — Austin; (2); 1883; Dr. Gregory L. Fenves. | 3,280 | 51,312 | ** | ** |
| **University of Texas at Arlington, The** — Arlington; (2); 1895 (as Arlington College; as state-run Grubbs Vocational College, 1917; as North Texas Agricultural and Mechanical College, 1923; as Arlington State College, 1949; current name, 1967); Dr. Vistasp M. Karbhari. | 1,491 | 34,868 | 11,164 | 7,468 |
| **University of Texas at Brownsville, The** — (2); 1973 (as branch of Pan American College; as University of Texas–Pan American at Brownsville, 1989; present name, 1991); Dr. William R. Fannin. | ** | 8,009 | 7,653 | 1,651 |

| Name of Institution — Location; (*type or ownership, if private sectarian institution); date of founding; president (unless otherwise noted) | Number of Faculty † 2012 | Enrollment | | |
|---|---|---|---|---|
| | | Fall Term 2014 | Summer Sessions 2012 § | Extesion or Contining Education 2012 |
| University of Texas at Dallas, The — Richardson; (2); 1961 (as Graduate Research of the Southwest; as Southwest Center for Advanced Studies, 1967; joined UT System with current name, 1969; full undergraduate program, 1975); Dr. Bryan Hobson Wildenthal, interim. | 890 | 23,095 | ** | NA |
| University of Texas at El Paso, The — El Paso; (2); 1913 (as Texas College of Mines and Metallurgy; as Texas Western College of UT, 1949; current name, 1967); Dr. Diana S. Natalicio. | 1,174 | 23,043 | 8,716 | 2,921 |
| University of Texas–Pan American, The — Edinburg; (2); 1927 (as Edinburg Junior College; as 4-yr. Pan American College, 1952; as Pan American University, 1971; current name, 1991); Dr. Havidan Rodriguez. | 783 | 21,015 | 15,165 | 50 |
| University of Texas of the Permian Basin, The — Odessa; (2); 1969 (as 2-yr., upper-level institution; expanded to 4-yr., 1991); Dr. W. David Watts. | 207 | 5,560 | 2,156 | 140 |
| University of Texas at San Antonio, The — San Antonio; (2); 1969; Dr. Ricardo Romo. | 1,422 | 28,628 | ** | ** |
| University of Texas at Tyler, The — Tyler; (2); 1971 (as Tyler State College; as Texas Eastern University, 1975; joined UT System, 1979); Dr. Rodney H. Mabry. | 434 | 8,036 | 2,169 | NA |
| University of Texas Health Science Center at Houston, The — Houston; (4); 1972; includes Dental Branch (1905); Graduate School of Biomedical Sciences (1963); Medical School (1970); School of Allied Health Sciences (1973); School of Nursing (1972); School of Public Health (1967); Division of Continuing Education (1958); Dr. Giuseppe N. Colasurdo. | 1,538 | 4,556 | 2,306 | 24,875 |
| University of Texas Health Science Center at San Antonio, The — San Antonio; (4) 1968; includes Dental School (1970); Graduate School of Biomedical Sciences (1970); Health Science Center (1972); Medical School (1959 as South Texas Medical School of UT; present name, 1966); School of Allied Health Sciences (1976); School of Nursing (1969); Dr. William L. Henrich. | 1,696 | 3,147 | NA | NA |
| University of Texas Health Science Center at Tyler, The — Tyler; (4); 1949 (as East Texas Tuberculosis Sanatorium; as East Texas Chest Hospital, 1971; joined UT system with current name, 1977); Dr. Kirk A. Calhoun. | 88 | 19 | NA | NA |
| University of Texas M.D. Anderson Cancer Center, The — Houston; (4); 1941; Dr. Ronald DePinho. | 2,007 | 303 | NA | 2,252 |
| University of Texas Medical Branch at Galveston, The — Galveston; (4) 1891; includes Graduate School of Biomedical Sciences (1952); Medical School (1891); School of Allied Health Sciences (1968); School of Nursing (1890); Dr. David L. Callender. | 1,215 | 3,211 | NA | NA |
| University of Texas Southwestern Medical Center at Dallas, The — Dallas; (4); 1943 (as private institution; as Southwestern Medical College of UT, 1948; as UT South-western Medical School at Dallas, 1967; joined UT Health Science Center at Dallas, 1972; includes Graduate School of Biomedical Sciences (1947); School of Allied Health Sciences (1968); Southwestern Medical School (1943); Dr. Daniel K. Podolsky. | 2,146 | 2,310 | NA | NA |
| Vernon College — Vernon; (7); 1970; includes Wichita Falls campus; Dr. Dusty R. Johnston. | 139 | 2,989 | 2,180 | 930 |
| Victoria College, The — Victoria; (7); 1925; Dr. Thomas Butler. | 241 | 4,125 | 1,596 | 832 |
| Wayland Baptist University — Plainview; (3–Southern Baptist); 1910; Dr. Paul Armes. | 329 | 3,851 | 4,516 | NA |
| Weatherford College — Weatherford; (7); 1869 (as branch of Southwestern University; as denominational junior college, 1922; as municipal junior college, 1949); Dr. Kevin Eaton. | 225 | 5,610 | 2,319 | 1,012 |
| Western Texas College — Snyder; (7); 1969; Dr. Barbara Beebe. | 72 | 2,069 | 1,099 | 876 |
| Wharton County Junior College — Wharton; (7); 1946; Dr. Betty A. McCrohan. | 293 | 7,152 | 4,006 | 300 |
| Wiley College — Marshall; (3–Methodist); 1873; Dr. Haywood L. Strickland. | 85 | 1,355 | 182 | 20 |

# Key to Table Symbols

*Type: (1) Public University System
(2) Public University
(3) Independent Senior College or University
(4) Public Medical School or Health Science Center
(5) Independent Medical, Dental or Chiropractic School

(6) Public Technical College System
(7) Public Community College
(8) Independent Junior College
(9) Public Community College System
(10) Public Lower-Level Institution

NA — Not applicable
† Unless otherwise noted, faculty count includes pro-fessors, associate professors, adjunct professors, instructors and tutors, both full- and part-time, but does not include voluntary instructors. These are 2012 figures.
Name of president and number of students enrolled in fall 2014 obtained from the institution's website or the Texas Higher Education Coordinating Board website: www.txhighereddata.org/Interactive/Insti-tutions.cfm.

# Includes faculty and enrollment at all branches..
§ Figure may combine multiple summer sessions.
¶ Full-time faculty only.
** Information not supplied by institution.
†† Approximate count.
§§ Latest figures available from institution's website were for 2013–2014 school year.
§§§ Enrollment in online courses only.
~ Number of students in extension courses or con-tinuing education for all of fiscal year 2012.

# Business

*Computer giant Dell, Inc., was founded in 1984. The headquarters is in Round Rock in Williamson County. Dell photo.*

## Economy and Employment
## Banking, Insurance, Construction
## Commercial Fishing and Tourism
## Electric Grids, Oil, Gas
## Minerals and Media

# Texas Economy: Steady Expansion

Source: Excerpted from the State of Texas Annual Cash Report 2013, Comptroller of Public Accounts.

In 2013 the Texas economy continued its steady post-recession expansion, adding 274,700 nonfarm jobs, for an increase of 2.5 percent. Private sector employment grew by 2.9 percent, while government employment (federal, state, and local) grew by 0.8 percent.

Pre-recession Texas employment peaked at 10,635,700 in August 2008, a level that was surpassed in September 2011, and since that point Texas has added an additional 548,000 jobs.

In addition to adding more new jobs than any state last year, Texas had the lowest unemployment rate among the 10 most populous states at the end of 2013.

The comparatively vibrant economic conditions, especially during a slow national recovery, have resulted in an influx of new residents into Texas, with 216,000 net migrants (inbound less outbound migrants) arriving during the year, and has motivated previously discouraged job seekers to rejoin the labor force to search for work.

## Consumer Spending

Consumer spending is a major component of a healthy Texas economy. As measured by state sales tax collections in the retail trade sector, consumer spending dropped in the recession years of fiscal 2009 and 2010, then recovered in 2011 and 2012, growing by 5.5 and 6.6 percent, respectively.

Fiscal 2013 state sales tax collections in retail trade were up by 4.3 percent.

The Consumer Confidence Index serves as a monthly measure of the level of consumer optimism, an important factor affecting the sales of housing, automobiles, and other major purchases. The index levels fluctuated during fiscal 2013, but ended the year considerably higher for both the nation (up 33 percent) and the four-state West South Central (WSC) Region that includes Texas (up 18 percent).

During the year the WSC index surpassed the 1985 baseline level of 100 for the first time since February 2008, although the final WSC index level for 2013 was only 88.5. The national index ended the year at 81.5.

## Exports

According to the U.S. Census Bureau, Texas is the nation's leading export state, a position held since 2002.

Those exports provided a major boost to Texas manufacturing, notably for companies producing chemicals, computers and electronics, petroleum products, industrial machinery and transportation equipment.

The value of Texas exports in fiscal 2013 reached an estimated $272 billion, a record amount and 4 percent more than fiscal 2012.

The gross state product attributable to Texas manufacturing activity was estimated at $218 billion in fiscal 2013, up by 5.6 percent from $207 billion in 2012.

## Oil and gas

The mining and logging industry has been an important factor in Texas' post-recession economic performance, and will remain important for the foreseeable future.

In addition to Texas being the home for many of the nation's oil and natural gas companies, the industry was again the fastest growing major Texas industry in fiscal 2013.

This was due to firm market prices for oil and natural gas and the broad implementation of improved exploration technologies.

Following the recession-induced 17 percent employment loss for the Texas industry in 2009, the num-

## Gross Domestic Product in Current Dollars

| | Millions of $ dollars | | | Percent of U.S. total | | | GDP* 2013 | |
|---|---|---|---|---|---|---|---|---|
| | 2007 | 2011 | 2012 | 2007 | 2011 | 2012 | United States | 16,720,000 |
| **United States** | **13,743,021** | **14,981,020** | **15,566,077** | **100.0** | **100.0** | **100.0** | European Union | 15,830,000 |
| 1. California | 1,883,679 | 1,958,904 | 2,003,479 | 13.5 | 13.1 | 12.9 | China | 13,370,000 |
| **2. Texas** | **1,140,030** | **1,308,132** | **1,397,369** | **8.2** | **8.7** | **9.0** | India | 4,962,000 |
| 3. New York | 1,088,169 | 1,157,969 | 1,205,930 | 7.8 | 7.7 | 7.7 | Japan | 4,729,000 |
| 4. Florida | 758,776 | 754,255 | 777,164 | 5.4 | 5.0 | 5.0 | Germany | 3,227,000 |
| 5. Illinois | 630,277 | 670,727 | 695,238 | 4.5 | 4.5 | 4.5 | Russia | 2,553,000 |
| 6. Pennsylvania | 534,620 | 578,839 | 600,897 | 3.8 | 3.9 | 3.9 | Brazil | 2,422,000 |
| 7. Ohio | 471,119 | 483,962 | 509,393 | 3.4 | 3.2 | 3.3 | United Kingdom | 2,378,000 |
| 8. New Jersey | 474,487 | 486,989 | 508,003 | 3.4 | 3.3 | 3.3 | France | 2,273,000 |
| 9. North Carolina | 396,832 | 439,862 | 455,973 | 2.8 | 2.9 | 2.9 | Mexico | 1,845,000 |
| 10. Virginia | 389,319 | 428,909 | 445,876 | 2.8 | 2.9 | 2.9 | Italy | 1,805,000 |

Source: Bureau of Economic Analysis, U.S. Department of Commerce, 2014.

*Estimated GDP in millions of U.S. dollars from the World Factbook of the CIA.

ber of industry jobs has doubled to reach 288,900 in August 2013, the highest level ever.

The 35-year slide in Texas oil production ended in 2008, and production has since surged. The number of operating drilling rigs in Texas has remained well above 800 for over two years.

As in fiscal 2011 and 2012, mining and logging again had the highest rate of job growth in fiscal 2013, 5.5 percent, adding 15,000 jobs. The state's two fastest growing metropolitan areas in fiscal 2013 were Odessa and Midland, both with economies dominated by the energy industry.

Odessa's employment increased by 5.2 percent and Midland's by 4.6 percent, considerably above the statewide average of 2.5 percent.

## Construction

The Texas construction employment began to recover in fiscal 2012, increasing by 20,300. In 2013, construction gained another 24,200 jobs (up 4.1 percent) to reach 611,300 in August 2013. Specialty trade contractor employment increased the most of any construction sector, growing by 20,100. Employment in construction of buildings also increased substantially, up 9,500 (7.3 percent).

Concurrent with residential construction employment growth, housing activity also increased substantially. Total single-family building permits issued in the year ending August 2013 were up 18 percent from the year ending August 2012, while multi-family permits were up 6 percent.

The value of Texas nonbuilding construction (e.g., highways, power/heat/cooling facilities, water/sewer systems and bridges) increased by 13 percent in fiscal 2013.

## Services

Texas' service-providing industries, which accounted for more than 84 percent of the state's total nonfarm employment, had job growth of 2.5 percent in fiscal 2013, following annual increases of 2.0 and 2.1 percent in fiscal 2011 and 2012, respectively.

Services employment growth accounted for 85 percent of the nonfarm jobs added during the year.

The professional and business services industry was the service-producing industry with both the largest absolute and percentage gains in employment, increasing by 58,200 jobs or 4.1 percent.

The industry, with 13 percent of the state's nonfarm employment, accounted for 21 percent of the state's employment growth in fiscal 2013.

The education and health services industry, composed of the private education, health care, social assistance, and child day care services sectors, added 39,700 jobs in fiscal 2013, a growth rate of 2.7 percent.

The large health care and social assistance sector grew at a 3.6 percent rate (46,900 jobs).

Within the health care and social assistance sector, home health care services had both the highest growth rate (6.0 percent), and the highest absolute gain (14,800), while child day care services had the largest decline (2,200 jobs, or 2.0 percent).

Overall, education and health services employment

in Texas reached 1,501,300 in August 2013.

## Trade, Transportation and Utilities

The trade, transportation and utilities industry, the state's largest industry employer with 20 percent of total nonfarm jobs in August 2013, added 51,300 jobs (up 2.4 percent) during the year. Both retail trade and wholesale trade employment increased, while transportation, warehousing, and utilities employment decreased slightly.

Overall, the trade, transportation and utilities industry provided 2,230,500 Texas jobs in August 2013.

## Information

The information industry is a collection of diverse sectors, some old-economy (newspaper publishing, data processing, television broadcasting, and wired telephone services) and some that are technologically newer (cellular telephone providers, Internet and DSL providers, and software).

During the second half of the 1990s the international speculative internet stock (or the "dot-com") boom took off, and as a result at its peak in 2000, the Texas information industry had increased its employment by over 50 percent.

In that year the bubble burst. Over the next decade Texas information employment fell by a third. Industry employment growth resumed in 2011, and in fiscal 2013 employment increased by a substantial 3.2 percent (6,300). The renewed growth has been in data processing, host
ing, and related services (up 6.5 percent) and telecommunications (2.5 percent), while newspapers and general publishing (down 1.7 percent) continued to lose jobs. Total information industry employment in August 2013 was 202,500.

## Leisure and Hospitality

For the third year in a row, the leisure and hospitality industry had strong job growth in fiscal 2013, adding 43,000 jobs (up 3.9 percent) and accounting for almost 16 percent of total nonfarm employment gains.

More than three-quarters of the industry's job gains occurred in the food services and drinking places sector which added 32,800 jobs (up 3.7 percent).

Amusement, gambling, and recreation industries (7.0 percent) and accommodation services (6.6 percent) also saw significant employment increases. Total leisure and hospitality employment in August 2013 was 1,132,700, or 10 percent of total employment.

## Government

Following job losses in fiscal 2011 and 2012, government employment in the aggregate expanded by 0.8 percent in fiscal 2013. Jobs in state government increased by 5,900 jobs and local government jobs increased by 15,000, including a 0.3 percent expansion in local government education services.

Federal government employment, however, fell by 6,200 jobs, including a 3,300 job reduction in Department of Defense civilian employment. Total government employment in Texas increased by 14,700 jobs, to reach 1,810,700 in August 2013. ☆

# Texas Gross Domestic Product, 2005–2014, By Industry (in millions)

| Industry | 2005 | 2006 | 2007 | 2008 | 2009 | 2010 | 2011 | 2012 | 2013 | 2014 |
|---|---|---|---|---|---|---|---|---|---|---|
| **Agriculture, Forestry, Fishing/Hunting** | $8,492 | $7,650 | $8,506 | $7,464 | $5,964 | $9,709 | $9,804 | $10,194 | $13,375 | $13,192 |
| % change* | (14.0) | (9.9) | 11.2 | (12.3) | (20.1) | 62.8 | 1.0 | 4.0 | 31.2 | (1.4) |
| **Natural Resources and Mining** | 99,803 | 116,161 | 137,043 | 182,889 | 119,696 | 134,618 | 171,134 | 190,156 | 206,214 | 221,997 |
| % change | 36.0 | 16.4 | 18.0 | 33.5 | (34.6) | 12.5 | 27.1 | 11.1 | 8.4 | 7.7 |
| **Construction** | 53,096 | 59,574 | 64,581 | 64,340 | 61,603 | 60,096 | 61,758 | 67,535 | 72,595 | 76,763 |
| % change | 10.5 | 12.2 | 8.4 | (0.4) | (4.3) | (2.4) | 2.8 | 9.4 | 7.5 | 5.7 |
| **Manufacturing** | 147,275 | 168,625 | 181,273 | 163,627 | 153,204 | 178,942 | 210,312 | 228,050 | 233,194 | 245,699 |
| % change | 4.3 | 14.5 | 7.5 | (9.7) | (6.4) | 16.8 | 17.5 | 8.4 | 2.3 | 5.4 |
| **Trade, Transportation, Utilities** | 186,102 | 203,909 | 213,600 | 220,989 | 213,255 | 226,093 | 240,696 | 267,490 | 278,953 | 294,620 |
| % change | 7.3 | 9.6 | 4.8 | 3.5 | (3.5) | 6.0 | 6.5 | 11.1 | 4.3 | 5.6 |
| **Information** | 41,070 | 41,602 | 43,326 | 43,986 | 41,877 | 41,167 | 42,150 | 44,816 | 46,153 | 48,722 |
| % change | 1.7 | 1.3 | 4.1 | 1.5 | (4.8) | (1.7) | 2.4 | 6.3 | 3.0 | 5.6 |
| **Financial Activities** | 141,719 | 150,992 | 158,527 | 165,722 | 167,303 | 175,302 | 183,743 | 196,497 | 207,101 | 213,896 |
| % change | 6.9 | 6.5 | 5.0 | 4.5 | 1.0 | 4.8 | 4.8 | 6.9 | 5.4 | 3.3 |
| **Professional and Business Services** | 96,392 | 106,761 | 118,225 | 128,510 | 122,764 | 128,971 | 138,121 | 148,440 | 153,192 | 167,452 |
| % change | 9.6 | 10.8 | 10.7 | 8.7 | (4.5) | 5.1 | 7.1 | 7.5 | 5.2 | 7.2 |
| **Educational and Health Services** | 59,293 | 62,493 | 65,731 | 70,915 | 77,579 | 80,979 | 83,898 | 88,329 | 92,557 | 96,743 |
| % change | 3.9 | 7.2 | 5.2 | 7.9 | 9.4 | 4.4 | 3.6 | 5.3 | 4.8 | 4.5 |
| **Leisure and Hospitality Services** | 32,280 | 34,800 | 35,994 | 36,722 | 37,452 | 38,593 | 40,211 | 43,215 | 45,592 | 48,047 |
| % change | 4.5 | 7.8 | 3.4 | 2.0 | 2.0 | 3.0 | 4.2 | 7.5 | 5.5 | 5.4 |
| **Other Private Services** | 22,713 | 24,387 | 25,255 | 25,496 | 26,077 | 26,644 | 27,200 | 28,815 | 29,903 | 30,432 |
| % change | 6.4 | 7.4 | 3.6 | 1.0 | 2.3 | 2.2 | 2.1 | 5.9 | 3.8 | 1.8 |
| **Government and Schools** | 110,857 | 116,839 | 124,900 | 132,671 | 140,460 | 147,402 | 148,296 | 149,464 | 150,775 | 153,233 |
| % change | 5.5 | 5.4 | 6.9 | 6.2 | 5.9 | 4.9 | 0.6 | 0.8 | 0.9 | 1.6 |
| **TOTAL** | $998,093 | $1,093,794 | $1,176,962 | $1,243,331 | $1,167,232 | $1,248,516 | $1,357,322 | $1,463,003 | $1,532,605 | $1,610,796 |
| % change | 8.4 | 9.6 | 7.6 | 5.6 | (6.1) | 7.0 | 8.7 | 7.8 | 4.8 | 5.1 |
| **TOTAL (in 2009 chained** dollars)** | $1,056,502 | $1,118,319 | $1,165,041 | $1,173,481 | $1,167,233 | $1,201,991 | $1,252,008 | $1,338,578 | $1,387,598 | $1,447,826 |
| % change | 2.0 | 5.9 | 4.2 | 0.7 | (0.5) | 3.0 | 4.2 | 6.9 | 3.7 | 4.3 |

*Percent change from the previous year. ** In 1996, the U.S. Department of Commerce introduced the chained-dollar measure. The new measure is based on the average weights of goods and services in successive pairs of years. It is "chained" because the second year in each pair, with its weights, becomes the first year of the next pair. *Source: 2014 Comprehensive Annual Financial Report for the State of Texas.*

# Per Capita Income by County, 2013

Below are listed data for 2013 for total personal income and per capita income by county. Total income is reported in millions of dollars. The middle column indicates the percent of change in total personal income from 2012 to 2013.

In the far right column is the county's rank in the state for per capita income. Midland County is first with $87,897. The lowest per capita income is in Starr County, along the Rio Grande, at $20,811.

*Source: Bureau of Economic Analysis, U.S. Department of Commerce, 2014.*

| County | Total Income ($ mil) | % change 12/13 | Per capita income | Rank in State |
|---|---|---|---|---|
| **United States** | $14,151,427 | 1.3 | $ 44,765 | – |
| Metropolitan | 12,463,711 | 1.1 | 46,177 | – |
| Nonmetro | 1,687,716 | 2.2 | 36,517 | – |
| | | | | |
| **Texas** | $ 1,160,079 | 2.9 | $ 43,862 | – |
| Metropolitan | 1,044,932 | 1.2 | 44,608 | – |
| Nonmetro | 115,147 | 2.3 | 38,083 | – |
| | | | | |
| Anderson | $ 1,742 | 1.5 | $ 30,065 | 239 |
| Andrews | 840 | 6.7 | 49,997 | 44 |
| Angelina | 3,158 | – 1.3 | 36,112 | 175 |
| Aransas | 1,147 | 2.7 | 47,075 | 61 |
| Archer | 465 | 1.5 | 53,578 | 28 |
| Armstrong | 91 | 5.7 | 46,513 | 64 |
| Atascosa | 1,698 | 2.6 | 36,060 | 177 |
| Austin | 1,256 | 1.6 | 43,550 | 87 |
| Bailey | 269 | 2.4 | 37,877 | 145 |
| Bandera | 871 | 2.0 | 42,262 | 95 |
| Bastrop | 2,392 | 3.5 | 31,552 | 228 |
| Baylor | 146 | 3.0 | 40,331 | 121 |
| Bee | 1,021 | 5.4 | 31,135 | 232 |
| Bell | 12,844 | – 0.3 | 39,298 | 131 |
| Bexar | 70,896 | 2.7 | 39,005 | 135 |
| Blanco | 580 | 4.3 | 54,051 | 25 |
| Borden | 39 | – 0.5 | 61,289 | 11 |
| Bosque | 658 | 2.5 | 36,838 | 164 |
| Bowie | 3,367 | – 1.2 | 36,016 | 179 |
| Brazoria | 13,788 | 2.1 | 41,751 | 99 |
| Brazos | 6,550 | 3.0 | 32,241 | 219 |
| Brewster | 377 | 2.3 | 40,558 | 115 |
| Briscoe | 67 | 22.3 | 43,606 | 85 |
| Brooks | $ 239 | 0.4 | $ 33,003 | 210 |
| Brown | 1,274 | 2.6 | 33,760 | 208 |
| Burleson | 693 | 2.0 | 40,348 | 119 |
| Burnet | 2,075 | 2.5 | 47,354 | 59 |
| Caldwell | 1,157 | 3.0 | 29,483 | 243 |
| Calhoun | 782 | 1.9 | 35,858 | 181 |
| Callahan | 499 | 2.4 | 26,892 | 162 |
| Cameron | 10,349 | 2.1 | 24,802 | 250 |
| Camp | 440 | 2.6 | 35,458 | 186 |
| Carson | 286 | 6.3 | 47,640 | 57 |
| Cass | 1,030 | – 0.2 | 33,946 | 206 |
| Castro | 331 | – 11.3 | 41,188 | 107 |
| Chambers | 2,006 | 1.9 | 54,496 | 23 |
| Cherokee | 1,623 | 1.3 | 31,893 | 223 |
| Childress | 203 | 12.3 | 28,561 | 245 |
| Clay | 537 | 0.8 | 51,237 | 39 |
| Cochran | 129 | 10.7 | 42,759 | 93 |

| County | Total Income ($ mil) | % change 12/13 | Per capita income | Rank in State |
|---|---|---|---|---|
| Coke | 119 | 0.8 | 36,991 | 158 |
| Coleman | 310 | 0.2 | 36,322 | 172 |
| Collin | 47,458 | 3.6 | 55,520 | 17 |
| Collingsworth | 138 | 11.3 | 44,534 | 79 |
| Colorado | 914 | 1.8 | 44,021 | 83 |
| Comal | 5,742 | 4.6 | 48,466 | 52 |
| Comanche | 504 | 2.6 | 37,013 | 157 |
| Concho | 116 | 6.1 | 28,814 | 244 |
| Cooke | 2,262 | 1.8 | 58,815 | 13 |
| Coryell | 2,811 | – 1.5 | 36,900 | 161 |
| Cottle | 60 | 0.3 | 41,652 | 103 |
| Crane | 219 | 4.0 | 45,803 | 71 |
| Crockett | 155 | 5.4 | 40,585 | 113 |
| Crosby | 298 | 16.9 | 49,814 | 45 |
| Culberson | $ 85 | 5.9 | $37,359 | 150 |
| Dallam | 349 | 8.2 | 49,518 | 46 |
| Dallas | 120,638 | 2.5 | 48,638 | 49 |
| Dawson | 480 | 10.7 | 34,782 | 194 |
| Deaf Smith | 698 | – 3.8 | 36,401 | 169 |
| Delta | 163 | 2.8 | 31,172 | 230 |
| Denton | 33,237 | 3.4 | 45,605 | 74 |
| DeWitt | 941 | 3.9 | 45,919 | 69 |
| Dickens | 77 | 4.3 | 33,780 | 207 |
| Dimmit | 478 | 7.1 | 43,890 | 84 |
| Donley | 153 | 21.5 | 43,555 | 86 |
| Duval | 470 | 4.0 | 40,347 | 120 |
| Eastland | 1,283 | 4.4 | 70,322 | 6 |
| Ector | 6,598 | 4.2 | 44,168 | 82 |
| Edwards | 67 | – 1.1 | 35,384 | 189 |
| Ellis | 5,867 | 2.4 | 37,616 | 147 |
| El Paso | 25,788 | 1.2 | 31,156 | 231 |
| Erath | 1,301 | 2.3 | 32,800 | 212 |
| Falls | 560 | 2.2 | 32,019 | 222 |
| Fannin | 1,102 | 3.6 | 32,728 | 213 |
| Fayette | 1,125 | 1.7 | 45,338 | 75 |
| Fisher | 185 | 29.1 | 48,096 | 54 |
| Floyd | 278 | 6.8 | 44,677 | 78 |
| Foard | 46 | 0.6 | 35,656 | 184 |
| Fort Bend | 35,043 | 3.9 | 53,717 | 27 |
| Franklin | 391 | 2.8 | 36,679 | 166 |
| Freestone | 717 | 1.6 | 36,516 | 167 |
| Frio | 587 | 4.0 | 32,501 | 216 |
| Gaines | 699 | 4.9 | 36,931 | 160 |
| Galveston | 14,476 | 2.2 | 47,186 | 60 |
| Garza | 390 | 8.8 | 61,667 | 10 |
| Gillespie | 1,383 | 1.6 | 54,527 | 22 |
| Glasscock | 98 | 13.9 | 78,659 | 3 |
| Goliad | 269 | 3.1 | 36,019 | 178 |

| County | Total Income ($ mil) | % change 12/13 | Per capita income | Rank in State | County | Total Income ($ mil) | % change 12/13 | Per capita income | Rank in State |
|---|---|---|---|---|---|---|---|---|---|
| Gonzales | 755 | 4.9 | 37,183 | 154 | Leon | 661 | 2.4 | 39,468 | 129 |
| Gray | 1,055 | 2.4 | 45,773 | 72 | Liberty | 2,830 | 1.9 | 36,799 | 165 |
| Grayson | 4,417 | 3.4 | 36,098 | 176 | Limestone | 810 | 2.0 | 34,746 | 195 |
| Gregg | 5,897 | 2.8 | 47,934 | 55 | Lipscomb | 181 | 1.9 | 51,805 | 36 |
| Grimes | 935 | 1.3 | 34,808 | 193 | Live Oak | 545 | 4.6 | 45,926 | 68 |
| Guadalupe | 5,784 | 2.9 | 40,399 | 116 | Llano | 803 | 2.1 | 41,275 | 106 |
| Hale | 1,059 | 0.6 | 29,606 | 242 | Loving | 4 | 16.1 | 40,358 | 117 |
| Hall | 133 | 26.4 | 41,184 | 108 | Lubbock | 11,084 | 3.4 | 38,311 | 141 |
| Hamilton | 316 | 1.8 | 37,972 | 144 | Lynn | 266 | 26.8 | 46,496 | 65 |
| Hansford | 310 | − 5.5 | 55,742 | 16 | Madison | 424 | 5.4 | 30,731 | 235 |
| Hardeman | 150 | 4.8 | 37,303 | 152 | Marion | 360 | 2.2 | 35,216 | 190 |
| Hardin | 2,252 | 0.0 | 40,638 | 111 | Martin | 259 | 11.7 | 48,843 | 48 |
| Harris | 230,463 | 3.6 | 53,141 | 32 | Mason | 155 | 3.2 | 37,500 | 149 |
| Harrison | 3,170 | 2.2 | 47,391 | 58 | Matagorda | 1,296 | 3.0 | 35,426 | 188 |
| Hartley | 311 | − 5.3 | 50,931 | 40 | Maverick | 1,311 | 2.8 | 23,440 | 251 |
| Haskell | 230 | 11.4 | 39,164 | 134 | McCulloch | 360 | 1.9 | 43,200 | 90 |
| Hays | 6,148 | 5.5 | 34,927 | 192 | McLennan | 8,743 | 1.7 | 36,205 | 174 |
| Hemphill | 323 | 0.5 | 77,681 | 4 | McMullen | 55 | 8.7 | 71,840 | 5 |
| Henderson | 2,787 | 1.6 | 35,429 | 187 | Medina | 1,719 | 2.4 | 36,259 | 173 |
| Hidalgo | 18,828 | 2.6 | 23,073 | 252 | Menard | 66 | − 0.8 | 30,524 | 237 |
| Hill | 1,239 | 2.2 | 35,572 | 185 | Midland | 13,314 | 5.1 | 87,897 | 1 |
| Hockley | 1,184 | 7.5 | 50,312 | 42 | Milam | 912 | 1.8 | 37,727 | 146 |
| Hood | $ 2,384 | 2.5 | $45,061 | 76 | Mills | $ 188 | 3.7 | $38,274 | 142 |
| Hopkins | 1,251 | 3.4 | 35,172 | 191 | Mitchell | 291 | 5.6 | 30,950 | 234 |
| Houston | 753 | 2.4 | 32,863 | 211 | Montague | 976 | 4.9 | 50,047 | 43 |
| Howard | 1,341 | 2.7 | 37,092 | 156 | Montgomery | 26,550 | 3.0 | 53,192 | 31 |
| Hudspeth | 103 | − 3.2 | 31,118 | 233 | Moore | 795 | − 0.6 | 35,924 | 180 |
| Hunt | 3,002 | 3.0 | 34,491 | 199 | Morris | 478 | 0.7 | 37,281 | 153 |
| Hutchinson | 916 | 1.3 | 41,967 | 97 | Motley | 46 | 4.6 | 38,574 | 139 |
| Irion | 88 | 2.9 | 54,776 | 19 | Nacogdoches | 2,064 | 1.67 | 31,592 | 226 |
| Jack | 439 | 6.8 | 48,085 | 47 | Navarro | 1,777 | 2.6 | 36,985 | 159 |
| Jackson | 542 | 3.3 | 37,136 | 155 | Newton | 425 | − 1.0 | 30,049 | 240 |
| Jasper | 1,233 | − 0.1 | 34,573 | 196 | Nolan | 572 | 2.9 | 38,072 | 143 |
| Jeff Davis | 89 | 0.1 | 39,670 | 126 | Nueces | 14,842 | 3.3 | 42,151 | 96 |
| Jefferson | 10,084 | 0.0 | 39,958 | 124 | Ochiltree | 591 | 2.9 | 54,671 | 20 |
| Jim Hogg | 206 | 2.0 | 39,276 | 133 | Oldham | 111 | − 2.1 | 52,776 | 34 |
| Jim Wells | 1,871 | 0.3 | 44,885 | 77 | Orange | 3,313 | − 0.2 | 39,941 | 125 |
| Johnson | 5,621 | 2.4 | 36,336 | 170 | Palo Pinto | 1,083 | 2.0 | 38,820 | 136 |
| Jones | 638 | 5.6 | 32,145 | 220 | Panola | 1,092 | 3.8 | 45,738 | 73 |
| Karnes | 582 | 7.7 | 38,597 | 138 | Parker | 5,568 | 6.3 | 45,856 | 70 |
| Kaufman | 3,944 | 2.8 | 36,325 | 171 | Parmer | 384 | − 2.7 | 38,530 | 140 |
| Kendall | 2,447 | 3.3 | 64,797 | 9 | Pecos | 498 | 0.4 | 31,723 | 224 |
| Kenedy | 27 | 4.5 | 65,500 | 8 | Polk | 1,908 | 1.7 | 41,659 | 101 |
| Kent | 32 | 1.3 | 40,164 | 122 | Potter | 4,345 | 2.3 | 35,712 | 183 |
| Kerr | 2,343 | 1.6 | 46,898 | 63 | Presidio | 246 | 0.9 | 34,222 | 204 |
| Kimble | 177 | − 0.2 | 39,572 | 127 | Rains | 360 | 3.1 | 32,531 | 215 |
| King | 15 | 17.2 | 52.095 | 35 | Randall | 5,495 | 1.6 | 43,444 | 89 |
| Kinney | 116 | − 0.9 | 32,329 | 218 | Reagan | 172 | 5.3 | 47,777 | 56 |
| Kleberg | 1,198 | 1.6 | 37,334 | 151 | Real | 112 | 3.2 | 33,319 | 209 |
| Knox | 149 | 8.5 | 39,505 | 128 | Red River | 425 | 0.4 | 34,111 | 205 |
| Lamar | 1,804 | 2.5 | 36,509 | 168 | Reeves | 358 | 3.3 | 25,630 | 249 |
| Lamb | 448 | 4.8 | 32,489 | 217 | Refugio | 339 | 1.4 | 46,429 | 66 |
| Lampasas | 1,071 | 0.1 | 52,983 | 33 | Roberts | 45 | 1.4 | 53,953 | 26 |
| La Salle | 301 | 15.0 | 40,858 | 110 | Robertson | 687 | 5.5 | 41,656 | 102 |
| Lavaca | 852 | 2.2 | 43,525 | 88 | Rockwall | 4,550 | 3.3 | 53,379 | 29 |
| Lee | 737 | 0.6 | 44,324 | 81 | Runnels | 356 | 5.7 | 34,548 | 197 |

| County | Total Income ($ mil) | % change 12/13 | Per capita income | Rank in State | County | Total Income ($ mil) | % change 12/13 | Per capita income | Rank in State |
|---|---|---|---|---|---|---|---|---|---|
| Rusk | 1,852 | 2.0 | 34,541 | 198 | Tyler | 657 | 0.2 | 30,602 | 236 |
| Sabine | 356 | – 3.0 | 34,370 | 201 | Upshur | 1,569 | 2.3 | 39,349 | 130 |
| San Augustine | 277 | 0.5 | 31,590 | 227 | Upton | 206 | 7.9 | 61,179 | 12 |
| San Jacinto | 925 | 0.4 | 34,441 | 200 | Uvalde | 1,058 | 1.7 | 39,286 | 132 |
| San Patricio | 2,748 | 2.2 | 41,545 | 104 | Val Verde | 1,563 | – 0.4 | 32,137 | 221 |
| San Saba | 196 | 1.7 | 32,590 | 214 | Van Zandt | 1,935 | 1.7 | 36,878 | 163 |
| Schleicher | 124 | 7.4 | 38,755 | 137 | Victoria | 4,235 | 5.0 | 47,041 | 62 |
| Scurry | 980 | 10.4 | 56,643 | 14 | Walker | 1,931 | 2.4 | 28,055 | 246 |
| Shackelford | 294 | 6.8 | 87,115 | 2 | Waller | 1,429 | 2.2 | 31,605 | 225 |
| Shelby | 924 | 1.5 | 35,812 | 182 | Ward | 521 | 4.6 | 46,347 | 67 |
| Sherman | $150 | – 19.4 | $48,489 | 51 | Washington | 1,721 | 1.9 | 50,396 | 41 |
| Smith | 9,199 | 2.2 | 42,573 | 94 | Webb | 7,114 | 2.1 | 27,102 | 248 |
| Somervell | 361 | 2.3 | 41,667 | 100 | Wharton | 1,672 | 1.7 | 40,559 | 114 |
| Starr | 1,289 | 2.8 | 20,811 | 254 | Wheeler | 314 | 1.4 | 54,538 | 21 |
| Stephens | 503 | 2.5 | 54,430 | 24 | Wichita | 5,291 | 1.5 | 40,066 | 123 |
| Sterling | 69 | 6.7 | 56,435 | 15 | Wilbarger | 533 | 3.0 | 40,628 | 112 |
| Stonewall | 76 | 2.8 | 53,240 | 30 | Willacy | 596 | 0.8 | 27,196 | 247 |
| Sutton | 277 | 4.8 | 69,100 | 7 | Williamson | 20,153 | 3.5 | 42,786 | 92 |
| Swisher | 266 | – 1.7 | 34,329 | 202 | Wilson | 1,833 | 6.6 | 40,351 | 118 |
| Tarrant | 84,906 | 2.7 | 44,417 | 80 | Winkler | 327 | 5.1 | 43,004 | 91 |
| Taylor | 5,606 | 2.8 | 41,800 | 98 | Wise | 2,500 | 2.4 | 41,019 | 109 |
| Terrell | 44 | 0.3 | 48,375 | 53 | Wood | 1,448 | 2.3 | 34,231 | 203 |
| Terry | 478 | 4.7 | 37,535 | 148 | Yoakum | 452 | 1.8 | 55,226 | 18 |
| Throckmorton | 83 | – 2.9 | 51,733 | 37 | Young | 941 | 3.0 | 51,282 | 38 |
| Titus | 967 | 0.6 | 29,680 | 241 | Zapata | 435 | 2.4 | 30,223 | 238 |
| Tom Green | 4,751 | 2.8 | 41,329 | 105 | Zavala | 264 | 2.0 | 21,747 | 253 |
| Travis | 54,435 | 2.8 | 48,562 | 50 | | | | | |
| Trinity | 453 | 2.4 | 31,502 | 229 | | | | | |

# Average Work Hours and Earnings

The following table compares the **average weekly earnings**, **hours worked per week** and **average hourly wage** in Texas for production workers in selected industries in June 2015 and June 2014. Figures are provided by the Texas Workforce Commission.

| Industry | Avg. Weekly Earnings | | Avg. Weekly Hours | | Avg. Hourly Earnings | |
|---|---|---|---|---|---|---|
| | June 2015 | June 2014 | June 2015 | June 2014 | June 2015 | June 2014 |
| **Mining and Logging** | $ 1,217.37 | $ 1,,250.69 | 46.5 | 47.7 | $ 26.18 | $ 26.22 |
| Mining (including Oil & Gas) | 1,207.41 | 1,255.89 | 46.6 | 48.1 | 25.91 | 26.11 |
| **Manufacturing** | 917.54 | 947.41 | 42.4 | 44.5 | 21.64 | 21.29 |
| Durable Goods | 1,008.95 | 1,044.17 | 41.9 | 45.3 | 24.08 | 23.05 |
| Fabricated Metal Product Mfg. | 822.62 | 895.67 | 41.8 | 44.1 | 19.68 | 20.31 |
| Non-Durable Goods | 746.49 | 763.25 | 43.3 | 43.0 | 17.24 | 17.75 |
| **Trade, Transportation, Utilities** | | | | | | |
| Wholesale Trade | 886.80 | 918.27 | 40.0 | 42.2 | 22.17 | 21.76 |
| Machinery, Equipment, Supplies | 962.63 | 1,031.63 | 40.6 | 44.2 | 23.71 | 23.34 |
| Retail Trade | | | | | | |
| Auto Dealers/Parts | 704.97 | 696.50 | 39.1 | 39.8 | 18.03 | 17.50 |
| Building Material/Garden Equip. | 422.40 | 402.21 | 30.9 | 31.3 | 13.67 | 12.85 |
| Food/Beverage Stores | 363.21 | 380.46 | 33.2 | 34.4 | 10.94 | 11.06 |
| Gasoline Stations | 353.58 | 378.32 | 33.2 | 33.9 | 10.65 | 11.16 |
| Clothing/Accessories Stores | 277.72 | 244.03 | 23.9 | 22.7 | 11.62 | 10.75 |
| **Information** | | | | | | |
| Telecommunications | 811.82 | 643.77 | 37.9 | 34.5 | 21.42 | 18.66 |

# Employment in Texas by Industry

Employment in Texas reached 11,954,600 in June 2015, up from 11.578,200 in June 2014. The following table shows Texas Workforce Commission estimates of the nonagricultural labor force by industry for June 2014 and 2015. The column at the extreme right shows the percent change during the year in the number employed. *Source: Texas Workforce Commission. Additional information available at the website www.twc.state.ts.us.*

| Industry | 2015 | 2014 | Chng. |
|---|---|---|---|
| (in thousands, 000) | | | |
| **GOODS PRODUCING** | 1,838.9 | 1,847.0 | −2.4 |
| **Mining** | 297.1 | 306.5 | −3.1 |
| Oil & Gas Extraction | 102.8 | 101.7 | 1.1 |
| Support Activities | 182.7 | 192.2 | −4.9 |
| **Construction** | 674.2 | 652.4 | 3.3 |
| **Manufacturing** | 867.6 | 888.1 | −2.3 |
| Durable Goods | 573.0 | 589.9 | −2.9 |
| Wood Products | 21.8 | 21.5 | 1.4 |
| Furniture/Fixtures | 21.9 | 22.3 | −1.8 |
| Primary Metals | 23.7 | 23.3 | 1.7 |
| Fabricated Metal Industries | 136.7 | 141.9 | −3.7 |
| Machinery | 101.6 | 109.0 | −6.8 |
| Computers/Electronics | 92.9 | 96.4 | −3.6 |
| Electric/Appliances | 19.6 | 19.7 | −0.5 |
| Transportation Equipment | 88.0 | 90.1 | −2.3 |
| Misc. Manufacturing | 30.2 | 30.3 | −0.8 |
| Non-Durable Goods | 294.6 | 298.2 | −1.2 |
| Food | 83.3 | 84.7 | −1.7 |
| Beverage/Tobacco | 13.0 | 12.8 | 1.6 |
| Paper | 16.7 | 17.0 | −1.8 |
| Printing | 25.8 | 25.7 | 0.4 |
| Petroleum/Coal Products | 23.0 | 22.9 | 0.4 |
| Chemicals | 78.3 | 78.0 | 0.4 |
| Rubber/Plastic | 38.7 | 39.2 | −1.3 |
| **SERVICE PROVIDING** | 10,015.7 | 9,731.2 | 2.9 |
| **Trade/Transport/Utilities** | 2.365.6 | 2,301.2 | 2.8 |
| Wholesale Trade | 592.5 | 577.2 | 2.7 |
| Merchants/Durable Goods | 334.2 | 327.1 | 2.2 |
| Merchants/Non-Durable | 177.0 | 173.3 | 2.1 |
| Retail Trade | 1,281.5 | 1,249.1 | 2.6 |
| Building/Garden Supplies | 102.1 | 100.8 | 1.3 |
| General Merchandise | 293.3 | 286.6 | 2.3 |
| Food/Beverage Stores | 230.4 | 223.3 | 3.2 |
| Motor Vehicles/Parts | 181.6 | 171.1 | 6.1 |
| Clothing/Accessories | 112.9 | 113.5 | −0.5 |
| Furniture | 40.4 | 38.1 | 6.0 |
| Electronics/Appliances | 40.1 | 39.4 | 1.8 |
| Gasoline Stations | 84.5 | 80.7 | 4.7 |
| Sporting/Books/Music | 38.6 | 39.3 | −1.8 |
| Misc. Store Retailers | 64.7 | 63.1 | 2.5 |
| Nonstore Retailers | 21.2 | 20.1 | 5.5 |

| Industry | 2015 | 2014 | Chng. |
|---|---|---|---|
| Transportation/Utilities | 491.6 | 474.9 | 3.5 |
| Utilities | 50.0 | 49.3 | 1.4 |
| Transportation | 441.6 | 425.6 | 3.8 |
| Air | 54.6 | 53.3 | 2.4 |
| Trucking | 146.3 | 138.5 | 5.6 |
| Pipeline | 17.9 | 17.0 | 5.3 |
| Support Activities | 83.9 | 78.6 | 6.7 |
| Couriers/Messengers | 41.3 | 38.7 | 6.7 |
| Warehousing/Storage | 53.1 | 51.6 | 2.9 |
| Information | 206.7 | 204.5 | 1.1 |
| Publishing | 39.4 | 39.3 | 0.3 |
| Telecommunications | 86.0 | 86.7 | −0.8 |
| Data Processing, Hosting | 31.4 | 30.2 | 4.0 |
| **Financial Activities** | 716.3 | 700.5 | 2.3 |
| Finance/Insurance | 518.2 | 502.5 | 3.1 |
| Credit Intermediation | 250.7 | 254.1 | −1.3 |
| Securities/Investments | 66.0 | 60.7 | 8.7 |
| Insurance Carriers | 198.1 | 186.1 | 6.4 |
| Real Estate/Rental | 198.1 | 198.0 | 0.1 |
| Real Estate | 132.9 | 133.1 | −0.2 |
| Rental/Leasing | 60.1 | 62.5 | −3.8 |
| **Professional Services** | 1,601.6 | 1,546.9 | 3.5 |
| Scientific/Tech | 708.8 | 672.9 | 5.3 |
| Management/Enterprises | 110.2 | 110.7 | −0.5 |
| Administration/Support | 782.6 | 763.3 | 2.5 |
| **Education/Health** | 1,572.9 | 1,514.3 | 3.9 |
| Educational Services | 175.3 | 173.1 | 1.3 |
| Health Care | 1,397.6 | 1,341.2 | 4.2 |
| Ambulatory | 685.0 | 649.7 | 5.4 |
| Hospitals | 315.5 | 305.6 | 3.2 |
| Residential Care | 182.7 | 180.0 | 1.5 |
| Social Assistance | 214.4 | 2059 | 4.1 |
| **Leisure/Hospitality** | 1,287.2 | 1,225.3 | 5.1 |
| Accommodations | 126.3 | 120.2 | 5.1 |
| Food/Drinking Places | 1,016.0 | 965.6 | 5.2 |
| Amusements/Recreation | 106,0 | 100.0 | 6.0 |
| **Other Services** | 420.6 | 416.2 | 1.1 |
| Repair/Maintenance | 125.7 | 124.0 | 1.4 |
| Personal/Laundry | 107.7 | 103.4 | 4.2 |
| Religious/Civic | 187.2 | 188.8 | −0.8 |
| **Total Government** | 1,844.8 | 1,822.3 | 1.2 |
| Federal | 194.1 | 193.5 | 0.3 |
| State | 359.8 | 353.0 | 1.9 |
| Local | 1,290.9 | 1,275.8 | 1.2 |

# Cost of Living Index for Selected Metro Areas

The comparison standard of all values is for the **United States set at 100**. Data are an annual average for 2010. The overall composite is excluding taxes. The column at the far right refers to miscellaneous goods and services.

| Metro area | Overall | Groceries | Housing | Utilities | Transport | Health | Goods/Services |
|---|---|---|---|---|---|---|---|
| Austin | 95.5 | 89.3 | 85.1 | 110.7 | 100.2 | 100.3 | 100.4 |
| Brownsville | 85.8 | 88.6 | 71.0 | 93.1 | 95.0 | 96.5 | 91.4 |
| Corpus Christi | 90.8 | 82.4 | 79.6 | 113.5 | 93.3 | 92.8 | 96.0 |
| Dallas | 91.9 | 96.2 | 70.7 | 105.5 | 100.9 | 103.8 | 100.4 |
| El Paso | 90.4 | 99.9 | 86.0 | 88.1 | 97.0 | 95.4 | 88.5 |
| Fort Worth | 91.1 | 89.8 | 78,0 | 106.2 | 97.6 | 93.8 | 96.1 |
| Houston | 92.2 | 85.1 | 82.0 | 97.7 | 99.2 | 94.6 | 99.9 |
| Lubbock | 89.1 | 90.0 | 80.4 | 74.8 | 97.6 | 98.3 | 97.1 |
| San Antonio | 95.7 | 84.9 | 95.3 | 82.8 | 100.7 | 99.9 | 102.2 |

*Source: Statistical Abstract of the United States 2012.*

# Largest Banks Operating in Texas by Asset Size

Source: Texas Department of Banking, Dec. 31, 2014
Abbreviations: NA, not available; N.A. National Association.

| | Name | City | Class | Assets | Loans |
|---|---|---|---|---|---|
| | | | | (in thousands, 000) | |
| 1 | JP Morgan Chase Bank | New York NY | National | $ 163,792,000 | NA |
| 2 | Bank of America | Charlotte NC | National | 88,097,000 | NA |
| 3 | Comerica Bank | Dallas | State | 69,310,249 | $ 48,592,848 |
| 4 | USAA Federal Savings Bank | San Antonio | State | 67,301,249 | 43,397,265 |
| 5 | Wells Fargo Bank | San Francisco CA | National | 66,017,000 | NA |
| 6 | Compass Bank | Birmingham AL | State | 33,720,000 | NA |
| 7 | Frost Bank | San Antonio | State | 28,327,456 | 10,987,006 |
| 8 | Prosperity Bank | El Campo | State | 21,504,119 | 9,235,582 |
| 9 | Texas Capital Bank N.A. | Dallas | National | 15,892,596 | 14,257,012 |
| 10 | Amergy Bank N.A. | Houston | National | 13,888,144 | 10,076,555 |
| 11 | Capital One | New Orleans LA | National | 10,734,000 | NA |
| 12 | International Bank of Commerce | Laredo | State | 9,892,151 | 5,042,285 |
| 13 | Wells Fargo Bank South Central N.A. | Houston | National | 9,493,324 | 8,256,062 |
| 14 | PlainsCapital Bank | Dallas | State | 8,685,931 | 4,563,517 |
| 15 | First Financial Bank N.A. | Abilene | National | 5,816,065 | 2,929,187 |
| 16 | BOKF | Tulsa OK | National | 5,247,000 | NA |
| 17 | Southside Bank | Tyler | National | 4,821,186 | 2,182,466 |
| 18 | Woodforest National Bank | The Woodlands | National | 4,519,923 | 2,167,019 |
| 19 | LegacyTexas Bank | Plano | State | 4,162,830 | 3,418,473 |
| 20 | Independent Bank | McKinney | State | 4,127,466 | 3,200,598 |
| 21 | Regions Bank | Birmingham AL | State | 3,985,000 | NA |
| 22 | Amarillo National Bank | Amarillo | National | 3,891,248 | 3,091,058 |
| 23 | Citibank | Las Vegas NV | National | 3,510,000 | NA |
| 24 | Broadway National Bank | San Antonio | National | 3,208,577 | 1,384,198 |
| 25 | Branch Banking & Trust | Winston-Salem NC | State | 2,942,000 | NA |
| 26 | CommunityBank of Texas N.A. | Beaumont | National | 2,629,926 | 1,876,758 |
| 27 | American National Bank of Texas | Terrell | National | 2,590,121 | 1,643,172 |
| 28 | Happy State Bank | Happy | State | 2,570,931 | 1,936,105 |
| 29 | City Bank | Lubbock | State | 2,332,169 | 1,548,924 |
| 30 | American Bank of Texas | Sherman | State | 2,196,869 | 1,392,438 |
| 31 | Green Bank N.A. | Houston | National | 2,189,079 | 1,799,155 |
| 32 | TIB The Independent BankersBank | Farmers Branch | State | 2,180,805 | 829,651 |
| 33 | Cadence Bank N.A. | Birmingham AL | National | 2,174,000 | NA |
| 34 | Lone Star National Bank | Pharr | National | 2,155,074 | 1,224,318 |
| 35 | Beal Bank SSB | Plano | State | 2,086,312 | 1,750,870 |
| 36 | Texas Bank & Trust Company | Longview | National | 1,989,439 | 1,538,135 |
| 37 | Inter National Bank | McAllen | National | 1,887,221 | 909,585 |
| 38 | Inwood National Bank | Dallas | National | 1,853,227 | 1,331,311 |
| 39 | NexBank SSB | Dallas | State | 1,807,705 | 1,338,611 |
| 40 | Northstar Bank of Texas | Denton | State | 1,745,262 | 1,074,863 |
| 41 | Southwest Bank | Fort Worth | State | 1,617,450 | 1,362,110 |
| 42 | The Northern Trust | Chicago IL | State | 1,604,000 | NA |
| 43 | Austin Bank, Texas N.A. | Jacksonville | National | 1,532,354 | 1,111,679 |
| 44 | Jefferson Bank | San Antonio | National | 1,446,871 | 722,254 |
| 45 | Patriot Bank | Houston | National | 1,404,489 | 947,055 |
| 46 | First State Bank Central Texas | Austin | State | 1,358,365 | 595,415 |
| 47 | First State Bank of Uvalde | Uvalde | National | 1,356,785 | 226,814 |
| 48 | Citizens National Bank | Henderson | National | 1,348,525 | 729,326 |
| 49 | Guaranty Bank & Trust N.A. | Mount Pleasant | National | 1,333,577 | 788,229 |
| 50 | Extraco Banks N.A. | Temple | National | 1,308,045 | 796,056 |

# Deposits/Assets of Commercial Banks by County

Source: Federal Reserve Bank of Dallas as of Dec. 31, 2014.

**(thousands of dollars, 000)**

| County | Banks | Deposits | Assets | County | Banks | Deposits | Assets |
|---|---|---|---|---|---|---|---|
| Anderson | 1 | $ 45,242 | $ 47,490 | El Paso | 3 | 1,388,702 | 1,614,452 |
| Andrews | 2 | 696,580 | 772,960 | Erath | 2 | 97,991 | 109,393 |
| Angelina | 2 | 1,021,522 | 1,142,472 | Fannin | 2 | 207,888 | 241,177 |
| Atascosa | 3 | 323,376 | 365,267 | Fayette | 4 | 1,001,497 | 1,117,756 |
| Austin | 5 | 1,685,214 | 1,931,972 | Fisher | 1 | 66,360 | 78,807 |
| Bailey | 2 | 191,679 | 215,767 | Floyd | 1 | 100,949 | 112,670 |
| Bandera | 2 | 95,014 | 111,801 | Foard | 1 | 30,484 | 34,093 |
| Bastrop | 2 | 552,286 | 631,401 | Fort Bend | 1 | 562,532 | 629,231 |
| Baylor | 1 | 151,246 | 191,317 | Franklin | 1 | 161,451 | 210,333 |
| Bee | 1 | 292,041 | 318,698 | Frio | 2 | 581,349 | 656,487 |
| Bell | 4 | 2,569,178 | 3,103,086 | Galveston | 4 | 2,294,999 | 2,604,206 |
| Bexar | 7 | 29,332,398 | 34,332,765 | Gillespie | 1 | 660,784 | 797,769 |
| Blanco | 2 | 245,450 | 276,167 | Gonzales | 1 | 337,675 | 372,926 |
| Bosque | 2 | 204,553 | 225,673 | Gray | 1 | 31,725 | 36,605 |
| Bowie | 3 | 577,342 | 671,798 | Grayson | 4 | 2,282,440 | 2,649,219 |
| Brazoria | 7 | 930,808 | 1,067,381 | Gregg | 5 | 2,422,201 | 2,740,563 |
| Brazos | 2 | 1,137,081 | 1,458,389 | Grimes | 2 | 296,639 | 332,922 |
| Briscoe | 1 | 44,700 | 52,728 | Guadalupe | 3 | 428,105 | 478,460 |
| Brooks | 2 | 128,957 | 142,835 | Hale | 1 | 19,792 | 30,073 |
| Brown | 2 | 481,044 | 577,362 | Hall | 1 | 57,314 | 64,634 |
| Burleson | 1 | 395,419 | 443,170 | Hansford | 3 | 337,183 | 400,880 |
| Burnet | 1 | 211,684 | 240,520 | Hardeman | 2 | 84,624 | 96,674 |
| Caldwell | 2 | 246,388 | 274,912 | Harris | 25 | 30,423,867 | 36,220,109 |
| Calhoun | 1 | 226,107 | 254,407 | Harrison | 1 | 185,613 | 214,467 |
| Cameron | 4 | 1,435,925 | 1,895,389 | Haskell | 1 | 68,734 | 76,891 |
| Camp | 1 | 298,273 | 374,044 | Henderson | 2 | 425,671 | 478,046 |
| Carson | 1 | 37,657 | 40,970 | Hidalgo | 6 | 3,856,145 | 4,732,424 |
| Cass | 3 | 394,495 | 465,758 | Hill | 1 | 142,909 | 209,100 |
| Castro | 1 | 979,902 | 1,173,561 | Hockley | 2 | 211,224 | 226,705 |
| Chambers | 2 | 222,367 | 248,905 | Hood | 2 | 448,152 | 501,631 |
| Cherokee | 2 | 1,654,165 | 1,936,142 | Hopkins | 2 | 978,512 | 1,096,562 |
| Childress | 1 | 77,837 | 84,235 | Houston | 3 | 155,508 | 175,007 |
| Coke | 1 | 37,506 | 43,240 | Howard | 2 | 459,671 | 519,082 |
| Coleman | 2 | 133,831 | 149,751 | Hunt | 1 | 37,824 | 41,690 |
| Collin | 8 | 9,125,148 | 12,044,899 | Irion | 1 | 308,680 | 329,947 |
| Collingsworth | 1 | 224,168 | 249,274 | Jack | 1 | 219,935 | 248,885 |
| Colorado | 4 | 411,399 | 475,342 | Jackson | 1 | 57,890 | 62,100 |
| Comanche | 2 | 357,250 | 406,752 | Jasper | 1 | 226,511 | 259,305 |
| Concho | 2 | 174,967 | 195,608 | Jeff Davis | 1 | 63,745 | 71,378 |
| Cooke | 2 | 863,909 | 976,408 | Jefferson | 1 | 2,276,888 | 2,629,926 |
| Coryell | 3 | 594,530 | 661,553 | Jim Hogg | 1 | 124,950 | 143,418 |
| Cottle | 1 | 40,110 | 44,207 | Jim Wells | 1 | 318,032 | 411,965 |
| Crockett | 2 | 589,009 | 711,949 | Johnson | 2 | 643,167 | 748,358 |
| Crosby | 2 | 274,156 | 327,868 | Jones | 2 | 136,943 | 159,338 |
| Dallam | 1 | 59,818 | 66,556 | Karnes | 2 | 670,698 | 720,526 |
| Dallas | 27 | 85,356,779 | 103,657,693 | Kaufman | 2 | 2,374,578 | 2,645,691 |
| Dawson | 1 | 296,487 | 327,435 | Kendall | 1 | 98,016 | 121,771 |
| Deaf Smith | 1 | 131,243 | 146,018 | Kerr | 1 | 108,540 | 119,935 |
| Delta | 2 | 66,196 | 75,306 | Kimble | 2 | 93,417 | 104,622 |
| Denton | 5 | 2,134,362 | 2,508,004 | Kleberg | 1 | 394,081 | 494,726 |
| DeWitt | 2 | 369,642 | 416,331 | Lamar | 3 | 408,091 | 500,937 |
| Dickens | 1 | 39,229 | 44,180 | Lamb | 2 | 645,917 | 723,016 |
| Dimmit | 1 | 63,554 | 71,997 | Lampasas | 1 | 101,177 | 117,167 |
| Donley | 1 | 31,875 | 39,492 | La Salle | 1 | 120,352 | 128,981 |
| Duval | 2 | 113,170 | 123,211 | Lavaca | 2 | 756,221 | 840,626 |
| Ector | 2 | 702,120 | 774,423 | Lee | 1 | 166,188 | 184,766 |
| Edwards | 1 | 65,238 | 73,694 | Leon | 3 | 765,188 | 861,856 |
| Ellis | 5 | 979,629 | 1,111,232 | Liberty | 1 | 284,355 | 324,880 |

No independent banks
were reported in 52
counties.

Total bank assets in Dallas County were
$130.7 biillion in 2014. In Harris County
(Houston), assets were $36.2 billion and
in Bexar County (San Antonio), assets
were $34.3 billion.
Besides the three largest cities, banks
in three other counties had assets over
$10 billion, Wharton, Webb (Laredo) and
Collin (Plano).

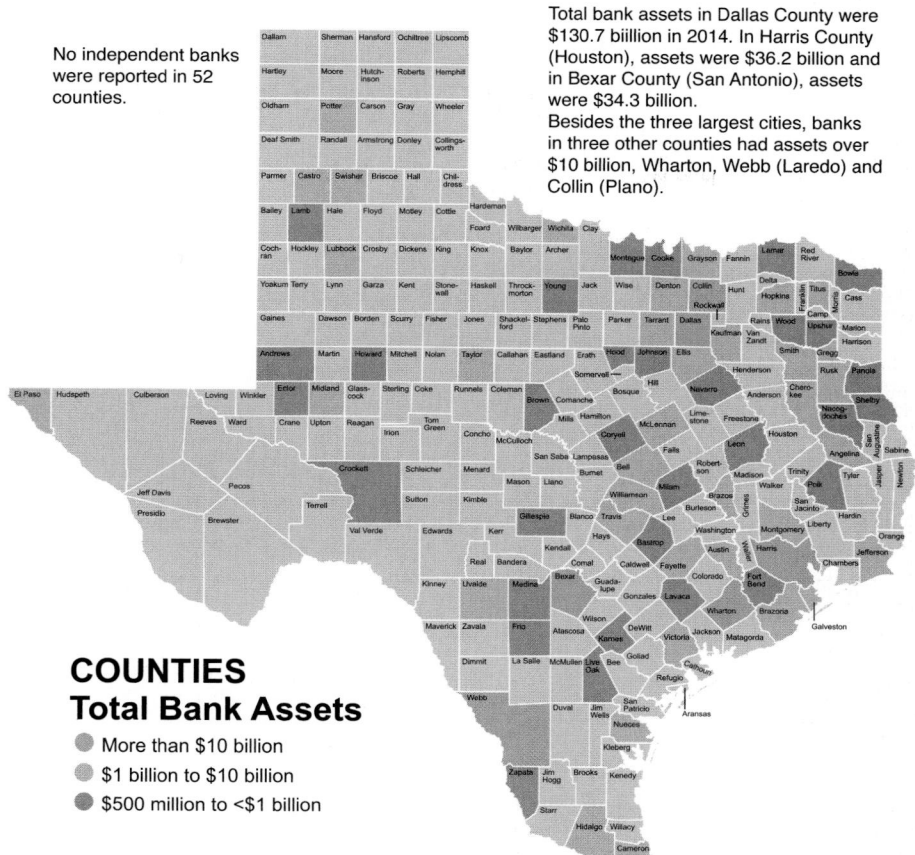

## COUNTIES
## Total Bank Assets

- More than $10 billion
- $1 billion to $10 billion
- $500 million to <$1 billion

| County | Banks | Deposits | Assets |
|--------|-------|----------|--------|
| Limestone | 3 | 256,758 | 293,430 |
| Live Oak | 2 | 469,367 | 536,764 |
| Llano | 2 | 266,184 | 298,538 |
| Lubbock | 9 | 5,985,079 | 6,880,790 |
| Lynn | 1 | 51,383 | 57,216 |
| Martin | 1 | 136,821 | 149,627 |
| Mason | 2 | 110,454 | 140,746 |
| McCulloch | 2 | 233,673 | 260,173 |
| McLennan | 12 | 2,940,034 | 3,326,961 |
| Medina | 3 | 506,935 | 562,293 |
| Menard | 1 | 29,557 | 34,029 |
| Midland | 5 | 3,845,393 | 4,302,806 |
| Milam | 3 | 676,936 | 754,211 |
| Mills | 1 | 251,152 | 282,261 |
| Mitchell | 2 | 158,658 | 172,941 |
| Montague | 1 | 527,524 | 617,102 |
| Montgomery | 2 | 4,399,321 | 4,891,733 |
| Morris | 2 | 171,134 | 207,702 |
| Nacogdoches | 1 | 460,231 | 530,892 |
| Navarro | 5 | 701,148 | 797,159 |
| Nolan | 2 | 248,777 | 277,801 |
| Nueces | 4 | 1,900,120 | 2,098,683 |
| Ochiltree | 1 | 169,955 | 188,464 |
| Orange | 1 | 160,262 | 175,595 |

| County | Banks | Deposits | Assets |
|--------|-------|----------|--------|
| Palo Pinto | 1 | 68,964 | 79,441 |
| Panola | 2 | 544,726 | 635,488 |
| Parker | 2 | 291,022 | 325,584 |
| Parmer | 1 | 110,105 | 125,286 |
| Pecos | 2 | 258,595 | 285,430 |
| Polk | 3 | 663,275 | 780,167 |
| Potter | 3 | 4,590,001 | 5,313,975 |
| Presidio | 1 | 102,338 | 118,421 |
| Rains | 1 | 93,416 | 113,502 |
| Randall | 1 | 129,943 | 147,096 |
| Reeves | 1 | 123,619 | 139,916 |
| Refugio | 1 | 56,787 | 62,075 |
| Rockwall | 2 | 117,376 | 132,175 |
| Runnels | 4 | 309,196 | 345,415 |
| Rusk | 2 | 1,486,794 | 1,697,444 |
| Sabine | 1 | 47,475 | 56,054 |
| San Jacinto | 2 | 132,032 | 145,953 |
| San Patricio | 1 | 124,153 | 136,484 |
| San Saba | 1 | 48,216 | 56,456 |
| Schleicher | 1 | 65,830 | 74,523 |
| Scurry | 2 | 252,360 | 282,724 |
| Shackelford | 1 | 425,913 | 486,698 |
| Shelby | 2 | 442,766 | 504,288 |
| Sherman | 1 | 188,668 | 225,425 |

| County | Banks | Deposits | Assets |
|--------|-------|----------|--------|
| Smith | 4 | 4,318,283 | 6,174,051 |
| Starr | 1 | 68,037 | 82,185 |
| Sterling | 1 | 154,568 | 166,493 |
| Stonewall | 1 | 48,844 | 60,114 |
| Sutton | 1 | 307,953 | 354,373 |
| Swisher | 2 | 2,297,351 | 2,610,133 |
| Tarrant | 12 | 3,718,609 | 4,374,190 |
| Taylor | 3 | 4,954,492 | 5,968,775 |
| Throckmorton | 1 | 33,586 | 36,437 |
| Titus | 2 | 1,160,176 | 1,429,486 |
| Tom Green | 1 | 229,211 | 259,645 |
| Travis | 2 | 1,223,986 | 1,472,174 |
| Trinity | 1 | 50,319 | 55,229 |
| Tyler | 1 | 127,033 | 142,791 |
| Upshur | 2 | 478,903 | 555,367 |
| Uvalde | 1 | 1,251,437 | 1,356,785 |
| Val Verde | 1 | 22,572 | 27,963 |

| County | Banks | Deposits | Assets |
|--------|-------|----------|--------|
| Van Zandt | 3 | 242,372 | 275,470 |
| Walker | 1 | 408,556 | 459,067 |
| Ward | 1 | 132,277 | 148,233 |
| Washington | 4 | 427,676 | 497,237 |
| Webb | 4 | 9,305,404 | 12,626,149 |
| Wharton | 4 | 18,878,249 | 22,786,549 |
| Wheeler | 1 | 81,257 | 90,659 |
| Wichita | 5 | 1,508,905 | 1,776,885 |
| Wilbarger | 1 | 234,415 | 272,990 |
| Williamson | 6 | 1,431,953 | 1,603,128 |
| Wilson | 1 | 40,411 | 48,718 |
| Wise | 3 | 404,001 | 462,167 |
| Wood | 2 | 672,105 | 783,163 |
| Young | 3 | 591,268 | 685,008 |
| Zapata | 2 | 467,218 | 659,413 |
| Zavala | 1 | 60,263 | 70,155 |

# Texas Total Bank Resources and Deposits: 1905–2014

On Dec. 31, 2014, Texas had 470 national and state banks, the lowest number since the first decade of the 20th century. In 1986, the number of independent banks in the state peaked at 1,972. In 2014, total assets were the hightest ever at more than $363 billion. Deposits peaked in 2012 at $302 billion. *Source: Federal Reserve Bank of Dallas.*

| Date | National Banks | | | State Banks | | | Combined Total | | |
|------|-------------|-----------------|------------------|-------------|-----------------|------------------|-------------|-----------------|------------------|
| | No. Banks | Assets (add 000) | Deposits (add 000) | No. Banks | Assets (add 000) | Deposits (add 000) | No. Banks | Assets (add 000) | Deposits (add 000) |
| Sept. 30, 1905 | 440 | $ 189,484 | $ 101,285 | 29 | $ 4,341 | $ 2,213 | 469 | $ 193,825 | $ 103,498 |
| Nov. 10, 1910 | 516 | 293,245 | 145,249 | 621 | 88,103 | 59,766 | 1,137 | 381,348 | 205,015 |
| Dec. 29, 1920 | 556 | 780,246 | 564,135 | 1,031 | 391,127 | 280,429 | 1,587 | 1,171,373 | 844,564 |
| Dec. 31, 1930 | 560 | 1,028,420 | 826,723 | 655 | 299,012 | 231,909 | 1,215 | 1,327,432 | 1,058,632 |
| Dec. 31, 1940 | 446 | 1,695,662 | 1,534,702 | 393 | 227,866 | 179,027 | 839 | 1,923,528 | 1,713,729 |
| Dec. 31, 1950 | 442 | 6,467,275 | 6,076,006 | 449 | 1,427,680 | 1,338,540 | 891 | 7,894,955 | 7,414,546 |
| Dec. 31, 1960 | 468 | 10,520,690 | 9,560,668 | 532 | 2,997,600 | 2,735,726 | 1,000 | 13,518,299 | 12,296,394 |
| Dec. 31, 1970 | 530 | 22,087,890 | 18,384,922 | 653 | 8,907,039 | 7,958,133 | 1,183 | 30,994,929 | 26,343,055 |
| Dec. 31, 1980 | 641 | 75,540,334 | 58,378,669 | 825 | 35,186,113 | 31,055,648 | 1,466 | 110,726,447 | 89,434,317 |
| Dec. 31, 1985 | 1,058 | 144,674,908 | 111,903,178 | 878 | 64,349,869 | 56,392,634 | 1,936 | 209,024,777 | 168,295,812 |
| Dec. 31, 1986 | 1,077 | 141,397,037 | 106,973,189 | 895 | 65,989,944 | 57,739,091 | 1,972 | 207,386,981 | 164,712,280 |
| Dec. 31, 1987 | 953 | 135,690,678 | 103,930,262 | 812 | 54,361,514 | 47,283,855 | 1,765 | 190,052,192 | 151,214,117 |
| Dec. 31, 1988 | 802 | 130,310,243 | 106,740,461 | 690 | 40,791,310 | 36,655,253 | 1,492 | 171,101,553 | 143,395,714 |
| Dec. 31, 1989 | 687 | 133,163,016 | 104,091,836 | 626 | 40,893,848 | 36,652,675 | 1,313 | 174,056,864 | 140,744,511 |
| Dec. 31, 1990 | 605 | 125,808,263 | 103,573,445 | 578 | 45,021,304 | 40,116,662 | 1,183 | 170,829,567 | 143,690,107 |
| Dec. 31, 1991 | 579 | 123,022,314 | 106,153,441 | 546 | 46,279,752 | 41,315,420 | 1,125 | 169,302,066 | 147,468,861 |
| Dec. 31, 1992 | 562 | 135,507,244 | 112,468,203 | 529 | 40,088,963 | 35,767,858 | 1,091 | 175,596,207 | 148,236,061 |
| Dec. 31, 1993 | 502 | 139,409,250 | 111,993,205 | 510 | 44,566,815 | 39,190,373 | 1,012 | 183,976,065 | 151,183,578 |
| Dec. 31, 1994 | 481 | 140,374,540 | 111,881,041 | 502 | 47,769,694 | 41,522,943 | 983 | 188,144,234 | 153,403,984 |
| Dec. 31, 1995 | 456 | 152,750,093 | 112,557,468 | 479 | 49,967,946 | 42,728,454 | 935 | 202,718,039 | 155,285,922 |
| Dec. 31, 1996 | 432 | 152,299,695 | 122,242,990 | 445 | 52,868,263 | 45,970,674 | 877 | 205,167,958 | 168,213,664 |
| Dec. 31, 1997 | 417 | 180,252,942 | 145,588,677 | 421 | 54,845,186 | 46,202,808 | 838 | 235,098,128 | 191,791,485 |
| Dec. 31, 1998 | 402 | 128,609,813 | 106,704,893 | 395 | 50,966,996 | 42,277,367 | 797 | 179,576,809 | 148,982,260 |
| Dec. 31, 1999 | 380 | 128,878,607 | 99,383,776 | 373 | 52,266,148 | 42,579,986 | 753 | 181,144,755 | 141,963,762 |
| Dec. 31, 2000 | 358 | 112,793,856 | 88,591,657 | 351 | 53,561,550 | 43,835,525 | 709 | 166,355,406 | 132,427,182 |
| Dec. 31, 2001 | 342 | 85,625,768 | 72,812,548 | 344 | 59,047,520 | 47,843,799 | 686 | 144,673,288 | 120,656,347 |
| Dec. 31, 2002 | 332 | 95,308,420 | 79,183,418 | 337 | 62,093,220 | 49,715,186 | 669 | 157,401,640 | 128,898,604 |
| Dec. 31, 2003 | 316 | 75,003,613 | 62,567,943 | 337 | 61,448,617 | 49,790,333 | 653 | 136,452,230 | 112,358,276 |
| Dec. 31, 2004 | 311 | 82,333,800 | 67,977,669 | 328 | 69,127,411 | 54,950,601 | 639 | 151,461,211 | 122,928,270 |
| Dec. 31, 2005 | 302 | 96,505,262 | 77,688,463 | 324 | 76,697,256 | 61,257,128 | 626 | 173,202,518 | 138,945,591 |
| Dec. 31, 2006 | 286 | 97,936,270 | 79,389,737 | 322 | 83,910,356 | 66,132,394 | 608 | 181,846,626 | 145,522,131 |
| Dec. 31, 2007 | 282 | 107,260,539 | 83,637,302 | 330 | 154,283,181 | 114,537,280 | 612 | 261,543,720 | 198,174,582 |
| Dec. 31, 2008 | 267 | 108,816,852 | 84,802,191 | 327 | 164,658,101 | 115,186,285 | 594 | 273,474,953 | 199,988,476 |
| Dec. 31, 2009 | 263 | 153,639,579 | 109,552,071 | 318 | 162,958,865 | 120,962,911 | 581 | 316,598,444 | 230,514,982 |
| Dec. 31, 2010 | 253 | 149,498,073 | 120,827,780 | 314 | 162,772,458 | 127,925,865 | 567 | 312,270,531 | 248,753,645 |
| Dec. 31, 2011 | 250 | 159,621,331 | 129,799,399 | 302 | 169,525,070 | 137,180,187 | 552 | 329,146,401 | 266,979,586 |
| Dec. 31, 2012 | 227 | 156,392,247 | 139,945,006 | 293 | 205,788,318 | 169,156,089 | 520 | 362,180,565 | 302,101,095 |
| Dec. 31, 2013 | 211 | 138,785,446 | 118,373,970 | 283 | 216,540,710 | 181,010,324 | 494 | 355,326,156 | 299,384,294 |
| Dec. 31, 2014 | 203 | $128,134,221 | $108,506,074 | 267 | $235,388,932 | $197,078,456 | 470 | $363,523,153 | $305,584,530 |

# Texas State Banks

Consolidated Statement, Foreign and Domestic
Offices, as of Dec. 31, 2014
*Source: Federal Reserve Bank of Dallas*

| Number of Banks | 267 |
|---|---|

**(thousands of dollars, 000)**

## Assets

Cash and balances due from banks:
Non-interest-bearing balances
and currency and coin................................... $ 4,887,035
Interest-bearing balances.............................. 16,957,059
Held-to-maturity securities.............................. 17,717,638
Available-for sale securities............................. 43,146,887
Federal funds sold in domestic offices ...................928,691
Securities purchases under agreements to resell .....27,687
Loans and lease financing receivables:
Loans and leases held for sale ....................... 1,577,029
Loans and leases, net of unearned income ..134,669,785
Less: allowance for loan and lease losses....... 1,571,240
Loans and leases, net.................................. 133,098,545
Trading Assets...................................................... 586,912
Premises and fixed assets.................................. 3,763,183
Other real estate owned...................................... 439,722
Investments in unconsolidated subsidiaries
and associated companies................................... 39,347
Direct/indirect investments in real estate ventures........ 467
Intangible assets:
Goodwill ...............................................................4,558,404
Other ..................................................................... 279,266
Other assets ................................................. _7,381,060_

**Total Assets** ........................................ **$ 235,388,932**

## Liabilities

Deposits:
In domestic offices .................................... $ 195,128,609
Non-interest-bearing.................................... 70,451,579
Interest-bearing ......................................... 124,677,030
In foreign offices, edge & agreement subsidiaries
and IBFs......................................................... 1,949,854
Non-interest-bearing.......................................232,269
Interest-bearing balances............................. 1,717,585
Federal funds purchased and securities sold under
agreements to repurchase:
funds in domestic offices.....................................362,261
securities sold under agreement to repurchase.2,824,931
Trading liabilities...................................................... 622,668
Other borrowed money (mortgages/leases)......... 4,466,939
Subordinated notes and debentures ................... 1,444,759
Other liabilities................................................ _2,043,105_

**Total Liabilities** ................................... **$ 208,843,126**

## Equity Capital

Perpetual preferred stock ......................................... $ 6,740
Common stock....................................................... 611,870
Surplus (exclude surplus related to
preferred stock) ............................................ 13,629,306
Retained earnings ............................................. 12,454,428
Accumulated other comprehensive income........... −165,828
Other equity capital components..................................3,189
Total bank equity capital .......................................26,539,705
Minority interest in cons. subsidiaries.............._6,101_

**Total Equity Capital** ............................... **$ 26,545,806**

**Total liabilities, minority interest and
equity capital** .......................................... **$ 235,388,932**

# Texas National Banks

Consolidated Statement, Foreign and Domestic
Offices, as of Dec. 31, 2014
*Source: Federal Reserve Bank of Dallas*

| Number of Banks | 203 |
|---|---|

**(thousands of dollars, 000)**

## Assets

Cash and balances due from banks:
Non-interest-bearing balances
and currency and coin................................... $ 3,423,870
Interest-bearing balances............................... 8,999,095
Held-to-maturity securities.............................. 2,977,852
Available-for sale securities............................. 21,977,852
Federal funds sold in domestic offices .................2,539,690
Securities purchases under agreements to resell ........8,000
Loans and lease financing receivables:
Loans and leases held for sale ........................... 224,852
Loans and leases, net of unearned income .... 84,184,636
Less: allowance for loan and lease losses........ 1,265,421
Loans and leases, net...................................... 82,919,215
Trading Assets.......................................................... 50,799
Premises and fixed assets................................... 1,748,983
Other real estate owned ...................................... 108,384
Investments in unconsolidated subsidiaries
and associated companies......................................14,671
Direct/indirect investments in real estate ventures........ − 00
Intangible assets:
Goodwill ............................................................. 1,342,873
Other ..................................................................... 99,309
Other assets ................................................. _2,639,851_

**Total Assets** ........................................ **$ 128,134,221**

## Liabilities

Deposits:
In domestic offices .....................................$ 107,864,843
Non-interest-bearing.................................... 32,795,537
Interest-bearing ......................................... 75,069,309
In foreign offices, edge & agreement subsidiaries
and IBFs......................................................... 641,231
Non-interest-bearing.......................................− 00
Interest-bearing balances................................. 641,231
Federal funds purchased and securities sold under
agreements to repurchase:
funds in domestic offices.....................................188,919
securities sold under agreement to repurchase....931,248
Trading liabilities......................................................71,089
Other borrowed money (mortgages/leases)..........2,964,675
Subordinated notes and debentures .......................225,000
Other liabilities................................................ _935,338_

**Total Liabilities** ................................... **$ 133,822,343**

## Equity Capital

Perpetual preferred stock ..................................... $ 386,750
Common stock....................................................... 420,351
Surplus (exclude surplus related to
preferred stock) ............................................ 6,413,278
Retained earnings ............................................. 6,912,737
Accumulated other comprehensive income............. 184,305
Other equity capital components........................... − 18,211
Total bank equity capital ..................................... 14,299,211
Minority interest in consolidated subsidiaries ....._12,667_

**Total Equity Capital** ............................... **$ 14,311,878**

**Total liabilities, minority interest and
equity capital** .......................................... **$ 128,134,221**

# Credit Unions: Mid-Year 2014

| | #Credit Unions | State | Federal | Members | Percent of Pop.* | Savings (000) | Loans (000) | Assets (000) |
|---|---|---|---|---|---|---|---|---|
| **Texas** | 490 | 187 | 303 | 8,277,551 | 31.2 | $73,226,007 | $57,920,542 | $85,123,659 |
| **U.S.** | 6,513 | 2,589 | 3,924 | 101,460,027 | 31.7 | $971,243,591 | $728,005,226 | $1,144,659,789 |

*\* Percent of population, each member counted once for every credit union they belong to. Source: Credit Union National Association.*

## U.S. Credit Union History

| Year | # Credit Unions | Members | Savings ($ millions) | Loans ($ millions) |
|---|---|---|---|---|
| 2013 | 6,795 | 98,379,068 | $ 930,008 | $ 659,436 |
| 2012 | 7,070 | 95,968,179 | 897,286 | 614,635 |
| 2011 | 7,351 | 93,933,798 | 845,898 | 586,616 |
| 2010 | 7,605 | 92,619,205 | 804,357 | 580,035 |
| 2009 | 7,831 | 91,997,528 | 770,055 | 587,125 |
| 2008 | 8,088 | 90,735,249 | 697,972 | 580,101 |
| 2005 | 9,198 | 86,987,764 | 591,388 | 449,891 |
| 2000 | 10,860 | 78,865,715 | 380,858 | 295,251 |
| 1995 | 12,230 | 69,305,876 | 278,813 | 198,337 |
| 1990 | 14,549 | 61,610,057 | 201,082 | 141,889 |
| 1980 | 21,465 | 43,930,569 | 61,724 | 48,703 |
| 1970 | 23,687 | 22,775,511 | 15,411 | 14,068 |
| 1960 | 20,094 | 12,025,393 | 4,976 | 4,376 |
| 1950 | 10,586 | 4,617,086 | 862 | 679 |

## Texas Credit Union History

| # Credit Unions | Members | Savings ($ millions) | Loans ($ millions) |
|---|---|---|---|
| 498 | 8,216,251 | $ 72,470 | $ 55,038 |
| 518 | 7,848,434 | 67,129 | 48,109 |
| 535 | 7,848,434 | 63,470 | 44,873 |
| 550 | 7,539,545 | 58,912 | 43,271 |
| 561 | 7,402,875 | 55,070 | 42,161 |
| 571 | 7,197,177 | 49,335 | 39,092 |
| 625 | 6,832,172 | 40,273 | 32,745 |
| 714 | 6,454,376 | 28,400 | 22,562 |
| 819 | 5,360,020 | 20,306 | 14,701 |
| 954 | 4,379,982 | 13,875 | 8,946 |
| 1,379 | 3,202,066 | 4,818 | 3,691 |
| 1,435 | 1,452,416 | 1,034 | 951 |
| 1,159 | 688,517 | 282 | 265 |
| 484 | 179,956 | 38 | 35 |

*Source: Credit Union National Association.*

# Credit Unions in Texas

*Source: Texas Credit Union Department, National Credit Union Administration and Credit Union National Association.*

Credit unions are chartered at federal and state levels. The National Credit Union Administration (NCUA) is the regulatory agency for the federal-chartered credit unions in Texas.

The Texas Credit Union Department is the regulatory agency for the state-chartered credit unions. It was established in 1969 as a separate agency by the 61st Legislature. In 2014, it supervised 187 active state-chartered credit unions.

These state-chartered credit unions served 3 million Texans and had approximately $32.3 billion in assets in 2014.

The department is supervised by the nine-member Texas Credit Union Commission, which is appointed by the governor to staggered terms of six years, with the terms of one-third of the members expiring Feb. 15 of each odd-numbered year.

The Texas Credit Union League has been the state association for federal and state chartered credit unions since October 1934.

The league's address is 4455 LBJ Freeway Ste. 909, Farmers Branch, 75244-5998.

The address for the Texas Credit Union Department is 914 East Anderson Lane, Austin, 78752-1699. Their Web site is www.tcud.state.tx.us. ☆

## Distribution of Consumer Savings

**$ billions. End-of-Year 2014**

| | Savings | Market share |
|---|---|---|
| Commercial banks | $ 7,589.7 | 74.5% |
| Money Market Mutual Funds | 857.8 | 8.4% |
| **Credit Unions** | 971.2 | **9.5%** |
| Savings Institutions | 592.6 | 5.8% |
| US Savings Securities | 176.0 | 1.7% |
| **Total** | $ 10,187.3 | |

## Credit Outstanding by Lenders

| | Outstanding | Market share |
|---|---|---|
| Commercial banks | $ 1224.7 | 36.4% |
| Pool of Securitized Assets | 49.8 | 1.5% |
| Finance Companies | 684.1 | 20.4% |
| **Credit Unions** | 345.6 | **10.3%** |
| Student Loans | 894.5 | 26.6% |
| Savings Institutions | 118.4 | 3.5% |
| Nonfinancial business | 43.0 | 1.3% |
| **Total** | $ 3,360.0 | |

*Source: Credit Union National Association.*

# Savings and Loan Associations in Texas

This table includes all thrifts that are not also classified as banks under federal law: that is, it includes federal savings and loan associations and federal savings banks. *Source: Texas Department of Savings and Mortgage Lending.*

| Year ending | Number of Inst. | Total Assets | Mortgage Loans | Cash/ Securities | Deposits | FHLB/ Borrowed Money | †Net Worth |
|---|---|---|---|---|---|---|---|
| | | | in thousands of dollars (000) | | | | |
| Dec. 31, 2014 | 8 | $ 71,253,195 | $ 45,943,853 | $ 29,164,768 | $ 62,899,043 | $ 379,957 | $ 6,470,089 |
| Dec. 31, 2013 | 8 | 66,605,862 | 41,812,008 | 34,083,458 | 59,101,594 | 196,784 | 5,941,114 |
| Dec. 31, 2012 | 12 | 64,448,340 | 41,967,892 | 20,925,955 | 57,004,423 | 579,846 | 5,645,916 |
| Dec. 31, 2011 | 12 | 57,857,491 | 40,757,220 | 15,671,590 | 50,819,345 | 657,598 | 5,079,133 |
| Dec. 31, 2010 | 19 | 53,980,441 | 17,005,657 | 14,230,550 | 46,935,007 | 987,211 | 4,840,466 |
| Dec. 31, 2009 | 19 | 46,524,327 | 17,810,587 | 9,702,023 | 40,272,742 | 973,610 | 4,254,794 |
| Dec. 31, 2008 | 22 | 87,572,855 | 49,816,471 | 31,763,898 | 52,606,655 | 27,137,730 | 6,582,759 |
| Dec. 31, 2007 | 21 | 74,346,114 | 38,795,098 | 15,444,116 | 43,442,843 | 23,264,570 | 5,628,255 |
| Dec. 31, 2006 | 20 | 64,692,927 | 22,908,898 | 12,709,276 | 39,661,286 | 18,817,750 | 4,993,335 |
| Dec. 31, 2005 | 19 | 55,755,096 | 42,027,293 | 9,140,789 | 30,565,411 | 11,299,136 | 4,228,103 |
| Dec. 31, 2004 | 20 | 51,000,806 | 40,740,030 | 6,648,858 | 26,526,138 | 12,786,086 | 3,647,046 |
| Dec. 31, 2003 | 21 | 45,941,356 | 16,840,610 | 17,362,664 | 23,954,623 | 10,725,209 | 3,130,442 |
| Dec. 31, 2002 | 24 | 43,940,058 | 31,604,285 | 4,900,880 | 23,264,510 | 11,662,118 | 3,189,629 |
| Dec. 31, 2001 | 24 | 42,716,060 | 35,823,258 | 9,542,688 | 22,182,152 | 15,531,159 | 3,608,222 |
| Dec. 31, 2000 | 25 | 55,709,391 | 43,515,610 | 1,512,444 | 28,914,234 | 17,093,369 | 4,449,097 |
| Dec. 31, 1995 | 45 | 52,292,519 | 27,509,933 | 5,971,364 | 28,635,799 | 15,837,632 | 3,827,249 |
| Dec. 31, 1994 | 50 | 50,014,102 | 24,148,760 | 6,790,416 | 29,394,433 | 15,973,056 | 3,447,110 |
| Dec. 31, 1990 § | 131 | 72,041,456 | 27,475,664 | 20,569,770 | 56,994,387 | 17,738,041 | -4,566,656 |
| Conservatorship | 51 | 14,952,402 | 6,397,466 | 2,188,820 | 16,581,525 | 4,304,033 | -6,637,882 |
| Privately Owned | 80 | 57,089,054 | 21,078,198 | 18,380,950 | 40,412,862 | 13,434,008 | 2,071,226 |
| Dec. 31, 1989 § | 196 | 90,606,100 | 37,793,043 | 21,218,130 | 70,823,464 | 27,158,238 | -9,356,209 |
| Conservatorship | 81 | 22,159,752 | 11,793,445 | 2,605,080 | 25,381,494 | 7,103,657 | -10,866,213 |
| Privately Owned | 115 | 68,446,348 | 25,999,598 | 18,613,050 | 45,441,970 | 20,054,581 | 1,510,004 |
| Dec. 31, 1988 | 204 | 110,499,276 | 50,920,006 | 26,181,917 | 83,950,314 | 28,381,573 | -4,088,355 |
| Dec. 31, 1985 | 273 | 91,798,890 | * 60,866,666 | 10,426,464 | 72,806,067 | 13,194,147 | 3,903,611 |
| Dec. 31, 1980 | 318 | 34,954,129 | $ 27,717,383 | $ 3,066,791 | $ 28,439,210 | $ 3,187,638 | $ 1,711,201 |

# Texas Savings Banks

The savings bank charter was approved by the Legislature in 1993 and the first savings bank was chartered in 1994. Savings banks operate similarly to savings and loans associations in that they are housing-oriented lenders. Under federal law a savings bank is categorized as a commercial bank and not a thrift. Therefore savings-bank information is also reported with state and national bank information. *Source: Texas Department of Savings and Mortgage Lending.*

| Year ending | Number of Inst. | Total Assets | Mortgage Loans | Cash/ Securities | Deposits | FHLB/ Borrowed Money | †Net Worth |
|---|---|---|---|---|---|---|---|
| | | | in thousands of dollars (000) | | | | |
| Dec. 31, 2014 | 29 | $ 11,031,064 | $ 8,211,320 | $ 2,947,322 | $ 8,257,801 | $ 659,216 | $ 1,977,443 |
| Dec. 31, 2013 | 30 | 10,194,983 | 7,148,798 | 3,389,771 | 7,739,381 | 499,261 | 1,812,736 |
| Dec. 31, 2012 | 30 | 10,142,623 | 6,816,212 | 2,630,941 | 7,610,074 | 699,816 | 1,674,039 |
| Dec. 31, 2011 | 30 | 9,530,011 | 6,132,972 | 2,650,324 | 7,247,147 | 568,547 | 1,543,269 |
| Dec. 31, 2010 | 29 | 8,559,443 | 4,568,866 | 4,164,611 | 6,720,417 | 332,684 | 1,329,943 |
| Dec. 31, 2009 | 29 | 8,372,892 | 4,283,372 | 1,237,215 | 6,330,896 | 307,494 | 1,201,409 |
| Dec. 31, 2008 | 28 | 3,988,377 | 1,980,651 | 538,162 | 3,119,082 | 411,119 | 434,893 |
| Dec. 31, 2007 | 26 | 9,967,678 | 6,471,833 | 1,027,709 | 6,162,709 | 2,328,467 | 1,372,231 |
| Dec. 31, 2006 | 22 | 9,393,482 | 6,444,178 | 836,821 | 5,721,314 | 2,453,757 | 1,138,780 |
| Dec. 31, 2005 | 19 | 8,720,497 | 5,605,678 | 985,535 | 5,308,639 | 1,967,673 | 1,352,882 |
| Dec. 31, 2004 | 22 | 12,981,650 | 6,035,081 | 1,654,978 | 8,377,409 | 3,000,318 | 1,482,078 |
| Dec. 31, 2003 | 23 | 17,780,413 | 8,396,606 | 3,380,565 | 11,901,441 | 3,315,544 | 2,422,317 |
| Dec. 31, 2002 | 24 | 15,445,211 | 7,028,139 | 3,147,381 | 10,009,861 | 3,422,600 | 1,910,660 |
| Dec. 31, 2001 | 25 | 11,956,074 | 5,845,605 | 1,305,731 | 8,742,372 | 1,850,076 | 1,270,273 |
| Dec. 31, 2000 | 25 | 11,315,961 | 9,613,164 | 514,818 | 8,644,826 | 1,455,497 | 1,059,638 |
| Dec. 31, 1995 | 13 | 7,348,647 | 5,644,591 | 1,106,557 | 4,603,026 | 2,225,793 | 519,827 |
| Dec. 31, 1994 | 8 | $ 6,347,505 | $ 2,825,012 | $ 3,139,573 | $ 3,227,886 | $ 2,628,847 | $ 352,363 |

† Net worth includes permanent stock and paid-in surplus general reserves, surplus and undivided profits. § In 1989 and 1990, the Office of Thrift Supervision, U.S. Department of the Treasury, separated data on savings and loans (thrifts) into two categories: those under the supervision of the Office of Thrift Supervision (Conservatorship Thrifts) and those still under private management (Privately Owned).

# Insurance in Texas

*Source: 2014 Annual Report, Texas Dept. of Insurance.*

The Texas Department of Insurance reported that on Aug. 31, 2014, there were 2,593 entities licensed to handle insurance business in Texas and 495,176 agents.

Under reforms in 1993-94, a three-member State Board of Insurance was replaced by the department with a Commissioner of Insurance appointed by the governor for a two-year term in each odd-numbered year and confirmed by the Texas Senate.

On Sept. 1, 2005, legislation passed by the 79th Legislature took effect, transferring functions of the Texas Workers' Compensation Commission to the department and creating within it the Division of Worker's Compensation.

Also established was the office of Commissioner of Workers' Compensation, appointed by the governor, to enforce and implement the Texas Workers' Compensation Act.

## Entities in Texas

The following table shows the number and kinds of insurance companies licensed in Texas on Aug. 31, 2014.

| Type of Insurance | Texas | Non-Texas | Non-U.S. | Total |
|---|---|---|---|---|
| Mutual Life | 1 | 27 | 0 | 28 |
| Life Port-of-Entry | 0 | 0 | 1 | 1 |
| Gov. Created Life | 1 | 0 | 0 | 1 |
| Retirement System.Pension | 0 | 1 | 0 | 1 |
| Stock Life | 97 | 424 | 4 | 525 |
| Stipulated Premium Life | 26 | 0 | 0 | 26 |
| Nonprofit Hospital Service | 1 | 0 | 0 | 1 |
| Mutual Fire | 1 | 0 | 0 | 1 |
| Stock Fire | 2 | 3 | 0 | 5 |
| Mutual Casualty | 1 | 9 | 0 | 10 |
| Stock Casualty | 12 | 148 | 0 | 160 |
| Mutual Fire/Casualty | 2 | 46 | 1 | 49 |
| Stock Fire/Casualty | 94 | 679 | 2 | 775 |
| Gov. Created Fire/Casualty | 3 | 0 | 0 | 3 |
| Mortgage Guaranty | 1 | 24 | 0 | 25 |
| Mexican Casualty | 0 | 0 | 13 | 13 |
| Lloyds | 47 | 0 | 0 | 47 |
| Reciprocal Exchanges | 7 | 16 | 0 | 23 |
| Joint Underwriting | 0 | 3 | 0 | 3 |
| Risk Retention Groups | 1 | 0 | 0 | 1 |
| County Mutual Fire | 23 | 0 | 0 | 23 |
| Fraternal Benefit Societies | 6 | 26 | 1 | 33 |
| Title Insurance | 7 | 18 | 0 | 23 |
| Nonprofit Legal Service | 2 | 0 | 0 | 2 |
| Basic HMOs | 37 | 4 | 0 | 41 |
| Single-Service HMOs | 2 | 0 | 0 | 2 |
| Limited HMOs | 14 | 0 | 0 | 14 |
| Local Mutual Aid | 2 | 0 | 0 | 2 |
| Local Mutual Burial | 2 | 0 | 0 | 2 |
| Exempt Associaitons | 6 | 0 | 0 | 6 |
| Farm Mutual Fire | 17 | 0 | 0 | 17 |
| **Total** | **415** | **1,428** | **22** | **1,865** |
| Continuing Care Reitrement | 29 | 4 | 0 | 33 |
| Multiple Employer Welfare | 4 | 1 | 0 | 5 |
| Workers' Comp. Self Insur. | 6 | 0 | 0 | 6 |
| Third-Party Admin. | 219 | 459 | 6 | 684 |
| **Total** | **258** | **464** | **6** | **728** |
| **Grand Total** | **673** | **1,892** | **28** | **2,593** |

## Premium Rates Compared

### Auto Insurance: Average for Coverage by State, 2015

The U.S. average is $1,311. Maine has the least expensive at $805. Selected states below:

| | |
|---|---|
| 1. Michigan | $ 2,476 |
| 2. Montana | 1,886 |
| 3. D.C. | 1,799 |
| 4. Louisiana | 1,774 |
| 5. Florida | 1,742 |
| 6. West Virginia | 1,716 |
| 7. Connecticut | 1,690 |
| 8. Rhode Island | 1,656 |
| 9. California | 1,643 |
| 10. New Jersey | 1,595 |
| 11. Maryland | 1,590 |
| 12. Mississippi | 1,584 |
| **17. Texas** | **1,449** |

*In dollars, twelve-month rates. Information not available from some states. Source: insure.com.*

### Homeowners Insurance: Average Premiums by State, 2014

Idaho has the least expensive at $405. Selected states below (survey did not have information on seven states):

| | |
|---|---|
| 1. Florida | $ 2,280 |
| 2. Oklahoma | 1,572 |
| 3. Louisiana | 1,483 |
| 4. Arkansas | 1,014 |
| 5. Kansas | 1,004 |
| **6. Texas** | **986** |
| 7. Missouri | 949 |
| 8. Alabama | 933 |
| 9. Minnesota | 926 |
| 10. Mississippi | 907 |

*In dollars, twelve-month rates. Information not available from some states. Source: statisticbrain.com.*

## Texas Premiums, Payments

| Year | Total Premiums | Claim Payments | Ratio |
|---|---|---|---|
| 2013 | $ 128.8 billion | $ 91.7 billion | 71.2 |
| 2012 | $ 120.7 billion | $86.7 billion | 71.8 |
| 2011 | $ 108.7 billion | $ 77.3 billion | 71.1 |
| 2010 | $ 102.9 billion | $ 70.8 billion | 68.8 |

## Capital/Surplus of Texas Companies

| |
|---|
| $ 1.1 trillion |
| $ 1.0 trillion |
| $ 931.0 billion |
| $ 933.8 billion |

## Texas Top 5 Auto Insurers / 2014

| Group | Premiums | % of market |
|---|---|---|
| 1. State Farm IL | $ 2,923,827,106 | 19.23 |
| 2. Allstate Ins. | $ 1,711,014,412 | 11.25 |
| 3. Farmers Ins. | $ 1,651,484,285 | 10.86 |
| 4. Progressive | $ 1,329,424,696 | 8.74 |
| 5. Berkshire Hathaway | $ 1,238,184,835 | 8.14 |

## Texas Top 5 Homeowners Insurers / 2014

| 1. State Farm | $ 1,920,865,990 | 26.76 |
|---|---|---|
| 2. Farmers | $ 851,138,540 | 11.86 |
| 3. Allstate | $ 839,608,318 | 11.70 |
| 4. USAA | $ 625,471,216 | 8.71 |
| 5. Liberty Mutual | $ 566,058,696 | 7.89 |

## Texas Top 5 Health Insurers / 2014

| 1. United Health Care | $ 9,184,383,015 | 18.06 |
|---|---|---|
| 2. Blue Cross/Blue Shield | $ 8,937,925,498 | 17.57 |
| 3. Humana | $ 4,074,399,911 | 8.01 |
| 4. Centene Corp | $ 4,027,847,045 | 7.92 |
| 5. Aetna | $ 3,594,119,483 | 7.07 |

## Texas Top 5 Life Insurers / 2014

| 1. Metropolitan | $ 812,822,193 | 7.75 |
|---|---|---|
| 2. New York Life | $ 563,856,012 | 5.37 |
| 3. Northwestern Mutual | $ 529,922,140 | 5.05 |
| 4. Prudential of Am. | $ 483,697,437 | 4.61 |
| 5. Lincoln National | $ 429,232,450 | 4.09 |

### Personal Auto

| | |
|---|---|
| Companies in state | 181 |
| Groups in state | 67 |
| New Companies | 12 |
| Vehicles (liability) | 17,141,155 |
| Total Premiums | $15,202,559,628 |

### Homeowners Insurance

| | |
|---|---|
| Companies in state | 129 |
| Groups in state | 58 |
| New Companies | 10 |
| Homeowner policies | 4,301,678 |
| Total Premiums | $7,177,732,856 |

### Health Insurance

| | |
|---|---|
| Companies in state | 495 |
| Groups in state | 183 |
| New Companies | 31 |
| Population est. 2011 | 26,422,511 |
| Texans with insurance | 21,064,835 |
| Texans without insurance | 5,357,675 |
| Total Premiums | $50,860,063,884 |

### Life Insurance

| | |
|---|---|
| Companies in state | 460 |
| Groups in state | 172 |
| New Companies | 1 |
| Total Premiums | $10,490,890,069 |

## Ten-year history, number of insurance companies operating in Texas

| | 2005 | 2006 | 2007 | 2008 | 2009 | 2010 | 2011 | 2012 | 2013 | 2014 |
|---|---|---|---|---|---|---|---|---|---|---|
| **Life/Health** | | | | | | | | | | |
| Texas | 190 | 186 | 175 | 170 | 161 | 161 | 157 | 153 | 149 | 146 |
| Non-Texas | 552 | 546 | 529 | 520 | 514 | 504 | 499 | 485 | 483 | 479 |
| Non-U.S. | 0 | 0 | 0 | 0 | 0 | 0 | 0 | 7 | 6 | 6 |
| subtotal | 742 | 732 | 704 | 690 | 675 | 665 | 656 | 645 | 638 | 638 |
| **Property/Casualty** | | | | | | | | | | |
| Texas | 250 | 248 | 252 | 250 | 250 | 243 | 238 | 236 | 225 | 224 |
| Non-Texas | 917 | 926 | 932 | 942 | 948 | 948 | 947 | 935 | 948 | 946 |
| Non-U.S. | 0 | 0 | 0 | 0 | 0 | 0 | 0 | 18 | 17 | 16 |
| subtotal | 1,167 | 1,174 | 1,184 | 1,192 | 1,198 | 1,191 | 1,185 | 1,189 | 1,190 | 1,186 |
| **Other*** | | | | | | | | | | |
| Texas | 352 | 341 | 341 | 348 | 353 | 350 | 332 | 324 | 301 | 303 |
| Non-Texas | 479 | 485 | 471 | 486 | 504 | 515 | 512 | 487 | 464 | 467 |
| Non-U.S. | 0 | 0 | 0 | 0 | 0 | 0 | 0 | 7 | 6 | 6 |
| subtotal | 831 | 826 | 812 | 834 | 857 | 865 | 844 | 818 | 771 | 776 |
| **Grand Total** | **2,740** | **2,732** | **2,700** | **2,716** | **2,730** | **2,721** | **2,685** | **2,652** | **2,599** | ****2,593** |

*Other includes: Non-profit legal services corporations, third party administrators, continuing care retirement communities and health maintenance organizations.

**Does not include 194 premium finance companies and their 10 branch offices.

# Construction: Texas Non-Residential Contract Awards

The chart below shows the total value of non-residential construction contract awards in Texas by month in billions of dollars (000,000). The **change over the period September 2013 to 2014** to the previous year was an increase of **9.6 percent**.

| Month | Total Awards | Month | Total Awards | Month | Total Awards |
|---|---|---|---|---|---|
| January 2009 | 1.458 | March 2012 | 1.170 | July 2013 | 2.253 |
| January 2010 | 1.364 | April 2012 | 1.032 | August 2013 | 1.225 |
| January 2011 | 0.983 | May 2012 | 1.005 | September 2013 | 2.153 |
| February 2011 | 0.942 | June 2012 | 1.440 | Ocdtober 2013 | 1.887 |
| March 2011 | 1.307 | July 2012 | 1.241 | November 2013 | 1.369 |
| April 2011 | 1.606 | August 2012 | 1.289 | December 2013 | 1.166 |
| May 2011 | 1.216 | September 2012 | 1.400 | January 2014 | 2.521 |
| June 2011 | 1.692 | October 2012 | 1.297 | February 2014 | 1.245 |
| July 2011 | 0.975 | November 2012 | 1.114 | March 2014 | 2.218 |
| August 2011 | 1.717 | December 2012 | 1.097 | April 2014 | 4.634 |
| September 2011 | 0.938 | January 2013 | 1.103 | May 2014 | 1.664 |
| October 2011 | 0.869 | February 2013 | 0.809 | June 2014 | 4.261 |
| November 2011 | 1.405 | March 2013 | 1.175 | July 2014 | 6.858 |
| December 2011 | 1.014 | April 2013 | 1.215 | August 2014 | 1.589 |
| January 2012 | 1.028 | May 2013 | 1.412 | September 2014 | 2.359 |
| February 2012 | 0.855 | June 2013 | 1.458 | | |

*Source: Texas State Comptroller, 2015.*

## State Expenditures for Highways

The chart below shows net expenditures for state highway construction and maintenance by fiscal year and percent change from the previous year.

| Year | Net Expenditures | Percent change |
|---|---|---|
| 2007 | $ 5,359,397,359 | 4.4 |
| 2008 | $ 5,208,591,565 | – 2.8 |
| 2009 | $ 4,252,879,534 | – 18.3 |
| 2010 | $ 3,353,467,064 | – 21.1 |
| 2011 | $ 3,774,008,186 | 12.5 |
| 2012 | $ 4,186,493,637 | 10.9 |
| 2013 | $ 4,491,601,827 | 7.3 |
| 2014 | $ 5,305,157,884 | 18.1 |

*Source: Texas Annual Cash Report 2014.*

## Federal Funds for Highways

The chart below shows fiscal 2013 dispersement of Federal Highway Administration funds for construction and maintenance in **thousands of dollars**. The column at right shows dollars per capita.

| State | Highway Funds | |
|---|---|---|
| | Total | Per capita |
| U.S. Total | $ 39,778,262 | $ 126 |
| 1. California | 3,810,280 | 99 |
| **2. Texas** | **3,099,376** | **117** |
| 3. New York | 2,011,024 | 102 |
| 4. Florida | 1,886,696 | 96 |
| 5. Pennsylvania | 1,635,411 | 128 |
| 6. Illinois | 1,411,285 | 109 |
| 7. Ohio | 1,313,749 | 114 |
| 8. Georgia | 1,269,819 | 127 |
| 9. New Jersey | 1,164,644 | 131 |
| 10. North Carolina | 1,130,009 | 115 |
| 11. Michigan | 1,047,257 | 106 |
| 12. Virginia | 1,013,632 | 127 |

*Source: Federal Highway Administration, 2015.*

## Texas Single-Family Building Permits

| Year | No. of Dwelling Units | | Avg. Value per Unit ($) | |
|---|---|---|---|---|
| | Units | % change | Value | % change |
| 1980 | 67,870 | – | $ 51.900 | – |
| 1981 | 66,161 | – 2.5 | 55,700 | 7.3 |
| 1982 | 78,714 | 19.0 | 53,800 | – 3.4 |
| 1983 | 103,252 | 31.2 | 63,400 | 17.8 |
| 1984 | 84,565 | – 18.1 | 68,000 | 7.3 |
| 1985 | 67,964 | – 19.6 | 71,000 | 4.4 |
| 1986 | 59,143 | – 13.0 | 72,200 | 1.7 |
| 1987 | 43,975 | – 25.6 | 77,700 | 7.6 |
| 1988 | 35,908 | – 18.3 | 83,900 | 8.0 |
| 1989 | 36,658 | 2.1 | 90,400 | 7.7 |
| 1990 | 38,233 | 4.3 | 95,500 | 5.6 |
| 1991 | 46,209 | 20.9 | 92,800 | – 2.8 |
| 1992 | 59,543 | 28.9 | 95,400 | 2.8 |
| 1993 | 69,964 | 17.5 | 96,400 | 1.0 |
| 1994 | 70,452 | 0.7 | 99,500 | 3.2 |
| 1995 | 70,421 | 0.0 | 100,300 | 0.8 |
| 1996 | 83,132 | 18.1 | 102,100 | 1.8 |
| 1997 | 82,228 | – 1.1 | 108,900 | 6.7 |
| 1998 | 99,912 | 21.5 | 112,800 | 3.6 |
| 1999 | 101,928 | 2.0 | 118,800 | 5.3 |
| 2000 | 108,782 | 6.7 | 127,100 | 7.0 |
| 2001 | 111,915 | 2.9 | 124,700 | – 1.9 |
| 2002 | 122,913 | 9.8 | 126,400 | 1.4 |
| 2003 | 137,493 | 11.9 | 128,800 | 1.9 |
| 2004 | 151,384 | 10.1 | 137,600 | 6.8 |
| 2005 | 166,203 | 9.8 | 144,300 | 4.9 |
| 2006 | 163,032 | – 1.9 | 155,100 | 7.5 |
| 2007 | 120,366 | – 26.2 | 169,000 | 9.0 |
| 2008 | 81,107 | – 32.6 | 174,100 | 3.0 |
| 2009 | 68,230 | – 15.9 | 167,900 | – 3.6 |
| 2010 | 68,170 | – 0.1 | 179,200 | 6.7 |
| 2011 | 67,254 | – 1.3 | 191,100 | 6.6 |
| 2012 | 81,926 | 21.8 | 192,300 | 0.6 |
| 2013 | 93,478 | 14.1 | 197,500 | 2.7 |
| 2014 | 103,045 | 10.2 | $ 208,900 | 5.8 |

*Real Estate Center at Texas A&M University, 2015.*

# Commercial Fishing in Texas

Total coastwide landings in 2012 were more than 90.5 million pounds, valued at more than $213 million. Shrimp accounted for most of the weight and value of all seafood landed (see chart a bottom).

The Coastal Fisheries Division of the Texas Parks and Wildlife Department manages the marine fishery resources of Texas' four million acres of saltwater, including the bays and estuaries and out to nine nautical miles in the Gulf of Mexico.

The division works toward sustaining fisheries populations at levels that are necessary to ensure replenishable stocks of commercially and recreationally important species.

It also focuses on habitat conservation and restoration and leads the agency research on all water-related issues, including assuring adequate in-stream flows for rivers and sufficient freshwater inflows for bays and estuaries. ☆

### Landings by State 2012

| Rank | States | Pounds (000) | Dollars (000) |
|---|---|---|---|
| | Total, U.S. | 9,286,517 | $5,109,570 |
| 1 | Alaska | 5,344,168 | 1,692,174 |
| 2 | Massachusetts | 297,561 | 618,247 |
| 3 | Maine | 262,588 | 448,578 |
| 4 | Louisiana | 856,665 | 309,956 |
| 5 | Washington | 213,578 | 275,585 |
| 6 | **Texas** | **90,558** | **$213,313** |

Source: National Maritime Fisheries Service, 2014.

### U.S. Ports in 2012

| Rank | Port | Fishery Landed Value Dollars (000,000) |
|---|---|---|
| 1 | New Bedford, MA | $411.1 |
| 2 | Kodiak, AK | 170.3 |
| 3 | Honolulu, HI | 100.1 |
| 4 | Empire-Venice, LA | 79.7 |
| 5 | **Galveston, TX** | **74.3** |
| 14 | **Brownsville–Port Isabel, TX** | **$53.6** |

Source: National Ocean Economics Program, 2014.

### Top Fishing Ports for Texas in 2012

| Rank | Port (Landing Weight) | Pounds (000) | Port (Landed Value) | Dollars (000) |
|---|---|---|---|---|
| 1 | Galveston | 27,000 | Galveston | $74,300 |
| 2 | Brownsville–Port Isabel | 23,000 | Brownsville–Port Isabel | 53,600 |
| 3 | Port Arthur | 20,000 | Port Arthur | 47,400 |
| 4 | Palacios | 9,000 | Palacios | $21,200 |

Source: National Ocean Economics Program, 2014.

*Shrimp boats docked in Brownsville. Photo by Robert Plocheck.*

### Texas Commercial Fishery Landings by Species

| Species | 2012 Pounds | 2012 Value | 2009 Pounds | 2009 Value | 2007 Pounds | 2007 Value |
|---|---|---|---|---|---|---|
| Shrimp, Brown | 43,707,869 | $92,254,541 | 65,297,755 | $86,812,353 | 42,841,648 | $84,258,622 |
| Shrimp, White | 24,100,143 | 62,970,321 | 23,590,484 | 40,846,270 | 27,160,444 | 56,847,983 |
| Oyster, Eastern | 5,817,191 | 21,302,111 | 2,733,150 | 9,375,720 | 5,187,631 | 17,759,573 |
| Snapper, Red | 1,122,665 | 4,447,884 | 850,932 | 2,398,100 | 1,214,664 | 3,769,518 |
| Shrimp, Dendrobranchiata | 1,023,748 | 4,021,505 | 790,484 | 3,071,621 | 1,051,026 | 3,127,202 |
| Crab, Blue | 2,849,739 | 2,875,694 | 2,844,263 | 2,454,370 | 3,309,044 | 2,660,051 |
| Drum, Black | 1,612,023 | 1,485,663 | 1,610,103 | 1,377,472 | 1,684,400 | 1,656,699 |
| Snapper, Vermilion | 511,224 | 1,433,985 | 561,013 | 1,232,502 | 664,095 | 1,535,104 |
| Croaker, Atlantic | 88,918 | 740,110 | 63,393 | 484,016 | 54,926 | 417,341 |
| **Total, including others** | **90,557,774** | **$213,313,076** | **99,497,064** | **$150,231,931** | **84,937,097** | **$174,346,556** |

Source: National Ocean Economics Program and National Maritime Fisheries Service, 2014.

# Tourism Impact Estimates by County, 2013

This analysis covers most travel in Texas including business, pleasure, shopping, to attend meetings and other destinations. Visitor **spending** is for purchases including lodging taxes and other applicable local and state taxes. **Earnings** are wages and salaries of employees and income of proprietors of businesses that receive travel expenditures. Employment associated with these businesses are listed under **jobs**. **Local tax** receipts are from hotel taxes, local sales taxes, auto rental taxes, etc, as separate from state tax receipts. *Source: Office of the Governor, Economic Development and Tourism.*

| County | Spending ($000) | Earnings ($000) | Jobs | Local tax ($000) | County | Spending ($000) | Earnings ($000) | Jobs | Local tax ($000) |
|---|---|---|---|---|---|---|---|---|---|
| Anderson | $ 56,970 | $ 13,610 | 710 | $ 920 | Cooke | 65,850 | 16,020 | 600 | 1,120 |
| Andrews | 24,180 | 5,520 | 340 | 450 | Coryell | 49,860 | 14,010 | 540 | 630 |
| Angelina | 132,670 | 26,640 | 1,400 | 1,770 | Cottle | 1,920 | 160 | 10 | 10 |
| Aransas | 101,690 | 30,760 | 1,340 | 2,020 | Crane | 2,660 | 650 | 20 | 40 |
| Archer | 1,820 | 330 | 20 | 20 | Crockett | 38,100 | 4,700 | 310 | 350 |
| Armstrong | 1,440 | 90 | 10 | 0 | Crosby | 1,490 | 390 | 20 | 10 |
| Atascosa* | 73,660 | 21,950 | 780 | 1,930 | Culberson | 39,030 | 4,430 | 160 | 400 |
| Austin | 42,960 | 9,070 | 390 | 370 | Dallam | 16,050 | 5,200 | 250 | 370 |
| Bailey | 4,240 | 1,110 | 70 | 80 | Dallas | 9,178,020 | 3,556,.280 | 81,190 | 226,650 |
| Bandera | 35,480 | 21,870 | 1,380 | 790 | Dawson | 18,910 | 3,320 | 220 | 240 |
| Bastrop | 143,830 | 54,250 | 1,640 | 3,620 | Deaf Smith | 16,410 | 3,160 | 170 | 260 |
| Baylor | 6,730 | 670 | 30 | 20 | Delta | 1,370 | 250 | 10 | 10 |
| Bee* | 47,670 | 13,410 | 590 | 980 | Denton | 702,930 | 207,650 | 6,090 | 13,540 |
| Bell | 408,000 | 106,770 | 4,730 | 7,470 | DeWitt* | 70,600 | 20,550 | 790 | 1,290 |
| Bexar | 7,168,840 | 1,853,110 | 60,960 | 163,690 | Dickens | 470 | 130 | 10 | 10 |
| Blanco | 14,010 | 3,530 | 180 | 280 | Dimmit* | 46,490 | 8,310 | 370 | 1,270 |
| Borden | 100 | 10 | 0 | 0 | Donley | 6,530 | 1,820 | 90 | 150 |
| Bosque | 13,230 | 5,510 | 150 | 230 | Duval | 13,310 | 1,340 | 80 | 170 |
| Bowie | 190,680 | 29,890 | 1,560 | 2,330 | Eastland | 16,380 | 3,910 | 220 | 340 |
| Brazoria | 339,960 | 89,120 | 4,410 | 5,950 | Ector | 388,710 | 97,310 | 3,020 | 10,370 |
| Brazos | 437,830 | 106,160 | 4,980 | 8,350 | Edwards | 960 | 210 | 10 | 10 |
| Brewster | 56,370 | 26,240 | 1,160 | 1,260 | Ellis | 147,840 | 33,560 | 970 | 2,350 |
| Briscoe | 1,400 | 150 | 10 | 0 | El Paso | 1,658,620 | 367,590 | 12,480 | 25,850 |
| Brooks | 15,240 | 2,030 | 100 | 200 | Erath | 48,890 | 11,840 | 500 | 740 |
| Brown | 50,010 | 14,550 | 610 | 1,030 | Falls | 10,310 | 2,050 | 100 | 170 |
| Burleson | 14,320 | 3,820 | 160 | 170 | Fannin | 12,850 | 1,830 | 90 | 120 |
| Burnet | 79,910 | 26,950 | 1,070 | 1,920 | Fayette | 44,150 | 8,640 | 440 | 620 |
| Caldwell | 33,150 | 7,180 | 200 | 390 | Fisher | 1,080 | 150 | 10 | 10 |
| Calhoun | 37,180 | 9,890 | 380 | 830 | Floyd | 5,870 | 710 | 40 | 30 |
| Callahan | 3,570 | 900 | 50 | 40 | Foard | 340 | 80 | 0 | 0 |
| Cameron | 823,740 | 175,900 | 8,110 | 17,780 | Fort Bend | 510,180 | 146,050 | 4,610 | 10,210 |
| Camp | 17,740 | 1,400 | 80 | 60 | Franklin | 9,340 | 1,720 | 100 | 110 |
| Carson | 7,140 | 400 | 30 | 10 | Freestone | 54,460 | 5,860 | 430 | 500 |
| Cass | 23,000 | 5,420 | 280 | 260 | Frio* | 47,210 | 12,250 | 520 | 1,180 |
| Castro | 3,130 | 520 | 30 | 20 | Gaines | 15,470 | 2,900 | 150 | 230 |
| Chambers | 33,770 | 6,840 | 220 | 860 | Galveston | 843,910 | 230,340 | 9,360 | 23,820 |
| Cherokee | 38,710 | 7,960 | 440 | 500 | Garza | 10,690 | 3,150 | 100 | 100 |
| Childress | 16,690 | 3,660 | 250 | 560 | Gillespie | 89,050 | 25,270 | 980 | 2,580 |
| Clay | 23,460 | 1,610 | 100 | 30 | Glasscock | 230 | 40 | 0 | 0 |
| Cochran | 890 | 180 | 10 | 10 | Goliad | 11,630 | 1,950 | 70 | 180 |
| Coke | 3,120 | 610 | 40 | 20 | Gonzales* | 35,650 | 8,400 | 380 | 780 |
| Coleman | 6,740 | 1,230 | 80 | 90 | Gray | 53,640 | 14,990 | 680 | 1,040 |
| Collin | 1,331,630 | 438,660 | 12,460 | 27,760 | Grayson | 215,980 | 33,110 | 1,460 | 2,550 |
| Collingswrth | 2,230 | 270 | 20 | 10 | Gregg | 246,780 | 61,450 | 2,750 | 3,830 |
| Colorado | 62,080 | 12,700 | 520 | 700 | Grimes | 19,970 | 5,230 | 230 | 330 |
| Comal | 382,130 | 112,320 | 3,720 | 8,170 | Guadalupe | 155,120 | 55,130 | 1,730 | 3,070 |
| Comanche | 13,810 | 2,260 | 120 | 140 | Hale | 53,570 | 12,300 | 780 | 880 |
| Concho | 1,410 | 770 | 30 | 20 | Hall | 2,480 | 270 | 10 | 20 |

*Oil and gas production in recent years may affect travel impact estimates.*

*Tourists view the exhibit at Palo Alto National Historic Site in the Rio Grande Valley. Photo by Robert Plocheck.*

## Top Places of Origin, 2013

The leading places of origin for visitors to Texas.
*Source: Survey for Office of Governor.*

| Rank | Metro Area | Percent |
|---|---|---|
| 1. | Oklahoma City | 6.1 |
| 2. | Los Angeles | 4.7 |
| 3. | New Orleans | 4.4 |
| 4. | Alburquerque-Santa Fe | 4.4 |
| 5. | New York | 3.3 |

| Rank | State | Percent |
|---|---|---|
| 1. | Louisiana | 11.1 |
| 2. | Oklahoma | 8.9 |
| 3. | California | 8.5 |
| 4. | Missouri | 5.2 |
| 5. | Florida | 5.2 |
| 6. | New Mexico | 4.6 |
| 7. | Mississippi | 4.3 |
| 8. | Illinois | 4.2 |

| County | Spending ($000) | Earnings ($000) | Jobs | Local tax ($000) |
|---|---|---|---|---|
| Hamilton | 5,590 | 1,550 | 50 | 90 |
| Hansford | 2,000 | 310 | 20 | 30 |
| Hardeman | 7,150 | 1,120 | 70 | 100 |
| Hardin | 42,260 | 8,970 | 470 | 590 |
| Harris | 13,706,590 | 4,472,120 | 102,580 | 305,280 |
| Harrison | 98,190 | 14,130 | 660 | 580 |
| Hartley | 1,240 | 240 | 20 | 10 |
| Haskell | 6,680 | 1,730 | 110 | 160 |
| Hays | 287,890 | 81,250 | 2,840 | 5,660 |
| Hemphill | 18,290 | 2,920 | 130 | 690 |
| Henderson | 124,590 | 19,610 | 490 | 930 |
| Hidalgo | 1,318,940 | 331,550 | 15,100 | 22,300 |
| Hill | 61,210 | 9,020 | 490 | 490 |
| Hockley | 26,240 | 6,450 | 350 | 280 |
| Hood | 60,490 | 14,440 | 470 | 1,060 |
| Hopkins | 70,070 | 11,350 | 500 | 590 |
| Houston | 38,740 | 6,450 | 290 | 260 |
| Howard | 120,050 | 19,220 | 970 | 2,230 |
| Hudspeth | 6,110 | 360 | 10 | 0 |
| Hunt | 114,470 | 25,450 | 750 | 1,230 |
| Hutchinson | 41,620 | 8,600 | 380 | 620 |
| Irion | 12,170 | 350 | 10 | 0 |

| County | Spending ($000) | Earnings ($000) | Jobs | Local tax ($000) |
|---|---|---|---|---|
| Jack | 5,550 | 880 | 50 | 70 |
| Jackson | 13,260 | 2,410 | 110 | 230 |
| Jasper | 36,130 | 9,390 | 470 | 630 |
| Jeff Davis | 9,130 | 3,680 | 120 | 0 |
| Jefferson | 507,990 | 105,090 | 5,420 | 7,860 |
| Jim Hogg | 5,840 | 1,370 | 60 | 60 |
| Jim Wells | 81,030 | 19,720 | 920 | 840 |
| Johnson | 162,910 | 30,410 | 1,020 | 1,920 |
| Jones | 8,600 | 2,140 | 110 | 90 |
| Karnes* | 43,120 | 9,860 | 340 | 700 |
| Kaufman | 150,290 | 23,540 | 730 | 1,360 |
| Kendall | 87,230 | 23,930 | 1,040 | 1,370 |
| Kenedy | 800 | 280 | 20 | 0 |
| Kent | 790 | 120 | 10 | 0 |
| Kerr | 91,910 | 34,210 | 1,590 | 1,870 |
| Kimble | 19,010 | 2,660 | 160 | 310 |
| King | 40 | 10 | 0 | 0 |
| Kinney | 5,410 | 1,710 | 110 | 60 |
| Kleberg | 59,260 | 14,330 | 560 | 880 |
| Knox | 3,590 | 490 | 20 | 30 |
| La Salle* | 44,470 | 21,610 | 890 | 1,630 |
| Lamar | 73,720 | 19,270 | 780 | 1,110 |

*Oil and gas production in recent years may affect travel impact estimates.

| County | Spending ($000) | Earnings ($000) | Jobs | Local tax ($000) | County | Spending ($000) | Earnings ($000) | Jobs | Local tax ($000) |
|---|---|---|---|---|---|---|---|---|---|
| Lamb | 13,800 | 1,660 | 100 | 100 | Robertson | 23,040 | 4,400 | 240 | 530 |
| Lampasas | 13,810 | 2,650 | 160 | 200 | Rockwall | 96,000 | 23,550 | 770 | 2,040 |
| Lavaca | 20,230 | 4,870 | 170 | 370 | Runnels | 7,040 | 1,150 | 70 | 60 |
| Lee | 25,620 | 5,540 | 230 | 230 | Rusk | 43,090 | 7,400 | 360 | 540 |
| Leon | 38,040 | 5,530 | 300 | 530 | Sabine | 11,570 | 2,060 | 120 | 30 |
| Liberty | 48,800 | 14,220 | 390 | 640 | S.Augustne | 7,740 | 1,740 | 100 | 60 |
| Limestone | 18,690 | 2,420 | 130 | 280 | SanJacinto | 12,630 | 2,760 | 140 | 50 |
| Lipscomb | 3,010 | 280 | 10 | 10 | SanPatricio | 120,110 | 28,400 | 1,190 | 2,340 |
| Live Oak* | 53,860 | 8,020 | 410 | 1,200 | San Saba | 3,800 | 840 | 60 | 30 |
| Llano | 94,830 | 36,860 | 2,080 | 2,130 | Schleicher | 460 | 120 | 10 | 10 |
| Loving | 30 | 10 | 0 | 0 | Scurry | 41,500 | 14,430 | 710 | 810 |
| Lubbock | 801,150 | 231,240 | 7,740 | 12,270 | Shackelford | 2,200 | 1,360 | 90 | 40 |
| Lynn | 1,120 | 230 | 20 | 10 | Shelby | 33,810 | 7,170 | 450 | 490 |
| Madison | 12,680 | 2,650 | 140 | 310 | Sherman | 6,160 | 470 | 30 | 20 |
| Marion | 7,230 | 1,670 | 100 | 100 | Smith | 370,960 | 80,080 | 3,530 | 5,660 |
| Martin | 22,420 | 2,220 | 140 | 40 | Somervell | 15,640 | 3,480 | 150 | 350 |
| Mason | 2,860 | 670 | 60 | 50 | Starr | 27,820 | 5,130 | 240 | 430 |
| Matagorda | 52,740 | 17,200 | 860 | 1,320 | Stephens | 6,670 | 1,600 | 80 | 110 |
| Maverick* | 61,520 | 13,190 | 600 | 1,260 | Sterling | 2,600 | 180 | 10 | 10 |
| McCulloch | 17,940 | 2,230 | 160 | 270 | Stonewall | 960 | 230 | 20 | 10 |
| McLennan | 510,660 | 109,620 | 5,160 | 7,520 | Sutton | 11,660 | 2,960 | 210 | 420 |
| McMullen* | 2,960 | 760 | 40 | 0 | Swisher | 3,850 | 800 | 40 | 30 |
| Medina | 45,500 | 7,530 | 340 | 400 | Tarrant | 7,201,710 | 3,012,440 | 65,350 | 111,420 |
| Menard | 3,060 | 330 | 20 | 20 | Taylor | 434,260 | 80,480 | 3,640 | 7,620 |
| Midland | 592,900 | 101,210 | 3,900 | 10,430 | Terrell | 1,090 | 190 | 10 | 0 |
| Milam | 31,780 | 6,900 | 310 | 380 | Terry | 14,050 | 3,980 | 250 | 360 |
| Mills | 2,860 | 440 | 20 | 20 | Throckmrton | 3,910 | 180 | 10 | 0 |
| Mitchell | 9,530 | 1,710 | 60 | 140 | Titus | 57,600 | 10,240 | 490 | 770 |
| Montague | 20,330 | 4,850 | 330 | 340 | Tom Green | 282,290 | 75,010 | 3,660 | 5,090 |
| Montgomery | 570,380 | 243,770 | 6,170 | 13,840 | Travis | 5,268,500 | 1,330,000 | 44,550 | 126,820 |
| Moore | 44,200 | 6,590 | 400 | 860 | Trinity | 10,950 | 5,180 | 220 | 140 |
| Morris | 5,360 | 850 | 40 | 40 | Tyler | 10,690 | 2,350 | 150 | 140 |
| Motley | 740 | 90 | 10 | 0 | Upshur | 22,860 | 3,010 | 150 | 170 |
| Nacgdoches | 76,750 | 18,960 | 1,050 | 1,510 | Upton | 3,100 | 740 | 50 | 70 |
| Navarro | 48,340 | 11,010 | 560 | 770 | Uvalde | 75,810 | 14,450 | 700 | 1,500 |
| Newton | 4,730 | 650 | 30 | 40 | Val Verde | 53,000 | 14,360 | 630 | 1,050 |
| Nolan | 26,560 | 8,060 | 390 | 870 | Van Zandt | 52,220 | 8,860 | 410 | 480 |
| Nueces | 1,136,110 | 316,350 | 13,370 | 29,510 | Victoria | 221,810 | 42,600 | 1,670 | 3,740 |
| Ochiltree | 31,810 | 6,140 | 370 | 910 | Walker | 106,110 | 21,130 | 1,110 | 1,340 |
| Oldham | 10,810 | 970 | 60 | 50 | Waller | 53,150 | 8,180 | 220 | 620 |
| Orange | 119,290 | 24,450 | 1,100 | 1,420 | Ward | 25,000 | 7,610 | 440 | 710 |
| Palo Pinto | 80,010 | 13,310 | 600 | 640 | Washington | 101,740 | 15,580 | 700 | 1,100 |
| Panola | 18,510 | 3,470 | 190 | 440 | Webb* | 597,720 | 141,890 | 5,840 | 9,720 |
| Parker | 126,620 | 25,470 | 820 | 1,350 | Wharton | 34,830 | 8,790 | 460 | 620 |
| Parmer | 5,480 | 650 | 30 | 40 | Wheeler | 29,260 | 5,320 | 310 | 550 |
| Pecos | 55,020 | 7,420 | 510 | 1,420 | Wichita | 227,530 | 51,600 | 3,130 | 4,170 |
| Polk | 56,400 | 15,220 | 710 | 630 | Wilbarger | 26,680 | 6,230 | 330 | 590 |
| Potter | 817,450 | 159,740 | 7,540 | 16,100 | Willacy | 26,290 | 3,620 | 150 | 190 |
| Presidio | 10,270 | 1,900 | 60 | 290 | Williamson | 550,340 | 132,680 | 4,700 | 11,210 |
| Rains | 7,990 | 2,330 | 90 | 80 | Wilson* | 39,830 | 8,480 | 370 | 640 |
| Randall | 117,580 | 20,360 | 1,080 | 1,270 | Winkler | 6,030 | 950 | 60 | 90 |
| Reagan | 5,920 | 1,510 | 100 | 20 | Wise | 62,860 | 17,520 | 890 | 1,060 |
| Real | 5,900 | 1,810 | 70 | 60 | Wood | 26,890 | 7,550 | 340 | 240 |
| Red River | 4,940 | 1,150 | 40 | 40 | Yoakum | 5,100 | 1,030 | 60 | 70 |
| Reeves | 84,090 | 15,600 | 1,060 | 2,520 | Young | 28,020 | 8,000 | 380 | 440 |
| Refugio | 25,420 | 2,450 | 120 | 200 | Zapata | 15,200 | 2,700 | 160 | 110 |
| Roberts | 1,190 | 30 | 0 | 0 | Zavala* | 14,730 | 2,510 | 120 | 340 |

*Oil and gas production in recent years may affect travel impact estimates.*

# Telecommunications Trends to High-Speed, Wireless

The chart below shows the move to wireless communications, and the decline in the number of telephone land lines in Texas and nationwide. The chart also shows the growth of high-speed Internet use in the state and in the United States. Sources: *Trends in Telephone Service, Federal Communications Commission, December 2013.*

| | 2000 | 2005 | 2007 | 2009 | 2011 | 2013 |
|---|---|---|---|---|---|---|
| **Mobile Wireless Telephone Subscribers (in thousands)** | | | | | | |
| Texas | 6,705 | 14,424 | 18,792 | 21,008 | 23,482 | 25,481 |
| U.S. | 90,643 | 192,053 | 238,230 | 261,284 | 290,304 | 310,691 |
| **Local Telephone Lines** | | | | | | |
| Texas | 13,657,444 | 10,945,498 | 9,692,891 | 8,948,577 | 7,046,000 | 5,160,000 |
| U.S. | 188,499,586 | 157,041,487 | 135,121,037 | 122,596,593 | 92,958,000 | 75,082,000 |
| **Internet Connections (in thousands)** | | | | | | |
| Texas | 253 | 2,943 | 6,856 | 7,484 | 17,487 | 23,612 |
| U.S. | 4,107 | 42,518 | 100,922 | 102,043 | 206,124 | 275,608 |

*Tablets and other handheld devices are an increasing part of everyday life. Photo by Mk2010 (CC).*

## Internet Lines by Technology as of June 2013 (in thousands)

| | DSL | Cable Modem | Fiber | Satellite | Fixed Wireless | Mobile Wireless | Total |
|---|---|---|---|---|---|---|---|
| Texas | 3,099 | 2,962 | 490 | * | 91 | 16,710 | 23,612 |
| U.S. | 31,009 | 52,760 | 7,261 | 1,623 | 810 | 181,365 | 275,608 |

*\* Data withheld to maintain firm confidentiality.*

## Type of Computer in Household: 2013 (in thousands)

| | Household with computer | | Desktop or laptop | Handheld | Internet connection | |
|---|---|---|---|---|---|---|
| | Total | Percent | Percent | Percent | Total | Broadband |
| Texas | 7,635 | 83.8 | NA | NA | 72.3 | 71.4 |
| South | 43,399 | 82.2 | 76.0 | 63.2 | 71.7 | 70.7 |
| U.S | 116,291 | 83.8 | 78.5 | 63.6 | 74.4 | 73.4 |

*Source: U.S. Census Bureau, June 2014 and Proximityone.com.*
*'Handheld computers (tablets), smartphones or other handheld wireless computers.*

# Texas Electric Grids: Demand and Capacity

- The Electric Reliability Council of Texas (**ERCOT**) operates the electric grid for 75 percent of the state.
- The Panhandle, South Plains and a small corner of Northeast Texas are under the Southwest Power Pool (**SPP**).
- El Paso and the far western corner of the Trans Pecos are under the Western Electric Coordinating Council (**WECC**).
- The southeast corner of Texas is under the **SERC** Reliability Corporation.

The councils were first formed in 1968 to ensure adequate bulk power supply.

| | **Actual** (in megawatts) | | | | | **Projections** | | | |
|---|---|---|---|---|---|---|---|---|---|
| | **2006** | **2008** | **2010** | **2011** | **2012** | **2013** | **2014** | **2015** | **2016** |
| **ERCOT** demand | 61,214 | 61,049 | 62,378 | 68,416 | 66,548 | 65,901 | 67,592 | 69,679 | 71,613 |
| capacity | 70,664 | 74,274 | 73,857 | 69,595 | 73,219 | 72,681 | 75,182 | 76,010 | 77,220 |
| % margin* | 13.4 | 17.8 | 12.8 | 1.7 | 9.1 | 9.3 | 10.7 | 8.3 | 7.3 |
| **SPP** demand | 41,982 | 42,906 | 51,942 | 54,991 | 53,177 | 53,177 | 54,080 | 54,722 | 55,433 |
| capacity | 45,831 | 48,110 | 63,337 | 62,044 | 72,802 | 73,337 | 72,768 | 73,071 | 72,924 |
| % margin | 8.4 | 10.8 | 18.0 | 11.4 | 27.0 | 27.5 | 25.7 | 25.1 | 24.0 |
| **WECC** demand | 139,402 | 130,916 | 126,944 | 117,755 | 130,465 | 129,278 | 128,200 | 129,553 | 133,150 |
| capacity | 162,288 | 167,860 | 158,407 | 147,147 | 147,527 | 155,044 | 172,443 | 174,960 | 175,673 |
| % margin | 14.1 | 22.0 | 19.9 | 20.0 | 11.6 | 16.6 | 25.7 | 26.0 | 24.2 |
| **SERC** demand | 196,196 | 196,711 | 160,896 | 161,995 | 158,041 | 152,949 | 152,843 | 157,287 | 159,684 |
| capacity | 223,630 | 228,169 | 200,511 | 201,103 | 198,140 | 196,660 | 197,116 | 194,447 | 194,830 |
| % margin | 12.3 | 13.8 | 19.8 | 19.4 | 20.2 | 22.2 | 22.5 | 19.1 | 18.0 |
| **U.S.** demand | 776,479 | 744,151 | 747,836 | 759,642 | 768,943 | 744,851 | 748,499 | 762,336 | 776,343 |
| capacity | 891,226 | 909,504 | 924,922 | 892,426 | 927,060 | 908,348 | 933,830 | 924,848 | 925,736 |
| % margin | 12.9 | 18.2 | 19.1 | 14.9 | 17.1 | 18.0 | 19.8 | 17.6 | 16.1 |

*Capacity Margin is the amount of unused available capability of an electric power system at **summer peak** load as a percentage of capacity resources. Source: Federal Energy Information Administration, Annual Report 2013.*

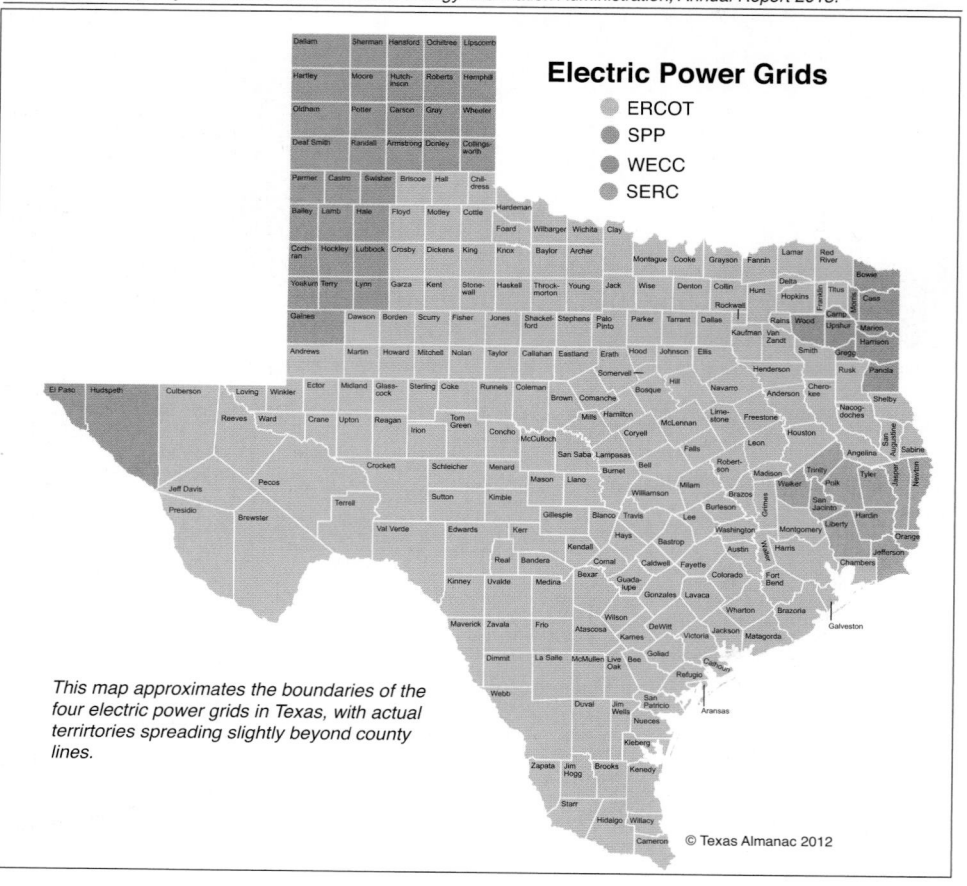

**Electric Power Grids**

- ERCOT
- SPP
- WECC
- SERC

*This map approximates the boundaries of the four electric power grids in Texas, with actual territories spreading slightly beyond county lines.*

© Texas Almanac 2012

*The Panther Creek wind farm in Howard County. Photo © 2014 Larry D. Moore (CC).*

# Wind Energy Continues Expansion in State

*Source: U.S. Energy Information Administration, 2015.*

Texas continues to lead the nation in installed wind capacity and generation. In 2015, Texas had 21 percent of the nation's installed wind capacity, reaching 14,208 megawatts. California was second in installed wind capacity, at 5,829 megawatts.

With Texas' significant increase, wind generation was responsible for 7.0 percent of total electricity generation in the state in 2010, and dipping slightly to 6.9 in 2011.

By the middle of 2015, U.S. installed wind capacity had grown to 66,008 MW.

The Texas plains continues to see rapid growth in wind farms, while more recently expansion has began offshore on the Gulf Coast. In all, Texas has six of the ten largest wind generation projects in the country. Roscoe Wind Farm, which stretches across Nolan, Mitchell, Scurry and Fisher counties, is the largest in the state, with a capacity of 782 MW. It is second in the nation to Alta Wind farm in California at 981 MW. ☆

| Installed Wind Capacity in megawatts (MW) | | |
|---|---|---|
| YEAR | Texas | U.S. |
| 2015 | 14,208 | 66,008 |
| 2014 | 14,098 | 65,879 |
| 2013 | 12,354 | 61,110 |
| 2012 | 10,648 | 49,802 |
| 2011 | 10,394 | 46,919 |
| 2010 | 10,089 | 40,267 |
| 2009 | 9,403 | 34,863 |
| 2008 | 7,427 | 24,651 |
| 2007 | 4,296 | 16,596 |
| 2005 | 1,995 | 9,149 |
| 2000 | 181 | 2,566 |
| *Source: U.S. Department of Energy.* | | |

## 2013 Renewable Energy as Portion of Net Generation of Electricity

[in thousand megawatthours.]

| State | Total All | Total Renewable | % Renewable | Hydroelectric | Wind |
|---|---|---|---|---|---|
| 1. Washington | 113,321 | 86,658 | 76.5 | 78,155 | 7,004 |
| 2. California | 199,998 | 61,105 | 30.6 | 23,755 | 12,822 |
| 3. Oregon | 60,165 | 41,984 | 69.8 | 33,098 | 7,456 |
| 4. Texas | 433,526 | 38,970 | 9.0 | 480 | 35,874 |
| 5. New York | 135,337 | 31,006 | 22.9 | 24,973 | 3,539 |
| 6. Iowa | 56,876 | 16.398 | 28.8 | 749 | 15,568 |
| United States | 4,058,209 | 522,464 | 12.9 | 268,565 | 167,840 |
| *No data reported. Source: Energy Information Administration, 2015.* | | | | | |

# Texas Oil Production History

The table shows the year of oil or gas discovery in each county, oil production in 2013 and 2014 and total oil production from date of discovery to Jan. 1, 2015. **The 16 counties omitted have not produced oil.**

The table has been compiled by the Texas Almanac from information provided in past years by the Texas Mid-Continent Oil & Gas Assoc., which used data from the U.S. Bureau of Mines and the Texas state comptroller. Since 1970, production figures have been compiled from records of the Railroad Commission of Texas. The figures in the final column are cumulative of all previously published figures. The change in sources, due to different techniques, may create some discrepancies in year-to-year comparisons among counties.

| County | Year of Discovery | Production in Barrels* 2013 | Production in Barrels* 2014 | Total Production to Jan. 1, 2015 | County | Year of Discovery | Production in Barrels* 2013 | Production in Barrels* 2014 | Total Production to Jan. 1, 2015 |
|---|---|---|---|---|---|---|---|---|---|
| Anderson | 1928 | 688,127 | 708,244 | 306,933,824 | Crockett | 1925 | 8,497,552 | 11,368,854 | 423,695,438 |
| Andrews | 1929 | 34,310,461 | 36,855,424 | 3,057,943,158 | Crosby | 1955 | 1,102,095 | 1,566,518 | 32,059,129 |
| Angelina | 1936 | 6,414 | 4,919 | 981,069 | Culberson | 1953 | 2,403,955 | 5,396,186 | 34,151,117 |
| Aransas | 1936 | 206,947 | 315,041 | 88,291,990 | Dallas | 1986 | 0 | 0 | 232 |
| Archer | 1911 | 1,269,023 | 1,306,487 | 505,121,557 | Dawson | 1934 | 4,157,370 | 4,122,858 | 420,106,947 |
| Atascosa | 1917 | 13,234,122 | 22,995,897 | 198,865,628 | Delta | 1984 | 0 | 0 | 65,089 |
| Austin | 1915 | 569,098 | 562,598 | 119,843,913 | Denton | 1937 | 415,357 | 453,075 | 10,881,558 |
| Bandera | 1995 | 867 | 1,759 | 37,754 | DeWitt | 1930 | 47,962,502 | 69,059,203 | 221,509,988 |
| Bastrop | 1913 | 138,507 | 113,517 | 18,342,783 | Dickens | 1953 | 679,666 | 646,172 | 27,658,765 |
| Baylor | 1924 | 128,155 | 157,584 | 59,084,084 | Dimmit | 1943 | 43,125,185 | 58,120,033 | 241,517,546 |
| Bee | 1929 | 540,633 | 601,585 | 113,173,664 | Donley | 1967 | 163 | 70 | 2,498 |
| Bell | 1980 | 0 | 0 | 446 | Duval | 1905 | 1,117,126 | 1,141,166 | 598,085,462 |
| Bexar | 1889 | 125,446 | 119,014 | 37,006,082 | Eastland | 1917 | 257,897 | 236,154 | 159,473,682 |
| Borden | 1949 | 3,774,148 | 3,621,556 | 441,851,810 | Ector | 1926 | 28,691,614 | 29,883,436 | 3,310,799,564 |
| Bosque | 2006 | 0 | 0 | 309 | Edwards | 1946 | 2,966 | 1,721 | 599,620 |
| Bowie | 1944 | 56,432 | 56,329 | 7,049,274 | Ellis | 1953 | 392 | 424 | 843,915 |
| Brazoria | 1902 | 3,368,787 | 3,445,226 | 1,297,013,377 | Erath | 1917 | 9,773 | 8,448 | 2,273,766 |
| Brazos | 1942 | 4,546,852 | 5,173,351 | 161,725,179 | Falls | 1937 | 5,650 | 3,225 | 886,720 |
| Brewster | 1969 | 0 | 0 | 56 | Fannin | 1980 | 0 | 0 | 13,354 |
| Briscoe | 1982 | 19 | 0 | 4,065 | Fayette | 1943 | 3,036,574 | 4,018,901 | 169,230,925 |
| Brooks | 1935 | 780,014 | 1,135,620 | 180,198,429 | Fisher | 1928 | 932,633 | 1,060,028 | 256,037,742 |
| Brown | 1917 | 126,930 | 138,795 | 54,486,347 | Floyd | 1952 | 1,006 | 98,441 | 267,504 |
| Burleson | 1938 | 1,769,893 | 3,314,617 | 212,898,934 | Foard | 1929 | 109,584 | 98,441 | 25,099,774 |
| Caldwell | 1922 | 1,721,908 | 1,558,221 | 293,473,184 | Fort Bend | 1919 | 1,775,294 | 1,720,574 | 709,505,118 |
| Calhoun | 1935 | 295,017 | 293,282 | 107,798,873 | Franklin | 1936 | 686,168 | 605,196 | 181,250,679 |
| Callahan | 1923 | 181,943 | 163,112 | 87,946,197 | Freestone | 1916 | 125,357 | 117,250 | 46,923,858 |
| Cameron | 1944 | 501 | 389 | 477,705 | Frio | 1934 | 3,832,645 | 5,252,130 | 162,943,312 |
| Camp | 1940 | 25 | 179,935 | 30,871,507 | Gaines | 1935 | 23,704,999 | 24,048,613 | 2,427,174,847 |
| Carson | 1921 | 1,225,315 | 208,781 | 183,439,591 | Galveston | 1922 | 517,975 | 533,089 | 463,422,492 |
| Cass | 1936 | 305,514 | 356,891 | 117,057,564 | Garza | 1926 | 2,892,566 | 2,822,346 | 368,094,068 |
| Chambers | 1916 | 3,236,972 | 3,760,314 | 924,593,147 | Glasscock | 1925 | 19,494,423 | 22,859,958 | 349,182,458 |
| Cherokee | 1926 | 411,309 | 487,554 | 73,895,199 | Goliad | 1930 | 335,680 | 327,842 | 88,147,279 |
| Childress | 1961 | 10,543 | 10,860 | 1,778,737 | Gonzales | 1902 | 42,329,668 | 46,252,698 | 164,708,946 |
| Clay | 1917 | 531,294 | 538,212 | 209,975,437 | Gray | 1925 | 1,047,068 | 1,022,387 | 683,354,828 |
| Cochran | 1936 | 3,337,469 | 3,302,086 | 539,365,262 | Grayson | 1930 | 1,708,288 | 1,826,965 | 269,119,753 |
| Coke | 1942 | 724,154 | 710,389 | 229,471,678 | Gregg | 1931 | 2,452,122 | 2,498,643 | 3,311,591,071 |
| Coleman | 1902 | 298,401 | 316,368 | 97,441,402 | Grimes | 1952 | 1,214,517 | 1,131,360 | 23,283,439 |
| Collin | 1963 | 0 | 0 | 53,000 | Guadalupe | 1922 | 966,636 | 891,176 | 214,653,857 |
| Collingswrth | 1936 | 14,541 | 8,504 | 1,283,004 | Hale | 1946 | 1,702,868 | 1,547,789 | 199,061,433 |
| Colorado | 1932 | 463,991 | 611,689 | 45,657,136 | Hamilton | 1938 | 1,435 | 355 | 163,109 |
| Comanche | 1918 | 41,958 | 66,199 | 6,185,153 | Hansford | 1937 | 222,633 | 216,232 | 41,310,431 |
| Concho | 1940 | 309,895 | 312,072 | 29,629,764 | Hardeman | 1944 | 887,202 | 815,787 | 92,949,441 |
| Cooke | 1924 | 2,717,224 | 2,131,492 | 412,949,186 | Hardin | 1893 | 1,801,224 | 1,587,258 | 457,552,012 |
| Coryell | 1964 | 0 | 0 | 1,100 | Harris | 1905 | 1,438,607 | 1,385,423 | 1,390,766,278 |
| Cottle | 1955 | 139,503 | 137,305 | 5,917,978 | Harrison | 1928 | 1,043,131 | 1,237,418 | 100,540,568 |
| Crane | 1926 | 10,180,974 | 10,461,720 | 1,836,601,473 | | | | | |

*Total includes condensate production.*

| County | Year of Discovery | Production in Barrels* 2013 | 2014 | Total Production to Jan. 1, 2015 |
|---|---|---|---|---|
| Hartley | 1937 | 356,434 | 402,400 | 10,150,412 |
| Haskell | 1929 | 515,076 | 604,519 | 120,499,083 |
| Hays | 1956 | 0 | 0 | 296 |
| Hemphill | 1955 | 4,228,560 | 3,965,037 | 59,257,550 |
| Henderson | 1934 | 259,998 | 385,073 | 180,962,495 |
| Hidalgo | 1934 | 1,476,034 | 1,539,136 | 132,526,134 |
| Hill | 1929 | 45 | 4 | 80,654 |
| Hockley | 1937 | 14,910,683 | 14,456,057 | 1,802,343,799 |
| Hood | 1958 | 164,956 | 144,927 | 2,516,171 |
| Hopkins | 1936 | 228,279 | 235,951 | 92,069,821 |
| Houston | 1934 | 1,531,191 | 10,063,660 | 74,148,576 |
| Howard | 1925 | 11,916,125 | 13,918,116 | 885,915,062 |
| Hudspeth | 2008 | 0 | 0 | 59 |
| Hunt | 1942 | 123 | 196 | 2,024,979 |
| Hutchinson | 1923 | 729,205 | 675,381 | 538,281,977 |
| Irion | 1928 | 10,651,499 | 15,501,559 | 145,838,548 |
| Jack | 1923 | 1,534,439 | 1,994,715 | 214,353,224 |
| Jackson | 1934 | 980,199 | 912,385 | 691,308,554 |
| Jasper | 1928 | 771,149 | 1,122,315 | 41,895,182 |
| Jeff Davis | 1980 | 0 | 0 | 20,866 |
| Jefferson | 1901 | 2,584,930 | 2,178,442 | 572,089,492 |
| Jim Hogg | 1921 | 90,778 | 89,426 | 114,023,384 |
| Jim Wells | 1931 | 144,917 | 119,319 | 464,138,036 |
| Johnson | 1962 | 22,745 | 23,065 | 498,608 |
| Jones | 1926 | 689,154 | 669,480 | 227,756,234 |
| Karnes | 1930 | 76,778,246 | 103,223,651 | 348,100,366 |
| Kaufman | 1948 | 97,333 | 87,918 | 25,391,526 |
| Kenedy | 1947 | 161,208 | 305,625 | 41,761,864 |
| Kent | 1946 | 3,947,231 | 3,802,030 | 611,342,684 |
| Kerr | 1982 | 0 | 0 | 78,946 |
| Kimble | 1939 | 264 | 284 | 101,033 |
| King | 1943 | 1,303,688 | 1,369,629 | 193,413,686 |
| Kinney | 1960 | 0 | 0 | 402 |
| Kleberg | 1919 | 427,621 | 646,849 | 340,827,632 |
| Knox | 1946 | 282,032 | 194,737 | 64,248,415 |
| Lamb | 1945 | 336,519 | 345,019 | 42,808,170 |
| Lampasas | 1985 | 0 | 0 | 111 |
| La Salle | 1940 | 49,747,975 | 71,215,846 | 179,839,798 |
| Lavaca | 1941 | 4,364,983 | 6,835,325 | 48,242,196 |
| Lee | 1939 | 1,182,868 | 1,635,292 | 146,356,065 |
| Leon | 1936 | 2,045,944 | 2,026,782 | 74,013,333 |
| Liberty | 1904 | 1,898,700 | 1,664,925 | 556,661,609 |
| Limestone | 1920 | 128,856 | 47,052 | 120,893,829 |
| Lipscomb | 1956 | 4,388,943 | 4,267,758 | 83,423,187 |
| Live Oak | 1930 | 15,229,114 | 21,283,629 | 138,267,405 |
| Llano | 1978 | 0 | 0 | 647 |
| Loving | 1921 | 7,474,171 | 13,439,506 | 144,488,545 |
| Lubbock | 1941 | 1,379,997 | 1,302,766 | 82,890,383 |
| Lynn | 1950 | 710,160 | 514,878 | 22,675,120 |
| Madison | 1946 | 4,211,556 | 4,304,656 | 49,300,960 |
| Marion | 1910 | 160,392 | 196,191 | 57,358,538 |
| Martin | 1945 | 27,737,617 | 33,299,143 | 454,939,818 |
| Matagorda | 1901 | 664,142 | 599,534 | 289,869,015 |
| Maverick | 1929 | 1,071,537 | 1,016,136 | 64,513,475 |
| McCulloch | 1938 | 47,500 | 52,832 | 2,429,695 |
| McLennan | 1902 | 821 | 414 | 347,885 |
| McMullen | 1922 | 31,521,619 | 47,129,924 | 207,264,674 |
| Medina | 1901 | 150,876 | 174,972 | 11,818,315 |
| Menard | 1946 | 192,336 | 156,179 | 8,818,778 |
| Midland | 1945 | 24,500,002 | 32,960,578 | 785,994,204 |
| Milam | 1921 | 684,823 | 631,878 | 25,533,086 |
| Mills | 1982 | 0 | 0 | 28,122 |
| Mitchell | 1920 | 4,239,247 | 3,811,332 | 261,445,703 |
| Montague | 1919 | 30,606,367 | 4,699,035 | 345,640,896 |
| Montgomery | 1931 | 1,029,590 | 1,057,451 | 785,600,843 |
| Moore | 1926 | 291,948 | 261,854 | 32,747,089 |
| Morris | 2004 | 1,292 | 1,283 | 18,474 |
| Motley | 1957 | 18,658 | 27,307 | 11,278,091 |
| Nacgdoches | 1866 | 144,800 | 128,059 | 6,962,910 |
| Navarro | 1894 | 323,756 | 339,310 | 221,750,126 |
| Newton | 1937 | 843,243 | 701,823 | 70,893,324 |
| Nolan | 1939 | 1,803,939 | 1,860,314 | 211,945,908 |
| Nueces | 1930 | 783,571 | 650,323 | 572,896,388 |
| Ochiltree | 1951 | 7,190,752 | 8,230,765 | 193,175,216 |
| Oldham | 1957 | 2,046,003 | 953,975 | 18,510,532 |
| Orange | 1913 | 1,273,883 | 1,172,430 | 168,129,528 |
| Palo Pinto | 1902 | 545,242 | 550,200 | 27,626,338 |
| Panola | 1917 | 2,197,751 | 2,188,566 | 114,466,034 |
| Parker | 1942 | 235,887 | 175,654 | 5,210,372 |
| Parmer | 1963 | 0 | 0 | 144,000 |
| Pecos | 1926 | 9,748,381 | 9,800,234 | 1,862,710,831 |
| Polk | 1930 | 1,408,572 | 1,261,365 | 138,914,684 |
| Potter | 1925 | 198,706 | 201,887 | 11,556,065 |
| Presidio | 1980 | 0 | 0 | 4,641 |
| Rains | 1955 | 0 | 0 | 148,911 |
| Reagan | 1923 | 15,240,034 | 23,109,852 | 596,670,210 |
| Real | 2003 | 353 | 918 | 28,894 |
| Red River | 1951 | 114,003 | 106,341 | 8,981,025 |
| Reeves | 1939 | 11,326,792 | 24,286,882 | 126,973,962 |
| Refugio | 1920 | 3,396,175 | 3,211,016 | 1,357,066,442 |
| Roberts | 1945 | 3,698,856 | 4,306,988 | 64,831,378 |
| Robertson | 1944 | 2,228,081 | 1,726,598 | 39,178,467 |
| Runnels | 1927 | 543,306 | 491,839 | 152,513,069 |
| Rusk | 1930 | 2,908,515 | 2,864,902 | 1,856,162,190 |
| Sabine | 1981 | 5,724 | 2,620 | 4,965,392 |
| S.Augustine | 1947 | 208,745 | 99,393 | 3,235,326 |
| San Jacinto | 1940 | 344,292 | 263,300 | 29,252,986 |
| SanPatricio | 1930 | 977,712 | 894,110 | 495,444,405 |
| San Saba | 1982 | 0 | 0 | 499,480 |
| Schleicher | 1934 | 493,330 | 496,714 | 92,587,586 |
| Scurry | 1923 | 15,574,371 | 16,905,131 | 2,185,155,616 |
| Shackelford | 1910 | 623,701 | 579,806 | 188,851,863 |
| Shelby | 1917 | 128,606 | 117,085 | 5,777,576 |
| Sherman | 1938 | 66,951 | 63,214 | 10,054,525 |
| Smith | 1931 | 1,418,232 | 1,521,542 | 278,848,254 |
| Somervell | 1978 | 6,340 | 4,927 | 80,812 |
| Starr | 1929 | 1,376,891 | 1,251,607 | 313,737,887 |
| Stephens | 1916 | 2,204,807 | 2,332,003 | 361,647,072 |
| Sterling | 1947 | 1,287,103 | 1,427,245 | 99,569,285 |
| Stonewall | 1938 | 1,821,468 | 2,327,510 | 275,123,833 |
| Sutton | 1948 | 148,534 | 106,011 | 8,868,296 |
| Swisher | 1981 | 0 | 0 | 6 |
| Tarrant | 1969 | 32,950 | 28,724 | 305,013 |

*Total includes condensate production.

| County | Year of Discovery | Production in Barrels* 2013 | 2014 | Total Production to Jan. 1, 2015 | County | Year of Discovery | Production in Barrels* 2013 | 2014 | Total Production to Jan. 1, 2015 |
|---|---|---|---|---|---|---|---|---|---|
| Taylor | 1929 | 411,330 | 414,325 | 148,703,896 | Webb | 1921 | 15,276,960 | 16,819,846 | 214,238,349 |
| Terrell | 1952 | 61,018 | 73,302 | 10,369,020 | Wharton | 1925 | 1,747,077 | 1,953,288 | 360,508,925 |
| Terry | 1940 | 4,374,558 | 4,202,888 | 480,182,643 | Wheeler | 1910 | 15,026,157 | 10,786,522 | 157,477,203 |
| Throckmrton | 1925 | 751,488 | 1,253,780 | 228,159,738 | Wichita | 1910 | 2,085,203 | 2,130,130 | 848,940,421 |
| Titus | 1936 | 557,125 | 587,601 | 216,039,558 | Wilbarger | 1915 | 821,827 | 914,224 | 270,923,436 |
| Tom Green | 1940 | 464,516 | 422,077 | 97,432,246 | Willacy | 1936 | 401,131 | 423,627 | 120,670,773 |
| Travis | 1934 | 2,999 | 2,895 | 776,224 | Williamson | 1915 | 11,335 | 17,579 | 9,641,833 |
| Trinity | 1946 | 50,693 | 48,255 | 1,540,879 | Wilson | 1941 | 3,858,884 | 3,686,390 | 60,999,531 |
| Tyler | 1937 | 2,004,205 | 1,739,450 | 68,529,951 | Winkler | 1926 | 4,923,447 | 4,608,359 | 1,111,779,945 |
| Upshur | 1931 | 378,712 | 359,852 | 292,588,769 | Wise | 1942 | 1,448,028 | 1,463,841 | 113,104,184 |
| Upton | 1925 | 26,594,561 | 33,979,117 | 1,010,477,149 | Wood | 1940 | 3,485,987 | 3,594,234 | 1,236,111,688 |
| Uvalde | 1950 | 0 | 0 | 1,814 | Yoakum | 1936 | 21,804,321 | 21,846,778 | 2,290,138,787 |
| Val Verde | 1935 | 1,594 | 2,982 | 156,159 | Young | 1917 | 1,268,809 | 1,328,687 | 322,045,729 |
| Van Zandt | 1929 | 550,450 | 594,306 | 557,241,137 | Zapata | 1919 | 202,704 | 206,105 | 50,293,817 |
| Victoria | 1931 | 648,489 | 713,247 | 260,114,498 | Zavala | 1937 | 5,133,523 | 6,787,657 | 65,125,749 |
| Walker | 1934 | 83,568 | 72,373 | 712,543 | | | | | |
| Waller | 1934 | 420,565 | 379,638 | 34,332,875 | | | | | |
| Ward | 1928 | 21,880,112 | 23,695,047 | 867,157,422 | | | | | |
| Washington | 1915 | 574,948 | 639,256 | 35,966,282 | | | | | |

Source: Railroad Commission, 2013–14 production reports.

*Total includes condensate production.

# Rig Counts and Wells Drilled by Year

| Year | Rotary rigs active* Texas | U.S. | Permits Texas | Texas wells completed Oil | Gas | Wells drilled** Texas |
|---|---|---|---|---|---|---|
| 1982 | 994 | 3,117 | 41,224 | 16,296 | 6,273 | 27,648 |
| 1985 | 680 | 1,980 | 30,878 | 16,543 | 4,605 | 27,124 |
| 1990 | 348 | 1,009 | 14,033 | 5,593 | 2,894 | 11,231 |
| 1991 | 315 | 860 | 12,494 | 6,025 | 2,755 | 11,295 |
| 1992 | 251 | 721 | 12,089 | 5,031 | 2,537 | 9,498 |
| 1993 | 264 | 754 | 11,612 | 4,646 | 3,295 | 9,969 |
| 1994 | 274 | 775 | 11,030 | 3,962 | 3,553 | 9,299 |
| 1995 | 251 | 723 | 11,244 | 4,334 | 3,778 | 9,785 |
| 1996 | 283 | 779 | 12,669 | 4,061 | 4,060 | 9,747 |
| 1997 | 358 | 945 | 13,933 | 4,482 | 4,594 | 10,778 |
| 1998 | 303 | 827 | 9,385 | 4,509 | 4,907 | 11,057 |
| 1999 | 226 | 622 | 8,430 | 2,049 | 3,566 | 6,658 |
| 2000 | 343 | 918 | 12,021 | 3,111 | 4,580 | 8,854 |
| 2001 | 462 | 1,156 | 12,227 | 3,082 | 5,787 | 10,005 |
| 2002 | 338 | 830 | 9,716 | 3,268 | 5,474 | 9,877 |
| 2003 | 449 | 1,032 | 12,664 | 3,111 | 6,336 | 10,420 |
| 2004 | 506 | 1,192 | 14,700 | 3,446 | 7,118 | 11,587 |
| 2005 | 614 | 1,381 | 16,914 | 3,454 | 7,197 | 11,154 |
| 2006 | 746 | 1,649 | 18,952 | 4,761 | 8,534 | 12,764 |
| 2007 | 834 | 1,769 | 19,994 | 5,084 | 8,643 | 13,778 |
| 2008 | 898 | 1,880 | 24,073 | 6,208 | 10,361 | 16,615 |
| 2009 | 432 | 1,086 | 12,212 | 5,860 | 8,706 | 14,585 |
| 2010 | 659 | 1,541 | 18,029 | 5,392 | 4,071 | 9,477 |
| 2011 | 838 | 1,875 | 22,480 | 5,380 | 3,008 | 8,391 |
| 2012 | 899 | 1,919 | 22,479 | 10,936 | 3,580 | 14,535 |
| 2013 | 835 | 1,761 | 21,471 | 19,249 | 4,917 | 24,166 |
| 2014 | 882 | 1,862 | 25,792 | 24,999 | 3,585 | 28,585 |

Texas Railroad Commission. *Source for rig count: Baker Hughes Inc. This is an annual average from monthly reports.
†Totals shown for 1988 and after are number of drilling permits issued; data for previous years were total drilling applications received.
**Wells drilled are oil and gas well **completions and dry holes** drilled/plugged.

# Top Oil Producing Counties since Discovery

There are 35 counties that have produced more than 500 million barrels of oil since discovery. The counties are ranked below. The column at right lists the number of regurlar producing oil wells in the county in February 2015.

| Rank | County | Barrels | Oil Wells | Rank | County | Barrels | Oil Wells |
|------|--------|---------|-----------|------|--------|---------|-----------|
| 1. | Gregg | 3,311,591,071 | 3,059 | 19. | Ward | 867,157,422 | 3,619 |
| 2. | Ector | 3,310,799,564 | 7,532 | 20. | Wichitia | 848,940,421 | 5,597 |
| 3. | Andrews | 3,057,943,158 | 10,671 | 21. | Midland | 785,994,204 | 6,787 |
| 4. | Gaines | 2,427,174,847 | 3,896 | 22. | Montgomery | 785,600,843 | 143 |
| 5. | Yoakum | 2,290,138,787 | 3,680 | 23. | Fort Bend | 709,505,118 | 341 |
| 6. | Scurry | 2,185,155,616 | 2,590 | 24. | Jackson | 691,308,554 | 198 |
| 7. | Pecos | 1,862,710,831 | 3,190 | 25. | Gray | 683,354,828 | 2,799 |
| 8. | Rusk | 1,856,162,190 | 1,735 | 26. | Kent | 611,342,684 | 621 |
| 9. | Crane | 1,826,601,473 | 4,535 | 27. | Duval | 598,085,462 | 687 |
| 10. | Hockley | 1,802,343,799 | 4,182 | 28. | Reagan | 596,670,210 | 5,433 |
| 11. | Harris | 1,357,066,442 | 330 | 29. | Nueces | 572,896,388 | 168 |
| 12. | Refugio | 1,357,066,442 | 686 | 30. | Jefferson | 572,089,492 | 212 |
| 13. | Brazoria | 1,297,013,377 | 271 | 31. | Van Zandt | 557,241,137 | 310 |
| 14. | Wood | 1,236,111,688 | 896 | 32. | Liberty | 556,661,609 | 624 |
| 15. | Winkler | 1,111,477,149 | 1,802 | 33. | Cochran | 539,365,262 | 1,861 |
| 16. | Upton | 1,010,477,149 | 5,457 | 34. | Hutchinson | 538,281,977 | 2,913 |
| 17. | Chambers | 924,593,147 | 184 | 35. | Archer | 505,121,557 | 3,258 |
| 18. | Howard | 885,915,062 | 4,502 | | Source: Texas Railroad Commission. | | |

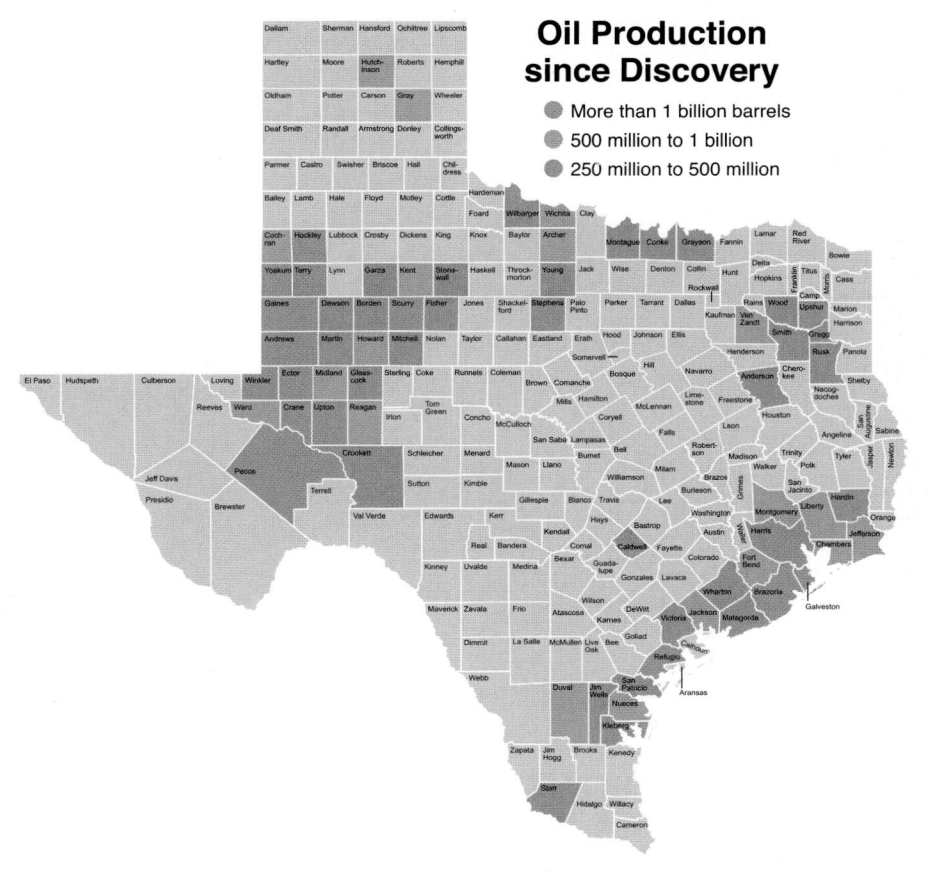

## Oil Production since Discovery

- More than 1 billion barrels
- 500 million to 1 billion
- 250 million to 500 million

# Oil and Gas Production by County, 2014

In 2014 in Texas, the total natural gas production from gas wells was 6,279,338,200 thousand cubic feet (MCF) and total crude oil production was 954,954,080 barrels (BBL). Total condensate was 144,890,378 barrels. Total casinghead production was 2,072,279,634 MCF. **Counties not listed in the chart below had no production in 2012.** *Source: Texas Railroad Commission.*

| County | Oil (BBL) | Casing-head (MCF) | GW Gas (MCF) | Conden-sate (BBL) | County | Oil (BBL) | Casing-head (MCF) | GW Gas (MCF) | Conden-sate (BBL) |
|---|---|---|---|---|---|---|---|---|---|
| Anderson | 666,737 | 1,271,158 | 2,690,356 | 41,507 | Eastland | 208,980 | 687,958 | 2,460,995 | 27,174 |
| Andrews | 36,849,734 | 57,826,670 | 641,734 | 5,690 | Ector | 29,864,923 | 68,687,859 | 3,934,909 | 18,513 |
| Angelina | 0 | 0 | 5,807,947 | 4,919 | Edwards | 1,592 | 0 | 7,607,759 | 126 |
| Aransas | 69,726 | 419,514 | 9,692,003 | 245,315 | Ellis | 424 | 0 | 5,247,775 | 0 |
| Archer | 1,306,404 | 526,509 | 9,439 | 83 | Erath | 1,061 | 13,097 | 4,438,509 | 5,387 |
| Atascosa | 22,973,574 | 19,187,479 | 2,970,029 | 22,323 | Falls | 3,225 | 0 | 0 | 0 |
| Austin | 529,975 | 201,507 | 3,131,905 | 32,623 | Fayette | 3,873,877 | 8,801,296 | 10,133,000 | 145,024 |
| Bandera | 1,759 | 0 | 22,115 | 0 | Fisher | 1,058,979 | 1,575,605 | 64,535 | 1,049 |
| Bastrop | 102,407 | 95,806 | 92,407 | 11,110 | Floyd | 927 | 0 | 0 | 0 |
| Baylor | 157,584 | 7,600 | 0 | 0 | Foard | 98441 | 12 | 94,346 | 0 |
| Bee | 331,332 | 661,541 | 19,016,489 | 270,253 | Fort Bend | 1,591,317 | 818,221 | 8,440,416 | 129,257 |
| Bexar | 119,014 | 24 | 0 | 0 | Franklin | 569,696 | 170,322 | 1,731,489 | 35,500 |
| Borden | 3,621,556 | 2,003,091 | 0 | 0 | Freestone | 42,052 | 97,048 | 155,665,065 | 75,198 |
| Bowie | 45,060 | 18,876 | 138,568 | 11,269 | Frio | 5,197,046 | 8,794,171 | 1,763,374 | 55,084 |
| Brazoria | 3,216,585 | 2,174,978 | 9,336,192 | 228,641 | Gaines | 24,034,310 | 21,087,488 | 6,172,628 | 14,303 |
| Brazos | 5,149,059 | 6,002,660 | 1,937,827 | 24,292 | Galveston | 397,756 | 326,745 | 2,998,197 | 135,333 |
| Brooks | 250,002 | 228,829 | 31,408,365 | 885,618 | Garza | 2,822,346 | 485,984 | 0 | 0 |
| Brown | 136,835 | 345,370 | 759,833 | 1,960 | Glasscock | 22,845,110 | 89,957,577 | 945,080 | 14,848 |
| Burleson | 3,283,740 | 7,680,081 | 1,293,819 | 30,877 | Goliad | 223,933 | 301,982 | 9,783,125 | 103,909 |
| Caldwell | 1,558,221 | 331,745 | 9,736 | 0 | Gonzales | 46,247,215 | 58,564,763 | 553,406 | 5,483 |
| Calhoun | 122,544 | 224,028 | 5,077,833 | 170,738 | Gray | 1,011,028 | 2,247,694 | 6,852,200 | 11,359 |
| Callahan | 160,687 | 290,478 | 564,161 | 2,425 | Grayson | 1,812,084 | 5,154,907 | 1,829,981 | 14,881 |
| Cameron | 0 | 0 | 276,900 | 389 | Gregg | 2,3125,945 | 2,891,185 | 27,814,786 | 182,698 |
| Camp | 179,927 | 0 | 555,521 | 8 | Grimes | 1,084,520 | 3,808,963 | 8,783,802 | 46,840 |
| Carson | 202,008 | 1,232,742 | 11,596,217 | 6,773 | Guadalupe | 891,176 | 43,544 | 0 | 0 |
| Cass | 339,622 | 391,698 | 545,867 | 17,269 | Hale | 1,547,789 | 1,362,721 | 0 | 0 |
| Chambers | 3,548,372 | 1,003,152 | 5,804,202 | 211,942 | Hamilton | 269 | 0 | 97,380 | 86 |
| Cherokee | 323,124 | 740,912 | 19,233,748 | 164,430 | Hansford | 200,057 | 1,000,142 | 12,382,347 | 16,175 |
| Childress | 10,860 | 0 | 0 | 0 | Hardeman | 815,787 | 681,519 | 0 | 0 |
| Clay | 535,131 | 1,067,328 | 98,155 | 3,081 | Hardin | 1,207,991 | 1,442,734 | 5,789,692 | 379,267 |
| Cochran | 3.301,443 | 2,033,414 | 125,718 | 643 | Harris | 1,190,657 | 620,046 | 12,281,995 | 194,766 |
| Coke | 709,141 | 3,107,569 | 203,053 | 1,248 | Harrison | 412,393 | 1,454,304 | 138,173,561 | 825,025 |
| Coleman | 313,654 | 498,453 | 596,186 | 2,714 | Hartley | 402,397 | 22,163 | 1,345,443 | 3 |
| Collingswth | 8,434 | 101,454 | 1,077,423 | 70 | Haskell | 604,504 | 284,911 | 0 | 15 |
| Colorado | 144,456 | 481,241 | 15,462,621 | 467,233 | Hemphill | 1,533,846 | 9,596,775 | 141,999,482 | 2,431,191 |
| Comanche | 65,175 | 146,379 | 504,486 | 1,024 | Henderson | 359,595 | 3,935,622 | 10,409,330 | 25,478 |
| Concho | 310,940 | 156,754 | 319,844 | 1,132 | Hidalgo | 44,314 | 52,548 | 97,023,710 | 1,494,822 |
| Cooke | 1,450,231 | 2,982,784 | 21,522,398 | 681,261 | Hill | 4 | 0 | 14,934,953 | 0 |
| Cottle | 76,788 | 20,262 | 4,180,835 | 60,517 | Hockley | 14,454,126 | 7,967,918 | 68,837 | 1,931 |
| Crane | 10,406,193 | 43,298,699 | 6,299,707 | 55,527 | Hood | 152 | 3,060 | 47,792,756 | 144,775 |
| Crockett | 11,182,236 | 43,204,270 | 59,259,239 | 186,618 | Hopkins | 231,257 | 122,685 | 163,443 | 4,694 |
| Crosby | 1,566,518 | 93,255 | 0 | 0 | Houston | 951,860 | 973,924 | 7,376,004 | 544,800 |
| Culberson | 2,063,671 | 12,487,954 | 39,609,347 | 3,332,515 | Howard | 13,913,642 | 37,364,984 | 262,722 | 4,474 |
| Dallas | 0 | 0 | 10,129,427 | 0 | Hutchinson | 666,727 | 3,649,872 | 5,911,824 | 8,654 |
| Dawson | 4,122,858 | 2,255,187 | 0 | 0 | Irion | 15,473,188 | 75,577,745 | 2,431,892 | 28,371 |
| Denton | 32,303 | 576,784 | 227,451,232 | 420,772 | Jack | 1,833,811 | 22,162,014 | 11,320,554 | 160,904 |
| DeWitt | 51,710,197 | 137,768,974 | 137,687,612 | 17,349,006 | Jackson | 716,143 | 810,098 | 6,411,433 | 196,242 |
| Dickens | 646,172 | 7,600 | 0 | 0 | Jasper | 142,943 | 271,444 | 11,582,270 | 979,372 |
| Dimmit | 31,353,951 | 70,177,076 | 200,983,102 | 26,766,082 | Jefferson | 1,079,053 | 974,921 | 17,502,098 | 979,372 |
| Donley | 0 | 0 | 10,768 | 70 | Jim Hogg | 27,159 | 86,851 | 7,340,040 | 62,267 |
| Duval | 1,070,400 | 178,450 | 15,224,116 | 70,766 | Jim Wells | 107,469 | 250,624 | 3,858,661 | 11,850 |

| County | Oil (BBL) | Casing-head (MCF) | GW Gas (MCF) | Conden-sate (BBL) | County | Oil (BBL) | Casing-head (MCF) | GW Gas (MCF) | Conden-sate (BBL) |
|---|---|---|---|---|---|---|---|---|---|
| Johnson | 0 | 0 | 326,334,355 | 23,065 | Red River | 106,341 | 0 | 0 | 0 |
| Jones | 669,288 | 340,010 | 29,348 | 192 | Reeves | 23,319,833 | 54,924,005 | 29,827,283 | 967,049 |
| Karnes | 82,291,077 | 116,562,562 | 125,472,610 | 20,932,574 | Refugio | 3,133,463 | 12,406,175 | 2,938,178 | 77,553 |
| Kaufman | 87,918 | 82,895 | 0 | 0 | Roberts | 2,911,336 | 16,602,966 | 58,202,487 | 1,395,652 |
| Kenedy | 119,409 | 419,601 | 25,573,229 | 186,216 | Robertson | 1,720,069 | 914,646 | 117,890,447 | 6,529 |
| Kent | 3,802,030 | 6,987,771 | 0 | 0 | Runnels | 487,367 | 1,268,702 | 249,199 | 4,472 |
| Kimble | 284 | 0 | 27,914 | 0 | Rusk | 1,901,204 | 2,471,057 | 117,161,755 | 963,698 |
| King | 1,368,347 | 146,600 | 424,210 | 1,282 | Sabine | 2,620 | 34,626 | 1,738,421 | 0 |
| Kleberg | 266,160 | 571,950 | 15,030,062 | 380,689 | S. Augustine | 15,786 | 320,568 | 75,276,945 | 83,607 |
| Knox | 194,737 | 34,568 | 0 | 0 | San Jacinto | 81,274 | 243,328 | 4,837,643 | 182,026 |
| La Salle | 66,956,916 | 121,258,961 | 114,807,048 | 4,258,930 | San Patricio | 481,135 | 720,878 | 11,708,650 | 412,975 |
| Lamb | 345,019 | 284,606 | 0 | 0 | Schleicher | 449,384 | 3,059,038 | 7,743,470 | 47,330 |
| Lampasas | 0 | 0 | 8,875 | 0 | Scurry | 16,905,131 | 36,677,259 | 0 | 0 |
| Lavaca | 6,465,624 | 11,159,267 | 26,524,629 | 369,701 | Shackelford | 571,414 | 638,211 | 1,400,532 | 8,392 |
| Lee | 1,611,153 | 6,562,852 | 1,336,050 | 45,240 | Shelby | 46,965 | 652,977 | 83,788,219 | 70,120 |
| Leon | 1,954,988 | 2,294,238 | 61,623,486 | 71,794 | Sherman | 59,652 | 69,293 | 16,839,169 | 3,562 |
| Liberty | 1,183,032 | 875,864 | 17,695,495 | 481,893 | Smith | 1,378,200 | 1,248,949 | 16,733,011 | 143,342 |
| Limestone | 79,008 | 1,812 | 51,131,487 | 45,240 | Somervell | 0 | 0 | 5,241,779 | 4,927 |
| Lipscomb | 2,798,871 | 19,905,140 | 43,817,212 | 1,468,887 | Starr | 471,943 | 1,221,101 | 54,358,697 | 779,664 |
| Live Oak | 13,569,528 | 32,587,236 | 86,190,749 | 7,714,101 | Stephens | 2,282,261 | 3,552,397 | 10,117,463 | 49,742 |
| Loving | 11,462,799 | 38,133,997 | 43,692,425 | 1,976,707 | Sterling | 1,403,391 | 8,210,143 | 2,923,375 | 23,854 |
| Lubbock | 1,302,766 | 90,394 | 0 | 0 | Stonewall | 2,327,510 | 2,668,980 | 0 | 0 |
| Lynn | 514,878 | 196,164 | 0 | 0 | Sutton | 68,604 | 87,979 | 33,928,091 | 37,407 |
| Madison | 4,018,330 | 9,372,636 | 3,842,290 | 286,326 | Tarrant | 0 | 0 | 682,213,054 | 28,724 |
| Marion | 152,598 | 162,263 | 2,241,944 | 43,593 | Taylor | 414,322 | 130,299 | 33,736 | 3 |
| Martin | 33,298,941 | 66,651,976 | 10,275 | 202 | Terrell | 22,483 | 245,691 | 29,718,573 | 50,819 |
| Matagorda | 247,889 | 421,750 | 19,997,979 | 351,645 | Terry | 4,202,8188 | 891,776 | 57,682 | 0 |
| Maverick | 759,517 | 254,276 | 3,555,740 | 256,619 | Throckmrton | 1,250,852 | 2,585,472 | 197,476 | 2,928 |
| McCulloch | 52,832 | 0 | 0 | 0 | Titus | 587,601 | 1,472 | 0 | 0 |
| McLennan | 414 | 0 | 0 | 0 | Tom Green | 414,626 | 1,749,689 | 936,193 | 2,928 |
| McMullen | 42,213,610 | 57,800,981 | 83,788,593 | 4,916,314 | Travis | 2,895 | 0 | 0 | 0 |
| Medina | 174,972 | 874 | 20,731 | 0 | Trinity | 47,480 | 17,692 | 197,637 | 775 |
| Menard | 156,128 | 10,972 | 44,731 | 0 | Tyler | 485,877 | 285,244 | 12,775,231 | 1,253,573 |
| Midland | 32,822,528 | 85,783,531 | 6,591,235 | 138,050 | Upshur | 134,444 | 54,592 | 24,760,064 | 225,408 |
| Milam | 631,590 | 317,887 | 36,641 | 288 | Upton | 33,666,348 | 109,075,847 | 18,661,463 | 312,769 |
| Mills | 0 | 0 | 4,413 | 0 | Val Verde | 2,970 | 2,863 | 6,579,309 | 12 |
| Mitchell | 3,811,332 | 975,525 | 0 | 0 | Van Zandt | 592,060 | 283,027 | 3,700,606 | 2,246 |
| Montague | 1,804,236 | 9,698,960 | 80,824,112 | 2,894,799 | Victoria | 644,064 | 846,297 | 4,355,050 | 69,183 |
| Montgomery | 1,024,883 | 2,434,547 | 3,662,678 | 32,568 | Walker | 57,880 | 1,360,443 | 946,340 | 14,493 |
| Moore | 257,555 | 1,736,853 | 25,891,271 | 4,299 | Waller | 379,638 | 8,698 | 3,339,815 | 24,756 |
| Morris | 1,283 | 0 | 0 | 0 | Ward | 23,644,255 | 48,119,040 | 16,253,269 | 50,792 |
| Motley | 27,307 | 1,870 | 0 | 0 | Washington | 561,359 | 2,914,045 | 8,136,922 | 77,897 |
| Nacgdoches | 11,599 | 58,877 | 81,162,724 | 116,460 | Webb | 785,918 | 2,010,184 | 607,648,701 | 16,033,928 |
| Navarro | 323,601 | 544,461 | 427,544 | 15,709 | Wharton | 1,384,480 | 1,105,791 | 23,931,316 | 568,808 |
| Newton | 455,471 | 1,417,162 | 4,989,503 | 246,352 | Wheeler | 4,120,006 | 17,568,378 | 212,322,237 | 6,666,516 |
| Nolan | 1,858,453 | 2,833,468 | 308,049 | 1,861 | Wichita | 2,180,180 | 307,414 | 0 | 0 |
| Nueces | 330,886 | 707,871 | 13,707,620 | 319,437 | Wilbarger | 914,224 | 91,869 | 0 | 0 |
| Ochiltree | 7,757,665 | 32,610,987 | 16,292,703 | 473,100 | Willacy | 316,959 | 181,935 | 8,728,780 | 106,668 |
| Oldham | 953,975 | 3,488,329 | 72,010 | 0 | Williamson | 17,579 | 0 | 0 | 0 |
| Orange | 562,853 | 1,328,420 | 12,559,092 | 609,577 | Wilson | 3,686,271 | 1,429,727 | 8,937 | 119 |
| Palo Pinto | 477,079 | 8,040,609 | 10,589,185 | 73,121 | Winkler | 4,551,035 | 12,846,009 | 14,316,358 | 57,324 |
| Panola | 402,k671 | 2,580,682 | 351,499,709 | 1,785,895 | Wise | 392,131 | 7,798,981 | 258,623,853 | 1,071,710 |
| Parker | 4,032 | 218,319 | 100,754,152 | 73,121 | Wood | 3,572,340 | 52,999,000 | 2,246,083 | 21,894 |
| Pecos | 9,722,545 | 31,696,360 | 81,873,361 | 77,689 | Yoakum | 21,846,778 | 26,193,719 | 277,228 | 0 |
| Polk | 597,440 | 241,456 | 19,265,391 | 663,965 | Young | 1,303,865 | 1,643,476 | 1,200,826 | 24,822 |
| Potter | 201,869 | 205,507 | 8,588,707 | 18 | Zapata | 118,729 | 14,526 | 110,468,680 | 87,376 |
| Rains | 0 | 0 | 2,647,198 | 0 | Zavala | 6,787,621 | 4,063,278 | 410,433 | 36 |
| Reagan | 23,086,620 | 78,737,577 | 1,260,106 | 23,232 | | | | | |
| Real | 918 | 0 | 24,657 | 0 | *Source: Texas Railroad Commission.* | | | | |

# Top Gas Producing Counties, 1993–2015

The top 37 natural gas-producing counties are listed in the chart below. The fourth column at the right lists the number of producing gas wells in the county in February 2015. Sixty-one counties have produced more than 500 billion cubic feet of natural gas since 1993 (see map). (**MCF** is thousand cubic feet.)

| Rank | County | Gas (MCF) | Gas Wells | Rank | County | Gas (MCF) | Gas Wells |
|------|--------|-----------|-----------|------|--------|-----------|-----------|
| 1. | Webb | 6,868,237,241 | 5,736 | 20. | Lavaca | 1,373,054,109 | 454 |
| 2. | Zapata | 5,861,049,055 | 2,985 | 21. | Limestone | 1,372,344,607 | 1,181 |
| 3. | Panola | 5,855,105,985 | 5,269 | 22. | Terrell | 1,303,625,834 | 674 |
| 4. | Tarrant | 5,320,218,174 | 3,980 | 23. | Duval | 1,228,943,267 | 479 |
| 5. | Hidalgo | 4,766,932,810 | 1,407 | 24. | Brooks | 1,175,122,819 | 419 |
| 6. | Freestone | 3,802,171,102 | 3,068 | 25. | Gregg | 1,141,039,634 | 916 |
| 7. | Pecos | 3,774,171,449 | 1,382 | 26. | Upshur | 1,118,897,099 | 743 |
| 8. | Johnson | 3,703,128,523 | 3,231 | 27. | Wharton | 1,089,960,334 | 373 |
| 9. | Wise | 3,254,344,893 | 4,548 | 28. | Leon | 1,088,318,229 | 591 |
| 10. | Starr | 2,734,806,624 | 1,226 | 29. | Moore | 1,046,517,170 | 1,298 |
| 11. | Denton | 2,590,514,996 | 2,936 | 30. | Lipscomb | 972,052,385 | 1,341 |
| 12. | Crockett | 2,351,011,886 | 5,790 | 31. | Parker | 962,406,798 | 1,821 |
| 13. | Hemphill | 2,346,352,296 | 2,579 | 32. | Loving | 936,299,289 | 244 |
| 14. | Robertson | 2,127,442,187 | 922 | 33. | Harris | 923,309,133 | 126 |
| 15. | Harrison | 2,107,441,909 | 2,540 | 34. | DeWitt | 914,677,365 | 584 |
| 16. | Wheeler | 2,077,687,748 | 2,013 | 35. | Nueces | 905,473,703 | 648 |
| 17. | Rusk | 2,051,577,715 | 2,516 | 36. | Shelby | 890,172,076 | 684 |
| 18. | Nacogdoches | 1,469,191,394 | 1,429 | 37. | Kenedy | 874,137,921 | 169 |
| 19. | Sutton | 1,395,290,019 | 5,872 | | *Source: Texas Railroad Commission.* | | |

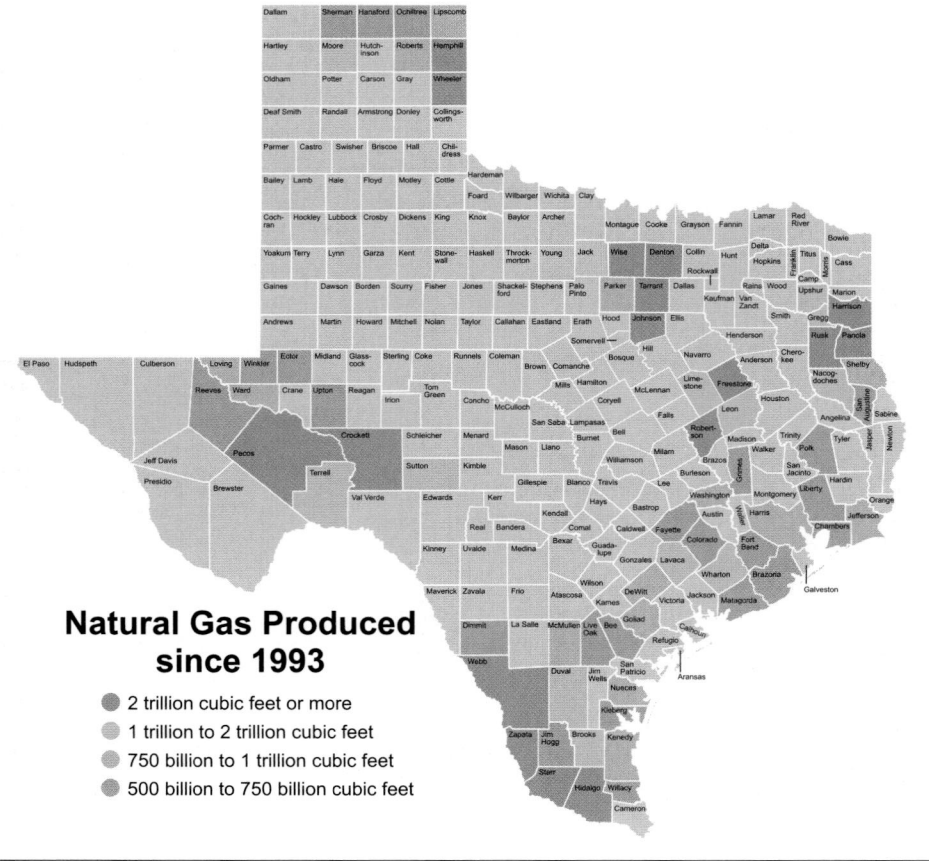

## Natural Gas Produced since 1993

- ● 2 trillion cubic feet or more
- ● 1 trillion to 2 trillion cubic feet
- ● 750 billion to 1 trillion cubic feet
- ● 500 billion to 750 billion cubic feet

# Petroleum Production and Income in Texas

| Year | Crude Oil | | | | Natural Gas | | |
|------|-----------|---|---|---|-------------|---|---|
| | Production (thousand barrels) | Value (add 000) | Average Price per barrel (nominal) | *Average price per barrel (2005 $) | Production (million cubic feet) | Value (add 000) | Wellhead Price (cents per **Mcf) |
| 1915 | 24,943 | $ 13,027 | $ 0 .52 | NA | 13,324 | $ 2,594 | 19.5 |
| 1925 | 144,648 | 262,270 | 1.81 | NA | 134,872 | 7,040 | 5.2 |
| 1935 | 392,666 | 367,820 | 0.94 | NA | 642,366 | 13,233 | 2.1 |
| 1945 | 754,710 | 914,410 | 1.21 | NA | 1,711,401 | 44,839 | 2.6 |
| 1955 | 1,053,297 | 2,989,330 | 2.84 | NA | 4,730,798 | 378,464 | 8.0 |
| 1965 | 1,000,749 | 2,962,119 | 2.96 | NA | 6,636,555 | 858,396 | 12.9 |
| 1970 | 1,249,697 | 4,104,005 | 3.28 | NA | 8,357,716 | 1,203,511 | 14.4 |
| 1975 | 1,221,929 | 9,336,570 | 7.64 | NA | 7,485,764 | 3,885,112 | 51.9 |
| 1978 | 1,074,050 | 9,980,333 | $ 9.29 | $ 23.00 | 6,548,184 | 6,515,443 | 99.5 |
| 1979 | 1,018,094 | 12,715,994 | 12.65 | 28.91 | 7,174,623 | 8,509,103 | 118.6 |
| 1980 | 977,436 | 21,259,233 | 21.84 | 47.74 | 7,115,889 | 10,673,834 | 150.0 |
| 1981 | 945,132 | 32,692,116 | 35.06 | 67.14 | 7,050,207 | 12,598,712 | 178.7 |
| 1982 | 923,868 | 29,074,126 | 31.77 | 57.33 | 6,497,678 | 13,567,151 | 208.8 |
| 1983 | 876,205 | 22,947,814 | 29.35 | 50.95 | 5,643,183 | 14,672,275 | 225.0 |
| 1984 | 874,079 | 25,138,520 | 28.87 | 48.31 | 5,864,224 | 13,487,715 | 230.0 |
| 1985 | 860,300 | 23,159,286 | 26.80 | 43.52 | 5,805,098 | 12,665,114 | 218.0 |
| 1986 | 813,620 | 11,976,488 | 14.73 | 23.40 | 5,663,491 | 8,778,410 | 155.0 |
| 1987 | 754,213 | 13,221,345 | 17.55 | 27.10 | 5,516,224 | 7,612,389 | 138.0 |
| 1988 | 727,928 | 10,729,660 | 14.71 | 21.96 | 5,702,643 | 7,983,700 | 141.0 |
| 1989 | 679,575 | 12,123,624 | 17.81 | 25.62 | 5,595,190 | 8,113,026 | 145.0 |
| 1990 | 672,081 | 15,047,902 | 22.37 | 30.98 | 5,533,771 | 8,281,372 | 149.7 |
| 1991 | 672,810 | 12,836,080 | 19.04 | 25.47 | 5,509,990 | 7,713,986 | 143.0 |
| 1992 | 642,059 | 11,820,306 | 18.32 | 23.94 | 5,436,408 | 8,643,888 | 174.0 |
| 1993 | 572,600 | 9,288,800 | 16.19 | 20.70 | 5,606,498 | 7,365,800 | 204.0 |
| 1994 | 533,900 | 7,977,500 | 14.98 | 18.76 | 5,675,748 | 6,220,300 | 185.0 |
| 1995 | 503,200 | 8,177,700 | 16.38 | 20.09 | 5,672,105 | 5,305,200 | 155.0 |
| 1996 | 478,100 | 9,560,800 | 20.31 | 24.44 | 5,770,255 | 6,945,000 | 217.0 |
| 1997 | 464,900 | 8,516,800 | 18.66 | 22.07 | 5,814,745 | 8,134,200 | 232.0 |
| 1998 | 440,600 | 5,472,400 | 12.28 | 14.36 | 5,772,080 | 6,362,900 | 196.0 |
| 1999 | 337,100 | 5,855,800 | 17.29 | 19.93 | 5,538,929 | 6,789,700 | 219.0 |
| 2000 | 348,900 | 10,037,300 | 28.60 | 32.26 | 5,645,972 | 12,837,600 | 368.0 |
| 2001 | 325,500 | 7,770,500 | 23.41 | 25.82 | 5,668,602 | 13,708,700 | 400.0 |
| 2002 | 335,600 | 8,150,400 | 23.77 | 25.80 | 5,611,958 | 9,840,800 | 295.0 |
| 2003 | 333,300 | 9,708,600 | 29.13 | 30.96 | 5,671,689 | 14,797,800 | 488.0 |
| 2004 | 327,910 | 12,762,650 | 38.79 | 40.08 | 5,817,227 | 17,077,700 | 546.0 |
| 2005 | 327,600 | 12,744,600 | 52.61 | 52.61 | 5,700,613 | 16,399,400 | 733.0 |
| 2006 | 314,600 | 19,353,500 | 61.31 | 59.38 | 6,077,786 | 23,500,800 | 639.0 |
| 2007 | 311,830 | 21,341,100 | 68.30 | 64.30 | 6,421,375 | 22,968,420 | 625.0 |
| 2008 | 315,896 | 30,409,170 | 96.85 | 89.28 | 7,271,815 | 34,415,890 | 797.0 |
| 2009 | 349,391 | 18,455,530 | 57.40 | 52.31 | 7,573,033 | 12,167,800 | 367.0 |
| 2010 | 369,953 | 26,054,900 | 76.23 | 68.88 | 7,246,042 | 11,796,700 | 448.0 |
| 2011 | 448,903 | 39,420,500 | 91.99 | 81.15 | 7,051,594 | 13,646,300 | 395.0 |
| 2012 | 607,708 | 55,145,600 | 92.50 | NA | 7,128,775 | 12,959,100 | 266.0 |
| 2013 | 749,876 | 73,666,700 | 95.80 | NA | 7,725,119 | 15,358,900 | NA |
| 2014 | 900,492 | $ 85,962,300 | $ 87.02 | NA | 8,171,230 | $ 18,034,000 | NA |

*In chained (2005) dollars, as calculated by the U.S. Energy Information Administration (EIA). (NA, not available.) **Mcf (thousand cubic feet).

Sources: Previously from the Texas Railroad Commission, Texas Mid-Continent Oil & Gas Association and, beginning in 1979, data are from Department of Energy. Data since 1993 are from the state comptroller and EIA and the railroad commission. Federal figures do not include gas that is vented or flared or used for pressure maintenance and repressuring, but do include non-hydrocarbon gases.

# Offshore Production History – Oil and Gas

The cumulative offshore natural gas production as of Jan. 1, 2015, was **4,180,771,918** thousand cubic feet (Mcf). The cumulative offshore oil production was **41,901,111** barrels.

## Production in Recent Years

| YEAR | Crude Oil BBL | Casing-head Mcf | Gas Well Gas Mcf | Conden-sate BBL |
|------|------|------|------|------|
| 2000 | 548,046 | 335,415 | 44,086,237 | 220,309 |
| 2001 | 530,261 | 408,163 | 53,526,532 | 475,387 |
| 2002 | 1,144,389 | 2,404,329 | 54,988,278 | 405,577 |
| 2003 | 760,824 | 1,370,696 | 52,572,194 | 436,442 |
| 2004 | 442,462 | 325,345 | 46,539,253 | 396,096 |
| 2005 | 450,378 | 389,301 | 28,589,312 | 452,049 |
| 2006 | 310,625 | 262,049 | 26,870,964 | 295,034 |
| 2007 | 232,602 | 124,942 | 30,051,725 | 410,375 |
| 2008 | 210,897 | 120,986 | 42,029,079 | 393,594 |
| 2009 | 480,514 | 1,673,140 | 37,235,149 | 918,357 |
| 2010 | 477,080 | 1,159,787 | 27,577,237 | 843,630 |
| 2011 | 522,307 | 925,166 | 23,573,021 | 566,413 |
| 2012 | 605,389 | 902,900 | 16,811,048 | 435,049 |
| 2013 | 500,209 | 460,876 | 15,083,228 | 369,599 |

## 2014 Production by Area

| Offshore Area | Crude Oil BBL | Casing-head Mcf | Gas Well Gas Mcf | Conden-sate BBL |
|------|------|------|------|------|
| Brazos-LB | 0 | 0 | 150,615 | 114 |
| Brazos-SB | 0 | 0 | 0 | 0 |
| Galveston-LB | 161,129 | 83,760 | 705,604 | 181,748 |
| Galveston-SB | 0 | 0 | 0 | 0 |
| High Island-LB | 185,941 | 400,266 | 5,293,260 | 36,132 |
| High Island-SB | 0 | 0 | 0 | 0 |
| Matagrda Is.-LB | 76,925 | 63,230 | 2,685,522 | 3,069 |
| Matagrda Is.-SB | 0 | 0 | 17,416 | 0 |
| Mustang Is.-LB | 0 | 0 | 981,811 | 13,709 |
| Mustang Is.-SB | 0 | 0 | 2,620,595 | 119,898 |
| N. Padre Is.-LB | 0 | 0 | 0 | 0 |
| Sabine Pass | 0 | 0 | 0 | 0 |
| **Total** | **424,102** | **547,256** | **12,454,823** | **354,670** |

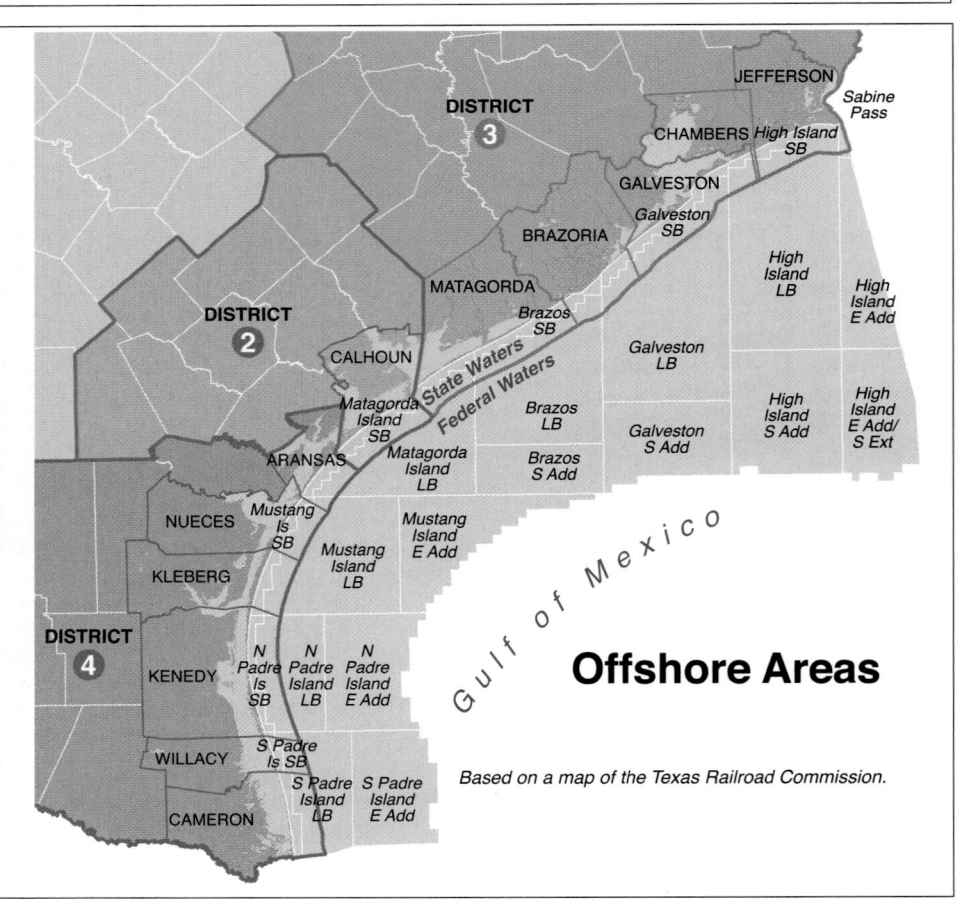

Offshore Areas

Based on a map of the Texas Railroad Commission.

# Receipts by Texas from Tidelands

The Republic of Texas had proclaimed its Gulf boundaries as three marine leagues, recognized by international law as traditional national boundaries. These boundaries were never seriously questioned when Texas joined the Union in 1845. But, in 1930 a congressional resolution authorized the U.S. Attorney General to file suit to establish offshore lands as properties of the federal government. Congress returned the disputed lands to Texas in 1953, and the U.S. Supreme Court confirmed Texas' ownership in 1960. In 1978, the federal government also granted states a "fair and equitable" share of the revenues from offshore leases within three miles of the states' outermost boundary. States did not receive any such revenue until 1986.

*The following table shows annual receipts from tidelands in the Gulf of Mexico by the Texas General Land Office from 1958 to Aug. 31, 2014. It does not include revenue from bays and other submerged area owned by Texas. Source: General Land Office.*

| From | To | Total | Bonus | Rental | Royalty | Lease |
|---|---|---|---|---|---|---|
| 7-01-1958 | 8-31-1959 | 771,064.75 | — | 143,857.00 | 627,207.75 | ... |
| 9-01-1959 | 8-31-1963 | 9,571,949.20 | 6,400,726.53 | 471,083.91 | 2,700,138.76 | ... |
| 9-01-1963 | 8-31-1964 | 3,656,236.75 | 2,435,244.36 | 525,315.00 | 695,677.39 | ... |
| 9-01-1964 | 8-31-1965 | 54,654,576.96 | 53,114,943.63 | 755,050.12 | 784,583.21 | ... |
| 9-01-1965 | 8-31-1966 | 22,148,825.44 | 18,223,357.84 | 3,163,475.00 | 761,992.60 | ... |
| 9-01-1966 | 8-31-1967 | 8,469,680.86 | 3,641,414.96 | 3,711,092.65 | 1,117,173.25 | ... |
| 9-01-1967 | 8-31-1968 | 6,305,851.00 | 1,251,852.50 | 2,683,732.50 | 2,370,266.00 | ... |
| 9-01-1968 | 8-31-1969 | 6,372,268.28 | 1,838,118.33 | 1,491,592.50 | 3,042,557.45 | ... |
| 9-01-1969 | 8-31-1970 | 10,311,030.48 | 5,994,666.32 | 618,362.50 | 3,698,001.66 | ... |
| 9-01-1970 | 8-31-1971 | 9,969,629.17 | 4,326,120.11 | 726,294.15 | 4,917,214.91 | ... |
| 9-01-1971 | 8-31-1972 | 7,558,327.21 | 1,360,212.64 | 963,367.60 | 5,234,746.97 | ... |
| 9-01-1972 | 8-31-1973 | 9,267,975.68 | 3,701,737.30 | 920,121.60 | 4,646,116.78 | ... |
| 9-01-1973 | 8-31-1974 | 41,717,670.04 | 32,981,619.28 | 1,065,516.60 | 7,670,534.16 | ... |
| 9-01-1974 | 8-31-1975 | 27,321,536.62 | 5,319,762.85 | 2,935,295.60 | 19,066,478.17 | ... |
| 9-01-1975 | 8-31-1976 | 38,747,074.09 | 6,197,853.00 | 3,222,535.84 | 29,326,685.25 | ... |
| 9-01-1976 | 8-31-1977 | 84,196,228.27 | 41,343,114.81 | 2,404,988.80 | 40,448,124.66 | ... |
| 9-01-1977 | 8-31-1978 | 118,266,812.05 | 49,807,750.45 | 4,775,509.92 | 63,683,551.68 | ... |
| 9-01-1978 | 8-31-1979 | 100,410,268.68 | 34,578,340.94 | 7,318,748.40 | 58,513,179.34 | ... |
| 9-01-1979 | 8-31-1980 | 200,263,803.03 | 34,733,270.02 | 10,293,153.80 | 155,237,379.21 | ... |
| 9-01-1980 | 8-31-1981 | 219,126,876.54 | 37,467,196.97 | 13,100,484.25 | 168,559,195.32 | ... |
| 9-01-1981 | 8-31-1982 | 250,824,581.69 | 27,529,516.33 | 14,214,478.97 | 209,080,586.39 | ... |
| 9-01-1982 | 8-31-1983 | 165,197,734.83 | 10,180,696.40 | 12,007,476.70 | 143,009,561.73 | ... |
| 9-01-1983 | 8-31-1984 | 152,755,934.29 | 32,864,122.19 | 8,573,996.87 | 111,317,815.23 | ... |
| 9-01-1984 | 8-31-1985 | 140,561,690.79 | 32,650,127.75 | 6,837,603.70 | 101,073,959.34 | ... |
| 9-01-1985 | 8-31-1986 | 516,503,771.08 | 6,365,426.23 | 4,241,892.75 | 78,289,592.27 | $427,606,859.83 |
| 9-01-1986 | 8-31-1987 | 60,066,571.05 | 4,186,561.63 | 1,933,752.50 | 44,691,907.22 | 9,254,349.70 |
| 9-01-1987 | 8-31-1988 | 56,875,069.22 | 14,195,274.28 | 1,817,058.90 | 28,068,202.53 | 12,794,533.51 |
| 9-01-1988 | 8-31-1989 | 61,793,380.04 | 12,995,892.74 | 1,290,984.37 | 35,160,568.40 | 12,345,934.53 |
| 9-01-1989 | 8-31-1990 | 68,701,751.51 | 7,708,449.54 | 1,289,849.87 | 40,331,537.06 | 19,371,915.04 |
| 9-01-1990 | 8-31-1991 | 90,885,856.99 | 3,791,832.77 | 1,345,711.07 | 70,023,601.01 | 15,724,712.14 |
| 9-01-1991 | 8-31-1992 | 51,154,511.34 | 4,450,850.00 | 1,123,585.54 | 26,776,191.35 | 18,803,884.45 |
| 9-01-1992 | 8-31-1993 | 60,287,712.60 | 3,394,230.00 | 904,359.58 | 34,853,679.68 | 21,135,443.34 |
| 9-01-1993 | 8-31-1994 | 57,825,043.59 | 3,570,657.60 | 694,029.30 | 32,244,987.95 | 21,315,368.74 |
| 9-01-1994 | 8-31-1995 | 62,143,227.78 | 8,824,722.93 | 674,479.79 | 34,691,023.35 | 17,951,001.71 |
| 9-01-1995 | 8-31-1996 | 68,166,645.51 | 13,919,246.80 | 1,102,591.39 | 32,681,315.73 | 20,463,491.59 |
| 9-01-1996 | 8-31-1997 | 90,614,935.93 | 22,007,378.46 | 1,319,614.78 | 41,605,792.50 | 25,682,150.19 |
| 9-01-1997 | 8-31-1998 | 104,016,006.75 | 36,946,312.49 | 2,070,802.90 | 38,760,320.91 | 26,238,570.45 |
| 9-01-1998 | 8-31-1999 | 53,565,810.30 | 5,402,171.00 | 2,471,128.47 | 23,346,515.93 | 22,345,994.90 |
| 9-01-1999 | 8-31-2000 | 55,465,763.99 | 3,487,564.80 | 2,171,636.35 | 24,314,241.99 | 25,492,320.85 |
| 9-01-2000 | 8-31-2001 | 68,226,347.58 | 9,963,608.68 | 1,830,378.11 | 23,244,034.74 | 33,188,326.05 |
| 9-01-2001 | 8-31-2002 | 30,910,283.91 | 9,286,015.20 | 1,545,583.01 | 13,369,771.56 | 6,708,914.14 |
| 9-01-2002 | 8-31-2003 | 50,881,515.90 | 15,152,092.40 | 1,071,377.60 | 19,648,641.39 | 15,009,404.51 |
| 9-01-2003 | 8-31-2004 | 54,379,791.20 | 14,448,555.70 | 1,094,201.41 | 25,199,635.21 | 13,637,398.88 |
| 9-01-2004 | 8-31-2005 | 53,594,809.87 | 9,148,220.20 | 1,624,666.50 | 32,406,328.78 | 10,415,594.39 |
| 9-01-2005 | 8-31-2006 | 60,829,271.63 | 22,565,845.14 | 1,605,090.30 | 23,287,994.53 | 13,370,341.66 |
| 9-01-2006 | 8-31-2007 | 52,513,621.85 | 15,879,784.44 | 2,022,859.80 | 18,785,626.55 | 15,825,351.06 |
| 9-01-2007 | 8-31-2008 | 86,705,980.28 | 4,632,175.50 | 1,485,080.97 | 68,408,943.01 | 12,179,780.80 |
| 9-01-2008 | 8-31-2009 | 65,835,625.76 | 3,896,795.20 | 1,020,204.33 | 53,166,364.50 | 7,752,261.73 |
| 09-01-2009 | 8-31-2010 | 49,647,832.14 | 3,352,431.20 | 603,406.00 | 41,901,754.81 | 3,790,240.13 |
| 09-01-2010 | 8-31-2011 | 50,360,843.36 | 4,088,819.06 | 546,404.80 | 43,602,027.62 | 2,123,591.88 |
| 09-01-2011 | 8-31-2012 | 37,561,595.54 | 2,436,420.00 | 217,356.00 | 33,327,417.09 | 1,580,402.45 |
| 09-01-2012 | 8-31-2013 | 32,676,026.13 | 1,079,400.00 | 339,941.00 | 30,353,820.49 | 902,864.64 |
| 09-01-2013 | 8-31-2014 | 28,103,953.40 | 217,000.00 | 193,125.00 | 26,665,893.97 | 1,027.934.53 |
| **Totals** | | $ 3,931,977,147.43 | $ 773,442,649.71 | $ 146,885,198.10 | $ 2,177,610,361.78 | $ 834,038,937.82 |
| Inside three-mile line | | $ 529,103,711.51 | $ 180,470,279.91 | $ 39,113,979.97 | $ 309,499,451.63 | 0 |
| Between three-mile and three marine-league line | | $ 2,566,029,132.50 | $ 590,320,285.41 | $ 107,597,936.94 | $1,868,110,910.15 | 0 |
| Outside three marine-league line | | $ 836,864,303.40 | $ 2,652,084.39 | $ 173,281.19 | 0 | $ 834,038,937.82 |

# Nonpetroleum Minerals

Source: U.S. Geological Survey; Bureau of Economic Geology, The University of Texas at Austin; www.beg.utexas.edu/

There are many nonpetroleum, or nonfuel, minerals found in Texas. Although they are overshadowed by production of petroleum, natural gas, and natural gas liquids, many are important to the economy.

In 2011, Texas nonfuel mineral production was valued at **$3.03 billion,** a 6.8-percent increase from the $2.84 billion in total value for 2010. Texas ranked **eighth among the 50 states** in total nonfuel mineral production value, down from sixth in 2009. Texas accounting for 4 percent of the total U.S. nonfuel mineral production value of $74.7 billion.

The top three mineral commodities produced were, in descending order of value, **portland cement, crushed stone,** and **construction sand and gravel,** which accounted for 73 percent of the total nonfuel mineral production value for the state in 2011.

Crushed stone was the only one of these mineral commodities to decrease in value in 2011, despite an increase in production. Other leading commodities in 2010 and 2011 were industrial sand and gravel, salt, and lime, in descending order of production value. Industrial sand had the biggest increases each year, up 41 percent by production value in 2010 and 67 percent in 2011, and 39 percent and 56 percent by production quantity. The table, below, shows production quantity and value for the major mineral commodities.

The **Bureau of Economic Geology,** which functions as the state geological survey of Texas, revised the following information about nonfuel minerals for this edition of the Texas Almanac. For more information about the bureau, go to **www.beg.utexas.edu/.** Bureau publications and maps are available at: **http://begstore.beg.utexas.edu/store/.**

Texas' nonfuel minerals are reported as follows:

**ALUMINUM** — No aluminum ores are mined in Texas, but three Texas plants process aluminum materials in one or more ways. Plants in San Patricio and Calhoun counties produce **aluminum oxide (alumina)** from imported raw ore **(bauxite),** and a plant in Milam County reduces the oxide to aluminum.

**ASBESTOS** — Small occurrences of amphibole-type asbestos have been found in the state. In West Texas, **richterite,** a white, long-fibered amphibole, is associated with some of the **talc deposits** northwest of **Allamoore** in Hudspeth County. Another type, **tremolite,** has been found in the **Llano Uplift** of Central Texas where it is associated with **serpentinite** in eastern Gillespie and western Blanco counties. No asbestos is mined in Texas.

**ASPHALT (Native)** — Asphalt-bearing Cretaceous limestones crop out in Burnet, Kinney, Pecos, Reeves, Uvalde, and other counties. The most significant deposit is in southwestern Uvalde County, where asphalt occurs naturally in pore spaces of the Anacacho Limestone. The material is quarried and used extensively as **road-paving material.** Asphalt-bearing sandstones occur in Anderson, Angelina, Cooke, Jasper, Maverick, Montague, Nacogdoches, Uvalde, Zavala, and other counties.

**BARITE** — Deposits of a heavy, nonmetallic mineral, barite (barium sulphate), have been found in many localities, including Baylor, Brown, Brewster, Culberson, Gillespie, Howard, Hudspeth, Jeff Davis, Kinney, Llano, Live Oak, Taylor, Val Verde, and Webb counties. During the 1960s, there was small, intermittent production in the **Seven Heart Gap** area of the **Apache Mountains** in Culberson County, where barite was mined from open pits. Most of the deposits are known to be relatively small, but the Webb County deposit has not been evaluated. Grinding plants, which prepare barite mined outside of Texas for use chiefly as a **weighting agent** in well-drilling muds and as a **filler,** are located in Browns-

## Nonfuel Raw Mineral Production and Value in Texas

Production as measured by mine shipments, sales, or marketable production, including consumption by producers. Production is in **thousand metric tons** and value is in **thousand dollars.**

| MINERAL | 2009 Production | 2009 Value | 2010 Production | 2010 Value | 2011 Production | 2011 Value |
|---|---|---|---|---|---|---|
| **Cement:** | | | | | | |
| Masonry | 382 | $ 50,700* | 368 | $ 52,100* | 274 | $ 40,300* |
| Portland | 11,300 | 1,070,000* | 10,900 | 1,060,000* | 11,100 | 1,110,000* |
| **Clays:** | | | | | | |
| Bentonite | 71 | 4,000 | 64 | 3,730 | 73 | 12,000 |
| Common | 2,360 | 12,600 | 1,950 | 12,600 ʳ | 2,070 | 13,700 |
| **Gemstones, natural** | NA | 202 | NA | 202 | NA | 202 |
| **Gypsum, crude** | 1,010 | 10,200 | 1,180 | 8,200 | 1,040 | 7,550 |
| **Lime** | 1,650 | 130,000 | 1,620 | 132,000 | 1,500 | 128,000 |
| **Salt** | 9,570 | 132,000 | 8,950 | 143,000 | 9,080 | 157,000 |
| **Sand and gravel:** | | | | | | |
| Construction | 99,500 | 603,000 | 95,900 ʳ | 654,000 ʳ | 87,700 | 627,000 |
| Industrial | 1,530 | 65,600 | 3,280 | 123,000 | 3,570 | 139,000 |
| **Stone:** | | | | | | |
| Crushed | 141,000 ʳ | 861,000 ʳ | 153,000 ʳ | 1,020,000 ʳ | 148,000 | 1,090,000 |
| Dimension | 233 ʳ | 30,100 ʳ | 243 ʳ | 31,600 ʳ | 269 | 27,700 |
| ‡Combined values | § | 68,200 | § | 72,100 | § | 77,700 |
| **Total Texas Values | § | $3,040,000 ʳ | § | $3,310,000 ʳ | § | $3,430,000 |

* Estimated. ʳRevised. **NA:** Not available. § Not applicable. ‡ Combined values of brucite, clays (ball, fuller's earth, kaolin), helium, talc (crude), and zeolites. **Data are rounded to no more than three significant digits; may not add to totals shown.

ville, Corpus Christi, El Paso, Galena Park, Galveston, and Houston.

**BASALT (TRAP ROCK)** — Masses of basalt — a hard, dark-colored, fine-grained igneous rock — crop out in Kinney, Travis, Uvalde, and several other counties along the **Balcones Fault Zone,** and also in the Trans-Pecos area of West Texas. Basalt is quarried near Knippa in Uvalde County for use as **road-building material, railroad ballast, and other aggregate.**

**BENTONITE** (see **CLAYS**).

**BERYLLIUM** — Occurrences of beryllium minerals at several Trans-Pecos localities have been recognized for several years.

**BRINE** (see also **SALT, SODIUM SULPHATE**) — Many wells in Texas produce brine by solution mining of subsurface salt deposits, mostly in West Texas counties such as Andrews, Crane, Ector, Loving, Midland, Pecos, Reeves, Ward, and others. These wells in the Permian Basin dissolve salt from the Salado Formation, an enormous salt deposit that extends in the subsurface from north of the Big Bend northward to Kansas, has an east-west width of 150 to 200 miles, and may have several hundred feet of net salt thickness. The majority of the brine is used in the petroleum industry, but it also is used in water softening, the chemical industry, and other uses. Three Gulf Coast counties, Fort Bend, Duval, and Jefferson, have brine stations that produce from salt domes.

**BUILDING STONE (DIMENSION STONE)** — **Granite** and **limestone** currently are quarried for use as dimension stone. The granite quarries are located in Burnet, Gillespie, Llano, and Mason counties; the limestone quarries are in Shackelford and Williamson counties. Past production of limestone for use as dimension stone has been reported in Burnet, Gillespie, Jones, Tarrant, Travis, and several other counties. There also has been production of **sandstone** in various counties for use as dimension stone.

**CEMENT MATERIALS** — Cement is currently manufactured in Bexar, Comal, Dallas, Ector, Ellis, Hays, McLennan, Nolan, and Potter counties. Many of these plants utilize Cretaceous limestones and shales or clays as raw materials for the cement. On the Texas High Plains, a cement plant near Amarillo uses impure **caliche** as the chief raw material. Iron oxide, also a constituent of cement, is available from the iron ore deposits of East Texas and from smelter slag. **Gypsum,** added to the cement as a retarder, is found chiefly in North-Central Texas, Central Texas, and the Trans-Pecos area.

**CHROMIUM** — Chromite-bearing rock has been found in several small deposits around the margin of the Coal Creek **serpentinite** mass in northeastern Gillespie County and northwestern Blanco County. Exploration has not revealed significant deposits.

**CLAYS** — Texas has an abundance and variety of ceramic and non-ceramic clays and is one of the country's leading producers of clay products.

Almost any kind of clay, ranging from common clay used to make brick and tile to clays suitable for manufacture of specialty whitewares, can be used for ceramic purposes. **Fire clay** suitable for use as **refractories** occurs chiefly in East and North-Central Texas; **ball clay,** a high-quality plastic ceramic clay, is found in East Texas.

Ceramic clay suitable for quality structural clay products, such as **structural building brick, paving brick, and drain tile,** is especially abundant in East and North-Central Texas. Common clay suitable for use in the manufacture of cement and ordinary brick is found in most counties of the state. Many of the Texas clays will expand or bloat upon rapid firing and are suitable for the manufacture of lightweight aggregate, which is used mainly in concrete blocks and highway surfacing.

Nonceramic clays are utilized without firing. They are used primarily as **bleaching and absorbent clays, fillers, coaters, additives, bonding clays, drilling muds, catalysts,** and potentially as sources of alumina. Most of the nonceramic clays in Texas are **bentonites** and **fuller's earth.** These occur extensively in the Coastal Plain and locally in the High Plains and Big Bend areas. **Kaolin clays** in parts of East Texas are potential sources of such nonceramic products as **paper coaters and fillers, rubber fillers, and drilling agents.** Relatively high in alumina, these clays also are a potential source of metallic aluminum.

**COAL** (see also **LIGNITE**) — **Bituminous coal**, which occurs in North-Central, South, and West Texas, was a significant energy source in Texas prior to the large-scale development of oil and gas. During the period from 1895–1943, Texas mines produced more than 25 million tons of coal. The mines were inactive for many years, but the renewed interest in coal as a major energy source prompted a revaluation of Texas' coal deposits. In the late 1970s, bituminous coal production resumed in the state on a limited scale when mines were opened in Coleman, Erath, and Webb counties.

Much of the state's bituminous coal occurs in North-Central Texas. Deposits are found there in Pennsylvanian rocks within a large area that includes Coleman, Eastland, Erath, Jack, McCulloch, Montague, Palo Pinto, Parker, Throckmorton, Wise, Young, and other counties. Before the general availability of oil and gas, underground coal mines near **Thurber, Bridgeport, Newcastle, Strawn,** and other points annually produced significant coal tonnages. Preliminary evaluations indicate substantial amounts of coal may remain in the North-Central Texas area. The coal seams there are generally no more than 30 inches thick and are commonly covered by well-consolidated overburden. Ash and sulphur content are high. Beginning in 1979, two bituminous coal mine operations in North-Central Texas — one in southern Coleman County and one in northwestern Erath County — produced coal to be used as fuel by the cement industry. Neither mine is currently operating.

In South Texas, bituminous coal occurs in the Eagle Pass district of Maverick County, and bituminous **cannel coal** is present in the **Santo Tomas district** of Webb County. The Eagle Pass area was a leading coal-producing district in Texas during the late 1800s and early 1900s. The bituminous coal in that area, which occurs in the Upper Cretaceous Olmos Formation, has a high ash content and a moderate moisture and sulfur content. According to reports, Maverick County coal beds range from four to seven feet thick.

The **cannel coals** of western Webb County occur near the Rio Grande in middle Eocene strata. They were mined for more than 50 years and used primarily as a boiler fuel. Mining ceased from 1939 until 1978, when a surface mine was opened 30 miles northwest of Laredo to produce cannel coal for use as fuel in the cement industry and for export. An additional mine has since been opened in that county. Tests show that the coals of the Webb County Santo Tomas district have a high hydrogen content and yield significant amounts of gas and oil when distilled. They also have a high sulfur content. A potential use might be as a source of various petrochemical products.

Coal deposits in the Trans-Pecos country of West Texas include those in the Cretaceous rocks of the Terlingua area of Brewster County, the Eagle Spring area of Hudspeth County, and the **San Carlos** area of Presidio County. The coal deposits in these areas are believed to have relatively little potential for development as a fuel. They have been sold in the past as a soil amendment (see **LEONARDITE**).

**COPPER** — Copper minerals have been found in

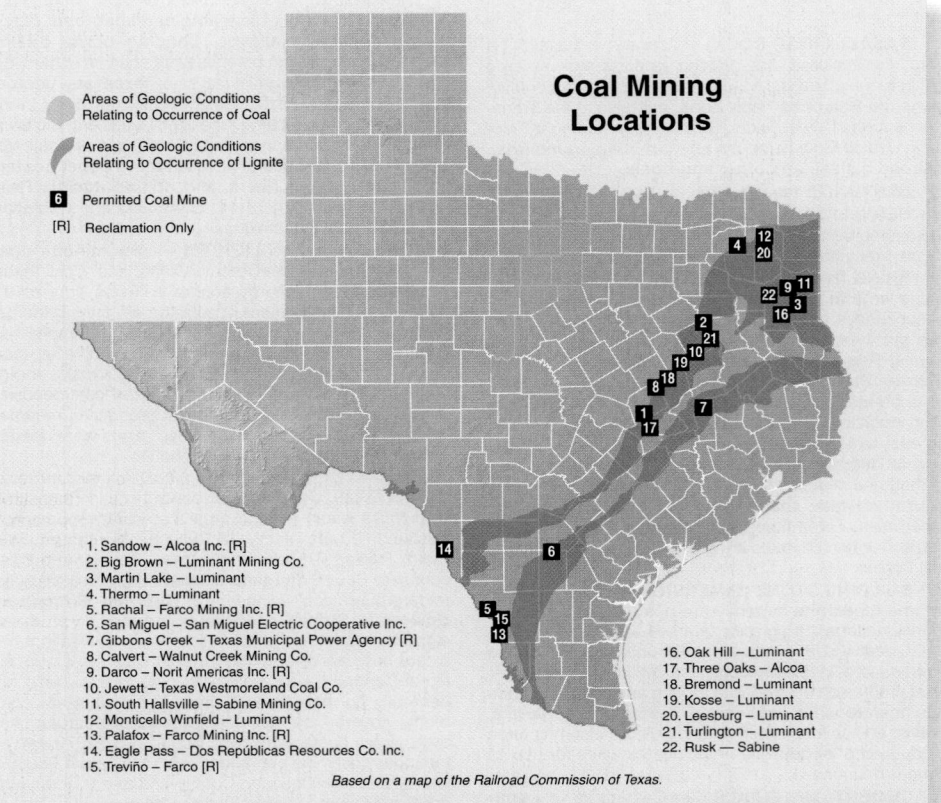

Coal Mining Locations

Areas of Geologic Conditions Relating to Occurrence of Coal

Areas of Geologic Conditions Relating to Occurrence of Lignite

6   Permitted Coal Mine

[R]   Reclamation Only

1. Sandow – Alcoa Inc. [R]
2. Big Brown – Luminant Mining Co.
3. Martin Lake – Luminant
4. Thermo – Luminant
5. Rachal – Farco Mining Inc. [R]
6. San Miguel – San Miguel Electric Cooperative Inc.
7. Gibbons Creek – Texas Municipal Power Agency [R]
8. Calvert – Walnut Creek Mining Co.
9. Darco – Norit Americas Inc. [R]
10. Jewett – Texas Westmoreland Coal Co.
11. South Hallsville – Sabine Mining Co.
12. Monticello Winfield – Luminant
13. Palafox – Farco Mining Inc. [R]
14. Eagle Pass – Dos Repúblicas Resources Co. Inc.
15. Treviño – Farco [R]

16. Oak Hill – Luminant
17. Three Oaks – Alcoa
18. Bremond – Luminant
19. Kosse – Luminant
20. Leesburg – Luminant
21. Turlington – Luminant
22. Rusk — Sabine

*Based on a map of the Railroad Commission of Texas.*

## Mine Production (in short tons)

| MINE | 2011 | CUMULATIVE |
|---|---|---|
| 1. Sandow | 0 | 150,966,982 |
| 2. Big Brown | 969,081 | 171,155,954 |
| 3. Martin Lake | 5,626,489 | 289,554,497 |
| 4. Monticello-Thermo | 1,338,548 | 42,130,159 |
| 5. Rachal | 0 | 963,827 |
| 6. San Miguel | 685,063 | 84,265,332 |
| San Miguel Area C | 2,519,090 | 8,720,743 |
| 7. Gibbons Creek | 0 | 30,431,174 |
| Gibbons Creek V | 0 | 12,547,611 |
| 8. Calvert | 1,826,445 | 40,186,243 |
| 9. Darco | 0 | 6,798,881 |
| 10. Jewett | 1,479,924 | 158,923,432 |
| Jewett E/F | 2,741,622 | 28,752,440 |
| 11. South Hallsville | 4,014,304 | 96,859,813 |
| 12. Monticello-Winfield | 1,373,844 | 273,978,766 |
| 13. Palafox | 0 | 5,355,519 |
| 14. Eagle Pass | 0 | 0 |
| 15. Treviño | 0 | 890,453 |
| 16. Oak Hill | 3,087,308 | 116,506,465 |
| 17. Three Oaks | 7,192,404 | 32,489,410 |
| 18. Bremond | 0 | 236 |
| 19. Kosse | 8,614,847 | 17,083,487 |
| 20. Leesburg | 0 | 0 |
| 21. Turlington | 2,765,429 | 2,765,429 |
| 22. Rusk | 0 | 0 |
| *Little Bull Creek (Coleman Co.)* | *No longer permitted* | 428,932 |
| *Powell Bend ( Bastrop Co.)* | *No longer permitted* | 1,569,875 |
| *Thurber (Erath Co.)* | *No longer permitted* | 465,984 |
| **Statewide** | **45,587,404** | **1,578,397,305** |

*Source: Railroad Commission of Texas, 2013*

### Coal Production by State, 2011
(million short tons)

| Total | United States | 1,095.6 |
|---|---|---|
| 1. | Wyoming | 438.7 |
| 2. | West Virginia | 134.7 |
| 3. | Kentucky | 108.8 |
| 4. | Pennsylvania | 59.2 |
| **5.** | **Texas** | **45.9** |
| 6. | Montana | 42.0 |
| 7. | Ilinois | 37.8 |
| 8. | Indiana | 37.4 |

*Source: U.S. Energy Information Administration*

### Texas Coal Production
(short tons)

| Year | Total |
|---|---|
| 2010 | 41,419,857 |
| 2009 | 37,099,067 |
| 2008 | 40,152,112 |
| 2007 | 38,403,681 |
| 2006 | 46,128,231 |
| 2005 | 47,168,916 |
| 2004 | 45,680,097 |
| 2003 | 48,179,875 |
| 2002 | 44,683,793 |
| pre-2002 | 1,143,894,272 |

*Source: Railroad Commission of Texas*

the **Trans-Pecos** area of West Texas, in the **Llano Uplift** area of Central Texas, and in redbed deposits of North Texas. No copper has been mined in Texas during recent years, and the total copper produced in the state has been relatively small. Past attempts to mine the North Texas and Llano Uplift copper deposits resulted in small shipments.

Practically all the copper production in the state has been from the **Van Horn–Allamoore** district of Culberson and Hudspeth counties in the Trans-Pecos area. Chief output was from the **Hazel copper-silver mine** of Culberson County that yielded over 1 million pounds of copper during 1891–1947. Copper ores and concentrates from outside of Texas are processed at **smelters** in El Paso and Amarillo.

**CRUSHED STONE** — Texas is among the leading states in the production of crushed stone. Most production consists of **limestone**; other kinds of crushed stone produced in the state include **basalt (trap rock), dolomite, granite, marble, rhyolite, sandstone, and serpentinite.** Large tonnages of crushed stone are used as **aggregate** in concrete, as **road material,** and in the manufacture of cement and lime. Some is used as **riprap, terrazzo, roofing chips, filter material, fillers,** as well as other purposes.

**DIATOMITE (DIATOMACEOUS EARTH)** — Diatomite is a very lightweight siliceous material consisting of the remains of microscopic aquatic plants (diatoms). It is used chiefly as a **filter and filler;** other uses are for **thermal insulation,** as an **abrasive,** as an **insecticide carrier,** as a **lightweight aggregate,** and for other purposes. The diatomite was deposited in shallow, freshwater lakes that were present in the High Plains during portions of the Pliocene and Pleistocene epochs. Deposits have been found in Armstrong, Crosby, Dickens, Ector, Hartley, and Lamb counties. No diatomite is mined in Texas.

**DOLOMITE ROCK** — Dolomite rock, which consists largely of the mineral dolomite (calcium-magnesium carbonate), commonly is associated with limestone in Texas. Areas in which dolomite rock occurs include Central Texas, the Callahan Divide, and parts of the Edwards Plateau, High Plains, and West Texas. Some of the principal deposits of dolomite rock are found in Bell, Brown, Burnet, Comanche, Edwards, El Paso, Gillespie, Lampasas, Mills, Nolan, Taylor, and Williamson counties. Dolomite rock can be used as crushed stone (although much of Texas dolomite is soft and not a good aggregate material), in the manufacture of lime, and as a source of **magnesium.**

**FELDSPAR** — Large crystals and crystal fragments of feldspar minerals occur in the Precambrian pegmatite rocks that crop out in the **Llano Uplift** area of Central Texas — including Blanco, Burnet, Gillespie, Llano, and Mason counties — and in the **Van Horn area** of Culberson and Hudspeth counties in West Texas. Feldspar has been mined in Llano County for use as **roofing granules** and as a **ceramic material.** Feldspar is currently mined in Burnet County for use as an aggregate.

**FLUORSPAR** — The mineral fluorite (calcium fluoride), which is known commercially as fluorspar, occurs in both Central and West Texas. In Central Texas, the deposits that have been found in Burnet, Gillespie, and Mason counties are not considered adequate to sustain mining operations. In West Texas, deposits have been found in Brewster, El Paso, Hudspeth, Jeff Davis, and Presidio counties. Fluorspar has been mined in the **Christmas Mountains** of Brewster County and processed in Marathon. Former West Texas mining activity in the **Eagle Mountains** district of Hudspeth County resulted in the production of approximately 15,000 short tons of fluorspar during the peak years of 1942–1950. No production has been reported in Hudspeth County

since that period. Imported fluorspar is processed in Brownsville, Eagle Pass, El Paso, and Houston. Fluorspar is used in the **steel, chemical, aluminum, magnesium, ceramics, and glass industries,** and for various other purposes.

**FULLER'S EARTH** (see **CLAY**).

**GOLD** — No major deposits of gold are known in Texas. Small amounts have been found in the **Llano Uplift** region of Central Texas and in West Texas; minor occurrences have been reported on the **Edwards Plateau** and the **Gulf Coastal Plain** of Texas. Nearly all of the gold produced in the state came as a by-product of silver and lead mining at **Presidio mine,** near **Shafter** in Presidio County. Additional small quantities were produced as a by-product of copper mining in Culberson County and from residual soils developed from gold-bearing quartz stringers in metamorphic rocks in Llano County. No gold mining has been reported in Texas since 1952. Total **gold production** in the state from 1889–1952 amounted to more than 8,419 troy ounces, according to U.S. Bureau of Mines figures. Most of the production — at least 73 percent and probably more — came from the Presidio mine.

**GRANITE** — Granites in shades of red and gray and related intrusive igneous rocks occur in the **Llano Uplift** of Central Texas and in the **Trans-Pecos** country of West Texas. Deposits are found in Blanco, Brewster, Burnet, El Paso, Gillespie, Hudspeth, Llano, McCulloch, Mason, Presidio, and other counties. Quarries in Burnet, Gillespie, Llano, and Mason counties produce Precambrian granite for a variety of uses as **dimension stone** and **crushed stone.**

**GRAPHITE** — Graphite, a soft, dark-gray mineral, is a form of very high-grade carbon. It occurs in Precambrian schist rocks of the **Llano Uplift** of Central Texas, notably in Burnet and Llano counties. Crystalline-flake graphite ore formerly was mined from open pits in the **Clear Creek area** of western Burnet County and processed at a plant near the mine. The mill now occasionally grinds imported material. Uses of natural crystalline graphite are **refractories, steel production, pencil leads, lubricants, foundry facings, and crucibles,** as well as other purposes.

**GRINDING PEBBLES (ABRASIVE STONES)** — Flint pebbles, suitable for use in **tube-mill grinding,** are found in the **Gulf Coastal Plain,** where they occur in gravel deposits along rivers and in upland areas. Grinding pebbles are produced from **Frio River terrace deposits** near the McMullen–Live Oak county line, but the area is now part of the Choke Canyon Reservoir area.

**GYPSUM** — Gypsum is widely distributed in Texas. Chief deposits are bedded gypsum in the area east of the **High Plains,** in the **Trans-Pecos** country, and in **Central Texas.** It also occurs in **salt-dome caprocks** of the Gulf Coast. The massive, granular variety, which is known as rock gypsum, is the kind most commonly used by industry. Other varieties include **alabaster, satin spar, and selenite.**

Gypsum is one of the important industrial minerals in Texas. Bedded gypsum is produced from surface mines in Culberson, Fisher, Gillespie, Hardeman, Hudspeth, Kimble, Nolan, and Stonewall counties. Gypsum was formerly mined at **Gyp Hill salt dome** in Brooks County and at **Hockley salt dome** in Harris County. Most of the gypsum is calcined and used in the manufacture of **gypsum wallboard, plaster, joint compounds,** and other construction products. Crude gypsum is used chiefly as **a retarder in portland cement** and as a **soil conditioner.**

**HELIUM** — Helium is a very light, nonflammable, chemically inert gas. The **U.S. Interior Department has ended its helium operation** near Masterson in the Panhandle. The storage facility at **Cliffside gas field** near Amarillo and the 425-mile pipeline system will remain in operation until the government sells its remaining unrefined, crude helium. Helium is used in **cryogenics, welding, pressurizing and purging, leak detection, synthetic breathing mixtures,** and for other purposes.

**IRON** — Iron oxide **(limonite, goethite, and hematite)** and **iron carbonate (siderite)** deposits occur widely in East Texas, notably in Cass, Cherokee, Marion, and Morris counties, and also in Anderson, Camp, Harrison, Henderson, Nacogdoches, Smith, Upshur, and other counties. **Magnetite (magnetic, black iron oxide)** occurs in Central Texas, including a deposit at **Iron Mountain** in Llano County. Hematite occurs in the **Trans-Pecos** area and in the **Llano Uplift** of Central Texas. The extensive deposits of **glauconite** (a complex silicate containing iron) that occur in East Texas and the hematitic and goethitic Cambrian sandstone that crops out in the northwestern Llano Uplift region are potential sources of low-grade iron ore.

Limonite and other East Texas iron ores are mined from open pits in Cherokee and Henderson counties for use in the preparation of **portland cement,** as a **weighting agent in well-drilling fluids,** as an **animal feed supplement,** and for other purposes. East Texas iron ores also were mined in the past for use in the iron-steel industry.

**KAOLIN** (see **CLAY**).

**LEAD AND ZINC** — The lead mineral **galena (lead sulfide)** commonly is associated with zinc and silver. It formerly was produced as a by-product of West Texas silver mining, chiefly from the **Presidio mine at Shafter** in Presidio County, although lesser amounts were obtained at several other mines and prospects. Deposits of galena also are known to occur in Blanco, Brewster, Burnet, Gillespie, and Hudspeth counties.

Zinc, primarily from the mineral **sphalerite (zinc sulphide),** was produced chiefly from the **Bonanza** and **Alice Ray** mines in the **Quitman Mountains** of Hudspeth County. In addition, small production was reported from several other areas, including the **Chinati** and **Montezuma mines** of Presidio County and the **Buck Prospect** in the **Apache Mountains** of Culberson County. Zinc mineralization also occurs in association with the lead deposits in Cambrian rocks of Central Texas.

**LEONARDITE** — Deposits of weathered (oxidized) low-Btu value bituminous coals, generally referred to as "leonardite," occur in Brewster County. The name leonardite is used for a mixture of chemical compounds that is high in humic acids. In the past, material from these deposits was sold as **soil conditioner.** Other uses of leonardite include **modification of viscosity of drill fluids and as sorbants in water-treatment.**

**LIGHTWEIGHT AGGREGATE** (see **CLAY, DIATOMITE, PERLITE, VERMICULITE**).

**LIGNITE** — Almost all current coal production in Texas is located in the Tertiary-aged lignite belts that extend across the Texas Gulf Coastal Plain from the Rio Grande in South Texas to the Arkansas and Louisiana borders in East Texas. The Railroad Commission of Texas (RRC) reported that in 2010, **Texas produced 41.4 million short tons of lignite from 14 mines.** Cumulative production in 2010 was 1.5 billion short tons of lignite and coal. The U.S. Energy Information Administration (EIA) ranked Texas as the sixth-largest coal-producing state.

The near-surface lignite resources, occurring at depths of less than 200 feet in seams of three feet or thicker, are estimated at 23 billion short tons. **Recoverable reserves of strippable lignite** — those that can be economically mined under current conditions of price and technology — are estimated by the EIA to be 722 million short tons.

Additional lignite resources of the Texas Gulf Coastal Plain occur as deep-basin deposits. Deep-basin resources, those that occur at depths of 200 to 2,000 feet in seams of five feet or thicker, are comparable in magnitude to near-surface resources. The deep-basin lignites are a potential energy resource that conceivably could be utilized by in situ (in place) recovery methods such as underground gasification.

As with bituminous coal, lignite production was significant prior to the general availability of oil and gas. Remnants of old underground mines are common throughout the area of lignite occurrence. Large reserves of strippable lignite have again attracted the attention of energy suppliers, and Texas is now the nation's **sixth leading producer of coal,** 99 percent of it lignite. Twelve large strip mines are now producing lignite that is burned for **mine-mouth electric-power generation,** and additional mines are planned. Mines are located in Atascosa, Franklin, Freestone, Harrison, Hopkins, Leon, Limestone, McMullen, Milam, Panola, Robertson, Rusk, and Titus counties.

**LIME MATERIAL — Limestones,** which are abundant in some areas of Texas, are heated to produce lime (calcium oxide) at a number of plants in the state. High-magnesium limestone and dolomite are used to prepare lime at a plant in Burnet County. Other lime plants are located in Bexar, Bosque, Comal, Hill, Johnson, and Travis counties. Lime production captive to the kiln's operator occurs in several Texas counties. Lime is used in **soil stabilization, water purification, paper and pulp manufacture, metallurgy, sugar refining, agriculture, construction, removal of sulfur from stack gases,** and for many other purposes.

**LIMESTONE** (see also **BUILDING STONE**) — Texas is one of the nation's leading producers of limestone, which is quarried in more than 60 counties. Limestone occurs in nearly all areas of the state with the exception of most of the Gulf Coastal Plain and High Plains. Although some of the limestone is quarried for use as **dimension stone,** most of the output is crushed for uses such as **bulk building materials (crushed stone, road base, concrete aggregate), chemical raw materials, fillers or extenders, lime and portland cement raw materials, agricultural limestone, and removal of sulfur from stack gases.**

**MAGNESITE** — Small deposits of magnesite (natural magnesium carbonate) have been found in Precambrian rocks in Llano and Mason counties of Central Texas. At one time, there was small-scale mining of magnesite in the area; some of the material was used as **agricultural stone** and as **terrazzo chips.** Magnesite also can be calcined to form magnesia, which is used in metallurgical furnace refractories and other products.

**MAGNESIUM** — On the Texas Gulf Coast in Brazoria County, magnesium chloride is **extracted from sea water** at a plant in Freeport and used to produce **magnesium compounds and magnesium metal.** During World War II, high-magnesium Ellenburger dolomite rock from Burnet County was used as magnesium ore at a plant near Austin.

**MANGANESE** — Deposits of manganese minerals, such as **braunite, hollandite, and pyrolusite,** have been found in several areas, including Jeff Davis, Llano, Mason, Presidio, and Val Verde counties. Known deposits are not large. Small shipments have been made from Jeff Davis, Mason, and Val Verde counties, but no manganese mining has been reported in Texas since 1954.

**MARBLE** — Metamorphic and sedimentary marbles suitable for **monument and building stone** are found in the **Llano Uplift** and nearby areas of Central Texas and the **Trans-Pecos** area of West Texas. Gray, white, black, greenish black, light green, brown, and cream-colored marbles occur in Central Texas in Burnet, Gillespie,

Llano, and Mason counties. West Texas metamorphic marbles include the bluish-white and the black marbles found southwest of Alpine in Brewster County and the white marble from **Marble Canyon** north of Van Horn in Culberson County. Marble can be used as **dimension stone, terrazzo, and roofing aggregate,** and for other purposes.

**MERCURY (QUICKSILVER)** — Mercury minerals, chiefly **cinnabar,** occur in the **Terlingua district** and nearby districts of southern Brewster and southeastern Presidio counties. Mining began there about 1894, and from 1905–1935, Texas was one of the nation's leading producers of quicksilver. Following World War II, a sharp drop in demand and price, along with depletion of developed ore reserves, caused abandonment of all the Texas mercury mines.

With a rise in the price, sporadic mining took place between 1951–1960. In 1965, when the price of mercury moved to a record high, renewed interest in the Texas mercury districts resulted in the reopening of several mines and the discovery of new ore reserves. By April 1972, however, the price had declined and the mines have reported no production since 1973.

**MICA** — Large crystals of flexible, transparent mica minerals in igneous pegmatite rocks and mica flakes in metamorphic schist rocks are found in the **Llano Uplift area** of Central Texas and the **Van Horn area** of West Texas. Most Central Texas deposits do not meet specifications for sheet mica, and although several attempts have been made to produce West Texas sheet mica in Culberson and Hudspeth counties, sustained production has not been achieved. A mica quarry operated for a short time in the early 1980s in the Van Horn Mountains of Culberson and Hudspeth counties to mine mica schist for use as an **additive in rotary drilling fluids.**

**MOLYBDENUM** — Small occurrences of molybdenite have been found in Burnet and Llano counties, and **wulfenite,** another molybdenum mineral, has been noted in rocks in the **Quitman Mountains** of Hudspeth County. Molybdenum minerals also occur at **Cave Peak** north of Van Horn in Culberson County, in the **Altuda Mountain area** of northwestern Brewster County, and in association with uranium ores of the Gulf Coastal Plain.

**PEAT** — This spongy organic substance forms in bogs from plant remains. It has been found in the **Gulf Coastal Plain** in several localities including Gonzales, Guadalupe, Lee, Milam, Polk, and San Jacinto counties. There has been intermittent, small-scale production of some of the peat for use as a **soil conditioner.**

**PERLITE** — Perlite, a glassy igneous rock, expands to a lightweight, porous mass when heated. It can be used as a **lightweight aggregate, filter aid, horticultural aggregate,** and for other purposes. Perlite occurs in Presidio County, where it has been mined in the **Pinto Canyon area** north of **the Chinati Mountains.** No perlite is currently mined in Texas, but perlite mined outside of Texas is expanded at plants in Bexar, Dallas, El Paso, Guadalupe, Harris, and Nolan counties.

**PHOSPHATE** — Rock phosphate is present in Paleozoic rocks in several areas of Brewster and Presidio counties in West Texas and in Central Texas, but the known deposits are not large. In Northeast Texas, sedimentary rock phosphate occurs in thin conglomeratic lenses in Upper Cretaceous and Tertiary rock units; possibly some of these low-grade phosphorites could be processed on a small scale for local use as a **fertilizer.** Imported phosphate rock is processed at a plant in Brownsville.

**POTASH** — The potassium mineral **polyhalite** is widely distributed in the subsurface Permian Basin of West Texas and has been found in many wells in that area. During 1927–1931, the federal government drilled a series of potash-test wells in Crane, Crockett, Ector, Glasscock, Loving, Reagan, Upton, and Winkler counties. In addition to polyhalite, which was found in all of the counties, these wells revealed the presence of the potassium minerals **carnallite and sylvite** in Loving County and carnallite in Winkler County. The known Texas potash deposits are not as rich as those in the New Mexico portion of the Permian Basin and have not been developed.

**PUMICITE (VOLCANIC ASH)** — Deposits of volcanic ash occur in Brazos, Fayette, Gonzales, Karnes, Polk, Starr, and other counties of the Texas Coastal Plain. Deposits also have been found in the Trans-Pecos area, High Plains, and in several counties east of the High Plains. Volcanic ash is used to prepare **pozzolan cement, cleansing and scouring compounds, and soaps and sweeping compounds;** as a **carrier for insecticides,** and for other purposes. It has been mined in Dickens, Lynn, Scurry, Starr, and other counties.

**QUICKSILVER** (see **MERCURY**).

**RARE-EARTH ELEMENTS AND METALS** — The term, "rare-earth elements," is commonly applied to elements of the **lanthanide** group (atomic numbers 57 through 71) plus **yttrium.** Yttrium, atomic number 39 and not a member of the lanthanide group, is included as a rare-earth element because it has similar properties to members of that group and usually occurs in nature with them. The metals **thorium and scandium** are sometimes termed "rare metals" because their occurence is often associated with the rare-earth elements.

The majority of rare-earth elements are consumed as **catalysts** in petroleum cracking and other chemical industries. Rare earths are widely used in the **glass industry for tableware, specialty glasses, optics, and fiber optics.** Cerium oxide has growing use as a **polishing compound** for glass, gem stones, cathode-ray tube faceplates, and other polishing. Rare earths are alloyed with various metals to produce materials used in the **aeronautic, space, and electronics** industries. The addition of rare-earth elements may improve resistance to metal fatigue at high temperatures, reduce potential for corrosion, and selectively increase conductivity and magnetism of the metal.

Various members of this group, including **thorium,** have anomalous concentrations in the **rhyolitic and related igneous rocks** of the **Quitman Mountains** and the **Sierra Blanca area** of Trans-Pecos.

**SALT (SODIUM CHLORIDE)** (see also **BRINES**) — Salt resources of Texas are virtually inexhaustible. Enormous deposits occur in the subsurface **Permian Basin** of West Texas and in the **salt domes of the Gulf Coastal Plain.** Salt also is found in the alkali **playa lakes** of the High Plains, the **alkali flats or salt lakes in the Salt Basin** of Culberson and Hudspeth counties, and along some of the bays and lagoons of the South Texas **Gulf Coast.**

Texas is one of the leading salt-producing states. **Rock salt** is obtained from underground mines in **salt domes at Grand Saline** in Van Zandt County and **Hockley Dome** in Harris County. Salt is produced from rock salt and by solution mining as brines from wells drilled into the underground salt deposits.

**SAND, INDUSTRIAL** — Sands used for special purposes, due to **high silica content** or to unique physical properties, command higher prices than common sand. Industrial sands in Texas occur mainly in the **Central Gulf Coastal Plain** and in **North-Central Texas.** They include **abrasive, blast, chemical, engine, filtration, foundry, glass, hydraulic-fracturing (propant), molding, and pottery sands.** Recent production of industrial sands has been from Atascosa, Colorado, Hardin, Harris, Liberty, Limestone, McCulloch, Newton, Smith, Somervell, and Upshur counties.

**SAND AND GRAVEL (CONSTRUCTION)** — Sand and gravel are among the most extensively utilized resources in Texas. Principal occurrence is along the major streams and in stream terraces. Sand and gravel are important **bulk construction materials, used as railroad ballast, base materials,** and for other purposes.

**SANDSTONE** — Sandstones of a variety of colors and textures are widely distributed in a number of geologic formations in Texas. Some of the sandstones have been quarried for use as **dimension stone** in El Paso, Parker, Terrell, Ward, and other counties. **Crushed sandstone** is produced in Freestone, Gaines, Jasper, McMullen, Motley, and other counties for use as **road-building material, terrazzo stone, and aggregate.**

**SERPENTINITE** — Several masses of serpentinite, which formed from the alteration of basic igneous rocks, are associated with other Precambrian metamorphic rocks of the **Llano Uplift.** The largest deposit is the **Coal Creek serpentinite mass** in northern Blanco and Gillespie counties from which **terrazzo chips** have been produced. Other deposits are present in Gillespie and Llano counties. (The features that are associated with surface and subsurface Cretaceous rocks in several counties in or near the **Balcones Fault Zone** and that are commonly known as **"serpentine plugs"** are not serpentine at all, but are altered igneous volcanic necks and pipes, and mounds of altered volcanic ash — **palagonite** — that accumulated around the former **submarine volcanic pipes.**)

**SHELL** — Oyster shells and other shells in shallow coastal waters and in deposits along the **Texas Gulf Coast** have been produced in the past chiefly by dredging. They were used to a limited extent as raw material in the **manufacture of cement, as concrete aggregate and road base,** and for other purposes. No shell has been produced in Texas since 1981.

**SILVER** — During the period 1885–1952, the production of silver in Texas, as reported by the U.S. Bureau of Mines, totaled about **33 million troy ounces.** For about 70 years, silver was the most consistently produced metal in Texas, although always in moderate quantities. All of the production came from the **Trans-Pecos country** of West Texas, where the silver was mined in Brewster County **(Altuda Mountain),** Culberson and Hudspeth counties **(Van Horn Mountains and Van Horn–Allamoore district),** Hudspeth County **(Quitman Mountains and Eagle Mountains),** and Presidio County **(Chinati Mountains area, Loma Plata mine, and Shafter district).**

Chief producer was the **Presidio mine in the Shafter district,** which began operations in the late 1800s, and, through September 1942, produced more than 30 million ounces of silver — more than 92 percent of Texas' total silver production. Water in the lower mine levels, lean ores, and low price of silver resulted in the closing of the mine in 1942. Another important silver producer was the **Hazel copper-silver mine** in the **Van Horn–Allamoore district** in Culberson County, which accounted for more than 2 million ounces.

An increase in the price of silver in the late 1970s stimulated prospecting for new reserves, and exploration began near the old **Presidio mine,** near the old **Plata Verde mine** in the Van Horn Mountains district, at the Bonanza mine in the **Quitman Mountains** district, and at the old **Hazel mine.** A decline in the price of silver in the early 1980s, however, resulted in reduction of exploration and mine development in the region. The recent rise in value of silver has sparked new interest in the Shafter mining district of West Texas.

**SOAPSTONE** (see **TALC AND SOAPSTONE**).

**SODIUM SULFATE (SALT CAKE)** — Sodium sulfate minerals occur in salt beds and brines of the alkali **playa lakes** of the High Plains in West Texas. In some lakes, the sodium sulfate minerals are present in deposits a few feet beneath the lakebeds. Sodium sulfate also is found in underground brines in the Permian Basin. Current production is from brines and dry salt beds at alkali lakes in Gaines and Terry counties. Past production was reported in Lynn and Ward counties. Sodium sulfate is used chiefly by the **detergent and paper and pulp industries.** Other uses are in the **preparation of glass and other products.**

**STONE** (see **BUILDING STONE** and **CRUSHED STONE**).

**STRONTIUM** — Deposits of the mineral **celestite (strontium sulfate)** have been found in a number of places, including localities in Brown, Coke, Comanche, Fisher, Lampasas, Mills, Nolan, Real, Taylor, Travis, and Williamson counties. Most of the occurrences are very minor, and no strontium is currently produced in the state.

**SULFUR** — Texas is **one of the world's principal sulfur-producing areas.** The sulfur is mined from deposits of native sulfur, and it is extracted from sour (sulfur-bearing) natural gas and petroleum. **Recovered sulfur** is a growing industry and accounted for approximately 60 percent of all 1987 sulfur production in the United States, but only approximately 40 percent of Texas production. Native sulfur is found in large deposits in the caprock of some of the **salt domes** along the Texas Gulf Coast and in some of the surface and subsurface Permian strata of West Texas, notably in Culberson and Pecos counties.

Native sulfur obtained from the underground deposits is known as **Frasch sulfur,** so-called because of Herman Frasch, the chemist who devised the method of drilling wells into the deposits, melting the sulfur with superheated water, and forcing the molten sulfur to the surface. Most of the production now goes to the users in molten form.

Frasch sulfur is produced from only one Gulf Coast salt dome in Wharton County and from West Texas underground Permian strata in Culberson County. Operations at several Gulf Coast domes have been closed in recent years. During the 1940s, acidic sulfur earth was produced in the **Rustler Springs district** in Culberson County for use as a **fertilizer and soil conditioner.** Sulfur is recovered from sour natural gas and petroleum at plants in numerous Texas counties.

Sulfur is used in the preparation of **fertilizers and organic and inorganic chemicals, in petroleum refining,** and for many other purposes.

**TALC AND SOAPSTONE** — Deposits of talc are found in the Precambrian metamorphic rocks of the **Allamoore area** of eastern Hudspeth and western Culberson counties. Soapstone, containing talc, occurs in the Precambrian metamorphic rocks of the **Llano Uplift** area, notably in Blanco, Gillespie, and Llano counties. Current production is from surface mines in the **Allamoore area.** Talc is used in **ceramic, roofing, paint, paper, plastic, synthetic rubber,** and other products.

**TIN** — Tin minerals have been found in El Paso and Mason counties. Small quantities were produced during the early 1900s in the Franklin Mountains north of El Paso. **Cassiterite (tin dioxide)** occurrences in Mason County are believed to be very minor. The **only tin smelter in the United States,** built at **Texas City** by the federal government during World War II and later sold to a private company, processes tin concentrates from ores mined outside of Texas, tin residues, and secondary tin-bearing materials.

**TITANIUM** — The titanium mineral **rutile** has been found in small amounts at the **Mueller prospect** in Jeff Davis County. Another titanium mineral, **ilmenite,** occurs in sandstones in Burleson, Fayette, Lee, Starr, and several other counties. Deposits that would be consid-

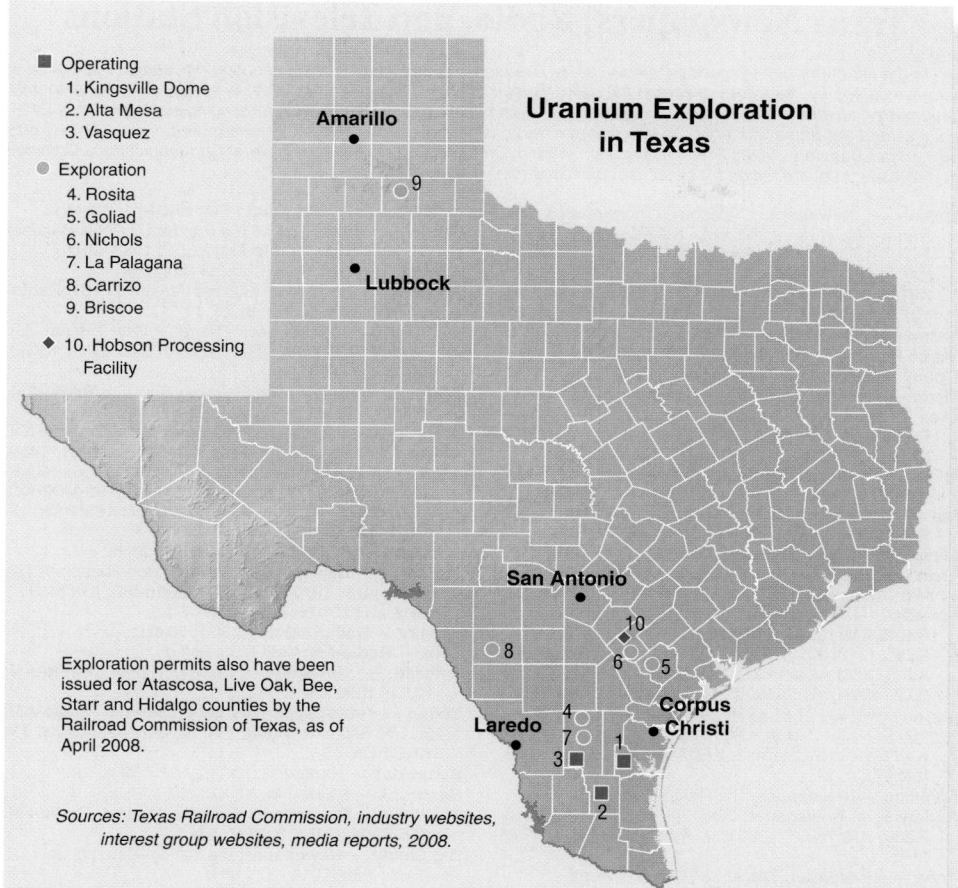

**Uranium Exploration in Texas**

Operating
1. Kingsville Dome
2. Alta Mesa
3. Vasquez

Exploration
4. Rosita
5. Goliad
6. Nichols
7. La Palangana
8. Carrizo
9. Briscoe

10. Hobson Processing Facility

Amarillo
Lubbock
San Antonio
Laredo
Corpus Christi

Exploration permits also have been issued for Atascosa, Live Oak, Bee, Starr and Hidalgo counties by the Railroad Commission of Texas, as of April 2008.

Sources: Texas Railroad Commission, industry websites, interest group websites, media reports, 2008.

ered commercial under present conditions have not been found.

**TRAP ROCK** (see **BASALT**).

**TUNGSTEN** — The tungsten mineral **scheelite** has been found in small deposits in Gillespie and Llano counties and in the **Quitman Mountains** in Hudspeth County. Small deposits of other tungsten minerals have been prospected in the **Cave Peak area** north of Van Horn in Culberson County.

**URANIUM** — Uranium deposits were discovered in the **Texas Coastal Plain** in 1954 when abnormal radioactivity was detected in the Karnes County area. A number of uranium deposits have since been discovered within a belt of strata extending more than 250 miles from the middle Coastal Plain southwestward to the Rio Grande.

Various uranium minerals also have been found in other areas of Texas, including the **Trans-Pecos**, the **Llano Uplift**, and the **High Plains**. With the exception of small shipments from the High Plains during the 1950s, all the uranium production in Texas has been from the Coastal Plain. Uranium has been obtained from surface mines extending from northern Live Oak County, southeastern Atascosa County, across northern Karnes County, and into southern Gonzales County. Uranium is produced by in-situ leaching, brought to the surface through wells, and stripped from the solution at recovery operations.

In 1999, uranium mining shut down because of

decreased value and demand. Production resumed in Texas in late 2004, when inventories were depleted and market prices rose to economic levels that allowed resumption of production. A total of 1.38 million pounds (606.5 tons) of $eU_3O_8$ was produced in South Texas in 2007.

**VERMICULITE** — Vermiculite, a mica-like mineral that expands when heated, occurs in Burnet, Gillespie, Llano, Mason, and other counties in the **Llano Uplift** region. It has been produced at a surface mine in Llano County. Vermiculite, mined outside of Texas, is exfoliated (expanded) at plants in Dallas, Houston, and San Antonio. Exfoliated vermiculite is used for **lightweight concrete aggregate, horticulture, insulation,** and other purposes.

**VOLCANIC ASH** (see **PUMICITE**).

**ZEOLITES** — The zeolite minerals **clinoptilolite** and **analcime** occur in Tertiary lavas and tuffs in Brewster, Jeff Davis, and Presidio counties in West Texas. Clinoptilolite also is found associated with Tertiary tuffs in the southern Texas Coastal Plain, including deposits in Karnes, McMullen, and Webb counties, and currently is produced in McMullen County. Zeolites, sometimes called **"molecular sieves,"** can be used in **ion-exchange processes to reduce pollution,** as a catalyst in **oil cracking,** in obtaining **high-purity oxygen and nitrogen** from air, in **water purification,** and for many other purposes.

**ZINC** (see **LEAD AND ZINC**). ☆

# Texas Newspapers, Radio, and Television Stations

*In the list of print and broadcast media, below, frequency of publication of subscription newspapers is indicated after the names by the following codes: (D) daily, (S) semiweekly, (TW) triweekly, (BW) biweekly, (SM) semimonthly, (M) monthly; all others are weeklies. The radio and TV stations are those with valid operating licenses as of July 2014. Not included are those with only construction permits or with applications pending. Newspaper Source: 2014 Texas Newspaper Directory, Texas Press Association, Austin; Broadcast Media Source: Federal Communications Commission website: http://transition.fcc.gov/mb/audio/index.html.*

**Abilene** — **Newspaper:** Abilene Reporter-News (D). **Radio-AM:** KSLI, 1280 kHz; KWKC, 1340; KYYW, 1470; KZQQ, 1560. **Radio-FM:** KGNZ, 88.1 MHz; KACU, 89.7; KAGT, 90.5; KAQD, 91.3; KULL, 92.5; KFGL, 100.7; KEAN, 105.1; KKHR, 106.3; KEYJ, 107.9. **TV:** KXVA-Ch. 15; KTAB-Ch. 24; KRBC-Ch. 29.

**Alamo** — **Radio-FM:** KJAV, 104.9 MHz.

**Alamo Heights** — **Radio-AM:** KDRY, 1100 kHz.

**Albany** — **Newspaper:** Albany News.

**Aledo** — **Newspaper:** The Community News.

**Alice** — **Newspaper:** Alice Echo-News Journal (TW). **Radio-AM:** KOPY, 1070 kHz. **Radio-FM:** KIFR, 88.3 MHz; KOPY, 92.1; KNDA, 102.9.

**Allen** — **Newspaper:** The Allen American. **Radio-FM:** KESN, 103.3 MHz.

**Alpine** — **Newspaper:** Alpine Avalanche. **Radio-AM:** KVLF, 1240 kHz. **Radio-FM:** KALP, 92.7 MHz.

**Alvarado** — **Newspapers:** Alvarado Post; Alvarado Star.

**Alvin** — **Newspaper:** Alvin Sun. **Radio-AM:** KTEK, 1110 kHz. **Radio-FM:** KACC, 89.7 MHz. **TV:** KFTH-Ch. 36.

**Amarillo** — **Newspaper:** Amarillo Globe-News (D). **Radio-AM:** KGNC, 710 kHz; KIXZ, 940; KTNZ, 1010; KZIP, 1310; KDJW, 1360; KPUR, 1440. **Radio-FM:** KJRT, 88.3 MHz; KXLV, 89.1; KACV, 89.9; KAVW, 90.7; KXRI, 91.9; KQIZ, 93.1; KMXJ, 94.1; KXSS, 96.9; KGNC, 99.7; KPRF, 98.7; KBZD, 99.7; KXGL, 100.9; KATP, 101.9; KRGN, 102.9; KJJP, 105.7. **TV:** KVII-Ch. 7; KACV-Ch. 8; KFDA-Ch. 10; KCIT-Ch. 15; KAMR-Ch. 19.

**Anahuac** — **Newspaper:** The Progress.

**Andrews** — **Newspaper:** Andrews County News (S). **Radio-AM:** KACT, 1360 kHz. **Radio-FM:** KACT, 105.5 MHz.

**Anna** — **Newspaper:** The Anna-Melissa Tribune.

**Anson** — **Newspaper:** Western Observer. **Radio-FM:** KTLT, 98.1 MHz.

**Aransas Pass** — **Newspapers:** Aransas Pass Progress; The Coastal Bend Herald. **Radio-FM:** KKWV, 88.1 MHz.

**Archer City** — **Newspaper:** Archer County News. **Radio-FM:** KPMA, 91.9 MHz.

**Arlington** — **Radio-FM:** KLTY, 94.9 MHz. **TV:** KPXD-Ch. 42.

**Aspermont** — **Newspaper:** Stonewall County Courier.

**Athens** — **Newspaper:** Athens Daily Review (D). **Radio-AM:** KLVQ, 1410 kHz. **Radio-FM:** KATG, 88.1 MHz.

**Atlanta** — **Newspaper:** Atlanta Citizens Journal (S). **Radio-AM:** KPYN, 900 kHz. **Radio-FM:** KNRB, 100.1 MHz.

**Austin** — **Newspapers:** Austin American-Statesman (D); Austin Business Journal; Daily Texan (D); Texas Observer (M); West Austin News; Westlake Picayune. **Radio-AM:** KLBJ, 590 kHz; KVET, 1300; KFON, 1490. **Radio-FM:** KAZI, 88.7 MHz; KMFA, 89.5; KUT, 90.5; KVRX, 91.7; KLBJ, 93.7; KKMJ, 95.5; KVET, 98.1; KASE, 100.7; KPEZ, 102.3. **TV:** KTBC-Ch. 7; KXAN-CH. 21; KLRU-Ch. 22; KVUE-CH. 33; KEYE-Ch. 43; KNVA-Ch. 49.

**Azle** — **Newspaper:** Azle News. **Radio-FM:** KTCY,101.7 MHz.

**Baird** — **Newspapers:** Baird Banner; Callahan County Star. **Radio-FM:** KORQ, 95.1 MHz.

**Balch Springs** — **Radio-AM:** KSKY, 660 kHz.

**Ballinger** — **Newspaper:** Ballinger Ledger. **Radio-AM:**

KRUN, 1400 kHz. **Radio-FM:** KKCN, 103.1 MHz.

**Bandera** — **Newspapers:** The Bandera Bulletin; Bandera County Courier. **Radio-FM:** KEEP, 103.1 MHz.

**Bartlett** — **Newspaper:** Tribune-Progress.

**Bastrop** — **Newspaper:** Bastrop Advertiser (S). **Radio-FM:** KHIB, 88.5 MHz; KLZT, 107.1.

**Bay City** — **Newspaper:** The Bay City Tribune (S). **Radio-FM:** KEDR, 88.1 MHz; KZBJ, 89.5; KXGJ, 101.7; KMKS, 102.5.

**Baytown** — **Newspaper:** Baytown Sun (D). **Radio-AM:** KWWJ, 1360 kHz. **TV:** KUBE-Ch. 41.

**Beaumont** — **Newspaper:** The Beaumont Enterprise (D). **Radio-AM:** KLVI, 560 kHz; KZZB, 990; KIKR, 1450. **Radio-FM:** KLBT, 88.1 MHz; KGHY, 88.5; KTXB, 89.7; KVLU, 91.3; KQXY, 94.1; KYKR, 95.1; KFNC, 97.5; KTCX, 102.5; KQQK, 107.9. **TV:** KBMT-Ch. 12; KFDM-Ch. 21; KITU-Ch. 33.

**Bee Cave** — **Radio-FM:** KTXX, 104.9 MHz.

**Beeville** — **Newspaper:** Beeville Bee-Picayune (S). **Radio-AM:** KIBL, 1490 kHz. **Radio-FM:** KVFM, 91.3 MHz; KTKO, 105.7; KRXB, 107.1.

**Bellaire** — **Radio-AM:** KGOW, 1560 kHz.

**Bells** — **Radio-FM:** KMKT, 93.1 MHz.

**Bellville** — **Newspaper:** Bellville Times. **Radio-AM:** KULF, 1090 kHz.

**Belton** — **Newspaper:** The Belton Journal. **Radio-AM:** KTON, 940 kHz. **Radio-FM:** KOOC, 106.3 MHz. **TV:** KNCT-Ch. 46.

**Benavides** — **Radio-FM:** KXTM, 107.7 MHz.

**Benbrook** — **Radio-FM:** KDXX, 107.1 MHz.

**Big Lake** — **Newspaper:** Big Lake Wildcat. **Radio-FM:** KPDB, 98.3 MHz; KWTR, 104.1.

**Big Sandy** — **Newspaper:** Big Sandy–Hawkins Journal. **Radio-FM:** KTAA, 90.7 MHz.

**Big Spring** — **Newspaper:** Big Spring Herald (D). **Radio-AM:** KBYG, 1400 kHz; KBST, 1490. **Radio-FM:** KPBD, 89.3 MHz; KBCX, 91.5; KBTS, 94.3; KBST, 95.7. **TV:** KWAB-Ch. 33.

**Bishop** — **Newspaper:** Kingsville Record and Bishop News. **Radio-FM:** KMZZ, 106.9 MHz.

**Blanco** — **Newspaper:** Blanco County News. **TV:** KNIC-Ch. 18.

**Bloomington** — **Radio-FM:** KHVT, 91.5 MHz; KLUB, 106.9.

**Boerne** — **Newspapers:** Boerne Star (S). **Radio-AM:** KBRN, 1500 kHz.

**Bogata** — **Newspaper:** Bogata News–Talco Times.

**Bonham** — **Radio-AM:** KFYN, 1420 kHz.

**Booker** — **Newspaper:** Booker News.

**Borger** — **Newspaper:** Borger News-Herald (D). **Radio-AM:** KQTY, 1490 kHz. **Radio-FM:** KASV, 88.7 MHz; KQFX, 104.3; KQTY, 106.7. **TV:** KEYU-Ch. 31.

**Bovina** — **Radio-FM:** KKNM, 96.5 MHz.

**Bowie** — **Newspaper:** Bowie News (S). **Radio-AM:** KNTX, 1410 kHz.

**Brackettville** — **Newspaper:** The Brackett News.

**Brady** — **Newspaper:** Brady Standard-Herald. **Radio-AM:** KNEL, 1490 kHz. **Radio-FM:** KNEL, 95.3 MHz.

**Breckenridge** — **Newspaper:** Breckenridge American (S). **Radio-AM:** KROO, 1430 kHz. **Radio-FM:** KQXB, 89.9 MHz; KLXK, 93.5.

**Bremond** — **Newspaper:** The Bremond Press.

**Brenham** — **Newspaper:** Brenham Banner-Press (D). **Radio-AM:** KWHI, 1280 kHz. **Radio-FM:** KUBJ, 89.7 MHz; KLTR, 94.1; KTTX, 106.1.

**Bridgeport** — **Newspaper:** Bridgeport Index. **Radio-FM:** KBOC, 98.3 MHz.

**Brookshire** — **Newspaper:** The Times Tribune. **Radio-AM:** KCHN, 1050 kHz.

**Brownfield** — **Newspaper:** Brownfield News (S). **Radio-AM:** KKUB, 1300 kHz. **Radio-FM:** KPBB, 88.5 MHz; KMLU, 90.7; KTTU, 104.3.

**Brownsboro** — **Newspaper:** Chandler & Brownsboro Statesman.

**Brownsville** — **Newspaper:** The Brownsville Herald (D). **Radio-AM:** KVNS, 1700 kHz. **Radio-FM:** KBNR, 88.3 MHz; KKPS, 99.5. **TV:** KVEO-Ch. 24.

**Brownwood** — **Newspaper:** Brownwood Bulletin (D). **Radio-AM:** KXYL, 1240 kHz; KBWD, 1380. **Radio-FM:** KPBE, 89.3 MHz; KBUB, 90.3; KHBW, 91.7; KQBZ, 96.9; KPSM, 99.3; KOXE, 101.3.

**Bruni** — **Radio-FM:** KMAE, 106.5 MHz.

**Bryan** — **Newspaper:** The Eagle (D). **Radio-AM:** KTAM, 1240 kHz; KAGC, 1510. **Radio-FM:** KORA, 98.3 MHz; KNFX, 99.5; KKYS, 104.7. **TV:** KAMU-Ch.12; KYLE-Ch. 28; KBTX-Ch. 50.

**Buda** — **Newspaper:** Hays Free Press. **Radio-FM:** KROX, 101.5 MHz.

**Buffalo** — **Newspapers:** Buffalo Express; The Buffalo Press.

**Bullard** — **Newspaper:** Bullard Banner News.

**Buna** — **Newspaper:** The Buna Beacon.

**Burkburnett** — **Newspaper:** Burkburnett Informer Star. **Radio-FM:** KYYI, 104.7 MHz.

**Burleson** — **Newspaper:** Burleson Star (S). **Radio-AM:** KCLE, 1460 kHz.

**Burnet** — **Newspapers:** Burnet Bulletin; Citizens Gazette. **Radio-AM:** KRHC, 1340 kHz. **Radio-FM:** KBEY, 92.5 MHz.

**Bushland** — **Radio-FM:** KTXP, 91.5 MHz.

**Byrne** — **Radio-FM:** KLRW, 88.5 MHz.

**Caldwell** — **Newspaper:** Burleson County Tribune. **Radio-FM:** KALD, 91.9 MHz; KAPN, 107.3.

**Callisburg** — **Radio-FM:** KPFC, 91.9 MHz.

**Cameron** — **Newspaper:** The Cameron Herald. **Radio-AM:** KTAE, 1330 kHz. **Radio-FM:** KMIL, 105.1 MHz.

**Campbell** — **Radio-FM:** KRVA, 107.1 MHz.

**Camp Wood** — **Radio-FM:** KAYG, 99.1 MHz.

**Canadian** — **Newspaper:** Canadian Record.

**Canton** — **Newspapers:** Canton Herald; Van Zandt News. **Radio-AM:** KRDH, 1510 kHz.

**Canyon** — **Newspaper:** The Canyon News (S). **Radio-AM:** KZRK, 1550 kHz. **Radio-FM:** KWTS, 91.1 MHz; KPUR, 107.1; KZRK, 107.9.

**Carrizo Springs** — **Newspaper:** Carrizo Springs Javelin. **Radio-AM:** KBEN, 1450 kHz. **Radio-FM:** KCZO, 92.1 MHz; KAJP, 93.5.

**Carrollton** — **Radio-AM:** KJON, 850 kHz.

**Carthage** — **Newspaper:** The Panola Watchman (S). **Radio-AM:** KGAS, 1590 kHz. **Radio-FM:** KTUX, 98.9 MHz; KGAS, 104.3.

**Castroville** — **Newspaper:** Castroville News Bulletin.

**Cedar Lake** — **Radio-FM:** KQVI, 89.9 MHz.

**Cedar Park** — **Newspaper:** Hill Country News Weekender. **Radio-FM:** KGSR, 93.3 MHz.

**Celina** — **Newspaper:** The Celina Record.

**Center** — **Newspaper:** The Light & Champion (TW). **Radio-AM:** KDET, 930 kHz. **Radio-FM:** KQBB, 100.5 MHz.

**Centerville** — **Newspaper:** Centerville News. **Radio-FM:** KUZN, 105.9 MHz.

**Charlotte** — **Radio-FM:** KSAQ, 102.3 MHz.

**Chico** — **Newspaper:** Chico Texan.

**Childress** — **Newspaper:** The Childress Index (S). **Radio-AM:** KCTX, 1510 kHz. **Radio-FM:** KFCH, 89.5 MHz; KCTX, 96.1.

**Cisco** — **Newspaper:** Cisco Press (S).

**Clarendon** — **Newspaper:** Clarendon Enterprise. **Radio-FM:** KEFH, 99.3 MHz.

**Clarksville** — **Newspaper:** Clarksville Times. **Radio-AM:** KCAR, 1350 kHz. **Radio-FM:** KGAP, 98.5 MHz.

**Claude** — **Newspaper:** The Claude News. **Radio-FM:** KARX, 95.7 MHz.

**Clear Lake** — **Newspaper:** The Bay Area Citizen.

**Cleburne** — **Newspaper:** Cleburne Times-Review (D). **Radio-AM:** KHFX, 1140 kHz.

**Cleveland** — **Newspaper:** Cleveland Advocate. **Radio-FM:** KTHT, 97.1 MHz.

**Clifton** — **Newspaper:** Clifton Record. **Radio-FM:** KWOW, 104.1 MHz.

**Clute** — **Newspaper:** The Facts (D).

**Clyde** — **Newspaper:** Clyde Journal.

**Coahoma** — **Radio-FM:** KXCS, 105.5 MHz.

**Cockrell Hill** — **Radio-AM:** KRVA, 1600 kHz.

**Coleman** — **Newspaper:** Chronicle & Democrat-Voice. **Radio-AM:** KSTA, 1000 kHz. **Radio-FM:** KXYL, 102.3 MHz.

**College Station** — **Newspaper:** The Battalion (D). **Radio-AM:** KZNE, 1150 kHz; WTAW, 1620. **Radio-FM:** KEOS, 89.1 MHz; KLGS, 89.9; KAMU, 90.9; KNDE, 95.1. **TV:** KAMU-Ch. 12.

**Colorado City** — **Newspaper:** Colorado City Record. **Radio-AM:** KVMC, 1320 kHz. **Radio-FM:** KAUM, 107.1 MHz.

**Columbus** — **Newspapers:** The Banner Press Newspaper; Colorado County Citizen. **Radio-FM:** KULM, 98.3 MHz.

**Comanche** — **Newspaper:** Comanche Chief. **Radio-AM:** KCOM, 1550 kHz. **Radio-FM:** KYOX, 94.3 MHz.

**Comfort** — **Newspaper:** The Comfort News. **Radio-FM:** KGSX, 95.1 MHz.

**Commerce** — **Newspaper:** Commerce Journal. **Radio-FM:** KETR, 88.9 MHz; KYJC, 91.3.

**Conroe** — **Newspaper:** The Courier (D). **Radio-AM:** KJOJ, 880 kHz; KYOK, 1140. **Radio-FM:** KAFR, 88.3 MHz; KHPT, 106.9. **TV:** KPXB-Ch. 32; KTBU-Ch. 42.

**Converse** — **Radio-AM:** KTMR, 1130 kHz.

**Cooper** — **Newspaper:** Cooper Review. **Radio-FM:** KPCO, 89.9 MHz.

**Coppell** — **Newspaper:** Citizens' Advocate.

**Copperas Cove** — **Newspaper:** Copperas Cove Leader-Press (S). **Radio-FM:** KSSM, 103.1 MHz.

**Corpus Christi** — **Newspapers:** Corpus Christi Caller-Times (D); Coastal Bend Legal & Business News (D). **Radio-AM:** KCTA, 1030 kHz; KCCT, 1150; KSIX, 1230; KKTX, 1360; KUNO, 1400; KEYS, 1440. **Radio-FM:** KKLM, 88.7 MHz; KEDT, 90.3; KBNJ, 91.7; KMXR, 93.9; KBSO, 94.7; KZFM, 95.5; KLTG, 96.5; KRYS, 99.1. **TV:** KIII-Ch. 8; KZTV-Ch. 10; KRIS-Ch. 13; KEDT-Ch. 23; KORO-Ch. 27; KUQI-Ch. 38.

**Corrigan** — **Newspaper:** Corrigan Times.

**Corsicana** — **Newspapers:** Corsicana Daily Sun (D); Navarro County Times. **Radio-AM:** KAND, 1340 kHz.

**Crane** — **Newspaper:** Crane News. **Radio-AM:** KXOI, 810 kHz. **Radio-FM:** KMMZ, 101.3 MHz.

**Creedmoor** — **Radio-AM:** KZNX, 1530 kHz.

**Crockett** — **Newspaper:** Houston County Courier (S). **Radio-AM:** KIVY, 1290 kHz. **Radio-FM:** KCKT, 88.5 MHz; KIVY, 92.7; KBHT, 93.5.

**Cross Plains** — **Newspaper:** Cross Plains Review.

**Crowell** — **Newspaper:** Foard County News.

**Crowley** — **Newspaper:** Crowley Star.

**Crystal Beach** — **Radio-FM:** KSTB, 101.5 MHz; KPTY, 105.3.

**Crystal City** — **Newspaper:** Zavala County Sentinel. **Radio-FM:** KHER, 94.3 MHz.

**Cuero** — **Newspaper:** Cuero Record. **Radio-FM:** KTLZ, 89.9 MHz.

**Cypress** — **Radio-AM:** KYND, 1520 kHz.

**Daingerfield** — **Newspaper:** The Bee. **Radio-AM:** KNGR, 1560 kHz.

**Dalhart** — **Newspaper:** Dalhart Texan (TW). **Radio-AM:** KXIT, 1240 kHz. **Radio-FM:** KTDA, 91.7 MHz; KPPC, 96.3.

**Dallas — Newspapers:** The Dallas Morning News (D); Dallas Business Journal; Daily Commercial Record (D); Park Cities News; Park Cities People; Texas Jewish Post; Texas Lawyer. **Radio-AM:** KLIF, 570 kHz; KGGR, 1040; KRLD, 1080; KFXR, 1190; KTCK, 1310; KNIT, 1480. **Radio-FM:** KNON, 89.3 MHz; KERA, 90.1; KCBI, 90.9; KKXT, 91.7; KZPS, 92.5; KBFB, 97.9; KLUV, 98.7; KJKK, 100.3; WRR, 101.1; KDMX, 102.9; KKDA, 104.5; KRLD, 105.3. **TV:** WFAA-Ch. 9; KERA-Ch. 14; KDAF-Ch. 32; KDFW-Ch. 35; KDFI-Ch. 36; KXTX-Ch. 40; KDTX-Ch. 45.

**Decatur — Newspaper:** Wise County Messenger (S). **Radio-FM:** KDKR, 91.3 MHz; KRNB, 105.7. **TV:** KMPX-Ch. 30.

**Deer Park — Radio-FM:** KAMA, 104.9 MHz.

**De Kalb — Newspaper:** De Kalb News (S).

**De Leon — Newspapers:** De Leon Free Press.

**Dell City — Newspaper:** Hudspeth County Herald.

**Del Mar Hills — Radio-AM:** KVOZ, 890 kHz.

**Del Rio — Newspaper:** Del Rio News-Herald (D). **Radio-AM:** KTJK, 1230 kHz; KWMC, 1490. **Radio-FM:** KDLI, 89.9 MHz; KDLK, 94.1; KTDR, 96.3.

**Del Valle — Radio-AM:** KIXL, 970 kHz.

**Denison — Radio-FM:** KYFB, 91.5 MHz.

**Denton — Newspaper:** Denton Record-Chronicle (D). **Radio-FM:** KFZO, 99.1 MHz; KHKS, 106.1. **TV:** KDTN-Ch. 43.

**Denver City — Newspaper:** Denver City Press.

**Deport — Newspaper:** Deport Times-Blossom Times.

**DeSoto — Newspapers:** Focus Daily News (D).

**Detroit — Newspaper:** Detroit Weekly.

**Devine — Newspaper:** Devine News. **Radio-FM:** KRPT, 92.5 MHz.

**Diboll — Newspaper:** Diboll Free Press. **Radio-AM:** KSML, 1260 kHz. **Radio-FM:** KAFX, 95.5 MHz.

**Dilley — Radio-FM:** KVWG, 95.3 MHz; KLMO, 98.9.

**Dimmitt — Newspaper:** Castro County News. **Radio-AM:** KDHN, 1470 kHz. **Radio-FM:** KNNK, 100.5 MHz.

**Doss — Radio-FM:** KGLF, 88.1 MHz.

**Dripping Springs — Newspapers:** Dripping Springs Century News; The News-Dispatch. **Radio-FM:** KLLR, 91.9 MHz.

**Dublin — Newspaper:** Dublin Citizen. **Radio-FM:** KSTV, 93.1 MHz.

**Dumas — Newspaper:** Moore County News-Press (S). **Radio-AM:** KDDD, 800 kHz. **Radio-FM:** KDDD, 95.3 MHz.

**Eagle Lake — Newspaper:** Eagle Lake Headlight.

**Eagle Pass — Radio-AM:** KEPS, 1270 kHz. **Radio-FM:** KEPI, 88.7 MHz; KEPX, 89.5; KINL, 92.7. **TV:** KVAW-Ch. 18.

**East Bernard — Newspaper:** East Bernard Express.

**Eastland — Newspaper:** Eastland Telegram (S). **Radio-FM:** KQXE, 91.1 MHz; KATX, 97.7.

**Eden — Newspaper:** The Eden Echo.

**Edgewood — Newspaper:** Edgewood Enterprise.

**Edinburg — Radio-AM:** KURV, 710 kHz. **Radio-FM:** KOIR, 88.5 MHz; KBFM, 104.1; KVLY, 107.9.

**Edna — Newspaper:** Jackson County Herald-Tribune. **Radio-FM:** KIOX, 96.1 MHz.

**El Campo — Newspaper:** El Campo Leader-News (S). **Radio-AM:** KULP, 1390 kHz. **Radio-FM:** KNTE, 96.9 MHz.

**Eldorado — Newspaper:** Eldorado Success. **Radio-FM:** KOPE, 88.9 MHz; KLDE, 104.9.

**Electra — Newspaper:** Electra Star-News. **Radio-FM:** KOLI, 94.9 MHz.

**Elgin — Newspaper:** Elgin Courier. **Radio-FM:** KXXS, 92.5 MHz.

**El Paso — Newspaper:** El Paso Times (D). **Radio-AM:** KROD, 600 kHz; KTSM, 690; KAMA, 750; KQBU, 920; KXPL, 1060; KHRO, 1150; KVIV, 1340; KHEY, 1380; KELP, 1590; KSVE, 1650. **Radio-FM:** KTEP, 88.5 MHz; KKLY; 89.5; KVER, 91.1; KOFX, 92.3; KSII,

93.1; KINT, 93.9; KYSE, 94.7; KLAQ, 95.5; KHEY, 96.3; KBNA, 97.5; KTSM, 99.9; KPRR, 102.1. **TV:** KVIA-Ch. 7; KTSM-Ch. 9; KCOS-Ch. 13; KFOX-CH. 15; KDBC-Ch. 18; KSCE-Ch. 39; KTFN-Ch. 51.

**Emory — Newspaper:** Rains County Leader.

**Encinal — Radio-FM:** KELT, 102.5 MHz.

**Ennis — Newspaper:** Ennis Daily News (D).

**Escobares — Radio-FM:** KERG, 104.7 MHz.

**Fabens — Radio-FM:** KPAS, 103.1 MHz.

**Fairfield — Newspapers:** Freestone County Times; The Fairfield Recorder. **Radio-FM:** KNES, 99.1 MHz.

**Falfurrias — Newspaper:** Falfurrias Facts. **Radio-AM:** KLDS, 1260 kHz. **Radio-FM:** KDFM, 103.3 MHz; KPSO, 106.3.

**Fannett — Radio-FM:** KZFT, 90.5 MHz.

**Farmersville — Newspaper:** Farmersville Times. **Radio-AM:** KFCD, 990 kHz. **Radio-FM:** KXEZ, 92.1 MHz.

**Farwell — Newspaper:** State Line Tribune. **Radio-AM:** KMUL, 830 kHz; KIJN, 1060. **Radio-FM:** KIJN, 92.3 MHz; KICA, 98.3. **TV:** KPTF-Ch. 18.

**Ferris — Newspaper:** The Ellis County Press. **Radio-AM:** KDFT, 540 kHz.

**Flatonia — Newspaper:** The Flatonia Argus.

**Floresville — Newspaper:** Wilson County News. **Radio-FM:** KJMA, 89.7 MHz; KTFM, 94.1.

**Flower Mound — Radio-FM:** WBAP, 96.7 MHz.

**Floydada — Newspaper:** Floyd County Hesperian-Beacon. **Radio-AM:** KFLP, 900 kHz. **Radio-FM:** KFLP, 106.1 MHz.

**Forney — Newspaper:** Forney Messenger.

**Fort Davis — Newspaper:** Jeff Davis County Mt. Dispatch.

**Fort Stockton — Newspaper:** Fort Stockton Pioneer. **Radio-AM:** KFST, 860 kHz. **Radio-FM:** KRAF, 88.3 MHz; KFST, 94.3.

**Fort Worth — Newspapers:** Fort Worth Business Press; Commercial Recorder (D); Fort Worth Star-Telegram (D); Texas Jewish Post. **Radio-AM:** WBAP, 820 kHz; KFJZ, 870; KHVN, 970; KFLC, 1270; KKGM, 1630. **Radio-FM:** KTCU, 88.7 MHz; KLNO, 94.1; KSCS, 96.3; KEGL, 97.1; KPLX, 99.5; KDGE, 102.1; KMVK, 107.5. **TV:** KFWD-Ch. 9; KTVT-Ch. 11; KTXA-Ch. 29; KXAS-Ch. 41.

**Franklin — Newspaper:** Franklin News Weekly. **Radio-FM:** KJXJ, 103.9 MHz.

**Frankston — Newspaper:** The Frankston Citizen. **Radio-FM:** KOYE, 96.7 MHz.

**Fredericksburg — Newspaper:** Standard-Radio Post. **Radio-AM:** KNAF, 910 kHz. **Radio-FM:** KBLC, 91.5 MHz; KNAF, 105.7. **TV:** KCWX-Ch. 5.

**Freeport — Radio-FM:** KJOJ, 103.3 MHz.

**Freer — Newspaper:** Freer Press. **Radio-FM:** KPBN, 90.7 MHz; KBRA, 95.9.

**Friendswood — Newspapers:** Friendswood Journal; Friendswood Reporter News.

**Friona — Newspaper:** Friona Star. **Radio-FM:** KGRW, 94.7 MHz.

**Frisco — Newspaper:** The Frisco Enterprise. **Radio-AM:** KATH, 910 kHz.

**Fritch — Newspaper:** The Eagle Press.

**Fulshear — Newspaper:** Fulshear Times.

**Gail — Newspaper:** Borden Star.

**Gainesville — Newspaper:** Gainesville Daily Register (D). **Radio-AM:** KGAF, 1580 kHz. **Radio-FM:** KSOC, 94.5 MHz.

**Galveston — Newspaper:** Galveston County Daily News (D). **Radio-AM:** KGBC, 1540 kHz. **Radio-FM:** KOVE, 106.5 MHz. **TV:** KLTJ-Ch. 23; KTMD-Ch. 48.

**Ganado — Radio-FM:** KHTZ, 104.7 MHz.

**Gardendale — Radio-FM:** KFZX, 102.1 MHz.

**Garland — Radio-AM:** KAAM, 770 kHz. **TV:** KUVN-Ch. 23.

**Garrison — Newspaper:** Garrison In The News.

Gatesville — Newspaper: Gatesville Messenger and Star Forum (S). Radio-FM: KVLW, 88.1 MHz.
Georgetown — Newspapers: Sunday Sun; Williamson County Sun. Radio-FM: KHFI, 96.7 MHz; KLJA, 107.7.
George West — Radio-FM: KGWT, 93.5 MHz.
Giddings — Newspaper: Giddings Times & News. Radio-FM: KANJ, 91.1 MHz.
Gilmer — Newspaper: Gilmer Mirror (S). Radio-AM: KOFY, 1060 kHz. Radio-FM: KFRO, 95.3 MHz.
Ginger — Radio-FM: KYFA, 91.5 MHz.
Gladewater — Newspaper: Gladewater Mirror. Radio-AM: KEES, 1430 kHz.
Glen Rose — Newspapers: Glen Rose Newspaper; Glen Rose Reporter. Radio-FM: KTFW, 92.1 MHz.
Goldsmith — Radio-FM: KTXO, 94.7 MHz.
Goldthwaite — Newspaper: Goldthwaite Eagle.
Goliad — Newspaper: The Texan Express. Radio-FM: KHMC, 95.9 MHz.
Gonzales — Newspaper: Gonzales Inquirer (S). Radio-AM: KCTI, 1450 kHz. Radio-FM: KZAR, 88.1 MHz; KMLR, 106.3.
Gorman — Newspaper: Gorman Progress.
Graford — Newspaper: Lake Country Sun.
Graham — Newspaper: The Graham Leader (S). Radio-AM: KSWA, 1330 kHz. Radio-FM: KWKQ, 94.7 MHz.
Granbury — Newspaper: Hood County News (S). Radio-AM: KPIR, 1420 kHz.
Grand Prairie — Radio-AM: KKDA, 730 kHz.
Grand Saline — Newspaper: Grand Saline Sun.
Grandview — Newspaper: Grandview Tribune.
Grapeland — Newspaper: The Messenger (S).
Greenville — Newspaper: Herald-Banner (D). Radio-AM: KGVL, 1400 kHz. Radio-FM: KTXG, 90.5 MHz; KIKT, 93.5. TV: KTAQ-Ch. 46.
Gregory — Radio-FM: KPUS, 104.5 MHz.
Groesbeck — Newspaper: Groesbeck Journal.
Groom — Newspaper: Groom News.
Groves — Radio-FM: KCOL, 92.5 MHz.
Groveton — Newspaper: Groveton News.
Gun Barrel City — Newspaper: Cedar Creek Pilot.

Hale Center — Newspaper: Hale Center American.
Hallettsville — Newspaper: Hallettsville Tribune-Herald. Radio-AM: KHLT, 1520 kHz. Radio-FM: KTXM, 99.9 MHz.
Haltom City — Radio-FM: KLIF, 93.3 MHz.
Hamilton — Newspaper: Hamilton Herald-News. Radio-AM: KCLW, 900 kHz. Radio-FM: KHHG, 107.7 MHz.
Hamlin — Newspaper: Hamlin Herald. Radio-FM: KCDD, 103.7 MHz.
Hardin — Radio-FM: KGBV, 90.7 MHz.
Harker Heights — Radio-FM: KUSJ, 105.5 MHz.
Harlingen — Newspaper: Valley Morning Star (D). Radio-AM: KGBT, 1530 kHz. Radio-FM: KMBH, 88.9 MHz; KFRQ, 94.5; KBTQ, 96.1. TV: KGBT-Ch. 31; KLUJ-Ch. 34; KMBH-Ch. 38.
Hart — Newspaper: Hart Beat. Radio-FM: KKFC, 89.3 MHz.
Haskell — Newspaper: Haskell Free Press. Radio-FM: KVRP, 97.1 MHz.
Hearne — Newspaper: Hearne–Robertson County News. Radio-FM: KEDC, 88.5 MHz; KVJM, 103.1.
Hebbronville — Newspapers: Hebbronville View; Jim Hogg County Enterprise. Radio-FM: KAZF, 91.9 MHz; KEKO, 101.7.
Helotes — Radio-FM: KONO, 101.1 MHz.
Hemphill — Newspaper: The Sabine County Reporter. Radio-AM: KPBL, 1240 kHz. Radio-FM: KTHP, 103.9 MHz.
Hempstead — Newspaper: Waller County News-Citizen. Radio-FM: KTWL, 105.3 MHz.
Henderson — Newspaper: Henderson Daily News (D). Radio-AM: KWRD, 1470 kHz.
Henrietta — Newspaper: Clay County Leader.

Hereford — Newspaper: Hereford Brand (D). Radio-AM: KPAN, 860 kHz. Radio-FM: KRLH, 90.9 MHz; KJNZ, 103.5; KPAN, 106.3.
Hewitt — Newspaper: Hometown News. Radio-FM: KDRW, 106.7 MHz.
Hico — Newspaper: Hico News Review.
Highland Park — Radio-AM: KVCE, 1160 kHz. Radio-FM: KVIL, 103.7 MHz.
Highlands — Newspaper: Highlands Star/Crosby Courier.
Highland Village — Radio-FM: KWRD, 100.7 MHz.
Hillsboro — Newspaper: Hillsboro Reporter (S). Radio-AM: KHBR, 1560 kHz. Radio-FM: KBRQ, 102.5 MHz.
Holliday — Radio-FM: KGVB, 90.9 MHz; KWFB, 100.9.
Hondo — Newspaper: Hondo Anvil Herald. Radio-AM: KCWM, 1460 kHz. Radio-FM: KZIC, 89.9 MHz; KMFR, 105.9.
Honey Grove — Newspaper: The Weekly Gazette.
Hooks — Radio-FM: KPWW, 95.9 MHz.
Hornsby — Radio-FM: KOOP, 91.7 MHz.
Houston — Newspapers: Houston Business Journal; Houston Chronicle (D); Daily Court Review (D); Houston Forward Times; Jewish Herald-Voice. Radio-AM: KILT, 610 kHz; KTRH, 740; KBME, 790; KEYH, 850; KPRC, 950; KLAT, 1010; KNTH, 1070; KQUE, 1230; KXYZ, 1320; KCOH, 1430; KMIC, 1590. Radio-FM: KUHF, 88.7 MHz; KPFT, 90.1; KTSU, 90.9; KUHA, 91.7; KKRW, 93.7; KTBZ, 94.5; KKHH, 95.7; KHMX, 96.5; KBXX, 97.9; KODA, 99.1; KILT, 100.3; KLOL, 101.1; KMJQ, 102.1; KLTN, 102.9; KRBE, 104.1; KHCB, 105.7. TV: KUHT-Ch. 8; KHOU-Ch. 11; KTRK-Ch. 13; KTXH-Ch. 19; KETH-Ch. 24; KRIV-Ch. 26; KPRC-Ch. 35; KIAH-Ch. 38; KZJL-Ch. 44.
Howe — Newspaper: Texoma Enterprise. Radio-FM: KHYI, 95.3 MHz.
Hubbard — Newspaper: Hubbard City News.
Hudson — Radio-FM: KZXL, 96.3 MHz.
Humble — Radio-AM: KGOL, 1180 kHz. Radio-FM: KSBJ, 89.3 MHz.
Huntington — Radio-FM: KSML, 101.9 MHz.
Hunt — Radio-FM: KRZS, 99.9 MHz.
Huntsville — Newspaper: Huntsville Item (D). Radio-AM: KM2XVL, 1220 kHz; KHCH, 1410; KHVL, 1490. Radio-FM: KSHU, 90.5 MHz; KSAM, 101.7.
Hurst — Radio-AM: KMNY, 1360 kHz.
Hutto — Radio-FM: KYLR, 92.1 MHz.

Idalou — Newspaper: Idalou Beacon. Radio-FM: KRBL, 105.7 MHz.
Ingleside — Newspaper: Ingleside Index. Radio-FM: KAJE, 107.3 MHz.
Ingram — Newspaper: West Kerr Current. Radio-FM: KTXI, 90.1 MHz; KSYY, 96.5.
Iowa Park — Newspaper: Iowa Park Leader. Radio-FM: KXXN, 96.3 MHz.
Irving — Newspaper: The Irving Rambler. TV: KSTR-Ch. 48.

Jacksboro — Newspapers: Jacksboro Gazette-News; The Jack County Herald. Radio-FM: KJKB, 95.5 MHz.
Jacksonville — Newspaper: Jacksonville Daily Progress (D). Radio-AM: KEBE, 1400 kHz. Radio-FM: KBJS, 90.3 MHz; KLJT, 102.3; KOOI, 106.5. TV: KETK-Ch. 22.
Jasper — Newspaper: The Jasper Newsboy. Radio-AM: KCOX, 1350 kHz. Radio-FM: KTXJ, 102.7 MHz; KJAS, 107.3.
Jefferson — Newspaper: Jefferson Jimplecute. Radio-FM: KHCJ, 91.9 MHz; KJTX, 104.5.
Jewett — Newspaper: Jewett Messenger.
Johnson City — Newspaper: Johnson City Record-Courier. Radio-FM: KFAN, 107.9 MHz.
Joshua — Newspaper: Joshua Star.
Jourdanton — Radio-FM: KLEY, 95.7 MHz.
Junction — Newspaper: Junction Eagle. Radio-AM:

KMBL, 1450 kHz. **Radio-FM:** KOOK, 93.5 MHz.

**Karnes City — Newspaper:** The Karnes Countywide. **Radio-AM:** KAML, 990 kHz. **Radio-FM:** KHHL, 103.1 MHz.
**Katy — Newspaper:** Katy Times. **TV:** KYAZ-Ch. 47.
**Kaufman — Newspaper:** The Kaufman Herald.
**Keene — Newspaper:** Keene Star. **Radio-FM:** KJRN; 88.3 MHz.
**Kempner — Radio-FM:** KHLE, 106.9 MHz.
**Kenedy — Radio-AM:** KAML, 990 kHz. **Radio-FM:** KTNR, 92.1 MHz.
**Kerens — Newspaper:** Kerens Tribune. **Radio-FM:** KRVF, 106.9 MHz.
**Kermit — Newspaper:** The Winkler County News. **Radio-AM:** KERB, 600 kHz. **Radio-FM:** KERB, 106.3 MHz.
**Kerrville — Newspapers:** Kerrville Daily Times (D); Hill Country Community Journal. **Radio-AM:** KERV, 1230 kHz. **Radio-FM:** KKER, 88.7 MHz; KHKV, 91.1; KRNH, 92.3; KRVL, 94.3; KKVR, 106.1. **TV:** KMYS-Ch. 32.
**Kilgore — Newspaper:** Kilgore News Herald (S). **Radio-AM:** KDOK, 1240 kHz. **Radio-FM:** KZLO, 88.7 MHz; KKTX, 96.1.
**Killeen — Newspaper:** Killeen Daily Herald (D). **Radio-AM:** KRMY, 1050 kHz. **Radio-FM:** KNCT, 91.3 MHz; KIIZ, 92.3. **TV:** KAKW-Ch. 13.
**Kingsville — Newspaper:** Kingsville Record & Bishop News (S). **Radio-AM:** KINE, 1330 kHz. **Radio-FM:** KTAI, 91.1 MHz; KKBA, 92.7; KFTX, 97.5.
**Kirbyville — Newspaper:** Kirbyville Banner.
**Knox City — Newspaper:** Knox County News.
**Kress — Newspaper:** Kress Chronicle.
**Krum — Radio-FM:** KNOR, 93.7 MHz.
**Kyle — Newspaper:** Hays Free Press.

**La Feria — Newspaper:** La Feria News.
**La Grange — Newspaper:** The Fayette County Record (S). **Radio-AM:** KVLG, 1570 kHz. **Radio-FM:** KBUK, 104.9 MHz.
**Lake Dallas — Newspaper:** The Lake Cities Sun. **TV:** KAZD-Ch. 39.
**Lake Jackson — Radio-FM:** KYBJ, 91.1 MHz; KGLK, 107.5.
**Lakeway — Newspaper:** Lake Travis View.
**Lamesa — Newspaper:** Lamesa Press Reporter (S). **Radio-AM:** KPET, 690 kHz. **Radio-FM:** KBKN, 91.3 MHz; KTXC, 104.7.
**Lampasas — Newspaper:** Lampasas Dispatch Record (S). **Radio-AM:** KCYL, 1450 kHz.
**La Porte — Radio-FM:** KHJK, 103.7 MHz.
**Laredo — Newspaper:** Laredo Morning Times (D). **Radio-AM:** KLAR, 1300 kHz; KLNT, 1490. **Radio-FM:** KHOY, 88.1 MHz; KBNL, 89.9; KJBZ, 92.7; KQUR, 94.9; KRRG, 98.1; KNEX, 106.1. **TV:** KVTV-Ch. 13; KLDO-Ch. 19.
**Laughlin AFB — Radio-FM:** KDRX, 106.9 MHz.
**La Vernia — Newspaper:** La Vernia News.
**League City — Radio-AM:** KHCB, 1400 kHz.
**Leakey — Radio-FM:** KBLT, 104.3 MHz.
**Leander — Radio-FM:** KXBT, 98.9 MHz.
**Leonard — Newspaper:** Leonard Graphic.
**Levelland — Newspaper:** Levelland & Hockley County News-Press (S). **Radio-AM:** KLVT, 1230 kHz. **Radio-FM:** KJDL, 105.3 MHz.
**Lewisville — Radio-FM:** KESS, 107.9 MHz.
**Lexington — Newspaper:** Lexington Leader.
**Liberty — Newspaper:** The Vindicator. **Radio-FM:** KSHN, 99.9 MHz.
**Liberty Hill — Newspaper:** The Liberty Hill Independent.
**Lindale — Newspapers:** Lindale News & Times.
**Linden — Newspaper:** Cass County Sun.
**Lindsay — Newspaper:** Lindsay Letter.
**Little Elm — Newspaper:** The Little Elm Journal.
**Littlefield — Newspaper:** Lamb County Leader-News

(S). **Radio-AM:** KZZN, 1490 kHz.
**Livingston — Newspaper:** Polk County Enterprise (S). **Radio-AM:** KETX, 1440 kHz. **Radio-FM:** KETX, 92.3 MHz.
**Llano — Newspapers:** Llano County Journal; The Llano News. **Radio-FM:** KAJZ, 96.3 MHz; KITY, 102.9. **TV:** KBVO-Ch. 27.
**Lockhart — Newspaper:** Lockhart Post-Register. **Radio-AM:** KFIT, 1060 kHz.
**Lometa — Radio-FM:** KACQ, 101.9 MHz.
**Longview — Newspaper:** Longview News-Journal (D). **Radio-AM:** KFRO, 1370 kHz. **Radio-FM:** KYKX, 105.7 MHz. **TV:** KFXK-Ch. 31; KCEB-Ch. 51.
**Lorena — Radio-FM:** KYAR, 98.3 MHz.
**Lorenzo — Radio-FM:** KKCL, 98.1 MHz.
**Los Ybañez — Radio-FM:** KBXJ, 98.5 MHz.
**Lovelady — Radio-FM:** KHMR, 104.3 MHz.
**Lubbock — Newspaper:** Lubbock Avalanche-Journal (D). **Radio-AM:** KRFE, 580 kHz; KFYO, 790; KJTV, 950; KKAM, 1340; KJDL, 1420; KBZO, 1460; KDAV, 1590. **Radio-FM:** KTXT, 88.1 MHz; KOHM, 89.1; KAMY, 90.1; KKLU, 90.9; KXTQ, 93.7; KFMX, 94.5; KLLL, 96.3; KQBR, 99.5; KONE, 101.1; KZII, 102.5; KEJS, 106.5. **TV:** KCBD-Ch. 11; KPTB-Ch. 16; KTXT-Ch. 39; KLBK-Ch. 40.
**Lufkin — Newspaper:** Lufkin Daily News (D). **Radio-AM:** KRBA, 1340 kHz. **Radio-FM:** KLDN, 88.9 MHz; KSWP, 90.9; KAVX, 91.9; KAGZ, 93.9; KYBI, 100.1; KYKS, 105.1. **TV:** KTRE-Ch. 9.
**Luling — Newspaper:** Luling Newsboy and Signal. **Radio-FM:** KAMX, 94.7 MHz.
**Lumberton — Radio-AM:** KSET, 1300 kHz.
**Lytle — Newspapers:** Leader News; Medina Valley Times. **Radio-FM:** KZLV, 91.3 MHz.

**Mabank — Newspaper:** The Monitor (S). **Radio-AM:** KTXV, 890 kHz.
**Madisonville — Newspaper:** Madisonville Meteor. **Radio-AM:** KMVL, 1220 kHz. **Radio-FM:** KHML, 91.5 MHz; KAGG, 96.1; KMVL, 100.5; KKLB, 107.7.
**Malakoff — Newspaper:** Malakoff News. **Radio-FM:** KCKL, 95.9 MHz.
**Manor — Radio-AM:** KELG, 1440 kHz.
**Marble Falls — Newspapers:** The Highlander (S); The River Cities Sunday Tribune. **Radio-FM:** KBMD, 88.5 MHz.
**Marfa — Newspaper:** The Big Bend Sentinel. **Radio-FM:** KRTS, 93.5 MHz.
**Marion — Radio-AM:** KBIB, 1000 kHz.
**Markham — Radio-FM:** KKHA, 92.5 MHz.
**Marlin — Newspaper:** The Marlin Democrat. **Radio-FM:** KRMX, 92.9 MHz.
**Marshall — Newspaper:** Marshall News Messenger (D). **Radio-AM:** KCUL, 1410 kHz; KMHT, 1450. **Radio-FM:** KBWC, 91.1 MHz; KCUL, 92.3; KMHT, 103.9.
**Mart — Newspaper:** Mart Messenger. **Radio-FM:** KSUR, 88.9 MHz.
**Mason — Newspaper:** Mason County News. **Radio-FM:** KOTY, 95.7 MHz; KYRT, 97.7; KZZM, 101.7; KHLB, 102.5.
**Matador — Newspaper:** Motley County Tribune.
**Mathis — Newspaper:** Mathis News.
**McAllen — Newspaper:** The Monitor (D). **Radio-AM:** KRIO, 910 kHz. **Radio-FM:** KHID, 88.1 MHz; KVMV, 96.9; KGBT, 98.5. **TV:** KNVO-Ch. 49.
**McCamey — Radio-FM:** KPBM, 95.3 MHz.
**McCook — Radio-FM:** KCAS, 91.5 MHz.
**McGregor — Newspaper:** McGregor Mirror & Crawford Sun.
**McKinney — Newspapers:** McKinney Courier-Gazette (D); Collin County Commercial Record. **Radio-FM:** KNTU, 88.1 MHz.
**McQueeney — Radio-FM:** KLTO, 97.7 MHz.
**Melissa — Newspaper:** The Anna-Melissa Tribune.
**Memphis — Newspaper:** Hall County Herald. **Radio-FM:**

KLSR, 105.3 MHz.

**Menard — Newspaper:** Menard News and Messenger.

**Mercedes — Newspaper:** Mercedes Enterprise. **Radio-FM:** KTEX, 100.3 MHz.

**Meridian — Newspaper:** Meridian Tribune. **Radio-FM:** KOME, 95.3 MHz.

**Merkel — Newspaper:** Merkel Mail. **Radio-AM:** KMXO, 1500 kHz. **Radio-FM:** KHXS, 102.7 MHz.

**Mertzon — Radio-FM:** KMEO, 91.9 MHz.

**Mesquite — Radio-FM:** KEOM, 88.5 MHz.

**Mexia — Newspaper:** The Mexia News (TW). **Radio-AM:** KLRK, 1590 kHz. **Radio-FM:** KWBT, 104.9 MHz.

**Miami — Newspaper:** Miami Chief.

**Midland — Newspaper:** Midland Reporter-Telegram (D). **Radio-AM:** KCRS, 550 kHz; KWEL, 1070; KLPF, 1150; KMND, 1510. **Radio-FM:** KPBJ, 90.1 MHz; KVDG, 90.9; KNFM, 92.3; KZBT, 93.3; KQRX, 95.1; KCRS, 103.3; KCHX, 106.7. **TV:** KUPB-Ch. 18.

**Midlothian — Newspaper:** Midlothian Mirror.

**Miles — Newspaper:** Miles Messenger.

**Mineola — Newspaper:** Mineola Monitor. **Radio-FM:** KMOO, 99.9 MHz.

**Mineral Wells — Newspaper:** Mineral Wells Index (D). **Radio-AM:** KVTT, 1110 kHz. **Radio-FM:** KFWR, 95.9 MHz.

**Mirando City — Radio-FM:** KBDR, 100.5 MHz.

**Mission — Newspaper:** Progress-Times. **Radio-AM:** KIRT, 1580 kHz. **Radio-FM:** KQXX, 105.5 MHz.

**Missouri City — Radio-AM:** KBRZ, 1460 kHz.

**Monahans — Newspaper:** The Monahans News (S). **Radio-AM:** KCKM, 1330 kHz. **Radio-FM:** KBAT, 99.9 MHz.

**Morton — Newspaper:** Morton Tribune. **Radio-FM:** KQOA, 91.1 MHz; KPGA, 91.9.

**Moulton — Newspaper:** Moulton Eagle.

**Mount Pleasant — Newspaper:** Daily Tribune (D). **Radio-AM:** KIMP, 960 kHz. **Radio-FM:** KYZQ, 88.3 MHz.

**Mount Vernon — Newspaper:** Mount Vernon Optic-Herald.

**Muenster — Newspaper:** Muenster Enterprise. **Radio-FM:** KZZA, 106.7 MHz.

**Muleshoe — Newspaper:** Muleshoe Journal. **Radio-FM:** KMUL, 103.1 MHz.

**Munday — Newspaper:** The Munday Courier.

**Murphy — Newspaper:** Murphy Monitor.

**Nacogdoches — Newspaper:** Nacogdoches Daily Sentinel (D). **Radio-AM:** KSFA, 860 kHz. **Radio-FM:** KSAU, 90.1 MHz; KJCS, 103.3; KTBQ, 107.7. **TV:** KYTX-Ch. 18.

**Naples — Newspaper:** The Monitor.

**Natalia — Radio-FM:** KYRQ, 90.3 MHz.

**Navasota — Newspaper:** The Navasota Examiner. **Radio-AM:** KWBC, 1550 kHz. **Radio-FM:** KWUP, 92.5 MHz.

**Nederland — Radio-AM:** KBED, 1510 kHz.

**Needville — Newspaper:** The Gulf Coast Tribune.

**New Boston — Newspaper:** Bowie County Citizen Tribune (S). **Radio-AM:** KLBW, 1530 kHz. **Radio-FM:** KEWL, 95.1 MHz; KZRB, 103.5; KTTY, 105.1.

**New Braunfels — Newspaper:** Herald-Zeitung (D). **Radio-AM:** KGNB, 1420 kHz. **Radio-FM:** KNBT, 92.1 MHz.

**New Deal — Radio-FM:** KLZK, 97.3 MHz.

**Newton — Newspaper:** Newton County News.

**New Ulm — Newspaper:** New Ulm Enterprise. **Radio-FM:** KNRG, 92.3 MHz.

**Nixon — Newspaper:** Cow Country Courier.

**Nocona — Newspaper:** Nocona News.

**Nolanville — Radio-FM:** KLFX, 107.3 MHz.

**Normangee — Newspaper:** Normangee Star.

**Odem — Newspaper:** Odem-Edroy Times. **Radio-FM:** KMJR, 98.3 MHz.

**Odessa — Newspaper:** Odessa American (D). **Radio-AM:** KFLB, 920 kHz; KOZA, 1230; KRIL, 1410. **Radio-FM:** KBMM, 89.5 MHz; KLVW, 90.5; KOCV, 91.3; KMRR, 96.1; KMCM, 96.9; KODM, 97.9; KHKX, 99.1; KQLM, 107.9. **TV:** KOSA-Ch. 7; KPEJ-Ch. 23; KWWT-Ch. 30; KPBT-Ch. 38; KMLM-Ch. 42.

**O'Donnell — Newspaper:** O'Donnell Index-Press.

**Olney — Newspaper:** The Olney Enterprise.

**Olton — Newspaper:** Olton Enterprise.

**Orange — Newspaper:** The Orange Leader (D). **Radio-AM:** KOGT, 1600 kHz. **Radio-FM:** KKMY, 104.5 MHz; KIOC, 106.1.

**Ore City — Radio-FM:** KAZE, 106.9 MHz.

**Overland — Radio-FM:** KKVI, 89.9 MHz.

**Overton — Newspaper:** Overton Press. **Radio-FM:** KPXI, 100.7 MHz.

**Ozona — Newspaper:** Ozona Stockman. **Radio-FM:** KYXX, 94.3 MHz.

**Paducah — Newspaper:** Paducah Post.

**Paint Rock — Newspaper:** Concho Herald.

**Palacios — Newspaper:** Palacios Beacon. **Radio-FM:** KROY, 99.7 MHz.

**Palestine — Newspaper:** Palestine Herald Press (D). **Radio-AM:** KNET, 1450 kHz. **Radio-FM:** KYFP, 89.1 MHz; KYYK, 98.3.

**Pampa — Newspaper:** The Pampa News (D). **Radio-AM:** KGRO, 1230 kHz. **Radio-FM:** KAVO, 90.9 MHz; KOMX, 100.3; KDRL, 103.3.

**Panhandle — Newspaper:** Panhandle Herald White Deer News.

**Paris — Newspaper:** Paris News (D). **Radio-AM:** KZHN, 1250 kHz; KPLT, 1490. **Radio-FM:** KHCP, 89.3 MHz; KOYN, 93.9; KBUS, 101.9; KPLT, 107.7.

**Pasadena — Newspaper:** The Pasadena Citizen (S). **Radio-AM:** KIKK, 650 kHz; KLVL, 1480. **Radio-FM:** KFTG, 88.1 MHz; KKBQ, 92.9.

**Pearland — Newspapers:** Pearland Journal; Pearland Reporter News.

**Pearsall — Newspaper:** Frio-Nueces Current. **Radio-AM:** KVWG, 1280 kHz. **Radio-FM:** KSAG, 103.3 MHz; KSAH, 104.1.

**Pecan Grove — Radio-AM:** KREH, 900 kHz.

**Pecos — Newspaper:** Pecos Enterprise (S). **Radio-AM:** KIUN, 1400 kHz. **Radio-FM:** KPKO, 91.3 MHz; KGEE, 97.3; KPTX, 98.3.

**Perryton — Newspaper:** Perryton Herald (S). **Radio-AM:** KEYE, 1400 kHz. **Radio-FM:** KEYE, 96.1 MHz.

**Pflugerville — Newspaper:** Pflugerville Pflag. **Radio-AM:** KOKE, 1600 kHz.

**Pharr — Newspaper:** Advance News Journal. **Radio-AM:** KVJY, 840 kHz.

**Pilot Point — Newspaper:** Pilot Point Post-Signal. **Radio-FM:** KZMP, 104.9 MHz.

**Pittsburg — Newspaper:** Pittsburg Gazette. **Radio-FM:** KGWP, 91.1 MHz; KPIT, 91.7; KSCN, 96.9; KMPA, 103.1.

**Plains — Radio-FM:** KPHS, 90.3 MHz.

**Plainview — Newspaper:** Plainview Daily Herald (D). **Radio-AM:** KVOP, 1090 kHz; KREW, 1400. **Radio-FM:** KPMB, 88.5 MHz; KBAH, 90.5; KWLD, 91.5; KRIA, 103.9; KKYN, 106.9.

**Plano — Newspaper:** Plano Star Courier (S). **Radio-AM:** KMKI, 620 kHz.

**Pleasanton — Newspaper:** Pleasanton Express. **Radio-AM:** KWMF, 1380 kHz.

**Pleasant Valley — Radio-FM:** KZAM, 98.7 MHz.

**Point Comfort — Radio-FM:** KJAZ, 94.1 MHz.

**Port Aransas — Newspaper:** Port Aransas South Jetty.

**Port Arthur — Newspaper:** The Port Arthur News (D). **Radio-AM:** KDEI, 1250 kHz; KOLE, 1340. **Radio-FM:** KQBU, 93.3 MHz; KTJM, 98.5.

**Port Isabel — Newspaper:** Port Isabel/South Padre Press (S). **Radio-FM:** KNVO, 101.1 MHz.

**Portland — Newspaper:** Portland News; The Coastal

Bend Herald. **Radio-FM:** KSGR, 91.1 MHz; KLHB, 105.5.

**Port Lavaca — Newspaper:** Port Lavaca Wave (S). **Radio-FM:** KITE, 93.3 MHz.

**Port Neches — Radio-AM:** KBPO, 1150 kHz.

**Port O'Connor — Radio-FM:** KHPO, 91.9 MHz.

**Post — Newspaper:** Post Dispatch. **Radio-FM:** KSSL, 107.3 MHz.

**Prairie View — Radio-FM:** KPVU, 91.3 MHz.

**Premont — Radio-FM:** KLBD, 88.1 MHz; KMFM, 100.7.

**Presidio — Newspaper:** The International Presidio Paper.

**Princeton — Newspaper:** Princeton Herald.

**Quanah — Newspaper:** Quanah Tribune-Chief. **Radio-AM:** KOLJ, 1150 kHz.

**Quinlan — Newspaper:** The Quinlan-Tawakoni News.

**Quitaque — Newspaper:** Valley Tribune.

**Quitman — Newspaper:** Wood County Democrat.

**Ralls — Newspaper:** Crosby County News. **Radio-AM:** KCLR, 1530 kHz.

**Ranger — Newspaper:** Ranger Times (S). **Radio-FM:** KWBY, 98.5 MHz.

**Rankin — Newspaper:** Pecos River Dispatch.

**Raymondville — Newspaper:** Chronicle/Willacy County News. **Radio-AM:** KSOX, 1240 kHz. **Radio-FM:** KBUC, 102.1 MHz; KBIC, 105.7.

**Red Oak — Newspapers:** Ellis County Chronicle; Red Oak Record.

**Refugio — Newspaper:** Refugio County Press. **Radio-FM:** KRIK, 100.5 MHz; KOUL, 103.7; KYRK, 106.1.

**Reno — Radio-FM:** KLOW, 98.9 MHz.

**Richardson — Radio-AM:** KKLF, 1700 kHz.

**Richmond — Radio-AM:** KRTX, 980 kHz.

**Riesel — Newspaper:** Riesel Rustler.

**Rio Grande City — Radio-FM:** KRGX, 95.1 MHz; KQBO, 107.5. **TV:** KTLM-Ch. 40.

**Rising Star — Newspaper:** Rising Star.

**Robert Lee — Newspaper:** Observer/Enterprise.

**Robinson — Radio-FM:** KWPW, 107.9 MHz.

**Robstown — Newspaper:** Nueces County Record-Star. **Radio-AM:** KROB, 1510 kHz. **Radio-FM:** KLUX, 89.5 MHz; KSAB, 99.9; KMIQ, 104.9.

**Rockdale — Newspaper:** Rockdale Reporter. **Radio-FM:** KRXT, 98.5 MHz.

**Rockport — Newspapers:** Rockport Pilot (S); The Coastal Bend Herald. **Radio-FM:** KKPN, 102.3 MHz.

**Rocksprings — Newspaper:** Texas Mohair Weekly.

**Rockwall — Newspaper:** Rockwall County News.

**Rollingwood — Radio-AM:** KJCE, 1370 kHz.

**Roma — Newspaper:** South Texas Reporter. **Radio-FM:** KRIO, 97.7 MHz.

**Rosebud — Newspaper:** Rosebud News.

**Rosenberg — Newspaper:** Rosenberg Herald & Texas Coaster (D). **Radio-AM:** KRTX, 980 kHz. **TV:** KXLN-Ch. 45.

**Rotan — Newspaper:** Rotan Advance-Star-Record.

**Round Rock — Newspaper:** Round Rock Leader (TW). **Radio-FM:** KNLE, 88.1 MHz; KFMK, 105.9.

**Rowena — Newspaper:** Rowena Press.

**Rowlett — Newspaper:** The Rowlett Lakeshore Times.

**Rudolph — Radio-FM:** KTER, 90.7 MHz.

**Rusk — Newspaper:** Cherokeean Herald. **Radio-AM:** KTLU, 1580 kHz. **Radio-FM:** KWRW, 97.7 MHz.

**Sachse — Newspaper:** Sachse News.

**Saint Jo — Newspaper:** Saint Jo Tribune.

**Salado — Newspaper:** Salado Village Voice.

**San Angelo — Newspaper:** San Angelo Standard-Times (D). **Radio-AM:** KGKL, 960 kHz; KKSA, 1260; KCRN, 1340. **Radio-FM:** KNAR, 89.3 MHz; KNCH, 90.1; KLTP, 90.9; KDCD, 92.9; KCRN, 93.9; KIXY, 94.7; KGKL, 97.5; KELI, 98.7; KCLL, 100.1; KWFR, 101.9; KMDX, 106.1; KSJT, 107.5. **TV:** KLST-Ch. 11; KSAN-

Ch. 16; KIDY-Ch. 19.

**San Antonio — Newspapers:** San Antonio Business Journal; Commercial Recorder (D); Express-News (D); Hart Beat (TW); Today's Catholic (BW). **Radio-AM:** KTSA, 550 kHz; KSLR, 630; KKYX, 680; KTKR, 760; KONO, 860; KRDY, 1160; WOAI, 1200; KZDC, 1250; KAHL, 1310; KCOR, 1350; KCHL, 1480; KEDA, 1540. **Radio-FM:** KPAC, 88.3 MHz; KSTX, 89.1; KSYM, 90.1; KYFS, 90.9; KRTU, 91.7; KROM, 92.9; KXXM, 96.1; KAJA, 97.3; KISS, 99.5; KCYY, 100.3; KQXT, 101.9; KJXK, 102.7; KZEP, 104.5; KXTN, 107.5. **TV:** KLRN-Ch. 9; KSAT-Ch. 12; KHCE-Ch. 16; KABB-Ch. 30; KVDA-Ch. 38; KENS-Ch. 39; KWEX-Ch. 41; WOAI-Ch. 48.

**San Augustine — Newspaper:** San Augustine Tribune. **Radio-FM:** KDET, 92.5 MHz.

**San Benito — Newspaper:** San Benito News (S). **Radio-FM:** KHKZ, 106.3 MHz.

**San Diego — Radio-FM:** KUKA, 105.9 MHz.

**Sanger — Newspaper:** Sanger Courier. **Radio-FM:** KVRK, 89.7 MHz; KTDK, 104.1.

**San Juan — Radio-AM:** KUBR, 1210 kHz.

**San Marcos — Newspaper:** San Marcos Daily Record (D). **Radio-FM:** KUOL, 1470 kHz. **Radio-FM:** KTSW, 89.9 MHz; KBPA, 103.5.

**San Saba — Newspaper:** San Saba News & Star. **Radio-AM:** KNVR, 1410 kHz. **Radio-FM:** KNUZ, 106.1 MHz.

**Santa Fe — Radio-FM:** KJIC, 90.5 MHz.

**Savoy — Radio-FM:** KQDR, 107.3 MHz.

**Schertz — Radio-FM:** KBBT, 98.5 MHz.

**Schulenburg — Newspaper:** Schulenburg Sticker.

**Seabrook — Radio-AM:** KROI, 92.1 MHz.

**Seadrift — Radio-FM:** KMAT, 105.1 MHz.

**Seagoville — Newspaper:** Suburbia News.

**Seagraves — Newspaper:** Tri County Tribune.

**Sealy — Newspaper:** The Sealy News. **Radio-FM:** KQLC, 90.7 MHz.

**Seguin — Newspaper:** Seguin Gazette-Enterprise (D). **Radio-AM:** KWED, 1580 kHz. **Radio-FM:** KSMG, 105.3 MHz.

**Seminole — Newspaper:** Seminole Sentinel (S). **Radio-AM:** KIKZ, 1250 kHz. **Radio-FM:** KSEM, 106.3 MHz.

**Seymour — Newspaper:** Baylor County Banner. **Radio-AM:** KSEY, 1230 kHz. **Radio-FM:** KSEY, 94.3 MHz.

**Shamrock — Newspaper:** County News-Star.

**Shepherd — Newspaper:** San Jacinto News-Times.

**Shenandoah — Radio-AM:** KRCM, 1380 kHz.

**Sherman — Newspaper:** Herald Democrat (D). **Radio-AM:** KJIM, 1500 kHz. **TV:** KXII-Ch. 20.

**Shiner — Newspaper:** The Shiner Gazette.

**Silsbee — Newspaper:** Silsbee Bee. **Radio-FM:** KAYD, 101.7 MHz.

**Silverton — Newspaper:** Briscoe County News.

**Sinton — Newspaper:** San Patricio County News. **Radio-AM:** KDAE, 1590 kHz. **Radio-FM:** KNCN, 101.3 MHz.

**Slaton — Newspaper:** Slaton Slatonite. **Radio-FM:** KJAK, 92.7 MHz.

**Smithville — Newspaper:** Smithville Times.

**Snyder — Newspaper:** Snyder Daily News (D). **Radio-AM:** KSNY, 1450 kHz. **Radio-FM:** KGWB, 91.1 MHz; KLYD, 98.9; KSNY, 101.5. **TV:** KPCB-Ch. 17.

**Somerset — Radio-AM:** KYTY, 810 kHz.

**Somerville — Radio-FM:** KUTX, 88.1 MHz.

**Sonora — Newspaper:** Devil's River News. **Radio-FM:** KHOS, 92.1 MHz.

**South Padre Island — Radio-FM:** KESO, 92.7 MHz; KZSP, 95.3.

**Spearman — Newspaper:** Hansford County Reporter-Statesman. **Radio-FM:** KTOT, 89.5 MHz; KXDJ, 98.3.

**Springtown — Newspaper:** Springtown Epigraph. **Radio-FM:** KSQX, 89.1 MHz.

**Spur — Newspaper:** Texas Spur.

**Stamford — Newspapers:** The New Stamford American; The Stamford Star. **Radio-AM:** KVRP, 1400 kHz. **Radio-FM:** KLGD, 106.9 MHz.

Stanton — **Newspaper:** Martin County Messenger. **Radio-FM:** KFLB, 88.1 MHz; KKJW, 105.9.
Stephenville — **Newspaper:** Stephenville Empire Tribune (D). **Radio-AM:** KSTV, 1510 kHz. **Radio-FM:** KQXS, 89.1 MHz; KEQX, 89.7; KTRL, 90.5.
Sterling City — **Radio-FM:** KNRX, 96.5 MHz.
Stratford — **Newspaper:** Stratford Star.
Sulphur Bluff — **Radio-FM:** KETE, 99.7 MHz.
Sulphur Springs — **Newspaper:** News-Telegram (D). **Radio-AM:** KSST, 1230 kHz. **Radio-FM:** KGPF, 91.1 MHz; KZRF, 91.9; KSCH, 95.9.
Sweetwater — **Newspaper:** Sweetwater Reporter (D). **Radio-AM:** KXOX, 1240 kHz. **Radio-FM:** KXOX, 96.7. **TV:** KTXS-Ch. 20.

Taft — **Newspaper:** Taft Tribune.
Tahoka — **Newspaper:** Lynn County News. **Radio-FM:** KMMX, 100.3 MHz; KAMZ, 103.5.
Tatum — **Newspaper:** Trammel Trace Tribune. **Radio-FM:** KZQX, 100.3 MHz.
Taylor — **Newspaper:** Taylor Daily Press (D). **Radio-AM:** KWNX, 1260 kHz. **Radio-FM:** KLQB, 104.3 MHz.
Teague — **Newspaper:** Teague Chronicle.
Temple — **Newspaper:** Temple Daily Telegram (D). **Radio-AM:** KTEM, 1400 kHz. **Radio-FM:** KVLT, 88.5 MHz; KBDE, 89.9; KLTD, 101.7. **TV:** KCEN-Ch. 9.
Terrell — **Newspaper:** Terrell Tribune (S). **Radio-AM:** KPYK, 1570 kHz.
Terrell Hills — **Radio-AM:** KLUP, 930 kHz. **Radio-FM:** KTKX, 106.7 MHz.
Texarkana — **Newspaper:** Texarkana Gazette (D). **Radio-AM:** KCMC, 740 kHz; KTFS, 940; KKTK, 1400. **Radio-FM:** KTXK, 91.5 MHz; KTAL, 98.1; KKYR, 102.5. **TV:** KTAL-Ch. 15.
Texas City — **Radio-AM:** KYST, 920 kHz.
Thorndale — **Newspaper:** Thorndale Champion. **Radio-FM:** KLGO, 99.3 MHz.
Three Rivers — **Newspaper:** The Progress. **Radio-FM:** KEMA, 94.5 MHz.
Throckmorton — **Newspaper:** Throckmorton Tribune.
Timpson — **Newspaper:** Timpson & Tenaha News.
Tomball — **Radio-AM:** KSEV, 700 kHz.
Tom Bean — **Radio-FM:** KLAK, 97.5 MHz.
Trenton — **Newspaper:** Trenton Tribune.
Trinity — **Newspaper:** Trinity Standard.
Tulia — **Newspapers:** Swisher County News; Tulia Herald. **Radio-AM:** KTUE, 1260 kHz. **Radio-FM:** KBTE, 104.9 MHz.
Tuscola — **Newspaper:** Jim Ned Journal (BW).
Tye — **Radio-FM:** KBCY, 99.7 MHz.
Tyler — **Newspapers:** Tyler Morning Telegraph (D). **Radio-AM:** KTBB, 600 kHz; KGLD, 1330; KYZS, 1490. **Radio-FM:** KVNE, 89.5 MHz; KGLY, 91.3; KTBB, 92.1; KTYL, 93.1; KNUE, 101.5; KKUS, 104.1. **TV:** KLTV-Ch. 7.

Umbarger — **Radio-FM:** KRBG, 88.7 MHz.
Universal City — **Radio-AM:** KSAH, 720 kHz.
University Park — **Radio-AM:** KTNO, 1440 kHz; KZMP, 1540.
Uvalde — **Newspaper:** Uvalde Leader-News (S). **Radio-AM:** KVOU, 1400 kHz. **Radio-FM:** KBNU, 93.9 MHz; KUVA, 102.3; KVOU, 104.9. **TV:** KPXL-Ch. 26.

Valley Mills — **Newspaper:** Valley Mills Progress.
Valley View — **Radio-FM:** KQFZ, 89.1 MHz.
Van — **Newspaper:** Van Banner.
Van Alstyne — **Newspaper:** Van Alstyne Leader.
Van Horn — **Newspaper:** Van Horn Advocate. **Radio-FM:** KVHR, 91.5 MHz.
Vega — **Newspaper:** Vega Enterprise.
Vernon — **Newspaper:** Vernon Daily Record (D). **Radio-AM:** KVWC, 1490 kHz. **Radio-FM:** KVED, 88.5 MHz; KVWC, 103.1.
Victoria — **Newspaper:** Victoria Advocate (D). **Radio-**

**AM:** KVNN, 1340 kHz; KNAL, 1410. **Radio-FM:** KAYK, 88.5 MHz; KXBJ, 89.3; KVRT, 90.7; KQVT, 92.3; KVIC, 95.1; KTXN, 98.7; KBAR, 100.9; KIXS, 107.9. **TV:** KAVU-Ch. 15.
Vidor — **Newspaper:** Vidor Vidorian.

Waco — **Newspapers:** The Suburban Courier. The Waco Citizen; Waco Tribune-Herald (D); **Radio-AM:** KBBW, 1010 kHz; KWTX, 1230; KRZI, 1660. **Radio-FM:** KBCT, 94.5; KBGO, 95.7; KWTX, 97.5; WACO, 99.9; KWBU, 103.3. **TV:** KDYW-Ch 20; KXXV-Ch. 26; KWKT-Ch. 44; KWTX-Ch. 53.
Wake Village — **Radio-FM:** KHTA, 92.5 MHz.
Wallis — **Newspaper:** Wallis News-Review.
Waskom — **Radio-FM:** KQHN, 97.3 MHz.
Waxahachie — **Newspaper:** Waxahachie Daily Light (D). **Radio-AM:** KBEC, 1390 kHz.
Weatherford — **Newspaper:** Weatherford Democrat (D). **Radio-AM:** KZEE, 1220 kHz. **Radio-FM:** KMQX, 88.5 MHz; KYQX, 89.5.
Weimar — **Newspaper:** Weimar Mercury.
Wells — **Radio-FM:** KVLL, 94.7 MHz.
Wellington — **Newspaper:** Wellington Leader.
Weslaco — **Radio-AM:** KRGE, 1290 kHz. **TV:** KRGV-Ch. 13.
West — **Newspaper:** The West News.
West Lake Hills — **Radio-AM:** KTXZ, 1560 kHz.
West Odessa — **Radio-FM:** KFRI, 88.7 MHz.
Wharton — **Newspaper:** Wharton Journal-Spectator (S). **Radio-AM:** KANI, 1500 kHz.
Wheeler — **Newspaper:** The Wheeler Times. **Radio-FM:** KLXL, 88.3 MHz; KPDR, 90.3.
Whitehouse — **Newspaper:** Tri County Leader. **Radio-FM:** KISX, 107.3 MHz.
White Oak — **Newspaper:** White Oak Independent. **Radio-FM:** KZTK, 99.3 MHz.
Whitesboro — **Newspaper:** Whitesboro News-Record. **Radio-FM:** KMAD, 102.5 MHz.
Whitewright — **Newspaper:** Whitewright Sun.
Whitney — **Newspaper:** Lake Whitney Views (M).
Wichita Falls — **Newspaper:** Times-Record-News (D). **Radio-AM:** KWFS, 1290. **Radio-FM:** KMCU, 88.7 MHz; KMOC, 89.5; KZKL, 90.5; KNIN, 92.9; KLUR, 99.9; KWFS, 102.3; KQXC, 103.9; KBZS, 106.3. **TV:** KJTL-Ch. 15; KAUZ-Ch. 22; KFDX-Ch. 28.
Willis — **Radio-FM:** KVST, 99.7 MHz.
Wills Point — **Newspaper:** Wills Point Chronicle.
Wimberley — **Newspaper:** Wimberley View (S).
Winfield — **Radio-FM:** KALK, 97.7 MHz.
Winnie — **Newspaper:** The Hometown Press. **Radio-FM:** KKHT, 100.7 MHz.
Winnsboro — **Newspaper:** Winnsboro News. **Radio-FM:** KWNS, 104.7 MHz.
Winona — **Radio-FM:** KBLZ, 102.7 MHz.
Winters — **Newspaper:** Winters Enterprise. **Radio-FM:** KFNA, 96.1 MHz.
Wixon Valley — **Radio-FM:** KBXT, 101.9 MHz.
Wolfe City — **Newspaper:** Wolfe City Mirror.
Wolfforth — **Radio-FM:** KAIQ, 95.5 MHz. **TV:** KLCW-Ch. 43.
Woodville — **Newspaper:** Tyler County Booster. **Radio-AM:** KWUD, 1490 kHz.
Wylie — **Newspaper:** The Wylie News. **Radio-AM:** KHSE, 700 kHz.

Yoakum — **Newspaper:** Yoakum Herald-Times. **Radio-FM:** KYKM, 92.5 MHz.
Yorktown — **Newspaper:** Yorktown News-View. **Radio-FM:** KGGB, 96.3 MHz.

Zapata — **Newspaper:** Zapata County News. **Radio-FM:** KBAW, 93.5 MHz; KJJS, 103.9. ☆

# Transportation

*Long exposure of San Antonio at the Interstate-10 and Charles William Anderson Loop interchange. Photo by Russell Harrison.*

**Railroads**
**Highways and Motor Vehicles**
**Freight Gateways**
**Consulates and Foreign Trade Zones**
**Ports and Aviation**

# Freight Railroads in Texas

In Texas in 2012 there were 49 railroad companies operating, carrying close to 300 million tons of freight. A complete list of railroads is in the Counties section on page 239. *Source: Association of American Railroads.*

| Railroads in State | Miles Operated |
|---|---|
| **Class I** (3 – *see chart at right*) | 12,367 |
| Regional | 0 |
| Local (22) | 1,289 |
| Switching & Terminal (20) | 1,031 |
| **Total** | **14,687** |
| **Total excluding trackage rights\*** | **10,469** |

| Railroads in State | Miles Operated |
|---|---|
| **Class I** | |
| Union Pacific Railroad Co. | 6,317 |
| BNSF Railway Co. | 5,122 |
| Kansas City Southern Railway Co. | 928 |

*\*Trackage rights — track provided by another railroad. Numbers in parentheses represent the number of railroad companies in each category.*

| Freight Traffic in Texas by Kind – 2012 | | | | | |
|---|---|---|---|---|---|
| **Carloads originated** | | **Tons** | **Carloads terminated** | | **Tons** |
| Chemicals | 408,300 | 35.1 million | Coal | 517,300 | 62.3 million |
| Gravel, crushed stone | 191,900 | 17.2 million | Gravel, crushed stone | 355,700 | 36.6 million |
| Petroleum | 58,000 | 7.5 million | Chemicals | 294,400 | 25.2 million |
| Intermodal | 432,900 | 6.9 million | Farm products | 170,200 | 17.7 million |
| Coke | 33,100 | 3.1 million | Food products | 173,000 | 12.5 million |
| All Other | 778,200 | 23.8 million | All Other | 1,606,500 | 52.3 million |
| **Total** | **1,902,200** | **92.9 million** | **Total** | **3,117,400** | **206.6 million** |

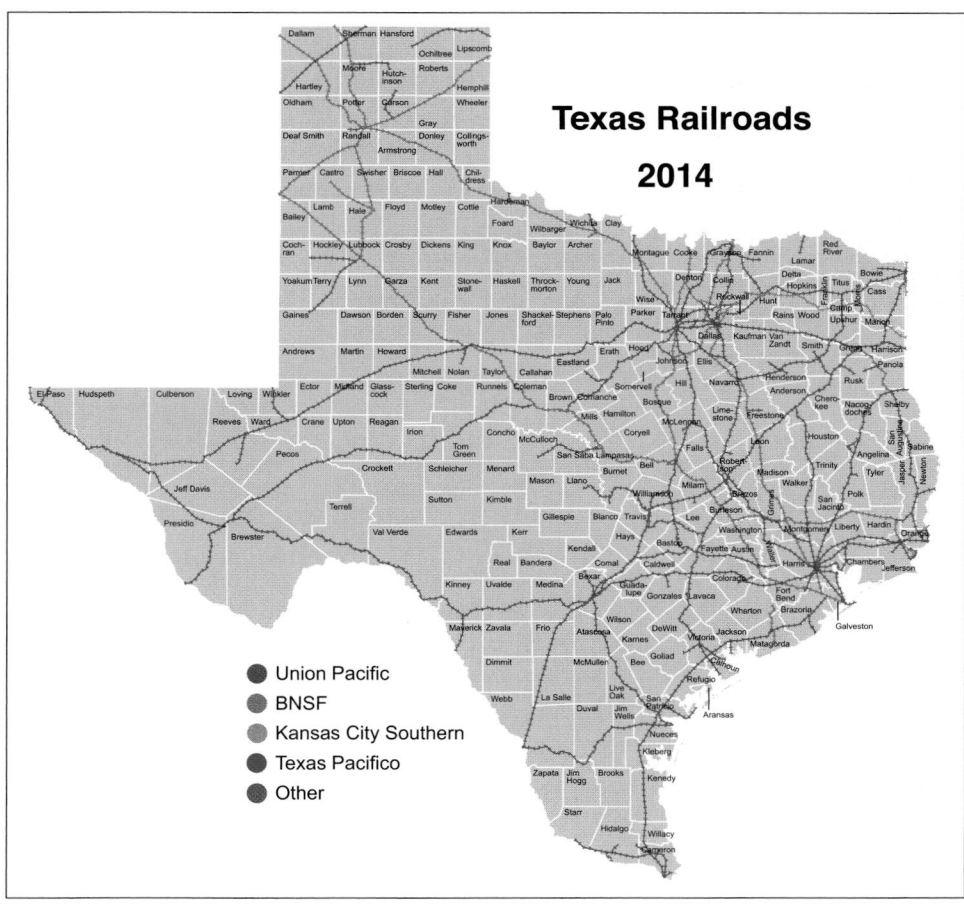

**Texas Railroads 2014**

- ● Union Pacific
- ● BNSF
- ● Kansas City Southern
- ● Texas Pacifico
- ● Other

*Interstate 35E through Dallas. Photo by Yinan Chen (CC).*

# Highway Miles, Construction, Maintenance, Vehicles: 2014

Texans drove more than 23.8 million motor vehicles in 2014 over 300,000 miles of roadways, including city- and county-maintained roads. That driving is calculated to have included more than 499 million miles driven daily on the 199,295 miles of state-maintained highways alone.

The Texas Department of Transportation (TxDOT) is responsible for state highway construction and maintenance, planning for future road expansion, administering Texas tollways and toll tags, and operating the state's 12 official Texas Travel Information Centers and 100 safety rest areas.

*Mileage, maintenance and construction figures (listed by county) refer only to roads that are maintained by the state: Interstates, U.S. highways, state highways, farm-to-market roads and some loops around urban areas. Not included are city- or county-maintained streets and roads. A lane mile is one lane for one mile; i.e., one mile of four-lane highway equals four lane miles. Sources: Texas Department of Transportation and Department of Motor Vehicles, 2015.*

| County | Vehicles Registered | Lane Miles of Highway | Vehicle Miles Driven Daily | State Construction Expenditures | Combined Construction Maintenance Expenditures | Total Vehicle Registration Fees | State Net Receipts | County Net Receipts |
|---|---|---|---|---|---|---|---|---|
| Anderson | 50,974 | 991 | 1,173,965 | 10,141,437 | 16,841,773 | 3,485,834 | $ 2,515,780 | 967,731 |
| Andrews | 21,966 | 554 | 837,650 | 2,591,348 | 5,409,017 | 1,966,915 | 1,474,074 | 491,832 |
| Angelina | 87,145 | 947 | 2,151,557 | 14,966,488 | 46,971,355 | 6,227,359 | 4,776,785 | 1,446,527 |
| Aransas | 27,296 | 203 | 402,466 | 21,460,288 | 22,359,853 | 1,683,147 | 1,120,687 | 558,431 |
| Archer | 11,928 | 549 | 387,274 | 7,792,522 | 10,614,303 | 784,958 | 323,238 | 460,796 |
| Armstrong | 2,913 | 379 | 418,134 | 1,718,625 | 8,682,159 | 174,661 | 5,627 | 168,936 |
| Atascosa | 49,000 | 1,012 | 2,263,351 | 13,986,727 | 26,202,316 | 3,634,520 | 2,691,806 | 940,386 |
| Austin | 41,130 | 628 | 1,331,445 | 5,453,862 | 18,856,448 | 2,761,730 | 1,938,030 | 820,627 |
| Bailey | 6,902 | 490 | 209,698 | 533,545 | 7,214,116 | 479,147 | 91,275 | 387,678 |
| Bandera | 27,147 | 416 | 367,066 | 777,877 | 2,097,883 | 1,535,740 | 910,371 | 622,201 |
| Bastrop | 81,984 | 803 | 2,076,372 | 8,620,299 | 34,310,530 | 5,450,004 | 4,059,716 | 1,382,095 |
| Baylor | 4,509 | 498 | 230,732 | 16,709,979 | 19,002,235 | 282,858 | 34,236 | 248,302 |
| Bee | 24,979 | 675 | 749,565 | 5,506,343 | 11,268,573 | 1,725,430 | 1,074,279 | 649,562 |
| Bell | 291,023 | 1,549 | 6,683,398 | 135,257,438 | 193,436,676 | 19,496,368 | 14,982,996 | 4,489,832 |
| Bexar | 1,517,285 | 3,414 | 29,898,455 | 112,494,618 | 204,469,907 | 127,112,924 | 89,382,479 | 37,609,974 |
| Blanco | 16,269 | 462 | 543,147 | 1,545,338 | 11,045,428 | 1,100,773 | 652,707 | 445,733 |
| Borden | 1,162 | 343 | 70,511 | - | 2,167,338 | 55,683 | 2,567 | 53,073 |
| Bosque | 23,017 | 696 | 444,500 | 1,280,305 | 5,062,320 | 1,289,950 | 690,896 | 597,492 |
| Bowie | 91,157 | 1,209 | 3,013,772 | 17,741,071 | 32,686,047 | 5,972,685 | 4,486,767 | 1,478,554 |
| Brazoria | 316,281 | 1,366 | 4,492,895 | 31,073,602 | 64,111,006 | 21,272,676 | 16,985,705 | 4,258,186 |
| Brazos | 145,164 | 962 | 3,332,470 | 24,100,377 | 40,452,364 | 10,534,517 | 8,079,159 | 2,428,809 |

| County | Vehicles Registered | Lane Miles of Highway | Vehicle Miles Driven Daily | State Construction Expenditures | Combined Construction Maintenance Expenditures | Total Vehicle Registration Fees | State Net Receipts | County Net Receipts |
|--------|--------|--------|--------|--------|--------|--------|--------|--------|
| Brewster | 10,982 | 609 | 176,161 | 883,998 | 8,342,168 | 662,170 | 299,683 | 357,203 |
| Briscoe | 2,129 | 326 | 58,531 | 1,153,754 | 3,393,192 | 120,243 | 4,582 | 115,529 |
| Brooks | 7,367 | 317 | 724,699 | 24,253,472 | 29,819,618 | 423,826 | 130,424 | 292,927 |
| Brown | 42,418 | 767 | 727,293 | 7,358,239 | 11,615,621 | 2,943,446 | 2,082,560 | 858,306 |
| Burleson | 23,637 | 527 | 681,146 | 3,091,507 | 8,181,800 | 1,566,805 | 943,999 | 621,281 |
| Burnet | 53,269 | 805 | 1,339,934 | 1,648,047 | 15,536,361 | 3,540,297 | 2,530,657 | 1,003,192 |
| Caldwell | 37,527 | 720 | 1,351,470 | 4,578,997 | 17,348,451 | 2,384,148 | 1,628,458 | 753,530 |
| Calhoun | 23,722 | 406 | 462,405 | 671,366 | 6,131,656 | 1,853,133 | 1,219,816 | 631,343 |
| Callahan | 16,814 | 746 | 828,488 | 422,674 | 4,623,011 | 1,195,221 | 615,897 | 578,260 |
| Cameron | 294,026 | 1,816 | 5,815,053 | 18,777,823 | 37,624,709 | 23,521,927 | 16,381,074 | 7,131,126 |
| Camp | 18,123 | 265 | 261,178 | 202,690 | 2,396,165 | 1,440,871 | 967,986 | 472,304 |
| Carson | 7,877 | 776 | 764,269 | 2,875,240 | 11,897,736 | 523,699 | 110,400 | 412,958 |
| Cass | 35,104 | 987 | 962,417 | 8,043,001 | 17,760,442 | 2,095,849 | 1,355,465 | 738,837 |
| Castro | 8,509 | 533 | 305,028 | 810,146 | 3,743,116 | 667,367 | 206,645 | 460,457 |
| Chambers | 44,805 | 819 | 2,512,691 | 1,742,586 | 10,489,980 | 3,095,915 | 2,263,436 | 828,329 |
| Cherokee | 48,048 | 1,147 | 1,210,993 | 5,114,162 | 13,448,073 | 3,058,692 | 2,145,696 | 910,724 |
| Childress | 6,939 | 479 | 595,042 | 1,793,579 | 4,410,246 | 416,647 | 75,466 | 340,818 |
| Clay | 13,886 | 777 | 845,311 | 1,606,561 | 7,750,843 | 869,560 | 341,611 | 526,770 |
| Cochran | 3,369 | 468 | 88,747 | 496,708 | 1,550,820 | 218,192 | 7,458 | 210,438 |
| Coke | 4,561 | 370 | 207,175 | 35,475 | 1,247,675 | 266,514 | 37,508 | 228,808 |
| Coleman | 11,577 | 753 | 357,749 | 600,411 | 2,675,810 | 669,350 | 192,674 | 476,144 |
| Collin | 729,624 | 1,374 | 7,327,362 | 175,844,294 | 204,277,675 | 52,699,748 | 40,912,365 | 11,682,677 |
| Collingsworth | 3,573 | 454 | 230,550 | 1,864,630 | 4,818,203 | 221,517 | 7,235 | 213,985 |
| Colorado | 29,647 | 759 | 1,802,832 | 1,895,051 | 8,737,868 | 2,023,198 | 1,329,914 | 691,151 |
| Comal | 145,316 | 693 | 3,815,182 | 31,306,975 | 49,861,473 | 12,114,964 | 9,491,222 | 2,601,695 |
| Comanche | 17,125 | 741 | 456,672 | 2,049,389 | 7,891,858 | 1,112,290 | 555,243 | 556,290 |
| Concho | 3,562 | 480 | 270,060 | 162,926 | 2,205,663 | 203,310 | 7,655 | 195,477 |
| Cooke | 57,787 | 849 | 1,720,744 | 1,904,884 | 12,219,864 | 4,520,960 | 3,494,263 | 1,022,928 |
| Coryell | 58,376 | 687 | 986,347 | 18,100,120 | 25,868,473 | 3,222,869 | 2,244,221 | 974,807 |
| Cottle | 1,894 | 390 | 85,341 | 4,718,747 | 12,319,020 | 101,327 | 4,097 | 97,120 |
| Crane | 5,800 | 318 | 318,144 | 369,370 | 1,197,155 | 423,950 | 196,284 | 227,578 |
| Crockett | 6,125 | 783 | 667,332 | 502,879 | 2,148,441 | 396,625 | 89,819 | 306,553 |
| Crosby | 6,366 | 569 | 170,007 | 1,259,652 | 3,823,409 | 366,443 | 38,642 | 327,273 |
| Culberson | 2,312 | 749 | 607,896 | 689,352 | 5,881,932 | 143,695 | 5,101 | 138,452 |
| Dallam | 7,992 | 681 | 386,474 | 3,899,906 | 10,001,667 | 699,042 | 247,257 | 451,614 |
| Dallas | 2,064,783 | 3,366 | 37,269,886 | 909,853,612 | 937,987,361 | 159,421,392 | 129,948,342 | 29,297,223 |
| Dawson | 12,493 | 712 | 471,880 | 2,491,084 | 14,439,645 | 1,089,984 | 514,717 | 573,005 |
| Deaf Smith | 20,923 | 602 | 402,863 | 841,211 | 6,237,347 | 1,833,101 | 1,209,805 | 621,951 |
| Delta | 6,796 | 353 | 172,450 | 3,980,934 | 9,142,846 | 358,180 | 81,618 | 276,272 |
| Denton | 603,332 | 1,489 | 9,186,357 | 330,603,907 | 353,255,643 | 41,082,122 | 32,080,223 | 8,918,983 |
| Dewitt | 27,504 | 662 | 874,652 | 3,013,647 | 16,161,416 | 1,755,503 | 1,097,125 | 657,062 |
| Dickens | 3,029 | 468 | 99,940 | 1,007,301 | 4,589,027 | 154,332 | 5,452 | 148,858 |
| Dimmit | 13,894 | 507 | 1,062,757 | 2,882,015 | 14,696,844 | 1,202,287 | 787,946 | 413,865 |
| Donley | 3,653 | 459 | 574,401 | 980,150 | 5,289,566 | 226,402 | 8,896 | 217,308 |
| Duval | 13,455 | 637 | 561,852 | 2,391,820 | 7,083,021 | 985,144 | 513,459 | 471,290 |
| Eastland | 24,686 | 1,026 | 1,356,032 | 3,917,217 | 22,056,559 | 1,797,767 | 1,142,591 | 654,200 |
| Ector | 178,905 | 970 | 2,616,204 | 4,158,750 | 20,543,755 | 16,684,760 | 13,849,624 | 2,828,572 |
| Edwards | 3,139 | 499 | 100,355 | 1,210,332 | 2,891,854 | 166,910 | 5,782 | 161,063 |
| Ellis | 165,813 | 1,524 | 4,631,440 | 19,551,872 | 41,476,205 | 10,836,048 | 8,552,367 | 2,271,606 |
| El Paso | 638,673 | 1,687 | 10,463,985 | 254,840,989 | 302,390,631 | 50,690,099 | 35,950,541 | 14,712,164 |
| Erath | 40,785 | 822 | 1,014,886 | 11,427,218 | 17,920,727 | 2,647,481 | 1,830,146 | 814,250 |
| Falls | 17,394 | 746 | 758,023 | 3,676,838 | 15,291,421 | 1,053,054 | 507,447 | 544,971 |
| Fannin | 37,166 | 986 | 772,227 | 18,389,429 | 32,240,379 | 2,394,968 | 1,588,541 | 804,177 |
| Fayette | 35,313 | 1,025 | 1,726,145 | 5,010,178 | 16,759,701 | 2,220,375 | 1,464,174 | 752,989 |
| Fisher | 5,220 | 556 | 149,841 | 769,564 | 4,505,856 | 280,186 | 9,498 | 270,477 |
| Floyd | 7,384 | 704 | 180,184 | 963,542 | 10,947,884 | 506,924 | 103,915 | 402,349 |
| Foard | 1,700 | 298 | 70,188 | 1,256,402 | 2,610,834 | 99,183 | 3,297 | 95,864 |
| Fort Bend | 551,551 | 1,224 | 6,480,792 | 66,454,246 | 84,010,380 | 40,386,820 | 32,001,465 | 8,319,027 |
| Franklin | 12,843 | 339 | 466,558 | 1,124,645 | 6,515,516 | 713,386 | 301,512 | 411,183 |

| County | Vehicles Registered | Lane Miles of Highway | Vehicle Miles Driven Daily | State Construction Expenditures | Combined Construction Maintenance Expenditures | Total Vehicle Registration Fees | State Net Receipts | County Net Receipts |
|---|---|---|---|---|---|---|---|---|
| Freestone | 24,789 | 825 | 1,446,562 | 1,853,787 | 13,870,576 | 1,757,949 | 1,116,190 | 640,902 |
| Frio | 16,163 | 762 | 1,614,876 | 1,854,641 | 13,909,923 | 1,399,856 | 882,537 | 516,675 |
| Gaines | 20,428 | 662 | 681,872 | 397,805 | 2,489,303 | 1,432,361 | 1,017,857 | 413,315 |
| Galveston | 286,017 | 1,086 | 4,527,940 | 13,323,194 | 34,733,735 | 18,958,209 | 15,002,840 | 3,921,868 |
| Garza | 5,625 | 457 | 415,790 | 379,796 | 2,649,163 | 389,912 | 98,399 | 291,086 |
| Gillespie | 34,399 | 690 | 684,166 | 1,528,805 | 15,048,210 | 2,071,904 | 1,298,256 | 768,757 |
| Glasscock | 2,809 | 295 | 443,061 | 11,331,790 | 12,576,214 | 166,195 | 8,429 | 157,613 |
| Goliad | 9,454 | 535 | 432,323 | 917,604 | 4,850,219 | 482,718 | 119,754 | 362,254 |
| Gonzales | 25,111 | 883 | 1,612,017 | 8,628,726 | 22,872,076 | 1,642,105 | 1,013,575 | 627,439 |
| Gray | 26,378 | 769 | 780,584 | 900,071 | 4,689,806 | 1,915,863 | 1,225,542 | 688,068 |
| Grayson | 128,526 | 1,261 | 3,081,504 | 17,341,343 | 35,543,216 | 8,607,992 | 6,603,367 | 1,987,711 |
| Gregg | 134,302 | 808 | 2,713,372 | 5,730,871 | 23,666,195 | 11,408,224 | 9,360,188 | 2,038,865 |
| Grimes | 33,594 | 615 | 940,678 | 4,824,380 | 22,446,703 | 2,119,829 | 1,382,958 | 734,848 |
| Guadalupe | 138,385 | 1,006 | 3,134,295 | 9,315,468 | 27,577,455 | 9,343,143 | 7,096,818 | 2,231,386 |
| Hale | 30,573 | 1,055 | 819,420 | 9,115,122 | 16,647,437 | 2,183,711 | 1,452,363 | 729,689 |
| Hall | 3,686 | 459 | 266,446 | 1,067,400 | 3,196,899 | 222,624 | 7,720 | 214,729 |
| Hamilton | 11,451 | 583 | 367,459 | 2,143,458 | 13,383,914 | 690,415 | 214,492 | 475,235 |
| Hansford | 7,454 | 525 | 143,334 | 1,441,012 | 4,473,654 | 530,401 | 119,960 | 410,138 |
| Hardeman | 4,364 | 466 | 408,028 | 681,472 | 5,834,281 | 265,828 | 9,284 | 256,315 |
| Hardin | 60,187 | 579 | 1,268,215 | 2,285,091 | 8,825,956 | 4,386,094 | 3,191,100 | 1,191,329 |
| Harris | 3,500,829 | 5,009 | 57,639,386 | 756,744,369 | 942,668,340 | 276,644,896 | 221,239,301 | 55,026,369 |
| Harrison | 73,083 | 1,187 | 2,774,030 | 5,830,559 | 26,028,430 | 4,997,914 | 3,746,630 | 1,245,786 |
| Hartley | 6,893 | 540 | 410,794 | 3,245,774 | 9,974,898 | 578,361 | 225,213 | 352,633 |
| Haskell | 6,691 | 669 | 218,739 | 2,628,926 | 5,581,711 | 451,914 | 79,750 | 371,661 |
| Hays | 158,389 | 714 | 4,510,518 | 26,072,222 | 50,673,391 | 11,014,555 | 8,595,968 | 2,395,880 |
| Hemphill | 6,824 | 391 | 326,505 | 2,294,622 | 9,251,717 | 465,244 | 127,467 | 337,141 |
| Henderson | 89,375 | 1,037 | 1,599,991 | 9,433,194 | 23,044,478 | 5,442,112 | 4,082,346 | 1,354,451 |
| Hidalgo | 564,625 | 2,430 | 9,969,860 | 55,610,782 | 92,479,447 | 47,405,618 | 34,026,952 | 13,357,360 |
| Hill | 43,124 | 1,091 | 2,081,519 | 20,584,860 | 42,978,676 | 2,974,921 | 2,141,450 | 830,516 |
| Hockley | 27,356 | 751 | 626,231 | 2,262,808 | 5,176,364 | 2,006,291 | 1,333,034 | 669,463 |
| Hood | 65,871 | 402 | 919,756 | 1,624,003 | 4,980,804 | 4,626,834 | 3,419,063 | 1,201,019 |
| Hopkins | 40,944 | 961 | 1,582,630 | 7,507,547 | 19,277,080 | 2,725,565 | 1,893,672 | 829,819 |
| Houston | 23,718 | 868 | 647,838 | 3,605,012 | 24,846,583 | 1,350,904 | 746,974 | 602,243 |
| Howard | 32,459 | 858 | 1,099,438 | 11,731,025 | 25,147,112 | 2,153,296 | 1,428,139 | 723,603 |
| Hudspeth | 3,840 | 826 | 1,313,176 | 3,530,965 | 12,245,850 | 218,148 | 8,072 | 209,873 |
| Hunt | 93,199 | 1,354 | 2,659,440 | 9,283,750 | 33,277,613 | 6,178,332 | 4,572,740 | 1,599,462 |
| Hutchinson | 26,738 | 488 | 395,104 | 1,822,662 | 5,796,582 | 1,850,821 | 1,231,003 | 617,922 |
| Irion | 3,843 | 246 | 439,117 | 152,179 | 3,696,060 | 330,801 | 97,684 | 232,847 |
| Jack | 12,482 | 576 | 378,709 | 856,703 | 6,211,368 | 935,672 | 483,954 | 451,178 |
| Jackson | 18,504 | 637 | 938,331 | 1,559,813 | 8,332,554 | 1,165,994 | 611,215 | 553,910 |
| Jasper | 41,927 | 775 | 1,059,491 | 882,478 | 5,340,887 | 2,709,638 | 1,873,422 | 834,707 |
| Jeff Davis | 2,955 | 469 | 180,663 | 695,039 | 2,110,759 | 177,984 | 36,917 | 140,326 |
| Jefferson | 220,898 | 1,132 | 4,953,483 | 14,172,036 | 51,916,834 | 15,891,230 | 12,635,356 | 3,238,561 |
| Jim Hogg | 5,204 | 288 | 161,934 | 3,152,941 | 7,385,094 | 366,605 | 108,215 | 258,186 |
| Jim Wells | 51,317 | 712 | 1,285,366 | 9,973,645 | 25,355,507 | 4,326,305 | 3,328,445 | 995,677 |
| Johnson | 168,964 | 995 | 2,770,093 | 22,673,593 | 44,421,403 | 12,838,221 | 10,139,977 | 2,686,401 |
| Jones | 18,221 | 1,010 | 462,896 | 2,843,903 | 6,978,084 | 1,342,753 | 749,391 | 591,675 |
| Karnes | 19,097 | 696 | 1,059,801 | 19,846,967 | 33,563,011 | 1,303,500 | 745,458 | 557,613 |
| Kaufman | 109,180 | 1,202 | 3,461,699 | 15,914,121 | 32,096,451 | 7,394,875 | 5,543,252 | 1,844,495 |
| Kendall | 55,974 | 455 | 993,278 | 2,263,067 | 5,225,578 | 4,508,741 | 3,226,135 | 1,271,218 |
| Kenedy | 873 | 191 | 453,762 | 4,730,742 | 13,392,294 | 39,576 | 1,692 | 37,840 |
| Kent | 1,210 | 325 | 52,347 | 172,856 | 3,633,402 | 62,050 | 4,009 | 57,922 |
| Kerr | 57,597 | 710 | 1,136,884 | 3,202,179 | 8,930,475 | 3,926,072 | 2,851,083 | 1,063,866 |
| Kimble | 6,550 | 684 | 514,899 | 306,413 | 2,867,212 | 378,632 | 77,526 | 300,540 |
| King | 567 | 206 | 93,393 | 6,063,344 | 9,587,801 | 20,880 | 888 | 19,954 |
| Kinney | 3,746 | 407 | 198,812 | 812,499 | 2,882,428 | 226,080 | 56,308 | 169,485 |
| Kleberg | 27,856 | 373 | 732,439 | 12,124,772 | 14,915,657 | 2,000,052 | 1,372,831 | 625,024 |
| Knox | 4,868 | 465 | 148,300 | 2,968,839 | 8,812,181 | 334,373 | 48,026 | 285,836 |
| Lamar | 52,652 | 1,001 | 1,179,251 | 3,048,571 | 18,345,632 | 3,701,823 | 2,684,856 | 1,014,589 |

| County | Vehicles Registered | Lane Miles of Highway | Vehicle Miles Driven Daily | State Construction Expenditures | Combined Construction Maintenance Expenditures | Total Vehicle Registration Fees | State Net Receipts | County Net Receipts |
|---|---|---|---|---|---|---|---|---|
| Lamb | 14,682 | 800 | 443,697 | 862,906 | 4,588,876 | 966,234 | 440,165 | 525,156 |
| Lampasas | 24,719 | 512 | 559,361 | 6,416,928 | 11,336,846 | 1,636,471 | 949,696 | 684,710 |
| La Salle | 8,382 | 649 | 1,469,848 | 24,424,076 | 39,625,320 | 673,150 | 324,149 | 348,710 |
| Lavaca | 28,987 | 659 | 710,276 | 11,398,336 | 17,740,249 | 1,829,271 | 1,171,538 | 655,698 |
| Lee | 24,290 | 531 | 703,276 | 1,579,625 | 13,265,667 | 1,618,712 | 1,021,066 | 596,574 |
| Leon | 25,225 | 837 | 1,379,973 | 1,634,093 | 14,435,681 | 1,611,583 | 1,007,946 | 602,418 |
| Liberty | 80,728 | 853 | 1,988,752 | 4,910,645 | 23,006,352 | 5,630,084 | 4,326,541 | 1,300,098 |
| Limestone | 25,121 | 771 | 650,607 | 3,232,691 | 15,091,117 | 1,499,548 | 871,117 | 627,469 |
| Lipscomb | 4,578 | 412 | 153,463 | 6,183,812 | 12,473,085 | 325,051 | 39,605 | 285,206 |
| Live Oak | 17,160 | 1,007 | 1,711,978 | 13,198,523 | 31,052,518 | 1,165,970 | 622,172 | 542,761 |
| Llano | 26,835 | 499 | 468,520 | 3,390,761 | 11,334,062 | 1,582,140 | 916,056 | 662,120 |
| Loving | 212 | 68 | 103,090 | - | 188,636 | 9,140 | 391 | 8,749 |
| Lubbock | 240,982 | 1,728 | 3,726,569 | 39,268,977 | 53,763,664 | 18,878,445 | 15,064,225 | 3,760,874 |
| Lynn | 6,702 | 715 | 378,749 | 134,966 | 2,646,435 | 375,218 | 43,119 | 331,042 |
| Madison | 14,228 | 576 | 885,727 | 2,290,619 | 12,781,168 | 1,270,115 | 779,659 | 489,966 |
| Marion | 11,452 | 329 | 315,835 | 1,024,949 | 3,515,946 | 702,996 | 260,500 | 442,154 |
| Martin | 7,647 | 578 | 665,540 | 8,106,571 | 11,583,996 | 664,416 | 210,864 | 453,248 |
| Mason | 6,374 | 423 | 171,853 | 171,496 | 3,318,325 | 335,618 | 65,163 | 269,927 |
| Matagorda | 39,105 | 690 | 734,811 | 344,507 | 6,278,264 | 2,477,575 | 1,675,403 | 799,510 |
| Maverick | 43,540 | 499 | 935,450 | 2,720,013 | 11,056,275 | 3,192,462 | 2,351,324 | 839,497 |
| McCulloch | 10,321 | 609 | 338,109 | 828,073 | 7,741,069 | 703,556 | 240,494 | 462,148 |
| McLennan | 216,653 | 1,703 | 5,942,513 | 96,666,777 | 146,944,986 | 15,791,371 | 12,336,971 | 3,437,326 |
| McMullen | 2,884 | 317 | 656,294 | 7,053,217 | 13,703,185 | 216,008 | 44,820 | 170,895 |
| Medina | 52,303 | 766 | 1,279,203 | 1,829,066 | 13,210,069 | 3,531,467 | 2,529,217 | 999,620 |
| Menard | 3,075 | 349 | 165,304 | 942,761 | 6,057,982 | 157,469 | 12,868 | 144,382 |
| Midland | 196,865 | 1,075 | 3,395,464 | 23,858,942 | 37,274,502 | 17,957,523 | 15,050,027 | 2,888,687 |
| Milam | 30,702 | 692 | 797,424 | 1,684,499 | 13,616,057 | 1,826,525 | 1,133,723 | 691,225 |
| Mills | 7,440 | 451 | 274,907 | 205,240 | 3,921,418 | 440,472 | 82,973 | 357,023 |
| Mitchell | 8,288 | 660 | 560,320 | 413,720 | 2,749,342 | 501,069 | 108,132 | 392,453 |
| Montague | 27,168 | 853 | 841,090 | 1,385,491 | 17,386,097 | 1,820,505 | 1,152,402 | 666,511 |
| Montgomery | 473,702 | 1,251 | 9,270,606 | 94,135,804 | 119,247,566 | 32,873,889 | 26,447,147 | 6,363,773 |
| Moore | 23,125 | 472 | 593,711 | 5,250,129 | 8,619,766 | 1,729,274 | 1,160,397 | 568,077 |
| Morris | 15,347 | 359 | 489,199 | 1,324,926 | 7,923,347 | 960,413 | 518,966 | 440,995 |
| Motley | 1,653 | 330 | 60,081 | 3,396,211 | 5,779,252 | 85,107 | 3,477 | 81,587 |
| Nacogdoches | 58,902 | 981 | 1,749,105 | 7,751,085 | 17,622,200 | 3,983,852 | 2,878,347 | 1,100,732 |
| Navarro | 51,056 | 1,193 | 2,068,729 | 10,375,844 | 35,883,457 | 3,425,378 | 2,454,614 | 968,159 |
| Newton | 15,164 | 552 | 373,710 | 2,108,188 | 11,358,850 | 846,837 | 332,589 | 513,815 |
| Nolan | 15,714 | 689 | 900,603 | 4,669,927 | 18,103,140 | 1,079,109 | 546,008 | 531,537 |
| Nueces | 300,564 | 1,523 | 5,418,066 | 74,285,109 | 109,824,489 | 22,632,799 | 18,145,156 | 4,464,982 |
| Ochiltree | 14,845 | 429 | 330,738 | 3,353,146 | 13,129,344 | 1,208,143 | 665,556 | 541,789 |
| Oldham | 3,105 | 467 | 713,046 | 179,401 | 4,481,572 | 223,158 | 39,245 | 183,803 |
| Orange | 86,157 | 626 | 2,497,318 | 6,702,533 | 43,009,560 | 5,518,638 | 4,161,238 | 1,351,335 |
| Palo Pinto | 35,583 | 831 | 965,515 | 2,747,355 | 9,792,014 | 2,435,816 | 1,717,504 | 716,445 |
| Panola | 30,950 | 780 | 1,121,245 | 2,431,207 | 11,228,810 | 1,920,109 | 1,473,783 | 445,000 |
| Parker | 143,469 | 884 | 2,927,380 | 13,974,218 | 33,825,192 | 10,801,612 | 8,493,107 | 2,291,060 |
| Parmer | 10,936 | 614 | 433,425 | 480,770 | 5,712,933 | 816,163 | 327,851 | 487,971 |
| Pecos | 18,017 | 1,681 | 958,562 | 1,922,248 | 10,112,333 | 1,453,705 | 893,625 | 559,070 |
| Polk | 58,248 | 860 | 1,879,109 | 5,890,703 | 20,233,821 | 4,513,759 | 3,370,584 | 1,139,993 |
| Potter | 104,742 | 901 | 2,869,911 | 4,567,408 | 15,974,334 | 8,032,647 | 6,381,737 | 1,638,613 |
| Presidio | 8,383 | 546 | 172,028 | 5,217,417 | 7,412,993 | 549,274 | 208,506 | 340,344 |
| Rains | 13,941 | 270 | 291,192 | 854,357 | 4,626,816 | 854,836 | 410,977 | 442,992 |
| Randall | 132,874 | 891 | 1,471,219 | 12,235,899 | 26,980,785 | 10,018,114 | 7,754,225 | 2,241,351 |
| Reagan | 5,567 | 319 | 417,067 | 2,898,060 | 6,142,174 | 468,862 | 146,635 | 321,997 |
| Real | 4,339 | 296 | 99,112 | 679,339 | 2,880,769 | 264,272 | 54,313 | 209,392 |
| Red River | 15,256 | 752 | 403,315 | 1,320,571 | 14,591,990 | 838,426 | 324,219 | 513,819 |
| Reeves | 12,064 | 1,175 | 1,032,914 | 330,387 | 6,107,909 | 1,088,791 | 588,259 | 499,857 |
| Refugio | 9,237 | 462 | 716,519 | 653,515 | 3,043,429 | 607,574 | 264,464 | 342,399 |
| Roberts | 1,531 | 243 | 131,888 | 670,261 | 1,608,949 | 81,273 | 3,355 | 77,852 |
| Robertson | 19,839 | 659 | 855,009 | 1,428,044 | 7,250,492 | 1,239,870 | 650,471 | 588,340 |

| County | Vehicles Registered | Lane Miles of Highway | Vehicle Miles Driven Daily | State Construction Expenditures | Combined Construction Maintenance Expenditures | Total Vehicle Registration Fees | State Net Receipts | County Net Receipts |
|---|---|---|---|---|---|---|---|---|
| Rockwall | 82,515 | 346 | 1,896,236 | 19,626,501 | 26,735,796 | 5,965,743 | 4,572,127 | 1,382,772 |
| Runnels | 13,482 | 735 | 345,022 | 462,657 | 2,922,119 | 919,068 | 420,720 | 497,380 |
| Rusk | 54,717 | 1,185 | 1,416,124 | 2,762,105 | 13,999,951 | 3,481,763 | 2,505,072 | 973,533 |
| Sabine | 13,497 | 484 | 290,049 | 926,245 | 8,225,698 | 799,964 | 333,215 | 466,004 |
| SanAugustine | 9,870 | 540 | 276,937 | 2,282,554 | 8,453,667 | 637,903 | 222,918 | 414,554 |
| San Jacinto | 28,549 | 527 | 728,307 | 1,843,178 | 10,108,283 | 1,816,455 | 1,119,340 | 695,572 |
| San Patricio | 68,376 | 987 | 1,996,714 | 11,631,871 | 29,159,821 | 4,645,018 | 3,371,684 | 1,267,930 |
| San Saba | 7,820 | 436 | 146,958 | 133,167 | 3,141,722 | 458,440 | 83,805 | 374,301 |
| Schleicher | 4,569 | 361 | 151,333 | 3,503,233 | 3,132,252 | 277,740 | 53,575 | 223,967 |
| Scurry | 27,097 | 686 | 648,331 | 792,372 | 8,922,425 | 2,458,584 | 1,801,880 | 655,727 |
| Shackelford | 5,550 | 357 | 154,571 | 971,957 | 3,976,179 | 483,608 | 155,875 | 327,338 |
| Shelby | 31,977 | 878 | 808,839 | 10,199,918 | 30,778,580 | 1,935,327 | 1,209,521 | 724,733 |
| Sherman | 3,383 | 429 | 313,956 | 1,335,959 | 4,082,498 | 238,067 | 8,517 | 229,413 |
| Smith | 216,905 | 1,603 | 4,967,593 | 15,715,132 | 38,738,064 | 15,729,072 | 12,156,240 | 3,554,044 |
| Somervell | 11,064 | 198 | 230,044 | 108,969 | 5,241,269 | 598,636 | 289,606 | 307,898 |
| Starr | 55,063 | 526 | 1,034,431 | 9,681,481 | 18,065,137 | 3,570,218 | 2,594,734 | 972,344 |
| Stephens | 12,071 | 561 | 217,947 | 844,325 | 6,429,884 | 831,530 | 396,976 | 433,844 |
| Sterling | 2,730 | 283 | 285,944 | 2,682,258 | 3,345,337 | 146,981 | 34,287 | 112,650 |
| Stonewall | 2,314 | 329 | 89,303 | 853,289 | 2,207,569 | 123,456 | 3,586 | 119,826 |
| Sutton | 6,925 | 591 | 507,036 | 3,600,637 | 6,689,224 | 496,559 | 179,537 | 316,639 |
| Swisher | 7,522 | 805 | 395,905 | 1,455,289 | 4,384,295 | 483,624 | 92,172 | 390,666 |
| Tarrant | 1,637,874 | 3,290 | 30,301,087 | 535,741,619 | 612,914,932 | 128,534,615 | 105,109,202 | 23,155,634 |
| Taylor | 130,994 | 1,211 | 2,321,697 | 4,492,670 | 27,840,063 | 9,669,142 | 7,582,125 | 2,075,106 |
| Terrell | 1,373 | 374 | 72,101 | 383,098 | 1,539,614 | 66,967 | 2,754 | 64,117 |
| Terry | 12,310 | 636 | 480,290 | 1,809,904 | 8,775,860 | 832,706 | 328,483 | 503,169 |
| Throckmorton | 2,358 | 343 | 73,191 | 656,644 | 2,440,458 | 127,743 | 4,953 | 122,746 |
| Titus | 31,536 | 541 | 1,075,094 | 970,242 | 9,233,977 | 2,388,124 | 1,620,993 | 765,708 |
| Tom Green | 118,094 | 1,042 | 1,761,780 | 9,268,532 | 15,329,707 | 8,725,640 | 6,636,848 | 2,077,175 |
| Travis | 1,070,670 | 2,096 | 18,068,121 | 186,547,686 | 259,768,163 | 71,040,473 | 56,027,074 | 14,836,512 |
| Trinity | 16,034 | 443 | 342,141 | 937,091 | 5,554,799 | 957,320 | 454,260 | 502,320 |
| Tyler | 22,728 | 520 | 551,713 | 1,962,556 | 6,073,216 | 1,337,363 | 720,923 | 615,570 |
| Upshur | 43,382 | 792 | 954,327 | 1,869,931 | 22,796,995 | 2,618,159 | 1,779,037 | 837,323 |
| Upton | 5,187 | 391 | 377,776 | 2,268,331 | 4,504,248 | 356,163 | 114,572 | 241,319 |
| Uvalde | 27,197 | 760 | 715,594 | 2,709,386 | 13,491,397 | 1,925,689 | 1,306,327 | 617,731 |
| Val Verde | 45,603 | 739 | 480,034 | 7,236,957 | 12,372,282 | 3,164,815 | 2,274,923 | 885,584 |
| Van Zandt | 64,196 | 1,162 | 1,848,068 | 4,500,059 | 18,457,443 | 3,861,779 | 2,723,654 | 1,135,362 |
| Victoria | 99,448 | 906 | 2,027,159 | 11,604,047 | 28,922,704 | 7,592,049 | 5,929,374 | 1,654,411 |
| Walker | 52,989 | 804 | 2,006,531 | 8,884,122 | 27,327,701 | 3,369,015 | 2,369,317 | 995,105 |
| Waller | 49,840 | 587 | 1,808,739 | 7,120,537 | 14,746,648 | 3,462,354 | 2,539,020 | 920,279 |
| Ward | 15,427 | 665 | 729,012 | 1,862,080 | 7,140,919 | 1,232,328 | 922,668 | 308,992 |
| Washington | 44,091 | 659 | 1,099,030 | 7,071,513 | 15,436,888 | 3,129,178 | 2,245,147 | 879,866 |
| Webb | 190,761 | 1,200 | 3,448,560 | 33,650,819 | 43,500,243 | 17,363,833 | 12,459,525 | 4,896,395 |
| Wharton | 49,489 | 893 | 1,690,515 | 5,146,528 | 19,434,811 | 3,735,327 | 2,786,653 | 946,046 |
| Wheeler | 9,084 | 673 | 687,796 | 1,264,517 | 3,681,879 | 572,558 | 141,965 | 429,949 |
| Wichita | 116,800 | 1,136 | 2,200,794 | 3,641,958 | 12,913,241 | 8,126,357 | 6,314,076 | 1,803,739 |
| Wilbarger | 13,807 | 723 | 640,029 | 603,025 | 4,934,336 | 935,514 | 394,925 | 539,314 |
| Willacy | 15,746 | 518 | 516,494 | 11,355,421 | 14,435,031 | 1,009,823 | 484,665 | 524,595 |
| Williamson | 402,711 | 1,688 | 7,829,346 | 75,028,436 | 111,253,736 | 29,311,661 | 22,705,261 | 6,536,433 |
| Wilson | 53,303 | 747 | 1,200,367 | 5,828,613 | 8,203,076 | 3,334,925 | 2,382,821 | 949,349 |
| Winkler | 9,371 | 293 | 359,469 | 1,307,071 | 2,543,326 | 702,595 | 383,060 | 319,267 |
| Wise | 83,797 | 911 | 2,434,045 | 7,628,192 | 24,333,226 | 6,568,500 | 5,161,121 | 1,403,255 |
| Wood | 51,592 | 907 | 856,295 | 2,014,880 | 12,521,764 | 3,160,876 | 2,203,115 | 954,343 |
| Yoakum | 11,782 | 430 | 283,171 | 1,631,702 | 3,603,217 | 966,619 | 469,940 | 496,146 |
| Young | 24,366 | 708 | 405,600 | 1,940,725 | 6,493,988 | 1,672,013 | 1,038,542 | 631,669 |
| Zapata | 13,783 | 270 | 365,522 | 11,246,132 | 20,026,127 | 1,042,362 | 631,938 | 410,208 |
| Zavala | 9,153 | 542 | 461,121 | 2,394,789 | 18,860,202 | 602,542 | 246,374 | 355,871 |
| | | | | $ | $ | $ | $ | $ |
| **Total** | 23,875,821 | 199,295 | 499,867,599 | 5,154,558,471 | 8,846,602,400 | 1,779,977,762 | 1,344,148,017 | 433,432,603 |

# Texas Toll Roads, Bridges

| Facilities | Authority | 2006 | 2008 | 2010 | 2012 |
|---|---|---|---|---|---|
| **Roads** | (**Tolls Collected** in thousands of dollars, 000) | | | | |
| Camino Colombia Toll Road | TxDOT | $ 566 | $ 668 | $ 3,352 | $ 347 |
| Central Texas Toll Facilities[1] | Central Texas Turnpike System and Regional Mobility Authority | – | 99,837 | 90,006 | 113,237 |
| Fort Bend Toll Road | Fort Bend Toll Road Authority | 11,643 | 15,155 | 15,675 | 17,487 |
| Harris County Toll Facilities[2] | Harris County Toll Road Authority | 354,460 | 428,022 | 464,269 | 485,932 |
| North Texas Toll Facilities | North Texas Tollway Authority | 200,865 | 241,609 | 399,054 | 485,838 |
| **Bridges** | | | | | |
| Cameron County International Toll | Cameron County | $ 17,867 | $ 14,972 | $ 22,102 | $ 15,066 |
| Del Rio International | City of Del Rio | 4,610 | 4,986 | 4,144 | 4,978 |
| Eagle Pass International | City of Eagle Pass | 7,784 | 8,751 | 8,106 | 7,979 |
| Laredo International | City of Laredo | 39,047 | 45,452 | 41,449 | 44,412 |
| McAllen International Toll | City of McAllen | 11,643 | 12,203 | 11,036 | 11,491 |
| Pharr International Toll | City of Pharr | 7,658 | 8,140 | 10,639 | 10,233 |
| Roma International Toll | Starr County | 2,673 | 2,447 | 2,081 | 1,764 |
| San Luis Pass–Vacek | Galveston County | 675 | 731 | 1,265 | 516 |
| Zaragosa | City of El Paso | 14,262 | 16,677 | 16,094 | 16,384 |
| **Total tolls collected, roads & bridges** | | **$ 673,366** | **$ 785,291** | **$ 1,089,272** | **$ 1,215,644** |

[1]Including U.S. 183A. [2]Including Jesse Jones Memorial Toll Bridge. *Estimate. NA, not available.
Source: Highway Statistics annual, Federal Highway Administration; and local toll authorities.

# Driver Licenses

The following list shows the number of licensed drivers by year for Texas and for all the states. Sources are the Texas Department of Public Safety (for state figures) and the Federal Highway Administration, 2015.

| Year | Texas licensed drivers | Total U.S. licensed drivers | Year | Texas licensed drivers | Total U.S. licensed drivers |
|---|---|---|---|---|---|
| 2013 | 16,230,209 | 212,159,728 | 1993 | 11,876,268 | 173,149,313 |
| 2012 | 15,950,297 | 211,814,830 | 1992 | 11,437,571 | 173,125,396 |
| 2011 | 16,880,877 | 211,874,649 | 1991 | 11,293,184 | 168,995,076 |
| 2010 | 16,808,359 | 210,114,939 | 1990 | 11,136,694 | 167,015,250 |
| 2009 | 16,602,416 | 209,618,386 | 1989 | 11,103,511 | 165,555,295 |
| 2008 | 16,551,156 | 208,320,601 | 1988 | 11,080,702 | 162,853,255 |
| 2007 | 16,330,825 | 205,741,845 | 1987 | 11,153,472 | 161,818,461 |
| 2006 | 16,096,985 | 202,810,438 | 1986 | 11,129,193 | 159,487,000 |
| 2005 | 15,831,852 | 200,548,972 | 1985 | 10,809,078 | 156,868,277 |
| 2004 | 15,562,484 | 198,888,912 | 1984 | 10,855,549 | 155,423,709 |
| 2003 | 15,091,776 | 196,165,666 | 1983 | 11,406,433 | 154,389,178 |
| 2002 | 14,639,132 | 194,295,633 | 1982 | 10,154,386 | 150,233,659 |
| 2001 | 14,303,799 | 191,275,719 | 1981 | 9,673,885 | 147,075,169 |
| 2000 | 14,024,305 | 190,625,023 | 1980 | 9,287,286 | 145,295,036 |
| 1999 | 13,718,319 | 187,170,420 | 1975 | 7,509,497 | 129,790,666 |
| 1998 | 13,419,288 | 184,980,177 | 1970 | 6,380,057 | 111,542,787 |
| 1997 | 12,833,603 | 182,709,204 | 1965 | 5,413,887 | 98,502,152 |
| 1996 | 12,568,265 | 179,539,340 | 1960 | 4,352,168 | 87,252,563 |
| 1995 | 12,369,243 | 176,628,482 | 1955 | 3,874,834 | 74,685,949 |
| 1994 | 12,109,960 | 175,403,465 | 1950 | 2,687,349 | 59,322,278 |

# Motor Vehicles Crashes, Losses in Texas

| Year | Number killed | Number injured | Crashes by Kind | | | | Vehicle Miles Traveled | | Economic loss (000,000) |
|------|------|------|------|------|------|------|------|------|------|
| | | | Fatal | Injury | Non-injury | Total | Number (000,000) | Deaths per 100 mill miles | |
| 1960 | 2,254 | 127,980 | 1,842 | 71,100 | 239,300 | 312,242 | 46,353 | 4.9 | $ 350 |
| 1965 | 3,028 | 186,062 | 2,460 | 103,368 | 365,160 | 470,988 | * 52,163 | 5.8 | 498 |
| 1966 | 3,406 | 208,310 | 2,784 | 115,728 | 406,460 | 524,972 | 55,261 | 6.2 | 557 |
| 1970 | 3,560 | 223,000 | 2,965 | 124,000 | 886,000 | 1,012,965 | * 68,031 | 5.2 | 1,042 |
| 1975 | 3,429 | 138,962 | 2,945 | 92,510 | 373,141 | 468,596 | 84,575 | 4.1 | 1,440 |
| 1976 | 3,230 | 145,282 | 2,780 | 96,348 | 380,075 | 479,203 | 91,279 | 3.5 | 1,485 |
| 1977 | 3,698 | 161,635 | 3,230 | 106,923 | 393,848 | 504,001 | 96,998 | 3.8 | 1,960 |
| 1978 | ‡ 3,980 | 178,228 | ‡ 3,468 | 117,998 | § 304,830 | 426,296 | 102,624 | 3.9 | 2,430 |
| 1979 | 4,229 | 184,550 | 3,685 | 122,793 | 322,336 | 448,814 | 101,909 | 4.1 | 2,580 |
| 1980 | 4,424 | 185,964 | 3,863 | 123,577 | 305,500 | 432,940 | 103,255 | 4.3 | 3,010 |
| 1981 | 4,701 | 206,196 | 4,137 | 136,396 | 317,484 | 458,017 | 111,036 | 4.2 | 3,430 |
| 1982 | 4,271 | 204,666 | 3,752 | 135,859 | 312,159 | 451,770 | * 124,910 | 3.4 | 3,375 |
| 1983 | ‡ 3,823 | 208,157 | ‡ 3,328 | 137,695 | 302,876 | 443,899 | 129,309 | 3.0 | 3,440 |
| 1984 | 3,913 | 220,720 | 3,466 | 145,543 | 293,285 | 442,294 | 137,280 | 2.9 | ¶ 3,795 |
| 1985 | 3,682 | 231,009 | 3,270 | 151,657 | 300,531 | 452,188 | 143,500 | 2.6 | 3,755 |
| 1986 | 3,568 | 234,120 | 3,121 | 154,514 | 298,079 | 452,593 | 150,474 | 2.4 | 3,782 |
| 1987 | 3,261 | 226,895 | 2,881 | 146,913 | 246,175 | 395,969 | 151,221 | 2.2 | 3,913 |
| 1988 | 3,395 | 238,845 | 3,004 | 152,004 | 237,703 | 392,711 | 152,819 | 2.2 | 4,515 |
| 1989 | 3,361 | 243,030 | 2,926 | 153,356 | 233,967 | 390,249 | 159,679 | 2.1 | 4,873 |
| 1990 | 3,243 | 262,576 | 2,882 | 162,424 | 216,140 | 381,446 | 163,103 | 2.0 | 4,994 |
| 1991 | 3,079 | 263,430 | 2,690 | 161,470 | 207,288 | 371,448 | 162,780 | 1.9 | 5,604 |
| 1992 | 3,057 | 282,025 | 2,690 | 170,513 | 209,152 | 382,355 | 162,769 | 1.9 | 6,725 |
| 1993 | 3,037 | 298,891 | 2,690 | 178,194 | 209,533 | 390,417 | 167,988 | 1.8 | ¶ 11,784 |
| 1994 | 3,142 | 326,837 | 2,710 | 192,014 | 219,890 | 414,614 | 172,976 | 1.8 | 12,505 |
| 1995 | 3,172 | 334,259 | 2,790 | 196,093 | 152,190 | 351,073 | 183,103 | 1.7 | 13,005 |
| 1996 | 3,738 | 350,397 | 3,247 | 204,635 | § 90,261 | 298,143 | 187,064 | 2.0 | ¶ 7,766 |
| 1997 | 3,508 | 347,881 | 3,079 | 205,595 | 97,315 | 305,989 | 194,665 | 1.8 | 7,662 |
| 1998 | 3,576 | 338,661 | 3,160 | 202,223 | 102,732 | 308,115 | 201,989 | 1.8 | 8,780 |
| 1999 | 3,519 | 339,448 | 3,106 | 203,220 | 105,375 | 311,701 | 213,847 | 1.6 | 8,729 |
| 2000 | 3,775 | 341,097 | 3,247 | 205,569 | 110,174 | 318,990 | 210,340 | 1.8 | 9,163 |
| 2001 | 3,739 | 340,554 | 3,319 | 207,043 | 113,596 | 323,958 | 216,276 | 1.73 | 9,348 |
| 2002 | 3,826 | 315,061 | 3,544 | 196,211 | 113,089 | ** 324,651 | 215,873 | 1.77 | ¶ 21,100 |
| 2003 | 3,823 | 308,543 | 3,372 | 190,926 | § 245,607 | †† 460,025 | 218,209 | 1.75 | 20,700 |
| 2004 | 3,725 | 288,715 | 3,286 | 180,556 | 245,000 | 447,691 | 229,345 | 1.62 | 19,400 |
| 2005 | 3,559 | 293,583 | 3,157 | 184,093 | 257,532 | 464,541 | 234,232 | 1.52 | 19,200 |
| 2006 | 3,523 | 272,779 | 3,120 | 173,861 | 243,970 | 439,027 | 236,852 | 1.49 | 20,400 |
| 2007 | 3,463 | 267,305 | 3,098 | 173,052 | 264,098 | 459,689 | 241,746 | 1.43 | 20,600 |
| 2008 | 3,477 | 243,547 | 3,116 | 159,760 | 257,154 | 438,996 | 234,593 | 1.48 | 22,900 |
| 2009 | 3,108 | 234,704 | 2,807 | 154,685 | 251,850 | 428,273 | 232,055 | 1.34 | 20,300 |
| 2010 | 3,050 | 217,381 | 2,772 | 141,554 | 233,573 | 391,101 | 234,261 | 1.30 | 22,200 |
| 2011 | 3,015 | 211,006 | 2,751 | 138,624 | 226,949 | 381,463 | 235,602 | 1.28 | 21,900 |
| 2012 | 3,417 | 230,957 | 3,037 | 152,301 | 247,679 | 417,707 | 237,831 | 1.44 | 26,000 |
| 2013 | 3,408 | 232,599 | 3,065 | 154,458 | 272,601 | 445,829 | 244,536 | 1.39 | 27,800 |
| 2014 | 3,534 | 237,941 | 3,189 | 158,833 | 297,934 | 476,875 | 248,824 | 1.42 | $ 28,800 |

(Note: The highest death rate was in 1966 at 6.2.)

*Method of calculating vehicle miles traveled revised. Last changed in 1982 by TxDOT.

†In August 1967, amended estimating formula received from National Safety Council (NCS). Starting 1972, actual reported injuries are listed rather than estimates.

‡Change in counting fatalities. In 1978, counted when injury results in death within 90 days of accident. In 1983, counted when injury results in death within 30 days.

§Change in counting Non-injury accidents. For 1996–2002, only crashes having at least **one vehicle towed** were tabulated.

¶Economic loss formula changed. Last changed in 2002, when figures are calculated using NCS Average Calculable Cost on a per death basis figure for the year identified. Figures are rounded to the nearest hundred million. For 1996–2001, only property damage in crashes having at least one vehicle towed was tabulated.

**Beginning with 2002 data, the "Total" crash figure includes "Unknown Severity Crashes" which are not included on this chart. Prior to 2002 these crashes were counted in the Non-injury or Injury category.

††Beginning with 2003 crashes, only those resulting in injury or death or damage to property to the apparent extent of $1,000 are tabulated.

*Source: Texas Department of Transportation (TxDOT) since 2001. Earlier statistics are from the Texas Department of Public Safety (DPS).*

# Foreign Consulates in Texas

In the list below, these abbreviations appear after the name of the city: (CG) Consulate General; (C) Consulate; (VC) Vice Consulate. The letter "H" before the designation indicates honorary status. Compiled from "Foreign Consular Offices in the United States," U.S. Dept. of State, April 2012, and recent Internet sources.

**Albania**: Houston (HC); 10 Waterway Ct., Ste. 401, The Woodlands, 77380. (281) 548-4740.
**Angola**: Houston (CG); 3040 Post Oak Blvd., Ste. 780, 77056. (713) 212-3840.
**Argentina**: Houston (CG); 2200 S. West Loop, Ste. 1025, 77027. (713) 871-1034.
**Australia**: Houston (HC); 4623 Feagan St., 77007. (713) 782-6009.
**Austria**: Houston (HCG); 800 Wilcrest, Ste 340, 77042. (713) 723-9979.
**Barbados**: Houston (HC); 3027 Sleepy Hollow Dr., Sugar Land 77479. (832) 725-5566.
**Belgium**: Houston (HC); 2009 Lubbock St., 77007. (713) 426-3933.
Fort Worth (HC); 6201 South Fwy., 76134. (817) 551-8389.
San Antonio (HC); 106 S. St. Mary's, Ste. 200, 78205. (210) 271-8820.
**Belize**: Houston (HCG); 7101 Breen, 77086. (713) 999-4484.
Dallas (HCA); 8035 East R.L. Thorton Fwy, Ste. 2221, Dallas, 75228.
**Bolivia**: Houston (HCG); 800 Wilcrest, Ste. 100, 77042 (713) 977-2344.
Dallas (HC); 1881 Sylvan Ave., Ste. 110, 75208. (214) 571-6131.
**Brazil**: Houston (CG); 1233 West Loop South, Ste. 1150, 77027. (281) 384-4966.
**Cameroon**: Houston (HC); 1319 Gamma, Crosby 77532. (713) 499-3502.
**Canada**: Dallas (CG); 500 N. Akard St., Ste. 2900, 75201. (214) 922-9806.
Houston (C); 5847 San Felipe St., Ste. 1700, 77057. (713) 821-1440.
San Antonio (HCG); 106 S. St. Mary's, Ste. 800, 78205. (210) 299-3525.
**Chile**: Houston (CG):1360 Post Oak Blvd., Ste. 1130, 77056; (713) 963-9066.
Dallas (HC); 3500 Oak Lawn, Ste. 570, 75248.
**China**: Houston (CG); 3417 Montrose, Ste. 700, 77006. (713) 524-0780.
**Colombia**: Houston (CG); 5851 San Felipe, Ste. 300, 77057; (713) 527-8919.
**Costa Rica**: Houston (CG); 3000 Wilcrest, Ste. 112, 77042. (713) 266-0484.
Austin (C); 1730 E. Oltorf, 78741. (512) 445-0023.
Dallas (HC); 7777 Forest Lane, Ste. B-445, 75230. (972) 566-7020.
**Cyprus**: Houston (HC); 4307 Mildred St., Bellaire, 77401.
**Czech Republic**: Houston (HC); 11748 Heritage Pkwy., West, 76691. (713) 629-6963.
**Denmark**: Dallas (HC); 2100 McKinney Ave., Ste. 700, 75201. (214) 661-8399.
Houston (HC); 4545 Post Oak Place, Ste. 345, 77027. (713) 622-9018.
**Ecuador**: Houston (CG); 4200 Westheimer, Ste. 218, 77027. (713) 622-1787.
Dallas (HCG); 7510 Acorn Lane, Frisco, 75034. (972) 712-9106.
**Egypt**: Houston (CG); 5718 Westheimer, Ste. 1350, 77057. (713) 961-4915.
**El Salvador**: Dallas (CG); 1555 W. Mockingbird Lane, Ste. 216, 75235. (214) 637-1018.
Houston (CG); 10301 Harwin St. Ste. B. 77036. (713) 270-6239.
**Equatorial Guinea**: Houston (CG); 6401 Southwest Fwy.,

77074.
**Estonia**: Houston (HC); 1912 Buschong Rd., 77039.
**Ethiopia**: Houston (HC); 9301 Southwest Freeway, Ste. 250, 77074. (713) 271-7567.
**Fiji**: Dallas (HC); 3400 Carlisle, Ste. 310, 75204. (214) 954-9993.
**Finland**: Dallas (HC); 1601 Elm, Ste. 3000, 75201. (214) 999-4472.
Houston (HC); 14 Greenway Plaza, Ste. 22R, 77046. (713) 552-1722.
**France**: Houston (CG); 777 Post Oak Blvd. Ste. 600, 77056. (713) 572-2799.
Austin (HC); 515 Congress Ave, 78701. (512) 480-5605.
Dallas (HC); 12720 Hillcrest, Ste. 730, 75230. (972) 789-9305.
San Antonio (HC); 215 W. Travis, 78205. (210) 225-6742.
**Georgia**: Houston (HC); 3040 Post Oak Blvd., Ste. 700, 77056. (281) 633-3500.
**Germany**: Houston (CG); 1330 Post Oak Blvd., Ste. 1850, 77056. (713) 627-7770.
Dallas (HC); 325 N. St. Paul, Ste. 2300, 75201. (214) 748-8500.
San Antonio (HC); 310 S. St. Mary's, 78205. (210) 226-1788.
**Ghana**: Houston (HC); 3434 Locke Lane, 77027. (713) 960-8806.
**Greece**: Houston (CG); 520 Post Oak Blvd., Ste. 450, 77027. (713) 840-7522.
**Guatemala**: Houston (CG); 3013 Fountain View, Ste 210, 77057. (713) 953-9531.
McAllen (CG); 709 S. Broadway St., 78501.
San Antonio (HVC); 4840 Whirlwind, 78217.
**Guyana**: Houston (HC); 11110 Bellaire Blvd., 77072. (832) 448-0113.
**Haiti**: Houston (HC); 3535 Sage Rd., 77027.
**Honduras**: Houston (CG); 7400 Harwin Dr., Floor 2nd, 77036. (713) 667-4693.
**Hungary**: Houston (HCG); 11850 Hempstead, Ste. 230, 77092. (713) 977-8604.
**Iceland**: Dallas (HC); 15305 Dallas Pkwy., Ste. 1000, Addison, 75001.
Houston (HC); 2028 Buffalo Terrace, 77019.
**India**: Houston (CG); 4300 Scotland St., 77007, (713) 626-2148.
**Indonesia**: Houston (CG); 10900 Richmond Ave., 77042.
**Ireland**: Houston (HC); 2630 Sutton Ct., 77027. (713) 961-5363.
**Israel**: Houston (CG); 24 Greenway Plz., Ste. 1500, 77046. (713) 627-3780.
**Italy**: Houston (CG); 1300 Post Oak Blvd., Ste. 775, 77056. (713) 850-7520.
**Ivory Coast**: Houston (HCG); 412 Hawthorne, 77006. (713) 529-4928.
**Jamaica**: Houston (HC); 6001 Savoy Dr., Suite 509, 77036. (713) 541-3333.
Dallas (HC); 3068 Forest Lane, 75234. (972) 396-7969.
**Japan**: Houston (CG); 909 Fannin, Ste. 3000, 77010. (713) 652-2977.
Dallas (HCG); 5819 Edinburgh St., 75252. (972) 713-8683.
**Kazakhstan**: Houston (HC); 27211 Skiers Crossing Dr., Katy, 77493. (281) 574-8489.

**Korea**: Houston (CG); 1990 Post Oak Blvd., Ste. 1250, 77056. (713) 961-0186.
Dallas (HC); 13111 N. Central Expy., 75243. (214) 454-1112.

**Kyrgyzstan**: Houston (HCG); 15600 Barkers Landing Rd., Apt. 1, 77079. (281) 920-1841.

**Latvia**: Houston (HC); 5847 San Felipe, Ste. 3400, 77057. (713) 785-0807.

**Lebanon**: Houston (HC); 2400 Augusta Dr., Ste. 308, 77057. (713) 268-1640.

**Lithuania**: Houston (HC); 4030 Case, 77005 (713) 665-4218.

**Luxembourg**: Fort Worth (HC); 48 Valley Ridge Rd., 76107. (817) 738-8600.

**Malta**: Houston (HCG); 2602 Commonwealth, 77006. (713) 654-7900.
Dallas (HC); PO Box 830688, SM-24, Richardson, 75083. (972) 883-4785.

**Mexico**: Austin (CG); 410 Baylor St., 78703. (512) 478,2803.
Brownsville (C); 301 Mexico Blvd., Ste. F2, 78520. (956) 542-4431.
Dallas (CG); 8855 N. Stemmons Fwy, 75247. (214) 522-9740.
Del Rio (C); 2398 Spur 239, 78840. (830) 774-5031.
Eagle Pass (C); 2252 E. Garrison, 78852. (830) 773-9255.
El Paso (CG); 910 E. San Antonio Ave., 79901. (915) 533-3644.
Houston (CG); 4507 San Jacinto St., 77004. (713) 271-6800.
Laredo (CG); 1612 Farragut St., 78040. (956) 723-6369.
McAllen (C); 600 S. Broadway, 78501. (956) 686-0243.
Midland (C); 511 W. Ohio St., Ste. 121, 79701.
Presidio (C); 319 W. De Marzo St., 79845. (915) 229-2788.
San Antonio (CG); 127 Navarro St., 78205. (210) 227-9145.
San Antonio (Office of Mexican Attorney General); 613 NW Loop 410 Ste. 610, 78216. (210) 344-1131.

**Moldova**: Austin (HC); 100 Commons Rd. Ste. 7-343, 78701. (512) 308-6190.

**Monaco**: Dallas (HC); 8350 N. Central Expressway, Ste. 1900, 75206. (214) 234-4124.

**Mongolia**: Houston (HCG); 1221 Lamar, Ste. 1201, 77010. (713) 759-1922.

**Netherlands**: Houston (HC); 5177 Richmond Ave., Ste. 725, 77056. (713) 622-8000.

**New Zealand**: Houston (HC); 246 Warrenton Dr., 77024. (713) 973-8680.

**Nicaragua**: Houston (CG); 8989 Westheimer, Ste. 103, 77063. (713) 789-2762.

**Norway**: Houston (CG); 3410 W. Dallas St., Ste. 100, 77019. (713) 620-4200.
Dallas (HC); 2000 McKinney Ave., Apt. 700, 75201. (214) 932-6830.

**Pakistan**: Houston (C); 11850 Jones Rd. 77070. (281) 890-8525.

**Panama**: Houston (CG); 24 Greenway Plaza, Ste. 1307, 77046. (713) 622-4451.

**Papua New Guinea**: Houston (HCG); 4900 Woodway Dr. Ste. 1200, 77056. (713) 966-2500.

**Paraguay**: Houston (HC); 4707 Welford Dr., Bellaire, 77401. (713) 444-9887.

**Peru**: Houston (CG); 5177 Richmond Ave., Ste. 695, 77056. (713) 355-9438.
Dallas (CG); 13601 Preston Rd. Ste. E650, 75240.

**Poland**: Houston (HC); 35 Harbor View, Sugar Land, 77479. (281) 565-1507.

**Portugal**: Houston (HC); 4544 Post Oak Place, Ste. 350, 77027. (713) 759-1188.

**Qatar**: Houston (CG); 1990 Post Oak Blvd, Ste. 810, 77056. (713) 355-8221.

**Romania**: Dallas (HC); 112 Main St., Ste. 1800, 75202. (214) 740-8608.
Houston (HCG); 4265 San Felipe, Ste. 220, 77027. (713) 629-1551.

**Russia**: Houston (CG); 1333 West Loop South, Ste. 1300, 77027. (713) 337-3300.

**Rwanda**: Houston (HCG); 70 Terra Bella Dr., Manvel, 77578.

**Saint Kitts/Nevis**: Dallas (HC); 6336 Greenville Ave., 75206.

**Saudi Arabia**: Houston (CG); 5718 Westheimer, Ste. 1500, 77057. (713) 785-5577.

**Senegal**: Houston (CG); 9701 Richmond, Ste. 212, 77042.

**Sierra Leone**: Houston (HCG); 1330 Post Oak Blvd., Ste. 2200, 77056. (713) 965-5100.

**Slovak Republic**: Dallas (HC); 10830 N. Central Expwy., Ste. 400, 75231.

**Slovenia**: Houston (HC); 2925 Briar Park, Floor 7, 77042. (713) 430-7350.

**South Africa**: Dallas (HC); 400 S. Zang, Ste. 806, 75208.

**Spain**: Houston (CG); 1800 Bering Dr., Ste. 660, 77057. (713) 783-6200.
Corpus Christi (HC); 7517 Yorkshire Blvd., 78413 (361) 994-7517.
Dallas (HC); 5499 Glen Lakes Dr., Ste. 209, 75231. (214) 373-1200.
El Paso (HC); 867 Braodmoor Dr., 79912.

**Sri Lanka**: Houston (HCG); 9001 Airport Blvd., Ste. 503, 77061.

**Sweden**: Houston (HCG); 2909 Hillcroft, Ste. 515, 77057. (713) 953-1417.
Dallas: (HC); 6600 LBJ Fwy, Ste. 183, 75240. (972) 991-8013.

**Switzerland**: Houston (HC); 11922 Taylorcrest, 77024. (713) 467-9889.
Dallas (HC); 2651 N. Harwood, Ste. 455, 75201. (214) 965-1025.

**Syria**: Houston (HCG); 5433 Westheimer Rd., Ste. 1020, 77056. (713) 622-8860.

**Thailand**: Houston (HCG); 600 Travis St., Ste. 2800, 77002. (713) 229-8733.
Dallas (HCG); 1717 Main St., Ste. 4100, 75201.

**Trinidad/Tobago**: Houston (HC); 2400 Augusta, Ste. 250, 77057. (713) 840-1100.

**Tunisia**: Dallas (HC); 4227 N. Capistrano Dr., 75287. (972) 267-4191.
Houston (HC); 12527 Mossycup, 77024. (713) 935-9427.

**Turkey**: Houston (CG); 1990 Post Oak Blvd., Ste.1300, 77056. (713) 622-5849.

**Uganda**: Dallas (HC); 5720 LBJ Fwy., Ste. 470, 75240. (972) 387-7860.

**Ukraine**: Houston (HC); 5433 Westheimer Rd. Ste. 200, 77056. (281) 242-2842.

**United Kingdom**: Houston (CG); 1000 Louisiana St., Ste. 1900, 77002. (713) 659-6270.
Dallas (HC); 2911 Turtle Creek, Ste. 940, 75219. (214) 637-3600.
San Antonio (HC); 254 Spencer Lane, 78201. (210) 735-9393.

**Uruguay**: Houston (HCG); 1220 S. Ripple Creek Dr., 77057. (713) 974-7855.

**Venezuela** : Houston (CG); 2401 Fountain View Dr., Ste. 220, 77057. (713) 961-5141.

**Vietnam**: Houston (CG); 5251 Westheimer Rd., Ste. 1100, 77056. (713) 871-0312. ☆

# Foreign Trade Zones in Texas

Source: U.S. Department of Commerce.

Foreign-trade-zone status endows a domestic site with certain customs privileges, causing it to be considered outside customs territory and therefore available for activities that might otherwise be carried on overseas.

Operated as public utilities for qualified corporations, the zones are established under grants of authority from the Foreign-Trade Zones board, which is chaired by the U.S. Secretary of Commerce. Zone facilities are available for operations involving storage, repacking, inspection, exhibition, assembly, manufacturing and other processing.

A foreign-trade zone is especially suitable for export processing or manufacturing operations when foreign components or materials with a high U.S. duty are needed to make the end product competitive in markets abroad.

Source: U.S. Department of Commerce

There were 32 Foreign-Trade Zones in Texas as of November 2012.

**Amarillo,** FTZ 252
City of Amarillo
801 S. Fillmore, Ste. 2205, Amarillo 79101

**Athens,** FTZ 269
Athens Economic Development Corp.
100 W. Tyler St., Athens 75751

**Austin,** FTZ 183
FTZ of Central Texas Inc.
535 E. 5th St., Austin 78701

**Beaumont,** FTZ 115
**Port Arthur,** FTZ 116
**Orange,** FTZ 117
FTZ of Southeast Texas Inc.
P.O. Drawer 2297, Beaumont 77704

**Bowie County,** FTZ 258
Red River Redevelopment Authority
107 Chapel Lane, New Boston 75570

**Brownsville,** FTZ 62
Brownsville Navigation District
1000 Foust Road, Brownsville 78521

**Calhoun/Victoria Counties** FTZ 155
Calhoun-Victoria FTZ Inc.
P.O. Drawer 397, Point Comfort 77978

**Conroe,** FTZ 265
City of Conroe
PO Box 3066, Conroe 77305

**Corpus Christi,** FTZ 122
Port of Corpus Christi Authority
1305 N. Shoreline Blvd.
Corpus Christi 78403

**Dallas/Ft.Worth,** FTZ 39
D/FW International Airport Board
Drawer 619428,
D/FW Airport 75261

**Dallas/Fort Worth,** FTZ 168
FTZ Operating Company of Texas
P.O. Box 742916, Dallas 75374

**Eagle Pass,** FTZ 96
Maverick County Development Corp.
P.O. Box 3693, Eagle Pass 78853

**Ellis County,** FTZ 113
Ellis County Trade Zone Corp.
P.O. Box 788
Midlothian 76065

**El Paso,** FTZ 68
City of El Paso
501 George Perry, Ste. I,
El Paso 79906

**El Paso,** FTZ 150
Westport Economic Dev. Corp.
1865 Northwestern Dr.. El Paso 79912

**Fort Worth,** FTZ 196
Alliance Corridor Inc.
13600 Heritage Pkwy., Ste. 200
Fort Worth 76177

**Freeport,** FTZ 149
Port Freeport
200 W. 2nd, Ste. 301,
Freeport 77541

**Galveston,** FTZ 36
Port of Galveston
P.O. Box 328, Galveston 77553

**Gregg County,** FTZ 234
Gregg County
269 Terminal Circle, Longview 75603

**Harris County,** FTZ 84
Port of Houston Authority
111 East Loop North, Houston 77029

**Laredo,** FTZ 94
Laredo International Airport
5210 Bob Bullock Loop, Laredo 78041

**Liberty County,** FTZ 171
Liberty Co. Economic Dev. Corp.
P.O. Box 857, Liberty 77575

**Lubbock,** FTZ 260
City of Lubbock
1500 Broadway, 6th Floor,
Lubbock 79401

**McAllen,** FTZ 12
McAllen Economic Dev. Corp.
6401 South 33rd St., McAllen 78501

**Midland,** FTZ 165
City of Midland
P.O. Box 60305, Midland 79711

**San Antonio,** FTZ 80
City of San Antonio
P.O. Box 839966, San Antonio 78283

**Starr County,** FTZ 95
Starr County Industrial Foundation
P.O. Box 502, Rio Grande City 78582

**Texas City,** FTZ 199
Texas City Harbor FTZ Corp.
P.O. Box 2608, Texas City 77592

**Waco,** FTZ 246
City of Waco
P.O. Box 1220, Waco 76703

**Weslaco,** FTZ 156
City of Weslaco
255 S. Kansas Ave., Weslaco 78596

*A tugboat passes storage tanks on the Houston Ship Channel. Photo by Robert Plocheck.*

# Annual Tonnage Handled by Major/Minor Texas Ports

Table below gives consolidated tonnage (x1,000) handled by Texas ports. All figures are in short tons (2,000 lbs.). Note that " - " indicates no commerce was reported, "0" means tonnage reported was less than 500 tons. *Source: U.S. Corps of Engineers.*

| Port | 2013 | 2010 | 2005 | 2000 | 1995 | 1990 | 1985 |
|------|------|------|------|------|------|------|------|
| Beaumont | 94,404 | 76,959 | 78,887 | 76,894 | 20,937 | 26,729 | 26,842 |
| Brownsville | 5,543 | 4,616 | 5,105 | 3,268 | 2,656 | 1,372 | 1,443 |
| Corpus Christi | 76,157 | 73,663 | 77,637 | 81,164 | 70,218 | 60,165 | 41,057 |
| Freeport | 19,716 | 26,676 | 33,602 | 28,966 | 19,662 | 14,526 | 12,918 |
| Galveston | 11,407 | 13,949 | 8,008 | 10,402 | 10,465 | 9,620 | 7,792 |
| Houston | 229,247 | 227,133 | 211,666 | 186,567 | 135,231 | 126,178 | 90,669 |
| Matagorda Channel (Port Lavaca) | 10,888 | 8,879 | 11,607 | 10,552 | 9,237 | 6,097 | 4,366 |
| Port Arthur | 34,699 | 30,232 | 26,385 | 20,524 | 49,800 | 30,681 | 15,755 |
| Sabine Pass | 500 | 2,494 | 641 | 910 | 231 | 631 | 547 |
| Texas City | 49,674 | 56,591 | 57,839 | 58,109 | 50,403 | 48,052 | 33,441 |
| Victoria Channel | 5,520 | 2,792 | 3,224 | 5,104 | 4,624 | 3,740 | 3,414 |
| Anahuac | - | - | - | - | - | 0 | 53 |
| Aransas Pass | 705 | 173 | 128 | 6 | 181 | 169 | 10 |
| Arroyo Colorado | 538 | 411 | 791 | 837 | 994 | 765 | 692 |
| Port Isabel | - | 0 | - | 5 | 130 | 269 | 280 |
| Cedar Bayou | 1,794 | 931 | 1,172 | 1,002 | 473 | 219 | 219 |
| Chocolate Bayou | 1,288 | 1,005 | 3,537 | 3,488 | 3,480 | 3,463 | 4,077 |
| Clear Creek | - | - | - | - | - | 0 | 0 |
| Colorado River | 1,128 | 671 | 501 | 445 | 576 | 476 | 480 |
| Dickinson | 163 | 93 | 688 | 904 | 657 | 556 | 195 |
| Double Bayou | - | - | 257 | 0 | - | 0 | 21 |
| Greens Bayou | 7,438 | 5,523 | 3,768 | 0 | 0 | 0 | 0 |
| Harbor Island (Port Aransas) | 1 | 1 | 10 | 151 | 209 | na | na |
| Liberty Channel | 12 | 5 | - | - | - | 0 | 0 |
| Orange | 759 | 684 | 627 | 681 | 693 | 710 | 648 |
| Palacios | - | - | - | - | - | 0 | 10 |
| Port Mansfield | 2 | - | - | - | 20 | 102 | 204 |
| Rockport | - | - | - | - | - | 644 | 0 |
| San Bernard River | 367 | 371 | 773 | 633 | 653 | 534 | 519 |
| Other Ports | 0 | 0 | 0 | 0 | 0 | 0 | 307 |
| **TOTAL\*** | **492,659** | **486,658** | **487,100** | **452,991** | **371,021** | **335,312** | **245,959** |

*\*Excludes duplication.*

## Foreign/Domestic Commerce: Breakdown for 2013

Data below represent inbound and outbound tonnage for major ports. Note that "-" means no tonnage was reported. *Does not include Canadian. Source: U.S. Corps of Engineers*
**(All figures in short tons x1000)**

| Port | Foreign* | | Domestic | | | | Local |
|------|------|------|------|------|------|------|------|
| | Imports | Exports | Coastwise Receipts | Coastwise Shipments | Internal Receipts | Internal Shipments | |
| Beaumont | 48,498 | 11,124 | 2,635 | 4,516 | 11,640 | 12,477 | 2,103 |
| Brownsville | 2,064 | 340 | 1,440 | 421 | 596 | 639 | 32 |
| Corpus Christi | 28,435 | 14,942 | 488 | 14,429 | 3,941 | 9,311 | 3,741 |
| Freeport | 61 | - | 1,205 | 441 | 4,115 | 1,466 | 4 |
| Galveston | 1,621 | 2,578 | 66 | 1,505 | 2,637 | 2,865 | 48 |
| Houston | 75,943 | 81,974 | 2,813 | 2,867 | 29,629 | 19,249 | 15,137 |
| Matagorda Chl. (Port Lavaca) | 5,223 | 1,715 | 34 | 534 | 378 | 2,199 | - |
| Port Arthur | 9,498 | 14,938 | 1,111 | 2,477 | 2,575 | 3,229 | 148 |
| Sabine Pass | 131 | - | - | - | 7,638 | 12 | - |
| Texas City | 18,977 | 11,007 | 1,919 | 4,108 | 5,66 | 7,158 | 433 |
| Victoria | - | - | - | - | 1,335 | 4,185 | - |

## Gulf Intracoastal Waterway by Commodity (Texas portion)

**(All figures in short tons x1000)** *Source: U.S. Army Corps of Engineers*

| Commodity | 2013 | 2010 | 2005 | 2000 | 1995 |
|-----------|------|------|------|------|------|
| Coal | 70 | 93 | 335 | 121 | 162 |
| Petroleum products | 54,959 | 49,219 | 39,538 | 34,816 | 40,496 |
| Chemicals | 17,360 | 17,553 | 20,668 | 21,382 | 26,818 |
| Raw materials | 3,400 | 3,123 | 4,898 | 5,822 | 6,544 |
| Manufactured goods | 2,087 | 1,646 | 2,449 | 2,301 | 2,056 |
| Food, farm products | 549 | 574 | 473 | 960 | 1,216 |
| **Total** | **79,174** | **72,917** | **69,549** | **66,440** | **78,386** |

### U.S. ports ranked by tonnage, 2013
(millions)

1. S. Louisiana ............. 238.6
2. **Houston ................. 229.2**
3. New York ................. 123.3
4. **Beaumont ................ 94.4**
5. Long Beach ............... 84.5
6. New Orleans ............. 77.2
7. **Corpus Christi .......... 76.2**
8. Baton Rouge ............. 63.9
9. Los Angeles .............. 57.9
10. Plaquemines LA ....... 56.9

### States ranked by tonnage, 2013
(x1,000)

1. Louisiana ............. 501,077
2. **Texas ................... 492,659**
3. California ............. 226,174
4. New Jersey .......... 145,991
5. Washington ........... 112,212
6. Kentucky .............. 100,323
7. Florida .................. 93,925
8. Ohio ...................... 93,749
9. Illinois .................... 92,015
10. Virginia ................. 83,834

# Aviation: Enplanements Rise at Major Airports

Air transportation is a vital and vigorous part of the Texas economy, and Texans are major users of air transportation. The state's airport system ranks as one of the busiest and largest in the nation.

The state's 49,614 active pilots represent 8.36 percent of the nation's pilots. The number of active general aviation aircraft in the state total 16,811, 8.41 percent of the nation's total. Collectively they flew nearly 2.24 million hours.

In 2013, Texas' commercial service airports with scheduled passenger service enplaned 70,311,549 passengers, a 2.6 percent increase from 2011; scheduled carriers served 27 Texas airports in 25 Texas cities; and more than 90 percent of the state's population lived within 50 miles of an airport with scheduled air passenger service.

Dallas/Fort Worth International, Dallas Love Field, Houston George Bush Intercontinental, and Houston's William P. Hobby together accounted for 81 percent of the passengers, or 56,937,546 enplanements.

Twenty-seven airports continue to provide commercial service to Texas communities including the Texarkana Regional Airport which is physically located in Arkansas. Fourteen airports saw their enplanements increase with 13 airports experiencing a decrease.

Of the seven largest airports in the state, all but El Paso International experienced increases in passenger enplanements. Houston Hobby and Austin-Bergstrom International lead with increases of 12.20 percent and 9.08 percent respectively. Among the smaller airports, double-digit increases were seen at Beaumont, College Station, Tyler and Wichita Falls.

Of the 13 airports losing enplanements, three airports experienced double-digit loses including Del Rio, Victoria, and Lubbock with declines of 26.63 percent, 17.81 percent, and 10.04 percent, respectively.

Air service continues to be an area of concern for some communities as the airlines have worked to remove excess capacity from the system in an effort to return to profitability. This has been exacerbated by the global economic recession that officially began in late 2007.

While the economy has continued to improve slowly, some small communities remain vulnerable to decreases in air service. In 2012, Southeast Regional Airport in Beaumont saw its air service eliminated and

## Public Administration

*Source: Texas Transportation Institute*

In 1945, the Texas Aeronautics Commission (TAC) was created and directed by the legislature to encourage, foster, and assist in the development of aeronautics within the state, and to encourage the establishment of airports and air navigational facilities.

The Commission's first annual report of Dec. 31, 1946, stated that Texas had 592 designated airports and 7,756 civilian aircraft.

The commitment to providing air transportation was strengthened in 1989 when the TAC became the Texas Department of Aviation (TDA). And on Sept. 1, 1991, when the Texas Department of Transportation (TxDOT) was created, the TDA became the Aviation Division within the department.

The primary responsibilities of the Aviation Division include providing engineering and technical services for planning, constructing, and maintaining aeronautical facilities in the state. It is also responsible for long-range aviation facility development planning (statewide system of airports), and applying for, receiving, and disbursing federal funds.

One of TxDOT's goals is to develop a statewide system of airports that will provide adequate air access to the population and economic centers of the state.

In the Texas Airport System Plan, TxDOT has identified 294 airports and three heliports that are needed to meet the forecast aviation demand and to maximize access by aircraft to the state's population, business, and agricultural and mineral resource centers.

Of these 294 airports, 27 are commercial service airports, 24 are reliever airports, and 243 are general aviation airports.

Additionally, TxDOT's-Aviation Division has requested Federal Aviation Administration Reliever status for five airports. These include the privately owned Austin Executive and Houston Executive airports, as well as the publicly owned New Braunfels Municipal, Mid-Way Regional, and Cleburne Municipal airports.

Commercial service airports provide scheduled passenger service. Reliever airports are a special class of general aviation airports designated by the Federal Aviation Administration (FAA). They provide alternative landing facilities in the metropolitan areas separate from the commercial service airports, and, together with the business/corporate airports, provide access for business and executive turbine-powered aircraft.

The community service and basic service airports provide access for single- and multi-engine, piston-powered aircraft to smaller communities throughout the state. Some community service airports are also capable of accommodating light jets.

TxDOT is charged by the legislature with planning, programming, and implementing improvement projects at the general aviation airports. In carrying out these responsibilities, TxDOT channels the Airport Improvement Program (AIP) funds provided by the FAA for all general aviation airports in Texas.

Since 1993, TxDOT has participated in the FAA's state block grant demonstration program. Under this program, TxDOT assumes most of the FAA's responsibility for the administration of the AIP funds for general aviation airports.

The Aviation Facilities Development Program (AFDP) oversees planning and research, assists with engineering and technical services, and provides financial assistance through state grants to public bodies operating airports for the purpose of establishing, constructing, reconstructing, enlarging, or repairing airports, airstrips, or navigational facilities.

The 83rd Legislature appropriated funds to TxDOT who subsequently allocated a portion of those funds to the Aviation Division. TxDOT allocated approximately $16.5 million annually for the 2014-2015 biennium to the Aviation Division to help implement and administer the AFDP. These funds are in addition to the block grant funds received through the FAA's AIP.

*American Airlines planes at DFW International Airport. Photo by Grant Wickes (CC).*

replaced with bus service to George Bush Intercontinental Airport.

The air service, previously to Houston, was restored in early February 2013 with service provided to Dallas/Fort Worth International Airport by American Airlines. Enplanements increased markedly and have exceeded 2009 levels.

Consolidation and restructuring in the airline industry continued in 2014 with both capacity and demand growing but still below 2007 levels. Nationwide, enplanements increased 2.1 percent in from 2013 to 2014 and load factors increased to 83.4 percent.

Airlines continued their efforts to generate additional revenue through fees that typically have been included in the airfare, such as meals and baggage, as well as those services that have not typically been provided such as premium boarding. Despite economic uncertainty in the Europe and Japan and slow recovery from economic recession in the United States since 2008, thee airlines posted their fifth straight year of profits.

The U.S. airline industry has become adept at adjusting capacity up or down to minimize losses or take advantage of opportunities. Recent drops in fuel prices are expected to further bolster the economic position of the airlines.

The current industry data reflect the recovery from the challenges it faced as a result of the global economic recession. Worldwide aircraft shipments increased in 2014 with total piston deliveries up to 1,129 from 1,030 in 2013, 908 in 2012, and 898 in 2011.

Total turbine shipments increased in 2014 to 1,325 from 1,323 in 2013, 1,256 in 2012, and 1,222 in 2011. Overall, total shipments were up to 2,454 from 2,353 in 2013, 2,164 in 2012 and 2,120 in 2011. This is up markedly from the low in 2010 but still down significantly from the all-time high set in 2007. The industry has experienced very difficult times in the past several years but has shown signs of stabilizing and even improving. Corporate profits are improving and the economy is recovering, which are both positive indicators for general aviation.

Billings for general aviation aircraft worldwide also increased in 2014 but at a greater pace than ship-

ments. Total billings increased from $23.450 billion in 2013 to $24.499 billion in 2014 after dropping from an all-time high of $24.845 billion in 2008. This slight year-over-year increase is due to an increase in turbine aircraft billings, which make up the vast majority of total billings.

Total airplane shipments for those manufactured in the U.S. showed a slight increase in 2014 to 1,631 from 1,615 in 2013 and 1,518 in 2012. Billings increased as well but at a higher rate to $11.688 billion from $11.069 billion in 2013 and $8.017 billion in 2012.

As with their global counterparts, the market for general aviation aircraft has been a challenging one reflected in shipments and billings that are only recently beginning to recover from the declines that began in 2008 and 2009 respectively, and were further compounded by a global economic downturn and a slow recovery.

In both worldwide and U.S. manufacturing, piston aircraft showed an increase in shipments in 2014 from 2013, while turbine shipments increased slightly for worldwide manufactured aircraft and decreased for U.S. manufactured aircraft over the same period. Overall, shipments increased 4.29 percent and .99 percent for aircraft manufactured worldwide and in the U.S., respectively.

Billings also increased 4.47 percent for aircraft manufactured worldwide and 5.59 percent for U.S. manufactured aircraft. Billings of U.S manufactured aircraft exported out of the country decreased 3.52 percent from 2013 to 2014 to $5.419 billion.

Shipments increased 0.72 percent to 696 units. U.S. exports accounted for 42.7 percent of the total U.S. manufactured shipments and 46.4 percent of the billings. It is clear the global marketplace remains significant to U.S. aircraft manufacturers.

*Sources: Federal Aviation Administration, General Aviation and Part 135 Activity Survey - CY2013; U.S. Civil Airmen Statistics 2014; General Aviation Manufacturer's Association 2014 General Aviation Statistical Databook and 2015 Industry Outlook; FAA Terminal Area Forecasts 2014; Texas Department of Transportation, Aviation Division; FAA Aerospace Forecasts 2015-2035; The Economic Impact of Civil Aviation on the U.S. Economy, Federal Aviation Administration, January 2015.*

# Passenger Enplanement by Airport

| Airport | 2003 | 2005 | 2007 | 2009 | 2011 | Percent change* | 2011 |
|---|---|---|---|---|---|---|---|
| Abilene | 46,166 | 75,414 | 90,507 | 81,451 | 80,030 | −1.48% | 78,847 |
| Amarillo | 384,829 | 442,327 | 455,539 | 404,903 | 399,997 | −6.51% | 373,946 |
| Austin | 3,157,961 | 3,600,331 | 4,112,023 | 4,019,088 | 4,409,094 | 9.08% | 4,809,436 |
| Beaumont | 43,931 | 55,484 | 35,352 | 22,310 | 14,323 | 82.01% | 26,070 |
| Brownsville | 60,087 | 73,361 | 91,262 | 77,438 | 84,465 | 4.53% | 88,292 |
| Brownwood** | 2,008 | 603 | - | - | - | - | - |
| College Station | 67,459 | 84,039 | 89,830 | 73,462 | 70,869 | 19.06% | 84,379 |
| Corpus Christi | 358,843 | 413,363 | 418,674 | 353,868 | 327,534 | −5.53% | 309,409 |
| D/FW | 24,601,481 | 27,960,344 | 28,395,711 | 26,548,401 | 27,464,158 | 5.34% | 28,931,046 |
| Dallas/Love | 2,783,787 | 2,977,048 | 3,912,856 | 3,704,594 | 3,841,785 | 3.37% | 3,971,064 |
| Del Rio | 0 | 7,638 | 17,386 | 13,851 | 9,331 | −26.63% | 6,846 |
| El Paso | 1,418,974 | 1,614,404 | 1,676,738 | 1,489,619 | 1,469,168 | −6.22% | 1,377,812 |
| Harlingen | 392,733 | 429,541 | 442,117 | 374,232 | 361,494 | −3.07% | 350,399 |
| Houston/Bush | 15,934,088 | 18,638,471 | 20,717,170 | 19,168,962 | 19,491,854 | −3.44% | 18,821,924 |
| Houston/Hobby | 3,691,967 | 3,947,543 | 4,219,867 | 4,032,037 | 4,646,710 | 12.20% | 5,213,512 |
| Houston/Ellington | 45,748 | 3,021 | - | - | - | - | - |
| Killeen† | 92,106 | - | - | - | - | - | - |
| Fort Hood/Gray† | 3,159 | 153,930 | 193,722 | 202,226 | 189,330 | −7.04% | 175,992 |
| Laredo | 73,210 | 93,541 | 110,971 | 100,308 | 105,631 | 0.57% | 106,236 |
| Longview | 29,022 | 23,250 | 26,076 | 24,201 | 21,360 | −5.40% | 20,207 |
| Lubbock | 504,916 | 545,377 | 575,774 | 533,635 | 505,381 | −10.04% | 454,661 |
| McAllen | 263,431 | 341,910 | 411,431 | 360,608 | 335,008 | −0.67% | 332,769 |
| Midland | 399,334 | 439,507 | 489,845 | 435,979 | 472,177 | 6.38% | 502,303 |
| San Angelo | 42,688 | 63,785 | 69,738 | 60,315 | 55,304 | 8.72% | 60,127 |
| San Antonio | 3,121,545 | 3,521,538 | 3,907,118 | 3,809,114 | 3,967,764 | 0.71% | 3,995,774 |
| Texarkana | 25,634 | 33,573 | 35,280 | 27,530 | 28,626 | 9.04% | 31,214 |
| Tyler | 53,854 | 81,723 | 77,117 | 73,177 | 73,334 | 10.83% | 81,277 |
| Victoria | 10,775 | 11,115 | 8,829 | 6,113 | 5,115 | −17.81% | 4,204 |
| Waco | 49,915 | 70,942 | 75,496 | 66,116 | 60,479 | −1.11% | 59,809 |
| Wichita Falls | 39,608 | 47,126 | 46,297 | 43,376 | 38,941 | 12.98% | 43,994 |
| **Total** | **57,699,259** | **65,750,249** | **70,702,726** | **66,106,914** | **68,529,262** | **2.60%** | **70,311,549** |

*Percent change 2011 to 2013. **Not a commercial airport. †Killeen-Fort Hood Regional/Robert Gray AAF replaced Killeen Municipal as the commercial service airport in the area. Calendar year data. Source: FAA Terminal Area Forecast 2014.

## Texas Air History

Passengers enplaned in Texas by scheduled carriers. (Texarkana not included.) Fiscal year data. *Source: Federal Aviation Administration.*

| | |
|---|---|
| 1950 | 1,169,051 |
| 1960 | 3,113,582 |
| 1965 | 5,757,689 |
| 1970 | 10,256,691 |
| 1975 | 13,182,957 |
| 1980 | 26,216,873 |
| 1985 | 40,659,223 |
| 1990 | 49,245,445 |
| 1995 | 57,036,900 |
| 2000 | 64,965,396 |
| 2001 | 63,397,450 |
| 2004 | 62,701,663 |
| 2005 | 65,713,052 |
| 2006 | 69,251,113 |
| 2007 | 70,667,446 |
| 2008 | 69,894,717 |
| 2009 | 66,146,132 |
| 2010 | 66,843,803 |
| 2011 | 68,473,435 |
| 2012 | 69,057,281 |
| 2013 | 70,280,335 |

### Leading U.S. Routes, 2014

| Rank | Route | Daily Passengers* |
|---|---|---|
| 1. | New York to-from Los Angeles | 3,531 |
| 2. | Los Angeles to-from San Francisco | 2,757 |
| 3. | New York to-from Chicago | 2,654 |
| 4. | New York to-from San Francisco | 2,569 |
| 5. | Atlanta to-from New York | 2,072 |
| 6. | Honolulu to-from Kahului | 1,913 |
| 24. | **Dallas/Fort Worth** to-from Chicago | 1,398 |

*Average/Each Way. Includes all commercial airports in a metro area.
Source: Airlines for America.

### Leading U.S. Airlines, 2014

| Rank | Airline | Passengers | Planes |
|---|---|---|---|
| 1. | American/US Airways | 146,700,000 | 983 |
| 2. | **Southwest** | 142,600,000 | 665 |
| 3. | Delta | 128,700,000 | 786 |
| 4. | United | 90,500,000 | 691 |
| 5. | JetBlue | 32,200,000 | 203 |
| 6 | ExpressJet | 31,000,000 | 388 |
| 7. | SkyWest | 27,900,000 | 341 |
| 8. | Alaska | 21,600,000 | 137 |
| 9. | **Envoy** | 16,200,000 | 223 |
| 10. | Spirit | 14,300,000 | 65 |

Source: Airlines for America. Note: Texas-based airlines in bold type.
Passengers are cheduled service only. Departures include all services.

# U.S. Freight Gateways, 2013

[**In billions of dollars** ($212.9 represents $212,900,000,000)]. Top gateways ranked by value of shipments, with Texas gateways highlighted. *Source: U.S. Bureau of Transportation Statistics, National Transportation Statistics, annual.*

| Rank | Port | Mode | Exports | Imports | Total trade | Exports as a percent of total |
|------|------|------|---------|---------|-------------|-------------------------------|
| 1 | Los Angeles, CA | Water | $ 42.6 | $ 170.2 | $ 212.9 | 20.03% |
| 2 | Port of New York/New Jersey, NY/NJ | Water | 52.4 | 149.5 | 201.9 | 25.96% |
| 3 | John F. Kennedy, NY | Air | 96.4 | 93.4 | 189.7 | 50.79% |
| 4 | Long Beach, CA | Water | 37.3 | 143.6 | 180.9 | 20.63% |
| 5 | Laredo, TX | Land | 82.4 | 91.6 | 174.0 | 47.35% |
| 6 | Houston, TX | Water | 93.1 | 74.4 | 167.5 | 55.59% |
| 7 | Detroit, MI | Land | 64.0 | 58.9 | 122.9 | 52.07% |
| 8 | Chicago, IL | Air | 38.9 | 83.3 | 122.2 | 31.81% |
| 9 | Los Angeles International Airport, CA | Air | 41.8 | 45.8 | 87.6 | 47.72% |
| 10 | Port Huron, MI | Land | 40.2 | 41.6 | 81.8 | 49.18% |
| 11 | Buffalo-Niagara Falls, NY | Land | 43.4 | 37.5 | 80.9 | 53.59% |
| 12 | Norfolk, VA | Water | 33.8 | 37.5 | 71.3 | 47.40% |
| 13 | Savannah, GA | Water | 27.8 | 43.3 | 71.1 | 39.07% |
| 14 | New Orleans International Airport, LA | Air | 26.3 | 41.9 | 68.2 | 38.54% |
| 15 | Miami International Airport, FL | Air | 39.6 | 27.8 | 67.4 | 58.77% |
| 16 | Charleston, SC | Water | 24.4 | 40.7 | 65.2 | 37.49% |
| 17 | El Paso, TX | Land | 30.3 | 34.0 | 64.2 | 47.14% |
| 18 | Baltimore, MD | Water | 20.9 | 31.8 | 52.7 | 39.63% |
| 19 | San Francisco International Airport, CA | Air | 28.1 | 23.0 | 51.1 | 54.92% |
| 20 | Tacoma, WA | Water | 11.6 | 39.4 | 51.0 | 22.79% |
| 21 | Dallas-Fort Worth Airport, TX | Air | 17.4 | 32.6 | 50.0 | 34.78% |
| 22 | Oakland, CA | Water | 19.9 | 27.5 | 47.4 | 41.91% |
| 23 | Cleveland, OH | Air | 25.7 | 18.1 | 43.8 | 58.66% |
| | | | | | | |
| 28 | Beaumont, TX | Water | 6.6 | 25.9 | 32.6 | 20.39% |
| 30 | Hidalgo, TX | Land | 10.7 | 16.6 | 27.3 | 39.16% |
| 34 | Corpus Christi, TX | Water | 10.9 | 14.7 | 25.6 | 42.51% |
| 40 | Texas City, TX | Water | 9.6 | 12.0 | 21.7 | 44.48% |
| 41 | Eagle Pass, TX | Land | 7.1 | 14.3 | 21.4 | 33.14% |
| 47 | Port Arthur, TX | Water | 7.9 | 10.7 | 18.6 | 42.53% |
| 50 | Houston International Airport, TX | Air | 9.5 | 7.6 | 17.1 | 55.58% |

# Border Crossings at U.S. Ports of Entry, 2010 and 2014

Below are statistics for selected states as to incoming border traffic at ports of entry into the United States. *Data are from the U.S. Bureau of Transportation Statistics.* (**Total in thousands.** Percent of U.S. total listed with Texas.)

| Entering at border (thousands 000) | U.S. total | Texas | % | California | New York | Arizona | Michigan |
|-----------------------------------|-----------|-------|-----|-----------|----------|---------|----------|
| **2010** | | | | | | | |
| **Vehicle passengers** | 152,519 | 53,356 | 35.0 | 45,611 | 18,189 | 14,726 | 12,251 |
| **Personal vehicles** | 92,920 | 31,349 | 33.7 | 25,260 | 8,573 | 6,651 | 6,566 |
| **Pedestrians** | 40,310 | 17,156 | 42.6 | 14,740 | 262 | 7,648 | 17 |
| **Trucks** | 10,187 | 3,194 | 31.4 | 1,089 | 1,452 | 373 | 2,165 |
| **Containers (truck)** | 7,346 | 2,149 | 29.3 | 678 | 1,145 | 291 | 1,805 |
| **2014** | | | | | | | |
| **Vehicle passengers** | 188,908 | 61,838 | 32.7 | 49,327 | 18,301 | 16,367 | 12,659 |
| **Personal vehicles** | 101,603 | 32,690 | 32.2 | 27,593 | 8,690 | 8,519 | 6,945 |
| **Pedestrians** | 41,647 | 16,707 | 40.1 | 17,763 | 277 | 6,311 | 0 |
| **Trucks** | 11,217 | 3,745 | 33.4 | 1,188 | 1,514 | 381 | 2,371 |
| **Containers (truck)** | 8,007 | 2,602 | 32.5 | 815 | 1,211 | 295 | 1,809 |

# Agriculture

*A vast herd of cattle moves across a section of the 825,000-acre King Ranch in South Texas. Photo courtesy of King Ranch.*

**Principal Crops**

**Vegetable Crops**

**Fruits and Nuts**

**Livestock and Their Products**

*King Ranch Sponsors the Agriculture Section*

# Agriculture in Texas

*Information was provided by Texas A&M AgriLife Extension specialists, Texas Agricultural Statistics Service, U.S. Department of Agriculture, and U.S. Department of Commerce. It was coordinated by Caroline Gleaton, Office Associate; John Robinson, Professor and Extension Specialist–Cotton Marketing; and Mark Welch, Extension Economist–Grain Marketing, Texas A&M AgriLife Extension Service. All references are to Texas unless otherwise specified.*

## Importance of Agriculture to the Texas Economy

Agribusiness, the combined phases of food and fiber production, processing, transporting, and marketing, is a leading Texas industry. Most of this article is devoted to the **phase of production on farms and ranches.**

Agriculture is one of the most important industries in Texas. Many businesses, financial institutions, and individuals are involved in providing supplies, credit, and services to farmers and ranchers, and in processing and marketing agricultural commodities.

Texas agriculture is a strong industry. **Cash receipts** were estimated at **$21.6 billion in 2013** and **$23.7 billion in 2012.**

The potential for further growth is favorable. With the increasing demand for food and fiber throughout the world, and because of the importance of agricultural exports to the United States' trade balance, agriculture in Texas plays a vital role.

Major efforts of research and educational programs by the Texas A&M University System are directed toward developing the state's agricultural industry to its fullest potential. The goal is to capitalize on natural advantages that agriculture has in Texas because of the relatively warm climate, productive soils, and availability of excellent export and transportation facilities.

### Texas Farms

The number and nature of farms have changed over time. The number of farms in Texas has decreased from 420,000 in 1940 to **245,500 in 2012,** with an **average size of 530 acres.** The number of small farms is increasing but many are operated by part-time farmers and ranchers.

Mechanization of farming continues as new and larger machines replace manpower. Although machinery price tags are high relative to times past, machines are technologically advanced and efficient. Tractors, mechanical harvesters, and numerous cropping machines have virtually eliminated menial tasks that for many years were traditional to farming.

Revolutionary agricultural chemicals and generally engineered traits have appeared along with improved plants and animals. Many of the natural hazards of farming and ranching have been reduced by better use of weather information, machinery, and other improvements; but rising costs, labor availability, and high energy costs have added to the concerns of farmers and ranchers.

Changes in Texas agriculture over the last 50 years include:

1. More detailed record keeping that assists in management and marketing decisions;
2. More restrictions on choice or inputs/practices;
3. Precision agriculture takes on new dimensions through the use of satellites, computers, Global Positioning Systems (GPS), and other high-tech tools to help producers manage inputs, such as seed, fertilizers, pesticides, and water.

Farms have become fewer, larger, specialized, and much more expensive to own and operate, but are also far more productive. The number of small farms operated by part-time farmers is increasing. Land ownership is becoming more of a lifestyle used mostly for recreational purposes. The number of off-farm landowners is increasing.

Irrigation has become an important factor in crop production. Crops and livestock have made major changes in production areas, as in the concentration of cotton on the High Plains and increased livestock production in Central and East Texas.

Pest and disease control methods have improved, and herbicides are relied upon for weed control.

Feedlot finishing, commercial broiler production, artificial insemination, improved pastures and brush control, and reduced feed requirements have greatly increased livestock and poultry efficiency. Biotechnology and genetic engineering promise new breakthroughs in reaching even higher levels of productivity. Horticultural plant and nursery businesses have expanded. Improved wildlife management has increased deer, turkey, and other wildlife populations. The use of land for recreation and ecotourism is growing.

Farmers and ranchers are better educated and informed, and more science- and business-oriented. Today, agriculture operates in a global, high-tech, consumer-driven environment.

Cooperation among farmers in marketing, promotion, and other fields has increased.

Agricultural producers also have become increasingly dependent on off-the-farm services to supply production inputs, such as feeds, chemicals, credit, and other essentials.

### Agribusiness

Texas farmers and ranchers have developed considerable dependence on agribusiness. With many producers specializing in the production of certain crops and livestock, they look beyond the farm and ranch for supplies and services. On the input side, they rely on suppliers of production needs and services, and on the output side, they need assemblers, processors, and distributors.

Since 1940, the proportion of Texans whose livelihood is linked to agriculture has changed greatly. In 1940, about 23 percent were producers on farms and ranches, and about 17 percent were suppliers or were engaged in assembly, processing, and distribution of agricultural products. The agribusiness alignment in 2008

*An NRCS employee, left, visits a West Texas producer on his farm to talk about conservation plans. Photo courtesy of USDA/Natural Resources Conservation Service.*

was less than 2 percent on farms and ranches, with about 15 percent of the labor force providing production or marketing supplies and services, and retailing food and fiber products.

## Cash Receipts

Farm and ranch **cash receipts in 2013 totaled $21.57 billion,** with estimates of $1.125 billion for government payments. Realized gross farm income totaled $27.35 billion. With farm production expenses of $23.23 billion, net farm income totaled $4.12 billion. The value of inventory adjustment was $176 million.

## Percent of Income from Products

Livestock and livestock products accounted for 71.3 percent of the $21.57 billion cash receipts from farm marketings in 2013, with the remaining 28.7 percent from crops.

Receipts from livestock have trended up largely because of increased feeding operations and reduced crop acreage associated with farm programs and low prices. However, these relationships change because of variations in commodity prices and volume of marketings.

Cattle, calves, and hogs accounted for 47.8 percent of total cash receipts (excluding government payments) received by Texas farmers and ranchers in 2013. Most of these receipts were from cattle and calf sales. Milk made up 9.1 percent of receipts; poultry and eggs, 12.8 percent; and miscellaneous livestock, 1.6 percent.

Cotton accounted for 7.8 percent of total receipts; feed crops, 9.8 percent; food grains, 3 percent; vegetables and melons, 2.3 percent; oil crops, 1.1 percent; fruits and nuts, 0.68 percent; and other crops, 4.1 percent.

## Texas' Rank Among the States

Measured by cash receipts from crops and livestock, **Texas ranked fourth in 2013,** behind California, first; Iowa, second; and Nebraska, third.

Texas normally leads all other states in numbers of farms and ranches, farm and ranch land, cattle slaughtered, cattle on feed, calf births, sheep and lambs, goats, cash receipts from livestock marketings, cattle and calves, beef cows, wool production, mohair production, and exports of fats, oils, and greases.

The state also usually leads in production of cotton.

## Texas' Agricultural Exports

The value of Texas' share of **agricultural exports in fiscal year 2013 was $5.6 billion. Following are primary products and their share of exports:**

Cotton accounted for $1.403 billion of the exports; corn and processed grain products, $281.9 million; wheat, $329 million; vegetable oils, $10.9 million; rice, $137 million; hides and skins, $350.8 million; beef, veal, and pork, $962.1 million; poultry products, $398.1 million; fresh fruits, $25.5 million; processed fruits and nuts, $60.8 million; soybeans and soybean meal, $19.2 million; fresh and processed vegetables, $154.5 million; dairy products, $326 million; and miscellaneous and other products, $1.15 billion.

In 2012, Texas' exports of $6.504 billion of farm and ranch products compares with $6.648 billion in 2011 and $5.821 billion in 2010.

## Hunting

The management of wildlife as an economic enterprise through leasing for hunting makes a significant contribution to the economy of many Texas counties.

# Cash Receipts by Commodities, 2009–2013

| COMMODITIES | 2009 | 2010 | 2011 | 2012 | 2013 | Percent of 2013 |
|---|---|---|---|---|---|---|
| (All values in thousands of dollars) | | | | | | |
| **All Commodities:** | 16,313,630 | 19,726,172 | 22,299,871 | 23,744,693 | 21,567,307 | 100.00% |
| Livestock & products | 10,590,950 | 11,787,557 | 15,695,777 | 14,513,189 | 15,378,700 | 71.31% |
| Crops, fruits & others | 5,722,680 | 7,938,614 | 6,604,094 | 9,231,504 | 6,188,607 | 28.69% |
| **Livestock & Products** | 10,590,950 | 11,787,557 | 15,695,777 | 14,513,189 | 15,378,700 | 71.31% |
| Meat animals | 7,072,210 | 7,742,111 | 11,200,786 | 10,170,348 | 10,313,488 | 47.82% |
| Cattle & calves | 6,938,721 | 7,647,699 | 11,050,080 | 9,884,326 | 10,104,422 | 46.85% |
| Hogs | 133,489 | 94,412 | 150,706 | 286,022 | 209,067 | 0.97% |
| Dairy products, Milk | 1,172,262 | 1,505,313 | 1,986,816 | 1,789,964 | 1,955,544 | 9.07% |
| Poultry & eggs | 2,023,008 | 2,177,332 | 2,126,824 | 2,212,337 | 2,768,479 | 12.84% |
| Broilers | 1,650,227 | 1,757,083 | 1,678,517 | 1,747,250 | 2,181,358 | 10.11% |
| Misc. livestock † | 323,469 | 362,801 | 381,351 | 340,541 | 341,189 | 1.58% |
| **Crops** | 5,722,680 | 7,938,614 | 6,604,094 | 9,231,504 | 6,188,607 | 28.69% |
| Food grains | 442,639 | 692,368 | 570,265 | 797,919 | 639,298 | 2.96% |
| Rice | 170,293 | 160,269 | 181,244 | 170,498 | 189,465 | 0.88% |
| Wheat | 268,430 | 530,089 | 387,621 | 625,202 | 448,777 | 2.08% |
| Feed crops | 1,840,605 | 2,143,395 | 1,434,694 | 2,491,367 | 2,118,263 | 9.82% |
| Corn | 1,048,278 | 1,275,144 | 816,911 | 1,507,316 | 1,212,388 | 5.62% |
| Cotton | 1,768,561 | 3,211,369 | 2,151,174 | 3,377,079 | 1,690,800 | 7.84% |
| Oil crops | 236,840 | 198,843 | 202,484 | 210,123 | 225,571 | 1.05% |
| Vegetables & melons | 467,245 | 584,827 | 396,973 | 468,682 | 494,576 | 2.29% |
| Fruits & nuts | 161,156 | 276,183 | 174,163 | 180,790 | 145,592 | 0.68% |
| All other crops ‡ | 805,633 | 831,628 | 1,674,340 | 1,705,544 | 874,508 | 4.05% |

† Includes sheep and lambs, wool and mohair, milkfat, turkey eggs, equine, goats, goat milk, catfish, honey, farm chickens and other poultry, and livestock.

‡ Includes miscellaneous vegetables and other field crops.

Values are rounded to the nearest thousand. Sub-categories may not sum to total because not all sub-categories are reported.

**Sources:** Various issues of Texas Ag Statistics, USDA/TASS; USDA/ERS Farm Income and Wealth Statistics.

Leasing the right of ingress on a farm or ranch for the purpose of hunting is the service marketed. After the leasing, the consumer — the hunter — goes onto the land to seek the harvest of the wildlife commodity. **Hunting lease income to farmers and ranchers in 2014 was estimated at $630 million.**

The demand for hunting opportunities is growing, while the land capable of producing huntable wildlife is decreasing. As a result, farmers and ranchers are placing more emphasis on wildlife management practices to help meet requests for hunting leases.

## Irrigation

Agricultural irrigation in Texas peaked in 1974 at 8.6 million acres. Over the next 20 years, irrigation declined due to many factors including poor farm economics, falling water tables in certain regions, energy costs for irrigation pumping, and the movement of much of the vegetable production from South Texas to Mexico.

For the past 15 years, total irrigated area has stabilized, fluctuating from year to year between **6 million and 6.4 million acres.** This puts Texas third in the nation, behind California and Nebraska, in agricultural irrigation.

Although some irrigation is practiced in nearly every county of the state, about 60 percent of the total irrigated acreage is on the High Plains of Texas.

Other concentrated areas of irrigation are the Upper Gulf Coast rice-producing area, the Lower Rio Grande Valley, the Winter Garden area of South Texas, and the Trans-Pecos area of West Texas.

**Sprinkler irrigation** is used on about 70 percent of the total irrigated acreage, with surface irrigation methods, primarily **furrow and surge methods,** being used on the remaining irrigated area.

Texas growers are continuing the switch to center pivot irrigation machines. Texas farmers lead the nation in the adoption of efficient irrigation technologies, particularly **LEPA** (low energy precision application) and **LESA** (low elevation spray application) **center pivot systems,** both of which were developed by Texas A&M AgriLife Research and the Texas A&M AgriLife Extension Service.

The use of **drip irrigation** continues to increase but still accounts for less than 10 percent of the total irrigated acreage. Drip irrigation is routinely used on vegetables and tree crops, such as citrus, pecans, and peaches. Some drip irrigation of cotton, forages, and peanuts is being practiced in West Texas. Farmers continue to experiment with drip irrigation, but the relatively high costs and management requirements are limiting more widespread use.

Agricultural irrigation uses about 60 percent of all fresh water in the state, and landscape irrigation accounts for about 40 percent of the total municipal water use.

Texas is one of only a handful of states that require a state irrigator's license for the design and installation of landscape and residential irrigation systems. Cities of 20,000 persons or larger are required to have irrigation inspectors to ensure that landscape irrigation systems meet state design and installation requirements. However, no license or certification is required for the design or installation of agricultural irrigation systems.

To meet future water demand for our rapidly growing cities and industries, several regions of the state are looking at water transfers from agriculture.

Texas water planning documents estimate that as much as 30 percent of future water demand could be met through agricultural irrigation conservation. However, state funding for such programs continues to decline.

In about 20 percent of the irrigated area, water is delivered to farms by irrigation and other types of water districts, and by river authorities through canals and pipelines. Many of these delivery networks are aging, in poor condition, and have high seepage losses. Estimates are that over 30 percent of all water diverted to irrigation districts is lost in the conveyance systems.

Approximately 80 percent of the state's irrigated acreage is supplied with water pumped from wells. Surface water sources supply the remaining area. The severe drought of recent years has greatly impacted wa-

# Realized Gross Income* and Net Income from Farming 1980–2013

| Year | **Realized Gross Farm Income | Farm Production Expenses | Net Change In Farm Inventories | ***Total Net Farm Income | ***Total Net Income Per Farm |
|------|------|------|------|------|------|
| | — Millions of Dollars — | | | | Dollars |
| 1980 | 9,611.4 | 9,081.1 | −542.5 | 456.9 | 2,331.0 |
| 1981 | 11,545.7 | 9,643.1 | 699.9 | 1,902.6 | 9,756.8 |
| 1982 | 11,404.5 | 10,008.2 | −127.8 | 1,396.3 | 7,197.6 |
| 1983 | 11,318.1 | 9,778.9 | −590.7 | 1,539.2 | 7,933.8 |
| 1984 | 11,692.6 | 10,257.3 | 186.1 | 1,435.3 | 7,398.3 |
| 1985 | 11,375.3 | 9,842.8 | −9.0 | 1,532.5 | 7,981.9 |
| 1986 | 10,450.1 | 9,272.8 | −349.0 | 1,177.3 | 6,196.6 |
| 1987 | 12,296.6 | 10,038.7 | 563.2 | 2,257.9 | 12,010.1 |
| 1988 | 12,842.3 | 10,331.7 | −128.4 | 2,510.6 | 13,076.2 |
| 1989 | 12,843.1 | 10,328.4 | −798.6 | 2,514.7 | 12,962.1 |
| 1990 | 14,421.5 | 11,012.9 | 343.9 | 3,408.6 | 17,391.0 |
| 1991 | 14,376.4 | 11,270.3 | 150.0 | 3,106.1 | 15,767.0 |
| 1992 | 14,482.5 | 10,617.6 | 464.1 | 3,864.9 | 19,519.8 |
| 1993 | 15,817.0 | 11,294.6 | 197.0 | 4,522.5 | 20,745.4 |
| 1994 | 15,394.5 | 11,134.7 | 107.7 | 4,259.9 | 19,363.0 |
| 1995 | 15,678.9 | 12,537.3 | 243.7 | 3,141.6 | 14,151.3 |
| 1996 | 15,025.0 | 12,006.6 | −290.1 | 3,018.4 | 13,475.1 |
| 1997 | 16,430.7 | 12,718.5 | 709.2 | 3,712.3 | 16,498.9 |
| 1998 | 15,506.0 | 12,047.4 | −817.1 | 3,458.6 | 15,269.7 |
| 1999 | 17,469.5 | 12,441.9 | 196.0 | 5,027.6 | 22,099.3 |
| 2000 | 16,810.1 | 12,707.8 | −50.2 | 4,102.3 | 17,968.9 |
| 2001 | 18,089.1 | 13,106.6 | 113.4 | 4,982.5 | 21,795.7 |
| 2002 | 16,567.7 | 11,372.8 | 436.8 | 5,195.1 | 22,686.0 |
| 2003 | 20,105.7 | 13,687.6 | −137.7 | 6,418.1 | 28,026.6 |
| 2004 | 21,826.4 | 14,343.8 | 539.0 | 7,482.5 | 32,674.7 |
| 2005 | 21,928.5 | 15,371.6 | 306.7 | 6,556.8 | 28,507.8 |
| 2006 | 20,329.6 | 16,010.9 | −753.8 | 4,318.7 | 18,777.0 |
| 2007 | 24,738.0 | 19,800.2 | 948.6 | 4,937.7 | 19,950.3 |
| 2008 | 22,503.0 | 20,390.0 | −1,095.7 | 2,113.0 | 14,282.1 |
| 2009 | 21,038.0 | 19,741.5 | −775.6 | 1,296.6 | 9,133.8 |
| 2010 | 24,060.0 | 19,912.5 | −125.8 | 4,147.5 | 22,404.4 |
| 2011 | 28,186.6 | 21,820.9 | −949.4 | 6,365.6 | 21,811.9 |
| 2012 | 26,195.2 | 22,023.4 | −2,423.6 | 4,171.8 | NA |
| 2013 | 27,353.7 | 23,232.4 | 176.0 | 4,121.3 | NA |

*Details for items may not add to totals because of rounding.
**Cash receipts from farm marketings, government payments, value of home consumption, and gross rental value of farm dwellings.
***Farm income of farm operators.
**NOTE:** A positive value of inventory change represents current-year production not sold by Dec. 31. A negative value is an offset to production from prior years included in current-year sales.
**Sources:** "Economic Indicators of the Farm Sector, State Financial Summary, 1985, 1987, 1989, 1993," USDA/ERS; "Farm Business Economics Report," August 1996; "Texas Agricultural Statistics Service, October 2010"; USDA/ERS.
NA= Not available.

ter availability from surface sources, such as rivers and reservoirs. As a result, groundwater wells are increasing rapidly throughout South and West Texas, which could impact future water availability.

Declining groundwater levels in several of the major aquifers is a serious problem, particularly in the Ogallala Aquifer in the Texas High Plains, and the southern portion of the Carizo-Wilcox formation. **See Major Aquifers of Texas, page 92.**

Texas common law grants the landowner with broad rights to exploit the underlying groundwater. Laws and regulations governing groundwater use enacted in Texas over the last 50 years attempt to recognize the landowner's right to beneficially use the water, while giving water districts certain powers to manage and restrict water use. Legal battles are ongoing between these two interests.

An increasing number of groundwater conservation districts, however, are establishing water use limits for agricultural irrigation.

The Edwards Aquifer Authority has a voluntary irrigation "opt-out" program, the first of its kind in Texas, where farmers receive payments in exchanging for not irrigating during drought years.

Irrigation is an important factor in the productivity of Texas agriculture. The value of crop production from irrigated acreage is 50–60 percent of the total value of all crop production, although only about 30 percent of the

# Export Shares of Commodities

| Commodity* | 2010 | 2011 | 2012 | 2013 | 2013 % of U.S. Total |
|------|------|------|------|------|------|
| | Millions of Dollars | | | | |
| Beef and veal | 608.7 | 961.0 | 823.8 | 908.0 | 14.71 |
| Pork | 25.2 | 42.7 | 81.9 | 54.1 | 0.89 |
| Hides and skins | 255.9 | 355.4 | 321.2 | 350.8 | 11.20 |
| Other animal products | 241.4 | 291.8 | 243.0 | 222.3 | 6.18 |
| Dairy products | 177.0 | 240.6 | 247.5 | 326.0 | 4.86 |
| Poultry products | 301.6 | 339.2 | 364.1 | 398.1 | 6.17 |
| Vegetables, fresh | 61.9 | 43.9 | 50.9 | 55.2 | 2.30 |
| Vegetables, processed | 96.4 | 71.3 | 95.5 | 99.3 | 2.30 |
| Fruits, fresh | 49.7 | 31.9 | 31.4 | 25.5 | 0.50 |
| Fruits and nuts, processed | 100.6 | 68.0 | 68.3 | 60.8 | 0.50 |
| Rice | 117.5 | 139.7 | 114.1 | 137.0 | 6.26 |
| Wheat | 321.2 | 309.7 | 305.9 | 329.0 | 3.15 |
| Corn | 248.0 | 167.2 | 186.1 | 125.4 | 1.96 |
| Grain products, processed | 158.1 | 101.2 | 159.9 | 156.5 | 3.06 |
| Feeds and fodder | 243.7 | 142.6 | 228.6 | 269.3 | 2.91 |
| Soybeans | 28.6 | 9.4 | 23.5 | 15.3 | 0.07 |
| Soybean meal | 5.4 | 1.7 | 4.7 | 3.9 | 0.07 |
| Vegetable oils | 16.2 | 16.6 | 13.3 | 10.9 | 0.47 |
| Cotton | 2,312.7 | 2,308.8 | 2,019.9 | 1,402.7 | 24.92 |
| † Other plant products | 451.3 | 1,005.7 | 1,120.3 | 659.2 | 3.49 |
| **Total** animal products | 1,609.8 | 2,230.6 | 2,081.5 | 2,259.2 | 7.03 |
| **Total** plant products | 4,211.2 | 4,417.6 | 4,422.5 | 3,350.0 | 2.98 |
| **GRAND TOTAL** | 5,821.0 | 6,648.2 | 6,504.0 | 5,609.2 | 3.89 |

*Totals may not add due to rounding.
**NOTE:** Commodity coverage in this update of State Export Data differs from earlier versions because of changes in the coverage of the U.S. farm cash receipts data.
† Includes sugar products, planting seeds, other oilseeds and oilseed products, other horticulture products, and other processed foods.
**Source:** USDA/ERS; USDA/FAS (Global Agricultural Trade System).

# Principal Crops

In most recent years, the value of crop production in Texas is less than 40 percent of the total value of the state's agricultural output.

Cash receipts from farm sales of crops are reduced somewhat because some grain and roughage is fed to livestock on farms where it is produced. Drought also has reduced receipts in recent years.

**Receipts from all Texas crops totaled $6.189 billion in 2013;** $9.232 billion in 2012; and $6.604 billion in 2011.

Cotton, corn, grain sorghum, and wheat account for a large part of the total crop receipts. In 2013, cotton contributed about 27.3 percent of the crop total; corn, 19.6 percent; and wheat, 7.3 percent. Hay, cottonseed, vegetables, peanuts, rice, soybeans, and grain sorghum are other important cash crops.

# Value of Cotton & Cottonseed 1900–2014

| Crop Year | Upland Cotton | | Cottonseed | |
|---|---|---|---|---|
| | Production (Bales) | Value | Production (Tons) | Value |
| | (All Figures in Thousands) | | | |
| 1900 | 3,438 | $157,306 | 1,531 | $20,898 |
| 1910 | 3,047 | 210,260 | 1,356 | 31,050 |
| 1920 | 4,345 | 376,080 | 1,934 | 41,350 |
| 1930 | 4,037 | 194,080 | 1,798 | 40,820 |
| 1940 | 3,234 | 162,140 | 1,318 | 31,852 |
| 1950 | 2,946 | 574,689 | 1,232 | 111,989 |
| 1960 | 4,346 | 612,224 | 1,821 | 75,207 |
| 1970 | 3,191 | 314,913 | 1,242 | 68,310 |
| 1980* | 3,320 | 1,091,616 | 1,361 | 161,959 |
| 1981 | 5,645 | 1,259,964 | 2,438 | 207,230 |
| 1982 | 2,700 | 664,848 | 1,122 | 90,882 |
| 1983 | 2,380 | 677,443 | 1,002 | 162,324 |
| 1984 | 3,680 | 927,360 | 1,563 | 157,863 |
| 1985 | 3,910 | 968,429 | 1,635 | 102,156 |
| 1986 | 2,535 | 560,945 | 1,053 | 82,118 |
| 1987 | 4,635 | 1,325,981 | 1,915 | 157,971 |
| 1988 | 5,215 | 1,291,651 | 2,131 | 238,672 |
| 1989 | 2,870 | 812,784 | 1,189 | 141,491 |
| 1990 | 4,965 | 1,506,182 | 1,943 | 225,388 |
| 1991 | 4,710 | 1,211,789 | 1,903 | 134,162 |
| 1992 | 3,265 | 769,495 | 1,346 | 145,368 |
| 1993 | 5,095 | 1,308,396 | 2,147 | 255,493 |
| 1994 | 4,915 | 1,642,003 | 2,111 | 215,322 |
| 1995 | 4,460 | 1,597,037 | 1,828 | 201,080 |
| 1996 | 4,345 | 1,368,154 | 1,784 | 230,136 |
| 1997 | 5,140 | 1,482,787 | 1,983 | 226,062 |
| 1998 | 3,600 | 969,408 | 1,558 | 204,098 |
| 1999 | 5,050 | 993,840 | 1,987 | 160,947 |
| 2000 | 3,940 | 868,061 | 1,589 | 162,078 |
| 2001 | 4,260 | 580,723 | 1,724 | 159,470 |
| 2002 | 5,040 | 967,680 | 1,855 | 191,065 |
| 2003 | 4,330 | 1,199,237 | 1,616 | 202,000 |
| 2004 | 7,740 | 1,493,510 | 2,895 | 301,080 |
| 2005 | 8,440 | 1,879,757 | 2,869 | 289,739 |
| 2006 | 5,800 | 1,288,992 | 2,066 | 243,776 |
| 2007 | 8,250 | 2,391,840 | 2,861 | 443,409 |
| 2008 | 4,450 | 935,568 | 1,547 | 351,192 |
| 2009 | 4,620 | 1,328,342 | 1,634 | 254,904 |
| 2010 | 7,840 | 3,006,797 | 2,685 | 413,490 |
| 2011 | 3,500 | 1,375,920 | 1,228 | 354,892 |
| 2012 | 5,000 | 1,675,200 | 1,669 | 442,285 |
| 2013 | 4,170 | 1,493,194 | 1,368 | 347,472 |
| 2014 | 6,175 | 1,753,814 | 1,959 | 363,629 |

\* Beginning in 1971, the basis for cotton prices was changed from 500 pound gross weight to 480 pound net weight bale; to compute comparable prices for previous years multiply price times 1.04167.

**Sources:** Texas Agricultural Facts@, USDA/NASS Crop Production Annual Summary, January; and Crop Values Annual Summary, February. USDA/NASS Quick Stats data system.

state's total harvested cropland acreage is irrigated.

## Cotton

Cotton has been a major crop in Texas for more than a century. Since 1880, Texas has led all states in cotton production in most years, and today the annual Texas cotton harvest amounts to around 40 percent of total production in the United States. The annual Texas cotton crop has averaged 5.37 million bales since 1996.

Value of upland cotton produced in Texas in 2014 was $1.754 billion. Cottonseed value in 2014 was $363.63 million, making the **value of the Texas crop around $2.117 billion.**

**Upland cotton** was harvested from 4.6 million acres in 2014, and **American-Pima** from 16,000 acres, for a total of 4.616 million acres. Yield for upland cotton in 2014 was 644 pounds per harvested acre, with American-Pima yielding 840 pounds per acre.

In 2013, total cotton acreage was 3.109 million acres. Upland cotton was harvested from 3.1 million acres, with a yield of 646 pounds per acre. American-Pima was harvested from 8,500 acres with a yield of 847 pounds per acre.

**Total cotton production amounted to 6.203 million bales in 2014** and 4.185 million bales in 2013.

Cotton is the raw material for processing operations at gins, oil mills, compresses, and a small number of textile mills in Texas. Cotton in Texas is machine harvested. Field storage of harvested seed cotton is a common practice as gins decline in number.

**Most of the Texas cotton crop is exported.** China, Turkey, Mexico, and various Pacific Rim countries are major buyers. With the continuing development of fiber-spinning technology and the improved quality of Texas cotton, the export demand for Texas cotton has grown.

Spinning techniques can efficiently produce high-quality yarn from relatively strong, short or longer staple upland cotton with fine mature fiber.

## Grain Sorghum

Grain sorghum in 2014 **ranked second nationally in value of production,** with Kansas ranked first. Much of the grain is exported, as well as being used in livestock and poultry feed throughout Texas. Ethanol production is another demand source for Texas sorghum.

Total production of grain sorghum in 2014 was 137.25 million bushels, with 61 bushels per acre yield. With an average price of $7.20 per cwt. **(hundredweight),** the total value reached $553.4 million.

In 2013, 2.3 million acres of grain sorghum were harvested, yielding an average of 56 pounds per acre for a total production of 128.8 million bushels. It was valued at $8.33 per cwt., for a total value of $600.8 million.

In 2012, 1.9 million acres were harvested with an average of 59 bushels per acre, or 112.1 million bushels. The season's average price was $11.20 per cwt. for a total value of $703.1 million.

Lynn County producer Kevin Mitchell stands in his irrigated cotton crop planted in wheat stubble. At right is a close up of the cotton seedlings growing out of the terminated wheat cover. This practice combines the benefits of crop rotation and soil and water conservation. Photos courtesy of USDA/ Natural Resources Conservation Service.

Although grown to some extent in all counties where crops are important, the largest concentrations are in the High Plains, Coastal Bend, and the Lower Rio Grande Valley areas.

Research continues to develop high-yielding hybrids resistant to diseases and insect damage. *A history of grain sorghum appeared in the 1972–1973 edition of the Texas Almanac and can be found at www. TexasAlmanac.com/archive.*

## Rice

Rice, which is grown in about 20 counties on the Coastal Prairie of Texas, ranked third in value among Texas crops for many years. However, in 2014, cotton, corn, hay, grain sorghum, and wheat outranked rice.

Rice farms are highly mechanized, producing rice through irrigation and using airplanes for much of the planting, fertilizing, and application of insecticides and herbicides.

Texas farmers grow **long- and medium-grain rice** only. The Texas rice industry, which has grown from 110 acres in 1850 to a high of 642,000 planted acres in 1954, has been marked by significant yield increases and improved varieties. Record production was in 1981, with 27.24 million cwt. harvested. Highest yield was 8,370 pounds per acre in 2012.

Several different types of rice milling procedures are in use today. The simplest and oldest method produces a product known as regular milled white rice, the most prevalent on the market today.

During this process, rice grains are subjected to additional cleaning to remove chaff, dust, and foreign seed, and then husks are removed from the grains. This results in a product that is the whole unpolished grain of rice with only the outer hull and a small amount of bran removed. This product is called **brown rice** and is sometimes sold without further treatment other than grading. It has a delightful nutlike flavor and a slightly chewy texture.

When additional layers of the bran are removed, the rice becomes white in color and begins to appear as it is normally recognized at retail level. The removal of the bran layer from the grain is performed in a number of steps using two or three types of machines.

After the bran is removed, the product is ready for classification as to size. Rice is more valuable if the grains are not broken. In many cases, additional vitamins are added to the grains to produce what is called "**enriched rice.**"

Another process may be used in rice milling to produce a product called **parboiled rice.** In this process, the rice is subjected to a combination of steam and pressure prior to the time it is milled. This process gelatinizes the starch in the grain, which aids in the retention of much of the natural vitamin and mineral content. After cooking, parboiled rice tends to be fluffy, more separate, and plump.

Still another type of rice is **precooked rice,** which is actually milled rice that, after milling, has been cooked. Then the moisture is removed through a dehydration process. Precooked rice requires a minimum of preparation time since it needs merely to have the moisture restored.

The United States produces only a small part of the world's total rice, but it is **one of the leading exporters.** American rice is popular abroad and is exported to more than 100 foreign countries.

Texas rice production in 2014 totaled 10.791 million cwt. from 147,000 harvested acres, for a yield of 7,340 pounds per acre. Crop value totaled $158.63 million.

In 2013, rice production was 11.145 million cwt. in 2013 on 144,000 harvested acres, yielding 7,740 pounds per acre. Total value in 2013 was $182.78 million. In 2012, rice production was 11.217 million cwt. on 134,000 harvested acres. Production in 2012 was valued at $170.5 million, with a yield of 8,370 pounds per acre.

## Wheat

Wheat for grain is **one of the state's most valuable cash crops.** In 2014, wheat was exceeded in value by cotton, corn, hay, and grain sorghum. Wheat pastures also provide considerable winter forage for cattle that is reflected in the value of livestock produced.

Texas wheat production totaled 67.5 million bushels in 2014 as yield averaged 30 bushels per acre. Planted acreage totaled 6 million acres, and 2.25 million acres were harvested. With an average price of $6.40 per bushel, **the 2014 wheat value totaled $432 million.**

In 2013, Texas wheat growers planted 6.3 million acres and harvested 2.35 million acres. The yield was 29 bushels per acre for 2013, with total production of 68.15 million bushels at $7.11 per bushel, which was valued at $484.6 million.

Texas wheat growers planted 5.6 million acres in 2012 and harvested grain from 2.9 million acres. The yield was 33 bushels per acre for a total production of 95.7 million bushels, valued at $643.1 million or $6.72

### Texas Crop Production, 2014

| Crop | Harvested Acres (000) | Yield Per Acre | Unit | Total Production (000) | Value (000) |
|---|---|---|---|---|---|
| Corn, grain | 1,990 | 148 | bushel | 294,520 | 1,310,614 |
| Corn, silage | 210 | 22 | ton | 4,620 | — |
| Cotton, American-Pima | 16 | 840 | lb. bale | 28 | 25.344 |
| Cotton, Upland | 4,600 | 644 | lb. bale | 6,175 | 1,753,814 |
| Cottonseed | — | — | ton | 1,959 | 363,629 |
| Grapefruit * | 17 | 335 | box | — | 48,040 |
| Hay, Alfalfa | 140 | 4.4 | ton | 616.0 | 149,072 |
| Hay, Other | 5,300 | 2.1 | ton | 11,130 | 829,185 |
| Hay, all | 5,440 | 2.2 | ton | 11,746 | 978,257 |
| Oats | 45 | 38 | bushel | 1,710 | 10,175 |
| Oranges † | 8 | 222 | box | — | 23.815 |
| Peaches | 3.1 | 1.23 | ton | 3.8 | — |
| Peanuts | 127 | 3,850 | lb. | 488,950 | 135,439 |
| Pecans | — | — | lb. | 60,000 | 110,040 |
| Potatoes (all) | 20.6 | 330 | cwt. | 6,798 | 115,556 |
| Rice | 147 | 7,340 | lb:cwt. | 10,791 | 158,628 |
| Sorghum, grain | 2,250 | 61 | lb:cwt. | 137,250 | 553,392 |
| Sorghum, silage | 100 | 14 | ton | 1,400 | — |
| Soybeans | 140 | 38 | bushel | 5,390 | 51,475 |
| Sugar cane | 33.1 | 37.9 | ton | 1,255 | †† |
| Sunflowers | 92 | 1,493 | lb. | 137,400 | 35,440 |
| Sweet potatoes | 0.9 | 155 | cwt. | 140 | 4,144 |
| Vegetables (commercial): | | | | | |
| Fresh market | 52.2 | — | cwt. | 11,337 | 213,212 |
| Processing | 8.5 | — | cwt. | 75,270 | 16,306 |
| Wheat, winter | 2,250 | 30 | bushel | 67,500 | 432,000 |
| **Total of Listed Crops** | **22,990.4** | **—** | **—** | **—** | **7,317,577** |

*Grapefruit, Texas 80-lb./box, reflects 13/14 crop year. †Oranges, Texas 85-lb./box, reflects 13/14 crop year.*
††*Sugarcane value will be published in Agricultural Prices released July 2015.*
**Source:** *USDA/NASS, annual crop production, January, annual crop values, February.*

per bushel.

Wheat was **first grown commercially in Texas near Sherman about 1833.** The acreage expanded greatly in North-Central Texas after 1850 because of rapid settlement of the state and introduction of the well-adapted Mediterranean strain of wheat. A major family flour industry was developed in the Fort Worth–Dallas–Sherman area between 1875 and 1900. Now, around half of the state acreage is planted on the High Plains and about a third of this is irrigated. Most of the Texas wheat acreage is of the **hard red winter class.** Because of the development of varieties with improved disease resistance and the use of wheat for winter pasture, there has been a sizable expansion of acreage in Central and South Texas.

Most all wheat harvested for grain is used in some phase of the milling industry. The better-quality hard red winter wheat is used in the production of **commercial bakery flour.** Lower grades and varieties of **soft red winter wheat** are used in family flours. By-products of milled wheat are used for feed.

## Corn

Interest in corn production throughout the state has increased since the 1970s as yields improved with new varieties. Once the principal grain crop, corn acreage declined as plantings of grain sorghum increased. Only 500,000 acres were harvested annually until the mid-1970s, when development of new hybrids occurred.

Harvested acreage was 1.99 million in 2014; 1.95 million in 2013; and 1.55 million in 2012. Yields were 130 bushels per acre in 2014, 93 bushels per acre in 2013, and 145 bushels per acre in 2012.

Most of the acreage and yield increase has occurred in Central and South Texas. **In 2014, corn ranked second in value among the state's crops.** It was valued at $1.311 billion in 2014; $1.363 billion in 2013; and $1.423 billion in 2012. The grain is largely used for livestock feed, but **other important uses are for ethanol and in food products.**

## Oats

Oats are grown extensively in Texas for winter pasture, hay, silage, and greenchop feeding, and some acreage is harvested for grain.

Of the 450,000 acres planted to oats in 2014, 45,000 acres were harvested. The average yield was 38 bushels per acre. Production totaled 1.71 million bushels with a value of $10.175 million. In 2013, 450,000 acres were planted. From the plantings, 40,000 acres were harvested, with an average yield of 46 bushels per acre for a total production of 1.84 million bushels. Average price per bushel was $3.63, and total production value was $6.679 million.

Texas farmers planted 500,000 acres of oats in 2012. They harvested 65,000 acres that averaged 49 bushels per acre for a total production of 3.185 million bushels at an average price of $5.94 per bushel. The estimated value was $18.92 million. Most of the acreage was used for grazing.

**Almost all oat grain produced in Texas is utilized as feed for livestock** within the state. A small acreage is grown exclusively for planting seed.

## Sugarcane

Sugarcane is grown from seed cane planted in late summer or fall. It is harvested 12 months later and milled to produce **raw sugar and molasses.** Raw sugar requires additional refining before it is in final form and can be offered to consumers.

The **sugarcane grinding mill operated at Santa Rosa in Cameron County** is one of the most modern mills in the United States. Texas sugarcane-producing counties include Cameron, Hidalgo, and Willacy.

At a yield of 37.9 tons per acre, sugarcane production in 2014 totaled 1.194 million tons from 31,500 harvested acres. In 2013, 34,100 acres were harvested for total production of 1.446 million tons valued at $27.185 million. The yield was 42.4 tons per acre.

In 2012, 43,000 acres were harvested, from which 1.544 million tons of sugarcane were milled. The yield averaged 35.9 tons per acre for a total value of $46.166 million.

## Hay, Silage, and Other Forage Crops

A large proportion of Texas' agricultural land is devoted to forage crop production. This acreage produces forage needs and provides essentially the total feed requirements for most of the state's large domestic livestock population as well as game animals.

Approximately 90.3 million acres of pasture and rangeland, which are primarily in the western half of Texas, provide **grazing for beef cattle, sheep, goats, horses, and game animals.** An additional 9.8 million acres are devoted to cropland used only for pasture or grazing. The average annual acreage of forage land used for hay, silage, and other forms of machine-harvested forage is around 5 million acres.

All hay accounts for a large amount of this production with some corn and sorghum silage produced. **The most important hay crops are annual and perennial grasses and alfalfa.** Production in 2014 totaled 11.746 million tons of hay from 5.44 million harvested acres at a yield of 2.16 tons per acre. Value of hay was $978 million, or $107 per ton. In 2013, 8.88 million tons of

*Red grain sorghum stretches to the horizon on Joe Reed's farm near Edmonson in Hale County. Photo courtesy of USDA/Natural Resources Conservation Service.*

*Mature wheat is planted on terrace ridges in a cotton field south of Lubbock. Photo courtesy of USDA/Natural Resources Conservation Service.*

hay was produced from 5.64 million harvested acres at a yield of 1.57 tons per acre. The value in 2013 was $884.8 million or $120 per ton. In 2012, the production of hay was 9.46 million tons from 5.1 million harvested acres with a value of $1 billion, or $121 per ton, at a yield of 1.85 tons per acre.

Alfalfa hay production in 2014 totaled 616,000 tons with 140,000 acres harvested and a yield of 4.4 tons per acre. At a value of $242 per ton, total value was $149 million. In 2013, 630,000 tons of alfalfa hay was harvested from 140,000 acres at a yield of 4.5 tons per acre. Value was $150.6 million, or $239 per ton. Alfalfa hay was harvested from 100,000 acres in 2012, producing an average of 4.6 tons per acre for total production of 460,000 tons valued at $109.48 million or $238 per ton.

An additional sizable acreage of annual forage crops is grazed, as well as much of the small grain acreage. Alfalfa, sweet corn, vetch, arrowleaf clover, grasses, and other forage plants also provide income as seed crops.

## Peanuts

Well over three-fourths of the annual peanut production is from irrigated acreage. **Texas ranked fourth nationally in production of peanuts in 2014.** Among Texas crops, peanuts rank eighth in value.

Until 1973, essentially all of the Texas acreage was planted to the **Spanish type,** which was favored because of earlier maturity and better drought tolerance than other types. The Spanish variety is also preferred for some uses due to its distinctive flavor. The **Florunner variety,** a runner market type, is now planted on a sizable proportion of the acreage where soil moisture is favorable. The variety is later maturing but better yielding than Spanish varieties under good growing conditions. Florunner peanuts have acceptable quality to compete with the Spanish variety in most products.

In 2014, peanut production totaled 488.9 million pounds from 127,000 harvested acres, yielding 3,850 pounds per acre. At 27.7 cents per pound, value of the crop was estimated at $135.4 million.

In 2013, peanut production amounted to 423.5 million pounds from 120,000 acres planted and 117,000 harvested. Average yield of 3,620 pounds per acre and average price of 32.1 cents per pound combined for a 2013 value of $135.95 million.

Production in 2012 amounted to 525.6 million pounds of peanuts from 150,000 acres planted and 146,000 acres harvested. Average yield of 3,600 pounds per harvested acre and a value of 37.5 cents per pound added up to a total value of $197.1 million.

## Soybeans

Production is largely in the Upper Coast, irrigated High Plains, and Red River Valley of Northeast Texas. Soybeans are adapted to the same general soil climate conditions as corn, cotton, or grain sorghum, provided moisture, disease, and insects are not limiting factors.

In low-rainfall areas, yields have been too low or inconsistent for profitable production under dryland conditions. **Soybeans' need for moisture in late summer** minimizes economic crop possibilities in the Blacklands and Rolling Plains.

In the Blacklands, cotton root rot seriously hinders soybean production. Limited moisture at critical growth stages may occasionally prevent economical yields, even in high-rainfall areas of Northeast Texas and the Coastal Prairie.

Because of day length sensitivity, soybeans should be planted in Texas during the long days of May and June to obtain sufficient vegetative growth for optimum yields. Varieties planted during this period usually cease vegetative development and initiate reproductive processes during the hot, usually dry months of July and August.

When moisture is insufficient during the blooming and fruiting period, yields are drastically reduced. In most areas of the state, July and August rainfall is insufficient to permit economical dryland production. The risk of dryland soybean production in the Coastal Prairie and Northeast Texas is considerably less when compared to other dryland areas because moisture is available more often during the critical fruiting period.

The 2014 soybean crop totaled 5.39 million bushels and was valued at $51.48 million, or $9.55 per bushel. Of the 155,000 acres planted, 140,000 were harvested with an average yield of 38.5 bushels per acre. In 2013, the Texas soybean crop averaged 25.5 bushels per acre from 92,000 acres harvested. Total production of 2.35 million bushels was valued at $29.56 million, or $12.60 per bushel. In 2012, the Texas soybean crop averaged 26 bushels per acre from 110,000 acres harvested. Total production of 2.86 million bushels was valued at $40.76 million, or $14.60 per bushel.

## Sunflowers

Sunflowers constitute **one of the most important annual oilseed crops** in the world. The cultivated types, which are thought to be descendants of the common wild sunflower native to Texas, have been successfully grown in several countries including Russia, Argentina, Romania, Bulgaria, Uruguay, Western Canada, and portions of the northern United States. Extensive trial plantings conducted in the Cotton Belt states since 1968 showed sunflowers have considerable potential as an oilseed crop in much of this area, including Texas.

This crop exhibits good cold and drought tolerance, is adapted to a wide range of soil and climate conditions, and tolerates higher levels of hail, wind, and sand abrasion than other crops normally grown in the state.

In 2014, sunflower production totaled 137.4 million pounds and was harvested from 92,000 acres at a yield of 1,493 pounds per acre. With an average price of $25.90 per cwt., the crop was valued at $35.54 million. In 2013, 85,000 of the 114,000 acres planted to sunflowers were harvested with an average yield of 1,344 pounds per acre. Total production of 114.25 million pounds was valued at $26.87 million, or $23.50 per cwt.

In 2012, of 95,000 acres planted to sunflowers, 85,000 acres were harvested, yielding 1,200 pounds per acre for a total yield of 102 million pounds valued at $31.908 million, or $31.50 per cwt.

Reasons for growing sunflowers include the need for an additional cash crop with low water and plant nutrient requirements, the development of sunflower hybrids, and interest by food processors in **Texas sunflower oil,** which has high oleic acid content. Commercial users have found many advantages in this high oleic oil, including excellent cooking stability, particularly for use as a deep-frying medium for potato chips, corn chips, and similar products.

**Sunflower meal** is a high-quality protein source free of nutritional toxins that can be included in rations for swine, poultry, and ruminants (cud-chewing animals). The hulls constitute a source of roughage, which can also be included in livestock rations.

## Nursery Crops

The trend to increase production of nursery crops continues to rise as transportation costs on long-distance hauling increases. This has resulted in a marked increase in the production of container-grown plants within the state. This increase is noted especially in the production of **bedding plants, foliage plants, sod, and the woody landscape plants.**

Plant rental services have become a multi-million dollar business. This service provides the plants and maintains them in office buildings, shopping malls, public buildings, and even in some homes for a fee. The response has been good as evidenced by the growth of companies providing these services.

The interest in plants for interior landscapes is popular among all age groups, as both retail nurseries and florist shops report that people of all ages are buying their plants — from the elderly in retirement homes to high school and college students in dormitory rooms and apartments.

Texas A&M AgriLife Extension specialists estimated cash receipts from nursery crops to be around $1.6 billion in 2014. Texans are creating colorful and green surroundings by improving their landscape plantings.

## Forest Products

For information on Texas forest products, ***see Texas Forest Resources, page 118.***

# Vegetable Crops

Some **market vegetables** are produced in almost all Texas counties. Hidalgo County was the leading Texas county in vegetable acres harvested, followed by Frio and Uvalde counties. Other leading producing counties are: Zavala, Cameron, Yoakum, Terry, Hale, and Medina.

Texas is one of the seven leading states in the production of fresh market vegetables. Nationally in 2014, Texas ranked seventh in production, exceeded by California, Arizona, Florida, Washington, Georgia, and Oregon, and seventh in value of fresh-market vegetables.

In 2014, fresh **market vegetable production of 11.34 million cwt. was valued at $213.21 million** from 52,230 acres harvested. In 2013, Texas growers harvested total fresh market vegetable crops valued at $241 million from 54,085 acres with a production of 13.12 million cwt.

In 2012, Texas growers harvested 12.34 million cwt. of fresh market vegetable crops from 58,520 acres, valued at $228.46 million.

## Onions

Onion production in 2014 totaled 2.34 million cwt. from 9,000 harvested acres and was valued at $56.16 million, at a yield of 260 cwt. per acre.

In 2013, 3.49 million cwt. of onions were harvested from 9,700 acres and valued at $83.1 million, at a yield of 360 cwt. per acre. A total of 3.1 million cwt. of onions were produced from 10,300 harvested acres and valued at $69.5 million in 2012, yielding 300 cwt. per acre.

## Carrots

Carrot production in 2014 totaled 378,000 cwt. from 1,400 harvested acres at a yield of 270 cwt. per acre. Production was valued at $7.56 million. In 2013, carrots were harvested from 1,600 acres with a value of $7.39 million. At a yield of 210 cwt. per acre, 2013 production was 336,000 cwt. Carrot production was valued at $8.45 million in 2012 from 1,300 acres harvested. Production was 325,000 cwt. at a yield of 250 cwt. per acre.

The winter carrot production from South Texas accounts for about three-fourths of total production during the winter season.

*Felix Arreguin empties a bag of canteloupe melons at the Mandujano Brothers canteloupe farm near Coyanosa in Pecos County. Photo by Heather Leiphart; Odessa American.*

*Bags of onions, right, bear the "Pecos Fresh" brand of brothers Tony, Junior, Mando, and Beto Mandujano, who run a diversified operation that also includes watermelons, peppers, and hay. Photo by Mark Matson.*

## All Potatoes

In 2014, all potatoes were harvested from 20,600 acres with production of 6.798 million cwt. were valued at $115.56 million and a yield of 330 cwt. per acre.

In 2013, all potatoes were harvested from 17,700 acres with production of 8.142 million cwt. Yielding 460 cwt. per acre, they were valued at $131.1 million. In 2012, 20,100 acres were harvested, valued at $105.7 million. Production was 7.478 million cwt. and a yield of 372 cwt. per acre.

## Cantaloupes and Honeydews

Cantaloupe production in 2014 totaled 265,000 cwt. from 2,300 harvested acres and was valued at $8.215 million with a yield of 115 cwt. per acre.

In 2013, cantaloupes were harvested from 1,900 acres for total production of 228,000 cwt. valued at $7.07 million and yielding 120 cwt. per acre. Of the 2,700 harvested acres in 2012, 351,000 cwt. cantaloupes were produced at a yield of 130 cwt. per acre and a total value of $11.723 million.

Honeydew production in 2014 totaled 99,000 cwt.

and was valued at $2.871 million at a yield of 220 cwt. per acre. In 2013, 182,000 cwt. of honeydew melons were harvested from 650 acres for total value of $5.205 million, yielding 280 cwt. per acre.

In 2012, honeydew melons valued at $8.928 million were harvested on 1,000 acres, producing a yield of 310 cwt. per acre for a total production of 310,000 cwt.

## Cabbage

In 2014, 6,200 acres were harvested and yielded total production of 1.55 million cwt. that was valued at $33.32 million. Yield was 250 cwt. per acre. In 2013, 6,100 acres of cabbage were harvested yielding total production of 2.07 million cwt., or 340 cwt. per acre, valued at $37.12 million. The 6,000 acres of cabbage harvested in Texas in 2012 brought a value of $30.42 million. At a yield of 260 cwt. per acre, total production was 1.56 million cwt.

## Watermelons

Watermelon production in 2014 was 5.2 million cwt. from 20,000 acres with a value of $49.92 million, yielding 260 cwt. per acre. In 2013, at a yield of 240 cwt. per acre, 5.52 million cwt. of watermelons were harvested

## Vegetable Production, 2014

| Crop | Harvested Acres (000) | Yield Per Acre, Cwt. | Production (000) Cwt. | Value (000) |
|---|---|---|---|---|
| Cabbage | 6,200 | 250 | 1,550 | 33,325 |
| Cantaloupes | 2,300 | 115 | 265 | 8,215 |
| Carrots | 1,400 | 270 | 378 | 7,560 |
| Chile Peppers ‡ | 3,100 | 60 | 185 | 9,693 |
| Cucumbers | 2,400 | 118 | 283 | 5,264 |
| Honeydew Melons | 450 | 220 | 99 | 2,871 |
| Onions, Spring | 9,000 | 260 | 2,340 | 56,160 |
| Squash | 1,500 | 90 | 135 | 7,425 |
| Sweet Corn | 2,950 | 95 | 280 | 6,160 |
| Watermelons | 20,000 | 260 | 5,200 | 49,920 |
| **Total Fresh Market\*** | **49,300** | **—** | **10,715** | **186,593** |

\* Includes some quantities processed.

‡ Chile peppers are defined as all peppers, excluding bell peppers. Estimates include both fresh and dry product combined.

**Sources:** USDA/NASS, Annual Vegetable Summary, January 2015; "2014 State Agriculture Overview, Texas".

from 23,000 acres and valued at $53.54 million. In 2012, watermelon production was 5.4 million cwt. from 23,500 acres, with a value of $51.89 million and a yield of 230 cwt. per acre.

### Sweet Potatoes

In 2014, 140,000 cwt. of sweet potatoes were harvested from 900 acres at a yield of 155 cwt. per acre. Sweet potatoes in 2013 produced 140,000 cwt. from 800 harvested acres with a yield of 100 cwt. per acre. This compared with 150,000 cwt. produced in 2012 at a yield of 150 cwt. from 1,000 harvested acres.

### Spinach

Spinach production is primarily concentrated in the Winter Garden area of South Texas. The 2014 production value of spinach was estimated at $9.9 million. Production of 225,000 cwt. was harvested from 1,500 acres with a yield of 150 cwt. per acre.

In 2013, 1,300 acres were harvested with a value of $10 million. At a yield of 200 cwt. per acre, production was 260,000 cwt. The 1,500 acres harvested in 2012 produced 224,000 cwt. at a yield of 149 cwt. per acre and valued at $7.48 million.

### Cucumbers

In 2014, 2,400 acres of cucumbers were harvested. Production totaled 283,000 cwt. and was valued at $5.26 million. Yield was 118 cwt. per acre.

In 2013, 2,000 acres of cucumbers were harvested with a value of $5.17 million. Production was 230,000 cwt., with a yield of 115 cwt. per acre. At a yield of 120 cwt. per acre, the 252,000 cwt. cucumber crop in Texas during 2012 was harvested from 2,100 acres and valued at $6.3 million.

### Sweet Corn

In 2014, 280,000 cwt. of sweet corn was harvested from 2,950 acres. Value of production was estimated at $6.16 million with a yield of 95 cwt. per acre.

In 2013, 158,000 cwt. of sweet corn was produced from 2,100 harvested acres at a yield of 75 cwt. per acre and valued at $3.45 million. In 2012, sweet corn was harvested from 3,200 acres valued at $4.68 million. Production was 240,000 cwt. at a yield of 75 cwt. per acre.

## Fruits and Nuts

Texas is noted for producing a wide variety of fruits. The pecan is the only commercial nut crop in the state. The **pecan** is native to most of the state's river valleys and is the Texas state tree.

**Citrus** is produced commercially in the three southernmost counties in the Lower Rio Grande Valley. **Peaches** are the next most important Texas fruit crop, and an increase in apple growing.

### Citrus

Texas ranks with Florida, California, and Arizona as leading states in the production of citrus. Most of the Texas production is in Cameron, Hidalgo, and Willacy counties of the Lower Rio Grande Valley.

In the 2013–2014 growing season, **grapefruit** utilized production was estimated at 5.7 million boxes at $8.43 per box or $48.04 million.

Grapefruit production in 2012–2013 was 6.1 million boxes at $7.06 per box for a total value of $43.06 million. Production in 2011–2012 was 4.8 million boxes at $7.61 per box with a value of $36.54 million.

Production of **oranges** in 2013–2014 was 1.78 million boxes at $13.41 per box for a total value of $23.8 million. In 2012–2013, production was 1.79 million boxes at $12.20 per box for a total value of $21.8 million. Production in 2011–2012 was 1.42 million boxes at $13.57 per box for a value of $19.26 million.

### Peaches

Primary production areas are East Texas, the Hill Country, and the West Cross Timbers. Production varies due to adverse weather conditions. Low-chilling varieties for early marketings are being grown in Atascosa, Frio, Webb, Karnes, and Duval counties.

The Texas peach crop's utilized production totaled 3,300 tons in 2014 for a value of $6.6 million, or $2,000 per ton. In 2013, utilized production was 7,500 tons. Value of production was $19.27 million, or $2,570 per ton. In 2012, utilized production was 8,400 tons that was valued at $15.54 million, or $1,850 per ton.

The demand for high-quality Texas peaches greatly exceeds the supply. Leading Texas counties in production are Gillespie, Parker, Montague, Comanche, Limestone, and Eastland.

### Pecans

The pecan, **the state tree,** is one of the most widely distributed trees in Texas. It is native to over 150 counties and is grown commercially in 30 more counties.

The pecan is also widely used as a dual-purpose yard tree. The commercial plantings of pecans have accelerated in Central and West Texas, with many of the new orchards being irrigated.

In 2014, utilized pecan production totaled 60 million pounds and was valued at $110 million or $1.83 per pound. In 2013, 28 million pounds were produced. Total value was estimated at $44.78 million as price averaged $1.60 per pound. The 2012 crop totaled 55 million pounds valued at $74.76 million or $1.36 per pound.

Nationally, Texas ranked third behind Georgia and New Mexico in utilized pecan production in 2014. Leading Texas counties in pecan production are Hood, El Paso, Pecos, San Saba, Mills, Comanche, Wharton, and Gonzales.

Longhorn on Stasney's Cook Ranch near Albany in Shackelford County; www.stasneyscookranch.com. Photo courtesy of USDA/Natural Resources Conservation Service.

# Livestock and Their Products

Livestock and their products accounted for about 71.3 percent of the agricultural cash receipts in Texas in 2013. The state **ranks first nationally** in all cattle, beef cattle, cattle on feed, sheep and lambs, wool, goats, and mohair.

Cattle, calves, and hogs account for around 47.8 percent of cash receipts from marketings of livestock and their products. Sales of livestock and products in 2013 totaled $15.38 billion, up from $14.51 billion in 2012.

**Cattle and calves** dominate livestock production in Texas, contributing around 46.9 percent of cash receipts from livestock and products each year. The Jan. 1, 2015, inventory of all cattle and calves in Texas totaled 11.8 million head, valued at $17.94 billion, compared to 11.1 million head as of Jan. 1, 2014, valued at $12.77 billion.

On Jan. 1, 2015, the **sheep and lamb** inventory stood at 720,000 head, valued at $126 million, compared with 730,000 head as of Jan. 1, 2014, val-

ued at $118.99 million. Sheep and lambs numbered 3.214 million on Jan. 1, 1973, down from a high of 10.829 million in 1943. Sheep and lamb production fell from 148.3 million pounds in 1973 to 32.42 million pounds on Jan. 1, 2011.

Wool production decreased from 26.35 million pounds valued at $23.2 million in 1973 to 2.6 million pounds valued at $3.3 million in 2014. Production was 2.1 million pounds in 2013 valued at $4.05 million. The price of wool per pound was 88 cents in 1973, $1.57 in 2014, and $1.76 in 2013.

**Mohair production** in Texas has dropped from a 1965 high of 31.584 million pounds to 580,000 pounds in 2014. Production was valued at $3.654 million or $6.30 per pound. In 2013, production was 490,000 pounds valued at $2.7 million or $5.50 per pound. Mohair production in 2012 was 470,000 pounds valued at $2.256 million or $4.80 per pound.

### Beef Cattle

Raising beef cattle is the **most extensive agricultural operation in Texas.** In 2013, cattle and calves comprised 46.9 percent of total cash receipts — $10.1 billion of $21.6 billion — compared with $9.9 billion of $23.7 billion in 2012 (41.6%) and $11 billion of $22.3

billion in 2011 (49.6%). The next leading commodity is poultry and eggs.

Nearly all of the 254 counties in Texas derive more revenue from cattle than from any other agricultural commodity, and those that don't usually rank cattle second in importance.

Within the boundaries of Texas are **13.1 percent**

**of all the cattle in the United States,** as are 14.1 percent of the beef breeding cows, and 11.9 percent of the calf crop as of the Jan. 1, 2015, inventory.

The number of all cattle in Texas on Jan. 1, 2015, totaled 11.8 million, compared with 11.1 million on Jan. 1, 2014, and 11.6 million in 2013.

Calves born on Texas farms and ranches as of Jan. 1, 2015, totaled 4 million compared with 3.8 million in 2014; and 3.95 million in 2013.

### Livestock Industries

A large portion of Texas livestock is sold through local **auction markets.** In 2009, the Texas Animal Health Commission reported 145 livestock auctions.

Auctions sold 4.4 million head of cattle and calves; 27,000 hogs; and 869,000 sheep and goats in 2010. This compares with 4.53 million cattle and calves; 28,000 hogs; and 928,000 sheep and goats in 2009. Figures for 2008 were 4.2 million cattle and calves; 32,000 hogs; 1.03 million sheep and goats.

During 2010, the commission reported 871,503 cattle and calves shipped from Texas to other states and 1.37 million shipped in; compared with 813,145 shipped out and 1.85 million shipped in during 2009; and 720,000 shipped out and 2 million shipped in during 2008. (Figures exclude cattle shipped directly to slaughter, where no health certificates are required.)

During 2010, Texas shipped out 72,756 sheep and lambs and shipped in 11,425; compared with 62,132 shipped out and 21,779 shipped in during 2009; and 26,000 shipped out and 12,000 shipped in during 2008.

### Feedlot Production

Feedlot production of livestock, mainly cattle, is a major industry in Texas. Annual fed cattle marketings totaled 5.73 million for 1,000 head-and-over feedlot capacity in 2008.

Texas lots marketed a total of 5.7 million head of grain-fed cattle in 2007, compared with 5.78 million in 2006; and 5.76 million in 2005. In recent years, more cattle have been fed in Texas than any other state in the United States. **State-level numbers are only published in conjunction with the Census of Agriculture every five years.**

During 2008, there were 128 feedlots in Texas with capacity of 1,000 animals or more. This compared with 128 in 2007, 130 in 2006, and 130 in 2005.

Slaughter plants in Texas numbered 103 in 2010. This compared with 111 in 2009 and 121 in 2008. In 2009, the number of federally inspected cattle slaughtered in Texas totaled 6.6 million cattle, 352,000 hogs, 21,000 sheep and lambs, and 43,000 calves. That compares with 2008 figures of 6.72 million cattle, 369,000 hogs, 5,000 sheep and lambs, and 19,000 calves; and 6.1 million cattle, 357,000 hogs, 3,000 sheep and lambs, and 11,000 calves in 2007.

Feeding of cattle in commercial feedlots is a major economic development that has stimulated the establishment and expansion of beef slaughtering plants.

## Texas Cattle Marketed by Size of Feedlots, 1965–2007

| Year | Under 1,000 | 1,000–1,999 | 2,000–3,999 | 4,000–7,999 | 8,000–15,999 | 16,000 & Over | Total |
|---|---|---|---|---|---|---|---|
| | | | Cattle Marketed — 1,000 head — | | | | |
| 1965 | 104 | 108 | 205 | 324 | 107 | 246 | 1,094 |
| 1970 | 98 | 53 | 112 | 281 | 727 | 1,867 | 3,138 |
| 1975 | 50 | 22 | 51 | 134 | 485 | 2,325 | 3,067 |
| 1976 | 60 | 33 | 62 | 170 | 583 | 3,039 | 3,947 |
| 1977 | 146 | 22 | 38 | 206 | 604 | 3,211 | 4,277 |
| 1978 | 80 | 20 | 50 | 242 | 697 | 3,826 | 4,915 |
| 1979 | 54 | 19 | 46 | 227 | 556 | 3,543 | 4,445 |
| 1980 | 51 | 18 | 47 | 226 | 533 | 3,285 | 4,160 |
| 1981 | 50 | 20 | 50 | 220 | 510 | 3,110 | 3,960 |
| 1982 | 55 | 20 | 60 | 210 | 540 | 3,190 | 4,075 |
| 1983 | 100 | 20 | 80 | 130 | 490 | 3,580 | 4,400 |
| 1984 | 60 | 20 | 180 | 150 | 540 | 4,140 | 5,090 |
| 1985 | 70 | 10 | 20 | 170 | 620 | 4,140 | 5,030 |
| 1986 | 90 | 10 | 40 | 180 | 550 | 4,390 | 5,260 |
| 1987 | 90 | 20 | 35 | 170 | 625 | 4,375 | 5,255 |
| 1988 | 30 | 15 | 35 | 185 | 650 | 4,120 | 5,035 |
| 1989 | 40 | 15 | 40 | 165 | 675 | 3,810 | 4,745 |
| 1990 | 35 | 24 | 56 | 180 | 605 | 3,940 | 4,840 |
| 1991 | 35 | 25 | 45 | 225 | 500 | 4,250 | 5,080 |
| 1992 | 50 | 10 | 25 | 140 | 505 | 4,065 | 4,795 |
| 1993 | 30 | 20 | 70 | 160 | 640 | 4,370 | 5,290 |
| 1994 | 14 | 13 | 55 | 173 | 725 | 4,680 | 5,660 |
| 1995 | 12 | 24 | 43 | 166 | 630 | 4,665 | 5,540 |
| 1996 | NA | 17 | 43 | 180 | 460 | 4,800 | 5,500 |
| 1997 | NA | 17 | 48 | 250 | 485 | 5,000 | 5,800 |
| 1998 | NA | 10 | 20 | 140 | 420 | 5,470 | 6,060 |
| 1999 | NA | 10 | 20 | 140 | 385 | 5,510 | 6,065 |
| 2000 | NA | 8 | 17 | 125 | 470 | 5,570 | 6,190 |
| 2001 | NA | 8 | 22 | 90 | 450 | 5,460 | 6,030 |
| 2002 | NA | 10 | 15 | 85 | 390 | 5,480 | 5,980 |
| 2003 | NA | 10 | 15 | 75 | 420 | 5,450 | 5,970 |
| 2004* | NA | 20 | | 485 | | 5,180 | 5,685 |
| 2005 | NA | 20 | | 475 | | 5,260 | 5,755 |
| 2006 | NA | 25 | | 470 | | 5,280 | 5,755 |
| 2007 | NA | 20 | | 400 | | 5,265 | 5,685 |

Number of feedlots with 1,000 head or more capacity is number of lots operating any time during the year. Number under 1,000 head capacity and total number of all feedlots is number at end of year.

\* Beginning in 2004 report, cattle marketed as 1,000–3,999 and 4,000–15,999 in feedlot capacity.

**Sources:** *"Texas Agricultural Facts, 1997," Texas Agricultural Statistics Service, September 1998.* Numbers for 1986, 1987, 1988, 1989, 1990, 1991, 1992.: *1993 Texas Livestock Statistics, Bulletin 252, August 1994; Cattle on Feed annual summary, USDA/NASS, February 2009.*

Most of this development is in the Northern High Plains area of Northwest Texas. This area alone accounts for around 91 percent of the cattle fed in the state as of Jan. 1, 2009.

Total feedlot marketings represented about 26 percent of total U.S. fed cattle marketings as of Jan. 1, 2009. Large amounts of capital are required for feedlot operations, which has forced many lots to become custom feeding facilities.

Feedlots are concentrated on the High Plains largely because of extensive supplies of corn, sorghum, and other feed. Beef breeding herds have increased the most in East Texas, where the acreage for grazing is abundant.

## Dairy Manufacturing

The **major dairy products** manufactured in Texas include condensed, evaporated, and dry milk; creamer; butter; and cheese. However, these data are not available because of the small number of manufacturing plants producing these products.

*These spotted Boer goats are raised by Henri and Carol DeLobbe on their Bon Joli Farm north of Fredericksburg. Photo courtesy of Bon Joli Farm; www.bonjolifarm.com.*

## Dairying

All the cow's milk sold by Texas dairy farmers is marketed under the terms of **Federal Marketing Orders.** Most Texas dairymen are members of one of four marketing cooperatives. Associate Milk Producers, Inc., is the largest, representing the majority of the state's milk producers.

Texas dairy farmers received an average price for milk of $24.60 per hundred pounds in 2014, $20.40 in 2013, and $18.70 in 2012. A total of 10.282 billion pounds of milk was sold to plants and dealers in 2014, bringing in cash receipts from milk to dairy farmers of $2.53 billion.

This compared with 9.59 billion pounds sold in 2013 that brought in $1.96 billion in cash receipts. In 2012, Texas dairymen sold 9.57 billion pounds of milk, which brought in cash receipts of $1.79 billion.

The annual average number of milk cows in Texas was 470,000 head as of the Jan. 1, 2015, inventory. This compared with 440,000 head as of Jan. 1, 2014, and 435,000 as of Jan. 1, 2013.

Average milk production per cow in the state has increased steadily over the past several decades. The average milk production per cow in 2014 was 22,268 pounds. Milk per cow was 21,991 pounds in 2013; and 22,009 pounds in 2012. Total milk production in Texas was 10.31 billion pounds in 2014; 9.61 billion pounds in 2013; and 9.6 billion pounds in 2012.

There were 985 farms reporting milk cows in Texas

in 2012. In 2007, 1,293 farms reported milk cows, and in 2006, 1,300 farms reported milk cows in Texas.

## Swine

Texas had 760,000 head of swine on hand as of Dec. 1, 2014 — only 1.15 percent of the U.S. swine herd. Swine producers in the state produce about 660,000 head marketed annually. Although the number of farms producing hogs has steadily decreased, **the size of production units has increased substantially.**

In 2014, 2.17 million head of hogs were marketed in Texas, producing 309.4 million pounds of pork valued at $241.8 million.

In 2013, 1.83 million head of hogs were marketed, producing 287.8 million pounds of pork valued at $197.89 million. Comparable figures for 2012 were 1.6 million head marketed, and 207.5 million pounds of pork produced with a value of $174.73 million.

## Goats and Mohair

Goats in Texas numbered 928,000 on Jan. 1, 2015. This compares with 906,000 on Jan. 1, 2014, and 940,000 on Jan. 1, 2013.

**Angora goats are raised for mohair production.** Angora goats totaled 85,000 as of Jan. 1, 2015; 76,000 as of Jan. 1, 2014; and 72,000 as of Jan. 1, 2013.

Mohair production during 2014 totaled 580,000 pounds. This compares with 490,000 pounds in 2013 and 470,000 pounds in 2012. Average price per pound in 2014 was $6.30 from 92,000 goats clipped for a total value of $3.654 million.

In 2013, producers received $5.50 per pound from 80,000 goats clipped for a total value of $2.7 million. In 2012, producers received $4.80 per pound from 75,000 goats clipped for a total value of $2.26 million.

**Over half of the world's mohair** and more than 55 percent of the U.S. clip are produced in Texas.

## Goats and Mohair 1900–2015

| Year | Goats | | Mohair | |
|---|---|---|---|---|
| | Number | Farm Value | Production (lbs) | Value |
| 1900 | 627,000 | $924,000 | 961,000 | $268,000 |
| 1910 | 1,135,000 | 2,514,000 | 1,998,000 | 468,000 |
| 1920 | 1,753,000 | 9,967,000 | 6,786,000 | 1,816,000 |
| 1930 | 2,965,000 | 14,528,000 | 14,800,000 | 4,995,000 |
| 1940 | 3,300,000 | 10,560,000 | 18,250,000 | 9,308,000 |
| 1950 | 2,295,000 | 13,082,000 | 12,643,000 | 9,735,000 |
| 1960 | 3,339,000 | 29,383,000 | 23,750,000 | 21,375,000 |
| 1970 | 2,572,000 | 19,033,000 | 17,985,000 | 7,032,000 |
| 1980 | 1,400,000 | 64,400,000 | 8,800,000 | 30,800,000 |
| 1981 | 1,380,000 | 53,130,000 | 10,100,000 | 35,350,000 |
| 1982 | 1,410,000 | 57,810,000 | 10,000,000 | 25,500,000 |
| 1983 | 1,420,000 | 53,250,000 | 10,600,000 | 42,930,000 |
| 1984 | 1,450,000 | 82,215,000 | 10,600,000 | 48,160,000 |
| 1985 | 1,590,000 | 76,797,000 | 13,300,000 | 45,885,000 |
| 1986 | 1,770,000 | 70,977,000 | 16,000,000 | 40,160,000 |
| 1987 | 1,780,000 | 82,592,000 | 16,200,000 | 42,606,000 |
| 1988 | 1,800,000 | 108,180,000 | 15,400,000 | 29,876,000 |
| 1989 | 1,850,000 | 100,270,000 | 15,400,000 | 24,794,000 |
| 1990 | 1,900,000 | 93,100,000 | 14,500,000 | 13,775,000 |
| 1991 | 1,830,000 | 73,200,000 | 14,800,000 | 19,388,000 |
| 1992 | 2,000,000 | 84,000,000 | 14,200,000 | 12,354,000 |
| 1993 | 1,960,000 | 84,280,000 | 13,490,000 | 11,197,000 |
| 1994 | 1,960,000 | 74,480,000 | 11,680,000 | 30,602,000 |
| 1995 | 1,850,000 | 81,400,000 | 11,319,000 | 20,940,000 |
| 1996 | 1,900,000 | 89,300,000 | 7,490,000 | 14,606,000 |
| 1997 | 1,650,000 | 70,950,000 | 6,384,000 | 14,556,000 |
| 1998 | 1,400,000 | 71,400,000 | 4,650,000 | 12,044,000 |
| 1999 | 1,350,000 | 71,550,000 | 2,550,000 | 9,384,000 |
| 2000 | 1,300,000 | 74,100,000 | 2,346,000 | 10,088,000 |
| 2001 | 1,400,000 | 105,000,000 | 1,716,000 | 3,775,000 |
| 2002 | 1,250,000 | 106,250,000 | 1,944,000 | 3,110,400 |
| 2003 | 1,200,000 | 110,400,000 | 1,680,000 | 2,856,000 |
| 2004 | 1,200,000 | 115,200,000 | 1,620,000 | 3,402,000 |
| 2005 | 1,270,000 | 138,430,000 | 1,250,000 | 3,750,000 |
| 2006 | 1,310,000 | 137,388,000 | 1,100,000 | 4,400,000 |
| 2007 | 1,300,000 | 147,552,000 | 960,000 | 3,840,000 |
| 2008 | 1,185,000 | 120,870,000 | 820,000 | 3,116,000 |
| 2009 | 1,090,000 | 129,920,000 | 700,000 | 2,170,000 |
| 2010 | 1,020,000 | 108,290,000 | 730,000 | 3,066,000 |
| 2011 | 980,000 | NA | 530,000 | 2,703,000 |
| 2012 | 905,000 | NA | 470,000 | 2,256,000 |
| 2013 | 872,000 | NA | 490,000 | 2,695,000 |
| 2014 | 906,000 | NA | 580,000 | 3,654,000 |
| 2015 | 928,000 | NA | NA | NA |

NA = not available.
**Sources:** "1985 Texas Livestock, Dairy and Poultry Statistics", USDA Bulletin 235, June 1986. "Texas Agricultural Facts," Crop and Livestock Reporting Service, various years; "1993 Texas Livestock Statistics", Texas Agricultural Statistics Service, Bulletin 252, August 1994; "Texas Agricultural Statistics, 2009", October 2010; "Texas Ag Facts", February and March 2011. USDA/TASS Texas Goat Inventory, January 30, 2015.

## Sheep and Wool

Sheep and lambs in Texas numbered 720,000 head on Jan. 1, 2015, compared to 730,000 as of Jan. 1, 2014, and 700,000 as of Jan. 1, 2013. All sheep were valued at $126 million on Jan. 1, 2015, compared with $119 million as of Jan. 1, 2014, and $99.4 million as of Jan. 1, 2011.

Breeding ewes 1 year old and older numbered 435,000 as of Jan. 1, 2015, 440,000 as of Jan. 1, 2014, and 420,000 as of Jan. 1, 2013. Replacement lambs less than 1 year old totaled 105,000 head as of Jan. 1, 2015, 105,000 as of Jan. 1, 2014; and 90,000 as of Jan. 1, 2013.

## Hog Production 1960–2014

| Year | Production (1,000 Pounds) | Avg. Market Wt. (Pounds) | Avg. Price Per Cwt. (Dollars) | Gross Income (1,000 Dollars) |
|---|---|---|---|---|
| 1960 | 288,844 | 228 | $14.70 | $44,634 |
| 1970 | 385,502 | 241 | 22.50 | 75,288 |
| 1980 | 315,827 | 259 | 35.90 | 111,700 |
| 1981 | 264,693 | 256 | 41.70 | 121,054 |
| 1982 | 205,656 | 256 | 49.60 | 112,726 |
| 1983 | 209,621 | 256 | 45.20 | 95,343 |
| 1984 | 189,620 | 262 | 45.50 | 95,657 |
| 1985 | 168,950 | 266 | 43.40 | 72,512 |
| 1986 | 176,660 | 269 | 47.30 | 82,885 |
| 1987 | 216,834 | NA | 50.60 | 103,983 |
| 1988 | 236,658 | NA | 41.30 | 100,029 |
| 1989 | 224,229 | NA | 39.90 | 93,178 |
| 1990 | 196,225 | NA | 48.20 | 92,222 |
| 1991 | 207,023 | NA | 45.10 | 97,398 |
| 1992 | 217,554 | NA | 36.40 | 79,436 |
| 1993 | 221,130 | NA | 39.90 | 90,561 |
| 1994 | 224,397 | NA | 35.10 | 78,394 |
| 1995 | 221,323 | NA | 35.50 | 81,509 |
| 1996 | 203,761 | NA | 45.90 | 93,526 |
| 1997 | 224,131 | NA | 47.40 | 106,238 |
| 1998 | 270,977 | NA | 30.70 | 83,190 |
| 1999 | 274,572 | NA | 27.50 | 71,604 |
| 2000 | 328,732 | NA | 36.60 | 115,105 |
| 2001 | 260,875 | NA | 39.10 | 105,217 |
| 2002 | 223,441 | NA | 28.70 | 67,255 |
| 2003 | 197,876 | NA | 33.60 | 67,998 |
| 2004 | 202,199 | NA | 44.90 | 90,349 |
| 2005 | 223,375 | NA | 45.40 | 105,989 |
| 2006 | 259,989 | NA | 40.80 | 109,318 |
| 2007 | 273,213 | NA | 39.70 | 95,581 |
| 2008 | 317,446 | NA | 40.50 | 133,488 |
| 2009 | 302,578 | NA | 37.60 | 130,951 |
| 2010 | 154,540 | NA | 50.20 | 88,434 |
| 2011 | 203,312 | NA | NA | 123,298 |
| 2012 | 267,523 | NA | NA | 179,668 |
| 2013 | 285,822 | NA | NA | 240,322 |
| 2014 | 309,408 | NA | NA | 255,705 |

NA = not available.
**Sources:** "1985 Texas Livestock, Dairy and Poultry Statistics", USDA, Bulletin 235, June 1986, pp. 32, 46; 1991 "Texas Livestock Statistics"; USDA, "Meat Animals - Prod., Dips., & Income", April 2010 and April 2011; "1993 Texas Livestock Statistics", Bulletin 252, Texas Agricultural Statistics Service, August 1994; "Texas Agricultural Facts, 2009", October, 2010; "Texas Ag Facts", various years. (December 1 previous year); USDA/NASS Quick Stats.

Sheep and lamb operations in Texas were estimated to be 10,674 as of Jan. 1, 2012, compaired to 8,700 in 2007.

Texas wool production in 2014 was 2.1 million pounds from 290,000 sheep. Value totaled $3.3 million or $1.57 per pound. This compared with 2.3 million pounds of wool from 310,000 sheep in 2013 valued at $4.05 million or $1.76 per pound; and 2.1 million pounds from 290,000 sheep valued at $3.51 million or $1.67 per pound in 2012.

Most sheep and lambs in Texas are concentrated in the **Edwards Plateau** area of West-Central Texas and nearby counties.

**San Angelo** long has been the largest sheep and wool market in the nation, and the center for wool and mohair warehouses, scouring plants, and slaughterhouses.

## Poultry and Eggs

Poultry and eggs annually contributed about 12.84 percent to the average yearly cash receipts of Texas farmers in 2013. On Jan. 1, 2014, **Texas ranked sixth among the states in broilers produced and fifth in eggs produced.**

In 2013, cash receipts to Texas producers from the production of poultry and eggs totaled $2.77 billion. This compares with $2.21 billion in 2012, and $2.13 in 2011.

Broiler production in 2014 totaled 591.8 million birds, compared with 610.1 million in 2013, and 602.6 million in 2012.

## Horses

Nationally, Texas ranks as **one of the leading states in horse numbers** and is the headquarters for many national horse organizations. The largest single breed registry in America, the American Quarter Horse Association, has its headquarters in Amarillo.

The National Cutting Horse Association and the American Paint Horse Association are both located in Fort Worth. In addition to these national associations, Texas also has active state associations that include Palominos, Arabians, Thoroughbreds, Appaloosa, and ponies.

Horses are still used to support the state's giant beef cattle and sheep industries. The largest horse numbers within the state, however, are near urban and suburban areas where they are mostly used for recreational activities.

Horses are most abundant in the heavily populated areas of the state. State participation activities consist of horse shows, trail rides, play days, rodeos, polo, and horse racing.

Residential subdivisions have been developed within the state to provide facilities for urban and suburban horse owners. ☆

# Sheep and Wool Production
# 1850–2015

| Year | Sheep | | Wool | | Year | Sheep | | Wool | |
|------|*Number|Value|Production (lbs)|Value| |*Number|Value|Production (lbs)|Value|
| 1850 | 100,530 | N A | 131,917 | N A | 1988 | 2,040,000 | 155,040,000 | 18,200,000 | 35,854,000 |
| 1860 | 753,363 | N A | 1,493,363 | N A | 1989 | 1,870,000 | 133,445,000 | 18,000,000 | 27,180,000 |
| 1870 | 1,223,000 | $2,079,000 | N A | N A | 1990 | 2,090,000 | 133,760,000 | 17,400,000 | 19,662,000 |
| 1880 | 6,024,000 | 12,048,000 | N A | N A | 1991 | 2,000,000 | 108,000,000 | 16,700,000 | 13,861,000 |
| 1890 | 4,752,000 | 7,128,000 | N A | N A | 1992 | 2,140,000 | 111,280,000 | 17,600,000 | 16,896,000 |
| 1900 | 2,416,000 | 4,590,000 | 9,630,000 | N A | 1993 | 2,040,000 | 118,320,000 | 17,000,000 | 11,050,000 |
| 1910 | 1,909,000 | 5,536,000 | 8,943,000 | $1,699,170 | 1994 | 1,895,000 | 106,120,000 | 14,840,000 | 15,582,000 |
| 1920 | 3,360,000 | 33,600,000 | 22,813,000 | 5,019,000 | 1995 | 1,700,000 | 100,300,000 | 13,468,000 | 15,488,000 |
| 1930 | 6,304,000 | 44,758,000 | 48,262,000 | 10,135,000 | 1996 | 1,650,000 | 108,900,000 | 9,900,000 | 8,316,000 |
| 1940 | 10,069,000 | 49,413,000 | 79,900,000 | 23,171,000 | 1997 | 1,400,000 | 100,800,000 | 10,950,000 | 11,607,000 |
| 1950 | 6,756,000 | 103,877,000 | 51,480,000 | 32,947,000 | 1998 | 1,530,000 | 122,400,000 | 9,230,000 | 5,815,000 |
| 1960 | 5,938,000 | 85,801,000 | 51,980,000 | 21,832,000 | 1999 | 1,350,000 | 95,850,000 | 7,956,000 | 3,898,000 |
| 1970 | 3,708,000 | 73,602,000 | 30,784,000 | 11,082,000 | 2000 | 1,200,000 | 94,800,000 | 7,506,000 | 3,678,000 |
| 1973 | 3,214,000 | 64,280,000 | 26,352,000 | 23,190,000 | 2001 | 1,150,000 | 92,000,000 | 6,003,000 | 3,122,000 |
| 1974 | 3,090,000 | 80,340,000 | 23,900,000 | 15,535,000 | 2002 | 1,130,000 | 88,140,000 | 5,950,000 | 4,046,000 |
| 1975 | 2,715,000 | 63,803,000 | 23,600,000 | 14,868,000 | 2003 | 1,040,000 | 82,160,000 | 5,600,000 | 5,040,000 |
| 1976 | 2,600,000 | 81,900,000 | 22,000,000 | 17,380,000 | 2004 | 1,100,000 | 105,600,000 | 5,600,000 | 5,712,000 |
| 1977 | 2,520,000 | 93,240,000 | 21,000,000 | 17,220,000 | 2005 | 1,070,000 | 112,350,000 | 5,550,000 | 5,328,000 |
| 1978 | 2,460,000 | 111,930,000 | 18,500,000 | 15,355,000 | 2006 | 1,090,000 | 124,260,000 | 4,900,000 | 4,459,000 |
| 1979 | 2,415,000 | 152,145,000 | 19,075,000 | 18,503,000 | 2007 | 1,050,000 | 111,300,000 | 4,500,000 | 5,445,000 |
| 1980 | 2,400,000 | 138,000,000 | 18,300,000 | 17,751,000 | 2008 | 960,000 | 97,920,000 | 4,200,000 | 4,872,000 |
| 1981 | 2,360,000 | 116,820,000 | 20,500,000 | 24,600,000 | 2009 | 870,000 | 87,870,000 | 3,500,000 | 3,640,000 |
| 1982 | 2,400,000 | 100,800,000 | 19,300,000 | 16,212,000 | 2010 | 830,000 | 83,000,000 | 3,450,000 | 5,451,000 |
| 1983 | 2,225,000 | 86,775,000 | 18,600,000 | 15,438,000 | 2011 | 850,000 | 109,650,000 | 2,600,000 | 5,746,000 |
| 1984 | 1,970,000 | 76,830,000 | 17,500,000 | 16,100,000 | 2012 | 670,000 | 102,510,000 | 2,100,000 | 3,507,000 |
| 1985 | 1,930,000 | 110,975,000 | 16,200,000 | 13,284,000 | 2013 | 700,000 | 99,400,000 | 2,300,000 | 4,048,000 |
| 1986 | 1,850,000 | 107,300,000 | 16,400,000 | 13,284,000 | 2014 | 730,000 | 118,990,000 | 2,100,000 | 3,297,000 |
| 1987 | 2,050,000 | 133,250,000 | 16,400,000 | 19,844,000 | 2015 | 720,000 | 126,000,000 | NA | NA |

*NA = not available*

**Sources:** *"1985 Texas Livestock, Dairy and Poultry Statistics", USDA Bulletin 235, June 1986. "Texas Agricultural Facts" Annual Summary, Crop and Livestock Reporting Service, various years, "1993 Texas Livestock Statistics", Texas Agricultural Statistics Service, Bulletin 252, August 1994; "Texas Agricultural Statistics, 2009", October 2010, "Texas Ag Fact", February and March 2011; Texas Sheep and Wool report, NASS/TASS Quick Stats.*

# Appendix

*Working pens on a ranch near Stanton in Martin County. Photo courtesy of USDA/Natural Resources Conservation Service.*

**Pronunciation Guide**

**Texas Obituaries**

**Index of Entries**

# Texas Almanac Pronunciation Guide

Texas' rich cultural diversity is reflected nowhere better than in the names of places. Standard pronunciation is used in many cases, but purely colloquial pronunciation often is used, too.

In the late 1940s, George Mitchel Stokes, a graduate student at Baylor University, developed a list of pronunciations of 2,300 place names across the state. Stokes earned his doctorate and eventually was the director of the speech division in the communications studies department at Baylor University. He retired in 1983.

In the following list based on Stokes longer list, pronunciation is by respelling and diacritical marking. Respelling is employed as follows: "ah" as in the exclamation, ah, or the "o" in tot; "ee" as in meet; "oo" as in moot; "yoo" as in use; "ow" as in cow; "oi" as in oil; "uh" as in mud.

Note that ah, uh and the apostrophe(') are used for varying degrees of neutral vowel sounds, the apostrophe being used where the vowel is barely sounded. Diacritical markings are used as follows: bāle, băd, lĕt, rīse, rĭll, ōak, brōōd, fŏŏt.

The stressed syllable is capitalized. Secondary stress is indicated by an underline as in Atascosa — ăt uhs KŌ suh.

## A

Abbott — Ă buht
Abernathy — Ă ber nă thĭ
Abilene — ĂB uh leen
Acala — uh KĀ luh
Ackerly — ĂK er lĭ
Acme — ĂK mĭ
Acton — ĂK t'n
Acuff — Ă kuhf
Adamsville — Ă d'mz vĭl
Addicks — Ă dĭks
Addielou — ă dĭ LŌŌ
Addison — A di s'n
Adkins — ĂT kĭnz
Adrian — Ă drĭ uhn
Afton — ĂF t'n
Agua Dulce — ah wuh DŌŌL sĭ
Agua Nueva — ah wuh nyōō Ā vuh
Aiken — Ā kĭn
Alamo — ĂL uh mō
Alamo Heights — ăl uh mō HĪTS
Alanreed — ĂL uhn reed
Alba — ĂL buh
Albany — AWL buh nĭ
Albert — ĂL bert
Aledo — uh LEE dō
Alexander — ĕl ĭg ZĂN der
Alfred — ĂL frĕd
Algoa — ăl GŌ uh
Alice — Ă lĭs
Alief — Ā leef
Allen — Ă lĭn
Allenfarm — ălĭn FAHRM
Alleyton — Ă lĭ t'n
Allison — ĂL uh s'n
Alma — AHL muh
Alpine — ĂL pīn
Altair — awl TĂR
Alto — ĂL tō
Altoga — ăl TŌ guh
Alvarado — ăl vuh RĀ dō
Alvin — ĂL vĭn
Alvord — ĂL vord
Amarillo — ăm uh RĬL ō
Amherst — AM herst
Ammannsville — ĂM 'nz vĭl

Anahuac — ĂN uh wăk
Anderson — ĂN der s'n
Andice — ĂN dīs
Andrews — ĂN drōōz
Angelina — ăn juh LEE nuh
Angleton — ĂNG g'l t'n
Anna — ĂN uh
Annona — ă NŌ nuh
Anson — ĂN s'n
Antelope — ĂNT uh lōp
Anton — ĂNT n
Appleby — Ă p'l bĭ
Apple Springs — ă p'l SPRĬNGZ
Aquilla — uh KWĬL uh
Aransas — uh RĂN zuhs
Aransas Pass — uh răn zuhs PĂS
Arbala — ahr BĂ luh
Arcadia — ahr KĀ dĭ uh
Archer — AHR cher
Archer City — ahr cher SĬT ĭ
Arcola — ahr KŌ luh
Argo — AHR gō
Argyle — ahr GĪL
Arlington — AHR lĭng t'n
Arneckeville — AHR nĭ kĭ vĭl
Arnett — AHR nĭt
Arp — ahrp
Artesia Wells — ahr tee zh' WĔLZ
Arthur City — ahr ther SĬT ĭ
Asherton — ĂSH er t'n
Aspermont — ĂS per mahnt
Atascosa — ăt uhs KŌ suh
Athens — Ă thĕnz
Atlanta — ăt LĂN tuh
Atlas — ĂT l's
Attoyac — AT uh yăk
Aubrey — AW brĭ
Augusta — aw GUHS tuh
Austin — AWS t'n
Austonio — aws TŌ nĭ ō
Austwell — AWS wĕl
Avalon — ĂV uhl n
Avery — Ā vuh rĭ
Avinger — Ă vĭn jer
Avoca — uh VŌ kuh
Axtell — ĂKS t'l
Azle — Ā z'l

## B

Bagwell — BĂG w'l
Bailey — BĀ lĭ
Baileyboro — BĀ lĭ ber ruh
Baileyville — BĀ lĭ vĭl
Baird — bărd
Bakersfield — BĀ kers feeld
Balch Springs — bawlch or bawlk SPRĬNGZ
Ballinger — BĂL ĭn jer
Balmorhea — băl muh RĀ
Bandera — băn DĔR uh
Bangs — băngz
Banquete — băn KĔ tĭ
Barclay — BAHRK lĭ
Bardwell — BAHRD w'l
Barker — BAHR ker
Barksdale — BAHRKS dāl
Barnhart — BAHRN hahrt
Barnum — BAHR n'm
Barry — BĂ rĭ
Barstow — BAHRS tō
Bartlett — BAHRT lĭt
Bassett — BĂ sĭt
Bastrop — BĂS trahp
Batesville — BĀTS v'l
Batson — BĂT s'n
Baxter — BĂKS ter
Bay City — ba SĬT ĭ
Baylor — BĀ ler
Bayside — BĀ sīd
Baytown — BĀ town
Beasley — BEEZ lĭ
Beaukiss — bō KĬS
Beaumont — BŌ mahnt
Bebe — bee bee
Beckville — BĔK v'l
Becton — BĔK t'n
Bedias — BEE dīs
Bee — bee
Beehouse — BEE hows
Beeville — BEE vĭl
Belcherville — BĔL cher vĭl
Bell — bĕl
Bellaire — bĕl ĂR
Bellevue — BĔL vyōō

---

Bellmead — bĕl MEED
Bells — bĕlz
Bellville — BĔL vĭl
Belmont — BĔL mahnt
Belton — BĔL t'n
Ben Arnold — bĕn AHR n'ld
Benavides — bĕn uh VEE d's
Ben Bolt — bĕn BŌLT
Benbrook — BĬN brŏŏk
Benchley — BĔNCH lĭ
Bend — bĕnd
Ben Franklin — bĕn FRĂNGk lĭn
Ben Hur — bĕn HER
Benjamin — BĔN juh m'n
Bennett — BĔN ĭt
Bentonville — BĔNT n vĭl
Ben Wheeler — bĭn HWEE ler
Berclair — ber KLĂR
Bertram — BERT r'm
Bessmay — bĕs MĀ
Best — bĕst
Bettie — BĔT ĭ
Bexar — BA är or bär
Beyersville — BĪRZ vĭl
Biardstown — BĂRDZ t'n
Bigfoot — BĬG fŏŏt
Big Lake — bĭg LĀK
Big Sandy — bĭg SĂN dĭ
Big Spring — bĭg SPRĬNG
Big Wells — bĭg WĔLZ
Birdville — BERD vĭl
Birome — bī RŌM
Birthright — BERTH rĭt
Bishop — BĬ sh'p
Bivins — BĬ vĭnz
Black — blăk
Blackfoot — BLĂK fŏŏt
Blackwell — BLĂK w'l
Blair — blăr
Blanchard — BLĂN cherd
Blanco — BLĂNG kō
Blanket — BLĂNG kĭt
Bleakwood — BLEEK wŏŏd
Bledsoe — BLĔD sō
Blessing — BLĔ sĭng
Blewett — BLŌŌ ĭt
Blooming Grove — blŏŏ mĭng
  GRŌV
Bloomington — BLŌŌM ĭng t'n
Blossom — BLAH s'm
Blue Grove — blŏŏ GRŌV
Blue Ridge — blŏŏ RĬJ
Bluff Dale — BLUHF dāl
Bluffton — BLUHF t'n
Blum — bluhm
Boerne — BER nĭ
Bogata — buh GŌ duh
Boling — BŌL ĭng
Bolivar — BAH lĭ ver
Bomarton — BŌ mer t'n
Bonham — BAH n'm
Bonita — bō NEE tuh
Bonney — BAH nĭ
Bonus — BŌ n's
Bon Wier — bahn WEER

Booker — BŌŌ ker
Boonsville — BŌŌNZ vĭl
Booth — bŏŏth
Borden — BAWRD n
Borger — BŌR ger
Bosque — BAHS kĭ
Boston — BAWS t'n
Bovina — bō VEE nuh
Bowie — BŌŌ Ĭ
Boxelder — bahks ĔL der
Boyce — bawĭs
Boyd — boĭd
Brachfield — BRĂCH feeld
Bracken — BRĂ kĭn
Brackettville — BRĂ kĭt vĭl
Bradford — BRĂD ferd
Bradshaw — BRĂD shaw
Brady — BRĂ dĭ
Brandon — BRĂN d'n
Brashear — bruh SHĬR
Brazoria — bruh ZŌ rĭ uh
Brazos — BRĂZ uhs
Breckenridge — BRĔK uhn rĭj
Bremond — bree MAHND
Brenham — BRĔ n'm
Brewster — BRŌŌ ster
Brice — brīs
Bridgeport — BRĬJ pōrt
Briggs — brĭgz
Briscoe — BRĬS kō
Britton — BRĬT n
Broaddus — BRAW d's
Brock — brahk
Bronson — BRAHN s'n
Bronte — brahnt
Brookeland — BRŎŎK l'nd
Brookesmith — BRŎŎK smith
Brooks — brŏŏks
Brookshire — BRŎŎK sher
Brookston — BRŎŎKS t'n
Brown — brown
Browndel — brown DĔL
Brownfield — BROWN feeld
Brownsboro — BROWNZ buh ruh
Brownsville — BROWNZ vĭl
Brownwood — BROWN wŏŏd
Bruceville — BRŌŎS v'l
Brundage — BRUHN dĭj
Bruni — BRŌŌ nĭ
Brushy Creek — bruh shĭ KREEK
Bryan — BRĪ uhn
Bryans Mill — brī 'nz MĬL
Bryarly — BRĪ er lĭ
Bryson — BRĪ s'n
Buchanan Dam — buhk hăn uhn
  DĂM
Buckholts — BUHK hōlts
Buckhorn — BUHK hawrn
Buda — BYŌŌ duh
Buena Vista — bwā nuh VEES tuh
Buffalo — BUHF uh lō
Buffalo Gap — buhf uh lō GĂP
Buffalo Springs — buhf uh lō
  SPRĬNGZ
Bula — BYŌŌ luh

Bullard — BŌŌL erd
Bulverde — bŏŏl VER dĭ
Buna — BYŌŌ nuh
Burkburnett — berk ber NET
Burkett — BER kĭt
Burkeville — BERK vĭl
Burleson — BER luh s'n
Burlington — BER lĭng t'n
Burnet — BER nĕt
Burton — BERT n
Bushland — BŌŌSH l'nd
Bustamante — buhs tuh MAHN tĭ
Butler — BUHT ler
Byers — BĪ erz
Bynum — BĪ n'm
Byrd — berd

## C

Cactus — KĂK t's
Caddo Mills — kă dō MĬLZ
Calallen — kăl ĂL ĭn
Calaveras — kăl uh VĔR's
Caldwell — KAHL wĕl
Calhoun — kăl HŌŌN
Call — kawl
Calliham — KĂL uh hăm
Callisburg — KĂ lĭs berg
Call Junction — kawl JUHNGK sh'n
Calvert — KĂL vert
Camden — KĂM dĭn
Cameron — KĂM uh r'n
Camilla — kuh MEEL yuh
Camp — kămp
Campbell — KĂM uhl
Campbellton — KĂM uhl t'n
Camp Wood — kămp WŎŎD
Canadian — kuh NĀ dĭ uhn
Candelaria — kăn duh LĔ rĭ uh
Canton — KĂNT n
Canyon — KĂN y'n
Caplen — KĂP lĭn
Caps — kăps
Caradan — KĂR uh dăn
Carbon — KAHR b'n
Carey — KĂ rĭ
Carlisle — KAHR lĭl
Carlsbad — KAHR uhlz băd
Carlton — KAHR uhl t'n
Carmine — kahr MEEN
Carmona — kahr MŌ nuh
Caro — KAH rō
Carrizo Springs — kuh ree zuh
  SPRĬNGZ
Carrollton — KĂR 'l t'n
Carson — KAHR s'n
Carthage — KAHR thĭj
Cash — kăsh
Cason — KĂ s'n
Cass — käs
Castell — käs TĔL
Castro — KĂS trō
Castroville — KĂS tro vĭl
Catarina — kăt uh REE nuh
Cat Spring — kăt SPRĬNG
Caviness — KĂ vĭ nĕs

Diacritical markings are used as follows: bāle, băd, lĕt, rīse, rĭll, ōak, brŏŏd, fŏŏt. The stressed syllable is capitalized. Secondary stress is indicated by an underline as in Atascosa — ăt uhs KŌ suh. TEXAS ALMANAC ©.

*The town square in Jayton, Kent County. Photo by Robert Plocheck.*

Cayuga — kā YOŌ guh
Cedar Bayou — <u>see</u> der BĪ ō
Cedar Creek — <u>see</u> der KREEK
Cedar Hill — <u>see</u> der HĬL
Cedar Lake — <u>see</u> der LĀK
Cedar Lane — <u>see</u> der LĀN
Cedar Park — <u>see</u> der PAHRK
Cedar Valley — <u>see</u> der VA lĭ
Cee Vee — <u>see</u> VEE
Celeste — suh LĔST
Celina — suh LĪ nuh
Center — SENT er
Center City — sĕn ter SĬT ĭ
Center Point — sĕn ter POINT
Centerville — sĕn ter vĭl
Centralia — sĕn TRĀL yuh
Chalk — chawlk
Chalk Mountain — chawlk MOWNT n
Chambers — CHĀM berz
Chandler — CHĂND ler
Channelview — <u>chăn</u> uhl VYOŌ
Channing — CHĂN ĭng
Chapman Ranch — chăp m'n RĂNCH
Chappell Hill — chă p'l HĬL
Charco — CHAHR kō
Charleston — CHAHR uhls t'n
Charlie — CHAHR lĭ
Charlotte — SHAHR l't
Chatfield — CHĂT feeld
Cheapside — CHEEP sīd
Cheek — cheek
Cherokee — CHĔR uh <u>kee</u>
Chester — CHĔS ter
Chico — CHEE kō

Chicota — chĭ KŌ tuh
Childress — CHĬL drĕs
Chillicothe — <u>chĭl</u> ĭ KAH thĭ
Chilton — CHĬL t'n
China — CHĪ nuh
China Spring — chī nuh SPRĬNG
Chireno — sh' REE nō
Chisholm — CHĬZ uhm
Chita — CHEE tuh
Chocolate Bayou — <u>chah</u> kuh lĭt BĪ ō
Choice — chois
Chriesman — KRĬS m'n
Christine — krĭs TEEN
Christoval — krĭs TŌ v'l
Cibolo — SEE bō lō
Circle Back — SER k'l băk
Circleville — SER k'l vĭl
Cisco — SĬS kō
Cistern — SĬS tern
Clairemont — KLĀR mahnt
Clairette — klăr ĭ ĔT
Clarendon — KLĀR ĭn d'n
Clareville — KLĀR vĭl
Clarksville — KLAHRKS vĭl
Clarkwood — KLAHRK wŏŏd
Claude — klawd
Clawson — KLAW s'n
Clay — klā
Clayton — KLĀT n
Clear Lake — KLĬR läk
Clear Spring — klĭr SPRĬNG
Cleburne — KLEE bern
Clemville — KLĔM vĭl
Cleveland — KLEEV l'nd
Clifton — KLĬF t'n

Cline — klīn
Clint — klĭnt
Clodine — klaw DEEN
Clute — klōōt
Clyde — klīd
Coahoma — kuh HŌ muh
Cockrell Hill — kahk ruhl HĬL
Coke — kōk
Coldspring — KŌLD sprĭng
Coleman — KŌL m'n
Colfax — KAHL fäks
Collegeport — kah lĭj PŌRT
College Station — <u>kah</u> lĭj STĀ sh'n
Collin — KAH lĭn
Collingsworth — KAH lĭnz werth
Collinsville — KAH lĭnz vĭl
Colmesneil — KŌL m's neel
Colorado — <u>kahl</u> uh RAH dō
Colorado City — kah luh <u>rā</u> duh or kah luh <u>rah</u> duh SĬT ĭ
Columbus — kuh LUHM b's
Comal — KŌ măl
Comanche — kuh MĂN chĭ
Combes — kōmz
Comfort — KUHM fert
Commerce — KAH mers
Como — KŌ mō
Comstock — KAHM stahk
Concan — KAHN kăn
Concepcion — kuhn sep sĭ ŌN
Concho — KAHN chō
Concord — KAHN kawrd
Concrete — kahn KREET
Cone — kōn
Conlen — KAHN lĭn
Conroe — KAHN rō

Diacritical markings are used as follows: bāle, băd, lĕt, rīse, rĭll, ōak, brōōd, fŏŏt. The stressed syllable is capitalized. Secondary stress is indicated by an underline as in Atascosa — ăt uhs KŌ suh. TEXAS ALMANAC ©.

Converse — KAHN vers
Conway — KAHN wā
Cooke — kŏŏk
Cookville — KŎŎK vĭl
Coolidge — KŌŌ lĭj
Cooper — KŌŌ per
Copeville — KŌP v'l
Coppell — kahp pĕl  or  kuhp PĔL
Copperas Cove — kahp ruhs KŌV
Corbett — KAWR bĭt
Cordele — kawr DĔL
Corinth — KAH rĭnth
Corley — KAWR lĭ
Corpus Christi — <u>kawr</u> p's KRĬS tĭ
Corrigan — KAWR uh g'n
Corsicana — <u>kawr</u> sĭ KĂN uh
Coryell — kō rĭ ĔL
Cost — kawst
Cottle — KAH t'l
Cotton Center — <u>kaht</u> n SĔNT er
Cotton Gin — KAHT n jĭn
Cottonwood — KAHT n wŏŏd
Cotulla — kuh TŌŌ luh
Coupland — KŌP l'n
Courtney — KŌRT nĭ
Covington — KUHV ĭng t'n
Coy City — koi SĬT ĭ
Craft — krăft
Crafton — KRĂF t'n
Crandall — KRĂN d'l
Crane — krān
Cranfills Gap — krăn f'lz GĂP
Crawford — KRAW ferd
Creedmoor — KREED mŏr
Cresson — KRĔ s'n
Crisp — krĭsp
Crockett — KRAH kĭt
Crosby — KRAWZ bĭ
Crosbyton — KRAWZ bĭ t'n
Cross — kraws
Cross Cut — KRAWS kuht
Cross Plains — kraws PLĀNZ
Cross Roads — KRAWS rōdz
Crow — krō
Crowell — KRŌ uhl
Crowley — KROW li
Crystal City — krĭs t'l SĬT ĭ
Crystal Falls — krĭs t'l FAWLZ
Cuero — KWĔR o
Culberson — KUHL ber s'n
Cumby — KUHM bĭ
Cuney — KYŌŌ nĭ
Cunningham — KUHN ĭng hăm
Currie — KER rĭ
Cushing — KŌŌ shĭng
Cuthand — KUHT hănd
Cyclone — SĪ klōn
Cypress — SĪ prĕs

**D**

Dabney — DĂB nĭ
Dacosta — duh KAHS tuh
Dacus — DĂ k's
Daingerfield — DĂN jer feeld
Daisetta — dā ZĔT uh

Dalby Springs — dĂl bĭ SPRĬNGZ
Dale — dāl
Dalhart — DĂL hahrt
Dallam — DĂL uhm
Dallas — DĂ luhs
Damon — DĂ m'n
Danbury — DĂN bĕrĭ
Danciger — DĂN sĭ ger
Danevang — DĂN uh văng
Darrouzett — dăr uh ZĔT
Davilla — duh VĬL uh
Dawn — dawn
Dawson — DAW s'n
Dayton — DĀT n
Deadwood — DĔD wŏŏd
Deaf Smith — dĕf SMĬTH
Deanville — DEEN vĭl
DeBerry — duh BĔ rĭ
Decatur — <u>dee</u> KĀT er
Deer Park — dĭr PAHRK
De Kalb — dĭ KĂB
De Leon — da lee AHN
Del Rio — dĕl REE ō
Delta — DĔL tuh
Del Valle — dĕl VĂ lĭ
Delwin — DĔL wĭn
Denhawken — DĬN haw kĭn
Denison — DĔN uh s'n
Denning — DĔN ĭng
Dennis — DĔ nĭs
Denton — DĔNT n
Denver City — <u>dĕn</u> ver SĬT ĭ
Deport — DEE pōrt  or  dĭ PŌRT
Derby — DER bĭ
Desdemona — <u>dĕz</u> dĭ MŌ nuh
DeSoto — dĭ SŌ tuh
Detroit — dee TROIT
Devers — DĔ vers
Devine — duh VĬN
Dew — dyŏŏ
Deweyville — DYŌŌ ĭ vĭl
DeWitt — dĭ WĬT
Dewville — DYŌŌ vĭl
Dexter — DĔKS ter
D'Hanis — duh HĂ nĭs
Dialville — DĪ uhl vil
Diboll — DĪ bawl
Dickens — DĬK Ĭnz
Dickinson — DĬK ĭn s'n
Dike — dĭk
Dilley — DĬL i
Dilworth — DĬL <u>werth</u>
Dimebox — dĭm BAHKS
Dimmit — DĬM ĭt
Dinero — dĭ NĔ rō
Direct — duh RĔKT
Dixon — DĬK s'n
Dobbin — DAH bĭn
Dobrowolski — <u>dah</u> bruh WAHL skĭ
Dodd City — dahd SĬT ĭ
Dodge — DAH j
Dodson — DAHD s'n
Donie — DŌ nĭ
Donley — DAHN lĭ
Donna — dah nuh
Doole — DOO lĭ

Dorchester — dawr CHĔS ter
Doss — daws
Doucette — DŌŌ sĕt
Dougherty — DAHR tĭ
Douglass — DUHG l's
Douglassville — DUHG lĭs vĭl
Downing — DOWN ĭng
Downsville — DOWNZ vĭl
Dozier — DŌ zher
Draw — draw
Driftwood — DRĬFT wŏŏd
Dripping Springs — drĭp ĭng
  SPRĬNGZ
Driscoll — DRĬS k'l
Dryden — DRĪD n
Dublin — DUHB lĭn
Duffau — DUHF ō
Dumas — DŌŌ m's
Dumont — DYŌŌ mahnt
Dundee — DUHN dĭ
Dunlap — DUHN lăp
Dunlay — DUHN lĭ
Dunn — duhn
Durango — duh RĂNG gō
Duval — DŌŌ vawl

**E**

Eagle — EE g'l
Eagle Lake — <u>ee</u> g'l LĀK
Eagle Pass — <u>ee</u> g'l PĂS
Earth — erth
East Bernard — <u>eest</u> ber NAHRD
Easterly — EES ter lĭ
Eastland — EEST l'nd
Easton — EES t'n
Ector — ĔK ter
Edcouch — ĕd KOWCH
Eddy — E di
Eden — EED n
Edge — ĕj
Edgewood — ĔJ wŏŏd
Edinburg — ĔD n <u>berg</u>
Edmonson — ĔD m'n s'n
Edna — ED nuh
Edom — EE d'm
Edroy — ĔD roi
Edwards — ĔD werdz
Egan — EE g'n
Egypt — EE juhpt
Elbert — ĔL bert
El Campo — ĕl KĂM pō
Eldorado — <u>ĕl</u> duh RĂ duh
Electra — ĭ LĔK truh
Elgin — ĔL gĭn
Eliasville — <u>ee</u> LĪ uhs vĭl
El Indio — ĕl ĬN dĭ ō
Elkhart — ĔLK hahrt
Ellinger — ĔL ĭn jer
Elliott — ĔL ĭ 't
Ellis — ĔL uhs
Elmendorf — ĔLM 'n dawrf
Elm Mott — ĕl MAHT
Elmo — ĔL mō
Eloise — ĔL o eez
El Paso — ĕl PĂS ō

Elsa — ĔL suh
Elysian Fields — uh lee zh'n FEELDZ
Emhouse — ĔM hows
Emory — ĔM uh rĭ
Encinal — ĕn suh NAHL
Encino — ĕn SEE nō
Energy — ĔN er jĭ
Engle — ĔN g'l
English — ĬNG glĭsh
Enloe — ĔN lō
Ennis — ĔN ĭs
Enochs — EE nuhks
Eola — ee Ō luh
Era — EE ruh
Erath — EE räth
Esperanza — ĕs per RĂN zuh
Estelline — ĔS tuh leen
Etoile — ĭ TOIL
Etter — ĔT er
Eula — YŌŌ luh
Euless — YŌŌ lĭs
Eureka — yōō REE kuh
Eustace — YŌŌS t's
Evadale — EE vuh dāl
Evant — EE vănt
Evergreen — Ĕ ver green
Everman — Ĕ ver m'n

**F**

Fabens — FĀ b'nz
Fairbanks — FĂR bangks
Fairfield — FĂR feeld
Fairlie — FĂR lee
Fair Play — fär PLĀ
Fairview — FĂR vyōō
Fairy — FĀ rĭ
Falfurrias — făl FYŌŌ rĭ uhs
Falls — fawlz
Falls City — fawlz SĬT ĭ
Fannett — fă NĔT
Fannin — FĂN ĭn
Fargo — FAHR gō
Farmers Branch — fahr merz BRĂNCH
Farmersville — FAHRM erz vĭl
Farnsworth — FAHRNZ werth
Farrar — FĂR uh
Farrsville — FAHRZ vĭl
Farwell — FAHR w'l
Fashing — FĂ shĭng
Fate — fāt
Fayette — fă ĔT
Fayetteville — FĀ uht vĭl
Fentress — FĔN trĭs
Ferris — FĔR ĭs
Field Creek — feeld KREEK
Fieldton — FEEL t'n
Fife — fīf
Fischer — FĬ sher
Fisher — FĬSH er
Fisk — fĭsk
Flagg — flăg
Flat — flăt
Flatonia — flă TŌN yuh

Flint — flĭnt
Flomot — FLŌ maht
Florence — FLAH ruhns
Floresville — FLŌRZ vil
Florey — FLŌ ri
Floyd — floid
Floydada — floi DĀ duh
Fluvanna — flōō VĂN uh
Flynn — flĭn
Foard — förd
Foard City — förd SĬT ĭ
Fodice — FŌ dĭs
Follett — fah LĔT
Fordtran — förd TRĂN
Forest — FAW rĕst
Forestburg — FAW rĕst berg
Forney — FAWR nĭ
Forreston — FAW rĕs t'n
Forsan — FŌR săn
Fort Bend — fört BĔND
Fort Chadbourne — fört CHĂD bern
Fort Davis — fört DĀ vĭs
Fort Griffin — fört GRĬF ĭn
Fort Hancock — fört HĂN kahk
Fort McKavett — fört muh KĀ vĕt
Fort Stockton — fört STAHK t'n
Fort Worth — fört WERTH
Fowlerton — FOW ler t'n
Francitas — frän SEE t's
Franklin — FRĂNGK lĭn
Frankston — FRĂNGS t'n
Fred — frĕd
Fredericksburg — FRĔD er rĭks berg
Fredonia — free DŌN yuh
Freeport — FREE pört
Freer — FREE er
Freestone — FREE stōn
Frelsburg — FRĔLZ berg
Fresno — FRĔZ nō
Friday — FRĪ dĭ
Friendswood — FRĔNZ wŏŏd
Frio — FREE ō
Friona — free Ō nuh
Frisco — FRĬS kō
Fritch — frĭch
Frost — frawst
Fruitland — FRŌŌT länd
Fruitvale — FRŌŌT väl
Frydek — FRĪ dĕk
Fulbright — FŎŎL brīt
Fulshear — FUHL sher
Fulton — FŎŎL t'n

**G**

Gail — gāl
Gaines — gānz
Gainesville — GĀNZ vuhl
Galena Park — guh lee nuh PAHRK
Gallatin — GĂL uh t'n
Galveston — GĂL vĕs t'n
Ganado — guh NĀ dō
Garceno — gahr SĀ nō
Garciasville — gahr SEE uhs vĭl
Garden City — GAHRD n sĭt ĭ

Gardendale — GAHRD n dāl
Garden Valley — gahrd n VĂ lĭ
Garland — GAHR l'nd
Garner — GAHR ner
Garrett — GĂR ĭt
Garrison — GĂ rĭ s'n
Garwood — GAHR wŏŏd
Gary — GĔ rĭ
Garza — GAHR zuh
Gatesville — GĀTS vil
Gause — gawz
Gay Hill — gā HĬL
Geneva — juh NEE vuh
Georgetown — JAWRJ town
George West — jawrj WĔST
Geronimo — juh RAH nĭ mō
Giddings — GĬD ĭngz
Gillespie — guh LĔS pĭ
Gillett — juh LĔT
Gilliland — GĬL ĭ l'nd
Gilmer — GĬL mer
Ginger — JĬN jer
Girard — juh RAHRD
Girvin — GER vĭn
Gladewater — GLĂD wah ter
Glasscock — GLĂS kahk
Glazier — GLĀ zher
Glen Cove — glĕn KŌV
Glendale — GLĔN dāl
Glenfawn — glĕn FAWN
Glen Flora — glĕn FLŌ ruh
Glenn — glĕn
Glen Rose — GLĔN rōz
Glidden — GLĬD n
Gober — GŌ ber
Godley — GAHD lĭ
Golden — GŌL d'n
Goldfinch — GŌLD fĭnch
Goldsboro — GŌLZ buh ruh
Goldsmith — GŌL smith
Goldthwaite — GŌLTH wāt
Goliad — GŌ lĭ ăd
Golinda — gō LĬN duh
Gonzales — guhn ZAH l's
Goodland — GŎŎD l'n
Goodlett — GŎŎD lĕt
Goodnight — GŎŎD nīt
Goodrich — GŎŎD rĭch
Gordon — GAWRD n
Gordonville — GAWRD n vĭl
Goree — GŌ ree
Gorman — GAWR m'n
Gouldbusk — GŌŌLD buhsk
Graford — GRĀ ferd
Graham — GRĀ 'm
Granbury — GRĂN bĕ rĭ
Grandfalls — gränd FAWLZ
Grand Saline — grän suh LEEN
Grandview — GRĂN vyōō
Granger — GRĂN jer
Grapeland — GRĀP l'nd
Grapevine — GRĀP vīn
Grassland — GRĂS l'nd
Grassyville — GRĀ sĭ vĭl
Gray — grā
Grayburg — GRĀ berg

*The shop at a lavender farm in Kendall County. Photo by Robert Plocheck.*

Grayson — GRA s'n
Green — green
Greenville — GREEN v'l
Greenwood — GREEN wŏŏd
Gregg — grĕg
Gregory — GRĔG uh rĭ
Grimes — grīmz
Groesbeck — GRŌZ bĕk
Groom — grŏŏm
Groveton — GRŌV t'n
Grow — grō
Gruene — green
Grulla — GRŌŌL yuh
Gruver — GRŌŌ ver
Guadalupe — gwah duh LŌŌ pĭ  or
  gwah duh LŌŌ pā
Guerra — GWĔ ruh
Gunter — GUHN ter
Gustine — GUHS teen
Guthrie — GUHTH rĭ
Guy — gī

### H

Hackberry — HĂK bĕ rĭ
Hagansport — HĂ gĭnz pōrt
Hainesville — HĂNZ v'l
Hale — hāl
Hale Center — hāl SĔNT er
Hall — hawl
Hallettsville — HĂL ĕts vĭl
Hallsville — HAWLZ vĭl
Hamilton — HĂM uhl t'n
Hamlin — HĂM lĭn
Hammond — HĂM 'nd

Hamon — HĂ m'n
Hamshire — HĂM sher
Handley — HĂND lĭ
Hankamer — HĂN kăm er
Hansford — HĂNZ ferd
Happy — HĂ pĭ
Hardeman — HAHR duh m'n
Hardin — HAHRD n
Hare — hăr
Hargill — HAHR gĭl
Harleton — HAHR uhl t'n
Harlingen — HAHR lĭn juhn
Harper — HAHR per
Harris — HĂ rĭs
Harrison — HĂ rĭ s'n
Harrold — HĂR 'ld
Hart — hahrt
Hartburg — HAHRT berg
Hartley — HAHRT lĭ
Harwood — HAHR wŏŏd
Haskell — HĂS k'l
Haslam — HĂZ l'm
Haslet — HĂS lĕt
Hasse — HĂ sĭ
Hatchell — HĂ ch'l
Hawkins — HAW kĭnz
Hawley — HAW lĭ
Hays — hăz
Hearne — hern
Heath — heeth
Hebbronville — HĔB r'n vĭl
Hebron — HEE br'n
Hedley — HĔD lĭ
Heidenheimer — HĪD n hīmer
Helena — HĔL uh nuh

Helotes — hĕl Ō tĭs
Hemphill — HĔMP hĭl
Hempstead — HĔM stĕd
Henderson — HĔN der s'n
Henly — HĔN lĭ
Henrietta — hĕn rĭ Ĕ tuh
Hereford — HER ferd
Hermleigh — HER muh lee
Hewitt — HYŌŌ ĭt
Hicks — hĭks
Hico — HĪ kō
Hidalgo — hĭ DĂL gō
Higgins — HĪ gĭnz
High — hī
Highbank — HĪ băngk
High Island — hī Ī l'nd
Highlands — HĪ l'ndz
Hightower — HĪ tow er
Hill — hĭl
Hillister — HĬL ĭs ter
Hillsboro — HĬLZ buh ruh
Hindes — hĭndz
Hiram — HĪ r'm
Hitchcock — HĬCH kahk
Hitchland — HĬCH l'nd
Hobson — HAHB s'n
Hochheim — HŌ hĭm
Hockley — HAHK lĭ
Holland — HAHL 'nd
Holliday — HAH luh dā
Hondo — HAHN dō
Honey Grove — HUHN ĭ grŏv
Honey Island — huhn ĭ Ī l'nd
Honey Springs — huhn ĭ SPRĬNGZ
Hood — hŏŏd

---

Hooks — hŏŏks
Hopkins — HAHP kĭnz
Houston — HYŌŌS t'n or YŌŌS t'n
Howard — HOW erd
Howe — how
Howland — HOW l'nd
Hubbard — HUH berd
Huckabay — HUHK uh bĭ
Hudspeth — HUHD sp'th
Huffman — HUHF m'n
Hufsmith — HUHF smĭth
Hughes Springs — hyōōz SPRĬNGZ
Hull — huhl
Humble — UHM b'l
Hungerford — HUHNG ger ferd
Hunt — huhnt
Hunter — HUHNT er
Huntington — HUHNT ĭng t'n
Huntsville — HUHNTS v'l
Hurlwood — HERL wŏŏd
Hutchins — HUH chĭnz
Hutchinson — HUH chĭn s'n
Hutto — HUH tō
Hye — hī
Hylton — HĬL t'n

**I**

Iago — ī Ā gō
Idalou — Ĭ duh lōō
Imperial — ĭm PĬR ĭ uhl
Inadale — Ĭ nuh dāl
Independence — ĭn duh PĔN d'ns
Indian Creek — ĭn dĭ uhn KREEK
Indian Gap — ĭn dĭ uhn GĂP
Industry — ĬN duhs trī
Inez — ī NĔZ
Ingleside — ĬNG g'l sīd
Ingram — ĬNG gr'm
Iola — ī Ō luh
Iowa Park — ī uh wuh PAHRK
Ira — Ī ruh
Iraan — ī ruh ĂN
Iredell — Ī ruh děl
Ireland — Ī rī l'nd
Irene — ī REEN
Irion — ĬR i uhn
Ironton — ĪRN t'n
Irving — ER vĭng
Italy — ĬT uh lĭ
Itasca — ī TĂS kuh
Ivan — Ī v'n
Ivanhoe — Ī v'n hō

**J**

Jack — jăk
Jacksboro — JĂKS buh ruh
Jackson — JĂK s'n
Jacksonville — JĂK s'n vĭl
Jamestown — JĂMZ town
Jardin — JAHRD n
Jarrell — JĂR uhl
Jasper — JĂS per
Jayton — JĀT n
Jean — jeen

Jeddo — JĔ dō
Jeff Davis — <u>jĕf</u> DA vĭs
Jefferson — JĔF er s'n
Jericho — JĔ rĭ kō
Jermyn — JER m'n
Jewett — JŌŌ ĭt
Jiba — HEE buh
Jim Hogg — jĭm HAWG
Jim Wells — jĭm WĔLZ
Joaquin — waw KEEN
Johnson — JAHN s'n
Johnson City — <u>jahn</u> s'n SĬT ĭ
Johntown — JAHN town
Johnsville — JAHNZ vĭl
Joinerville — JOI ner vĭl
Jolly — JAH lĭ
Jollyville — JAH lĭ vĭl
Jonah — JŌ nuh
Jones — jōnz
Jonesboro — JŌNZ <u>buh</u> ruh
Jonesville — JŌNZ vĭl
Josephine — JŌ suh <u>feen</u>
Joshua — JAH sh' wa
Jourdanton — JERD n t'n
Joy — joi
Joyce — jawĭs
Juliff — JŌŌ lĭf
Junction — JUHNGK sh'n
Juno — JŌŌ nō
Justiceburg — JUHS tĭs berg
Justin — JUHS tĭn

**K**

Kalgary — KĂL gĕ rĭ
Kamay — KĀ ĭm ā
Kanawha — KAHN uh wah
Karnack — KAHR năk
Karnes — kahrnz
Karnes City — kahrnz SĬT ĭ
Katemcy — kuh TĔM sĭ
Katy — KĀ tĭ
Kaufman — KAWF m'n
Keechi — KEE chī
Keene — keen
Kellerville — KĔL er vĭl
Kemah — KEE muh
Kemp — kĕmp or kĭmp
Kemp City — kĕmp SĬT ĭ
Kempner — KĔMP ner
Kendalia — kĔn DĀL yuh
Kenedy — KĔN uh dĭ
Kennard — kuh NAHRD
Kennedale — KĔN uh dāl
Kent — kĕnt
Kerens — KER 'nz
Kermit — KER mĭt
Kerr — ker
Kerrville — KER vĭl
Kildare — KĬL dăr
Kilgore — KĬL gōr
Killeen — kuh LEEN
Kimble — KĬM b'l
King — kĭng
Kingsbury — KĬNGZ bĕ rĭ

Kingsland — KĬNGZ l'nd
Kingsmill — kĭngz MĬL
Kingston — KĬNGZ t'n
Kingsville — KĬNGZ vĭl
Kinney — KĬN ĭ
Kirby — KER bĭ
Kirbyville — KER bĭ vĭl
Kirkland — KERK l'nd
Kirvin — KER vĭn
Kleberg — KLĀ berg
Klondike — KLAHN dīk
Knickerbocker — NĬK uh <u>bah</u> ker
Knippa — kuh NĬP uh
Knott — naht
Knox — nahks
Knox City — nahks SĬT ĭ
Kosciusko — kuh SHŌŌS kō
Kosse — KAH sĭ
Kountze — kōōntz
Kress — kres
Krum — kruhm
Kurten — KER t'n
Kyle — kīl

**L**

La Blanca — lah BLAHN kuh
La Coste — luh KAWST
Ladonia — luh DŌN yuh
LaFayette — lah fĭ ĔT
Laferia — luh FĔ rĭ uh
Lagarto — luh GAHR tō
La Gloria — lah GLŌ rĭ uh
La Grange — luh GRĀNJ
Laguna — luh GŌŌ nuh
Laird Hill — lărd HĬL
La Joya — luh HŌ yuh
Lake Creek — lăk KREEK
Lake Dallas — <u>lăk</u> DĂL uhs
Lake Jackson — lăk JĂK s'n
Laketon — LĂK t'n
Lake Victor — lăk VĬK ter
Lakeview — LĂK vyōō
Lamar — luh MAHR
La Marque — luh MAHRK
Lamasco — luh MĂS kō
Lamb — lăm
Lamesa — luh MEE suh
Lamkin — LĂM kĭn
Lampasas — lăm PĂ s's
Lancaster — LĂNG k's ter
Laneville — LĂN s'n vĭl
Langtry — LĂNG trĭ
Lanier — luh NĬR
La Paloma — <u>lah</u> puh LŌ muh
La Porte — luh PŌRT
La Pryor — luh PRĪ er
Laredo — luh RĀ dō
Lariat — LĂ ri uht
Larue — luh RŌŌ
La Salle — luh SĂL
Lasara — luh SĔ ruh
Lassater — LĂ sĭ ter
Latch — lĂch
Latexo — luh TĔKS ō

---

Diacritical markings are used as follows: bāle, băd, lĕt, rīse, rĭll, ōak, brŏŏd, fŏŏt. The stressed syllable is capitalized. Secondary stress is indicated by an underline as in Atascosa — <u>ăt</u> uhs KŌ suh. TEXAS ALMANAC ©.

Lavaca — luh VĂ kuh
La Vernia — luh VER nĭ uh
La Villa — lah VĬL uh
Lavon — luh VAHN
La Ward — luh WAWRD
Lawn — lawn
Lawrence — LAH r'ns
Lazbuddie — LĂZ buh dĭ
League City — <u>leeg</u> SĬT ĭ
Leakey — LĀ kĭ
Leander — lee ĂN der
Leary — LĬ er ĭ
Ledbetter — LĔD bĕt er
Lee — lee
Leesburg — LEEZ berg
Leesville — LEEZ vĭl
Lefors — lĭ FŌRZ
Leggett — LĔ gĭt
Leigh — lee
Lela — LEE luh
Lelia Lake — <u>leel</u> yuh LĀK
Leming — LĔ mĭng
Lenorah — lĕ NŌ ruh
Leo — LEE ō
Leon — lee AHN
Leona — <u>lee</u> Ō nuh
Leonard — LĔN erd
Leon Springs — lee ahn SPRĬNGZ
Leroy — LEE roi
Levelland — LĔ v'l lănd
Levita — luh VĬ tuh
Lewisville — LOO ĭs vĭl
Lexington — LĔKS ĭng t'n
Liberty — LĬB er tĭ
Liberty Hill — <u>lĬ</u> ber tĭ HĬL
Lillian — LĬL yuhn
Limestone — LĬM stōn
Lincoln — LĬNG k'n
Lindale — LĬN dāl
Linden — LĬN d'n
Lindenau — lĭn duh NOW
Lindsay — LĬN zĭ
Lingleville — LĬNG g'l vĭl
Linn — lĭn
Lipan — lĭ PĂN
Lipscomb — LĬPS k'm
Lissie — LĬ sĭ
Little Elm — <u>lĭt</u> l ĔLM
Littlefield — LĬT uhl feeld
Little River — <u>lĭt</u> uhl RĬV er
Live Oak — LĬV ōk
Liverpool — LĬ ver pōōl
Livingston — LĬV ĭngz t'n
Llano — LĂ nō
Locker — LAH ker
Lockett — LAH kĭt
Lockhart — LAHK hahrt
Lockney — LAHK nĭ
Lodi — LŌ dĭ
Lohn — lahn
Lolita — lō LEE tuh
Loma Alto — <u>lō</u> muh ĂL tō
Lometa — lō MEE tuh
London — LUHN d'n
Lone Grove — lōn GRŌV
Lone Oak — LŌN ōk

Long Branch — lawng BRĂNCH
Long Mott — lawng MAHT
Longview — LAWNG vyōō
Longworth — LAWNG werth
Loop — lōōp
Lopeno — lō PEE nō
Loraine — lō RĀN
Lorena — lō REE nuh
Los Angeles — laws AN juh l's
Los Ebanos — lōs ĔB uh nōs
Los Fresnos — lōs FRĔZ nōs
Los Indios — lōs ĬN dĭ ōs
Losoya — luh SAW yuh
Lott — laht
Louise — LŌŌ eez
Lovelady — LUHV lā dĭ
Loving — LUH vĭng
Lubbock — LUH buhk   or   LUH b'k
Lueders — LŌŌ derz
Luella — lōō ĔL uh
Lufkin — LUHF kĭn
Luling — LŌŌ lĭng
Lund — luhnd
Lutie — LŌŌ tĭ
Lyford — LĬ ferd
Lynn — lĭn
Lyons — LĬ 'nz
Lytton Springs — lĬt n SPRĬNGZ

# M

Mabank — MĀ băngk
Macune — muh KŌŌN
Madison — MĂ dĭ s'n
Madisonville — MĂ duh s'n vĭl
Magnolia — măg NŌL yuh
Magnolia Springs — măg nol yuh
   SPRINGZ
Malakoff — MĂL uh kawf
Malone — muh LŌN
Malta — MAWL tuh
Manchaca — MĂN shăk
Manchester — MĂN chĕs ter
Manheim — MĂN hīm
Mankins — MĂN kĭnz
Manor — MĂ ner
Mansfield — MĂNZ feeld
Manvel — MĂN v'l
Maple — MĂ puhl
Marathon — MĂR uh th'n
Marble Falls — mahr b'l FAWLZ
Marfa — MAHR fuh
Margaret — MAHR guh rĭt
Marietta — mĕ rĭ Ĕ tuh
Marion — MĔ rĭ uhn
Markham — MAHR k'm
Marlin — MAHR lĭn
Marquez — mahr KĀ
Marshall — MAHR sh'l
Mart — mahrt
Martin — MAHRT n
Martindale — MAHRT n dāl
Martinsville — MAHRT nz vĭl
Maryneal — mā rĭ NEEL
Marysville — MĂ rĭz vĭl
Mason — MĂ s'n

Matador — MĂT uh dōr
Matagorda — măt uh GAWR duh
Mathis — MĂ thĭs
Maud — mawd
Mauriceville — maw REES vĭl
Maverick — MĂV rĭk
Maxey — MĂKS ĭ
Maxwell — MĂKS w'l
May — mā
Maydell — MĀ dĕl
Maypearl — <u>mā</u> PERL
Maysfield — MĀZ feeld
McAdoo — MĂK uh dōō
McAllen — măk ĂL ĭn
McCamey — muh KĀ mĭ
McCaulley — muh KAW lĭ
McCoy — muh KOI
McCulloch — muh KUH luhk
McFaddin — măk FĂD n
McGregor — muh GRĔ ger
McKinney — muh KĬN ĭ
McLean — muh KLĀN
McLennan — muhk LĔN uhn
McLeod — măk LOWD
McMahan — măk MĂN
McMullen — măk MUHL ĭn
McNary — măk NĂ rĭ
McNeil — măk NEEL
McQueeney — muh KWEE nĭ
Meadow — MĔ dō
Medicine Mound — <u>mĕd</u> uhs n
   MOWND
Medill — mĕ DĬL
Medina — muh DEE nuh
Megargel — muh GAHR g'l
Melissa — muh LĬS uh
Melrose — MĔL rōz
Melvin — MĔL vĭn
Memphis — MĔM fĭs
Menard — muh NAHRD
Mendoza — mĕn DŌ zuh
Mentone — mĕn TŌN
Mercedes — <u>mer</u> SĀ deez
Mercury — MER kyuh ri
Mereta — muh RĔT uh
Meridian — muh RĬ dĭ uhn
Merit — MĔR ĭt
Merkel — MER k'l
Mertens — <u>mer</u> TĔNZ
Mertzon — MERTS n
Mesquite — muhs KEET
Mexia — muh HĀ uh
Meyersville — MĪRZ vĭl
Miami — mĭ ĂM uh or mĭ ĂM ĭ
Mico — MEE kō
Middleton — MĬD uhl t'n
Midfields — MĬD feeldz
Midland — MĬD l'nd
Midlothian — <u>mĭd</u> LŌ thĭ n
Midway — MĬD wā
Milam — MĪ l'm
Milano — mĭ LĂ nō
Mildred — MĬL drĕd
Miles — mīlz
Milford — MĬL ferd
Miller Grove — mĭl er GRŌV

Diacritical markings are used as follows: bāle, băd, lĕt, rīse, rĬll, ōak, brōōd, fŏŏt. The stressed syllable is capitalized. Secondary stress
is indicated by an underline as in Atascosa — <u>ăt</u> uhs KŌ suh. TEXAS ALMANAC ©.

Millersview — MĬL erz vyōō
Millett — MĬL ĭt
Millheim — MĬL hīm
Millican — MĬL uh kuhn
Mills — mĭlz
Millsap — MĬL săp
Minden — MĬN d'n
Mineola — mĭn ĭ Ō luh
Mineral — MĬN er uhl
Mineral Wells — mĭn er uhl WĔLZ
Minerva — mĭ NER vuh
Mingus — MĬNG guhs
Minter — MĬNT er
Mirando City — mĭ răn duh SĬT ĭ
Mission — MĬSH uhn
Mission Valley — mĭsh uhn VĂ lĭ
Missouri City — muh zōōr uh SĬT ĭ
Mitchell — MĬ ch'l
Mobeetie — mō BEE tĭ
Moline — mō LEEN
Monahans — MAH nuh hănz
Monaville — MŌ nuh vĭl
Monkstown — MUHNGKS town
Monroe — MAHN rō
Monroe City — mahn rō SĬT ĭ
Montague — mahn TĀG
Montalba — mahnt ĂL buh
Mont Belvieu — mahnt BĔL vyōō
Montell — mahn TĔL
Montgomery — mahnt GUHM er ĭ
Monthalia — mahn THĀL yuh
Moody — MŌŌ dĭ
Moore — mōr
Morales — muh RAH lĕs
Moran — mō RĂN
Morgan — MAWR g'n
Morgan Mill — mawr g'n MĬL
Morse — mawrs
Morton — MAWRT n
Moscow — MAHS kow
Mosheim — MŌ shĭm
Moss Bluff — maws BLUHF
Motley — MAHT lĭ
Moulton — MŌL t'n
Mound — mownd
Mountain Home — mownt n HŌM
Mount Calm — mownt KAHM
Mount Enterprise — mownt ĔN ter prīz
Mount Pleasant — mownt PLĔ z'nt
Mount Selman — mownt SĔL m'n
Mount Sylvan — mownt SĬL v'n
Mount Vernon — mownt VER n'n
Muenster — MYŌŌNS ter
Muldoon — muhl DŌŌN
Muleshoe — MYŌŌL shōō
Mullin — MUHL ĭn
Mumford — MUHM ferd
Munday — MUHN dĭ
Murchison — MER kuh s'n
Murphy — MER fĭ
Mykawa—mĭ KAH wuh
Myra — MĪ ruh
Myrtle Springs — mert l SPRĬNGZ

## N

Nacogdoches — năk uh DŌ chĭs
Nada — NĀ duh
Naples — NĀ p'lz
Nash — năsh
Natalia — nuh TĂL yuh
Navarro — nuh VĂ rō
Navasota — năv uh SŌ tuh
Nazareth — NĂZ uh r'th
Neches — NĀ chĭs
Nederland — NEE der l'nd
Needville — NEED vĭl
Nelsonville — NĔL s'n vĭl
Neuville — NYŌŌ v'l
Nevada — nuh VĂ duh
Newark — NŌŌ erk
New Baden — nyōō BĀD n
New Berlin — nyōō BER lin
New Boston — nyōō BAWS t'n
New Braunfels — nyōō BRAHN f'ls
   or  BROWN fĕlz
Newby — NYŌŌ bĭ
New Caney — nyōō KĀ nĭ
Newcastle — NYŌŌ kăs uhl
New Gulf — nyōō GUHLF
New Home — NYŌŌ hōm
New Hope — nyōō HŌP
Newlin — NYŌŌ lĭn
New London — nyōō LUHN d'n
Newman — NYŌŌ m'n
Newport — NYŌŌ pōrt
New Salem — nyōō SĀ l'm
Newsome — NYŌŌ s'm
New Summerfield — nyōō SUHM er feeld
Newton — NYŌŌT n
New Ulm — nyōō UHLM
New Waverly — nyōō WĀ ver lĭ
New Willard — nyōō WĬL erd
Nimrod — NĬM rahd
Nineveh — NĬN uh vuh
Nixon — NĬKS uhn
Nocona — nō KŌ nuh
Nolan — NŌ l'n
Nolanville — NŌ l'n vĭl
Nome — nōm
Noonday — NŌŌN dā
Nopal — NŌ păl
Nordheim — NAWRD hīm
Normandy — NAWR m'n dĭ
Normangee — NAWR m'n jee
Normanna — nawr MĂN uh
Northrup — NAWR thr'p
North Zulch — nawrth ZŌŌLCH
Norton — NAWRT n
Novice — NAH vĭs
Nueces — nyōō Ā sĭs
Nugent — NYŌŌ j'nt
Nursery — NER suh rĭ

## O

Oakalla — ō KĂL uh
Oak Grove — ŏk GRŌV
Oak Hill — ŏk HĬL

Oakhurst — ŌK herst
Oakland — ŌK l'nd
Oakville — ŌK vĭl
Oakwood — ŌK wŏŏd
O'Brien — ō BRĪ uhn
Ochiltree — AH k'l tree
Odell — Ō dĕl or ō DĚL
Odem — Ō d'm
Odessa — ō DĔS uh
O'Donnell — ō DAH n'l
Oenaville — ō EEN uh v'l
Oglesby — Ō g'lz bĭ
Oilton — OIL t'n
Oklaunion — ōk luh YŌŌN y'n
Olden — ŌL d'n
Oldenburg — ŌL dĭn berg
Oldham — ŌL d'm
Old Glory — ōld GLŌ rĭ
Olivia — ō LĬV ĭ uh
Olmito — awl MEE tuh
Olmos Park — ahl m's PAHRK
Olney — AHL nĭ
Olton — ŌL t'n
Omaha — Ō muh haw
Omen — Ō mĭn
Onalaska — uhn uh LĂS kuh
Oplin — AHP lĭn
Orange — AHR ĭnj
Orangefield — AHR ĭnj feeld
Orange Grove — AHR ĭnj GRŌV
Orchard — AWR cherd
Ore City — ōr SĬT ĭ
Osceola — ō sĭ Ō luh
Otey — Ō tĭ
Otis Chalk — ō tĭs CHAWLK
Ottine — ah TEEN
Otto — AH tō
Ovalo — ō VĂL uh
Overton — Ō ver t'n
Owens — Ō ĭnz
Ozona — ō ZŌ nuh

## P

Paducah — puh DYŌŌ kuh
Paige — pāj
Paint Rock — pănt RAHK
Palacios — puh LĂ sh's
Palestine — PAL uhs teen
Palito Blanco — p' lee to BLAHNG kō
Palmer — PAH mer
Palo Pinto — pă lō PĬN tō
Paluxy — puh LUHK sĭ
Pampa — PĂM puh
Pandora — păn DŌR uh
Panhandle — PĂN hăn d'l
Panna Maria — păn uh muh REE uh
Papalote — pah puh LŌ tĭ
Paradise — PĂR uh dīs
Paris — PĂ rĭs
Parker — PAHR ker
Parmer — PAH mer
Parnell — pahr NĔL
Parsley Hill — pahrs lĭ HĬL

Pasadena — păs uh DEE nuh
Patricia — puh TRĬ shuh
Patroon — puh TROŌN
Pattison — PĂT uh s'n
Pattonville — PĂT n vĭl
Pawnee — paw NEE
Paxton — PĂKS t'n
Peacock — PEE kahk
Pearl — perl
Pearland — PĂR lănd
Pearsall — PEER sawl
Peaster — PEES ter
Pecan Gap — pĭ kahn GĂP
Pecos — PĀ k's
Penelope — puh NĔL uh pĭ
Penitas — puh NEE t's
Pennington — PĔN ĭng t'n
Penwell — PĬN wĕl
Peoria — pee Ō rĭ uh
Percilla — per SĬL uh
Perrin — PĔR ĭn
Perry — PĔ rĭ
Perryton — PĔ rĭ t'n
Peters — PEET erz
Petersburg — PEET erz berg
Petrolia — puh TRŌL yuh
Petteway — PĔT uh wā
Pettit — PĔT ĭt
Pettus — PĔT uhs
Petty — PĔT ĭ
Pflugerville — FLOŌ ger vĭl
Pharr — fahr
Phelps — fĕlps
Phillips — FĬL uhps
Pickton — PĬK t'n
Pidcoke — PĬD kŏk
Piedmont — PEED mahnt
Pierce — PĬ ers
Pilot Point — pī l't POINT
Pine Forest — pĭn FAW rĕst
Pine Hill — pĭn HĬL
Pinehurst — PĬN herst
Pineland — PĬN land
Pine Mills — pĭn MĬLZ
Pine Springs — pĭn SPRĬNGZ
Pioneer — pī uh NĬR
Pipecreek — pīp KREEK
Pittsburg — PĬTS berg
Placedo — PLĂS ĭ dō
Placid — PLĂ sĭd
Plains — plānz
Plainview — PLĀN vyoō
Plano — PLĀ nō
Plantersville — PLĂN terz vĭl
Plaska — PLĂS kuh
Plateau — plă TŌ
Pleasant Grove—plĕ z'nt GRŌV
Pleasanton — PLĔZ uhn t'n
Pledger — PLĔ jer
Plum — pluhm
Point — point
Pointblank — pint BLĂNGK
Polk — pōlk
Pollock — PAHL uhk
Ponder — PAHN der

Ponta — pahn TĀ
Pontotoc — PAHNT uh tahk
Poolville — POŌL vĭl
Port Aransas — pōrt uh RĂN zuhs
Port Arthur — pōrt AHR ther
Port Bolivar — pōrt BAH lĭ ver
Porter Springs — pōr ter SPRĬNGZ
Port Isabel — pōrt ĬZ uh bĕl
Portland — PŌRT l'nd
Port Lavaca — pōrt luh VĂ kuh
Port Neches — pōrt NĀ chĬs
Port O'Connor — pōrt ō KAH ner
Posey — PŌ zĭ
Post — pōst
Postoak — PŌST ōk
Poteet — pō TEET
Poth — pōth
Potosi — puh TŌ sĭ
Potter — PAHT er
Pottsboro — PAHTS buh ruh
Pottsville — PAHTS vĭl
Powderly — POW der lĭ
Powell — POW w'l
Poynor — POI ner
Prairie Dell — prĕr ĭ DĔL
Prairie Hill — prĕr ĭ HĬL
Prairie Lea — prĕr ĭ LEE
Prairie View — prĕr ĭ VYOŌ
Prairieville — PRĔR ĭ vĭl
Premont — PREE mahnt
Presidio — pruh SĬ dĭ ō
Priddy — PRĬ dĭ
Primera — pree MĔ ruh
Princeton — PRĬNS t'n
Pritchett — PRĬ chĭt
Proctor — PRAHK ter
Progreso — prō GRĔ sō
Prosper — PRAHS per
Purdon — PERD n
Purley — PER lĭ
Purmela — per MEE luh
Putnam — PUHT n'm
Pyote — PĬ ōt

## Q

Quail — kwāl
Quanah — KWAH nuh
Queen City — kween SĬT ĭ
Quemado — kuh MAH dō
Quihi — KWEE hee
Quinlan — KWĬN l'n
Quintana — kwĭn TAH nuh
Quitaque — KĬT uh kwa
Quitman — KWĬT m'n

## R

Rainbow — RĂN bō
Rains — rānz
Ralls — rahlz
Randall — RĂN d'l
Randolph — RĂN dahlf
Ranger — RĂN jer
Rangerville — RĂN jer vĭl
Rankin — RĂNG kĭn

Ratcliff — RĂT klĭf
Ravenna — rĭ VĔN uh
Rayburn — RĀ bern
Raymondville — RĀ m'nd vĭl
Raywood — RĀ woōd
Reagan — RĀ g'n
Real — REE awl
Realitos — ree uh LEE t's
Redford — RĔD ferd
Red Oak — RĔD ōk
Red River — rĕd RĬ ver
Red Rock — rĕd RAHK
Red Springs — rĕd SPRĬNGZ
Red Water — RĔD wah ter
Reeves — reevz
Refugio — rĕ FYOŌ rĭ ō
Reilly Springs — rī lĭ SPRĬNGZ
Reklaw — RĔK law
Reno — REE nō
Rhineland — RĪN l'nd
Rhome — rōm
Rhonesboro — RŌNZ buh ruh
Ricardo — rĭ KAHR dō
Rice — rĭs
Richards — RĬCH erdz
Richardson — RĬCH erd s'n
Richland — RĬCH l'nd
Richland Springs — rĭch l'nd
    SPRĬNGZ
Richmond — RĬCH m'nd
Ridge — rĭj
Ridgeway — RĬJ wā
Riesel — REE s'l
Ringgold — RĬNG gōld
Rio Frio — ree ō FREE ō
Rio Grande City — ree ō grahn dĭ
    or ree ō grän SĬT ĭ
Rio Hondo — ree ō HAHN dō
Riomedina — ree ō muh DEE nuh
Rios — REE ōs
Rio Vista — ree ō VĬS tuh
Rising Star — rī zĭng STAHR
River Oaks — rĭ ver ŌKS
Riverside — RĬ ver sĭd
Riviera — ruh VĬR uh
Roane — rōn
Roanoke — RŌN ōk or RŌ uh
    nōk
Roans Prairie — rōnz PRĔR Ĭ
Roaring Springs — rōr ĭng
    SPRĬNGZ
Robert Lee — rah bert LEE
Roberts — RAH berts
Robertson — RAH bert s'n
Robinson — RAH bĭn s'n
Robstown — RAHBZ town
Roby — RŌ bĭ
Rochelle — rō SHĔL
Rochester — RAH chĕs ter
Rockdale — RAHK dāl
Rock Island — rahk Ī l'nd
Rockland — RAHK l'nd
Rockport — rahk PŌRT
Rocksprings — rahk SPRĬNGZ
Rockwall — rahk WAWL

---

Diacritical markings are used as follows: bāle, băd, lĕt, rīse, rĭll, ōak, broōd, foŏt. The stressed syllable is capitalized. Secondary stress is indicated by an underline as in Atascosa — ăt uhs KŌ suh. TEXAS ALMANAC ©.

*Some of the eclectic architecture of Marathon, Brewster County. Photo by Robert Plocheck.*

Rockwood — RAHK wŏŏd
Roganville — RŌ g'n vĭl
Rogers — RAH jerz
Roma — RŌ muh
Romayor — rō MĀ er
Roosevelt — RŌ suh v'lt or RŌŌ suh v'lt
Ropesville — RŌPS vĭl
Rosanky — rō ZĂNG kĭ
Roscoe — RAHS kō
Rosebud — RŌZ b'd
Rose Hill — rōz HĬL
Rosenberg — RŌZ n berg
Rosenthal — RŌZ uhn thawl
Rosewood — RŌZ wŏŏd
Rosharon — rō SHĔ r'n
Rosita — rō SEE tuh
Ross — raws
Rosser — RAW ser
Rosston — RAWS t'n
Rossville — RAWS vĭl
Roswell — RAHZ w'l
Rotan — rō TĂN
Round Rock — ROWND rahk
Round Top — ROWN tahp
Rowena — rō EE nuh
Rowlett — ROW lĭt
Roxton — RAHKS t'n
Royalty — ROI uhl tĭ
Royse City — roi SĪT ĭ
Royston — ROIS t'n
Rugby — RUHG bĭ
Ruidosa — ree uh DŌ suh
Rule — rŏŏl
Runge — RUHNG ĭ
Runnels — RUHN 'lz
Rural Shade — rŏŏr uhl SHĀD
Rusk — ruhsk
Rutersville — RŌŌ ter vĭl
Rye — rī

## S

Sabinal — SĂB uh năl
Sabine — suh BEEN

Sabine Pass — suh <u>been</u> PĂS
Sabinetown — suh <u>been</u> TOWN
Sachse — SĂK sĭ
Sacul — SĂ k'l
Sadler — SĂD ler
Sagerton — SĂ ger t'n
Saginaw — SĂ guh naw
Saint Jo — sănt JŌ
Saint Paul — sănt PAWL
Salado — suh LĂ dō
Salesville — SĂLZ vĭl
Salineno — suh LEEN yō
Salmon — SĂL m'n
Salt Gap — sawlt GĂP
Saltillo — săl TĬL ō
Samfordyce — săm FOR dis
Sample — SĂM p'l
Samnorwood — săm NAWR wŏŏd
San Angelo — <u>săn</u> ĂN juh lō
San Antonio — <u>săn</u> ăn TŌ nĭ ō
San Augustine — <u>săn</u> AW g's teen
San Benito — săn buh NEE tuh
Sanderson — SĂN der s'n
Sandia — săn DEE uh
San Diego — <u>săn</u> dĭ Ā gō
Sandy Point — săn dĭ POINT
San Elizario — săn ĕl ĭ ZAH rĭ ō
San Felipe — <u>săn</u> fuh LEEP
Sanford — SĂN ferd
San Gabriel — săn GĀ brĭ uhl
Sanger — SĂNG er
San Jacinto — <u>săn</u> juh SĬN tuh or juh SĬN tō
San Juan — săn WAHN
San Marcos — <u>săn</u> MAHR k's
San Patricio — <u>săn</u> puh TRĬSH ĭ ō
San Perlita — <u>săn</u> per LEE tuh
San Saba — <u>săn</u> SĂ buh
Santa Anna — <u>săn</u> tuh ĂN uh
Santa Elena — săn tuh LEE nuh
Santa Maria — <u>săn</u> tuh muh REE uh
Santa Rosa — <u>săn</u> tuh RŌ suh
Santo — SĂN tō

San Ygnacio — <u>săn</u> ĭg NAH sĭ ō
Saragosa — <u>sĕ</u> ruh GŌ suh
Saratoga — <u>sĕ</u> ruh TŌ guh
Sargent — SAHR juhnt
Sarita — suh REE tuh
Saspamco — suh SPĂM kō
Satin — SĂT n
Savoy — suh VOI
Schattel — SHĂT uhl
Schertz — sherts
Schleicher — SHLĪ ker
Schroeder — SHRĀ der
Schulenburg — SHŌŌ lĭn berg
Schwertner — SWERT ner
Scotland — SKAHT l'nd
Scottsville — SKAHTS vĭl
Scranton — SKRĂNT n
Scurry — SKUH rĭ
Scyene — sī EEN
Seabrook — SEE brŏŏk
Seadrift — SEE drĭft
Seagoville — SEE gō vĭl
Seagraves — SEE grăvz
Seale — seel
Sealy — SEE lĭ
Sebastopol — suh BĂS tuh pŏŏl
Sebastian — suh BĂS tĭ 'n
Security — sĭ KYŌŌR ĭ tĭ
Segno — SĔG nō
Segovia — sĭ GŌ vĭ uh
Seguin — sĭ GEEN
Selfs — sĕlfs
Selma — SĔL muh
Seminole — SĔM uh nōl
Seymour — SEE mōr
Shackelford — SHĂK uhl ferd
Shady Grove — shā dĭ GRŌV
Shafter — SHĂF ter
Shallowater — SHĂL uh wah ter
Shamrock — SHĂM rahk
Shannon — SHĂN uhn
Sharp — shahrp
Sheffield — SHĔ feeld
Shelby — SHĔL bĭ

---

Shelbyville — SHĔL bǐ vǐl
Sheldon — SHĔL d'n
Shepherd — SHĔ perd
Sheridan — SHĔ rǐ dn
Sherman — SHER m'n
Sherwood — SHER wood
Shiner — SHĪ ner
Shiro — SHĪ rō
Shive — shǐv
Sidney — SĬD nǐ
Sierra Blanca — sǐer ruh BLĂNG kuh
Siloam — suh LŌM
Silsbee — SĬLZ bǐ
Silver Lake — sǐl ver LĀK
Silverton — SĬL ver t'n
Silver Valley — sǐl ver VĂ lǐ
Simms — sǐmz
Simonton — SĪ m'n t'n
Singleton — SĬNG g'l t'n
Sinton — SĬNT n
Sipe Springs — SEEP sprǐngz
Sisterdale — SĬS ter dāl
Sivells Bend — sǐ v'lz BĔND
Skellytown — SKĔ lǐ town
Skidmore — SKĬD mōr
Slaton — SLĀT n
Slayden — SLĀD n
Slidell — slī DĔL
Slocum — SLŌ k'm
Smiley — SMĪ lǐ
Smith — smǐth
Smithfield — SMĬTH feeld
Smithland — SMĬTH l'nd
Smithson Valley — smǐth s'n VĂ lǐ
Smithville — SMĬTH vǐl
Smyer — SMĪ er
Snook — snōōk
Snyder — SNĪ der
Somerset — SUH mer sĕt
Somervell — SUH mer vĕl
Somerville — SUH mer vǐl
Sonora — suh NŌ ruh
Sour Lake — sowr LĀK
South Bend — sowth BĔND
South Bosque — sowth BAHS kǐ
South Houston — sowth HYŌŌS t'n
Southland — SOWTH l'nd
Southmayd — sowth MĀD
South Plains — sowth PLĀNZ
Spade — spād
Spanish Fort — spă nǐsh FŌRT
Sparenberg — SPĂR ǐn berg
Speaks — speeks
Spearman — SPĬR m'n
Spicewood — SPĪS wōōd
Splendora — splĕn DŌ ruh
Spofford — SPAH ferd
Spring — sprǐng
Springdale — SPRĬNG dāl
Springlake — sprǐng LĀK
Springtown — SPRĬNG town
Spur — sper
Spurger — SPER ger
Stacy — STĀ sǐ
Stafford — STĂ ferd

Stamford — STĂM ferd
Stanton — STĂNT n
Staples — STĀ p'lz
Starr — stahr
Stephens — STEE vĕnz
Stephenville — STEEV n vǐl
Sterley — STER lǐ
Sterling — STER lǐng
Sterling City — ster lǐng SĬT ǐ
Stiles — stīlz
Stinnett — stǐ NĔT
Stockdale — STAHK dāl
Stoneburg — STŌN berg
Stoneham — STŌN uhm
Stone Point — stōn POINT
Stonewall — STŌN wawl
Stout — stowt
Stowell — STO w'l
Stranger — STRĂN jer
Stratford — STRĂT ferd
Strawn — strawn
Streeter — STREET er
Streetman — STREET m'n
Study Butte — styōō dǐ BYŌŌT
Sublime — s'b LĬM
Sudan — SŌŌ dän
Sugar Land — SHŌŌ ger länd
Sullivan City — suh luh v'n SĬT ǐ
Sulphur Bluff — suhl fer BLUHF
Sulphur Springs — suhl fer SPRĬNGZ
Summerfield — SUHM er feeld
Sumner — SUHM ner
Sundown — SUHN down
Suniland — SUH nǐ länd
Sunny Side — SUH nǐ sīd
Sunray — SUHN rä
Sunset — SUHN sĕt
Sutherland Springs — suh ther l'nd SPRĬNGZ
Sutton — SUHT n
Swan — swahn
Sweeny — SWEE nǐ
Sweet Home — sweet HŌM
Sweetwater — SWEET wah ter
Swenson — SWĔN s'n
Swift — swǐft
Swisher — SWĬ sher
Sylvester — sǐl VES ter

# T

Taft — tăft
Tahoka — tuh HŌ kuh
Talco — TĂL kō
Talpa — TĂL puh
Tanglewood — TĂNG g`l wōōd
Tankersley — TĂNG kers lǐ
Tarrant — TAR uhnt
Tarzan — TAHR z'n
Tascosa — täs KŌ suh
Tatum — TĂ t'm
Tavener — TĂV uh ner
Taylor — TĂ ler
Teague — teeg
Tehuacana — tuh WAW kuh nuh

Telephone — TĔL uh fōn
Telferner — TĔLF ner
Tell — tĕl
Temple — TĔM p'l
Tenaha — TĔN uh haw
Tennyson — TĔN uh s'n
Terlingua — TER lǐng guh
Terrell — TĔR uhl
Terrell Hills — ter uhl HILZ
Terry — TĔR ǐ
Texarkana — tĕks ahr KĂN uh
Texas City — tĕks ĕz SĬT ǐ
Texhoma — tĕks Ō muh
Texline — TĔKS līn
Texon — tĕks AHN
Thalia — THĂL yuh
The Grove — th' GRŌV
Thicket — THĬ kǐt
Thomaston — TAHM uhs t'n
Thompsons — TAHMP s'nz
Thorndale — THAWRN dāl
Thornton — THAWRN t'n
Thorp Spring — thawrp SPRING
Thrall — thrawl
Three Rivers — three RĬ verz
Throckmorton — THRAHK mawrt n
Thurber — THER ber
Tilden — TĬL d'n
Timpson — TĬM s'n
Tioga — tǐ Ō guh
Titus — TĬT uhs
Tivoli — tǐ VŌ luh
Tokio — TŌ kǐ ō
Tolar — TŌ ler
Tolbert — TAHL bert
Tolosa — tuh LŌ suh
Tomball — TAHM bawl
Tom Bean — tahm BEEN
Tom Green — tahm GREEN
Tool — tōōl
Topsey — TAHP sǐ
Tornillo — tawr NEE yō
Tow — tow
Toyah — TOI yuh
Toyahvale — TOI yuh väl
Trawick — TRĂ wǐk
Travis — TRĂ vǐs
Trent — trĕnt
Trenton — TRĔNT n
Trickham — TRĬK uhm
Trinidad — TRĬN uh dăd
Trinity — TRĬN ǐ tǐ
Troup — trōōp
Troy — TRAW ǐ
Truby — TRŌŌ bǐ
Trumbull — TRUHM b'l
Truscott — TRUHS k't
Tucker — TUHK er
Tuleta — tōō LEE tuh
Tulia — TŌŌL yuh
Tulsita — tuhl SEE tuh
Tundra — TUHN druh
Tunis — TŌŌ nǐs
Turkey — TER kǐ
Turlington — TER lǐng t'n
Turnersville — TER nerz vǐl

---

Diacritical markings are used as follows: bāle, băd, lĕt, rīse, rǐll, ōak, brōōd, fōŏt. The stressed syllable is capitalized. Secondary stress is indicated by an underline as in Atascosa — ăt uhs KŌ suh. TEXAS ALMANAC ©.

Turnertown — TER ner town
Turney — TER nĭ
Tuscola — tuhs KŌ luh
Tuxedo — TUHKS ĭ dō
Twin Sisters — twĭn SĬS terz
Twitty — TWĬ tĭ
Tye — tī
Tyler — TĪ ler
Tynan — TĪ nuhn

## U

Uhland — YŌŌ l'nd
Umbarger — UHM bahr ger
Union — YŌŌN y'n
Upshur — UHP sher
Upton — UHP t'n
Urbana — er BĀ nuh
Utley — YŌŌT lĭ
Utopia — yōō TŌ pĭ uh
Uvalde — yōō VĂL dĭ

## V

Valdasta — văl DĂS tuh
Valentine — VĂL uhn tīn
Valera — vuh LĬ ruh
Valley Mills — vă lĭ MĬLZ
Valley Spring — vă lĭ SPRĬNG
Valley View — vă lĭ VYŌŌ
Van — văn
Van Alstyne — văn AWLZ teen
Vancourt — VĂN kŏrt
Vanderbilt — VĂN der bĭlt
Vanderpool — VĂN der pōōl
Van Horn — văn hawrn
Van Vleck — văn VLĔK
Van Zandt — văn ZĂNT
Vashti — VĂSH tī
Vaughan — vawn
Vega — VĀ guh
Velasco — vuh LĂS kō
Venus — VEE n's
Vera — VĬ ruh
Veribest — VĔR ĭ bĕst
Verhalen — ver HĂ lĭn
Vernon — VER n'n
Vickery — VĬK er ĭ
Victoria — vĭk TŌ rĭ uh
Vidor — VĬ der
Vienna — vee ĔN uh
View — vyōō
Village Mills — vĭl ĭj MĬLZ
Vincent — VĬN s'nt
Vinegarone — vĭn er guh RŌN
Vineyard — VĬN yerd
Violet — VĪ ō lĕt
Voca — VŌ kuh
Von Ormy — vahn AHR mĭ
Voss — vaws
Votaw — VŌ taw

## W

Waco — WĀ kō
Wadsworth — WAHDZ werth
Waelder — WĔL der

Waka — WAH kuh
Walberg — WAWL berg
Waldeck — WAWL dĕk
Walker — WAWL ker
Wall — wawl
Waller — WAW ler
Wallis — WAH lĭs
Wallisville — WAH lĭs vĭl
Walnut Springs — wawl n't SPRĬNGZ
Walton — WAWL t'n
Warda — WAWR duh
Ward — wawrd
Waring — WĂR ĭng
Warren — WAW rĭn
Warrenton — WAW rĭn t'n
Washburn — WAHSH bern
Washington — WAHSH ĭng t'n
Waskom — WAHS k'm
Wastella — wahs TĔL uh
Watauga — wuh TAW guh
Water Valley — wah ter VĂ lĭ
Waxahachie — wawks uh HĂ chĭ
Wayland — WĀ l'nd
Weatherford — WĔ ther ferd
Weaver — WEE ver
Webb — wĕb
Webberville — WĔ ber vĭl
Webster — WĔBS ter
Weches — WEE chĭz
Weesatche — WEE săch
Weimar — WĬ mer
Weinert — WĬ nert
Weir — weer
Welch — wĕlch
Welcome — WĔL k'm
Weldon — WĔL d'n
Wellborn — WĔL bern
Wellington — WĔL ĭng t'n
Wellman — WĔL m'n
Wells — wĕlz
Weser — WEE zer
Weslaco — WĔS luh kō
West — wĕst
Westbrook — WĔST brŏŏk
Westfield — WĔST feeld
Westhoff — WĔS tawf
Westminster — wĕst MĬN ster
Weston — WĔS t'n
Westover — WĔS tō ver
Westphalia — wĕst FĂL yuh
West Point — wĕst POINT
Wharton — HWAWRT n
Wheeler — HWEE ler
Wheelock — HWEE lahk
White Deer — HWĬT Deer
Whiteface — HWĬT făs
Whiteflat — hwĭt FLĂT
Whitehouse — HWĬT hows
Whitesboro — HWĬTS buh ruh
Whitewright — HWĬT rīt
Whitharral — HWĬT hăr uhl
Whitney — HWĬT nĭ
Whitsett — HWĬT sĭt
Whitson — HWĬT s'n
Whitt — hwĭt

Whon — hwahn
Wichita — WĬCH ĭ taw
Wichita Falls — wĭch ĭ taw FAWLZ
Wickett — WĬ kĭt
Wiergate — WEER gāt
Wilbarger — WĬL bahr ger
Wildorado — wĭl duh RĀ dō
Willacy — WĬL uh sĭ
Williamson — WĬL yuhm s'n
Willis — WĬ lĭs
Wills Point — wĭlz POINT
Wilmer — WĬL mer
Wilson — WĬL s'n
Wimberley — WĬM ber lĭ
Winchester — WĬN ches ter
Windom — WĬN d'm
Windthorst — WĬN thr'st
Winfield — WĬN feeld
Wingate — WĬN gāt
Wink — wĭngk
Winkler — WĬNGK ler
Winnie — WĬ nĭ
Winnsboro — WĬNZ buh ruh
Winona — wĭ NŌ nuh
Winterhaven — WĬN ter hă v'n
Winters — WĬN terz
Wise — wīz
Wizard Wells — wĭ zerd WĔLZ
Woden — WŌD n
Wolfe City — wŏŏlf SĬT ĭ
Wolfforth — WŎŎL forth
Wood — wŏŏd
Woodbine — WŎŎD bīn
Woodlake — wŏŏd LĀK
Woodland — WŎŎD l'nd
Woodlawn — wŏŏd LAWN
Woodrow — WŎŎD rō
Woodsboro — WŎŎDZ buh ruh
Woodson — WŎŎD s'n
Woodville — WŎŎD v'l
Wortham — WERTH uhm
Wright City — rīt SĬT ĭ
Wrightsboro — RĪTS buh ruh
Wylie — WĪ lĭ

## Y

Yancey — YĂN sĭ
Yantis — YĂN tĭs
Yoakum — YŌ k'm
Yorktown — YAWRK town
Young — yuhng
Youngsport — YUHNGZ pŏrt
Ysleta — ĭs LĔT uh

## Z

Zapata — zuh PAH tuh
Zavalla — zuh VĂL uh
Zephyr — ZĔF er
Zuehl — ZEE uhl

---

Diacritical markings are used as follows:  băle, băd, lĕt, rīse, rĭll, ōak, brōōd, fŏŏt. The stressed syllable is capitalized. Secondary stress is indicated by an underline as in Atascosa — ăt uhs KŌ suh. TEXAS ALMANAC ©.

# Obituaries: July 2013 – July 2015

**Adams, Bud, 90**; oilman who was one of the founders of the American Football League in 1960 and owner of the Houston Oilers, he moved the franchise to Tennessee in 1997; in Houston, Oct. 21, 2013.

**Albritton, Ford D. 93**; businessman, A&M Class of 1943, served as A&M regent 1968-75 and as president of former students, donated the landmark bell tower on campus in 1984; in Dallas, Jan. 26, 2014.

**Alger, Bruce, 96**; staunch conservative member of Congress for 10 years from Dallas, the lone Republican in the Texas delegation when elected in 1954, led a group of demonstrators that in 1960 accosted Lyndon Johnson and Lady Bird at a campaign appearance in Dallas; in Florida, April 13, 2015.

**Anderson, Carl, 83**: Taylor native, A&M professor of agricultural economics, considered one of state's leading cotton analysts, provided the Texas Almanac with agriculture analysis from 1978-2010; in College Station, Aug. 30, 2014.

**Arhos, Bill, 80**; founder of *Austin City Limits* in 1974, Teague native raised in Bryan, Rice University graduate, began working with Austin's public TV station in 1961; in Austin, April 11, 2015.

**Armstrong, Bob, 82**; former state land commissioner (1970-82), Austin Democrat served 8 years in the Legislature; lost primary in run for governor in 1982; in Austin, March 1, 2015.

**Banks, Ernie, 83**: Dallas native, attended Booker T. Washington High School where he played softball (there was no baseball team) and other sports, but during high school summers toured with semi-pro baseball Amarillo Colts; in Chicago, Jan. 23, 2014.

**Bass, Richard D., 85**; scion of Dallas oil family, adventurer and mountain climber, co-wrote in 1986 *Seven Summits* chronicling his being the first to climb highest peak of every continent, graduate of Highland Park High School; in Dallas, July 26, 2015.

**Beaty, Zelmo, 73**; Hillister native, attended school in Woodville, Prairie View A&M basketball star who left the NBA in 1970 to lead the Utah Stars to the ABA championship; in Bellevue, Wash., Aug. 27, 2013.

**Berman, Leo, 79**; Brooklyn native, son of Jewish immigrants from Europe, became city council member in Arlington and from 1999-2012 conservative GOP legislator from Tyler; in Tyler, May 23, 2015.

**Birdwell, Lloyd, 70**; Comfort native grew up in Dallas, St. Mark's grad, free-spirited artist founded Austin's annual Eeyore's Birthday Party in 1963; in Dallas, Jan. 9, 2014.

**Blanton, William W. "Bill," 90**; five-term legislator 1977-87, sponsored bills for free summer school and standardized graduation testing; in Carrollton, April 11, 2014.

**Brown, Charles, 83**: basketball player who was the first black athlete at Texas Western (UTEP) a decade before the *Glory Road* 1966 championship team; became school administrator in San Francisco; in California, May 11, 2014.

**Burns, Marilyn, 65**; actress best known as the heroine in *The Texas Chainsaw Massacre*, grew up in Houston, 1971 drama graduate of UT-Austin, film debut was in Robert Altman's *Brewster McCloud*; in Houston, Aug. 5, 2014.

**Carpenter, Scott, 88**; one of the original seven astronauts and the second to orbit the Earth, after his astronaut years he continued in administration at the NASA center in Houston until 1967; in Denver, Oct. 10, 2013.

**Carson, L.M. Kit, 73**; actor, writer, film director and producer, well-known in the independent film world, *David Holzman's Diary* was his first film in 1967, raised in Irving, co-founded in 1970 the USA Film Festival; in Dallas, Oct. 20, 2014.

**Cates, Jean, 77**; National Cowgirl Hall of Fame inductee who with her sister became the first two women to win the Western Heritage chuckwagon cook-off in 1992; in Amarillo, April 28, 2015.

**Cavazos, Bobby, 82**; son of a King Ranch foreman, star running back for Texas Tech in the 1950s, achieved a winning record that helped the school get into the Southwest Conference; in San Antonio, Nov. 16, 2013.

**Cisneros, Elvira Munguia, 90**; San Antonio community leader, including Alamo Area Council of Governments, mother of city's mayor Henry Cisneros (1981-89); in San Antonio, Nov. 22, 2014.

**Clark, Harvey, 78**; as a UT cheerleader introduced the "Hook 'em Horns" hand sign in 1955, as a state district judge issued the 1987 landmark decision that declared the state's public school finance system unconstitutional; in Dripping Springs, Oct. 9, 2014.

**Clement, Jack, 82**; music producer was Tennessee native and Sun Records veteran who moved to Beaumont in 1961 where he supported George Jones, Charlie Pride, and other country singers in their early years, added mariachi horns to Johnny Cash's "Ring of Fire" in 1963; in Nashville, Aug. 8, 2013.

**Coffey, Lucy, 108**; left her job at a

*San Antonio resident Ann B. Davis, left, with Bob Cummings.. NBC photo (CC). Country music fiddle legend Johnny Gimble, center. Stephen Kniatt photo (CC). Actress Martha Hyer, right. Studio photo (CC).*

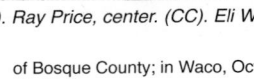

*Robert Strauss, left. Hugh16 photo (CC). Ray Price, center. (CC). Eli Wallach, right. Studio photo (CC).*

Dallas A&P after Pearl Harbor was bombed in 1941 to join the WACs, was the nation's oldest woman veteran when she died; in San Antonio, March 19, 2015.

**Coleman, Ornette, 85**; alto saxophonist and composer was master of "free jazz," introducing those innovations in the 1950s and 1960s; Fort Worth native attended I.M. Terrell High School; in New York, June 11, 2015.

**Connor, Namoi, 114**; raised on a farm, she was the oldest living Texan when she died; in McGregor, Oct. 18, 2013.

**Crow, John David, 79**; Heisman Trophy-winning running back (1957) for A&M where he played for Bear Bryant, after playing for the NFL Cardinals he was A&M athletic director and served in other positions until 2001; in College Station, June 17, 2015.

**Cuellar, Frank Jr., 84**; civic leader born in Terrell, served in a variety of management positions in the family's El Chico Mexican restaurant business; in Dallas, Jan. 4, 2014.

**Cuellar, Yolanda Montañes, 95**; last of the El Chico chain's founding family members, Mexico City native married Mack Jr. there, although the chain was known for its Tex-Mex she taught cooking classes on the cuisine of Mexico City; in Dallas, Nov. 5, 2014.

**Cullen, Roy H., 84**; grandson of oilman Hugh Roy Cullen and a philanthropist who headed the Cullen Foundation which gave millions in grants to health and cultural institutions; in Houston, April 4, 2014.

**Davis, Ann B., 88**; character actress best known as the housekeeper on *The Brady Bunch*, also *The Bob Cummings Show*; in San Antonio, where she moved in 1996, on June 1, 2014.

**DiNino, Vincent R., 95**; legendary director of the University of Texas Longhorn Band beginning in 1955, which previously had been entirely student-run, he built it into the "Showband of the Southwest," continued involvement with the marching band into the 2010s; in Bay City, Sept. 9, 2014.

**Fehrenbach, T.R., 88**; San Benito native, noted Texas historian and columnist, his most famous work was *Lone Star: A History of Texas and Texans*; in San Antonio, Dec. 1, 2013.

**Fromholz, Steve, 68**; singer-songwriter born in Temple, wrote "I'd Have to Be Crazy" and "Texas Trilogy" about his ancestral Bosque County, poet laureate of Texas in 2007, attended UNT; in Scheicher County in a hunting accident, Jan. 19, 2014.

**Gage, Freddie, 81**; a one-time Houston gang leader and drug addict who embraced religion and became a leading Baptist evangelist; in Houston, Sept. 12, 2014.

**Gimble, Johnny, 88**; fiddle legend played with country music stars from Bob Wills to George Strait, born on a farm near Tyler, grew up in Bascom, began playing with the Rose City Swingers when he was 12; in Marble Falls, May 9, 2015.

**Goodwyn, Lawrence, 85**: reporter and editor with the *Texas Observer* in the 1950s and 1960s, helped create a coalition that supported Ralph Yarborough and Don Yarborough in their campaigns, in 1976 wrote *Democratic Promise: The Populist Movement in America* which became a standard text in colleges, A&M graduate worked on his doctorate at UT; in North Carolina where he taught at Duke for 32 years, Sept. 29, 2013.

**Graves, John, 92**; Fort Worth native, prolific writer's most famous work, *Goodbye to a River* was an account of his trip down the Brazos in 1957; at his home near Glen Rose, July 31, 2013.

**Harbin, Jack, 97**; Waxahachie native joined Halliburton Co. in 1948 and eventually became chairman and CEO in the 1970s-80s; philanthropist gave millions to medical research and UT-Austin; in Dallas, July 27, 2014.

**Hardesty, Robert, 82**; speechwriter for President Lyndon Johnson, president of Southwest Texas State University (now Texas State U.) from 1981-88; in Austin, July 8, 2013.

**Harris, Don, 75**; radio personality in Dallas-Fort Worth market on WBAP for more than 30 years; grew up in the Lake Whitney area of Bosque County; in Waco, Oct. 21, 2013.

**Harrison, Charles "Tex," 81**; for nearly 20 years a player on the Harlem Globetrotters and for decades later he served as a coach and advisor to the team; in Houston, his home since 1933 when his parents moved there from Indiana, Nov. 20, 2014.

**Harrison, Frank, 99**; Dallas native, SMU graduate, taught pathology and anatomy at UT Southwestern Medical Center in Dallas, president of UT-Arlington 1969-72, first president of the UT Health Science Center at San Antonio 1972-85; in Dallas, Aug. 8, 2013.

**Harrison, William, 79**; author who adapted his fiction into films *Rollerball* in 1975 and *Mountains of the Moon* in 1990, Dallas native was a graduate of Texas Christian; in Fayetteville, Ark., Oct. 22, 2013.

**Hartsfield, Henry Jr. "Hank," 80**; flew on three space shuttles, commander of maiden mission of the Discovery, pilot of the final test flight of the Columbia; in El Lago, July 17, 2014.

**Hay, Jess, 84**; a fundraising champion for Texas Democrats for decades, a committeeman for the national party, UT regent for 12 years including serving as chairman, SMU grad grew up in Orange; in Dallas, April 20, 2015.

**Haynes, Marques, 90**; Harlem Globetrotter for a half century 1946-97 playing more than 12,000 games, in 1997 he moved to the Dallas area where he ran a heating and air conditioning business; in Plano, May 22, 2015.

**Heard, Robert, 84**: Big Spring native reported for decades from Austin on state government, politics, and sports for AP, he was wounded in the 1966 UT tower shootings; in Austin, April 15, 2014.

**Henderson, Wayne, 74**; trombonist and composer, Houston native was a founder of the Jazz Crusaders in 1961 when they performed in Gulf Coast clubs and bars playing jazz he described as "a combination of southeast Texas and Louisiana;" in Culver City, Calif., April 4, 2014.

**Herkimer, Lawrence, 89**; called the "grandfather of modern cheerleading," after being SMU's head cheerleader, in 1948 he started his first cheerleading camp, began a cheerleading magazine and co-wrote a book on the subject; in Dallas, July 1, 2015.

**Hightower, Jack, 86**; Texas Supreme Court justice, Memphis (Tex.) native served in the Legislature and for six terms as a Democrat in Congress beginning in 1975; in Austin, Aug. 3, 2013.

**Hobby, Diana, 83**; wife of former Lt. Gov. Bill Hobby, book editor of the *Houston Post* in the 1950s-60s, served on many Houston civic boards, conservationist who was a founding board member of the Lady Bird Johnson Wildflower Center; in Houston, July 4, 2014.

**Hunt, N. Bunker, 88**; second son of oil wildcatter H.L. Hunt, grew up in Tyler and Dallas, in the 1960s-70s one of the world's richest men, but lost much of his fortune after trying to corner the world's silver market just before the price collapsed; in Dallas, Oct. 21,2014.

**Hutchison, Ray, 81**; attorney instrumental in creation of DFW Airport, GOP state chairman, legislator, gubernatorial candidate, Dallas native graduated from SMU, husband of Sen. Kay Bailey Hutchison; March 30. 2014.

**Hyer, Martha, 89**; Fort Worth native, Arlington Heights graduate, received an Oscar nomination for best supporting actress for her role in the 1958 film *Some Came Running* opposite Frank Sinatra; in Santa Fe, May 31, 2014.

**Jacobs, Mike, 89**; born Mendel Jakubowicz in Poland, he survived five years in concentration camps, came to Dallas in 1951, recounted his story to generations of children, founded the Dallas Holocaust Museum; in Dallas, July 28, 2014.

**Kennedy, Rod, 84**; entertainment producer who in 1972 started the Kerrville Folk Festival as an offshoot of the Texas State Arts & Crafts Fair; moved to Houston as a teen in the late 1940s; in Kerrville, April 14, 2014.

**Keys, Bobby, 70**; Rolling Stones saxophonist grew up in Slaton, as a kid hung out with Buddy Holly and the Crickets, met Stones on tour in San Antonio in the mid-1960s, when he objected to their covering Buddy's "Not Fade Away," a friendly, professional bond followed; in Tennessee, Dec. 2, 2014.

**King, Betty, 89**; secretary of the Texas Senate 1977-2001, before that worked in the state Capitol for 30 years in various posts; in Austin, Dec. 1, 2014.

**Kinzler, Jack, 94**; considered "Mr. Fix-It" at NASA where he worked for decades as chief of technical services, credited with saving the Skylab space station when the thermal shield failed in 1973; in a

Houston suburb, March 4, 2014.

**Kraddick, David "Kidd," 53**; radio and TV host of morning program heard in many U.S. markets as well as worldwide on the Armed Forces Radio Network; suddenly in New Orleans while at a charity golf event, July 27, 2013.

**Lancarte, Esperanza "Hope," 86**; grande dame of the Fort Worth restaurant trade and mother of seven children, ran her family's iconic Joe T. Garcia's for decades; in Fort Worth, Nov. 20, 2014.

**Lanier, Bob, 89**; real estate developer who was elected Houston mayor in 1991 on a promise to reduce the crime rate which plunged in his first term, served three terms; in Houston, Dec. 20, 2014.

**Loftis, Jack, 80**; Hillsboro native, editor of the *Houston Chronicle* 1986-2002, which in the early years included adding news bureaus across Texas and in Latin America; in Bellaire, Dec. 29, 2014.

**Mack, Gary, 68**; Kennedy assassination expert who was curator at the Sixth Floor Museum at Dealey Plaza, broadcaster joined Dallas' KXAS in 1981, became archivist at the museum in 1994 and appeared on many documentaries on the events of November 1963; in Arlington, July 15, 2015.

**Marcus, Lawrence, 96**; with his more high-profile brother Stanley in 1950 took over the family department store founded by their father and aunt Carrie Neiman; in Dallas, Nov. 1, 2013.

**Marsh, Stanley 3, 76**; scion of oil family, banker and television executive, patron of the arts including iconic Cadillac Ranch sculpture outside Amarillo; in Amarillo, June 17, 2014.

**Mauldin, Joe B., 74**; Rock and Roll Hall of Famer joined Buddy Holly and the Crickets in 1957 as their bass player at the age of 16, went on to become a recording engineer; in Nashville, Feb. 7, 2015.

**McDuffie, Glenn, 86**; believed to be the sailor kissing the nurse in the famous World War II-era photo, later a mail carrier and semi-pro baseball player; in Dallas, where he had lived since 2009, on March 9, 2014.

**McLagan, Ian, 69**; Rock and Roll Hall of Fame keyboardist and 20-year Austin resident, toured and recorded with Bob Dylan, Rolling Stones and Bruce Springsteen, London native played with the Faces in 1960s; in Austin, Dec. 3, 2014.

**Mitchell, George, 94**; Galveston native, son of Greek immigrant became prominent independent oilman; pioneer in hydraulic fracking, developer of The Woodlands community north of Houston; in Galveston, July 26, 2013.

**Montgomery, Bob, 77**; first sang with

Buddy Holly at Hutchinson Junior High in Lubbock in 1949 as "Buddy and Bob," co-wrote some Holly songs as well as "Misty Blue" and the Patsy Cline hit, "Back in Baby's Arms;" in Missouri, Dec. 4, 2014.

**Moroles, Jesús, 64**; noted Rockport sculptor was named State Artist in 2011, born to cotton farmers near Corpus Christi; in a traffic accident near Jarrell, June 15, 2015.

**Newhouse, Robert, 64**; running back played in three Super Bowls for the Dallas Cowboys, threw the game-winning touchdown against the Denver Broncos in Super Bowl XII; at the Mayo Clinic in Minnesota while being treated following a stroke, July 22, 2014.

**Platte, Claude Jr., 92**; Denison native was instructor for the Tuskegee airmen in World War II, after the war he became the first black commissioned an officer at Randolph AFB in San Antonio; in Fort Worth, Sept. 27, 2013.

**Porter, G. Robert "Bob," 85**; longtime entertainment writer for the *Dallas Times Herald*, co-founded the video oral history collection at the Sixth Floor Museum; in Dallas, Nov. 14, 2013.

**Powell, Maxine, 98**; was Motown's "Maven of Style" heading the label's in-house finishing school; born in Texarkana; outside Detroit, Oct. 14, 2013.

**Price, Ray, 87**: ballad singer who reshaped country music adding lush strings, hits included "Make the World Go Away" and "Crazy Arms;" Perryville native died in Mount Pleasant, Dec. 16, 2013.

**Pugh, Jethro, 70**; pillar of the Dallas Cowboys Doomsday Defense 1965-78 including the Ice Bowl game with Green Bay in 1967, played in four Super Bowls; in Dallas, Jan. 7, 2015.

**Sample, Joe, 75**; jazz great was one of the founders with Wayne Henderson (above) of the Jazz Crusaders, pianist and keyboardist was Houston native attended Texas Southern University; in Houston, Sept. 12, 2014.

**Scharbauer, Clarence Jr., 88**; rancher and philanthropist of prominent Permian Basin family, donor to hospital, sports complex, a horse-racing enthusiast; in Midland, Feb. 21, 2014.

**Senterfitt, Reuben, 96;** native of San Saba County served as Texas House Speaker 1951-55, in 1941 co-sponsor of bill establishing M.D. Anderson Hospital in Houston, in 1949 sponsored veterans' land legislation; in Buda, Nov. 20, 2013.

**Sherrill, Robert, 89**; journalist and author received master's in English from UT-Austin in 1956, was associate editor of the *Texas Observer* beginning in 1960, wrote in 1967 *The Accidental President*, a critical portrait of Lyndon Johnson; in Florida, Aug. 19, 2014.

**Shine, Billy Joe, 75**; singer with the Dallas band Nightcaps, he wrote the 1959 rock and roll classic "Wine, Wine, Wine," he said, while sitting in a study hall at Jesuit Prep; in Dallas, March 23, 2015.

**Shipp, Bert, 85**; 40-year career in Dallas broadcasting included interviewing the Beatles in 1964 in their dressing room, and the first televised accounts of the JFK assassination directly from the WFAA newsroom; in Dallas, April 20, 2015.

**Snelson, W.E. "Pete," 91**; conservative Democratic state senator from Midland 1964-1983, raised in a ranching family in Grandfalls; in Georgetown, April 26, 2014.

**Snow, Clyde, 86**; world-renowned forensic anthropologist who worked on cases from JFK to mass graves in Argentina to King Tut, Texas Tech graduate was raised in Ralls where his father was a physician and his mother a nurse; in Norman, Okla., May 16, 2014.

**Strauss, Robert S., 95**; political deal maker and advisor to presidents; Dallas attorney, Lockhart native, grew up in Stamford; led national Democratic Party in the 1970s; in Washington, March 19, 2014.

**Strauss, Ted, 89**; Hamlin native, businessman, banker, and philanthropist, younger brother of Robert Strauss, husband of Annette Strauss who was Dallas mayor 1987-91; in Dallas, Sept. 5, 2014.

**Street, James, 65**: as quarterback he led the UT Longhorns over Arkansas win the college national title in 1969, Longview native went on to a career in finance; in Austin, Sept. 30, 2013.

**Swayze, Patsy, 86**; Houston dance instructor for her son Patrick, as well as for Tommy Tune, Debbie Allen, Randy Quaid, and Jaclyn Smith; choreographed the 1980 film *Urban Cowboy*; in California, Sept. 16, 2013.

**Taylor, Dallas, 66**; drummer for Crosby, Stills, Nash & Young, as well as John Sebastian, grew up in San Antonio, overcame drug addiction to become counselor for other addicts; in Los Angeles, Jan. 18, 2015.

**Temple, Arthur III "Buddy," 73**; part of a dynasty of East Texas lumbermen, served in Legislature 1973-81 where he worked for nature conservation, ran for governor in 1982; in Lufkin, April 14, 2015.

**Tijerina, Reies Lopez, 88**; Chicano movement leader born to migrant farmworkers in Falls City, formed a group in 1963 to reclaim Spanish and Mexican land grants for Latinos; led a group that occupied a courthouse in northern New Mexico in 1967; in El Paso, Jan. 19, 2015.

**Truhill, Jerri Sloan, 85**; test pilot was one of the Mercury 13, a shadow group of women, privately financed, who in the 1960s went through astronaut testing to see if they had the "right stuff," received media attention when Clare Boothe Luce criticized NASA in a *Life* article for excluding women while the Soviets had already sent women into space; in Irving, Nov. 18, 2013.

**Wallach, Eli, 98**; Brooklyn-born actor came to study drama at UT-Austin in the 1930s because of the low tuition and, he said, it was in Texas that he learned to ride horses; in New York, June 24, 2014.

**Walton, Cedar, 79**; pianist who played with John Coltrane and who composed many jazz standards, Dallas native was first taught by his mother, an aspiring concert pianist, he was in the band at Lincoln High School in Dallas; in Brooklyn, Aug. 19, 2013.

**Welch, Christopher Evan, 48**; actor best known as venture capitalist Gregory on HBO's *Silicon Valley*, a graduate of Irving MacArthur High School and the University of Dallas; in Santa Monica, Calif., of lung cancer, Dec. 2, 2013.

**Wilson, Burton, 95**; New Englander studied photograpy at UT-Austin, his photos of the Austin music scene in the 1970s, including the Armadillo World Headquarters and Vulcan Gas Company, became lasting historical documents; in Austin, June 2, 2014.

**Winter, Johnny, 70**; blues guitar legend from Beaumont, known for lightning-fast riffs and for collaborations with Jimi Hendrix and childhood hero Muddy Waters; in Zurich while on a European tour, July 16, 2014.

**Woolf, Jack R., 90**; described as "the founding father" of UT-Arlington, he was president 1959-68 during tremendous growth, steered its transfer from A&M to UT system; in Arlington, June 10, 2014.

**Woolley, Bryan, 77**; newspaperman for several Texas papers including the *Dallas Times Herald* and the *Dallas Morning News* and an author who grew up in Fort Davis, his 1983 *November 22*, a fictional account of the JFK assassination, was praised as the best depiction of what Dallas was like in 1963; in Dallas, Jan. 9, 2015.

**Wright, Jim, 92**; long time member of Congress from Fort Worth, elected majority leader in 1976 and Speaker in 1987, resigned in 1989, started political career in 1947 in the Legislature at the age of 23, then became mayor of Weatherford before he went to Congress in 1954; in Fort Worth, May 6, 2015. ☆

*Johnny Winter. Chascar photo (CC).*

*Jim Wright. U.S. House photo (CC).*

# ADVERTISER INDEX

# GENERAL INDEX

For cities and towns not listed in the index, see lists on pages *416–447* and pages *515–524*.
For full information about cities, see "Cities and towns" entry in this index. For full information about counties, also look under the cities and towns in the county, as well as the "Counties" index entry.

For CITIES and TOWNS not listed in the Index, see complete list on pages 416–447.

---

**For CITIES and TOWNS not listed in the Index, see complete list on pages 416–447.**

---

---

**For CITIES and TOWNS not listed in the Index, see complete list on pages 416–447.**

---

**For CITIES and TOWNS not listed in the Index, see complete list on pages 416–447.**

For **CITIES** and **TOWNS** not listed in the Index, see complete list on pages 416–447.

For CITIES and TOWNS not listed in the Index, see complete list on pages 416–447.

For CITIES and TOWNS not listed in the Index, see complete list on pages 416–447.

**For CITIES and TOWNS not listed in the Index, see complete list on pages 416–447.**

For CITIES and TOWNS not listed in the Index, see complete list on pages 416–447.

For CITIES and TOWNS not listed in the Index, see complete list on pages 416–447.

For CITIES and TOWNS not listed in the Index, see complete list on pages 416–447.

---

**For CITIES and TOWNS not listed in the Index, see complete list on pages 416–447.**

For CITIES and TOWNS not listed in the Index, see complete list on pages 416–447.

For CITIES and TOWNS not listed in the Index, see complete list on pages 416–447.

**For CITIES and TOWNS not listed in the Index, see complete list on pages 416–447.**

**For CITIES and TOWNS not listed in the Index, see complete list on pages 416–447.**

---

**For CITIES and TOWNS not listed in the Index, see complete list on pages 416–447.**

For CITIES and TOWNS not listed in the Index, see complete list on pages 416–447.

---

**For CITIES and TOWNS not listed in the Index, see complete list on pages 416–447.**

For CITIES and TOWNS not listed in the Index, see complete list on pages 416–447.

---

*Horses graze at Miss M's Equestrian Center in Flower Mound in Denton County. Photo by Elizabeth Cruce Alvarez.*

**For CITIES and TOWNS not listed in the Index, see complete list on pages 416–447.**

# Texas Lakes

**Bodies of water with a normal capacity of 5,000 acre-feet or larger. Italicized reservoirs usually dry.**

## ● PANHANDLE PLAINS
1. Palo Duro Reservoir
2. Lake Rita Blanca
3. Lake Meredith
4. Bivins Lake
5. *Buffalo Lake*
6. Mackenzie Reservoir
7. Greenbelt Lake
8. Baylor Creek Lake
9. White River Lake
10. Lake Alan Henry
11. Lake J.B. Thomas
12. Sulphur Springs Draw Reservoir
13. *Natural Dam Lake*
14. Red Draw Reservoir
15. Lake Colorado City
16. Champion Creek Reservoir
17. Mitchell County Reservoir
18. Lake Sweetwater
19. E.V. Spence Reservoir
20. Oak Creek Reservoir
21. O.C. Fisher Lake
22. Twin Buttes Reservoir
23. Lake Nasworthy
24. Lake Ballinger/ Moonen
25. O.H. Ivie Reservoir
26. Hords Creek Lake
27. Lake Winters
28. Lake Abilene
29. Lake Coleman
30. Lake Brownwood
31. Lake Clyde
32. Lake Kirby
33. Lake Fort Phantom Hill
34. Lake Stamford
35. Lake Davis
36. Truscott Brine Lake
37. Santa Rosa Lake
38. Lake Electra
39. Lake Kemp
40. Lake Diversion
41. Lake Kickapoo
42. North Fork Buffalo Creek Reservoir
43. Lake Wichita
44. Lake Arrowhead
45. Millers Creek Reservoir
46. Lake Cooper/Olney
47. Lake Graham
48. Lost Creek Reservoir
49. Possum Kingdom Lake
50. Hubbard Creek Reservoir
51. Lake Daniel
52. Lake Cisco
53. Lake Palo Pinto
54. Lake Leon
55. Proctor Lake

## ● BIG BEND
56. Red Bluff Reservoir
57. Balmorhea Lake
58. Imperial Reservoir
59. Amistad International Reservoir

## ● HILL COUNTRY
60. Brady Creek Reservoir
61. Lake Buchanan
62. Inks Lake
63. Lake Lyndon B. Johnson
64. Lake Marble Falls
65. Lake Travis
66. Lake Austin
67. Town Lake
68. Lake Walter E. Long
69. Lake Georgetown
70. Granger Lake
71. Canyon Lake
72. Medina Lake

## ● PRAIRIES AND LAKES
73. Lake Nocona
74. Hubert H. Moss Lake
75. Lake Texoma
76. Randell Lake
77. Valley Lake
78. Lake Bonham
79. Coffee Mill Lake
80. Pat Mayse Lake
81. Lake Crook
82. River Crest Lake
83. Big Creek Reservoir
84. Cooper Lake
85. Lake Sulphur Springs
86. Lake Cypress Springs
87. Greenville City Lakes
88. Lake Tawakoni
89. Terrell City Lake
90. Lake Lavon
91. Lake Ray Hubbard
92. Lake Kiowa
93. Lake Ray Roberts
94. Lewisville Lake
95. Grapevine Lake
96. North Lake
97. White Rock Lake
98. Mountain Creek Lake
99. Joe Pool Reservoir
100. Lake Arlington
101. Lake Worth
102. Eagle Mountain Lake
103. Lake Weatherford
104. Lake Amon G. Carter
105. Lake Bridgeport
106. Lake Mineral Wells
107. Benbrook Lake
108. Lake Granbury
109. Squaw Creek Reservoir
110. Lake Pat Cleburne
111. Lake Waxahachie
112. Bardwell Lake
113. Cedar Creek Reservoir
114. Forest Grove Reservoir
115. Lake Athens
116. Trinidad Lake
117. Lake Halbert
118. Richland-Chambers Reservoir
119. Fairfield Lake
120. Navarro Mills Lake
121. Aquilla Lake
122. Lake Whitney
123. Lake Waco
124. Tradinghouse Creek Reservoir
125. Lake Creek Lake
126. Belton Lake
127. Stillhouse Hollow Lake
128. Alcoa Lake
129. Lake Limestone
130. Twin Oaks Reservoir
131. Camp Creek Lake
132. Bryan Lake
133. Gibbons Creek Reservoir
134. Somerville Lake
135. Lake Bastrop
136. Fayette County Reservoir
137. Lake Dunlap
138. Lake Gonzales
139. Eagle Lake

## ● PINEYWOODS
140. Wright Patman Lake
141. Monticello Reservoir
142. Lake Winnsboro
143. Lake Bob Sandlin
144. Welsh Reservoir
145. Ellison Creek Reservoir
146. Lake O' the Pines
147. Johnson Creek Reservoir
148. Caddo Lake
149. Lake Fork Reservoir
150. Lake Quitman
151. Lake Holbrook
152. Lake Hawkins
153. Gilmer Reservoir
154. Lake Gladewater
155. Eastman Lakes
156. Brandy Branch Reservoir
157. Lake Cherokee
158. Martin Creek Lake